ABC



With t… [illegible] Thumb Index at the edge of this page you can quickly find the letter you are looking for in the German-English or English-German section of this dictionary.

You place your thumb on the letter you want at the edge of this page, then flick through the dictionary till you come to the appropriate pages in the German-English or English-German section.

Left-handed people should use the ABC Thumb Index at the end of the book.

A B C D E F G H I J K L M N O P Q R S T U V W X Y Z

# Langenscheidt's Pocket Dictionary

# German

## German-English
## English-German

*Completely revised edition in the new German spelling*

Edited by the
Langenscheidt Editorial Staff

LANGENSCHEIDT
NEW YORK · BERLIN · MUNICH · VIENNA · ZURICH

*Neither the presence nor the absence of a designation that any entered word constitutes a trademark should be regarded as affecting the legal status of any trademark.*



*Printed in Germany*

## Preface

This edition of Langenscheidt's "Pocket German Dictionary" has been completely revised.

Languages are in a constant process of change. Therefore many words which have entered the German and English languages in the last few years have been included in the vocabulary, e.g. *abgasfrei*, *Bankleitzahl* (*BLZ*), *gefriergetrocknet*, *genetischer Fingerabdruck*, *Handy*, *Informatiker(in)*, *Katalysator*, *Lauschangriff*, *Nährwert*, *Ozonloch*, *Ozonwerte*; *data transfer*, *end user*, *gene*, *low-calorie*, *low-emission*, *hype*, *cellular phone*, *solar energy*, *solar panel* etc.

Easy-to-read, clearly laid out typography makes for good readability and allows the user to find words and expressions and their translations more quickly. The **new German spelling** has been used and detailed notes for the user have been included.

The A–Z part of this dictionary now contains many important German and English proper names and abbreviations. Another feature is the special quick-reference sections listing the States of Germany and Austria and the Cantons of Switzerland, the German and future European currency, German weights and measures, examples of German declension and conjugation and alphabetical lists of German and English irregular verbs etc.

Designed for the widest possible variety of uses, this dictionary, now with more than 55,000 references, will be of great value to students, teachers and tourists, and will find a place in home and office libraries alike.

# Contents

# Guide for the User

This dictionary endeavors to do everything it can to help you find the words and translations you are looking for as quickly and as easily as possible.

To enable you to get the most out of your dictionary, you will be shown exactly where and how to find the information that will help you choose the right translation in every situation – whether at school or at home, in your profession, when writing letters, or in everyday conversation.

## 1. German and English headwords

**1.1** When you are looking for a particular word it is important to know that the dictionary entries are arranged in strict **alphabetical order:**

A**al** – a**b**
b**e**ugen – b**i**egen
ha**y** – ha**z**e

In the German-English section the umlauts *ä ö ü* are treated as *a o u*. *ß* is treated as *ss*.

**1.2** Besides the headwords and their derivatives and compounds, the past tense and past participle of irregular German verbs are also given as individual entries in alphabetical order in the German-English section, e.g. **ging, gegangen.**

**1.3** Many German and English proper names and abbreviations are included in the vocabulary.

**1.4** How then do you go about finding a particular word? Take a look at the words in bold print at the top of each page. These are the so-called **catchwords** and they serve as a guide to tracing your word as quickly as possible. The catchword on the top left gives you the first headword on the left-hand page, while the one on the top right gives you the last word on the right-hand page, e.g.

**Gesundheit – Glanz**

**1.5** What about entries comprising hyphenated expressions or two or more words, such as **D-Zug, left-handed** or **mass media?** Expressions of this kind are treated in the same way as single words and thus appear in strict alphabetical order. Should you be unable to find a compound in the dictionary, just break it down into its components and look these up separately. In this way the meaning of many compound expressions can be derived indirectly.

When using the dictionary you will notice many 'word families', or groups of words stemming from a common root, which have been collated within one article in order to save space:

**Einkaufs... – ~bummel – ~preis – ~wagen – ~zentrum**
**amend – amendment – amends**

## 2. Spelling

**2.1** Where American and British spelling of a word differs, the American spelling is given first as in

**center,** *Br* **centre**
**center** (*Br* **centre**) **forward**
**dialog,** *Br* **dialogue**
**analy|ze,** *Br* **-se** etc.

or in the English-German section as a separate headword, e.g. **theater, defense** etc.

A 'u' or an 'l' in parentheses in a word also indicates variant spellings:

**colo(u)red** means: American **colored,** British **coloured**
**travel(l)er** means: American **traveler,** British **traveller**

**2.2** Word division in a German word is possible after each syllable, e.g.

**ein-hül-len, Zu-cker, ba-cken, tes-ten**

In the English-German section the centered dots within a headword indicate syllabification breaks.

## 3. The different typefaces and their functions

**3.1 Bold type** is used for the German and English headwords and for Arabic numerals separating different parts of speech (nouns, transitive and intransitive verbs, adjectives and adverbs etc.) and different grammatical forms of a word:

**bieten 1.** *v/t* ... **2.** *v/i* ...
**hängen 1.** *v/i* (*irr*, *ge-*, *h*) hang (**an** *dat* on...); **2.** *v/t* (*ge-*, *h*) hang (**an** *acc* on)
**feed 1.** Futter *n*; ... **2.** *v/t* füttern

**3.2** *Italics* are used for

a) grammatical and other abbreviations: *v/t*, *v/i*, *adj*, *adv*, *appr*, *fig* etc.
b) gender labels (masculine, feminine and neuter): *m*, *f*, *n*
c) grammatical references in brackets in the German-English section
d) any additional information preceding or following a translation (including dative or accusative objects):

**knacken** *v/t and v/i* ... *twig*: snap; *fire*, *radio*: crackle
**Etikett** *n* ... label (*a. fig*)
**Gedanke** *m* (*-n*; *-n*) ...
**geben** (*irr*, *ge-*, *h*) ...
**befolgen** ... follow, take (*advice*); observe (*rule etc*)
**file** ... *Briefe etc* ablegen
**labored** schwerfällig (*style etc*); mühsam (*breathing etc*)

**3.3** ***Boldface italics*** are used for phraseology etc., notes on German grammar and prepositions taken by the headword:

**Lage** *f* ... ***in der ~ sein zu*** *inf* be able to *inf*
**BLZ** ... ABBR *of* ***Bankleitzahl***
**abheben** (*irr*, ***heben***, *sep*, *-ge-*, *h*)
**abfahren** ... (*irr*, ***fahren***, *sep*, *-ge-*, *sein*) leave, depart (*both*: ***nach*** for)
**line** ... ***hold the ~*** TEL bleiben Sie am Apparat
**agree** ... sich einigen (***on*** über *acc*)

**3.4** Normal type is used for translations of the headwords.

## 4. Pronunciation

When you have found the headword you are looking for in the German-English section, you will notice that very often this word is followed by certain symbols enclosed in square brackets. This is the phonetic transcription of the word, which tells you how it is pronounced. And one phonetic alphabet has come to be used internationally, namely that of the International Phonetic Association. This phonetic system is known by the abbreviation **IPA.** The symbols used in this dictionary are listed in the following tables on page 9 and 10.

**4.1** The length of vowels is indicated by [ː] following the vowel symbol.

**4.1.1** Stress is indicated by [ˈ] or [ˌ] preceding the stressed syllable. [ˈ] stands for strong stress, [ˌ] for weak stress:

**Kabel** [ˈkaːbəl] – **Kabine** [kaˈbiːnə]
**ˈnachsehen – Beˈsitz – beˈsprechen**
**Jusˈtizminisˌterium – Miˈnisterpräsiˌdent**

**4.1.2** The glottal stop [ʔ] is the forced stop between one word or syllable and a following one beginning with a vowel, as in

**Analphabet** [anʔalfaˈbeːt]
**beeindrucken** [bəˈʔaindrʊkən]

**4.2** No transcription of compounds is given if the parts appear as separate entries. Each individual part should be looked up, as with

**ˈBlumenbeet** (= **Blume** and **Beet**)

**4.2.1** If only part of the pronunciation changes or if a compound word consists of a new component, only the pronunciation of the changed or new part is given:

**Demonstrant** [demɔnˈstrant]
**Demonstration** [-straˈtsjoːn]
**ˈKinderhort** [-hɔrt]

## 4.3 Guide to pronunciation for the German-English section

### A. Vowels

[a] as in French *carte*: ***Mann*** [man]
[a:] as in *father*: ***Wagen*** ['va:gən]
[e] as in *bed*: ***Tenor*** [te'no:ɐ]
[e:] resembles the first sound in English [eɪ]: ***Weg*** [ve:k]
[ə] unstressed e as in *ago*: ***Bitte*** ['bɪtə]
[ɛ] as in *fair*: ***männlich*** ['mɛnlɪç], ***Geld*** [gɛlt]
[ɛ:] same sound but long: ***zählen*** ['tsɛ:lən]
[ɪ] as in *it*: ***Wind*** [vɪnt]
[i] short, otherwise like [i:]: ***Kapital*** [kapi'ta:l]
[i:] long, as in *meet*: ***Vieh*** [fi:]
[ɔ] as in *long*: ***Ort*** [ɔrt]
[o] as in *molest*: ***Moral*** [mo'ra:l]
[o:] resembles the English sound in *go* [gəʊ] but without the [ʊ]: ***Boot*** [bo:t]
[ø:] as in French *feu*. The sound may be acquired by saying [e] through closely rounded lips: ***schön*** [ʃø:n]
[ø] same sound but short: ***ökumenisch*** [øku'me:nɪʃ]
[œ] as in French *neuf*. The sound resembles the English vowel in *her*. Lips, however, must be well rounded as for [ɒ]: ***öffnen*** ['œfnən]
[ʊ] as in *book*: ***Mutter*** ['mʊtɐ]
[u] short, otherwise like [u:]: ***Musik*** [mu'zi:k]
[u:] long, as in *boot*: ***Uhr*** [u:ɐ]
[ʏ] short, opener than [y:]: ***Hütte*** ['hʏtə]
[y] almost like the French u as in *sur*. It may be acquired by saying [ɪ] through fairly closely rounded lips: ***Büro*** [by'ro:]
[y:] same sound but long: ***führen*** ['fy:rən]

### B. Diphthongs

[aɪ] as in *like*: ***Mai*** [maɪ]
[aʊ] as in *mouse*: ***Maus*** [maʊs]
[ɔʏ] as in *boy*: ***Beute*** ['bɔʏtə], ***Läufer*** ['lɔʏfɐ]

### C. Consonants

[b] as in *better*: ***besser*** ['bɛsɐ]
[d] as in *dance*: ***du*** [du:]
[f] as in *find*: ***finden*** ['fɪndən], ***Vater*** ['fa:tɐ], ***Philosoph*** [filo'zo:f]
[g] as in *gold*: ***Gold*** [gɔlt]
[ʒ] as in *measure*: ***Genie*** [ʒe'ni:]
[h] as in *house* but not aspirated: ***Haus*** [haʊs]
[ç] an approximation to this sound may be acquired by assuming the mouth-configuration for [ɪ] and emitting a strong current of breath: ***Licht*** [lɪçt], ***Mönch*** [mœnç], ***lustig*** ['lʊstɪç]
[x] as in Scottish *loch*. Whereas [ç] is pronounced at the front of the mouth, [x] is pronounced in the throat: ***Loch*** [lɔx]
[j] as in *year*: ***ja*** [ja:]
[k] as in *kick*: ***keck*** [kɛk], ***Tag*** [ta:k], ***Chronik*** ['kro:nɪk], ***Café*** [ka'fe:]
[l] as in *lump*. Pronounced like English initial "clear l": ***lassen*** ['lasən]
[m] as in *mouse*: ***Maus*** [maʊs]
[n] as in *not*: ***nein*** [naɪn]
[ŋ] as in *sing*, *drink*: ***singen*** ['zɪŋən], ***trinken*** ['trɪŋkən]
[p] as in *pass*: ***Pass*** [pas], ***Trieb*** [tri:p], ***obgleich*** [ɔp'glaɪç]
[r] as in *rot*. There are two pronunciations: the frontal or lingual r: ***rot*** [ro:t] and the uvular r [ʁ] (unknown in the

English language): ***Mauer*** ['mauɐ]

[s] as in *miss*. Unvoiced when final, doubled, or next a voiceless consonant: ***Glas*** [gla:s], ***Masse*** ['masə], ***Mast*** [mast], ***nass*** [nas]

[z] as in *zero*. S voiced when initial in a word or syllable: ***Sohn*** [zo:n], ***Rose*** ['ro:zə]

[ʃ] as in *ship*: ***Schiff*** [ʃɪf], ***Charme*** [ʃarm], ***Spiel*** [ʃpi:l], ***Stein*** [ʃtaɪn]

[t] as in *tea*: ***Tee*** [te:], ***Thron*** [tro:n], ***Stadt*** [ʃtat], ***Bad*** [ba:t], ***Findling*** ['fɪntlɪŋ], ***Wind*** [vɪnt]

[v] as in *vast*: ***Vase*** ['va:ze], ***Winter*** ['vɪntɐ]

[ã, ɛ̃, õ] are nasalized vowels. Examples: ***Ensemble*** [ã'sã:bəl], ***Terrain*** [tɛ'rɛ̃:], ***Bonbon*** [bõ'bõ:]

## 4.3.1 Phonetic changes in plurals

| singular | | plural | | example |
|---|---|---|---|---|
| -g | [-k] | -ge | [-gə] | Flug – Flüge |
| -d | [-t] | -de | [-də] | Grund – Gründe, Abend – Abende |
| -b | [-p] | -be | [-bə] | Stab – Stäbe |
| -s | [-s] | -se | [-zə] | Los – Lose |
| -ch | [-x] | -che | [-çə] | Bach – Bäche |
| -iv | [-i:f] | -ive | [-i:və] | Stativ – Stative |

## 4.3.2 The German alphabet

a [a:], b [be:], c [tse:], d [de:], e [e:], f [ɛf], g [ge:], h [ha:], i [i:], j [jɔt], k [ka:], l [ɛl], m [ɛm], n [ɛn], o [o:], p [pe:], q [ku:], r [ɛr], s [ɛs], t [te:], u [u:], v [fau], w [ve:], x [ɪks], y ['ʏpsilɔn], z [tsɛt]

## 4.3.3 List of suffixes

The German suffixes are not transcribed unless they are parts of headwords.

| | | | |
|---|---|---|---|
| -bar | [-ba:ɐ] | -isch | [-ɪʃ] |
| -chen | [-çən] | -ist | [-ɪst] |
| -d | [-t] | -keit | [-kaɪt] |
| -de | [-də] | -lich | [-lɪç] |
| -ei | [-aɪ] | -ling | [-lɪŋ] |
| -en | [-ən] | -losigkeit | [-lo:zɪçkaɪt] |
| -end | [-ənt] | -nis | [-nɪs] |
| -er | [-ɐ] | -sal | [-za:l] |
| -haft | [-haft] | -sam | [-za:m] |
| -heit | [-haɪt] | -schaft | [-ʃaft] |
| -icht | [-ɪçt] | -sieren | [-zi:rən] |
| -ie | [-i:] | -ste | [-stə] |
| -ieren | [-i:rən] | -tät | [-tɛ:t] |
| -ig | [-ɪç] | -tum | [-tu:m] |
| -ik | [-ɪk] | -ung | [-ʊŋ] |
| -in | [-ɪn] | -ungs- | [-ʊŋs-] |
| | | -wärts | [-vɛrts] |

## 5. The tilde (~)

**5.1** A symbol you will repeatedly come across in the dictionary articles is the so-called tilde (~), which serves as a replacement mark. For reasons of space, related words are often combined in groups with the help of the tilde. In these cases, the tilde represents either the complete headword or that part of the word up to a vertical line (|):

**Ski ... ~fahrer(in)** (= ***Skifahrer, Skifahrerin***)
**Ess|löffel ... ~stäbchen** (= ***Essstäbchen***)
**jet ... ~ engine** (= ***jet engine***)
**natural| resources ... ~ science** (= ***natural science***)

**5.2** In the case of the phrases in boldface italics, the tilde represents the headword immediately preceding, which itself may also have been formed with the help of a tilde:

**kommen ...** ***zu spät ~*** (= **kommen**)
**ange|bracht ... ~gossen ...** ***wie ~*** (= ***angegossen***) ***sitzen***
**foreign ... ~** (= ***foreign***) ***affairs***
**break ...** ***take a ~*** (= ***break***)

**6. Abbreviations** of grammatical terms and subject areas are designed to help the user choose the appropriate headword or translation of a word.

In the dictionary words which are predominantly used in British English are marked by the abbreviation *Br*:

**Bürgersteig** *m* sidewalk, *Br* pavement
**girl guide** *Br* Pfadfinderin *f*

## List of abbreviations

*a.* *also*, auch

ABBR *abbreviation*, Abkürzung

*acc* *accusative* (*case*), Akkusativ

*adj* *adjective*, Adjektiv

*adv* *adverb*, Adverb

AGR *agriculture*, Landwirtschaft

*Am* *American English*, amerikanisches Englisch

ANAT *anatomy*, Anatomie

*appr* *approximately*, etwa

ARCH *architecture*, Architektur

*art* *article*, Artikel

ASTR *astrology*, Astrologie; *astronomy*, Astronomie

*attr* *attributively*, attributiv

AVIAT *aviation*, Luftfahrt

BIOL *biology*, Biologie

BOT *botany*, Botanik

*Br* *British English*, britisches Englisch

CHEM *chemistry*, Chemie

*cj* *conjunction*, Konjunktion

*coll* *collectively*, als Sammelwort

*comp* *comparative*, Komparativ

*contp* *contemptuously*, verächtlich

*cpds* *compounds*, Zusammensetzungen

*dat* *dative* (*case*), Dativ

ECON *economy*, Wirtschaft

EDP *electronic data processing*, Elektronische Datenverarbeitung

*e-e* *a*(*n*), eine

e.g. *for example*, zum Beispiel

ELECTR *electrical engineering*, Elektrotechnik

*e-m* *einem*, to a(n)

*e-n* *einen*, a(n)

*e-r* *einer*, of a(n), to a(n)

*e-s* *eines*, of a(n)

*esp.* *especially*, besonders

et., *et.* etwas, *something*

*etc* *et cetera*, *and so on*, usw., und so weiter

F *colloquial*, umgangssprachlich

*f* *feminine*, weiblich

*fig* *figuratively*, übertragen

GASTR *gastronomy*, Kochkunst

*gen* *genitive* (*case*), Genitiv

GEOGR *geography*, Geografie

GEOL *geology*, Geologie

*ger* *gerund*, Gerundium

GR *grammar*, Grammatik

*h* *haben*, have

HIST *history*, Geschichte

HUMOR *humorous*, humorvoll

*impers* *impersonal*, unpersönlich

*indef* *indefinite*, unbestimmt

*inf* *infinitive* (*mood*), Infinitiv

*int* *interjection*, Interjektion

*interr* *interrogative*, fragend

*irr* *irregular*, unregelmäßig

*j-m* *jemandem*, to someone

*j-n* *jemanden*, someone

*j-s* *jemandes*, someone's

JUR *jurisprudence*, Recht

LING *linguistics*, Sprachwissenschaft

LIT *literary*, nur in der Schriftsprache vorkommend

*m* *masculine*, männlich

MAR *maritime term*, Schifffahrt

MATH *mathematics*, Mathematik

*m-e* *my*, meine

MED *medicine*, Medizin

METEOR *meteorology*, Meteorologie

MIL *military term*, militärisch

MOT *motoring*, Kraftfahrwesen

*m-r* *meiner*, of my, to my

*mst* *mostly*, *usually*, meistens

MUS *music*, Musik

*n* *neuter*, sächlich

*neg!* *negative*, *usually considered offensive*, kann als beleidigend empfunden werden

*nom* *nominative* (*case*), Nominativ

*num* *numeral*, Zahlwort

OPT *optics*, Optik

o.s., *o.s.* *oneself*, sich

PAINT *painting*, Malerei

PARL *parliamentary term*, parlamentarischer Ausdruck

| | |
|---|---|
| *pass* | *passive voice*, Passiv |
| PED | *pedagogy*, Schulwesen |
| *pers* | *personal*, persönlich |
| PHARM | *pharmacy*, Pharmazie |
| PHIL | *philosophy*, Philosophie |
| PHOT | *photography*, Fotografie |
| PHYS | *physics*, Physik |
| *pl* | *plural*, Plural |
| POET | *poetry*, Dichtung |
| POL | *politics*, Politik |
| *poss* | *possessive*, besitzanzeigend |
| POST | *post and telecommunications*, Postwesen |
| *pp* | *past participle*, Partizip Perfekt |
| *pred* | *predicative*, prädikativ |
| *pres* | *present*, Präsens |
| *pres p* | *present participle*, Partizip Präsens |
| *pret* | *preterit(e)*, Präteritum |
| PRINT | *printing*, Druckwesen |
| *pron* | *pronoun*, Pronomen |
| *prp* | *preposition*, Präposition |
| PSYCH | *psychology*, Psychologie |
| RAIL | *railroad*, *railway*, Eisenbahn |
| *refl* | *reflexive*, reflexiv |
| REL | *religion*, Religion |
| RHET | *rhetoric*, Rhetorik |
| *s-e* | *seine*, his, one's |
| *sep* | *separable*, abtrennbar |
| *sg* | *singular*, Singular |
| *sl* | *slang*, Slang |
| *s-m* | *seinem*, to his, to one's |
| *s-n* | *seinen*, his, one's |
| s.o., *s.o.* | *someone*, jemand(en) |
| SPORT | *sports*, Sport |
| *s-r* | *seiner*, of his, of one's, to his, to one's |
| *s-s* | *seines*, of his, of one's |
| s.th., *s.th.* | *something*, etwas |
| *su* | *substantive*, Substantiv |
| *subj* | *subjunctive (mood)*, Konjunktiv |
| *sup* | *superlative*, Superlativ |
| TECH | *technology*, Technik |
| TEL | *telegraphy*, Telegrafie; *telephony*, Fernsprechwesen |
| THEA | *theater*, Theater |
| TV | *television*, Fernsehen |
| u., *u.* | *und*, and |
| UNIV | *university*, Hochschulwesen, Studentensprache |
| V | *vulgar*, vulgär, unanständig |
| *v/aux* | *auxiliary verb*, Hilfsverb |
| *vb* | *verb*, Verb |
| VET | *veterinary medicine*, Veterinärmedizin, Tiermedizin |
| *v/i* | *intransitive verb*, intransitives Verb |
| *v/refl* | *reflexive verb*, reflexives Verb |
| *v/t* | *transitive verb*, transitives Verb |
| ZO | *zoology*, Zoologie |
| → | *see*, *refer to*, siehe |
| ® | *registered trademark*, eingetragenes Markenzeichen |

## 7. Translations and phraseology

After the boldface headword in the German-English section, the phonetic transcription of this word, its part of speech label, and its grammar, we finally come to the most important part of the entry: **the translation(s).**

**7.1** It is quite rare for a headword to be given just one translation. Usually a word will have several related translations, which are separated by a **comma.**

**7.2** Different senses of a word are indicated by

a) **semicolons:**

**Fest** ... celebration; party; REL festival
**balance** ... Waage *f*; Gleichgewicht *n*

b) italics for **definitions:**

**Läufer** ... runner (*a. carpet*); *chess*: bishop
**call** ... Berufung *f* (**to** in *ein Amt*; auf *einen Lehrstuhl*)
**cake** ... Tafel *f Schokolade*, Stück *n Seife*

c) **abbreviations** of subject areas:

**Bug** *m* ... MAR bow; AVIAT nose
**Gespräch** *n* talk (*a.* POL); ... TEL call
**daisy** BOT Gänseblümchen *n*
**duck** ... ZO Ente *f*

**7.2.1** Where a word has fundamentally different meanings, it very often appears as two or more separate entries distinguished by **exponents** or raised figures:

**betreten¹** *v/t* ... step on; enter
**betreten²** *adj* embarrassed
**Bauer¹** *m* ... farmer
**Bauer²** *n, m* ... (bird)cage
**chap¹** ... Riss *m*
**chap²** ... *Br* F Bursche *m*

This does not apply to senses which have directly evolved from the primary meaning of the word.

**7.3** When a headword can be several different parts of speech, these are distinguished by boldface **Arabic numerals** (see also the section on p.7, paragraph 3.1 concerning the different typefaces):

| | |
|---|---|
| **geräuschlos** | **1.** *adj* noiseless (*adjective*)<br>**2.** *adv* without a sound (*adverb*) |
| **work** | **1.** Arbeit *f* (*noun*)<br>**2.** *v/i* arbeiten (*verb*) |
| **green** | **1.** grün (*adjective*)<br>**2.** Grün *n* (*noun*) |

**7.3.1** In the German-English section boldface Arabic numerals are also used to distinguish between transitive, intransitive and reflexive verbs (if this affects their translation) and to show that where there is a change of meaning a verb may be differently conjugated:

**fahren** (*irr*, *ge-*) **1.** *v/i* (*sein*) go; *bus etc*: run; ... **2.** *v/t* (*h*) drive (*car etc*) ...

If grammatical indications come before the subdivision they refer to all translations that follow:

**bauen** (*ge-*, *h*) **1.** *v/t* build ...; **2.** *fig v/i*: ~ ***auf*** ...

**7.3.2** Boldface Arabic numerals are also used to indicate the different meanings of nouns which can occur in more than one gender and to show that where there is a change of meaning a noun may be differently inflected:

**Halfter 1.** *m*, *n* (*-s*; -) halter; **2.** *n* (*-s*; -), *f* (-; *-n*) holster

**7.4 Illustrative phrases** in boldface italics are generally given within the respective categories of the dictionary article:

**baden 1.** *v/i* ... ~ ***gehen*** go swimming; **2.** *v/t* ...
**good 1.** ... ***real*** ~ F echt gut (= *adjective*); **2.** ... ***for*** ~ für immer (= *noun*)

## 8. Grammatical references

Knowing what to do with the grammatical information available in the dictionary will enable the user to get the most out of this dictionary.

**8.1 verbs** (see the list of irregular German verbs on page 656).

Verbs have been treated in the following ways:

a) **bändigen** *v/t* (*ge-*, *h*)

The past participle of this word is formed by means of the prefix *ge-* and the auxiliary verb *haben*: ***er hat gebändigt.***

b) **abfassen** *v/t* (*sep*, *-ge-*, *h*)

In conjugation the prefix *ab* must be separated from the primary verb *fassen*: ***sie fasst ab; sie hat abgefasst.***

c) **finden** *v/t* (*irr*, *ge-*, *h*)

*irr* following a verb means that it is an irregular verb. The principal parts of this particular word can be found as an individual headword in the main part of the German-English section and in the list of irregular German verbs on page 656: ***sie fand; sie hat gefunden.***

d) **abfallen** *v/i* (*irr*, ***fallen***, *sep*, *-ge-*, *sein*)

A reference such as *irr*, ***fallen*** indicates that the compound word ***abfallen*** is conjugated in exactly the same way as the primary verb ***fallen*** as given in the list of irregular German verbs on page 656: ***er fiel ab; er ist abgefallen.***

e) **senden** *v/t* ([*irr*,] *ge-*, *h*)

The square brackets indicate that ***senden*** can be treated as a regular or an irregular verb: ***sie sandte*** or ***sie sendete; sie hat gesandt*** or ***sie hat gesendet.***

### 8.2 nouns

The inflectional forms (*genitive singular*; *nominative plural*) follow immediately after the indication of gender. No forms are given for compounds if the parts appear as separate headwords.

The horizontal stroke replaces the part of the word which remains unchanged in the inflection:

**Affäre** *f* (-; *-n*)
**Keks** *m*, *n* (*-es*; *-e*)
**Bau** *m* (-[*e*]*s*; *Bauten*)
**Blatt** *n* (-[*e*]*s*; *Blätter* ['blɛtɐ])

The inflectional forms of German nouns ending in ***-in*** are given in the following ways:

**Ärztin** *f* (-; *-nen*)
**Chemiker(in)** (*-s*; *-/-*; *-nen*) = **Chemiker** *m* (*-s*; -) and **Chemikerin** *f* (-; *-nen*)

### 8.3 Prepositions

If, for instance, a headword (verb, adjective or noun) is governed by certain prepositions, these are given in boldface italics and in brackets together with their English or German translations and placed next to the appropriate translation. If the German or English preposition is the same for all or several translations, it is given only once before or after the first translation and then also applies to the translations which follow it:

**abrücken ... 1.** *v/t* (*h*) move away (***von*** from)
**befestigen** *v/t* (*no -ge-*, *h*) fasten (***an*** *dat* to), fix (to), attach (to)
**dissent ... 2.** anderer Meinung sein (***from*** als)
**dissimilar** (***to***) unähnlich (*dat*); verschieden (von)

With German prepositions which can take the dative or the accusative, the case is given in brackets:

**fürchten** ... ***sich ~*** ... be afraid (***vor*** *dat* of)
**bauen ...** ***~ auf*** (*acc*) rely *or* count on

We hope that this somewhat lengthy introduction has shown you that this dictionary contains a great deal more than simple one-to-one translations, and that you are now well-equipped to make the most of all it has to offer.

PART I

# GERMAN-ENGLISH DICTIONARY

# A

**à** [a] *prp* ***5 Karten ~ DM 20*** 5 tickets at 20 marks each *or* a piece
**Aal** [aːl] *m* (-[*e*]*s*; -*e*) zo eel
**aalen** [ˈaːlən] *v/refl* (*ge-, h*) ***sich in der Sonne ~*** bask in the sun
**ˈaalˈglatt** *fig adj* (as) slippery as an eel
**Aas** [aːs] *n* (-[*e*]*s*) a) *no pl* carrion, b) F *contp pl* ***Äser*** beast, *sl* bastard
**ˈAasgeier** *m* zo vulture (*a. fig*)
**ab** [ap] *prp and adv*: ***München ~ 13.55*** departure from Munich (at) 1.55; ***~ 7 Uhr*** from 7 o'clock (on); ***~ morgen (1. März)*** starting tomorrow (March 1st); ***von jetzt ~*** from now on; ***~ und zu*** now and then; ***ein Film ~ 18*** an X(-rated) film; ***ein Knopf ist ~*** a button has come off
**ˈabarbeiten** *v/t* (*sep, -ge-, h*) work out *or* off (*debts*); ***sich ~*** wear o.s. out
**Abart** [ˈapˀart] *f* (-; -*en*) variety
**abartig** [ˈapˀartɪç] *adj* abnormal
**Abb.** ABBR *of* ***Abbildung*** fig., illustration
**ˈAbbau** *m* (-[*e*]*s*; *no pl*) mining; TECH dismantling; *fig* overcoming (*of prejudices etc*); reduction (*of expenditure, staff etc*); **ˈabbauen** *v/t* (*sep, -ge-, h*) mine; TECH dismantle; *fig* overcome (*prejudices etc*); reduce (*expenditure, staff etc*); ***sich ~*** BIOL break down
**ˈabbeißen** *v/t* (*irr,* ***beißen****, sep, -ge-, h*) bite off
**ˈabbeizen** *v/t* (*sep, -ge-, h*) remove *old paint etc* with corrosives
**ˈabbekommen** *v/t* (*irr,* ***kommen****, sep, no -ge-, h*) get off; ***s-n Teil*** *or* ***et. ~*** get one's share; ***et. ~*** *fig* get hurt, get damaged
**ˈabberufen** *v/t* (*irr,* ***rufen****, sep, no -ge-, h*), **ˈAbberufung** *f* recall
**ˈabbestellen** *v/t* (*sep, no -ge-, h*) cancel one's subscription (*or* order) for
**ˈAbbestellung** *f* cancellation
**ˈabbiegen** *v/i* (*irr,* ***biegen****, sep, -ge-, sein*) turn (off); ***nach rechts (links) ~*** turn right (left)
**ˈabbilden** *v/t* (*sep, -ge-, h*) show, depict
**ˈAbbildung** *f* (-; -*en*) picture, illustration
**ˈAbbitte** *f* apology; ***j-m ~ leisten wegen*** apologize to s.o. for
**ˈabblasen** F *v/t* (*irr,* ***blasen****, sep, -ge-, h*) call off, cancel
**ˈabblättern** *v/i* (*sep, -ge-, sein*) *paint etc*: flake off
**ˈabblenden 1.** *v/t* (*sep, -ge-, h*) dim; **2.** *v/i* MOT dim (*Br* dip) the headlights
**ˈAbblendlicht** *n* MOT dimmed (*Br* dipped) headlights *pl*, low beam
**ˈabbrechen** *v/t* (*irr,* ***brechen****, sep, -ge-*) **1.** *v/t* (*h*) break off (*a. fig*); pull down, demolish (*building etc*); strike (*camp, tent*); **2.** *v/i* a) (*sein*) break off, b) (*h*) *fig* stop; **ˈabbremsen** *v/t* (*sep, -ge-, h*) slow down; **ˈabbrennen** *v/t* (*irr,* ***brennen****, sep, -ge-*) **1.** *v/i* (*sein*) burn down; **2.** *v/t* (*h*) burn down (*building etc*); let *or* set off (*fireworks*); **ˈabbringen** *v/t* (*irr,* ***bringen****, sep, -ge-, h*) ***j-n von e-r Sache ~*** talk s.o. out of (doing) s.th.; ***j-n vom Thema ~*** get s.o. off a subject
**ˈAbbruch** *m* (-[*e*]*s*; *no pl*) breaking off; demolition; **ˈabbruchreif** *adj* derelict, due for demolition
**ˈabbuchen** *v/t* (*sep, -ge-, h*) debit (**von** to); **ˈAbbuchung** *f* debit
**ˈabbürsten** *v/t* (*sep, -ge-, h*) brush off (*dust etc*); brush (*coat etc*)
**Abc** [aːbeːˈtseː] *n* (-; *no pl*) ABC, alphabet; **ABC-Waffen** *pl* MIL nuclear, biological and chemical weapons
**ˈabdanken** *v/i* (*sep, -ge-, h*) resign; *king etc*: abdicate; **ˈAbdankung** *f* (-; -*en*) resignation; abdication
**ˈabdecken** *v/t* (*sep, -ge-, h*) uncover; untile (*roof*); unroof (*house*); clear (*the table*); ECON cover (up)
**ˈabdichten** *v/t* (*sep, -ge-, h*) TECH seal
**ˈabdrängen** *v/t* (*sep, -ge-, h*) push aside
**ˈabdrehen 1.** *v/t* (*sep, -ge-, h*) turn *or* switch off (*light, water etc*); **2.** *v/i* (*a. sein*) *ship, plane*: change one's course
**ˈAbdruck** *m* print, mark
**ˈabdrucken** *v/t* (*sep, -ge-, h*) print
**ˈabdrücken** (*sep, -ge-, h*) **1.** *v/t* fire (*gun*); **2.** *v/i* pull the trigger

**Abend** ['a:bənt] *m* (*-s*; *-e*) evening; ***am ~*** in the evening, at night; ***heute ~*** tonight; ***morgen*** (***gestern***) ~ tomorrow (last) night; → ***bunt, essen***; **~brot** *n* (*-[e]s*; *no pl*), **~essen** *n* supper, dinner, *Br a.* high tea; **~kasse** *f* THEA *etc* box office; **~kleid** *n* evening dress *or* gown; **~kurs** *m* evening classes *pl*

**'Abendland** *n* (*-[e]s*; *no pl*) West, Occident; **'abendländisch** [~lɛndɪʃ] *adj* Western, Occidental

**'Abendmahl** *n* (*-[e]s*; *no pl*) *the* (Holy) Communion, *the* Lord's Supper; ***das ~ empfangen*** receive Communion

**abends** ['a:bənts] *adv* in the evening, at night; ***dienstags ~*** (on) Tuesday evenings

**'Abendschule** *f* evening classes *pl*, night school

**Abenteuer** ['a:bəntɔʏɐ] *n* (*-s*; *-*) adventure (*a. in cpds ...ferien, ...spielplatz*)

**'abenteuerlich** *adj* adventurous; *fig* risky; fantastic

**Abenteurer** ['a:bəntɔʏrɐ] *m* (*-s*; *-*) adventurer; **'Abenteurerin** [~rərɪn] *f* (*-*; *-nen*) adventuress

**aber** ['a:bɐ] *cj and adv* but; ***oder ~*** or else; *~, ~!* now then!; ***~ nein!*** not at all!

**'Aberglaube** *m* superstition

**abergläubisch** ['a:bɐglɔʏbɪʃ] *adj* superstitious

**'aberkennen** *v/t* (*irr*, ***kennen***, *sep*, *no -ge-*, *h*) ***j-m et.*** ~ deprive s.o. of s.th. (*a.* JUR); **'Aberkennung** *f* (*-*; *-en*) deprivation (*a.* JUR)

**abermalig** ['a:bɐma:lɪç] *adj* repeated

**abermals** ['a:bɐma:ls] *adv* once more *or* again

**'aber'tausend** *adj*: ***tausende und ~e*** thousands upon thousands

**'abfahren** (*irr*, ***fahren***, *sep*, *-ge-*) **1.** *v/i* (*sein*) leave, depart (*both*: ***nach*** for); F (***voll***) ***~ auf*** (*acc*) really go for; **2.** *v/t* (*h*) carry *or* cart away

**'Abfahrt** *f* departure (***nach*** for), start (for); *skiing*: descent

**'Abfahrts|lauf** *m* downhill skiing (*or* race); **~zeit** *f* (time of) departure

**'Abfall** *m* waste, refuse, garbage, trash, *Br a.* rubbish; **~beseitigung** *f* waste disposal; **~eimer** *m* → ***Mülleimer***

**'abfallen** *v/i* (*irr*, ***fallen***, *sep*, *-ge-*, *sein*) fall (off); *terrain*: slope (down); *fig* fall away (***von*** from); *esp* POL secede (from); ***vom Glauben ~*** renounce one's faith; ***~ gegen*** compare badly with

**'abfällig 1.** *adj* derogatory; **2.** *adv*: ***~ von j-m sprechen*** run s.o. down

**'Abfallpro,dukt** *n* waste product

**'abfälschen** *v/t* (*sep*, *-ge-*, *h*) SPORT deflect; **'abfangen** *v/t* (*irr*, ***fangen***, *sep*, *-ge-*, *h*) catch, intercept; MOT, AVIAT right; **'abfärben** *v/i* (*sep*, *-ge-*, *h*) *color etc*: run, *material*: *a.* bleed; *fig* ***~ auf*** (*acc*) rub off on; **'abfassen** *v/t* (*sep*, *-ge-*, *h*) compose, word, write

**'abfertigen** *v/t* (*sep*, *-ge-*, *h*) dispatch; *customs*: clear; serve (*customers*); check in (*passengers etc*); ***j-n kurz ~*** be short with s.o.; **'Abfertigung** *f* dispatch; clearance; check-in

**'abfeuern** *v/t* (*sep*, *-ge-*, *h*) fire (off); launch (*rocket*)

**'abfinden** *v/t* (*irr*, ***finden***, *sep*, *-ge-*, *h*) ECON pay off (*creditor*); buy out (*partner*); compensate; ***sich mit e-r Sache ~*** put up with s.th.; **'Abfindung** *f* (*-*; *-en*) ECON satisfaction; compensation

**'abflachen** *v/t and v/refl* (*sep*, *-ge-*, *h*) flatten; **'abflauen** *v/i* (*sep*, *-ge-*, *sein*) *wind etc*: drop (*a. fig*); **'abfliegen** *v/i* (*irr*, ***fliegen***, *sep*, *-ge-*, *sein*) AVIAT leave, depart; **'abfließen** *v/i* (*irr*, ***fließen***, *sep*, *-ge-*, *sein*) flow off, drain (off *or* away)

**'Abflug** *m* AVIAT departure

**'Abfluss** *m* (*-es*; *Abflüsse*) a) *no pl* flowing off, b) TECH drain

**'Abflussrohr** *n* wastepipe, drain(pipe)

**'abfragen** *v/t* (*sep*, *-ge-*, *h*) quiz *or* question *s.o.* (***über*** *acc* about), test *s.o.* orally

**Abfuhr** ['apfu:ɐ] *f* (*-*; *-en*) removal; ***j-m e-e ~ erteilen*** rebuff (F SPORT lick) s.o.

**'abführen** (*sep*, *-ge-*, *h*) **1.** *v/t* lead *or* take away; ECON pay (over) (***an*** *acc* to); **2.** *v/i* MED move one's bowels; act as a laxative; **'abführend** *adj*, **'Abführmittel** *n* MED laxative

**'abfüllen** *v/t* (*sep*, *-ge-*, *h*) bottle; can

**'Abgabe** *f* (*-*; *-n*) a) *no pl* handing in, b) SPORT pass, c) ECON rate; duty

**'abgabenfrei** *adj* tax-free

**'abgabenpflichtig** *adj* dutiable

**'Abgang** *m* (*-[e]s*; *Abgänge*) a) *no pl* departure; *Am* graduation, *Br* school-leaving; THEA exit (*a. fig*), b) SPORT dismount; **Abgänger** ['apgɛŋɐ] *m* (*-s*; *-*) *Am* graduate, *Br* school-leaver

'**Abgas** *n* waste gas; *pl* emission(s *pl*); MOT exhaust fumes *pl*
'**abgasfrei** *adj* emission-free
'**Abgasuntersuchung** *f* MOT *Am* emissions test, *Br* exhaust emission test
'**abgearbeitet** *adj* worn out
'**abgeben** *v/t* (*irr*, ***geben***, *sep*, *-ge-*, *h*) leave (***bei*** with); hand in; deposit (*one's baggage etc*), hand over (*ticket etc*) (***an*** *acc* to); cast (*vote*); pass (*ball*); give off, emit (*heat etc*); make (*offer*, *statement etc*); ***j-m et. ~ von*** share s.th. with s.o.; ***sich ~ mit*** concern o.s. with *s.th.*, associate with *s.o.*
'**abge|brannt** *adj* burnt down; F *fig* broke; **~brüht** *fig adj* hard-boiled; **~droschen** *adj* hackneyed; **~fahren** *adj tires*: worn out; **~griffen** *adj* worn; **~hackt** *fig adj* disjointed; **~hangen** *adj*: ***gut ~es Fleisch*** well-hung meat; **~härtet** *adj* hardened (***gegen*** to)
'**abgehen** *v/i* (*irr*, ***gehen***, *sep*, *-ge-*, *sein*) *train etc*: leave; *mail*, *goods*: get off; THEA go off (stage); *button etc*: come off; *path etc*: branch off; ***von der Schule ~*** leave school; ***~ von*** drop (*plan etc*); ***von s-r Meinung ~*** change one's mind *or* opinion; ***ihm geht ... ab*** he lacks ...; ***gut ~*** end well, pass off well
'**abge|hetzt, ~kämpft** *adj* exhausted, worn out; **~kartet** ['apgəkartət] F *adj*: ***~e Sache*** put-up job; **~legen** *adj* remote, distant; **~macht** *adj* fixed; ***~!*** it's a deal!; **~magert** *adj* emaciated; **~neigt** *adj*: ***e-r Sache ~ sein*** be averse to s.th.; ***ich wäre nicht ~, et. zu tun*** I wouldn't mind doing s.th.; **~nutzt** *adj* worn out
**Abgeordnete** ['apgəʔɔrdnətə] *m*, *f* (*-n*; *-n*) *Am* representative, congress|man (-woman), *Br* Member of Parliament (ABBR MP); '**Abgeordnetenhaus** *n Am* House of Representatives, *Br* House of Commons
'**abgepackt** *adj* prepack(ag)ed
'**abgeschieden** *adj* secluded
'**Abgeschiedenheit** *f* (-; *no pl*) seclusion
'**abge|schlossen** *adj* completed; ***~e Wohnung*** self-contained apartment (*Br* flat); **~sehen** *adj*: ***~ von*** aside (*Br a.* apart) from; ***ganz ~ von*** not to mention, let alone; **~spannt** *adj* exhausted, weary; **~standen** *adj* stale; **~storben** *adj* dead (*tree etc*); numb (*leg etc*); **~stumpft** *adj* insensitive, indifferent (***gegen*** to); **~tragen, ~wetzt** *adj* worn out; threadbare, shabby
**abgewöhnen** *v/t* (*sep*, *-ge-*, *h*) ***j-m et. ~*** make s.o. give up s.th.; ***sich*** (*dat*) ***das Rauchen ~*** stop *or* give up smoking
'**Abgott** *m* idol (*a. fig*); **abgöttisch** ['apgœtɪʃ] *adv*: ***j-n ~ lieben*** idolize s.o.
'**abgrasen** *v/t* (*sep*, *-ge-*, *h*) graze; *fig* scour
'**abgrenzen** *v/t* (*sep*, *-ge-*, *h*) mark off; delimit (***gegen*** from)
'**Abgrund** *m* abyss, chasm, gulf (*all a. fig*); ***am Rande des ~s*** *fig* on the brink of disaster; '**abgrund'tief** *adj* abysmal
'**abgucken** F *v/t* (*sep*, *-ge-*, *h*) ***j-m et. ~*** learn s.th. from (watching) s.o.; → ***abschreiben***
'**Abguss** *m* cast
'**abhaben** F *v/t* (*irr*, ***haben***, *sep*, *-ge-*, *h*) ***willst du et. ~?*** do you want some (of it)? '**abhacken** *v/t* (*sep*, *-ge-*, *h*) chop *or* cut off; '**abhaken** *v/t* (*sep*, *-ge-*, *h*) check (*Br* tick) off; F forget; '**abhalten** *v/t* (*irr*, ***halten***, *sep*, *-ge-*, *h*) hold (*meeting etc*); ***j-n von der Arbeit ~*** keep s.o. from his work; ***j-n davon ~, et. zu tun*** keep s.o. from doing s.th.
'**abhandeln** *v/t* (*sep*, *-ge-*, *h*) treat (*subject etc*); ***j-m et. ~*** make a deal with s.o. for s.th.; '**Abhandlung** *f* treatise (***über*** *acc* on)
'**Abhang** *m* slope
'**abhängen**[1] *v/t* (*sep*, *-ge-*, *h*) take down (*picture etc*); RAIL *etc* uncouple; F shake *s.o.* off
'**abhängen**[2] *v/i* (*irr*, ***hängen***, *sep*, *-ge-*, *h*) ***~ von*** depend on; ***das hängt davon ab*** that depends
**abhängig** ['aphɛŋɪç] *adj*: ***~ von*** dependent on; *a.* addicted to *drugs etc*
'**Abhängigkeit** *f* (-; *-en*) dependence (***von*** on); addiction (to)
'**abhärten** *v/t* (*sep*, *-ge-*, *h*) ***sich ~*** harden o.s. (***gegen*** to)
'**abhauen** (*irr*, ***hauen***, *sep*, *-ge-*) **1.** *v/t* (*h*) cut *or* chop off; **2.** F *v/i* (*sein*) make off (***mit*** with), run away (with); ***hau ab!*** beat it!, scram!
'**abheben** (*irr*, ***heben***, *sep*, *-ge-*, *h*) **1.** *v/t* lift *or* take off; pick up (*receiver*); (with)draw (*money*); cut (*cards*); ***sich ~*** stand out (***von*** among, from), *fig a.*

contrast with; **2.** *v/i* cut the cards; answer the phone; *plane*: take (*esp rocket*: lift) off

'**abheften** *v/t* (*sep*, *-ge-*, *h*) file

'**abheilen** *v/i* (*sep*, *-ge-*, *sein*) heal (up)

'**abhetzen** *v/refl* (*sep*, *-ge-*, *h*) wear o.s. out

'**Abhilfe** *f* remedy; ~ ***schaffen*** take remedial measures

'**Abholdienst** *m* pickup service

'**abholen** *v/t* (*sep*, *-ge-*, *h*) pick up, collect; ***j-n von der Bahn*** ~ meet s.o. at the station; '**abholzen** *v/t* (*sep*, *-ge-*, *h*) fell, cut down (*trees*); deforest (*area*); '**abhorchen** *v/t* (*sep*, *-ge-*, *h*) MED auscultate, sound; '**abhören** *v/t* (*sep*, *-ge-*, *h*) listen in on, tap (*telephone conversation*), F bug; → ***abfragen***

'**Abhörgerät** *n* bugging device, F bug

**Abitur** [abi'tu:ɐ] *n* (*-s*; *-e*) school-leaving examination (qualifying for university entrance)

'**abjagen** *v/t* (*sep*, *-ge-*, *h*) ***j-m et.*** ~ recover s.th. from s.o.; '**abkanzeln** F *v/t* (*sep*, *-ge-*, *h*) tell *s.o.* off; '**abkaufen** *v/t* (*sep*, *-ge-*, *h*) ***j-m et.*** ~ buy s.th. from s.o.

**Abkehr** ['apke:ɐ] *f* (*-*; *no pl*) break (***von*** with); '**abkehren** *v/refl* (*sep*, *-ge-*, *h*) ***sich*** ~ ***von*** turn away from

'**abklingen** *v/i* (*irr*, ***klingen***, *sep*, *-ge-*, *sein*) fade away; *pain etc*: ease off

'**abklopfen** *v/t* (*sep*, *-ge-*, *h*) MED sound

'**abknallen** F *v/t* (*sep*, *-ge-*, *h*) pick off

'**abknicken** *v/t* (*sep*, *-ge-*, *h*) snap *or* break off; bend

'**abkochen** *v/t* (*sep*, *-ge-*, *h*) boil

'**abkomman,dieren** *v/t* (*sep*, *no -ge-*, *h*) MIL detach (***zu*** for)

'**abkommen** *v/i* (*irr*, ***kommen***, *sep*, *-ge-*, *sein*) ~ ***von*** get off; drop (*plan etc*); ***vom Thema*** ~ stray from the point; → ***Weg***

'**Abkommen** *n* (*-s*; *-*) agreement, treaty; ***ein*** ~ ***schließen*** make an agreement

**Abkömmling** ['apkœmlɪŋ] *m* (*-s*; *-e*) descendant

'**abkoppeln** *v/t* (*sep*, *-ge-*, *h*) uncouple (***von*** from); undock (*spacecraft*)

'**abkratzen** (*sep*, *-ge-*) **1.** *v/t* (*h*) scrape off; **2.** F *v/i* (*sein*) kick the bucket

'**abkühlen** *v/t and v/refl* (*sep*, *-ge-*, *h*) cool down (*a. fig*)

'**Abkühlung** *f* cooling

'**abkürzen** *v/t* (*sep*, *-ge-*, *h*) shorten; abbreviate; ***den Weg*** ~ take a short cut

'**Abkürzung** *f* abbreviation; short cut

'**abladen** *v/t* (*irr*, ***laden***, *sep*, *-ge-*, *h*) unload; dump (*waste etc*)

'**Ablage** *f* (*-*; *-n*) a) *no pl* filing, b) filing tray, c) *Swiss* → ***Zweigstelle***

'**ablagern** (*sep*, *-ge-*, *h*) **1.** *v/t* season (*wood*); let *wine* age; GEOL *etc* deposit; ***sich*** ~ settle, be deposited; **2.** *v/i* (*a. sein*) season; age; '**Ablagerung** *f* (*-*; *-en*) CHEM, GEOL deposit, sediment

'**ablassen** (*irr*, ***lassen***, *sep*, *-ge-*, *h*) **1.** *v/t* drain off (*liquid*); let off (*steam*); drain (*pond etc*); **2.** *v/i*: ***von et.*** (***j-m***) ~ stop doing s.th. (leave s.o. alone)

'**Ablauf** *m* (*-[e]s*; *Abläufe*) a) course; process; order of events, b) *no pl* expiration, *Br* expiry, c) → ***Abfluss***

'**ablaufen** (*irr*, ***laufen***, *sep*, *-ge-*) **1.** *v/i* (*sein*) *water etc*: run off; *performance etc*: go, proceed; come to an end; *period*, *passport etc*: expire; *time*, *record*, *tape*: run out; *clock*: run down; ***gut*** ~ turn out well; **2.** *v/t* (*h*) wear down

'**ablecken** *v/t* (*sep*, *-ge-*, *h*) lick (off)

'**ablegen** (*sep*, *-ge-*, *h*) **1.** *v/t* take off (*clothes*); file (*letters etc*); give up (*habit etc*); take (*examination*, *oath*); ***abgelegte Kleider*** cast-offs *pl*; **2.** *v/i* take off one's (hat and) coat; MAR put out, sail

'**Ableger** *m* (*-s*; *-*) BOT layer; offshoot (*a. fig*)

'**ablehnen** *v/t* (*sep*, *-ge-*, *h*) refuse; turn down (*application etc*); PARL reject; object to; condemn; **~d** *adj* negative

'**Ablehnung** *f* (*-*; *-en*) refusal; rejection; objection (*gen* to)

'**ableiten** *v/t* (*sep*, *-ge-*, *h*) divert; LING, MATH derive (***aus*** *dat*, ***von*** from) (*a. fig*)

'**Ableitung** *f* diversion; LING, MATH derivation (*a. fig*)

'**ablenken** *v/t* (*sep*, *-ge-*, *h*) divert (***von*** from); *soccer*: turn away (*ball*); deflect (*rays etc*); ***j-n von der Arbeit*** ~ distract s.o. from his work; ***er lässt sich leicht*** ~ he is easily diverted

'**Ablenkung** *f* diversion

'**ablesen** *v/t* (*irr*, ***lesen***, *sep*, *-ge-*, *h*) read

'**abliefern** *v/t* (*sep*, *-ge-*, *h*) deliver (***bei*** to, at); hand over (to)

'**ablösbar** *adj* detachable; '**ablösen** *v/t* (*sep*, *-ge-*, *h*) detach; take off; take *s.o.'s* place, take over from *s.o.*; *esp* MIL relieve; replace; ***sich*** ~ take turns (*driving*

*etc*); '**Ablösesumme** *f* SPORT transfer fee; '**Ablösung** *f* relief
'**abmachen** *v/t* (*sep*, *-ge-*, *h*) remove, take off; settle, arrange
'**Abmachung** *f* (-; *-en*) arrangement, agreement, deal
'**abmagern** *v/i* (*sep*, *-ge-*, *sein*) get thin
'**Abmagerung** *f* (-; *-en*) emaciation
'**Abmagerungskur** *f* slimming diet
'**abmähen** *v/t* (*sep*, *-ge-*, *h*) mow
'**abmalen** *v/t* (*sep*, *-ge-*, *h*) copy
'**Abmarsch** *m* (-[*e*]*s*; *no pl*) start; MIL marching off; '**abmarˌschieren** *v/i* (*sep*, *no -ge-*, *sein*) start; MIL march off
'**abmelden** *v/t* (*sep*, *-ge-*, *h*) cancel the registration of (*car etc*); cancel s.o.'s membership (*in a club etc*); give notice of s.o.'s withdrawal (from school); ***sich*** ~ give notice of change of address; report off duty; '**Abmeldung** *f* notice of withdrawal; notice of change of address
'**abmessen** *v/t* (*irr*, ***messen***, *sep*, *-ge-*, *h*) measure; '**Abmessung** *f* measurement; *pl* dimensions
'**abmonˌtieren** *v/t* (*sep*, *no -ge-*, *h*) take off; take down; TECH dismantle
'**abmühen** *v/refl* (*sep*, *-ge-*, *h*) work very hard; try hard (*to do s.th.*); struggle (***mit*** with)
'**abnagen** *v/t* (*sep*, *-ge-*, *h*) gnaw (at)
**Abnahme** ['apnaːmə] *f* (-; *-n*) reduction, decrease; loss (*a. of weight*); ECON purchase; TECH acceptance
'**abnehmbar** *adj* removable
'**abnehmen** (*irr*, ***nehmen***, *sep*, *-ge-*, *h*) **1.** *v/t* take off (*a.* MED), remove; pick up (*receiver*); TECH accept; ECON buy; ***j-m et.*** ~ take s.th. (away) from s.o.; **2.** *v/i* decrease, diminish; lose weight; answer the phone; *moon*: wane
'**Abnehmer** *m* (*-s*; -) buyer; customer
'**Abneigung** *f* (***gegen***) dislike (of, for); aversion (to)
**abnorm** [ap'nɔrm] *adj* abnormal; exceptional, unusual; **Abnormität** [apnɔrmi'tɛːt] *f* (-; *-en*) abnormality
'**abnutzen**, '**abnützen** *v/t and v/refl* (*sep*, *-ge-*, *h*) wear out
'**Abnutzung**, '**Abnützung** *f* (-; *no pl*) wear (and tear) (*a. fig*)
**Abonnement** [abɔnə'mãː] *n* (*-s*; *-s*) subscription (***auf*** *acc* to); **Abonnent** [abɔ'nɛnt] *m* (*-en*; *-en*) subscriber; THEA season-ticket holder; **abonnieren** [abɔ'niːrən] *v/t* (*no -ge-*, *h*) subscribe to
**Abordnung** *f* (-; *-en*) delegation
**Abort** [a'bɔrt] *m* (-[*e*]*s*; *-e*) lavatory, toilet
'**abpassen** *v/t* (*sep*, *-ge-*, *h*) watch *or* wait for (*s.o.*, *s.th.*); waylay *s.o.* (*a. fig*)
'**abpfeifen** *v/t and v/i* (*irr*, ***pfeifen***, *sep*, *-ge-*, *h*) SPORT blow the final whistle; stop the game
'**abplagen** *v/refl* (*sep*, *-ge-*, *h*) struggle (***mit*** with)
'**abprallen** *v/i* (*sep*, *-ge-*, *sein*) rebound, bounce (off); *bullet*: ricochet
'**abputzen** *v/t* (*sep*, *-ge-*, *h*) wipe off; clean
'**abraten** *v/i* (*irr*, ***raten***, *sep*, *-ge-*, *h*) ***j-m ~ von*** advise *or* warn s.o. against
'**abräumen** *v/t* (*sep*, *-ge-*, *h*) clear away; clear (*the table*)
'**abreaˌgieren** *v/t* (*sep*, *no -ge-*, *h*) work off (*one's anger etc*) (**an** *dat* on); ***sich*** ~ F let off steam
'**abrechnen** (*sep*, *-ge-*, *h*) **1.** *v/t* deduct, subtract; claim (*expenses*); **2.** *v/i*: ***mit j-m*** ~ settle accounts (*fig a.* get even) with s.o.; '**Abrechnung** *f* settlement; F *fig* showdown
'**abreiben** *v/t* (*irr*, ***reiben***, *sep*, *-ge-*, *h*) rub off; rub down (*body*); polish
'**Abreise** *f* departure (***nach*** for)
'**abreisen** *v/i* (*sep*, *-ge-*, *sein*) depart, leave, start, set out (*all*: ***nach*** for)
'**abreißen** (*irr*, ***reißen***, *sep*, *-ge-*) **1.** *v/t* (*h*) tear *or* pull off; pull down (*building*); **2.** *v/i* (*sein*) break; *button etc*: come off
'**Abreißkaˌlender** *m* tear-off calendar
'**abrichten** *v/t* (*sep*, *-ge-*, *h*) train (*animal*), *a.* break *a horse* in
'**abriegeln** *v/t* (*sep*, *-ge-*, *h*) block off, cordon off
'**Abriss** *m* (*-es*; *-e*) a) (*no pl*) demolition, b) outline, summary
'**abrollen** *v/i* (*sep*, *-ge-*, *sein*) *and v/t* (*h*) unroll (*a. fig*)
'**abrücken** (*sep*, *-ge-*) **1.** *v/t* (*h*) move away (***von*** from); **2.** *v/i* (*sein*) draw away (***von*** from); MIL march off
'**Abruf** *m*: ***auf*** ~ ECON on call
'**abrufen** *v/t* (*irr*, ***rufen***, *sep*, *-ge-*, *h*) call away; EDP recall, fetch, retrieve
'**abrunden** *v/t* (*sep*, *-ge-*, *h*) round (off)
'**abrupfen** *v/t* (*sep*, *-ge-*, *h*) pluck (off)

**abrupt** [ap'rʊpt] *adj* abrupt
'**abrüsten** *v/i* (*sep*, *-ge-*, *h*) MIL disarm
'**Abrüstung** *f* (-; *no pl*) MIL disarmament
'**abrutschen** *v/i* (*sep*, *-ge-*, *sein*) slide down; slip (off) (***von*** from)
**ABS** [a:be:'ɛs] → ***Antiblockiersystem***
**Absage** ['apza:gə] *f* (-; *-n*) refusal; cancellation; '**absagen** (*sep*, *-ge-*, *h*) **1.** *v/t* call off, cancel (*event etc*); **2.** *v/i* call off; ***j-m ~ a.*** cancel one's appointment with s.o.; decline (the invitation)
'**absägen** *v/t* (*sep*, *-ge-*, *h*) saw off; F *fig* oust, sack *s.o.*
'**absahnen** F *v/i* (*sep*, *-ge-*, *h*) cash in
'**Absatz** *m* paragraph; ECON sales *pl*; *shoe*: heel; *stairs*: landing
'**abschaben** *v/t* (*sep*, *-ge-*, *h*) scrape off
'**abschaffen** *v/t* (*sep*, *-ge-*, *h*) do away with, abolish; repeal (*law*); put an end to (*abuses etc*); '**Abschaffung** *f* (-; *no pl*) abolition; repeal
'**abschalten** (*sep*, *-ge-*, *h*) **1.** *v/t* switch *or* turn off; **2.** F *v/i* relax, switch off
'**abschätzen** *v/t* (*sep*, *-ge-*, *h*) estimate; assess; size up; **abschätzig** ['apʃɛtsɪç] *adj* contemptuous; derogatory
**Abschaum** *m* (*-s*; *no pl*) scum (*a. fig*)
'**Abscheu** *m* (*-s*; *no pl*) disgust (***vor***, ***gegen*** at, for); ***e-n ~ haben vor*** abhor, detest; '**abscheuerregend** *adj* revolting, repulsive
**ab'scheulich** *adj* abominable, despicable (*a. person*), *a.* atrocious (*crime*)
'**abschicken** *v/t* (*sep*, *-ge-*, *h*) → ***absenden***
'**abschieben** *fig v/t* (*irr*, ***schieben***, *sep*, *-ge-*, *h*) push away; get rid of; deport; ***et. auf j-n ~*** shove s.th. off on (to) s.o.
**Abschied** ['apʃi:t] *m* (*-[e]s*; *-e*) parting, farewell; ***~ nehmen*** (***von***) say goodbye (to), take leave (of); ***s-n ~ nehmen*** resign, retire
'**Abschiedsfeier** *f* farewell party
'**Abschiedskuss** *m* goodbye kiss
'**abschießen** *v/t* (*irr*, ***schießen***, *sep*, *-ge-*, *h*) shoot off (AVIAT down); launch (*rocket*); shoot, kill (*deer*); F pick *s.o.* off; *fig* oust; get rid of *s.o.*
'**abschirmen** *v/t* (*sep*, *-ge-*, *h*) shield (***gegen*** from); *fig* protect (***gegen*** against, from); '**Abschirmung** *f* (-; *-en*) shield, screen; *fig* protection
'**abschlachten** *v/t* (*sep*, *-ge-*, *h*) slaughter (*a. fig*)
'**Abschlag** *m* SPORT kickout; ECON down payment; '**abschlagen** *v/t* (*irr*, ***schlagen***, *sep*, *-ge-*, *h*) knock off; cut off (*head*); cut down (*tree*); refuse (*request etc*), turn *s.th.* down
'**abschleifen** *v/t* (*irr*, ***schleifen***, *sep*, *-ge-*, *h*) grind off; sand(paper), smooth
'**Abschleppdienst** *m* MOT emergency road (*Br* breakdown) service
'**abschleppen** *v/t* (*sep*, *-ge-*, *h*) MOT (give *s.o.* a) tow; *police*: tow away
'**Abschlepp|seil** *n* towrope; **~wagen** *m Am* tow truck, *Br* breakdown lorry
'**abschließen** (*irr*, ***schließen***, *sep*, *-ge-*, *h*) **1.** *v/t* lock (up); close, finish; complete; take out (*insurance*); conclude (*research etc*); ***e-n Handel ~*** strike a bargain; ***sich ~*** shut o.s. off; → ***Wette***; **2.** *v/i* close, finish; **~d 1.** *adj* concluding; final; **2.** *adv*: ***~ sagte er*** he concluded by saying
'**Abschluss** *m* conclusion, close; **~prüfung** *f* final examination, finals *pl*, *esp Am a.* graduation; ***s-e ~ machen*** graduate (***an*** *dat* from); **~zeugnis** *n Am* diploma, *Br* school-leaving certificate
'**abschmecken** *v/t* (*sep*, *-ge-*, *h*) season
'**abschmieren** *v/t* (*sep*, *-ge-*, *h*) TECH lubricate, grease
'**abschminken** *v/t* (*sep*, *-ge-*, *h*) ***sich ~*** remove one's make-up
'**abschnallen** *v/t* (*sep*, *-ge-*, *h*) undo; take off (*skis*); ***sich ~*** MOT, AVIAT unfasten one's seat belt
'**abschneiden** (*irr*, ***schneiden***, *sep*, *-ge-*, *h*) **1.** *v/t* cut (off) (*a. fig*); ***j-m das Wort ~*** cut s.o. short; **2.** *v/i*: ***gut ~*** come off well
'**Abschnitt** *m* passage, section (*of book etc*); paragraph; MATH, BIOL segment; period (*of time*), stage (*of journey*), phase (*of development*); coupon, slip, stub (*of check etc*)
'**abschnittweise** *adv* section by section
'**abschrauben** *v/t* (*sep*, *-ge-*, *h*) unscrew
'**abschrecken** *v/t* (*sep*, *-ge-*, *h*) deter (***von*** from); GASTR douse *eggs etc* with cold water; **~d** *adj* deterrent; ***~es Beispiel*** warning example
'**Abschreckung** *f* (-; *-en*) deterrence
'**abschreiben** *v/t* (*irr*, ***schreiben***, *sep*, *-ge-*, *h*) copy; PED crib; ECON write off (*a.* F *fig*); '**Abschrift** *f* copy, duplicate
'**abschürfen** *v/t* (*sep*, *-ge-*, *h*) graze

**'Abschürfung** *f* (-; *-en*) abrasion
**Abschuss** *m* launch(ing) (*of rocket*); AVIAT shooting down, downing; kill; **~basis** *f* MIL launching base
**abschüssig** ['apʃʏsɪç] *adj* sloping; steep
**'Abschussliste** F *f*: ***auf der ~ stehen*** be on the hit list
**'Abschussrampe** *f* MIL launching pad
**'abschütteln** *v/t* (*sep*, *-ge-*, *h*) shake off
**'abschwächen** *v/t* (*sep*, *-ge-*, *h*) lessen, diminish
**'abschweifen** *fig v/i* (*sep*, *-ge-*, *sein*) digress (***von*** from)
**'Abschweifung** *f* (-; *-en*) digression
**absehbar** ['apze:ba:ɐ] *adj* foreseeable; ***in ~er*** (***auf ~e***) ***Zeit*** in the (for the) foreseeable future
**'absehen** *v/t* (*irr*, ***sehen***, *sep*, *-ge-*, *h*) foresee; ***es ist kein Ende abzusehen*** there is no end in sight; ***es abgesehen haben auf*** (*acc*) be after; ***~ von*** refrain from
**'abseilen** *v/refl* (*sep*, *-ge-*, *h*) descend by a rope, *Br a.* abseil; F make a getaway
**abseits** ['apzaɪts] *adv and prp* away *or* remote from; ***~ stehen*** *soccer*: be offside; *fig* be left out
**'Abseitsfalle** *f soccer*: offside trap
**'absenden** *v/t* ([*irr*, ***senden***,] *sep*, *-ge-*, *h*) send (off), dispatch; mail, *esp Br* post (*letter etc*)
**'Absender** *m* (*-s*; -) sender
**absetzbar** ['apzɛtsba:ɐ] *adj*: ***steuerlich ~*** deductible from tax
**'absetzen** (*sep*, *-ge-*, *h*) **1.** *v/t* take off (*hat*, *glasses etc*); set *or* put down (*bag etc*); drop (*passenger*); dismiss (*employee*); THEA, *film*: take off; deduct (*from tax*); depose (*king etc*); ECON sell; ***sich ~*** CHEM, GEOL settle, be deposited; **2.** *v/i*: ***ohne abzusetzen*** without stopping
**'Absetzung** *f* (-; *-en*) dismissal; deposition; THEA, *film*: withdrawal
**'Absicht** *f* (-; *-en*) intention; ***mit ~*** on purpose; **'absichtlich 1.** *adj* intentional; **2.** *adv* on purpose
**'absitzen** (*irr*, ***sitzen***, *sep*, *-ge-*) **1.** *v/i* (*sein*) dismount (***von*** from); **2.** *v/t* (*h*) serve (*sentence*); F sit out (*play etc*)
**absolut** [apzo'lu:t] *adj* absolute
**Absolvent** [apzɔl'vɛnt] *m* (*-en*; *-en*), **Absol'ventin** *f* (-; *-nen*) graduate; **absolvieren** [apzɔl'vi:rən] *v/t* (*no -ge-*, *h*) attend (*school*); complete (*studies*); graduate from (*college etc*)
**'absondern** *v/t* (*sep*, *-ge-*, *h*) separate; MED, BIOL secrete; ***sich ~*** cut o.s. off (***von*** from); **'Absonderung** *f* (-; *-en*) separation; MED, BIOL secretion
**absorbieren** [apzɔr'bi:rən] *v/t* (*no -ge-*, *h*) absorb (*a. fig*)
**'abspeichern** *v/t* (*sep*, *-ge-*, *h*) EDP store, save
**abspenstig** ['apʃpɛnstɪç] *adj*: ***j-m die Freundin ~ machen*** steal s.o.'s girlfriend
**absperren** *v/t* (*sep*, *-ge-*, *h*) lock; turn off (*water*, *gas etc*); block off (*road*); cordon off; **'Absperrung** *f* (-; *-en*) barrier; cordon
**'abspielen** *v/t* (*sep*, *-ge-*, *h*) play (*record etc*); SPORT pass (*the ball*); ***sich ~*** happen, take place
**'Absprache** *f* agreement
**'absprechen** *v/t* (*irr*, ***sprechen***, *sep*, *-ge-*, *h*) agree upon; arrange; ***j-m die Fähigkeit*** *etc* ***~*** dispute s.o.'s ability *etc*
**'abspringen** *v/i* (*irr*, ***springen***, *sep*, *-ge-*, *sein*) jump off; AVIAT jump, bail out; *fig* back out (***von*** of)
**'Absprung** *m* jump; SPORT take-off; *fig* ***den ~ schaffen*** make it
**'abspülen** *v/t* (*sep*, *-ge-*, *h*) rinse; wash up
**abstammen** *v/i* (*sep*, *no past participle*) be descended (***von*** from); CHEM, LING derive; **'Abstammung** *f* (-; *no pl*) descent; derivation; **'Abstammungslehre** *f* theory of the origin of species
**'Abstand** *m* distance (*a. fig*); interval; ***~ halten*** keep one's distance; *fig* ***mit ~*** by far
**abstatten** ['apʃtatən] *v/t* (*sep*, *-ge-*, *h*) ***j-m e-n Besuch ~*** pay a visit to s.o.
**'abstauben** *v/t* (*sep*, *-ge-*, *h*) dust; F *fig* sponge; swipe
**'Abstauber** F *m* (*-s*; -), **'Abstaubertor** *n* SPORT opportunist goal
**'abstechen** (*irr*, ***stechen***, *sep*, *-ge-*, *h*) **1.** *v/t* stick (*pig etc*); **2.** *v/i* contrast (***von*** with); **'Abstecher** *m* (*-s*; -) side-trip, excursion (*a. fig*)
**'abstecken** *v/t* (*sep*, *-ge-*, *h*) mark out
**'abstehen** *v/i* (*irr*, ***stehen***, *sep*, *-ge-*, *h*) stick out, protrude; → ***abgestanden***
**'absteigen** *v/i* (*irr*, ***steigen***, *sep*, *-ge-*, *sein*) get off (*a horse etc*); climb down;

stay (**in** *dat* at); SPORT *Am* be moved down to a lower division, *Br* be relegated; **'Absteiger** *m* (*-s*; -) SPORT *Br* relegated club
**'abstellen** *v/t* (*sep*, *-ge-*, *h*) put down; leave (*s.th. with s.o.*); turn off (*gas etc*); park (*car*); *fig* put an end to *s.th.*
**'Abstellgleis** *n* RAIL siding; ***j-n aufs ~ schieben*** F push s.o. aside
**'Abstellraum** *m* storeroom
**'abstempeln** *v/t* (*sep*, *-ge-*, *h*) stamp
**'absterben** *v/i* (*irr*, ***sterben***, *sep*, *-ge-*, *sein*) die off; *limb*: go numb
**Abstieg** ['apʃtiːk] *m* (*-[e]s*; *-e*) descent; *fig* decline; SPORT *Br* relegation
**'abstimmen** *v/i* (*sep*, *-ge-*, *h*) vote (**über** *acc* on)
**'Abstimmung** *f* vote; *radio*: tuning
**Abstinenzler** [apsti'nɛntslɐ] *m* (*-s*; -) teetotal(l)er
**'Abstoß** *m* SPORT goal-kick
**'abstoßen** *v/t* (*irr*, ***stoßen***, *sep*, *-ge-*, *h*) repel; MED reject; push off (*boat*); F get rid of *s.th.*; **~d** *fig adj* repulsive
**abstrakt** [ap'strakt] *adj* abstract
**'abstreiten** *v/t* (*irr*, ***streiten***, *sep*, *-ge-*, *h*) deny
**'Abstrich** *m* MED smear; *pl* ECON cuts; *fig* reservations
**'abstufen** *v/t* (*sep*, *-ge-*, *h*) graduate; gradate (*colors*)
**'abstumpfen** (*sep*, *-ge-*) **1.** *v/t* (*h*) blunt, dull (*a. fig*); **2.** *fig v/i* (*sein*) become unfeeling
**'Absturz** *m*, **'abstürzen** *v/i* (*sep*, *-ge-*, *sein*) fall; AVIAT, EDP crash
**'absuchen** *v/t* (*sep*, *-ge-*, *h*) search (***nach*** for)
**absurd** [ap'zʊrt] *adj* absurd, preposterous
**Abszess** [aps'tsɛs] *m* (*-es*; *-e*) MED abscess
**Abt** [apt] *m* (*-[e]s*; *Äbte* ['ɛptə]) REL abbot
**'abtasten** *v/t* (*sep*, *-ge-*, *h*) feel (for); MED palpate; frisk; TECH, EDP scan
**'abtauen** *v/t* (*sep*, *-ge-*, *h*) defrost
**Abtei** [ap'tai] *f* (-; *-en*) REL abbey
**Abteil** [ap'tail] *n* (*-[e]s*; *-e*) RAIL compartment
**'abteilen** *v/t* (*sep*, *-ge-*, *h*) divide; ARCH partition off
**Ab'teilung** *f* (-; *-en*) department (*a.* ECON); ward (*of hospital*); MIL detachment; **Ab'teilungsleiter** *m* head of (a) department; *Am* floorwalker, *Br* shopwalker
**Äbtissin** [ɛp'tɪsɪn] *f* (-; *-nen*) REL abbess
**'abtöten** *v/t* (*sep*, *-ge-*, *h*) kill (*bacteria etc*); *fig* deaden (*feelings etc*)
**'abtragen** *v/t* (*irr*, ***tragen***, *sep*, *-ge-*, *h*) wear out (*clothes*); clear away (*dishes etc*); pay off (*debt*)
**'Abtrans,port** *m* transportation
**'abtreiben** (*irr*, ***treiben***, *sep*, *-ge-*) **1.** *v/i* MED (*h*) have an abortion; MAR, AVIAT (*sein*) be blown off course; **2.** *v/t* (*h*) MED abort; **'Abtreibung** *f* (-; *-en*) abortion; ***e-e ~ vornehmen*** perform an abortion
**'abtrennen** *v/t* (*sep*, *-ge-*, *h*) detach; separate; MED sever
**'abtreten** (*irr*, ***treten***, *sep*, *-ge-*) **1.** *v/t* (*h*) wear down (*heels*); wipe (*one's feet*); *fig* give up (***an*** *acc* to); **2.** *v/i* (*sein*) resign; THEA exit; **'Abtreter** *m* (*-s*; -) doormat
**'abtrocknen** (*sep*, *-ge-*, *h*) **1.** *v/t* dry; ***sich ~*** dry o.s. off; **2.** *v/i* dry the dishes, *Br a.* dry up
**abtrünnig** ['aptrʏnɪç] *adj* unfaithful, disloyal; **'Abtrünnige** [-nɪgə] *m*, *f* (*-n*; *-n*) renegade, turncoat
**abtun** *v/t* (*irr*, ***tun***, *sep*, *-ge-*, *h*) dismiss (***als*** as), brush *s.o.*, *s.th.* aside
**abwägen** ['apvɛːgən] *v/t* (*irr*, ***wägen***, *sep*, *-ge-*, *h*) weigh (**gegen** against)
**'abwählen** *v/t* (*sep*, *-ge-*, *h*) vote out
**'abwälzen** *v/t* (*sep*, *-ge-*, *h*) ***et. auf j-n ~*** shove s.th. off on (to) s.o.
**'abwandeln** *v/t* (*sep*, *-ge-*, *h*) vary, modify
**'abwandern** *v/i* (*sep*, *-ge-*, *sein*) migrate (**von** from; ***nach*** to); **'Abwanderung** *f* migration
**'Abwandlung** *f* modification, variation
**'Abwärme** *f* TECH waste heat
**Abwart** ['apvart] *m* (*-s*; *-e*) *Swiss* → ***Hausmeister***
**'abwarten** (*sep*, *-ge-*, *h*) **1.** *v/t* wait for, await; **2.** *v/i* wait; ***warten wir ab!*** let's wait and see!; ***wart nur ab!*** just wait!
**abwärts** ['apvɛrts] *adv* down, downward(s)
**Abwasch** ['apvaʃ] *m* (*-[e]s*; *no pl*) ***den ~ machen*** do the washing-up
**'abwaschbar** *adj* washable
**'abwaschen** (*irr*, ***waschen***, *sep*, *-ge-*, *h*) **1.** *v/t* wash off; **2.** *v/i* do the dishes, *Br a.* wash up

'**Abwaschwasser** *n* dishwater
'**Abwasser** *n* TECH waste water, sewage; **~aufbereitung** *f* TECH sewage treatment
'**abwechseln** *v/i* (*sep*, *-ge-*, *h*) alternate; ***sich mit j-m ~*** take turns (***bei et.*** at [doing] s.th.); **~d** *adv* by turns
'**Abwechslung** *f* (-; *-en*) change; ***zur ~*** for a change; '**abwechslungsreich** *adj* varied; colo(u)rful
'**Abweg** *m*: ***auf ~e geraten*** go astray
**abwegig** ['apveːgɪç] *adj* absurd, unrealistic
'**Abwehr** *f* (-; *no pl*) defen|se, *Br* -ce (*a.* SPORT); warding off (*of blow etc*); save (*of ball*)
'**abwehren** *v/t* (*sep*, *-ge-*, *h*) ward off (*blow etc*); beat off; SPORT block
'**Abwehr|fehler** *m* SPORT defensive error; **~kräfte** *pl* MED resistance; **~spieler** *m* SPORT defender; **~stoffe** *pl* MED antibodies
'**abweichen** *v/i* (*irr*, **weichen**, *sep*, *-ge-*, *sein*) deviate (**von** from); digress
'**Abweichung** *f* (-; *-en*) deviation
'**abweisen** *v/t* (*irr*, **weisen**, *sep*, *-ge-*, *h*) turn away; rebuff; decline, turn down (*request*, *offer etc*); **~d** *adj* unfriendly
'**abwenden** *v/t* ([*irr*, **wenden**,] *sep*, *-ge-*, *h*) turn away (*a.* **sich ~**) (**von** from); avert (*tragedy etc*)
'**abwerfen** *v/t* (*irr*, **werfen**, *sep*, *-ge-*, *h*) throw off; AVIAT drop; BOT shed (*leaves*); ECON yield (*profit*)
'**abwerten** *v/t* (*sep*, *-ge-*, *h*) ECON devalue; **~d** *fig adj* disparaging
'**Abwertung** *f* ECON devaluation
'**abwesend** *adj* absent
'**Abwesenheit** *f* (-; *no pl*) absence
**abwickeln** *v/t* (*sep*, *-ge-*, *h*) unwind; ECON handle; transact (*business*)
'**abwiegen** *v/t* (*irr*, **wiegen**, *sep*, *-ge-*, *h*) weigh (out)
'**abwischen** *v/t* (*sep*, *-ge-*, *h*) wipe (off)
'**Abwurf** *m* dropping; *soccer*: throw-out
'**abwürgen** F *v/t* (*sep*, *-ge-*, *h*) MOT stall; *fig* stifle; '**abzahlen** *v/t* (*sep*, *-ge-*, *h*) make *monthly etc* payments for; pay off; '**abzählen** *v/t* (*sep*, *-ge-*, *h*) count
'**Abzahlung** *f*: ***et. auf ~ kaufen*** *Am* buy s.th. on the instalment plan (*Br* on hire purchase)
'**abzapfen** *v/t* (*sep*, *-ge-*, *h*) tap, draw off
'**Abzeichen** *n* badge; medal
'**abzeichnen** *v/t* (*sep*, *-ge-*, *h*) copy, draw; sign, initial; ***sich ~*** (begin to) show; stand out (***gegen*** against)
'**Abziehbild** *n* *Am* decal, *Br* transfer
'**abziehen** (*irr*, **ziehen**, *sep*, *-ge-*) **1.** *v/t* (*h*) take off, remove; MATH subtract; strip (*bed*); take out (*key*); ***das Fell ~*** skin; **2.** *v/i* (*sein*) go away; MIL withdraw; *smoke*: escape; *storm*, *clouds*: move off
'**Abzug** *m* ECON deduction; discount; MIL withdrawal; PRINT copy; PHOT print; *gun*: trigger; TECH vent, outlet; cooker hood
**abzüglich** ['aptsyːklɪç] *prp* less, minus
'**abzweigen** (*sep*, *-ge-*) **1.** *v/t* (*h*) divert (*resources etc*) (**für** to); **2.** *v/i* (*sein*) *path etc*: branch off
'**Abzweigung** *f* (-; *-en*) junction
**ach** [ax] *int* oh!; ***~ je!*** oh dear!; ***~ so!*** I see; ***~ was!*** *surprised*: really?, *annoyed*: of course not!, nonsense!
**Achse** ['aksə] *f* (-; *-n*) TECH axle; MATH *etc* axis; F ***auf ~ sein*** be on the move
**Achsel** ['aksəl] *f* (-; *-n*) ANAT shoulder; ***die ~n zucken*** shrug one's shoulders
'**Achselhöhle** *f* ANAT armpit
**acht** [axt] *adj* eight; ***heute in ~ Tagen*** a week from today, *esp Br* today week; (***heute***) ***vor ~ Tagen*** a week ago (today)
**Acht** *f*: ***~ geben*** be careful; pay attention (***auf*** *acc* to); take care (***auf*** *acc* of); ***gib ~!*** look *or* watch out!, be careful!; ***außer ~ lassen*** disregard; ***sich in ~ nehmen*** be careful, look *or* watch out (***vor*** *dat* for)
**achte** ['axtə] *adj* eighth
'**achteckig** *adj* octagonal
**Achtel** ['axtəl] *n* (*-s*; -) eighth (part)
**achten** (*ge-*, *h*) **1.** *v/t* respect; **2.** *v/i*: ***~ auf*** (*acc*) pay attention to; keep an eye on; watch; be careful with; ***darauf ~, dass*** see to it that
**ächten** ['ɛçtən] *v/t* (*ge-*, *h*) ban; *esp* HIST outlaw
**Achter** ['axtɐ] *m* (*-s*; -) *rowing*: eight
'**Achterbahn** *f* roller coaster
'**achtfach** *adj and adv* eightfold
'**achtlos** *adj* careless, heedless
'**Achtung** *f* (-; *no pl*) respect (***vor*** *dat* for); ***~!*** look out!; MIL attention!; ***~! ~!*** attention please!; ***~! Fertig! Los!*** On your marks! Get set! Go!; ***~ Stufe!*** *Am* caution: step!, *Br* mind the step!

**'achtzehn** *adj* eighteen
**'achtzehnte** *adj* eighteenth
**achtzig** ['axtsıç] *adj* eighty; ***die ~er Jahre*** the eighties; **~ste** *adj* eightieth
**ächzen** ['ɛçtsən] *v/i (ge-, h)* groan (***vor*** *dat* with)
**Acker** ['akɐ] *m (-s; Äcker* ['ɛkɐ]) field; **~bau** *m (-[e]s; no pl)* agriculture; farming; ***~ und Viehzucht*** crop and stock farming; **~land** *n (-[e]s; no pl)* farmland
**'ackern** F *v/i (ge-, h)* slog (away)
**Adapter** [a'daptɐ] *m (-s; -)* TECH adapter
**addieren** [a'di:rən] *v/t (no -ge-, h)* add (up); **Addition** [adi'tsio:n] *f (-; -en)* addition, adding up
**Adel** ['a:dəl] *m (-s; no pl)* aristocracy
**'adeln** *v/t (ge-, h)* ennoble (*a. fig*); *Br* knight
**Ader** ['a:dɐ] *f (-; -n)* ANAT blood vessel, vein
**Adjektiv** ['atjɛkti:f] *n (-s; -e)* LING adjective
**Adler** ['a:dlɐ] *m (-s; -)* ZO eagle
**adlig** ['a:dlıç] *adj* noble; **Adlige** ['a:dlıgə] *m, f (-n; -n)* noble|man (-woman)
**Admiral** [atmi'ra:l] *m (-s; -e)* MAR admiral
**adoptieren** [adɔp'ti:rən] *v/t (no -ge-, h)* adopt; **Adoptivkind** [adɔp'ti:f-] *n* adopted child
**Adressbuch** [a'drɛs-] *n* directory
**Adresse** [a'drɛsə] *f (-; -n)* address
**adressieren** [adrɛ'si:rən] *v/t (no -ge-, h)* address (***an*** *acc* to)
**Advent** [at'vɛnt] *m (-[e]s; no pl)* REL Advent; Advent Sunday
**Ad'ventszeit** *f* Christmas season
**Adverb** [at'vɛrp] *n (-s; Adverbien* [at'vɛrbĭən]) LING adverb
**Aerobic** [ɛ'ro:bık] *n (-s; no pl)* aerobics
**Affäre** [a'fɛ:rə] *f (-; -n)* affair
**Affe** ['afə] *m (-n; -n)* ZO monkey; ape
**Affekt** [a'fɛkt] *m (-[e]s; -e)* ***im ~*** in the heat of passion (*a.* JUR)
**affektiert** [afɛk'ti:ɐt] *adj* affected
**Afrika** ['a:frika] Africa; **Afrikaner** [afri'ka:nɐ] *m (-s; -)*, **Afri'kanerin** [-nərın] *f (-; -nen)*, **afri'kanisch** *adj* African
**After** ['aftɐ] *m (-s; -)* ANAT anus
**AG** ABBR *of* ***Aktiengesellschaft*** *Am* (stock) corporation, *Br* PLC, public limited company

**Agent** [a'gɛnt] *m (-en; -en)*, **A'gentin** *f (-; -nen)* agent; POL (secret) agent
**Agentur** [agɛn'tu:ɐ] *f (-; -en)* agency
**Aggression** [agrɛ'sĭo:n] *f (-; -en)* aggression; **aggressiv** [agrɛ'si:f] *adj* aggressive; **Aggressivität** [agrɛsivi'tɛ:t] *f (-; no pl)* aggressiveness
**Agitator** [agi'ta:to:ɐ] *m (-s; -en* [-ta'to:rən]) agitator
**ah** [a:] *int* ah!
**äh** [ɛ:] *int* er; *disgusted*: ugh!
**aha** [a'ha] *int* I see!, oh!
**A'ha-Erlebnis** *n* aha-experience
**Ahn** [a:n] *m (-[e]s, -en; -en)* ancestor, *pl a.* forefathers
**ähneln** ['ɛ:nəln] *v/i (ge-, h)* resemble, look like
**ahnen** ['a:nən] *v/t (ge-, h)* suspect; foresee, know
**ähnlich** ['ɛ:nlıç] *adj* similar (*dat* to); ***j-m ~ sehen*** look like s.o.
**'Ähnlichkeit** *f (-; -en)* likeness, resemblance, similarity (***mit*** to)
**'Ahnung** *f (-; -en)* presentiment, *a.* foreboding; notion, idea; ***ich habe keine ~*** I have no idea; **'ahnungslos** *adj* unsuspecting, innocent
**Ahorn** ['a:hɔrn] *m (-s, -e)* BOT maple
**Ähre** ['ɛ:rə] *f (-; -n)* BOT ear; spike
**Aids** [eıdz] *n (-; no pl)* MED AIDS
**'Aids|-Kranke** *m, f* MED AIDS victim *or* sufferer; **~test** *m* MED AIDS test
**Airbag** ['ɛəbæg] *m (-s; -s)* MOT airbag
**Akademie** [akade'mi:] *f (-; -n)* academy, college; **Akademiker(in)** [aka'de:mikɐ (-kərın)] *(-s; -/-; -nen)* university graduate; **akademisch** [-'de:mıʃ] *adj* academic
**akklimatisieren** [aklimati'zi:rən] *v/refl (no -ge-, h)* acclimatize (***an*** *acc* to)
**Akkord** [a'kɔrt] *m (-[e]s; -e)* MUS chord; ***im ~*** ECON by the piece *or* job; **~arbeit** *f* ECON piecework; **~arbeiter(in)** ECON pieceworker
**Akkordeon** [a'kɔrdeɔn] *n (-s; -s)* MUS accordion
**Ak'kordlohn** *m* ECON piece wages
**Akku** ['aku] F *m (-s; -s)*, **Akkumulator** [akumu'la:to:ɐ] *m (-s; -en* [-la'to:rən]) TECH (storage) battery, *Br a.* accumulator
**Akkusativ** ['akuzati:f] *m (-s; -e)* LING accusative (case)
**Akne** ['aknə] *f (-; -n)* MED acne

**Akrobat** [akro'ba:t] *m* (*-en*; *-en*), **Akro'batin** *f* (-; *-nen*) acrobat; **akro'batisch** *adj* acrobatic
**Akt** [akt] *m* (-[*e*]*s*; *-e*) act(ion); THEA act; PAINT, PHOT nude
**Akte** ['aktə] *f* (-; *-n*) file; *pl* files, records; ***zu den ~n legen*** file
**'Akten|deckel** *m* folder; **~koffer** *m* attaché case; **~ordner** *m* file; **~tasche** *f* briefcase; **~zeichen** *n* reference (number)
**Aktie** ['aktsĭə] *f* (-; *-n*) ECON share, *esp Am* stock; **'Aktiengesellschaft** *f Am* corporation, *Br* joint-stock company
**Aktion** [ak'tsĭo:n] *f* (-; *-en*) campaign, drive; MIL *etc* operation; ***in ~*** in action
**Aktionär** [aktsĭo'nɛ:ɐ] *m* (*-s*; *-e*), **Ak-tio'närin** *f* (-; *-nen*) ECON shareholder, *esp Am* stockholder
**aktiv** [ak'ti:f] *adj* active
**Aktiv** ['akti:f] *n* (*-s*; *no pl*) LING active voice; **Aktivist** [akti'vist] *m* (*-en*; *-en*) *esp* POL activist
**Ak'tivurlaub** *m* activity vacation
**aktualisieren** [aktŭali'zi:rən] *v/t* (*no -ge-*, *h*) update
**aktuell** [aktŭ'ɛl] *adj* topical; current; up-to-date; TV, *radio*: ***e-e ~e Sendung*** a current affairs *or* news feature
**Akupunktur** [akupʊŋk'tu:ɐ] *f* (-; *-en*) MED acupuncture
**Akustik** [a'kʊstɪk] *f* (-; *no pl*) acoustics
**a'kustisch** *adj* acoustic
**akut** [a'ku:t] *adj* urgent (*problem etc*); *a.* MED acute
**Akzent** [ak'tsɛnt] *m* (-[*e*]*s*; *-e*) accent; stress (*a. fig*)
**akzeptabel** [aktsɛp'ta:bəl] *adj* acceptable; reasonable (*price etc*)
**akzeptieren** [aktsɛp'ti:rən] *v/t* (*no -ge-*, *h*) accept
**Alarm** [a'larm] *m* (-[*e*]*s*; *-e*) alarm; ***~ schlagen*** sound the alarm; **~anlage** *f* alarm system; **~bereitschaft** *f*: ***in ~*** on standby, on the alert
**alarmieren** [alar'mi:rən] *v/t* (*no -ge-*, *h*) call; alert; **~d** *adj* alarming
**albern** ['albɐn] *adj* silly, foolish
**Album** ['albʊm] *n* (*-s*; *Alben* ['albən]) album (*a. record*)
**Algen** ['algən] *pl* BOT algae; **~pest** *f* plague of algae, algal bloom
**Algebra** ['algəbra] *f* (-; *no pl*) MATH algebra
**Alibi** ['a:libi] *n* (*-s*; *-s*) JUR alibi
**Alimente** [ali'mɛntə] *pl* JUR alimony
**Alkohol** ['alkoho:l] *m* (*-s*; *no pl*) alcohol; **'alkoholfrei** *adj* nonalcoholic, soft; **Alkoholiker(in)** [alko'ho:likɐ (-kərɪn)] (*-s*; *-/-*; *-nen*) alcoholic; **alko'holisch** *adj* alcoholic; **Alkoholismus** [alkoho'lɪsmʊs] *m* (-; *no pl*) alcoholism; **alkoholsüchtig** *adj* addicted to alcohol; **Alkoholtest** *m* MOT breath test
**all** [al] *indef pron and adj* all; ***~es*** everything; ***~es*** (***Beliebige***) anything; ***~e*** (***Leute***) everybody; anybody; ***~e beide*** both of them; ***wir ~e*** all of us; ***~es in ~em*** all in all; ***auf ~e Fälle*** in any case; ***~e drei Tage*** every three days; → ***Art, Gute, vor***
**All** *n* (*-s*; *no pl*) universe; (outer) space
**alle** ['alə] F *adj*: ***~ sein*** be all gone; ***mein Geld ist ~*** I'm out of money
**Allee** [a'le:] *f* (-; *-n*) avenue
**allein** [a'lain] *adj and adv* alone; lonely; by o.s.; ***ganz ~*** all alone; ***er hat es ganz ~ gemacht*** he did it all by himself; ***~ stehend*** single
**Al'lein|erziehende** *m*, *f* (*-n*; *-n*) single parent; **~gang** *m*: ***im ~*** single-handedly, solo
**alleinig** [a'lainɪç] *adj* sole
**Al'leinsein** *n* (*-s*; *no pl*) loneliness
**Allerbeste** ['alɐ'bɛstə]: ***der*** (***die***, ***das***) ***~*** the best of all, the very best
**allerdings** ['alɐ'dɪŋs] *adv* however, though; ***~!*** certainly!, *esp Am* F sure!
**'aller'erste** *adj* very first
**Allergie** [alɛr'gi:] *f* (-; *-n*) MED allergy (***gegen*** to); **allergisch** [a'lɛrgɪʃ] *adj* allergic (***gegen*** to)
**'aller'hand** F *adj* a good deal (of); ***das ist ja ~!*** that's a bit much!
**'Aller'heiligen** *n* REL All Saints' Day
**allerlei** ['alɐ'lai] *adj* all kinds *or* sorts of
**'aller|'letzte** *adj* last of all, very last; **~'liebst 1.** *adj* (most) lovely; **2.** *adv*: ***am ~en mögen*** like best of all; **~'meiste** *adj* (by far the) most; **~'nächste** *adj* very next; ***in ~r Zeit*** in the very near future; **~'neu(e)ste** *adj* very latest
**'Aller'seelen** *n* REL All Souls' Day
**allerseits** ['alɐ'zaits] *adv* F: ***Tag ~!*** hi, everybody!
**'aller'wenigst** *adv*: ***am ~en*** least of all
**allesamt** ['alə'zamt] *adv* all together

**'allge'mein** 1. *adj* general; common; universal; 2. *adv*: ***im Allgemeinen*** in general, generally; ***~ verständlich*** intelligible (to all), popular
**'Allge'meinbildung** *f* general education
**'Allge'meinheit** *f* (-; *no pl*) (general) public
**All'heilmittel** *n* cure-all (*a. fig*)
**Allianz** [a'ljants] *f* (-; *-en*) alliance
**Alligator** [ali'ga:to:ɐ] *m* (*-s*; *-en*) alligator
**Alliierte** [ali'i:ɐtə]: ***die ~n*** *pl* POL the Allies
**'all|'jährlich** *adv* every year; ***~ stattfindend*** annual; **~'mächtig** *adj* omnipotent; Almighty (*God*)
**allmählich** [al'mɛ:lɪç] 1. *adj* gradual; 2. *adv* gradually
**'Allradantrieb** *m* MOT four-wheel drive
**allseitig** ['alzaitɪç] *adv*: ***~ interessiert sein*** have all-round interests
**'Alltag** *m* everyday life
**'all|'täglich** *adj* everyday; *fig a.* ordinary; **~'wissend** *adj* omniscient
**'allzu** *adv* (all) too; ***~ viel*** too much
**Alm** [alm] *f* (-; *-en*) alpine pasture, alp
**Almosen** ['almo:zən] *n* (*-s*; -) alms
**'Alpdruck** *m* (-[*e*]*s*; *no pl*) nightmare (*a. fig*)
**Alphabet** [alfa'be:t] *n* (-[*e*]*s*; *-e*] alphabet; **alpha'betisch** *adj* alphabetical
**alpin** [al'pi:n] *adj* alpine
**'Alptraum** *m* nightmare (*a. fig*)
**als** [als] *cj time*: when; while; *after comp*: than; ***~ ich ankam*** when I arrived; ***~ Kind (Geschenk)*** as a child (present); ***älter ~*** older than; ***~ ob*** as if, as though; ***nichts ~*** nothing but
**also** ['alzo] *cj* so, therefore; F well, you know; ***~ gut!*** very well (then)!, all right (then)!; ***~ doch*** so ... after all; ***du willst ~ gehen*** *etc?* so you want to go *etc?*
**alt** [alt] *adj* old; HIST ancient; classical (*language*); ***ein 12 Jahre ~er Junge*** a twelve-year-old boy
**Alt** *m* (*-s*; *no pl*) MUS alto
**Altar** [al'ta:ɐ] *m* (*-s*; *Altäre* [al'tɛ:rə]) REL altar
**'Alte** *m, f* (*-n*; *-n*) ***der ~*** the old man (*a. fig*); the boss; ***die ~*** the old woman (*a. fig*); ***die ~n*** *pl* the old
**'Altenheim** *n* → ***Altersheim***
**'Altenpfleger(in)** geriatric nurse
**Alter** ['altɐ] *n* (*-s*; *no pl*) age; old age; ***im ~ von ...*** at the age of ...; ***er ist in deinem ~*** he's your age
**älter** ['ɛltɐ] *adj* older; ***mein ~er Bruder*** my elder brother; ***ein ~er Herr*** an elderly gentleman
**'altern** *v/i* (*ge-*, *sein*) grow old, age
**alternativ** [altɛrna'ti:f] *adj* alternative; POL ecological, green; *a.* counterculture (*movement etc*)
**Alternative**[1] [altɛrna'ti:və] *f* (-; *-n*) alternative; option, choice
**Alterna'tive**[2] *m, f* (*-n*; *-n*) ecologist, member of the counterculture movement
**'Alters|grenze** *f* age limit; retirement age; **~heim** *n* old people's home; **~rente** *f* old-age pension; **~schwäche** *f* (-; *no pl*) infirmity; ***an ~ sterben*** die of old age; **~versorgung** *f* old age pension (scheme)
**'Altertum** *n* (*-s*; *no pl*) antiquity
**'Altglascon,tainer** *m Am* glass recycling bin, *Br* bottle bank
**'altklug** *adj* precocious
**'Altlasten** *pl* residual pollution
**'Altme,tall** *n* scrap (metal)
**'altmodisch** *adj* old-fashioned
**'Altöl** *n* waste oil
**'Altpa,pier** *n* waste paper
**'altsprachlich** *adj*: ***~es Gymnasium*** *appr* classical secondary school
**'Altstadt** *f* old town; **~sa,nierung** *f* town-cent|er (*Br* -re) rehabilitation
**'Altwarenhändler** *m* second-hand dealer
**Alt'weibersommer** *m* Indian summer; gossamer
**Aluminium** [alu'mi:njʊm] *n* (*-s*; *no pl*) alumin(i)um
**am** [am] *prp* at the (*window etc*); *time*: in the (*morning etc*); at the (*weekend etc*); on (*Sunday etc*); ***~ 1. Mai*** on May 1st; ***~ Tage*** during the day; ***~ Himmel*** in the sky; ***~ meisten*** most; ***~ Leben*** alive
**Amateur** [ama'tø:ɐ] *m* (*-s*; *-e*) amateur; **~funker** *m* radio amateur, F radio ham
**Amboss** ['ambɔs] *m* (*-es*; *-e*) anvil
**ambulant** [ambu'lant] *adv*: ***~ behandelt werden*** MED get outpatient treatment
**Ambulanz** [ambu'lants] *f* (-; *-en*) MED outpatients' department; MOT ambulance
**Ameise** ['a:maizə] *f* (-; *-n*) ZO ant

'**Ameisenhaufen** *m* ZO anthill
**Amerika** [a'me:rika] America
**Amerikaner** [ameri'ka:nɐ] *m* (*-s*; -), **Ameri'kanerin** [-nərɪn] *f* (-; *-nen*), **ameri'kanisch** *adj* American
**Amnestie** [amnɛs'ti:] *f* (-; *-n*), **amnes'tieren** *v/t* (*no -ge-*, *h*) JUR amnesty
**Amok** ['a:mɔk] *m*: ~ ***laufen*** run amok
**Ampel** ['ampəl] *f* (-; *-n*) traffic light(s)
**Amphibie** [am'fi:bjə] *f* (-; *-n*) ZO amphibian
**Ampulle** [am'pʊlə] *f* (-; *-n*) ampoule
**Amputation** [amputa'tsjo:n] *f* (-; *-en*) MED amputation; **amputieren** [ampu'ti:rən] *v/t* (*no -ge-*, *h*) MED amputate
**Amsel** ['amzəl] *f* (-; *-n*) ZO blackbird
**Amt** [amt] *n* (-[*e*]*s*; *Ämter* ['ɛmtɐ]) office, department, *esp Am* bureau; position; duty, function; TEL exchange
'**amtlich** *adj* official
'**Amts|arzt** *m* medical examiner (*Br* officer); **~einführung** *f* inauguration; **~geheimnis** *n* official secret; **~geschäfte** *pl* official duties; **~zeichen** *n* TEL dial (*Br* dialling) tone; **~zeit** *f* term (of office)
**Amulett** [amu'lɛt] *n* (-[*e*]*s*; *-e*) amulet, (lucky) charm
**amüsant** [amy'zant] *adj* amusing, entertaining
**amüsieren** [amy'zi:rən] *v/t* (*no -ge-*, *h*) amuse; ***sich*** ~ enjoy o.s., have a good time; ***sich*** ~ ***über*** (*acc*) laugh at
**an** [an] **1.** *prp*: ~ ***der Themse*** (***Küste***, ***Wand***) on the Thames (coast, wall); ~ ***s-m Schreibtisch*** at his desk; ~ ***der Hand*** by the hand; ~ ***der Arbeit*** at work; ~ ***den Hausaufgaben sitzen*** sit over one's homework; ***et. schicken*** ~ (*acc*) send s.th. to; ***sich lehnen*** ~ (*acc*) lean against; ~ ***die Tür*** *etc* ***klopfen*** knock at the door *etc*; ~ ***e-m Sonntagmorgen*** on a Sunday morning; ~ ***dem Tag, ...*** on the day ...; ~ ***Weihnachten*** *etc* at Christmas *etc*; → ***Mangel, Stelle, sterben***; **2.** *adv* on (*a. light etc*); ***von jetzt*** (***da***, ***heute***) ~ from now (that time, today) on; ***München*** ~ ***16.45*** arrival Munich 4.45 p.m.
**Anabolikum** [ana'bo:likʊm] *n* (*-s*; *-ka*) PHARM anabolic steroid
**analog** [ana'lo:k] *adj* analogous
**Ana'log...** *in cpds* analog(ue) (*computer etc*)
**Analphabet** [anˀalfa'be:t] *m* (*-en*; *-en*), **Analpha'betin** *f* (-; *-nen*) illiterate (person)
**Analyse** [ana'ly:zə] *f* (-; *-n*) analysis
**analysieren** [analy'zi:rən] *v/t* (*no -ge-*, *h*) analy|ze, *Br* -se
**Ananas** ['ananas] *f* (-; -, *-se*) BOT pineapple
**Anarchie** [anar'çi:] *f* (-; *-n*) anarchy
**Anatomie** [anato'mi:] *f* (-; *-n*) anatomy
**anatomisch** [ana'to:mɪʃ] *adj* anatomical
'**anbahnen** *v/t* (*sep*, *-ge-*, *h*) pave the way for; ***sich*** ~ be developing; be impending
'**Anbau** *m* (-[*e*]*s*; *-ten*) a) AGR (*no pl*) cultivation, b) ARCH annex, extension
'**anbauen** *v/t* (*sep*, *-ge-*, *h*) AGR cultivate, grow; ARCH add (***an*** *acc* to), build on
'**anbehalten** *v/t* (*irr*, ***halten***, *sep*, *no -ge-*, *h*) keep on
**an'bei** *adv* ECON enclosed
'**anbeißen** (*irr*, ***beißen***, *sep*, *-ge-*, *h*) **1.** *v/t* take a bite of; **2.** *v/i fish*: bite; *fig* take the bait; '**anbellen** *v/t* (*sep*, *-ge-*, *h*) bark at; '**anbeten** *v/t* (*sep*, *-ge-*, *h*) adore, worship (*a. fig*)
'**Anbetracht** *m*: ***in*** ~ (***dessen***, ***dass***) considering (that)
'**anbetteln** *v/t* (*sep*, *-ge-*, *h*) ***j-n um et.*** ~ beg s.o. for s.th.; '**anbiedern** [-bi:dɐn] *v/refl* (*sep*, *-ge-*, *h*) curry favo(u)r (***bei*** with); '**anbieten** *v/t* (*irr*, ***bieten***, *sep*, *-ge-*, *h*) offer; '**anbinden** *v/t* (*irr*, ***binden***, *sep*, *-ge-*, *h*) tie up; ~ ***an*** (*acc or dat*) tie to
'**Anblick** *m* sight; '**anblicken** *v/t* (*sep*, *-ge-*, *h*) look at; glance at
'**anbohren** *v/t* (*sep*, *-ge-*, *h*) tap
'**anbrechen** (*irr*, ***brechen***, *sep*, *-ge-*) **1.** *v/t* (*h*) break into (*supplies*); open; **2.** *v/i* (*sein*) begin; *day*: break; *night*: fall
'**anbrennen** *v/i* (*irr*, ***brennen***, *sep*, *-ge-*, *sein*) burn (*a.* ~ ***lassen***)
'**anbringen** *v/t* (*irr*, ***bringen***, *sep*, *-ge-*, *h*) fix (***an*** *dat* to)
'**Anbruch** *m* (-[*e*]*s*; *no pl*) beginning; ***bei*** ~ ***der Nacht*** at nightfall
'**anbrüllen** *v/t* (*sep*, *-ge-*, *h*) roar at
**Andacht** ['andaxt] *f* (-; *-en*) REL a) (*no pl*) devotion, b) service; prayers
**andächtig** ['andɛçtɪç] *adj* REL devout
'**andauern** *v/i* (*sep*, *-ge-*, *h*) continue, go

on, last; **~d** *adj and adv* → **dauernd**
**'Andenken** *n* (-*s*; -) keepsake; souvenir (*both*: **an** *acc* of); **zum ~ an** (*acc*) in memory of
**andere** ['andərə] *adj and indef pron* other; different; **mit ~n Worten** in other words; **am ~n Morgen** the next morning; **et.** (**nichts**) **~s** s.th. (nothing) else; **nichts ~s als** nothing but; **die ~n** the others; **alle ~n** everybody else
**andererseits** ['andərɐ'zaits] *adv* on the other hand
**ändern** ['ɛndɐn] *v/t* (*ge-*, *h*) change; alter (*clothes*); **ich kann es nicht ~** I can't help it; **sich ~** change
**'andern'falls** *adv* otherwise
**anders** ['andɐs] *adv* different(ly); **jemand ~** somebody else; **~ werden** change; **~ sein** (**als**) be different (from); **es geht nicht ~** there is no other way; **~herum 1.** *adv* the other way round; **2.** F *adj* queer; **~wo(hin)** *adv* elsewhere
**anderthalb** ['andɐt'halp] *adj* one and a half
**'Änderung** *f* (-; -*en*) change; alteration
**'andeuten** *v/t* (*sep*, *-ge-*, *h*) hint (at), suggest; indicate; **j-m ~, dass** give s.o. a hint that
**'Andeutung** *f* (-; -*en*) hint, suggestion
**'Andrang** *m* (-[*e*]*s*; *no pl*) crush; ECON rush (**nach** for), run (**zu**, **nach** on)
**'andrehen** *v/t* (*sep*, *-ge-*, *h*) turn on; F **j-m et. ~** fob s.th. off on s.o.
**'androhen** *v/t* (*sep*, *-ge-*, *h*) **j-m et. ~** threaten s.o. with s.th.
**'aneignen** *v/refl* (*sep*, *-ge-*, *h*) acquire; *esp* JUR appropriate
**anei'nander** *adv tie etc* together; **~ denken** think of each other; **~ geraten** clash (**mit** with)
**Anekdote** [anɛk'do:tə] *f* (-; -*n*) anecdote
**'anekeln** *v/t* (*sep*, *-ge-*, *h*) disgust, sicken; **es ekelt mich an** it makes me sick
**'anerkannt** *adj* acknowledged, recognized
**'anerkennen** *v/t* (*irr*, **kennen**, *sep*, *no -ge-*, *h*) acknowledge, recognize; appreciate; **~d** *adj* appreciative
**'Anerkennung** *f* (-; -*en*) acknowledg(e)ment, recognition; appreciation
**'anfahren** (*irr*, **fahren**, *sep*, *-ge-*) **1.** *v/i* (*sein*) start; **2.** *v/t* (*h*) deliver; MOT *etc* hit, *car etc*: *a.* run into; *fig* **j-n ~** jump on s.o.; **'Anfahrt** *f* journey, ride
**'Anfall** *m* MED fit, attack
**'anfallen** *v/t* (*irr*, **fallen**, *sep*, *-ge-*, *h*) attack, assault; *dog*: go for
**'anfällig** *adj* delicate; **~ für** susceptible to
**'Anfang** *m* beginning, start; **am ~** at the beginning; **~ Mai** early in May; **~ nächsten Jahres** early next year; **~ der neunziger Jahre** in the early nineties; **er ist ~ 20** he is in his early twenties; **von ~ an** from the beginning *or* start;
**'anfangen** *v/t and v/i* (*irr*, **fangen**, *sep*, *-ge-*, *h*) begin, start; do; **'Anfänger** *m* (-*s*; -), **'Anfängerin** *f* (-; -*nen*) beginner
**'anfangs** *adv* at first
**'Anfangs|buchstabe** *m* initial (letter); **großer ~** capital (letter); **~stadium** *n*: **im ~** at an early stage
**'anfassen** *v/t* (*sep*, *-ge-*, *h*) touch; take (hold of); **sich ~** take each other by the hands; F **zum Anfassen** everyman's
**'anfechtbar** *adj* contestable; **'anfechten** *v/t* (*irr*, **fechten**, *sep*, *-ge-*, *h*) contest; **'Anfechtung** *f* (-; -*en*) contesting
**'anfertigen** *v/t* (*sep*, *-ge-*, *h*) make, manufacture
**'anfeuchten** *v/t* (*sep*, *-ge-*, *h*) moisten
**'anfeuern** *fig v/t* (*sep*, *-ge-*, *h*) cheer
**'anflehen** *v/t* (*sep*, *-ge-*, *h*) implore
**'anfliegen** *v/t* (*irr*, **fliegen**, *sep*, *-ge-*, *h*) AVIAT approach; fly (regularly) to
**'Anflug** *m* AVIAT approach; *fig* touch
**'anfordern** *v/t* (*sep*, *-ge-*, *h*) demand; request; **'Anforderung** *f* (-; -*en*) demand; request; *pl* requirements, qualifications
**'Anfrage** *f* (-; -*n*) inquiry
**'anfragen** *v/i* (*sep*, *-ge-*, *h*) inquire (**bei j-m nach et.** of s.o. about s.th.)
**'anfreunden** *v/refl* (*sep*, *-ge-*, *h*) make friends (**mit** with)
**'anfühlen** *v/refl* (*sep*, *-ge-*, *h*) feel; **es fühlt sich weich an** it feels soft
**'anführen** *v/t* (*sep*, *-ge-*, *h*) lead; state; F fool; **'Anführer(in)** leader
**'Anführungszeichen** *pl* quotation marks, inverted commas
**'Angabe** *f* (-; -*n*) statement; indication; F big talk; *tennis*: service; *pl* information, data; TECH specifications
**'angeben** (*irr*, **geben**, *sep*, *-ge-*, *h*) **1.** *v/t* give, state; *customs*: declare; indicate; quote (*price*); **2.** *v/i* F *fig* brag, show off; *tennis*: serve; **'Angeber** F *m* (-*s*; -)

braggart, show-off; **Angeberei** [ange:bə'rai] F *f* (-; *no pl*) bragging, showing off

**angeblich** ['ange:plıç] *adj* alleged; ~ ***ist er ...*** he is said to be ...

'**angeboren** *adj* innate, inborn; MED congenital

'**Angebot** *n* (-[*e*]*s*, -*e*) offer (*a.* ECON); ~ ***und Nachfrage*** supply and demand

'**ange|bracht** *adj* appropriate; **~bunden** *adj*: ***kurz*** ~ curt; **~gossen** F *adj*: ***wie*** ~ ***sitzen*** fit like a glove; **~heitert** *adj* tipsy, *Br a.* (slightly) merry

'**angehen** (*irr*, ***gehen***, *sep*, *-ge-*, *sein*) **1.** F *v/i light etc*: go on; **2.** *v/t* concern; ***das geht dich nichts an*** that is none of your business; **~d** *adj* future; ***~er Arzt*** doctor-to-be

'**angehören** *v/i* (*sep*, *no -ge-*, *h*) belong to; '**Angehörige** *m*, *f* (-*n*; -*n*) relative; member; ***die nächsten ~n*** the next of kin

'**Angeklagte** *m*, *f* (-*n*; -*n*) JUR defendant

**Angel** ['aŋəl] *f* (-; -*n*) fishing tackle; TECH hinge

'**Angelegenheit** *f* (-; -*en*) matter, affair

**angelehnt** *adj door etc*: ajar

'**angelernt** *adj* semi-skilled (*worker*)

'**Angelhaken** *m* fishhook

'**angeln** (*ge-*, *h*) **1.** *v/i* (***nach*** for) fish, angle (*both a. fig*); **2.** *v/t* catch, hook

'**Angelrute** *f* fishing rod

'**Angelsachse** [-zaksə] *m* (-*n*; -*n*), '**angelsächsisch** [-zɛksıʃ] *adj* Anglo-Saxon

'**Angelschein** *m* fishing permit

'**Angelschnur** *f* fishing line

**angemessen** *adj* proper, suitable; just (*punishment*); reasonable (*price*)

'**angenehm** *adj* pleasant, agreeable; *~!* pleased to meet you

'**ange|nommen** *cj* (let's) suppose, supposing; **~regt** *adj* animated; lively; **~schrieben** *adj*: ***bei j-m gut*** (***schlecht***) ~ ***sein*** be in s.o.'s good (bad) books; **~sehen** *adj* respected

'**angesichts** *prp* (*gen*) in view of

'**Angestellte** *m*, *f* (-*n*; -*n*) employee (***bei*** with), *pl* the staff

'**ange|tan** *adj*: ***ganz*** ~ ***sein von*** be taken with; **~trunken** *adj* (slightly) drunk; ***in ~em Zustand*** under the influence of alcohol; **~wandt** *adj* applied; **~wiesen** *adj*: ~ ***auf*** (*acc*) dependent (up)on

'**angewöhnen** *v/t* (*sep*, *no -ge-*, *h*) ***sich*** (***j-m***) ~, ***et. zu tun*** get (s.o.) used to doing s.th.; ***sich das Rauchen*** ~ take to smoking; '**Angewohnheit** *f* habit

**Angina** [aŋ'gi:na] *f* (-; -*nen*) MED tonsillitis

'**angleichen** *v/t* (*irr*, ***gleichen***, *sep*, *-ge-*, *h*) adjust (***an*** *acc* to)

**Angler** ['aŋlɐ] *m* (-*s*; -) angler

**Anglist** [aŋ'glıst] *m* (-*en*; -*en*), **An'glistin** *f* (-; -*nen*) student of (*or* graduate in) English

'**angreifen** *v/t* (*irr*, ***greifen***, *sep*, *-ge-*, *h*) attack (*a.* SPORT *and fig*); affect (*health etc*); touch (*supplies*)

'**Angreifer** *m* (-*s*; -) attacker, SPORT *a.* offensive player; *esp* POL aggressor

'**angrenzend** *adj* adjacent (***an*** *acc* to)

'**Angriff** *m* attack (*a.* SPORT *and fig*); MIL assault, charge; ***in*** ~ ***nehmen*** set about

'**angriffslustig** *adj* aggressive

**Angst** [aŋst] *f* (-; *Ängste* ['ɛŋstə]) fear (***vor*** *dat* of); ~ ***haben*** (***vor*** *dat*) be afraid *or* scared (of); ***j-m*** ~ ***einjagen*** frighten *or* scare s.o.; (***hab***) ***keine Angst!*** don't be afraid!; **~hase** F *m* chicken

**ängstigen** ['ɛŋstıgən] *v/t* (*ge-*, *h*) frighten, scare; ***sich*** ~ be afraid (***vor*** *dat* of); be worried (***um*** about)

**ängstlich** ['ɛŋstlıç] *adj* timid, fearful; anxious

'**anhaben** F *v/t* (*irr*, ***haben***, *sep*, *-ge-*, *h*) have on (*a. light etc*), *a.* wear, be wearing (*dress etc*)

'**anhalten** (*irr*, ***halten***, *sep*, *-ge-*, *h*) **1.** *v/t* stop; ***den Atem*** ~ hold one's breath; **2.** *v/i* stop; continue; **~d** *adj* continual

'**Anhalter** *m* (-*s*; -) hitchhiker; F ***per*** ~ ***fahren*** hitchhike

'**Anhaltspunkt** *m* clue

**an'hand** *prp* (*gen*) by means of

'**Anhang** *m* a) appendix, b) (*no pl*) relations; '**anhängen** *v/t* (*sep*, *-ge-*, *h*) add; hang up; RAIL, MOT couple (***an*** *acc* to); '**Anhänger** *m* (-*s*; -) follower, supporter (*a.* SPORT); pendant; label, tag; MOT trailer; '**anhänglich** *adj* affectionate; *contp* clinging

'**anhäufen** *v/t and v/refl* (*sep*, *-ge-*, *h*) heap up, accumulate

'**Anhäufung** *f* (-; -*en*) accumulation

'**anheben** *v/t* (*irr*, ***heben***, *sep*, *-ge-*, *h*) lift, raise (*a. price*); MOT jack up

'**anheften** *v/t* (*sep*, *-ge-*, *h*) attach, tack (*both*: ***an*** *acc* to)

**Anhieb** *m*: ***auf ~*** on the first try
'**anhimmeln** F *v/t* (*sep*, *-ge-*, *h*) idolize, worship
'**Anhöhe** *f* rise, hill, elevation
**anhören** *v/t* (*sep*, *-ge-*, *h*) listen to; ***mit ~*** overhear; ***es hört sich ... an*** it sounds ...; '**Anhörung** *f* (-; *-en*) hearing
**animieren** [ani'mi:rən] *v/t* (*no -ge-*, *h*) encourage; stimulate
'**ankämpfen** *v/i* (*sep*, *-ge-*, *h*) ***~ gegen*** fight *s.th.*
'**Ankauf** *m* purchase
**Anker** ['aŋkɐ] *m* (*-s*; -) MAR anchor; ***vor ~ gehen*** drop anchor
'**ankern** *v/i* (*ge-*, *h*) MAR anchor
'**anketten** *v/t* (*sep*, *-ge-*, *h*) chain up
'**Anklage** *f* (-; *no pl*) JUR accusation, charge (*a. fig*); '**anklagen** *v/t* (*sep*, *-ge-*, *h*) JUR accuse (***wegen*** of), charge (with) (*both a. fig.*)
'**anklammern** *v/t* (*sep*, *-ge-*, *h*) clip *s.th.* on; ***sich ~*** (***an*** *acc*) cling (to)
**Anklang** *m*: ***~ finden*** meet with approval
'**ankleben** *v/t* (*sep*, *-ge-*, *h*) stick on (***an*** *dat or acc* to)
'**anklicken** *v/t* (*sep*, *-ge-*, *h*) EDP click
'**anklopfen** *v/i* (*sep*, *-ge-*, *h*) knock (***an*** *dat or acc* at)
'**anknipsen** *v/t* (*sep*, *-ge-*, *h*) switch on
'**anknüpfen** *v/t* (*sep*, *-ge-*, *h*) tie (***an*** *acc* to); *fig* begin; ***Beziehungen ~*** (***zu***) establish contacts (with)
'**ankommen** *v/i* (*irr*, ***kommen***, *sep*, *-ge-*, *sein*) arrive; ***nicht gegen j-n ~*** be no match for s.o.; ***es kommt*** (***ganz***) ***darauf an*** it (all) depends; ***es kommt darauf an, dass*** what matters is; ***darauf kommt es nicht an*** that doesn't matter; ***es darauf ~ lassen*** take a chance; ***gut ~*** (***bei***) *fig* go down well (with)
'**ankündigen** *v/t* (*sep*, *-ge-*, *h*) announce; advertise; '**Ankündigung** *f* announcement; advertisement
**Ankunft** ['ankʊnft] *f* (-; *no pl*) arrival
'**anlächeln**, '**anlachen** *v/t* (*sep*, *-ge-*, *h*) smile at
'**Anlage** *f* arrangement; facility; plant; TECH system; (stereo *etc*) set; ECON investment; enclosure; *fig* gift; *pl* park, gardens; ***sanitäre ~n*** sanitary facilities
**Anlass** ['anlas] *m* (*-es*; *Anlässe* ['anlɛsə]) occasion; cause
'**anlassen** *v/t* (*irr*, ***lassen***, *sep*, *-ge-*, *h*) MOT start; F keep on, leave on (*a. light etc*); '**Anlasser** *m* (*-s*; -) MOT starter
**anlässlich** ['anlɛslɪç] *prp* (*gen*) on the occasion of
'**Anlauf** *m* SPORT run-up; *fig* start
'**anlaufen** (*irr*, ***laufen***, *sep*, *-ge-*) **1.** *v/i* (*sein*) run up; *fig* start; *metal*: tarnish; *glasses etc*: steam up; **2.** *v/t* (*h*) MAR call or touch at
'**anlegen** (*sep*, *-ge-*, *h*) **1.** *v/t* put on (*dress etc*); lay out (*garden etc*); build (*road etc*); invest (*money*); found (*town etc*); MED apply (*dressing etc*); lay in (*supplies*); ***sich mit j-m ~*** pick a quarrel with s.o.; **2.** *v/i* MAR land; moor; ***es ~ auf*** (*acc*) aim at; '**Anleger** *m* (*-s*; -) ECON investor; MAR landing stage
'**anlehnen** *v/t* (*sep*, *-ge-*, *h*) lean (***an*** *acc* against); leave *door etc* ajar; ***sich ~ an*** (*acc*) lean against, *fig* lean on *s.o.*
**Anleihe** ['anlaiə] *f* (-; *-n*) ECON loan
'**Anleitung** *f* (-; *-en*) guidance, instruction; *written* instructions
'**Anliegen** *n* (*-s*; -) request; message (*of a film etc*)
**Anlieger** ['anli:gɐ] *m* (*-s*; -) resident
'**anlocken** *v/t* (*sep*, *-ge-*, *h*) attract, lure
'**anmachen** *v/t* (*sep*, *-ge-*, *h*) light (*fire etc*); turn on (*light etc*); dress (*salad*); F chat *s.o.* up; turn *s.o.* on
'**anmalen** *v/t* (*sep*, *-ge-*, *h*) paint
'**Anmarsch** *m*: ***im ~*** on the way
**anmaßen** *v/t* (*sep*, *-ge-*, *h*) ***sich ~*** assume; claim (*right*); ***sich ~, et. zu tun*** presume to do s.th.; ***~d*** *adj* arrogant
'**anmelden** *v/t* (*sep*, *-ge-*, *h*) announce (*visitor*); register (*birth etc*); *customs*: declare; ***sich ~*** enrol(l) (*for classes etc*); register (*at a hotel*); ***sich ~ bei*** make an appointment with (*doctor etc*)
'**Anmeldung** *f* announcement; registration, enrol(l)ment
'**anmerken** *v/t* (*sep*, *-ge-*, *h*) ***j-m et. ~*** notice s.th. in s.o.; ***sich et.*** (***nichts***) ***~ lassen*** (not) let it show; '**Anmerkung** *f* (-; *-en*) note; annotation, footnote
**Anmut** ['anmu:t] *f* (-; *no pl*) grace
'**anmutig** *adj* graceful
'**annähen** *v/t* (*sep*, *-ge-*, *h*) sew on (***an*** *acc* to)
'**annähernd** *adv* approximately
'**Annäherung** *f* (-; *-en*) approach (***an*** *acc* to); '**Annäherungsversuche** *pl* advances, F pass

**Annahme** ['anna:mə] *f* (-; *-n*) a) (*no pl*) acceptance (*a. fig*), b) assumption
**'annehmbar** *adj* acceptable; reasonable (*price etc*); **'annehmen** *v/t* (*irr*, ***nehmen***, *sep*, *-ge-*, *h*) accept; suppose; adopt (*child*, *name*); take (*ball*); take on (*color*, *look etc*); ***sich e-r Sache*** *or* ***j-s*** ~ take care of s.th. *or* s.o.; **'Annehmlichkeiten** *pl* comforts, amenities
**Annonce** [a'nõ:sə] *f* (-; *-n*) advertisement
**annullieren** [anʊ'li:rən] *v/t* (*no -ge-*, *h*) annul; ECON cancel
**anöden** ['anˀø:dən] F *v/t* (*sep*, *-ge-*, *h*) bore *s.o.* to death
**anonym** [ano'ny:m] *adj* anonymous
**Anonymität** [anonymi'tɛ:t] *f* (-; *no pl*) anonymity
**Anorak** ['anorak] *m* (*-s*; *-s*) anorak
**'anordnen** *v/t* (*sep*, *-ge-*, *h*) arrange; give order(s), order; **'Anordnung** *f* (-; *-en*) arrangement; direction, order
**'anorganisch** *adj* CHEM inorganic
**'anpacken** F *fig* (*sep*, *-ge-*, *h*) **1.** *v/t* tackle; **2.** *v/i*: ***mit*** ~ lend a hand
**'anpassen** *v/t* (*sep*, *-ge-*, *h*) adapt, adjust (*both a.* ***sich*** ~) (*dat*, ***an*** *acc* to)
**'Anpassung** *f* (-; *-en*) adaptation, adjustment
**'anpassungsfähig** *adj* adaptable
**'Anpassungsfähigkeit** *f* adaptability
**'Anpfiff** *m* SPORT starting whistle; F *fig* dressing-down
**'anpflanzen** *v/t* (*sep*, *-ge-*, *h*) cultivate, plant; **'Anpflanzung** *f* cultivation
**'anpöbeln** *v/t* (*sep*, *-ge-*, *h*) accost; shout abuse at; **anprangern** ['anpraŋɐn] *v/t* (*sep*, *-ge-*, *h*) denounce; **'anpreisen** *v/t* (*irr*, ***preisen***, *sep*, *-ge-*, *h*) push; plug; **'anpro͵bieren** *v/t* (*no -ge-*, *h*) try on; **'anpumpen** F *v/t* (*sep*, *-ge-*, *h*) touch *s.o.* (***um*** for); **'anraten** *v/t* (*irr*, ***raten***, *sep*, *-ge-*, *h*) advise; **'anrechnen** *v/t* (*sep*, *-ge-*, *h*) charge; allow
**'Anrecht** *n*: ***ein ~ haben auf*** (*acc*) be entitled to
**'Anrede** *f* address; **'anreden** *v/t* (*sep*, *-ge-*, *h*) address (***mit Namen*** by name)
**'anregen** *v/t* (*sep*, *-ge-*, *h*) stimulate; suggest; **~d** *adj* stimulating
**'Anregung** *f* stimulation; suggestion
**'Anregungsmittel** *n* PHARM stimulant
**'Anreiz** *m* incentive
**'anrichten** *v/t* (*sep*, *-ge-*, *h*) GASTR prepare, dress; cause, do (*damage etc*)
**anrüchig** ['anrʏçɪç] *adj* disreputable
**'Anruf** *m* call (*a.* TEL); **~beantworter** *m* TEL answering machine
**'anrufen** *v/t* (*irr*, ***rufen***, *sep*, *-ge-*, *h*) TEL call *or* ring up, phone
**'anrühren** *v/t* (*sep*, *-ge-*, *h*) touch; mix
**'Ansage** *f* announcement; **'ansagen** *v/t* (*sep*, *-ge-*, *h*) announce; **Ansager** ['anza:gɐ] *m* (*-s*; -), **'Ansagerin** [-gərɪn] *f* (-; *-nen*) announcer
**'ansammeln** *v/t and v/refl* (*sep*, *-ge-*, *h*) accumulate; **'Ansammlung** *f* collection, accumulation; crowd
**'Ansatz** *m* start (***zu*** of); attempt (***zu*** at); approach; TECH attachment; MATH set-up; *pl* first signs
**'anschaffen** *v/t* (*sep*, *-ge-*, *h*) get; ***sich et.*** ~ buy *or* get (o.s.) s.th.
**'Anschaffung** *f* (-; *-en*) purchase, buy
**'anschauen** *v/t* (*sep*, *-ge-*, *h*) → ***ansehen***; **'anschaulich** *adj* graphic (*account etc*); **'Anschauung** *f* (-; *-en*) (***von***) view (of), opinion (about, of)
**'Anschauungsmateri͵al** *n* PED visual aids
**'Anschein** *m* (*-[e]s*; *no pl*) appearance; ***allem ~ nach*** to all appearances; ***den ~ erwecken, als*** (***ob***) give the impression of ...; **'anscheinend** *adv* apparently
**'anschieben** *v/t* (*irr*, ***schieben***, *sep*, *-ge-*, *h*) give a push (*a.* MOT)
**'Anschlag** *m* attack; poster; bill, notice; *typewriter*: stroke; MUS, *swimming*: touch; ***e-n ~ auf j-n verüben*** make an attempt on s.o.'s life; **~brett** *n* bulletin (*esp Br* notice) board
**'anschlagen** (*irr*, ***schlagen***, *sep*, *-ge-*, *h*) **1.** *v/t* post; MUS strike; chip (*cup etc*); **2.** *v/i dog*: bark; take (effect) (*a.* MED); *swimming*: touch the wall
**'anschließen** *v/t* (*irr*, ***schließen***, *sep*, *-ge-*, *h*) ELECTR, TECH connect; ***sich*** ~ follow; agree with; ***sich j-m or e-r Sache*** ~ join s.o. *or* s.th.; **~d** **1.** *adj* following; **2.** *adv* then, afterwards
**'Anschluss** *m* connection; ***im ~ an*** (*acc*) following; ~ ***finden*** (***bei***) make contact *or* friends (with); ~ ***bekommen*** TEL get through
**'anschmiegen** *v/refl* (*sep*, *-ge-*, *h*) snuggle up (***an*** *acc* to)
**'anschmiegsam** *adj* affectionate

**'anschnallen** *v/t* (*sep*, *-ge-*, *h*) strap on, put on (*a. ski*); **sich ~** AVIAT, MOT fasten one's seat belt; **'anschnauzen** F *v/t* (*sep*, *-ge-*, *h*) tell *s.o.* off, *Am a.* bawl *s.o.* out; **'anschneiden** *v/t* (*irr*, ***schneiden***, *sep*, *-ge-*, *h*) cut; *fig* bring up; **'anschrauben** *v/t* (*sep*, *-ge-*, *h*) screw on (***an*** *acc* to); **'anschreiben** *v/t* (*irr*, ***schreiben***, *sep*, *-ge-*, *h*) write on the (black)board; ***j-n*** **~** write to s.o.; (***et.***) **~** ***lassen*** buy (s.th.) on credit; → ***angeschrieben***; **'anschreien** *v/t* (*irr*, ***schreien***, *sep*, *-ge-*, *h*) shout at

**'Anschrift** *f* address

**'Anschuldigung** *f* (-; *-en*) accusation

**'anschwellen** *v/i* (*irr*, ***schwellen***, *sep*, *-ge-*, *sein*) swell (*a. fig*); **'anschwemmen** *v/t* (*sep*, *-ge-*, *h*) wash ashore

**'ansehen** *v/t* (*irr*, ***sehen***, *sep*, *-ge-*, *h*) look at, have *or* take a look at; watch; see (*all a.* ***sich*** [*dat*] **~**); **~ *als*** look upon as; ***et. mit*** **~** watch *or* witness s.th.; ***man sieht ihm an, dass ...*** one can see that ...; **'Ansehen** *n* (*-s*; *no pl*) reputation

**ansehnlich** ['anze:nlıç] *adj* considerable

**'anseilen** *v/t and v/refl* (*sep*, *-ge-*, *h*) rope

**'ansetzen** (*sep*, *-ge-*, *h*) **1.** *v/t* put (***an*** *acc* to); put on, add; fix, set (*date etc*); ***Fett*** *etc* **~** put on weight *etc*; **2.** *v/i*: **~ *zu*** prepare for (*landing etc*)

**'Ansicht** *f* (-; *-en*) view, *a.* opinion, *a.* sight; ***der ~ sein, dass ...*** be of the opinion that ...; ***meiner ~ nach*** in my opinion; ***zur ~*** ECON on approval

**'Ansichts|karte** *f* picture postcard; **~sache** *f* matter of opinion

**'anspannen** *v/t* (*sep*, *-ge-*, *h*) strain

**'Anspannung** *f* (-; *-en*) strain, exertion

**'anspielen** *v/i* (*sep*, *-ge-*, *h*) *soccer*: kick off; **~ *auf*** (*acc*) allude to, hint at

**'Anspielung** *f* (-; *-en*) allusion, hint

**'anspitzen** *v/t* (*sep*, *-ge-*, *h*) sharpen

**'Ansporn** *m* (-[*e*]*s*; *no pl*) incentive

**'anspornen** *v/t* (*sep*, *-ge-*, *h*) encourage, spur *s.o.* on

**'Ansprache** *f* address, speech; ***e-e ~ halten*** deliver an address

**'ansprechen** *v/t* (*irr*, ***sprechen***, *sep*, *-ge-*, *h*) address, speak to; *fig* appeal to; **~d** *adj* attractive

**'Ansprechpartner** *m* s.o. to talk to, contact

**'anspringen** (*irr*, ***springen***, *sep*, *-ge-*) **1.** *v/i* (*sein*) *engine*: start; **2.** *v/t* (*h*) jump (up)on

**'anspritzen** *v/t* (*sep*, *-ge-*, *h*) spatter

**'Anspruch** *m* claim (***auf*** *acc* to) (*a.* JUR); **~ *haben auf*** (*acc*) be entitled to; **~ *erheben auf*** (*acc*) claim; ***Zeit in ~ nehmen*** take up time

**'anspruchslos** *adj* modest; light, undemanding (*reading etc*); *contp* trivial

**'anspruchsvoll** *adj* demanding; sophisticated, refined (*tastes etc*)

**Anstalt** ['anʃtalt] *f* (-; *-en*) establishment, institution; mental hospital; **~*en machen zu*** get ready for

**'Anstand** *m* (-[*e*]*s*; *no pl*) decency; manners; **'anständig** *adj* decent (*a. fig*)

**'anstandslos** *adv* unhesitatingly; without difficulty

**'anstarren** *v/t* (*sep*, *-ge-*, *h*) stare at

**an'statt** *prp* (*gen*) *and cj* instead of

**'anstechen** *v/t* (*irr*, ***stechen***, *sep*, *-ge-*, *h*) tap (*barrel*)

**'anstecken** *v/t* (*sep*, *-ge-*, *h*) stick on; put on (*ring*); light; set fire to; MED infect; ***sich bei j-m ~*** MED catch s.th. from s.o.; **~d** *adj* MED infectious, contagious, catching (*all a. fig*)

**'Anstecknadel** *f* pin, button

**'Ansteckung** *f* (-; *no pl*) MED infection, contagion

**'anstehen** *v/i* (*irr*, ***stehen***, *sep*, *-ge-*, *h*) (***nach*** for) stand in line, *Br* queue up

**'ansteigen** *v/i* (*irr*, ***steigen***, *sep*, *-ge-*, *sein*) rise

**'anstellen** *v/t* (*sep*, *-ge-*, *h*) engage, employ; TV *etc*: turn on; MOT start; F be up to (*s.th. illegal etc*); make (*inquiries etc*); ***sich ~*** line up (***nach*** for), *Br* queue up (for); F (make a) fuss

**'Anstellung** *f* job, position; ***e-e ~ finden*** find employment

**Anstieg** ['anʃti:k] *m* (-[*e*]*s*; *no pl*) rise, increase

**'anstiften** *v/t* (*sep*, *-ge-*, *h*) incite

**'Anstifter** *m* instigator

**'Anstiftung** *f* incitement

**'anstimmen** *v/t* (*sep*, *-ge-*, *h*) MUS strike up

**'Anstoß** *m soccer*: kickoff; *fig* initiative, impulse; offen|se, *Br* -ce; **~ *erregen*** give offense (***bei*** to); **~ *nehmen an*** take offense at; ***den ~ zu et. geben*** start s.th., initiate s.th.; **'anstoßen** (*irr*, ***sto-***

**ßen,** *sep, -ge-*) **1.** *v/t* (*h*) nudge *s.o.*; **2.** *v/i* a) (*sein*) knock, bump, b) (*h*) clink glasses; **~ *auf*** (*acc*) drink to *s.o. or s.th.*
**anstößig** ['anʃtøːsɪç] *adj* offensive
**'anstrahlen** *v/t* (*sep, -ge-, h*) illuminate; beam at *s.o.*
**'anstreichen** *v/t* (*irr,* ***streichen,*** *sep, -ge-, h*) paint; PED mark (*mistakes etc*)
**'Anstreicher** *m* (house)painter
**'anstrengen** *v/refl* (*sep, -ge-, h*) try (hard), make an effort; **~d** *adj* strenuous, hard
**'Anstrengung** *f* (-; *-en*) exertion, strain; effort
**Ansturm** *fig m* (-[*e*]*s*; *no pl*) rush (***auf*** *acc* for)
**'Anteil** *m* share (*a.* ECON), portion; ***~ nehmen an*** (*dat*) take an interest in; sympathize with; **~nahme** [-naːmə] *f* (-; *no pl*) sympathy; interest
**Antenne** [an'tɛnə] *f* (-; *-n*) antenna, *Br* aerial
**Anti..., anti...** *in cpds* anti...
**Anti|alko'holiker** *m* teetotal(l)er; **~'babypille** F *f* birth control pill, F the pill; **~'biotikum** *n* MED antibiotic; **~blo'ckiersys͵tem** *n* MOT anti-lock braking system
**antik** [an'tiːk] *adj* antique, HIST *a.* ancient; **An'tike** *f* (-; *no pl*) ancient world
**'Antikörper** *m* MED antibody
**Antilope** [anti'loːpə] *f* (-; *-n*) ZO antelope
**Antipathie** [antipa'tiː] *f* (-; *-n*) antipathy
**Antiquariat** [antikva'rjaːt] *n* (-[*e*]*s*; *-e*) second-hand bookshop
**antiquarisch** [anti'kvaːrɪʃ] *adj and adv* second-hand
**Antiquitäten** [antikvi'tɛːtən] *pl* antiques; **~laden** *m* antique shop
**Antisemit** [-ze'miːt] *m* (*-en*; *-en*) anti-Semite; **antise'mitisch** *adj* anti-Semitic; **Antisemitismus** [-zemi'tɪsmʊs] *m* (-; *no pl*) anti-Semitism
**Antrag** ['antraːk] *m* (-[*e*]*s*; *Anträge* ['antrɛːgə]) application; PARL motion; proposal; ***~ stellen auf*** (*acc*) make an application for; PARL move for; **~steller(in)** [-ʃtɛlɐ (-lərɪn)] *m* (*-s*; *-/-*; *-nen*) applicant; PARL mover
**'antreiben** (*irr,* ***treiben,*** *sep, -ge-*) **1.** *v/t* (*h*) TECH drive; urge *s.o.* (on); **2.** *v/i* (*sein*) float ashore
**'antreten** (*irr,* ***treten,*** *sep, -ge-*) **1.** *v/t* (*h*) enter upon (*office etc*); take up (*position*); set out on (*journey*); **2.** *v/i* (*sein*) take one's place; MIL line up
**'Antrieb** *m* TECH drive (*a. fig*), propulsion; *fig* motive, impulse; ***aus eigenem ~*** of one's own accord
**'antun** *v/t* (*irr,* ***tun,*** *sep, -ge-, h*) ***j-m et. ~*** do s.th. to s.o.; ***sich et. ~*** lay hands on o.s.
**Antwort** ['antvɔrt] *f* (-; *-en*) answer (***auf*** *acc* to), reply (to)
**'antworten** *v/i* (*ge-, h*) answer (***j-m*** s.o., ***auf et.*** s.th.), reply (to s.o. *or* s.th.)
**'anvertrauen** *v/t* (*sep, no -ge-, h*) ***j-m et. ~*** (en)trust s.o. with s.th.; confide s.th. to s.o.
**'anwachsen** *v/i* (*irr,* ***wachsen,*** *sep, -ge-, sein*) BOT take root; *fig* increase
**Anwalt** ['anvalt] *m* (-[*e*]*s*; *Anwälte* ['anvɛltə]) → ***Rechtsanwalt***
**'Anwärter** *m* candidate (***auf*** *acc* for)
**'anweisen** *v/t* (*irr,* ***weisen,*** *sep, -ge-, h*) instruct; direct, order
**'Anweisung** *f* instruction; order
**'anwenden** *v/t* ([*irr,* ***wenden,***] *sep, -ge-, h*) use; apply (***auf*** *acc* to)
**'Anwendung** *f* use; application
**'anwerben** *v/t* (*irr,* ***werben,*** *sep, -ge-, h*) recruit (*a. fig*)
**'Anwesen** *n* (*-s*; -) estate; property
**'anwesend** *adj* present
**'Anwesenheit** *f* (-; *no pl*) presence; PED attendance; ***die ~ feststellen*** call the roll; **'Anwesenheitsliste** *f* attendance record (*Br* list)
**anwidern** ['anviːdɐn] *v/t* (*sep, -ge-, h*) make *s.o.* sick
**'Anzahl** *f* (-; *no pl*) number, quantity
**'anzahlen** *v/t* (*sep, -ge-, h*) pay on account; **'Anzahlung** *f* down payment
**'anzapfen** *v/t* (*sep, -ge-, h*) tap
**'Anzeichen** *n* symptom (*a.* MED), sign
**Anzeige** ['antsaigə] *f* (-; *-n*) advertisement; announcement; JUR information; EDP display; TECH reading
**'anzeigen** *v/t* (*sep, -ge-, h*) announce; report to the police; TECH indicate, show
**'anziehen** *v/t* (*irr,* ***ziehen,*** *sep, -ge-, h*) put on (*dress etc*); dress *s.o.*; *fig* attract, draw; tighten (*screw*); pull (*lever etc*); ***sich ~*** get dressed; dress; **~d** *adj* attractive
**'Anziehung** *f* (-; *no pl*), **'Anziehungskraft** *f* (-; *no pl*) PHYS attraction, *fig a.* appeal

**'Anzug** *m* suit
**anzüglich** ['antsy:klıç] *adj* suggestive (*joke*); personal, offensive (*remark etc*)
**'anzünden** *v/t* (*sep*, *-ge-*, *h*) light; set on fire
**apart** [a'part] *adj* striking
**Apartment** [a'partmənt] *n* (*-s*; *-s*) studio (apartment *or Br* flat)
**apathisch** [a'pa:tıʃ] *adj* apathetic
**Apfel** ['apfəl] *m* (*-s*; *Äpfel* ['ɛpfəl]) BOT apple; **~mus** *n* GASTR apple sauce
**Apfelsine** [apfəl'zi:nə] *f* (*-*; *-n*) BOT orange
**'Apfelwein** *m* cider
**Apostel** [a'pɔstəl] *m* (*-s*; *-*) REL apostle
**Apostroph** [apo'strɔf] *m* (*-s*; *-e*) apostrophe
**Apotheke** [apo'te:kə] *f* (*-*; *-n*) pharmacy, drugstore, *Br* chemist's
**Apotheker** [apo'te:kɐ] *m* (*-s*; *-*), **Apo'thekerin** *f* (*-*; *-nen*) pharmacist, druggist, *Br* chemist
**App.** ABBR *of* ***Apparat*** TEL ext., extension
**Apparat** [apa'ra:t] *m* (*-[e]s*; *-e*) apparatus; device; (tele)phone; radio; TV set; camera; POL *etc* machine(ry); ***am ~!*** TEL speaking!; ***am ~ bleiben*** TEL hold the line
**Appell** [a'pɛl] *m* (*-s*; *-e*) appeal (***an*** *acc* to); MIL roll call
**appellieren** [apɛ'li:rən] *v/i* (*no -ge-*, *h*) (make an) appeal (***an*** *acc* to)
**Appetit** [ape'ti:t] *m* (*-[e]s*; *no pl*) appetite (***auf*** *acc* for); ***~ auf et. haben*** feel like s.th.; ***guten ~!*** enjoy your meal!
**appe'titanregend** *adj* appetizing
**Appe'tithappen** *m* GASTR appetizer
**appe'titlich** *adj* appetizing, savo(u)ry, *fig a.* inviting
**applaudieren** [aplau'di:rən] *v/i* (*no -ge-*, *h*) applaud; **Applaus** [a'plaus] *m* (*-es*; *no pl*) applause
**Aprikose** [apri'ko:zə] *f* (*-*; *-n*) BOT apricot
**April** [a'prıl] *m* (*-[s]*; *no pl*) April; ***~! ~!*** April fool!
**Aquaplaning** [akva'pla:nıŋ] *n* (*-[s]*; *no pl*) MOT hydroplaning, *Br* aquaplaning
**Aquarell** [akva'rɛl] *n* (*-s*; *-e*) watercolo(u)r
**Aquarium** [a'kva:rjʊm] *n* (*-s*; *-ien*) aquarium
**Äquator** [ɛ'kva:to:ɐ] *m* (*-s*; *no pl*) equator

**Ära** ['ɛ:ra] *f* (*-*; *no pl*) era
**Araber** ['arabɐ] *m* (*-s*; *-*), **'Araberin** [-bərın] *f* (*-*; *-nen*) Arab
**arabisch** [a'ra:bıʃ] *adj* Arabian; Arabic
**Arbeit** ['arbait] *f* (*-*; *-en*) work, ECON, POL *a.* labo(u)r; employment, job; PED test; *scientific etc* paper; workmanship; ***bei der ~*** at work; ***zur ~ gehen*** *or* ***fahren*** go to work; ***gute ~ leisten*** make a good job of it; ***sich an die ~ machen*** set to work; **'arbeiten** *v/i* (*ge-*, *h*) work (***an*** *dat* at, on)
**'Arbeiter** *m* (*-s*; *-*), **'Arbeiterin** *f* (*-*; *-nen*) worker
**'Arbeitgeber** *m* (*-s*; *-*) employer
**'Arbeitnehmer** *m* (*-s*; *-*) employee
**'Arbeits|amt** *n Am* labor office, *Br* job centre; **~blatt** *n* PED worksheet; **~erlaubnis** *f* green card, *Br* work permit
**'arbeitsfähig** *adj* fit for work
**'Arbeits|gang** *m* TECH operation; **~gemeinschaft** *f* work *or* study group; **~gericht** *n* JUR labor court, *Br* industrial tribunal; **~hose** *f* overalls; **~kleidung** *f* working clothes; **~kräfte** *pl* workers, labo(u)r
**'arbeitslos** *adj* unemployed, out of work; **'Arbeitslose** *m, f* (*-n*; *-n*) ***die ~n*** *pl* the unemployed
**'Arbeitslosengeld** *n* unemployment compensation (*Br* benefit); ***~ beziehen*** F be on the dole
**'Arbeitslosigkeit** *f* (*-*; *no pl*) unemployment
**'Arbeits|markt** *m* labo(u)r market; **~mi,nister** *m Am* Secretary of Labor; *Br* Minister of Labour; **~niederlegung** *f* strike, walkout; **~pause** *f* break, intermission; **~platz** *m* workplace; job
**'arbeitsscheu** *adj* work-shy
**'Arbeits|speicher** *m* EDP main memory; **~suche** *f*: ***er ist auf ~*** he is looking for a job; **~süchtige** *m, f* workaholic; **~tag** *m* workday
**'arbeitsunfähig** *adj* unfit for work; *permanently* disabled
**'Arbeits|weise** *f* method (of working); **~zeit** *f* (***gleitende*** flexible) working hours; **~zeitverkürzung** *f* fewer working hours; **~zimmer** *n* study
**Archäologe** [arçɛo'lo:gə] *m* (*-n*; *-n*) arch(a)eologist; **Archäologie** [arçɛolo'gi:] *f* (*-*; *no pl*) arch(a)eology; **Ar-**

**chäo'login** *f* (-; *-nen*) arch(a)eologist
**Arche** ['arçə] *f* (-; *-n*) ark; ***die ~ Noah*** Noah's ark
**Architekt** [arçi'tɛkt] *m* (*-en*; *-en*), **Ar-chi'tektin** *f* (-; *-nen*) architect; **archi-tektonisch** [-tɛk'to:nɪʃ] *adj* architectural; **Architektur** [-tɛk'tu:ɐ] *f* (-; *-en*) architecture
**Archiv** [ar'çi:f] *n* (*-s*; *-e*) archives; record office
**Arena** [a're:na] *f* (-; *-nen*) ring
**Ärger** ['ɛrgɐ] *m* (*-s*; *no pl*) anger (***über*** *acc* at); trouble; F ***j-m ~ machen*** cause s.o. trouble; **'ärgerlich** *adj* angry (***über***, ***auf*** *acc* at *s.th.*; with *s.o.*); annoying; **'ärgern** *v/t* (*ge-*, *h*) annoy; ***sich ~*** be annoyed (***über*** *acc* at, about *s.th.*, with *s.o.*); **'Ärgernis** *n* (*-ses*; *-se*) nuisance
**arglos** ['arklo:s] *adj* innocent
**Argwohn** ['arkvo:n] *m* (*-[e]s*; *no pl*) suspicion (***gegen*** of)
**'argwöhnisch** [-vø:nɪʃ] *adj* suspicious
**Arie** ['a:rjə] *f* (-; *-n*) MUS aria
**Aristokratie** [arɪstokra'ti:] *f* (-; *-n*) aristocracy
**arm** [arm] *adj* poor; ***die Armen*** the poor
**Arm** *m* (*-[e]s*; *-e*) ANAT arm; GEOGR branch; F ***j-n auf den ~ nehmen*** pull s.o.'s leg
**Armaturen** [arma'tu:rən] *pl* TECH instruments; (plumbing) fixtures; **~brett** *n* MOT dashboard
**'Armband** *n* bracelet
**'Armbanduhr** *f* wrist-watch
**Armee** [ar'me:] *f* (-; *-n*) MIL armed forces; army
**Ärmel** ['ɛrməl] *m* (*-s*; -) sleeve
**ärmlich** ['ɛrmlɪç] *adj* poor (*a. fig*); shabby
**'Armreif(en)** *m* bangle
**'armselig** *adj* wretched, miserable
**Armut** ['armu:t] *f* (-; *no pl*) poverty; ***~ an*** (*dat*) lack of
**Aroma** [a'ro:ma] *n* (*-s*; *-men*) flavo(u)r; aroma
**Arrest** [a'rɛst] *m* (*-[e]s*; *-e*) PED detention; ***~ bekommen*** be kept in
**arrogant** [aro'gant] *adj* arrogant, conceited
**Arsch** [arʃ] V *m* (*-es*; *Ärsche* ['ɛrʃə]) ass, *Br* arse; **~loch** V *n* asshole, *Br* arsehole
**Art** [art] *f* (-; *-en*) way, manner; kind, sort; BIOL species; ***auf diese ~*** (in) this way; ***e-e ~*** ... a sort of ...; ***Geräte aller ~*** all kinds *or* sorts of tools
**'Artenschutz** *m* protection of endangered species
**Arterie** [ar'te:rjə] *f* (-; *-n*) ANAT artery
**Ar'terienverkalkung** *f* MED arteriosclerosis
**Arthritis** [ar'tri:tɪs] *f* (-; *-tiden*) MED arthritis
**artig** ['artɪç] *adj* good, well-behaved; ***sei ~!*** be good!, be a good boy (*or* girl)!
**Artikel** [ar'ti:kəl] *m* (*-s*; -) article
**Artillerie** ['artɪləri:] *f* (-; *no pl*) MIL artillery
**Artist** [ar'tɪst] *m* (*-en*; *-en*), **Ar'tistin** *f* (-; *-nen*) acrobat, (circus) performer
**Arznei** [a:ɐts'nai] *f* (-; *-en*), **~mittel** *n* medicine, drug
**Arzt** [a:ɐtst] *m* (*-es*; *Ärzte* ['ɛ:ɐtstə]) doctor, physician; **Ärztin** ['ɛ:ɐtstɪn] *f* (-; *-nen*) (lady) doctor *or* physician
**'ärztlich** *adj* medical; ***sich ~ behandeln lassen*** undergo treatment
**As** [as] *n* (-; -) MUS A flat
**Asbest** [as'bɛst] *m* (*-[e]s*; *-e*) asbestos
**Asche** ['aʃə] *f* (-; *-n*) ash(es)
**'Aschen|bahn** *f* SPORT cinder-track, MOT dirt track; **~becher** *m* ashtray
**Ascher'mittwoch** *m* Ash Wednesday
**äsen** ['ɛ:zən] *v/i* (*ge-*, *h*) HUNT feed, browse
**Asiat** [a'zja:t] *m* (*-en*; *-en*), **Asi'atin** *f* (-; *-nen*) Asian; **asi'atisch** *adj* Asian, Asiatic; **Asien** ['a:zjən] *n* (*-s*; *no pl*) Asia
**Asket** [as'ke:t] *m* (*-en*; *-en*), **as'ketisch** *adj* ascetic
**'asozial** *adj* antisocial
**Asphalt** [as'falt] *m* (*-s*; *-e*) asphalt
**asphaltieren** [asfal'ti:rən] *v/t* (*no -ge-*, *h*) (cover with) asphalt
**Ass** [as] *n* (*-es*; *-e*) ace (*a. tennis and fig*)
**aß** [a:s] *pret of* ***essen***
**Assistent** [asɪs'tɛnt] *m* (*-en*; *-en*), **Assis'tentin** *f* (-; *-nen*) assistant
**Assis'tenzarzt** *m Am* intern, *Br* houseman
**Ast** [ast] *m* (*-es*; *Äste* ['ɛstə]) BOT branch
**Astronaut** [astro'naut] *m* (*-en*; *-en*), **Astro'nautin** *f* (-; *-nen*) astronaut
**Astronom** [astro'no:m] *m* (*-en*; *-en*) astronomer; **Astronomie** [-no'mi:] *f* (-; *no pl*) astronomy
**ASU** ['a:zu] ABBR *of* ***Abgas-Sonder-Un-***

***tersuchung*** MOT *Am* emissions test, *Br* exhaust emission test
**Asyl** [a'zy:l] *n* (*-s*; *-e*) asylum; **Asylant** [azy'lant] *m* (*-en*; *-en*), **Asy'lantin** *f* (-; *-nen*) asylum seeker, (political) refugee
**A'syl|bewerber(in)** asylum seeker; **~recht** *n* right of (political) asylum
**Atelier** [ate'lje:] *n* (*-s*; *-s*) studio
**Atem** ['a:təm] *m* (*-s*; *no pl*) breath; ***außer ~*** out of breath; (***tief***) ***~ holen*** take a (deep) breath; **'atemberaubend** *adj* breathtaking; **'Atemgerät** *n* MED respirator; **'atemlos** *adj* breathless; **'Atempause** *f* F breather; **'Atemzug** *m* breath
**Äther** ['ɛ:tɐ] *m* (*-s*; *no pl*) CHEM ether; *radio etc*: air
**Athlet** [at'le:t] *m* (*-en*; *-en*), **Ath'letin** *f* (-; *-nen*) SPORT athlete
**ath'letisch** *adj* athletic
**Atlas** ['atlas] *m* (*-ses*; *-se*, *Atlanten*) atlas
**atmen** ['a:tmən] *v/i and v/t* (*ge-*, *h*) breathe
**Atmosphäre** [atmo'sfɛ:rə] *f* (-; *-n*) atmosphere
**'Atmung** *f* (-; *no pl*) breathing, respiration
**Atoll** [a'tɔl] *n* (*-s*; *-e*) atoll
**Atom** [a'to:m] *n* (*-s*; *-e*) atom
**A'tom...** *in cpds -energie*, *-forschung*, *-kraft*, *-krieg*, *-müll*, *-rakete*, *-reaktor*, *-waffen etc* nuclear ...
**atomar** [ato'ma:ɐ] *adj* atomic, nuclear
**A'tombombe** *f* MIL atom(ic) bomb
**A'tomkern** *m* PHYS (atomic) nucleus
**a'tomwaffenfrei** *adj* nuclear-free
**Attentat** ['atənta:t] *n* (*-[e]s*; *-e*) assassination attempt, attempt on *s.o.'s* life; ***Opfer e-s ~s werden*** be assassinated
**'Attentäter** *m* (*-s*; -) assassin
**Attest** [a'tɛst] *n* (*-[e]s*; *-e*) (doctor's) certificate
**Attraktion** [atrak'tsjo:n] *f* (-; *-en*) attraction; **attraktiv** [-'ti:f] *adj* attractive
**Attrappe** [a'trapə] *f* (-; *-n*) dummy
**Attribut** [atri'bu:t] *n* (*-[e]s*; *-e*) LING attribute (*a. fig*)
**ätzend** ['ɛtsənt] *adj* corrosive, caustic (*a. fig*); F gross; ***das ist echt ~*** it's the pits
**au** [au] *int* ouch!; ***~ fein!*** oh, good!
**Aubergine** [obɛr'ʒi:nə] *f* (-; *-n*) BOT eggplant, *Br* aubergine
**auch** [aux] *cj* also, too, as well; ***ich ~*** so am (*or* do) I, F me too; ***~ nicht*** not ... either; ***wenn ~*** even if; ***wo ~*** (***immer***) wherever; ***ist es ~ wahr?*** is it really true?
**Audienz** [au'djɛnts] *f* (-; *-en*) audience (***bei*** with)
**auf** [auf] *prp* (*dat and acc*) *and adv* on; in; at; open; up; ***~ Seite 20*** on page 20; ***~ der Straße*** on (*Br* in) the street; on the road; ***~ der Welt*** in the world; ***~ See*** at sea; ***~ dem Lande*** in the country; ***~ dem Bahnhof*** *etc* at the station *etc*; ***~ Urlaub*** on vacation; ***die Uhr stellen ~*** (*acc*) set the watch to; ***~ deutsch*** in German; ***~ deinen Wunsch*** at your request; ***~ die Sekunde genau*** to the second; ***~ und ab*** up and down
**'auf|arbeiten** *v/t* (*sep*, *-ge-*, *h*) catch up on (*backlog*); refurbish; **~atmen** *v/i* (*sep*, *-ge-*, *h*) heave a sigh of relief
**'Aufbau** *m* (*-[e]s*; *no pl*) building (up); structure; **'aufbauen** *v/t* (*sep*, *-ge-*, *h*) build (up) (*a. fig*); set up; construct
**'auf|bauschen** *v/t* (*sep*, *-ge-*, *h*) exaggerate; **~bekommen** *v/t* (*irr*, ***kommen***, *sep*, *no -ge-*, *h*) get *door etc* open; be given (*a task etc*); **~bereiten** *v/t* (*sep*, *no -ge-*, *h*) process, clean, treat; **~bessern** *v/t* (*sep*, *-ge-*, *h*) raise (*salary etc*); **~bewahren** *v/t* (*sep*, *no -ge-*, *h*) keep; **~bieten** *v/t* (*irr*, ***bieten***, *sep*, *-ge-*, *h*) muster; **~blasen** *v/t* (*irr*, ***blasen***, *sep*, *-ge-*, *h*) blow up; **~bleiben** *v/i* (*irr*, ***bleiben***, *sep*, *-ge-*, *sein*) stay up; *door etc*: remain open; **~blenden** *v/i* (*sep*, *-ge-*, *h*) MOT turn the headlights up; **~blicken** *v/i* (*sep*, *-ge-*, *h*) look up (***zu*** at) (*a. fig*); **~blitzen** *v/i* (*sep*, *-ge-*, *h*, *sein*) flash (*a. fig*)
**'aufbrausen** *v/i* (*sep*, *-ge-*, *sein*) fly into a temper; **~d** *adj* irascible
**'aufbrechen** (*irr*, ***brechen***, *sep*, *-ge-*) **1.** *v/t* (*h*) break *or* force open; **2.** *v/i* (*sein*) burst open; *fig* leave (***nach*** for)
**'aufbringen** *v/t* (*irr*, ***bringen***, *sep*, *-ge-*, *h*) raise (*money*); muster (*courage etc*); start (*fashion etc*); → ***aufgebracht***
**'Aufbruch** *m* (*-[e]s*; *no pl*) departure, start
**'auf|brühen** *v/t* (*sep*, *-ge-*, *h*) make; **~bürden** *v/t* (*sep*, *-ge-*, *h*) ***j-m et. ~*** burden s.o. with s.th.; **~decken** *v/t* (*sep*, *-ge-*, *h*) uncover; **~drängen** *v/t* (*sep*, *-ge-*, *h*) ***j-m et. ~*** force s.th. on s.o.;

***sich j-m ~*** impose on s.o.; ***sich ~*** *fig* suggest itself; **~drehen** F (*sep*, *-ge-*, *h*) **1.** *v/t* turn on; **2.** *v/i* MOT step on the gas

**'aufdringlich** *adj* obtrusive

**'Aufdruck** *m* imprint; *on stamps*: overprint, surcharge

**aufei'nander** *adv* on top of each other; one after another; ***~folgend*** successive

**Aufenthalt** ['aufɛnthalt] *m* (-[*e*]*s*; *-e*) stay; RAIL stop

**'Aufenthalts|genehmigung** *f* residence permit; **~raum** *m* lounge, recreation room

**'auferstehen** *v/i* (*irr*, ***stehen,*** *sep*, *no -ge-*, *sein*) rise (from the dead)

**'Auferstehung** *f* (-; *-en*) REL resurrection

**'aufessen** *v/t* (*irr*, ***essen,*** *sep*, *-ge-*, *h*) eat up

**'auffahren** *v/i* (*irr*, ***fahren,*** *sep*, *-ge-*, *sein*) crash (***auf*** *acc* into); *fig* start up; **'Auffahrt** *f* approach; driveway, *Br* drive; **'Auffahrunfall** *m* MOT rear-end collision; pileup

**'auffallen** *v/i* (*irr*, ***fallen,*** *sep*, *-ge-*, *sein*) attract attention; ***j-m ~*** strike s.o.

**'auffallend, 'auffällig** *adj* striking; conspicuous; flashy (*clothes*)

**'auffangen** *v/t* (*irr*, ***fangen,*** *sep*, *-ge-*, *h*) catch (*a. fig*)

**'auffassen** *v/t* (*sep*, *-ge-*, *h*) understand (***als*** as)

**'Auffassung** *f* view; interpretation

**'auffinden** *v/t* (*irr*, ***finden,*** *sep*, *-ge-*, *h*) find, discover

**'auffordern** *v/t* (*sep*, *-ge-*, *h*) ***j-n ~, et. zu tun*** ask (*or* tell) s.o. to do s.th.

**'Aufforderung** *f* request; demand

**'auffrischen** *v/t* (*sep*, *-ge-*, *h*) freshen up; brush up

**'aufführen** *v/t* (*sep*, *-ge-*, *h*) THEA *etc* perform, present; state; ***sich ~*** behave

**'Aufführung** *f* THEA *etc* performance; *film*: showing

**'Aufgabe** *f* task, job; duty; PED task, assignment; MATH problem; *fig* surrender; ***es sich zur ~ machen*** make it one's business

**'Aufgang** *m* staircase; AST rising

**'aufgeben** (*irr*, ***geben,*** *sep*, *-ge-*, *h*) **1.** *v/t* give up; mail, send, *Br* post; check (*baggage*); PED set, give, assign (*homework etc*); ECON place (*order etc*); **2.** *v/i* give up *or* in

**'aufge|bracht** *adj* furious; **~dreht** F *adj* excited; **~dunsen** ['aufgədʊnzən] *adj* puffed(-up)

**'aufgehen** *v/i* (*irr*, ***gehen,*** *sep*, *-ge-*, *sein*) open; *sun, dough etc*: rise; MATH come out even; ***in Flammen ~*** go up in flames

**'aufge|hoben** *fig adj*: ***gut ~ sein bei*** be in good hands with; **~legt** *adj*: ***zu et. ~ sein*** feel like (doing) s.th.; ***gut*** (***schlecht***) ~ in a good (bad) mood; **~regt** *adj* excited; nervous; **~schlossen** *fig adj* open-minded; ***~ für*** open to; **~weckt** *fig adj* bright

**'aufgreifen** *v/t* (*irr*, ***greifen,*** *sep*, *-ge-*, *h*) pick up

**auf'grund** (*gen*) because of

**'auf|haben** F *v/t* (*irr*, ***haben,*** *sep*, *-ge-*, *h*) have on, wear; PED have *homework etc* to do; **~halten** *v/t* (*irr*, ***halten,*** *sep*, *-ge-*, *h*) stop, hold up (*a. traffic, thief etc*); keep open; ***sich ~*** (***bei j-m***) stay (with s.o.); **~hängen** *v/t* (*sep*, *-ge-*, *h*) hang (up); ***j-n ~*** hang s.o.; **~heben** *v/t* (*irr*, ***heben,*** *sep*, *-ge-*, *h*) pick up; keep; abolish (*law etc*); break up (*meeting etc*); ***sich gegenseitig ~*** neutralize each other; → ***aufgehoben***

**'Aufheben** *n* (*-s*; *no pl*) ***viel ~s machen*** make a fuss (***von*** about)

**'auf|heitern** *v/t* (*sep*, *-ge-*, *h*) cheer up; ***sich ~*** *weather*: clear up; **~helfen** *v/i* (*irr*, ***helfen,*** *sep*, *-ge-*, *h*) help *s.o.* up; **~hellen** *v/t and v/refl* (*sep*, *-ge-*, *h*) brighten; **~hetzen** *v/t* (*sep*, *-ge-*, *h*) ***j-n ~ gegen*** set s.o. against; **~holen** (*sep*, *-ge-*, *h*) **1.** *v/t* make up for; **2.** *v/i* catch up (***gegen*** with); **~horchen** *v/i* (*sep*, *-ge-*, *h*) prick (up) one's ears; ***~ lassen*** make *s.o.* sit up; **~hören** *v/i* (*sep*, *-ge-*, *h*) stop, end, finish, quit; ***mit et. ~*** stop (doing) s.th.; ***hör(t) auf!*** stop it!; **~kaufen** *v/t* (*sep*, *-ge-*, *h*) buy up

**'aufklären** *v/t* (*sep*, *-ge-*, *h*) clear up, *a.* solve (*crime*); ***j-n ~ über*** (*acc*) inform s.o. about; ***j-n*** (***sexuell***) ~ F tell s.o. the facts of life; **'Aufklärung** *f* (-; *no pl*) clearing up, solution; information; sex education; PHILOS Enlightenment; MIL reconnaissance

**'aufkleben** *v/t* (*sep*, *-ge-*, *h*) paste *or* stick on; **'Aufkleber** *m* (*-s*; -) sticker

**'aufknöpfen** *v/t* (*sep*, *-ge-*, *h*) unbutton

**'aufkommen** *v/i* (*irr*, ***kommen,*** *sep*,

*-ge-, sein*) come up; come into fashion *or* use; *rumo(u)r etc*: arise; ~ **für** pay (for)

'**aufladen** *v/t* (*irr*, **laden**, *sep*, *-ge-*, *h*) load; ELECTR charge

'**Auflage** *f* edition; circulation

'**auf|lassen** F *v/t* (*irr*, **lassen**, *sep*, *-ge-*, *h*) leave *door etc* open; keep *one's hat etc* on; **~lauern** *v/i* (*sep*, *-ge-*, *h*) ***j-m*** **~** waylay s.o.

'**Auflauf** *m* crowd; GASTR soufflé, pudding

'**auf|laufen** *v/i* (*irr*, **laufen**, *sep*, *-ge-*, *sein*) MAR run aground; **~leben** *v/i* (*sep*, *-ge-*, *sein*) *a.* (**wieder**) **~ lassen** revive; **~legen** (*sep*, *-ge-*, *h*) **1.** *v/t* put on, lay on; **2.** *v/i* TEL hang up

'**auflehnen** *v/t and v/refl* (*sep*, *-ge-*, *h*) lean (**auf** *acc* on); ***sich*** ~ rebel, revolt (**gegen** against); '**Auflehnung** *f* (-; *-en*) rebellion, revolt

'**auf|lesen** *v/t* (*irr*, **lesen**, *sep*, *-ge-*, *h*) pick up (*a. fig*); **~leuchten** *v/i* (*sep*, *-ge-*, *h*) flash (up); **~listen** *v/t* (*sep*, *-ge-*, *h*) list (*a.* EDP); **~lockern** *v/t* (*sep*, *-ge-*, *h*) loosen up; *fig* liven up

'**auflösen** *v/t* (*sep*, *-ge-*, *h*) dissolve; solve (*a.* MATH); disintegrate; '**Auflösung** *f* (dis)solution; disintegration

'**aufmachen** F *v/t* (*sep*, *-ge-*, *h*) open; ***sich*** ~ set out; '**Aufmachung** *f* (-; *-en*) get-up

'**aufmerksam** *adj* attentive (**auf** *acc* to); thoughtful; ***j-n ~ machen auf*** (*acc*) call s.o.'s attention to

'**Aufmerksamkeit** *f* (-; *-en*) a) (*no pl*) attention, b) small present

'**aufmuntern** *v/t* (*sep*, *-ge-*, *h*) encourage; cheer up

**Aufnahme** ['aufna:mə] *f* (-; *-n*) taking up; reception (*a.* MED *etc*); admission; photo(graph); recording; *film*: shooting

'**aufnahmefähig** *adj* receptive (**für** of)

'**Aufnahme|gebühr** *f* admission fee; **~prüfung** *f* entrance exam(ination)

'**aufnehmen** *v/t* (*irr*, **nehmen**, *sep*, *-ge-*, *h*) take up (*a. post etc*); pick up; put *s.o.* up; hold; take *s.th.* in; receive; PED *etc* admit; PHOT take a picture of; record; take (*the ball*); ***es ~ mit*** be a match for

'**aufpassen** *v/i* (*sep*, *-ge-*, *h*) pay attention; take care; ~ **auf** (*acc*) take care of, look after; keep an eye on; ***pass auf!*** look out!

'**Aufprall** *m* (-[*e*]*s*; *no pl*) impact

'**aufprallen** *v/i* (*sep*, *-ge-*, *sein*) ~ **auf** (*dat or acc*) hit

'**aufpumpen** *v/t* (*sep*, *-ge-*, *h*) pump up

'**aufputschen** *v/t* (*sep*, *-ge-*, *h*) pep up

'**Aufputschmittel** *n* PHARM stimulant, pep pill

'**auf|raffen** *v/refl* (*sep*, *-ge-*, *h*) ***sich ~ zu*** bring o.s. to *do s.th.*; **~räumen** *v/t* (*sep*, *-ge-*, *h*) tidy up; clear

'**aufrecht** *adj and adv* upright (*a. fig*); **~erhalten** *v/t* (*irr*, **halten**, *sep*, *no -ge-*, *h*) maintain, keep up

'**aufregen** *v/t* (*sep*, *-ge-*, *h*) excite, upset; ***sich*** ~ get excited *or* upset (**über** *acc* about); **~d** *adj* exciting

'**Aufregung** *f* excitement; fuss

'**aufreiben** *fig v/t* (*irr*, **reiben**, *sep*, *-ge-*, *h*) wear down; **~d** *adj* stressful

'**aufreißen** *v/t* (*irr*, **reißen**, *sep*, *-ge-*, *h*) tear open; fling *door etc* open; open *one's eyes* wide; F pick *s.o.* up

'**aufreizend** *adj* provocative

'**aufrichten** *v/t* (*sep*, *-ge-*, *h*) put up, raise; ***sich*** ~ straighten up; sit up

'**aufrichtig** *adj* sincere; frank

'**Aufrichtigkeit** *f* (-; *no pl*) sincerity; frankness

'**Aufriss** *m* (*-es*; *-e*) ARCH elevation

'**aufrollen** *v/t and v/refl* (*sep*, *-ge-*, *h*) roll up

'**Aufruf** *m* call; appeal (**zu** for)

'**aufrufen** *v/t* (*irr*, **rufen**, *sep*, *-ge-*, *h*) call on

**Aufruhr** ['aufru:ɐ] *m* (*-s*; *no pl*) revolt; riot; turmoil; '**Aufrührer** *m* (*-s*; -) rebel; rioter; **aufrührerisch** ['aufry:rərɪʃ] *adj* rebellious

'**aufrunden** *v/t* (*sep*, *-ge-*, *h*) round off

'**aufrüsten** *v/t and v/i* (*sep*, *-ge-*, *h*) (re)arm; '**Aufrüstung** *f* (re)armament

'**auf|rütteln** *fig v/t* (*sep*, *-ge-*, *h*) shake up, rouse; **~sagen** *v/t* (*sep*, *-ge-*, *h*) say; *a.* recite (*poem*)

**aufsässig** ['aufzɛsɪç] *adj* rebellious

'**Aufsatz** *m* PED essay, *Am a.* theme; (*newspaper etc*) article; TECH top

'**auf|saugen** *v/t* (*sep*, *-ge-*, *h*) absorb (*a. fig*); **~scheuern** *v/t* (*sep*, *-ge-*, *h*) chafe; **~schichten** *v/t* (*sep*, *-ge-*, *h*) pile up; **~schieben** *fig v/t* (*irr*, **schieben**, *sep*, *-ge-*, *h*) put off, postpone; delay

'**Aufschlag** *m* impact; ECON extra charge; lapel; cuff, *Br* turnup; *tennis*:

service; **'aufschlagen** (*irr*, ***schlagen***, *sep*, *-ge-*, *h*) **1.** *v/t* open (*book*, *eyes etc*); pitch (*tent*); cut (*one's knee etc*); ***Seite 3*** **~** open at page 3; **2.** *v/i tennis*: serve; ***auf dem Boden*** **~** hit the ground

**'auf|schließen** *v/t* (*irr*, ***schließen***, *sep*, *-ge-*, *h*) unlock, open; **~schlitzen** *v/t* (*sep*, *-ge-*, *h*) slit *or* rip open

**'Aufschluss** *m* information (***über*** *acc* on)

**'auf|schnappen** F *fig v/t* (*sep*, *-ge-*, *h*) pick up; **~schneiden** (*irr*, ***schneiden***, *sep*, *-ge-*, *h*) **1.** *v/t* cut open; GASTR cut up; **2.** F *fig v/i* brag, boast, talk big

**'Aufschnitt** *m* (*-[e]s*; *no pl*) GASTR cold cuts, *Br* (slices of) cold meat

**'auf|schnüren** *v/t* (*sep*, *-ge-*, *h*) untie; unlace; **~schrauben** *v/t* (*sep*, *-ge-*, *h*) unscrew; **~schrecken** (*sep*, *-ge-*) **1.** *v/t* (*h*) startle; **2.** *v/i* (*sein*) start (up)

**'Aufschrei** *m* yell; scream, outcry (*a. fig*)

**'auf|schreiben** *v/t* (*irr*, ***schreiben***, *sep*, *-ge-*, *h*) write down; **~schreien** *v/i* (*irr*, ***schreien***, *sep*, *-ge-*, *h*) cry out, scream

**'Aufschrift** *f* inscription

**'Aufschub** *m* postponement; delay; adjournment; respite

**'Aufschwung** *m* SPORT swing-up; *esp* ECON recovery, upswing; boom

**'Aufsehen** *n* (*-s*; *no pl*) **~** ***erregen*** attract attention; cause a sensation; **~** ***erregend*** sensational

**'Aufseher** *m* (*-s*; *-*), **'Aufseherin** *f* (*-*; *-nen*) guard

**'aufsetzen** (*sep*, *-ge-*, *h*) **1.** *v/t* put on; draw up (*letter etc*); ***sich*** **~** sit up; **2.** *v/i* AVIAT touch down

**'Aufsetzer** *m* (*-s*; *-*) SPORT awkward bouncing ball

**'Aufsicht** *f* (*-*; *no pl*) supervision, control; **~** ***führen*** PED *etc* be on (break) duty; proctor, *Br* invigilate

**'Aufsichts|behörde** *f* supervisory board; **~rat** *m* ECON board of directors; supervisory board

**'auf|sitzen** *v/i* (*irr*, ***sitzen***, *sep*, *-ge-*, *sein*) mount; **~spannen** *v/t* (*sep*, *-ge-*, *h*) stretch; put up (*umbrella*); spread; **~sparen** *v/t* (*sep*, *-ge-*, *h*) save; **~sperren** *v/t* (*sep*, *-ge-*, *h*) unlock; F open wide; **~spielen** *v/refl* (*sep*, *-ge-*, *h*) show off; ***sich*** **~** ***als*** play; **~spießen** *v/t* (*sep*, *-ge-*, *h*) spear, skewer; *animal*: gore; **~springen** *v/i* (*irr*, ***springen***, *sep*, *-ge-*, *sein*) jump up; *door etc*: fly open; *lips etc*: chap; **~spüren** *v/t* (*sep*, *-ge-*, *h*) track down; **~stacheln** *v/t* (*sep*, *-ge-*, *h*) goad (*s.o. into doing s.th.*); **~stampfen** *v/i* (*sep*, *-ge-*, *h*) stamp (one's foot)

**'Aufstand** *m* revolt, rebellion

**'Aufständische** *m*, *f* (*-n*; *-n*) rebel

**'auf|stapeln** *v/t* (*sep*, *-ge-*, *h*) pile up; **~stechen** *v/t* (*irr*, ***stechen***, *sep*, *-ge-*, *h*) puncture, prick open; MED lance; **~stecken** *v/t* (*sep*, *-ge-*, *h*) put up (*hair*); F *fig* give up; **~stehen** *v/i* (*irr*, ***stehen***, *sep*, *-ge-*, *sein*) get up, rise; **~steigen** *v/i* (*irr*, ***steigen***, *sep*, *-ge-*, *sein*) rise (*a. fig*); get on (*horse*, *bicycle*); be promoted, SPORT *Am a.* be moved up to a higher division

**'aufstellen** *v/t* (*sep*, *-ge-*, *h*) set up, put up; post (*guard*); set (*trap*, *record etc*); nominate *s.o.*; draw up (*table*, *list etc*)

**'Aufstellung** *f* putting up; nomination; list; SPORT line-up

**Aufstieg** ['aufʃtiːk] *m* (*-[e]s*; *-e*) ascent, *fig a.* rise

**'auf|stöbern** *fig v/t* (*sep*, *-ge-*, *h*) ferret out; **~stoßen** (*irr*, ***stoßen***, *sep*, *-ge-*, *h*) **1.** *v/t* push open; **2.** *v/i* belch; **~stützen** *v/refl* (*sep*, *-ge-*, *h*) lean (***auf*** *acc or dat* on); **~suchen** *v/t* (*sep*, *-ge-*, *h*) visit; see

**'Auftakt** *m* MUS upbeat; *fig* prelude

**'auf|tanken** *v/t* (*sep*, *-ge-*, *h*) fill up; MOT, AVIAT refuel; **~tauchen** *v/i* (*sep*, *-ge-*, *sein*) appear; MAR surface; **~tauen** *v/t* (*sep*, *-ge-*, *h*) thaw; GASTR defrost; **~teilen** *v/t* (*sep*, *-ge-*, *h*) divide (up)

**Auftrag** ['auftraːk] *m* (*-[e]s*; *Aufträge* ['auftrɛːgə]) instructions, order (*a.* ECON); MIL mission; ***im*** **~** ***von*** on behalf of; **auftragen** *v/t* (*irr*, ***tragen***, *sep*, *-ge-*, *h*) serve (up) (*food*); apply (*paint*); ***j-m et.*** **~** ask (*or* tell) s.o. to do s.th.; F ***dick*** **~** exaggerate; **'Auftraggeber** *m* (*-s*; *-*) principal; customer

**'auf|treffen** *v/i* (*irr*, ***treffen***, *sep*, *-ge-*, *sein*) strike, hit; **~treiben** F *v/t* (*irr*, ***treiben***, *sep*, *-ge-*, *h*) get hold of; raise (*money*); **~trennen** *v/t* (*sep*, *-ge-*, *h*) undo (*seam*), cut open; **~treten** *v/i* (*irr*, ***treten***, *sep*, *-ge-*, *sein*) THEA *etc* appear (***als*** as); behave, act; occur

**'Auftreten** *n* (*-s*; *no pl*) appearance; behavio(u)r; occurrence

**'Auftrieb** *m* (-[*e*]*s*; *no pl*) PHYS buoyancy (*a. fig*); AVIAT lift; *fig* impetus
**'Auftritt** *m* THEA entrance
**'auf|tun** *v/refl* (*irr*, ***tun***, *sep*, *-ge-*, *h*) open (*a. fig*); *abyss*: yawn; **~türmen** *v/t* (*sep*, *-ge-*, *h*) pile *or* heap up; ***sich*** ~ pile up; **~wachen** *v/i* (*sep*, *-ge-*, *sein*) wake up; **~wachsen** *v/i* (*irr*, ***wachsen***, *sep*, *-ge-*, *sein*) grow up
**Aufwand** ['aufvant] *m* (-[*e*]*s*; *no pl*) expenditure (***an*** *dat* of), *a.* expense; pomp
**aufwändig** ['aufwɛndɪç] *adj* costly; extravagant (*lifestyle*)
**'aufwärmen** *v/t* (*sep*, *-ge-*, *h*) warm up; F *fig contp* bring up
**aufwärts** ['aufvɛrts] *adv* upward(s); ~ ***gehen*** *fig* improve
**'auf|wecken** *v/t* (*sep*, *-ge-*, *h*) wake (up); **~weichen** *v/t* (*sep*, *-ge-*, *h*) soften; soak; **~weisen** *v/t* (*irr*, ***weisen***, *sep*, *-ge-*, *h*) show, have; **~wenden** *v/t* ([*irr*, ***wenden***,] *sep*, *-ge-*, *h*) spend (***für*** on); ***Mühe*** ~ take pains
**aufwendig** → ***aufwändig***
**'aufwerfen** *v/t* (*irr*, ***werfen***, *sep*, *-ge-*, *h*) raise (*question etc*)
**'aufwerten** *v/t* (*sep*, *-ge-*, *h*) ECON revalue; *fig* increase the value of
**'Aufwertung** *f* revaluation
**'aufwickeln** *v/t and v/refl* (*sep*, *-ge-*, *h*) wind up, roll up; put *hair* in curlers
**aufwiegeln** ['aufvi:gəln] *v/t* (*sep*, *-ge-*, *h*) stir up, incite, instigate
**'aufwiegen** *v/t* (*irr*, ***wiegen***, *sep*, *-ge-*, *h*) make up for
**Aufwiegler** ['aufvi:glɐ] *m* (*-s*; -) agitator; instigator
**'Aufwind** *m* upwind; ***im*** ~ *fig* on the upswing
**'auf|wirbeln** *v/t* (*sep*, *-ge-*, *h*) whirl up; *fig* (***viel***) ***Staub*** ~ make (quite) a stir; **~wischen** *v/t* (*sep*, *-ge-*, *h*) wipe up; **~wühlen** *fig v/t* (*sep*, *-ge-*, *h*) stir, move
**'aufzählen** *v/t* (*sep*, *-ge-*, *h*) name (one by one), list; **'Aufzählung** *f* enumeration, list
**'aufzeichnen** *v/t* (*sep*, *-ge-*, *h*) TV, *radio etc*: record, tape; draw; **'Aufzeichnung** *f* recording; *pl* notes
**'aufzeigen** *v/t* (*sep*, *-ge-*, *h*) show; demonstrate; point out (*mistake etc*)
**'aufziehen** (*irr*, ***ziehen***, *sep*, *-ge-*) **1.** *v/t* (*h*) draw *or* pull up; (pull) open; bring up (*child*); wind (up) (*clock*); mount (*photo etc*); ***j-n*** ~ tease s.o.; **2.** *v/i* (*sein*) come up; **'Aufzug** *m* elevator, *Br* lift; THEA act; F *contp* get-up
**'aufzwingen** *v/t* (*irr*, ***zwingen***, *sep*, *-ge-*, *h*) ***j-m et.*** ~ force s.th. upon s.o.
**Augapfel** ['auk-] *m* ANAT eyeball
**Auge** ['augə] *n* (*-s*; *-n*) ANAT eye; ***ein blaues*** ~ a black eye; ***mit bloßem*** ~ with the naked eye; ***mit verbundenen*** **~*n*** blindfold; ***in meinen*** **~*n*** in my view; ***mit anderen*** **~*n*** in a different light; ***aus den*** **~*n verlieren*** lose sight of; ***ein*** ~ ***zudrücken*** turn a blind eye; ***unter vier*** **~*n*** in private; F ***ins*** ~ ***gehen*** go wrong
**'Augenarzt** *m* eye specialist
**'Augenblick** *m* moment, instant
**'augenblicklich 1.** *adj* present; immediate; momentary; **2.** *adv* at present, at the moment; immediately
**'Augen|braue** *f* eyebrow; **~licht** *n* (-[*e*]*s*; *no pl*) eyesight; **~lid** *n* eyelid; **~maß** *n*: ***ein gutes*** ~ a sure eye; ***nach dem*** ~ by the eye; **~merk** *n*: ***sein*** ~ ***richten auf*** (*acc*) turn one's attention to, *fig a.* have in view; **~schein** *m* (*-s*; *no pl*) appearance; ***in*** ~ ***nehmen*** examine, inspect; **~zeuge** *m* eyewitness
**August** [au'gʊst] *m* (-; *no pl*) August
**Auktion** [auk'tsjo:n] *f* (-; *-en*) auction
**Auktionator** [auktsjo'na:to:ɐ] *m* (*-s*; *-en* [-na'to:rən]) auctioneer
**Aula** ['aula] *f* (-; *-s*, *Aulen*) auditorium, *Br* (assembly) hall
**aus** [aus] *prp* (*dat*) *and adv mst* out of, from; of (*silk etc*); out of (*spite etc*); *light etc*: out, off; *play etc*: over, finished; SPORT out; ~ ***dem Fenster*** *etc* out of the window *etc*; ~ ***München*** from Munich; ~ ***Holz*** (made) of wood; ~ ***Mitleid*** out of pity; ~ ***Spaß*** for fun; ~ ***Versehen*** by mistake; ~ ***diesem Grunde*** for this reason; ***von hier*** ~ from here; F ***von mir*** **~*!*** I don't care!; ~ ***der Mode*** out of fashion; F ~ ***sein*** be over; be out; ~ ***sein auf*** (*acc*) be out for; be after (*s.o.'s money etc*); ***die Schule*** (***das Spiel***) ***ist*** ~ school (the game) is over; ***ein/***~ TECH on/off
**Aus** *n*: ***im*** ~ *ball*: out of play
**'aus|arbeiten** *v/t* (*sep*, *-ge-*, *h*) work out; prepare; **~arten** *v/i* (*sep*, *-ge-*, *sein*) get out of hand; **~atmen** *v/t and v/i* (*sep*, *-ge-*, *h*) breathe out; **~baden** F *v/t*

(*sep*, *-ge-*, *h*) ***et. ~ müssen*** take the rap for s.th.

'**Ausbau** *m* (-[*e*]*s*; *no pl*) extension; completion; removal; '**ausbauen** *v/t* (*sep*, *-ge-*, *h*) extend; complete; remove; improve; '**ausbaufähig** *adj*: ***et. ist ~*** there is potential for growth *or* development

'**ausbessern** *v/t* (*sep*, *-ge-*, *h*) mend, repair, F *a.* fix; '**Ausbesserung** *f* (-; *-en*) repair(ing)

'**Ausbeute** *f* (-; *no pl*) gain, profit; yield; '**ausbeuten** *v/t* (*sep*, *-ge-*, *h*) exploit (*a. contp*); '**Ausbeutung** *f* (-; *no pl*) exploitation

'**ausbilden** *v/t* (*sep*, *-ge-*, *h*) train, instruct; ***j-n ~ zu*** train s.o. to be

'**Ausbilder** *m* (*-s*; -) instructor

'**Ausbildung** *f* (-; *-en*) training, instruction

'**ausbleiben** *v/i* (*irr*, ***bleiben***, *sep*, *-ge-*, *sein*) stay out; fail to come; ***es konnte nicht ~*** it was inevitable

'**Ausblick** *m* view (***auf*** *acc* of); *fig* outlook (for)

'**ausbrechen** *v/i* (*irr*, ***brechen***, *sep*, *-ge-*, *sein*) break out (*a. fig*); ***in Tränen ~*** burst into tears; '**Ausbrecher** *m* (*-s*; -) escaped prisoner

'**ausbreiten** *v/t* (*sep*, *-ge-*, *h*) spread (out); ***sich ~*** spread; '**Ausbreitung** *f* (-; *no pl*) spreading

'**ausbrennen** *v/t* (*irr*, ***brennen***, *sep*, *-ge-*, *sein*) burn out

'**Ausbruch** *m* escape, breakout; outbreak (*of fire etc*); eruption (*of volcano*); (out)burst (*of resentment etc*)

'**ausbrüten** *v/t* (*sep*, *-ge-*, *h*) hatch (*a. fig*)

'**Ausdauer** *f* perseverance, stamina, *esp* SPORT *a.* staying power; '**ausdauernd** *adj* persevering; SPORT tireless

'**ausdehnen** *v/t and v/refl* (*sep*, *-ge-*, *h*) stretch; *fig* expand, extend

'**Ausdehnung** *f* expansion; extension

'**ausdenken** *v/t* (*irr*, ***denken***, *sep*, *-ge-*, *h*) think *s.th.* up; invent (*a. fig*)

'**Ausdruck** *m* expression, term; EDP print-out; '**ausdrucken** *v/t* (*sep*, *-ge-*, *h*) EDP print out

'**ausdrücken** *v/t* (*sep*, *-ge-*, *h*) stub out (*cigarette etc*); *fig* express

**ausdrücklich** ['ausdrʏklɪç] *adj* express, explicit

'**ausdrucks|los** *adj* expressionless, blank; **~voll** *adj* expressive

'**Ausdrucksweise** *f* language, style

'**Ausdünstung** *f* (-; *-en*) exhalation; perspiration; odo(u)r

**auseinander** [ausʔai'nandɐ] *adv* apart; separate(d); ***~ bringen*** separate, ***~ gehen*** part; *meeting etc*: break up; *opinions etc*: differ; *married couple*: separate; ***~ halten*** tell apart; ***~ nehmen*** take apart (*a. fig*); ***~ setzen*** explain; ***sich ~ setzen mit*** deal with; argue with *s.o.*

**Ausei'nandersetzung** *f* (-; *-en*) argument

'**auserlesen** *adj* choice, exquisite

'**ausfahren** (*irr*, ***fahren***, *sep*, *-ge-*) **1.** *v/i* (*sein*) go for a drive *or* ride; **2.** *v/t* (*h*) take *s.o.* out; AVIAT extend (*landing gear*); '**Ausfahrt** *f* drive, ride; MOT exit

'**Ausfall** *m* TECH, MOT, SPORT failure; loss

'**ausfallen** *v/i* (*irr*, ***fallen***, *sep*, *-ge-*, *sein*) fall out; not take place, be cancelled; TECH, MOT break down, fail; ***gut*** *etc* ***~*** turn out well *etc*; ***~ lassen*** cancel; ***die Schule fällt aus*** there is no school

'**ausfallend**, '**ausfällig** *adj* insulting

'**ausfertigen** *v/t* (*sep*, *-ge-*, *h*) draw up (*contract etc*); make out (*check etc*)

'**Ausfertigung** *f* drawing up; copy; ***in doppelter ~*** in duplicate

'**ausfindig** *adj*: ***~ machen*** find

**ausflippen** ['ausflɪpən] F *v/i* (*sep*, *-ge-*, *sein*) freak out

**Ausflüchte** ['ausflʏçtə] *pl* excuses

'**Ausflug** *m* trip, excursion, outing

**Ausflügler** ['ausfly:klɐ] *m* (*-s*; -) day-tripper

'**Ausfluss** *m* TECH outlet; MED discharge

'**aus|fragen** *v/t* (*sep*, *-ge-*, *h*) question (***über*** *acc* about); sound out; **~fransen** *v/i* (*sep*, *-ge-*, *sein*) fray; **~fressen** F *v/t* (*irr*, ***fressen***, *sep*, *-ge-*, *h*) ***et. ~*** be up to no good

**Ausfuhr** ['ausfu:ɐ] *f* (-; *-en*) ECON export(ation); '**ausführbar** *adj* practicable; '**ausführen** *v/t* (*sep*, *-ge-*, *h*) take *s.o.* out; carry out (*task etc*); ECON export; explain

**ausführlich** ['ausfy:ɐlɪç] **1.** *adj* detailed; comprehensive; **2.** *adv* in detail; '**Ausführlichkeit** *f*: ***in aller ~*** in great detail

'**Ausführung** *f* execution, performance; type, model, design

**'ausfüllen** *v/t* (*sep*, *-ge-*, *h*) fill out (*Br* in) (*form*)
**'Ausgabe** *f* distribution; edition; expense; issue; EDP output
**'Ausgang** *m* exit, way out; end; result, outcome; TECH, ELECTR output, outlet
**'Ausgangs|punkt** *m* starting point; **~sperre** *f* POL curfew
**'ausgeben** *v/t* (*irr*, **geben**, *sep*, *-ge-*, *h*) give out; spend; F **j-m e-n ~** buy s.o. a drink; **sich ~ als** pass o.s. off as
**'ausge|beult** *adj* baggy; **~bildet** *adj* trained, skilled; **~bucht** *adj* booked up; **~dehnt** *adj* extensive; **~dient** *adj*: **~ haben** *fig* have had its day; **~fallen** *adj* odd, unusual; **~glichen** *adj* (well-)balanced
**'ausgehen** *v/i* (*irr*, **gehen**, *sep*, *-ge-*, *sein*) go out; end; *hair*: fall out; *money*, *supplies*: run out; **leer ~** get nothing; **~ von** start from *or* at; come from; **davon ~, dass** assume that; **ihm ging das Geld aus** he ran out of money
**'ausge|kocht** *fig adj* cunning; out-and--out (*villain etc*); **~lassen** *fig adj* cheerful; hilarious; **~ sein** be in high spirits; **~macht** *adj* agreed(-on); downright (*nonsense*); **~prägt** *adj* marked, pronounced; **~rechnet** *adv*: **~ er** he of all people; **~ heute** today of all days; **~schlossen** *adj* out of the question; **~storben** *adj* extinct; **~sucht** *adj* select, choice; **~wachsen** *adj* full--grown; **~wogen** *adj* (well-)balanced; **~zeichnet** *adj* excellent
**ausgiebig** ['ausgi:bɪç] *adj* extensive, thorough; substantial (*meal*)
**'ausgießen** *v/t* (*irr*, **gießen**, *sep*, *-ge-*, *h*) pour out
**'Ausgleich** *m* (-[*e*]*s*; *no pl*) compensation; SPORT even score, *Br* equalization; *tennis*: deuce; **'ausgleichen** *v/t and v/i* (*irr*, **gleichen**, *sep*, *-ge-*, *h*) compensate; equalize (*Br a.* SPORT); ECON balance; SPORT make the score even
**'Ausgleichs|sport** *m* remedial exercises; **~tor** *n*, **~treffer** *m* SPORT tying point, *Br* equalizer
**'ausgraben** *v/t* (*irr*, **graben**, *sep*, *-ge-*, *h*) dig out *or* up (*a. fig*)
**'Ausgrabungen** *pl* excavations
**'ausgrenzen** *v/t* (*sep*, *-ge-*, *h*) isolate
**'Ausguss** *m* (kitchen) sink
**'aushalten** (*irr*, **halten**, *sep*, *-ge-*, *h*) **1.** *v/t* bear, stand; keep (*mistress etc*); **nicht auszuhalten sein** be unbearable; **2.** *v/i* hold out
**aushändigen** ['aushɛndɪgən] *v/t* (*sep*, *-ge-*, *h*) hand over
**'Aushang** *m* notice; bulletin
**'aushängen** *v/t* (*sep*, *-ge-*, *h*) hang out, put up; unhinge (*door*)
**'aus|heben** *v/t* (*irr*, **heben**, *sep*, *-ge-*, *h*) dig (*trench*); raid (*place etc*); **~helfen** *v/i* (*irr*, **helfen**, *sep*, *-ge-*, *h*) help out
**'Aushilfe** *f* (temporary) help
**'Aushilfs...** *in cpds -kellner etc*: temporary
**'aus|holen** *v/i* (*sep*, *-ge-*, *h*) **zum Schlag ~** swing (to strike); *fig* **weit ~** go far back; **~horchen** *v/t* (*sep*, *-ge-*, *h*) sound (**über** *acc* on); **~hungern** *v/t* (*sep*, *-ge-*, *h*) starve out; **~kennen** *v/refl* (*irr*, **kennen**, *sep*, *-ge-*, *h*) **sich ~** (**in** *dat*) know one's way (about); *fig* know a lot (about); **~klingen** *v/i* (*irr*, **klingen**, *sep*, *-ge-*, *sein*) draw to a close; **~klopfen** *v/t* (*sep*, *-ge-*, *h*) knock out; **~kommen** *v/i* (*irr*, **kommen**, *sep*, *-ge-*, *sein*) get by; **~ mit** manage with *s.th.*; get along with *s.o.*
**Auskunft** ['auskʊnft] *f* (-; *Auskünfte* ['auskʏnftə]) a) information, b) (*no pl*) information desk; TEL inquiries
**'aus|lachen** *v/t* (*sep*, *-ge-*, *h*) laugh at (**wegen** for); **~laden** *v/t* (*irr*, **laden**, *sep*, *-ge-*, *h*) unload
**'Auslage** *f* window display; *pl* expenses
**'Ausland** *n* (-[*e*]*s*; *no pl*) **das ~** foreign countries; **ins ~, im ~** abroad
**Ausländer** ['auslɛndɐ] *m* (-*s*; -) foreigner; **~feindlichkeit** *f* hostility to foreigners, xenophobia
**Ausländerin** ['auslɛndərɪn] *f* (-; *-nen*) foreigner
**'ausländisch** [-lɛndɪʃ] *adj* foreign
**'Auslands|gespräch** *n* international call; **~korrespondent(in)** foreign correspondent
**'auslassen** *v/t* (*irr*, **lassen**, *sep*, *-ge-*, *h*) leave out; melt (*butter etc*); let out (*seam*); **s-n Zorn an j-m ~** take it out on s.o.; **sich ~ über** (*acc*) express o.s. on
**'Auslassung** *f* (-; *-en*) omission
**'Auslassungszeichen** *n* LING apostrophe
**'Auslauf** *m* room to move about; *dog*: exercise; **'auslaufen** *v/i* (*irr*, **laufen**,

*sep*, *-ge-*, *sein*) MAR leave port; *pot etc*: leak; *liquid etc*: run out; **'Ausläufer** *m* METEOR ridge, trough; *pl* GEOGR foothills; **'Auslaufmo,dell** *n* ECON close-out (*Br* phase-out) model

**'auslegen** *v/t* (*sep*, *-ge-*, *h*) lay out; carpet; line (*with paper etc*); display (*goods*); interpret (*text etc*); advance (*money*)

**'Auslegung** *f* (-; *-en*) interpretation

**'aus|leihen** *v/t* (*irr*, ***leihen***, *sep*, *-ge-*, *h*) lend (out), loan; ***sich*** (*dat*) ***et.*** ~ borrow s.th.; **~lernen** *v/i* (*sep*, *-ge-*, *h*) complete one's training; ***man lernt nie aus*** we live and learn

**'Auslese** *f* choice, selection; *fig* pick

**'auslesen** *v/t* (*irr*, ***lesen***, *sep*, *-ge-*, *h*) pick out, select; finish (*book etc*)

**'ausliefern** *v/t* (*sep*, *-ge-*, *h*) hand *or* turn over, deliver (up); POL extradite; **'Auslieferung** *f* delivery; extradition

**'aus|liegen** *v/i* (*irr*, ***liegen***, *sep*, *-ge-*, *h*) be laid out; **~löschen** *v/t* (*sep*, *-ge-*, *h*) put out; *fig* wipe out; **~losen** *v/t* (*sep*, *-ge-*, *h*) draw (lots) for

**'auslösen** *v/t* (*sep*, *-ge-*, *h*) TECH release; ransom, redeem; cause, start, trigger *s.th.* off; **'Auslöser** *m* (PHOT shutter) release; trigger

**'ausmachen** *v/t* (*sep*, *-ge-*, *h*) put out (*fire*); turn off (*light etc*); arrange (*date etc*); agree on (*price etc*); make up; amount to; settle (*dispute*); sight, spot; ***macht es Ihnen et. aus*** (***, wenn***...)**?** do you mind (if ...)?; ***es macht mir nichts aus*** I don't mind; ***das macht*** (***gar***) ***nichts aus*** that doesn't matter (at all)

**'ausmalen** *v/t* (*sep*, *-ge-*, *h*) paint; ***sich et.*** ~ imagine s.th.

**'Ausmaß** *n* extent; *pl* proportions

**aus|merzen** ['ausmɛrtsən] *v/t* (*sep*, *-ge-*, *h*) eliminate; **~messen** *v/t* (*irr*, ***messen***, *sep*, *-ge-*, *h*) measure

**Ausnahme** ['ausnaːmə] *f* (-; *-n*) exception; **~zustand** *m* POL state of emergency

**'ausnahmslos** *adv* without exception

**'ausnahmsweise** *adv* by way of exception; just this once

**'ausnehmen** *v/t* (*irr*, ***nehmen***, *sep*, *-ge-*, *h*) clean (*chicken etc*); except; F *contp* fleece *s.o.*; **~d** *adv* exceptionally

**'aus|nutzen** *v/t* (*sep*, *-ge-*, *h*) use; take advantage of (*a. contp*); exploit; **~packen** (*sep*, *-ge-*, *h*) **1.** *v/t* unpack; **2.** F *v/i* talk; **~pfeifen** *v/t* (*irr*, ***pfeifen***, *sep*, *-ge-*, *h*) boo, hiss; **~plaudern** *v/t* (*sep*, *-ge-*, *h*) blab out; **~plündern** *v/t* (*sep*, *-ge-*, *h*) plunder, rob; **~pro,bieren** *v/t* (*sep*, *no -ge-*, *h*) try (out), test

**'Auspuff** *m* MOT exhaust; **~gase** *pl* MOT exhaust fumes; **~rohr** *n* MOT exhaust pipe; **~topf** *m* MOT muffler, *Br* silencer

**'aus|quar,tieren** *v/t* (*sep*, *no -ge-*, *h*) move out; **~ra,dieren** *v/t* (*sep*, *no -ge-*, *h*) erase; *fig* wipe out; **~ran,gieren** *v/t* (*sep*, *no -ge-*, *h*) discard; **~rauben** *v/t* (*sep*, *-ge-*, *h*) rob; **~räumen** *v/t* (*sep*, *-ge-*, *h*) empty; clear out (*room etc*); *fig* clear up (*doubt etc*); **~rechnen** *v/t* (*sep*, *-ge-*, *h*) work out

**'Ausrede** *f* excuse

**'ausreden** (*sep*, *-ge-*, *h*) **1.** *v/i* finish speaking; ***j-n ~ lassen*** hear s.o. out; **2.** *v/t*: ***j-m et.*** ~ talk s.o. out of s.th.

**'ausreichen** *v/t* (*sep*, *-ge-*, *h*) be enough; **~d** *adj* sufficient, enough; *grade*: (barely) passing, only average, weak, D

**'Ausreise** *f* departure; **'ausreisen** *v/i* (*sep*, *-ge-*, *sein*) leave (a *or* one's country); **'Ausreisevisum** *n* exit visa

**'ausreißen** (*irr*, ***reißen***, *sep*, *-ge-*) **1.** *v/t* (*h*) pull *or* tear out; **2.** F *v/i* (*sein*) run away; **'Ausreißer** *m* (*-s*; -) runaway

**'aus|renken** *v/t* (*sep*, *-ge-*, *h*) MED dislocate; **~richten** *v/t* (*sep*, *-ge-*, *h*) tell *s.o. s.th.*; deliver (*message*); accomplish; arrange (*party etc*); ***richte ihr e-n Gruß von mir aus!*** give her my regards!; ***kann ich et. ~?*** can I take a message

**'ausrotten** *v/t* (*sep*, *-ge-*, *h*) exterminate

**'Ausrottung** *f* (-; *-en*) extermination

**'ausrücken** *v/i* (*sep*, *-ge-*, *sein*) F run away; MIL march out

**'Ausruf** *m* cry, shout; **'ausrufen** *v/t* (*irr*, ***rufen***, *sep*, *-ge-*, *h*) cry, shout, exclaim; call out (*name*); POL proclaim; **'Ausrufung** *f* (-; *-en*) POL proclamation; **'Ausrufungszeichen** *n* LING exclamation mark

**'ausruhen** *v/i*, *v/t and v/refl* (*sep*, *-ge-*, *h*) rest

**'ausrüsten** *v/t* (*sep*, *-ge-*, *h*) equip; **'Ausrüstung** *f* equipment

**'ausrutschen** *v/i* (*sep*, *-ge-*, *sein*) slip

**'Aussage** *f* statement; JUR evidence

**'aussagen** *v/t* (*sep*, *-ge-*, *h*) state, declare; JUR testify
**ausschalten** *v/t* (*sep*, *-ge-*, *h*) switch off; *fig* eliminate
**'Ausschau** *f*: ~ ***halten nach*** → **'ausschauen** *v/i* (*sep*, *-ge-*, *h*) ~ ***nach*** look out for, watch out for
**'ausscheiden** (*irr*, ***scheiden***, *sep*, *-ge-*) **1.** *v/i* (*sein*) be ruled out; SPORT *etc* drop out (***aus*** *dat* of); retire (***aus*** *dat* from *office etc*); ~ ***aus*** (*dat*) leave (*a firm etc*); **2.** *v/t* (*h*) eliminate; MED *etc* secrete, exude; **'Ausscheidung** *f* elimination (*a.* SPORT); MED secretion
**'Ausscheidungs...** *in cpds ...spiel etc*: SPORT qualifying ...
**'aus|schlachten** *fig v/t* (*sep*, *-ge-*, *h*) salvage, *Br a.* cannibalize; *contp* exploit; **~schlafen** (*irr*, ***schlafen***, *sep*, *-ge-*, *h*) **1.** *v/i* sleep in; **2.** *v/t* sleep off
**'Ausschlag** *m* MED rash; TECH deflection; ***den ~ geben*** decide it
**'ausschlagen** (*irr*, ***schlagen***, *sep*, *-ge-*, *h*) **1.** *v/t* knock out (*tooth etc*); *fig* refuse, decline (*offer etc*); **2.** *v/i horse*: kick; BOT bud; TECH deflect
**'ausschlaggebend** *adj* decisive
**'ausschließen** *v/t* (*irr*, ***schließen***, *sep*, *-ge-*, *h*) lock out; *fig* exclude; expel; SPORT disqualify
**'ausschließlich** *adj* exclusive
**'Ausschluss** *m* exclusion; expulsion; SPORT disqualification; ***unter ~ der Öffentlichkeit*** in closed session
**'aus|schmücken** *v/t* (*sep*, *-ge-*, *h*) decorate; *fig* embellish; **~schneiden** *v/t* (*irr*, ***schneiden***, *sep*, *-ge-*, *h*) cut out
**'Ausschnitt** *m clothing*: neck; (*press*) clipping (*Br* cutting); *fig* part; extract; ***mit tiefem ~*** low-necked
**'ausschreiben** *v/t* (*irr*, ***schreiben***, *sep*, *-ge-*, *h*) write out (*a. check etc*); advertise (*post etc*); **'Ausschreibung** *f* advertisement
**'Ausschreitungen** *pl* violence, riots
**'Ausschuss** *m* committee, board; TECH (*no pl*) refuse, waste, rejects
**'aus|schütteln** *v/t* (*sep*, *-ge-*, *h*) shake out; **~schütten** *v/t* (*sep*, *-ge-*, *h*) pour out (*a. fig*); spill; ECON pay; ***sich vor Lachen ~*** split one's sides
**'ausschweifend** *adj* dissolute
**'Ausschweifung** *f* (-; *-en*) debauchery, excess
**'aussehen** *v/i* (*irr*, ***sehen***, *sep*, *-ge-*, *h*) look; ***krank*** (***traurig***) ~ look ill (sad); ~ ***wie ...*** look like ...; ***wie sieht er aus?*** what does he look like? **'Aussehen** *n* (*-s*; *no pl*) look(s), appearance
**außen** ['ausən] *adv* outside; ***nach ~*** (***hin***) outward(s); *fig* outwardly
**'Außenbordmotor** *m* outboard motor
**aussenden** *v/t* ([*irr*, ***senden***,] *sep*, *-ge-*, *h*) send out
**'Außen|dienst** *m* field service; **~handel** *m* foreign trade; **~mi,nister** *m Am* Secretary of State, *Br* Foreign Secretary; **~minis,terium** *n Am* State Department, *Br* Foreign Office; **~poli,tik** *f* foreign affairs; foreign policy
**'außenpo,litisch** *adj* foreign-policy
**'Außenseite** *f* outside
**'Außenseiter** [-zaitɐ] *m* (*-s*; -) outsider
**'Außen|spiegel** *m* MOT outside rearview mirror; **~stände** *pl* ECON receivables; **~stelle** *f* branch; **~stürmer** *m* SPORT winger; **~welt** *f* outside world
**außer** ['ausɐ] **1.** *prp* (*dat*) out of; aside from, *Br* beside(s); except; ~ ***sich sein*** be beside o.s. (***vor Freude*** with joy); ***alle ~ e-m*** all but one; → ***Betrieb***, ***Gefahr***; **2.** *cj*: ~ ***dass*** except that; ~ ***wenn*** unless
**'außerdem** *cj* besides, moreover
**äußere** ['ɔʏsərə] *adj* exterior, outer, outward; **'Äußere** *n* (*-n*; *no pl*) exterior, outside; (outward) appearance
**'außergewöhnlich** *adj* unusual
**'außerhalb** *prp* (*gen*) *and adv* outside; out of; beyond
**'außerirdisch** *adj* extraterrestrial
**'äußerlich** *adj* external, outward
**'Äußerlichkeit** *f* (-; *-en*) formality; minor detail
**äußern** ['ɔʏsɐn] *v/t* (*ge-*, *h*) utter, express; ***sich ~*** say s.th.; ***sich ~ zu*** *or* ***über*** (*acc*) express o.s. on
**'außer'ordentlich** *adj* extraordinary
**'außerplanmäßig** *adj* unscheduled
**äußerst** ['ɔʏsɐst] **1.** *adj* outermost; *fig* extreme; ***im ~en Fall*** at (the) worst; at (the) most **2.** *adv* extremely
**außer'stande** *adj*: ~ ***sein*** be unable
**'Äußerung** *f* (-; *-en*) utterance, remark
**'aussetzen** (*sep*, *-ge-*, *h*) **1.** *v/t* abandon; expose (*dat* to); ***et. auszusetzen haben an*** (*dat*) find fault with; **2.** *v/i* stop, break off; MOT, TECH fail

**'Aussicht** *f* view (***auf*** *acc* of); *fig* prospect (of), chance (***auf Erfolg*** of success); **'aussichtslos** *adj* hopeless, desperate; **'Aussichtspunkt** *m* vantage point; **'aussichtsreich** *adj* promising; **'Aussichtsturm** *m* lookout tower
**'Aussiedler** *m* resettler, evacuee
**'aussitzen** *v/t* (*irr*, ***sitzen***, *sep*, *-ge-*, *h*) sit *s.th.* out
**aussöhnen** ['auszø:nən] *v/refl* (*sep*, *-ge-*, *h*) ***sich*** ~ (***mit***) become reconciled (with), F make it up (with)
**'Aussöhnung** *f* (-; *-en*) reconciliation
**'aus|sor,tieren** *v/t* (*sep*, *no -ge-*, *h*) sort out; **~spannen** (*sep*, *-ge-*, *h*) **1.** *v/t* unharness; **2.** *fig v/i* (take a) rest, relax
**'aussperren** *v/t* (*sep*, *-ge-*, *h*) lock out (*a.* ECON); **'Aussperrung** *f* (-; *-en*) ECON lock-out
**'aus|spielen** (*sep*, *-ge-*, *h*) **1.** *v/t* play; ***j-n gegen j-n*** ~ play s.o. off against s.o.; **2.** *v/i card game*: lead; ***er hat ausgespielt*** *fig* he is done for; **~spio,nieren** *v/t* (*sep*, *no -ge-*, *h*) spy out
**'Aussprache** *f* pronunciation; discussion; *private* heart-to-heart (talk)
**'aussprechen** *v/t* (*irr*, ***sprechen***, *sep*, *-ge-*, *h*) pronounce; express; ***sich ~ für*** (***gegen***) speak for (against); ***sich mit j-m gründlich*** ~ have a heart-to-heart talk with s.o.
**'Ausspruch** *m* saying; remark
**'aus|spucken** *v/i and v/t* (*sep*, *-ge-*, *h*) spit out; **~spülen** *v/t* (*sep*, *-ge-*, *h*) rinse
**'Ausstand** *m* strike, F walkout
**'ausstatten** *v/t* (*sep*, *-ge-*, *h*) fit out, equip, furnish; **'Ausstattung** *f* (-; *-en*) equipment, furnishings; design
**'aus|stechen** *v/t* (*irr*, ***stechen***, *sep*, *-ge-*, *h*) GASTR cut out (*a. fig*); put out (*eyes*); **~stehen** (*irr*, ***stehen***, *sep*, *-ge-*, *h*) **1.** *v/t* stand, endure; F ***ich kann ihn*** (***es***) ***nicht*** ~ I can't stand him (it); **2.** *v/i*: (***noch***) ~ be outstanding *or* overdue
**'aussteigen** *v/i* (*irr*, ***steigen***, *sep*, *-ge-*, *sein*) get out (***aus*** *dat* of); (*a.* ~ ***aus*** *dat*) get off *a bus*, *train*; F *fig* drop out; **'Aussteiger** F *m* (*-s*; -) drop-out
**'ausstellen** *v/t* (*sep*, *-ge-*, *h*) exhibit, display, show; make out (*check etc*); issue (*passport*); **'Aussteller** *m* (*-s*; -) exhibitor; issuer; drawer (*of check*)
**'Ausstellung** *f* exhibition, show
**'aussterben** *v/i* (*irr*, ***sterben***, *sep*, *-ge-*, *sein*) die out, become extinct (*both a. fig*)
**'Aussteuer** *f* trousseau; dowry
**'aussteuern** *v/t* (*sep*, *-ge-*, *h*) ELECTR modulate; **'Aussteuerung** *f* ELECTR modulation; level control
**Ausstieg** ['ausʃti:k] *m* (-[*e*]*s*; *-e*) exit; *fig* withdrawal (***aus*** *dat* from)
**'ausstopfen** *v/t* (*sep*, *-ge-*, *h*) stuff; pad
**'Ausstoß** *m* TECH, PHYS discharge, ejection; ECON output
**'ausstoßen** *v/t* (*irr*, ***stoßen***, *sep*, *-ge-*, *h*) TECH, PHYS give off, eject, emit; ECON turn out; give (*cry*, *sigh*); expel
**'aus|strahlen** *v/t* (*sep*, *-ge-*, *h*) radiate (*happiness etc*); TV, *radio*: broadcast, transmit; **'Ausstrahlung** *f* radiation; broadcast; *fig* magnetism, charisma
**'aus|strecken** *v/t* (*sep*, *-ge-*, *h*) stretch (out); **~streichen** *v/t* (*irr*, ***streichen***, *sep*, *-ge-*, *h*) strike out; **~strömen** *v/i* (*sep*, *-ge-*, *sein*) escape (***aus*** *dat* from); **~suchen** *v/t* (*sep*, *-ge-*, *h*) choose, pick
**'Austausch** *m* (-[*e*]*s*; *no pl*) exchange
**'austauschbar** *adj* exchangeable
**'austauschen** *v/t* (*sep*, *-ge-*, *h*) exchange (***gegen*** for)
**'Austauschschüler(in)** exchange student
**'austeilen** *v/t* (*sep*, *-ge-*, *h*) distribute, hand out; deal (out) (*cards*, *blows*)
**Auster** ['austɐ] *f* (-; *-n*) ZO oyster
**'austragen** *v/t* (*irr*, ***tragen***, *sep*, *-ge-*, *h*) deliver (*mail*); settle (*dispute etc*); hold (*contest etc*); ***das Kind*** ~ have the baby
**'Austragungsort** *m* SPORT venue
**Australien** [aus'tra:ljən] Australia
**Australier** [aus'tra:ljɐ] *m* (*-s*; -), **Aust'ralierin** [-ljərɪn] *f* (-; *-nen*), **aust'ralisch** *adj* Australian
**'aus|treiben** *v/t* (*irr*, ***treiben***, *sep*, *-ge-*, *h*) exorcise; F ***j-m et.*** ~ cure s.o. of s.th.; **~treten** (*irr*, ***treten***, *sep*, *-ge-*) **1.** *v/t* (*h*) tread *or* stamp out (*fire*); wear out (*shoes*); **2.** *v/i* (*sein*) escape (***aus*** *dat* from); F go to the bathroom (*Br* toilet); ~ ***aus*** (*dat*) leave (*a club etc*); resign from; **~trinken** *v/t* (*irr*, ***trinken***, *sep*, *-ge-*, *h*) drink up; empty
**'Austritt** *m* leaving; resignation; escape
**'austrocknen** *v/t* (*sep*, *-ge-*, *h*) *and v/i* (*sein*) dry up
**'ausüben** *v/t* (*sep*, *-ge-*, *h*) practi|ce, *Br* -se; hold (*office*); exercise (*power etc*);

exert (*pressure etc*); '**Ausübung** *f* (-; *no pl*) practice; exercise

'**Ausverkauf** *m* ECON (clearance) sale

'**ausverkauft** *adj* ECON, THEA sold out; ***vor ~em Haus spielen*** play to a full house

'**Auswahl** *f* choice, selection (*both a.* ECON); SPORT representative team

'**auswählen** *v/t* (*sep, -ge-, h*) choose, select

'**Auswanderer** *m* emigrant

'**auswandern** *v/i* (*sep, -ge-, sein*) emigrate; '**Auswanderung** *f* emigration

**auswärtig** ['ausvɛrtıç] *adj* out-of-town; POL foreign

'**auswärts** *adv* out of town

'**Auswärts|sieg** *m* SPORT away victory; **~spiel** *n* SPORT away game

'**auswechseln** *v/t* (*sep, -ge-, h*) exchange (***gegen*** for); change (*tire*); replace; ***A gegen B ~*** SPORT substitute B for A; ***wie ausgewechselt*** (like) a different person; '**Auswechselspieler** *m* SPORT substitute

'**Ausweg** *m* way out; '**ausweglos** *adj* hopeless; '**Ausweglosigkeit** *f* (-; *no pl*) hopelessness

'**ausweichen** *v/i* (*irr*, ***weichen***, *sep, -ge-, sein*) make way (*dat* for); *fig* avoid *s.o.*; evade (*question*); **~d** *adj* evasive

'**ausweinen** *v/refl* (*sep, -ge-, h*) have a good cry

**Ausweis** ['ausvais] *m* (*-es; -e*) identification (card); card

'**ausweisen** *v/t* (*irr*, ***weisen***, *sep, -ge-, h*) expel; ***sich ~*** identify o.s.

'**Ausweispa,piere** *pl* documents

'**Ausweisung** *f* (-; *-en*) expulsion

'**ausweiten** *fig v/t* (*sep, -ge-, h*) expand

'**auswendig** *adv* by heart; ***et. ~ können*** know s.th. by heart; ***~ lernen*** memorize; learn by heart

'**auswerfen** *v/t* (*irr*, ***werfen***, *sep, -ge-, h*) throw out; cast (*anchor*); TECH eject

'**auswerten** *v/t* (*sep, -ge-, h*) evaluate, analyze, interpret; utilize, exploit; '**Auswertung** *f* evaluation; utilization

'**auswickeln** *v/t* (*sep, -ge-, h*) unwrap

'**auswirken** *v/refl* (*sep, -ge-, h*) ***sich ~ auf*** (*acc*) affect; ***sich positiv ~*** have a favo(u)rable effect; '**Auswirkung** *f* effect

'**auswischen** *v/t* (*sep, -ge-, h*) wipe out

'**auswringen** *v/t* (*irr*, ***wringen***, *sep, -ge-, h*) wring out

'**Auswuchs** *m* (*-es; Auswüchse* ['ausvy:ksə]) excrescence; *fig pl* excesses

'**aus|wuchten** *v/t* (*sep, -ge-, h*) TECH balance; **~zahlen** *v/t* (*sep, -ge-, h*) pay (out); pay *s.o.* off; ***sich ~*** pay; **~zählen** *v/t* (*sep, -ge-, h*) count; *boxing*: count out

'**Auszahlung** *f* payment; paying off

'**auszeichnen** *v/t* (*sep, -ge-, h*) price, mark (out) (*goods*); ***sich ~*** distinguish o.s.; ***j-n mit et. ~*** award s.th. to s.o.; '**Auszeichnung** *f* marking; *fig* distinction, hono(u)r; award; decoration

'**ausziehen** (*irr*, ***ziehen***, *sep, -ge-*) **1.** *v/t* (*h*) take off (*coat etc*); pull out (*table etc*); ***sich ~*** undress; **2.** *v/i* (*sein*) move out

'**Auszubildende** *m, f* (*-n; -n*) apprentice, trainee

'**Auszug** *m* move, removal; extract, excerpt; statement (of account)

**authentisch** [au'tɛntıʃ] *adj* authentic, genuine

**Autismus** [au'tısmʊs] *m* PSYCH autism

**autistisch** [au'tıstıʃ] *adj* PSYCH autistic

**Auto** ['auto] *n* (*-s; -s*) car, auto(mobile); (***mit dem***) ***~ fahren*** drive, go by car

'**Autobahn** *f Am* expressway, *Br* motorway; **~dreieck** *n* interchange; **~gebühr** *f* toll; **~kreuz** *n* interchange

**Autobiogra'phie** *f* autobiography

'**Auto|bombe** *f* car bomb; **~bus** *m* → ***Bus***; **~fähre** *f* car ferry; **~fahrer(in)** motorist, driver; **~fahrt** *f* drive; **~friedhof** F *m* car dump, auto junkyard

**Autogramm** [auto'gram] *n* autograph; **~jäger** *m* autograph hunter

'**Auto|karte** *f* road map; **~kino** *n* drive-in theater (*Br* cinema)

**Automat** [auto'ma:t] *m* (*-en; -en*) vending (*Br a.* slot) machine; TECH robot; → ***Spielautomat***; **Automatik** [auto'ma:tık] *f* (-; *no pl*) automatic (system *or* control); MOT automatic transmission; automatic; **Automation** [automa'tsjo:n] *f* (-; *no pl*) automation; **auto'matisch** *adj* automatic

'**Autome,chaniker** *m* car mechanic

**autonom** [auto'no:m] *adj* autonomous

'**Autonummer** *f* license (*Br* licence) number

B

**Autor** ['auto:ɐ] *m* (*-s*; *-en* [au'to:rən]) author
'**Autorepara͵turwerkstatt** *f* garage, car repair shop
**Autorin** [au'to:rɪn] *f* (-; *-nen*) author(ess)
**autorisieren** [autori'zi:rən] *v/t* (*no -ge-*, *h*) authorize; **autoritär** [autori'tɛ:ɐ] *adj* authoritarian; **Autorität** [autori'tɛ:t] *f* (-; *-en*) authority
'**Auto|tele͵fon** *n* car phone; **~vermietung** *f* car rental (*Br* hire) service; **~waschanlage** *f* car wash
**Axt** [akst] *f* (-; *Äxte* ['ɛkstə]) ax(e)

# B

**Bach** [bax] *m* (-[*e*]*s*; *Bäche* ['bɛçə]) brook, stream, *Am a.* creek
'**Backblech** *n* baking sheet
'**Backbord** *n* (*-s*; *no pl*) MAR port
**Backe** ['bakə] *f* (-; *-n*) ANAT cheek
**backen** *v/t and v/i* ([*irr*, **backen**,] *-ge-*, *h*) bake
'**Backenzahn** *m* ANAT molar (tooth)
**Bäcker** ['bɛkɐ] *m* (*-s*; -) baker; ***beim ~*** at the baker's; **Bäckerei** [bɛkə'rai] *f* (-; *-en*) bakery, baker's (shop)
'**Back|form** *f* baking tin; **~hendl** ['bakhɛndl] *Austrian n* (*-s*; *-n*) fried chicken; **~obst** *n* dried fruit; **~ofen** *m* oven; **~pflaume** *f* prune; **~pulver** *n* baking powder; **~stein** *m* brick
**backte** ['baktə] *pret of* **backen**
'**Backwaren** *pl* breads and pastries
**Bad** [ba:t] *n* (-[*e*]; *Bäder* ['bɛ:dɐ]) bath; swim; bathroom; → ***Badeort***; ***ein ~ nehmen*** → ***baden*** 1
'**Bade|anstalt** *f* swimming pool, public baths; **~anzug** *m* swimsuit; **~hose** *f* bathing trunks; **~kappe** *f* bathing cap; **~mantel** *m* bathrobe; **~meister** *m* pool *or* bath attendant
**baden** ['ba:dən] (*ge-*, *h*) **1.** *v/i* bathe, take *or* have a bath; swim; ***~ gehen*** go swimming; **2.** *v/t* bathe (*a.* MED); *Br a.* bath
'**Bade|ort** *m* seaside (*or* health) resort; **~tuch** *n* bath towel; **~wanne** *f* bathtub; **~zimmer** *n* bathroom
**baff** [baf] *adj*: F ***~ sein*** be flabbergasted
**Bagatelle** [baga'tɛlə] *f* (-; *-n*) trifle
**Baga'tellschaden** *m* superficial damage
**Bagger** ['bagɐ] *m* (*-s*; -) TECH excavator; dredge(r); '**baggern** *v/i* (*ge-*, *h*) TECH excavate; dredge
**Bahn** [ba:n] *f* (-; *-en*) railroad, *Br* railway; train; way, path, course; SPORT track; ***mit der ~*** by rail; ***~ frei!*** make way!; *cpds* → *a.* ***Eisenbahn***
'**bahnbrechend** *adj* epoch-making
'**Bahndamm** *m* railroad (*Br* railway) embankment
'**bahnen** *v/t* (*ge-*, *h*) ***den Weg ~*** clear the way (*dat* for *s.o. or s.th.*); ***sich e-n Weg ~*** force *or* work one's way
'**Bahn|hof** *m* (railroad, *Br* railway) station; **~linie** *f* railroad (*Br* railway) line; **~steig** [-ʃtaik] *m* (-[*e*]*s*; *-e*) platform; **~übergang** *m* grade (*Br* level) crossing
**Bahre** ['ba:rə] *f* (-; *-n*) stretcher; bier
**Baisse** ['bɛ:sə] *f* (-; *-n*) ECON fall, slump
**Bakterien** [bak'te:rjən] *pl* MED bacteria, germs
**balancieren** [balã'si:rən] *v/t and v/i* (*no -ge-*, *h*) balance
**bald** [balt] *adv* soon; F almost, nearly; ***so ~ wie möglich*** as soon as possible
**baldig** ['baldɪç] *adj* speedy; ***~e Antwort*** ECON early reply; ***auf (ein) ~es Wiedersehen!*** see you again soon!
**balgen** ['balgən] *v/refl* (*ge-*, *h*) scuffle (***um*** for)
**Balken** ['balkən] *m* (*-s*; -) beam
**Balkon** [bal'kɔŋ] *m* (*-s*; *-s*, *-e* [-'ko:nə]) balcony; **~tür** *f* French window
**Ball** [bal] *m* (-[*e*]*s*; *Bälle* ['bɛlə]) ball; dance; ***am ~ sein*** SPORT have the ball; ***am ~ bleiben*** *fig* stick to it
**Ballade** [ba'la:də] *f* (-; *-n*) ballad
**Ballast** ['balast] *m* (-[*e*]*s*; *no pl*) ballast,

B

*fig a.* burden; **~stoffe** *pl* MED roughage, bulk
**ballen** ['balən] *v/t* (*ge-*, *h*) clench (*fist*)
'**Ballen** *m* (*-s*; -) bale; ANAT ball
**Ballett** [ba'lɛt] *n* (*-[e]s*; *-e*) ballet
**Ballon** [ba'lɔŋ] *m* (*-s*; *-s*) balloon
'**Ballungs|raum** *m*, **~zentrum** *n* congested area, conurbation
**Balsam** ['balzaːm] *m* (*-s*; *no pl*) balm
**Bambus** ['bambʊs] *m* (*-ses*, -; *-se*) BOT bamboo; **~rohr** *n* BOT bamboo (cane)
**banal** [ba'naːl] *adj* banal, trite
**Banane** [ba'naːnə] *f* (-; *-n*) BOT banana
**Banause** [ba'nauzə] *m* (*-n*; *-n*) philistine
**band** [bant] *pret of* ***binden***
**Band**[1] *n* (*-[e]s*; *Bänder* ['bɛndɐ]) ribbon; tape; (*hat*) band; ANAT ligament; *fig* tie, link; ***auf ~ aufnehmen*** tape; ***am laufenden ~*** *fig* continuously
**Band**[2] *m* (*-[e]s*; *Bände* ['bɛndə]) volume
**Bandage** [ban'daːʒə] *f* (-; *-n*) bandage
**bandagieren** [banda'ʒiːrən] *v/t* (*no -ge-*, *h*) bandage (up)
'**Bandbreite** *f* ELECTR bandwidth; *fig* range
**Bande** ['bandə] *f* (-; *-n*) gang; *billiards*: cushions; *ice hockey*: boards; *bowling*: gutter
'**Bänderriss** *m* MED torn ligament
**bändigen** ['bɛndigən] *v/t* (*ge-*, *h*) tame (*a. fig*); restrain, control (*children etc*)
**Bandit** [ban'diːt] *m* (*-en*; *-en*) bandit, outlaw
'**Band|maß** *n* tape measure; **~scheibe** *f* ANAT (intervertebral) disk (*Br* disc); **~scheibenschaden** *m*, **~scheibenvorfall** *m* MED slipped disk; **~wurm** *m* ZO tapeworm
**bange** ['baŋə] *adj* afraid; anxious
'**Bange** *f*: ***j-m ~ machen*** frighten *or* scare s.o.; ***keine ~!*** (have) no fear!
'**bangen** *v/i* (*ge-*, *h*) be anxious *or* worried (***um*** about)
**Bank**[1] [baŋk] *f* (-; *Bänke* ['bɛŋkə]) bench; F ***durch die ~*** without exception; ***auf die lange ~ schieben*** put off
**Bank**[2] *f* (-; *-en*) bank; ***auf der ~*** in the bank
'**Bankangestellte** *m*, *f* bank clerk *or* employee
'**Bankauto͵mat** *m* → ***Geldautomat***
**Bankett** [baŋ'kɛt] *n* (*-[e]s*; *-e*) banquet
'**Bankgeschäfte** *pl* banking transactions
**Bankier** [baŋ'kjeː] *m* (*-s*; *-s*) banker
'**Bank|konto** *n* bank(ing) account; **~leitzahl** *f* A.B.A. number, *Br* bank (sorting) code; **~note** *f* bill, *Br* (bank) note; **~raub** *m* bank robbery
**bankrott** [baŋ'krɔt] *adj* ECON bankrupt
**Bank'rott** *m* (*-[e]s*; *-e*) ECON bankruptcy; ~ ***machen*** go bankrupt
'**Bankverbindung** *f* account(s), account details
**Bann** [ban] *m* (*-[e]s*; *no pl*) ban; spell
'**bannen** *v/t* (*ge-*, *h*) ward off; (***wie***) ***gebannt*** spellbound
**Banner** ['banɐ] *n* (*-s*; -) banner (*a. fig*)
**bar** [baːɐ] *adj* (in) cash; ***gegen ~*** for cash
**Bar** *f* (-; *-s*) bar; nightclub
**Bär** [bɛːɐ] *m* (*-en*; *-en*) ZO bear
**Baracke** [ba'rakə] *f* (-; *-n*) hut; *contp* shack
**Barbar** [bar'baːɐ] *m* (*-en*; *-en*) barbarian; **barbarisch** [bar'baːrɪʃ] *adj* barbarous, *a.* atrocious (*crime etc*)
'**Bardame** *f* barmaid
'**barfuß** *adj and adv* barefoot
**barg** [bark] *pret of* ***bergen***
'**Bargeld** *n* cash
'**bargeldlos** *adj* noncash
'**Barhocker** *m* bar stool
**Bariton** ['baːritɔn] *m* (*-s*; *-e* [-toːnə]) MUS baritone
**Barkasse** [bar'kasə] *f* (-; *-n*) MAR launch
**barm'herzig** *adj* merciful; charitable
**Barm'herzigkeit** *f* (-; *no pl*) mercy; charity
'**Barmixer** *m* barman
**Barometer** [baro'meːtɐ] *n* (*-s*; -) barometer
**Baron** [ba'roːn] *m* (*-s*; *-e*) baron
**Ba'ronin** *f* (-; *-nen*) baroness
**Barren** ['barən] *m* (*-s*; -) bar, ingot, *a. gold, silver* bullion; SPORT parallel bars
**Barriere** [ba'rjeːrə] *f* (-; *-n*) barrier
**Barrikade** [bari'kaːdə] *f* (-; *-n*) barricade
**barsch** [barʃ] *adj* rough, gruff, brusque
**Barsch** *m* (*-[e]s*; *-e*) ZO perch
'**Barscheck** *m* (negotiable) check, *Br* open cheque
**barst** [barst] *pret of* ***bersten***
**Bart** [baːɐt] *m* (*-[e]s*; *Bärte* ['bɛːɐtə]) beard; TECH bit; ***sich e-n ~ wachsen lassen*** grow a beard
**bärtig** ['bɛːɐtɪç] *adj* bearded
'**Barzahlung** *f* cash payment

**Basar** [ba'zaːɐ] *m* (*-s*; *-e*) bazaar
**Base** ['baːzə] *f* (*-*; *-n*) cousin; CHEM base
**basieren** [ba'ziːrən] *v/i* (*no -ge-*, *h*) ~ ***auf*** (*dat*) be based on
**Basis** ['baːzɪs] *f* (*-*; *Basen*) basis; MIL, ARCH base
**Baskenmütze** ['baskən-] *f* beret
**Bass** [bas] *m* (*-es*; *Bässe* ['bɛsə]) MUS bass
**Bassin** [ba'sɛ̃ː] *n* (*-s*; *-s*) basin; (swimming) pool
**Bassist** [ba'sɪst] *m* (*-en*; *-en*) MUS bass singer *or* player
**Bast** [bast] *m* (*-[e]s*; *-e*) bast; HUNT velvet
**Bastard** ['bastart] *m* (*-s*; *-e*) BIOL hybrid; mongrel; V bastard
**basteln** ['bastəln] (*ge-*, *h*) **1.** *v/i* make *or* repair things o.s.; **2.** *v/t* build, make
**Bastler** ['bastlɐ] *m* (*-s*; *-*) home handyman, do-it-yourselfer
**bat** [baːt] *pret of* ***bitten***
**Batik** ['baːtɪk] *m* (*-s*; *-en*), *f* (*-*; *-en*) batik
**Batist** [ba'tɪst] *m* (*-[e]s*; *-e*) cambric
**Batterie** [batə'riː] *f* (*-*; *-n*) ELECTR, MIL battery
**Bau** [bau] *m* (*-[e]s*; *Bauten*) a) (*no pl*) building, construction; build, frame, b) building, c) ZO (*pl Baue*) hole, den; ***im*** ~ under construction; **~arbeiten** *pl* construction work; road works; **~arbeiter** *m* construction worker; **~art** *f* style (of construction); type, model
**Bauch** [baux] *m* (*-[e]s*; *Bäuche* ['bɔʏçə]) belly (*a. fig*); ANAT abdomen; F tummy
'**bauchig** *adj* bulgy
'**Bauch|landung** *f* AVIAT belly landing; **~redner** *m* ventriloquist; **~schmerzen** *pl* stomachache; **~tanz** *m* belly dancing
**bauen** ['bauən] (*ge-*, *h*) **1.** *v/t* build, construct, *a.* make (*furniture etc*); **2.** *fig v/i*: ~ ***auf*** (*acc*) rely *or* count on
**Bauer**[1] ['bauɐ] *m* (*-n*; *-n*) farmer; *chess*: pawn
'**Bauer**[2] *n*, *m* (*-s*; *-*) (bird)cage
**Bäuerin** ['bɔʏərɪn] *f* (*-*; *-nen*) farmer's wife; farmer
**bäuerlich** ['bɔʏɐlɪç] *adj* rural; rustic
'**Bauern|fänger** *contp m* trickster, conman; **~haus** *n* farmhouse; **~hof** *m* farm; **~möbel** *pl* rustic furniture
'**baufällig** *adj* dilapidated
'**Bau|firma** *f* builders and contractors; **~genehmigung** *f* building permit; **~gerüst** *n* scaffold(ing); **~herr** *m* owner; **~holz** *n* lumber, *Br a.* timber; **~inge|nieur** *m* civil engineer; **~jahr** *n* year of construction; ~ ***1995*** 1995 model; **~kasten** *m* box of building blocks (*Br* bricks); TECH construction set; kit; **~leiter** *m* building supervisor
'**baulich** *adj* structural
**Baum** [baum] *m* (*-[e]s*; *Bäume* ['bɔʏmə]) BOT tree
'**Baumarkt** *m* do-it-yourself superstore
**baumeln** ['bauməln] *v/i* (*ge-*, *h*) dangle, swing; ***mit den Beinen*** ~ dangle one's legs
'**Baum|schule** *f* nursery; **~stamm** *m* trunk; log; **~wolle** *f* cotton
'**Bau|plan** *m* architectural drawing; blueprints; **~platz** *m* building site
**Bausch** [bauʃ] *m* (*-[e]s*; *-e*) wad, ball; ***in*** ~ ***und Bogen*** lock, stock and barrel
'**Bausparkasse** *f* building and loan association, *Br* building society
'**Bau|stein** *m* brick; (building) block; *fig* element; **~stelle** *f* building site; MOT construction zone, *Br* roadworks; **~stil** *m* (architectural) style; **~stoff** *m* building material; **~techniker** *m* engineer; **~teil** *n* component (part), unit, module; **~unternehmer** *m* building contractor; **~vorschriften** *pl* building regulations; **~werk** *n* building; **~zaun** *m* hoarding; **~zeichner** *m* draftsman, *Br* draughtsman
**Bayern** ['baiɐn] Bavaria; **Bayer** ['baiɐ] *m* (*-n*; *-n*), **Bayerin** ['baiərɪn] *f* (*-*; *-nen*), **bay(e)risch** ['bai(ə)rɪʃ] *adj* Bavarian
**Bazillus** [ba'tsɪlʊs] *m* (*-*; *-len*) MED bacillus, germ
**beabsichtigen** [bə'ˀapzɪçtɪgən] *v/t* (*no -ge-*, *h*) intend, plan; ***es war beabsichtigt*** it was intentional
**be'achten** *v/t* (*no -ge-*, *h*) pay attention to; observe, follow (*rule etc*); ~ ***Sie, dass ...*** note that ...; ***nicht*** ~ take no notice of; disregard; **be'achtlich** *adj* remarkable; considerable
**Be'achtung** *f* (*-*; *no pl*) attention; consideration; observance
**Beamte** [bə'ˀamtə] *m* (*-n*; *-n*), **Be'amtin** *f* (*-*; *-nen*) official; (*police etc*) officer; civil servant
**be'ängstigend** *adj* alarming
**beanspruchen** [bə'ˀanʃprʊxən] *v/t* (*no -ge-*, *h*) claim; take up (*time etc*); TECH

stress; **Be'anspruchung** *f* (-; *-en*) claim; TECH stress, strain (*a. fig*)
**beanstanden** [bə'ʔanʃtandən] *v/t* (*no -ge-*, *h*) complain about; object to
**beantragen** [bə'ʔantra:gən] *v/t* (*no -ge-*, *h*) apply for; JUR, PARL move (for); propose
**be'antworten** *v/t* (*no -ge-*, *h*) answer, reply to
**be'arbeiten** *v/t* (*no -ge-*, *h*) work; AGR till; hew (*stone*); process; be in charge of (*a case etc*); treat (*subject*); revise; THEA adapt (***nach*** from); *esp* MUS arrange; F ***j-n ~*** work on s.o.
**Be'arbeitung** *f* (-; *-en*) working; revision; THEA adaptation; *esp* MUS arrangement; TECH processing, treatment
**be'atmen** *v/t* (*no -ge-*, *h*) MED give artificial respiration to *s.o.*
**beaufsichtigen** [bə'ʔaufzɪçtɪgən] *v/t* (*no -ge-*, *h*) supervise; look after; **Be'aufsichtigung** *f* (-; *-en*) supervision; looking after
**be'auftragen** *v/t* (*no -ge-*, *h*) commission; instruct; ***~ mit*** put *s.o.* in charge of; **Be'auftragte** [-tra:ktə] *m*, *f* (*-n*; *-n*) agent; representative; commissioner
**be'bauen** *v/t* (*no -ge-*, *h*) build on; AGR cultivate
**beben** ['be:bən] *v/i* (*ge-*, *h*) shake, tremble; shiver (*all*: ***vor*** with); *earth*: quake
**bebildern** [bə'bɪldɐn] *v/t* (*no -ge-*, *h*) illustrate
**Becher** ['bɛçɐ] *m* (*-s*; -) cup, mug
**Becken** ['bɛkən] *n* (*-s*; -) basin, bowl; pool; ANAT pelvis; MUS cymbal(s)
**bedacht** [bə'daxt] *adj*: ***darauf ~ sein zu*** *inf* be anxious to *inf*
**bedächtig** [bə'dɛçtɪç] *adj* deliberate; measured
**bedang** [bə'daŋ] *pret of* ***bedingen***
**be'danken** *v/refl* (*no -ge-*, *h*) ***sich bei j-m für et. ~*** thank s.o. for s.th.
**Bedarf** [bə'darf] *m* (*-[e]s*; *no pl*) need (***an*** *dat* of), want (of); ECON demand (for); ***bei ~*** if necessary
**Be'darfshaltestelle** *f* request stop
**bedauerlich** [bə'dauɐlɪç] *adj* regrettable; **be'dauerlicher'weise** *adv* unfortunately
**be'dauern** *v/t* (*no -ge-*, *h*) feel *or* be sorry for *s.o.*, pity *s.o.*; regret *s.th.*; **Be'dauern** *n* (*-s*; *no pl*) regret (***über*** *acc* at); **be'dauernswert** *adj* pitiable, deplorable
**be'decken** *v/t* (*no -ge-*, *h*) cover
**be'deckt** *adj* METEOR overcast
**be'denken** *v/t* (*irr*, ***denken,*** *no -ge-*, *h*) consider, think *s.th.* over; **Be'denken** *pl* doubts; scruples; objections
**be'denkenlos** *adv* unhesitatingly; without scruples
**be'denklich** *adj* doubtful; serious, critical; alarming
**Be'denkzeit** *f*: ***e-e Stunde ~*** one hour to think it over
**be'deuten** *v/t* (*no -ge-*, *h*) mean; **~d** *adj* important; considerable; distinguished
**Be'deutung** *f* (-; *-en*) meaning; importance; **be'deutungslos** *adj* insignificant; meaningless; **be'deutungsvoll** *adj* significant; meaningful
**be'dienen** (*no -ge-*, *h*) **1.** *v/t* serve, wait on *s.o.*; TECH operate, work; ***sich ~*** help o.s.; ***~ Sie sich!*** help yourself! **2.** *v/i* serve; wait (at table); *card games*: follow suit; **Be'dienung** *f* (-; *-en*) a) (*no pl*) service, b) waiter, waitress; shop assistant, clerk, c) TECH operation, control; **Be'dienungsanleitung** *f* operating instructions
**bedingen** [bə'dɪŋən] *v/t* ([*irr*,] *no -ge-*, *h*) require; cause; imply, involve; **be'dingt** *adj*: ***~ durch*** caused by, due to
**Be'dingung** *f* (-; *-en*) condition; *pl* ECON terms; requirements; conditions; ***unter einer ~*** on one condition
**be'dingungslos** *adj* unconditional
**be'drängen** *v/t* (*no -ge-*, *h*) press (hard)
**be'drohen** *v/t* (*no -ge-*, *h*) threaten, menace; **be'drohlich** *adj* threatening; **Be'drohung** *f* threat, menace (*gen* to)
**be'drücken** *v/t* (*no -ge-*, *h*) depress, sadden
**bedungen** [bə'dʊŋən] *pp of* ***bedingen***
**Bedürfnis** [bə'dʏrfnɪs] *n* (*-ses*; *-se*) need, necessity (***für***, ***nach*** for); **~anstalt** *f* comfort station, *Br* public convenience (*or* toilets)
**be'dürftig** *adj* needy, poor
**be'eilen** *v/refl* (*no -ge-*, *h*) hurry (up)
**beeindrucken** [bə'ʔaindrʊkən] *v/t* (*no -ge-*, *h*) impress
**beeinflussen** [bə'ʔainflʊsən] *v/t* (*no -ge-*, *h*) influence; affect
**beeinträchtigen** [bə'ʔaintrɛçtɪgən] *v/t* (*no -ge-*, *h*) affect, impair

**be'end(ig)en** *v/t* (*no -ge-, h*) (bring to an) end, finish, conclude, close
**beengen** [bə'ɛŋən] *v/t* (*no -ge-, h*) make *s.o.* (feel) uncomfortable; **be'engt** *adj*: ~ ***wohnen*** live in cramped quarters
**be'erben** *v/t* (*no -ge-, h*) ***j-n*** ~ be s.o.'s heir
**beerdigen** [bə'ˀeːɐdɪgən] *v/t* (*no -ge-, h*) bury; **Be'erdigung** *f* (-; *-en*) burial, funeral
**Beere** ['beːrə] *f* (-; *-n*) BOT berry; grape
**Beet** [beːt] *n* (-[*e*]*s*; *-e*) bed, patch
**befähigen** [bə'fɛːɪgən] *v/t* (*no -ge-, h*) enable; qualify (***für, zu*** for); **be'fähigt** *adj* (cap)able; ***zu et.*** ~ fit *or* qualified for s.th.; **Be'fähigung** *f* (-; *no pl*) qualification(s), (cap)ability
**befahl** [bə'faːl] *pret of* ***befehlen***
**be'fahrbar** *adj* passable, practicable; MAR navigable
**be'fahren** *v/t* (*irr*, ***fahren****, no -ge-, h*) drive *or* travel on; MAR navigate
**be'fallen** *v/t* (*irr*, ***fallen****, no -ge-, h*) attack, seize (*a. fig*)
**be'fangen** *adj* self-conscious; prejudiced, JUR *a.* bias(s)ed
**Be'fangenheit** *f* (-; *no pl*) self-consciousness; JUR bias, prejudice
**be'fassen** *v/refl* (*no -ge-, h*) ***sich*** ~ ***mit*** engage *or* occupy o.s. with; work on *s.th.*; deal with *s.o., s.th.*
**Befehl** [bə'feːl] *m* (-[*e*]*s*; *-e*) order; command (***über*** *acc* of); **be'fehlen** *v/t* (*irr, no -ge-, h*) order; command
**Be'fehlshaber** *m* (-*s*; -) MIL commander
**be'festigen** *v/t* (*no -ge-, h*) fasten (***an*** *dat* to), fix (to), attach (to); MIL fortify; **Be'festigung** *f* (-; *-en*) fixing, fastening; MIL fortification
**be'feuchten** *v/t* (*no -ge-, h*) moisten, damp
**be'finden** *v/refl* (*irr*, ***finden****, no -ge-, h*) be (situated); **Be'finden** *n* (-*s*; *no pl*) (state of) health
**be'flecken** *v/t* (*no -ge-, h*) stain; *fig a.* sully
**befohlen** [bə'foːlən] *pp of* ***befehlen***
**be'folgen** *v/t* (*no -ge-, h*) follow, take (*advice*); observe (*rule etc*); REL keep; **Be'folgung** *f* (-; *no pl*) following; observance
**be'fördern** *v/t* (*no -ge-, h*) carry, transport; haul, ship; promote (***zu*** to)
**Be'förderung** *f* (-; *-en*) a) (*no pl*) transport(ation); shipment, b) promotion
**be'fragen** *v/t* (*no -ge-, h*) question, interview
**be'freien** *v/t* (*no -ge-, h*) free, liberate; rescue; exempt (***von*** from); **Be'freiung** *f* (-; *no pl*) liberation; exemption
**Befremden** [bə'frɛmdən] *n* (-*s*; *no pl*) irritation, displeasure; **be'fremdet** *adj* irritated, displeased
**befreunden** [bə'frɔʏndən] *v/refl* (*no -ge-, h*) ***sich*** ~ ***mit*** make friends with; *fig* warm to; **be'freundet** *adj* friendly; ~ ***sein*** be friends
**befriedigen** [bə'friːdɪgən] *v/t* (*no -ge-, h*) satisfy; ***sich selbst*** ~ masturbate; **~d** *adj* satisfactory; *grade*: fair
**befriedigt** [bə'friːdɪçt] *adj* satisfied, pleased
**Be'friedigung** *f* (-; *no pl*) satisfaction
**be'fristet** *adj* limited (***auf*** *acc* to), temporary
**be'fruchten** *v/t* (*no -ge-, h*) BIOL fertilize, inseminate; **Be'fruchtung** *f* (-; *-en*) BIOL fertilization, insemination
**Befugnis** [bə'fuːknɪs] *f* (-; *-se*) authority; *esp* JUR competence; **befugt** [bə'fuːkt] *adj* authorized; competent
**be'fühlen** *v/t* (*no -ge-, h*) feel, touch
**Be'fund** *m* finding(s) (*a.* MED, JUR)
**be'fürchten** *v/t* (*no -ge-, h*) fear, be afraid of; suspect; **Be'fürchtung** *f* (-; *-en*) fear, suspicion
**befürworten** [bə'fyːɐvɔrtən] *v/t* (*no -ge-, h*) advocate, speak *or* plead for; **Be'fürworter** *m* (-*s*; -) advocate
**begabt** [bə'gaːpt] *adj* gifted, talented
**Be'gabung** *f* (-; *-en*) gift, talent(s)
**begann** [bə'gan] *pret of* ***beginnen***
**be'geben** *v/refl* (*irr*, ***geben****, no -ge-, h*) ***sich in Gefahr*** ~ expose o.s. to danger
**Be'gebenheit** *f* (-; *-en*) incident, event
**begegnen** [bə'geːgnən] *v/i* (*no -ge-, sein*) meet (*a. fig* ***mit*** with); ***sich*** ~ meet
**Be'gegnung** *f* (-; *-en*) meeting, encounter (*a.* SPORT)
**be'gehen** *v/t* (*irr*, ***gehen****, no -ge-, h*) walk (on); celebrate (*birthday etc*); commit (*crime*); make (*mistake*); ***ein Unrecht*** ~ do wrong
**begehren** [bə'geːrən] *v/t* (*no -ge-, h*) desire; **be'gehrenswert** *adj* desirable
**be'gehrlich** *adj* desirous, covetous
**begehrt** [bə'geːɐt] *adj* (very) popular, (much) in demand

**begeistern** [bə'gaistɐn] *v/t* (*no -ge-, h*) fill with enthusiasm; carry away (*audience*); ***sich ~ für*** be enthusiastic about
**be'geistert** *adj* enthusiastic
**Be'geisterung** *f* (-; *no pl*) enthusiasm
**Begierde** [bə'giːɐdə] *f* (-; *-n*) desire (***nach*** for), appetite (for)
**be'gierig** *adj* greedy; eager (***nach***, ***auf*** *acc* for; ***zu*** *inf* to *inf*)
**be'gießen** *v/t* (*irr*, ***gießen,*** *no -ge-, h*) water; GASTR baste; F *fig* celebrate *s.th.* (with a drink)
**Beginn** [bə'gɪn] *m* (-[*e*]*s*; *no pl*) beginning, start; ***zu ~*** at the beginning
**be'ginnen** *v/t and v/i* (*irr, no -ge-, h*) begin, start
**beglaubigen** [bə'glaubɪgən] *v/t* (*no -ge-, h*) attest, certify; **Be'glaubigung** *f* (-; *-en*) attestation, certification
**be'gleichen** *v/t* (*irr*, ***gleichen,*** *no -ge-, h*) pay, settle
**be'gleiten** *v/t* (*no -ge-, h*) accompany (*a.* MUS ***auf*** *dat* on); ***j-n nach Hause ~*** see s.o. home; **Be'gleiter(in)** (*-s*; *-/-*; *-nen*) companion; MUS accompanist
**Be'gleit|erscheinung** *f* concomitant; MED side effect; **~schreiben** *n* covering letter
**Be'gleitung** *f* (-; *-en*) company; *esp* MIL escort; MUS accompaniment
**be'glückwünschen** *v/t* (*no -ge-, h*) congratulate (***zu*** on)
**begnadigen** [bə'gnaːdɪgən] *v/t* (*no -ge-, h*), **Be'gnadigung** *f* (-; *-en*) JUR pardon; amnesty
**begnügen** [bə'gnyːgən] *v/refl* (*no -ge-, h*) ***sich ~ mit*** be satisfied with; make do with
**begonnen** [bə'gɔnən] *pp of* ***beginnen***
**be'graben** *v/t* (*irr*, ***graben,*** *no -ge-, h*) bury (*a. fig*); **Begräbnis** [bə'grɛːpnɪs] *n* (*-ses*; *-se*) burial; funeral
**begradigen** [bə'graːdɪgən] *v/t* (*no -ge-, h*) straighten
**be'greifen** *v/t* (*irr*, ***greifen,*** *no -ge-, h*) comprehend, understand
**be'greiflich** *adj* understandable
**be'grenzen** *v/t* (*no -ge-, h*) limit, restrict (***auf*** *acc* to); **be'grenzt** *adj* limited
**Be'griff** *m* (-[*e*]*s*; *-e*) idea, notion; term (*a.* MATH); ***im ~ sein zu*** *inf* be about to *inf*; **be'griffsstutzig** *contp adj* F slow on the uptake
**be'gründen** *v/t* (*no -ge-, h*) give reasons for; **be'gründet** *adj* well-founded, justified; **Be'gründung** *f* (-; *-en*) reasons, arguments
**be'grünen** *v/t* (*no -ge-, h*) landscape
**be'grüßen** *v/t* (*no -ge-, h*) greet, welcome (*a. fig*); **Be'grüßung** *f* (-; *-en*) greeting, welcome
**begünstigen** [bə'gʏnstɪgən] *v/t* (*no -ge-, h*) favo(u)r
**be'gutachten** *v/t* (*no -ge-, h*) give an (expert's) opinion on; examine; ***~ lassen*** obtain expert opinion on
**begütert** [bə'gyːtɐt] *adj* wealthy
**be'haart** *adj* hairy
**behäbig** [bə'hɛːbɪç] *adj* slow; portly
**be'haftet** *adj*: ***mit Fehlern ~*** flawed
**behagen** [bə'haːgən] *v/i* (*no -ge-, h*) ***j-m ~*** please *or* suit s.o.; **Be'hagen** *n* (*-s*; *no pl*) pleasure, enjoyment; **behaglich** [bə'haːklɪç] *adj* comfortable; cozy, snug
**be'halten** *v/t* (*irr*, ***halten,*** *no -ge-, h*) keep (*fig* ***für sich*** to o.s.); remember
**Behälter** [bə'hɛltɐ] *m* (*-s*; *-*) container, receptacle
**be'handeln** *v/t* (*no -ge-, h*) handle; treat (*a.* MED); ***sich*** (***ärztlich***) ***~ lassen*** undergo (medical) treatment
**Be'handlung** *f* (-; *-en*) handling; *a.* MED treatment
**beharren** [bə'harən] *v/i* (*no -ge-, h*) insist (***auf*** *dat* on)
**be'harrlich** *adj* persistent
**behaupten** [bə'hauptən] *v/t* (*no -ge-, h*) claim; pretend; **Be'hauptung** *f* (-; *-en*) statement, claim
**be'heben** *v/t* (*irr*, ***heben,*** *no -ge-, h*) repair (*damage etc*)
**be'heizen** *v/t* (*no -ge-, h*) heat
**be'helfen** *v/refl* (*irr*, ***helfen,*** *no -ge-, h*) ***sich ~ mit*** make do with; ***sich ~ ohne*** do without
**Be'helfs...** *in cpds mst* temporary
**beherbergen** [bə'hɛrbɛrgən] *v/t* (*no -ge-, h*) accommodate
**be'herrschen** *v/t* (*no -ge-, h*) rule (over), govern; ECON dominate, control; have (a good) command of (*language*); ***sich ~*** control o.s.; **Be'herrschung** *f* (-; *no pl*) command, control
**beherzigen** [bə'hɛrtsɪgən] *v/t* (*no -ge-, h*) take to heart, mind
**be'hilflich** *adj*: ***j-m ~ sein*** help s.o. (***bei*** with, in)

**be'hindern** *v/t* (*no -ge-*, *h*) hinder; obstruct (*a.* SPORT); **be'hindert** *adj* MED handicapped; disabled
**Be'hinderung** *f* (-; *-en*) obstruction; MED handicap
**Behörde** [bə'hø:ɐdə] *f* (-; *-n*) authority, *mst the* authorities; board
**be'hüten** *v/t* (*no -ge-*, *h*) guard (**vor** *dat* from)
**behutsam** [bə'hu:tza:m] *adj* careful; gentle
**bei** [bai] *prp* (*dat*) near; at; with; by; *time*: during; at; ~ ***München*** near Munich; ***wohnen*** ~ stay (*or* live) with; ~ ***mir*** (***ihr***) at my (her) place; ~ ***uns*** (***zu Hause***) at home; ***arbeiten*** ~ work for; ***e-e Stelle*** ~ a job with; ~ ***der Marine*** in the navy; ~ ***Familie Müller*** at the Müllers'; ~ ***Müller*** c/o Müller; ***ich habe kein Geld*** ~ ***mir*** I have no money with *or* on me; ~ ***e-r Tasse Tee*** over a cup of tea; ***wir haben Englisch*** ~ ***Herrn X*** we have Mr X for English; ~ ***Licht*** by light; ~ ***Tag*** during the day; ~ ***Nacht*** (***Sonnenaufgang***) at night (sunrise); ~ ***s-r Geburt*** at his birth; ~ ***Regen*** (***Gefahr***) in case of rain (danger); ~ ***100 Grad*** at a hundred degrees; → ***Arbeit, beim, weit***
**'beibehalten** *v/t* (*irr*, ***halten***, *sep*, *no -ge-*, *h*) keep up, retain
**'beibringen** *v/t* (*irr*, ***bringen***, *sep*, *no -ge-*, *h*) teach; tell; inflict (*dat* on)
**Beichte** ['baiçtə] *f* (-; *-n*) REL confession
**'beichten** *v/t and v/i* (*ge-*, *h*) REL confess (*a. fig*)
**'Beichtstuhl** *m* REL confessional
**beide** ['baidə] *adj and pron* both; ***m-e*** ~***n Brüder*** my two brothers; ***wir*** ~ the two of us; both of us; ***keiner von*** ~***n*** neither of them; ***30*** ~ *tennis*: 30 all
**beiei'nander** *adv* together
**'Beifahrer** *m* front(-seat) passenger
**'Beifall** *m* (-[*e*]*s*; *no pl*) applause; *fig* approval
**'Beifallssturm** *m* (standing) ovation
**'beifügen** *v/t* (*sep*, *-ge-*, *h*) enclose (*dat* with)
**beige** [be:ʃ] *adj* beige
**'beigeben** (*irr*, ***geben***, *sep*, *-ge-*, *h*) **1.** *v/t* add; **2.** F *v/i*: ***klein*** ~ knuckle under
**'Bei|geschmack** *m* smack (**von** of) (*a. fig*); ~**hilfe** *f* aid, allowance; JUR aiding and abetting
**Beil** [bail] *n* (-[*e*]*s*; *-e*) hatchet; ax(e)
**'Beilage** *f* supplement; GASTR side dish; vegetables
**'beiläufig** *adj* casual
**'beilegen** *v/t* (*sep*, *-ge-*, *h*) add (*dat* to); enclose (with); settle (*dispute*)
**'Beilegung** *f* (-; *-en*) settlement
**'Beileid** *n* (-[*e*]*s*; *no pl*) condolence; ***herzliches*** ~ my deepest sympathy
**'beiliegen** *v/i* (*irr*, ***liegen***, *sep*, *-ge-*, *h*) be enclosed (*dat* with)
**beim** [baim] *prp*: ~ ***Bäcker*** at the baker's; ~ ***Sprechen*** *etc* while speaking *etc*; ~ ***Spielen*** at play; → *a.* ***bei***
**'beimessen** *v/t* (*irr*, ***messen***, *sep*, *-ge-*, *h*) attach *importance etc* (*dat* to)
**Bein** [bain] *n* (-[*e*]*s*; *-e*) ANAT leg; bone
**beinah(e)** ['baina:(ə)] *adv* almost, nearly
**'Beinbruch** *m* MED fracture of the leg
**'beipflichten** *v/i* (*sep*, *-ge-*, *h*) agree (*dat* with)
**be'irren** *v/t* (*no -ge-*, *h*) confuse
**beisammen** [bai'zamən] *adv* together
**Bei'sammensein** *n*: ***geselliges*** ~ get-together
**'Beischlaf** *m* JUR sexual intercourse
**bei'seite** *adv* aside; ~ ***schaffen*** remove; liquidate *s.o.*
**'beisetzen** *v/t* (*sep*, *-ge-*, *h*) bury
**'Beisetzung** *f* (-; *-en*) funeral
**'Beispiel** *n* (-[*e*]*s*; *-e*) example; ***zum*** ~ for example, for instance; ***sich an j-m ein*** ~ ***nehmen*** follow s.o.'s example
**'beispiel|haft** *adj* exemplary; ~**los** *adj* unprecedented, unparalleled
**'beispielsweise** *adv* such as
**beißen** ['baisən] *v/t and v/i* (*irr*, *-ge-*, *h*) bite (*a. fig*); ***sich*** ~ *colors*: clash; ~**d** *adj* biting, pungent (*both a. fig*)
**'Beistand** *m* (-[*e*]*s*; *no pl*) assistance
**'bei|stehen** *v/i* (*irr*, ***stehen***, *sep*, *-ge-*, *h*) ***j-m*** ~ assist *or* help s.o.; ~**steuern** *v/t* (*sep*, *-ge-*, *h*) contribute (**zu** to)
**Beitrag** ['baitra:k] *m* (-[*e*]*s*; *Beiträge* ['baitrɛ:gə]) contribution; dues, *Br* subscription; **'beitragen** *v/t* (*irr*, ***tragen***, *sep*, *-ge-*, *h*) contribute (***zu*** to)
**'beitreten** *v/i* (*irr*, ***treten***, *sep*, *-ge-*, *sein*) join; **'Beitritt** *m* (-[*e*]*s*; *-e*) joining
**'Beiwagen** *m* MOT sidecar
**bei'zeiten** *adv* early, in good time
**beizen** ['baitsən] *v/t* (*ge-*, *h*) stain (*wood*); pickle (*meat*)
**bejahen** [bə'ja:ən] *v/t* (*no -ge-*, *h*) an-

swer in the affirmative, affirm; **~d** *adj* affirmative
**be'kämpfen** *v/t* (*no -ge-*, *h*) fight (against)
**bekannt** [bə'kant] *adj* (well-)known; familiar; ***et. ~ geben*** announce s.th.; ***j-n mit j-m ~ machen*** introduce s.o. to s.o.; **Be'kannte** *m, f* (*-n*; *-n*) acquaintance, *mst* friend
**be'kanntlich** *adv* as you know
**Be'kanntmachung** *f* (*-*; *-en*) announcement
**Be'kanntschaft** *f* (*-*; *-en*) acquaintance
**be'kehren** *v/t* (*no -ge-*, *h*) convert
**be'kennen** *v/t* (*irr*, ***kennen***, *no -ge-*, *h*) confess (*a.* REL); admit; ***sich schuldig ~*** JUR plead guilty; ***sich ~ zu*** profess *s.th.*; claim responsibility for; **Be'kennerbrief** *m* letter claiming responsibility
**Be'kenntnis** *n* (*-ses*; *-se*) confession, REL *a.* denomination
**be'klagen** *v/t* (*no -ge-*, *h*) deplore; ***sich ~*** complain (***über*** *acc* about)
**be'klagenswert** *adj* deplorable
**be'kleben** *v/t* (*no -ge-*, *h*) stick (*or* paste) on *s.th.*; ***mit Etiketten ~*** label *s.th.*
**be'kleckern** F *v/t* (*no -ge-*, *h*) stain; ***sich ~ mit*** spill *s.th.* over o.s.
**Be'kleidung** *f* (*-*; *-en*) clothing, clothes
**be'kommen** (*irr*, ***kommen***, *no -ge-*) **1.** *v/t* (*h*) get, receive; MED catch; be having (*baby*); **2.** *v/i* (*sein*) ***j-m*** (***gut***) ~ agree with s.o.; **bekömmlich** [bə'kœmlıç] *adj* wholesome
**be'kräftigen** *v/t* (*no -ge-*, *h*) confirm
**be'kreuzigen** *v/refl* (*no -ge-*, *h*) cross o.s.
**bekümmert** [bə'kʏmɐt] *adj* worried
**be'laden** *v/t* (*irr*, ***laden***, *no -ge-*, *h*) load, *fig a.* burden
**Belag** [bə'la:k] *m* (*-[e]s*; *Beläge* [bə'lɛ:gə]) covering; TECH coat(ing); MOT lining; (*road*) surface; MED fur; plaque; GASTR topping; spread; (sandwich) filling
**be'lagern** *v/t* (*no -ge-*, *h*) MIL besiege (*a. fig*); **Be'lagerung** *f* (*-*; *-en*) MIL siege
**be'lassen** *v/t* (*irr*, ***lassen***, *no -ge-*, *h*) leave; ***es dabei ~*** leave it at that
**be'langlos** *adj* irrelevant
**be'lastbar** *adj* resistant to strain *or* stress; TECH loadable; **be'lasten** *v/t* (*no -ge-*, *h*) load; *fig* burden; JUR incriminate; pollute; damage; ***j-s Konto ~ mit*** charge *s.th.* to s.o.'s account
**belästigen** [bə'lɛstıgən] *v/t* (*no -ge-*, *h*) molest; annoy; disturb, bother; **Be'lästigung** *f* (*-*; *-en*) molestation; annoyance; disturbance
**Be'lastung** *f* (*-*; *-en*) load (*a.* TECH); *fig* burden; strain; stress; JUR incrimination; pollution, contamination
**Be'lastungszeuge** *m* JUR witness for the prosecution
**be'laufen** *v/refl* (*irr*, ***laufen***, *no -ge-*, *h*) ***sich ~ auf*** (*acc*) amount to
**be'lauschen** *v/t* (*no -ge-*, *h*) eavesdrop on
**be'leben** *fig v/t* (*no -ge-*, *h*) stimulate; **~d** *adj* stimulating
**belebt** [bə'le:pt] *adj* busy, crowded
**Beleg** [bə'le:k] *m* (*-[e]s*; *-e*) proof; receipt; document; **be'legen** *v/t* (*no -ge-*, *h*) cover; reserve (*seat*); prove; enrol(l) for, take (*classes*); GASTR put s.th. on; ***den ersten*** *etc* ***Platz ~*** SPORT take first *etc* place
**Be'legschaft** *f* (*-*; *-en*) staff
**be'legt** *adj* taken, occupied; *hotel etc*: full; TEL busy, *Br* engaged; MED coated; ***~es Brot*** sandwich
**be'lehren** *v/t* (*no -ge-*, *h*) teach, instruct, inform; ***sich ~ lassen*** take advice
**beleidigen** [bə'laidıgən] *v/t* (*no -ge-*, *h*) offend (*a. fig*), insult; **~d** *adj* offensive, insulting
**Be'leidigung** *f* (*-*; *-en*) offense, *Br* offence, insult
**be'lesen** *adj* well-read
**be'leuchten** *v/t* (*no -ge-*, *h*) light (up), illuminate (*a. fig*); *fig* throw light on
**Be'leuchtung** *f* (*-*; *-en*) light(ing); illumination
**Belgien** ['bɛlgjən] Belgium; **Belgier** ['bɛlgjɐ] *m* (*-s*; *-*), **'Belgierin** [-gjərın] *f* (*-*; *-nen*), **'belgisch** *adj* Belgian
**be'lichten** *v/t* (*no -ge-*, *h*) PHOT expose
**Be'lichtungsmesser** *m* PHOT exposure meter
**Be'lieben** *n*: ***nach ~*** at will
**beliebig** [bə'li:bıç] *adj* any; optional; ***jeder ~e*** anyone
**beliebt** [bə'li:pt] *adj* popular (***bei*** with)
**Be'liebtheit** *f* (*-*; *no pl*) popularity
**be'liefern** *v/t* (*no -ge-*, *h*) supply, furnish (***mit*** with); **Be'lieferung** *f* supply
**bellen** ['bɛlən] *v/i* (*ge-*, *h*) bark (*a. fig*)

**be'lohnen** *v/t* (*no -ge-, h*) reward
**Be'lohnung** *f* (-; *-en*) reward; ***zur*** ~ as a reward
**be'lügen** *v/t* (*irr, **lügen**, no -ge-, h*) ***j-n*** ~ lie to s.o.
**belustigen** [bə'lʊstɪgən] *v/t* (*no -ge-, h*) amuse; **be'lustigt** [-tɪçt] *adj* amused; **Be'lustigung** *f* (-; *-en*) amusement
**bemächtigen** [bə'mɛçtɪgən] *v/refl* (*no -ge-, h*) get hold of, seize
**be'malen** *v/t* (*no -ge-, h*) paint
**bemängeln** [bə'mɛŋəln] *v/t* (*no -ge-, h*) find fault with
**bemannt** [bə'mant] *adj* manned
**be'merkbar** *adj* noticeable; ***sich*** ~ ***machen*** draw attention to o.s.; begin to show; **be'merken** *v/t* (*no -ge-, h*) notice; remark; **be'merkenswert** *adj* remarkable; **Be'merkung** *f* (-; *-en*) remark (***über*** *acc* about)
**be'mitleiden** *v/t* (*no -ge-, h*) pity, feel sorry for; **be'mitleidenswert** *adj* pitiable
**be'mühen** *v/refl* (*no -ge-, h*) try (hard); ***sich*** ~ ***um*** try to get *s.th.*; try to help *s.o.*; ***bitte*** ~ ***Sie sich nicht!*** please don't bother; **Be'mühung** *f* (-; *-en*) effort; ***danke für Ihre*** ~***en!*** thank you for your trouble
**be'muttern** *v/t* (*no -ge-, h*) mother *s.o.*
**be'nachbart** *adj* neighbo(u)ring
**benachrichtigen** [bə'na:xrɪçtɪgən] *v/t* (*no -ge-, h*) inform, notify
**Be'nachrichtigung** *f* (-; *-en*) information, notification
**benachteiligen** [bə'na:xtailɪgən] *v/t* (*no -ge-, h*) place *s.o.* at a disadvantage; discriminate against *s.o.*; **benachteiligt** [bə'na:xtailɪçt] *adj* disadvantaged; ***die Benachteiligten*** the underprivileged; **Be'nachteiligung** *f* (-; *-en*) disadvantage; discrimination
**be'nehmen** *v/refl* (*irr, **nehmen**, no -ge-, h*) behave (o.s.); **Be'nehmen** *n* (*-s; no pl*) behavio(u)r; manners
**be'neiden** *v/t* (*no -ge-, h*) ***j-n um et.*** ~ envy s.o. s.th.
**be'neidenswert** *adj* enviable
**BENELUX** ['be:nelʊks] ABBR *of **Belgien, Niederlande, Luxemburg*** Belgium, the Netherlands and Luxembourg
**be'nennen** *v/t* (*irr, **nennen**, no -ge-, h*) name
**Bengel** ['bɛŋəl] *m* (*-s*; -) (little) rascal, urchin
**benommen** [bə'nɔmən] *adj* dazed, F dopey
**be'noten** *v/t* (*no -ge-, h*) grade, *Br* mark
**be'nötigen** *v/t* (*no -ge-, h*) need, want, require
**be'nutzen** *v/t* (*no -ge-, h*) use
**Be'nutzer** *m* (*-s*; -) user
**be'nutzerfreundlich** *adj* user-friendly
**Be'nutzeroberfläche** *f* EDP user interface
**Be'nutzung** *f* use
**Benzin** [bɛn'tsi:n] *n* (*-s; -e*) gasoline, F gas, *Br* petrol
**beobachten** [bə'ʔo:baxtən] *v/t* (*no -ge-, h*) watch; observe
**Be'obachter** *m* (*-s*; -) observer
**Be'obachtung** *f* (-; *-en*) observation
**be'pflanzen** *v/t* (*no -ge-, h*) plant (***mit*** with)
**bequem** [bə'kve:m] *adj* comfortable; easy; lazy; **be'quemen** *v/refl* (*no -ge-, h*) ***sich*** ~ ***zu*** *inf* bring o.s. to *inf*
**Be'quemlichkeit** *f* (-; *-en*) a) comfort; ***alle*** ~***en*** all conveniences, b) (*no pl*) laziness
**be'raten** *v/t* (*irr, **raten**, no -ge-, h*) advise *s.o.*; debate, discuss *s.th.*; ***sich*** ~ confer (***mit j-m*** with s.o.; ***über et.*** on s.th.); **Be'rater** *m* (*-s*; -) adviser, consultant; **Be'ratung** *f* (-; *-en*) advice (*a.* MED); debate; consultation, conference; **Be'ratungsstelle** *f* counsel(l)ing center (*Br* centre)
**be'rauben** *v/t* (*no -ge-, h*) rob
**be'rauschend** *adj* intoxicating; F *fig* ***nicht gerade*** ~***!*** not so hot!; **be'rauscht** *fig adj*: ~ ***von*** drunk with
**be'rechnen** *v/t* (*no -ge-, h*) calculate; ECON charge (***zu*** at); ~**d** *adj* calculating
**Be'rechnung** *f* calculation (*a. fig*)
**berechtigen** [bə'rɛçtɪgən] *v/t*: ***j-n*** ~ ***zu*** entitle (*or* authorize) s.o. to; **be'rechtigt** [-tɪçt] *adj* entitled (***zu*** to); authorized (to); legitimate; **Be'rechtigung** *f* (-; *no pl*) right (***zu*** to); authority
**Beredsamkeit** [bə're:tza:mkait] *f* (-; *no pl*) eloquence
**beredt** [bə're:t] *adj* eloquent (*a. fig*)
**Be'reich** *m* (*-[e]s; -e*) area; range; field
**bereichern** [bə'raɪçɐn] *v/t* (*no -ge-, h*) enrich; ***sich*** ~ get rich (***an*** *dat* on);

**Be'reicherung** [bə'raiçərʊŋ] *f* (-; *no pl*) enrichment
**Be'reifung** *f* (-; *-en*) (set of) tires (*Br* tyres)
**be'reinigen** *v/t* (*no -ge-, h*) settle
**be'reisen** *v/t* (*no -ge-, h*) tour; cover
**bereit** [bə'rait] *adj* ready, prepared; willing; **be'reiten** *v/t* (*no -ge-, h*) prepare; cause; **be'reithalten** *v/t* (*irr*, ***halten***, *sep, -ge-, h*) have *s.th.* ready; ***sich ~*** stand by; **be'reits** *adv* already; **Be'reitschaft** *f* (-; *no pl*) readiness; ***in ~*** on standby; **Be'reitschaftsdienst** *m*: ***~ haben*** *doctor etc*: be on call; **be'reitstellen** *v/t* (*sep, -ge-, h*) provide; **be'reitwillig** *adj* ready, willing
**be'reuen** *v/t* (*no -ge-, h*) repent (of); regret
**Berg** [bɛrk] *m* (-[*e*]*s*; *-e*) mountain; ***~e von*** F loads of; ***die Haare standen ihm zu ~e*** his hair stood on end
**berg'ab** *adv* downhill (*a. fig*)
**'Bergarbeiter** *m* miner
**berg'auf** *adv* uphill
**'Berg|bahn** *f* mountain railroad (*Br* railway); **~bau** *m* (-[*e*]*s*; *no pl*) mining
**bergen** ['bɛrgən] *v/t* (*irr, ge-, h*) rescue, save *s.o.*; salvage *s.th.*; recover (*body*)
**'Bergführer** *m* mountain guide
**bergig** ['bɛrgɪç] *adj* mountainous
**'Berg|kette** *f* mountain range; **~mann** *m* (-[*e*]*s*; *-leute*) miner; **~rutsch** *m* landslide; **~schuhe** *pl* mountain(eering) boots; **~spitze** *f* (mountain) peak; **~steigen** *n* mountaineering, (mountain) climbing; **~steiger** *m* (-*s*; -) mountaineer, (mountain) climber
**'Bergung** *f* (-; *-en*) recovery; rescue
**'Bergungsarbeiten** *pl* rescue work; salvage operations
**'Bergwacht** *f* alpine rescue service
**'Bergwerk** *n* mine
**Bericht** [bə'rɪçt] *m* (-[*e*]*s*; *-e*) report (***über*** *acc* on), account (of)
**be'richten** *v/t and v/i* (*no -ge-, h*) report (***über*** *acc* on); ***j-m et. ~*** inform s.o. of s.th.; tell s.o. about s.th.
**Be'richt|erstatter** *m* (-*s*; -) reporter; correspondent; **~erstattung** *f* (-; *-en*) report(ing)
**berichtigen** [bə'rɪçtɪgən] *v/t* (*no -ge-, h*) correct; **Be'richtigung** *f* (-; *-en*) correction
**be'rieseln** *v/t* (*no -ge-, h*) sprinkle
**Bernstein** ['bɛrnʃtain] *m* (-*s*; *no pl*) amber
**bersten** ['bɛrstən] *v/i* (*irr, ge-, sein*) burst (*fig* ***vor*** *dat* with)
**berüchtigt** [bə'rʏçtɪçt] *adj* notorious (***wegen*** for)
**berücksichtigen** [bə'rʏkzɪçtɪgən] *v/t* (*no -ge-, h*) take into consideration; ***nicht ~*** disregard
**Be'rücksichtigung** *f*: ***unter ~*** (*gen*) in consideration of
**Be'ruf** *m* (-[*e*]*s*; *-e*) job, occupation; trade; profession; **be'rufen** *v/t* (*irr*, ***rufen***, *no -ge-, h*) appoint (***zu*** [as] *s.o.*; to *s.th.*); ***sich ~ auf*** (*acc*) refer to
**be'ruflich** *adj* professional; ***~ unterwegs*** away on business
**Be'rufs...** *in cpds ...sportler etc*: professional ...; **~ausbildung** *f* vocational (*or* professional) training; **~berater** *m* careers advisor; **~beratung** *f* careers guidance; **~bezeichnung** *f* job designation *or* title; **~kleidung** *f* work clothes; **~krankheit** *f* occupational disease; **~schule** *f* vocational school
**be'rufstätig** *adj*: ***~ sein*** (go to) work, have a job; **Be'rufstätige** *m, f* (-*n*; -*n*) working person, *pl* working people
**Be'rufsverkehr** *m* rush-hour traffic
**Be'rufung** *f* (-; *-en*) appointment (***zu*** to); JUR appeal (***bei*** to); ***unter ~ auf*** (*acc*) with reference to; on the grounds of
**be'ruhen** *v/i* (*no -ge-, h*) ***~ auf*** (*dat*) be based on; ***et. auf sich ~ lassen*** let s.th. rest
**beruhigen** [bə'ruːɪgən] *v/t* (*no -ge-, h*) quiet(en), calm, soothe; reassure *s.o.*; ***sich ~*** calm down; **~d** *adj* reassuring; MED sedative
**Be'ruhigung** *f* (-; *-en*) calming (down); soothing; relief; **Be'ruhigungsmittel** *n* MED sedative; tranquil(l)izer
**berühmt** [bə'ryːmt] *adj* famous (***wegen*** for); **Be'rühmtheit** *f* (-; *-en*) a) (*no pl*) fame, b) celebrity, star
**be'rühren** *v/t* (*no -ge-, h*) touch (*a. fig*); concern; **Be'rührung** *f* (-; *-en*) touch; ***in ~ kommen*** come into contact
**Be'rührungs|angst** *f* fear of contact; **~punkt** *m* point of contact
**besänftigen** [bə'zɛnftɪgən] *v/t* (*no -ge-, h*) appease, calm, soothe
**Be'satzung** *f* (-; *-en*) AVIAT, MAR crew; MIL occupying forces

**Be'satzungs|macht** *f* MIL occupying power; **~truppen** *pl* MIL occupying forces

**be'saufen** F *v/refl* (*irr*, ***saufen***, *no -ge-*, *h*) get drunk, get bombed

**be'schädigen** *v/t* (*no -ge-*, *h*) damage

**Be'schädigung** *f* (-; *-en*) damage

**be'schaffen** *v/t* (*no -ge-*, *h*) provide, get; raise (*money*); **Be'schaffenheit** *f* (-; *no pl*) state, condition

**beschäftigen** [bəˈʃɛftɪgən] *v/t* (*no -ge-*, *h*) employ; keep *s.o.* busy; ***sich ~*** occupy o.s.; **be'schäftigt** [-tɪçt] *adj* busy, occupied; **Be'schäftigte** *m, f* (*-n*; *-n*) employed person, *pl* employed people; **Be'schäftigung** *f* (-; *-en*) employment; occupation

**be'schämen** *v/t* (*no -ge-*, *h*) shame *s.o.*, make *s.o.* feel ashamed; **~d** *adj* shameful; humiliating

**be'schämt** *adj* ashamed (***über*** *acc* of)

**be'schatten** *fig v/t* (*no -ge-*, *h*) shadow, F tail

**Bescheid** [bəˈʃait] *m* (-[*e*]*s*; *-e*) answer; JUR decision; information (***über*** *acc* on, about); ***sagen Sie mir ~*** let me know; (***gut***) ***~ wissen über*** (*acc*) know all about

**be'scheiden** *adj* modest (*a. fig*); humble; **Be'scheidenheit** *f* (-; *no pl*) modesty

**bescheinigen** [bəˈʃainɪgən] *v/t* (*no -ge-*, *h*) certify

**Be'scheinigung** *f* (-; *-en*) a) (*no pl*) certification, b) certificate

**be'scheißen** V *v/t* (*irr*, ***scheißen***, *no -ge-*, *h*) cheat; ***j-n ~ um*** do s.o. out of

**be'schenken** *v/t* (*no -ge-*, *h*) ***j-n*** (***reich***) ***~*** give s.o. (shower s.o. with) presents

**Be'scherung** *f* (-; *-en*) distribution of (Christmas) presents; F *fig* mess

**be'schichten** *v/t* (*no -ge-*, *h*) TECH coat

**Be'schichtung** *f* (-; *-en*) TECH coat

**be'schießen** *v/t* (*irr*, ***schießen***, *no -ge-*, *h*) MIL fire *or* shoot at; bombard (*a.* PHYS), shell

**be'schimpfen** *v/t* (*no -ge-*, *h*) abuse, insult; swear at; **Be'schimpfung** *f* (-; *-en*) abuse, insult

**be'schissen** V *adj* lousy, rotten

**Be'schlag** *m* TECH metal fitting(s); ***in ~ nehmen*** *fig* monopolize *s.o.*; bag; occupy; **be'schlagen** (*irr*, ***schlagen***, *no -ge-*) **1.** *v/t* (*h*) cover; TECH fit, mount; shoe (*horse*); **2.** *v/i* (*sein*) *window etc*: steam up; **3.** *adj* steamed-up; *fig* well-versed (***auf***, ***in*** *dat* in)

**Be'schlagnahme** [bəˈʃlaːknaːmə] *f* (-; *-n*) confiscation; **be'schlagnahmen** *v/t* (*no -ge-*, *h*) confiscate

**beschleunigen** [bəˈʃlɔʏnɪgən] *v/t and v/i* (*no -ge-*, *h*) accelerate, speed up; **Be'schleunigung** *f* (-; *-en*) acceleration

**be'schließen** *v/t* (*irr*, ***schließen***, *no -ge-*, *h*) decide (on); pass (*law*); conclude; **Be'schluss** *m* decision

**be'schmieren** *v/t* (*no -ge-*, *h*) smear, soil; scrawl all over; cover *wall etc* with graffiti; spread (*toast etc*)

**be'schmutzen** *v/t* (*no -ge-*, *h*) soil (*a. fig*), dirty

**be'schneiden** *v/t* (*irr*, ***schneiden***, *no -ge-*, *h*) clip, cut (*a. fig*); prune; MED circumcise

**be'schönigen** [bəˈʃøːnɪgən] *v/t* (*no -ge-*, *h*) gloss over

**beschränken** [bəˈʃrɛŋkən] *v/t* (*no -ge-*, *h*) confine, limit, restrict; ***sich ~ auf*** (*acc*) confine o.s. to; **be'schränkt** *adj* limited; *contp* dense; narrow-minded

**Be'schränkung** *f* (-; *-en*) limitation, restriction

**be'schreiben** *v/t* (*irr*, ***schreiben***, *no -ge-*, *h*) describe; write on

**Be'schreibung** *f* (-; *-en*) description

**be'schriften** *v/t* (*no -ge-*, *h*) inscribe; mark (*goods*); **Be'schriftung** *f* (-; *-en*) inscription

**beschuldigen** [bəˈʃʊldɪgən] *v/t* (*no -ge-*, *h*) blame; ***j-n e-r Sache ~*** accuse s.o. of s.th. (*a.* JUR); **Be'schuldigung** *f* (-; *-en*) accusation

**be'schummeln** F *v/t* (*no -ge-*, *h*) cheat

**Be'schuss** *m*: ***unter ~*** MIL under fire

**be'schützen** *v/t* (*no -ge-*, *h*) protect, shelter, guard (***vor*** *dat* from)

**Be'schützer** *m* (*-s*; -) protector

**Beschwerde** [bəˈʃveːɐdə] *f* (-; *-n*) complaint (***über*** *acc* about; ***bei*** to); *pl* MED complaints, trouble

**beschweren** [bəˈʃveːrən] *v/t* (*no -ge-*, *h*) weight *s.th.*; ***sich ~*** complain (***über*** *acc* about; ***bei*** to)

**be'schwerlich** *adj* hard, arduous

**beschwichtigen** [bəˈʃvɪçtɪgən] *v/t* (*no -ge-*, *h*) appease (*a.* POL), calm

**be'schwindeln** *v/t* (*no -ge-*, *h*) tell a fib *or* lie; cheat
**beschwingt** [bə'ʃvɪŋt] *adj* buoyant; MUS lively, swinging
**beschwipst** [bə'ʃvɪpst] F *adj* tipsy
**be'schwören** *v/t* (*irr*, ***schwören***, *no -ge-*, *h*) swear to; implore; conjure up
**beseitigen** [bə'zaitɪgən] *v/t* (*no -ge-*, *h*) remove (*a. s.o.*), *a.* dispose of (*waste etc*); eliminate; POL liquidate
**Be'seitigung** *f* (-; *no pl*) removal; disposal; elimination
**Besen** ['be:zən] *m* (*-s*; -) broom
**'Besenstiel** *m* broomstick
**besessen** [bə'zesən] *adj* obsessed (**von** by, with); ***wie ~*** like mad
**be'setzen** *v/t* (*no -ge-*, *h*) occupy (*a.* MIL); fill (*post etc*); THEA cast; trim; squat in; **be'setzt** *adj* occupied; *seat*: taken; *bus etc*: full up; TEL busy, *Br* engaged; **Be'setztzeichen** *n* TEL busy signal, *Br* engaged tone; **Be'setzung** *f* (-; *-en*) THEA cast; MIL occupation
**besichtigen** [bə'zɪçtɪgən] *v/t* (*no -ge-*, *h*) visit, see the sights of; inspect
**Be'sichtigung** *f* (-; *-en*) sightseeing; visit (*gen* to); inspection (of)
**be'siedeln** *v/t* (*no -ge-*, *h*) settle; colonize; populate; **be'siedelt** *adj*: ***dicht*** (***dünn***) ~ densely (sparsely) populated; **Be'siedlung** *f* (-; *-en*) settlement; colonization; population
**be'siegeln** *v/t* (*no -ge-*, *h*) seal
**be'siegen** *v/t* (*no -ge-*, *h*) defeat, beat; conquer (*a. fig*)
**besinnen** *v/refl* (*irr*, ***sinnen***, *no -ge-*, *h*) remember; think (***auf*** *acc* about); ***sich anders ~*** change one's mind
**be'sinnlich** *adj* contemplative
**Be'sinnung** *f* (-; *no pl*) MED consciousness; (***wieder***) ***zur ~ kommen*** MED come round; *fig* come to one's senses
**be'sinnungslos** *adj* MED unconscious
**Be'sitz** *m* (*-es*; *no pl*) possession; property; ***~ ergreifen von*** take possession of; **be'sitzanzeigend** *adj* LING possessive; **be'sitzen** *v/t* (*irr*, ***sitzen***, *no -ge-*, *h*) possess, own; **Be'sitzer** *m* (*-s*; -) possessor, owner; ***den ~ wechseln*** change hands
**besoffen** [bə'zɔfən] F *adj* drunk, plastered, stoned
**besohlen** [bə'zo:lən] *v/t* (*no -ge-*, *h*) ~ ***lassen*** have (re)soled
**Be'soldung** *f* (-; *-en*) pay; salary
**besondere** [bə'zɔndərə] *adj* special, particular; peculiar
**Be'sonderheit** *f* (-; *-en*) peculiarity
**be'sonders** *adv* especially, particularly; chiefly, mainly
**be'sonnen** *adj* prudent, level-headed
**be'sorgen** *v/t* (*no -ge-*, *h*) get, buy; → ***erledigen***; **Besorgnis** [bə'zɔrknɪs] *f* (-; *-se*) concern, alarm, anxiety (***über*** *acc* about, at); ***~ erregend*** alarming; **besorgt** [bə'zɔrkt] *adj* worried, concerned; **Be'sorgung** *f* (-; *-en*) ***~en machen*** go shopping
**be'spielen** *v/t* (*no -ge-*, *h*) make a recording on
**be'spitzeln** *v/t* (*no -ge-*, *h*) spy on *s.o.*
**be'sprechen** *v/t* (*irr*, ***sprechen***, *no -ge-*, *h*) discuss, talk *s.th.* over; review (*book etc*); **Be'sprechung** *f* (-; *-en*) discussion, talk(s); meeting, conference; review
**be'spritzen** *v/t* (*no -ge-*, *h*) spatter
**besser** ['bɛsɐ] *adj and adv* better; ***es ist ~, wir fragen ihn*** we had better ask him; ***immer ~*** better and better; ***es geht ihm ~*** he is better; ***oder ~ gesagt*** or rather; ***es ~ wissen*** know better; ***es ~ machen als*** do better than; ***~ ist ~*** just to be on the safe side
**'bessern** *v/refl* (*ge-*, *h*) improve, get better; **'Besserung** *f* (-; *no pl*) improvement; ***auf dem Wege der ~*** on the way to recovery; ***gute ~!*** get better soon
**'Besserwisser** [-vɪsɐ] *m* (*-s*; -) F smart aleck
**Be'stand** *m* a) (*no pl*) (continued) existence, b) stock; ***~ haben*** last, be lasting
**be'ständig** *adj* constant, steady (*a. character*); settled; ***...beständig*** *in cpds* ...-resistant, ...proof
**Be'standsaufnahme** *f* ECON stocktaking (*a. fig*); ***~ machen*** take stock (*a. fig*)
**Be'standteil** *m* part, component
**be'stärken** *v/t* (*no -ge-*, *h*) confirm, strengthen, encourage (***in*** *dat* in)
**bestätigen** [bə'ʃtɛ:tɪgən] *v/t* (*no -ge-*, *h*) confirm; certify; acknowledge (*receipt*); ***sich ~*** prove (to be) true; come true; ***sich bestätigt fühlen*** feel affirmed; **Be'stätigung** *f* (-; *-en*) confirmation; certificate; acknowledg(e)ment; letter of confirmation

**bestatten** [bə'ʃtatən] *v/t* (*no -ge-, h*) bury; **Be'stattungsinsti,tut** *n* funeral home, *Br* undertakers

**be'stäuben** *v/t* (*no -ge-, h*) dust; BOT pollinate

**beste** ['bɛstə] *adj and adv* best; ***am ~n*** best; ***welches gefällt dir am ~n?*** which one do you like best?; ***am ~n nehmen Sie den Bus*** it would be best to take a bus; **Beste** *m, f* (*-n; -n*), *n* (*-n; no pl*) *the* best; ***das ~ geben*** do one's best; ***das ~ machen aus*** make the best of; (***nur***) ***zu deinem ~n*** for your own good

**be'stechen** *v/t* (*irr*, ***stechen***, *no -ge-, h*) bribe; fascinate (***durch*** by)

**be'stechlich** *adj* corrupt

**Be'stechung** *f* (*-; -en*) bribery, corruption; **Be'stechungsgeld** *n* bribe

**Besteck** [bə'ʃtɛk] *n* (*-[e]s; -e*) (set of) knife, fork and spoon; cutlery

**be'stehen** (*irr*, ***stehen***, *no -ge-, h*) **1.** *v/t* pass (*examination etc*); **2.** *v/i* be, exist; ***~ auf*** (*dat*) insist on; ***~ aus*** (***in***) (*dat*) consist of (in); ***~ bleiben*** last, survive

**Be'stehen** *n* (*-s; no pl*) existence

**be'stehlen** *v/t* (*irr*, ***stehlen***, *no -ge-, h*) ***j-n ~*** steal s.o.'s money *etc*

**be'steigen** *v/t* (*irr*, ***steigen***, *no ge-, h*) climb; get on *a bus etc*; ascend (*the throne*)

**be'stellen** *v/t* (*no -ge-, h*) order; book (*room etc*); reserve (*seat etc*); call (*taxi*); give, send (*message etc*); AGR cultivate; ***kann ich et. ~?*** can I take a message?; ***~ Sie ihm bitte, ...*** please tell him ...

**Be'stellschein** *m* ECON order form

**Be'stellung** *f* (*-; -en*) booking; reservation; ECON order; ***auf ~*** to order

**'bestenfalls** *adv* at best

**'bestens** *adv* very well

**bestialisch** [bɛs'tja:lɪʃ] *adj fig* bestial

**Bestie** ['bɛstjə] *f* (*-; -n*) beast, *fig a.* brute

**be'stimmen** *v/t* (*no -ge-, h*) determine, decide; define; choose, pick; ***zu ~ haben*** be in charge, F be the boss; ***bestimmt für*** meant for; **be'stimmt 1.** *adj* determined, firm; LING definite (*article*); ***~e Dinge*** certain things; **2.** *adv* certainly; ***ganz ~*** definitely; ***er ist ~ ...*** he must be ...; **Be'stimmung** *f* (*-; -en*) regulation; destiny

**Be'stimmungsort** *m* destination

**'Bestleistung** *f* SPORT (personal) record

**be'strafen** *v/t* (*no -ge-, h*) punish

**Be'strafung** *f* (*-; -en*) punishment

**be'strahlen** *v/t* (*no -ge-, h*) irradiate (*a.* MED); **Be'strahlung** *f* (*-; -en*) irradiation; MED ray treatment, radiotherapy

**be'streichen** *v/t* (*irr*, ***streichen***, *no -ge-, h*) spread; **be'streiten** *v/t* (*irr*, ***streiten***, *no -ge-, h*) challenge; deny; pay for, finance; **be'streuen** *v/t* (*no -ge-, h*) sprinkle (***mit*** with); **be'stürmen** *v/t* (*no -ge-, h*) urge; bombard

**be'stürzt** *adj* dismayed (***über*** *acc* at); **Be'stürzung** *f* (*-; no pl*) consternation, dismay

**Besuch** [bə'zu:x] *m* (*-[e]s; -e*) visit (*gen*, ***bei***, ***in*** *dat* to); call (***bei*** on; ***in*** *dat* at); attendance (*gen* at); ***~ haben*** have company *or* guests; **be'suchen** *v/t* (*no -ge-, h*) visit; call on, (go to) see; look *s.o.* up; attend (*meeting etc*); go to (*pub etc*); **Be'sucher(in)** (*-s; -/-; -nen*) visitor, guest; **Be'suchszeit** *f* visiting hours; **be'sucht** *adj*: ***gut*** (***schlecht***) ***~*** well (poorly) attended; much (little) frequented

**betagt** [bə'ta:kt] *adj* aged

**be'tasten** *v/t* (*no -ge-, h*) touch, feel

**be'tätigen** *v/t* (*no -ge-, h*) TECH operate; apply (*brake*); ***sich ~*** be active

**Be'tätigung** *f* (*-; -en*) activity

**betäuben** [bə'tɔʏbən] *v/t* (*no -ge-, h*) stun (*a. fig*), daze; MED an(a)esthetize

**Be'täubung** *f* (*-; -en*) MED an(a)esthetization; an(a)esthesia; *fig* daze, stupor

**Be'täubungsmittel** *n* MED an(a)esthetic; narcotic

**Bete** ['be:tə] *f* (*-; -n*) ***rote ~*** BOT beet, *Br* beetroot

**beteiligen** [bə'tailɪgən] *v/t* (*no -ge-, h*) ***j-n ~*** give s.o. a share (***an*** *dat* in); ***sich ~*** take part (***an*** *dat*, ***bei*** in), participate (in) (*a.* JUR); **beteiligt** [bə'tailɪçt] *adj* concerned; ***~ sein an*** (*dat*) be involved in; ECON have a share in; **Be'teiligung** *f* (*-; -en*) participation (*a.* JUR, ECON); involvement; share (*a.* ECON)

**beten** ['be:tən] *v/i* (*ge-, h*) pray (***um*** for), say one's prayers; say grace

**beteuern** [bə'tɔʏɐn] *v/t* (*no -ge-, h*) protest (*one's innocence etc*)

**Beton** [be'tɔŋ] *m* (*-s; -s, -e* [be'to:nə]) concrete

**betonen** [bə'to:nən] *v/t* (*no -ge-, h*) stress, *fig a.* emphasize

**betonieren** [beto'ni:rən] *v/t* (*no -ge-*, *h*) (cover with) concrete
**Be'tonung** *f* (-; *-en*) stress; *fig* emphasis
**betören** [bə'tø:rən] *v/t* (*no -ge-*, *h*) infatuate, bewitch
**Betr.** ABBR *of* ***betrifft*** re
**Betracht** [bə'traxt] *m*: ***in ~ ziehen*** take into consideration; ***nicht in ~ kommen*** be out of the question
**be'trachten** *v/t* (*no -ge-*, *h*) look at, *fig a.* view; ***~ als*** look upon *or* regard as, consider; **Be'trachter** *m* (*-s*; -) viewer
**beträchtlich** [bə'trɛçtlıç] *adj* considerable
**Be'trachtung** *f* (-; *-en*) view; ***bei näherer ~*** on closer inspection
**Betrag** [bə'tra:k] *m* (-[*e*]*s*; *Beträge* [bə'trɛ:gə]) amount, sum; **be'tragen** (*irr*, ***tragen***, *no -ge-*, *h*) **1.** *v/t* amount to; **2.** *v/refl* behave (o.s.); **Be'tragen** *n* (*-s*; *no pl*) behavio(u)r, conduct
**be'trauen** *v/t* (*no -ge-*, *h*) entrust (***mit*** with)
**be'treffen** *v/t* (*irr*, ***treffen***, *no -ge-*, *h*) concern; refer to; ***was ... betrifft*** as for ..., as to ...; ***betrifft*** (ABBR ***Betr.***) re; **~d** *adj* concerning; ***die ~en Personen*** *etc* the people *etc* concerned
**be'treiben** *v/t* (*irr*, ***treiben***, *no -ge-*, *h*) operate, run; go in for (*sport etc*)
**be'treten[1]** *v/t* (*irr*, ***treten***, *no -ge-*, *h*) step on; enter; ***Betreten*** (***des Rasens***) ***verboten!*** keep out! (keep off the grass!)
**be'treten[2]** *adj* embarrassed
**betreuen** [bə'trɔʏən] *v/t* (*no -ge-*, *h*) look after, take care of; **Be'treuung** *f* (-; *no pl*) care (*gen* of, for)
**Betrieb** [bə'tri:p] *m* (-[*e*]*s*; *-e*) a) business, firm, company, b) (*no pl*) operation, running, c) (*no pl*) rush; ***in ~ sein*** (***setzen***) be in (put into) operation; ***außer ~*** out of order; ***im Geschäft war viel ~*** the shop was very busy
**Be'triebs|anleitung** *f* operating instructions; **~berater** *m* business consultant; **~ferien** *pl* company (*Br a.* works) holiday; **~fest** *n* annual company fête; **~kapi,tal** *n* working capital; **~klima** *n* working atmosphere; **~kosten** *pl* operating costs; **~leitung** *f* management; **~rat** *m* works council
**be'triebssicher** *adj* safe to operate
**Be'triebs|störung** *f* TECH breakdown; **~sys,tem** *n* EDP operating system; **~unfall** *m* industrial accident; **~wirtschaft** *f* business administration
**be'trinken** *v/refl* (*irr*, ***trinken***, *no -ge-*, *h*) get drunk
**betroffen** [bə'trɔfən] *adj* affected, concerned; dismayed, shocked; **Be'troffenheit** *f* (-; *no pl*) dismay, shock
**betrübt** [bə'try:pt] *adj* sad, grieved (***über*** *acc* at)
**Betrug** [bə'tru:k] *m* (-[*e*]*s*; *no pl*) cheat; JUR fraud; deceit; **be'trügen** *v/t* (*irr*, ***trügen***, *no -ge-*, *h*) deceive; cheat (***beim Kartenspiel*** at cards); swindle, trick (***um et.*** out of s.th.); be unfaithful to; **Be'trüger(in)** (*-s*; -/-; *-nen*) swindler, trickster
**betrunken** [bə'trʊŋkən] *adj* drunken; ***~ sein*** be drunk
**Be'trunkene** *m, f* (*-n*; *-n*) drunk
**Bett** [bɛt] *n* (-[*e*]*s*; *-en*) bed; ***am ~*** at the bedside; ***ins ~ gehen*** (***bringen***) go (put) to bed; **~bezug** *m* comforter case, *Br* duvet cover; **~decke** *f* blanket; quilt
**betteln** ['bɛtəln] *v/i* (*ge-*, *h*) beg (***um*** for)
**'Bettgestell** *n* bedstead
**'bettlägerig** [-lɛ:gərıç] *adj* bedridden
**'Bettlaken** *n* sheet
**Bettler** ['bɛtlɐ] *m* (*-s*; -) beggar
**'Bett|nässer** [-nɛsɐ] *m* (*-s*; -) MED bed wetter; **~ruhe** *f* bed rest; ***j-m ~ verordnen*** tell s.o. to stay in bed; **~vorleger** *m* bedside rug; **~wäsche** *f* bed linen; **~zeug** *n* bedding, bedclothes
**beugen** ['bɔʏgən] *v/t* (*ge-*, *h*) bend; LING inflect; ***sich ~*** (***vor*** *dat* to) bend, bow
**Beule** ['bɔʏlə] *f* (-; *-n*) MED bump; MOT dent
**beunruhigen** [bə'ʔʊnru:ıgən] *v/t* (*no -ge-*, *h*) alarm, worry
**beurlauben** [bə'ʔu:ɐlaubən] *v/t* give *s.o.* leave *or* time off; suspend; ***sich ~ lassen*** ask for leave; **be'urlaubt** [-laupt] *adj* on leave
**be'urteilen** *v/t* (*no -ge-*, *h*) judge (***nach*** by); rate; **Be'urteilung** *f* (-; *-en*) judg(e)ment; evaluation
**Beute** ['bɔʏtə] *f* (-; *no pl*) booty, loot; ZO prey (*a. fig*); HUNT bag; *fig a.* victim
**Beutel** ['bɔʏtəl] *m* (*-s*; -) bag; pouch
**bevölkern** [bə'fœlkɐn] *v/t* (*no -ge-*, *h*) populate; **be'völkert** *adj* → ***besiedelt***; **Be'völkerung** *f* (-; *-en*) population

**bevollmächtigen** [bəˈfɔlmɛçtɪɡən] *v/t* (*no -ge-*, *h*) authorize
**beˈvor** *cj* before
**bevor|munden** [bəˈfoːɐmʊndən] *v/t* (*no -ge-*, *h*) patronize; **~stehen** *v/i* (*irr*, ***stehen***, *sep*, *-ge-*, *h*) be approaching; lie ahead; be imminent; ***j-m*** **~** be in store for s.o., await s.o.
**beˈvorzugen** [-tsuːɡən] *v/t* (*no -ge-*, *h*) prefer; favo(u)r; **Beˈvorzugung** *f* (-; *-en*) preferential treatment
**beˈwachen** *v/t* (*no -ge-*, *h*) guard, watch over; **Beˈwacher** *m* (*-s*; -) guard; SPORT marker; **Beˈwachung** *f* (-; *-en*) a) (*no pl*) guarding; SPORT marking, b) guard
**bewaffnen** [bəˈvafnən] *v/t* (*no -ge-*, *h*) arm (*a. fig*); **Beˈwaffnung** *f* (-; *-en*) armament; arms
**beˈwahren** *v/t* (*no -ge-*, *h*) keep; **~** ***vor*** (*dat*) keep *or* save from
**beˈwähren** *v/refl* (*no -ge-*, *h*) prove successful; ***sich*** **~** ***als*** prove to be
**bewährt** [bəˈvɛːɐt] *adj* (well-)tried, reliable; experienced; **Beˈwährung** *f* (-; *-en*) JUR probation
**Beˈwährungs|frist** *f* JUR (period of) probation; **~helfer** *m* JUR probation officer; **~probe** *f* (acid) test
**bewaldet** [bəˈvaldət] *adj* wooded, woody
**bewältigen** [bəˈvɛltɪɡən] *v/t* (*no -ge-*, *h*) manage, cope with; cover (*distance*)
**beˈwandert** *adj* (well-)versed (***in*** *dat* in)
**beˈwässern** *v/t* (*no -ge-*, *h*) irrigate; **Beˈwässerung** *f* (-; *-en*) irrigation
**bewegen** [bəˈveːɡən] *v/t and v/refl* (*no -ge-*, *h*) move (*a. fig*); ***nicht*** **~!** don't move!; (*irr*) ***j-n zu et.*** **~** get s.o. to do s.th.
**Beˈweggrund** *m* motive
**beweglich** [bəˈveːklɪç] *adj* movable; agile; flexible; TECH moving (*parts*); **Beˈweglichkeit** *f* (-; *no pl*) mobility; agility; **beˈwegt** *adj* rough (*sea*); choked (*voice*); eventful (*life*); *fig* moved, touched; **Beˈwegung** *f* (-; *-en*) movement (*a.* POL); motion (*a.* PHYS); exercise; *fig* emotion; ***in*** **~** ***setzen*** set in motion; **Beˈwegungsfreiheit** *f* (-; *no pl*) freedom of movement (*fig a.* of action); **beˈwegungslos** *adj* motionless
**Beweis** [bəˈvais] *m* (*-es*; *-e*) proof (***für*** of); **~(e)** evidence (*esp* JUR)
**beˈweisen** *v/t* (*irr*, ***weisen***, *no -ge-*, *h*) prove; show
**Beˈweismittel** *n* JUR (piece of) evidence
**Beˈweisstück** *n* (piece of) evidence, JUR exhibit
**beˈwenden** *v/i*: ***es dabei*** **~** ***lassen*** leave it at that
**beˈwerben** *v/refl* (*irr*, ***werben***, *no -ge-*, *h*) ***sich*** **~** ***um*** apply for; **Beˈwerber(in)** (*-s*; *-/-*; *-nen*) applicant; **Beˈwerbung** *f* (-; *-en*) application; **Beˈwerbungsschreiben** *n* (letter of) application
**beˈwerten** *v/t* (*no -ge-*, *h*) assess; judge; **Beˈwertung** *f* (-; *-en*) assessment
**bewilligen** [bəˈvɪlɪɡən] *v/t* (*no -ge-*, *h*) grant, allow; **beˈwirken** *v/t* (*no -ge-*, *h*) cause; **bewirten** [bəˈvɪrtən] *v/t* (*no -ge-*, *h*) entertain
**beˈwirtschaften** *v/t* (*no -ge-*, *h*) run; AGR farm; **beˈwirtschaftet** *adj* open (to the public)
**Beˈwirtung** *f* (-; *-en*) catering; service; hospitality
**bewog** [bəˈvoːk] *pret of* ***bewegen***
**bewogen** [bəˈvoːɡən] *pp of* ***bewegen***
**beˈwohnen** *v/t* (*no -ge-*, *h*) live in; inhabit; **Beˈwohner(in)** (*-s*; *-/-*; *-nen*) inhabitant; occupant; **beˈwohnt** *adj* inhabited; occupied
**bewölken** [bəˈvœlkən] *v/refl* (*no -ge-*, *h*) METEOR cloud over (*a. fig*); **beˈwölkt** *adj* METEOR cloudy, overcast
**Beˈwölkung** *f* (-; *no pl*) METEOR clouds
**Bewunderer** [bəˈvʊndərɐ] *m* (*-s*; -) admirer; **beˈwundern** *v/t* (*no -ge-*, *h*) admire (***wegen*** for); **beˈwundernswert** *adj* admirable; **Beˈwunderung** *f* (-; *no pl*) admiration
**bewusst** [bəˈvʊst] *adj* conscious; intentional; ***sich e-r Sache*** **~** ***sein*** be conscious *or* aware of s.th., realize s.th.; ***j-m et.*** **~** ***machen*** make s.o. realize s.th.
**beˈwusstlos** *adj* MED unconscious
**Beˈwusstsein** *n* (*-s*; *no pl*) MED consciousness; ***bei*** **~** conscious
**beˈzahlen** *v/t* (*no -ge-*, *h*) pay; pay for (*a. fig*); **beˈzahlt** *adj*: **~*er Urlaub*** paid leave; ***es macht sich*** **~** it pays; **Beˈzahlung** *f* (-; *no pl*) payment; pay
**beˈzaubern** *v/t* (*no -ge-*, *h*) charm; **~d** *adj* charming, F sweet, darling
**beˈzeichnen** *v/t* (*no -ge-*, *h*) **~** ***als*** call, describe as; **~d** *adj* characteristic, typical (***für*** of)

**Be'zeichnung** *f* (-; *-en*) name, term
**be'zeugen** *v/t* (*no -ge-, h*) JUR testify to
**be'ziehen** *v/t* (*irr*, ***ziehen***, *no -ge-, h*) cover; put clean sheets on (*bed*); move into; receive; subscribe to (*paper etc*); ~ ***auf*** (*acc*) relate to; ***sich*** ~ cloud over; ***sich*** ~ ***auf*** (*acc*) refer to; **Be'ziehung** *f* (-; *-en*) relation (***zu*** to *s.th.*; with *s.o.*); connection (***zu*** with); relationship; respect; ~***en haben*** have connections
**be'ziehungsweise** *cj* respectively; or; or rather
**Bezirk** [bə'tsɪrk] *m* (-[*e*]*s*; *-e*) precinct, *Br a.* district
**Bezug** [bə'tsu:k] *m* (-[*e*]*s*; *Bezüge* [bə'tsy:gə]) a) cover(ing); case, slip, b) (*no pl*) ECON purchase; subscription (*gen* to), c) *pl* earnings; ~ ***nehmen auf*** (*acc*) refer to; ***in*** ~ ***auf*** (*acc*) → ***bezüglich***
**bezüglich** [bə'tsy:klɪç] *prp* (*gen*) regarding, concerning
**Be'zugs|per,son** *f* PSYCH person to relate to, role model; ~**punkt** *m* reference point; ~**quelle** *f* source (of supply)
**be'zwecken** *v/t* (*no -ge-, h*) aim at, intend; **be'zweifeln** *v/t* (*no -ge-, h*) doubt, question; **be'zwingen** *v/t* (*irr*, ***zwingen***, *no -ge-, h*) conquer, defeat
**Bibel** ['bi:bəl] *f* (-; *-n*) Bible
**Biber** ['bi:bɐ] *m* (*-s*; -) ZO beaver
**Bibliothek** [biblio'te:k] *f* (-; *-en*) library
**Bibliothekar** [bibliote'ka:ɐ] *m* (*-s*; *-e*), **Bibliothe'karin** *f* (-; *-nen*) librarian
**biblisch** ['bi:blɪʃ] *adj* biblical
**bieder** ['bi:dɐ] *adj* honest; square
**biegen** ['bi:gən] *v/t* (*irr*, *ge-, h*) *and v/i* (*sein*) bend (*a.* ***sich*** ~), *road*: *a.* turn; ***um die Ecke*** ~ turn (round) the corner
**biegsam** ['bi:kza:m] *adj* flexible
**'Biegung** *f* (-; *-en*) curve
**Biene** ['bi:nə] *f* (-; *-n*) ZO bee
**'Bienen|königin** *f* ZO queen (bee); ~**korb** *m*, ~**stock** *m* (bee)hive; ~**wachs** *n* beeswax
**Bier** [bi:ɐ] *n* (-[*e*]*s*; *-e*) beer; ~ ***vom Faß*** draft (*Br* draught) beer; ~**deckel** *m* coaster, beer mat; ~**krug** *m* beer mug, stein
**Biest** [bi:st] F *fig n* (-[*e*]*s*; *-er*) beast; (***kleines***) ~ brat, little devil, stinker
**bieten** ['bi:tən] (*irr*, *ge-, h*) **1.** *v/t* offer; ***sich*** ~ present itself; **2.** *v/i auction*: (make a) bid
**Bigamie** [biga'mi:] *f* (-; *-n*) bigamy
**Bikini** [bi'ki:ni] *m* (*-s*; *-s*) bikini
**Bilanz** [bi'lants] *f* (-; *-en*) ECON balance; *fig* result; ~ ***ziehen aus*** (*dat*) *fig* take stock of
**Bild** [bɪlt] *n* (-[*e*]*s*; *-er* ['bɪldɐ]) picture; image; ***sich ein*** ~ ***machen von*** get an idea of; ~**ausfall** *m* TV blackout; ~**bericht** *m* photo(graphic) essay (*Br* report)
**bilden** ['bɪldən] *v/t* (*ge-, h*) form (*a.* ***sich*** ~); shape; *fig* educate (***sich*** o.s.); be, constitute
**'Bilderbuch** *n* picture book
**'Bildfläche** *f*: F ***auf der*** ~ ***erscheinen*** (***von der*** ~ ***verschwinden***) appear on (disappear from) the scene
**'Bildhauer** *m* (*-s*; -), **'Bildhauerin** *f* (-; *-nen*) sculptor
**'bildlich** *adj* graphic; figurative
**'Bildnis** *n* (*-ses*; *-se*) portrait
**'Bildplatte** *f* videodisk (*Br* -disc)
**'Bildröhre** *f* picture tube
**'Bildschirm** *m* TV screen, EDP *a.* display, monitor; ~**arbeitsplatz** *m* workstation; ~**gerät** *n* visual display unit, VDU; ~**schoner** *m* (*-s*; -) screen saver; ~**text** *m* videotext, *Br* viewdata
**'bild'schön** *adj* most beautiful
**'Bildung** *f* (-; *-en*) a) (*no pl*) education, b) formation
**'Bildungs...** *in cpds ...chancen, ...reform, ...urlaub etc*: educational ...; ~**lücke** *f* gap in one's knowledge
**'Bildunterschrift** *f* caption
**Billard** ['bɪljart] *n* (*-s*; *-e*) billiards, pool; ~**kugel** *f* billiard ball; ~**stock** *m* cue
**Billett** [bɪl'jɛt] *n* (-[*e*]*s*; *-e*) *Swiss* ticket
**billig** ['bɪlɪç] *adj* cheap (*a. contp*), inexpensive
**billigen** ['bɪlɪgən] *v/t* (*ge-, h*) approve of; **'Billigung** *f* (-; *no pl*) approval
**Billion** [bɪ'ljo:n] *f* (-; *-en*) trillion
**bimmeln** ['bɪməln] F *v/i* (*ge-, h*) jingle; TEL ring
**binär** [bi'nɛ:ɐ] *adj* MATH, PHYS *etc* binary
**Binde** ['bɪndə] *f* (-; *-n*) bandage; sling; → ***Damenbinde***; ~**gewebe** *n* ANAT connective tissue; ~**glied** *n* (connecting) link
**'Bindehaut** *f* ANAT conjunctiva; ~**entzündung** *f* MED conjunctivitis
**binden** (*irr*, *ge-, h*) **1.** *v/t* bind (*a. book*), tie (***an*** *acc* to); make (*wreath etc*); knot (*tie*); ***sich*** ~ bind *or* commit o.s.; **2.** *v/i* bind

'**Bindestrich** *m* LING hyphen
'**Bindewort** *n* LING conjunction
**Bindfaden** ['bınt-] *m* string
'**Bindung** *f* (-; *-en*) tie, link, bond; *skiing*: binding
**Binnen|hafen** ['bınən-] *m* inland port; **~handel** *m* domestic trade; **~markt** *m*: ***Europäischer*** ~ European single market; **~schifffahrt** *f* inland navigation; **~verkehr** *m* inland traffic *or* transport
**Binse** ['bınzə] *f* (-; *-n*) BOT rush
'**Binsenweisheit** *f* (-; *-en*) truism
**Bio..., bio...** [bio-] *in cpds ...chemie, ...dynamisch, ...sphäre etc*: bio...
**Biografie, Biographie** [biogra'fi:] *f* (-; *-n*) biography
**bio'grafisch, bio'graphisch** *adj* biographic(al)
**Bioladen** ['bi:o-] *m* health food shop *or* store
**Biologe** [bio'lo:gə] *m* (*-n*; *-n*) biologist
**Biologie** [biolo'gi:] *f* (-; *no pl*) biology
**Bio'login** *f* (-; *-nen*) biologist
**biologisch** [bio'lo:gıʃ] *adj* biological; AGR organic; ~ ***abbaubar*** biodegradable
'**Biorhythmus** *m* biorhythms
'**Biotechnik** *f* (-; *no pl*) biotechnology
**Biotop** [bio'to:p] *n* (*-s*; *-e*) biotope
**Birke** ['bırkə] *f* (-; *-n*) BOT birch (tree)
**Birne** ['bırnə] *f* (-; *-n*) BOT pear; ELECTR (light) bulb
**bis** [bıs] *prp* (*acc*) *and adv and cj time*: till, until, (up) to; *space*: (up) to, as far as; ***von ... ~ ...*** from ... to ...; ~ ***auf*** (*acc*) except; ~ ***zu*** up to; ~ ***später!*** see you later!; ~ ***jetzt*** up to now, so far; ~ ***Montag*** by Monday; ***zwei ~ drei*** two or three; ***wie weit ist es ~ ...?*** how far is it to ...?
**Bischof** ['bıʃɔf] *m* (*-s*; *Bischöfe* ['bıʃœfə]) REL bishop
**bisexuell** [bizɛ'ksuɛl] *adj* bisexual
**bis'her** *adv* up to now, so far; ***wie*** ~ as before
**bisherig** [bıs'he:rıç] *adj* previous
**Biskuit** [bıs'kvi:t] *n* (*-[e]s*; *-e*) sponge cake (mix)
**biss** [bıs] *pret of* ***beißen***
**Biss** *m* (*-es*; *-e*) bite (*a. fig*)
**bisschen** ['bısçən] *adj and adv*: ***ein*** ~ a little, a (little) bit (of); ***nicht ein*** ~ not in the least
**Bissen** ['bısən] *m* (*-s*; -) bite; ***keinen*** ~ not a thing
**bissig** ['bısıç] *adj fig* cutting; ***ein ~er Hund*** a dog that bites; ***Vorsicht, ~er Hund!*** beware of the dog!
**Bistum** ['bıstu:m] *n* (*-s*; *Bistümer* ['bısty:mɐ]) REL bishopric, diocese
**bis'weilen** *adv* at times, now and then
**Bit** [bıt] *n* (*-[s]*; *-[s]*) EDP bit
**bitte** ['bıtə] *adv* please; ~ ***nicht!*** please don't!; ~ (***schön***)***!*** that's all right, not at all, you're welcome; here you are; (***wie***) ***~?*** pardon?; ~ ***sehr?*** can I help you?; '**Bitte** *f* (-; *-n*) request (***um*** for); ***ich habe e-e ~*** (***an dich***) I have a favo(u)r to ask of you; '**bitten** *v/t* (*irr, ge-, h*) ***j-n um et. ~*** ask s.o. for s.th.; ***darf ich ~?*** may I have (the pleasure of) this dance?; → ***Erlaubnis***
**bitter** ['bıtɐ] *adj* bitter (*a. fig*), *a.* biting (*cold*); **~'kalt** *adj* bitterly cold
**blähen** ['blɛ:ən] *v/refl* (*ge-, h*) swell
'**Blähungen** *pl* MED flatulence, *Br a.* wind
**blamabel** [bla'ma:bəl] *adj* embarrassing; **Blamage** [bla'ma:ʒə] *f* (-; *-n*) disgrace, shame; **blamieren** [bla'mi:rən] *v/t* (*no -ge-, h*) ***j-n*** ~ make s.o. look like a fool; ***sich*** ~ make a fool of o.s.
**blank** [blaŋk] *adj* shining, shiny, bright; polished; F broke
**Blanko...** ['blaŋko] *in cpds* ECON blank
**Bläschen** ['blɛ:sçən] *n* (*-s*; -) MED vesicle, small blister
**Blase** ['bla:zə] *f* (-; *-n*) bubble; ANAT bladder; MED blister
'**Blasebalg** *m* (pair of) bellows
'**blasen** *v/t* (*irr, ge-, h*) blow (*a.* MUS)
'**Blas|instru,ment** *n* MUS wind instrument; **~ka,pelle** *f* brass band; **~rohr** *n* blowpipe
**blass** [blas] *adj* pale (***vor*** with); ~ ***werden*** turn pale; **Blässe** ['blɛsə] *f* (-; *no pl*) paleness, pallor
**Blatt** [blat] *n* (*-[e]s*; *Blätter* ['blɛtɐ]) BOT leaf; piece, sheet (*a.* MUS); (news)paper; *card games*: hand; **blättern** ['blɛtɐn] *v/i* (*ge-, h*) ~ ***in*** (*dat*) leaf through
'**Blätterteig** *m* puff pastry
**blau** [blau] *adj* blue; F loaded, stoned; ***~es Auge*** black eye; ***~er Fleck*** bruise; ***Fahrt ins Blaue*** mystery tour
'**blauäugig** [-ɔygıç] *adj* blue-eyed; *fig* starry-eyed

**'Blaubeere** *f* BOT blueberry, *Br* bilberry
**'blaugrau** *adj* bluish-gray (*Br* -grey)
**bläulich** ['blɔʏlɪç] *adj* bluish
**'Blaulicht** *n* (-[*e*]*s*; -*er*) flashing light(s)
**'Blauhelme** *pl* MIL UN soldiers
**'blaumachen** F *v/i* (*sep*, -*ge*-, *h*) stay away from work *or* school
**'Blausäure** *f* CHEM prussic acid
**Blech** [blɛç] *n* (-[*e*]*s*; -*e*) sheet metal; *in cpds ...dach, ...löffel etc*: tin ...; *...instrument*: MUS brass ...
**'blechen** F *v/t and v/i* (*ge*-, *h*) shell out
**'Blech|büchse, ~dose** *f* can, *Br a.* tin; **~schaden** *m* MOT bodywork damage
**Blei** [blai] *n* (-[*e*]*s*; -*e*) lead; **aus ~** leaden
**Bleibe** ['blaibə] *f* (-; -*n*) place to stay
**'bleiben** *v/i* (*irr*, *ge*-, *sein*) stay, remain; **~ *bei*** stick to; F ***et. ~ lassen*** not do s.th.; ***lass das ~!*** stop that!; ***das wirst du schön ~ lassen!*** you'll do nothing of the sort!; → ***Apparat, ruhig***; **~d** *adj* lasting, permanent
**bleich** [blaiç] *adj* pale (***vor*** *dat* with)
**'bleichen** *v/t* ([*irr*,] *ge*-, *h*) bleach
**bleiern** ['blaiɐn] *adj* lead(en *fig*)
**'bleifrei** *adj* MOT unleaded
**'Bleistift** *m* pencil; **~spitzer** *m* pencil sharpener
**Blende** ['blɛndə] *f* (-; -*n*) blind; PHOT aperture; (***bei***) **~ *8*** (at) f-8
**'blenden** *v/t* (*ge*-, *h*) blind, dazzle (*both a. fig*); **~d** *adj* dazzling (*a. fig*); brilliant; **~ *aussehen*** look great
**'blendfrei** *adj* OPT antiglare
**blich** [blɪç] *pret of* ***bleichen***
**Blick** [blɪk] *m* (-[*e*]*s*; -*e*) look (***auf*** *acc* at); view (of); ***flüchtiger ~*** glance; ***auf den ersten ~*** at first sight; **'blicken** *v/i* (*ge*-, *h*) look, glance (*both*: ***auf*** *acc*, ***nach*** at)
**'Blickfang** *m* eye-catcher
**'Blickfeld** *n* field of vision
**blieb** [bliːp] *pret of* ***bleiben***
**blies** [bliːs] *pret of* ***blasen***
**blind** [blɪnt] *adj* blind (*a. fig* ***gegen, für*** to; ***vor*** *dat* with); dull (*mirror etc*); ***~er Alarm*** false alarm; ***~er Passagier*** stowaway; ***auf e-m Auge ~*** blind in one eye; ***ein Blinder*** a blind man; ***e-e Blinde*** a blind woman; ***die Blinden*** the blind
**'Blinddarm** *m* ANAT appendix; **~entzündung** *f* MED appendicitis; **~operation** *f* MED appendectomy
**Blinden|hund** ['blɪndən-] *m* seeing eye (*Br* guide) dog; **~schrift** *f* braille
**'Blindgänger** [-gɛŋɐ] *m* (-*s*; -) MIL dud
**'Blindheit** *f* (-; *no pl*) blindness
**blindlings** ['blɪntlɪŋs] *adv* blindly
**'Blindschleiche** *f* ZO blindworm
**blinken** ['blɪŋkən] *v/i* (*ge*-, *h*) sparkle, shine; twinkle; flash (a signal); MOT indicate; **Blinker** ['blɪŋkɐ] *m* (-*s*; -) MOT turn signal, *Br* indicator
**blinzeln** ['blɪntsəln] *v/i* (*ge*-, *h*) blink (one's eyes)
**Blitz** [blɪts] *m* (-*es*; -*e*) (flash of) lightning; PHOT flash; **~ableiter** *m* (-*s*; -) lightning conductor
**'blitzen** *v/i* (*ge*-, *h*) flash; ***es blitzt*** it's lightening
**'Blitz|gerät** *n* PHOT (electronic) flash; **~lampe** *f* PHOT flashbulb; flash cube; **~licht** *n* (-[*e*]*s*; -*er*) PHOT flash(light); **~schlag** *m* lightning stroke
**'blitz'schnell** *adj and adv* like a flash; *attr* split-second
**Block** [blɔk] *m* (-[*e*]*s*; *Blöcke* ['blœkə]) block; POL, ECON bloc; (*writing*) pad
**Blockade** [blɔ'kaːdə] *f* (-; -*n*) MAR, MIL blockade
**'Blockflöte** *f* recorder
**'Blockhaus** *n* log cabin
**blockieren** [blɔ'kiːrən] *v/t and v/i* (*no -ge-*, *h*) block; MOT lock
**'Blockschrift** *f* block letters
**blöde** ['bløːdə] F *adj* silly, stupid
**'blödeln** *v/i* (*ge*-, *h*) fool *or* clown around
**Blödheit** ['bløːthait] *f* (-; *no pl*) stupidity
**'Blödsinn** F *m* (-[*e*]*s*; *no pl*) rubbish, nonsense
**'blödsinnig** F *adj* stupid, idiotic
**blöken** ['bløːkən] *v/i* (*ge*-, *h*) ZO bleat
**blond** [blɔnt] *adj* blond, fair
**Blondine** [blɔn'diːnə] *f* (-; -*n*) blonde
**bloß** [bloːs] **1.** *adj* bare; naked (*eye*); mere; **2.** *adv* only, just, merely
**Blöße** ['bløːsə] *f* (-; -*n*) nakedness; ***sich e-e ~ geben*** lay o.s. open to attack *or* criticism
**'bloß|legen** *v/t* (*sep*, -*ge*-, *h*) lay bare, expose; **~stellen** *v/t* (*sep*, -*ge*-, *h*) expose, compromise, unmask; ***sich ~*** compromise o.s.
**blühen** ['blyːən] *v/i* (*ge*-, *h*) (be in) bloom; (be in) blossom; *fig* flourish
**Blume** ['bluːmə] *f* (-; -*n*) flower; GASTR bouquet; head, froth

**'Blumen|beet** *n* flowerbed; **~händler** *m* florist; **~kohl** *m* BOT cauliflower; **~laden** *m* flower shop, florist's; **~strauß** *m* bunch of flowers; bouquet; **~topf** *m* flowerpot; **~vase** *f* vase
**Bluse** ['blu:zə] *f* (-; *-n*) blouse
**Blut** [blu:t] *n* (-[*e*]*s*; *no pl*) blood
**'blutarm** *adj* MED an(a)emic (*a. fig*)
**'Blut|armut** *f* MED an(a)emia; **~bad** *n* massacre; **~bahn** *f* ANAT bloodstream; **~bank** *f* (-; *-en*) MED blood bank
**'blutbefleckt** *adj* bloodstained
**'Blut|bild** *n* MED blood count; **~blase** *f* MED blood blister; **~druck** *m* MED blood pressure
**Blüte** ['bly:tə] *f* (-; *-n*) flower; bloom (*a. fig*); blossom; *fig* height, heyday; ***in*** (***voller***) **~** in (full) bloom
**'Blutegel** *m* ZO leech
**'bluten** *v/i* (*ge-*, *h*) bleed (***aus*** *dat* from)
**'Blüten|blatt** *n* petal; **~staub** *m* pollen
**Bluter** ['blu:tɐ] *m* (*-s*; -) MED h(a)emophiliac
**'Blut|erguss** *m* bruise; MED h(a)ematoma; **~gefäß** *n* ANAT blood vessel; **~gerinnsel** *n* MED blood clot; **~gruppe** *f* MED blood group; **~hund** *m* ZO bloodhound
**'blutig** *adj* bloody; ***~er Anfänger*** rank beginner, F greenhorn
**'Blut|körperchen** *n* MED blood corpuscle; **~kreislauf** *m* MED (blood) circulation; **~lache** *f* pool of blood
**'blutleer** *adj* bloodless
**'Blutprobe** *f* MED blood test
**'blutrünstig** [-rynstıç] *adj* bloodthirsty, gory
**'Blutschande** *f* JUR incest
**'Blutspender** *m* blood donor
**'Blutsverwandte** *m, f* blood relation
**'Blutübertragung** *f* MED blood transfusion
**'Blutung** *f* (-; *-en*) MED bleeding, h(a)emorrhage
**'blutunterlaufen** *adj* bloodshot
**'Blut|vergießen** *n* (*-s*; *no pl*) bloodshed; **~vergiftung** *f* MED blood poisoning; **~wurst** *f* black sausage (*Br* pudding)
**BLZ** [be:ɛl'tsɛt] ABBR *of* ***Bankleitzahl*** A.B.A. number, *Br* bank (sorting) code
**Bö** [bø:] *f* (-; *-en*) gust, squall
**Bob** [bɔp] *m* (*-s*; *-s*) bob(sled); **~bahn** *f* bob run; **~fahrer** *m* bobber
**Bock** [bɔk] *m* (-[*e*]*s*; *Böcke* ['bœkə]) ZO buck; he-goat, billy-goat; ram; SPORT buck; F ***e-n ~ schießen*** (make a) blunder; F ***keinen*** (*or* ***null***) **~ *auf et. haben*** have zero interest in s.th.
**'bocken** *v/i* (*ge-*, *h*) buck; sulk
**'bockig** *adj* obstinate; sulky
**'Bockspringen** *n* leapfrog
**Boden** ['bo:dən] *m* (*-s*; *Böden* ['bø:dən]) ground; AGR soil; bottom; floor; attic
**'Boden|perso,nal** *n* AVIAT ground crew; **~re,form** *f* land reform; **~schätze** *pl* mineral resources; **~sta-ti,on** *f* AVIAT ground control; **~turnen** *n* floor exercises
**Body** ['bɔdi] *m* (*-s*; *-s*) bodysuit
**bog** [bo:k] *pret of* ***biegen***
**Bogen** ['bo:gən] *m* (*-s*; *Bögen* ['bø:gən]) bend, curve; MATH arc; ARCH arch; *skiing*: turn; bow; sheet; **~schießen** *n* archery; **~schütze** *m* archer
**Bohle** ['bo:lə] *f* (-; *-n*) plank
**Bohne** ['bo:nə] *f* (-; *-n*) BOT bean; ***grüne ~n*** green (*Br a.* French) beans
**'Bohnenstange** *f* beanpole (*a.* F)
**bohnern** ['bo:nɐn] *v/t* (*ge-*, *h*) polish, wax; **'Bohnerwachs** *n* floor polish
**bohren** ['bo:rən] *v/t* (*ge-*, *h*) bore, drill (*a. dentist*); **~d** *fig adj* piercing (*look*); insistent (*questions etc*)
**Bohrer** ['bo:rɐ] *m* (*-s*; -) TECH drill
**'Bohr|insel** *f* oil rig; **~loch** *n* borehole, well(head); **~ma,schine** *f* (electric) drill; **~turm** *m* derrick
**'Bohrung** *f* (-; *-en*) drilling; bore
**Boje** ['bo:jə] *f* (-; *-n*) MAR buoy
**Bolzen** ['bɔltsən] *m* (*-s*; -) TECH bolt
**bombardieren** [bɔmbar'di:rən] *v/t* (*no -ge-*, *h*) bomb; *fig* bombard
**Bombe** ['bɔmbə] *f* (-; *-n*) bomb; *fig* bombshell
**'Bomben|angriff** *m* air raid; **~anschlag** *m* bomb attack; **~erfolg** F *m* roaring success; THEA *etc* smash hit; **~geschäft** F *n* super deal
**'Bombenleger** *m* (*-s*; -) bomber
**'bombensicher** *adj* bombproof
**Bomber** ['bɔmbɐ] F *m* (*-s*; -) MIL bomber (*a.* SPORT)
**Bon** [bɔŋ] *m* (*-s*; *-s*) coupon, voucher
**Bonbon** [bɔŋ'bɔŋ] *m, n* (*-s*; *-s*) candy, *Br* sweet
**Boot** [bo:t] *n* (-[*e*]*s*; *-e*) boat
**'Bootsmann** *m* (-[*e*]*s*; *-leute*) boatswain

B

**Bord**[1] [bɔrt] *n* (-[*e*]*s*; -*e*) shelf
**Bord**[2] *m*: ***an ~*** AVIAT, MAR on board; ***über ~*** MAR overboard; ***von ~ gehen*** MAR disembark
**Bordell** [bɔr'dɛl] *n* (-*s*; -*e*) brothel, F whorehouse
**'Bordkarte** *f* AVIAT boarding pass
**'Bordstein** *m* curb, *Br* kerb
**borgen** ['bɔrgən] *v/t* (*ge-*, *h*) borrow; ***sich et. von j-m ~*** borrow s.th. from s.o.; ***j-m et. ~*** lend s.th. to s.o.
**Borke** ['bɔrkə] *f* (-; -*n*) BOT bark
**borniert** [bɔr'niːɐt] *adj* narrow-minded
**Börse** ['bœrzə] *f* (-; -*n*) ECON stock exchange
**'Börsen|bericht** *m* market report; **~kurs** *m* quotation; **~makler** *m* stockbroker; **~speku,lant** *m* stock-jobber
**Borste** ['bɔrstə] *f* (-; -*n*) bristle
**'borstig** *adj* bristly
**Borte** ['bɔrtə] *f* (-; -*n*) border; braid, lace
**bösartig** ['bøːs-] *adj* vicious; MED malignant
**Böschung** ['bœʃʊŋ] *f* (-; -*en*) slope, bank; RAIL embankment
**böse** ['bøːzə] *adj* bad, evil, wicked; angry (***über*** *acc* about; ***auf j-n*** with s.o.), mad (***auf*** *acc* at); ***er meint es nicht ~*** he means no harm
**'Böse** *n* (-*n*; *no pl*) (the) evil
**'Bösewicht** *m* (-[*e*]*s*; -*er*) villain
**boshaft** ['boːshaft] *adj* malicious
**Bosheit** ['boːshait] *f* (-; *no pl*) malice
**'böswillig** *adj* malicious, JUR *a.* wil(l)ful
**bot** [boːt] *pret of* ***bieten***
**Botanik** [bo'taːnɪk] *f* (-; *no pl*) botany
**Bo'taniker** *m* (-*s*; -) botanist
**bo'tanisch** *adj* botanical
**Bote** ['boːtə] *m* (-*n*; -*n*) messenger
**'Botengang** *m* errand; ***Botengänge machen*** run errands
**Botschaft** ['boːtʃaft] *f* (-; -*en*) message; POL embassy
**'Botschafter** *m* (-*s*; -) POL ambassador (***in*** *dat* to); **'Botschafterin** *f* (-; -*nen*) POL ambassadress (***in*** *dat* to)
**Bottich** ['bɔtɪç] *m* (-*s*; -*e*) tub, vat
**Bouillon** [bʊl'jɔŋ] *f* (-; -*s*) consommé, bouillon, broth
**Boulevard|blatt** [bulə'vaːɐ-] *n*, **~zeitung** *f* tabloid
**Bowle** ['boːlə] *f* (-; -*n*) (cold) punch; bowl
**boxen** ['bɔksən] (*ge-*, *h*) **1.** *v/i* box; **2.** *v/t* punch; **'Boxen** *n* (-*s*; *no pl*) boxing;
**Boxer** ['bɔksɐ] *m* (-*s*; -) boxer
**'Box|handschuh** *m* boxing glove; **~kampf** *m* boxing match, fight; **~sport** *m* boxing
**Boykott** [bɔʏ'kɔt] *m* (-[*e*]*s*; -*e*), **boykottieren** [bɔʏkɔ'tiːrən] *v/t* (*no -ge-*, *h*) boycott
**brach** [braːx] *pret of* ***brechen***
**brachliegend** *adj* AGR fallow
**brachte** ['braxtə] *pret of* ***bringen***
**Branche** ['brãːʃə] *f* (-; -*n*) ECON line (of business); **'Branchenverzeichnis** *n* TEL yellow pages
**Brand** [brant] *m* (-[*e*]*s*, *Brände* ['brɛndə]) fire; ***in ~ geraten*** catch fire; ***in ~ stecken*** set fire to; **~blase** *f* MED blister
**branden** ['brandən] *v/i* (*ge-*, *sein*) surge (***gegen*** against)
**'Brand|fleck** *m* burn; **~mal** *n* brand
**'brandmarken** *fig v/t* (*ge-*, *h*) brand, stigmatize
**'Brand|mauer** *f* fire wall; **~stätte** *f*, **~stelle** *f* scene of fire; **~stifter** *m* arsonist; **~stiftung** *f* arson
**'Brandung** *f* (-; *no pl*) surf, surge, breakers
**'Brandwunde** *f* MED burn; scald
**brannte** ['brantə] *pret of* ***brennen***
**'Branntwein** *m* brandy, spirits
**braten** ['braːtən] *v/t* (*irr*, *ge-*, *h*) roast; grill, broil; fry; ***am Spieß ~*** roast on a spit, barbecue
**'Braten** *m* (-*s*; -) roast (meat); joint; **~fett** *n* dripping; **~soße** *f* gravy
**'Brat|fisch** *m* fried fish; **~huhn** *n* roast chicken; **~kar,toffeln** *pl* fried potatoes; **~ofen** *m* oven; **~pfanne** *f* frying pan
**Bratsche** ['braːtʃə] *f* (-; -*n*) MUS viola
**'Bratwurst** *f* grilled sausage
**Brauch** [braux] *m* (-[*e*]*s*; *Bräuche* ['brɔʏçə]) custom; habit, practice
**'brauchbar** *adj* useful
**'brauchen** *v/t* (*ge-*, *h*) need; require; take (*time*); use; ***wie lange wird er ~?*** how long will it take him?; ***du brauchst es nur zu sagen*** just say the word; ***ihr braucht es nicht zu tun*** you don't have to do it; ***er hätte nicht zu kommen ~*** he need not have come
**brauen** ['brauən] *v/t* (*ge-*, *h*) brew
**Brauerei** [brauə'rai] *f* (-; -*en*) brewery
**braun** [braun] *adj* brown; (sun)tanned; ***~ werden*** (get a) tan

**Bräune** ['brɔʏnə] *f* (-; *no pl*) (sun)tan
**'bräunen** (*ge-*, *h*) **1.** *v/t* brown, tan; **2.** *v/i* (get a) tan
**'Braunkohle** *f* brown coal, lignite
**'bräunlich** *adj* brownish
**Brause** ['brauzə] *f* (-; *-n*) shower; → ***Limonade***; **'brausen** *v/i* a) (*ge-*, *h*) roar, b) (*sein*) rush, c) (*h*) → ***duschen***
**Braut** [braut] *f* (-; *Bräute* ['brɔʏtə]) bride; fiancée; **Bräutigam** ['brɔʏtɪgam] *m* (-*s*; -*e*) (bride)groom; fiancé
**'Braut|jungfer** *f* bridesmaid; **~kleid** *n* wedding-dress; **~paar** *n* bride and (bride)groom; engaged couple
**brav** [bra:f] *adj* good; honest; ***sei(d) ~!*** be good!
**BRD** [be:ʔɛr'de:] ABBR *of* ***Bundesrepublik Deutschland*** FRG, Federal Republic of Germany
**brechen** ['brɛçən] (*irr*, *ge-*) **1.** *v/t* (*h*) break (*a. fig*); MED vomit; ***sich ~*** OPT be refracted; ***sich den Arm ~*** break one's arm; **2.** *v/i* a) (*h*) MED vomit, F throw up, *Br a.* be sick; ***mit j-m ~*** break with s.o; ***~d voll*** crammed, packed, b) (*sein*) break, get broken, fracture
**'Brechreiz** *m* MED nausea
**'Brechstange** *f* crowbar
**'Brechung** *f* (-; *-en*) OPT refraction
**Brei** [brai] *m* (-[*e*]*s*; -*e*) pulp, mash; pap; porridge; pudding
**'breiig** *adj* pulpy, mushy
**breit** [brait] *adj* wide; broad (*a. fig*); F ***sich ~ machen*** spread o.s., take up room
**'breitbeinig** *adj* with legs (wide) apart
**Breite** ['braitə] *f* (-; *-n*) width, breadth; ASTR, GEOGR latitude
**'breiten** *v/t* (*ge-*, *h*) spread
**'Breiten|grad** *m* degree of latitude; **~kreis** *m* parallel (of latitude)
**'Breitwand** *f film*: wide screen
**Bremsbelag** ['brɛms-] *m* brake lining
**Bremse** ['brɛmzə] *f* (-; *-n*) TECH brake; ZO gadfly; **'bremsen** (*ge-*, *h*) **1.** *v/i* MOT brake, put on the brake(s); slow down; **2.** *v/t* MOT brake; *fig* curb
**'Brems|licht** *n* (-[*e*]*s*; -*er*) MOT stop light; **~pe,dal** *n* MOT brake pedal; **~spur** *f* MOT skid marks; **~weg** *m* MOT stopping distance
**'brennbar** *adj* combustible; (in)flammable; **brennen** ['brɛnən] (*irr*, *ge-*, *h*) **1.** *v/t* burn; distil(l) (*whisky etc*); bake (*bricks*); **2.** *v/i* burn; be on fire; *wound, eyes*: smart, burn; F ***darauf ~ zu inf*** be dying to *inf*; ***es brennt!*** fire!; **Brenner** ['brɛnɐ] *m* (-*s*; -) burner
**'Brenn|holz** *n* firewood; **~materi,al** *n* fuel; **~nessel** *f* BOT (stinging) nettle; **~punkt** *m* focus, focal point; **~spiritus** *m* methylated spirit; **~stab** *m* TECH fuel rod; **~stoff** *m* fuel
**brenzlig** ['brɛntslɪç] *adj* burnt; *fig* hot
**Bresche** ['brɛʃə] *f* (-; *-n*) breach (*a. fig*), gap
**Brett** [brɛt] *n* (-[*e*]*s*; -*er*] board
**'Bretterzaun** *m* wooden fence
**'Brettspiel** *n* board game
**Brezel** ['bre:tsəl] *f* (-; *-n*) pretzel
**Brief** [bri:f] *m* (-[*e*]*s*; -*e*] letter; **~beschwerer** *m* (-*s*; -) paperweight; **~bogen** *m* sheet of (note)paper; **~freund(in)** pen pal (*Br* friend); **~kasten** *m* mailbox, *Br* letterbox
**'brieflich** *adj and adv* by letter
**'Brief|marke** *f* (postage) stamp; **~markensammlung** *f* stamp collection; **~öffner** *m* letter opener, *Br* paper knife; **~pa,pier** *n* stationery; **~tasche** *f* wallet; **~taube** *f* ZO carrier pigeon; **~träger(in)** (-*s*; -/-; -*nen*) mailman (mailwoman), *Br* postman (postwoman); **~umschlag** *m* envelope; **~wahl** *f* postal vote; **~wechsel** *m* correspondence
**briet** [bri:t] *pret of* ***braten***
**Brikett** [bri'kɛt] *n* (-*s*; -*s*) briquet(te)
**brillant** [brɪl'jant] *adj* brilliant
**Bril'lant** *m* (-*en*; -*en*) (cut) diamond
**Bril'lantring** *m* diamond ring
**Brille** ['brɪlə] *f* (-; *-n*) (pair of) glasses, spectacles; goggles; toilet seat
**'Brillen|etui** *n* eyeglass (*Br* spectacle) case; **~träger(in)** (-*s*; -/-; -*nen*) ***~ sein*** wear glasses
**bringen** ['brɪŋən] *v/t* (*irr*, *ge-*, *h*) bring; take; cause; make (*sacrifice*); yield (*profit*); ***j-n nach Hause ~*** see (*or* take) s.o. home; ***in Ordnung ~*** put in order; ***das bringt mich auf e-e Idee*** that gives me an idea; ***j-n dazu ~, et. zu tun*** get s.o. to do s.th.; ***et. mit sich ~*** involve s.th.; ***j-n um et. ~*** deprive s.o. of s.th.; ***j-n zum Lachen ~*** make s.o. laugh; ***j-n wieder zu sich ~*** bring s.o. round ; ***es zu et.*** (***nichts***) ***~*** go far (get nowhere); F ***es ~*** make it; ***das bringt nichts*** it's no use

B

**Brise** ['bri:zə] *f* (-; *-n*) breeze
**Brite** ['brɪtə] *m* (*-n*; *-n*), '**Britin** *f* (-; *-nen*) Briton; ***die Briten*** *pl* the British
'**britisch** *adj* British
**bröckeln** ['brœkəln] *v/i* (*ge-*, *h*, *sein*) crumble
**Brocken** ['brɔkən] *m* (*-s*; -) piece; lump; rock; GASTR chunk; morsel; ***ein paar ~ Englisch*** a few scraps of English; F ***ein harter ~*** a hard nut to crack
**Brombeere** ['brɔm-] *f* BOT blackberry
**Bronchitis** [brɔn'çi:tɪs] *f* (-; *-tiden* [brɔnçi'ti:dən]) MED bronchitis
**Bronze** ['brõ:sə] *f* (-; *-n*) bronze; **~zeit** *f* (-; *no pl*) HIST Bronze Age
**Brosche** ['brɔʃə] *f* (-; *-n*) brooch, pin
**broschiert** [brɔ'ʃi:ɐt] *adj* paperback
**Broschüre** [brɔ'ʃy:rə] *f* (-; *-n*) pamphlet; brochure
**Brot** [bro:t] *n* (*-[e]s*; *-e*) bread; sandwich; ***ein*** (***Laib***) ***~*** a loaf (of bread); ***e-e Scheibe ~*** a slice of bread; ***sein ~ verdienen*** earn one's living
**Brötchen** ['brø:tçən] *n* (*-s*; -) roll
'**Brot|rinde** *f* crust; **~(schneide)ma,schine** *f* bread cutter
**Bruch** [brʊx] *m* (*-[e]s*; *Brüche* ['brʏçə]) break; MED fracture; hernia; MATH fraction; GEOL fault; *fig* breach (*of promise etc*); JUR violation; ***zu ~ gehen*** be wrecked; **~bude** F *f* dump, hovel
**brüchig** ['brʏçɪç] *adj* brittle
'**Bruch|landung** *f* AVIAT crash landing; **~rechnung** *f* MATH fractional arithmetic, F fractions
'**bruchsicher** *adj* breakproof
'**Bruch|strich** *m* MATH fraction bar; **~stück** *n* fragment; **~teil** *m* fraction; ***im ~ e-r Sekunde*** in a split second; **~zahl** *f* MATH fraction(al) number
**Brücke** ['brʏkə] *f* (-; *-n*) bridge (*a.* SPORT); rug; '**Brückenpfeiler** *m* pier
**Bruder** ['bru:dɐ] *m* (*-s*; *Brüder* ['bry:dɐ]) brother (*a.* REL); **~krieg** *m* civil war
**brüderlich** ['bry:dɐlɪç] **1.** *adj* brotherly; **2.** *adv*: ***~ teilen*** share and share alike
'**Brüderlichkeit** *f* (-; *no pl*) brotherhood
'**Brüderschaft** *f*: ***~ trinken*** *agree to use the familiar 'du' form of address*
**Brühe** ['bry:ə] *f* (-; *-n*) broth; stock; F dishwater; slops; F filthy water, bilge
'**Brühwürfel** *m* beef cube
**brüllen** ['brʏlən] *v/i* (*ge-*, *h*) roar (***vor Lachen*** with laughter); ZO bellow; F bawl; **~*des Gelächter*** roars of laughter
**brummen** ['brʊmən] *v/i* (*ge-*, *h*) growl; ZO hum, buzz (*a. engine etc*); *head*: be buzzing; '**brummig** *adj* grumpy
**brünett** [bry'nɛt] *adj* brunette, dark-haired
**Brunnen** ['brʊnən] *m* (*-s*; -) well, spring, fountain
**Brunstzeit** ['brʊnst-] *f* ZO rutting season
**Brust** [brʊst] *f* (-; *Brüste* ['brʏstə]) ANAT a) (*no pl*) chest, b) breast(s), bosom; **~bein** *n* ANAT breastbone; **~beutel** *m* neck pouch, *Br* money bag
**brüsten** ['brʏstən] *v/refl* (*ge-*, *h*) boast, brag (***mit*** of)
'**Brust|kasten** *m*, **~korb** *m* ANAT chest, thorax; **~schwimmen** *n* breaststroke
'**Brüstung** *f* (-; *-en*) parapet
'**Brustwarze** *f* ANAT nipple
**Brut** [bru:t] *f* (-; *-en*) ZO brooding; brood (*a.* F), hatch; fry
**brutal** [bru'ta:l] *adj* brutal; **Brutalität** [brutali'tɛ:t] *f* (-; *-en*) brutality
'**Brutappa,rat** *m* ZO incubator
**brüten** ['bry:tən] *v/i* (*ge-*, *h*) ZO brood, sit (on eggs); ***~ über*** (*dat*) *fig* brood over
'**Brutkasten** *m* MED incubator
**brutto** ['brʊto] *adv* ECON gross
'**Brutto|einkommen** *n* ECON gross earnings; **~sozi,alpro,dukt** *n* ECON gross national product
**Bube** ['bu:bə] *m* (*-n*; *-n*) boy, lad; *card game*: knave, jack
**Buch** [bu:x] *n* (*-[e]s*; *Bücher* ['by:çɐ]) book; **~binder** *m* (*-s*; -) (book)binder; **~drucker** *m* printer; **~druckerei** *f* print shop, *Br* printing office
**Buche** ['bu:xə] *f* (-; *-n*) BOT beech
'**buchen** *v/t* (*ge-*, *h*) book; ECON enter
**Bücherbord** ['by:çɐ-] *n* bookshelf
**Bücherei** [by:çə'rai] *f* (-; *-en*) library
'**Bücherre,gal** *n* bookshelf
'**Bücherschrank** *m* bookcase
'**Buch|fink** *m* ZO chaffinch; **~halter(in)** bookkeeper; **~haltung** *f* (-; *no pl*) bookkeeping; **~händler(in)** bookseller; **~handlung** *f* bookstore, *Br* bookshop; **~macher** *m* bookmaker
**Büchse** ['bʏksə] *f* (-; *-n*) can, *Br* tin; box; rifle
'**Büchsen|fleisch** *n* canned (*Br* tinned)

meat; **~öffner** *m* can (*Br* tin) opener

**Buchstabe** ['bu:xʃta:bə] *m* (*-n; -n*) letter; ***großer*** (***kleiner***) ~ capital (small) letter; **buchstabieren** [bu:xʃta'bi:rən] *v/t* (*no -ge-, h*) spell; **buchstäblich** ['bu:xʃtɛ:plıç] *adv* literally

**'Buchstütze** *f* bookend

**Bucht** ['bʊxt] *f* (*-; -en*) bay; creek, inlet

**'Buchung** *f* (*-; -en*) booking; ECON entry

**Buckel** ['bʊkəl] *m* (*-s; -*) hump, hunch; ***e-n ~ machen*** hump *or* hunch one's back

**bücken** ['bʏkən] *v/refl* (*ge-, h*) bend (down), stoop

**bucklig** ['bʊklıç] *adj* hunchbacked

**Bucklige** ['bʊklıgə] *m, f* (*-n; -n*) hunchback

**Bückling** ['bʏklıŋ] *m* (*-s; -e*) smoked herring, *Br* kipper

**Buddhismus** [bʊ'dısmʊs] *m* (*-; no pl*) Buddhism; **Buddhist** [bʊ'dıst] *m* (*-en; -en*), **bud'dhistisch** *adj* Buddhist

**Bude** ['bu:də] *f* (*-n; -n*) stall, booth; hut; F pad, *Br* digs; *contp* shack, dump, hole

**Budget** [bʏ'dʒe:] *n* (*-s; -s*) budget

**Büfett** [by'fɛt] *n* (*-[e]s; -s, -e*) counter, bar, buffet; sideboard, cupboard; ***kaltes*** ~ GASTR cold buffet (meal)

**Büffel** ['bʏfəl] *m* (*-s; -*) ZO buffalo

**'büffeln** F *v/i* (*ge-, h*) grind, cram, swot

**Bug** [bu:k] *m* (*-[e]s; -e*) MAR bow; AVIAT nose; ZO, GASTR shoulder

**Bügel** ['by:gəl] *m* (*-s; -*) hanger; bow; **~brett** *n* ironing board; **~eisen** *n* iron; **~falte** *f* crease

**'bügelfrei** *adj* no(n)-iron

**'bügeln** *v/t* (*ge-, h*) iron, press

**buh** [bu:] *int* boo!

**buhen** ['bu:ən] *v/i* (*ge-, h*) boo

**Bühne** ['by:nə] *f* (*-; -n*) stage, *fig a.* scene

**'Bühnen|bild** *n* (stage) set(ting); **~bildner(in)** (*-s; -/-; -nen*) stage designer

**'Buhrufe** *pl* boos

**Bullauge** ['bʊl-] *n* MAR porthole

**'Bulldogge** *f* ZO bulldog

**Bulle** ['bʊlə] *m* (*-n; -n*) ZO bull (*a. fig*); F *contp* cop, *pl the* fuzz

**Bummel** ['bʊməl] F *m* (*-s; -*) stroll; **Bummelei** [bʊmə'lai] *f* (*-; no pl*) F *contp* dawdling; slackness; **'bummeln** F *v/i* a) (*ge-, sein*) stroll, saunter, b) (*ge-, h*) *contp* dawdle; ECON go slow; **'Bummelstreik** *m* ECON slowdown, *Br* go-slow (strike); **Bummler** ['bʊmlɐ] F *m* (*-s; -*) stroller; *contp* dawdler, slowpoke, *Br* slowcoach

**bumsen** ['bʊmzən] *v/i and v/t* (*ge-, h*) F → ***krachen***; V screw

**Bund**[1] [bʊnt] *m* (*-[e]s; Bünde* ['bʏndə]) union, federation, alliance; association; (waist)band; ***der*** ~ POL the Federal Government; F → ***Bundeswehr***

**Bund**[2] *n* (*-[e]s; -e*) bundle; bunch

**Bündel** ['bʏndəl] *n* (*-s; -*) bundle

**'bündeln** *v/t* (*ge-, h*) bundle (up)

**Bundes...** ['bʊndəs-] *in cpds* Federal ...; German ...; **~bahn** *f* Federal Railroad(s); **~genosse** *m* ally; **~kanzler** *m* Federal Chancellor; **~land** *n appr* (federal) state, Land; **~liga** *f* SPORT First Division; **~post** *f* Federal Postal Administration; **~präsi,dent** *m* Federal President; **~rat** *m* Bundesrat, Upper House of German Parliament; **~repu,blik** *f* Federal Republic; **~staat** *m* federal state; confederation; **~straße** *f* Federal Highway **~tag** *m* (*-[e]s; no pl*) Bundestag, Lower House of German Parliament; **~trainer** *m* coach of the (German) national team; **~verfassungsgericht** *n* Federal Constitutional Court, *Am appr* Supreme Court; **~wehr** *f* (*-; no pl*) MIL (German Federal) Armed Forces

**bündig** ['bʏndıç] *adj* TECH flush; ***kurz und*** ~ terse(ly); point-blank

**Bündnis** ['bʏntnıs] *n* (*-ses; -se*) alliance

**Bunker** ['bʊŋkɐ] *m* (*-s; -*) air-raid shelter, bunker

**bunt** [bʊnt] *adj* colo(u)red; multicolo(u)red; colo(u)rful (*a. fig*); varied; ***~er Abend*** evening of entertainment; F ***mir wird's zu*** ~ that's all I can take

**'Buntstift** *m* colo(u)red pencil, crayon

**Bürde** ['bʏrdə] *f* (*-; -n*) burden (***für j-n*** to s.o.)

**Burg** [bʊrk] *f* (*-; -en*) castle

**Bürge** ['bʏrgə] *m* (*-n; -n*) JUR guarantor (*a. fig*); **'bürgen** *v/i* (*ge-, h*) ***für j-n*** ~ JUR stand surety for s.o.; ***für et.*** ~ guarantee s.th.

**Bürger** ['bʏrgɐ] *m* (*-s; -*), **'Bürgerin** *f* (*-; -nen*) citizen; **~initia,tive** *f* (citizen's *or* local) action group; **~krieg** *m* civil war

**'bürgerlich** *adj* civil; middle-class; *esp contp* bourgeois; ***~e Küche*** home cooking; '**Bürgerliche** *m, f* (*-n*; *-n*) commoner

'**Bürger|meister** *m* mayor; **~rechte** *pl* civil rights; **~steig** [-ʃtaik] *m* (*-[e]s*; *-e*) sidewalk, *Br* pavement

'**Bürgschaft** *f* (*-*; *-en*) JUR surety; bail

**Büro** [by'ro:] *n* (*-s*; *-s*) office; **~angestellte** *m, f* (*-n*; *-n*) clerk, office worker; **~klammer** *f* (paper) clip

**Bürokrat** [byro'kra:t] *m* (*-en*; *-en*) bureaucrat; **Bürokratie** [byrokra'ti:] *f* (*-*; *-n*) bureaucracy; *contp* red tape

**Bü'rostunden** *pl* office hours

**Bursche** ['bʊrʃə] *m* (*-n*; *-n*) fellow, guy

**burschikos** [bʊrʃi'ko:s] *adj* (tom)boyish, pert

**Bürste** ['bʏrstə] *f* (*-*; *-n*) brush

'**bürsten** *v/t* (*ge-*, *h*) brush

'**Bürstenschnitt** *m* crew cut

**Bus** [bʊs] *m* (*-ses*; *-se*) bus; coach

**Busch** [bʊʃ] *m* (*-[e]s*; *Büsche* ['bʏʃə]) BOT bush, shrub

**Büschel** ['bʏʃəl] *n* (*-s*; *-*) bunch; tuft

'**buschig** *adj* bushy

**Busen** ['bu:zən] *m* (*-s*; *-*) ANAT bosom, breast(s)

'**Busfahrer** *m* bus driver

'**Bushaltestelle** *f* bus stop

**Bussard** ['bʊsart] *m* (*-s*; *-e*) ZO buzzard

**Buße** ['bu:sə] *f* (*-*; *-n*) REL penance; repentance; **~ *tun*** do penanc

**büßen** ['by:sən] *v/t* (*ge-*, *h*) pay *or* suffer for *s.th.*; REL repent

'**Bußgeld** *n* fine, penalty

'**Bußtag** *m* REL day of repentance

**Büste** ['by:stə] *f* (*-*; *-n*) bust

'**Büstenhalter** *m* bra

**Butter** ['bʊtɐ] *f* (*-*; *no pl*) butter; **~blume** *f* BOT buttercup; **~brot** *n* (slice *or* piece of) bread and butter; F ***für ein ~*** for a song; **~brotpa,pier** *n* greaseproof paper; **~dose** *f* butter dish; **~milch** *f* buttermilk

**b.w.** ABBR *of* ***bitte wenden*** PTO, please turn over

**bzw.** ABBR *of* ***beziehungsweise*** resp., respectively

# C

**C** ABBR *of* ***Celsius*** C, Celsius, centigrade

**ca.** ABBR *of* ***circa*** approx., approximately

**Café** [ka'fe:] *n* (*-s*; *-s*) café, coffee house

**campen** ['kɛmpən] *v/i* (*ge-*, *h*) camp

**Camper** ['kɛmpɐ] *m* (*-s*; *-*) camper

**Camping...** ['kɛmpɪŋ-] *in cpds ...bett, ...tisch etc* camp ...; **~bus** *m* camper (van *Br*); **~platz** *m* campground, *Br* campsite

**Catcher** ['kɛtʃɐ] *m* (*-s*; *-*) wrestler

**CD** [tse:'de:] *f* (*-*; *-s*), **C'D-Platte** *f* CD, compact disk (*Br* disc); **C'D-ROM** CD-ROM; **C'D-Spieler** *m* CD player

**Cellist** [tʃɛ'lɪst] *m* (*-en*; *-en*), **Cel'listin** *f* (*-*; *-nen*) MUS cellist

**Cello** ['tʃɛlo] *n* (*-s*; *-s*, *Celli*) MUS Cello

**Celsius** ['tsɛlzjʊs] ***5 Grad ~*** (ABBR **5° C**) five degrees centigrade *or* Celsius

**Cembalo** ['tʃɛmbalo] *n* (*-s*; *-s*, *-li*) MUS harpsichord

**Champagner** [ʃam'panjɐ] *m* (*-s*; *-*) champagne

**Champignon** ['ʃampɪnjɔŋ] *m* (*-s*; *-s*) BOT mushroom

**Chance** ['ʃã:sə] *f* (*-*; *-n*) chance; ***die ~n stehen gleich*** (***3 zu 1***) the odds are even (three to one); '**Chancengleichheit** *f* equal opportunities

**Chaos** ['ka:ɔs] *n* (*-*; *no pl*) chaos

**Chaot** [ka'o:t] *m* (*-en*; *-en*) chaotic person; POL anarchist, *pl a.* lunatic fringe

**cha'otisch** *adj* chaotic

**Charakter** [ka'raktɐ] *m* (*-s*; *-e* [-'te:rə]) character, nature; **charakterisieren** [-teri'zi:rən] *v/t* (*no -ge-*, *h*) characterize, describe (***als*** as); **charakteristisch** [-te'rɪstɪʃ] *adj* characteristic, typical (***für*** of); **Cha'rakterzug** *m* trait

**charmant** [ʃar'mant] *adj* charming

**Charme** [ʃarm] *m* (*-s*; *no pl*) charm

**Chassis** [ʃa'si:] *n* (*-*; *-*) TECH chassis

**Chauffeur** [ʃɔ'føːɐ] *m* (*-s*; *-e*) chauffeur, driver
**Chauvi** ['ʃoːvi] *m* (*-s*; *-s*) F male chauvinist (pig)
**Chauvinismus** [ʃovi'nɪsmʊs] *m* (*-*; *no pl*) chauvinism, POL *a.* jingoism
**Chef** [ʃɛf] *m* (*-s*; *-s*) head, chief, F boss; **~arzt** *m* medical director, *Br* senior consultant; **~sekre'tärin** *f* executive secretary
**Chemie** [çe'miː] *f* (*-*; *no pl*) chemistry; **~faser** *f* synthetic fiber (*Br* fibre)
**Chemikalien** [çemi'kaːljən] *pl* chemicals; **Chemiker(in)** ['çeːmikɐ (-kərɪn)] (*-s*; *-/-*; *-nen*) (analytical) chemist; **chemisch** ['çeːmɪʃ] *adj* chemical; **~e Reinigung** dry cleaning
**Chemothera'pie** [çemo-] *f* MED chemotherapy
**Chiffre** ['ʃɪfrə] *f* (*-*; *-n*) code, cipher; box (number); **chiffrieren** [ʃɪ'friːrən] *v/t* (*no -ge-*, *h*) (en)code
**China** ['çiːna] China; **Chinese** [çi'neːzə] *m* (*-n*; *-n*), **Chi'nesin** *f* (*-*; *-nen*), **chi'nesisch** *adj* Chinese
**Chinin** [çi'niːn] *n* (*-s*; *no pl*) PHARM quinine
**Chip** [tʃɪp] *m* (*-s*; *-s*) *a.* EDP chip; GASTR *pl* chips, *Br* crisps
**Chirurg** [çi'rʊrk] *m* (*-en*; *-en*) surgeon
**Chirurgie** [çirʊr'giː] *f* (*-*; *-n*) surgery
**Chirurgin** [çi'rʊrgɪn] *f* (*-*; *-nen*) surgeon
**chirurgisch** [çi'rʊrgɪʃ] *adj* surgical
**Chlor** [kloːɐ] *n* (*-s*; *no pl*) CHEM chlorine
**chloren** ['kloːrən] *v/t* (*ge-*, *h*) chlorinate
**Cholera** ['koːlera] *f* (*-*; *no pl*) MED cholera; **cholerisch** [ko'leːriʃ] *adj* choleric
**Cholesterin** [çolɛste'riːn] *n* (*-s*; *no pl*) MED cholesterol
**Chor** [koːɐ] *m* (*-[e]s*; *Chöre* ['køːrə]) MUS choir (*a.* ARCH); ***im ~*** in chorus
**Choral** [ko'raːl] *m* (*-s*; *Choräle* [ko'rɛːlə]) MUS, REL chorale, hymn
**Christ** [krɪst] *m* (*-en*; *-en*) REL Christian; **~baum** *m* Christmas tree
**'Christenheit:** ***die ~*** REL Christendom
**'Christentum** *n* (*-s*; *no pl*) REL Christianity
**Christin** ['krɪstɪn] *f* (*-*; *-nen*) REL Christian
**'Christkind** *n* Infant Jesus; Father Christmas, Santa Claus
**'christlich** *adj* REL Christian
**Christus** ['krɪstʊs] REL Christ; ***vor ~*** B.C.; ***nach ~*** A.D.
**Chrom** [kroːm] *n* (*-s*; *no pl*) chrome, CHEM *a.* chromium
**Chromosom** [kromo'zoːm] *n* (*-s*; *-en*) BIOL chromosome
**Chronik** ['kroːnɪk] *f* (*-*; *-en*) chronicle
**chronisch** ['kroːnɪʃ] *adj* MED chronic
**chronologisch** [krono'loːgɪʃ] *adj* chronological
**circa** → ***zirka***
**City** ['sɪtɪ] *f* (*-*; *-s*) downtown, (city) center, *Br* centre
**Clique** ['klɪkə] *f* (*-*; *-n*) F group, set; *contp* clique
**Clou** [kluː] F *m* (*-s*; *-s*) highlight, climax; ***der ~ daran*** the whole point of it
**Compactdisc** ['kəmpæktdɪsk] *f* (*-*; *-s*) compact disk (*Br* disc)
**Computer** [kɔm'pjuːtɐ] *m* (*-s*; *-*) computer; **~ausdruck** *m* computer printout
**com'puter|gesteuert** *adj* computer-controlled; **~gestützt** *adj* computer-aided
**Com'putergrafik** *f* computer graphics
**computerisieren** [kɔmpjutəri'ziːrən] *v/t* (*no -ge-*, *h*) computerize
**Com'puter|spiel** *n* computer game; **~virus** *m* EDP computer virus
**Conférencier** [kõferɑ̃'sjeː] *m* (*-s*; *-s*) master of ceremonies, F emcee, MC, *Br* compère
**Cord** *etc* → ***Kord*** *etc*
**Couch** [kautʃ] *f* (*-*; *-s*) couch
**Coupé** [ku'peː] *n* (*-s*; *-s*) MOT coupé
**Coupon** → ***Kupon***
**Cousin** [ku'zɛ̃ː] *m* (*-s*; *-s*), **Cousine** [ku'ziːnə] *f* (*-*; *-n*) cousin
**Creme** [kreːm] *f* (*-*; *-s*) cream (*a. fig*)
**Curry** ['kari] *m* (*-s*; *-s*) curry powder
**Cursor** ['kɜːsə] *m* (*-s*; *-s*) EDP cursor

# D

D

**da** [daː] **1.** *adv space*: there; here; *time*: then, at that time; ~ ***drüben*** (***draußen***, ***hinten***) over (out, back) there; ***von*** ~ ***aus*** from there; ***das ...*** ~ that ... (over there) ; ~ ***kommt er*** here he comes; ~ ***bin ich*** here I am; ~ ***sein*** be there; exist; ***ist noch ...*** ~**?** is any ... left?; ***noch nie*** ~ ***gewesen*** unprecedented; ***er ist gleich wieder*** ~ he'll be right back; ***von*** ~ ***an*** *or* ***ab*** from then on; **2.** *cj* as, since, because

**'dabehalten** *v/t* (*irr*, ***halten***, *sep*, *no -ge-*, *h*) keep; ***j-n*** ~ keep s.o. in

**dabei** [da'bai] *adv* there, present; near *or* close by; at the same time; included with it; ~ ***sein*** be there; take part; be in on it; ***ich bin*** ~**!** count me in!; ***er ist gerade*** ~ ***zu gehen*** he's just leaving; ***es ist nichts*** ~ there's nothing to it; there's no harm in it; ***was ist schon*** ~**?** (so) what of it?; ***lassen wir es*** ~**!** let's leave it at that!; **~bleiben** *v/i* (*irr*, ***bleiben***, *sep*, *-ge-*, *sein*) stick to it; **~haben** F *v/t* (*irr*, ***haben***, *sep*, *-ge-*, *h*) have with (*or* on) one

**'dableiben** *v/i* (*irr*, ***bleiben***, *sep*, *-ge-*, *sein*) stay

**Dach** [dax] *n* (-[*e*]*s*; *Dächer* ['dɛçɐ]) roof

**'Dach|boden** *m* attic; **~decker** [-dekɐ] *m* (*-s*; -) roofer; **~fenster** *n* dormer window; **~gepäckträger** *m* MOT roof-rack

**'Dachgeschoss** *n*, **'Dachgeschoß** *Austrian n* attic; **~wohnung** *f* loft apartment, *Br* attic flat

**'Dach|kammer** *f* garret; **~luke** *f* skylight; **~pappe** *f* roofing felt; **~rinne** *f* gutter

**Dachs** [daks] *m* (*-es*; *-e*) ZO badger

**'Dachstuhl** *m* roof framework

**dachte** ['daxtə] *pret of* ***denken***

**'Dachter,rasse** *f* roof terrace

**'Dachverband** *m* ECON *etc* umbrella organization

**Dackel** ['dakəl] *m* (*-s*; -) ZO dachshund

**'dadurch** *adv and cj* this *or* that way; for this reason, so; ~**,** ***dass*** due to the fact that

**dafür** [da'fyːɐ] *adv* for it, for that; instead; in return, in exchange; ~ ***sein*** be in favo(u)r of it; ***er kann nichts*** ~ it is not his fault; ~ ***sorgen, dass*** see to it that

**da'gegen** *adv and cj* against it; however, on the other hand; ~ ***sein*** be against (*or* opposed to) it; ***haben Sie et.*** ~**,** ***dass ich ...?*** do you mind if I ...?; ***wenn Sie nichts*** ~ ***haben*** if you don't mind; ***... ist nichts*** ~ ... can't compare

**da'heim** *adv* at home

**'daher** *adv and cj* from there; that's why

**da'hin** *adv* there, to that place; gone, past; ***bis*** ~ till then; up to there

**da'hinten** *adv* back there

**da'hinter** *adv* behind it; ***es steckt nichts*** ~ there is nothing to it; F ~ ***kommen*** find out (about it)

**'dalassen** F *v/t* (*irr*, ***lassen***, *sep*, *-ge-*, *h*) leave behind

**damalig** ['daːmaːlɪç] *adj* then

**damals** ['daːmaːls] *adv* then, at that time

**Dame** ['daːmə] *f* (-; *-n*) lady; partner; *cards*, *chess*: queen; checkers, *Br* draughts

**'Damen...** *in cpds* ladies' ...; SPORT women's ...; **~binde** *f* sanitary napkin (*Br* towel)

**'damenhaft** *adj* ladylike

**'Damen|toi,lette** *f* ladies' room (*Br* toilet), *the* ladies; **~wahl** *f* ladies' choice

**damit 1.** ['daːmɪt] *adv* with it *or* that; by it, with it; ***was will er*** ~ ***sagen?*** what's he trying to say?; ***wie steht es*** ~**?** how about it?; ~ ***einverstanden sein*** have no objections; **2.** [da'mɪt] *cj* so that; in order to *inf*; ~ ***nicht*** so as not to *inf*

**Damm** [dam] *m* (-[*e*]*s*; *Dämme* ['dɛmə]) dam; embankment

**dämmerig** ['dɛmərɪç] *adj* dim

**'Dämmerlicht** *n* (-[*e*]*s*; *no pl*) twilight

**dämmern** ['dɛmɐn] *v/i* (*ge-*, *h*) dawn (*a.* F ***j-m*** on s.o.); get dark *or* dusky

**'Dämmerung** *f* (-; *-en*) dusk; dawn

**Dämon** ['dɛːmɔn] *m* (*-s*; *-en* [dɛ'moːnən]) demon; **dämonisch** [dɛ'moːnɪʃ] *adj* demoniac(al)

**Dampf** [dampf] *m* (-[*e*]*s*; *Dämpfe* ['dɛmpfə]) steam; PHYS vapo(u)r

**'dampfen** *v/i* (*ge-*, *h and sein*) steam

**dämpfen** ['dɛmpfən] *v/t* (*ge-*, *h*) deaden; muffle (*voice*); soften (*light*, *sound*, *blow*); GASTR steam, stew; steam-iron; *fig* put a damper on; curb (*a.* ECON)
**Dampfer** ['dampfɐ] *m* (*-s*; *-*) steamer, steamship
**'Dampf|kochtopf** *m* pressure cooker; **~ma,schine** *f* steam engine; **~schiff** *n* steamer, steamship
**da'nach** *adv* after it *or* that; afterwards; for it; according to it; ***ich fragte ihn ~*** I asked him about it; F ***mir ist nicht ~*** I don't feel like it
**Däne** ['dɛːnə] *m* (*-n*; *-n*) Dane
**da'neben** *adv* next to it, beside it; besides, as well, at the same time; beside the mark; **~benehmen** F *v/refl* (*irr*, ***nehmen***, *sep*, *no -ge-*, *h*) step out of line; **~gehen** F *v/i* (*irr*, ***gehen***, *sep*, *-ge-*, *sein*) miss (the target); F misfire
**'Dänemark** Denmark
**Dänin** ['dɛːnɪn] *f* (*-*; *-nen*) Danish woman *or* girl; **'dänisch** *adj* Danish
**dank** [daŋk] *prp* (*gen*) thanks to
**Dank** *m* (*-[e]s*; *no pl*) thanks; ***Gott sei ~!*** thank God!; ***vielen ~!*** many thanks!
**'dankbar** *adj* grateful (***j-m*** to s.o.); rewarding (*task etc*)
**'Dankbarkeit** *f* (*-*; *no pl*) gratitude
**'danken** *v/i* (*ge-*, *h*) thank (***j-m für et.*** s.o. for s.th.); ***danke*** (***schön***) thank you (very much); (***nein***,) ***danke*** no, thank you; ***nichts zu ~*** not at all
**dann** [dan] *adv* then; ***~ und wann*** (every) now and then
**daran** [da'ran] *adv* on it; *die*, *think etc* of it; *believe etc* in it; *suffer etc* from it; → ***liegen***
**darauf** [da'rauf] *adv* on (top of) it; after (that); *listen*, *drink etc* to it; *proud etc* of it; *wait etc* for it; ***am Tage ~*** the day after; ***zwei Jahre ~*** two years later; ***~ kommt es an*** that's what matters
**darauf'hin** *adv* after that; as a result
**daraus** [da'raus] *adv* from (*or* out of) it; ***was ist ~ geworden?*** what has become of it?; ***~ wird nichts!*** F nothing doing!
**Darbietung** ['daːɐbiːtʊŋ] *f* (*-*; *-en*) presentation; performance
**darin** [da'rɪn] *adv* in it; ['daːrɪn] in that
**darlegen** ['daːɐ-] *v/t* (*sep*, *-ge-*, *h*) explain, set out
**Darlehen** ['daːɐleːən] *n* (*-s*; *-*) loan; ***ein ~ geben*** grant a loan
**Darm** [darm] *m* (*-[e]s*; *Därme* ['dɛrmə]) ANAT bowel(s), intestine(s); GASTR skin; **~grippe** *f* MED intestinal flu
**darstellen** ['daːɐ-] *v/t* (*sep*, *-ge-*, *h*) represent, show, depict; describe; THEA play, do; trace, graph; **'Darsteller(in)** (*-s*; *-/-*; *-nen*) THEA performer, actor (actress); **'Darstellung** *f* (*-*; *-en*) representation; description; account; portrayal
**darüber** [da'ryːbɐ] *adv* over *or* above it; across it; in the meantime; *write*, *talk etc* about it; ***... und ~*** ... and more; ***~ werden Jahre vergehen*** that will take years
**darum** [da'rʊm] *adv and cj* (a)round it; because of it, that's why; ***~ bitten*** ask for it; → ***gehen***
**darunter** [da'rʊntɐ] *adv* under *or* below it, underneath; among them; including; ***... und ~*** ... and less; ***was verstehst du ~?*** what do you understand by it?
**das** [das] → ***der***
**'Dasein** *n* (*-s*; *no pl*) life, existence
**dass** [das] *cj* that; so (that); ***es sei denn, ~*** unless; ***nicht ~ ich wüsste*** not that I know of
**'dastehen** *v/i* (*irr*, ***stehen***, *sep*, *-ge-*, *h*) stand (there)
**Datei** [da'tai] *f* (*-*; *-en*) EDP file; **~verwaltung** *f* EDP file management
**Daten** ['daːtən] *pl* data (*a.* EDP), facts; particulars; **~bank** *f* (*-*; *-en*) EDP database, data bank; **~schutz** *m* JUR data protection; **~speicher** *m* data memory *or* storage; **~träger** *m* data medium *or* carrier; **~übertragung** *f* data transfer; **~verarbeitung** *f* data processing
**datieren** [da'tiːrən] *v/t and v/i* (*no -ge-*, *h*) date
**Dativ** ['daːtiːf] *m* (*-s*; *-e*) dative (case)
**Dattel** ['datəl] *f* (*-*; *-n*) BOT date
**Datum** ['daːtʊm] *n* (*-s*; *Daten* ['daːtən]) date; ***welches ~ haben wir heute?*** what's the date today?
**Dauer** ['dauɐ] *f* (*-*; *no pl*) duration; continuance; ***auf die ~*** in the long run; ***für die ~ von*** for a period *or* term of; ***von ~ sein*** last; **~arbeitslosigkeit** *f* long-term unemployment; **~auftrag** *m* ECON standing order; **~geschwindigkeit** *f* MOT *etc* cruising speed
**'dauerhaft** *adj* lasting; durable

D

D

**'Dauer|karte** *f* season ticket; **~lauf** *m* SPORT jogging; ***im ~*** at a jog; **~lutscher** *m* lollipop
**dauern** *v/i* (*ge-*, *h*) last, take; → ***lange***
**'Dauerwelle** *f* permanent, *Br* perm
**Daumen** ['daumən] *m* (*-s*; *-*) ANAT thumb; F ***j-m den ~ halten*** keep one's fingers crossed (for s.o.); ***am ~ lutschen*** suck one's thumb
**Daunen** ['daunən] *pl* down
**'Daunendecke** *f* eiderdown
**da'von** *adv* (away) from it; by it; about it; away; of it *or* them; ***et. ~ haben*** get s.th. out of it; ***das kommt ~!*** there you are!, that will teach you!; **~kommen** *v/i* (*irr*, ***kommen***, *sep*, *-ge-*, *sein*) escape, get away; **~laufen** *v/i* (*irr*, ***laufen***, *sep*, *-ge-*, *sein*) run away
**da'vor** *adv* before it; in front of it; *be afraid*, *warn s.o. etc* of it
**da'zu** *adv* for it, for that purpose; in addition; ***noch ~*** into the bargain; ***~ ist es da*** that's what it's there for; ***Salat ~?*** a salad with it?; → ***kommen***, ***Lust***; **~gehören** *v/i* (*sep*, *no -ge-*, *h*) belong to it, be part of it; **~gehörig** *adj* belonging to it; **~kommen** *v/i* (*irr*, ***kommen***, *sep*, *-ge-*, *sein*) join *s.o.*; be added
**da'zwischen** *adv* between (them); in between; among them; **~kommen** *v/i* (*irr*, ***kommen***, *sep*, *-ge-*, *sein*) intervene, happen; ***wenn nichts dazwischenkommt*** if all goes well
**DB** [deː'beː] ABBR *of* ***Deutsche Bahn*** German Rail
**dealen** ['diːlən] *v/i* (*ge-*, *h*) F push drugs
**Dealer** ['diːlɐ] *m* (*-s*; *-*) drug dealer, F pusher
**Debatte** [de'batə] *f* (*-*; *-n*) debate
**debattieren** [deba'tiːrən] *v/i* (*no -ge-*, *h*) debate (***über*** *acc* on)
**Debüt** [de'byː] *n* (*-s*; *-s*) debut; ***sein ~ geben*** make your debut
**dechiffrieren** [deʃɪ'friːrən] *v/t* (*no -ge-*, *h*) decipher, decode
**Deck** [dɛk] *n* (*-[e]s*; *-s*) MAR deck
**Decke** ['dɛkə] *f* (*-*; *-n*) blanket; quilt; ARCH ceiling
**Deckel** ['dɛkəl] *m* (*-s*; *-*) lid, cover, top
**'decken** *v/t and v/i* (*ge-*, *h*) cover (*a.* ZO), SPORT *a.* mark; ***sich ~*** (***mit***) coincide (with); → ***Tisch***
**'Deckung** *f* (*-*; *no pl*) cover; *boxing*: guard; ***in ~ gehen*** take cover
**defekt** [de'fɛkt] *adj* defective, faulty; TECH out of order; **De'fekt** *m* (*-[e]s*; *-e*) defect, fault
**defensiv** [defɛn'siːf] *adj*, **Defensive** [-'ziːvə] *f* (*-*; *no pl*) defensive
**definieren** [defi'niːrən] *v/t* (*no -ge-*, *h*) define; **Definition** [defini'tsjoːn] *f* (*-*; *-en*) definition
**Defizit** ['deːfitsɪt] *n* (*-s*; *-e*) deficit; deficiency
**Degen** ['deːgən] *m* (*-s*; *-*) sword; *fencing*: épée
**degradieren** [degra'diːrən] *v/t* (*no -ge-*, *h*) degrade (*a. fig*)
**dehnbar** ['deːnbaːɐ] *adj* flexible, elastic (*a. fig*); **dehnen** ['deːnən] *v/t* (*ge-*, *h*) stretch (*a. fig*)
**Deich** [daiç] *m* (*-[e]s*; *-e*) dike
**Deichsel** ['daiksəl] *f* (*-*; *-n*) pole, shaft
**dein** [dain] *poss pron* your; **~er, ~e, ~(e)s** yours; **deinerseits** ['dainɐ'zaits] *adv* on your part; **deines'gleichen** ['dainəs-] *pron contp* the likes of you
**deinetwegen** ['dainət'veːgən] *adv* for your sake; because of you
**Dekan** [de'kaːn] *m* (*-s*; *-e*), **De'kanin** *f* (*-*; *-nen*) REL, UNIV dean
**Deklination** [deklina'tsjoːn] *f* (*-*; *-en*) LING declension; **deklinieren** [dekli'niːrən] *v/t* (*no -ge-*, *h*) decline
**Dekolleté** [dekɔl'teː] *n* (*-s*; *-s*) low neckline
**Dekorateur** [dekora'tøːɐ] *m* (*-s*; *-e*), **Dekora'teurin** *f* (*-*; *-nen*) decorator; window dresser; **Dekoration** [-'tsjoːn] *f* (*-*; *-en*) decoration; (window) display; THEA scenery; **dekorativ** [-'tiːf] *adj* decorative; **dekorieren** [deko'riːrən] *v/t* (*no -ge-*, *h*) decorate; dress
**Delfin** → ***Delphin***
**delikat** [deli'kaːt] *adj* delicious, exquisite; *fig* delicate, ticklish
**Delikatesse** [delika'tɛsə] *f* (*-*; *-n*) delicacy; **Delika'tessenladen** *m* delicatessen, F deli
**Delphin** [dɛl'fiːn] *m* (*-s*; *-e*) ZO dolphin
**Dementi** [de'mɛnti] *n* (*-s*; *-s*) (official) denial; **dementieren** [demɛn'tiːrən] *v/t* (*no -ge-*, *h*) deny (officially)
**dementsprechend, demgemäß** ['deːm-] *adv* accordingly
**'demnach** *adv* according to that
**'demnächst** *adv* shortly, before long
**Demo** ['deːmo] F *f* (*-*; *-s*) demo

**Demokrat** [demo'kra:t] *m* (*-en*; *-en*) democrat; **Demokratie** [demokra'ti:] *f* (-; *-n*) democracy; **Demo'kratin** *f* (-; *-nen*) democrat; **demo'kratisch** *adj* democratic

**demolieren** [demo'li:rən] *v/t* (*no -ge-*, *h*) demolish, wreck

**Demonstrant** [demɔn'strant] *m* (*-en*; *-en*), **Demon'strantin** *f* (-; *-nen*) demonstrator; **Demonstration** [-stra-'tsjo:n] *f* (-; *-en*) demonstration; **demonstrieren** [-'stri:rən] *v/t and v/i* (*no -ge-*, *h*) demonstrate

**demontieren** [demɔn'ti:rən] *v/t* (*no -ge-*, *h*) dismantle

**demoralisieren** [demorali'zi:rən] *v/t* (*no -ge-*, *h*) demoralize

**Demoskopie** [demosko'pi:] *f* (-; *-n*) public opinion research

**Demut** ['de:mu:t] *f* (-; *no pl*) humility, humbleness; **demütig** ['de:my:tɪç] *adj* humble; **demütigen** ['de:my:tɪgən] *v/t* (*ge-*, *h*) humiliate; **'Demütigung** *f* (-; *-en*) humiliation

**denkbar** ['dɛŋkba:ɐ] **1.** *adj* conceivable; **2.** *adv*: ~ ***einfach*** most simple

**denken** ['dɛŋkən] *v/t and v/i* (*irr*, *ge-*, *h*) think (***an*** *acc*, ***über*** *acc* of, about); ***daran*** ~ (***zu*** *inf*) remember (to *inf*)

**'Denkfa,brik** *f* think tank

**'Denkmal** *n* monument; memorial

**'denkwürdig** *adj* memorable

**denn** [dɛn] *cj and adv* for, because; ***es sei*** ~, ***dass*** unless; ***mehr*** ~ ***je*** more than ever; **dennoch** ['dɛnnɔx] *cj* yet, still, nevertheless

**Denunziant** [denʊn'tsjant] *m* (*-en*; *-en*) informer; **denunzieren** [-'tsi:rən] *v/t* (*no -ge-*, *h*) inform on *or* against

**Deodorant** [deˀodo'rant] *n* (*-s*; *-e*, *-s*) deodorant

**Deponie** [depo'ni:] *f* (-; *-n*) dump, waste disposal site

**deponieren** [depo'ni:rən] *v/t* (*no -ge-*, *h*) deposit, leave

**Depot** [de'po:] *n* (*-s*; *-s*) depot (*a.* MIL); *Swiss*: deposit

**Depression** [deprɛ'sjo:n] *f* (-; *-en*) depression (*a.* ECON)

**depressiv** [deprɛ'si:f] *adj* depressive

**deprimieren** [depri'mi:rən] *v/t* (*no -ge-*, *h*) depress; **~d** *adj* depressing

**deprimiert** [depri'mi:ɐt] *adj* depressed

**der** [de:ɐ], **die** [di:], **das** [das] **1.** *art* the; **2.** *dem pron* that, this; he, she, it; ***die*** *pl* these, those, they; **3.** *rel pron* who, which, that; **'derartig 1.** *adv* so (much); like that; **2.** *adj* such (as this)

**derb** [dɛrp] *adj* coarse; tough, sturdy

**'der'gleichen** *dem pron*: ***nichts*** ~ nothing of the kind

**'der-, 'die-, 'dasjenige** [-je:nɪgə] *dem pron* the one; ***diejenigen*** *pl* the ones, those

**dermaßen** ['de:ɐ'ma:sən] *adv* so (much), like that

**Dermatologe** [dɛrmato'lo:gə] *m* (*-n*; *-n*), **Dermato'login** *f* (-; *-nen*) dermatologist

**der-, die-, dasselbe** [-'zɛlbə] *dem pron* the same

**Deserteur** [dezɛr'tø:ɐ] *m* (*-s*; *-e*) MIL deserter; **desertieren** [dezɛr'ti:rən] *v/i* (*no -ge-*, *sein*) MIL desert

**deshalb** ['dɛs'halp] *cj and adv* therefore, for that reason, that is why, so

**Desinfektionsmittel** [dɛsˀɪnfɛk-'tsjo:ns-] *n* MED disinfectant

**desinfizieren** [dɛsˀɪnfi'tsi:rən] *v/t* (*no -ge-*, *h*) MED disinfect

**'Desinteresse** *n* (*-s*; *no pl*) indifference

**'desinteres,siert** *adj* uninterested, indifferent

**destillieren** [dɛstɪ'li:rən] *v/t* (*no -ge-*, *h*) distil(l)

**desto** ['dɛsto] *cj and adv* → ***je***

**'des'wegen** *cj and adv* → ***deshalb***

**Detail** [de'tai] *n* (*-s*; *-s*) detail

**detailliert** [deta'ji:ɐt] *adj* detailed

**Detektiv** [detɛk'ti:f] *m* (*-s*; *-e*) detective

**deuten** ['dɔʏtən] (*ge-*, *h*) **1.** *v/t* interpret; **2.** *v/i*: ~ ***auf*** (*acc*) point at

**'deutlich** *adj* clear, distinct, plain

**deutsch** [dɔʏtʃ] *adj* German; ***auf Deutsch*** in German

**'Deutsche** *m*, *f* (*-n*; *-n*) German

**'Deutschland** Germany

**Devise** [de'vi:zə] *f* (-; *-n*) motto

**De'visen** *pl* ECON foreign currency

**Dezember** [de'tsɛmbɐ] *m* (*-[s]*; -) December

**dezent** [de'tsɛnt] *adj* discreet, unobtrusive; conservative (*clothes etc*); soft (*music etc*)

**Dezimal...** [detsi'ma:l-] MATH *in cpds ...bruch*, *...system etc*: decimal ...; **~stelle** *f* MATH decimal (place)

**DGB** [de:ge:'be:] ABBR *of* ***Deutscher Ge-***

***werkschaftsbund*** Federation of German Trade Unions
**d.h.** ABBR *of* ***das heißt*** i.e., that is
**Dia** ['di:a] *n* (*-s*; *-s*) PHOT slide
**Diagnose** [dia'gno:zə] *f* (*-*; *-n*) diagnosis
**diagonal** [diago'na:l] *adj*, **Diago'nale** *f* (*-*; *-n*) diagonal
**Dialekt** [dia'lɛkt] *m* (*-[e]s*; *-e*) dialect
**Dialog** [dia'lo:k] *m* (*-[e]s*; *-e*) dialog, *Br* dialogue
**Diamant** [dia'mant] *m* (*-en*; *-en*) diamond
**'Diapro,jektor** *m* slide projector
**Diät** [di'ɛ:t] *f* (*-*; *-en*) diet; ***e-e ~ machen*** (***Diät leben***) be on (keep to) a diet
**Di'äten** *pl* PARL allowance
**dich** [dɪç] *pers pron* you; *~* (***selbst***) yourself
**dicht** [dɪçt] **1.** *adj* dense, *a.* thick (*fog*); heavy (*traffic*); F closed, shut; **2.** *adv*: ***~ an*** (*dat*) *or* ***bei*** close to
**'dichten** *v/t and v/i* (*ge-*, *h*) write (poetry); **Dichter(in)** ['dɪçtɐ (-tərɪn)] (*-s*; *-/-*; *-nen*) poet; writer; **dichterisch** ['dɪçtərɪʃ] *adj* poetic; ***~e Freiheit*** poetic licen|se, *Br* -ce
**'dichthalten** F *v/i* (*irr*, ***halten***, *sep*, *-ge-*, *h*) keep mum
**'Dichtung¹** *f* (*-*; *-en*) TECH seal(ing)
**'Dichtung²** *f* (*-*; *-en*) poetry
**dick** [dɪk] *adj* thick; fat; ***es macht ~*** it's fattening
**'Dicke** *f* (*-*; *-n*) thickness; fatness;
**'dickfellig** F *adj* thick-skinned
**'dickflüssig** *adj* thick; TECH viscous
**Dickicht** ['dɪkɪçt] *n* (*-[e]s*; *-e*) thicket
**'Dick|kopf** *m* stubborn *or* pig-headed person; **~milch** *f* soured milk
**Dieb** [di:p] *m* (*-[e]s*; *-e* ['di:bə]), **Diebin** ['di:bɪn] *f* (*-*; *-nen*) thief
**diebisch** ['di:bɪʃ] *adj* thievish; *fig* malicious (*glee etc*)
**Diebstahl** ['di:pʃta:l] *m* (*-[e]s*; *-stähle* [-ʃtɛ:lə]) theft; JUR *mst* larceny
**Diele** ['di:lə] *f* (*-*; *-n*) board, plank; hallway, *Br a.* hall
**dienen** ['di:nən] *v/i* (*ge-*, *h*) serve (***j-m*** s.o.; ***als*** as); **Diener** ['di:nɐ] *m* (*-s*; *-*) servant; *fig* bow (***vor*** *dat* to)
**Dienst** [di:nst] *m* (*-[e]s*; *-e*) service; work; ***~ haben*** be on duty; ***im*** (***außer***) *~* on (off) duty; ***~ tuend*** on duty; ***~...*** *in cpds ...wagen, ....wohnung etc*: official ..., company ..., business ...
**'Dienstag** *m* (*-[e]s*; *-e*) Tuesday
**'Dienstalter** *n* seniority, length of service
**'dienstbereit** *adj* on duty
**diensteifrig** *adj* (*contp* over-)eager
**'Dienstgrad** *m* grade, rank (*a.* MIL)
**'Dienstleistung** *f* service
**'dienstlich** *adj* official
**'Dienstreise** *f* business trip
**'Dienststunden** *pl* office hours
**'Dienstweg** *m* official channels
**dies** [di:s], **dieser** ['di:zɐ], **diese** ['di:zə], **dieses** ['di:zəs] *dem pron* this; this one; ***diese*** *pl* these
**diesig** ['di:zɪç] *adj* hazy, misty
**'diesjährig** [-jɛ:rɪç] *adj* this year's
**'diesmal** *adv* this time
**'diesseits** [-zaits] *prp* (*gen*) on this side of; **'Diesseits** *n* (*-*; *no pl*) this life *or* world
**Dietrich** ['di:trɪç] *m* (*-s*; *-e*) TECH picklock, skeleton key
**Differenz** [dɪfə'rɛnts] *f* (*-*; *-en*) difference; disagreement
**differenzieren** [dɪfərɛn'tsi:rən] *v/i* (*no -ge-*, *h*) distinguish
**Digital...** [digi'ta:l] *in cpds ...anzeige, ...uhr etc*: digital ...
**Diktat** [dɪk'ta:t] *n* (*-[e]s*; *-e*) dictation; **Diktator** [dɪk'ta:to:ɐ] *m* (*-s*; *-en* [dɪkta'to:rən]) dictator; **diktatorisch** [dɪkta'to:rɪʃ] *adj* dictatorial; **Diktatur** [dɪkta'tu:ɐ] *f* (*-*; *-en*) dictatorship; **diktieren** [dɪk'ti:rən] *v/t and v/i* (*no -ge-*, *h*) dictate
**Dik'tiergerät** *n* Dictaphone®
**Dilettant** [dilɛ'tant] *m* (*-en*; *-en*) amateur; **dilet'tantisch** *adj* amateurish
**DIN** [di:n] ABBR *of* ***Deutsches Institut für Normung*** German Institute for Standardization
**Ding** [dɪŋ] *n* (*-[e]s*; *-e*) thing; ***vor allen ~en*** above all; F ***ein ~ drehen*** pull a job
**'Dings(bums)** *m, f, n*, **Dingsda** *m, f, n* F thingamajig, whatchamacallit
**Dinosaurier** [dino'zaurjɐ] *m* (*-s*; *-*) ZO dinosaur
**Dioxid** ['di:ʔɔksy:t] *n* (*-s*; *-e*) CHEM dioxide
**Dioxin** [diɔ'ksi:n] *n* (*-s*; *-e*) CHEM dioxin
**Diphtherie** [dɪfte'ri:] *f* (*-*; *-n*) MED diphtheria
**Diplom** [di'plo:m] *n* (*-s*; *-e*) diploma, degree; ***~...*** *in cpds ...ingenieur etc*: qualified ..., graduate ...

**Diplomat** [diplo'ma:t] *m* (*-en*; *-en*) diplomat; **Diplomatie** [diploma'ti:] *f* (-; *no pl*) diplomacy; **Diplo'matin** *f* (-; *-nen*) diplomat; **diplo'matisch** *adj* diplomatic (*a. fig*)

**dir** [di:ɐ] *pers pron* (to) you; ~ (***selbst***) yourself

**direkt** [di'rɛkt] **1.** *adj* direct; TV live; **2.** *adv* direct; *fig* directly, right; TV live; ~ ***gegenüber*** (***von***) right across

**Direktion** [dirɛk'tsjo:n] *f* (-; *-en*) management

**Direktor** [di'rɛkto:ɐ] *m* (*-s*; *-en* [dirɛk'to:rən]) director, manager; PED principal, *Br* headmaster; **Direktorin** [dirɛk'to:rɪn] (-; *-nen*) director, manager; PED principal, *Br* headmistress

**Di'rektübertragung** *f* TV live transmission *or* broadcast

**Dirigent** [diri'gɛnt] *m* (*-en*; *-en*) conductor; **dirigieren** [diri'gi:rən] *v/t and v/i* (*no -ge-, h*) MUS conduct; *fig* direct

**Dirne** ['dɪrnə] *f* (-; *-n*) prostitute, whore

**Disharmo'nie** [dɪs-] *f* MUS dissonance (*a. fig*); **dishar'monisch** *adj* MUS discordant

**Diskette** [dɪs'kɛtə] *f* (-; *-n*) EDP diskette, floppy (disk); **Dis'kettenlaufwerk** *n* EDP disk drive

**Disko** ['dɪsko] *f* (-; *-s*) disco

**Diskont** [dɪs'kɔnt] *m* (*-s*; *-e*) ECON discount

**Diskothek** [dɪsko'te:k] (-; *-en*) disco, discotheque

**diskret** [dɪs'kre:t] *adj* discreet; **Diskretion** [dɪskre'tsjo:n] *f* (-; *no pl*) discretion

**diskriminieren** [dɪskrimi'ni:rən] *v/t* (*no -ge-, h*) discriminate against

**Diskrimi'nierung** *f* (-; *-en*) discrimination (***von*** against)

**Diskussion** [dɪskʊ'sjo:n] *f* (-; *-en*) discussion, debate

**Diskussi'ons|leiter** *m* (panel) chairman; **~runde** *f*, **~teilnehmer** *pl* panel

**Diskuswerfen** ['dɪskʊs-] *n* (*-s*; *no pl*) SPORT discus throwing

**diskutieren** [dɪsku'ti:rən] *v/t and v/i* (*no -ge-, h*) discuss

**Disqualifikati'on** *f* SPORT disqualification (***wegen*** for); **disqualifi'zieren** *v/t* (*no -ge-, h*) SPORT disqualify

**Dissident** [dɪsi'dɛnt] *m* (*-en*; *-en*), **Dissi'dentin** *f* (-; *-nen*) POL dissident

**Distanz** [dɪs'tants] *f* (-; *-en*) distance

**distanzieren** [dɪstan'tsi:rən] *v/refl* (*no -ge-, h*) distance o.s. (***von*** from)

**Distel** ['dɪstəl] *f* (-; *-n*) BOT thistle

**Distrikt** [dɪs'trɪkt] *m* (*-[e]s*; *-e*) district

**Disziplin** [dɪstsi'pli:n] *f* (-; *-en*) a) (*no pl*) discipline, b) SPORT event; **diszipliniert** [dɪstsipli'ni:ɐt] *adj* disciplined

**divers** [di'vɛrs] *adj* various; several

**Dividende** [divi'dɛndə] *f* (-; *-n*) ECON dividend

**dividieren** [divi'di:rən] *v/t* (*no -ge-, h*) MATH divide (***durch*** by)

**Division** [divi'zjo:n] *f* (-; *-en*) MATH, MIL division

**DJH** [de:jɔt'ha:] ABBR *of* ***Deutsches Jugendherbergswerk*** German Youth Hostel Association

**DM** [de:'ɛm] ABBR *of* ***Deutsche Mark*** German mark(s)

**doch** [dɔx] *cj and adv* but, however, yet; ***kommst du nicht*** (***mit***)***? - ~!*** aren't you coming? - (oh) yes, I am!; ***ich war es nicht - ~!*** I didn't do it - yes, you did!; ***er kam also ~?*** so he did come after all?; ***du kommst ~?*** you're coming, aren't you?; ***kommen Sie ~ herein!*** do come in!; ***wenn ~ ...!*** if only ...!

**Docht** [dɔxt] *m* (*-[e]s*; *-e*) wick

**Dock** [dɔk] *n* (*-s*; *-s*) MAR dock

**Dogge** ['dɔgə] *f* (-; *-n*) ZO mastiff; Great Dane

**Dogma** ['dɔgma] *n* (*-s*; *Dogmen* ['dɔgmən]) dogma; **dogmatisch** [dɔg'ma:tɪʃ] *adj* dogmatic

**Dohle** ['do:lə] *f* (-; *-n*) ZO (jack)daw

**Doktor** ['dɔkto:ɐ] *m* (*-s*; *-en* [dɔk'to:rən]) doctor; UNIV doctor's degree; **~arbeit** *f* UNIV (doctoral *or* PhD) thesis

**Dokument** [doku'mɛnt] *n* (*-[e]s*; *-e*) document

**Dokumentar...** [dokumɛn'ta:ɐ-] *in cpds ...spiel etc*: documentary ...; **~film** *m* documentary (film)

**Dolch** [dɔlç] *m* (*-[e]s*; *-e*) dagger

**Dollar** ['dɔlar] *m* (*-[s]*; *-s*) dollar

**dolmetschen** ['dɔlmɛtʃən] *v/i* (*ge-, h*) interpret; **'Dolmetscher**(**in**) (*-s*; *-/-*; *-nen*) interpreter

**Dom** [do:m] *m* (*-[e]s*; *-e*) cathedral

**dominierend** [domi'ni:rənt] *adj* (pre-)dominant

**Dompteur** [dɔmp'tø:ɐ] *m* (*-s*; *-e*), **Dompteuse** [dɔmp'tø:zə] *f* (-; *-n*) animal tamer *or* trainer

**Donner** ['dɔnɐ] *m* (-*s*; *no pl*) thunder
**'donnern** *v/i* (*ge-*, *h*) thunder (*a. fig*)
**'Donnerstag** *m* (-[*e*]*s*; -*e*) Thursday
**'Donnerwetter** F *n* (-*s*; -) dressing-down; **~!** wow!
**doof** [do:f] F *adj* stupid, dumb
**Doppel** ['dɔpəl] *n* (-*s*; -) duplicate; *tennis etc*: doubles; **~...** *in cpds ...bett, ...zimmer etc*: double ...
**'Doppeldecker** [-dɛkɐ] *m* (-*s*; -) AVIAT biplane; MOT double-decker (bus)
**'Doppelgänger** [-gɛŋɐ] *m* (-*s*; -) double, look-alike
**'Doppelhaus** *n* duplex, *Br* pair of semis; **~hälfte** *f* semidetached (house)
**'Doppel|pass** *m* *soccer*: wall pass; **~punkt** *m* LING colon; **~stecker** *m* ELECTR two-way adapter
**doppelt** *adj* double; **~ *so viel* (*wie*)** twice as much (as)
**'Doppelverdiener** *pl* two-income family
**Dorf** [dɔrf] *n* (-[*e*]*s*; *Dörfer* ['dœrfɐ]) village; **~bewohner** *m* villager
**Dorn** [dɔrn] *m* (-[*e*]*s*; -*en*) BOT thorn (*a. fig*); TECH tongue; spike
**'dornig** *adj* thorny (*a. fig*)
**Dorsch** [dɔrʃ] *m* (-[*e*]*s*; -*e*) ZO cod(fish)
**dort** [dɔrt] *adv* there
**'dorther** *adv* from there
**'dorthin** *adv* there
**Dose** ['do:zə] *f* (-; -*n*) can, *Br a.* tin
**'Dosen...** *in cpds* canned, *Br a.* tinned
**dösen** ['dø:zən] F *v/i* (*ge-*, *h*) doze
**'Dosenöffner** *m* can (*Br* tin) opener
**Dosis** ['do:zɪs] *f* (-; *Dosen*) MED dose
**Dotter** ['dɔtɐ] *m*, *n* (-*s*; -) yolk
**Double** ['du:bəl] *n* (-*s*; -*s*) *film*: stunt man (*or* woman)
**Dozent** [do'tsɛnt] *m* (-*en*; -*en*), **Do'zentin** *f* (-; -*nen*) (university) lecturer, assistant professor
**Dr.** ABBR *of* ***Doktor*** Dr., Doctor
**Drache** ['draxə] *m* (-*n*; -*n*) dragon
**'Drachen** *m* (-*s*; -) kite; SPORT hang glider; ***e-n ~ steigen lassen*** fly a kite; **~fliegen** *n* SPORT hang gliding
**Draht** [dra:t] *m* (-[*e*]*s*; *Drähte* ['drɛ:tə]) wire; F ***auf ~ sein*** be on the ball
**drahtig** ['dra:tɪç] *fig adj* wiry
**'drahtlos** *adj* wireless
**'Drahtseil** *n* TECH cable; *circus*: tightrope; **~bahn** *f* cable railway
**'Drahtzieher** *fig m* (-*s*; -) wirepuller
**drall** [dral] *adj* buxom, strapping
**Drall** *m* (-[*e*]*s*; *no pl*) twist, spin
**Drama** ['dra:ma] *n* (-*s*; *Dramen*) drama
**Dramatiker** [dra'ma:tikɐ] *m* (-*s*; -) dramatist, playwright
**dra'matisch** *adj* dramatic
**dran** [dran] F *adv* → ***daran***; ***du bist ~*** it's your turn; *fig* you're in for it
**drang** [draŋ] *pret of* ***dringen***
**Drang** *m* (-[*e*]*s*; *no pl*) urge, drive (***nach*** for)
**drängeln** ['drɛŋəln] F *v/t and v/i* (*ge-*, *h*) push, shove
**drängen** ['drɛŋən] *v/t and v/i* (*ge-*, *h*) push, shove; ***j-n zu et. ~*** press *or* urge s.o. to do s.th.; ***sich ~*** press; force one's way; **~d** *adj* pressing
**'drankommen** F *v/i* (*irr*, ***kommen***, *sep*, *-ge-*, *sein*) have one's turn; ***als erster ~*** be first
**drastisch** ['drastɪʃ] *adj* drastic
**drauf** [drauf] F *adv* → ***darauf***; ***~ und dran sein, et. zu tun*** be just about to do s.th.; **'Draufgänger** [-gɛŋɐ] *m* (-*s*; -) daredevil
**draus** [draus] F *adv* → ***daraus***
**draußen** ['drausən] *adv* outside; outdoors; ***da ~*** out there; ***bleib*(*t*) *~!*** keep out!
**drechseln** ['drɛksəln] *v/t* (*ge-*, *h*) turn (on a lathe)
**Drechsler** ['drɛkslɐ] *m* (-*s*; -) turner
**Dreck** [drɛk] F *m* (-[*e*]*s*; *no pl*) dirt; filth (*a. fig*); mud; *fig* trash; **dreckig** ['drɛkɪç] F *adj* dirty; filthy (*both a. fig*)
**Dreh|arbeiten** ['dre:-] *pl film*: shooting; **~bank** *f* (-; -*bänke*) TECH lathe
**'drehbar** *adj* revolving, rotating
**'Drehbuch** *n film*: script
**drehen** ['dre:ən] *v/t* (*ge-*, *h*) turn; *film*: shoot; roll; ***sich ~*** turn, rotate; spin; ***sich ~ um*** *fig* be about; → ***Ding***
**Dreher** ['dre:ɐ] *m* (-*s*; -) TECH turner
**'Dreh|kreuz** *n* turnstile; **~orgel** *f* barrel-organ; **~ort** *m* *film*: location; **~strom** *m* ELECTR three-phase current; **~stuhl** *m* swivel chair; **~tür** *f* revolving door
**'Drehung** *f* (-; -*en*) turn; rotation
**'Drehzahl** *f* TECH (number of) revolutions; **~messer** *m* MOT rev(olution) counter
**drei** [drai] *adj* three
**Drei** *f* (-; -*en*) three; *grade*: fair, C

**'drei|beinig** *adj* three-legged; **~dimensio,nal** *adj* three-dimensional
**'Dreieck** *n* (-[*e*]*s*; -*e*) triangle
**'dreieckig** *adj* triangular
**dreierlei** ['draiɐ'lai] *adj* three kinds of
**'dreifach** *adj* threefold, triple
**'Drei|gang...** TECH *in cpds* three-speed ...; **~kampf** *m* SPORT triathlon; **~rad** *n* tricycle; **~satz** *m* (-*es*; *no pl*) MATH rule of three; **~sprung** *m* (-[*e*]*s*; *no pl*) SPORT triple jump
**dreißig** ['draisɪç] *adj* thirty
**'dreißigste** *adj* thirtieth
**dreist** [draist] *adj* brazen, impertinent
**'dreistufig** [-ʃtu:fɪç] *adj* three-stage
**'dreizehn(te)** *adj* thirteen(th)
**Dresche** ['drɛʃə] F *f* (-; *no pl*) thrashing
**'dreschen** *v/t and v/i* (*irr, ge-, h*) AGR thresh; thrash; **'Dreschma,schine** *f* AGR threshing machine
**dressieren** [drɛ'si:rən] *v/t* (*no -ge-, h*) train
**Dressman** ['drɛsmən] *m* (-*s*; -*men*) male model
**Dressur** [drɛ'su:ɐ] *f* (-; -*en*) training; act; **~reiten** *n* dressage
**dribbeln** ['drɪbəln] *v/i* (*ge-, h*), **Dribbling** *n* (-*s*; -*s*) SPORT dribble
**drillen** ['drɪlən] *v/t* (*ge-, h*) MIL drill (*a. fig*)
**Drillinge** ['drɪlɪŋə] *pl* triplets
**drin** [drɪn] F *adv* → ***darin***; ***das ist nicht ~!*** no way!
**dringen** ['drɪŋən] *v/i* (*irr, ge-, h*) **~ *auf*** (*acc*) insist on; **~ *aus*** come from; **~ *durch*** force one's way through, penetrate, pierce; **~ *in*** (*acc*) penetrate into; ***darauf ~, dass*** urge that; **~d** *adj* urgent, pressing; strong (*suspicion etc*)
**drinnen** ['drɪnən] F *adv* inside; indoors
**dritte** ['drɪtə] *adj* third; ***wir sind zu dritt*** there are three of us; ***die Dritte Welt*** the Third World; **'Drittel** *n* (-*s*; -) third; **'drittens** *adv* thirdly; **'Dritte-Welt--Laden** *m* third world shop
**Droge** ['dro:gə] *f* (-; -*n*) drug
**'drogenabhängig** *adj* addicted to drugs; **~ *sein*** be a drug addict
**'Drogen|abhängige** *m, f* (-*n*; -*n*) drug addict; **~missbrauch** *m* drug abuse
**'drogensüchtig** → ***drogenabhängig***
**'Drogentote** *m, f* drug victim
**Drogerie** [drogə'ri:] *f* (-; -*n*) drugstore, *Br* chemist's (shop)
**Drogist** [dro'gɪst] *m* (-*en*; -*en*), **Dro'gistin** *f* (-; -*nen*) chemist
**drohen** ['dro:ən] *v/i* (*ge-, h*) threaten, menace
**dröhnen** ['drø:nən] *v/i* (*ge-, h*) roar
**'Drohung** *f* (-; -*en*) threat (***gegen*** to)
**drollig** ['drɔlɪç] *adj* funny, droll
**Dromedar** [dromə'da:ɐ] *n* (-*s*; -*e*) ZO dromedary
**drosch** [drɔʃ] *pret of* ***dreschen***
**Drossel** ['drɔsəl] *f* (-; -*n*) ZO thrush
**'drosseln** *v/t* (*ge-, h*) TECH throttle
**drüben** ['dry:bən] *adv* over there (*a. fig*)
**drüber** ['drybɐ] F *adv* → ***darüber, drunter***
**Druck** [drʊk] *m* (-[*e*]*s*; -*e*) pressure; printing; print
**'Druckbuchstabe** *m* block letter
**Drückeberger** ['drʏkəbɛrgɐ] F *m* (-*s*; -) shirker
**'drucken** *v/t* (*ge-, h*) print; ***et. ~ lassen*** have s.th. printed *or* published
**drücken** ['drʏkən] (*ge-, h*) **1.** *v/t* press; push; *fig* force down; ***j-m die Hand ~*** shake hands with s.o.; **2.** *v/i* pinch; **3.** F *v/refl*: ***sich vor et. ~*** shirk (doing) s.th.; **~d** *adj* heavy, oppressive
**Drucker** ['drʊkɐ] *m* (-*s*; -) printer (*a.* EDP)
**Drücker** ['drʏkɐ] *m* (-*s*; -) latch; trigger; F hawker
**Druckerei** [drʊkə'rai] *f* (-; -*en*) printers
**'Druck|fehler** *m* misprint; **~kammer** *f* pressurized cabin; **~knopf** *m* snap fastener, *Br* press stud; TECH (push) button; **~luft** *f* TECH compressed air; **~sache** *f* printed (*or* second-class) matter; **~schrift** *f* block letters; **~taste** *f* TECH push button
**drunter** ['drʊntɐ] F *adv* → ***darunter***; ***es ging ~ und drüber*** it was absolutely chaotic
**Drüse** ['dry:zə] *f* (-; -*n*) ANAT gland
**Dschungel** ['dʒʊŋəl] *m* (-*s*; -) jungle (*a. fig*)
**Dschunke** ['dʒʊŋkə] *f* (-; -*n*) MAR junk
**du** [du:] *pers pron* you
**Dübel** ['dy:bəl] *m* (-*s*; -), **'dübeln** *v/t* (*ge-, h*) TECH dowel
**ducken** ['dʊkən] *v/refl* (*ge-, h*) duck; *fig* cringe (***vor*** *dat* before); crouch
**Duckmäuser** ['dʊkmɔʏzɐ] *m* (-*s*; -) coward; yes-man
**Dudelsack** ['du:dəlzak] *m* MUS bagpipes

D

**Duell** [du'ɛl] *n* (*-s*; *-e*) duel; **duellieren** [duɛ'li:rən] *v/refl* (*no -ge-*, *h*) fight a duel
**Duett** [du'ɛt] *n* (*-[e]s*; *-e*) MUS duet
**Duft** [dʊft] *m* (*-[e]s*; *Düfte* ['dʏftə]) scent, fragrance, smell (**nach** of); '**duften** *v/i* (*ge-*, *h*) smell (**nach** of); '**duftend** *adj* fragrant; '**duftig** *adj* dainty
**dulden** ['dʊldən] *v/t* (*ge-*, *h*) tolerate, put up with; suffer
**duldsam** ['dʊltza:m] *adj* tolerant
**dumm** [dʊm] *adj* stupid, F dumb
'**Dummheit** *f* (*-*; *-en*) a) (*no pl*) stupidity, ignorance, b) stupid *or* foolish thing
'**Dummkopf** *m contp* fool, blockhead
**dumpf** [dʊmpf] *adj* dull; *fig* vague
**Düne** ['dy:nə] *f* (*-*; *-n*) (sand) dune
**Dung** [dʊŋ] *m* (*-[e]s*; *no pl*) dung, manure
**düngen** ['dʏŋən] *v/t* (*ge-*, *h*) fertilize; manure; **Dünger** ['dʏŋɐ] *m* (*-s*; *-*) fertilizer; manure
**dunkel** ['dʊŋkəl] *adj* dark (*a. fig*)
'**Dunkelheit** *f* (*-*; *no pl*) dark(ness)
'**Dunkel|kammer** *f* PHOT darkroom; **~ziffer** *f* number of unreported cases
**dünn** [dʏn] *adj* thin; weak (*coffee etc*)
**Dunst** [dʊnst] *m* (*-[e]s*; *Dünste* ['dʏnstə]) haze, mist; CHEM vapo(u)r; **dünsten** ['dʏnstən] *v/t* (*ge-*, *h*) GASTR stew, braise; '**dunstig** *adj* hazy, misty
**Duplikat** [dupli'ka:t] *n* (*-[e]s*; *-e*) duplicate; copy
**Dur** [du:ɐ] *n* (*-*; *no pl*) MUS major (key)
**durch** [dʊrç] *prp* (*acc*) *and adv* through; across; MATH divided by; GASTR (well) done; **~ j-n** (**et.**) by s.o. (s.th.); **~ und ~** through and through
'**durcharbeiten** (*sep*, *-ge-*, *h*) **1.** *v/t* study thoroughly; **sich ~ durch** work (one's way) through *a text etc*; **2.** *v/i* work without a break
**durch'aus** *adv* absolutely, quite; **~ nicht** by no means
'**durchblättern** *v/t* (*sep*, *-ge-*, *h*) leaf *or* thumb through
'**Durchblick** *fig m* grasp *of s.th.*
'**durchblicken** *v/i* (*sep*, *-ge-*, *h*) look through; **~ lassen** give to understand; ***ich blicke*** (***da***) ***nicht durch*** I don't get it
**durch'bohren** *v/t* (*no -ge-*, *h*) pierce; perforate
'**durchbraten** *v/t* (*irr*, **braten**, *sep*, *-ge-*, *h*) roast thoroughly
'**durchbrechen¹** (*irr*, **brechen**, *sep*, *-ge-*) **1.** *v/t* (*h*) break (in two); **2.** *v/i* (*sein*) break through *or* apart
**durch'brechen²** *v/t* (*irr*, **brechen**, *no -ge-*, *h*) break through
'**durch|brennen** *v/i* (*irr*, **brennen**, *sep*, *-ge-*, *sein*) ELECTR blow; *reactor*: melt down; F run away
'**durchbringen** *v/t* (*irr*, **bringen**, *sep*, *-ge-*, *h*) get (MED pull) *s.o.* through; go through *one's money*; support (*family*)
'**Durchbruch** *m* breakthrough (*a. fig*)
**durch'dacht** *adj* (well) thought-out
'**durchdrehen** (*sep*, *-ge-*, *h*) **1.** *v/i wheels*: spin; F *fig* crack up, flip; **2.** *v/t* GASTR grind, *Br* mince
'**durchdringend** *adj* piercing
**durchei'nander** *adv* confused; (in) a mess; **~ bringen** confuse, mix up; mess up; **Durchei'nander** *n* (*-s*; *no pl*) confusion, mess
**durch'fahren¹** *v/t* (*irr*, **fahren**, *no -ge-*, *h*) go (*or* pass, drive) through
'**durchfahren²** *v/i* (*irr*, **fahren**, *sep*, *-ge-*, *sein*) go (*or* pass, drive) through
'**Durchfahrt** *f* passage; **~ verboten** no thoroughfare
'**Durchfall** *m* MED diarrh(o)ea
'**durch|fallen** *v/i* (*irr*, **fallen**, *sep*, *-ge-*, *sein*) fall through; fail, F flunk (*test etc*); F be a flop; **j-n ~ lassen** fail (F flunk) s.o.; **~fragen** *v/refl* (*sep*, *-ge-*, *h*) ask one's way (**nach**, **zu** to)
'**durchführbar** *adj* practicable, feasible
'**durchführen** *v/t* (*sep*, *-ge-*, *h*) carry out, do
'**Durchgang** *m* passage
'**Durchgangs...** *in cpds ...verkehr etc*: through ...; *...lager etc*: transit ...
'**durchgebraten** *adj* well done
'**durchgehen** (*irr*, **gehen**, *sep*, *-ge-*, *sein*) **1.** *v/i* go through (*a.* RAIL *and* PARL); *fig* run away (**mit** with); *horse*: bolt; **2.** *v/t* go *or* look through; **~ lassen** tolerate ; **~d** *adj* continuous; **~er Zug** through train; **~ geöffnet** open all day
'**durchgreifen** *fig v/i* (*irr*, **greifen**, *sep*, *-ge-*, *h*) take drastic measures; **~d** *adj* drastic; radical
'**durchhalten** (*irr*, **halten**, *sep*, *-ge-*, *h*) **1.** *v/t* keep up; **2.** *v/i* hold out
'**durchhängen** *v/i* (*irr*, **hängen**, *sep*, *-ge-*, *h*) sag; F have a low
'**durchkämpfen** *v/t* (*sep*, *-ge-*, *h*) fight out; **sich ~** fight one's way through

**'durchkommen** *v/i* (*irr*, ***kommen***, *sep*, *-ge-*, *sein*) come through (*a.* MED); get through; get along; get away (***mit e-r Lüge*** *etc* with a lie *etc*)

**durch'kreuzen** *v/t* (*no -ge-*, *h*) cross, thwart

**'durchlassen** *v/t* (*irr*, ***lassen***, *sep*, *-ge-*, *h*) let pass, let through

**'durchlässig** *adj* permeable (***für*** to)

**'durchlaufen¹** (*irr*, ***laufen***, *sep*, *-ge-*) **1.** *v/i* (*sein*) run through; **2.** *v/t* (*h*) wear through

**durch'laufen²** *v/t* (*irr*, ***laufen***, *no -ge-*, *h*) pass through

**'Durchlauferhitzer** *m* (*-s*; -) (instant) water heater, *Br a.* geyser

**'durchlesen** *v/t* (*irr*, ***lesen***, *sep*, *-ge-*, *h*) read through

**durch|'leuchten** *v/t* (*no -ge-*, *h*) MED X-ray; *fig* screen; **~löchern** [-'lœçɐn] *v/t* (*no -ge-*, *h*) perforate, make holes in

**'durchmachen** F *v/t* (*sep*, *-ge-*, *h*) go through; ***viel ~*** suffer a lot; ***die Nacht ~*** make a night of it

**'Durchmesser** *m* (*-s*; -) diameter

**durch'nässen** *v/t* (*no -ge-*, *h*) soak

**'durchnehmen** *v/t* (*irr*, ***nehmen***, *sep*, *-ge-*, *h*) PED do, deal with

**'durchpausen** *v/t* (*sep*, *-ge-*, *h*) trace

**durch'queren** *v/t* (*no -ge-*, *h*) cross

**'Durchreiche** *f* (-; *-n*) hatch

**'Durchreise** *f*: ***ich bin nur auf der ~*** I'm only passing through; **'durchreisen** *v/i* (*sep*, *-ge-*, *sein*) travel through

**'Durchreisevisum** *n* transit visa

**'durch|reißen** (*irr*, ***reißen***, *sep*, *-ge-*) **1.** *v/t* (*h*) tear (in two); **2.** *v/i* (*sein*) tear, break; **~ringen** *v/refl* (*irr*, ***ringen***, *sep*, *-ge-*, *h*) ***sich ~, et. zu tun*** bring o.s. to do s.th.

**'Durchsage** *f* announcement

**durch'schauen** *v/t* (*no -ge-*, *h*) see through *s.o. or s.th.*

**'durchscheinen** *v/i* (*irr*, ***scheinen***, *sep*, *-ge-*, *h*) shine through; **~d** *adj* transparent

**'durchscheuern** *v/t* (*sep*, *-ge-*, *h*) chafe; wear through

**'durchschlafen** *v/i* (*irr*, ***schlafen***, *sep*, *-ge-*, *h*) sleep through

**'Durchschlag** *m* (carbon) copy

**durch'schlagen¹** *v/t* (*irr*, ***schlagen***, *no -ge-*, *h*) cut in two; *bullet etc*: go through, pierce

**'durchschlagen²** (*irr*, ***schlagen***, *sep*, *-ge-*) **1.** *v/refl* (*h*): ***sich ~ nach*** make one's way to; **2.** *v/i* (*sein*) come through (*a. fig*); **~d** *adj* sweeping; effective

**'Durch|schlagpa,pier** *n* carbon paper; **~schlagskraft** *fig f* force, impact

**'durchschneiden** *v/t* (*irr*, ***schneiden***, *sep*, *-ge-*, *h*) cut (through)

**'Durchschnitt** *m* average; ***im*** (***über***, ***unter dem***) ~ on an (above, below) average; ***im ~ betragen*** (***verdienen*** *etc*) average

**'durchschnittlich** **1.** *adj* average; ordinary; **2.** *adv* on an average

**'Durchschnitts...** *in cpds* average ...

**'Durchschrift** *f* (carbon) copy

**'durch|sehen** *v/t* (*irr*, ***sehen***, *sep*, *-ge-*, *h*) look *or* go through; check; **~setzen** *v/t* (*sep*, *-ge-*, *h*) put (*or* push) *s.th.* through; ***s-n Kopf ~*** have one's way; ***sich ~*** get one's way; be successful; ***sich ~ können*** have authority (***bei*** over)

**durch'setzt** *adj*: ***~ mit*** interspersed with

**'durchsichtig** *adj* transparent (*a. fig*); clear; see-through

**'durchsickern** *v/i* (*sep*, *-ge-*, *sein*) seep through; *fig* leak out

**'durchstarten** *v/i* (*sep*, *-ge-*, *sein*) AVIAT climb and reaccelerate

**durch'stechen** *v/t* (*irr*, ***stechen***, *no -ge-*, *h*) pierce

**'durch|stecken** *v/t* (*sep*, *-ge-*, *h*) stick through; **~stehen** *v/t* (*irr*, ***stehen***, *sep*, *-ge-*, *h*) go through

**durch'stoßen** *v/t* (*irr*, ***stoßen***, *no -ge-*, *h*) break through

**'durchstreichen** *v/t* (*irr*, ***streichen***, *sep*, *-ge-*, *h*) cross out

**durch'suchen** *v/t* (*no -ge-*, *h*) search, F frisk; **Durch'suchung** *f* (-; *-en*) search; **Durch'suchungsbefehl** *m* search warrant

**durch|trieben** [-'triːbən] *adj* cunning, sly; **~'wachsen** *adj* GASTR streaky

**'Durchwahl** *f* (-; *no pl*) TEL direct dial(l)ing; **'durchwählen** *v/i* (*sep*, *-ge-*, *h*) TEL dial direct

**'durchweg** [-vɛk] *adv* without exception

**durch'weicht** *adj* soaked, drenched

**durch'wühlen** *v/t* (*no -ge-*, *h*) rummage through

**'durch|zählen** *v/t* (*sep*, *-ge-*, *h*) count off (*Br* up); **~ziehen** (*irr*, ***ziehen***, *sep*,

D

*-ge-)* **1.** *v/i* (*sein*) pass through; **2.** *v/t* (*h*) pull *s.th.* through; *fig* carry *s.th.* through (to the end)
**durch'zucken** *v/t* (*no -ge-, h*) flash through
**'Durchzug** *m* (*-[e]s; no pl*) draft, *Br* draught
**dürfen** ['dʏrfən] **1.** *v/aux* (*irr, no -ge-, h*) be allowed *or* permitted to *inf*; ***darf ich gehen?*** may I go?; ***ja(, du darfst)*** yes, you may; ***du darfst nicht*** you must not, you aren't allowed to; ***dürfte ich ...?*** could I ...?; ***das dürfte genügen*** that should be enough; **2.** *v/i* (*irr, ge-, h*) ***er darf*** (***nicht***) he is (not) allowed to *inf*
**durfte** ['dʊrftə] *pret of* ***dürfen***
**dürftig** ['dʏrftɪç] *adj* poor; scanty
**dürr** [dʏr] *adj* dry; barren, arid; skinny
**Dürre** ['dʏrə] *f* (-; *-n*) a) drought, b) (*no pl*) barrenness
**Durst** [dʊrst] *m* (*-[e]s; no pl*) thirst (***auf*** *acc* for); ~ ***haben*** be thirsty
**'durstig** *adj* thirsty
**Dusche** ['dʊʃə] *f* (-; *-n*) shower
**'duschen** *v/refl and v/i* (*ge-, h*) have *or* take a shower
**Düse** ['dyːzə] *f* (-; *-n*) TECH nozzle; jet
**'düsen** F *v/i* (*ge-, sein*) jet
**'Düsen|antrieb** *m* jet propulsion; ***mit*** ~ jet-propelled; **~flugzeug** *n* jet (plane); **~jäger** *m* MIL jet fighter; **~triebwerk** *n* jet engine
**düster** ['dyːstɐ] *adj* dark, gloomy (*both a. fig*); dim (*light*); *fig* dismal
**Dutzend** ['dʊtsənt] *n* (*-s; -e*) dozen
**'dutzendweise** *adv* by the dozen
**duzen** ['duːtsən] *v/t* (*ge-, h*) use the familiar 'du' with s.o.; ***sich*** ~ be on 'du' terms
**Dynamik** [dy'naːmɪk] *f* (-; *no pl*) PHYS dynamics; *fig* dynamism
**dy'namisch** *adj* dynamic
**Dynamit** [dyna'miːt] *n* (*-s; no pl*) dynamite
**Dynamo** [dy'naːmo] *m* (*-s; -s*) ELECTR dynamo, generator
**D-Zug** ['deː-] *m* express train

# E

**Ebbe** ['ɛbə] *f* (-; *-n*) ebb, low tide
**eben** ['eːbən] **1.** *adj* even; flat; MATH plane; ***zu ~er Erde*** on the first (*Br* ground) floor; **2.** *adv* just; ***an ~ dem Tag*** on that very day; ***so ist es*** ~ that's the way it is; ***gerade ~ so*** *or* ***noch*** just barely
**'Ebenbild** *n* image
**'ebenbürtig** [-bʏrtɪç] *adj*: ***j-m ~ sein*** be a match for s.o., be s.o.'s equal
**Ebene** ['eːbənə] *f* (-; *-n*) GEOGR plain; MATH plane; *fig* level
**'ebenerdig** *adj and adv* at street level; on the first (*Br* ground) floor
**'ebenfalls** *adv* as well, too
**'Ebenholz** *n* ebony
**'Ebenmaß** *n* (*-es; no pl*) symmetry; harmony; regularity; **'ebenmäßig** *adj* symmetrical; harmonious; regular
**'ebenso** *adv and cj* just as; as well; ~ ***wie*** in the same way as; ~ ***gern,*** ~ ***gut*** just as well; ~ ***sehr,*** ~ ***viel*** just as much; ~ ***wenig*** just as little *or* few
**Eber** ['eːbɐ] *m* (*-s; -*) ZO boar
**ebnen** ['eːbnən] *v/t* (*ge-, h*) even, level; *fig* smooth
**Echo** ['ɛço] *n* (*-s; -s*) echo; *fig* response
**echt** [ɛçt] *adj* genuine (*a. fig*), real; true; pure; fast (*color*); authentic; F ~ ***gut*** real good; **'Echtheit** *f* (-; *no pl*) genuineness; authenticity
**Eckball** ['ɛk-] *m* SPORT corner (kick)
**Ecke** ['ɛkə] *f* (-; *-n*) corner; edge; SPORT ***lange*** (***kurze***) ~ far (near) corner; → ***Eckball***; **eckig** ['ɛkɪç] *adj* square, angular; *fig* awkward
**'Eckzahn** *m* canine tooth
**edel** ['eːdəl] *adj* noble; MIN precious
**'Edelme,tall** *n* precious metal
**'Edelstahl** *m* stainless steel
**'Edelstein** *m* precious stone; gem
**EDV** [eːdeː'fau] ABBR *of* ***Elektronische***

***Datenverarbeitung*** EDP, electronic data processing
**Efeu** ['eːfɔʏ] *m* (*-s; no pl*) BOT ivy
**Effekt** [ɛ'fɛkt] *m* (*-[e]s; -e*) effect
**effektiv** [ɛfɛk'tiːf] **1.** *adj* effective; **2.** *adv* actually; **Effektivität** [ɛfɛktivi'tɛːt] *f* (*-; no pl*) effectiveness
**ef'fektvoll** *adj* effective, striking
**Effet** [ɛ'feː] *m* (*-s; -s*) SPORT spin
**EG** [eː'geː] HIST ABBR *of* ***Europäische Gemeinschaft*** EC, European Community
**egal** [e'gaːl] F *adj*: ~ ***ob*** (***warum, wer*** *etc*) no matter if (why, who, *etc*); ***das ist*** ~ it doesn't matter; ***das ist mir*** ~ I don't care, it's all the same to me
**Egge** ['ɛgə] *f* (*-; -n*), **'eggen** *v/t* (*ge-, h*) AGR harrow
**Egoismus** [ego'ɪsmʊs] *m* (*-; no pl*) ego(t)ism; **Egoist(in)** [ego'ɪst(ɪn)] (*-en; -en/-; -nen*) ego(t)ist; **ego'istisch** *adj* selfish, ego(t)istic(al)
**ehe** ['eːə] *cj* before; ***nicht*** ~ not until
**Ehe** ['eːə] *f* (*-; -n*) marriage (***mit*** to); **~beratung** *f* marriage counseling (*Br* guidance); **~brecher** *m* (*-s; -*) adulterer; **~brecherin** *f* (*-; -nen*) adulteress
**'ehebrecherisch** *adj* adulterous
**'Ehe|bruch** *m* adultery; **~frau** *f* wife; **~leute** *pl* married couple
**'ehelich** *adj* conjugal; JUR legitimate
**ehemalig** ['eːəmaːlɪç] *adj* former, ex-...
**ehemals** ['eːəmaːls] *adv* formerly
**'Ehemann** *m* husband
**'Ehepaar** *n* (married) couple
**eher** ['eːɐ] *adv* earlier, sooner; ***je*** ~, ***desto lieber*** the sooner the better; ***nicht*** ~ ***als*** not until *or* before
**'Ehering** *m* wedding ring
**ehrbar** ['eːɐbaːɐ] *adj* respectable
**Ehre** ['eːrə] *f* (*-; -n*) hono(u)r; ***zu*** **~*n*** (***von***) in hono(u)r of
**'ehren** *v/t* (*ge-, h*) hono(u)r; respect
**'ehrenamtlich** *adj* honorary
**'Ehren|bürger** *m* honorary citizen; **~doktor** *m* UNIV honorary doctor; **~gast** *m* guest of hono(u)r; **~kodex** *m* code of hono(u)r; **~mann** *m* man of hono(u)r; **~mitglied** *n* honorary member; **~platz** *m* place of hono(u)r; **~rechte** *pl* civil rights; **~rettung** *f* rehabilitation
**'ehrenrührig** *adj* defamatory
**'Ehren|runde** *f esp* SPORT lap of hono(u)r; **~sache** *f* point of hono(u)r; **~tor** *n*, **~treffer** *m* SPORT consolation goal
**'ehrenwert** *adj* hono(u)rable
**'Ehrenwort** *n* (*-[e]s; -e*) word of hono(u)r; F **~!** cross my heart!
**ehrerbietig** ['eːɐʔɛɐbiːtɪç] *adj* respectful
**Ehrfurcht** ['eːɐ-] *f* (*-; no pl*) respect (***vor*** *dat* for); awe (of); ~ ***gebietend*** awe-inspiring, awesome; **'ehrfürchtig** [-fʏrçtɪç] *adj* respectful
**'Ehrgefühl** *n* (*-[e]s; no pl*) sense of hono(u)r
**'Ehrgeiz** *m* ambition; **'ehrgeizig** *adj* ambitious
**'ehrlich** *adj* honest; frank; fair; **'Ehrlichkeit** *f* (*-; no pl*) honesty; fairness
**'Ehrung** *f* (*-; -en*) hono(u)r(ing)
**'ehrwürdig** *adj* venerable
**Ei** [ai] *n* (*-[e]s; Eier* ['aiɐ]) egg; V *pl* balls
**Eiche** ['aiçə] *f* (*-; -n*) oak(-tree)
**Eichel** ['aiçəl] *f* (*-; -n*) BOT acorn; *card games*: club(s); ANAT glans (penis)
**eichen** ['aiçən] *v/t* (*ge-, h*) ga(u)ge
**Eichhörnchen** ['aiçhœrnçən] *n* (*-s; -*) ZO squirrel
**Eid** [ait] *m* (*-[e]s; -e*) oath; ***e-n*** ~ ***ablegen*** take an oath
**Eidechse** ['aidɛksə] *f* (*-; -n*) ZO lizard
**eidesstattlich** ['aidəs-] *adj*: **~*e Erklärung*** JUR statutory declaration
**'Eidotter** *m, n* (egg) yolk
**'Eier|becher** *m* eggcup; **~kuchen** *m* pancake; **~li͵kör** *m* eggnog; **~schale** *f* eggshell; **~stock** *m* ANAT ovary; **~uhr** *f* egg timer
**Eifer** ['aifɐ] *m* (*-s; no pl*) zeal, eagerness; ***glühender*** ~ ardo(u)r
**'Eifersucht** *f* (*-; no pl*) jealousy
**'eifersüchtig** *adj* jealous (***auf*** *acc* of)
**eifrig** *adj* eager, zealous; ardent
**'Eigelb** *n* (*-[e]s; -e*) (egg) yolk
**eigen** ['aigən] *adj* own, of one's own; peculiar; particular, F fussy; **...eigen** *in cpds staats~ etc*: ...-owned
**'Eigenart** *f* peculiarity
**'eigenartig** *adj* peculiar; strange
**'Eigenbedarf** *m* personal needs
**'Eigengewicht** *n* dead weight
**'eigenhändig** [-hɛndɪç] **1.** *adj* personal; **2.** *adv* personally, with one's own hands
**'Eigen|heim** *n* home (of one's own); **~liebe** *f* self-love; **~lob** *n* self-praise

E

**'eigenmächtig** *adj* arbitrary
**'Eigenname** *m* proper noun
**'Eigennutz** *m* (*-es; no pl*) self-interest
**'eigennützig** [-nʏtsɪç] *adj* selfish
**'eigens** *adv* (e)specially, expressly
**'Eigenschaft** *f* (*-; -en*) quality; TECH, PHYS, CHEM property; ***in s-r ~ als*** in his capacity as; **'Eigenschaftswort** *n* (*-[e]s; -wörter*) LING adjective
**'Eigensinn** *m* (*-[e]s; no pl*) stubbornness; **'eigensinnig** *adj* stubborn, obstinate
**eigentlich** ['aigəntlɪç] **1.** *adj* actual, true, real; exact; **2.** *adv* actually, really; originally
**'Eigentor** *n* SPORT own goal (*a. fig*)
**'Eigentum** *n* (*-[e]s; no pl*) property
**Eigentümer** ['aɪgənty:mɐ] *m* (*-s; -*), **'Eigentümerin** *f* (*-; -nen*) owner, proprietor (proprietress)
**'eigentümlich** [-ty:mlɪç] *adj* peculiar; strange, odd; **'Eigentümlichkeit** *f* (*-; -en*) peculiarity
**'Eigentumswohnung** *f* condominium, F condo, *Br* owner-occupied flat
**'eigenwillig** *adj* wil(l)ful; individual, original (*style etc*)
**eignen** ['aignən] *v/refl* (*ge-, h*) ***sich ~ für*** be suited *or* fit for; **'Eignung** *f* (*-; no pl*) suitability; aptitude, qualification
**'Eignungs|prüfung** *f*, **~test** *m* aptitude test
**Eil|bote** ['ail-] *m*: ***durch ~n*** by special delivery; **~brief** *m* special delivery (*Br* express) letter
**Eile** ['ailə] *f* (*-; no pl*) haste, hurry; **'eilen** *v/i* a) (*ge-, sein*) hurry, hasten, rush, b) (*ge-, h*) be urgent; **'eilig** *adj* hurried, hasty; urgent; ***es ~ haben*** be in a hurry
**Eimer** ['aimɐ] *m* (*-s; -*) bucket, pail
**ein** [ain] **1.** *adj* one; **2.** *indef art* a, an; **3.** *adv*: „ ***ein/aus***" "on/off"; ***~ und aus gehen*** come and go; ***nicht mehr ~ noch aus wissen*** be at one's wits' end
**einander** [ai'nandɐ] *pron* each other, one another
**'einarbeiten** *v/t* (*sep, -ge-, h*) train, acquaint *s.o.* with his work, F break *s.o.* in; ***sich ~*** work o.s. in
**'einarmig** [-armɪç] *adj* one-armed
**einäschern** ['ain?ɛʃɐn] *v/t* (*sep, -ge-, h*) cremate; **Einäscherung** ['ain?ɛʃərʊŋ] *f* (*-; -en*) cremation
**'einatmen** *v/t* (*sep, -ge-, h*) inhale, breathe
**'einäugig** [-ɔʏgɪç] *adj* one-eyed
**'Einbahnstraße** *f* one-way street
**einbalsamieren** ['ainbalzami:rən] *v/t* (*no -ge-, h*) embalm
**'Einband** *m* (*-[e]s; -bände*) binding, cover
**'Einbau** *m* (*-[e]s; -bauten*) installation, fitting; **~...** *in cpds ...möbel etc*: built-in ...; **'einbauen** *v/t* (*sep, -ge-, h*) build in, instal(l), fit
**'einberufen** *v/t* (*irr,* ***rufen****, sep, no -ge-, h*) MIL draft, *Br* call up; call (*meeting etc*); **'Einberufung** *f* (*-; -en*) MIL draft, *Br* call-up
**'ein|beziehen** *v/t* (*irr,* ***ziehen****, sep, no -ge-, h*) include; **~biegen** *v/i* (*irr,* ***biegen****, sep, -ge-, sein*) turn (***in*** *acc* into)
**'einbilden** *v/refl* (*sep, -ge-, h*) imagine; ***sich et. ~ auf*** (*acc*) be conceited about
**'Einbildung** *f* (*-; no pl*) imagination, fancy; conceit
**'einblenden** *v/t* (*sep, -ge-, h*) TV fade in
**'Einblick** *m* insight (***in*** *acc* into)
**'einbrechen** *v/i* (*irr,* ***brechen****, sep, -ge-, sein*) collapse; *winter*: set in; ***~ in*** (*acc*) break into, burgle; fall through (the ice); **'Einbrecher** *m* (*-s; -*) burglar
**'einbringen** *v/t* (*irr,* ***bringen****, sep, -ge-, h*) bring in; yield (*profit etc*)
**'Einbruch** *m* burglary; ***bei ~ der Nacht*** at nightfall
**'einbürgern** [-bʏrgɐn] *v/t* (*sep, -ge-, h*) naturalize; ***sich ~*** *fig* come into use
**'Einbürgerung** *f* (*-; -en*) naturalization
**'Einbuße** *f* (*-; -n*) loss
**'einbüßen** *v/t* (*sep, -ge-, h*) lose
**'eindämmen** [-dɛmən] *v/t* (*sep, -ge-, h*) dam (up), *fig a.* get under control
**'eindecken** *fig v/t* (*sep, -ge-, h*) provide (***mit*** with)
**'eindeutig** [-dɔʏtɪç] *adj* clear
**'eindrehen** *v/t* (*sep, -ge-, h*) put *hair* in curlers
**'eindringen** *v/i* (*irr,* ***dringen****, sep, -ge-, sein*) ***~ in*** (*acc*) enter (*a. fig*); force one's way into; MIL invade; **'eindringlich** *adj* urgent; **'Eindringling** *m* (*-s; -e*) intruder; MIL invader
**'Eindruck** *m* impression; **'eindrücken** *v/t* (*sep, -ge-, h*) break *or* push in
**'eindrucksvoll** *adj* impressive
**eineiig** ['ain?aiɪç] *adj* identical (*twins*)

**'einein'halb** *adj* one and a half
**einengen** ['ain?ɛŋən] *v/t* (*sep*, *-ge-*, *h*) confine, restrict
**einer** ['ainɐ], **eine** ['ainə], **ein(e)s** ['ain(ə)s] *indef pron* one
**'Einer** *m* (*-s*; *-*) MATH unit; *rowing*: single sculls
**einerlei** ['ainɐ'lai] *adj*: ***ganz ~*** all the same; ***~ ob*** no matter if; **'Einer'lei** *n*: ***das tägliche ~*** the daily grind *or* rut
**'einer'seits** *adv* on the one hand
**'einfach** *adj* simple; easy; plain; one-way (*Br* single) (*ticket*)
**'Einfachheit** *f* (*-*; *no pl*) simplicity
**'einfädeln** [-fɛːdəln] *v/t* (*sep*, *-ge-*, *h*) thread; F start, set afoot; MOT merge
**'einfahren** (*irr*, ***fahren***, *sep*, *-ge-*) **1.** *v/t* (*h*) MOT run in; bring in (*harvest*); **2.** *v/i* (*sein*) come in, RAIL *a.* pull in
**'Einfahrt** *f* entrance, way in
**'Einfall** *m* idea; MIL invasion
**'einfallen** *v/i* (*irr*, ***fallen***, *sep*, *-ge-*, *sein*) fall in; collapse; MUS join in; ***~ in*** (*acc*) MIL invade; ***ihm fiel ein, dass*** it came to his mind that; ***mir fällt nichts ein*** I have no ideas; ***es fällt mir nicht ein*** I can't think of it; ***dabei fällt mir ein*** that reminds me; ***was fällt dir ein?*** what's the idea?
**einfältig** ['ainfɛltɪç] *adj* simple-minded; stupid
**Einfa'milienhaus** *n* detached house
**'einfarbig** *adj* solid-colored, *Br* self-coloured
**'ein|fassen** *v/t* (*sep*, *-ge-*, *h*) border; **~fetten** *v/t* (*sep*, *-ge-*, *h*) grease; **~finden** *v/refl* (*irr*, ***finden***, *sep*, *-ge-*, *h*) appear, arrive; **~flechten** *fig v/t* (*irr*, ***flechten***, *sep*, *-ge-*, *h*) work in; **~fliegen** *v/t* (*irr*, ***fliegen***, *sep*, *-ge-*, *h*) fly in; **~fließen** *v/i* (*irr*, ***fließen***, *sep*, *-ge-*, *sein*) *fig* ***et. ~ lassen*** slip s.th. in; **~flößen** *v/t* (*sep*, *-ge-*, *h*) pour (***j-m*** into s.o.'s mouth); *fig* fill with (*awe etc*)
**'Einfluss** *fig m* influence
**'einflussreich** *adj* influential
**'einförmig** [-fœrmɪç] *adj* uniform
**'einfrieren** (*irr*, ***frieren***, *sep*, *-ge-*) **1.** *v/i* (*sein*) freeze (in); **2.** *v/t* (*h*) freeze (*a. fig*)
**'einfügen** *v/t* (*sep*, *-ge-*, *h*) put in; *fig* insert; ***sich ~*** fit in; adjust (o.s.) (***in*** *acc* to); **'Einfügetaste** *f* EDP insert key
**einfühlsam** ['ainfyːlzaːm] *adj* sympathetic; **'Einfühlungsvermögen** *n* (*-s*; *no pl*) empathy
**Einfuhr** ['ainfuːɐ] *f* (*-*; *-en*) ECON a) (*no pl*) importation, b) import
**'einführen** *v/t* (*sep*, *-ge-*, *h*) introduce; instal(l) *s.o.*; insert; ECON import
**'Einfuhrstopp** *m* ECON import ban
**'Einführung** *f* (*-*; *-en*) introduction
**'Einführungs...** *in cpds ...kurs*, *...preis etc*: introductory ...
**'Eingabe** *f* petition; EDP input; **~taste** *f* EDP enter *or* return key
**'Eingang** *m* entrance; ECON arrival; receipt; **'eingängig** *adj* catchy (*tune etc*)
**'eingangs** *adv* at the beginning
**'eingeben** *v/t* (*irr*, ***geben***, *sep*, *-ge-*, *h*) MED administer (*dat* to); EDP feed, enter
**'eingebildet** *adj* imaginary; conceited (***auf*** *acc* of)
**'Eingeborene** *m*, *f* (*-n*; *-n*) native
**'Eingebung** *f* (*-*; *-en*) inspiration; impulse
**'eingefallen** *adj* sunken, hollow
**'eingefleischt** *adj* confirmed
**'eingehen** (*irr*, ***gehen***, *sep*, *-ge-*, *sein*) **1.** *v/i* ECON come in, arrive; BOT, ZO die; *fabric*: shrink; ***~ auf*** (*acc*) agree to; go into (*detail*); listen to *s.o.*; **2.** *v/t* enter into (*a contract etc*); make (*a bet*); take (*a risk etc*); **~d** *adj* thorough; detailed
**'eingemacht** *adj* preserved
**eingemeinden** ['aingəmaindən] *v/t* (*sep*, *no -ge-*, *h*) incorporate (***in*** *acc* into)
**'einge|nommen** *adj* partial (***für*** to); prejudiced (***gegen*** against); ***von sich ~*** full of o.s.; **~schlossen** *adj* locked in; trapped; ECON included; **~schnappt** F *adj* in a huff; **~schrieben** *adj* registered; **~spielt** *adj*: (***gut***) ***aufeinander ~ sein*** work well together, be a good team; **~stellt** *adj*: ***~ auf*** (*acc*) prepared for; ***~ gegen*** opposed to
**Eingeweide** ['aingəvaidə] *pl* ANAT intestines, guts
**'Eingeweihte** *m*, *f* (*-n*; *-n*) insider
**'eingewöhnen** *v/refl* (*sep*, *no -ge-*, *h*) ***sich ~ in*** (*acc*) get used to, settle in
**'eingießen** *v/t* (*irr*, ***gießen***, *sep*, *-ge-*, *h*) pour
**'eingleisig** [-glaizɪç] *adj* single-track
**'eingliedern** *v/t* (*sep*, *-ge-*, *h*) integrate
**'Eingliederung** *f* integration
**'ein|graben** *v/t* (*irr*, ***graben***, *sep*, *-ge-*,

E

*h*) bury; **~graˌvieren** *v/t* (*sep, no -ge-, h*) engrave
**'eingreifen** *v/i* (*irr*, ***greifen***, *sep*, *-ge-*, *h*) step in, interfere; **'Eingriff** *m* intervention, interference; MED operation
**'einhaken** *v/t* (*sep*, *-ge-*, *h*) hook in; ***sich ~*** link arms, take s.o.'s arm
**'Einhalt** *m*: ***~ gebieten*** put a stop (*dat* to); **'einhalten** *v/t* (*irr*, ***halten***, *sep*, *-ge-*, *h*) keep
**'einhängen** (*sep*, *-ge-*, *h*) **1.** *v/t* hang in; TEL hang up (*receiver*); ***sich ~ → einhaken***; **2.** *v/i* TEL hang up
**'einheimisch** *adj* native, local; ECON home, domestic; **'Einheimische** *m*, *f* (*-n*; *-n*) local, native
**'Einheit** *f* (-; *-en*) unit; POL unity
**'einheitlich** *adj* uniform; homogeneous
**'Einheits...** *in cpds ...preis etc*: standard
**einhellig** ['ainhɛlıç] *adj* unanimous
**'einholen** *v/t* (*sep*, *-ge-*, *h*) catch up with (*a. fig*); make up for *lost time*; make (*inquiries*) (***über*** *acc* about); seek (*advice*) (***bei*** from); ask for *permission etc*; strike (*sail*); ***~ gehen*** go shopping
**'Einhorn** *n* MYTH unicorn
**'einhüllen** *v/t* (*sep*, *-ge-*, *h*) wrap (up); *fig* shroud
**einig** ['ainıç] *adj*: ***sich ~ sein*** agree; ***sich nicht ~ sein*** disagree, differ
**einige** ['ainıgə] *indef pron* some, a few, several
**einigen** ['ainıgən] *v/t* (*ge-*, *h*) ***sich ~ über*** (*acc*) agree on
**einigermaßen** ['ainıgɐ'ma:sən] *adv* quite, fairly; not too bad
**'einiges** *indef pron* some, something; quite a lot
**'Einigkeit** *f* (-; *no pl*) unity; agreement
**'Einigung** *f* (-; *-en*) agreement, settlement; POL unification
**'einjagen** *v/t* (*sep*, *-ge-*, *h*) ***j-m e-n Schrecken ~*** give s.o. a fright, frighten *or* scare s.o.
**'einjährig** [-jɛ:rıç] *adj* one-year-old; ***~e Pflanze*** annual
**'einkalkuˌlieren** *v/t* (*no -ge-*, *h*) take into account, allow for
**'Einkauf** *m* purchase; ***Einkäufe machen → einkaufen*** 2; **'einkaufen** (*sep*, *-ge-*, *h*) **1.** *v/t* buy, ECON *a.* purchase; **2.** *v/i* go shopping
**'Einkaufs...** *in cpds* shopping ...; **~bummel** *m* shopping spree; **~preis** *m* ECON purchase price; **~wagen** *m* grocery *or* shopping cart, *Br* (supermarket) trolley; **~zentrum** *n* (shopping) mall, *Br* shopping centre
**'ein|kehren** *v/i* (*sep*, *-ge-*, *sein*) stop (***in*** *dat* at); **~klammern** *v/t* (*sep*, *-ge-*, *h*) put in brackets
**'Einklang** *m* (-[*e*]*s*; *no pl*) MUS unison; *fig* harmony
**'ein|kleiden** *v/t* (*sep*, *-ge-*, *h*) clothe (*a. fig*); **~klemmen** *v/t* (*sep*, *-ge-*, *h*) squeeze, jam; ***eingeklemmt sein*** be stuck, be jammed; **~kochen** (*sep*, *-ge-*) **1.** *v/t* (*h*) preserve; **2.** *v/i* (*sein*) boil down
**'Einkommen** *n* (*-s*; -) income; **~steuererklärung** *f* income-tax return
**'einkreisen** *v/t* (*sep*, *-ge-*, *h*) encircle, surround
**Einkünfte** ['ainkʏnftə] *pl* income
**'einladen** *v/t* (*irr*, ***laden***, *sep*, *-ge-*, *h*) invite; load; **~d** *adj* inviting
**'Einladung** *f* (-; *-en*) invitation
**'Einlage** *f* (-; *-n*) ECON investment; MED arch support; THEA, MUS interlude
**Einlass** ['ainlas] *m* (*-es*; *no pl*) admission, admittance; **'einlassen** *v/t* (*irr*, ***lassen***, *sep*, *-ge-*, *h*) let in; run (*a bath*); ***sich ~ auf*** (*acc*) get involved in; let o.s. in for; agree to; ***sich mit j-m ~*** get involved with s.o.
**'Einlauf** *m* SPORT finish; MED enema
**'einlaufen** (*irr*, ***laufen***, *sep*, *-ge-*) **1.** *v/i* (*sein*) come in (*a.* SPORT); *water*: run in; MAR enter port; *fabric*: shrink; **2.** *v/t* (*h*) break *new shoes* in; ***sich ~*** warm up
**'einleben** *v/refl* (*sep*, *-ge-*, *h*) settle in
**'einlegen** *v/t* (*sep*, *-ge-*, *h*) put in; set (*hair*); GASTR pickle; MOT change into
**'Einlegesohle** *f* insole
**'einleiten** *v/t* (*sep*, *-ge-*, *h*) start; introduce; MED induce; TECH dump, discharge (*sewage*); **~d** *adj* introductory
**'Einleitung** *f* introduction
**'ein|lenken** *v/i* (*sep*, *-ge-*, *h*) come round; **~leuchten** *v/i* (*sep*, *-ge-*, *h*) be evident, be obvious; ***das leuchtet mir*** (***nicht***) ***ein*** that makes (doesn't make) sense to me; **~liefern** *v/t* (*sep*, *-ge-*, *h*) take (***ins Gefängnis*** to prison; ***in die Klinik*** to [the] hospital); **~lösen** *v/t* (*sep*, *-ge-*, *h*) redeem; cash (*check*); **~machen** *v/t* (*sep*, *-ge-*, *h*) preserve
**'einmal** *adv* once; some *or* one day,

sometime; ***auf*** ~ suddenly; at the same time, at once; ***noch*** ~ once more *or* again; ***noch*** ~ ***so*** ... (***wie***) twice as ... (as); ***es war*** ~ once (upon a time) there was; ***haben Sie schon*** ~ ...? have you ever ...?; ***schon*** ~ ***dort gewesen sein*** have been there before; ***nicht*** ~ not even

**'Einmal...** *in cpds* disposable ...

**Einmal'eins** *n* (-; *no pl*) multiplication table

**einmalig** ['ainma:lıç] *adj* single; *fig* unique; F fabulous

**'Einmann...** *in cpds* one-man ...

**'Einmarsch** *m* entry; MIL invasion

**'einmar,schieren** *v/i* (*no -ge-, sein*) march in; ~ ***in*** (*acc*) MIL invade

**'einmischen** *v/refl* (*sep, -ge-, h*) meddle (***in*** *acc* in, with), interfere (with)

**'Einmündung** *f* junction

**'einmütig** [-my:tıç] *adj* unanimous

**'Einmütigkeit** *f* (-; *no pl*) unanimity

**Einnahmen** ['ainna:mən] *pl* takings, receipts; **'einnehmen** *v/t* (*irr*, ***nehmen***, *sep, -ge-, h*) take (*a.* MIL); earn, make; **'einnehmend** *adj* engaging

**'einnicken** *v/i* (*sep, -ge-, sein*) doze off

**'einnisten** *v/refl* (*sep, -ge-, h*) ***sich bei j-m*** ~ park o.s. on s.o.

**'Einöde** *f* (-; *-n*) desert, wilderness

**'ein|ordnen** *v/t* (*sep, -ge-, h*) put in its proper place; file; ***sich*** ~ MOT get in lane; **~packen** *v/t* (*sep, -ge-, h*) pack (up); wrap up; **~parken** *v/t and v/i* (*sep, -ge-, h*) park (between two cars); **~pferchen** *v/t* (*sep, -ge-, h*) pen in; coop up; **~pflanzen** *v/t* (*sep, -ge-, h*) plant; *fig* implant (*a.* MED); **~planen** *v/t* (*sep, -ge-, h*) allow for; **~prägen** *v/t* (*sep, -ge-, h*) impress; ***sich et.*** ~ keep s.th. in mind; memorize s.th.; **~quar,tieren** F *v/t* (*no -ge-, h*) put *s.o.* up (***bei j-m*** at s.o.'s place); ***sich*** ~ ***bei*** (*dat*) move in with; **~rahmen** *v/t* (*sep, -ge-, h*) frame; **~räumen** *v/t* (*sep, -ge-, h*) put away; furnish; *fig* grant, concede; **~reden** (*sep, -ge-, h*) **1.** *v/t*: ***j-m et.*** ~ talk s.o. into (believing) s.th.; **2.** *v/i*: ***auf j-n*** ~ keep on at s.o.; **~reiben** *v/t* (*irr*, ***reiben***, *sep, -ge-, h*) rub; **~reichen** *v/t* (*sep, -ge-, h*) hand *or* send in; **~reihen** *v/t* (*sep, -ge-, h*) place (among); ***sich*** ~ take one's place

**'einreihig** [-raiıç] *adj* single-breasted

**'Einreise** *f* entry (*a. in cpds*)

**'einreisen** *v/i* (*sep, -ge-, sein*) enter (***in ein Land*** a country)

**'ein|reißen** (*irr*, ***reißen***, *sep, -ge-*) **1.** *v/t* (*h*) tear; pull down; **2.** *v/i* (*sein*) tear; *fig* spread; **~renken** *v/t* (*sep, -ge-, h*) MED set; *fig* straighten out

**'einrichten** *v/t* (*sep, -ge-, h*) furnish; establish; arrange; ***sich*** ~ furnish one's home; ***sich*** ~ ***auf*** (*acc*) prepare for; **'Einrichtung** *f* (-; *-en*) furnishings; fittings; TECH installation(s), facilities; institution, facility

**'einrücken** (*sep, -ge-*) **1.** *v/i* (*sein*) MIL join the forces; march in; **2.** *v/t* (*h*) PRINT indent

**eins** [ains] *pron and adj* one; one thing; ***es ist alles*** ~ it's all the same (thing)

**Eins** *f* (-; *-en*) one; *grade*: excellent, A

**einsam** ['ainza:m] *adj* lonely, lonesome; solitary; **'Einsamkeit** *f* (-; *no pl*) loneliness; solitude

**'einsammeln** *v/t* (*sep, -ge-, h*) collect

**'Einsatz** *m* TECH inset, insert; stake(s) (*a. fig*); MUS entry; *fig* effort(s), zeal; use, employment; MIL action, mission; deployment; ***im*** ~ in action; ***unter*** ~ ***des Lebens*** at the risk of one's life

**'einsatz|bereit** *adj* ready for action; **~freudig** *adj* dynamic, zealous

**'einschalten** *v/t* (*sep, -ge-, h*) ELECTR switch *or* turn on; call *s.o.* in; ***sich*** ~ step in; **'Einschaltquote** *f* TV rating

**'ein|schärfen** *v/t* (*sep, -ge-, h*) urge (***j-m et.*** s.o. to do s.th.); **~schätzen** *v/t* (*sep, -ge-, h*) estimate; judge, rate; ***falsch*** ~ misjudge; **~schenken** *v/t* (*sep, -ge-, h*) pour (out); **~schicken** *v/t* (*sep, -ge-, h*) send in; **~schieben** *v/t* (*irr*, ***schieben***, *sep, -ge-, h*) slip in; insert; **~schlafen** *v/i* (*irr*, ***schlafen***, *sep, -ge-, sein*) fall asleep, go to sleep; **~schläfern** [-ʃlɛ:fɐn] *v/t* (*sep, -ge-, h*) put to sleep

**einschl.** ABBR *of* ***einschließlich*** incl., including

**'Einschlag** *m* strike, impact; *fig* touch

**'einschlagen** (*irr*, ***schlagen***, *sep, -ge-, h*) **1.** *v/t* knock in (*or* out); break (in), smash; wrap up; take (*road etc*); turn (*wheels*); → ***Laufbahn***; **2.** *v/i lightning etc*: strike; *fig* be a success

**'einschlägig** [-ʃlɛ:gıç] *adj* relevant

**'ein|schleusen** *fig v/t* (*sep, -ge-, h*) infiltrate (***in*** *acc* into); **~schließen** *v/t* (*irr*, ***schließen,*** *sep*, *-ge-*, *h*) lock in *or* up; enclose; MIL surround, encircle; *fig* include; **~schließlich** *prp* (*gen*) including, ... included; **~schmeicheln** *v/refl* (*sep*, *-ge-*, *h*) ***sich ~ bei*** ingratiate o.s. with; **~schnappen** *v/i* (*sep*, *-ge-*, *sein*) snap shut; *fig* go into a huff; → ***eingeschnappt***

E

**'einschneidend** *fig adj* drastic; far-reaching; **'Einschnitt** *m* cut; notch; *fig* break

**'einschränken** *v/t* (*sep*, *-ge-*, *h*) restrict, reduce (*both*: ***auf*** *acc* to); cut down on; ***sich ~*** economize; **'Einschränkung** *f* (-; *-en*) restriction, reduction, cut; ***ohne ~*** without reservation

**'Einschreibebrief** *m* registered letter

**'einschreiben** *v/t* (*irr*, ***schreiben,*** *sep*, *-ge-*, *h*) enter; book; enrol(l) (*a.* MIL); (***sich***) ***~ lassen*** (***für***) enrol(l) (o.s.) (for)

**'einschreiten** *fig v/i* (*irr*, ***schreiten,*** *sep*, *-ge-*, *sein*) step in, intervene; ***~*** (***gegen***) take (legal) measures (against)

**'einschüchtern** *v/t* (*sep*, *-ge-*, *h*) intimidate; bully; **'Einschüchterung** *f* (-; *-en*) intimidation

**'einschulen** *v/t* (*sep*, *-ge-*, *h*) ***eingeschult werden*** start school

**'Einschuss** *m* bullet hole

**'einschweißen** *v/t* (*sep*, *-ge-*, *h*) shrink-wrap

**'einsegnen** *v/t* (*sep*, *-ge-*, *h*) REL consecrate; confirm; **'Einsegnung** *f* (-; *-en*) REL consecration; confirmation

**'einsehen** *v/t* (*irr*, ***sehen,*** *sep*, *-ge-*, *h*) see, realize; ***das sehe ich nicht ein!*** I don't see why!; **'Einsehen** *n*: ***ein ~ haben*** show some understanding

**'einseifen** *v/t* (*sep*, *-ge-*, *h*) soap; lather; F *fig* ***j-n ~*** take s.o. for a ride

**'einseitig** [-zaitɪç] *adj* one-sided; MED, POL, JUR unilateral

**'einsenden** *v/t* ([*irr*, ***senden,***] *sep*, *-ge-*, *h*) send in; **'Einsendeschluss** *m* closing date (for entries)

**'einsetzen** (*sep*, *-ge-*, *h*) **1.** *v/t* put in, insert; appoint; use, employ; TECH put into service; ECON invest, stake; bet; risk; ***sich ~*** try hard, make an effort; ***sich ~ für*** stand up for; **2.** *v/i* set in, start

**'Einsicht** *f* (-; *-en*) a) insight, b) (*no pl*) understanding; ***zur ~ kommen*** listen to reason; ***~ nehmen in*** (*acc*) take a look at; **'einsichtig** *adj* understanding; reasonable

**'Einsiedler** *m* (*-s*; -) hermit

**'einsilbig** [-zɪlbɪç] *adj* monosyllabic; *fig* taciturn

**'ein|spannen** *v/t* (*sep*, *-ge-*, *h*) harness; TECH clamp, fix; F rope *s.o.* in; **~sparen** *v/t* (*sep*, *-ge-*, *h*) save, economize on; **~sperren** *v/t* (*sep*, *-ge-*, *h*) lock *or* shut up; **~spielen** *v/t* (*sep*, *-ge-*, *h*) bring in; ***sich ~*** warm up; *fig* get going; → ***eingespielt***

**'Einspielergebnisse** *pl film*: box-office returns

**'einspringen** *v/i* (*irr*, ***springen,*** *sep*, *-ge-*, *sein*) ***für j-n ~*** take s.o.'s place

**'Einspritz...** *in cpds* MOT fuel-injection

**'Einspruch** *m* objection (*a.* JUR), protest; POL veto; appeal

**'einspurig** [-ʃpuːrɪç] *adj* RAIL single-track; MOT single-lane

**einst** [ainst] *adv* once, at one time

**'Einstand** *m* start; *tennis*: deuce

**'ein|stecken** *v/t* (*sep*, *-ge-*, *h*) pocket (*a. fig*); ELECTR plug in; mail, post; *fig* take; **~stehen** *v/i* (*irr*, ***stehen,*** *sep*, *-ge-*, *h*) ***~ für*** stand up for; **~steigen** *v/i* (*irr*, ***steigen,*** *sep*, *-ge-*, *sein*) get in; get on (*bus etc*); ***alles ~!*** RAIL all aboard!; **~stellen** *v/t* (*sep*, *-ge-*, *h*) engage, employ, hire; give up; stop; SPORT equal; TECH adjust (***auf*** *acc* to); *radio*: tune in (to); OPT, PHOT focus (on); ***die Arbeit ~*** (go on) strike, walk out; ***das Feuer ~*** MIL cease fire; ***sich ~ auf*** (*acc*) adjust to; be prepared for

**'Einstellung** *f* attitude (***zu*** towards); employment; cessation; TECH adjustment; OPT, PHOT focus(s)ing; *film*: take

**'Einstellungsgespräch** *n* interview

**Einstieg** ['ainʃtiːk] *m* (*-[e]s*; *-e*) entrance, entry (*a.* POL, ECON)

**'Einstiegsdroge** *f* gateway drug

**einstig** ['ainstɪç] *adj* former, one-time

**'einstimmen** *v/i* (*sep*, *-ge-*, *h*) MUS join in

**'einstimmig** [-ʃtɪmɪç] *adj* unanimous

**'einstöckig** [-ʃtœkɪç] *adj* one-storied, *Br* one-storey(ed)

**'ein|stuˌdieren** *v/t* (*no -ge-*, *h*) THEA rehearse; **~stufen** *v/t* (*sep*, *-ge-*, *h*) grade, rate

**'Einstufungsprüfung** *f* placement test

**'einstufig** [-ʃtuːfɪç] *adj* single-stage

'**Einsturz** *m*, '**einstürzen** *v/i* (*sep*, *-ge-*, *sein*) collapse
'**einst'weilen** *adv* for the present
'**einstweilig** [-vailɪç] *adj* temporary
'**ein|tauschen** *v/t* (*sep*, *-ge-*, *h*) exchange (***gegen*** for); **~teilen** *v/t* (*sep*, *-ge-*, *h*) divide (***in*** *acc* into); organize
'**einteilig** [-tailɪç] *adj* one-piece
'**Einteilung** *f* (-; *-en*) division; organization; arrangement
'**eintönig** [-tøːnɪç] *adj* monotonous
'**Eintönigkeit** *f* (-; *no pl*) monotony
'**Eintopf** *m* GASTR stew
'**Eintracht** *f* (-; *no pl*) harmony, unity
'**einträchtig** *adj* harmonious, peaceful
**Eintrag** ['aintraːk] *m* (-[*e*]*s*; *Einträge* ['aintrɛːgə]) entry (*a.* ECON), registration; '**eintragen** *v/t* (*irr*, ***tragen***, *sep*, *-ge-*, *h*) enter (***in*** *acc* in); register (***bei*** with); enrol(l) (with); *fig* earn; ***sich ~*** register, *hotel*: *a.* check in
**einträglich** ['aintrɛːklɪç] *adj* profitable
'**ein|treffen** *v/i* (*irr*, ***treffen***, *sep*, *-ge-*, *sein*) arrive; happen; come true; **~treiben** *fig v/t* (*irr*, ***treiben***, *sep*, *-ge-*, *h*) collect; **~treten** (*irr*, ***treten***, *sep*, *-ge-*) **1.** *v/i* (*sein*) enter; happen, take place; ***~ für*** stand up for, support; ***~ in*** (*acc*) join (*club etc*); **2.** *v/t* (*h*) kick in (*door etc*); ***sich et. ~*** run s.th. into one's foot
'**Eintritt** *m* entry; admission; ***~ frei!*** admission free!; ***~ verboten!*** keep out!
'**Eintritts|geld** *n* entrance *or* admission (fee); **~karte** *f* (admission) ticket
'**einüben** *v/t* (*sep*, *-ge-*, *h*) practise; rehearse
'**einverstanden** *adj*: ***~ sein*** agree (***mit*** to); ***~!*** agreed!; '**Einverständnis** *n* (*-ses*; *no pl*) agreement
**Einwand** ['ainvant] *m* (-[*e*]*s*; *Einwände* ['ainvɛndə]) objection (***gegen*** to)
'**Einwanderer** *m*, '**Einwanderin** *f* immigrant; '**einwandern** *v/i* (*sep*, *-ge-*, *sein*) immigrate; '**Einwanderung** *f* immigration
'**einwandfrei** *adj* perfect, faultless
**einwärts** ['ainvɛrts] *adv* inward(s)
'**Einweg...** *...rasierer*, *...spritze etc*: disposable; **~flasche** *f* non-returnable bottle; **~packung** *f* throwaway pack
'**einweichen** *v/t* (*sep*, *-ge-*, *h*) soak
'**einweihen** *v/t* (*sep*, *-ge-*, *h*) dedicate, *Br* inaugurate; ***j-n ~ in*** (*acc*) F let s.o. in on; '**Einweihung** *f* (-; *-en*) dedication, *Br* inauguration
'**einweisen** *v/t* (*irr*, ***weisen***, *sep*, *-ge-*, *h*) ***j-n ~ in*** (*acc*) send (*esp* JUR commit) s.o. to; instruct s.o. in, brief s.o. on
'**einwenden** *v/t* ([*irr*, ***wenden***,] *sep*, *-ge-*, *h*) object (***gegen*** to)
'**Einwendung** *f* (-; *-en*) objection
'**einwerfen** *v/t* (*irr*, ***werfen***, *sep*, *-ge-*, *h*) throw in (*a. fig*, SPORT *a. v/i*); break (*window*); mail, *Br* post; insert (*coin*)
'**einwickeln** *v/t* (*sep*, *-ge-*, *h*) wrap (up); F take *s.o.* in
'**Einwickelpa,pier** *n* wrapping-paper
**einwilligen** ['ainvɪlɪgən] *v/i* (*sep*, *-ge-*, *h*) consent (***in*** *acc* to), agree (to)
'**Einwilligung** *f* (-; *-en*) consent (***in*** *acc* to), agreement
'**einwirken** *v/i* (*sep*, *-ge-*, *h*) ***~ auf*** (*acc*) act (up)on; *fig* work on *s.o.*
'**Einwirkung** *f* effect, influence
**Einwohner** ['ainvoːnɐ] *m* (*-s*; -), '**Einwohnerin** *f* (-; *-nen*) inhabitant; '**Einwohnermeldeamt** *n* registration office
'**Einwurf** *m* slot; SPORT throw-in
'**Einzahl** *f* (-; *no pl*) LING singular
'**einzahlen** *v/t* (*sep*, *-ge-*, *h*) pay in
'**Einzahlung** *f* payment, deposit
**einzäunen** ['aintsɔʏnən] *v/t* (*sep*, *-ge-*, *h*) fence in
**Einzel** ['aintsəl] *n* (*-s*; -) *tennis*: singles
'**Einzel...** *in cpds ...bett*, *...zimmer etc*: single ...; **~fall** *m* special case; **~gänger** [-gɛŋɐ] *m* (*-s*; -) F loner; **~haft** *f* solitary confinement; **~handel** *m* retail trade; **~händler** *m* retailer; **~haus** *n* detached house
'**Einzelheit** *f* (-; *-en*) detail
'**einzeln** *adj* single; odd (*shoe etc*); ***Einzelne*** *pl* several, some; ***der Einzelne*** the individual; ***~ eintreten*** enter one at a time; ***~ angeben*** specify; ***im Einzelnen*** in detail; ***jeder Einzelne*** each and every one
'**einziehen** (*irr*, ***ziehen***, *sep*, *-ge-*) **1.** *v/t* (*h*) draw in; *esp* TECH retract; duck; strike (*sail etc*); MIL draft, *Br* call up; confiscate; withdraw (*license etc*); make (*inquiries*); **2.** *v/i* (*sein*) move in; march in; soak in
**einzig** ['aintsɪç] *adj* only; single; ***kein Einziger ...*** not a single ...; ***das Einzige*** the only thing; ***der*** (***die***) ***Einzige*** the only one; **~artig** *adj* unique, singular

**'Einzug** *m* moving in; entry
**Eis** [ais] *n* (*-es; no pl*) ice; GASTR ice cream; ~ ***am Stiel*** ice lolly; **~bahn** *f* skating rink; **~bär** *m* ZO polar bear; **~becher** *m* sundae; **~bein** *n* GASTR (pickled) pork knuckles; **~berg** *m* iceberg; **~brecher** *m* (*-s; -*) MAR icebreaker; **~diele** *f* ice-cream parlo(u)r
**Eisen** ['aizən] *n* (*-s; -*) iron
**'Eisenbahn** *f* railroad, *Br* railway; train set; **'Eisenbahner** [-ba:nɐ] *m* (*-s; -*) railroadman, *Br* railwayman
**'Eisenbahnwagen** *m* (railroad) car, *Br* coach, railway carriage
**'Eisen|erz** *n* iron ore; **~gießerei** *f* iron foundry; **~hütte** *f* TECH ironworks
**'Eisenwaren** *pl* hardware, ironware; **~handlung** *f* hardware store, *Br* ironmonger's
**eisern** ['aizɐn] *adj* iron (*a. fig*), of iron
**'eisgekühlt** *adj* iced
**'Eishockey** *n* hockey, *Br* ice hockey
**eisig** ['aiziç] *adj* icy (*a. fig*)
**'eis'kalt** *adj* ice-cold
**'Eiskunst|lauf** *m* (*-[e]s; no pl*) figure skating; **~läufer(in)** figure skater
**'Eis|meer** *n* polar sea; **~re͵vue** *f* ice show; **~schnelllauf** *m* speed skating; **~scholle** *f* ice floe; **~verkäufer** *m* iceman; **~würfel** *m* ice cube; **~zapfen** *m* icicle; **~zeit** *f* (*-; no pl*) GEOL ice age
**eitel** ['aitəl] *adj* vain; **'Eitelkeit** *f* (*-; no pl*) vanity
**Eiter** ['aitɐ] *m* (*-s; no pl*) MED pus
**'Eiterbeule** *f* MED abscess, boil
**'eitern** *v/i* (*ge-, h*) MED fester
**eitrig** ['aitriç] *adj* MED purulent, festering
**'Eiweiß** *n* (*-es; no pl*) white of egg; BIOL protein
**'eiweiß|arm** *adj* low in protein, low-protein; **~reich** *adj* rich in protein, high-protein
**'Eizelle** *f* BIOL egg cell, ovum
**Ekel** ['e:kəl] **1.** *m* (*-s; no pl*) disgust (***vor*** *dat* at), loathing (for); ~ ***erregend*** → ***ekelhaft***; **2.** F *n* (*-s; -*) beast
**'ekelhaft, 'ek(e)lig** *adj* sickening, disgusting, repulsive
**'ekeln** *v/refl and v/impers* (*ge-, h*) ***ich ekle mich davor*** it makes me sick
**Ekstase** [ɛk'sta:zə] *f* (*-; -n*) ecstasy
**Elan** [e'la:n] *m* (*-s; no pl*) vigo(u)r
**elastisch** [e'lastɪʃ] *adj* elastic, flexible
**Elch** [ɛlç] *m* (*-[e]s; -e*) ZO elk; moose
**Elefant** [ele'fant] *m* (*-en; -en*) ZO elephant; **Ele'fantenhochzeit** F *f* ECON jumbo merger
**elegant** [ele'gant] *adj* elegant
**Eleganz** [ele'gants] *f* (*-; no pl*) elegance
**Elektriker** [e'lɛktrɪkɐ] *m* (*-s; -*) electrician; **elektrisch** [e'lɛktrɪʃ] *adj* electrical; electric; **elektrisieren** [elɛktri'zi:rən] *v/t* (*no -ge-, h*) electrify
**Elektrizität** [elɛktritsi'tɛ:t] *f* (*-; no pl*) electricity; **Elektrizi'tätswerk** *n* (electric) power station
**Elektrogerät** [e'lɛktro-] *n* electric appliance
**Elektronik** [elɛk'tro:nɪk] *f* electronics; electronic system; **elektronisch** [elɛk'tro:nɪʃ] *adj* electronic
**E'lektrora͵sierer** *m* (*-s; -*) electric razor
**Elektro|'technik** *f* electrical engineering; **~'techniker** *m* electrical engineer
**Element** [ele'mɛnt] *n* (*-[e]s; -e*) element
**elementar** [elemɛn'ta:ɐ] *adj* elementary
**elend** ['e:lɛnt] *adj* miserable
**'Elend** *n* (*-s; no pl*) misery
**'Elendsviertel** *n* slums
**elf** [ɛlf] *adj* eleven
**Elf** *f* (*-; -en*) eleven; *soccer*: team
**Elfe** ['ɛlfə] *f* (*-; -n*) elf, fairy
**'Elfenbein** *n* ivory
**Elf'meter** *m* (*-s; -*) *soccer*: penalty; **~punkt** *m* penalty spot; **~schießen** *n* penalty shoot-out
**'elfte** *adj* eleventh
**Elite** [e'li:tə] *f* (*-; -n*) elite
**Ellbogen** ['ɛl-] *m* ANAT elbow
**Elster** ['ɛlstɐ] *f* (*-; -n*) ZO magpie
**elterlich** ['ɛltɐlɪç] *adj* parental
**Eltern** ['ɛltɐn] *pl* parents
**'Elternhaus** *n* (one's parents') home
**'elternlos** *adj* orphan(ed)
**'Eltern|teil** *m* parent; **~vertretung** *f* *appr* Parent-Teacher Association
**Email** [e'mai] *n* (*-s; -s*), **Emaille** [e'maljə] *f* (*-; -n*) enamel
**Emanze** [e'mantsə] F *f* (*-; -n*) women's libber; **Emanzipation** [emantsipa'tsjo:n] *f* (*-; -en*) emancipation; women's lib(eration); **emanzipieren** [emantsi'pi:rən] *v/refl* (*no -ge-, h*) become emancipated
**Embargo** [ɛm'bargo] *n* (*-s; -s*) ECON embargo

**Embolie** [ɛmbo'li:] *f* (-; *-n*) MED embolism

**Embryo** ['ɛmbryo] *m* (*-s*; *-en* [ɛmbry'o:nən]) BIOL embryo

**Emigrant** [emi'grant] *m* (*-en*; *-en*), **Emi'grantin** *f* (-; *-nen*) emigrant, *esp* POL refugee; **Emigration** [emigra'tsjo:n] *f* (-; *-en*) emigration; ***in der* ~** in exile; **emigrieren** [emi'gri:rən] *v/i* (*no -ge-*, *sein*) emigrate

**Emission** [emɪ'sjo:n] *f* (-; *-en*) PHYS emission; ECON issue

**empfahl** [ɛm'pfa:l] *pret of* ***empfehlen***

**Empfang** [ɛm'pfaŋ] *m* (-[*e*]*s*; *Empfänge* [ɛm'pfɛŋə]) reception (*a. radio, hotel*), welcome; receipt (***nach***, ***bei*** on)

**emp'fangen** *v/t* (*irr*, ***fangen***, *no -ge-*, *h*) receive; welcome; **Emp'fänger(in)** (*-s*; *-/-*; *-nen*) receiver (*m a. radio*); addressee

**emp'fänglich** *adj* susceptible (***für*** to)

**Empfängnis** [ɛm'pfɛŋnɪs] *f* (-; *no pl*) MED conception; **~verhütung** *f* MED contraception, birth control

**Emp'fangs|bescheinigung** *f* receipt; **~dame** *f* receptionist

**empfehlen** [ɛm'pfe:lən] *v/t* (*irr*, *no -ge-*, *h*) recommend; **emp'fehlenswert** *adj* advisable; **Emp'fehlung** *f* (-; *-en*) recommendation

**empfinden** [ɛm'pfɪndən] *v/t* (*irr*, ***finden***, *no -ge-*, *h*) feel (***als*** ... to be ...); **empfindlich** [ɛm'pfɪntlɪç] *adj* sensitive (***für***, ***gegen*** to) (*a.* PHOT, CHEM); tender, delicate; touchy; irritable (*a.* MED); severe (*punishment etc*); ***~e Stelle*** sore spot

**Emp'findlichkeit** *f* (-; *-en*) sensitivity; PHOT speed; delicacy; touchiness

**empfindsam** [ɛm'pfɪntza:m] *adj* sensitive

**Emp'findung** *f* (-; *-en*) sensation; perception; feeling, emotion

**empfohlen** [ɛm'pfo:lən] *pp of* ***empfehlen***

**empor** [ɛm'po:ɐ] *adv* up, upward(s)

**empören** [ɛm'pø:rən] *v/t* (*no -ge-*, *h*) outrage; shock; ***sich* ~** (***über*** *acc*) be outraged *or* shocked (at); **~d** *adj* shocking, outrageous

**Em'porkömmling** [-kœmlɪŋ] *contp m* (*-s*; *-e*) upstart

**empört** [ɛm'pø:ɐt] *adj* indignant (***über*** *acc* at), shocked (at); **Em'pörung** *f* (-; *no pl*) indignation

**emsig** ['ɛmzɪç] *adj* busy; **'Emsigkeit** *f* (-; *no pl*) activity

**Ende** ['ɛndə] *n* (*-s*; *no pl*) end; *film*: ending; ***am* ~** at the end; in the end, finally; ***zu* ~** over; *time*: up; ***zu* ~ *gehen*** come to an end; ***zu* ~ *lesen*** finish reading; ***er ist* ~ *zwanzig*** he is in his late twenties; **~ *Mai*** at the end of May; **~ *der achtziger Jahre*** in the late eighties; *radio*: **~!** over!; **'enden** *v/i* (*ge-*, *h*) (come to an) end; stop, finish; F **~ *als*** end up as

**'Endergebnis** *n* final result

**'endgültig** *adj* final, definitive

**Endlagerung** ['ɛnt-] *f* final disposal (*of radioactive waste*)

**'endlich** *adv* finally, at last

**'endlos** *adj* endless

**'End|runde** *f*, **~spiel** *n* SPORT final(s); **~spurt** *m* SPORT final spurt (*a. fig*); **~stati,on** *f* RAIL terminus, terminal; **~summe** *f* (sum) total

**'Endung** *f* (-; *-en*) LING ending

**Energie** [enɛr'gi:] *f* (-; *-n*) energy; TECH, ELECTR power

**ener'giebewusst** *adj* energy-conscious

**Ener'giekrise** *f* energy crisis

**ener'gielos** *adj* lacking in energy

**Ener'gie|quelle** *f* source of energy; **~sparen** *n* energy saving, conservation of energy; **~versorgung** *f* power supply

**energisch** [e'nɛrgɪʃ] *adj* energetic, vigorous

**eng** [ɛŋ] *adj* narrow; tight; cramped; *fig* close; **~ *beieinander*** close(ly) together

**Engagement** [ãgaʒə'mã:] *n* (*-s*; *-s*) THEA *etc* engagement; POL commitment; **engagieren** [ãga'ʒi:rən] *v/t* (*no -ge-*, *h*) engage; ***sich* ~ *für*** be very involved in; **engagiert** [ãga'ʒi:ɐt] *adj* involved, committed

**Enge** ['ɛŋə] *f* (-; *no pl*) narrowness; cramped conditions; ***in die* ~ *treiben*** drive into a corner

**Engel** ['ɛŋəl] *m* (*-s*; -) angel

**'England** England; **Engländer** ['ɛŋlɛndɐ] *m* (*-s*; -) Englishman; ***die* ~** *pl* the English; **Engländerin** ['ɛŋlɛndərɪn] *f* (-; *-nen*) Englishwoman

**'englisch** *adj* English; ***auf Englisch*** in English

**'Englischunterricht** *m* English lesson(s) *or* class(es); teaching of English

**'Engpass** *m* bottleneck (*a. fig*)
**'engstirnig** [-ʃtɪrnɪç] *adj* narrow-minded
**Enkel** ['ɛŋkəl] *m* (*-s*; -) grandchild; grandson
**'Enkelin** *f* (-; *-nen*) granddaughter
**enorm** [e'nɔrm] *adj* enormous; F terrific
**Ensemble** [ã'sã:bl] *n* (*-s*; *-s*) THEA company; cast
**entarten** [ɛnt'ʔa:ʁtən] *v/i* (*no -ge-, sein*), **ent'artet** *adj* degenerate; **Ent'artung** *f* (-; *-en*) degeneration
**entbehren** [ɛnt'be:rən] *v/t* (*no -ge-, h*) do without; spare; miss; **entbehrlich** [ɛnt'be:ʁlɪç] *adj* dispensable; superfluous; **Ent'behrung** *f* (-; *-en*) want, privation
**ent'binden** (*irr*, ***binden***, *no -ge-, h*) **1.** *v/i* MED have the baby; **2.** *v/t*: ***j-n ~ von*** *fig* relieve s.o. of; ***entbunden werden von*** MED give birth to
**Ent'bindung** *f* (-; *-en*) MED delivery
**Ent'bindungsstati,on** *f* MED maternity ward
**entblößen** [ɛnt'blø:sən] *v/t* (*no -ge-, h*) bare, uncover
**ent'decken** *v/t* (*no -ge-, h*) discover
**Ent'decker** *m* (*-s*; -), **Ent'deckerin** *f* (-; *-nen*) discoverer
**Ent'deckung** *f* (-; *-en*) discovery
**Ente** ['ɛntə] *f* (-; *-n*) ZO duck; F *fig* hoax
**ent'ehren** *v/t* (*no -ge-, h*) dishono(u)r
**enteignen** [ɛnt'ʔaignən] *v/t* (*no -ge-, h*) expropriate; dispossess *s.o.*
**Ent'eignung** *f* (-; *-en*) expropriation; dispossession
**ent'erben** *v/t* (*no -ge-, h*) disinherit
**entern** ['ɛntɐn] *v/t* (*ge-, h*) MAR board
**ent|fachen** [ɛnt'faxən] *v/t* (*no -ge-, h*) kindle, *fig a.* rouse; **~fallen** *v/i* (*irr*, ***fallen***, *no -ge-, sein*) be cancelled; ***~ auf*** (*acc*) fall to s.o.('s share); ***es ist mir ~*** it has slipped my memory; **~falten** *v/t* (*no -ge-, h*) unfold; *fig* develop; ***sich ~*** unfold; *fig* develop (**zu** into)
**entfernen** [ɛnt'fɛrnən] *v/t* (*no -ge-, h*) remove (*a. fig*); ***sich ~*** leave; **ent'fernt** *adj* distant (*a. fig*); ***weit*** (***zehn Meilen***) ~ far (10 miles) away; **Ent'fernung** *f* (-; *-en*) distance; removal
**Ent'fernungsmesser** *m* (*-s*; -) PHOT range finder
**ent'flammbar** *adj* (in)flammable
**entfremden** [ɛnt'frɛmdən] *v/t* (*no -ge-, h*) estrange (*dat* from); **Ent'fremdung** *f* (-; *-en*) estrangement, alienation
**ent'führen** *v/t* (*no -ge-, h*) kidnap; AVIAT hijack; **Ent'führer** *m* (*-s*; -) kidnapper; AVIAT hijacker; **Ent'führung** *f* (-; *-en*) kidnapping; AVIAT hijacking
**ent'gegen** *prp* (*dat*) *and adv* contrary to; toward(s); **~gehen** *v/i* (*irr*, ***gehen***, *sep, -ge-, sein*) go to meet
**ent'gegengesetzt** *adj* opposite
**ent'gegenkommen** *v/i* (*irr*, ***kommen***, *sep, -ge-, sein*) come to meet; *fig* ***j-m ~*** meet s.o. halfway; **~d** *fig adj* obliging
**ent'gegen|nehmen** *v/t* (*irr*, ***nehmen***, *sep, -ge-, h*) accept, receive; **~sehen** *v/i* (*irr*, ***sehen***, *sep, -ge-, h*) await; look forward to *s.th.*; **~setzen** *v/t* (*sep, -ge-, h*) ***j-m Widerstand ~*** put up resistance to s.o.; **~treten** *v/i* (*irr*, ***treten***, *sep, -ge-, sein*) walk towards; oppose; face
**entgegnen** [ɛnt'ge:gnən] *v/i* (*no -ge-, h*) reply, answer; retort
**Ent'gegnung** *f* (-; *-en*) reply; retort
**ent'gehen** *v/i* (*irr*, ***gehen***, *no -ge-, sein*) escape; miss
**entgeistert** [ɛnt'gaistɐt] *adj* aghast
**Entgelt** [ɛnt'gɛlt] *n* (*-[e]s*; *-e*) remuneration; fee
**ent|giften** [ɛnt'gɪftən] *v/t* (*no -ge-, h*) decontaminate; **~gleisen** [ɛnt'glaizən] *v/i* (*no -ge-, sein*) RAIL be derailed; *fig* blunder; **~'gleiten** *fig v/i* (*irr*, ***gleiten***, *no -ge-, sein*) get out of control; **~gräten** [ɛnt'grɛ:tən] *v/t* (*no -ge-, h*) bone, fil(l)et
**ent'halten** *v/t* (*irr*, ***halten***, *no -ge-, h*) contain, hold; include; ***sich ~*** (*gen*) abstain *or* refrain from; **ent'haltsam** *adj* abstinent; moderate; **Ent'haltsamkeit** *f* (-; *no pl*) abstinence; moderation
**Ent'haltung** *f* (-; *-en*) abstention
**ent'härten** *v/t* (*no -ge-, h*) soften
**enthaupten** [ɛnt'hauptən] *v/t* (*no -ge-, h*) behead, decapitate
**ent'hüllen** *v/t* (*no -ge-, h*) uncover; unveil; *fig* reveal, disclose; **Ent'hüllung** *f* (-; *-en*) unveiling; *fig* revelation, disclosure
**Enthusiasmus** [ɛntu'zjasmʊs] *m* (-; *no pl*) enthusiasm; **Enthusiast(in)** [-'zjast(ɪn)] (*-en*; *-en*/-; *-nen*) enthusiast; *film*, SPORT F fan; **enthusi'astisch** *adj* enthusiastic
**ent|'kleiden** *v/t and v/refl* (*no -ge-, h*)

undress, strip; **~'kommen** *v/i* (*irr*, ***kommen***, *no -ge-*, *sein*) escape (*dat* from); **~'korken** *v/t* (*no -ge-*, *h*) uncork
**entkräften** [ɛnt'krɛftən] *v/t* (*no -ge-*, *h*) weaken (*a. fig*); **Ent'kräftung** *f* (-; *-en*) weakening, exhaustion
**ent'laden** *v/t* (*irr*, ***laden***, *no -ge-*, *h*) unload; *esp* ELECTR discharge; ***sich ~*** *esp* ELECTR discharge; *fig* explode
**Ent'ladung** *f* (-; *-en*) unloading; *esp* ELECTR discharge; *fig* explosion
**ent'lang** *prp* (*dat*) *and adv* along; ***hier ~, bitte!*** this way, please!; ***die Straße*** *etc* ~ along the street *etc*
**entlarven** [ɛnt'larfən] *v/t* (*no -ge-*, *h*) unmask, expose
**ent'lassen** *v/t* (*irr*, ***lassen***, *no -ge-*, *h*) dismiss, F fire, give *s.o.* the sack; MED discharge; JUR release
**Ent'lassung** *f* (-; *-en*) dismissal; MED discharge; JUR release
**ent'lasten** *v/t* (*no -ge-*, *h*) relieve *s.o.* of some of his work; JUR exonerate, clear *s.o.* of a charge; ***den Verkehr ~*** relieve the traffic congestion; **Ent'lastung** *f* (-; *-en*) relief; JUR exoneration
**Ent'lastungszeuge** *m* JUR witness for the defense (*Br* defence)
**ent'laufen** *v/i* (*irr*, ***laufen***, *no -ge-*, *sein*) run away (*dat* from)
**ent'legen** *adj* remote, distant
**ent|'locken** *v/t* (*no -ge-*, *h*) draw, elicit (*dat* from); **~'lohnen** *v/t* (*no -ge-*, *h*) pay (off); **~'lüften** *v/t* (*no -ge-*, *h*) ventilate; **~machten** [ɛnt'maxtən] *v/t* (*no -ge-*, *h*) deprive *s.o.* of *his* power; **~militarisieren** [ɛntmilitari'ziːrən] *v/t* (*no -ge-*, *h*) demilitarize; **~mündigen** [ɛnt'mʏndɪgən] *v/t* (*no -ge-*, *h*) JUR place under disability; **~mutigen** [ɛnt'muːtɪgən] *v/t* (*no -ge-*, *h*) discourage; **~'nehmen** *v/t* (*irr*, ***nehmen***, *no -ge-*, *h*) take (*dat* from); ***~ aus*** (with)draw from; *fig* gather *or* learn from; **~'puppen** *v/refl* (*no -ge-*, *h*) ***sich ~ als*** turn out to be; **~'rahmen** *v/t* (*no -ge-*, *h*) skim; **~'reißen** *v/t* (*irr*, ***reißen***, *no -ge-*, *h*) snatch (away) (*dat* from); **~'rinnen** *v/i* (*irr*, ***rinnen***, *no -ge-*, *sein*) escape (*dat* from); **~'rollen** *v/t* (*no -ge-*, *h*) unroll
**ent'rüsten** *v/t* (*no -ge-*, *h*) fill with indignation; ***sich ~*** become indignant (***über*** *acc* at *s.th.*, with *s.o.*); **ent'rüstet** *adj* indignant (***über*** *acc* at *s.th.*, with *s.o.*); **Ent'rüstung** *f* (-; *-en*) indignation
**Entsafter** [ɛnt'zaftɐ] *m* (*-s*; -) juice extractor
**ent'salzen** *v/t* (*no -ge-*, *h*) desalinize
**ent'schädigen** *v/t* (*no -ge-*, *h*) compensate; **Ent'schädigung** *f* (-; *-en*) compensation
**ent'schärfen** *v/t* (*no -ge-*, *h*) defuse (*a. fig*)
**ent'scheiden** *v/t and v/i and v/refl* (*irr*, ***scheiden***, *no -ge-*, *h*) decide (***für*** on, in favo[u]r of; ***gegen*** against); settle; ***er kann sich nicht ~*** he can't make up his mind; **~d** *adj* decisive; crucial
**Ent'scheidung** *f* (-; *-en*) decision
**entschieden** [ɛnt'ʃiːdən] *adj* decided, determined, resolute; ***~ dafür*** strongly in favo(u)r of it; **Ent'schiedenheit** *f* (-; *no pl*) determination
**ent'schließen** *v/refl* (*irr*, ***schließen***, *no -ge-*, *h*) decide, determine, make up one's mind; **Ent'schließung** *f* (-; *-en*) POL resolution
**entschlossen** [ɛnt'ʃlɔsən] *adj* determined, resolute; **Ent'schlossenheit** *f* (-; *no pl*) determination, resoluteness
**Ent'schluss** *m* decision, resolution
**entschlüsseln** [ɛnt'ʃlʏsəln] *v/t* (*no -ge-*, *h*) decipher, decode
**entschuldigen** [ɛnt'ʃʊldɪgən] *v/t* (*no -ge-*, *h*) excuse; ***sich ~*** apologize (***bei*** to; ***für*** for); excuse o.s.; ***~ Sie!*** (I'm) sorry!; excuse me!; **Ent'schuldigung** *f* (-; *-en*) excuse; apology; ***um ~ bitten*** apologize; ***~!*** (I'm) sorry!; excuse me!
**ent'setzen** *v/t* (*no -ge-*, *h*) shock; horrify; **Ent'setzen** *n* (*-s*; *no pl*) horror, terror; **ent'setzlich** *adj* horrible, dreadful, terrible; atrocious; **ent'setzt** *adj* shocked; horrified
**ent|'sichern** *v/t* (*no -ge-*, *h*) release the safety catch of; **~'sinnen** *v/refl* (*irr*, ***sinnen***, *no -ge-*, *h*) remember, recall
**ent'sorgen** *v/t* (*no -ge-*, *h*) dispose of
**Ent'sorgung** *f* (-; *-en*) (waste) disposal
**ent'spannen** *v/t and v/refl* (*no -ge-*, *h*) relax; ***sich ~*** *a.* take it easy; *fig* ease (up); **ent'spannt** *adj* relaxed
**Ent'spannung** *f* (-; *-en*) relaxation; POL détente
**ent'spiegelt** *adj* OPT non-glare
**ent'sprechen** *v/i* (*irr*, ***sprechen***, *no -ge-*, *h*) correspond to; answer to *a de-*

*scription*; meet (*requirements etc*); **~d** *adj* corresponding (*dat* to); appropriate
**Ent'sprechung** *f* (-; *-en*) equivalent
**ent'springen** *v/i* (*irr*, **springen**, *no -ge-*, *sein*) *river*: rise
**entstehen** *v/i* (*irr*, **stehen**, *no -ge-*, *sein*) come into being; arise; emerge, develop; **~ aus** originate from
**Ent'stehung** *f* (-; *-en*) origin
**ent'stellen** *v/t* (*no -ge-*, *h*) disfigure, deform; *fig* distort; **Ent'stellung** *f* (-; *-en*) disfigurement, deformation, distortion (*a. fig*)
**entstört** [ɛnt'ʃtøːɐt] *adj* ELECTR interference-free
**ent'täuschen** *v/t* (*no -ge-*, *h*) disappoint; **Ent'täuschung** *f* (-; *-en*) disappointment
**entwaffnen** [ɛnt'vafnən] *v/t* (*no -ge-*, *h*) disarm
**Ent'warnung** *f* all clear (signal)
**ent'wässern** *v/t* (*no -ge-*, *h*) drain; **Ent'wässerung** *f* (-; *-en*) drainage; CHEM dehydration
**'entweder** *cj*: **~ ... oder** either ... or
**ent|'weichen** *v/i* (*irr*, **weichen**, *no -ge-*, *sein*) escape (**aus** from); **~'weihen** *v/t* (*no -ge-*, *h*) desecrate; **~'wenden** *v/t* (*no -ge-*, *h*) pilfer, steal; **~'werfen** *v/t* (*irr*, **werfen**, *no -ge-*, *h*) design; draw up
**ent'werten** *v/t* (*no -ge-*, *h*) lower the value of (*a. fig*); cancel; **Ent'wertung** *f* (-; *-en*) devaluation; cancellation
**ent'wickeln** *v/t and v/refl* (*no -ge-*, *h*) develop (*a.* PHOT) (**zu** into); **Ent'wicklung** *f* (-; *-en*) development, BIOL *a.* evolution; adolescence, age of puberty
**Ent'wicklungs|helfer** *m*, **~helferin** *f* POL, ECON development aid volunteer; Peace Corps volunteer, *Br* VSO worker; **~hilfe** *f* development aid; **~land** *n* POL developing country
**ent|wirren** [ɛnt'vɪrən] *v/t* (*no -ge-*, *h*) disentangle (*a. fig*); **~'wischen** *v/i* (*no -ge-*, *sein*) get away
**ent'würdigend** *adj* degrading
**Ent'wurf** *m* outline, (rough) draft, plan; design; sketch
**ent|'wurzeln** *v/t* (*no -ge-*, *h*) uproot; **~'ziehen** *v/t* (*irr*, **ziehen**, *no -ge-*, *h*) take away (*dat* from); revoke (*license etc*); deprive of *rights etc*; CHEM extract; **sich j-m (e-r Sache) ~** evade s.o. (s.th.)
**Ent'ziehungs|anstalt** *f* substance (*Br* drug) abuse clinic; **~kur** *f* detoxi(fi)cation (treatment), *a.* F drying out
**entziffern** [ɛnt'tsɪfɐn] *v/t* (*no -ge-*, *h*) decipher, make out
**ent'zücken** *v/t* (*no -ge-*, *h*) charm, delight; **Ent'zücken** *n* (*-s*; *no pl*) delight; **ent'zückend** *adj* delightful, charming, F sweet; **ent'zückt** *adj* delighted (**über** *acc*, **von** at, with)
**Ent'zug** *m* withdrawal; revocation
**Ent'zugserscheinung** *f* MED withdrawal symptom
**entzündbar** [ɛnt'tsʏntbaːɐ] *adj* (in-) flammable; **ent'zünden** *v/refl* (*no -ge-*, *h*) catch fire; MED become inflamed; **Ent'zündung** *f* (-; *-en*) MED inflammation
**ent'zwei** *adv* in two, to pieces
**Enzyklopädie** [ɛntsyklopɛ'diː] *f* (-; *-n*) encyclop(a)edia
**Epidemie** [epide'miː] *f* (-; *-n*) MED epidemic (disease)
**Epilog** [epi'loːk] *m* (*-[e]s*; *-e* [epi'loːgə]) epilog, *Br* epilogue
**episch** ['eːpɪʃ] *adj* epic
**Episode** [epi'zoːdə] *f* (-; *-n*) episode
**Epoche** [e'pɔxə] *f* (-; *-n*) epoch, period, era
**Epos** ['eːpɔs] *n* (-; *Epen* ['eːpən]) epic (poem)
**er** [eːɐ] *pers pron* he; it
**Er'achten** *n*: **meines ~s** in my opinion
**Erbanlage** ['ɛrp-] *f* BIOL genes, genetic code
**erbarmen** [ɛɐ'barmən] *v/refl* (*no -ge-*, *h*) **sich j-s ~** take pity on s.o.
**erbärmlich** [ɛɐ'bɛrmlɪç] *adj* pitiful, pitiable; miserable; mean
**er'barmungslos** *adj* pitiless, merciless
**er'bauen** *v/t* (*no -ge-*, *h*) build, construct; **Er'bauer** *m* (*-s*; -) builder, constructor
**er'baulich** *adj* edifying; **Er'bauung** *fig f* (-; *-en*) edification, uplift
**Erbe** ['ɛrbə] **1.** *m* (*-n*; *-n*) heir; **2.** *n* (*-s*; *no pl*) inheritance, heritage
**erben** ['ɛrbən] *v/t* (*ge-*, *h*) inherit
**erbeuten** [ɛɐ'bɔʏtən] *v/t* (*no -ge-*, *h*) MIL capture; *thief*: get away with
**'Erbfaktor** *m* BIOL gene
**Erbin** ['ɛrbɪn] *f* (-; *-nen*) heir, heiress
**er'bitten** *v/t* (*irr*, **bitten**, *no -ge-*, *h*) ask for, request
**erbittert** [ɛɐ'bɪtɐt] *adj* fierce, furious

**'Erbkrankheit** *f* MED hereditary disease
**erblich** ['ɛrplɪç] *adj* hereditary
**er'blicken** *v/t* (*no -ge-, h*) see, catch sight of
**erblinden** [ɛɐ'blɪndən] *v/i* (*no -ge-, sein*) go blind
**er'brechen** *v/t and v/refl* (*irr*, ***brechen***, *no -ge-, h*) MED vomit
**Erbschaft** ['ɛrpʃaft] *f* (-; *-en*) inheritance, heritage
**Erbse** ['ɛrpsə] *f* (-; *-n*) BOT pea; (***grüne***) **~n** green peas
**'Erbstück** *n* heirloom
**Erd|apfel** ['eːɐt-] *Austrian m* potato; **~ball** *m* (-[*e*]*s*; *no pl*) globe; **~beben** *n* (-*s*; -) earthquake; **~beere** *f* BOT strawberry; **~boden** *m* earth, ground
**Erde** ['eːɐdə] *f* (-; *-n*) a) (*no pl*) earth, b) ground, soil; → ***eben***; **'erden** *v/t* (*ge-, h*) ELECTR earth, ground
**erdenklich** [ɛɐ'dɛŋklɪç] *adj* imaginable
**Erd|gas** ['eːɐt-] *n* natural gas; **~geschoss** *n*, **~geschoß** *Austrian n* first (*Br* ground) floor
**er'dichten** *v/t* (*no -ge-, h*) invent, make up; **er'dichtet** *adj* invented, made-up
**erdig** ['eːɐdɪç] *adj* earthy
**'Erd|klumpen** *m* clod, lump of earth; **~kruste** *f* earth's crust; **~kugel** *f* globe; **~kunde** *f* (-; *no pl*) geography; **~leitung** *f* ELECTR ground (*Br* earth) connection; underground pipe(line); **~nuss** *f* BOT peanut; **~öl** *n* (mineral) oil, petroleum; **~reich** *n* ground, earth
**erdreisten** [ɛɐ'draistən] *v/refl* (*no -ge-, h*) F have the nerve
**er'drosseln** *v/t* (*no -ge-, h*) throttle
**er'drücken** *v/t* (*no -ge-, h*) crush (to death); **~d** *fig adj* overwhelming
**'Erd|rutsch** *m* (-[*e*]*s*; *-e*) landslide (*a.* POL); **~teil** *m* GEOGR continent
**er'dulden** *v/t* (*no -ge-, h*) suffer, endure
**'Erdumlaufbahn** *f* earth orbit
**'Erdung** *f* (-; *-en*) ELECTR grounding, *Br* earthing
**'Erdwärme** *f* GEOL geothermal energy
**er'eifern** *v/refl* (*no -ge-, h*) get excited
**ereignen** [ɛɐ'ˀaignən] *v/refl* (*no -ge-, h*) happen, occur; **Ereignis** [ɛɐ'ˀaignɪs] *n* (-*ses*; *-se*) event, occurrence
**er'eignisreich** *adj* eventful
**Erektion** [erɛk'tsjoːn] *f* (-; *-en*) erection
**Eremit** [ere'miːt] *m* (-*en*; *-en*) hermit, anchorite

**er'fahren¹** *v/t* (*irr*, ***fahren***, *no -ge-, h*) hear; learn; experience
**er'fahren²** *adj* experienced
**Er'fahrung** *f* (-; *-en*) (work) experience
**Er'fahrungsaustausch** *m* exchange of experience; **er'fahrungsgemäß** *adv* as experience shows
**er'fassen** *v/t* (*no -ge-, h*) grasp; record, register; cover, include; EDP collect
**er'finden** *v/t* (*irr*, ***finden***, *no -ge-, h*) invent; **Er'finder(in)** (-*s*; -/-; *-nen*) inventor; **erfinderisch** [ɛɐ'fɪndərɪʃ] *adj* inventive; **Er'findung** *f* (-; *-en*) invention; **Er'findungskraft** *f* (-; *no pl*) inventiveness
**Erfolg** [ɛɐ'fɔlk] *m* (-[*e*]*s*; *-e*) success; result; ***viel ~!*** good luck!; ***~ versprechend*** promising; **er'folgen** *v/i* (*no -ge-, sein*) happen, take place; **er'folglos** *adj* unsuccessful; futile; **Er'folglosigkeit** *f* (-; *no pl*) lack of success; **er'folgreich** *adj* successful; **Er'folgserlebnis** *n* sense of achievement
**erforderlich** [ɛɐ'fɔrdɐlɪç] *adj* necessary, required; **er'fordern** *v/t* (*no -ge-, h*) require, demand; **Erfordernis** [ɛɐ'fɔrdɐnɪs] *n* (-*ses*; *-se*) requirement, demand
**er'forschen** *v/t* (*no -ge-, h*) explore; investigate, study; **Er'forscher** *m* explorer; **Er'forschung** *f* exploration
**er'freuen** *v/t* (*no -ge-, h*) please
**erfreulich** [ɛɐ'frɔʏlɪç] *adj* pleasing, pleasant; gratifying
**er'freut** *adj* pleased (***über*** *acc* at, about); ***sehr ~!*** pleased to meet you
**er'frieren** *v/i* (*irr*, ***frieren***, *no -ge-, sein*) freeze to death; **Er'frierung** *f* (-; *-en*) MED frostbite
**er'frischen** *v/t and v/refl* (*no -ge-, h*) refresh (o.s.); **~d** *adj* refreshing
**Er'frischung** *f* (-; *-en*) refreshment
**erfroren** [ɛɐ'froːrən] *adj* frostbitten; BOT killed by frost
**er'füllen** *fig v/t* (*no -ge-, h*) fulfil(l); keep (*promise etc*); serve (*purpose etc*); meet (*requirements etc*); ***~ mit*** fill with; ***sich ~*** be fulfilled, come true; **Er'füllung** *f* (-; *-en*) fulfil(l)ment; ***in ~ gehen*** come true
**ergänzen** [ɛɐ'gɛntsən] *v/t* (*no -ge-, h*) complement (***einander*** each other); supplement, add; **~d** *adj* complementary, supplementary
**Er'gänzung** *f* (-; *-en*) completion; supplement, addition

**ergattern** [ɛɐ'gatɐn] F *v/t* (*no -ge-, h*) (manage to) get hold of
**er'geben** (*irr*, ***geben***, *no -ge-, h*) **1.** *v/t* amount *or* come to; **2.** *v/refl* surrender; *fig* arise; ***sich ~ aus*** result from; ***sich ~ in*** (*acc*) resign o.s. to
**Er'gebenheit** *f* (-; *no pl*) devotion
**Ergebnis** [ɛɐ'ge:pnɪs] *n* (*-ses*; *-se*) result, SPORT *a.* score; outcome
**er'gebnislos** *adj* without result
**er'gehen** *v/i* (*irr*, ***gehen***, *no -ge-, sein*) *order etc*: be issued (***an*** *acc* to); ***wie ist es dir ergangen?*** how did things go with you?; ***et. über sich ~ lassen*** (patiently) endure s.th.
**ergiebig** [ɛɐ'gi:bɪç] *adj* productive, rich; **Er'giebigkeit** *f* (-; *no pl*) (high) yield; productiveness
**er'gießen** *v/refl* (*irr*, ***gießen***, *no -ge-, h*) ***sich ~ über*** (*acc*) pour down on
**er'grauen** *v/i* (*no -ge-, sein*) turn gray (*Br* grey)
**er'greifen** *v/t* (*irr*, ***greifen***, *no -ge-, h*) seize, grasp, take hold of; take (*measures etc*); take up; *fig* move, touch
**ergriffen** [ɛɐ'grɪfən] *fig adj* moved
**Er'griffenheit** *f* (-; *no pl*) emotion
**er'gründen** *v/t* (*no -ge-, h*) find out, fathom
**er'haben** *adj* raised, elevated; *fig* sublime; ***~ sein über*** (*acc*) be above
**er'halten**[1] *v/t* (*irr*, ***halten***, *no -ge-, h*) get, receive; keep, preserve; protect; support, maintain (*family etc*)
**er'halten**[2] *adj*: ***gut ~*** in good condition
**erhältlich** [ɛɐ'hɛltlɪç] *adj* obtainable, available
**Er'haltung** *f* (-; *no pl*) preservation; upkeep
**er'hängen** *v/t* (*no -ge-, h*) hang (***sich*** o.s.)
**er'heben** *v/t* (*irr*, ***heben***, *no -ge-, h*) raise (*a. voice*), lift; ***sich ~*** rise up (***gegen*** against)
**erheblich** [ɛɐ'he:plɪç] *adj* considerable
**Er'hebung** *f* (-; *-en*) survey; revolt
**erheitern** [ɛɐ'haitɐn] *v/t* (*no -ge-, h*) cheer up, amuse; **erhellen** [ɛɐ'hɛlən] *v/t* (*no -ge-, h*) light up; *fig* throw light upon; **erhitzen** [ɛɐ'hɪtsən] *v/t* (*no -ge-, h*) heat; ***sich ~*** get hot; **er'hoffen** *v/t* (*no -ge-, h*) hope for
**erhöhen** [ɛɐ'hø:ən] *v/t* (*no -ge-, h*) raise; increase; **Er'höhung** *f* (-; *-en*) increase
**er'holen** *v/refl* (*no -ge-, h*) recover; relax, rest; **erholsam** [ɛɐ'ho:lza:m] *adj* restful, relaxing; **Er'holung** *f* (-; *no pl*) recovery; relaxation
**Er'holungsheim** *n* rest home
**erinnern** [ɛɐ'ʔɪnɐn] *v/t* (*no -ge-, h*) ***j-n ~ an*** (*acc*) remind s.o. of; ***sich ~ an*** (*acc*) remember, recall; **Erinnerung** [ɛɐ'ɪnərʊŋ] *f* (-; *-en*) memory (***an*** *acc* of); remembrance, souvenir; keepsake; ***zur ~ an*** (*acc*) in memory of
**erkalten** [ɛɐ'kaltən] *v/i* (*no -ge-, sein*) cool down (*a. fig*)
**erkälten** [ɛɐ'kɛltən] *v/refl* (*no -ge-, h*) ***sich ~*** catch (a) cold; (***stark***) ***erkältet sein*** have a (bad) cold; **Er'kältung** *f* (-; *-en*) cold
**erkennbar** [ɛɐ'kɛnba:ɐ] *adj* recognizable; **er'kennen** *v/t* (*irr*, ***kennen***, *no -ge-, h*) recognize (***an*** *dat* by), know (by); see, realize; **er'kenntlich** *adj*: ***sich (j-m) ~ zeigen*** show (s.o.) one's gratitude; **Er'kenntnis** *f* (-; *-se*) realization; discovery; *pl* findings
**Er'kennungs|dienst** *m* (police) records department; **~melo,die** *f* signature tune; **~zeichen** *n* badge; AVIAT markings
**Erker** ['ɛrkɐ] *m* (*-s*; -) ARCH bay; **~fenster** *n* ARCH bay window
**er'klären** *v/t* (*no -ge-, h*) explain (***j-m*** to s.o.); declare; ***j-n*** (*offiziell*) ***für ... ~*** pronounce s.o. ...; **~d** *adj* explanatory
**erklärlich** [ɛɐ'klɛ:ɐlɪç] *adj* explainable; **er'klärt** *adj* declared; **Er'klärung** *f* (-; *-en*) explanation; declaration; definition; ***e-e ~ abgeben*** make a statement
**er'klingen** *v/i* (*irr*, ***klingen***, *no -ge-, sein*) (re)sound, ring (out)
**erkranken** [ɛɐ'kraŋkən] *v/i* (*no -ge-, sein*) fall ill, get sick; ***~ an*** (*dat*) get; **Er'krankung** *f* (-; *-en*) illness, sickness
**erkunden** [ɛɐ'kʊndən] *v/t* (*no -ge-, h*) explore
**erkundigen** [ɛɐ'kʊndɪgən] *v/refl* (*no -ge-, h*) inquire (***nach*** about *s.th.*; after *s.o.*); make inquiries (about); ***sich*** (***bei j-m***) ***nach dem Weg ~*** ask (s.o.) the way; **Er'kundigung** *f* (-; *-en*) inquiry
**Er'kundung** *f* (-; *-en*) exploration; MIL reconnaissance
**Erlagschein** [ɛɐ'la:k-] *Austrian m* money-order form
**er'lahmen** *v/i* (*no -ge-, sein*) flag

**Erlass** [ɛɐ'las] *m* (*-es*; *-e*) decree; JUR remission; **er'lassen** *v/t* (*irr*, ***lassen***, *no -ge-*, *h*) issue; enact (*bill etc*); ***j-m et.*** ~ release s.o. from s.th.
**erlauben** [ɛɐ'laubən] *v/t* (*no -ge-*, *h*) allow, permit; ***sich et.*** ~ permit o.s. (*or* dare) to do s.th.; treat o.s. to s.th.
**Erlaubnis** [ɛɐ'laupnɪs] *f* (-; *no pl*) permission; authority; ***um ~ bitten*** ask s.o.'s permission; **~schein** *m* permit
**erläutern** [ɛɐ'lɔʏtɐn] *v/t* (*no -ge-*, *h*) explain, illustrate; **Er'läuterung** *f* (-; *-en*) explanation; annotation
**Erle** ['ɛrlə] *f* (-, *-n*) BOT alder
**er'leben** *v/t* (*no -ge-*, *h*) experience; go through; see; have; ***das werden wir nicht mehr*** ~ we won't live to see that
**Erlebnis** [ɛɐ'le:pnɪs] *n* (*-ses*; *-se*) experience; adventure
**er'lebnisreich** *adj* eventful
**erledigen** [ɛɐ'le:dɪgən] *v/t* (*no -ge-*, *h*) take care of, do, handle; settle; F finish *s.o.* (*a.* SPORT); do *s.o.* in; **erledigt** [ɛɐ'le:dɪçt] *adj* finished, settled; F worn out; F ***der ist ~!*** he is done for
**Er'ledigung** *f* (-; *-en*) a) (*no pl*) settlement, b) *pl* things to do, shopping
**er'legen** *v/t* (*no -ge-*, *h*) HUNT shoot
**erleichtern** [ɛɐ'laɪçtɐn] *v/t* (*no -ge-*, *h*) ease, relieve; **er'leichtert** *adj* relieved; **Er'leichterung** [-tərʊŋ] *f* (-; *no pl*) relief (***über*** *acc* at)
**er'leiden** *v/t* (*irr*, ***leiden***, *no -ge-*, *h*) suffer
**er'lesen** *adj* choice, select
**er'leuchten** *v/t* (*no -ge-*, *h*) illuminate
**er'liegen** *v/i* (*irr*, ***liegen***, *no -ge-*, *sein*) succumb to
**Er'liegen** *n*: ***zum ~ kommen*** (***bringen***) come (bring) to a standstill
**erlogen** [ɛɐ'lo:gən] *adj* false; ~ ***sein*** be a lie
**Erlös** [ɛɐ'lø:s] *m* (*-es*; *-e*) proceeds; profit(s)
**erlosch** [ɛɐ'lɔʃ] *pret of* ***erlöschen***
**erloschen** [ɛɐ'lɔʃən] **1.** *pp of* ***erlöschen***; **2.** *adj* extinct (*volcano*)
**er'löschen** *v/i* (*irr*, *no -ge-*, *sein*) go out; *fig* die; JUR lapse, expire
**er'lösen** *v/t* (*no -ge-*, *h*) deliver, free (*both*: ***von*** from); **Erlöser** [ɛɐ'lø:zɐ] *m* (*-s*; *no pl*) REL Savio(u)r; **Er'lösung** *f* (-; *no pl*) REL salvation; relief
**ermächtigen** [ɛɐ'mɛçtɪgən] *v/t* (*no -ge-*, *h*) authorize; **Er'mächtigung** *f* (-; *-en*) authorization; authority
**er'mahnen** *v/t* (*no -ge-*, *h*) admonish; reprove, warn (*a.* SPORT)
**Er'mahnung** *f* (-; *-en*) admonition; warning; *esp* SPORT (first) caution
**Er'mangelung** *f*: ***in ~*** (*gen*) for want of
**ermäßigt** [ɛɐ'mɛ:sɪçt] *adj* reduced, cut; **Er'mäßigung** *f* (-; *-en*) reduction, cut
**er'messen** *v/t* (*irr*, ***messen***, *no -ge-*, *h*) assess; judge; **Er'messen** *n* (*-s*; *no pl*) discretion; ***nach eigenem*** ~ at one's own discretion
**er'mitteln** (*no -ge- h*) **1.** *v/t* find out; determine; **2.** *v/i esp* JUR investigate; **Er'mittlung** *f* (-; *-en*) finding; JUR investigation
**er'möglichen** *v/t* (*no -ge-*, *h*) make possible
**er'morden** *v/t* (*no -ge-*, *h*) murder; *esp* POL assassinate; **Er'mordung** *f* (-; *-en*) murder; *esp* POL assassination
**ermüden** [ɛɐ'my:dən] (*no -ge-*) **1.** *v/t* (*h*) tire, fatigue; **2.** *v/i* (*sein*) tire, get tired, fatigue (*a.* TECH); **Er'müdung** *f* (-; *no pl*) fatigue, tiredness
**er'muntern** [ɛɐ'mʊntɐn] *v/t* (*no -ge-*, *h*) encourage; stimulate; **Er'munterung** *f* (-; *-en*) encouragement; incentive
**ermutigen** [ɛɐ'mu:tɪgən] *v/t* (*no -ge-*, *h*) encourage; **~d** *adj* encouraging
**Er'mutigung** *f* (-; *-en*) encouragement
**er'nähren** *v/t* (*no -ge-*, *h*) feed; support (*family etc*); ***sich ~ von*** live on; **Er'nährer** *m* (*-s*; -) breadwinner, supporter; **Er'nährung** *f* (-; *no pl*) nutrition, food, diet
**er'nennen** *v/t* (*irr*, ***nennen***, *no -ge-*, *h*) ***j-n ~ zu*** appoint s.o. (to be)
**Er'nennung** *f* (-; *-en*) appointment
**erneuern** [ɛɐ'nɔʏɐn] *v/t* (*no -ge-*, *h*) renew; **Er'neuerung** *f* (-; *-en*) renewal
**er'neut 1.** *adj* renewed **2.** *adv* once more
**erniedrigen** [ɛɐ'ni:drɪgən] *v/t* (*no -ge-*, *h*) humiliate; ***sich*** ~ degrade o.s.
**Er'niedrigung** *f* (-; *-en*) humiliation
**ernst** [ɛrnst] *adj* serious, earnest; ***~ nehmen*** take *s.o. or s.th.* seriously
**Ernst** *m* (*-es*; *no pl*) seriousness, earnest; ***im ~(?)*** seriously(?); ***ist das dein ~?*** are you serious?
**'ernsthaft, 'ernstlich** *adj* serious
**Ernte** ['ɛrntə] *f* (-; *-n*) harvest; crop(s)

**'Erntedankfest** *n* Thanksgiving (Day), *Br* harvest festival
**'ernten** *v/t* (*ge-*, *h*) harvest, reap (*a. fig*)
**er'nüchtern** *v/t* (*no -ge-*, *h*) sober, *fig a.* disillusion; **Er'nüchterung** *f* (-; *-en*) sobering up; *fig* disillusionment
**Eroberer** [ɛɐ'ʔoːbərɐ] *m* (*-s*; -) conqueror; **erobern** [ɛɐ'ʔoːbɐn] *v/t* (*no -ge-*, *h*) conquer; **Er'oberung** *f* (-; *-en*) conquest (*a. fig*)
**er'öffnen** *v/t* (*no -ge-*, *h*) open; inaugurate; disclose *s.th.* (***j-m*** to s.o.)
**Er'öffnung** *f* (-; *-en*) opening; inauguration; disclosure
**erörtern** [ɛɐ'ʔœrtɐn] *v/t* (*no -ge-*, *h*) discuss; **Er'örterung** *f* (-; *-en*) discussion
**Erotik** [e'roːtɪk] *f* (-; *no pl*) eroticism
**erotisch** [e'roːtɪʃ] *adj* erotic
**er'pressen** *v/t* (*no -ge-*, *h*) blackmail; extort; **Er'presser(in)** (*-s*; -/-; *-nen*) blackmailer; **Er'pressung** *f* (-; *-en*) blackmail(ing); extortion
**er'proben** *v/t* (*no -ge-*, *h*) try, test
**er'raten** *v/t* (*irr*, ***raten***, *no -ge-*, *h*) guess
**er'rechnen** *v/t* (*no -ge-*, *h*) calculate, work *s.th.* out
**erregbar** [ɛɐ'reːkbaːɐ] *adj* excitable; irritable
**er'regen** *v/t* (*no -ge-*, *h*) excite, *sexually*: *a.* arouse; *fig* rouse; cause; ***sich*** ~ get excited; **~d** *adj* exciting, thrilling
**Er'reger** *m* (*-s*; -) MED germ, virus
**Er'regung** *f* (-; *-en*) excitement
**erreichbar** [ɛɐ'raiçbaːɐ] *adj* within reach (*a. fig*); available; ***leicht*** ~ within easy reach; ***nicht*** ~ out of reach; not available; **er'reichen** *v/t* (*no -ge-*, *h*) reach; catch (*train etc*); ***es*** **~, *dass ...*** succeed in *doing s.th.*; ***et.*** ~ get somewhere; ***telefonisch zu ~ sein*** have a (*Br* be on the) phone
**er'richten** *v/t* (*no -ge-*, *h*) put up, erect; *fig* found, *esp* ECON set up
**Er'richtung** *f* (-; *-en*) erection; *fig* establishment
**er'ringen** *v/t* (*irr*, ***ringen***, *no -ge-*, *h*) win, gain; achieve
**er'röten** *v/i* (*no -ge-*, *sein*) blush
**Errungenschaft** [ɛɐ'rʊŋənʃaft] *f* (-; *-en*) achievement; ***m-e neueste*** ~ my latest acquisition
**Ersatz** [ɛɐ'zats] *m* (*-es*; *no pl*) replacement; substitute; surrogate; compensation; damages; ***als ~ für*** in exchange for; **~dienst** *m* → ***Zivildienst***; **~mann** *m* (*-[e]s*; *-leute*) substitute (*a.* SPORT); **~mine** *f* refill; **~reifen** *m* MOT spare tire (*Br* tyre); **~spieler** *m* SPORT substitute; **~teil** *n* TECH spare part
**er'schaffen** *v/t* (*irr*, ***schaffen***, *no -ge-*, *h*) create
**er'schallen** *v/i* ([*irr*, ***schallen***,] *no -ge-*, *sein*) (re)sound, ring (out)
**er'scheinen** *v/i* (*irr*, ***scheinen***, *no -ge-*, *sein*) appear, F turn up; be published; **Er'scheinen** *n* (*-s*; *no pl*) appearance; publication; **Er'scheinung** *f* (-; *-en*) appearance; apparition; phenomenon
**er'schießen** *v/t* (*irr*, ***schießen***, *no -ge-*, *h*) shoot (dead); **erschlaffen** [ɛɐ'ʃlafən] *v/i* (*no -ge-*, *sein*) go limp; *fig* weaken; **er'schlagen** *v/t* (*irr*, ***schlagen***, *no -ge-*, *h*) kill; **er'schließen** *v/t* (*irr*, ***schließen***, *no -ge-*, *h*) open up; develop
**erschollen** [ɛɐ'ʃɔlən] *pp of* ***erschallen***
**er'schöpfen** *v/t* (*no -ge-*, *h*) exhaust; **er'schöpft** *adj* exhausted
**Er'schöpfung** *f* (-; *no pl*) exhaustion
**erschrak** [ɛɐ'ʃraːk] *pret of* ***erschrecken*** 2
**er'schrecken 1.** *v/t* (*no -ge-*, *h*) frighten, scare; **2.** *v/i* (*irr*, *no -ge-*, *sein*) be frightened (***über*** *acc* at); **~d** *adj* alarming; terrible
**erschrocken** [ɛɐ'ʃrɔkən] *pp of* ***erschrecken*** 2
**erschüttern** [ɛɐ'ʃʏtɐn] *v/t* (*no -ge-*, *h*) shake; *fig a.* shock; *fig* move
**Er'schütterung** *f* (-; *-en*) shock (*a. fig*); TECH vibration
**erschweren** [ɛɐ'ʃveːrən] *v/t* (*no -ge-*, *h*) make more difficult; aggravate
**er'schwindeln** *v/t* (*no -ge-*, *h*) obtain *s.th.* by fraud; (***sich***) ***et. von j-m*** ~ swindle s.o. out of s.th.
**er'schwingen** *v/t* (*irr*, ***schwingen***, *no -ge-*, *h*) afford; **er'schwinglich** *adj* within one's means, affordable; reasonable (*price*)
**er'sehen** *v/t* (*irr*, ***sehen***, *no -ge-*, *h*) see, learn, gather (*all*: ***aus*** from)
**ersetzbar** [ɛɐ'zɛtsbaːɐ] *adj* replaceable; reparable; **er'setzen** *v/t* (*no -ge-*, *h*) replace (***durch*** by); compensate for; ***j-m et.*** ~ reimburse s.o. for s.th.
**er'sichtlich** *adj* evident, obvious
**er'sparen** *v/t* (*no -ge-*, *h*) save; ***j-m et.*** ~ spare s.o. s.th.

**Ersparnisse** [ɛɐ'ʃpa:ɐnɪsə] *pl* savings
**erst** [e:ɐrst] *adv* first; at first; ~ ***jetzt*** (***gestern***) only now (yesterday); ~ ***nächste Woche*** not before *or* until next week; ***es ist*** ~ ***neun Uhr*** it's only nine o'clock; ***eben*** ~ just (now); ~ ***recht*** all the more; ~ ***recht nicht*** even less; → ***einmal***
**er'starren** *v/i* (*no -ge-*, *sein*) stiffen; *fig* freeze; **er'starrt** *adj* stiff; numb
**erstatten** [ɛɐ'ʃtatən] *v/t* (*no -ge-*, *h*) refund, reimburse (***j-m et.*** s.o. for s.th.); ***Bericht*** ~ (give a) report (***über*** *acc* on); ***Anzeige*** ~ report to the police
**'Erstaufführung** *f* THEA first night *or* performance, premiere, *film*: *a.* first run
**er'staunen** *v/t* (*no -ge-*, *h*) surprise, astonish; **Er'staunen** *n* (*-s*; *no pl*) surprise, astonishment; ***in*** ~ (***ver***)***setzen*** astonish; **er'staunlich** *adj* surprising, astonishing; **er'staunt** *adj* astonished
**'Erstausgabe** *f* first edition
**'erst'beste** *adj* first; any old
**'erste** *adj* first; ***auf den*** ~***n Blick*** at first sight; ***fürs Erste*** for the time being; ***als Erste***(***r***) first; ***zum*** ~***n Mal***(***e***) for the first time; ***am Ersten*** on the first
**er'stechen** *v/t* (*irr*, ***stechen,*** *no -ge-*, *h*) stab
**'erstens** *adv* first(ly), in the first place
**'Erstere:** ***der*** (***die, das***) ~ the former
**er'sticken** *v/t* (*no -ge-*, *h*) *and v/i* (*sein*) choke, suffocate; **Er'stickung** *f* (-; *no pl*) suffocation
**'erst|klassig** [-klasɪç] *adj* first-class, F *a.* super; **~malig** [-ma:lɪç] *adj* first; **~mals** [-ma:ls] *adv* for the first time
**er'streben** *v/t* (*no -ge-*, *h*) strive after
**er'strebenswert** *adj* desirable
**er'strecken** *v/refl* (*no -ge-*, *h*) extend, stretch (***bis***, ***auf*** *acc* to; ***über*** *acc* over); ***sich*** ~ ***über*** (*acc*) *a.* cover
**'Erstschlag** *m* MIL first strike
**er'suchen** *v/t* (*no -ge-*, *h*) request
**er'tappen** *v/t* (*no -ge-*, *h*) catch; → ***Tat***
**er'tönen** *v/i* (*no -ge-*, *sein*) (re)sound
**Ertrag** [ɛɐ'tra:k] *m* (-[*e*]*s*; *Erträge* [ɛɐ'trɛ:gə]) AGR yield, produce, TECH *a.* output; ECON proceeds, returns
**er'tragen** *v/t* (*irr*, ***tragen,*** *no -ge-*, *h*) bear, endure; stand
**erträglich** [ɛɐ'trɛ:klɪç] *adj* bearable, tolerable
**er'tränken** *v/t* (*no -ge-*, *h*) drown
**er'trinken** *v/i* (*irr*, ***trinken,*** *no -ge-*, *sein*) drown
**erübrigen** [ɛɐ'ʔy:brɪgən] *v/t* (*no -ge-*, *h*) spare; ***sich*** ~ be unnecessary
**er'wachen** *v/i* (*no -ge-*, *sein*) wake (up); *esp fig* awake, awaken
**Erw.** ABBR *of* ***Erwachsene***(***r***) adult(s)
**er'wachsen¹** *v/i* (*irr*, ***wachsen,*** *no -ge-*, *sein*) arise (***aus*** from)
**er'wachsen²** *adj* grown-up, adult
**Er'wachsene** *m, f* (*-n*; *-n*) adult; ***nur für*** ~***!*** adults only!; **Er'wachsenenbildung** *f* adult education
**erwägen** [ɛɐ'vɛ:gən] *v/t* (*irr*, ***wägen,*** *no -ge-*, *h*) consider, think *s.th.* over; **Er'wägung** *f* (-; *-en*) consideration; ***in*** ~ ***ziehen*** take into consideration
**erwähnen** [ɛɐ'vɛ:nən] *v/t* (*no -ge-*, *h*) mention; **Er'wähnung** *f* (-; *-en*) mention(ing)
**er'wärmen** *v/t and v/refl* (*no -ge-*, *h*) warm (up); *fig* ***sich*** ~ ***für*** warm to
**Er'wärmung** *f* (-; *-en*) warming up; ~ ***der Erdatmosphäre*** global warming
**er'warten** *v/t* (*no -ge-*, *h*) expect; wait for, await; **Er'wartung** *f* (-; *-en*) expectation, anticipation
**er'wartungsvoll** *adj and adv* full of expectation, expectant(ly)
**er'wecken** *fig v/t* (*no -ge-*, *h*) awaken; arouse; → ***Anschein***
**er'weisen** *v/t* (*irr*, ***weisen,*** *no -ge-*, *h*) do (*service etc*); show (*respect etc*); ***sich*** ~ ***als*** prove to be
**erweitern** [ɛɐ'vaitɐn] *v/t and v/refl* (*no -ge-*, *h*) extend, enlarge; *esp* ECON expand; **Er'weiterung** *f* (-; *-en*) extension, enlargement, expansion
**Erwerb** [ɛɐ'vɛrp] *m* (-[*e*]*s*; *-e*) acquisition; purchase; income; **er'werben** *v/t* (*irr*, ***werben,*** *no -ge-*, *h*) acquire (*a. fig*); purchase
**er'werbs|los** *adj* unemployed; **~tätig** *adj* (gainfully) employed, working; **~unfähig** *adj* unable to work
**Er'werbung** *f* (-; *-en*) acquisition; purchase
**erwidern** [ɛɐ'vi:dɐn] *v/t* (*no -ge-*, *h*) reply, answer; return (*visit etc*)
**Er'widerung** *f* (-; *-en*) reply, answer; return
**er'wischen** *v/t* (*no -ge-*, *h*) catch, get; ***ihn hat's erwischt*** he's had it

**er'wünscht** *adj* desired; desirable; welcome
**er'würgen** *v/t* (*no -ge-, h*) strangle
**Erz** [eːɐts] *n* (*-es; -e*) ore
**er'zählen** *v/t* (*no -ge-, h*) tell; narrate; ***man hat mir erzählt*** I was told
**Er'zähler** *m* (*-s; -*), **Er'zählerin** *f* (*-; -nen*) narrator
**Er'zählung** *f* (*-; -en*) (short) story, tale
**'Erzbischof** *m* REL archbishop
**'Erzbistum** *n* REL archbishopric
**'Erzengel** *m* REL archangel
**er'zeugen** *v/t* (*no -ge-, h*) ECON produce (*a. fig*); TECH make, manufacture; ELECTR generate; *fig* cause, create; **Er'zeuger** *m* (*-s; -*) ECON producer; **Er'zeugnis** *n* (*-ses; -se*) ECON product (*a. fig*); **Er'zeugung** *f* (*-; -en*) ECON production
**er'ziehen** *v/t* (*irr*, ***ziehen***, *no -ge-, h*) bring up, raise; educate; ***j-n zu et. ~*** teach s.o. to be *or* to do s.th.
**Erzieher** [ɛɐ'tsiːɐ] *m* (*-s; -*), **Erzieherin** [ɛɐ'tsiːərɪn] *f* (*-; -nen*) educator; teacher; (qualified) kindergarten teacher; **er'zieherisch** *adj* educational, pedagogic(al); **Er'ziehung** *f* (*-; no pl*) upbringing; education
**Er'ziehungs|anstalt** *f* reform (*Br* approved) school; **~berechtigte** *m, f* (*-n; -n*) parent or guardian; **~wesen** *n* (*-s; no pl*) educational system
**er'zielen** *v/t* (*no -ge-, h*) achieve; SPORT score
**erzogen** [ɛɐ'tsoːgən] *adj*: ***gut ~ sein*** be well-bred; ***schlecht ~ sein*** be ill-bred
**er'zwingen** *v/t* (*irr*, ***zwingen***, *no -ge-, h*) (en)force
**es** [ɛs] *pers pron* it; he; she; ***~ gibt*** there is, there are; ***ich bin ~*** it's me; ***ich hoffe ~*** I hope so; ***ich kann ~*** I can (do it)
**Esche** ['ɛʃə] *f* (*-; -n*) BOT ash (tree)
**Esel** ['eːzəl] *m* (*-s; -*) ZO donkey, ass (*a.* F)
**'Eselsbrücke** *f* mnemonic
**'Eselsohr** *fig n* dog-ear
**Eskorte** [ɛs'kɔrtə] *f* (*-; -n*) MIL escort, MAR *a.* convoy
**essbar** ['ɛsbaːɐ] *adj* eatable; edible
**essen** ['ɛsən] *v/t and v/i* (*irr, ge-, h*) eat; ***zu Mittag ~*** (have) lunch; ***zu Abend ~*** have supper (*or* dinner); ***~ gehen*** eat *or* dine out; **'Essen** *n* (*-s; -*) food; meal; dish; dinner
**'Essens|marke** *f* meal ticket; **~zeit** *f* lunchtime; dinner *or* supper time
**Essig** ['ɛsɪç] *m* (*-s; -e*) vinegar
**'Essiggurke** *f* pickled gherkin, pickle
**Ess|löffel** *m* tablespoon; **~stäbchen** *pl* chopsticks; **~tisch** *m* dining table; **~zimmer** *n* dining room
**Estrich** ['ɛstrɪç] *m* (*-s; -e*) ARCH flooring, subfloor; *Swiss*: loft, attic, garret
**etablieren** [eta'bliːrən] *v/refl* (*no -ge-, h*) establish o.s.
**Etage** [e'taːʒə] *f* (*-; -n*) floor, stor(e)y; ***auf der ersten ~*** on the second (*Br* first) floor; **E'tagenbett** *n* bunk bed
**Etappe** [e'tapə] *f* (*-; -n*) stage, SPORT *a.* leg
**Etat** [e'taː] *m* (*-s; -s*) budget
**Ethik** ['eːtɪk] *f* (*-; no pl*) ethics
**ethisch** ['eːtɪʃ] *adj* ethical
**ethnisch** ['ɛtnɪʃ] *adj* ethnic
**Etikett** [eti'kɛt] *n* (*-[e]s; -e[n]*) label (*a. fig*); (price) tag; **Eti'kette** *f* (*-; -n*) etiquette; **etikettieren** [etikɛ'tiːrən] *v/t* (*no -ge-, h*) label
**etliche** ['ɛtlɪçə] *indef pron* several, quite a few
**Etui** [ɛt'viː] *n* (*-s; -s*) case
**etwa** ['ɛtva] *adv* about, around; perhaps, by any chance; ***nicht ~, dass*** not that; **etwaig** ['ɛtvaɪç] *adj* any
**etwas** ['ɛtvas] **1.** *indef pron* something; anything; **2.** *adj* some; any; **3.** *adv* a little, somewhat
**EU** [eː'uː] ABBR *of* ***Europäische Union*** EU, European Union
**euch** [ɔʏç] *pers pron* you; ***~ (selbst)*** yourselves; **euer** ['ɔʏɐ] *poss pron* your; ***der (die, das) Eu(e)re*** yours
**Eule** ['ɔʏlə] *f* (*-; -n*) ZO owl; ***~n nach Athen tragen*** carry coals to Newcastle
**euresgleichen** ['ɔʏrəs'glaɪçən] *pron* people like you, F *contp* the likes of you
**Euro...** ['ɔʏro] *in cpds ...cheque etc*: Euro...
**Europa** [ɔʏ'roːpa] Europe; ***~...*** *in cpds* European; **Europäer** [ɔʏro'pɛːɐ] *m* (*-s; -*), **Europäerin** [-'pɛːərɪn] *f* (*-; -nen*), **euro'päisch** *adj* European; ***Europäische Gemeinschaft*** European Community
**Euter** ['ɔʏtɐ] *n* (*-s; -*) udder
**ev.** ABBR *of* ***evangelisch*** Prot., Protestant
**evakuieren** [evaku'iːrən] *v/t* (*no -ge-, h*) evacuate

**evangelisch** [evaŋ'ge:lɪʃ] *adj* REL Protestant; **~-lutherisch** Lutheran
**Evangelium** [evaŋ'ge:ljʊm] *n* (-*s*; -*lien*) Gospel
**eventuell** [evɛntu'ɛl] **1.** *adj* possible; **2.** *adv* possibly, perhaps
**evtl.** ABBR *of* **eventuell** poss., possibly
**ewig** ['e:vɪç] *adj* eternal; F constant, endless; **auf ~** for ever; **'Ewigkeit** *f* (-; *no pl*) eternity; F **eine ~** (for) ages
**exakt** [ɛ'ksakt] *adj* exact, precise
**Ex'aktheit** *f* (-; *no pl*) exactness, precision
**Examen** [ɛ'ksa:mən] *n* (-*s*; *Examina* [ɛ'ksa:mina]) exam, examination
**Exekutive** [ɛkseku'ti:və] *f* (-; -*n*) POL executive (power)
**Exemplar** [ɛksɛm'pla:ɐ] *n* (-*s*; -*e*) specimen; copy
**exerzieren** [ɛksɛr'tsi:rən] *v/i* (*no -ge-*, *h*) MIL drill
**Exil** [ɛ'ksi:l] *n* (-*s*; -*e*) exile
**Existenz** [ɛksɪs'tɛnts] *f* (-; -*en*) existence; living, livelihood; **~kampf** *m* struggle for survival; **~minimum** *n* subsistence level
**existieren** [ɛksɪs'ti:rən] *v/i* (*no -ge-*, *h*) exist; live (**von** on)
**exklusiv** [ɛksklu'zi:f] *adj* exclusive, select
**exotisch** [ɛ'kso:tɪʃ] *adj* exotic
**Expansion** [ɛkspan'zjo:n] *f* (-; -*en*) expansion
**Expedition** [ɛkspedi'tsjo:n] *f* (-; -*en*) expedition
**Experiment** [ɛksperi'mɛnt] *n* (-[*e*]*s*; -*e*), **experimentieren** [ɛksperimɛn'ti:rən] *v/i* (*no -ge-*, *h*) experiment
**Experte** [ɛks'pɛrtə] *m* (-*n*; -*n*), **Ex'pertin** *f* (-; -*nen*) expert (**für** on)
**explodieren** [ɛksplo'di:rən] *v/i* (*no -ge-*, *sein*) explode (*a. fig*), burst; **Explosion** [ɛksplo'zjo:n] *f* (-; -*en*) explosion (*a. fig*); **explosiv** [-'zi:f] *adj* explosive
**Export** [ɛks'pɔrt] *m* (-[*e*]*s*; -*e*) a) (*no pl*) export(ation), b) exports
**exportieren** [ɛkspɔr'ti:rən] *v/t* (*no -ge-*, *h*) export
**Express** [ɛks'prɛs] *m* (-*es*; *no pl*) RAIL express; **per ~** by special delivery, *Br* express
**extra** ['ɛkstra] *adv* extra; separately; F on purpose; **~ für dich** especially for you
**Extra** *n* (-*s*; -*s*), **~blatt** *n* extra
**Extrakt** [ɛks'trakt] *m* (-[*e*]*s*; -*e*) extract
**extravagant** [ɛkstrava'gant] *adj* flamboyant
**extrem** [ɛks'tre:m] *adj*, **Ex'trem** *n* (-*s*; -*e*) extreme; **Extremist(in)** [ɛkstre'mɪst(ɪn)] (-*en*; -*en*/-; -*nen*), **extre'mistisch** *adj* extremist, ultra
**Exzellenz** [ɛkstsɛ'lɛnts] *f* (-; -*en*) Excellency
**exzentrisch** [ɛks'tsɛntrɪʃ] *adj* eccentric
**Exzess** [ɛks'tsɛs] *m* (-*ses*; -*se*) excess

# F

**Fa.** ABBR *of* **Firma** firm; Messrs.
**Fabel** ['fa:bəl] *f* (-; -*n*) fable (*a. fig*)
**'fabelhaft** *adj* fantastic, wonderful
**Fabrik** [fa'bri:k] *f* (-; -*en*) factory, works, shop; **Fabrikant** [fabri'kant] *m* (-*en*; -*en*) factory owner; manufacturer
**Fa'brikarbeiter** *m* factory worker
**Fabrikat** [fabri'ka:t] *n* (-[*e*]*s*; -*e*) make, brand; product
**Fabrikation** [fabrika'tsjo:n] *f* (-; -*en*) manufacturing, production
**Fabrikati'onsfehler** *m* flaw
**Fa'brik|besitzer** *m* factory owner; **~ware** *f* manufactured product(s)
**Fach** [fax] *n* (-[*e*]*s*; *Fächer* ['fɛçɐ]) compartment; pigeonhole; shelf; PED, UNIV subject; → **Fachgebiet**; **~arbeiter** *m* skilled worker; **~arzt** *m*, **~ärztin** *f* specialist (**für** in); **~ausbildung** *f* professional training; **~ausdruck** *m* technical term; **~buch** *n* specialist book
**Fächer** ['fɛçɐ] *m* (-*s*; -) fan
**'Fach|frau** *f* expert; **~gebiet** *n* line, field; trade, business; **~geschäft** *n*

dealer (specializing in ...); **~hochschule** *f appr* (technical) college, *esp Br* polytechnic; **~kenntnisse** *pl* specialized knowledge
**'fachkundig** *adj* competent, expert
**'fachlich** *adj* professional, specialized
**'Fach|litera,tur** *f* specialized literature; **~mann** *m* (-[*e*]*s*; *-leute*) expert
**'fachmännisch** [-mɛnɪʃ] *adj* expert
**'Fachschule** *f* technical school *or* college
**fachsimpeln** ['faxzɪmpəln] *v/i* (*ge-*, *h*) talk shop
**'Fach|werk** *n* framework; **~werkhaus** *n* half-timbered house; **~zeitschrift** *f* (professional *or* specialist) journal
**Fackel** ['fakəl] *f* (-; *-n*) torch; **~zug** *m* torchlight procession
**fade** ['fa:də] *adj* GASTR tasteless, flat; stale; *fig* dull, boring
**Faden** ['fa:dən] *m* (*-s*; *Fäden* ['fɛ:dən]) thread (*a. fig*); **'fadenscheinig** *adj* threadbare; *fig* flimsy (*excuse etc*)
**fähig** ['fɛ:ɪç] *adj* capable (**zu** of [*doing*] *s.th.*), able (to *do s.th.*); **'Fähigkeit** *f* (-; *-en*) (cap)ability; talent, gift
**fahl** [fa:l] *adj* pale; ashen (*face*)
**fahnden** ['fa:ndən] *v/i* (*ge-*, *h*) search (***nach*** for); **'Fahndung** *f* (-; *-en*) search; **'Fahndungsliste** *f* wanted list
**Fahne** ['fa:nə] *f* (-; *-n*) flag; *mst fig* banner; F ***e-e ~ haben*** reek of alcohol
**'Fahnen|flucht** *f* (-; *no pl*) MIL desertion; **~stange** *f* flagpole, flagstaff
**Fahrbahn** ['fa:ɐ-] *f* road(way), pavement; MOT lane
**'fahrbar** *adj* mobile
**Fähre** ['fɛ:rə] *f* (-; *-n*) ferry(boat)
**fahren** ['fa:rən] (*irr*, *ge-*) **1.** *v/i* (*sein*) go; *bus etc*: run; leave; MOT drive; ride; ***mit dem Auto*** (***Zug, Bus*** *etc*) ~ go by car (train, bus *etc*); ***über e-e Brücke*** *etc* ~ cross a bridge *etc*; ***mit der Hand über et.*** ~ run one's hand over s.th.; ***was ist denn in dich gefahren?*** what's got into you?; **2.** *v/t* (*h*) drive (*car etc*); ride (*bicycle etc*); carry
**Fahrer** ['fa:rɐ] *m* (*-s*; -) driver; **~flucht** *f* hit-and-run offense (*Br* offence)
**'Fahrerin** *f* (-; *-nen*) driver
**Fahr|gast** ['fa:ɐ-] *m* passenger; **~geld** *n* fare; **~gelegenheit** *f* means of transport(ation); **~gemeinschaft** *f* car pool; **~gestell** *n* MOT chassis; AVIAT → ***Fahrwerk***; **~karte** *f* ticket
**'Fahrkarten|auto,mat** *m* ticket machine; **~entwerter** *m* (*-s*; -) ticket-cancel(l)ing machine; **~schalter** *m* ticket window
**'fahrlässig** *adj* careless, reckless (*a.* JUR); ***grob*** ~ grossly negligent
**'Fahrlehrer** *m* driving instructor
**'Fahrplan** *m* timetable, schedule
**'fahrplanmäßig 1.** *adj* scheduled; **2.** *adv* according to schedule; on time
**'Fahr|preis** *m* fare; **~prüfung** *f* driving test; **~rad** *n* bicycle, F bike; **~schein** *m* ticket; **~schule** *f* driving school; **~schüler** *m* MOT student driver, *Br* learner (driver); PED non-local student; **~stuhl** *m* elevator, *Br* lift; **~stunde** *f* driving lesson
**Fahrt** [fa:ɐt] *f* (-; *-en*) ride, MOT *a.* drive; trip, journey, MAR voyage, cruise; speed (*a.* MOT); ***in voller*** ~ at full speed
**Fährte** ['fɛ:ɐtə] *f* (-; *-n*) track (*a. fig*)
**'Fahrtenschreiber** *m* MOT tachograph
**'Fahrwasser** *n* MAR fairway
**'Fahrwerk** *n* AVIAT landing gear
**'Fahrzeug** *n* (-[*e*]*s*; *-e*) vehicle
**Fairness** ['fɛ:ɐnɪs] *f* (-; *no pl*) fair play
**Faktor** ['fakto:ɐ] *m* (*-s*; *-en* [fak'to:rən]) factor
**Fakultät** [fakʊl'tɛ:t] *f* (-; *-en*) UNIV faculty, department
**Falke** ['falkə] *m* (*-n*; *-n*) ZO hawk, falcon
**Fall** [fal] *m* (-[*e*]*s*; *Fälle* ['fɛlə]) fall; LING, JUR, MED case; ***auf jeden*** ~ in any case; ***auf keinen*** ~ on no account; ***für den*** ~, ***dass*** ... in case ...; ***gesetzt den*** ~, ***dass*** suppose (that); ***zu*** ~ ***bringen*** *fig* defeat
**Falle** ['falə] *f* (-; *-n*) trap (*a. fig*)
**fallen** ['falən] *v/i* (*irr*, *ge-*, *sein*) fall (*a. rain etc*), drop; ~ ***lassen*** drop (*a. fig*); MIL be killed (in action); ***ein Tor fiel*** SPORT a goal was scored
**fällen** ['fɛlən] *v/t* (*ge-*, *h*) fell, cut down (*tree*); JUR pass (*sentence*); make (*a decision etc*)
**fällig** ['fɛlɪç] *adj* due; payable
**'Fall|obst** *n* windfall; **~rückzieher** *m soccer*: overhead kick
**falls** [fals] *cj* if, in case; ~ ***nicht*** unless
**'Fallschirm** *m* parachute; **~jäger** *m* MIL paratrooper; **~springen** *n* MIL parachuting; SPORT skydiving; **~springer** *m* MIL parachutist; SPORT skydiver
**'Falltür** *f* trapdoor

**falsch** [falʃ] *adj and adv* wrong; false (*a. fig*); forged; ~ ***gehen*** *watch*: be wrong; ***et.*** ~ ***aussprechen*** (***schreiben***, ***verstehen*** *etc*) mispronounce (misspell, misunderstand *etc*) s.th.; ~ ***verbunden!*** TEL sorry, wrong number
**fälschen** ['fɛlʃən] *v/t* (*ge-*, *h*) forge, fake; counterfeit; '**Fälscher** *m* (*-s*; -) forger
'**Falsch|geld** *n* counterfeit *or* false money; **~münzer** [-mʏntsɐ] *m* (*-s*; -) counterfeiter; **~spieler** *m* cheat
'**Fälschung** *f* (-; *-en*) forgery; counterfeit; '**fälschungssicher** *adj* forgery-proof
**Falt...** ['falt-] *in cpds ...bett, ...boot etc*: folding ...; **Falte** ['faltə] *f* (-; *-n*) fold; wrinkle; pleat; crease; '**falten** *v/t* (*ge-*, *h*) fold; '**Faltenrock** *m* pleated skirt
**Falter** ['faltɐ] *m* (*-s*; -) ZO butterfly
**faltig** ['faltɪç] *adj* wrinkled
**familiär** [fami'ljɛːɐ] *adj* personal; informal; ***~e Probleme*** family problems
**Familie** [fa'miːljə] *f* (-; *-n*) family (*a.* ZO, BOT)
**Fa'milien|angelegenheit** *f* family affair; **~anschluss** *m*: ~ ***haben*** live as one of the family; **~name** *m* family (*or* last) name, surname; **~packung** *f* family size (package); **~planung** *f* family planning; **~stand** *m* marital status; **~vater** *m* family man
**Fanatiker** [fa'naːtikɐ] *m* (*-s*; -), **Fa'natikerin** *f* (-; *-nen*), **fa'natisch** *adj* fanatic; **Fanatismus** [fana'tɪsmʊs] *m* (-; *no pl*) fanaticism
**fand** [fant] *pret of* ***finden***
**Fang** [faŋ] *m* (-[*e*]*s*; *Fänge* ['fɛŋə]) catch (*a. fig*); '**fangen** *v/t* (*irr*, *ge-*, *h*) catch (*a. fig*); ***sich wieder*** ~ get a grip on o.s. again; ***Fangen spielen*** play tag (*Br* catch); '**Fangzahn** *m* ZO fang
**Fantasie** [fanta'ziː] *f* (-; *-n*) imagination; fantasy; **fanta'sielos** *adj* unimaginative; **fanta'sieren** *v/i* (*no -ge-*, *h*) daydream; MED be delirious; F talk nonsense; **fanta'sievoll** *adj* imaginative; **Fantast** [fan'tast] *m* (*-en*; *-en*) dreamer; **fan'tastisch** *adj* fantastic, F *a.* great, terrific
**Farbband** ['farp-] *n* (typewriter) ribbon
**Farbe** ['farbə] *f* (-; *-n*) colo(u)r; paint; complexion; tan; *card games*: suit
'**farbecht** *adj* colo(u)r-fast
**färben** ['fɛrbən] *v/t* (*ge-*, *h*) dye; *esp fig* colo(u)r; ***sich rot*** ~ turn red; → ***abfärben***
'**farben|blind** *adj* colo(u)r-blind; **~froh**, **~prächtig** *adj* colo(u)rful
'**Farb|fernsehen** *n* colo(u)r television; **~fernseher** *m* colo(u)r TV set; **~film** *m* colo(u)r film; **~foto** *n* colo(u)r photo
**farbig** ['farbɪç] *adj* colo(u)red; stained (*glass*); *fig* colo(u)rful; **Farbige** ['farbɪgə] *m*, *f* (*-n*; *-n*) → ***Schwarze***
'**Farbkasten** *m* paintbox
'**farblos** *adj* colo(u)rless (*a. fig*)
'**Farbstift** *m* colo(u)red pencil, crayon
'**Farbstoff** *m* dye; GASTR colo(u)ring
'**Farbton** *m* shade, tint
'**Färbung** *f* (-; *-en*) colo(u)ring; hue
**Farnkraut** ['farn-] *n* BOT fern
**Fasan** [fa'zaːn] *m* (-[*e*]*s*; *-e*[*n*]) ZO pheasant
**Faschismus** [fa'ʃɪsmʊs] *m* (-; *no pl*) POL fascism; **Faschist** [fa'ʃɪst] *m* (*-en*; *-en*), **fa'schistisch** *adj* POL fascist
**faseln** ['faːzəln] F *v/i* (*ge-*, *h*) drivel
**Faser** ['faːzɐ] *f* (-; *-n*) fiber, *Br* fibre; grain; **faserig** ['faːzərɪç] *adj* fibrous; '**fasern** *v/i* (*ge-*, *h*) fray
**Fass** [fas] *n* (*-es*; *Fässer* ['fɛsɐ]) cask, barrel; ***vom*** ~ on tap
**Fassade** [fa'saːdə] *f* (-; *-n*) ARCH facade, front (*a. fig*)
'**Fassbier** *n* draft (*Br* draught) beer
**fassen** ['fasən] (*ge-*, *h*) **1.** *v/t* take hold of, grasp; seize; catch (*criminal*); hold, take; set (*jewels*); *fig* grasp, understand; pluck up (*courage*); make (*a decision*); ***sich*** ~ compose o.s.; ***sich kurz*** ~ be brief; ***es ist nicht zu*** ~ that's incredible **2.** *v/i*: ~ ***nach*** reach for
'**Fassung** *f* (-; *-en*) a) setting; frame (*of glasses*); ELECTR socket; draft(ing); wording, version, b) (*no pl*) composure; ***die*** ~ ***verlieren*** lose one's composure; ***j-n aus der*** ~ ***bringen*** put s.o. out
'**fassungslos** *adj* stunned; speechless
'**Fassungsvermögen** *n* capacity
**fast** [fast] *adv* almost, nearly; ~ ***nie*** (***nichts***) hardly ever (anything)
**fasten** ['fastən] *v/i* (*ge-*, *h*) fast
'**Fastenzeit** *f* REL Lent
'**Fastnacht** *f* → ***Karneval***
**fatal** [fa'taːl] *adj* unfortunate; awkward; disastrous
**fauchen** ['fauxən] *v/i* (*ge-*, *h*) ZO hiss
**faul** [faul] *adj* rotten, bad, GASTR *a.*

F

spoiled; *fig* lazy; F fishy; **~e Ausrede** lame excuse; **'faulen** *v/i (ge-, h, sein)* rot, go bad; decay
**faulenzen** ['faulɛntsən] *v/i (ge-, h)* laze, loaf (about); **'Faulenzer(in)** [-tsɐ (-tsərɪn)] *(-s; -/-; -nen)* lazybones; *contp* loafer
**'Faulheit** *f (-; no pl)* laziness
**faulig** ['faulɪç] *adj* rotten
**Fäulnis** ['fɔʏlnɪs] *f (-; no pl)* rottenness, decay *(a. fig)*
**'Faulpelz** F *m* → ***Faulenzer***
**'Faultier** *n* ZO sloth
**Faust** [faust] *f (-; Fäuste* ['fɔʏstə]) fist; ***auf eigene ~*** on one's own initiative; **~handschuh** *m* mitten; **~regel** *f (**als ~** as a)* rule of thumb; **~schlag** *m* punch
**Favorit** [favo'ri:t] *m (-en; -en)*, **Favo'ritin** *f (-; -nen)* favo(u)rite
**Fax** [faks] *n (-; -[e])* fax; fax machine
**faxen** ['faksən] *v/i and v/t (ge-, h)* fax, send a fax (to)
**'Faxgerät** *n* fax machine
**FCKW** [ɛftse:ka:'ve:] ABBR *of* ***Fluorchlorkohlenwasserstoff*** chlorofluorocarbon, CFC
**Feber** ['fe:bɐ] *Austrian m (-s; -)*, **Februar** ['fe:brua:ɐ] *m (-s; -e)* February
**fechten** ['fɛçtən] *v/i (irr, ge-, h)* SPORT fence; *fig* fight; **'Fechten** *n (-s; no pl)* SPORT fencing; **Fechter(in)** ['fɛçtɐ (-tərɪn)] *(-s; -/-; -nen)* SPORT fencer
**Feder** ['fe:dɐ] *f (-; -n)* feather; plume; nib; TECH spring; **~ball** *m* SPORT badminton; shuttlecock; **~bett** *n* comforter, *Br* duvet; **~gewicht** *n* SPORT featherweight; **~halter** *m* penholder
**'feder'leicht** *adj* (as) light as a feather
**'Federmäppchen** [-mɛpçən] *n (-s; -)* pencil case
**'federn** *(ge-, h)* **1.** *v/i* be springy; **2.** *v/t* TECH spring; **~d** *adj* springy, elastic
**'Federstrich** *m* stroke of the pen
**Federung** ['fe:dərʊŋ] *f (-; -en)* springs; MOT suspension; ***e-e gute ~ haben*** be well sprung
**'Federzeichnung** *f* pen-and-ink drawing
**Fee** [fe:] *f (-; -n)* fairy
**fegen** ['fe:gən] *v/t (ge-, h) and fig v/i (sein)* sweep
**fehl** [fe:l] *adj*: ***~ am Platze*** out of place
**'Fehlbetrag** *m* deficit
**'fehlen** *v/i (ge-, h)* be missing; be absent; ***ihm fehlt (es an)*** ... he is lacking ...; ***du fehlst uns*** we miss you; ***was dir fehlt, ist ...*** what you need is ...; ***was fehlt Ihnen?*** what's wrong with you?
**Fehler** ['fe:lɐ] *m (-s; -)* mistake; fault, TECH *a.* defect, flaw; EDP error
**'fehlerfrei** *adj* faultless, flawless
**'fehlerhaft** *adj* faulty; full of mistakes; TECH defective
**'Fehlermeldung** *f* EDP error message
**'Fehl|ernährung** *f* malnutrition; **~geburt** *f* MED miscarriage; **~griff** *m* mistake; wrong choice
**'Fehlschlag** *m* failure; **'fehlschlagen** *v/i (irr, **schlagen**, sep, -ge-, sein)* fail
**'Fehl|start** *m* false start; **~tritt** *m* slip; *fig* lapse; **~zündung** *f* MOT backfire *(a. **~ haben**)*
**Feier** ['faiɐ] *f (-; -n)* celebration; party
**'Feierabend** *m* end of a day's work; closing time; evening (at home); ***~ machen*** finish (work), F knock off; ***nach ~*** after work
**'feierlich** *adj* solemn; festive
**'Feierlichkeit** *f (-; -en)* a) *(no pl)* solemnity, b) ceremony
**'feiern** *v/t and v/i (ge-, h)* celebrate; have a party
**'Feiertag** *m* holiday; ***gesetzlicher ~*** public *(or* legal, *Br a.* bank) holiday
**feig** [faik], **feige** ['faigə] *adj* cowardly; ***~ sein*** be a coward
**Feige** ['faigə] *f (-; -n)* BOT fig
**'Feigheit** *f (-; no pl)* cowardice
**'Feigling** *m (-s; -e)* coward
**Feile** ['failə] *f (-; -n)*, **'feilen** *v/t and v/i (ge-, h)* file
**feilschen** ['failʃən] *v/i (ge-, h)* haggle (***um*** about, over)
**fein** [fain] *adj* fine; choice, excellent; keen *(ear)*; delicate; distinguished, F posh; ***~!*** good!, okay!
**Feind** [faint] *m (-[e]s; -e* ['faində]) enemy *(a. fig)*; **~bild** *n* enemy image
**Feindin** ['faindɪn] *f (-; -nen)* enemy
**'feindlich** *adj* hostile; MIL enemy
**'Feindschaft** *f (-; no pl)* hostility
**'feindselig** *adj* hostile (***gegen*** to)
**'Feindseligkeit** *f (-; no pl)* hostility
**feinfühlig** ['fainfy:lɪç] *adj* sensitive
**'Feingefühl** *n (-[e]s; no pl)* sensitiveness
**'Feinheit** *f (-; -en)* a) *(no pl)* fineness; keenness; delicacy, b) *pl* niceties

'**Fein|kostgeschäft** *n* delicatessen; **~me,chaniker** *m* precision mechanic
'**Feinschmecker** *m* (-*s*; -) gourmet
**feist** [faist] *adj* fat, stout
**Feld** [fɛlt] *n* (-[*e*]*s*; -*er* ['fɛldɐ]) field (*a. fig*); *chess*: square; **~arbeit** *f* AGR work in the fields; fieldwork; **~bett** *n* cot, *Br* camp bed; **~flasche** *f* water bottle, canteen; **~lerche** *f* ZO skylark; **~marschall** *m* MIL field marshal
'**Feldstecher** [-ʃtɛçɐ] *m* (-*s*; -) field glasses
'**Feldwebel** [-veːbəl] *m* (-*s*; -) MIL sergeant
'**Feldzug** *m* MIL campaign (*a. fig*)
**Felge** ['fɛlgə] *f* (-; -*n*) rim; SPORT circle
**Fell** [fɛl] *n* (-[*e*]*s*; -*e*) ZO coat; skin, fur
**Fels** [fɛls] *m* (-*en*; -*en*) rock
'**Felsbrocken** *m* boulder
**Felsen** ['fɛlzən] *m* (-*s*; -) rock
**felsig** ['fɛlzɪç] *adj* rocky
'**Felsspalte** *f* crevice
'**Felsvorsprung** *m* ledge
**feminin** [femi'niːn] *adj* feminine (*a.* LING); *contp* effeminate; **Feminismus** [femi'nɪsmʊs] *m* (-; *no pl*) feminism; **Feministin** [femi'nɪstɪn] *f* (-; -*nen*), **femi'nistisch** *adj* feminist
**Fenchel** ['fɛnçəl] *m* (-*s*; *no pl*) BOT fennel
**Fenster** ['fɛnstɐ] *n* (-*s*; -) window; **~bank** *f* (-; -*bänke*), **~brett** *n* windowsill; **~flügel** *m* casement; **~laden** *m* shutter; **~rahmen** *m* window frame; **~scheibe** *f* (window)pane
**Ferien** ['feːrjən] *pl* vacation, *esp Br* holiday(s *pl*); **~ *haben*** be on vacation; **~haus** *n* vacation home, cottage; **~lager** *n* summer camp; **~wohnung** *f* vacation rental, *Br* holiday apartment
**Ferkel** ['fɛrkəl] *n* (-*s*; -) ZO piglet; F pig
**fern** [fɛrn] *adj and adv* far(away), far-off, distant; ***von*** ~ from a distance; ~ ***halten*** keep away (***von*** from); ***es liegt mir ~ zu*** far be it from me to
'**Fernamt** *n* telephone exchange
'**Fernbedienung** *f* remote control
'**fernbleiben** *v/i* (*irr*, ***bleiben***, *sep*, -*ge*-, *sein*) stay away (*dat* from)
**Ferne** ['fɛrnə] *f* (-; *no pl*) distance; ***aus der*** ~ from a distance
**ferner** ['fɛrnɐ] *adv* further(more); in addition, also
'**Fern|fahrer** *m* long-haul truck driver, F trucker, *Br* long-distance lorry driver; **~gespräch** *n* TEL long-distance call
'**ferngesteuert** *adj* remote-controlled; MIL guided (*missile etc*)
'**Fern|glas** *n* binoculars; **~heizung** *f* district heating; **~ko,pierer** *m* fax machine; **~kurs** *m* correspondence course; **~laster** F *m* (-*s*; -) MOT long-haul truck, *Br* long-distance lorry; **~lenkung** *f* remote control; **~licht** *n* MOT full (*or* high) beam
'**Fernmelde|satel,lit** *m* communications satellite; **~technik** *f*, **~wesen** *n* (-*s*; *no pl*) telecommunications
'**Fern|rohr** *n* telescope; **~schreiben** *n*, **~schreiber** *m* telex
'**fernsehen** *v/i* (*irr*, ***sehen***, *sep*, -*ge*-, *h*) watch television; '**Fernsehen** *n* (-*s*; *no pl*) television (***im*** on); '**Fernseher** F *m* (-*s*; -) TV (set); TV viewer
'**Fernseh|schirm** *m* (TV) screen; **~sendung** *f* TV program(me)
**Fernsprechamt** *n* telephone exchange
'**Fernsteuerung** *f* remote control
'**Fernverkehr** *m* long-distance traffic
**Ferse** ['fɛrzə] *f* (-; -*n*) ANAT heel (*a. fig*)
**fertig** ['fɛrtɪç] *adj* ready; finished; ~ ***bringen*** manage; *iro* be capable of; ~ ***machen*** finish (*a.* F *s.o.*); get *s.th.* ready; F give *s.o.* hell, do *s.o.* in; ***sich ~ machen*** get ready; (***mit et.***) ~ ***sein*** have finished (s.th.); ***mit et.*** ~ ***werden*** cope with *a problem etc*; F ***völlig*** ~ dead beat
'**Fertig|gericht** *n* ready(-to-serve) meal; **~haus** *n* prefabricated house, F prefab
'**Fertigkeit** *f* (-; -*en*) skill
'**Fertigstellung** *f* (-; *no pl*) completion
**fesch** [fɛʃ] *Austrian adj* smart, chic
**Fessel** ['fɛsəl] *f* (-; -*n*) shackle (*a. fig*); ANAT ankle; '**fesseln** *v/t* (*ge*-, *h*) bind, tie (up); *fig* fascinate
**fest** [fɛst] *adj* firm (*a. fig*); solid; fast; *fig* fixed (*date etc*); sound (*sleep*); steady (*girlfriend etc*); ~ ***schlafen*** be fast asleep
**Fest** *n* (-[*e*]*s*; -*e*) celebration; party; REL festival, feast; → ***froh***
'**festbinden** *v/t* (*irr*, ***binden***, *sep*, -*ge*-, *h*) fasten, tie (***an*** *dat* to)
'**Festessen** *n* banquet, feast
'**festfahren** *v/refl* (*irr*, ***fahren***, *sep*, -*ge*-, *h*) get stuck
'**Festhalle** *f* (festival) hall
'**festhalten** (*irr*, ***halten***, *sep*, -*ge*-, *h*) **1.**

F

*v/i*: ~ ***an*** (*dat*) stick to; **2.** *v/t* hold on to; hold *s.o. or s.th.* tight; ***sich*** ~ ***an*** (*dat*) hold on to
**festigen** ['fɛstɪgən] *v/t* (*ge-*, *h*) strengthen; ***sich*** ~ grow firm *or* strong
**Festigkeit** ['fɛstɪçkait] *f* (-; *no pl*) firmness; strength
**'Festland** *n* mainland; *the* Continent
**'festlegen** *v/t* (*sep*, *-ge-*, *h*) fix, set; ***sich*** ~ ***auf*** (*acc*) commit o.s. to *s.th.*
**'festlich** *adj* festive
**'festmachen** *v/t* (*sep*, *-ge-*, *h*) fasten, fix (***an*** *dat* to); MAR moor; ECON fix
**'Festnahme** [-na:mə] *f* (-; *-n*), **'festnehmen** *v/t* (*irr*, ***nehmen***, *sep*, *-ge-*, *h*) arrest
**'Festplatte** *f* EDP hard disk
**'fest|schrauben** *v/t* (*sep*, *-ge-*, *h*) screw (on) tight; **~setzen** *v/t* (*sep*, *-ge-*, *h*) fix; **~sitzen** *v/i* (*irr*, ***sitzen***, *sep*, *-ge-*, *h*) be stuck; be (left) stranded
**'Festspiele** *pl* festival
**'feststehen** *v/i* (*irr*, ***stehen***, *sep*, *-ge-*, *h*) be certain; *date etc*: be fixed; **~d** *adj* established (*fact etc*); set (*phrase etc*)
**'feststellen** *v/t* (*sep*, *-ge-*, *h*) find (out); establish; see, notice; state; TECH lock, arrest; **'Feststellung** *f* (-; *-en*) finding(s); realization; statement
**'Festtag** *m* holiday; REL religious holiday; F red-letter day
**'Festung** *f* (-; *-en*) fortress
**'Festwertspeicher** *m* EDP read-only memory, ROM
**'Festzug** *m* procession
**fett** [fɛt] *adj* fat (*a. fig*); PRINT bold; ~ ***gedruckt*** boldface, in bold type (*or* print); **Fett** *n* (-[*e*]*s*; *-e*) fat; dripping; shortening; TECH grease; **'fettarm** *adj* low-fat, *pred* low in fat; **'Fettfleck** *m* grease spot; **fettig** ['fɛtɪç] *adj* greasy
**'Fettnäpfchen** *n*: ***ins*** ~ ***treten*** put one's foot in it
**Fetzen** ['fɛtsən] *m* (*-s*; -) shred; rag; scrap (*of paper etc*)
**feucht** [fɔʏçt] *adj* moist, damp; humid
**Feuchtigkeit** ['fɔʏçtɪçkait] *f* (-; *no pl*) moisture; dampness; humidity
**feudal** [fɔʏ'da:l] *adj* POL feudal; F posh, *Br* swish
**Feuer** ['fɔʏɐ] *n* (*-s*; -) fire (*a. fig*); ***j-m*** ~ ***geben*** give s.o. a light; ~ ***fangen*** catch fire; *fig* fall for *s.o.*; **~a͵larm** *m* fire alarm; **~bestattung** *f* cremation; **~eifer** *m* ardo(u)r
**'feuerfest** *adj* fireproof, fire-resistant
**'Feuergefahr** *f* danger of fire
**'feuergefährlich** *adj* inflammable
**'Feuer|leiter** *f* fire escape; **~löscher** [-lœʃɐ] *m* (*-s*; -) fire extinguisher; **~melder** [-mɛldɐ] *m* (*-s*; -) fire alarm
**feuern** ['fɔʏɐn] *v/i and v/t* (*ge-*, *h*) fire (*a.* F *s.o.*)
**'feuer'rot** *adj* blazing red; crimson
**'Feuer|schiff** *n* lightship; **~stein** *m* flint; **~wache** *f* fire station; **~waffe** *f* firearm, gun; **~wehr** *f* (-; *-en*) fire brigade (*or* department); fire truck (*Br* engine); **~wehrmann** *m* (-[*e*]*s*, *-männer*, *-leute*) fireman, fire fighter; **~werk** *n* fireworks; **~werkskörper** *m* firework, firecracker; **~zeug** *n* (cigarette) lighter
**feurig** ['fɔʏrɪç] *adj* fiery, ardent
**Fiasko** ['fjasko] *n* (*-s*; *-s*) fiasco, (complete) failure
**Fibel** ['fi:bəl] *f* (-; *-n*) primer, first reader
**Fiber** ['fi:bɐ] *f* fiber, *Br* fibre; **~glas** *n* fiberglass, *Br* fibreglass
**Fichte** ['fɪçtə] *f* (-; *-n*) BOT spruce, F *mst* pine *or* fir (tree)
**ficken** ['fɪkən] V *v/i and v/t* (*ge-*, *h*) fuck
**Fieber** ['fi:bɐ] *n* (*-s*; *no pl*) MED temperature, fever (*a. fig*); ~ ***haben*** (***messen***) have a (take *s.o.'s*) temperature; ~ ***senkend*** MED antipyretic
**'fieberhaft** *adj* MED feverish (*a. fig*)
**'fiebern** *v/i* (*ge-*, *h*) MED have *or* run a temperature; ~ ***nach*** *fig* crave for
**'Fieberthermo͵meter** *n* fever (*Br* clinical) thermometer
**fiel** [fi:l] *pret of* ***fallen***
**fies** [fi:s] F *adj* mean, nasty
**Figur** [fi'gu:ɐ] *f* (-; *-en*) figure
**Filet** [fi'le:] *n* (*-s*; *-s*) GASTR fil(l)et
**Filiale** [fi'lja:lə] *f* (-; *-n*) branch
**Film** [film] *m* (-[*e*]*s*; *-e*) film; movie, *esp Br* (motion) picture; *the* movies, *Br the* cinema; ***e-n*** ~ ***einlegen*** PHOT load a camera; **~aufnahme** *f* filming, shooting; take, shot
**filmen** ['filmən] (*ge-*, *h*) **1.** *v/t* film, shoot; **2.** *v/i* make a film
**'Film|gesellschaft** *f* motion-picture (*Br* film) company; **~kamera** *f* motion-picture (*Br* film) camera; **~kas͵sette** *f* film magazine, cartridge; **~pro͵jektor** *m* film (*or* movie) projec-

tor; **~regis̩seur** *m* film director; **~schauspieler(in)** film (*or* screen, movie) actor (actress); **~studio** *n* film studio(s); **~the̩ater** *n* → ***Kino***; **~verleih** *m* film distributors; **~vorführer** *m* (*-s*; -) projectionist
**Filter** ['fɪltɐ] *m*, *esp* TECH *n* (*-s*; -) filter
**'Filterkaffee** *m* filter coffee
**'filtern** *v/t* (*ge-*, *h*) filter
**'Filterziga̩rette** *f* filter(-tipped) cigarette, filter tip
**Filz** [fɪlts] *m* (*-es*; *-e*) felt; F POL corruption, sleaze; **'filzen** F *v/t* (*ge-*, *h*) frisk
**'Filz|schreiber** [-ʃraibɐ] *m* (*-s*; -), **~stift** *m* felt(-tipped) pen
**Finale** [fi'na:lə] *n* (*-s*; -) finale; SPORT final(s)
**Finanz|amt** [fi'nants-] *n* tax office; Internal (*Br* Inland) Revenue; **~beamte** *m* tax officer
**Finanzen** [fi'nantsən] *pl* finances
**finanziell** [finan'tsjɛl] *adj* financial
**finanzieren** [finan'tsi:rən] *v/t* (*no -ge-*, *h*) finance
**Fi'nanz|mi̩nister** *m* minister of finance; Secretary of the Treasury, *Br* Chancellor of the Exchequer; **~minis̩terium** *n* ministry of finance; Treasury Department, *Br* Treasury; **~wesen** *n* (*-s*; *no pl*) finance
**Findelkind** ['fɪndəl-] *n* JUR foundling
**finden** *v/t* (*irr*, *ge-*, *h*) find; think, believe; ***ich finde ihn nett*** I think he's nice; ***wie ~ Sie ...?*** how do you like ...?; ***~ Sie (nicht)?*** do (don't) you think so?; ***das wird sich ~*** we'll see
**Finder** ['fɪndɐ] *m* (*-s*; -) finder
**'Finderlohn** *m* finder's reward
**findig** ['fɪndɪç] *adj* clever
**fing** [fɪŋ] *pret of* ***fangen***
**Finger** ['fɪŋɐ] *m* (*-s*; -) ANAT finger; **~abdruck** *m* fingerprint; **~fertigkeit** *f* (-; *no pl*) manual skill; **~hut** *m* thimble; BOT foxglove; **~nagel** *m* ANAT fingernail; **~spitze** *f* fingertip; **~spitzengefühl** *n* (*-[e]s*; *no pl*) sure instinct; tact
**fingiert** [fɪŋ'gi:ɐt] *adj* faked; fictitious
**Fink** [fɪŋk] *m* (*-en*; *-en*) ZO finch
**Finne** ['fɪnə] *m* (*-n*; *-n*), **Finnin** ['fɪnɪn] *f* (-; *-nen*) Finn; **'finnisch** *adj* Finnish
**Finnland** ['fɪn-] Finland
**finster** ['fɪnstɐ] *adj* dark, gloomy; *fig* grim; shady
**'Finsternis** *f* (-; *-se*) darkness, gloom
**Finte** ['fɪntə] *f* (-; *-n*) trick; SPORT feint
**Firma** ['fɪrma] *f* (-; *-men*) firm, company
**firmen** ['fɪrmən] *v/t* (*ge-*, *h*) REL confirm
**'Firmung** *f* (-; *-en*) REL confirmation
**First** [fɪrst] *m* (*-[e]s*; *-e*) ARCH ridge
**Fisch** [fɪʃ] *m* (*-[e]s*; *-e*) ZO fish; *pl* ASTR Pisces; ***er ist (ein) ~*** he's (a) Pisces
**'Fischdampfer** *m* trawler
**fischen** ['fɪʃən] *v/t and v/i* (*ge-*, *h*) fish
**Fischer** ['fɪʃɐ] *m* (*-s*; -) fisherman; **~...** *in cpds ...boot*, *...dorf etc*: fishing ...
**Fischerei** [fɪʃə'rai] *f* (-; *no pl*) fishing
**'Fisch|fang** *m* (*-[e]s*; *no pl*) fishing; **~gräte** *f* fishbone; **~grätenmuster** *n* herring-bone (pattern); **~gründe** *pl* fishing grounds; **~händler** *m* fish dealer, *esp Br* fishmonger; **~kutter** *m* smack; **~laich** *m* spawn; **~stäbchen** *n* GASTR fish stick (*Br* finger); **~zucht** *f* fish farming; **~zug** *m* catch, haul (*both a. fig*)
**Fisole** [fi'zo:lə] *Austrian f* (-; *-n*) BOT string bean
**Fistel** ['fɪstəl] *f* (-; *-n*) MED fistula
**'Fistelstimme** *f* falsetto
**fit** [fɪt] *adj* fit; ***sich ~ halten*** keep fit
**'Fitness** *f* (-; *no pl*) fitness; **~center** *n* health club, fitness center, gym
**fix** [fɪks] *adj* ECON fixed; F quick; F smart, bright; F ***~ und fertig sein*** be dead beat; be a nervous wreck; ***~e Idee*** PSYCH obsession
**fixen** ['fɪksən] F *v/i* (*ge-*, *h*) shoot, fix; be a junkie; **Fixer** ['fɪksɐ] F *m* (*-s*; -) junkie, mainliner
**fixieren** [fɪ'ksi:rən] *v/t* (*no -ge-*, *h*) fix (*a.* PHOT); stare at *s.o.*
**'Fixstern** *m* ASTR fixed star
**FKK** [ɛfka:'ka:] ABBR *of* ***Freikörperkultur*** nudism
**FK'K-Strand** *m* nudist beach
**flach** [flax] *adj* flat; level, even, plane; *fig* shallow
**Fläche** ['flɛçə] *f* (-; *-n*) surface (*a.* MATH); area (*a.* MATH); expanse, space
**'flächendeckend** *adj* exhaustive
**'Flächen|inhalt** *m* MATH (surface) area; **~maß** *n* square *or* surface measure
**'Flachland** *n* (*-[e]s*; *no pl*) lowland, plain
**Flachs** [flaks] *m* (*-es*; *no pl*) BOT flax
**flackern** ['flakɐn] *v/i* (*ge-*, *h*) flicker
**Fladenbrot** ['fla:dən-] *n* round flat bread (*or* loaf)

F

**Flagge** ['flagə] *f* (-; *-n*) flag
**'flaggen** *v/i* (*ge-*, *h*) fly a flag *or* flags
**Flak** [flak] *f* (-; -) MIL anti-aircraft gun
**Flamme** ['flamə] *f* (-; *-n*) flame (*a. fig*)
**Flanell** [fla'nɛl] *m* (*-s*; *-e*) flannel
**Flanke** ['flaŋkə] *f* (-; *-n*) flank, side; *soccer*: cross; SPORT flank vault
**flankieren** [flaŋ'ki:rən] *v/t* (*no -ge-*, *h*) flank
**Flasche** ['flaʃə] *f* (-; *-n*) bottle; baby's bottle; F *contp* dead loss
**'Flaschen|bier** *n* bottled beer; **~hals** *m* neck of a bottle; **~öffner** *m* bottle opener; **~pfand** *n* (bottle) deposit; **~zug** *m* TECH block and tackle, pulley
**flatterhaft** ['flatɐhaft] *adj* fickle, flighty
**flattern** ['flatɐn] *v/i* (*ge-*, *sein*) flutter; TECH (*h*) wobble
**flau** [flau] *adj* queasy; *fig* flat; ECON slack
**Flaum** [flaum] *m* (*-[e]s*; *no pl*) down, fluff, fuzz
**Flausch** [flauʃ] *m* (*-es*; *-e*) fleece
**flauschig** ['flauʃıç] *adj* fleecy, fluffy
**Flausen** ['flauzən] F *pl* (funny) ideas
**Flaute** ['flautə] *f* (-; *-n*) MAR calm; ECON slack period
**Flechte** ['flɛçtə] *f* (-; *-n*) plait, braid; BOT, MED lichen; **'flechten** *v/t* (*irr*, *ge-*, *h*) plait, braid (*hair*); weave (*basket*)
**Fleck** [flɛk] *m* (*-[e]s*; *-e*) stain, mark; speck; dot; blot(ch); *fig* place, spot; patch; ***blauer ~*** bruise; ***vom ~ weg*** on the spot; ***nicht vom ~ kommen*** not get anywhere; **'Flecken** *m* → ***Fleck***
**'Fleckenentferner** *m* stain remover
**'fleckenlos** *adj* spotless (*a. fig*)
**fleckig** ['flɛkıç] *adj* spotted; stained
**Fledermaus** ['fle:dɐ-] *f* ZO bat
**Flegel** ['fle:gəl] *m* (*-s*; -) lout, boor
**'flegelhaft** *adj* loutish
**'Flegeljahre** *pl* awkward age
**'flegeln** F *contp v/refl* (*ge-*, *h*) lounge
**flehen** ['fle:ən] *v/i* (*ge-*, *h*) beg; pray (***um*** for); **flehentlich** ['fle:əntlıç] *adj* imploring, entreating
**Fleisch** [flaiʃ] *n* (*-[e]s*; *no pl*) flesh (*a. fig*); GASTR meat; ***~ fressend*** BOT, ZO carnivorous; **~brühe** *f* (meat) broth, consommé
**Fleischer** ['flaiʃɐ] *m* (*-s*; -) butcher
**Fleischerei** [flaiʃə'rai] *f* (-; *-en*) butcher's (shop)
**'Fleischhauer** [-hauɐ] *Austrian m* (*-s*; -) butcher
**fleischig** ['flaiʃıç] *adj* fleshy
**'Fleisch|klößchen** *n* (*-s*; -) meatball; **~konˌserven** *pl* canned (*Br* tinned) meat
**'fleischlos** *adj* meatless
**'Fleischwolf** *m* meat grinder, *Br* mincer
**Fleiß** [flais] *m* (*-es*; *no pl*) diligence, hard work; **fleißig** ['flaisıç] *adj* diligent, hard-working; ***~ sein*** work hard
**fletschen** ['flɛtʃən] *v/t* (*ge-*, *h*) bare
**flexibel** [flɛ'ksi:bəl] *adj* flexible
**Flexibilität** [flɛksibili'tɛ:t] *f* (-; *no pl*) flexibility
**flicken** ['flıkən] *v/t* (*ge-*, *h*) mend, repair, *a. fig* patch (up); **'Flicken** *m* (*-s*; -) patch; **'Flickwerk** *n* patchwork (*a. fig*); **'Flickzeug** *n* TECH repair kit
**Flieder** ['fli:dɐ] *m* (*-s*; -) BOT lilac
**Fliege** ['fli:gə] *f* (-; *-n*) ZO fly; bow tie
**'fliegen** *v/i* (*irr*, *ge-*, *sein*) *and v/t* (*h*) fly (*a.* ***~ lassen***); F fall; F be fired, F get the sack; be kicked out *of school*; F ***~ auf*** (*acc*) really go for; F ***in die Luft ~*** blow up
**'Fliegen** *n* (*-s*; *no pl*) flying; aviation
**'Fliegen|fänger** *m* flypaper; **~fenster** *n* flyscreen; **~gewicht** *n* SPORT flyweight; **~gitter** *n* wire mesh (screen); **~klatsche** *f* flyswatter; **~pilz** *m* BOT fly agaric
**Flieger** ['fli:gɐ] *m* (*-s*; -) MIL airman; F plane; *cycling*: sprinter; **~aˌlarm** *m* air-raid warning
**fliehen** ['fli:ən] *v/i* (*irr*, *ge-*, *sein*) flee, run away (*both*: ***vor*** *dat* from)
**'Fliehkraft** *f* PHYS centrifugal force
**Fliese** ['fli:zə] *f* (-; *-n*), **'fliesen** *v/t* (*ge-*, *h*) tile; **'Fliesenleger** *m* (*-s*; -) tiler
**Fließband** ['fli:s-] *n* (*-[e]s*; *-bänder*) TECH assembly line; conveyor belt
**fließen** ['fli:sən] *v/i* (*irr*, *ge-*, *sein*) flow (*a. fig*); run; **~d 1.** *adj* flowing; running; LING fluent; **2.** *adv*: ***er spricht ~ Englisch*** he speaks English fluently *or* fluent English
**'Fließheck** *n* MOT fastback
**flimmern** ['flımɐn] *v/i* (*ge-*, *h*) shimmer; *film*: flicker
**flink** [flıŋk] *adj* quick, nimble
**Flinte** ['flıntə] *f* (-; *-n*) shotgun; F gun
**Flipper** ['flıpɐ] F *m* (*-s*; -) pinball machine; **'flippern** *v/i* (*ge-*, *h*) play pinball
**Flirt** [flœrt] *m* (*-s*; *-s*) flirtation
**flirten** ['flœrtən] *v/i* (*ge-*, *h*) flirt

**Flittchen** ['flɪtçən] F *n* (-*s*; -) floozie
**Flitter** ['flɪtɐ] *m* (-*s*; -) tinsel (*a. fig*), spangles; **~wochen** *pl* honeymoon
**flitzen** ['flɪtsən] F *v/i* (*ge-*, *sein*) flit, whizz, shoot
**flocht** [flɔxt] *pret of* ***flechten***
**Flocke** ['flɔkə] *f* (-; -*n*) flake
**flockig** ['flɔkɪç] *adj* fluffy, flaky
**flog** [flo:k] *pret of* ***fliegen***
**floh** [flo:] *pret of* ***fliehen***
**Floh** *m* (-[*e*]*s*; *Flöhe* ['flø:ə]) ZO flea
'**Flohmarkt** *m* flea market
**Florett** [flo'rɛt] *n* (-[*e*]*s*; -*e*) foil
**florieren** [flo'ri:rən] *v/i* (*no -ge-*, *h*) flourish, prosper
**Floskel** ['flɔskəl] *f* (-; -*n*) empty *or* cliché(d) phrase
**floss** [flɔs] *pret of* ***fließen***
**Floß** [flo:s] *n* (-*es*; *Flöße* ['flø:sə]) raft, float
**Flosse** ['flɔsə] *f* (-; -*n*) ZO fin, *a.* SPORT flipper
**Flöte** ['flø:tə] *f* (-; -*n*) MUS flute; recorder
**flott** [flɔt] *adj* brisk (*pace*); F smart, chic; MAR afloat
**Flotte** ['flɔtə] *f* (-; -*n*) MAR fleet; navy
'**Flottenstützpunkt** *m* MIL naval base
**Fluch** [flu:x] *m* (-[*e*]*s*; *Flüche* ['fly:çə]) curse; swear word; **fluchen** ['flu:xən] *v/i* (*ge-*, *h*) swear, curse
**Flucht** [flʊxt] *f* (-; -*en*) flight (***vor*** *dat* from); escape, getaway (***aus*** *dat* from)
'**fluchtartig** *adv* hastily
'**Fluchtauto** *n* getaway car
**flüchten** ['flʏçtən] *v/i* (*ge-*, *sein*) flee (***nach***, ***zu*** to), run away; escape, get away; **flüchtig** ['flʏçtɪç] *adj* quick; superficial; careless; fugitive, *criminal etc*: on the run, at large; ***~er Blick*** glance; ***~er Eindruck*** glimpse
'**Flüchtigkeitsfehler** *m* slip
**Flüchtling** ['flʏçtlɪŋ] *m* fugitive; POL refugee
'**Flüchtlingslager** *n* refugee camp
**Flug** [flu:k] *m* (-[*e*]*s*; *Flüge* ['fly:gə]) flight; ***im*** **~(e)** rapidly, quickly; **~abwehrra,kete** *f* MIL anti-aircraft missile; **~bahn** *f* trajectory; **~ball** *m tennis*: volley; **~begleiter(in)** flight attendant; **~blatt** *n* handbill, leaflet; **~dienst** *m* air service
**Flügel** ['fly:gəl] *m* (-*s*; -) ZO wing (*a.* SPORT); TECH blade; *windmill*: sail; MUS grand piano; **~mutter** *f* TECH wing nut; **~schraube** *f* TECH thumb screw; **~stürmer** *m* SPORT wing forward; **~tür** *f* folding door
'**Fluggast** *m* (air) passenger
**flügge** ['flʏgə] *adj* full-fledged
'**Flug|gesellschaft** *f* airline; **~hafen** *m* airport; **~linie** *f* air route; → ***Fluggesellschaft***; **~lotse** *m* air traffic controller; **~plan** *m* air schedule; **~platz** *m* airfield, airport; **~schein** *m* (flight) ticket; **~schreiber** *m* (-*s*; -) flight recorder, black box; **~sicherung** *f* air traffic control; **~verkehr** *m* air traffic
'**Flugzeug** *n* (-[*e*]*s*; -*e*) (air)plane, aircraft, *Br a.* aeroplane; ***mit dem*** ~ by air *or* plane; **~absturz** *m* air *or* plane crash; **~entführung** *f* hijacking, skyjacking; **~halle** *f* hangar; **~träger** *m* MAR MIL aircraft carrier
**Flunder** ['flʊndɐ] *f* (-; -*n*) ZO flounder
**flunkern** ['flʊŋkɐn] *v/i* (*ge-*, *h*) fib; brag
**Fluor** ['flu:o:ɐ] *n* (-*s*; *no pl*) CHEM fluorine; fluoride
'**Fluorchlorkohlenwasserstoff** *m* CHEM chlorofluorocarbon, CFC
**Flur** [flu:ɐ] *m* (-[*e*]*s*; -*e*) hall; corridor
**Fluss** [flʊs] *m* (-*es*; *Flüsse* ['flʏsə]) river; stream; ***im*** ~ *fig* in (a state of) flux
**fluss'abwärts** *adv* downstream
**fluss'aufwärts** *adv* upstream
'**Flussbett** *n* river bed
**flüssig** ['flʏsɪç] *adj* liquid; melted; *fig* fluent; ECON available; '**Flüssigkeit** *f* (-; -*en*) a) liquid, b) (*no pl*) liquidity; *fig* fluency; '**Flüssigkris,tallanzeige** *f* liquid crystal display, LCD
'**Fluss|lauf** *m* course of a river; **~pferd** *n* ZO hippopotamus, F hippo; **~ufer** *n* riverbank, riverside
**flüstern** ['flʏstɐn] *v/i and v/t* (*ge-*, *h*) whisper
**Flut** [flu:t] *f* (-; -*en*) flood (*a. fig*); high tide; ***es ist*** ~ the tide is in; **~licht** *n* floodlights; **~welle** *f* tidal wave
**focht** [fɔxt] *pret of* ***fechten***
**Fohlen** ['fo:lən] *n* (-*s*; -) ZO foal; colt; filly
**Föhn¹** [fø:n] *m* (-[*e*]*s*; -*e*) hairdrier
**Föhn²** *m* (-[*e*]*s*; -*e*) METEOR foehn, föhn
**föhnen** ['fø:nən] *v/t* (*ge-*, *h*) blow-dry
**Folge** ['fɔlgə] *f* (-; -*n*) result, consequence; effect; succession; order; series; TV *etc*: sequel, episode; aftermath; MED aftereffect

**folgen** ['fɔlgən] *v/i* (*ge-*, *sein*) follow; obey; ***hieraus folgt, dass*** from this it follows that; ***wie folgt*** as follows; **~d** *adj* following, subsequent
**folgendermaßen** ['fɔlgəndɐ'ma:sən] *adv* as follows
**'folgenschwer** *adj* momentous
**'folgerichtig** *adj* logical; consistent
**folgern** ['fɔlgɐn] *v/t* (*ge-*, *h*) conclude (***aus*** *dat* from); **Folgerung** ['fɔlgəruŋ] *f* (-; *-en*) conclusion
**folglich** ['fɔlklıç] *cj* consequently, thus, therefore
**folgsam** ['fɔlkza:m] *adj* obedient
**Folie** ['fo:ljə] *f* (-; *-n*) foil; transparency
**Folter** ['fɔltɐ] *f* (-; *-n*) torture; ***auf die ~ spannen*** tantalize; **'foltern** *v/t* (*ge-*, *h*) torture, *fig a.* torment
**Fön®** *m* → ***Föhn***[1]
**Fonds** [fõ:] *m* (-; -) ECON fund
**fönen** *v/t* → ***föhnen***
**Fontäne** [fɔn'tɛ:nə] *f* (-; *-n*) jet, spout; gush
**Förder|band** ['fœrdɐ-] *n* TECH conveyor belt; **~korb** *m mining*: cage
**fordern** ['fɔrdɐn] *v/t* (*ge-*, *h*) demand, *esp* JUR *a.* claim; ECON ask, charge
**fördern** ['fœrdɐn] *v/t* (*ge-*, *h*) promote; support (*a.* UNIV), sponsor; PED tutor, provide remedial classes for; TECH mine
**Forderung** ['fɔrdəruŋ] *f* (-; *-en*) demand; claim (*a.* JUR); ECON charge
**Förderung** ['fœrdəruŋ] *f* (-; *-en*) promotion, advancement; support, sponsorship; UNIV *etc*: grant; PED tutoring, remedial classes; TECH mining
**Forelle** [fo'rɛlə] *f* (-; *-n*) ZO trout
**Form** [fɔrm] *f* (-; *-en*) form, shape, SPORT *a.* condition; TECH mo(u)ld; ***gut in ~*** in great form; **formal** [fɔr'ma:l] *adj* formal; **Formalität** [fɔrmali'tɛ:t] *f* (-; *-en*) formality
**Format** [fɔr'ma:t] *n* (-[*e*]*s*; *-e*) size; format; *fig* caliber, *Br* calibre
**formatieren** [fɔrma'ti:rən] *v/t* (*no -ge-*, *h*) EDP format; **Forma'tierung** *f* (-; *-en*) EDP formatting
**Formel** ['fɔrməl] *f* (-; *-n*) formula
**formell** [fɔr'mɛl] *adj* formal
**formen** ['fɔrmən] *v/t* (*ge-*, *h*) shape, form; *fig* mo(u)ld
**'Formfehler** *m* irregularity
**formieren** [fɔr'mi:rən] *v/t and v/refl* (*no -ge-*, *h*) form (up)
**förmlich** ['fœrmlıç] **1.** *adj* formal; *fig* regular; **2.** *adv* formally; *fig* literally
**'formlos** *adj* shapeless; *fig* informal
**'formschön** *adj* well-designed
**Formular** [fɔrmu'la:ɐ] *n* (*-s*; *-e*) form, blank
**formulieren** [fɔrmu'li:rən] *v/t* (*no -ge-*, *h*) word, phrase; formulate; express
**Formu'lierung** *f* (-; *-en*) wording, phrasing; formulation; expression, phrase
**forsch** [fɔrʃ] *adj* dashing
**forschen** ['fɔrʃən] *v/i* (*ge-*, *h*) research, do research; **~ *nach*** search for
**Forscher** ['fɔrʃɐ] *m* (*-s*; -), **'Forscherin** *f* (-; *-nen*) explorer; (research) scientist; **Forschung** ['fɔrʃuŋ] *f* (-; *-en*) research (work)
**Forst** [fɔrst] *m* (-[*e*]*s*; *-e*[*n*]) forest
**Förster** ['fœrstɐ] *m* (*-s*; -) forester; forest ranger
**'Forstwirtschaft** *f* (-; *no pl*) forestry
**fort** [fɔrt] *adv* off, away; gone; missing
**Fort** [fo:ɐ] *n* (*-s*; *-s*) MIL fort
**'fortbestehen** *v/i* (*irr*, ***stehen***, *sep*, *no -ge-*, *h*) continue
**'fortbewegen** *v/refl* (*sep*, *no -ge-*, *h*) move; **'Fortbewegung** *f* moving; (loco)motion
**'Fortbildung** *f* (-, *no pl*) further education *or* training
**'fort|fahren** *v/i* (*irr*, ***fahren***, *sep*, *-ge-*) a) (*sein*) leave, go away, MOT *a.* drive off, b) (*h*) continue, go *or* keep on (***et. zu tun*** doing s.th.); **~führen** *v/t* (*sep*, *-ge-*, *h*) continue, carry on; **~gehen** *v/i* (*irr*, ***gehen***, *sep*, *-ge-*, *sein*) go away, leave
**'fortgeschritten** *adj* advanced
**'fortlaufend** *adj* consecutive, successive
**'fortpflanzen** *v/refl* (*sep*, *-ge-*, *h*) BIOL reproduce; *fig* spread; **'Fortpflanzung** *f* BIOL reproduction
**'fortschreiten** *v/i* (*irr*, ***schreiten***, *sep*, *-ge-*, *sein*) advance, proceed, progress; **~d** *adj* progressive
**'Fortschritt** *m* progress
**'fortschrittlich** *adj* progressive
**'fortsetzen** *v/t* (*sep*, *-ge-*, *h*) continue, go on with; **'Fortsetzung** *f* (-; *-en*) continuation; *film etc*: sequel; ***~ folgt*** to be continued; **'Fortsetzungsro,man** *m* serialized novel
**'fortwährend** *adj* continual, constant

**fossil** [fɔ'si:l] *adj*, **Fos'sil** *n* (-*s*; -*ien*) GEOL fossil (*a. fig* F)
**Foto** ['fo:to] *n* (-*s*; -*s*) photo(graph); ***ein ~ machen (von)*** take a photo (of)
'**Fotoalbum** *n* photo album
'**Fotoappa,rat** *m* camera
**Fotograf** [foto'gra:f] *m* (-*en*; -*en*) photographer; **Fotografie** [fotogra'fi:] *f* (-; -*n*) a) (*no pl*) photography, b) photograph, picture; **fotografieren** [fotogra'fi:rən] *v/t and v/i* (*no -ge-, h*) take a photo(graph) *or* picture (of); ***sich ~ lassen*** have one's picture taken; **Foto'grafin** *f* (-; -*nen*) photographer
**Fotoko'pie** *f* photocopy; **fotoko'pieren** *v/t* (*no -ge-, h*) (photo)copy
'**Fotomo,dell** *n* model
'**Fotozelle** *f* photoelectric cell
**Fotze** ['fɔtsə] V *f* (-; -*n*) cunt
**Foul** [faul] *n* (-*s*; -*s*) SPORT foul; **foulen** ['faulən] *v/t and v/i* (*ge-, h*) SPORT foul
**Foyer** [foa'je:] *n* (-*s*; -*s*) foyer, lobby, lounge
**Fr.** ABBR *of* ***Frau*** Mrs, Ms
**Fracht** [fraxt] *f* (-; -*en*) freight, load, MAR, AVIAT *a.* cargo; ECON freight, *Br* carriage; **~brief** *m* RAIL bill of lading (*a.* MAR), *Br* consignment note
**Frachter** ['fraxtɐ] *m* (-*s*; -) MAR freighter
**Frack** [frak] *m* (-[*e*]*s*; *Fräcke* ['frɛkə]) tails, tailcoat
**Frage** ['fra:gə] *f* (-; -*n*) question; ***e-e ~ stellen*** ask a question; → ***infrage***
'**Fragebogen** *m* question(n)aire
'**fragen** *v/t and v/i* (*ge-, h*) ask (***nach*** for; ***wegen*** about); ***nach dem Weg (der Zeit) ~*** ask the way (time); ***sich ~*** wonder
'**Frage|wort** *n* LING interrogative; **~zeichen** *n* LING question mark
**fraglich** ['fra:klɪç] *adj* doubtful, uncertain; ... in question
**fraglos** ['fra:klo:s] *adv* undoubtedly, unquestionably
**Fragment** [fra'gmɛnt] *n* (-[*e*]*s*; -*e*) fragment
**fragwürdig** ['fra:k-] *adj* dubious, F shady
**Fraktion** [frak'tsjo:n] *f* (-; -*en*) (parliamentary) group *or* party
**Frakti'onsführer** *m* PARL floor leader, *Br* chief whip
**Franc** [frã:] *m* (-; -*s*), **Franken** ['fraŋkən] *m* (-; -) franc
**frankieren** [fraŋ'ki:rən] *v/t* (*no -ge-, h*) stamp; frank
**Frankreich** ['fraŋkraiç] France
**Franse** ['franzə] *f* (-; -*n*) fringe
**fransig** ['franzɪç] *adj* frayed
**Franzose** [fran'tso:zə] *m* (-*n*; -*n*) Frenchman; ***die ~n pl*** the French
**Französin** [fran'tsø:zɪn] *f* (-; -*nen*) Frenchwoman
**französisch** [fran'tsø:zɪʃ] *adj* French
**fraß** [fra:s] *pret of* ***fressen***
**Fraß** F *contp m* (-*es*; *no pl*) muck
**Fratze** ['fratsə] *f* (-; -*n*) grimace
'**fratzenhaft** *adj* distorted
**Frau** [frau] *f* (-; -*en*) woman; wife; ***~ X*** Mrs (*or* Ms) X
**Frauchen** ['frauçən] *n* mistress (*of dog*)
'**Frauen|arzt** *m*, **~ärztin** *f* gyn(a)ecologist; **~bewegung** *f*: ***die ~*** POL women's lib(eration)
'**frauenfeindlich** *adj* sexist
'**Frauen|haus** *n* women's shelter (*Br* refuge); **~klinik** *f* gyn(a)ecological hospital; **~rechtlerin** [-rɛçtlərɪn] *f* (-; -*nen*) feminist
**Fräulein** ['frɔʏlain] *n* (-*s*; -) Miss
'**fraulich** *adj* womanly, feminine
**frech** [frɛç] *adj* sassy, *Br* cheeky
'**Frechheit** *f* (-; *no pl*) F *Br* cheek
**frei** [frai] *adj* free (***von*** from, of); independent; freelance; vacant; candid, frank; SPORT unmarked; ***ein ~er Tag*** a day off; ***morgen haben wir ~*** there is no school tomorrow; ***im Freien*** outdoors; → ***Fuß***
'**Freibad** *n* open-air swimming-pool
'**freibekommen** *v/t* (*irr*, ***kommen***, *sep*, *no -ge-, h*) get *a day etc* off
'**freiberuflich** *adj* freelance, self-employed
'**Freiexem,plar** *n* free copy
'**Freigabe** *f* (-; *no pl*) release
'**freigeben** (*irr*, ***geben***, *sep*, *-ge-, h*) **1.** *v/t* release; ***e-n Tag*** *etc* **~** give a day *etc* off; **2.** *v/i*: ***j-m ~*** give s.o. time off
'**freigebig** [-ge:bɪç] *adj* generous
'**Freigepäck** *n* AVIAT baggage allowance
'**freihaben** F *v/i* (*irr*, ***haben***, *sep*, *-ge-, h*) have a day off (*Br a.* a holiday)
'**Freihafen** *m* free port
'**freihalten** *v/t* (*irr*, ***halten***, *sep*, *-ge-, h*) keep, save (*seat etc*); treat (*s.o.*)

F

'**Frei|handel** *m* free trade; **~handelszone** *f* free trade area
'**freihändig** [-hɛndɪç] *adv* with no hands
'**Freiheit** *f* (-; *-en*) freedom, liberty; ***sich ~en herausnehmen gegen*** take liberties with
'**Freiheitsstrafe** *f* JUR prison sentence
'**Freikarte** *f* free ticket
'**freikaufen** *v/t* (*sep*, *-ge-*, *h*) ransom
'**Freikörperkul,tur** *f* (-; *no pl*) nudism
'**freilassen** *v/t* (*irr*, ***lassen***, *sep*, *-ge-*, *h*) release, set free; '**Freilassung** *f* (-; *-en*) release
'**Freilauf** *m* freewheel (*a.* ***im ~ fahren***)
'**freilich** *adv* indeed, of course
'**Freilicht...** *in cpds* open-air ...
'**freimachen** *v/t* (*sep*, *-ge-*, *h*) *post*: stamp; ***sich ~*** undress; ***sich ~ von*** free o.s. from; → ***Oberkörper***
'**Freimaurer** *m* freemason
'**freimütig** [-myːtɪç] *adj* candid, frank
'**freischaffend** *adj* freelance
'**freischwimmen** *v/refl* (*irr*, ***schwimmen***, *sep*, *-ge-*, *h*) pass a 15-minute swimming test
'**freisprechen** *v/t* (*irr*, ***sprechen***, *sep*, *-ge-*, *h*) *esp* REL absolve (***von*** from); JUR acquit (of); '**Freispruch** *m* JUR acquittal
'**Freistaat** *m* POL free state
'**frei|stehen** *v/i* (*irr*, ***stehen***, *sep*, *-ge-*, *h*) be unoccupied; SPORT be unmarked; ***es steht dir frei zu*** *inf* you are free to *inf*; **~stellen** *v/t* (*sep*, *-ge-*, *h*) ***j-n ~*** exempt s.o. (***von*** from) (*a.* MIL); ***j-m et. ~*** leave s.th. (up) to s.o.
'**Frei|stil** *m* freestyle; **~stoß** *m soccer*: free kick; **~stunde** *f* PED free period; **~tag** *m* Friday; **~tod** *m* suicide; **~treppe** *f* outdoor stairs; **~übungen** *pl* exercises; **~wild** *fig n* fair game
'**freiwillig** *adj* voluntary; ***sich ~ melden*** volunteer (***zu*** for); **Freiwillige** ['fraivɪlɪgə] *m, f* (*-n*; *-n*) volunteer
'**Freizeit** *f* free *or* leisure time; **~gestaltung** *f* leisure-time activities; **~kleidung** *f* leisurewear; **~park** *m* amusement park; **~zentrum** *n* leisure center (*Br* centre)
'**freizügig** *adj* permissive; *film etc*: explicit
**fremd** [frɛmt] *adj* strange; foreign; unknown; ***ich bin auch ~ hier*** I'm a stranger here myself; '**fremdartig** *adj* strange, exotic; **Fremde** ['frɛmdə] *m, f* (*-n*; *-n*) stranger; foreigner
'**Fremden|führer** *m*, **~führerin** *f* (-; *-nen*) (tourist) guide; **~hass** *m* xenophobia; **~legi,on** *f* Foreign Legion; **~verkehr** *m* tourism; **~verkehrsbü,ro** *n* tourist office; **~zimmer** *n* guest room; **~** (***zu vermieten***) rooms to let
'**fremdgehen** F *v/i* (*irr*, ***gehen***, *sep*, *-ge-*, *sein*) be unfaithful (to one's wife *or* husband), play around
'**Fremd|körper** *m* MED foreign body; *fig* alien element; **~sprache** *f* foreign language; **~sprachensekre,tärin** *f* bilingual secretary
'**fremd|sprachig, ~sprachlich** *adj* foreign-language
'**Fremdwort** *n* (*-[e]s*; *-wörter*) foreign word
**Frequenz** [fre'kvɛnts] *f* (-; *-en*) PHYS frequency
**Fresse** ['frɛsə] V *f* (-; *-n*) big (fat) mouth
'**fressen** *v/t* (*irr*, *ge-*, *h*) ZO eat, feed on; F gobble (up); *fig* devour
**Freude** ['frɔydə] *f* (-; *-n*) joy, delight; pleasure; ***~ haben an*** (*dat*) take pleasure in
'**Freuden|geschrei** *n* shouts of joy, cheers; **~haus** F *n* brothel; **~tag** *m* red-letter day; **~tränen** *pl* tears of joy
'**freudestrahlend** *adj* radiant (with joy)
**freudig** ['frɔydɪç] *adj* joyful, cheerful; happy (*event etc*)
**freudlos** ['frɔyt-] *adj* joyless, cheerless
**freuen** ['frɔyən] *v/t* (*ge-*, *h*) ***es freut mich, dass*** I'm glad *or* pleased (that); ***sich ~ über*** (*acc*) be pleased *or* glad about; ***sich ~ auf*** (*acc*) look forward to
**Freund** [frɔynt] *m* (*-[e]s*; *-e* ['frɔyndə]) friend; boyfriend; **Freundin** ['frɔyndɪn] *f* (-; *-nen*) friend; girlfriend
'**freundlich** *adj* friendly, kind, nice; *fig* cheerful (*room etc*); '**Freundlichkeit** *f* (-; *no pl*) friendliness, kindness
'**Freundschaft** *f* (-; *-en*) friendship; ***~ schließen*** make friends
'**freundschaftlich** *adj* friendly
'**Freundschaftsspiel** *n* SPORT friendly (game)
**Frevel** ['freːfəl] *m* (*-s*; -) outrage (***an*** *dat*, ***gegen*** on)
**Frieden** ['friːdən] *m* (*-s*; *no pl*) peace; ***im***

~ in peacetime; ***lass mich in ~!*** leave me alone!
**'Friedens|bewegung** *f* peace movement; **~forschung** *f* peace studies; **~verhandlungen** *pl* peace negotiations *or* talks; **~vertrag** *m* peace treaty
**friedfertig** ['fri:t-] *adj* peaceable
**'Friedhof** *m* cemetery, graveyard
**'friedlich** *adj* peaceful
**'friedliebend** *adj* peace-loving
**frieren** ['fri:rən] *v/i* (*irr, ge-, h*) freeze; ***ich friere*** I am *or* feel cold; I'm freezing
**Fries** [fri:s] *m* (*-es; -e*) ARCH frieze
**Frikadelle** [frika'dɛlə] *f* (*-; -n*) meatball
**frisch** [frɪʃ] *adj* fresh; clean (*shirt etc*); ***~ gestrichen!*** wet (*or* fresh) paint!
**Frische** ['frɪʃə] *f* (*-; no pl*) freshness
**'Frischhalte|beutel** *m* polythene bag; **~folie** *f* plastic wrap, *Br.* cling film
**Friseur** [fri'zø:ɐ] *m* (*-s; -e*) hairdresser; barber; **~sa,lon** *m* hairdresser's (shop), barber's shop
**Friseuse** [fri'zø:zə] *f* (*-; -n*) hairdresser
**frisieren** [fri'zi:rən] *v/t* (*no -ge-, h*) do *s.o.'s* hair; F MOT soup up
**Frisör** *etc* → ***Friseur*** *etc*
**Frist** [frɪst] *f* (*-; -en*) (fixed) period of time; deadline; extension (*a.* ECON)
**fristen** ['frɪstən] *v/t* (*ge-, h*) ***sein Dasein ~*** scrape a living
**'fristlos** *adj* without notice
**Frisur** [fri'zu:ɐ] *f* (*-; -en*) hairstyle, hairdo
**Fritten** ['frɪtən] F *pl* fries, *Br* chips; **frittieren** [fri'ti:rən] *v/t* (*no -ge-, h*) deep-fry
**frivol** [fri'vo:l] *adj* frivolous; suggestive
**froh** [fro:] *adj* glad (***über*** *acc* about); cheerful; happy; ***~es Fest!*** happy holiday!; Merry Christmas!
**fröhlich** ['frø:lɪç] *adj* cheerful, happy; merry; **'Fröhlichkeit** *f* (*-; no pl*) cheerfulness, merriment
**fromm** [frɔm] *adj* pious, devout; meek; steady (*horse*); ***~er Wunsch*** pious hope
**Frömmigkeit** ['frœmɪçkait] *f* (*-; no pl*) religiousness, piety
**Fronleichnam** ['fro:n-] *m* (*-[e]s; no pl*) REL Corpus Christi
**Front** [frɔnt] *f* (*-; -en*) front (*a. fig*), ARCH *a.* face, MIL *a.* line; ***in ~ liegen*** SPORT be ahead
**frontal** [frɔn'ta:l] *adj* MOT head-on
**Fron'talzusammenstoß** *m* MOT head-on collision
**'Frontantrieb** *m* MOT front-wheel drive
**fror** [fro:ɐ] *pret of* ***frieren***
**Frosch** [frɔʃ] *m* (*-[e]s; Frösche* ['frœʃə]) ZO frog; **~mann** *m* frogman; **~perspek,tive** *f* worm's-eye view; **~schenkel** *pl* GASTR frog's legs
**Frost** [frɔst] *m* (*-[e]s; Fröste* ['frœstə]) frost; **~beule** *f* chilblain
**frösteln** ['frœstəln] *v/i* (*ge-, h*) feel chilly, shiver (*a. fig*)
**'frostig** *adj* frosty, *fig a.* chilly
**'Frostschutzmittel** *n* MOT antifreeze
**Frottee** [frɔ'te:] *n, m* (*-[s]; -s*) terry(cloth); **frottieren** [frɔ'ti:rən] *v/t* (*no -ge-, h*) rub down
**Frucht** [frʊxt] *f* (*-; Früchte* ['frʏçtə]) BOT fruit (*a. fig*); **'fruchtbar** *adj* BIOL fertile, *esp fig a.* fruitful; **'Fruchtbarkeit** *f* (*-; no pl*) fertility; *fig* fruitfulness
**'fruchtlos** *adj* fruitless, futile
**'Fruchtsaft** *m* fruit juice
**früh** [fry:] *adj and adv* early; ***zu ~ kommen*** be early; ***~ genug*** soon enough; ***heute*** (***morgen***) ~ this (tomorrow) morning; **'Frühaufsteher** *m* (*-s; -*) early riser (F bird); **Frühe** ['fry:ə] *f*: ***in aller ~*** (very) early in the morning
**früher** ['fry:ɐ] **1.** *adj* former; previous; **2.** *adv* in former times, at one time; ***~ oder später*** sooner or later; ***ich habe ~*** (***einmal***) ... I used to ...
**'frühestens** *adv* at the earliest
**'Früh|geburt** *f* MED premature birth; premature baby; **~jahr** *n* spring; **~jahrsputz** *m* spring cleaning
**früh'morgens** *adv* early in the morning
**'frühreif** *adj* precocious
**'Frühstück** *n* breakfast (***zum*** for)
**'frühstücken** *v/i* (*ge-, h*) (have) breakfast
**Frust** [frʊst] F *m* (*-[e]s; no pl*) frustration
**Frustration** [frʊstra'tsjo:n] *f* (*-; -en*) frustration; **frustrieren** [frʊs'tri:rən] *v/t* (*no -ge-, h*) frustrate
**frz.** ABBR *of* ***französisch*** Fr., French
**Fuchs** [fʊks] *m* (*-es; Füchse* ['fʏksə]) ZO fox (*a. fig*); sorrel; **~jagd** *f* foxhunt(ing); **~schwanz** *m* TECH handsaw
**'fuchs'teufels'wild** F *adj* hopping mad
**fuchteln** ['fʊxtəln] *v/i* (*ge-, h*) ***~ mit*** wave *s.th.* around
**Fuge** ['fu:gə] *f* (*-; -n*) TECH joint; MUS fugue

**fügen** ['fy:gən] *v/refl (ge-, h)* submit (***in*** *acc, dat* to *s.th.*)
**fühlbar** ['fy:l-] *fig adj* noticeable; considerable; **fühlen** ['fy:lən] *v/t and v/i and v/refl (ge-, h)* feel, *fig a.* sense; ***sich wohl*** ~ feel well
**Fühler** ['fy:lɐ] *m (-s; -)* ZO feeler (*a. fig*)
**fuhr** [fu:ɐ] *pret of* ***fahren***
**führen** ['fy:rən] *(ge-, h)* **1.** *v/t* lead; guide; take; run, manage; ECON sell, deal in; keep (*account, books etc*); have (*a talk etc*); bear (*name etc*); MIL command; ***j-n ~ durch*** show s.o. round; ***sich*** ~ conduct o.s.; **2.** *v/i* lead (***zu*** to, *a. fig*), SPORT *a.* be leading, be ahead; **~d** *adj* leading
**Führer** ['fy:rɐ] *m (-s; -)* leader (*a.* POL); guide; head, chief; guide(book)
'**Führerschein** *m* MOT driver's license, *Br* driving licence
'**Führung** *f (-; -en)* a) *(no pl)* leadership, control; ECON management, b) (guided) tour; ***gute*** ~ good conduct; ***in ~ gehen*** (***sein***) SPORT take (be in) the lead; '**Führungszeugnis** *n* certificate of (good) conduct
**Fuhrunternehmen** ['fu:ɐ-] *n* trucking company, *Br* haulage contractors
'**Fuhrwerk** *n* horse-drawn vehicle
**Fülle** ['fʏlə] *f (-; no pl)* crush; *fig* wealth, abundance; GASTR body
'**füllen** *v/t and v/refl (ge-, h)* fill (*a.* MED), stuff (*a.* GASTR)
**Füller** ['fʏlɐ] *m (-s; -)*, '**Füllfederhalter** *m* fountain pen
**füllig** ['fʏlɪç] *adj* stout, portly
'**Füllung** *f (-; -en)* filling (*a.* MED), stuffing (*a.* GASTR)
**fummeln** ['fʊməln] F *v/i (ge-, h)* fiddle, tinker (*both*: ***an*** *dat* with); F grope
**Fund** [fʊnt] *m (-[e]s; -e* ['fʊndə]) discovery; find
**Fundament** [fʊnda'mɛnt] *n (-[e]s; -e)* ARCH foundation(s), *fig a.* basis
**Fundamentalist** [fʊndamɛnta'lɪst] *m (-en; -en)* fundamentalist
'**Fundbü͵ro** *n* lost and found (office), *Br* lost-property office
'**Fundgrube** *fig f* treasure trove
**Fundi** ['fʊndi] F *m (-s; -s)* POL radical Green
**fundiert** [fʊn'di:ɐt] *adj* well-founded (*argument etc*); sound (*knowledge*)
**fünf** [fʏnf] *adj* five; *grade*: F, N, *Br* fail, poor, E; '**Fünfeck** *n (-[e]s; -e)* pentagon; '**fünffach** *adj* fivefold
'**Fünfkampf** *m* SPORT pentathlon
'**Fünflinge** *pl* quintuplets
'**fünfte** *adj* fifth; '**Fünftel** *n (-s; -)* fifth
'**fünftens** *adv* fifth(ly), in the fifth place
'**fünfzehn(te)** *adj* fifteen(th)
**fünfzig** ['fʏnftsɪç] *adj* fifty
'**fünfzigste** *adj* fiftieth
**fungieren** [fʊŋ'gi:rən] *v/i (no -ge-, h)* ~ ***als*** act as, function as
**Funk** [fʊŋk] *m (-s; no pl)* radio; ***über*** *or* ***durch*** ~ by radio
'**Funkama͵teur** *m* radio ham
**Funke** ['fʊŋkə] *m (-n; -n)* spark; *fig a.* glimmer; **funkeln** ['fʊŋkəln] *v/i (ge-, h)* sparkle, glitter; twinkle
'**funken** *v/t (ge-, h)* radio, transmit
**Funker** ['fʊŋkɐ] *m (-s; -)* radio operator
'**Funk|gerät** *n* radio set; **~haus** *n* broadcasting center (*Br* centre); **~sig͵nal** *n* radio signal; **~spruch** *m* radio message; **~stati͵on** *f* radio station; **~streife** *f* (radio) patrol car; **~tele͵fon** *n* cellular phone
**Funktion** [fʊŋk'tsjo:n] *f (-; -en)* function; **Funktionär** [fʊŋktsjo'nɛ:ɐ] *m (-s; -e)* functionary, official (*a.* SPORT); **funktionieren** [fʊŋktsjo'ni:rən] *v/i (no -ge-, h)* work
'**Funkturm** *m* radio tower
'**Funkverkehr** *m* radio communication
**für** [fy:ɐ] *prp (acc)* for; in favo(u)r of; on behalf of; ~ ***immer*** forever; ***Tag ~ Tag*** day by day; ***Wort ~ Wort*** word by word; ***jeder ~ sich*** everyone by himself; ***was ~ ...?*** what (kind *or* sort of) ...?; ***das Für und Wider*** the pros and cons
**Furche** ['fʊrçə] *f (-; -n)* furrow; rut
**Furcht** [fʊrçt] *f (-; no pl)* fear, dread (*both*: ***vor*** *dat* of); ***aus*** **~(*, dass*)** for fear (that); ~ ***erregend*** frightening
'**furchtbar** *adj* terrible, awful
**fürchten** ['fʏrçtən] *v/t and v/i (ge-, h)* fear, be afraid of; dread; ~ ***um*** fear for; ***sich*** ~ be scared; be afraid (***vor*** *dat* of); ***ich fürchte***, ... I'm afraid ...
**fürchterlich** ['fʏrçtɐlɪç] → ***furchtbar***
'**furcht|los** *adj* fearless; **~sam** *adj* timid
**fürei'nander** *adv* for each other
**Furnier** [fʊr'ni:ɐ] *n (-[e]s; -e)*, **furnieren** [fʊr'ni:rən] *v/t (no -ge-, h)* veneer
'**Fürsorge** *f (-; no pl)* care; ***öffentliche*** ~

(public) welfare (work); **~empfänger** *m* social security beneficiary
**'fürsorglich** [-zɔrklıç] *adj* considerate
**'Für|sprache** *f* intercession (***für*** for; ***bei*** with); **~sprech** *m* (-[*e*]*s*; -*e*) *Swiss*: lawyer; **~sprecher(in)** advocate (*a. fig*)
**Fürst** [fʏrst] *m* (-*en*; -*en*) prince
**'Fürstentum** *n* (-*s*; -*tümer* [-ty:mɐ]) principality
**'Fürstin** *f* (-; -*nen*) princess
**'fürstlich** *adj* princely (*a. fig*)
**Furt** [fʊrt] *f* (-; -*en*) ford
**Furunkel** [fu'rʊŋkəl] *m* (-*s*; -) MED boil, furuncle
**'Fürwort** *n* (-[*e*]*s*; -*wörter*) LING pronoun
**Furz** [fʊrts] *m* (-*es*; -*e*), **'furzen** *v/i* (*ge*-, *h*) fart
**Fusion** [fu'zjo:n] *f* (-; -*en*) ECON merger, amalgamation
**fusionieren** [fuzjo'ni:rən] *v/i* (*no -ge-*, *h*) ECON merge, amalgamate
**Fuß** [fu:s] *m* (-*es*; *Füße* ['fy:sə]) ANAT foot; stand; stem; ***zu ~*** on foot; ***zu ~ gehen*** walk; ***gut zu ~ sein*** be a good walker; ***~ fassen*** become established; ***auf freiem ~*** at large
**'Fußball** *m* a) (*no pl*) soccer, *Br* football, b) soccer ball, *Br* football
**'Fußballer** [-balɐ] *m* (-*s*; -) footballer
**'Fußball|feld** *n* football field; **~rowdy** *m* (football) hooligan; **~spiel** *n* soccer *or* football match; **~spieler(in)** football player, footballer; **~toto** *n* football pools
**'Fußboden** *m* floor; flooring; **~heizung** *f* underfloor heating
**'Fußbremse** *f* MOT footbrake
**Fussel** ['fʊsəl] *f* (-; -*n*), *m* (-*s*; -[*n*]) piece of lint (*Br* fluff); *pl* lint, *Br* fluff; **'fusselig** ['fʊsəlıç] *adj* linty, *Br* covered in fluff; **'fusseln** *v/i* (*ge*-, *h*) shed a lot of lint (*Br* fluff), F mo(u)lt
**'Fußgänger** [-gɛŋɐ] *m* (-*s*; -), **'Fußgängerin** *f* (-; -*nen*) pedestrian; **'Fußgängerzone** *f* (pedestrian *or* shopping) mall, *Br* pedestrian precinct
**'Fußgeher** *Austrian m* → ***Fußgänger***
**'Fuß|gelenk** *n* ANAT ankle; **~matte** *f* doormat; **~note** *f* footnote; **~pflege** *f* pedicure; MED podiatry, *Br* chiropody; **~pfleger(in)** podiatrist, *Br* chiropodist; **~pilz** *m* MED athlete's foot; **~sohle** *f* ANAT sole (of the foot); **~spur** *f* footprint; track; **~stapfen** *pl*: ***in j-s ~ treten*** follow in s.o.'s footsteps; **~tritt** *m* kick; **~weg** *m* foothpath; ***e-e Stunde ~*** an hour's walk
**Futter¹** ['fʊtɐ] *n* (-*s*; *no pl*) AGR feed, fodder, food
**'Futter²** *n* (-*s*; -) lining
**Futteral** [fʊtə'ra:l] *n* (-*s*; -*e*) case; cover
**füttern¹** ['fʏtɐn] *v/t* (*ge*-, *h*) AGR feed
**'füttern²** *v/t* (*ge*-, *h*) line
**'Futternapf** *m* (feeding) bowl
**Fütterung** ['fʏtərʊŋ] *f* (-; -*en*) feeding (time)
**Futur** [fu'tu:ɐ] *n* (-*s*; -*e*) future (*a.* LING)

# G

**gab** [ga:p] *pret of* ***geben***
**Gabe** ['ga:bə] *f* (-; -*n*) gift, present; MED dose; *fig* talent, gift; ***milde ~*** alms
**Gabel** ['ga:bəl] *f* (-; -*n*) fork; TEL cradle
**'gabeln** *v/refl* (*ge*-, *h*) fork, branch
**'Gabelstapler** [-ʃta:plɐ] *m* (-*s*; -) TECH fork-lift (truck)
**Gabelung** ['ga:bəlʊŋ] *f* (-; -*en*) fork(ing)
**gackern** ['gakɐn] *v/i* (*ge*-, *h*) cluck, cackle (*a. fig*)
**gaffen** ['gafən] *v/i* (*ge*-, *h*) gawk, gawp, F rubberneck; **Gaffer** ['gafɐ] *m* (-*s*; -) F rubberneck(er), *Br* nosy parker
**Gage** ['ga:ʒə] *f* (-; -*n*) fee
**gähnen** ['gɛ:nən] *v/i* (*ge*-, *h*) yawn
**Gala** ['ga:la] *f* (-; -*s*) gala
**galant** [ga'lant] *adj* gallant, courteous
**Galeere** [ga'le:rə] *f* (-; -*n*) MAR galley
**Galerie** [galə'ri:] *f* (-; -*n*) gallery
**Galgen** ['galgən] *m* (-*s*; -) gallows; **~frist** *f* reprieve; **~humor** *m* gallows humo(u)r; **~vogel** F *m* crook

**Galle** ['galə] *f* (-; *-n*) ANAT gall; bile
'**Gallen|blase** *f* ANAT gall bladder; **~stein** *m* MED gallstone
**Gallert** ['galɐt] *n* (-[*es*]; *-e*), **Gallerte** [ga'lɛrtə] *f* (-; *-n*) jelly
**Galopp** [ga'lɔp] *m* (*-s*; *-s*, *-e*) gallop
**galoppieren** [galɔ'piːrən] *v/i* (*no -ge-*, *sein*) gallop
**galt** [galt] *pret of* **gelten**
**gammeln** ['gaməln] F *v/i* (*ge-*, *h*) loaf (about), bum around; **Gammler(in)** ['gamlɐ (-lərɪn)] F (*-s*; *-/-*; *-nen*) loafer, bum
**Gämse** ['gɛmzə] *f* (-; *-n*) ZO chamois
**gang** [gaŋ] *adj*: **~ *und gäbe*** nothing unusual, (quite) usual
**Gang** [gaŋ] *m* (-[*e*]*s*; *Gänge* ['gɛŋə]) walk, gait, way *s.o.* walks; ARCH passage, *a.* AVIAT *etc* aisle; corridor; MOT gear; GASTR course; ***et. in ~ bringen*** get s.th. going, start s.th.; ***in ~ kommen*** get started; ***im ~(e) sein*** be (going) on, be in progress; ***in vollem ~(e)*** in full swing
**gängeln** ['gɛŋəln] *v/t* (*ge-*, *h*) lead *s.o.* by the nose
**gängig** ['gɛŋɪç] *adj* current; ECON sal(e)able
'**Gangschaltung** *f* MOT gears
**Ganove** [ga'noːvə] F *m* (*-n*; *-n*) crook
**Gans** [gans] *f* (-; *Gänse* ['gɛnzə]) ZO goose
**Gänse|blümchen** ['gɛnzə-] *n* BOT daisy; **~braten** *m* roast goose; **~haut** *f* (-; *no pl*) gooseflesh; ***dabei kriege ich e-e ~*** F it gives me the creeps; **~marsch** *m* (-[*e*]*s*; *no pl*) single *or* Indian file
**Gänserich** ['gɛnzərɪç] *m* (*-s*; *-e*) ZO gander
**ganz** [gants] **1.** *adj* whole, entire, total; F undamaged; full (*hour etc*); ***den ~en Tag*** all day; ***die ~e Zeit*** all the time; ***auf der ~en Welt*** all over the world; ***sein ~es Geld*** all his money; **2.** *adv* completely, totally; very; quite, rather, fairly; ***~ allein*** all by oneself; ***~ aus Holz*** *etc* all wood *etc*; ***~ und gar*** completely, totally; ***~ und gar nicht*** not at all, by no means; ***~ wie du willst*** just as you like; ***nicht ~*** not quite; → ***voll***
**Ganze** ['gantsə] *n* (*-n*; *no pl*) whole; ***das ~*** the whole thing; ***im ~n*** in all, altogether; ***im großen ~n*** on the whole; ***aufs ~ gehen*** go all out
**gänzlich** ['gɛntslɪç] *adv* completely, entirely

'**Ganztags|beschäftigung** *f* full-time job; **~schule** *f* all-day school(ing)
**gar** [gaːɐ] **1.** *adj* GASTR done; **2.** *adv*: ***~ nicht*** not at all; ***~ nichts*** nothing at all; ***~ zu ...*** (a bit) too ...
**Garage** [ga'raːʒə] *f* (-; *-n*) garage
**Garantie** [garan'tiː] *f* (-; *-n*) guarantee, *esp* ECON warranty; **garantieren** [garan'tiːrən] *v/t and v/i* (*no -ge-*, *h*) guarantee (***für et.*** s.th.)
**Garbe** ['garbə] *f* (-; *-n*) AGR sheaf
**Garde** ['gardə] *f* (-; *-n*) guard; MIL (the) Guards
**Garderobe** [gardə'roːbə] *f* (-; *-n*) a) (*no pl*) wardrobe, clothes, b) checkroom, *Br* cloakroom; THEA dressing room
**Garde'roben|frau** *f* checkroom (*Br* cloakroom) attendant; **~marke** *f* coatcheck (*Br* cloakroom) ticket; **~ständer** *m* coat stand *or* rack
**Gardine** [gar'diːnə] *f* (-; *-n*) curtain
**Gar'dinenstange** *f* curtain rod
**gären** ['gɛːrən] *v/i* ([*irr*,] *ge-*, *h*, *sein*) ferment, work
**Garn** [garn] *n* (-[*e*]*s*; *-e*) yarn; thread; cotton
**Garnele** [gar'neːlə] *f* (-; *-n*) ZO shrimp; prawn
**garnieren** [gar'niːrən] *v/t* (*no -ge-*, *h*) garnish (*a. fig*)
**Garnison** [garni'zoːn] *f* (-; *-en*) MIL garrison, post
**Garnitur** [garni'tuːɐ] *f* (-, *-en*) set; suite
**Garten** ['gartən] *m* (*-s*; *Gärten* ['gɛrtən]) garden; **~arbeit** *f* gardening; **~bau** *m* (-[*e*]*s*; *no pl*) horticulture; **~erde** *f* (garden) mo(u)ld; **~fest** *n* garden party; **~geräte** *pl* gardening tools; **~haus** *n* summerhouse; **~lo,kal** *n* beer garden; outdoor restaurant; **~schere** *f* pruning shears; **~stadt** *f* garden city; **~zwerg** *m* (garden) gnome
**Gärtner** ['gɛrtnɐ] *m* (*-s*; -) gardener
**Gärtnerei** [gɛrtnə'rai] *f* (-; *-en*) truck farm, *Br* market garden
'**Gärtnerin** *f* (-; *-nen*) gardener
**Gärung** ['gɛːrʊŋ] *f* (-; *-en*) fermentation
**Gas** [gaːs] *n* (*-es*; *-e* ['gaːzə]) gas; ***~ geben*** MOT accelerate, F step on the gas
'**gasförmig** [-fœrmɪç] *adj* gaseous
'**Gas|hahn** *m* gas valve (*or* cock, *Br* tap); **~heizung** *f* gas heating; **~herd** *m* gas cooker *or* stove; **~kammer** *f* gas chamber; **~la,terne** *f* gas (street)

lamp; **~leitung** *f* gas main; **~maske** *f* gas mask; **~ofen** *m* gas stove; **~peˌdal** *n* MOT gas pedal, *Br* accelerator (pedal)
**Gasse** ['gasə] *f* (-; *-n*) lane, alley
**Gast** [gast] *m* (-[*e*]*s*; *Gäste* ['gɛstə]) guest; visitor; customer
**'Gastarbeiter** *m*, **'Gastarbeiterin** *f* foreign worker
**Gästebuch** ['gɛstə-] *n* visitors' book
**'Gästezimmer** *n* guest (*or* spare) room
**'gastfreundlich** *adj* hospitable
**'Gastfreundschaft** *f* hospitality
**'Gastgeber** [-ge:bɐ] *m* (*-s*; -) host
**'Gastgeberin** [-ge:bərɪn] *f* (-; *-nen*) hostess
**'Gast|haus** *n*, **~hof** *m* restaurant, inn
**gastieren** [gas'ti:rən] *v/i* (*no -ge-*, *h*) give performances; THEA guest, give a guest performance
**'gastlich** *adj* hospitable
**'Gast|mannschaft** *f* SPORT visiting team; **~spiel** *n* THEA guest performance; **~stätte** *f* restaurant; **~stube** *f* taproom; restaurant; **~wirt** *m* landlord; **~wirtschaft** *f* restaurant, inn
**'Gaswerk** *n* TECH gasworks
**'Gaszähler** *m* TECH gas meter
**Gatte** ['gatə] *m* (*-n*; *-n*) husband
**Gatter** ['gatɐ] *n* (*-s*; -) fence; gate
**Gattin** ['gatɪn] *f* (-; *-nen*) wife
**Gattung** ['gatʊŋ] *f* (-; *-en*) type, class, sort; BIOL genus; species
**GAU** [gau] (ABBR *of* ***größter anzunehmender Unfall***) *m* (-[*s*]; *no pl*) worst case scenario, *Br* maximum credible accident, MCA
**Gaul** [gaul] *m* (-[*e*]*s*; *Gäule* ['gɔʏlə]) nag
**Gaumen** ['gaumən] *m* (*-s*; -) ANAT palate
**Gauner** ['gaunɐ] *m* (*-s*; -), **'Gaunerin** *f* (-; *-nen*) F crook
**Gaze** ['ga:zə] *f* (-; *-n*) gauze
**Gazelle** [ga'tsɛlə] *f* (-; *-n*) ZO gazelle
**geb.** ABBR *of* ***geboren*** b., born
**Gebäck** [gə'bɛk] *n* (-[*e*]*s*; *-e*) pastry; cookies, *Br* biscuits
**ge'backen** *pp of* ***backen***
**Gebälk** [gə'bɛlk] *n* (-[*e*]*s*; *-e*) timberwork, beams
**gebar** [gə'ba:ɐ] *pret of* ***gebären***
**Gebärde** [gə'bɛ:ɐdə] *f* (-; *-n*) gesture
**ge'bärden** *v/refl* (*no -ge-*, *h*) behave, act (***wie*** like)
**gebären** [gə'bɛ:rən] *v/t* (*irr*, *no -ge-*, *h*) give birth to; **Gebärmutter** [gə'bɛ:ɐ-] *f* ANAT uterus, womb
**Gebäude** [gə'bɔʏdə] *n* (*-s*; -) building, structure
**Ge'beine** *pl* bones, mortal remains
**geben** ['ge:bən] *v/t* (*irr*, *ge-*, *h*) give (***j-m et.*** s.o. s.th.); hand, pass; deal (*cards*); make; ***sich ~*** pass; get better; ***von sich ~*** utter, let out; ***j-m die Schuld ~*** blame s.o.; ***es gibt*** there is, there are; ***was gibt es?*** what's up?; what's for *lunch etc?*; TV *etc* what's on?; ***das gibt's nicht*** that can't be true; that's out
**Gebet** [gə'be:t] *n* (-[*e*]*s*; *-e*) prayer
**ge'beten** *pp of* ***bitten***
**Gebiet** [gə'bi:t] *n* (-[*e*]*s*; *-e*) region, area; *esp* POL territory; *fig* field
**ge'bieterisch** *adj* imperious
**ge'bietsweise** *adv* regionally; ***~ Regen*** local showers
**Gebilde** [gə'bɪldə] *n* (*-s*; -) thing, object
**gebildet** [gə'bɪldət] *adj* educated
**Gebirge** [gə'bɪrgə] *n* (*-s*; -) mountains
**gebirgig** [gə'bɪrgɪç] *adj* mountainous
**Ge'birgs|bewohner** *m* mountain-dweller; **~zug** *m* mountain range
**Ge'biss** *n* (*-es*; *-e*) (set of) teeth; (set of) false teeth, denture(s)
**ge'bissen** *pp of* ***beißen***
**Gebläse** [gə'blɛ:zə] *n* (*-s*; -) TECH blower, (MOT air) fan
**ge'blasen** *pp of* ***blasen***
**geblichen** [gə'blɪçən] *pp of* ***bleichen***
**geblieben** [gə'bli:bən] *pp of* ***bleiben***
**geblümt** [gə'bly:mt] *adj* floral
**gebogen** [gə'bo:gən] **1.** *pp of* ***biegen***; **2.** *adj* bent, curved
**geboren** [gə'bo:rən] **1.** *pp of* ***gebären***; **2.** *adj* born; ***ein ~er Deutscher*** German by birth; ***~e Smith*** née Smith; ***ich bin am ... ~*** I was born on the ...
**geborgen** [gə'bɔrgən] **1.** *pp of* ***bergen***; **2.** *adj* safe, secure; **Ge'borgenheit** *f* (-; *no pl*) safety, security
**geborsten** [gə'bɔrstən] *pp of* ***bersten***
**Gebot** [gə'bo:t] *n* (-[*e*]*s*; *-e*) REL commandment; *fig* rule; necessity; *auction etc*: bid
**geboten** [gə'bo:tən] *pp of* ***bieten***
**gebracht** [gə'braxt] *pp of* ***bringen***
**gebrannt** [gə'brant] *pp of* ***brennen***
**ge'braten** *pp of* ***braten***
**Ge'brauch** *m* (-[*e*]*s*; *no pl*) use; application; **ge'brauchen** *v/t* (*no -ge-*, *h*) use;

employ; ***gut*** (***nicht***) ***zu ~ sein*** be useful (useless); ***ich könnte ... ~*** I could do with ...; **gebräuchlich** [gəˈbrɔʏçlɪç] *adj* in use; common, usual; current
**Geˈbrauchsanweisung** *f* directions *or* instructions for use
**geˈbrauchsfertig** *adj* ready for use; instant (*coffee etc*)
**Geˈbrauchsgrafiker** *m* commercial artist
**geˈbraucht** *adj* used, ECON *a.* second-hand
**Geˈbrauchtwagen** *m* MOT used *or* second-hand car; **~händler** *m* used car dealer
**Geˈbrechen** *n* (*-s*; -) defect, handicap
**gebrechlich** [gəˈbrɛçlɪç] *adj* frail; infirm; **Geˈbrechlichkeit** *f* (-; *no pl*) frailty; infirmity
**gebrochen** [gəˈbrɔxən] *pp of* ***brechen***
**Geˈbrüder** *pl* brothers
**Gebrüll** [gəˈbrʏl] *n* (-[*e*]*s*; *no pl*) roar(ing)
**Gebühr** [gəˈbyːɐ] *f* (-; *-en*) charge (*a.* TEL), fee; postage; due; **gebührend** [gəˈbyːrənt] *adj* due; proper
**geˈbühren|frei** *adj* free of charge; TEL toll-free, *Br* nonchargeable; **~pflichtig** *adj* chargeable; ***~e Straße*** toll road; ***~e Verwarnung*** fine
**gebunden** [gəˈbʊndən] **1.** *pp of* ***binden***; **2.** *adj* bound, *fig a.* tied
**Geburt** [gəˈbuːɐt] *f* (-; *-en*) birth; ***Deutscher von ~*** German by birth
**Geˈburten|konˌtrolle** *f*, **~regelung** *f* birth control
**geˈburten|schwach** *adj* low-birthrate; **~stark** *adj*: ***~e Jahrgänge*** baby boom
**Geˈburtenziffer** *f* birthrate
**gebürtig** [gəˈbʏrtɪç] *adj* by birth
**Geˈburts|anzeige** *f* birth announcement; **~datum** *n* date of birth; **~fehler** *m* congenital defect; **~helfer(in)** obstetrician; **~jahr** *n* year of birth; **~land** *n* native country; **~ort** *m* birthplace; **~tag** *m* birthday; **~tagsfeier** *f* birthday party; **~tagskind** *n* birthday boy (*or* girl); **~urkunde** *f* birth certificate
**Gebüsch** [gəˈbʏʃ] *n* (-[*e*]*s*; *-e*) bushes, shrubbery
**gedacht** [gəˈdaxt] *pp of* ***denken***
**Gedächtnis** [gəˈdɛçtnɪs] *n* (*-ses*; *-se*) memory; ***aus dem ~*** from memory; ***zum ~ an*** (*acc*) in memory (*or* commemoration) of; ***im ~ behalten*** keep in mind, remember; **~lücke** *f* memory lapse; **~schwund** *m* MED amnesia; blackout; **~stütze** *f* memory aid
**Gedanke** [gəˈdaŋkə] *m* (*-n*; *-n*) thought; idea; ***was für ein ~!*** what an idea!; ***in ~n*** absorbed in thought; absent-minded; ***sich ~n machen über*** (*acc*) think about; be worried *or* concerned about; ***j-s ~n lesen*** read s.o.'s mind
**Geˈdanken|austausch** *m* exchange of ideas; **~gang** *m* train of thought
**geˈdankenlos** *adj* thoughtless
**Geˈdanken|strich** *m* dash; **~übertragung** *f* telepathy
**Gedeck** [gəˈdɛk] *n* (-[*e*]*s*; *-e*) cover; ***ein ~ auflegen*** set a place
**gedeihen** [gəˈdaiən] *v/i* (*irr*, *no -ge-*, *sein*) thrive, prosper; grow; flourish
**geˈdenken** *v/i* (*irr*, ***denken***, *no -ge-*, *h*) (*gen*) think of; commemorate; mention
**Gedenk|feier** [gəˈdɛŋk-] *f* commemoration; **~miˌnute** *f*: ***e-e ~*** a moment's (*Br* minute's) silence; **~stätte** *f*, **~stein** *m* memorial; **~tafel** *f* plaque
**Gedicht** [gəˈdɪçt] *n* (-[*e*]*s*; *-e*) poem
**gediegen** [gəˈdiːgən] *adj* solid; tasteful
**gedieh** [gəˈdiː] *pret of* ***gedeihen***
**gediehen** [gəˈdiːən] *pp of* ***gedeihen***
**Gedränge** [gəˈdrɛŋə] *n* (*-s*; -) crowd, F crush; **geˈdrängt** *fig adj* concise
**gedroschen** [gəˈdrɔʃən] *pp of* ***dreschen***
**geˈdrückt** *fig adj* depressed
**gedrungen** [gəˈdrʊŋən] **1.** *pp of* ***dringen***; **2.** *adj* squat, stocky; thickset
**Geduld** [gəˈdʊlt] *f* (-; *no pl*) patience; **geˈdulden** *v/refl* (*no -ge-*, *h*) wait (patiently); **geduldig** [gəˈdʊldɪç] *adj* patient; **Geˈduldspiel** *n* puzzle (*a. fig*)
**gedurft** [gəˈdʊrft] *pp of* ***dürfen***
**geehrt** [gəˈʔeːɐt] *adj* hono(u)red; ***Sehr ~er Herr N.*** Dear Mr N.
**geeignet** [gəˈʔaignət] *adj* suitable; suited, qualified; right
**Gefahr** [gəˈfaːɐ] *f* (-; *-en*) danger; threat; risk; ***auf eigene ~*** at one's own risk; ***außer ~*** out of danger, safe
**gefährden** [gəˈfɛːɐdən] *v/t* (*no -ge-*, *h*) endanger; risk, jeopardize
**geˈfahren** *pp of* ***fahren***
**gefährlich** [gəˈfɛːɐlɪç] *adj* dangerous; risky
**geˈfahrlos** *adj* without risk, safe

**Gefährte** [gə'fɛːɐtə] *m* (*-n*; *-n*), **Ge'fährtin** *f* (-; *-nen*) companion
**Gefälle** [gə'fɛlə] *n* (*-s*; -) fall, slope, descent; gradient (*a.* PHYS)
**ge'fallen 1.** *pp of* **fallen; 2.** *v/i* (*irr*, **fallen**, *no -ge-*, *h*) please; ***es gefällt mir*** (***nicht***) I (don't) like it; ***wie gefällt dir ...?*** how do you like ...?; ***sich et. ~ lassen*** put up with s.th.
**Ge'fallen**[1] *m* (*-s*; -) favo(u)r; ***j-n um e-n ~ bitten*** ask a favo(u)r of s.o.
**Ge'fallen**[2] *n*: ***~ finden an*** (*dat*) enjoy, like
**ge'fällig** *adj* pleasant, agreeable; obliging, kind; ***j-m ~ sein*** do s.o. a favo(u)r
**Ge'fälligkeit** *f* (-; *-en*) a) (*no pl*) kindness, b) favo(u)r
**ge'fangen 1.** *pp of* **fangen; 2.** *adj* captive; imprisoned; ***~ halten*** keep *s.o.* prisoner; ***~ nehmen*** take *s.o.* prisoner; *fig* captivate; **Ge'fangene** *m*, *f* (*-n*; *-n*) prisoner; convict; **Ge'fangennahme** *f* (-; *no pl*) capture; **Ge'fangenschaft** *f* (-; *no pl*) captivity, imprisonment; ***in ~ sein*** be a prisoner of war
**Gefängnis** [gə'fɛŋnɪs] *n* (*-ses*; *-se*) prison, jail, *Br a.* gaol; ***ins ~ kommen*** go to jail *or* prison; **~di,rektor** *m* governor, warden; **~strafe** *f* (sentence *or* term of) imprisonment; **~wärter** *m* prison guard
**Gefäß** [gə'fɛːs] *n* (*-es*; *-e*) vessel (*a.* ANAT), container
**gefasst** [gə'fast] *adj* composed; ***~ auf*** (*acc*) prepared for
**Gefecht** [gə'fɛçt] *n* (*-[e]s*; *-e*) MIL combat, action
**gefedert** [gə'feːdɐt] *adj*: ***gut ~ sein*** MOT have good suspension
**gefeit** [gə'fait] *adj*: ***~ gegen*** immune to
**Gefieder** [gə'fiːdɐ] *n* (*-s*; -) ZO plumage, feathers
**geflochten** [gə'flɔxtən] *pp of* **flechten**
**geflogen** [gə'floːgən] *pp of* **fliegen**
**geflohen** [gə'floːən] *pp of* **fliehen**
**geflossen** [gə'flɔsən] *pp of* **fließen**
**Ge'flügel** *n* (*-s*; *no pl*) poultry
**ge'flügelt** *adj*: ***~es Wort*** saying
**gefochten** [gə'fɔxtən] *pp of* **fechten**
**Ge'folge** *n* (*-s*; -) entourage, retinue, train; **Gefolgschaft** [gə'fɔlkʃaft] *f* (-; *-en*) followers
**gefragt** [gə'fraːkt] *adj* in demand, popular
**gefräßig** [gə'frɛːsɪç] *adj* greedy, voracious
**Gefreite** [gə'fraitə] *m* (*-n*; *-n*) MIL private first class, *Br* lance corporal
**ge'fressen** *pp of* **fressen**
**ge'frieren** *v/i* (*irr*, **frieren**, *no -ge-*, *sein*) freeze
**Gefrier|fach** [gə'friːɐ-] *n* freezer, freezing compartment; **~fleisch** *n* frozen meat
**ge'friergetrocknet** *adj* freeze-dried
**Ge'frier|punkt** *m* freezing point; **~truhe** *f* freezer, deep-freeze
**gefroren** [gə'froːrən] *pp of* **frieren**
**Ge'frorene** *Austrian n* (*-n*; *no pl*) ice cream
**Gefüge** [gə'fyːgə] *n* (*-s*; -) structure, texture
**gefügig** [gə'fyːgɪç] *adj* pliant
**Ge'fügigkeit** *f* (-; *no pl*) pliancy
**Gefühl** [gə'fyːl] *n* (*-[e]s*; *-e*) feeling; sense; sensation; emotion; **ge'fühllos** *adj* insensible, numb; unfeeling, heartless; **ge'fühlsbetont** *adj* (highly) emotional; **ge'fühlvoll** *adj* (full of) feeling; tender; sentimental
**gefunden** [gə'fʊndən] *pp of* **finden**
**gegangen** [gə'gaŋən] *pp of* **gehen**
**gegeben** [gə'geːbən] *pp of* **geben**
**gegen** ['geːgən] *prp* (*acc*) against, JUR, SPORT *a.* versus; about, around; (in return) for; MED *etc* for; compared with
**'Gegen...** *in cpds ...aktion*, *...angriff*, *...argument*, *...frage etc*: counter-...; **~besuch** *m* return visit
**Gegend** ['geːgənt] *f* (-; *-en*) region, area; countryside; neighbo(u)rhood
**gegenei'nander** *adv* against one another *or* each other
**'Gegen|fahrbahn** *f* MOT opposite *or* oncoming lane; **~gewicht** *n* counterweight; ***ein ~ bilden zu et.*** counterbalance s.th.; **~kandi,dat** *m* rival candidate; **~leistung** *f* quid pro quo; ***als ~*** in return; **~licht** *n* (*-[e]s*; *no pl*) PHOT back light; ***im*** *or* ***bei ~*** against the light; **~maßnahme** *f* countermeasure; **~mittel** *n* MED antidote (*a. fig*); **~par,tei** *f* other side; POL opposition; SPORT opposite side; **~richtung** *f* opposite direction
**'Gegensatz** *m* contrast; opposite; ***im ~ zu*** in contrast to *or* with; **'gegensätzlich** [-zɛtslɪç] *adj* contrary, opposite
**'Gegenseite** *f* opposite side

G

**'gegenseitig** [-zaitıç] *adj* mutual
**'Gegenseitigkeit** *f*: ***auf ~ beruhen*** be mutual
**'Gegen|spieler** *m*, **~spielerin** *f* SPORT opponent (*a. fig*); **~sprechanlage** *f* intercom (system)
**'Gegenstand** *m* object (*a. fig*); *fig* subject; **'gegenständlich** [-ʃtɛntlıç] *adj art*: representational; **'gegenstandslos** *adj* invalid; irrelevant; *art*: abstract, nonrepresentational
**'Gegen|stimme** *f* PARL vote against, no; ***nur drei ~n*** only three noes; **~stück** *n* counterpart
**'Gegenteil** *n* opposite; ***im ~*** on the contrary; **'gegenteilig** *adj* contrary, opposite
**gegen'über** *adv and prp* (*dat*) opposite; *fig* to, toward(s); compared with
**Gegen'über** *n* (-*s*; -) person opposite; neighbo(u)r across the street
**gegen'überstehen** *v/i* (*irr*, ***stehen***, *sep*, *-ge-*, *h*) face, be faced with
**Gegen'überstellung** *f* confrontation
**'Gegenverkehr** *m* oncoming traffic
**'Gegenwart** [-vart] *f* (-; *no pl*) present (time); presence; LING present (tense)
**'gegenwärtig** [-vɛrtıç] **1.** *adj* present, current; **2.** *adv* at present
**'Gegen|wehr** [-veːɐ] *f* (-; *no pl*) resistance; **~wert** *m* equivalent (value); **~wind** *m* head wind
**'gegenzeichnen** *v/t* (*sep*, *-ge-*, *h*) countersign
**'Gegenzug** *m* countermove; RAIL train coming from the opposite direction
**gegessen** [gə'gɛsən] *pp of* ***essen***
**geglichen** [gə'glıçən] *pp of* ***gleichen***
**geglitten** [gə'glıtən] *pp of* ***gleiten***
**geglommen** [gə'glɔmən] *pp of* ***glimmen***
**Gegner** ['geːgnɐ] *m* (-*s*; -), **'Gegnerin** *f* (-; *-nen*) opponent (*a.* SPORT), adversary; MIL enemy
**'gegnerisch** *adj* opposing; MIL (of the) enemy, hostile
**'Gegnerschaft** *f* (-; *-en*) opposition
**gegolten** [gə'gɔltən] *pp of* ***gelten***
**gegoren** [gə'goːrən] *pp of* ***gären***
**gegossen** [gə'gɔsən] *pp of* ***gießen***
**ge'graben** *pp of* ***graben***
**gegriffen** [gə'grıfən] *pp of* ***greifen***
**gehabt** [gə'haːpt] *pp of* ***haben***
**Gehackte** [gə'haktə] *n* → ***Hackfleisch***

G

**Gehalt** [gə'halt] **1.** *m* (-[*e*]*s*; *-e*) content; **2.** *n* (-[*e*]*s*; *Gehälter* [gə'hɛltɐ]) salary
**ge'halten** *pp of* ***halten***
**Ge'halts|empfänger** *m* salaried employee; **~erhöhung** *f* raise, *Br* increase *or* rise in salary
**ge'haltvoll** *adj* substantial; nutritious
**gehangen** [gə'haŋən] *pp of* ***hängen*** 1
**gehässig** [gə'hɛsıç] *adj* malicious, spiteful; **Ge'hässigkeit** *f* (-; *no pl*) malice, spite(fulness)
**ge'hauen** *pp of* ***hauen***
**Gehäuse** [gə'hɔyzə] *n* (-*s*; -) case, box; TECH casing; ZO shell; BOT core
**Gehege** [gə'heːgə] *n* (-*s*; -) enclosure
**geheim** [gə'haim] *adj* secret; ***et. ~ halten*** keep s.th. (a) secret
**Ge'heim|a,gent** *m* secret agent; **~dienst** *m* secret service
**Geheimnis** [gə'haimnıs] *n* (-*ses*; *-se*) secret; mystery
**ge'heimnisvoll** *adj* mysterious
**Ge'heim|nummer** *f* TEL unlisted (*Br* ex-directory) number; **~poli,zei** *f* secret police; **~schrift** *f* code, cipher
**ge'heißen** *pp of* ***heißen***
**gehemmt** [gə'hɛmt] *adj* inhibited, self-conscious
**gehen** ['geːən] *v/i* (*irr*, *ge-*, *sein*) go; walk; leave; TECH work (*a. fig*); ECON sell; *fig* last; ***einkaufen*** (***schwimmen***) ***~*** go shopping (swimming); ***~ wir!*** let's go!; ***wie geht es dir*** (***Ihnen***)***?*** how are you?; ***es geht mir gut*** (***schlecht***) I'm fine (not feeling well); ***~ in*** (*acc*) go into; ***~ nach*** *road etc*: lead to; *window etc*: face; *fig* go *or* judge by; ***das geht nicht*** that's impossible; ***das geht schon*** that's o.k.; ***es geht nichts über*** (*acc*) ... there is nothing like ...; ***worum geht es?*** what is it about?; ***darum geht es*** (***nicht***) that's (not) the point; ***sich ~ lassen*** let o.s. go
**geheuer** [gə'hɔyɐ] *adj*: ***nicht*** (***ganz***) ***~*** eerie, creepy, F fishy
**Geheul** [gə'hɔyl] *n* (-[*e*]*s*; *no pl*) howling
**Ge'hirn** *n* (-[*e*]*s*; *-e*) ANAT brain(s); **~erschütterung** *f* MED concussion (of the brain); **~schlag** *m* MED (cerebral) apoplexy; **~wäsche** *f* brainwashing
**gehoben** [gə'hoːbən] **1.** *pp of* ***heben***; **2.** *adj* elevated; high(er); ***~e Stimmung*** high spirits
**Gehöft** [gə'hœft] *n* (-[*e*]*s*; *-e*) farm(stead)

**geholfen** [gə'hɔlfən] *pp of* ***helfen***
**Gehölz** [gə'hœlts] *n (-es; -e)* wood, coppice, copse
**Gehör** [gə'hø:ɐ] *n (-[e]s; -e)* (sense of) hearing; ear; ***nach dem ~*** by ear; ***sich ~ verschaffen*** make o.s. heard
**ge'horchen** *v/i (no -ge-, h)* obey; ***nicht ~*** disobey
**ge'hören** *v/i (no -ge-, h)* belong (*dat or* ***zu*** to); ***gehört dir das?*** is this yours?; ***es gehört sich*** (***nicht***) it is proper *or* right (not done); ***das gehört nicht hierher*** that's not to the point
**ge'hörig 1.** *adj* due, proper; necessary; decent; ***zu et. ~*** belonging to s.th.; **2.** *adv* properly, thoroughly
**ge'hörlos** *adj* deaf; ***die Gehörlosen*** the deaf
**gehorsam** [gə'ho:ɐza:m] *adj* obedient
**Ge'horsam** *m (-s; no pl)* obedience
**'Gehsteig** *m*, **'Gehweg** *m* sidewalk, *Br* pavement
**Geier** ['gaiɐ] *m (-s; -)* ZO vulture, buzzard
**Geige** ['gaigə] *f (-; -n)* MUS violin, F fiddle; (***auf der***) ***~ spielen*** play (on) the violin
**'Geigen|bogen** *m* MUS (violin) bow; **~kasten** *m* MUS violin case
**'Geiger** ['gaigɐ] *m (-s; -)*, **Geigerin** ['gaigərɪn] *f (-; -nen)* MUS violinist
**'Geigerzähler** *m* PHYS Geiger counter
**geil** [gail] *adj* V hot, horny; *contp* lecherous, lewd; BOT rank; F awesome, *Br* brill, ace
**Geisel** ['gaizəl] *f (-; -n)* hostage; **~nehmer** [-ne:mɐ] *m (-s; -)* kidnap(p)er
**Geißel** ['gaisəl] *fig f (-; -n)* scourge
**Geist** [gaist] *m (-[e]s; -er)* a) (*no pl*) spirit; soul; mind; intellect; wit, b) ghost; ***der Heilige ~*** REL the Holy Ghost *or* Spirit
**Geister|bahn** ['gaistɐ-] *f* tunnel of horror, *Br* ghost train; **~fahrer** F *m* MOT wrong-way driver
**'geisterhaft** *adj* ghostly
**'geistesabwesend** *adj* absent-minded
**'Geistes|arbeiter** *m* brainworker; **~blitz** *m* brainstorm, *Br* brainwave
**'Geistesgegenwart** *f* presence of mind; **'geistesgegenwärtig** *adj* alert; quick-witted
**'geistesgestört** *adj* mentally disturbed, deranged
**'geisteskrank** *adj* mentally ill
**'Geisteskrankheit** *f* mental illness
**'geistesschwach** *adj* feeble-minded
**'Geisteswissenschaften** *pl the* arts, *the* humanities
**'Geisteszustand** *m* mental state
**geistig** ['gaistɪç] *adj* mental; intellectual; spiritual; ***~ behindert*** mentally handicapped; ***~e Getränke*** spirits
**'geistlich** *adj* religious; spiritual; ecclesiastical; clerical; **'Geistliche** *m (-n; -n)* clergyman; priest; minister; ***die ~n*** the clergy
**'geistlos** *adj* trivial, inane, silly
**'geistreich, 'geistvoll** *adj* witty, clever
**Geiz** [gaits] *m (-es; no pl)* stinginess
**'Geizhals** *m* miser, niggard
**geizig** ['gaitsɪç] *adj* stingy, miserly
**Ge'jammer** F *n (-s; no pl)* wailing, complaining
**gekannt** [gə'kant] *pp of* ***kennen***
**Gekläff** [gə'klɛf] F *n (-[e]s; no pl)* yapping
**Geklapper** [gə'klapɐ] F *n (-s; no pl)* clatter(ing)
**Geklimper** F *n (-s; no pl)* tinkling
**geklungen** [gə'klʊŋən] *pp of* ***klingen***
**gekniffen** [gə'knɪfən] *pp of* ***kneifen***
**ge'kommen** *pp of* ***kommen***
**gekonnt** [gə'kɔnt] **1.** *pp of* ***können***; **2.** *adj* masterly
**gekränkt** [gə'krɛŋkt] *adj* hurt, offended
**Gekritzel** [gə'krɪtsəl] *contp n (-s; no pl)* scrawl, scribble
**gekrochen** [gə'krɔxən] *pp of* ***kriechen***
**gekünstelt** [gə'kʏnstəlt] *adj* affected; artificial
**Gelächter** [gə'lɛçtɐ] *n (-s; no pl)* laughter
**ge'laden** *pp of* ***laden***
**Ge'lage** *n (-s; -)* feast; carouse
**Gelände** [gə'lɛndə] *n (-s; -)* area, country, ground; site; ***auf dem ~*** on the premises; **~...** *in cpds ...lauf, ...ritt, ...wagen etc*: cross-country ...
**Geländer** [gə'lɛndɐ] *n (-s; -)* banisters; handrail, rail(ing); parapet
**ge'lang** *pret of* ***gelingen***
**ge'langen** *v/i (no -ge-, sein)* ***~ an*** (*acc*) *or* ***nach*** reach, arrive at, get *or* come to; ***~ in*** (*acc*) get *or* come into; *fig* ***zu et. ~*** gain *or* win *or* achieve s.th.
**ge'lassen 1.** *pp of* ***lassen***; **2.** *adj* calm, composed, cool
**Gelatine** [ʒela'ti:nə] *f (-; no pl)* gelatin(e)

**ge'laufen** *pp of* ***laufen***
**ge'läufig** *adj* common, current; familiar
**gelaunt** [gə'launt] *adj*: ***schlecht*** **(*gut*)** ~ ***sein*** be in a bad (good) mood
**gelb** [gɛlp] *adj* yellow
**'gelblich** *adj* yellowish
**'Gelbsucht** *f* (-; *no pl*) MED jaundice
**Geld** [gɛlt] *n* (-[*e*]*s*; *-er* ['gɛldɐ]) money; ***zu ~ machen*** turn into cash
**'Geld|angelegenheiten** *pl* money *or* financial matters *or* affairs; **~anlage** *f* investment; **~ausgabe** *f* expense; **~auto,mat** *m* automatic teller machine, ATM, autoteller, *Br* cash dispenser; **~beutel** *m*, **~börse** *f* purse; **~buße** *f* fine, penalty; **~geber(in)** [-ge:bɐ (-bərɪn)] (*-s*; *-/-*; *-nen*) financial backer; investor
**'geldgierig** *adj* greedy for money
**'Geld|knappheit** *f*, **~mangel** *m* lack of money; ECON (financial) stringency; **~mittel** *pl* funds, means, resources; **~schein** *m* bill, *Br* (bank)note; **~schrank** *m* safe; **~sendung** *f* remittance; **~strafe** *f* fine; **~stück** *n* coin; **~verlegenheit** *f* financial embarrassment; **~verschwendung** *f* waste of money; **~waschanlage** *f* money laundering scheme; **~wechsel** *m* exchange of money; **~wechsler** [-vɛksl ɐ] *m* (*-s*; *-*) change machine
**Gelee** [ʒe'le:] *n*, *m* (*-s*; *-s*) jelly; gel
**ge'legen 1.** *pp of* ***liegen***; **2.** *adj* situated, located; *fig* convenient, opportune; **Ge'legenheit** *f* (-; *-en*) occasion; opportunity, chance; ***bei ~*** on occasion
**Ge'legenheits|arbeit** *f* casual *or* odd job; **~arbeiter** *m* casual labo(u)rer, odd-job man; **~kauf** *m* bargain
**gelegentlich** [gə'le:gəntlɪç] *adv* occasionally
**gelehrig** [gə'le:rɪç] *adj* docile
**Gelehrsamkeit** [gə'le:ɐza:mkait] *f* (-; *no pl*) learning; **gelehrt** [gə'le:ɐt] *adj* learned; **Ge'lehrte** *m*, *f* (*-n*; *-n*) scholar, learned man *or* woman
**Geleise** [gə'laizə] *n* → ***Gleis***
**Geleit** [gə'lait] *n* (-[*e*]*s*; *-e*) escort
**ge'leiten** *v/t* (*no -ge-*, *h*) accompany, conduct, escort
**Ge'leitzug** *m* MAR, MIL convoy
**Gelenk** [gə'lɛŋk] *n* (-[*e*]*s*; *-e*) ANAT, TECH joint; **ge'lenkig** *adj* flexible (*a.* TECH); lithe, supple
**gelernt** [gə'lɛrnt] *adj* skilled, trained
**ge'lesen** *pp of* ***lesen***
**geliebt** [gə'li:pt] *adj* (be)loved, dear
**Ge'liebte 1.** *m* (*-n*; *-n*) lover; **2.** *f* (*-n*; *-n*) mistress
**geliehen** [gə'li:ən] *pp of* ***leihen***
**gelingen** [gə'lɪŋən] *v/i* (*irr*, *no -ge-*, *sein*) succeed, manage; turn out well; ***es gelang mir*, *et. zu tun*** I succeeded in doing (I managed to do) s.th.; **Ge'lingen** *n* (*-s*; *no pl*) success; ***gutes ~!*** good luck!
**gelitten** [gə'lɪtən] *pp of* ***leiden***
**gelogen** [gə'lo:gən] *pp of* ***lügen***
**gelten** ['gɛltən] *v/i and v/t* (*irr*, *ge-*, *h*) be worth; *fig* count for; be valid; SPORT count; ECON be effective; ***~ für*** apply to; ***~ als*** be regarded *or* looked upon as, be considered *or* supposed to be; ***~ lassen*** accept (***als*** as); **~d** *adj* accepted; ***~ machen*** assert; ***s-n Einfluss*** **(*bei j-m*)** ***~ machen*** bring one's influence to bear (on s.o.)
**'Geltung** *f* (-; *no pl*) prestige; weight; ***zur ~ kommen*** show to advantage
**'Geltungsbedürfnis** *n* (*-ses*; *no pl*) need for recognition
**Gelübde** [gə'lʏpdə] *n* (*-s*; *-*) vow
**gelungen** [gə'lʊŋən] **1.** *pp of* ***gelingen***; **2.** *adj* successful, a success
**gemächlich** [gə'mɛ:çlɪç] *adj* leisurely
**ge'mahlen** *pp of* ***mahlen***
**Gemälde** [gə'mɛ:ldə] *n* (*-s*; *-*) painting, picture; **~gale,rie** *f* art (*or* picture) gallery
**gemäß** [gə'mɛ:s] *prp* (*dat*) according to
**gemäßigt** [gə'mɛ:sɪçt] *adj* moderate; temperate (*climate etc*)
**gemein** [gə'main] *adj* mean; dirty, filthy (*joke etc*); BOT, ZO common
**Gemeinde** [gə'maində] *f* (-; *-n*) POL municipality; local government; REL parish; congregation; **~rat** *m* (member of the) city (*Br* local) council; **~rätin** [-rɛ:tɪn] *f* (-; *-nen*) member of the city (*Br* local) council; **~steuern** *pl* local taxes, *Br* (local) rates
**ge'meingefährlich** *adj*: ***~er Mensch*** public enemy
**Ge'meinheit** *f* (-; *-en*) a) (*no pl*) meanness, b) mean thing (to do *or* say), F dirty trick
**ge'meinnützig** [-nʏtsɪç] *adj* non-profit, *Br* non-profitmaking

**Ge'meinplatz** *m* commonplace
**ge'meinsam** **1.** *adj* common, joint; mutual; **2.** *adv* together
**Ge'meinschaft** *f* (-; *-en*) community
**Ge'meinschafts|arbeit** *f* teamwork; **~kunde** *f* (-; *no pl*) PED social studies; **~produkti͵on** *f* coproduction; **~raum** *m* recreation room, lounge
**Ge'meinsinn** *m* (-[*e*]*s*; *no pl*) public spirit; (sense of) solidarity
**ge'meinverständlich** *adj* popular
**Ge'meinwohl** *n* public welfare
**ge'messen** **1.** *pp of* ***messen***; **2.** *adj* measured; formal; grave
**Gemetzel** [gə'mɛtsəl] *n* (-*s*; -) slaughter, massacre
**gemieden** [gə'mi:dən] *pp of* ***meiden***
**Gemisch** [gə'mɪʃ] *n* (-[*e*]*s*; -*e*) mixture (*a.* CHEM)
**gemocht** [gə'mɔxt] *pp of* ***mögen***
**gemolken** [gə'mɔlkən] *pp of* ***melken***
**Gemse** → ***Gämse***
**Gemurmel** [gə'murməl] *n* (-*s*; *no pl*) murmur, mutter
**Gemüse** [gə'my:zə] *n* (-*s*; -) vegetable(s); greens; **~händler** *m* greengrocer('s)
**gemusst** [gə'mʊst] *pp of* ***müssen***
**Gemüt** [gə'my:t] *n* (-[*e*]*s*; -*er*) mind, soul; heart; nature, mentality
**ge'mütlich** *adj* comfortable, snug, cozy, *Br* cosy; peaceful, pleasant, relaxed; ***mach es dir*** ~ make yourself at home; **Ge'mütlichkeit** *f* (-; *no pl*) snugness, coziness, *Br* cosiness; cozy (*Br* cosy) *or* relaxed atmosphere
**Ge'mütsbewegung** *f* emotion
**ge'mütskrank** *adj* emotionally disturbed
**Ge'mütszustand** *m* state of mind
**Gen** [ge:n] *n* (-*s*; -*e*) BIOL gene
**genannt** [gə'nant] *pp of* ***nennen***
**genas** [gə'na:s] *pret of* ***genesen*** 1
**genau** [gə'nau] **1.** *adj* exact, precise, accurate; careful, close; strict; ***Genaueres*** further details; **2.** *adv*: ~ ***um 10 Uhr*** at 10 o'clock sharp; ~ ***der ...*** that very ...; ~ ***zuhören*** listen closely; ***es*** ~ ***nehmen*** (***mit et.***) be particular (about s.th.); **Ge'nauigkeit** *f* (-; *no pl*) accuracy, precision, exactness
**ge'nauso** *adv* → ***ebenso***
**genehmigen** [gə'ne:mɪgən] *v/t* (*no -ge-*, *h*) permit, allow; approve
**Ge'nehmigung** *f* (-; -*en*) permission; approval; permit; licen|se, *Br* -ce
**geneigt** [gə'naikt] *adj* inclined (***zu*** to)
**General** [genə'ra:l] *m* (-*s*; *Generäle* [genə'rɛ:lə]) MIL general; **~di͵rektor** *m* ECON president, *Br* chairman; **~konsul** *m* consul general; **~konsu͵lat** *n* consulate general; **~probe** *f* THEA dress rehearsal; **~sekre͵tär** *m* secretary-general; **~stab** *m* MIL general staff; **~streik** *m* general strike; **~versammlung** *f* general meeting; **~vertreter** *m* ECON sole agent
**Generation** [genəra'tsjo:n] *f* (-; -*en*) generation; **Generati'onenkon͵flikt** *m* generation gap
**Generator** [genə'ra:to:ɐ] *m* (-*s*; -*en* [-ra'to:rən]) ELECTR generator
**generell** [genə'rɛl] *adj* general, universal
**genesen** [gə'ne:zən] **1.** *v/i* (*irr*, *no -ge-*, *sein*) recover (***von*** from), get well; **2.** *pp of* ***genesen*** 1
**Ge'nesung** *f* (-; *no pl*) recovery
**Genetik** [ge'ne:tɪk] *f* (-; *no pl*) BIOL genetics; **ge'netisch** *adj* BIOL genetic; ***~er Fingerabdruck*** genetic fingerprint
**genial** [ge'nja:l] *adj* brilliant, of genius
**Genialität** [genjali'tɛ:t] *f* (-; *no pl*) genius
**Genick** [gə'nɪk] *n* (-[*e*]*s*; -*e*) ANAT (back *or* nape of the) neck
**Genie** [ʒe'ni:] *n* (-*s*; -*s*) genius
**genieren** [ʒe'ni:rən] *v/refl* (*no -ge-*, *h*) be embarrassed
**genießen** [gə'ni:sən] *v/t* (*irr*, *no -ge-*, *h*) enjoy
**Genießer** [gə'ni:sɐ] *m* (-*s*; -) gourmet
**Genitiv** ['ge:niti:f] *m* (-*s*; -*e*) LING genitive *or* possessive (case)
**genommen** [gə'nɔmən] *pp of* ***nehmen***
**genormt** [gə'nɔrmt] *adj* standardized
**genoss** [gə'nɔs] *pret of* ***genießen***
**Genosse** [gə'nɔsə] *m* (-*n*; -*n*) POL comrade; F pal, buddy, *Br* mate
**genossen** [gə'nɔsən] *pp of* ***genießen***
**Ge'nossenschaft** *f* (-; -*en*) cooperative
**Ge'nossin** *f* (-; -*nen*) POL comrade
**'Gentechnik** *f*, **'Gentechnolo͵gie** *f* genetic engineering
**genug** [gə'nu:k] *adj* enough, sufficient
**Genüge** [gə'ny:gə] *f*: ***zur*** ~ (well) enough, sufficiently
**ge'nügen** *v/i* (*no -ge-*, *h*) be enough, be

sufficient; ***das genügt*** that will do; **~d** *adj* enough, sufficient; plenty of
**genügsam** [gə'ny:kza:m] *adj* easily satisfied; frugal; modest; **Ge'nügsamkeit** *f* (-; *no pl*) modesty; frugality
**Ge'nugtuung** *f* (-; *no pl*) satisfaction
**Genus** ['ge:nʊs] *n* (-; *Genera* ['ge:nera]) LING gender
**Genuss** [gə'nʊs] *m* (*-es*; *Genüsse* [gə'nʏsə]) a) pleasure, b) (*no pl*) consumption; ***ein ~*** a real treat; *food*: *a.* delicious; **~mittel** *n* excise item, *Br* (semi-)luxury
**Geografie, Geographie** [geogra'fi:] *f* (-; *no pl*) geography; **geografisch, geographisch** [geo'gra:fɪʃ] *adj* geographic(al)
**Geologe** [geo'lo:gə] *m* (*-n*; *-n*) geologist; **Geologie** [geolo'gi:] *f* (-; *no pl*) geology; **Geo'login** *f* (-; *-nen*) geologist; **geologisch** [geo'lo:gɪʃ] *adj* geologic(al)
**Geometrie** [geome'tri:] *f* (-; *no pl*) geometry; **geometrisch** [geo'me:trɪʃ] *adj* geometric(al)
**Gepäck** [gə'pɛk] *n* (*-[e]s*; *no pl*) baggage, luggage; **~ablage** *f* baggage (*or* luggage) rack; **~aufbewahrung** *f* baggage room, *Br* left-luggage office; **~kon,trolle** *f* baggage check, *Br* luggage inspection; **~schalter** *m* baggage (*or* luggage) counter; **~schein** *m* baggage check, *Br* luggage ticket; **~träger** *m* porter; *bicycle*: carrier
**gepanzert** [gə'pantsɐt] *adj* MOT armo(u)red
**Gepard** ['ge:part] *m* (*-s*; *-e*) ZO cheetah
**gepfiffen** [gə'pfɪfən] *pp of* ***pfeifen***
**gepflegt** [gə'pfle:kt] *adj* well-groomed, neat; *fig* cultivated
**Gepflogenheit** [gə'pflo:gənhait] *f* (-; *-en*) habit, custom
**Geplapper** [gə'plapɐ] F *n* (*-s*; *no pl*) babbling, chatter(ing)
**Geplauder** [gə'plaudɐ] *n* (*-s*; *no pl*) chat(ting)
**Gepolter** [gə'pɔltɐ] *n* (*-s*; *no pl*) rumble
**gepriesen** [gə'pri:zən] *pp of* ***preisen***
**Gequassel** [gə'kvasəl] F *n* (*-s*; *no pl*), **Gequatsche** [gə'kvatʃə] F *n* (*-s*; *no pl*) blather, blabber
**gequollen** [gə'kvɔlən] *pp of* ***quellen***
**gerade** [gə'ra:də] **1.** *adj* straight (*a. fig*); even (*number*); direct; upright, erect (*posture*); **2.** *adv* just; ***nicht ~*** not exactly; ***das ist es ja ~!*** that's just it!; ***~ deshalb*** that's just why; ***~ rechtzeitig*** just in time; ***warum ~ ich?*** why me of all people?; ***da wir ~ von ... sprechen*** speaking of ...; **Ge'rade** *f* (*-n*; *-n*) MATH (straight) line; SPORT straight; ***linke*** (***rechte***) ***~*** *boxing*: straight left (right)
**gerade|'aus** *adv* straight on *or* ahead; **~he'raus** *adj* straightforward, frank
**ge'radestehen** *v/i* (*irr*, ***stehen***, *sep*, *-ge-*, *h*) stand straight; ***~ für*** answer for
**ge'radewegs** *adv* straight, directly
**ge'radezu** *adv* simply
**gerannt** [gə'rant] *pp of* ***rennen***
**Gerät** [gə'rɛ:t] *n* (*-[e]s*; *-e*) device; F gadget; appliance; (kitchen) utensil; *radio*, TV set; *coll*, *a.* SPORT *etc* equipment; SPORT apparatus; TECH tool; instrument
**ge'raten** **1.** *pp of* ***raten***; **2.** *v/i* (*irr*, ***raten***, *no -ge-*, *sein*) turn out (***gut*** well); ***~ an*** (*acc*) come across; ***~ in*** (*acc*) get into; ***in Brand ~*** catch fire
**Ge'räteturnen** *n* apparatus gymnastics
**Ge'ratewohl** *n*: ***aufs ~*** at random
**geräumig** [gə'rɔʏmɪç] *adj* spacious, roomy
**Geräusch** [gə'rɔʏʃ] *n* (*-[e]s*; *-e*) sound, noise; **ge'räuschlos** **1.** *adj* noiseless (*a.* TECH); **2.** *adv* without a sound; **ge'räuschvoll** *adj* noisy
**gerben** ['gɛrbən] *v/t* (*ge-*, *h*) tan
**Gerberei** [gɛrbə'rai] *f* (-; *-en*) tannery
**ge'recht** *adj* just, fair; (*j-m*, *e-r Sache*) ***~ werden*** do justice to; meet (*demands etc*); **Ge'rechtigkeit** *f* (-; *no pl*) justice
**Ge'rede** F *n* (*-s*; *no pl*) talk; gossip
**gereizt** [gə'raitst] *adj* irritable
**Ge'reiztheit** *f* (-; *no pl*) irritability
**Gericht**[1] [gə'rɪçt] *n* (*-[e]s*; *-e*) GASTR dish
**Ge'richt**[2] *n* (*-[e]s*; *-e*) JUR court; ***vor ~ stehen*** (***stellen***) stand (bring to) trial; ***vor ~ gehen*** go to court
**ge'richtlich** *adj* JUR judicial, legal
**Ge'richtsbarkeit** *f* (-; *no pl*) JUR jurisdiction
**Ge'richts|gebäude** *n* JUR law court(s), courthouse; **~hof** *m* JUR law court; **~medi,zin** *f* JUR forensic medicine; **~saal** *m* JUR courtroom; **~verfahren** *n* JUR lawsuit; **~verhandlung** *f* JUR hearing; trial; **~vollzieher** [-fɔltsi:ɐ] *m* (*-s*; -) JUR marshal, *Br* bailiff
**gerieben** [gə'ri:bən] *pp of* ***reiben***

**gering** [gəˈrɪŋ] *adj* little, small; slight, minor; low; ~ ***schätzen*** think little of
**geˈringfügig** *adj* slight, minor; petty
**geˈringschätzig** [-ʃɛtsɪç] *adj* contemptuous
**geˈringst** *adj* least; ***nicht im Geringsten*** not in the least
**geˈrinnen** *v/i* (*irr*, ***rinnen,*** *no -ge-*, *sein*) coagulate; curdle; clot
**Geˈrippe** *n* (*-s*; -) skeleton (*a. fig*); TECH framework
**gerissen** [gəˈrɪsən] **1.** *pp of* ***reißen*; 2.** F *adj* cunning, smart
**geritten** [gəˈrɪtən] *pp of* ***reiten***
**germanisch** [gɛrˈmaːnɪʃ] *adj* Germanic; **Germanist(in)** [gɛrmaˈnɪst(ɪn)] (*-en*; *-en*/-; *-nen*) student of (*or* graduate in) German
**gern** [gɛrn] *adv* willingly, gladly; ~ ***haben*** like, be fond of; ***et.*** (***sehr***) ~ ***tun*** like (love) to do s.th. *or* doing s.th.; ***ich möchte*** ~ I'd like (to); ~ ***geschehen!*** not at all, (you're) welcome
**gerochen** [gəˈrɔxən] *pp of* ***riechen***
**Geröll** [gəˈrœl] *n* (*-[e]s*; *-e*) scree; boulders
**geronnen** [gəˈrɔnən] *pp of* ***rinnen***
**Gerste** [ˈgɛrstə] *f* (-; *-n*) BOT barley
**ˈGerstenkorn** *n* MED sty(e)
**Gerte** [ˈgɛrtə] *f* (-; *-n*) switch, rod, twig
**Geruch** [gəˈrʊx] *m* (*-[e]s*; *Gerüche* [gəˈrʏçə]) smell; odo(u)r; scent
**geˈruchlos** *adj* odo(u)rless
**Geˈruchssinn** *m* (sense of) smell
**Gerücht** [gəˈrʏçt] *n* (*-[e]s*; *-e*) rumo(u)r
**geˈrufen** *pp of* ***rufen***
**gerührt** [gəˈryːɐt] *adj* touched, moved
**Gerümpel** [gəˈrʏmpəl] *n* (*-s*; *no pl*) lumber, junk
**Gerundium** [geˈrʊndiʊm] *n* (*-s*; *-ien*) LING gerund
**gerungen** [gəˈrʊŋən] *pp of* ***ringen***
**Gerüst** [gəˈrʏst] *n* (*-[e]s*; *-e*) frame(work); scaffold(ing); stage
**geˈsalzen** *pp of* ***salzen***
**gesamt** [gəˈzamt] *adj* whole, entire, total, all
**Geˈsamt...** *in cpds ...ergebnis etc*: *mst* total ...; **~ausgabe** *f* complete edition; **~schule** *f* comprehensive school
**gesandt** [gəˈzant] *pp of* ***senden***
**Gesandte** [gəˈzantə] *m*, *f* (*-n*; *-n*) POL envoy; **Geˈsandtschaft** *f* (-; *-en*) legation, mission
**Gesang** [gəˈzaŋ] *m* (*-[e]s*; *Gesänge* [gəˈzɛŋə]) singing; song; voice; **~buch** *n* REL hymn book; **~(s)lehrer(in)** singing teacher; **~verein** *m* choral society, glee club
**Gesäß** [gəˈzɛːs] *n* (*-es*; *-e*) ANAT buttocks, bottom
**geˈschaffen** *pp of* ***schaffen***[1]
**Geschäft** [gəˈʃɛft] *n* (*-[e]s*; *-e*) business; store, *Br* shop; bargain
**geˈschäftig** *adj* busy, active
**Geˈschäftigkeit** *f* (-; *no pl*) activity
**geˈschäftlich 1.** *adj* business ...; commercial; **2.** *adv* on business
**Geˈschäfts|brief** *m* business letter; **~frau** *f* businesswoman; **~freund** *m* business friend; **~führer** *m* manager; **~führung** *f* management; **~inhaber** *m* proprietor; **~mann** *m* businessman
**geˈschäftsmäßig** *adj* businesslike
**Geˈschäfts|ordnung** *f* PARL standing orders; rules (of procedure); **~partner** *m* (business) partner; **~räume** *pl* (business) premises; **~reise** *f* business trip; **~schluss** *m* closing time; ***nach*** ~ ***a.*** after business hours; **~stelle** *f* office; **~straße** *f* shopping street; **~träger** *m* POL chargé d'affaires
**ˈgeˈschäftstüchtig** *adj* efficient, smart
**Geˈschäfts|verbindung** *f* business connection; **~viertel** *n* commercial district; downtown; **~zeit** *f* office *or* business hours; **~zweig** *m* branch *or* line (of business)
**geschah** [gəˈʃaː] *pret of* ***geschehen*** 1
**geschehen** [gəˈʃeːən] **1.** *v/i* (*irr*, *no -ge-*, *sein*) happen, occur, take place; be done; ***es geschieht ihm recht*** it serves him right; **2.** *pp of* ***geschehen*** 1
**gescheit** [gəˈʃait] *adj* clever, bright, F brainy
**Geschenk** [gəˈʃɛŋk] *n* (*-[e]s*; *-e*) present, gift; **~packung** *f* gift box
**Geschichte** [gəˈʃɪçtə] *f* (-; *-n*) a) story, b) (*no pl*) history, c) F business, thing
**geˈschichtlich** *adj* historical
**Geˈschichts|schreiber** *m* (*-s*; -), **~wissenschaftler** *m* historian
**Geschick** [gəˈʃɪk] *n* (*-[e]s*; *-e*) fate, destiny; → **Geˈschicklichkeit** *f* (-; *no pl*) skill; dexterity; **geˈschickt** *adj* skil(l)ful, skilled; dext(e)rous; clever
**geschieden** [gəˈʃiːdən] **1.** *pp of* ***scheiden*; 2.** *adj* divorced, *marriage*: dissolved

G

**geschienen** [gə'ʃi:nən] *pp of* ***scheinen***
**Geschirr** [gə'ʃɪr] *n* (-[*e*]*s*; -*e*) a) dishes, china, b) (*no pl*) kitchen utensils, pots and pans, crockery, c) harness; ~ ***spülen*** wash *or* do the dishes
**Ge'schirrspüler** *m* (-*s*; -) dishwasher
**geschissen** [gə'ʃɪsən] *pp of* ***scheißen***
**ge'schlafen** *pp of* ***schlafen***
**ge'schlagen** *pp of* ***schlagen***
**Geschlecht** [gə'ʃlɛçt] *n* (-[*e*]*s*; -*er*) a) (*no pl*) sex, b) kind, species, c) family, line(age); generation, d) LING gender
**Ge'schlechts|krankheit** *f* MED venereal disease; **~reife** *f* puberty; **~teile** *pl* genitals; **~trieb** *m* sexual instinct *or* urge; **~verkehr** *m* (sexual) intercourse; **~wort** *n* LING article
**geschlichen** [gə'ʃlɪçən] *pp of* ***schleichen***
**geschliffen** [gə'ʃlɪfən] **1.** *pp of* ***schleifen²***; **2.** *adj* cut; *fig* polished
**geschlossen** [gə'ʃlɔsən] **1.** *pp of* ***schließen***; **2.** *adj* closed
**geschlungen** [gə'ʃlʊŋən] *pp of* ***schlingen***
**Geschmack** [gə'ʃmak] *m* (-[*e*]*s*; *Geschmäcke* [gə'ʃmɛkə]) taste (*a. fig*); flavo(u)r; ~ ***finden an*** (*dat*) develop a taste for; **ge'schmacklos** *adj a. fig* tasteless; **Ge'schmacklosigkeit** *f* (-; *no pl*) tastelessness; ***das war e-e*** ~ that was in bad taste; **Ge'schmack(s)sache** *f* matter of taste; **ge'schmackvoll** *adj* tasteful, in good taste
**geschmeidig** [gə'ʃmaidɪç] *adj* supple, pliant
**geschmissen** [gə'ʃmɪsən] *pp of* ***schmeißen***
**geschmolzen** [gə'ʃmɔltsən] *pp of* ***schmelzen***
**geschnitten** [gə'ʃnɪtən] *pp of* ***schneiden***
**geschoben** [gə'ʃo:bən] *pp of* ***schieben***
**Geschöpf** [gə'ʃœpf] *n* (-[*e*]*s*; -*e*) creature
**geschoren** [gə'ʃo:rən] *pp of* ***scheren***
**Geschoss** [gə'ʃɔs] *n* (-*es*; -*e*), **Geschoß** [gə'ʃo:s] *Austrian n* (-*es*; -*e*) projectile, missile; stor(e)y, floor
**ge'schossen** *pp of* ***schießen***
**Ge'schrei** F *n* (-*s*; *no pl*) shouting, yelling; screams; crying; *fig* fuss
**geschrieben** [gə'ʃri:bən] *pp of* ***schreiben***
**geschrie(e)n** [gə'ʃri:(ə)n] *pp of* ***schreien***
**geschritten** [gə'ʃrɪtən] *pp of* ***schreiten***
**geschunden** [gə'ʃʊndən] *pp of* ***schinden***
**Geschütz** [gə'ʃʏts] *n* (-*es*; -*e*) MIL gun, cannon
**Geschwader** [gə'ʃva:dɐ] *n* (-*s*; -) MIL MAR squadron; AVIAT group, *Br* wing
**Geschwätz** [gə'ʃvɛts] F *n* (-*es*; *no pl*) chatter, babble; gossip; *fig* nonsense
**ge'schwätzig** *adj* talkative; gossipy
**geschweige** [gə'ʃvaigə] *cj*: ~ (***denn***) let alone
**geschwiegen** [gə'ʃvi:gən] *pp of* ***schweigen***
**geschwind** [gə'ʃvɪnt] *adj* quick, swift
**Geschwindigkeit** [gə'ʃvɪndɪçkait] *f* (-; -*en*) speed; fastness, quickness; PHYS velocity; ***mit e-r*** ~ ***von ...*** at a speed *or* rate of ...
**Ge'schwindigkeits|begrenzung** *f* speed limit; **~überschreitung** *f* MOT speeding
**Geschwister** [gə'ʃvɪstɐ] *pl* brother(s) and sister(s); JUR siblings
**geschwollen** [gə'ʃvɔlən] **1.** *pp of* ***schwellen*** 1; **2.** *adj* MED swollen; *fig* bombastic, pretentious, pompous
**geschwommen** [gə'ʃvɔmən] *pp of* ***schwimmen***
**geschworen** [gə'ʃvo:rən] *pp of* ***schwören***; **Ge'schworene** *m, f* (-*n*; -*n*) member of a jury; ***die*** **~*n*** the jury
**Geschwulst** [gə'ʃvʊlst] *f* (-; *Geschwülste* [gə'ʃvʏlstə]) MED growth, tumo(u)r
**geschwunden** [gə'ʃvʊndən] *pp of* ***schwinden***
**geschwungen** [gə'ʃvʊŋən] *pp of* ***schwingen***
**Geschwür** [gə'ʃvy:ɐ] *n* (-*s*; -*e*) MED abscess, ulcer
**ge'sehen** *pp of* ***sehen***
**Geselchte** [gə'zɛlçtə] *Austrian n* (-*n*; *no pl*) GASTR smoked meat
**Geselle** [gə'zɛlə] *m* (-*n*; -*n*) journeyman
**ge'sellen** *v/refl* (*no -ge-, h*) ***sich zu j-m*** ~ join s.o.
**ge'sellig** *adj* sociable; ZO *etc* social; **~*es Beisammensein*** get-together
**Ge'sellin** *f* (-; -*nen*) trained woman *hairdresser etc*, journeywoman
**Gesellschaft** [gə'zɛlʃaft] *f* (-; -*en*) society; company; party; ECON company,

corporation; ***j-m ~ leisten*** keep s.o. company
**ge'sellschaftlich** *adj* social
**Ge'sellschafts...** *in cpds ...kritik, ...ordnung etc*: social ...; **~reise** *f* group tour; **~spiel** *n* parlo(u)r game; **~tanz** *m* ballroom dance
**gesessen** [gə'zɛsən] *pp of* ***sitzen***
**Gesetz** [gə'zɛts] *n* (*-es*; *-e*) JUR law; act; **~buch** *n* JUR code (of law); **~entwurf** *m* PARL bill
**ge'setzgebend** *adj* JUR legislative
**Ge'setzgeber** *m* (*-s*; *-*) JUR legislator
**Ge'setzgebung** *f* (*-*; *-en*) JUR legislation
**ge'setzlich 1.** *adj* legal; lawful; **2.** *adv*: **~** ***geschützt*** JUR patented, registered
**ge'setzlos** *adj* lawless
**ge'setzmäßig** *adj* legal, lawful
**gesetzt** [gə'zɛtst] **1.** *adj* staid, dignified; mature (*age*); **2.** *cj*: **~ *den Fall*(, *dass*) ...** supposing (that)
**ge'setzwidrig** *adj* illegal, unlawful
**Gesicht** [gə'zɪçt] *n* (*-[e]s*; *-er*) face; ***zu ~ bekommen*** catch sight of
**Ge'sichts|ausdruck** *m* look, expression; **~farbe** *f* complexion; **~punkt** *m* point of view, aspect, angle; **~zug** *m* feature
**Gesindel** [gə'zɪndəl] *n* (*-s*; *no pl*) trash, *the* riff-raff
**gesinnt** [gə'zɪnt] *adj* minded; ***j-m feindlich ~ sein*** be ill-disposed towards s.o.
**Ge'sinnung** *f* (*-*; *-en*) mind; attitude; POL conviction(s)
**ge'sinnungslos** *adj* unprincipled
**ge'sinnungstreu** *adj* loyal
**Ge'sinnungswechsel** *m* about-face, *Br* about-turn
**gesittet** [gə'zɪtət] *adj* civilized, well--mannered
**gesoffen** [gə'zɔfən] *pp of* ***saufen***
**gesogen** [gə'zoːgən] *pp of* ***saugen***
**gesotten** [gə'zɔtən] *pp of* ***sieden***
**gespalten** [gə'ʃpaltən] *pp of* ***spalten***
**Gespann** [gə'ʃpan] *n* (*-[e]s*; *-e*) team (*a. fig*)
**gespannt** [gə'ʃpant] *adj* tense (*a. fig*); ***~ sein auf*** (*acc*) be anxious to see; ***ich bin ~, ob*** (***wie***) I wonder if (how)
**Gespenst** [gə'ʃpɛnst] *n* (*-[e]s*; *-er*) ghost, apparition, *esp fig* specter, *Br* spectre
**ge'spenstisch** *adj* ghostly, F spooky
**gespie(e)n** [gə'ʃpiː(ə)n] *pp of* ***speien***
**Gespinst** [gə'ʃpɪnst] *n* (*-[e]s*; *-e*) web, tissue (*both a. fig*)
**gesponnen** [gə'ʃpɔnən] *pp of* ***spinnen***
**Gespött** [gə'ʃpœt] *n* (*-[e]s*; *no pl*) mockery, ridicule; ***j-n zum ~ machen*** make a laughingstock of s.o.
**Gespräch** [gə'ʃprɛːç] *n* (*-[e]s*; *-e*) talk (*a.* POL), conversation; TEL call
**ge'sprächig** *adj* talkative
**gesprochen** [gə'ʃprɔxən] *pp of* ***sprechen***
**gesprossen** [gə'ʃprɔsən] *pp of* ***sprießen***
**gesprungen** [gə'ʃprʊŋən] *pp of* ***springen***
**Gespür** [gə'ʃpyːɐ] *n* (*-s*; *no pl*) flair, nose
**Gestalt** [gə'ʃtalt] *f* (*-*; *-en*) shape, form; figure; **ge'stalten** *v/t* (*no -ge-*, *h*) arrange; design; **Ge'staltung** *f* (*-*; *-en*) arrangement; design; decoration
**gestanden** [gə'ʃtandən] *pp of* ***stehen***
**ge'ständig** *adj*: **~ *sein*** confess; have confessed
**Geständnis** [gə'ʃtɛntnɪs] *n* (*-ses*; *-se*) confession (*a. fig*)
**Gestank** [gə'ʃtaŋk] *m* (*-[e]s*; *no pl*) stench, stink
**gestatten** [gə'ʃtatən] *v/t* (*no -ge-*, *h*) allow, permit
**Geste** ['gɛstə] *f* (*-*; *-n*) gesture (*a. fig*)
**ge'stehen** *v/t and v/i* (*irr*, ***stehen***, *no -ge-*, *h*) confess
**Ge'stein** *n* (*-[e]s*; *-e*) rock, stone
**Gestell** [gə'ʃtɛl] *n* (*-[e]s*; *-e*) stand, base, pedestal; shelves; frame
**gestern** ['gɛstɐn] *adv* yesterday; **~ *Abend*** last night
**gestiegen** [gə'ʃtiːgən] *pp of* ***steigen***
**gestochen** [gə'ʃtɔxən] *pp of* ***stechen***
**gestohlen** [gə'ʃtoːlən] *pp of* ***stehlen***
**gestorben** [gə'ʃtɔrbən] *pp of* ***sterben***
**ge'stoßen** *pp of* ***stoßen***
**gestreift** [gə'ʃtraift] *adj* striped
**gestrichen** [gə'ʃtrɪçən] *pp of* ***streichen***
**gestrig** ['gɛstrɪç] *adj* yesterday's, of yesterday
**gestritten** [gə'ʃtrɪtən] *pp of* ***streiten***
**Gestrüpp** [gə'ʃtrʏp] *n* (*-[e]s*; *-e*) brushwood, undergrowth; *fig* jungle, maze
**gestunken** [gə'ʃtʊŋkən] *pp of* ***stinken***
**Gestüt** [gə'ʃtyːt] *n* (*-[e]s*; *-e*) stud
**Gesuch** [gə'zuːx] *n* (*-[e]s*; *-e*) application, request
**gesund** [gə'zʊnt] *adj* healthy; healthful, *fig a.* sound; ***~er Menschenverstand***

G

common sense; (***wieder***) ~ ***werden*** get well (again), recover; **Ge'sundheit** *f* (-; *no pl*) health; ***auf j-s ~ trinken*** drink to s.o.'s health; ***~!*** bless you!; **ge'sundheitlich 1.** *adj*: ***~er Zustand*** state of health; ***aus ~en Gründen*** for health reasons; **2.** *adv*: ***~ geht es ihm gut*** he is in good health

**Ge'sundheitsamt** *n* Public Health Department (*Br* Office)

**ge'sundheitsschädlich** *adj* bad for one's health

**Ge'sundheits|zeugnis** *n* health certificate; **~zustand** *m* state of health

**gesungen** [gə'zʊŋən] *pp of* ***singen***

**gesunken** [gə'zʊŋkən] *pp of* ***sinken***

**getan** [gə'ta:n] *pp of* ***tun***

**Getöse** [gə'tø:zə] *n* (-*s*; *no pl*) din, (deafening) noise

**ge'tragen** *pp of* ***tragen***

**Getränk** [gə'trɛŋk] *n* (-[*e*]*s*; -*e*) drink, beverage; **Ge'tränkeauto,mat** *m* drinks machine

**Getreide** [gə'traidə] *n* (-*s*; -) cereals, grain, *Br a.* corn; **~ernte** *f* grain harvest (*or* crop)

**ge'treten** *pp of* ***treten***

**Getriebe** [gə'tri:bə] *n* (-*s*; -) MOT transmission

**ge'trieben** [gə'tri:bən] *pp of* ***treiben***

**getroffen** [gə'trɔfən] *pp of* ***treffen***

**getrogen** [gə'tro:gən] *pp of* ***trügen***

**getrost** [gə'tro:st] *adv* safely

**getrunken** [gə'trʊŋkən] *pp of* ***trinken***

**Getue** [gə'tu:ə] F *n* (-*s*; *no pl*) fuss

**Getümmel** [gə'tʏməl] *n* (-*s*; -) turmoil

**Gewächs** [gə'vɛks] *n* (-*es*; -*e*) plant; MED growth

**ge'wachsen 1.** *pp of* ***wachsen***[1]; **2.** *fig adj*: ***j-m ~ sein*** be a match for s.o.; ***e-r Sache ~ sein*** be equal to s.th., be able to cope with s.th.

**Ge'wächshaus** *n* greenhouse, hothouse

**gewagt** [gə'va:kt] *adj* daring; *fig* risqué

**gewählt** [gə'vɛ:lt] *adj* refined

**Gewähr** [gə'vɛ:ɐ] *f*: ***~ übernehmen*** (***für***) guarantee; **ge'währen** *v/t* (*no -ge-, h*) grant, allow; **ge'währleisten** *v/t* (*no -ge-, h*) guarantee

**Gewahrsam** [gə'va:ɐza:m] *m*: ***et.*** (***j-n***) ***in ~ nehmen*** take s.th. in safekeeping (s.o. into custody)

**Gewalt** [gə'valt] *f* (-; -*en*) a) (*no pl*) force, violence, b) power; ***mit ~*** by force; ***höhere ~*** act of God; ***häusliche ~*** domestic violence; ***in s-e ~ bringen*** seize by force; ***die ~ verlieren über*** (*acc*) lose control over; **~herrschaft** *f* tyranny

**ge'waltig** *adj* powerful, mighty; enormous

**ge'waltlos** *adj* nonviolent; **Ge'waltlosigkeit** *f* (-; *no pl*) nonviolence

**ge'waltsam 1.** *adj* violent; **2.** *adv* by force; ***~ öffnen*** force open

**ge'walttätig** *adj* violent

**Ge'walttätigkeit** *f* (-; -*en*) a) (*no pl*) violence, b) act of violence

**Ge'waltverbrechen** *n* crime of violence

**Gewand** [gə'vant] *n* (-[*e*]*s*; *Gewänder* [gə'vɛndɐ]) robe, gown; REL vestment

**gewandt** [gə'vant] **1.** *pp of* ***wenden*** (*v/refl*); **2.** *adj* nimble; skil(l)ful; clever

**Ge'wandtheit** *f* (-; *no pl*) nimbleness; skill; ease

**gewann** [gə'van] *pret of* ***gewinnen***

**ge'waschen** *pp of* ***waschen***

**Gewässer** [gə'vɛsɐ] *n* (-*s*; -) body of water; *pl* waters

**Gewebe** [gə've:bə] *n* (-*s*; -) fabric; BIOL tissue

**Gewehr** [gə've:ɐ] *n* (-[*e*]*s*; -*e*) gun; rifle; shotgun; **~kolben** *m* (rifle) butt; **~lauf** *m* (rifle *or* gun) barrel

**Geweih** [gə'vai] *n* (-[*e*]*s*; -*e*) ZO antlers, horns

**Gewerbe** [gə'vɛrbə] *n* (-*s*; -) trade, business; **~schein** *m* trade licen|se, *Br* -ce; **~schule** *f* vocational *or* trade school

**gewerblich** [gə'vɛrplɪç] *adj* commercial, industrial; **gewerbsmäßig** [gə'vɛrps-] *adj* professional

**Gewerkschaft** [gə'vɛrkʃaft] *f* (-; -*en*) labor union, *Br* (trade) union

**Ge'werkschaft(l)er** *m* (-*s*; -), **Ge'werkschaft(l)erin** *f* (-; -*nen*) labor (*Br* trade) unionist; **ge'werkschaftlich** *adj*, **Ge'werkschafts...** *in cpds* labor (*Br* trade) union ...

**ge'wesen** *pp of* ***sein***[1]

**gewichen** [gə'vɪçən] *pp of* ***weichen***

**Gewicht** [gə'vɪçt] *n* (-[*e*]*s*; -*e*) weight; importance; ***~ legen auf*** (*acc*) stress

**gewiesen** [gə'vi:zən] *pp of* ***weisen***

**gewillt** [gə'vɪlt] *adj* willing, ready

**Gewimmel** [gə'vɪməl] *n* (-*s*; *no pl*) throng

**Gewinde** [gə'vɪndə] *n* (*-s*; -) TECH thread; ***ein ~ bohren in*** (*acc*) tap
**Gewinn** [gə'vɪn] *m* (*-[e]s*; *-e*) ECON profit (*a. fig*); gain(s); prize; winnings; ***~ bringend*** profitable
**ge'winnen** *v/t and v/i* (*irr, no -ge-, h*) win; gain; **~d** *fig adj* winning, engaging
**Gewinner** [gə'vɪnɐ] *m* (*-s*; -), **Ge'winnerin** *f* (-; *-nen*) winner
**Ge'winnzahl** *f* winning number
**Gewirr** [gə'vɪr] *n* (*-[e]s*; *no pl*) tangle; maze
**gewiss** [gə'vɪs] **1.** *adj* certain; **2.** *adv* certainly
**Ge'wissen** *n* (*-s*; -) conscience
**ge'wissenhaft** *adj* conscientious
**ge'wissenlos** *adj* unscrupulous
**Ge'wissens|bisse** *pl* pricks *or* pangs of conscience; **~frage** *f* question of conscience; **~gründe** *pl*: ***aus ~n*** for reasons of conscience
**Ge'wissheit** *f* (-; *no pl*) certainty; ***mit ~*** *know etc* for certain *or* sure
**Gewitter** [gə'vɪtɐ] *n* (*-s*; -) thunderstorm; **~regen** *m* thundershower; **~wolke** *f* thundercloud
**gewoben** [gə'vo:bən] *pp of* ***weben***
**gewogen** [gə'vo:gən] *pp of* ***wiegen¹*** *and* ***wägen***
**gewöhnen** [gə'vø:nən] *v/t and v/refl* (*no -ge-, h*) ***sich*** (***j-n***) ***~ an*** (*acc*) get (s.o.) used to; **Gewohnheit** [gə'vo:nhait] *f* (-; *-en*) habit (***et. zu tun*** of doing s.th.); **ge'wohnheitsmäßig** *adj* habitual
**gewöhnlich** [gə'vø:nlɪç] *adj* common, ordinary, usual; vulgar, F common
**gewohnt** [gə'vo:nt] *adj* usual; ***et.*** (***zu tun***) ***~ sein*** be used *or* accustomed to (doing) s.th.
**Gewölbe** [gə'vœlbə] *n* (*-s*; -) vault
**gewölbt** [gə'vœlpt] *adj* arched
**gewonnen** [gə'vɔnən] *pp of* ***gewinnen***
**geworben** [gə'vɔrbən] *pp of* ***werben***
**geworden** [gə'vɔrdən] *pp of* ***werden***
**geworfen** [gə'vɔrfən] *pp of* ***werfen***
**gewrungen** [gə'vrʊŋən] *pp of* ***wringen***
**Gewühl** [gə'vy:l] *n* (*-[e]s*; *no pl*) crowd, crush
**gewunden** [gə'vʊndən] **1.** *pp of* ***winden***; **2.** *adj* winding
**Gewürz** [gə'vʏrts] *n* (*-es*; *-e*) spice; **~gurke** *f* pickle(d gherkin)
**gewusst** [gə'vʊst] *pp of* ***wissen***
**gezackt** [gə'tsakt] *adj* jagged, serrated
**Ge'zeiten** *pl* tide(s)
**Gezeter** [gə'tse:tɐ] *contp n* (*-s*; *no pl*) (shrill) clamo(u)r; nagging
**geziert** [gə'tsi:ɐt] *adj* affected
**gezogen** [gə'tso:gən] *pp of* ***ziehen***
**Gezwitscher** [gə'tsvɪtʃɐ] *n* (*-s*; *no pl*) chirp(ing), twitter(ing)
**gezwungen** [gə'tsvʊŋən] **1.** *pp of* ***zwingen***; **2.** *adj* forced, unnatural
**Gicht** [gɪçt] *f* (-; *no pl*) MED gout
**Giebel** ['gi:bəl] *m* (*-s*; -) gable
**Gier** [gi:ɐ] *f* (-; *no pl*) greed(iness) (***nach*** for); **gierig** ['gi:rɪç] *adj* greedy (***nach***, ***auf*** *acc* for, after)
**gießen** ['gi:sən] *v/t and v/i* (*irr, ge-, h*) pour; TECH cast; water
**Gieße'rei** *f* (-; *-en*) TECH foundry
**'Gießkanne** *f* watering pot (*Br* can)
**Gift** [gɪft] *n* (*-[e]s*; *-e*) poison, ZO *a.* venom (*a. fig*); **'giftig** *adj* poisonous; venomous (*a. fig*); poisoned; MED toxic
**'Gift|müll** *m* toxic waste; **~mülldepo,nie** *f* toxic waste dump; **~schlange** *f* ZO poisonous *or* venomous snake; **~stoff** *m* poisonous *or* toxic substance; pollutant; **~zahn** *m* ZO poison fang
**Gigant** [gi'gant] *m* (*-en*; *-en*) giant
**gi'gantisch** *adj* gigantic
**ging** [gɪŋ] *pret of* ***gehen***
**Gipfel** ['gɪpfəl] *m* (*-s*; -) top, peak, summit, *fig a.* height; **~konfe,renz** *f* POL summit (meeting *or* conference)
**'gipfeln** *v/i* (*ge-, h*) culminate (***in*** *dat* in)
**Gips** [gɪps] *m* (*-es*; *-e*) plaster (of Paris); ***in ~*** MED in (a) plaster (cast); **~abdruck** *m*, **~abguss** *m* plaster cast
**'gipsen** *v/t* (*ge-, h*) plaster (*a.* F MED)
**'Gipsverband** *m* MED plaster cast
**Giraffe** [gi'rafə] *f* (-; *-n*) ZO giraffe
**Girlande** [gɪr'landə] *f* (-; *-n*) garland, festoon
**Girokonto** ['ʒi:ro-] *n* checking (*or* current) account; postal check(*Br* giro) account
**Gischt** [gɪʃt] *m* (*-[e]s*; *-e*), *f* (-; *-en*) (sea) spray, spindrift
**Gitarre** [gi'tarə] *f* (-; *-n*) MUS guitar
**Gitarrist** [gita'rɪst] *m* (*-en*; *-en*) guitarist
**Gitter** ['gɪtɐ] *n* (*-s*; -) lattice; grating; F ***hinter ~n*** (***sitzen***) (be) behind bars
**'Gitterbett** *n* crib, *Br* cot
**'Gitterfenster** *n* lattice (window)
**Glanz** [glants] *m* (*-es*; *no pl*) shine, gloss (*a.* TECH), luster, *Br* lustre, brilliance (*a. fig*); *fig* splendo(u)r, glamo(u)r

**glänzen** ['glɛntsən] *v/i* (*ge-*, *h*) shine, gleam; glitter, glisten; **~d** *adj* shining, shiny, bright; PHOT glossy; *fig* brilliant, excellent
'**Glanz|leistung** *f* brilliant achievement; **~zeit** *f* heyday
**Glas** [glaːs] *n* (*-es*; *Gläser* ['glɛːzɐ]) glass
**Glaser** ['glaːzɐ] *m* (*-s*; *-*) glazier
**gläsern** ['glɛːzɐn] *adj* (of) glass
'**Glas|faser** *f*, **~fiber** *f* glass fiber (*Br* fibre); **~hütte** *f* TECH glassworks
**glasieren** [gla'ziːrən] *v/t* (*no -ge-*, *h*) glaze; GASTR ice, frost
**glasig** ['glaːzɪç] *adj* glassy
'**glasklar** *adj* crystal-clear (*a. fig*)
'**Glasscheibe** *f* (glass) pane
**Glasur** [gla'zuːɐ] *f* (*-*; *-en*) glaze; GASTR icing
**glatt** [glat] *adj* smooth (*a. fig*); slippery; *fig* clear; F **~ gehen** work (out well), go (off) well; **Glätte** ['glɛtə] *f* (*-*; *no pl*) smoothness (*a. fig*); slipperiness
'**Glatteis** *n* (glare, *Br* black) ice; **es herrscht ~** the roads are icy; F **j-n aufs ~ führen** mislead s.o.
**glätten** ['glɛtən] *v/t* (*ge-*, *h*) smooth; *Swiss*: → **bügeln**
**Glatze** ['glatsə] *f* (*-*; *-n*) bald head; **e-e ~ haben** be bald
**Glaube** ['glaubə] *m* (*-ns*; *no pl*) belief, *esp* REL faith (*both*: **an** *acc* in)
'**glauben** *v/t and v/i* (*ge-*, *h*) believe; think, guess; **~ an** (*acc*) believe in (*a.* REL)
'**Glaubens|bekenntnis** *n* REL creed, profession *or* confession of faith; **~lehre** *f*, **~satz** *m* dogma, doctrine
**glaubhaft** ['glauphaft] *adj* credible, plausible
**gläubig** ['glɔʏbɪç] *adj* religious; devout; **die Gläubigen** the faithful
**Gläubiger** ['glɔʏbɪgɐ] *m* (*-s*; *-*), '**Gläubigerin** *f* (*-*; *-nen*) ECON creditor
'**glaubwürdig** *adj* credible; reliable
**gleich** [glaiç] **1.** *adj* same; equal (*right etc*); **auf die ~e Art** (in) the same way; **zur ~en Zeit** at the same time; **das ist mir ~** it's all the same to me; **ganz ~, wann** *etc* no matter when *etc*; **das Gleiche** the same; (**ist**) **~ ...** MATH equals ..., is ...; **~ bleibend** constant, steady; **~ gesinnt** like-minded; **~ lautend** identical; **2.** *adv* equally, alike; at once, right away; in a moment *or* minute; **~ groß** (**alt**) of the same size (age); **~ nach** (**neben**) right after (next to); **~ gegenüber** just opposite *or* across the street; **es ist ~ 5 Uhr** it's almost 5 o'clock; **~ aussehen** (**gekleidet sein**) look (be dressed) alike; **bis ~!** see you soon *or* later!; **gleichaltrig** ['glaiçʔaltrɪç] *adj* (of) the same age
'**gleichberechtigt** *adj* equal, having equal rights; '**Gleichberechtigung** *f* (*-*; *no pl*) equal rights
'**gleichen** *v/i* (*irr*, *ge-*, *h*) (*dat*) be *or* look like
'**gleichfalls** *adv* also, likewise; **danke, ~!** (thanks,) the same to you
'**gleichförmig** [-fœrmɪç] *adj* uniform
'**Gleichgewicht** *n* (*-[e]s*; *no pl*) balance (*a. fig*)
'**gleichgültig** *adj* indifferent (**gegen** to); careless; **das** (**er**) **ist mir ~** I don't care (for him); '**Gleichgültigkeit** *f* (*-*; *no pl*) indifference
'**Gleichheit** *f* (*-*; *no pl*) equality
'**gleichkommen** *v/i* (*irr*, **kommen**, *sep*, *-ge-*, *sein*) **e-r Sache ~** amount to s.th.; **j-m ~** equal s.o. (**an** *dat* in)
'**gleichmäßig** *adj* regular; constant; even
'**gleichnamig** [-naːmɪç] *adj* of the same name
'**Gleichnis** *n* (*-ses*; *-se*) parable
'**gleichsam** *adv* as it were, so to speak
'**gleichseitig** [-zaitɪç] *adj* MATH equilateral
'**gleich|setzen, ~stellen** *v/t* (*sep*, *-ge-*, *h*) equate (*dat* to, with); put *s.o.* on an equal footing (with)
'**Gleichstrom** *m* ELECTR direct current
'**Gleichung** *f* (*-*; *-en*) MATH equation
'**gleichwertig** *adj* equally good; **j-m ~ sein** be a match for s.o. (*a.* SPORT)
'**gleichzeitig** *adj* simultaneous; **beide ~** both at the same time
**Gleis** [glais] *n* (*-es*; *-e*) RAIL rail(s), track(s), line; platform, gate
**gleiten** ['glaitən] *v/i* (*irr*, *ge-*, *sein*) glide, slide; **~d** *adj*: **~e Arbeitszeit** flexible working hours, flextime, *Br a.* flexitime
'**Gleitflug** *m* glide
'**Gleitschirm|fliegen** *n* paragliding; **~flieger** *m* paraglider
**Gletscher** ['glɛtʃɐ] *m* (*-s*; *-*) glacier; **~spalte** *f* crevasse
**glich** [glɪç] *pret of* **gleichen**

**Glied** [gli:t] *n* (*-es*; *Glieder* ['gli:dɐ]) ANAT limb; penis; TECH link
**gliedern** ['gli:dɐn] *v/t* (*ge-*, *h*) structure; divide (***in*** *acc* into)
**Gliederung** ['gli:dərʊŋ] *f* (-; *-en*) structure, arrangement; outline
'**Gliedmaßen** *pl* ANAT limbs, extremities
**glimmen** ['glɪmən] *v/i* ([*irr*,] *ge-*, *h*) glow; smo(u)lder
'**Glimmstängel** F *m* (*-s*; -) cigarette, *Br sl* fag
**glimpflich** ['glɪmpflɪç] **1.** *adj* lenient, mild; **2.** *adv*: ~ ***davonkommen*** get off lightly
**glitschig** ['glɪtʃɪç] *adj* slippery
**glitt** [glɪt] *pret of* ***gleiten***
**glitzern** ['glɪtsɐn] *v/i* (*ge-*, *h*) glitter, sparkle, glint
**global** [glo'ba:l] *adj* global
**Globus** ['glo:bʊs] *m* (*-*[*ses*]; *-se*) globe
**Glocke** ['glɔkə] *f* (-; *-n*) bell
'**Glocken|blume** *f* bluebell; **~spiel** *n* chimes; **~turm** *m* bell tower, belfry
**glomm** [glɔm] *pret of* ***glimmen***
**glorreich** ['glo:ɐraiç] *adj* glorious
**Glotze** ['glɔtsə] F *f* (-; *-n*) TV *the* tube, *Br* goggle box; '**glotzen** F *v/i* (*ge-*, *h*) goggle, gape, stare
**Glück** [glʏk] *n* (-[*e*]*s*; *no pl*) (good) luck, fortune; happiness; ~ ***haben*** be lucky; ***zum*** ~ fortunately; ***viel ~!*** good luck!
**Glucke** ['glʊkə] *f* (-; *-n*) ZO sitting hen; *fig* hen
**gluckern** ['glʊkɐn] *v/i* (*ge-*, *h*) gurgle
'**glücklich** *adj* happy; ***~er Zufall*** lucky chance
'**glücklicher'weise** *adv* fortunately
'**Glücks|bringer** *m* (*-s*; -) lucky charm; **~fall** *m* lucky chance; **~pfennig** *m* lucky penny; **~pilz** *m* lucky fellow; **~spiel** *n* game of chance; *coll* gambling; **~spieler** *m* gambler; **~tag** *m* lucky day
'**glückstrahlend** *adj* radiant
'**Glückwunsch** *m* congratulations; ***herzlichen ~!*** congratulations!; happy birthday!
**Glühbirne** ['gly:-] *f* ELECTR light bulb
**glühen** ['gly:ən] *v/i* (*ge-*, *h*) glow (*a. fig*)
**glühend** ['gly:ənt] *adj* glowing; red-hot (*iron*); *fig* burning; ~ ***heiß*** blazing hot
'**Glühwein** *m* mulled wine
**Glut** [glu:t] *f* (-; *-en*) (glowing) fire; embers; live coals; *fig* ardo(u)r
'**Gluthitze** *f* blazing heat
**GmbH** [ge:ʔɛmbe:'ha:] ABBR *of* ***Gesellschaft mit beschränkter Haftung*** private limited liability company
**Gnade** ['gna:də] *f* (-; *-n*) mercy, *esp* REL *a.* grace; favo(u)r
'**Gnaden|frist** *f* reprieve; **~gesuch** *n* JUR petition for mercy
'**gnadenlos** *adj* merciless
**gnädig** ['gnɛ:dɪç] *adj* gracious; *esp* REL merciful
**Gold** [gɔlt] *n* (-[*e*]*s*; *no pl*) gold; **~barren** *m* gold bar *or* ingot; *coll* bullion
**golden** ['gɔldən] *adj* gold; *fig* golden
'**Goldfisch** *m* ZO goldfish
'**goldgelb** *adj* golden (yellow)
'**Gold|gräber** [-grɛ:bɐ] *m* (*-s*; -) gold digger; **~grube** *fig f* goldmine, bonanza
**goldig** ['gɔldɪç] F *adj* sweet, lovely, cute
'**Gold|mine** *f* goldmine; **~münze** *f* gold coin; **~schmied** *m* goldsmith; **~stück** *n* gold coin
**Golf**[1] [gɔlf] *m* (-[*e*]*s*; *-e*) GEOGR gulf
**Golf**[2] *n* (*-s*; *no pl*) SPORT golf; **~platz** *m* golf course; **~schläger** *m* golf club; **~spieler** *m* golfer
**Gondel** ['gɔndəl] *f* (-; *-n*) gondola; cabin
**Gong** ['gɔŋ-] *m* (*-s*; *-s*) gong
**gönnen** ['gœnən] *v/t* (*ge-*, *h*) ***j-m et.*** ~ not (be)grudge s.o. s.th.; ***j-m et. nicht*** ~ (be)grudge s.o. s.th.; ***sich et.*** ~ allow o.s. s.th., treat o.s. to s.th.
**gönnerhaft** ['gœnɐhaft] *adj* patronizing
**gor** [go:ɐ] *pret of* ***gären***
**Gorilla** [go'rɪla] *m* (*-s*; *-s*) ZO gorilla
**goss** [gɔs] *pret of* ***gießen***
**Gosse** ['gɔsə] *f* (-; *-n*) gutter (*a. fig*)
**Gotik** ['go:tɪk] *f* (-; *no pl*) ARCH Gothic style *or* period; '**gotisch** *adj* Gothic
**Gott** [gɔt] *m* (-[*e*]*s*; *Götter* ['gœtɐ]) REL God, Lord; MYTH god; ~ ***sei Dank***(*!*) thank God(!); ***um ~es Willen!*** for heaven's sake!; '**gottergeben** *adj* resigned (to the will of God)
'**Gottesdienst** *m* REL (divine) service
'**gottesfürchtig** [-fʏrçtɪç] *adj* god-fearing
'**Gotteslästerer** [-lɛstərɐ] *m* (*-s*; -) blasphemer; '**Gotteslästerung** *f* (-; *-en*) blasphemy
'**Gottheit** *f* (-; *-en*) deity, divinity
**Göttin** ['gœtɪn] *f* (-; *-nen*) goddess

**'göttlich** ['gœtlıç] *adj* divine
**gott'lob** *int* thank God *or* goodness!
**'gottlos** *adj* godless, wicked
**'gottverlassen** F *adj* godforsaken
**'Gottvertrauen** *n* trust in God
**Götze** ['gœtsə] *m* (*-n*; *-n*), **'Götzenbild** *n* idol
**Gouverneur** [guvɛr'nøːɐ] *m* (*-s*; *-e*) governor
**Grab** [graːp] *n* (*-[e]s*; *Gräber* ['grɛːbɐ]) grave; tomb
**graben** ['graːbən] *v/t and v/i* (*irr*, *ge-*, *h*) dig, ZO *a.* burrow; **'Graben** *m* (*-s*; *Gräben* ['grɛːbən]) ditch; MIL trench
**'Grab|mal** *n* monument; tomb; **~rede** *f* funeral address; **~schrift** *f* epitaph; **~stätte** *f* burial place; grave, tomb; **~stein** *m* tombstone, gravestone
**Grad** [graːt] *m* (*-[e]s*; *-e*) degree; MIL *etc* rank, grade; ***15 ~ Kälte*** 15 degrees below zero; **~einteilung** *f* graduation
**graduell** [gra'duɛl] *adj* in degree
**Graf** [graːf] *m* (*-en*; *-en*) count, *Br* earl
**Graffiti** [gra'fiːti] *pl* graffiti
**Grafik** ['graːfık] *f* (*-*; *-en*) a) (*no pl*) graphic arts, b) print, c) MATH, TECH graph, diagram, d) (*no pl*) art(work), illustrations, e) (*no pl*) EDP graphics
**'Grafiker** *m* (*-s*; *-*), **'Grafikerin** *f* (*-*; *-nen*) graphic artist
**Gräfin** ['grɛːfın] *f* (*-*; *-nen*) countess
**grafisch** ['graːfıʃ] *adj* graphic
**Grafologie** *f* → ***Graphologie***
**'Grafschaft** *f* (*-*; *-en*) county
**Gramm** [gram] *n* (*-s*; *-e*) gram
**Grammatik** [gra'matık] *f* (*-*; *-en*) grammar; **gram'matisch** *adj* grammatical
**Granat** [gra'naːt] *m* (*-[e]s*; *-e*) MIN garnet
**Gra'nate** *f* (*-*; *-n*) MIL shell
**Gra'nat|splitter** *m* MIL shell splinter; **~werfer** *m* MIL mortar
**grandios** [gran'djoːs] *adj* magnificent, grand
**Granit** [gra'niːt] *m* (*-s*; *-e*) granite
**Graphik** *f etc* → ***Grafik etc***
**Graphologie** [grafolo'giː] *f* (*-*; *no pl*) graphology
**Gras** [graːs] *n* (*-es*; *Gräser* ['grɛːzɐ]) grass; **grasen** ['graːzən] *v/i* (*ge-*, *h*) graze; **'Grashalm** *m* blade of grass
**grassieren** [gra'siːrən] *v/i* (*no -ge-*, *h*) rage, be rife
**grässlich** ['grɛslıç] *adj* hideous, atrocious
**Gräte** ['grɛːtə] *f* (*-*; *-n*) (fish)bone
**Gratifikation** [gratifika'tsjoːn] *f* (*-*; *-en*) gratuity, bonus
**gratis** ['graːtıs] *adv* free (of charge)
**Grätsche** ['grɛːtʃə] *f* (*-*; *-n*), **'grätschen** *v/i* (*ge-*, *h*) straddle; *soccer:* stride tackle
**Gratulant** [gratu'lant] *m* (*-en*; *-en*), **Gratu'lantin** *f* (*-*; *-nen*) congratulator; **Gratulation** [-la'tsjoːn] *f* (*-*; *-en*) congratulation; **gratulieren** [-'liːrən] *v/i* (*no -ge-*, *h*) congratulate (***j-m zu et.*** s.o. on s.th.); ***j-m zum Geburtstag ~*** wish s.o. many happy returns (of the day)
**grau** [grau] *adj* gray, *Br* grey
**'Graubrot** *n* rye bread
**Gräuel** ['grɔʏəl] *m* (*-s*; *-*) horror
**'Gräueltat** *f* atrocity
**'grauen** *v/i* (*ge-*, *h*) ***mir graut es vor*** (*dat*) I dread (the thought of)
**'Grauen** *n* (*-s*; *-*) horror
**'grauenhaft, 'grauenvoll** *adj* horrible, horrifying
**Graupel** ['graupəl] *f* (*-*; *-n*) sleet, soft hail
**grausam** ['grauzaːm] *adj* cruel
**'Grausamkeit** *f* (*-*; *-en*) cruelty
**grausig** ['grauzıç] *adj* → ***grauenhaft***
**'Grauzone** *f fig* gray (*Br* grey) area
**gravieren** [gra'viːrən] *v/t* (*no -ge-*, *h*) engrave; **~d** *adj* serious
**Gravur** [gra'vuːɐ] *f* (*-*; *-en*) engraving
**Grazie** ['graːtsjə] *f* (*-*; *no pl*) grace
**graziös** [gra'tsjøːs] *adj* graceful
**greifen** ['graifən] (*irr*, *ge-*, *h*) **1.** *v/t* seize, grasp, grab, take *or* catch hold of; **2.** *v/i fig* take effect; ***~ nach*** reach for; grasp at
**Greis** [grais] *m* (*-es*; *-e*) (very) old man; **greisenhaft** ['graizənhaft] *adj* senile (*a.* MED); **Greisin** ['graizın] *f* (*-*; *-nen*) (very) old woman
**grell** [grɛl] *adj* glaring; shrill
**Grenze** ['grɛntsə] *f* (*-*; *-n*) border; boundary; *fig* limit; **'grenzen** *v/i* (*ge-*, *h*) ***~ an*** (*acc*) border on
**'grenzenlos** *adj* boundless
**'Grenz|fall** *m* borderline case; **~land** *n* borderland, frontier; **~linie** *f* borderline, POL demarcation line; **~stein** *m* boundary stone; **~übergang** *m* frontier crossing (point), checkpoint
**Greuel** *m* → ***Gräuel***
**Grieche** ['griːçə] *m* (*-n*; *-n*) Greek;

**'Griechenland** Greece; **'Griechin** *f* (-; *-nen*), **'griechisch** *adj* Greek
**Grieß** [gri:s] *m* (*-es*; *-e*) semolina
**griff** [grɪf] *pret of* ***greifen***
**Griff** *m* (-[*e*]*s*; *-e*) grip, grasp; handle
**'griffbereit** *adj* at hand, handy
**Grill** [grɪl] *m* (*-s*; *-s*) grill
**Grille** ['grɪlə] *f* (-; *-n*) ZO cricket
**'grillen** *v/t* (*ge-*, *h*) grill, barbecue
**Grimasse** [gri'masə] *f* (-; *-n*) grimace; ***~n schneiden*** pull faces
**grimmig** [['grɪmɪç] *adj* grim
**grinsen** ['grɪnzən] *v/i* (*ge-*, *h*) grin (***über*** *acc* at); ***höhnisch*** *or* ***spöttisch ~*** (***über*** *acc*) sneer (at); **'Grinsen** *n* (*-s*; *no pl*) grin; ***höhnisches*** *or* ***spöttisches ~*** sneer
**Grippe** ['grɪpə] *f* (-; *-n*) MED influenza, F flu
**Grips** [grɪps] F *m* (*-es*; *no pl*) brains
**grob** [gro:p] **1.** *adj* coarse (*a. fig*); *fig* gross; crude; rude; rough; **2.** *adv*: ***~ geschätzt*** at a rough estimate
**'Grobheit** *f* (-; *no pl*) coarseness; roughness; rudeness
**grölen** ['grø:lən] F *v/t and v/i* (*ge-*, *h*) bawl
**Groll** [grɔl] *m* (-[*e*]*s*; *no pl*) grudge, ill will; **'grollen** *v/i* (*ge-*, *h*) ***j-m ~*** bear s.o. a grudge
**Groschen** ['grɔʃən] *m* (*-s*; -) *Austrian* groschen; F ten-pfennig piece, ten pfennigs
**groß** [gro:s] *adj* big; large (*a. family*); tall; grown-up; F big (*brother etc*); *fig* great (*a. fun, trouble, pain etc*); capital (*letter*); ***~es Geld*** bills, *Br* notes; ***~e Ferien*** summer vacation, *Br* summer holiday(s); ***Groß und Klein*** young and old; ***im Großen und Ganzen*** on the whole; F ***~ in et. sein*** be great at (doing) s.th.; ***wie ~ ist es?*** what size is it?; ***wie ~ bist du?*** how tall are you?
**'großartig** *adj* great, F *a.* terrific
**'Großaufnahme** *f film*: close-up
**Größe** ['grø:sə] *f* (-; *-n*) size; height; *esp* MATH quantity; *fig* greatness; celebrity
**'Großeltern** *pl* grandparents
**'großen'teils** *adv* to a large *or* great extent, largely
**'Größenwahn** *m* megalomania (*a. fig*)
**'Groß|fa,milie** *f* extended family; **~handel** *m* ECON wholesale (trade); **~händler** *m* ECON wholesale dealer, wholesaler; **~handlung** *f* ECON wholesale business; **~indus,trie** *f* big industry; big business; **~industri,elle** *m* big industrialist, F tycoon; **~macht** *f* POL great power; **~markt** *m* ECON hypermarket; wholesale market; **~maul** F *n* braggart; **~mutter** *f* grandmother; **~raum** *m* conurbation, metropolitan area; ***der ~ München*** Greater Munich, the Greater Munich area; **~raumflugzeug** *n* wide-bodied jet
**'großschreiben** *v/t* (*irr*, ***schreiben***, *sep*, *-ge-*, *h*) capitalize; **'Großschreibung** *f* (use of) capitalization
**'großsprecherisch** [-ʃprɛçərɪʃ] *adj* boastful
**'großspurig** [-ʃpu:rɪç] *adj* arrogant
**'Großstadt** *f* big city; **'großstädtisch** *adj* of *or* in a big city, urban
**'größten'teils** *adv* mostly, mainly
**'großtun** *v/i* (*irr*, ***tun***, *sep*, *-ge-*, *h*) show off; ***sich mit et. ~*** brag about s.th.
**'Großvater** *m* grandfather
**'Großverdiener** *m* (*-s*; -) big earner
**'Großwild** *n* big game
**'großziehen** *v/t* (*irr*, ***ziehen***, *sep*, *-ge-*, *h*) raise, rear; bring up
**'großzügig** *adj* generous, liberal; ... on a large scale; spacious
**'Großzügigkeit** *f* (-; *no pl*) generosity, liberality; spaciousness
**grotesk** [gro'tɛsk] *adj* grotesque
**Grotte** ['grɔtə] *f* (-; *-n*) grotto
**grub** [gru:p] *pret of* ***graben***
**Grübchen** ['gry:pçən] *n* (*-s*; -) dimple
**Grube** ['gru:bə] *f* (-; *-n*) pit; mine
**Grübelei** [gry:bə'lai] *f* (-; *-en*) pondering, musing
**grübeln** ['gry:bəln] *v/i* (*ge-*, *h*) ponder, muse (***über*** *acc* on, over)
**Gruft** [grʊft] *f* (-; *Grüfte* ['grʏftə]) tomb, vault
**grün** [gry:n] *adj* green; **Grün** *n* (*-s*; -) green; ***im ~en*** in the country
**'Grünanlage** *f* park
**Grund** [grʊnt] *m* (-[*e*]*s*; *Gründe* ['grʏndə]) reason; cause; ground, AGR *a.* soil; bottom; ***~ und Boden*** property, land; ***aus diesem ~(e)*** for this reason; ***von ~ auf*** entirely; ***im ~e*** (***genommen***) actually, basically; → ***aufgrund***; → ***zugrunde***
**'Grund...** *in cpds ...bedeutung*, *...bedingung*, *...regel*, *...prinzip*, *...wortschatz*

*etc*: *mst* basic ...; **~begriffe** *pl* basics, fundamentals; **~besitz** *m* property, land; **~besitzer** *m* landowner

**gründen** ['grʏndən] *v/t* (*ge-*, *h*) found (*a. family*), set up, establish; ***sich ~ auf*** (*dat*) be based *or* founded on

**Gründer** ['grʏndɐ] *m* (*-s*; -), **'Gründerin** *f* (-; *-nen*) founder

**'grund'falsch** *adj* absolutely wrong

**'Grund|fläche** *f* MATH base; ARCH area; **~gedanke** *m* basic idea; **~geschwindigkeit** *f* AVIAT ground speed; **~gesetz** *n* POL Basic (Constitutional) Law (for the Federal Republic of Germany); **~lage** *f* foundation, *fig a.* basis; *pl* (basic) elements

**'grundlegend** *adj* fundamental, basic

**gründlich** ['grʏntlıç] *adj* thorough

**'Grundlinie** *f tennis etc*: base line

**'grundlos** *adj* groundless, unfounded

**'Grundmauer** *f* foundation

**Grün'donnerstag** *m* REL Maundy *or* Holy Thursday

**'Grund|rechnungsart** *f* MATH basic arithmetical operation; **~riss** *m* ARCH ground plan; **~satz** *m* principle

**grundsätzlich** ['grʊntzɛtslıç] **1.** *adj* fundamental; **2.** *adv*: ***ich bin ~ dagegen*** I am against it on principle

**'Grund|schule** *f* elementary (*or* grade) school, *Br* primary (*or* junior) school; **~stein** *m* ARCH foundation stone; *fig* foundations; **~stück** *n* plot (of land), lot; (building) site; premises; **~stücksmakler** *m* realtor, *Br* real estate agent

**'Gründung** *f* (-; *-en*) foundation, establishment, setting up

**'grundver'schieden** *adj* totally different

**'Grund|wasser** *n* ground water; **~zahl** *f* cardinal number; **~zug** *m* main feature, characteristic

**Grüne** ['gry:nə] *m, f* (*-n*; *-n*) POL Green

**'Grünfläche** *f* green space

**'grünlich** *adj* greenish

**'Grünspan** *m* (-[*e*]*s*; *no pl*) verdigris

**grunzen** ['grʊntsən] *v/i and v/t* (*ge-*, *h*) grunt

**Gruppe** ['grʊpə] *f* (-; *-n*) group

**'Gruppenreise** *f* group tour

**gruppieren** [grʊ'pi:rən] *v/t* (*no -ge-*, *h*) group, arrange in groups; ***sich ~*** form groups

**Grusel...** ['gru:zəl-] *in cpds ...film etc*: horror ...; **'gruselig** *adj* eerie, creepy; spine-chilling; **'gruseln** *v/t and v/refl* (*ge-*, *h*) ***es gruselt mich*** F it gives me the creeps

**Gruß** [gru:s] *m* (*-es*; *Grüße* ['gry:sə]) greeting(s); MIL salute; ***viele Grüße an*** (*acc*) **...** give my regards (*or* love) to ...; ***mit freundlichen Grüßen*** yours sincerely; ***herzliche Grüße*** best wishes; love

**grüßen** ['gry:sən] *v/t* (*ge-*, *h*) greet, F say hello to; MIL salute; ***~ Sie ihn von mir*** give my regards (*or* love) to him

**gucken** ['gʊkən] *v/i* (*ge-*, *h*) look

**'Guckloch** *n* peephole

**Güggeli** ['gʏgəli] *n* (*-s*; -) *Swiss* chicken

**gültig** ['gʏltıç] *adj* valid; current

**'Gültigkeit** *f* (-; *no pl*) validity; ***s-e ~ verlieren*** expire

**Gummi** ['gʊmi] *m, n* (*-s*; -[*s*]) rubber; **~band** *n* (-[*e*]*s*; *-bänder*) rubber (*esp Br a.* elastic) band; **~bärchen** *pl* gummy bears; **~baum** *m* BOT rubber tree; rubber plant; **~bon,bon** *m, n* gumdrop

**gummieren** [gʊ'mi:rən] *v/t* (*no -ge-*, *h*) gum

**'Gummi|knüppel** *m* truncheon; **~stiefel** *m* rubber boot, *esp Br* wellington (boot); **~zug** *m* elastic

**Gunst** [gʊnst] *f* (-; *no pl*) favo(u)r, goodwill; → ***zugunsten***

**günstig** ['gʏnstıç] *adj* favo(u)rable (**für** to); convenient; ***im ~sten Fall*** at best; ***~e Gelegenheit*** chance

**Gurgel** ['gʊrgəl] *f* (-; *-n*) throat; ***j-m an die ~ springen*** fly at s.o.'s throat; **'gurgeln** *v/i* (*ge-*, *h*) MED gargle

**Gurke** ['gʊrkə] *f* (-; *-n*) BOT cucumber

**gurren** ['gʊrən] *v/i* (*ge-*, *h*) ZO coo

**Gurt** [gʊrt] *m* (-[*e*]*s*; *-e*) belt (*a.* MOT *and* AVIAT); strap

**Gürtel** ['gʏrtəl] *m* (*-s*; -) belt; **~reifen** *m* MOT radial (tire, *Br* tyre)

**GUS** [gʊs, ge:ʔu:'ʔɛs] ABBR *of* ***Gemeinschaft Unabhängiger Staaten*** CIS, Commonwealth of Independent States

**Guss** [gʊs] *m* (*-es*; *Güsse* ['gʏsə]) downpour; TECH casting; GASTR icing; *fig* ***aus e-m ~*** of a piece; **'Gusseisen** *n* cast iron; **'gusseisern** *adj* cast-iron

**gut** [gu:t] **1.** *adj* good; fine; ***ganz ~*** not bad; ***also ~!*** all right (then)!; ***schon ~!*** never mind!; (***wieder***) ***~ werden*** come right (again), be all right; ***~e Reise!***

have a nice trip!; ***sei bitte so ~ und ...*** would you be so good as to *or* good enough to ...; ***in et. ~ sein*** be good at (doing) s.th.; **2.** *adv* well; *look, taste etc* good; ***du hast es ~*** you are lucky; ***es ist ~ möglich*** it may well be; ***es gefällt mir ~*** I (do) like it; ***~ gebaut*** well-built; ***~ gelaunt*** in a good mood; ***~ gemacht!*** well done!; ***mach's ~!*** take care (of yourself)!; ***~ gehen*** go (off) well, work out well *or* all right; ***wenn alles ~ geht*** if nothing goes wrong; ***mir geht es ~*** I'm (doing) well; **Gut** *n* (-[*e*]*s*; *Güter* ['gy:tɐ]) estate; *pl* goods

'**Gutachten** *n* (-*s*; -) (expert) opinion; certificate; **Gutachter** ['gu:tˀaxtɐ] *m* (-*s*; -) expert

'**gutartig** *adj* good-natured; MED benign

**Gutdünken** ['gu:tdʏŋkən] *n*: ***nach ~*** at one's discretion

**Gute** ['gu:tə] *n* (-*n*; *no pl*) good; ***~s tun*** do good; ***alles ~!*** all the best!, good luck!

**Güte** ['gy:tə] *f* (-; *no pl*) goodness, kindness; ECON quality; F ***meine ~!*** good gracious!

**Güter|bahnhof** ['gy:tɐ-] *m* freight depot, *Br* goods station; **~gemeinschaft** *f* JUR community of property; **~trennung** *f* JUR separation of property; **~verkehr** *m* freight (*Br* goods) traffic; **~wagen** *m* freight car, *Br* goods wag(g)on; **~zug** *m* freight (*Br* goods) train

'**gutgläubig** *adj* credulous

'**Guthaben** *n* (-*s*; -) ECON credit (balance)

'**gutheißen** *v/t* (*irr*, ***heißen***, *sep*, -*ge*-, *h*) approve (of)

'**gutherzig** *adj* kind(-hearted)

**gütig** ['gy:tɪç] *adj* good, kind(ly)

**gütlich** ['gy:tlɪç] *adv*: ***sich ~ einigen*** come to an amicable settlement

'**gutmachen** *v/t* (*sep*, -*ge*-, *h*) make up for, repay

'**gutmütig** [-my:tɪç] *adj* good-natured

'**Gutmütigkeit** *f* (-; *no pl*) good nature

'**Gutsbesitzer** *m*, '**Gutsbesitzerin** *f* (-; -*nen*) estate owner

'**Gutschein** *m* coupon, *esp Br* voucher

'**gutschreiben** *v/t* (*irr*, ***schreiben***, *sep*, -*ge*-, *h*) ***j-m et. ~*** credit s.th. to s.o.'s account; '**Gutschrift** *f* credit

'**Gutshaus** *n* manor (house)

'**Gutshof** *m* estate, manor

'**Gutsverwalter** *m* steward, manager

'**gutwillig** *adj* willing

**Gymnasium** [gʏm'na:zjʊm] *n* (-*s*; -*ien*) high school, *Br appr* grammar school

**Gymnastik** [gʏm'nastɪk] *f* (-; *no pl*) exercises, gymnastics; **gym'nastisch** *adj*: ***~e Übungen*** physical exercises

**Gynäkologe** [gynɛko'lo:gə] *m* (-*n*; -*n*), **Gynäko'login** *f* (-; -*nen*) MED gyn(a)ecologist

# H

**Haar** [ha:ɐ] *n* (-[*e*]*s*; -*e* ['ha:rə]) hair; ***sich die ~e kämmen*** (***schneiden lassen***) comb one's hair (have one's hair cut); ***sich aufs ~ gleichen*** look absolutely identical; ***um ein ~*** by a hair's breadth

'**Haarausfall** *m* loss of hair

'**Haarbürste** *f* hairbrush

**haaren** ['ha:rən] *v/i and v/refl* (*ge*-, *h*) ZO lose its hair; *fur*: shed hairs

'**Haaresbreite** *f*: ***um ~*** by a hair's breadth

'**haarfein** *adj* (as) fine as a hair

'**Haarfestiger** *m* (-*s*; -) setting lotion

'**Haargefäß** *n* ANAT capillary (vessel)

'**haargenau** F *adv* precisely; (***stimmt***) ***~!*** dead right!

**haarig** ['ha:rɪç] *adj* hairy

'**haarklein** F *adv* to the last detail

'**Haar|klemme** *f* bobby pin, *Br* hair clip; **~nadel** *f* hairpin; **~nadelkurve** *f* hairpin bend; **~netz** *n* hair-net

'**haarscharf** F *adv* by a hair's breadth

'**Haar|schnitt** *m* haircut; **~spalterei** *f* (-; *no pl*) hair-splitting; **~spange** *f* barrette, *Br* (hair) slide; **~spray** *m*, *n* hairspray

'**haarsträubend** *adj* hair-raising
'**Haar|teil** *n* hairpiece; **~trockner** *m* hair dryer; **~wäsche** *f*, **~waschmittel** *n* shampoo; **~wasser** *n* hair tonic; **~wuchs** *m*: ***starken ~ haben*** have a lot of hair; **~wuchsmittel** *n* hair restorer
**haben** ['ha:bən] *v/t* (*irr*, *ge-*, *h*) have (got); ***Hunger ~*** be hungry; ***Durst ~*** be thirsty; ***Ferien*** (***Urlaub***) ***~*** be on vacation (*Br* holiday); ***er hat Geburtstag*** it's his birthday; ***welche Farbe hat ...?*** what colo(u)r is ...?; ***zu ~ sein*** be available; F ***sich ~*** make a fuss; F ***was hast du?*** what's the matter with you?; F ***da ~ wir's!*** there we are!; → ***Datum***
'**Haben** *n* (*-s*; *no pl*) ECON credit
**Habgier** ['ha:p-] *f* greed(iness)
'**habgierig** *adj* greedy
**Habicht** ['ha:bıçt] *m* (*-s*; *-e*) ZO hawk
'**Habseligkeiten** *pl* belongings
**Hacke** ['hakə] *f* (-; *-n*) AGR hoe; (pick-)axe; ANAT heel; '**hacken** *v/t* (*ge-*, *h*) chop; AGR hoe; ZO peck
'**Hackentrick** *m soccer*: backheeler
**Hacker** ['hakɐ] *m* (*-s*; -) EDP hacker
'**Hack|fleisch** *n* ground (*Br* minced) meat; **~ordnung** *f* ZO pecking order
**Hafen** ['ha:fən] *m* (*-s*; *Häfen* ['hɛ:fən]) harbo(u)r, port; **~arbeiter** *m* docker, longshoreman; **~stadt** *f* (sea)port
**Hafer** ['ha:fɐ] *m* (*-s*; -) BOT oats; **~brei** *m* oatmeal, *Br* porridge; **~flocken** *pl* (rolled) oats; **~schleim** *m* gruel
**Haft** [haft] *f* (-; *no pl*) JUR confinement, imprisonment; ***in ~*** under arrest
'**haftbar** *adj* responsible, JUR liable
'**Haftbefehl** *m* JUR warrant of arrest
'**haften** *v/i* (*ge-*, *h*) stick, adhere (***an*** *dat* to); ***~ für*** JUR answer for, be liable for
**Häftling** ['hɛftlıŋ] *m* (*-s*; *-e*) prisoner, convict
'**Haftpflicht** *f* JUR liability; **~versicherung** *f* liability insurance; MOT third party insurance
'**Haftung** *f* (-; *-en*) responsibility, JUR liability; ***mit beschränkter ~*** limited
**Hagel** ['ha:gəl] *m* (*-s*; *no pl*) hail, *fig a.* shower, volley; '**Hagelkorn** *n* hailstone; '**hageln** *v/i* (*ge-*, *h*) hail (*a. fig*); '**Hagelschauer** *m* hail shower
**hager** ['ha:gɐ] *adj* lean, gaunt, haggard
**Hahn** [ha:n] *m* (*-[e]s*; *Hähne* ['hɛ:nə]) ZO cock, rooster; TECH (water) tap, faucet
**Hähnchen** ['hɛ:nçən] *n* (*-s*; -) ZO chicken
'**Hahnenkamm** *m* ZO cockscomb
**Hai** [hai] *m* (*-[e]s*; *-e*), **~fisch** *m* ZO shark
**häkeln** ['hɛ:kəln] *v/t and v/i* (*ge-*, *h*) crochet
**Haken** ['ha:kən] *m* (*-s*; -) hook (*a. boxing*), peg; check, *Br* tick; F snag, catch
'**Hakenkreuz** *n* swastika
**halb** [halp] *adj and adv* half; ***e-e ~e Stunde*** half an hour; ***ein ~es Pfund*** half a pound; ***zum ~en Preis*** at half-price; ***auf ~em Wege*** (***entgegenkommen***) (meet) halfway; ***~ so viel*** half as much; F (***mit j-m***) ***halbe-halbe machen*** go halves *or* fifty-fifty (with s.o.); ***~ gar*** GASTR underdone
'**Halbbruder** *m* half-brother
'**Halbdunkel** *n* semi-darkness
**Halbe** ['halbə] *f* (*-n*; *-n*) pint (of beer)
'**halbfett** *adj* GASTR medium-fat; PRINT semi-bold
'**Halbfiˌnale** *n* SPORT semifinal
'**Halbgott** *m* demigod
'**halbherzig** *adj* half-hearted
**halbieren** [hal'bi:rən] *v/t* (*no -ge-*, *h*) halve; MATH bisect
'**Halbinsel** *f* peninsula
'**Halbjahr** *n* six months; '**halbjährig** [-jɛ:rıç] *adj* six-month; '**halbjährlich** **1.** *adj* half-yearly; **2.** *adv* half-yearly, twice a year
'**Halbkreis** *m* semicircle
'**Halbkugel** *f* hemisphere
'**halblaut** **1.** *adj* low, subdued; **2.** *adv* in an undertone
'**Halbleiter** *m* ELECTR semiconductor
'**halbmast** *adv* (at) half-mast
'**Halb|mond** *m* half-moon, crescent; **~pensiˌon** *f* (-; *no pl*) *esp Br* half board; **~schlaf** *m* doze; **~schuh** *m* (low) shoe; **~schwester** *f* half-sister
'**halbtags** *adv*: ***~ arbeiten*** work part-time; '**Halbtagsarbeit** *f* (-; *no pl*) part-time job; '**Halbtagskraft** *f* part-time worker, F part-timer
'**halbwegs** [-ve:ks] *adv* reasonably
'**Halbwüchsige** [-vy:ksıgə] *m*, *f* (*-n*; *-n*) adolescent
'**Halbzeit** *f* SPORT half (time); **~stand** *m* SPORT half-time score
**Halde** ['haldə] *f* (-; *-n*) slope; dump
**half** [half] *pret of* ***helfen***
**Hälfte** ['hɛlftə] *f* (-; *-n*) half; ***die ~ von*** half of

**Halfter** ['halftɐ] **1.** *m*, *n* (*-s*; -) halter; **2.** *n* (*-s*; -), *f* (-; *-n*) holster

**Halle** ['halə] *f* (-; *-n*) hall; lounge; ***in der*** ~ SPORT *etc* indoors

'**hallen** *v/i* (*ge-*, *h*) resound, reverberate

'**Hallenbad** *n* indoor swimming pool

'**Hallensport** *m* indoor sports

**Halm** [halm] *m* (*-[e]s*; *-e*) BOT blade; ha(u)lm, stalk; straw

**Hals** [hals] *m* (*-es*; *Hälse* ['hɛlzə]) ANAT neck; throat; ~ ***über Kopf*** helter-skelter; F ***sich vom*** ~ ***schaffen*** get rid of; F ***es hängt mir zum*** ~***(e)*** ***(he)raus*** I'm fed up with it; *fig* ***bis zum*** ~ up to one's neck; ~**band** *n* (*-[e]s*; *-bänder*) necklace; collar; ~**entzündung** *f* MED sore throat; ~**kette** *f* necklace; ~**schmerzen** *pl*: ~ ***haben*** have a sore throat

'**halsstarrig** [-ʃtarɪç] *adj* stubborn, obstinate

'**Halstuch** *n* neckerchief; scarf

**Halt** *m* (*-[e]s*; *-e*, *-s*) a) (*no pl*) hold; support (*a. fig*); *fig* stability, b) stop; ~ ***machen*** stop; *fig* ***vor nichts*** ~ ***machen*** stop at nothing

**halt** [halt] *int* stop!, MIL halt!

'**haltbar** *adj* durable; GASTR not perishable; *fig* tenable; ~ ***bis ...*** best before ...

'**Haltbarkeitsdatum** *n* best-by (*or* best-before) date

**halten** ['haltən] (*irr*, *ge-*, *h*) **1.** *v/t* hold; keep (*animal*, *promise etc*); make (*speech*); give (*lecture*); take (*Br a.* in) *a paper etc*; SPORT save; ~ ***für*** regard as; (mis)take for; ***viel*** (***wenig***) ~ ***von*** think highly (little) of; ***sich*** ~ last; GASTR keep; ***sich gut*** ~ *fig* do well; ***sich*** ~ ***an*** (*acc*) keep to; **2.** *v/i* hold, last; stop, halt; *ice*: bear; *rope etc*: hold; ~ ***zu*** stand by, F stick to; **Halter(in)** ['haltɐ (-tərɪn)] (*-s*; *-/-*; *-nen*) owner; TECH holder

'**Haltestelle** *f* stop, RAIL *a.* station

'**Halteverbot** *n* MOT no stopping (area)

'**haltlos** *adj* unsteady; *fig* baseless

'**Haltung** *f* (-; *-en*) posture; *fig* attitude (***zu*** towards)

**hämisch** ['hɛːmɪʃ] *adj* malicious, sneering

**Hammel** ['haməl] *m* (*-s*; -) ZO wether

'**Hammelfleisch** *n* GASTR mutton

**Hammer** ['hamɐ] *m* (*-s*; *Hämmer* ['hɛmɐ]) hammer (*a.* SPORT); **hämmern** ['hɛmɐn] *v/t and v/i* (*ge-*, *h*) hammer

**Hämorrhoiden, Hämorriden** [hɛmɔro'iːdən] *pl* MED h(a)emorrhoids, F *Br* piles

**Hampelmann** ['hampəl-] *m* jumping jack

**Hamster** ['hamstɐ] *m* (*-s*; -) ZO hamster

'**hamstern** *v/t and v/i* (*ge-*, *h*) hoard

**Hand** [hant] *f* (-; *Hände* ['hɛndə]) hand; ***von*** ~, ***mit der*** ~ by hand; ***an*** ~ ***von*** (*or gen*) by means of; ***zur*** ~ at hand; ***aus erster*** (***zweiter***) ~ first-hand (second-hand); ***an die*** ~ ***nehmen*** take by the hand; ***sich die*** ~ ***geben*** shake hands; ***aus der*** ~ ***legen*** lay aside; ~ ***voll*** handful; ***Hände hoch*** (***weg***)***!*** hands up (off)!; ~**arbeit** *f* a) (*no pl*) manual labo(u)r, b) needlework; ***es ist*** ~ it is handmade; ~**ball** *m* SPORT (European) handball; ~**betrieb** *m* TECH manual operation; ~**breit** *f* (-; -) hand's breadth; ~**bremse** *f* MOT handbrake; ~**buch** *n* manual, handbook

**Händedruck** ['hɛndə-] *m* (*-[e]s*; *-drücke*) handshake

**Handel** ['handəl] *m* (*-s*; *no pl*) commerce, business; trade; market; transaction, deal, bargain; ~ ***treiben*** ECON trade (***mit*** with *s.o.*); '**handeln** *v/i* (*ge-*, *h*) act, take action; bargain (***um*** for), haggle (over); ***mit j-m*** ~ ECON trade with s.o.; ~ ***mit*** deal in; ~ ***von*** deal with, be about; ***es handelt sich um*** it concerns, it is about; it is a matter of

'**Handels|abkommen** *n* trade agreement; ~**bank** *f* (-; *-banken*) commercial bank; ~**bi͵lanz** *f* balance of trade

'**handelseinig** *adj*: ~ ***werden*** come to terms

'**Handels|gesellschaft** *f* (trading) company; ~**kammer** *f* chamber of commerce; ~**schiff** *n* merchant ship; ~**schule** *f* commercial school; ~**vertreter** *m* (traveling) salesman, *Br* sales representative; ~**ware** *f* commodity, merchandise

'**Hand|feger** [-feːgɐ] *m* (*-s*; -) handbrush; ~**fertigkeit** *f* manual skill

'**handfest** *adj* solid

'**Handfläche** *f* ANAT palm

'**handgearbeitet** *adj* handmade

'**Hand|gelenk** *n* ANAT wrist; ~**gepäck** *n* hand baggage (*Br* luggage); ~**gra͵nate** *f* MIL hand grenade

'**handgreiflich** [-graiflɪç] *adj*: ~ ***werden*** turn violent, get tough

H

**'handhaben** *v/t* (*ge-*, *h*) handle, manage; TECH operate
**'Handkantenschlag** *m* chop
**Händler** ['hɛndlɐ] *m* (*-s*; -), **'Händlerin** *f* (-; *-nen*) dealer, trader
**'handlich** *adj* handy, manageable
**Handlung** ['handlʊŋ] *f* (-; *-en*) act, action; *film etc*: story, plot
**'Handlungs|reisende** *m* sales representative, travel(l)ing salesman; **~weise** *f* conduct, behavio(u)r
**'Hand|rücken** *m* ANAT back of the hand; **~schellen** *pl* handcuffs; ***j-m ~ anlegen*** handcuff s.o.; **~schlag** *m* handshake; **~schrift** *f* hand(writing)
**'handschriftlich** *adj* handwritten
**'Hand|schuh** *m* glove; **~spiel** *n soccer*: hand ball; **~stand** *m* handstand; **~tasche** *f* handbag, purse; **~tuch** *n* towel; **~wagen** *m* handcart; **~werk** *n* craft, trade
**'Handwerker** [-vɛrkɐ] *m* (*-s*; -) craftsman; workman
**'Handwerkszeug** *n* (kit of) tools
**'Handwurzel** *f* ANAT wrist
**Handy** ['hɛndi] *n* (*-s*; *-s*) mobile (phone)
**Hanf** [hanf] *m* (*-es*; *no pl*) BOT hemp; cannabis
**Hang** [haŋ] *m* (*-[e]s*; *Hänge* ['hɛŋə]) a) slope, b) (*no pl*) *fig* inclination (***zu*** for), tendency (towards)
**Hänge|brücke** ['hɛŋə-] *f* suspension bridge; **~lampe** *f* hanging lamp; **~matte** *f* hammock
**hängen** ['hɛŋən] **1.** *v/i* (*irr*, *ge-*, *h*) hang (***an*** *dat* on *the wall etc*; from *the ceiling etc*); ***~ bleiben*** get stuck (*a. fig*); ***~ bleiben an*** (*dat*) get caught on; ***~ an*** (*dat*) be fond of; be devoted to; ***alles, woran ich hänge*** everything that is dear to me; **2.** *v/t* (*ge-*, *h*) hang (***an*** *acc* on)
**hänseln** ['hɛnzəln] *v/t* (*ge-*, *h*) tease (***wegen*** about)
**Hanswurst** [hans'vʊrst] *m* (*-[e]s*; *-e*) fool, clown
**Hantel** ['hantəl] *f* (-; *-n*) dumbbell
**hantieren** [han'ti:rən] *v/i* (*no -ge-*, *h*) ***~ mit*** handle; ***~ an*** (*dat*) fiddle about with
**Happen** ['hapən] *m* (*-s*; -) morsel, bite; snack
**Hardware** ['hɑ:dwɛə] *f* (-; *-s*) EDP hardware
**Harfe** ['harfə] *f* (-; *-n*) MUS harp
**Harfenist** [harfə'nɪst] *m* (*-en*; *-en*), **Harfe'nistin** *f* (-; *-nen*) MUS harpist
**Harke** ['harkə] *f* (-; *-n*), **'harken** *v/t* (*ge-*, *h*) rake
**harmlos** ['harmlo:s] *adj* harmless
**Harmonie** [harmo'ni:] *f* (-; *-n*) harmony (*a.* MUS); **harmo'nieren** *v/i* (*no -ge-*, *h*) harmonize (***mit*** with); **harmonisch** [har'mo:nɪʃ] *adj* harmonious
**Harn** [harn] *m* (*-[e]s*; *-e*) MED urine
**'Harnblase** *f* ANAT (urinary) bladder
**'Harnröhre** *f* ANAT urethra
**Harpune** [har'pu:nə] *f* (-; *-n*) harpoon
**harpunieren** [harpu'ni:rən] *v/t* (*no -ge-*, *h*) harpoon
**hart** [hart] **1.** *adj* hard, F *a.* tough; SPORT rough; severe; ***~ gekocht*** hard-boiled; **2.** *adv* hard
**Härte** ['hɛrtə] *f* (-; *-n*) hardness; toughness; roughness; severity; *esp* JUR hardship; **~fall** *m* case of hardship
**'härten** *v/t* (*ge-*, *h*) harden
**'Hartfaserplatte** *f* hardboard
**'Hartgeld** *n* coin(s)
**'hartgesotten** [-gəzɔtən] *adj* hard-boiled
**'hartherzig** *adj* hard-hearted
**'hartnäckig** [-nɛkɪç] *adj* stubborn, obstinate; persistent
**Harz** [ha:ɐts] *n* (*-es*; *-e*) resin; rosin
**'harzig** *adj* resinous
**Hasch** [haʃ] F *n* (*-s*; *no pl*) hash
**'haschen** F *v/i* (*ge-*, *h*) smoke hash
**Haschisch** ['haʃɪʃ] *n* (*-[s]*; *no pl*) hashish
**Hase** ['ha:zə] *m* (*-n*; *-n*) ZO hare
**Haselmaus** ['ha:zəl-] *f* ZO dormouse
**'Haselnuss** *f* BOT hazelnut
**'Hasenscharte** *f* MED harelip
**Hass** [has] *m* (*-es*; *no pl*) hatred, hate (***auf*** *acc*, ***gegen*** of, for)
**hassen** ['hasən] *v/t* (*ge-*, *h*) hate
**hässlich** ['hɛslɪç] *adj* ugly, *fig a.* nasty
**Hast** [hast] *f* (-; *no pl*) hurry, haste; rush
**hasten** ['hastən] *v/i* (*ge-*, *sein*) hurry, hasten, rush
**'hastig** *adj* hasty, hurried
**hätscheln** ['hɛ:tʃəln] *v/t* (*ge-*, *h*) fondle; *contp* pamper
**hatte** ['hatə] *pret of* ***haben***
**Haube** ['haubə] *f* (-; *-n*) bonnet (*a. Br* MOT); cap; ZO crest; MOT hood
**Hauch** [haux] *m* (*-[e]s*; *-e*) breath; whiff; *fig* touch, trace; **hauchen** ['hauxən] *v/t* (*ge-*, *h*) breathe
**hauen** F *v/t* ([*irr*,] *ge-*, *h*) hit, beat,

thrash; TECH hew; ***sich ~*** (have a) fight

**Haufen** ['haufən] *m* (*-s*; -) heap, pile (*both a.* F); F crowd; **häufen** ['hɔʏfən] *v/t* (*ge-*, *h*) heap (up), pile (up); ***sich ~*** *fig* become more frequent, be on the increase; **häufig** ['hɔʏfɪç] **1.** *adj* frequent; **2.** *adv* frequently, often

**Haupt** [haupt] *n* (-[*e*]*s*; *Häupter* ['hɔʏptɐ]) head, *fig a.* leader; **~bahnhof** *m* main *or* central station; **~beschäftigung** *f* chief occupation; **~bestandteil** *m* chief ingredient; **~darsteller(in)** leading actor (actress), lead

**Häuptelsa͵lat** ['hɔʏptəl-] *Austrian m* BOT lettuce

**'Haupt|fach** *n* UNIV major, *Br* main subject; **~film** *m* feature (film); **~gericht** *n* GASTR main course; **~gewinn** *m* first prize; **~grund** *m* main reason; **~leitung** *f* TECH main

**Häuptling** ['hɔʏptlɪŋ] *m* (*-s*; *-e*) chief

**'Haupt|mann** *m* (-[*e*]*s*; *-leute*) MIL captain; **~me͵nü** *n* EDP main menu; **~merkmal** *n* chief characteristic; **~per͵son** F *f* center (*Br* centre) of attention; **~quar͵tier** *n* headquarters; **~rolle** *f* THEA *etc* lead(ing part)

**'Hauptsache** *f* main thing *or* point

**'hauptsächlich** *adj* main, chief, principal

**'Haupt|satz** *m* LING main clause; **~sendezeit** *f* TV prime time, *Br* peak time (*or* viewing hours); **~speicher** *m* EDP main memory; **~stadt** *f* capital; **~straße** *f* main street; main road; **~verkehrsstraße** *f* arterial road; **~verkehrszeit** *f* rush *or* peak hour(s); **~versammlung** *f* general meeting; **~wohnsitz** *m* main place of residence; **~wort** *n* (-[*e*]*s*; *-wörter*) LING noun

**Haus** [haus] *n* (*-es*; *Häuser* ['hɔʏzɐ]) house; building; ***zu ~e*** at home, in; ***nach ~e kommen*** (***bringen***) come *or* get (take) home; **~angestellte** *m*, *f* domestic (servant); **~apo͵theke** *f* medicine cabinet; **~arbeit** *f* housework; **~arzt** *m*, **~ärztin** *f* family doctor; **~aufgaben** *pl* PED homework, assignment; ***s-e ~n machen*** *a. fig* do one's homework; **~bar** *f* cocktail cabinet; **~besetzer** *m* (*-s*; -) squatter; **~besetzung** *f* squatting; **~besitzer** *m* house owner; **~einweihung** *f* house-warming (party)

**hausen** ['hauzən] *v/i* (*ge-*, *h*) live; *fig* play havoc

**'Hausflur** *m* (entrance) hall, hallway

**'Hausfrau** *f* housewife

**'Hausfriedensbruch** *m* JUR trespass

**'hausgemacht** *adj* homemade

**'Haushalt** *m* (-[*e*]*s*; *-e*) household; PARL budget; (***j-m***) ***den ~ führen*** keep house (for s.o.); **'Haushälterin** [-hɛltərɪn] *f* (-; *-nen*) housekeeper

**'Haushalts|geld** *n* housekeeping money; **~plan** *m* PARL budget; **~waren** *pl* household articles

**'Haus|herr** *m* head of the household; host; **~herrin** *f* lady of the house; hostess

**'haushoch** *adj* huge; crushing (*defeat etc*)

**hausieren** [hau'ziːrən] *v/i* (*no -ge-*, *h*) peddle, hawk (***mit et.*** s.th.) (*a. fig*); **Hau'sierer** *m* (*-s*; -) pedlar, hawker

**häuslich** ['hɔʏslɪç] *adj* domestic; home-loving

**'Haus|mädchen** *n* (house)maid; **~mann** *m* house husband; **~mannskost** *f* plain fare; **~meister** *m* caretaker, janitor; **~mittel** *n* household remedy; **~ordnung** *f* house rules; **~rat** *m* (-[*e*]*s*; *no pl*) household effects; **~schlüssel** *m* front-door key; **~schuh** *m* slipper

**Hausse** ['hoːs(ə)] *f* (-; *-n*) ECON rise, boom

**'Haus|suchung** *f* (-; *-en*) house search; **~tier** *n* domestic animal; **~tür** *f* front door; **~verwaltung** *f* property management; **~wirt** *m* landlord; **~wirtin** *f* landlady; **~wirtschaft** *f* (-; *no pl*) housekeeping; **~wirtschaftslehre** *f* domestic science, home economics; **~wirtschaftsschule** *f* domestic science (*or* home economics) school

**Haut** [haut] *f* (-; *Häute* ['hɔʏtə]) skin; complexion; ***bis auf die ~ durchnässt*** soaked to the skin; **~abschürfung** *f* MED abrasion; **~arzt** *m*, **~ärztin** *f* dermatologist; **~ausschlag** *m* MED rash

**'hauteng** *adj* skin-tight

**'Haut|farbe** *f* colo(u)r of the skin; complexion; **~krankheit** *f* skin disease; **~pflege** *f* skin care; **~schere** *f* cuticle scissors

**Hbf.** ABBR *of* ***Hauptbahnhof*** cent. sta., central station

H

**H-Bombe** ['ha:bɔmbə] *f* MIL H-bomb
**Hebamme** ['he:pˀamə] *f* (-; -*n*) midwife
**Hebebühne** ['he:bə-] *f* MOT car hoist
**Hebel** ['he:bəl] *m* (-*s*; -) TECH lever
**heben** ['he:bən] *v/t* (*irr*, *ge-*, *h*) lift, raise (*a. fig*); heave; hoist; *fig a.* improve; ***sich*** ~ rise, go up
**Hecht** [hɛçt] *m* (-[*e*]*s*; -*e*) ZO pike
'**hechten** *v/i* (*ge-*, *sein*) dive (***nach*** for); SPORT do a long-fly
**Heck** [hɛk] *n* (-[*e*]*s*; -*e*) MAR stern; AVIAT tail; MOT rear
**Hecke** ['hɛkə] *f* (-; -*n*) BOT hedge
'**Heckenrose** *f* BOT dogrose
'**Heckenschütze** *m* MIL sniper
'**Heckscheibe** *f* MOT rear window
**Heer** [he:ɐ] *n* (-[*e*]*s*; -*e*) MIL army, *fig a.* host
**Hefe** ['he:fə] *f* (-; -*n*) yeast
**Heft** [hɛft] *n* (-[*e*]*s*; -*e*) notebook; exercise book; booklet; issue, number
**heften** ['hɛftən] *v/t* (*ge-*, *h*) fix, fasten, attach (***an*** *acc* to); pin (to); tack, baste; stitch
**Hefter** ['hɛftɐ] *m* (-*s*; -) stapler; file
**heftig** ['hɛftɪç] *adj* violent, fierce; heavy
'**Heftklammer** *f* staple
'**Heftpflaster** *n* bandage, Band Aid®, *Br* (adhesive *or* sticking) plaster
**Hehl** [he:l] *n*: ***kein ~ aus et. machen*** make no secret of s.th.
**Hehler** ['he:lɐ] *m* (-*s*; -) JUR receiver of stolen goods, *sl* fence
**Hehlerei** [he:lə'rai] *f* (-; -*en*) JUR receiving stolen goods
**Heide**[1] ['haidə] *m* (-*n*; -*n*) REL heathen
'**Heide**[2] *f* (-; -*n*) heath(land)
'**Heidekraut** *n* (-[*e*]*s*; *no pl*) BOT heather, heath
'**Heiden|angst** F *f*: ***e-e ~ haben*** be scared stiff; **~geld** F *n*: ***ein*** ~ a fortune; **~lärm** F *m*: ***ein*** ~ a hell of a noise; **~spaß** F *m*: ***e-n ~ haben*** have a ball
'**Heidentum** *n* (-*s*; *no pl*) REL heathenism; **Heidin** ['haidɪn] *f* (-; -*nen*), '**heidnisch** ['haidnɪʃ] *adj* REL heathen
**heikel** ['haikəl] *adj* delicate, tricky; tender; F fussy
**heil** [hail] *adj* safe, unhurt; undamaged, whole, intact; **Heil** *n* (-*s*; *no pl*) REL grace; ***sein ~ versuchen*** try one's luck
**Heiland** ['hailant] *m* (-[*e*]*s*; *no pl*) REL Savio(u)r, Redeemer
'**Heilanstalt** *f* sanatorium, sanitarium; mental home
'**Heilbad** *n* health resort, spa
'**heilbar** *adj* curable
**heilen** ['hailən] **1.** *v/t* (*ge-*, *h*) cure; **2.** *v/i* (*ge-*, *sein*) heal (up)
'**Heilgym,nastik** *f* physiotherapy
**heilig** ['hailɪç] *adj* REL holy; sacred (*a. fig*); ~ ***sprechen*** canonize
**Heilig'abend** *m* Christmas Eve
**Heilige** ['hailɪgə] *m, f* (-*n*; -*n*) REL saint
**heiligen** ['hailɪgən] *v/t* (*ge-*, *h*) REL sanctify (*a. fig*), hallow
'**Heiligtum** *n* (-*s*; -*tümer* [-ty:mɐ]) REL sanctuary, shrine
'**Heilkraft** *f* healing *or* curative power; '**heilkräftig** *adj* curative
'**Heilkraut** *n* BOT medicinal herb
'**heillos** *fig adj* utter, hopeless
'**Heil|mittel** *n* remedy, cure (*both a. fig*); **~praktiker(in)** [-praktikɐ (-kərɪn)] (-*s*; -/-; -*nen*) nonmedical practitioner; **~quelle** *f* (medicinal) mineral spring
'**heilsam** *fig adj* salutary
'**Heilsar,mee** *f* Salvation Army
'**Heilung** *f* (-; -*en*) cure; healing
**heim** [haim] *adv* home
**Heim** *n* (-[*e*]*s*; -*e*) a) (*no pl*) home, b) hostel; **Heim...** *in cpds ...computer*, *...mannschaft*, *...sieg*, *...spiel etc*: home
**Heimat** ['haima:t] *f* (-; *no pl*) home; home country; home town; ***in der*** (***meiner***) ~ at home; '**heimatlos** *adj* homeless; '**Heimatstadt** *f* home town; '**Heimatvertriebene** *m, f* expellee
**heimisch** ['haimɪʃ] *adj* home, domestic; BOT, ZO *etc* native; *fig* homelike, hom(e)y; ***sich ~ fühlen*** feel at home
'**Heimkehr** [-ke:ɐ] *f* (-; *no pl*) return (home); '**heimkehren** *v/i* (*sep*, *-ge-*, *sein*) return home, come back
'**heimlich** *adj* secret; '**Heimlichkeit** *f* (-; -*en*) a) (*no pl*) secrecy, b) *pl* secrets
'**Heimreise** *f* journey home
'**heimsuchen** *v/t* (*sep*, *-ge-*, *h*) strike
'**heimtückisch** *adj* insidious (*a.* MED); treacherous
'**heimwärts** [-vɛrts] *adv* homeward(s)
'**Heimweg** *m* way home
'**Heimweh** *n* (-*s*; *no pl*) homesickness; ~ ***haben*** be homesick
'**Heimwerker** [-vɛrkɐ] *m* (-*s*; -) do-it--yourselfer
**Heirat** ['haira:t] *f* (-; -*en*) marriage
**heiraten** ['haira:tən] *v/t and v/i* (*ge-*, *h*) marry, get married (to)

**'Heirats|antrag** *m* proposal (of marriage); ***j-m e-n ~ machen*** propose to s.o.; **~schwindler** *m* marriage impostor; **~vermittler(in)** (*-s*; *-/-*; *-nen*) marriage broker; **~vermittlung** *f* marriage bureau

**heiser** ['haizɐ] *adj* hoarse, husky

**'Heiserkeit** *f* (-; *no pl*) hoarseness, huskiness

**heiß** [hais] *adj* hot, *fig a.* passionate, ardent; ***mir ist ~*** I am *or* feel hot

**heißen** ['haisən] *v/i* (*irr*, *ge-*, *h*) be called; mean; ***wie ~ Sie?*** what's your name?; ***wie heißt das?*** what do you call this?; ***was heißt ... auf Englisch?*** what is ... in English?; ***es heißt im Text*** it says in the text; ***das heißt*** that is (ABBR ***d.h.*** i.e.)

**heiter** ['haitɐ] *adj* cheerful; humorous (*film etc*); METEOR fair; *fig* ***aus ~em Himmel*** out of the blue; **'Heiterkeit** *f* (-; *no pl*) cheerfulness; amusement

**heizbar** ['haitsbaːɐ] *adj* heated; **heizen** ['haitsən] *v/t and v/i* (*ge-*, *h*) heat; ***mit Kohlen ~*** burn coal; **Heizer** ['haitsɐ] *m* (*-s*; -) MAR, RAIL stoker

**'Heiz|kessel** *m* boiler; **~kissen** *n* electric cushion; **~körper** *m* radiator; **~kraftwerk** *n* thermal power-station; **~materi|al** *n* fuel; **~öl** *n* fuel oil

**'Heizung** *f* (-; *-en*) heating

**Held** [hɛlt] *m* (*-en*; *-en* ['hɛldən]) hero

**heldenhaft** ['hɛldənhaft] *adj* heroic

**'Heldentat** *f* heroic deed

**'Heldentum** *n* (*-s*; *no pl*) heroism

**Heldin** ['hɛldɪn] *f* (-; *-nen*) heroine

**helfen** ['hɛlfən] *v/i* (*irr*, *ge-*, *h*) help, aid; assist; ***j-m bei et. ~*** help s.o. with *or* in (doing) s.th.; ***~ gegen*** MED *etc* be good for; ***er weiß sich zu ~*** he can manage; ***es hilft nichts*** it's no use

**Helfer** ['hɛlfɐ] *m* (*-s*; -), **'Helferin** *f* (-; *-nen*) helper, assistant

**'Helfershelfer** *contp m* accomplice

**hell** [hɛl] *adj* bright (*light*, *flame etc*); light (*color etc*); light-colo(u)red (*dress etc*); clear (*voice etc*); pale (*beer*); *fig* bright, clever; ***es wird schon ~*** it's getting light already; **~blau** *adj* light blue; **~blond** *adj* very fair; **~hörig** *adj* quick of hearing; ARCH poorly soundproofed; ***~ werden*** prick up one's ears

**'Hellseher** *m* (*-s*; -), **'Hellseherin** *f* (-; *-nen*) clairvoyant

**Helm** [hɛlm] *m* (*-[e]s*; *-e*) helmet

**Hemd** [hɛmt] *n* (*-[e]s*; *-en* ['hɛmdən]) shirt; vest; **~bluse** *f* shirt; **~blusenkleid** *n* shirtwaist, *Br* shirt-waister

**Hemisphäre** [hemi'sfɛːrə] *f* (-; *-n*) hemisphere

**hemmen** ['hɛmən] *v/t* (*ge-*, *h*) check, stop; hamper; **'Hemmung** *f* (-; *-en*) PSYCH inhibition; scruple

**'hemmungslos** *adj* unrestrained; unscrupulous

**Hengst** [hɛŋst] *m* (*-[e]s*; *-e*) ZO stallion

**Henkel** ['hɛŋkəl] *m* (*-s*; -) handle

**Henker** ['hɛŋkɐ] *m* (*-s*; -) hangman, executioner

**Henne** ['hɛnə] *f* (-; *-n*) ZO hen

**her** [heːɐ] *adv* here; ***das ist lange ~*** that was a long time ago

**herab** [hɛ'rap] *adv* down; **~lassen** *fig v/refl* (*irr*, ***lassen***, *sep*, *-ge-*, *h*) condescend; **~lassend** *adj* condescending; **~sehen** *fig v/i* (*irr*, ***sehen***, *sep*, *-ge-*, *h*) ***~ auf*** (*acc*) look down upon; **~setzen** *v/t* (*sep*, *-ge-*, *h*) reduce; *fig* disparage

**heran** [hɛ'ran] *adv* close, near; ***~ an*** (*acc*) up *or* near to; **~gehen** *v/i* (*irr*, ***gehen***, *sep*, *-ge-*, *sein*) ***~ an*** (*acc*) walk up to; *fig* set about *a task etc*; **~kommen** *v/i* (*irr*, ***kommen***, *sep*, *-ge-*, *sein*) come near (*a. fig*); **~wachsen** *v/i* (*irr*, ***wachsen***, *sep*, *-ge-*, *sein*) grow (up) (***zu*** into)

**He'ranwachsende** *m*, *f* (*-n*; *-n*) adolescent

**he'ranwinken** *v/t* (*sep*, *-ge-*, *h*) hail (*taxi etc*)

**herauf** [hɛ'rauf] *adv* up (here); upstairs; **~beschwören** *v/t* (*irr*, ***schwören***, *sep*, *no -ge-*, *h*) call up; bring on, provoke

**heraus** [hɛ'raus] *adv* out; *fig* ***aus*** (*dat*) ***... ~*** out of ...; ***zum Fenster ~*** out of the window; ***~ mit der Sprache!*** speak out!, out with it!; **~bekommen** *v/t* (*irr*, ***kommen***, *sep*, *no -ge-*, *h*) get out; get back (*change*); *fig* find out; **~bringen** *v/t* (*irr*, ***bringen***, *sep*, *-ge-*, *h*) bring out; PRINT publish; THEA stage; *fig* find out; **~finden** (*irr*, ***finden***, *sep*, *-ge-*, *h*) **1.** *v/t* find; *fig* find out, discover; **2.** *v/i* find one's way out

**He'rausforderer** *m* (*-s*; -) challenger; **he'rausfordern** *v/t* (*sep*, *-ge-*, *h*) challenge; provoke, F ask for it; **He'rausforderung** *f* challenge; provocation

**he'rausgeben** *v/t* (*irr*, ***geben***, *sep*,

H

*-ge-, h)* give back; give up; PRINT publish; issue; give change (***auf** acc* for); **He'rausgeber(in)** [-ge:bɐ (-bərɪn)] (*-s; -/-; -nen*) publisher

**he'raus|kommen** *v/i* (*irr*, ***kommen,*** *sep, -ge-, sein*) come out; *book*: be published; *stamps*: be issued; **~ *aus*** get out of; F ***groß ~*** be a great success; **~nehmen** *v/t* (*irr*, ***nehmen,*** *sep, -ge-, h*) take out; SPORT take *s.o.* off the team; *fig* ***sich et. ~*** take liberties, go too far; **~putzen** *v/t and v/refl* (*sep, -ge-, h*) spruce (o.s.) up; **~reden** *v/refl* (*sep, -ge-, h*) make excuses; talk one's way out; **~stellen** *v/t* (*sep, -ge-, h*) put out; *fig* emphasize; ***sich ~ als*** turn out *or* prove to be; **~strecken** *v/t* (*sep, -ge-, h*) stick out; **~suchen** *v/t* (*sep, -ge-, h*) pick out; ***j-m et. ~*** find s.o. s.th.

**herb** [hɛrp] *adj* tart; dry (*wine etc*); *fig* harsh; bitter

**her'bei** *adv* up, over, here; **~eilen** *v/i* (*sep, -ge-, sein*) come running up; **~führen** *fig v/t* (*sep, -ge-, h*) cause, bring about

**Herberge** ['hɛrbɛrgə] *f* (*-; -n*) inn; lodging; hostel

**Herbst** [hɛrpst] *m* (*-[e]s; -e*) fall, autumn

**Herd** [he:ɐt] *m* (*-[e]s; -e* ['he:ɐdə]) cooker, stove; *fig* center, *Br* centre; MED focus, seat

**Herde** ['he:ɐdə] *f* (*-; -n*) ZO herd (*a. fig contp*); flock (*of sheep, geese etc*)

**herein** [hɛ'rain] *adv* in (here); **~*!*** come in!; **~brechen** *v/i* (*irr*, ***brechen,*** *sep, -ge-, sein*) *night*: fall; **~ *über*** (*acc*) befall *s.o.*; **~fallen** F *v/i* (*irr*, ***fallen,*** *sep, -ge-, sein*) be taken in (***auf** acc* by); **~legen** F *v/t* (*sep, -ge-, h*) take *s.o.* in

**'herfallen** *v/i* (*irr*, ***fallen,*** *sep, -ge-, sein*) **~ *über*** (*acc*) attack (*a. fig*)

**'Hergang** *m*: ***j-m den ~ schildern*** tell s.o. what happened

**'hergeben** *v/t* (*irr*, ***geben,*** *sep, -ge-, h*) give up, part with; ***sich ~ zu*** lend o.s. to

**Hering** ['he:rɪŋ] *m* (*-s; -e*) ZO herring

**'herkommen** *v/i* (*irr*, ***kommen,*** *sep, -ge-, sein*) come (here); **~ *von*** come from, *fig a.* be caused by

**'herkömmlich** [-kœmlɪç] *adj* conventional (*a.* MIL)

**'Herkunft** [-kʊnft] *f* (*-; no pl*) origin; birth, descent

**heroisch** [he'ro:ɪʃ] *adj* heroic

**Herr** [hɛr] *m* (*-n; -en*) gentleman; master; REL *the* Lord; **~ *Brown*** Mr Brown; **~ *der Lage*** master of the situation

**'Herren|bekleidung** *f* menswear; **~doppel** *n tennis*: men's doubles; **~einzel** *n tennis*: men's singles

**'herrenlos** *adj* abandoned; stray (*dog*)

**'Herrentoi,lette** *f* men's restroom (*Br* toilet *or* lavatory)

**'herrichten** *v/t* (*sep, -ge-, h*) get ready, F fix

**herrisch** ['hɛrɪʃ] *adj* imperious

**herrlich** ['hɛrlɪç] *adj* marvel(l)ous, wonderful, F fantastic; **'Herrlichkeit** *f* (*-; -en*) glory

**'Herrschaft** *f* (*-; no pl*) rule, power, control (*a. fig*) (***über** acc* over); ***die ~ verlieren über*** (*acc*) lose control of

**herrschen** ['hɛrʃən] *v/i* (*ge-, h*) rule; ***es herrschte ...*** there was ...; **Herrscher(in)** ['hɛrʃɐ (-ʃərɪn)] (*-s; -/-; -nen*) ruler; sovereign, monarch; **'herrschsüchtig** *adj* domineering, F bossy

**'herrühren** *v/i* (*sep, -ge-, h*) **~ *von*** come from, be due to

**'herstellen** *v/t* (*sep, -ge-, h*) make, produce; *fig* establish; **'Herstellung** *f* (*-; no pl*) production; *fig* establishment; **'Herstellungskosten** *pl* production cost(s)

**herüber** [hɛ'ry:bɐ] *adv* over (here), across

**herum** [hɛ'rʊm] *adv* (a)round; F ***anders ~*** the other way round; **~führen** *v/t* (*sep, -ge-, h*) ***j-n*** (***in der Stadt*** *etc*) **~** show s.o. (a)round (the town *etc*); **~kommen** F *v/i* (*irr*, ***kommen,*** *sep, -ge-, sein*) (***weit*** *or* ***viel***) **~** get around; ***um et. ~*** *fig* get (a)round s.th.; **~kriegen** F *v/t* (*sep, -ge-, h*) ***j-n zu et. ~*** get s.o. round to (doing) s.th.; **~lungern** F *v/i* (*sep, -ge-, h*) loaf *or* hang around; **~reichen** *v/t* (*sep, -ge-, h*) pass *or* hand round; **~sprechen** *v/refl* (*irr*, ***sprechen,*** *sep, -ge-, h*) get around; **~treiben** F *v/refl* (*irr*, ***treiben,*** *sep, -ge-, h*) gad *or* knock about

**He'rumtreiber** F *m* (*-s; -*), **He'rumtreiberin** F *f* (*-; -nen*) tramp, loafer

**herunter** [hɛ'rʊntɐ] *adv* down; downstairs; **~gekommen** *adj* run-down; seedy, shabby; **~hauen** F *v/t* (*sep, -ge-, h*) ***j-m e-e ~*** smack *or* slap s.o.('s face); **~machen** F *v/t* (*sep, -ge-, h*) run *s.o. or*

*s.th.* down; **~spielen** F *v/t* (*sep*, *-ge-*, *h*) play *s.th.* down
**hervor** [hɛɐ'foːɐ] *adv* out of *or* from, forth; **~bringen** *v/t* (*irr*, ***bringen***, *sep*, *-ge-*, *h*) bring out, produce (*a. fig*); yield; utter; **~gehen** *v/i* (*irr*, ***gehen***, *sep*, *-ge-*, *sein*) **~ aus** (*dat*) follow from; ***als Sieger ~*** come off victorious; **~heben** *v/t* (*irr*, ***heben***, *sep*, *-ge-*, *h*) stress, emphasize; **~ragend** *adj* outstanding, excellent, superior; prominent, eminent; **~rufen** *v/t* (*irr*, ***rufen***, *sep*, *-ge-*, *h*) cause, bring about; create; **~stechend** *adj* striking; **~tretend** *adj* prominent; protruding, bulging; **~tun** *v/refl* (*irr*, ***tun***, *sep*, *-ge-*, *h*) distinguish o.s. (***als*** as)
**Herz** [hɛrts] *n* (*-ens*; *-en*) ANAT heart (*a. fig*); *cards*: heart(s); ***j-m das ~ brechen*** break s.o.'s heart; ***sich ein ~ fassen*** take heart; ***mit ganzem ~en*** wholeheartedly; ***schweren ~ens*** with a heavy heart; ***sich et. zu ~en nehmen*** take s.th. to heart; ***es nicht übers ~ bringen zu*** *inf* not have the heart to *inf*; ***et. auf dem ~en haben*** have s.th. on one's mind; ***ins ~ schließen*** take to one's heart; **~anfall** *m* heart attack
'**Herzens|lust** *f*: ***nach ~*** to one's heart's content; **~wunsch** *m* heart's desire, dearest wish
'**Herzfehler** *m* cardiac defect
'**herzhaft** *adj* hearty; savo(u)ry
'**herzig** *adj* sweet, lovely, cute
'**Herz|in͵farkt** *m* MED cardiac infarct(ion), F *mst* heart attack, coronary; **~klopfen** *n* (*-s*; *no pl*) palpitation; ***er hatte ~*** (***vor*** *dat*) his heart was throbbing (with)
'**herzkrank** *adj* suffering from (a) heart disease
'**herzlich 1.** *adj* cordial, hearty; warm, friendly; **2.** *adv*: ***~ gern*** with pleasure
'**herzlos** *adj* heartless
**Herzog** ['hɛrtsoːk] *m* (*-s*; *Herzöge* ['hɛrtsøːgə]) duke; **Herzogin** ['hɛrtsoːgɪn] *f* (*-*; *-nen*) duchess
'**Herz|schlag** *m* heartbeat; MED heart failure; **~schrittmacher** *m* MED (cardiac) pacemaker; **~transplantati͵on** *f* MED heart transplant
'**herzzerreißend** *adj* heart-rending
**Hetze** ['hɛtsə] *f* (*-*; *no pl*) hurry, rush; POL *etc* agitation, campaign(ing) (***gegen*** against); '**hetzen 1.** *v/t* (*ge-*, *h*) rush; ZO hunt, chase; ***e-n Hund auf j-n ~*** set a dog on s.o.; **2.** *v/i* a) (*ge-*, *sein*) hurry, rush, b) (*ge-*, *h*) POL *etc* agitate (***gegen*** against); '**hetzerisch** *adj* inflammatory; '**Hetzjagd** *f* hunt(ing), chase (*a. fig*); *fig* rush; '**Hetzkam͵pagne** *f* POL smear campaign
**Heu** [hɔʏ] *n* (*-[e]s*; *no pl*) hay
'**Heuboden** *m* hayloft
**Heuchelei** [hɔʏçə'lai] *f* (*-*; *-en*) hypocrisy; cant; **heucheln** ['hɔʏçəln] *v/i and v/t* (*ge-*, *h*) feign, simulate; **Heuchler(in)** ['hɔʏçlɐ (-lərɪn)] (*-s*; *-/-*; *-nen*) hypocrite; **heuchlerisch** ['hɔʏçlərɪʃ] *adj* hypocritical
**heuer** ['hɔʏɐ] *Austrian adv* this year
**Heuer** ['hɔʏɐ] *f* (*-*; *-n*) MAR pay; '**heuern** *v/t* (*ge-*, *h*) hire, MAR *a.* sign on
**heulen** ['hɔʏlən] *v/i* (*ge-*, *h*) howl; F *contp* bawl; MOT roar; *siren*: whine
'**Heuschnupfen** *m* MED hay fever
'**Heuschrecke** *f* (*-*; *-n*) ZO grasshopper; locust
**heute** ['hɔʏtə] *adv* today; ***~ Abend*** this evening, tonight; ***~ früh***, ***~ Morgen*** this morning; ***~ in acht Tagen*** a week from now; ***~ vor acht Tagen*** a week ago today; **heutig** ['hɔʏtɪç] *adj* today's; of today, present(-day); '**heutzutage** *adv* nowadays, these days
**Hexe** ['hɛksə] *f* (*-*; *-n*) witch (*a. fig*); ***alte ~*** (old) hag; '**hexen** *v/i* (*ge-*, *h*) practice witchcraft; F work miracles
'**Hexen|kessel** *m* inferno; **~schuss** *m* (*-es*; *no pl*) MED lumbago
**hieb** [hiːp] *pret of* ***hauen***
**Hieb** [hiːp] *m* (*-[e]s*; *-e* ['hiːbə]) blow, stroke; punch; lash, cut; *pl* beating; thrashing
**hielt** [hiːlt] *pret of* ***halten***
**hier** [hiːɐ] *adv* here, in this place; present; ***~ entlang!*** this way!
**hieran** ['hiː'ran] *adv* from *or* in this; **hierauf** ['hiː'rauf] *adv* on it *or* this; after this, then; **hieraus** ['hiː'raus] *adv* from *or* out of this; '**hier'bei** *adv* here, in this case; on this occasion; '**hier'durch** *adv* by this, hereby, this way; '**hier'für** *adv* for this; '**hier'her** *adv* (over) here, this way; ***bis ~*** so far; **hierin** ['hiː'rɪn] *adv* in this; '**hier'mit** *adv* with this; '**hier'nach** *adv* after this; according to this; **hierüber** ['hiː'ryːbɐ] *adv* about this (subject);

H

**hierunter** ['hiː'rʊntɐ] *adv* under this; among these; *understand etc* by this *or* that; **'hier'von** *adv* of *or* from this; **'hier'zu** *adv* for this; to this
**hiesig** ['hiːzɪç] *adj* local; ***ein Hiesiger*** one of the locals
**hieß** [hiːs] *pret of* ***heißen***
**Hilfe** ['hɪlfə] *f* (-; *-n*) help; aid (*a.* ECON), assistance (*a.* MED), relief (***für*** to); ***erste ~*** first aid; ***um ~ rufen*** cry for help; ***~!*** help!; → ***mithilfe***; **~meˌnü** *n* EDP help menu; **~ruf** *m* call (*or* cry) for help; **~stellung** *f* support (*a. fig*)
**'hilf|los** *adj* helpless; **~reich** *adj* helpful
**'Hilfsaktiˌon** *f* relief action
**'Hilfsarbeiter** *m*, **'Hilfsarbeiterin** *f* unskilled worker
H
**'hilfsbedürftig** *adj* needy
**'hilfsbereit** *adj* helpful, ready to help; **'Hilfsbereitschaft** *f* (-; *no pl*) readiness to help, helpfulness
**'Hilfs|mittel** *n* aid, TECH *a.* device; **~orˌganisatiˌon** *f* relief organization; **~verb** *n* LING auxiliary (verb)
**Himbeere** ['hɪmbeːrə] *f* BOT raspberry
**Himmel** ['hɪməl] *m* (*-s*; -) sky; REL heaven (*a. fig*); ***um ~s willen*** for Heaven's sake; → ***heiter***
**'Himmelfahrt** REL Ascension (Day)
**'Himmels|körper** *m* AST celestial body; **~richtung** *f* direction; cardinal point
**himmlisch** ['hɪmlɪʃ] *adj* heavenly, *fig a.* marvel(l)ous
**hin** [hɪn] **1.** *adv* there; ***bis ~ zu*** as far as; ***noch lange ~*** still a long way off; ***auf s-e Bitte*** (***s-n Rat***) ***~*** at his request (advice); ***~ und her*** to and fro, back and forth; ***~ und wieder*** now and then; ***~ und zurück*** there and back; RAIL round trip, round-trip ticket, *esp Br* return (ticket); **2.** F *pred adj* ruined; done for; gone
**hi'nab** *adv* → ***hinunter***
**'hinarbeiten** *v/i* (*sep*, *-ge-*, *h*) ***~ auf*** (*acc*) work towards
**hi'nauf** *adv* up (there); upstairs; ***die Straße*** *etc* ***~*** up the street *etc*; **~gehen** *v/i* (*irr*, ***gehen***, *sep*, *-ge-*, *sein*) go up, *fig a.* rise
**hi'naus** *adv* out; ***aus ... ~*** out of ...; ***in*** (*acc*) ***... ~*** out into ...; ***~ (mit dir)!*** (get) out!, out you go!; **~gehen** *v/i* (*irr*, ***gehen***, *sep*, *-ge-*, *sein*) go out(side); ***~ über*** (*acc*) go beyond; ***~ auf*** (*acc*) *window etc:* look out onto; **~laufen** *v/i* (*irr*, ***laufen***, *sep*, *-ge-*, *sein*) run out(side); ***~ auf*** (*acc*) come *or* amount to; **~schieben** *v/t* (*irr*, ***schieben***, *sep*, *-ge-*, *h*) put off, postpone; **~stellen** *v/t* (*sep*, *-ge-*, *h*) SPORT send *s.o.* off (the field); **~werfen** *v/t* (*irr*, ***werfen***, *sep*, *-ge-*, *h*) throw out (***aus*** of), *fig a.* kick out; (give *s.o.* the) sack, fire; **~wollen** *v/i* (*sep*, *-ge-*, *h*) ***~ auf*** (*acc*) aim (*or* drive *or* get) at; ***hoch ~*** aim high
**'Hinblick** *m*: ***im ~ auf*** (*acc*) in view of, with regard to
**'hinbringen** *v/t* (*irr*, ***bringen***, *sep*, *-ge-*, *h*) take there
**hinderlich** ['hɪndɐlɪç] *adj* hindering, impeding; ***j-m ~ sein*** be in s.o.'s way
**hindern** ['hɪndɐn] *v/t* (*ge-*, *h*) hinder, hamper; ***~ an*** (*dat*) prevent from
**Hindernis** ['hɪndɐnɪs] *n* (*-ses*; *-se*) obstacle (*a. fig*); **~rennen** *n* steeplechase
**Hindu** ['hɪndu] *m* (*-[s]*; *-[s]*) Hindu
**Hinduismus** [hɪndu'ɪsmʊs] *m* (-; *no pl*) hinduism
**hin'durch** *adv* through; ***das ganze Jahr*** *etc* ***~*** throughout the year *etc*
**hi'nein** *adv* in; ***~ mit dir!*** in you go!; **~gehen** *v/i* (*irr*, ***gehen***, *sep*, *-ge-*, *sein*) go in; ***~ in*** (*acc*) go into
**'hinfallen** *v/i* (*irr*, ***fallen***, *sep*, *-ge-*, *sein*) fall (down)
**'hinfällig** *adj* frail, infirm; invalid
**hing** [hɪŋ] *pret of* ***hängen*** 1
**'Hingabe** *f* (-; *no pl*) devotion (***an*** *acc* to); **'hingeben** *v/t* (*irr*, ***geben***, *sep*, *-ge-*, *h*) give (up); ***sich ~*** (*dat*) give o.s. to; devote o.s. to
**'hinhalten** *v/t* (*irr*, ***halten***, *sep*, *-ge-*, *h*) hold out; ***j-n ~*** put s.o. off
**hinken** ['hɪŋkən] *v/i* a) (*ge-*, *h*) (walk with a) limp, b) (*ge-*, *sein*) limp
**'hin|kommen** *v/i* (*irr*, ***kommen***, *sep*, *-ge-*, *sein*) get there; **~kriegen** F *v/t* (*sep*, *-ge-*, *h*) manage
**'hinlänglich** *adj* sufficient
**'hin|legen** *v/t* (*sep*, *-ge-*, *h*) lay *or* put down; ***sich ~*** lie down; **~nehmen** *v/t* (*irr*, ***nehmen***, *sep*, *-ge-*, *h*) put up with
**'hinreißen** *v/t* (*irr*, ***reißen***, *sep*, *-ge-*, *h*) carry away; **~d** *adj* entrancing; breathtaking
**'hinrichten** *v/t* (*sep*, *-ge-*, *h*) execute; **'Hinrichtung** *f* (-; *-en*) execution

**'hinsetzen** *v/t* (*sep*, *-ge-*, *h*) set *or* put down; ***sich*** ~ sit down
**'Hinsicht** *f* (*-*; *no pl*) respect; ***in gewisser*** ~ in a way; **'hinsichtlich** *prp* (*gen*) with respect *or* regard to
**'Hinspiel** *n* SPORT first leg
**'hinstellen** *v/t* (*sep*, *-ge-*, *h*) put (down); ~ ***als*** make *s.o. or s.th.* appear to be
**hinten** ['hɪntən] *adv* at the back; MOT in the back; ***von*** ~ from behind
**hinter** ['hɪntɐ] *prp* (*dat*) behind
**'Hinter...** *in cpds ...achse*, *...eingang*, *...rad etc*: rear ...; **~bein** *n* hind leg
**Hinterbliebenen** [-'bli:bənən] *pl the* bereaved; *esp* JUR surviving dependents
**hinterei'nander** *adv* one after the other; ***dreimal*** ~ three times in a row
**'Hintergedanke** *m* ulterior motive
**hinter'gehen** *v/t* (*irr*, ***gehen***, *no -ge-*, *h*) deceive
**'Hintergrund** *m* background (*a. fig*)
**'Hinterhalt** *m* ambush; **'hinterhältig** [-hɛltɪç] *adj* insidious, underhand(ed)
**'Hinterhaus** *n* rear building
**hinter'her** *adv* behind, after; afterwards
**'Hinterhof** *m* backyard
**'Hinterkopf** *m* back of the head
**hinter'lassen** *v/t* (*irr*, ***lassen***, *no -ge-*, *h*) leave (behind); **Hinter'lassenschaft** *f* (*-*; *-en*) property (left), estate
**hinter'legen** *v/t* (*no -ge-*, *h*) deposit (***bei*** with)
**'Hinterlist** *f* deceit(fulness); (underhanded) trick; **'hinterlistig** *adj* deceitful; underhand(ed)
**'Hintermann** *m* person (car *etc*) behind (one); *fig mst pl* person behind the scenes, brain(s), mastermind
**'Hintern** F *m* (*-s*; *-*) bottom, backside, behind, *Br* bum
**'hinterrücks** [-rʏks] *adv* from behind
**'Hinter|seite** *f* back; **~teil** F *n* → ***Hintern***; **~treppe** *f* back stairs; **~tür** *f* back door
**hinter'ziehen** *v/t* (*irr*, ***ziehen***, *no -ge-*, *h*) evade (*taxes*)
**'Hinterzimmer** *n* back room
**hi'nüber** *adv* over, across; ~ ***sein*** F be ruined; GASTR be spoilt
**hi'nunter** *adv* down; downstairs; ***die Straße*** ~ down the road
**Hinweg** ['hɪnve:k] *m* way there
**hinweg** [hɪn'vɛk] *adv*: ***über*** (*acc*) ... ~ over ...; **~kommen** *v/i* (*irr*, ***kommen*** *sep*, *-ge-*, *sein*) ~ ***über*** (*acc*) get over; **~sehen** *v/i* (*irr*, ***sehen***, *sep*, *-ge-*, *h*) ~ ***über*** (*acc*) ignore; **~setzen** *v/refl* (*sep*, *-ge-*, *h*) ***sich*** ~ ***über*** (*acc*) ignore, disregard
**Hinweis** ['hɪnvais] *m* (*-es*; *-e*) reference (***auf*** *acc* to); hint, tip (as to, regarding); indication (of), clue (as to); **'hinweisen** (*irr*, ***weisen***, *sep*, *-ge-*, *h*) **1.** *v/t*: ***j-n*** ~ ***auf*** (*acc*) draw *or* call s.o.'s attention to; **2.** *v/i*: ~ ***auf*** (*acc*) point at *or* to, indicate; *fig* point out, indicate; hint at
**'Hinweis|schild** *n*, **~tafel** *f* sign, notice
**'hin|werfen** *v/t* (*irr*, ***werfen***, *sep*, *-ge-*, *h*) throw down; **~ziehen** *v/refl* (*irr*, ***ziehen***, *sep*, *-ge-*, *h*) extend (***bis zu*** to), stretch (to); drag on
**hin'zu|fügen** *v/t* (*sep*, *-ge-*, *h*) add (***zu*** to) (*a. fig*); **~kommen** *v/i* (*irr*, ***kommen***, *sep*, *-ge-*, *sein*) be added; ***hinzu kommt***, ***dass*** add to this ..., and what is more, ...; **~ziehen** *v/t* (*irr*, ***ziehen***, *sep*, *-ge-*, *h*) call in, consult
**Hirn** [hɪrn] *n* (*-[e]s*; *-e*) ANAT brain; *fig* brain(s), mind; **~gespinst** *n* fantasy
**Hirsch** [hɪrʃ] *m* (*-[e]s*; *-e*) ZO stag; **~geweih** *n* ZO antlers; **~kuh** *f* ZO hind
**Hirse** ['hɪrzə] *f* (*-*; *-n*) BOT millet
**Hirte** ['hɪrtə] *m* (*-n*; *-n*) herdsman; shepherd (*a. fig*)
**hissen** ['hɪsən] *v/t* (*ge-*, *h*) hoist
**Historiker** [hɪs'to:rikɐ] *m* (*-s*; *-*), **His'torikerin** *f* (*-*; *-nen*) historian; **his'torisch** *adj* historical; historic (*event etc*)
**Hitliste** ['hɪtlɪstə] *f* top 40 *etc*, charts
**Hitze** ['hɪtsə] *f* (*-*; *no pl*) heat
**'Hitzewelle** *f* heat wave
**'hitzig** *adj* hot-tempered, peppery; heated (*debate etc*)
**'Hitzkopf** *m* hothead
**'Hitzschlag** *m* MED heatstroke
**HIV|-negativ** [ha:ʔi:'fau-] *adj* MED HIV negative; **~-positiv** *adj* MED HIV positive; **~-Positive** *m*, *f* (*-n*; *-n*) MED HIV carrier
**H-Milch** ['ha:-] *f Br* long-life milk
**hob** [ho:p] *pret of* ***heben***
**Hobby** ['hɔbi] *n* (*-s*; *-s*) hobby
**'Hobby...** *in cpds* amateur ...
**Hobel** ['ho:bəl] *m* (*-s*; *-*) TECH plane
**'Hobelbank** *f* (*-*; *-bänke*) TECH carpenter's bench

**'hobeln** *v/t* (*ge-*, *h*) TECH plane
**hoch** [hoːx] *adj and adv* high; tall; *fig* heavy (*fine etc*); distinguished (*guest*); great, old (*age*); deep (*snow*); ***10 ~ 4*** MATH 10 to the power of 4; ***3000 Meter*** *~ fly etc* at an altitude of 3,000 meters; ***in hohem Maße*** highly, greatly; ***~ verschuldet*** heavily in debt; F ***das ist mir zu ~*** that's above me
**Hoch** *n* (*-s*; *-s*) METEOR high (*a. fig*)
**'Hochachtung** *f* (deep) respect (***vor*** *dat* for); **'hochachtungsvoll** *adv* Yours sincerely
**'Hoch|bau** *m* (*-[e]s*; *no pl*) ***Hoch- und Tiefbau*** structural and civil engineering; **~betrieb** F *m* (*-[e]s*; *no pl*) rush
**'hochdeutsch** *adj* High *or* standard German
**'Hoch|druck** *m* high pressure (*a. fig*); **~ebene** *f* plateau, tableland; **~form** *f*: ***in ~*** in top form *or* shape; **~fre,quenz** *f* ELECTR high frequency; **~gebirge** *n* high mountains; **~genuss** *m* real treat
**'hochgezüchtet** *adj* ZO, TECH highbred, TECH *a.* sophisticated; MOT tuned up, F souped up
**'hochhackig** [-hakıç] *adj* high-heeled
**'Hoch|haus** *n* high rise, tower block; **~konjunk,tur** *f* ECON boom; **~land** *n* highlands; **~leistungs...** *in cpds ...sport etc*: high-performance ...
**'Hochmut** *m* arrogance; **'hochmütig** [-myːtıç] *adj* arrogant
**'Hochofen** *m* TECH blast furnace
**'hochpro,zentig** *adj* high-proof
**'Hoch|rechnung** *f* projection; POL computer prediction; **~sai,son** *f* peak (*or* height of the) season; **~schulabschluss** *m* degree; **~schulausbildung** *f* higher education; **~schule** *f* university; college; academy; **~seefischerei** *f* deep-sea fishing; **~sommer** *m* midsummer; **~spannung** *f* ELECTR high tension (*a. fig*) *or* voltage; **~sprung** *m* SPORT high jump
**höchst** [høːçst] **1.** *adj* highest, *fig a.* supreme; extreme; **2.** *adv* highly, most, extremely; **'Höchst...** *in cpds mst* maximum ..., top ...
**'Hochstapler** [-ʃtaːplɐ] *m* (*-s*; *-*), **'Hochstaplerin** *f* (*-*; *-nen*) impostor, swindler
**'höchstens** *adv* at (the) most, at best
**'Höchst|form** *f* SPORT top form *or* shape; **~geschwindigkeit** *f* top speed (***mit*** at); speed limit; **~leistung** *f* SPORT record (performance); TECH maximum output; **~maß** *n* maximum (***an*** *dat* of)
**'höchstwahr'scheinlich** *adv* most likely *or* probably
**'Hochtechnolo,gie** *f* high technology, hi tech
**'hochtrabend** *adj* pompous
**'Hochverrat** *m* high treason
**'Hochwasser** *n* high tide; flood
**'hochwertig** [-veːɐtıç] *adj* high-grade, high-quality
**Hochzeit** ['hɔxtsait] *f* (*-*; *-en*) wedding
**'Hochzeits...** *in cpds ...geschenk, ...kleid, ...tag etc*: wedding ...; **~reise** *f* honeymoon
**Hocke** ['hɔkə] *f* (*-*; *-n*) crouch, squat
**'hocken** *v/i* (*ge-*, *h*) squat, crouch; F sit
**Hocker** ['hɔkɐ] *m* (*-s*; *-*) stool
**Höcker** ['hœkɐ] *m* (*-s*; *-*) ZO hump
**Hockey** ['hɔki] *n* (*-s*; *no pl*) SPORT field hockey, *Br* hockey
**Hoden** ['hoːdən] *m* (*-s*; *-*) ANAT testicle
**Hof** [hoːf] *m* (*-[e]s*; *Höfe* ['høːfə]) yard; AGR farm; court(yard); court; **~dame** *f* lady-in-waiting
**hoffen** ['hɔfən] *v/i and v/t* (*ge-*, *h*) hope (***auf*** *acc* for); trust (in); ***das Beste ~*** hope for the best; ***ich hoffe es*** I hope so; ***ich hoffe nicht, ich will es nicht ~*** I hope not; **'hoffentlich** *adv* I hope, let's hope, hopefully; **'Hoffnung** *f* (*-*; *-en*) hope (***auf*** *acc* of); ***sich ~en machen*** have hopes; ***die ~ aufgeben*** lose hope
**'hoffnungslos** *adj* hopeless
**'hoffnungsvoll** *adj* hopeful; promising
**höflich** ['høːflıç] *adj* polite, courteous (***zu*** to); **'Höflichkeit** *f* (*-*; *no pl*) politeness, courtesy
**Höhe** ['høːə] *f* (*-*; *-n*) height; AVIAT, MATH, ASTR, GEOGR altitude; peak (*a. fig*); *fig* amount; level; extent (*of damage etc*); MUS pitch; ***auf gleicher ~ mit*** on a level with; ***in die ~*** up; F ***ich bin nicht ganz auf der ~*** I'm not feeling up to the mark
**Hoheit** ['hoːhait] *f* (*-*; *no pl*) POL sovereignty; Highness
**'Hoheits|gebiet** *n* territory; **~gewässer** *pl* territorial waters; **~zeichen** *n* national emblem
**'Höhen|luft** *f* mountain air; **~messer** *m* altimeter; **~ruder** *n* AVIAT elevator;

**~sonne** *f* MED ultraviolet lamp, sunlamp; **~zug** *m* mountain chain
'**Höhepunkt** *m* climax, culmination, height, peak; highlight
**hohl** [ho:l] *adj* hollow (*a. fig*)
**Höhle** ['hø:lə] *f* (-; -*n*) cave, cavern; ZO hole, burrow; den, lair
'**Hohl|maß** *n* measure of capacity; **~raum** *m* hollow, cavity; **~spiegel** *m* concave mirror
**Hohn** [ho:n] *m* (-[*e*]*s*; *no pl*) derision, scorn; '**Hohngelächter** *n* jeers, jeering laughter; **höhnisch** ['hø:nɪʃ] *adj* derisive, scornful; ***~es Lächeln*** sneer
**holen** ['ho:lən] *v/t* (*ge-*, *h*) (go and) get, fetch, go for; draw (*breath*); call (*s.o., the police etc*); ***~ lassen*** send for; ***sich ~*** catch, get (*a cold etc*); seek (*advice*)
**Holland** ['hɔlant] Holland, *the* Netherlands; **Holländer** ['hɔlɛndɐ] *m* (-*s*; -) Dutchman; '**Hol'länderin** [-dərɪn] *f* (-; -*nen*) Dutchwoman; '**holländisch** *adj* Dutch
**Hölle** ['hœlə] *f* (-; *no pl*) hell
'**Höllenlärm** F *m a* hell of a noise
**Holler** ['hɔlɐ] *Austrian m* (-*s*; -) BOT elder
**höllisch** ['hœlɪʃ] *adj* infernal, F hellish
**holperig** ['hɔlpərɪç] *adj* bumpy (*a. fig*), rough, uneven; *fig* clumsy (*style etc*)
**holpern** ['hɔlpɐn] *v/i* (*ge-*, *sein*) jolt, bump; *fig* be bumpy
**Holunder** [ho'lʊndɐ] *m* (-*s*; -) BOT elder
**Holz** [hɔlts] *n* (-*es*; *Hölzer* ['hœltsɐ]) wood; lumber, *Br a.* timber; ***aus ~*** (made) of wood, wooden; ***~ hacken*** chop wood; **~blasinstru,ment** *n* MUS woodwind (instrument)
**hölzern** ['hœltsɐn] *adj* wooden, *fig a.* clumsy
'**Holz|fäller** [-fɛlɐ] *m* (-*s*; -) woodcutter, lumberjack; **~hammer** *m* mallet; *fig* sledgehammer
**holzig** ['hɔltsɪç] *adj* woody; stringy
'**Holz|kohle** *f* charcoal; **~schnitt** *m* woodcut; **~schnitzer** *m* wood carver; **~schuh** *m* clog; **~weg** *fig m*: ***auf dem ~ sein*** be barking up the wrong tree; **~wolle** *f* wood shavings, excelsior; **~wurm** *m* ZO woodworm
**homöopathisch** [homøo'pa:tɪʃ] *adj* hom(o)eopathic
**homosexuell** [homozɛ'ksuɛl] *adj*, **Homosexu'elle** *m,f* (-*n*; -*n*) homosexual
**Honig** ['ho:nɪç] *m* (-*s*; -*e*) honey
'**Honigwabe** *f* honeycomb
**Honorar** [hono'ra:ɐ] *n* (-*s*; -*e*) fee
**honorieren** [hono'ri:rən] *v/t* (*no -ge-*, *h*) pay (a fee to); *fig* appreciate, reward
**Hopfen** ['hɔpfən] *m* (-*s*; -) BOT hop; *brewing*: hops
**hoppla** ['hɔpla] *int* (wh)oops!
**hopsen** ['hɔpsən] F *v/i* (*ge-*, *sein*) hop, jump
**Hörappa,rat** ['hø:ɐ-] *m* hearing aid
**hörbar** ['hø:ɐba:ɐ] *adj* audible
**horchen** ['hɔrçən] *v/i* (*ge-*, *h*) listen (***auf*** *acc* to); eavesdrop; **Horcher** ['hɔrçɐ] *m* (-*s*; -) eavesdropper
**Horde** ['hɔrdə] *f* (-; -*n*) horde (*a.* ZO), *contp a.* mob, gang
**hören** ['hø:rən] *v/i and v/t* (*ge-*, *h*) hear; listen to; obey, listen; ***~ auf*** (*acc*) listen to; ***von j-m ~*** hear from (*or* of, about) s.o.; ***er hört schwer*** his hearing is bad; ***hör(t) mal!*** listen!; look (here)!; ***nun*** *or* ***also hör(t) mal!*** wait a minute!, now look *or* listen here!; **Hörer** ['hø:rɐ] *m* (-*s*; -) listener; TEL receiver; '**Hörerin** [-rərɪn] *f* (-; -*nen*) listener
**Hör|fehler** ['hø:ɐ-] *m* MED hearing defect; **~gerät** *n* hearing aid
**hörig** ['hø:rɪç] *adj*: ***j-m ~ sein*** be s.o.'s slave
**Horizont** [hori'tsɔnt] *m* (-[*e*]*s*; -*e*) horizon (*a. fig*); ***s-n ~ erweitern*** broaden one's mind; ***das geht über meinen ~*** that's beyond me; **horizontal** [horitsɔn'ta:l] *adj* horizontal
**Hormon** [hɔr'mo:n] *n* (-*s*; -*e*) hormone
**Horn** [hɔrn] *n* (-[*e*]*s*; *Hörner* ['hœrnɐ]) horn; **~haut** *f* horny skin, callus(es); ANAT cornea
**Hornisse** [hɔr'nɪsə] *f* (-; -*n*) ZO hornet
**Horoskop** [horo'sko:p] *n* (-*s*; -*e*) horoscope
**Hör|rohr** ['hø:ɐ-] *n* MED stethoscope; **~saal** *m* lecture hall, auditorium; **~spiel** *n* radio play; **~weite** *f*: ***in*** (***außer***) **~** within (out of) earshot
**Höschen** ['hø:sçən] *n* (-*s*; -) panties
**Hose** ['ho:zə] *f* (-; -*n*) (**e-e ~** a pair of) pants, *Br* trousers; slacks; shorts
'**Hosen|anzug** *m* pants (*Br* trouser) suit; **~rock** *m* (***ein ~*** a pair of) culottes; **~schlitz** *m* fly; **~tasche** *f* trouser pocket; **~träger** *pl* (a pair of) suspenders *or Br* braces

H

**Hospital** [hɔspi'taːl] *n* (-*s*; -*täler* [-'tɛːlɐ]) hospital
**Hostie** ['hɔstjə] *f* (-; -*n*) REL host
**Hotel** [ho'tɛl] *n* (-*s*; -*s*) hotel; **~diˌrektor** *m* hotel manager; **~fach** *n* (-[*e*]*s*; *no pl*) hotel business; **~zimmer** *n* hotel room
**HP** ABBR *of* ***Halbpension*** half-board
**Hr(n).** ABBR *of* ***Herrn*** Mr
**Hubraum** ['huːp-] *m* MOT cubic capacity
**hübsch** [hʏpʃ] *adj* pretty, nice(-looking), cute; *fig* nice, lovely
**Hubschrauber** ['huːpʃraubɐ] *m* (-*s*; -) helicopter; **~landeplatz** *m* heliport
**Huf** [huːf] *m* (-[*e*]*s*; -*e*) ZO hoof
**'Hufeisen** *n* horseshoe
**Hüfte** ['hʏftə] *f* (-; -*n*) ANAT hip
**'Hüftgelenk** *n* ANAT hip joint
**'Hüftgürtel** *m* girdle
**Hügel** ['hyːgəl] *m* (-*s*; -) hill; **'hügelig** *adj* hilly; **'Hügelland** *n* downs
**Huhn** [huːn] *n* (-[*e*]*s*; *Hühner* ['hyːnɐ]) ZO chicken; hen; **Hühnchen** ['hyːnçən] *n* (-*s*; -) chicken; F ***mit j-m ein ~ zu rupfen haben*** have a bone to pick with s.o.
**'Hühner|auge** *n* MED corn; **~brühe** *f* chicken broth; **~ei** *n* hen's egg; **~farm** *f* poultry *or* chicken farm; **~hof** *m* poultry *or* chicken yard; **~leiter** *f* chicken ladder; **~stall** *m* henhouse
**huldigen** ['hʊldɪgən] *v/i* (*ge-*, *h*) pay homage to; *fig* indulge in
**Hülle** ['hʏlə] *f* (-; -*n*) cover(ing), wrap(ping); jacket, *Br* sleeve; sheath; ***in ~ und Fülle*** in abundance; **'hüllen** *v/t* (*ge-*, *h*) **~ *in*** (*acc*) wrap (up) in, cover in
**Hülse** ['hʏlzə] *f* (-; -*n*) BOT pod; husk; TECH case; **'Hülsenfrüchte** *pl* pulse
**human** [hu'maːn] *adj* humane
**humanitär** [humani'tɛːɐ] *adj* humanitarian; **Humanität** [humani'tɛːt] *f* (-; *no pl*) humanity
**Hummel** ['hʊməl] *f* (-; -*n*) ZO bumblebee
**Hummer** ['hʊmɐ] *m* (-*s*; -) ZO lobster
**Humor** [hu'moːɐ] *m* (-*s*; *no pl*) humo(u)r; (***keinen***) **~ *haben*** have a (no) sense of humo(u)r; **Humorist** [humo'rɪst] *m* (-*en*; -*en*) humorist; **humo'ristisch, hu'morvoll** *adj* humorous
**humpeln** ['hʊmpəln] *v/i* a) (*ge-*, *h*) hobble, b) (*ge-*, *sein*) limp
**Hund** [hʊnt] *m* (-[*e*]*s*; -*e*) ZO dog
**Hunde|hütte** ['hʊndə-] *f* doghouse, *Br* kennel; **~kuchen** *m* dog biscuit; **~leine** *f* lead, leash
**'hunde'müde** *adj* dog-tired
**hundert** ['hʊndɐt] *adj* a *or* one hundred; ***zu hunderten*** by the hundreds
**'hundertfach** *adj* hundredfold
**Hundert'jahrfeier** *f* centenary, centennial; **'hundertjährig** [-jɛːrɪç] *adj* a hundred years old; a hundred years of
**'hundertste** *adj* hundredth
**Hündin** ['hʏndɪn] *f* (-; -*nen*) ZO bitch
**hündisch** ['hʏndɪʃ] *adj* doglike, slavish
**Hüne** ['hyːnə] *m* (-*n*; -*n*) giant
**'Hünengrab** *n* dolmen
**Hunger** ['hʊŋɐ] *m* (-*s*; *no pl*) hunger; **~ *bekommen*** get hungry; **~ *haben*** be hungry; ***vor ~ sterben*** die of starvation, starve to death
**'Hungerlohn** *m* starvation wages
**'hungern** *v/i* (*ge-*, *h*) go hungry, starve
**'Hungersnot** *f* famine
**'Hungerstreik** *m* hunger strike
**'Hungertod** *m* (death from) starvation
**hungrig** ['hʊŋrɪç] *adj* hungry (***nach***, ***auf*** *acc* for)
**Hupe** ['huːpə] *f* (-; -*n*) MOT horn
**'hupen** *v/i* (*ge-*, *h*) MOT sound one's horn, hoot, honk
**hüpfen** ['hʏpfən] *v/i* (*ge-*, *sein*) hop, skip; *ball etc*: bounce
**Hürde** ['hʏrdə] *f* (-; -*n*) hurdle, *fig a.* obstacle; ZO fold, pen
**'Hürdenlauf** *m* SPORT hurdles
**'Hürdenläufer** *m*, **'Hürdenläuferin** *f* SPORT hurdler
**Hure** ['huːrə] *f* (-; -*n*) whore, prostitute
**huschen** ['hʊʃən] *v/i* (*ge-*, *sein*) flit, dart
**hüsteln** ['hyːstəln] *v/i* (*ge-*, *h*) cough slightly; *iro* hem; **husten** ['huːstən] *v/i* (*ge-*, *h*), **'Husten** *m* (-*s*; *no pl*) cough
**'Husten|bonˌbon** *m*, *n* cough drop; **~saft** *m* PHARM cough syrup
**Hut**[1] [huːt] *m* (-[*e*]*s*; *Hüte* ['hyːtə]) hat; ***den ~ aufsetzen*** (***abnehmen***) put on (take off) one's hat
**Hut**[2] *f*: ***auf der ~ sein*** be on one's guard (***vor*** *dat* against)
**hüten** ['hyːtən] *v/t* (*ge-*, *h*) guard, protect, watch over; ZO herd, mind; look after; ***das Bett ~*** be confined to (one's) bed; ***sich ~ vor*** (*dat*) beware of; ***sich ~, et. zu tun*** be careful not to do s.th.
**'Hutkrempe** *f* (hat) brim
**hutschen** ['hʊtʃən] *Austrian v/t and v/i* → ***schaukeln***
**Hütte** ['hʏtə] *f* (-; -*n*) hut; *contp* shack;

cottage, cabin; mountain hut; TECH ironworks
**Hyäne** ['hyɛːnə] *f* (-; *-n*) ZO hy(a)ena
**Hyazinthe** [hya'tsɪntə] *f* (-; *-n*) BOT hyacinth
**Hydrant** [hy'drant] *m* (*-en*; *-en*) hydrant
**hydraulisch** [hy'draulɪʃ] *adj* hydraulic
**Hydrokultur** ['hyːdro-] *f* hydroponics
**Hygiene** [hy'gjeːnə] *f* (-; *no pl*) hygiene
**hygienisch** [hy'gjeːnɪʃ] *adj* hygienic
**Hypnose** [hʏp'noːzə] *f* (-; *-n*) hypnosis; **Hypnotiseur** [hʏpnoti'zøːɐ] *m* (*-s*; *-e*) hypnotist; **hypnotisieren** [hʏpnoti'ziːrən] *v/t* (*no -ge-*, *h*) hypnotize
**Hypotenuse** [hypote'nuːzə] *f* (-; *-n*) MATH hypotenuse
**Hypothek** [hypo'teːk] *f* (-; *-en*) ECON mortgage; ***e-e* ~ *aufnehmen*** take out a mortgage
**Hypothese** [hypo'teːzə] *f* (-; *-n*) hypothesis, supposition; **hypothetisch** [hypo'teːtɪʃ] *adj* hypothetical
**Hysterie** [hʏste'riː] *f* (-; *-n*) hysteria
**hysterisch** [hʏs'teːrɪʃ] *adj* hysterical

# I

**i.A.** ABBR *of* ***im Auftrag*** p.p., per procuration
**ICE** [iːtseː'ˀeː] ABBR *of* ***Intercityexpresszug*** intercity express (train)
**ich** [ɪç] *pers pron* I; ***~ selbst*** (I) myself; ***~ bin's*** it's me
**ideal** [ide'aːl] *adj*, **Ide'al** *n* (*-s*; *-e*) ideal; **Idealismus** [idea'lɪsmʊs] *m* (-; *no pl*) idealism; **Idea'list(in)** (*-en*; *-en*/-; *-nen*) idealist
**Idee** [i'deː] *f* (-; *-n*) idea
**identifizieren** [idɛntifi'tsiːrən] *v/t* (*no -ge-*, *h*) identify; ***sich ~ mit*** identify with; **identisch** [i'dɛntɪʃ] *adj* identical
**Identitätskarte** [idɛnti'tɛːts-] *Austrian f* identity card
**Ideologe** [ideo'loːgə] *m* (*-n*; *-n*) ideologist; **Ideologie** [ideolo'giː] *f* (-; *-n*) ideology; **ideo'logisch** *adj* ideological
**idiomatisch** [idio'maːtɪʃ] *adj* LING idiomatic; ***~er Ausdruck*** idiom
**Idiot** [i'djoːt] *m* (*-en*; *-en*) idiot
**Idi'otenhügel** F *m skiing*: nursery slope
**idi'otisch** *adj* idiotic
**Idol** [i'doːl] *n* (*-s*; *-e*) idol
**Idyll** [i'dʏl] *n* (*-s*; *-e*), **I'dylle** *f* (-; *-n*) idyl(l); **i'dyllisch** *adj* idyllic
**Igel** ['iːgəl] *m* (*-s*; -) ZO hedgehog
**Iglu** ['iːglu] *m* (*-s*; *-s*) igloo
**ignorieren** [ɪgno'riːrən] *v/t* (*no -ge-*, *h*) ignore, disregard
**i.H.** ABBR *of* ***im Hause*** on the premises
**ihr** [iːɐ] *poss pron* her; *pl* their; ***Ihr*** your; **ihrerseits** ['iːrɐzaits] *adv* on her (*pl* their) part; **ihresgleichen** ['iːrəs-] *indef pron* her (*pl* their) equals, people like herself (*pl* themselves); **ihretwegen** ['iːrət-] *adv* for her (*pl* their) sake
**Ikone** [i'koːnə] *f* (-; *-n*) icon (*a.* EDP)
**illegal** ['ɪlegaːl] *adj* JUR illegal
**illegitim** [ɪlegi'tiːm] *adj* JUR illegitimate
**Illusion** [ɪlu'zjoːn] *f* (-; *-en*) illusion
**illusorisch** [ɪlu'zoːrɪʃ] *adj* illusory
**Illustration** [ɪlʊstra'tsjoːn] *f* (-; *-en*) illustration; **illustrieren** [ɪlʊs'triːrən] *v/t* (*no -ge-*, *h*) illustrate; **Illustrierte** [ɪlʊs'triːɐtə] *f* (*-n*; *-n*) magazine
**im** [ɪm] *prep* in the; ***~ Bett*** in bed; ***~ Kino*** *etc* at the cinema *etc*; ***~ Erdgeschoss*** on the first (*Br* ground) floor; ***~ Mai*** in May; ***~ Jahre 1997*** in (the year) 1997; ***~ Stehen*** (while) standing up; → ***in***
**imaginär** [imagi'nɛːɐ] *adj* imaginary
**Imbiss** ['ɪmbɪs] *m* (*-es*; *-e*) snack
**'Imbissstube** *f* snack bar
**imitieren** [imi'tiːrən] *v/t* (*no -ge-*, *h*) imitate
**Imker** ['ɪmkɐ] *m* (*-s*; -) beekeeper
**immatrikulieren** [ɪmatriku'liːrən] *v/t and v/refl* (*no -ge-*, *h*) UNIV enrol(l), register
**immer** ['ɪmɐ] *adv* always, all the time; ***~ mehr*** more and more; ***~ wieder*** again and again; ***für ~*** for ever, for good
**'Immergrün** *n* BOT evergreen
**'immer'hin** *adv* after all

**'immer'zu** *adv* all the time, constantly
**Immigrant** [ɪmi'grant] *m* (*-en*; *-en*), **Immi'grantin** *f* (-; *-nen*) immigrant
**Immissionen** [ɪmɪ'sjo:nən] *pl* (harmful effects of) noise, pollutants *etc*
**Immobilien** [ɪmo'bi:liən] *pl* real estate; **~makler** *m* realtor, real estate agent
**immun** [ɪ'mu:n] *adj* immune (***gegen*** to, against, from); **~ *machen*** → **immunisieren** [ɪmuni'zi:rən] *v/t* (*no -ge-*, *h*) immunize; **Immunität** [ɪmuni'tɛ:t] *f* (-; *no pl*) immunity; **Im'munschwäche** *f* (-; *-n*) ***Erworbene ~*** MED AIDS
**Imperativ** ['ɪmperati:f] *m* (*-s*; *-e*) LING imperative (mood)
**Imperfekt** ['ɪmpɛrfɛkt] *n* (*-s*; *-e*) LING past (tense)
**Imperialismus** [ɪmperja'lɪsmʊs] *m* (-; *no pl*) imperialism; **Imperialist** [ɪmperja'lɪst] *m* (*-en*; *-en*), **imperia'listisch** *adj* imperialist
**impfen** ['ɪmpfən] *v/t* (*ge-*, *h*) MED vaccinate
**'Impf|pass** *m* MED vaccination card; **~schein** *m* MED vaccination certificate; **~stoff** *m* MED vaccine, serum
**'Impfung** *f* (-; *-en*) MED vaccination
**imponieren** [ɪmpo'ni:rən] *v/i* (*no -ge-*, *h*) ***j-m ~*** impress s.o.
**Import** [ɪm'pɔrt] *m* (*-[e]s*; *-e*) ECON import(ation); **Importeur** [ɪmpɔr'tø:ɐ] *m* (*-s*; *-e*) ECON importer; **importieren** [-'ti:rən] *v/t* (*no -ge-*, *h*) ECON import
**imposant** [ɪmpo'zant] *adj* impressive, imposing
**imprägnieren** [ɪmprɛ'gni:rən] *v/t* (*no -ge-*, *h*), **imprägniert** [ɪmprɛ'gni:ɐt] *adj* waterproof
**improvisieren** [ɪmprovi'zi:rən] *v/t and v/i* (*no -ge-*, *h*) improvise
**Impuls** [ɪm'pʊls] *m* (*-es*; *-e*) impulse; stimulus
**impulsiv** [ɪmpʊl'zi:f] *adj* impulsive
**imstande** [ɪm'ʃtandə] *adj*: ***~ sein zu inf*** be capable of *ger*
**in** [ɪn] *prp* (*dat and acc*) **1.** in, at; within, inside; into, in; ***überall ~*** all over; ***~ der Stadt*** in town; ***~ der Schule*** at school; ***~ die Schule*** to school; ***~s Kino*** to the cinema; ***~s Bett*** to bed; ***warst du schon mal ~ ...?*** have you ever been to ...?; → ***im***; **2.** in, at, during; ***~ dieser*** (***der nächsten***) ***Woche*** this (next) week; ***~ diesem Alter*** (***Augenblick***) at this age (moment); ***~ der Nacht*** at night; ***heute ~ acht Tagen*** a week from now; ***heute ~ e-m Jahr*** this time next year; → ***im***; **3.** in, at; ***gut sein ~*** (*dat*) be good at; ***~ Eile*** in a hurry; ***~ Behandlung*** (***Reparatur***) under treatment (repair); ***~s Deutsche*** into German; → ***im***; **4.** F ***~ sein*** be in
**'Inbegriff** *m* epitome
**'inbegriffen** *adj* ECON included
**in'dem** *cj* while, as; by *doing s.th.*
**Inder** ['ɪndɐ] *m* (*-s*; -), **Inderin** ['ɪndərɪn] *f* (-; *-nen*) Indian
**Indian** ['ɪndja:n] *Austrian m* (*-s*; *-e*) ZO turkey (cock)
**Indianer** [ɪn'dja:nɐ] *m* (*-s*; -), **Indianerin** [ɪn'dja:nərɪn] *f* (-; *-nen*) Native American, (American) Indian
**Indien** ['ɪndjən] India
**Indikativ** ['ɪndikati:f] *m* (*-s*; *-e*) LING indicative (mood)
**indirekt** ['ɪndirɛkt] *adj* indirect, LING *a.* reported
**indisch** ['ɪndɪʃ] *adj* Indian
**indiskret** ['ɪndɪskre:t] *adj* indiscreet
**Indiskretion** [ɪndɪskre'tsjo:n] *f* (-; *-en*) indiscretion
**indiskutabel** [ɪndɪsku'ta:bəl] *adj* out of the question
**individuell** [ɪndivi'duɛl] *adj*, **Individuum** [ɪndi'vi:duʊm] *n* (*-s*; *-en*) individual
**Indiz** [ɪn'di:ts] *n* (*-es*; *-ien*) indication, sign; *pl* JUR circumstantial evidence
**industrialisieren** [ɪndʊstriali'zi:rən] *v/t* (*no -ge-*, *h*) industrialize; **Industriali'sierung** *f* (-; *no pl*) industrialization
**Industrie** [ɪndʊs'tri:] *f* (-; *-n*) industry
**Indus'triegebiet** *n* industrial area
**industriell** [ɪndʊstri'ɛl] *adj* industrial
**Industri'elle** *m* (*-n*; *-n*) industrialist
**inei'nander** *adv* into one another; ***~ verliebt*** in love with each other; ***~ greifen*** TECH interlock (*a. fig*)
**Infanterie** ['ɪnfantəri:] *f* (-; *-n*) MIL infantry; **Infanterist** ['ɪnfantərɪst] *m* (*-en*; *-en*) MIL infantryman
**Infektion** [ɪnfɛk'tsjo:n] *f* (-; *-en*) MED infection; **Infekti'onskrankheit** *f* infectious disease
**Infinitiv** ['ɪnfiniti:f] *m* (*-s*; *-e*) LING infinitive (mood)
**infizieren** [ɪnfi'tsi:rən] *v/t* (*no -ge-*, *h*) MED infect
**Inflation** [ɪnfla'tsjo:n] *f* (-; *-en*) inflation

**in'folge** *prp (gen)* owing to, due to
**infolge'dessen** *adv* consequently
**Informatik** [ɪnfɔr'ma:tɪk] *f (-; no pl)* computer science; **Infor'matiker(in)** [ɪnfɔr'ma:tikɐ (-kərɪn)] *(-s; -/-; -nen)* computer scientist
**Information** [ɪnfɔrma'tsjo:n] *f (-; -en)* information; ***die neuesten ~en*** the latest information
**informieren** [ɪnfɔr'mi:rən] *v/t (no -ge-, h)* inform; ***falsch ~*** misinform
**in'frage: *~ stellen*** question; put in jeopardy; ***~ kommen*** be possible (*person*: eligible); ***nicht ~ kommen*** be out of the question
**infrarot** ['ɪnfra-] *adj* PHYS infrared
**'Infrastruk,tur** *f* infrastructure
**Ing.** ABBR *of* ***Ingenieur*** eng., engineer
**Ingenieur** [ɪnʒe'njø:ɐ] *m (-s; -e)*, **Inge'nieurin** *f (-; -nen)* engineer
**Ingwer** ['ɪŋvɐ] *m (-s; no pl)* ginger
**Inhaber** ['ɪnha:bɐ] *m (-s; -)*, **'Inhaberin** *f (-; -nen)* owner, proprietor (proprietress); holder
**Inhalt** ['ɪnhalt] *m (-[e]s; -e)* contents; volume, capacity; *fig* meaning
**'Inhalts|angabe** *f* summary; **~verzeichnis** *n* table of contents
**Initiative** [initsja'ti:və] *f (-; -n)* initiative; ***die ~ ergreifen*** take the initiative
**inklusive** [ɪnklu'zi:və] *prp* ECON including
**inkonsequent** ['ɪnkɔnzekvɛnt] *adj* inconsistent
**In-'Kraft-Treten** *n (-s; no pl)* coming into force, taking effect
**'Inland** *n (-[e]s; no pl)* home (country); **~flug** *m* domestic (*or* internal) flight
**inländisch** ['ɪnlɛndɪʃ] *adj* domestic, home, inland
**Inlett** ['ɪnlɛt] *n (-[e]s; -e)* ticking
**in'mitten** *prp (gen)* in the middle of
**innen** ['ɪnən] *adv* inside; ***nach ~*** inwards
**'Innen|archi,tekt** *m*, **~archi,tektin** *f* interior designer; **~architek,tur** *f* interior design; **~mi,nister(in)** minister of the interior; Secretary of the Interior, *Br* Home Secretary; **~minis,terium** *n* ministry of the interior; Department of the Interior, *Br* Home Office; **~poli,tik** *f* domestic politics
**'innenpo,litisch** *adj* domestic, internal
**'Innenseite** *f*: ***auf der ~*** (on the) inside
**'Innenstadt** *f* downtown, (city *or* town) center *or Br* centre
**inner** ['ɪnɐ] *adj* inside; *fig* inner; MED, POL internal; **Innere** ['ɪnərə] *n (-n; no pl)* interior, inside
**Innereien** [ɪnə'raiən] *pl* GASTR offal
**'innerhalb** *prp (gen)* within
**'innerlich** *adj* internal (*a.* MED)
**innert** ['ɪnɐt] *Swiss prp (gen or dat)* within
**innig** ['ɪnɪç] *adj* tender, affectionate
**Innung** ['ɪnʊŋ] *f (-; -en)* guild
**'inoffiziell** *adj* unofficial
**ins** [ɪns] → ***in***
**Insasse** ['ɪnzasə] *m (-n; -n)* inmate; MOT passenger; **'Insassenversicherung** *f* MOT passenger insurance; **'Insassin** *f (-; -nen)* inmate; MOT passenger
**insbe'sondere** *adv* (e)specially, particularly
**'Inschrift** *f* inscription, legend
**Insekt** [ɪn'zɛkt] *n (-s; -en)* ZO insect, bug
**In'sektenstich** *m* insect bite
**Insel** ['ɪnzəl] *f (-; -n)* island
**'Inselbewohner** *m* islander
**Inserat** [ɪnze'ra:t] *n (-[e]s; -e)* advertisement, F ad; **inserieren** [ɪnze'ri:rən] *v/t and v/i (no -ge-, h)* advertise
**insge'heim** *adv* secretly
**insge'samt** *adv* altogether, in all
**inso'fern 1.** *adv* as far as that goes; **2.** *cj*: ***~ als*** in so far as
**Inspektion** [ɪnspɛk'tsjo:n] *f (-; -en)* inspection; MOT service
**Inspektor** [ɪn'spɛkto:ɐ] *m (-s; -en* [ɪnspɛk'to:rən]*)*, **Inspek'torin** *f (-; -nen)* inspector
**inspizieren** [ɪnspi'tsi:rən] *v/t (no -ge-, h)* inspect
**Installateur** [ɪnstala'tø:ɐ] *m (-s; -e)* plumber; (gas *or* electrical) fitter
**installieren** [ɪnsta'li:rən] *v/t (no -ge-, h)* put in, fit, instal(l)
**instand** [ɪn'ʃtant] *adv*: ***~ halten*** keep in good condition *or* repair; TECH maintain; ***~ setzen*** repair
**In'standhaltung** *f (-; no pl)* maintenance
**'inständig** *adv*: ***j-n ~ bitten*** implore s.o.
**In'standsetzung** *f (-; -en)* repair
**Instanz** [ɪn'stants] *f (-; -en)* authority; JUR instance
**Instinkt** [ɪn'stɪŋkt] *m (-[e]s; -e)* instinct
**instinktiv** [ɪnstɪŋk'ti:f] *adv* instinctively
**Institut** [ɪnsti'tu:t] *n (-[e]s; -e)* institute

**Institution** [ɪnstitu'tsjoːn] *f* (-; *-en*) institution

**Instrument** [ɪnstru'mɛnt] *n* (-[*e*]*s*; *-e*) instrument

**inszenieren** [ɪnstse'niːrən] *v/t* (*no -ge-*, *h*) (put on) stage; *film*: direct; *fig* stage

**Insze'nierung** *f* (-; *-en*) production

**intellektuell** [ɪntɛlɛk'tuɛl] *adj*, **Intellektu'elle** *m*, *f* (*-n*; *-n*) intellectual, F highbrow

**intelligent** [ɪntɛli'gɛnt] *adj* intelligent

**Intelligenz** [ɪntɛli'gɛnts] *f* (-; *-en*) intelligence; **~quoti͵ent** *m* I.Q.

**Intendant** [ɪntɛn'dant] *m* (*-en*; *-en*), **Inten'dantin** *f* (-; *-nen*) THEA *etc* director

**intensiv** [ɪntɛn'ziːf] *adj* intensive; intense; **Inten'sivkurs** *m* crash course

**interessant** [ɪntərɛ'sant] *adj* interesting; **Interesse** [ɪntə'rɛsə] *n* (*-s*; *-n*) interest (***an*** *dat*, ***für*** in)

**Inte'ressengebiet** *n* field of interest

**Interessent** [ɪntərɛ'sɛnt] *m* (*-en*; *-en*), **Interes'sentin** *f* (-; *-nen*) interested person; ECON prospect, *Br* prospective buyer

**interessieren** [ɪntərɛ'siːrən] *v/t* (*no -ge-*, *h*) interest (***für*** in); ***sich ~ für*** take an interest in; be interested in

**intern** [ɪn'tɛrn] *adj* internal

**Internat** [ɪntɐ'naːt] *n* (-[*e*]*s*; *-e*) boarding school

**internatio'nal** [ɪntɐ-] *adj* international

**Internist** [ɪntɐ'nɪst] *m* (*-en*; *-en*), **Inter'nistin** *f* (-; *-nen*) MED internist

**Interpretation** [ɪntɐpreta'tsjoːn] *f* (-; *-en*) interpretation; analysis

**interpretieren** [ɪntɐpre'tiːrən] *v/t* (*no -ge-*, *h*) interpret, ana|lyze, *Br* -lyse

**Interpunktion** [ɪntɐpʊŋk'tsjoːn] *f* (-; *no pl*) punctuation

**Intervall** [ɪntɐ'val] *n* (-[*e*]*s*; *-e*) interval

**intervenieren** [ɪntɐve'niːrən] *v/i* (*no -ge-*, *h*) intervene

**Interview** ['ɪntɐvjuː] *n* (*-s*; *-s*), **interviewen** [ɪntɐ'vjuːən] *v/t* (*no -ge-*, *h*) interview

**intim** [ɪn'tiːm] *adj* intimate (***mit*** with) (*a. sexually*); **Intimität** [ɪntimi'tɛːt] *f* (-; *no pl*) intimacy; **In'timsphäre** *f* privacy

**intolerant** ['ɪntolerant] *adj* intolerant (***gegen*** of); **Intoleranz** ['ɪntolerants] *f* (-; *no pl*) intolerance

**intransitiv** ['ɪntranzitiːf] *adj* LING intransitive

**Intrige** [ɪn'triːgə] *f* (-; *-n*) intrigue, scheme, plot; **intrigieren** [ɪntri'giːrən] *v/i* (*no -ge-*, *h*) (plot and) scheme

**Invalide** [ɪnva'liːdə] *m* (*-n*; *-n*) invalid; **Inva'lidenrente** *f* disability pension

**Invalidität** [ɪnvalidi'tɛːt] *f* (-; *no pl*) disablement, disability

**Inventar** [ɪnvɛn'taːɐ] *n* (*-s*; *-e*) inventory, stock

**Inventur** [ɪnvɛn'tuːɐ] *f* (-; *-en*) ECON stocktaking; ***~ machen*** take stock

**investieren** [ɪnvɛs'tiːrən] *v/t* (*no -ge-*, *h*) ECON invest (*a. fig*); **Investition** [ɪnvɛsti'tsjoːn] *f* (-; *-en*) ECON investment

**inwiefern** [ɪnvi'fɛrn] *cj and adv* in what respect *or* way

**inwie'weit** *cj and adv* to what extent

**'Inzucht** *f* inbreeding

**in'zwischen** *adv* meanwhile, in the meantime; by now

**irdisch** ['ɪrdɪʃ] *adj* earthly, worldly

**Ire** ['iːrə] *m* (*-n*; *-n*) Irishman; *pl* the Irish

**irgend** ['ɪrgənt] *adv in cpds*: some...; any...; ***wenn ~ möglich*** if at all possible; ***wenn du ~ kannst*** if you possibly can; F ***~ so ein ...*** some ...; **~'ein(e)** *indef pron* some(one); any(one); **~'ein(e)s** *indef pron* some; any; **~etwas** something; anything; **~jemand** someone, somebody; anyone, anybody; **~'wann** *adv* sometime (or other); (at) any time; **~'wie** *adv* somehow (or other); **~'wo** *adv* somewhere; anywhere

**Irin** ['iːrɪn] *f* (-; *-nen*) Irishwoman; **irisch** ['iːrɪʃ] *adj* Irish; **Irland** ['ɪrlant] Ireland

**Ironie** [iro'niː] *f* (-; *no pl*) irony

**ironisch** [i'roːnɪʃ] *adj* ironic(al)

**irre** ['ɪrə] *adj* mad, crazy, insane; confused; F super, terrific

**'Irre** *m*, *f* (*-n*; *-n*) madman (madwoman), lunatic; ***wie ein ~r*** like mad *or* a madman

**'irreführen** *v/t* (*sep*, *-ge-*, *h*) mislead, lead astray; **~d** *adj* misleading

**'irre|gehen** *v/i* (*irr*, ***gehen***, *sep*, *-ge-*, *sein*) go astray, *fig a.* be wrong; **~machen** *v/t* (*sep*, *-ge-*, *h*) confuse

**irren** ['ɪrən] **1.** *v/refl* (*ge-*, *h*) be wrong, be mistaken; ***sich ~*** be wrong; ***sich in et. ~*** get s.th. wrong; **2.** *v/i* (*ge-*, *sein*) wander, stray, err

**irritieren** [iri'tiːrən] *v/t* (*no -ge-*, *h*) irritate; F confuse

**'Irrlicht** *n* (-[*e*]*s*; *-er*) will-o'-the-wisp
**'Irrsinn** *m* (-[*e*]*s*; *no pl*) madness
**'irrsinnig** *adj* insane, mad; F terrific
**Irrtum** ['ɪrtu:m] *m* (*-s*; *Irrtümer* ['ɪrty:mɐ]) error, mistake; ***im ~ sein*** be mistaken; **'irrtümlich** *adv* by mistake
**Ischias** ['ɪʃjas] *m*, *n*, *f* (-; *no pl*) MED sciatica
**Islam** [ɪs'la:m] *m* (-[*s*]; *no pl*) Islam
**Island** ['i:slant] Iceland
**Isländer** ['i:slɛndɐ] *m* (*-s*; -), **'Isländerin** [-dərɪn] *f* (-; *-nen*) Icelander
**'isländisch** *adj* Icelandic
**Isolierband** [izo'li:ɐ-] *n* (-[*e*]*s*; *-bänder*) insulating tape; **isolieren** [izo'li:rən] *v/t* (*no -ge-*, *h*) isolate; ELECTR, TECH insulate; **Iso'lierstati,on** *f* MED isolation ward; **Iso'lierung** *f* (-; *-en*) isolation; ELECTR, TECH insulation
**Israel** ['ɪsrae:l] Israel
**Israeli** [ɪsra'e:li] *m* (-[*s*]; -[*s*]), *f* (-; -[*s*]), **israelisch** [ɪsra'e:lɪʃ] *adj* Israeli
**Italien** [i'ta:ljən] Italy; **Italiener** [ita'lje:nɐ] *m* (*-s*; -), **Itali'enerin** [-nərɪn] *f* (-; *-nen*), **itali'enisch** *adj* Italian

# J

**ja** [ja:] *adv* yes, F *a.* yeah; PARL yea, aye; ***wenn ~*** if so; ***da ist er ~!*** well, there he is!; ***ich sagte es Ihnen ~*** I told you so; ***ich bin ~*** (***schließlich***) ***...*** after all, I am ...; ***tut es 'ja nicht!*** don't you dare do it!; ***sei 'ja vorsichtig!*** do be careful!; ***vergessen Sie es 'ja nicht!*** be sure not to forget it!; ***~, weißt du nicht?*** why, don't you know?; ***du kommst doch, ~?*** you're coming, aren't you?
**Jacht** [jaxt] *f* (-; *-en*) MAR yacht
**Jacke** ['jakə] *f* (-; *-n*) jacket; coat
**Jackett** [ʒa'kɛt] *n* (*-s*; *-s*) jacket, coat
**Jagd** [ja:kt] *f* (-; *-en*) hunt(ing) (*a. fig*); shoot(ing); *fig* chase; → ***Jagdrevier***; ***auf*** (***die***) ***~ gehen*** go hunting *or* shooting; ***~ machen auf*** (*acc*) hunt (for); *a.* chase *s.o.*; **~aufseher** *m* gamekeeper; **~flugzeug** *n* MIL fighter (plane); **~hund** *m* ZO hound; **~hütte** *f* (hunting) lodge; **~re,vier** *n* hunting ground; **~schein** *m* hunting *or* shooting licen|se, *Br* -ce
**jagen** ['ja:gən] *v/t and v/i* (*ge-*, *h*) hunt; shoot; *fig* race, dash; hunt, chase; ***j-n aus dem Haus*** *etc* ***~*** drive *or* chase s.o. out of the house *etc*
**Jäger** ['jɛ:gɐ] *m* (*-s*; -) hunter, huntsman
**Jaguar** ['ja:gua:ɐ] *m* (*-s*; *-e*) ZO jaguar
**jäh** [jɛ:] *adj* sudden; steep
**Jahr** [ja:ɐ] *n* (-[*e*]*s*; *-e* ['ja:rə]) year; ***ein drei viertel ~*** nine months; ***einmal im ~*** once a year; ***im ~e 1995*** in (the year) 1995; ***ein 10 ~e altes Auto*** a ten-year--old car; ***mit 18 ~en, im Alter von 18 ~en*** at (the age of) eighteen; ***heute vor e-m ~*** a year ago today; ***die 80er-Jahre*** the eighties
**jahr'aus** *adv*: ***~, jahrein*** year in, year out; year after year
**'Jahrbuch** *n* yearbook, annual
**jahrelang** ['ja:rəlaŋ] **1.** *adj* longstanding, (many) years of; **2.** *adv* for (many) years
**Jahres...** ['ja:rəs-] *in cpds ...bericht*, *...bilanz*, *...einkommen etc*: annual ...; **~anfang** *m* beginning of the year; **~ende** *n* end of the year; **~tag** *m* anniversary; **~wechsel** *m* turn of the year; **~zahl** *f* date, year; **~zeit** *f* season, time of (the) year
**'Jahrgang** *m* age group; PED year, class (***1995*** of '95); GASTR vintage
**Jahr'hundert** *n* (*-s*; *-e*) century; **~wende** *f* turn of the century
**jährlich** ['jɛ:ɐlɪç] **1.** *adj* annual, yearly; **2.** *adv* every year, yearly, once a year
**'Jahrmarkt** *m* fair
**Jahr'tausend** *n* (*-s*; *-e*) millennium
**Jahr'zehnt** *n* (-[*e*]*s*; *-e*) decade
**'Jähzorn** *m* violent (fit of) temper
**'jähzornig** *adj* hot-tempered
**Jalousie** [ʒalu'zi:] *f* (-; *-n*) (venetian) blind

**Jammer** ['jamɐ] *m* (*-s*; *no pl*) misery; ***es ist ein ~*** it is a pity; **jämmerlich** ['jɛmɐlɪç] *adj* miserable, wretched; pitiful, sorry; ***~ versagen*** fail miserably; **'jammern** *v/i* (*ge-*, *h*) moan, lament (***über*** *acc* over, about); complain (of, about); **jammer'schade** *adj*: ***es ist ~, dass*** it's a crying shame that

**Janker** ['jaŋkɐ] *Austrian m* (*-s*; *-*) jacket

**Jänner** ['jɛnɐ] *Austrian m* (*-s*; *-*), **Januar** ['janua:ɐ] *m* (*-[s]*; *-e*) January

**Japan** ['ja:pan] Japan; **Japaner** [ja'pa:nɐ] *m* (*-s*; *-*), **Ja'panerin** [-nərɪn] *f* (*-*; *-nen*), **ja'panisch** *adj* Japanese

**Jargon** [ʒar'gõ:] *m* (*-s*; *-s*) jargon; slang

**'Jastimme** *f* PARL aye, yea

**jäten** ['jɛ:tən] *v/t* (*ge-*, *h*) weed

**Jauche** ['jauxə] *f* (*-*; *-n*) liquid manure

**jauchzen** ['jauxtsən] *v/i* (*ge-*, *h*) shout for *or* with joy; exult, rejoice

**Jause** ['jauzə] *Austrian f* (*-*; *-n*) snack

**ja'wohl** *adv* (that's) right, (yes,) indeed

**je** [je:] *adv and cj* ever; each; per; ***der beste Film***, ***den ich ~ gesehen habe*** the best film I have ever seen; ***~ zwei*** (***Pfund***) two (pounds) each; ***drei Mark ~ Kilo*** three marks per kilo; ***~ nach Größe*** (***Geschmack***) according to size (taste); ***~ nachdem***(***, wie***) it depends (on how); ***~ ..., desto ...*** the ... the ...

**Jeans** [dʒi:nz] *pl*, *a. f* (*-*; *-*) (***e-e ~*** a pair of) jeans; **~jacke** *f* denim jacket

**jede** ['je:də], **jeder** ['je:dɐ], **jedes** ['je:dəs] *indef pron* every; any; each; either; ***jeder weiß*** (***das***) everybody knows; ***du kannst jeden fragen*** (you can) ask anyone; ***jeder von uns*** (***euch***) each of us (you); ***jeder***, ***der*** whoever; ***jeden zweiten Tag*** every other day; ***jeden Augenblick*** any moment now; ***jedes Mal*** every time; ***jedes Mal wenn*** whenever

**'jeden'falls** *adv* in any case, anyhow

**'jedermann** *indef pron* everyone, everybody

**'jeder'zeit** *adv* any time, always

**je'doch** *cj* however

**je'her** *adv*: ***von ~*** always

**jemals** ['je:ma:ls] *adv* ever

**jemand** ['je:mant] *indef pron* someone, somebody; anyone, anybody

**jene** ['je:nə], **jener** ['je:nɐ], **jenes** ['je:nəs] *dem pron* that (one); *pl* those; ***dies und jenes*** this and that

**jenseitig** ['je:nzaitɪç] *adj* opposite

**jenseits** ['je:nzaits] *adv and prp* (*gen*) on the other side (of), beyond (*a. fig*)

**'Jenseits** *n* (*-*; *no pl*) next world, hereafter

**jetzig** ['jɛtsɪç] *adj* present; existing

**jetzt** [jɛtst] *adv* now, at present; ***bis ~*** up to now, so far; ***erst ~*** only now; ***~ gleich*** right now *or* away; ***für ~*** for the present; ***von ~ an*** from now on

**jeweilig** ['je:'vailɪç] *adj* respective

**jeweils** ['je:'vails] *adv* each; at a time

**Jh.** ABBR *of* ***Jahrhundert*** cent., century

**Jochbein** ['jɔx-] *n* ANAT cheekbone

**Jockei** ['dʒɔke] *m* (*-s*; *-s*) jockey

**Jod** [jo:t] *n* (*-[e]s*; *no pl*) CHEM iodine

**jodeln** ['jo:dəln] *v/i* (*ge-*, *h*) yodel

**Joga** → ***Yoga***

**joggen** ['dʒɔgən] *v/i* (*ge-*, *h*) jog

**Jogger** ['dʒɔgɐ] *m* (*-s*; *-*) jogger

**Jogging** ['dʒɔgɪŋ] *n* (*-s*; *no pl*) jogging; **~anzug** *m* tracksuit; **~hose** *f* tracksuit trousers

**Joghurt, Jogurt** ['jo:gʊrt] *m*, *n* (*-[s]*; *-[s]*) yog(h)urt, yoghourt

**Johannisbeere** [jo'hanɪs-] *f*: ***rote ~*** redcurrant; ***schwarze ~*** blackcurrant

**johlen** ['jo:lən] *v/i* (*ge-*, *h*) howl, yell

**Jolle** ['jɔlə] *f* (*-*; *-n*) MAR dinghy

**Jongleur** [ʒõ'glø:ɐ] *m* (*-s*; *-e*) juggler

**jonglieren** [ʒõ'gli:rən] *v/t and v/i* (*no -ge-*, *h*) juggle

**Joule** [dʒu:l] *n* (*-[s]*; *-*) PHYS joule

**Journalismus** [ʒʊrna'lɪsmʊs] *m* (*-*; *no pl*) journalism; **Journalist(in)** [ʒʊrna'lɪst(ɪn)] (*-en*; *-en*/*-*; *-nen*) journalist

**jr.** → ***jun.***

**Jubel** ['ju:bəl] *m* (*-s*; *no pl*) cheering, cheers; rejoicing; **'jubeln** *v/i* (*ge-*, *h*) cheer, shout for joy; rejoice

**Jubiläum** [jubi'lɛ:ʊm] *n* (*-s*; *-läen*) anniversary; ***50-jähriges ~*** fiftieth anniversary, (golden) jubilee

**jucken** ['jʊkən] *v/t and v/i* (*ge-*, *h*) itch; ***es juckt mich am ...*** my ... itches

**Jude** ['ju:də] *m* (*-n*; *-n*) Jewish person; ***er ist ~*** he is Jewish; **Jüdin** ['jy:dɪn] *f* (*-*; *-nen*) Jewish woman *or* girl; ***sie ist ~*** she is Jewish; **jüdisch** ['jy:dɪʃ] *adj* Jewish

**Judo** ['ju:do] *n* (*-[s]*; *no pl*) SPORT judo

**Jugend** ['ju:gənt] *f* (*-*; *no pl*) youth; ***die ~*** young people; **~amt** *n* youth welfare office; **~arbeitslosigkeit** *f* youth unemployment

**'jugendfrei** *adj*: **~er Film** G(-rated) (*Br* U[-rated]) film; **nicht ~** X-rated
**'Jugend|fürsorge** *f* youth welfare; **~gericht** *n* JUR juvenile court; **~herberge** *f* youth hostel; **~klub** *m* youth club; **~kriminali,tät** *f* juvenile delinquency
**'jugendlich** *adj* youthful, young
**'Jugendliche** *m, f* (*-n*; *-n*) young person, *m a.* youth, JUR *a.* juvenile
**'Jugend|stil** *m* (*-s*; *no pl*) Art Nouveau; **~strafanstalt** *f* detention center (*Br* centre), reformatory; **~verbot** *n* for adults only; → ***jugendfrei***; **~zentrum** *n* youth center (*Br* centre)
**Juli** ['ju:li] *m* (*-[s]*; *-s*) July
**Jumbojet** ['jʊmbo-] *m* jumbo (jet)
**jun.** ABBR *of* ***junior*** Jun., jun., Jnr., Jr., junior
**jung** [jʊŋ] *adj* young
**Junge¹** ['jʊŋə] *m* (*-n*; *-n*) boy; lad; *cards*: jack, knave
**'Junge²** *n* (*-n*; *-n*) ZO young; puppy; kitten; cub; ***~ bekommen*** *or* ***werfen*** have young
**'jungenhaft** *adj* boyish
**'Jungenstreich** *m* boyish prank
**jünger** ['jʏŋɐ] *adj* younger
**'Jünger** *m* (*-s*; *-*) REL disciple (*a. fig*)
**Jungfer** ['jʊŋfɐ] *f* (*-*; *-n*) ***alte ~*** old maid
**'Jungfern|fahrt** *f* MAR maiden voyage; **~flug** *m* AVIAT maiden flight
**'Jung|frau** *f* virgin; ASTR Virgo; ***er ist ~*** he's (a) Virgo; **~geselle** *m* bachelor, single (man); **~gesellin** *f* bachelor girl, single (woman); *esp* JUR spinster
**jüngste** ['jʏŋstə] *adj* youngest; *fig* latest; ***in ~r Zeit*** lately, recently; ***das Jüngste Gericht*** the Last Judg(e)ment; ***der Jüngste Tag*** Doomsday
**Juni** ['ju:ni] *m* (*-[s]*; *-s*) June
**junior** ['ju:njo:ɐ] *adj*, **'Junior** *m* (*-s*; *-en* [ju'njo:rən]), **Juni'orin** *f* (*-*; *-nen*) junior (*a.* SPORT)
**Jupe** [ʒy:p] *Swiss m* (*-s*; *-s*) skirt
**Jura** ['ju:ra]: ***~ studieren*** study (the) law
**juridisch** [ju'ri:dɪʃ] *Austrian* → ***juristisch***; **Jurist(in)** [ju'rɪst(ɪn)] (*-en*; *-en*/*-*; *-nen*) lawyer; law student; **ju'ristisch** *adj* legal
**Jurorenkomitee** [ju'ro:rən-] *Austrian n* → ***Jury***
**Jury** [ʒy'ri:] *f* (*-*; *-s*) jury
**justieren** [jʊs'ti:rən] *v/t* (*no -ge-*, *h*) TECH adjust, set
**Justiz** [jʊs'ti:ts] *f* (*-*; *no pl*) (administration of) justice, (the) law; **~beamte** *m* judicial officer; **~irrtum** *m* error of justice; **~mi,nister** *m* minister of justice; Attorney General, *Br* Lord Chancellor; **~minis,terium** *n* ministry of justice; Department of Justice
**Jute** ['ju:tə] *f* (*-*; *no pl*) jute
**Juwel** [ju've:l] *m, n* (*-s*; *-en*) jewel, gem (*both a. fig*); *pl* jewel(le)ry
**Juwelier** [juve'li:ɐ] *m* (*-s*; *-e*) jewel(l)er



# K

**Kabarett** [kaba'rɛt] *n* (*-s*; *-s*) (political) revue
**Kabel** ['ka:bəl] *n* (*-s*; *-*) cable
**'Kabelfernsehen** *n* cable TV
**Kabeljau** ['ka:bəljau] *m* (*-s*; *-e*, *-s*) ZO cod(fish)
**Kabine** [ka'bi:nə] *f* (*-*; *-n*) cabin; cubicle; SPORT dressing room; TECH car; TEL *etc* booth; **Ka'binenbahn** *f* cable railway
**Kabinett** [kabi'nɛt] *n* (*-s*; *-e*) POL cabinet
**Kabis** ['ka:bɪs] *Swiss m* (*-*; *no pl*) green cabbage
**Kabriolett** [kabrio'lɛt] *n* (*-s*; *-s*) MOT convertible
**Kachel** ['kaxəl] *f* (*-*; *-n*), **'kacheln** *v/t* (*ge-*, *h*) tile; **'Kachelofen** *m* tiled stove
**Kadaver** [ka'da:vɐ] *m* (*-s*; *-*) carcass
**Kadett** [ka'dɛt] *m* (*-en*; *-en*) MIL cadet
**Käfer** ['kɛ:fɐ] *m* (*-s*; *-*) ZO beetle, bug
**Kaffee** ['kafe] *m* (*-s*; *-s*) coffee; ***~ kochen*** make coffee; ***~ mit Milch*** white coffee; **~auto,mat** *m* coffee machine; **~bohne** *f* coffee bean; **~haus** [ka'fe:-] *Austrian n* café, coffee house; **~kanne**

*f* coffee pot; **~maˌschine** *f* coffeemaker; **~mühle** *f* coffee grinder
**Käfig** ['kɛːfɪç] *m* (*-s*; *-e*) cage (*a. fig*)
**kahl** [kaːl] *adj* bald; *fig* bare (*rock, wall etc*); barren, bleak (*landscape*)
**Kahn** [kaːn] *m* (*-[e]s*; *Kähne* ['kɛːnə]) boat; barge
**Kai** [kai] *m* (*-s*; *-s*) quay, wharf
**Kaiser** ['kaizɐ] *m* (*-s*; *-*) emperor
**Kaiserin** ['kaizərɪn] *f* (*-*; *-nen*) empress
'**Kaiserreich** *n* empire
**Kajüte** [ka'jyːtə] *f* (*-*; *-n*) MAR cabin
**Kakao** [ka'kau] *m* (*-s*; *-s*) cocoa; (hot) chocolate; chocolate milk
**Kaktee** [kak'teːə] *f* (*-*; *-n*), **Kaktus** ['kaktʊs] *m* (*-*; *Kakteen*) BOT cactus
**Kalb** [kalp] *n* (*-[e]s*; *Kälber* ['kɛlbɐ]) ZO calf; **kalben** ['kalbən] *v/i* (*ge-, h*) calve
'**Kalbfleisch** *n* veal
'**Kalbs|braten** *m* roast veal; **~schnitzel** *n* veal cutlet; escalope (of veal)
**Kaldaunen** [kal'daunən] *pl* GASTR tripe
**Kalender** [ka'lɛndɐ] *m* (*-s*; *-*) calendar; **~jahr** *n* calendar year
**Kali** ['kaːli] *n* (*-s*; *no pl*) CHEM potash
**Kaliber** [ka'liːbɐ] *n* (*-s*; *-*) caliber, *Br* calibre (*a. fig*)
**Kalk** [kalk] *m* (*-[e]s*; *-e*) lime; GEOL limestone, chalk; MED calcium; '**kalken** *v/t* (*ge-, h*) whitewash; AGR lime; '**kalkig** *adj* limy; '**Kalkstein** *m* limestone
**Kalorie** [kalo'riː] *f* (*-*; *-n*) calorie
**kalo'rien|arm** *adj*, **~reduˌziert** *adj* low-calorie, low in calories; **~reich** *adj* high-calorie, high *or* rich in calories
**kalt** [kalt] *adj* cold; ***mir ist ~*** I'm cold; ***es*** (***mir***) ***wird ~*** it's (I'm) getting cold; ***~ bleiben*** *fig* keep (one's) cool; ***das lässt mich kalt*** that leaves me cold
'**kaltblütig** [-blyːtɪç] **1.** *adj* cold-blooded (*a. fig*); **2.** *adv* in cold blood
**Kälte** ['kɛltə] *f* (*-*; *no pl*) cold; *fig* coldness; ***vor ~ zittern*** shiver with cold; ***fünf Grad ~*** five degrees below zero; **~einbruch** *m* cold snap; **~grad** *m* degree below zero; **~periˌode** *f* cold spell
'**kaltmachen** F *v/t* (*sep, -ge-, h*) bump off
**kam** [kaːm] *pret of* ***kommen***
**Kamee** [ka'meːə] *f* (*-*; *-n*) cameo
**Kamel** [ka'meːl] *n* (*-s*; *-e*) ZO camel
**Ka'melhaar** *n* (*-[e]s*; *no pl*) camelhair
**Kamera** ['kaməra] *f* (*-*; *-s*) camera
**Kamerad** [kamə'raːt] *m* (*-en*; *-en* [-'raːdən]) companion, F mate, pal, buddy;
**Kameradin** [-'raːdɪn] *f* (*-*; *-nen*) companion
**Kame'radschaft** *f* (*-*; *no pl*) comradeship
'**Kameramann** *m* cameraman
'**Kamerareˌkorder** *m* (*-s*; *-*) camcorder
**Kamille** [ka'mɪlə] *f* (*-*; *-n*) BOT camomile
**Kamin** [ka'miːn] *m* (*-s*; *-e*) fireplace; chimney (*a.* MOUNT); ***am ~*** by the fire(side); **~kehrer** [-keːrɐ] *m* (*-s*; *-*) chimney sweep; **~sims** *m, n* mantelpiece
**Kamm** [kam] *m* (*-[e]s*; *Kämme* ['kɛmə]) comb, ZO *a.* crest (*a. fig*)
**kämmen** ['kɛmən] *v/t* (*ge-, h*) comb; ***sich*** (***die Haare***) ***~*** comb one's hair
**Kammer** ['kamɐ] *f* (*-*; *-n*) (small) room; storeroom, closet; garret; POL, ECON chamber; JUR division
'**Kammermuˌsik** *f* chamber music
'**Kammgarn** *n* worsted (yarn)
**Kampagne** [kam'panjə] *f* (*-*; *-n*) campaign
**Kampf** [kampf] *m* (*-[e]s*; *Kämpfe* ['kɛmpfə]) fight (*a. fig*), struggle (*a. fig*), *esp* MIL combat, battle (*a. fig*); SPORT contest, match; *boxing*: fight, bout; *fig* conflict; '**kampfbereit** *adj* ready for battle (MIL combat); **kämpfen** ['kɛmpfən] *v/i* (*ge-, h*) fight (***gegen*** against; ***mit*** with; ***um*** for) (*a. fig*); struggle (*a. fig*); *fig* contend, wrestle
**Kampfer** ['kampfɐ] *m* (*-s*; *no pl*) CHEM camphor
**Kämpfer** ['kɛmpfɐ] *m* (*-s*; *-*), '**Kämpferin** *f* (*-*; *-nen*) fighter (*a. fig*); **kämpferisch** ['kɛmpfərɪʃ] *adj* fighting, aggressive (*a.* SPORT)
'**Kampf|flugzeug** *n* MIL combat aircraft; **~kraft** *f* (*-*; *no pl*) fighting strength; **~richter** *m* SPORT judge; **~sportarten** *pl* martial arts
**Kanada** ['kanada] Canada; **Kanadier** [ka'naːdjɐ] *m* (*-s*; *-*), **Ka'nadierin** [-djərɪn] *f* (*-*; *-nen*), **ka'nadisch** *adj* Canadian
**Kanal** [ka'naːl] *m* (*-s*; *Kanäle* [ka'nɛːlə]) canal; channel (*a.* TV, TECH, *fig*); sewer, drain; ***der ~*** the (English) Channel
**Kanalisation** [kanaliza'tsjoːn] *f* (*-*; *-en*) sewerage (system); canalization
**kanalisieren** [kanali'ziːrən] *v/t* (*no -ge-, h*) sewer; canalize; *fig* channel

**Ka'naltunnel** *m* Channel Tunnel, F Chunnel

**Kanarienvogel** [ka'na:rjən-] *m* canary

**Kandidat** [kandi'da:t] *m* (*-en*; *-en*), **Kandi'datin** *f* (-; *-nen*) candidate; **Kandidatur** [kandida'tu:ɐ] *f* (-; *-en*) candidacy, *Br a.* candidature; **kandidieren** [kandi'di:rən] *v/i* (*no -ge-*, *h*) stand *or* run for election; **~ für ...** run for the office of ...

**Känguru, Känguruh** ['kɛŋguru] *n* (*-s*; *-s*) ZO kangaroo

**Kaninchen** [ka'ni:nçən] *n* (*-s*; -) ZO rabbit

**Kanister** [ka'nɪstɐ] *m* (*-s*; -) (fuel) can

**Kanne** ['kanə] *f* (-; *-n*) pot; can

**Kannibale** [kani'ba:lə] *m* (*-n*; *-n*) cannibal

**kannte** ['kantə] *pret of* ***kennen***

**Kanon** ['ka:nɔn] *m* (*-s*; *-s*) MUS canon, round

**Kanone** [ka'no:nə] *f* (-; *-n*) MIL gun; cannon; F ace, *esp* SPORT *a.* crack

**Kante** ['kantə] *f* (-; *-n*) edge; **'kanten** *v/t* (*ge-*, *h*) set on edge, tilt; edge (*skis*)

**'Kanten** *m* (*-s*; -) crust

**kantig** ['kantɪç] *adj* angular, square(d)

**Kantine** [kan'ti:nə] *f* (-; *-n*) canteen

**Kanton** [kan'to:n] *m* (*-s*; *-e*) POL canton

**Kanu** ['ka:nu] *n* (*-s*; *-s*) canoe

**Kanüle** [ka'ny:lə] *f* (-; *-n*) MED cannula, (drain) tube

**Kanzel** ['kantsəl] *f* (-; *-n*) REL pulpit; AVIAT cockpit

**Kanzlei** [kants'lai] *f* (-; *-en*) office

**Kanzler** ['kantslɐ] *m* (*-s*; -) chancellor

**Kap** [kap] *n* (*-s*; *-s*) cape, headland

**Kapazität** [kapatsi'tɛ:t] *f* (-; *-en*) capacity; *fig* authority

**Kapelle** [ka'pɛlə] *f* (-; *-n*) REL chapel; MUS band

**Ka'pellmeister** *m* MUS conductor

**kapern** ['ka:pɐn] *v/t* (*ge-*, *h*) MAR capture, seize

**kapieren** [ka'pi:rən] F *v/t* (*no -ge-*, *h*) get; ***kapiert?*** got it?

**Kapital** [kapi'ta:l] *n* (*-s*; *-e*, *-ien*) ECON capital, funds; **~anlage** *f* investment

**Kapitalismus** [kapita'lɪsmʊs] *m* (-; *no pl*) capitalism; **Kapita'list** *m* (*-en*; *-en*), **kapita'listisch** *adj* capitalist

**Kapi'talverbrechen** *n* capital crime, JUR felony

**Kapitän** [kapi'tɛ:n] *m* (*-s*; *-e*) captain (*a.* SPORT)

**Kapitel** [ka'pɪtəl] *n* (*-s*; -) chapter (*a. fig*); F *fig* story

**Kapitulation** [kapitula'tsjo:n] *f* (-; *-en*) capitulation, surrender (*a. fig*)

**kapitulieren** [kapitu'li:rən] *v/i* (*no -ge-*, *h*) capitulate, surrender (*a. fig*)

**Kaplan** [ka'pla:n] *m* (*-s*; *Kapläne* [ka'plɛ:nə]) REL curate

**Kappe** ['kapə] *f* (-; *-n*) cap, TECH *a.* top, hood; **'kappen** *v/t* (*ge-*, *h*) cut (*rope*); lop, top (*tree*)

**Kapsel** ['kapsəl] *f* (-; *-n*) capsule

**kaputt** [ka'pʊt] F *adj* broken (*a. fig*); TECH out of order; *fig* dead beat; ruined; **~gehen** F *v/i* (*irr*, ***gehen***, *sep*, *-ge-*, *sein*) break; MOT *etc* break down; *fig* break up; **~machen** F *v/t* (*sep*, *-ge-*, *h*) break, wreck (*a. fig*), ruin (*a. fig*)

**Kapuze** [ka'pu:tsə] *f* (-; *-n*) hood; cowl

**Karabiner** [kara'bi:nɐ] *m* (*-s*; -) carbine; **~haken** *m* karabiner, snaplink

**Karaffe** [ka'rafə] *f* (-; *-n*) decanter

**Karambolage** [karambo'la:ʒə] *f* (-; *-n*) collision, crash

**Karat** [ka'ra:t] *n* (-[*e*]*s*; *-e*) carat

**Karate** [ka'ra:tə] *n* (-[*s*]; *no pl*) SPORT karate

**Karawane** [kara'va:nə] *f* (-; *-n*) caravan

**Kardinal** [kardi'na:l] *m* (*-s*; *Kardinäle* [kardi'nɛ:lə]) REL cardinal

**Karfiol** [kar'fjo:l] *Austrian m* (*-s*; *no pl*) BOT cauliflower

**Kar'freitag** [ka:ɐ-] *m* REL Good Friday

**karg** [kark], **kärglich** ['kɛrklɪç] *adj* meag|er, *Br* -re, scanty; frugal; poor

**kariert** [ka'ri:ɐt] *adj* checked, checkered, *Br* chequered; squared

**Karies** ['ka:rjɛs] *f* (-; *no pl*) MED (dental) caries

**Karikatur** [karika'tu:ɐ] *f* (-; *-en*) *mst* cartoon, *esp fig* caricature; **Karikaturist** [karikatu'rɪst] *m* (*-en*; *-en*) cartoonist

**karikieren** [kari'ki:rən] *v/t* (*no -ge-*, *h*) caricature

**Karneval** ['karnəval] *m* (*-s*; *-e*, *-s*) carnival

**Karo** ['ka:ro] *n* (*-s*; *-s*) square, check; *cards*: diamonds

**Karosserie** [karɔsə'ri:] *f* (-; *-n*) MOT body

**Karotte** [ka'rɔtə] *f* (-; *-n*) BOT carrot

**Karpfen** ['karpfən] *m* (*-s*; -) ZO carp

**Karre** ['karə] *f* (-; *-n*), **'Karren** *m* (*-s*; -) cart; wheelbarrow; F MOT jalopy
**Karriere** [ka'rje:rə] *f* (-; *-n*) career; ~ ***machen*** work one's way up, get to the top
**Karte** ['kartə] *f* (-; *-n*) card; ticket; GEOGR map; chart; GASTR menu; ***gute*** (***schlechte***) ~***n*** a good (bad) hand
**Kartei** [kar'tai] *f* (-; *-en*) card index; **~karte** *f* index *or* file card
**'Karten|haus** *n* house of cards (*a. fig*); MAR chartroom; **~spiel** *n* card game; deck (*Br* pack) of cards; **~tele,fon** *n* cardphone; **~vorverkauf** *m* advance booking; box office
**Kartoffel** [kar'tɔfəl] *f* (-; *-n*) BOT potato; **~brei** *m* mashed potatoes; **~chips** *pl* (potato) chips, *Br* crisps; **~kloß** *m*, **~knödel** *m* potato dumpling; **~puffer** *m* potato fritter; **~schalen** *pl* potato peelings; **~schäler** *m* potato peeler
**Karton** [kar'tɔŋ] *m* (*-s*; *-s*) cardboard; pasteboard; cardboard box
**Karussell** [karʊ'sɛl] *n* (*-s*; *-s*) car(r)ousel, roundabout, merry-go-round
**Karwoche** ['ka:ɐ-] *f* REL Holy Week
**Kaschmir** ['kaʃmi:ɐ] *m* (*-s*; *-e*) cashmere
**Käse** ['kɛ:zə] *m* (*-s*; -) cheese
**Kaserne** [ka'zɛrnə] *f* (-; *-n*) barracks
**Ka'sernenhof** *m* barrack square
**käsig** ['kɛ:zɪç] *adj* cheesy; pasty
**Kasino** [ka'zi:no] *n* (*-s*; *-s*) casino; MIL (officers') mess
**Kasperle** ['kaspɐlə] *n*, *m* (*-s*; -) Punch; **~the,ater** *n* Punch and Judy show
**Kassa** ['kasa] *Austrian f* (-; *Kassen*), **Kasse** ['kasə] *f* (-; *-n*) till; cash register; checkout (counter); cash desk; cashier's counter; THEA *etc* box office; F ***gut*** (***knapp***) ***bei Kasse sein*** be flush (be a bit hard up)
**'Kassen|beleg** *m*, **~bon** *m* sales slip, *Br* receipt; **~erfolg** *m* THEA *etc* box-office success; **~pati,ent** *m* MED health plan (*Am* medicaid, *Br* NHS) patient; **~schlager** F *m* blockbuster; **~wart** [-vart] *m* (*-[e]s*; *-e*) treasurer
**Kassette** [ka'sɛtə] *f* (-; *-n*) box, case; MUS, TV, PHOT *etc* cassette; casket
**Kas'setten...** *in cpds ...rekorder etc*: cassette ...
**kassieren** [ka'si:rən] *v/t and v/i* (*no -ge-*, *h*) collect, take (the money)
**Kassierer** [ka'si:rɐ] *m* (*-s*; -), **Kas'siererin** *f* (-; *-nen*) cashier; teller; collector
**Kastanie** [kas'ta:njə] *f* (-; *-n*) BOT chestnut
**Kasten** ['kastən] *m* (*-s*; *Kästen* ['kɛstən]) box (*a.* F TV, SPORT *etc*); case; chest
**kastrieren** [kas'tri:rən] *v/t* (*no -ge-*, *h*) MED, VET castrate
**Kasus** ['ka:zʊs] *m* (-; -) LING case
**Katalog** [kata'lo:k] *m* (*-[e]s*; *-e*) catalog(ue *Br*)
**Katalysator** [kataly'za:to:ɐ] *m* (*-s*; *-en* [-za'to:rən]) CHEM catalyst; MOT catalytic converter
**Katapult** [kata'pʊlt] *m*, *n* (*-[e]s*; *-e*), **katapultieren** [katapʊl'ti:rən] *v/t* (*no -ge-*, *h*) catapult
**katastrophal** [katastro'fa:l] *adj* disastrous (*a. fig*); **Katastrophe** [katas'tro:fə] *f* (-; *-n*) catastrophe, disaster (*a. fig*)
**Kata'strophen|gebiet** *n* disaster area; **~schutz** *m* disaster control
**Katechismus** [katɛ'çɪsmʊs] *m* (-; *-men*) REL catechism
**Kategorie** [katego'ri:] *f* (-; *-n*) category
**Kater** ['ka:tɐ] *m* (*-s*; -) ZO male cat, tomcat; F hangover
**kath.** ABBR *of* ***katholisch*** Cath., Catholic
**Kathedrale** [kate'dra:lə] *f* (-; *-n*) cathedral
**Katholik** [kato'li:k] *m* (*-en*; *-en*), **Katho'likin** *f* (-; *-nen*), **katholisch** [ka'to:lɪʃ] *adj* (Roman) Catholic
**Kätzchen** ['kɛtsçən] *n* (*-s*; -) ZO kitten, pussy (*a.* BOT)
**Katze** ['katsə] *f* (-; *-n*) ZO cat; kitten
**Kauderwelsch** ['kaudɐvɛlʃ] *n* (*-[s]*; *no pl*) gibberish
**kauen** ['kauən] *v/t and v/i* (*ge-*, *h*) chew
**kauern** ['kauɐn] *v/i and v/refl* (*ge-*, *h*) crouch, squat
**Kauf** [kauf] *m* (*-[e]s*; *Käufe* ['kɔʏfə]) purchase (*a.* ECON), F buy; purchasing, buying; ***ein guter*** ~ a bargain, F a good buy; ***zum*** ~ ***anbieten*** offer for sale
**'kaufen** *v/t* (*ge-*, *h*) buy (*a. fig*), purchase
**Käufer** ['kɔʏfɐ] *m* (*-s*; -), **'Käuferin** *f* (-; *-nen*) buyer; customer
**'Kauffrau** *f* (-; *-en*) businesswoman
**'Kauf|haus** *n* department store; **~kraft** *f* (-; *no pl*) ECON purchasing power
**käuflich** ['kɔʏflɪç] *adj* for sale; *fig* venal

K

'**Kaufmann** *m* (-[*e*]*s*; *-leute*) businessman; dealer, trader, merchant; storekeeper, *Br mst* shopkeeper; grocer
'**kaufmännisch** [-mɛnɪʃ] *adj* commercial, business; **~er Angestellter** clerk
'**Kaufvertrag** *m* contract of sale
'**Kaugummi** *m* (*-s*; *-s*) chewing gum
**kaum** [kaum] *adv* hardly; **~ zu glauben** hard to believe
**Kaution** [kau'tsjo:n] *f* (-; *-en*) security; JUR bail
**Kautschuk** ['kautʃʊk] *m* (*-s*; *-e*) (india) rubber
**Kavalier** [kava'li:ɐ] *m* (*-s*; *-e*) gentleman
**Kaviar** ['ka:vjar] *m* (*-s*; *-e*) caviar(e)
**keck** [kɛk] *adj* cheeky, saucy, pert
**Kegel** ['ke:gəl] *m* (*-s*; -) skittle, pin; MATH, TECH cone; **~bahn** *f* bowling (*esp Br* skittle) alley
'**kegelförmig** [-fœrmɪç] *adj* conical
'**Kegelkugel** *f* bowling (*esp Br* skittle) ball
'**kegeln** *v/i* (*ge-*, *h*) bowl, go bowling, *esp Br* play (at) skittles *or* ninepins
**Kehle** ['ke:lə] *f* (-; *-n*) ANAT throat
'**Kehlkopf** *m* ANAT larynx
**Kehre** ['ke:rə] *f* (-; *-n*) (sharp) bend
'**kehren** *v/t* (*ge-*, *h*) sweep; **j-m den Rücken ~** turn one's back on s.o.
**Kehricht** ['ke:rɪçt] *m* (*-s*; *no pl*) sweepings; **~schaufel** *f* dustpan
**kehrtmachen** ['ke:ɐt-] *v/i* (*sep*, *-ge-*, *h*) turn back
**keifen** ['kaifən] *v/i* (*ge-*, *h*) nag, bitch
**Keil** [kail] *m* (-[*e*]*s*; *-e*) wedge; gusset
**Keiler** ['kailɐ] *m* (*-s*; -) ZO wild boar
'**Keilriemen** *m* MOT fan belt
**Keim** [kaim] *m* (-[*e*]*s*; *-e*) BIOL, MED germ; BOT bud, sprout; *fig* seed(s)
'**keimen** *v/i* (*ge-*, *h*) BOT germinate, sprout; *fig* form, grow; stir
'**keimfrei** *adj* MED sterile
'**keimtötend** *adj* MED germicidal
'**Keimzelle** *f* BIOL germ cell
**kein** [kain] *indef pron* **1.** *adj*: **~(e)** no, not any; **~ anderer** no one else; **~(e) ... mehr** not any more ...; **~ Geld** (**~e Zeit**) **mehr** no money (time) left; **~ Kind mehr** no longer a child; **2.** *su*: **~er, ~e, ~(e)s** none, no one, nobody; **~er von beiden** neither (of the two); **~er von uns** none of us; '**keines'falls** *adv* by no means, under no circumstances; '**keineswegs** [-'ve:ks] *adv* by no means, not in the least; '**keinmal** *adv* not once, not a single time
**Keks** [ke:ks] *m*, *n* (*-es*; *-e*) cookie, *Br* biscuit
**Kelch** [kɛlç] *m* (-[*e*]*s*; *-e*) cup (*a.* BOT); REL chalice
**Kelle** ['kɛlə] *f* (-; *-n*) GASTR ladle, scoop; TECH trowel; signaling disk
**Keller** ['kɛlɐ] *m* (*-s*; -) cellar; → **~geschoss** *n*, **~geschoß** *Austrian n* basement; **~wohnung** *f* basement (apartment, *esp Br* flat)
**Kellner** ['kɛlnɐ] *m* (*-s*; -) waiter
**Kellnerin** ['kɛlnərɪn] *f* (-; *-nen*) waitress
**keltern** ['kɛltɐn] *v/t* (*ge-*, *h*) press
**kennen** ['kɛnən] *v/t* (*irr*, *ge-*, *h*) know, be acquainted with; **~ lernen** get to know, become acquainted with; meet *s.o.*; **als ich ihn ~ lernte** when I first met him; **Kenner** ['kɛnɐ] *m* (*-s*; -), '**Kennerin** *f* (-; *-nen*) expert; **kenntlich** ['kɛntlɪç] *adj* recognizable (**an** *dat* by); **Kenntnis** *f* (-; *-se*) knowledge; **gute ~se in** (*dat*) a good knowledge of
'**Kennwort** *n* password
'**Kennzeichen** *n* mark, sign; (distinguishing) feature, characteristic; MOT license (*Br* registration) number
'**kennzeichnen** *v/t* (*ge-*, *h*) mark; *fig* characterize
**kentern** ['kɛntɐn] *v/i* (*ge-*, *sein*) MAR capsize
**Keramik** [ke'ra:mɪk] *f* (-; *-en*) ceramics
**Kerbe** ['kɛrbə] *f* (-; *-n*) notch
**Kerker** ['kɛrkɐ] *m* (*-s*; -) dungeon
**Kerl** [kɛrl] F *m* (*-s*; *-e*) fellow, guy; **armer ~** poor devil; **ein anständiger ~** a decent sort
**Kern** [kɛrn] *m* (-[*e*]*s*; *-e*) BOT pip, seed, stone, kernel; TECH core (*a. fig*); PHYS nucleus ; **~...** *in cpds ...energie*, *...forschung*, *...physik*, *...reaktor*, *...technik etc*: nuclear ...; **~fach** *n* PED basic subject; **~fa,milie** *f* nuclear family; **~gehäuse** *n* BOT core
'**kernge'sund** *adj* F (as) sound as a bell
**kernig** ['kɛrnɪç] *adj* full of seeds (*Br* pips); *fig* robust; pithy
'**Kernkraft** *f* PHYS nuclear power; **~gegner** *m* anti-nuclear activist; **~werk** *n* nuclear power station *or* plant
'**kernlos** *adj* BOT seedless
'**Kernspaltung** *f* PHYS nuclear fission

'**Kernwaffen** *pl* MIL nuclear weapons; '**kernwaffenfrei** *adj*: ***~e Zone*** MIL nuclear-free zone; '**Kernwaffenversuch** *m* MIL nuclear test
'**Kernzeit** *f* ECON core time
**Kerze** ['kɛrtsə] *f* (-; -*n*) candle; SPORT shoulder stand
**kess** [kɛs] F *adj* cheeky, saucy, pert
**Kessel** ['kɛsəl] *m* (-*s*; -) kettle; TECH boiler; tank
**Kette** ['kɛtə] *f* (-; -*n*) chain (*a. fig*); necklace; ***e-e ~ bilden*** form a line
'**Ketten...** *in cpds ...antrieb, ...laden, ...rauchen, ...raucher, ...reaktion etc*: chain ...
'**ketten** *v/t* (*ge-, h*) chain (***an*** *acc* to)
'**Kettenfahrzeug** *n* tracked vehicle
**Ketzer** ['kɛtsɐ] *m* (-*s*; -) heretic
**Ketzerei** [kɛtsə'rai] *f* (-; -*en*) heresy
**keuchen** ['kɔyçən] *v/i* (*ge-, h*) pant, gasp
'**Keuchhusten** *m* MED whooping cough
**Keule** ['kɔylə] *f* (-; -*n*) club; GASTR leg
**keusch** [kɔyʃ] *adj* chaste
'**Keuschheit** *f* (-; *no pl*) chastity
**Kfz** [ka:ʔɛfʔtsɛt] ABBR *of* ***Kraftfahrzeug*** motor vehicle; **Kf'z-Brief** *m*, **Kf'z-Schein** *m* vehicle registration document; **Kf'z-Steuer** *f* road *or* automobile tax; **Kf'z-Werkstatt** *f* garage
**KG** [ka:'ge:] ABBR *of* ***Kommanditgesellschaft*** ECON limited partnership
**kichern** ['kıçɐn] *v/i* (*ge-, h*) giggle
**Kiebitz** ['ki:bıts] *m* (-*es*; -*e*) ZO peewit, lapwing; F kibitzer
**Kiefer**[1] ['ki:fɐ] *m* (-*s*; -) ANAT jaw(bone)
'**Kiefer**[2] *f* (-; -*n*) BOT pine(tree)
**Kiel** [ki:l] *m* (-[*e*]*s*; -*e*) MAR keel; **~flosse** *f* AVIAT tail fin; **~raum** *m* MAR bilge; **~wasser** *n* (-*s*; -) MAR wake (*a. fig*)
**Kieme** ['ki:mə] *f* (-*n*; -*n*) ZO gill
**Kies** [ki:s] *m* (-*es*; -*e*) gravel (*a.* ***mit ~ bestreuen***); F dough
**Kiesel** ['ki:zəl] *m* (-*s*; -) pebble
**Kilo** ['ki:lo] *n* (-*s*; -) → ***Kilogramm***
**Kilo|'gramm** [kilo-] *n* kilogram(me); **~hertz** [-'hɛrts] *n* (-; -) kilohertz; **~'meter** *m* kilometer, *Br* kilometre; **~'watt** *n* ELECTR kilowatt
**Kind** [kınt] *n* (-[*e*]*s*; -*er* ['kındɐ]) child; ***ein ~ erwarten*** be expecting a baby
'**Kinder|arzt** *m*, **~ärztin** *f* p(a)ediatrician; **~garten** *m* kindergarten, nursery school; **~gärtnerin** [-gɛrtnərın] *f* (-; -*nen*) nursery-school *or* kindergarten teacher; **~geld** *n* child benefit; **~hort** [-hɔrt] *m* (-[*e*]*s*; -*e*), **~krippe** *f* day nursery; **~lähmung** *f* MED polio(myelitis)
'**kinderlieb** *adj* fond of children
'**kinderlos** *adj* childless
'**Kinder|mädchen** *n* nurse(maid), nanny; **~spiel** *fig n*: ***ein ~ sein*** be child's play; **~stube** *fig f* manners, upbringing; **~wagen** *m* baby carriage, buggy, *Br* pram; **~zimmer** *n* children's room
**Kindes|alter** ['kındəs-] *n* childhood; infancy; **~entführung** *f* kidnap(p)ing; **~misshandlung** *f* child abuse
'**Kindheit** *f* (-; *no pl*) (***von ~ an*** from) childhood
**kindisch** ['kındıʃ] *adj* childish
'**kindlich** *adj* childlike
**Kinn** [kın] *n* (-[*e*]*s*; -*e*) ANAT chin; **~backe** *f*, **~backen** *m* (-*s*; -) ANAT jaw(bone); **~haken** *m* *boxing*: hook (to the chin), uppercut
**Kino** ['ki:no] *n* (-*s*; -*s*) a) (*no pl*) motion pictures, *esp Br* cinema, F *the* movies, b) movie theater, *esp Br* cinema
'**Kinobesucher** *m*, '**Kinogänger** [-gɛŋɐ] *m* (-*s*; -) moviegoer, *Br* cinemagoer
**Kippe** ['kıpə] *f* (-; -*n*) F butt, *esp Br* stub; SPORT upstart
'**kippen 1.** *v/i* (*ge-, sein*) tip *or* topple (over); **2.** *v/t* (*ge-, h*) tilt, tip over *or* up
**Kirche** ['kırçə] *f* (-; -*n*) church; ***in die ~ gehen*** go to church
'**Kirchen|buch** *n* parish register; **~diener** *m* sexton; **~gemeinde** *f* parish; **~jahr** *n* Church *or* ecclesiastical year; **~lied** *n* hymn; **~mu,sik** *f* sacred *or* church music; **~schiff** *n* ARCH nave; **~steuer** *f* church tax; **~stuhl** *m* pew; **~tag** *m* church congress
'**Kirchgang** *m* churchgoing; '**Kirchgänger** [-gɛŋɐ] *m* (-*s*; -) churchgoer
'**kirchlich** *adj* church, ecclesiastical
'**Kirchturm** *m* steeple; spire; church tower
**Kirsche** ['kırʃə] *f* (-; -*n*) BOT cherry
**Kissen** ['kısən] *n* (-*s*; -) pillow; cushion; **~bezug** *m*, **~hülle** *f* pillowcase, pillowslip
**Kiste** ['kıstə] *f* (-; -*n*) box, chest; crate
**Kitsch** [kıtʃ] *m* (-[*e*]*s*; *no pl*) kitsch; trash; F slush
'**kitschig** *adj* kitschy; trashy; slushy

K

**Kitt** [kɪt] *m* (-[*e*]*s*; -*e*) cement; putty
**Kittel** ['kɪtəl] *m* (-*s*; -) smock; overall; MED (white) coat
'**kitten** *v/t* (*ge-*, *h*) cement; putty
**Kitzel** ['kɪtsəl] *m* (-*s*; -) tickle, *fig a.* thrill, kick; '**kitzeln** *v/i and v/t* (*ge-*, *h*) tickle; **Kitzler** ['kɪtslɐ] *m* (-*s*; -) ANAT clitoris; **kitzlig** ['kɪtslɪç] *adj* ticklish (*a. fig*)
**kläffen** ['klɛfən] *v/i* (*ge-*, *h*) yap, yelp
**klaffend** ['klafənt] *adj* gaping; yawning
**Klage** ['kla:gə] *f* (-; -*n*) complaint; lament; JUR action, (law)suit
'**klagen** *v/i* (*ge-*, *h*) complain (***über*** *acc* of, about; ***bei*** to); lament; JUR go to court; ***gegen j-n*** ~ JUR sue s.o.
**Kläger** ['klɛ:gɐ] *m* (-*s*; -), '**Klägerin** *f* (-; -*nen*) JUR plaintiff
**kläglich** ['klɛ:klɪç] → ***jämmerlich***
**Klamauk** [kla'mauk] *m* (-*s*; *no pl*) racket; THEA *etc* slapstick
**klamm** [klam] *adj* numb; clammy
**Klammer** ['klamɐ] *f* (-; -*n*) TECH cramp, clamp; clip; clothespin, *Br* (clothes) peg; MED brace; MATH, PRINT bracket(s); '**klammern** *v/t* (*ge-*, *h*) fasten *or* clip together; ***sich ~ an*** (*acc*) cling to
**klang** [klaŋ] *pret of* ***klingen***
**Klang** *m* (-[*e*]*s*; *Klänge* ['klɛŋə]) sound; tone; clink; ringing
'**klangvoll** *adj* sonorous; *fig* illustrious
**Klappe** ['klapə] *f* (-; -*n*) flap; hinged lid; MOT tailgate, *Br* tailboard; TECH, BOT, ANAT valve; F trap; '**klappen** (*ge-*, *h*) **1.** *v/t*: ***nach oben*** ~ lift up, raise; put *or* fold up; ***nach unten*** ~ lower, put down; ***es lässt sich*** (***nach hinten***) ~ it folds (backward); **2.** *v/i* clap, clack; F work, work out (well)
**Klapper** ['klapɐ] *f* (-; -*n*) rattle
'**klappern** *v/i* (*ge-*, *h*) clatter, rattle (***mit et.*** s.th.)
'**Klapperschlange** *f* ZO rattlesnake
**Klapp|fahrrad** ['klap-] *n* folding bicycle; **~fenster** *n* top-hung window; **~messer** *n* jack knife, clasp knife
**klapprig** ['klaprɪç] *adj* MOT rattly, ramshackle; F shaky
'**Klappsitz** *m* folding *or* tip-up seat
'**Klappstuhl** *m* folding chair
'**Klapptisch** *m* folding table
**Klaps** [klaps] *m* (-*es*; -*e*) slap, pat; smack
**klar** [kla:ɐ] *adj* clear (*a. fig*); ***ist dir ~, dass ...?*** do you realize that ...?; ***das ist mir*** (***nicht ganz***) ~ I (don't quite) understand; (***na***) ***~!*** of course!; ***alles ~?*** everything okay?
**Kläranlage** ['klɛ:ɐ-] *f* sewage works
**klären** ['klɛ:rən] *v/t* (*ge-*, *h*) TECH purify, treat; *fig* clear up; settle; SPORT clear
'**Klarheit** *f* (-; *no pl*) clearness, *fig a.* clarity
**Klarinette** [klari'nɛtə] *f* (-; -*n*) MUS clarinet
'**Klarsicht...** *in cpds* transparent
**Klasse** ['klasə] *f* (-; -*n*) class (*a.* POL), PED *a.* grade, *Br* form; classroom; F ***~ sein*** be super, be fantastic
'**Klassen|arbeit** *f* (classroom) test; **~buch** *n* classbook, *Br* (class) register; **~kame,rad** *m* classmate; **~lehrer(in)** homeroom teacher, *Br* form teacher, *a.* form master (mistress); **~sprecher** *m* class representative; **~zimmer** *n* classroom
**klassifizieren** [klasifi'tsi:rən] *v/t* (*no -ge-*, *h*) classify; '**Klassifi'zierung** *f* (-; -*en*) classification
**Klassiker** ['klasikɐ] *m* (-*s*; -) classic
**klassisch** ['klasɪʃ] *adj* classic(al)
**Klatsch** [klatʃ] F *m* (-*es*; *no pl*) gossip
'**Klatschbase** *f* gossip
'**klatschen** *v/i and v/t* (*ge-*, *h*) clap, applaud; F slap, bang; splash; F gossip; ***in die Hände ~*** clap one's hands
'**klatschhaft** *adj* gossipy
'**Klatschmaul** F *n* (old) gossip
'**klatsch'nass** F *adj* soaking wet
**klauben** ['klaubən] *Austrian v/t* (*ge-*, *h*) pick; gather
**Klaue** ['klauə] *f* (-; -*n*) ZO claw; *pl fig* clutches
**klauen** ['klauən] F *v/t* (*ge-*, *h*) pinch
**Klausel** ['klauzəl] *f* (-; -*n*) JUR clause; condition
**Klausur** [klau'zu:ɐ] *f* (-; -*en*) test (paper), exam(ination)
**Klavier** [kla'vi:ɐ] *n* (-*s*; -*e*) MUS piano; ***~ spielen*** play the piano; **~kon,zert** *n* MUS piano concerto; piano recital
**Klebeband** ['kle:bə-] *n* (-[*e*]*s*; -*bänder*) adhesive tape; **kleben** ['kle:bən] (*ge-*, *h*) **1.** *v/t* glue, paste; stick; **2.** *v/i* stick, cling (***an*** *dat* to) (*a. fig*); **klebrig** ['kle:brɪç] *adj* sticky
**Kleb|stoff** ['kle:p-] *m* adhesive; glue; **~streifen** *m* adhesive tape
**kleckern** ['klɛkɐn] F (*ge-*, *h*) **1.** *v/i* make a mess; **2.** *v/t* spill

K

**Klecks** [klɛks] F *m* (*-es*; *-e*) (ink)blot; blob; **klecksen** ['klɛksən] F *v/i* (*ge-*, *h*) blot, make blots
**Klee** [kleː] *m* (*-s*; *no pl*) BOT clover
'**Kleeblatt** *n* cloverleaf
**Kleid** [klait] *n* (*-[e]s*; *-er* ['klaidɐ]) dress; *pl* clothes; **kleiden** ['klaidən] *v/t* (*ge-*, *h*) dress, clothe; ***j-n gut*** ~ suit s.o.; ***sich gut*** *etc* ~ dress well *etc*
**Kleider|bügel** ['klaidɐ-] *m* (coat) hanger; **~bürste** *f* clothes brush; **~haken** *m* coat hook; **~schrank** *m* wardrobe; **~ständer** *m* coat stand; **~stoff** *m* dress material
'**kleidsam** *adj* becoming
'**Kleidung** *f* (*-*; *no pl*) clothes, clothing
'**Kleidungsstück** *n* article of clothing
**Kleie** ['klaiə] *f* (*-*; *-n*) AGR bran
**klein** [klain] *adj* small, *esp* F little (*a. finger*, *brother*); short; ***von ~ auf*** from an early age; ***ein ~ wenig*** a little bit; ***Groß und Klein*** young and old; ***die Kleinen*** the little ones; ***~ schneiden*** cut up (into small pieces)
'**Klein|anzeige** *f* want ad, *Br* small ad; **~bildkamera** *f* 35 mm camera; **~fa|milie** *f* nuclear family; **~geld** *n* (small) change; **~holz** *n* matchwood
**Kleinigkeit** ['klainɪçkait] *f* (*-*; *-en*) little thing, trifle; little something; ***e-e ~ sein*** be nothing, be child's play
'**Kleinkind** *n* baby, infant
'**Kleinkram** F *m* odds and ends
'**kleinlaut** *adj* subdued
'**kleinlich** *adj* small-minded, petty; mean; pedantic, fussy
'**Kleinstadt** *f* small town; '**kleinstädtisch** *adj* small-town, provincial
'**Kleintrans|porter** *m* MOT pick-up
'**Kleinwagen** *m* MOT small *or* compact car, F runabout
**Kleister** ['klaistɐ] *m* (*-s*; *-*) paste
**Klemme** ['klɛmə] *f* (*-*; *-n*) TECH clamp; (hair) clip; F ***in der ~ sitzen*** be in a fix *or* tight spot; '**klemmen** *v/i and v/t* (*ge-*, *h*) jam; stick; be stuck, be jammed; ***sich*** ~ jam one's finger *or* hand
**Klempner** ['klɛmpnɐ] *m* (*-s*; *-*) plumber
**Klepper** ['klɛpɐ] *m* (*-s*; *-*) ZO nag
**Klerus** ['kleːrʊs] *m* (*-*; *no pl*) REL clergy
**Klette** ['klɛtə] *f* (*-*; *-n*) BOT bur(r); *fig* leech
**klettern** ['klɛtɐn] *v/i* (*ge-*, *sein*) climb; ***auf e-n Baum*** ~ climb (up) a tree
'**Kletterpflanze** *f* BOT climber
**Klient** [kli'ɛnt] *m* (*-en*; *-en*), **Kli'entin** *f* (*-*; *-nen*) client
**Klima** ['kliːma] *n* (*-s*; *-s*) climate, *fig a.* atmosphere
'**Klimaanlage** *f* air-conditioning
**klimatisch** [kli'maːtɪʃ] *adj* climatic
**klimpern** ['klɪmpɐn] *v/i* (*ge-*, *h*) jingle, chink (***mit et.*** s.th.); F MUS strum (away) (***auf*** *dat* on)
**Klinge** ['klɪŋə] *f* (*-*; *-n*) blade
**Klingel** ['klɪŋəl] *f* (*-*; *-n*) bell
'**Klingelknopf** *m* bell (push)
'**klingeln** *v/i* (*ge-*, *h*) ring (the bell); ***es klingelt*** the (door)bell is ringing
'**klingen** *v/i* (*irr*, *ge-*, *h*) sound; *bell*, *metal etc*: ring; *glasses etc*: clink
**Klinik** ['kliːnɪk] *f* (*-*; *-en*) hospital; clinic
**klinisch** ['kliːnɪʃ] *adj* clinical
**Klinke** ['klɪŋkə] *f* (*-*; *-n*) (door) handle
**Klippe** ['klɪpə] *f* (*-*; *-n*) cliff, rock(s); *fig* obstacle
**klirren** ['klɪrən] *v/i* (*ge-*, *h*) *window*: rattle; *glasses etc*: clink; *broken glass*: tinkle; *swords*: clash; *keys*, *coins*: jingle
**Klischee** [kli'ʃeː] *n* (*-s*; *-s*) cliché
**klobig** ['kloːbɪç] *adj* bulky, clumsy
**klopfen** ['klɔpfən] (*ge-*, *h*) **1.** *v/i heart etc*: beat, throb; knock (***an*** *acc* at, on); tap; pat; ***es klopft*** there's a knock at the door; **2.** *v/t* beat; knock; drive (*nail etc*)
**Klosett** [klo'zɛt] *n* (*-s*; *-s*) lavatory, toilet; **~brille** *f* toilet seat; **~pa|pier** *n* toilet paper
**Kloß** [kloːs] *m* (*-es*; *Klöße* ['kløːsə]) clod, lump (*a. fig*); GASTR dumpling
**Kloster** ['kloːstɐ] *n* (*-s*; *Klöster* ['kløːstɐ]) REL monastery; convent
**Klotz** [klɔts] *m* (*-es*; *Klötze* ['klœtsə]) block; log
**Klub** [klʊb] *m* (*-s*; *-s*) club
'**Klubsessel** *m* lounge chair
**Kluft** [klʊft] *f* (*-*; *Klüfte* ['klʏftə]) gap (*a. fig*); abyss
**klug** [kluːk] *adj* intelligent, clever, F bright, smart; wise; ***daraus*** (***aus ihm***) ***werde ich nicht*** ~ I don't know what to make of it (him)
'**Klugheit** *f* (*-*; *no pl*) intelligence, cleverness, F brains; good sense; knowledge
**Klumpen** ['klʊmpən] *m* (*-s*; *-*) lump; clod; nugget; '**Klumpfuß** *m* MED club

foot; **'klumpig** *adj* lumpy; cloddish
**knabbern** ['knabɐn] *v/t and v/i* (*ge-*, *h*) nibble, gnaw
**Knabe** ['kna:bə] *m* (*-n*; *-n*) boy
**'knabenhaft** *adj* boyish
**Knäckebrot** ['knɛkə-] *n* crispbread
**knacken** ['knakən] *v/t and v/i* (*ge-*, *h*) crack; *twig*: snap; *fire*, *radio*: crackle
**Knacks** F *m* (*-es*; *-e*) crack; *fig* defect
**Knall** [knal] *m* (*-[e]s*; *-e*) bang; crack, report; pop; F ***e-n ~ haben*** be nuts
**'Knallbon,bon** *m*, *n* cracker
**'knallen** *v/i and v/t* (*ge-*, *h*) bang; slam; crack; pop; F crash (***gegen*** into); F ***j-m e-e ~*** slap s.o.('s face)
**'knallig** F *adj* flashy, loud
**'Knallkörper** *m* firecracker
**knapp** [knap] *adj* scarce; scanty, meager, *Br* meagre (*food, pay etc*); bare (*a. majority etc*); limited (*time etc*); narrow (*escape etc*); tight (*dress etc*); brief; ***~ an Geld*** (***Zeit*** *etc*) short of money (time *etc*); ***mit ~er Not*** only just, barely; ***j-n ~ halten*** keep s.o. short
**Knappe** ['knapə] *m* (*-n*; *-n*) miner
**'Knappheit** *f* (*-*; *no pl*) shortage
**Knarre** ['knarə] *f* (*-*; *-n*) rattle; F gun
**'knarren** *v/i* (*ge-*, *h*) creak
**Knast** [knast] F *m* (*-[e]s*; *Knäste* ['knɛstə]) *sl* clink; **~bruder** F *m* jailbird
**knattern** ['knatɐn] *v/i* (*ge-*, *h*) crackle; MOT roar
**Knäuel** ['knɔʏəl] *m*, *n* (*-s*; *-*) ball; tangle
**Knauf** [knauf] *m* (*-[e]s*; *Knäufe* ['knɔʏfə]) knob; pommel
**knaus(e)rig** ['knauz(ə)rɪç] F *adj* stingy
**knautschen** ['knautʃən] *v/t and v/i* (*ge-*, *h*) crumple
**'Knautschzone** *f* MOT crumple zone
**Knebel** ['kne:bəl] *m* (*-s*; *-*), **'knebeln** *v/t* (*ge-*, *h*) gag (*a. fig*)
**Knecht** [knɛçt] *m* (*-[e]s*; *-e*) farmhand; *fig* slave; **~schaft** *fig f* (*-*; *no pl*) slavery
**kneifen** ['knaifən] *v/t and v/i* (*irr*, *ge-*, *h*) pinch (***j-m in den Arm*** s.o.'s arm); F chicken out; **'Kneifzange** *f* pincers
**Kneipe** ['knaipə] F *f* (*-*; *-n*) saloon, bar, *esp Br* pub
**kneten** ['kne:tən] *v/t* (*ge-*, *h*) knead; mo(u)ld; **'Knetmasse** *f* Plasticine®, Play-Doh®
**Knick** [knɪk] *m* (*-[e]s*; *-e*, *-s*) fold, crease; bend; **'knicken** *v/t* (*ge-*, *h*) fold, crease; bend; break; ***nicht ~!*** do not bend!
**Knicks** [knɪks] *m* (*-es*; *-e*) curts(e)y; ***e-n ~ machen*** → **'knicksen** *v/i* (*ge-*, *h*) curts(e)y (***vor*** *dat* to)
**Knie** [kni:] *n* (*-s*; *-* ['kni:ə, kni:]) ANAT knee; **~beuge** *f* SPORT knee bend; **~kehle** *f* ANAT hollow of the knee
**knien** [kni:n] *v/i* (*ge-*, *h*) kneel, be on one's knees (***vor*** *dat* before)
**'Kniescheibe** *f* ANAT kneecap
**'Kniestrumpf** *m* knee(-length) sock
**kniff** [knɪf] *pret of* ***kneifen***
**Kniff** *m* (*-[e]s*; *-e*) crease, fold; pinch; trick, knack
**kniff(e)lig** ['knɪf(ə)lɪç] *adj* tricky
**knipsen** ['knɪpsən] *v/t and v/i* (*ge-*, *h*) F PHOT take a picture (of); punch, clip
**Knirps** [knɪrps] *m* (*-es*; *-e*) little guy
**knirschen** ['knɪrʃən] *v/i* (*ge-*, *h*) crunch; ***mit den Zähnen ~*** grind *or* gnash one's teeth
**knistern** ['knɪstɐn] *v/i* (*ge-*, *h*) crackle; rustle
**knittern** ['knɪtɐn] *v/t and v/i* (*ge-*, *h*) crumple, crease, wrinkle
**Knoblauch** ['kno:plaux] *m* (*-[e]s*; *no pl*) BOT garlic
**Knöchel** ['knœçəl] *m* (*-s*; *-*) ANAT ankle; knuckle
**Knochen** ['knɔxən] *m* (*-s*; *-*) ANAT bone
**'Knochenbruch** *m* MED fracture
**knochig** ['knɔxɪç] *adj* bony
**Knödel** ['knø:dəl] *m* (*-s*; *-*) dumpling
**Knolle** ['knɔlə] *f* (*-*; *-n*) BOT tuber; bulb
**Knopf** [knɔpf] *m* (*-es*; *Knöpfe* ['knœpfə]), **knöpfen** ['knœpfən] *v/t* (*ge-*, *h*) button
**'Knopfloch** *n* buttonhole
**Knorpel** ['knɔrpəl] *m* (*-s*; *-*) GASTR gristle; ANAT cartilage
**knorrig** ['knɔrɪç] *adj* gnarled, knotted
**Knospe** ['knɔspə] *f* (*-*; *-n*), **'knospen** *v/i* (*ge-*, *h*) BOT bud
**knoten** [kno:tən] *v/t* (*ge-*, *h*) knot, make a knot in; **'Knoten** *m* (*-s*; *-*) knot (*a. fig*); **'Knotenpunkt** *m* center, *Br* centre; RAIL junction
**knüllen** ['knʏlən] *v/t and v/i* (*ge-*, *h*) crumple
**Knüller** ['knʏlɐ] F *m* (*-s*; *-*) smash (hit); scoop
**knüpfen** ['knʏpfən] *v/t* (*ge-*, *h*) tie; weave
**Knüppel** ['knʏpəl] *m* (*-s*; *-*) stick, cudgel; truncheon; **~schaltung** *f* MOT floor shift

**knurren** ['knʊrən] *v/i* (*ge-*, *h*) growl, snarl; *fig* grumble (**über** *acc* at); *stomach*: rumble
**knusp(e)rig** ['knʊsp(ə)rɪç] *adj* crisp, crunchy
**knutschen** ['knu:tʃən] F *v/i* (*ge-*, *h*) pet, neck, smooch
**k.o.** [ka:'ʔo:] *adj* knocked out; *fig* beat
**Kobold** ['ko:bɔlt] *m* (-[*e*]*s*; -*e*) (hob)goblin, imp (*a. fig*)
**Koch** [kɔx] *m* (-[*e*]*s*; *Köche* ['kœçə]) cook; chef; **~buch** *n* cookbook, *Br* cookery book
'**kochen** (*ge-*, *h*) **1.** *v/t* cook; boil (*eggs etc*); make (*coffee etc*); **2.** *v/i* cook, do the cooking; boil (*a. fig*); ***gut ~*** be a good cook; F ***vor Wut ~*** boil with rage; ***~d heiß*** boiling hot
**Kocher** ['kɔxɐ] *m* (-*s*; -) ELECTR cooker
**Köchin** ['kœçɪn] *f* (-; -*nen*) cook; chef
'**Koch|löffel** *m* (wooden) spoon; **~nische** *f* kitchenette; **~platte** *f* hotplate; **~salz** *n* common salt; **~topf** *m* saucepan, pot

K

**Köder** ['kø:dɐ] *m* (-*s*; -) bait, decoy (*both a. fig*), lure; '**ködern** *v/t* (*ge-*, *h*) bait, decoy (*both a. fig*)
**Kodex** ['ko:dɛks] *m* (-*es*; -, -*e*) code
**kodieren** [ko'di:rən] *v/t* (*no -ge-*, *h*) (en)code; **Ko'dierung** *f* (-; -*en*) (en-)coding
**Koffein** [kɔfe'i:n] *n* (-*s*; *no pl*) caffeine
**Koffer** ['kɔfɐ] *m* (-*s*; -) (suit)case; trunk; **~radio** *n* portable (radio); **~raum** *m* MOT trunk, *Br* booth
**Kognak** ['kɔnjak] *m* (-*s*; -*s*) (French) brandy, cognac
**Kohl** [ko:l] *m* (-[*e*]*s*; -*e*) BOT cabbage
**Kohle** ['ko:lə] *f* (-; -*n*) coal; ELECTR carbon; F dough
'**Kohlehy,drat** *n* carbohydrate
'**Kohlen...** *in cpds ...dioxid etc*: CHEM carbon ...; **~bergwerk** *n* coalmine, colliery; **~ofen** *m* coal-burning stove
'**Kohlensäure** *f* CHEM carbonic acid; GASTR F fizz; '**kohlensäurehaltig** *adj* carbonated, F fizzy
'**Kohlen|stoff** *m* CHEM carbon; **~wasserstoff** *m* CHEM hydrocarbon
'**Kohle|pa,pier** *n* carbon paper; **~zeichnung** *f* charcoal drawing
'**Kohlkopf** *m* BOT (head of) cabbage
**Kohlrabi** [-'ra:bi] *m* (-*s*; -*s*) BOT kohlrabi
**Koje** ['ko:jə] *f* (-; -*n*) MAR berth, bunk
**Kokain** [koka'i:n] *n* (-*s*; *no pl*) cocaine
**kokett** [ko'kɛt] *adj* coquettish
**kokettieren** [kokɛ'ti:rən] *v/i* (*no -ge-*, *h*) flirt; *fig* ***~ mit*** toy with
**Kokosnuss** ['ko:kɔs-] *f* BOT coconut
**Koks** [ko:ks] *m* (-*es*; *no pl*) coke; F dough; *sl* coke, snow
**Kolben** ['kɔlbən] *m* (-*s*; -) butt; TECH piston; **~stange** *f* TECH piston rod
**Kolibri** ['ko:libri] *m* (-*s*; -*s*) ZO humming bird
**Kolleg** [kɔ'le:k] *n* (-*s*; -*s*) UNIV course (of lectures)
**Kollege** [kɔ'le:gə] *m* (-*n*; -*n*), **Kol'legin** *f* (-; -*nen*) colleague
**Kollegium** [kɔ'le:gjʊm] *n* (-*s*; -*ien*) UNIV faculty, *Br* teaching staff
**Kollekte** [kɔ'lɛktə] *f* (-; -*n*) REL collection
**Kollektion** [kɔlɛk'tsjo:n] *f* (-; -*en*) ECON collection; range
**kollektiv** [kɔlɛk'ti:f] *adj*, **Kollek'tiv** *n* (-*s*; -*e*) collective (*a. in cpds*)
**Koller** ['kɔlɐ] F *m* (-*s*; -) fit; rage
**kollidieren** [kɔli'di:rən] *v/i* (*no -ge-*, *sein*) collide; **Kollision** [kɔli'zjo:n] *f* (-; -*en*) collision, *fig a.* clash, conflict
**Kölnischwasser** ['kœlnɪʃ-] *n* (-*s*; -) (eau de) cologne
**Kolonie** [kolo'ni:] *f* (-; -*n*) colony
**kolonisieren** [koloni'zi:rən] *v/t* (*no -ge-*, *h*) colonize; **Koloni'sierung** *f* (-; -*en*) colonization
**Kolonne** [ko'lɔnə] *f* (-; -*n*) column; MIL convoy; gang, crew
**Koloss** [ko'lɔs] *m* (-*es*; -*e*) colossus, *fig a.* giant (of a man)
**kolossal** [kolɔ'sa:l] *adj* gigantic
**Kombi** ['kɔmbi] *m* (-[*s*]; -*s*) MOT station wagon, *Br* estate (car)
**Kombination** [kɔmbina'tsjo:n] *f* (-; -*en*) combination; set; coveralls, *Br* overalls; flying suit; *soccer*: combined move
**kombinieren** [kɔmbi'ni:rən] (*no -ge-*, *h*) **1.** *v/t* combine; **2.** *v/i* reason
**Kombüse** [kɔm'by:zə] *f* (-; -*n*) MAR galley
**Komet** [ko'me:t] *m* (-*en*; -*en*) ASTR comet
**Komfort** [kɔm'fo:ɐ] *m* (-*s*; *no pl*) (modern) conveniences; luxury
**komfortabel** [kɔmfɔr'ta:bəl] *adj* comfortable; well-appointed; luxurious
**Komik** ['ko:mɪk] *f* (-; *no pl*) humo(u)r; comic effect; **Komiker** ['ko:mikɐ] *m*

(-*s*; -) comedian; **komisch** ['ko:mɪʃ] *adj* comic(al), funny; strange, odd
**Komitee** [komi'te:] *n* (-*s*; -*s*) committee
**Komma** ['kɔma] *n* (-*s*; -*s*, -*ta*) comma; ***sechs ~ vier*** six point four
**Kommandant** [kɔman'dant] *m* (-*en*; -*en*), **Kommandeur** [kɔman'dø:ɐ] *m* (-*s*; -*e*) MIL commander, commanding officer; **kommandieren** [kɔman'di:rən] *v/i and v/t* (*no -ge-, h*) command, be in command of; **Kommando** [kɔ'mando] *n* (-*s*; -*s*) command; order; MIL commando; **Komm'mandobrücke** *f* MAR (navigating) bridge
**kommen** ['kɔmən] *v/i* (*irr, ge-, sein*) come; arrive; get; reach; ***zu spät ~*** be late; ***weit ~*** get far; ***zur Schule ~*** start school; ***ins Gefängnis ~*** go to jail; ***~ lassen*** send for *s.o.*, call *s.o.*; order *s.th.*; ***~ auf*** (*acc*) think of, hit upon; remember; ***hinter et. ~*** find s.th. out; ***um et. ~*** lose s.th.; miss s.th.; ***zu et. ~*** come by s.th.; ***wieder zu sich ~*** come round *or* to; ***wohin kommt ...?*** where does ... go?; ***daher kommt es, dass*** that's why; ***woher kommt es, dass ...?*** why is it that ...?, F how come ...?
**Kommentar** [kɔmɛn'ta:ɐ] *m* (-*s*; -*e*) commentary; ***kein ~!*** no comment
**Kommentator** [kɔmɛn'ta:to:ɐ] *m* (-*s*; -*en* [-ta'to:rən]), **Kommentatorin** [-ta'to:rɪn] *f* (-; -*nen*) commentator
**kommentieren** [kɔmɛn'ti:rən] *v/t* (*no -ge-, h*) comment (on)
**kommerzialisieren** [kɔmɛrtsjali'zi:rən] *v/t* (*no -ge-, h*) commercialize
**Kommissar** [kɔmɪ'sa:ɐ] *m* (-*s*; -*e*) commissioner; superintendent
**Kommission** [kɔmɪ'sjo:n] *f* (-; -*en*) commission; committee
**Kommode** [kɔ'mo:də] *f* (-; -*n*) bureau, *Br* chest (of drawers)
**Kommunal...** [kɔmu'na:l-] *in cpds ...politik etc*: local ...; **Kommune** [kɔ'mu:nə] *f* (-; -*n*) commune
**Kommunikation** [kɔmunika'tsjo:n] *f* (-; *no pl*) communication
**Kommunion** [kɔmu'njo:n] *f* (-; -*en*) REL (Holy) Communion
**Kommunismus** [kɔmu'nɪsmʊs] *m* (-; *no pl*) POL communism; **Kommunist** [kɔmu'nɪst] *m* (-*en*; -*en*), **Kommu'nistin** *f* (-; -*nen*), **kommu'nistisch** *adj* POL communist
**Komödie** [ko'mø:djə] *f* (-; -*n*) comedy; ***~ spielen*** put on an act, play-act
**kompakt** [kɔm'pakt] *adj* compact
**Kom'paktanlage** *f* stereo system, music center (*Br* centre)
**Kompanie** [kɔmpa'ni:] *f* (-; -*n*) MIL company
**Kompass** ['kɔmpas] *m* (-*es*; -*e*) compass
**kompatibel** [kɔmpa'ti:bəl] *adj* compatible (*a.* EDP)
**komplett** [kɔm'plɛt] *adj* complete
**Komplex** [kɔm'plɛks] *m* (-*es*; -*e*) complex (*a.* PSYCH)
**Kompliment** [kɔmpli'mɛnt] *n* (-[*e*]*s*; -*e*) compliment; ***j-m ein ~ machen*** pay s.o. a compliment
**Komplize** [kɔm'pli:tsə] *m* (-*n*; -*n*) accomplice
**komplizieren** [kɔmpli'tsi:rən] *v/t* (*no -ge-, h*) complicate; **kompliziert** [kɔmpli'tsi:ɐt] *adj* complicated, complex
**Kom'plizin** *f* (-; -*nen*) accomplice
**Komplott** [kɔm'plɔt] *n* (-[*e*]*s*; -*e*) plot, conspiracy
**komponieren** [kɔmpo'ni:rən] *v/t and v/i* (*no -ge-, h*) MUS compose; write; **Komponist** [kɔmpo'nɪst] *m* (-*en*; -*en*) MUS composer; **Komposition** [kɔmpozi'tsjo:n] *f* (-; -*en*) MUS composition
**Kompott** [kɔm'pɔt] *n* (-[*e*]*s*; -*e*) GASTR compot(e), stewed fruit
**Kompresse** [kɔm'prɛsə] *f* (-; -*n*) MED compress
**komprimieren** [kɔmpri'mi:rən] *v/t* (*no -ge-, h*) compress
**Kompromiss** [kɔmpro'mɪs] *m* (-*es*; -*e*) compromise; **kompro'misslos** *adj* uncompromising
**kompromittieren** [kɔmpromɪ'ti:rən] *v/t* (*no -ge-, h*) compromise (***sich*** o.s.); **~d** *adj* compromising
**Kondensator** [kɔndɛn'za:to:ɐ] *m* (-*s*; -*en* [-za'to:rən]) ELECTR capacitor; TECH condenser; **kondensieren** [kɔndɛn'zi:rən] *v/t* (*no -ge-, h*) condense
**Kondensmilch** [kɔn'dɛns-] *f* condensed milk
**Kondition** [kɔndi'tsjo:n] *f* (-; -*en*) a) condition, b) (*no pl*) SPORT condition, shape, form; ***gute ~*** (great) stamina
**konditional** [kɔnditsjo'na:l] *adj* LING conditional
**Konditi'onstraining** *n* fitness training

K

**Konditor** [kɔn'diːtoːɐ] *m* (*-s*; *-en* [-di'toː-rən]) confectioner, pastrycook
**Konditorei** [kɔndito'rai] *f* (-; *-en*) cake shop; café, tearoom; **~waren** *pl* confectionery
**Kondom** [kɔn'doːm] *n*, *m* (*-s*; *-e*) condom
**Kondukteur** [kɔndʊk'tøːɐ] *Swiss m* (*-s*; *-e*) → ***Schaffner***
**Konfekt** [kɔn'fɛkt] *n* (*-[e]s*; *-e*) sweets, chocolates
**Konfektion** [kɔnfɛk'tsjoːn] *f* (-; *no pl*) ready-made clothing; **Konfekti'ons...** *in cpds* ready-made ..., off-the-peg ...
**Konferenz** [kɔnfe'rɛnts] *f* (-; *-en*) conference
**Konfession** [kɔnfɛ'sjoːn] *f* (-; *-en*) religion, denomination; **konfessionell** [kɔnfɛsjo'nɛl] *adj* confessional, denominational; **Konfessi'onsschule** *f* denominational school
**Konfirmand** [kɔnfɪr'mant] *m* (*-en*; *-en*), **Konfir'mandin** *f* (-; *-nen*) REL confirmand; **Konfirmation** [kɔnfɪrma'tsjoːn] *f* (-; *-en*) REL confirmation; **konfirmieren** [kɔnfɪr'miːrən] *v/t* (*no -ge-*, *h*) confirm
**konfiszieren** [kɔnfɪs'tsiːrən] *v/t* (*no -ge-*, *h*) JUR confiscate
**Konfitüre** [kɔnfi'tyːrə] *f* (-; *-n*) jam
**Konflikt** [kɔn'flɪkt] *m* (*-[e]s*; *-e*) conflict
**konfrontieren** [kɔnfrɔn'tiːrən] *v/t* (*no -ge-*, *h*) confront
**konfus** [kɔn'fuːs] *adj* confused, mixed-up
**Kongress** [kɔn'grɛs] *m* (*-es*; *-e*) convention, *Br* congress
**König** ['køːnɪç] *m* (*-s*; *-e*) king
**Königin** ['køːnɪgɪn] *f* (-; *-nen*) queen
**königlich** ['køːnɪklɪç] *adj* royal
**Königreich** ['køːnɪk-] *n* kingdom
**Konjugation** [kɔnjuga'tsjoːn] *f* (-; *-en*) LING conjugation; **konjugieren** [kɔnju'giːrən] *v/t* (*no -ge-*, *h*) LING conjugate
**Konjunktiv** ['kɔnjʊŋktiːf] *m* (*-s*; *-e*) LING subjunctive (mood)
**Konjunktur** [kɔnjʊŋk'tuːɐ] *f* (-; *-en*) economic situation
**konkret** [kɔn'kreːt] *adj* concrete
**Konkurrent** [kɔnkʊ'rɛnt] *m* (*-en*; *-en*), **Konkur'rentin** *f* (-; *-nen*) competitor, rival; **Konkurrenz** [kɔnkʊ'rɛnts] *f* (-; *no pl*) competition; ***die ~*** one's competitors; ***außer ~*** not competing; → ***konkurrenzlos***
**konkur'renzfähig** *adj* competitive
**Konkur'renzkampf** *m* competition
**konkur'renzlos** *adj* without competition, unrival(l)ed
**konkurrieren** [kɔnkʊ'riːrən] *v/i* (*no -ge-*, *h*) compete
**Konkurs** [kɔn'kʊrs] *m* (*-es*; *-e*) ECON, JUR bankruptcy; ***in ~ gehen*** go bankrupt; **~masse** *f* JUR bankrupt's estate
**können** ['kœnən] *v/t and v/i* (*irr*, *ge-*, *h*), *v/aux* (*irr*, *no -ge-*, *h*) can, be able to; may, be allowed to; ***kann ich gehen etc?*** can *or* may I go *etc?*; ***du kannst nicht*** you cannot *or* can't; ***ich kann nicht mehr*** I can't go on; I can't manage *or* eat any more; ***es kann sein*** it may be; ***ich kann nichts dafür*** it's not my fault; ***e-e Sprache ~*** know *or* speak a language
**'Können** *n* (*-s*; *no pl*) ability, skill
**Könner** ['kœnɐ] *m* (*-s*; -), **'Könnerin** *f* (-; *-nen*) master, expert; *esp* SPORT ace, crack
**konnte** ['kɔntə] *pret of* ***können***
**konsequent** [kɔnze'kvɛnt] *adj* consistent; **Konsequenz** [kɔnze'kvɛnts] *f* (-; *-en*) a) (*no pl*) consistency, b) consequence
**konservativ** [kɔnzɛrva'tiːf] *adj* conservative
**Konserven** [kɔn'zɛrvən] *pl* canned (*Br a.* tinned) foods; **~büchse** *f*, **~dose** *f* can, *Br a.* tin; **~fa,brik** *f* cannery
**konservieren** [kɔnzɛr'viːrən] *v/t* (*no -ge-*, *h*) preserve; **Konser'vierungsmittel** *n* preservative
**Konsonant** [kɔnzo'nant] *m* (*-en*; *-en*) LING consonant
**konstruieren** [kɔnstru'iːrən] *v/t* (*no -ge-*, *h*) construct; design
**Konstrukteur** [kɔnstrʊk'tøːɐ] *m* (*-s*; *-e*) TECH designer; **Konstruktion** [kɔnstrʊk'tsjoːn] *f* (-; *-en*) construction
**Konsul** ['kɔnzʊl] *m* (*-s*; *-n*) consul
**Konsulat** [kɔnzu'laːt] *n* (*-[e]s*; *-e*) consulate
**konsultieren** [kɔnzʊl'tiːrən] *v/t* (*no -ge-*, *h*) consult
**Konsum**[1] [kɔn'zuːm] *m* (*-s*; *no pl*) consumption
**Konsum**[2] ['kɔnzuːm] *m* (*-s*; *-s*) cooperative (society *or* store), F co-op
**Konsument** [kɔnzu'mɛnt] *m* (*-en*; *-en*), **Konsu'mentin** *f* (-; *-nen*) consumer;

**Kon'sumgesellschaft** *f* consumer society; **konsumieren** [kɔnzu'miːrən] *v/t* (*no -ge-*, *h*) consume
**Kontakt** [kɔn'takt] *m* (-[*e*]*s*; -*e*) contact (*a.* ELECTR); ~ ***aufnehmen*** get in touch; ~ ***haben*** *or* ***in*** ~ ***stehen mit*** be in contact *or* touch with; ***den*** ~ ***verlieren*** lose touch; **kon'taktfreudig** *adj* sociable
**Kon'taktlinsen** *pl* OPT contact lenses
**Konter** ['kɔntɐ] *m* (-*s*; -), **'kontern** *v/i* (*ge-*, *h*) counter (*a. fig*)
**Kontinent** [kɔnti'nɛnt] *m* (-[*e*]*s*; -*e*) continent
**Konto** ['kɔnto] *n* (-*s*; *Konten*) account
**'Kontoauszug** *m* (bank) statement
**Kontrast** [kɔn'trast] *m* (-[*e*]*s*; -*e*) contrast (*a.* PHOT, TV *etc*)
**Kontrolle** [kɔn'trɔlə] *f* (-; -*n*) control; supervision; check(up)
**Kontrolleur** [kɔntrɔ'løːɐ] *m* (-*s*; -*e*), **Kontrol'leurin** *f* (-; -*nen*) inspector, RAIL *a.* conductor
**kontrollieren** [kɔntrɔ'liːrən] *v/t* (*no -ge-*, *h*) check; check up on *s.o.*; control
**Kon'trollpunkt** *m* checkpoint
**Kontroverse** [kɔntro'vɛrzə] *f* (-; -*n*) controversy
**konventionell** [kɔnvɛntsjo'nɛl] *adj* conventional
**Konversation** [kɔnvɛrza'tsjoːn] *f* (-; -*en*) conversation; **Konversati'onslexikon** *n* encyclop(a)edia
**Konzentration** [kɔntsɛntra'tsjoːn] *f* (-; -*en*) concentration
**Konzentrati'onslager** *n* concentration camp
**konzentrieren** [kɔntsɛn'triːrən] *v/t and v/refl* (*no -ge-*, *h*) concentrate; ***sich auf et.*** ~ concentrate on s.th.
**Konzept** [kɔn'tsɛpt] *n* (-[*e*]*s*; -*e*) (rough) draft; conception; ***j-n aus dem*** ~ ***bringen*** put s.o. out
**Konzern** [kɔn'tsɛrn] *m* (-[*e*]*s*; -*e*) ECON combine, group
**Konzert** [kɔn'tsɛrt] *n* (-[*e*]*s*; -*e*) MUS concert; concerto; **~halle** *f*, **~saal** *m* concert hall, auditorium
**Konzession** [kɔntsɛ'sjoːn] *f* (-; -*en*) concession; license, *Br* licence
**Kopf** [kɔpf] *m* (-[*e*]*s*; *Köpfe* ['kœpfə]) head (*a. fig*); top; *fig a.* brains, mind; ~ ***hoch!*** chin up!; ***j-m über den*** ~ ***wachsen*** outgrow s.o.; *fig* be too much for s.o.; ***sich den*** ~ ***zerbrechen*** (***über*** *acc*) rack one's brains (over); ***sich et. aus dem*** ~ ***schlagen*** put s.th. out of one's mind; ~ ***an*** ~ neck and neck; **~ball** *m* SPORT header; headed goal; **~bedeckung** *f* headgear; ***ohne*** ~ bareheaded
**köpfen** ['kœpfən] *v/t* (*ge-*, *h*) behead, decapitate; SPORT head (***ins Tor*** home)
**'Kopf|ende** *n* head; **~hörer** *pl* headphones; **~jäger** *m* headhunter; **~kissen** *n* pillow
**'kopflos** *adj* headless; *fig* panicky
**'Kopf|rechnen** *n* mental arithmetic; **~sa,lat** *m* BOT lettuce; **~schmerzen** *pl* headache; **~sprung** *m* SPORT header; **~stand** *m* SPORT headstand; **~tuch** *n* scarf, (head)kerchief
**kopf'über** *adv* headfirst (*a. fig*)
**'Kopfweh** *n* → ***Kopfschmerzen***
**'Kopfzerbrechen** *n*: ***j-m*** ~ ***machen*** give s.o. a headache
**Kopie** [ko'piː] *f* (-; -*n*), **ko'pieren** *v/t* (*no -ge-*, *h*) copy; **Kopiergerät** [ko'piːɐ-] *n* copier; **Ko'pierstift** *m* indelible pencil
**Koppel**[1] ['kɔpəl] *f* (-; -*n*) paddock
**'Koppel**[2] *n* (-*s*; -) MIL belt
**'koppeln** *v/t* (*ge-*, *h*) couple; dock
**Koralle** [ko'ralə] *f* (-; -*n*) ZO coral
**Korb** [kɔrp] *m* (-[*e*]*s*; *Körbe* ['kœrbə]) basket; **~möbel** *pl* wicker furniture
**Kord** [kɔrt] *m* (-[*e*]*s*; -*e*) corduroy
**Kordel** ['kɔrdəl] *f* (-; -*n*) cord
**'Kordhose** *f* corduroys
**Korinthe** [ko'rɪntə] *f* (-; -*n*) currant
**Kork** [kɔrk] *m* (-[*e*]*s*; -*e*) BOT cork
**'Korkeiche** *f* BOT cork oak
**Korken** ['kɔrkən] *m* (-*s*; -) cork; **~zieher** [-tsiːɐ] *m* (-*s*; -) corkscrew
**Korn**[1] [kɔrn] *n* (-[*e*]*s*; *Körner* ['kœrnɐ]) BOT a) grain; seed, b) (*no pl*) grain, *Br a.* corn, c) (*pl* -*e*) TECH front sight
**Korn**[2] F *m* (-[*e*]*s*; -*e*) (grain) schnapps
**körnig** ['kœrnɪç] *adj* grainy
**Körper** ['kœrpɐ] *m* (-*s*; -) body (*a.* PHYS, CHEM ), MATH *a.* solid; **~bau** *m* (-[*e*]*s*; *no pl*) build, physique
**'körperbehindert** *adj* (physically) disabled *or* handicapped
**'Körper|geruch** *m* body odo(u)r, BO; **~größe** *f* height; **~kraft** *f* physical strength
**'körperlich** *adj* physical
**'Körperpflege** *f* personal hygiene

**'Körperschaft** *f* (-; *-en*) corporation, (corporate) body
**'Körper|teil** *m* part of the body; **~verletzung** *f* JUR bodily injury
**korrekt** [kɔ'rɛkt] *adj* correct
**Korrektur** [kɔrɛk'tu:ɐ] *f* (-; *-en*) correction; PED *etc* grading, *Br* marking
**Korrespondent** [kɔrɛspɔn'dɛnt] *m* (*-en*; *-en*), **Korrespon'dentin** *f* (-; *-nen*) correspondent; **Korrespondenz** [-'dɛnts] *f* (-; *-en*) correspondence; **korrespondieren** [-'di:rən] *v/i* (*no -ge-*, *h*) correspond (***mit*** with)
**Korridor** ['kɔrido:ɐ] *m* (*-s*; *-e*) corridor; hall
**korrigieren** [kɔri'gi:rən] *v/t* (*no -ge-*, *h*) correct; PED *etc* grade, *Br* mark
**korrupt** [kɔ'rʊpt] *adj* corrupt(ed)
**Korruption** [kɔrʊp'tsjo:n] *f* (-; *-en*) corruption
**Korsett** [kɔr'zɛt] *n* (*-s*; *-s*) corset (*a. fig*)
**Kosename** ['ko:zə-] *m* pet name
**Kosmetik** [kɔs'me:tɪk] *f* (-; *no pl*) beauty culture; cosmetics, toiletries
**Kosmetikerin** [kɔs'me:tikərɪn] *f* (-; *-nen*) beautician, cosmetician
**Kost** [kɔst] *f* (-; *no pl*) food, diet; board
**'kostbar** *adj* precious, valuable; costly
**'Kostbarkeit** *f* (-; *-en*) precious object, treasure (*a. fig*)
**kosten**[1] ['kɔstən] *v/t* (*ge-*, *h*) cost, be; *fig* take (*time etc*); ***was*** *or* ***wie viel kostet ...?*** how much is ...?
**'kosten**[2] *v/t* (*ge-*, *h*) taste, try
**'Kosten** *pl* cost(s); price; expenses; charges; ***auf j-s ~*** at s.o.'s expense
**'kostenlos 1.** *adj* free; **2.** *adv* free of charge
**köstlich** ['kœstlɪç] *adj* delicious; *fig* priceless; ***sich ~ amüsieren*** have great fun, F have a ball
**'Kostprobe** *f* taste, sample (*a. fig*)
**'kostspielig** *adj* expensive, costly
**Kostüm** [kɔs'ty:m] *n* (*-s*; *-e*) costume, dress; suit; **~fest** *n* fancy-dress ball
**Kot** [ko:t] *m* (*-[e]s*; *no pl*) excrement, ZO *a.* droppings
**Kotelett** [kotə'lɛt] *n* (*-s*; *-s*) chop, cutlet
**Koteletten** [kotə'lɛtən] *pl* sideburns
**'Kotflügel** *m* MOT fender, *Br* wing
**kotzen** ['kɔtsən] V *v/i* (*ge-*, *h*) puke
**Krabbe** ['krabə] *f* (-; *-n*) ZO shrimp; prawn
**krabbeln** ['krabəln] *v/i* (*ge-*, *sein*) crawl
**Krach** [krax] *m* (*-[e]s*; *Kräche* ['krɛçə]) a) crash, bang, b) (*no pl*) noise, c) F quarrel, fight
**'krachen** *v/i* (*ge-*, *h*) crack, bang, crash
**Kracher** ['kraxɐ] *m* (*-s*; -) (fire)cracker
**krächzen** ['krɛçtsən] *v/t and v/i* (*ge-*, *h*) croak
**Kraft** [kraft] *f* (-; *Kräfte* ['krɛftə]) strength, force (*a.* POL), power (*a.* ELECTR, TECH, POL); ***in ~ sein*** (***setzen, treten***) JUR *etc* be in (put into, come into) force; **~brühe** *f* GASTR consommé, clear soup; **~fahrer(in)** driver, motorist; **~fahrzeug** *n* motor vehicle
**kräftig** ['krɛftɪç] *adj* strong (*a. fig*), powerful; substantial (*food*); good
**'kraftlos** *adj* weak, feeble
**'Kraft|probe** *f* test of strength; **~stoff** *m* MOT fuel; **~verschwendung** *f* waste of energy; **~werk** *n* power station
**Kragen** ['kra:gən] *m* (*-s*; -) collar
**Krähe** ['krɛ:ə] *f* (-; *-n*) ZO crow
**krähen** ['krɛ:ən] *v/i* (*ge-*, *h*) crow
**Krake** ['kra:kə] *m* (*-n*; *-n*) ZO octopus
**Kralle** ['kralə] *f* (-; *-n*) ZO claw (*a. fig*)
**'krallen** *v/refl* (*ge-*, *h*) cling (***an*** *acc* on), clutch (at)
**Kram** [kra:m] F *m* (*-[e]s*; *no pl*) stuff, (one's) things
**Krampf** [krampf] *m* (*-[e]s*; *Krämpfe* ['krɛmpfə]) MED cramp; spasm, convulsion; **~ader** *f* MED varicose vein
**'krampfhaft** *fig adj* forced (*smile etc*); desperate (*attempt etc*)
**Kran** [kra:n] *m* (*-[e]s*; *Kräne* ['krɛ:nə]) TECH crane
**Kranich** ['kra:nɪç] *m* (*-s*; *-e*) ZO crane
**krank** [kraŋk] *adj* ill, sick; ***~ werden*** get sick, *Br* fall ill; **'Kranke** *m, f* (*-n*; *-n*) sick person, patient; ***die ~n*** the sick
**kränken** ['krɛŋkən] *v/t* (*ge-*, *h*) hurt (*s.o.'s* feelings), offend
**'Kranken|bett** *n* sickbed; **~geld** *n* sickness benefit; **~gym,nastik** *f* physiotherapy; **~haus** *n* hospital; **~kasse** *f* health insurance scheme; ***in e-r ~ sein*** be a member of a health insurance scheme *or* plan; **~pflege** *f* nursing; **~pfleger** *m* male nurse; **~schein** *m* health insurance certificate; **~schwester** *f* nurse; **~versicherung** *f* health insurance; **~wagen** *m* ambulance; **~zimmer** *n* sickroom

'**krankhaft** *adj* morbid (*a. fig*)
'**Krankheit** *f* (-; *-en*) illness, sickness, disease
'**Krankheitsserreger** *m* germ
**kränklich** ['krɛŋklɪç] *adj* sickly, ailing
**Kränkung** ['krɛŋkʊŋ] *f* (-; *-en*) insult, offense, *Br* offence
**Kranz** [krants] *m* (*-es*; *Kränze* ['krɛntsə]) wreath; *fig* ring, circle
**krass** [kras] *adj* crass, gross; blunt
**Krater** ['kra:tɐ] *m* (*-s*; -) crater
**kratzen** ['kratsən] *v/t and v/refl* (*ge-*, *h*) scratch (o.s.); scrape (***von*** off)
**Kratzer** ['kratsɐ] *m* (*-s*; -) scratch (*a.* MED)
**kraulen**['kraulən] **1.** *v/t* (*ge-*, *h*) stroke; run one's fingers through; **2.** *v/i* (*ge-*, *sein*) SPORT do the crawl
**kraus** [kraus] *adj* curly (*hair*); wrinkled
**Krause** ['krauzə] *f* (-; *-n*) ruff; friz(z)
**kräuseln** ['krɔʏzəln] *v/t and v/refl* (*ge-*, *h*) curl, friz(z); *water*: ripple
**Kraut** [kraut] *n* (*-[e]s*; *Kräuter* ['krɔʏtɐ]) BOT herb; tops, leaves; cabbage
**Krawall** [kra'val] *m* (*-s*; *-e*) riot; F row, racket
**Krawatte** [kra'vatə] *f* (-; *-n*) tie
**kreativ** [krea'ti:f] *adj* creative
**Kreativität** [kreativi'tɛ:t] *f* (-; *no pl*) creativity
**Kreatur** [krea'tu:ɐ] *f* (-; *-en*) creature
**Krebs** [kre:ps] *m* ZO crayfish; MED cancer; AST Cancer; ***sie ist*** (***ein***) ~ she's (a) Cancer; ~ ***erregend*** MED carcinogenic
**Krebs...** MED cancerous; **~geschwulst** *f* MED carcinoma; **~kranke** *m, f* cancer patient
**Kredit** [kre'di:t] *m* (*-[e]s*; *-e*) ECON credit; loan; **~hai** *m* loan shark; **~karte** *f* credit card, *pl coll* F plastic money
**Kreide** ['kraidə] *f* (-; *-n*) chalk; crayon
**Kreis** [krais] *m* (*-es*; *-e*) circle (*a. fig*); POL district, county; **~bahn** *f* AST orbit
**kreischen** ['kraiʃən] *v/i* (*ge-*, *h*) screech; squeal
**Kreisel** ['kraizəl] *m* (*-s*; -) (spinning) top; PHYS gyro(scope); '**kreiseln** *v/i* (*ge-*, *h*, *sein*) spin around
**kreisen** ['kraizən] *v/i* (*ge-*, *h*, *sein*) (move in a) circle, revolve, rotate; circulate
'**kreisförmig** [-fœrmɪç] *adj* circular
'**Kreislauf** *m* MED, ECON circulation; BIOL cycle (*a. fig*), TECH, ELECTR *a.* circuit; **~störungen** *pl* MED circulatory trouble
'**Kreis|säge** *f* circular saw; **~verkehr** *m* traffic circle, *Br* roundabout
**Krempe** ['krɛmpə] *f* (-; *-n*) brim
**Kren** [kre:n] *Austrian m* (*-[e]s*; *no pl*) GASTR horseradish
**Krepp** [krɛp] *m* (*-s*; *-s*) crepe
**Kreuz** [krɔʏts] *n* (*-es*; *-e*) cross (*a. fig*); ANAT (small of the) back; *cards*: club(s); MUS sharp; ***über*** ~ crosswise; F ***j-n aufs*** ~ ***legen*** take s.o. in; **kreuzen** ['krɔʏtsən] **1.** *v/t and v/refl* (*ge-*, *h*) cross; clash; **2.** *v/i* (*ge-*, *sein*) MAR cruise
**Kreuzer** ['krɔʏtsɐ] *m* (*-s*; -) MAR cruiser
'**Kreuzfahrer** *m* HIST crusader
'**Kreuzfahrt** *f* MAR cruise
**kreuzigen** ['krɔʏtsɪgən] *v/t* (*ge-*, *h*) crucify; '**Kreuzigung** *f* (-; *-en*) crucifixion
'**Kreuzotter** *f* ZO adder
'**Kreuzschmerzen** *pl* backache
'**Kreuzung** *f* (-; *-en*) RAIL, MOT crossing, junction; intersection, crossroads; BIOL cross(breed)ing; cross(breed); *fig* cross
'**Kreuzverhör** *n* JUR cross-examination; ***ins*** ~ ***nehmen*** cross-examine
'**kreuzweise** *adv* crosswise, crossways
'**Kreuz|worträtsel** *n* crossword (puzzle); **~zug** HIST *m* crusade
**kriechen** ['kri:çən] *v/i* (*irr*, *ge-*, *sein*) creep, crawl; *fig* ***vor j-m*** ~ toady to s.o.
**Kriecher** ['kri:çɐ] *contp m* (*-s*; -) toady
'**Kriechspur** *f* MOT slow lane
**Krieg** [kri:k] *m* (*-[e]s*; *-e* ['kri:gə]) war; ~ ***führen gegen*** be at war with
**kriegen** ['kri:gən] F *v/t* (*ge-*, *h*) get; catch
**Krieger** ['kri:gɐ] *m* (*-s*; -) warrior
'**Kriegerdenkmal** *n* war memorial
**kriegerisch** ['kri:gərɪʃ] *adj* warlike, martial
'**Kriegführung** *f* (-; *no pl*) warfare
'**Kriegs|beil** *fig n*: ***das*** ~ ***begraben*** bury the hatchet; **~dienstverweigerer** *m* (*-s*; -) conscientious objector; **~erklärung** *f* declaration of war; **~gefangene** *m* prisoner of war, P.O.W.; **~gefangenschaft** *f* captivity; **~recht** *n* JUR martial law; **~schauplatz** *m* theater (*Br* theatre) of war; **~schiff** *n* warship; **~teilnehmer** *m* (war) veteran, *Br* ex-serviceman; **~treiber** [-traibɐ] *m* (*-s*; -) POL warmonger; **~verbrechen** *n* war crime; **~verbrecher** *m* war criminal
**Krimi** ['kri:mi] F *m* (*-s*; *-s*) (crime) thriller, detective novel

**Kriminal|beamte** [krimi'na:l-] *m* detective, plain-clothesman; **~polizei** *f* criminal investigation department; **~roman** *m* → ***Krimi***
**kriminell** [krimi'nɛl] *adj*, **Krimi'nelle** *m, f (-n; -n)* criminal
**Krippe** ['krɪpə] *f (-; -n)* crib, manger (*a.* REL); REL crèche, *Br* crib
**Krise** ['kri:zə] *f (-; -n)* crisis
**'Krisenherd** *m esp* POL trouble spot
**Kristall¹** [krɪs'tal] *m (-s; -e)* crystal
**Kris'tall²** *n (-s; no pl)*, **~glas** *n* crystal
**kristallisieren** [krɪstali'zi:rən] *v/i and v/refl (no -ge-, h)* crystallize
**Kriterium** [kri'te:rjʊm] *n (-s; -ien)* criterion (***für*** of)
**Kritik** [kri'ti:k] *f (-; -en)* criticism; THEA, MUS *etc* review, critique; ***gute ~en*** a good press; ***~ üben an*** (*dat*) criticize; **Kritiker(in)** ['kri:tikɐ (-kərɪn)] *(-s; -/-; -nen)* critic; **kri'tiklos** *adj* uncritical; **kritisch** ['kri:tɪʃ] *adj* critical (*a. fig*) (***gegenüber*** of); **kritisieren** [kriti'zi:rən] *v/t (no -ge-, h)* criticize
**kritzeln** ['krɪtsəln] *v/t and v/i (ge-, h)* scrawl, scribble
**kroch** [krɔx] *pret of* ***kriechen***
**Krokodil** [kroko'di:l] *n (-s; -e)* ZO crocodile
**Krone** ['kro:nə] *f (-; -n)* crown; coronet
**krönen** ['krø:nən] *v/t (ge-, h)* crown; ***j-n zum König ~*** crown s.o. king
**'Kronleuchter** *m* chandelier
**'Kronprinz** *m* crown prince
**'Kronprin,zessin** *f* crown princess
**'Krönung** *f (-; -en)* coronation; *fig* crowning event, climax, high point
**Kropf** [krɔpf] *m (-[e]s; Kröpfe* ['krœpfə]) MED goiter, *Br* goitre; ZO crop
**Kröte** ['krø:tə] *f (-; -n)* ZO toad
**Krücke** ['krʏkə] *f (-; -n)* crutch
**Krug** [kru:k] *m (-[e]s; Krüge* ['kry:gə]) jug, pitcher; mug, stein; tankard
**Krümel** ['kry:məl] *m (-s; -)* crumb
**krümelig** ['kry:məlɪç] *adj* crumbly
**'krümeln** *v/t and v/i (ge-, h)* crumble
**krumm** [krʊm] *adj* crooked (*a. fig*), bent
**'krummbeinig** [-bainɪç] *adj* bow-legged
**krümmen** ['krʏmən] *v/t (ge-, h)* bend (*a.* TECH), crook; ***sich ~*** bend; writhe (with pain); **'Krümmung** *f (-; -en)* bend, curve; GEOGR, MATH, MED curvature
**Krüppel** ['krʏpəl] *m (-s; -)* cripple
**Kruste** ['krʊstə] *f (-; -n)* crust

**Kto.** ABBR *of* ***Konto*** a/c, account
**Kübel** ['ky:bəl] *m (-s; -)* bucket, pail; tub
**Kubik|meter** [ku'bi:k-] *n, m* cubic meter (*Br* metre); **~wurzel** *f* MATH cube root
**Küche** ['kʏçə] *f (-; -n)* kitchen; GASTR cooking, cuisine; ***kalte*** (***warme***) **~** cold (hot) meals
**Kuchen** ['ku:xən] *m (-s; -)* cake; tart, pie
**'Küchen|geräte** *pl* kitchen utensils (*or* appliances); **~geschirr** *n* kitchen crockery, kitchenware; **~herd** *m* cooker; **~schrank** *m* (kitchen) cupboard
**Kuckuck** ['kʊkʊk] *m (-s; -s)* ZO cuckoo
**Kufe** ['ku:fə] *f (-; -n)* runner; AVIAT skid
**Kugel** ['ku:gəl] *f (-; -n)* ball; bullet; MATH, GEOGR sphere; SPORT shot
**'kugelförmig** [-fœrmɪç] *adj* ball-shaped, *esp* ASTR, MATH spheric(al)
**'Kugelgelenk** *n* TECH, ANAT ball (and socket) joint
**'Kugellager** *n* TECH ball bearing
**'kugeln** *v/i (ge-, sein) and v/t (h)* roll
**'Kugelschreiber** [-ʃraibɐ] *m (-s; -)* ballpoint (pen)
**'kugelsicher** *adj* bulletproof
**'Kugelstoßen** *n (-s; no pl)* SPORT shot put(ting); **'Kugelstoßer** [-ʃto:sɐ] *m (-s; -)*, **'Kugelstoßerin** [-ʃto:sərɪn] *f (-; -nen)* SPORT shot-putter
**Kuh** [ku:] *f (-; Kühe* ['ky:ə]) ZO cow
**kühl** [ky:l] *adj* cool (*a. fig*); **'Kühle** *f (-; no pl)* cool(ness); **'kühlen** *v/t (ge-, h)* cool; chill; refrigerate; refresh
**Kühler** ['ky:lɐ] *m (-s; -)* MOT radiator
**'Kühlerhaube** *f* MOT hood, *Br* bonnet
**'Kühlmittel** *n* coolant
**'Kühlraum** *m* cold-storage room
**'Kühlschrank** *m* fridge, refrigerator
**'Kühltruhe** *f* deep-freeze, freezer
**'Kühlwasser** *n* MOT cooling water
**kühn** [ky:n] *adj* bold
**'Kühnheit** *f (-; no pl)* boldness
**'Kuhstall** *m* cowshed
**Küken** ['ky:kən] *n (-s; -)* ZO chick (*a. fig*)
**Kukuruz** ['kʊkurʊts] *Austrian m* → ***Mais***
**Kuli** ['ku:li] F *m (-s; -s)* ballpoint
**Kulissen** [ku'lɪsən] *pl* THEA wings; scenery; ***hinter den ~*** backstage, *esp fig* behind the scenes
**Kult** [kʊlt] *m (-[e]s; -e)* cult; rite, ritual (act)

**kultivieren** [kʊlti'viːrən] *v/t* (*no -ge-, h*) cultivate
**Kultur** [kʊl'tuːɐ] *f* (-; *-en*) culture (*a.* BIOL), civilization; AGR cultivation
**Kul'turbeutel** *m* toilet bag
**kulturell** [kʊltu'rɛl] *adj* cultural
**Kul'tur|geschichte** *f* history of civilization; **~volk** *n* civilized people; **~zentrum** *n* cultural center (*Br* centre)
**Kultusmi,nister** ['kʊltʊs-] *m* minister of education and cultural affairs
**Kummer** ['kʊmɐ] *m* (*-s*; *no pl*) grief, sorrow; trouble, worry; **~ *haben mit*** have trouble *or* problems with
**kümmerlich** ['kʏmɐlɪç] *adj* miserable; poor, scanty; **kümmern** ['kʏmɐn] *v/refl and v/t* (*ge-, h*) ***sich ~ um*** look after, take care of, mind; care *or* worry about, be interested in
**Kumpel** ['kʊmpəl] *m* (*-s*; -) miner; F mate, buddy, pal
**Kunde** ['kʊndə] *m* (*-n*; *-n*) customer, client; **'Kundendienst** *m* after-sales service; (customer) service; service department; TECH servicing
**Kundgebung** ['kʊntgeːbʊŋ] *f* (-; *-en*) meeting, rally, demonstration
**kündigen** ['kʏndɪgən] *v/i and v/t* (*ge-, h*) cancel; ***j-m* ~** give s.o. his/her/one's notice; dismiss s.o., F sack *or* fire s.o.
**'Kündigung** *f* (-; *-en*) cancellation; (period of) notice
**Kundin** ['kʊndɪn] *f* (-; *-nen*) customer, client
**Kundschaft** ['kʊntʃaft] *f* (-; *-en*) customers, clients
**Kunst** [kʊnst] *f* (-; *Künste* ['kʏnstə]) art; skill; **~...** *in cpds ...herz, ...leder, ...licht etc*: artificial ...; **~akade,mie** *f* academy of arts; **~ausstellung** *f* art exhibition; **~dünger** *m* AGR artificial fertilizer; **~erziehung** *f* PED art (education); **~faser** *f* man-made *or* synthetic fiber (*Br* fibre); **~fehler** *m* professional blunder; **~fliegen** *n* stunt flying, aerobatics; **~geschichte** *f* history of art; **~gewerbe** *n*, **~handwerk** *n* arts and crafts
**Künstler** ['kʏnstlɐ] *m* (*-s*; -), **Künstlerin** ['kʏnstlərɪn] *f* (-; *-nen*) artist, MUS, THEA *a.* performer
**künstlerisch** ['kʏnstlərɪʃ] *adj* artistic
**künstlich** ['kʏnstlɪç] *adj* artificial; false; synthetic; man-made
**'Kunst|schwimmen** *n* water ballet; **~seide** *f* rayon; **~springen** *n* springboard diving; **~stoff** *m* plastic; **~stück** *n* trick, stunt, *esp fig* feat; **~turnen** *n* gymnastics; **~turner** *m* gymnast
**'kunstvoll** *adj* artistic; elaborate
**'Kunstwerk** *n* work of art
**Kupfer** ['kʊpfɐ] *n* (*-s*; *no pl*) copper (***aus*** of); **~stich** *m* copperplate (engraving)
**Kupon** [ku'põː] *m* (*-s*; *-s*) coupon
**Kuppe** ['kʊpə] *f* (-; *-n*) (rounded) hilltop; ANAT head
**Kuppel** ['kʊpəl] *f* (-; *-n*) ARCH dome; cupola
**Kuppelei** [kʊpə'lai] *f* (-; *-en*) JUR procuring
**'kuppeln** *v/i* (*ge-, h*) MOT put the clutch in *or* out; **Kupplung** ['kʊplʊŋ] *f* (-; *-en*) MOT clutch
**Kur** [kuːɐ] *f* (-; *-en*) course of treatment; cure
**Kür** [kyːɐ] *f* (-; *-en*) SPORT free skating; free exercises
**Kurbel** ['kʊrbəl] *f* (-; *-n*) crank, handle; **'kurbeln** *v/t* (*ge-, h*) crank; wind (up *etc*); **'Kurbelwelle** *f* TECH crankshaft
**Kürbis** ['kʏrbɪs] *m* (*-ses*; *-se*) BOT pumpkin, gourd, squash
**'Kurgast** *m* visitor
**kurieren** [ku'riːrən] *v/t* (*no -ge-, h*) cure (***von*** of)
**kurios** [ku'rjoːs] *adj* curious, odd, strange
**'Kürlauf** *m* SPORT free skating
**'Kurort** *m* health resort, spa
**Kurpfuscher** ['kuːɐpfʊʃɐ] *m* (*-s*; -) quack (doctor)
**Kurs** [kʊrs] *m* (*-es*; *-e*) AVIAT, MAR course (*a. fig*); PED *etc* class(es); ECON (exchange) rate; (stock) price; **~buch** *n* railroad (*Br* railway) guide
**Kürschner** ['kʏrʃnɐ] *m* (*-s*; -) furrier
**kursieren** [kʊr'ziːrən] *v/i* (*no -ge-, h*) circulate (*a. fig*)
**Kurve** ['kʊrvə] *f* (-; *-n*) curve (*a.* MATH *and fig*); bend, turn; **'kurvenreich** *adj* winding, full of bends; F curvaceous
**kurz** [kʊrts] *adj* short; brief; ***~e Hose*** shorts; (***bis***) ***vor ~em*** (until) recently; (***erst***) ***seit ~em*** (only) for a short time; ***~ vorher*** (***darauf***) shortly before (after[wards]); ***~ vor uns*** just ahead of us; ***~ nacheinander*** in quick succession; ***~ fortgehen etc*** go away for a short time

*or* a moment; ***sich ~ fassen*** be brief, put it briefly; ***~ gesagt*** in short; ***zu ~ kommen*** go short; ***~ angebunden*** curt
'**Kurzarbeit** *f* ECON short time
'**kurzarbeiten** *v/i* (*sep*, *ge-*, *h*) ECON work short time
'**kurzatmig** [-ʔaːtmɪç] *adj* short of breath
**Kürze** ['kʏrtsə] *f* (-; *no pl*) shortness; brevity; ***in ~*** soon, shortly, before long
'**kürzen** *v/t* (*ge-*, *h*) shorten (***um*** by); abridge; cut, reduce (*a.* MATH)
**kurzerhand** ['kʊrtsɐ'hant] *adv* without hesitation, on the spot
'**kurzfristig 1.** *adj* short-term; **2.** *adv* at short notice
'**Kurzgeschichte** *f* short story
'**kurzlebig** [-leːbɪç] *adj* short-lived
**kürzlich** ['kʏrtslɪç] *adv* recently, not long ago
'**Kurz|nachrichten** *pl* news summary; **~schluss** *m* ELECTR short circuit, F short; **~schrift** *f* shorthand
'**kurzsichtig** *adj* nearsighted, *Br* short-sighted
'**Kurzstrecke** *f* short distance
'**Kürzung** *f* (-; *-en*) cut, reduction (*a.* MATH)
'**Kurzwaren** *pl* notions, *Br* haberdashery
'**kurzweilig** [-vailɪç] *adj* entertaining
'**Kurzwelle** *f* PHYS, *radio*: short wave
**kuschelig** ['kʊʃəlɪç] F *adj* cozy, *Br* cosy, snug; **kuscheln** ['kʊʃəln] *v/refl* (*ge-*, *h*) snuggle, cuddle (***an*** *acc* up to; ***in*** *acc* in)
**Kusine** *f* → ***Cousine***
**Kuss** [kʊs] *m* (*-es*; *Küsse* ['kʏsə]) kiss
'**kussecht** *adj* kiss-proof
**küssen** ['kʏsən] *v/t* (*ge-*, *h*) kiss
**Küste** ['kʏstə] *f* (-; *-n*) coast, shore; ***an der ~*** on the coast; ***an die ~*** ashore
'**Küsten|gewässer** *pl* coastal waters; **~schifffahrt** *f* coastal shipping; **~schutz** *m*, **~wache** *f* coast guard
**Küster** ['kʏstɐ] *m* (*-s*; -) REL verger, sexton
**Kutsche** ['kʊtʃə] *f* (-; *-n*) carriage, coach; **Kutscher** ['kʊtʃɐ] *m* (*-s*; -) coachman
**Kutte** ['kʊtə] *f* (-; *-n*) (monk's) habit
**Kutteln** ['kʊtəln] *pl* GASTR tripe
**Kutter** ['kʊtɐ] *m* (*-s*; -) MAR cutter
**Kuvert** [ku'veːɐ] *n* (*-s*; *-s*) envelope
**Kybernetik** [kybɛr'neːtɪk] *f* (-; *no pl*) cybernetics

# L

**labil** [la'biːl] *adj* unstable
**Labor** [la'boːɐ] *n* (*-s*; *-e*) laboratory, F lab; **Laborant(in)** [labo'rant(ɪn)] (*-en*; *-en*/-; *-nen*) laboratory assistant
**Labyrinth** [laby'rɪnt] *n* (-[*e*]*s*; *-e*) labyrinth, maze (*both a. fig*)
**Lache** ['laxə] *f* (-; *-n*) pool, puddle
**lächeln** ['lɛçəln] *v/i* (*ge-*, *h*), '**Lächeln** *n* (*-s*; *no pl*) smile
**lachen** ['laxən] *v/i* (*ge-*, *h*) laugh (***über*** *acc* at); '**Lachen** *n* (*-s*; *no pl*) laugh(ter); ***j-n zum ~ bringen*** make s.o. laugh; **lächerlich** ['lɛçɐlɪç] *adj* ridiculous; ***~ machen*** ridicule, make fun of; ***sich ~ machen*** make a fool of o.s.
**Lachs** [laks] *m* (*-es*; *-e*) ZO salmon
**Lack** [lak] *m* (-[*e*]*s*; *-e*) varnish; lacquer; MOT paint(work)
**lackieren** [la'kiːrən] *v/t* (*no -ge-*, *h*) varnish; lacquer; paint (*a.* MOT)
'**Lackschuhe** *pl* patent-leather shoes
**Ladefläche** ['laːdə-] *f* loading space
'**Ladegerät** *n* ELECTR battery charger
'**Ladehemmung** *f* MIL jam
**laden** ['laːdən] *v/t* (*irr*, *ge-*, *h*) load; ELECTR charge; EDP boot (up); *fig* ***et. auf sich ~*** burden o.s. with s.th.
'**Laden** *m* (*-s*; *Läden* ['lɛːdən]) store, *Br* shop; shutter; **~dieb** *m* shoplifter; **~diebstahl** *m* shoplifting; **~inhaber** *m* storekeeper, *Br* shopkeeper; **~kasse** *f* till; **~schluss** *m* closing time; ***nach ~*** after hours; **~tisch** *m* counter
'**Laderampe** *f* loading platform *or* ramp
'**Laderaum** *m* loading space; MAR hold

**'Ladung** *f* (-; *-en*) load, freight; AVIAT, MAR cargo; ELECTR, MIL charge; ***e-e ~ ...*** a load of ...
**lag** [la:k] *pret of* ***liegen***
**Lage** ['la:gə] *f* (-; *-n*) situation, position (*both a. fig*); location; layer; round (*of beer etc*); ***in schöner*** (***ruhiger***) ~ beautifully (peacefully) situated; ***in der ~ sein zu*** *inf* be able to *inf*, be in a position to *inf*
**Lager** ['la:gɐ] *n* (*-s*; -) bed; camp (*a. fig*); ECON stock, store; GEOL deposit; TECH bearing; ***et. auf ~ haben*** have s.th. in store (*a. fig for s.o.*); **~feuer** *n* campfire; **~haus** *n* warehouse
**'lagern** (*ge-*, *h*) **1.** *v/i* camp; ECON be stored; **2.** *v/t* store, keep; MED lay, rest; ***kühl ~*** keep in a cool place
**'Lagerraum** *m* storeroom
**Lagerung** ['la:gərʊŋ] *f* (-; *no pl*) storage
**Lagune** [la'gu:nə] *f* (-; *-n*) lagoon
**lahm** [la:m] *adj* lame; ***~ legen*** → ***lähmen***; **lahmen** ['la:mən] *v/i* (*ge-*, *h*) be lame (***auf*** *dat* in)
**lähmen** ['lɛ:mən] *v/t* (*ge-*, *h*) paralyze, *Br* paralyse; bring *traffic etc* to a standstill
**'Lähmung** *f* (-; *-en*) MED paralysis
**Laib** [laip] *m* (*-[e]s*; *-e* ['laibə]) loaf
**Laich** [laiç] *m* (*-[e]s*; *-e*), **laichen** ['laiçən] *v/i* (*ge-*, *h*) spawn
**Laie** ['laɪə] *m* (*-n*; *-n*) layman; amateur
**'laienhaft** *adj* amateurish
**'Laienspiel** *n* amateur play
**Laken** ['la:kən] *n* (*-s*; -) sheet; bath towel
**Lakritze** [la'krɪtsə] *f* (-; *-n*) liquorice
**lallen** ['lalən] *v/i and v/t* (*ge-*, *h*) speak drunkenly; *baby*: babble
**Lamm** [lam] *n* (*-[e]s*; *Lämmer* ['lɛmɐ]) ZO lamb; **~fell** *n* lambskin
**Lampe** ['lampə] *f* (-; *-n*) lamp, light; bulb
**'Lampenfieber** *n* stage fright
**'Lampenschirm** *m* lampshade
**Lampion** [lam'pjõ:] *m* (*-s*; *-s*) Chinese lantern
**Land** [lant] *n* (*-[e]s*; *Länder* ['lɛndɐ]) land; country; AGR ground, soil; ECON land, property; ***an ~ gehen*** MAR go ashore; ***auf dem ~e*** in the country; ***aufs ~ fahren*** go into the country; ***außer ~es gehen*** go abroad; **~arbeiter** *m* farmhand; **~bevölkerung** *f* country *or* rural population
**Landebahn** ['landə-] *f* AVIAT runway
**land'einwärts** *adv* up-country, inland
**landen** ['landən] *v/i* (*ge-*, *sein*) land; *fig* ***~ in*** (*dat*) end up in
**'Landenge** *f* neck of land, isthmus
**'Landeplatz** *m* AVIAT landing field
**Länderspiel** ['lɛndɐ-] *n* SPORT international match
**'Landes|grenze** *f* national border; **~innere** *n* interior; **~re,gierung** *f* Land (*Austrian* Provincial) government; **~sprache** *f* national language
**'landesüblich** *adj* customary
**'Landes|verrat** *m* treason; **~verräter** *m* traitor (to one's country); **~verteidigung** *f* national defen|se, *Br* -ce
**'Land|flucht** *f* rural exodus; **~friedensbruch** *m* JUR breach of the public peace; **~gericht** *n* JUR *appr* regional superior court; **~gewinnung** *f* reclamation of land; **~haus** *n* country house, cottage; **~karte** *f* map; **~kreis** *m* district
**'landläufig** *adj* customary, current, common
**ländlich** ['lɛntlɪç] *adj* rural; rustic
**'Land|rat** *m*, **~rätin** [-rɛ:tɪn] *f* (-; *-nen*) *appr* District Administrator; **~ratte** F *f* MAR landlubber
**'Landschaft** *f* (-; *-en*) countryside; scenery; *esp* PAINT landscape
**'landschaftlich** *adj* scenic
**'Landsmann** *m* (*-[e]s*; *-leute*) (fellow) countryman; **'Landsmännin** [-mɛnɪn] *f* (-; *-nen*) fellow countrywoman
**'Land|straße** *f* country (*or* ordinary) road; **~streicher(in)** tramp; **~streitkräfte** *pl* MIL land forces; **~tag** *m* Land parliament
**'Landung** *f* (-; *-en*) landing, AVIAT *a.* touchdown
**'Landungssteg** *m* MAR gangway
**'Land|vermesser** [-fɛɐmɛsɐ] *m* (*-s*; -) land surveyor; **~vermessung** *f* (-; *-en*) land surveying; **~weg** *m*: ***auf dem ~e*** by land; **~wirt(in)** farmer
**'Landwirtschaft** *f* (-; *no pl*) agriculture, farming; **'landwirtschaftlich** *adj* agricultural
**'Landzunge** *f* GEOGR promontory, spit
**lang** [laŋ] *adj and adv* long; F tall; ***drei Jahre*** (***einige Zeit***) ~ for three years (some time); ***den ganzen Tag ~*** all day

long; ***seit ~em*** for a long time; ***vor ~er Zeit*** (a) long (time) ago; ***über kurz oder ~*** sooner or later; ***~ ersehnt*** long-hoped-for; ***~ erwartet*** long-awaited; ***gleich ~*** the same length

'**langatmig** [-ˀa:tmɪç] *adj* long-winded

**lange** ['laŋə] *adv* (for a) long (time); ***es ist schon ~ her***(, ***seit***) it has been a long time (since); (***noch***) ***nicht ~ her*** not long ago; ***noch ~ hin*** still a long way off; ***es dauert nicht ~*** it won't take long; ***ich bleibe nicht ~ fort*** I won't be long; ***wie ~ noch?*** how much longer?

**Länge** ['lɛŋə] *f* (-; -*n*) length; GEOGR longitude; ***der ~ nach*** (at) full length; (***sich***) ***in die ~ ziehen*** stretch (*a. fig*)

**langen** ['laŋən] F *v/i* (*ge-*, *h*) reach (***nach*** for); be enough; ***mir langt es*** I've had enough, *fig a.* I'm sick of it

'**Längen|grad** *m* GEOGR degree of longitude; **~maß** *n* linear measure

'**Langeweile** *f* (-; *no pl*) boredom; ***~ haben*** be bored; ***aus ~*** to pass the time

'**langfristig** *adj* long-term

'**langjährig** [-jɛ:rɪç] *adj* longstanding; ***~e Erfahrung*** many years of experience

'**Langlauf** *m* (-[*e*]*s*; *no pl*) SPORT cross--country (skiing)

'**langlebig** [-le:bɪç] *adj* long-lived

**länglich** ['lɛŋlɪç] *adj* longish, oblong

**längs** [lɛŋs] **1.** *prp* (*gen*) along(side); **2.** *adv* lengthwise

'**langsam** *adj* slow; ***~er werden*** *or* ***fahren*** slow down

'**Lang|schläfer** [-ʃlɛ:fɐ] *m* (-*s*; -), **~schläferin** [-fərɪn] *f* (-; -*nen*) late riser; **~spielplatte** *f* long-playing record, *mst* LP

**längst** [lɛŋst] *adv* long ago *or* before; ***~ vorbei*** long past; ***ich weiß es ~*** I have known it for a long time; **längstens** ['lɛŋstəns] *adv* at (the) most

'**Langstrecken...** *in cpds* long-distance ...; AVIAT, MIL long-range ...

'**langweilen** *v/t* (*ge-*, *h*) bore; ***sich ~*** be bored; '**langweilig** [-vailɪç] *adj* boring, dull; ***~e Person*** bore

'**Langwelle** *f* PHYS, *radio*: long wave

'**langwierig** [-vi:rɪç] *adj* lengthy, protracted (*a.* MED)

**Lanze** ['lantsə] *f* (-; -*n*) lance, spear

**Lappalie** [la'pa:ljə] *f* (-; -*n*) trifle

**Lappen** ['lapən] *m* (-*s*; -) (piece of) cloth; rag (*a. fig*)

**läppisch** ['lɛpɪʃ] *adj* silly; ridiculous

**Lärche** ['lɛrçə] *f* (-; -*n*) BOT larch

**Lärm** [lɛrm] *m* (-*s*; *no pl*) noise

**lärmen** ['lɛrmən] *v/i* (*ge-*, *h*) be noisy; **~d** *adj* noisy

**Larve** ['larfə] *f* (-; -*n*) mask; ZO larva

**las** [la:s] *pret of* ***lesen***

**lasch** [laʃ] F *adj* slack, lax

**Lasche** ['laʃə] *f* (-; -*n*) flap; tongue

**Laser** ['le:zɐ] *m* (-*s*; -) PHYS laser; **~drucker** *m* EDP laser printer; **~strahl** *m* PHYS laser beam; **~technik** *f* laser technology

**lassen** ['lasən] *v/t* (*irr*, *ge-*, *h*) *and v/aux* (*irr*, *no -ge-*, *h*) let, leave; ***j-n et. tun ~*** let s.o. do s.th.; allow s.o. to do s.th.; make s.o. do s.th.; ***j-n*** (***et.***) ***zu Hause ~*** leave s.o. (s.th.) at home; ***j-n allein*** (***in Ruhe***) ***~*** leave s.o. alone; ***sich die Haare schneiden ~*** have *or* get one's hair cut; ***sein Leben ~*** (***für***) lose (give) one's life (for); ***rufen ~*** send for, call in; ***es lässt sich machen*** it can be done; ***lass alles so***, ***wie*** (***wo***) ***es ist*** leave everything as (where) it is; ***er kann das Rauchen*** *etc* ***nicht ~*** he can't stop smoking *etc*; ***lass das!*** stop it! → ***grüßen, kommen***

**lässig** ['lɛsɪç] *adj* casual; careless

**Last** [last] *f* (-; -*en*) load, burden, weight (*all a. fig*); ***j-m zur ~ fallen*** be a burden to s.o.; ***j-m et. zur ~ legen*** charge s.o. with s.th.; **lasten** ['lastən] *v/i* (*ge-*, *h*) ***~ auf*** (*dat*) *a. fig* weigh *or* rest (up)on

'**Lastenaufzug** *m* freight elevator, *Br* goods lift

**Laster**[1] ['lastɐ] *m* (-*s*; -) → ***Lastwagen***

'**Laster**[2] *n* (-*s*; -) vice

**lästern** ['lɛstɐn] *v/i* (*ge-*, *h*) ***~ über*** (*acc*) run down

**lästig** ['lɛstɪç] *adj* troublesome, annoying; (***j-m***) ***~ sein*** be a nuisance (to s.o.)

'**Last|kahn** *m* barge; **~tier** *n* pack animal; **~wagen** *m* MOT truck, *Br a.* lorry; **~wagenfahrer** *m* MOT truck (*Br a.* lorry) driver, trucker

**Latein** [la'tain] *n* (-*s*; *no pl*) Latin

**La'teina͵merika** Latin America; **La'teinameri͵kaner(in)**, **la'teinameri͵kanisch** *adj* Latin American

**la'teinisch** *adj* Latin

**Laterne** [la'tɛrnə] *f* (-; -*n*) lantern; streetlight

**La'ternenpfahl** *m* lamppost

**Latte** ['latə] *f* (-; -*n*) lath; pale; SPORT bar

'**Lattenzaun** *m* paling, picket fence
**Lätzchen** ['lɛtsçən] *n* (*-s*; -) bib
**Laub** [laup] *n* (*-[e]s*; *no pl*) foliage, leaves; '**Laubbaum** *m* deciduous tree
**Laube** ['laubə] *f* (-; *-n*) arbo(u)r
'**Laubfrosch** *m* ZO tree frog
'**Laubsäge** *f* fretsaw
**Lauch** [laux] *m* (*-[e]s*; *-e*) BOT leek
**Lauer** ['lauɐ] *f*: ***auf der ~ liegen** or **sein*** lie in wait; '**lauern** *v/i* (*ge-*, *h*) lurk; ***~ auf*** (*acc*) lie in wait for
**Lauf** [lauf] *m* (*-[e]s*; *Läufe* ['lɔʏfə]) run; course; *gun*: barrel; ***im ~(e) der Zeit*** in the course of time; **~bahn** *f* career; **~diszi͵plin** *f* SPORT track event
**laufen** ['laufən] *v/i and v/t* (*irr*, *ge-*, *sein*) run (*a.* TECH, MOT, ECON); walk; *fig* work, run; ***j-n ~ lassen*** let s.o. go; let s.o. off; **~d 1.** *fig adj* present, current (*a.* ECON); continual; ***auf dem Laufenden sein*** be up to date; **2.** *adv* continuously; regularly; always
**Läufer** ['lɔʏfɐ] *m* (*-s*; -) runner (*a. carpet*); *chess*: bishop; '**Läuferin** *f* (-; *-nen*) runner
'**Lauf|gitter** *n* playpen; **~masche** *f* run, *Br* ladder; **~schritt** *m*: ***im ~*** on the double; **~schuhe** *pl* walking shoes; SPORT trainers; **~steg** *m* footbridge; TECH, *fashion*: catwalk; MAR gangway
**Lauge** ['laugə] *f* (-; *-n*) suds; CHEM lye
**Laune** ['launə] *f* (-; *-n*) mood, temper; ***gute** (**schlechte**) **~ haben*** be in a good (bad) mood *or* temper; **launenhaft,** '**launisch** *adj* moody; bad-tempered
**Laus** [laus] *f* (-; *Läuse* ['lɔʏzə]) ZO louse
**Lauschangriff** ['lauʃ-] *m* bugging operation; **lauschen** ['lauʃən] *v/i* (*ge-*, *h*) listen (*dat* to); eavesdrop
**lauschig** ['lauʃɪç] *adj* snug, cozy, *Br* cosy
**laut**[1] [laut] **1.** *adj* loud; noisy; **2.** *adv* loud(ly); ***~ vorlesen*** read (out) aloud; (***sprich***) ***~er, bitte!*** speak up, please!
**laut**[2] *prp* (*gen or dat*) according to
**Laut** *m* (*-[e]s*; *-e*) sound, noise
**lauten** ['lautən] *v/i* (*ge-*, *h*) read; be
**läuten** ['lɔʏtən] *v/i and v/t* (*ge-*, *h*) ring; ***es läutet** (**an der Tür**)* the (door)bell is ringing
**lauter** ['lautɐ] *adv* sheer (*nonsense etc*); nothing but; (so) many
'**lautlos** *adj* silent, soundless; hushed
'**Lautschrift** *f* phonetic transcription
'**Lautsprecher** *m* TECH (loud)speaker
'**Lautstärke** *f* loudness, ELECTR *a.* (sound) volume; ***mit voller ~*** (at) full blast; **~regler** *m* volume control
**lauwarm** ['lau-] *adj* lukewarm (*a. fig*)
**Lava** ['la:va] *f* (-; *Laven*) GEOL lava
**Lavabo** [la'va:bo] *Swiss n* → ***Waschbecken***
**Lavendel** [la'vɛndəl] *m* (*-s*; -) BOT lavender
**Lawine** [la'vi:nə] *f* (-; *-n*) avalanche
**Lazarett** [latsa'rɛt] *n* (*-[e]s*; *-e*) (military) hospital
**leben** ['le:bən] (*ge-*, *h*) **1.** *v/i* live; be alive; ***von et. ~*** live on s.th.; **2.** *v/t* live; '**Leben** *n* (*-s*; -) life; ***am ~ bleiben*** stay alive; survive; ***am ~ sein*** be alive; ***ums ~ bringen*** kill; ***sich das ~ nehmen*** take one's (own) life, commit suicide; ***ums ~ kommen*** lose one's life, be killed; ***um sein ~ laufen** (**kämpfen**)* run (fight) for one's life; ***das tägliche ~*** everyday life; ***mein ~ lang*** all my life; '**lebend** *adj* living; **lebendig** [le'bɛndɪç] *adj* living, alive; *fig* lively
'**Lebens|abend** *m* old age, the last years of one's life; **~bedingungen** *pl* living conditions; **~dauer** *f* life-span; TECH (service) life; **~erfahrung** *f* experience of life; **~erwartung** *f* life expectancy
'**lebensfähig** *adj* MED viable (*a. fig*)
'**Lebensgefahr** *f* mortal danger; ***in** (**unter**) **~*** in danger (at the risk) of one's life; '**lebensgefährlich** *adj* dangerous (to life), perilous
'**lebensgroß** *adj* life-size(d)
'**Lebensgröße** *f*: ***e-e Statue in ~*** a life-size(d) statue
'**Lebenshaltungskosten** *pl* cost of living
'**lebenslänglich 1.** *adj* lifelong; ***~e Freiheitsstrafe*** JUR life sentence; **2.** *adv* for life
'**Lebenslauf** *m* personal record, curriculum vitae
'**lebenslustig** *adj* fond of life
'**Lebensmittel** *pl* food(stuffs); groceries; **~geschäft** *n* grocery, supermarket
'**lebensmüde** *adj* tired of life
'**Lebens|notwendigkeit** *f* vital necessity; **~retter(in)** lifesaver, rescuer; **~standard** *m* standard of living; **~unterhalt** *m* livelihood; ***s-n ~ verdienen***

earn one's living (***als*** as; ***mit*** out of, by); **~versicherung** *f* life insurance; **~weise** *f* way of life

**'lebenswichtig** *adj* vital, essential

**'Lebenszeichen** *n* sign of life

**'Lebenszeit** *f* lifetime; ***auf ~*** for life

**Leber** ['le:bɐ] *f* (-; *-n*) ANAT liver; **~fleck** *m* mole; **~tran** *m* cod-liver oil

**'Lebewesen** *n* living being, creature

**lebhaft** ['le:phaft] *adj* lively; heavy (*traffic etc*)

**'Lebkuchen** *m* gingerbread

**'leblos** *adj* lifeless (*a. fig*)

**'Lebzeiten** *pl*: ***zu s-n ~*** in his lifetime

**lechzen** ['lɛçtsən] *v/i* (*ge-, h*) ***~ nach*** thirst for

**leck** [lɛk] *adj* leaking, leaky

**Leck** *n* (-[*e*]*s*; *-s*) leak

**lecken**[1] ['lɛkən] *v/t and v/i* (*ge-, h*) *a.* ***~ an*** (*dat*) lick

**'lecken**[2] *v/i* (*ge-, h*) leak

**lecker** ['lɛkɐ] *adj* delicious, tasty, F yummy; **'Leckerbissen** *m* delicacy, treat (*a. fig*)

**Leder** ['le:dɐ] *n* (*-s*; -) leather; **'ledern** *adj* leather(n); **'Lederwaren** *pl* leather goods

**ledig** ['le:dɪç] *adj* single, unmarried

**lediglich** ['le:dɪklɪç] *adv* only, merely

**Lee** [le:] *f* (-; *no pl*) MAR lee; ***nach ~*** leeward

**leer** [le:ɐ] **1.** *adj* empty (*a. fig*); vacant (*house etc*); blank (*page etc*); ELECTR dead, *Br* flat; ***~ stehend*** unoccupied, vacant; **2.** *adv*: ***~ laufen*** TECH idle; **Leere** ['le:rə] *f* (-; *no pl*) emptiness (*a. fig*); **'leeren** *v/t and v/refl* (*ge-, h*) empty; **'Leergut** *n* empties; **'Leerlauf** *m* TECH idling; neutral (gear); *fig* running on the spot; **'Leertaste** *f* space bar; **'Leerung** *f* (-; *-en*) *post* collection

**legal** [le'ga:l] *adj* legal, lawful

**legalisieren** [legali'zi:rən] *v/t* (*no -ge-, h*) legalize; **Legali'sierung** *f* (-; *-en*) legalization

**Legasthenie** [legaste'ni:] *f* (-; *-n*) PSYCH dyslexia, F word blindness

**Legastheniker** [legas'te:nikɐ] *m* (*-s*; -), **Legas'thenikerin** *f* (-; *-nen*) PSYCH dyslexic

**legen** ['le:gən] *v/t and v/i* (*ge-, h*) lay (*a. eggs*); place, put; set (*hair*); ***sich ~*** lie down; *fig* calm down; *pain*: wear off

**Legende** [le'gɛndə] *f* (-; *-n*) legend

**leger** [le'ʒe:ɐ] *adj* casual, informal

**Legislative** [legɪsla'ti:və] *f* (-; *-n*) legislative power

**legitim** [legi'ti:m] *adj* legitimate

**Lehm** [le:m] *m* (-[*e*]*s*; *-e*) loam; clay

**lehmig** ['le:mɪç] *adj* loamy, F muddy

**Lehne** ['le:nə] *f* (-; *-n*) back(rest); arm(rest); **'lehnen** *v/t and v/i* lean (*a.* ***sich ~***) rest (***an*** *acc*, ***gegen*** against; ***auf*** *acc* on); ***sich aus dem Fenster ~*** lean out of the window; **'Lehnsessel** *m*, **'Lehnstuhl** *m* armchair, easy chair

**Lehrbuch** ['le:ɐ-] *n* textbook

**Lehre** ['le:rə] *f* (-; *-n*) science; theory; REL, POL teachings, doctrine; moral; ECON apprenticeship; ***in der ~ sein*** be apprenticed (***bei*** to); ***das wird ihm e-e ~ sein*** that will teach him a lesson

**'lehren** *v/t* (*ge-, h*) teach, instruct; show

**Lehrer** ['le:rɐ] *m* (*-s*; -) teacher, instructor, *Br a.* master; **~ausbildung** *f* teacher training

**Lehrerin** ['le:rərɪn] *f* (-; *-nen*) (lady) teacher, *Br a.* mistress

**'Lehrer|kol,legium** *n* (teaching) staff; **~zimmer** *n* staff *or* teachers' room

**'Lehr|gang** *m* course (of instruction *or* study); training course; **~herr** *m* master; **~jahr** *n* year (of apprenticeship)

**Lehrling** ['le:ɐlɪŋ] *m* (*-s*; *-e*) apprentice, trainee

**'Lehr|meister** *m*, **~meisterin** *f* master; *fig* teacher; **~mittel** *pl* teaching aids; **~plan** *m* curriculum, syllabus; **~probe** *f* demonstration lesson

**'lehrreich** *adj* informative, instructive

**'Lehr|stelle** *f* apprenticeship; vacancy for an apprentice; **~stuhl** *m* professorship; **~tochter** *Swiss f* apprentice; **~vertrag** *m* indenture(s); **~zeit** *f* apprenticeship

**Leib** [laip] *m* (-[*e*]*s*; *Leiber* ['laibɐ]) body; belly, ANAT abdomen; stomach; ***bei lebendigem ~e*** alive; ***mit ~ und Seele*** (with) heart and soul

**Leibes|erziehung** ['laibəs-] *f* PED physical education, ABBR PE; **~kräfte** *pl*: ***aus ~n*** with all one's might

**'Leibgericht** *n* GASTR favo(u)rite dish

**leibhaftig** [laip'haftɪç] *adj*: ***der ~e Teufel*** the devil incarnate; ***~es Ebenbild*** living image; ***ich sehe ihn noch ~ vor mir*** I can see him (before me) now

**'leiblich** *adj* physical

'**Leib|rente** *f* life annuity; **~wache** *f*, **~wächter** *m* bodyguard; **~wäsche** *f* underwear
**Leiche** ['laiçə] *f* (-; -*n*) (dead) body, corpse
'**leichen'blass** *adj* deadly pale
'**Leichen|halle** *f* mortuary; **~schauhaus** *n* morgue; **~verbrennung** *f* cremation; **~wagen** *m* hearse
**leicht** [laiçt] *adj* light (*a. fig*); easy, simple; slight, minor; TECH light(weight); **~** ***möglich*** quite possible; **~** ***gekränkt*** easily offended; ***es fällt mir*** (***nicht***) **~** (***zu*** *inf*) I find it easy (difficult) (to *inf*); ***das ist ~ gesagt*** it's not as easy as that; ***es geht ~ kaputt*** it breaks easily; ***et. ~ nehmen*** not worry about s.th.; make light of s.th.; ***nimm's ~!*** never mind!, don't worry about it!; **~** ***verständlich*** easy to understand
'**Leicht|ath,let** *m* SPORT (track-and--field) athlete; **~ath,letik** *f* SPORT track and field (events), athletics; **~ath,letin** *f* SPORT (track-and-field) athlete; **~gewicht** *n* SPORT lightweight
'**leichtgläubig** *adj* credulous
**Leichtigkeit** ['laiçtıçkait] *f*: ***mit ~*** easily, with ease
'**leichtlebig** [-le:bıç] *adj* happy-go--lucky
'**Leichtme,tall** *n* light metal
'**Leichtsinn** *m* (-[*e*]*s*; *no pl*) carelessness; recklessness; '**leichtsinnig** *adj* careless; reckless
**Leid** [lait] *n* (-[*e*]*s*; *no pl*) sorrow, grief; pain; ***es tut mir ~*** I'm sorry (***um*** for; ***wegen*** about; ***dass ich zu spät komme*** for being late)
**leiden** ['laidən] *v/t and v/i* (*irr*, *ge-*, *h*) suffer (***an*** *dat*, ***unter*** *dat* from); ***j-n gut ~ können*** like s.o.; ***ich kann ... nicht ~*** I don't like ...; I can't stand ...; '**Leiden** *n* (-*s*; -) suffering(s); MED disease
'**Leidenschaft** *f* (-; -*en*) passion
'**leidenschaftlich** *adj* passionate; vehement
'**Leidensgenosse** *m*, '**Leidensgenossin** *f* fellow sufferer
**leider** ['laidɐ] *adv* unfortunately; **~** ***ja*** (***nein***) I'm afraid so (not)
'**leidlich** *adj* passable, F so-so
'**Leidtragende** *m*, *f* (-*n*; -*n*) mourner; ***er ist der ~ dabei*** he is the one who suffers for it
'**Leidwesen** *n*: ***zu m-m ~*** to my regret
**Leierkasten** ['laiɐ-] *m* barrel organ; **~mann** *m* organ grinder
**leiern** ['laiɐn] *v/i and v/t* (*ge-*, *h*) crank (up); *fig* drone
**Leihbücherei** ['lai-] *f* public library
**leihen** ['laiən] *v/t* (*irr*, *ge-*, *h*) lend; rent (*Br* hire) out; borrow (***von*** from); rent, hire
'**Leih|gebühr** *f* rental, lending fee; **~haus** *n* pawnshop, pawnbroker's (shop); **~mutter** F *f* surrogate mother; **~wagen** *m* MOT rented (*Br* hire) car
'**leihweise** *adv* on loan
**Leim** [laim] *m* (-[*e*]*s*; -*e*), **leimen** ['laimən] *v/t* (*ge-*, *h*) glue
**Leine** ['lainə] *f* (-; -*n*) line; lead, leash
**Leinen** ['lainən] *n* (-*s*; -) linen; canvas; ***in ~ gebunden*** clothbound
'**Leinenschuh** *m* canvas shoe
'**Lein|samen** *m* BOT linseed; **~tuch** *n* (linen) sheet; **~wand** *f* linen; PAINT canvas; screen
**leise** ['laizə] *adj* quiet, *a.* low, soft (*voice*, *a. music etc*); *fig* slight, faint; ***~r stellen*** turn (the volume) down
**Leiste** ['laistə] *f* (-; -*n*) ledge; ANAT groin
'**leisten** *v/t* (*ge-*, *h*) do, work; achieve, accomplish; render (*service etc*); take (*oath*); ***gute Arbeit ~*** do a good job; ***sich et. ~*** treat o.s. to s.th.; ***ich kann es mir*** (***nicht***) **~** I can('t) afford it
'**Leistung** *f* (-; -*en*) performance; achievement, PED *a.* (piece of) work, result, TECH *a.* output; service; benefit
'**Leistungsdruck** *m* (-[*e*]*s*; *no pl*) pressure, stress
'**leistungsfähig** *adj* efficient; (physically) fit; '**Leistungsfähigkeit** *f* (-; *no pl*) efficiency (*a.* TECH, ECON); fitness
'**Leistungs|kon,trolle** *f* (achievement *or* proficiency) test; **~kurs** *m* PED *appr* special subject; **~sport** *m* competitive sport(s)
**Leitar,tikel** ['lait-] *m* editorial, *esp Br* leader, leading article
**leiten** ['laitən] *v/t* (*ge-*, *h*) lead, guide (*a. fig*), conduct (*a.* PHYS, MUS); run (*a.* PED), be in charge of, manage; TV *etc* direct; host; **~d** *adj* leading; PHYS conductive; ***~e Stellung*** key position; ***~er Angestellter*** executive
**Leiter**[1] ['laitɐ] *f* (-; -*n*) ladder
'**Leiter**[2] *m* (-*s*; -) leader; conductor (*a.*

L

PHYS, MUS); ECON *etc* head, manager; chairman; → ***Schulleiter***
**Leiterin** ['laitərın] *f* (-; *-nen*) leader; head; chairwoman
**'Leit|faden** *m* manual, guide; **~planke** *f* MOT guardrail, *Br* crash barrier; **~spruch** *m* motto
**'Leitung** *f* (-; *-en*) ECON management; head office; administration; chairmanship; organization; THEA *etc* direction; TECH main, pipe(s); ELECTR, TEL line; ***die ~ haben*** be in charge; ***unter der ~ von*** MUS conducted by
**'Leitungsrohr** *n* pipe
**'Leitungswasser** *n* tap water
**Lektion** [lɛk'tsjoːn] *f* (-; *-en*) lesson
**Lektüre** [lɛk'tyːrə] *f* (-; *-n*) reading (matter); PED reader
**Lende** ['lɛndə] *f* (-; *-n*) ANAT loin; GASTR sirloin
**lenken** ['lɛŋkən] *v/t* (*ge-*, *h*) steer, drive; *fig* guide *s.o.*; direct (*traffic etc*)
**Lenker** ['lɛŋkɐ] *m* (*-s*; -) handlebar
**'Lenkrad** *n* MOT steering wheel
**'Lenkung** *f* (-; *-en*) MOT steering (system)
**Leopard** [leo'part] *m* (*-en*; *-en*) ZO leopard
**Lerche** ['lɛrçə] *f* (-; *-n*) ZO lark
**lernen** ['lɛrnən] *v/t and v/i* (*ge-*, *h*) learn; study; ***er lernt leicht*** he is a quick learner; ***lesen ~*** learn (how) to read
**'Lernmittelfreiheit** *f* free books *etc*
**lesbar** ['leːsbaːɐ] *adj* readable
**Lesbierin** ['lɛsbjərın] *f* (-; *-nen*), **lesbisch** ['lɛsbıʃ] *adj* lesbian
**Lesebuch** ['leːzə-] *n* reader
**'Leselampe** *f* reading lamp
**lesen** ['leːzən] *v/i and v/t* (*irr*, *ge-*, *h*) read; AGR harvest
**'lesenswert** *adj* worth reading
**Leser** ['leːzɐ] *m* (*-s*; -) reader
**'Leseratte** F *f* bookworm
**'Leserbrief** *m* letter to the editor
**'Leserin** *f* (-; *-nen*) reader
**'leserlich** *adj* legible
**'Lesestoff** *m* reading matter
**'Lesezeichen** *n* bookmark
**'Lesung** *f* (-; *-en*) reading (*a.* PARL)
**Letzt** [lɛtst] *f*: ***zu guter ~*** in the end
**letzte** ['lɛtstə] *adj* last; latest; ***zum ~n Mal(e)*** for the last time; ***in ~r Zeit*** recently; ***als Letzter ankommen*** *etc* arrive *etc* last; ***Letzter sein*** be last (*a.* SPORT); ***das ist das Letzte!*** that's the limit!; **'letztens** *adv* finally; ***erst ~*** just recently; **letztere** ['lɛtstərə] *adj* latter; ***der*** (***die***, ***das***) ***Letztere*** the latter
**Leuchtanzeige** ['lɔʏçt-] *f* luminous *or* LED display light; **leuchten** ['lɔʏçtən] *v/i* (*ge-*, *h*) shine; glow; **'Leuchten** *n* (*-s*; *no pl*) shining; glow; **'leuchtend** *adj* shining (*a. fig*); bright; **Leuchter** ['lɔʏçtɐ] *m* (*-s*; -) candlestick
**'Leucht|farbe** *f* luminous paint; **~reˌklame** *f* neon sign(s); **~(stoff)röhre** *f* ELECTR fluorescent lamp; **~turm** *m* lighthouse; **~ziffer** *f* luminous figure
**leugnen** ['lɔʏgnən] *v/t and v/i* (*ge-*, *h*) deny (***et. getan zu haben*** having done s.th.)
**Leute** ['lɔʏtə] *pl* people, F folks
**Leutnant** ['lɔʏtnant] *m* (*-s*; *-s*) MIL second lieutenant
**Lexikon** ['lɛksikɔn] *n* (*-s*; *-ka*, *-ken*) encyclop(a)edia; dictionary
**Libelle** [li'bɛlə] *f* (-; *-n*) ZO dragonfly
**liberal** [libe'raːl] *adj* liberal
**Libero** ['liːbero] *m* (*-s*; *-s*) *soccer*: sweeper
**licht** ['lıçt] *adj* bright; *fig* lucid
**Licht** *n* (*-[e]s*; *-er* ['lıçtɐ]) a) light, b) (*no pl*) brightness; ***~ machen*** switch *or* turn on the light(s)
**'Licht|bild** *n* photo(graph); slide; **~bildervortrag** *m* slide lecture; **~blick** *m* ray of hope; bright moment
**'lichtempfindlich** *adj* sensitive to light; PHOT sensitive; **'Lichtempfindlichkeit** *f* (light) sensitivity; PHOT speed
**lichten** ['lıçtən] *v/t* (*ge-*, *h*) clear; ***den Anker ~*** MAR weigh anchor; ***sich ~*** get thin(ner); *fig* be thinning (out)
**'Licht|geschwindigkeit** *f* speed of light; **~griffel** *m* light pen; **~hupe** *f* MOT (headlight) flash(er); ***die ~ betätigen*** flash one's lights; **~jahr** *n* light year; **~maˌschine** *f* MOT generator; **~orgel** *f* colo(u)r organ; **~pause** *f* blueprint; **~schacht** *m* well; **~schalter** *m* (light) switch
**'lichtscheu** *fig adj* shady
**'Licht|schutzfaktor** *m* sun protection factor, SPF; **~strahl** *m* ray *or* beam of light (*a. fig*)
**'Lichtung** *f* (-; *-en*) clearing
**Lid** [liːt] *n* (*-[e]s*; *Lider* ['liːdɐ]) ANAT (eye)lid; **~schatten** *m* eye shadow

**lieb** [li:p] *adj* dear; sweet; nice, kind; good; ~ ***gewinnen*** get fond of; ~ ***haben*** love, be fond of; **Liebe** ['li:bə] *f* (-; *no pl*) love (***zu*** of, for); ***aus ~ zu*** out of love for; ~ ***auf den ersten Blick*** love at first sight; '**lieben** *v/t* (*ge-*, *h*) love, *a.* be in love with *s.o.*; make love to

'**liebenswert** *adj* lovable, charming, sweet

'**liebenswürdig** *adj* kind; '**Liebenswürdigkeit** *f* (-; *no pl*) kindness

**lieber** ['li:bɐ] *adv* rather, sooner; ~ ***haben*** prefer, like better; ***ich möchte*** ~ (***nicht***) ... I'd rather (not) ...; ***du solltest*** ~ (***nicht***) ... you had better (not) ...

'**Liebes|brief** *m* love letter; **~erklärung** *f*: ***j-m e-e ~ machen*** declare one's love to s.o.; **~kummer** *m*: ~ ***haben*** be lovesick; **~paar** *n* lovers

'**liebevoll** *adj* loving, affectionate

**Liebhaber** ['li:pha:bɐ] *m* (-*s*; -) lover (*a. fig*); **~...** *in cpds ...preis, ...stück etc*: collector's ...; **Liebhaberei** [li:pha:bə'rai] *f* (-; *-en*) hobby

**Liebkosung** [li:p'ko:zʊŋ] *f* (-; *-en*) caress

'**lieblich** *adj* lovely, charming, sweet (*a. wine*)

'**Liebling** *m* (-*s*; -*e*) darling; favo(u)rite

'**Lieblings...** *in cpds mst* favo(u)rite

'**lieblos** *adj* unloving, cold; unkind (*words etc*); *fig* careless

**Lied** [li:t] *n* (-[*e*]*s*; -*er* ['li:dɐ]) song; tune

**liederlich** ['li:dɐlɪç] *adj* slovenly, sloppy

**Liedermacher** ['li:dɐ-] *m* (-*s*; -) singer-songwriter

**lief** [li:f] *pret of* ***laufen***

**Lieferant** [lifə'rant] *m* (-*en*; -*en*) ECON supplier; **lieferbar** ['li:fɐba:ɐ] *adj* ECON available; '**Lieferfrist** *f* ECON term of delivery; **liefern** ['li:fɐn] *v/t* (*ge-*, *h*) ECON deliver; ***j-m et.*** ~ supply s.o. with s.th.; **Lieferung** ['li:fərʊŋ] *f* (-; *-en*) ECON delivery; supply

'**Lieferwagen** *m* MOT (delivery) van

**Liege** ['li:gə] *f* (-; *-n*) couch

**liegen** ['li:gən] *v/i* (*irr*, *ge-*, *h*) lie, *a.* be (situated); (***krank***) ***im Bett*** ~ be (ill) in bed; ***nach Osten*** (***der Straße***) ~ face east (the street); ***daran liegt es***(, ***dass***) that's (the reason) why; ***es*** (***er***) ***liegt mir nicht*** F it (he) is not my cup of tea; ***mir liegt viel*** (***wenig***) ***daran*** it means a lot (doesn't mean much) to me; ~ ***bleiben*** stay in bed; be left behind; ~ ***lassen*** leave (behind); F ***j-n links ~ lassen*** ignore s.o., give s.o. the cold shoulder

'**Liege|sitz** *m* reclining seat; **~stuhl** *m* deckchair; **~stütz** *m* (-*es*; -*e*) SPORT push-up, *Br* press-up; **~wagen** *m* RAIL couchette

**lieh** [li:] *pret of* ***leihen***

**ließ** [li:s] *pret of* ***lassen***

**Lift** [lɪft] *m* (-[*e*]*s*; -*e*, -*s*) elevator, *Br* lift; ski lift

**Liga** ['li:ga] *f* (-; *Ligen*) league, SPORT *a.* division

**Likör** [li'kø:ɐ] *m* (-*s*; -*e*) liqueur

**lila** ['li:la] *adj* purple, violet

**Lilie** ['li:ljə] *f* (-; *-n*) BOT lily

**Liliputaner** [lilipu'ta:nɐ] *m* (-*s*; -) dwarf, midget

**Limonade** [limo'na:də] *f* (-; *-n*) pop; lemon soda, *Br* lemonade

**Limousine** [limu'zi:nə] *f* (-; *-n*) MOT sedan, *Br* saloon car; limousine

**Linde** ['lɪndə] *f* (-; *-n*) BOT lime (tree), linden

**lindern** ['lɪndɐn] *v/t* (*ge-*, *h*) relieve, ease, alleviate; **Linderung** ['lɪndərʊŋ] *f* (-; *no pl*) relief, alleviation

**Lineal** [line'a:l] *n* (-*s*; -*e*) ruler

**Linie** ['li:njə] *f* (-; *-n*) line; ***auf s-e*** ~ ***achten*** watch one's weight

'**Linien|flug** *m* AVIAT scheduled flight; **~richter** *m* SPORT linesman

'**linientreu** *adj* POL: ~ ***sein*** follow the party line

**linieren** [li'ni:rən], **liniieren** [lini'i:rən] *v/t* (*no -ge-*, *h*) rule, line

**linke** ['lɪŋkə] *adj* left (*a.* POL); ***auf der ~n Seite*** on the left(-hand side); '**Linke** *m*, *f* (-*n*; -*n*) POL leftist, left-winger

**linkisch** ['lɪŋkɪʃ] *adj* awkward, clumsy

**links** [lɪŋks] *adv* on the left (*a.* POL); on the wrong side; ***nach*** ~ (to the) left; ~ ***von*** to the left of

**Links...** *in cpds ...verkehr etc*: left-hand

**Links'außen** *m* (-; -) SPORT outside left, left wing

'**Linkshänder** [-hɛndɐ] *m* (-*s*; -), '**Linkshänderin** *f* (-; *-nen*) left-hander

'**Linksradi,kale** *m*, *f* (-*n*; -*n*) POL left-wing extremist

**Linse** ['lɪnzə] *f* (-; *-n*) BOT lentil; OPT lens

**Lippe** ['lɪpə] *f* (-; *-n*) ANAT lip

'**Lippenstift** *m* lipstick

**liquidieren** [likvi'di:rən] *v/t* (*no -ge-, h*) ECON liquidate (*a.* POL)
**lispeln** ['lɪspəln] *v/i* (*ge-, h*) (have a) lisp
**List** [lɪst] *f* (-; *-en*) a) trick, b) (*no pl*) cunning
**Liste** ['lɪstə] *f* (-; *-n*) list; roll
**listig** ['lɪstɪç] *adj* cunning, tricky, sly
**Liter** ['li:tɐ] *n, m* (*-s*; -) liter, *Br* litre
**literarisch** [lɪtə'ra:rɪʃ] *adj* literary
**Literatur** [lɪtəra'tu:ɐ] *f* (-; *-en*) literature; **~...** *in cpds ...kritik etc*: *mst* literary
**Litfaßsäule** ['lɪtfas-] *f* advertising pillar
**litt** [lɪt] *pret of* ***leiden***
**Lizenz** [li'tsɛnts] *f* (-; *-en*) license, *Br* licence
**Lkw, LKW** ['ɛlkave] *m* (*-[s]*; -) ABBR *of* ***Lastkraftwagen*** truck, *Br a.* lorry
**Lob** [lo:p] *n* (*-[e]s*; *no pl*), **loben** ['lo:bən] *v/t* (*ge-, h*) praise; **'lobenswert** *adj* praiseworthy, laudable
**Loch** [lɔx] *n* (*-[e]s*; *Löcher* ['lœçɐ]) hole (*a. fig*); puncture; **lochen** ['lɔxən] *v/t* (*ge-, h*) punch (*a.* TECH); **Locher** ['lɔxɐ] *m* (*-s*; -) punch
**Locke** ['lɔkə] *f* (-; *-n*) curl; lock
**locken¹** ['lɔkən] *v/t and v/refl* (*ge-, h*) curl
**locken²** *v/t* (*ge-, h*) lure, entice, *fig a.* attract, tempt
**'Locken|kopf** *m* curly head; **~wickler** [-vɪklɐ] *m* (*-s*; -) curler, roller
**locker** ['lɔkɐ] *adj* loose; slack; *fig* relaxed; **'lockern** *v/t* (*ge-, h*) loosen, slacken; relax (*a. fig*); ***sich ~*** loosen, (be)come loose; SPORT limber up; *fig* relax
**lockig** ['lɔkɪç] *adj* curly, curled
**'Lockvogel** *m* decoy (*a. fig*)
**lodern** ['lo:dɐn] *v/i* (*ge-, h*) blaze, flare
**Löffel** ['lœfəl] *m* (*-s*; -) spoon; ladle
**'löffeln** *v/t* (*ge-, h*) spoon up
**log** [lo:k] *pret of* ***lügen***
**Logbuch** ['lɔk-] *n* MAR log
**Loge** ['lo:ʒə] *f* (-; *-n*) THEA box; lodge
**Logik** ['lo:gɪk] *f* (-; *no pl*) logic
**logisch** ['lo:gɪʃ] *adj* logical
**'logischer'weise** *adv* obviously
**Lohn** [lo:n] *m* (*-[e]s*; *Löhne* ['lø:nə]) ECON wages, pay(ment); *fig* reward; **~empfänger** *m* wageworker, *Br* wage earner
**lohnen** ['lo:nən] *v/refl* (*ge-, h*) be worth(while), pay; ***es (die Mühe) lohnt sich*** it's worth it (the trouble); ***das Buch (der Film) lohnt sich*** the book (film) is worth reading (seeing); **~d** *adj* paying; *fig* rewarding
**'Lohn|erhöhung** *f* raise, *Br* increase in wages, rise; **~steuer** *f* income tax; **~stopp** *m* wage freeze; **~tüte** *f* pay packet
**Loipe** ['lɔʏpə] *f* (-; *-n*) (cross-country) course
**Lokal** [lo'ka:l] *n* (*-s*; *-e*) restaurant; bar, saloon, *esp Br* pub
**Lo'kal...** *in cpds mst* local
**Lok** [lɔk] *f* (-; *-s*) → ***Lokomotive***; **~führer** *m* RAIL engineer, *Br* train driver
**Lokomotive** [lokomo'ti:və] *f* (-; *-n*) RAIL engine
**Lorbeer** ['lɔrbe:ɐ] *m* (*-s*; *-en*) BOT laurel; GASTR bay leaf
**Lore** ['lo:rə] *f* (-; *-n*) TECH tipcart
**los** [lo:s] *adj and adv* off; *dog etc*: loose; ***~ sein*** be rid of; ***was ist ~?*** what's the matter?, F what's up?; what's going on (here)?; ***hier ist nicht viel ~*** there's nothing much going on here; F ***da ist was ~!*** that's where the action is!; F ***also ~!*** okay, let's go!
**Los** [lo:s] *n* (*-es*; *-e* ['lo:zə]) lot, *fig a.* fate; (lottery) ticket, number
**'losbinden** *v/t* (*irr*, ***binden***, *sep*, *-ge-, h*) untie
**Löschblatt** ['lœʃ-] *n* blotting paper
**löschen** ['lœʃən] *v/t* (*ge-, h*) extinguish, put out; quench (*thirst*); blot (*ink*); wipe off *the blackboard*; erase, EDP *a.* delete; slake (*lime*); MAR unload
**'Löschpa,pier** *n* blotting paper
**lose** ['lo:zə] *adj* loose
**Lösegeld** ['lø:zə-] *n* ransom
**losen** ['lo:zən] *v/i* (*ge-, h*) draw lots (***um*** for)
**lösen** ['lø:zən] *v/t* (*ge-, h*) undo (*knot etc*); loosen, relax; TECH release; take off; solve (*problem etc*); settle (*conflict etc*); buy, get (*ticket etc*); dissolve (*a.* CHEM); ***sich ~*** come loose *or* undone; *fig* free o.s. (***von*** from)
**'los|fahren** *v/i* (*irr*, ***fahren***, *sep*, *-ge-, sein*) leave; drive off; **~gehen** *v/i* (*irr*, ***gehen***, *sep*, *-ge-, sein*) leave; start, begin; *shot etc*: go off; ***auf j-n ~*** go for s.o.; ***ich gehe jetzt los*** I'm off now; **~ketten** *v/t* (*sep*, *-ge-, h*) unchain; **~kommen** *v/i* (*irr*, ***kommen***, *sep*, *-ge-, sein*) get away (***von*** from); **~lassen** *v/t* (*irr*, ***lassen***, *sep*, *-ge-, h*) let go; ***den Hund ~***

***auf*** (*acc*) set the dog on; **~legen** F *v/i* (*sep*, *-ge-*, *h*) get cracking
**löslich** ['løːslıç] *adj* CHEM soluble
'**los|machen** *v/t* (*sep*, *-ge-*, *h*) → ***lösen***; **~reißen** *v/t* (*irr*, ***reißen***, *sep*, *-ge-*, *h*) tear off; ***sich*** ~ break away; *esp fig* tear o.s. away (*both*: ***von*** from); **~sagen** *v/refl* (*sep*, *-ge-*, *h*) ***sich*** ~ ***von*** break with; **~schlagen** *v/i* (*irr*, ***schlagen***, *sep*, *-ge-*, *h*) strike (***auf j-n*** out at s.o.); **~schnallen** *v/t* (*sep*, *-ge-*, *h*) unbuckle; ***sich*** ~ MOT, AVIAT unfasten one's seatbelt; **~stürzen** *v/i* (*sep*, *-ge-*, *sein*) ~ ***auf*** (*acc*) rush at
**Losung** ['loːzʊŋ] *f* (-; *-en*) MIL password; *fig* slogan
**Lösung** ['løːzʊŋ] *f* (-; *-en*) solution (*a. fig*); settlement
'**Lösungsmittel** *n* solvent
'**loswerden** *v/t* (*irr*, ***werden***, *sep*, *-ge-*, *sein*) get rid of; spend (*money*); lose
'**losziehen** *v/i* (*irr*, ***ziehen***, *sep*, *-ge-*, *sein*) set out, take off, march away
**Lot** [loːt] *n* (-[*e*]*s*; *-e*) plumbline
**löten** ['løːtən] *v/t* (*ge-*, *h*) TECH solder
**Lotion** [lo'tsjoːn] *f* (-; *-en*) lotion
**Lotse** ['loːtsə] *m* (*-n*; *-n*), '**lotsen** *v/t* (*ge-*, *h*) MAR pilot
**Lotterie** [lɔtə'riː] *f* (-; *-n*) lottery; **~gewinn** *m* prize; **~los** *n* lottery ticket
**Lotto** ['lɔto] *n* (*-s*; *-s*) lotto, bingo; *Br* national lottery; *in Germany*: Lotto; (***im***) ~ ***spielen*** do Lotto; **~schein** *m* Lotto coupon; **~ziehung** *f* Lotto draw
**Löwe** ['løːvə] *m* (*-n*; *-n*) ZO lion; AST Leo; ***er ist*** (***ein***) ~ he's (a) Leo
'**Löwenzahn** *m* BOT dandelion
**Löwin** ['løːvın] *f* (-; *-nen*) ZO lioness
**loyal** [loa'jaːl] *adj* loyal, faithful
**Luchs** [lʊks] *m* (*-es*; *-e*) ZO lynx
**Lücke** ['lʏkə] *f* (-; *-n*) gap (*a. fig*); '**Lückenbüßer** *m* stopgap; '**lückenhaft** *adj* full of gaps; *fig* incomplete; '**lückenlos** *adj* without a gap; *fig* complete; '**Lückentest** *m* PSYCH completion *or* fill-in test
**lud** [luːt] *pret of* ***laden***
**Luft** [lʊft] *f* (-; *no pl*) air; ***an der frischen*** ~ (out) in the fresh air; (***frische***) ~ ***schöpfen*** get a breath of fresh air; ***die*** ~ ***anhalten*** catch (*esp fig a.* hold) one's breath; ***tief*** ~ ***holen*** take a deep breath; ***in die*** ~ ***sprengen*** (F ***fliegen***) blow up
'**Luft|angriff** *m* air raid; **~ballon** *m* balloon; **~bild** *n* aerial photograph *or* view; **~blase** *f* air bubble; **~brücke** *f* airlift
'**luftdicht** *adj* airtight
'**Luftdruck** *m* (-[*e*]*s*; *no pl*) PHYS, TECH air pressure
**lüften** ['lʏftən] *v/t and v/i* (*ge-*, *h*) air, ventilate; *fig* reveal
'**Luft|fahrt** *f* (-; *no pl*) aviation, aeronautics; **~feuchtigkeit** *f* (atmospheric) humidity; **~gewehr** *n* airgun
'**luftig** *adj* airy; breezy; light (*dress etc*)
'**Luft|kissen** *n* air cushion; **~kissenfahrzeug** *n* hovercraft; **~krankheit** *f* air-sickness; **~krieg** *m* air warfare; **~kurort** *m* (climatic) health resort
'**luftleer** *adj*: ***~er Raum*** vacuum
'**Luft|linie** *f*: ***50 km*** ~ 50 km as the crow flies; **~post** *f* air mail; **~pumpe** *f* air pump; bicycle pump; **~röhre** *f* ANAT windpipe, trachea; **~schlange** *f* streamer; **~schloss** *n* castle in the air; **~sprünge** *pl*: ~ ***machen vor Freude*** jump for joy
'**Lüftung** *f* (-; *-en*) airing; TECH ventilation
'**Luft|veränderung** *f* change of air; **~verkehr** *m* air traffic; **~verschmutzung** *f* air pollution; **~waffe** *f* MIL air force; **~weg** *m*: ***auf dem*** ~ by air; **~zug** *m* draft, *Br* draught
**Lüge** ['lyːgə] *f* (-; *-n*) lie; '**lügen** *v/i* (*irr*, *ge-*, *h*) lie, tell a lie *or* lies; ***das ist gelogen*** that's a lie; **Lügner**(**in**) ['lyːgnɐ (-nərın)] (*-s*; *-/-*; *-nen*) liar; '**lügnerisch** [-nərıʃ] *adj* false
**Luke** ['luːkə] *f* (-; *-n*) hatch; skylight
**Lümmel** ['lʏməl] F *m* (*-s*; -) rascal
**lumpen** ['lʊmpən] F *v/t*: ***sich nicht*** ~ ***lassen*** be generous
'**Lumpen** *m* (*-s*; -) rag; ***in*** ~ in rags; **~pack** F *n sl* bastards
**lumpig** ['lʊmpıç] F *adj*: ***für ~e zwei Mark*** for a paltry two marks
**Lunge** ['lʊŋə] *f* (-; *-n*) ANAT lungs; (***auf***) ~ ***rauchen*** inhale
'**Lungen|entzündung** *f* MED pneumonia; **~flügel** *m* ANAT lung; **~zug** *m*: ***e-n*** ~ ***machen*** inhale
**Lupe** ['luːpə] *f* (-; *-n*) magnifying glass; ***unter die*** ~ ***nehmen*** scrutinize (closely)
**Lust** [lʊst] *f* (-; *Lüste* ['lʏstə]) a) (*no pl*) desire, interest; pleasure, delight, b) lust; ~ ***haben auf et.*** (***et. zu tun***) feel

like (doing) s.th.; ***hättest du ~ auszugehen?*** would you like to go out?, how about going out?; ***ich habe keine ~*** I don't feel like it, I'm not in the mood for it; ***die ~ an et. verlieren*** (***j-m die ~ an et. nehmen***) (make s.o.) lose all interest in s.th.
**lüstern** ['lʏstɐn] *adj* greedy (***nach*** for)
**lustig** ['lʊstɪç] *adj* funny; cheerful; ***er ist sehr ~*** he is full of fun; ***es war sehr ~*** it was great fun; ***sich ~ machen über*** (*acc*) make fun of
**'lustlos** *adj* listless, indifferent
**'Lustmord** *m* sex murder
**'Lustspiel** *n* THEA comedy
**lutschen** ['lʊtʃən] *v/i and v/t* (*ge-, h*) suck
**Luv** [lu:f] *f* (-; *no pl*) MAR windward, weather side
**luxuriös** [lʊksu'rjø:s] *adj* luxurious
**Luxus** ['lʊksʊs] *m* (-; *no pl*) luxury; **~ar,tikel** *m* luxury (article); **~ausführung** *f* deluxe version; **~ho,tel** *n* five-star (*or* luxury) hotel
**Lymphdrüse** ['lʏmf-] *f* ANAT lymph gland
**lynchen** ['lʏnçən] *v/t* (*ge-, h*) lynch
**Lyrik** ['ly:rɪk] *f* (-; *no pl*) poetry
**Lyriker** ['ly:rikɐ] *m* (-*s*; -), **'Lyrikerin** *f* (-; -*nen*) (lyric) poet
**lyrisch** ['ly:rɪʃ] *adj* lyrical (*a. fig*)

# M

**machbar** ['maxba:ɐ] *adj* feasible
**machen** ['maxən] *v/t* (*ge-, h*) do; make; GASTR make, prepare; fix (*a. fig*); be, come to, amount to; take, pass (*test etc*); make, go on (*a trip etc*); ***Hausaufgaben ~*** do one's homework; ***da(gegen) kann man nichts ~*** it can't be helped; ***mach, was du willst!*** do as you please!; ***(nun) mach mal*** *or* ***schon!*** hurry up!, come on *or* along now!; ***mach's gut!*** take care (of yourself)!, good luck!; (***das***) ***macht nichts*** it doesn't matter; ***mach dir nichts d(a)raus!*** never mind!, don't worry!; ***das macht mir nichts aus*** I don't mind *or* care; ***was*** *or* ***wie viel macht das?*** how much is it?; ***sich et.*** (***nichts***) ***~ aus*** (not) care about; (not) care for
**'Machenschaften** *pl* machinations; ***unsaubere ~*** sleaze (*esp* POL)
**Macher** ['maxɐ] *m* (-*s*; -) man of action, doer
**Macho** ['matʃo] *m* (-*s*; -*s*) macho
**Macht** [maxt] *f* (-; *Mächte* ['mɛçtə]) power (***über*** *acc* of); ***an der ~*** in power; ***mit aller ~*** with all one's might
**'Machthaber** [-ha:bɐ] *m* (-*s*; -) POL ruler
**mächtig** ['mɛçtɪç] *adj* powerful, mighty (*a.* F); enormous, huge
**'Machtkampf** *m* struggle for power
**'machtlos** *adj* powerless
**'Macht|missbrauch** *m* abuse of power; **~poli,tik** *f* power politics; **~übernahme** *f* takeover; **~wechsel** *m* transition of power
**Mädchen** ['mɛ:tçən] *n* (-*s*; -) girl; maid
**'mädchenhaft** *adj* girlish
**'Mädchen|name** *m* girl's name; maiden name; **~schule** *f* girls' school
**Made** ['ma:də] *f* (-; -*n*) ZO maggot; worm
**Mädel** ['mɛ:dəl] *n* (-*s*; -*s*) girl
**'madig** *adj* maggoty, worm-eaten; F ***j-m et. ~ machen*** spoil s.th. for s.o.
**Magazin** [maga'tsi:n] *n* (-*s*; -*e*) magazine (*a.* MIL, PHOT, TV); store(room), warehouse
**Magd** [ma:kt] *f* (-; *Mägde* ['mɛ:ktə]) (female) farmhand
**Magen** ['ma:gən] *m* (-*s*; *Mägen* ['mɛ:gən]) ANAT stomach; **~beschwerden** *pl* MED stomach trouble; **~geschwür** *n* MED (stomach) ulcer; **~schmerzen** *pl* stomachache
**mager** ['ma:gɐ] *adj* lean, thin, skinny; GASTR low-fat (*cheese*), lean (*meat*), skim (*milk*); *fig* meager, *Br* meagre
**Magie** [ma'gi:] *f* (-; *no pl*) magic
**magisch** ['ma:gɪʃ] *adj* magic(al)
**Magister** [ma'gɪstɐ] *m* (-*s*; -) UNIV Mas-

ter of Arts *or* Science; *Austrian* → ***Apotheker***
**Magistrat** [magɪs'tra:t] *m* (-[*e*]*s*; -*e*) municipal council
**Magnet** [ma'gne:t] *m* (-[*e*]*s*, -*en*; -*e*[*n*]) magnet (*a. fig*); **~...** *in cpds ...band, ...feld, ...nadel etc*: magnetic ...
**mag'netisch** *adj* magnetic (*a. fig*)
**magnetisieren** [magneti'zi:rən] *v/t* (*no -ge-, h*) magnetize
**Mahagoni** [maha'go:ni] *n* (-*s*; *no pl*) mahogany
**mähen** ['mɛ:ən] *v/t* (*ge-, h*) mow; cut; AGR reap; **'Mähdrescher** [-drɛʃɐ] *m* (-*s*; -) AGR combine (harvester)
**mahlen** ['ma:lən] *v/t* (*irr, ge-, h*) grind; mill
**'Mahlzeit** *f* (-; -*en*) meal; feed(ing)
**Mähne** ['mɛ:nə] *f* (-; -*n*) ZO mane (*a.* F)
**mahnen** ['ma:nən] *v/t* (*ge-, h*) remind; ECON send *s.o.* a reminder
**'Mahngebühr** *f* reminder fee
**'Mahnmal** *n* memorial
**'Mahnung** *f* (-; -*en*) reminder
**Mai** [mai] *m* (-[*e*]*s*; -*e*) May; ***der Erste ~*** May Day; **~baum** *m* maypole; **~glöckchen** *n* BOT lily of the valley; **~käfer** *m* ZO cockchafer
**Mais** [mais] *m* (-*es*; -*e*) BOT corn, *Br* maize
**Majestät** [majɛs'tɛ:t] *f*: ***Seine*** (***Ihre***, ***Eure***) ~ His (Her, Your) Majesty
**majes'tätisch** *adj* majestic
**Majonäse** *f* → ***Mayonnaise***
**Major** [ma'jo:ɐ] *m* (-*s*; -*e*) MIL major
**makaber** [ma'ka:bɐ] *adj* macabre
**Makel** ['ma:kəl] *m* (-*s*; -) blemish (*a. fig*)
**mäkelig** ['mɛ:kəlɪç] F *adj* picky, *esp Br* choos(e)y
**'makellos** *adj* immaculate (*a. fig*)
**mäkeln** ['mɛ:kəln] F *v/i* (*ge-, h*) carp, pick, nag (***an*** *dat* at)
**Makler** ['ma:klɐ] *m* (-*s*; -) ECON real estate agent; broker; **~gebühr** *f* fee, commission
**'Maklerin** *f* (-; -*nen*) ECON → ***Makler***
**mal** [ma:l] *adv* MATH times, multiplied by; by; F → ***einmal***; ***12 ~ 5 ist*** (***gleich***) ***60*** 12 times *or* multiplied by 5 is *or* equals 60; ***ein 7 ~ 4 Meter großes Zimmer*** a room 7 meters by 4
**Mal**[1] *n* (-[*e*]*s*; -*e*) time; ***zum ersten*** (***letzten***) **~(*e*)** for the first (last) time; ***mit e-m*** **~(*e*)** all of a sudden; ***ein für alle*** **~(*e*)** once and for all
**Mal**[2] *n* mark
**malen** ['ma:lən] *v/t* (*ge-, h*) paint
**Maler** ['ma:lɐ] *m* (-*s*; -) painter
**Malerei** [ma:lə'rai] *f* (-; -*en*) painting
**Malerin** ['ma:lərɪn] *f* (-; -*nen*) (woman) painter
**'malerisch** *fig adj* picturesque
**'Malkasten** *m* paintbox
**'malnehmen** → ***multiplizieren***
**Malz** [malts] *n* (-*es*; *no pl*) malt
**'Malzbier** *n* malt beer
**Mama** ['mama] F *f* (-; -*s*) mom(my), *Br* mum(my)
**Mammut** ['mamʊt] *n* (-*s*; -*e*, -*s*) ZO mammoth
**man** [man] *indef pron* you, one; they, people; ***wie schreibt ~ das?*** how do you spell it?; ***~ sagt, dass*** they *or* people say (that); ***~ hat mir gesagt*** I was told
**Manager** ['mɛnɪdʒɐ] *m* (-*s*; -), **'Managerin** *f* (-; -*nen*) ECON executive; SPORT manager
**manch** [manç], **~er** ['mançɐ], **~e** ['mançə], **~es** ['mançəs] *indef pron* (*mst pl*) some; quite a few, many
**'manchmal** *adv* sometimes, occasionally
**Mandant** [man'dant] *m* (-*en*; -*en*), **Man'dantin** *f* (-; -*nen*) JUR client
**Mandarine** [manda'ri:nə] *f* (-; -*n*) BOT tangerine
**Mandat** [man'da:t] *n* (-[*e*]*s*; -*e*) POL mandate; seat; **Mandatar** [manda'ta:ɐ] *Austrian m* → ***Abgeordnete***
**Mandel** ['mandəl] *f* (-; -*n*) BOT almond; ANAT tonsil; **~entzündung** *f* MED tonsillitis
**Manege** [ma'ne:ʒə] *f* (-; -*n*) (circus) ring
**Mangel**[1] ['maŋəl] *m* (-*s*; *Mängel* ['mɛŋəl]) a) (*no pl*) lack (***an*** *dat* of), shortage, b) TECH defect, fault; shortcoming; ***aus ~ an*** (*dat*) for lack of
**'Mangel**[2] *f* (-; -*n*) mangle
**'mangelhaft** *adj* poor (*quality etc*); defective (*goods etc*); PED poor, unsatisfactory, failing
**'mangeln** *v/t* (*ge-, h*) mangle
**'mangels** *prp* (*gen*) for lack *or* want of
**'Mangelware** *f*: ***~ sein*** be scarce
**Manie** [ma'ni:] *f* (-; -*n*) mania (*a. fig*)
**Manieren** [ma'ni:rən] *pl* manners
**manierlich** [ma'ni:ɐlɪç] *adv*: ***sich ~ betragen*** behave (decently)

M

**Manifest** [mani'fɛst] *n* (-[*e*]*s*; -*e*) manifesto
**manipulieren** [manipu'li:rən] *v/t* (*no -ge-*, *h*) manipulate
**Mann** [man] *m* (-[*e*]*s*; *Männer* ['mɛnɐ]) man; husband
**Männchen** ['mɛnçən] *n* (-*s*; -) ZO male
'**Manndeckung** *f* SPORT man-to-man marking
**Mannequin** ['manəkɛ̃:] *n* (-*s*; -*s*) model
**mannigfach** ['manɪçfax], '**mannigfaltig** *adj* many and various
**männlich** ['mɛnlɪç] *adj* BIOL male; masculine (*a.* LING)
'**Mannschaft** *f* (-; -*en*) SPORT team; MAR, AVIAT crew
**Manöver** [ma'nø:vɐ] *n* (-*s*; -), **manövrieren** [manø'vri:rən] *v/i* (*no -ge-*, *h*) maneuver, *Br* manoeuvre
**Mansarde** [man'zardə] *f* (-; -*n*) room *or* apartment in the attic
**Manschette** [man'ʃɛtə] *f* (-; -*n*) cuff; TECH gasket
**Man'schettenknopf** *m* cuff-link
**Mantel** ['mantəl] *m* (-*s*; *Mäntel* ['mɛntəl]) coat; *tire*: casing, *bicycle*: tire (*Br* tyre) cover; TECH jacket, shell
**Manuskript** [manu'skrɪpt] *n* (-[*e*]*s*; -*e*) manuscript; copy
**Mappe** ['mapə] *f* (-; -*n*) briefcase; school bag, satchel; folder
M
**Märchen** ['mɛ:ɐçən] *n* (-*s*; -) fairytale (*a. fig*); **~land** *n* (-[*e*]*s*; *no pl*) fairyland
**Marder** ['mardɐ] *m* (-*s*; -) ZO marten
**Margarine** [marga'ri:nə] *f* (-; *no pl*) margarine
**Margerite** [margə'ri:tə] *f* (-; -*n*) BOT marguerite
**Marienkäfer** [ma'ri:ən-] *m* ZO lady bug, *Br* ladybird
**Marihuana** [mari'hua:na] *n* (-*s*; *no pl*) marijuana, *sl* grass; **~ziga͵rette** *f sl* joint
**Marille** [ma'rɪlə] *Austrian f* (-; -*n*) BOT apricot
**Marine** [ma'ri:nə] *f* (-; -*n*) MIL navy
**ma'rineblau** *adj* navy blue
**Marionette** [marjo'nɛtə] *f* (-; -*n*) puppet (*a. fig*); **Mario'nettenthe͵ater** *n* puppet show
**Mark**[1] [mark] *f* (-; -) mark
**Mark**[2] *n* (-[*e*]*s*; *no pl*) marrow; BOT pulp
**Marke** ['markə] *f* (-; -*n*) ECON brand; TECH make; trademark; stamp; badge, tag; mark; **markieren** [mar'ki:rən] *v/t* (*no -ge-*, *h*) mark (*a.* SPORT); F *fig* act;
**Mar'kierung** *f* (-; -*en*) mark
**Markise** [mar'ki:zə] *f* (-; -*n*) awning, sun blind
**Markt** [markt] *m* (-[*e*]*s*; *Märkte* ['mɛrktə]) ECON market; ***auf den ~ bringen*** put on the market; **~platz** *m* market place; **~wirtschaft** *f* market economy
**Marmelade** [marmə'la:də] *f* (-; -*n*) jam
**Marmor** ['marmo:ɐ] *m* (-*s*; -*e*) marble
**Marsch**[1] [marʃ] *m* (-[*e*]*s*; *Märsche* ['mɛrʃə]) march (*a.* MUS)
**Marsch**[2] *f* (-; -*en*) GEOGR marsh, fen
**Marschall** ['marʃal] *m* (-*s*; *Marschälle* ['marʃɛlə]) MIL marshal
'**Marschbefehl** *m* MIL marching orders
**marschieren** [mar'ʃi:rən] *v/i* (*no -ge-*, *sein*) march
**Marsmensch** ['mars-] *m* Martian
**Marter** ['martɐ] *f* (-; -*n*) torture
'**martern** *v/t* (*ge-*, *h*) torture
'**Marterpfahl** *m* stake
**Martinshorn** ['marti:ns-] *n* (police *etc*) siren
**Märtyrer** ['mɛrtyrɐ] *m* (-*s*; -), '**Märtyrerin** *f* (-; -*nen*) martyr (*a. fig*)
**Marxismus** [mar'ksɪsmʊs] *m* (-; *no pl*) POL Marxism; **Marxist** [mar'ksɪst] *m* (-*en*; -*en*), **mar'xistisch** *adj* POL Marxist
**März** [mɛrts] *m* (-[*es*]; -*e*) March
**Marzipan** [martsi'pa:n] *n* (-*s*; -*e*) marzipan
**Masche** ['maʃə] *f* (-; -*n*) stitch; mesh; F trick
'**Maschendraht** *m* wire netting
**Maschine** [ma'ʃi:nə] *f* (-; -*n*) machine; MOT engine; AVIAT plane; motorcycle; ***~ schreiben*** type
**Ma'schinen|bau** *m* (-[*e*]*s*; *no pl*) mechanical engineering; **~gewehr** *n* MIL machinegun
**ma'schinenlesbar** *adj* EDP machine-readable
**Ma'schinen|öl** *n* engine oil; **~pis͵tole** *f* MIL submachine gun, machine pistol; **~schaden** *m* engine trouble *or* failure; **~schlosser** *m* (engine) fitter
**Masern** ['ma:zɐn] *pl* MED measles
**Maserung** ['ma:zərʊŋ] *f* (-; -*en*) grain
**Maske** ['maskə] *f* (-; -*n*) mask (*a.* EDP)
'**Maskenball** *m* fancy-dress ball
'**Maskenbildner** [-bɪldnɐ] *m* (-*s*; -),

'**Maskenbildnerin** *f* (-; *-nen*) THEA *etc* make-up artist
**maskieren** [mas'ki:rən] *v/t* (*no -ge-, h*) mask; ***sich*** ~ put on a mask
**maskulin** [masku'li:n] *adj* masculine (*a.* LING)
**maß** [ma:s] *pret of* ***messen***
**Maß**[1] *n* (*-es; -e*) measure (**für** of); dimensions, measurements, size; *fig* extent, degree; ***~e und Gewichte*** weights and measures; ***nach*** ~ (***gemacht***) made to measure; ***in gewissem*** (***hohem***) ***~e*** to a certain (high) degree; ***in zunehmendem ~e*** increasingly; ~ ***halten*** be moderate (***in*** *dat* in)
**Maß**[2] *f* (-; -[*e*]) liter (*Br* litre) of beer
**Massage** [ma'sa:ʒə] *f* (-; *-n*) massage
**Massaker** [ma'sa:kɐ] *n* (*-s*; -) massacre
**Masse** ['masə] *f* (-; *-n*) mass; substance; bulk; F ***e-e*** ~ *Geld etc* loads *or* heaps of; ***die*** (***breite***) ~, POL ***die ~n*** *pl* the masses
'**Maßeinheit** *f* unit of measure(ment)
'**Massen...** *in cpds ...medien, ...mörder etc*: mass ...; **~andrang** *m* crush
'**massenhaft** F *adv* masses *or* loads of
'**Massen|karambo,lage** *f* MOT pileup; **~produkti,on** *f* ECON mass production
**Masseur** [ma'sø:ɐ] *m* (*-s; -e*) masseur
**Masseurin** [ma'sø:rɪn] *f* (-; *-nen*), **Masseuse** [ma'sø:zə] *f* (-; *-n*) masseuse
'**maßgebend**, '**maßgeblich** [-ge:plɪç] *adj* authoritative
**massieren** [ma'si:rən] *v/t* (*no -ge-, h*) massage
**massig** ['masɪç] *adj* massive, bulky
**mäßig** ['mɛ:sɪç] *adj* moderate; poor
**mäßigen** ['mɛ:sɪgən] *v/t and v/refl* (*ge-, h*) moderate; '**Mäßigung** *f* (-; *no pl*) moderation; restraint
**massiv** [ma'si:f] *adj* solid
**Mas'siv** *n* (*-s; -e*) GEOL massif
'**Maßkrug** *m* beer mug, stein
'**maßlos** *adj* immoderate; gross (*exaggeration*)
'**Maßnahme** [-na:mə] *f* (-; *-n*) measure, step
'**Maßregel** *f* rule; '**maßregeln** *v/t* (*ge-, h*) reprimand; discipline
'**Maßstab** *m* scale; *fig* standard; ***im*** ~ ***1:10*** on the scale of 1:10
**maßstabgetreu** *adj* true to scale
'**maßvoll** *adj* moderate
**Mast**[1] [mast] *m* (-[*e*]*s; -en*) MAR, TECH mast
**Mast**[2] *f* (-; *-en*) AGR fattening
'**Mastdarm** *m* ANAT rectum
**mästen** ['mɛstən] *v/t* (*ge-, h*) AGR fatten; F stuff *s.o.*
**masturbieren** [mastʊr'bi:rən[ *v/i* (*no -ge-, h*) masturbate
**Match** [mɛtʃ] *n* (-[*e*]*s; -s, -e*) game, *Br* match; **~ball** *m tennis*: match point
**Material** [mate'rja:l] *n* (*-s; -ien*) material (*a. fig*); TECH materials
**Materialismus** [materja'lɪsmʊs] *m* (-; *no pl*) PHILOS materialism; **Materialist** [-'lɪst] *m* (*-en; -en*) materialist; **materia'listisch** *adj* materialistic
**Materie** [ma'te:rjə] *f* (-; *-n*) matter (*a. fig*); *fig* subject (matter); **materiell** [mate'rjɛl] *adj* material
**Mathematik** [matema'ti:k] *f* (-; *no pl*) mathematics; **Mathematiker** [mate'ma:tikɐ] *m* (*-s*; -) mathematician; **mathe'matisch** *adj* mathematical
**Matinee** [mati'ne:] *f* (-; *-n*) THEA *etc* morning performance
**Matratze** [ma'tratsə] *f* (-; *-n*) mattress
**Matrize** [ma'tri:tsə] *f* (-; *-n*) stencil
**Matrose** [ma'tro:zə] *m* (*-n; -n*) MAR sailor, seaman
**Matsch** [matʃ] F *m* (-[*e*]*s; no pl*) mud, slush; '**matschig** *adj* muddy, slushy
**matt** [mat] *adj* weak; exhausted, worn out; dull, pale (*color*); PHOT mat(t); frosted (*glass*); *chess*: checkmate
**Matte** ['matə] *f* (-; *-n*) mat
**Mattigkeit** ['matɪçkait] *f* (-; *no pl*) exhaustion, weakness
'**Mattscheibe** *f* screen; PHOT focus(s)ing screen; F (boob) tube, *Br* telly, box
**Matura** [ma'tu:ra] *Austrian, Swiss f* → ***Abitur***
**Mauer** ['mauɐ] *f* (-; *-n*) wall; **~blümchen** *fig n* wallflower; **~werk** *n* (-[*e*]*s; no pl*) masonry, brickwork
'**mauern** *v/i* (*ge-, h*) lay bricks
**Maul** [maul] *n* (-[*e*]*s; Mäuler* ['mɔʏlɐ]) ZO mouth; *sl* ***halt's ~!*** shut up!
**maulen** ['maulən] F *v/i* (*ge-, h*) grumble, sulk, pout
'**Maul|korb** *m* muzzle (*a. fig*); **~tier** *n* mule; **~wurf** *m* ZO mole; **~wurfshaufen** *m*, **~wurfshügel** *m* molehill
**Maurer** ['maurɐ] *m* (*-s*; -) bricklayer; **~kelle** *f* trowel; **~meister** *m* master bricklayer; **~po,lier** *m* foreman bricklayer

M

**Maus** [maus] *f* (-; *Mäuse* ['mɔʏzə]) ZO mouse (*a.* EDP)
**'Mausefalle** ['mauzə-] *f* mousetrap
**Mauser** ['mauzɐ] *f* (-; *no pl*) ZO mo(u)lt (-ing); ***in der ~ sein*** be mo(u)lting
**Maut** [maut] *Austrian f* (-; *-en*) toll; **~straße** *f* turnpike, toll road
**maximal** [maksi'ma:l] **1.** *adj* maximum; **2.** *adv* at (the) most; **Maximum** ['maksimʊm] *n* (-*s*; -*ma*) maximum
**Mayonnaise** [majɔ'nɛ:zə] *f* (-; -*n*) GASTR mayonnaise
**Mäzen** [mɛ'tse:n] *m* (-*s*; -*e*) patron; SPORT sponsor
**Mechanik** [me'ça:nɪk] *f* (-; -*en*) a) (*no pl*) PHYS mechanics, b) TECH mechanism; **Mechaniker** [me'ça:nikɐ] *m* (-*s*; -) mechanic; **mechanisch** [me'ça:nɪʃ] *adj* TECH mechanical; **mechanisieren** [meçani'zi:rən] *v/t* (*no -ge-*, *h*) mechanize; **Mechani'sierung** *f* (-; -*en*) mechanization; **Mechanismus** [meça'nɪsmʊs] *m* (-; -*men*) TECH mechanism; works
**meckern** ['mɛkɐn] *v/i* (*ge-*, *h*) ZO bleat; F grumble, bitch (***über*** *acc* at, about)
**Medaille** [me'daljə] *f* (-; -*n*) medal
**Me'daillengewinner** *m* medal(l)ist
**Medaillon** [medal'jõ:] *n* (-*s*; -*s*) locket
**Medien** ['me:djən] *pl* mass media; teaching aids; audio-visual aids
**Medikament** [medika'mɛnt] *n* (-[*e*]*s*; -*e*) drug; medicine
**meditieren** [medi'ti:rən] *v/i* (*no -ge-*, *h*) meditate (***über*** *acc* on)
**Medizin** [medi'tsi:n] *f* (-; -*en*) a) (*no pl*) (science of) medicine, b) medicine, remedy (***gegen*** for)
**Mediziner** [medi'tsi:nɐ] *m* (-*s*; -), **Medi'zinerin** *f* (-; -*nen*) (medical) doctor; UNIV medical student
**medizinisch** [medi'tsi:nɪʃ] *adj* medical
**Meer** [me:ɐ] *n* (-[*e*]*s*; -*e* ['me:rə]) sea (*a. fig*), ocean; **~enge** *f* GEOGR straits
**Meeres|boden** ['me:rəs-] *m* seabed; **~früchte** *pl* GASTR seafood; **~spiegel** *m* sea level
**'Meerjungfrau** *f* MYTH mermaid
**'Meerrettich** *m* (-*s*; -*e*) horseradish
**'Meerschweinchen** [-ʃvainçən] *n* (-*s*; -) ZO guinea pig
**Megabyte** [mega'bait] *n* EDP megabyte
**Mehl** [me:l] *n* (-[*e*]*s*; -*e*) flour; meal
**mehlig** ['me:lɪç] *adj* mealy
**'Mehlspeise** *Austrian f* sweet (dish)
**mehr** [me:ɐ] *indef pron and adv* more; ***immer ~*** more and more; ***nicht ~*** no longer, not any longer (*or* more); ***noch ~*** even more; ***es ist kein ... ~ da*** there isn't any ... left
**'mehrdeutig** [-dɔʏtɪç] *adj* ambiguous
**mehrere** ['me:rərə] *adj and indef pron* several
**'Mehrheit** *f* (-; -*en*) majority
**'Mehrkosten** *pl* extra costs
**'mehrmals** *adv* several times
**'Mehr|wegflasche** *f* returnable (*or* deposit) bottle; **~wertsteuer** *f* ECON value-added tax (ABBR VAT); **~zahl** *f* (-; *no pl*) majority; LING plural (form)
**'Mehrzweck...** *in cpds ...fahrzeug etc*: multi-purpose ...
**meiden** ['maidən] *v/t* (*irr*, *ge-*, *h*) avoid
**Meile** ['mailə] *f* (-; -*n*) mile
**'meilenweit** *adv* (for) miles
**mein** [main] *poss pron and adj* my; ***das ist ~er*** (***~e***, ***~***[***e***]***s***) that's mine
**'Meineid** *m* JUR perjury
**meinen** ['mainən] *v/t* (*ge-*, *h*) think, believe; mean; say; ***~ Sie*** (***wirklich***)***?*** do you (really) think so?; ***wie ~ Sie das?*** what do you mean by that?; ***sie ~ es gut*** they mean well; ***ich habe es nicht so gemeint*** I didn't mean it; ***wie ~ Sie?*** (I beg your) pardon?
**meinet'wegen** ['mainət-] *adv* for my sake; because of me; F I don't mind *or* care!
**'Meinung** *f* (-; -*en*) opinion (***über*** *acc*, ***von*** about, of); ***meiner ~ nach*** in my opinion; ***der ~ sein***, ***dass*** be of the opinion that, feel *or* believe that; ***s-e ~ äußern*** express one's opinion; ***s-e ~ ändern*** change one's mind; ***ich bin Ihrer*** (***anderer***) ***~*** I (don't) agree with you; ***j-m die ~ sagen*** give s.o. a piece of one's mind
**'Meinungs|austausch** *m* exchange of views (***über*** *acc* on); **~forscher** *m* pollster; **~freiheit** *f* (-; *no pl*) freedom of speech *or* opinion; **~umfrage** *f* opinion poll; **~verschiedenheit** *f* disagreement (***über*** *acc* about)
**Meise** ['maizə] *f* (-; -*n*) ZO titmouse
**Meißel** ['maisəl] *m* (-*s*; -) chisel
**'meißeln** *v/t and v/i* (*ge-*, *h*) chisel, carve
**meist** [maist] **1.** *adj* most; ***das ~e*** (***davon***) most of it; ***die ~en*** (***von ihnen***)

most of them; ***die ~en Leute*** most people; ***die ~e Zeit*** most of the time; **2.** *adv* → ***meistens***; ***am ~en*** (the) most; most (of all); **meistens** ['maistəns] *adv* usually; most of the time

**Meister** ['maistɐ] *m* (*-s*; -) master (*a. fig*); SPORT champion, F champ

'**meisterhaft** **1.** *adj* masterly; **2.** *adv* in a masterly manner *or* way

'**Meisterin** *f* (-; *-nen*) master (*a. fig*); SPORT champion

**meistern** ['maistɐn] *v/t* (*ge-*, *h*) master

'**Meisterschaft** *f* (-; *-en*) a) (*no pl*) mastery, b) SPORT championship, cup; title

'**Meister|stück** *n*, **~werk** *n* masterpiece

**Melancholie** [melaŋko'li:] *f* (-; *-n*) melancholy; **melancholisch** [melaŋ-'ko:lɪʃ] *adj* melancholy; ~ ***sein*** feel depressed, F have the blues

**Melange** [me'lã:ʒə] *Austrian f* (-; *-n*) coffee with milk

**melden** ['mɛldən] (*ge-*, *h*) **1.** *v/t* report *s.th. or s.o.* (***bei*** to); *radio etc*: announce, report; ***j-m et.*** ~ notify s.o. of s.th.; **2.** *v/refl*: ***sich*** ~ report (***bei*** to, ***für***, ***zu*** for); register (***bei*** with); PED *etc*: put up one's hand; TEL answer the phone; SPORT enter (***für, zu*** for); volunteer (***für, zu*** for)

'**Meldung** *f* (-; *-en*) report, news, announcement; information, notice; notification; registration (***bei*** with); SPORT entry (***für***, ***zu*** for)

**melken** ['mɛlkən] *v/t* ([*irr*,] *ge-*, *h*) milk

**Melodie** [melo'di:] *f* (-; *-n*) MUS melody, tune; **melodisch** [me'lo:dɪʃ] *adj* MUS melodious, melodic

**Melone** [me'lo:nə] *f* (-; *-n*) BOT melon; F derby, *Br* bowler (hat)

**Memoiren** [me'moa:rən] *pl* memoirs

**Menge** ['mɛŋə] *f* (-; *-n*) amount, quantity; MATH set; F ***e-e ~ Geld*** plenty (*or* lots) of money; → ***Menschenmenge***

'**Mengenlehre** *f* (-; *no pl*) MATH set theory; PED new math(ematics)

**Mensa** ['mɛnza] *f* (-; *-s*, *Mensen*) cafeteria, *Br* refectory, canteen

**Mensch** [mɛnʃ] *m* (*-en*; *-en*) human being; man; person, individual; *pl* people; mankind; ***kein*** ~ nobody; **~!** wow!

'**Menschen|affe** *m* ZO ape; **~fresser** *m* cannibal; **~freund** *m* philanthropist; **~handel** *m* slave trade; **~kenntnis** *f*: ~ ***haben*** know human nature; **~leben** *n* human life

'**menschenleer** *adj* deserted

'**Menschen|menge** *f* crowd; **~rechte** *pl* human rights; **~seele** *f*: ***keine*** ~ not a (living) soul

'**menschenunwürdig** *adj* degrading; *housing etc*: unfit for human beings

'**Menschen|verstand** *m*: ***gesunder*** ~ common sense; **~würde** *f* human dignity

**Menschheit:** ***die*** ~ mankind, the human race

'**menschlich** *adj* human; humane

'**Menschlichkeit** *f* (-; *no pl*) humanity

**Menstruation** [mɛnstrua'tsjo:n] *f* (-; *-en*) MED menstruation

**Mentalität** [mɛntali'tɛ:t] *f* (-; *-en*) mentality

**Menü** [me'ny:] *n* (*-s*; *-s*) set meal (*or* lunch); EDP menu

**Meridian** [meri'dja:n] *m* (*-s*; *-e*) GEOGR, ASTR meridian

**merkbar** ['mɛrkba:ɐ] *adj* marked, distinct; noticeable; '**Merkblatt** *n* leaflet; **merken** ['mɛrkən] *v/t* (*ge-*, *h*) notice; feel; find (out), discover; ***sich et.*** ~ remember s.th., keep *or* bear s.th. in mind; '**merklich** *adj* → ***merkbar***; '**Merkmal** *n* sign; feature, trait

'**merkwürdig** *adj* strange, odd, curious

'**merkwürdiger'weise** *adv* strangely enough

**messbar** ['mɛsba:ɐ] *adj* measurable

'**Messbecher** *m* measuring cup

**Messe** ['mɛsə] *f* (-; *-n*) ECON fair; REL mass; MIL, MAR mess

**messen** ['mɛsən] *v/t* (*irr*, *ge-*, *h*) measure; take (*temperature etc*); ***sich nicht mit j-m ~ können*** be no match for s.o.; ***gemessen an*** (*dat*) compared with

**Messer** ['mɛsɐ] *n* (*-s*; -) knife; ***bis aufs ~*** to the knife; ***auf des ~s Schneide stehen*** be on a razor edge, be touch and go (***ob*** whether)

**Messerstecherei** [-ʃtɛçə'rai] *f* (-; *-en*) knife fight

'**Messerstich** *m* stab (with a knife)

**Messing** ['mɛsɪŋ] *n* (*-s*; *-e*) brass

'**Messinstru,ment** *n* measuring instrument

'**Messung** *f* (-; *-en*) measuring; reading

**Metall** [me'tal] *n* (*-s*; *-e*) metal

**metallen** [me'talən], **me'tallisch** *adj* metallic

M

**Me'tallwaren** *pl* hardware
**Metamorphose** [metamɔr'fo:zə] *f* (-; -*n*) metamorphosis
**Metastase** [meta'sta:zə] *f* (-; -*n*) MED metastasis
**Meteor** [mete'o:ɐ] *m* (-*s*; -*e*) ASTR meteor
**Meteorit** [meteo'ri:t] *m* (-*en*; -*e*[*n*]) ASTR meteorite
**Meteorologe** [meteoro'lo:gə] *m* (-*n*; -*n*) meteorologist; **Meteorologie** [meteorolo'gi:] *f* (-; *no pl*) meteorology; **Meteoro'login** *f* (-; -*nen*) meteorologist
**Meter** ['me:tɐ] *n*, *m* (-*s*; -) meter, *Br* metre; **~maß** *n* tape measure
**Methode** [me'to:də] *f* (-; -*n*) method, TECH *a.* technique; **methodisch** [me'to:dɪʃ] *adj* methodical
**metrisch** ['me:trɪʃ] *adj* metric; **~es Maßsystem** metric system
**Metropole** [metro'po:lə] *f* (-; -*n*) metropolis
**Metzger** ['mɛtsgɐ] *m* (-*s*; -) butcher
**Metzgerei** [mɛtsgə'rai] *f* (-; -*en*) butcher's (shop)
**Meute** ['mɔʏtə] *f* (-; -*n*) pack (of hounds); *fig* mob, pack
**Meuterei** [mɔʏtə'rai] *f* (-; -*en*) mutiny; **Meuterer** ['mɔʏtərɐ] *m* (-*s*; -) mutineer; **meutern** ['mɔʏtɐn] *v/i* (*ge*-, *h*) mutiny (***gegen*** against)
**MEZ** ABBR *of* ***Mitteleuropäische Zeit*** CET, Central European Time
**miau** [mi'au] *int* ZO meow, *Br* miaow
**miauen** [mi'auən] *v/i* (*no -ge-*, *h*) ZO meow, *Br* miaow
**mich** [mɪç] *pers pron* me; **~ (*selbst*)** myself
**mied** [mi:t] *pret of* ***meiden***
**Mieder** ['mi:dɐ] *n* (-*s*; -) corset(s); bodice; **~höschen** *n* pantie girdle; **~waren** *pl* foundation garments
**Miene** ['mi:nə] *f* (-; -*n*) expression, look, air; ***gute ~ zum bösen Spiel machen*** grin and bear it
**mies** [mi:s] F *adj* rotten, lousy
**Miete** ['mi:tə] *f* (-; -*n*) rent; hire charge; ***zur ~ wohnen*** be a tenant; lodge (***bei*** with); **'mieten** *v/t* (*ge*-, *h*) rent; (take on) lease; AVIAT, MAR charter; ***ein Auto etc ~*** rent (*Br* hire) a car *etc*; **Mieter(in)** ['mi:tɐ (-tərɪn)] (-*s*; -/-; -*nen*) tenant, lodger
**'Mietshaus** *n* apartment building *or* house, *Br* block of flats, tenement
**'Mietvertrag** *m* lease (contract)
**'Mietwohnung** *f* apartment, *Br* (rented) flat
**Migräne** [mi'grɛ:nə] *f* (-; -*n*) MED migraine
**Mikro** ['mi:kro] F *n* (-*s*; -*s*) mike
**Mikro...** ['mi:kro-] *in cpds ...chip, ...computer, ...elektronik, ...film, ...prozessor etc*: micro...
**Mikrofon** [mikro'fo:n] *n* (-*s*; -*e*) microphone
**Mikroskop** [mikro'sko:p] *n* (-*s*; -*e*) microscope; **mikro'skopisch** *adj* microscopic(al)
**Mikrowelle** ['mi:kro-] F *f*, **'Mikrowellenherd** *m* microwave oven
**Milbe** ['mɪlbə] *f* (-; -*n*) ZO mite
**Milch** [mɪlç] *f* (-; *no pl*) milk; **~geschäft** *n* dairy, creamery; **~glas** *n* frosted glass
**milchig** ['mɪlçɪç] *adj* milky
**'Milch|kaffee** *m* white coffee; **~kännchen** *n* (milk) jug; **~kanne** *f* milk can; **~mann** F *m* milkman; **~mixgetränk** *n* milk shake; **~pro,dukte** *pl* dairy products; **~pulver** *n* powdered milk; **~reis** *m* rice pudding; **~straße** *f* ASTR Milky Way, Galaxy; **~tüte** *f* milk carton; **~wirtschaft** *f* dairy farming; **~zahn** *m* milk tooth
**mild** [mɪlt] *adj* mild, soft; gentle
**milde** ['mɪldə] *adv* mildly; **~ *ausgedrückt*** to put it mildly
**'Milde** *f* (-; *no pl*) mildness, gentleness; leniency, mercy
**mildern** ['mɪldɐn] *v/t* (*ge*-, *h*) lessen, soften; **~d** *adj*: ***~e Umstände*** JUR mitigating circumstances
**'mildtätig** *adj* charitable
**Milieu** [mi'ljø:] *n* (-*s*; -*s*) environment; social background
**Militär** [mili'tɛ:ɐ] *n* (-*s*; *no pl*) *the* military, armed forces; army; **~dienst** *m* (-[*e*]*s*; *no pl*) military service; **~dikta,tur** *f* military dictatorship; **~gericht** *n* court martial
**militärisch** [mili'tɛ:rɪʃ] *adj* military
**Militarismus** [milita'rɪsmʊs] *m* (-; *no pl*) militarism; **Militarist** [milita'rɪst] *m* (-*en*; -*en*) militarist; **milita'ristisch** *adj* militaristic
**'Mili'tärre'gierung** *f* military government

**Milliarde** [mɪ'ljardə] *f* (-; *-n*) billion, *Br old use a.* a thousand million(s)
**Millimeter** ['mɪlimeːtɐ] *n, m* (*-s*; -) millimet|er, *Br* -re; **~pa,pier** *n* graph paper
**Million** [mɪ'lioːn] *f* (-; *-en*) million
**Millionär** [mɪljo'nɛːɐ] *m* (*-s*; *-e*), **Millio'närin** *f* (-; *-nen*) millionaire
**Milz** [mɪlts] *f* (-; *no pl*) ANAT spleen
**Mimik** ['miːmɪk] *f* (-; *no pl*) facial expression
**minder** ['mɪndɐ] **1.** *adj* → ***geringer***, ***weniger***; **2.** *adv* less; ***nicht*** ~ no less
**'Minderheit** *f* (-; *-en*) minority
**'minderjährig** [-jɛːrɪç] *adj*: ~ ***sein*** be under age, be a minor; **'Minderjährige** [-jɛːrɪgə] *m, f* (*-n*; *-n*) minor
**'Minderjährigkeit** *f* (-; *no pl*) minority
**'minderwertig** *adj* inferior, of inferior quality; **'Minderwertigkeit** *f* (-; *no pl*) inferiority; ECON inferior quality
**'Minderwertigkeitskom,plex** *m* PSYCH inferiority complex
**mindest** ['mɪndəst] *adj* least; ***das Mindeste*** the (very) least; ***nicht im 2en*** not in the least, not at all
**'Mindest...** *in cpds ...alter, ...einkommen, ...lohn etc*: minimum ...
**mindestens** ['mɪndəstəns] *adv* at least
**'Mindest|haltbarkeitsdatum** *n* pull date, *Br* best-before (*or* best-by, sell-by) date; **~maß** *n* minimum; ***auf ein ~ herabsetzen*** reduce to a minimum
**Mine** ['miːnə] *f* (-; *-n*) mine (*a.* MAR, MIL); lead; cartridge; refill
**Mineral** [minə'raːl] *n* (*-s*; *-e*, *-ien*) mineral; **Mineralogie** [mineralo'giː] *f* (-; *no pl*) mineralogy
**Mine'ralöl** *n* mineral oil
**Mine'ralwasser** *n* mineral water
**Miniatur** [minja'tuːɐ] *f* (-; *-en*) miniature
**Minigolf** ['mɪni-] *n* miniature (*Br* crazy) golf
**minimal** [mini'maːl] *adj, adv* minimal; minimum; at least; **Minimum** ['miːnimʊm] *n* (*-s*; *-ma*) minimum
**Minirock** ['mɪni-] *m* miniskirt
**Minister** [mi'nɪstɐ] *m* (*-s*; -), **Mi'nisterin** *f* (-; *-nen*) minister, secretary, *Br a.* secretary of state
**Ministerium** [minɪs'teːriʊm] *n* (*-s*; *-ien*) ministry, department, *Br a.* office
**Mi'nisterpräsi,dent** *m*, **Mi'nisterpräsi,dentin** *f* prime minister
**minus** ['miːnʊs] *adv* MATH minus; ***bei 10 Grad*** ~ at 10 degrees below zero
**Minute** [mi'nuːtə] *f* (-; *-n*) minute
**Mi'nutenzeiger** *m* minute hand
**Mio** ABBR *of* ***Million(en)*** m, million
**mir** [miːɐ] *pers pron* (to) me
**Mischbatte,rie** ['mɪʃ-] *f* mixing faucet, *Br* mixer tap
**'Mischbrot** *n* wheat and rye bread
**mischen** ['mɪʃən] *v/t* (*ge-*, *h*) mix; blend (*tea etc*); shuffle (*cards*); ***sich*** ~ mingle *or* mix (***unter*** with)
**'Mischling** *m* (*-s*; *-e*) *esp contp* half-caste; BOT, ZO hybrid; mongrel
**'Mischmasch** F *m* (*-[e]s*; *-e*) hotchpotch, jumble
**'Misch|ma,schine** *f* TECH mixer; **~pult** *n radio*, TV: mixer, mixing console
**'Mischung** *f* (-; *-en*) mixture; blend; assortment
**'Mischwald** *m* mixed forest
**miserabel** [mizə'raːbəl] F *adj* lousy, rotten
**miss'achten** [mɪs-] *v/t* (*no -ge-*, *h*) disregard, ignore; despise
**Miss'achtung** *f* disregard; contempt; neglect (*all*: *gen* of)
**'Missbildung** *f* (-; *-en*) deformity, malformation
**miss'billigen** *v/t* (*no -ge-*, *h*) disapprove of
**'Missbrauch** *m* abuse (*a.* JUR); misuse; **miss'brauchen** *v/t* (*no -ge-*, *h*) abuse; misuse
**miss'deuten** *v/t* (*no -ge-*, *h*) misinterpret
**'Misserfolg** *m* failure; F flop
**'Missernte** *f* bad harvest, crop failure
**miss'fallen** *v/i* (*irr*, ***fallen***, *no -ge-*, *h*) ***j-m*** ~ displease s.o.; **'Missfallen** *n* (*-s*; *no pl*) displeasure, dislike
**'missgebildet** *adj* deformed, malformed; **'Missgeburt** *f* deformed child *or* animal; freak
**'Missgeschick** *n* (*-[e]s*; *-e*) mishap
**miss'glücken** *v/i* (*no -ge-*, *sein*) fail
**miss'gönnen** *v/t* (*no -ge-*, *h*) ***j-m et.*** ~ envy s.o. s.th.
**'Missgriff** *m* mistake
**miss'handeln** *v/t* (*no -ge-*, *h*) ill-treat, maltreat (*a. fig*); batter
**Miss'handlung** *f* ill-treatment, maltreatment, *esp* JUR assault and battery
**Mission** [mɪ'sjoːn] *f* (-; *-en*) mission (*a.* POL *and fig*); **Missionar(in)** [mɪsjo-

M

'naːɐ (-'naːrɪn)] (*-s*; *-e*/*-*; *-nen*) missionary

**'Missklang** *m* dissonance, discord (*both a. fig*)

**'Misskreˌdit** *m* discredit

**misslang** [mɪs'laŋ] *pret of* ***misslingen***; **misslingen** [mɪs'lɪŋən] *v/i* (*irr*, *no -ge-*, *sein*) fail; **misslungen** [mɪs'lʊŋən] *pp of* ***misslingen***; ***das ist mir*** ~ I've bungled it

**'missmutig** *adj* bad-tempered, grumpy, glum

**miss'raten 1.** *v/i* (*irr*, ***raten***, *no -ge-*, *sein*) fail; turn out badly; **2.** *adj* wayward

**miss'trauen** *v/i* (*no -ge-*, *h*) distrust; **'Misstrauen** *n* (*-s*; *no pl*) distrust, suspicion (*both*: ***gegenüber*** of)

**'Misstrauens|antrag** *m* PARL motion of no confidence; **~votum** *n* PARL vote of no confidence

**misstrauisch** ['mɪstrauɪʃ] *adj* distrustful, suspicious

**'Missverhältnis** *n* disproportion

**'Missverständnis** *n* (*-ses*; *-se*) misunderstanding; **'missverstehen** *v/t* (*irr*, ***stehen***, *no -ge-*, *h*) misunderstand

**'Misswahl** *f* beauty contest *or* competition

**Mist** [mɪst] *m* (*-[e]s*; *no p*) AGR dung, manure; F trash, rubbish

**'Mistbeet** *n* AGR hotbed

**Mistel** ['mɪstəl] *f* (*-*; *-n*) BOT mistletoe

**'Mistgabel** *f* AGR dung fork

**'Misthaufen** *m* AGR manure heap

**mit** [mɪt] *prp* (*dat*) *and adv* with; ~ ***Gewalt*** by force; ~ ***Absicht*** on purpose; ~ ***dem Auto*** (***der Bahn*** *etc*) by car (train *etc*); ~ ***20 Jahren*** at (the age of) 20; ~ ***100 Stundenkilometern*** at 100 kilometers per hour; ~ ***einem Mal***(***e***) all of a sudden; (all) at the same time; ~ ***lauter Stimme*** in a loud voice; ~ ***anderen Worten*** in other words; ***ein Mann*** ~ ***dem Namen ...*** a man by the name of ...; ***j-n*** ~ ***Namen kennen*** know s.o. by name; ~ ***der Grund dafür***, ***dass*** one of the reasons why; ~ ***der Beste*** one of the best

**'Mitarbeit** *f* cooperation; assistance; PED activity, class participation

**'Mitarbeiter** *m*, **'Mitarbeiterin** *f* colleague; employee; assistant; ***freie***(***r***) ***Mitarbeiter***(***in***) freelance

**'mit|bekommen** F *v/t* (*irr*, ***kommen***, *sep*, *no -ge-*, *h*) get; catch; **~benutzen** *v/t* (*sep*, *no -ge-*, *h*) share

**'Mit|bestimmungsrecht** *n* (right of) codetermination, worker participation; **~bewerber(in)** (rival) competitor; fellow applicant; **~bewohner(in)** roommate, *Br* flatmate

**'mitbringen** *v/t* (*irr*, ***bringen***, *sep*, *-ge-*, *h*) bring *s.th. or s.o.* with one; ***j-m et.*** ~ bring s.o. s.th.; **Mitbringsel** ['mɪtbrɪŋzəl] F *n* (*-s*; *-*) little present; souvenir

**'Mitbürger** *m*, **'Mitbürgerin** *f* fellow citizen

**mitei'nander** *adv* with each other, with one another; together, jointly

**'miterleben** *v/t* (*sep*, *no -ge-*, *h*) live to see

**'Mitesser** *m* MED blackhead

**'mitfahren** *v/i* (*irr*, ***fahren***, *sep*, *-ge-*, *sein*) ***mit j-m*** ~ drive *or* go with s.o.; ***j-n*** ~ ***lassen*** give s.o. a lift

**'Mitfahr|gelegenheit** *f* lift; **~zenˌtrale** *f* car pool(ing) service

**'mitfühlend** *adj* sympathetic

**'mitgeben** *v/t* (*irr*, ***geben***, *sep*, *-ge-*, *h*) ***j-m et.*** ~ give s.o. s.th. (to take along)

**'Mitgefühl** *n* (*-[e]s*; *no pl*) sympathy

**'mitgehen** *v/i* (*irr*, ***gehen***, *sep*, *-ge-*, *sein*) ***mit j-m*** ~ go *or* come along with s.o.; F ***et.*** ~ ***lassen*** walk off with s.th.

**'Mitgift** *f* (*-*; *-en*) dowry

**'Mitglied** *n* member (***bei*** of)

**'Mitgliedsbeitrag** *m* subscription

**'Mitgliedschaft** *f* (*-*; *-en*) membership

**'mithaben** *v/t* (*irr*, ***haben***, *sep*, *-ge-*, *h*) ***ich habe kein Geld mit*** I haven't got any money with me *or* on me

**'Mithilfe** *f* (*-*; *no pl*) assistance, help, cooperation (***bei*** in; ***von*** of)

**mit'hilfe** *prp*: ~ ***von*** (*or gen*) with the help of, *fig a.* by means of

**'mithören** *v/t* (*sep*, *-ge-*, *h*) listen in to; overhear

**'Mitinhaber** *m*, **'Mitinhaberin** *f* joint owner

**'mitkommen** *v/i* (*irr*, ***kommen***, *sep*, *-ge-*, *sein*) come along (***mit*** with); *fig* keep pace (***mit*** with), follow; PED get on, keep up (with the class)

**'Mitlaut** *m* LING consonant

**'Mitleid** *n* (*-[e]s*; *no pl*) pity (***mit*** for); ***aus*** ~ out of pity; ~ ***haben mit*** feel sorry for

**mitleidig** ['mɪtlaidɪç] *adj* compassionate, sympathetic

**'mitleidslos** *adj* pitiless
**'mitmachen** (*sep*, *-ge-*, *h*) **1.** *v/i* join in; **2.** *v/t* take part in; follow (*a fashion etc*); F go through
**'Mitmenschen:** ***die*** ~ one's fellow human beings; people
**'mitnehmen** *v/t* (*irr*, ***nehmen***, *sep*, *-ge-*, *h*) take *s.th. or s.o.* with one; ***j-n*** (***im Auto***) ~ give s.o. a lift
**'mitreden** *v/t* (*sep*, *-ge-*, *h*) ***et. mitzureden haben*** (***bei***) have a say (in)
**'mitreißen** *v/t* (*irr*, ***reißen***, *sep*, *-ge-*, *h*) drag along; *fig* carry away (*mst passive*); **~d** *fig adj* electrifying (*speech etc*)
**'mitschneiden** *v/t* (*irr*, ***schneiden***, *sep*, *-ge-*, *h*) *radio*, TV record, tape(-record)
**'mitschreiben** (*irr*, ***schreiben***, *sep*, *-ge-*, *h*) **1.** *v/t* take down; take, do (*a test*); **2.** *v/i* take notes
**'Mitschuld** *f* (-; *no pl*) partial responsibility; **'mitschuldig** *adj*: ~ ***sein*** be partly to blame (***an*** *dat* for)
**'Mitschüler** *m*, **'Mitschülerin** *f* classmate; schoolmate, fellow student
**'mitspielen** *v/i* (*sep*, *-ge-*, *h*) SPORT, MUS play; join in *a game etc*; ***in e-m Film*** *etc* ~ be *or* appear in a film *etc*
**'Mitspieler** *m*, **'Mitspielerin** *f* partner, SPORT *a.* team-mate
**Mittag** ['mɪta:k] *m* (*-s*; *-e*) noon, midday; ***heute*** ~ at noon today; ***zu*** ~ ***essen*** (have) lunch; **~essen** *n* lunch; ***was gibt es zum ~?*** what's for lunch?
**'mittags** *adv* at noon; ***12 Uhr*** ~ 12 o'clock noon
**'Mittags|pause** *f* lunch break; **~ruhe** *f* midday rest; **~schlaf** *m* after-dinner nap; **~zeit** *f* lunchtime
**Mitte** ['mɪtə] *f* (-; *no pl*) middle; center, *Br* centre (*a.* POL); ~ ***Juli*** in the middle of July; ~ ***dreißig*** in one's mid thirties
**'mitteilen** *v/t* (*sep*, *-ge-*, *h*) ***j-m et.*** ~ inform s.o. of s.th.; **'mitteilsam** *adj* communicative; **'Mitteilung** *f* (-; *-en*) report, information, message
**Mittel** ['mɪtəl] *n* (*-s*; -) means, way; measure; PHARM remedy (***gegen*** for) (*a. fig*); average; MATH mean; PHYS medium; *pl* means, money
**'Mittelalter** *n* (*-s*; *no pl*) Middle Ages
**'mittelalterlich** *adj* medi(a)eval
**'Mittel|ding** *n* cross (***zwischen*** between); **~feld** *n* SPORT midfield; **~feldspieler(in)** midfield player, midfielder; **~finger** *m* ANAT middle finger
**'mittelfristig** *adj* medium-term
**'Mittelgewicht** *n* (*-[e]s*; *no pl*) SPORT middleweight (class)
**'mittelgroß** *adj* of medium height; medium-sized
**'Mittel|klasse** *f* middle class (*a.* MOT); **~linie** *f* SPORT halfway line
**'mittellos** *adj* without means
**'mittelmäßig** *adj* average
**'Mittelpunkt** *m* center, *Br* centre (*a. fig*)
**'mittels** *prp* (*gen*) by (means of), through
**'Mittelschule** *f* → ***Realschule***
**'Mittel|strecke** *f* SPORT middle distance; **~streckenra,kete** *f* MIL medium-range missile; **~streifen** *m* MOT median strip, *Br* central reservation; **~stufe** *f* PED junior highschool, *Br* middle school; **~stürmer(in)** SPORT center (*Br* centre) forward; **~weg** *m* middle course; **~welle** *f radio*: medium wave (ABBR AM); **~wort** *n* (*-[e]s*; *-wörter*) LING participle
**mitten** ['mɪtən] *adv*: ~ ***in*** (***auf***, ***unter*** *dat*) in the midst *or* middle of
**mitten'drin** F *adv* right in the middle
**mitten'durch** F *adv* right through (the middle); right in two
**Mitternacht** ['mɪtɐ-] *f* midnight
**mittlere** ['mɪtlərə] *adj* middle, central; average, medium
**mittlerweile** ['mɪtlɐ'vailə] *adv* meanwhile, (in the) meantime
**Mittwoch** ['mɪtvɔx] *m* (*-[s]*; *-e*) Wednesday
**mit'unter** *adv* now and then
**'Mitverantwortung** *f* share of the responsibility
**'mitwirken** *v/i* (*sep*, *-ge-*, *h*) take part (***bei*** in); **'Mitwirkende** *m*, *f* (*-n*; *-n*) THEA, MUS performer; *pl* THEA the cast; **'Mitwirkung** *f* (-; *no pl*) participation
**mixen** ['mɪksən] *v/t* (*ge-*, *h*) mix
**'Mixbecher** *m* shaker; **Mixer** ['mɪksɐ] *m* (*-s*; -) mixer; **'Mixgetränk** *n* mixed drink, cocktail, shake
**Möbel** ['mø:bəl] *pl* furniture; **~spedi,tion** *f* removal firm; **~stück** *n* piece of furniture; **~wagen** *m* moving (*Br* furniture) van
**mobil** [mo'bi:l] *adj* mobile; ~ ***machen*** MIL mobilize
**Mobiliar** [mobi'lja:ɐ] *n* (*-s*; *no pl*) furniture

M

**Mo'biltele,fon** *n* mobile phone
**möblieren** [mø'bli:rən] *v/t* (*no -ge-, h*) furnish
**mochte** ['mɔxtə] *pret of* ***mögen***
**Mode** ['mo:də] *f* (-; *-n*) fashion; ***in*** ~ in fashion; ~ ***sein*** be in fashion, F be in; ***die neueste*** ~ the latest fashion; ***mit der*** ~ ***gehen*** follow the fashion; ***in*** (***aus der***) ~ ***kommen*** come into (go out of) fashion
**Modell** [mo'dɛl] *n* (*-s*; *-e*) model; ***j-m*** ~ ***stehen*** *or* ***sitzen*** pose *or* sit for s.o.; **~bau** *m* model construction; **~baukasten** *m* model construction kit; **~eisenbahn** *f* model railway
**modellieren** [modɛ'li:rən] *v/t* (*no -ge-, h*) model
**Modem** ['mo:dɛm] *m, n* (*-s*; *-s*) EDP modem
**'Modenschau** *f* fashion show
**Moderator** [mode'ra:to:ɐ] *m* (*-s*; *-en* [modera'to:rən]), **Modera'torin** *f* (-; *-nen*) TV *etc* presenter, host, anchorman (anchorwoman)
**moderieren** [mode'ri:rən] *v/t* (*no -ge-, h*) TV *etc* present, host
**moderig** ['mo:dərɪç] *adj* musty, mo(u)ldy
**modern**[1] ['mo:dɐn] *v/i* (*ge-, h, sein*) mo(u)ld, rot, decay
**modern**[2] [mo'dɛrn] *adj* modern; fashionable
**modernisieren** [modɛrni'zi:rən] *v/t* (*no -ge-, h*) modernize, bring up to date
**'Mode|schmuck** *m* costume jewel(le)ry; **~schöpfer(in)** fashion designer; **~waren** *pl* fashionwear; **~wort** *n* (-[*e*]*s*; *-wörter*) vogue word, F in word; **~zeichner(in)** fashion designer; **~zeitschrift** *f* fashion magazine
**modisch** ['mo:dɪʃ] *adj* fashionable, stylish
**Modul**[1] [mo'du:l] *n* (*-s*; *-e*) EDP module
**Modul**[2] ['mo:dʊl] *m* (*-s*; *-n*) MATH, TECH module
**Mofa** ['mo:fa] *n* (*-s*; *-s*) (small) moped, motorized bicycle
**mogeln** ['mo:gəln] F *v/i* (*ge-, h*) cheat; crib
**mögen** ['mø:gən] *v/t* (*irr, ge-, h*) *and v/aux* (*irr, no -ge-, h*) like; ***er mag sie*** (***nicht***) he likes (doesn't like) her; ***lieber*** ~ like better, prefer; ***nicht*** ~ dislike; ***was möchten Sie?*** what would you like?; ***ich möchte, dass du es weißt*** I'd like you to know (it); ***ich möchte lieber bleiben*** I'd rather stay; ***es mag sein*** (, ***dass***) it may be (that)
**möglich** ['mø:klɪç] **1.** *adj* possible; ***alle ~en*** all sorts of; ***sein Möglichstes tun*** do what one can; do one's utmost; ***nicht ~!*** you don't say (so)!; ***so bald*** (***schnell, oft***) ***wie*** ~ as soon (quickly, often) as possible; **2.** *adv*: ***~st bald*** *etc* as soon *etc* as possible; **'möglicher'weise** *adv* possibly; **'Möglichkeit** *f* (-; *-en*) possibility; opportunity; chance; ***nach*** ~ if possible
**Mohammedaner** [mohame'da:nɐ] *m* (*-s*; -), **mohamme'danisch** *adj* Muslim
**Mohn** [mo:n] *m* (-[*e*]*s*; *-e*) BOT poppy
**Möhre** ['mø:rə] *f* (-; *-n*), **Mohrrübe** ['mo:ɐ-] *f* BOT carrot
**Molch** [mɔlç] *m* (-[*e*]*s*; *-e*) ZO salamander
**Mole** ['mo:lə] *f* (-; *-n*) MAR mole, jetty
**Molekül** [mole'ky:l] *n* (*-s*; *-e*) CHEM molecule
**molk** [mɔlk] *pret of* ***melken***
**Molkerei** [mɔlkə'rai] *f* (-; *-en*) dairy
**Moll** [mɔl] *n* (-; *no pl*) MUS minor (key); ***a-Moll*** A minor
**mollig** ['mɔlɪç] F *adj* snug, cozy, *Br* cosy; plump, chubby
**Moment** [mo'mɛnt] *m* (-[*e*]*s*; *-e*) moment; (***e-n***) ~ ***bitte!*** just a moment please!; ***im*** ~ at the moment
**Monarch** [mo'narç] *m* (*-en*; *-en*) monarch; **Monarchie** [monar'çi:] *f* (-; *-n*) monarchy; **Monarchin** [mo'narçɪn] *f* (-; *-nen*) monarch; **Monarchist** [monar'çɪst] *m* (*-en*; *-en*) monarchist
**Monat** ['mo:nat] *m* (-[*e*]*s*; *-e*) month; ***zweimal im*** *or* ***pro*** ~ twice a month
**'monatelang** *adv* for months
**'monatlich** *adj and adv* monthly
**'Monats|binde** *f* sanitary napkin (*Br* towel); **~karte** *f* commuter ticket, *Br* (monthly) season ticket
**Mönch** [mœnç] *m* (-[*e*]*s*; *-e*) monk; friar
**Mond** [mo:nt] *m* (-[*e*]*s*; *-e* ['mo:ndə]) moon; **~finsternis** *f* lunar eclipse
**'mondhell** *adj* moonlit
**'Mond|landefähre** *f* lunar module; **~landung** *f* moon landing; **~oberfläche** *f* moon surface, lunar soil; **~schein** *m* (-[*e*]*s*; *no pl*) moonlight; **~sichel** *f* crescent; **~umkreisung** *f*, **~umlaufbahn** *f* lunar orbit

**Monitor** ['mo:nito:ɐ] *m* (*-s*; *-en* [moni'to:rən]) TV *etc* monitor
**Monolog** [mono'lo:k] *m* (*-[e]s*; *-e*) monolog(ue *Br*)
**Monopol** [mono'po:l] *n* (*-s*; *-e*) ECON monopoly
**monoton** [mono'to:n] *adj* monotonous
**Monotonie** [monoto'ni:] *f* (*-*; *-n*) monotony
**Monoxid** ['mo:nɔksi:t] *n* CHEM monoxide
**Monster** ['mɔnstɐ] *n* (*-s*; *-*) monster
**Montag** ['mo:nta:k] *m* (*-[e]s*; *-e*) Monday
**Montage** [mɔn'ta:ʒə] *f* (*-*; *-n*) TECH assembly; installation; ***auf ~ sein*** be away on a field job; **~band** *n* (*-[e]s*; *-bänder*) TECH assembly line; **~halle** *f* TECH assembly shop
**Monteur** [mɔn'tø:ɐ] *m* (*-s*; *-e*) TECH fitter; *esp* MOT, AVIAT mechanic
**montieren** [mɔn'ti:rən] *v/t* (*no -ge-*, *h*) TECH assemble; fit, attach; instal(l)
**Moor** [mo:ɐ] *n* (*-[e]s*; *-e*) bog, moor(land); **moorig** ['mo:rıç] *adj* boggy
**Moos** [mo:s] *n* (*-es*; *-e*) BOT moss
**moosig** ['mo:zıç] *adj* mossy
**Moped** ['mo:pɛt] *n* (*-s*; *-s*) moped
**Mops** [mɔps] *m* (*-es*; *Möpse* ['mœpsə]) ZO pug(dog)
**Moral** [mo'ra:l] *f* (*-*; *no pl*) morals, moral standards; MIL *etc* morale; **mo'ralisch** *adj* moral; **moralisieren** [morali'zi:rən] *v/i* (*no -ge-*, *h*) moralize
**Morast** [mo'rast] *m* (*-[e]s*; *-e*) morass; mire, mud
**Mord** [mɔrt] *m* (*-[e]s*; *-e* ['mɔrdə]) murder (***an*** *dat* of); ***e-n ~ begehen*** commit murder; **~anschlag** *m esp* POL assassination attempt
**Mörder** ['mœrdɐ] *m* (*-s*; *-*), **'Mörderin** *f* (*-*; *-nen*) murderer; (hired) killer; *esp* POL assassin
**'Mord|kommissi,on** *f* homicide division, *Br* murder squad; **~pro,zess** *m* JUR murder trial
**'Mords|angst** F *f*: ***e-e ~ haben*** be scared stiff; **~glück** F *n* stupendous luck; **~kerl** F *m* devil of a fellow; **~wut** F *f*: ***e-e ~ haben*** be in a hell of a rage
**'Mord|verdacht** *m* suspicion of murder; **~versuch** *m* attempted murder
**morgen** ['mɔrgən] *adv* tomorrow; ***~ Abend*** (***früh***) tomorrow night (morning); ***~ Mittag*** at noon tomorrow; ***~ in e-r Woche*** a week from tomorrow; ***~ um diese Zeit*** this time tomorrow; ***... von ~*** tomorrow's ..., ... of tomorrow
**'Morgen** *m* (*-s*; *-*) morning; AGR acre; ***heute ~*** this morning; ***am*** (***frühen***) ***~*** (early) in the morning; ***am nächsten ~*** the next morning; **~essen** *Swiss n* breakfast; **~grauen** *n* dawn; ***im*** *or* ***bei ~*** at dawn; **~land** *n* (*-[e]s*; *no pl*) Orient; **~mantel** *m*, **~rock** *m* dressing gown
**'morgens** *adv* in the morning; ***von ~ bis abends*** from morning till night
**morgig** ['mɔrgıç] *adj* tomorrow's ...
**Morphium** ['mɔrfjʊm] *n* (*-s*; *no pl*) PHARM morphine
**morsch** [mɔrʃ] *adj* rotten; ***~ werden*** rot
**Morsealpha,bet** ['mɔrzə-] *n* Morse code
**Mörser** ['mœrzɐ] *m* (*-s*; *-*) mortar (*a.* MIL)
**'Morsezeichen** *n* Morse signal
**Mörtel** ['mœrtəl] *m* (*-s*; *-*) mortar
**Mosaik** [moza'i:k] *n* (*-s*; *-en*) mosaic
**Mosa'ikstein** *m* piece
**Moschee** [mɔ'ʃe:] *f* (*-*; *-n*) mosque
**Moskito** [mɔs'ki:to] *m* (*-s*; *-s*) ZO mosquito
**Moslem** ['mɔslɛm] *m* (*-s*; *-s*), **moslemisch** [mɔs'le:mıʃ] *adj*, **Moslime** [-'li:mə] *f* (*-*; *-n*) Muslim
**Most** [mɔst] *m* (*-[e]s*; *-e*) grape juice; cider
**Motiv** [mo'ti:f] *n* (*-s*; *-e*) motive; PAINT, MUS motif; **Motivation** [motiva'tsjo:n] *f* (*-*; *-en*) motivation; **motivieren** [moti'vi:rən] *v/t* (*no -ge-*, *h*) motivate
**Motor** ['mo:to:ɐ, mo'to:ɐ] *m* (*-s*; *-en* [mo'to:rən]) motor, engine; **~boot** *n* motor boat; **~haube** *f* hood, *Br* bonnet
**motorisieren** [motori'zi:rən] *v/t* (*no -ge-*, *h*) motorize
**'Motor|leistung** *f* (engine) performance; **~rad** *n* motorcycle, F motorbike; ***~ fahren*** ride a motorcycle; **~radfahrer(in)** motorcyclist, biker; **~roller** *m* (motor) scooter; **~säge** *f* power saw; **~schaden** *m* engine trouble (*or* failure)
**Motte** ['mɔtə] *f* (*-*; *-n*) ZO moth
**'Mottenkugel** *f* mothball
**'mottenzerfressen** *adj* moth-eaten
**Motto** ['mɔto] *n* (*-s*; *-s*) motto
**Möwe** ['mø:və] *f* (*-*; *-n*) ZO (sea)gull

**Mücke** ['mʏkə] *f* (-; *-n*) ZO gnat, midge, mosquito; ***aus e-r ~ e-n Elefanten machen*** make a mountain out of a molehill; **'Mückenstich** *m* gnat bite
**müde** ['my:də] *adj* tired; weary; sleepy; ***~ sein*** (***werden***) be (get) tired (*fig* ***e-r Sache*** of s.th.)
**'Müdigkeit** *f* (-; *no pl*) tiredness
**Muff** [mʊf] *m* (-[*e*]*s*; *-e*) muff
**Muffe** ['mʊfə] *f* (-; *-n*) TECH sleeve, socket
**Muffel** ['mʊfəl] F *m* (*-s*; -) sourpuss
**muff(e)lig** ['mʊf(ə)lɪç], **muffig** ['mʊfɪç] F *adj* musty; *contp* sulky, sullen
**Mühe** ['my:ə] *f* (-; *-n*) trouble; effort; difficulty (***mit*** with *s.th.*); (***nicht***) ***der ~ wert*** (not) worth the trouble; ***j-m ~ machen*** give s.o. trouble; ***sich ~ geben*** try hard; ***sich die ~ sparen*** save o.s. the trouble; ***mit ~ und Not*** (just) barely
**'mühelos** *adv* without difficulty
**mühen** ['my:ən] *v/refl* (*ge-*, *h*) struggle, work hard
**'mühevoll** *adj* laborious
**Mühle** ['my:lə] *f* (-; *-n*) mill; morris
**Mühsal** ['my:za:l] *f* (-; *-e*) toil
**mühsam** ['my:za:m], **'mühselig 1.** *adj* laborious; **2.** *adv* with difficulty
**Mulatte** [mu'latə] *m* (*-n*; *-n*), **Mu'lattin** *f* (-; *-nen*) mulatto
**Mulde** ['mʊldə] *f* (-; *-n*) hollow
**Mull** [mʊl] *m* (-[*e*]*s*; *-e*) muslin; *esp* MED gauze
**Müll** [mʏl] *m* (*-s*; *no pl*) garbage, trash, *Br* refuse, rubbish; **~abfuhr** *f* garbage (*Br* refuse) collection; **~beseitigung** *f* waste disposal; **~beutel** *m* garbage bag, *Br* dustbin liner
**'Mullbinde** *f* MED gauze bandage
**'Müll|con,tainer** *m* garbage (*Br* rubbish) skip; **~depo,nie** *f* dump; **~eimer** *m* garbage can, *Br* dustbin; **~fahrer** *m* garbage man, *Br* dustman; **~halde** *f* dump; **~haufen** *m* garbage (*Br* rubbish) heap; **~kippe** *f* dump; **~schlucker** *m* garbage (*Br* refuse) chute; **~tonne** *f* garbage can, *Br* dustbin; **~verbrennungsanlage** *f* (waste) incineration plant; **~wagen** *m* garbage truck, *Br* dustcart
**Multiplikation** [mʊltiplika'tsjo:n] *f* (-; *-en*) MATH multiplication; **multiplizieren** [mʊltipli'tsi:rən] *v/t* (*no -ge-*, *h*) MATH multiply (***mit*** by)

**Mumie** ['mu:mjə] *f* (-; *-n*) mummy
**Mumps** [mʊmps] *m*, *f* (-; *no pl*) MED mumps
**Mund** [mʊnt] *m* (-[*e*]*s*; *Münder* ['mʏndɐ]) mouth; F ***den ~ voll nehmen*** talk big; ***halt den ~!*** shut up!; **~art** *f* dialect
**münden** ['mʏndən] *v/i* (*ge-*, *h*, *sein*) ***~ in*** (*acc*) *river etc*: flow into; *road etc*: lead into
**'Mundgeruch** *m* bad breath
**'Mundhar,monika** *f* MUS mouth organ, harmonica
**mündig** ['mʏndɪç] *adj* emancipated; ***~*** (***werden***) JUR (come) of age
**mündlich** ['mʏntlɪç] *adj* oral; verbal
**'Mundstück** *n* mouthpiece; tip
**'Mündung** *f* (-; *-en*) *river*: mouth; *gun*: muzzle
**'Mund|wasser** *n* mouthwash; **~werk** F *n*: ***ein gutes ~ haben*** have the gift of the gab; ***ein loses ~*** a loose tongue; **~winkel** *m* corner of the mouth
**'Mund-zu-'Mund-Beatmung** *f* (-; *-en*) MED mouth-to-mouth resuscitation, F kiss of life
**Munition** [muni'tsjo:n] *f* (-; *-en*) ammunition
**munkeln** ['mʊŋkəln] F *v/t* (*ge-*, *h*) ***man munkelt, dass*** rumo(u)r has it that
**Münster** ['mʏnstɐ] *n* (*-s*; -) cathedral, minster
**munter** ['mʊntɐ] *adj* awake; lively; merry
**Münze** ['mʏntsə] *f* (-; *-n*) coin; medal
**'Münz|einwurf** *m* (coin) slot; **~fernsprecher** *m* pay phone; **~tank(auto,mat)** *m* coin-operated (gas, *Br* petrol) pump; **~wechsler** *m* (*-s*; -) change machine
**mürbe** ['mʏrbə] *adj* tender; brittle; GASTR crisp; **'Mürbeteig** *m* short pastry; shortcake
**Murmel** ['mʊrməl] *f* (-; *-n*) marble
**'murmeln** *v/t and v/i* (*ge-*, *h*) murmur
**'Murmeltier** *n* ZO marmot
**murren** ['mʊrən] *v/i* (*ge-*, *h*) complain (***über*** *acc* about)
**mürrisch** ['mʏrɪʃ] *adj* sullen; grumpy
**Mus** [mu:s] *n* (*-es*; *-e*) mush; stewed fruit
**Muschel** ['mʊʃəl] *f* (-; *-n*) ZO mussel; shell
**Museum** [mu'ze:ʊm] *n* (*-s*; *Museen*) museum
**Musik** [mu'zi:k] *f* (-; *no pl*) music

**musikalisch** [muzi'ka:lɪʃ] *adj* musical
**Mu'sik|anlage** *f* hi-fi *or* stereo set; **~auto,mat** *m*, **~box** *f* juke box
**Musiker** ['mu:zikɐ] *m* (*-s*; -), **'Musikerin** *f* (-; *-nen*) musician
**Mu'sik|instru,ment** *n* musical instrument; **~ka,pelle** *f* band; **~kas,sette** *f* music cassette; **~lehrer(in)** music teacher; **~stunde** *f* music lesson
**musisch** ['mu:zɪʃ] *adv*: **~ *interessiert*** (***begabt***) fond of (gifted for) fine arts and music
**musizieren** [muzi'tsi:rən] *v/i* (*no -ge-*, *h*) make music
**Muskat** [mʊs'ka:t] *m* (*-[e]s*; *-e*), **~nuss** *f* BOT nutmeg
**Muskel** ['mʊskəl] *m* (*-s*; *-n*) ANAT muscle; **~kater** F *m* aching muscles; **~zerrung** *f* MED pulled muscle
**muskulös** [mʊsku'lø:s] *adj* muscular, brawny
**Müsli** ['my:sli] *n* (*-s*; -) GASTR granola, *Br* muesli
**Muss** *n* (-; *no pl*) necessity; ***es ist ein ~*** it is a must
**Muße** ['mu:sə] *f* (-; *no pl*) leisure; spare time
**müssen** ['mʏsən] *v/i* (*irr*, *ge-*, *h*) *and v/aux* (*irr*, *no -ge-*, *h*) must, have (got) to; ***du musst den Film sehen!*** you must see the film!; ***ich muss jetzt*** (***m-e***) ***Hausaufgaben machen*** I have (got) to do my homework now; ***sie muss krank sein*** she must be ill; ***du musst es nicht tun*** you need not do it; ***das müsstest du*** (***doch***) ***wissen*** you ought to know (that); ***sie müsste zu Hause sein*** she should (ought to) be (at) home; ***das müsste schön sein!*** that would be nice!; ***du hättest ihm helfen ~*** you ought to have helped him
**müßig** ['my:sɪç] *adj* idle; useless
**musste** ['mʊstə] *pret of* ***müssen***
**Muster** ['mʊstɐ] *n* (*-s*; -) pattern; sample; model
**'muster|gültig, ~haft** *adj* exemplary; ***sich ~ benehmen*** behave perfectly
**'Musterhaus** *n* showhouse
**'mustern** *v/t* (*ge-*, *h*) eye *s.o.*; size *s.o.* up; MIL ***gemustert werden*** F have one's medical; **Musterung** ['mʊstərʊŋ] *f* (-; *-en*) MIL medical (examination for military service)
**Mut** [mu:t] *m* (*-[e]s*; *no pl*) courage; ***j-m ~ machen*** encourage s.o.; ***den ~ verlieren*** lose courage; → ***zumute***
**mutig** ['mu:tɪç] *adj* courageous, brave
**'mutlos** *adj* discouraged
**'mutmaßen** *v/t* (*ge-*, *h*) speculate
**'mutmaßlich** *adj* probable; presumed
**'Mutprobe** *f* test of courage
**Mutter** ['mʊtɐ] *f* (-; *Mütter* ['mʏtɐ]) mother; TECH nut; **~boden** *m*, **~erde** *f* AGR topsoil
**mütterlich** ['mʏtɐlɪç] *adj* motherly
**'mütterlicherseits** *adv*: ***Onkel** etc* **~** maternal uncle *etc*
**'Mutterliebe** *f* motherly love
**'mutterlos** *adj* motherless
**'Mutter|mal** *n* birthmark, mole; **~milch** *f* mother's milk; **~schaftsurlaub** *m* maternity leave; **~schutz** *m* JUR legal protection of expectant and nursing mothers; **~söhnchen** *contp n* sissy; **~sprache** *f* mother tongue; **~sprachler** [-ʃpra:xlɐ] *m* (*-s*; -) native speaker; **~tag** *m* Mother's Day
**Mutti** ['mʊti] F *f* (-; *-s*) mom(my), *esp Br* mum(my)
**'mutwillig** *adj* wanton
**Mütze** ['mʏtsə] *f* (-; *-n*) cap
**MwSt** ABBR *of* ***Mehrwertsteuer*** VAT, value-added tax
**mysteriös** [mʏste'rjø:s] *adj* mysterious
**mystisch** ['mʏstɪʃ] *adj* mystic(al)
**mythisch** ['my:tɪʃ] *adj* mythical
**Mythologie** [mytolo'gi:] *f* (-; *-n*) mythology
**Mythos** ['my:tɔs] *m* (-; *Mythen*) myth

# N

**N** ABBR *of* ***Nord*(*en*)** N, north

**na** [na] *int* well; **~ *und?*** so what?; **~ *gut!*** all right then; **~ *ja*** (oh) well; **~(, ~)!** come on!, come now!; **~ *so* (*et*)*was!*** what do you know!, *Br* I say!; **~, *dann nicht!*** oh, forget it!; **~ *also!*** there you are!; **~, *warte!*** just you wait!

**Nabe** [ˈnaːbə] *f* (-; *-n*) TECH hub

**Nabel** [ˈnaːbəl] *m* (*-s*; -) ANAT navel

**ˈNabelschnur** *f* ANAT umbilical chord

**nach** [naːx] *prp* (*dat*) *and adv* to, toward(s), for; after; *time*: after, past; according to, by; **~ *Hause*** home; ***abfahren* ~** leave for; **~ *rechts* (*Süden*)** to the right (south); **~ *oben*** up(stairs); **~ *unten*** down(stairs); **~ *vorn* (*hinten*)** to the front (back); ***der Reihe* ~** one after the other; ***s-e Uhr* ~ *dem Radio stellen*** set one's watch by the radio; **~ *m-r Uhr*** by my watch; ***suchen* (*fragen*) ~** look (ask) for; **~ *Gewicht* (*Zeit*)** by weight (the hour); ***riechen* (*schmecken*) ~** smell (taste) of; **~ *und* ~** gradually; **~ *wie vor*** as before, still

**ˈnachahmen** [-aːmən] *v/t* (*sep*, *-ge-*, *h*) imitate, copy; take off

**ˈNachahmung** *f* (-; *-en*) imitation

**Nachbar** [ˈnaxbaːɐ] *m* (*-n*; *-n*), **ˈNachbarin** *f* (-; *-nen*) neighbo(u)r; **ˈNachbarschaft** *f* (-; *no pl*) neighbo(u)rhood, vicinity

**ˈNachbau** *m* (-[*e*]*s*; *-ten*) TECH reproduction; **ˈnachbauen** *v/t* (*sep*, *-ge-*, *h*) copy, reproduce

**ˈNachbildung** *f* (-; *-en*) copy, imitation; replica; dummy

**ˈnachblicken** *v/i* (*sep*, *-ge-*, *h*) look after

**nachˈdem** *cj* after, when; ***je* ~ *wie*** depending on how

**ˈnachdenken** *v/i* (*irr*, ***denken***, *sep*, *-ge-*, *h*) think; **~ *über*** (*acc*) think about, think *s.th.* over

**ˈnachdenklich** *adj* thoughtful; ***es macht e-n* ~** it makes you think

**ˈNachdruck**[1] *m* (-[*e*]*s*; *no pl*) emphasis, stress

**ˈNachdruck**[2] (-[*e*]*s*; *-e*) reprint

**ˈnachdrucken** *v/t* (*sep*, *-ge-*, *h*) reprint

**ˈnachdrücklich** [-drʏklɪç] *adj* emphatic; forceful; **~ *raten* (*empfehlen*)** advise (recommend) strongly

**ˈnacheifern** *v/i* (*sep*, *-ge-*, *h*) ***j-m* ~** emulate s.o.

**nacheiˈnander** *adv* one after the other, in (*or* by) turns

**ˈnacherzählen** *v/t* (*sep*, *no -ge-*, *h*) retell; **ˈNacherzählung** *f* (-; *-en*) PED reproduction

**ˈNachfolge** *f* (-; *no pl*) succession; ***j-s* ~ *antreten*** succeed s.o.; **ˈnachfolgen** *v/i* (*sep*, *-ge-*, *sein*) (*dat*) succeed *s.o.*; **ˈNachfolger(in)** [-fɔlgɐ (-gərɪn)] (*-s*; -/-; *-nen*) successor

**ˈnachforschen** *v/i* (*sep*, *-ge-*, *h*) investigate; **ˈNachforschung** *f* (-; *-en*) investigation, inquiry

**ˈNachfrage** *f* (-; *-n*) inquiry; ECON demand; **ˈnachfragen** *v/i* (*sep*, *-ge-*, *h*) inquire, ask

**ˈnach|fühlen** *v/t* (*sep*, *-ge-*, *h*) ***j-m et.* ~** understand how s.o. feels; **~füllen** *v/t* (*sep*, *-ge-*, *h*) refill; **~geben** *v/i* (*irr*, ***geben***, *sep*, *-ge-*, *h*) give (way); *fig* give in

**ˈNachgebühr** *f* (-; *-en*) *post* surcharge

**ˈnachgehen** *v/i* (*irr*, ***gehen***, *sep*, *-ge-*, *sein*) follow (*a. fig*); *watch*: be slow; ***e-r Sache* ~** investigate s.th.; ***s-r Arbeit* ~** go about one's work

**ˈNachgeschmack** *m* (-[*e*]*s*; *no pl*) aftertaste (*a. fig*)

**ˈnachgiebig** [-giːbɪç] *adj* yielding, soft (*both a. fig*); **ˈNachgiebigkeit** *f* (-; *no pl*) yieldingness, softness (*both a. fig*)

**ˈnachhaltig** [-haltɪç] *adj* lasting, enduring

**nachˈhause** *Austrian adv* home

**nachˈher** *adv* afterwards; ***bis* ~!** see you later!, so long!

**ˈNachhilfe** *f* help, assistance; PED → **~stunden** *pl*, **~unterricht** *m* PED private lesson(s), coaching

**ˈnachholen** *v/t* (*sep*, *-ge-*, *h*) make up for, catch up on

**ˈNachkomme** *m* (*-n*; *-n*) descendant, *pl esp* JUR issue; **ˈnachkommen** *v/i* (*irr*, ***kommen***, *sep*, *-ge-*, *sein*) follow, come later; (*dat*) comply with

**ˈNachkriegs...** *in cpds* postwar ...

**Nachlass** [ˈnaːxlas] *m* (*-es*; *-lässe* [-lɛsə]) ECON reduction, discount; JUR estate

**'nachlassen** *v/i* (*irr*, ***lassen***, *sep*, *-ge-*, *h*) decrease, diminish, go down; *effect etc*: wear off; *student etc*: slacken one's effort; *interest etc*: flag; *health etc*: fail, deteriorate

**'nachlässig** *adj* careless, negligent

**'nach|laufen** *v/i* (*irr*, ***laufen***, *sep*, *-ge-*, *sein*) run after; **~lesen** *v/t* (*irr*, ***lesen***, *sep*, *-ge-*, *h*) look up; **~machen** *v/t* (*sep*, *-ge-*, *h*) imitate, copy; counterfeit, forge

**'Nachmittag** *m* afternoon; ***heute ~*** this afternoon

**'nachmittags** *adv* in the afternoon

**Nachnahme** ['na:xna:mə] *f* (-; *-n*) ECON cash on delivery; ***per ~ schicken*** send C.O.D.

**'Nach|name** *m* surname, last (*or* family) name; **~porto** *n* surcharge

**'nachprüfen** *v/t* (*sep*, *-ge-*, *h*) check (up), make sure (of)

**'nachrechnen** *v/t* (*sep*, *-ge-*, *h*) check

**'Nachrede** *f*: ***üble ~*** malicious gossip; JUR defamation (of character), slander

**Nachricht** ['na:xrɪçt] *f* (-; *-en*) news; message; report; information, notice; *pl* news (report), newscast; ***e-e gute*** (***schlechte***) ***~*** good (bad) news; ***Sie hören ~en*** here is the news

**'Nachrichten|dienst** *m* news service; MIL intelligence service; **~satel,lit** *m* communications satellite; **~sprecher(in)** newscaster, *esp Br* newsreader; **~technik** *f* telecommunications

**'Nachruf** *m* obituary

**'nach|rüsten** *v/i* (*sep*, *-ge-*, *h*) POL, MIL close the armament gap; **~sagen** *v/t* (*sep*, *-ge-*, *h*) ***j-m Schlechtes ~*** speak badly of s.o.; ***man sagt ihm nach, dass er ...*** he is said to *inf*

**'Nachsai,son** *f* off-peak season; ***in der ~*** out of season

**'nachschlagen** (*irr*, ***schlagen***, *sep*, *-ge-*, *h*) **1.** *v/t* look up; **2.** *v/i*: ***~ in*** (*dat*) consult; **'Nachschlagewerk** *n* reference book

**'Nach|schlüssel** *m* duplicate (*or* skeleton) key; **~schrift** *f* postcript; dictation; **~schub** *m esp* MIL supplies

**'nach|sehen** (*irr*, ***sehen***, *sep*, *-ge-*, *h*) **1.** *v/i* follow with one's eyes; (have a) look; ***~ ob*** (go and) see whether; **2.** *v/t* look *or* go over *or* through; correct, mark; check (*a.* TECH); **~senden** *v/t* ([*irr*, ***senden***,] *sep*, *-ge-*, *h*) send on, forward; ***bitte ~!*** *post* please forward!

**'Nachsilbe** *f* LING suffix

**'nachsitzen** *v/i* (*irr*, ***sitzen***, *sep*, *-ge-*, *h*) stay in (after school), be kept in; ***~ lassen*** keep in, detain

**'Nachspann** *m* (-[*e*]*s*; *-e*) *film*: credits *pl*

**'Nachspiel** *n* sequel, consequences

**'nachspielen** *v/i* (*sep*, *-ge-*, *h*) SPORT ***5 Minuten ~ lassen*** allow 5 minutes for injury time; **'Nachspielzeit** *f esp soccer*: injury time

**'nach|spio,nieren** *v/i* (*no -ge-*, *h*) spy (up)on; **~sprechen** *v/t* (*irr*, ***sprechen***, *sep*, *-ge-*, *h*) ***j-m et. ~*** say *or* repeat s.th. after s.o.

**nächst'beste** ['nɛ:çst-] *adj* first, F any old; next-best, second-best

**nächste** ['nɛ:çstə] *adj* next; nearest (*a. relative*); ***in den ~n Tagen*** (***Jahren***) in the next few days (years); ***in ~r Zeit*** in the near future; ***was kommt als Nächstes?*** what comes next?; ***der Nächste, bitte!*** next please!

**'nachstehen** *v/i* (*irr*, ***stehen***, *sep*, *-ge-*, *h*) ***j-m in nichts ~*** be in no way inferior to s.o.

**'nachstellen** (*sep*, *-ge-*, *h*) **1.** *v/t* put back (*watch*); TECH (re)adjust; **2.** *v/i*: ***j-m ~*** be after s.o.; **'Nachstellung** *f* (-; *-en*) persecution

**'Nächstenliebe** *f* charity

**Nacht** [naxt] *f* (-; *Nächte* ['nɛçtə]) night; ***Tag und ~*** night and day; ***die ganze ~*** all night (long); ***heute Nacht*** tonight; last night

**'Nachtdienst** *m* night duty; ***~ haben*** PHARM be open all night

**'Nachteil** *m* disadvantage, drawback; ***im ~ sein*** be at a disadvantage (***gegenüber*** compared with); **'nachteilig** [-tailɪç] *adj* disadvantageous

**'Nacht|essen** *Swiss n* → ***Abendbrot***; **~falter** *m* ZO moth; **~hemd** *n* nightgown, nightdress, F nightie; nightshirt

**Nachtigall** ['naxtigal] *f* (-; *-en*) ZO nightingale

**'Nachtisch** *m* (-[*e*]*s*; *no pl*) dessert; sweet

**nächtlich** ['nɛçtlɪç] *adj* nightly; at *or* by night

**'Nachtlo,kal** *n* nightclub

**Nachtrag** ['na:xtra:k] *m* (-[*e*]*s*; *-träge* [-trɛ:gə]) supplement; **'nachtragen**

*fig v/t* (*irr*, ***tragen***, *sep*, *-ge-*, *h*) ***j-m et.*** ~ bear s.o. a grudge; '**nachtragend** *adj* unforgiving; '**nachträglich** [-trɛ:klıç] *adj* additional; later; belated

**nachts** *adv* at night, in the night(time)

'**Nachtschicht** *f* night shift; ~ ***haben*** be on night shift

'**nachtschlafend** *adj*: ***zu ~er Zeit*** in the middle of the night

'**Nachttisch** *m* bedside table

'**Nachttopf** *m* chamber pot

'**Nachtwächter** *m* night watchman

'**nachwachsen** *v/i* (*irr*, ***wachsen***, *sep*, *-ge-*, *sein*) grow again

'**Nachwahl** *f* PARL special election, *Br* by-election

**Nachweis** ['na:xvais] *m* (*-es*; *-e*) proof, evidence; '**nachweisbar** *adj* demonstrable; *esp* CHEM *etc* detectable

'**nachweisen** *v/t* (*irr*, ***weisen***, *sep*, *-ge-*, *h*) prove; *esp* CHEM *etc* detect

'**nachweislich** *adv* as can be proved

'**Nach|welt** *f* (-; *no pl*) posterity; **~wirkung** *f* aftereffect(s), *pl a.* aftermath; **~wort** *n* (-[*e*]*s*; *-worte*) epilog(ue)

'**Nachwuchs** *m* (*-es*; *no pl*) young talent, F new blood; **~...** *in cpds ...autor*, *...schauspieler etc*: talented *or* promising young ..., up-and-coming ...

'**nach|zahlen** *v/t* (*sep*, *-ge-*, *h*) pay extra; **~zählen** *v/t* (*sep*, *-ge-*, *h*) count over (again), check

'**Nachzahlung** *f* additional *or* extra payment

**Nachzügler** ['na:xtsy:klɐ] *m* (*-s*; -) straggler, latecomer

**Nacken** ['nakən] *m* (*-s*; -) ANAT (back *or* nape of the) neck; **~stütze** *f* headrest

**nackt** [nakt] *adj* naked; *esp* PAINT, PHOT nude; bare (*a. fig*); *fig* plain; ***völlig*** ~ stark naked; ***sich ~ ausziehen*** strip; ~ ***baden*** swim in the nude; ***j-n ~ malen*** paint s.o. in the nude

**Nadel** ['na:dəl] *f* (-; *-n*) needle; pin; brooch; **~baum** *m* BOT conifer(ous tree); **~öhr** *n* eye of a needle; **~stich** *m* pinprick (*a. fig*)

**Nagel** ['na:gəl] *m* (*-s*; *Nägel* ['nɛ:gəl]) nail; ***an den Nägeln kauen*** bite one's nails; **~lack** *m* nail varnish *or* polish

'**nageln** *v/t* (*ge-*, *h*) nail (***an*** *acc*, ***auf*** *acc* to)

'**nagel'neu** F *adj* brand-new

'**Nagelpflege** *f* manicure

**nagen** ['na:gən] (*ge-*, *h*) **1.** *v/i* gnaw (***an*** *dat* at); ***an e-m Knochen*** ~ pick a bone; **2.** *v/t* gnaw; '**Nagetier** *n* ZO rodent

'**Nahaufnahme** *f* PHOT *etc* close-up

**nahe** [na:ə] *adj* near, close (***bei*** to); nearby; ***j-m ~ gehen*** affect s.o. deeply; ~ ***kommen*** (*dat*) come close to; ~ ***legen*** suggest; ~ ***liegen*** seem likely; ~ ***liegend*** likely, obvious; **Nähe** ['nɛ:ə] *f* (-; *no pl*) nearness; neighbo(u)rhood, vicinity; ***in der ~ des Bahnhofs*** near the station; ***ganz in der*** ~ quite near, close by; ***in deiner*** ~ near you

**nahen** ['na:ən] *v/i* (*ge-*, *sein*) approach

**nähen** ['nɛ:ən] *v/t and v/i* (*ge-*, *h*) sew; make

**Nähere** ['nɛ:ərə] *n* (*-n*; *no pl*) details, particulars

**nähern** ['nɛ:ɐn] *v/refl* (*ge-*, *h*) approach, get near(er) *or* close(r) (*dat* to)

'**nahezu** *adv* nearly, almost

'**Nähgarn** *n* (sewing) cotton

'**Nahkampf** *m* MIL close combat

**nahm** [na:m] *pret of* ***nehmen***

'**Nähma͜schine** *f* sewing machine

'**Nähnadel** *f* (sewing) needle

**nähren** ['nɛ:rən] *v/t* (*ge-*, *h*) feed; *fig* nurture

**nahrhaft** ['na:ɐhaft] *adj* nutritious, nourishing

**Nährstoff** ['nɛ:ɐ-] *m* nutrient

**Nahrung** ['na:rʊŋ] *f* (-; *no pl*) food, nourishment; AGR feed; diet

'**Nahrungsmittel** *pl* food(stuffs)

**Nährwert** ['nɛ:ɐ-] *m* nutritional value

**Naht** [na:t] *f* (-; *Nähte* ['nɛ:tə]) seam; MED suture

'**Nahverkehr** *m* local traffic; '**Nahverkehrszug** *m* local *or* commuter train

'**Nähzeug** *n* sewing kit

**naiv** [na'i:f] *adj* naive; **Naivität** [naivi'tɛ:t] *f* (-; *no pl*) naivety

**Name** ['na:mə] *m* (*-ns*; *-n*) name; ***im ~n von*** on behalf of; ***nur dem ~n nach*** in name only; '**namenlos** *adj* nameless, *fig a.* unspeakable; '**namens** *adv* by (the) name of, named, called

'**Namens|tag** *m* name day; **~vetter** *m* namesake; **~zug** *m* signature

**namentlich** ['na:məntlıç] *adj and adv* by name

**nämlich** ['nɛ:mlıç] *adv* that is (to say), namely; you see *or* know

**nannte** ['nantə] *pret of* ***nennen***

**Napf** [napf] *m* (-[*e*]*s*; *Näpfe* ['nɛpfə]) bowl, basin
**Narbe** ['narbə] *f* (-; -*n*) scar
**narbig** ['narbɪç] *adj* scarred
**Narkose** [nar'ko:zə] *f* (-; -*n*) MED an(a)esthesia; ***in ~*** under an an(a)esthetic
**Narr** [nar] *m* (-*en*; -*en*) fool; ***j-n zum ~en halten*** fool s.o.; '**narrensicher** *adj* foolproof; **närrisch** ['nɛrɪʃ] *adj* foolish; ***~ vor*** (*dat*) mad with
**Narzisse** [nar'tsɪsə] *f* (-; -*n*) BOT daffodil
**nasal** [na'za:l] *adj* nasal
**naschen** ['naʃən] *v/i and v/t* (*ge-*, *h*) nibble (***an*** *dat* at); ***gern ~*** have a sweet tooth; **Naschereien** [naʃə'raiən] *pl* dainties, goodies, sweets; '**naschhaft** *adj* sweet-toothed
**Nase** ['na:zə] *f* (-; -*n*) ANAT nose (*a. fig*); ***sich die ~ putzen*** blow one's nose; ***in der ~ bohren*** pick one's nose; F ***die ~ voll haben*** (***von***) be fed up (with)
'**Nasen|bluten** *n* MED nosebleed; **~loch** *n* nostril; **~spitze** *f* tip of the nose
**Nashorn** *n* ZO rhinoceros, F rhino
**nass** [nas] *adj* wet; ***triefend ~*** soaking (wet); **Nässe** ['nɛsə] *f* (-; *no pl*) wetness; '**nässen** (*ge-*, *h*) **1.** *v/t* wet; **2.** *v/i* MED weep
'**nasskalt** *adj* damp and cold, raw
**Nation** [na'tsjo:n] *f* (-; -*en*) nation
**national** [natsjo'na:l] *adj* national
**Natio'nalhymne** *f* national anthem
**Nationalismus** [natsjona'lɪsmʊs] *m* (-; *no pl*) nationalism; **Nationalität** [natsjonali'tɛ:t] *f* (-; -*en*) nationality
**Natio'nal|mannschaft** *f* SPORT national team; **~park** *m* national park
**Natio'nalsozia,lismus** *m* HIST National Socialism, *contp* Nazism; **Natio'nalsozia,list** *m*, **natio'nalsozia,listisch** *adj* HIST National Socialist, *contp* Nazi
**Natter** ['natɐ] *f* (-; -*n*) ZO adder, viper (*a. fig*)
**Natur** [na'tu:ɐ] *f* (-; -*en*) nature; ***von ~*** (***aus***) by nature
**Naturalismus** [natura'lɪsmʊs] *m* (-; *no pl*) naturalism
**Na'tur|ereignis** *n*, **~erscheinung** *f* natural phenomenon; **~forscher** *m* naturalist; **~geschichte** *f* natural history; **~gesetz** *n* law of nature
**na'turgetreu** *adj* true to life; lifelike
**Na'turkata,strophe** *f* (natural) catastrophe *or* disaster, act of God
**natürlich** [na'ty:ɐlɪç] **1.** *adj* natural; **2.** *adv* naturally, of course
**Na'tur|schätze** *pl* natural resources; **~schutz** *m* nature conservation; ***unter ~*** protected; **~schützer** [-ʃʏtsɐ] *m* (-*s*; -) conservationist; **~schutzgebiet** *n* nature reserve; national park; **~volk** *n* primitive race; **~wissenschaft** *f* (natural) science
**n. Chr.** ABBR *of* ***nach Christus*** AD, anno domini
**Nebel** ['ne:bəl] *m* (-*s*; -) fog; mist; haze; smoke; **~horn** *n* foghorn; **~leuchte** *f* MOT fog light
**neben** ['ne:bən] *prp* (*dat and acc*) beside, next to; besides, apart from; compared with; ***~ anderem*** among other things; ***setz dich ~ mich*** sit by me *or* by my side
**neben'an** *adv* next door
**neben'bei** *adv* in addition, at the same time; ***~*** (***gesagt***) by the way
'**Nebenberuf** *m* second job, sideline; '**nebenberuflich** *adv* as a sideline
'**Nebenbuhler** [-bu:lɐ] *m* (-*s*; -), '**Nebenbuhlerin** *f* (-; -*nen*) rival
'**nebenei'nander** *adv* side by side; next (door) to each other; ***~ bestehen*** coexist
'**Neben|einkünfte** *pl*, **~einnahmen** *pl* extra money; **~fach** *n* PED *etc* minor (subject), *Br* subsidiary subject; **~fluss** *m* tributary; **~gebäude** *n* next-door *or* adjoining building; annex(e); **~haus** *n* house next door; **~kosten** *pl* extras; **~mann** *m*: ***dein ~*** the person next to you; **~pro,dukt** *n* by-product; **~rolle** *f* THEA supporting role, minor part (*a. fig*); cameo (role); **~sache** *f* minor matter; ***das ist ~*** that's of little *or* no importance
'**nebensächlich** *adj* unimportant
'**Neben|satz** *m* LING subordinate clause; **~stelle** *f* TEL extension; **~straße** *f* side street; minor road; **~strecke** *f* RAIL branch line; **~tisch** *m* next table; **~verdienst** *m* extra earnings; **~wirkung** *f* side effect; **~zimmer** *n* adjoining room
**neblig** ['ne:blɪç] *adj* foggy; misty; hazy
**necken** ['nɛkən] *v/t* (*ge-*, *h*) tease
**Neckerei** [nɛkə'rai] *f* (-; -*en*) teasing
'**neckisch** *adj* playful, teasing

**Neffe** ['nɛfə] *m* (*-n*; *-n*) nephew
**negativ** ['ne:gati:f] *adj* negative
'**Negativ** *n* (*-s*; *-e*) PHOT negative
**Neger** ['ne:gɐ] *m* (*-s*; -), **Negerin** ['ne:gərɪn] *f* (-; *-nen*) → ***Schwarze***
**nehmen** ['ne:mən] *v/t* (*irr*, *ge-*, *h*) take (*a.* ***sich*** ~); ***j-m et.*** ~ take s.th. (away) from s.o. (*a. fig*); ***sich e-n Tag frei*** ~ take a day off; ***j-n an die Hand*** ~ take s.o. by the hand
**Neid** [nait] *m* (*-es*; *no pl*) envy; ***reiner*** ~ sheer envy; **neidisch** ['naidɪʃ] *adj* envious (***auf*** *acc* of)
**Neige** ['naigə] *f*: ***zur*** ~ ***gehen*** draw to its close; run out
'**neigen** (*ge-*, *h*) **1.** *v/t and refl* bend, incline; **2.** *v/i*: ***zu et.*** ~ tend to (do) s.th.
'**Neigung** *f* (-; *-en*) inclination (*a. fig*), slope, incline; *fig* tendency
**nein** [nain] *adv* no
**Nektar** ['nɛkta:ɐ] *m* (*-s*; *-e*) BOT nectar
**Nelke** ['nɛlkə] *f* (-; *-n*) BOT carnation; GASTR clove
**nennen** ['nɛnən] *v/t* (*irr*, *ge-*, *h*) name, call; mention; ***sich*** ~ call o.s., be called; ***man nennt ihn ...*** he is called ...; ***das nenne ich ...!*** that's what I call ...!
'**nennenswert** *adj* worth mentioning
**Nenner** ['nɛnɐ] *m* (*-s*; -) MATH denominator
'**Nennwert** *m* ECON nominal *or* face value; ***zum*** ~ at par
**Neo..., neo...** [neo-] *in cpds ...faschist etc*: neo-...
**Neon** ['ne:ɔn] *n* (*-s*; *no pl*) CHEM neon
'**Neonröhre** *f* neon tube
**Nepp** [nɛp] F *m* (*-s*; *no pl*) rip-off
**neppen** ['nɛpən] F *v/t* (*ge-*, *h*) fleece, rip *s.o.* off
**Nerv** [nɛrf] *m* (*-s*; *-en*) ANAT nerve; ***j-m auf die*** ~***en fallen*** *or* ***gehen*** get on s.o.'s nerves; ***die*** ~***en behalten*** (***verlieren***) keep (lose) one's head
**nerven** ['nɛrfən] F *v/t and v/i* (*ge-*, *h*) be a pain in the neck (***j-n*** to s.o.)
'**Nervenarzt** *m*, '**Nervenärztin** *f* neurologist
'**nervenaufreibend** *adj* nerve-racking
'**Nerven|belastung** *f* nervous strain; ~**kitzel** *m* thrill, F kick(s)
'**nervenkrank** *adj* mentally ill
'**Nerven|säge** F *f* pain in the neck; ~**sys,tem** *n* nervous system; ~**zusammenbruch** *m* nervous breakdown
**nervös** [nɛr'vø:s] *adj* nervous
**Nervosität** [nɛrvozi'tɛ:t] *f* (-; *no pl*) nervousness
**Nerz** [nɛrts] *m* (*-es*; *-e*) ZO mink
**Nessel** ['nɛsəl] *f* (-; *-n*) BOT nettle
**Nest** [nɛst] *n* (*-[e]s*; *-er* ['nɛstɐ]) ZO nest; F *contp* one-horse town
**nett** [nɛt] *adj* nice; kind; ***so*** ~ ***sein und et.*** (*or* ***et. zu***) ***tun*** be so kind as to do s.th.
**netto** ['nɛto] *adv* ECON net
**Netz** [nɛts] *n* (*-es*; *-e*) net; RAIL, TEL, EDP network; ELECTR mains; ***am*** ~ ***sein*** EDP be in the network; ~**haut** *f* ANAT retina; ~**karte** *f* RAIL area season ticket
**neu** [nɔʏ] *adj* new; fresh; *fig* modern; ***neuere Sprachen*** modern languages; ***neueste Nachrichten*** (***Mode***) latest news (fashion); ***von neuem*** anew, afresh; ***seit neu***(***st***)***em*** since (very) recently; ***viel Neues*** a lot of new things; ***was gibt es Neues?*** what's the news?, what's new?; '**neuartig** *adj* novel
'**Neubau** *m* (*-[e]s*; *-ten*) new building; ~**gebiet** *n* new housing estate
**neuerdings** ['nɔʏɐ'dɪŋs] *adv* lately, recently
**Neuerer** ['nɔʏərɐ] *m* (*-s*; -) innovator; '**Neuerung** *f* (-; *-en*) innovation
'**Neugestaltung** *f* reorganization, reformation
'**Neugier** *f*, **Neugierde** ['nɔʏgi:ɐdə] *f* (-; *no pl*) curiosity; '**neugierig** *adj* curious (***auf*** *acc* about); F *contp* nos(e)y; ***ich bin*** ~, ***ob*** I wonder if; '**Neugierige** [-gi:rɪgə] *contp pl* rubbernecks
'**Neuheit** *f* (-; *-en*) novelty
**Neuigkeit** ['nɔʏɪçkait] *f* (-; *-en*) (piece of) news
'**Neujahr** *n* New Year('s Day); ***Prost*** ~**!** Happy New Year!
'**neulich** *adv* the other day
**Neuling** ['nɔʏlɪŋ] *m* (*-s*; *-e*) newcomer, F greenhorn
'**neumodisch** *contp adj* newfangled
'**Neumond** *m* new moon
**neun** [nɔʏn] *adj* nine; '**neunte** *adj* ninth; '**Neuntel** *n* (*-s*; -) ninth (part); '**neuntens** *adv* ninthly; '**neunzehn** *adj* nineteen; '**neunzehnte** *adj* nineteenth; '**neunzig** *adj* ninety; '**neunzigste** *adj* ninetieth
**Neurose** [nɔʏ'ro:zə] *f* (-; *-n*) MED neurosis; **neurotisch** [nɔʏ'ro:tɪʃ] *adj* MED neurotic

**'neusprachlich** *adj* modern-language
**neutral** [nɔʏ'tra:l] *adj* neutral
**Neutralität** [nɔʏtrali'tɛ:t] *f* (-; *no pl*) neutrality
**Neutronen...** [nɔʏ'tro:nən-] PHYS *in cpds ...bombe etc*: neutron ...
**Neutrum** ['nɔʏtrʊm] *n* (-*s*; -*tra*) LING neuter
**'Neuverfilmung** *f* remake
**'neuwertig** *adj* as good as new
**'Neuzeit** *f* (-; *no pl*) modern times
**nicht** [nɪçt] *adv* not; ***überhaupt*** ~ not at all; ~ ***(ein)mal, gar*** ~ ***erst*** not even; ~ ***mehr*** not any more *or* longer; ***sie ist nett*** (***wohnt hier***), ~ (***wahr***)***?*** she's nice (lives here), isn't (doesn't) she?; ~ ***so ... wie*** not as ... as; ***noch*** ~ not yet; ~ ***besser*** (***als***) no (*or* not any) better (than); ***ich*** (***auch***) ~ I don't *or* I'm not (either); (***bitte***) ~***!*** (please) don't!
**'Nicht...** *in cpds ...mitglied, ...schwimmer etc*: *mst* non-...; **~beachtung** *f* disregard; non-observance
**Nichte** ['nɪçtə] *f* (-; -*n*) niece
**nichtig** ['nɪçtɪç] *adj* trivial; JUR void, invalid
**'Nichtraucher** *m*, **'Nichtraucherin** *f* non-smoker
**nichts** *indef pron* nothing, not anything; ~ (***anderes***) ***als*** nothing but; ***gar*** ~ nothing at all; F ***das ist*** ~ that's no good; ~ ***sagend*** meaningless; **Nichts** *n* (-*s*; *no pl*) nothing(ness); ***aus dem*** ~ *appear etc* from nowhere; *build etc* from nothing
**nichtsdesto'weniger** *adv* nevertheless
**'nichtsnutzig** [-nʊtsɪç] *adj* good-for--nothing, worthless
**'Nichtstuer** [-tu:ɐ] *m* (-*s*; -) do-nothing, F bum
**nicken** ['nɪkən] *v/i* (*ge-*, *h*) nod (one's head)
**nie** [ni:] *adv* never, at no time; ***fast*** ~ hardly ever; ~ ***und nimmer*** never ever
**nieder** ['ni:dɐ] **1.** *adj* low; **2.** *adv* down
**'Niedergang** *m* (-[*e*]*s*; *no pl*) decline
**'niedergeschlagen** *adj* depressed, (feeling) down
**'Niederlage** *f* defeat, F beating
**'niederlassen** *v/refl* (*irr*, ***lassen,*** *sep*, *-ge-*, *h*) settle (down); ECON set up (***als*** as); **'Niederlassung** *f* (-; -*en*) ECON establishment; branch
**'nieder|legen** *v/t* (*sep*, *-ge-*, *h*) lay down (*a. office etc*); ***die Arbeit*** ~ (go on) strike, down tools, F walk out; ***sich*** ~ lie down; go to bed; **~metzeln** *v/t* (*sep*, *-ge-*, *h*) massacre
**'Niederschlag** *m* METEOR rain(fall); PHYS fallout; CHEM precipitate; *boxing*: knock-down; **'niederschlagen** *v/t* (*irr*, ***schlagen,*** *sep*, *-ge-*, *h*) knock down; cast down (*eyes*); *fig* put down (*revolt etc*); JUR quash; ***sich*** ~ CHEM precipitate
**'niederschmettern** *fig v/t* (*sep*, *-ge-*, *h*) shatter, crush
**'niederträchtig** *adj* base, mean
**Niederung** ['ni:dərʊŋ] *f* (-; -*en*) lowland(s)
**niedlich** ['ni:tlɪç] *adj* pretty, sweet, cute
**niedrig** ['ni:drɪç] *adj* low (*a. fig*); *fig* light (*sentence etc*); ~ ***fliegen*** fly low
**niemals** ['ni:ma:ls] → ***nie***
**niemand** ['ni:mant] *indef pron* nobody, no one, not anybody; ~ ***von ihnen*** none of them; **'Niemandsland** *n* (-[*e*]*s*; *no pl*) no-man's-land
**Niere** ['ni:rə] *f* (-; -*n*) ANAT kidney
**nieseln** ['ni:zəln] *v/i* (*ge-*, *h*) drizzle
**'Nieselregen** *m* drizzle
**niesen** ['ni:zən] *v/i* (*ge-*, *h*) sneeze
**Niete[1]** ['ni:tə] *f* (-; -*n*) TECH rivet
**'Niete[2]** *f* (-; -*n*) blank; F failure
**Nikolaustag** ['nɪkolaus-] *m* St. Nicholas' Day
**Nikotin** [niko'ti:n] *n* (-*s*; *no pl*) CHEM nicotine
**Nilpferd** ['ni:l-] *n* ZO hippopotamus, F hippo
**Nippel** ['nɪpəl] *m* (-*s*; -) TECH nipple
**nippen** ['nɪpən] *v/i* (*ge-*, *h*) sip (***an*** *dat* at)
**nirgends** ['nɪrgənts] *adv* nowhere
**Nische** ['ni:ʃə] *f* (-; -*n*) niche, recess
**nisten** ['nɪstən] *v/i* (*ge-*, *h*) ZO nest
**'Nistplatz** *m* ZO nesting place
**Niveau** [ni'vo:] *n* (-*s*; -*s*) level, *fig a.* standard
**Nixe** ['nɪksə] *f* (-; -*n*) water nymph, mermaid
**noch** [nɔx] *adv* still; ~ ***nicht*** not yet; ~ ***nie*** never before; ***er hat nur*** ~ ***5 Mark*** (***Minuten***) he has only 5 marks (minutes) left; (***sonst***) ~ ***et.?*** anything else?; ***ich möchte*** ~ ***et.*** (***Tee***) I'd like some more (tea); ~ ***ein***(***e, -n***)***..., bitte*** another ..., please; ~ ***einmal*** once more *or* again; ~ ***zwei Stunden*** another two hours, two

N

hours to go; ~ ***besser*** (***schlimmer***) even better (worse); ~ ***gestern*** only yesterday; ***und wenn es ~ so ... ist*** however (*or* no matter how) ... it may be
**'nochmalig** [-maːlɪç] *adj* new, renewed
**'nochmals** *adv* once more *or* again
**Nockerl** ['nɔkɐl] *Austrian n* (*-s*; *-n*) GASTR small dumpling
**Nomade** [no'maːdə] *m* (*-n*; *-n*), **No'madin** *f* (-; *-nen*) nomad
**Nominativ** ['noːminatiːf] *m* (*-s*; *-e*) LING nominative (case)
**nominieren** [nomi'niːrən] *v/t* (*no -ge-*, *h*) nominate
**Nonne** ['nɔnə] *f* (-; *-n*) REL nun
**'Nonnenkloster** *n* REL convent
**Norden** ['nɔrdən] *m* (*-s*; *no pl*) north; ***nach*** ~ north(wards); **nordisch** ['nɔrdɪʃ] *adj* northern; SPORT ***~e Kombination*** Nordic Combined
**nördlich** ['nœrtlɪç] **1.** *adj* north(ern); northerly; **2.** *adv*: ~ ***von*** north of
**Nordlicht** ['nɔrt-] *n* (*-[e]s*; *-er*) ASTR northern lights
**Nord'osten** *m* northeast; **nord'östlich** *adj* northeast(ern); northeasterly
**'Nordpol** *m* North Pole
**Nord'westen** *m* northwest
**nord'westlich** *adj* northwest(ern); northwesterly
**'Nordwind** *m* north wind
**nörgeln** ['nœrgəln] *v/i* (*ge-*, *h*) nag (***an*** *dat* at)
**Nörgler** ['nœrglɐ] *m* (*-s*; -), **'Nörglerin** *f* (-; *-nen*) nagger
**Norm** [nɔrm] *f* (-; *-en*) standard, norm
**normal** [nɔr'maːl] *adj* normal; F ***nicht ganz*** ~ not quite right in the head
**Nor'mal...** *esp* TECH *in cpds* *...maß*, *...zeit etc*: standard ...; **~ben'zin** *n* regular (gas, *Br* petrol)
**normalerweise** [nɔr'maːlɐ'vaizə] *adv* normally, usually
**normalisieren** [nɔrmali'ziːrən] *v/refl* (*no -ge-*, *h*) return to normal
**normen** ['nɔrmən] *v/t* (*ge-*, *h*) standardize
**Norwegen** ['nɔrveːgən] Norway
**Norweger** ['nɔrveːgɐ] *m* (*-s*; -), **'Norwegerin** [-gərɪn] *f* (-; *-nen*), **'norwegisch** *adj* Norwegian
**Not** [noːt] *f* (-; *Nöte* ['nøːtə]) need; want; poverty; hardship, misery; difficulty; emergency; distress; ~ ***leidend*** needy; ***in ~ sein*** be in trouble; ***zur*** ~ if need be, if necessary
**Notar** [no'taːɐ] *m* (*-s*; *-e*), **No'tarin** *f* (-; *-nen*) JUR notary (public)
**'Not|aufnahme** *f* MED emergency room, *Br* casualty; **~ausgang** *m* emergency exit; **~behelf** *m* (*-[e]s*; *-e*) makeshift, expedient; **~bremse** *f* emergency brake; **~dienst** *m* emergency duty
**'notdürftig** *adj* scanty; temporary
**Note** ['noːtə] *f* (-; *-n*) note (*a.* MUS *and* POL); ECON bill, *esp Br* (bank)note; PED grade, *Br* mark; *pl* MUS (sheet) music; ***~n lesen*** read music
**Notebook** ['noʊtbʊk] *n* (*-s*; *-s*) EDP notebook
**'Notendurchschnitt** *m* PED *etc* average
**'Notenständer** *m* music stand
**'Notfall** *m* emergency
**'notfalls** *adv* if necessary
**'notgedrungen** *adv*: ***et. ~ tun*** be forced to do s.th.
**notieren** [no'tiːrən] *v/t* (*no -ge-*, *h*) make a note of, note (down); ECON quote
**nötig** ['nøːtɪç] *adj* necessary; ~ ***haben*** need; ~ ***brauchen*** need badly; ***das Nötigste*** the (bare) necessities *or* essentials; **nötigen** ['nøːtɪgən] *v/t* (*ge-*, *h*) force, compel; press, urge; **'Nötigung** *f* (-; *-en*) coercion; JUR intimidation
**Notiz** [no'tiːts] *f* (-; *-en*) note; ***keine ~ nehmen von*** take no notice of, ignore; ***sich ~en machen*** take notes; **~block** *m* memo pad, *Br* notepad; **~buch** *n* notebook
**'Notlage** *f* awkward (*or* difficult) situation; difficulties; emergency
**'notlanden** *v/i* (*-ge-*, *sein*) AVIAT make an emergency landing; **'Notlandung** *f* AVIAT emergency landing
**'Notlösung** *f* expedient
**'Notlüge** *f* white lie
**notorisch** [no'toːrɪʃ] *adj* notorious
**'Not|ruf** *m* TEL emergency call; **~rufsäule** *f* TEL emergency phone; **~sig'nal** *n* emergency *or* distress signal; **~stand** *m* state of (national) emergency; **~standsgebiet** *n* disaster area; ECON depressed area; **~standsgesetze** *pl* POL emergency laws; **~verband** *m* MED emergency dressing
**'Notwehr** *f* (-; *no pl*) JUR self-defense, *Br* self-defence

'**notwendig** *adj* necessary
'**Notwendigkeit** *f* (-; *-en*) necessity
'**Notzucht** *f* (-; *no pl*) JUR rape
**Novelle** [no'vɛlə] *f* (-; *-n*) novella; PARL amendment
**November** [no'vɛmbɐ] *m* (-[*s*]; -) November
**Nr.** ABBR *of* ***Nummer*** No., no., number
**Nu** [nu:] *m*: ***im ~*** in no time
**Nuance** ['nyã:sə] *f* shade
**nüchtern** ['nʏçtɐn] *adj* sober (*a. fig*); matter-of-fact; ***auf ~en Magen*** on an empty stomach; ***~ werden*** (***machen***) sober up
'**Nüchternheit** *f* (-; *no pl*) sobriety
**Nudel** ['nu:dəl] *f* (-; *-n*) noodle
**nuklear** [nukle'a:ɐ] *adj* nuclear
**null** [nʊl] *adj* zero, *Br* nought; TEL 0; SPORT nil, nothing; *tennis*: love; ***~ Grad*** zero degrees; ***~ Fehler*** no mistakes; ***gleich Null sein*** be nil
'**Null|di,ät** *f* low-calorie (*or* F starvation) diet; **~punkt** *m* zero (point *or fig* level); **~ta,rif** *m* free fare(s); ***zum ~*** free (of charge)
**Numerus clausus** ['nu:merʊs 'klauzʊs] *m* (-; *no pl*) UNIV restricted admission(s)
**Nummer** ['nʊmɐ] *f* (-; *-n*) number; issue; size; **nummerieren** [nʊmə'ri:rən] *v/t* (*no -ge-, h*) number
'**Nummernschild** *n* MOT license plate, *Br* numberplate
**nun** [nu:n] *adv* now; well
**nur** [nu:ɐ] *adv* only, just; merely; nothing but; ***er tut ~ so*** he's just pretending; ***~ so*** (***zum Spaß***) just for fun; ***warte ~!*** just you wait!; ***mach ~!***, ***~ zu!*** go ahead!; → ***Erwachsene***
**Nuss** [nʊs] *f* (-; *Nüsse* ['nʏsə]) BOT nut; **~baum** *m* walnut (tree); **~knacker** *m* nutcracker; **~schale** *f* nutshell
**Nüstern** ['nʏstɐn] *pl* ZO nostrils
**Nutte** ['nʊtə] F *f* (-; *-n*) hooker, *sl* tart
**Nutzanwendung** ['nʊts-] *f* practical application; '**nutzbar** *adj* usable; ***~ machen*** utilize; exploit; harness; '**nutzbringend** *adj* profitable, useful
**nütze** ['nʏtsə] *adj* useful; ***zu nichts ~ sein*** be (of) no use; be good for nothing
**Nutzen** ['nʊtsən] *m* (*-s*; -) use; profit, gain; advantage; ***~ ziehen aus*** (*dat*) benefit *or* profit from *or* by; ***zum ~ von*** (*or gen*) for the benefit of
'**nutzen,** '**nützen** (*ge-, h*) **1.** *v/i*: ***j-m ~*** be of use to s.o.; ***es nützt nichts*** (***es zu tun***) it's no use (doing it); **2.** *v/t* use, make use of; take advantage of
**nützlich** ['nʏtslɪç] *adj* useful, helpful; advantageous; ***sich ~ machen*** make o.s. useful
'**nutzlos** *adj* useless, (of) no use
'**Nutzung** *f* (-; *-en*) use, utilization
**Nylon**® ['nailɔn] *n* (*-s*; *no pl*) nylon; **~strümpfe** *pl* nylon stockings
**Nymphe** ['nʏmfə] *f* (-; *-n*) nymph

O

# O

**O** ABBR *of* ***Osten*** E, east
**o** *int* oh!; ***o weh!*** oh dear!
**o. Ä.** ABBR *of* ***oder Ähnliche(s)*** or the like
**Oase** [o'a:zə] *f* (-; *-n*) oasis (*a. fig*)
**ob** [ɔp] *cj* whether, if; ***als ~*** as if, as though; ***und ~!*** and how!, you bet!
**Obacht** ['o:baxt] *f*: ***~ geben auf*** (*acc*) pay attention to; (***gib***) ***~!*** watch out!
**Obdach** ['ɔpdax] *n* (*-[e]s*; *no pl*) shelter
'**obdachlos** *adj* homeless, without shelter; '**Obdachlose** *m, f* (*-n*; *-n*) homeless person; '**Obdachlosena,syl** *n* shelter for the homeless
**Obduktion** [ɔpdʊk'tsjo:n] *f* (-; *-en*) MED autopsy
**obduzieren** [ɔpdu'tsi:rən] *v/t* (*no -ge-, h*) MED perform an autopsy on
**oben** ['o:bən] *adv* above; up; on (the) top; at the top (*a. fig*); on the surface; upstairs; ***da ~*** up there; ***von ~ bis unten*** from top to bottom (*or* toe); ***links ~*** (at the) top left; ***siehe ~*** see above; F ***~ ohne*** topless; ***von ~ herab*** *fig* patroniz-

ing(ly), condescending(ly); ~ ***erwähnt*** *or* ***genannt*** above-mentioned; **~'an** *adv* at the top; **~'auf** *adv* on the top; on the surface; F feeling great; **~'drein** *adv* besides, into the bargain, at that; **~'hin** *adv* superficially

**Ober** ['o:bɐ] *m* (-*s*; -) waiter

**'Ober|arm** *m* ANAT upper arm; **~arzt** *m*, **~ärztin** *f* assistant medical director; **~befehl** *m* MIL supreme command; **~begriff** *n* generic term; **~bürgermeister** *m* mayor, *Br* Lord Mayor

**obere** ['o:bərə] *adj* upper, top, *fig a.* superior

**'Oberfläche** *f* surface (*a. fig*) (***an*** *dat* on); **'oberflächlich** *adj* superficial

**'oberhalb** *prp* (*gen*) above

**'Ober|hand** *f*: ***die ~ gewinnen*** (***über*** *acc*) get the upper hand (of); **~haupt** *n* head, chief; **~haus** *n* (-*es*; *no pl*) *Br* PARL House of Lords; **~hemd** *n* shirt; **~herrschaft** *f* (-; *no pl*) supremacy

**Oberin** ['o:bərɪn] *f* (-; -*nen*) REL Mother Superior

**'oberirdisch** *adj* above ground; ELECTR overhead

**'Ober|kellner** *m* head waiter; **~kiefer** *m* ANAT upper jaw; **~körper** *m* upper part of the body; ***den ~ freimachen*** strip to the waist; **~leder** *n* uppers; **~leitung** *f* chief management; ELECTR overhead contact line; **~lippe** *f* ANAT upper lip

O

**Obers** ['o:bɐs] *Austrian n* (-; *no pl*) GASTR cream

**'Oberschenkel** *m* ANAT thigh

**'Oberschule** *f appr* highschool, *Br* grammar school

**Oberst** ['o:bɐst] *m* (-*en*; -*en*) MIL colonel

**oberste** ['o:bɐstə] *adj* up(per)most, top(most); highest; *fig* chief, first

**'Ober|stufe** *f appr* senior highschool, *Br appr* senior classes; **~teil** *n* top

**ob'gleich** *cj* (al)though

**Obhut** ['ɔphu:t] *f* (-; *no pl*) care, charge; ***in s-e ~ nehmen*** take care *or* charge of

**obig** ['o:bɪç] *adj* above(-mentioned)

**Objekt** [ɔp'jɛkt] *n* (-[*e*]*s*; -*e*) object (*a.* LING); ECON property

**objektiv** [ɔpjɛk'ti:f] *adj* objective; impartial, unbias(s)ed

**Objek'tiv** *n* (-*s*; -*e*) PHOT (object) lens

**Objektivität** [ɔpjɛktivi'tɛ:t] *f* (-; *no pl*) objectivity; impartiality

**Oblate** [o'bla:tə] *f* (-; -*n*) wafer; REL host

**obligatorisch** [obliga'to:rɪʃ] *adj* compulsory

**Oboe** [o'bo:ə] *f* (-; -*n*) MUS oboe

**Oboist** [obo'ɪst] *m* (-*en*; -*en*) MUS oboist

**Observatorium** [ɔpzɛrva'to:rjʊm] *n* (-*s*; -*ien*) ASTR observatory

**Obst** [o:pst] *n* (-[*e*]*s*; *no pl*) fruit; **~garten** *m* orchard; **~kon͵serven** *pl* canned fruit; **~laden** *m* fruit store, *esp Br* fruiterer's (shop); **~torte** *f* fruit pie (*Br* flan)

**obszön** [ɔps'tsø:n] *adj* obscene, filthy

**ob'wohl** *cj* (al)though

**Occasion** [ɔka'zjo:n] *Swiss f* (-; -*en*) bargain, good buy

**Ochse** ['ɔksə] *m* (-*n*; -*n*) ZO ox, bullock; F blockhead

**od.** ABBR *of* ***oder*** or

**öde** ['ø:də] *adj* deserted, desolate; waste; *fig* dull, dreary, tedious

**oder** ['o:dɐ] *cj* or; ***~ aber*** or else, otherwise; ***~ vielmehr*** or rather; ***~ so*** or so; ***er kommt doch, ~?*** he's coming, isn't he?; ***du kennst ihn ja nicht, ~ doch?*** you don't know him, or do you?

**Ofen** ['o:fən] *m* (-*s*; *Öfen* ['ø:fən]) stove; oven; TECH furnace; **~heizung** *f* stove heating; **~rohr** *n* stovepipe

**offen** ['ɔfən] **1.** *adj* open (*a. fig*); vacant (*post*); *fig* frank; **2.** *adv*: ***~ gesagt*** frankly (speaking); ***~ s-e Meinung sagen*** speak one's mind (freely); ***~ stehen*** be open (*fig* ***j-m*** to s.o.); ECON be outstanding

**'offenbar** *adj* obvious, evident; apparent; **offenbaren** [-'ba:rən] *v/t* (*ge-*, *h*) reveal, disclose, show; **Offen'barung** *f* (-; -*en*) revelation

**'Offenheit** *f* (-; *no pl*) openness, frankness

**'offenherzig** *adj* open-hearted, frank, candid; *fig* revealing (*dress*)

**'offensichtlich** *adj* → ***offenbar***

**offensiv** [ɔfɛn'zi:f] *adj*, **Offensive** [ɔfɛn'zi:və] *f* (-; -*n*) offensive

**öffentlich** ['œfəntlɪç] *adj* public; ***~e Verkehrsmittel*** *pl* public transport; ***~e Schulen*** *pl* public (*Br* state) schools; ***~ auftreten*** appear in public

**'Öffentlichkeit** *f* (-; *no pl*) *the* public; ***in aller ~*** in public, openly; ***an die ~ bringen*** make public

**offiziell** [ɔfi'tsjɛl] *adj* official

**Offizier** [ɔfi'tsiːɐ] *m* (*-s*; *-e*) MIL (commissioned) officer

**öffnen** ['œfnən] *v/t and v/refl* (*ge-*, *h*) open; **Öffner** ['œfnɐ] *m* (*-s*; *-*) opener; **'Öffnung** *f* (*-*; *-en*) opening

**'Öffnungszeiten** *pl* business *or* office hours

**oft** [ɔft] *adv* often, frequently

**oh** [oː] *int* o(h)!

**ohne** ['oːnə] *prp* (*acc*) *and cj* without; ~ ***mich!*** count me out!; ~ ***ein Wort*** (***zu sagen***) without (saying) a word

**ohne|'gleichen** *adv* unequal(l)ed, unparalleled; **~'hin** *adv* anyhow, anyway

**Ohnmacht** ['oːnmaxt] *f* (*-*; *-en*) MED unconsciousness; *fig* helplessness; ***in ~ fallen*** faint, pass out; **'ohnmächtig** *adj* MED unconscious; *fig* helpless; ~ ***werden*** faint, pass out

**Ohr** [oːɐ] *n* (*-[e]s*; *-en* ['oːrən]) ANAT ear; F ***j-n übers ~ hauen*** cheat s.o.; ***bis über die ~en verliebt*** (***verschuldet***) head over heels in love (over your head in debt)

**Öhr** [øːɐ] *n* (*-[e]s*; *-e* ['øːrə]) eye

**Ohrenarzt** ['oːrən-] *m* ear specialist

**'ohrenbetäubend** *adj* deafening

**'Ohren|schmerzen** *pl* earache; **~schützer** *pl* earmuffs; **~zeuge** *m* earwitness

**'Ohrfeige** *f* slap in the face (*a. fig*); **'ohrfeigen** [-faigən] *v/t* (*ge-*, *h*) ***j-n*** ~ slap s.o.'s face

**'Ohr|läppchen** [-lɛpçən] *n* (*-s*; *-*) ANAT earlobe; **~ring** *m* earring

**oje** [o'jeː] *int* oh dear!, dear me!

**Ökologe** [øko'loːgə] *m* (*-n*; *-n*) ecologist; **Ökologie** [økolo'giː] *f* (*-*; *no pl*) ecology; **ökologisch** [øko'loːgɪʃ] *adj* ecological

**Ökonomie** [økono'miː] *f* (*-*; *no pl*) economy; ECON economics; **ökonomisch** [øko'noːmɪʃ] *adj* economical; ECON economic

**Ökosys,tem** ['øːko-] *n* ecosystem

**Oktave** [ɔk'taːvə] *f* (*-*; *-n*) MUS octave

**Oktober** [ɔk'toːbɐ] *m* (*-[s]*; *-*) October

**ökumenisch** [øku'meːnɪʃ] *adj* REL ecumenical

**Öl** [øːl] *n* (*-[e]s*; *Öle*) oil; petroleum; ***nach ~ bohren*** drill for oil; ***auf ~ stoßen*** strike oil; **'Ölbaum** *m* BOT olive (tree)

**Oldtimer** ['oʊldtaɪmə] *m* (*-s*; *-*) MOT veteran car

**ölen** ['øːlən] *v/t* (*ge-*, *h*) oil, TECH *a.* lubricate

**'Öl|farbe** *f* oil (paint); **~feld** *n* oilfield; **~förderland** *n* oil-producing country; **~förderung** *f* oil production; **~gemälde** *n* oil painting; **~heizung** *f* oil heating

**ölig** ['øːlɪç] *adj* oily, greasy (*both a. fig*)

**oliv** [o'liːf] *adj* olive

**Olive** [o'liːvə] *f* (*-*; *-n*) BOT olive

**'Öl|leitung** *f* (oil) pipeline; **~messstab** *m* MOT dipstick; **~pest** *f* oil pollution; **~quelle** *f* oil well; **~sar,dine** *f* canned (*Br a.* tinned) sardine; **~tanker** *m* MAR oil tanker; **~teppich** *m* oil slick; **~stand** *m* oil level

**'Ölung** *f* (*-*; *no pl*) oiling, TECH *a.* lubrication; ***Letzte*** ~ REL extreme unction

**'Öl|wanne** *f* MOT oil pan, *Br* sump; **~wechsel** *m* MOT oil change; **~zeug** *n* oilskins

**Olympia...** [o'lʏmpja-] *in cpds ...mannschaft*, *...medaille etc*: Olympic ...

**Olympiade** [olʏm'pjaːdə] *f* (*-*; *-n*) SPORT Olympic Games, Olympics

**Oma** ['oːma] F *f* (*-*; *-s*) grandma

**Omi** ['oːmi] F *f* (*-*; *-s*) granny

**Omnibus** ['ɔmnibʊs] *m* → ***Bus***

**onanieren** [ona'niːrən] *v/i* (*no -ge-*, *h*) masturbate

**Onkel** ['ɔŋkəl] *m* (*-s*; *-*) uncle

**Online...** ['ɔnlain-] EDP online ...

**Opa** ['oːpa] F *m* (*-s*; *-s*) grandpa

**Oper** ['oːpɐ] *f* (*-*; *-n*) MUS opera; opera (house)

**Operation** [opəra'tsjoːn] *f* (*-*; *-en*) MED operation; ***e-e ~ vornehmen*** perform an operation; **Operati'onssaal** *m* MED operating room (*Br* theatre)

**Operette** [opə'rɛtə] *f* (*-*; *-n*) MUS operetta

**operieren** [opə'riːrən] (*no -ge-*, *h*) **1.** *v/t* MED ***j-n*** ~ operate on s.o. (***wegen*** for); ***operiert werden*** be operated on, have an operation; ***sich ~ lassen*** undergo an operation; **2.** *v/i* MED, MIL operate; proceed

**'Opernsänger(in)** opera singer

**Opfer** ['ɔpfɐ] *n* (*-s*; *-*) sacrifice; offering; victim; ***ein ~ bringen*** make a sacrifice; (*dat*) ***zum ~ fallen*** fall victim to

**'opfern** *v/t and v/i* (*ge-*, *h*) sacrifice

**Opium** ['oːpjʊm] *n* (*-s*; *no pl*) opium

**Opposition** [ɔpozi'tsjoːn] *f* (*-*; *-en*) opposition (*a.* PARL)

**Optik** ['ɔptik] *f* (-; *no pl*) optics; PHOT optical system
**Optiker** ['ɔptikɐ] *m* (-s; -), **'Optikerin** *f* (-; *-nen*) optician
**optimal** [ɔpti'ma:l] *adj* optimum, best
**Optimismus** [ɔpti'mɪsmʊs] *m* (-; *no pl*) optimism; **Optimist(in)** [ɔpti'mɪst(ɪn)] (*-en*; *-en*/-; *-nen*) optimist; **opti'mistisch** *adj* optimistic
**Option** [ɔp'tsjo:n] *f* (-; *-en*) option
**optisch** ['ɔptɪʃ] *adj* optical
**Orange** [o'rã:ʒə] *f* (-; *-n*) BOT orange
**Orchester** [ɔr'kɛstɐ] *n* (*-s*; -) MUS orchestra
**Orchidee** [ɔrçi'de:] *f* (-; *-n*) BOT orchid
**Orden** ['ɔrdən] *m* (*-s*; -) medal, decoration; *esp* REL order
**'Ordensschwester** *f* REL sister, nun
**ordentlich** ['ɔrdəntlɪç] **1.** *adj* tidy, neat, orderly; proper; thorough; decent (*a.* F); respectable; full (*member etc*); JUR ordinary; reasonable (*performance etc*); F good, sound; **2.** *adv*: ***s-e Sache ~ machen*** do a good job; ***sich ~ benehmen*** (***anziehen***) behave (dress) properly *or* decently
**ordinär** [ɔrdi'nɛ:ɐ] *adj* vulgar; common
**ordnen** ['ɔrdnən] *v/t* (*ge-*, *h*) put in order; arrange, sort (out); file; settle
**Ordner** ['ɔrdnɐ] *m* (*-s*; -) file; folder; attendant, guard
**'Ordnung** *f* (-; *no pl*) order; orderliness, tidiness; arrangement; system, set-up; class; ***in ~*** all right; TECH *etc* in (good) order; ***in ~ bringen*** put right (*a. fig*); tidy up; repair, fix (*a. fig*); (***in***) ***~ halten*** keep (in) order; ***et. ist nicht in ~*** (***mit***) there is s.th. wrong (with)
**'ordnungsgemäß 1.** *adj* correct, regular; **2.** *adv* duly, properly
**'Ordnungs|strafe** *f* JUR fine, penalty; **~zahl** *f* MATH ordinal number
**Organ** [ɔr'ga:n] *n* (*-s*; *-e*) organ; **~empfänger** *m* MED organ recipient; **~handel** *m* sale of (transplant) organs
**Organisation** [ɔrganiza'tsjo:n] *f* (-; *-en*) organization; **Organisator** [ɔrgani'za:to:ɐ] *m* (*-s*; *-en* [-za'to:rən]) organizer; **Organisa'torin** *f* (-; *-nen*) organizer; **organisatorisch** [-za'to:rɪʃ] *adj* organizational
**organisch** [ɔr'ga:nɪʃ] *adj* organic
**organisieren** [ɔrgani'zi:rən] *v/t* organize; F get (hold of); ***sich ~*** organize; ECON unionize; **organisiert** [ɔrgani'zi:ɐt] *adj* organized; ECON unionized
**Organismus** [ɔrga'nɪsmʊs] *m* (-; *-men*) BIOL organism
**Organist** [ɔrga'nɪst] *m* (*-en*; *-en*), **Orga'nistin** *f* (-; *-nen*) MUS organist
**Or'ganspender** *m* MED (organ) donor
**Orgasmus** [ɔr'gasmʊs] *m* (-; *-men*) orgasm
**Orgel** ['ɔrgəl] *f* (-; *-n*) MUS organ
**'Orgelpfeife** *f* MUS organ pipe
**Orgie** ['ɔrgjə] *f* (-; *-n*) orgy
**Orientale** [orjɛn'ta:lə] *m* (*-n*; *-n*), **Orien'talin** *f* (-; *-nen*), **orien'talisch** *adj* oriental
**orientieren** [orjɛn'ti:rən] *v/t* (*no -ge-*, *h*) inform (***über*** *acc* about), brief (on); ***sich ~*** orient(ate) o.s. (*a. fig*) (***nach*** by); inform o.s.; **Orien'tierung** *f* (-; *no pl*) orientation, *fig a.* information; ***die ~ verlieren*** lose one's bearings
**Orien'tierungssinn** *m* (-[*e*]*s*; *no pl*) sense of direction
**original** [origi'na:l] *adj* original; real, genuine; TV live; **Origi'nal** *n* (*-s*; *-e*) original; *fig* real (*or* quite a) character
**Origi'nal...** *in cpds ...aufnahme*, *...ausgabe etc*: original ...; **~übertragung** *f* live broadcast *or* program(me)
**originell** [origi'nɛl] *adj* original; ingenious; witty
**Orkan** [ɔr'ka:n] *m* (-[*e*]*s*; *-e*) hurricane
**or'kanartig** *adj* violent; *fig* thunderous
**Ort** [ɔrt] *m* (-[*e*]*s*; *-e*) place; village, (small) town; spot, point; scene; ***vor ~*** *mining*: at the (pit) face; *fig* in the field, on the spot
**orten** ['ɔrtən] *v/t* (*ge-*, *h*) locate, spot
**orthodox** [ɔrto'dɔks] *adj* orthodox
**Orthographie** [ɔrtogra'fi:] *f* (-; *-n*) orthography
**Orthopäde** [ɔrto'pɛ:də] *m* (*-n*; *-n*), **Ortho'pädin** *f* (-; *-nen*) MED orthop(a)edic specialist
**örtlich** ['œrtlɪç] *adj* local
**'Ortsbestimmung** *f* AVIAT, MAR location; LING adverb of place
**'Ortschaft** *f* → ***Ort***
**'Ortsgespräch** *n* TEL local call
**'Ortskenntnis** *f*: ***~ besitzen*** know a place
**'Ortsnetz** *n* TEL local exchange
**'Ortszeit** *f* local time
**Öse** ['ø:zə] *f* (-; *-n*) eye; eyelet

O

**Ostblock** ['ɔst-] *m* (-[*e*]*s*; *no pl*) HIST POL East(ern) Bloc
**Osten** ['ɔstən] *m* (-*s*; *no pl*) east; POL *the* East; ***nach*** ~ east(wards)
**Oster|ei** ['o:stɐ-] *n* Easter egg; **~hase** *m* Easter bunny *or* rabbit
**Ostern** ['o:stɐn] *n* (-; -) Easter (***zu***, ***an*** at); ***frohe*** **~!** Happy Easter!
**Österreicher** ['ø:stəraiçɐ] *m* (-*s*; -), **'Österreicherin** [-raiçərın] *f* (-; -*nen*), **'österreichisch** *adj* Austrian
**östlich** ['œstlıç] **1.** *adj* east(ern); easterly; **2.** *adv*: ~ ***von*** (to the) east of
**ostwärts** ['ɔstvɛrts] *adv* east(wards)
**'Ostwind** *m* east wind
**Otter** ['ɔtɐ] ZO **1.** *m* (-*s*; -) otter; **2.** *f* (-; -*n*) adder, viper
**outen** ['autən] *v/t* (*ge*-, *h*) out
**Ouvertüre** [uvɛr'ty:rə] *f* (-; -*n*) MUS overture
**oval** [o'va:l] *adj*, **O'val** *n* (-*s*; -*e*) oval
**Oxid** [ɔ'ksi:t] *n* (-[*e*]*s*; -*e* [ɔ'ksi:də]) CHEM oxide; **oxidieren** [ɔksi'di:rən] *v/t* (*no* -*ge*-, *h*) *and v/i* (*h*, *sein*) CHEM oxidize;
**Oxyd** *n* → ***Oxid***
**Ozean** ['o:tsea:n] *m* (-*s*; -*e*) ocean, sea
**Ozon** [o'tso:n] *n* (-*s*; *no pl*) CHEM ozone
**o'zonfreundlich** *adj* ozone-friendly
**O'zon|loch** *n* ozone hole; **~schicht** *f* ozone layer; **~schild** *m* ozone shield; **~werte** *pl* ozone levels

# P

**paar** [pa:ɐ] *indef pron*: ***ein*** ~ a few, some, F a couple of; ***ein*** ~ ***Mal*** a few times
**Paar** *n* (-[*e*]*s*; -*e*) pair; couple; ***ein*** ~ (***neue***) ***Schuhe*** a (new) pair of shoes
**paaren** ['pa:rən] *v/t and v/refl* (*ge*-, *h*) ZO mate; *fig* combine
**'Paarlauf** *m* SPORT pair skating
**'Paarung** *f* (-; -*en*) ZO mating, copulation; SPORT matching
**'paarweise** *adv* in pairs, in twos
**Pacht** [paxt] *f* (-; -*en*) lease; rent
**'pachten** *v/t* (*ge*-, *h*) (take on) lease
**Pächter** ['pɛçtɐ] *m* (-*s*; -), **'Pächterin** *f* (-; -*nen*) leaseholder; AGR tenant
**'Pacht|vertrag** *m* lease; **~zins** *m* rent
**Pack**[1] [pak] *m* → ***Packen***
**Pack**[2] *contp n* (-[*e*]*s*; *no pl*) rabble
**Päckchen** ['pɛkçən] *n* (-*s*; -) pack, *Br* packet; small parcel; **packen** ['pakən] *v/t and v/i* (*ge*-, *h*) pack; make up (*parcel etc*); grab, seize (***an*** *dat* by); *fig* grip; **'Packen** *m* (-*s*; -) pack, pile (*a. fig*); **Packer** ['pakɐ] *m* (-*s*; -) packer; removal man; **'Packpa,pier** *n* packing *or* brown paper; **'Packung** *f* (-; -*en*) package, box; pack, *Br* packet
**Pädagoge** [pɛda'go:gə] *m* (-*n*; -*n*), **Päda'gogin** *f* (-; -*nen*) teacher; education(al)ist
**päda'gogisch** *adj* pedagogic, educational; **~*e Hochschule*** college of education
**Paddel** ['padəl] *n* (-*s*; -) paddle
**'Paddelboot** *n* canoe
**'paddeln** *v/i* (*ge*-, *h*, *sein*) paddle, canoe
**Page** ['pa:ʒə] *m* (-*n*; -*n*) page(boy)
**Paket** [pa'ke:t] *n* (-[*e*]*s*; -*e*) package; parcel; **~karte** *f* parcel post slip, *Br* parcel mailing form; **~post** *f* parcel post; **~schalter** *m* parcel counter; **~zustellung** *f* parcel delivery
**Pakt** [pakt] *m* (-[*e*]*s*; -*e*) POL pact
**Palast** [pa'last] *m* (-[*e*]*s*; *Paläste* [pa'lɛstə]) palace
**Palme** ['palmə] *f* (-; -*n*) BOT palm (tree)
**Palm'sonntag** *m* REL Palm Sunday
**Pampelmuse** ['pampəlmu:zə] *f* (-; -*n*) BOT grapefruit
**paniert** [pa'ni:ɐt] *adj* GASTR breaded
**Panik** ['pa:nık] *f* (-; -*en*) panic; ***in*** ~ ***geraten*** (***versetzen***) panic; ***in*** ~ panic-stricken, F panicky; **panisch** ['pa:nıʃ] *adj*: **~*e Angst*** mortal terror
**Panne** ['panə] *f* (-; -*n*) breakdown, MOT *a.* engine trouble; *fig* mishap
**'Pannenhilfe** *f* MOT breakdown service
**Panter, Panther** ['pantɐ] *m* (-*s*; -) ZO panther

P

**Pantoffel** [pan'tɔfəl] *m* (*-s*; *-n*) slipper; **~held** F *m* henpecked husband

**Pantomime** [panto'mi:mə] THEA **1.** *f* (*-*; *-n*) mime, dumb show; **2.** *m* (*-n*; *-n*) mime (artist); **panto'mimisch** *adv*: **~ *darstellen*** mime

**Panzer** ['pantsɐ] *m* (*-s*; *-*) armo(u)r (*a. fig*); MIL tank; ZO shell; **~glas** *n* bullet-proof glass

**'panzern** *v/t* (*ge-*, *h*) armo(u)r; → ***gepanzert***

**'Panzerschrank** *m* safe

**Panzerung** ['pantsərʊŋ] *f* (*-*; *-en*) armo(u)r plating

**Papa** [pa'pa:] F *m* (*-s*; *-s*) dad(dy), pa

**Papagei** [papa'gai] *m* (*-en*; *-en*) ZO parrot

**Papeterie** [papɛtə'ri:] *Swiss f* (*-*; *-n*) stationer('s shop)

**Papier** [pa'pi:ɐ] *n* (*-s*; *-e*) paper; *pl* papers, documents; identification (paper)

**Pa'pier...** *in cpds ...geld, ...handtuch, ...serviette, ...tüte etc*: *mst* paper ...; **~geschäft** *n* stationer('s store, *Br* shop); **~korb** *m* wastepaper basket; **~krieg** F *m* red tape; **~schnitzel** *pl* scraps of paper; **~waren** *pl* stationery

**Pappe** ['papə] *f* (*-*; *-n*) cardboard, pasteboard

**Pappel** ['papəl] *f* (*-*; *-n*) BOT poplar

**'Papp|kar,ton** *m* cardboard box, carton; **~teller** *m* paper plate

**Paprika** ['paprika] *m* (*-s*; *-[s]*) a) BOT sweet pepper, b) (*no pl*) GASTR paprika

**Papst** [pa:pst] *m* (*-[e]s*; *Päpste* ['pɛ:pstə]) pope; **'päpstlich** *adj* papal

**Parade** [pa'ra:də] *f* (*-*; *-n*) parade; *soccer etc*: save; *boxing*, *fencing*: parry

**Paradeiser** [para'daizɐ] *Austrian m* (*-s*; *-*) BOT tomato

**Paradies** [para'di:s] *n* (*-es*; *-e*) paradise

**paradiesisch** [para'di:zɪʃ] *fig adj* heavenly, delightful

**paradox** [para'dɔks] *adj* paradoxical

**Paragraph** [para'gra:f] *m* (*-en*; *-en*) JUR article, section; paragraph

**parallel** [para'le:l] *adj*, **Paral'lele** *f* (*-*; *-n*) parallel

**Parasit** [para'zi:t] *m* (*-en*; *-en*) parasite

**Parfüm** [par'fy:m] *n* (*-s*; *-s*) perfume, *Br a.* scent; **Parfümerie** [parfymə'ri:] *f* (*-*; *-n*) perfumery; **parfümieren** [parfy'mi:rən] *v/t* (*no -ge-*, *h*) perfume, scent; ***sich* ~** put on perfume

**parieren** [pa'ri:rən] *v/t and v/i* (*no -ge-*, *h*) SPORT parry, *fig a.* counter (***mit*** with); pull up (*horse*); obey

**Park** [park] *m* (*-s*; *-s*) park

**parken** ['parkən] *v/i and v/t* (*ge-*, *h*) MOT park; ***Parken verboten!*** no parking!

**Parkett** [par'kɛt] *n* (*-[e]s*; *-e*, *-s*) parquet (floor); THEA orchestra, *Br* stalls; dance floor

**'Park|gebühr** *f* parking fee; **~(hoch)haus** *n* parking garage, *Br* multi-storey car park

**parkieren** [par'ki:rən] *Swiss v/t and v/i* → ***parken***

**'Park|kralle** *f* wheel clamp; **~lücke** *f* parking space; **~platz** *m* parking lot, *Br* car park; → ***Parklücke; e-n ~ suchen*** (***finden***) look for (find) somewhere to park the car; **~scheibe** *f* parking disk (*Br* disc); **~sünder** *m* parking offender; **~uhr** *f* MOT parking meter; **~wächter** *m* park keeper; MOT parking lot (*Br* car park) attendant

**Parlament** [parla'mɛnt] *n* (*-[e]s*; *-e*) parliament; **parlamentarisch** [parlamɛn'ta:rɪʃ] *adj* parliamentary

**Parodie** [paro'di:] *f* (*-*; *-n*), **paro'dieren** *v/t* (*no -ge-*, *h*) parody

**Parole** [pa'ro:lə] *f* (*-n*; *-n*) MIL password; *fig* watchword, POL *a.* slogan

**Partei** [par'tai] *f* (*-*; *-en*) party (*a.* POL); ***j-s ~ ergreifen*** take sides with s.o., side with s.o.; **par'teiisch** *adj* partial (***für*** to); prejudiced (***gegen*** against)

**par'teilos** *adj* POL independent

**Par'tei|mitglied** *n* POL party member; **~pro,gramm** *n* POL platform; **~tag** *m* POL convention; **~zugehörigkeit** *f* POL party membership

**Parterre** [par'tɛrə] *n* (*-s*; *-s*) first (*Br* ground) floor

**Partie** [par'ti:] *f* (*-*; *-n*) game, SPORT *a.* match; part, passage (*a.* MUS); ***e-e gute*** *etc* **~ *sein*** be a good *etc* match

**Partisan** [parti'za:n] *m* (*-s*, *-en*; *-en*), **Parti'sanin** *f* (*-*; *-nen*) MIL partisan, guerilla

**Partitur** [parti'tu:ɐ] *f* (*-*; *-en*) MUS score

**Partizip** [parti'tsi:p] *n* (*-s*; *-ien*) LING participle

**Partner** ['partnɐ] *m* (*-s*; *-*), **'Partnerin** *f* (*-*; *-nen*) partner

**'Partnerschaft** *f* (*-*; *-en*) partnership

**'Partnerstadt** *f* twin town

**paschen** ['paʃən] *Austrian v/t and v/i* (*ge-*, *h*) smuggle; **Pascher** ['paʃɐ] *Austrian m* (*-s*; -) smuggler
**Pass** [pas] *m* (*-es*; *Pässe* ['pɛsə]) passport; SPORT, GEOGR pass; ***langer ~*** SPORT long ball
**Passage** [pa'sa:ʒə] *f* (-; *-n*) passage
**Passagier** [pasa'ʒi:ɐ] *m* (*-s*; *-e*) passenger; **~flugzeug** *n* passenger plane; airliner
**Passa'gierin** *f* (-; *-nen*) passenger
**Passah** ['pasa] *n* (*-s*; *no pl*), **'Passahfest** *n* REL Passover
**Passant** [pa'sant] *m* (*-en*; *-en*), **Pas'santin** *f* (-; *-nen*) passerby
**'Passbild** *n* passport photo(graph)
**passen** ['pasən] **1.** *v/i* (*ge-*, *h*) fit (***j-m*** s.o.; ***auf*** *or* ***für*** *or* ***zu et.*** s.th.); suit (***j-m*** s.o.), be convenient; *cards*, SPORT pass; ***~ zu*** go with, match; ***sie ~ gut zueinander*** they are well suited to each other; ***passt es Ihnen morgen?*** would tomorrow suit you *or* be all right (with you)?; ***das*** (***er***) ***passt mir gar nicht*** I don't like that (him) at all; ***das passt*** (***nicht***) ***zu ihm*** that's just like him (not like him, not his style); **~d** *adj* fitting; matching; suitable, right
**passierbar** [pa'si:ɐba:ɐ] *adj* passable
**passieren** [pa'si:rən] (*no -ge-*) **1.** *v/i* (*sein*) happen; **2.** *v/t* (*h*) pass (through)
**Pas'sierschein** *m* pass, permit
**Passion** [pa'sjo:n] *f* (-; *-en*) passion; REL Passion
**passiv** ['pasi:f] *adj* passive
**'Passiv** *n* (*-s*; *no pl*) LING passive (voice)
**Paste** ['pastə] *f* (-; *-n*) paste
**Pastell** [pas'tɛl] *n* (*-[e]s*; *-e*) PAINT pastel
**Pastete** [pas'te:tə] *f* (-; *-n*) GASTR pie
**Pate** ['pa:tə] *m* (*-n*; *-n*) godfather; **'Patenkind** *n* godchild
**'Patenschaft** *f* (-; *-en*) sponsorship
**Patent** [pa'tɛnt] *n* (*-[e]s*; *-e*) patent; MIL commission; **~amt** *n* patent office; **~anwalt** *m* JUR patent agent
**patentieren** [patɛn'ti:rən] *v/t* (*no -ge-*, *h*) patent; (***sich***) ***et. ~ lassen*** take out a patent for s.th.
**Pa'tentinhaber** *m* patentee
**pathetisch** [pa'te:tɪʃ] *adj* pompous
**Patient** [pa'tsjɛnt] *m* (*-en*; *-en*), **Pa'tientin** *f* (-; *-nen*) MED patient
**Patin** ['pa:tɪn] *f* (-; *-nen*) godmother
**Patriot** [patri'o:t] *m* (*-en*; *-en*) patriot
**patri'otisch** *adj* patriotic
**Patrone** [pa'tro:nə] *f* (-; *-n*) cartridge
**Patrouille** [pa'trʊljə] *f* (-; *-n*) MIL patrol; **patroullieren** [patrʊl'ji:rən] *v/i* (*no -ge-*, *h*) MIL patrol
**Patsche** ['patʃə] F *f*: ***in der ~ sitzen*** be in a fix *or* jam
**'patschen** F *v/i* (*ge-*, *h*) (s)plash
**'patsch'nass** *adj* soaking wet
**patzen** ['patsən] F *v/i* (*ge-*, *h*), **Patzer** ['patsɐ] F *m* (*-s*; -) blunder
**Pauke** ['paukə] *f* (-; *-n*) MUS bass drum; kettledrum
**'pauken** F *v/i and v/t* (*ge-*, *h*) cram
**Pauschale** [pau'ʃa:lə] *f* (-; *-n*) lump sum
**Pau'schal|gebühr** *f* flat rate; **~reise** *f* package tour; **~urteil** *n* sweeping judg(e)ment
**Pause**[1] ['pauzə] *f* (-; *-n*) recess, *Br* break, *esp* THEA, SPORT intermission, *Br* interval; pause; rest (*a.* MUS)
**'Pause**[2] *f* (-; *-n*) TECH tracing
**'pausen** *v/t* (*ge-*, *h*) TECH trace
**'pausenlos** *adj* uninterrupted, nonstop
**'Pausenzeichen** *n radio*: interval signal; PED bell
**pausieren** [pau'zi:rən] *v/i* (*no -ge-*, *h*) pause, rest
**Pavian** ['pa:vja:n] *m* (*-s*; *-e*) ZO baboon
**Pavillon** ['pavɪljɔŋ] *m* (*-s*; *-s*) pavilion
**Pazifist** [patsi'fɪst] *m* (*-en*; *-en*), **Pazi'fistin** *f* (-; *-nen*), **pazi'fistisch** *adj* pacifist
**PC** [pe:'tse:] *m* (*-[s]*; *-[s]*) ABBR *of* ***personal computer*** PC
**Pech** [pɛç] *n* (*-s*; *no pl*) pitch; F bad luck; **~strähne** F *f* run of bad luck; **~vogel** F *m* unlucky fellow
**pedantisch** [pe'dantɪʃ] *adj* pedantic, fussy
**Pegel** ['pe:gəl] *m* (*-s*; -) level (*a. fig*)
**peilen** ['pailən] *v/t* (*ge-*, *h*) sound
**peinigen** ['painɪgən] *v/t* (*ge-*, *h*) torment
**Peiniger** ['painɪgɐ] *m* (*-s*; -) tormentor
**peinlich** ['painlɪç] *adj* embarrassing; ***~ genau*** meticulous (***bei***, ***in*** *dat* in); ***es war mir ~*** I was *or* felt embarrassed
**Peitsche** ['paitʃə] *f* (-; *-n*), **'peitschen** *v/t* (*ge-*, *h*) whip
**'Peitschenhieb** *m* lash
**Pelle** ['pɛlə] *f* (-; *-n*) skin; peel; **'pellen** *v/t* (*ge-*, *h*) peel; **'Pellkar,toffeln** *pl* potatoes (boiled) in their jackets
**Pelz** [pɛlts] *m* (*-es*; *-e*) fur; skin

'**pelzgefüttert** *adj* fur-lined
'**Pelzgeschäft** *n* fur(rier's) store (*Br* shop)
**pelzig** ['pɛltsɪç] *adj* furry; MED furred
'**Pelzmantel** *m* fur coat
'**Pelztiere** *pl* furred animals, furs
**Pendel** ['pɛndəl] *n* (*-s*; -) pendulum
'**pendeln** *v/i* (*ge-*, *h*) swing; RAIL *etc* shuttle; commute
'**Pendeltür** *f* swing door
'**Pendelverkehr** *m* RAIL *etc* shuttle service; commuter traffic; **Pendler(in)** ['pɛndlɐ (-lərɪn)] (*-s*; -/-; *-nen*) RAIL *etc* commuter
**Penis** ['pe:nɪs] *m* (*-s*; *-se*) ANAT penis
**Penner** ['pɛnɐ] F *m* (*-s*; -) tramp, bum
**Pension** [pã'sjo:n] *f* (-; *-en*) (old age) pension; boarding-house, private hotel; ***in ~ sein*** be retired; **Pensionär(in)** [pãsjo'nɛ:ɐ (-'nɛ:rɪn)] (*-s*; *-e*/-; *-nen*) (old age) pensioner; boarder; **Pensionat** [pãsjo'na:t] *n* (*-[e]s*; *-e*) boarding school
**pensionieren** [pãsjo'ni:rən] *v/t* (*no -ge-*, *h*) pension (off); ***sich ~ lassen*** retire; **Pensio'nierung** *f* (-; *-en*) retirement
**Pensionist** [pãsjo'nɪst] *Austrian*, *Swiss* *m* (*-en*; *-en*) (old age) pensioner
**Pensi'onsgast** *m* boarder
**Pensum** ['pɛnzʊm] *n* (*-s*; *Pensen*, *Pensa*) (work) quota, stint
**per** [pɛr] *prp* (*acc*) per; by
**perfekt** [pɛr'fɛkt] *adj* perfect; ***~ machen*** settle
'**Perfekt** *n* (*-s*; *-e*) LING present perfect
**Pergament** [pɛrga'mɛnt] *n* (*-[e]s*; *-e*) parchment
**Periode** [pe'rjo:də] *f* (-; *-n*) period, MED *a.* menstruation
**periodisch** [pe'rjo:dɪʃ] *adj* periodic(al)
**Peripherie** [perife'ri:] *f* (-; *-n*) periphery, outskirts; **~geräte** *pl* EDP peripheral equipment
**Perle** ['pɛrlə] *f* (-; *-n*) pearl; bead
'**perlen** *v/i* (*ge-*, *h*) sparkle, bubble
'**Perlenkette** *f* pearl necklace
'**Perlmuschel** *f* ZO pearl oyster
**Perlmutt** ['pɛrlmʊt] *n* (*-s*; *no pl*) mother-of-pearl
**Perron** [pɛ'rõ:] *m* (*-s*; *-s*) *Swiss* platform
**Perser** ['pɛrzɐ] *m* (*-s*; -) Persian; Persian carpet; **Perserin** ['pɛrzərɪn] *f* (-; *-nen*) Persian (woman); **Persien** ['pɛrzjən] Persia; **persisch** ['pɛrzɪʃ] *adj* Persian
**Person** [pɛr'zo:n] *f* (-; *-en*) person, THEA *etc a.* character; ***ein Tisch für drei ~en*** a table for three
**Personal** [pɛrzo'na:l] *n* (*-s*; *no pl*) staff, personnel; ***zu wenig ~ haben*** be understaffed; **~abbau** *m* staff reduction; **~abteilung** *f* personnel department; **~ausweis** *m* identity card; **~chef** *m* staff manager
**Personalien** [pɛrzo'na:ljən] *pl* particulars, personal data
**Perso'nalpro,nomen** *n* LING personal pronoun
**Per'sonen|(kraft)wagen** (ABBR **PKW**) *m* (*Br a.* motor)car, auto(mobile); **~zug** *m* passenger train; local *or* commuter train
**personifizieren** [pɛrzonifi'tsi:rən] *v/t* (*no -ge-*, *h*) personify
**persönlich** [pɛr'zø:nlɪç] *adj* personal
**Per'sönlichkeit** *f* (-; *-en*) personality
**Perücke** [pe'rʏkə] *f* (-; *-n*) wig
**pervers** [pɛr'vɛrs] *adj* perverted; ***~er Mensch*** pervert
**Pessimismus** [pɛsi'mɪsmʊs] *m* (-; *no pl*) pessimism; **Pessimist(in)** [pɛsi'mɪst(ɪn)] (*-en*; *-en*/-; *-nen*) pessimist; **pessi'mistisch** *adj* pessimistic
**Pest** [pɛst] *f* (-; *no pl*) MED plague
**Pestizid** [pɛsti'tsi:t] *n* (*-s*; *-e*) pesticide
**Petersilie** [pe:tɐ'zi:ljə] *f* (-; *-n*) BOT parsley
**Petroleum** [pe'tro:leʊm] *n* (*-s*; *no pl*) kerosene, *Br* paraffin; **~lampe** *f* kerosene (*Br* paraffin) lamp
**petzen** ['pɛtsən] F *v/i* (*ge-*, *h*) tell tales, *Br a.* sneak
**Pfad** [pfa:t] *m* (*-[e]s*; *-e* ['pfa:də]) path, track; **~finder** *m* boy scout; **~finderin** [-fɪndərɪn] *f* (-; *-nen*) girl scout, *Br* girl guide
**Pfahl** [pfa:l] *m* (*-[e]s*; *Pfähle* ['pfɛ:lə]) stake; post; pole
**Pfand** [pfant] *n* (*-[e]s*; *Pfänder* ['pfɛndɐ]) security; pawn, pledge; deposit; forfeit
'**Pfandbrief** *m* ECON mortgage bond
**pfänden** ['pfɛndən] *v/t* (*ge-*, *h*) seize
'**Pfandhaus** *n* → ***Leihhaus***
'**Pfandleiher** [-laiɐ] *m* (*-s*; -) pawnbroker
'**Pfandschein** *m* pawn ticket
'**Pfändung** *f* (-; *-en*) JUR seizure
**Pfanne** ['pfanə] *f* (-; *-n*) pan, skillet

**'Pfannkuchen** *m* pancake
**Pfarrbezirk** ['pfar-] *m* parish
**Pfarrer** ['pfarɐ] *m* (*-s*; -) vicar; pastor; (parish) priest
**'Pfarr|gemeinde** *f* parish; **~haus** *n* parsonage; rectory, vicarage; **~kirche** *f* parish church
**Pfau** [pfau] *m* (*-[e]s*; *-en*) ZO peacock
**Pfeffer** ['pfɛfɐ] *m* (*-s*; -) pepper; **~kuchen** *m* gingerbread; **~minze** [-mɪntsə] *f* (-; *no pl*) BOT peppermint
**'pfeffern** *v/t* (*ge-*, *h*) pepper
**'Pfefferstreuer** *m* (*-s*; -) pepper caster
**pfeffrig** ['pfɛfrɪç] *adj* peppery
**Pfeife** ['pfaifə] *f* (-; *-n*) whistle; pipe (*a.* MUS); **'pfeifen** *v/i and v/t* (*irr*, *ge-*, *h*) whistle (***j-m*** to s.o.); F **~ auf** (*acc*) not give a damn about
**Pfeil** [pfail] *m* (*-[e]s*; *-e*) arrow
**Pfeiler** ['pfailɐ] *m* (*-s*; -) pillar; pier
**Pfennig** ['pfɛnɪç] *m* (*-s*; *-e*) pfennig; *fig* penny
**Pferch** [pfɛrç] *m* (*-[e]s*; *-e*) fold, pen
**'pferchen** *v/t* (*ge-*, *h*) cram (***in*** *acc* into)
**Pferd** [pfeːɐt] *n* (*-[e]s*; *-e*) ZO horse (*a.* SPORT); ***zu ~e*** on horseback
**Pferde|geschirr** ['pfeːɐdə-] *n* harness; **~koppel** *f* paddock; **~rennen** *n* horserace; **~stall** *m* stable; **~stärke** *f* TECH horsepower; **~wagen** *m* (horse-drawn) carriage
**pfiff** [pfɪf] *pret of* ***pfeifen***
**Pfiff** *m* (*-[e]s*; *-e*) whistle
**pfiffig** ['pfɪfɪç] *adj* smart
**Pfingsten** ['pfɪŋstən] *n* (-; -) REL Pentecost, *Br* Whitsun (**zu**, **an** at)
**Pfingst'montag** *m* REL Whit Monday
**'Pfingstrose** *f* BOT peony
**Pfingst'sonntag** *m* REL Pentecost, *Br* Whit Sunday
**Pfirsich** ['pfɪrzɪç] *m* (*-s*; *-e*) BOT peach
**Pflanze** ['pflantsə] *f* (-; *-n*) plant; ***~n fressend*** ZO herbivorous
**'pflanzen** *v/t* (*ge-*, *h*) plant
**'Pflanzenfett** *n* vegetable fat
**'pflanzlich** *adj* vegetable
**'Pflanzung** *f* (-; *-en*) plantation
**Pflaster** ['pflastɐ] *n* (*-s*; -) pavement; MED Band-Aid®, *Br* plaster
**'pflastern** *v/t* (*ge-*, *h*) pave
**'Pflasterstein** *m* paving stone
**Pflaume** ['pflaumə] *f* (-; *-n*) BOT plum
**Pflege** ['pfleːgə] *f* (-; *no pl*) care; MED nursing; *fig* cultivation; TECH maintenance; ***j-n in ~ nehmen*** take s.o. into one's care; **~...** *in cpds ...eltern*, *...kind*, *...sohn etc*: foster ...; *...heim*, *...kosten*, *...personal etc*: nursing ...
**'pflegebedürftig** *adj* needing care
**'Pflegefall** *m* constant-care patient
**'pflegeleicht** *adj* wash-and-wear, easy-care
**'pflegen** *v/t* (*ge-*, *h*) care for, look after, *esp* MED *a.* nurse; TECH maintain; *fig* cultivate; keep up (*custom etc*); ***sie pflegte zu sagen*** she used to *or* would say; **Pfleger** ['pfleːgɐ] *m* (*-s*; -) male nurse; **Pflegerin** ['pfleːgərɪn] *f* (-; *-nen*) nurse; **'Pflegestelle** *f* nursing place
**Pflicht** [pflɪçt] *f* (-; *-en*) duty (***gegen*** to); SPORT compulsory events
**'pflichtbewusst** *adj* conscientious
**'Pflicht|bewusstsein** *n* sense of duty; **~erfüllung** *f* performance of one's duty; **~fach** *n* PED compulsory subject
**'pflicht|gemäß**, **~getreu** *adj* dutiful; **~vergessen** *adv*: ***~ handeln*** neglect one's duty
**'Pflichtversicherung** *f* compulsory insurance
**Pflock** ['pflɔk] *m* (*-[e]s*; *Pflöcke* ['pflœkə]) peg, pin; plug
**pflücken** ['pflʏkən] *v/t* (*ge-*, *h*) pick, gather
**Pflug** [pfluːk] *m* (*-[e]s*; *Pflüge* ['pflyːgə]), **pflügen** ['pflyːgən] *v/t and v/i* (*ge-*, *h*) plow, *Br* plough
**Pforte** ['pfɔrtə] *f* (-; *-n*) gate, door, entrance; **Pförtner** ['pfœrtnɐ] *m* (*-s*; -) doorman, doorkeeper, porter
**Pfosten** ['pfɔstən] *m* (*-s*, -) post
**Pfote** ['pfoːtə] *f* (-; *-n*) ZO paw (*a.* F)
**pfropfen** ['pfrɔpfən] *v/t* (*ge-*, *h*) stopper; cork; plug; AGR graft; F cram, stuff
**'Pfropfen** *m* (*-s*; -) stopper; cork; plug; MED clot
**pfui** [pfui] *int* ugh!; *audience*: boo!
**Pfund** [pfʊnt] *n* (*-[e]s*; *-e* ['pfʊndə]) pound (*453,59 g*); pound (sterling); ***10 ~*** ten pounds
**'pfundweise** *adv* by the pound
**pfuschen** ['pfʊʃən] F *v/i* (*ge-*, *h*), **Pfuscherei** [pfʊʃə'rai] F *f* (-; *-en*) bungle, botch
**Pfütze** ['pfʏtsə] *f* (-; *-n*) puddle, pool
**Phänomen** [fɛno'meːn] *n* (*-s*; *-e*) phenomenon; **phänomenal** [fɛnome'naːl] *adj* phenomenal

P

**Phantasie** *etc* → ***Fantasie*** *etc*
**pharmazeutisch** [farma'tsɔʏtɪʃ] *adj* pharmaceutic(al)
**Phase** ['fa:zə] *f* (-; *-n*) phase (*a.* ELECTR), stage
**Philosoph** [filo'zo:f] *m* (*-en*; *-en*) philosopher; **Philosophie** [filozo'fi:] *f* (-; *-n*) philosophy; **philosophieren** [filozo'fi:rən] *v/i* (*no -ge-*, *h*) philosophize (***über*** *acc* on); **Philo'sophin** *f* (-; *-nen*) (woman) philosopher; **philosophisch** [filo'zo:fɪʃ] *adj* philosophical
**phlegmatisch** [flɛ'gma:tɪʃ] *adj* phlegmatic
**Phonetik** [fo'ne:tɪk] *f* (-; *no pl*) phonetics; **pho'netisch** *adj* phonetic
**Phosphor** ['fɔsfo:ɐ] *m* (*-s*; *-e*) CHEM phosphorus
**Photo...** → ***Foto...***
**Phrase** ['fra:zə] *contp f* (-; *-n*) cliché (phrase)
**Physik** [fy'zi:k] *f* (-; *no pl*) physics
**physikalisch** [fyzi'ka:lɪʃ] *adj* physical
**Physiker** ['fy:zikɐ] *m* (*-s*; -), **'Physikerin** *f* (-; *-nen*) physicist
**physisch** ['fy:zɪʃ] *adj* physical
**Pianist** [pja'nɪst] *m* (*-en*; *-en*), **Pia'nistin** *f* (-; *-nen*) MUS pianist
**Piano** ['pja:no] *n* (*-s*; *-s*) MUS piano
**Picke** ['pɪkə] *f* (-; *-n*) TECH pick(axe)
**Pickel**[1] ['pɪkəl] *m* (*-s*; -) TECH pick(axe)
**'Pickel**[2] *m* (*-s*; -) MED pimple; **pickelig** ['pɪkəlɪç] *adj* MED pimpled, pimply
**picken** ['pɪkən] *v/i and v/t* (*ge-*, *h*) ZO peck, pick
**Picknick** ['pɪknɪk] *n* (*-s*; *-e*, *-s*) picnic
**'picknicken** *v/i* (*ge-*, *h*) (have a) picnic
**piekfein** ['pi:k-] F *adj* posh
**piep(s)en** ['pi:p(s)ən] *v/i* (*ge-*, *h*) chirp, cheep; ELECTR bleep
**Pietät** [pje'tɛ:t] *f* (-; *no pl*) reverence; piety; **pie'tätlos** *adj* irreverent; **pie'tätvoll** *adj* reverent
**Pik** [pi:k] *n* (-[*s*]; -[*s*]) *cards*: spade(s)
**pikant** [pi'kant] *adj* piquant, spicy (*both a. fig*)
**Pilger** ['pɪlgɐ] *m* (*-s*; -) pilgrim; **'Pilgerfahrt** *f* pilgrimage; **'Pilgerin** *f* (-; *-nen*) pilgrim; **'pilgern** *v/i* (*ge-*, *sein*) (go on a) pilgrimage
**Pille** ['pɪlə] *f* (-; *-n*) pill; F ***die ~ nehmen*** be on the pill
**Pilot** [pi'lo:t] *m* (*-en*; *-en*), **Pi'lotin** *f* (-; *-nen*) pilot
**Pilz** [pɪlts] *m* (*-es*; *-e*) BOT mushroom (*a. fig*); toadstool; MED fungus; ***~e suchen*** (***gehen***) go mushrooming
**Pinguin** ['pɪŋgui:n] *m* (*-s*; *-e*) ZO penguin
**pinkeln** ['pɪŋkəln] F *v/i* (*ge-*, *h*) (have a) pee, piddle
**Pinsel** ['pɪnzəl] *m* (*-s*; -) (paint)brush
**'Pinselstrich** *m* brushstroke
**Pinzette** [pɪn'tsɛtə] *f* (-; *-n*) tweezers
**Pionier** [pjo'ni:ɐ] *m* (*-s*; *-e*) pioneer, MIL *a.* engineer
**Pirat** [pi'ra:t] *m* (*-en*; *-en*) pirate
**Pisse** ['pɪsə] V *f* (-; *no pl*), **'pissen** V *v/i* (*ge-*, *h*) piss
**Piste** ['pɪstə] *f* (-; *-n*) course; AVIAT runway
**Pistole** [pɪs'to:lə] *f* (-; *-n*) pistol, gun
**Pkw, PKW** ['pe:ka:ve:] ABBR *of* ***Personenkraftwagen*** (*Br a.* motor)car, automobile
**Plache** ['plaxə] *Austrian f* (-; *-n*) awning, tarpaulin
**placieren** *etc* → ***platzieren*** *etc*
**plädieren** [plɛ'di:rən] *v/i* (*no -ge-*, *h*) JUR plead (***für*** for); **Plädoyer** [plɛdoa'je:] *n* (*-s*; *-s*) JUR final speech, pleading
**Plage** ['pla:gə] *f* (-; *-n*) trouble, misery; plague; nuisance, F pest; **'plagen** *v/t* (*ge-*, *h*) trouble; bother; pester; ***sich ~*** toil, drudge
**Plakat** [pla'ka:t] *n* (-[*e*]*s*; *-e*) poster, placard, bill
**Plakette** [pla'kɛtə] *f* (-; *-n*) plaque, badge
**Plan** [pla:n] *m* (-[*e*]*s*; *Pläne* ['plɛ:nə]) plan; intention
**Plane** ['pla:nə] *f* (-; *-n*) awning, tarpaulin
**'planen** *v/t* (*ge-*, *h*) plan, make plans for
**Planet** [pla'ne:t] *m* (*-en*; *-en*) ASTR planet
**planieren** [pla'ni:rən] *v/t* (*no -ge-*, *h*) TECH level, plane, grade
**Planke** ['plaŋkə] *f* (-; *-n*) plank, (thick) board
**plänkeln** ['plɛŋkəln] *v/i* (*ge-*, *h*) skirmish
**'planlos** *adj* without plan; aimless
**'planmäßig 1.** *adj* scheduled (*arrival etc*); **2.** *adv* according to plan
**Plan(t)schbecken** ['planʃ-] *n* paddling pool
**plan(t)schen** ['planʃən] *v/i* (*ge-*, *h*) splash
**Plantage** [plan'ta:ʒə] *f* (-; *-n*) plantation
**Plappermaul** ['plapɐ-] F *n* chatterbox

**plappern** ['plapɐn] F *v/i* (*ge-*, *h*) chatter, prattle, babble, jabber
**plärren** ['plɛrən] F *v/i and v/t* (*ge-*, *h*) blubber; bawl; *radio*: blare
**Plastik**[1] ['plastɪk] *f* (-; *-en*) sculpture
'**Plastik**[2] *n* (*-s*; *no pl*) plastic; **~...** *in cpds ...besteck etc*: plastic ...
**plastisch** ['plastɪʃ] *adj* plastic; three-dimensional; *fig* graphic
**Platin** ['pla:ti:n] *n* (*-s*; *no pl*) platinum
**plätschern** ['plɛtʃɐn] *v/i* (*ge-*, *h*) ripple (*a. fig*), splash
**platt** [plat] *adj* flat, level, even; *fig* trite; F flabbergasted
**Platte** ['platə] *f* (-; *-n*) sheet, plate; slab; board; panel; MUS record, disk, *Br* disc; EDP disk; GASTR dish; F bald pate; ***kalte ~*** GASTR plate of cold cuts (*Br* meats)
**plätten** ['plɛtən] *v/t* (*ge-*, *h*) iron, press
'**Platten|spieler** *m* record player; **~teller** *m* turntable
'**Plattform** *f* platform
'**Plattfuß** *m* MED flat foot
'**Plattheit** *fig f* (-; *-en*) triviality; platitude
**Plättli** ['plɛtli] *Swiss n* (*-s*; *-s*) tile
**Platz** [plats] *m* (*-es*; *Plätze* ['plɛtsə]) place, spot; site; room, space; square; circus; seat; ***es ist*** (***nicht***) ***genug ~*** there's (there isn't) enough room; ***~ machen für*** make room for; make way for; ***~ nehmen*** take a seat, sit down; ***ist dieser ~ noch frei?*** is this seat taken?; ***j-n vom ~ stellen*** SPORT send s.o. off; ***auf eigenem ~*** SPORT at home; ***auf die Plätze, fertig, los!*** SPORT on your marks, get set, go!
'**Platz|anweiser** *m* (*-s*; -) usher; **~anweiserin** *f* (-; *-nen*) usherette
**Plätzchen** ['plɛtsçən] *n* (*-s*; -) (little) place, spot; GASTR cookie, *Br* biscuit
**platzen** ['platsən] *v/i* (*ge-*, *sein*) burst (*a. fig*); crack, split; explode (*a. fig* ***vor*** *dat* with), blow up; F come to grief *or* nothing, fall through, blow up, *sl* go phut; break up
**platzieren** [pla'tsi:rən] *v/t* (*no -ge-*, *h*) place; ***sich ~*** SPORT be placed
**Plat'zierung** *f* (-; *-en*) place, placing
'**Platzkarte** *f* reservation (ticket)
**Plätzli** ['plɛtsli] *Swiss n* (*-s*; -) cutlet
'**Platz|pa,trone** *f* blank (cartridge); **~regen** *m* cloudburst, downpour; **~reser,vierung** *f* seat reservation; **~verweis** *m*: ***e-n ~ erhalten*** SPORT be sent off; **~wart** *m* (*-s*; *-e*) SPORT groundkeeper, *Br* groundsman; **~wunde** *f* MED cut, laceration
**Plauderei** [plaudə'rai] *f* (-; *-en*) chat
**plaudern** ['plaudɐn] *v/i* (*ge-*, *h*) (have a) chat
**plauschen** ['plauʃən] *Austrian v/i* (have a) chat
**pleite** ['plaitə] F *adj* broke; ***~ gehen*** go broke
'**Pleite** F *f* (-; *-n*) bankruptcy; *fig* flop
**Plombe** ['plɔmbə] *f* (-; *-n*) TECH seal; MED filling; **plombieren** [plɔm'bi:rən] *v/t* (*no -ge-*, *h*) TECH seal; MED fill
**plötzlich** ['plœtslɪç] **1.** *adj* sudden; **2.** *adv* suddenly, all of a sudden
**plump** [plʊmp] *adj* clumsy; **plumps** *int* thud, plop; **plumpsen** ['plʊmpsən] *v/i* (*ge-*, *sein*) thud, plop, flop
**Plunder** ['plʊndɐ] F *m* (*-s*; *no pl*) trash, junk
**Plünderer** ['plʏndərɐ] *m* (*-s*; -) looter, plunderer; **plündern** ['plʏndɐn] *v/i and v/t* (*ge-*, *h*) plunder, loot
**Plural** ['plu:ra:l] *m* (*-s*; *-e*) LING plural
**plus** [plʊs] *adv* plus
**Plusquamperfekt** ['plʊskvampɛrfɛkt] *n* (*-s*; *-e*) LING past perfect
**Pneu** [pnɔʏ] *Swiss m* (*-s*; *-s*) tire, *Br* tyre
**Po** [po:] F *m* (*-s*; *-s*) bottom, behind
**Pöbel** ['pø:bəl] *m* (*-s*; *no pl*) mob, rabble
**pochen** ['pɔxən] *v/i* (*ge-*, *h*) knock, rap (*both*: ***an*** *acc* at)
**Pocke** ['pɔkə] *f* (-; *-n*) MED pock
'**Pocken** *pl* MED smallpox; **~impfung** *f* MED smallpox vaccination
**Podest** [po'dɛst] *n*, *m* (*-[e]s*; *-e*) platform; *fig* pedestal
**Podium** ['po:djʊm] *n* (*-s*; *-ien*) podium, platform; '**Podiumsdiskussi,on** *f* panel discussion
**Poesie** [poe'zi:] *f* (-; *-n*) poetry
**Poet** [po'e:t] *m* (*-en*; *-en*), **Po'etin** *f* (-; *-nen*) poet
**poetisch** [po'e:tɪʃ] *adj* poetic(al)
**Pointe** ['poɛ̃:tə] *f* (-; *-n*) point, punch line
**Pokal** [po'ka:l] *m* (*-s*; *-e*) goblet; SPORT cup; **~endspiel** *n* SPORT cup final; **~sieger** *m* SPORT cup winner; **~spiel** *n* SPORT cup tie
**pökeln** ['pø:kəln] *v/t* (*ge-*, *h*) salt
**Pol** [po:l] *m* (*-s*; *-e*) GEOGR pole
**polar** [po'la:ɐ] *adj* polar

**Pole** ['po:lə] *m* (-*n*; -*n*) Pole
**'Polen** Poland
**Polemik** [po'le:mɪk] *f* (-; -*en*) polemic(s); **po'lemisch** *adj* polemic(al)
**polemisieren** [polemi'zi:rən] *v/i* (*no -ge-*, *h*) polemize
**Police** [po'li:sə] *f* (-; -*n*) policy
**Polier** [po'li:ɐ] *m* (-*s*; -*e*) TECH foreman
**polieren** [po'li:rən] *v/t* (*no -ge-*, *h*) polish
**Polin** ['po:lɪn] *f* (-; -*nen*) Pole, Polish woman
**Politik** [poli'ti:k] *f* (-; *no pl*) politics; policy (*a. fig*); **Politiker(in)** [po'li:tikɐ (-kərɪn)] (-*s*; -/-; -*nen*) politician; **politisch** [po'li:tɪʃ] *adj* political; **politisieren** [politi'zi:rən] *v/i* (*no -ge-*, *h*) talk politics
**Polizei** [poli'tsai] *f* (-; *no pl*) police; **~auto** *n* police car; **~beamt|e** *m*, **-in** *f* police officer
**poli'zeilich** *adj* (of *or* by the) police
**Poli'zei|prä,sidium** *n* police headquarters; **~re,vier** *n* police station; precinct, *Br* district; **~schutz** *m*: ***unter ~*** under police guard; **~streife** *f* police patrol; **~stunde** *f* closing time; **~wache** *f* police station
**Polizist** [poli'tsɪst] *m* (-*en*; -*en*) policeman; **Poli'zistin** *f* (-; -*nen*) policewoman
**polnisch** ['pɔlnɪʃ] *adj* Polish
**Polster** ['pɔlstɐ] *n* (-*s*; -) upholstery; cushion; pad(ding); *fig* bolster; **~garni,tur** *f* three-piece suite; **~möbel** *pl* upholstered furniture
**'polstern** *v/t* (*ge-*, *h*) upholster; pad
**'Polster|sessel** *m* easy chair, armchair; **~stuhl** *m* upholstered chair
**Polsterung** ['pɔlstərʊŋ] *f* (-; -*en*) upholstery; padding
**poltern** ['pɔltɐn] *v/i* (*ge-*, *h*) rumble; *fig* bluster
**Pommes frites** [pɔm'frɪt] *pl* French fries, French fried potatoes, *Br* chips
**Pomp** [pɔmp] *m* (-[*e*]*s*; *no pl*) pomp
**pompös** [pɔm'pø:s] *adj* showy
**Pony**[1] ['pɔni] *n* (-*s*; -*s*) ZO pony
**'Pony**[2] *m* (-*s*; -*s*) fringe, bangs
**Popgruppe** ['pɔp-] *f* MUS pop group
**'Popmu,sik** *f* pop music
**populär** [popu'lɛ:ɐ] *adj* popular
**Popularität** [populari'tɛ:t] *f* (-; *no pl*) popularity
**Pore** ['po:rə] *f* (-; -*n*) pore
**Porno** ['pɔrno] F *m* (-*s*; -*s*), **~film** *m* porn (film), blue movie; **~heft** *n* porn magazine
**porös** [po'rø:s] *adj* porous
**Portemonnaie** [pɔrtmɔ'ne:] *n* (-*s*; -*s*) purse
**Portier** [pɔr'tje:] *m* (-*s*; -*s*) doorman, porter
**Portion** [pɔr'tsjo:n] *f* (-; -*en*) portion, share; helping, serving
**Portmonee** *n* → ***Portemonnaie***
**Porto** ['pɔrto] *n* (-*s*; -*s*, -*ti*) postage
**Porträt** [pɔr'trɛ:] *n* (-*s*; -*s*) portrait
**porträtieren** [pɔrtrɛ'ti:rən] *v/t* (*no -ge-*, *h*) portray
**Portugal** ['pɔrtugal] Portugal
**Portugiese** [pɔrtu'gi:zə] *m* (-*n*; -*n*), **Portu'giesin** *f* (-; -*nen*), **portu'giesisch** *adj* Portuguese
**Porzellan** [pɔrtsɛ'la:n] *n* (-*s*; -*e*) china, porcelain
**Posaune** [po'zaunə] *f* (-; -*n*) MUS trombone; *fig* trumpet
**Pose** ['po:zə] *f* (-; -*n*) pose, attitude
**Position** [pozi'tsjo:n] *f* (-; -*en*) position (*a. fig*)
**positiv** ['po:ziti:f] *adj* positive
**possessiv** [pɔsɛ'si:f] *adj* LING possessive; **Posses'sivpro,nomen** *n* LING possessive pronoun
**Post** [pɔst] *f* (-; *no pl*) mail, *esp Br* post; letters; ***mit der ~*** by post *or* mail; **~amt** *n* post office; **~anweisung** *f* money order; **~beamt|e** *m*, **-in** *f* post office clerk; **~bote** *m* mailman, *Br* postman
**Posten** ['pɔstən] *m* (-*s*; -) post; job, position; MIL sentry; ECON item; lot, parcel
**'Postfach** *n* (PO) box
**postieren** [pɔs'ti:rən] *v/t* (*no -ge-*, *h*) post, station, place; ***sich ~*** station o.s.
**'Postkarte** *f* postcard
**'Postkutsche** *f* stagecoach
**'postlagernd** *adj* (in care of) general delivery, *Br* poste restante
**'Post|leitzahl** *f* zip code, *Br* post(al) code; **~mi,nister** *m* Postmaster General; **~scheck** *m* postal check (*Br* cheque); **~sparbuch** *n* post-office savings book; **~stempel** *m* postmark
**'postwendend** *adv* by return mail, *Br* by return (of post)
**'Post|wertzeichen** *n* (postage) stamp; **~zustellung** *f* postal *or* mail delivery

P

**Potenz** [po'tɛnts] *f* (-; *-en*) a) (*no pl*) MED potency, b) MATH power

**Pracht** [praxt] *f* (-; *no pl*) splendo(u)r, magnificence

**prächtig** ['prɛçtıç] *adj* splendid, magnificent, *fig a.* great, super

**Prädikat** [prɛdi'ka:t] *n* (-[*e*]*s*; *-e*) LING predicate

**prägen** ['prɛ:gən] *v/t* (*ge-*, *h*) stamp, coin (*a. fig*)

**prahlen** ['pra:lən] *v/i* (*ge-*, *h*) brag, boast (*both*: ***mit*** of), talk big, show off; **Prahler** ['pra:lɐ] *m* (*-s*; -) boaster, braggart; **Prahlerei** [pra:lə'rai] *f* (-; *-en*) boasting, bragging; **'prahlerisch** *adj* boastful; showy

**Praktikant** [prakti'kant] *m* (*-en*; *-en*), **Prakti'kantin** *f* (-; *-nen*) trainee; **Praktiken** ['praktikən] *pl* practices; **'Praktikum** *n* (*-s*; *-ka*) practical training; **'praktisch 1.** *adj* practical; useful, handy; ***~er Arzt*** general practitioner; **2.** *adv* practically; virtually; **praktizieren** [prakti'tsi:rən] *v/t* (*no -ge-*, *h*) practice (*Br* practise) medicine *or* law

**Prälat** [prɛ'la:t] *m* (*-en*; *-en*) REL prelate

**Praline** [pra'li:nə] *f* (-; *-n*) chocolate

**prall** [pral] *adj* tight; well-rounded; bulging; blazing (*sun*)

**prallen** ['pralən] *v/i* (*ge-*, *sein*) ***~ gegen*** (*or* ***auf*** *acc*) crash *or* bump into

**Prämie** ['prɛ:mjə] *f* (-; *-n*) premium; prize; bonus; **prämieren** [prɛ'mi:rən], **prämiieren** [prɛmi'i:rən] *v/t* (*no -ge-*, *h*) award a prize to

**Pranke** ['praŋkə] *f* (-; *-n*) ZO paw (*a.* F)

**Präparat** [prɛpa'ra:t] *n* (-[*e*]*s*; *-e*) preparation

**präparieren** [prɛpa'ri:rən] *v/t* (*no -ge-*, *h*) prepare; MED, BOT, ZO dissect

**Präposition** [prɛpozi'tsjo:n] *f* (-; *-en*) LING preposition

**Prärie** [prɛ'ri:] *f* (-; *-n*) prairie

**Präsens** ['prɛ:zɛns] *n* (-; *-sentia* [prɛ'zɛntsja]) LING present (tense)

**präsentieren** [prɛzɛn'ti:rən] *v/t* (*no -ge-*, *h*) present; offer

**Präservativ** [prɛzɛrva'ti:f] *n* (*-s*; *-e*) condom

**Präsident** [prɛzi'dɛnt] *m* (*-en*; *-en*), **Präsi'dentin** *f* (-; *-nen*) president; chairman (chairwoman); **präsidieren** [prɛzi'di:rən] *v/i* preside (***in*** *dat* over)

**Präsidium** [prɛ'zi:djʊm] *n* (*-s*; *-ien*) presidency

**prasseln** ['prasəln] *v/i* (*ge-*, *h*) *rain etc*: patter; *fire*: crackle

**Präteritum** [prɛ'te:ritʊm] *n* (*-s*; *-ta*) LING past (tense)

**Praxis** ['praksıs] *f* (-; *Praxen*) a) (*no pl*) practice (*a.* MED, JUR), b) MED doctor's office, *Br* surgery

**Präzedenzfall** [prɛtse'dɛnts-] *m* precedent

**präzis** [prɛ'tsi:s], **präzise** [prɛ'tsi:zə] *adj* precise; **Präzision** [prɛtsi'zjo:n] *f* (-; *no pl*) precision

**predigen** ['pre:dıgən] *v/i and v/t* (*ge-*, *h*) preach

**Prediger** ['pre:dıgɐ] *m* (*-s*; -), **'Predigerin** *f* (-; *-nen*) preacher

**Predigt** ['pre:dıçt] *f* (-; *-en*) sermon

**Preis** [prais] *m* (*-es*; *-e*) price (*a. fig*); prize; *film etc*: award; reward; ***um jeden ~*** at all costs

**'Preisausschreiben** *n* competition

**Preiselbeere** ['praizəl-] *f* BOT cranberry

**preisen** ['praizən] *v/t* (*irr*, *ge-*, *h*) praise

**'Preiserhöhung** *f* rise *or* increase in price(s)

**'preisgeben** *v/t* (*irr*, ***geben***, *sep*, *-ge-*, *h*) abandon; reveal, give away

**'preisgekrönt** *adj* prize-winning; *film etc*: award-winning

**'Preis|gericht** *n* jury; **~lage** *f* price range; **~liste** *f* price list; **~nachlass** *m* discount; **~rätsel** *n* competition; **~richter(in)** judge; **~schild** *n* price tag; **~stopp** *m* price freeze; **~träger(in)** prizewinner

**'preiswert** *adj* cheap

**prellen** ['prɛlən] *v/t* (*ge-*, *h*) *fig* cheat (***um*** out of); ***sich et. ~*** MED bruise s.th.; **'Prellung** *f* (-; *-en*) MED contusion, bruise

**Premiere** [prə'mje:rə] *f* (-; *-n*) THEA *etc* first night, première

**Premiermi͵nister** [prə'mje:-] *m*, **Pre'miermi͵nisterin** *f* prime minister

**Presse** ['prɛsə] *f* (-; *-n*) a) (*no pl*) press, b) squeezer; **~...** *in cpds ...agentur*, *...konferenz*, *...fotograf etc*: press ...; **~freiheit** *f* freedom of the press; **~meldung** *f* news item

**'pressen** *v/t* (*ge-*, *h*) press; squeeze

P

'**Presse|tri,büne** *f* press box; **~vertreter** *m* reporter
'**Pressluft** *f* compressed air; **~...** *in cpds ...bohrer, ...hammer etc*: pneumatic ...
**Prestige** [prɛs'tiːʒə] *n* (*-s*; *no pl*) prestige; **~verlust** *m* loss of prestige *or* face
**Preuße** ['prɔʏsə] *m* (*-n*; *-n*), '**Preußin** *f* (*-*; *-nen*), '**preußisch** *adj* Prussian
**prickeln** ['prɪkəln] *v/i* (*ge-*, *h*) prickle; tingle
**pries** [priːs] *pret of* ***preisen***
**Priester** ['priːstɐ] *m* (*-s*; *-*) priest; **Priesterin** ['priːstərɪn] *f* (*-*; *-nen*) priestess; '**priesterlich** *adj* priestly
**prima** ['priːma] F *adj* great, super
**primär** [pri'mɛːɐ] *adj* primary
**Primar|arzt** [pri'maːɐ-] *Austrian m* → ***Oberarzt***; **~schule** *Swiss f* → ***Grundschule***
**Primel** ['priːməl] *f* (*-*; *-n*) BOT primrose
**primitiv** [primi'tiːf] *adj* primitive
**Prinz** [prɪnts] *m* (*-en*; *-en*) prince
**Prinzessin** [prɪn'tsɛsɪn] *f* (*-*; *-nen*) princess
'**Prinzgemahl** *m* prince consort
**Prinzip** [prɪn'tsiːp] *n* (*-s*; *-ien*) principle (***aus*** on; ***im*** in); **prinzipiell** [prɪntsi'pjɛl] *adv* as a matter of principle
**Prise** ['priːzə] *f* (*-*; *-n*) ***e-e ~ Salz*** *etc* a pinch of salt *etc*
**Prisma** ['prɪsma] *n* (*-s*; *-men*) prism
**Pritsche** ['prɪtʃə] *f* (*-*; *-n*) plank bed; MOT platform
**privat** [pri'vaːt] *adj* private; personal
**Pri'vat...** *in cpds ...leben, ...schule, ...detektiv etc*: private ...; **~angelegenheit** *f* personal *or* private matter *or* affair; ***das ist m-e ~*** that's my own business
**Privileg** [privi'leːk] *n* (*-[e]s*; *-gien* [privi'leːgjən]) privilege
**pro** [proː] *prp* (*acc*) per; ***2 Mark ~ Stück*** two marks each
**Pro** *n*: ***das ~ und Kontra*** the pros and cons
**Probe** ['proːbə] *f* (*-*; *-n*) trial, test; sample; THEA rehearsal; MATH proof; ***auf ~*** on probation; ***auf die ~ stellen*** put to the test; **~a,larm** *m* test alarm, fire drill; **~aufnahmen** *pl film*: screen test; **~fahrt** *f* test drive; **~flug** *m* test flight
'**proben** *v/i and v/t* (*ge-*, *h*) THEA *etc* rehearse
'**probeweise** *adv* on trial; on probation
'**Probezeit** *f* (time of) probation
**probieren** [pro'biːrən] *v/t* (*no -ge-*, *h*) try; taste
**Problem** [pro'bleːm] *n* (*-s*; *-e*) problem
**problematisch** [proble'maːtɪʃ] *adj* problematic(al)
**Produkt** [pro'dʊkt] *n* (*-[e]s*; *-e*) product (*a.* MATH); result
**Produktion** [prodʊk'tsjoːn] *f* (*-*; *-en*) production; output
**produktiv** [prodʊk'tiːf] *adj* productive
**Produktivität** [prodʊktivi'tɛːt] *f* (*-*; *no pl*) productivity
**Produzent** [produ'tsɛnt] *m* (*-en*; *-en*), **Produ'zentin** *f* (*-*; *-nen*) producer; **produzieren** [produ'tsiːrən] *v/t* (*no -ge-*, *h*) produce
**professionell** [profɛsjo'nɛl] *adj* professional
**Professor** [pro'fɛsoːɐ] *m* (*-s*; *-en* [profɛ'soːrən]), **Profes'sorin** *f* (*-*; *-nen*) professor
**Professur** [profɛ'suːɐ] *f* (*-*; *-en*) professorship, chair (***für*** of)
**Profi** ['proːfi] *m* (*-s*; *-s*) pro; **~...** *in cpds ...boxer, ...fußballer etc*: professional
**Profil** [pro'fiːl] *n* (*-s*; *-e*) profile; MOT tread; **profilieren** [profi'liːrən] *v/refl* (*no -ge-*, *h*) distinguish o.s.
**Profit** [pro'fiːt] *m* (*-[e]s*; *-e*) profit
**profitieren** [profi'tiːrən] *v/i* (*no -ge-*, *h*) profit (***von*** *or* ***bei et.*** from *or* by s.th.)
**Prognose** [pro'gnoːzə] *f* (*-*; *-n*) prediction; METEOR forecast; MED prognosis
**Programm** [pro'gram] *n* (*-s*; *-e*) program(me *Br*), TV *a.* channel; EDP program; **~fehler** *m* EDP program error, bug
**programmieren** [progra'miːrən] *v/t* (*no -ge-*, *h*) program (*a.* EDP)
**Programmierer** [progra'miːrɐ] *m* (*-s*; *-*), **Program'miererin** *f* (*-*; *-nen*) EDP programmer
**Projekt** [pro'jɛkt] *n* (*-[e]s*; *-e*) project
**Projektion** [projɛk'tsjoːn] *f* (*-*; *-en*) projection; **Projektor** [pro'jɛktoːɐ] *m* (*-s*; *-en* [projɛk'toːrən]) projector
**proklamieren** [prokla'miːrən] *v/t* (*no -ge-*, *h*) proclaim
**Prokurist** [proku'rɪst] *m* (*-en*; *-en*), **Proku'ristin** *f* (*-*; *-nen*) authorized signatory
**Proletarier** [prole'taːrjɐ] *m* (*-s*; *-*), **proletarisch** [-'taːrɪʃ] *adj* proletarian

**Prolog** [pro'lo:k] *m* (-[*e*]*s*; -*e*) prologue
**Promillegrenze** [pro'mılə-] *f* (blood) alcohol limit
**prominent** [promi'nɛnt] *adj* prominent
**Prominenz** [promi'nɛnts] *f* (-; *no pl*) notables; high society
**Promotion** [promo'tsjo:n] *f* (-; -*en*) UNIV doctorate; **promovieren** [promo'vi:rən] *v/i* (*no -ge-*, *h*) do one's doctorate
**prompt** [prɔmpt] *adj* prompt; quick
**Pronomen** [pro'no:mən] *n* (-*s*; -*mina*) LING pronoun
**Propeller** [pro'pɛlɐ] *m* (-*s*; -) propeller
**Prophet** [pro'fe:t] *m* (-*en*; -*en*) prophet; **pro'phetisch** *adj* prophetic
**prophezeien** [profe'tsaiən] *v/t* (*no -ge-*, *h*) prophesy, predict; **Prophe'zeiung** *f* (-; -*en*) prophecy, prediction
**Proportion** [propɔr'tsjo:n] *f* (-; -*en*) proportion
**Proporz** [pro'pɔrts] *m* (-*es*; -*e*) POL proportional representation
**Prosa** ['pro:za] *f* (-; *no pl*) prose
**Prospekt** [pro'spɛkt] *m* (-[*e*]*s*; -*e*) prospectus; brochure, pamphlet
**prost** [pro:st] *int* cheers!
**Prostituierte** [prostitu'i:ɐtə] *f* (-*n*; -*n*) prostitute
**Protest** [pro'tɛst] *m* (-[*e*]*s*; -*e*) protest; ***aus*** ~ in (*or* as a) protest
**Protestant** [protɛs'tant] *m* (-*en*; -*en*), **Protes'tantin** *f* (-; -*nen*), **protes'tantisch** *adj* REL Protestant
**protestieren** [protɛs'ti:rən] *v/i* (*no -ge-*, *h*) protest
**Prothese** [pro'te:zə] *f* (-; -*n*) MED artificial limb; denture
**Protokoll** [proto'kɔl] *n* (-*s*; -*e*) record, minutes; protocol; (***das***) ~ ***führen*** take *or* keep the minutes; ***zu*** ~ ***nehmen*** JUR record; **~führer** *m* keeper of the minutes
**protokollieren** [protokɔ'li:rən] *v/t and v/i* (*no -ge-*, *h*) take the minutes (of); JUR record
**protzen** ['prɔtsən] F *v/i* (*ge-*, *h*) show off (***mit et***. s.th.)
**protzig** ['prɔtsıç] *adj* showy, flashy
**Proviant** [pro'vjant] *m* (-*s*; *no pl*) provisions, food
**Provinz** [pro'vınts] *f* (-; -*en*) province; *fig* country; **provinziell** [provın'tsjɛl] *adj* provincial (*a. contp*)
**Provision** [provi'zjo:n] *f* (-; -*en*) ECON commission
**provisorisch** [provi'zo:rıʃ] *adj* provisional, temporary
**provozieren** [provo'tsi:rən] *v/t* (*no -ge-*, *h*) provoke
**Prozent** [pro'tsɛnt] *n* (-[*e*]*s*; -*e*) per cent; F *pl* discount; **~satz** *m* percentage
**prozentual** [protsɛn'tua:l] *adj* proportional; ***~er Anteil*** percentage
**Prozess** [pro'tsɛs] *m* (-*es*; -*e*) process (*a.* TECH, CHEM *etc*); JUR action; lawsuit, case; trial; ***j-m den*** ~ ***machen*** take s.o. to court; ***e-n*** ~ ***gewinnen*** (***verlieren***) win (lose) a case; **prozessieren** [protsɛ'si:rən] *v/i* (*no -ge-*, *h*) JUR go to court; ***gegen j-n*** ~ bring an action against s.o., take s.o. to court
**Prozession** [protsɛ'sjo:n] *f* (-; -*en*) procession
**Prozessor** [pro'tsɛso:ɐ] *m* (-*s*; -*en* [protsɛ'so:rən]) EDP processor
**prüde** ['pry:də] *adj* prudish; ~ ***sein*** be a prude
**prüfen** ['pry:fən] *v/t* (*ge-*, *h*) PED *etc* examine, test (*a.* TECH); check; inspect (*a.* TECH); *fig* consider; **~d** *adj* searching
**Prüfer** ['pry:fɐ] *m* (-*s*; -), **'Prüferin** *f* (-; -*nen*) PED *etc* examiner; *esp* TECH tester
**Prüfling** ['pry:flıŋ] *m* (-*s*; -*e*) candidate
**'Prüfstein** *m* touchstone (***für*** of)
**'Prüfung** *f* (-; -*en*) examination, F exam; test; check(ing), inspection; ***e-e*** ~ ***machen*** (***bestehen, nicht bestehen***) take (pass, fail) an exam(ination)
**'Prüfungsarbeit** *f* examination *or* test paper
**Prügel** ['pry:gəl] F *pl* (***e-e Tracht***) ~ ***bekommen*** get a (good) beating *or* hiding *or* thrashing; **Prüge'lei** F *f* (-; -*en*) fight; **'prügeln** F *v/t* (*ge-*, *h*) beat, flog; ***sich*** ~ (have a) fight; **'Prügelstrafe** *f* corporal punishment
**Prunk** [prʊŋk] *m* (-[*e*]*s*; *no pl*) splendo(u)r, pomp; **'prunkvoll** *adj* splendid, magnificent
**PS** [pe:'ʔɛs] ABBR *of* ***Pferdestärke*** horsepower, HP
**Psalm** [psalm] *m* (-*s*; -*en*) REL psalm
**Pseudonym** [psɔʏdo'ny:m] *n* (-*s*; -*e*) pseudonym
**pst** [pst] *int* sh!, ssh!; psst!
**Psyche** ['psy:çə] *f* (-; -*n*) mind, psyche
**Psychiater** [psy'çja:tɐ] *m* (-*s*; -),

**Psy'chiaterin** *f* (-; *-nen*) psychiatrist; **psychiatrisch** [psy'çja:trɪʃ] *adj* psychiatric

**psychisch** ['psy:çɪʃ] *adj* mental, MED *a.* psychic

**Psychoana'lyse** [psyço-] *f* psychoanalysis

**Psychologe** [psyço'lo:gə] *m* (*-n*; *-n*) psychologist (*a. fig*); **Psychologie** [psyçolo'gi:] *f* (-; *no pl*) psychology; **Psycho'login** *f* (-; *-nen*) psychologist; **psycho'logisch** *adj* psychological

**Psychose** [psy'ço:zə] *f* (-; *-n*) MED psychosis

**psychosomatisch** [psyçozo'ma:tɪʃ] *adj* MED psychosomatic

**Pubertät** [pubɛr'tɛ:t] *f* (-; *no pl*) puberty

**Publikum** ['pu:blikʊm] *n* (*-s*; *no pl*) audience, TV *a.* viewers, *radio*: *a.* listeners; SPORT crowd, spectators; ECON customers; public

**publizieren** [publi'tsi:rən] *v/t* (*no -ge-*, *h*) publish

**Pudding** ['pʊdɪŋ] *m* (*-s*; *-e*, *-s*) pudding, *esp Br* blancmange

**Pudel** ['pu:dəl] *m* (*-s*; -) ZO poodle

**Puder** ['pu:dɐ] *m* (*-s*; -) powder

'**Puderdose** *f* powder compact

'**pudern** *v/t* (*ge-*, *h*) powder; ***sich ~*** powder one's face

'**Puderzucker** *m* confectioner's (*Br* icing) sugar

**Puff**[1] [pʊf] F *m* (*-s*; *-s*) brothel

**Puff**[2] *m* (*-[e]s*; *Püffe* ['pʏfə]) hump; poke

**Puffer** ['pʊfɐ] *m* (*-s*; -) RAIL buffer (*a. fig*)

'**Puffmais** *m* popcorn

**Pulli** ['pʊli] F *m* (*-s*; *-s*) (light) sweater

**Pullover** [pʊ'lo:vɐ] *m* (*-s*; -) sweater, pullover

**Puls** [pʊls] *m* (*-es*; *-e*) MED pulse; pulse rate; **~ader** *f* ANAT artery

**pulsieren** [pʊl'zi:rən] *v/i* (*no -ge-*, *h*) MED pulsate (*a. fig*)

**Pult** [pʊlt] *n* (*-[e]s*; *-e*) desk

**Pulver** ['pʊlvɐ] *n* (*-s*; -) powder; F cash, *sl* dough; **pulv(e)rig** ['pʊlv(ə)rɪç] *adj* powdery; **pulverisieren** [pʊlveri'zi:rən] *v/t* (*no -ge-*, *h*) pulverize

'**Pulverkaffee** *m* instant coffee

'**Pulverschnee** *m* powder snow

**pumm(e)lig** ['pʊm(ə)lɪç] F *adj* chubby, plump, tubby

**Pumpe** ['pʊmpə] *f* (-; *-n*) TECH pump

'**pumpen** *v/i and v/t* TECH pump; F lend; borrow

**Punker** ['paŋkɐ] F *m* (*-s*; -), '**Punkerin** *f* (-; *-nen*) punk

**Punkt** [pʊŋkt] *m* (*-[e]s*; *-e*) point (*a. fig*); dot; full stop, period; *fig* spot, place; ***um ~ zehn (Uhr)*** at ten (o'clock) sharp; ***nach ~en gewinnen*** *etc* SPORT win *etc* on points

**punktieren** [pʊŋk'ti:rən] *v/t* (*no -ge-*, *h*) dot; MED puncture

**pünktlich** ['pʏŋktlɪç] *adj* punctual; ***~ sein*** be on time; '**Pünktlichkeit** *f* (-; *no pl*) punctuality

'**Punkt|sieger** *m* SPORT winner on points; **~spiel** *n* SPORT league game

**Pupille** [pu'pɪlə] *f* (-; *-n*) ANAT pupil

**Puppe** ['pʊpə] *f* (-; *-n*) doll, F *a.* chick; THEA puppet (*a. fig*); MOT dummy; ZO chrysalis, pupa

'**Puppen|spiel** *n* puppet show; **~stube** *f* doll's house; **~wagen** *m* doll carriage, *Br* doll's pram

**pur** [pu:ɐ] *adj* pure (*a. fig*); *whisky etc*: straight, *Br* neat

**Purpur** ['pʊrpʊr] *m* (*-s*; *no pl*) crimson

'**purpurrot** *adj* crimson

**Purzelbaum** ['pʊrtsəl-] *m* somersault; ***e-n ~ schlagen*** turn a somersault

**purzeln** ['pʊrtsəln] *v/i* (*ge-*, *sein*) tumble

**Pute** ['pu:tə] *f* (-; *-n*) ZO turkey (hen)

**Puter** ['pu:tɐ] *m* (*-s*; -) ZO turkey (cock)

**Putsch** [pʊtʃ] *m* (*-[e]s*; *-e*) putsch, coup (d'état); '**putschen** *v/i* (*ge-*, *h*) revolt, make a putsch

**Putz** [pʊts] *m* (*-es*; *no pl*) ARCH plaster(ing); ***unter ~*** ELECTR concealed

**putzen** ['pʊtsən] (*ge-*, *h*) **1.** *v/t* clean; polish; wipe; ***sich die Nase ~*** blow one's nose; ***sich die Zähne ~*** brush one's teeth; **2.** *v/i* do the cleaning; ***~ (gehen)*** work as a cleaner

'**Putzfrau** *f* cleaner, cleaning woman *or* lady

**putzig** ['pʊtsɪç] *adj* funny, cute

'**Putzlappen** *m* cleaning rag

'**Putzmittel** *n* clean(s)er; polish

**Puzzle** ['pazəl] *n* (*-s*; *-s*) jigsaw (puzzle)

**Pyjama** [py'dʒa:ma] *m* (*-s*; *-s*) pajamas, *Br* pyjamas

**Pyramide** [pyra'mi:də] *f* (-; *-n*) pyramid

# Q

**Quacksalber** ['kvakzalbɐ] *m* (*-s*; *-*) quack (doctor)
**Quadrat** [kva'dra:t] *n* (*-[e]s*; *-e*) square; ***ins ~ erheben*** MATH square; **~...** *in cpds ...meile*, *...meter*, *...wurzel*, *...zahl etc*: square ...; **qua'dratisch** *adj* square; MATH quadratic
**quaken** ['kva:kən] *v/i* (*ge-*, *h*) *duck*: quack; *frog*: croak
**quäken** ['kvɛ:kən] *v/i* (*ge-*, *h*) squeak
**Qual** [kva:l] *f* (*-*; *-en*) pain, torment, agony; anguish
**quälen** ['kvɛ:lən] *v/t* (*ge-*, *h*) torment (*a. fig*); torture; *fig* pester, plague
**Qualifikation** [kvalifika'tsjo:n] *f* (*-*; *-en*) qualification; **Qualifikati'ons...** *in cpds ...spiel etc*: qualifying ...
**qualifizieren** [kvalifi'tsi:rən] *v/t and v/refl* (*no -ge-*, *h*) qualify
**Qualität** [kvali'tɛ:t] *f* (*-*; *-en*) quality
**qualitativ** [kvalita'ti:f] *adj and adv* in quality
**Quali'täts...** *in cpds ...arbeit*, *...waren etc*: high-quality ...
**Qualm** [kvalm] *m* (*-[e]s*; *no pl*) (thick) smoke; **qualmen** ['kvalmən] *v/i* (*ge-*, *h*) smoke; F be a heavy smoker
**'qualvoll** *adj* very painful; agonizing
**Quantität** [kvanti'tɛ:t] *f* (*-*; *-en*) quantity; **quantitativ** [kvantita'ti:f] *adj and adv* in quantity
**Quantum** ['kvantʊm] *n* (*-s*; *Quanten*) amount, *fig a.* share
**Quarantäne** [karan'tɛ:nə] *f* (*-*; *-n*) (***unter ~ stellen*** put in) quarantine
**Quark** [kvark] *m* (*-s*; *no pl*) curd, cottage cheese
**Quartal** [kvar'ta:l] *n* (*-s*; *-e*) quarter (of a year)
**Quartett** [kvar'tɛt] *n* (*-[e]s*; *-e*) MUS quartet(te)
**Quartier** [kvar'ti:ɐ] *n* (*-s*; *-e*) accommodation; *Swiss*: quarter
**Quarz** [kva:ɐts] *m* (*-es*; *-e*) MIN quartz
**Quatsch** [kvatʃ] F *m* (*-[e]s*; *no pl*) nonsense, rubbish, *sl* rot, crap, bullshit; ***~ machen*** fool around; joke, F kid
**quatschen** ['kvatʃən] F *v/i* (*ge-*, *h*) talk rubbish; chat
**Quecksilber** ['kvɛkzɪlbɐ] *n* (*-s*; *no pl*) mercury, quicksilver
**Quelle** ['kvɛlə] *f* (*-*; *-n*) spring, source (*a. fig*), well, *fig a.* origin; **'quellen** *v/i* (*irr*, *ge-*, *sein*) pour (***aus*** from)
**'Quellenangabe** *f* reference
**quengeln** ['kvɛŋəln] F *v/i* (*ge-*, *h*) whine
**quer** [kve:ɐ] *adv* across; crosswise; ***kreuz und ~*** all over the place; ***kreuz und ~ durch Deutschland fahren*** travel all over Germany; **Quere** ['kve:rə] *f*: F ***j-m in die ~ kommen*** get in s.o.'s way
**Querfeld'einlauf** *m* SPORT cross-country race
**'Querlatte** *f* SPORT crossbar
**'Querschläger** *m* MIL ricochet
**'Querschnitt** *m* cross-section (*a. fig*)
**'querschnitt(s)gelähmt** *adj* MED paraplegic
**'Querstraße** *f* intersecting road; ***zweite ~ rechts*** second turning on the right
**Querulant** [kveru'lant] *m* (*-en*; *-en*), **Queru'lantin** *f* (*-*; *-nen*) querulous person
**quetschen** ['kvɛtʃən] *v/t and v/refl* (*ge-*, *h*) squeeze; MED bruise (o.s.)
**'Quetschung** *f* (*-*; *-en*) MED bruise
**quiek(s)en** ['kvi:k(s)ən] *v/i* (*ge-*, *h*) squeak, squeal
**quietschen** ['kvi:tʃən] *v/i* (*ge-*, *h*) squeal; screech; squeak, creak
**quitt** [kvɪt] *adj*: ***mit j-m ~ sein*** be quits *or* even with s.o. (*a. fig*)
**quittieren** [kvɪ'ti:rən] *v/t* (*no -ge-*, *h*) ECON give a receipt for
**'Quittung** *f* (*-*; *-en*) receipt; *fig* answer
**quoll** [kvɔl] *pret of* ***quellen***
**Quote** ['kvo:tə] *f* (*-*; *-n*) quota; share; rate
**'Quotenregelung** *f* quota system
**Quotient** [kvo'tsjɛnt] *m* (*-en*; *-en*) MATH quotient

# R

**Rabatt** [ra'bat] *m* (-[*e*]*s*; -*e*) ECON discount, rebate
**Rabe** ['ra:bə] *m* (-*n*; -*n*) ZO raven
**rabiat** [ra'bja:t] *adj* rough, tough
**Rache** ['raxə] *f* (-; *no pl*) revenge; ***aus ~ für*** in revenge for
**Rachen** ['raxən] *m* (-*s*; -) ANAT throat
**rächen** ['rɛçən] *v/t* (*ge*-, *h*) avenge *s.th.*; revenge *s.o.*; ***sich an j-m für et. ~*** revenge o.s. *or* take revenge on s.o. for s.th.; **Rächer** ['rɛçɐ] *m* (-*s*; -) avenger
**rachsüchtig** ['rax-] *adj* revengeful, vindictive
**Rad** [ra:t] *n* (-[*e*]*s*; *Räder* ['rɛ:dɐ]) wheel; bicycle, F bike; ***~ fahren*** cycle, ride a bicycle, F bike; ***ein ~ schlagen*** *peacock*: spread its tail; SPORT turn a (cart)wheel
**Radar** [ra'da:ɐ] *m*, *n* (-*s*; -*e*) radar; **~falle** *f* MOT speed trap; **~kon,trolle** *f* MOT radar speed check; **~schirm** *m* radar screen; **~stati,on** *f* radar station
**radeln** ['ra:dəln] F *v/i* (*ge*-, *sein*) bike
**Rädelsführer** ['rɛ:dəls-] *m* ringleader
**Räderwerk** ['rɛ:dɐ-] *n* TECH gearing
**'Radfahrer** *m* (-*s*; -), **'Radfahrerin** *f* (-; -*nen*) cyclist
**radieren** [ra'di:rən] *v/t* (*no* -*ge*-, *h*) erase, rub out; *art*: etch
**Radiergummi** [ra'di:ɐ-] *m* eraser, *Br a.* rubber
**Ra'dierung** *f* (-; -*en*) *art*: etching
**Radieschen** [ra'di:sçən] *n* (-*s*; -) BOT (red) radish
**radikal** [radi'ka:l] *adj*, **Radi'kale** *m*, *f* (-*n*; -*n*) radical; **Radikalismus** [radika'lɪsmʊs] *m* (-; *no pl*) radicalism
**Radio** ['ra:djo] *n* (-*s*; -*s*) radio; ***im ~*** on the radio; ***~ hören*** listen to the radio
**radioak'tiv** [radjo-] *adj* PHYS radioactive; ***~er Niederschlag*** fall-out
**Radioaktivi'tät** *f* (-; *no pl*) radioactivity
**'Radiowecker** *m* clock radio
**Radius** ['ra:djʊs] *m* (-*s*; *Radien*) radius
**'Rad|kappe** *f* hubcap; **~rennbahn** *f* cycling track; **~rennen** *n* cycle race; **~sport** *m* cycling; **~sportler** *m* cyclist; **~weg** *m* cycle track *or* path, bikeway
**raffen** ['rafən] *v/t* (*ge*-, *h*) gather up; ***an sich ~*** grab
**Raffinerie** [rafinə'ri:] *f* (-; -*n*) CHEM refinery
**Raffinesse** [rafi'nɛsə] *f* (-; -*n*) a) (*no pl*) shrewdness, b) refinement
**raffiniert** [rafi'ni:ɐt] *adj* refined (*a. fig*); *fig* shrewd, clever
**ragen** ['ra:gən] *v/i* (*ge*-, *h*) tower (up), rise (high)
**Rahe** ['ra:ə] *f* (-; -*n*) MAR yard
**Rahm** [ra:m] *m* (-[*e*]*s*; *no pl*) cream
**rahmen** ['ra:mən] *v/t* (*ge*-, *h*) frame; PHOT mount; **'Rahmen** *m* (-*s*; -) frame; *fig* framework; setting; scope; ***aus dem ~ fallen*** be out of the ordinary
**Rakete** [ra'ke:tə] *f* (-; -*n*) rocket, MIL *a.* missile; ***ferngelenkte ~*** guided missile; ***e-e ~ abfeuern*** (***starten***) launch a rocket *or* missile
**Ra'keten|antrieb** *m* rocket propulsion; ***mit ~*** rocket-propelled; **~basis** *f* MIL rocket *or* missile base *or* site
**rammen** ['ramən] *v/t* (*ge*-, *h*) ram; MOT *etc* hit, collide with
**Rampe** ['rampə] *f* (-; -*n*) (loading) ramp
**'Rampenlicht** *n* (-[*e*]*s*; *no pl*) THEA footlights; *fig* limelight
**Ramsch** [ramʃ] F *m* (-*es*; *no pl*) junk
**Rand** [rant] *m* (-[*e*]*s*; *Ränder* ['rɛndɐ]) edge, border; brink (*a. fig*); rim; brim; margin; ***am ~(e) des Ruins*** *etc* on the brink of ruin *etc*
**randalieren** [randa'li:rən] *v/i* (*no* -*ge*-, *h*) kick up a racket; **Randalierer** [randa'li:rɐ] *m* (-*s*; -) rowdy, hooligan
**'Rand|bemerkung** *f* marginal note; *fig* comment; **~gruppe** *f* fringe group
**'randlos** *adj* rimless
**'Randstreifen** *m* MOT shoulder
**rang** [raŋ] *pret of* ***ringen***
**Rang** *m* (-[*e*]*s*; *Ränge* ['rɛŋə]) position, rank (*a.* MIL); THEA balcony, *Br* circle; *pl* SPORT terraces
**rangieren** [raŋ'ʒi:rən] (*no* -*ge*-, *h*) **1.** *v/t* RAIL switch, *Br* shunt; **2.** *fig v/i* rank (***vor j-m*** before s.o.)
**'Rangordnung** *f* hierarchy
**Ranke** ['raŋkə] *f* (-; -*n*) BOT tendril
**'ranken** *v/refl* (*ge*-, *h*) BOT creep, climb
**rann** [ran] *pret of* ***rinnen***
**rannte** ['rantə] *pret of* ***rennen***

**Ranzen** ['rantsən] *m* (*-s*; -) knapsack; satchel

**ranzig** ['rantsıç] *adj* rancid, rank

**Rappe** ['rapə] *m* (*-n*; *-n*) ZO black horse

**rar** [ra:ɐ] *adj* rare, scarce

**Rarität** [rari'tɛ:t] *f* (-; *-en*) a) curiosity, b) (*no pl*) rarity

**rasch** [raʃ] *adj* quick, swift; prompt

**rascheln** ['raʃəln] *v/i* (*ge-*, *h*) rustle

**rasen** ['ra:zən] *v/i* a) (*ge-*, *sein*) F MOT race, tear, speed, b) (*ge-*, *h*) rage; ~ ***vor Begeisterung*** roar with enthusiasm

**'Rasen** *m* (*-s*; -) lawn, grass

**'rasend** *adj* breakneck; raging; agonizing; splitting; thunderous

**'Rasen|mäher** *m* lawn mower; **~platz** *m* lawn; *tennis*: grass court

**Raserei** [ra:zə'rai] *f* (-; *-en*) a) (*no pl*) frenzied rage; frenzy, madness, b) F MOT reckless driving

**Rasier|appa,rat** [ra'zi:ɐ-] *m* (safety) razor; *esp* ***elektrischer*** ~ shaver; **~creme** *f* shaving cream

**rasieren** [ra'zi:rən] *v/t and v/refl* (*no -ge-*, *h*) shave

**Ra'sier|klinge** *f* razor blade; **~messer** *n* (straight) razor; **~pinsel** *m* shaving brush; **~seife** *f* shaving soap; **~wasser** *n* aftershave (lotion)

**Rasse** ['rasə] *f* (-; *-n*) race; ZO breed

**'Rassehund** *m* ZO pedigree dog

**Rassel** ['rasəl] *f* (-; *-n*), **'rasseln** *v/i* (*ge-*, *h*) rattle

**'Rassen...** *in cpds ...diskriminierung*, *...konflikt*, *...probleme etc*: *mst* racial ...; **~trennung** *f* POL (racial) segregation; HIST apartheid; **~unruhen** *pl* race riots

**rassig** ['rasıç] *adj* classy

**rassisch** ['rasıʃ] *adj* racial

**Rassismus** [ra'sısmʊs] *m* (-; *no pl*) POL racism; **Ras'sist(in)** (*-en*; *-en*/-; *-nen*), **ras'sistisch** *adj* POL racist

**Rast** [rast] *f* (-; *-en*) rest, stop; break; **rasten** ['rastən] *v/i* (*ge-*, *h*) rest, stop, take a break; **'rastlos** *adj* restless

**'Rastplatz** *m* resting place; MOT rest area, *Br* lay-by

**'Raststätte** *f* MOT service area

**Rasur** [ra'zu:ɐ] *f* (-; *-en*) shave

**Rat** [ra:t] *m* (-[*e*]*s*; *Räte* ['rɛ:tə]) a) (*no pl*) (piece of) advice, b) council; ***j-n um ~ fragen*** ask s.o.'s advice; ***j-s ~ befolgen*** take s.o.'s advice

**Rate** ['ra:tə] *f* (-; *-n*) rate; ECON instal(l)ment; ***auf ~n*** by instal(l)ments

**raten** ['ra:tən] *v/t and v/i* (*irr*, *ge-*, *h*) advise; guess; solve; ***j-m zu et.*** ~ advise s.o. to do s.th.; ***rate mal!*** (have a) guess!

**'Ratenzahlung** *f* → ***Abzahlung***

**'Rateteam** *n* TV *etc* panel

**'Ratgeber** [-ge:bɐ] *m* (*-s*; -), **'Ratgeberin** *f* (-; *-nen*) adviser, counsel(l)or; *m* guide (***über*** *acc* to)

**'Rathaus** *n* city (*Br* town) hall

**ratifizieren** [ratifi'tsi:rən] *v/t* (*no -ge-*, *h*) ratify

**Ration** [ra'tsjo:n] *f* (-; *-en*) ration

**rational** [ratsjo'na:l] *adj* rational

**rationell** [ratsjo'nɛl] *adj* efficient; economical

**rationieren** [ratsjo'ni:rən] *v/t* (*no -ge-*, *h*) ration

**'ratlos** *adj* at a loss

**'ratsam** *adj* advisable, wise

**'Ratschlag** *m* piece of advice; ***ein paar gute Ratschläge*** some good advice

**Rätsel** ['rɛ:tsəl] *n* (*-s*; -) puzzle; riddle (*both a. fig*); mystery

**'rätselhaft** *adj* puzzling; mysterious

**Ratte** ['ratə] *f* (-; *-n*) ZO rat (*a. contp*)

**rattern** ['ratɐn] *v/i* (*ge-*, *h*, *sein*) rattle, clatter

**rau** [rau] *adj* rough, rugged (*both a. fig*); harsh; chapped; sore

**Raub** [raup] *m* (-[*e*]*s*; *no pl*) robbery; loot, booty; prey; **~bau** *m* (-[*e*]*s*; *no pl*) overexploitation (***an*** *dat* of); ~ ***mit s-r Gesundheit treiben*** ruin one's health

**rauben** ['raubən] *v/t* (*ge-*, *h*) rob, steal; kidnap; ***j-m et.*** ~ rob s.o. of s.th. (*a. fig*)

**Räuber** ['rɔʏbɐ] *m* (*-s*; -) robber

**'Raub|fisch** *m* predatory fish; **~mord** *m* murder with robbery; **~mörder** *m* murderer and robber; **~tier** *n* beast of prey; **~überfall** *m* holdup, (armed) robbery; mugging; **~vogel** *m* bird of prey; **~zug** *m* raid

**Rauch** [raux] *m* (-[*e*]*s*; *no pl*) smoke; CHEM *etc* fume; **rauchen** ['rauxən] *v/i and v/t* (*ge-*, *h*) smoke; CHEM *etc* fume; ***Rauchen verboten!*** no smoking; ***Pfeife*** ~ smoke a pipe; **Raucher(in)** ['rauxɐ (-xərın)] (*-s*; -/-; *-nen*) smoker (*m a.* RAIL)

**Räucher...** ['rɔʏçɐ-] *in cpds ...aal*, *...speck etc*: smoked ...

**'räuchern** *v/t* (*ge-*, *h*) smoke
**'Räucherstäbchen** *n* joss stick
**'Rauchfahne** *f* trail of smoke
**rauchig** ['rauxıç] *adj* smoky
**'Rauch|waren** *pl* tobacco products; furs; **~zeichen** *n* smoke signal
**Räude** ['rɔʏdə] *f* (-; *-n*) VET mange
**'räudig** *adj* VET mangy
**raufen** ['raufən] (*ge-*, *h*) **1.** *v/t*: ***sich die Haare ~*** tear one's hair; **2.** *v/i* fight, scuffle; **Rauferei** [raufə'rai] *f* (-; *-en*) fight, scuffle
**Raum** [raum] *m* (*-[e]s*; *Räume* ['rɔʏmə]) room; space; area; (outer) space; **~anzug** *m* spacesuit; **~deckung** *f* SPORT zone marking
**räumen** ['rɔʏmən] *v/t* (*ge-*, *h*) leave, move out of; check out of; clear (***von*** of); evacuate (*a.* MIL); ***s-e Sachen in ...*** (*acc*) *~* put one's things (away) in ...
**'Raum|fahrer** F *m* spaceman; **~fahrt** *f* (-; *no pl*) space travel *or* flight; astronautics; **~fahrt...** *in cpds ...technik, ...zentrum etc*: space ...; **~fähre** *f* space shuttle; **~flug** *m* space flight; **~inhalt** *m* volume; **~kapsel** *f* space capsule; **~la,bor** *n* space lab
**räumlich** ['rɔʏmlıç] *adj* three-dimensional
**'Raum|schiff** *n* spacecraft; spaceship; **~sonde** *f* space probe; **~stati,on** *f* space station
**'Räumung** *f* (-; *-en*) clearance; evacuation (*a.* MIL); JUR eviction
**'Räumungsverkauf** *m* ECON clearance sale
**raunen** ['raunən] *v/i* (*ge-*, *h*) whisper, murmur
**Raupe** ['raupə] *f* (-; *-n*) ZO caterpillar, TECH *a.* track; **'Raupenschlepper** *m* MOT caterpillar tractor
**'Raureif** *m* hoarfrost
**raus** [raus] F *int* get out (of here)!
**Rausch** [rauʃ] *m* (*-es*; *Räusche* ['rɔʏʃə]) drunkenness, intoxication; F high; *fig* ecstasy; ***e-n ~ haben*** be drunk; ***s-n ~ ausschlafen*** sleep it off
**rauschen** ['rauʃən] *v/i* a) (*ge-*, *h*) *water etc*: rush; *brook*: murmur; *storm*: roar, b) (*ge-*, *sein*) sweep; **~d** *adj* thunderous (*applause*); ***~es Fest*** lavish celebration
**'Rauschgift** *n* drug(s), narcotic(s); **~dezer,nat** *n* narcotics *or* drugs squad; **~handel** *m* drug traffic(king); **~händler** *m* drug trafficker, F pusher
**räuspern** ['rɔʏspɐn] *v/refl* (*ge-*, *h*) clear one's throat
**Razzia** ['ratsja] *f* (-; *-ien*) raid, roundup
**Reagenzglas** [rea'gɛnts-] *n* CHEM test tube
**reagieren** [rea'gi:rən] *v/i* (*no -ge-*, *h*) CHEM, MED react (***auf*** *acc* to), *fig a.* respond (to); **Reaktion** [reak'tsjo:n] *f* (-; *-en*) CHEM, MED, PHYS, POL reaction (***auf*** *acc* to), *fig a.* response (to)
**Reaktor** [re'akto:ɐ] *m* (*-s*; *-en* [reak'to:rən]) PHYS (nuclear *or* atomic) reactor
**real** [re'a:l] *adj* real; concrete
**realisieren** [reali'zi:rən] *v/t* (*no -ge-*, *h*) realize
**Realismus** [rea'lısmʊs] *m* (-; *no pl*) realism; **rea'listisch** *adj* realistic
**Realität** [reali'tɛ:t] *f* (-; *no pl*) reality
**Re'alschule** *f appr* (junior) highschool, *Br* secondary (modern) school
**Rebe** ['re:bə] *f* (-; *-n*) BOT vine
**Rebell** [re'bɛl] *m* (*-en*; *-en*) rebel
**rebellieren** [rebɛ'li:rən] *v/i* (*no -ge-*, *h*) rebel, revolt, rise (*all*: ***gegen*** against)
**Re'bellin** *f* (-; *-nen*) rebel
**re'bellisch** *adj* rebellious
**Rebhuhn** ['re:p-] *n* ZO partridge
**'Rebstock** *m* BOT vine
**Rechen** ['rɛçən] *m* (*-s*; -), **'rechen** *v/t* (*ge-*, *h*) rake
**'Rechen|aufgabe** *f* MATH (arithmetical) problem; **~fehler** *m* MATH arithmetical error, miscalculation; **~ma,schine** *f* calculator; computer
**'Rechenschaft** *f*: ***~ ablegen über*** (*acc*) account for; ***zur ~ ziehen*** call to account (***wegen*** for)
**'Rechen|schieber** *m* MATH slide rule; **~werk** *n* EDP arithmetic unit; **~zentrum** *n* computer center (*Br* centre)
**rechnen** ['rɛçnən] *v/i and v/t* (*ge-*, *h*) calculate, reckon; work out, do sums; count; ***~ mit*** *fig* expect; count on; ***mit mir kannst du nicht ~!*** count me out!
**'Rechnen** *n* (*-s*; *no pl*) arithmetic
**Rechner** ['rɛçnɐ] *m* (*-s*; -) calculator; computer
**'rechnerabhängig** *adj* EDP online
**rechnerisch** ['rɛçnərıʃ] *adj* arithmetical
**'rechnerunabhängig** *adj* EDP offline
**'Rechnung** *f* (-; *-en*) MATH calculation; problem, sum; ECON invoice, bill, check; ***die ~, bitte!*** can I have the

check, please?; ***das geht auf m-e ~*** that's on me

**recht** [rɛçt] **1.** *adj* right; correct; POL right-wing; ***auf der ~en Seite*** on the right(-hand side); ***mir ist es ~*** I don't mind; **2.** *adv* right(ly), correctly; rather, quite; ***ich weiß nicht ~*** I don't really know; ***es geschieht ihm ~*** it serves him right; ***erst ~*** all the more; ***erst ~ nicht*** even less; ***du kommst gerade ~*** (***zu***) you're just in time (for)

**Recht** *n* (-[*e*]*s*; -*e*) a) right, claim (*both*: ***auf*** *acc* to), b) (*no pl*) JUR law; justice; ***gleiches ~*** equal rights; ***~ haben*** be right; ***j-m ~ geben*** agree with s.o.; ***im ~ sein*** be in the right; ***er hat es mit*** (***vollem***) ***~ getan*** he was (perfectly) right to do so; ***ein ~ auf et. haben*** be entitled to s.th.

**'Rechteck** *n* (-[*e*]*s*; -*e*) rectangle

**'rechteckig** *adj* rectangular

**'rechtfertigen** *v/t* (*ge-*, *h*) justify

**'Rechtfertigung** *f* (-; -*en*) justification

**'rechtlich** *adj* JUR legal

**'rechtlos** *adj* without rights; outcast

**'rechtmäßig** *adj* JUR lawful; legitimate; legal; **'Rechtmäßigkeit** *f* (-; *no pl*) JUR lawfulness, legitimacy

**rechts** [rɛçts] *adv* on the right(-hand side); ***nach ~*** to the right

**Rechts...** *in cpds* POL right-wing ...; **~anspruch** *m* legal claim (***auf*** *acc* to); **~anwalt** *m*, **~anwältin** [-anvɛltɪn] *f* (-; -*nen*) lawyer

**Rechts'außen** *m* (-; -) *soccer*: outside right

**'rechtschaffen** *adj* honest

**'Recht|schreibfehler** *m* spelling mistake; **~schreibung** *f* (-; *no pl*) spelling, orthography

**'rechtsextre,mistisch** *adj* POL extreme right

**'Rechtsfall** *m* JUR (law) case

**'Rechtshänder** [-hɛndɐ] *m* (-*s*; -), **'Rechtshänderin** *f* (-; -*nen*) right-handed person; ***sie ist Rechtshänderin*** she is right-handed

**'Rechtsprechung** *f* (-; *no pl*) jurisdiction

**'rechtsradi,kal** *adj* POL extreme right-wing

**'Rechtsschutz** *m* legal protection; legal costs insurance

**'rechtswidrig** *adj* JUR illegal, unlawful

**'rechtwink(e)lig** *adj* rectangular

**'rechtzeitig** **1.** *adj* punctual; **2.** *adv* in time (***zu*** for)

**Reck** [rɛk] *n* (-[*e*]*s*; -*e*) horizontal bar

**recken** ['rɛkən] *v/t* (*ge-*, *h*) stretch; ***sich ~*** stretch o.s.

**recyceln** [ri'saikəln] *v/t* (*no -ge-*, *h*) recycle; **Recyclingpa,pier** [ri'saiklɪŋ-] *n* recycled paper

**Redakteur** [redak'tøːɐ] *m* (-*s*; -*e*), **Redak'teurin** *f* (-; -*nen*) editor

**Redaktion** [redak'tsjoːn] *f* (-;-*en*) a) (*no pl*) editing, b) editorial staff, editors, c) editorial office *or* department

**redaktionell** [redaktsjo'nɛl] *adj* editorial

**Rede** ['reːdə] *f* (-; -*n*) speech, address; talk (***von*** of); ***e-e ~ halten*** make a speech; ***direkte*** (***indirekte***) ***~*** LING direct (reported *or* indirect) speech; ***j-n zur ~ stellen*** take s.o. to task; ***nicht der ~ wert*** not worth mentioning

**'redegewandt** *adj* eloquent

**reden** ['reːdən] *v/i and v/t* (*ge-*, *h*) talk, speak (*both*: ***mit*** to; ***über*** *acc* about, of); ***ich möchte mit dir ~*** I'd like to talk to you; ***die Leute ~*** people talk; ***j-n zum Reden bringen*** make s.o. talk

**'Redensart** *f* saying, phrase

**redlich** ['reːtlɪç] *adj* upright, honest; ***sich ~(e) Mühe geben*** do one's best

**Redner** ['reːdnɐ] *m* (-*s*; -), **'Rednerin** *f* (-; -*nen*) speaker

**'Rednerpult** *n* speaker's desk

**redselig** ['reːtzeːlɪç] *adj* talkative

**reduzieren** [redu'tsiːrən] *v/t* (*no -ge-*, *h*) reduce (***auf*** *acc* to)

**Reeder** ['reːdɐ] *m* (-*s*; -) shipowner

**Reederei** [reːdə'rai] *f* (-; -*en*) shipping company

**reell** [re'ɛl] *adj* reasonable, fair (*price*); real (*chance*); solid (*firm*)

**Referat** [refe'raːt] *n* (-[*e*]*s*; -*e*) paper; report; lecture; ***ein ~ halten*** read a paper

**Referendar** [referɛn'daːɐ] *m* (-*s*; -*e*), **Referen'darin** *f* (-; -*nen*) *appr* trainee teacher

**Referent** [refe'rɛnt] *m* (-*en*; -*en*), **Refe'rentin** *f* (-; -*nen*) speaker; **Referenz** [refe'rɛnts] *f* (-; -*en*) reference; **referieren** [refe'riːrən] *v/i* (*no -ge-*, *h*) (give a) report *or* lecture (***über*** *acc* on)

**reflektieren** [reflɛk'tiːrən] *v/t and v/i* (*no -ge-*, *h*) reflect (*fig* ***über*** *acc* [up]on)

R

**Reflex** [re'flɛks] *m* (*-es*; *-e*) reflex
**reflexiv** [reflɛ'ksi:f] *adj* LING reflexive
**Reform** [re'fɔrm] *f* (*-*; *-en*) reform
**Reformator** [refɔr'ma:to:ɐ] *m* (*-s*; *-en* [-ma'to:rən]), **Reformer(in)** [re'fɔrmɐ (-mərɪn)] (*-s*; *-/-*; *-nen*) reformer
**Re'formhaus** *n* health food store (*Br* shop)
**reformieren** [refɔr'mi:rən] *v/t* (*no -ge-*, *h*) reform
**Refrain** [rə'frɛ̃:] *m* (*-s*; *-s*) refrain, chorus
**Regal** [re'ga:l] *n* (*-s*; *-e*) shelf (unit), shelves
**rege** ['re:gə] *adj* lively; busy; active
**Regel** ['re:gəl] *f* (*-*; *-n*) rule; MED period, menstruation; ***in der ~*** as a rule
**'regelmäßig** *adj* regular
**regeln** ['re:gəln] *v/t* (*ge-*, *h*) regulate, TECH *a.* adjust; ECON settle
**'regelrecht** *adj* regular (*a.* F)
**'Regeltechnik** *f* control engineering
**'Regelung** *f* (*-*; *-en*) regulation; adjustment; ECON settlement; TECH control
**'regelwidrig** *adj* against the rule(s); SPORT unfair; ***~es Spiel*** foul play
**regen** ['re:gən] *v/t and v/refl* (*ge-*, *h*) move, stir
**'Regen** *m* (*-s*; *-*) rain; ***starker ~*** heavy rain(fall); **~bogen** *m* rainbow; **~bogenhaut** *f* ANAT iris; **~guss** *m* (heavy) shower, downpour; **~mantel** *m* raincoat; **~schauer** *m* shower; **~schirm** *m* umbrella; **~tag** *m* rainy day; **~tropfen** *m* raindrop; **~wald** *m* rain forest; **~wasser** *n* rainwater; **~wetter** *n* rainy weather; **~wurm** *m* ZO earthworm; **~zeit** *f* rainy season, the rains
**Regie** [re'ʒi:] *f* (*-*; *no pl*) THEA, *film etc*: direction; ***unter der ~ von*** directed by
**Re'gieanweisung** *f* stage direction
**regieren** [re'gi:rən] (*no -ge-*, *h*) **1.** *v/i* reign; **2.** *v/t* govern (*a.* LING), rule
**Re'gierung** *f* (*-*; *-en*) government, administration; reign
**Re'gierungs|bezirk** *m* administrative district; **~chef** *m* head of government; **~wechsel** *m* change of government
**Regime** [re'ʒi:m] *n* (*-s*; *-*) POL regime
**Re'gimekritiker** *m* POL dissident
**Regiment** [regi'mɛnt] *n* (*-[e]s*; *-er*) a) (*no pl*) rule (*a. fig*), b) MIL regiment
**Regisseur** [reʒɪ'sø:ɐ] *m* (*-s*; *-e*), **Regis'seurin** *f* (*-*; *-nen*) THEA, *film etc*: director, THEA *Br a.* producer

R

**Register** [re'gɪstɐ] *n* (*-s*; *-*) register (*a.* MUS), record; index; **registrieren** [regɪs'tri:rən] *v/t* (*no -ge-*, *h*) register, record; *fig* note; **Registrierkasse** [regɪs'tri:ɐ-] *f* cash register
**Reglement** [reglə'mã:] *n* (*-s*; *-s*) regulation, order, rule
**Regler** ['re:glɐ] *m* (*-s*; *-*) TECH control
**regnen** ['re:gnən] *v/i* (*ge-*, *h*) rain (*a. fig*); ***es regnet in Strömen*** it's pouring with rain; **'regnerisch** *adj* rainy
**regulär** [regu'lɛ:ɐ] *adj* regular; normal
**regulierbar** [regu'li:ɐba:ɐ] *adj* adjustable; controllable
**regulieren** [regu'li:rən] *v/t* (*no -ge-*, *h*) regulate, adjust; control
**'Regung** *f* (*-*; *-en*) movement, motion; emotion; impulse
**'regungslos** *adj* motionless
**Reh** [re:] *n* (*-[e]s*; *-e*) ZO deer, roe; doe; GASTR venison
**rehabilitieren** [rehabili'ti:rən] *v/t* (*no -ge-*, *h*) rehabilitate
**'Reh|bock** *m* ZO (roe)buck; **~keule** *f* GASTR leg of venison; **~kitz** *n* ZO fawn
**Reibe** ['raibə] *f* (*-*; *-n*), **Reibeisen** ['raip-] *n* (*-s*; *-*) grater, rasp
**reiben** ['raibən] *v/i and v/t* (*irr*, *ge-*, *h*) rub; grate, grind; ***sich die Augen*** (***Hände***) *~* rub one's eyes (hands)
**'Reibung** *f* (*-*; *-en*) TECH *etc* friction
**'reibungslos** *adj* TECH *etc* frictionless; *fig* smooth
**reich** [raiç] *adj* rich (***an*** *dat* in), wealthy; abundant
**Reich** *n* (*-[e]s*; *-e*) empire, kingdom (*a.* REL, BOT, ZO); *fig* world
**reichen** ['raiçən] (*ge-*, *h*) **1.** *v/t* reach; hand, pass; give, hold out (*one's hand*); **2.** *v/i* last, do; ***~ bis*** reach *or* come up to; ***das reicht*** that will do; F ***mir reicht's!*** I've had enough
**'reichhaltig** *adj* rich
**'reichlich** **1.** *adj* rich, plentiful; plenty of; **2.** *adv* rather; generously
**'Reichtum** *m* (*-s*; *no pl*) wealth (***an*** *dat* of) (*a. fig*)
**'Reichweite** *f* reach; AVIAT, MIL *etc* range; ***in*** (***außer***) (***j-s***) *~* within (out of) (s.o.'s) reach
**reif** [raif] *adj* ripe, *esp fig* mature
**Reif** *m* (*-[e]s*; *no pl*) white frost, hoarfrost
**Reife** ['raifə] *f* (*-*; *no pl*) ripeness, *esp fig*

maturity; **'reifen** *v/i* (*ge-*, *sein*) ripen, mature (*both a. fig*)

**Reifen** ['raifən] *m* (*-s*; -) hoop; MOT *etc* tire, *Br* tyre; **~panne** *f* MOT flat tire (*Br* tyre), puncture, F flat

**'Reifeprüfung** *f* → ***Abitur***

**'reiflich** *adj* careful

**Reihe** ['raiə] *f* (-; *-n*) line, row; number; series; ***der ~ nach*** in turn; ***ich bin an der ~*** it's my turn

**'Reihenfolge** *f* order

**'Reihenhaus** *n* row (*Br* terraced) house

**'reihenweise** *adv* in rows; F *fig* by the dozen

**Reiher** ['raiɐ] *m* (*-s*; -) ZO heron

**Reim** [raim] *m* (*-[e]s*; *-e*) rhyme

**reimen** ['raimən] *v/t and v/refl* (*ge-*, *h*) rhyme (***auf*** *acc* with)

**rein** [rain] *adj* pure (*a. fig*); clean; *fig* clear (*conscience*); plain (*truth*); mere, sheer, nothing but

**'Reinfall** F *m* flop; let-down

**'Reingewinn** *m* ECON net profit

**'reinhauen** F *v/i* (*sep*, *-ge-*, *h*) tuck in

**'Reinheit** *f* (-; *no pl*) purity (*a. fig*); cleanness

**reinigen** ['rainɪgən] *v/t* (*ge-*, *h*) clean; cleanse (*a.* MED); dry-clean; *fig* purify

**'Reinigung** *f* (-; *-en*) clean(s)ing; *fig* purification; (dry) cleaners; ***chemische ~*** dry cleaning; dry cleaner's

**'Reinigungsmittel** *n* cleaning agent, cleaner, detergent

**'reinlich** *adj* clean; cleanly

**'reinrassig** *adj* ZO purebred, pedigree; thoroughbred

**'Reinschrift** *f* fair copy

**Reis** [rais] *m* (*-es*; *-e*) BOT rice

**Reise** ['raizə] *f* (-; *-n*) trip; journey; tour; MAR voyage; ***auf ~n sein*** be travel(l)ing; ***e-e ~ machen*** take a trip; ***gute ~!*** have a nice trip!; **~andenken** *n* souvenir; **~bü͵ro** *n* travel agency *or* bureau; **~führer** *m* guide(book); **~gesellschaft** *f* tourist party; tour operator; **~kosten** *pl* travel(l)ing expenses; **~krankheit** *f* travel sickness; **~leiter(in)** tour guide *or* manager, *Br* courier

**'reisen** *v/i* (*ge-*, *sein*) travel; ***durch Frankreich ~*** tour France; ***ins Ausland ~*** go abroad; **'Reisende** *m, f* (*-n*; *-n*) travel(l)er; tourist; passenger

**'Reise|pass** *m* passport; **~scheck** *m* travel(l)er's check (*Br* cheque); **~tasche** *f* travel(l)ing bag, holdall

**Reisig** ['raizɪç] *n* (*-s*; *no pl*) brushwood

**Reißbrett** ['rais-] *n* drawing board

**reißen** ['raisən] (*irr*, *ge-*) **1.** *v/t* (*h*) tear (***in Stücke*** to pieces), rip; pull, drag; ZO kill; F crack (*jokes*); SPORT knock down; ***an sich ~*** seize, snatch, grab; **2.** *v/i* (*sein*) break, burst; ***sich um et. ~*** scramble for (*or* to get) s.th.; **~d** *adj* torrential

**Reißer** ['raisɐ] F *m* (*-s*; -) thriller; hit

**reißerisch** ['raisərɪʃ] *adj* sensational, loud

**'Reiß|verschluss** *m* zipper; ***den ~ an et. öffnen*** (***schließen***) unzip (zip up) s.th.; **~zwecke** *f* thumbtack, *Br* drawing pin

**reiten** ['raitən] (*irr*, *ge-*) **1.** *v/i* (*sein*) ride, go on horseback; **2.** *v/t* (*h*) ride

**'Reiten** *n* (*-s*; *no pl*) horseback riding

**Reiter** ['raitɐ] *m* (*-s*; -) rider, horseman

**Reiterin** ['raitərɪn] *f* (-; *-nen*) rider, horsewoman

**'Reitpferd** *n* saddle *or* riding horse

**Reiz** [raits] *m* (*-es*; *-e*) charm, attraction, appeal; thrill; MED, PSYCH stimulus; (***für j-n***) ***den ~ verlieren*** lose one's appeal (for s.o.); **'reizbar** *adj* irritable, excitable; **reizen** ['raitsən] (*ge-*, *h*) **1.** *v/t* irritate (*a.* MED), annoy; ZO bait; provoke; appeal to, attract; tempt; challenge; **2.** *v/i cards*: bid; **'reizend** *adj* charming, delightful; lovely, sweet, cute; **'reizlos** *adj* unattractive

**'Reizung** *f* (-; *-en*) irritation (*a.* MED)

**'reizvoll** *adj* attractive; challenging

**'Reizwort** *n* (*-[e]s*; *-wörter*) emotive word

**rekeln** ['rɛːkəln] F *v/refl* (*ge-*, *h*) loll

**Reklamation** [reklama'tsjoːn] *f* (-; *-en*) complaint

**Reklame** [re'klaːmə] *f* (-; *-n*) advertising, publicity; advertisement, F ad; ***~ machen für*** advertise, promote

**reklamieren** [rekla'miːrən] *v/i* (*no -ge-*, *h*) complain (***wegen*** about), protest (against)

**Rekord** [re'kɔrt] *m* (*-[e]s*; *-e*) record; ***e-n ~ aufstellen*** set *or* establish a record

**Rekrut** [re'kruːt] *m* (*-en*; *-en*) MIL recruit

**rekrutieren** [rekru'tiːrən] *v/t* (*no -ge-*, *h*) recruit

**Rektor** ['rɛktoːɐ] *m* (*-s*; *-en* [rɛk'toːrən])

principal, *Br* headmaster; UNIV president, *Br* rector; **Rektorin** [rɛk'to:rɪn] *f* (-; *-nen*) principal, *Br* headmistress; UNIV president, *Br* rector
**relativ** [rela'ti:f] *adj* relative
**Relief** [re'ljɛf] *n* (*-s*; *-s*) relief
**Religion** [reli'gjo:n] *f* (-; *-en*) religion
**religiös** [reli'gjø:s] *adj* religious
**Reling** ['re:lɪŋ] *f* (-; *-s*) MAR rail
**Reliquie** [re'li:kvjə] *f* (-; *-n*) relic
**Rempelei** [rɛmpə'lai] F *f* (-; *-en*), **rempeln** ['rɛmpəln] F *v/t* (*ge-*, *h*) jostle
**Rennbahn** ['rɛn-] *f* racecourse, racetrack; cycling track
**'Rennboot** *n* racing boat; speedboat
**rennen** ['rɛnən] *v/i and v/t* (*irr*, *ge-*, *sein*) run; **'Rennen** *n* (*-s*; -) race (*a. fig*); heat
**'Renn|fahrer** *m*, **~fahrerin** *f* racing driver; racing cyclist; **~läufer** *m* ski racer; **~pferd** *n* racehorse, racer; **~rad** *n* racing bicycle, racer; **~sport** *m* racing; **~stall** *m* racing stable; **~wagen** *m* race (*Br* racing) car, racer
**renommiert** [renɔ'mi:ɐt] *adj* renowned
**renovieren** [reno'vi:rən] *v/t* (*no -ge-*, *h*) renovate, F do up; redecorate
**rentabel** [rɛn'ta:bəl] *adj* ECON profitable, paying
**Rente** ['rɛntə] *f* (-; *-n*) (old age) pension; ***in ~ gehen*** retire
**'Renten|alter** *n* retirement age; **~versicherung** *f* pension scheme
**Rentier** ['rɛnti:ɐ] *n* (*-s*; *-e*) ZO reindeer
**rentieren** [rɛn'ti:rən] *v/refl* (*no -ge-*, *h*) ECON pay; *fig* be worth it
**Rentner** ['rɛntnɐ] *m* (*-s*; -), **'Rentnerin** [-nərɪn] *f* (-; *-nen*) (old age) pensioner
**Reparatur** [repara'tu:ɐ] *f* (-; *-en*) repair; **~werkstatt** *f* repair shop; MOT garage
R
**reparieren** [repa'ri:rən] *v/t* (*no -ge-*, *h*) repair, mend, F fix
**Reportage** [repɔr'ta:ʒə] *f* (-; *-n*) report
**Reporter** [re'pɔrtɐ] *m* (*-s*; -), **Re'porterin** *f* (-; *-nen*) reporter
**Repräsentant** [reprɛzɛn'tant] *m* (*-en*; *-en*) representative; **Repräsentantenhaus** *n* PARL House of Representatives; **Repräsen'tantin** *f* (-; *-nen*) representative; **repräsentieren** [reprɛzɛn'ti:rən] *v/t* (*no -ge-*, *h*) represent
**Repressalie** [reprɛ'sa:ljə] *f* (-; *-n*) reprisal
**Reproduktion** [reprodʊk'tsjo:n] *f* (-; *-en*) reproduction, print
**reproduzieren** [reprodu'tsi:rən] *v/t* (*no -ge-*, *h*) reproduce
**Reptil** [rɛp'ti:l] *n* (*-s*; *-ien*) ZO reptile
**Republik** [repu'bli:k] *f* (-; *-en*) republic
**Republikaner** [republi'ka:nɐ] *m* (*-s*; -), **Republi'kanerin** *f* (-; *-nen*), **republi'kanisch** *adj* POL republican
**Reservat** [rezɛr'va:t] *n* (*-[e]s*; *-e*) (p)reserve; reservation
**Reserve** [re'zɛrvə] *f* (-; *-n*) reserve (*a.* MIL); **~...** *in cpds ...kanister*, *...rad etc*: spare ...
**reservieren** [rezɛr'vi:rən] *v/t* (*no -ge-*, *h*) reserve (*a.* ***~ lassen***); ***j-m e-n Platz ~*** keep *or* save a seat for s.o.; **reserviert** [rezɛr'vi:ɐt] *adj* reserved (*a. fig*); aloof; **Reser'viertheit** *f* (-; *no pl*) aloofness
**Residenz** [rezi'dɛnts] *f* (-; *-en*) residence
**Resignation** [rezɪgna'tsjo:n] *f* (-; *no pl*) resignation; **resignieren** [rezɪ'gni:rən] *v/i* (*no -ge-*, *h*) give up; **resigniert** [rezɪ'gni:ɐt] *adj* resigned
**Resoziali'sierung** *f* (-; *-en*) rehabilitation
**Respekt** [re'spɛkt] *m* (*-[e]s*; *no pl*) respect (***vor*** *dat* for); **respektieren** [respɛk'ti:rən] *v/t* (*no -ge-*, *h*) respect
**re'spektlos** *adj* irreverent, disrespectful; **re'spektvoll** *adj* respectful
**Ressort** [rɛ'so:ɐ] *n* (*-s*; *-s*) department, province
**Rest** [rɛst] *m* (*-[e]s*; *-e*) rest; *pl* remains, remnants; GASTR leftovers; F ***das gab ihm den ~*** that finished him (off)
**Restaurant** [rɛsto'rã:] *n* (*-s*; *-s*) restaurant
**restaurieren** [rɛsto'ri:rən] *v/t* (*no -ge-*, *h*) restore
**'Restbetrag** *m* remainder
**'restlich** *adj* remaining
**'restlos** *adv* completely
**Resultat** [rezʊl'ta:t] *n* (*-[e]s*; *-e*) result (*a.* SPORT), outcome
**Retorte** [re'tɔrtə] *f* (-; *-n*) CHEM retort
**Re'tortenbaby** F *n* test-tube baby
**retten** ['rɛtən] *v/t* (*ge-*, *h*) save, rescue (*both*: ***aus*** *dat*, ***vor*** *dat* from)
**Retter** ['rɛtɐ] *m* (*-s*; -), **'Retterin** *f* (-; *-nen*) rescuer
**Rettich** ['rɛtɪç] *m* (*-s*; *-e*) BOT radish
**'Rettung** *f* (-; *-en*) rescue (***aus*** *dat*, ***vor*** *dat* from); ***das war s-e ~*** that saved him
**'Rettungs|boot** *n* lifeboat; **~mannschaft** *f* rescue party; **~ring** *m* life belt,

life buoy; **~schwimmer** *m* lifeguard
**Reue** ['rɔʏə] *f* (-; *no pl*) remorse, repentance (*both*: **über** *acc* for)
**reumütig** ['rɔʏmyːtɪç] *adj* repentant
**Revanche** [re'vãːʃ(ə)] *f* (-; *-n*) revenge
**revanchieren** [revã'ʃiːrən] *v/refl* (*no -ge-*, *h*) have one's revenge (**bei, an** *dat* on); make it up (**bei j-m** to s.o.)
**Revers** [re'veːɐ] *n*, *m* (-; -) lapel
**revidieren** [revi'diːrən] *v/t* (*no -ge-*, *h*) revise; ECON audit
**Revier** [re'viːɐ] *n* (*-s*; *-e*) district; ZO territory (*a. fig*); → **Polizeirevier**
**Revision** [revi'zjoːn] *f* (-; *-en*) revision; ECON audit; JUR appeal
**Revolte** [re'vɔltə] *f* (-; *-n*), **revoltieren** [revɔl'tiːrən] *v/i* (*no -ge-*, *h*) revolt
**Revolution** [revolu'tsjoːn] *f* (-; *-en*) revolution; **revolutionär** [revolutsjo'nɛːɐ] *adj*, **Revolutio'när(in)** (*-s*; *-e*/-; *-nen*) revolutionary
**Revolver** [re'vɔlvɐ] *m* (*-s*; -) revolver, F gun
**Revue** [re'vyː] *f* (-; *-n*) THEA (musical) show
**Rezept** [re'tsɛpt] *n* (*-[e]s*; *-e*) MED prescription; GASTR recipe (*a. fig*)
**Rezession** [retsɛ'sjoːn] *f* (-; *-en*) ECON recession
**Rhabarber** [ra'barbɐ] *m* (*-s*; *no pl*) BOT rhubarb
**rhetorisch** [re'toːrɪʃ] *adj* rhetorical
**Rheuma** ['rɔʏma] *n* (*-s*; *no pl*) MED rheumatism
**rhythmisch** ['rʏtmɪʃ] *adj* rhythmic(al)
**Rhythmus** ['rʏtmʊs] *m* (-; *-men*) rhythm
**Ribisel** ['riːbiːzəl] *Austrian f* (-; *-[n]*) → **Johannisbeere**
**richten** ['rɪçtən] *v/t* (*ge-*, *h*) fix; get *s.th.* ready, prepare; do (*room, one's hair*); (**sich**) **~ an** (*acc*) address (o.s.) to; put *a question* to; **~ auf** (*acc*) direct *or* turn to; point *or* aim *camera, gun etc* at; **~ gegen** direct against; **sich ~ nach** go by, act according to; follow (*fashion etc*); depend on; **ich richte mich ganz nach dir** I leave it to you
**Richter** ['rɪçtɐ] *m* (*-s*; -), **'Richterin** *f* (-; *-nen*) judge
**'richterlich** *adj* judicial
**'Richtgeschwindigkeit** *f* MOT recommended speed
**richtig** ['rɪçtɪç] **1.** *adj* right; correct, proper; true; real; **2.** *adv*: **~ nett** (**böse**) really nice (angry); **et. ~ machen** do s.th. right; **m-e Uhr geht ~** my watch is right; *fig* **~ stellen** put *or* set right
**'Richtigkeit** *f* (-; *no pl*) correctness
**'Richt|linien** *pl* guidelines; **~preis** *m* ECON recommended price
**'Richtung** *f* (-; *-en*) direction; POL leaning; PAINT *etc* style; **'richtungslos** *adj* aimless, disorient(at)ed
**'richtungweisend** *adj* pioneering
**rieb** [riːp] *pret of* **reiben**
**riechen** ['riːçən] *v/i and v/t* (*irr*, *ge-*, *h*) smell (**nach** of; **an** *dat* at)
**rief** [riːf] *pret of* **rufen**
**Riegel** ['riːgəl] *m* (*-s*; -) bolt, bar
**Riemen** ['riːmən] *m* (*-s*; -) strap; TECH belt; MAR oar
**Riese** ['riːzə] *m* (*-n*; *-n*) giant (*a. fig*)
**rieseln** ['riːzəln] *v/i* (*ge-*, *sein*) trickle; *rain*: drizzle; *snow*: fall gently
**'Riesen...** *in cpds mst* giant ..., gigantic ..., enormous ...; **~erfolg** *m* huge success, *film etc*: *a.* smash hit
**'riesengroß, 'riesenhaft** → **riesig**
**'Riesenrad** *n* Ferris wheel
**riesig** ['riːzɪç] *adj* enormous, gigantic, giant
**'Riesin** *f* (-; *-nen*) giantess (*a. fig*)
**riet** [riːt] *pret of* **raten**
**Riff** [rɪf] *n* (*-[e]s*; *-e*) GEOGR reef
**Rille** ['rɪlə] *f* (-; *-n*) groove
**Rind** [rɪnt] *n* (*-[e]s*; *-er* ['rɪndɐ]) ZO cow, *pl* cattle; GASTR beef
**Rinde** ['rɪndə] *f* (-; *-n*) BOT bark; GASTR rind; crust
**Rinder|braten** ['rɪndɐ-] *m* roast beef; **~herde** *f* herd of cattle
**'Rind|fleisch** *n* GASTR beef; **~(s)leder** *n* cowhide; **~vieh** *n* ZO cattle
**Ring** [rɪŋ] *m* (*-[e]s*; *-e*) ring (*a. fig*); MOT ring road; *subway etc*: circle (line)
**'Ringbuch** *n* loose-leaf *or* ring binder
**ringeln** ['rɪŋəln] *v/refl* (*ge-*, *h*) curl, coil (*a.* ZO)
**'Ringelnatter** *f* ZO grass snake
**'Ringelspiel** *Austrian n* → **Karussell**
**ringen** ['rɪŋən] (*irr*, *ge-*, *h*) **1.** *v/i* SPORT wrestle (**mit** with), *fig a.* struggle (against, with; **um** for); **nach Atem ~** gasp (for breath); **2.** *v/t* wring
**'Ringen** *n* (*-s*; *no pl*) SPORT wrestling
**Ringer** ['rɪŋɐ] *m* (*-s*; -) SPORT wrestler
**'ringförmig** [-fœrmɪç] *adj* circular

'**Ringkampf** *m* SPORT wrestling match
'**Ringrichter** *m* SPORT referee
**rings** *adv*: ~ ***um*** around
'**ringshe'rum,** '**rings'um,** '**rings-um'her** *adv* all around; everywhere
**Rinne** ['rɪnə] *f* (-; *-n*) groove, channel; gutter; '**rinnen** *v/i* (*irr, ge-, sein*) run; flow, stream; **Rinnsal** ['rɪnza:l] *n* (*-s; -e*) trickle
'**Rinnstein** *m* gutter
**Rippe** ['rɪpə] *f* (-; *-n*) ANAT rib
'**Rippenfell** *n* ANAT pleura; **~entzündung** *f* MED pleurisy
'**Rippenstoß** *m* nudge in the ribs
**Risiko** ['ri:ziko] *n* (*-s; -s, -ken*) risk; ***ein*** (***kein***) ~ ***eingehen*** take a risk (no risks); ***auf eigenes*** ~ at one's own risk
**riskant** [rɪs'kant] *adj* risky
**riskieren** [rɪs'ki:rən] *v/t* (*no -ge-, h*) risk
**riss** [rɪs] *pret of* ***reißen***
**Riss** *m* (*-es; -e*) tear, rip, split (*a. fig*); crack; MED chap, laceration; **rissig** ['rɪsɪç] *adj* chapped; cracky, cracked
**Rist** [rɪst] *m* (*-es; -e*) ANAT instep
**ritt** [rɪt] *pret of* ***reiten***
**Ritt** *m* (*-[e]s; -e*) ride (on horseback)
**Ritter** ['rɪtɐ] *m* (*-s; -*) knight; ***j-n zum ~ schlagen*** knight s.o.
'**ritterlich** *fig adj* chivalrous
**Ritz** [rɪts] *m* (*-es; -e*), **Ritze** ['rɪtsə] *f* (-; *-n*) crack, chink; gap
**Rivale** [ri'va:lə] *m* (*-n; -n*), **Ri'valin** *f* (-; *-nen*) rival; **rivalisieren** [rivali'zi:rən] *v/i* (*no -ge-, h*) compete; **Rivalität** [rivali'tɛ:t] *f* (-; *-en*) rivalry
**rk., r.-k.** ABBR *of* ***römisch-katholisch*** RC, Roman Catholic
**Robbe** ['rɔbə] *f* (-; *-n*) ZO seal
**Robe** ['ro:bə] *f* (-; *-n*) robe, gown
**Roboter** ['rɔbɔtɐ] *m* (*-s; -*) robot
**robust** [ro'bʊst] *adj* robust, strong, tough
**roch** [rɔx] *pret of* ***riechen***
**röcheln** ['rœçəln] (*ge-, h*) **1.** *v/i* moan; **2.** *v/t* gasp
**Rock** [rɔk] *m* (*-[e]s; Röcke* ['rœkə]) skirt
**Rodelbahn** ['ro:dəl-] *f* toboggan run
**rodeln** ['ro:dəln] *v/i* (*ge-, sein*) sled(ge), coast; SPORT toboggan
'**Rodelschlitten** *m* sled(ge); toboggan
**roden** ['ro:dən] *v/t* (*ge-, h*) clear; stub
**Rogen** ['ro:gən] *m* (*-s; -*) (hard) roe
**Roggen** ['rɔgən] *m* (*-s; -*) BOT rye
**roh** [ro:] *adj* raw; rough; *fig* brutal; ***mit ~er Gewalt*** with brute force
'**Rohbau** *m* (*-[e]s; -ten*) carcass
'**Rohkost** *f* raw vegetables and fruit
'**Rohling** *m* (*-s; -e*) TECH blank; *fig* brute
'**Rohmateri͵al** *n* raw material
'**Rohöl** *n* crude (oil)
**Rohr** [ro:ɐ] *n* (*-[e]s; -e* ['ro:rə]) TECH pipe, tube; duct; BOT reed; cane
**Röhre** ['rø:rə] *f* (-; *-n*) pipe, tube (*a.* TV), TV *etc* valve
'**Rohr|leitung** *f* duct, pipe(s); plumbing; pipeline; **~stock** *m* cane; **~zucker** *m* cane sugar
'**Rohstoff** *m* raw material
**Rollbahn** ['rɔl-] *f* AVIAT runway
**Rolle** ['rɔlə] *f* (-; *-n*) roll (*a.* SPORT), TECH *a.* roller; coil; caster, castor; THEA part, role (*both a. fig*); ***e-e ~ Garn*** a spool of thread, *Br* a reel of cotton; ***das spielt keine ~*** that doesn't matter, that makes no difference; ***Geld spielt k-e ~*** money is no object
'**rollen** *v/i* (*ge-, sein*) *and v/t* (*ge-, h*) roll
**Roller** ['rɔlɐ] *m* (*-s; -*) (motor) scooter
'**Roll|film** *m* PHOT roll film; **~kragen** *m* turtleneck, *esp Br* polo neck; **~laden** *m* rolling shutter
**Rollo** ['rɔlo] *n* (*-s; -s*) shades, *Br* (roller) blind
'**Rollschuh** *m* roller skate; ***~ laufen*** roller-skate; **~bahn** *f* roller-skating rink; **~läufer** *m* roller skater
'**Rollstuhl** *m* wheelchair
'**Rolltreppe** *f* escalator
**Roman** [ro'ma:n] *m* (*-s; -e*) novel
**Romanik** [ro'ma:nɪk] *f* (-; *no pl*) ARCH Romanesque (style *or* period)
**romanisch** [ro'ma:nɪʃ] *adj* LING Romance; ARCH Romanesque
**Romanist** [roma'nɪst] *m* (*-en; -en*), **Roma'nistin** *f* (-; *-nen*) student of Romance languages
**Ro'manschriftsteller** *m*, **Ro'manschriftstellerin** *f* novelist
**Romantik** [ro'mantɪk] *f* (-; *no pl*) romance; HIST Romanticism
**romantisch** [ro'mantɪʃ] *adj* romantic
**Römer** ['rø:mɐ] *m* (*-s; -*), '**Römerin** *f* (-; *-nen*), **römisch** ['rø:mɪʃ] *adj* Roman
**Rommee** ['rɔme] *n* (*-s; -s*) rummy
**röntgen** ['rœntgən] *v/t* (*ge-, h*) MED X-ray
'**Röntgen|appa͵rat** *m* MED X-ray apparatus; **~aufnahme** *f*, **~bild** *n* MED X-

ray; **~strahlen** *pl* PHYS X-rays; **~untersuchung** *f* MED X-ray
**rosa** ['ro:za] *adj* pink; *fig* rose-colo(u)red; **Rose** ['ro:zə] *f* (-; *-n*) BOT rose
**'Rosenkohl** *m* BOT Brussels sprouts
**'Rosenkranz** *m* REL rosary
**rosig** ['ro:zıç] *adj* rosy (*a. fig*)
**Rosine** [ro'zi:nə] *f* (-; *-n*) raisin
**'Rosshaar** *n* (-[*e*]*s*; *no pl*) horsehair
**Rost** [rɔst] *m* (-[*e*]*s*; *-e*) a) (*no pl*) CHEM rust, b) TECH grate; GASTR grid(iron), grill; **rosten** ['rɔstən] *v/i* (*ge-*, *sein*) rust
**rösten** ['rœstən] *v/t* (*ge-*, *h*) roast (*a.* F); toast; fry
**'Rostfleck** *m* rust stain; **'rostfrei** *adj* rustproof, stainless; **'rostig** *adj* rusty
**rot** [ro:t] *adj* red (*a.* POL); *~ glühend* red-hot; *~ werden* blush; *in den ~en Zahlen* ECON in the red
**Rot** *n* (-*s*; -) red; ***die Ampel steht auf ~*** the lights are red; ***bei ~*** at red
**'rotblond** *adj* sandy(-haired)
**Röte** ['rø:tə] *f* (-; *no pl*) redness, red (colo[u]r); *fig* blush
**Röteln** ['rø:təln] *pl* MED German measles
**röten** ['rø:tən] *v/refl* (*ge-*, *h*) redden; flush
**'rothaarig** *adj* red-haired
**'Rothaarige** *m*, *f* (*-n*; *-n*) redhead
**rotieren** [ro'ti:rən] *v/i* (*no -ge-*, *h*) rotate
**'Rotkehlchen** *n* (-*s*; -) ZO robin
**'Rotkohl** *m* BOT red cabbage
**rötlich** ['rø:tlıç] *adj* reddish
**'Rot|stift** *m* red crayon *or* pencil; **~wein** *m* red wine; **~wild** *n* ZO (red) deer
**Rotznase** [rɔts-] F *f* snotty nose
**Route** ['ru:tə] *f* (-; *-n*) route
**Routine** [ru'ti:nə] *f* (-; *no pl*) routine; experience; **~sache** *f* routine (matter)
**routiniert** [ruti'ni:ɐt] *adj* experienced
**Rübe** ['ry:bə] *f* (-; *-n*) BOT turnip; (sugar) beet
**Rubin** [ru'bi:n] *m* (-*s*; *-e*) MIN ruby
**Rübli** ['ry:pli] *Swiss n* (-*s*; -) BOT carrot
**Rubrik** [ru'bri:k] *f* (-; *-en*) heading; column
**Ruck** [rʊk] *m* (-[*e*]*s*; *-e*) jerk, jolt, start; *fig* POL swing
**Rückantwortschein** ['rʏk-] *m* reply coupon
**'ruckartig** *adj* jerky, abrupt
**'rückbezüglich** *adj* LING reflexive
**'Rückblende** *f* flashback (***auf*** *acc* to)
**'Rückblick** *m* review (***auf*** *acc* of); ***im ~*** in retrospect
**rücken** ['rʏkən] **1.** *v/t* (*ge-*, *h*) move, shift, push; **2.** *v/i* (*ge-*, *sein*) move; move over; ***näher ~*** approach
**'Rücken** *m* (-*s*; -) ANAT back (*a. fig*); **~deckung** *fig f* backing, support; **~lehne** *f* back(rest); **~mark** *n* ANAT spinal cord; **~schmerzen** *pl* backache; **~schwimmen** *n* backstroke; **~wind** *m* following wind, tailwind; **~wirbel** *m* ANAT dorsal vertebra
**'Rück|erstattung** *f* (-; *-en*) refund; **~fahrkarte** *f* round-trip ticket, *Br a.* return (ticket); **~fahrt** *f* return trip; ***auf der ~*** on the way back; **~fall** *m* relapse
**'rückfällig** *adj*: ***~ werden*** relapse
**'Rückflug** *m* return flight
**'Rückgabe** *f* (-; *no pl*) return
**'Rückgang** *m* drop, fall; ECON recession
**'rückgängig** *adj*: ***~ machen*** cancel
**'Rück|gewinnung** *f* (-; *no pl*) recovery; **~grat** *n* ANAT spine, backbone (*both a. fig*); **~halt** *m* (-[*e*]*s*; *no pl*) support; **~hand** *f*, **~handschlag** *m tennis*: backhand; **~kauf** *m* ECON repurchase
**Rückkehr** ['rʏkke:ɐ] *f* (-; *no pl*) return; ***nach s-r ~ aus ...*** on his return from ...
**'Rück|kopplung** *f* ELECTR feedback (*a. fig*); **~lage** *f* (-; *-n*) reserve(s); savings; **~lauf** *m* TECH rewind
**'rückläufig** *adj* falling, downward
**'Rücklicht** *n* (-[*e*]*s*; *-er*) MOT rear light, taillight
**rücklings** ['rʏklıŋs] *adv* backward(s); from behind
**'Rückporto** *n* return postage
**'Rückreise** *f* → ***Rückfahrt***
**Rucksack** ['rʊkzak] *m* rucksack, backpack; **~tou,rismus** *m* backpacking; **~tou,rist** *m* backpacker
**'Rück|schlag** *m* SPORT return; *fig* setback; **~schluss** *m* conclusion; **~schritt** *m fig* step back(ward); **~seite** *f* back; reverse; flip side; **~sendung** *f* return
**'Rücksicht** *f* (-; *-en*) consideration, regard; ***aus*** (***ohne***) ***~ auf*** (*acc*) out of (without any) consideration *or* regard for; ***~ nehmen auf*** (*acc*) show consideration for; **'rücksichtslos** *adj* inconsiderate (***gegen*** of), thoughtless (of); ruthless; reckless; **'rücksichtsvoll** *adj* considerate (***gegen*** of), thoughtful
**'Rück|sitz** *m* MOT back seat; **~spiegel** *m* MOT rear-view mirror; **~spiel** *n*

R

SPORT return match; **~stand** *m* CHEM residue; ***mit der Arbeit* (*e-m Tor*) *im ~ sein*** be behind with one's work (down by one goal)
**'rückständig** *adj* backward; underdeveloped; ***~e Miete*** arrears of rent
**'Rück|stau** *m* MOT tailback; **~stelltaste** *f* backspace key; **~tritt** *m* resignation; withdrawal; TECH → **~trittbremse** *f* coaster (*Br* back-pedal) brake
**rückwärts** ['rYkvɛrts] *adv* backward(s); ***~ aus*** (*dat*) ***... fahren*** back out of ...; ***~ in*** (*acc*) ***... fahren*** back into ...
**'Rückwärtsgang** *m* MOT reverse (gear)
**'Rückweg** *m* way back
**'ruckweise** *adv* jerkily, in jerks
**'rückwirkend** *adj* retroactive
**'Rück|wirkung** *f* reaction (***auf*** *acc* upon); **~zahlung** *f* repayment; **~zieher** *m* (*-s*; *-*) *soccer*: overhead kick; F ***e-n ~ machen*** back (*or* chicken) out (***von*** of); **~zug** *m* retreat
**Rüde** ['ry:də] *m* (*-n*; *-n*) ZO male (dog *etc*)
**Rudel** ['ru:dəl] *n* (*-s*; *-*) ZO pack; herd
**Ruder** ['ru:dɐ] *n* (*-s*; *-*) AVIAT, MAR rudder; SPORT oar; ***am ~*** at the helm (*a. fig*); **~boot** *n* rowing boat, rowboat
**Ruderer** ['ru:dərɐ] *m* (*-s*; *-*) rower, oarsman; **'Ruderin** *f* (*-*; *-nen*) rower, oarswoman; **'rudern** *v/i and v/t* (*ge-*, *h*) row
**'Ruder|re,gatta** *f* (rowing) regatta, boat race; **~sport** *m* rowing
**Ruf** [ru:f] *m* (*-[e]s*; *-e*) call (*a. fig*); cry, shout; *fig* reputation; **'rufen** *v/i and v/t* (*irr*, *ge-*, *h*) call (*a. doctor etc*); cry, shout; ***~ nach*** call for (*a. fig*); ***~ lassen*** send for; ***um Hilfe ~*** call *or* cry for help
**'Rufnummer** *f* telephone number
**'Rufweite** *f*: ***in* (*außer*) *~*** within (out of) call(ing distance)
**Rüge** ['ry:gə] *f* (*-*; *-n*) reproof, reproach (*both*: ***wegen*** for); **'rügen** *v/t* (*ge-*, *h*) reprove, reproach
**Ruhe** ['ru:ə] *f* (*-*; *no pl*) quiet, calm; silence; rest; peace; calm(ness); ***zur ~ kommen*** come to rest; ***j-n in ~ lassen*** leave s.o. in peace; ***lass mich in ~!*** leave me alone!; ***et. in ~ tun*** take one's time (doing s.th.); ***die ~ behalten*** F keep (one's) cool, play it cool; ***sich zur ~ setzen*** retire; ***~, bitte!*** (be) quiet, please!; **'ruhelos** *adj* restless
**'ruhen** *v/i* (*ge-*, *h*) rest (***auf*** *dat* on)
**'Ruhe|pause** *f* break; **~stand** *m* (*-[e]s*; *no pl*) retirement; **~störer** *m* (*-s*; *-*) *esp* JUR disturber of the peace; **~tag** *m* a day's rest; ***Montag ~*** closed on Mondays
**ruhig** ['ru:ɪç] *adj* quiet; silent; calm; cool; TECH smooth; ***~ bleiben*** F keep (one's) cool, play it cool
**Ruhm** [ru:m] *m* (*-[e]s*; *no pl*) fame, *esp* POL, MIL *etc* glory; **rühmen** ['ry:mən] *v/t* (*ge-*, *h*) praise (***wegen*** for); ***sich e-r Sache ~*** boast of s.th.; **rühmlich** ['ry:mlɪç] *adj* laudable, praiseworthy
**'ruhmlos** *adj* inglorious
**'ruhmreich** *adj* glorious
**Ruhr** [ru:ɐ] *f* (*-*; *no pl*) MED dysentery
**Rühreier** ['ry:ɐʔaiɐ] *pl* scrambled eggs
**rühren** ['ry:rən] *v/t* (*ge-*, *h*) stir; move (*a. fig*); *fig* touch, affect; ***das rührt mich gar nicht*** that leaves me cold; ***rührt euch!*** MIL (stand) at ease!; **~d** *fig adj* touching, moving; very kind
**rührig** ['ry:rɪç] *adj* active, busy
**rührselig** ['ry:ɐ-] *adj* sentimental
**'Rührung** *f* (*-*; *no pl*) emotion
**Ruin** [ru'i:n] *m* (*-s*; *no pl*) ruin
**Ruine** [ru'i:nə] *f* (*-*; *-n*) ruin
**ruinieren** [rui'ni:rən] *v/t* (*no -ge-*, *h*) ruin
**rülpsen** ['rYlpsən] *v/i* (*ge-*, *h*), **Rülpser** ['rYlpsɐ] *m* (*-s*; *-*) belch
**Rumäne** [ru'mɛ:nə] *m* (*-n*; *-n*) Romanian; **Rumänien** Romania; **Ru'mänin** *f* (*-*; *-nen*), **ru'mänisch** *adj* Romanian
**Rummel** ['rʊməl] F *m* (*-s*; *no pl*) (hustle and) bustle; F ballyhoo; **~platz** F *m* amusement park, fairground
**rumoren** [ru'mo:rən] *v/i* (*no -ge-*, *h*) rumble
**Rumpelkammer** ['rʊmpəl-] F *f* lumber room
**rumpeln** ['rʊmpəln] F *v/i* (*ge-*, *h*, *sein*) rumble
**Rumpf** [rʊmpf] *m* (*-es*; *Rümpfe* ['rYmpfə]) ANAT trunk; MAR hull; AVIAT fuselage
**rümpfen** ['rYmpfən] *v/t* (*ge-*, *h*) ***die Nase ~*** turn up one's nose (***über*** *acc* at), sneer (at)
**rund** [rʊnt] **1.** *adj* round (*a. fig*); **2.** *adv* about; ***~ um*** (a)round; **'Rundblick** *m* panorama; **Runde** ['rʊndə] *f* (*-*; *-n*)

R

round (*a. fig and* SPORT); *racing*: lap; ***s-e ~ machen in*** (*dat*) patrol; ***die ~ machen*** go the round(s)
'**Rundfahrt** *f* tour (***durch*** round)
'**Rundfunk** *m* (*-s*; *no pl*) radio; broadcasting corporation; ***im ~*** on the radio; ***im ~ übertragen*** *or* ***senden*** broadcast; **~hörer(in)** listener, *pl a.* (radio) audience; **~sender** *m* broadcasting *or* radio station
'**Rundgang** *m* tour (***durch*** of)
'**rundhe'raus** *adv* frankly, plainly
'**rundhe'rum** *adv* all around
'**rundlich** *adj* plump, chubby
'**Rund|reise** *f* tour (***durch*** of); **~schau** *f* review; **~schreiben** *n* circular (letter); **~spruch** *Swiss m* → ***Rundfunk***
'**Rundung** *f* (-; *-en*) curve
'**rundweg** [-'vɛk] *adv* flatly, plainly
**runter** ['rʊntɐ] F *adv* → ***herunter***
**Runzel** ['rʊntsəl] *f* (-; *-n*) wrinkle
**runz(e)lig** ['rʊnts(ə)lɪç] *adj* wrinkled
'**runzeln** *v/t* (*ge-*, *h*) ***die Stirn ~*** frown (***über*** *acc* at)
**Rüpel** ['ry:pəl] *m* (*-s*; -) lout
**rupfen** ['rʊpfən] *v/t* (*ge-*, *h*) pluck
**Rüsche** ['ry:ʃə] *f* (-; *-n*) frill, ruffle
**Ruß** ['ru:s] *m* (*-es*; *no pl*) soot
**Russe** ['rʊsə] *m* (*-n*; *-n*) Russian
**Rüssel** ['rʏsəl] *m* (*-s*; -) ZO trunk; snout
**rußen** ['ru:sən] *v/i* (*ge-*, *h*) smoke
**rußig** ['ru:sɪç] *adj* sooty
**Russin** ['rʊsɪn] *f* (-; *-nen*), **russisch** ['rʊsɪʃ] *adj* Russian
'**Russland** Russia
**rüsten** ['rʏstən] (*ge-*, *h*) **1.** *v/i* MIL arm; **2.** *v/refl* get ready, prepare (***zu***, ***für*** for); arm o.s. (***gegen*** for)
**rüstig** ['rʏstɪç] *adj* vigorous, sprightly
**rustikal** [rʊsti'ka:l] *adj* rustic
'**Rüstung** *f* (-; *-en*) MIL armament; armo(u)r
'**Rüstungs|indus,trie** *f* armament industry; **~wettlauf** *m* arms race
'**Rüstzeug** *n* equipment
**Rute** ['ru:tə] *f* (-; *-n*) rod (*a. fig*), switch
**Rutschbahn** ['rʊtʃ-] *f*, **Rutsche** ['rʊtʃə] *f* (-; *-n*) slide, chute; '**rutschen** *v/i* (*ge-*, *sein*) slide, slip; glide; MOT *etc* skid; **rutschig** ['rʊtʃɪç] *adj* slippery
'**rutschsicher** *adj* MOT *etc* non-skid
**rütteln** ['rʏtəln] (*ge-*, *h*) **1.** *v/t* shake; **2.** *v/i* jolt; ***an der Tür ~*** rattle at the door

# S

**S** ABBR *of* ***Süd(en)*** S, south
**S.** ABBR *of* ***Seite*** p., page
**s.** ABBR *of* ***siehe*** see
**Saal** [za:l] *m* (*-[e]s*; *Säle* ['zɛ:lə]) hall
**Saat** [za:t] *f* (-; *-en*) a) (*no pl*) sowing, b) seed(s) (*a. fig*); crop(s)
**Sabbat** ['zabat] *m* (*-s*; *-e*) sabbath (day)
**sabbern** ['zabɐn] F *v/i* (*ge-*, *h*) slobber, slaver
**Säbel** ['zɛ:bəl] *m* (*-s*; -) saber, *Br* sabre (*a.* SPORT), sword; '**säbeln** F *v/t* (*ge-*, *h*) cut, hack
**Sabotage** [zabo'ta:ʒə] *f* (-; *-n*) sabotage; **Saboteur** [zabo'tø:ɐ] *m* (*-s*; *-e*) saboteur; **sabotieren** [zabo'ti:rən] *v/t* (*no -ge-*, *h*) sabotage
**Sach|bearbeiter** ['zax-] *m*, **~bearbeiterin** *f* official in charge; **~beschädigung** *f* damage to property; **~buch** *n* specialized book, *pl coll* nonfiction
'**sachdienlich** *adj*: ***~e Hinweise*** relevant information
**Sache** ['zaxə] *f* (-; *-n*) thing; matter, business; issue, problem, question; cause; JUR matter, case; *pl* things, clothes; ***zur ~ kommen*** (***bei der ~ bleiben***) come (keep) to the point; ***nicht zur ~ gehören*** be irrelevant
'**sachgerecht** *adj* proper
'**Sachkenntnis** *f* expert knowledge
'**sachkundig** *adj* expert
'**sachlich** *adj* matter-of-fact, businesslike; unbias(s)ed, objective; practical, technical; ***~ richtig*** factually correct
**sächlich** ['zɛçlɪç] *adj* LING neuter
'**Sachre,gister** *n* (subject) index

**'Sachschaden** *m* damage to property
**sacht** [zaxt] *adj* soft, gentle; slow
**'Sach|verhalt** *m* (-[*e*]*s*; -*e*) facts (of the case); **~verstand** *m* know-how; **~verständige** *m, f* (-*n*; -*n*) expert; JUR expert witness; **~wert** *m* (-[*e*]*s*; *no pl*) real value; **~zwänge** *pl* inherent necessities
**Sack** [zak] *m* (-[*e*]*s*; *Säcke* ['zɛkə]) sack, bag; V balls; **sacken** ['zakən] F *v/i* (*ge-, sein*) sink; **'Sackgasse** *f* blind alley (*a. fig*), dead end (*a. fig*), *fig* impasse
**Sadismus** [za'dɪsmʊs] *m* (-; *no pl*) sadism; **Sadist** [za'dɪst] *m* (-*en*; -*en*) sadist; **sa'distisch** *adj* sadistic
**säen** ['zɛ:ən] *v/t and v/i* (*ge-, h*) sow (*a. fig*)
**Safari** [za'fa:ri] *f* (-; -*s*) safari; **~park** *m* wildlife reserve, safari park
**Saft** [zaft] *m* (-[*e*]*s*; *Säfte* ['zɛftə]) juice; BOT sap (*both a. fig*); **saftig** ['zaftɪç] *adj* juicy (*a. fig*); lush; F fancy (*prices etc*)
**Sage** ['za:gə] *f* (-; -*n*) legend, myth
**Säge** ['zɛ:gə] *f* (-; -*n*) saw
**'Sägemehl** *n* sawdust
**sagen** ['za:gən] *v/i and v/t* (*ge-, h*) say; ***j-m et.*** ~ tell s.o. s.th.; ***die Wahrheit*** ~ tell the truth; ***er lässt dir*** ~ he asked me to tell you; ~ ***wir ...*** (let's) say ...; ***man sagt, er sei reich*** he is said to be rich; ***er lässt sich nichts*** ~ he will not listen to reason; ***das hat nichts zu*** ~ it doesn't matter; ***et.*** (***nichts***) ***zu*** ~ ***haben*** (***bei***) have a say (no say) (in); ~ ***wollen mit*** mean by; ***das sagt mir nichts*** it doesn't mean anything to me; ***unter uns gesagt*** between you and me
**sägen** ['zɛ:gən] *v/t and v/i* (*ge-, h*) saw
**'sagenhaft** *adj* legendary; F fabulous, incredible, fantastic
**'Sägespäne** *pl* sawdust
**'Sägewerk** *n* sawmill
**sah** [za:] *pret of* ***sehen***
**Sahne** ['za:nə] *f* (-; *no pl*) cream
**Saison** [zɛ'zõ:] *f* (-; -*s*) season; ***in der*** ~ in season
**sai'sonbedingt** *adj* seasonal
**Saite** ['zaitə] *f* (-; -*n*) MUS string, chord (*a. fig*); **'Saiteninstru,ment** *n* MUS string(ed) instrument
**Sakko** ['zako] *m, n* (-*s*; -*s*) (sports) jacket, sport(s) coat
**Sakristei** [zakrɪs'tai] *f* (-; -*en*) REL vestry, sacristy
**Salat** [za'la:t] *m* (-[*e*]*s*; -*e*) BOT lettuce; GASTR salad; **~sauce** *f* salad dressing
**Salbe** ['zalbə] *f* (-; -*n*) ointment
**'Salbung** *f* (-; -*en*) unction
**'salbungsvoll** *adj* unctuous
**Saldo** ['zaldo] *m* (-*s*; -*s*, -*di*) ECON balance
**Salon** [za'lõ:] *m* (-*s*; -*s*) salon; MAR saloon; drawing room
**salopp** [za'lɔp] *adj* casual; *contp* sloppy
**Salpeter** [zal'pe:tɐ] *m* (-*s*; *no pl*) CHEM salt|peter (*Br* -petre), niter, *Br* nitre
**Salto** ['zalto] *m* (-*s*; -*s*, -*ti*) somersault
**Salut** [za'lu:t] *m* (-[*e*]*s*; -*e*) MIL salute; ~ ***schießen*** fire a salute
**salutieren** [zalu'ti:rən] *v/i* (*no -ge-, h*) MIL (give a) salute
**Salve** ['zalvə] *f* (-; -*n*) MIL volley (*a. fig*); salute
**Salz** [zalts] *n* (-*es*; -*e*) salt
**'Salzbergwerk** *n* salt mine
**salzen** ['zaltsən] *v/t* ([*irr*,] *ge-, h*) salt
**salzfrei** ['zaltsfrai] *adj* salt-free, no-salt *diet*
**salzig** ['zaltsɪç] *adj* salty
**'Salz|kar,toffeln** *pl* boiled potatoes; **~säure** *f* (-; *no pl*) CHEM hydrochloric acid; **~stange** *f* pretzel (*Br* salt) stick; **~streuer** *m* (-*s*; -) salt shaker, *Br* salt cellar; **~wasser** *n* salt water
**Same** ['za:mə] *m* (-*n*; -*n*), **'Samen** *m* (-*s* -) BOT seed (*a. fig*); BIOL sperm, semen
**'Samen|bank** *f* (-; -*en*) MED, VET sperm bank; **~erguss** *m* ejaculation; **~korn** *n* BOT seedcorn
**Sammel...** ['zaməl-] *in cpds ...begriff, ...bestellung, ...konto etc*: collective ...; **~büchse** *f* collecting box
**'sammeln** *v/t* (*ge-, h*) collect; gather, pick; accumulate; ***sich*** ~ assemble; *fig* compose o.s.
**Sammler** ['zamlɐ] *m* (-*s*; -), **'Sammlerin** *f* (-; -*nen*) collector
**'Sammlung** *f* (-; -*en*) collection
**Samstag** ['zamsta:k] *m* (-[*e*]*s*; -*e*) Saturday
**samt** [zamt] *prp* (*dat*) together *or* along with
**Samt** *m* (-[*e*]*s*; -*e*) velvet
**sämtlich** ['zɛmtlɪç] *adj*: **~e** *pl* all the; the complete *works etc*
**Sanatorium** [zana'to:rjʊm] *n* (-*s*; -*ien*) sanatorium, sanitarium
**Sand** [zant] *m* (-[*e*]*s*; -*e*) sand

**Sandale** [zan'daːlə] *f* (-; *-n*) sandal
**Sandalette** [zanda'lɛtə] *f* (-; *-n*) high-heeled sandal
'**Sand|bahn** *f* SPORT dirt track; **~bank** *f* (-; *-bänke*) sandbank; **~boden** *m* sandy soil; **~burg** *f* sandcastle
**sandig** ['zandɪç] *adj* sandy
'**Sand|mann** *m*, **~männchen** *n* sandman; **~pa͵pier** *n* sandpaper; **~sack** *m* sand bag; **~stein** *m* sandstone; **~strand** *m* sandy beach
**sandte** ['zantə] *pret of* ***senden***
'**Sanduhr** *f* hourglass
**sanft** [zanft] *adj* gentle, soft; mild; easy (*death*)
'**sanftmütig** [-myːtɪç] *adj* gentle, mild
**sang** [zaŋ] *pret of* ***singen***
**Sänger** ['zɛŋɐ] *m* (*-s*; -), **Sängerin** ['zɛŋərɪn] *f* (-; *-nen*) singer
**sanieren** [za'niːrən] *v/t* (*no -ge-*, *h*) redevelop (*a.* ECON), rehabilitate (*a.* ARCH)
**Sa'nierung** *f* (-; *-en*) redevelopment, rehabilitation; **Sa'nierungsgebiet** *n* redevelopment area
**sanitär** [zani'tɛːɐ] *adj* sanitary
**Sanitäter** [zani'tɛːtɐ] *m* (*-s*; -) paramedic; MIL medic, *Br* medical orderly
**sank** [zaŋk] *pret of* ***sinken***
**Sankt** [zaŋkt] Saint, ABBR St
**Sardelle** [zar'dɛlə] *f* (-; *-n*) ZO anchovy
**Sardine** [zar'diːnə] *f* (-; *-n*) ZO sardine
**Sarg** [zark] *m* (-[*e*]*s*; *Särge* ['zɛrgə]) casket, *esp Br* coffin
**Sarkasmus** [zar'kasmʊs] *m* (-; *no pl*) sarcasm; **sar'kastisch** *adj* sarcastic
**saß** [zaːs] *pret of* ***sitzen***
**Satan** ['zaːtan] *m* (*-s*; *-e*) Satan; *fig* devil
**Satellit** [zatɛ'liːt] *m* (*-en*; *-en*) satellite (*a. fig*); ***über*** **~** by *or* via satellite
**Satel'liten...** *in cpds* ...*bild*, ...*staat*, ...*stadt*, ...*-TV*: satellite ...
**Satin** [za'tɛ̃ː] *m* (*-s*; *-s*) satin; sateen
**Satire** [za'tiːrə] *f* (-; *-n*) satire (***auf*** *acc* upon); **Satiriker** [za'tiːrikɐ] *m* (*-s*; -) satirist; **sa'tirisch** *adj* satiric(al)
**satt** [zat] *adj* F full (up); ***ich bin ~*** I've had enough, F I'm full (up); ***sich ~ essen*** eat one's fill (***an*** *dat* of); F ***~ haben*** be tired *or* F sick of, be fed up with
**Sattel** ['zatəl] *m* (*-s*; *Sättel* ['zɛtəl]) saddle; '**satteln** *v/t* (*ge-*, *h*) saddle; '**Sattelschlepper** *m* MOT semi-trailer truck, *Br* articulated lorry
**sättigen** ['zɛtɪgən] (*ge-*, *h*) **1.** *v/t* satisfy; feed; CHEM, PHYS saturate; **2.** *v/i* be substantial, be filling; '**Sättigung** *f* (-; *-en*) satiety; CHEM, ECON saturation (*a. fig*)
**Sattler** ['zatlɐ] *m* (*-s*; -) saddler
**Sattlerei** [zatlə'rai] *f* (-; *-en*) saddlery
**Satz** [zats] *m* (*-es*; *Sätze* ['zɛtsə]) leap; LING sentence; *tennis etc*: set; ECON rate; MUS movement; **~aussage** *f* LING predicate; **~bau** *m* (-[*e*]*s*; *no pl*) LING syntax; construction; **~gegenstand** *m* LING subject
**Satzung** ['zatsʊŋ] *f* (-; *-en*) statute
'**Satzzeichen** *n* LING punctuation mark
**Sau** [zau] *f* (-; *Säue* ['zɔʏə]) ZO sow; HUNT wild sow; F swine, pig
**sauber** ['zaubɐ] *adj* clean (*a.* F *fig*); pure; neat (*a. fig*), tidy; decent; *iro* fine, nice; ***~ halten*** keep clean (***sich*** o.s.); ***~ machen*** clean (up); '**Sauberkeit** *f* (-; *no pl*) clean(li)ness; tidiness, neatness; purity; decency; **säubern** ['zɔʏbɐn] *v/t* (*ge-*, *h*) clean (up); cleanse (*a.* MED); ***~ von*** clear (POL *a.* purge) of
'**Säuberung(sakti͵on)** *f* POL purge
**sauer** ['zauɐ] *adj* sour (*a. fig*), acid (*a.* CHEM); GASTR pickled; F mad (***auf*** *acc* at), cross (with); ***~ werden*** turn sour; F get mad; ***saurer Regen*** acid rain
**säuerlich** ['zɔʏɐlɪç] *adj* sharp; F wry
'**Sauerstoff** *m* (-[*e*]*s*; *no pl*) CHEM oxygen; **~gerät** *n* MED oxygen apparatus; **~zelt** *n* MED oxygen tent
'**Sauerteig** *m* leaven
**saufen** ['zaufən] *v/t and v/i* (*irr*, *ge-*, *h*) ZO drink; F booze; **Säufer(in)** ['zɔʏfɐ (-fərɪn)] F (*-s*; *-/-*; *-nen*) drunkard, F boozer
**saugen** ['zaugən] *v/i and v/t* ([*irr*,] *ge-*, *h*) suck (***an et.*** [at] s.th.)
**säugen** ['zɔʏgən] *v/t* (*ge-*, *h*) suckle (*a.* ZO), nurse, breastfeed
'**Säugetier** *n* mammal
**saugfähig** ['zauk-] *adj* absorbent
**Säugling** ['zɔʏklɪŋ] *m* (*-s*; *-e*) baby, infant
'**Säuglings|heim** *n* (baby) nursery; **~pflege** *f* infant care; **~schwester** *f* baby nurse; **~stati͵on** *f* neonatal care unit; **~sterblichkeit** *f* infant mortality
**Säule** ['zɔʏlə] *f* (-; *-n*) column; pillar (*a. fig*); '**Säulengang** *m* colonnade
**Saum** [zaum] *m* (-[*e*]*s*; *Säume* ['zɔʏmə])

hem(line); seam; **säumen** ['zɔʏmən] *v/t* (*ge-, h*) hem; border, edge; line
**Sauna** ['zauna] *f* (-; *-s, Saunen*) sauna
**Säure** ['zɔʏrə] *f* (-; *-n*) CHEM acid
**'säurehaltig** [-haltıç] *adj* acid
**sausen** ['zauzən] *v/i* a) (*ge-, sein*) F rush, dash, b) (*ge-, h*) *ears*: buzz; *wind*: howl
**'Saustall** *m* pigsty (*a.* F *contp*)
**Saxophon** [zakso'fo:n] *n* (*-s; -e*) MUS saxophone, F sax
**S-Bahn** ['ɛsba:n] *f* rapid transit, *Br* suburban train
**Schabe** ['ʃa:bə] *f* (-; *-n*) ZO cockroach
**'schaben** *v/t* (*ge-, h*) scrape (***von*** from)
**schäbig** ['ʃɛ:bıç] *adj* shabby, *fig a.* mean
**Schablone** [ʃa'blo:nə] *f* (-; *-n*) stencil; *fig* stereotype
**Schach** [ʃax] *n* (*-s; no pl*) chess; ***~!*** check!; ***~ und matt!*** checkmate!; ***j-n in ~ halten*** keep s.o. in check; **~brett** *n* chessboard; **~feld** *n* square; **~fi,gur** *f* chessman, piece
**schach'matt** *adj*: ***j-n ~ setzen*** checkmate s.o.
**'Schachspiel** *n* (game of) chess; chessboard and men
**Schacht** [ʃaxt] *m* (-[*e*]*s*; *Schächte* ['ʃɛçtə]) shaft, *mining*: *a.* pit
**Schachtel** ['ʃaxtəl] *f* (-; *-n*) box; carton; ***e-e ~ Zigaretten*** a pack (*esp Br* packet) of cigarettes
**'Schachzug** *m* move (*a. fig*)
**schade** ['ʃa:də] *pred adj*: ***es ist ~*** it's a pity; ***wie ~!*** what a pity *or* shame!; ***zu ~ sein für*** be too good for
**Schädel** ['ʃɛ:dəl] *m* (*-s*; -) ANAT skull; **~bruch** *m* MED fracture of the skull
**schaden** ['ʃa:dən] *v/i* (*ge-, h*) damage, do damage to, harm, hurt; ***der Gesundheit ~*** be bad for one's health; ***das schadet nichts*** it doesn't matter; ***es könnte ihm nicht ~*** it wouldn't hurt him
**'Schaden** *m* (*-s*; *Schäden* ['ʃɛ:dən]) damage (***an*** *dat* to); *esp* TECH trouble, defect (*a.* MED); *fig* disadvantage; ECON loss; ***j-m ~ zufügen*** do s.o. harm; **~ersatz** *m* damages; ***~ leisten*** pay damages; **~freude** *f*: ***~ empfinden über*** (*acc*) gloat over
**'schadenfroh** *adv* gloatingly
**schadhaft** ['ʃa:thaft] *adj* damaged; defective, faulty; leaking (*pipes*)
**schädigen** ['ʃɛ:dıgən] *v/t* (*ge-, h*) damage, harm
**schädlich** ['ʃɛ:tlıç] *adj* harmful, injurious; bad (for your health)
**Schädling** ['ʃɛ:tlıŋ] *m* (*-s*; *-e*) BIOL pest
**'Schädlings|bekämpfung** *f* pest control; **~bekämpfungsmittel** *n* pesticide
**Schadstoff** ['ʃa:t-] *m* harmful substance; pollutant
**'schadstoffarm** *adj* MOT low-emission
**Schaf** [ʃa:f] *n* (-[*e*]*s*; *-e*) ZO sheep
**'Schafbock** *m* ZO ram
**Schäfer** ['ʃɛ:fɐ] *m* (*-s*; -) shepherd; **~hund** *m* sheepdog; ***Deutscher ~*** German shepherd, *esp Br* Alsatian
**'Schaffell** *n* sheepskin; ZO fleece
**schaffen**[1] ['ʃafən] *v/t* (*irr, ge-, h*) create
**'schaffen**[2] (*ge-, h*) **1.** *v/t* cause, bring about; manage, get *s.th.* done; take; ***es ~*** make it, *a.* succeed; **2.** *v/i* work; ***j-m zu ~ machen*** cause s.o. trouble; ***sich zu ~ machen an*** (*dat*) tamper with
**Schaffner** ['ʃafnɐ] *m* (*-s*; -), **'Schaffnerin** *f* (-; *-nen*) conductor; *Br* RAIL guard
**Schafott** [ʃa'fɔt] *n* (-[*e*]*s*; *-e*) scaffold
**Schaft** [ʃaft] *m* (-[*e*]*s*; *Schäfte* ['ʃɛftə]) shaft; stock; shank; leg
**'Schafwolle** *f* sheep's wool
**'Schafzucht** *f* sheep breeding
**schäkern** ['ʃɛ:kɐn] *v/i* (*ge-, h*) joke; flirt
**schal** [ʃa:l] *adj* stale, flat, *fig a.* empty
**Schal** *m* (*-s*; *-s*) scarf
**Schale** ['ʃa:lə] *f* (-; *-n*) bowl, dish; GASTR shell; peel, skin; **schälen** ['ʃɛ:lən] *v/t* (*ge-, h*) peel, pare; ***sich ~*** *skin*: peel (off)
**Schall** [ʃal] *m* (-[*e*]*s*; *-e*) sound; **~dämpfer** *m* silencer (*a. Br* MOT), MOT muffler
**'schalldicht** *adj* soundproof
**schallen** ['ʃalən] *v/i* ([*irr,*] *ge-, h*) sound; ring (out); ***~des Gelächter*** roars of laughter
**'Schall|geschwindigkeit** *f* speed of sound; **~mauer** *f* sound barrier; **~platte** *f* record, disk, *Br* disc; **~welle** *f* PHYS sound wave
**schalten** ['ʃaltən] *v/i and v/t* (*ge-, h*) switch, turn; MOT shift (*esp Br* change) gear; F get it; react; **Schalter** ['ʃaltɐ] *m* (*-s*; -) counter; RAIL ticket window; AVIAT desk; ELECTR switch
**'Schalt|hebel** *m* MOT gear lever; TECH, AVIAT control lever; ELECTR switch lever; **~jahr** *n* leap year; **~tafel** *f*

S

ELECTR switchboard, control panel; **~uhr** *f* time switch
'**Schaltung** *f* (-; *-en*) MOT gearshift; ELECTR circuit
**Scham** [ʃaːm] *f* (-; *no pl*) shame; ***vor ~*** with shame; **schämen** ['ʃɛːmən] *v/refl* (*ge-*, *h*) be *or* feel ashamed (*gen*, ***wegen*** of); ***du solltest dich*** (***was***) ***~!*** you ought to be ashamed of yourself!
'**Scham|gefühl** *n* (-[*e*]*s*; *no pl*) sense of shame; **~haare** *pl* pubic hair
'**schamhaft** *adj* bashful
'**schamlos** *adj* shameless; indecent
**Schande** ['ʃandə] *f* (-; *no pl*) shame, disgrace; **schänden** ['ʃɛndən] *v/t* (*ge-*, *h*) disgrace; desecrate; rape
**Schandfleck** ['ʃant-] *m* eyesore
**schändlich** ['ʃɛntlɪç] *adj* disgraceful
'**Schandtat** *f* atrocity
**Schanze** ['ʃantsə] *f* (-; *-n*) SPORT ski jump
**Schar** [ʃaːɐ] *f* (-; *-en* ['ʃaːrən]) troop, band; F horde; crowd; ZO flock
'**scharen** *v/refl* (*ge-*, *h*) ***sich ~ um*** gather round
**scharf** [ʃarf] *adj* sharp (*a. fig*), PHOT *a.* in focus; clear; savage, fierce (*dog*); live (*ammunition*), armed (*bomb etc*); GASTR hot; F hot, sexy; F ***~ sein auf*** (*acc*) be keen on; ***~*** (***ein***)***stellen*** PHOT focus; F ***~e Sachen*** hard liquor
**Schärfe** ['ʃɛrfə] *f* (-; *-n*) sharpness (*a.* PHOT); *fig* severity, fierceness
'**schärfen** *v/t* (*ge-*, *h*) sharpen
'**Scharf|richter** *m* executioner; **~schütze** *m* sharpshooter; sniper
'**scharfsichtig** *adj* sharp-sighted; *fig* clear-sighted
'**Scharfsinn** *m* (-[*e*]*s*; *no pl*) acumen
'**scharfsinnig** *adj* sharp-witted, shrewd
**Scharlach** ['ʃarlax] *m* (*-s*; *no pl*) scarlet; MED scarlet fever
'**scharlachrot** *adj* scarlet
**Scharlatan** ['ʃarlatan] *m* (*-s*; *-e*) charlatan, fraud
**Scharnier** [ʃar'niːɐ] *n* (*-s*; *-e*) TECH hinge
**Schärpe** ['ʃɛrpə] *f* (-; *-n*) sash
**scharren** ['ʃarən] *v/i* (*ge-*, *h*) scrape, scratch
**schartig** ['ʃartɪç] *adj* jagged, notchy
**Schaschlik** ['ʃaʃlɪk] *m*, *n* (*-s*; *-s*) GASTR shish kebab
**Schatten** ['ʃatən] *m* (*-s*; -) shadow (*a. fig*); shade; ***im ~*** in the shade
'**schattenhaft** *adj* shadowy
**Schattierung** [ʃa'tiːrʊŋ] *f* (-; *-en*) shade; *fig* colo(u)r
**schattig** ['ʃatɪç] *adj* shady
**Schatz** [ʃats] *m* (*-es*; *Schätze* ['ʃɛtsə]) treasure; *fig* darling; **~amt** *n* POL Treasury Department, *Br* Treasury
**schätzen** ['ʃɛtsən] *v/t* (*ge-*, *h*) estimate, value (*both*: ***auf*** *acc* at); appreciate; think highly of; F reckon, guess
'**Schatz|kammer** *f* treasury (*a. fig*); **~kanzler** *m* Chancellor of the Exchequer; **~meister(in)** treasurer
'**Schätzung** *f* (-; *-en*) estimate; valuation
**Schau** [ʃau] *f* (-; *-en*) show, exhibition; ***zur ~ stellen*** exhibit, display
**Schauder** ['ʃaudɐ] *m* (*-s*; -) shudder
'**schauderhaft** *adj* horrible, dreadful
'**schaudern** *v/i* (*ge-*, *h*) shudder, shiver (*both*: ***vor*** *dat* with)
**schauen** ['ʃauən] *v/i* (*ge-*, *h*) look (***auf*** *acc* at)
**Schauer** ['ʃauɐ] *m* (*-s*; -) METEOR shower; shudder, shiver; **~geschichte** *f* horror story (*a. fig*)
'**schauerlich** *adj* dreadful, horrible
**Schaufel** ['ʃaufəl] *f* (-; *-n*) shovel; dustpan; '**schaufeln** *v/t* (*ge-*, *h*) shovel; dig
'**Schaufenster** *n* shop window; **~auslage** *f* window display; **~bummel** *m*: ***e-n ~ machen*** go window-shopping; **~dekorati,on** *f* window dressing
**Schaukel** ['ʃaukəl] *f* (-; *-n*) swing
'**schaukeln** (*ge-*, *h*) **1.** *v/i* swing; *boat etc*: rock; **2.** *v/t* rock
'**Schaukel|pferd** *n* rocking horse; **~stuhl** *m* rocking chair, rocker
'**Schaulustige** [-lʊstɪgə] *pl* (curious) onlookers, F rubbernecks
**Schaum** [ʃaum] *m* (-[*e*]*s*; *Schäume* ['ʃɔʏmə]) foam; GASTR froth, head; lather; spray; **schäumen** ['ʃɔʏmən] *v/i* (*ge-*, *h*) foam (*a. fig*), froth; lather; spray
'**Schaumgummi** *m* foam rubber
**schaumig** ['ʃaumɪç] *adj* foamy, frothy
'**Schaumlöscher** *m* foam extinguisher
'**Schauplatz** *m* scene
'**Schaupro,zess** *m* JUR show trial
**schaurig** ['ʃaurɪç] *adj* creepy; horrible
'**Schauspiel** *n* THEA play; *fig* spectacle
'**Schauspieler(in)** actor (actress)
'**Schauspielschule** *f* drama school
'**Schausteller** [-ʃtɛlɐ] *m* (*-s*; -) showman

S

**Scheck** [ʃɛk] *m* (*-s*; *-s*) ECON check, *Br* cheque; **~heft** *n* checkbook, *Br* chequebook
**scheckig** ['ʃɛkɪç] *adj* spotty
'**Scheckkarte** *f* check cashing (*Br* cheque) card
**scheffeln** ['ʃɛfəln] F *v/t* (*ge-*, *h*) rake in
**Scheibe** ['ʃaibə] *f* (*-*; *-n*) disk, *Br* disc; slice; pane; target
'**Scheiben|bremse** *f* MOT disk (*Br* disc) brake; **~wischer** *m* MOT windshield (*Br* windscreen) wiper
**Scheide** ['ʃaidə] *f* (*-*; *-n*) sheath; scabbard; ANAT vagina; '**scheiden** (*irr*, *ge-*) **1.** *v/t* (*h*) separate, part (*both*: ***von*** from); divorce; ***sich ~ lassen*** get a divorce, ***von j-m:*** divorce s.o.; **2.** *v/i* (*sein*) part; ***~ aus*** (*dat*) retire from
'**Scheideweg** *m* crossroads
'**Scheidung** *f* (*-*; *-en*) divorce
'**Scheidungsklage** *f* JUR divorce suit
**Schein**[1] [ʃain] *m* (*-[e]s*; *-e*) certificate; blank, *Br* form; bill, *Br* note
**Schein**[2] *m* (*-[e]s*; *no pl*) light; *fig* appearance; ***et.*** (***nur***) ***zum ~ tun*** (only) pretend to do s.th.
'**scheinbar** *adj* seeming, apparent
**scheinen** ['ʃainən] *v/i* (*irr*, *ge-*, *h*) shine; *fig* seem, appear, look
'**scheinheilig** *adj* hypocritical
'**Scheinwerfer** *m* searchlight; MOT headlight; THEA spotlight
**Scheiß...** ['ʃais-] V *in cpds* damn ..., fucking ..., *esp Br* bloody ...
**Scheiße** ['ʃaisə] V *f* (*-*; *no pl*), '**scheißen** V *v/i* (*irr*, *ge-*, *h*) shit, crap
**Scheit** [ʃait] *n* (*-[e]s*; *-e*) piece of wood
**Scheitel** ['ʃaitəl] *m* (*-s*; *-*) parting
'**scheiteln** *v/t* (*ge-*, *h*) part
**Scheiterhaufen** ['ʃaitɐ-] *m* pyre; HIST stake
**scheitern** ['ʃaitɐn] *v/i* (*ge-*, *sein*) fail, go wrong
**Schelle** ['ʃɛlə] *f* (*-*; *-n*) (little) bell; TECH clamp, clip
**Schellfisch** ['ʃɛl-] *m* ZO haddock
**Schelm** [ʃɛlm] *m* (*-[e]s*; *-e*) rascal
**schelmisch** ['ʃɛlmɪʃ] *adj* impish
**Schema** ['ʃeːma] *n* (*-s*; *-s*, *-ta*) pattern, system; **schematisch** [ʃe'maːtɪʃ] *adj* schematic; mechanical
**Schemel** ['ʃeːməl] *m* (*-s*; *-*) stool
**schemenhaft** ['ʃeːmən-] *adj* shadowy
**Schenkel** ['ʃɛŋkəl] *m* (*-s*; *-*) ANAT thigh; shank; MATH leg
**schenken** ['ʃɛŋkən] *v/t* (*ge-*, *h*) give (as a present) (***zu*** for)
'**Schenkung** *f* (*-*; *-en*) JUR donation
**Scherbe** ['ʃɛrbə] *f* (*-*; *-n*), '**Scherben** *m* (*-s*; *-*) (broken) piece, fragment
**Schere** ['ʃeːrə] *f* (*-*; *-n*) scissors; ZO claw
**scheren**[1] ['ʃeːrən] *v/t* (*irr*, *ge-*, *h*) ZO shear; BOT clip; cut
'**scheren**[2] *v/refl* (*ge-*, *h*) ***sich ~ um*** bother about
**Scherereien** [ʃeːrə'raiən] *pl* trouble, bother
**Schermaus** ['ʃeːɐ-] *Austrian f* ZO mole
**Scherz** [ʃɛrts] *m* (*-es*; *-e*) joke; ***im*** (***zum***) ***~*** for fun; **scherzen** ['ʃɛrtsən] *v/i* (*ge-*, *h*) joke (***über*** *acc* at); '**scherzhaft** *adj* joking; ***~ gemeint*** meant as a joke
**scheu** [ʃɔʏ] *adj* shy (*a.* ZO); bashful; ***~ machen*** frighten; **Scheu** *f* (*-*; *no pl*) shyness; awe; **scheuen** ['ʃɔʏən] (*ge-*, *h*) **1.** *v/i* shy (***vor*** *dat* at), take fright (at); **2.** *v/t* shun, avoid; fear; ***sich ~, et. zu tun*** be afraid of doing s.th.
**scheuern** ['ʃɔʏɐn] *v/t and v/i* (*ge-*, *h*) scrub, scour; chafe
'**Scheuertuch** *n* floor cloth
'**Scheuklappen** *pl* blinders, *Br* blinkers (*both a. fig*)
**Scheune** ['ʃɔʏnə] *f* (*-*; *-n*) barn
**Scheusal** ['ʃɔʏzaːl] *n* (*-s*; *-e*) monster (*a. fig*); *fig* beast
**scheußlich** ['ʃɔʏslɪç] *adj* horrible (*a.* F), atrocious
**Schicht** [ʃɪçt] *f* (*-*; *-en*) layer; coat; film; ECON shift; class; **schichten** ['ʃɪçtən] *v/t* (*ge-*, *h*) arrange in layers, pile up
'**schichtweise** *adv* in layers
**schick** [ʃɪk] *adj* smart, chic, stylish
**schicken** ['ʃɪkən] *v/t* (*ge-*, *h*) send (***nach***, ***zu*** to); ***das schickt sich nicht*** that isn't done
**Schickeria** [ʃɪkə'riːa] F *f* (*-*; *no pl*) smart set, beautiful people, trendies
**Schickimicki** [ʃɪki'mɪki] F *contp m* (*-s*; *-s*) trendy
**Schicksal** ['ʃɪkzaːl] *n* (*-s*; *-e*) fate, destiny; lot
**Schiebe|dach** ['ʃiːbə-] *n* MOT sliding roof, sunroof; **~fenster** *n* sliding window; sash window
**schieben** ['ʃiːbən] *v/t* (*irr*, *ge-*, *h*) push
**Schieber** ['ʃiːbɐ] *m* (*-s*; *-*) TECH slide; bolt; F profiteer

S

'**Schiebetür** *f* sliding door
'**Schiebung** F *f* (-; *-en*) swindle, fix (*a.* SPORT)
**schied** [ʃi:t] *pret of* ***scheiden***
**Schiedsrichter** ['ʃi:ts-] *m*, '**Schiedsrichterin** *f soccer*: referee; *tennis*: umpire; judge, *esp pl a.* jury
**schief** [ʃi:f] *adj* crooked, not straight; sloping, oblique (*a.* MATH); leaning; *fig* false; F ~ ***gehen*** go wrong
**Schiefer** ['ʃi:fɐ] *m* (*-s*; -) GEOL slate
'**Schiefertafel** *f* slate
**schielen** ['ʃi:lən] *v/i* (*ge-*, *h*) squint, be cross-eyed
**schien** [ʃi:n] *pret of* ***scheinen***
**Schienbein** ['ʃi:n-] *n* ANAT shin(bone)
**Schiene** ['ʃi:nə] *f* (-; *-n*) TECH *etc* rail; MED splint
'**schienen** *v/t* (*ge-*, *h*) MED splint
**Schießbude** ['ʃi:s-] *f* shooting gallery
**schießen** ['ʃi:sən] *v/i and v/t* (*irr*, *ge-*, *h*) shoot, fire (*both*: ***auf*** *acc* at); SPORT score; **Schießerei** [ʃi:sə'rai] *f* (-; *-en*) shooting; gunfight
'**Schieß|pulver** *n* gunpowder; **~scharte** *f* MIL loophole, embrasure; **~scheibe** *f* target; **~stand** *m* shooting range
**Schiff** [ʃɪf] *n* (-[*e*]*s*; *-e*) MAR ship, boat; ARCH nave; ***mit dem*** ~ by boat
**Schiffahrt** *f* → ***Schifffahrt***
'**schiffbar** *adj* navigable
'**Schiffbau** *m* (-[*e*]*s*; *no pl*) shipbuilding
'**Schiffbruch** *m* shipwreck (*a. fig*); ~ ***erleiden*** be shipwrecked
**Schiffer** ['ʃɪfɐ] *m* (*-s*; -) sailor; skipper
'**Schifffahrt** *f* (-; *no pl*) shipping, navigation
'**Schiffs|junge** *m* ship's boy; **~ladung** *f* shipload; cargo; **~schraube** *f* (ship's) propeller; **~werft** *f* shipyard
**Schikane** [ʃi'ka:nə] *f* (-; *-n*) *a. pl* harassment; ***aus reiner*** ~ out of sheer spite; F ***mit allen ~n*** with all the trimmings
**schikanieren** [ʃika'ni:rən] *v/t* (*no -ge-*, *h*) harass; bully
**Schild**[1] [ʃɪlt] *n* (-[*e*]*s*; *-er* ['ʃɪldɐ]) sign, plate
**Schild**[2] *m* (-[*e*]*s*; *-e*) shield
'**Schilddrüse** *f* ANAT thyroid (gland)
**schildern** ['ʃɪldɐn] *v/t* (*ge-*, *h*) describe; depict, portray
**Schilderung** ['ʃɪldərʊŋ] *f* (-; *-en*) description, portrayal; account
'**Schildkröte** *f* ZO tortoise; turtle
**Schilf** [ʃɪlf] *n* (-[*e*]*s*; *no pl*) BOT reed(s)
**schillern** ['ʃɪlɐn] *v/i* (*ge-*, *h*) be iridescent; **~d** *adj* iridescent; *fig* dubious
**Schimmel** ['ʃɪməl] *m* ZO white horse; BOT mo(u)ld; **schimm(e)lig** ['ʃɪm(ə)lɪç] *adj* mo(u)ldy, musty; '**schimmeln** *v/i* (*ge-*, *h*, *sein*) go mo(u)ldy
**Schimmer** ['ʃɪmɐ] *m* (*-s*; -) glimmer (*a. fig*), gleam, *fig a.* trace, touch
'**schimmern** *v/i* (*ge-*, *h*) shimmer, glimmer, gleam
**Schimpanse** [ʃɪm'panzə] *m* (*-n*; *-n*) ZO chimpanzee
**schimpfen** ['ʃɪmpfən] *v/i and v/t* (*ge-*, *h*) scold (***mit j-m*** s.o.); F tell *s.o.* off, bawl *s.o.* out; ~ ***über*** (*acc*) complain about
'**Schimpfwort** *n* swearword
**Schindel** ['ʃɪndəl] *f* (-; *-n*) shingle
**schinden** ['ʃɪndən] *v/t* (*irr*, *ge-*, *h*) maltreat; slave-drive; ***sich*** ~ drudge, slave away; **Schinder** ['ʃɪndɐ] *m* (*-s*; -) slave driver; **Schinderei** [ʃɪndə'rai] *f* (-; *-en*) slavery, drudgery
**Schinken** ['ʃɪŋkən] *m* (*-s*; -) ham
**Schippe** ['ʃɪpə] *f* (-; *-n*), '**schippen** *v/t* (*ge-*, *h*) shovel
**Schirm** [ʃɪrm] *m* (-[*e*]*s*; *-e*) umbrella; sunshade; TV, EDP *etc*: screen; shade; peak, visor; **~herr(in)** patron, sponsor; **~herrschaft** *f* patronage, sponsorship; ***unter der*** ~ ***von*** under the auspices of; **~mütze** *f* peaked cap; **~ständer** *m* umbrella stand
**schiss** [ʃɪs] *pret of* scheißen
**Schlacht** [ʃlaxt] *f* (-; *-en*) battle (***bei*** of)
'**schlachten** *v/t* (*ge-*, *h*) slaughter, kill, butcher
**Schlachter** ['ʃlaxtɐ] *m* (*-s*; -) butcher
'**Schlacht|feld** *n* MIL battlefield, battleground; **~haus** *n*, **~hof** *m* slaughterhouse; **~plan** *m* MIL plan of action (*a. fig*); **~schiff** *n* MIL battleship
**Schlacke** ['ʃlakə] *f* (-; *-n*) cinders; GEOL, METALL slag
**Schlaf** [ʃla:f] *m* (-[*e*]*s*; *no pl*) sleep; ***e-n leichten*** (***festen***) ~ ***haben*** be a light (sound) sleeper; F *fig* ***im*** ~ blindfold
'**Schlafanzug** *m* pajamas, *Br* pyjamas
**Schläfe** ['ʃlɛ:fə] *f* (-; *-n*) ANAT temple
**schlafen** ['ʃla:fən] *v/i* (*irr*, *ge-*, *h*) sleep (*a. fig*); ~ ***gehen***, ***sich*** ~ ***legen*** go to bed; ***fest*** ~ be fast asleep; ***j-n*** ~ ***legen*** put s.o. to bed *or* to sleep
**schlaff** [ʃlaf] *adj* slack (*a. fig*); flabby; limp

S

**'Schlaf|gelegenheit** *f* sleeping accommodation; **~krankheit** *f* MED sleeping sickness; **~lied** *n* lullaby
**'schlaflos** *adj* sleepless
**'Schlaflosigkeit** *f* (-; *no pl*) sleeplessness, MED insomnia
**'Schlafmittel** *n* MED sleeping pill(s)
**'Schlafmütze** *fig f* sleepyhead; slowpoke, *Br* slowcoach
**schläfrig** ['ʃlɛːfrɪç] *adj* sleepy, drowsy
**'Schlaf|saal** *m* dormitory; **~sack** *m* sleeping bag; **~ta,blette** *f* sleeping pill
**'schlaftrunken** *adj* (very) drowsy
**'Schlaf|wagen** *m* RAIL sleeping car, sleeper; **~wandler(in)** [-vandlɐ (-lərɪn)] (*-s*; *-/-*; *-nen*) sleepwalker, somnambulist; **~zimmer** *n* bedroom
**Schlag** [ʃlaːk] *m* (*-[e]s*; *Schläge* ['ʃlɛːgə]) blow (*a. fig*); slap; punch; pat, tap; *a. tennis*: stroke; ELECTR shock (*a. fig*); MED beat; *pl* beating; → ***Schlaganfall***; **~ader** *f* ANAT artery; **~anfall** *m* MED (apoplectic) stroke
**'schlagartig 1.** *adj* sudden, abrupt; **2.** *adv* all of a sudden, abruptly
**'Schlagbaum** *m* barrier
**'Schlagbohrer** *m* TECH percussion drill
**schlagen** ['ʃlaːgən] (*irr*, *ge-*, *h*) **1.** *v/t* hit, beat (*a.* GASTR *and fig*), strike, knock; fell, cut (down); ***sich ~*** fight (***um*** over); ***sich geschlagen geben*** admit defeat; **2.** *v/i* hit, beat (*a. heart etc*), strike (*a. clock*), knock; ***an*** *or* ***gegen et. ~*** hit s.th., bump *or* crash into s.th.
**Schlager** ['ʃlaːgɐ] *m* (*-s*; *-*) MUS hit (*a. fig*), (pop) song
**Schläger** ['ʃlɛːgɐ] *m* (*-s*; *-*) *tennis etc*: racket; *table tennis, cricket, baseball*: bat; *golf*: club; *hockey*: stick; *contp* thug; **Schlägerei** [ʃlɛːgə'rai] *f* (*-*; *-en*) fight, brawl
**'schlagfertig** *adj* quick-witted; ***~e Antwort*** (witty) repartee
**'Schlag|instru,ment** *n* MUS percussion instrument; **~kraft** *f* (*-*; *no pl*) striking power (*a.* MIL); **~loch** *n* pot-hole; **~obers** *Austrian n*, **~sahne** *f* whipped cream; **~seite** *f* MAR list; ***~ haben*** be listing; **~stock** *m* baton, truncheon; **~wort** *n* catchword, slogan; **~zeile** *f* headline
**'Schlagzeug** *n* MUS drums
**'Schlagzeuger** [-tsɔygɐ] *m* (*-s*; *-*) MUS drummer

**schlaksig** ['ʃlaːksɪç] *adj* lanky, gangling
**Schlamm** [ʃlam] *m* (*-[e]s*; *-e*) mud
**schlammig** ['ʃlamɪç] *adj* muddy
**Schlampe** ['ʃlampə] F *f* (*-*; *-n*) slut
**schlampig** ['ʃlampɪç] F *adj* sloppy
**schlang** [ʃlaŋ] *pret of* ***schlingen***
**Schlange** ['ʃlaŋə] *f* (*-*; *-n*) ZO snake, serpent (*a. fig*); *fig* line, *esp Br* queue; ***~ stehen*** line up, stand in line, *esp Br* queue (up) (***nach*** for); **schlängeln** ['ʃlɛŋəln] *v/refl* (*ge-*, *h*) wind *or* weave (one's way), *person*: worm one's way
**'Schlangenlinie** *f* serpentine line; ***in ~n fahren*** weave
**schlank** [ʃlaŋk] *adj* slim, slender; ***j-n ~ machen*** make s.o. look slim; ***~e Unternehmensstruktur*** ECON lean management; **'Schlankheitskur** *f*: ***e-e ~ machen*** be slimming
**schlapp** [ʃlap] F *adj* worn out; weak;
**Schlappe** ['ʃlapə] F *f* (*-*; *-n*) setback, beating; **'schlappmachen** F *v/i* (*sep*, *-ge-*, *h*) flake out; **'Schlappschwanz** F *m* weakling, wimp
**schlau** [ʃlau] *adj* clever, smart, bright; sly, cunning, crafty
**Schlauch** [ʃlaux] *m* (*-[e]s*; *Schläuche* ['ʃlɔyçə]) tube; hose; **~boot** *n* (inflatable *or* rubber) dinghy
**Schlaufe** ['ʃlaufə] *f* (*-*; *-n*) loop
**schlecht** [ʃlɛçt] *adj* bad; poor; ***mir ist*** (***wird***) ~ I feel (I'm getting) sick to my stomach; ***~ aussehen*** look ill; ***sich ~ fühlen*** feel bad; ***~ werden*** GASTR go bad; ***es geht ihm sehr ~*** he is in a bad way; ***~ gelaunt*** in a bad temper *or* mood, bad-tempered; F ***j-n ~ machen*** run s.o. down, backbite s.o.
**schleichen** ['ʃlaiçən] *v/i* (*irr*, *ge-*, *sein*) creep (*a. fig*), sneak; **'Schleichweg** *m* secret path; **'Schleichwerbung** *f* plugging; ***für et. ~ machen*** plug s.th.
**Schleier** ['ʃlaiɐ] *m* (*-s*; *-*) veil (*a. fig*); haze; **'schleierhaft** *adj*: F ***es ist mir ~*** it's a mystery to me
**Schleife** ['ʃlaifə] *f* (*-*; *-n*) bow; ribbon; AVIAT, EDP, ELECTR, GEOGR loop
**schleifen**[1] ['ʃlaifən] *v/t and v/i* (*ge-*, *h*) drag (along); rub
**'schleifen**[2] *v/t* (*irr*, *ge-*, *h*) grind (*a.* TECH), sharpen; sand(paper); cut; F drill *s.o.* hard
**Schleifer** ['ʃlaifɐ] *m* (*-s*; *-*), **'Schleifma,schine** *f* TECH grinder

S

'**Schleifpa,pier** *n* sandpaper
'**Schleifstein** *m* grindstone; whetstone
**Schleim** [ʃlaim] *m* (-[*e*]*s*; -*e*) slime; MED mucus; '**Schleimhaut** *f* ANAT mucous membrane; **schleimig** ['ʃlaimıç] *adj* slimy (*a. fig*); MED mucous
**schlemmen** ['ʃlɛmən] *v/i* (*ge-*, *h*) feast
**schlendern** ['ʃlɛndɐn] *v/i* (*ge-*, *sein*) stroll, saunter, amble
**schlenkern** ['ʃlɛŋkɐn] *v/i and v/t* (*ge-*, *h*) dangle, swing (***mit den Armen*** one's arms)
**schleppen** ['ʃlɛpən] *v/t* (*ge-*, *h*) drag (*a. fig*); MOT, MAR tow; ***sich ~*** drag (on); **~d** *adj* dragging; *fig* drawling
**Schlepper** ['ʃlɛpɐ] *m* (-*s*; -) MAR tug; MOT tractor
'**Schlepp|lift** *m* T-bar (lift), drag lift, ski tow; **~tau** *n* tow-rope; ***im*** (***ins***) **~** in tow (*a. fig*)
**Schleuder** ['ʃlɔʏdɐ] *f* (-; -*n*) catapult, slingshot; TECH spin drier
'**schleudern** (*ge-*, *h*) **1.** *v/t* fling, hurl (*both a. fig*); spin-dry; **2.** *v/i* MOT skid
'**Schleudersitz** *m* AVIAT ejection (*esp Br* ejector) seat
**schleunigst** ['ʃlɔʏnıçst] *adv* immediately
**Schleuse** ['ʃlɔʏzə] *f* (-; -*n*) sluice; lock
**schlich** [ʃlıç] *pret of* ***schleichen***
**schlicht** [ʃlıçt] *adj* plain, simple
**schlichten** ['ʃlıçtən] *v/t* (*ge-*, *h*) settle
'**Schlichtung** *f* (-; -*en*) settlement
**schlief** [ʃli:f] *pret of* ***schlafen***
**schließen** ['ʃli:sən] *v/t and v/i* (*irr*, *ge-*, *h*) shut, close (down); *fig* close, finish; **~ *aus*** (*dat*) conclude from; ***nach ... zu ~*** judging by ...
**Schließfach** ['ʃli:s-] *n* safe-deposit box; RAIL *etc*: (left luggage) locker
**schließlich** ['ʃli:slıç] *adv* finally; eventually, in the end; after all
**schliff** [ʃlıf] *pret of* ***schleifen***[2]
**Schliff** *m* (-[*e*]*s*; -*e*) cut; polish (*a. fig*)
**schlimm** [ʃlım] *adj* bad; awful; ***das ist nicht*** *or* ***halb so ~*** it's not as bad as that; ***das Schlimme daran*** the bad thing about it
'**schlimmsten'falls** *adv* at (the) worst
**Schlinge** ['ʃlıŋə] *f* (-; -*n*) loop; noose; HUNT snare (*a. fig*); MED sling
**Schlingel** ['ʃlıŋəl] *m* (-*s*; -) rascal
**schlingen** ['ʃlıŋən] *v/t* (*irr*, *ge-*, *h*) wind, twist; tie; wrap (***um*** [a]round); gobble; ***sich um et. ~*** wind (a)round s.th.
**schlingern** ['ʃlıŋɐn] *v/i* (*ge-*, *h*) MAR roll
'**Schlingpflanze** *f* BOT creeper, climber
**Schlips** [ʃlıps] *m* (-*es*; -*e*) necktie, *esp Br* tie
**schlitteln** ['ʃlıtəln] *Swiss v/i* (*ge-*, *sein*) go sledging, go tobogganing
**Schlitten** ['ʃlıtən] *m* (-*s*; -) sled, *Br* sledge; sleigh; SPORT toboggan; **~ *fahren*** go sledging, go tobogganing
**Schlittschuh** ['ʃlıt-] *m* ice-skate (*a.* **~ *laufen***); **~läufer(in)** ice-skater
**Schlitz** [ʃlıts] *m* (-*es*; -*e*) slit; slot
**schlitzen** ['ʃlıtsən] *v/t ge-*, *h*) slit, slash
**schloss** [ʃlɔs] *pret of* ***schließen***
**Schloss** *n* (-*es*; *Schlösser* ['ʃlœsɐ]) TECH lock; ARCH castle, palace; ***ins ~ fallen*** *door*: slam shut; ***hinter ~ und Riegel*** locked up, under lock and key
**Schlosser** ['ʃlɔsɐ] *m* (-*s*; -) metalworker; locksmith; **Schlosserei** [ʃlɔsə'rai] *f* (-; -*en*) metalwork shop
**schlottern** ['ʃlɔtɐn] *v/i* (*ge-*, *h*) shake, tremble (*both*: ***vor*** *dat* with); bag
**Schlucht** [ʃlʊxt] *f* (-; -*en*) canyon, gorge, ravine
**schluchzen** ['ʃlʊxtsən] *v/i* (*ge-*, *h*), **Schluchzer** ['ʃlʊxtsɐ] *m* (-*s*; -) sob
**Schluck** [ʃlʊk] *m* (-[*e*]*s*; -*e*) draught, swallow; sip; gulp; '**Schluckauf** *m* (-*s*; *no pl*) hiccups; **(*e-n*) ~ *haben*** have (the) hiccups; **schlucken** ['ʃlʊkən] *v/t and v/i* (*ge-*, *h*) swallow (*a. fig*)
'**Schluckimpfung** *f* MED oral vaccination
**schlug** [ʃlu:k] *pret of* ***schlagen***
**Schlummer** ['ʃlʊmɐ] *m* (-*s*; *no pl*) slumber; '**schlummern** *v/i* (*ge-*, *h*) lie asleep; *fig* slumber
**schlüpfen** ['ʃlʏpfən] *v/i* (*ge-*, *sein*) slip, slide; ZO hatch (out); **Schlüpfer** ['ʃlʏpfɐ] *m* (-*s*; -) briefs, panties
**schlüpfrig** ['ʃlʏpfrıç] *adj* slippery; *contp* risqué, off-colo(u)r
**Schlupfwinkel** ['ʃlʊpf-] *m* hiding place
**schlurfen** ['ʃlʊrfən] *v/i* (*ge-*, *sein*) shuffle (along)
**schlürfen** ['ʃlʏrfən] *v/t and v/i* (*ge-*, *h*) slurp
**Schluss** [ʃlʊs] *m* (-*es*; *no pl*) end; conclusion; ending; **~ *machen*** finish; break up; **~ *machen mit*** stop *s.th.*, put an end to *s.th.*; ***zum ~*** finally; **(*ganz*) *bis zum ~*** to the (very) end; **~ *für heute!*** that's all for today!

**Schlüssel** ['ʃlʏsəl] *m* (*-s*; -) key (***für, zu*** to); **~bein** *n* ANAT collarbone; **~blume** *f* BOT cowslip, primrose; **~bund** *m, n* bunch of keys; **~kind** F *n* latchkey child; **~loch** *n* keyhole; **~wort** *n* keyword, EDP *a.* password
'**Schlussfolgerung** *f* conclusion
**schlüssig** ['ʃlʏsɪç] *adj* conclusive; ***sich ~ werden*** make up one's mind (***über*** *acc* about)
'**Schluss|licht** *n* MOT *etc*: tail-light; **~pfiff** *m* SPORT final whistle; **~phase** *f* final stage(s); **~verkauf** *m* ECON (end-of-season) sale
**schmächtig** ['ʃmɛçtɪç] *adj* slight, thin, frail
**schmackhaft** ['ʃmakhaft] *adj* tasty
**schmal** [ʃma:l] *adj* narrow; thin, slender (*a. fig*); **schmälern** ['ʃmɛ:lɐn] *v/t* (*ge-, h*) detract from
'**Schmalfilm** *m* cinefilm
'**Schmalspur** *f* RAIL narrow ga(u)ge
'**Schmalspur...** *fig in cpds* small-time ...
**Schmalz** [ʃmalts] *n* (*-es; -e*) grease; lard
**schmalzig** ['ʃmaltsɪç] F *adj* schmaltzy, mushy, *Br* soapy
**schmarotzen** [ʃma'rɔtsən] F *v/i* (*no -ge-, h*) sponge (***bei*** on)
**Schmarotzer** [ʃma'rɔtsɐ] *m* (*-s*; -) BOT, ZO parasite, *fig a.* sponger
**schmatzen** ['ʃmatsən] *v/i* smack (one's lips), eat noisily
**schmecken** ['ʃmɛkən] *v/i and v/t* (*ge-, h*) taste (***nach*** of); ***gut*** (***schlecht***) **~** taste good (bad); (***wie***) ***schmeckt dir ...?*** (how) do you like ...? (*a. fig*); ***es schmeckt süß*** (***nach nichts***) it has a sweet (no) taste
**Schmeichelei** [ʃmaiçə'lai] *f* (-; *-en*) flattery; '**schmeichelhaft** *adj* flattering; '**schmeicheln** *v/i* (*ge-, h*) flatter (***j-m*** s.o.); **Schmeichler(in)** ['ʃmaiçlɐ (-lərɪn)] (*-s; -/-; -nen*) flatterer; **schmeichlerisch** ['ʃmaiçlərɪʃ] *adj* flattering
**schmeißen** ['ʃmaisən] F *v/t and v/i* (*irr, ge-, h*) throw, chuck; slam; ***mit Geld um sich ~*** throw one's money about
'**Schmeißfliege** *f* ZO blowfly, bluebottle
**schmelzen** ['ʃmɛltsən] *v/i* (*irr, ge-, sein*) *and v/t* (*h*) melt; thaw; TECH smelt
'**Schmelz|ofen** *m* (s)melting furnace; **~tiegel** *m* melting pot (*a. fig*)

**Schmerz** [ʃmɛrts] *m* (*-es; -en*) pain (*a. fig*), ache; *fig* grief, sorrow
**schmerzen** ['ʃmɛrtsən] *v/i and v/t* (*ge-, h*) hurt (*a. fig*), ache; *esp fig* pain
'**schmerzfrei** *adj* without pain
'**schmerzhaft** *adj* painful
'**schmerzlich** *adj* painful, sad
'**schmerzlos** *adj* painless
'**Schmerzmittel** *n* PHARM painkiller
'**schmerzstillend** *adj* painkilling
**Schmetterling** ['ʃmɛtɐlɪŋ] *m* (*-s; -e*) ZO butterfly
**schmettern** ['ʃmɛtɐn] (*ge-, h*) **1.** *v/t* smash (*a. tennis*); F MUS belt out; **2.** *v/i* a) (*sein*) crash, slam, b) MUS blare
**Schmied** [ʃmi:t] *m* (*-[e]s; -e*) (black-)smith; **Schmiede** ['ʃmi:də] *f* (-; *-n*) forge, smithy; '**Schmiedeeisen** *n* wrought iron; '**schmieden** *v/t* (*ge-, h*) forge; *fig* make (*plans etc*)
**schmiegen** ['ʃmi:gən] *v/refl* (*ge-, h*) ***sich ~ an*** (*acc*) snuggle up to; *dress etc*: cling to
**Schmiere** ['ʃmi:rə] *f* (-; *-n*) grease
'**schmieren** *v/t* (*ge-, h*) TECH grease, oil, lubricate; spread (*butter etc*); *contp* scribble, scrawl; **Schmiererei** [ʃmi:rə'rai] *f* (-; *-en*) scrawl; graffiti
**schmierig** ['ʃmi:rɪç] *adj* greasy; dirty; filthy; *contp* slimy
**Schmiermittel** ['ʃmi:ɐ-] *n* TECH lubricant
**Schminke** ['ʃmɪŋkə] *f* (-; *-n*) make-up (*a.* THEA); '**schminken** *v/t* (*ge-, h*) make *s.o.* up; ***sich ~*** make o.s. *or* one's face up
**Schmirgelpa,pier** ['ʃmɪrgəl-] *n* emery paper
**schmiss** [ʃmɪs] *pret of* ***schmeißen***
**schmollen** ['ʃmɔlən] *v/i* (*ge-, h*) sulk, be sulky, pout
**schmolz** [ʃmɔlts] *pret of* ***schmelzen***
**schmoren** ['ʃmo:rən] *v/t and v/i* (*ge-, h*) GASTR braise, stew (*a. fig*)
**Schmuck** [ʃmʊk] *m* (*-[e]s; no pl*) jewel(le)ry, jewels; decoration(s), ornament(s); **schmücken** ['ʃmʏkən] *v/t* (*ge-, h*) decorate; '**schmucklos** *adj* unadorned; plain; '**Schmuckstück** *n* piece of jewel(le)ry; *fig* gem
**Schmuggel** ['ʃmʊgəl] *m* (-; *no pl*), **Schmuggelei** [ʃmʊgə'lai] *f* (-; *-en*) smuggling; '**schmuggeln** *v/t and v/i* (*ge-, h*) smuggle; '**Schmuggelware** *f*

S

smuggled goods; **Schmuggler** ['ʃmʊglɐ] *m* (*-s*; -) smuggler
**schmunzeln** ['ʃmʊntsəln] *v/i* (*ge-*, *h*) smile to o.s.
**schmusen** ['ʃmu:zən] F *v/i* (*ge-*, *h*) (kiss and) cuddle, smooch
**Schmutz** [ʃmʊts] *m* (*-es*; *no pl*) dirt, filth, *fig a.* smut; **~fleck** *m* smudge
**schmutzig** ['ʃmʊtsɪç] *adj* dirty, filthy (*both a. fig*); ***~ werden, sich ~ machen*** get dirty
**Schnabel** ['ʃna:bəl] *m* (*-s*; *Schnäbel* ['ʃnɛ:bəl]) ZO bill, beak
**Schnalle** ['ʃnalə] *f* (-; *-n*) buckle
'**schnallen** *v/t* (*ge-*, *h*) buckle; ***et. ~ an*** (*acc*) strap s.th. to
**schnalzen** ['ʃnaltsən] *v/i* (*ge-*, *h*) snap one's fingers; click one's tongue
**schnappen** ['ʃnapən] (*ge-*, *h*) **1.** *v/i* snap, snatch (*both*: ***nach*** at); F ***nach Luft ~*** gasp for breath; **2.** F *v/t* catch
'**Schnappschuss** *m* PHOT snapshot
**Schnaps** [ʃnaps] *m* (*-es*; *Schnäpse* ['ʃnɛpsə]) spirits, schnapps, F booze
**schnarchen** ['ʃnarçən] *v/i* (*ge-*, *h*) snore
**schnarren** ['ʃnarən] *v/i* (*ge-*, *h*) rattle; *voice*: rasp
**schnattern** ['ʃnatɐn] *v/i* (*ge-*, *h*) ZO cackle; chatter (*a.* F)
**schnauben** ['ʃnaubən] *v/i and v/t* (*ge-*, *h*) snort; ***sich die Nase ~*** blow one's nose
**schnaufen** ['ʃnaufən] *v/i* (*ge-*, *h*) breathe hard, pant, puff
**Schnauze** ['ʃnautsə] *f* (-; *-n*) ZO snout, mouth, muzzle; F AVIAT, MOT nose; TECH spout; V trap, kisser; V ***die ~ halten*** keep one's trap shut
**Schnecke** ['ʃnɛkə] *f* (-; *-n*) ZO snail; slug
'**Schnecken|haus** *n* ZO snail shell; **~tempo** *n*: ***im ~*** at a snail's pace
**Schnee** [ʃne:] *m* (*-s*; *no pl*) snow (*a. sl*); ***~ räumen*** remove snow; **~ball** *m* snowball; **~ballschlacht** *f* snowball fight
'**schneebedeckt** *adj* snow-capped
'**Schnee|fall** *m* snowfall; **~flocke** *f* snowflake; **~gestöber** [-gəʃtø:bɐ] *n* (*-s*; -) snow flurry; **~glöckchen** *n* BOT snowdrop; **~grenze** *f* snow line; **~mann** *m* snowman; **~matsch** *m* slush; **~mo,bil** *n* snowmobile; **~pflug** *m* snowplow, *Br* snowplough; **~regen** *m* sleet; **~sturm** *m* snowstorm, blizzard; **~verwehung** *f* snowdrift
'**schnee'weiß** *adj* snow-white
**Schneewittchen** [ʃne:'vɪtçən] *n* (*-s*; *no pl*) Snow White
**Schneid** [ʃnait] F *m* (*-[e]s*; *no pl*) grit, guts; **~brenner** *m* TECH cutting torch
**Schneide** ['ʃnaidə] *f* (-; *-n*) edge
'**schneiden** *v/t and v/i* (*irr*, *ge-*, *h*) cut (*a. fig*), *film etc*: *a.* edit; GASTR carve
**Schneider** ['ʃnaidɐ] *m* (*-s*; -) tailor; **Schneiderei** [ʃnaidə'rai] *f* (-; *-en*) a) (*no pl*) tailoring, dressmaking, b) tailor's *or* dressmaker's shop; '**Schneiderin** *f* (-; *-nen*) dressmaker; seamstress; '**schneidern** *v/i and v/t* (*ge-*, *h*) do dressmaking; make, sew
'**Schneidezahn** *m* incisor
**schneidig** ['ʃnaidɪç] *adj* dashing; smart
**schneien** ['ʃnaiən] *v/i* (*ge-*, *h*) snow
**schnell** [ʃnɛl] *adj* fast, quick; prompt; rapid; ***es geht ~*** it won't take long; (***mach[t]***) **~!** hurry up!
'**Schnell...** *in cpds ...dienst*, *...paket*, *...zug etc*: *mst* express ...
**schnellen** ['ʃnɛlən] *v/t* (*ge-*, *h*) *and v/i* (*ge-*, *sein*) shoot, spring
'**Schnellhefter** *m* folder
**Schnelligkeit** ['ʃnɛlɪçkait] *f* (-; *no pl*) speed; quickness, rapidity
'**Schnell|imbiss** *m* snack bar; **~straße** *f* expressway, thruway, *Br* motorway
**schnetzeln** ['ʃnɛtsəln] *esp Swiss v/t* (*ge-*, *h*) GASTR chop up
**Schnippchen** ['ʃnɪpçən] *n*: F ***j-m ein ~ schlagen*** outwit s.o.
**schnippisch** ['ʃnɪpɪʃ] *adj* sassy, pert
**schnipsen** ['ʃnɪpsən] *v/i* (*ge-*, *h*) snap one's fingers
**schnitt** [ʃnɪt] *pret of* ***schneiden***
**Schnitt** *m* (*-[e]s*; *-e*) cut (*a. fig*); average
'**Schnittblumen** *pl* cut flowers
**Schnitte** ['ʃnɪtə] *f* (-; *-n*) slice; open sandwich
**schnittig** ['ʃnɪtɪç] *adj* stylish; MOT sleek
**Schnitt|lauch** *m* BOT chives; **~muster** *n* pattern; **~punkt** *m* (point of) intersection; **~stelle** *f film etc*: cut; EDP interface; **~wunde** *f* MED cut
**Schnitzel**[1] ['ʃnɪtsəl] *n* (*-s*; -) GASTR cutlet; ***Wiener ~*** schnitzel
'**Schnitzel**[2] *n*, *m* (*-s*; -) chip; scrap
**schnitzen** ['ʃnɪtsən] *v/t* (*ge-*, *h*) carve, cut (in wood); **Schnitzer** ['ʃnɪtsɐ] *m* (*-s*; -) (wood) carver; **Schnitzerei** [ʃnɪtsə'rai] *f* (-; *-en*) (wood) carving

S

**Schnorchel** ['ʃnɔrçəl] *m* (*-s*; -), '**schnorcheln** *v/i* (*ge-*, *h*) snorkel
**Schnörkel** ['ʃnœrkəl] *m* (*-s*; -) flourish; ARCH scroll
**schnorren** ['ʃnɔrən] F *v/t* (*ge-*, *h*) mooch, *Br* cadge
**schnüffeln** ['ʃnʏfəln] *v/i* (*ge-*, *h*) sniff (***an*** *dat* at); F snoop (about *or* around)
**Schnuller** ['ʃnʊlɐ] *m* (*-s*; -) pacifier, *Br* dummy
**Schnulze** ['ʃnʊltsə] F *f* (-; *-n*) tearjerker; schmal(t)zy song
'**Schnulzensänger** F *m*, '**Schnulzensängerin** *f* crooner
**schnulzig** ['ʃnʊltsɪç] F *adj* schmal(t)zy
**Schnupfen** ['ʃnʊpfən] *m* (*-s*; -) MED cold; ***e-n ~ haben*** (***bekommen***) have a (catch [a]) cold
'**Schnupftabak** *m* snuff
**schnuppern** ['ʃnʊpɐn] *v/i* (*ge-*, *h*) sniff (***an et.*** [at] s.th.)
**Schnur** [ʃnu:ɐ] *f* (-; *Schnüre* ['ʃny:rə]) string, cord; ELECTR flex
**Schnürchen** ['ʃny:ɐçən] *n*: ***wie am ~*** like clockwork
**schnüren** ['ʃny:rən] *v/t* (*ge-*, *h*) lace (up); tie up
'**schnurgerade** *adv* dead straight
'**schnurlos** *adj*: ***~es Telefon*** cordless phone
**Schnürlsamt** ['ʃny:ɐl-] *Austrian m* corduroy
**Schnurrbart** ['ʃnʊr-] *m* m(o)ustache
**schnurren** ['ʃnʊrən] *v/i* (*ge-*, *h*) purr
**Schnür|schuh** ['ʃny:ɐ-] *m* laced shoe; **~senkel** [-zɛŋkəl] *m* (*-s*; -) shoestring, *Br* shoelace
**schnurstracks** ['ʃnu:ɐ'ʃtraks] *adv* direct(ly), straight; straight away
**schob** [ʃo:p] *pret of* ***schieben***
**Schober** ['ʃo:bɐ] *m* (*-s*; -) haystack, hayrick; barn
**Schock** [ʃɔk] *m* (*-[e]s*; *-s*) MED shock; ***unter ~ stehen*** be in (a state of) shock
**schocken** ['ʃɔkən] F *v/t* (*ge-*, *h*) shock
**schockieren** [ʃɔ'ki:rən] *v/t* (*no -ge-*, *h*) shock
**Schokolade** [ʃoko'la:də] *f* (-; *-n*) chocolate; ***e-e Tafel ~*** a bar of chocolate
**scholl** [ʃɔl] *pret of* ***schallen***
**Scholle** ['ʃɔlə] *f* (-; *-n*) clod; (ice)floe; ZO flounder, *Br* plaice
**schon** [ʃo:n] *adv* already; ever; even; ***~ damals*** even then; ***~ 1968*** as early as 1968; ***~ der Gedanke*** the very idea; ***ist sie ~ da*** (***zurück***)? has she come (is she back) yet?; ***habt ihr ~ gegessen?*** have you eaten yet?; ***bist du ~ einmal dort gewesen?*** have you ever been there?; ***ich wohne hier ~ seit zwei Jahren*** I've been living here for two years now; ***ich kenne ihn ~, aber*** I do know him, but; ***er macht das ~*** he'll do it all right; ***~ gut!*** never mind!, all right!
**schön** [ʃø:n] **1.** *adj* beautiful, lovely; METEOR *a.* fine, fair; nice (*a.* F *iro*); (***na,***) ***~*** all right; **2.** *adv*: ***~ warm*** (***kühl***) nice and warm (cool); ***ganz ~ teuer*** (***schnell***) pretty expensive (fast); ***j-n ganz ~ erschrecken*** (***überraschen***) give s.o. quite a start (surprise)
**schonen** ['ʃo:nən] *v/t* (*ge-*, *h*) take care of, go easy on (*a.* TECH); spare; ***sich ~*** take it easy; save o.s. *or* one's strength; **~d 1.** *adj* gentle; mild; **2.** *adv*: ***~ umgehen mit*** take (good) care of; handle with care; go easy on
'**Schönheit** *f* (-; *-en*) beauty
'**Schönheitspflege** *f* beauty care
'**Schonung** *f* (-; *-en*) a) (*no pl*) (good) care; rest; preservation, b) tree nursery
'**schonungslos** *adj* relentless, brutal
**schöpfen** ['ʃœpfən] *v/t* (*ge-*, *h*) scoop, ladle; draw (*water*); → ***Luft***, ***Verdacht***
**Schöpfer** ['ʃœpfɐ] *m* (*-s*; -), '**Schöpferin** *f* (-; *-nen*) creator
**schöpferisch** ['ʃœpfərɪʃ] *adj* creative
'**Schöpfung** *f* (-; *-en*) creation
**schor** [ʃo:ɐ] *pret of* ***scheren***
**Schorf** [ʃɔrf] *m* (*-[e]s*; *-e*) MED scab
**Schornstein** ['ʃɔrnʃtain] *m* chimney; MAR, RAIL funnel; **~feger** *m* chimneysweep
**schoss** [ʃɔs] *pret of* ***schießen***
**Schoß** [ʃo:s] *m* (*-es*; *Schöße* ['ʃø:sə]) lap; womb
**Schote** ['ʃo:tə] *f* (-; *-n*) BOT pod, husk
**Schotte** ['ʃɔtə] *m* (*-n*; *-n*) Scot(sman); *pl* the Scots, the Scottish (people)
**Schotter** ['ʃɔtɐ] *m* (*-s*; -) gravel, road metal
**Schottin** ['ʃɔtɪn] *f* (-; *-nen*) Scotswoman
'**schottisch** *adj* Scots, Scottish; Scotch
'**Schottland** Scotland
**schräg** [ʃrɛ:k] **1.** *adj* slanting, sloping, oblique; diagonal; **2.** *adv*: ***~ gegenüber*** diagonally opposite
**Schramme** ['ʃramə] *f* (-; *-n*), '**schram-**

**men** *v/t and v/i (ge-, h)* scratch (*a.* MED)
**Schrank** [ʃraŋk] *m* (-[*e*]*s*; *Schränke* ['ʃrɛŋkə]) cupboard; closet; wardrobe
**Schranke** ['ʃraŋkə] *f* (-; -*n*) barrier (*a. fig*), RAIL *a.* gate; JUR bar; *pl* limits, bounds
'**schrankenlos** *fig adj* boundless
'**Schrankenwärter** *m* RAIL gatekeeper
'**Schrankwand** *f* wall units
**Schraube** ['ʃraubə] *f* (-; -*n*), '**schrauben** *v/t (ge-, h)* TECH screw
'**Schrauben|schlüssel** *m* TECH spanner, wrench; **~zieher** *m* TECH screwdriver
**Schraubstock** ['ʃraup-] *m* vise, *Br* vice
**Schreck** [ʃrɛk] *m* (-[*e*]*s*; -*e*) fright, shock; ***j-m e-n ~ einjagen*** give s.o. a fright, scare s.o.
**Schrecken** ['ʃrɛkən] *m* (-*s*; -) terror, fright; horror(s); '**Schreckensnachricht** *f* dreadful news
'**schreckhaft** *adj* jumpy; skittish
'**schrecklich** *adj* awful, terrible; horrible, dreadful, atrocious
**Schrei** [ʃrai] *m* (-[*e*]*s*; -*e*) cry, shout, yell, scream (*all*: ***um***, ***nach*** for)
**schreiben** ['ʃraibən] *v/t and v/i (irr, ge-, h)* write (***j-m*** to s.o.; ***über*** *acc* about); type; spell; ***falsch ~*** misspell; ***wie schreibt man ...?*** how do you spell ...?
'**Schreiben** *n* (-*s*; -) letter
'**Schreib|fehler** *m* spelling mistake; **~heft** *n* exercise book; **~kraft** *f* typist; **~ma,schine** *f* typewriter; **~materi,al** *n* writing materials, stationery; **~schutz** *m* EDP write *or* file protection; **~tisch** *m* desk
'**Schreibung** *f* (-; -*en*) spelling
'**Schreibwaren** *pl* stationery; **~geschäft** *n* stationer's, stationery shop
'**Schreibzen,trale** *f* typing pool
**schreien** ['ʃraiən] *v/i and v/t (irr, ge-, h)* cry, shout, yell, scream (*all*: ***um***, ***nach*** [out] for); ***~ vor Schmerz*** (***Angst***) cry out with pain (in terror); ***es war zum Schreien*** it was a scream; **~d** *fig adj* loud (*colors*); flagrant (*abuse etc*), glaring (*injustices etc*)
**Schreiner** ['ʃrainɐ] *m* (-*s*; -) → ***Tischler***
**schreiten** ['ʃraitən] *v/i (irr, ge-, sein)* stride
**schrie** [ʃriː] *pret of* ***schreien***
**schrieb** [ʃriːp] *pret of* ***schreiben***
**Schrift** [ʃrɪft] *f* (-; -*en*) (hand)writing, hand; PRINT type; character, letter; *pl* works, writings; ***die Heilige ~*** REL the Scriptures; **~art** *f* script; PRINT typeface; **~deutsch** *n* standard German
'**schriftlich** *adj* written; ***~ übersetzen*** translate in writing
'**Schriftsteller** [-ʃtɛlɐ] *m* (-*s*; -), '**Schriftstellerin** *f* (-; -*nen*) author, writer
'**Schrift|verkehr** *m*, **~wechsel** *m* correspondence; **~zeichen** *n* character, letter
**schrill** [ʃrɪl] *adj* shrill (*a. fig*), piercing
**schritt** [ʃrɪt] *pret of* ***schreiten***
**Schritt** *m* (-[*e*]*s*; -*e*) step (*a. fig*); pace; *fig* ***~e unternehmen*** take steps; ***~ fahren!*** MOT dead slow; **~macher** *m* SPORT pacemaker (*a.* MED), pacesetter
'**schrittweise** *adv* step by step, gradually
**schroff** [ʃrɔf] *adj* steep; jagged; *fig* gruff
**Schrot** [ʃroːt] *m, n* (-[*e*]*s*; -*e*) a) (*no pl*) coarse meal, b) HUNT (small) shot; pellet; **~flinte** *f* shotgun
**Schrott** [ʃrɔt] *m* (-[*e*]*s*; -*e*) scrap (metal)
'**Schrotthaufen** *m* scrap heap
'**Schrottplatz** *m* scrapyard
**schrubben** ['ʃrʊbən] *v/t (ge-, h)* scrub, scour
**schrumpfen** ['ʃrʊmpfən] *v/i (ge-, sein)* shrink
**Schub** [ʃuːp] *m* (-[*e*]*s*; *Schübe* ['ʃyːbə]) → ***Schubkraft***; **~fach** *n* drawer; **~karren** *m* wheelbarrow; **~kasten** *m* drawer; **~kraft** *f* PHYS, TECH thrust; **~lade** *f* drawer
**Schubs** [ʃʊps] F *m* (-*es*; -*e*), **schubsen** ['ʃʊpsən] F *v/t (ge-, h)* push
**schüchtern** ['ʃʏçtɐn] *adj* shy, bashful
'**Schüchternheit** *f* (-; *no pl*) shyness, bashfulness
**schuf** [ʃuːf] *pret of* ***schaffen***[1]
**Schuft** [ʃʊft] *m* (-[*e*]*s*; -*e*) *contp* bastard
**schuften** ['ʃʊftən] F *v/i (ge-, h)* slave away, drudge
**Schuh** [ʃuː] *m* (-[*e*]*s*; -*e*) shoe; ***j-m et. in die ~e schieben*** put the blame for s.th. on s.o.; **~anzieher** *m* shoehorn; **~creme** *f* shoe polish; **~geschäft** *n* shoe store (*Br* shop); **~löffel** *m* shoehorn; **~macher** *m* shoemaker; **~putzer** [-pʊtsɐ] *m* (-*s*; -) shoeshine boy
'**Schul|abbrecher** *m* (-*s*; -) dropout; **~abgänger** [-apgɛŋɐ] *m* (-*s*; -) school

S

leaver; **~amt** *n* school board, *Br* education authority; **~arbeit** *f* schoolwork; *pl* homework; **~besuch** *m* (school) attendance; **~bildung** *f* education; **~buch** *n* textbook

**Schuld** [ʃʊlt] *f* (-; *-en* ['ʃʊldən]) a) (*no pl*) JUR guilt, *esp* REL sin, b) *mst pl* debt; ***j-m die ~ (an et.) geben*** blame s.o. (for s.th.); ***es ist (nicht) deine ~*** it is(n't) your fault; ***~en haben (machen)*** be in (run into) debt; → ***zuschulden***; **'schuldbewusst** *adj*: ***~e Miene*** guilty look; **schulden** ['ʃʊldən] *v/t* (*ge-*, *h*) ***j-m et. ~*** owe s.o. s.th.; **schuldig** ['ʃʊldɪç] *adj esp* JUR guilty (***an*** *dat* of); responsible *or* to blame (for); ***j-m et. ~ sein*** owe s.o. s.th.; **Schuldige** ['ʃʊldɪgə] *m,f* (*-n*; *-n*) culprit; JUR guilty person, offender

**'schuldlos** *adj* innocent

**Schuldner** ['ʃʊldnɐ] *m* (*-s*; -); **'Schuldnerin** *f* (-; *-nen*) debtor

**'Schuldschein** *m* ECON promissory note, IOU (= I owe you)

**Schule** ['ʃuːlə] *f* (-; *-n*) school (*a. fig*); ***höhere ~*** *appr* (senior) high school, *Br* secondary school; ***auf*** *or* ***in der ~*** at school; ***in die*** *or* ***zur ~ gehen (kommen)*** go to (start) school

**'schulen** *v/t* (*ge-*, *h*) train, school

**Schüler** ['ʃyːlɐ] *m* (*-s*; -) student, schoolboy, *esp Br a.* pupil; **~austausch** *m* student exchange (program[me])

**Schülerin** ['ʃyːlərɪn] *f* (-; *-nen*) student, schoolgirl, *esp Br a.* pupil

**'Schülervertretung** *f appr* student government (*Br* council)

**'Schul|ferien** *pl* vacation, *Br* holidays; **~fernsehen** *n* educational TV; **~funk** *m* schools programmes; **~gebäude** *n* school (building); **~geld** *n* school fee(s), tuition; **~heft** *n* exercise book; **~hof** *m* school yard, playground; **~kame,rad** *m* schoolfellow; **~leiter** *m* principal, *Br* headmaster, head teacher; **~leiterin** *f* principal, *Br* headmistress; **~mappe** *f* schoolbag; satchel; **~ordnung** *f* school regulations

**'schulpflichtig** *adj*: ***~es Kind*** school-age child

**'Schul|schiff** *n* training ship; **~schluss** *m* end of school (*or* term); ***nach ~*** after school; **~schwänzer** [-ʃvɛntsɐ] *m* (*-s*; -) truant; **~stunde** *f* lesson, class, period; **~tasche** *f* schoolbag

**Schulter** ['ʃʊltɐ] *f* (-; *-n*) ANAT shoulder

**'Schulterblatt** *n* ANAT shoulder-blade

**'schulterfrei** *adj* strapless

**'schultern** *v/t* (*ge-*, *h*) shoulder

**'Schultertasche** *f* shoulder bag

**'Schulwesen** *n* (*-s*; *no pl*) education(al system)

**schummeln** ['ʃʊməln] F *v/i* (*ge-*, *h*) cheat

**Schund** [ʃʊnt] *m* (*-[e]s*; *no pl*) trash, rubbish, junk

**schund** [ʃʊnt] *pret of* ***schinden***

**Schuppe** ['ʃʊpə] *f* (-; *-n*) ZO scale; *pl* MED dandruff

**'Schuppen** *m* (*-s*; -) shed, *esp* F *contp* shack

**schuppig** ['ʃʊpɪç] *adj* ZO scaly

**schüren** ['ʃyːrən] *v/t* (*ge-*, *h*) stir up (*a. fig*)

**schürfen** ['ʃʏrfən] *v/i* (*ge-*, *h*) prospect (***nach*** for)

**'Schürfwunde** *f* MED graze, abrasion

**Schurke** ['ʃʊrkə] *m* (*-n*; *-n*) *esp* THEA *etc* villain

**Schurwolle** ['ʃuːɐ-] *f* virgin wool

**Schürze** ['ʃʏrtsə] *f* (-; *-n*) apron

**Schuss** [ʃʊs] *m* (*-es*; *Schüsse* ['ʃʏsə]) shot; GASTR dash; SPORT shot, *soccer*: *a.* strike; *skiing*: schuss (*a.* ***~ fahren***); *sl* shot, fix; F ***gut in ~ sein*** be in good shape

**Schüssel** ['ʃʏsəl] *f* (-; *-n*) bowl, dish; basin

**'Schuss|waffe** *f* firearm; **~wunde** *f* MED gunshot *or* bullet wound

**Schuster** ['ʃuːstɐ] *m* (*-s*; -) shoemaker

**Schutt** [ʃʊt] *m* (*-[e]s*; *no pl*) rubble, debris

**'Schüttelfrost** *m* MED shivering fit, *the* shivers

**schütteln** ['ʃʏtəln] *v/t* (*ge-*, *h*) shake

**schütten** ['ʃʏtən] *v/t* (*ge-*, *h*) pour; throw

**Schutz** [ʃʊts] *m* (*-es*; *no pl*) protection (***gegen***, ***vor*** *dat* against), defense, *Br* defence (against, from); shelter (from); safeguard (against); cover; **~blech** *n* fender, *Br* mudguard; **~brille** *f* goggles

**Schütze** ['ʃʏtsə] *m* (*-n*; *-n*) MIL rifleman; hunter; SPORT scorer; ASTR Sagittarius; ***er ist (ein) ~*** he's (a) Sagittarius; ***ein guter ~*** a good shot

**schützen** ['ʃʏtsən] *v/t* (*ge-*, *h*) protect

S

(***gegen, vor*** *dat* against, from), defend (against, from), guard (against, from); shelter (from); safeguard

'**Schutzengel** *m* guardian angel

'**Schützengraben** *m* MIL trench

'**Schutzgeld** *n* protection money; **~erpressung** *f* protection racket

'**Schutz|haft** *f* JUR protective custody; **~heilige** *m, f* patron (saint); **~impfung** *f* MED protective inoculation; vaccination; **~kleidung** *f* protective clothing

**Schützling** ['ʃʏtslɪŋ] *m* (*-s*; *-e*) protégé(e)

'**schutzlos** *adj* unprotected; defenseless, *Br* defenceless

'**Schutz|maßnahme** *f* safety measure; **~pa,tron** *m* REL patron (saint); **~umschlag** *m* dust cover; **~zoll** *m* ECON protective duty (*or* tariff)

**schwach** [ʃvax] *adj* weak (*a. fig*); poor; faint; delicate, frail; ***schwächer werden*** grow weak; decline; fail; fade

**Schwäche** ['ʃvɛçə] *f* weakness (*a. fig*); MED infirmity; *fig* drawback, shortcoming; ***e-e ~ haben für*** be partial to; '**schwächen** *v/t* (*ge-, h*) weaken (*a. fig*); lessen; '**schwächlich** *adj* weakly, feeble; delicate, frail; '**Schwächling** *m* (*-s*; *-e*) weakling (*a. fig*), softy, sissy

'**schwachsinnig** *adj* feeble-minded; F stupid, idiotic

'**Schwachstrom** *m* ELECTR low-voltage current

**Schwager** ['ʃva:gɐ] *m* (*-s*; *Schwäger* ['ʃvɛ:gɐ]) brother-in-law; **Schwägerin** ['ʃvɛ:gərɪn] *f* (*-*; *-nen*) sister-in-law

**Schwalbe** ['ʃvalbə] *f* (*-*; *-n*) ZO swallow; *soccer*: dive

**Schwall** [ʃval] *m* (*-[e]s*; *-e*) gush, *esp fig a.* torrent

**schwamm** [ʃvam] *pret of* ***schwimmen***

**Schwamm** *m* (*-[e]s*; *Schwämme* ['ʃvɛmə]) sponge; BOT fungus; F dry rot

**Schwammerl** ['ʃvamɐl] *Austrian m* (*-s*; *-[n]*) → ***Pilz***

**schwammig** ['ʃvamɪç] *adj* spongy; puffy; *fig* woolly

**Schwan** [ʃva:n] *m* (*-[e]s*; *Schwäne* ['ʃvɛ:nə]) ZO swan

**schwand** [ʃvant] *pret of* ***schwinden***

**schwang** [ʃvaŋ] *pret of* ***schwingen***

**schwanger** ['ʃvaŋɐ] *adj* pregnant

'**Schwangerschaft** *f* (*-*; *-en*) pregnancy; '**Schwangerschaftsabbruch** *m* abortion

**schwanken** ['ʃvaŋkən] *v/i* (*ge-, h*) sway, roll (*a.* MAR); stagger; *fig* ***~ zwischen ... und ...*** waver between ... and ...; *prices*: range from ... to ...; '**Schwankung** *f* (*-*; *-en*) change, variation (*a.* ECON)

**Schwanz** [ʃvants] *m* (*-es*; *Schwänze* ['ʃvɛntsə]) ZO tail (*a.* AVIAT, ASTR); V cock

**schwänzen** ['ʃvɛntsən] *v/i and v/t* (*ge-, h*) (***die Schule***) ~ play truant (F hooky)

**Schwarm** [ʃvarm] *m* (*-[e]s*; *Schwärme* ['ʃvɛrmə]) swarm; crowd, F bunch; ZO shoal, school; F dream; idol

**schwärmen** ['ʃvɛrmən] *v/i* a) (*ge-, sein*) ZO swarm, b) (*ge-, h*) ***~ für*** be mad about; dream of; have a crush on *s.o.*; ***~ von*** rave about

**Schwarte** ['ʃvartə] *f* (*-*; *-n*) rind; F *contp* (old) tome

**schwarz** [ʃvarts] *adj* black (*a. fig*); ***~es Brett*** bulletin board, *Br* notice board; ***~ auf weiß*** in black and white

'**Schwarzarbeit** *f* (*-*; *no pl*) illicit work

'**Schwarzbrot** *n* rye bread

**Schwarze** ['ʃvartsə] *m, f* (*-n*; *-n*) black (man *or* woman); *pl* the Blacks

**schwärzen** ['ʃvɛrtsən] *v/t* (*ge-, h*) blacken

'**Schwarz|fahrer** *m* fare dodger; **~händler** *m* black marketeer; **~markt** *m* black market; **~seher** *m* pessimist; (TV) license (*Br* licence) dodger

**Schwarz'weiß...** *in cpds ...film, ...fernseher etc*: black-and-white ...

**schwatzen** ['ʃvatsən], **schwätzen** ['ʃvɛtsən] *v/i* (*ge-, h*) chat(ter); PED talk

**Schwätzer** ['ʃvɛtsɐ] *contp m* (*-s*; *-*), '**Schwätzerin** *f* (*-*; *-nen*) loudmouth

**schwatzhaft** ['ʃvatshaft] *adj* chatty

**Schwebe|bahn** ['ʃve:bə-] *f* cableway, ropeway; **~balken** *m* SPORT beam

**schweben** ['ʃve:bən] *v/i* (*ge-, h*) be suspended; ZO, AVIAT hover (*a. fig*); glide; *esp* JUR be pending; ***in Gefahr ~*** be in danger

**Schwede** ['ʃve:də] *m* (*-n*; *-n*) Swede

**Schweden** ['ʃve:dən] Sweden

**Schwedin** ['ʃve:dɪn] *f* (*-*; *-nen*) Swede

'**schwedisch** *adj* Swedish

**Schwefel** ['ʃve:fəl] *m* (*-s*; *no pl*) CHEM sulfur, *Br* sulphur; **~säure** *f* CHEM sulfuric (*Br* sulphuric) acid

**Schweif** [ʃvaif] *m* (-[*e*]*s*; -*e*) ZO tail (*a.* ASTR); **schweifen** [ˈʃvaifən] *v/i* (*ge-*, *sein*) wander (*a. fig*), roam
**schweigen** [ˈʃvaigən] *v/i* (*irr*, *ge-*, *h*) be silent; ˈ**Schweigen** *n* (-*s*; *no pl*) silence; ˈ**schweigend** *adj* silent
**schweigsam** [ˈʃvaikza:m] *adj* quiet, taciturn, reticent
**Schwein** [ʃvain] *n* (-[*e*]*s*; -*e*) ZO pig, hog; F *contp* (filthy) pig; swine, bastard; F **~ *haben*** be lucky; ˈ**Schweinebraten** *m* roast pork; ˈ**Schweinefleisch** *n* pork; **Schweinerei** [ʃvainəˈrai] F *f* (-; -*en*) mess; *fig* dirty trick; dirty *or* crying shame; filth(y story *or* joke)
ˈ**Schweinestall** *m* pigsty (*a. fig*)
ˈ**schweinisch** F *adj* filthy, obscene
ˈ**Schweinsleder** *n* pigskin
**Schweiß** [ʃvais] *m* (-*es*; *no pl*) sweat, perspiration
**schweißen** *v/t* (*ge-*, *h*) TECH weld
**Schweißer** *m* (-*s*; -) TECH welder
ˈ**schweißgebadet** *adj* soaked in sweat
ˈ**Schweißgeruch** *m* body odo(u)r, BO
**Schweiz** [ʃvaits] Switzerland
**Schweizer** [ˈʃvaitsɐ] *m* (-*s*; -), *adj* Swiss
**Schweizerin** [ˈʃvaitsərɪn] *f* (-; -*nen*) Swiss woman *or* girl
**schweizerisch** [ˈʃvaitsərɪʃ] *adj* Swiss
**schwelen** [ˈʃve:lən] *v/i* (*ge-*, *h*) smo(u)lder (*a. fig*)
**schwelgen** [ˈʃvɛlgən] *v/i* (*ge-*, *h*) **~ *in*** (*dat*) revel in
**Schwelle** [ˈʃvɛlə] *f* (-; -*n*) threshold (*a. fig*); RAIL tie, *Br* sleeper
ˈ**schwellen 1.** *v/i* (*irr*, *ge-*, *sein*) swell; **2.** *v/t* (*ge-*, *h*) swell
ˈ**Schwellung** *f* (-; -*en*) MED swelling
**Schwemme** [ˈʃvɛmə] *f* (-; -*n*) ECON glut, oversupply; ˈ**schwemmen** *v/t* (*ge-*, *h*) ***an Land* ~** wash ashore
**Schwengel** [ˈʃvɛŋəl] *m* (-*s*; -) clapper; handle
**schwenken** [ˈʃvɛŋkən] *v/t* (*ge-*, *h*) *and* *v/i* (*ge-*, *sein*) swing, wave
**schwer** [ʃve:ɐ] **1.** *adj* heavy; *fig* difficult, hard; GASTR strong, rich; MED *etc* serious, severe; heavy, violent (*storm etc*); ***~e Zeiten*** hard times; ***es ~ haben*** have a bad time; ***100 Pfund ~ sein*** weigh a hundred pounds; **2.** *adv*: ***~ arbeiten*** work hard; → ***hören***; ***~ beschädigt*** seriously disabled; ***j-m ~ fallen*** be difficult for s.o.; ***es fällt ihm ~ zu ...*** he finds it difficult to ...; ***~ verdaulich*** indigestible, heavy (*both a. fig*); ***~ verständlich*** difficult *or* hard to understand; ***~ verwundet*** seriously wounded
**Schwere** [ˈʃve:rə] *f* (-; *no pl*) weight (*a. fig*); *fig* seriousness
ˈ**schwerfällig** *adj* awkward, clumsy
ˈ**Schwergewicht** *n* (-[*e*]*s*; *no pl*) heavyweight; *fig* (main) emphasis
ˈ**schwerhörig** *adj* hard of hearing
ˈ**Schwer|indusˌtrie** *f* heavy industry; **~kraft** *f* (-; *no pl*) PHYS gravity; **~meˌtall** *n* heavy metal
ˈ**schwermütig** [-my:tɪç] *adj* melancholy; ***~ sein*** have the blues
ˈ**Schwerpunkt** *m* center (*Br* centre) of gravity; *fig* (main) emphasis
**Schwert** [ʃve:ɐt] *n* (-[*e*]*s*; -*er*) sword
ˈ**Schwerverbrecher** *m* dangerous criminal, JUR felon
ˈ**schwerwiegend** *fig adj* weighty, serious
**Schwester** [ˈʃvɛstɐ] *f* (-; -*n*) sister, REL *a.* nun; MED nurse
**schwieg** [ʃvi:k] *pret of* ***schweigen***
**Schwieger...** [ˈʃvi:gɐ-] *in cpds ...eltern*, *...mutter*, *...sohn etc*: ...-in-law
**Schwiele** [ˈʃvi:lə] *f* (-; -*n*) MED callus
**schwielig** [ˈʃvi:lɪç] *adj* horny
**schwierig** [ˈʃvi:rɪç] *adj* difficult, hard
ˈ**Schwierigkeit** *f* (-; -*en*) difficulty, trouble; ***in ~en geraten*** get *or* run into trouble; ***~en haben, et. zu tun*** have difficulty in doing s.th.
**Schwimmbad** [ˈʃvɪm-] *n* (indoor) swimming pool; **schwimmen** [ˈʃvɪmən] *v/i* (*irr*, *ge-*, *sein*) swim; float; ***~ gehen*** go swimming
ˈ**Schwimm|flosse** *f* swimfin, *Br* flipper; **~gürtel** *m* swimming belt; **~haut** *f* ZO web; **~lehrer** *m* swimming instructor; **~weste** *f* life jacket
**Schwindel** [ˈʃvɪndəl] *m* (-*s*; *no pl*) MED giddiness, dizziness; F swindle, fraud; ***~ erregend*** dizzy
ˈ**schwindeln** F *v/i* (*ge-*, *h*) fib, tell fibs
**schwinden** [ˈʃvɪndən] *v/i* (*irr*, *ge-*, *sein*) dwindle, decline
**Schwindler** [ˈʃvɪndlɐ] F *m* (-*s*; -), ˈ**Schwindlerin** *f* (-; -*nen*) swindler, crook; liar
**schwindlig** [ˈʃvɪndlɪç] *adj* MED dizzy, giddy; ***mir ist ~*** I feel dizzy
**Schwinge** [ˈʃvɪŋə] *f* (-; -*n*) ZO wing

S

**'schwingen** *v/i and v/t* (*irr, ge-, h*) swing; wave; PHYS oscillate; vibrate
**'Schwingung** *f* (-; *-en*) PHYS oscillation; vibration
**Schwips** [ʃvɪps] F *m*: ***e-n ~ haben*** be tipsy
**schwirren** ['ʃvɪrən] *v/i* a) (*ge-, sein*) whirr, whizz, *esp* ZO buzz (*a. fig*), b) (*ge-, h*) ***mir schwirrt der Kopf*** my head is buzzing
**schwitzen** ['ʃvɪtsən] *v/i* (*ge-, h*) sweat, perspire
**schwoll** [ʃvɔl] *pret of* **schwellen** 1
**schwor** [ʃvoːɐ] *pret of* **schwören**
**schwören** ['ʃvøːrən] *v/t and v/i* (*irr, ge-, h*) swear; JUR take an *or* the oath; *fig* **~ *auf*** (*acc*) swear by
**schwul** [ʃvuːl] F *adj* gay; *contp* queer
**schwül** [ʃvyːl] *adj* sultry (*a. fig*), close
**schwülstig** ['ʃvʏlstɪç] *adj* bombastic, pompous
**Schwung** [ʃvʊŋ] *m* (*-[e]s; Schwünge* ['ʃvʏŋə]) swing; *fig* verve, pep; drive; ***in ~ kommen*** get going; ***et. in ~ bringen*** get s.th. going; **'schwungvoll** *adj* full of energy *or* verve; MUS swinging
**Schwur** [ʃvuːɐ] *m* (*-[e]s; Schwüre* ['ʃvyːrə]) oath; **~gericht** *n* JUR jury court
**sechs** [zɛks] *adj* six; *grade*: F, *Br a.* poor; **'Sechseck** *n* (*-[e]s; -e*) hexagon; **'sechseckig** *adj* hexagonal; **'sechsfach** *adj* sixfold; **'sechsmal** *adv* six times; **Sechs'tagerennen** *n* SPORT six-day race; **'sechstägig** [-tɛːgɪç] *adj* lasting *or* of six days; **'sechste** *adj* sixth; **Sechstel** ['zɛkstəl] *n* (*-s; -*) sixth (part); **'sechstens** *adv* sixthly, in the sixth place; **sechzehn(te)** ['zɛçtseːn(tə)] *adj* sixteen(th); **sechzig** ['zɛçtsɪç] *adj* sixty; **'sechzigste** *adj* sixtieth
**See¹** [zeː] *m* (*-s; -n*) lake
**See²** *f* (-; *no pl*) sea, ocean; ***auf ~*** at sea; ***auf hoher ~*** on the high seas; ***an der ~*** at the seaside; ***zur ~ gehen*** (***fahren***) go to sea (be a sailor); ***in ~ stechen*** put to sea; **~bad** *n* seaside resort; **~fahrt** *f* navigation; **~gang** *m* (*-[e]s; no pl*): ***hoher ~*** heavy sea; **~hafen** *m* seaport; **~hund** *m* ZO seal; **~karte** *f* nautical chart
**'seekrank** *adj* seasick
**'Seekrankheit** *f* seasickness
**Seele** ['zeːlə] *f* (-; *-n*) soul (*a. fig*)
**'seelenlos** *adj* soulless
**'Seelenruhe** *f* peace of mind; ***in aller ~*** as cool as you please
**seelisch** ['zeːlɪʃ] *adj* mental
**'Seelsorge** *f* (-; *no pl*) pastoral care
**'Seelsorger** [-zɔrgɐ] *m* (*-s; -*), **'Seelsorgerin** *f* (-; *-nen*) pastor
**'See|macht** *f* sea power; **~mann** *m* (*-[e]s; -leute*) seaman, sailor; **~meile** *f* nautical mile; **~not** *f* (-; *no pl*) distress (at sea); **~notkreuzer** *m* MAR rescue cruiser; **~räuber** *m* pirate; **~reise** *f* voyage, cruise; **~rose** *f* BOT water lily; **~sack** *m* kit bag; **~schlacht** *f* MIL naval battle; **~streitkräfte** *pl* MIL naval forces, navy
**'seetüchtig** *adj* seaworthy
**'See|warte** *f* naval observatory; **~weg** *m* sea route; ***auf dem ~*** by sea; **~zeichen** *n* seamark; **~zunge** *f* ZO sole
**Segel** ['zeːgəl] *n* (*-s; -*) sail; **~boot** *n* sailboat, *Br* sailing boat; **~fliegen** *n* gliding; **~flugzeug** *n* glider
**'segeln** *v/i* (*ge-, sein*) sail, SPORT *a.* yacht
**'Segel|schiff** *n* sailing ship; sailing vessel; **~sport** *m* sailing, yachting; **~tuch** *n* canvas, sailcloth
**Segen** ['zeːgən] *m* (*-s; -*) blessing (*a. fig*)
**Segler** ['zeːglɐ] *m* (*-s; -*) yachtsman
**Seglerin** ['zeːglərɪn] *f* (-; *-nen*) yachtswoman
**segnen** ['zeːgnən] *v/t* (*ge-, h*) bless
**'Segnung** *f* (-; *-nen*) blessing
**Sehbeteiligung** ['zeː-] *f* (TV) ratings
**sehen** ['zeːən] *v/i and v/t* (*irr, ge-, h*) see; watch; notice; **~ *nach*** look after; look for; ***sich ~ lassen*** show up; ***das sieht man*** (***kaum***) it (hardly) shows; ***siehst du*** (you) see; I told you; ***siehe oben*** (***unten, Seite ...***) see above (below, page ...); **'sehenswert** *adj* worth seeing; **'Sehenswürdigkeit** *f* (-; *-en*) place *etc* worth seeing, sight, *pl* sights
**'Sehkraft** *f* (-; *no pl*) eyesight, vision
**Sehne** ['zeːnə] *f* (-; *-n*) ANAT sinew; string
**sehnen** ['zeːnən] *v/refl* (*ge-, h*) long (***nach*** for), yearn (for); ***sich danach ~ zu*** *inf* be longing to *inf*
**'Sehnerv** *m* ANAT optic nerve
**sehnig** ['zeːnɪç] *adj* sinewy, GASTR *a.* stringy
**sehnlichst** ['zeːnlɪçst] *adj* dearest
**'Sehnsucht** *f*, **'sehnsüchtig** *adj* longing, yearning

**sehr** [zeːɐ] *adv before adj and adv*: very; *with verbs*: very much, greatly
**'Sehtest** *m* sight test
**seicht** [zaiçt] *adj* shallow (*a. fig*)
**Seide** ['zaidə] *f* (-; -*n*), **'seiden** *adj* silk
**'Seidenpa,pier** *n* tissue paper
**'Seidenraupe** *f* ZO silkworm
**seidig** ['zaidɪç] *adj* silky
**Seife** ['zaifə] *f* (-; -*n*) soap
**'Seifen|blase** *f* soap bubble; **~lauge** *f* (soap)suds; **~oper** *f* TV soap opera; **~schale** *f* soap dish; **~schaum** *m* lather
**seifig** ['zaifɪç] *adj* soapy
**Seil** [zail] *n* (-[*e*]*s*; -*e*) rope
**'Seilbahn** *f* cable railway
**'seilspringen** *v/i* (*only inf*) skip
**sein¹** [zain] *v/i* (*irr*, *ge-*, *sein*) be; exist; ***et. ~ lassen*** stop *or* quit (doing) s.th.
**sein²** *poss pron* his, her, its; **~er, ~e, ~(e)s** his, hers
**Sein** *n* (-*s*; *no pl*) being; existence
**seiner|seits** ['zainɐzaits] *adv* for his part; **~'zeit** *adv* then, in those days
**seines'gleichen** ['zainəs-] *pron* his equals
**seinet'wegen** ['zainət-] → ***meinetwegen***
**seit** [zait] *prp and cj* since; ***~ 1982*** since 1982; ***~ drei Jahren*** for three years (now); ***~ langem*** (***kurzem***) for a long (short) time; **~'dem 1.** *adv* since then, since that time, ever since; **2.** *cj* since
**Seite** ['zaitə] *f* (-; -*n*) side (*a. fig*); page; ***auf der linken ~*** on the left(-hand side); *fig* ***auf der e-n*** (***anderen***) ***~*** on the one (other) hand
**'Seiten|ansicht** *f* side view, profile; **~blick** *m* sidelong glance; **~hieb** *m* sideswipe; **~linie** *f esp soccer*: touchline
**seitens** ['zaitəns] *prp* (*gen*) on the part of, by
**'Seitensprung** F *m*: ***e-n ~ machen*** cheat (on one's wife *or* husband)
**'Seitenstechen** *n* (-*s*; *no pl*) MED a stitch (in the side)
**'seitlich** *adj* side ..., at the side(s)
**'seitwärts** [-vɛrts] *adv* sideways, to the side
**Sekretär** [zekre'tɛːɐ] *m* (-*s*; -*e*) secretary; bureau; **Sekretariat** [-ta'rjaːt] *n* (-[*e*]*s*; -*e*) (secretary's) office; **Sekretärin** [-'tɛːrɪn] *f* (-; -*nen*) secretary
**Sekt** [zɛkt] *m* (-[*e*]*s*; -*e*) sparkling wine, champagne
**Sekte** ['zɛktə] *f* (-; -*n*) sect
**Sektion** [zɛk'tsjoːn] *f* (-; -*en*) section; MED autopsy
**Sektor** ['zɛktoːɐ] *m* (-*s*; -*en* [zɛk'toːrən]) sector; *fig* field
**Sekunde** [ze'kʊndə] *f* (-; -*n*) second; ***auf die ~*** to the second
**Se'kundenzeiger** *m* second(s) hand
**selbe** ['zɛlbə] *adj* same
**selber** ['zɛlbɐ] *pron* → ***selbst*** 1
**selbst** [zɛlbst] **1.** *pron*: ***ich*** (***du*** *etc*) ***~*** I (you *etc*) myself (yourself *etc*); ***mach es ~*** do it yourself; ***et. ~ tun*** do s.th. by oneself; ***von ~*** by itself; ***~ gemacht*** homemade; **2.** *adv* even
**'Selbstachtung** *f* self-respect
**'selbständig** *etc* → ***selbstständig*** *etc*
**'Selbst|bedienung(sladen** *m*) *f* self-service (store, *Br* shop); **~befriedigung** *f* masturbation; **~beherrschung** *f* self-control; **~bestimmung** *f* self-determination
**'selbstbewusst** *adj* self-confident, self-assured; **'Selbstbewusstsein** *n* self-confidence
**'Selbst|bildnis** *n* self-portrait; **~erhaltungstrieb** *m* survival instinct; **~erkenntnis** *f* (-; *no pl*) self-knowledge
**'selbstgerecht** *adj* self-righteous
**'Selbst|hilfe** *f* self-help; **~hilfegruppe** *f* self-help group; **~kostenpreis** *m*: ***zum ~*** ECON at cost (price)
**'selbstkritisch** *adj* self-critical
**'Selbstlaut** *m* LING vowel
**'selbstlos** *adj* unselfish
**'Selbst|mord** *m*, **~mörder(in)** suicide
**'selbstmörderisch** *adj* suicidal
**'selbstsicher** *adj* self-confident, self-assured
**'selbstständig** *adj* independent, self-reliant; self-employed; **'Selbstständigkeit** *f* (-; *no pl*) independence
**'Selbststudium** *n* (-*s*; *no pl*) self-study
**'selbst|süchtig** *adj* selfish, ego(t)istic(al); **~tätig** *adj* automatic
**'Selbsttäuschung** *f* self-deception
**'selbstverständlich 1.** *adj* natural; ***das ist ~*** that's a matter of course; **2.** *adv* of course, naturally; **~!** *a.* by all means!; **'Selbstverständlichkeit** *f* (-; -*en*) matter of course
**'Selbst|verteidigung** *f* self-defense, *Br* self-defence; **~vertrauen** *n* self-confidence, self-reliance; **~verwaltung** *f*

S

self-government, autonomy; **~wähldienst** *m* TEL automatic long-distance dial(l)ing service
**'selbstzufrieden** *adj* self-satisfied
**selchen** ['zɛlçən] *Austrian* → **räuchern**
**selig** ['ze:lıç] *adj* REL blessed; late; *fig* overjoyed
**Sellerie** ['zɛləri] *m* (-*s*; -[*s*]), *f* (-; -) BOT celeriac; celery
**selten** ['zɛltən] **1.** *adj* rare; **~ sein** be rare, be scarce; **2.** *adv* rarely, seldom
**'Seltenheit** *f* (-; *no pl*) rarity
**seltsam** ['zɛltza:m] *adj* strange, odd
**Semester** [ze'mɛstɐ] *n* (-*s*; -) UNIV semester, *esp Br* term
**Semikolon** [zemi'ko:lɔn] *n* (-*s*; -*s*) LING semicolon
**Seminar** [zemi'na:ɐ] *n* (-*s*; -*e*) UNIV department; seminar; REL seminary; teacher training college
**sen.** ABBR *of* **senior** sen., Sen., Sr, Snr, senior
**Senat** [ze'na:t] *m* (-[*e*]*s*; -*e*) senate
**Senator** [ze'na:to:ɐ] *m* (-*s*; -*en* [zena'to:rən]), **Sena'torin** *f* (-; -*nen*) senator
**Sendemast** *m* ELECTR mast
**senden** ['zɛndən] *v/t* ([*irr*,] *ge*-, *h*) send (**mit der Post** by mail, *Br* by post); ELECTR broadcast, transmit, *a.* televise
**Sender** ['zɛndɐ] *m* (-*s*; -) radio *or* television station; ELECTR transmitter
**'Sende|reihe** *f* TV *or* radio series; **~schluss** *m* close-down, F sign-off; **~zeichen** *n* call letters (*Br* sign); **~zeit** *f* air time
**'Sendung** *f* (-; -*en*) broadcast, program(me), *a.* telecast; ECON consignment, shipment; **auf ~ sein** be on the air
**Senf** [zɛnf] *m* (-[*e*]*s*; -*e*) mustard (*a.* BOT)
**senil** [ze'ni:l] *adj* senile; **Senilität** [zenili'tɛ:t] *f* (-; *no pl*) senility
**Senior** ['ze:njo:ɐ] **1.** *m* (-*s*; -*en* [ze'njo:rən]) senior (*a.* SPORT); senior citizen; **2.** *adj* senior
**Seni'orenheim** *n* old people's home
**Seni'orin** *f* (-; -*nen*) senior citizen
**Senke** ['zɛŋkə] *f* (-; -*n*) GEOGR depression, hollow; **'senken** *v/t* (*ge*-, *h*) lower (*a. one's voice*), *a.* bow (*one's head*); ECON *a.* reduce, cut; **sich ~** drop, go *or* come down
**'senkrecht** *adj* vertical
**Sensation** [zɛnza'tsjo:n] *f* (-; -*en*) sensation; **sensationell** [zɛnzatsjo'nɛl] *adj*,
**Sensati'ons...** *in cpds* ...*blatt etc*: sensational (...)
**Sense** ['zɛnzə] *f* (-; -*n*) AGR scythe
**sensibel** [zɛn'zi:bəl] *adj* sensitive
**sensibilisieren** [zɛnzibili'zi:rən] *v/t* (*no -ge*-, *h*) sensitize (**für** to)
**sentimental** [zɛntimɛn'ta:l] *adj* sentimental; **Sentimentalität** [zɛntimɛntali'tɛ:t] *f* (-; -*en*) sentimentality
**September** [zɛp'tɛmbɐ] *m* (-[*s*]; -) September
**Serenade** [zere'na:də] *f* (-; -*n*) MUS serenade
**Serie** ['ze:rjə] *f* (-; -*n*) series, TV *etc a.* serial; set; **in ~** *produce etc* in series
**'serienmäßig** *adj* series(-produced); standard
**'Serien|nummer** *f* serial number; **~wagen** *m* MOT standard-type car
**seriös** [ze'rjø:s] *adj* respectable; honest; serious
**Serum** ['ze:rʊm] *n* (-*s*; -*ren*, -*ra*) serum
**Service¹** [zɛr'vi:s] *n* (-[*s*]; -) set; service
**Service²** ['zø:ɐvıs] *m*, *n* (-; -*s*) service
**servieren** [zɛr'vi:rən] *v/t* (*no -ge*-, *h*) serve; **Serviererin** [zɛr'vi:rərın] *f* (-; -*nen*) waitress; **Serviertochter** [zɛr'vi:ɐ-] *Swiss f* waitress
**Serviette** [zɛr'vjɛtə] *f* (-; -*n*) napkin, *esp Br* serviette
**Servo|bremse** ['zɛrvo-] *f* MOT servo *or* power brake; **~lenkung** *f* MOT servo(-assisted) *or* power steering
**Sessel** ['zɛsəl] *m* (-*s*; -) armchair, easy chair; **~lift** *m* chair lift
**sesshaft** ['zɛshaft] *adj*: **~ werden** settle (down)
**Set** [zɛt] *n*, *m* (-*s*; -*s*) place mat
**setzen** ['zɛtsən] *v/t and v/i* (*ge*-, *h*) put, set (*a.* PRINT, AGR, MAR), AGR *a.* plant; place; seat *s.o.*; **~ über** (*acc*) jump over; cross (*river*); **~ auf** (*acc*) bet on, back; **sich ~** sit down; CHEM *etc* settle; **sich ~ auf** (*acc*) get on, mount; **sich ~ in** (*acc*) get into; **sich zu j-m ~** sit beside *or* with s.o.; **~ Sie sich bitte!** take *or* have a seat!
**Setzer** ['zɛtsɐ] *m* (-*s*; -) PRINT compositor, typesetter; **Setzerei** [zɛtsə'rai] *f* (-; -*en*) PRINT composing room
**Seuche** ['zɔʏçə] *f* (-; -*n*) epidemic (disease)
**seufzen** ['zɔʏftsən] *v/i* (*ge*-, *h*), **Seufzer** ['zɔʏftsɐ] *m* (-*s*; -) sigh

**Sexismus** [zɛ'ksɪsmʊs] *m* (-; *no pl*) sexism; **Sexist** [zɛ'ksɪst] *m* (*-en*; *-en*), **se'xistisch** *adj* sexist

**Sexual...** [zɛ'ksua:l-] *in cpds ...erziehung, ...leben, ...trieb etc*: sex(ual) ...; **~verbrechen** *n* sex crime

**sexuell** [zɛ'ksuɛl] *adj* sexual; ***~e Belästigung*** (sexual) harassment

**sexy** ['zɛksi] *adj* sexy

**sezieren** [ze'tsi:rən] *v/t* (*no -ge-*, *h*) MED dissect (*a. fig*); perform an autopsy on

**Showgeschäft** ['ʃou-] *n* (*-[e]s*; *no pl*) show business

**sich** [zɪç] *refl pron* oneself; himself, herself, itself; *pl* themselves; yourself, *pl* yourselves; ***~ ansehen*** look at oneself; look at each other

**Sichel** ['zɪçəl] *f* (-; *-n*) AGR sickle; ASTR crescent

**sicher** ['zɪçɐ] **1.** *adj* safe (***vor*** *dat* from), secure (from); *esp* TECH proof (***gegen*** against); *fig* certain, sure; reliable; (***sich***) ***~ sein*** be sure (***e-r Sache*** of s.th.; ***dass*** that); **2.** *adv* safely; ***~!*** of course, sure(ly); certainly; probably; ***du hast*** (***bist***) ***~ ...*** you must have (be) ...

**'Sicherheit** *f* (-; *-en*) a) (*no pl*) security (*a.* MIL, POL, ECON); safety (*a.* TECH); *fig* certainty; skill; (***sich***) ***in ~ bringen*** get to safety, b) ECON cover

**'Sicherheits...** *esp* TECH *in cpds ...glas, ...nadel, ...schloss etc*: safety ...; **~gurt** *m* seat belt, safety belt; **~maßnahme** *f* safety (POL security) measure

**'sicherlich** *adv* → ***sicher*** 2

**'sichern** *v/t* (*ge-*, *h*) protect, safeguard; secure (*a.* MIL, TECH); EDP save; ***sich ~*** secure o.s. (***gegen***, ***vor*** *dat* against, from); **'sicherstellen** *v/t* (*sep*, *-ge-*, *h*) secure; guarantee; **Sicherung** ['zɪçərʊŋ] *f* (-; *-en*) securing; safeguard(ing); TECH safety device; ELECTR fuse

**'Sicherungs|kasten** *m* ELECTR fuse box; **~koˌpie** *f* EDP backup; ***e-e ~ machen*** (***von***) back up

**Sicht** [zɪçt] *f* (-; *no pl*) visibility; view; ***in ~ kommen*** come into sight *or* view; ***auf lange ~*** in the long run; **'sichtbar** *adj* visible; **sichten** ['zɪçtən] *v/t* (*ge-*, *h*) sight; *fig* sort (through *or* out)

**'Sichtkarte** *f* season ticket

**'sichtlich** *adv* visibly

**'Sichtweite** *f* visibility; ***in*** (***außer***) ***~*** within (out of) sight

**sickern** ['zɪkɐn] *v/i* (*ge-*, *sein*) trickle, ooze, seep

**sie** [zi:] *pers pron* she; it; *pl* they; ***Sie*** you

**Sieb** [zi:p] *n* (*-[e]s*; *-e*) sieve; strainer

**sieben**[1] ['zi:bən] *v/t* (*ge-*, *h*) sieve, sift

**'sieben**[2] *adj* seven

**Sieben'meter** *m* SPORT penalty shot *or* throw

**siebte** ['zi:ptə] *adj*, **'Siebtel** *n* (*-s*; -) seventh; **siebzehn(te)** ['zi:p-] *adj* seventeen(th); **siebzig** ['zi:ptsɪç] *adj* seventy; **'siebzigste** *adj* seventieth

**siedeln** ['zi:dəln] *v/i* (*ge-*, *h*) settle

**sieden** ['zi:dən] *v/t and v/i* (*[irr,] ge-*, *h*) boil, simmer

**'Siedepunkt** *m* boiling point (*a. fig*)

**Siedler** ['zi:dlɐ] *m* (*-s*; -) settler

**Siedlung** ['zi:dlʊŋ] *f* (-; *-en*) settlement; housing development

**Sieg** [zi:k] *m* (*-[e]s*; *-e*) victory, SPORT *a.* win

**Siegel** ['zi:gəl] *n* (*-s*; -) seal, signet

**'Siegellack** *m* sealing wax

**'siegeln** *v/t* (*ge-*, *h*) seal

**siegen** ['zi:gən] *v/i* (*ge-*, *h*) win

**Sieger** ['zi:gɐ] *m* (*-s*; -), **Siegerin** ['zi:gərɪn] *f* (-; *-nen*) winner

**'siegreich** *adj* winning; victorious

**Signal** [zɪ'gna:l] *n* (*-s*; *-e*), **signalisieren** [zɪgnali'zi:rən] *v/t* (*no -ge-*, *h*) signal

**signieren** [zɪ'gni:rən] *v/t* (*no -ge-*, *h*) sign

**Silbe** ['zɪlbə] *f* (-; *-n*) syllable

**'Silbentrennung** *f* LING syllabification

**Silber** ['zɪlbɐ] *n* (*-s*; *no pl*) silver; silverware; **'silbergrau** *adj* silver-gray (*Br* -grey); **'Silberhochzeit** *f* silver wedding; **'silbern** *adj* silver

**Silhouette** [zi'luɛtə] *f* (-; *-n*) silhouette; skyline

**Silikon** [zili'ko:n] *n* (*-s*; *-e*) CHEM silicone

**Silizium** [zi'li:tsjʊm] *n* (*-s*; *no pl*) CHEM silicon

**Silvester** [zɪl'vɛstɐ] *n* (*-s*; -) New Year's Eve

**Sims** [zɪms] *m*, *n* (*-es*; *-e*) ledge; windowsill

**simulieren** [zimu'li:rən] *v/t and v/i* TECH *etc* simulate; sham

**simultan** [zimʊl'ta:n] *adj* simultaneous

**Sinfonie** [zɪnfo'ni:] *f* (-; *-n*) MUS symphony

**singen** ['zɪŋən] *v/t and v/i* (*irr*, *ge-*, *h*)

sing (***richtig*** [***falsch***] in [out of] tune)
**Singular** ['zɪŋgulaːɐ] *m* (*-s*; *-e*) LING singular
**Singvogel** ['zɪŋ-] *m* ZO songbird
**sinken** ['zɪŋkən] *v/i* (*irr*, *ge-*, *sein*) sink (*a. fig*), go down (*a.* ECON), ASTR *a.* set; *prices etc*: fall, drop
**Sinn** [zɪn] *m* (*-[e]s*; *-e*) sense (***für*** of); mind; meaning; point, idea; ***im ~ haben*** have in mind; ***es hat keinen ~*** (***zu warten*** *etc*) it's no use *or* good (waiting *etc*); '**Sinnbild** *n* symbol
'**sinnentstellend** *adj* distorting
**Sinnes|organ** ['zɪnəs-] *n* sense organ; **~täuschung** *f* hallucination; **~wandel** *m* change of mind
'**sinnlich** *adj* sensuous; sensory; sensual; '**Sinnlichkeit** *f* (*-*; *no pl*) sensuality
'**sinnlos** *adj* senseless; useless
'**sinnverwandt** *adj* synonymous
'**sinnvoll** *adj* meaningful; useful; wise, sensible
**Sintflut** ['zɪnt-] *f the* Flood
**Sippe** ['zɪpə] *f* (*-*; *-n*) (extended) family, clan
**Sirene** [zi'reːnə] *f* (*-*; *-n*) siren
**Sirup** ['ziːrʊp] *m* (*-s*; *-e*) sirup, *Br* syrup; treacle, molasses
**Sitte** ['zɪtə] *f* (*-*; *-n*) custom, tradition; *pl* morals; manners
'**Sittenlosigkeit** *f* (*-*; *no pl*) immorality
'**Sittenpoliˌzei** *f* vice squad
'**sittenwidrig** *adj* immoral
'**Sittlichkeitsverbrechen** *n* sex crime
**Situation** [zitua'tsjoːn] *f* (*-*; *-en*) situation; position
**Sitz** [zɪts] *m* (*-es*; *-e*) seat; fit; **~bloˌckade** *f* sit-down demonstration
**sitzen** ['zɪtsən] *v/i* (*irr*, *ge-*, *h*) sit (***an*** *dat* at; ***auf*** *dat* on); be; fit; F do time; ***~ bleiben*** keep one's seat; PED have to repeat a year; F ***~ bleiben auf*** (*dat*) be left with; F ***j-n ~ lassen*** leave s.o. in the lurch, let s.o. down
'**Sitzplatz** *m* seat
'**Sitzstreik** *m* sit-down strike
'**Sitzung** *f* (*-*; *-en*) session (*a.* PARL), meeting, conference
**Skala** ['skaːla] *f* (*-*; *-en*) scale, *fig a.* range
**Skalp** [skalp] *m* (*-s*; *-e*), **skalpieren** [skal'piːrən] *v/t* (*no -ge-*, *h*) scalp
**Skandal** [skan'daːl] *m* (*-s*; *-e*) scandal; ***ein ~ sein*** be scandalous; **skandalös** [skanda'løːs] *adj* scandalous, shocking
**Skelett** [ske'lɛt] *n* (*-[e]s*; *-e*) skeleton
**Skepsis** ['skɛpsɪs] *f* (*-*; *no pl*) skepticism, *Br* scepticism; **Skeptiker** ['skɛptikɐ] *m* (*-s*; *-*) skeptic, *Br* sceptic; **skeptisch** ['skɛptɪʃ] *adj* skeptical, *Br* sceptical
**Ski** [ʃiː] *m* (*-s*; *-er* ['ʃiːɐ]) ski; ***~ laufen*** *or* ***fahren*** ski; **~fahrer(in)** skier; **~fliegen** *n* ski flying; **~lift** *m* ski lift; **~piste** *f* ski run; **~schuh** *m* ski boot; **~sport** *m* skiing; **~springen** *n* ski jumping
**Skizze** ['skɪtsə] *f* (*-*; *-n*), **skizzieren** [skɪ'tsiːrən] *v/t* (*no -ge-*, *h*) sketch
**Sklave** ['sklaːvə] *m* (*-n*; *-n*) slave (*a. fig*); **Sklaverei** [sklaːvə'rai] *f* (*-*; *no pl*) slavery; '**Sklavin** *f* (*-*; *-nen*) slave (*a. fig*); '**sklavisch** *adj* slavish (*a. fig*)
**Skonto** ['skɔnto] *m*, *n* (*-s*; *-s*) ECON (cash) discount
**Skorpion** [skɔr'pjoːn] *m* (*-s*; *-e*) ZO scorpion; ASTR Scorpio; ***er ist*** (***ein***) ~ he's (a) Scorpio
**Skrupel** ['skruːpəl] *m* (*-s*; *-*) scruple, qualm; '**skrupellos** *adj* unscrupulous
**Skulptur** [skʊlp'tuːɐ] *f* (*-*; *-en*) sculpture
**Slalom** ['slaːlɔm] *m* (*-s*; *-s*) slalom
**Slawe** ['slaːvə] *m* (*-n*; *-n*), '**Slawin** *f* (*-*; *-nen*) Slav; '**slawisch** *adj* Slav(ic)
**Slip** [slɪp] *m* (*-s*; *-s*) briefs, panties
'**Slipeinlage** *f* panty liner
**Slipper** ['slɪpɐ] *m* (*-s*; *-*) loafer, *esp Br* slip-on (shoe)
**Slowake** [slo'vaːkə] *m* (*-n*; *-n*) Slovak
**Slowakei** [slova'kai] *f* Slovakia
**Slo'wakin** *f* (*-*; *-nen*), **slo'wakisch** *adj* Slovak
**Smaragd** [sma'rakt] *m* (*-[e]s*; *-e*) MIN, **sma'ragdgrün** *adj* emerald
**Smoking** ['smoːkɪŋ] *m* (*-s*; *-s*) tuxedo, *Br* dinner jacket
**Snob** [snɔp] *m* (*-s*; *-s*) snob; **Snobismus** [sno'bɪsmʊs] *m* (*-*; *no pl*) snobbery; **sno'bistisch** *adj* snobbish
**so** [zoː] **1.** *adv* so; like this *or* that, this *or* that way; thus; such; (***nicht***) ***~ groß wie*** (not) as big as; ***~ ein***(***e***) such a; ***~ sehr*** so (F that) much; ***und ~ weiter*** and so on; ***oder ~ et.*** or s.th. like that; ***oder ~*** or so; ***~, fangen wir an!*** well *or* all right, let's begin!; F ***~ weit sein*** be ready; ***es ist ~ weit*** it's time; ***~ genannt*** so-called; ***doppelt ~ viel*** twice as much; ***~ viel wie möglich*** as much as possible; **2.** *cj* so, therefore; ***~ dass*** so that; **3.** *int*: ***~!*** all right!, o.k.!; that's it!; ***ach ~!*** I see

**s.o.** ABBR *of* ***siehe oben*** see above
**so'bald** [zo-] *cj* as soon as
**Socke** ['zɔkə] *f* (-; -*n*) sock
**Sockel** ['zɔkəl] *m* (-*s*; -) base; pedestal
**Sodbrennen** ['zo:t-] *n* (-*s*; *no pl*) MED heartburn
**soeben** [zo'e:bən] *adv* just (now)
**Sofa** ['zo:fa] *n* (-*s*; -*s*) sofa, settee, davenport
**sofern** [zo'fɛrn] *cj* if, provided that; ~ ***nicht*** unless
**soff** [zɔf] *pret of* ***saufen***
**sofort** [zo'fɔrt] *adv* at once, immediately, right away
**So'fortbildkamera** *f* PHOT instant camera
**Software** ['zɔftwɛ:ɐ] *f* EDP software; **~pa͵ket** *n* software package
**sog** [zo:k] *pret of* ***saugen***
**Sog** *m* (-[*e*]*s*; -*e*) suction, MAR *a.* wake
**sogar** [zo'ga:ɐ] *adv* even
**Sohle** ['zo:lə] *f* (-; -*n*) sole; *mining*: floor
**Sohn** [zo:n] *m* (-[*e*]*s*; *Söhne* ['zø:nə]) son
**Sojabohne** ['zo:ja-] *f* BOT soybean
**so'lange** [zo-] *cj* as long as
**Solar...** [zo'la:ɐ-] *in cpds ...energie etc*: solar ...
**solch** [zɔlç] *dem pron* such, like this *or* that
**Sold** [zɔlt] *m* (-[*e*]*s*; -*e*) MIL pay
**Soldat** [zɔl'da:t] *m* (-*en*; -*en*), **Sol'datin** *f* (-; -*nen*) soldier
**Söldner** ['zœldnɐ] *m* (-*s*; -) MIL mercenary
**Sole** ['zo:lə] *f* (-; -*n*) brine, salt water
**solidarisch** [zoli'da:rɪʃ] *adj*: ***sich ~ erklären mit*** declare one's solidarity with
**solide** [zo'li:də] *adj* solid, *fig a.* sound; reasonable (*prices*); steady (*person*)
**Solist** [zo'lɪst] *m* (-*en*; -*en*), **So'listin** *f* (-; -*nen*) soloist
**Soll** [zɔl] *n* (-[*s*]; -[*s*]) ECON debit; target, quota; ~ ***und Haben*** debit and credit
**sollen** ['zɔlən] *v/i* (*ge-*, *h*) *and v/aux* (*irr*, *no -ge-*, *h*) be to; be supposed to; (***was***) ***soll ich ...?*** (what) shall I ...?; ***du solltest*** (***nicht***) ***...*** you should(n't) ...; you ought(n't) to; ***was soll das?*** what's the idea?
**Solo** ['zo:lo] *n* (-*s*, -*s*, *Soli*) *esp* MUS solo; SPORT solo attempt *etc*
**so'mit** [zo-] *cj* thus, so, consequently
**Sommer** ['zɔmɐ] *m* (-*s*; -) summer (time); ***im*** ~ in (the) summer; **~ferien** *pl* summer vacation (*Br* holidays); **~frische** *f* summer resort
**'sommerlich** *adj* summery
**'Sommersprosse** *f* freckle
**'sommersprossig** *adj* freckled
**'Sommerzeit** *f* summertime; daylight saving (*Br* summer) time
**Sonate** [zo'na:tə] *f* (-; -*n*) MUS sonata
**Sonde** ['zɔndə] *f* (-; -*n*) probe (*a.* MED)
**Sonder...** ['zɔndɐ-] *in cpds ...angebot, ...ausgabe, ...flug, ...preis, ...wunsch, ...zug etc*: special ...
**'sonderbar** *adj* strange, F funny
**'Sonderling** *m* (-*s*; -*e*) eccentric
**'Sondermüll** *m* hazardous (*or* special toxic) waste; **~depo͵nie** *f* special waste dump
**sondern** ['zɔndɐn] *cj* but; ***nicht nur ..., ~ auch ...*** not only ... but also ...
**'Sonderschule** *f* special school (for the handicapped *etc*)
**Sonnabend** ['zɔn-] *m* Saturday
**Sonne** ['zɔnə] *f* (-; -*n*) sun
**sonnen** ['zɔnən] *v/refl* (*ge-*, *h*) sunbathe
**'Sonnenaufgang** *m* (***bei*** ~ at) sunrise
**'Sonnen|bad** *n*: ***ein ~ nehmen*** sunbathe; **~bank** *f* (-; -*bänke*) sunbed; **~blume** *f* BOT sunflower; **~brand** *m* sunburn; **~bräune** *f* suntan; **~brille** *f* sunglasses; **~creme** *f* suntan lotion, *Br* sun cream; **~ener͵gie** *f* solar energy; **~finsternis** *f* solar eclipse
**'sonnen'klar** F *adj* (as) clear as daylight
**'Sonnen|kol͵lektor** *m* solar panel; **~licht** *n* (-[*e*]*s*, *no pl*) sunlight; **~öl** *n* suntan oil; **~schein** *m* sunshine; **~schirm** *m* sunshade; **~schutz** *m* suntan lotion; **~seite** *f* sunny side (*a. fig*); **~stich** *m* sunstroke; **~strahl** *m* sunbeam; **~sys͵tem** *n* solar system; **~uhr** *f* sundial; **~untergang** *m* sunset
**sonnig** ['zɔnɪç] *adj* sunny (*a. fig*)
**Sonntag** ['zɔn-] *m* Sunday; (***am***) ~ on Sunday; **'sonntags** *adv* on Sundays
**'Sonntagsfahrer** *contp m* MOT Sunday driver
**sonst** [zɔnst] *adv* else; otherwise, or (else); normally, usually; ***~ noch et.*** (***jemand***)***?*** anything (anyone) else?; ***~ noch Fragen?*** any other questions?; ***~ nichts*** nothing else; ***alles wie ~*** everything as usual; ***nichts ist wie ~*** nothing is as it used to be; **'sonstig** *adj* other

S

**Sopran** [zo'pra:n] *m* (*-s*; *-e*) MUS, **Sopranistin** [zopra'nıstın] *f* (-; *-nen*) MUS soprano

**Sorge** ['zɔrgə] *f* (-; *-n*) worry; sorrow; trouble; care; ***sich ~n machen*** (***um***) worry *or* be worried (about); ***keine ~!*** don't worry!; **sorgen** ['zɔrgən] (*ge-*, *h*) **1.** *v/i*: ***~ für*** care for, take care of; ***dafür ~, dass*** see (to it) that; **2.** *v/refl*: ***sich ~ um*** worry *or* be worried about

'**Sorgenkind** *n* problem child

**Sorgfalt** ['zɔrkfalt] *f* (-; *no pl*) care

**sorgfältig** ['zɔrkfɛltıç] *adj* careful

**sorglos** ['zɔrk-] *adj* carefree; careless

**Sorte** ['zɔrtə] *f* (-; *-n*) sort, kind, type; **sortieren** [zɔr'ti:rən] *v/t* (*no -ge-*, *h*) sort; arrange; **Sortiment** [zɔrti'mɛnt] *n* (-[*e*]*s*; *-e*) ECON assortment

**Soße** ['zo:sə] *f* (-; *-n*) sauce; gravy

**sott** [zɔt] *pret of* ***sieden***

**Souffleur** [zu'flø:ɐ] *m* (*-s*; *-e*), **Souffleuse** [zu'flø:zə] *f* (-; *-n*) THEA prompter; **soufflieren** [zu'fli:rən] *v/i* (*no -ge-*, *h*) THEA prompt (***j-m*** s.o.)

**souverän** [zuvə'rɛ:n] *adj* POL sovereign

**Souveränität** [zuvərɛni'tɛ:t] *f* (-; *no pl*) POL sovereignty

**so'viel** [zo-] *cj* as far as; → ***so***; **so'weit** *cj* as far as; → ***so***; **so'wie** *cj* as well as, and ... as well; as soon as; **sowie'so** *adv* anyway, anyhow, in any case

**Sowjet** [zɔ'vjɛt] *m* (*-s*; *-s*), **sow'jetisch** *adj* HIST Soviet

**so'wohl** [zo-] *cj*: ***~ Lehrer als*** (***auch***) ***Schüler*** both teachers and students

**sozial** [zo'tsja:l] *adj* social

**Sozi'al...** *in cpds ...arbeiter*, *...demokrat*, *...versicherung etc*: social ...; ***~hilfe*** *f* welfare, *Br* social security; ***~ beziehen*** be on welfare (*Br* social security)

**Sozialismus** [zotsja'lısmʊs] *m* (-; *no pl*) socialism; **Sozialist(in)** (*-en*/-; *-en*/*-nen*), **sozia'listisch** *adj* socialist

**Sozi'alkunde** *f* PED social studies

**Sozi'alstaat** *m* welfare state

**Soziologe** [zotsjo'lo:gə] *m* (*-n*; *-n*) sociologist; **Soziologie** [zotsjolo'gi:] *f* (-; *no pl*) sociology; **Sozio'login** *f* (-; *-nen*) sociologist; **soziologisch** [zotsjo'lo:gıʃ] *adj* sociological

**sozu'sagen** *adv* so to speak

**Spagat** [ʃpa'ga:t] *m*: ***~ machen*** do the splits

**Spalier** [ʃpa'li:ɐ] *n* (*-s*; *-e*) BOT espalier; MIL *etc* lane

**Spalt** [ʃpalt] *m* (-[*e*]*s*; *-e*) crack, gap; **Spalte** ['ʃpaltə] *f* (-; *-n*) → ***Spalt***; PRINT column; '**spalten** *v/t* ([*irr*,] *ge-*, *h*) split (*a. fig*); POL divide; ***sich ~*** split (up); '**Spaltung** *f* (-; *-en*) split(ting); PHYS fission; *fig* split; POL division

**Span** [ʃpa:n] *m* (-[*e*]*s*; *Späne* ['ʃpɛ:nə]) chip; *pl* TECH shavings

**Spange** ['ʃpaŋə] *f* (-; *-n*) clasp

**Spaniel** ['ʃpa:njəl] *m* (*-s*; *-s*) ZO spaniel

**Spanien** ['ʃpa:njən] Spain

**Spanier** ['ʃpa:njɐ] *m* (*-s*; -), **Spanierin** ['ʃpa:njərın] *f* (-; *-nen*) Spaniard

**spanisch** ['ʃpa:nıʃ] *adj* Spanish

**spann** [ʃpan] *pret of* ***spinnen***

**Spann** *m* (-[*e*]*s*; *-e*) ANAT instep

**Spanne** ['ʃpanə] *f* (-; *-n*) span

'**spannen** (*ge-*, *h*) **1.** *v/t* stretch, tighten; put up (*line*); cock (*gun*); draw, bend (*bow*); **2.** *v/i* be (too) tight; ***~d*** *adj* exciting, thrilling, gripping

'**Spannung** *f* (-; *-en*) tension (*a.* TECH, POL, PSYCH); ELECTR voltage; *fig* suspense, excitement

'**Spannweite** *f* span, *fig a.* range

**Spar|buch** ['ʃpa:ɐ-] *n* savings book; ***~büchse*** *f esp Br* money box

**sparen** ['ʃpa:rən] *v/i and v/t* (*ge-*, *h*) save; economize; ***~ für*** *or* ***auf*** (*acc*) save up for; **Sparer(in)** ['ʃpa:rɐ (-rərın)] (*-s*; -/-; *-nen*) saver

'**Sparschwein(chen)** *n* piggy bank

**Spargel** ['ʃpargəl] *m* (*-s*; -) BOT asparagus

'**Sparkasse** *f* savings bank

'**Sparkonto** *n* savings account

**spärlich** ['ʃpɛ:ɐlıç] *adj* sparse, scant; scanty; poor (*attendance*)

**sparsam** ['ʃpa:ɐza:m] *adj* economical (***mit*** of); ***~ leben*** lead a frugal life; ***~ umgehen mit*** use sparingly; go easy on

'**Sparsamkeit** *f* (-; *no pl*) economy

**Spaß** [ʃpa:s] *m* (*-es*; *Späße* ['ʃpɛ:sə]) fun; joke; ***aus*** (***nur zum***) ***~*** (just) for fun; ***es macht viel*** (***keinen***) ***~*** it's great (no) fun; ***j-m den ~ verderben*** spoil s.o.'s fun; ***er macht nur ~*** he is only joking (F kidding); ***keinen ~ verstehen*** have no sense of humo(u)r

**spaßen** ['ʃpa:sən] *v/i* (*ge-*, *h*) joke

**spaßig** ['ʃpa:sıç] *adj* funny

'**Spaßvogel** *m* joker

**spät** [ʃpɛ:t] *adj and adv* late; ***am ~en***

***Nachmittag*** late in the afternoon; ***wie ~ ist es?*** what time is it?; ***von früh bis ~*** from morning till night; ***(fünf Minuten) zu ~ kommen*** be (five minutes) late; ***bis ~er!*** see you (later)!; → ***früher***
**Spaten** ['ʃpa:tən] *m* (*-s*; -) spade
'**spätestens** *adv* at the latest
**Spatz** [ʃpats] *m* (*-en*; *-en*) ZO sparrow
**spazieren** [ʃpa'tsi:rən]: ***~ fahren*** go (take *s.o.*) for a drive; take *s.o.* out; ***~ gehen*** go for a walk
**Spazierfahrt** [ʃpa'tsi:ɐ-] *f* drive, ride
**Spa'ziergang** *m* walk; ***e-n ~ machen*** go for a walk; **Spa'ziergänger(in)** [-gɛŋɐ (-ŋərɪn)] (*-s*; *-/-*; *-nen*) walker
**Specht** [ʃpɛçt] *m* (*-[e]s*; *-e*) ZO woodpecker
**Speck** [ʃpɛk] *m* (*-[e]s*; *-e*) bacon
**speckig** ['ʃpɛkɪç] *fig adj* greasy
**Spediteur** [ʃpedi'tø:ɐ] *m* (*-s*; *-e*) shipping agent; remover
**Spedition** [ʃpedi'tsjo:n] *f* (-; *-en*) shipping agency; moving (*Br* removal) firm
**Speer** [ʃpe:ɐ] *m* (*-[e]s*; *-e*) spear; SPORT javelin
**Speiche** ['ʃpaiçə] *f* (-; *-n*) spoke
**Speichel** ['ʃpaiçəl] *m* (*-s*; *no pl*) saliva, spit
**Speicher** ['ʃpaiçɐ] *m* (*-s*; -) storehouse; tank, reservoir; ARCH attic; EDP memory, store; **~dichte** *f* EDP bit density; **~kapazi,tät** *f* EDP memory capacity
'**speichern** *v/t* (*ge-*, *h*) store (up)
**Speicherung** ['ʃpaiçərʊŋ] *f* (-; *-en*) storage
**speien** ['ʃpaiən] *v/t* (*irr*, *ge-*, *h*) spit; spout; *volcano etc*: belch
**Speise** ['ʃpaizə] *f* (-; *-n*) food; dish; **~eis** *n* ice cream; **~kammer** *f* larder, pantry; **~karte** *f* menu
'**speisen** (*ge-*, *h*) **1.** *v/i* dine; **2.** *v/t* feed (*a.* ELECTR *etc*)
'**Speise|röhre** *f* ANAT gullet; **~saal** *m* dining hall; **~wagen** *m* RAIL diner, *esp Br* dining car
**Spekulant** [ʃpeku'lant] *m* (*-en*; *-en*) ECON speculator
**Spekulation** [ʃpekula'tsjo:n] *f* (-; *-en*) speculation, ECON *a.* venture
**spekulieren** [ʃpeku'li:rən] *v/i* (*no -ge-*, *h*) ECON speculate (***auf*** *acc* on; ***mit*** in)
**Spende** ['ʃpɛndə] *f* (-; *-n*) gift; contribution; donation; '**spenden** *v/t* (*ge-*, *h*) give (*a. fig*); donate (*a.* MED); **Spender** ['ʃpɛndɐ] *m* (*-s*; -) giver; donor (*a.* MED), **Spenderin** *f* (-; *-nen*) donor (*a.* MED)
**spendieren** [ʃpɛn'di:rən] *v/t* (*no -ge-*, *h*) ***j-m et. ~*** treat s.o. to s.th.
**Spengler** ['ʃpɛŋlɐ] *Austrian m* → ***Klempner***
**Sperling** ['ʃpɛrlɪŋ] *m* (*-s*; *-e*) ZO sparrow
**Sperre** ['ʃpɛrə] *f* (-; *-n*) barrier, RAIL *a.* gate; *fig* stop; TECH lock(ing device); barricade; SPORT suspension; PSYCH mental block; ECON embargo
'**sperren** *v/t* (*ge-*, *h*) close; ECON embargo; cut off; stop (*check*); SPORT suspend; obstruct; ***~ in*** (*acc*) lock (up) in
'**Sperr|holz** *n* plywood; **~müllabfuhr** *f* removal of bulky refuse
'**Sperrung** *f* (-; *-en*) closing
**Spesen** ['ʃpe:zən] *pl* expenses
**Spezi** ['ʃpe:tsi] F *m* (*-s*; *-[s]*) buddy, pal
**Spezial|ausbildung** [ʃpe'tsja:l-] *f* special training; **~gebiet** *n* special field, special(i)ty; **~geschäft** *n* specialized shop *or* store
**spezialisieren** [ʃpetsjali'zi:rən] *v/refl* (*no -ge-*, *h*) specialize (***auf*** *acc* in); **Spezialist(in)** [ʃpetsja'lɪst(ɪn)] (*-en*; *-en/-*; *-nen*) specialist; **Spezialität** [ʃpetsjali'tɛ:t] *f* (-; *-en*) special(i)ty; **speziell** [ʃpe'tsjɛl] *adj* specific, particular
**spezifisch** [ʃpe'tsi:fɪʃ] *adj* specific; ***~es Gewicht*** specific gravity
**Sphäre** ['sfɛ:rə] *f* (-; *-n*) sphere (*a. fig*)
**spicken** ['ʃpɪkən] (*ge-*, *h*) **1.** *v/t* GASTR lard (*a. fig*); **2.** F *v/i* PED crib
**spie** [ʃpi:] *pret of* ***speien***
**Spiegel** ['ʃpi:gəl] *m* (*-s*; -) mirror (*a. fig*)
'**Spiegelbild** *n* reflection (*a. fig*)
'**Spiegelei** *n* GASTR fried egg
'**spiegel'glatt** *adj* glassy; icy
'**spiegeln** *v/i and v/t* (*ge-*, *h*) reflect (*a. fig*); shine; ***sich ~*** be reflected (*a. fig*)
'**Spiegelung** *f* (-; *-en*) reflection
**Spiel** [ʃpi:l] *n* (*-[e]s*; *-e*) game (*a. fig*); match; play (*a.* THEA *etc*); gambling; *fig* gamble; ***auf dem ~ stehen*** be at stake; ***aufs ~ setzen*** risk; **spielen** ['ʃpi:lən] *v/i and v/t* (*ge-*, *h*) play (*a. fig*) (***um*** for); THEA act; perform; gamble; do (*the pools etc*); ***Klavier*** *etc* ~ play the piano *etc*; '**spielend** *fig adv* easily; **Spieler** ['ʃpi:lɐ] *m* (*-s*; -), **Spielerin** ['ʃpi:lərɪn] *f* (-; *-nen*) player; gambler
'**Spiel|feld** *n* (playing) field, pitch;

S

**~film** *m* feature film; **~halle** *f* amusement arcade, game room; **~kame,rad(in)** playmate; **~karte** *f* playing card; **~ka,sino** *n* casino; **~marke** *f* counter, chip; **~plan** *m* THEA *etc* program(me); **~platz** *m* playground; **~raum** *fig m* play, scope; **~regel** *f* rule (of the game); **~sachen** *pl* toys; **~stand** *m* score; **~uhr** *f* music (*Br* musical) box; **~verderber(in)** (*-s*; -/-; *-nen*) spoilsport; **~waren** *pl* toys; **~zeit** *f* THEA, SPORT season; playing (*film*: running) time

**'Spielzeug** *n* toy(s); **~...** *in cpds ...pistole etc*: toy ...

**Spieß** [ʃpiːs] *m* (*-es*; *-e*) MIL spear; GASTR spit; skewer

**spießen** ['ʃpiːsən] *v/t* (*ge-*, *h*) skewer

**Spießer** ['ʃpiːsɐ] F *contp m* (*-s*; -), **'spießig** F *contp adj* philistine

**Spinat** [ʃpi'naːt] *m* (*-[e]s*; *-e*) BOT spinach

**Spind** [ʃpɪnt] *n*, *m* (*-[e]s*; *-e*) locker

**Spindel** ['ʃpɪndəl] *f* (-; *-n*) spindle

**Spinne** ['ʃpɪnə] *f* (-; *-n*) ZO spider

**'spinnen** (*irr*, *ge-*, *h*) **1.** *v/t* spin (*a. fig*); **2.** F *contp v/i* be nuts; talk nonsense

**Spinner** ['ʃpɪnɐ] *m* (*-s*; -), **'Spinnerin** *f* (-; *-nen*) spinner; F *contp* nut, crackpot

**'Spinnrad** *n* spinning wheel

**'Spinnwebe** *f* (-; *-n*) cobweb

**Spion** [ʃpjoːn] *m* (*-s*; *-e*) spy

**Spionage** [ʃpjo'naːʒə] *f* (-; *no pl*) espionage; **spionieren** [ʃpjo'niːrən] *v/i* (*no -ge-*, *h*) spy; F snoop

**Spi'onin** *f* (-; *-nen*) spy

**Spirale** [ʃpi'raːlə] *f* (-; *-n*), **spi'ralförmig** [-fœrmɪç] *adj* spiral

**Spirituosen** [ʃpiri'tuoːzən] *pl* spirits

**Spiritus** ['ʃpiːritʊs] *m* spirit

**Spital** [ʃpi'taːl] *Austrian, Swiss n* (*-s*; *Spitäler* [ʃpi'tɛːlɐ]) hospital

**spitz** [ʃpɪts] *adj* pointed (*a. fig*); MATH acute; **~e Zunge** sharp tongue

**'Spitzbogen** *m* ARCH pointed arch

**Spitze** ['ʃpɪtsə] *f* (-; *-n*) point; tip; ARCH spire; BOT, GEOGR top; head (*a. fig*); lace; F MOT top speed; **~ sein** F be super, be (the) tops; **an der ~** at the top (*a. fig*)

**Spitzel** ['ʃpɪtsəl] *m* (*-s*; -) informer, F stoolpigeon

**spitzen** ['ʃpɪtsən] *v/t* (*ge-*, *h*) point, sharpen; purse; ZO prick up (*its ears*)

**'Spitzen...** *in cpds* top ...; hi-tech ...; **~technolo,gie** *f* high technology, hi tech

**'spitzfindig** *adj* quibbling

**'Spitzfindigkeit** *f* (-; *-en*) subtlety

**'Spitzhacke** *f* pickax(e), pick

**'Spitzname** *m* nickname

**Splitter** ['ʃplɪtɐ] *m* (*-s*; -), **'splittern** *v/i* (*ge-*, *h*, *sein*) splinter

**'splitter'nackt** F *adj* stark naked

**sponsern** ['ʃpɔnzɐn] *v/t* (*ge-*, *h*) sponsor

**Sponsor** ['ʃpɔnzɐ] *m* (*-s*; *-en* [ʃpɔn'zoːrən]) sponsor

**spontan** [ʃpɔn'taːn] *adj* spontaneous

**Sporen** ['ʃpoːrən] *pl* spurs (*a.* ZO); BIOL spores

**Sport** [ʃpɔrt] *m* (*-[e]s*; *no pl*) sport(s); PED physical education; **~ treiben** do sports

**'Sport...** *in cpds ...ereignis*, *...geschäft*, *...hemd*, *...verein*, *...zentrum etc*: *mst* sports ...; **~kleidung** *f* sportswear

**'Sportler** ['ʃpɔrtlɐ] *m* (*-s*; -), **Sportlerin** ['ʃpɔrtlərɪn] *f* (-; *-nen*) athlete

**'sportlich** *adj* athletic; casual, sporty

**'Sport|nachrichten** *pl* sports news; **~platz** *m* sports grounds; **~tauchen** *n* scuba diving; **~wagen** *m* stroller, *Br* pushchair; MOT sports car

**Spott** [ʃpɔt] *m* (*-[e]s*, *no pl*) mockery; derision

**'spott'billig** F *adj* dirt cheap

**spotten** ['ʃpɔtən] *v/i* (*ge-*, *h*) mock (**über** *acc* at), scoff (at); make fun (of)

**Spötter** ['ʃpœtɐ] *m* (*-s*; -) mocker, scoffer; **'spöttisch** *adj* mocking, derisive

**'Spottpreis** *m*: **für e-n ~** dirt cheap

**sprach** [ʃpraːx] *pret of* **sprechen**

**Sprache** ['ʃpraːxə] *f* (-; *-n*) language (*a. fig*); speech; **zur ~ kommen** (**bringen**) come up (bring *s.th.* up)

**'Sprach|fehler** *m* speech defect; **~gebrauch** *m* usage; **~la,bor** *n* language laboratory; **~lehre** *f* grammar; **~lehrer(in)** language teacher

**'sprachlich 1.** *adj* language ...; **2.** *adv*: **~ richtig** grammatically correct

**'sprachlos** *adj* speechless

**'Sprach|rohr** *fig n* mouthpiece; **~unterricht** *m* language teaching; **~wissenschaft** *f* linguistics

**sprang** [ʃpraŋ] *pret of* **springen**

**Spraydose** ['ʃpreː-] *f* spray can, aerosol (can)

**Sprechanlage** ['ʃprɛç-] *f* intercom

**sprechen** ['ʃprɛçən] *v/t and v/i* (*irr*, *ge-*,

S

*h*) speak (***j-n, mit j-m*** to s.o.); talk (to) (*both*: ***über*** *acc*, ***von*** about, of); ***nicht zu ~ sein*** be busy; **Sprecher(in)** ['ʃprɛçɐ (-çərɪn)] (*-s*; *-/-*; *-nen*) speaker; announcer; spokesman (spokeswoman); '**Sprechstunde** *f* office hours; MED office (*Br* consulting) hours, *Br* surgery; '**Sprechzimmer** *n* office, *Br a.* consulting room

**spreizen** ['ʃpraitsən] *v/t* (*ge-*, *h*) spread

**sprengen** ['ʃprɛŋən] *v/t* (*ge-*, *h*) blow up; blast; sprinkle; water; *fig* break up

'**Sprengkopf** *m* MIL warhead

'**Sprengstoff** *m* MIL explosive

'**Sprengung** *f* (*-*; *-en*) blasting; blowing up

**sprenkeln** ['ʃprɛŋkəln] *v/t* (*ge-*, *h*) speck(le), spot, dot

**Spreu** [ʃprɔʏ] *f* (*-*; *no pl*) chaff (*a. fig*)

**Sprichwort** ['ʃprɪç-] *n* proverb, saying

'**sprichwörtlich** *adj* proverbial (*a. fig*)

**sprießen** ['ʃpri:sən] *v/i* (*irr*, *ge-*, *sein*) BOT sprout

'**Springbrunnen** *m* fountain

**springen** ['ʃprɪŋən] *v/i* (*irr*, *ge-*, *sein*) jump, leap; *ball etc*: bounce; SPORT dive; *glass etc*: crack; break; burst; ***in die Höhe*** (***zur Seite***) *~* jump up (aside)

**Springer** ['ʃprɪŋɐ] *m* (*-s*; *-*) jumper; diver; *chess*: knight

'**Springflut** *f* spring tide

'**Springreiten** *n* show jumping

**Spritze** ['ʃprɪtsə] *f* (*-*; *-n*) MED injection, F shot; syringe; '**spritzen 1.** *v/i and v/t* (*ge-*, *h*) splash; spray (*a.* TECH, AGR); MED inject; give *s.o.* an injection of; **2.** *v/i* (*ge-*, *sein*) spatter; gush (***aus*** from); **Spritzer** ['ʃprɪtsɐ] *m* (*-s*; *-*) splash; dash

'**Spritzpis,tole** *f* TECH spray gun

'**Spritztour** F *f* MOT spin

**spröde** ['ʃprø:də] *adj* brittle (*a. fig*); rough

**spross** [ʃprɔs] *pret of* ***sprießen***

**Sprosse** ['ʃprɔsə] *f* (*-*; *-n*) rung

**Spruch** [ʃprʊx] *m* (*-[e]s*; *Sprüche* ['ʃprʏçə]) saying; decision; **~band** *n* banner

**Sprudel** ['ʃpru:dəl] *m* (*-s*; *-*) mineral water; '**sprudeln** *v/i* (*ge-*, *sein*) bubble

**Sprühdose** ['ʃpry:-] *f* spray can, aerosol (can); **sprühen** ['ʃpry:ən] *v/t and v/i* (*ge-*, *h*) spray; throw out (*sparks*)

'**Sprühregen** *m* drizzle

**Sprung** [ʃprʊŋ] *m* (*-[e]s*; *Sprünge* ['ʃprʏŋə]) jump, leap; SPORT dive; crack, fissure; **~brett** *n* SPORT diving board; springboard; *fig* stepping stone; **~schanze** *f* ski jump

**Spucke** ['ʃpʊkə] F *f* (*-*; *no pl*) spit

'**spucken** *v/i and v/t* (*ge-*, *h*) spit; F throw up

**Spuk** [ʃpu:k] *m* (*-[e]s*; *-e*) apparition, ghost; **spuken** ['ʃpu:kən] *v/i* (*ge-*, *h*) *~* ***in*** (*dat*) haunt; ***hier spukt es*** this place is haunted

**Spule** ['ʃpu:lə] *f* (*-*; *-n*) spool, reel; bobbin; ELECTR coil; '**spulen** *v/t* (*ge-*, *h*) spool, wind, reel

**spülen** ['ʃpy:lən] *v/t and v/i* (*ge-*, *h*) wash up, do the dishes; rinse; flush the toilet

'**Spülma,schine** *f* dishwasher

**Spur** [ʃpu:ɐ] *f* (*-*; *-en*) track(s); trail; print; lane; trace (*a. fig*); ***j-m auf der ~ sein*** be on s.o.'s trail; **spüren** ['ʃpy:rən] *v/t* (*ge-*, *h*) feel, sense; notice

'**spurlos** *adv* without leaving a trace

'**Spurweite** *f* RAIL ga(u)ge; MOT track

**St.** ABBR *of* ***Sankt*** St, Saint

**Staat** [ʃta:t] *m* (*-[e]s*; *-en*) state; POL government; '**Staatenbund** *m* confederacy, confederation; '**staatenlos** *adj* stateless; '**staatlich 1.** *adj* state ...; public, national; **2.** *adv*: ***~ geprüft*** qualified, registered

'**Staats|angehörige** *m*, *f* national, citizen, subject; **~angehörigkeit** *f* (*-*; *no pl*) nationality; **~anwalt** *m* JUR district attorney, *Br* (public) prosecutor; **~besuch** *m* official *or* state visit; **~bürger(in)** citizen; **~chef** *m* head of state; **~dienst** *m* civil (*or* public) service

'**staatseigen** *adj* state-owned

'**Staatsfeind** *m* public enemy

'**staatsfeindlich** *adj* subversive

'**Staats|haushalt** *m* budget; **~kasse** *f* treasury; **~mann** *m* statesman; **~oberhaupt** *n* head of (the) state; **~sekre,tär(in)** undersecretary of state; **~streich** *m* coup d'état; **~vertrag** *m* treaty; **~wissenschaft** *f* political science

**Stab** [ʃta:p] *m* (*-[e]s*; *Stäbe* ['ʃtɛ:bə]) staff (*a. fig*); bar; SPORT, MUS baton; SPORT pole

**Stäbchen** ['ʃtɛ:pçən] *pl* chopstick

'**Stabhochsprung** *m* SPORT pole vault

**stabil** [ʃta'bi:l] *adj* stable (*a.* ECON, POL); solid, strong; sound; **stabilisieren**

S

[ʃtabili'ziːrən] *v/t* (*no -ge-, h*) stabilize; **Stabilität** [-'tɛːt] *f* (-; *no pl*) stability
**stach** [ʃtaːx] *pret of* ***stechen***
**Stachel** ['ʃtaxəl] *m* (-*s*; -*n*) BOT, ZO spine, prick; ZO sting; **~beere** *f* BOT gooseberry; **~draht** *m* barbed wire
**stachelig** ['ʃtaxəlɪç] *adj* prickly
'**Stachelschwein** *n* ZO porcupine
**Stadel** ['ʃtaːdəl] *Austrian m* (-*s*; -[*n*]) barn
**Stadion** ['ʃtaːdjɔn] *n* (-*s*; -*ien*) stadium
**Stadium** ['ʃtaːdjʊm] *n* (-*s*; -*ien*) stage, phase
**Stadt** [ʃtat] *f* (-; *Städte* ['ʃtɛːtə]) town; city; ***die ~ Berlin*** the city of Berlin; ***in die ~ fahren*** go downtown, *esp Br* go (in)to town; **~bahn** *f* urban railway
**Städter** ['ʃtɛːtɐ] *m* (-*s*; -), '**Städterin** *f* (-; -*nen*) city dweller, F townie, *often contp* city slicker
'**Stadt|gebiet** *n* urban area; **~gespräch** *fig n* talk of the town
**städtisch** ['ʃɛːtɪʃ] *adj* urban; POL municipal
'**Stadt|plan** *m* city map; **~rand** *m* outskirts; **~rat** *m* town council; city councilman, *Br* town council(l)or; **~rundfahrt** *f* sightseeing tour; **~streicher(in)** city vagrant; **~teil** *m*, **~viertel** *n* quarter
**Staffel** ['ʃtafəl] *f* (-; -*n*) SPORT relay race *or* team; MIL, AVIAT squadron
**Staffelei** [ʃtafə'lai] *f* (-; -*en*) PAINT easel
'**staffeln** *v/t* (*ge-, h*) grade, scale
**stahl** [ʃtaːl] *pret of* ***stehlen***
**Stahl** *m* (-[*e*]*s*; *Stähle* ['ʃtɛːlə]) steel
'**Stahlwerk** *n* steelworks
**stak** [ʃtaːk] *pret of* ***stecken*** 2
**Stall** [ʃtal] *m* (-[*e*]*s*; *Ställe* ['ʃtɛlə]) stable
'**Stallknecht** *m* stableman
**Stamm** [ʃtam] *m* (-[*e*]*s*; *Stämme* ['ʃtɛmə]) BOT stem (*a.* LING), trunk; tribe, stock; *fig* regulars; **~...** *in cpds ...gast, ...kunde, ...spieler etc*: regular ...; **~baum** *m* family tree; ZO pedigree
**stammeln** ['ʃtaməln] *v/t* (*ge-, h*) stammer
**stammen** ['ʃta,ən] *v/i* (*ge-, h*) ***~ aus*** (***von***) come from; be from; ***~ von*** *work of art etc*: be by
'**Stammformen** *pl* LING principal parts, *mst* tenses
**stämmig** ['ʃtɛmɪç] *adj* sturdy; stout
'**Stammkneipe** F *f Br* local
**stampfen** ['ʃtampfən] (*ge-, h*) **1.** *v/t* mash; **2.** *v/i* stamp (***mit dem Fuß*** one's foot)
**stand** [ʃtant] *pret of* ***stehen***
**Stand** *m* (-[*e*]*s*; *Stände* ['ʃtɛndə]) a) (*no pl*) stand(ing), standing *or* upright position; footing, foothold; ASTR position; TECH *etc*: height, level (*a. fig*); reading; SPORT score; *racing*: standings; *fig* state; social standing, status, b) stand, stall, c) class; profession; ***auf den neuesten ~ bringen*** bring up to date; ***e-n schweren ~ haben*** have a hard time (of it); → ***außerstande***; → ***imstande***; → ***instand***; → ***zustande***
**Standard** ['ʃtandart] *m* (-*s*; -*s*) standard
'**Standbild** *n* statue
**Ständchen** ['ʃtɛntçən] *n* (-*s*; -) MUS serenade
**Ständer** ['ʃtɛndɐ] *m* (-*s*; -) stand; rack
**Standesamt** ['ʃtandəs-] *n* marriage license bureau, *Br* registry office; '**standesamtlich** *adj*: ***~e Trauung*** civil marriage; '**Standesbeamt|e** *m*, **-in** *f* civil magistrate, *Br* registrar
'**Standfoto** *n* still
'**standhaft** *adj* steadfast, firm; ***~ bleiben*** resist temptation
'**standhalten** *v/i* (*irr*, ***halten***, *sep, -ge-, h*) withstand, resist
**ständig** ['ʃtɛndɪç] *adj* constant; permanent (*address*)
'**Stand|licht** *n* (-[*e*]*s*; *no pl*) MOT parking light; **~ort** *m* position; location; MIL post, garrison; **~pauke** F *f*: ***j-m e-e ~ halten*** give s.o. a talking-to; **~platz** *m* stand; **~punkt** *m* (point of) view, standpoint; **~recht** *n* (-[*e*]*s*; *no pl*) MIL martial law; **~spur** *f* MOT (*Br* hard) shoulder; **~uhr** *f* grandfather clock
**Stange** ['ʃtaŋə] *f* (-; -*n*) pole; staff; rod, bar; carton (*of cigarettes*)
**Stängel** ['ʃtɛŋəl] *m* (-*s*; -) BOT stalk, stem
**stank** [ʃtaŋk] *pret of* ***stinken***
**Stanniol** [ʃta'njoːl] *n* (-*s*; -*e*) tin foil
**Stanze** ['ʃtantsə] *f* (-; -*n*), '**stanzen** *v/t* (*ge-, h*) TECH punch
**Stapel** ['ʃtaːpəl] *m* (-*s*; -) pile, stack; heap; ***vom ~ lassen*** MAR launch (*a. fig*); ***vom ~ laufen*** MAR be launched
'**Stapellauf** *m* MAR launch
'**stapeln** *v/t* (*ge-, h*) pile (up), stack
**stapfen** ['ʃtapfən] *v/i* (*ge-, sein*) trudge

**Star¹** [ʃtaːɐ] *m* (-[*e*]*s*; -*e*) ZO starling; MED cataract
**Star²** *m* (-*s*; -*s*) THEA *etc*: star
**starb** [ʃtarp] *pret of* ***sterben***
**stark** [ʃtark] **1.** *adj* strong (*a.* GASTR); powerful; *fig* heavy; F super, great; **2.** *adv*: **~ *beeindruckt*** greatly impressed; **~ *beschädigt*** badly damaged; **Stärke** ['ʃtɛrkə] *f* (-; -*n*) a) (*no pl*) strength, power; intensity, b) degree, c) CHEM starch; **'stärken** *v/t* (*ge-*, *h*) strengthen (*a. fig*); starch; ***sich* ~** take some refreshment; **'Starkstrom** *m* ELECTR high-voltage (*or* heavy) current; **Stärkung** *f* (-; -*en*) strengthening; refreshment; **'Stärkungsmittel** *n* MED tonic
**starr** [ʃtar] *adj* stiff; rigid (*a.* TECH); frozen (*face*); **~*er Blick*** (fixed) stare; **~ *vor Kälte* (*Entsetzen*)** frozen (scared) stiff; **'starren** *v/i* (*ge-*, *h*) stare (***auf*** *acc* at); **'starrköpfig** [-kœpfɪç] *adj* stubborn, obstinate; **'Starrsinn** *m* (-[*e*]*s*; *no pl*) stubbornness, obstinacy
**Start** [ʃtart] *m* (-[*e*]*s*; -*s*) start (*a. fig*); AVIAT take-off; *rocket*: lift-off
**'Startbahn** *f* AVIAT runway
**'startbereit** *adj* ready to start; AVIAT ready for take-off
**starten** ['ʃtartən] *v/i* (*ge-*, *sein*) *and v/t* (*ge-*, *h*) start (*a.* F); AVIAT take off; lift off; launch (*a. fig*)
**Station** [ʃta'tsjoːn] *f* (-; -*en*) station; MED ward; **stationär** [ʃtatsjo'nɛːɐ] *adj*: **~*er Patient*** MED in-patient; **stationieren** [ʃtatsjo'niːrən] *v/t* (*no -ge-*, *h*) MIL station; deploy; **Stationsvorsteher** *m* RAIL stationmaster
**Statist** [ʃta'tɪst] *m* (-*en*; -*en*) THEA extra
**Statistik** [ʃta'tɪstɪk] *f* (-; -*en*) statistics; **Sta'tistiker** [-tikɐ] *m* (-*s*; -) statistician; **sta'tistisch** *adj* statistical
**Stativ** [ʃta'tiːf] *n* (-*s*; -*e*) PHOT tripod
**statt** [ʃtat] *prp* instead of; **~ *et. zu tun*** instead of doing s.th.; **~'dessen** instead
**Stätte** ['ʃtɛtə] *f* (-; -*n*) place; scene
**'stattfinden** *v/i* (*irr*, ***finden***, *sep*, -*ge-*, *h*) take place; happen
**'stattlich** *adj* imposing; handsome
**Statue** ['ʃtaːtuə] *f* (-; -*n*) statue
**Statur** [ʃta'tuːɐ] *f* (-; -*en*) build
**Status** ['ʃtaːtʊs] *m* (-; -) state; status; **~sym͵bol** *n* status symbol; **~zeile** *f* EDP status line

**Stau** [ʃtau] *m* (-[*e*]*s*; -*s*, -*e*) MOT traffic jam *or* congestion
**Staub** [ʃtaup] *m* (-[*e*]*s*; TECH -*e*, *Stäube* ['ʃtɔʏbə]) dust (*a.* **~ *wischen***)
**'Staubecken** *n* reservoir
**stauben** ['ʃtaubən] *v/i* (*ge-*, *h*) give off *or* make dust; **staubig** ['ʃtaubɪç] *adj* dusty; **'staubsaugen** *v/i and v/t* (*ge-*, *h*) vacuum, F *Br* hoover; **'Staubsauger** *m* vacuum cleaner, F *Br* hoover; **'Staubtuch** *n* duster
**'Staudamm** *m* dam
**Staude** ['ʃtaudə] *f* (-; -*n*) BOT herbacious plant
**stauen** ['ʃtauən] *v/t* (*ge-*, *h*) dam up; ***sich* ~** MOT *etc* be stacked up
**staunen** ['ʃtaunən] *v/i* (*ge-*, *h*) be astonished *or* surprised (***über*** *acc* at)
**'Staunen** *n* (-*s*; *no pl*) astonishment, amazement
**Staupe** ['ʃtaupə] *f* (-; -*n*) VET distemper
**'Stausee** *m* reservoir
**stechen** ['ʃtɛçən] *v/i and v/t* (*irr*, *ge-*, *h*) prick; ZO sting, bite; stab; pierce; ***mit et.* ~ *in*** (*acc*) stick s.th. in(to); ***sich* ~** prick o.s.; **~*d*** *fig adj* piercing (*look*); stabbing (*pain*)
**'Stechuhr** *f* time clock
**Steckbrief** ['ʃtɛk-] *m* JUR "wanted" poster
**'steckbrieflich** *adv*: ***er wird* ~ *gesucht*** JUR a warrant is out against him
**'Steckdose** *f* ELECTR (wall) socket
**stecken** ['ʃtɛkən] (*ge-*, *h*) **1.** *v/t* stick; put; *esp* TECH insert (***in*** *acc* into); pin (***an*** *acc* to, on); AGR set, plant; **2.** *v/i* ([*irr*]) be; stick, be stuck; **~ *bleiben*** get stuck (*a. fig*)
**'Steckenpferd** *n* hobby horse; *fig* hobby
**Stecker** ['ʃtɛkɐ] *m* (-*s*; -) ELECTR plug
**'Steck|kon͵takt** *m* ELECTR plug (connection); **~nadel** *f* pin; **~platz** *m* EDP slot
**Steg** [ʃteːk] *m* (-[*e*]*s*; -*e*) footbridge
**Stegreif** ['ʃteːkraif] *m*: ***aus dem* ~** extempore, ad-lib; ***aus dem* ~ *sprechen*** *or* ***spielen*** *etc* extemporize, ad-lib
**stehen** ['ʃteːən] *v/i* (*irr*, *ge-*, *h*) stand; be; stand up; ***es steht ihr*** it suits (*or* looks well on) her; ***wie steht es*** (*or* ***das Spiel***)*?* what's the score?; ***hier steht, dass*** it says here that; ***wo steht das?*** where does it say so *or* that?; ***sich gut***

S

(***schlecht***) ~ be well (badly) off; F ***sich gut mit j-m*** ~ get along well with s.o.; ***wie steht es mit ...?*** what about ...?; F ***darauf stehe ich*** it turns me on; ~ ***bleiben*** stop; *esp* TECH come to a standstill (*a. fig*); ~ ***lassen*** leave (untouched); leave behind; ***alles*** ~ ***und liegen lassen*** drop everything; ***sich e-n Bart*** ~ ***lassen*** grow a beard

**'Steh|kragen** *m* stand-up collar; **~lampe** *f* floor (*Br* standard) lamp; **~leiter** *f* step ladder

**stehlen** ['ʃteːlən] *v/t and v/i* (*irr, ge-, h*) steal (*a. fig* **sich** ~)

**'Stehplatz** *m* standing ticket; *pl* standing room

**steif** [ʃtaif] *adj* stiff (***vor*** *dat* with)

**Steigbügel** ['ʃtaik-] *m* stirrup

**steigen** ['ʃtaigən] *v/i* (*irr, ge-, sein*) go, step; climb (*a.* AVIAT); *fig* rise, go up; ~ ***in*** (***auf***) (*acc*) get on (*bus, bike etc*); ~ ***aus*** (***von***) get off (*bus, horse etc*); ***aus dem Bett*** ~ get out of bed

**steigern** ['ʃtaigɐn] *v/t* (*ge-, h*) raise, increase; heighten; improve; LING compare; ***sich*** ~ improve, get better

**Steigerung** ['ʃtaigərʊŋ] *f* (-; *-en*) rise, increase; heightening; improvement; LING comparison

**'Steigung** *f* (-; *-en*) gradient; slope

**steil** [ʃtail] *adj* steep (*a. fig*)

**Stein** [ʃtain] *m* (-[*e*]*s*; *-e*) stone (*a.* BOT, MED), rock; **~bock** *m* ZO rock goat; ASTR Capricorn; ***er ist*** (***ein***) ~ he's (a) Capricorn; **~bruch** *m* quarry

**steinern** ['ʃtainɐn] *adj* (of) stone; *fig* stony

**'Steingut** *n* (-[*e*]*s*; *-e*) earthenware

**steinig** ['ʃtainɪç] *adj* stony

**steinigen** ['ʃtainɪgən] *v/t* (*ge-, h*) stone

**'Steinkohle** *f* (hard) coal

**'Steinmetz** [-mɛts] *m* (*-en*; *-en*) stonemason

**'Steinzeit** *f* (-; *no pl*) Stone Age

**Stellage** [ʃtɛ'laːʒə] *Austrian f* (-; *-n*) stand, rack, shelf

**Stelle** ['ʃtɛlə] *f* (-; *-n*) place; spot; point; job; authority; MATH figure; ***freie*** ~ vacancy, opening; ***auf der*** (***zur***) ~ on the spot; ***an erster*** ~ ***stehen*** (***kommen***) be (come) first; ***an j-s*** ~ in s.o.'s place; ***ich an deiner*** ~ if I were you

**'stellen** *v/t* (*ge-, h*) put; set (*trap, clock, task etc*); turn (*up, down etc*); ask (*question*); provide; corner, hunt down (*criminal etc*); **sich** ~ give o.s. up, turn o.s. in; ***sich gegen*** (***hinter***) ***j-n*** ~ *fig* oppose (back) s.o.; ***sich schlafend*** *etc* ~ pretend to be asleep *etc*; ***stell dich dorthin!*** (go and) stand over there!

**'Stellen|angebot** *n* vacancy; ***ich habe ein*** ~ I was offered a job; **~anzeige** *f* job ad(vertisement), employment ad; **~gesuch** *n* application for a job

**'stellenweise** *adv* partly, in places

**'Stellung** *f* (-; *-en*) position; post, job; ~ ***nehmen zu*** comment on, give one's opinion of; **~nahme** [-naːmə] *f* (-; *-n*) comment, opinion (*both*: **zu** on)

**'stellungslos** *adj* unemployed, jobless

**'stellvertretend** *adj* acting, deputy, vice-...; **'Stellvertreter(in)** (*-s*; *-/-*; *-nen*) representative; deputy

**Stelze** ['ʃtɛltsə] *f* (-; *-n*) stilt

**'stelzen** *v/i* (*ge-, sein*) stalk

**stemmen** ['ʃtɛmən] *v/t* (*ge-, h*) lift (*weight*); ***sich*** ~ ***gegen*** press o.s. against; *fig* resist *or* oppose *s.th.*

**Stempel** ['ʃtɛmpəl] *m* (*-s*; -) stamp; postmark; hallmark; BOT pistil

**'Stempelkissen** *n* ink pad

**'stempeln** (*ge-, h*) **1.** *v/t* stamp; cancel; hallmark; **2.** F *v/i*: ~ ***gehen*** be on the dole

**Stengel** → ***Stängel***

**Stenografie** [ʃtenogra'fiː] *f* (-; *-n*) shorthand; **stenogra'fieren** *v/t* (*no -ge-, h*) take down in shorthand

**Stenogramm** [ʃteno'gram] *n* (-[*e*]*s*; *-e*) shorthand notes; **Stenotypistin** [-ty'pɪstɪn] *f* (-; *-nen*) shorthand typist

**Steppdecke** ['ʃtɛp-] *f* quilt; **steppen** ['ʃtɛpən] (*ge-, h*) **1.** *v/t* quilt; stitch; **2.** *v/i* tap dance; **'Stepptanz** *m* tap dancing

**Sterbebett** ['ʃtɛrbə-] *n* deathbed

**'Sterbeklinik** *f* MED hospice

**sterben** ['ʃtɛrbən] *v/i* (*irr, ge-, sein*) die (***an*** *dat* of) (*a. fig*); ***im Sterben liegen*** be dying

**sterblich** ['ʃtɛrplɪç] *adj* mortal

**'Sterblichkeit** *f* (-; *no pl*) mortality

**Stereo** ['ʃteːreo] *n* (*-s*; *-s*) stereo

**steril** [ʃte'riːl] *adj* sterile; **Sterilisation** [ʃteriliza'tsjoːn] *f* (-; *-en*) sterilization; **sterilisieren** [ʃterili'ziːrən] *v/t* (*no -ge-, h*) sterilize

**Stern** [ʃtɛrn] *m* (-[*e*]*s*; *-e*) star (*a. fig*)

**'Sternbild** *n* ASTR constellation; sign of the zodiac

**'Sternchen** *n* (-*s*; -) PRINT asterisk
**'Sternenbanner** *n* Star-Spangled Banner, Stars and Stripes
**'Sternenhimmel** *m* starry sky
**'sternklar** *adj* starry
**'Stern|kunde** *f* (-; *no pl*) astronomy; **~schnuppe** *f* (-; -*n*) shooting *or* falling star; **~warte** *f* (-; -*n*) observatory
**stetig** ['ʃteːtɪç] *adj* continual, constant; steady; **stets** [ʃteːts] *adv* always
**Steuer**[1] ['ʃtɔʏɐ] *n* (-*s*; -) MOT (steering) wheel; MAR helm, rudder
**'Steuer**[2] *f* (-; -*n*) tax (***auf*** *acc* on)
**'Steuer|beamte** *m* revenue officer; **~berater** *m* tax adviser
**'Steuerbord** *n* MAR starboard
**'Steuer|erklärung** *f* tax return; **~ermäßigung** *f* tax allowance
**'steuerfrei** *adj* tax-free
**'Steuerhinterziehung** *f* tax evasion
**'Steuer|knüppel** *m* AVIAT control column *or* stick; **~mann** *m* MAR helmsman; *rowing*: cox, coxswain
**'steuern** *v/t and v/i* (*ge-, h*) steer, AVIAT, MAR *a.* navigate, pilot, MOT *a.* drive; TECH control (*a. fig*); *fig* direct
**'steuerpflichtig** *adj* taxable
**'Steuerrad** *n* MOT steering wheel
**'Steuerruder** *n* MAR helm, rudder
**'Steuersenkung** *f* tax reduction
**Steuerung** ['ʃtɔʏərʊŋ] *f* (-; -*en*) steering (system); ELECTR, TECH control (*a. fig*)
**'Steuerzahler** *m*, **'Steuerzahlerin** *f* taxpayer
**Stich** [ʃtɪç] *m* (-[*e*]*s*; -*e*) prick; ZO sting, bite; stab; stitch; *cards*: trick; engraving; ***im ~ lassen*** desert *or* abandon *s.o., s.th.*, leave *s.o.* in the lurch, let *s.o.* down
**Stichelei** [ʃtɪçə'lai] F *f* (-; -*en*) dig, gibe
**sticheln** ['ʃɪçəln] F *v/i* (*ge-, h*) make digs, gibe (***gegen*** at)
**'Stichflamme** *f* jet of flame
**'stichhaltig** *adj* valid, sound; watertight; ***nicht ~ sein*** F not hold water
**'Stich|probe** *f* spot check; **~tag** *m* cut-off date; deadline; **~wahl** *f* POL run-off; **~wort** *n* a) (-[*e*]*s*; -*e*) THEA cue, b) (-[*e*]*s*; -*wörter*) headword; **~e** *pl* notes; ***das Wichtigste in ~en*** an outline of the main points; **~wortverzeichnis** *n* index; **~wunde** *f* MED stab
**sticken** ['ʃtɪkən] *v/t and v/i* (*ge-, h*) embroider; **Stickerei** [ʃtɪkə'rai] *f* (-; -*en*) embroidery
**stickig** ['ʃtɪkɪç] *adj* stuffy
**'Stickstoff** *m* (-[*e*]*s*; *no pl*) CHEM nitrogen
**Stief...** [ʃtiːf-] *in cpds ...mutter etc*: step...
**Stiefel** ['ʃtiːfəl] *m* (-*s*; -) boot
**'Stiefmütterchen** [-mʏtɐçən] *n* (-*s*; -) BOT pansy
**stieg** [ʃtiːk] *pret of* ***steigen***
**Stiege** ['ʃtiːgə] *Austrian f* (-; -*n*) → ***Treppe***
**Stiel** [ʃtiːl] *m* (-[*e*]*s*; -*e*) handle; stick; stem; BOT stalk
**Stier** [ʃtiːɐ] *m* (-[*e*]*s*; -*e*) ZO bull; ASTR Taurus; ***er ist*** (***ein***) ~ he's (a) Taurus
**'Stierkampf** *m* bullfight
**stieß** [ʃtiːs] *pret of* ***stoßen***
**Stift** [ʃtɪft] *m* (-[*e*]*s*; -*e*) pen; pencil; crayon; TECH pin; peg
**stiften** ['ʃtɪftən] *v/t* (*ge-, h*) donate; *fig* cause; **'Stiftung** *f* (-; -*en*) donation
**Stil** [ʃtiːl] *m* (-[*e*]*s*; -*e*) style (*a. fig*); ***in großem ~*** in (grand) style; *fig* on a large scale; **stilistisch** [ʃti'lɪstɪʃ] *adj* stylistic
**still** [ʃtɪl] *adj* quiet, silent; still; ***sei***(***d***) ***~!*** be quiet!; ***halt ~!*** keep still!; ***sich ~ verhalten*** keep quiet (*or* still)
**Stille** ['ʃtɪlə] *f* (-; *no pl*) silence, quiet(ness); ***in aller ~*** quietly; secretly
**Stilleben** *n* → ***Stillleben***
**stillen** ['ʃtɪlən] *v/t* (*ge-, h*) nurse, breastfeed; *fig* relieve (*pain*); satisfy (*curiosity etc*); quench (*one's thirst*)
**'stillhalten** *v/i* (*irr*, ***halten***, *sep*, *-ge-, h*) keep still
**'Stillleben** *n* PAINT still life
**'stilllegen** *v/t* (*sep, -ge-, h*) close down
**'stillos** *adj* lacking style, tasteless
**'stillschweigend** *adj* tacit
**'Stillstand** *m* (-[*e*]*s*; *no pl*) standstill, stop, *fig a.* stagnation (*a.* ECON); deadlock; **'stillstehen** *v/i* (*irr*, ***stehen***, *sep, -ge-, h*) (have) stop(ped), (have) come to a standstill
**'Stilmöbel** *pl* period furniture
**'stilvoll** *adj* stylish; ***~ sein*** have style
**'Stimmband** *n* ANAT vocal cord
**'stimmberechtigt** *adj* entitled to vote
**Stimme** ['ʃtɪmə] *f* (-; -*n*) voice; POL vote; ***sich der ~ enthalten*** abstain
**'stimmen** (*ge-, h*) **1.** *v/i* be right, be true, be correct; POL vote (***für*** for; ***gegen*** against); ***es stimmt et. nicht*** (***damit*** *or* ***mit ihm***) there's s.th. wrong (with it *or*

S

him); **2.** *v/t* MUS tune; ***j-n traurig*** *etc* ~ make s.o. sad *etc*
**'Stimmenthaltung** *f* abstention
**'Stimmrecht** *n* right to vote
**'Stimmung** *f* (-; *-en*) mood; atmosphere; feeling
**'stimmungsvoll** *adj* atmospheric
**'Stimmzettel** *m* ballot (paper)
**stinken** ['ʃtɪŋkən] *v/i* (*irr, ge-, h*) stink (*a. fig*) (***nach*** of)
**Stipendium** [ʃti'pɛndjʊm] *n* (*-s*; *-ien*) UNIV scholarship, grant
**stippen** ['ʃtɪpən] *v/t* (*ge-, h*) dip
**'Stippviˌsite** F *f* flying visit
**Stirn** [ʃtɪrn] *f* (-; *-en*) ANAT forehead; ***die ~ runzeln*** frown
**stöbern** ['ʃtøːbɐn] F *v/i* (*ge-, h*) rummage (about)
**stochern** ['ʃtɔxɐn] *v/i* (*ge-, h*) ***im Feuer*** ~ poke the fire; ***im Essen*** ~ pick at one's food; ***in den Zähnen*** ~ pick one's teeth
**Stock** [ʃtɔk] *m* (-[*e*]*s*; *Stöcke* ['ʃtœkə]) stick; cane; ARCH stor(e)y, floor; ***im ersten*** ~ on the second (*Br* first) floor
**'stock'dunkel** F *adj* pitch-dark
**stocken** ['ʃtɔkən] *v/i* (*ge-, h*) stop (short); falter; *traffic*: be jammed; **~d** **1.** *adj* halting; **2.** *adv*: ***~ lesen*** stumble through a text; ***~ sprechen*** speak haltingly
**'Stockfleck** *m* mo(u)ld stain
**'Stockung** *f* (-; *-en*) holdup, delay
**'Stockwerk** *n* stor(e)y, floor
**Stoff** [ʃtɔf] *m* (-[*e*]*s*; *-e*) material, stuff (*a.* F); fabric, textile; cloth; CHEM, PHYS *etc* substance; *fig* subject (matter)
**'stofflich** *adj* material
**'Stofftier** *n* soft toy animal
**'Stoffwechsel** *m* BIOL metabolism
**stöhnen** ['ʃtøːnən] *v/i* (*ge-, h*) groan, moan (*a. fig*)
**Stollen** ['ʃtɔlən] *m* (*-s*; -) tunnel, gallery
**stolpern** ['ʃtɔlpɐn] *v/i* (*ge-, sein*) stumble (***über*** *acc* over), trip (over) (*both a. fig*)
**stolz** [ʃtɔlts] *adj* proud (***auf*** *acc* of)
**Stolz** *m* (*-es*; *no pl*) pride (***auf*** *acc* in)
**stolzieren** [ʃtɔl'tsiːrən] *v/i* (*no -ge-, sein*) strut, stalk
**stopfen** ['ʃtɔpfən] *v/t* (*ge-, h*) darn, mend; stuff, fill (*a. pipe*)
**Stoppel** ['ʃtɔpəl] *f* (-; *-n*) stubble
**'Stoppelbart** F *m* stubbly beard
**'stoppelig** *adj* stubbly, bristly
**'Stoppelzieher** *Austrian m* corkscrew
**stoppen** ['ʃtɔpən] *v/i and v/t* (*ge-, h*) stop (*a. fig*); *esp* SPORT time
**'Stopp|licht** *n* (-[*e*]*s*; *-er*) MOT stop light; **~schild** *n* stop sign; **~uhr** *f* stopwatch
**Stöpsel** ['ʃtœpsəl] *m* (*-s*; -) stopper; plug
**Storch** [ʃtɔrç] *m* (-[*e*]*s*; *Störche* ['ʃtœrçə]) ZO stork
**stören** ['ʃtøːrən] *v/t and v/i* (*ge-, h*) disturb; trouble; bother, annoy; be in the way; ***lassen Sie sich nicht ~!*** don't let me disturb you!; ***darf ich Sie kurz ~?*** may I trouble you for a minute?; ***es*** (***er***) ***stört mich nicht*** it (he) doesn't bother me, I don't mind (him); ***stört es Sie***(***, wenn ich rauche***)***?*** do you mind (my smoking *or* if I smoke)?
**'Störenfried** [-friːt] *m* (-[*e*]*s*; *-e*) troublemaker; intruder
**Störfall** ['ʃtøːɐ-] *m* TECH accident
**störrisch** ['ʃtœrɪʃ] *adj* stubborn, obstinate
**'Störung** *f* (-; *-en*) disturbance; trouble (*a.* TECH); TECH breakdown; TV, *radio*: interference
**Stoß** [ʃtoːs] *m* (*-es*; *Stöße* ['ʃtøːsə]) push, shove; thrust; kick; butt; blow, knock; shock; MOT jolt; bump, *esp* TECH, PHYS impact; pile, stack; **'Stoßdämpfer** *m* MOT shock absorber; **stoßen** ['ʃtoːsən] *v/t* (*irr, ge-, h*) *and v/i* (*sein*) push, shove; thrust; kick; butt; knock, strike; pound; ***~ gegen*** *or* ***an*** (*acc*) bump *or* run into *or* against; ***sich den Kopf ~*** (***an*** *dat*) knock one's head (against); ***~ auf*** (*acc*) strike (*oil etc*); *fig* come across; meet with; **'stoßgesichert** *adj* shockproof, shock-resistant; **'Stoßstange** *f* MOT bumper; **'Stoßzahn** *m* ZO tusk; **'Stoßzeit** *f* rush hour, peak hours
**stottern** ['ʃtɔtɐn] *v/i and v/t* (*ge-, h*) stutter
**Str.** ABBR *of* ***Straße*** St, Street; Rd, Road
**'Strafanstalt** *f* prison, penitentiary; **'strafbar** *adj* punishable, penal; ***sich ~ machen*** commit an offense (*Br* offence); **Strafe** ['ʃtraːfə] *f* (-; *-n*) punishment; JUR, ECON, SPORT penalty (*a. fig*); fine; ***20 Mark ~ zahlen müssen*** be fined 20 marks; ***zur ~*** as a punishment; **'strafen** *v/t* (*ge-, h*) punish
**straff** [ʃtraf] *adj* tight; *fig* strict

S

**'straffrei** *adj*: ~ ***ausgehen*** go unpunished
**'Straf|gefangene** *m, f* prisoner, convict; **~gesetz** *n* criminal law
**sträflich**['ʃtrɛːflɪç] **1.** *adj* inexcusable; **2.** *adv*: ~ ***vernachlässigen*** neglect badly
**'Straf|mi,nute** *f* SPORT penalty minute; **~pro,zess** *m* JUR criminal action, trial; **~raum** *m* SPORT penalty area (F box); **~stoß** *m* SPORT penalty kick; **~tat** *f* JUR criminal offense (*Br* offence); crime; **~zettel** *m* ticket
**Strahl** [ʃtraːl] *m* (-[*e*]*s*, -*en*) ray (*a. fig*); beam; flash; jet; **strahlen** ['ʃtraːlən] *v/i* (*ge-*, *h*) radiate; shine (brightly); *fig* beam (***vor*** with); **'Strahlen...** *in cpds* PHYS *...schutz etc*: radiation ...
**'Strahlung** *f* (-; -*en*) PHYS radiation
**Strähne** ['ʃtrɛːnə] *f* (-; -*n*) strand; streak
**stramm** ʃtram] *adj* tight; **~stehen** MIL stand to attention
**strampeln** ['ʃtrampəln] *v/i* (*ge-*, *h*) kick
**Strand** [ʃtrant] *m* (-[*e*]*s*; *Strände* ['ʃtrɛndə]) beach; ***am*** ~ on the beach
**stranden** ['ʃtrandən] *v/i* (*ge-*, *sein*) MAR strand; *fig* fail
**'Strand|gut** *n* flotsam and jetsam (*a. fig*); **~korb** *m* roofed wicker beach chair
**Strang** [ʃtraŋ] *m* (-[*e*]*s*; *Stränge* ['ʃtrɛŋə]) rope; *esp* ANAT cord
**Strapaze** [ʃtra'paːtsə] *f* (-; -*n*) strain, exertion, hardship; **strapazieren** [ʃtrapa'tsiːrən] *v/t* (*no -ge-*, *h*) wear *s.o. or s.th.* out, be hard on; **strapazierfähig** *adj* longwearing, *Br* hardwearing
**strapaziös** [ʃtrapa'tsjøːs] *adj* strenuous
**Straße** ['ʃtraːsə] *f* (-; -*n*) road; street; GEOGR strait; ***auf der*** ~ on the road; on (*Br a.* in) the street
**'Straßen|arbeiten** *pl* roadworks; **~bahn** *f* streetcar, *Br* tram; **~ca,fé** *n* sidewalk (*Br* pavement) café; **~karte** *f* road map; **~kehrer** [-keːrɐ] *m* (-*s*; -) street sweeper; **~kreuzung** *f* crossroads; intersection; **~lage** *f* MOT roadholding; **~rand** *m* roadside; ***am*** ~ at *or* by the roadside; **~sperre** *f* road block
**strategisch** [ʃtra'teːgɪʃ] *adj* strategic
**sträuben** ['ʃtrɔʏbən] *v/t and v/refl* (*ge-*, *h*) ruffle (up); bristle (up); ***sich*** ~ ***gegen*** struggle against
**Strauch** [ʃtraux] *m* (-[*e*]*s*; *Sträucher* ['ʃtrɔʏçɐ]) BOT shrub, bush
**straucheln** ['ʃtrauxəln] *v/i* (*ge-*, *sein*) stumble
**Strauß**[1] [ʃtraus] *m* (-*es*; -*e*) ZO ostrich
**Strauß**[2] *m* (-*es*; *Sträuße* ['ʃtrɔʏsə]) bunch, bouquet
**Strebe** ['ʃtreːbə] *f* (-; -*n*) prop, stay (*a.* AVIAT, MAR); **'streben** *v/i* (*ge-*, *h*) strive (***nach*** for, after); **Streber** ['ʃtreːbɐ] *m* (-*s*; -) pusher; PED *etc* grind, *Br* swot; **strebsam** ['ʃtreːp-] *adj* ambitious
**Strecke** ['ʃtrɛkə] *f* (-; -*n*) distance (*a.* SPORT, MATH), way; route; RAIL line; SPORT course; stretch; ***zur*** ~ ***bringen*** kill; *esp fig* hunt down; **'strecken** *v/t* (*ge-*, *h*) stretch (out), extend
**Streich** [ʃtraiç] *m* (-[*e*]*s*; -*e*) trick, prank, practical joke; ***j-m e-n*** ~ ***spielen*** play a trick *or* joke on s.o.
**streicheln** ['ʃtraiçəln] *v/t* (*ge-*, *h*) stroke, caress
**streichen** ['ʃtraiçən] *v/t and v/i* (*irr*, *ge-*, *h*) paint; spread; cross out; cancel; MAR strike; MUS bow; ***mit der Hand*** ~ ***über*** (*acc*) run one's hand over; ~ ***durch*** roam (*acc*); **Streicher(in)** ['ʃtraiçɐ (-çərɪn)] (-*s*; -/-; -*nen*) MUS string player, *pl the* strings
**'Streich|holz** *n* match; **~instru,ment** *n* MUS string instrument; **~or,chester** *n* MUS string orchestra
**'Streichung** *f* (-; -*en*) cancellation; cut
**Streife** ['ʃtraifə] *f* (-; -*n*) patrol; ***auf*** ~ ***gehen*** go on patrol; ***auf*** ~ ***sein in*** (*dat*) patrol
**'streifen** *v/t and v/i* (*ge-*, *h*) touch, brush (against); MOT scrape against; graze; slip (***von*** off); *fig* touch on; ~ ***durch*** roam (*acc*), wander through
**'Streifen** *m* (-*s*; -) stripe; strip
**'Streifenwagen** *m* squad (*Br* patrol) car
**'Streifschuss** *m* MED graze
**'Streifzug** *m* tour (***durch*** of)
**Streik** [ʃtraik] *m* (-[*e*]*s*; -*s*) strike, walkout; ***wilder*** ~ wildcat strike
**'Streikbrecher** *m* strikebreaker, *Br* blackleg, *contp* scab
**streiken** ['ʃtraikən] *v/i* (*ge-*, *h*) (go *or* be on) strike; F *fig* refuse (to work *etc*)
**'Streikende** *m, f* (-*n*; -*n*) striker
**'Streikposten** *m* picket
**Streit** [ʃtrait] *m* (-[*e*]*s*; -*e*) quarrel; argument; fight; POL *etc* dispute; ~ ***anfangen*** pick a fight *or* quarrel; ~ ***suchen*** be

looking for trouble; **streiten** ['ʃtraitən] *v/i and v/refl* (*irr*, *ge-*, *h*) quarrel, argue, fight (*all*: ***wegen***, ***über*** *acc* about, over); ***sich ~ um*** fight for

'**Streitfrage** *f* (point at) issue

**streitig** ['ʃtraitɪç] *adj*: ***j-m et. ~ machen*** dispute s.o.'s right to s.th.

'**Streitkräfte** *pl* MIL (armed) forces

'**streitsüchtig** *adj* quarrelsome

**streng** [ʃtrɛŋ] *adj* strict; severe; harsh; rigid; ***~ genommen*** strictly speaking

**Strenge** ['ʃtrɛŋə] *f* (-; *no pl*) strictness; severity; harshness; rigidity

'**strenggläubig** *adj* REL orthodox

**Stress** [ʃtrɛs] *m* (*-es*; *no pl*) stress; ***im ~*** under stress

**Streu** [ʃtrɔʏ] *f* (-; *-en*) AGR litter

'**streuen** *v/t and v/i* (*ge-*, *h*) scatter (*a.* PHYS); spread; sprinkle; grit

**streunen** ['ʃtrɔʏnən] *v/i* (*ge-*, *sein*), **~d** *adj* stray

**strich** [ʃtrɪç] *pret of* ***streichen***

**Strich** *m* (-[*e*]*s*; *-e*) line; stroke; F red-light district; F ***auf den ~ gehen*** walk the streets; **~kode** *m* bar code; **~junge** F *m* male prostitute

'**strichweise** *adv* in parts; ***~ Regen*** scattered showers

**Strick** [ʃtrɪk] *m* (-[*e*]*s*; *-e*) cord; rope

**stricken** ['ʃtrɪkən] *v/t and v/i* (*ge-*, *h*) knit

'**Strick|jacke** *f* cardigan; **~leiter** *f* rope ladder; **~nadel** *f* knitting needle; **~waren** *pl* knitwear; **~zeug** *n* knitting (things)

**Striemen** ['ʃtri:mən] *m* (*-s*; -) welt, weal

**stritt** [ʃtrɪt] *pret of* ***streiten***

**strittig** ['ʃtrɪtɪç] *adj* controversial; ***~er Punkt*** point at issue

**Stroh** [ʃtro:] *n* (-[*e*]*s*; *no pl*) straw; thatch; **~dach** *n* thatch(ed) roof; **~halm** *m* straw; **~hut** *m* straw hat; **~witwe** F *f* grass widow; **~witwer** F *m* grass widower

**Strom** [ʃtro:m] *m* (-[*e*]*s*; *Ströme* ['ʃtrø:mə]) (large) river; current (*a.* ELECTR); ***ein ~ von*** a stream of (*a. fig*); ***es gießt in Strömen*** it's pouring (with rain)

**strom'ab(wärts)** *adv* downstream

**strom'auf(wärts)** *adv* upstream

'**Stromausfall** *m* ELECTR power failure, blackout

**strömen** ['ʃtrø:mən] *v/i* (*ge-*, *sein*) stream (*a. fig*), flow, run; pour (*a. fig*)

'**Stromkreis** *m* ELECTR circuit

'**stromlinienförmig** *adj* streamlined

'**Stromschnelle** *f* (-; *-n*) GEOGR rapid

'**Stromstärke** *f* ELECTR amperage

'**Strömung** *f* (-; *-en*) current, *fig a.* trend

**Strophe** ['ʃtro:fə] *f* (-; *-n*) stanza, verse

**strotzen** ['ʃtrɔtsən] *v/i* (*ge-*, *h*) ***~ von*** be full of, abound with; ***~ vor*** (*dat*) be bursting with

**Strudel** ['ʃtru:dəl] *m* (*-s*; -) whirlpool (*a. fig*), eddy

**Struktur** [ʃtrʊk'tu:ɐ] *f* (-; *-en*) structure, pattern

**Strumpf** [ʃtrʊmpf] *m* (-[*e*]*s*; *Strümpfe* ['ʃtrʏmpfə]) stocking

'**Strumpfhose** *f* pantyhose, *Br* tights

**struppig** ['ʃtrʊpɪç] *adj* shaggy

**Stück** [ʃtʏk] *n* (-[*e*]*s*; *-e*) piece; part; lump; AGR head (*a. pl*); THEA play; ***2 Mark das ~*** 2 marks each; ***im*** *or* ***am ~*** in one piece; ***in ~e schlagen*** (***reißen***) smash (tear) to pieces; '**stückweise** *adv* bit by bit (*a. fig*); ECON by the piece

**Student** [ʃtu'dɛnt] *m* (*-en*; *-en*), **Stu'dentin** *f* (-; *-nen*) student; **Studie** ['ʃtu:djə] *f* (-; *-n*) study (***über*** *acc* of); '**Studienplatz** *m* university *or* college place; **studieren** [ʃtu'di:rən] *v/t and v/i* (*no -ge-*, *h*) study, be a student (of) (***an*** *dat* at); **Studium** ['ʃtu:djʊm] *n* (*-s*; *-ien*) studies; ***das ~ der Medizin*** *etc* the study of medicine *etc*

**Stufe** ['ʃtu:fə] *f* (-; *-n*) step; level; stage

'**Stufenbarren** *m* SPORT uneven parallel bars

**Stuhl** [ʃtu:l] *m* (-[*e*]*s*; *Stühle* ['ʃty:lə]) chair; MED stool; **~gang** *m* (-[*e*]*s*; *no pl*) MED (bowel) movement; **~lehne** *f* back of a chair

**stülpen** ['ʃtʏlpən] *v/t* (*ge-*, *h*) put (***auf*** *acc*, ***über*** *acc* over, on)

**stumm** [ʃtʊm] *adj* dumb, mute; *fig* silent

**Stummel** ['ʃtʊməl] *m* (*-s*; -) stub, stump, butt

'**Stummfilm** *m* silent film

**Stümper** ['ʃtʏmpɐ] F *m* (*-s*; -) bungler

**stumpf** [ʃtʊmpf] *adj* blunt, dull (*a. fig*)

**Stumpf** *m* (-[*e*]*s*; *Stümpfe* ['ʃtʏmpfə]) stump, stub

'**stumpfsinnig** *adj* dull; monotonous

**Stunde** ['ʃtʊndə] *f* (-; *-n*) hour; PED class, lesson; period

'**Stundenkilo,meter** *m* kilometer (*Br* kilometre) per hour

'**stundenlang 1.** *adj*: ***nach ~em Warten***

after hours of waiting; **2.** *adv* for hours (and hours)
'**Stunden|lohn** *m* hourly wage; **~plan** *m* schedule, *Br* timetable
'**stundenweise** *adv* by the hour
'**Stundenzeiger** *m* hour hand
**stündlich** ['ʃtʏntlɪç] **1.** *adj* hourly; **2.** *adv* hourly, every hour
**Stupsnase** ['ʃtʊps-] F *f* snub nose
**stur** [ʃtuːɐ] F *adj* pigheaded
**Sturm** [ʃtʊrm] *m* (-[*e*]*s*; *Stürme* ['ʃtʏrmə]) storm (*a. fig*); **stürmen** ['ʃtʏrmən] *v/t* (*ge-*, *h*) *and v/i* (*ge-*, *sein*) storm; SPORT attack; rush; **Stürmer(in)** ['ʃtʏrmɐ (-mərɪn)] (*-s*; *-/-*; *-nen*) SPORT forward; *esp soccer*: striker; **stürmisch** ['ʃtʏrmɪʃ] *adj* stormy; *fig* wild, vehement
**Sturz** [ʃtʊrts] *m* (*-es*; *Stürze* ['ʃtʏrtsə]) fall (*a. fig*); POL *etc*: overthrow
**stürzen** ['ʃtʏrtsən] **1.** *v/i* (*ge-*, *sein*) fall; crash; rush, dash; ***schwer ~*** have a bad fall; **2.** *v/t* (*ge-*, *h*) throw; POL *etc*: overthrow; ***j-n ins Unglück ~*** ruin s.o.; ***sich stürzen aus*** throw o.s. out of; ***sich ~ auf*** (*acc*) throw o.s. at
'**Sturzflug** *m* AVIAT nosedive
'**Sturzhelm** *m* crash helmet
**Stute** ['ʃtuːtə] *f* (-; *-n*) ZO mare
**Stütze** ['ʃtʏtsə] *f* (-; *-n*) support, prop; *fig a.* aid
**stutzen** ['ʃtʊtsən] (*ge-*, *h*) **1.** *v/t* trim, clip; **2.** *v/i* stop short; (begin to) wonder
**stützen** ['ʃtʏtsən] *v/t* (*ge-*, *h*) support (*a. fig*); ***sich ~ auf*** (*acc*) lean on; *fig* be based on
'**Stütz|pfeiler** *m* ARCH supporting column; **~punkt** *m* MIL base (*a. fig*)
**Styropor**® [ʃtyro'poːɐ] *n* (*-s*; *no pl*) Styrofoam®, *Br* polystyrene
**s.u.** ABBR *of* ***siehe unten*** see below
**Subjekt** [zʊp'jɛkt] *n* (-[*e*]*s*; *-e*) LING subject; *contp* character
**subjektiv** [zʊpjɛk'tiːf] *adj* subjective
**Substantiv** ['zʊpstantiːf] *n* (*-s*; *-e*) LING noun
**Substanz** [zʊp'stants] *f* (-; *-en*) substance (*a. fig*)
**subtrahieren** [zʊptra'hiːrən] *v/t* (*no -ge-*, *h*) MATH subtract; **Subtraktion** [zʊptrak'tsjoːn] *f* (-; *-en*) MATH subtraction
**subventionieren** [zʊpvɛntsjo'niːrən] *v/t* (*no -ge-*, *h*) subsidize

**Suche** ['zuːxə] *f* (-; *no pl*) search (***nach*** for); ***auf der ~ nach*** in search of; '**suchen** *v/t and v/i* (*ge-*, *h*) look for; search for; ***gesucht: ...*** wanted: ...; ***was hat er hier zu ~?*** what's he doing here?; ***er hat hier nichts zu ~*** he has no business to be here; **Sucher** ['zuːxɐ] *m* (*-s*; -) PHOT viewfinder
**Sucht** [zʊxt] *f* (-; *Süchte* ['zʏçtə]) addiction (***nach*** to); mania (for); **süchtig** ['zʏçtɪç] *adj*: ***~ sein*** be addicted to *drugs etc*, be a *drug etc* addict; **Süchtige** ['zʏçtɪgə] *m*, *f* (*-n*; *-n*) addict
**Süden** ['zyːdən] *m* (*-s*; *no pl*) south; ***nach ~*** south(wards)
**Südfrüchte** ['zyːt-] *pl* tropical *or* southern fruits
'**südlich 1.** *adj* south(ern); southerly; **2.** *adv*: ***~ von*** (to the) south of
**Süd'osten** *m* southeast; **süd'östlich** *adj* southeast(ern); southeasterly
'**Südpol** *m* South Pole
'**südwärts** [-vɛrts] *adv* southward(s)
**Süd'westen** *m* southwest; **süd'westlich** *adj* southwest(ern); southwesterly
'**Südwind** *m* south wind
**Sülze** ['zʏltsə] *f* (-; *-n*) GASTR jellied meat
**Summe** ['zʊmə] *f* (-; *-n*) sum (*a. fig*); amount; (sum) total
**summen** ['zʊmən] *v/i and v/t* (*ge-*, *h*) buzz, hum
**summieren** [zʊ'miːrən] *v/refl* (*no -ge-*, *h*) add up (***auf*** *acc* to)
**Sumpf** [zʊmpf] *m* (*-es*; *Sümpfe* ['zʏmpfə]) swamp, bog
'**sumpfig** *adj* swampy, marshy
**Sünde** ['zʏndə] *f* (-; *-n*) sin (*a. fig*)
'**Sündenbock** F *m* scapegoat
**Sünder** ['zʏndɐ] *m* (*-s*; -), '**Sünderin** *f* (-; *-nen*) sinner
**sündig** ['zʏndɪç] *adj* sinful; **sündigen** ['zʏndɪgən] *v/i* (*ge-*, *h*) (commit a) sin
**Super...** ['zuːpɐ-] *in cpds ...macht etc*: *mst* super...
'**Super** *n* (*-s*; *no pl*), **~ben,zin** *n* super *or* premium (gasoline), *Br* four-star (petrol)
**Superlativ** ['zuːpɐlatiːf] *m* (*-s*; *-e*) LING superlative (*a. fig*)
'**Supermarkt** *m* supermarket
**Suppe** ['zʊpə] *f* (-; *-n*) soup
'**Suppen...** *in cpds ...löffel*, *...teller*, *...küche etc*: soup ...
**Surfbrett** ['zøːɐf-] *n* sail board; surf-

board; '**surfen** *v/i* (*ge-*, *h*) go surfing

**surren** ['zʊrən] *v/i* (*ge-*, *h*) whirr; buzz

**süß** [zy:s] *adj* sweet, sugary (*both a. fig*)

**Süße** ['zy:sə] *f* (-; *no pl*) sweetness

'**süßen** *v/t* (*ge-*, *h*) sweeten

**Süßigkeiten** ['zy:sıçkaitən] *pl* sweets, candy

'**süßlich** *adj* sweetish; *contp* mawkish, sugary

'**süß'sauer** *adj* GASTR sweet-and-sour

'**Süßstoff** *m* sweetener

'**Süßwasser** *n* fresh water

**Symbol** [zʏm'bo:l] *n* (-*s*; -*e*) symbol; **Symbolik** [zʏm'bo:lık] *f* (-; *no pl*) symbolism; **sym'bolisch** *adj* symbolic(al)

**Symmetrie** [zʏme'tri:] *f* (-; -*n*) symmetry; **symmetrisch** [zʏ'me:trıʃ] *adj* symmetric(al)

**Sympathie** [zʏmpa'ti:] *f* (-; -*n*) liking (***für*** for); sympathy; **Sympathisant(in)** [zʏmpati'zant(ın)] (-*en*; -*en*/-; -*nen*) sympathizer; **sympathisch** [zʏm'pa:tıʃ] *adj* nice, likable; ***er ist mir ~*** I like him

**Symphonie** [zʏmfo'ni:] *f* (-; -*n*) *etc* → ***Sinfonie***

**Symptom** [zʏmp'to:m] *n* (-*s*; -*e*) symptom

**Synagoge** [zyna'go:gə] *f* (-; -*n*) synagogue

**synchron** [zʏn'kro:n] *adj* TECH synchronous; **synchronisieren** [zʏnkroni'zi:rən] *v/t* (*no -ge-*, *h*) synchronize; *film etc*: dub

**synonym** [zyno'ny:m] *adj* synonymous

**Syno'nym** *n* (-*s*; -*e*) synonym

**Synthese** [zʏn'te:zə] *f* (-; -*n*) synthesis

**synthetisch** [zʏn'te:tıʃ] *adj* synthetic

**System** [zʏs'te:m] *n* (-*s*; -*e*) system

**systematisch** [zʏste'ma:tıʃ] *adj* systematic, methodical

**Sys'temfehler** *m* EDP system error

**Szene** ['stse:nə] *f* (-; -*n*) scene (*a. fig*)

**Szenerie** [stsenə'ri:] *f* (-; -*n*) scenery; setting

# T

**Tabak** ['ta:bak] *m* (-*s*; -*e*) tobacco; **~geschäft** *n* tobacconist's; **~waren** *pl* tobacco products

**Tabelle** [ta'bɛlə] *f* (-; -*n*) table (*a.* MATH, SPORT)

**Ta'bellen|kalkulati͵on** *f* EDP spreadsheet; **~platz** *m* SPORT position

**Tablett** [ta'blɛt] *n* (-[*e*]*s*; -*s*) tray

**Tablette** [ta'blɛtə] *f* (-; -*n*) tablet

**tabu** [ta'bu:] *adj*, **Ta'bu** *n* (-*s*; -*s*) taboo

**Tabulator** [tabu'la:to:ɐ] *m* (-*s*; -*en* [-la'to:rən]) tabulator

**Tachometer** [taxo'me:tɐ] *m*, *n* (-*s*; -) MOT speedometer

**Tadel** ['ta:dəl] *m* (-*s*; -) blame; censure, reproof, rebuke; '**tadellos** *adj* faultless; blameless; excellent; perfect

'**tadeln** *v/t* (*ge-*, *h*) criticize, blame; censure, reprove, rebuke (*all*: ***wegen*** for)

**Tafel** ['ta:fəl] *f* PED *etc*: blackboard; (bulletin, *esp Br* notice) board; sign; tablet, plaque; GASTR bar (*of chocolate*)

**täfeln** ['tɛ:fəln] *v/t* (*ge-*, *h*) panel

'**Täfelung** *f* (-; -*en*) panel(l)ing

**Taft** [taft] *m* (-[*e*]*s*; -*e*) taffeta

**Tag** [ta:k] *m* (-[*e*]*s*; -*e* ['ta:gə]) day; daylight; ***welchen ~ haben wir heute?*** what day is it today?; ***heute*** (***morgen***) ***in 14 ~en*** two weeks from today (tomorrow); ***e-s ~es*** one day; ***den ganzen ~*** all day; ***am ~e*** during the day; ***~ und Nacht*** night and day; ***am helllichten ~*** in broad daylight; ***ein freier ~*** a day off; ***guten ~!*** hello!, hi!; how do you do?; (***j-m***) ***guten ~ sagen*** say hello (to s.o.); F ***sie hat ihre ~e*** she has her period; ***unter ~e*** underground; → ***zutage***

**Tage|bau** ['ta:gə-] *m* (-[*e*]*s*; -*e*) opencast mining; **~buch** *n* diary; ***~ führen*** keep a diary

'**tagelang** *adv* for days

'**tagen** *v/i* (*ge-*, *h*) meet, hold a meeting; JUR be in session

T

**'Tages|anbruch** *m*: ***bei*** ~ at daybreak, at dawn; **~gespräch** *n* talk of the day; **~karte** *f* day ticket; GASTR menu for the day; **~licht** *n* (-[*e*]*s*; *no pl*) daylight; **~mutter** *f* childminder; **~ordnung** *f* agenda; **~stätte** *f* day care center (*Br* centre); **~tour** *f* day trip; **~zeit** *f* time of day; ***zu jeder*** ~ at any hour; **~zeitung** *f* daily (paper)
**'tageweise** *adv* by the day
**täglich** ['tɛːklɪç] *adj and adv* daily
**'Tagschicht** *f* ECON day shift
**'tagsüber** *adv* during the day
**'Tagung** *f* (-; *-en*) conference
**Taille** ['taljə] *f* (-; *-n*) waist; waistline
**tailliert** [ta'jiːɐt] *adj* waisted, tapered
**Takelage** [takə'laːʒə] *f* (-; *-n*) MAR rigging
**Takt** [takt] *m* (-[*e*]*s*; *-e*) a) (*no pl*) MUS time, measure, beat, b) MUS bar, c) MOT stroke, d) (*no pl*) tact; ***den*** ~ ***halten*** MUS keep time
**Taktik** ['taktɪk] *f* (-; *-en*) MIL tactics (*a. fig*); **'taktisch** *adj* tactical
**'taktlos** *adj* tactless
**'Taktstock** *m* MUS baton
**'Taktstrich** *m* MUS bar
**'taktvoll** *adj* tactful
**Tal** [taːl] *n* (-[*e*]*s*; *Täler* ['tɛːlɐ]) valley
**Talar** [ta'laːɐ] *m* (*-s*; *-e*) robe, gown
**Talent** [ta'lɛnt] *n* (-[*e*]*s*; *-e*) talent (*a. person*), gift; **talentiert** [talɛn'tiːɐt] *adj* talented, gifted
**Talg** [talk] *m* (-[*e*]*s*; *-e*) tallow; GASTR suet
**Talisman** ['taːlɪsman] *m* (*-s*; *-e*) talisman, charm
**Talk|master** ['tɔːk-] *m* (*-s*; -) TV talk (*Br* chat) show host; **~show** [-ʃoʊ] *f* (-; *-s*) TV talk (*Br* chat) show
**'Talsperre** *f* dam, barrage
**Tampon** ['tampɔn] *m* (*-s*; *-s*) tampon
**Tandler** ['tandlɐ] *Austrian m* (*-s*; -) second-hand dealer
**Tang** [taŋ] *m* (-[*e*]*s*; *-e*) BOT seaweed
**Tank** [taŋk] *m* (*-s*; *-s*) tank; **tanken** ['taŋkən] *v/t* (*ge-*, *h*) get some gasoline (*Br* petrol), fill up; **Tanker** ['taŋkɐ] *m* (*-s*; -) MAR tanker; **'Tankstelle** *f* filling (*or* gas, *Br* petrol) station; **'Tankwart** *m* (-[*e*]*s*; *-e*) gas station (*Br* petrol pump) attendant
**Tanne** ['tanə] *f* (-; *-n*) BOT fir (tree)
**'Tannenbaum** *m* Christmas tree
**'Tannenzapfen** *m* BOT fir cone
**Tante** ['tantə] *f* (-; *-n*) aunt; ~ ***Lindy*** Aunt Lindy; **~-Emma-Laden** F *m* mom-and-pop store, *Br* corner shop
**Tantiemen** [tã'tjeːmən] *pl* royalties
**Tanz** [tants] *m* (*-es*; *Tänze* ['tɛntsə]), **tanzen** ['tantsən] *v/i* (*ge-*, *h*, *sein*) *and v/t* (*ge-*, *h*) dance; **Tänzer** ['tɛntsɐ] *m* (*-s*; -), **Tänzerin** ['tɛntsərɪn] *f* (-; *-nen*) dancer
**'Tanz|fläche** *f* dance floor; **~kurs** *m* dancing lessons; **~mu,sik** *f* dance music; **~schule** *f* dancing school
**Tapete** [ta'peːtə] *f* (-; *-n*), **tapezieren** [tape'tsiːrən] *v/t* (*no -ge-*, *h*) wallpaper
**tapfer** ['tapfɐ] *adj* brave; courageous
**'Tapferkeit** *f* (-; *no pl*) bravery; courage
**Tarif** [ta'riːf] *m* (-[*e*]*s*; *-e*) rate(s), tariff; (wage) scale; **~lohn** *m* standard wage(s); **~verhandlungen** *pl* wage negotiations, collective bargaining
**tarnen** ['tarnən] *v/t* (*ge-*, *h*) camouflage; *fig* disguise
**'Tarnung** *f* (-; *-en*) camouflage
**Tasche** ['taʃə] *f* (-; *-n*) bag; pocket
**'Taschen|buch** *n* paperback; **~dieb** *m* pickpocket; **~geld** *n* allowance, *Br* pocket money; **~lampe** *f* flashlight, *Br* torch; **~messer** *n* penknife, pocketknife; **~rechner** *m* pocket calculator; **~schirm** *m* telescopic umbrella; **~tuch** *n* handkerchief, F hankie; **~uhr** *f* pocket watch
**Tasse** ['tasə] *f* (-; *-n*) cup; **e-e** ~ ***Tee*** *etc* a cup of tea *etc*
**Tastatur** [tasta'tuːɐ] *f* (-; *-en*) keyboard, keys; **Taste** ['tastə] *f* (-; *-n*) key
**tasten** ['tastən] (*ge-*, *h*) **1.** *v/i* grope (***nach*** for), feel (for); fumble (for); **2.** *v/t* touch, feel; ***sich*** ~ feel *or* grope (*a. fig*) one's way
**'Tastentele,fon** *n* push-button phone
**'Tastsinn** *m* (-[*e*]*s*; *no pl*) sense of touch
**tat** [taːt] *pret of* ***tun***
**Tat** *f* (-; *-en*) act, deed; action; JUR offense, *Br* offence; ***j-n auf frischer*** ~ ***ertappen*** catch s.o. in the act
**'tatenlos** *adj* inactive, passive
**Täter** ['tɛːtɐ] *m* (*-s*; -), **'Täterin** *f* (-; *-nen*) culprit; JUR offender
**tätig** ['tɛːtɪç] *adj* active; busy; ~ ***sein bei*** be employed with; ~ ***werden*** act, take action; **'Tätigkeit** *f* (-; *-en*) activity; work; occupation, job; ***in*** ~ in action

**'Tatkraft** *f* (-; *no pl*) energy
**'tatkräftig** *adj* energetic, active
**tätlich** ['tɛ:tlɪç] *adj* violent; *~ **werden gegen*** assault; **'Tätlichkeiten** *pl* (acts of) violence; JUR assault (and battery)
**'Tatort** *m* JUR scene of the crime
**tätowieren** [tɛto'vi:rən] *v/t* (*no -ge-, h*), **Täto'wierung** *f* (-; *-en*) tattoo
**'Tatsache** *f* fact
**'tatsächlich 1.** *adj* actual, real; **2.** *adv* actually, in fact; really
**tätscheln** ['tɛ:tʃəln] *v/t* (*ge-, h*) pat, pet
**Tatze** ['tatsə] *f* (-; *-n*) ZO paw (*a. fig*)
**Tau**[1] [tau] *n* (-[*e*]*s*; *-e*) rope
**Tau**[2] *m* (-[*e*]*s*; *no pl*) dew
**taub** [taup] *adj* deaf (*fig **gegen*** to); numb, benumbed
**Taube** ['taubə] *f* (-; *-n*) ZO pigeon; *esp fig* dove; **'Taubenschlag** *m* pigeonhouse
**'Taubheit** *f* (-; *no pl*) deafness; numbness
**'taubstumm** *adj* deaf-and-dumb
**'Taubstumme** *m, f* (*-n*; *-n*) deaf mute
**tauchen** ['tauxən] **1.** *v/i* (*ge-, h, sein*) dive (***nach*** for); SPORT skin-dive; *submarine*: *a.* submerge; stay underwater; **2.** *v/t* (*h*) dip (***in** accc* into); duck; **Taucher** ['tauxɐ] *m* (*-s*; *-*) (SPORT skin) diver; **'Tauchsport** *m* skin diving
**tauen** ['tauən] *v/i* (*ge-, sein*) *and v/t* (*ge-, h*) thaw, melt
**Taufe** ['taufə] *f* (-; *-n*) baptism, christening; **'taufen** *v/t* (*ge-, h*) baptize, christen; **'Taufpate** *m* godfather; **'Taufpatin** *f* godmother; **'Taufschein** *m* certificate of baptism
**taugen** ['taugən] *v/i* (*ge-, h*) be good *or* fit *or* of use *or* suited (*all*: ***zu, für*** for); ***nichts** ~* be no good; F ***taugt es was?*** is it any good?; **tauglich** ['tauklɪç] *adj esp* MIL fit (for service)
**Taumel** ['tauməl] *m* (*-s*; *no pl*) dizziness; rapture, ecstasy; **'taumelig** *adj* dizzy; **'taumeln** *v/i* (*ge-, sein*) stagger, reel
**Tausch** [tauʃ] *m* (-[*e*]*s*; *-e*) exchange, F swap; **tauschen** ['tauʃən] *v/t* (*ge-, h*) exchange, F swap (*both*: ***gegen*** for); switch; change; ***ich möchte nicht mit ihm** ~* I wouldn't like to be in his shoes
**täuschen** ['tɔʏʃən] *v/t* (*ge-, h*) deceive, fool; delude; cheat; *a.* SPORT feint; ***sich** ~* deceive o.s.; be mistaken; ***sich ~ lassen von*** be taken in by; ***~de Ähnlichkeit*** striking similarity; **'Täuschung** *f* (-; *-en*) deception; delusion; JUR deceit; *a.* PED cheating
**tausend** ['tauzənt] *adj* a thousand
**'tausendst** *adj* thousandth
**'Tausendstel** *n* (*-s*; *-*) thousandth (part)
**'Tautropfen** *m* dewdrop
**'Tauwetter** *n* thaw
**'Tauziehen** *n* (*-s*; *no pl*) SPORT tug-of-war (*a. fig*)
**Taxi** ['taksi] *n* (*-s*; *-s*) taxi(cab), cab
**taxieren** [ta'ksi:rən] *v/t* (*no -ge-, h*) rate, estimate (***auf** acc* at)
**'Taxistand** *m* cabstand, *esp Br* taxi rank
**Technik** ['tɛçnɪk] *f* (-; *-en*) a) (*no pl*) technology, engineering, b) technique (*a.* SPORT *etc*), MUS execution
**Techniker** ['tɛçnikɐ] *m* (*-s*; *-*), **'Technikerin** *f* (-; *-nen*) engineer; technician (*a.* SPORT *etc*)
**technisch** ['tɛçnɪʃ] *adj* technical; technological; ***~e Hochschule*** school *etc* of technology
**Technologie** [tɛçnolo'gi:] *f* (-; *-n*) technology; **technologisch** [tɛçno'lo:gɪʃ] *adj* technological
**Tee** [te:] *m* (*-s*; *-s*) tea; ***(e-n) ~ trinken*** have some tea; ***(e-n) ~ machen** or **kochen*** make some tea; **~beutel** *m* teabag; **~kanne** *f* teapot; **~löffel** *m* teaspoon
**Teer** [te:ɐ] *m* (-[*e*]*s*; *-e*), **teeren** ['te:rən] *v/t* (*ge-, h*) tar
**'Teesieb** *n* tea strainer
**'Teetasse** *f* teacup
**Teich** [taiç] *m* (-[*e*]*s*; *-e*) pool, pond
**Teig** [taik] *m* (-[*e*]*s*; *-e*) dough, paste
**teigig** ['taigɪç] *adj* doughy, pasty
**'Teigwaren** *pl* pasta
**Teil** [tail] *m, n* (-[*e*]*s*; *-e*) part; portion, share; component; ***zum** ~* partly, in part; **~...** *in cpds ...erfolg etc*: partial ...
**'teilbar** *adj* divisible
**'Teilchen** *n* (*-s*; *-*) particle
**teilen** ['tailən] *v/t* (*ge-, h*) divide; share
**'teilhaben** *v/i* (*irr*, ***haben***, *sep, -ge-, h*) *~ **an*** (*dat*) (have a) share in; **'Teilhaber(in)** [-ha:bɐ (-bərɪn)] (*-s*; *-/-*; *-nen*) ECON partner
**'Teilnahme** [-na:mə] *f* (-; *no pl*) participation (***an** dat* in); *fig* interest (in); sympathy (for)
**'teilnahmslos** *adj* indifferent; *esp* MED

T

apathetic; '**Teilnahmslosigkeit** *f* (-; *no pl*) indifference; apathy
'**teilnehmen** *v/i* (*irr*, ***nehmen***, *sep*, *-ge-*, *h*) ~ ***an*** (*dat*) take part *or* participate in; share (in); '**Teilnehmer(in)** [-neːmɐ (-mərɪn)] (*-s*; *-/-*; *-nen*) participant; UNIV student; SPORT competitor
**teils** *adv* partly
'**Teilstrecke** *f* stage, leg
'**Teilung** *f* (-; *-en*) division
'**teilweise** *adv* partly, in part
'**Teilzahlung** *f* → ***Abzahlung***, ***Rate***
**Teint** [tɛ̃ː] *m* (*-s*; *-s*) complexion
**Tel.** ABBR *of* ***Telefon*** tel., telephone
**Telefon** [tele'foːn] *n* (*-s*; *-e*) telephone, phone; ***am*** ~ on the (tele)phone; ~ ***haben*** have a (*Br* be on the) (tele)phone; ***ans*** ~ ***gehen*** answer the (tele)phone; **~anruf** *m* (tele)phone call; **~anschluss** *m* telephone connection; **~appa,rat** *m* telephone, phone
**Telefonat** [telefo'naːt] *n* (*-[e]s*; *-e*) → ***Telefongespräch***
**Tele'fon|buch** *n* telephone directory, phone book; **~gebühr** *f* telephone charge; **~gespräch** *n* (tele)phone call
**telefonieren** [telefo'niːrən] *v/i* (*no -ge-*, *h*) (tele)phone; be on the phone; ***mit j-m*** ~ talk to s.o. on the phone
**telefonisch** [tele'foːnɪʃ] **1.** *adj* telephonic, telephone ...; **2.** *adv* by (tele)phone, over the (tele)phone
**Telefonist** [telefo'nɪst] *m* (*-en*; *-en*), **Telefo'nistin** *f* (-; *-nen*) (telephone) operator
**Tele'fon|karte** *f* phonecard; **~leitung** *f* telephone line; **~netz** *n* telephone network; **~nummer** *f* (tele)phone number; **~zelle** *f* (tele)phone booth, *esp Br* (tele)phone box, *Br* call box; **~zen,trale** *f* switchboard
**telegrafieren** [telegra'fiːrən] *v/t and v/i* (*no -ge-*, *h*) telegraph, wire; cable
**telegrafisch** [tele'graːfɪʃ] *adj and adv* by telegraph, by wire, by cable
**Telegramm** [tele'gram] *n* (*-s*; *-e*) telegram, wire, cable(gram)
**Teleobjektiv** ['teːlə-] *n* telephoto lens
**Telephon** *n* → ***Telefon***
**Teletext** ['teːlə-] *m* teletext
**Teller** ['tɛlɐ] *m* (*-s*; -) plate; **~wäscher** [-vɛʃɐ] *m* (*-s*; -) dishwasher
**Tempel** ['tɛmpəl] *m* (*-s*; -) temple
**Temperament** [tɛmpəra'mɛnt] *n* (*-[e]s*; *-e*) temper(ament); life, F pep
**tempera'ment|los** *adj* lifeless, dull; **~voll** *adj* full of life *or* F pep
**Temperatur** [tɛmpəra'tuːɐ] *f* (-; *-en*) temperature; ***j-s*** ~ ***messen*** take s.o.'s temperature
**Tempo** ['tɛmpo] *n* (*-s*; *-s*, *-pi*) speed; MUS time; ***mit*** ~ ***...*** at a speed of ... an hour
**Tendenz** [tɛn'dɛnts] *f* (-; *-en*) tendency, trend; leaning; **tendenziös** [tɛndɛn'tsjøːs] *adj* tendentious; **tendieren** [tɛn'diːrən] *v/i* (*no -ge-*, *h*) tend (***zu*** towards; ***dazu, et. zu tun*** to do s.th.)
**Tennis** ['tɛnɪs] *n* (-; *no pl*) tennis; **~platz** *m* tennis court; **~schläger** *m* tennis racket; **~spieler(in)** tennis player
**Tenor** [te'noːɐ] *m* (*-s*; *Tenöre* [te'nøːrə]) MUS tenor
**Teppich** ['tɛpɪç] *m* (*-s*; *-e*) carpet
'**Teppichboden** *m* fitted carpet, wall-to-wall carpeting
**Termin** [tɛr'miːn] *m* (*-s*; *-e*) date; deadline; engagement; ***e-n*** ~ ***vereinbaren*** (***einhalten, absagen***) make (keep, cancel) an appointment
**Terminal** ['tøːɐminəl] a) *m*, *n* (*-s*; *-s*) AVIAT terminal, b) *n* (*-s*; *-s*) EDP terminal
**Terrasse** [tɛ'rasə] *f* (-; *-n*) terrace
**ter'rassenförmig** [-fœrmɪç] *adj* terraced, in terraces
**Terrine** [tɛ'riːnə] *f* (-; *-n*) tureen
**Territorium** [tɛri'toːrjʊm] *n* (*-s*; *-ien*) territory
**Terror** ['tɛroːɐ] *m* (*-s*; *no pl*) terror
**terrorisieren** [tɛrori'ziːrən] *v/t* (*no -ge-*, *h*) terrorize
**Terrorismus** [tɛro'rɪsmʊs] *m* (-; *no pl*) terrorism; **Terrorist(in)** [-'rɪst(ɪn)] (*-en*; *-en*/-; *-nen*), **terro'ristisch** *adj* terrorist
**Testament** [tɛsta'mɛnt] *n* (*-[e]s*; *-e*) (last) will; JUR last will and testament
**testamentarisch** [tɛstamɛn'taːrɪʃ] *adv* by will
**Testa'mentsvollstrecker** *m* executor
**Testbild** ['tɛst-] *n* TV test card
**testen** ['tɛstən] *v/t* (*no -ge-*, *h*) test
'**Testpi,lot** *m* test pilot
**Tetanus** ['teːtanʊs] *m* (-; *no pl*) MED tetanus
**teuer** ['tɔʏɐ] *adj* expensive; ***wie*** ~ ***ist es?*** how much is it?
**Teufel** ['tɔʏfəl] *m* (*-s*; -) devil (*a. fig*);

***wer*** (***wo, was***) ***zum ~ ...?*** who (where, what) the hell ...? **'Teufelskerl** F *m* devil of a fellow; **'Teufelskreis** *m* vicious circle; **teuflisch** ['tɔʏflɪʃ] *adj* devilish, diabolic(al)

**Text** [tɛkst] *m* (-[*e*]*s*; -*e*) text; MUS words, lyrics

**Texter** ['tɛkstɐ] *m* (-*s*; -), **'Texterin** *f* (-; -*nen*) MUS songwriter

**Textil...** [tɛks'ti:l-] *in cpds* textile ...

**Textilien** [tɛks'ti:ljən] *pl* textiles

**'Textverarbeitung** *f* EDP word processing; **'Textverarbeitungsgerät** *n* EDP word processor

**Theater** [te'a:tɐ] *n* (-*s*; -) theater, *Br* theatre; F ***~ machen*** (***um***) make a fuss (about); **~besucher** *m* theatergoer, *Br* theatregoer; **~karte** *f* theater (*Br* theatre) ticket; **~kasse** *f* box office; **~stück** *n* play

**Thema** ['te:ma] *n* (-*s*; *Themen*) subject, topic; MUS theme; ***das ~ wechseln*** change the subject

**Theologe** [teo'lo:gə] *m* (-*n*; -*n*) theologian; **Theologie** [teolo'gi:] *f* (-; -*n*) theology; **Theo'login** *f* (-; -*nen*) theologian; **theo'logisch** *adj* theological

**Theoretiker** [teo're:tikɐ] *m* (-*s*; -) theorist; **theo'retisch** *adj* theoretical

**Theorie** [teo'ri:] *f* (-; -*n*) theory

**Therapeut** [tera'pɔʏt] *m* (-*en*; -*en*), **Thera'peutin** *f* (-; -*nen*) therapist; **Therapie** [-'pi:] *f* (-; -*n*) therapy

**Thermometer** [tɛrmo'me:tɐ] *n* (-*s*; -) thermometer

**Thermosflasche®** ['tɛrmɔs-] *f* thermos®

**These** ['te:zə] *f* (-; -*n*) thesis

**Thon** [to:n] *Swiss m* (-*s*; -*s*) tuna (fish)

**Thrombose** [trɔm'bo:zə] *f* (-; -*n*) MED thrombosis

**Thron** [tro:n] *m* (-[*e*]*s*; -*e*) throne

**'Thronfolger** [-fɔlgɐ] *m* (-*s*; -), **'Thronfolgerin** [-fɔlgərɪn] *f* (-; -*nen*) successor to the throne

**Thunfisch** ['tu:n-] *m* tuna (fish)

**Tick** [tɪk] F *m* (-[*e*]*s*; -*s*) quirk

**ticken** ['tɪkən] *v/i* (*ge*-, *h*) tick

**Tiebreak, Tie-Break** ['taɪbreɪk] *m*, *n tennis*: tiebreak(er)

**tief** [ti:f] *adj* deep (*a. fig*); low

**Tief** *n* (-*s*; -*s*) METEOR depression (*a.* PSYCH, ECON), low (*a. fig*)

**Tiefe** ['ti:fə] *f* (-; -*n*) depth (*a. fig*)

**'Tief|ebene** *f* lowland(s); **~flieger** *m* low-flying air plane; **~gang** *m* MAR draft, *Br* draught; *fig* depth; **~ga'rage** *f* parking *or* underground garage, *Br* underground car park

**'tiefgekühlt** *adj* deep-frozen

**'Tiefkühl|fach** *n* freezing compartment; **~schrank** *m*, **~truhe** *f* freezer, deep-freeze; **~kost** *f* frozen foods

**Tier** [ti:ɐ] *n* (-[*e*]*s*; -*e*) animal; F ***hohes ~*** bigwig, big shot; **~arzt** *m*, **-ärztin** *f* veterinarian, *Br* veterinary surgeon, F vet; **~freund** *m* animal lover; **~garten** *m* → ***Zoo***; **~heim** *n* animal shelter

**tierisch** ['ti:rɪʃ] *adj* animal; *fig* bestial, brutish

**'Tierkreis** *m* ASTR zodiac; **~zeichen** *n* sign of the zodiac

**'Tiermedi'zin** *f* veterinary medicine

**Tierquäle'rei** *f* cruelty to animals

**'Tier|reich** *n* animal kingdom; **~schutz** *m* protection of animals; **~schutzverein** *m* society for the prevention of cruelty to animals; **~versuch** *m* MED experiment with animals

**Tiger** ['ti:gɐ] *m* (-*s*; -) ZO tiger

**Tigerin** ['ti:gərɪn] *f* (-; -*nen*) ZO tigress

**tilgen** ['tɪlgən] *v/t* (*ge*-, *h*) ECON pay off

**Tinte** ['tɪntə] *f* (-; -*n*) ink

**'Tintenfisch** *m* ZO squid

**Tipp** [tɪp] *m* (-*s*; -*s*) hint, tip; tip-off; ***j-m e-n ~ geben*** tip s.o. off

**tippen** ['tɪpən] *v/i and v/t* (*ge*-, *h*) tap; type; F guess; do *lotto etc*

**Tisch** [tɪʃ] *m* (-[*e*]*s*; -*e*) table; ***am ~ sitzen*** sit at the table; ***bei ~*** at table; ***den ~ decken*** (***abräumen***) lay (clear) the table; **~decke** *f* tablecloth; **~gebet** *n* REL grace: ***das ~ sprechen*** say grace

**Tischler** ['tɪʃlɐ] *m* (-*s*; -) joiner; cabinet-maker

**'Tisch|platte** *f* tabletop; **~rechner** *m* desktop computer; **~tennis** *n* table tennis; **~tuch** *n* tablecloth

**Titel** ['ti:təl] *m* (-*s*; -) title; **~bild** *n* cover picture; **~blatt** *n*, **~seite** *f* title page; cover, front page

**Toast** [to:st] *m* (-[*e*]*s*; -*s*), **toasten** ['to:stən] *v/t* (*ge*-, *h*) toast

**toben** ['to:bən] *v/i* (*ge*-, *h*) rage (*a. fig*); romp; **tobsüchtig** ['to:p-] *adj* raving mad; **'Tobsuchtsanfall** *m* tantrum

**Tochter** ['tɔxtɐ] *f* (-; *Töchter* ['tœçtɐ]) daughter; **~gesellschaft** *f* ECON subsidiary (company)

**Tod** [to:t] *m* (-[*e*]*s*; *no pl*) death (*a. fig*) (***durch*** from); **tod...** *in cpds ...ernst, ...müde, ...sicher*: dead ...
**Todes|ängste** ['to:dəs-] *pl*: ~ ***ausstehen*** be scared to death; **~anzeige** *f* obituary (notice); **~fall** *m* (case of) death; **~kampf** *m* agony; **~opfer** *n* casualty; **~strafe** *f* JUR capital punishment; death penalty; **~ursache** *f* cause of death; **~urteil** *n* JUR death sentence
**'Todfeind** *m* deadly enemy
**'tod'krank** *adj* mortally ill
**tödlich** ['tø:tlıç] *adj* fatal; deadly; *esp fig* mortal
**'Todsünde** *f* mortal *or* deadly sin
**Toilette** [toa'lɛtə] *f* (-; *-n*) bathroom, *Br* toilet, lavatory; *pl* rest rooms, *Br* ladies' *or* men's rooms
**Toi'letten...** *in cpds ...papier, ...seife etc*: toilet ...; **~tisch** *m* dressing table
**tolerant** [tole'rant] *adj* tolerant (***gegen*** of, towards); **Toleranz** [tole'rants *f* (-; *-en*) tolerance (*a.* TECH); **tolerieren** [tole'ri:rən] *v/t* (*no -ge-, h*) tolerate
**toll** [tɔl] *adj* wild; F great, fantastic
**'tollkühn** *adj* daredevil
**'Tollwut** *f* VET rabies; **'tollwütig** [-vy:tıç] *adj* VET rabid
**Tomate** [to'ma:tə] *f* (-; *-n*) BOT tomato
**Ton¹** [to:n] *m* (-[*e*]*s*; *-e*) clay
**Ton²** *m* (-[*e*]*s*; *Töne* ['tø:nə]) tone (*a.* MUS, PAINT), PAINT *a.* shade; sound (*a.* TV, *film*); note; stress; ***kein*** ~ not a word; **~abnehmer** *m* ELECTR pickup; **~art** *f* MUS key; **~band** *n* (-[*e*]*s*; *-bänder*) (recording) tape; **~bandgerät** *n* tape recorder
**tönen** ['tø:nən] (*ge-, h*) **1.** *v/i* sound, ring; **2.** *v/t* tinge, tint, shade
**'Ton|fall** *m* tone (of voice); accent; **~film** *m* sound film; **~kopf** *m* ELECTR (magnetic) head; **~lage** *f* MUS pitch; **~leiter** *f* MUS scale
**Tonne** ['tɔnə] *f* (-; *-n*) barrel; (metric) ton
**'Tontechniker** *m* sound engineer
**'Tönung** *f* (-; *-en*) tint, tinge, shade
**Topf** [tɔpf] *m* (-[*e*]*s*; *Töpfe* ['tœpfə]) pot; saucepan
**Topfen** ['tɔpfən] *Austrian m* (*-s*; *no pl*) GASTR curd(s)
**Töpfer** ['tœpfɐ] *m* (*-s*; -) potter
**Töpferei** [tœpfə'rai] *f* (-; *-en*) pottery
**'Töpferin** *f* (-; *-nen*) potter
**'Töpferscheibe** *f* potter's wheel
**'Töpferware** *f* pottery, earthenware
**Tor** [to:ɐ] *n* (-[*e*]*s*; *-e*) gate; *soccer etc*: goal; ***ein ~ schießen*** score (a goal); ***im ~ stehen*** keep goal
**Torf** [tɔrf] *m* (-[*e*]*s*; *-e*) peat
**'Torfmull** *m* peat dust
**'Torhüter** [-hy:tɐ] *m* → ***Torwart***
**torkeln** ['tɔrkəln] F *v/i* (*ge-, h, sein*) reel, stagger
**'Torlatte** *f* SPORT crossbar
**'Torlinie** *f* SPORT goal line
**torpedieren** [tɔrpe'di:rən] *v/t* (*no -ge-, h*) MIL torpedo (*a. fig*)
**'Tor|pfosten** *m* SPORT goalpost; **~raum** *m* SPORT goalmouth; **~schuss** *m* SPORT shot at goal; **~schütze** *m* SPORT scorer
**Torte** ['tɔrtə] *f* (-; *-n*) pie, *esp Br* flan; cream cake, gateau
**'Torwart** [-vart] *m* (-[*e*]*s*; *-e*) SPORT goalkeeper, F goalie
**tosen** ['to:zən] *v/i* (*ge-, h*) roar; thunder; **~d** *adj* thunderous (*applause*)
**tot** [to:t] *adj* dead (*a. fig*); late; ***~ geboren*** MED stillborn; ***~ umfallen*** drop dead
**total** [to'ta:l] *adj* total, complete
**totalitär** [totali'tɛ:ɐ] *adj* POL totalitarian
**'Tote** *m, f* (*-n*; *-n*) dead man *or* woman; (dead) body, corpse; *mst pl* casualty; *pl the* dead; **töten** ['tø:tən] *v/t* (*ge-, h*) kill
**'Totenbett** *n* deathbed
**'toten'blass** *adj* deadly pale
**'Toten|gräber** [-grɛ:bɐ] *m* (*-s*; -) gravedigger; **~kopf** *m* skull; skull and crossbones; **~maske** *f* death mask; **~messe** *f* REL mass for the dead, requiem (*a.* MUS); **~schädel** *m* skull; **~schein** *m* death certificate
**'toten'still** *adj* deathly still
**'totlachen** F *v/refl* (*sep, -ge-, h*) kill o.s. laughing
**Toto** ['to:to] *m*, F *n* (*-s*; *-s*) football pools
**'Totschlag** *m* (-[*e*]*s*; *no pl*) JUR manslaughter; **'totschlagen** *v/t* (*irr*, ***schlagen***, *sep, -ge-, h*) kill; ***j-n ~*** beat s.o. to death; ***die Zeit ~*** kill time
**'totschweigen** *v/t* (*irr*, ***schweigen***, *sep, -ge-, h*) hush up
**Toupet** [tu'pe:] *n* (*-s*; *-s*) toupee
**toupieren** [tu'pi:rən] *v/t* (*no -ge-, h*) *Br* backcomb
**Tour** [tu:ɐ] *f* (-; *-en*) tour (***durch*** of), trip;

T

excursion; TECH turn, revolution; ***auf ~en kommen*** MOT pick up speed; F ***krumme ~en*** underhand methods
**Touren...** ['tu:rən-] *in cpds ..rad etc*: touring ...
**Tourismus** [tu'rɪsmʊs] *m* (-; *no pl*) tourism; **~geschäft** *n* tourist industry
**Tourist** [tu'rɪst] *m* (-*en*; -*en*), **Tou'ristin** *f* (-; -*nen*) tourist; **tou'ristisch** *adj* touristic
**Tournee** [tʊr'ne:] *f* (-; -*s*, -*n*) tour; ***auf ~ gehen*** go on tour
**Trab** [tra:p] *m* (-[*e*]*s*; *no pl*) trot
**Trabant** [tra'bant] *m* (-*en*; -*en*) ASTR satellite; **Tra'bantenstadt** *f* satellite town
**traben** ['tra:bən] *v/i* (*ge*-, *sein*) trot
**Traber** ['tra:bɐ] *m* (-*s*; -) ZO trotter
'**Trabrennen** *n* trotting race
**Tracht** [traxt] *f* (-; -*en*) costume; uniform; dress; F ***e-e ~ Prügel*** a thrashing
**trächtig** ['trɛçtɪç] *adj* ZO with young, pregnant
**Tradition** [tradi'tsjo:n] *f* (-; -*en*) tradition; **traditionell** [traditsjo'nɛl] *adj* traditional
**traf** [tra:f] *pret of* ***treffen***
**Trafik** [tra'fɪk] *Austrian f* (-; -*en*) → ***Tabakgeschäft***; **Trafikant** [trafi'kant] *Austrian m* (-*en*; -*en*) tobacconist
**Tragbahre** ['tra:k-] *f* stretcher
'**tragbar** *adj* portable; wearable; *fig* bearable; *person*: acceptable
**Trage** ['tra:gə] *f* (-; -*n*) stretcher
**träge** ['trɛ:gə] *adj* lazy, indolent; PHYS inert (*a. fig*)
**tragen** [tra:gən] (*irr*, *ge*-, *h*) **1.** *v/t* carry; wear; *fig* bear; ***sich gut ~*** wear well; **2.** *v/i* BOT bear fruit; *fig* hold; **~d** *adj* ARCH supporting; THEA leading
**Träger** ['trɛ:gɐ] *m* (-*s*; -) carrier; porter; (shoulder) strap; TECH support; ARCH girder; *fig* bearer
'**trägerlos** *adj* strapless
'**Tragetasche** *f* carrier bag; carrycot
'**tragfähig** *adj* load-bearing; *fig* sound
'**Tragfläche** *f* AVIAT wing
**Trägheit** ['trɛ:khait] *f* (-; *no pl*) laziness, indolence; PHYS inertia (*a. fig*)
**Tragik** ['tra:gɪk] *f* (-; *no pl*) tragedy
**tragisch** ['tra:gɪʃ] *adj* tragic
**Tragödie** [tra'gø:djə] *f* (-; -*n*) tragedy
'**Tragriemen** *m* strap; sling
'**Tragweite** *f* range; *fig* significance
**Trainer** ['trɛ:nɐ] *m* (-*s*; -), '**Trainerin** *f* (-; -*nen*) SPORT trainer, coach; **trainieren** [trɛ'ni:rən] *v/i and v/t* (*no -ge-*, *h*) SPORT train, coach
'**Training** *n* (-*s*; -*s*) training
'**Trainingsanzug** *m* track suit
**Traktor** ['trakto:ɐ] *m* (-*s*; -*en* [trak'to:rən]) MOT tractor
**trällern** ['trɛlɐn] *v/t and v/i* (*ge*-, *h*) warble, trill
**Tram** [tram] *Austrian f* (-; -*s*), *Swiss n* (-*s*; -*s*) streetcar, *Br* tram
**trampeln** ['trampəln] *v/i* (*ge*-, *h*) trample, stamp
'**Trampelpfad** *m* beaten track
**trampen** ['trɛmpən] *v/i* (*ge*-, *sein*) hitchhike; **Tramper(in)** ['trɛmpɐ (-pərɪn)] (-*s*; -/-; -*nen*) hitchhiker
**Träne** ['trɛ:nə] *f* (-; -*n*) tear; ***in ~n ausbrechen*** burst into tears; '**tränen** *v/i* (*ge*-, *h*) water; '**Tränengas** *n* tear gas
**trank** [traŋk] *pret of* ***trinken***
**Tränke** ['trɛŋkə] *f* (-; -*n*) watering place
'**tränken** *v/t* (*ge*-, *h*) ZO water; soak, drench
**Transfer** [trans'fe:ɐ] *m* (-*s*; -*s*) transfer (*a.* SPORT)
**Transformator** [transfɔr'ma:to:ɐ] *m* (-*s*; -*en* [-ma'to:rən]) ELECTR transformer
**Transfusion** [transfu'zjo:n] *f* (-; -*en*) MED transfusion
**Transistor** [tran'zɪsto:ɐ] *m* (-*s*; -*en* [-zɪs'to:rən]) ELECTR transistor
**Transit** [tran'zi:t] *m* (-*s*; -*e*) transit
**transitiv** ['tranziti:f] *adj* LING transitive
**transparent** [transpa'rɛnt] *adj* transparent
**Transpa'rent** *n* (-[*e*]*s*; -*e*) banner
**Transplantation** [transplanta'tsjo:n] *f* (-; -*en*), **transplantieren** [-'ti:rən] *v/t* (*no -ge-*, *h*) MED transplant
**Transport** [trans'pɔrt] *m* (-[*e*]*s*; -*e*) transport; shipment; **transportabel** [transpɔr'ta:bəl], **trans'portfähig** *adj* transportable; **transportieren** [transpɔr'ti:rən] *v/t* (*no -ge-*, *h*) transport, ship, carry, MOT *a.* haul
**Trans'port|mittel** *n* (means of) transport(ation); **~unternehmen** *n* hauler, *Br* haulier
**Trapez** [tra'pe:ts] *n* (-*es*; -*e*) MATH trapezoid, *Br* trapezium; SPORT trapeze
**trappeln** ['trapəln] *v/i* (*ge*-, *sein*) clatter; patter

**trat** [traːt] *pret of* ***treten***
**Traube** ['traubə] *f* (-; *-n*) BOT bunch of grapes; grape; *pl* grapes; *fig* cluster
**Traubensaft** *m* grape juice
'**Traubenzucker** *m* glucose
**trauen** ['trauən] (*ge-*, *h*) **1.** *v/t* marry; **2.** *v/i* trust (***j-m*** s.o.); ***sich ~, et. zu tun*** dare (to) do s.th.; ***ich traute meinen Augen nicht*** I couldn't believe my eyes
**Trauer** ['trauɐ] *f* (-; *no pl*) grief, sorrow; mourning; ***in ~*** in mourning; **~fall** *m* death; **~feier** *f* funeral service; **~marsch** *m* MUS funeral march
'**trauern** *v/i* (*ge-*, *h*) mourn (***um*** for)
'**Trauerrede** *f* funeral oration
'**Trauerzug** *m* funeral procession
**träufeln** ['trɔʏfəln] *v/t* (*ge-*, *h*) drip, trickle
**Traum** [traum] *m* (-[*e*]*s*; *Träume* ['trɔʏmə]) dream (*a. fig*); **~...** *in cpds ...beruf, ...mann etc*: dream ..., ... of one's dreams; **träumen** ['trɔʏmən] *v/i and v/t* (*ge-*, *h*) dream (*a. fig*) (***von*** about, of); ***schlecht ~*** have bad dreams; **Träumer** ['trɔʏmɐ] *m* (-*s*; -) dreamer (*a. fig*); **Träumerei** [trɔʏmə'rai] *fig f* (day)dream(s), reverie (*a.* MUS)
**träumerisch** ['trɔʏmərɪʃ] *adj* dreamy
**traurig** ['traurɪç] *adj* sad (***über*** *acc*, ***wegen*** about)
'**Traurigkeit** *f* (-; *no pl*) sadness
**Trauring** ['trau-] *m* wedding ring
'**Trauschein** *m* marriage certificate
'**Trauung** *f* (-; *-en*) marriage, wedding
'**Trauzeuge** *m*, '**Trauzeugin** *f* witness to a marriage
**Trecker** ['trɛkɐ] *m* (-*s*; -) MOT tractor
**Treff** [trɛf] F *m* (-*s*; -*s*) meeting place
**treffen** ['trɛfən] *v/t and v/i* (*irr*, *ge-*, *h*) hit (*a. fig*); hurt; meet *s.o.*; take (*measures etc*); ***nicht ~*** miss; ***sich ~*** (***mit j-m***) meet (s.o.); ***gut ~*** PHOT *etc*: capture well; '**Treffen** *n* (-*s*; -) meeting; '**treffend 1.** *adj* apt (*remark etc*); **2.** *adv*: ***~ gesagt*** well put; **Treffer** ['trɛfɐ] *m* (-*s*; -) hit (*a. fig*); SPORT goal; win; '**Treffpunkt** *m* meeting place
**Treibeis** ['traip-] *n* drift ice
**treiben** ['traibən] (*irr*, *ge-*) **1.** *v/t* (*h*) drive (*a.* TECH *and fig*); SPORT *etc*: do; push, press *s.o.*; BOT put forth; F do, be up to; **2.** *v/i* (*sein*) drift (*a. fig*), float; BOT shoot (up); ***sich ~ lassen*** drift along (*a. fig*); ***~de Kraft*** driving force;
'**Treiben** *n* (-*s*; *no pl*) doings, goings-on; ***geschäftiges ~*** bustle
'**Treib|haus** *n* hothouse; **~hauseffekt** *m* greenhouse effect; **~holz** *n* driftwood; **~riemen** *m* TECH driving belt; **~sand** *m* quicksand; **~stoff** *m* fuel
**trennen** ['trɛnən] *v/t* (*ge-*, *h*) separate; sever; part; divide (*a.* LING, POL); segregate; TEL disconnect; ***sich ~*** separate (***von*** from), part (*a. fig*); ***sich ~ von*** part with *s.th.*; leave *s.o.*; '**Trennung** *f* (-; *-en*) separation; division; segregation
'**Trennwand** *f* partition
**Treppe** ['trɛpə] *f* (-; *-n*) staircase, stairs
'**Treppen|absatz** *m* landing; **~geländer** *n* banisters; **~haus** *n* staircase; hall
**Tresor** [tre'zoːɐ] *m* (-*s*; -*e*) safe; strongroom, vault
**treten** ['treːtən] *v/i and v/t* (*irr*, *ge-*, *h*) kick; step (***aus*** out of; ***in*** *acc* into; ***auf*** *acc* on[to]); pedal (away)
**treu** [trɔʏ] *adj* faithful (*a. fig*); loyal; devoted; **Treue** ['trɔʏə] *f* (-; *no pl*) fidelity, faithfulness, loyalty
'**Treuhänder** [-hɛndɐ] *m* (-*s*; -) JUR trustee
'**treulos** *adj* faithless, disloyal, unfaithful (*all*: ***gegen*** to)
**Tribüne** [tri'byːnə] *f* (-; *-n*) platform; stand
**Trichter** ['trɪçtɐ] *m* (-*s*; -) funnel; crater
**Trick** [trɪk] *m* (-*s*; -*s*) trick; **~aufnahme** *f* trick shot; **~betrüger(in)** confidence trickster
**trieb** [triːp] *pret of* ***treiben***
**Trieb** *m* (-[*e*]*s*; -*e* ['triːbə]) BOT (young) shoot, sprout; *fig* impulse, drive; sex drive; **~feder** *f* mainspring (*a. fig*)
**triefen** ['triːfən] *v/i* (*ge-*, *h*) drip, be dripping (***von*** with)
**triftig** ['trɪftɪç] *adj* weighty; good
**Trikot** [tri'koː] *n* (-*s*; -*s*) SPORT shirt, jersey; leotard
**Triller** ['trɪlɐ] *m* (-*s*; -) MUS trill; '**trillern** *v/i and v/t* (*ge-*, *h*) trill; ZO warble
**trimmen** ['trɪmən] *v/refl* (*ge-*, *h*) keep fit
'**Trimmpfad** *m* fitness trail
**trinkbar** ['trɪŋkbaːɐ] *adj* drinkable
**trinken** ['trɪŋkən] *v/t and v/i* (*irr*, *ge-*, *h*) drink (***auf*** *acc* to); have; ***et. zu ~*** a drink; **Trinker(in)** ['trɪŋkɐ (-kərɪn)] (-*s*; -/-; -*nen*) drinker, alcoholic
'**Trink|geld** *n* tip; ***j-m*** (***e-e Mark***) ***~ ge-***

***ben*** tip s.o. (one mark); **~spruch** *m* toast; **~wasser** *n* drinking water
**Trio** ['tri:o] *n* (-*s*; -*s*) MUS trio (*a. fig*)
**trippeln** ['trɪpəln] *v/i* (*ge-*, *sein*) mince
**Tripper** ['trɪpɐ] *m* (-*s*; -) MED gonorrh(o)ea
**Tritt** [trɪt] *m* (-[*e*]*s*; -*e*) kick; step
'**Trittbrett** *n* step; MOT running board
'**Trittleiter** *f* stepladder
**Triumph** [tri'ʊmf] *m* (-[*e*]*s*; -*e*) triumph
**triumphal** [triʊm'fa:l] *adj* triumphant
**triumphieren** [triʊm'fi:rən] *v/i* (*no -ge-*, *h*) triumph (***über*** *acc* over)
**trocken** ['trɔkən] *adj* dry (*a. fig*)
'**Trocken...** *in cpds* dried ...; drying ...
'**Trockenhaube** *f* hairdryer
'**Trockenheit** *f* (-; *no pl*) dryness; AGR drought
'**trockenlegen** *v/t* (*sep*, *-ge-*, *h*) drain; change (*a baby*)
**trocknen** ['trɔknən] *v/t* (*ge-*, *h*) *and v/i* (*sein*) dry
**Trockner** ['trɔknɐ] *m* (-*s*; -) dryer
**Troddel** ['trɔdəl] *f* (-; -*n*) tassel
**Trödel** ['trø:dəl] *m* (-*s*; *no pl*) junk
**trödeln** ['trø:dəln] *v/i* (*ge-*, *h*) dawdle
**Trödler** ['trø:dlɐ] *m* (-*s*; -) junk dealer; dawdler
**trog** [tro:k] *pret of* ***trügen***
**Trog** *m* (-[*e*]*s*; *Tröge* ['trø:gə]) trough
**Trommel** ['trɔməl] *f* (-; -*n*) MUS drum (*a.* TECH); **~fell** *n* ANAT eardrum
'**trommeln** *v/i and v/t* (*ge-*, *h*) drum
**Trommler** ['trɔmlɐ] *m* (-*s*; -) drummer
**Trompete** [trɔm'pe:tə] *f* (-; -*n*) MUS trumpet; **trom'peten** *v/i and v/t* (*no -ge-*, *h*) trumpet (*a.* ZO); **Trompeter** [trɔm'pe:tɐ] *m* (-*s*; -) trumpeter
**Tropen** ['tro:pən]: ***die ~*** *pl* the tropics
'**Tropen...** *in cpds* tropical ...
**Tropf** [trɔpf] *m* (-[*e*]*s*; *Tröpfe* ['trœpfə]) MED drip
**Tröpfchen** ['trœpfçən] *n* (-*s*; -) droplet
**tröpfeln** ['trœpfəln] *v/i and v/t* (*ge-*, *h*) drip; ***es tröpfelt*** it's spitting
**tropfen** ['trɔpfən] *v/i and v/t* (*ge-*, *h*) drip, drop; '**Tropfen** *m* (-*s*; -) drop (*a. fig*); ***ein ~ auf den heißen Stein*** a drop in the bucket; '**tropfenweise** *adv* in drops, drop by drop
**Trophäe** [tro'fɛ:ə] *f* (-; -*n*) trophy (*a. fig*)
**tropisch** ['tro:pɪʃ] *adj* tropical
**Trosse** ['trɔsə] *f* (-; -*n*) cable
**Trost** [tro:st] *m* (-[*e*]*s*; *no pl*) comfort, consolation; ***ein schwacher ~*** cold comfort
**trösten** ['trø:stən] *v/t* (*ge-*, *h*) comfort, console; ***sich ~*** console o.s. (***mit*** with)
**tröstlich** ['trø:stlɪç] *adj* comforting
'**trostlos** *adj* miserable; desolate
**Trott** [trɔt] *m* (-[*e*]*s*; -*e*) trot; F ***der alte ~*** the old routine
**Trottel** ['trɔtəl] F *m* (-*s*; -) dope
**trottelig** ['trɔtəlɪç] F *adj* dopey
**trotten** ['trɔtən] *v/i* (*ge-*, *sein*) trot
**Trottinett** ['trɔtinɛt] *Swiss n* (-*s*; -*e*) scooter
**Trottoir** [trɔ'toa:ɐ] *Swiss n* (-*s*; -*e*, -*s*) sidewalk, *Br* pavement
**trotz** [trɔts] *prp* (*gen*) in spite of, despite
**Trotz** *m* (-*es*; *no pl*) defiance; ***j-m zum ~*** to spite s.o.
'**trotzdem** *adv* in spite of it, nevertheless, F anyhow, anyway
**trotzen** ['trɔtsən] *v/i* (*ge-*, *h*) defy (*dat s.o. or s.th.*); sulk
**trotzig** ['trɔtsɪç] *adj* defiant; sulky
**trüb** [try:p], **trübe** ['try:bə] *adj* cloudy; muddy; dim; dull, *fig a.* gloomy
**Trubel** ['tru:bəl] *m* (-*s*; *no pl*) (hustle and) bustle
**trüben** ['try:bən] *v/t* (*ge-*, *h*) cloud; *fig* spoil, mar
**Trübsal** ['try:pza:l] *f*: ***~ blasen*** mope
'**trübselig** *adj* sad, gloomy; dreary
'**Trübsinn** *m* (-[*e*]*s*; *no pl*) melancholy, gloom, low spirits; '**trübsinnig** *adj* melancholy, gloomy
**trug** [tru:k] *pret of* ***tragen***
**trügen** ['try:gən] (*irr*, *ge-*, *h*) **1.** *v/t* deceive; **2.** *v/i* be deceptive
**trügerisch** ['try:gərɪʃ] *adj* deceptive
'**Trugschluss** *m* fallacy
**Truhe** ['tru:ə] *f* (-; -*n*) chest
**Trümmer** ['trʏmɐ] *pl* ruins; debris; pieces, bits
**Trumpf** [trʊmpf] *m* (-[*e*]*s*; *Trümpfe* ['trʏmpfə]) trump (card) (*a. fig*); ***~ sein*** be trumps; *fig* ***s-n ~ ausspielen*** play one's trump card
**Trunkenheit** ['trʊŋkənhait] *f* (-; *no pl*) *esp* JUR: ***~ am Steuer*** drunk (*Br* drink) driving
'**Trunksucht** *f* (-; *no pl*) alcoholism
**Trupp** [trʊp] *m* (-*s*; -*s*) band, party; group; **Truppe** ['trʊpə] *f* (-; -*n*) MIL troop, *pl* troops, forces; THEA company, troupe

**'Truppen|gattung** *f* MIL branch (of service); **~übungsplatz** *m* training area
**Truthahn** ['tru:t-] *m* ZO turkey
**Tscheche** ['tʃɛçə] *m* (*-n*; *-n*) Czech; **Tschechien** ['tʃɛçjən] Czech Republic; **'Tschechin** *f* (*-*; *-nen*) Czech; **'tschechisch** *adj* Czech; ***Tschechische Republik*** Czech Republic
**Tube** ['tu:bə] *f* (*-*; *-n*) tube
**Tuberkulose** [tubɛrku'lo:zə] *f* (*-*; *-n*) MED tuberculosis
**Tuch** [tu:x] *n* (*-[e]s*) a) (*pl -e*) cloth, b) (*pl Tücher* ['ty:çɐ]) scarf
**'Tuchfühlung** *f*: ***auf ~*** in close contact
**tüchtig** ['tʏçtɪç] *adj* (cap)able, competent; skil(l)ful; efficient; F *fig* good
**'Tüchtigkeit** *f* (*-*; *no pl*) (cap)ability, qualities; skill; efficiency
**tückisch** ['tʏkɪʃ] *adj* malicious; MED insidious; treacherous
**tüfteln** ['tʏftəln] F *v/i* (*ge-*, *h*) puzzle (***an*** *dat* over)
**Tugend** ['tu:gənt] *f* (*-*; *-en*) virtue (*a. fig*)
**Tulpe** ['tʊlpə] *f* (*-*; *-n*) BOT tulip
**Tumor** ['tu:mo:ɐ] *m* (*-s*; *-en* [tu'mo:rən]) MED tumo(u)r
**Tümpel** ['tʏmpəl] *m* (*-s*; *-*) pool
**Tumult** [tu'mʊlt] *m* (*-[e]s*; *-e*) tumult, uproar
**tun** [tu:n] *v/t and v/i* (*irr*, *ge-*, *h*) do; take (*a step etc*); F put; ***zu ~ haben*** have work to do; be busy; ***ich weiß (nicht), was ich ~ soll*** *or* ***muss*** I (don't) know what to do; ***so ~, als ob*** pretend to *inf*
**Tünche** ['tʏnçə] *f* (*-*; *-n*), **'tünchen** *v/t* (*ge-*, *h*) whitewash
**Tunfisch** *m* → ***Thunfisch***
**Tunke** ['tʊŋkə] *f* (*-*; *-n*) sauce
**Tunnel** ['tʊnəl] *m* (*-s*; *-*) tunnel
**Tüpfelchen** ['tʏpfəlçən] *n*: ***das ~ auf dem i*** the icing on the cake
**tupfen** ['tʊpfən] *v/t* (*ge-*, *h*) dab
**'Tupfen** *m* (*-s*; *-*) dot, spot
**Tupfer** ['tʊpfɐ] *m* (*-s*; *-*) MED swab
**Tür** [ty:ɐ] *f* (*-*; *-en* ['ty:rən]) door (*a. fig*); ***die ~(en) knallen*** slam the door(s); F ***j-n vor die ~ setzen*** throw s.o. out; ***Tag der offenen ~*** open house (*Br* day)
**Turban** ['tʊrba:n] *m* (*-s*; *-e*) turban
**Turbine** [tʊr'bi:nə] *f* (*-*; *-n*) TECH turbine
**Turbolader** ['tʊrbola:dɐ] *m* (*-s*; *-*) MOT turbo(charger)
**Türke** ['tʏrkə] *m* (*-n*; *-n*) Turk; **Türkei** [tʏr'kai] *f* Turkey; **Türkin** ['tʏrkɪn] *f* (*-*; *-nen*) Turk(ish woman); **'türkisch** *adj* Turkish
**'Tür|klingel** *f* doorbell; **~klinke** *f* door handle; **~knauf** *m* doorknob
**Turm** [tʊrm] *m* (*-[e]s*; *Türme* ['tʏrmə]) tower; steeple; *chess*: castle, rook
**türmen** ['tʏrmən] *v/t* (*ge-*, *h*) pile up (*a.* ***sich ~***)
**'Turmspitze** *f* spire
**'Turmspringen** *n* SPORT platform diving
**turnen** ['tʊrnən] *v/i* (*ge-*, *h*) SPORT do gymnastics; **'Turnen** *n* (*-s*; *no pl*) SPORT gymnastics; PED physical education (ABBR PE); **Turner** ['tʊrnɐ] *m* (*-s*; *-*), **Turnerin** ['tʊrnərɪn] *f* (*-*; *-nen*) SPORT gymnast
**'Turnhalle** *f* gymnasium, F gym
**'Turnhemd** *n* gym shirt
**'Turnhose** *f* gym shorts
**Turnier** [tʊr'ni:ɐ] *n* (*-s*; *-e*) tournament
**Tur'niertanz** *m* ballroom dancing
**'Turn|lehrer(in)** gym(nastics) *or* PE teacher; **~schuh** *m* sneaker, *Br* trainer; **~verein** *m* gymnastics club
**'Tür|pfosten** *m* doorpost; **~rahmen** *m* doorframe; **~schild** *n* doorplate; **~sprechanlage** *f* entryphone
**Tusche** ['tʊʃə] *f* (*-*; *-n*) Indian ink; watercolo(u)r
**'Tuschkasten** *m* paintbox
**Tüte** ['ty:tə] *f* (*-*; *-n*) (paper *or* plastic) bag; ***e-e ~ ...*** a bag of ...
**TÜV** [tʏf] ABBR *of* ***Technischer Überwachungs-Verein*** *Br appr* MOT (test), compulsory car inspection; ***(nicht) durch den ~ kommen*** pass (fail) its *or* one's MOT
**Typ** [ty:p] *m* (*-s*; *-en*) type; model; F fellow, guy; **Type** ['ty:pə] *f* (*-*; *-n*) TECH type; F character
**Typhus** ['ty:fʊs] *m* (*-*; *no pl*) MED typhoid (fever)
**typisch** ['ty:pɪʃ] *adj* typical (***für*** of)
**Tyrann** [ty'ran] *m* (*-en*; *-en*) tyrant
**Tyrannei** [tyra'nai] *f* (*-*; *-en*) tyranny
**tyrannisch** [ty'ranɪʃ] *adj* tyrannical
**tyrannisieren** [tyrani'zi:rən] *v/t* (*no -ge-*, *h*) tyrannize, bully

T

# U

**u.a.** ABBR *of* ***unter anderem*** among other things; ***und andere*** and others
**U-Bahn** ['u:ba:n] *f* underground, subway, *in London*: tube
**übel** ['y:bəl] *adj* bad; ***mir ist ~*** I feel sick; ***et. ~ nehmen*** be offended by s.th.; ***~ riechend*** foul-smelling, foul
**'Übel** *n* (*-s*; -) evil
**'Übelkeit** *f* (-; *-en*) nausea
**'Übeltäter** *m*, **'Übeltäterin** *f esp iro* culprit
**üben** ['y:bən] *v/t and v/i* (*ge-, h*) practice, *Br* practise; ***Klavier*** *etc* **~** practice the piano *etc*
**über** ['y:bɐ] *prp* (*dat or acc*) over; above (*a. fig*); more than; across; *fig* about, of, *lecture etc a.* on; ***sprechen*** (***nachdenken*** *etc*) **~** (*acc*) talk (think *etc*) about; ***~ Nacht bleiben*** stay overnight; ***~ München nach Rom*** to Rome via Munich
**über'all** *adv* everywhere; ***~ in ...*** (*dat*) *a.* throughout ..., all over ...
**über'anstrengen** *v/t and v/refl* (*no -ge-, h*) overstrain (o.s.)
**über'arbeiten** *v/t* (*no -ge-, h*) revise; ***sich ~*** overwork o.s.
**'überaus** *adv* most, extremely
**'überbelichten** *v/t* (*no -ge-, h*) PHOT overexpose
**über'bieten** *v/t* (*irr*, ***bieten***, *no -ge-, h*) *at auction*: outbid (***um*** by); *fig* beat, *a.* outdo *s.o.*
**'Überblick** *m* view; *fig* overview (***über*** *acc* of); general idea, outline
**über|'blicken** *v/t* (*no -ge-, h*) overlook; *fig* be able to calculate
**über'bringen** *v/t* (*irr*, ***bringen***, *no -ge-, h*) deliver; **Über'bringer(in)** (*-s*; -/-; *-nen*) ECON bearer
**über|'brücken** *v/t* (*no -ge-, h*) bridge (*a. fig*); **~dacht** [-'daxt] *adj* roofed, covered; **~'dauern** *v/t* (*no -ge-, h*) outlast, survive; **~'denken** *v/t* (*irr*, ***denken***, *no -ge-, h*) think *s.th.* over
**'überdimensio,nal** *adj* oversized
**'Überdosis** *f* MED overdose
**'überdrüssig** [-drʏsɪç] *adj*: ***~ sein*** be weary *or* sick (*gen* of)
**'über|durchschnittlich** *adj* above-average; **~eifrig** *adj* overzealous
**über'eilen** *v/t* (*no -ge-, h*) rush; ***nichts ~!*** don't rush things!; **über'eilt** *adj* rash, hasty
**überei'nander** *adv* on top of each other; *talk etc* about one another; ***die Beine ~ schlagen*** cross one's legs
**über'einkommen** *v/i* (*irr*, ***kommen***, *sep, -ge-, sein*) agree; **Über'einkommen** *n* (*-s*; -), **Über'einkunft** *f* (-; *-künfte*) agreement
**über'einstimmen** *v/i* (*sep, -ge-, h*) tally, correspond (with); ***mit j-m ~*** agree with s.o. (***in*** *dat* on); **Über'einstimmung** *f* (-; *-en*) agreement; correspondence; ***in ~ mit*** in accordance with
**über'fahren** *v/t* (*irr*, ***fahren***, *no -ge-, h*) run *s.o.* over, knock *s.o.* down
**'Überfahrt** *f* MAR crossing
**'Überfall** *m* assault (***auf*** *acc* on); hold-up (on, of); mugging (of); MIL raid (on); invasion (of); **über'fallen** *v/t* (*irr*, ***fallen***, *no -ge-, h*) attack, assault; hold up; mug; MIL raid; invade
**'überfällig** *adj* overdue
**über'fliegen** *v/t* (*irr*, ***fliegen***, *no -ge-, h*) fly over *or* across; *fig* glance over, skim (through)
**'überfließen** *v/i* (*irr*, ***fließen***, *sep, -ge-, sein*) overflow
**'Überfluss** *m* (*-es*; *no pl*) abundance (***an*** *dat* of); affluence; ***im ~ haben*** abound in; **'überflüssig** *adj* superfluous
**über|'fluten** *v/t* (*no -ge-, h*) flood (*a. fig*); **~'fordern** *v/t* (*no -ge-, h*) overtax
**überfragt** [-'fra:kt] *adj*: F ***da bin ich ~*** you've got me there
**über'führen** *v/t* (*no -ge-, h*) transport; JUR convict (***e-r Tat*** of a crime)
**Über'führung** *f* (-; *-en*) transfer; JUR conviction; MOT overpass, *Br* flyover; footbridge
**über'füllt** *adj* overcrowded, packed
**über'füttern** *v/t* (*no -ge-, h*) overfeed
**'Übergang** *m* crossing; *fig* transition
**über'geben** *v/t* (*irr*, ***geben***, *no -ge-, h*) hand over; MIL surrender; ***sich ~*** vomit
**über'gehen¹** *v/t* (*irr*, ***gehen***, *no -ge-, h*) pass over, ignore
**'übergehen²** *v/i* (*irr*, ***gehen***, *sep, -ge-,*

*sein*) pass (***zu*** on to); ~ ***in*** (*acc*) change *or* turn (in)to
**'übergeschnappt** F *adj* cracked
**'Übergewicht** *n* (~ ***haben*** be) overweight; *fig* predominance
**'übergewichtig** *adj* overweight
**'überglücklich** *adj* overjoyed
**'übergreifen** *v/i* (*irr*, ***greifen***, *sep*, *-ge-*, *h*) ~ ***auf*** (*acc*) spread to
**'Übergriff** *m* infringement (***auf*** *acc* of); (act of) violence
**'Übergröße** *f* outsize; ***in*** ~***n*** outsized, oversize(d)
**über'hand:** ~ ***nehmen*** become rampant
**über'häufen** *v/t* (*no -ge-*, *h*) swamp; shower
**über'haupt** *adv* ... at all; anyway; ~ ***nicht*** (***nichts***) not (nothing) at all
**überheblich** [-'heːplɪç] *adj* arrogant
**Über'heblichkeit** *f* (-; *no pl*) arrogance
**über|'hitzen** *v/t* (*no -ge-*, *h*) overheat (*a. fig*); ~**'höht** [-'høːt] *adj* excessive; ~**'holen** *v/t* (*no -ge-*, *h*) pass, overtake (*a.* SPORT); TECH overhaul, service; ~**'holt** *adj* outdated, antiquated; ~**'hören** *v/t* (*no -ge-*, *h*) miss, not catch *or* get; ignore
**'überirdisch** *adj* supernatural
**über'kleben** *v/t* (*no -ge-*, *h*) paste up, cover
**'überkochen** *v/i* (*sep*, *-ge-*, *sein*) boil over
**über|'kommen** *v/t* (*irr*, ***kommen***, *no -ge-*, *h*) ... ***überkam ihn*** he was seized with *or* overcome by ...; ~**'laden** *v/t* (*irr*, ***laden***, *no -ge-*, *h*) overload (*a.* ELECTR); *fig* clutter; ~**'lassen** *v/t* (*irr*, ***lassen***, *no -ge-*, *h*) ***j-m et.*** ~ let s.o. have s.th., leave s.th. to s.o. (*a. fig*); ***j-n sich selbst*** ~ leave s.o. to himself; ***j-n s-m Schicksal*** ~ leave s.o. to his fate; ~**'lasten** *v/t* (*no -ge-*, *h*) overload (*a.* ELECTR); *fig* overburden
**'überlaufen**[1] *v/i* (*irr*, ***laufen***, *sep*, *-ge-*, *sein*) run *or* flow over; MIL desert
**über'laufen**[2] *v/t* (*irr*, ***laufen***, *no -ge-*, *h*) ***es überlief mich heiß und kalt*** I went hot and cold
**über'laufen**[3] *adj* overcrowded
**'Überläufer** *m* MIL deserter; POL defector
**über'leben** *v/t and v/i* (*no -ge-*, *h*) survive (*a. fig*); live through *s.th.*
**Über'lebende** *m, f* (*-n*; *-n*) survivor
**'überlebensgroß** *adj* larger than life
**über'legen**[1] *v/t and v/i* (*no -ge-*, *h*) think about *s.th.*, think *s.th.* over; consider; ***lassen Sie mich*** ~ let me think; ***ich habe es mir*** (***anders***) ***überlegt*** I've made up (changed) my mind
**über'legen**[2] *adj* superior (***j-m*** to s.o.)
**Über'legenheit** *f* (-; *no pl*) superiority
**über'legt** *adj* deliberate; prudent
**Über'legung** *f* (-; *-en*) consideration, reflection
**'überleiten** *v/i* (*sep*, *-ge-*, *h*) ~ ***zu*** lead up *or* over to
**über'liefern** *v/t* (*no -ge-*, *h*) hand down, pass on; **Über'lieferung** *f* (-; *-en*) tradition
**über'listen** *v/t* (*no -ge-*, *h*) outwit
**'Übermacht** *f* (-; *no pl*) superiority; *esp* MIL superior forces; ***in der*** ~ ***sein*** be superior in numbers; **'übermächtig** *adj* superior; *fig* overpowering
**'Übermaß** *n* (*-es*; *no pl*) excess (***an*** *dat* of); **'übermäßig** *adj* excessive
**'übermenschlich** *adj* superhuman
**über'mitteln** *v/t* (*no -ge-*, *h*) convey
**'übermorgen** *adv* the day after tomorrow
**über'müdet** *adj* overtired
**'übermütig** [-myːtɪç] *adj* high-spirited
**'übernächst** *adj the* next but one; ~***e Woche*** the week after next
**übernachten** [-'naxtən] *v/i* (*no -ge-*, *h*) stay overnight (***bei j-m*** at s.o.'s [house], with s.o.), spend the night (at, with)
**Über'nachtung** *f* (-; *-en*) night; ~ ***und Frühstück*** bed and breakfast
**Übernahme** ['yːbɐnaːmə] *f* (-; *-n*) taking (over); adoption
**'übernaˌtürlich** *adj* supernatural
**über'nehmen** *v/t* (*irr*, ***nehmen***, *no -ge-*, *h*) take over; adopt; take (*responsibility etc*); undertake *to do*
**über'prüfen** *v/t* (*no -ge-*, *h*) check, examine; verify; *esp* POL screen
**Über'prüfung** *f* check, examination; verification; screening
**über|'queren** *v/t* (*no -ge-*, *h*) cross; ~**'ragen** *v/t* (*no -ge-*, *h*) tower above (*a. fig*); ~**'ragend** *adj* outstanding
**überraschen** [yːbɐ'raʃən] *v/t* (*no -ge-*, *h*) surprise; ***j-n bei et.*** ~ *a.* catch s.o. doing s.th.; **Über'raschung** *f* (-; *-en*) surprise

**über'reden** *v/t* (*no -ge-*, *h*) persuade (***et. zu tun*** to do s.th.); ***j-n zu et.*** ~ talk s.o. into (doing) s.th.; **Über'redung** *f* (-; *no pl*) persuasion

**'überregio,nal** *adj* national

**über|'reichen** *v/t* (*no -ge-*, *h*) present, hand *s.th.* over (*dat* to); **~'reizen** *v/t* (*no -ge-*, *h*) overexcite; **~'reizt** *adj* overwrought, F on edge

**'Überrest** *m* remains; *pl* relics; GASTR leftovers

**über|'rumpeln** *v/t* (*no -ge-*, *h*) (take *s.o.* by) surprise; **~'runden** *v/t* (*no -ge-*, *h*) SPORT lap

**übersät** [-'zɛːt] *adj*: ~ ***mit*** strewn with *garbage*; studded with *stars*

**übersättigt** [-'zɛtɪçt] *adj* sated, surfeited

**'Überschall...** *in cpds* supersonic ...

**über|'schatten** *v/t* (*no -ge-*, *h*) overshadow (*a. fig*); **~'schätzen** *v/t* (*no -ge-*, *h*) overrate, overestimate

**'Überschlag** *m* AVIAT loop; SPORT somersault; ECON rough estimate

**'überschlagen¹** (*irr*, ***schlagen***, *sep*, *-ge-*) **1.** *v/t* (*h*) cross (*one's legs*); **2.** *v/i* (*sein*) *fig* ~ ***in*** (*acc*) turn into

**über'schlagen²** (*no -ge-*, *h*) **1.** *v/t* skip; ECON make a rough estimate of; **2.** *v/refl* turn (right) over; go head over heels; *voice*: break

**'überschnappen** F *v/i* (*no -ge-*, *sein*) crack up

**über|'schneiden** *v/refl* (*irr*, ***schneiden***, *no -ge-*, *h*) overlap (*a. fig*); intersect; **~'schreiben** *v/t* (*irr*, ***schreiben***, *no -ge-*, *h*) make *s.th.* over (*dat* to); **~'schreiten** *v/t* (*irr*, ***schreiten***, *no -ge-*, *h*) cross; *fig* go beyond; pass; break (*the speed limit etc*)

**'Überschrift** *f* heading, title; headline; caption

**'Überschuss** *m*, **'überschüssig** [-ʃʏsɪç] *adj* surplus

**über'schütten** *v/t* (*no -ge-*, *h*) ~ ***mit*** cover with; shower with; heap *s.th.* on

**'überschwänglich** [-ʃvɛŋlɪç] *adj* effusive

**über'schwemmen** *v/t* (*no -ge-*, *h*), **Über'schwemmung** *f* (-; *-en*) flood

**'überschwenglich** → ***überschwänglich***

**'Übersee:** ***in*** (***nach***) ~ oversea

**über'sehen** *v/t* (*irr*, ***sehen***, *no -ge-*, *h*) overlook; ignore

**über'setzen¹** *v/t* (*no -ge-*, *h*) translate (***in*** *acc* into)

**'übersetzen²** (*sep*, *-ge-*) **1.** *v/i* (*h*, *sein*) cross (***über e-n Fluss*** a river); **2.** *v/t* (*h*) take over

**Übersetzer** [-'zɛtsɐ] *m* (*-s*; -), **Über'setzerin** *f* (-; *-nen*) translator

**Über'setzung** *f* (-; *-en*) translation (***aus*** *dat* from; ***in*** *acc* into)

**'Übersicht** *f* (-; *-en*) overview (***über*** *acc* of); outline, summary

**'übersichtlich** *adj* clear(ly arranged)

**'übersiedeln** *v/i* (*sep*, *-ge-*, *sein*) move (***nach*** to); **'Übersied(e)lung** *f* move

**über'spannen** *v/t* (*no -ge-*, *h*) span

**über'spannt** *fig adj* eccentric; extravagant

**über'spielen** *v/t* (*no -ge-*, *h*) record; tape; *fig* cover up

**über'spitzt** *adj* exaggerated

**über'springen** *v/t* (*irr*, ***springen***, *no -ge-*, *h*) jump (over), *esp* SPORT *a.* clear; *fig* skip

**über'stehen¹** *v/t* (*irr*, ***stehen***, *no -ge-*, *h*) get over; survive (*a. fig*), live through

**'überstehen²** *v/i* (*irr*, ***stehen***, *sep*, *-ge-*, *h*) jut out

**über|'steigen** *fig v/t* (*irr*, ***steigen***, *no -ge-*, *h*) exceed; **~'stimmen** *v/t* (*no -ge-*, *h*) outvote

**'über|streifen** *v/t* (*sep*, *-ge-*, *h*) slip *s.th.* on; **~strömen** *v/i* (*sep*, *-ge-*, *sein*) overflow (***vor*** *dat* with)

**'Überstunden** *pl* overtime; ~ ***machen*** work overtime

**über|'stürzen** *v/t* (*no -ge-*, *h*) ***et.*** ~ rush things; ***sich*** ~ *events*: follow in rapid succession; **~'stürzt** *adj* (over)hasty; rash; **~'teuert** *adj* overpriced; **~'tönen** *v/t* (*no -ge-*, *h*) drown (out)

**über'tragbar** *adj* transferable; MED contagious

**über'tragen¹** *adj* figurative

**über'tragen²** *v/t* (*irr*, ***tragen***, *no -ge-*, *h*) broadcast, *a.* televise; translate; MED, TECH transmit; MED transfuse (*blood*); JUR, ECON transfer

**Über'tragung** *f* (-; *-en*) *radio*, TV broadcast; transmission; translation; MED transfusion; JUR, ECON transfer

**über'treffen** *v/t* (*irr*, ***treffen***, *no -ge-*, *h*) outstrip, outdo, surpass, beat

**über'treiben** *v/i and v/t* (*irr*, ***treiben***, *no -ge-*, *h*) exaggerate; overdo

Ü

**Über'treibung** *f* (-; *-en*) exaggeration

**'übertreten¹** *v/i* (*irr*, **treten**, *sep*, *-ge-*, *sein*) ~ **zu** go over to, REL convert to

**über'treten²** (*irr*, **treten**, *no -ge-*, *h*) **1.** *v/t* break, violate; **2.** *v/i* SPORT foul (a jump *or* throw); **Über'tretung** *f* (-; *-en*) violation, JUR *a.* offen|se, *Br* -ce

**'Übertritt** *m* change (**zu** to); REL, POL conversion (to)

**übervölkert** [-'fœlkɐt] *adj* overpopulated

**über'wachen** *v/t* (*no -ge-*, *h*) supervise, oversee; control; observe

**Über'wachung** *f* (-; *-en*) supervision, control; observance; surveillance

**überwältigen** [-'vɛltɪgən] *v/t* (*no -ge-*, *h*) overwhelm, overpower, *fig a.* overcome; **~d** *adj* overwhelming, overpowering

**über'weisen** *v/t* (*irr*, **weisen**, *no -ge-*, *h*) ECON transfer (**an j-n** to s.o.'s account); remit; MED refer (**an** *acc* to)

**Über'weisung** *f* (-; *-en*) ECON transfer; remittance; MED referral

**'überwerfen¹** *v/t* (*irr*, **werfen**, *sep*, *-ge-*, *h*) slip *s.th.* on

**über'werfen²** *v/refl* (*irr*, **werfen**, *no -ge-*, *h*) **sich** ~ (**mit j-m**) fall out with each other (with s.o.)

**über'wiegen** *v/i* (*irr*, **wiegen**, *no -ge-*, *h*) predominate; **~d** *adj* predominant; vast (*majority*)

**über|'winden** *v/t* (*irr*, **winden**, *no -ge-*, *h*) overcome (*a. fig*); defeat; **sich ~ zu** *inf* bring o.s. to *inf*; **~wintern** [-'vɪntɐn] *v/i* (*no -ge-*, *h*) spend the winter (**in** *dat* in); **~'wuchern** *v/t* (*no -ge-*, *h*) overgrow

**'Überzahl** *f* (-; *no pl*) majority; **in der ~ sein** outnumber *s.o.*

**über'zeugen** *v/t* (*no -ge-*, *h*) convince (**von** of), persuade; **sich ~, dass** make sure that; **sich selbst ~** (go and) see for o.s.; **überzeugt** [-'tsɔʏkt] *adj* convinced; **~ sein** *a.* be *or* feel (quite) sure; **Über'zeugung** *f* (-; *-en*) conviction

**'überziehen¹** *v/t* (*irr*, **ziehen**, *sep*, *-ge-*, *h*) put *s.th.* on

**über'ziehen²** *v/t* (*irr*, **ziehen**, *no -ge-*, *h*) TECH *etc* cover; ECON overdraw

**Über'ziehungskre,dit** *m* ECON overdraft (facility)

**'Überzug** *m* cover; coat(ing)

**üblich** ['y:plɪç] *adj* usual, normal; **es ist ~** it's the custom; **wie ~** as usual

**'U-Boot** *n* submarine

**übrig** ['y:brɪç] *adj* remaining; **die Übrigen** *pl* the others, the rest; **~ sein** (**haben**) be (have) left; **~ bleiben** be left, remain; **es bleibt mir nichts anderes ~** (**als zu** *inf*) there is nothing else I can do (but *inf*); **~ lassen** leave

**übrigens** ['y:brɪgəns] *adv* by the way

**Übung** ['y:bʊŋ] *f* (-; *-en*) exercise; practice; **in** (**aus der**) **~** in (out of) practice

**Ufer** ['u:fɐ] *n* (*-s*; -) shore; bank; **ans ~** ashore

**Uhr** [u:ɐ] *f* (-; *-en* ['u:rən]) clock; watch; **um vier ~** at four o'clock

**'Uhr|armband** *n* watchstrap; **~macher** *m* (*-s*; -) watchmaker; **~werk** *n* clockwork; **~zeiger** *m* hand; **~zeigersinn** *m*: **im ~** clockwise; **entgegen dem ~** counterclockwise, *Br* anticlockwise

**Uhu** ['u:hu] *m* (*-s*; *-s*) ZO eagle owl

**UKW** [u:ka:'ve:] ABBR *of* **Ultrakurzwelle** VHF, very high frequency

**Ulk** [ʊlk] *m* (*-s*; *-e*) joke; hoax

**ulkig** ['ʊlkɪç] *adj* funny

**Ulme** ['ʊlmə] *f* (-; *-n*) BOT elm

**Ultimatum** [ʊlti'ma:tʊm] *n* (*-s*; *-ten*) ultimatum; **j-m ein ~ stellen** deliver an ultimatum to s.o.

**um** [ʊm] *prp* (*acc*) *and cj* (a)round; at; about, around; **~ Geld** for money; **~ e-e Stunde** (**10 cm**) by an hour (10 cm); **~ ... willen** for the sake of ...; **~ zu** *inf* (in order) to *inf*; **~ sein** F be over; **die Zeit ist ~** time's up; → **umso**

**umarmen** [ʊm'ˀarmən] *v/t* (*no -ge-*, *h*) (*a.* **sich ~**) embrace, hug

**Um'armung** *f* (-; *-en*) embrace, hug

**'Umbau** *m* (-[*e*]*s*; *-e*, *-ten*) rebuilding, reconstruction; **'umbauen** *v/t* (*sep*, *-ge-*, *h*) rebuild, reconstruct

**'um|binden** *v/t* (*irr*, **binden**, *sep*, *-ge-*, *h*) put *s.th.* on; **~blättern** *v/i* (*sep*, *-ge-*, *h*) turn (over) the page; **~bringen** *v/t* (*irr*, **bringen**, *sep*, *-ge-*, *h*) kill; **sich ~** kill o.s.; **~buchen** *v/t* (*sep*, *-ge-*, *h*) change; ECON transfer (**auf** *acc* to); **~denken** *v/i* (*irr*, **denken**, *sep*, *-ge-*, *h*) change one's way of thinking; **~dispo,nieren** *v/i* (*sep*, *no -ge-*, *h*) change one's plans; **~drehen** *v/t* (*sep*, *-ge-*, *h*) turn (round); **sich ~** turn round

**Um'drehung** *f* (-; *-en*) turn; PHYS, TECH rotation, revolution
**umei'nander** *adv care etc* about *or* for each other
**'umfahren**[1] *v/t* (*irr*, ***fahren***, *sep*, *-ge-*, *h*) run down
**um'fahren**[2] *v/t* (*irr*, ***fahren***, *no -ge-*, *h*) drive (MAR sail) round
**'umfallen** *v/i* (*irr*, ***fallen***, *sep*, *-ge-*, *sein*) fall down *or* over; collapse; ***tot ~*** drop dead
**'Umfang** *m* circumference; size; extent; ***in großem ~*** on a large scale
**'umfangreich** *adj* extensive; voluminous
**um'fassen** *fig v/t* (*no -ge-*, *h*) cover; include; **~d** *adj* comprehensive; complete
**'umformen** *v/t* (*sep*, *-ge-*, *h*) turn, change; ELECTR, LING, MATH *a.* transform, convert (*all*: ***in*** *acc* [in]to)
**'Umformer** *m* (*-s*; -) ELECTR converter
**'Umfrage** *f* opinion poll
**'Umgang** *m* (-[*e*]*s*; *no pl*) company; ***~ haben mit*** associate with; ***beim ~ mit*** when dealing with
**'umgänglich** [-gɛŋlɪç] *adj* sociable
**'Umgangs|formen** *pl* manners; **~sprache** *f* colloquial speech; ***die englische ~*** colloquial English
**um'geben** *v/t* (*irr*, ***geben***, *no -ge-*, *h*) surround (***mit*** with); **Um'gebung** *f* (-; *-en*) surroundings; environment
**'umgehen**[1] *v/i* (*irr*, ***gehen***, *sep*, *-ge-*, *sein*) ***~ mit*** deal with, handle; ***~ können mit*** have a way with, be good with
**um'gehen**[2] *v/t* (*irr*, ***gehen***, *no -ge-*, *h*) avoid; bypass
**'umgehend** *adv* immediately
**Um'gehungsstraße** *f* bypass; beltway, *Br* ring road
**umgekehrt** ['ʊmgəkeːɐt] **1.** *adj* reverse; opposite; (***genau***) **~** (just) the other way round; **2.** *adv* the other way round; ***und ~*** and vice versa
**'umgraben** *v/t* (*irr*, ***graben***, *sep*, *-ge-*, *h*) dig (up), break up
**'Umhang** *m* cape; **'umhängen** *v/t* (*sep*, *-ge-*, *h*) put around *or* over s.o.'s shoulders *etc*; rehang
**'umhauen** *v/t* (*irr*, ***hauen***, *sep*, *-ge-*, *h*) fell, cut down; F knock *s.o.* out
**um'her** *adv* (a)round, about
**um'herstreifen** *v/i* (*sep*, *-ge-*, *sein*) roam *or* wander around
**'umkehren** (*sep*, *-ge-*) **1.** *v/i* (*sein*) turn back; **2.** *v/t* (*h*) reverse
**'Umkehrung** *f* (-; *-en*) reversal (*a. fig*)
**'umkippen** (*sep*, *-ge-*) **1.** *v/t* (*h*) tip over, upset; **2.** *v/i* (*sein*) fall down *or* over, overturn
**um'klammern** *v/t* (*no -ge-*, *h*), **Um'klammerung** *f* (-; *-en*) clasp, clutch, clench
**'Umkleide|ka,bine** *f* changing cubicle; **~raum** *m esp* SPORT changing *or* locker room; THEA dressing room
**'umkommen** *v/i* (*irr*, ***kommen***, *sep*, *-ge-*, *sein*) be killed (***bei*** in), die (in); F ***~ vor*** (*dat*) be dying with
**'Umkreis** *m*: ***im ~ von*** within a radius of; **um'kreisen** *v/t* (*no -ge-*, *h*) circle; ASTR revolve around; *satellite etc*: orbit
**'umkrempeln** *v/t* (*sep*, *-ge-*, *h*) roll up
**'Umlauf** *m* circulation; PHYS, TECH rotation; ECON circular; ***im*** (***in***) ***~ sein*** (***bringen***) be in (put into) circulation, circulate; **~bahn** *f* ASTR orbit
**'um|laufen** *v/i* (*irr*, ***laufen***, *sep*, *-ge-*, *sein*) circulate; **~legen** *v/t* (*sep*, *-ge-*, *h*) put on; move; share (*expenses etc*); TECH pull; F do *s.o.* in, bump *s.o.* off
**'umleiten** *v/t* (*sep*, *-ge-*, *h*) divert; **'Umleitung** *f* (-; *-en*) detour, *Br* diversion
**'umliegend** *adj* surrounding
**'umpacken** *v/t* (*sep*, *-ge-*, *h*) repack
**'umpflanzen** *v/t* (*sep*, *-ge-*, *h*) repot
**umranden** [ʊm'randən] *v/t* (*no -ge-*, *h*), **Um'randung** *f* (-; *-en*) edge, border
**'umräumen** *v/t* (*sep*, *-ge-*, *h*) rearrange
**'umrechnen** *v/t* (*sep*, *-ge-*, *h*) convert (***in*** *acc* into); **'Umrechnung** *f* (-; *-en*) conversion; **'Umrechnungskurs** *m* exchange rate
**'umreißen** *v/t* (*irr*, ***reißen***, *sep*, *-ge-*, *h*) knock *s.o.* down
**um'ringen** *v/t* (*no -ge-*, *h*) surround
**'Umriss** *m* outline (*a. fig*), contour
**'um|rühren** *v/t* (*sep*, *-ge-*, *h*) stir; **~rüsten** *v/t* (*sep*, *-ge-*, *h*) TECH convert (***auf*** *acc* to); **~satteln** F *v/i* (*sep*, *-ge-*, *h*) ***~ von ... auf*** (*acc*) ... switch from ... to ...
**'Umsatz** *m* ECON sales
**'umschalten** *v/t and v/i* (*sep*, *-ge-*, *h*) switch (over) (***auf*** *acc* to) (*a. fig*)
**'Umschlag** *m* envelope; cover, wrapper; jacket; cuff, *Br* turn-up; MED compress; ECON handling; **'umschlagen**

(*irr*, **schlagen**, *sep*, *-ge-*) **1.** *v/t* (*h*) cut down, fell; turn up; turn down; ECON handle; **2.** *v/i* (*sein*) turn over; *fig* change (suddenly).

**'Umschlagplatz** *m* trading center (*Br* centre)

**'umschnallen** *v/t* (*sep*, *-ge-*, *h*) buckle on

**'umschreiben¹** *v/t* (*irr*, **schreiben**, *sep*, *-ge-*, *h*) rewrite

**um'schreiben²** *v/t* (*irr*, **schreiben**, *no -ge-*, *h*) paraphrase

**Um'schreibung** *f* (-; *-en*) paraphrase

**'Umschrift** *f* transcription

**'umschulen** *v/t* (*sep*, *-ge-*, *h*) retrain; transfer to another school

**umschwärmt** [ʊm'ʃvɛrmt] *adj* idolized

**'Umschwung** *m* (drastic) change, *esp* POL *a.* swing

**um'segeln** *v/t* (*no -ge-*, *h*) sail round; circumnavigate

**'um|sehen** *v/refl* (*irr*, **sehen**, *sep*, *-ge-*, *h*) look around (**in e-m Laden** a shop; **nach** for); look back (**nach** at); **sich ~ nach** be looking for; **~setzen** *v/t* (*sep*, *-ge-*, *h*) move (*a.* PED); ECON sell; **~ in** (*acc*) convert (in)to; **in die Tat ~** put into action; **sich ~** change places

**'umsiedeln** *v/i* (*sep*, *-ge-*, *sein*) *and v/t* (*h*) resettle; → **umziehen**

**'Umsied(e)lung** *f* (-; *-en*) resettlement

**'Umsiedler** *m* (*-s*; -) resettler

**'umso 1. je später** *etc*, **~ schlechter** *etc* the later *etc* the worse *etc*; **2. ~ besser** so much the better

**um'sonst** *adv* free (of charge), for nothing; F for free; *fig* in vain

**um'spannen** *v/t* (*no -ge-*, *h*) span (*a. fig*)

**'umspringen** *v/i* (*irr*, **springen**, *sep*, *-ge-*, *sein*) shift, change (suddenly) (*a. fig*); **~ mit** treat (badly)

**'Umstand** *m* circumstance; fact; detail; **unter diesen** (**keinen**) **Umständen** under the (no) circumstances; **unter Umständen** possibly; **keine Umstände machen** not cause *s.o.* any trouble; not go to any trouble, not put o.s. out; **in anderen Umständen sein** be expecting

**umständlich** ['ʊmʃtɛntlɪç] *adj* awkward; complicated; long-winded; **das ist** (**mir**) **viel zu ~** that's far too much trouble (for me)

**'Umstands|kleid** *n* maternity dress; **~wort** *n* (*-[e]s*; *-wörter*) LING adverb

**'Umstehende: die ~n** *pl* the bystanders

**'umsteigen** *v/i* (*irr*, **steigen**, *sep*, *-ge-*, *sein*) change (**nach** for), RAIL *a.* change trains (for)

**'umstellen** *v/t* (*sep*, *-ge-*, *h*) change (**auf** *acc* to), make a change *or* changes in, *esp* TECH *a.* switch (over) (to), convert (to); adjust (to); rearrange (*a. furniture*), reorganize; reset (*watch*); **sich ~ auf** (*acc*) change *or* switch (over) to; adjust (o.s.) to, get used to

**'Umstellung** *f* (-; *-en*) change; switch, conversion; adjustment; rearrangement, reorganization

**'umstimmen** *v/t* (*sep*, *-ge-*, *h*) **j-n ~** change s.o.'s mind

**'umstoßen** *v/t* (*irr*, **stoßen**, *sep*, *-ge-*, *h*) knock over, upset (*a. fig*)

**umstritten** [ʊm'ʃtrɪtən] *adj* controversial

**'Umsturz** *m* overthrow; **'umstürzen** *v/i* (*sep*, *-ge-*, *sein*) overturn, fall over

**'Umtausch** *m*, **'umtauschen** *v/t* (*sep*, *-ge-*, *h*) exchange (**gegen** for)

**'umwälzend** *adj* revolutionary

**'Umwälzung** *f* (-; *-en*) radical change

**'umwandeln** *v/t* (*sep*, *-ge-*, *h*) turn (**in** *acc* into), transform (into), *esp* CHEM, ELECTR, PHYS *a.* convert ([in]to)

**'Umwandlung** *f* (-; *-en*) transformation, conversion

**'Umweg** *m* roundabout route *or* way (*a. fig*), *esp* MOT *a.* detour; **ein ~ von 10 Minuten** ten minutes out of the way; *fig* **auf ~en** in a roundabout way

**'Umwelt** *f* (-; *no pl*) environment

**'Umwelt...** *in cpds mst* environmental ...; **~forschung** *f* ecology

**'umwelt|freundlich** *adj* environment-friendly, non-polluting; **~schädlich** *adj* harmful, noxious, polluting

**'Umwelt|schutz** *m* conservation, environmental protection, pollution control; **~schützer** *m* environmentalist, conservationist; **~schutzpa,pier** *n* recycled paper; **~sünder** *m* (environmental) polluter; **~verschmutzer** *m* (*-s*; -) polluter; **~verschmutzung** *f* (environmental) pollution; **~zerstörung** *f* ecocide

**'umziehen** (*irr*, **ziehen**, *sep -ge-*) **1.** *v/i* (*sein*) move (**nach** to); **2.** *v/refl* (*h*) change (one's clothes)

U

**umzingeln** [ʊmˈtsɪŋəln] *v/t* (*no -ge-*, *h*) surround, encircle
ˈ**Umzug** *m* move (***nach*** to), removal (to); parade
**unabhängig** [ˈʊn-] *adj* independent (***von*** of); ~ ***davon, ob*** (***was***) regardless of whether (what); ˈ**Unabhängigkeit** *f* (-; *no pl*) independence (***von*** from)
ˈ**unabsichtlich** *adj* unintentional; ***et.*** ~ ***tun*** do s.th. by mistake
**unabˈwendbar** *adj* inevitable
ˈ**unachtsam** *adj* careless, negligent
ˈ**Unachtsamkeit** *f* (-; *no pl*) carelessness, negligence
**unanˈfechtbar** *adj* incontestable
ˈ**un|angebracht** *adj* inappropriate; ~ ***sein*** be out of place; **~angemessen** *adj* unreasonable; inadequate; **~angenehm** *adj* unpleasant; embarrassing
**unanˈnehmbar** *adj* unacceptable
**Unannehmlichkeiten** [ˈʊnʔanneːmlɪçkaitən] *pl* trouble, difficulties
ˈ**unansehnlich** *adj* unsightly
ˈ**unanständig** *adj* indecent, obscene
**unanˈtastbar** *adj* inviolable
ˈ**unappetitlich** *adj* unappetizing
**Unart** [ˈʊnʔart] *f* (-; *-en*) bad habit
ˈ**unartig** *adj* naughty, bad
ˈ**unaufdringlich** *adj* unobtrusive
ˈ**unauffällig** *adj* inconspicuous, unobtrusive
**unaufˈfindbar** *adj* not to be found, untraceable
ˈ**unaufgefordert** *adv* without being asked, of one's own accord
**unaufhörlich** [ʊnʔaufˈhøːɐlɪç] *adj* continuous
ˈ**unaufmerksam** *adj* inattentive
ˈ**Unaufmerksamkeit** *f* (-; *no pl*) inattention, inattentiveness
ˈ**unaufrichtig** *adj* insincere
**unaus|löschlich** [ʊnʔausˈlœʃlɪç] *adj* indelible; **~stehlich** [-ˈʃteːlɪç] *adj* unbearable
ˈ**unbarmherzig** *adj* merciless
ˈ**un|beabsichtigt** *adj* unintentional; **~beachtet** *adj* unnoticed; **~beaufsichtigt** *adj* unattended; **~bebaut** *adj* undeveloped; **~bedacht** [-bədaxt] *adj* thoughtless; **~bedenklich 1.** *adj* safe; **2.** *adv* without hesitation; **~bedeutend** *adj* insignificant; minor; **~bedingt 1.** *adj* unconditional, absolute; **2.** *adv* by all means, absolutely; *need etc* badly; **~befahrbar** *adj* impassable; **~befangen** *adj* unprejudiced, unbias(s)ed; unembarrassed; **~befriedigend** *adj* unsatisfactory; **~befriedigt** *adj* dissatisfied; **~begabt** *adj* untalented; **~begreiflich** *adj* inconceivable, incomprehensible; **~begrenzt** *adj* unlimited, boundless; **~begründet** *adj* unfounded
ˈ**Unbehagen** *n* (*-s*; *no pl*) uneasiness, discomfort; ˈ**unbehaglich** *adj* uneasy, uncomfortable
**unbehelligt** [ʊnbəˈhɛlɪçt] *adj* unmolested
ˈ**un|beherrscht** *adj* uncontrolled, lacking self-control; **~beholfen** [-bəhɔlfən] *adj* clumsy, awkward; **~beirrt** *adj* unwavering; **~bekannt** *adj* unknown
ˈ**Unbekannte** *f* (-; *-n*) MATH unknown quantity
ˈ**un|bekümmert** *adj* light-hearted, cheerful; **~belehrbar** *adj*: ***er ist*** ~ he'll never learn; **~beliebt** *adj* unpopular; ***er ist überall*** ~ nobody likes him; **~bemannt** *adj* unmanned; **~bemerkt** *adj* unnoticed; **~benutzt** *adj* unused; **~bequem** *adj* uncomfortable; inconvenient; **~berechenbar** *adj* unpredictable; **~berechtigt** *adj* unauthorized; unjustified; **~beschädigt** *adj* undamaged; **~bescheiden** *adj* immodest
**un|beˈschränkt** *adj* unlimited; absolute (*power*); **~beschreiblich** [-bəˈʃraiplɪç] *adj* indescribable; **~beˈsehen** *adv* unseen; **~besiegbar** [-bəˈziːkbaːɐ] *adj* invincible
ˈ**un|besonnen** *adj* thoughtless, imprudent; rash; **~beˈspielbar** *adj* SPORT unplayable; **~beständig** *adj* unstable; METEOR changeable, unsettled; **~bestätigt** *adj* unconfirmed
**unbeˈstechlich** *adj* incorruptible
ˈ**unbestimmt** *adj* indefinite (*a.* LING); uncertain; vague
**un|beˈstreitbar** *adj* indisputable; **~bestritten** [-bəˈʃtrɪtən] *adj* undisputed
ˈ**un|beteiligt** *adj* not involved; indifferent; **~betont** *adj* unstressed
**unbeugsam** [ʊnˈbɔʏkzaːm] *adj* inflexible
ˈ**un|bewacht** *adj* unwatched, unguarded (*a. fig*); **~bewaffnet** *adj* unarmed; **~beweglich** *adj* immovable; motionless

**unbe'wohnbar** *adj* uninhabitable
**'unbewohnt** *adj* uninhabited; unoccupied, vacant
**'unbewusst** *adj* unconscious
**unbe'zahlbar** *fig adj* invaluable, priceless; **'unbezahlt** *adj* unpaid
**'unblutig 1.** *adj* bloodless; **2.** *adv* without bloodshed
**'unbrauchbar** *adj* useless
**und** [ʊnt] *cj* and; F ***na ~?*** so what?
**'undankbar** *adj* ungrateful (***gegen*** to); thankless; **'Undankbarkeit** *f* (-; *no pl*) ingratitude, ungratefulness
**undefi'nierbar** *adj* undefinable
**un'denkbar** *adj* unthinkable
**'undeutlich** *adj* indistinct; inarticulate; *fig* vague
**'undicht** *adj* leaky
**'unduldsam** *adj* intolerant; **'Unduldsamkeit** *f* (-; *no pl*) intolerance
**undurch|'dringlich** *adj* impenetrable; **~'führbar** *adj* impracticable
**'undurch|lässig** *adj* impervious, impermeable; **~sichtig** *adj* opaque; *fig* mysterious
**'uneben** *adj* uneven; **'Unebenheit** *f* a) (-; *no pl*) unevenness, b) (-; *-en*) bump
**'unecht** *adj* false; artificial; imitation ...; F *contp* fake, phon(e)y
**'unehelich** *adj* illegitimate
**'unehrenhaft** *adj* dishono(u)rable
**'unehrlich** *adj* dishonest
**'uneigennützig** *adj* unselfish
**'uneinig** *adj*: (***sich***) ~ ***sein*** disagree (***über*** *acc* on); **'Uneinigkeit** *f* (-; *no pl*) disagreement; dissension
**unein'nehmbar** *adj* impregnable
**'un|empfänglich** *adj* insusceptible (***für*** to); **~empfindlich** *adj* insensitive (***gegen*** to)
**un'endlich** *adj* infinite; endless, never-ending; **Un'endlichkeit** *f* (-; *no pl*) infinity (*a. fig*)
**unent|behrlich** [ʊnˀɛnt'beːɐlɪç] *adj* indispensable; **~geltlich** [-'gɛltlɪç] *adj and adv* free (of charge)
**'unentschieden** *adj* undecided; ~ ***enden*** SPORT end in a draw *or* tie; ***es steht*** ~ the score is even; **'Unentschieden** *n* (-*s*; -) SPORT draw, tie
**'unentschlossen** *adj* irresolute
**unent'schuldbar** *adj* inexcusable
**unentwegt** [ʊnˀɛnt'veːkt] *adv* untiringly; continuously
**'un|erfahren** *adj* inexperienced; **~erfreulich** *adj* unpleasant; **~erfüllt** *adj* unfulfilled; **~ergiebig** *adj* unproductive; **~erheblich** *adj* irrelevant (***für*** to); insignificant
**unerhört** ['ʊnˀɛːɐ'høːɐt] *adj* outrageous
**'un|erkannt** *adj* unrecognized; **~erklärlich** *adj* inexplicable; **~erlässlich** *adj* essential, indispensable; **~erlaubt** *adj* unallowed; unauthorized; **~erledigt** *adj* unsettled (*a.* ECON)
**uner'messlich** *adj* immeasurable
**unermüdlich** [ʊnˀɛɐ'myːtlɪç] *adj* indefatigable; untiring
**uner'reichbar** *adj* inaccessible; *esp fig* unattainable; **uner'reicht** *adj* unequal(l)ed
**unersättlich** [ʊnˀɛɐ'zɛtlɪç] *adj* insatiable
**'unerschlossen** *adj* undeveloped
**uner|schöpflich** [ʊnˀɛɐ'ʃœpflɪç] *adj* inexhaustible; **~schütterlich** [-'ʃʏtɐlɪç] *adj* imperturbable; **~schwinglich** [-'ʃvɪŋlɪç] *adj* exorbitant; ***für j-n ~ sein*** be beyond s.o.'s means; **~setzlich** [-'zɛtslɪç] *adj* irreplaceable; **~träglich** [-'trɛːklɪç] *adj* unbearable
**'unerwartet** *adj* unexpected
**'unerwünscht** *adj* unwanted
**'unfähig** *adj* incompetent; incapable (***zu tun*** of doing), unable (to *inf*)
**'Unfähigkeit** *f* (-; *no pl*) incompetence; incapacity, inability
**'Unfall** *m* accident; crash
**'Unfallstelle** *f* scene of the accident
**un'fehlbar** *adj* infallible (*a.* REL); unfailing
**unförmig** ['ʊnfœrmɪç] *adj* shapeless; misshapen; monstrous
**'unfrankiert** *adj* unstamped
**'unfrei** *adj* not free; *post* unpaid
**'unfreiwillig** *adj* involuntary; unconscious (*humor*)
**'unfreundlich** *adj* unfriendly (***zu*** to), unkind (to); *fig* cheerless
**'Unfrieden** *m* (-*s*; *no pl*) discord; ~ ***stiften*** make mischief
**'unfruchtbar** *adj* infertile; **'Unfruchtbarkeit** *f* (-; *no pl*) infertility
**Unfug** ['ʊnfuːk] *m* (-[*e*]*s*; *no pl*) nonsense; ~ ***treiben*** be up to mischief, fool around
**Ungar** ['ʊŋgar] *m* (-*n*; -*n*), **'Ungarin** *f* (-; -*nen*), **'ungarisch** *adj* Hungarian; **'Ungarn** Hungary

'**ungastlich** *adj* inhospitable
'**un|geachtet** *prp* (*gen*) regardless of; despite; **~geahnt** *adj* unthought-of; **~gebeten** *adj* uninvited, unasked; **~gebildet** *adj* uneducated; **~geboren** *adj* unborn; **~gebräuchlich** *adj* uncommon, unusual; **~gebührlich** [-gəby:ɐlɪç] *adj* unseemly; **~gebunden** *fig adj* free, independent; ***frei und ~*** footloose and fancy-free; **~gedeckt** *adj* ECON uncovered; SPORT unmarked
'**Ungeduld** *f* (-; *no pl*) impatience
'**ungeduldig** *adj* impatient
'**ungeeignet** *adj* unfit; unqualified; inappropriate
**ungefähr** ['ʊngəfɛ:ɐ] **1.** *adj* approximate; rough; **2.** *adv* approximately, roughly, about, around, ... or so; ***so ~*** something like that
'**ungefährlich** *adj* harmless; safe
'**ungeheuer** *adj* enormous (*a. fig*), huge, vast
'**Ungeheuer** *n* (-*s*; -) monster (*a. fig*)
**unge'heuerlich** *adj* monstrous
'**ungehindert** *adj and adv* unhindered
'**ungehobelt** *fig adj* uncouth, rough
'**ungehörig** *adj* improper, unseemly
'**ungehorsam** *adj* disobedient
**Ungehorsam** *m* (-*s*; *no pl*) disobedience
'**un|gekocht** *adj* uncooked; **~gekünstelt** *adj* unaffected; **~gekürzt** *adj* unabridged; **~gelegen** *adj* inconvenient; ***j-m ~ kommen*** be inconvenient for s.o.
**ungelenk** ['ʊngəlɛŋk] *adj* awkward, clumsy
'**ungelernt** *adj* unskilled
'**ungemütlich** *adj* uncomfortable; F ***~ werden*** get nasty
'**ungenau** *adj* inaccurate; *fig* vague; '**Ungenauigkeit** *f* (-; -*en*) inaccuracy
**ungeniert** ['ʊnʒeni:ɐt] *adj* uninhibited
'**un|genießbar** *adj* uneatable; undrinkable; F unbearable; **~genügend** *adj* insufficient; PED poor, unsatisfactory; *grade*: *a.* F; **~gepflegt** *adj* neglected; untidy, unkempt; **~gerade** *adj* uneven; odd; **~gerecht** *adj* unfair, unjust
'**Ungerechtigkeit** *f* (-; *no pl*) injustice, unfairness
'**ungern** *adv* unwillingly; ***et. ~ tun*** hate *or* not like to do s.th.
'**un|geschehen** *adj*: ***~ machen*** undo; **~geschickt** *adj* awkward, clumsy; **~geschliffen** *adj* uncut (*diamond etc*); unpolished (*a. fig*); **~geschminkt** *adj* without make-up; *fig* unvarnished, plain (*truth*); **~gesetzlich** *adj* illegal, unlawful; **~gestört** *adj* undisturbed; **~gestraft** *adj*: ***~ davonkommen*** get off unpunished (F scot-free); **~gesund** *adj* unhealthy (*a. fig*); **~geteilt** *adj* undivided (*a. fig*)
**Ungetüm** ['ʊngəty:m] *n* (-*s*; -*e*) monster, *fig a.* monstrosity
'**ungewiss** *adj* uncertain; ***j-n im Ungewissen lassen*** keep s.o. in the dark (***über*** *acc* about); '**Ungewissheit** *f* (-; *no pl*) uncertainty
'**ungewöhnlich** *adj* unusual
'**ungewohnt** *adj* strange, unfamiliar;
**Ungeziefer** ['ʊngətsi:fɐ] *n* (-*s*; *no pl*) vermin
'**ungezogen** *adj* naughty, bad; spoilt
'**ungezwungen** *adj* relaxed, informal; easygoing
'**ungläubig** *adj* incredulous, unbelieving (*a.* REL)
**unglaublich** [ʊn'glauplɪç] *adj* incredible, unbelievable
'**unglaubwürdig** *adj* implausible; unreliable (*witness etc*)
'**ungleich** *adj* unequal, different; unlike; **~mäßig** *adj* uneven; irregular
'**Unglück** *n* (-[*e*]*s*; -*e*) a) (*no pl*) bad luck, misfortune; misery, b) accident; disaster; '**unglücklich** *adj* unhappy, miserable; unfortunate; '**unglücklicherweise** *adv* unfortunately
'**ungültig** *adj* invalid; ***für ~ erklären*** JUR invalidate
'**Ungunst** *f*: ***zu ~en*** → ***zuungunsten***; '**ungünstig** *adj* unfavo(u)rable; disadvantageous
'**ungut** *adj*: ***~es Gefühl*** misgivings (***bei et.*** about s.th.); ***nichts für ~!*** no offense (*Br* offence) meant!
'**unhaltbar** *adj* untenable; intolerable; SPORT unstoppable
'**unhandlich** *adj* unwieldy
'**unhar,monisch** *adj* MUS discordant
'**Unheil** *n* (-*s*; *no pl*) mischief; evil; disaster; '**unheilbar** *adj* MED incurable
'**unheilvoll** *adj* disastrous; sinister
'**unheimlich** *adj* creepy, spooky, eerie; F tremendous; F ***~ gut*** terrific, fantastic
'**unhöflich** *adj* impolite; rude
'**Unhöflichkeit** *f* (-; *no pl*) impoliteness; rudeness

U

**un'hörbar** *adj* inaudible
**'unhygienisch** *adj* insanitary
**Uniform** [uni'fɔrm] *f* (-; *-en*) uniform
**'uninteressant** *adj* uninteresting
**uninteressiert** ['ʊnʔɪntərɛsiːɐt] *adj* uninterested (**an** *dat* in)
**Union** [u'njoːn] *f* (-; *-en*) union
**Universität** [univɛrzi'tɛːt] *f* (-; *-en*) university
**Universum** [uni'vɛrzʊm] *n* (*-s*; *no pl*) universe
**Unke** ['ʊŋkə] *f* (-; *-n*) ZO toad
**'unkenntlich** *adj* unrecognizable
**'Unkenntnis** *f* (-; *no pl*) ignorance
**'unklar** *adj* unclear; uncertain; confused, muddled; ***im Unklaren sein*** (***lassen***) be (leave *s.o.*) in the dark
**'unklug** *adj* imprudent, unwise
**'Unkosten** *pl* expenses, costs
**'Unkraut** *n* (-[*e*]*s*; *no pl*) weed(s); ***~ jäten*** weed (the garden)
**unkündbar** ['ʊnkʏntbaːɐ] *adj* permanent (*post*)
**'unlängst** *adv* lately, recently
**'unleserlich** *adj* illegible
**'unlogisch** *adj* illogical
**un'lösbar** *adj* insoluble
**'unmännlich** *adj* unmanly, effeminate
**'unmäßig** *adj* excessive
**'Unmenge** *f* vast quantity *or* number(s) (***von*** of), F loads (of), tons (of)
**'Unmensch** *m* monster, brute
**'unmenschlich** *adj* inhuman, cruel
**'Unmenschlichkeit** *f* (-; *-en*) a) (*no pl*) inhumanity, b) cruelty
**un'merklich** *adj* imperceptible
**'unmissverständlich** *adj* unmistakable
**'unmittelbar 1.** *adj* immediate, direct; **2.** *adv*: ***~ nach*** (***hinter***) right after (behind)
**'unmöbliert** *adj* unfurnished
**'unmodern** *adj* out of fashion *or* style
**'unmöglich 1.** *adj* impossible; **2.** *adv*: ***ich kann es ~ tun*** I can't possibly do it
**'unmoralisch** *adj* immoral
**'unmündig** *adj* JUR under age
**'unmusikalisch** *adj* unmusical
**'unnachahmlich** *adj* inimitable
**'unnachgiebig** *adj* unyielding
**'unnachsichtig** *adj* strict, severe
**unnahbar** [ʊn'naːbaːɐ] *adj* standoffish, cold
**'unnatürlich** *adj* unnatural (*a. fig*); affected
**'unnötig** *adj* unnecessary, needless
**unnütz** ['ʊnnʏts] *adj* useless
**'unordentlich** *adj* untidy; ***~ sein*** *room etc*: be (in) a mess; **'Unordnung** *f* (-; *no pl*) disorder, mess
**'unparteiisch** *adj* impartial, unbias(s)ed; **'Unparteiische** *m, f* (*-n*; *-n*) SPORT referee
**'unpassend** *adj* unsuitable; improper; inappropriate
**'unpassierbar** *adj* impassable
**unpässlich** ['ʊnpɛslɪç] *adj* indisposed
**'unpersönlich** *adj* impersonal (*a.* LING)
**'unpolitisch** *adj* unpolitical
**'unpraktisch** *adj* impractical
**'unpünktlich** *adj* unpunctual
**'unrecht** *adj* wrong; ***j-m ~ tun*** do s.o. wrong; **'Unrecht** *n* (-[*e*]*s*; *no pl*) injustice, wrong; ***zu ~*** wrong(ful)ly; ***~ haben*** be wrong
**'unrechtmäßig** *adj* unlawful
**'unregelmäßig** *adj* irregular (*a.* LING)
**'Unregelmäßigkeit** *f* (-; *-en*) irregularity
**'unreif** *adj* unripe; *fig* immature
**'Unreife** *fig f* immaturity
**'unrein** *adj* unclean; impure (*a.* REL)
**'Unreinheit** *f* (-; *-en*) impurity
**'unrichtig** *adj* incorrect, wrong
**'Unruhe** *f* (-; *-n*) a) (*no pl*) restlessness, unrest (*a.* POL); anxiety, alarm, b) *pl* disturbances, riots
**'unruhig** *adj* restless; uneasy; worried, alarmed; MAR rough
**uns** [ʊns] *pers pron* (to) us; each other; ~ (***selbst***) (to) ourselves; ***ein Freund von ~*** a friend of ours
**'un|sachgemäß** *adj* improper; **~sachlich** *adj* unobjective; **~sanft** *adj* rude, rough; **~sauber** *adj* unclean, *esp fig a.* impure; SPORT unfair; *fig* underhand; **~schädlich** *adj* harmless; **~scharf** *adj* PHOT blurred, out of focus
**un'schätzbar** *adj* inestimable, invaluable
**'un|scheinbar** *adj* inconspicuous; plain; **~schicklich** *adj* indecent; **~schlüssig** *adj* irresolute; undecided; **~schön** *adj* unsightly; *fig* unpleasant
**'Unschuld** *f* (-; *no pl*) innocence; *fig* virginity
**'unschuldig** *adj* innocent (***an*** *dat* of)

**'unselbstständig** *adj* dependent on others; **'Unselbstständigkeit** *f* lack of independence, dependence on others
**unser** ['ʊnzɐ] *poss pron* our; **~er, ~e, ~es** ours
**'unsicher** *adj* unsafe, insecure; self-conscious; uncertain; **'Unsicherheit** *f* (-; *-en*) a) (*no pl*) insecurity, unsafeness; self-consciousness, b) uncertainty
**'unsichtbar** *adj* invisible
**'Unsinn** *m* (-[*e*]*s*; *no pl*) nonsense
**'unsinnig** *adj* nonsensical, stupid; absurd
**'Unsitte** *f* bad habit; abuse
**'unsittlich** *adj* immoral, indecent
**'unsozial** *adj* unsocial
**'unsportlich** *adj* unathletic; *fig* unfair
**'unsterblich 1.** *adj* immortal (*a. fig*); **2.** *adv*: **~ *verliebt*** madly in love (***in*** *acc* with); **'Unsterblichkeit** *f* immortality
**'Unstimmigkeit** *f* (-; *-en*) discrepancy; *pl* disagreements
**'unsympathisch** *adj* disagreeable; ***er*** (***es***) ***ist mir*** ~ I don't like him (it)
**'untätig** *adj* inactive; idle; **'Untätigkeit** *f* (-; *no pl*) inactivity
**'untauglich** *adj* unfit (*a.* MIL); incompetent
**un'teilbar** *adj* indivisible
**unten** ['ʊntən] *adv* (down) below, down (*a.* ***nach*** ~); downstairs; ~ ***auf*** (*dat*) at the bottom of *the page etc*; ***siehe*** ~ see below; ***von oben bis*** ~ from top to bottom
**unter** ['ʊntɐ] *prp* under; below (*a. fig*); among; *fig* less than; ~ ***anderem*** among other things; ~ ***uns*** (***gesagt***) between you and me; ~ ***Wasser*** underwater
**'Unterarm** *m* ANAT forearm
**'unter|belichtet** *adj* PHOT underexposed; **~besetzt** *adj* understaffed
**'Unterbewusstsein** *n* subconscious; ***im*** ~ subconsciously
**unter|'bieten** *v/t* (*irr*, ***bieten,*** *no -ge-*, *h*) underbid; undercut; beat (*record*); **~'binden** *fig v/t* (*irr*, ***binden,*** *no -ge-*, *h*) put a stop to; prevent
**unter'brechen** *v/t* (*irr*, ***brechen,*** *no -ge-*, *h*) interrupt; **Unter'brechung** *f* (-; *-en*) interruption
**'unterbringen** *v/t* (*irr*, ***bringen,*** *sep*, *-ge-*, *h*) accommodate, put *s.o.* up; find a place for, put (***in*** *acc* into); **'Unterbringung** *f* (-; *-en*) accommodation
**unter'dessen** *adv* in the meantime, meanwhile
**unter'drücken** *v/t* (*no -ge-*, *h*) oppress; suppress; **Unter'drücker** *m* (*-s*; -) oppressor; **Unter'drückung** *f* (-; *-en*) oppression; suppression
**untere** ['ʊntərə] *adj* lower (*a. fig*)
**'unterentwickelt** *adj* underdeveloped
**'unterernährt** *adj* undernourished, underfed; **'Unterernährung** *f* (-; *no pl*) undernourishment, malnutrition
**Unter'führung** *f* (-; *-en*) underpass, *Br a.* subway
**'Untergang** *m* ASTR setting; MAR sinking; *fig* downfall; decline; fall; **'untergehen** *v/i* (*irr*, ***gehen,*** *sep*, *-ge-*, *sein*) go down (*a. fig*), ASTR *a.* set, MAR *a.* sink
**'untergeordnet** *adj* subordinate, inferior; secondary
**'Untergewicht** *n* (-[*e*]*s*; *no pl*), **'untergewichtig** *adj* underweight
**unter'graben** *fig v/t* (*irr*, ***graben,*** *no -ge-*, *h*) undermine
**'Untergrund** *m* subsoil; POL underground; ***in den*** ~ ***gehen*** go underground; **~bahn** *f* → ***U-Bahn***
**'unterhalb** *prp* (*gen*) below, under
**'Unterhalt** *m* (-[*e*]*s*; *no pl*) support, maintenance (*a.* JUR); **unter'halten** *v/t* (*irr*, ***halten,*** *no -ge-*, *h*) entertain; support; ***sich*** ~ (***mit***) talk (to, with); ***sich*** (***gut***) ~ enjoy o.s., have a good time; **unter'haltsam** *adj* entertaining; **Unter'haltung** *f* (-; *-en*) talk, conversation; entertainment; **Unter'haltungsindusˌtrie** *f* show business
**'Unter|händler** *m* negotiator; **~haus** *n* (*-es*; *no pl*) *Br* PARL House of Commons; **~hemd** *n* undershirt, *Br* vest; **~holz** *n* (*-es*; *no pl*) undergrowth; **~hose** *f* shorts, *esp Br* underpants, panties, *Br* pants; ***e-e lange*** **~, *lange*** **~*n*** (a pair of) long johns
**'unterirdisch** *adj* underground
**'Unterkiefer** *m* ANAT lower jaw
**'Unterkleid** *n* slip
**'unterkommen** *v/i* (*irr*, ***kommen,*** *sep*, *-ge-*, *sein*) find accommodation; find work *or* a job (***bei*** with)
**Unterkunft** ['ʊntɐkʊnft] *f* (-; *-künfte* [-kʏnftə]) accommodation, lodging(s); MIL quarters; ~ ***und Verpflegung*** board and lodging

**'Unterlage** *f* TECH base; *pl* documents; data
**unter'lassen** *v/t* (*irr*, ***lassen***, *no -ge-*, *h*) omit, fail to do *s.th.*; stop *or* quit doing *s.th.*; **Unter'lassung** *f* (-; *-en*) omission (*a.* JUR)
**'unterlegen¹** *v/t* (*sep*, *-ge-*, *h*) underlay
**unter'legen²** *adj* inferior (*dat* to)
**Unter'legenheit** *f* (-; *no pl*) inferiority
**'Unterleib** *m* ANAT abdomen, belly
**unter'liegen** *v/i* (*irr*, ***liegen***, *no -ge-*, *sein*) be defeated (***j-m*** by s.o.), lose (to s.o.); *fig* be subject to
**'Unterlippe** *f* ANAT lower lip
**'Untermieter** *m*, **'Untermieterin** *f* roomer, *Br* lodger
**unter'nehmen** *v/t* (*irr*, ***nehmen***, *no -ge-*, *h*) make, take, go on *a trip etc*; **et. ~** do s.th. (***gegen*** about *s.th.*), take action (against *s.o.*); **Unter'nehmen** *n* (*-s*; -) firm, business; venture; undertaking, enterprise; MIL operation; **Unter'nehmensberater(in)** management consultant; **Unter'nehmer** *m* (*-s*; -) businessman, entrepreneur; employer; **Unter'nehmerin** *f* (-; *-nen*) businesswoman; **unter'nehmungslustig** *adj* active, dynamic; adventurous
**'Unteroffizier** *m* MIL non-commissioned officer
**'unterordnen** *v/t and v/refl* (*sep*, *-ge-*, *h*) subordinate (o.s.) (*dat* to)
**Unter'redung** *f* (-; *-en*) talk(s)
**Unterricht** ['ʊntɐrɪçt] *m* (*-[e]s*; *no pl*) instruction, teaching; PED school, classes, lessons; **unter'richten** *v/i and v/t* (*no -ge-*, *h*) teach; give lessons; inform (***über*** *acc* of); **'Unterrichtsstunde** *f* lesson, PED *a.* class, period
**'Unterrock** *m* slip
**unter'sagen** *v/t* (*no -ge-*, *h*) prohibit
**unter'schätzen** *v/t* (*no -ge-*, *h*) underestimate; underrate
**unter'scheiden** *v/t and v/i* (*irr*, ***scheiden***, *no -ge-*, *h*) distinguish (***zwischen*** between; ***von*** from); tell apart; ***sich ~*** differ (***von*** from; ***in*** *dat* in; ***durch*** by); **Unter'scheidung** *f* (-; *-en*) distinction; **Unterschied** ['ʊntɐʃiːt] *m* (*-[e]s*; *-e*) difference; ***im ~ zu*** unlike, as opposed to; **'unterschiedlich** *adj* different; varying
**unter'schlagen** *v/t* (*irr*, ***schlagen***, *no -ge-*, *h*) embezzle; **Unter'schlagung** *f* (-; *-en*) embezzlement
**Unterschlupf** ['ʊntɐʃlʊpf] *m* (*-[e]s*; *no pl*) hiding place
**unter'schreiben** *v/t and v/i* (*irr*, ***schreiben***, *no -ge-*, *h*) sign
**'Unterschrift** *f* signature; caption
**'Unterseeboot** *n* → ***U-Boot***
**Untersetzer** ['ʊntɐzɛtsɐ] *m* (*-s*; -) coaster; saucer
**unter'setzt** *adj* thickset, stocky
**'Unterstand** *m* shelter, MIL *a.* dugout
**unter'stehen** (*irr*, ***stehen***, *no -ge-*, *h*) **1.** *v/i* (*dat*) be under (the control of); **2.** *v/refl* dare; ***~ Sie sich*** (***et. zu tun***)***!*** don't you dare ([to] do s.th.)!
**'unterstellen¹** *v/t* (*sep*, *-ge-*, *h*) put *s.th.* in; store; ***sich ~*** take shelter
**unter'stellen²** *v/t* (*no -ge-*, *h*) assume; ***j-m ~, dass er ...*** insinuate that s.o. ...; **Unter'stellung** *f* (-; *-en*) insinuation
**unter'streichen** *v/t* (*irr*, ***streichen***, *no -ge-*, *h*) underline (*a. fig*)
**unter'stützen** *v/t* (*no -ge-*, *h*) support; back (up); **Unter'stützung** *f* (-; *-en*) support; aid; welfare (payments)
**unter'suchen** *v/t* (*no -ge-*, *h*) examine (*a.* MED), investigate (*a.* JUR); search; CHEM analyze; **Unter'suchung** *f* (-; *-en*) examination (*a.* MED), investigation (*a.* JUR), *a.* (medical) checkup; CHEM analysis
**Unter'suchungs|gefangene** *m, f* JUR prisoner on remand; **~gefängnis** *n* JUR remand prison; **~haft** *f*: ***in ~ sein*** JUR be on remand; **~richter** *m* JUR examining magistrate
**Untertan** ['ʊntɐtaːn] *m* (*-s*; *-en*) subject
**'Untertasse** *f* saucer
**'untertauchen** (*sep*, *-ge-*) **1.** *v/i* (*sein*) dive, submerge; *fig* disappear; *esp* POL go underground; **2.** *v/t* (*h*) duck
**'Unterteil** *n, m* lower part, bottom
**unter'teilen** *v/t* (*no -ge-*, *h*) subdivide; **Unter'teilung** *f* (-; *-en*) subdivision
**'Untertitel** *m* subtitle, *film*: *a.* caption
**'Unterton** *m* undertone
**Unter'treibung** *f* (-; *-en*) understatement
**'untervermieten** *v/t* (*no -ge-*, *h*) sublet
**unter'wandern** *v/t* (*no -ge-*, *h*) infiltrate
**'Unterwäsche** *f* underwear
**'Unterwasser...** *in cpds* underwater ...

**unterwegs** [ʊntɐ'veːks] *adv* on the *or* one's way (***nach*** to)

**unter'weisen** *v/t* (*irr*, ***weisen***, *no -ge-*, *h*) instruct; **Unter'weisung** *f* (-; *-en*) instruction

**'Unterwelt** *f* (-; *no pl*) underworld

**unter'werfen** *v/t* (*irr*, ***werfen***, *no -ge-*, *h*) subject (*dat* to); subjugate; ***sich ~*** submit (to); **Unter'werfung** *f* (-; *-en*) subjection; submission (***unter*** *acc* to)

**unterwürfig** [ʊntɐ'vʏrfɪç] *adj* servile

**unter'zeichnen** *v/t* (*no -ge-*, *h*) sign; **Unter'zeichnete** *m*, *f* (*-n*; *-n*) *the* undersigned; **Unter'zeichnung** *f* (-; *-en*) signing

**'unterziehen¹** *v/t* (*irr*, ***ziehen***, *sep*, *-ge-*, *h*) put *s.th.* on underneath

**unter'ziehen²** *v/t* (*irr*, ***ziehen***, *no -ge-*, *h*) ***sich*** *e-r Behandlung*, *Prüfung etc* ***~*** undergo (*treatment etc*), take (*an examination etc*)

**'Untiefe** *f* shallow, shoal

**un|'tragbar** *adj* unbearable, intolerable; **~'trennbar** *adj* inseparable

**'untreu** *adj* unfaithful (*dat* to)

**un|'tröstlich** *adj* inconsolable; **~trüglich** [ʊn'tryːklɪç] *adj* unmistakable

**'Untugend** *f* vice, bad habit

**'unüber|legt** *adj* thoughtless; **~sichtlich** *adj* blind (*bend etc*)

**unüber|trefflich** [ʊnʔyːbɐ'trɛflɪç] *adj* unsurpassable, matchless; **~troffen** [-'trɔfən] *adj* unequal(l)ed; **~windlich** [-'vɪntlɪç] *adj* insuperable, invincible

**unum|gänglich** [ʊnʔʊm'gɛŋlɪç] *adj* inevitable; **~schränkt** [-'ʃrɛŋkt] *adj* unlimited; POL absolute; **~stritten** [-'ʃtrɪtən] *adj* undisputed; **~wunden** [-'vʊndən] *adv* straight out, frankly

**ununterbrochen** ['ʊnʔʊntɐbrɔxən] *adj* uninterrupted; continuous

**un|ver'änderlich** *adj* unchanging; **~ver'antwortlich** *adj* irresponsible; **~ver'besserlich** *adj* incorrigible; **~ver'bindlich** *adj* noncommittal, ECON not binding; **~ver'daulich** *adj* indigestible (*a. fig*)

**'unverdient** *adj* undeserved

**'unverdünnt** *adj* undiluted; straight

**unver'einbar** *adj* incompatible

**'unverfälscht** *adj* unadulterated

**'unverfänglich** *adj* harmless

**'unverfroren** *adj* brazen, impertinent

**'unvergänglich** *adj* immortal, eternal

**unver'gesslich** *adj* unforgettable

**'unver'gleichlich** *adj* incomparable

**'unverhältnismäßig** *adv* disproportionately; ***~ hoch*** excessive

**'unverheiratet** *adj* unmarried, single

**unverhofft** ['ʊnfɛɐhɔft] *adj* unhoped-for; unexpected

**unverhohlen** ['ʊnfɛɐhoːlən] *adj* undisguised, open

**'unverkäuflich** *adj* not for sale; unsal(e)able

**unver'kennbar** *adj* unmistakable

**'unverletzt** *adj* unhurt

**unvermeidlich** [ʊnfɛɐ'maitlɪç] *adj* inevitable

**'unvermindert** *adj* undiminished

**'unvermittelt** *adj* abrupt, sudden

**'Unvermögen** *n* (*-s*; *no pl*) inability, incapacity

**'unvermutet** *adj* unexpected

**'unvernünftig** *adj* unreasonable; foolish

**'unverschämt** *adj* rude, impertinent; outrageous (*price etc*); **'Unverschämtheit** *f* (-; *-en*) impertinence; ***die ~ haben zu*** *inf* have the nerve to *inf*

**'unverschuldet** *adj* through no fault of one's own

**unversehens** ['ʊnfɛɐzeːəns] *adv* unexpectedly, all of a sudden

**'un|versehrt** *adj* unhurt; undamaged; **~versöhnlich** *adj* irreconcilable (*a. fig*), implacable; **~versorgt** *adj* unprovided for; **~verständlich** *adj* unintelligible; ***es ist mir ~*** I can't see how *or* why, F it beats me; **~versucht** *adj*: ***nichts ~ lassen*** leave nothing undone

**unver'wundbar** *adj* invulnerable

**unver|wüstlich** [ʊnfɛɐ'vyːstlɪç] *adj* indestructible; **~zeihlich** [-'tsailɪç] *adj* inexcusable; **~züglich** [-'tsyːklɪç] **1.** *adj* immediate, prompt; **2.** *adv* immediately, without delay

**'unvollendet** *adj* unfinished

**'unvollkommen** *adj* imperfect

**'unvollständig** *adj* incomplete

**'unvorbereitet** *adj* unprepared

**'unvoreingenommen** *adj* unprejudiced, unbias(s)ed

**'unvorhergesehen** *adj* unforeseen

**'unvorhersehbar** *adj* unforeseeable

**'unvorsichtig** *adj* careless; **'Unvorsichtigkeit** *f* (-; *no pl*) carelessness

**unvor'stellbar** *adj* unthinkable

**'unvorteilhaft** *adj* unbecoming
**'unwahr** *adj* untrue; **'Unwahrheit** *f* untruth; **'unwahrscheinlich** *adj* improbable, unlikely; F fantastic
**unwegsam** ['ʊnveːkzaːm] *adj* difficult, rough (*terrain*)
**unweigerlich** [ʊn'vaigɐlıç] *adv* inevitably
**'unweit** *prp* (*gen*) not far from
**'Unwetter** *n* (*-s*; -) disastrous (thunder)storm
**'unwichtig** *adj* unimportant
**unwider|legbar** [ʊnviːdɐ'leːkbaːɐ] *adj* irrefutable; **~ruflich** [-'ruːflıç] *adj* irrevocable; **~stehlich** [-'ʃteːlıç] *adj* irresistible
**'Unwille(n)** *m* indignation (**über** *acc* at); **'unwillig** *adj* indignant (**über** *acc* at); unwilling, reluctant
**'unwillkürlich** *adj* involuntary
**'unwirklich** *adj* unreal
**'unwirksam** *adj* ineffective
**unwirsch** ['ʊnvırʃ] *adj* surly, gruff
**unwirtlich** ['ʊnvırtlıç] *adj* inhospitable
**'unwirtschaftlich** *adj* uneconomic(al)
**'unwissend** *adj* ignorant
**'Unwissenheit** *f* (-; *no pl*) ignorance
**'unwohl** *adj* unwell; uneasy
**'unwürdig** *adj* unworthy (*gen* of)
**unzählig** [ʊn'tsɛːlıç] *adj* innumerable, countless
**unzer'brechlich** *adj* unbreakable
**unzer'reißbar** *adj* untearable
**unzer'störbar** *adj* indestructible
**unzer'trennlich** *adj* inseparable
**'Unzucht** *f* (-; *no pl*) sexual offense (*Br* offence); **'unzüchtig** *adj* indecent; obscene
**'unzufrieden** *adj* discontent(ed) (**mit** with), dissatisfied (with); **'Unzufriedenheit** *f* discontent, dissatisfaction
**'unzugänglich** *adj* inaccessible
**'unzulänglich** *adj* inadequate
**'unzulässig** *adj* inadmissible
**unzu'mutbar** *adj* unacceptable; unreasonable
**'unzurechnungsfähig** *adj* JUR irresponsible; **'Unzurechnungsfähigkeit** *f* (-; *no pl*) JUR irresponsibility
**'unzureichend** *adj* insufficient
**'unzusammenhängend** *adj* incoherent
**'unzuverlässig** *adj* unreliable, untrustworthy; uncertain
**üppig** ['ʏpıç] *adj* luxuriant, lush (*both a. fig*); voluptuous, luscious; opulent; rich
**uralt** ['uːɐˀalt] *adj* ancient (*a. iro*)
**Uran** [u'raːn] *n* (*-s*; *no pl*) uranium
**'Uraufführung** *f* première, first performance (*film*: showing)
**urbar** ['uːɐbaːɐ] *adj* arable; **~ machen** cultivate; reclaim
**'Urbevölkerung** *f*, **'Ureinwohner** *pl* aboriginal inhabitants; *in Australia*: Aborigines
**'Urenkel** *m* great-grandson
**'Urenkelin** *f* great-granddaughter
**'Urgroß...** *in cpds ...eltern*, *...mutter*, *...vater*: great-grand...
**Urheberrechte** ['uːɐheːbɐ-] *pl* copyright (**an** *dat* on, for)
**Urin** [u'riːn] *m* (*-s*; *-e*) urine; **urinieren** [uri'niːrən] *v/i* (*no -ge-*, *h*) urinate
**Urkunde** ['uːɐkʊndə] *f* (-; *-n*) document; diploma; **'Urkundenfälschung** *f* forgery of documents
**Urlaub** ['uːɐlaup] *m* (-[*e*]*s*; *-e*) vacation, *Br* holiday(s); MIL leave; ***in*** *or* ***im ~ sein*** (***auf ~ gehen***) be (go) on vacation (*Br* holiday); ***e-n Tag*** (***ein paar Tage***) ***~ nehmen*** take a day (a few days) off; **Urlauber(in)** ['uːɐlaubɐ (-bərın)] (*-s*; *-/-*; *-nen*) vacationist, vacationer, *Br* holidaymaker
**Urne** ['ʊrnə] *f* (-; *-n*) urn; ballot box
**'Ursache** *f* (-; *-n*) cause; reason; ***keine ~!*** not at all, you're welcome
**'Ursprung** *m* origin
**ursprünglich** ['uːɐʃprʏŋlıç] *adj* original; natural, unspoilt
**Urteil** ['ʊrtail] *n* (-[*e*]*s*; *-e*) judg(e)ment; JUR sentence; ***sich ein ~ bilden*** form a judg(e)ment (***über*** *acc* about)
**'urteilen** *v/i* (*ge-*, *h*) judge (***über j-n, et.*** s.o., s.th.; ***nach*** by)
**'Urwald** *m* primeval forest; jungle
**urwüchsig** ['uːɐvyːksıç] *adj* coarse, earthy
**'Urzeit** *f* prehistoric times
**usw.** ABBR *of* ***und so weiter*** etc, and so on
**Utensilien** [utɛn'ziːljən] *pl* utensils
**Utopie** [uto'piː] *f* (-; *-n*) illusion
**utopisch** [u'toːpıʃ] *adj* utopian; fantastic

U

# V

**Vagabund** [vaga'bʊnt] *m* (*-en*; *-en*) vagabond, tramp, F bum
**vage** ['va:gə] *adj* vague
**Vakuum** ['va:kuʊm] *n* (*-s*; *-kua*, *-kuen*) vacuum
**Vampir** ['vampi:ɐ] *m* (*-s*; *-e*) ZO vampire (*a. fig*)
**Vanille** [va'nɪljə] *f* (*-*; *no pl*) vanilla
**variabel** [va'rja:bəl] *adj* variable
**Variante** [va'rjantə] *f* (*-*; *-n*) variant
**Variation** [varja'tsio:n] *f* (*-*; *-en*) variation
**Varietee,** *a.* **Varieté** [varje'te:] *n* (*-s*; *-s*) vaudeville, *Br* variety theatre, music hall
**variieren** [vari'i:rən] *v/i and v/t* (*no -ge-*, *h*) vary
**Vase** ['va:zə] *f* (*-*; *-n*) vase
**Vater** ['fa:tɐ] *m* (*-s*; *Väter* ['fɛ:tɐ]) father
**'Vaterland** *n* native country
**'Vaterlandsliebe** *f* patriotism
**väterlich** ['fɛ:tɐlɪç] *adj* fatherly, paternal
**'Vaterschaft** *f* (*-*; *-en*) JUR paternity
**'Vater'unser** *n* (*-s*; *-*) REL Lord's Prayer
**v. Chr.** ABBR *of* ***vor Christus*** BC, before Christ
**V-Ausschnitt** ['fau-] *m* V-neck
**Vegetarier** [vege'ta:rjɐ] *m* (*-s*; *-*), **Vege'tarierin** *f* (*-*; *-nen*), **vegetarisch** [vege'ta:rɪʃ] *adj* vegetarian
**Vegetation** [vegeta'tsjo:n] *f* (*-*; *-en*) vegetation; **vegetieren** [vege'ti:rən] *v/i* (*no -ge-*, *h*) vegetate
**Veilchen** ['failçən] *n* (*-s*; *-*) BOT violet
**Velo** ['ve:lo] *Swiss n* (*-s*; *-s*) bicycle, F bike
**Ventil** [vɛn'ti:l] *n* (*-s*; *-e*) TECH valve; *fig* vent, outlet
**Ventilation** [vɛntila'tsjo:n] *f* (*-*; *-en*) ventilation; **Ventilator** [vɛnti'la:to:ɐ] *m* (*-s*; *-en* [-la'to:rən]) fan
**verabreden** [fɛɐ'ʔap-] *v/t* (*no -ge-*, *h*) agree (up)on, arrange; appoint, fix; ***sich*** **~** make a date (*or* an appointment) (***mit*** with); **Ver'abredung** *f* (*-*; *-en*) appointment; date
**ver'ab|reichen** *v/t* (*no -ge-*, *h*) give; MED administer; **~scheuen** *v/t* (*no -ge-*, *h*) loathe, detest
**verabschieden** [fɛɐ'ʔapʃi:dən] *v/t* (*no -ge-*, *h*) say goodbye to (*a.* ***sich*** **~** ***von***); dismiss; JUR pass; **Ver'abschiedung** *f* (*-*; *-en*) dismissal; JUR passing
**ver'achten** *v/t* (*no -ge-*, *h*) despise; **verächtlich** [fɛɐ'ʔɛçtlɪç] *adj* contemptuous; **Ver'achtung** *f* (*-*; *no pl*) contempt
**verallgemeinern** [fɛɐ'ʔalgə'mainɐn] *v/t* (*no -ge-*, *h*) generalize
**ver'altet** *adj* antiquated, out of date
**Veranda** [ve'randa] *f* (*-*; *-den*) porch, *Br* veranda(h)
**veränderlich** [fɛɐ'ʔɛndɐlɪç] *adj* changeable (*a.* METEOR), variable (*a.* MATH, LING); **ver'ändern** *v/t and v/refl* (*no -ge-*, *h*), **Ver'änderung** *f* change
**verängstigt** [fɛɐ'ʔɛŋstɪçt] *adj* frightened, scared
**ver'anlagen** *v/t* (*no -ge-*, *h*) ECON assess; **veranlagt** [fɛɐ'ʔanla:kt] *adj* inclined (***zu, für*** to); ***künstlerisch*** (***musikalisch***) **~** ***sein*** have a gift *or* bent for art (music); **Ver'anlagung** *f* (*-*; *-en*) (pre)disposition (*a.* MED); talent, gift; ECON assessment
**ver'anlassen** *v/t* (*no -ge-*, *h*) make arrangements (*or* arrange) for *s.th.*; ***j-n zu et.*** **~** make s.o. do s.th.
**Ver'anlassung** *f* (*-*; *-en*) cause (***zu*** for)
**ver|'anschaulichen** *v/t* (*no -ge-*, *h*) illustrate; **~'anschlagen** *v/t* (*no -ge-*, *h*) estimate (***auf*** *acc* at)
**ver'anstalten** *v/t* (*no -ge-*, *h*) arrange, organize; hold, give (*concert*, *party etc*); **Ver'anstaltung** *f* (*-*; *-en*) event, SPORT *a.* meet, *Br* meeting
**ver'antworten** *v/t* (*no -ge-*, *h*) take the responsibility for; **ver'antwortlich** *adj* responsible; ***j-n*** **~** ***machen für*** hold s.o. responsible for; **Ver'antwortung** *f* (*-*; *no pl*) responsibility; ***auf eigene*** **~** at one's own risk; ***j-n zur*** **~** ***ziehen*** call s.o. to account; **Ver'antwortungsgefühl** *n* (*-[e]s*; *no pl*) sense of responsibility; **ver'antwortungslos** *adj* irresponsible
**ver|'arbeiten** *v/t* (*no -ge-*, *h*) process; *fig* digest; ***et.*** **~** ***zu*** manufacture (*or* make) s.th. into; **~'ärgern** *v/t* (*no -ge-*, *h*) make *s.o.* angry, annoy

**ver'armt** *adj* impoverished
**ver'arschen** *v/t* (*no -ge-, h*) ***j-n ~*** take the piss out of s.o.
**Verb** [vɛrp] *n* (*-s; -en* ['vɛrbən]) LING verb
**Verband** [fɛɐ'bant] *m* (*-es; Verbände* [fɛɐ'bɛndə]) MED dressing, bandage; ECON association; MIL formation, unit; **~(s)kasten** *m* MED first-aid kit *or* box; **~(s)zeug** *n* MED dressing material
**ver'bannen** *v/t* (*no -ge-, h*) banish (*a. fig*), exile; **Ver'bannung** *f* (*-; -en*) banishment, exile
**verbarrika'dieren** *v/t* (*no -ge-, h*) barricade; block
**ver'bergen** *v/t* (*irr,* ***bergen,*** *no -ge-, h*) hide (*a.* ***sich ~***), conceal
**ver'bessern** *v/t* (*no -ge-, h*) improve; correct; **Ver'besserung** *f* (*-; -en*) improvement; correction
**ver'beugen** *v/refl* (*no -ge-, h*), **Ver'beugung** *f* (*-; -en*) bow (***vor*** to)
**ver|'biegen** *v/t* (*irr,* ***biegen,*** *no -ge-, h*) twist; **~'bieten** *v/t* (*irr,* ***bieten,*** *no -ge-, h*) forbid; prohibit; → ***verboten***
**ver'billigen** *v/t* (*no -ge-, h*) reduce in price; **verbilligt** [-'bɪlɪçt] *adj* reduced, at reduced prices
**verbinden** *v/t* (*irr,* ***binden,*** *no -ge-, h*) MED dress, bandage; bandage *s.o.* up; *a.* TECH connect, join, link (up); TEL put *s.o.* through (***mit*** to); combine (*a.* CHEM ***sich ~***); *fig* unite; associate; ***j-m die Augen ~*** blindfold s.o.; ***damit sind beträchtliche Kosten verbunden*** that involves considerable cost(s *pl*); ***falsch verbunden!*** wrong number!
**verbindlich** [fɛɐ'bɪntlɪç] *adj* obligatory, compulsory (*a.* PED); obliging
**Ver'bindlichkeit** *f* (*-; -en*) a) (*no pl*) obligingness, b) *pl* ECON liabilities
**Ver'bindung** *f* (*-; -en*) connection; combination; CHEM compound; UNIV fraternity, *Br* society; ***sich in ~ setzen mit*** get in touch with; ***in ~ stehen*** (***bleiben***) be (keep) in touch
**verbissen** [fɛɐ'bɪsən] *adj* dogged
**ver'bittert** *adj* bitter, embittered
**verblassen** [fɛɐ'blasən] *v/i* (*no -ge-, sein*) fade (*a. fig*)
**Verbleib** [fɛɐ'blaip] *m* (*-[e]s; no pl*) whereabouts; **ver'bleiben** *v/i* (*irr,* ***bleiben,*** *no -ge-, sein*) remain
**verbleit** [fɛɐ'blait] *adj* leaded
**ver'blendet** *fig adj* blind
**Ver'blendung** *fig f* (*-; -en*) blindness
**verblichen** [fɛɐ'blɪçən] *adj* faded
**verblüffen** [fɛɐ'blʏfən] *v/t* (*no -ge-, h*) amaze, F flabbergast
**Ver'blüffung** *f* (*-; -en*) amazement
**ver'blühen** *v/i* (*no -ge-, sein*) fade, wither (*both a. fig*)
**ver'bluten** *v/i* (*no -ge-, sein*) MED bleed to death
**verborgen** [fɛɐ'bɔrgən] *adj* hidden, concealed; ***im Verborgenen*** in secret
**Verbot** [fɛɐ'bo:t] *n* (*-[e]s; -e*) prohibition, ban (on *s.th.*); **ver'boten** *adj*: ***Rauchen ~*** no smoking
**Ver'brauch** *m* (*-[e]s; no pl*) consumption (***an*** *dat* of); **ver'brauchen** *v/t* (*no -ge-, h*) consume, use up
**Verbraucher** [fɛɐ'brauxɐ] *m* (*-s; -*), **Ver'braucherin** *f* (*-; -nen*) consumer; **~schutz** *m* consumer protection
**Ver'brechen** *n* (*-s; -*) crime; ***ein ~ begehen*** commit a crime; **Ver'brecher(in)** (*-s; -/-; -nen*), **ver'brecherisch** *adj* criminal
**ver'breiten** *v/t and v/refl* (*no -ge-, h*) spread (***in*** *dat*, ***über*** *acc* over, through); circulate
**verbreitern** [fɛɐ'braitɐn] *v/t and v/refl* (*no -ge-, h*) widen, broaden
**Ver'breitung** *f* (*-; no pl*) spread(ing); circulation
**ver'brennen** *v/i* (*irr,* ***brennen,*** *no -ge-, sein*) *and v/t* (*h*) burn (up); cremate
**Ver'brennung** *f* (*-; -en*) burning; cremation; TECH combustion; MED burn
**ver'bringen** *v/t* (*irr,* ***bringen,*** *no -ge-, h*) spend, pass
**verbrüdern** [fɛɐ'bry:dɐn] *v/refl* (*no -ge-, h*) fraternize; **Verbrüderung** [fɛɐ'bry:dərʊŋ] *f* (*-; -en*) fraternization
**ver'brühen** *v/t* (*no -ge-, h*) scald
**ver'buchen** *v/t* (*no -ge-, h*) book
**verbünden** [fɛɐ'bʏndən] *v/refl* (*no -ge-, h*) ally o.s. (***mit*** to, with)
**Ver'bündete** *m, f* (*-n; -n*) ally (*a. fig*)
**ver'bürgen** *v/refl* (*no -ge-, h*) ***sich ~ für*** vouch for, guarantee
**ver'büßen** *v/t* (*no -ge-, h*) ***e-e Strafe ~*** serve a sentence, serve time
**verchromt** [fɛɐ'kro:mt] *adj* chromium-plated
**Verdacht** [fɛɐ'daxt] *m* (*-[e]s; -e*) suspicion; ***~ schöpfen*** become suspicious

**verdächtig** [fɛɐ'dɛçtıç] *adj* suspicious, suspect; **Verdächtige** [fɛɐ'dɛçtıgə] *m, f* (*-n*; *-n*) suspect; **ver'dächtigen** *v/t* (*no -ge-, h*) suspect (***j-n e-r Tat*** s.o. of [doing] s.th.); **Ver'dächtigung** *f* (-; *-en*) suspicion

**verdammen** [fɛɐ'damən] *v/t* (*no -ge-, h*) condemn (***zu*** to), damn (*a.* REL); **Ver'dammnis** *f* (-; *no pl*) REL damnation; **ver'dammt 1.** *adj* damned, F *a.* damn, darn(ed), *Br sl a.* bloody; F **~** (***noch mal***)**!** damn (it)!; **2.** *adv*: **~ *gut*** *etc* damn (*Br sl a.* bloody) good *etc*; **Ver'dammung** *f* (-; *-en*) condemnation; REL damnation

**ver'dampfen** *v/t* (*no -ge-, h*) *and v/i* (*sein*) evaporate

**ver'danken** *v/t* (*no -ge-, h*) ***j-m*** (***e-m Umstand***) ***et.*** **~** owe s.th. to s.o. (s.th.)

**verdarb** [fɛɐ'darp] *pret of* ***verderben***

**verdauen** [fɛɐ'dauən] *v/t* (*no -ge-, h*) digest (*a. fig*)

**ver'daulich** *adj* digestible; ***leicht*** (***schwer***) **~** easy (hard) to digest

**Ver'dauung** *f* (-; *no pl*) digestion

**Ver'deck** *n* (-[*e*]*s*; *-e*) top; **ver'decken** *v/t* (*no -ge-, h*) cover (up) (*a. fig*)

**ver'denken** *v/t* (*irr*, ***denken***, *no -ge-, h*) ***ich kann es ihm nicht ~(, dass er ...)*** I can't blame him (for *doing*)

**verderben** [fɛɐ'dɛrbən] (*irr, no -ge-*) **1.** *v/i* (*sein*) spoil (*a. fig*); GASTR go bad; **2.** *v/t* (*h*) spoil (*a. fig*), ruin; ***sich den Magen*** **~** upset one's stomach

**Ver'derben** *n* (*-s*; *no pl*) ruin

**verderblich** [fɛɐ'dɛrplıç] *adj* perishable; ***leicht ~e Lebensmittel*** perishables

**ver'dichten** *v/t* (*no -ge-, h*) compress, condense

**ver'dienen** *v/t* (*no -ge-, h*) earn, make; *fig* deserve

**Ver'dienst**[1] *m* (-[*e*]*s*; *-e*) earnings; salary; wages; gain, profit

**Ver'dienst**[2] *n* (-[*e*]*s*; *-e*) merit; ***es ist sein ~, dass*** it is thanks to him that

**ver'dient** *adj* (well-)deserved

**ver'doppeln** *v/t and v/refl* (*no -ge-, h*) double

**verdorben** [fɛɐ'dɔrbən] **1.** *pp of* ***verderben***; **2.** *adj* GASTR spoilt, bad (*both a. fig*); MED upset

**ver|dorren** [fɛɐ'dɔrən] *v/i* (*no -ge-, sein*) wither, dry up; **~'drängen** *v/t* (*no -ge-, h*) supplant, supersede; replace; PHYS displace; PSYCH repress, suppress; **~'drehen** *v/t* (*no -ge-, h*) twist, *fig a.* distort; ***die Augen ~*** roll one's eyes; ***j-m den Kopf ~*** turn s.o.'s head; **~'dreht** F *fig adj* mixed up; **~'dreifachen** *v/t and v/refl* (*no -ge-, h*) treble, triple

**verdrießen** [fɛɐ'dri:sən] *v/t* (*irr, no -ge-, h*) annoy; **verdrießlich** [fɛɐ'dri:slıç] *adj* glum, morose, sullen; **verdross** [fɛɐ'drɔs] *pret of* ***verdrießen***; **verdrossen** [fɛɐ'drɔsən] **1.** *pp of* ***verdrießen***; **2.** *adj* grumpy, sullen; **Verdruss** [fɛɐ'drʊs] *m* (*-es*; *-e*) annoyance

**ver'dummen** (*no -ge-*) **1.** *v/t* (*h*) make stupid, stultify; **2.** *v/i* (*sein*) become stultified

**ver'dunkeln** *v/t and v/refl* (*no -ge-, h*) darken; black out; *fig* obscure

**Ver'dunk(e)lung** *f* (-; *-en*) darkening; blackout; JUR collusion

**ver'dünnen** *v/t* (*no -ge-, h*) dilute

**ver'dunsten** *v/i* (*no -ge-, sein*) evaporate

**ver'dursten** *v/i* (*no -ge-, sein*) die of thirst

**verdutzt** [fɛɐ'dʊtst] *adj* puzzled

**ver'edeln** *v/t* (*no -ge-, h*) BOT graft; TECH process, refine; **Ver'ed(e)lung** *f* (-; *-en*) BOT grafting; TECH processing, refinement

**ver'ehren** *v/t* (*no -ge-, h*) admire; adore, worship (*both a. fig*), *esp* REL *a.* revere, venerate; **Ver'ehrer(in)** (*-s*; -/ -; *-nen*) admirer, *esp film etc*: *a.* fan; **Ver'ehrung** *f* (-; *no pl*) admiration; adoration, worship; *esp* REL reverence, veneration

**vereidigen** [fɛɐ'ʔaidıgən] *v/t* (*no -ge-, h*) swear *s.o.* in; JUR put *s.o.* under an oath

**Verein** [fɛɐ'ʔain] *m* (-[*e*]*s*; *-e*) club (*a.* SPORT); society, association

**vereinbar** [fɛɐ'ʔainba:ɐ] *adj* compatible (***mit*** with); **vereinbaren** [fɛɐ'ʔainba:rən] *v/t* (*no -ge-, h*) agree (up)on, arrange; **Ver'einbarung** *f* (-; *-en*) agreement, arrangement

**ver'einen** → ***vereinigen***

**ver'einfachen** *v/t* (*no -ge-, h*) simplify

**Ver'einfachung** *f* (-; *-en*) simplification

**ver'einheitlichen** *v/t* (*no -ge-, h*) standardize

**ver'einigen** *v/t and v/refl* (*no -ge-*, *h*) unite (***zu*** into); combine, join
**Ver'einigung** *f* (-; *-en*) union; combination; alliance
**ver'einsamen** *v/i* (*no -ge-*, *sein*) become lonely *or* isolated
**vereinzelt** [fɛɐ'ˀaintsəlt] *adj* occasional, odd; ~ ***Regen*** scattered showers
**ver|'eiteln** *v/t* (*no -ge-*, *h*) prevent; frustrate; **~'enden** *v/i* (*no -ge-*, *sein*) *esp* ZO die, perish; **~'engen** *v/t and v/refl* (*no -ge-*, *h*) narrow
**ver'erben** *v/t* (*no -ge-*, *h*) ***j-m et.*** ~ leave (BIOL transmit) s.th. to s.o.; ***sich*** ~ (***auf*** *acc*) be passed on *or* down (to) (*a.* BIOL *and fig*); **Ver'erbung** *f* (-; *no pl*) BIOL heredity; **Ver'erbungslehre** *f* BIOL genetics
**verewigen** [fɛɐ'ˀeːvɪgən] *v/t* (*no -ge-*, *h*) immortalize
**ver'fahren** (*irr*, ***fahren***, *no -ge-*) **1.** *v/i* (*sein*) proceed; ~ ***mit*** deal with; **2.** *v/refl* (*h*) MOT get lost
**Ver'fahren** *n* (*-s*; -) procedure, method, *esp* TECH *a.* technique, way; JUR (legal) proceedings (***gegen*** against)
**Ver'fall** *m* (*-[e]s*; *no pl*) decay (*a. fig*); dilapidation; *fig* decline; ECON *etc* expiry; **ver'fallen** (*irr*, ***fallen***, *no -ge-*, *sein*) **1.** *v/i* decay (*a. fig*), dilapidate; *esp fig* decline; ECON expire; MED waste away; become addicted to; (***wieder***) ~ ***in*** (*acc*) fall (back) into; ~ ***auf*** (*acc*) hit (up)on; **2.** *adj* decayed; dilapidated; ***j-m*** ~ ***sein*** be s.o.'s slave; **Ver'fallsdatum** *n* expiry date; GASTR pull date, *Br* best-before (*or* best-by) date; PHARM sell-by date
**ver'fälschen** *v/t* (*no -ge-*, *h*) falsify; distort; GASTR adulterate
**verfänglich** [fɛɐ'fɛŋlɪç] *adj* delicate, tricky; embarrassing, compromising
**ver'färben** *v/refl* (*no -ge-*, *h*) discolo(u)r
**ver'fassen** *v/t* (*no -ge-*, *h*) write
**Verfasser** [fɛɐ'fasɐ] *m* (*-s*; -), **Ver'fasserin** *f* (-; *-nen*) author
**Ver'fassung** *f* (-; *-en*) state (of health *or* of mind), condition; POL constitution
**ver'fassungs|mäßig** *adj* POL constitutional; **~widrig** *adj* unconstitutional
**ver'faulen** *v/i* (*no -ge-*, *sein*) rot, decay
**ver'fechten** *v/t* (*irr*, ***fechten***, *no -ge-*, *h*), **Ver'fechter(in)** (*-s*; *-/-*; *-nen*) advocate
**ver'fehlen** *v/t* (*no -ge-*, *h*) miss (***sich*** each other); **Ver'fehlung** *f* (-; *-en*) offense, *Br* offence
**verfeinden** [fɛɐ'faindən] *v/refl* (*no -ge-*, *h*) become enemies; **ver'feindet** *adj* hostile; ~ ***sein*** be enemies
**verfeinern** [fɛɐ'fainɐn] *v/t and v/refl* (*no -ge-*, *h*) refine
**ver'filmen** *v/t* (*no -ge-*, *h*) film; **Ver'filmung** *f* (-; *-en*) filming; film version
**ver'flechten** *v/t* (*irr*, ***flechten***, *no -ge-*, *h*) intertwine (*a.* ***sich*** ~)
**ver'fluchen** *v/t* (*no -ge-*, *h*) curse
**ver'flucht** → ***verdammt***
**ver'folgen** *v/t* (*no -ge-*, *h*) pursue (*a. fig*); chase, hunt (*both a. fig*); POL, REL persecute; follow (*track etc*); *fear etc*: haunt *s.o.*; ***j-n gerichtlich*** ~ prosecute s.o.; **Verfolger** [fɛɐ'fɔlgɐ] *m* (*-s*; -) pursuer; persecutor; **Ver'folgung** *f* (-; *-en*) pursuit (*a. cycling*); chase, hunt; persecution; ***gerichtliche*** ~ prosecution
**ver'frachten** *v/t* (*no -ge-*, *h*) freight, ship; F bundle *s.o.*, *s.th.* (***in*** *acc* into)
**verfremden** [fɛɐ'frɛmdən] *v/t* (*no -ge-*, *h*) *esp art*: alienate
**ver'früht** *adj* premature
**verfügbar** [fɛɐ'fyːkbaːɐ] *adj* available; **ver'fügen** (*no -ge-*, *h*) **1.** *v/t* decree, order; **2.** *v/i*: ~ ***über*** (*acc*) have at one's disposal; **Ver'fügung** *f* (-; *-en*) a) decree, order, b) (*no pl*) disposal; ***j-m zur*** ~ ***stehen*** (***stellen***) be (place) at s.o.'s disposal
**ver'führen** *v/t* (*no -ge-*, *h*) seduce (***et. zu tun*** into doing s.th.); **Ver'führer** *m* (*-s*; -) seducer; **Ver'führerin** *f* (-; *-nen*) seductress; **ver'führerisch** *adj* seductive; tempting; **Ver'führung** *f* (-; *-en*) seduction
**vergangen** [fɛɐ'gaŋən] *adj* gone, past; ***im ~en Jahr*** last year; **Ver'gangenheit** *f* (-; *no pl*) past; LING past tense
**vergänglich** [fɛɐ'gɛŋlɪç] *adj* transitory, transient
**vergasen** [fɛɐ'gaːzən] *v/t* (*no -ge-*, *h*) gas; CHEM gasify; **Vergaser** [fɛɐ'gaːzɐ] *m* (*-s*; -) MOT carburet(t)or
**vergaß** [fɛɐ'gaːs] *pret of* ***vergessen***
**ver'geben** *v/t* (*irr*, ***geben***, *no -ge-*, *h*) give away (*a. fig*); award (*prize etc*); forgive; **ver'gebens** *adv* in vain; **vergeblich** [fɛɐ'geːplɪç] **1.** *adj* futile; **2.** *adv* in vain; **Ver'gebung** *f* (-; *-en*) forgiveness, pardon

V

**ver'gehen** (*irr*, **gehen**, *no -ge-*, *sein*) **1.** *v/i time etc*: go by, pass; *pain*, *effect etc*: wear off; **~ vor** (*dat*) be dying with; ***wie die Zeit vergeht!*** how time flies!; **2.** *v/refl* ***sich ~ an*** (*dat*) violate; rape

**Vergehen** *n* (*-s*; -) JUR offen|se, *Br* -ce

**ver'gelten** *v/t* (*irr*, **gelten**, *no -ge-*, *h*) repay; reward; **Ver'geltung** *f* (-; *-en*) retaliation (*a.* MIL)

**vergessen** [fɛɐ'gɛsən] **1.** *v/t* (*irr*, *no -ge-*, *h*) forget; leave; **2.** *pp of* **vergessen** 1; **Ver'gessenheit** *f*: ***in ~ geraten*** fall into oblivion; **vergesslich** [fɛɐ'gɛslɪç] *adj* forgetful

**vergeuden** [fɛɐ'gɔʏdən] *v/t* (*no -ge-*, *h*), **Ver'geudung** *f* (-; *-en*) waste

**vergewaltigen** [fɛɐgə'valtɪgən] *v/t* (*no -ge-*, *h*) rape, violate (*a. fig*)

**Verge'waltigung** *f* (-; *-en*) rape, violation (*a. fig*)

**vergewissern** [fɛɐgə'vɪsɐn] *v/refl* (*no -ge-*, *h*) make sure (***e-r Sache*** of s.th.; ***ob*** whether; ***dass*** that)

**ver'gießen** *v/t* (*irr*, **gießen**, *no -ge-*, *h*) shed (*blood*, *tears*); spill

**ver'giften** *v/t* (*no -ge-*, *h*) poison (*a. fig*); contaminate; **Ver'giftung** *f* (-; *-en*) poisoning (*a. fig*); contamination

**ver'gittert** *adj* barred (*window etc*)

**Ver'gleich** *m* (-[*e*]*s*; *-e*) comparison; JUR compromise; **ver'gleichbar** *adj* comparable (***mit*** to, with); **ver'gleichen** *v/t* (*irr*, **gleichen**, *no -ge-*, *h*) compare (***mit*** with *or* to); ***... ist nicht zu ~ mit ...*** cannot be compared to; ... cannot compare with; ***verglichen mit*** compared to *or* with; **ver'gleichsweise** *adv* comparatively, relatively

**ver'glühen** *v/i* (*no -ge-*, *sein*) burn out (*or* up)

**vergnügen** [fɛɐ'gny:gən] *v/refl* (*no -ge-*, *h*) enjoy o.s. (***mit et.*** doing s.th.)

**Ver'gnügen** *n* (*-s*; -) pleasure, enjoyment, fun; ***mit ~*** with pleasure; ***viel ~!*** have fun!, have a good time!

**vergnügt** [fɛɐ'gny:kt] *adj* cheerful

**Ver'gnügung** *f* (-; *-en*) pleasure, amusement, entertainment

**Ver'gnügungspark** *m* amusement park

**ver'gnügungssüchtig** *adj* pleasure-seeking

**Ver'gnügungsviertel** *n* nightlife district

**ver|'golden** *v/t* (*no -ge-*, *h*) gild; **~göttern** [fɛɐ'gœtɐn] *v/t* (*no -ge-*, *h*) idolize, adore; **~'graben** *v/t* (*irr*, **graben**, *no -ge-*, *h*) bury (*a. fig*)

**ver'greifen** *v/refl* (*irr*, **greifen**, *no -ge-*, *h*) ***sich ~ an*** (*dat*) lay hands on

**vergriffen** [fɛɐ'grɪfən] *adj* out of print

**vergrößern** [fɛɐ'grø:sɐn] *v/t* (*no -ge-*, *h*) enlarge (*a.* PHOT); increase; OPT magnify; ***sich ~*** increase, grow, expand; **Ver'größerung** *f* (-; *-en*) increase; PHOT enlargement; OPT magnification; **Ver'größerungsglas** *n* OPT magnifying glass

**Vergünstigung** [fɛɐ'gʏnstɪgʊŋ] *f* (-; *-en*) privilege

**vergüten** [fɛɐ'gy:tən] *v/t* (*no -ge-*, *h*) reimburse, pay (for); **Ver'gütung** *f* (-; *-en*) reimbursement

**ver'haften** *v/t* (*no -ge-*, *h*), **Ver'haftung** *f* (-; *-en*) arrest

**ver'halten**[1] *v/refl* (*irr*, **halten**, *no -ge-*, *h*) behave, conduct o.s., act; ***sich ruhig ~*** keep quiet

**ver'halten**[2] *adj* restrained; subdued

**Ver'halten** *n* (*-s*; *no pl*) behavio(u)r, conduct; **Ver'haltensforschung** *f* behavio(u)ral science; **ver'haltensgestört** *adj* disturbed, maladjusted

**Verhältnis** [fɛɐ'hɛltnɪs] *n* (*-ses*; *-se*) relationship, relations; attitude; proportion, relation, *esp* MATH ratio; F affair; *pl* circumstances, conditions; ***über j-s ~se*** beyond s.o.'s means; **ver'hältnismäßig** *adv* comparatively, relatively

**Ver'hältniswort** *n* (-[*e*]*s*; *-wörter*) LING preposition

**ver'handeln** *no* (*-ge-*, *h*) **1.** *v/i* negotiate; **2.** *v/t* JUR hear; **Ver'handlung** *f* (-; *-en*) negotiation, talk; JUR hearing; trial; **Ver'handlungsbasis** *f* ECON asking price

**ver'hängen** *v/t* (*no -ge-*, *h*) cover (***mit*** with); impose (***über*** *acc* on)

**Verhängnis** [fɛɐ'hɛŋnɪs] *n* (*-ses*; *-se*) fate; disaster; **ver'hängnisvoll** *adj* fatal, disastrous

**verharmlosen** [fɛɐ'harmlo:zən] *v/t* (*no -ge-*, *h*) play *s.th.* down

**verhärmt** [fɛɐ'hɛrmt] *adj* careworn

**ver'hasst** *adj* hated; hateful

**ver'hätscheln** *v/t* (*no -ge-*, *h*) coddle, pamper, spoil

**ver'hauen** F *v/t* (*no -ge-*, *h*) spank

**verheerend** [fɛɐ'he:rənt] *adj* disastrous
**ver'heilen** *v/i* (*no -ge-*, *sein*) heal (up)
**verheimlichen** [fɛɐ'haimlɪçən] *v/t* (*no -ge-*, *h*) hide, conceal
**ver'heiraten** *v/t* (*no -ge-*, *h*) marry (*s.o.* off) (***mit*** to); ***sich ~*** get married
**ver'heiratet** *adj* married (***mit*** to)
**ver'heißungsvoll** *adj* promising
**ver'helfen** *v/i* (*irr*, ***helfen,*** *no -ge-*, *h*) ***j-m zu et. ~*** help s.o. to get s.th.
**ver'herrlichen** *v/t* (*no -ge-*, *h*) glorify, *contp a.* idolize; **Ver'herrlichung** *f* (-; *-en*) glorification
**ver'hexen** *v/t* (*no -ge-*, *h*) bewitch
**ver'hindern** *v/t* (*no -ge-*, *h*) prevent (***dass j. et. tut*** s.o. from doing s.th.); **ver'hindert** *adj* unable to come; F ***ein ~er ...*** a would-be ...; **Ver'hinderung** *f* (-; *-en*) prevention
**ver'höhnen** *v/t* (*no -ge-*, *h*) deride, mock (at), jeer (at)
**Verhör** [fɛɐ'hø:ɐ] *n* (-[*e*]*s*; *-e*) JUR interrogation; **ver'hören** (*no -ge-*, *h*) **1.** *v/t* interrogate, question; **2.** *v/refl* get it wrong
**ver'hüllen** *v/t* (*no -ge-*, *h*) cover, veil
**ver'hungern** *v/i* (*no -ge-*, *sein*) die of hunger, starve (to death)
**Ver'hungern** *n* (-*s*; *no pl*) starvation
**ver'hüten** *v/t* (*no -ge-*, *h*) prevent
**Ver'hütung** *f* (-; *-en*) prevention
**Ver'hütungsmittel** *n* MED contraceptive
**ver'irren** *v/refl* (*no -ge-*, *h*) get lost, lose one's way, go astray (*a. fig*)
**Ver'irrung** *f* (-; *-en*) aberration
**ver'jagen** *v/t* (*no -ge-*, *h*) chase *or* drive away
**verjähren** [fɛɐ'jɛ:rən] *v/i* (*no -ge-*, *sein*) JUR come under the statute of limitations; **ver'jährt** *adj* JUR statute-barred
**verjüngen** [fɛɐ'jʏŋən] *v/t* (*no -ge-*, *h*) make *s.o.* (look) younger, rejuvenate; ***sich ~*** ARCH, TECH taper (off)
**ver'kabeln** *v/t* (*no -ge-*, *h*) ELECTR cable
**Ver'kauf** *m* sale; **ver'kaufen** *v/t* (*no -ge-*, *h*) sell; ***zu ~*** for sale; ***sich gut ~*** sell well; **Ver'käufer** *m* (-*s*; -) (sales)clerk, salesman, *Br* shop assistant; ECON seller; **Ver'käuferin** *f* (-; *-nen*) (sales)clerk, saleslady, *Br* shop assistant; **ver'käuflich** *adj* for sale; ***schwer ~*** hard to sell
**Verkehr** [fɛɐ'ke:ɐ] *m* (-*s*; *no pl*) traffic; transportation, *Br* transport; *fig* contact, dealings; intercourse; circulation; ***starker*** (***schwacher***) ~ heavy (light) traffic; **ver'kehren** (*no -ge-*, *h*) **1.** *v/i bus etc*: run; ***~ in*** (*dat*) frequent; ***~ mit*** associate *or* mix with; have intercourse with; **2.** *v/t* turn (***in*** *acc* into); ***ins Gegenteil ~*** reverse
**Ver'kehrs|ader** *f* arterial road; **~ampel** *f* traffic light(s); **~behinderung** *f* holdup, delay; JUR obstruction of traffic; **~de,likt** *n* traffic offense (*Br* offence); **~flugzeug** *n* airliner; **~funk** *m* traffic bulletin; **~insel** *f* traffic island; **~meldung** *f* traffic announcement, flash; **~mi,nister** *m* minister of transportation; **~minis,terium** *n* ministry of transportation; **~mittel** *n* means of transportation; ***öffentliche ~*** public transportation; **~opfer** *n* road casualty; **~poli,zei** *f* traffic police; **~rowdy** *m* F road hog
**ver'kehrssicher** *adj* MOT roadworthy
**Ver'kehrs|sicherheit** *f* MOT road safety; roadworthiness; **~stau** *m* traffic jam; **~sünder(in)** F traffic offender; **~teilnehmer(in)** road user; **~unfall** *m* traffic accident; (car) crash; **~unterricht** *m* traffic instruction; **~zeichen** *n* traffic sign
**ver'kehrt** *adj and adv* wrong; upside down; inside out
**ver|'kennen** *v/t* (*irr*, ***kennen,*** *no -ge-*, *h*) mistake, misjudge; **~'klagen** *v/t* (*no -ge-*, *h*) JUR sue (***auf*** *acc*, ***wegen*** for); **~'klappen** *v/t* (*no -ge-*, *h*) dump (into the sea); **~'kleben** *v/t* (*no -ge-*, *h*) glue (together)
**ver'kleiden** *v/t* (*no -ge-*, *h*) disguise (***als*** as), dress *s.o.* up (as); TECH cover, (en)case; panel; ***sich ~*** disguise o.s., dress (o.s.) up; **Ver'kleidung** *f* (-; *-en*) disguise; TECH cover, encasement; panel(l)ing; MOT fairing
**verkleinern** [fɛɐ'klainɐn] *v/t* (*no -ge-*, *h*) make smaller, reduce, diminish; **Ver'kleinerung** [fɛɐ'klainərʊŋ] *f* (-; *-en*) reduction
**ver'klingen** *v/i* (*irr*, ***klingen,*** *no -ge-*, *sein*) die away
**ver'knallt** F *adj*: ***~ sein in*** (*acc*) be madly in love with, have a crush on
**ver|'knoten** *v/t* (*no -ge-*, *h*) knot; **~'knüpfen** *v/t* (*no -ge-*, *h*) knot togeth-

er; *fig* connect, combine; **~'kohlen** *v/i* (*no -ge-, sein*) char; **~'kommen 1.** *v/i* (*irr,* ***kommen,*** *no -ge-, sein*) become run-down *or* dilapidated; go to seed; GASTR go bad; **2.** *adj* run-down, dilapidated; neglected; depraved, rotten (to the core); **~'korken** *v/t* (*no -ge-, h*) cork (up); **~'körpern** *v/t* (*no -ge-, h*) personify; embody; *esp* THEA impersonate; **~'kriechen** *v/refl* (*irr,* ***kriechen,*** *no -ge-, h*) hide; **~'krümmt** *adj* crooked, curved (*a.* MED); **~'krüppelt** *adj* crippled; **~'kümmern** *v/i* (*no -ge-, sein*) BIOL become stunted; **~'kümmert** *adj* BIOL stunted

**verkünden** [fɛɐ'kʏndən] *v/t* (*no -ge-, h*) announce; proclaim; JUR pronounce; REL preach; **Ver'kündung** *f* (-; *-en*) announcement; proclamation; JUR pronouncement; REL preaching

**ver|'kürzen** *v/t* (*no -ge-, h*) shorten; reduce; **~'laden** *v/t* (*irr,* ***laden,*** *no -ge-, h*) load (***auf*** *acc* onto; ***in*** *acc* into)

**Verlag** [fɛɐ'la:k] *m* (-[*e*]*s*; *-e* [-'la:gə]) publishing house *or* company, publisher(s)

**ver'lagern** *v/t and v/refl* (*no -ge-, h*) shift (***auf*** *acc* to)

**ver'langen** *v/t* (*no -ge-, h*) ask for; demand; claim; charge; take, call for; **Ver'langen** *n* (-*s*; -) desire (***nach*** for); longing (for), yearning (for); ***auf ~*** by request; ECON on demand

**verlängern** [fɛɐ'lɛŋɐn] *v/t* (*no -ge-, h*) lengthen, make longer; prolong, extend (*a.* ECON); **Verlängerung** [fɛɐ'lɛŋərʊŋ] *f* (-; *-en*) lengthening; prolongation, extension; SPORT overtime, *Br* extra time

**ver'langsamen** *v/t and v/refl* (*no -ge-, h*) slacken, slow down (*both a. fig*)

**ver'lassen** (*irr,* ***lassen,*** *no -ge-, h*) **1.** *v/t* leave; abandon, desert; **2.** *v/refl*: ***sich ~ auf*** (*acc*) rely *or* depend on

**verlässlich** [fɛɐ'lɛslɪç] *adj* reliable, dependable

**Ver'lauf** *m* course; **ver'laufen** (*irr,* ***laufen,*** *no -ge-*) **1.** *v/i* (*sein*) run; go; end (up); **2.** *v/refl* (*h*) get lost, lose one's way

**ver'leben** *v/t* (*no -ge-, h*) spend; have

**ver'legen¹** *v/t* (*no -ge-, h*) move; mislay; TECH lay; put off, postpone; publish

**ver'legen²** *adj* embarrassed

**Ver'legenheit** *f* (-; *-en*) a) (*no pl*) embarrassment, b) embarrassing situation

**Verleger** [fɛɐ'le:gɐ] *m* (-*s*; -), **Ver'legerin** *f* (-; *-nen*) publisher

**Verleih** [fɛɐ'lai] *m* (-[*e*]*s*; *-e*) a) (*no pl*) hire, rental, b) *film*: distributor(s)

**ver'leihen** *v/t* (*irr,* ***leihen,*** *no -ge-, h*) lend, loan; MOT *etc* rent (*Br* hire) out; award (*prize etc*); grant (*privilege etc*); **Ver'leihung** *f* (-; *-en*) award(ing), presentation; grant(ing)

**ver'leiten** *v/t* (*no -ge-, h*) ***j-n zu et. ~*** make s.o. do s.th., lead s.o. to do s.th.

**ver'lernen** *v/t* (*no -ge-, h*) forget

**ver'lesen** (*irr,* ***lesen,*** *no -ge-, h*) **1.** *v/t* read (*or* call) out; **2.** *v/refl* make a slip (in reading); misread *s.th.*

**verletzen** [fɛɐ'lɛtsən] *v/t* (*no -ge-, h*) hurt, injure, *fig a.* offend; ***sich ~*** hurt o.s., get hurt; **~d** *adj* offensive

**Ver'letzte** *m, f* (-*n*; -*n*) injured person; *pl the* injured; **Ver'letzung** *f* (-; *-en*) injury, *esp pl a.* hurt; JUR violation

**ver'leugnen** *v/t* (*no -ge-, h*) deny; renounce

**verleumden** [fɛɐ'lɔʏmdən] *v/t* (*no -ge-, h*) defame; JUR slander, libel; **ver'leumderisch** *adj* JUR slanderous, libel(l)ous; **Ver'leumdung** *f* (-; *-en*) JUR slander; libel

**ver'lieben** *v/refl* (*no -ge-, h*) fall in love (***in*** *acc* with); **verliebt** [fɛɐ'li:pt] *adj* in love (***in*** *acc* with); amorous (*look etc*); **Ver'liebte** *m, f* (-*n*; -*n*) lover

**verlieren** [fɛɐ'li:rən] *v/t and v/i* (*irr, no -ge-, h*) lose; **Ver'lierer(in)** (-*s*; -/-; *-nen*) loser

**ver'loben** *v/refl* (*no -ge-, h*) get engaged (***mit*** to); **Verlobte** [fɛɐ'lo:ptə] **1.** *m* (-*n*; -*n*) fiancé; **2.** *f* (-*n*; -*n*) fiancée; **Ver'lobung** *f* (-; *-en*) engagement

**ver'locken** *v/t* (*no -ge-, h*) tempt; **~d** *adj* tempting

**Ver'lockung** *f* (-; *-en*) temptation

**verlogen** [fɛɐ'lo:gən] *adj* untruthful, lying

**verlor** [fɛɐ'lo:ɐ] *pret of* ***verlieren***

**verloren** [fɛɐ'lo:rən] **1.** *pp of* ***verlieren;*** **2.** *adj* lost; wasted; ***~ gehen*** be *or* get lost

**ver'losen** *v/t* (*no -ge-, h*) raffle (off); **Ver'losung** *f* (-; *-en*) raffle

**Verlust** [fɛɐ'lʊst] *m* (-[*e*]*s*; *-e*) loss (*a. fig*); *pl esp* MIL casualties

**ver'machen** *v/t* (*no -ge-, h*) leave, will
**Vermächtnis** [fɛɐ'mɛçtnɪs] *n* (*-ses; -se*) legacy (*a. fig*)
**ver'markten** *v/t* (*no -ge-, h*) market, merchandize; **Ver'marktung** *f* (-; *-en*) marketing, merchandizing
**ver'mehren** *v/t and v/refl* increase (***um*** by), multiply (by) (*a.* BIOL); BIOL reproduce, *esp* ZO *a.* breed; **Ver'mehrung** *f* (-; *-en*) increase; BIOL reproduction
**vermeidbar** [fɛɐ'maitbaːɐ] *adj* avoidable; **ver'meiden** *v/t* (*irr,* ***meiden,*** *no -ge-, h*) avoid
**vermeintlich** [fɛɐ'maintlɪç] *adj* supposed, alleged
**ver'mengen** *v/t* (*no -ge-, h*) mix, mingle, blend
**Vermerk** [fɛɐ'mɛrk] *m* (-[*e*]*s; -e*) note
**ver'merken** *v/t* (*no -ge-, h*) make a note of
**ver'messen**[1] *v/t* (*irr,* ***messen,*** *no -ge-, h*) measure; survey
**ver'messen**[2] *adj* presumptuous
**Ver'messung** *f* (-; *-en*) measuring; survey(ing)
**ver'mieten** *v/t* (*no -ge-, h*) let, rent, lease (out); rent (*Br* hire) out (*cars etc*); ***zu ~*** for rent, *Br* to let, for hire
**Ver'mieter** *n* (*-s*; -) landlord
**Ver'mieterin** *f* (-; *-nen*) landlady
**Ver'mietung** *f* (-; *-en*) letting, renting
**ver'mischen** *v/t and v/refl* (*no -ge-, h*) mix, mingle, blend (***mit*** with); **ver'mischt** *adj* mixed; miscellaneous
**vermissen** [fɛɐ'mɪsən] *v/t* (*no -ge-, h*) miss; **ver'misst** *adj* missing; ***die Vermissten*** *pl* the missing
**ver'mitteln** (*no -ge-, h*) **1.** *v/t* arrange; give, convey (*impression etc*); ***j-m et. ~*** get *or* find s.o. s.th.; **2.** *v/i* mediate (***zwischen*** between); **Ver'mittler** *m* (*-s*; -) mediator, go-between; ECON agent, broker; **Ver'mittlung** *f* (-; *-en*) mediation; arrangement; agency, office; (telephone) exchange; operator
**ver'modern** *v/i* (*no -ge-, sein*) rot, mo(u)lder
**Ver'mögen** *n* (*-s*; -) fortune, property, possessions; ECON assets
**ver'mögend** *adj* well-to-do, well-off
**vermummen** [fɛɐ'mʊmən] *v/refl* (*no -ge-, h*) mask o.s., disguise o.s.
**vermuten** [fɛɐ'muːtən] *v/t* (*no -ge-, h*) suppose, expect, think, guess; **ver'mutlich** *adv* probably; **Ver'mutung** *f* (-; *-en*) supposition; speculation
**vernachlässigen** [fɛɐ'naːxlɛsɪgən] *v/t* (*no -ge-, h*), **Ver'nachlässigung** *f* (-; *-en*) neglect
**ver'narben** *v/i* (*no -ge-, sein*) scar over; *fig* heal
**ver'narrt** *adj*: ***~ in*** (*acc*) mad *or* crazy about
**ver'nehmen** *v/t* (*irr,* ***nehmen,*** *no -ge-, h*) JUR question, interrogate
**ver'nehmlich** *adj* clear, distinct
**Ver'nehmung** *f* (-; *-en*) JUR interrogation, examination
**ver'neigen** *v/refl* (*no -ge-, h*), **Ver'neigung** *f* (-; *-en*) bow (***vor*** *dat* to) (*a. fig*)
**ver'neinen** (*no -ge-, h*) **1.** *v/t* deny; **2.** *v/i* say no, answer in the negative; **~d** *adj* negative
**Ver'neinung** *f* (-; *-en*) denial, negative (*a.* LING)
**ver'nichten** *v/t* (*no -ge-, h*) destroy; **~d** *adj* devastating (*a. fig*); crushing
**Ver'nichtung** *f* (-; *-en*) destruction; extermination
**Vernunft** [fɛɐ'nʊnft] *f* (-; *no pl*) reason; ***~ annehmen*** listen to reason; ***j-n zur ~ bringen*** bring s.o. to reason
**vernünftig** [fɛɐ'nʏnftɪç] *adj* sensible, reasonable (*a.* ECON); F decent
**ver'öden** *v/i* (*no -ge-, sein*) become deserted
**ver'öffentlichen** *v/t* (*no -ge-, h*) publish; **Ver'öffentlichung** *f* (-; *-en*) publication
**ver'ordnen** *v/t* (*no -ge-, h*) order, MED *a.* prescribe (***gegen*** for); **Ver'ordnung** *f* (-; *-en*) order; MED prescription
**ver'pachten** *v/t* (*no -ge-, h*) lease
**Ver'pächter** *m* lessor
**ver'packen** *v/t* (*no -ge-, h*) pack (up); TECH package; wrap up
**Ver'packung** *f* (-; *-en*) pack(ag)ing; wrapping; **Ver'packungsmüll** *m* superfluous packaging
**ver|'passen** *v/t* (*no -ge-, h*) miss; **~'patzen** F *v/t* (*no -ge-, h*) mess up, spoil; **~pesten** [fɛɐ'pɛstən] *v/t* (*no -ge-, h*) pollute, foul, contaminate; stink up (*Br* out); **~'petzen** F *v/t* (*no -ge-, h*) ***j-n ~*** tell on s.o. (***bei*** to); **~'pfänden** *v/t* (*no -ge-, h*) pawn; *fig* pledge
**ver'pflanzen** *v/t* (*no -ge-, h*), **Ver'pflanzung** *f* (-; *-en*) transplant (*a.* MED)

**ver'pflegen** *v/t* (*no -ge-*, *h*) feed
**Ver'pflegung** *f* (-; *-en*) food
**ver'pflichten** *v/t* (*no -ge-*, *h*) oblige; engage; ***sich ~, et. zu tun*** undertake (ECON agree) to do s.th.; **ver'pflichtet** *adj*: ***~ sein*** (***sich ~ fühlen***) ***et. zu tun*** be (feel) obliged to do s.th.; **Ver'pflichtung** *f* (-; *-en*) obligation; duty; ECON, JUR liability; engagement, commitment
**ver'pfuschen** F *v/t* (*no -ge-*, *h*) bungle, botch
**ver'plappern** *v/refl* (*no -ge-*, *h*) blab
**verpönt** [fɛɐ'pøːnt] *adj* taboo
**ver'prügeln** F *v/t* (*no -ge-*, *h*) beat *s.o.* up
**Ver'putz** *m* (*-es*; *no pl*), **ver'putzen** *v/t* (*no -ge-*, *h*) ARCH plaster
**verquollen** [fɛɐ'kvɔlən] *adj face etc*: puffy, swollen; *wood*: warped
**Verrat** [fɛɐ'raːt] *m* (-[*e*]*s*; *no pl*) betrayal (***an*** *dat* of); treachery (to); JUR treason (to); **ver'raten** *v/t* (*irr*, ***raten***, *no -ge-*, *h*) betray, give away (*both a. fig*); ***sich ~*** betray o.s., give o.s. away
**Verräter** [fɛɐ'rɛːtɐ] *m* (*-s*; -), **Ver'räterin** *f* (-; *-nen*) traitor
**verräterisch** [fɛɐ'rɛːtərɪʃ] *adj* treacherous; *fig* telltale
**ver'rechnen** (*no -ge-*, *h*) **1.** *v/t* offset (***mit*** against); **2.** *v/refl* miscalculate, make a mistake (*a. fig*); ***sich um e-e Mark ~*** be one mark out
**Ver'rechnungsscheck** *m* ECON voucher check, *Br* crossed cheque
**ver'regnet** *adj* rainy
**ver'reisen** *v/i* (*no -ge-*, *sein*) go away (***geschäftlich*** on business); **ver'reist** *adj* away (***geschäftlich*** on business)
**verrenken** [fɛɐ'rɛŋkən] *v/t* (*no -ge-*, *h*) MED dislocate, luxate; ***sich et. ~*** MED dislocate s.th.; ***sich den Hals ~*** crane one's neck; **Ver'renkung** *f* (-; *-en*) MED dislocation, luxation
**ver'richten** *v/t* (*no -ge-*, *h*) do, perform, carry out
**ver'riegeln** *v/t* (*no -ge-*, *h*) bolt, bar
**verringern** [fɛɐ'rɪŋɐn] *v/t* (*no -ge-*, *h*) decrease, lessen (*both a.* ***sich ~***), reduce, cut down; **Ver'ringerung** *f* (-; *-en*) reduction, decrease
**ver'rosten** *v/t* (*no -ge-*, *sein*) rust, get rusty (*a. fig*)
**verrotten** [fɛɐ'rɔtən] *v/i* (*no -ge-*, *sein*) rot; **ver'rottet** *adj* rotten
**ver'rücken** *v/t* (*no -ge-*, *h*) move, shift
**ver'rückt** *adj* mad, crazy (*both a. fig* ***nach*** about); ***wie ~*** like mad; ***~ werden*** go mad, go crazy; ***j-n ~ machen*** drive s.o. mad; **Ver'rückte** *m,f* (*-n*; *-n*) madman (madwoman), lunatic, maniac (*all a.* F); **Ver'rücktheit** *f* (-; *-en*) a) (*no pl*) madness, craziness, b) crazy thing
**Ver'ruf** *m*: ***in ~ bringen*** bring discredit (up)on; ***in ~ kommen*** get into discredit
**ver'rufen** *adj* disreputable, notorious
**ver'rutschen** *v/i* (*no -ge-*, *sein*) slip, get out of place
**Vers** [fɛrs] *m* (*-es*; *-e* ['fɛrzə]) verse; line
**ver'sagen** (*no -ge-*, *h*) **1.** *v/i* fail (*a.* MED), MOT *etc a.* break down; *gun etc*: misfire; **2.** *v/t* deny, refuse; **Ver'sagen** *n* (*-s*; *no pl*) failure; **Ver'sager** *m* (*-s*; -) failure
**ver'salzen** *v/t* (*no -ge-*, *h*) oversalt
**ver'sammeln** *v/t* (*no -ge-*, *h*) gather, assemble; ***sich ~*** *a.* meet; **Ver'sammlung** *f* (-; *-en*) assembly, meeting
**Versand** [fɛɐ'zant] *m* (-[*e*]*s*; *no pl*) dispatch, shipment; ***~...*** *in cpds ...haus, ...katalog etc*: mail-order ...
**ver'säumen** *v/t* (*no -ge-*, *h*) miss; ***~ et. zu tun*** fail to do s.th.; **Versäumnis** [fɛɐ'zɔʏmnɪs] *n* (*-ses*; *-se*) omission
**ver|'schaffen** *v/t* (*no -ge-*, *h*) get, find; ***sich ~*** *a.* obtain; **~'schämt** *adj* bashful; **~'schanzen** *v/refl* (*no -ge-*, *h*) entrench o.s. (*a. fig* ***hinter*** behind); **~'schärfen** *v/t* (*no -ge-*, *h*) aggravate; tighten up; increase; ***sich ~*** get worse; **~'schenken** *v/t* (*no -ge-*, *h*) give away (*a. fig*); **~'scherzen** *v/t* (*no -ge-*, *h*) forfeit; **~'scheuchen** *v/t* (*no -ge-*, *h*) chase away (*a. fig*); **~'schicken** *v/t* (*no -ge-*, *h*) send off, *esp* ECON *a.* dispatch
**ver'schieben** *v/t* (*irr*, ***schieben***, *no -ge-*, *h*) move, shift (*a.* ***sich ~***); postpone, put off; **Ver'schiebung** *f* (-; *-en*) shift(ing); postponement
**verschieden** [fɛɐ'ʃiːdən] *adj* different (***von*** from); ***~e ...*** *pl* various ..., several...; **~artig** *adj* different; various
**Ver'schiedenheit** *f* (-; *-en*) difference
**ver'schiedentlich** *adv* repeatedly
**ver'schiffen** *v/t* (*no -ge-*, *h*) ship
**Ver'schiffung** *f* (-; *-en*) shipment
**ver|'schimmeln** *v/i* (*no -ge-*, *sein*) get mo(u)ldy; **~'schlafen** (*irr*, ***schlafen***, *no -ge-*, *h*) **1.** *v/i* oversleep; **2.** *v/t* sleep through; **3.** *adj* sleepy (*a. fig*)

**Ver'schlag** *m* shed
**ver'schlagen¹** *v/t* (*irr*, ***schlagen***, *no -ge-*, *h*) ***j-m den Atem*** ~ take s.o.'s breath away; ***j-m die Sprache*** ~ leave s.o. speechless; ***es hat ihn nach X*** ~ he ended up in X
**ver'schlagen²** *adj* sly, cunning
**verschlechtern** [fɛɐ'ʃlɛçtɐn] *v/t and v/refl* (*no -ge-*, *h*) make (*refl* get) worse, worsen, deteriorate
**Ver'schlechterung** *f* (-; *-en*) deterioration; change for the worse
**ver'schleiern** *v/t* (*no -ge-*, *h*) veil (*a. fig*)
**Verschleiß** [fɛɐ'ʃlais] *m* (*-es*; *no pl*) wear (and tear); **ver'schleißen** *v/t* (*irr*, *no -ge-*, *h*) wear out
**ver|'schleppen** *v/t* (*no -ge-*, *h*) carry off; POL displace; draw out, delay; MED neglect; **~'schleudern** *v/t* (*no -ge-*, *h*) waste; ECON sell dirt cheap; **~'schließen** *v/t* (*irr*, ***schließen***, *no -ge-*, *h*) close (*a. fig one's eyes*); lock (up)
**ver'schlingen** *v/t* (*irr*, ***schlingen***, *no -ge-*, *h*) devour (*a. fig*); gulp (down)
**verschliss** [fɛɐ'ʃlɪs] *pret of* ***verschleißen***; **verschlissen** [fɛɐ'ʃlɪsən] *pp of* ***verschleißen***
**verschlossen** [fɛɐ'ʃlɔsən] *adj* closed; *fig* aloof, reserved; **Ver'schlossenheit** *f* (-; *no pl*) aloofness
**ver'schlucken** (*no -ge-*, *h*) **1.** *v/t* swallow (*fig* up); **2.** *v/refl* choke; ***ich habe mich verschluckt*** it went down the wrong way
**Ver'schluss** *m* fastener; clasp; catch; lock; cover, lid; cap, top; PHOT shutter; ***unter*** ~ under lock and key
**ver'schlüsseln** *v/t* (*no -ge-*, *h*) (en)-code, (en)cipher
**verschmähen** [fɛɐ'ʃmɛːən] *v/t* (*no -ge-*, *h*) disdain, scorn
**ver'schmelzen** *v/i* (*irr*, ***schmelzen***, *no -ge-*, *sein*) *and v/t* (*h*) merge, fuse (*both a.* ECON, POL *etc*), melt; **Ver'schmelzung** *f* (-; *-en*) fusion (*a. fig*)
**ver|'schmerzen** *v/t* (*no -ge-*, *h*) get over *s.th.*; **~'schmieren** *v/t* (*no -ge-*, *h*) smear, smudge
**verschmitzt** [fɛɐ'ʃmɪtst] *adj* mischievous
**ver|'schmutzen** (*no -ge-*) **1.** *v/t* (*h*) soil, dirty; pollute; **2.** *v/i* (*sein*) get dirty; get polluted; **~'schnaufen** F *v/i and v/refl* (*no -ge-*, *h*) stop for breath
**ver'schneit** *adj* snow-covered, snowy
**Ver'schnitt** *m* blend; waste
**verschnupft** [fɛɐ'ʃnʊpft] *adj*: ~ ***sein*** MED have a cold; F be in a huff
**ver'schnüren** *v/t* (*no -ge-*, *h*) tie up
**verschollen** [fɛɐ'ʃɔlən] *adj* missing; JUR presumed dead
**ver'schonen** *v/t* (*no -ge-*, *h*) spare; ***j-n mit et.*** ~ spare s.o. s.th.
**verschönern** [fɛɐ'ʃøːnɐn] *v/t* (*no -ge-*, *h*) embellish; **Verschönerung** [fɛɐ'ʃøːnərʊŋ] *f* (-; *-en*) embellishment
**verschossen** [fɛɐ'ʃɔsən] *adj* faded; F ~ ***sein in*** (*acc*) have a crush on
**verschränken** [fɛɐ'ʃrɛŋkən] *v/t* (*no -ge-*, *h*) fold; cross (*one's legs*)
**ver'schreiben** (*irr*, ***schreiben***, *no -ge-*, *h*) **1.** *v/t* MED prescribe (***gegen*** for); **2.** *v/refl* make a slip of the pen
**ver'schreibungspflichtig** *adj* PHARM available on prescription only
**verschroben** [fɛɐ'ʃroːbən] *adj* eccentric, odd
**ver'schrotten** *v/t* (*no -ge-*, *h*) scrap
**ver'schüchtert** *adj* intimidated
**ver'schulden** *v/t* (*no -ge-*, *h*) be responsible for, cause, be the cause of; ***sich*** ~ get into debt; **ver'schuldet** *adj* in debt
**ver'schütten** *v/t* (*no -ge-*, *h*) spill; bury *s.o.* (alive)
**verschwägert** [fɛɐ'ʃvɛːgɐt] *adj* related by marriage
**ver'schweigen** *v/t* (*irr*, ***schweigen***, *no -ge-*, *h*) keep *s.th.* a secret, hide
**verschwenden** [fɛɐ'ʃvɛndən] *v/t* (*no -ge-*, *h*) waste; **Verschwender** [fɛɐ'ʃvɛndɐ] *m* (*-s*; -) spendthrift; **verschwenderisch** [fɛɐ'ʃvɛndərɪʃ] *adj* wasteful, extravagant; lavish; **Ver'schwendung** *f* (-; *-en*) waste
**verschwiegen** [fɛɐ'ʃviːgən] *adj* discreet; hidden, secret; **Ver'schwiegenheit** *f* (-; *no pl*) secrecy, discretion
**ver'schwimmen** *v/i* (*irr*, ***schwimmen***, *no -ge-*, *sein*) become blurred
**ver'schwinden** *v/i* (*irr*, ***schwinden***, *no -ge-*, *sein*) disappear, vanish; F ***verschwinde!*** beat it!; **Ver'schwinden** *n* (*-s*; *no pl*) disappearance
**verschwommen** [fɛɐ'ʃvɔmən] *adj* blurred (*a.* PHOT), *fig a.* vague, hazy
**ver'schwören** *v/refl* (*irr*, ***schwören***, *no -ge-*, *h*) conspire, plot; **Verschwörer**

[fɛɐ'ʃvøːrɐ] *m* (*-s*; -) conspirator; **Ver'schwörung** *f* (-; *-en*) conspiracy, plot
**verschwunden** [fɛɐ'ʃvʊndən] *adj* missing
**ver'sehen** (*irr*, ***sehen***, *no -ge-*, *h*) **1.** *v/t* hold (*an office etc*); ~ ***mit*** provide with; **2.** *v/refl* make a mistake; **Ver'sehen** *n* (*-s*; -) mistake, error; ***aus*** ~ → **versehentlich** [fɛɐ'zeːəntlɪç] *adv* by mistake, unintentionally
**Versehrte** [fɛɐ'zeːɐtə] *m, f* (*-n*; *-n*) disabled person
**ver|'sengen** *v/t* (*no -ge-*, *h*) singe, scorch; **~'senken** *v/t* (*no -ge-*, *h*) sink; ***sich*** ~ ***in*** (*acc*) become absorbed in
**versessen** [fɛɐ'zɛsən] *adj*: ~ ***auf*** (*acc*) keen on, mad *or* crazy about
**ver'setzen** *v/t* (*no -ge-*, *h*) move, shift; transfer; PED promote, *Br* move *s.o.* up; give (*s.o. a kick etc*); pawn; AGR transplant; F ***j-n*** ~ stand s.o. up; ***j-n in die Lage*** ~ ***zu*** *inf* put s.o. in a position to *inf*, enable s.o. to *inf*; ***sich in j-s Lage*** ~ put o.s. in s.o.'s place; **Ver'setzung** *f* (-; *-en*) transfer; PED promotion
**ver'seuchen** *v/t* (*no -ge-*, *h*) contaminate; **Ver'seuchung** *f* (-; *-en*) contamination
**ver'sichern** *v/t* (*no -ge-*, *h*) ECON insure (***bei*** with); assure (***j-m et.*** s.o. of s.th.), assert; ***sich*** ~ insure o.s.; make sure (***dass*** that); **Ver'sicherte** *m, f* (*-n*; *-n*) *the* insured; **Ver'sicherung** *f* (-; *-en*) insurance; assurance, assertion
**Ver'sicherungs|gesellschaft** *f* insurance company; **~po,lice** *f*, **~schein** *m* insurance policy
**ver|'sickern** *v/i* (*no -ge-*, *sein*) trickle away; **~'siegeln** *v/t* (*no -ge-*, *h*) seal; **~'siegen** *v/i* (*no -ge-*, *sein*) dry up, run dry; **~'silbern** *v/t* (*no -ge-*, *h*) silver-plate; F turn *s.th.* into cash; **~'sinken** *v/i* (*irr*, ***sinken***, *no -ge-*, *sein*) sink; → ***versunken***
**Version** [vɛr'zjoːn] *f* (-; *-en*) version
**'Versmaß** *n* meter, *Br* metre
**versöhnen** [fɛɐ'zøːnən] *v/t* (*no -ge-*, *h*) reconcile; ***sich*** (***wieder***) ~ make it up (***mit*** with); **ver'söhnlich** *adj* conciliatory; **Ver'söhnung** *f* (-; *-en*) reconciliation; *esp* POL appeasement
**ver'sorgen** *v/t* (*no -ge-*, *h*) provide (***mit*** with), supply (with); support; take care of, look after; **Ver'sorgung** *f* (-; *no pl*) supply (***mit*** with); support; care
**ver'späten** *v/refl* (*no -ge-*, *h*) be late; **ver'spätet** *adj* belated, late, RAIL *etc a.* delayed; **Ver'spätung** *f* (-; *-en*) being *or* coming late, RAIL *etc* delay; ***20 Minuten*** ~ ***haben*** be 20 minutes late
**ver'speisen** *v/t* (*no -ge-*, *h*) eat (up)
**ver'sperren** *v/t* (*no -ge-*, *h*) bar, block (up), obstruct (*a. view*); lock
**ver'spielen** *v/t* (*no -ge-*, *h*) lose; **ver'spielt** *adj* playful
**ver'spotten** *v/t* (*no -ge-*, *h*) make fun of, ridicule
**ver'sprechen** (*irr*, ***sprechen***, *no -ge-*, *h*) **1.** *v/t* promise (*a. fig*); ***sich zu viel*** ~ (***von***) expect too much (of); **2.** *v/refl* make a mistake *or* slip; **Ver'sprechen** *n* (*-s*; -) promise; ***ein*** ~ ***geben*** (***halten***, ***brechen***) make (keep, break) a promise; **Ver'sprecher** F *m* (*-s*; -) slip (of the tongue)
**ver'staatlichen** *v/t* (*no -ge-*, *h*) ECON nationalize; **Ver'staatlichung** *f* (-; *-en*) ECON nationalization
**Verstädterung** [fɛɐ'ʃtɛːtərʊŋ] *f* (-; *-en*) urbanization
**Verstand** [fɛɐ'ʃtant] *m* (*-[e]s*; *no pl*) mind, intellect; reason, (common) sense; intelligence, brains; ***nicht bei*** ~ out of one's mind, not in one's right mind; ***den*** ~ ***verlieren*** go out of one's mind; **verstandesmäßig** [fɛɐ'ʃtandəsmɛːsɪç] *adj* rational
**ver'ständig** *adj* reasonable, sensible
**verständigen** [fɛɐ'ʃtɛndɪgən] *v/t* (*no -ge-*, *h*) inform (***von*** of), notify (of); call (*doctor, police etc*); ***sich*** ~ communicate; come to an agreement (***über*** *acc* on); **Ver'ständigung** *f* (-; *no pl*) communication (*a.* TEL); agreement
**verständlich** [fɛɐ'ʃtɛntlɪç] *adj* audible; intelligible; comprehensible; understandable; ***schwer*** (***leicht***) ~ difficult (easy) to understand; ***j-m et.*** ~ ***machen*** make s.th. clear to s.o.; ***sich*** ~ ***machen*** make o.s. understood
**Verständnis** [fɛɐ'ʃtɛntnɪs] *n* (*-ses*; *no pl*) comprehension, understanding; sympathy; (***viel***) ~ ***haben*** be (very) understanding; ~ ***haben für*** understand; appreciate
**ver'ständnislos** *adj* uncomprehending; blank (*look etc*)
**ver'ständnisvoll** *adj* understanding,

sympathetic; knowing (*look etc*)
**ver'stärken** *v/t* (*no -ge-, h*) reinforce (*a.* TECH, MIL); strengthen (*a.* TECH); *radio*, PHYS amplify; intensify; **Ver'stärker** *m* (*-s; -*) amplifier; **Ver'stärkung** *f* (*-; -en*) strengthening; reinforcement(s MIL); amplification; intensification
**ver'stauben** *v/i* (*no -ge-, sein*) get dusty
**verstauchen** [fɛɐ'ʃtauxən] *v/t* (*no -ge-, h*), **Ver'stauchung** *f* (*-; -en*) MED sprain
**ver'stauen** *v/t* (*no -ge-, h*) stow away
**Versteck** [fɛɐ'ʃtɛk] *n* (*-[e]s; -e*) hiding place, hideout, hideaway
**ver'stecken** *v/t and v/refl* (*no -ge-, h*) hide (*a. fig*); ***Verstecken spielen*** play (at) hide-and-seek
**ver'stehen** *v/t* (*irr*, ***stehen, no -ge-, h***) understand, F get; catch; see; realize; know; ***es ~ zu*** *inf* know how to *inf*; ***zu ~ geben*** give *s.o.* to understand, suggest; ***ich verstehe!*** I see!; ***falsch ~*** misunderstand; ***was ~ Sie unter ...?*** what do you mean *or* understand by ...?; ***sich*** (***gut***) ~ get along (well) (***mit*** with); ***es versteht sich von selbst*** it goes without saying
**ver'steifen** (*no -ge-, h*) **1.** *v/t* stiffen (*a.* ***sich ~***); TECH strut, brace; **2.** *v/refl*: ***sich auf et. ~*** insist on (doing) s.th.
**ver'steigern** *v/t* (*no -ge-, h*) auction off
**Ver'steigerung** *f* (*-; -en*) auction (sale)
**ver'steinern** *v/i* (*no -ge-, sein*) petrify (*a. fig*)
**ver'stellbar** *adj* adjustable
**ver'stellen** *v/t* (*no -ge-, h*) block; move; set *s.th.* wrong *or* the wrong way; TECH adjust, regulate; disguise (*one's voice etc*); ***sich ~*** pretend
**Ver'stellung** *f* (*-; no pl*) disguise, make-believe, (false) show
**ver'steuern** *v/t* (*no -ge-, h*) pay duty *or* tax on
**verstiegen** [fɛɐ'ʃti:gən] *adj* high-flown
**ver'stimmen** *v/t* (*no -ge-, h*) MUS put out of tune; *fig* annoy; **ver'stimmt** *adj* annoyed; MUS out of tune; MED upset; **Ver'stimmung** *f* (*-; -en*) annoyance
**ver|stockt** [fɛɐ'ʃtɔkt] *adj* stubborn, obstinate; **~stohlen** [fɛɐ'ʃto:lən] *adj* furtive, stealthy
**ver'stopfen** *v/t* (*no -ge-, h*) plug (up); block, jam; MED constipate; **ver'stopft** *adj* MED constipated; **Ver'stopfung** *f* (*-; -en*) block(age); MED constipation
**verstorben** [fɛɐ'ʃtɔrbən] *adj* late, deceased; **Ver'storbene** *m, f* (*-n; -n*) *the* deceased; ***die ~n*** the deceased
**verstört** [fɛɐ'ʃtø:ɐt] *adj* upset; distracted; wild (*look etc*)
**Ver'stoß** *m* offense, *Br* offence (***gegen*** against), violation (of)
**ver'stoßen** (*irr*, ***stoßen, no -ge-, h***) **1.** *v/t* expel (***aus*** from); disown; **2.** *v/i*: ***~ gegen*** offend against, violate
**ver'strahlt** *adj* (radioactively) contaminated
**ver'streichen** (*irr*, ***streichen, no -ge-***) **1.** *v/i* (*sein*) *time*: pass, go by; *date*: expire; **2.** *v/t* (*h*) spread
**ver'streuen** *v/t* (*no -ge-, h*) scatter
**verstümmeln** [fɛɐ'ʃtʏməln] *v/t* (*no -ge-, h*) mutilate (*a. fig*); **Ver'stümmelung** *f* (*-; -en*) mutilation (*a. fig*)
**ver'stummen** *v/i* (*no -ge-, sein*) grow silent; stop; die down
**Versuch** [fɛɐ'zu:x] *m* (*-[e]s; -e*) attempt, try; trial, test; PHYS experiment; ***mit et.*** (***j-m***) ***e-n ~ machen*** give s.th. (s.o.) a try; **ver'suchen** *v/t* (*no -ge-, h*) try, attempt; taste; REL tempt; ***es ~*** have a try (at it)
**Ver'suchs...** *in cpds ...bohrung etc*: test ..., trial ...; **~ka͵ninchen** *n* guinea pig; **~stadium** *n* experimental stage; **~tier** *n* laboratory *or* test animal
**ver'suchsweise** *adv* by way of trial
**Ver'suchung** *f* (*-; -en*) temptation; ***j-n in ~ führen*** tempt s.o.
**versunken** [fɛɐ'zʊŋkən] *fig adj*: ***~ in*** (*acc*) absorbed *or* lost in
**ver'süßen** *v/t* (*no -ge-, h*) sweeten
**ver'tagen** *v/t and v/refl* (*no -ge-, h*) adjourn; **Ver'tagung** *f* (*-; -en*) adjournment
**ver'tauschen** *v/t* (*no -ge-, h*) exchange (***mit*** for)
**verteidigen** [fɛɐ'taidɪgən] *v/t* (*no -ge-, h*) defend (***sich*** o.s.); **Verteidiger(in)** [fɛɐ'taidɪgɐ (-gərɪn)] (*-s; -/-; -nen*) defender, SPORT *a.* back; *fig* advocate; **Ver'teidigung** *f* (*-; -en*) defense, *Br* defence
**Ver'teidigungs...** *in cpds ...politik etc*: *mst* defense ..., *Br* defence ...; **~mi͵nister** *m* Secretary of Defense, *Br* Minister of Defence; **~minis͵terium** *n* Department of Defense, *Br* Ministry of Defence

**ver'teilen** *v/t* (*no -ge-*, *h*) distribute; hand out; **Ver'teiler** *m* (*-s*; *-*) distributor; **Ver'teilung** *f* (*-*; *-en*) distribution
**ver'tiefen** *v/t and v/refl* (*no -ge-*, *h*) deepen (*a. fig*); ***sich ~ in*** (*acc*) become absorbed in; **Ver'tiefung** *f* (*-*; *-en*) hollow, depression, dent; *fig* deepening
**vertikal** [vɛrti'ka:l] *adj*, **Verti'kale** *f* (*-*; *-n*) vertical
**ver'tilgen** *v/t* (*no -ge-*, *h*) exterminate; F consume; **Ver'tilgung** *f* (*-*; *no pl*) extermination
**vertonen** [fɛɐ'to:nən] *v/t* (*no -ge-*, *h*) set to music
**Vertrag** [fɛɐ'tra:k] *m* (*-[e]s*; *Verträge* [fɛɐ'trɛ:gə]) contract; POL treaty
**ver'tragen** *v/t* (*irr*, ***tragen***, *no -ge-*, *h*) endure, bear, stand; ***ich kann ... nicht ~*** ... doesn't agree with me; I can't stand ...; ***er kann viel ~*** he can take a lot; he can hold his drink; F ***ich*** (***es***) ***könnte ... ~*** I (it) could do with ...; ***sich*** (***gut***) ***~*** get along (well) (***mit*** with); ***sich wieder ~*** make it up
**ver'traglich** *adv* by contract
**verträglich** [fɛɐ'trɛ:klɪç] *adj* easy to get on with; GASTR (easily) digestible
**ver'trauen** *v/i* (*no -ge-*, *h*) trust (***auf*** *acc* in); **Ver'trauen** *n* (*-s*; *no pl*) confidence, trust, faith; ***im ~*** (***gesagt***) between you and me; ***wenig ~ erweckend aussehen*** inspire little confidence
**Ver'trauens|frage** *f*: ***die ~ stellen*** PARL ask for a vote of confidence; **~sache** *f*: ***das ist ~*** that is a matter of confidence; **~stellung** *f* position of trust
**ver'trauensvoll** *adj* trustful, trusting
**Ver'trauensvotum** *n* PARL vote of confidence
**ver'trauenswürdig** *adj* trustworthy
**ver'traulich** *adj* confidential; familiar
**ver'traut** *adj* familiar; close
**Ver'traute** *m*, *f* (*-n*; *-n*) confidant(e *f*)
**Ver'trautheit** *f* (*-*; *no pl*) familiarity
**ver'treiben** *v/t* (*irr*, ***treiben***, *no -ge-*, *h*) drive *or* chase away (*a. fig*); pass (*the time*); ECON sell; ***~ aus*** drive out of; **Ver'treibung** *f* (*-*; *-en*) expulsion (***aus*** from)
**ver'treten** *v/t* (*irr*, ***treten***, *no -ge-*, *h*) substitute for, replace, stand in for; POL, ECON represent, PARL *a.* sit for; JUR act for *s.o.*; ***j-s Sache ~*** JUR plead s.o.'s cause; ***die Ansicht ~, dass*** argue that; ***sich den Fuß ~*** sprain one's ankle; F ***sich die Beine ~*** stretch one's legs
**Ver'treter** *m* (*-s*; *-*), **Ver'treterin** *f* (*-*; *-nen*) substitute, deputy; POL, ECON representative, ECON *a.* agent; MED locum
**Ver'tretung** *f* (*-*; *-en*) substitution, replacement; substitute, stand-in, *a.* supply teacher; ECON, POL representation
**Vertrieb** [fɛɐ'tri:p] *m* (*-[e]s*; *no pl*) ECON sale, distribution
**Vertriebene** [fɛɐ'tri:bənə] *m*, *f* (*-n*; *-n*) POL expellee, refugee
**ver|'trocknen** *v/i* (*no -ge-*, *sein*) dry up; **~'trödeln** F *v/t* (*no -ge-*, *h*) dawdle away, waste; **~'trösten** *v/t* (*no -ge-*, *h*) put *s.o.* off; **~'tuschen** F *v/t* (*no -ge-*, *h*) cover up; **~'übeln** *v/t* (*no -ge-*, *h*) take amiss; ***ich kann es ihr nicht ~*** I can't blame her for it; **~'üben** *v/t* (*no -ge-*, *h*) commit
**verunglücken** [fɛɐ'ʔʊnglʏkən] *v/i* (*no -ge-*, *sein*) have an accident; *fig* go wrong; ***tödlich ~*** die in an accident
**ver'ursachen** *v/t* (*no -ge-*, *h*) cause
**ver'urteilen** *v/t* (*no -ge-*, *h*) condemn (***zu*** to) (*a. fig*), sentence (to), convict (***wegen*** of); **Ver'urteilung** *f* (*-*; *-en*) condemnation (*a. fig*)
**ver'vielfachen** *v/t* (*no -ge-*, *h*) multiply
**vervielfältigen** [fɛɐ'fi:lfɛltɪgən] *v/t* (*no -ge-*, *h*) copy, duplicate; **Ver'vielfältigung** *f* (*-*; *-en*) duplication; copy
**ver'vollkommnen** *v/t* (*no -ge-*, *h*) perfect; improve
**vervollständigen** [fɛɐ'fɔlʃtɛndɪgən] *v/t* (*no -ge-*, *h*) complete
**ver|'wachsen** *adj* MED deformed, crippled; *fig* ***~ mit*** deeply rooted in, bound up with; **~'wackelt** F *adj* PHOT blurred
**ver'wahren** *v/t* (*no -ge-*, *h*) keep (in a safe place); ***sich ~ gegen*** protest against
**verwahrlost** [fɛɐ'va:ɐlo:st] *adj* uncared-for, neglected
**ver'walten** *v/t* (*no -ge-*, *h*) manage, *esp* POL *a.* administer; **Ver'walter** *m* (*-s*; *-*) manager; administrator; **Ver'waltung** *f* (*-*; *-en*) administration, management; **Ver'waltungs...** *in cpds ...gericht*, *...kosten etc*: administrative ...
**ver'wandeln** *v/t* (*no -ge-*, *h*) change, turn (*both a.* ***sich ~***), *esp* PHYS, CHEM *a.* transform, convert (*all*: ***in*** *acc* into);

**Ver'wandlung** *f* (-; *-en*) change, transformation; conversion
**verwandt** [fɛɐ'vant] *adj* related (***mit*** to); **Ver'wandte** *m, f* (*-n*; *-n*) relative; (***alle***) ***m-e ~n*** (all) my relatives *or* relations; ***der nächste ~*** the next of kin; **Ver'wandtschaft** *f* (-; *-en*) a) relationship, b) (*no pl*) relations
**ver'warnen** *v/t* (*no -ge-, h*) *Br* caution; SPORT book; **Ver'warnung** *f* (-; *-en*) *Br* caution; SPORT booking
**ver'waschen** *adj* washed-out
**ver'wässern** *v/t* (*no -ge-, h*) water down (*a. fig*)
**ver'wechseln** *v/t* (*no -ge-, h*) confuse (***mit*** with), mix up (with), mistake (for)
**Ver'wechs(e)lung** *f* (-; *-en*) mistake, F mix-up
**ver'wegen** *adj* daring, bold
**Ver'wegenheit** *f* (-; *no pl*) boldness, daring
**ver'weichlicht** *adj* soft
**ver'weigern** *v/t* (*no -ge-, h*) refuse; disobey; **Ver'weigerung** *f* (-; *-en*) denial, refusal
**ver'weilen** *v/i* (*no -ge-, h*) stay; *fig* rest
**Verweis** [fɛɐ'vais] *m* (*-es*; *-e*) reprimand, reproof; reference (***auf*** *acc* to)
**ver'weisen** *v/t* (*irr*, ***weisen***, *no -ge-, h*) refer (***auf*** *acc*, ***an*** *acc* to); expel (*gen* from)
**ver'welken** *v/i* (*no -ge-, sein*) wither, *fig a.* fade
**ver'wenden** *v/t* (*no -ge-, h*) use; spend (*time etc*) (***auf*** *acc* on); **Ver'wendung** *f* (-; *-en*) use; ***keine ~ haben für*** have no use for
**ver'werfen** *v/t* (*irr*, ***werfen***, *no -ge-, h*) drop, give up; reject
**ver'werten** *v/t* (*no -ge-, h*) use, make use of
**verwesen** [fɛɐ've:zən] *v/i* (*no -ge-, sein*), **Ver'wesung** *f* (-; *no pl*) decay
**ver'wickeln** *fig v/t* (*no -ge-, h*) involve; ***sich ~ in*** (*acc*) get caught in; **ver'wickelt** *fig adj* complicated; ***~ sein*** (***werden***) ***in*** (*acc*) be (get) involved in; **Ver'wicklung** *fig f* (-; *-en*) involvement; complication
**ver'wildern** *v/i* (*no -ge-, sein*) grow (*or* run) wild; **ver'wildert** *adj* wild (*a. fig*), overgrown
**ver'winden** *v/t* (*irr*, ***winden***, *no -ge-, h*) get over *s.th.*
**ver'wirklichen** *v/t* (*no -ge-, h*) realize; ***sich ~*** come true; ***sich selbst ~*** fulfil(l) o.s.; **Ver'wirklichung** *f* (-; *-en*) realization
**ver'wirren** *v/t* (*no -ge-, h*) tangle (up); *fig* confuse; **ver'wirrt** *fig adj* confused; **Ver'wirrung** *fig f* (-; *-en*) confusion
**ver'wischen** *v/t* (*no -ge-, h*) blur (*a. fig*); cover (*track etc*)
**verwittern** [fɛɐ'vɪtɐn] *v/i* (*no -ge-, sein*) GEOL weather
**ver'witwet** *adj* widowed
**verwöhnen** [fɛɐ'vø:nən] *v/t* (*no -ge-, h*) spoil; **ver'wöhnt** *adj* spoilt
**verworren** [fɛɐ'vɔrən] *adj* confused, muddled; complicated
**verwundbar** [fɛɐ'vʊntba:ɐ] *adj* vulnerable (*a. fig*); **ver'wunden** *v/t* (*no -ge-, h*) wound
**ver'wunderlich** *adj* surprising
**Verwunderung** [fɛɐ'vʊndərʊŋ] *f* (-; *no pl*) (***zu m-r*** *etc* ***~*** to my *etc*) surprise
**Ver'wundete** *m, f* (*-n*; *-n*) wounded (person), casualty
**Ver'wundung** *f* (-; *-en*) wound, injury
**ver'wünschen** *v/t* (*no -ge-, h*), **Ver'wünschung** *f* (-; *-en*) curse
**ver'wüsten** *v/t* (*no -ge-, h*) lay waste, devastate, ravage; **Ver'wüstung** *f* (-; *-en*) devastation, ravage
**ver|'zählen** *v/refl* (*no -ge-, h*) count wrong; **~zärteln** [fɛɐ'tsɛrtəln] *v/t* (*no -ge-, h*) coddle, pamper; **~'zaubern** *v/t* (*no -ge-, h*) enchant, *fig a.* charm; ***~ in*** (*acc*) turn into; **~'zehren** *v/t* (*no -ge-, h*) consume (*a. fig*)
**ver'zeichnen** *v/t* (*no -ge-, h*) record, keep a record of, list; *fig* achieve; suffer; **Ver'zeichnis** *n* (*-ses*; *-se*) list, catalog(ue); record, register; index
**verzeihen** [fɛɐ'tsaiən] *v/t and v/i* (*irr*, *no -ge-, h*) forgive *s.o.*; pardon, excuse *s.th.*; **ver'zeihlich** *adj* pardonable; **Ver'zeihung** *f* (-; *no pl*) pardon; (***j-n***) ***um ~ bitten*** apologize (to s.o.); ***~!*** (I'm) sorry!; excuse me!
**ver'zerren** *v/t* (*no -ge-, h*) distort (*a. fig*); ***sich ~*** become distorted
**Ver'zerrung** *f* (-; *-en*) distortion
**Verzicht** [fɛɐ'tsɪçt] *m* (-[*e*]*s*; *-e*) renunciation (***auf*** *acc* of); *mst* giving up, doing without *etc*
**ver'zichten** *v/i* (*no -ge-, h*) ***~ auf*** (*acc*) do without; give up; renounce (*a.* JUR)

V

**verzieh** [fɛɐ'tsiː] *pret of* ***verzeihen***
**ver'ziehen** (*irr*, ***ziehen***, *no -ge-*) **1.** *v/i* (*sein*) move (***nach*** to); **2.** *v/t* (*h*) spoil; ***das Gesicht ~*** make a face; ***sich ~*** *wood*: warp; *storm etc*: pass (over); F disappear; **3.** *pp of* ***verzeihen***
**ver'zieren** *v/t* (*no -ge-*, *h*) decorate
**Ver'zierung** *f* (-; *-en*) decoration, ornament
**ver'zinsen** *v/t* (*no -ge-*, *h*) pay interest on; ***sich ~*** yield interest
**Ver'zinsung** *f* (-; *-en*) interest
**ver'zögern** *v/t* (*no -ge-*, *h*) delay; ***sich ~*** be delayed; **Ver'zögerung** *f* (-; *-en*) delay
**ver'zollen** *v/t* (*no -ge-*, *h*) pay duty on; ***et.*** (***nichts***) ***zu ~ haben*** have s.th. (nothing) to declare
**verzückt** [fɛɐ'tsʏkt] *adj* ecstatic; **Ver'zückung** *f* (-; *-en*) ecstasy; ***in ~ geraten*** go into ecstasies *or* raptures (***wegen***, ***über*** *acc* over)
**Verzug** [fɛɐ'tsuːk] *m* (-[*e*]*s*; *no pl*) delay; ECON default
**ver'zweifeln** *v/i* (*no -ge-*, *h*) despair (***an*** *dat* of); **ver'zweifelt** *adj* desperate, despairing
**Ver'zweiflung** *f* (-; *no pl*) despair; ***j-n zur ~ bringen*** drive s.o. to despair
**verzweigen** [fɛɐ'tsvaigən] *v/refl* (*no -ge-*, *h*) branch
**verzwickt** [fɛɐ'tsvɪkt] F *adj* tricky
**Veteran** [vete'raːn] *m* (*-en*; *-en*) MIL veteran (*a. fig*)
**Veterinär** [veteri'nɛːɐ] *m* (*-s*; *-e*), **Veteri'närin** *f* (-; *-nen*) veterinarian, *Br* veterinary surgeon, F vet
**Veto** ['veːto] *n* (*-s*; *-s*) veto; (**s**)***ein ~ einlegen gegen*** veto
**Vetter** ['fɛtɐ] *m* (*-s*; *-n*) cousin
**'Vetternwirtschaft** *f* (-; *no pl*) nepotism
**vgl.** ABBR *of* ***vergleiche*** cf., confer
**VHS** ABBR *of* ***Volkshochschule*** adult education program(me); adult evening classes
**Vibration** [vibra'tsjoːn] *f* (-; *-en*) vibration; **vibrieren** [vi'briːrən] *v/i* (*no -ge-*, *h*) vibrate
**Video** ['viːdeo] *n* (*-s*; *-s*) video (*a. in cpds ...aufnahme*, *...clip*, *...kamera*, *...kassette*, *...recorder etc*); ***auf ~ aufnehmen*** video(tape), tape; **~band** *n* videotape; **~text** *m* teletext
**Videothek** [video'teːk] *f* (-; *-en*) video(tape) library; video store (*Br* shop)
**Vieh** [fiː] *n* (-[*e*]*s*; *no pl*) cattle; ***20 Stück ~*** 20 head of cattle; **~bestand** *m* livestock; **~händler** *m* cattle dealer
**'viehisch** *contp adj* bestial, brutal
**'Vieh|markt** *m* cattle market; **~zucht** *f* cattle breeding, stockbreeding; **~züchter** *m* cattle breeder, stockbreeder
**viel** [fiːl] *adj and adv* a lot (of), plenty (of), F lots of; ***~e*** many; ***nicht ~*** not much; ***nicht ~e*** not many; ***sehr ~*** a great deal (of); ***sehr ~e*** very many, a lot (of); ***das ~e Geld*** all that money; ***ziemlich ~*** quite a lot (of); ***ziemlich ~e*** quite a few; ***~ besser*** much better; ***~ teurer*** much more expensive; ***e-r zu ~*** one too many; ***~ zu ~*** far too much; ***~ zu wenig*** not nearly enough; ***~ lieber*** much rather; ***wie ~*** how much (*pl* many); ***~ beschäftigt*** very busy; ***~ sagend*** meaningful; ***~ versprechend*** promising; **'vieldeutig** [-dɔʏtɪç] *adj* ambiguous; **vielerlei** ['fiːlɐ'lai] *adj* all kinds *or* sorts of; **'vielfach 1.** *adj* multiple; **2.** *adv* in many cases, (very) often; **'Vielfalt** *f* (-; *no pl*) (great) variety (*gen* of); **'vielfarbig** *adj* multicolo(u)red
**vielleicht** [fi'laiçt] *adv* perhaps, maybe; ***~ ist er ...*** he may *or* might be ...
**'vielmals** *adv*: (***ich***) ***danke*** (***Ihnen***) ***~*** thank you very much; ***entschuldigen Sie ~*** I'm very sorry, I do apologize
**viel'mehr** *cj* rather
**'vielseitig** [-zaitɪç] *adj* versatile
**'Vielseitigkeit** *f* (-; *no pl*) versatility
**vier** [fiːɐ] *adj* four; ***zu viert sein*** be four; ***auf allen ~en*** on all fours; ***unter ~ Augen*** in private, privately
**'Vierbeiner** [-bainɐ] *m* (*-s*; -) ZO quadruped, four-legged animal
**'vierbeinig** *adj* four-legged
**'Viereck** *n* quadrangle, quadrilateral
**'viereckig** *adj* quadrangular, square
**Vierer** ['fiːrɐ] *m* (*-s*; -) *rowing*: four
**'vierfach** *adj* fourfold; ***~e Ausfertigung*** four copies
**'vierfüßig** [-fyːsɪç] *adj* four-footed
**'Vierfüßler** [-fyːslɐ] *m* (*-s*; -) ZO quadruped
**'vierhändig** [-hɛndɪç] *adj* MUS four-handed
**'vierjährig** [-jɛːrɪç] *adj* four-year-old, of four
**Vierlinge** ['fiːɐlɪŋə] *pl* quadruplets, quads

**'viermal** *adv* four times
**'Vierradantrieb** *m* MOT four-wheel drive
**'vierseitig** [-zaitıç] *adj* MATH quadrilateral
**'vierspurig** [-ʃpu:rıç] *adj* MOT four-lane
**'vierstöckig** [-ʃtœkıç] *adj* four-storied, *Br* four-storey ...
**'Viertaktmotor** *m* four-stroke engine
**vierte** ['fi:ɐtə] *adj* fourth
**Viertel** ['fırtəl] *n* (*-s*; -) fourth (part); quarter; (***ein***) ~ ***vor*** (***nach***) (a) quarter to (past); **~fiˌnale** *n* SPORT quarter finals
**Viertel'jahr** *n* three months
**'vierteljährlich 1.** *adj* quarterly; **2.** *adv* every three months, quarterly
**vierteln** ['fırtəln] *v/t* (*ge-*, *h*) quarter
**'Viertel|note** *f* MUS quarter note, *Br* crotchet; **~pfund** *n* quarter of a pound
**Viertel'stunde** *f* quarter of an hour
**viertens** ['fi:ɐtəns] *adv* fourthly
**vierzehn** ['fırtse:n] *adj* fourteen; ~ ***Tage*** two weeks, *esp Br a.* a fortnight
**'vierzehnte** *adj* fourteenth
**vierzig** ['fırtsıç] *adj* forty
**'vierzigste** *adj* fortieth
**Villa** ['vıla] *f* (-; *Villen*) villa
**violett** [vio'lɛt] *adj* violet, purple
**Violine** [vio'li:nə] *f* (-; *-n*) MUS violin
**Virtuelle Realität** [vır'tuɛlə] *f* EDP virtual reality, Cyberspace
**virtuos** [vır'tuo:s] *adj* virtuoso ..., masterly; **Virtuose** [vır'tuo:zə] *m* (*-n*; *-n*) virtuoso; **Virtuosität** [vırtuozi'tɛ:t] *f* (-; *no pl*) virtuosity
**Virus** ['vi:rʊs] *n*, *m* (-; *Viren*) MED virus
**Visier** [vi'zi:ɐ] *n* (*-s*; *-e*) sights; visor
**Vision** [vi'zjo:n] *f* (-; *-en*) vision
**Visite** [vi'zi:tə] *f* (-; *-n*) MED round
**Vi'sitenkarte** *f* (visiting) card
**Visum** ['vi:zʊm] *n* (*-s*; *Visa*) visa
**vital** [vi'ta:l] *adj* vigorous; **Vitalität** [vitali'tɛ:t] *f* (-; *no pl*) vigo(u)r
**Vitamin** [vita'mi:n] *n* (*-s*; *-e*) vitamin
**Vitrine** [vi'tri:nə] *f* (-; *-n*) (glass) cabinet; showcase
**Vize...** ['fi:tsə-] *in cpds ...präsident etc*: vice(-)...
**Vogel** ['fo:gəl] *m* (*-s*; *Vögel* ['fø:gəl]) ZO bird; F ***den ~ abschießen*** take the cake
**'Vogelbauer** *n* birdcage
**'vogelfrei** *adj* outlawed
**'Vogel|futter** *n* birdseed; **~kunde** *f* ornithology; **~käfig** *m* birdcage
**vögeln** ['fø:gəln] V *v/t and v/i* (*ge-*, *h*) screw
**'Vogel|nest** *n* bird's nest; **~perspekˌtive** *f* bird's-eye view; **~scheuche** *f* scarecrow (*a. fig*); **~schutzgebiet** *n* bird sanctuary; **~warte** *f* ornithological station; **~zug** *m* bird migration
**Vokabel** [vo'ka:bəl] *f* (-; *-n*) word; *pl* → **Vokabular** [vokabu'la:ɐ] *n* (*-s*; *-e*) vocabulary
**Vokal** [vo'ka:l] *m* (*-s*; *-e*) LING vowel
**Volant** [vo'lã:] *Austrian m* → ***Lenkrad***
**Volk** [fɔlk] *n* (*-[e]s*; *Völker* ['fœlkɐ]) people, nation; *the* people; ZO swarm; ***ein Mann aus dem ~e*** a man of the people
**Völker|kunde** ['fœlkɐ-] *f* ethnology; **~mord** *m* genocide; **~recht** *n* (*-[e]s*; *no pl*) international law; **~wanderung** *f* migration of peoples; F mass exodus
**'Volks|abstimmung** *f* POL referendum; **~fest** *n* funfair; **~hochschule** *f* adult evening classes; **~lied** *n* folk song; **~mund** *m*: ***im ~*** in the vernacular; **~muˌsik** *f* folk music; **~repuˌblik** *f* people's republic; **~schule** HIST *f* → ***Grundschule***; **~sport** *m* popular sport; **~sprache** *f* vernacular; **~stamm** *m* tribe, race; **~tanz** *m* folk dance; **~tracht** *f* national costume
**'volkstümlich** [-ty:mlıç] *adj* popular, folk ...; traditional
**'Volks|versammlung** *f* public meeting; **~wirt** *m* economist; **~wirtschaft** *f* (national) economy; → **~wirtschaftslehre** *f* economics; **~zählung** *f* census
**voll** [fɔl] **1.** *adj* full (*a. fig*); full up (*a.* F); F plastered; thick, rich (*hair*); ***~er*** full of, filled with, *a.* covered with *dirt etc*; **2.** *adv* fully; completely, totally, wholly; *pay etc* in full, the full price; *hit etc* full, straight, right; ~ ***entwickelt*** fully developed; ~ ***füllen*** (***gießen***) fill (up); ~ ***machen*** fill (up); F soil, dirty; ***um das Unglück ~ zu machen*** to crown it all; (***nicht***) ***für ~ nehmen*** (not) take seriously; ~ ***packen*** load (***mit*** with) (*a. fig*); ~ ***stopfen*** stuff, *fig a.* cram, pack (*all*: ***mit*** with); ***bitte ~ tanken!*** MOT fill her up, please!
**'vollauf** *adv* perfectly, quite
**'vollautoˌmatisch** *adj* fully automatic
**'Vollbart** *m* (full) beard
**'Vollbeschäftigung** *f* full employment

**'Vollblut...** *in cpds* full-blooded (*a. fig*)
**'Vollblüter** [-bly:tɐ] *m* (*-s*; -) ZO thoroughbred
**voll'bringen** *v/t* (*irr*, ***bringen***, *no -ge-*, *h*) accomplish, achieve; perform
**'Volldampf** *m* full steam; F ***mit*** ~ (at) full blast
**voll'enden** *v/t* (*no -ge-*, *h*) finish, complete; **voll'endet** *adj* completed; *fig* perfect; **vollends** ['fɔlɛnts] *adv* completely; **Voll'endung** *f* (-; *no pl*) finishing, completion; *fig* perfection
**voll'führen** *v/t* (*no -ge-*, *h*) perform
**'Vollgas** *n* (*-es*; *no pl*) MOT full throttle; ~ ***geben*** F step on it
**völlig** ['fœlɪç] **1.** *adj* complete, absolute, total; **2.** *adv* completely; ~ ***unmöglich*** absolutely impossible
**'volljährig** [-jɛ:rɪç] *adj* JUR ~ ***sein*** (***werden***) be (come) of age; ***noch nicht*** ~ under age; **'Volljährigkeit** *f* (-; *no pl*) JUR majority
**voll'kommen** *adj* perfect; → ***völlig***
**Voll'kommenheit** *f* (-; *no pl*) perfection
**'Voll|kornbrot** *n* wholemeal bread; **~macht** *f* (-; *-en*) full power(s), authority; JUR power of attorney; ~ ***haben*** be authorized; **~milch** *f* full-cream milk; **~mond** *m* full moon; **~pensi,on** *f* full board
**'vollschlank** *adj* plump
**'vollständig** *adj* complete; → ***völlig***
**voll'strecken** *v/t* (*no -ge-*, *h*) JUR execute; **Voll'streckung** *f* (-; *-en*) JUR execution
**'Voll|treffer** *m* direct hit; bull's eye (*a. fig*); **~versammlung** *f* plenary session
**'vollwertig** *adj* full
**'Vollwertkost** *f* wholefoods
**vollzählig** ['fɔltsɛ:lɪç] *adj* complete
**voll'ziehen** *v/t* (*irr*, ***ziehen***, *no -ge-*, *h*) execute; perform; ***sich*** ~ take place; **Voll'ziehung** *f* (-; *no pl*), **Voll'zug** *m* (-[*e*]*s*; *no pl*) execution
**Volontär** [volɔn'tɛ:ɐ] *m* (*-s*; *-e*), **Volon'tärin** *f* (-; *-nen*) unpaid trainee
**Volt** [vɔlt] *n* (-; -) ELECTR volt
**Volumen** [vo'lu:mən] *n* (*-s*; -, *-mina*) volume; size
**von** [fɔn] *prp* from; *instead of gen*: of; *passive*: by; about *s.o. or s.th.*; ***südlich*** ~ south of; ***weit*** ~ far from; ~ ***Hamburg*** from Hamburg; ~ ***nun an*** from now on; ***ein Freund*** ~ ***mir*** a friend of mine; ***die Freunde*** ~ ***Alice*** Alice's friends; ***ein Brief*** (***Geschenk***) ~ ***Tom*** a letter (gift) from Tom; ***ein Buch*** (***Bild***) ~ ***Orwell*** (***Picasso***) a book (painting) by Orwell (Picasso); ***der König*** (***Bürgermeister*** *etc*) ~ ***...*** the King (Mayor *etc*) of ...; ***ein Kind*** ~ ***10 Jahren*** a child of ten; ***müde*** ~ ***der Arbeit*** tired from work; ***es war nett*** (***gemein***) ~ ***dir*** it was nice (mean) of you; ***reden*** (***hören***) ~ talk (hear) about *or* of; ~ ***Beruf*** (***Geburt***) by profession (birth); ~ ***selbst*** by itself; ~ ***mir aus!*** I don't mind *or* care
**von'statten** *adv*: ~ ***gehen*** go, come off
**vor** [fo:ɐ] *prp* (*dat and acc*) in front of; outside; before; ... ago; with, for; ~ ***der Klasse*** in front of the class; ~ ***der Schule*** in front of *or* outside the school; before school; ~ ***kurzem*** (***e-r Stunde***) a short time (an hour) ago; ***5 Minuten*** ~ ***12*** five (minutes) to twelve; ~ ***j-m liegen*** be *or* lie ahead of s.o. (*a. fig and* SPORT); ~ ***sich hin*** *smile etc* to o.s.; ***sicher*** ~ safe from; ~ ***Kälte*** with cold; ~ ***Angst*** for fear; ~ ***allem*** above all; ~ ***sich gehen*** go on, happen
**'Vorabend** *m* eve (*a. fig*)
**'Vorahnung** *f* presentiment, foreboding
**voran** [fo'ran] *adv* at the head (*dat* of), in front (of), before; ***Kopf*** ~ head first; **~gehen** *v/i* (*irr*, ***gehen***, *sep*, *-ge-*, *sein*) go in front *or* first; *esp fig* lead the way; **~kommen** *v/i* (*irr*, ***kommen***, *sep*, *-ge-*, *sein*) get on *or* along (*a. fig*), make headway
**'Voranzeige** *f* preannouncement; *film*: trailer
**'vorarbeiten** *v/i* (*sep*, *-ge-*, *h*) work in advance; *fig* pave the way
**'Vorarbeiter** *m* foreman
**voraus** [fo'raus] *adv* ahead (*dat* of); ***im Voraus*** in advance, beforehand
**vo'rausgehen** *v/i* (*irr*, ***gehen***, *sep*, *-ge-*, *sein*) precede; → ***vorangehen***
**vo'rausgesetzt** *cj*: ~, ***dass*** provided that
**Vo'raussage** *f* (-; *-n*) prediction; METEOR forecast; **vo'raussagen** *v/t* (*sep*, *-ge-*, *h*) predict; forecast
**vo'raus|schicken** *v/t* (*sep*, *-ge-*, *h*) send on ahead; **~sehen** *v/t* (*irr*, ***sehen***, *sep*, *-ge-*, *h*) foresee, see *s.th.* coming

**vo'raussetzen** *v/t* (*sep*, *-ge-*, *h*) assume; take *s.th.* for granted
**Vo'raussetzung** *f* (-; *-en*) condition, prerequisite; assumption; ***die ~en erfüllen*** meet the requirements
**Vo'raussicht** *f* (-; *no pl*) foresight; ***aller ~ nach*** in all probability
**vo'raussichtlich** *adv* probably; ***er kommt ~ morgen*** he is expected to arrive tomorrow
**Vo'rauszahlung** *f* advance payment
**'Vorbedeutung** *f* omen
**'Vorbedingung** *f* prerequisite
**Vorbehalt** ['foːɐbəhalt] *m* (-[*e*]*s*; *-e*) reservation; **'vorbehalten 1.** *v/t* (*irr*, ***halten***, *sep*, *no -ge-*, *h*) ***sich*** (***das Recht***) ***~ zu*** *inf* reserve the right to *inf*; **2.** *adj* reserved; **'vorbehaltlos 1.** *adj* unconditional; **2.** *adv* without reservation
**vor'bei** *adv time*: over, past; finished; gone; *space*: past, by; ***jetzt ist alles ~*** it's all over now; ***~!*** missed!; **~fahren** *v/i* (*irr*, ***fahren***, *sep*, *-ge-*, *sein*) go (*or* drive) past (***an*** *dat s.o. or s.th.*), pass (*s.o. or s.th.*); **~gehen** *v/i* (*irr*, ***gehen***, *sep*, *-ge-*, *sein*) walk past; *a. fig* go by, pass; *shot etc*: miss; **~kommen** *v/i* (*irr*, ***kommen***, *sep*, *-ge-*, *sein*) pass (***an*** *dat s.th.*); get past (*an obstacle etc*); F drop in (***bei j-m*** on s.o.); *fig* avoid; **~lassen** *v/t* (*irr*, ***lassen***, *sep*, *-ge-*, *h*) let *s.o.* pass
**'Vorbemerkung** *f* preliminary remark
**'vorbereiten** *v/t and v/refl* (*sep*, *no -ge-*, *h*) prepare (***auf*** *acc* for); **'Vorbereitung** *f* (-; *-en*) preparation (***auf*** *acc* for)
**'vorbestellen** *v/t* (*sep*, *no -ge-*, *h*) book (*or* order) in advance; reserve (*room*, *seat etc*); **'Vorbestellung** *f* (-; *-en*) advance booking; reservation
**'vorbestraft** *adj*: ***~ sein*** have a police record
**'vorbeugen** (*sep*, *-ge-*, *h*) **1.** *v/i* prevent (***e-r Sache*** s.th.); **2.** *v/refl* bend forward; **~d** *adj* preventive, MED *a.* prophylactic
**'Vorbeugung** *f* (-; *-en*) prevention
**'Vorbild** *n* model, pattern; (***j-m***) ***ein ~ sein*** set an example (to s.o.); ***sich j-n zum ~ nehmen*** follow s.o.'s example
**'vorbildlich** *adj* exemplary
**'Vorbildung** *f* education(al background)
**'vor|bringen** *v/t* (*irr*, ***bringen***, *sep*, *-ge-*, *h*) bring forward; say, state; **~da,tieren** *v/t* (*no -ge-*, *h*) antedate; postdate
**Vorder...** ['fɔrdɐ-] *in cpds ...achse*, *...rad*, *...sitz*, *...tür*, *...zahn etc*: front ...
**vordere** ['fɔrdərə] *adj* front
**'Vorder|grund** *m* foreground (*a. fig*); **~mann** *m*: ***mein ~*** the man *or* boy in front of me; **~seite** *f* front (side); head
**'vor|dränge(l)n** *v/refl* (*sep*, *-ge-*, *h*) cut into line, *Br* jump the queue; **~dringen** *v/i* (*irr*, ***dringen***, *sep*, *-ge-*, *sein*) advance; ***~*** (***bis***) ***zu*** work one's way through to (*a. fig*); **~dringlich 1.** *adj* (most) urgent; **2.** *adv*: ***et. ~ behandeln*** give s.th. priority
**'Vordruck** *m* (-[*e*]*s*; *-e*) form, blank
**'voreilig** *adj* hasty, rash, precipitate; ***~e Schlüsse ziehen*** jump to conclusions
**'voreingenommen** *adj* prejudiced, bias(s)ed; **'Voreingenommenheit** *f* (-; *no pl*) prejudice, bias
**'vorenthalten** *v/t* (*irr*, ***halten***, *sep*, *no -ge-*, *h*) keep back, withhold (*both*: ***j-m et.*** s.th. from s.o.)
**'Vorentscheidung** *f* preliminary decision
**'vorerst** *adv* for the present, for the time being
**Vorfahr** ['foːɐfaːɐ] *m* (*-en*; *-en*) ancestor
**'vorfahren** *v/i* (*irr*, ***fahren***, *sep*, *-ge-*, *sein*) drive up (*or* on); **'Vorfahrt** *f* (-; *no pl*) right of way, priority
**'Vorfall** *m* incident, occurrence, event
**'vor|fallen** *v/i* (*irr*, ***fallen***, *sep*, *-ge-*, *sein*) happen, occur; **~finden** *v/t* (*irr*, ***finden***, *sep*, *-ge-*, *h*) find
**'Vorfreude** *f* anticipation
**'vorführen** *v/t* (*sep*, *-ge-*, *h*) show, present; perform (*trick etc*); demonstrate; JUR bring (***j-m*** before s.o.); **'Vorführer** *m* demonstrator; **'Vorführung** *f* presentation, show(ing); performance; demonstration; JUR production
**'Vorführwagen** *m* MOT demonstrator, *Br* demonstration car
**'Vorgabe** *f* handicap
**'Vorgang** *m* event, occurrence, happening; file, record(s); BIOL, TECH process; ***e-n ~ schildern*** give an account of what happened; **Vorgänger(in)** ['foːɐgɛŋɐ (-ŋərɪn)] (*-s*; *-/-*; *-nen*) predecessor
**'Vorgarten** *m* front yard (*Br* garden)
**'vorgeben** *v/t* (*irr*, ***geben***, *sep*, *-ge-*, *h*)

V

SPORT give; *fig* use *s.th.* as a pretext
**'Vorgebirge** *n* foothills
**'vorgefasst** *adj* preconceived
**'vorgefertigt** *adj* prefabricated
**'Vorgefühl** *n* presentiment
**'vorgehen** *v/i* (*irr*, ***gehen***, *sep*, *-ge-*, *sein*) go on; come first; act; JUR sue (***gegen j-n*** s.o.); proceed; *watch*: be fast; **'Vorgehen** *n* (*-s*; *no pl*) procedure
**'vorgeschichtlich** *adj* prehistoric
**'Vor|geschmack** *m* foretaste (***auf*** *acc* of); **~gesetzte** *m, f* (*-n*; *-n*) superior, F boss
**'vorgestern** *adv* the day before yesterday
**'vorgreifen** *v/i* (*irr*, ***greifen***, *sep*, *-ge-*, *h*) anticipate *s.o. or s.th.*
**'vorhaben** *v/t* (*irr*, ***haben***, *sep*, *-ge-*, *h*) plan, intend; ***haben Sie heute Abend et. vor?*** have you anything on tonight?; ***was hat er jetzt wieder vor?*** what is he up to now?; **'Vorhaben** *n* (*-s*; -) plan(s), intention; TECH, ECON *a.* project
**'Vorhalle** *f* (entrance) hall, lobby
**'vorhalten** (*irr*, ***halten***, *sep*, *-ge-*, *h*) **1.** *v/t*: ***j-m et. ~*** hold s.th. in front of s.o.; *fig* blame s.o. for (doing) s.th.; **2.** *v/i* last; **'Vorhaltungen** *pl* reproaches; ***j-m ~ machen*** (***für et.***) reproach s.o. (with s.th., for being ...)
**'Vorhand** *f* (-; *no pl*) *tennis*: forehand
**vorhanden** [foːɐ'handən] *adj* available; in existence; ***~ sein*** exist; ***es ist nichts mehr ~*** there's nothing left; **Vor'handensein** *n* (*-s*; *no pl*) existence
**'Vorhang** *m* curtain
**'Vorhängeschloss** *n* padlock
**vor'her** *adv* before, earlier; in advance, beforehand
**vor'herbestimmen** *v/t* (*sep*, *no -ge-*, *h*) predetermine
**vorherig** [foːɐ'heːrɪç] *adj* previous
**'Vorherrschaft** *f* (-; *no pl*) predominance; **'vorherrschen** *v/i* (*sep*, *-ge-*, *h*) predominate, prevail; **'vorherrschend** *adj* predominant, prevailing
**vor'hersehbar** *adj* foreseeable
**vor'hersehen** *v/t* (*irr*, ***sehen***, *sep*, *-ge-*, *h*) foresee
**vor'hin** *adv* a (little) while ago
**'Vorhut** *f* (-; *-en*) MIL vanguard
**vorig** ['foːrɪç] *adj* last; former, previous
**vorjährig** ['foːɐjɛːrɪç] *adj* of last year, last year's ...

**'Vorkämpfer** *m*, **'Vorkämpferin** *f* champion, pioneer
**Vorkehrungen** ['foːɐkeːrʊŋən] *pl*: ***~ treffen*** take precautions
**'Vorkenntnisse** *pl* previous knowledge *or* experience (***in*** *dat* of)
**'vorkommen** *v/i* (*irr*, ***kommen***, *sep*, *-ge-*, *sein*) be found; happen; ***es kommt mir ... vor*** it seems ... to me
**'Vorkommen** *n* (*-s*; -) MIN deposit(s)
**Vorkommnis** ['foːɐkɔmnɪs] *n* (*-ses*; *-se*) occurrence, incident, event
**'Vorkriegs...** *in cpds* prewar ...
**'vorladen** *v/t* (*irr*, ***laden***, *sep*, *-ge-*, *h*) JUR summon; **'Vorladung** *f* (-; *-en*) JUR summons
**'Vorlage** *f* model; pattern; copy; presentation; PARL bill; *soccer etc*: pass
**'vorlassen** *v/t* (*irr*, ***lassen***, *sep*, *-ge-*, *h*) let *s.o.* go first; let *s.o.* pass; ***vorgelassen werden*** be admitted (***bei*** to)
**'Vorlauf** *m* *recorder*: fast-forward; SPORT (preliminary) heat; **'Vorläufer** *m* forerunner, precursor; **'vorläufig 1.** *adj* provisional, temporary; **2.** *adv* for the present, for the time being
**'vorlaut** *adj* pert, cheeky
**'Vorleben** *n* (*-s*; *no pl*) former life, past
**'vorlegen** *v/t* (*sep*, *-ge-*, *h*) present; produce; show
**'Vorleger** *m* (*-s*; -) rug; mat
**'vorlesen** *v/t* (*irr*, ***lesen***, *sep*, *-ge-*, *h*) read out (aloud); ***j-m et. ~*** read s.th. to s.o.; **'Vorlesung** *f* (-; *-en*) lecture (***über*** *acc* on; ***vor*** *dat* to); ***e-e ~ halten*** (give a) lecture
**'vorletzte** *adj* last but one; ***~ Nacht*** (***Woche***) the night (week) before last
**vor'lieb:** ***~ nehmen mit*** make do with
**'Vorliebe** *f* (-;*-n*) preference, special liking
**'vorliegen** *v/i* (*irr*, ***liegen***, *sep*, *-ge-*, *h*) ***es liegen*** (***keine***) ***... vor*** there are (no) ...; ***was liegt gegen ihn vor?*** what is he charged with?; **~d** *adj* present, in question
**'vor|lügen** *v/t* (*irr*, ***lügen***, *sep*, *-ge-*, *h*) ***j-m et. ~*** tell s.o. lies; **~machen** *v/t* (*sep*, *-ge-*, *h*) ***j-m et. ~*** show s.th. to s.o., show s.o. how to do s.th.; *fig* fool s.o.
**'Vormachtstellung** *f* supremacy
**'Vormarsch** *m* MIL advance (*a. fig*)
**'vormerken** *v/t* (*sep*, *-ge-*, *h*) ***j-n ~*** put s.o.'s name down

ˈ**Vormittag** *m* morning; ***heute ~*** this morning
ˈ**vormittags** *adv* in the morning; ***sonntags ~*** on Sunday mornings
ˈ**Vormund** *m* (-[*e*]*s*; -*e*) JUR guardian; **~schaft** *f* (-; -*en*) JUR guardianship
**vorn** [fɔrn] *adv* in front; ***nach ~*** forward; ***von ~*** from the front; from the beginning; ***j-n von ~(e) sehen*** see s.o.'s face; ***noch einmal von ~(e) (anfangen)*** (start) all over again
ˈ**Vorname** *m* first *or* Christian name, forename
**vornehm** [ˈfoːɐneːm] *adj* distinguished; noble; fashionable, exclusive, F smart, posh; ***die ~e Gesellschaft*** (high) society; ***~ tun*** put on airs
ˈ**vornehmen** *v/t* (*irr*, ***nehmen***, *sep*, -*ge*-, *h*) carry out, do; make (*changes etc*); ***sich et. ~*** decide *or* resolve to do s.th.; make plans for s.th.; ***sich fest vorgenommen haben zu*** *inf* have the firm intention to *inf*, be determined to *inf*
ˈ**vornherein** *adv*: ***von ~*** from the start *or* beginning
ˈ**Vorort** *m* suburb; **~(s)zug** *m* suburban *or* local *or* commuter train
ˈ**Vorposten** *m* outpost (*a.* MIL)
ˈ**vorprogramˌmieren** *v/t* (*sep*, *no* -*ge*-, *sein*) (pre)program(me); *fig* ***das war vorprogrammiert*** that was bound to happen
ˈ**Vorrang** *m* (-[*e*]*s*; *no pl*) precedence (***vor*** *dat* over), priority (over)
ˈ**Vorrat** *m* (-[*e*]*s*; -*räte*) store, stock, supply (*all*: ***an*** *dat* of); GASTR provisions; ECON resources, reserves; ***e-n ~ anlegen an*** (*dat*) stockpile; **vorrätig** [ˈfoːɐrɛːtɪç] *adj* available; ECON in stock
ˈ**Vorrecht** *n* privilege
ˈ**Vorredner** *m* previous speaker
ˈ**Vorrichtung** *f* TECH device
ˈ**vorrücken** (*sep*, -*ge*-) **1.** *v/t* (*h*) move forward; **2.** *v/i* (*sein*) advance
ˈ**Vorrunde** *f* SPORT preliminary round
ˈ**vorsagen** *v/i* (*sep*, -*ge*-, *h*) ***j-m ~*** prompt s.o.
ˈ**Vorsaiˌson** *f* off-peak season
ˈ**Vorsatz** *m* resolution; intention; JUR intent; **vorsätzlich** [ˈfoːɐzɛtslɪç] *adj* intentional; *esp* JUR wil(l)ful
ˈ**Vorschau** *f* preview (***auf*** *acc* of), *film*, TV *a.* trailer
ˈ**Vorschein** *m*: ***zum ~ bringen*** produce; *fig* bring out; ***zum ~ kommen*** appear; *fig* come to light
ˈ**vor|schieben** *v/t* (*irr*, ***schieben***, *sep*, -*ge*-, *h*) push forward; slip (*bolt*); *fig* use as a pretext; **~schießen** F *v/t* (*irr*, ***schießen***, *sep*, -*ge*-, *h*) advance (*money*)
ˈ**Vorschlag** *m* suggestion, proposal (*a.* PARL *etc*); ***den ~ machen*** → ˈ**vorschlagen** *v/t* (*irr*, ***schlagen***, *sep*, -*ge*-, *h*) suggest, propose
ˈ**Vorschlussrunde** *f* SPORT semifinal
ˈ**vorschnell** *adj* hasty, rash
ˈ**vorschreiben** *fig v/t* (*irr*, ***schreiben***, *sep*, -*ge*-, *h*) prescribe; tell; ***ich lasse mir nichts ~*** I won't be dictated to; ˈ**Vorschrift** *f* rule, regulation; instruction, direction; ***Dienst nach ~ machen*** work to rule
ˈ**vorschrifts|mäßig** *adj* correct, proper; **~widrig** *adj and adv* contrary to regulations
ˈ**Vorschub** *m*: ***~ leisten*** (*dat*) encourage; JUR aid and abet
ˈ**Vorschul...** *in cpds* pre-school ...
ˈ**Vorschule** *f* preschool
ˈ**Vorschuss** *m* advance
ˈ**vorschützen** *v/t* (*sep*, -*ge*-, *h*) use *s.th.* as a pretext
ˈ**vorsehen** (*irr*, ***sehen***, *sep*, -*ge*-, *h*) **1.** *v/t* plan; JUR provide; ***~ für*** intend (*or* designate) for; **2.** *v/refl* be careful, take care, watch out (***vor*** *dat* for)
ˈ**Vorsehung** *f* (-; *no pl*) providence
ˈ**vorsetzen** *v/t* (*sep*, -*ge*-, *h*) ***j-m et. ~*** put s.th. before s.o.; offer s.o. s.th.
ˈ**Vorsicht** *f* (-; *no pl*) caution, care; ***~!*** look *or* watch out!, (be) careful!; ***~, Stufe!*** mind the step!; ˈ**vorsichtig** *adj* careful, cautious; ˈ**vorsichtshalber** [-halbɐ] *adv* to be on the safe side; ˈ**Vorsichtsmaßnahme** *f* precaution, precautionary measure; ***~n treffen*** take precautions
ˈ**Vorsilbe** *f* LING prefix
ˈ**vorsingen** *v/t and v/i* (*irr*, ***singen***, *sep*, -*ge*-, *h*) ***j-m et. ~*** sing s.th. to s.o.; (have an) audition
ˈ**Vorsitz** *m* chair(manship), presidency; ***den ~ haben (übernehmen)*** be in (take) the chair, preside (***bei*** over, at)
ˈ**Vorsitzende** *m, f* (-*n*; -*n*) chairman (chairwoman), president
ˈ**Vorsorge** *f* (-; *no pl*) precaution; ***~ treffen*** take precautions; **~untersu-**

**chung** *f* MED preventive checkup
**'vorsorglich 1.** *adj* precautionary; **2.** *adv* as a precaution
**'Vorspann** *m* (-[*e*]*s*; -*e*) *film etc*: credits
**'Vorspeise** *f* hors d'œuvre, *Br* starter
**'Vorspiel** *n* MUS prelude (*a. fig*); foreplay; **'vorspielen** *v/t* (*sep*, -*ge*-, *h*) ***j-m et.*** **~** play s.th. to s.o.
**'vorsprechen** (*irr*, ***sprechen,*** *sep*, -*ge*-, *h*) **1.** *v/t* pronounce (***j-m*** for s.o.); **2.** *v/i* call (***bei*** at); THEA (have an) audition
**'vorspringen** *fig v/i* (*irr*, ***springen,*** *sep*, -*ge*-, *sein*) project, protrude (*both a.* ARCH); **'Vorsprung** *m* ARCH projection; SPORT lead; ***e-n ~ haben*** be leading (***von*** by); *esp fig* ***e-n ~ von zwei Jahren haben*** be two years ahead
**'Vorstadt** *f* suburb
**'Vorstand** *m* ECON board (of directors); managing committee (*of a club etc*)
**'vorstehen** *v/i* (*irr*, ***stehen,*** *sep*, -*ge*-, *h*) project, protrude
**'vorstellen** *v/t* (*sep*, -*ge*-, *h*) introduce (***sich*** o.s.; ***j-n j-m*** s.o. to s.o.); put *watch* forward (***um*** by); *fig* mean; ***sich et.*** (***j-n als ...***) **~** imagine s.th. (s.o. as ...); ***so stelle ich mir ... vor*** that's my idea of ...; ***sich ~ bei*** have an interview with *a firm etc*; **'Vorstellung** *f* (-; -*en*) introduction; interview; THEA performance, *film etc*: *a.* show; idea; expectation
**'Vorstellungs|kraft** *f* (-; *no pl*), **~vermögen** *n* (-*s*; *no pl*) imagination
**Vorstopper** ['foːɐʃtɔpɐ] *m* (-*s*; -) SPORT center (*Br* centre) back
**'Vorstoß** *m* MIL advance; *fig* attempt
**'Vorstrafe** *f* previous conviction
**'vorstrecken** *v/t* (*sep*, -*ge*-, *h*) advance (*money*)
**'Vorstufe** *f* preliminary stage
**'vortäuschen** *v/t* (*sep*, -*ge*-, *h*) feign, fake
**'Vorteil** *m* advantage (*a.* SPORT); benefit, profit; ***die ~e und Nachteile*** the pros and cons; **'vorteilhaft** *adj* advantageous, profitable; **'Vorteilsregel** *f* SPORT advantage rule
**Vortrag** ['foːɐtraːk] *m* (-[*e*]*s*; *Vorträge* ['foːɐtrɛːgə]) talk, *esp* UNIV lecture; MUS *etc* recital; ***e-n ~ halten*** give a talk *or* lecture (***vor*** *dat* to; ***über*** *acc* on)
**'vortragen** *v/t* (*irr*, ***tragen,*** *sep*, -*ge*-, *h*) express, state; MUS *etc* perform, play; recite (*poem etc*)
**'vortreten** *v/i* (*irr*, ***treten,*** *sep*, -*ge*-, *sein*) step forward; *fig* protrude, stick out
**'Vortritt** *m* (-[*e*]*s*; *no pl*) precedence; ***j-m den ~ lassen*** let s.o. go first
**vorüber** [fo'ryːbɐ] *adv*: ***~ sein*** be over; **~gehen** *v/i* (*irr*, ***gehen,*** *sep*, -*ge*-, *sein*) pass, go by; **~gehend** *adj* temporary
**'Vorübung** *f* preparatory exercise
**'Voruntersuchung** *f* JUR, MED preliminary examination
**'Vorurteil** *n* prejudice; **'vorurteilslos** *adj* unprejudiced, unbias(s)ed
**'Vorverkauf** *m* THEA advance booking
**'vorverlegen** *v/t* (*sep*, *no* -*ge*-, *h*) advance
**'Vorwahl** *f* TEL area (*Br* STD *or* dialling) code; POL primary, *Br* preliminary election
**'Vorwand** *m* pretext, excuse
**vorwärts** ['foːɐvɛrts] *adv* forward, on(ward), ahead; **~!** come on!, let's go!; ***~ kommen*** make headway (*a. fig*)
**vorweg** [foːɐ'vɛk] *adv* beforehand
**vor'wegnehmen** *v/t* (*irr*, ***nehmen,*** *sep*, -*ge*-, *h*) anticipate
**'vor|weisen** *v/t* (*irr*, ***weisen,*** *sep*, -*ge*-, *h*) produce, show; ***et. ~ können*** boast s.th.; **~werfen** *fig v/t* (*irr*, ***werfen,*** *sep*, -*ge*-, *h*) ***j-m et. ~*** reproach s.o. with s.th.
**'vorwiegend** *adv* predominantly, chiefly, mainly, mostly
**'vorwitzig** *adj* cheeky, pert
**'Vorwort** *n* (-[*e*]*s*; -*e*) foreword; preface
**'Vorwurf** *m* reproach; ***j-m Vorwürfe machen*** (***wegen***) reproach s.o. (for); **'vorwurfsvoll** *adj* reproachful
**'Vorzeichen** *n* omen, sign (*a.* MATH)
**'vorzeigen** *v/t* (*sep*, -*ge*-, *h*) show; produce
**'vorzeitig** *adj* premature, early
**'vorziehen** *v/t* (*irr*, ***ziehen,*** *sep*, -*ge*-, *h*) draw; *fig* prefer
**'Vorzimmer** *n* anteroom; outer office; *Austrian* → ***Hausflur***
**'Vorzug** *m* advantage; merit
**vorzüglich** [foːɐ'tsyːklɪç] *adj* excellent, exquisite
**'vorzugsweise** *adv* preferably
**Votum** ['voːtʊm] *n* (-*s*; -*ta*, -*ten*) vote
**VP** ABBR *of* ***Vollpension*** full board; (full) board and lodging
**vulgär** [vʊl'gɛːɐ] *adj* vulgar
**Vulkan** [vʊl'kaːn] *m* (-*s*; -*e*) volcano; **~ausbruch** *m* volcanic eruption
**vul'kanisch** *adj* volcanic

V

# W

**W** ABBR *of* ***West*(*en*)** W, west; ***Watt*** W, watt(s)
**Waage** ['va:gə] *f* (-; *-n*) scale(s *Br*); balance; ASTR Libra; ***sich die ~ halten*** balance each other; ***er ist* (*e-e*) ~** he's (a) Libra; **'waagerecht** *adj* horizontal
**Waagschale** ['va:k-] *f* scale
**Wabe** ['va:bə] *f* (-; *-n*) honeycomb
**wach** [vax] *adj* awake; ***~ werden*** wake (up), *esp fig* awake
**Wache** ['vaxə] *f* (-; *-n*) guard (*a.* MIL); sentry; MAR, MED *etc* watch; police station; ***~ haben*** be on guard (MAR watch); ***~ halten*** keep watch; **'wachen** *v/i* (*ge-, h*) (keep) watch (***über*** *acc* over)
**'Wachhund** *m* watchdog
**'Wachmann** *m* (-[*e*]*s*; *-männer, -leute*) watchman; *Austrian* → ***Polizist***
**Wacholder** [va'xɔldɐ] *m* (-*s*; -) BOT juniper
**'wach|rufen** *v/t* (*irr*, ***rufen***, *sep, -ge-, h*) call up, evoke; **~rütteln** *v/t* (*sep, -ge-, h*) rouse (*a. fig*)
**Wachs** [vaks] *n* (-*es*; -*e*) wax
**wachsam** ['vaxza:m] *adj* watchful, on one's guard, vigilant; **'Wachsamkeit** *f* (-; *no pl*) watchfulness, vigilance
**wachsen¹** ['vaksən] *v/i* (*irr, ge-, sein*) grow (*a.* ***sich ~ lassen***), *fig a.* increase
**'wachsen²** *v/t* (*ge-, h*) wax
**'Wachs|fi͵gurenkabi͵nett** *n* waxworks; **~tuch** *n* oilcloth
**'Wachstum** *n* (-*s*; *no pl*) growth, *fig a.* increase
**Wachtel** ['vaxtəl] *f* (-; *-n*) ZO quail
**Wächter** ['vɛçtɐ] *m* (-*s*; -) guard
**'Wachtmeister** *m* (-*s*; *no pl*) patrolman, *Br* (police) constable
**'Wach(t)turm** *m* watchtower
**wackelig** ['vakəlɪç] *adj* shaky (*a. fig*); loose (*tooth*); **'wackeln** *v/i* (*ge-, h*) shake; *table etc*: wobble; *tooth*: be loose; PHOT move; ***~ mit*** waggle
**Wade** ['va:də] *f* (-; *-n*) ANAT calf
**Waffe** ['vafə] *f* (-; *-n*) weapon (*a. fig*), *pl a.* arms
**Waffel** ['vafəl] *f* (-; *-n*) waffle; wafer
**'Waffen|gewalt** *f*: ***mit ~*** by force of arms; **~schein** *m* gun license (*Br* licence); **~stillstand** *m* armistice (*a. fig*); truce
**wagen** ['va:gən] *v/t* (*ge-, h*) dare; risk; ***sich ~*** venture
**'Wagen** *m* (-*s*; -) MOT car; RAIL car, *Br* carriage
**wägen** ['vɛ:gən] *lit v/t* (*irr, ge-, h*) weigh (*one's words etc*)
**'Wagen|heber** *m* TECH jack; **~ladung** *f* cartload
**Waggon** [va'gõ:] *m* (-*s*; -*s*) (railroad) car, *Br* (railway) carriage; freight car, *Br* goods waggon
**Wagnis** ['va:knɪs] *n* (-*ses*; -*se*) venture, risk
**Wa'gon** *m* → ***Waggon***
**Wahl** [va:l] *f* (-; *-en*) choice; alternative; selection; POL election; voting, poll; vote; ***die ~ haben*** (***s-e ~ treffen***) have the (make one's) choice; ***keine*** (***andere***) ***~ haben*** have no choice *or* alternative; **'wahlberechtigt** *adj* POL entitled to vote; **'Wahlbeteiligung** *f* POL poll, (voter) turnout; ***hohe*** (***niedrige***) **~** heavy (light) poll; **'Wahlbezirk** *m* → ***Wahlkreis***
**wählen** ['vɛ:lən] *v/t and v/i* (*ge-, h*) choose, pick, select; POL vote (for); elect; TEL dial; **'Wähler** *m* (-*s*; -) voter
**'Wahlergebnis** *n* election result
**wählerisch** ['vɛ:lərɪʃ] *adj* F picky (***in*** *dat* about), *esp Br* choos(e)y
**'Wählerschaft** *f* (-; *-en*) electorate, voters
**'Wahl|fach** *n* PED *etc* elective, optional subject; **~ka͵bine** *f* voting (*esp Br* polling) booth; **~kampf** *m* election campaign; **~kreis** *m* electoral district, *Br* constituency; **~lo͵kal** *n* polling place (*Br* station)
**'wahllos** *adj* indiscriminate
**'Wahl|pro͵gramm** *n* election platform; **~recht** *n* (-[*e*]*s*; *no pl*) (right to) vote, suffrage, franchise; **~rede** *f* election speech
**'Wählscheibe** *f* TEL dial
**'Wahl|sieg** *m* election victory; **~sieger** *m* election winner; **~spruch** *m* motto; **~urne** *f* ballot box; **~versammlung** *f* election rally

**'Wahnsinn** *m* (-[*e*]*s*; *no pl*) madness (*a.* F), insanity
**'wahnsinnig 1.** *adj* mad (*a.* F), insane, F *a.* crazy; F awful, terrible; **2.** F *adv* terribly, awfully; madly (*in love*)
**'Wahnsinnige** *m*, *f* (-*n*; -*n*) madman (madwoman), lunatic, maniac (*all a.* F)
**'Wahnvorstellung** *f* delusion, hallucination
**wahr** [va:ɐ] *adj* true; real; genuine
**wahren** ['va:rən] *v/t* (*ge-*, *h*) protect; ***den Schein ~*** keep up appearances
**während** ['vɛ:rənt] **1.** *prp* (*gen*) during; **2.** *cj* while; whereas
**'wahrhaft, wahr'haftig** *adv* really, truly
**'Wahrheit** *f* (-; -*en*) truth
**'wahrheits|gemäß, ~getreu** *adj* true, truthful; **~liebend** *adj* truthful
**wahrnehmbar** ['va:ɐne:mba:ɐ] *adj* noticeable, perceptible; **'wahrnehmen** *v/t* (*irr*, ***nehmen***, *sep*, *-ge-*, *h*) perceive, notice; seize, take (*chance etc*); look after (*s.o.'s interests etc*); **'Wahrnehmung** *f* (-; -*en*) perception
**'wahrsagen** *v/i* (sep, -ge-, h) ***j-m ~*** tell s.o. his fortune; ***sich ~ lassen*** have one's fortune told; **'Wahrsager** [-za:gɐ] *m* (-*s*; -), **'Wahrsagerin** [-za:gərɪn] *f* (-; -*nen*) fortune-teller
**wahr'scheinlich 1.** *adj* probable, likely; **2.** *adv* probably, (very *or* most) likely; ***~ gewinnt er*** (***nicht***) he is (not) likely to win; **Wahr'scheinlichkeit** *f* (-; -*en*) probability, likelihood
**Währung** ['vɛ:rʊŋ] *f* (-; -*en*) currency
**'Währungs...** *in cpds ...politik, ...reform etc*: monetary ...
**'Wahrzeichen** *n* landmark
**Waise** ['vaizə] *f* (-; -*n*) orphan; ***~ werden*** be orphaned
**'Waisenhaus** *n* orphanage
**Wal** [va:l] *m* (-[*e*]*s*; -*e*) ZO whale
**Wald** [valt] *m* (-[*e*]*s*; *Wälder* ['vɛldɐ]) wood(s), forest; **~brand** *m* forest fire
**'waldreich** *adj* wooded
**'Waldsterben** *n* dying of forests
**'Walfang** *m* whaling
**'Walfänger** *m* whaler
**Walkman®** *m* (-*s*; -*men*) personal stereo, Walkman®
**Wall** [val] *m* (-[*e*]*s*; *Wälle* ['vɛlə]) mound; MIL rampart
**Wallach** ['valax] *m* (-[*e*]*s*; -*e*) ZO gelding
**wallen** ['valən] *v/i* (*ge-*, *sein*) flow
**'Wallfahrer** *m*, **'Wallfahrerin** *f* pilgrim
**'Wallfahrt** *f* pilgrimage
**'Walnuss** *f* BOT walnut
**'Walross** *n* ZO walrus
**Walze** ['valtsə] *f* (-; -*n*) roller; cylinder; TECH, MUS barrel
**'walzen** *v/t* (*ge-*, *h*) roll (*a.* TECH)
**wälzen** ['vɛltsən] *v/t* (*ge-*, *h*) roll (*a.* **sich ~**); *fig* turn *s.th.* over in one's mind
**Walzer** ['valtsɐ] *m* (-*s*; -) MUS waltz (*a.* ***~ tanzen***)
**wand** [vant] *pret of* ***winden***
**Wand** *f* (-; *Wände* ['vɛndə]) wall, *fig a.* barrier
**Wandale** [van'da:lə] *m* (-*n*; -*n*) vandal; **Wandalismus** [vanda'lɪsmʊs] *m* (-; *no pl*) vandalism
**Wandel** ['vandəl] *m* (-*s*; *no pl*), **'wandeln** *v/t and v/refl* (*ge-*, *h*) change
**Wanderer** ['vandərɐ] *m* (-*s*; -), **'Wanderin** *f* (-; -*nen*) hiker
**wandern** ['vandɐn] *v/i* (*ge-*, *sein*) hike; ramble (about); *eyes etc*: roam, wander
**'Wander|po,kal** *m* challenge cup; **~preis** *m* challenge trophy; **~schuhe** *pl* walking shoes; **~tag** *m* (school) outing *or* excursion
**'Wanderung** *f* (-; -*en*) walking tour, hike; ZO *etc* migration
**'Wand|gemälde** *n* mural; **~ka,lender** *m* wall calendar; **~karte** *f* wallchart
**Wandlung** ['vandlʊŋ] *f* (-; -*en*) change
**'Wand|schrank** *m* closet, *Br* built-in cupboard; **~tafel** *f* blackboard
**wandte** ['vantə] *pret of* ***wenden***
**'Wandteppich** *m* tapestry
**Wange** ['vaŋə] *f* (-; -*n*) ANAT cheek
**Wankelmotor** ['vaŋkəl-] *m* rotary piston *or* Wankel engine
**wankelmütig** ['vaŋkəlmy:tɪç] *adj* fickle
**wanken** ['vaŋkən] *v/i* (*ge-*, *sein*) stagger, reel; *fig* rock
**wann** [van] *interr adv* when, (at) what time; ***seit ~?*** (for) how long?, since when?
**Wanne** ['vanə] *f* (-; -*n*) tub (*a.* F); bath(tub)
**Wanze** ['vantsə] *f* (-; -*n*) ZO bug (*a.* F)
**Wapitihirsch** [va'pi:ti-] *m* ZO elk
**Wappen** ['vapən] *n* (-*s*; -) (coat of) arms
**'Wappenkunde** *f* heraldry
**wappnen** ['vapnən] *fig v/refl* (*ge-*, *h*) arm o.s.

**war** [vaːɐ] *pret of* ***sein***[1]
**warb** [varp] *pret of* ***werben***
**Ware** ['vaːrə] *f* (-; *-n*) *coll mst* goods; article; product
'**Waren|haus** *n* department store; **~lager** *n* stock; **~probe** *f* sample; **~zeichen** *n* trademark
**warf** [varf] *pret of* ***werfen***
**warm** [varm] *adj* warm (*a. fig*); GASTR hot; ***schön*** ~ nice and warm; ~ ***halten*** keep warm; ~ ***machen*** warm (up)
**Wärme** ['vɛrmə] *f* (-; *no pl*) warmth; PHYS heat; **~iso,lierung** *f* heat insulation
'**wärmen** *v/t* (*ge-*, *h*) warm
'**Wärmflasche** *f* hot-water bottle
'**warmherzig** *adj* warm-hearted
**Warm'wasser|bereiter** *m* (*-s*; -) water heater; **~versorgung** *f* hot-water supply
'**Warn|blinkanlage** *f* MOT warning flasher; **~dreieck** *n* MOT warning triangle
**warnen** ['varnən] *v/t* (*ge-*, *h*) warn (***vor*** *dat* of, against); ***j-n davor ~, et. zu tun*** warn s.o. not to do s.th.
'**Warn|schild** *n* danger sign; **~sig,nal** *n* warning signal; **~streik** *m* token strike
'**Warnung** *f* (-; *-en*) warning
**warten**[1] ['vartən] *v/i* (*ge-*, *h*) wait (***auf*** *acc* for); *j-n* ~ ***lassen*** keep *s.o.* waiting
'**warten**[2] *v/t* (*ge-*, *h*) TECH service, maintain
**Wärter** ['vɛrtɐ] *m* (*-s*; -), '**Wärterin** *f* (-; *-nen*) attendant; ZO keeper
'**Warte|liste** *f* waiting list; **~saal** *m*, **~zimmer** *n* waiting room
'**Wartung** *f* (-; *-en*) TECH maintenance
**warum** [va'rʊm] *interr adv* why
**Warze** ['vartsə] *f* (-; *-n*) MED wart
**was** [vas] **1.** *interr pron* what; ~ ***gibt's?*** what is it?, F what's up?; what's for lunch *etc*?; ~ ***soll's?*** so what?; ~ ***machen Sie?*** what are you doing?; what do you do?; ~ ***kostet ...?*** how much is ...?; ~ ***für ...?*** what kind *or* sort of ...?; ~ ***für e-e Farbe*** (***Größe***)***?*** what colo(u)r (size)?; ~ ***für ein Unsinn*** what nonsense!; ~ ***für e-e gute Idee!*** what a good idea!; **2.** *rel pron* what; ~ (***auch***) ***immer*** whatever; ***alles, ~ ich habe*** (***brauche***) all I have (need); ***ich weiß nicht, ~ ich tun*** (***sagen***) ***soll*** I don't know what to do (say); ***..., ~ mich ärgerte*** ..., which made me angry; **3.** F *indef pron* → ***etwas***
**waschbar** ['vaʃbaːɐ] *adj* washable
'**Waschbecken** *n* washbowl, *Br* washbasin
**Wäsche** ['vɛʃə] *f* (-; *-n*) a) washing, b) (*no pl*) laundry; linen; underwear; ***in der ~*** in the wash; ***schmutzige ~ waschen*** wash one's dirty linen in public
'**waschecht** *adj* washable; fast (*color*); *fig* trueborn, genuine
'**Wäsche|klammer** *f* clothespin, *Br* clothes peg; **~leine** *f* clothesline
**waschen** ['vaʃən] *v/t and v/refl* (*irr*, *ge-*, *h*) wash; ***sich die Haare*** (***Hände***) ~ wash one's hair (hands)
**Wäscherei** [vɛʃə'rai] *f* (-; *-en*) laundry
'**Wasch|lappen** *m* washcloth, *Br* flannel, facecloth; **~ma,schine** *f* washing machine, F washer
'**waschma,schinenfest** *adj* machine-washable
**Wasch|mittel** *n*, **~pulver** *n* washing powder; **~raum** *m* lavatory, washroom; **~sa,lon** *m* laundromat, *Br* launderette; **~straße** *f* MOT car wash
**Wasser** ['vasɐ] *n* (*-s*; -) water; **~ball** *m* beach ball; SPORT water polo; **~bett** *n* water bed; **~dampf** *m* steam
'**wasserdicht** *adj* waterproof; *esp* MAR watertight (*a. fig*)
'**Wasser|fall** *m* waterfall; falls; **~farbe** *f* water colo(u)r; **~flugzeug** *n* seaplane; **~graben** *m* SPORT water jump; **~hahn** *m* tap, faucet
**wässerig** ['vɛsərɪç] *adj* watery; ***j-m den Mund ~ machen*** make s.o.'s mouth water
'**Wasser|kessel** *m* kettle; **~klo,sett** *n* water closet, W.C.; **~kraft** *f* (-; *no pl*) water power; **~kraftwerk** *n* hydroelectric power station *or* plant; **~lauf** *m* watercourse; **~leitung** *f* waterpipe(s); **~mangel** *m* (*-s*; *no pl*) water shortage; **~mann** *m* (*-[e]s*; *no pl*) ASTR Aquarius; ***er ist*** (***ein***) ~ he's (an) Aquarius
'**wassern** *v/i* (*ge-*, *h*) AVIAT touch down on water; *spacecraft*: splash down
**wässern** ['vɛsɐn] *v/t* (*ge-*, *h*) water; AGR irrigate; GASTR soak; PHOT rinse
'**Wasserpflanze** *f* BOT aquatic plant
'**Wasserrohr** *n* TECH water pipe
'**Wasserscheide** *f* GEOGR watershed
'**wasserscheu** *adj* afraid of water

**'Wasser|ski 1.** *m* water ski; **2.** *n* (*-s; no pl*) water skiing; ~ ***fahren*** water-ski; **~spiegel** *m* water level; **~sport** *m* water *or* aquatic sports, aquatics; **~spülung** *f* TECH flushing cistern; ***Toilette mit*** ~ (flush) toilet, W.C.; **~stand** *m* water level; **~stoff** *m* (*-[e]s; no pl*) CHEM hydrogen; **~stoffbombe** *f* MIL hydrogen bomb, H-bomb; **~strahl** *m* jet of water; **~straße** *f* waterway; **~tier** *n* aquatic animal; **~verschmutzung** *f* water pollution; **~versorgung** *f* water supply; **~waage** *f* (*Br* spirit) level; **~weg** *m* waterway; ***auf dem*** ~ by water; **~welle** *f* water wave; **~werk(e** *pl*) *n* waterworks; **~zeichen** *n* watermark

**waten** ['va:tən] *v/i* (*ge-, sein*) wade

**watscheln** ['va:tʃəln] *v/i* (*ge-, sein*) waddle

**Watt¹** [vat] *n* (*-s; -*) ELECTR watt

**Watt²** *n* (*-[e]s; -en*) GEOGR mud flats

**Watte** ['vatə] *f* (*-; -n*) cotton wool

**wattiert** [va'ti:ɐt] *adj* padded; quilted

**weben** ['ve:bən] *v/t and v/i* (*[irr,] ge-, h*) weave; **Weber** ['ve:bɐ] *m* (*-s; -*) weaver; **Weberei** [ve:bə'rai] *f* (*-; -en*) weaving mill; **'Weberin** *f* (*-; -nen*) weaver; **Webstuhl** ['ve:p-] *m* loom

**Wechsel** ['vɛksəl] *m* (*-s; -*) change; exchange; ECON bill of exchange; allowance; **'Wechselgeld** *n* (small) change

**wechselhaft** *adj* changeable

**'Wechseljahre** *pl* MED menopause

**'Wechselkurs** *m* ECON exchange rate

**'wechseln** *v/t and v/i* (*ge-, h*) change; exchange; vary; **~d** *adj* varying

**'wechselseitig** [-zaitɪç] *adj* mutual, reciprocal

**'Wechsel|strom** *m* ELECTR alternating current; **~stube** *f* ECON exchange office; **~wirkung** *f* interaction

**wecken** ['vɛkən] *v/t* (*ge-, h*) wake (up), F call; *fig* awaken (*memories etc*); rouse (*s.o.'s curiosity etc*)

**Wecker** ['vɛkɐ] *m* (*-s; -*) alarm (clock)

**wedeln** ['ve:dəln] *v/i* (*ge-, h*) wave (***mit et.*** s.th.); *skiing*: wedel; ***mit dem Schwanz*** ~ wag its tail

**weder** ['ve:dɐ] *cj*: ~ ***... noch ...*** neither ... nor ...

**Weg** [ve:k] *m* (*-[e]s; -e* ['ve:gə]) way (*a. fig*); road (*a. fig*); path; route; walk; ***auf friedlichem*** (***legalem***) **~e** by peaceful (legal) means; ***j-m aus dem*** ~ ***gehen*** get (*fig* keep) out of s.o.'s way; ***j-n aus dem*** ~ ***räumen*** put s.o. out of the way; ***vom*** ~ ***abkommen*** lose one's way; → ***halb***

**weg** [vɛk] *adv* away; gone; off; F in raptures (***von*** over, about); ***Finger*** **~!** (keep your) hands off!; ***nichts wie*** **~!** let's get out of here!; F ~ ***sein*** be out; **~bleiben** F *v/i* (*irr,* ***bleiben,*** *sep, -ge-, sein*) stay away; be left out; **~bringen** F *v/t* (*irr,* ***bringen,*** *sep, -ge-, h*) take away; ~ ***von*** get *s.o.* away from

**wegen** ['ve'gən] *prp* (*gen*) because of; for the sake of; due *or* owing to; JUR for

**wegfahren** ['vɛk-] (*irr,* ***fahren,*** *sep, -ge-*) **1.** *v/i* (*sein*) leave; **2.** *v/t* (*h*) take away, remove

**'wegfallen** *v/i* (*irr,* ***fallen,*** *sep, -ge-, sein*) be dropped; stop, be stopped

**Weggang** ['vɛk-] *m* (*-[e]s; no pl*) leaving;

**'weggehen** *v/i* (*irr,* ***gehen,*** *sep, -ge-, sein*) go away (*a. fig*), leave; *stain etc*: come off; ECON sell

**weg|jagen** ['vɛk-] *v/t* (*sep, -ge-, h*) drive *or* chase away; **~kommen** F *v/i* (*irr,* ***kommen,*** *sep, -ge-, sein*) get away; get lost; ***gut*** ~ come off well; ***mach, dass du wegkommst!*** get out of here!, *sl* get lost!; **~lassen** *v/t* (*irr,* ***lassen,*** *sep, -ge-, h*) let *s.o.* go; leave *s.th.* out; **~laufen** *v/i* (*irr,* ***laufen,*** *sep, -ge-, sein*) run away ([***vor***] ***j-m*** from s.o.) (*a. fig*); **~legen** *v/t* (*sep, -ge-, h*) put away; **~nehmen** *v/t* (*irr,* ***nehmen,*** *sep, -ge-, h*) take away (***von*** from); take up (*room, time*); steal (*a. s.o.'s girlfriend etc*); ***j-m et.*** ~ take s.th. (away) from s.o.; **~räumen** *v/t* (*sep, -ge-, h*) clear away, remove; **~schaffen** *v/t* (*sep, -ge-, h*) remove; **~schicken** *v/t* (*sep, -ge-, h*) send away *or* off; **~sehen** *v/i* (*irr,* ***sehen,*** *sep, -ge-, h*) look away; **~setzen** *v/t* (*sep, -ge-, h*) move

**Wegweiser** ['ve:kvaizɐ] *m* (*-s; -*) signpost; *fig* guide

**Wegwerf...** ['vɛkvɛrf-] *in cpds ...geschirr, ...besteck, ...rasierer etc*: throwaway ..., disposable ...; *...flasche etc*: non-returnable ...; **'wegwerfen** *v/t* (*irr,* ***werfen,*** *sep, -ge-, h*) throw away

**weg|wischen** ['vɛk-] *v/t* (*sep, -ge-, h*) wipe off; **~ziehen** (*irr,* ***ziehen,*** *sep, -ge-*) **1.** *v/i* (*sein*) move away; **2.** *v/t* (*h*) pull away

**weh** [veː] *adv*: ~ ***tun*** → ***wehtun***
**wehen** ['veːən] *v/i* (*ge-*, *h*) blow; wave
'**Wehen** *pl* MED labo(u)r
**wehmütig** ['veːmyːtɪç] *adj* melancholy; wistful
**Wehr**[1] [veːɐ] *n* (-[*e*]*s*; -*e* ['veːrə]) weir
**Wehr**[2] *f*: ***sich zur ~ setzen*** → ***wehren***
'**Wehrdienst** *m* (-[*e*]*s*; *no pl*) military service; **~verweigerer** *m* (-*s*; -) conscientious objector
**wehren** ['veːrən] *v/refl* (*ge-*, *h*) defend o.s. (***gegen*** against), fight (*a. fig* ***gegen et.*** s.th.); '**wehrlos** *adj* defenseless, *Br* defenceless; *fig* helpless
'**Wehrpflicht** *f* (-; *no pl*) compulsory military service; '**wehrpflichtig** *adj* liable to military service; '**Wehrpflichtige** *m* (-*n*; -*n*) draftee, *Br* conscript
'**wehtun** hurt (***j-m*** s.o.; *fig* s.o.'s feelings); be aching; ***sich*** (***am Finger***) ~ hurt o.s. (hurt one's finger)
**Weib** [vaip] *n* (-[*e*]*s*; -*er* ['vaibɐ]) *contp* woman; bitch; '**Weibchen** *n* (-*s*; -) ZO female; **weibisch** ['vaibɪʃ] *adj* effeminate, F sissy; '**weiblich** *adj* female; feminine (*a.* LING)
**weich** [vaiç] *adj* soft (*a. fig*), tender; GASTR done; soft-boiled (*egg*); ~ ***werden*** soften; *fig* give in; F ***j-n ~ machen*** soften s.o. up
**Weiche** ['vaiçə] *f* (-; -*n*) RAIL switch, points
**weichen** ['vaiçən] *v/i* (*irr*, *ge-*, *sein*) give way (*dat* to), yield (to); go (away)
'**weichlich** *adj* soft, effeminate, F sissy
'**Weichling** *m* (-*s*; -*e*) weakling, F softy, sissy
'**Weichspüler** *m* (-*s*; -) fabric softener
'**Weichtier** *n* ZO mollusk, *Br* mollusc
**Weide**[1] ['vaidə] *f* (-; -*n*) BOT willow
'**Weide**[2] *f* (-; -*n*) AGR pasture; ***auf die*** (***der***) ~ to (at) pasture; '**Weideland** *n* pasture(land), range; '**weiden** *v/t and v/i* (*ge-*, *h*) graze, pasture; *fig* ***sich ~ an*** (*dat*) feast on; *contp* gloat over
**weigern** ['vaigɐn] *v/refl* (*ge-*, *h*) refuse
**Weigerung** ['vaigərʊŋ] *f* (-; -*en*) refusal
**Weihe** ['vaiə] *f* (-; -*n*) REL consecration; ordination; '**weihen** *v/t* (*ge-*, *h*) consecrate; ***zum Priester*** ~ ordain *s.o.* priest
**Weiher** ['vaiɐ] *m* (-*s*; -) pond
**Weihnachten** ['vainaxtən] *n* (-; -) Christmas, F Xmas
'**Weihnachts|abend** *m* Christmas Eve; **~baum** *m* Christmas tree; **~einkäufe** *pl* Christmas shopping; **~geschenk** *n* Christmas present; **~lied** *n* (Christmas) carol; **~mann** *m* Father Christmas, Santa Claus; **~markt** *m* Christmas fair; **~tag** *m* Christmas Day; ***zweiter*** ~ day after Christmas, *esp Br* Boxing Day; **~zeit** *f* Christmas season
'**Weih|rauch** *m* REL incense; **~wasser** *n* (-*s*; *no pl*) REL holy water
**weil** [vail] *cj* because; since, as
'**Weilchen** *n*: ***ein*** ~ a little while
**Weile** ['vailə] *f*: ***e-e*** ~ a while
**Wein** [vain] *m* (-[*e*]*s*; -*e*) wine; BOT vine; **~(an)bau** *m* (-[*e*]*s*; *no pl*) wine growing; **~beere** *f* grape; **~berg** *m* vineyard; **~brand** *m* brandy
**weinen** ['vainən] *v/i* (*ge-*, *h*) cry (***vor*** *dat* with; ***nach*** for; ***wegen*** about, over); weep (***um*** for, over; ***über*** *acc* at; ***vor*** *dat* for, with); **weinerlich** ['vainɐlɪç] *adj* tearful; whining
'**Wein|fass** *n* wine cask *or* barrel; **~flasche** *f* wine bottle; **~händler** *m* wine merchant; **~hauer** *Austrian m* → ***Winzer***; **~karte** *f* wine list; **~keller** *m* wine cellar *or* vault, vaults; **~kellerei** *f* winery; **~kenner** *m* wine connoisseur; **~lese** *f* vintage; **~presse** *f* wine press; **~probe** *f* wine tasting; **~rebe** *f* BOT vine
'**weinrot** *adj* claret
'**Weinstock** *m* BOT vine
'**Weintraube** *f* → ***Traube***
**weise** ['vaizə] *adj* wise
'**Weise** *f* (-; -*n*) way; MUS tune; ***auf diese*** (***die gleiche***) ~ this (the same) way; ***auf m-e*** (***s-e***) ~ my (his) way
**weisen** ['vaizən] *v/t and v/i* (*irr*, *ge-*, *h*) show; ***j-n von der Schule*** ~ expel s.o. from school; ~ ***auf*** (*acc*) point to *or* at; ***von sich*** ~ reject; repudiate
**Weisheit** ['vaishait] *f* (-; -*en*) wisdom; ***mit s-r ~ am Ende sein*** be at one's wit's end
'**Weisheitszahn** *m* wisdom tooth
**weismachen** ['vais-] F *v/t*: ***j-m ~, dass*** make s.o. believe that; ***du kannst mir nichts*** ~ you can't fool me
**weiß** [vais] *adj* white; ~ ***werden*** *or* ***machen*** whiten; '**Weißbrot** *n* white bread; '**Weiße** *m, f* (-*n*; -*n*) white, white man (woman), *pl the* whites

**'weißen** *v/t* (*ge-*, *h*) whitewash

**'Weißkohl** *m*, **'Weißkraut** *n* BOT (green, *Br* white) cabbage

**'weißlich** *adj* whitish

**'Weißwein** *m* white wine

**Weisung** ['vaizʊŋ] *f* (-; *-en*) instruction, directive

**weit** [vait] **1.** *adj* wide, *clothes*: *a.* big; long (*way*, *trip etc*); **2.** *adv* far, a long way (*a. time and fig*); ~ ***weg*** far away (***von*** from); ***von*** ~***em*** from a distance; ~ ***und breit*** far and wide; ***bei*** ~***em*** by far; ***bei*** ~***em nicht so ...*** not nearly as ...; ~ ***über*** (*acc*) well over; ~ ***besser*** far *or* much better; ***zu*** ~ ***gehen*** go too far; ***es*** ~ ***bringen*** go far; ***wir haben es*** ~ ***gebracht*** we have come a long way; ~ ***blickend*** *fig* farsighted; ~ ***reichend*** far-reaching; ~ ***verbreitet*** widespread

**'weit'ab** *adv* far away (***von*** from)

**'weit'aus** *adv* (by) far, much

**Weite** ['vaitə] *f* (-; *-n*) width; vastness, expanse; *esp* SPORT distance

**'weiten** *v/t and v/refl* (*ge-*, *h*) widen

**weiter** ['vaitɐ] *adv* on, further; (***mach***) ~***!*** go on!; (***geh***) ~***!*** move on!; ***und so*** ~ and so on *or* forth, et cetera; ***nichts*** ~ nothing else; **~arbeiten** *v/i* (*sep*, *-ge-*, *h*) go on working; **~bilden** *v/refl* (*sep*, *-ge-*, *h*) improve one's knowledge; continue one's education *or* training

**'Weiterbildung** *f* (-; *no pl*) further education *or* training

**weitere** ['vaitərə] *adj* further, additional; ***alles Weitere*** the rest; ***bis auf*** ~***s*** until further notice; ***ohne*** ~***s*** easily; ***Weiteres*** more, (further) details

**'weiter|geben** *v/t* (*irr*, ***geben***, *sep*, *-ge-*, *h*) pass (*dat*, ***an*** *acc* to) (*a. fig*); **~gehen** *v/i* (*irr*, ***gehen***, *sep*, *-ge-*, *sein*) move on; *fig* continue, go on

**'weiter'hin** *adv* further(more); ***et.*** ~ ***tun*** go on doing s.th., continue to do s.th.

**'weiter|kommen** *v/i* (*irr*, ***kommen***, *sep*, *-ge-*, *sein*) get on (*fig* in life); **~leben** *v/i* (*sep*, *-ge-*, *h*) live on, *fig a.* survive; **~machen** *v/t and v/i* (*sep*, *-ge-*, *h*) go *or* carry on, continue

**'Weiterverkauf** *m* resale

**'weit|gehend** **1.** *adj* considerable; **2.** *adv* largely; **~läufig** *adj* spacious; distant (*relative*); **~sichtig** *adj* MED farsighted (*a. fig*), *Br* longsighted

**'Weitsprung** *m* broad (*Br* long) jump

**'Weitwinkelobjek,tiv** *n* PHOT wide-angle lens

**Weizen** ['vaitsən] *m* (*-s*; -) BOT wheat

**welche** ['vɛlçə], **welcher** ['vɛlçɐ], **welches** ['vɛlçəs] **1.** *interr pron* what, which; ***welcher?*** which one?; ***welcher von beiden?*** which of the two?; **2.** *rel pron* who, that; which, that; **3.** F ***welche*** *indef pron* some, any

**welk** [vɛlk] *adj* faded, withered; flabby

**welken** ['vɛlkən] *v/i* (*ge-*, *sein*) fade, wither

**Wellblech** ['vɛl-] *n* corrugated iron

**Welle** ['vɛlə] *f* (-; *-n*) wave (*a.* PHYS *and fig*); TECH shaft; **'wellen** *v/t and v/refl* (*ge-*, *h*) wave

**'Wellenlänge** *f* ELECTR wavelength

**'Wellensittich** [-zɪtɪç] *m* (*-s*; *-e*) ZO budgerigar, F budgie

**wellig** ['vɛlɪç] *adj* wavy

**Welt** [vɛlt] *f* (-; *-en*) world; ***die ganze*** ~ the whole world; ***auf der ganzen*** ~ all over *or* throughout the world; ***das beste*** *etc* ***... der*** ~ the best *etc* ... in the world, the world's best *etc* ...; ***zur*** ~ ***kommen*** be born; ***zur*** ~ ***bringen*** give birth to

**'Weltall** *n* universe

**'weltberühmt** *adj* world-famous

**Weltergewicht** ['vɛltɐ-] *n* (-[*e*]*s*; *no pl*), **'Weltergewichtler** *m* (*-s*; -) SPORT welterweight

**'weltfremd** *adj* naive, unrealistic

**'Weltfriede(n)** *m* world peace

**'Weltgeschichte** *f* world history

**'weltklug** *adj* worldlywise

**'Weltkrieg** *m* world war; ***der Zweite*** ~ World War II

**'Weltkugel** *f* globe

**'weltlich** *adj* worldly

**'Welt|litera,tur** *f* world literature; **~macht** *f* POL world power; **~markt** *m* ECON world market; **~meer** *n* ocean; **~meister(in)** world champion; **~meisterschaft** *f* world championship; *esp soccer*: World Cup; **~raum** *m* (-[*e*]*s*; *no pl*) (outer) space; **~reich** *n* empire; **~reise** *f* world trip; **~re,kord** *m* world record; **~ruf** *m* (***von*** ~ of) worldwide reputation; **~stadt** *f* metropolis; **~untergang** *m* end of the world

**'weltweit** *adj* worldwide

**'Weltwirtschaft** *f* world economy

**'Weltwirtschaftskrise** *f* worldwide economic crisis

**'Weltwunder** *n* wonder of the world

**Wende** ['vɛndə] *f* (-; *-n*) turn (*a. swimming*); change; **~kreis** *m* ASTR, GEOGR tropic; MOT turning circle

**Wendeltreppe** ['vɛndəl-] *f* spiral staircase

**'wenden** *v/t and v/i* (*ge-, h*) *and v/refl* ([*irr*,] *ge-, h*) turn (***nach*** to; ***gegen*** against); MOT turn (round); GASTR turn over; ***sich an j-n um Hilfe ~*** turn to s.o. for help; ***bitte ~*** please turn over, pto

**'Wendepunkt** *m* turning point

**wendig** ['vɛndɪç] *adj* MOT, MAR maneuverable, *Br* manoeuvrable; *fig* nimble

**'Wendung** *f* (-; *-en*) turn, *fig a.* change; expression, phrase

**wenig** ['veːnɪç] *indef pron and adv* little; **~(e)** *pl* few; ***nur ~e*** only few; only a few; (***in***) ***~er als*** (in) less than; ***am ~sten*** least of all; ***er spricht ~*** he doesn't talk much; (***nur***) ***ein*** (***klein***) ~ (just) a little (bit)

**'wenigstens** *adv* at least

**wenn** [vɛn] *cj* when; if; ***~ ... nicht*** if ... not, unless; ***~ auch*** (al)though, even though; ***wie*** *or* ***als ~*** as though, as if; ***~ ich nur ... wäre!*** if only I were ...!; ***~ auch noch so ...*** no matter how ...; ***und ~ nun ...?*** what if ...?

**wer** [veːɐ] **1.** *interr pron* who, which; ***~ von euch?*** which of you?; **2.** *rel pron* who; ***~ auch*** (***immer***) who(so)ever; **3.** F *indef pron* somebody, anybody

**Werbe|abteilung** ['vɛrbə-] *f* publicity department; **~agen,tur** *f* advertising agency; **~feldzug** *m* advertising campaign; **~fernsehen** *n* commercial television; **~film** *m* promotion(al) film; **~funk** *m* radio commercials

**werben** ['vɛrbən] (*irr, ge-, h*) **1.** *v/i* advertise (***für et.*** s.th.), promote (s.th.), give *s.th. or s.o.* publicity; *esp* POL make propaganda (***für*** for), canvass (for); ***~ um*** court (*a. fig*); **2.** *v/t* recruit; canvass, solicit

**'Werbesendung** *f*, **'Werbespot** [-ʃpɔt] *m* (*-s; -s*) (TV) commercial

**'Werbung** *f* (-; *no pl*) advertising, (sales) promotion; *a.* POL *etc* publicity, propaganda; recruitment; ***~ machen für et.*** advertise s.th.

**Werdegang** ['veːɐdə-] *m* career

**werden** ['veːɐdən] *v/i* (*irr, ge-, sein*) *and v/aux* become, get; turn, go; grow; turn out; ***wir ~*** we will (*or* shall), we are going to; ***geliebt ~*** be loved (***von*** by); ***was willst du ~?*** what do you want to be?; ***mir wird schlecht*** I'm going to be sick; F ***es wird schon wieder*** (~) it'll be all right

**werfen** ['vɛrfən] *v/i and v/t* (*irr, ge-, h*) throw (*a.* ZO) ([***mit***] ***et. nach*** s.th. at); drop (*bombs*); cast (*shadow*)

**Werft** [vɛrft] *f* (-; *-en*) MAR shipyard, dockyard

**Werk** [vɛrk] *n* (-[*e*]*s*; *-e*) work, deed; TECH mechanism; ECON works, factory; ***ans ~ gehen*** set *or* go to work; **~bank** *f* (-; *-bänke*) TECH workbench; **~meister** *m* TECH foreman

**'Werkstatt** *f* (-; *-stätten*) workshop; MOT garage

**'Werktag** *m* workday

**'werktags** *adv* on workdays

**'werktätig** *adj* working

**'Werkzeug** *n* tool (*a. fig*); *coll* tools; instrument; **~macher** *m* toolmaker

**wert** [veːɐt] *adj* worth; ***die Mühe*** (***e-n Versuch***) ~ worth the trouble (a try); *fig* ***nichts ~*** no good; **Wert** *m* (-[*e*]*s*; *-e*) value, *esp fig a.* worth; use; *pl* data, figures; ***... im ~(e) von 20 Dollar*** 20 dollars' worth of ...; ***großen ~ legen auf*** (*acc*) set great store by

**werten** ['veːɐtən] *v/t* (*ge-, h*) value; *a.* SPORT rate, judge

**'Wertgegenstand** *m* article of value

**'wertlos** *adj* worthless

**'Wertpa,piere** *pl* securities

**'Wertsachen** *pl* valuables

**'Wertung** *f* (-; *-en*) valuation; *a.* SPORT rating, judging; score, points

**'wertvoll** *adj* valuable

**Wesen** ['veːzən] *n* (*-s*; -) being, creature; *fig* essence; nature, character; ***viel ~s machen um*** make a fuss about

**'wesentlich** *adj* essential; considerable; ***im Wesentlichen*** on the whole

**weshalb** [vɛs'halp] *interr adv* → ***warum***

**Wespe** ['vɛspə] *f* (-; *-n*) ZO wasp

**Weste** ['vɛstə] *f* (-; *-n*) vest, *Br* waistcoat

**Westen** ['vɛstən] *m* (*-s*; *no pl*) west; POL West

**Western** ['vɛstɐn] *m* (*-s*; -) western

**'westlich 1.** *adj* western; westerly; POL West(ern); **2.** *adv*: ***~ von*** (to the) west of

**'Westwind** *m* west(erly) wind

**Wettbewerb** ['vɛtbəvɛrp] *m* (-[*e*]*s*; -*e*) competition (*a.* ECON), contest

**'Wettbüˌro** *n* betting office

**Wette** ['vɛtə] *f* (-; -*n*) bet; ***e-e ~ abschließen*** make a bet; ***um die ~ laufen*** *etc* race (***mit j-m*** s.o.)

**'wetteifern** *v/i* (*ge-*, *h*) compete (***mit*** with; ***um*** for)

**'wetten** *v/i and v/t* (*ge-*, *h*) bet; ***mit j-m um 10 Dollar ~*** bet s.o. ten dollars; ***~ auf*** (*acc*) bet on, back

**Wetter** ['vɛtɐ] *n* (-*s*; -) weather

**'Wetterbericht** *m* weather report

**'Wetterfahne** *f* weather vane

**'wetterfest** *adj* weatherproof

**'Wetter|karte** *f* weather chart; **~lage** *f* weather situation; **~leuchten** *n* sheet lightning; **~vorhersage** *f* weather forecast; **~warte** *f* weather station

**'Wett|kampf** *m* competition, contest; **~kämpfer(in)** contestant, competitor; **~lauf** *m* race (*a. fig* ***mit*** against); **~läufer(in)** runner

**'wettmachen** *v/t* (*sep*, *-ge-*, *h*) make up for

**'Wettrennen** *n* race

**'Wettrüsten** *n* (-*s*; *no pl*) arms race

**'Wettstreit** *m* contest, competition

**wetzen** ['vɛtsən] *v/t* (*ge-*, *h*) whet, sharpen

**wich** [vɪç] *pret of* ***weichen***

**wichtig** ['vɪçtɪç] *adj* important

**'Wichtigkeit** *f* (-; *no pl*) importance

**'wickeln** *v/t* (*ge-*, *h*) change (*baby*); ***~ in*** (*acc*) wrap in; ***~ um*** wrap (a)round

**Widder** ['vɪdɐ] *m* (-*s*; -) ZO ram; ASTR Aries; ***er ist*** (***ein***) ***~*** he's (an) Aries

**wider** ['vi:dɐ] *prp* (*acc*) ***~ Willen*** against one's will; ***~ Erwarten*** contrary to expectations

**'Widerhaken** *m* barb

**'widerhallen** *v/i* (*sep*, *-ge-*, *h*) resound (***von*** with)

**wider'legen** *v/t* (*no -ge-*, *h*) refute, disprove

**'widerlich** *adj* sickening, disgusting

**'widerrechtlich** *adj* illegal, unlawful

**'Widerruf** *m* JUR revocation; withdrawal; **wider'rufen** *v/t* (*irr*, ***rufen***, *no -ge-*, *h*) revoke; withdraw

**Widersacher** ['vi:dɐzaxɐ] *m* (-*s*; -) adversary, rival

**'Widerschein** *m* reflection

**wider'setzen** *v/refl* (*no -ge-*, *h*) (*dat*) oppose, resist

**'widersinnig** *adj* absurd

**widerspenstig** ['vi:dɐʃpɛnstɪç] *adj* unruly, stubborn

**'widerspiegeln** *v/t* (*sep*, *-ge-*, *h*) reflect (*a. fig*); ***sich ~ in*** (*dat*) be reflected in

**wider'sprechen** *v/i* (*irr*, ***sprechen***, *no -ge-*, *h*) (*dat*) contradict

**'Widerspruch** *m* contradiction

**widersprüchlich** ['vi:dɐʃprʏçlɪç] *adj* contradictory

**'widerspruchslos** *adv* without contradiction

**'Widerstand** *m* resistance (*a.* ELECTR), opposition; ***~ leisten*** offer resistance (*dat* to); **'widerstandsfähig** *adj* resistant (*a.* TECH); **wider'stehen** *v/i* (*irr*, ***stehen***, *no -ge-*, *h*) (*dat*) resist

**wider'streben** *v/i* (*no -ge-*, *h*) ***es widerstrebt mir, dies zu tun*** I hate doing *or* to do that; **~d** *adv* reluctantly

**widerwärtig** ['vi:dɐvɛrtɪç] *adj* disgusting

**'Widerwille** *m* aversion (***gegen*** to), dislike (of, for); disgust (at)

**'widerwillig** *adj* reluctant, unwilling

**widmen** ['vɪtmən] *v/t* (ge-, h) dedicate; **'Widmung** *f* (-; -*en*) dedication

**wie** [vi:] **1.** *interr adv* how; ***~ geht es Gordon?*** how is Gordon?; ***~ ist er?*** what's he like?; ***~ ist das Wetter?*** what's the weather like?; ***~ heißen Sie?*** what's your name?; ***~ nennt man ...?*** what do you call ...?; ***~ wäre*** (***ist***, ***steht***) ***es mit ...?*** what *or* how about ...?; ***~ viele ...?*** how many ...?; **2.** *cj* like; as; ***~ neu*** (***verrückt***) like new (mad); ***doppelt so ... ~*** twice as ... as; ***~*** (***zum Beispiel***) such as, like; ***~ üblich*** as usual; ***~ er sagte*** as he said; ***ich zeige*** (***sage***) ***dir, ~*** (...) I'll show (tell) you how (...)

**wieder** ['vi:dɐ] *adv* again; *in cpds often* re...; ***immer ~*** again and again; ***~ aufbauen*** reconstruct; ***~ aufnehmen*** resume; ***~ beleben*** MED resuscitate, revive (*a. fig*); ***~ erkennen*** recognize (***an*** *dat* by); ***~ finden*** find (what one has lost); *fig* regain; ***~ gutmachen*** make up for; ***~ herstellen*** restore; ***~ sehen*** see *or* meet again; ***~ verwendbar*** reusable; ***~ verwerten*** TECH recycle

**Wieder|'aufbau** *m* (-[*e*]*s*; *no pl*) reconstruction, rebuilding; **~'aufbereitung**

*f* TECH recycling, reprocessing (*a.* NUCL); **~'aufbereitungsanlage** *f* TECH reprocessing plant; **~'aufleben** *n* (*-s; no pl*) revival; **~'aufnahme** *f* (*-; no pl*) resumption

**'wiederbekommen** *v/t* (*irr*, ***kommen***, *sep, no -ge-, h*) get back

**'Wieder|belebung** *f* (*-; -en*) MED resuscitation; **~belebungsversuch** *m* MED attempt at resuscitation

**'wiederbringen** *v/t* (*irr*, ***bringen***, *sep, -ge-, h*) bring back; return

**Wieder'einführung** *f* reintroduction

**'Wiederentdeckung** *f* rediscovery

**'Wiedergabe** *f* TECH reproduction, playback; **'wiedergeben** *v/t* (*irr*, ***geben***, *sep, -ge-, h*) give back, return; *fig* describe; TECH play back, reproduce

**Wieder'gutmachung** *f* (*-; -en*) reparation

**'wiederholen¹** *v/t* (*sep, -ge-, h*) (go and) get *s.o. or s.th.* back

**wieder'holen²** *v/t* (*no -ge-, h*) repeat; PED revise, review; THEA replay; ***sich ~*** repeat o.s. (*a. fig*); **wieder'holt** *adv* repeatedly, several times

**Wieder'holung** *f* (*-; -en*) repetition; PED review; TV *etc* rerun; SPORT replay

**Wiederkehr** ['vi:dɐke:ɐ] *f* (*-; no pl*) return; recurrence; **'wiederkehren** *v/i* (*sep, -ge-, sein*) return; recur

**'wiederkommen** *v/i* (*irr*, ***kommen***, *sep, -ge-, sein*) come back, return

**'Wiedersehen** *n* (*-s; -*) seeing *s.o.* again; reunion; ***auf ~!*** goodbye!

**wiederum** ['vi:dərʊm] *adv* again; on the other hand

**'Wieder|vereinigung** *f* reunion, *esp* POL *a.* reunification; **~verkauf** *m* resale; **~verwendung** *f* reuse; **~verwertung** *f* (*-; -en*) TECH recycling; **~wahl** *f* POL re-election

**Wiege** ['vi:gə] *f* (*-; -n*) cradle

**wiegen¹** ['vi:gən] *v/t and v/i* (*irr, ge-, h*) weigh

**'wiegen²** *v/t* (*ge-, h*) rock (***in den Schlaf*** to sleep)

**'Wiegenlied** *n* lullaby

**wiehern** ['vi:ɐn] *v/i* (*ge-, h*) ZO neigh

**wies** [vi:s] *pret of* ***weisen***

**Wiese** ['vi:zə] *f* (*-; -n*) meadow

**Wiesel** ['vi:zəl] *n* (*-s; -*) ZO weasel

**wieso** [vi'zo:] *interr adv* → ***warum***

**wievielt** [vi'fi:lt] *adj*: ***zum ~en Male?*** how many times?

**wild** [vɪlt] *adj* wild (*a. fig*) (F ***auf*** *acc* about); violent; ***~er Streik*** wildcat strike

**Wild** *n* (*-[e]s; no pl*) HUNT game; GASTR *mst* venison; **~bach** *m* torrent

**Wilde** ['vɪldə] *m, f* (*-n; -n*) savage; F ***wie ein ~r*** like mad

**Wilderer** ['vɪldərɐ] *m* (*-s; -*) poacher

**'wildern** *v/i* (*ge-, h*) poach

**'Wildhüter** *m* gamekeeper

**'Wildkatze** *f* ZO wild cat

**'Wildleder** *n* suede

**'Wildnis** *f* (*-; -se*) wilderness

**'Wild|park** *m*, **~reser,vat** *n* game park *or* reserve; **~schwein** *n* ZO wild boar

**Wille** ['vɪlə] *m* (*-ns; -n*) will; intention; ***s-n ~n durchsetzen*** have *or* get one's own way; ***j-m s-n ~n lassen*** let s.o. have his (own) way

**'willenlos** *adj* weak(-willed)

**'Willenskraft** *f* (*-; no pl*) willpower; ***durch ~ erzwingen*** will

**'willensstark** *adj* strong-willed

**willig** ['vɪlɪç] *adj* willing

**will'kommen** *adj* welcome (*a.* ***~ heißen***) (***in*** *dat* to)

**willkürlich** ['vɪlky:ɐlɪç] *adj* arbitrary; random

**wimmeln** ['vɪməln] *v/i* (*ge-, h*) ***~ von*** be teeming with

**wimmern** ['vɪmɐn] *v/i* (*ge-, h*) whimper

**Wimpel** ['vɪmpəl] *m* (*-s; -*) pennant

**Wimper** ['vɪmpɐ] *f* (*-; -n*) eyelash; ***ohne mit der ~ zu zucken*** without turning a hair; **'Wimperntusche** *f* mascara

**Wind** [vɪnt] *m* (*-[e]s; -e* ['vɪndə]) wind

**Winde** ['vɪndə] *f* (*-; -n*) winch,windlass, hoist

**Windel** ['vɪndəl] *f* (*-; -n*) diaper, *Br* nappy

**winden** ['vɪndən] *v/t* (*irr, ge-, h*) wind, TECH *a.* hoist; ***sich ~*** wind (one's way); writhe (*with pain etc*)

**'Windhund** *m* ZO greyhound

**windig** ['vɪndɪç] *adj* windy

**'Wind|mühle** *f* windmill; **~pocken** *pl* MED chickenpox; **~richtung** *f* direction of the wind; **~schutzscheibe** *f* MOT windshield, *Br* windscreen; **~stärke** *f* wind force

**'windstill** *adj*, **'Windstille** *f* calm

**'Windstoß** *m* gust

**'Windsurfen** *n* windsurfing

**'Windung** *f* (-; *-en*) bend, turn (*a.* TECH)
**Wink** [vɪŋk] *m* (-[*e*]*s*; *-e*) sign; *fig* hint
**Winkel** ['vɪŋkəl] *m* (-*s*; -) corner; MATH angle; **'winkelig** *adj* angular; crooked
**winken** ['vɪŋkən] *v/i* (*ge-*, *h*) wave (one's hand *etc*), signal; beckon
**winseln** ['vɪnzəln] *v/i* (*ge-*, *h*) whimper, whine
**Winter** ['vɪntɐ] *m* (-*s*; -) winter
**'winterlich** *adj* wintry
**'Winter|reifen** *m* MOT snow tire (*Br* tyre); **~schlaf** *m* ZO hibernation; **~spiele** *pl*: ***Olympische ~*** SPORT Winter Olympics; **~sport** *m* winter sports
**Winzer** ['vɪntsɐ] *m* (-*s*; -) winegrower
**winzig** ['vɪntsɪç] *adj* tiny, diminutive
**Wipfel** ['vɪpfəl] *m* (-*s*; -) (tree)top
**Wippe** ['vɪpə] *f* (-; *-n*), **'wippen** *v/i* (*ge-*, *h*) seesaw
**wir** [viːɐ] *pers pron* we; ***~ drei*** the three of us; F ***~ sind's!*** it's us!
**Wirbel** ['vɪrbəl] *m* (-*s*; -) whirl (*a. fig*); ANAT vertebra
**'wirbeln** *v/i* (*ge-*, *sein*) whirl
**'Wirbel|säule** *f* ANAT spinal column, spine; **~sturm** *m* cyclone, tornado; **~tier** *n* vertebrate; **~wind** *m* whirlwind
**wirken** ['vɪrkən] (*ge-*, *h*) **1.** *v/i* work; be effective (***gegen*** against); look; ***anregend*** *etc* **~** have a stimulating *etc* effect (***auf*** *acc* [up]on); ***~ als*** act as; **2.** *v/t* weave; *fig* work (*miracles etc*)
**wirklich** ['vɪrklɪç] *adj* real, actual; true, genuine; **'Wirklichkeit** *f* (-; *-en*) reality; ***in ~*** in reality, actually
**wirksam** ['vɪrkzaːm] *adj* effective
**'Wirkung** *f* (-; *-en*) effect
**'wirkungslos** *adj* ineffective
**'wirkungsvoll** *adj* effective
**wirr** [vɪr] *adj* confused, mixed-up; *hair*: tousled; **Wirren** ['vɪrən] *pl* disorder, confusion; **Wirrwarr** ['vɪrvar] *m* (-*s*; *no pl*) confusion, mess, welter
**Wirt** [vɪrt] *m* (-[*e*]*s*; *-e*) landlord; **'Wirtin** *f* (-; *-nen*) landlady; **'Wirtschaft** *f* (-; *-en*) ECON, POL economy; business; → ***Gastwirtschaft***; **'wirtschaften** *v/i* (*ge-*, *h*) keep house; manage one's money *or* affairs *or* business; economize; ***gut*** (***schlecht***) **~** be a good (bad) manager; **'Wirtschafterin** *f* (-; *-nen*) housekeeper; **'wirtschaftlich** *adj* economic; economical; **'Wirtschafts...** ECON *in cpds ...gemeinschaft*, *...gipfel*, *...krise*, *...system*, *...wunder etc*: economic ...
**'Wirtshaus** *n* → ***Gastwirtschaft***
**wischen** ['vɪʃən] *v/t* (*ge-*, *h*) wipe; ***Staub ~*** dust
**wispern** ['vɪspɐn] *v/t and v/i* (*ge-*, *h*) whisper
**wissbegierig** ['vɪs-] *adj* curious
**wissen** ['vɪsən] *v/t and v/i* (*irr*, *ge-*, *h*) know; ***ich möchte ~*** I'd like to know, I wonder; ***soviel ich weiß*** as far as I know; ***weißt du*** you know; ***weißt du noch?*** (do you) remember?; ***woher weißt du das?*** how do you know?; ***man kann nie ~*** you never know; ***ich will davon*** (***von ihm***) ***nichts ~*** I don't want anything to do with it (him)
**'Wissen** *n* (-*s*; *no pl*) knowledge; know-how; ***m-s ~s*** as far as I know
**'Wissenschaft** *f* (-; *-en*) science
**'Wissenschaftler** *m* (-*s*; -), **'Wissenschaftlerin** *f* (-; *-nen*) scientist
**'wissenschaftlich** *adj* scientific
**'wissenswert** *adj* worth knowing; ***Wissenswertes*** useful facts; ***alles Wissenswerte*** (***über*** *acc*) all you need to know (about)
**wittern** ['vɪtɐn] *v/t* (*ge-*, *h*) scent, smell (*both a. fig*)
**Witwe** ['vɪtvə] *f* (-; *-n*) widow
**Witwer** ['vɪtvɐ] *m* (-*s*; -) widower
**Witz** [vɪts] *m* (-*es*; *-e*) joke; ***~e reißen*** crack jokes
**witzig** ['vɪtsɪç] *adj* funny; witty
**wo** [voː] *adv* where; ***~ ... doch*** when, although
**wob** [voːp] *pret of* ***weben***
**wobei** [vo'bai] *adv*: ***~ bist du?*** what are you at?; ***~ mir einfällt*** which reminds me
**Woche** ['vɔxə] *f* (-; *-n*) week
**'Wochen...** *in cpds ...lohn*, *...markt*, *...zeitung etc*: weekly ...; **~ende** *n* weekend; ***am ~*** on (*Br* at) the weekend
**'wochenlang** **1.** *adj*: ***~es Warten*** (many) weeks of waiting; **2.** *adv* for weeks
**'Wochenschau** *f film*: newsreel
**'Wochentag** *m* weekday
**wöchentlich** ['vœçəntlɪç] **1.** *adj* weekly; **2.** *adv* weekly, every week; ***einmal ~*** once a week
**wodurch** [vo'dʊrç] *adv* how; through which

**wofür** [vo'fy:ɐ] *adv* for which; **~?** what (...) for?
**wog** [vo:k] *pret of* **wiegen¹** *and* **wägen**
**Woge** ['vo:gə] *f* (-; *-n*) wave, *esp fig a.* surge; breaker; **'wogen** *v/i* (*ge-*, *h*) surge, heave (*both a. fig*)
**woher** [vo'he:ɐ] *adv* where ... from; **~ *weißt du* (*das*)?** how do you know?
**wohin** [vo'hɪn] *adv* where (... to)
**wohl** [vo:l] *adv and cj* well; probably, I suppose; ***sich ~ fühlen*** be well; feel good; feel at home (***bei*** with); ***ich fühle mich nicht ~*** I don't feel well; ***j-m ~ tun*** do s.o. good; ***~ oder übel*** willy-nilly, whether you *etc* like it or not; ***~ kaum*** hardly
**Wohl** *n* (-[*e*]*s*; *no pl*) well-being; ***auf j-s ~ trinken*** drink to s.o.('s health); ***zum ~!*** to your health!; F cheers!
**'wohlbehalten** *adv* safely
**'Wohlfahrtsstaat** *m* welfare state
**'wohl|gemerkt** *adv* mind you; **~genährt** *adj* well-fed; **~gesinnt** *adj*: ***j-m ~ sein*** be well-disposed towards s.o.; **~habend** *adj* well-off, well-to-do
**wohlig** ['vo:lɪç] *adj* snug, cozy, *Br* cosy
**'Wohl|stand** *m* (-[*e*]*s*; *no pl*) prosperity, affluence; **~standsgesellschaft** *f* affluent society
**'Wohltat** *f* (-; *no pl*) pleasure; relief; blessing; **'Wohltäter(in)** benefactor (benefactress); **'wohltätig** *adj* charitable; ***für ~e Zwecke*** for charity
**'Wohltätigkeits...** *in cpds ...ball, ...konzert etc*: charity ...
**'wohlverdient** *adj* well-deserved
**'wohlwollend** *adj* benevolent
**wohnen** ['vo:nən] *v/i* (*ge-*, *h*) live (***in*** *dat* in; ***bei j-m*** with s.o.); stay (***in*** *dat* at; ***bei*** with)
**'Wohngebiet** *n* residential area
**'Wohngemeinschaft** *f*: (***mit j-m***) ***in e-r ~ leben*** share an apartment (*Br* a flat) *or* a house (with s.o.)
**wohnlich** ['vo:nlɪç] *adj* comfortable, snug, cozy, *Br* cosy
**'Wohnmo,bil** *n* (*-s*; *-e*) camper, motor home (*Br* caravan)
**'Wohn|siedlung** *f* housing development (*Br* estate); **~sitz** *m* residence; ***ohne festen ~*** of no fixed abode
**'Wohnung** *f* (-; *-en*) apartment, *Br* flat; ***m-e*** *etc* **~** my *etc* place
**'Wohnungs|amt** *n* housing office; **~bau** *m* (-[*e*]*s*; *no pl*) house building; **~not** *f* housing shortage
**'Wohnwagen** *m* trailer, *Br* caravan; mobile home
**'Wohnzimmer** *n* sitting *or* living room
**wölben** ['vœlbən] *v/refl* (*ge-*, *h*), **'Wölbung** *f* (-; *-en*) vault, arch
**Wolf** [vɔlf] *m* (-[*e*]*s*; *Wölfe* ['vœlfə]) zo wolf
**Wolke** ['vɔlkə] *f* (-; *-n*) cloud
**'Wolkenbruch** *m* cloudburst
**'Wolkenkratzer** *m* (*-s*; -) skyscraper
**'wolkenlos** *adj* cloudless
**wolkig** ['vɔlkɪç] *adj* cloudy, clouded
**Woll...** [vɔl-] *in cpds ...schal, ...socken etc*: wool(l)en ...; **~decke** *f* blanket
**Wolle** ['vɔlə] *f* (-; *-n*) wool
**wollen** ['vɔlən] *v/t and v/i* (*ge-*, *h*) *and v/aux* (*no -ge-*, *h*) want (to); ***lieber ~*** prefer; ***~ wir*** (***gehen*** *etc*)***?*** shall we (go *etc*)?; ***~ Sie bitte ...*** will *or* would you please ...; ***wie*** (***was, wann***) ***du willst*** as (whatever, whenever) you like; ***sie will, dass ich komme*** she wants me to come; ***ich wollte, ich wäre*** (***hätte***) ***...*** I wish I were (had) ...
**womit** [vo'mɪt] *adv* with which; **~?** what ... with?
**Wonne** ['vɔnə] *f* (-; *-n*) joy, delight
**woran** [vo'ran] *adv*: ***~ denkst du?*** what are you thinking of?; ***~ liegt es, dass ...?*** how is it that ...?; ***~ sieht man, welche*** (***ob***) ***...?*** how can you tell which (if) ...?
**worauf** [vo'rauf] *adv* after which; on which; **~?** what ... on?; ***~ wartest du?*** what are you waiting for?
**woraus** [vo'raus] *adv* from which; ***~ ist es?*** what's it made of?
**worin** [vo'rɪn] *adv* in which; **~?** where?
**Wort** [vɔrt] *n* (-[*e*]*s*; *-e*, *Wörter* ['vœrtɐ]) word; ***mit anderen ~en*** in other words; ***sein ~ geben*** (***halten, brechen***) give (keep, break) one's word; ***j-n beim ~ nehmen*** take s.o. at his word; ***ein gutes ~ einlegen für*** put in a good word for; ***j-m ins ~ fallen*** cut s.o. short
**'Wortart** *f* LING part of speech
**Wörter|buch** ['vœrtɐ-] *n* dictionary; **~verzeichnis** *n* vocabulary, list of words
**'Wortführer** *m* spokesman; **'Wortführerin** *f* spokeswoman
**'wortkarg** *adj* taciturn

W

**wörtlich** ['vœrtlıç] *adj* literal; **~e Rede** LING direct speech
'**Wort|schatz** *m* vocabulary; **~spiel** *n* pun; **~stellung** *f* LING word order
**worüber** [vo'ry:bɐ] *adv* about which; **~ lachen Sie?** what are you laughing at *or* about?
**worum** [vo'rʊm] *adv* about which; **~ handelt es sich?** what is it about?
**worunter** [vo'rʊntɐ] *adv* among which; **~?** what ... under?
**wovon** [vo'fɔn] *adv* about which; **~ redest du?** what are you talking about?
**wovor** [vo'fo:ɐ] *adv* of which; **~ hast du Angst?** what are you afraid of?
**wozu** [vo'tsu:] *adv*: **~ er mir rät** what he advised me to do; **~?** what (...) for?; why?
**Wrack** [vrak] *n* (-[*e*]*s*; -*s*) MAR wreck (*a. fig*)
**wrang** [vraŋ] *pret of* **wringen**
**wringen** ['vrıŋən] *v/t* (*irr*, *ge*-, *h*) wring
**Wucher** ['vu:xɐ] *m* (-*s*; *no pl*) usury
**Wucherer** ['vu:xərɐ] *m* (-*s*; -) usurer
'**wuchern** *v/i* (*ge*-, *h*) grow (*fig* be) rampant; **Wucherung** ['vu:xərʊŋ] *f* (-; -*en*) MED growth
**Wuchs** [vu:ks] *m* (-*es*; *no pl*) growth; build
**wuchs** [vu:ks] *pret of* **wachsen**[1]
**Wucht** [vʊxt] *f* (-; *no pl*) force; impact
**wuchtig** ['vʊxtıç] *adj* massive; powerful
**wühlen** ['vy:lən] *v/i* (*ge*-, *h*) dig; ZO root; rummage (**in** *dat* in, through)
**Wulst** [vʊlst] *m* (-*es*; *Wülste* ['vylstə)], *f* (-; *Wülste*) bulge; roll (*of fat*)
**wulstig** ['vʊlstıç] *adj* bulging; thick
**wund** [vʊnt] *adj* MED sore; **~e Stelle** MED sore; **~er Punkt** *fig* sore point
**Wunde** ['vʊndə] *f* (-; -*n*) MED wound
**Wunder** ['vʊndɐ] *n* (-*s*; -) miracle, *fig a.* wonder; **~ wirken** work wonders; (**es ist**) **kein ~, dass du müde bist** no wonder you are tired; '**wunderbar** *adj* wonderful, marvel(l)ous
'**Wunderkind** *n* infant prodigy
'**wunderlich** *adj* funny, odd; senile
'**wundern** *v/refl* (*ge*-, *h*) be surprised *or* astonished (**über** *acc* at)
'**wundervoll** *adj* wonderful
'**Wundstarrkrampf** *m* (-*es*; *no pl*) MED tetanus
**Wunsch** [vʊnʃ] *m* (-[*e*]*s*; *Wünsche* ['vynʃə]) wish; request; **auf j-s ~** at s.o.'s request; **auf eigenen ~** at one's own request; (**je**) **nach ~** as desired
**wünschen** ['vynʃən] *v/t* (*ge*-, *h*) wish; **sich et.** (**zu Weihnachten** *etc*) **~** want s.th. (for Christmas *etc*); **das habe ich mir** (**schon immer**) **gewünscht** that's what I (always) wanted; **alles, was man sich nur ~ kann** everything one could wish for; **ich wünschte, ich wäre** (**hätte**) **...** I wish I were (had) ...
'**wünschenswert** *adj* desirable
**wurde** ['vʊrdə] *pret of* **werden**
**Würde** ['vyrdə] *f* (-; -*n*) dignity
'**würdelos** *adj* undignified
'**Würdenträger** *m* dignitary
'**würdevoll** *adj* dignified
**würdig** ['vyrdıç] *adj* worthy (*gen* of); dignified; **würdigen** ['vyrdıgən] *v/t* (*ge*-, *h*) appreciate; **j-n keines Blickes ~** ignore s.o. completely; '**Würdigung** *f* (-; -*en*) appreciation
**Wurf** [vʊrf] *m* (-[*e*]*s*; *Würfe* ['vyrfə]) throw; ZO litter
**Würfel** ['vyrfəl] *m* (-*s*; -) cube (*a.* MATH); dice; '**würfeln** *v/i* (*ge*-, *h*) throw dice (**um** for); play dice; GASTR dice; **e-e Sechs ~** throw a six
'**Würfelzucker** *m* lump sugar
'**Wurfgeschoss** *n* missile
**würgen** ['vyrgən] *v/i and v/t* (*ge*-, *h*) choke; throttle *s.o.*
**Wurm** [vʊrm] *m* (-[*e*]*s*; *Würmer* ['vyrmɐ]) ZO worm; **wurmen** ['vʊrmən] F *v/t* (*ge*-, *h*) gall *s.o.*; '**wurmstichig** ['vʊrmʃtıçıç] *adj* worm-eaten
**Wurst** [vʊrst] *f* (-; *Würste* ['vyrstə]) sausage
**Würstchen** ['vyrstçən] *n* (-*s*; -) small sausage, frankfurter, wiener; hot dog
**Würze** [vyrtsə] *f* (-; *n*) spice (*a. fig*)
**Wurzel** ['vʊrtsəl] *f* (-; -*n*) root (*a.* MATH); **~n schlagen** take root (*a. fig*)
'**wurzeln** *v/i* (*ge*-, *h*) **~ in** (*dat*) be rooted in (*a. fig*)
'**würzen** *v/t* (*ge*-, *h*) spice, season, flavo(u)r; **würzig** ['vyrtsıç] *adj* spicy, well-seasoned
**wusch** [vu:ʃ] *pret of* **waschen**
**wusste** ['vʊstə] *pret of* **wissen**
**Wust** [vu:st] F *m* (-[*e*]*s*; *no pl*) tangled mass
**wüst** [vy:st] *adj* waste; confused; wild, dissolute

**Wüste** ['vy:stə] *f* (-; *-n*) desert
**Wut** [vu:t] *f* (-; *no pl*) rage, fury; **e-e ~ *haben*** be furious (***auf*** *acc* with)
**'Wutanfall** *m* fit of rage
**wüten** ['vy:tən] *v/i* (*ge-, h*) rage (*a. fig*); **~d** *adj* furious (***auf*** *acc* with; ***über*** *acc* at), F mad (at)
**'wutschnaubend** *adj* fuming

# X, Y

**X-Beine** ['ɪksbainə] *pl* knock-knees
**x-beinig** ['ɪksbainɪç] *adj* knock-kneed
**x-be'liebig** *adj*: ***jede*(*r*, -*s*) ~*e* ...** any ... you like, F any old ...
**'x-mal** F *adv* umpteen times
**x-te** ['ɪkstə] *adj*: ***zum ~n Male*** for the umpteenth time
**Xylophon** [ksylo'fo:n] *n* (*-s*; *-e*) MUS xylophone
**Yacht** [jaxt] *f* (-; *-en*) MAR yacht
**Yoga** ['jo:ga] *m, n* (-[*s*]; *no pl*) yoga

# Z

**Zacke** ['tsakə] *f* (-; *-n*), **'Zacken** *m* (*-s*; -) (sharp) point; tooth; **zackig** ['tsakɪç] *adj* serrated; jagged; *fig* smart
**zaghaft** ['tsa:khaft] *adj* timid
**zäh** [tsɛ:] *adj* tough (*a. fig*); **~flüssig** *adj* thick, viscous; *fig* slow-moving (*traffic*)
**Zähigkeit** ['tsɛ:ɪçkait] *f* (-; *no pl*) toughness, *fig a.* stamina
**Zahl** [tsa:l] *f* (-; *-en*) number; figure
**'zahlbar** *adj* payable (***an*** *acc* to; ***bei*** at)
**zählbar** ['tsɛ:lba:ɐ] *adj* countable
**zahlen** ['tsa:lən] *v/i and v/t* (*ge-, h*) pay; **~, *bitte!*** the check (*Br* bill), please!
**zählen** ['tsɛ:lən] *v/t and v/i* (*ge-, h*) count (***bis*** up to; *fig* ***auf*** *acc* on); **~ *zu*** rank with *the best etc*
**'zahlenmäßig 1.** *adj* numerical; **2.** *adv*: ***j-m ~ überlegen sein*** outnumber s.o.
**Zähler** ['tsɛ:lɐ] *m* (*-s*; -) counter (*a.* TECH); MATH numerator; ELECTR *etc* meter
**'Zahlkarte** *f post* deposit (*Br* paying-in) slip
**'zahllos** *adj* countless
**'Zahlmeister** *m* MIL paymaster; MAR purser
**'zahlreich 1.** *adj* numerous; **2.** *adv* in great number
**'Zahltag** *m* payday
**'Zahlung** *f* (-; *-en*) payment
**'Zählung** *f* (-; *-en*) count; POL census
**'Zahlungs|aufforderung** *f* request for payment; **~bedingungen** *pl* terms of payment; **~befehl** *m* order to pay
**'zahlungsfähig** *adj* solvent
**'Zahlungs|frist** *f* term of payment; **~mittel** *n* currency; ***gesetzliches ~*** legal tender; **~schwierigkeiten** *pl* financial difficulties; **~ter,min** *m* date of payment
**'zahlungsunfähig** *adj* insolvent
**'Zählwerk** *n* TECH counter
**'Zahlwort** *n* LING numeral
**zahm** [tsa:m] *adj* tame (*a. fig*)
**zähmen** ['tsɛ:mən] *v/t* (*ge-, h*) tame (*a. fig*); **'Zähmung** *f* (-; *no pl*) taming
**Zahn** [tsa:n] *m* (-[*e*]*s*; *Zähne* ['tsɛ:nə]) tooth, TECH *a.* cog; **~arzt** *m*, **~ärztin** *f* dentist, dental surgeon; **~bürste** *f* toothbrush; **~creme** *f* toothpaste
**zahnen** ['tsa:nən] *v/i* (*ge-, h*) cut one's teeth, teethe

**'Zahnfleisch** *n* gums
**'zahnlos** *adj* toothless
**'Zahn|lücke** *f* gap between the teeth; **~medi,zin** *f* dentistry; **~pasta, ~paste** *f* toothpaste; **~radbahn** *f* rack railroad; **~schmerzen** *pl* toothache; **~spange** *f* MED brace; **~stein** *m* tartar; **~stocher** *m* (*-s*; -) toothpick
**Zange** ['tsaŋə] *f* (-; *-n*) TECH pliers; pincers; tongs; MED forceps; ZO pincer
**zanken** ['tsaŋkən] *v/refl* (*ge-*, *h*) quarrel (***wegen*** about; ***um*** over), fight, argue (about; over)
**zänkisch** ['tsɛŋkɪʃ] *adj* quarrelsome
**Zäpfchen** ['tsɛpfçən] *n* (*-s*; -) ANAT uvula; PHARM suppository
**zapfen** ['tsapfən] *v/t* (*ge-*, *h*) tap
**'Zapfen** *m* (*-s*; -) faucet, *Br* tap; TECH peg, pin; bung; tenon; pivot; BOT cone
**'Zapfenstreich** *m* MIL tattoo, taps
**'Zapf|hahn** *m* faucet, *Br* tap; MOT nozzle; **~säule** *f* MOT gasoline (*Br* petrol) pump
**zappelig** ['tsapəlɪç] *adj* fidgety
**zappeln** ['tsapəln] *v/i* (*ge-*, *h*) fidget, wriggle
**zappen** ['zɛpən] F *v/i* (*ge-*, *h*) TV zap
**zart** [tsa:ɐt] *adj* tender; gentle; ***~fühlend*** sensitive
**'Zartgefühl** *n* (*-[e]s*; *no pl*) delicacy (of feeling), sensitivity, tact
**zärtlich** ['tsɛ:ɐtlɪç] *adj* tender, affectionate (***zu*** with); **'Zärtlichkeit** *f* (-; *-en*) a) (*no pl*) tenderness, affection, b) caress
**Zauber** ['tsaubɐ] *m* (*-s*; -) magic, spell, charm (*all a. fig*), *fig* enchantment; **Zauberei** [tsaubə'rai] *f* (-; *-en*) magic, witchcraft; **Zauberer** ['tsaubərɐ] *m* (*-s*; -) magician, sorcerer, wizard (*a. fig*); **'zauberhaft** *fig adj* enchanting, charming; **Zauberin** ['tsaubərɪn] *f* (-; *-nen*) sorceress
**'Zauber|kraft** *f* magic power; **~künstler** *m* magician, conjurer; **~kunststück** *n* conjuring trick
**'zaubern** (*ge-*, *h*) **1.** *v/i* practise magic; do conjuring tricks; **2.** *v/t* conjure (up)
**'Zauberspruch** *m* spell
**zaudern** ['tsaudɐn] *v/i* (*ge-*, *h*) hesitate
**Zaum** [tsaum] *m* (*-[e]s*; *Zäume* ['tsɔʏmə]) bridle; ***im ~ halten*** control (***sich*** o.s.), keep in check
**zäumen** ['tsɔʏmən] *v/t* (*ge-*, *h*) bridle
**'Zaumzeug** *n* (*-[e]s*; *-e*) bridle
**Zaun** [tsaun] *m* (*-[e]s*; *Zäune* ['tsɔʏnə]) fence; **~gast** *m* onlooker; **~pfahl** *m* pale
**z.B.** ABBR *of* ***zum Beispiel*** e.g., for example, for instance
**Zebra** ['tse:bra] *n* (*-s*; *-s*) ZO zebra
**'Zebrastreifen** *m* MOT zebra crossing
**Zeche** ['tsɛçə] *f* (-; *-n*) check, *Br* bill; (coal) mine, pit; ***die ~ bezahlen müssen*** F have to foot the bill
**Zeh** [tse:] *m* (*-s*; *-en*), **Zehe** ['tse:ə] *f* (-; *-n*) ANAT toe; ***große*** (***kleine***) **~** big (little) toe; **'Zehennagel** *m* ANAT toenail
**'Zehenspitze** *f* tip of the toe; ***auf ~n gehen*** (walk on) tiptoe
**zehn** [tse:n] *adj* ten; **'zehnfach** *adj* tenfold; **'zehnjährig** [-jɛ:rɪç] *adj* ten-year-old (*boy etc*); ten-year *anniversary etc*; *absence etc* of ten years
**Zehnkampf** *m* SPORT decathlon
**'zehnmal** *adv* ten times; **'zehnte** *adj* tenth; **'Zehntel** *n* (*-s*; -) tenth; **'zehntens** *adv* tenthly
**Zeichen** ['tsaiçən] *n* (*-s*; -) sign; mark; signal; ***zum ~*** *gen* as a token of; **~block** *m* sketch pad; **~brett** *n* drawing board; **~dreieck** *n* MATH set square; **~folge** *f* EDP string; **~lehrer(in)** art teacher; **~setzung** *f* (-; *no pl*) LING punctuation; **~sprache** *f* sign language; **~trickfilm** *m* (animated) cartoon
**zeichnen** ['tsaiçnən] *v/i and v/t* (*ge-*, *h*) draw; mark (*a. fig*); sign; *fig* leave its mark on *s.o.*; **'Zeichnen** *n* (*-s*; *no pl*) drawing; PED art; **'Zeichner** ['tsaiçnɐ] *m* (*-s*; -) *mst* graphic artist; draftsman, *Br* draughtsman; **'Zeichnung** *f* (-; *-en*) drawing; diagram; ZO marking
**Zeigefinger** ['tsaigə-] *m* ANAT forefinger, index finger; **zeigen** ['tsaigən] (*ge-*, *h*) **1.** *v/t* show (*a.* ***sich ~***); **2.** *v/i*: ***~ nach*** point to; (***mit dem Finger***) ***~ auf*** (*acc*) point (one's finger) at; **Zeiger** ['tsaigɐ] *m* (*-s*; -) hand; TECH pointer, needle; **'Zeigestock** *m* pointer
**Zeile** ['tsailə] *f* (-; *-n*) line (*a.* TV); ***j-m ein paar ~n schreiben*** drop s.o. a line
**Zeit** [tsait] *f* (-; *-en*) time; age, era; LING tense; ***vor einiger ~*** some time ago, a while ago; ***in letzter ~*** lately, recently; ***in der*** (*or* ***zur***) ***~*** *gen* in the days of; ***... aller ~en*** ... of all time; ***die ~ ist um*** time's up; ***e-e ~ lang*** for some time, for a while; ***sich ~ lassen*** take one's time;

***es wird ~, dass ...*** it's time to *inf*; ***das waren noch ~en*** those were the days; → ***zurzeit***

**'Zeit|abschnitt** *m* period (of time); **~alter** *n* age; **~bombe** *f* time bomb (*a. fig*); **~druck** *m*: ***unter ~ stehen*** be pressed for time; **~fahren** *n* (*-s*; *no pl*) *cycling*: time trials

**'zeitgemäß** *adj* modern, up-to-date

**'Zeitgenosse** *m*, **'Zeitgenossin** *f*, **'zeitgenössisch** [-gənœsɪʃ] *adj* contemporary

**'Zeit|geschichte** *f* (-; *no pl*) contemporary history; **~gewinn** *m* (-[*e*]*s*; *no pl*) gain of time; **~karte** *f* season ticket

**zeit'lebens** *adv* all one's life

**'zeitlich 1.** *adj* time ...; **2.** *adv*: ***et. ~ planen*** or ***abstimmen*** time s.th.

**'zeitlos** *adj* timeless; classic

**'Zeit|lupe** *f*: ***in ~*** in slow motion; **~not** *f*: ***in ~ sein*** be pressed for time; **~punkt** *m* moment; **~raffer** *m*: ***im ~*** in quick motion

**'zeitraubend** *adj* time-consuming

**'Zeitraum** *m* period (of time)

**'Zeitschrift** *f* magazine

**Zeitung** ['tsaitʊŋ] *f* (-; *-en*) (news)paper

**'Zeitungs|abonne,ment** *n* subscription to a paper; **~ar,tikel** *m* newspaper article; **~ausschnitt** *m* (newspaper) clipping (*Br* cutting); **~junge** *m* paper boy; **~kiosk** *m* newspaper kiosk; **~no,tiz** *f* press item; **~pa,pier** *n* newspaper; **~stand** *m* newsstand; **~verkäufer(in)** newsdealer, *Br* news vendor

**'Zeitverlust** *m* (-[*e*]*s*; *no pl*) loss of time

**'Zeitverschiebung** *f* AVIAT time lag

**'Zeitverschwendung** *f* waste of time

**'Zeitvertreib** [-fɛɐtraip] *m* (-[*e*]*s*; *-e*) pastime; ***zum ~*** to pass the time

**zeitweilig** ['tsaitvailɪç] *adj* temporary

**'zeitweise** *adv* at times, occasionally

**'Zeitwort** *n* (-[*e*]*s*; *-wörter*) LING verb

**'Zeitzeichen** *n radio*: time signal

**'Zeitzünder** *m* MIL time fuse

**Zelle** ['tsɛlə] *f* (-; *-n*) cell

**Zellstoff** ['tsɛl-] *m*, **Zellulose** [tsɛlu'loːzə] *f* (-; *-n*) TECH cellulose

**Zelt** [tsɛlt] *n* (-[*e*]*s*; *-e*) tent; **zelten** ['tsɛltən] *v/i* (*ge-*, *h*) camp; **'Zeltlager** *n* camp; **'Zeltplatz** *m* campsite

**Zement** [tse'mɛnt] *m* (-[*e*]*s*; *-e*), **zementieren** [tsemɛn'tiːrən] *v/t* (*no -ge-*, *h*) cement

**Zenit** [tse'niːt] *m* (-[*e*]*s*; *no pl*) zenith

**zensieren** [tsɛn'ziːrən] *v/t* (*no -ge-*, *h*) censor; PED mark, grade; **Zensor** ['tsɛnzoːɐ] *m* (*-s*; *-en* [tsɛn'zoːrən]) censor; **Zensur** [tsɛn'zuːɐ] *f* (-; *-en* [tsɛn'zuːrən]) a) (*no pl*) censorship, b) PED mark, grade

**Zentimeter** [tsɛnti'meːtɐ] *n*, *m* (*-s*; -) centimeter, *Br* centimetre

**Zentner** ['tsɛntnɐ] *m* (*-s*; -) 50 kilograms, metric hundredweight

**zentral** [tsɛn'traːl] *adj* central

**Zentrale** [tsɛn'traːlə] *f* (-; *-n*) head office; headquarters; TEL switchboard; TECH control room

**Zen'tral|heizung** *f* central heating; **~verriegelung** *f* MOT central locking

**Zentrum** ['tsɛntrʊm] *n* (*-s*; *Zentren*) center, *Br* centre

**Zepter** ['tsɛptɐ] *n* (*-s*; -) scepter, *Br* sceptre

**zer'brechen** *v/i* (*irr*, ***brechen***, *no -ge-*, *sein*) *and v/t* (*h*) break ; → ***Kopf***

**zer'brechlich** *adj* fragile

**zer'bröckeln** *v/t* (*no -ge-*, *h*) *and v/i* (*sein*) crumble

**zer'drücken** *v/t* (*no -ge-*, *h*) crush

**Zeremonie** [tseremo'niː] *f* (-; *-n*) ceremony

**zeremoniell** [tseremo'njɛl] *adj*, **Zeremoni'ell** *n* (*-s*; *-e*) ceremonial

**Zer'fall** *m* (-[*e*]*s*; *no pl*) disintegration, decay; **zer'fallen** *v/i* (*irr*, ***fallen***, *no -ge-*, *sein*) disintegrate, decay; ***~ in*** (*acc*) break up into

**zer|'fetzen** *v/t* (*no -ge-*, *h*) tear to pieces; **~'fressen** *v/t* (*irr*, ***fressen***, *no -ge-*, *h*) eat (holes in); CHEM corrode; **~'gehen** *v/i* (*irr*, ***gehen***, *no -ge-*, *sein*) melt, dissolve; **~'hacken** *v/t* (*no -ge-*, *h*) chop (*a.* ELECTR)

**zerknirscht** [tsɛɐ'knɪrʃt] *adj* remorseful

**zer|'knittern** *v/t* (*no -ge-*, *h*) (c)rumple, crease; **~'knüllen** *v/t* (*no -ge-*, *h*) crumple up; **~'kratzen** *v/t* (*no -ge-*, *h*) scratch; **~'krümeln** *v/t* (*no -ge-*, *h*) crumble; **~'lassen** *v/t* (*irr*, ***lassen***, *no -ge-*, *h*) melt; **~'legen** *v/t* (*no -ge-*, *h*) take apart *or* to pieces; TECH dismantle; GASTR carve; CHEM, LING, *fig* analyze, *Br* analyse

**zer'lumpt** *adj* ragged, tattered

**zer'mahlen** *v/t* (*no -ge-*, *h*) grind

**zer'mürben** *v/t* (*no -ge-*, *h*) wear down

**zer'quetschen** *v/t* (*no -ge-*, *h*) crush
**Zerrbild** ['tsɛɐ-] *n* caricature
**zer'reiben** *v/t* (*irr*, ***reiben,*** *no -ge-*, *h*) rub to powder, pulverize
**zer'reißen** (*irr*, ***reißen,*** *no -ge-*) **1.** *v/t* (*h*) tear up *or* to pieces; ***sich die Hose ~*** tear one's trousers; **2.** *v/i* (*sein*) tear; break
**zerren** ['tsɛrən] (*ge-*, *h*) **1.** *v/t* tug, drag, pull (*a.* MED); **2.** *v/i*: ***~ an*** (*dat*) tug (*or* strain) at
**'Zerrung** *f* (-; *-en*) MED pulled muscle
**zerrütten** [tsɛɐ'rʏtən] *v/t* (*no -ge-*, *h*) ruin; **zer'rüttet** *adj*: ***~e Ehe*** (***Verhältnisse***) broken marriage (home)
**zer|'sägen** *v/t* (*no -ge-*, *h*) saw up; **~schellen** [-'ʃɛlən] *v/i* (*no -ge-*, *sein*) be smashed, AVIAT *a.* crash; **~'schlagen** **1.** *v/t* (*irr*, ***schlagen,*** *no -ge-*, *h*) smash (to pieces); *fig* smash; ***sich ~*** come to nothing; **2.** *adj*: ***sich ~ fühlen*** be (all) worn out, F be dead beat; **~'schmettern** *v/t* (*no -ge-*, *h*) smash (to pieces), shatter (*a. fig*); **~'schneiden** *v/t* (*irr*, ***schneiden,*** *no -ge-*, *h*) cut (up); **~'setzen** *v/t* (*no -ge-*, *h*) CHEM decompose (*a.* ***sich ~***); *fig* corrupt, undermine; **~'splittern** *v/t* (*no -ge-*, *h*) *and v/i* (*sein*) split (up), splinter; shatter; **~'springen** *v/i* (*irr*, ***springen,*** *no -ge-*, *sein*) crack; shatter; **~'stampfen** *v/t* (*no -ge-*, *h*) pound; GASTR mash
**zer'stäuben** *v/t* (*no -ge-*, *h*) spray; **Zerstäuber** [tsɛɐ'ʃtɔʏbɐ] *m* (*-s*; -) atomizer, sprayer
**zer'stören** *v/t* (*no -ge-*, *h*) destroy, ruin (*both a. fig*); **Zer'störer** *m* (*-s*; -) destroyer (*a.* MAR); **zer'störerisch** *adj* destructive; **Zer'störung** *f* (-; *-en*) destruction
**zer'streuen** *v/t and v/refl* (*no -ge-*, *h*) scatter, disperse; break up (*crowd etc*); *fig* take s.o.'s (*refl* one's) mind off things; **zer'streut** *fig adj* absent-minded; **Zer'streutheit** *f* (-; *no pl*) absent-mindedness; **Zer'streuung** *fig f* (-; *-en*) diversion, distraction
**zer'stückeln** *v/t* (*no -ge-*, *h*) cut up *or* (in)to pieces; dismember (*body*)
**Zertifikat** [tsɛrtifi'ka:t] *n* (-[*e*]*s*; *-e*) certificate
**zer'treten** *v/t* (*irr*, ***treten,*** *no -ge-*, *h*) crush (*a. fig*)
**zer'trümmern** *v/t* (*no -ge-*, *h*) smash
**zerzaust** [tsɛɐ'tsaust] *adj* tousled, dishevel(l)ed
**Zettel** ['tsɛtəl] *m* (*-s*; -) slip (of paper); note; label, sticker
**Zeug** [tsɔʏk] *n* (-[*e*]*s*; *-e*) stuff (*a.* F); things; ***er hat das ~ dazu*** he's got what it takes; ***dummes ~*** nonsense
**Zeuge** ['tsɔʏgə] *m* (*-n*; *-n*) witness
**'zeugen¹** *v/i* (*ge-*, *h*) JUR give evidence (***für*** for); *fig* ***~ von*** testify to
**'zeugen²** *v/t* (*ge-*, *h*) BIOL procreate; father
**'Zeugen|aussage** *f* JUR testimony, evidence; **~bank** *f* (-; *-bänke*) JUR witness stand (*Br* box)
**'Zeugin** *f* (-; *-nen*) JUR (female) witness
**Zeugnis** ['tsɔʏknɪs] *n* (*-ses*; *-se*) report card, *Br* (school) report; certificate, diploma; reference; *pl* credentials
**'Zeugung** *f* (-; *-en*) BIOL procreation
**z. H(d).** ABBR *of* ***zu Händen*** attn, attention
**Zickzack** ['tsɪktsak] *m* (-[*e*]*s*; *-e*) (*a.* ***im ~ fahren***) zigzag
**Ziege** ['tsi:gə] *f* (-; *-n*) ZO (nanny) goat; F *contp* (***blöde***) **~** (silly old) cow
**Ziegel** ['tsi:gəl] *m* (*-s*; -) brick; tile
**'Ziegeldach** *n* tiled roof
**Ziegelei** [tsi:gə'lai] *f* (-; *-en*) brickyard
**'Ziegelstein** *m* brick
**'Ziegen|bock** *m* ZO billy goat; **~leder** *n* kid (leather); **~peter** [-pe:tɐ] *m* (*-s*; -) MED mumps
**ziehen** ['tsi:ən] (*irr*, *-ge-*) **1.** *v/t* (*h*) pull, draw; take off *one's hat* (**vor** *dat* to) (*a. fig*); AGR grow; pull *or* take out (***aus*** of); ***j-n ~ an*** (*dat*) pull s.o. by; ***auf sich ~*** attract (*attention etc*); ***sich ~*** run; stretch; → ***Länge***, ***Erwägung***; **2.** *v/i* a) (*h*) pull (**an** *dat* at), b) (*sein*) move; ZO *etc* migrate; go; travel; wander, roam; ***es zieht*** there's a draft (*Br* draught)
**Ziehharmonika** ['tsi:harmo:nika] *f* (-; *-s*) MUS accordion
**'Ziehung** *f* (-; *-en*) draw
**Ziel** [tsi:l] *n* (-[*e*]*s*; *-e*) aim, target, mark (*all a. fig*), *fig a.* goal, objective; destination; SPORT finish; ***sich ein ~ setzen*** set o.s. a goal; ***sein ~ erreichen*** reach one's goal; ***sich zum ~ gesetzt haben, et. zu tun*** aim to do *or* at doing s.th.
**'Zielband** *n* (-[*e*]*s*; *-bänder*) SPORT tape
**zielen** ['tsi:lən] *v/i* (*ge-*, *h*) (take) aim (***auf*** *acc* at)

'**Ziellinie** *f* SPORT finishing line
'**ziellos** *adj* aimless
'**Zielscheibe** *f* target, *fig a.* object
**zielstrebig** ['tsiːlʃtreːbɪç] *adj* purposeful, determined
**ziemlich** ['tsiːmlɪç] **1.** *adj* quite a; **2.** *adv* rather, fairly, quite, F pretty; ~ ***viele*** quite a few
**Zierde** ['tsiːɐdə] *f* (-; *-n*) (**zur** as a) decoration; **zieren** ['tsiːrən] *v/t* (*ge-*, *h*) decorate; ***sich*** ~ be coy; make a fuss
**zierlich** ['tsiːɐlɪç] *adj* dainty; petite
**Zierpflanze** ['tsiːɐ-] *f* ornamental plant
**Ziffer** ['tsɪfɐ] *f* (-; *-n*) figure
'**Zifferblatt** *n* dial, face
**Zigarette** [tsiga'rɛtə] *f* (-; *-n*) cigarette
**Ziga'retten|auto,mat** *m* cigarette machine; **~stummel** *m* cigarette end, stub, butt
**Zigarre** [tsi'garə] *f* (-; *-n*) cigar
**Zigeuner** [tsi'gɔʏnɐ] *m* (*-s*; -), **Zi'geunerin** [-nərɪn] *f* (-; *-nen*) gypsy, *Br* gipsy
**Zimmer** ['tsɪmɐ] *n* (*-s*; -) room; apartment; **~einrichtung** *f* furniture; **~mädchen** *n* (chamber)maid; **~mann** *m* carpenter
'**zimmern** *v/t* (*ge-*, *h*) build, make
'**Zimmer|pflanze** *f* indoor plant; **~service** *m* room service; **~suche** *f*: ***auf ~ sein*** be looking (*or* hunting) for a room; **~vermittlung** *f* accommodation office
**zimperlich** ['tsɪmpɐlɪç] *adj* prudish; soft, F sissy
**Zimt** [tsɪmt] *m* (-[*e*]*s*; *-e*) cinnamon
**Zink** ['tsɪŋk] *n* (-[*e*]*s*; *no pl*) CHEM zinc
**Zinke** ['tsɪŋkə] *f* (-; *-n*) tooth; prong
**Zinn** [tsɪn] *n* (-[*e*]*s*; *no pl*) CHEM tin; pewter
**Zins** [tsɪns] *m* (*-es*; *-en*) ECON interest (*a. pl*); ***3% ~en bringen*** bear interest at 3%; '**zinslos** *adj* ECON interest-free; '**Zinssatz** *m* ECON interest rate
**Zipfel** ['tsɪpfəl] *m* (*-s*; -) corner; point; tail; GASTR end; **~mütze** *f* pointed cap
**zirka** ['tsɪrka] *adv* about, approximately
**Zirkel** ['tsɪrkəl] *m* (*-s*; -) circle (*a. fig*); MATH compasses, dividers
**zirkulieren** [tsɪrku'liːrən] *v/i* (*no -ge-*, *h*) circulate
**Zirkus** ['tsɪrkʊs] *m* (-; *-se*) circus
**zirpen** ['tsɪrpən] *v/i* (*ge-*, *h*) chirp
**zischen** ['tsɪʃən] *v/i and v/t* (*ge-*, *h*) hiss; *fat etc*: sizzle; *fig* whiz(z)
**ziselieren** [tsizə'liːrən] *v/t* (*no -ge-*, *h*) TECH chase
**Zitat** [tsi'taːt] *n* (-[*e*]*s*; *-e*) quotation, F quote; **zitieren** [tsi'tiːrən] *v/t* (*no -ge-*, *h*) quote, cite (*a.* JUR), JUR summon
**Zitrone** [tsi'troːnə] *f* (-; *-n*) BOT lemon
**Zi'tronen|limo,nade** *f* lemon soda *or* pop, *Br* (fizzy) lemonade; **~saft** *m* lemon juice; **~schale** *f* lemon peel
**zitterig** ['tsɪtərɪç] *adj* shaky; **zittern** ['tsɪtɐn] *v/i* (*ge-*, *h*) tremble, shake (*both*: ***vor*** *dat* with)
**zivil** [tsi'viːl] *adj* civil, civilian
**Zi'vil** *n* (*-s*; *no pl*) civilian clothes; ***Polizist in ~*** plainclothes policeman
**Zi'vildienst** *m* MIL alternative service (*in lieu of military service*)
**Zivilisation** [tsiviliza'tsjoːn] *f* (-; *-en*) civilization; **zivilisieren** [tsivili'ziːrən] *v/t* (*no -ge-*, *h*) civilize
**Zivilist** [tsivi'lɪst] *m* (*-en*; *-en*) civilian
**Zi'vilrecht** *n* (-[*e*]*s*; *no pl*) JUR civil law
**Zi'vilschutz** *m* civil defen|se, *Br* -ce
**Znüni** ['tsnyːni] *Swiss m*, *n* (*-s*; -) midmorning snack, tea (*or* coffee) break
**zog** [tsoːk] *pret of* ***ziehen***
**zögern** ['tsøːgɐn] *v/i* (*ge-*, *h*) hesitate; '**Zögern** *n* (*-s*; *no pl*) hesitation
**Zoll¹** [tsɔl] *m* (-[*e*]*s*; -) inch
**Zoll²** *m* (-[*e*]*s*; *Zölle* ['tsœlə]) a) (*no pl*) customs, b) duty
'**Zollabfertigung** *f* customs clearance
'**Zollbeamte** *m* customs officer
'**Zollerklärung** *f* customs declaration
'**zollfrei** *adj* duty-free
'**Zollkon,trolle** *f* customs examination
'**zollpflichtig** *adj* liable to duty
'**Zollstock** *m* (folding) rule
**Zone** ['tsoːnə] *f* (-; *-n*) zone
**Zoo** [tsoː] *m* (*-s*; *-s*) zoo
'**Zoohandlung** *f* pet shop
**Zoologe** [tsoo'loːgə] *m* (*-n*; *-n*) zoologist; **Zoologie** [tsoolo'giː] *f* (-; *no pl*) zoology; **Zoo'login** *f* (-; *-nen*) zoologist; **zoo'logisch** *adj* zoological
**Zopf** [tsɔpf] *m* (-[*e*]*s*; *Zöpfe* ['tsœpfə]) plait; pigtail
**Zorn** [tsɔrn] *m* (-[*e*]*s*; *no pl*) anger
**zornig** ['tsɔrnɪç] *adj* angry
**Zote** ['tsoːtə] *f* (-; *-n*) filthy joke, obscenity
**zottelig** ['tsɔtəlɪç] *adj* shaggy
**z.T.** ABBR *of* ***zum Teil*** partly
**zu** [tsuː] **1.** *prp* (*dat*) to, toward(s); at;

*purpose*: for; **~ *Fuß*** (***Pferd***) on foot (horseback); **~ *Hause*** (***Ostern*** *etc*) at home (Easter *etc*); **~ *Weihnachten*** *give etc* for Christmas; ***Tür*** (***Schlüssel***) **~ ...** door (key) to ...; **~ *m-r Überraschung*** to my surprise; ***wir sind* ~ *dritt*** there are three of us; **~ *zweien*** two by two; **~ *e-r Mark*** at *or* for one mark; SPORT ***1* ~ *1*** one all; ***2* ~ *1 gewinnen*** win two one, win by two goals *etc* to one; → ***zum, zur***; **2.** *adv* too; F closed, shut; ***ein* ~ *großes Risiko*** too much of a risk; **~ *viel*** too much, too many; **~ *wenig*** too little, too few; **3.** *cj* to; ***es ist* ~ *erwarten*** it is to be expected

**Zubehör** ['tsu:bəhø:ɐ] *n* (*-[e]s*; *-e*) accessories

'**zubereiten** *v/t* (*sep*, *no -ge-*, *h*) prepare; '**Zubereitung** *f* (*-*; *-en*) preparation

'**zu|binden** *v/t* (*irr*, ***binden***, *sep*, *-ge-*, *h*) tie (up); **~bleiben** *v/i* (*irr*, ***bleiben***, *sep*, *-ge-*, *sein*) stay shut; **~blinzeln** *v/i* (*sep*, *-ge-*, *h*) (*dat*) wink at

'**Zubringer** *m* (*-s*; *-*), **~straße** *f* MOT feeder (road), access road

**Zucht** [tsʊxt] *f* (*-*; *-en*) breed; ZO breeding; BOT cultivation; **züchten** ['tsʏçtən] *v/t* (*ge-*, *h*) ZO breed; BOT grow, cultivate; **Züchter(in)** ['tsʏçtɐ (-tərɪn)] *m* (*-s*; *-/-*; *-nen*) ZO breeder; BOT grower

'**Zuchtperle** *f* culture(d) pearl

**zucken** ['tsʊkən] *v/i* (*ge-*, *h*) jerk; twitch (***mit et.*** s.th.); wince; *lightning*: flash

**zücken** ['tsʏkən] *v/t* (*ge-*, *h*) draw (*weapon*); F pull out (*one's wallet etc*)

**Zucker** ['tsʊkɐ] *m* (*-s*; *-*) sugar; **~dose** *f* sugar bowl; **~guss** *m* icing, frosting

'**zuckerkrank** *adj*, '**Zuckerkranke** *m*, *f* (*-n*; *-n*) MED diabetic

'**Zuckerkrankheit** *f* MED diabetes

'**Zuckermais** *m* sweet corn

'**zuckern** *v/t* (*ge-*, *h*) sugar

'**Zuckerrohr** *n* BOT sugarcane

'**Zuckerrübe** *f* BOT sugar beet

'**Zuckerwatte** *f* candy floss

'**Zuckerzange** *f* sugar tongs

'**Zuckung** *f* (*-*; *-en*) twitch(ing); tic; convulsion, spasm

'**zudecken** *v/t* (*sep*, *-ge-*, *h*) cover (up)

**zudem** [tsu'de:m] *adv* besides, moreover

'**zudrehen** *v/t* (*sep*, *-ge-*, *h*) turn off; ***j-m den Rücken* ~** turn one's back on s.o.

'**zudringlich** *adj*: **~ *werden*** F get fresh (***j-m gegenüber*** with s.o.)

'**zudrücken** *v/t* (*sep*, *-ge-*, *h*) close, push *s.th.* shut; → ***Auge***

**zuerst** [tsu'ʔe:ɐst] *adv* first; at first; first (of all), to begin with

'**Zufahrt** *f* approach; drive(way)

'**Zufahrtsstraße** *f* access road

'**Zufall** *m* chance; ***durch* ~** by chance, by accident; '**zufallen** *v/i* (*irr*, ***fallen***, *sep*, *-ge-*, *sein*) *door etc*: slam (shut); *fig* fall to *s.o.*; ***mir fallen die Augen zu*** I can't keep my eyes open; '**zufällig 1.** *adj* accidental, chance ...; **2.** *adv* by accident, by chance; **~ *tun*** happen to do

'**Zuflucht** *f*: **~ *suchen*** (***finden***) look for (find) refuge *or* shelter (***vor*** *dat* from; ***bei*** with); (***s-e***) **~ *nehmen zu*** resort to

**zufrieden** [tsu'fri:dən] *adj* content(ed), satisfied; ***sich* ~ *geben mit*** content o.s. with; ***j-n* ~ *lassen*** leave s.o. alone; **~ *stellen*** satisfy; **~ *stellend*** satisfactory;

**Zu'friedenheit** *f* (*-*; *no pl*) contentment, satisfaction

'**zufrieren** *v/i* (*irr*, ***frieren***, *sep*, *-ge-*, *sein*) freeze up *or* over

'**zufügen** *v/t* (*sep*, *-ge-*, *h*) do, cause; ***j-m Schaden* ~ *a.*** harm s.o.

**Zufuhr** ['tsu:fu:ɐ] *f* (*-*; *-en*) supply

**Zug** [tsu:k] *m* (*-[e]s*; *Züge* ['tsy:gə]) RAIL train; procession, line; parade; *fig* feature; trait; tendency; *chess etc*: move (*a. fig*); *swimming*: stroke; pull (*a.* TECH), PHYS *a.* tension; *smoking*: puff; draft, *Br* draught; PED stream; ***im* ~*e*** *gen* in the course of; ***in e-m* ~** at one go; **~ *um* ~** step by step; ***in groben Zügen*** in broad outlines

'**Zugabe** *f* addition; THEA encore

'**Zugang** *m* access (*a. fig*); '**zugänglich** [-gɛŋlɪç] *adj* accessible (***für*** to) (*a. fig*)

'**Zugbrücke** *f* drawbridge

'**zugeben** *v/t* (*irr*, ***geben***, *sep*, *-ge-*, *h*) add; *fig* admit

'**zugehen** *v/i* (*irr*, ***gehen***, *sep*, *-ge-*, *sein*) F *door etc*: close, shut; **~ *auf*** (*acc*) walk up to, approach (*a. fig*); ***es geht auf 8 Uhr zu*** it's getting on for 8; ***es ging lustig zu*** we had a lot of fun

'**Zugehörigkeit** *f* (*-*; *no pl*) membership

**Zügel** ['tsy:gəl] *m* (*-s*; *-*) rein (*a. fig*)

'**zügeln 1.** *v/t* (*ge-*, *h*) curb, control, bridle; **2.** *Swiss v/i* (*ge-*, *sein*) move

'**Zugeständnis** *n* concession

**'zugestehen** *v/t* (*irr*, ***stehen,*** *sep*, *no -ge-*, *h*) concede, grant
**'zugetan** *adj* attached (*dat* to)
**'Zugführer** *m* RAIL conductor, *Br* guard
**zugig** ['tsu:gıç] *adj* drafty, *Br* draughty
**'Zugkraft** *f* a) TECH traction, b) (*no pl*) attraction, draw, appeal
**'zugkräftig** *adj*: ~ ***sein*** be a draw
**zu'gleich** [tsu-] *adv* at the same time
**'Zugluft** *f* (-; *no pl*) draft, *Br* draught
**'Zugma,schine** *f* MOT tractor
**'zugreifen** *v/i* (*irr*, ***greifen,*** *sep*, *-ge-*, *h*) grab (at) it; *fig* grab the opportunity; ***greifen Sie zu!*** help yourself!; ***mit*** ~ lend a hand
**'Zugriffscode** *m* EDP access code
**'Zugriffszeit** *f* EDP access time
**zugrunde** [tsu'grʊndə] *adv*: ~ ***gehen*** (***an*** *dat*) perish (of); ***e-r Sache et.*** ~ ***legen*** base s.th. on s.th.; ~ ***richten*** ruin
**zugunsten** [tsu'gʊnstən] *prp* (*gen*) in favo(u)r of
**zu'gute** [tsu-] *adv*: ***j-m et.*** ~ ***halten*** give s.o. credit for s.th.; make allowances for s.o.'s ...; ***j-m*** ~ ***kommen*** be for the benefit of s.o.
**'Zugvogel** *m* ZO bird of passage
**'zuhalten** *v/t* (*irr*, ***halten,*** *sep*, *-ge-*, *h*) keep shut; ***sich die Ohren*** (***Augen***) ~ cover one's ears (eyes) with one's hands; ***sich die Nase*** ~ hold one's nose
**Zuhälter** ['tsu:hɛltɐ] *m* (*-s*; -) pimp
**Zuhause** [tsu'hauzə] *n* (*-s*; *no pl*) home
**zu'hause** *Austrian adv* at home
**'zuhören** *v/i* (*sep*, *-ge-*, *h*) listen (*dat* to)
**'Zuhörer** *m*, **'Zuhörerin** *f* listener, *pl a. the* audience
**'zujubeln** *v/i* (*sep*, *-ge-*, *h*) cheer
**'zukleben** *v/t* (*sep*, *-ge-*, *h*) seal
**'zuknöpfen** *v/t* (*sep*, *-ge-*, *h*) button (up)
**'zukommen** *v/i* (*irr*, ***kommen,*** *sep*, *-ge-*, *sein*) ~ ***auf*** (*acc*) come up to; *fig* be ahead of; ***die Dinge auf sich*** ~ ***lassen*** wait and see
**Zukunft** ['tsu:kʊnft] *f* (-; *no pl*) future (*a.* LING)
**'zukünftig 1.** *adj* future; **2.** *adv* in future
**'zulächeln** *v/i* (*sep*, *-ge-*, *h*) smile at
**'Zulage** *f* bonus
**'zulangen** F *v/i* (*sep*, *-ge-*, *h*) tuck in
**'zulassen** *v/t* (*irr*, ***lassen,*** *sep*, *-ge-*, *h*) F keep *s.th.* closed; *fig* allow; MOT *etc* license, register; ***j-n zu et.*** ~ admit s.o. to s.th.; **'zulässig** *adj* admissible (*a.* JUR); ~ ***sein*** be allowed; **'Zulassung** *f* (-; *-en*) admission; MOT *etc* license, *Br* licence
**'zulegen** *v/t* (*sep*, *-ge-*, *h*) add; F ***sich ...*** ~ get o.s. *s.th.*; adopt (*name*)
**zu'letzt** [tsu-] *adv* in the end; *come etc* last; finally; ***wann hast du ihn*** ~ ***gesehen?*** when did you last see him?
**zu'liebe** [tsu-] *adv*: ***j-m*** ~ for s.o.'s sake
**zum** [tsʊm] *prp* ***zu dem*** → ***zu;*** ~ ***ersten Mal*** for the first time; *et.* ~ ***Kaffee*** *s.th.* with one's coffee; ~ ***Schwimmen*** *etc* ***gehen*** go swimming *etc*
**'zumachen** F (*sep*, *-ge-*, *h*) **1.** *v/t* close, shut; button (up); **2.** *v/i* close (down)
**'zumauern** *v/t* (*sep*, *-ge-*, *h*) brick *or* wall up
**zumutbar** ['tsu:mu:tba:ɐ] *adj* reasonable; **zu'mute** [tsu-] *adv*: ***mir ist ...*** ~ I feel ...; **'zumuten** *v/t* (*sep*, *-ge-*, *h*) ***j-m et.*** ~ expect s.th. of s.o.; ***sich zu viel*** ~ overtax o.s.; **'Zumutung** *f*: ***das ist e-e*** ~ that's asking *or* expecting a bit much
**zu'nächst** [tsu-] *adv* → ***zuerst***
**'zunageln** *v/t* (*sep*, *-ge-*, *h*) nail up
**'zunähen** *v/t* (*sep*, *-ge-*, *h*) sew up
**Zunahme** ['tsu:na:mə] *f* (-; *-n*) increase
**'Zuname** *m* surname
**zünden** ['tsʏndən] *v/i* (*ge-*, *h*) kindle; ELECTR, MOT ignite, fire; **~d** *fig adj* stirring
**Zünder** ['tsʏndɐ] *m* (*-s*; -) MIL fuse; *pl Austrian* matches
**Zünd|holz** ['tsʏnt-] *n* match; **~kerze** *f* MOT spark plug; **~schlüssel** *m* MOT ignition key; **~schnur** *f* fuse
**'Zündung** *f* (-; *-en*) MOT ignition
**'zunehmen** *v/i* (*irr*, ***nehmen,*** *sep*, *-ge-*, *h*) increase (***an*** *dat* in); put on weight; *moon*: wax; *days*: grow longer
**'Zuneigung** *f* (-; *-en*) affection
**Zunft** [tsʊnft] HIST *f* (-; *Zünfte* ['tsʏnftə]) guild
**Zunge** [tsʊŋə] *f* (-; *-n*) ANAT tongue; ***es liegt mir auf der*** ~ it's on the tip of my tongue
**züngeln** ['tsʏŋəln] *v/i* (*ge-*, *h*) *flames*: lick, flicker
**'Zungenspitze** *f* tip of the tongue
**'zunicken** *v/i* (*sep*, *-ge-*, *h*) (*dat*) nod at
**zunutze** [tsu'nʊtsə] *adv*: ***sich et.*** ~ ***machen*** make (good) use of s.th.; take advantage of s.th.

**zupfen** [tsʊpfən] *v/t and v/i* (*ge-*, *h*) pull (**an** *dat* at), pick, pluck (at) (*a.* MUS)
**zur** [tsu:ɐ] *prp* ***zu der*** → ***zu***; ~ ***Schule*** (***Kirche***) ***gehen*** go to school (church); ~ ***Hälfte*** half (of it *or* them); ~ ***Belohnung*** *etc* as a reward *etc*
**'zurechnungsfähig** *adj* JUR responsible; **'Zurechnungsfähigkeit** *f* (-, *no pl*) JUR responsibility
**zu'recht|finden** *v/refl* (*irr*, ***finden***, *sep*, *-ge-*, *h*) find one's way; *fig* cope, manage; **~kommen** *v/i* (*irr*, ***kommen***, *sep*, *-ge-*, *sein*) get along (***mit*** with); cope (with); **~legen** *v/t* (*sep*, *-ge-*, *h*) arrange; *fig* ***sich et.*** ~ think s.th. out; **~machen** F *v/t* (*sep*, *-ge-*, *h*) get ready, prepare, fix; ***sich*** ~ do o.s. up; **~rücken** *v/t* (*sep*, *-ge-*, *h*) put *s.th.* straight (*a. fig*)
**zu'rechtweisen** *v/t* (*irr*, ***weisen***, *sep*, *-ge-*, *h*), **Zu'rechtweisung** *f* reprimand
**'zu|reden** *v/i* (*sep*, *-ge-*, *h*) ***j-m*** ~ encourage s.o.; **~reiten** *v/t* (*irr*, ***reiten***, *sep*, *-ge-*, *h*) break in; **~richten** F *fig v/t* (*sep*, *-ge-*, *h*) ***übel*** ~ batter, *a.* beat *s.o.* up badly, *a.* make a mess of *s.th.*, ruin
**zurück** [tsu'rʏk] *adv* back; behind (*a. fig*); **~behalten** *v/t* (*irr*, ***halten***, *sep*, *no -ge-*, *h*) keep back, retain; **~bekommen** *v/t* (*irr*, ***kommen***, *sep*, *no -ge-*, *h*) get back; **~bleiben** *v/i* (*irr*, ***bleiben***, *sep*, *-ge-*, *sein*) stay behind, be left behind; fall behind (*a.* PED *etc*); **~blicken** *v/i* (*sep*, *-ge-*, *h*) look back (***auf*** *acc* at, *fig* on); **~bringen** *v/t* (*irr*, ***bringen***, *sep*, *-ge-*, *h*) bring *or* take back, return; **~da͵tieren** *v/t* (*sep*, *no -ge-*, *h*) backdate (***auf*** *acc* to); **~fallen** *fig v/i* (*irr*, ***fallen***, *sep*, *-ge-*, *sein*) fall behind, SPORT *a.* drop back; **~finden** *v/i* (*irr*, ***finden***, *sep*, *-ge-*, *h*) find one's way back (***nach***, ***zu*** to); *fig* return (to); **~fordern** *v/t* (*sep*, *-ge-*, *h*) reclaim; **~führen** *v/t* (*sep*, *-ge-*, *h*) lead back; ~ ***auf*** (*acc*) attribute to; **~geben** *v/t* (*irr*, ***geben***, *sep*, *-ge-*, *h*) give back, return; **~geblieben** *fig adj* backward; retarded; **~gehen** *v/i* (*irr*, ***gehen***, *sep*, *-ge-*, *sein*) go back, return; *fig* decrease; go down, drop; **~gezogen** *fig adj* secluded; **~greifen** *v/i* (*irr*, ***greifen***, *sep*, *-ge-*, *h*) ~ ***auf*** (*acc*) fall back (up)on
**zu'rückhalten** (*irr*, ***halten***, *sep*, *-ge-*, *h*) **1.** *v/t* hold back; **2.** *v/refl* control o.s.; be careful; **~d** *adj* reserved
**Zu'rückhaltung** *f* (-; *no pl*) reserve
**zu'rück|kehren** *v/i* (*sep*, *-ge-*, *sein*) return; **~kommen** *v/i* (*irr*, ***kommen***, *sep*, *-ge-*, *sein*) come back, return (*both fig* ***auf*** *acc* to); **~lassen** *v/t* (*irr*, ***lassen***, *sep*, *-ge-*, *h*) leave (behind); **~legen** *v/t* (*sep*, *-ge-*, *h*) put back; put aside, save (*money*); cover, do (*miles*); **~nehmen** *v/t* (*irr*, ***nehmen***, *sep*, *-ge-*, *h*) take back (*a. fig*); **~rufen** (*irr*, ***rufen***, *sep*, *-ge-*, *h*) **1.** *v/t* call back (*a.* TEL); ECON recall; ***ins Gedächtnis*** ~ recall; **2.** *v/i* TEL call back; **~schlagen** (*irr*, ***schlagen***, *sep*, *-ge-*, *h*) **1.** *v/t* beat off; *tennis*: return; fold back; **2.** *v/i* hit back; MIL retaliate (*a. fig*); **~schrecken** *v/i* (*sep*, *-ge-*, *sein*) ~ ***vor*** (*dat*) shrink from; ***vor nichts*** ~ stop at nothing; **~setzen** *v/t* (*sep*, *-ge-*, *h*) MOT back (up); *fig* neglect *s.o.*; **~stehen** *v/i* (*irr*, ***stehen***, *sep*, *-ge-*, *h*) stand aside; **~stellen** *v/t* (*sep*, *-ge-*, *h*) put back (*a. watch*); put aside; MIL defer; **~strahlen** *v/t* (*sep*, *-ge-*, *h*) reflect; **~treten** *v/i* (*irr*, ***treten***, *sep*, *-ge-*, *sein*) step *or* stand back; resign (***von e-m Amt*** [***Posten***] one's office [post]); ECON, JUR withdraw (***von*** from); **~weichen** *v/i* (*irr*, ***weichen***, *sep*, *-ge-*, *sein*) fall back (*a.* MIL); **~weisen** *v/t* (*irr*, ***weisen***, *sep*, *-ge-*, *h*) turn down; JUR dismiss; **~zahlen** *v/t* (*sep*, *-ge-*, *h*) pay back (*a. fig*); **~ziehen** *v/t* (*irr*, ***ziehen***, *sep*, *-ge-*, *h*) draw back; *fig* withdraw; ***sich*** ~ retire, withdraw, MIL *a.* retreat
**'Zuruf** *m* shout; **'zurufen** *v/t* (*irr*, ***rufen***, *sep*, *-ge-*, *h*) ***j-m et.*** ~ shout s.th. to s.o.
**zur'zeit** *adv* at the moment, at present
**'Zusage** *f* promise; assent
**'zusagen** *v/i and v/t* (*sep*, *-ge-*, *h*) accept (an invitation); (*dat*) suit, appeal to; ***s-e Hilfe*** ~ promise to help
**zusammen** [tsu'zamən] *adv* together; ***alles*** ~ (all) in all; ***das macht*** ~ ... that makes ... altogether
**Zu'sammenarbeit** *f* (-; *no pl*) cooperation; ***in*** ~ ***mit*** in collaboration with; **zu'sammenarbeiten** *v/i* (*sep*, *-ge-*, *h*) cooperate, collaborate
**zu'sammenbeißen** *v/t* (*irr*, ***beißen***, *sep*, *-ge-*, *h*) ***die Zähne*** ~ clench one's teeth
**zu'sammenbrechen** *v/i* (*irr*, ***brechen***,

Z

*sep*, *-ge-*, *sein*) break down, collapse (*both a. fig*); **Zu'sammenbruch** *m* breakdown, collapse

**zu'sammen|fallen** *v/i* (*irr*, ***fallen***, *sep*, *-ge-*, *sein*) coincide; **~falten** *v/t* (*sep*, *-ge-*, *h*) fold up

**zu'sammenfassen** *v/t* (*sep*, *-ge-*, *h*) summarize, sum up; **Zu'sammenfassung** *f* (-; *-en*) summary

**zu'sammen|fügen** *v/t* (*sep*, *-ge-*, *h*) join (together); **~gesetzt** *adj* compound; **~halten** *v/i and v/t* (*irr*, ***halten***, *sep*, *-ge-*, *h*) hold together (*a. fig*); F stick together

**Zu'sammenhang** *m* (-[*e*]*s*; *-hänge*) connection; context; ***im ~ stehen*** (***mit***) be connected (with)

**zu'sammenhängen** *v/i* (*irr*, ***hängen***, *sep*, *-ge-*, *h*) be connected; **~d** *adj* coherent

**zu'sammenhang(s)los** *adj* incoherent, disconnected

**zu'sammen|klappen** *v/i* (*sep*, *-ge-*, *sein*) *and v/t* (*h*) TECH fold up; F break down; **~kommen** *v/i* (*irr*, ***kommen***, *sep*, *-ge-*, *sein*) meet

**Zu'sammenkunft** [-kʊnft] *f* (-; *-künfte* [-kʏnftə]) meeting

**zu'sammen|legen** (*sep*, *-ge-*, *h*) **1.** *v/t* combine; fold up; **2.** *v/i* club together; **~nehmen** *v/t* (*irr*, ***nehmen***, *sep*, *-ge-*, *h*) muster (up); ***sich ~*** pull o.s. together; **~packen** *v/t* (*sep*, *-ge-*, *h*) pack up; **~passen** *v/i* (*sep*, *-ge-*, *h*) harmonize; match; **~rechnen** *v/t* (*sep*, *-ge-*, *h*) add up; **~reißen** F *v/refl* (*irr*, ***reißen***, *sep*, *-ge-*, *h*) pull o.s. together; **~rollen** *v/t* (*sep*, *-ge-*, *h*) roll up; ***sich ~*** coil up; **~rotten** [-rɔtən] *v/refl* (*sep*, *-ge-*, *h*) band together; **~rücken** (*sep*, *-ge-*) **1.** *v/t* (*h*) move closer together; **2.** *v/i* (*sein*) move up; **~schlagen** *v/t* (*irr*, ***schlagen***, *sep*, *-ge-*, *h*) clap (*hands*); click (*one's heels*); beat *s.o.* up; smash (up)

**zu'sammenschließen** *v/refl* (*irr*, ***schließen***, *sep*, *-ge-*, *h*) join, unite; **Zu'sammenschluss** *m* union

**zu'sammen|schreiben** *v/t* (*irr*, ***schreiben***, *sep*, *-ge-*, *h*) write in one word; **~schrumpfen** *v/i* (*sep*, *-ge-*, *sein*) shrink

**zu'sammensetzen** *v/t* (*sep*, *-ge-*, *h*) put together; TECH assemble; ***sich ~ aus*** (*dat*) consist of, be composed of; **Zu'sammensetzung** *f* (-; *-en*) composition; CHEM, LING compound; TECH assembly

**zu'sammenstellen** *v/t* (*sep*, *-ge-*, *h*) put together; arrange

**Zu'sammenstoß** *m* collision (*a. fig*), crash; impact; *fig* clash; **zu'sammenstoßen** *v/i* (*irr*, ***stoßen***, *sep*, *-ge-*, *sein*) collide (*a. fig*); *fig* clash; ***~ mit*** run *or* bump into; *fig* have a clash with

**zu'sammentreffen** *v/i* (*irr*, ***treffen***, *sep*, *-ge-*, *sein*) meet, encounter; coincide (***mit*** with); **Zu'sammentreffen** *n* (*-s*; -) meeting; coincidence; encounter

**zu'sammen|treten** *v/i* (*irr*, ***treten***, *sep*, *-ge-*, *sein*) meet; **~tun** *v/refl* (*irr*, ***tun***, *sep*, *-ge-*, *h*) join (forces), F team up; **~wirken** *v/i* (*sep*, *-ge-*, *h*) combine; **~zählen** *v/t* (*sep*, *-ge-*, *h*) add up; **~ziehen** (*irr*, ***ziehen***, *sep*, *-ge-*) **1.** *v/t and v/refl* (*h*) contract; **2.** *v/i* (*sein*) move in (***mit*** with); **~zucken** *v/i* (*sep*, *-ge-*, *sein*) wince, flinch

**'Zusatz** *m* addition; *chemical etc* additive; ***~...*** *in cpds mst* additional ..., supplementary ...; auxiliary ...; **zusätzlich** ['tsu:zɛtslɪç] *adj* additional, extra

**'zuschauen** *v/i* (*sep*, *-ge-*, *h*) look on (***bei et.*** at s.th.); ***j-m ~*** watch s.o. (***bei et.*** doing s.th.)

**Zuschauer** ['tsu:ʃauɐ] *m* (*-s*; -), **'Zuschauerin** *f* (-; *-nen*) spectator; TV viewer, *pl a. the* audience

**'Zuschauerraum** *m* auditorium

**'Zuschlag** *m* extra charge; RAIL *etc* excess fare; bonus; *auction*: knocking down; **'zuschlagen** *v/i* (*irr*, ***schlagen***, *sep*, *-ge-*, *sein*) *and v/t* (*h*) *door etc*: slam *or* bang shut; *boxing etc*: hit, strike (a blow); *fig* act; ***j-m et. ~*** *auction*: knock s.th. down to s.o.

**'zu|schließen** *v/t* (*irr*, ***schließen***, *sep*, *-ge-*, *h*) lock (up); **~schnallen** *v/t* (*sep*, *-ge-*, *h*) buckle (up); **~schnappen** *v/i* (*sep*, *-ge-*) a) (*h*) *dog*: snap, b) (*sein*) *door etc*: snap shut; **~schneiden** *v/t* (*irr*, ***schneiden***, *sep*, *-ge-*, *h*) cut out; cut (to size); **~schnüren** *v/t* (*sep*, *-ge-*, *h*) tie (*or* lace) up; **~schrauben** *v/t* (*sep*, *-ge-*, *h*) screw shut; **~schreiben** *v/t* (*irr*, ***schreiben***, *sep*, *-ge-*, *h*) ascribe *or* attribute (*dat* to)

**'Zuschrift** *f* letter

**zuschulden** [tsu'ʃʊldən] *adv*: ***sich et.***

(**nichts**) ~ **kommen lassen** do s.th. (nothing) wrong
'**Zuschuss** *m* allowance; subsidy
'**zuschütten** *v/t* (*sep*, *-ge-*, *h*) fill up
'**zusehen** → **zuschauen**
**zusehends** ['tsuːseːənts] *adv* noticeably; rapidly
'**zusetzen** (*sep*, *-ge-*, *h*) **1.** *v/t* add; lose (*money*); **2.** *v/i* lose money; **j-m** ~ press s.o. (hard)
'**zuspielen** *v/t* (*sep*, *-ge-*, *h*) SPORT pass
'**zuspitzen** *v/t* (*sep*, *-ge-*, *h*) point; **sich** ~ become critical
'**Zuspruch** *m* (-[*e*]*s*; *no pl*) encouragement; words of comfort
'**Zustand** *m* condition, state, F shape
**zustande** [tsu'ʃtandə] *adv*: ~ **bringen** bring about, manage (to do); ~ **kommen** come about; **es kam nicht** ~ it didn't come off
'**zuständig** *adj* responsible (**für** for), in charge (of)
'**zustehen** *v/i* (*irr*, **stehen**, *sep*, *-ge-*, *h*) **j-m steht et.** (**zu tun**) **zu** s.o. is entitled to (do) s.th.
'**zustellen** *v/t* (*sep*, *-ge-*, *h*) *post*: deliver; '**Zustellung** *f post*: delivery
'**zustimmen** *v/i* (*sep*, *-ge-*, *h*) agree (*dat* to *s.th.*; with *s.o.*); '**Zustimmung** *f* approval, consent; (**j-s**) ~ **finden** meet with (s.o.'s) approval
'**zustoßen** *v/i* (*irr*, **stoßen**, *sep*, *-ge-*, *sein*) **j-m** ~ happen to s.o.
**zutage** [tsu'taːgə] *adv*: ~ **bringen** (**kommen**) bring (come) to light
'**Zutaten** *pl* ingredients
'**zuteilen** *v/t* (*sep*, *-ge-*, *h*) assign, allot; '**Zuteilung** *f* (-; *-en*) allotment; ration
'**zutragen** *v/refl* (*irr*, **tragen**, *sep*, *-ge-*, *h*) happen
'**zutrauen** *v/t* (*sep*, *-ge-*, *h*) **j-m et.** ~ credit s.o. with s.th.; **sich zu viel** ~ overrate o.s.
**zutraulich** ['tsuːtraulɪç] *adj* trusting; zo friendly
'**zutreffen** *v/i* (*irr*, **treffen**, *sep*, *-ge-*, *h*) be true; ~ **auf** (*acc*) apply to, go for; **~d** *adj* true, correct
'**zutrinken** *v/i* (*irr*, **trinken**, *sep*, *-ge-*, *h*) **j-m** ~ drink to s.o.
'**Zutritt** *m* (-[*e*]*s*; *no pl*) admission; access; ~ **verboten!** no admittance!
**zu'ungunsten** *adv* to *s.o.'s* disadvantage
**zuverlässig** ['tsuːfɛɐlɛsɪç] *adj* reliable, dependable; safe; '**Zuverlässigkeit** *f* (-; *no pl*) reliability, dependability
**Zuversicht** ['tsuːfɛɐzɪçt] *f* (-; *no pl*) confidence; '**zuversichtlich** *adj* confident, optimistic
**zuviel** → **zu**
**zu'vor** [tsu-] *adv* before, previously; first
**zu'vorkommen** *v/i* (*irr*, **kommen**, *sep*, *-ge-*, *sein*) anticipate; prevent; **j-m** ~ *a.* F beat s.o. to it; **~d** *adj* obliging; polite
**Zuwachs** ['tsuːvaks] *m* (*-es*; *no pl*) increase, growth; '**zuwachsen** *v/i* (*irr*, **wachsen**, *sep*, *-ge-*, *sein*) become overgrown; MED close
**zu'weilen** [tsu-] *adv* occasionally, now and then
'**zuweisen** *v/t* (*irr*, **weisen**, *sep*, *-ge-*, *h*) assign
'**zuwenden** *v/t and v/refl* ([*irr*, **wenden**,] *sep*, *-ge-*, *h*) turn to (*a. fig*)
'**Zuwendung** *f* (-; *-en*) a) payment, b) (*no pl*) attention; (loving) care, love, affection
**zuwenig** → **zu**
'**zuwerfen** *v/t* (*irr*, **werfen**, *sep*, *-ge-*, *h*) slam (shut); **j-m et.** ~ throw s.o. s.th.; **j-m e-n Blick** ~ cast a glance at s.o.
**zu'wider** [tsu-] *adj*: **... ist mir** ~ I hate *or* detest ...; **~handeln** *v/i* (*sep*, *-ge-*, *h*) (*dat*) act contrary to; violate
'**zu|winken** *v/i* (*sep*, *-ge-*, *h*) wave to; signal to; **~zahlen** *v/t* (*sep*, *-ge-*, *h*) pay extra; **~ziehen** (*irr*, **ziehen**, *sep*, *-ge-*) **1.** *v/t* (*h*) draw (*curtains etc*); pull tight; *fig* consult; **sich** ~ MED catch; **2.** *v/i* (*sein*) move in
**zuzüglich** ['tsuːtsyːklɪç] *prp* (*gen*) plus
**Zvieri** ['tsfiːri] *Swiss m, n* (*-s*; *-s*) afternoon snack, tea *or* coffee break
**zwang** [tsvaŋ] *pret of* **zwingen**
**Zwang** *m* (-[*e*]*s*; *Zwänge* ['tsvɛŋə]) compulsion, constraint; restraint; coercion; force; ~ **sein** be compulsory; **zwängen** ['tsvɛŋən] *v/t* (*ge-*, *h*) press, squeeze, force; '**zwanglos** *adj* informal; casual; '**Zwanglosigkeit** *f* (-; *no pl*) informality
'**Zwangs|arbeit** *f* JUR hard labo(u)r; **~herrschaft** *f* (-; *no pl*) despotism, tyranny; **~lage** *f* predicament
'**zwangsläufig** *adv* inevitably
'**Zwangs|maßnahme** *f* sanction; **~vollstreckung** *f* JUR compulsory ex-

ecution; **~vorstellung** *f* PSYCH obsession

**'zwangsweise** *adv* by force

**zwanzig** ['tsvantsɪç] *adj* twenty

**'zwanzigste** *adj* twentieth

**zwar** [tsvaːɐ] *adv*: ***ich kenne ihn ~, aber ...*** I do know him, but ..., I know him all right, but ...; ***und ~*** that is (to say), namely

**Zweck** [tsvɛk] *m* (-[*e*]*s*; -*e*) purpose, aim; ***s-n ~ erfüllen*** serve its purpose; ***es hat keinen ~ (zu warten*** *etc*) it's no use (waiting *etc*); **'zwecklos** *adj* useless

**'zweckmäßig** *adj* practical; wise; TECH, ARCH functional; **'Zweckmäßigkeit** *f* (-; *no pl*) practicality, functionality

**zwecks** *prp* (*gen*) for the purpose of

**zwei** [tsvai] *adj* two

**'zweibeinig** [-bainɪç] *adj* two-legged

**'Zweibettzimmer** *n* twin-bedded room

**'zweideutig** [-dɔʏtɪç] *adj* ambiguous; off-colo(u)r

**Zweier** ['tsvaiɐ] *m* (-*s*; -) *rowing*: pair

**zweierlei** ['tsvaiɐ'lai] *adj* two kinds of

**'zweifach** *adj* double, twofold

**Zweifa'milienhaus** *n* duplex, *Br* two--family house

**Zweifel** ['tsvaifəl] *m* (-*s*; -) doubt

**'zweifelhaft** *adj* doubtful, dubious

**'zweifellos** *adv* undoubtedly, no *or* without doubt

**'zweifeln** *v/i* (*ge-*, *h*) ~ ***an*** (*dat*) doubt *s.th.*, have one's doubts about

**Zweig** [tsvaik] *m* (-[*e*]*s*; -*e*) BOT branch (*a. fig*); twig; **~geschäft** *n*, **~niederlassung** *f*, **~stelle** *f* branch

**'zweijährig** [-jɛːrɪç] *adj* two-year-old, of two (years)

**'Zweikampf** *m* duel

**'zweimal** *adv* twice

**'zweimalig** *adj* (twice) repeated

**'zwei|motorig** [-motoːrɪç] *adj* twin-engined; **~reihig** [-raiɪç] *adj* double-breasted (*suit*); **~schneidig** *adj* double-edged, two-edged (*both a. fig*); **~seitig** [-zaitɪç] *adj* two-sided; reversible; POL bilateral; EDP double-sided

**'Zweisitzer** [-zɪtsɐ] *m* (-*s*; -) *esp* MOT two-seater

**'zwei|sprachig** [-ʃpraːxɪç] *adj* bilingual; **~stimmig** [-ʃtɪmɪç] *adj* MUS ... for two voices; **~stöckig** [-ʃtœkɪç] *adj* two--storied, *Br* two-storey ...

**zweit** [tsvait] *adj* second; ***ein ~er ...*** another ...; ***jede(r, -s) ~e ...*** every other ...; ***aus ~er Hand*** second-hand; ***wir sind zu ~*** there are two of us

**'zweitbeste** *adj* second-best

**'zweiteilig** *adj* two-piece (*suit etc*)

**zweitens** ['tsvaitəns] *adv* secondly

**'zweitklassig** [-klasɪç] *adj*, **'zweitrangig** [-raŋɪç] *adj* second-class *or* -rate

**Zwerchfell** ['tsvɛrç-] *n* ANAT diaphragm

**Zwerg** [tsvɛrk] *m* (-[*e*]*s*; -*e* ['tsvɛrgə]) dwarf; gnome; *fig* midget; **~...** *in cpds* BOT dwarf ...; ZO pygmy ...

**Zwetsch(g)e** ['tsvɛtʃ(g)ə] *f* (-; -*n*) BOT plum

**zwicken** ['tsvikən] *v/t and v/i* (*ge-*, *h*) pinch, nip

**Zwieback** ['tsviːbak] *m* (-[*e*]*s*; -*e*, -*bäcke* [-bɛkə]) rusk, zwieback

**Zwiebel** ['tsviːbəl] *f* (-; -*n*) GASTR onion; BOT bulb

**Zwiegespräch** ['tsviː-] *n* dialog(ue)

**'Zwielicht** *n* (-[*e*]*s*; *no pl*) twilight

**'Zwiespalt** *m* (-[*e*]*s*; -*e*) conflict

**'zwiespältig** [-ʃpɛltɪç] *adj* conflicting

**'Zwietracht** *f* (-; *no pl*) discord

**Zwilling** ['tsvɪlɪŋ] *m* (-*s*; -*e*) twin; *pl* ASTR Gemini; ***er ist (ein) ~*** he's (a) Gemini

**'Zwillings|bruder** *m* twin brother; **~schwester** *f* twin sister

**Zwinge** ['tsvɪŋə] *f* (-; -*n*) TECH clamp

**zwingen** ['tsvɪŋən] *v/t* (*irr*, *ge-*, *h*) force, compel; **~d** *adj* compelling; cogent

**Zwinger** ['tsvɪŋɐ] *m* (-*s*; -) kennels

**zwinkern** ['tsvɪŋkɐn] *v/i* (*ge-*, *h*) wink, blink

**Zwirn** [tsvɪrn] *m* (-[*e*]*s*; -*e*) thread, yarn, twist

**zwischen** ['tsvɪʃən] *prp* (*dat and acc*) between; among

**'zwischen'durch** F *adv* in between

**'Zwischen|ergebnis** *n* intermediate result; **~fall** *m* incident; **~händler** *m* ECON middleman; **~landung** *f* AVIAT stopover; ***ohne ~*** nonstop

**'Zwischen|raum** *m* space, interval; **~ruf** *m* (loud) interruption; *pl* heckling; **~rufer** *m* (-*s*; -) heckler; **~spiel** *n* interlude; **~stati͵on** *f* stop(over); ***~ machen (in*** *dat*) stop over (in); **~wand** *f* partition (wall); **~zeit** *f*: ***in der ~*** in the meantime, meanwhile

**Zwist** [tsvɪst] *m* (-[*e*]*s*; -*e*) discord

**zwitschern** ['tsvɪtʃɐn] *v/i* (*ge-*, *h*) twitter, chirp

**Zwitter** ['tsvɪtɐ] *m* (-*s*; -) BIOL hermaphrodite
**zwölf** [tsvœlf] *adj* twelve; ***um ~ (Uhr)*** at twelve (o'clock); at noon; at midnight
'**zwölfte** *adj* twelfth
**Zyankali** [tsyaːn'kaːli] *n* (-*s*; *no pl*) CHEM potassium cyanide
**Zyklus** ['tsyːklʊs] *m* (-; -*klen*) cycle; series, course
**Zylinder** [tsi'lɪndɐ] *m* (-*s*; -) top hat; MATH, TECH cylinder; **zylindrisch** [tsi'lɪndrɪʃ] *adj* cylindrical
**Zyniker** ['tsyːnikɐ] *m* (-*s*; -) cynic
**zynisch** ['tsyːnɪʃ] *adj* cynical
**Zynismus** [tsy'nɪsmʊs] *m* (-; -*men*) cynicism
**Zypresse** [tsy'prɛsə] *f* (-; -*n*) BOT cypress
**Zyste** ['tsʏstə] *f* (-; -*n*) MED cyst
**z.Z(t).** ABBR *of* ***zur Zeit*** at the moment, at present

## PART II

# ENGLISH-GERMAN DICTIONARY

# A

**A, a** A, a *n*; ***from A to Z*** von A bis Z
**A** *grade* Eins
**a** *before vowel*: **an** *indef art* ein(e); per, pro, je; ***not a(n)*** kein(e); ***all of a size*** alle gleich groß; ***100 dollars a year*** 100 Dollar im Jahr; ***twice a week*** zweimal die *or* in der Woche
**a·back: *taken ~*** überrascht, verblüfft; bestürzt
**a·ban·don** aufgeben, preisgeben; verlassen; überlassen; ***be found ~ed*** MOT *etc* verlassen aufgefunden werden
**a·base** erniedrigen, demütigen
**a·base·ment** Erniedrigung *f*, Demütigung *f*
**a·bashed** verlegen
**ab·at·toir** *Br* Schlachthof *m*
**ab·bess** REL Äbtissin *f*
**ab·bey** REL Kloster *n*; Abtei *f*
**ab·bot** REL Abt *m*
**ab·bre·vi·ate** (ab)kürzen
**ab·bre·vi·a·tion** Abkürzung *f*, Kurzform *f*
**ABC** Abc *n*, Alphabet *n*
**ab·di·cate** *Amt*, *Recht etc* aufgeben, verzichten auf (*acc*); ***~ (from) the throne*** abdanken
**ab·di·ca·tion** Verzicht *m*; Abdankung *f*
**ab·do·men** ANAT Unterleib *m*
**ab·dom·i·nal** ANAT Unterleibs...
**ab·duct** JUR *j-n* entführen
**ab·er·ra·tion** Verirrung *f*
**a·bet** → ***aid*** 1
**ab·hor** verabscheuen
**ab·hor·rence** Abscheu *m* (***of*** vor *dat*)
**ab·hor·rent** zuwider (***to*** *dat*); abstoßend
**a·bide** *v/i*: ***~ by the law*** *etc* sich an das Gesetz *etc* halten; *v/t*: ***he can't ~ him*** er kann ihn nicht ausstehen
**a·bil·i·ty** Fähigkeit *f*
**ab·ject** verächtlich, erbärmlich; ***in ~ poverty*** in äußerster Armut
**ab·jure** abschwören; entsagen (*dat*)
**a·blaze** in Flammen; *fig* glänzend, funkelnd (***with*** vor *dat*)
**a·ble** fähig; geschickt; ***be ~ to*** *inf* in der Lage sein zu *inf*, können
**a·ble-bod·ied** kräftig
**ab·norm·al** abnorm, ungewöhnlich; anomal
**a·board** an Bord; ***all ~!*** MAR alle Mann *or* Reisenden an Bord!; RAIL alles einsteigen!; ***~ a bus*** in e-m Bus; ***go ~ a train*** in e-n Zug einsteigen
**a·bode** *a.* ***place of ~*** Aufenthaltsort *m*, Wohnsitz *m*; ***of*** *or* ***with no fixed ~*** ohne festen Wohnsitz
**a·bol·ish** abschaffen, aufheben
**ab·o·li·tion** Abschaffung *f*, Aufhebung *f*
**A-bomb** → ***atom(ic) bomb***
**a·bom·i·na·ble** abscheulich, scheußlich; **a·bom·i·nate** verabscheuen; **a·bom·i·na·tion** Abscheu *m*
**ab·o·rig·i·nal 1.** eingeboren, Ur...; **2.** Ureinwohner *m*
**ab·o·rig·i·ne** Ureinwohner *m*
**a·bort** *v/t* abbrechen (*a.* MED *Schwangerschaft*); MED *Kind* abtreiben; *v/i* fehlschlagen, scheitern; MED e-e Fehlgeburt haben; **a·bor·tion** MED Fehlgeburt *f*; Schwangerschaftsabbruch *m*, Abtreibung *f*; ***have an ~*** abtreiben (lassen)
**a·bor·tive** misslungen, erfolglos
**a·bound** reichlich vorhanden sein; Überfluss haben, reich sein (***in*** an *dat*); voll sein (***with*** von)
**a·bout 1.** *prp* um (... herum); bei (*dat*); (irgendwo) herum in (*dat*); um, gegen, etwa; im Begriff, dabei; über (*acc*); ***I had no money ~ me*** ich hatte kein Geld bei mir; **2.** *adv* herum, umher; in der Nähe; etwa, ungefähr
**a·bove 1.** *prp* über (*dat or acc*), oberhalb (*gen*); *fig* über, erhaben über (*acc*); ***~ all*** vor allem; **2.** *adv* oben; darüber; **3.** *adj* obig, oben erwähnt
**a·breast** nebeneinander; ***keep ~ of, be ~ of*** *fig* Schritt halten mit
**a·bridge** (ab-, ver)kürzen
**a·bridg(e)·ment** Kürzung *f*; Kurzfassung *f*
**a·broad** im *or* ins Ausland; über-

all(hin); ***the news soon spread*** ~ die Nachricht verbreitete sich rasch

**a·brupt** abrupt; jäh; schroff

**ab·scess** MED Abszess *m*

**ab·sence** Abwesenheit *f*; Mangel *m*

**ab·sent 1.** abwesend; fehlend; nicht vorhanden; ***be*** ~ fehlen (***from school*** in der Schule; ***from work*** am Arbeitsplatz); **2.** ~ ***o.s. from*** fernbleiben (*dat*) *or* von; **ab·sent-mind·ed** zerstreut, geistesabwesend

**ab·so·lute** absolut; unumschränkt; vollkommen; unbedingt; CHEM rein, unvermischt

**ab·so·lu·tion** REL Absolution *f*

**ab·solve** freisprechen, lossprechen

**ab·sorb** absorbieren, aufsaugen, einsaugen; *fig* ganz in Anspruch nehmen

**ab·sorb·ing** *fig* fesselnd, packend

**ab·stain** sich enthalten (***from*** *gen*)

**ab·ste·mi·ous** enthaltsam; mäßig

**ab·sten·tion** Enthaltung *f*; POL Stimmenthaltung *f*

**ab·sti·nence** Abstinenz *f*, Enthaltsamkeit *f*

**ab·sti·nent** abstinent, enthaltsam

**ab·stract 1.** abstrakt; **2.** *das* Abstrakte; Auszug *m*; **3.** abstrahieren; entwenden

**ab·stract·ed** *fig* zerstreut

**ab·strac·tion** Abstraktion *f*; abstrakter Begriff

**ab·surd** absurd; lächerlich

**a·bun·dance** Überfluss *m*; Fülle *f*; Überschwang *m*

**a·bun·dant** reich, reichlich

**a·buse 1.** Missbrauch *m*; Beschimpfung(en *pl*) *f*; ~ ***of drugs*** Drogenmissbrauch *m*; ~ ***of power*** Machtmissbrauch *m*; **2.** missbrauchen; beschimpfen; **a·bu·sive** beleidigend, Schimpf...

**a·but** (an)grenzen (***on*** an *acc*)

**a·byss** Abgrund *m* (*a. fig*)

**ac·a·dem·ic 1.** Hochschullehrer *m*; **2.** akademisch; **a·cad·e·mi·cian** Akademiemitglied *n*; **a·cad·e·my** Akademie *f*; ~ ***of music*** Musikhochschule *f*

**ac·cede:** ~ ***to*** zustimmen (*dat*); *Amt* antreten; *Thron* besteigen

**ac·cel·e·rate** *v/t* beschleunigen; *v/i* schneller werden, MOT *a.* beschleunigen, Gas geben

**ac·cel·e·ra·tion** Beschleunigung *f*

**ac·cel·e·ra·tor** MOT Gaspedal *n*

**ac·cent 1.** Akzent *m* (*a.* LING); **2.** → **ac·cen·tu·ate** akzentuieren, betonen

**ac·cept** annehmen; akzeptieren; hinnehmen; **ac·cept·a·ble** annehmbar; *person*: tragbar; **ac·cept·ance** Annahme *f*; Aufnahme *f*

**ac·cess** Zugang *m* (***to*** zu); *fig* Zutritt *m* (***to*** bei, zu); EDP Zugriff *m* (***to*** auf *acc*); ***easy of*** ~ zugänglich (*person*)

**ac·ces·sa·ry** → ***accessory***

**ac·cess code** EDP Zugriffskode *m*

**ac·ces·si·ble** (leicht) zugänglich

**ac·ces·sion** (Neu)Anschaffung *f* (***to*** für); Zustimmung *f* (***to*** zu); Antritt *m* (*e-s Amtes*); ~ ***to power*** Machtübernahme *f*; ~ ***to the throne*** Thronbesteigung *f*

**ac·ces·so·ry** JUR Komplize *m*, Komplizin *f*, Mitschuldige *m, f*; *mst pl* Zubehör *n*, *fashion*: *a.* Accessoires *pl*, TECH *a.* Zubehörteile *pl*

**ac·cess| road** Zufahrts- *or* Zubringerstraße *f*; ~ **time** EDP Zugriffszeit *f*

**ac·ci·dent** Unfall *m*, Unglück *n*, Unglücksfall *m*; NUCL Störfall *m*; ***by*** ~ zufällig

**ac·ci·den·tal** zufällig; versehentlich

**ac·claim** feiern (***as*** als)

**ac·cla·ma·tion** lauter Beifall; Lob *n*

**ac·cli·ma·tize** (sich) akklimatisieren *or* eingewöhnen

**ac·com·mo·date** unterbringen; Platz haben für, fassen; anpassen (***to*** *dat or* an *acc*)

**ac·com·mo·da·tion** Unterkunft *f*, Unterbringung *f*; ~ **of·fice** Zimmervermittlung *f*

**ac·com·pa·ni·ment** MUS Begleitung *f*

**ac·com·pa·ny** begleiten (*a.* MUS)

**ac·com·plice** JUR Komplize *m*, Komplizin *f*, Helfershelfer(in)

**ac·com·plish** erreichen; leisten

**ac·com·plished** fähig, tüchtig

**ac·com·plish·ment** Fähigkeit *f*, Talent *n*

**ac·cord 1.** Übereinstimmung *f*; ***of one's own*** ~ von selbst; ***with one*** ~ einstimmig; **2.** übereinstimmen (***with*** mit)

**ac·cord·ance:** ***in*** ~ ***with*** entsprechend (*dat*)

**ac·cord·ing:** ~ ***to*** laut; nach

**ac·cord·ing·ly** folglich, also; (dem)entsprechend

**ac·cost** *j-n* ansprechen

**ac·count 1.** ECON Rechnung *f*, Berechnung *f*; Konto *n*; Rechenschaft *f*; Bericht *m*; ***by all ~s*** nach allem, was man so hört; ***of no ~*** ohne Bedeutung; ***on no ~*** auf keinen Fall; ***on ~ of*** wegen; ***take into ~, take ~ of*** in Betracht *or* Erwägung ziehen, berücksichtigen; ***turn s.th. to (good) ~*** et. (gut) ausnutzen; ***keep ~s*** die Bücher führen; ***call to ~*** zur Rechenschaft ziehen; ***give (an) ~ of*** Rechenschaft ablegen über (*acc*); ***give an ~ of*** Bericht erstatten über (*acc*); **2.** *v/i*: ***~ for*** Rechenschaft über *et.* ablegen; (sich) erklären

**ac·count·a·ble** verantwortlich; erklärlich

**ac·coun·tant** ECON Buchhalter(in)

**ac·count·ing** ECON Buchführung *f*

**acct** ABBR *of* ***account*** Konto *n*

**ac·cu·mu·late** (sich) (an)häufen *or* ansammeln

**ac·cu·mu·la·tion** Ansammlung *f*

**ac·cu·mu·la·tor** ELECTR Akkumulator *m*

**ac·cu·ra·cy** Genauigkeit *f*

**ac·cu·rate** genau

**ac·cu·sa·tion** Anklage *f*; Anschuldigung *f*, Beschuldigung *f*

**ac·cu·sa·tive** *a.* ***~ case*** LING Akkusativ *m*

**ac·cuse** JUR anklagen; beschuldigen (***of*** *gen*); ***the ~d*** der *or* die Angeklagte, die Angeklagten *pl*

**ac·cus·er** JUR Ankläger(in)

**ac·cus·ing** anklagend, vorwurfsvoll

**ac·cus·tom** gewöhnen (***to*** an *acc*)

**ac·cus·tomed** gewohnt, üblich; gewöhnt (***to*** an *acc*, zu *inf*)

**ace** Ass *n* (*a. fig*); ***have an ~ in the hole*** (*Br* ***up one's sleeve***) *fig* (noch) e-n Trumpf in der Hand haben; ***within an ~*** um ein Haar

**ache 1.** schmerzen, wehtun; **2.** *anhaltender* Schmerz

**a·chieve** zustande bringen; *Ziel* erreichen; **a·chieve·ment** Zustandebringen *n*, Leistung *f*, Ausführung *f*

**ac·id 1.** sauer; *fig* beißend, bissig; **2.** CHEM Säure *f*; **a·cid·i·ty** Säure *f*

**ac·id rain** saurer Regen

**ac·knowl·edge** anerkennen; zugeben; *Empfang* bestätigen

**ac·knowl·edg(e)·ment** Anerkennung *f*; (Empfangs)Bestätigung *f*; Eingeständnis *n*

**a·corn** BOT Eichel *f*

**a·cous·tics** Akustik *f*

**ac·quaint** bekannt machen; ***~ s.o. with s.th.*** j-m et. mitteilen; ***be ~ed with*** kennen; **ac·quaint·ance** Bekanntschaft *f*; Bekannte *m*, *f*

**ac·quire** erwerben; sich aneignen

**ac·qui·si·tion** Erwerb *m*; Anschaffung *f*, Errungenschaft *f*

**ac·quit** JUR freisprechen (***of*** von); ***~ o.s. well*** s-e Sache gut machen

**ac·quit·tal** JUR Freispruch *m*

**a·cre** Acre *m* (*4047 qm*)

**ac·rid** scharf, beißend

**ac·ro·bat** Akrobat(in)

**ac·ro·bat·ic** akrobatisch

**a·cross 1.** *adv* hinüber, herüber; (quer) durch; drüben, auf der anderen Seite; über Kreuz; **2.** *prp* (quer) über (*acc*); (quer) durch; auf der anderen Seite von (*or gen*), jenseits (*gen*); über (*dat*); ***come ~, run ~*** *fig* stoßen auf (*acc*)

**act 1.** *v/i* handeln; sich verhalten *or* benehmen; (ein)wirken; funktionieren; (Theater) spielen; *v/t* THEA spielen (*a. fig*), *Stück* aufführen; ***~ as*** fungieren als; **2.** Handlung *f*, Tat *f*; JUR Gesetz *n*; THEA Akt *m*; **act·ing** THEA Spiel(en) *n*

**ac·tion** Handlung *f* (*a.* THEA), Tat *f*; *film etc*: Action *f*; Funktionieren *n*; (Ein-) Wirkung *f*; JUR Klage *f*, Prozess *m*; MIL Gefecht *n*, Einsatz *m*; ***take ~*** handeln

**ac·tive** aktiv; tätig, rührig; lebhaft (*a.* ECON), rege; wirksam

**ac·tiv·ist** *esp* POL Aktivist(in)

**ac·tiv·i·ty** Tätigkeit *f*; Aktivität *f*; Betriebsamkeit *f*; *esp* ECON Lebhaftigkeit *f*; **~ va·ca·tion** Aktivurlaub *m*

**ac·tor** Schauspieler *m*

**ac·tress** Schauspielerin *f*

**ac·tu·al** wirklich, tatsächlich, eigentlich

**ac·u·men** Scharfsinn *m*

**ac·u·punc·ture** MED Akupunktur *f*

**a·cute** akut (*shortage, pain etc*); brennend (*problem etc*); scharf (*hearing etc*); scharfsinnig; MATH spitz (*angle*)

**ad** F → ***advertisement***

**ad·a·mant** unerbittlich

**a·dapt** anpassen (***to*** *dat or* an *acc*); *Text* bearbeiten (***from*** nach); TECH umstellen (***to*** auf *acc*); umbauen (***to*** für)

**a·dapt·a·ble** anpassungsfähig

**ad·ap·ta·tion** Anpassung *f*; Bearbeitung *f*

**a·dapt·er, a·dapt·or** ELECTR Adapter *m*
**add** *v/t* hinzufügen; **~ up** zusammenzählen, addieren; *v/i*: **~ to** vermehren, beitragen zu, hinzukommen zu; **~ up** MATH ergeben; F sich summieren; *fig* e-n Sinn ergeben; **~ up to** *fig* hinauslaufen auf (*acc*)
**ad·der** ZO Natter *f*
**ad·dict** Süchtige *m, f*; **alcohol (drug) ~** Alkoholsüchtige (Drogen- *or* Rauschgiftsüchtige); (*Fußball- etc*)Fanatiker(in), (*Film- etc*)Narr *m*
**ad·dic·ted** süchtig, abhängig (**to** von); **be ~ to alcohol (drugs)** alkoholsüchtig (drogenabhängig *or* -süchtig) sein
**ad·dic·tion** Sucht *f*, Süchtigkeit *f*
**ad·di·tion** Hinzufügen *n*; Zusatz *m*; Zuwachs *m*; ARCH Anbau *m*; MATH Addition *f*; **in ~** außerdem; **in ~ to** außer (*dat*)
**ad·di·tion·al** zusätzlich
**ad·dress 1.** *Worte* richten (**to** an *acc*), *j-n* anreden *or* ansprechen; **2.** Adresse *f*, Anschrift *f*; Rede *f*, Ansprache *f*
**ad·dress·ee** Empfänger(in)
**ad·ept** erfahren, geschickt (**at, in** in *dat*)
**ad·e·qua·cy** Angemessenheit *f*
**ad·e·quate** angemessen
**ad·here** (**to**) kleben, haften (an *dat*); *fig* festhalten (an *dat*); **ad·her·ence** Anhaften *n*; *fig* Festhalten *n*; **ad·her·ent** Anhänger(in)
**ad·he·sive 1.** klebend; **2.** Klebstoff *m*; **~ plas·ter** MED Heftpflaster *n*; **~ tape** Klebeband *n*, Klebstreifen *m*; MED Heftpflaster *n*
**ad·ja·cent** angrenzend, anstoßend (**to** an *acc*); benachbart
**ad·jec·tive** LING Adjektiv *n*, Eigenschaftswort *n*
**ad·join** (an)grenzen an (*acc*)
**ad·journ** *v/t* verschieben, (*v/i* sich) vertagen; **ad·journ·ment** Vertagung *f*, Verschiebung *f*
**ad·just** anpassen; TECH einstellen, regulieren; **ad·just·a·ble** TECH verstellbar, regulierbar; **ad·just·ment** Anpassung *f*; TECH Einstellung *f*
**ad-lib** aus dem Stegreif (sprechen *or* spielen)
**ad·min·is·ter** verwalten; PHARM geben, verabreichen; **~ justice** Recht sprechen
**ad·min·is·tra·tion** Verwaltung *f*; POL Regierung *f*; Amtsperiode *f*
**ad·min·is·tra·tive** Verwaltungs...
**ad·min·is·tra·tor** Verwaltungsbeamte *m*
**ad·mi·ra·ble** bewundernswert; großartig
**ad·mi·ral** MAR Admiral *m*
**ad·mi·ra·tion** Bewunderung *f*
**ad·mire** bewundern; verehren
**ad·mir·er** Verehrer *m*
**ad·mis·si·ble** zulässig
**ad·mis·sion** Eintritt *m*, Zutritt *m*; Aufnahme *f*; Eintrittsgeld *n*; Eingeständnis *n*; **~ free** Eintritt frei
**ad·mit** *v/t* zugeben; (her)einlassen (**to, into** in *acc*), eintreten lassen; zulassen (**to** zu); **ad·mit·tance** Einlass *m*, Eintritt *m*, Zutritt *m*; **no ~** Zutritt verboten
**ad·mon·ish** ermahnen; warnen (**of, against** vor *dat*)
**a·do** Getue *n*, Lärm *m*; **without more** *or* **further ~** ohne weitere Umstände
**ad·o·les·cence** Jugend *f*, Adoleszenz *f*
**ad·o·les·cent 1.** jugendlich, heranwachsend; **2.** Jugendliche *m, f*
**a·dopt** adoptieren; übernehmen; **~ed child** Adoptivkind *n*
**a·dop·tion** Adoption *f*
**a·dop·tive par·ents** Adoptiveltern *pl*
**a·dor·a·ble** F bezaubernd, entzückend
**ad·o·ra·tion** Anbetung *f*, Verehrung *f*
**a·dore** anbeten, verehren
**a·dorn** schmücken, zieren
**a·dorn·ment** Schmuck *m*, Verzierung *f*
**a·droit** geschickt
**ad·ult 1.** erwachsen; **2.** Erwachsene *m, f*; **~s only** nur für Erwachsene!; **~ ed·u·ca·tion** Erwachsenenbildung *f*
**a·dul·ter·ate** verfälschen, *Wein* panschen
**a·dul·ter·er** Ehebrecher *m*
**a·dul·ter·ess** Ehebrecherin *f*
**a·dul·ter·ous** ehebrecherisch
**a·dul·ter·y** Ehebruch *m*
**ad·vance 1.** *v/i* vordringen, vorrücken (*a. time*); Fortschritte machen; *v/t* vorrücken; *Termin etc* vorverlegen; *Argument etc* vorbringen; *Geld* vorstrecken, F vorschießen; (be)fördern; *Preis* erhöhen; *Wachstum etc* beschleunigen; **2.** Vorrücken *n*, Vorstoß *m* (*a. fig*); Fortschritt *m*; ECON Vorschuss *m*; Erhöhung *f*; **in ~** im Voraus
**ad·vanced** fortgeschritten; **~ for one's years** weit *or* reif für sein Alter

**ad·vance·ment** Fortschritt *m*, Verbesserung *f*
**ad·van·tage** Vorteil *m* (*a.* SPORT); **~ *rule*** SPORT Vorteilsregel *f*; ***take ~ of*** ausnutzen
**ad·van·ta·geous** vorteilhaft
**ad·ven·ture** Abenteuer *n*, Wagnis *n*
**ad·ven·tur·er** Abenteurer *m*
**ad·ven·tur·ess** Abenteu(r)erin *f*
**ad·ven·tur·ous** abenteuerlich; verwegen, kühn
**ad·verb** LING Adverb *n*, Umstandswort *n*
**ad·ver·sa·ry** Gegner(in)
**ad·ver·tise** ankündigen, bekannt machen; inserieren; Reklame machen (für)
**ad·ver·tise·ment** Anzeige *f*, Inserat *n*
**ad·ver·tis·ing 1.** Reklame *f*, Werbung *f*; **2.** Reklame..., Werbe...; **~ a·gen·cy** Werbeagentur *f*; **~ cam·paign** Werbefeldzug *m*
**ad·vice** Rat(schlag) *m*; ECON Benachrichtigung *f*; ***take medical ~*** e-n Arzt zu Rate ziehen; ***take my ~*** hör auf mich
**ad·vice| cen·ter,** *Br* **~ cen·tre** Beratungsstelle *f*
**ad·vis·ab·le** ratsam
**ad·vise** *v/t j-n* beraten; *j-m* raten; *esp* ECON benachrichtigen, avisieren; *v/i* sich beraten
**ad·vis·er** *esp Br*, **ad·vis·or** Berater *m*
**ad·vi·so·ry** beratend
**ad·vo·cate 1.** befürworten, verfechten; **2.** Befürworter(in), Verfechter(in)
**aer·i·al 1.** luftig; Luft...; **2.** Antenne *f*
**aer·i·al| pho·to·graph, ~ view** Luftaufnahme *f*, Luftbild *n*
**aer·o...** Aero..., Luft...
**aer·o·bics** SPORT Aerobic *n*
**aer·o·drome** *esp Br* Flugplatz *m*
**aer·o·dy·nam·ic** aerodynamisch
**aer·o·dy·nam·ics** Aerodynamik *f*
**aer·o·nau·tics** Luftfahrt *f*
**aer·o·plane** *Br* Flugzeug *n*
**aer·o·sol** Spraydose *f*, Sprühdose *f*
**aes·thet·ic** *etc* → ***esthetic*** *etc*
**a·far:** ***from ~*** von weit her
**af·fair** Angelegenheit *f*, Sache *f*; F Ding *n*, Sache *f*; Affäre *f*
**af·fect** beeinflussen; MED angreifen, befallen; bewegen, rühren; e-e Vorliebe haben für; vortäuschen
**af·fec·tion** Liebe *f*, Zuneigung *f*
**af·fec·tion·ate** liebevoll, herzlich
**af·fil·i·ate** *als Mitglied* aufnehmen; angliedern
**af·fin·i·ty** Affinität *f*; (geistige) Verwandtschaft; Neigung *f* (***for, to*** zu)
**af·firm** versichern; beteuern; bestätigen; **af·fir·ma·tion** Versicherung *f*; Beteuerung *f*; Bestätigung *f*
**af·fir·ma·tive 1.** bejahend; **2.** ***answer in the ~*** bejahen
**af·fix** (***to***) anheften, ankleben (an *acc*), befestigen (an *dat*); beifügen, hinzufügen (*dat*)
**af·flict** heimsuchen, plagen; ***~ed with*** geplagt von, leidend an (*dat*)
**af·flic·tion** Gebrechen *n*; Elend *n*, Not *f*
**af·flu·ence** Überfluss *m*; Wohlstand *m*
**af·flu·ent** reich, reichlich; **~ so·ci·e·ty** Wohlstandsgesellschaft *f*
**af·ford** sich leisten; gewähren, bieten; ***I can ~ it*** ich kann es mir leisten
**af·front 1.** beleidigen; **2.** Beleidigung *f*
**a·float** MAR flott, schwimmend; ***set ~*** MAR flottmachen; *fig Gerücht etc* in Umlauf setzen
**a·fraid:** ***be ~ of*** sich fürchten *or* Angst haben vor (*dat*); ***I'm ~ she won't come*** ich fürchte, sie wird nicht kommen; ***I'm ~ I must go now*** leider muss ich jetzt gehen
**a·fresh** von neuem
**Af·ri·ca** Afrika *n*; **Af·ri·can 1.** afrikanisch; **2.** Afrikaner(in)
**af·ter 1.** *adv* hinterher, nachher, danach; **2.** *prp* nach; hinter (*dat*) (... her); ***~ all*** schließlich (doch); **3.** *cj* nachdem; **4.** *adj* später; Nach...; **~ ef·fect** MED Nachwirkung *f* (*a. fig*)
**af·ter·glow** Abendrot *n*
**af·ter·math** Nachwirkungen *pl*, Folgen *pl*
**af·ter·noon** Nachmittag *m*; ***this ~*** heute Nachmittag; ***good ~!*** guten Tag!
**af·ter·taste** Nachgeschmack *m*
**af·ter·thought** nachträglicher Einfall
**af·ter·ward,** *Br* **af·ter·wards** nachher, später
**a·gain** wieder; wiederum; ferner; ***~ and ~, time and ~*** immer wieder; ***as much ~*** noch einmal so viel
**a·gainst** gegen; an (*dat or acc*); ***as ~*** verglichen mit; ***he was ~ it*** er war dagegen
**age 1.** (Lebens)Alter *n*; Zeit(alter *n*) *f*;

Menschenalter *n*; (***old***) ~ (hohes) Alter; ***at the ~ of*** im Alter von; *s.o.* ***your ~*** in deinem *or* Ihrem Alter; (***come***) ***of ~*** mündig *or* volljährig (werden); ***be over ~*** die Altersgrenze überschritten haben; ***under ~*** minderjährig; unmündig; ***wait for ~s*** F e-e Ewigkeit warten; **2.** alt werden *or* machen

**a·ged**[1] alt, betagt

**aged**[2]: ~ ***twenty*** 20 Jahre alt

**age·less** zeitlos; ewig jung

**a·gen·cy** Agentur *f*; Geschäftsstelle *f*, Büro *n*

**a·gen·da** Tagesordnung *f*

**a·gent** Agent *m* (*a.* POL), Vertreter *m*; (*Grundstücks- etc*)Makler *m*; CHEM Wirkstoff *m*, Mittel *n*

**ag·glom·er·ate** (sich) zusammenballen; (sich) (an)häufen

**ag·gra·vate** erschweren, verschlimmern; F ärgern

**ag·gre·gate 1.** sich belaufen auf (*acc*); **2.** gesamt; **3.** Gesamtmenge *f*, Summe *f*; TECH Aggregat *n*

**ag·gres·sion** Angriff *m*

**ag·gres·sive** aggressiv, Angriffs...; *fig* energisch

**ag·gres·sor** Angreifer *m*

**ag·grieved** verletzt, gekränkt

**a·ghast** entgeistert, entsetzt

**ag·ile** flink, behend

**a·gil·i·ty** Flinkheit *f*, Behendigkeit *f*

**ag·i·tate** *v/t fig* aufregen, aufwühlen; *Flüssigkeit* schütteln; *v/i* POL agitieren, hetzen (***against*** gegen)

**ag·i·ta·tion** Aufregung *f*; POL Agitation *f*

**ag·i·ta·tor** POL Agitator *m*

**a·glow: *be*** ~ strahlen (***with*** vor)

**a·go: *a year*** ~ vor e-m Jahr

**ag·o·ny** Qual *f*; Todeskampf *m*

**a·gree** *v/i* übereinstimmen; sich vertragen; einig werden, sich einigen (***on*** über *acc*); übereinkommen; ~ ***to*** zustimmen (*dat*), einverstanden sein mit

**a·gree·a·ble** (***to***) angenehm (für); übereinstimmend (mit)

**a·gree·ment** Übereinstimmung *f*; Vereinbarung *f*; Abkommen *n*

**ag·ri·cul·tur·al** landwirtschaftlich

**ag·ri·cul·ture** Landwirtschaft *f*

**a·ground** MAR gestrandet; ***run ~*** stranden, auf Grund laufen

**a·head** vorwärts, voraus; vorn; ***go ~!*** nur zu!, mach nur!; ***straight ~*** geradeaus

**aid 1.** unterstützen, *j-m* helfen (***in*** bei); fördern; ***he was accused of ~ing and abetting*** JUR er wurde wegen Beihilfe angeklagt; **2.** Hilfe *f*, Unterstützung *f*

**AIDS, Aids** MED Aids *n*; ***person with ~*** Aids-Kranke *m, f*

**ail** kränklich sein; **ail·ment** Leiden *n*

**aim 1.** *v/i* zielen (***at*** auf *acc*, nach); ~ ***at*** *fig* beabsichtigen; ***be ~ing to do s.th.*** vorhaben, et. zu tun; *v/t*: ~ ***at*** *Waffe etc* richten auf *or* gegen (*acc*); **2.** Ziel *n* (*a. fig*); Absicht *f*; ***take ~ at*** zielen auf (*acc*) *or* nach; **aim·less** ziellos

**air**[1] **1.** Luft *f*; Luftzug *m*; Miene *f*, Aussehen *n*; ***by ~*** auf dem Luftwege; ***in the open ~*** im Freien; ***on the ~*** im Rundfunk *or* Fernsehen; ***be on the ~*** senden; in Betrieb sein; ***go off the ~*** die Sendung beenden (*person*); sein Programm beenden (*station*); ***give o.s. ~s, put on ~s*** vornehm tun; **2.** (aus)lüften; *fig* an die Öffentlichkeit bringen; erörtern

**air**[2] MUS Arie *f*, Weise *f*, Melodie *f*

**air·bag** MOT Airbag *m*

**air·base** MIL Luftstützpunkt *m*

**air·bed** Luftmatratze *f*

**air·borne** AVIAT in der Luft; MIL Luftlande...

**air·brake** TECH Druckluftbremse *f*

**air·bus** AVIAT Airbus *m*, Großraumflugzeug *n*

**air-con·di·tioned** mit Klimaanlage

**air-con·di·tion·ing** Klimaanlage *f*

**air·craft car·ri·er** MAR, MIL Flugzeugträger *m*

**air·field** Flugplatz *m*

**air force** MIL Luftwaffe *f*

**air host·ess** AVIAT Stewardess *f*

**air jack·et** Schwimmweste *f*

**air·lift** AVIAT Luftbrücke *f*

**air·line** AVIAT Fluggesellschaft *f*

**air·lin·er** AVIAT Verkehrsflugzeug *n*

**air·mail** Luftpost *f*; ***by ~*** mit Luftpost

**air·man** MIL Flieger *m*

**air·plane** Flugzeug *n*

**air·pock·et** AVIAT Luftloch *n*

**air pol·lu·tion** Luftverschmutzung *f*

**air·port** Flughafen *m*

**air raid** MIL Luftangriff *m*

**air-raid| pre·cau·tions** MIL Luftschutz *m*; ~ **shel·ter** MIL Luftschutzraum *m*

**air route** AVIAT Flugroute *f*

**air·sick** luftkrank
**air·space** Luftraum *m*
**air·strip** (behelfsmäßige) Start- und Landebahn
**air ter·mi·nal** Flughafenabfertigungsgebäude *n*
**air·tight** luftdicht
**air time** Sendezeit *f*
**air traf·fic** AVIAT Flugverkehr *m*
**air-traf·fic| con·trol** AVIAT Flugsicherung *f*; **~ con·trol·ler** AVIAT Fluglotse *m*
**air·way** AVIAT Fluggesellschaft *f*
**air·wor·thy** AVIAT flugtüchtig
**air·y** luftig
**aisle** ARCH Seitenschiff *n*; Gang *m*
**a·jar** halb offen, angelehnt
**a·kin** verwandt (***to*** mit)
**a·lac·ri·ty** Bereitwilligkeit *f*
**a·larm 1.** Alarm(zeichen *n*) *m*; Wecker *m*; Angst *f*; **2.** alarmieren; beunruhigen; **~ clock** Wecker *m*
**al·bum** Album *n* (*a. record*)
**al·bu·mi·nous** BIOL eiweißhaltig
**al·co·hol** Alkohol *m*; **al·co·hol·ic 1.** alkoholisch; **2.** Alkoholiker(in)
**al·co·hol·ism** Alkoholismus *m*, Trunksucht *f*
**a·lert 1.** wachsam; munter; **2.** Alarm *m*; Alarmbereitschaft *f*; ***on the ~*** auf der Hut; in Alarmbereitschaft; **3.** warnen (***to*** vor *dat*), alarmieren
**al·ga** BOT Alge *f*
**al·ge·bra** MATH Algebra *f*
**al·i·bi** JUR Alibi *n*
**a·li·en 1.** ausländisch; fremd; **2.** Ausländer(in); Außerirdische *m, f*
**a·li·en·ate** veräußern; entfremden; *esp art*: verfremden; **a·li·en·a·tion** Entfremdung *f*; *esp art*: Verfremdung *f*
**a·light 1.** in Flammen; **2.** aussteigen; absteigen, absitzen; ZO sich niederlassen; AVIAT landen
**a·lign** (sich) ausrichten (***with*** nach)
**a·like 1.** *adj* gleich; **2.** *adv* gleich, ebenso
**al·i·men·ta·ry** nahrhaft; **~ ca·nal** ANAT Verdauungskanal *m*
**al·i·mo·ny** JUR Unterhalt *m*
**a·live** lebendig; (noch) am Leben; lebhaft; ***~ and kicking*** gesund und munter; ***be ~ with*** wimmeln von
**all 1.** *adj* all; ganz; jede(r, -s); **2.** *pron* alles; alle *pl*; **3.** *adv* ganz, völlig; ***~ at once*** auf einmal; ***~ the better*** desto besser; ***~ but*** beinahe, fast; ***~ in*** F fertig, ganz erledigt; ***~ right*** in Ordnung; ***for ~ that*** dessen ungeachtet, trotzdem; ***for ~ I know*** soviel ich weiß; ***at ~*** überhaupt; ***not at ~*** überhaupt nicht; ***the score was two ~*** das Spiel stand zwei zu zwei
**all-A·mer·i·can** typisch amerikanisch; die ganzen USA vertretend
**al·lay** beruhigen; lindern
**al·le·ga·tion** *unerwiesene* Behauptung
**al·lege** behaupten
**al·leged** angeblich, vermeintlich
**al·le·giance** Treue *f*
**al·ler·gic** MED allergisch (***to*** gegen)
**al·ler·gy** MED Allergie *f*
**al·le·vi·ate** mildern, lindern
**al·ley** (enge *or* schmale) Gasse; Garten-, Parkweg *m*; *bowling*: Bahn *f*
**al·li·ance** Bündnis *n*
**al·li·ga·tor** ZO Alligator *m*
**al·lo·cate** zuteilen, anweisen
**al·lo·ca·tion** Zuteilung *f*
**al·lot** zuteilen, an-, zuweisen
**al·lot·ment** Zuteilung *f*; Parzelle *f*
**al·low** erlauben, bewilligen, gewähren; zugeben; ab-, anrechnen, vergüten; ***~ for*** einplanen, berücksichtigen (*acc*)
**al·low·a·ble** erlaubt, zulässig
**al·low·ance** Erlaubnis *f*; Bewilligung *f*; Taschengeld *n*, Zuschuss *m*; Vergütung *f*; *fig* Nachsicht *f*; ***make ~(s) for s.th.*** et. berücksichtigen
**al·loy** TECH **1.** Legierung *f*; **2.** legieren
**all-round** vielseitig
**all-round·er** Alleskönner *m*; Allroundsportler *m*, -spieler *m*
**al·lude** anspielen (***to*** auf *acc*)
**al·lure** locken, an-, verlocken
**al·lure·ment** Verlockung *f*
**al·lu·sion** Anspielung *f*
**all-wheel drive** MOT Allradantrieb *m*
**al·ly 1.** (sich) vereinigen, verbünden (***to, with*** mit); **2.** Verbündete *m, f*, Bundesgenosse *m*, Bundesgenossin *f*; ***the Allies*** MIL die Alliierten *pl*
**al·might·y** allmächtig; ***the Almighty*** REL der Allmächtige
**al·mond** BOT Mandel *f*
**al·most** fast, beinah(e)
**alms** Almosen *n*
**a·loft** (hoch) (dr)oben
**a·lone** allein; ***let ~, leave ~*** in Ruhe lassen, bleiben lassen; ***let ~ ...*** geschweige denn ...

**a·long 1.** *adv* weiter, vorwärts; da; dahin; ***all** ~* die ganze Zeit; *~ **with*** (zusammen) mit; ***come** ~* mitkommen, mitgehen; ***get** ~* vorwärts kommen, weiterkommen; auskommen, sich vertragen (***with s.o.*** mit j-m); ***take** ~* mitnehmen; **2.** *prp* entlang (*dat*), längs (*gen*)
**a·long·side** Seite an Seite; neben
**a·loof** abseits; reserviert, zurückhaltend, verschlossen; **a·loof·ness** Reserviertheit *f*; Verschlossenheit *f*
**a·loud** laut
**al·pha·bet** Alphabet *n*
**al·pine** (Hoch)Gebirgs..., alpin
**al·read·y** bereits, schon
**al·right** → ***all right***
**Al·sa·tian** *esp Br* ZO Deutscher Schäferhund
**al·so** auch, ferner
**al·tar** REL Altar *m*
**al·ter** ändern, sich (ver)ändern; ab-, umändern; **al·ter·a·tion** Änderung *f* (***to*** an *dat*), Veränderung *f*
**al·ter·nate 1.** abwechseln (lassen); **2.** abwechselnd; **al·ter·nat·ing cur·rent** ELECTR Wechselstrom *m*
**al·ter·na·tion** Abwechslung *f*; Wechsel *m*
**al·ter·na·tive 1.** alternativ, wahlweise; **2.** Alternative *f*, Wahl *f*, Möglichkeit *f*
**al·though** obwohl, obgleich
**al·ti·tude** Höhe *f*; ***at an** ~ **of*** in e-r Höhe von
**al·to·geth·er** im Ganzen, insgesamt; ganz (und gar), völlig
**al·u·min·i·um** *Br*, **a·lu·mi·num** Aluminium *n*
**al·ways** immer, stets
**am, AM** ABBR *of **before noon*** (*Latin **ante meridiem***) morgens, vorm., vormittags
**a·mal·gam·ate** (sich) zusammenschließen, ECON *a.* fusionieren
**a·mass** anhäufen, aufhäufen
**am·a·teur** Amateur(in); Dilettant(in); Hobby...
**a·maze** in Erstaunen setzen, verblüffen; **a·maze·ment** Staunen *n*, Verblüffung *f*; **a·maz·ing** erstaunlich
**am·bas·sa·dor** POL Botschafter *m* (***to*** in *e-m Land*); **am·bas·sa·dress** POL Botschafterin *f* (***to*** in *e-m Land*)
**am·ber** Bernstein *m*
**am·bi·gu·i·ty** Zwei-, Mehrdeutigkeit *f*
**am·big·u·ous** zwei-, mehr-, vieldeutig
**am·bi·tion** Ehrgeiz *m*
**am·bi·tious** ehrgeizig, strebsam
**am·ble 1.** Passgang *m*; **2.** im Passgang gehen *or* reiten; schlendern
**am·bu·lance** Krankenwagen *m*
**am·bush 1.** Hinterhalt *m*; ***be or lie in** ~ **for s.o.*** j-m auflauern; **2.** auflauern (*dat*); überfallen
**a·men** *int* REL amen
**a·mend** verbessern, berichtigen; PARL abändern, ergänzen; **a·mend·ment** Bess(e)rung *f*; Verbesserung *f*; PARL Abänderungsantrag *m*, Ergänzungsantrag *m*; Zusatzartikel *m* zur Verfassung; **a·mends** (Schaden)Ersatz *m*; ***make** ~* Schadenersatz leisten, es wieder gutmachen; ***make** ~ **to s.o. for s.th.*** j-n für et. entschädigen
**a·men·i·ty** *often pl* Annehmlichkeiten *pl*
**A·mer·i·ca** Amerika *n*; **A·mer·i·can 1.** amerikanisch; **2.** Amerikaner(in)
**A·mer·i·can·is·m** LING Amerikanismus *m*
**A·mer·i·can·ize** (sich) amerikanisieren
**A·mer·i·can plan** Vollpension *f*
**a·mi·a·ble** liebenswürdig, freundlich
**am·i·ca·ble** freundschaftlich, *a.* JUR gütlich
**a·mid(st)** inmitten (*gen*), (mitten) in *or* unter
**a·miss** verkehrt, falsch, übel; ***take s.th.** ~* et. übel nehmen, et. verübeln
**am·mo·ni·a** CHEM Ammoniak *n*
**am·mu·ni·tion** Munition *f*
**am·nes·ty** JUR **1.** Amnestie *f*; **2.** begnadigen
**a·mok: *run** ~* Amok laufen
**a·mong(st)** (mitten) unter, zwischen
**am·o·rous** verliebt
**a·mount 1.** (***to***) sich belaufen (auf *acc*); hinauslaufen (auf *acc*); **2.** Betrag *m*, (Gesamt)Summe *f*; Menge *f*
**am·per·age** ELECTR Stromstärke *f*
**am·ple** weit, groß, geräumig; reich, reichlich, beträchtlich
**am·pli·fi·ca·tion** Erweiterung *f*; PHYS Verstärkung *f*
**am·pli·fi·er** ELECTR Verstärker *m*
**am·pli·fy** erweitern; ELECTR verstärken
**am·pli·tude** Umfang *m*, Weite *f*, Fülle *f*; ELECTR, PHYS Amplitude *f*
**am·pu·tate** MED amputieren

**a·muck** → ***amok***
**a·muse** (***o.s.*** sich) amüsieren, unterhalten, belustigen
**a·muse·ment** Unterhaltung *f*, Vergnügen *n*, Zeitvertreib *m*; ~ **park** Vergnügungspark *m*, Freizeitpark *m*
**a·mus·ing** amüsant, unterhaltend
**an** → ***a***
**an·a·bol·ic ster·oid** PHARM Anabolikum *n*
**a·nae·mi·a** *Br* → ***anemia***
**an·aes·thet·ic** *Br* → ***anesthetic***
**a·nal** ANAT anal, Anal...
**a·nal·o·gous** analog, entsprechend
**a·nal·o·gy** Analogie *f*, Entsprechung *f*
**an·a·lyse** *esp Br*, **an·a·lyze** analysieren; zerlegen
**a·nal·y·sis** Analyse *f*
**an·arch·y** Anarchie *f*, Gesetzlosigkeit *f*; Chaos *n*
**a·nat·o·mize** MED zerlegen; zergliedern; **a·nat·o·my** MED Anatomie *f*; Zergliederung *f*, Analyse *f*
**an·ces·tor** Vorfahr *m*, Ahn *m*
**an·ces·tress** Vorfahrin *f*, Ahnfrau *f*
**an·chor** MAR **1.** Anker *m*; ***at*** ~ vor Anker; **2.** verankern
**an·chor·man** TV Moderator *m*
**an·chor·wom·an** TV Moderatorin *f*
**an·cho·vy** ZO Anschovis *f*, Sardelle *f*
**an·cient 1.** alt, antik; uralt; **2.** ***the*** ~***s*** HIST die Alten, die antiken Klassiker
**and** und
**an·ec·dote** Anekdote *f*
**a·ne·mi·a** MED Blutarmut *f*, Anämie *f*
**an·es·thet·ic** MED **1.** betäubend, Narkose...; **2.** Betäubungsmittel *n*
**an·gel** Engel *m*
**an·ger 1.** Zorn *m*, Ärger *m* (***at*** über *acc*); **2.** erzürnen, (ver)ärgern
**an·gle**[1] Winkel *m* (*a.* MATH)
**an·gle**[2] angeln (***for*** nach)
**an·gler** Angler(in)
**An·gli·can** REL **1.** anglikanisch; **2.** Anglikaner(in)
**An·glo-Sax·on 1.** angelsächsisch; **2.** Angelsachse *m*
**an·gry** zornig, verärgert, böse (***at, with*** über *acc*, mit *dat*)
**an·guish** Qual *f*, Schmerz *m*
**an·gu·lar** winkelig; knochig
**an·i·mal 1.** Tier *n*; **2.** tierisch; ~ **lov·er** Tierfreund *m*; ~ **shel·ter** Tierheim *n*
**an·i·mate** beleben; aufmuntern, anregen
**an·i·mat·ed** lebendig; lebhaft, angeregt; ~ **car·toon** Zeichentrickfilm *m*
**an·i·ma·tion** Lebhaftigkeit *f*; Animation *f*, Herstellung *f* von (Zeichen)Trickfilmen; EDP bewegtes Bild
**an·i·mos·i·ty** Animosität *f*, Feindseligkeit *f*
**an·kle** ANAT (Fuß)Knöchel *m*
**an·nals** Jahrbücher *pl*
**an·nex 1.** anhängen; annektieren; **2.** Anhang *m*; ARCH Anbau *m*
**an·ni·ver·sa·ry** Jahrestag *m*; Jahresfeier *f*
**an·no·tate** mit Anmerkungen versehen; kommentieren
**an·nounce** ankündigen; bekannt geben; *radio*, TV ansagen; durchsagen; **an·nounce·ment** Ankündigung *f*; Bekanntgabe *f*; *radio*, TV Ansage *f*; Durchsage *f*; **an·nounc·er** *radio*, TV Ansager(in), Sprecher(in)
**an·noy** ärgern; belästigen
**an·noy·ance** Störung *f*, Belästigung *f*; Ärgernis *n*
**an·noy·ing** ärgerlich, lästig
**an·nu·al 1.** jährlich, Jahres...; **2.** einjährige Pflanze; Jahrbuch *n*
**an·nu·i·ty** (Jahres)Rente *f*
**an·nul** für ungültig erklären, annullieren; **an·nul·ment** Annullierung *f*, Aufhebung *f*
**an·o·dyne** MED **1.** schmerzstillend; **2.** schmerzstillendes Mittel
**a·noint** REL salben
**a·nom·a·lous** anomal
**a·non·y·mous** anonym
**an·o·rak** Anorak *m*
**an·oth·er** ein anderer; ein Zweiter; noch eine(r, -s)
**an·swer 1.** *v/t et.* beantworten; *j-m* antworten; entsprechen (*dat*); *Zweck* erfüllen; TECH *dem Steuer* gehorchen; JUR *e-r Vorladung* Folge leisten; *e-r Beschreibung* entsprechen; ~ ***the bell or door*** (die Tür) aufmachen; ~ ***the telephone*** ans Telefon gehen; *v/i* antworten (***to*** auf *acc*); entsprechen (***to*** *dat*); ~ ***s.o. back*** freche Antworten geben; widersprechen; ~ ***for*** einstehen für; **2.** Antwort *f* (***to*** auf *acc*)
**an·swer·a·ble** verantwortlich
**an·swer·ing ma·chine** TEL Anrufbeantworter *m*
**ant** ZO Ameise *f*

**an·tag·o·nism** Feindschaft *f*
**an·tag·o·nist** Gegner(in)
**an·tag·o·nize** bekämpfen; sich *j-n* zum Feind machen
**Ant·arc·tic** antarktisch
**an·te·ced·ent** vorhergehend, früher (*to* als)
**an·te·lope** ZO Antilope *f*
**an·ten·na¹** ZO Fühler *m*
**an·ten·na²** ELECTR Antenne *f*
**an·te·ri·or** vorhergehend, früher (*to* als); vorder
**an·them** MUS Hymne *f*
**an·ti...** Gegen..., gegen ... eingestellt, Anti..., anti...
**an·ti·air·craft** MIL Fliegerabwehr..., Flugabwehr...
**an·ti·bi·ot·ic** MED Antibiotikum *n*
**an·ti·bod·y** BIOL Antikörper *m*, Abwehrstoff *m*
**an·tic·i·pate** voraussehen, ahnen; erwarten; zuvorkommen; vorwegnehmen; **an·tic·i·pa·tion** (Vor)Ahnung *f*; Erwartung *f*; Vorwegnahme *f*; Vorfreude *f*; ***in** ~* im Voraus
**an·ti·clock·wise** *Br* entgegen dem Uhrzeigersinn
**an·tics** Mätzchen *pl*
**an·ti·dote** Gegengift *n*, Gegenmittel *n*
**an·ti·for·eign·er vi·o·lence** Gewalt *f* gegen Ausländer
**an·ti·freeze** Frostschutzmittel *n*
**an·ti-lock brak·ing sys·tem** MOT Antiblockiersystem *n* (ABBR ***ABS***)
**an·ti·mis·sile** MIL Raketenabwehr...
**an·ti·nu·cle·ar ac·tiv·ist** Kernkraftgegner(in)
**an·tip·a·thy** Abneigung *f*
**an·ti·quat·ed** veraltet
**an·tique 1.** antik, alt; **2.** Antiquität *f*
**an·tique| deal·er** Antiquitätenhändler(in); **~ shop** *esp Br*, **~ store** Antiquitätenladen *m*
**an·tiq·ui·ty** Altertum *n*, Vorzeit *f*
**an·ti·sep·tic** MED **1.** antiseptisch; **2.** antiseptisches Mittel
**ant·lers** ZO Geweih *n*
**a·nus** ANAT After *m*
**an·vil** Amboss *m*
**anx·i·e·ty** Angst *f*, Sorge *f*
**anx·ious** besorgt, beunruhigt (***about*** wegen); begierig, gespannt (***for*** auf *acc*); bestrebt (***to do*** zu tun)
**an·y 1.** *adj and pron* (irgend)eine(r, -s), (irgend)welche(r, -s); (irgend)etwas; jede(r, -s) (beliebige); einige *pl*, welche *pl*; ***not** ~* keiner; **2.** *adv* irgend(wie), ein wenig, (noch) etwas
**an·y·bod·y** (irgend)jemand; jeder
**an·y·how** irgendwie; trotzdem, jedenfalls; wie dem auch sei
**an·y·one** → ***anybody***
**an·y·thing** (irgend)etwas; alles; ***~ but*** alles andere als; ***~ else?*** sonst noch etwas?; ***not** ~* nichts
**an·y·way** → ***anyhow***
**an·y·where** irgendwo(hin); überall
**a·part** einzeln, für sich; beiseite; ***~ from*** abgesehen von
**a·part·heid** POL Apartheid *f*, Politik *f* der Rassentrennung
**a·part·ment** Wohnung *f*; **~ build·ing, ~ house** Mietshaus *n*
**ap·a·thet·ic** apathisch, teilnahmslos, gleichgültig; **ap·a·thy** Apathie *f*, Teilnahmslosigkeit *f*
**ape** ZO (Menschen)Affe *m*
**ap·er·ture** Öffnung *f*
**a·pi·a·ry** Bienenhaus *n*
**a·piece** für jedes Stück, pro Stück, je
**a·pol·o·gize** sich entschuldigen (***for*** für; ***to*** bei); **a·pol·o·gy** Entschuldigung *f*; Rechtfertigung *f*; ***make an ~ (for s.th.)*** sich (für et.) entschuldigen
**ap·o·plex·y** MED Schlaganfall *m*, F Schlag *m*
**a·pos·tle** REL Apostel *m*
**a·pos·tro·phe** LING Apostroph *m*
**ap·pal(l)** erschrecken, entsetzen
**ap·pal·ling** erschreckend, entsetzlich
**ap·pa·ra·tus** Apparat *m*, Vorrichtung *f*, Gerät *n*
**ap·par·ent** offenbar; anscheinend; scheinbar
**ap·pa·ri·tion** Erscheinung *f*, Gespenst *n*
**ap·peal 1.** JUR Berufung *or* Revision einlegen, Einspruch erheben, Beschwerde einlegen; appellieren, sich wenden (***to*** an *acc*); ***~ to*** gefallen (*dat*), zusagen (*dat*), wirken auf (*acc*); *j-n* dringend bitten (***for*** um); **2.** JUR Revision *f*, Berufung *f*; Beschwerde *f*; Einspruch *m*; Appell *m* (***to*** an *acc*), Aufruf *m*; Wirkung *f*, Reiz *m*; Bitte *f* (***to*** an *acc*; ***for*** um); ***~ for mercy*** JUR Gnadengesuch *n*
**ap·peal·ing** flehend; ansprechend

**ap·pear** (er)scheinen; sich zeigen; *öffentlich* auftreten; sich ergeben *or* herausstellen; **ap·pear·ance** Erscheinen *n*; Auftreten *n*; Äußere *n*, Erscheinung *f*, Aussehen *n*; Anschein *m*, äußerer Schein; ***keep up ~s*** den Schein wahren; ***to*** *or* ***by all ~s*** allem Anschein nach

**ap·pease** besänftigen, beschwichtigen; *Durst etc* stillen; *Neugier* befriedigen

**ap·pend** an-, hinzu-, beifügen

**ap·pend·age** Anhang *m*; Anhängsel *n*

**ap·pen·di·ci·tis** MED Blinddarmentzündung *f*

**ap·pen·dix** Anhang *m*; *a.* ***vermiform ~*** ANAT Wurmfortsatz *m*, Blinddarm *m*

**ap·pe·tite** (***for***) Appetit *m* (auf *acc*); *fig* Verlangen *n* (nach)

**ap·pe·tiz·er** Appetithappen *m*, appetitanregendes Gericht *or* Getränk

**ap·pe·tiz·ing** appetitanregend

**ap·plaud** applaudieren, Beifall spenden; loben

**ap·plause** Applaus *m*, Beifall *m*

**ap·ple** BOT Apfel *m*

**ap·ple cart:** ***upset s.o.'s ~*** F j-s Pläne über den Haufen werfen

**ap·ple pie** (*warmer*) gedeckter Apfelkuchen; **ap·ple-pie or·der:** F ***in ~*** in schönster Ordnung

**ap·ple sauce** Apfelmus *n*; *sl* Schmus *m*, Quatsch *m*

**ap·pli·ance** Vorrichtung *f*; Gerät *n*; Mittel *n*

**ap·plic·a·ble** anwendbar (***to*** auf *acc*)

**ap·pli·cant** Antragsteller(in), Bewerber(in) (***for*** um)

**ap·pli·ca·tion** Anwendung *f* (***to*** auf *acc*); Bedeutung *f* (***to*** für); Gesuch *n* (***for*** um); Bewerbung *f* (***for*** um)

**ap·ply** *v/t* (***to***) (auf)legen, auftragen (auf *acc*); anwenden (auf *acc*); verwenden (für); ***~ o.s. to*** sich widmen (*dat*); *v/i* (***to***) passen, zutreffen, sich anwenden lassen (auf *acc*); gelten (für); sich wenden (an *acc*); ***~ for*** sich bewerben um, *et.* beantragen

**ap·point** bestimmen, festsetzen; verabreden; ernennen (***s.o.*** *governor* j-n zum ...); berufen (***to*** auf *e-n Posten*)

**ap·point·ment** Bestimmung *f*; Verabredung *f*; Termin *m*; Ernennung *f*, Berufung *f*; Stelle *f*; **~ book** Terminkalender *m*

**ap·por·tion** verteilen, zuteilen

**ap·prais·al** (Ab)Schätzung *f*

**ap·praise** (ab)schätzen, taxieren

**ap·pre·cia·ble** nennenswert, spürbar

**ap·pre·ci·ate** *v/t* schätzen, würdigen; dankbar sein für; *v/i* im Wert steigen

**ap·pre·ci·a·tion** Würdigung *f*; Dankbarkeit *f*; (richtige) Beurteilung; ECON Wertsteigerung *f*

**ap·pre·hend** ergreifen, fassen; begreifen; befürchten; **ap·pre·hen·sion** Ergreifung *f*, Festnahme *f*; Besorgnis *f*; **ap·pre·hen·sive** ängstlich, besorgt (***for*** um; ***that*** dass)

**ap·pren·tice** **1.** Auszubildende *m, f*, Lehrling *m*, *Swiss* Lehrtochter *f*; **2.** in die Lehre geben; **ap·pren·tice·ship** Lehrzeit *f*, Lehre *f*, Ausbildung *f*

**ap·proach** **1.** *v/i* näher kommen, sich nähern; *v/t* sich nähern (*dat*); herangehen *or* herantreten an (*acc*); **2.** (Heran)Nahen *n*; Einfahrt *f*, Zufahrt *f*, Auffahrt *f*; Annäherung *f*; Methode *f*

**ap·pro·ba·tion** Billigung *f*, Beifall *m*

**ap·pro·pri·ate** **1.** sich aneignen; verwenden; PARL bewilligen; **2.** (***for, to***) angemessen (*dat*), passend (für, zu)

**ap·prov·al** Billigung *f*; Anerkennung *f*, Beifall *m*; **ap·prove** billigen, anerkennen; **ap·proved** bewährt

**ap·prox·i·mate** annähernd, ungefähr

**a·pri·cot** BOT Aprikose *f*

**A·pril** (ABBR ***Apr***) April *m*

**a·pron** Schürze *f*; **~ strings:** ***be tied to one's mother's ~*** an Mutters Schürzenzipfel hängen

**apt** geeignet, passend; treffend; begabt; ***~ to*** geneigt zu

**ap·ti·tude** (***for***) Begabung *f* (für), Befähigung *f* (für), Talent *n* (zu)

**ap·ti·tude test** Eignungsprüfung *f*

**aq·ua·plan·ing** *Br* MOT Aquaplaning *n*

**a·quar·i·um** Aquarium *n*

**A·quar·i·us** ASTR Wassermann *m*; ***he*** (***she***) ***is*** (***an***) ***~*** er (sie) ist (ein) Wassermann

**a·quat·ic** Wasser...

**a·quat·ic plant** Wasserpflanze *f*

**a·quat·ics, a·quat·ic sports** Wassersport *m*

**aq·ue·duct** Aquädukt *m*

**Ar·ab** Araber(in); **A·ra·bi·a** Arabien *n*

**Ar·a·bic** **1.** arabisch; **2.** LING Arabisch *n*

**ar·a·ble** AGR anbaufähig; Acker...

**ar·bi·tra·ry** willkürlich, eigenmächtig

**ar·bi·trate** entscheiden, schlichten
**ar·bi·tra·tion** Schlichtung *f*
**ar·bi·tra·tor** Schiedsrichter *m*; Schlichter *m*
**ar·bo(u)r** Laube *f*
**arc** Bogen *m*; ELECTR Lichtbogen *m*
**ar·cade** Arkade *f*; Lauben-, Bogengang *m*; Durchgang *m*, Passage *f*
**arch**[1] **1.** Bogen *m*; Gewölbe *n*; **2.** (sich) wölben; krümmen
**arch**[2] erste(r, -s), oberste(r, -s), Haupt..., Erz...
**arch**[3] schelmisch
**ar·cha·ic** veraltet
**arch·an·gel** Erzengel *m*
**arch·bish·op** REL Erzbischof *m*
**ar·cher** Bogenschütze *m*
**ar·cher·y** Bogenschießen *n*
**ar·chi·tect** Architekt(in)
**ar·chi·tec·ture** Architektur *f*
**ar·chives** Archiv *n*
**arch·way** (Bogen)Gang *m*
**arc·tic** arktisch, nördlich, Polar...
**ar·dent** feurig, glühend; *fig* leidenschaftlich, heftig; eifrig
**ar·do(u)r** Leidenschaft *f*, Glut *f*, Feuer *n*; Eifer *m*
**are** *du* bist, *wir or sie or Sie* sind, *ihr* seid
**ar·e·a** (Boden)Fläche *f*; Gegend *f*, Gebiet *n*; Bereich *m*
**ar·e·a code** TEL Vorwahl(nummer) *f*
**Ar·gen·ti·na** Argentinien *n*
**Ar·gen·tine 1.** argentinisch; **2.** Argentinier(in)
**a·re·na** Arena *f*
**ar·gue** argumentieren; streiten; diskutieren; **ar·gu·ment** Argument *n*; Wortwechsel *m*, Auseinandersetzung *f*
**ar·id** dürr, trocken (*a. fig*)
**Ar·ies** ASTR Widder *m*; ***he (she) is (an)*** ~ er (sie) ist (ein) Widder
**a·rise** entstehen; auftauchen, auftreten
**ar·is·toc·ra·cy** Aristokratie *f*, Adel *m*
**ar·is·to·crat** Aristokrat(in), Adlige *m*, *f*
**ar·is·to·crat·ic** aristokratisch, adlig
**a·rith·me·tic**[1] Rechnen *n*
**ar·ith·met·ic**[2] arithmetisch, Rechen...
**ar·ith·met·ic u·nit** EDP Rechenwerk *n*
**ark** Arche *f*; ***Noah's*** ~ die Arche Noah
**arm**[1] ANAT Arm *m*; Armlehne *f*; ***keep s.o. at ~'s length*** sich j-n vom Leibe halten
**arm**[2] MIL (sich) bewaffnen; (auf)rüsten
**ar·ma·ment** MIL Bewaffnung *f*; Aufrüstung *f*
**arm·chair** Lehnstuhl *m*, Sessel *m*
**ar·mi·stice** MIL Waffenstillstand *m*
**ar·mo(u)r 1.** MIL Rüstung *f*, Panzer *m* (*a. fig*, ZO); **2.** panzern
**ar·mo(u)red car** gepanzertes Fahrzeug
**arm·pit** ANAT Achselhöhle *f*
**arms** Waffen *pl*; Waffengattung *f*; **~ con·trol** Rüstungskontrolle *f*; **~ race** Wettrüsten *n*, Rüstungswettlauf *m*
**ar·my** MIL Armee *f*, Heer *n*
**a·ro·ma** Aroma *n*, Duft *m*
**ar·o·mat·ic** aromatisch, würzig
**a·round 1.** *adv* (rings)herum, (rund-) herum, ringsumher, überall; umher, herum; in der Nähe; da; **2.** *prp* um, um... herum, rund um; in (*dat*) ... herum; ungefähr, etwa
**a·rouse** (auf)wecken; *fig* aufrütteln, erregen
**ar·range** (an)ordnen; festlegen, festsetzen; arrangieren (*a.* MUS); vereinbaren; MUS, THEA bearbeiten
**ar·range·ment** Anordnung *f*; Vereinbarung *f*; Vorkehrung *f*; MUS Arrangement *n*, Bearbeitung *f* (*a.* THEA)
**ar·rears** Rückstand *m*, Rückstände *pl*
**ar·rest** JUR **1.** Verhaftung *f*, Festnahme *f*; **2.** verhaften, festnehmen
**ar·riv·al** Ankunft *f*; Erscheinen *n*; Ankömmling *m*; **~s** AVIAT, RAIL *etc* ‚Ankunft' (*timetable*); **ar·rive** (an)kommen, eintreffen, erscheinen; ~ ***at*** *fig* erreichen (*acc*), kommen zu
**ar·ro·gance** Arroganz *f*, Überheblichkeit *f*
**ar·ro·gant** arrogant, überheblich
**ar·row** Pfeil *m*
**ar·row·head** Pfeilspitze *f*
**ar·se·nic** CHEM Arsen *n*
**ar·son** JUR Brandstiftung *f*
**art 1.** Kunst *f*; **2.** Kunst...; ~ ***exhibition*** Kunstausstellung *f*; → ***arts***
**ar·ter·i·al** ANAT Schlagader...
**ar·te·ri·al road** Hauptverkehrsstraße *f*, Verkehrsader *f*
**ar·ter·i·o·scle·ro·sis** MED Arteriosklerose *f*, Arterienverkalkung *f*
**ar·te·ry** ANAT Arterie *f*, Schlagader *f*; (Haupt)Verkehrsader *f*
**art·ful** schlau, verschmitzt
**art gal·le·ry** Gemäldegalerie *f*

**ar·thri·tis** MED Arthritis *f*, Gelenkentzündung *f*
**ar·ti·choke** BOT Artischocke *f*
**ar·ti·cle** Artikel *m* (*a.* LING)
**ar·tic·u·late 1.** deutlich (aus)sprechen; **2.** deutlich ausgesprochen; gegliedert
**ar·tic·u·lat·ed** Gelenk...; ~ ***lorry*** *Br* MOT Sattelschlepper *m*
**ar·tic·u·la·tion** (deutliche) Aussprache; TECH Gelenk *n*
**ar·ti·fi·cial** künstlich, Kunst...; ~ ***person*** juristische Person
**ar·til·le·ry** MIL Artillerie *f*
**ar·ti·san** Handwerker *m*
**art·ist** Künstler(in)
**ar·tis·tic** künstlerisch, Kunst...
**art·less** schlicht; naiv
**arts** Geisteswissenschaften *pl*; ***Arts Department,*** *Br* ***Faculty of Arts*** philosophische Fakultät
**as 1.** *adv* so, ebenso; wie; als; **2.** *cj* (gerade) wie, so wie; ebenso wie; als, während; obwohl, obgleich; da, weil; ~ ***...*** ~ (eben)so ... wie; ~ ***for,*** ~ ***to*** was ... (an)betrifft; ~ ***from*** von *e-m Zeitpunkt* an, ab; ~ ***it were*** sozusagen; ~ ***Hamlet*** THEA als Hamlet
**as·bes·tos** Asbest *m*
**as·cend** (auf)steigen; ansteigen; besteigen; **as·cen·dan·cy, as·cen·den·cy** Überlegenheit *f*; Einfluss *m*
**as·cen·sion** Aufsteigen *n* (*esp* ASTR); Aufstieg *m*; **As·cen·sion (Day)** REL Himmelfahrt(stag *m*) *f*
**as·cent** Aufstieg *m*; Besteigung *f*; Steigung *f*
**as·cet·ic** asketisch
**a·sep·tic** MED **1.** aseptisch, keimfrei; **2.** aseptisches Mittel
**ash**[1] BOT Esche *f*; Eschenholz *n*
**ash**[2] *a.* ***ashes*** Asche *f*
**a·shamed** beschämt; ***be*** ~ ***of*** sich schämen für (*or gen*)
**ash·en** Aschen...; aschfahl, aschgrau
**a·shore** am *or* ans Ufer *or* Land
**ash·tray** Asch(en)becher *m*
**Ash Wednes·day** Aschermittwoch *m*
**A·sia** Asien *n*; **A·sian, A·si·at·ic 1.** asiatisch; **2.** Asiat(in)
**a·side** beiseite (*a.* THEA), seitwärts; ~ ***from*** abgesehen von
**ask** *v/t* fragen (***s.th.*** nach et.); verlangen (***of, from s.o.*** von j-m); bitten (***s.o.*** [***for***] ***s.th.*** j-n um et.; ***that*** darum, dass); erbitten; ~ (***s.o.***) ***a question*** (j-m) e-e Frage stellen; *v/i* ~ ***for*** bitten um; fragen nach; ***he*** ~***ed for it*** *or* ***for trouble*** er wollte es ja so haben; ***to be had for the*** ~***ing*** umsonst zu haben sein
**a·skance:** ***look*** ~ ***at s.o.*** j-n schief *or* misstrauisch ansehen
**a·skew** schief
**a·sleep** schlafend; ***be*** (***fast, sound***) ~ (fest) schlafen; ***fall*** ~ einschlafen
**as·par·a·gus** BOT Spargel *m*
**as·pect** Lage *f*; Aspekt *m*, Seite *f*, Gesichtspunkt *m*
**as·phalt 1.** Asphalt *m*; **2.** asphaltieren
**as·pic** GASTR Aspik *m*, Gelee *n*
**as·pi·rant** Bewerber(in)
**as·pi·ra·tion** Ambition *f*, Bestrebung *f*
**as·pire** streben (***to, after*** nach)
**ass** ZO Esel *m*
**as·sail** angreifen; ***be*** ~***ed with doubts*** von Zweifeln befallen werden
**as·sail·ant** Angreifer(in)
**as·sas·sin** (*esp* politischer) Mörder, Attentäter *m*; **as·sas·sin·ate** *esp* POL ermorden; ***be*** ~***d*** e-m Attentat *or* Mordanschlag zum Opfer fallen; **as·sas·sin·a·tion** (***of***) (*esp* politischer) Mord (an *dat*), Ermordung *f* (*gen*), Attentat *n* (auf *acc*)
**as·sault 1.** Angriff *m*, Überfall *m*; **2.** angreifen, überfallen
**as·sem·blage** Ansammlung *f*; TECH Montage *f*; **as·sem·ble** (sich) versammeln; TECH montieren
**as·sem·bly** Versammlung *f*, Gesellschaft *f*; TECH Montage *f*; ~ **line** TECH Fließband *n*
**as·sent 1.** Zustimmung *f*; **2.** (***to***) zustimmen (*dat*); billigen (*acc*)
**as·sert** behaupten; geltend machen; ~ ***o.s.*** sich behaupten, sich durchsetzen
**as·ser·tion** Behauptung *f*; Erklärung *f*; Geltendmachung *f*
**as·sess** *Kosten etc* festsetzen; *Einkommen etc* (zur Steuer) veranlagen (***at*** mit); *fig* abschätzen, beurteilen
**as·sess·ment** Festsetzung *f*; (Steuer)Veranlagung *f*; *fig* Einschätzung *f*
**as·set** ECON Aktivposten *m*; *fig* Plus *n*, Gewinn *m*; *pl* ECON Aktiva *pl*; JUR Vermögen(smasse *f*) *n*; Konkursmasse *f*
**as·sid·u·ous** emsig, fleißig
**as·sign** an-, zuweisen; bestimmen; zuschreiben; **as·sign·ment** An-, Zuwei-

sung *f*; Aufgabe *f*; Auftrag *m*; JUR Abtretung *f*, Übertragung *f*
**as·sim·i·late** (sich) angleichen *or* anpassen (***to, with*** *dat*)
**as·sim·i·la·tion** Assimilation *f*, Angleichung *f*, Anpassung *f* (*all*: ***to*** an *acc*)
**as·sist** *j-m* beistehen, helfen; *j-n* unterstützen; **as·sist·ance** Beistand *m*, Hilfe *f*; **as·sist·ant 1.** stellvertretend, Hilfs...; **2.** Assistent(in), Mitarbeiter(in); (***shop***) ~ *Br* Verkäufer(in)
**as·so·ci·ate 1.** vereinigen, verbinden, zusammenschließen; assoziieren; ~ ***with*** verkehren mit; **2.** Teilhaber(in)
**as·so·ci·a·tion** Vereinigung *f*, Verbindung *f*; Verein *m*
**as·sort** sortieren, aussuchen, zusammenstellen; **as·sort·ment** ECON (***of***) Sortiment *n* (von), Auswahl *f* (an *dat*)
**as·sume** annehmen, voraussetzen; übernehmen
**as·sump·tion** Annahme *f*, Voraussetzung *f*; Übernahme *f*; ***the Assumption*** REL Mariä Himmelfahrt *f*
**as·sur·ance** Zusicherung *f*, Versicherung *f*; *esp Br* (Lebens)Versicherung *f*; Sicherheit *f*, Gewissheit *f*; Selbstsicherheit *f*; **as·sure** *j-m* versichern; *esp Br j-s Leben* versichern; **as·sured 1.** sicher; **2.** *esp Br* Versicherte *m, f*; **as·sur·ed·ly** ganz gewiss
**as·te·risk** PRINT Sternchen *n*
**asth·ma** MED Asthma *n*
**as·ton·ish** in Erstaunen setzen; ***be ~ed*** erstaunt sein (***at*** über *acc*)
**as·ton·ish·ing** erstaunlich
**as·ton·ish·ment** (Er)Staunen *n*, Verwunderung *f*
**as·tound** verblüffen
**a·stray:** ***go ~*** vom Weg abkommen; *fig* auf Abwege geraten; irregehen; ***lead ~*** *fig* irreführen; verleiten
**a·stride** rittlings (***of*** auf *dat*)
**as·trin·gent** MED **1.** adstringierend; **2.** Adstringens *n*
**as·trol·o·gy** Astrologie *f*
**as·tro·naut** Astronaut *m*, (Welt)Raumfahrer *m*
**as·tron·o·my** Astronomie *f*
**as·tute** scharfsinnig; schlau
**a·sun·der** auseinander, entzwei
**a·sy·lum** Asyl *n*; ***right of ~*** Asylrecht *n*
**a·sy·lum seek·er** Asylant(in), Asylbewerber(in)
**at** *prp place*: in, an, bei, auf; *direction*: auf, nach, gegen, zu; *occupation*: bei, beschäftigt mit, in; *manner*, *state*: in, bei, zu, unter; *price etc*: für, um; *time*, *age*: um, bei; ***~ the baker's*** beim Bäcker; ***~ the door*** an der Tür; ***~ school*** in der Schule; ***~ 10 dollars*** für 10 Dollar; ***~ 18*** mit 18 (Jahren); ***~ the age of*** im Alter von; ***~ 8 o'clock*** um 8 Uhr
**a·the·ism** Atheismus *m*
**ath·lete** SPORT (Leicht)Athlet(in)
**ath·let·ic** SPORT athletisch
**ath·let·ics** SPORT (Leicht)Athletik *f*
**At·lan·tic 1.** *a.* ***~ Ocean*** *der* Atlantik; **2.** atlantisch
**at·mo·sphere** Atmosphäre *f* (*a. fig*)
**at·mo·spher·ic** atmosphärisch
**at·oll** Atoll *n*
**at·om** Atom *n*; **~ bomb** Atombombe *f*
**a·tom·ic** atomar, Atom...; **~ age** Atomzeitalter *n*; **~ bomb** Atombombe *f*; **~ en·er·gy** Atomenergie *f*; **~ pile** Atomreaktor *m*; **~ pow·er** Atomkraft *f*; **~-pow·ered** atomgetrieben; **~ waste** Atommüll *m*; **~ weight** CHEM Atomgewicht *n*
**at·om·ize** atomisieren; *Flüssigkeit* zerstäuben; **at·om·iz·er** Zerstäuber *m*
**a·tone:** ***~ for*** büßen für, *et.* sühnen
**a·tone·ment** Buße *f*, Sühne *f*
**a·tro·cious** scheußlich, grässlich; grausam
**a·troc·i·ty** Scheußlichkeit *f*; Greueltat *f*
**at·tach** *v/t* (***to***) anheften, ankleben (an *acc*), befestigen, anbringen (an *dat*); *Wert, Wichtigkeit etc* beimessen (*dat*); ***be ~ed to*** *fig* hängen an; **at·tach·ment** Befestigung *f*; Bindung *f* (***to*** an *acc*); Anhänglichkeit *f* (***to*** an *acc*)
**at·tack 1.** angreifen; **2.** Angriff *m*; MED Anfall *m*
**at·tempt 1.** versuchen; **2.** Versuch *m*; ***an ~ on s.o.'s life*** ein Mordanschlag *or* Attentat auf j-n
**at·tend** *v/t* (ärztlich) behandeln; *Kranke* pflegen; teilnehmen an (*dat*), *Schule, Vorlesung etc* besuchen; *fig* begleiten; *v/i* anwesend sein; erscheinen; ***~ to*** *j-n* (*im Laden*) bedienen; ***are you being ~ed to?*** werden Sie schon bedient?; ***~ to s.th.*** etwas erledigen; **at·tend·ance** Dienst *m*, Bereitschaft *f*; Pflege *f*; Anwesenheit *f*, Erscheinen *n*; Besucher *pl*, Teilnehmer *pl*; Besuch(erzahl *f*) *m*, Be-

teiligung *f*; **at·tend·ant** Begleiter(in); Aufseher(in); (*Tank*)Wart *m*
**at·ten·tion** Aufmerksamkeit *f* (*a. fig*); ***pay*** ~ aufpassen
**at·ten·tive** aufmerksam
**at·tic** Dachboden *m*; Dachkammer *f*
**at·ti·tude** (Ein)Stellung *f*; Haltung *f*
**at·tor·ney** Bevollmächtigte *m*, *f*; JUR (Rechts)Anwalt *m*, (Rechts)Anwältin *f*; ***power of*** ~ Vollmacht *f*
**At·tor·ney Gen·e·ral** JUR Justizminister; *Br* erster Kronanwalt
**at·tract** anziehen; *Aufmerksamkeit* erregen; *fig* reizen; **at·trac·tion** Anziehung *f*, Anziehungskraft *f*, Reiz *m*; Attraktion *f*, THEA *etc* Zugnummer *f*, Zugstück *n*; **at·trac·tive** anziehend; attraktiv; reizvoll
**at·trib·ute¹** zuschreiben (***to*** *dat*); zurückführen (***to*** auf *acc*)
**at·tri·bute²** Attribut *n* (*a.* LING), Eigenschaft *f*, Merkmal *n*
**at·tune:** ~ ***to*** *fig* einstellen auf (*acc*)
**au·ber·gine** BOT Aubergine *f*
**au·burn** kastanienbraun
**auc·tion 1.** Auktion *f*, Versteigerung *f*; **2.** *mst* ~ ***off*** versteigern
**auc·tion·eer** Auktionator *m*
**au·da·cious** unverfroren, dreist
**au·dac·i·ty** Unverfrorenheit *f*, Dreistigkeit *f*
**au·di·ble** hörbar
**au·di·ence** Publikum *n*, Zuhörer *pl*, Zuschauer *pl*, Besucher *pl*, Leser(kreis *m*) *pl*; Audienz *f*
**au·di·o·vis·u·al aids** audiovisuelle Unterrichtsmittel *pl*
**au·dit** ECON **1.** Buchprüfung *f*; **2.** prüfen
**au·di·tion** MUS Vorsingen *n*; THEA Vorsprechen *n*; ***have an*** ~ vorsingen, THEA vorsprechen
**au·di·tor** ECON Buchprüfer *m*; UNIV Gasthörer(in)
**au·di·to·ri·um** Zuhörer-, Zuschauerraum *m*; Vortrags-, Konzertsaal *m*
**Aug** ABBR *of* ***August*** Aug., August *m*
**au·ger** TECH großer Bohrer
**Au·gust** (ABBR ***Aug***) August *m*
**aunt** Tante *f*
**au pair (girl)** Au-pair-Mädchen *n*
**aus·pic·es:** ***under the*** ~ ***of*** unter der Schirmherrschaft (*gen*)
**aus·tere** streng; enthaltsam; dürftig; einfach, schmucklos
**Aus·tra·li·a** Australien; **Aus·tra·li·an 1.** australisch; **2.** Australier(in)
**Aus·tri·a** Österreich *n*
**Aus·tri·an 1.** österreichisch; **2.** Österreicher(in)
**au·then·tic** authentisch; zuverlässig; echt
**au·thor** Urheber(in); Autor(in), Verfasser(in), Schriftsteller(in)
**au·thor·ess** Autorin *f*, Verfasserin *f*, Schriftstellerin *f*
**au·thor·i·ta·tive** gebieterisch, herrisch; maßgebend
**au·thor·i·ty** Autorität *f*; Nachdruck *m*, Gewicht *n*; Vollmacht *f*; Einfluss *m* (***over*** auf *acc*); Ansehen *n*; Quelle *f*; Autorität *f*, Kapazität *f*; *mst pl* Behörde *f*
**au·thor·ize** *j-n* autorisieren, ermächtigen, bevollmächtigen
**au·thor·ship** Urheberschaft *f*
**au·to** Auto *n*
**au·to...** auto..., selbst..., Auto..., Selbst...
**au·to·bi·og·ra·phy** Autobiografie *f*
**au·to·graph** Autogramm *n*
**au·to·mat®** Automatenrestaurant *n*
**au·to·mate** automatisieren
**au·to·mat·ic 1.** automatisch; **2.** Selbstladepistole *f*, -gewehr *n*; Auto *n* mit Automatik; ~ **tel·ler ma·chine** (ABBR ***ATM***) Geld-, Bankautomat *m*
**au·to·ma·tion** TECH Automation *f*
**au·tom·a·ton** Roboter *m*
**au·to·mo·bile** Auto *n*, Automobil *n*
**au·ton·o·my** POL Autonomie *f*
**au·top·sy** MED Autopsie *f*
**au·to·tel·ler** Geld-, Bankautomat *m*
**au·tumn** Herbst *m*
**au·tum·nal** herbstlich, Herbst...
**aux·il·i·a·ry** helfend, Hilfs...
**a·vail:** ***to no*** ~ vergeblich
**a·vail·a·ble** verfügbar, vorhanden; erreichbar; ECON lieferbar, vorrätig, erhältlich
**av·a·lanche** Lawine *f*
**av·a·rice** Habsucht *f*
**av·a·ri·cious** habgierig
**a·venge** rächen; **a·veng·er** Rächer(in)
**av·e·nue** Allee *f*; Boulevard *m*, Prachtstraße *f*
**av·e·rage 1.** Durchschnitt *m*; **2.** durchschnittlich, Durchschnitts...
**a·verse** abgeneigt (***to*** *dat*)

**a·ver·sion** Widerwille *m*, Abneigung *f*
**a·vert** abwenden (*a. fig*)
**a·vi·a·ry** Vogelhaus *n*, Voliere *f*
**a·vi·a·tion** Luftfahrt *f*
**a·vi·a·tor** Flieger *m*
**av·id** gierig (***for*** nach); begeistert
**av·o·ca·do** BOT Avocado *f*
**a·void** (ver)meiden; ausweichen
**a·void·ance** Vermeidung *f*
**a·vow·al** Bekenntnis *n*, (Ein)Geständnis *n*
**a·wait** erwarten, warten auf (*acc*)
**a·wake 1.** wach, munter; **2.** *a.* **a·wak·en** *v/t* (auf)wecken; *v/i* aufwachen, erwachen; **a·wak·en·ing** Erwachen *n*
**a·ward 1.** Belohnung *f*; Preis *m*, Auszeichnung *f*; **2.** zuerkennen, *Preis etc* verleihen
**a·ware:** ***be ~ of s.th.*** von etwas wissen, sich e-r Sache bewusst sein; ***become ~ of s.th.*** etwas merken
**a·way** weg, fort; (weit) entfernt; immer weiter, d(a)rauflos; SPORT Auswärts...; ***~ match*** SPORT Auswärtsspiel *n*
**awe 1.** (Ehr)Furcht *f*, Scheu *f*; **2.** *j-m* (Ehr)Furcht *or* großen Respekt einflößen
**aw·ful** furchtbar, schrecklich
**awk·ward** ungeschickt, linkisch; unangenehm; unhandlich, sperrig; ungünstig, ungelegen
**awl** Ahle *f*, Pfriem *m*
**aw·ning** Plane *f*; Markise *f*
**a·wry** schief
**ax(e)** Axt *f*, Beil *n*
**ax·is** MATH *etc* Achse *f*
**ax·le** TECH (Rad)Achse *f*, Welle *f*
**ay(e)** PARL Jastimme *f*
**A-Z** *Br appr* Stadtplan *m*
**az·ure** azurblau, himmelblau

# B

**B, b** B, b *n*
**b** ABBR *of* ***born*** geb., geboren
**bab·ble 1.** stammeln; plappern, schwatzen; plätschern; **2.** Geplapper *n*, Geschwätz *n*
**babe** kleines Kind, Baby *n*; F Puppe *f*
**ba·boon** ZO Pavian *m*
**ba·by 1.** Baby *n*, Säugling *m*, kleines Kind; F Puppe *f*; **2.** Baby..., Kinder...; klein; **~ bug·gy, ~ car·riage** Kinderwagen *m*
**ba·by·hood** Säuglingsalter *n*
**ba·by·ish** *contp* kindisch
**ba·by-mind·er** *Br* Tagesmutter *f*
**ba·by·sit** babysitten
**ba·by·sit·ter** Babysitter(in)
**bach·e·lor** Junggeselle *m*
**back 1.** Rücken *m*; Rückseite *f*; (Rück)Lehne *f*; hinterer *or* rückwärtiger Teil; SPORT Verteidiger *m*; **2.** *adj* Hinter..., Rück..., hintere(r, -s), rückwärtig; ECON rückständig; alt, zurückliegend; **3.** *adv* zurück, rückwärts; **4.** *v/t* mit e-m Rücken versehen; wetten *or* setzen auf (*acc*); *a.* ***~ up*** unterstützen; zurückbewegen; MOT zurückstoßen mit; ***~ up*** EDP e-e Sicherungskopie machen von; *v/i often* ***~ up*** sich rückwärts bewegen, zurückgehen *or* -fahren, MOT *a.* zurückstoßen; ***~ in(to a parking space)*** MOT rückwärts einparken; ***~ up*** EDP e-e Sicherungskopie machen
**back·ache** Rückenschmerzen *pl*
**back·bite** verleumden, schlecht machen
**back·bone** ANAT Rückgrat *n* (*a. fig*)
**back·break·ing** erschöpfend, mörderisch
**back·chat** *Br* freche Antwort(en *pl*)
**back·comb** *Br* toupieren
**back door** Hintertür *f*; *fig* Hintertürchen *n*
**back·er** Unterstützer *m*, Geldgeber *m*
**back·fire** MOT Früh- *or* Fehlzündung haben; *fig* fehlschlagen
**back·ground** Hintergrund *m*
**back·hand** SPORT Rückhand *f*, Rückhandschlag *m*
**back·heel·er** *soccer*: Hackentrick *m*
**back·ing** Unterstützung *f*
**back num·ber** alte Nummer

**back·pack** *großer* Rucksack
**back·pack·er** Rucksacktourist(in)
**back·pack·ing** Rucksacktourismus *m*
**back-ped·al brake** *Br* Rücktritt *m*, Rücktrittbremse *f*
**back seat** MOT Rücksitz *m*
**back·side** Gesäß *n*, F Hintern *m*, Po *m*
**back·space (key)** EDP Rücktaste *f*
**back stairs** Hintertreppe *f*
**back street** Seitenstraße *f*
**back·stroke** Rückenschwimmen *n*
**back talk** freche Antwort(en *pl*)
**back·track** *fig* e-n Rückzieher machen
**back·up** Unterstützung *f*; TECH Ersatzgerät *n*; EDP Backup *n*, Sicherungskopie *f*; MOT Rückstau *m*
**back·ward** **1.** *adj* Rück..., Rückwärts...; zurückgeblieben; rückständig; ***a ~ glance*** ein Blick zurück; **2.** *adv a.* ***backwards*** rückwärts, zurück
**back·yard** Garten *m* hinter dem Haus; *Br* Hinterhof *m*
**ba·con** Speck *m*
**bac·te·ri·a** BIOL Bakterien *pl*
**bad** schlecht, böse, schlimm; ***go ~*** schlecht werden, verderben; ***he is in a ~ way*** es geht ihm schlecht; ***he is ~ly off*** es geht ihm finanziell schlecht; ***~ly wounded*** schwer verwundet; ***want ~ly*** dringend brauchen
**badge** Abzeichen *n*; Dienstmarke *f*
**bad·ger** **1.** ZO Dachs *m*; **2.** *j-n* plagen, *j-m* zusetzen
**bad·min·ton** Federball(spiel *n*) *m*, SPORT Badminton *n*
**bad-tempered** schlecht gelaunt
**bag** **1.** Beutel *m*, Sack *m*; Tüte *f*; Tasche *f*; ***~ and baggage*** (mit) Sack und Pack; **2.** in e-n Beutel *etc* tun; in Beutel verpacken *or* abfüllen; HUNT zur Strecke bringen; schlottern; *a.* ***~ out*** sich bauschen
**bag·gage** (Reise)Gepäck *n*; **~ car** RAIL Gepäckwagen *m*; **~ check** Gepäckschein *m*; **~ claim** AVIAT Gepäckausgabe *f*; **~ room** RAIL Gepäckaufbewahrung *f*
**bag·gy** bauschig; ausgebeult
**bag·pipes** MUS Dudelsack *m*
**bail** **1.** Bürge *m*; JUR Kaution *f*; ***be out on ~*** gegen Kaution auf freiem Fuß sein; ***go or stand ~ for s.o.*** für j-n Kaution stellen; **2.** ***~ out*** JUR *j-n* gegen Kaution freibekommen; AVIAT (mit dem Fallschirm) abspringen
**bai·liff** (Guts)Verwalter *m*; *Br* JUR Gerichtsvollzieher *m*
**bait** **1.** Köder *m* (*a. fig*); **2.** mit e-m Köder versehen; *fig* ködern
**bake** backen, im (Back)Ofen braten; TECH brennen; dörren
**bak·er** Bäcker *m*
**bak·er·y** Bäckerei *f*
**bak·ing pow·der** Backpulver *n*
**bal·ance** **1.** Waage *f*; Gleichgewicht *n* (*a. fig*); ECON Bilanz *f*; Saldo *m*, Kontostand *m*, Guthaben *n*; Restbetrag *m*; ***keep one's ~*** das Gleichgewicht halten; ***lose one's ~*** das Gleichgewicht verlieren; *fig* die Fassung verlieren; ***~ of payments*** ECON Zahlungsbilanz *f*; ***~ of power*** POL Kräftegleichgewicht *n*; ***~ of trade*** ECON Handelsbilanz *f*; **2.** *v/t* abwägen; im Gleichgewicht halten, balancieren; ECON ausgleichen; *v/i* balancieren; ECON sich ausgleichen; ***~ each other*** sich die Waage halten
**bal·ance sheet** ECON Bilanz *f*
**bal·co·ny** Balkon *m* (*a.* THEA)
**bald** kahl
**bale**[1] ECON Ballen *m*
**bale**[2]**:** ***~ out*** *Br* AVIAT (mit dem Fallschirm) abspringen
**bale·ful** hasserfüllt
**balk** **1.** Balken *m*; **2.** stutzen; scheuen
**ball**[1] **1.** Ball *m*; Kugel *f*; ANAT (Hand-, Fuß)Ballen *m*; Knäuel *m*, *n*; Kloß *m*; ***start the ~ rolling*** den Stein ins Rollen bringen; ***play ~*** F mitmachen; ***long ~*** SPORT langer Pass; **2.** ballen; sich zusammenballen
**ball**[2] Ball *m*, Tanzveranstaltung *f*
**bal·lad** Ballade *f*
**bal·last** **1.** Ballast *m*; **2.** mit Ballast beladen
**ball bear·ing** TECH Kugellager *n*
**bal·let** Ballett *n*
**bal·lis·tics** MIL Ballistik *f*
**bal·loon** **1.** Ballon *m*; Sprech-, Denkblase *f*; **2.** sich (auf)blähen
**bal·lot** **1.** Stimmzettel *m*; (geheime) Wahl; **2.** (***for***) stimmen (für), (in geheimer Wahl) wählen (*acc*); **~ box** Wahlurne *f*; **~ pa·per** Stimmzettel *m*
**ball·point (pen)** Kugelschreiber *m*, F Kuli *m*
**ball·room** Ballsaal *m*, Tanzsaal *m*
**balls** V Eier *pl*

B

**balm** Balsam *m* (*a. fig*)
**balm·y** lind, mild
**ba·lo·ney** F Quatsch *m*
**bal·us·trade** Balustrade *f*, Brüstung *f*, Geländer *n*
**bam·boo** BOT Bambus(rohr *n*) *m*
**bam·boo·zle** F betrügen, *j-n* übers Ohr hauen
**ban 1.** (amtliches) Verbot, Sperre *f*; REL Bann *m*; **2.** verbieten
**ba·nal** banal, abgedroschen
**ba·na·na** BOT Banane *f*
**band 1.** Band *n*; Streifen *m*; Schar *f*, Gruppe *f*; *contp* Bande *f*; (Musik)Kapelle *f*, (Tanz-, Unterhaltungs)Orchester *n*, (*Jazz-*, *Rock*)Band *f*; **2. ~ *together*** sich zusammentun *or* -rotten
**ban·dage** MED **1.** Bandage *f*; Binde *f*; Verband *m*; (Heft)Pflaster *n*; **2.** bandagieren; verbinden
**'Band-Aid**® MED (Heft)Pflaster *n*
**b & b, B & B** ABBR *of* ***bed and breakfast*** Übernachtung *f* mit Frühstück
**ban·dit** Bandit *m*
**band·lead·er** MUS Bandleader *m*
**band·mas·ter** MUS Kapellmeister *m*
**ban·dy** krumm
**ban·dy-legged** säbelbeinig, o-beinig
**bang 1.** heftiger Schlag; Knall *m*; *mst pl* Pony *m*; **2.** dröhnend (zu)schlagen
**ban·gle** Armreif *m*, Fußreif *m*
**ban·ish** verbannen
**ban·ish·ment** Verbannung *f*
**ban·is·ter** *a. pl* Treppengeländer *n*
**ban·jo** MUS Banjo *n*
**bank**[1] ECON **1.** Bank *f* (*a.* MED); **2.** *v/t* bei e-r Bank einzahlen; *v/i* ein Bankkonto haben (***with*** bei)
**bank**[2] (Erd)Wall *m*; Böschung *f*; (*Fluss- etc*)Ufer *n*; (*Sand-*, *Wolken*)Bank *f*
**bank ac·count** Bankkonto *n*
**bank bill** Banknote *f*, Geldschein *m*
**bank·book** Sparbuch *n*
**bank code** ECON Bankleitzahl *f*
**bank·er** Bankier *m*, Banker *m*; **~*'s card*** Scheckkarte *f*
**bank hol·i·day** *Br* gesetzlicher Feiertag *m*
**bank·ing** ECON **1.** Bankgeschäft *n*, Bankwesen *n*; **2.** Bank...
**bank note** *Br* → ***bank bill***
**bank rate** ECON Diskontsatz *m*
**bank·rupt** JUR **1.** Konkursschuldner *m*; **2.** bankrott; ***go*** ~ in Konkurs gehen, Bankrott machen; **3.** *j-n*, *Unternehmen* Bankrott machen; **bank·rupt·cy** JUR Bankrott *m*, Konkurs *m*
**bank sort·ing code** → ***bank code***
**ban·ner** Transparent *n*
**banns** Aufgebot *n*
**ban·quet** Bankett *n*
**ban·ter** necken
**bap·tism** REL Taufe *f*
**bap·tize** REL taufen
**bar 1.** Stange *f*, Stab *m*; SPORT (Tor-, Quer-, Sprung)Latte *f*; Riegel *m*; Schranke *f*, Sperre *f*; *fig* Hindernis *n*; (*Gold- etc*)Barren *m*; MUS Taktstrich *m*; *ein* Takt *m*; dicker Strich; JUR (Gerichts)Schranke *f*; JUR Anwaltschaft *f*; Bar *f*; Lokal *n*, Imbissstube *f*; *pl* Gitter *n*; ***a ~ of chocolate*** ein Riegel *or* e-e Tafel Schokolade; ***a ~ of soap*** ein Stück Seife; **2.** zuriegeln, verriegeln; versperren; einsperren; (ver)hindern; ausschließen
**barb** Widerhaken *m*
**bar·bar·i·an 1.** barbarisch; **2.** Barbar(in)
**bar·be·cue 1.** Bratrost *m*, Grill *m*; Barbecue *n*; **2.** auf dem Rost *or* am Spieß braten, grillen
**barbed wire** Stacheldraht *m*
**bar·ber** (Herren)Friseur *m*, (-)Frisör *m*
**bar code** Strichkode *m*
**bare 1.** nackt, bloß; kahl; leer; **2.** entblößen
**bare·faced** unverschämt, schamlos
**bare·foot, bare·foot·ed** barfuß
**bare·head·ed** barhäuptig
**bare·ly** kaum
**bar·gain 1.** Geschäft *n*, Handel *m*; vorteilhaftes Geschäft, Gelegenheitskauf *m*; ***a*** (***dead***) ~ spottbillig; ***it's a ~!*** abgemacht!; ***into the ~*** obendrein; **2.** (ver)handeln; **~ *sale*** Verkauf *m* zu herabgesetzten Preisen; Ausverkauf *m*
**barge 1.** Lastkahn *m*; **2. ~ *in*** F hereinplatzen (***on*** bei)
**bark**[1] BOT Borke *f*, Rinde *f*
**bark**[2] **1.** bellen; **~ *up the wrong tree*** F auf dem Holzweg sein; an der falschen Adresse sein; **2.** Bellen *n*
**bar·ley** BOT Gerste *f*; Graupe *f*
**barn** Scheune *f*; (Vieh)Stall *m*
**ba·rom·e·ter** Barometer *n*
**bar·on** Baron *m*; Freiherr *m*
**bar·on·ess** Baronin *f*; Freifrau *f*

**bar·racks** MIL Kaserne *f*; *contp* Mietskaserne *f*
**bar·rage** Staudamm *m*; MIL Sperrfeuer *n*; *fig* (Wort- *etc*)Schwall *m*
**bar·rel** Fass *n*, Tonne *f*; (*Gewehr*)Lauf *m*; TECH Trommel *f*, Walze *f*
**bar·rel or·gan** MUS Drehorgel *f*
**bar·ren** unfruchtbar; trocken
**bar·rette** Haarspange *f*
**bar·ri·cade 1.** Barrikade *f*; **2.** verbarrikadieren; sperren
**bar·ri·er** Schranke *f* (*a. fig*), Barriere *f*, Sperre *f*; Hindernis *n*
**bar·ris·ter** *Br* JUR Barrister *m*
**bar·row** Karre *f*
**bar·ter 1.** Tausch(handel) *m*; **2.** tauschen (***for*** gegen)
**base[1]** gemein
**base[2] 1.** Basis *f*; Grundlage *f*; Fundament *n*; Fuß *m*; MIL Standort *m*; MIL Stützpunkt *m*; **2.** gründen, stützen (***on*** auf *acc*)
**base[3]** CHEM Base *f*
**base·ball** SPORT Baseball(spiel *n*) *m*
**base·board** Scheuerleiste *f*
**base·less** grundlos
**base·line** *tennis etc*: Grundlinie *f*
**base·ment** ARCH Fundament *n*; Kellergeschoss *n*
**bash·ful** scheu, schüchtern
**ba·sic[1] 1.** Grund..., grundlegend; **2.** *pl* Grundlagen *pl*
**ba·sic[2]** CHEM basisch
**ba·sic·al·ly** im Grunde
**ba·sin** Becken *n*, Schale *f*, Schüssel *f*; Tal-, Wasser-, Hafenbecken *n*
**ba·sis** Basis *f*; Grundlage *f*
**bask** sich sonnen (*a. fig*)
**bas·ket** Korb *m*
**bas·ket·ball** SPORT Basketball(spiel *n*) *m*
**bass[1]** MUS Bass *m*
**bass[2]** ZO (Fluss-, See)Barsch *m*
**bas·tard** Bastard *m*
**baste[1]** GASTR mit Fett begießen
**baste[2]** (an)heften
**bat[1]** ZO Fledermaus *f*; ***as blind as a ~*** stockblind
**bat[2]** *baseball*, *cricket* **1.** Schlagholz *n*, Schläger *m*; F ***right off the ~*** sofort; **2.** am Schlagen sein
**batch** Stapel *m*, Stoß *m*; **~ pro·cess·ing** EDP Stapelverarbeitung *f*
**bate: *with ~d breath*** mit angehaltenem Atem
**bath 1.** (Wannen)Bad *n*; *pl* Bad *n*, Badeanstalt *f*; Badeort *m*; ***have a ~*** *Br*, ***take a ~*** baden, ein Bad nehmen; **2.** *Br* *v/t* *j-n* baden; *v/i* baden, ein Bad nehmen
**bathe** *v/t* baden (*a.* MED); *v/i* baden, ein Bad nehmen; schwimmen
**bath·ing 1.** Baden *n*; **2.** Bade...
**bath·ing suit → *swimsuit***
**bath·robe** Bademantel *m*; Morgenrock *m*, Schlafrock *m*
**bath·room** Badezimmer *n*; Toilette *f*
**bath·tub** Badewanne *f*
**bat·on** Stab *m*; MUS Taktstock *m*; Schlagstock *m*, Gummiknüppel *m*
**bat·tal·i·on** MIL Bataillon *n*
**bat·ten** Latte *f*
**bat·ter[1]** heftig schlagen; misshandeln; verbeulen; ***~ down, ~ in*** einschlagen
**bat·ter[2]** GASTR Rührteig *m*
**bat·ter[3]** *baseball*, *cricket*: Schläger *m*, Schlagmann *m*
**bat·ter·y** ELECTR Batterie *f*; JUR Tätlichkeit *f*, Körperverletzung *f*; ***assault and ~*** JUR tätliche Beleidigung
**bat·ter·y charg·er** ELECTR Ladegerät *n*
**bat·ter·y-op·e·rat·ed** ELECTR batteriebetrieben
**bat·tle 1.** MIL Schlacht *f* (***of*** bei); *fig* Kampf *m* (***for*** um); **2.** kämpfen
**bat·tle·field, bat·tle·ground** MIL Schlachtfeld *n*
**bat·tle·ments** ARCH Zinnen *pl*
**bat·tle·ship** MIL Schlachtschiff *n*
**baulk → *balk***
**Ba·va·ri·a** Bayern *n*
**Ba·var·i·an 1.** bay(e)risch; **2.** Bayer(in)
**bawd·y** obszön
**bawl** brüllen, schreien; ***~ s.o. out*** mit j-m schimpfen
**bay[1]** GEOGR Bai *f*, Bucht *f*; ARCH Erker *m*
**bay[2]** *a.* ***~ tree*** BOT Lorbeer(baum) *m*
**bay[3] 1.** ZO bellen, Laut geben; **2. *hold*** *or* ***keep at ~*** *j-n* in Schach halten; *et.* von sich fern halten
**bay[4] 1.** rotbraun; **2.** ZO Braune *m*
**bay·o·net** MIL Bajonett *n*
**bay·ou** GEOGR sumpfiger Flussarm
**bay win·dow** ARCH Erkerfenster *n*
**ba·zaar** Basar *m*
**BC** ABBR *of* ***before Christ*** v.Chr., vor Christus
**be** sein; *to form the passive*: werden; stattfinden; ***he wants to ~ a doctor*** *etc*

er möchte Arzt *etc* werden; ***how much are the shoes?*** was kosten die Schuhe?; ***that's five dollars*** das macht *or* kostet fünf Dollar; ***she is reading*** sie liest gerade; ***there is, there are*** es gibt

**beach** Strand *m*; ~ **ball** Wasserball *m*; ~ **bug·gy** MOT Strandbuggy *m*

**beach·wear** Strandkleidung *f*

**bea·con** Leucht-, Signalfeuer *n*

**bead** (*Glas-, Schweiß- etc*)Perle *f*; *pl* REL Rosenkranz *m*

**bead·y** klein, rund und glänzend

**beak** ZO Schnabel *m*; TECH Tülle *f*

**beam 1.** Balken *m*; (Licht)Strahl *m*; AVIAT *etc* Peil-, Leit-, Richtstrahl *m*; **2.** ausstrahlen; strahlen (*a. fig* ***with*** vor *dat*)

**bean** BOT Bohne *f*; ***be full of ~s*** F aufgekrazt sein; → ***spill*** 1

**bear¹** ZO Bär *m*

**bear²** tragen; zur Welt bringen, gebären; ertragen, aushalten; ***I can't ~ him*** (***it***) ich kann ihn (es) nicht ausstehen *or* leiden; ~ ***out*** bestätigen

**bear·a·ble** erträglich

**beard** Bart *m*; BOT Grannen *pl*

**beard·ed** bärtig

**bear·er** Träger(in); ECON Überbringer(in), Inhaber(in)

**bear·ing** Ertragen *n*; Betragen *n*; (Körper)Haltung *f*; *fig* Beziehung *f*; Lage *f*, Richtung *f*, Orientierung *f*; ***take one's ~s*** sich orientieren; ***lose one's ~s*** die Orientierung verlieren

**beast** (*a. wildes*) Tier; Bestie *f*

**beast·ly** scheußlich

**beast of prey** ZO Raubtier *n*

**beat 1.** schlagen; (ver)prügeln; besiegen; übertreffen; F ~ ***s.o. to it*** j-m zuvorkommen; ~ ***it!*** F hau ab!; ***that ~s all!*** das ist doch der Gipfel *or* die Höhe!; ***that ~s me*** F das ist mir zu hoch; ~ ***about the bush*** wie die Katze um den heißen Brei herumschleichen; ~ ***down*** ECON drücken, herunterhandeln; ~ ***s.o. up*** j-n zusammenschlagen; **2.** Schlag *m*; MUS Takt(schlag) *m*; *jazz*: Beat *m*; Pulsschlag *m*; Runde *f*, Revier *n*; **3.** (***dead***) ~ F wie erschlagen, fix und fertig

**beat·en track** Trampelpfad *m*; ***off the ~*** ungewohnt, ungewöhnlich

**beat·ing** (Tracht *f*) Prügel *pl*

**beau·ti·cian** Kosmetikerin *f*

**beau·ti·ful** schön

**beaut·y** Schönheit *f*; ***Sleeping Beauty*** Dornröschen *n*; ~ **care** Schönheitspflege *f*; ~ **par·lo(u)r,** ~ **sal·on** Schönheitssalon *m*

**bea·ver** ZO Biber *m*; Biberpelz *m*

**be·cause** weil; ~ ***of*** wegen (*gen*)

**beck·on** (zu)winken (*dat*)

**be·come** *v/i* werden (***of*** aus); *v/t* sich schicken für; *j-m* stehen, *j-n* kleiden

**be·com·ing** passend; schicklich; kleidsam

**bed 1.** Bett *n*; ZO Lager *n*; AGR Beet *n*; Unterlage *f*; ~ ***and breakfast*** Zimmer *n* mit Frühstück; **2.** ~ ***down*** sein Nachtlager aufschlagen

**bed·clothes** Bettwäsche *f*

**bed·ding** Bettzeug *n*; AGR Streu *f*

**bed·lam** Tollhaus *n*

**bed·rid·den** bettlägerig

**bed·room** Schlafzimmer *n*

**bed·side:** ***at the ~*** am (*a. Kranken*)Bett

**bed·side lamp** Nachttischlampe *f*

**bed·sit** F, **bed·sit·ter, bed·sit·ting room** *Br* möbliertes Zimmer; Einzimmerappartement *n*

**bed·spread** Tagesdecke *f*

**bed·stead** Bettgestell *n*

**bed·time** Schlafenszeit *f*

**bee** ZO Biene *f*; ***have a ~ in one's bonnet*** F e-n Fimmel *or* Tick haben

**beech** BOT Buche *f*

**beech·nut** BOT Buchecker *f*

**beef** GASTR Rindfleisch *n*

**beef·bur·ger** GASTR *Br* Hamburger *m*

**beef tea** GASTR (Rind)Fleischbrühe *f*

**beef·y** F bullig

**bee·hive** Bienenkorb *m*, Bienenstock *m*

**bee·keep·er** Imker *m*

**bee·line:** ***make a ~ for*** F schnurstracks losgehen auf (*acc*)

**beep·er** TECH Piepser *m*

**beer** Bier *n*

**beet** BOT Runkelrübe *f*, Rote Bete, Rote Rübe

**bee·tle** ZO Käfer *m*

**beet·root** BOT *Br* Rote Bete, Rote Rübe

**be·fore 1.** *adv space*: vorn, voran; *time*: vorher, früher, schon (früher); **2.** *cj* bevor, ehe, bis; **3.** *prp* vor; **be·fore·hand** zuvor, im Voraus, vorweg

**be·friend** sich *j-s* annehmen

**beg** *v/t et.* erbitten (***of s.o.*** von j-m); betteln um; *j-n* bitten; *v/i* betteln; (dringend) bitten

**be·get** (er)zeugen
**beg·gar 1.** Bettler(in); F Kerl *m*; **2.** ***it ~s all description*** es spottet jeder Beschreibung
**be·gin** beginnen, anfangen
**be·gin·ner** Anfänger(in)
**be·gin·ning** Beginn *m*, Anfang *m*
**be·grudge** missgönnen
**be·guile** täuschen; betrügen (***of, out of*** um); sich *die Zeit* vertreiben
**be·half:** ***in*** (*Br* ***on***) ***~ of*** im Namen von (*or gen*)
**be·have** sich (gut) benehmen
**be·hav·io(u)r** Benehmen *n*, Betragen *n*, Verhalten *n*
**be·hav·io(u)r·al sci·ence** PSYCH Verhaltensforschung *f*
**be·head** enthaupten
**be·hind 1.** *adv* hinten, dahinter; zurück; **2.** *prp* hinter (*dat or acc*); **3.** F Hinterteil *n*, Hintern *m*
**beige** beige
**be·ing** Sein *n*, Dasein *n*, Existenz *f*; (Lebe)Wesen *n*, Geschöpf *n*; *j-s* Wesen *n*, Natur *f*
**be·lat·ed** verspätet
**belch 1.** aufstoßen, rülpsen; *a.* ***~ out*** speien, ausstoßen; **2.** Rülpser *m*
**bel·fry** Glockenturm *m*, -stuhl *m*
**Bel·gium** Belgien *n*
**Bel·gian 1.** belgisch; **2.** Belgier(in)
**be·lief** Glaube *m* (***in*** an *acc*)
**be·liev·a·ble** glaubhaft
**be·lieve** glauben (***in*** an *acc*); ***I couldn't ~ my ears*** (***eyes***) ich traute m-n Ohren (Augen) nicht
**be·liev·er** REL Gläubige *m, f*
**be·lit·tle** *fig* herabsetzen
**bell** Glocke *f*; Klingel *f*
**bell·boy** *Br*, **bell·hop** (Hotel)Page *m*
**bel·lig·er·ent** kriegerisch; streitlustig, aggressiv; Krieg führend
**bel·low 1.** brüllen; **2.** Gebrüll *n*
**bel·lows** Blasebalg *m*
**bel·ly 1.** Bauch *m*; Magen *m*; **2.** ***~ out*** (an)schwellen lassen; bauschen
**bel·ly·ache** F Bauchweh *n*
**be·long** gehören; ***~ to*** gehören *dat or* zu
**be·long·ings** Habseligkeiten *pl*, Habe *f*
**be·loved 1.** (innig) geliebt; **2.** Geliebte *m, f*
**be·low 1.** *adv* unten; **2.** *prp* unter (*dat or acc*)
**belt 1.** Gürtel *m*; Gurt *m*; GEOGR Zone *f*, Gebiet *n*; TECH (Treib)Riemen *m*; **2.** ***~ out*** MUS schmettern; *a.* ***~ up*** den Gürtel (*gen*) zumachen; ***~ up*** MOT sich anschnallen; **belt·ed** mit e-m Gürtel
**belt·way** Umgehungsstraße *f*; Ringstraße *f*
**be·moan** betrauern, beklagen
**bench** Sitzbank *f*, Bank *f* (*a.* SPORT); TECH Werkbank *f*; JUR Richterbank *f*; Richter *m or pl*
**bend 1.** Biegung *f*, Kurve *f*; ***drive s.o. round the ~*** F j-n noch wahnsinnig machen; **2.** (sich) biegen *or* krümmen; neigen; beugen; *fig* richten (***to, on*** auf *acc*)
**be·neath** → ***below***
**ben·e·dic·tion** REL Segen *m*
**ben·e·fac·tor** Wohltäter *m*
**be·nef·i·cent** wohltätig
**ben·e·fi·cial** wohltuend, zuträglich, nützlich
**ben·e·fit 1.** Nutzen *m*, Vorteil *m*; Wohltätigkeitsveranstaltung *f*; (*Sozial-, Versicherungs- etc*)Leistung *f*; (*Arbeitslosen- etc*)Unterstützung *f*; (*Kranken- etc*)Geld *n*; **2.** nützen; ***~ by, ~ from*** Vorteil haben von *or* durch, Nutzen ziehen aus
**be·nev·o·lence** Wohlwollen *n*
**be·nev·o·lent** wohltätig; wohlwollend
**be·nign** MED gutartig
**bent 1.** ***~ on doing*** entschlossen zu tun; **2.** Hang *m*, Neigung *f*; Veranlagung *f*
**ben·zene** CHEM Benzol *n*
**ben·zine** CHEM Leichtbenzin *n*
**be·queath** JUR vermachen
**be·quest** JUR Vermächtnis *n*
**be·reave** berauben
**be·ret** Baskenmütze *f*
**ber·ry** BOT Beere *f*
**berth 1.** MAR Liege-, Ankerplatz *m*; Koje *f*; RAIL (Schlafwagen)Bett *n*; **2.** MAR festmachen, anlegen
**be·seech** (inständig) bitten (um); anflehen
**be·set** heimsuchen; ***~ with difficulties*** mit vielen Schwierigkeiten verbunden
**be·side** *prp* neben (*dat or acc*); ***~ o.s.*** außer sich (***with*** vor); ***~ the point, ~ the question*** nicht zur Sache gehörig
**be·sides 1.** *adv* außerdem; **2.** *prp* abgesehen von, außer (*dat*)
**be·siege** belagern
**be·smear** beschmieren
**be·spat·ter** bespritzen

**best 1.** *adj* beste(r, -s) höchste(r, -s), größte(r, -s), meiste; **~ before** GASTR haltbar bis; **2.** *adv* am besten; **3.** *der, die, das* Beste; ***all the ~!*** alles Gute!, viel Glück!; ***to the ~ of ...*** nach bestem ...; ***make the ~ of*** das Beste machen aus (*dat*); ***at ~*** bestenfalls; ***be at one's ~*** in Hoch- *or* Höchstform sein
**best-be·fore date, best-by date** Mindesthaltbarkeitsdatum *n*
**bes·ti·al** *fig* tierisch, bestialisch
**be·stow** geben, verleihen (***on*** *dat*)
**best-sell·er** Bestseller *m*
**bet 1.** Wette *f*; ***make a ~*** e-e Wette abschließen; **2.** wetten; ***~ s.o. ten dollars*** mit j-m um zehn Dollar wetten; ***you ~*** F und ob!
**be·tray** verraten (*a. fig*); verleiten
**be·tray·al** Verrat *m*
**be·tray·er** Verräter(in)
**bet·ter 1.** *adj* besser; ***he is ~*** es geht ihm besser; ***~ and ~*** immer besser; **2.** *das* Bessere; ***get the ~ of*** die Oberhand gewinnen über (*acc*); *et.* überwinden; **3.** *adv* besser; mehr; ***do ~ than*** es besser machen als; ***know ~*** es besser wissen; ***so much the ~*** desto besser; ***you had ~ go*** *Br*, F ***you ~ go*** es wäre besser, wenn du gingest; ***~ off*** (finanziell) besser gestellt; ***he is ~ off than I am*** es geht ihm besser als mir; **4.** *v/t* verbessern; *v/i* sich bessern
**be·tween 1.** *adv* dazwischen; ***in ~*** zwischendurch; F ***few and far ~*** (ganz) vereinzelt; **2.** *prp* zwischen (*dat or acc*); unter (*dat*); ***~ you and me*** unter uns *or* im Vertrauen (gesagt)
**bev·el** TECH abkanten, abschrägen
**bev·er·age** Getränk *n*
**bev·y** ZO Schwarm *m*, Schar *f*
**be·ware** (***of***) sich in Acht nehmen (vor *dat*), sich hüten (vor *dat*); ***~ of the dog!*** Vorsicht, bissiger Hund!
**be·wil·der** verwirren
**be·wil·der·ment** Verwirrung *f*
**be·witch** bezaubern, verhexen
**be·yond 1.** *adv* darüber hinaus; **2.** *prp* jenseits (*gen*); über ... (*acc*) hinaus
**bi...** zwei, zweifach, zweimal
**bi·as** Neigung *f*; Vorurteil *n*
**bi·as(s)ed** voreingenommen; JUR befangen
**bi·ath·lete** SPORT Biathlet *m*
**bi·ath·lon** SPORT Biathlon *n*
**bib** (Sabber)Lätzchen *n*
**Bi·ble** Bibel *f*
**bib·li·cal** biblisch, Bibel...
**bib·li·og·ra·phy** Bibliografie *f*
**bi·car·bon·ate** *a.* ***~ of soda*** CHEM doppeltkohlensaures Natron
**bi·cen·te·na·ry** *Br*, **bi·cen·ten·ni·al** Zweihundertjahrfeier *f*
**bi·ceps** ANAT Bizeps *m*
**bick·er** sich zanken *or* streiten
**bi·cy·cle** Fahrrad *n*
**bid 1.** *auction*: bieten; **2.** ECON Gebot *n*, Angebot *n*
**bi·en·ni·al** zweijährlich; BOT zweijährig; **bi·en·ni·al·ly** alle zwei Jahre
**bier** (Toten)Bahre *f*
**big** groß; dick, stark; ***talk ~*** F den Mund voll nehmen
**big·a·my** Bigamie *f*
**big busi·ness** Großunternehmertum *n*
**big·head** F Angeber *m*
**big shot, big·wig** F hohes Tier
**bike** F **1.** (Fahr)Rad *n*; **2.** Rad fahren
**bik·er** Motorradfahrer(in); Radfahrer(in), Radler(in)
**bi·lat·er·al** bilateral
**bile** Galle *f* (*a. fig*)
**bi·lin·gual** zweisprachig
**bill[1]** ZO Schnabel *m*
**bill[2]** ECON Rechnung *f*; POL (Gesetzes)Vorlage *f*; JUR (An)Klageschrift *f*; Plakat *n*; Banknote *f*, (Geld)Schein *m*
**bill·board** Reklametafel *f*
**bill·fold** Brieftasche *f*
**bil·li·ards** Billard(spiel) *n*
**bil·li·on** Milliarde *f*
**bill| of de·liv·er·y** ECON Lieferschein *m*; **~ of ex·change** ECON Wechsel *m*; **~ of sale** JUR Verkaufsurkunde *f*
**bil·low 1.** Woge *f*; (*Rauch- etc*) Schwaden *m*; **2.** *a.* ***~ out*** sich bauschen *or* blähen
**bil·ly goat** ZO Ziegenbock *m*
**bin** (großer) Behälter
**bi·na·ry** MATH, PHYS *etc* binär, Binär...
**bi·na·ry code** EDP Binärcode *m*
**bi·na·ry num·ber** MATH Binärzahl *f*
**bind** *v/t* (an-, ein-, um-, auf-, fest-, ver)binden; *a.* vertraglich binden, verpflichten; einfassen; *v/i* binden
**bind·er** (*esp Buch*)Binder(in); Einband *m*; Aktendeckel *m*
**bind·ing 1.** bindend, verbindlich; **2.** Einband *m*; Einfassung *f*, Borte *f*

**bin·go** Bingo *n*
**bi·noc·u·lars** Feldstecher *m*, Fern-, Opernglas *n*
**bi·o·chem·is·try** Biochemie *f*
**bi·o·de·gra·da·ble** biologisch abbaubar, umweltfreundlich
**bi·og·ra·pher** Biograf *m*
**bi·og·ra·phy** Biografie *f*
**bi·o·log·i·cal** biologisch
**bi·ol·o·gist** Biologe *m*, Biologin *f*
**bi·ol·o·gy** Biologie *f*
**bi·o·rhythms** Biorhythmus *m*
**bi·o·tope** Biotop *n*
**bi·ped** ZO Zweifüßer *m*
**birch** BOT Birke *f*
**bird** ZO Vogel *m*
**bird·cage** Vogelkäfig *m*
**bird of pas·sage** ZO Zugvogel *m*
**bird of prey** ZO Raubvogel *m*
**bird sanc·tu·a·ry** Vogelschutzgebiet *n*
**bird·seed** Vogelfutter *n*
**bird's-eye view** Vogelperspektive *f*
**bi·ro**® Kugelschreiber *m*
**birth** Geburt *f*; Herkunft *f*; ***give ~ to*** gebären, zur Welt bringen
**birth cer·tif·i·cate** Geburtsurkunde *f*
**birth con·trol** Geburtenregelung *f*; **~ pill** MED Antibabypille *f*
**birth·day** Geburtstag *m*; ***happy ~!*** alles Gute *or* herzlichen Glückwunsch zum Geburtstag!
**birth·mark** Muttermal *n*
**birth·place** Geburtsort *m*
**birth·rate** Geburtenziffer *f*
**bis·cuit** *Br* Keks *m*, *n*, Plätzchen *n*
**bi·sex·u·al** bisexuell
**bish·op** REL Bischof *m*; *chess*: Läufer *m*
**bish·op·ric** REL Bistum *n*
**bi·son** ZO Bison *m*; Wisent *m*
**bit** Bisschen *n*, Stück(chen) *n*; Gebiss *n* (*am Zaum*); (Schlüssel)Bart *m*; EDP Bit *n*; ***a*** (***little***) **~** ein (kleines) bisschen
**bitch** ZO Hündin *f*; F *contp* Miststück *n*, Schlampe *f*
**bit den·si·ty** EDP Speicherdichte *f*
**bite 1.** Beißen *n*; Biss *m*; Bissen *m*, Happen *m*; TECH Fassen *n*, Greifen *n*; **2.** (an)beißen; ZO stechen; GASTR brennen; *fig* schneiden (*cold etc*); beißen (*smoke etc*); TECH fassen, greifen
**bit·ter** bitter; *fig* verbittert
**bit·ters** GASTR Magenbitter *m*
**biz** F → ***business***
**black 1.** schwarz; dunkel; finster; ***have s.th. in ~ and white*** et. schwarz auf weiß haben *or* besitzen; ***be ~ and blue*** blaue Flecken haben; ***beat s.o. ~ and blue*** j-n grün und blau schlagen; **2.** schwärzen; ***~ out*** verdunkeln; **3.** Schwarz *n*; Schwärze *f*; Schwarze *m*, *f*
**black·ber·ry** BOT Brombeere *f*
**black·bird** ZO Amsel *f*
**black·board** (Schul-, Wand)Tafel *f*
**black box** AVIAT Flugschreiber *m*
**black cur·rant** BOT schwarze Johannisbeere
**black·en** *v/t* schwärzen; *fig* anschwärzen; *v/i* schwarz werden
**black eye** blaues Auge, Veilchen *n*
**black·head** MED Mitesser *m*
**black ice** Glatteis *n*
**black·ing** schwarze Schuhwichse
**black·leg** *Br* Streikbrecher *m*
**black·mail 1.** Erpressung *f*; **2.** *j-n* erpressen; **black·mail·er** Erpresser(in)
**black mar·ket** Schwarzmarkt *m*
**black·ness** Schwärze *f*
**black·out** Verdunkelung *f*; Black-out *n*, *m*; ELECTR Stromausfall *m*; Ohnmacht *f*
**black pud·ding** GASTR Blutwurst *f*
**black sheep** *fig* schwarzes Schaf
**black·smith** Schmied *m*
**blad·der** ANAT Blase *f*
**blade** TECH Blatt *n*, Schaufel *f*; Klinge *f*; Schneide *f*; BOT Halm *m*
**blame 1.** Tadel *m*; Schuld *f*; **2.** tadeln; ***be to ~ for*** schuld sein an (*dat*)
**blame·less** untadelig
**blanch** *v/t* bleichen; GASTR blanchieren; *v/i* erbleichen, bleich werden
**blank 1.** leer; unausgefüllt, unbeschrieben; ECON Blanko...; verdutzt; **2.** Leere *f*; leerer Raum, Lücke *f*; unbeschriebenes Blatt, Formular *n*; *lottery*: Niete *f*; **~ car·tridge** Platzpatrone *f*; **~ check** (*Br* **cheque**) ECON Blankoscheck *m*
**blan·ket 1.** (Woll)Decke *f*; **2.** zudecken
**blare** brüllen, plärren (*radio etc*), schmettern (*trumpet*)
**blas·pheme** lästern
**blas·phe·my** Gotteslästerung *f*
**blast 1.** Windstoß *m*; MUS Ton *m*; TECH Explosion *f*; Druckwelle *f*; Sprengung *f*; **2.** sprengen; *fig* zunichte machen; ***~ off*** (***into space***) in den Weltraum schießen; ***~ off*** abheben, starten (*rocket*); ***~!*** verdammt!; ***~ you!*** der Teufel soll dich holen!; ***~ed*** verdammt, verflucht

**blast fur·nace** TECH Hochofen *m*
**blast-off** Start *m* (*of a rocket*)
**bla·tant** offenkundig, eklatant
**blaze 1.** Flamme(n *pl*) *f*, Feuer *n*; heller Schein; *fig* Ausbruch *m*; **2.** brennen, lodern; leuchten
**blaz·er** Blazer *m*
**bla·zon** Wappen *n*
**bleach** bleichen
**bleak** öde, kahl; rau; *fig* trüb, freudlos, finster
**blear·y** trübe, verschwommen
**bleat** ZO **1.** Blöken *n*; **2.** blöken
**bleed** *v/i* bluten; *v/t* MED zur Ader lassen; F schröpfen
**bleed·ing** MED Blutung *f*; Aderlass *m*
**bleep 1.** Piepton *m*; **2.** *j-n* anpiepsen
**bleep·er** *Br* F Piepser *m*
**blem·ish 1.** (*a.* Schönheits)Fehler *m*; Makel *m*; **2.** entstellen
**blend 1.** (sich) (ver)mischen; GASTR verschneiden; **2.** Mischung *f*; GASTR Verschnitt *m*
**blend·er** Mixer *m*, Mixgerät *n*
**bless** segnen; preisen; ***be ~ed with*** gesegnet sein mit; **(God)** ***~ you!*** alles Gute!; Gesundheit!; ***~ me!, ~ my heart!, ~ my soul!*** F du meine Güte!
**bless·ed** selig, gesegnet; F verflixt
**bless·ing** Segen *m*
**blight** BOT Mehltau *m*
**blind 1.** blind (*fig* ***to*** gegen[über]); unübersichtlich; **2.** Rouleau *n*, Rollo *n*; ***the ~*** die Blinden *pl*; **3.** blenden; *fig* blind machen (***to*** für, gegen)
**blind al·ley** Sackgasse *f*
**blind·ers** Scheuklappen *pl*
**blind·fold 1.** blindlings; **2.** *j-m* die Augen verbinden; **3.** Augenbinde *f*
**blind·ly** *fig* blindlings
**blind·ness** Blindheit *f*; Verblendung *f*
**blind·worm** ZO Blindschleiche *f*
**blink 1.** Blinzeln *n*; **2.** blinzeln, zwinkern; blinken
**blink·ers** *Br* Scheuklappen *pl*
**bliss** Seligkeit *f*, Wonne *f*
**blis·ter** MED, TECH **1.** Blase *f*; **2.** Blasen hervorrufen auf (*dat*); Blasen ziehen *or* TECH werfen
**blitz** MIL **1.** heftiger Luftangriff; **2.** schwer bombardieren
**bliz·zard** Blizzard *m*, Schneesturm *m*
**bloat·ed** (an)geschwollen, (auf)gedunsen; *fig* aufgeblasen
**bloat·er** GASTR Bückling *m*
**blob** Klecks *m*
**block 1.** Block *m*, Klotz *m*; Baustein *m*, (Bau)Klötzchen *n*; (*Schreib-, Notiz-*) Block *m*; (Häuser)Block *m*; TECH Verstopfung *f*; *fig geistige etc* Sperre; ***~ (of flats)*** *Br* Wohn-, Mietshaus *n*; **2.** *a.* ***~ up*** (ab-, ver)sperren, blockieren, verstopfen
**block·ade 1.** Blockade *f*; **2.** blockieren
**block·bust·er** F Kassenmagnet *m*, Kassenschlager *m*
**block·head** F Dummkopf *m*
**block let·ters** Blockschrift *f*
**blond 1.** Blonde *m*; **2.** blond; hell (*skin*)
**blonde 1.** blond; **2.** Blondine *f*
**blood** Blut *n*; ***in cold ~*** kaltblütig; **~ bank** MED Blutbank *f*; **~ clot** MED Blutgerinnsel *n*; **~ cor·pus·cle** MED Blutkörperchen *n*
**blood·cur·dling** grauenhaft
**blood do·nor** MED Blutspender(in)
**blood group** MED Blutgruppe *f*
**blood·hound** ZO Bluthund *m*
**blood pres·sure** MED Blutdruck *m*
**blood·shed** Blutvergießen *n*
**blood·shot** blutunterlaufen
**blood·thirst·y** blutdürstig
**blood ves·sel** ANAT Blutgefäß *n*
**blood test** MED Blutprobe *f*
**blood·y** blutig; *Br* F verdammt, verflucht
**bloom 1.** Blume *f*, Blüte *f*; *fig* Blüte(zeit) *f*; **2.** blühen; *fig* (er)strahlen
**blos·som 1.** Blüte *f*; **2.** blühen; *fig* ***~ into*** erblühen zu
**blot 1.** Klecks *m*; *fig* Makel *m*; **2.** beklecksen
**blotch** Klecks *m*; Hautfleck *m*
**blotch·y** fleckig
**blot·ter** (Tinten)Löscher *m*
**blot·ting pa·per** Löschpapier *n*
**blouse** Bluse *f*
**blow**[1] Schlag *m* (*a. fig*), Stoß *m*
**blow**[2] *v/i* blasen, wehen; keuchen, schnaufen; explodieren; platzen (*tire*); ELECTR durchbrennen; ***~ up*** in die Luft fliegen; explodieren; *v/t*: ***~ one's nose*** sich die Nase putzen; ***~ one's top*** F an die Decke gehen (*vor Wut*); ***~ out*** ausblasen; ***~ up*** sprengen; PHOT vergrößern
**blow-dry** föhnen
**blow·fly** ZO Schmeißfliege *f*

**blow·pipe** Blasrohr *n*
**blow-up** PHOT Vergrößerung *f*
**blud·geon** Knüppel *m*
**blue 1.** blau; F melancholisch, traurig, schwermütig; **2.** Blau *n*; ***out of the ~*** *fig* aus heiterem Himmel
**blue·ber·ry** BOT Blau-, Heidelbeere *f*
**blue·bot·tle** ZO Schmeißfliege *f*
**blue-col·lar work·er** Arbeiter(in)
**blues** MUS Blues *m*; F Melancholie *f*; ***have the ~*** F den Moralischen haben
**bluff**[1] Steilufer *n*
**bluff**[2] **1.** Bluff *m*; **2.** bluffen
**blu·ish** bläulich
**blun·der 1.** Fehler *m*, F Schnitzer *m*; **2.** e-n (groben) Fehler machen; verpfuschen, F verpatzen
**blunt** stumpf; *fig* offen
**blunt·ly** freiheraus
**blur** [blɜː] **1.** *v/t* verwischen; verschmieren; PHOT, TV verwackeln, verzerren; *fig* trüben; **2.** *v/i* verschwimmen (*a. fig*)
**blurt:** ***~ out*** herausplatzen mit
**blush 1.** Erröten *n*, Schamröte *f*; **2.** erröten, rot werden
**blus·ter** brausen (*wind*); *fig* poltern, toben
**BMX** ABBR *of* ***bicycle motocross*** Querfeldeinrennen *n*; ***~ bike*** BMX-Rad *n*
**BO** ABBR → ***body odo(u)r***
**boar** ZO Eber *m*; Keiler *m*
**board 1.** Brett *n*; (Anschlag)Brett *n*; Konferenztisch *m*; Ausschuss *m*, Kommission *f*; Behörde *f*; Verpflegung *f*; Pappe *f*, Karton *m*; SPORT (Surf)Board *n*; ***on ~ a train*** in e-m Zug; **2.** *v/t* dielen, verschalen; beköstigen; an Bord gehen; MAR entern; RAIL *etc* einsteigen in; *v/i* in Kost sein, wohnen
**board·er** Kostgänger(in); Pensionsgast *m*; Internatsschüler(in)
**board game** Brettspiel *n*
**board·ing| card** AVIAT Bordkarte *f*; **~ house** Pension *f*, Fremdenheim *n*; **~ school** Internat *n*
**board of di·rec·tors** ECON Aufsichtsrat *m*
**Board of Trade** Handelskammer *f*; *Br* Handelsministerium *n*
**board·walk** Strandpromenade *f*
**boast 1.** Prahlerei *f*; **2.** (***of, about***) sich rühmen (*gen*), prahlen (mit)
**boat** Boot *n*; Schiff *n*
**bob 1.** Knicks *m*; kurzer Haarschnitt; *Br* HIST F Schilling *m*; **2.** *v/t Haar* kurz schneiden; *v/i* sich auf und ab bewegen; knicksen
**bob·bin** Spule *f* (*a.* ELECTR)
**bob·sleigh** SPORT Bob *m*
**bod·ice** Mieder *n*; Oberteil *n*
**bod·i·ly** körperlich
**bod·y** Körper *m*, Leib *m*; Leiche *f*; JUR Körperschaft *f*; Hauptteil *m*; MOT Karosserie *f*; MIL Truppenkörper *m*
**bod·y·guard** Leibwache *f*; Leibwächter *m*
**bod·y| o·do(u)r** (ABBR ***BO***) Körpergeruch *m*; **~ stock·ing** Body *m*
**bod·y·work** MOT Karosserie *f*
**Boer 1.** Bure *m*; **2.** Buren...
**bog** Sumpf *m*, Morast *m*
**bo·gus** falsch; Schwindel...
**boil**[1] MED Geschwür *n*, Furunkel *m*, *n*
**boil**[2] **1.** kochen, sieden; **2.** Kochen *n*, Sieden *n*
**boil·er** (Dampf)Kessel *m*; Boiler *m*
**boil·er suit** Overall *m*
**boil·ing point** Siedepunkt *m* (*a. fig*)
**bois·ter·ous** ungestüm; heftig, laut; lärmend
**bold** kühn, verwegen; keck, dreist, unverschämt; steil; PRINT fett; ***as ~ as brass*** F frech wie Oskar; *words* ***in ~ print*** fett gedruckt; **bold·ness** Kühnheit *f*, Verwegenheit *f*; Dreistigkeit *f*
**bol·ster 1.** Keilkissen *n*; **2.** ***~ up*** *fig* (unter)stützen, *j-m* Mut machen
**bolt 1.** Bolzen *m*; Riegel *m*; Blitz(strahl) *m*; plötzlicher Satz, Fluchtversuch *m*; **2.** *adv*: ***~ upright*** kerzengerade; **3.** *v/t* verriegeln; F hinunterschlingen; *v/i* davonlaufen, ausreißen; ZO scheuen, durchgehen
**bomb 1.** Bombe *f*; ***the ~*** die Atombombe; **2.** bombardieren; **bom·bard** bombardieren; **bomb·er** AVIAT Bomber *m*; Bombenleger *m*
**bomb·proof** bombensicher
**bomb·shell** Bombe *f* (*a. fig*)
**bo·nan·za** *fig* Goldgrube *f*
**bond** Bund *m*, Verbindung *f*; ECON Schuldverschreibung *f*, Obligation *f*; ***in ~*** ECON unter Zollverschluss
**bond·age** Hörigkeit *f*
**bonds** *fig* Bande *pl*
**bone 1.** ANAT Knochen *m*, *pl a.* Gebeine *pl*; ZO Gräte *f*; ***~ of contention*** Zankapfel *m*; ***have a ~ to pick with s.o.*** mit j-m

ein Hühnchen zu rupfen haben; ***make no ~s about*** nicht lange fackeln mit; **2.** die Knochen auslösen (aus); entgräten
**bon·fire** Feuer *n* im Freien; Freudenfeuer *n*
**bon·net** Haube *f*; *Br* Motorhaube *f*
**bo·nus** ECON Bonus *m*, Prämie *f*; Gratifikation *f*
**bon·y** knöchern; knochig
**boo** *int* buh!; THEA ***~ off the stage,*** *soccer:* ***~ off the park*** auspfeifen
**boobs** *sl* Titten *pl*
**boo·by** F Trottel *m*
**book 1.** Buch *n*; Heft *n*; Liste *f*; Block *m*; **2.** buchen; eintragen; SPORT verwarnen; *Fahrkarte etc* lösen; *Platz etc* (vor)bestellen, reservieren lassen; *Gepäck* aufgeben; ***~ in*** *esp Br* sich (*im Hotel*) eintragen; ***~ in at*** absteigen in (*dat*); ***~ed up*** ausgebucht, ausverkauft, belegt
**book·case** Bücherschrank *m*
**book·ing** Buchen *n*, (Vor)Bestellung *f*; SPORT Verwarnung *f*; **~ clerk** Schalterbeamte *m*, -beamtin *f*; **~ of·fice** Fahrkartenausgabe *f*, -schalter *m*; THEA Kasse *f*
**book·keep·er** ECON Buchhalter(in)
**book·keep·ing** ECON Buchhaltung *f*, Buchführung *f*
**book·let** Büchlein *n*, Broschüre *f*
**book·mak·er** Buchmacher *m*
**book·mark(·er)** Lesezeichen *n*
**book·sell·er** Buchhändler(in)
**book·shelf** Bücherregal *n*
**book·shop** *esp Br*, **book·store** Buchhandlung *f*
**book·worm** *fig* Bücherwurm *m*
**boom**[1] ECON **1.** Boom *m*, Aufschwung *m*, Hochkonjunktur *f*, Hausse *f*; **2.** e-n Boom erleben
**boom**[2] MAR Baum *m*, Spiere *f*; TECH (Kran)Ausleger *m*; *film*, TV (Mikrofon)Galgen *m*
**boom**[3] dröhnen, donnern
**boor·ish** ungehobelt
**boost 1.** hochschieben; ECON in die Höhe treiben; ankurbeln; ELECTR verstärken; TECH erhöhen; *fig* stärken, Auftrieb geben (*dat*); **2.** Erhöhung *f*; Auftrieb *m*; ELECTR Verstärkung *f*
**boot**[1] Stiefel *m*; *Br* MOT Kofferraum *m*
**boot**[2]**:** **~ (*up*)** EDP laden
**boot**[3]**:** ***to ~*** obendrein
**boot·ee** (*Damen*)Halbstiefel *m*
**booth** (Markt- *etc*)Bude *f*; (Messe-)Stand *m*; (Wahl- *etc*)Kabine *f*; (Telefon)Zelle *f*
**boot·lace** Schnürsenkel *m*
**boot·y** Beute *f*
**booze** F **1.** saufen; **2.** Zeug *n*; Sauferei *f*
**bor·der 1.** Rand *m*, Saum *m*, Einfassung *f*; Rabatte *f*; Grenze *f*; **2.** einfassen; (um)säumen; grenzen (**on** an *acc*)
**bore**[1] **1.** Bohrloch *n*; TECH Kaliber *n*; **2.** bohren
**bore**[2] **1.** Langweiler *m*; langweilige *or* lästige Sache; **2.** *j-n* langweilen; ***be ~d*** sich langweilen
**bore·dom** Lang(e)weile *f*
**bor·ing** langweilig
**bo·rough** Stadtteil *m*; Stadtgemeinde *f*; Stadtbezirk *m*
**bor·row** (sich) *et.* borgen *or* (aus)leihen
**bos·om** Busen *m*; *fig* Schoß *m*
**boss** F **1.** Boss *m*, Chef *m*; **2.** *a.* ***~ about, ~ around*** herumkommandieren
**boss·y** F herrisch
**bo·tan·i·cal** botanisch
**bot·a·ny** Botanik *f*
**botch 1.** Pfusch *m*; **2.** verpfuschen
**both** beide(s); ***~ ... and ...*** sowohl ... als (auch) ...
**both·er 1.** Belästigung *f*, Störung *f*, Plage *f*, Mühe *f*; **2.** belästigen, stören, plagen; ***don't ~!*** bemühen Sie sich nicht!
**bot·tle 1.** Flasche *f*; **2.** in Flaschen abfüllen; **~ bank** *Br* Altglascontainer *m*
**bot·tle·neck** *fig* Engpass *m*
**bot·tle o·pen·er** Flaschenöffner *m*
**bot·tom** unterster Teil, Boden *m*, Fuß *m*, Unterseite *f*; Grund *m*; F Hintern *m*, Popo *m*; ***be at the ~ of s.th.*** hinter e-r Sache stecken; ***get to the ~ of s.th.*** e-r Sache auf den Grund gehen
**bough** Ast *m*, Zweig *m*
**boul·der** Geröllblock *m*, Findling *m*
**bounce 1.** aufprallen *or* aufspringen (lassen); springen, hüpfen, stürmen; ECON F platzen (*check*); **2.** Sprung *m*, Satz *m*; F Schwung *m*
**bounc·ing** kräftig, stramm
**bound**[1] unterwegs (**for** nach)
**bound**[2] *mst pl* Grenze *f*, *fig a.* Schranke *f*
**bound**[3] **1.** Sprung *m*, Satz *m*; **2.** springen, hüpfen; auf-, abprallen
**bound·a·ry** Grenze *f*

**bound·less** grenzenlos

**boun·te·ous, boun·ti·ful** freigebig, reichlich

**boun·ty** Freigebigkeit *f*; großzügige Spende *f*; Prämie *f*

**bou·quet** Bukett *n* (*a.* GASTR), Strauß *m*; GASTR Blume *f*

**bout** SPORT (*Box-*, *Ring*)Kampf *m*; MED Anfall *m*

**bou·tique** Boutique *f*

**bow**[1] **1.** Verbeugung *f*; **2.** *v/i* sich verbeugen *or* verneigen (**to** vor *dat*); *fig* sich beugen *or* unterwerfen (**to** *dat*); *v/t* biegen; beugen, neigen

**bow**[2] MAR Bug *m*

**bow**[3] Bogen *m*; Schleife *f*

**bow·els** ANAT Darm *m*; Eingeweide *pl*

**bowl**[1] Schale *f*, Schüssel *f*, Napf *m*; (*Zucker*)Dose *f*; Becken *n*; (*Pfeifen-*) Kopf *m*

**bowl**[2] **1.** (*Bowling-*, *Kegel- etc*)Kugel *f*; **2.** kegeln; rollen (*bowling ball*); *cricket*: werfen

**bow-leg·ged** o-beinig

**bowl·er**[1] Bowlingspieler(in); Kegler(in)

**bowl·er**[2], *a.* ~ **hat** *esp Br* Bowler *m*, F Melone *f*

**bowl·ing** Bowling *n*; Kegeln *n*; ***go*** ~ kegeln; ~ **al·ley** Kegelbahn *f*; ~ **ball** Kegelkugel *f*

**box**[1] Kasten *m*, Kiste *f*; Büchse *f*, Dose *f*, Kästchen *n*; Schachtel *f*; Behälter *m*; TECH Gehäuse *n*; Postfach *n*; *Br* (Telefon)Zelle *f*; JUR Zeugenstand *m*; THEA Loge *f*; MOT, ZO Box *f*

**box**[2] **1.** SPORT boxen; F ~ ***s.o.'s ears*** j-n ohrfeigen; **2.** F ***a*** ~ ***on the ear*** e-e Ohrfeige

**box**[3] [bɒks] BOT Buchsbaum *m*

**box·er** Boxer *m*

**box·ing** Boxen *n*, Boxsport *m*

**Box·ing Day** *Br* der zweite Weihnachtsfeiertag

**box num·ber** Chiffre(nummer) *f*

**box of·fice** Theaterkasse *f*

**boy** Junge *m*, Knabe *m*, Bursche *m*

**boy·cott 1.** boykottieren; **2.** Boykott *m*

**boy·friend** Freund *m*

**boy·hood** Knabenjahre *pl*, Jugend(zeit) *f*

**boy·ish** jungenhaft

**boy scout** Pfadfinder *m*

**bra** BH *m* (*Büstenhalter*)

**brace 1.** TECH Strebe *f*, Stützbalken *m*; (Zahn)Klammer *f*, (-)Spange *f*; **2.** TECH verstreben, versteifen, stützen

**brace·let** Armband *n*

**brac·es** *Br* Hosenträger *pl*

**brack·et** TECH Träger *m*, Halter *m*, Stütze *f*; PRINT Klammer *f*; (*esp Alters-*, *Steuer*)Klasse *f*; ***lower income*** ~ niedrige Einkommensgruppe

**brack·ish** brackig, salzig

**brag** prahlen (***about*** mit)

**brag·gart** Prahler *m*, F Angeber *m*

**braid 1.** Zopf *m*; Borte *f*, Tresse *f*; **2.** flechten; mit Borte besetzen

**brain** ANAT Gehirn *n*, *often pl fig a.* Verstand *m*, Intelligenz *f*, Kopf *m*

**brain·storm** Geistesblitz *m*

**brain·wash** *j-n* e-r Gehirnwäsche unterziehen

**brain·wash·ing** Gehirnwäsche *f*

**brain·wave** *Br* Geistesblitz *m*

**brain·y** F gescheit

**braise** GASTR schmoren

**brake** TECH **1.** Bremse *f*; **2.** bremsen

**brake·light** MOT Bremslicht *n*

**bram·ble** BOT Brombeerstrauch *m*

**bran** AGR Kleie *f*

**branch 1.** Ast *m*, Zweig *m*; *fig* Fach *n*; Linie *f* (*des Stammbaumes*); ECON Zweigstelle *f*, Filiale *f*; **2.** sich verzweigen; abzweigen

**brand 1.** ECON (Schutz-, Handels)Marke *f*, Warenzeichen *n*; Markenname *m*; Sorte *f*, Klasse *f*; Brandmal *n*; **2.** einbrennen; brandmarken

**bran·dish** schwingen

**brand name** ECON Markenname *m*

**brand-new** nagelneu

**bran·dy** Kognak *m*, Weinbrand *m*

**brass** Messing *n*; F Unverschämtheit *f*

**brass band** MUS Blaskapelle *f*

**bras·sière** Büstenhalter *m*

**brat** *contp* Balg *m*, *n*, Gör *n*

**brave 1.** tapfer, mutig, unerschrocken; **2.** trotzen; mutig begegnen (*dat*)

**brav·er·y** Tapferkeit *f*

**brawl 1.** Krawall *m*; Rauferei *f*; **2.** Krawall machen; raufen

**brawn·y** muskulös

**bray 1.** ZO Eselsschrei *m*; **2.** ZO schreien; *fig* wiehern

**bra·zen** unverschämt, unverfroren, frech

**Bra·zil** Brasilien *n*; **Bra·zil·ian 1.** brasilianisch; **2.** Brasilianer(in)

**breach 1.** Bruch *m*; *fig* Verletzung *f*; MIL Bresche *f*; **2.** e-e Bresche schlagen in (*acc*)
**bread** Brot *n*; ***brown ~*** Schwarzbrot *n*; ***know which side one's ~ is buttered*** F s-n Vorteil (er)kennen
**breadth** Breite *f*
**break 1.** Bruch *m*; Lücke *f*; Pause *f* (*Br a.* PED), Unterbrechung *f*; (plötzlicher) Wechsel, Umschwung *m*; (*Tages*)Anbruch *m*; ***bad ~*** F Pech *n*; ***lucky ~*** F Dusel *m*, Schwein *n*; ***give s.o. a ~*** F j-m e-e Chance geben; ***take a ~*** e-e Pause machen; ***without a ~*** ununterbrochen; **2.** *v/t* (ab-, auf-, durch-, zer)brechen; zerschlagen, kaputtmachen; ZO *a.* ***~ in*** zähmen, abrichten, zureiten; *Gesetz, Vertrag etc* brechen; *Kode etc* knacken; *schlechte Nachricht* (schonend) beibringen; *v/i* brechen (*a. fig*); (zer)brechen, (zer)reißen, kaputtgehen; anbrechen (*Tag*); METEOR umschlagen; *fig* ausbrechen (***into*** in *Tränen etc*); ***~ away*** ab-, losbrechen; sich losmachen *or* losreißen; ***~ down*** ein-, niederreißen, *Haus* abbrechen; zusammenbrechen (*a. fig*); versagen; MOT e-e Panne haben; *fig* scheitern; ***~ in*** einbrechen, eindringen; ***~ into*** einbrechen in (*ein Haus etc*); ***~ off*** abbrechen, *fig a.* Schluss machen mit; ***~ out*** ausbrechen; ***~ through*** durchbrechen; *fig* den Durchbruch schaffen; ***~ up*** abbrechen, beenden, schließen; (sich) auflösen; *fig* zerbrechen, auseinander gehen
**break·a·ble** zerbrechlich
**break·age** Bruch *m*
**break·a·way 1.** Trennung *f*; **2.** Splitter...
**break·down** Zusammenbruch *m* (*a. fig*); TECH Maschinenschaden *m*; MOT Panne *f*; ***nervous ~*** MED Nervenzusammenbruch *m*; **~ lor·ry** *Br* MOT Abschleppwagen *m*; **~ ser·vice** *Br* MOT Pannendienst *m*, Pannenhilfe *f*; **~ truck** *Br* MOT Abschleppwagen *m*
**break·fast 1.** Frühstück *n*; ***have ~*** → **2.** frühstücken
**break·through** *fig* Durchbruch *m*
**break·up** Aufhebung *f*; Auflösung *f*
**breast** ANAT Brust *f*; Busen *m*; *fig* Herz *n*; ***make a clean ~ of s.th.*** et. offen (ein)gestehen
**breast·stroke** Brustschwimmen *n*
**breath** Atem(zug) *m*; Hauch *m*; ***be out of ~*** außer Atem sein; ***waste one's ~*** in den Wind reden
**breath·a·lyse** *Br*, **breath·a·lyze** F (ins Röhrchen) blasen *or* pusten lassen
**breath·a·lys·er**® *Br*, **breath·a·lyz·er**® Alkoholtestgerät *n*, F Röhrchen *n*
**breathe** atmen
**breath·less** atemlos
**breath·tak·ing** atemberaubend
**breech·es** Kniebund-, Reithosen *pl*
**breed 1.** ZO Rasse *f*, Zucht *f*; **2.** *v/t* BOT, ZO züchten; *v/i* BIOL sich fortpflanzen
**breed·er** Züchter(in); Zuchttier *n*; PHYS Brüter *m*
**breed·ing** BIOL Fortpflanzung *f*; (Tier)Zucht *f*; *fig* Erziehung *f*; (gutes) Benehmen
**breeze** Brise *f*
**breth·ren** *esp* REL Brüder *pl*
**brew** brauen; *Tee* zubereiten, aufbrühen
**brew·er** (Bier)Brauer *m*
**brew·er·y** Brauerei *f*
**bri·ar** → ***brier***
**bribe 1.** Bestechungsgeld *n*, -geschenk *n*; Bestechung *f*; **2.** bestechen
**brib·er·y** Bestechung *f*
**brick 1.** Ziegel(stein) *m*, Backstein *m*; *Br* Baustein *m*, (Bau)Klötzchen *n*
**brick·lay·er** Maurer *m*
**brick·yard** Ziegelei *f*
**brid·al** Braut...; **bride** Braut *f*
**bride·groom** Bräutigam *m*
**brides·maid** Brautjungfer *f*
**bridge 1.** Brücke *f*; **2.** e-e Brücke schlagen über (*acc*); *fig* überbrücken
**bri·dle 1.** Zaum *m*; Zügel *m*; **2.** (auf)zäumen; zügeln; **~ path** Reitweg *m*
**brief 1.** kurz, bündig; **2.** instruieren, genaue Anweisungen geben (*dat*)
**brief·case** Aktenmappe *f*
**briefs** Slip *m*
**bri·er** BOT Dornstrauch *m*; Wilde Rose
**bri·gade** MIL Brigade *f*
**bright** hell, glänzend; klar; heiter; lebhaft; gescheit
**bright·en** *v/t a.* ***~ up*** heller machen, aufhellen, erhellen; aufheitern; *v/i a.* ***~ up*** sich aufhellen
**bright·ness** Helligkeit *f*; Glanz *m*; Heiterkeit *f*; Gescheitheit *f*
**bril·liance, bril·lian·cy** Glanz *m*; *fig* Brillanz *f*

**bril·liant 1.** glänzend; hervorragend, brillant; **2.** Brillant *m*
**brim 1.** Rand *m*; Krempe *f*; **2.** bis zum Rande füllen *or* voll sein
**brim·ful(l)** randvoll
**brine** Sole *f*; Lake *f*
**bring** bringen, mitbringen, herbringen; *j-n* dazu bringen (***to do*** zu tun); ~ ***about*** zustande bringen; bewirken; ~ ***forth*** hervorbringen; ~ ***off*** *et.* fertig bringen, schaffen; ~ ***on*** verursachen; ~ ***out*** herausbringen; ~ ***round*** *Ohnmächtigen* wieder zu sich bringen; *Kranken* wieder auf die Beine bringen; ~ ***up*** auf-, großziehen; erziehen; zur Sprache bringen
**brink** Rand *m* (*a. fig*)
**brisk** flott; lebhaft; frisch
**bris·tle 1.** Borste *f*; (Bart)Stoppel *f*; **2.** *a.* ~ ***up*** sich sträuben; zornig werden; strotzen, wimmeln (***with*** von)
**bris·tly** stoppelig, Stoppel...
**Brit** F Brite *m*, Britin *f*
**Brit·ain** Britannien *n*
**Brit·ish** britisch; ***the*** ~ die Briten *pl*
**Brit·on** Brite *m*, Britin *f*
**brit·tle** spröde, zerbrechlich
**broach** *Thema* anschneiden
**broad** breit; weit; hell; deutlich (*hint etc*); derb (*humor etc*); stark (*accent*); allgemein; weitherzig; liberal
**broad·cast 1.** im Rundfunk *or* Fernsehen bringen, ausstrahlen, übertragen; senden; **2.** *radio*, TV Sendung *f*
**broad·cast·er** Rundfunk-, Fernsehsprecher(in)
**broad·en** verbreitern, erweitern
**broad jump** SPORT Weitsprung *m*
**broad·mind·ed** liberal
**bro·cade** Brokat *m*
**bro·chure** Broschüre *f*, Prospekt *m*
**brogue** fester Straßenschuh
**broil** grillen
**broke** F pleite, abgebrannt
**bro·ken** zerbrochen, kaputt; gebrochen (*a. fig*); zerrüttet
**brok·en-heart·ed** verzweifelt, untröstlich
**bro·ker** ECON Makler *m*
**bron·chi·tis** MED Bronchitis *f*
**bronze 1.** Bronze *f*; **2.** bronzefarben; Bronze...
**brooch** Brosche *f*
**brood** ZO **1.** Brut *f*; **2.** Brut...; **3.** brüten (*a. fig*)
**brook** Bach *m*
**broom** Besen *m*
**broth** GASTR Fleischbrühe *f*
**broth·el** Bordell *n*
**broth·er** Bruder *m*; ~(**s**) ***and sister***(**s**) Geschwister *pl*
**broth·er·hood** REL Bruderschaft *f*
**broth·er-in-law** Schwager *m*
**broth·er·ly** brüderlich
**brow** ANAT (Augen)Braue *f*; Stirn *f*; GEOGR Rand *m*
**brow·beat** einschüchtern
**brown 1.** braun; **2.** Braun *n*; **3.** bräunen; braun werden
**browse** grasen, weiden; *fig* schmökern
**bruise 1.** MED Quetschung *f*, blauer Fleck; **2.** quetschen; anstoßen; MED e-e Quetschung *or* e-n blauen Fleck bekommen
**brunch** Brunch *m*
**brush 1.** Bürste *f*; Pinsel *m*; ZO (*Fuchs*)Rute *f*; Scharmützel *n*; Unterholz *n*; **2.** bürsten; fegen; streifen; ~ ***against s.o.*** j-n streifen; ~ ***away***, ~ ***off*** wegbürsten, abwischen; ~ ***aside***, ~ ***away*** *et.* abtun; ~ ***up*** (***on***) *fig* aufpolieren, auffrischen
**brush·wood** Gestrüpp *n*, Unterholz *n*
**brusque** brüsk, barsch
**Brus·sels sprouts** BOT Rosenkohl *m*
**bru·tal** brutal, roh
**bru·tal·i·ty** Brutalität *f*
**brute 1.** brutal; ***with*** ~ ***force*** mit roher Gewalt; **2.** Vieh *n*; F Untier *n*, Scheusal *n*; Rohling *m*; **brut·ish** *fig* tierisch
**bub·ble 1.** Blase *f*; **2.** sprudeln
**buck¹ 1.** ZO Bock *m*; **2.** bocken
**buck² F** Dollar *m*
**buck·et** Eimer *m*, Kübel *m*
**buck·le 1.** Schnalle *f*, Spange *f*; **2.** *a.* ~ ***up*** zu-, festschnallen; ~ ***on*** anschnallen
**buck·skin** Wildleder *n*
**bud 1.** BOT Knospe *f*; *fig* Keim *m*; **2.** knospen, keimen
**bud·dy** F Kamerad *m*; Kumpel *m*, Spezi *m*
**budge** *v/i* sich (von der Stelle) rühren; *v/t* (vom Fleck) bewegen
**bud·ger·i·gar** ZO Wellensittich *m*
**bud·get** Budget *n*, Etat *m*; PARL Haushaltsplan *m*
**bud·gie** F → ***budgerigar***
**buf·fa·lo** ZO Büffel *m*
**buff·er** TECH Puffer *m*

B

**buf·fet¹** schlagen; ~ ***about*** durchrütteln, durchschütteln
**buf·fet²** Büfett *n*, Anrichte *f*
**buf·fet³** (*Frühstücks- etc*)Büfett *n*; Theke *f*
**bug 1.** ZO Wanze *f* (*a.* F *fig*); Insekt *n*; EDP Programmfehler *m*; **2.** F Wanzen anbringen in (*dat*); F ärgern
**bug·ging| de·vice** Abhörgerät *n*; ~ **op·e·ra·tion** Lauschangriff *m*
**bug·gy** Kinderwagen *m*; MOT Buggy *m*
**bu·gle** MUS Wald-, Signalhorn *n*
**build 1.** (er)bauen, errichten; **2.** Körperbau *m*, Figur *f*, Statur *f*; **build·er** Erbauer *m*; Bauunternehmer *m*
**build·ing 1.** (Er)Bauen *n*; Bau *m*, Gebäude *n*; **2.** Bau...; ~ **site** Baustelle *f*
**built-in** eingebaut, Einbau...
**built-up:** ~ ***area*** bebautes Gelände *or* Gebiet; geschlossene Ortschaft
**bulb** BOT Zwiebel *f*, Knolle *f*; ELECTR (Glüh)Birne *f*
**bulge 1.** (Aus)Bauchung *f*, Ausbuchtung *f*; **2.** sich (aus)bauchen; hervorquellen
**bulk** Umfang *m*, Größe *f*, Masse *f*; Großteil *m*; ***in*** ~ ECON lose, unverpackt; en gros; **bulk·y** sperrig
**bull** ZO Bulle *m*, Stier *m*
**bull·dog** ZO Bulldogge *f*
**bull·doze** planieren; F einschüchtern
**bull·doz·er** TECH Bulldozer *m*, Planierraupe *f*
**bul·let** Kugel *f*
**bul·le·tin** Bulletin *n*, Tagesbericht *m*
**bul·le·tin board** schwarzes Brett
**bul·let·proof** kugelsicher
**bull·fight** Stierkampf *m*
**bul·lion** Gold-, Silberbarren *m*
**bul·lock** ZO Ochse *m*
**bull's-eye:** ***hit the*** ~ ins Schwarze treffen (*a. fig*)
**bul·ly 1.** tyrannische Person, Tyrann *m*; **2.** einschüchtern, tyrannisieren
**bul·wark** Bollwerk *n* (*a. fig*)
**bum** F **1.** Gammler *m*; Tippelbruder *m*, Vagabund *m*; Nichtstuer *m*; **2.** *v/t* schnorren; ~ ***around*** herumgammeln
**bum·ble·bee** ZO Hummel *f*
**bump 1.** heftiger Schlag *or* Stoß; Beule *f*; Unebenheit *f*; **2.** stoßen; rammen, auf *ein Auto* auffahren; zusammenstoßen; holpern; ~ ***into*** *fig j-n* zufällig treffen; F ~ ***s.o. off*** j-n umlegen
**bump·er** MOT Stoßstange *f*
**bump·y** holp(e)rig
**bun** süßes Brötchen; (Haar)Knoten *m*
**bunch** Bund *n*, Bündel *n*; F Verein *m*, Haufen *m*; ~ ***of flowers*** Blumenstrauß *m*; ~ ***of grapes*** Weintraube *f*; ~ ***of keys*** Schlüsselbund *m*, *n*
**bun·dle 1.** Bündel *n* (*a. fig*), Bund *n*; **2.** *v/t a.* ~ ***up*** bündeln
**bun·ga·low** Bungalow *m*
**bun·gee** elastisches Seil
**bun·gee jump·ing** Bungeespringen *n*
**bun·gle 1.** Pfusch *m*; **2.** (ver)pfuschen
**bunk** Koje *f*; → ~ **bed** Etagenbett *n*
**bun·ny** Häschen *n*
**buoy 1.** MAR Boje *f*; **2.** ~ ***up*** *fig* Auftrieb geben (*dat*)
**bur·den 1.** Last *f*; Bürde *f*; **2.** belasten
**bu·reau** *Br* Schreibtisch *m*; (Spiegel-)Kommode *f*; Büro *n*
**bu·reauc·ra·cy** Bürokratie *f*
**burg·er** GASTR Hamburger *m*
**bur·glar** Einbrecher *m*
**bur·glar·ize** einbrechen in (*acc*)
**bur·glar·y** Einbruch *m*
**bur·gle** *Br* → ***burglarize***
**bur·i·al** Begräbnis *n*
**bur·ly** stämmig, kräftig
**burn 1.** MED Verbrennung *f*, Brandwunde *f*; verbrannte Stelle; **2.** (ver-, an)brennen; ~ ***down*** ab-, niederbrennen; ~ ***out*** ausbrennen; ~ ***up*** auflodern; verbrennen; verglühen (*rocket etc*)
**burn·ing** brennend (*a. fig*)
**burp** F rülpsen, aufstoßen; ein Bäuerchen machen (lassen)
**bur·row 1.** ZO Bau *m*; **2.** graben; sich eingraben *or* vergraben
**burst 1.** Bersten *n*; Riss *m*; *fig* Ausbruch *m*; **2.** *v/i* bersten, (zer)platzen; zerspringen; explodieren; ~ ***from*** sich losreißen von; ~ ***in on*** *or* ***upon s.o.*** bei j-m hereinplatzen; ~ ***into tears*** in Tränen ausbrechen; ~ ***out*** *fig* herausplatzen; *v/t* (auf)sprengen
**bur·y** begraben, vergraben; beerdigen
**bus** Omnibus *m*, Bus *m*
**bus driv·er** Busfahrer *m*
**bush** Busch *m*; Gebüsch *n*
**bush·el** Bushel *m*, Scheffel *m* (*Am 35,24 l, Br 36,37 l*)
**bush·y** buschig
**busi·ness** Geschäft *n*; Arbeit *f*, Beschäftigung *f*, Beruf *m*, Tätigkeit *f*; An-

gelegenheit *f*; Sache *f*, Aufgabe *f*; ~ ***of the day*** Tagesordnung *f*; ***on*** ~ geschäftlich, beruflich; ***you have no*** ~ ***doing*** (*or* ***to do***) ***that*** Sie haben kein Recht, das zu tun; ***that's none of your*** ~ das geht Sie nichts an; → ***mind*** 2

**busi·ness hours** Geschäftszeit *f*

**busi·ness·like** geschäftsmäßig, sachlich

**busi·ness·man** Geschäftsmann *m*

**busi·ness trip** Geschäftsreise *f*

**busi·ness·wom·an** Geschäftsfrau *f*

**bus stop** Bushaltestelle *f*

**bust**[1] Büste *f*

**bust**[2]: ***go*** ~ F Pleite gehen

**bus·tle 1.** geschäftiges Treiben; **2.** ~ ***about*** geschäftig hin und her eilen

**bus·y 1.** beschäftigt; geschäftig; fleißig (***at*** bei, an *dat*); belebt (*street*); arbeitsreich (*day*); TEL besetzt; **2.** (*mst* ~ ***o.s.*** sich) beschäftigen (***with*** mit)

**bus·y·bod·y** aufdringlicher Mensch, Gschaftlhuber *m*

**bus·y sig·nal** TEL Besetztzeichen *n*

**but 1.** *cj* aber, jedoch; sondern; außer, als; ohne dass; dennoch; ~ ***then*** and(e)rerseits; ***he could not*** ~ ***laugh*** er musste einfach lachen; **2.** *prp* außer (*dat*); ***all*** ~ ***him*** alle außer ihm; ***the last*** ~ ***one*** der Vorletzte; ***the next*** ~ ***one*** der Übernächste; ***nothing*** ~ nichts als; ~ ***for*** wenn nicht ... gewesen wäre, ohne; **3.** der (die *or* das) nicht; ***there is no one*** ~ ***knows*** es gibt niemand, der es nicht weiß; **4.** *adv* nur; erst, gerade; ***all*** ~ fast, beinahe

**butch·er 1.** Fleischer *m*, Metzger *m*; **2.** (*fig* ab)schlachten

**but·ler** Butler *m*

**butt**[1] **1.** (*Gewehr*)Kolben *m*; (*Zigarren- etc*)Stummel *m*, (*Zigaretten*)Kippe *f*; (Kopf)Stoß *m*; **2.** (mit dem Kopf) stoßen; ~ ***in*** F sich einmischen (***on*** in *acc*)

**butt**[2] Wein-, Bierfaß *n*; Regentonne *f*

**but·ter 1.** Butter *f*; **2.** mit Butter bestreichen

**but·ter·cup** BOT Butterblume *f*

**but·ter·fly** ZO Schmetterling *m*, Falter *m*

**but·tocks** ANAT Gesäß *n*, F *or* ZO Hinterteil *n*

**but·ton 1.** Knopf *m*; Button *m*, (Ansteck)Plakette *f*, Abzeichen *n*; **2.** *mst* ~ ***up*** zuknöpfen

**but·ton·hole** Knopfloch *n*

**but·tress** Strebepfeiler *m*

**bux·om** drall, stramm

**buy 1.** F Kauf *m*; **2.** (an-, ein)kaufen (***of, from*** von; ***at*** bei); *Fahrkarte* lösen; ~ ***out*** *j-n* abfinden, auszahlen; *Firma* aufkaufen; ~ ***up*** aufkaufen

**buy·er** Käufer(in); ECON Einkäufer(in)

**buzz 1.** Summen *n*, Surren *n*; Stimmengewirr *n*; **2.** *v/i* summen, surren; ~ ***off!*** F schwirr ab!, hau ab!

**buz·zard** ZO Bussard *m*

**buzz·er** ELECTR Summer *m*

**by 1.** *prp* (nahe *or* dicht) bei *or* an, neben (***side*** ~ ***side*** Seite an Seite); vorbei *or* vorüber an; *time*: bis um, bis spätestens (***be back*** ~ ***9.30*** sei um 9 Uhr 30 zurück); während, bei (~ ***day*** bei Tage); per, mit (~ ***bus*** mit dem Bus; ~ ***rail*** per Bahn); nach, ...weise (~ ***the dozen*** dutzendweise); nach, gemäß (~ ***my watch*** nach *or* auf m-r Uhr); von (~ ***nature*** von Natur aus); von, durch (***a play*** ~ ***...*** ein Stück von ...; ~ ***o.s.*** allein); um (~ ***an inch*** um e-n Zoll); MATH mal (**2** ~ **4**); *geteilt* durch (**6** ~ **3**); **2.** *adv* vorbei, vorüber (***go*** ~ vorbeigehen, -fahren; *time*: vergehen); beiseite (***put*** ~ beiseite legen, zurücklegen); ~ ***and large*** im Großen und Ganzen

**by...** Neben...; Seiten...

**bye, bye-bye** *int* F Wiedersehen!, tschüs(s)!

**by-e·lec·tion** PARL Nachwahl *f*

**by·gone 1.** vergangen; **2.** ***let*** ~***s be*** ~***s*** lass(t) das Vergangene ruhen

**by·pass 1.** Umgehungsstraße *f*; MED Bypass *m*; **2.** umgehen; vermeiden

**by-prod·uct** Nebenprodukt *n*

**by·road** Nebenstraße *f*

**by·stand·er** Zuschauer(in), *pl die* Umstehenden *pl*

**byte** EDP Byte *n*

**by·way** Nebenstraße *f*

**by·word** Inbegriff *m*; ***be a*** ~ ***for*** stehen für

C

# C

**C, c** C, c *n*

**C** ABBR *of* ***Celsius*** C, Celsius; ***centigrade*** hundertgradig

**c** ABBR *of* ***cent(s)*** Cent *m or pl*; ***century*** Jh., Jahrhundert *n*; ***circa*** ca., zirca, ungefähr; ***cubic*** Kubik...

**cab** Droschke *f*, Taxi *n*; RAIL Führerstand *m*; MOT Fahrerhaus *n*, *a.* TECH Führerhaus *n*

**cab·a·ret** Varieteedarbietung(en *pl*) *f*

**cab·bage** BOT Kohl *m*

**cab·in** Hütte *f*; MAR Kabine *f*, Kajüte *f*; AVIAT Kanzel *f*

**cab·i·net** Schrank *m*, Vitrine *f*; POL Kabinett *n*

**cab·i·net-mak·er** Kunsttischler *m*

**cab·i·net meet·ing** POL Kabinettssitzung *f*

**ca·ble 1.** Kabel *n*; (Draht)Seil *n*; **2.** telegrafieren; *j-m Geld* telegrafisch anweisen; TV verkabeln

**ca·ble car** Kabine *f*; Wagen *m*

**ca·ble·gram** (Übersee)Telegramm *n*

**ca·ble| rail·way** Drahtseil-, Kabinenbahn *f*; **~ tel·e·vi·sion, ~ TV** Kabelfernsehen *n*

**cab rank, cab·stand** Taxi-, Droschkenstand *m*

**cack·le** ZO **1.** Gegacker *n*, Geschnatter *n*; **2.** gackern, schnattern

**cac·tus** BOT Kaktus *m*

**ca·dence** MUS Kadenz *f*; (Sprech-) Rhythmus *m*

**ca·det** MIL Kadett *m*

**cadge** *Br* F schnorren

**caf·é, caf·e** Café *n*

**caf·e·te·ri·a** Cafeteria *f*, Selbstbedienungsrestaurant *n*, *a.* Kantine *f*, UNIV Mensa *f*

**cage 1.** Käfig *m*; *mining*: Förderkorb *m*; **2.** einsperren

**cake 1.** Kuchen *m*, Torte *f*; Tafel *f Schokolade*, Stück *n Seife*; F ***take the ~*** den Vogel abschießen; **2. *~d with mud*** schmutzverkrustet

**ca·lam·i·ty** großes Unglück, Katastrophe *f*

**cal·cu·late** *v/t* kalkulieren; be-, aus-, errechnen; F vermuten; *v/i*: ***~ on*** rechnen mit *or* auf (*acc*), zählen auf (*acc*)

**cal·cu·la·tion** Berechnung *f* (*a. fig*); ECON Kalkulation *f*; *fig* Überlegung *f*

**cal·cu·la·tor** TECH (Taschen)Rechner *m*

**cal·en·dar** Kalender *m*

**calf[1]** ANAT Wade *f*

**calf[2]** ZO Kalb *n*

**calf·skin** Kalb(s)fell *n*

**cal·i·ber,** *esp Br* **cal·i·bre** Kaliber *n*

**call 1.** Ruf *m*; TEL Anruf *m*, Gespräch *n*; Ruf *m*, Berufung *f* (***to*** in *ein Amt*; auf *e-n Lehrstuhl*); Aufruf *m*, Aufforderung *f*; Signal *n*; (kurzer) Besuch; ***on ~*** auf Abruf; ***be on ~*** MED Bereitschaftsdienst haben; ***make a ~*** telefonieren; **2.** *v/t* (herbei)rufen; (ein)berufen; TEL *j-n* anrufen; *j-n* berufen, ernennen (***to*** zu); nennen; *Aufmerksamkeit* lenken (***to*** auf *acc*); ***be ~ed*** heißen; ***~ s.o. names*** j-n beschimpfen, j-n beleidigen; *v/i* rufen; TEL anrufen; e-n (kurzen) Besuch machen (***on s.o., at s.o.'s [house]*** bei j-m); ***~ at a port*** MAR e-n Hafen anlaufen; ***~ for*** rufen nach; *et.* anfordern; *et.* abholen; ***to be ~ed for*** postlagernd; ***~ on*** sich an *j-n* wenden (***for*** wegen); appellieren an (*acc*) (***to do*** zu tun); ***~ on s.o.*** j-n besuchen

**call box** *Br* Telefonzelle *f*

**call·er** Besucher(in); TEL Anrufer(in)

**call girl** Callgirl *n*

**call-in** → ***phone-in***

**call·ing** Berufung *f*; Beruf *m*

**cal·lous** schwielig; *fig* gefühllos

**cal·lus** Schwiele *f*

**calm 1.** still, ruhig; **2.** (Wind)Stille *f*, Ruhe *f*; **3.** *often* ***~ down*** besänftigen, (sich) beruhigen

**cal·o·rie** Kalorie *f*; ***high*** *or* ***rich in ~s*** kalorienreich; ***low in ~s*** kalorienarm, kalorienreduziert

**cal·o·rie-con·scious** kalorienbewusst

**calve** ZO kalben

**cam·cor·der** Camcorder *m*, Kamerarekorder *m*

**cam·el** ZO Kamel *n*

**cam·e·o** Kamee *f*; THEA, *film*: kleine Nebenrolle, kurze Szene

**cam·e·ra** Kamera *f*, Fotoapparat *m*

**cam·o·mile** BOT Kamille *f*

**cam·ou·flage 1.** Tarnung *f*; **2.** tarnen
**camp 1.** (*Zelt- etc*)Lager *n*; **2.** lagern; ~ ***out*** zelten, campen
**cam·paign 1.** MIL Feldzug *m* (*a. fig*); *fig* Kampagne *f*, Aktion *f*; POL Wahlkampf *m*; **2.** *fig* kämpfen (***for*** für; ***against*** gegen)
**camp bed** *Br*, **camp cot** Feldbett *n*
**camp·er (van)** Campingbus *m*, Wohnmobil *n*
**camp·ground, camp·site** Lagerplatz *m*; Zeltplatz *m*, Campingplatz *m*
**cam·pus** Campus *m*, Universitätsgelände *n*
**can**[1] *v/aux ich* kann, *du* kannst *etc*; dürfen, können
**can**[2] **1.** Kanne *f*; (Blech-, Konserven-) Dose *f*, (-)Büchse *f*; **2.** einmachen, eindosen
**Can·a·da** Kanada *n*; **Ca·na·di·an 1.** kanadisch; **2.** Kanadier(in)
**ca·nal** Kanal *m* (*a.* ANAT)
**ca·nar·y** ZO Kanarienvogel *m*
**can·cel** (durch-, aus)streichen; entwerten; rückgängig machen; absagen; ***be ~(l)ed*** ausfallen
**Can·cer** ASTR Krebs *m*; ***he*** (***she***) ***is*** (***a***) ~ er (sie) ist (ein) Krebs
**can·cer** MED Krebs *m*
**can·cer·ous** MED Krebs..., krebsbefallen
**can·cer pa·tient** MED Krebskranke *m,f*
**can·did** aufrichtig, offen
**can·di·date** Kandidat(in) (***for*** für), Bewerber(in) (***for*** um)
**can·died** kandiert
**can·dle** Kerze *f*; Licht *n*; ***burn the ~ at both ends*** mit s-r Gesundheit Raubbau treiben
**can·dle·stick** Kerzenleuchter *m*, Kerzenständer *m*
**can·do(u)r** Aufrichtigkeit *f*, Offenheit *f*
**can·dy 1.** Kandis(zucker) *m*; Süßigkeiten *pl*; **2.** kandieren; **~ floss** Zuckerwatte *f*; **~ store** Süßwarengeschäft *n*
**cane** BOT Rohr *n*; (Rohr)Stock *m*
**ca·nine** Hunde...
**canned** Dosen..., Büchsen...; ***~ fruit*** Obstkonserven *pl*
**can·ne·ry** Konservenfabrik *f*
**can·ni·bal** Kannibale *m*
**can·non** MIL Kanone *f*
**can·ny** schlau
**ca·noe 1.** Kanu *n*, Paddelboot *n*; **2.** Kanu fahren, paddeln
**can·on** Kanon *m*; Regel *f*
**can o·pen·er** Dosen-, Büchsenöffner *m*
**can·o·py** Baldachin *m*
**cant** Jargon *m*; Phrase(n *pl*) *f*
**can·tan·ker·ous** F zänkisch, mürrisch
**can·teen** *esp Br* Kantine *f*; MIL Feldflasche *f*; Besteck(kasten *m*) *n*
**can·ter 1.** Kanter *m*; **2.** kantern
**can·vas** Segeltuch *n*; Zelt-, Packleinwand *f*; Segel *pl*; PAINT Leinwand *f*; Gemälde *n*
**can·vass 1.** POL Wahlfeldzug *m*; ECON Werbefeldzug *m*; **2.** *v/t* eingehend untersuchen *or* erörtern *or* prüfen; POL werben um (*Stimmen*); *v/i* POL e-n Wahlfeldzug veranstalten
**can·yon** GEOGR Cañon *m*, Schlucht *f*
**cap 1.** Kappe *f*; Mütze *f*; Haube *f*; Zündkapsel *f*; **2.** (mit e-r Kappe *etc*) bedecken; *fig* krönen; übertreffen
**ca·pa·bil·i·ty** Fähigkeit *f*
**cap·a·ble** fähig (***of*** zu)
**ca·pac·i·ty** (Raum)Inhalt *m*; Fassungsvermögen *n*; Kapazität *f*; Aufnahmefähigkeit *f*; (TECH Leistungs)Fähigkeit *f* (***for*** *ger* zu *inf*); ***in my ~ as*** in meiner Eigenschaft als
**cape**[1] GEOGR Kap *n*, Vorgebirge *n*
**cape**[2] Cape *n*, Umhang *m*
**ca·per 1.** Kapriole *f*, Luftsprung *m*; ***cut ~s*** → **2.** Freuden- *or* Luftsprünge machen
**ca·pil·la·ry** ANAT Haar-, Kapillargefäß *n*
**cap·i·tal 1.** ECON Kapital *n*; Hauptstadt *f*; Großbuchstabe *m*; **2.** Kapital...; Tod(es)...; Haupt...; großartig, prima; **~ crime** JUR Kapitalverbrechen *n*
**cap·i·tal·ism** ECON Kapitalismus *m*
**cap·i·tal·ist** ECON Kapitalist *m*
**cap·i·tal·ize** großschreiben; ECON kapitalisieren
**cap·i·tal| let·ter** Großbuchstabe *m*; **~ pun·ish·ment** JUR Todesstrafe *f*
**ca·pit·u·late** kapitulieren (***to*** vor *dat*)
**ca·pri·cious** launisch
**Cap·ri·corn** ASTR Steinbock *m*; ***he*** (***she***) ***is*** (***a***) ~ er (sie) ist (ein) Steinbock
**cap·size** MAR *v/i* kentern; *v/t* zum Kentern bringen
**cap·sule** Kapsel *f*
**cap·tain** (An)Führer *m*; MAR, ECON Kapitän *m*; AVIAT Flugkapitän *m*; MIL

C

Hauptmann *m*; SPORT (Mannschafts-) Kapitän *m*, Spielführer *m*

**cap·tion** Überschrift *f*, Titel *m*; Bildunterschrift *f*; *film*: Untertitel *m*

**cap·ti·vate** *fig* gefangen nehmen, fesseln; **cap·tive 1.** gefangen; gefesselt; ***hold ~*** gefangen halten; **2.** Gefangene *m*, *f*; **cap·tiv·i·ty** Gefangenschaft *f*

**cap·ture 1.** Eroberung *f*; Gefangennahme *f*; **2.** fangen, gefangen nehmen; erobern; erbeuten; MAR kapern

**car** Auto *n*, Wagen *m*; (Eisenbahn-, Straßenbahn)Wagen *m*; Gondel *f* (*of a balloon etc*); Kabine *f*; ***by ~*** mit dem Auto, im Auto

**car·a·mel** Karamell *m*; Karamelle *f*

**car·a·van** Karawane *f*; *Br* Wohnwagen *m*; **~ site** Campingplatz *m* für Wohnwagen

**car·a·way** BOT Kümmel *m*

**car·bine** MIL Karabiner *m*

**car·bo·hy·drate** CHEM Kohle(n)hydrat *n*

**car bomb** Autobombe *f*

**car·bon** CHEM Kohlenstoff *m*; → ***carbon copy, carbon paper***

**car·bon cop·y** Durchschlag *m*

**car·bon pa·per** Kohlepapier *n*

**car·bu·ret·(t)or** MOT Vergaser *m*

**car·case** *Br*, **car·cass** Kadaver *m*, Aas *n*; GASTR Rumpf *m*

**car·cin·o·genic** MED karzinogen, Krebs erregend

**car·ci·no·ma** MED Krebsgeschwulst *f*

**card** Karte *f*; ***play ~s*** Karten spielen; ***have a ~ up one's sleeve*** *fig* (noch) e-n Trumpf in der Hand haben

**card·board** Pappe *f*; **~ box** Pappschachtel *f*, Pappkarton *m*

**car·di·ac** MED Herz...; **~ pace·mak·er** MED Herzschrittmacher *m*

**car·di·gan** Strickjacke *f*

**car·di·nal 1.** Grund..., Haupt..., Kardinal...; scharlachrot; **2.** REL Kardinal *m*

**car·di·nal num·ber** MATH Kardinalzahl *f*, Grundzahl *f*

**card in·dex** Kartei *f*

**card phone** Kartentelefon *n*

**card·sharp·er** Falschspieler *m*

**car dump** Autofriedhof *m*

**care 1.** Sorge *f*; Sorgfalt *f*; Vorsicht *f*; Obhut *f*, Pflege *f*; ***needing ~*** MED pflegebedürftig; ***medical ~*** ärztliche Behandlung; ***take ~ of*** aufpassen auf (*acc*); versorgen; ***with ~!*** Vorsicht!; **2.** Lust haben (***to*** *inf* zu *inf*); **~ *about*** sich kümmern um; **~ *for*** sorgen für, sich kümmern um; sich etwas machen aus; ***I don't ~!*** F meinetwegen!; ***I couldn't ~ less*** F es ist mir völlig egal

**ca·reer 1.** Karriere *f*, Laufbahn *f*; **2.** Berufs...; Karriere...; **3.** rasen

**ca·reers| ad·vice** Berufsberatung *f*; **~ ad·vi·sor** Berufsberater *m*; **~ guid·ance** Berufsberatung *f*; **~ of·fice** Berufsberatungsstelle *f*; **~ of·fi·cer** Berufsberater *m*

**care·free** sorgenfrei, sorglos

**care·ful** vorsichtig; sorgsam bedacht (***of*** auf *acc*); sorgfältig; ***be ~!*** pass auf!

**care·less** nachlässig, unachtsam; leichtsinnig, unvorsichtig; sorglos

**care·less·ness** Nachlässigkeit *f*, Unachtsamkeit *f*; Leichtsinn *m*; Sorglosigkeit *f*

**ca·ress 1.** Liebkosung *f*; Zärtlichkeit *f*; **2.** liebkosen, streicheln

**care·tak·er** Hausmeister *m*; (Haus- *etc*)Verwalter *m*

**care·worn** abgehärmt, verhärmt

**car fer·ry** Autofähre *f*

**car·go** Ladung *f*

**car hire** *Br* Autovermietung *f*

**car·i·ca·ture 1.** Karikatur *f*, Zerrbild *n*; **2.** karikieren

**car·i·ca·tur·ist** Karikaturist *m*

**car·ies**, *a.* ***dental ~*** MED Karies *f*

**car me·chan·ic** Automechaniker *m*

**car·mine** Karmin(rot) *n*

**car·na·tion** BOT Nelke *f*

**car·nap·per** F Autoentführer *m*

**car·ni·val** Karneval *m*

**car·niv·o·rous** ZO Fleisch fressend

**car·ol** Weihnachtslied *n*

**carp**[1] ZO Karpfen *m*

**carp**[2] nörgeln

**car park** *esp Br* Parkplatz *m*; Parkhaus *n*

**car·pen·ter** Zimmermann *m*

**car·pet 1.** Teppich *m*; ***fitted ~*** Teppichboden *m*; ***sweep s.th. under the ~*** *fig* et. unter den Teppich kehren; **2.** mit Teppich(boden) auslegen

**car phone** Autotelefon *n*

**car pool** Fahrgemeinschaft *f*

**car pool(·ing) ser·vice** Mitfahrzentrale *f*

**car·port** MOT überdachter Abstellplatz

**car rent·al** Autovermietung *f*
**car re·pair shop** Autoreparaturwerkstatt *f*
**car·riage** Beförderung *f*, Transport *m*; Transportkosten *pl*; Kutsche *f*; *Br* RAIL (Personen)Wagen *m*; (Körper)Haltung *f*
**car·riage·way** Fahrbahn *f*
**car·ri·er** Spediteur *m*; Gepäckträger *m* (*on a bicycle*); MIL Flugzeugträger *m*
**car·ri·er bag** *Br* Trag(e)tasche *f*, -tüte *f*
**car·ri·on 1.** Aas *n*; **2.** Aas...
**car·rot** BOT Karotte *f*, Mohrrübe *f*
**car·ry** *v/t* bringen, führen, tragen (*a. v/i*), fahren, befördern; (bei sich) haben *or* tragen; *Ansicht* durchsetzen; *Gewinn, Preis* davontragen; *Ernte, Zinsen* tragen; (weiter)führen, *Mauer* ziehen; *Antrag* durchbringen; ***be carried*** PARL *etc* angenommen werden; ***~ the day*** den Sieg davontragen; ***~ s.th. too far*** et. übertreiben, et. zu weit treiben; ***get carried away*** *fig* die Kontrolle über sich verlieren; sich hinreißen lassen; ***~ forward, ~ over*** ECON übertragen; ***~ on*** fortsetzen, weiterführen; ECON betreiben; ***~ out, ~ through*** aus-, durchführen
**car·ry·cot** *Br* (Baby)Trag(e)tasche *f*
**cart 1.** Karren *m*; Wagen *m*; Einkaufswagen *m*; ***put the ~ before the horse*** *fig* das Pferd beim Schwanz aufzäumen; **2.** karren
**car·ti·lage** ANAT Knorpel *m*
**cart·load** Wagenladung *f*
**car·ton** Karton *m*; ***a ~ of cigarettes*** e-e Stange Zigaretten
**car·toon** Cartoon *m, n*; Karikatur *f*; Zeichentrickfilm *m*
**car·toon·ist** Karikaturist *m*
**car·tridge** Patrone *f* (*a.* MIL); (Film-)Patrone *f*, (Film)Kassette *f*; Tonabnehmer *m*
**cart·wheel:** ***turn ~s*** Rad schlagen
**carve** GASTR vorschneiden, zerlegen; TECH schnitzen; meißeln
**carv·er** (Holz)Schnitzer *m*; Bildhauer *m*; GASTR Tranchierer *m*; Tranchiermesser *n*; **carv·ing** Schnitzerei *f*
**car wash** Autowäsche *f*; (Auto)Waschanlage *f*, Waschstraße *f*
**cas·cade** Wasserfall *m*
**case[1] 1.** Behälter *m*; Kiste *f*, Kasten *m*; Etui *n*; Gehäuse *n*; Schachtel *f*; (*Glas-*)Schrank *m*; (*Kissen*)Bezug *m*; TECH Verkleidung *f*; **2.** in ein Gehäuse *or* Etui stecken; TECH verkleiden
**case[2]** Fall *m* (*a.* JUR), LING *a.* Kasus *m*; MED (Krankheits)Fall *m*, Patient(in); Sache *f*, Angelegenheit *f*
**case·ment** Fensterflügel *m*; → **~ window** Flügelfenster *n*
**cash 1.** Bargeld *n*; Barzahlung *f*; ***~ down*** gegen bar; ***~ on delivery*** Lieferung *f* gegen bar; (per) Nachnahme *f*; **2.** einlösen
**cash·book** ECON Kassenbuch *n*
**cash desk** Kasse *f*
**cash dis·pens·er** *esp Br* Geld-, Bankautomat *m*
**cash·ier** Kassierer(in)
**cash·less** bargeldlos
**cash ma·chine** Geld-, Bankautomat *m*
**cash·mere** Kaschmir *m*
**cash·point** *Br* → ***cash machine***
**cash reg·is·ter** Registrierkasse *f*
**cas·ing** (Schutz)Hülle *f*; Verschalung *f*, Verkleidung *f*, Gehäuse *n*
**cask** Fass *n*
**cas·ket** Kästchen *n*; Sarg *m*
**cas·sette** (*Film-, Band-, Musik*)Kassette *f*; **~ deck** Kassettendeck *n*; **~ player** Kassettenrekorder *m*; **~ ra·di·o** Radiorekorder *m*; **~ re·cord·er** Kassettenrekorder *m*
**cas·sock** REL Soutane *f*
**cast 1.** Wurf *m*; TECH Guss(form *f*) *m*; Abguss *m*, Abdruck *m*; Schattierung *f*, Anflug *m*; Form *f*, Art *f*; Auswerfen *n* (*of a fishing line etc*); THEA Besetzung *f*; **2.** (ab-, aus-, hin-, um-, weg)werfen; ZO abwerfen (*skin*); verlieren (*teeth*); verwerfen; gestalten; TECH gießen; *a.* ***~ up*** ausrechnen, zusammenzählen; THEA *Stück* besetzen; *Rollen* verteilen (***to*** an *acc*); ***~ lots*** losen (***for*** um); ***~ away*** wegwerfen; ***be ~ down*** niedergeschlagen sein; ***~ off*** *Kleidung* ausrangieren; MAR losmachen; *Freund etc* fallen lassen; *knitting*: abketten; *v/i*: ***~ about for, ~ around for*** suchen (nach), *fig a.* sich umsehen nach
**cas·ta·net** Kastagnette *f*
**cast·a·way** Schiffbrüchige *m, f*
**caste** Kaste *f* (*a. fig*)
**cast·er** Laufrolle *f*; *Br* (*Salz-, Zucker-etc*)Streuer *m*
**cast i·ron** Gusseisen *n*
**cast-i·ron** gusseisern

C

**cas·tle** Burg *f*, Schloss *n*; *chess*: Turm *m*
**cast·or** → ***caster***
**cast·or oil** PHARM Rizinusöl *n*
**cas·trate** kastrieren
**cas·u·al** zufällig; gelegentlich; flüchtig; lässig
**cas·u·al·ty** Unfall *m*; Verunglückte *m, f*, Opfer *n*; MIL Verwundete *m*; Gefallene *m*; ***casualties*** Opfer *pl*, MIL *mst* Verluste *pl*; **~ (de·part·ment)** MED Notaufnahme *f*; **~ ward** MED Unfallstation *f*
**cas·u·al wear** Freizeitkleidung *f*
**cat** ZO Katze *f*
**cat·a·log,** *esp Br* **cat·a·logue 1.** Katalog *m*; Verzeichnis *n*, Liste *f*; **2.** katalogisieren
**cat·a·lyt·ic con·vert·er** MOT Katalysator *m*
**cat·a·pult** *Br* Schleuder *f*; Katapult *n, m*
**cat·a·ract** Wasserfall *m*; Stromschnelle *f*; MED grauer Star
**ca·tarrh** MED Katarr(h) *m*
**ca·tas·tro·phe** Katastrophe *f*
**catch 1.** Fangen *n*; Fang *m*, Beute *f*; Halt *m*, Griff *m*; TECH Haken *m* (*a. fig*); (Tür)Klinke *f*; Verschluss *m*; **2.** *v/t* (auf-, ein)fangen; packen, fassen, ergreifen; überraschen, ertappen; *Blick etc* auffangen; F *Zug etc* (noch) kriegen, erwischen; *et.* erfassen, verstehen; *Atmosphäre etc* einfangen; sich *e-e Krankheit* holen; **~ (*a*) *cold*** sich erkälten; **~ *the eye*** ins Auge fallen; **~ *s.o.'s eye*** j-s Aufmerksamkeit auf sich lenken; **~ *s.o. up*** j-n einholen; ***be caught up in*** verwickelt sein in (*acc*); *v/i* sich verfangen, hängen bleiben; fassen, greifen; TECH ineinander greifen; klemmen; einschnappen; **~ *up with*** einholen
**catch·er** Fänger *m*
**catch·ing** packend; MED ansteckend (*a. fig*)
**catch·word** Schlagwort *n*; Stichwort *n*
**catch·y** MUS eingängig
**cat·e·chis·m** REL Katechismus *m*
**cat·e·go·ry** Kategorie *f*
**ca·ter: ~ *for*** Speisen und Getränke liefern für; *fig* sorgen für
**cat·er·pil·lar** ZO Raupe *f*
**Cat·er·pil·lar**® MOT Raupenfahrzeug *n*; **~ trac·tor**® MOT Raupenschlepper *m*
**cat·gut** MUS Darmsaite *f*
**ca·the·dral** Dom *m*, Kathedrale *f*
**Cath·o·lic** REL **1.** katholisch; **2.** Katholik(in)
**cat·kin** BOT Kätzchen *n*
**cat·tle** Vieh *n*; **~ breed·er** Viehzüchter *m*; **~ breed·ing** Viehzucht *f*; **~ deal·er** Viehhändler *m*; **~ mar·ket** Viehmarkt *m*
**ca(u)l·dron** großer Kessel
**cau·li·flow·er** BOT Blumenkohl *m*
**cause 1.** Ursache *f*; Grund *m*; Sache *f*; **2.** verursachen; veranlassen
**cause·less** grundlos
**cau·tion 1.** Vorsicht *f*; Warnung *f*; Verwarnung *f*; **2.** warnen; verwarnen; JUR belehren
**cau·tious** behutsam, vorsichtig
**cav·al·ry** HIST MIL Kavallerie *f*
**cave 1.** Höhle *f*; **2.** *v/i*: **~ *in*** einstürzen
**cav·ern** (große) Höhle
**cav·i·ty** Höhle *f*; MED Loch *n*
**caw** ZO **1.** krächzen; **2.** Krächzen *n*
**CD** ABBR *of* ***compact disk*** CD(-Platte) *f*
**CD play·er** CD-Spieler *m*
**CD-ROM** ABBR *of* ***compact disk read-only memory*** CD-ROM
**CD vid·e·o** CD-Video *n*
**cease** aufhören; beenden
**cease·fire** MIL Feuereinstellung *f*; Waffenruhe *f*
**cease·less** unaufhörlich
**cei·ling** (Zimmer)Decke *f*; ECON Höchstgrenze *f*, oberste Preisgrenze
**cel·e·brate** feiern; **cel·e·brat·ed** gefeiert, berühmt (***for*** für, wegen)
**cel·e·bra·tion** Feier *f*
**ce·leb·ri·ty** Berühmtheit *f*
**cel·e·ry** BOT Sellerie *m, f*
**ce·les·ti·al** himmlisch
**cel·i·ba·cy** Ehelosigkeit *f*
**cell** BIOL Zelle *f*, ELECTR *a.* Element *n*
**cel·lar** Keller *m*
**cel·list** MUS Cellist(in)
**cel·lo** MUS (Violon)Cello *n*
**cel·lo·phane**® Cellophan® *n*
**cel·lu·lar** BIOL Zell(en)...
**cel·lu·lar phone** Funktelefon *n*
**Cel·tic** keltisch
**ce·ment 1.** Zement *m*; Kitt *m*; **2.** zementieren; (ver)kitten
**cem·e·tery** Friedhof *m*
**cen·sor 1.** Zensor *m*; **2.** zensieren
**cen·sor·ship** Zensur *f*
**cen·sure 1.** Tadel *m*, Verweis *m*; **2.** tadeln

**cen·sus** Volkszählung *f*
**cent** Hundert *n*; Cent *m* (*1/100 Dollar*); ***per ~*** Prozent *n*
**cen·te·na·ry** Hundertjahrfeier *f*, hundertjähriges Jubiläum
**cen·ten·ni·al** **1.** hundertjährig; **2.** → ***centenary***
**cen·ter** **1.** Zentrum *n*, Mittelpunkt *m*; *soccer*: Flanke *f*; **2.** (sich) konzentrieren; zentrieren; **~ back** *soccer*: Vorstopper *m*; **~ for·ward** SPORT Mittelstürmer(in); **~ of grav·i·ty** PHYS Schwerpunkt *m*
**cen·ti·grade:** ***10 degrees ~*** 10 Grad Celsius
**cen·ti·me·ter,** *Br* **cen·ti·me·tre** Zentimeter *m*, *n*
**cen·ti·pede** ZO Tausendfüß(l)er *m*
**cen·tral** zentral; Haupt..., Zentral...; Mittel...; **~ heat·ing** Zentralheizung *f*
**cen·tral·ize** zentralisieren
**cen·tral| lock·ing** MOT Zentralverriegelung *f*; **~ res·er·va·tion** *Br* MOT Mittelstreifen *m*
**cen·tre** *Br* → ***center***
**cen·tu·ry** Jahrhundert *n*
**ce·ram·ics** Keramik *f*, keramische Erzeugnisse *pl*
**ce·re·al** **1.** Getreide...; **2.** BOT Getreide *n*; Getreidepflanze *f*; GASTR Getreideflocken *pl*, Frühstückskost *f*
**cer·e·bral** ANAT Gehirn...
**cer·e·mo·ni·al** **1.** zeremoniell; **2.** Zeremoniell *n*
**cer·e·mo·ni·ous** zeremoniell; förmlich
**cer·e·mo·ny** Zeremonie *f*; Feier *f*, Feierlichkeit *f*; Förmlichkeit(en *pl*) *f*
**cer·tain** sicher, gewiss; zuverlässig; bestimmt; gewisse(r, -s); **cer·tain·ly** sicher, gewiss; *int* sicherlich, bestimmt, natürlich; **cer·tain·ty** Sicherheit *f*, Bestimmtheit *f*, Gewissheit *f*
**cer·tif·i·cate** Zeugnis *n*; Bescheinigung *f*; ***~ of (good) conduct*** Führungszeugnis *n*; ***General Certificate of Education advanced level (A level)*** *Br* PED *appr* Abitur(zeugnis) *n*; ***General Certificate of Education ordinary level (O level)*** *Br* PED *appr* mittlere Reife; ***medical ~*** ärztliches Attest
**cer·ti·fy** *et.* bescheinigen; beglaubigen
**cer·ti·tude** Sicherheit *f*, Bestimmtheit *f*, Gewissheit *f*
**CET** ABBR *of* ***Central European Time*** MEZ, mitteleuropäische Zeit
**cf** (*Latin* ***confer***) ABBR *of* ***compare*** vgl., vergleiche
**CFC** ABBR *of* ***chlorofluorocarbon*** FCKW, Fluorchlorkohlenwasserstoff *m*
**chafe** *v/t* warm reiben; aufreiben, wund reiben; *v/i* (sich durch)reiben, scheuern
**chaff** AGR Spreu *f*; Häcksel *n*
**chaf·finch** ZO Buchfink *m*
**chag·rin** **1.** Ärger *m*; **2.** ärgern
**chain** **1.** Kette *f*; *fig* Fessel *f*; **2.** (an)ketten; fesseln
**chain re·ac·tion** Kettenreaktion *f*
**chain-smoke** F Kette rauchen
**chain-smok·er** Kettenraucher(in)
**chain-smok·ing** Kettenrauchen *n*
**chain store** Kettenladen *m*
**chair** Stuhl *m*; UNIV Lehrstuhl *m*; ECON *etc* Vorsitz *m*; ***be in the ~*** den Vorsitz führen; **~ lift** Sessellift *m*
**chair·man** Vorsitzende *m*, Präsident *m*; Diskussionsleiter *m*; ECON *Br* Generaldirektor *m*
**chair·man·ship** Vorsitz *m*
**chair·wom·an** Vorsitzende *f*, Präsidentin *f*; Diskussionsleiterin *f*
**chal·ice** REL Kelch *m*
**chalk** **1.** Kreide *f*; **2.** mit Kreide schreiben *or* zeichnen
**chal·lenge** **1.** Herausforderung *f*; **2.** herausfordern
**chal·len·ger** Herausforderer *m*
**cham·ber** TECH, PARL *etc* Kammer *f*
**cham·ber·maid** Zimmermädchen *n*
**cham·ber of com·merce** ECON Handelskammer *f*
**cham·ois** ZO Gämse *f*
**cham·ois (leath·er)** Fensterleder *n*
**champ** F SPORT → ***champion***
**cham·pagne** Champagner *m*
**cham·pi·on** **1.** Verfechter(in), Fürsprecher(in); SPORT Meister(in); **2.** verfechten, eintreten für; **cham·pi·on·ship** SPORT Meisterschaft *f*
**chance** **1.** Zufall *m*; Chance *f*, (günstige) Gelegenheit; Aussicht *f* (***of*** auf *acc*); Möglichkeit *f*; Risiko *n*; ***by ~*** zufällig; ***take a ~*** es darauf ankommen lassen; ***take no ~s*** nichts riskieren (wollen); **2.** zufällig; **3.** F riskieren
**chan·cel·lor** Kanzler *m*
**chan·de·lier** Kronleuchter *m*
**change** **1.** Veränderung *f*, Wechsel *m*;

C

Abwechslung *f*; Wechselgeld *n*; Kleingeld *n*; ***for a ~*** zur Abwechslung; ***~ for the better*** (***worse***) Bess(e)rung *f* (Verschlechterung *f*); **2.** *v/t* (ver)ändern, umändern; (aus)wechseln; (aus-, ver-) tauschen (***for*** gegen); umbuchen; MOT, TECH schalten; ***~ over*** umschalten; umstellen; ***~ trains*** umsteigen; *v/i* sich (ver)ändern, wechseln; sich umziehen
**change·a·ble** veränderlich
**change ma·chine** Münzwechsler *m*
**change·o·ver** Umstellung *f* (***to*** auf *acc*)
**chang·ing room** *esp* SPORT Umkleidekabine *f*, Umkleideraum *m*
**chan·nel 1.** Kanal *m* (*a. fig*); (*Fernseh- etc*)Kanal *m*, (*Fernseh- etc*)Programm *n*; *fig* Weg *m*; **2.** *fig* lenken
**Chan·nel Tun·nel** Kanaltunnel *m*, Eurotunnel *m*
**chant 1.** (Kirchen)Gesang *m*; Singsang *m*; **2.** in Sprechchören rufen
**cha·os** Chaos *n*
**chap**[1] **1.** Riss *m*; **2.** rissig machen *or* werden; aufspringen
**chap**[2] *Br* F Bursche *m*, Kerl *m*
**chap·el** ARCH Kapelle *f*; REL Gottesdienst *m*
**chap·lain** REL Kaplan *m*
**chap·ter** Kapitel *n*
**char** verkohlen
**char·ac·ter** Charakter *m*; Ruf *m*, Leumund *m*; Schriftzeichen *n*, Buchstabe *m*; *novel etc*: Figur *f*, Gestalt *f*; THEA Rolle *f*; **char·ac·ter·is·tic 1.** charakteristisch (***of*** für); **2.** Kennzeichen *n*; **char·ac·ter·ize** charakterisieren
**char·coal** Holzkohle *f*
**charge 1.** *v/t* ELECTR (auf)laden; *Gewehr etc* laden; *j-n* beauftragen (***with*** mit); *j-n* beschuldigen *or* anklagen (***with*** *e-r Sache*) (*a.* JUR); ECON berechnen, verlangen, fordern (***for*** für); MIL angreifen; stürmen; ***~ s.o. with s.th.*** ECON j-m et. in Rechnung stellen; *v/i*: ***~ at s.o.*** auf j-n losgehen; **2.** Ladung *f* (*a.* ELECTR *etc*); (Spreng)Ladung *f*; Beschuldigung *f*, *a.* JUR Anklage(punkt *m*) *f*; ECON Preis *m*; Forderung *f*; Gebühr *f*; *a. pl* Unkosten *pl*, Spesen *pl*; Verantwortung *f*; Schützling *m*, Mündel *n*, *m*; ***free of ~*** kostenlos; ***be in ~ of*** verantwortlich sein für; ***take ~ of*** die Leitung *etc* übernehmen, die Sache in die Hand nehmen

**char·i·ot** HIST Streit-, Triumphwagen *m*
**cha·ris·ma** Charisma *n*, Ausstrahlung *f*, Ausstrahlungskraft *f*
**char·i·ta·ble** wohltätig
**char·i·ty** Nächstenliebe *f*; Wohltätigkeit *f*; Güte *f*, Nachsicht *f*; milde Gabe
**char·la·tan** Scharlatan *m*; Quacksalber *m*, Kurpfuscher *m*
**charm 1.** Zauber *m*; Charme *m*, Reiz *m*; Talisman *m*, Amulett *n*; **2.** bezaubern, entzücken
**charm·ing** charmant, bezaubernd
**chart** (*See-*, *Himmels-*, *Wetter*)Karte *f*; Diagramm *n*, Schaubild *n*; *pl* MUS Charts *pl*, Hitliste(n *pl*) *f*
**char·ter 1.** Urkunde *f*; Charta *f*; Chartern *n*; **2.** chartern, mieten
**char·ter flight** Charterflug *m*
**char·wom·an** Putzfrau *f*, Raumpflegerin *f*
**chase 1.** Jagd *f*; Verfolgung *f*; **2.** *v/t* jagen, hetzen; Jagd machen auf (*acc*); TECH ziselieren; *v/i* rasen, rennen
**chasm** Kluft *f*, Abgrund *m*
**chaste** keusch; schlicht
**chas·tise** züchtigen
**chas·ti·ty** Keuschheit *f*
**chat 1.** Geplauder *n*, Schwätzchen *n*, Plauderei *f*; **2.** plaudern
**chat show** *Br* TV Talkshow *f*
**chat show host** *Br* TV Talkmaster *m*
**chat·ter 1.** plappern; schnattern; klappern; **2.** Geplapper *n*; Klappern *n*
**chat·ter·box** F Plappermaul *n*
**chat·ty** gesprächig
**chauf·feur** Chauffeur *m*
**chau·vi** F Chauvi *m*
**chau·vin·ist** Chauvinist *m*; F ***male ~ pig*** Chauvi *m*; *contp* Chauvischwein *n*
**cheap** billig; *fig* schäbig, gemein
**cheap·en** (sich) verbilligen; *fig* herabsetzen
**cheat 1.** Betrug *m*, Schwindel *m*; Betrüger(in); **2.** betrügen; F schummeln
**check 1.** Schach(stellung *f*) *n*; Hemmnis *n*, Hindernis *n* (***on*** für); Einhalt *m*; Kontrolle *f* (***on*** *gen*); Kontrollabschnitt *m*, -schein *m*; Gepäckschein *m*; Garderobenmarke *f*; ECON Scheck *m* (***for*** über); Häkchen *n* (*on a list etc*); ECON Kassenzettel *m*, Rechnung *f*; karierter Stoff; **2.** *v/i* (plötzlich) innehalten; ***~ in*** sich (*in e-m Hotel*) anmelden; einstempeln; AVIAT einchecken; ***~ out***

(*aus e-m Hotel*) abreisen; ausstempeln; ~ **up** (**on**) F (*e-e Sache*) nachprüfen, (*e-e Sache, j-n*) überprüfen; *v/t* hemmen, hindern, aufhalten; zurückhalten; checken, kontrollieren, überprüfen; *auf e-r Liste* abhaken; *Mantel etc* in der Garderobe abgeben; *Gepäck* aufgeben
**check card** ECON Scheckkarte *f*
**checked** kariert
**check·ers** Damespiel *n*
**check-in** Anmeldung *f*; Einstempeln *n*; AVIAT Einchecken *n*
**check-in| coun·ter,** ~ **desk** AVIAT Abfertigungsschalter *m*
**check·ing ac·count** ECON Girokonto *n*
**check·list** Check-, Kontrollliste *f*
**check·mate 1.** (Schach)Matt *n*; **2.** (schach)matt setzen
**check-out** Abreise *f*; Ausstempeln *n*
**check-out coun·ter** Kasse *f*
**check·point** Kontrollpunkt *m*
**check·room** Garderobe *f*; Gepäckaufbewahrung *f*
**check·up** Überprüfung *f*; MED Check-up *m*, Vorsorgeuntersuchung *f*
**cheek** ANAT Backe *f*, Wange *f*; *Br* Unverschämtheit *f*; **cheek·y** *Br* frech
**cheer 1.** Stimmung *f*, Fröhlichkeit *f*; Hoch *n*, Hochruf *m*, Beifall *m*, Beifallsruf *m*; *pl* SPORT Anfeuerungsrufe *pl*; ***three*** ~***s!*** dreimal hoch!; ~***s!*** prost!; **2.** *v/t* mit Beifall begrüßen; *a.* ~ ***on*** anspornen; *a.* ~ ***up*** aufheitern; *v/i* hoch rufen, jubeln; *a.* ~ ***up*** Mut fassen; ~ ***up!*** Kopf hoch!; **cheer·ful** vergnügt
**cheer·i·o** *int Br* F tschüs(s)!
**cheer·lead·er** SPORT Einpeitscher *m*, Cheerleader *m*
**cheer·less** freudlos; unfreundlich
**cheer·y** vergnügt
**cheese** Käse *m*
**chee·tah** ZO Gepard *m*
**chef** Küchenchef *m*; Koch *m*
**chem·i·cal 1.** chemisch; **2.** Chemikalie *f*
**chem·ist** Chemiker(in); Apotheker(in); Drogist(in)
**chem·is·try** Chemie *f*
**chem·ist's shop** Apotheke *f*; Drogerie *f*
**chem·o·ther·a·py** MED Chemotherapie *f*
**cheque** *Br* ECON Scheck *m*; ***crossed*** ~ Verrechnungsscheck *m*; ~ **ac·count** *Br* Girokonto *n*; ~ **card** *Br* Scheckkarte *f*
**cher·ry** BOT Kirsche *f*
**chess** Schach(spiel) *n*; ***a game of*** ~ e-e Partie Schach
**chess·board** Schachbrett *n*
**chess·man, chess·piece** Schachfigur *f*
**chest** Kiste *f*; Truhe *f*; ANAT Brust *f*, Brustkasten *m*; ***get s.th. off one's*** ~ F sich et. von der Seele reden
**chest·nut 1.** BOT Kastanie *f*; **2.** kastanienbraun
**chest of drawers** Kommode *f*
**chew** (zer)kauen
**chew·ing gum** Kaugummi *m*
**chic** schick, *Austrian* fesch
**chick** ZO Küken *n*, junger Vogel; F Biene *f*, Puppe *f* (*girl*)
**chick·en** ZO Huhn *n*; Küken *n*; GASTR (*Brat*)Hähnchen *n*, (*Brat*)Hühnchen *n*
**chick·en·heart·ed** furchtsam, feige
**chick·en pox** MED Windpocken *pl*
**chic·o·ry** BOT Chicorée *m, f*
**chief 1.** oberste(r, -s), Ober..., Haupt..., Chef...; wichtigste(r, -s); **2.** Chef *m*; Häuptling *m*
**chief·ly** hauptsächlich
**chil·blain** MED Frostbeule *f*
**child** Kind *n*; ***from a*** ~ von Kindheit an; ***with*** ~ schwanger; ~ **a·buse** JUR Kindesmisshandlung *f*; ~ **ben·e·fit** *Br* Kindergeld *n*
**child·birth** Geburt *f*, Niederkunft *f*
**child·hood** Kindheit *f*; ***from*** ~ von Kindheit an
**child·ish** kindlich; kindisch
**child·like** kindlich
**child·mind·er** Tagesmutter *f*
**chill 1.** kalt, frostig, kühl (*a. fig*); **2.** Frösteln *n*; Kälte *f*, Kühle *f* (*a. fig*); MED Erkältung *f*; **3.** abkühlen; *j-n* frösteln lassen; kühlen
**chill·y** kalt, frostig, kühl (*a. fig*)
**chime 1.** Glockenspiel *n*; Geläut *n*; **2.** läuten; schlagen (*clock*)
**chim·ney** Schornstein *m*
**chim·ney sweep** Schornsteinfeger *m*
**chimp** F, **chim·pan·zee** ZO Schimpanse *m*
**chin** ANAT Kinn *n*; ~ ***up!*** Kopf hoch!, halt die Ohren steif!
**chi·na** Porzellan *n*
**Chi·na** China *n*

C

**Chi·nese 1.** chinesisch; **2.** Chinese *m*, Chinesin *f*; LING Chinesisch *n*; ***the*** ~ die Chinesen *pl*
**chink** Ritz *m*, Spalt *m*
**chip 1.** Splitter *m*, Span *m*, Schnitzel *n*, *m*; dünne Scheibe; Spielmarke *f*; EDP Chip *m*; **2.** *v/t* schnitzeln; anschlagen, abschlagen; *v/i* abbröckeln
**chips** (Kartoffel)Chips *pl*; *Br* Pommes frites *pl*, F Fritten *pl*
**chi·rop·o·dist** Fußpfleger(in), Pediküre *f*
**chirp** ZO zirpen, zwitschern, piepsen
**chis·el 1.** Meißel *m*; **2.** meißeln
**chit-chat** Plauderei *f*
**chiv·al·rous** ritterlich
**chive(s)** BOT Schnittlauch *m*
**chlo·ri·nate** *Wasser etc* chloren
**chlo·rine** CHEM Chlor *n*
**chlo·ro·fluo·ro·car·bon** (ABBR ***CFC***) CHEM Fluorchlorkohlenwasserstoff *m* (ABBR ***FCKW***)
**chlor·o·form** MED **1.** Chloroform *n*; **2.** chloroformieren
**choc·o·late** Schokolade *f*; Praline *f*; *pl* Pralinen *pl*, Konfekt *n*
**choice 1.** Wahl *f*; Auswahl *f*; **2.** auserlesen, ausgesucht, vorzüglich
**choir** ARCH, MUS Chor *m*
**choke 1.** *v/t* (er)würgen, (*a. v/i*) ersticken; ~ ***back*** *Ärger etc* unterdrücken, *Tränen* zurückhalten; ~ ***down*** hinunterwürgen; *a.* ~ ***up*** verstopfen; **2.** MOT Choke *m*, Luftklappe *f*
**cho·les·te·rol** MED Cholesterin *n*
**choose** (aus)wählen, aussuchen
**choos·(e)y** *esp Br* wählerisch
**chop 1.** Hieb *m*, (Handkanten)Schlag *m*; GASTR Kotelett *n*; **2.** *v/t* (zer)hacken, hauen; ~ ***down*** fällen; *v/i* hacken
**chop·per** Hackmesser *n*, Hackbeil *n*; F Hubschrauber *m*
**chop·py** unruhig (*sea*)
**chop·stick** Essstäbchen *n*
**cho·ral** MUS Chor...
**cho·rale** MUS Choral *m*
**chord** MUS Saite *f*; Akkord *m*
**chore** schwierige *or* unangenehme Aufgabe; *pl* Hausarbeit *f*
**cho·rus** MUS Chor *m*; Kehrreim *m*, Refrain *m*; Tanzgruppe *f*
**Christ** REL Christus *m*
**chris·ten** REL taufen
**chris·ten·ing** REL **1.** Taufe *f*; **2.** Tauf...
**Chris·tian** REL **1.** christlich; **2.** Christ(in)
**Chris·ti·an·i·ty** REL Christentum *n*
**Chris·tian name** Vorname *m*
**Christ·mas** Weihnachten *n and pl*; ***at*** ~ zu Weihnachten; ~ **Day** erster Weihnachtsfeiertag; ~ **Eve** Heiliger Abend
**chrome** Chrom *n*
**chro·mi·um** CHEM Chrom *n*
**chron·ic** chronisch; ständig, (an)dauernd
**chron·i·cle** Chronik *f*
**chron·o·log·i·cal** chronologisch
**chro·nol·o·gy** Zeitrechnung *f*; Zeitfolge *f*
**chub·by** F rundlich, pumm(e)lig; pausbäckig
**chuck** F werfen, schmeißen; ~ ***out*** *j-n* rausschmeißen; *et.* wegschmeißen; ~ ***up*** *Job etc* hinschmeißen
**chuck·le 1.** ~ (***to o.s.***) (stillvergnügt) in sich hineinlachen; **2.** leises Lachen
**chum** F Kamerad *m*, Kumpel *m*
**chum·my** F dick befreundet
**chump** Holzklotz *m*; F Trottel *m*
**chunk** Klotz *m*, Klumpen *m*
**Chun·nel** F → ***Channel Tunnel***
**church 1.** Kirche *f*; **2.** Kirch..., Kirchen...
**church ser·vice** REL Gottesdienst *m*
**church·yard** Kirchhof *m*
**churl·ish** grob, flegelhaft
**churn 1.** Butterfass *n*; **2.** buttern; *Wellen* aufwühlen, peitschen
**chute** Stromschnelle *f*; Rutsche *f*, Rutschbahn *f*; F Fallschirm *m*
**ci·der** *a.* ***hard*** ~ Apfelwein *m*; (***sweet***) ~ Apfelmost *m*, Apfelsaft *m*
**ci·gar** Zigarre *f*
**cig·a·rette** Zigarette *f*
**cinch** F todsichere Sache
**cin·der** Schlacke *f*; *pl* Asche *f*
**Cin·de·rel·la** Aschenbrödel *n*, Aschenputtel *n*
**cin·der track** SPORT Aschenbahn *f*
**cin·e·cam·e·ra** (Schmal)Filmkamera *f*
**cin·e·film** Schmalfilm *m*
**cin·e·ma** *Br* Kino *n*; Film *m*
**cin·na·mon** Zimt *m*
**ci·pher** Geheimschrift *f*, Chiffre *f*; Null *f* (*a. fig*)
**cir·cle 1.** Kreis *m*; THEA Rang *m*; *fig* Kreislauf *m*; **2.** (um)kreisen
**cir·cuit** Kreislauf *m*; ELECTR Stromkreis

*m*; Rundreise *f*; SPORT Zirkus *m*; ***short ~*** ELECTR Kurzschluss *m*

**cir·cu·i·tous** gewunden; weitschweifig; ***~ route*** Umweg *m*

**cir·cu·lar 1.** kreisförmig; Kreis...; **2.** Rundschreiben *n*; Umlauf *m*; (Post-) Wurfsendung *f*

**cir·cu·late** *v/i* zirkulieren, im Umlauf sein; *v/t* in Umlauf setzen

**cir·cu·lat·ing li·bra·ry** Leihbücherei *f*

**cir·cu·la·tion** (*a.* Blut)Kreislauf *m*, Zirkulation *f*; ECON Umlauf *m*; *newspaper etc*: Auflage *f*

**cir·cum·fer·ence** (Kreis)Umfang *m*

**cir·cum·nav·i·gate** umschiffen, umsegeln

**cir·cum·scribe** MATH umschreiben; *fig* begrenzen

**cir·cum·spect** umsichtig, vorsichtig

**cir·cum·stance** Umstand *m*; *pl* (Sach-) Lage *f*, Umstände *pl*; Verhältnisse *pl*; ***in*** *or* ***under no ~s*** unter keinen Umständen, auf keinen Fall; ***in*** *or* ***under the ~s*** unter diesen Umständen

**cir·cum·stan·tial** ausführlich; umständlich; **~ ev·i·dence** JUR Indizien *pl*, Indizienbeweis *m*

**cir·cus** Zirkus *m*

**CIS** ABBR *of* ***Commonwealth of Independent States*** *die* GUS, *die* Gemeinschaft unabhängiger Staaten

**cis·tern** Wasserbehälter *m*; Spülkasten *m*

**ci·ta·tion** Zitat *n*; JUR Vorladung *f*

**cite** zitieren; JUR vorladen

**cit·i·zen** Bürger(in); Städter(in); Staatsangehörige *m, f*

**cit·i·zen·ship** Staatsangehörigkeit *f*

**cit·y 1.** (Groß)Stadt *f*; ***the City*** die (Londoner) City; **2.** städtisch, Stadt...; **~ cen·tre** *Br* Innenstadt *f*, City *f*; **~ coun·cil·(l)or** Stadtrat *m*, Stadträtin *f*; **~ hall** Rathaus *n*; Stadtverwaltung *f*; **~ slick·er** *often contp* Städter(in), Stadtmensch *m*; **~ va·grant** Stadtstreicher(in), Nichtsesshafte *m, f*

**civ·ic** städtisch, Stadt...

**civ·ics** PED Staatsbürgerkunde *f*

**civ·il** staatlich, Staats...; (staats)bürgerlich, Bürger...; zivil, Zivil...; JUR zivilrechtlich; höflich

**ci·vil·i·an** Zivilist *m*

**ci·vil·i·ty** Höflichkeit *f*

**civ·i·li·za·tion** Zivilisation *f*, Kultur *f*

**civ·i·lize** zivilisieren

**civ·il rights** (Staats)Bürgerrechte *pl*; **~ ac·tiv·ist** Bürgerrechtler(in); **~ move·ment** Bürgerrechtsbewegung *f*

**civ·il| ser·vant** Staatsbeamte *m*, -beamtin *f*; **~ ser·vice** Staatsdienst *m*; **~ war** Bürgerkrieg *m*

**clad** gekleidet

**claim 1.** Anspruch *m*; Anrecht *n* (***to*** auf *acc*); Forderung *f*; Behauptung *f*; Claim *m*; **2.** beanspruchen; fordern; behaupten

**clair·voy·ant 1.** hellseherisch; **2.** Hellseher(in)

**clam·ber** (mühsam) klettern

**clam·my** feuchtkalt, klamm

**clam·o(u)r 1.** Geschrei *n*, Lärm *m*; **2.** lautstark verlangen (***for*** nach)

**clamp** TECH Zwinge *f*

**clan** Clan *m*, Sippe *f*

**clan·des·tine** heimlich

**clang** klingen, klirren; erklingen lassen

**clank 1.** Gerassel *n*, Geklirr *n*; **2.** rasseln *or* klirren (mit)

**clap 1.** Klatschen *n*; Schlag *m*, Klaps *m*; **2.** schlagen *or* klatschen (mit)

**clar·et** roter Bordeaux(wein); Rotwein *m*

**clar·i·fy** *v/t* (auf)klären, klarstellen; *v/i* sich (auf)klären, klar werden

**clar·i·net** MUS Klarinette *f*

**clar·i·ty** Klarheit *f*

**clash 1.** Zusammenstoß *m*; Konflikt *m*; **2.** zusammenstoßen; *fig* nicht zusammenpassen *or* harmonieren

**clasp 1.** Haken *m*, Schnalle *f*; Schloss *n*, (Schnapp)Verschluss *m*; Umklammerung *f*; **2.** einhaken, zuhaken; ergreifen, umklammern

**clasp knife** Taschenmesser *n*

**class 1.** Klasse *f*; (Bevölkerungs-) Schicht *f*; (Schul)Klasse *f*; (Unterrichts)Stunde *f*; Kurs *m*; Jahrgang *m*; **2.** (in Klassen) einteilen, einordnen, einstufen

**clas·sic 1.** Klassiker *m*; **2.** klassisch

**clas·si·cal** klassisch

**clas·sic car** Klassiker *m*

**clas·si·fi·ca·tion** Klassifizierung *f*, Einteilung *f*

**clas·si·fied** klassifiziert; MIL, POL geheim; **~ ad** Kleinanzeige *f*

**clas·si·fy** klassifizieren, einstufen

**class·mate** Mitschüler(in)

C

**class·room** Klassenzimmer *n*
**clat·ter 1.** Geklapper *n*; **2.** klappern (mit)
**clause** JUR Klausel *f*, Bestimmung *f*; LING Satz(teil *n*) *m*
**claw 1.** ZO Klaue *f*, Kralle *f*; (*Krebs-*)Schere *f*; **2.** (zer)kratzen; umkrallen, packen
**clay** Ton *m*, Lehm *m*
**clean 1.** *adj* rein; sauber, glatt, eben; *sl* clean; **2.** *adv* völlig, ganz und gar; **3.** reinigen, säubern, putzen; **~ out** reinigen; **~ up** gründlich reinigen; aufräumen
**clean·er** Rein(e)machefrau *f*, (*Fenster- etc*)Putzer *m*; Reinigungsmittel *n*, Reiniger *m*; ***take to the ~s*** *et.* zur Reinigung bringen; F *j-n* ausnehmen
**clean·ing: *do the ~*** sauber machen, putzen; **~ la·dy, ~ wom·an** Putzfrau *f*
**clean·li·ness** Reinlichkeit *f*
**clean·ly 1.** *adv* sauber; **2.** *adj* reinlich
**cleanse** reinigen, säubern
**cleans·er** Putzmittel *n*, Reinigungsmittel *n*, Reiniger *m*
**clear 1.** klar; hell; rein; deutlich; frei (***of*** von); ECON Netto..., Rein...; **2.** *v/t* reinigen, säubern; *Wald* lichten, roden; wegräumen (*a.* **~ away**); *Tisch* abräumen; räumen, leeren; *Hindernis* nehmen; SPORT klären; ECON verzollen; JUR freisprechen; EDP löschen; *v/i* klar *or* hell werden; METEOR aufklaren; sich verziehen (*fog*); **~ out** aufräumen; ausräumen, entfernen; F abhauen; **~ up** aufräumen; *Verbrechen etc* aufklären; METEOR aufklaren
**clear·ance** Räumung *f*; TECH lichter Abstand; Freigabe *f*; **~ sale** ECON Räumungsverkauf *m*, Ausverkauf *m*
**clear·ing** Lichtung *f*
**cleave** spalten
**cleav·er** Hackmesser *n*
**clef** MUS Schlüssel *m*
**cleft** Spalt *m*, Spalte *f*
**clem·en·cy** Milde *f*, Nachsicht *f*
**clem·ent** mild (*a.* METEOR)
**clench** *Lippen etc* (fest) zusammenpressen; *Zähne* zusammenbeißen; *Faust* ballen
**cler·gy** REL Klerus *m*, *die* Geistlichen *pl*
**cler·gy·man** REL Geistliche *m*
**clerk** Verkäufer(in); (Büro- *etc*)Angestellte *m*, *f*, (Bank-, Post)Beamte *m*, (-)Beamtin *f*

**clev·er** klug, gescheit; geschickt
**click 1.** Klicken *n*; **2.** *v/i* klicken; zu-, einschnappen; *mit der Zunge* schnalzen; *v/t* klicken *or* einschnappen lassen; mit *der Zunge* schnalzen; **~ on** EDP anklicken
**cli·ent** JUR Klient(in), Mandant(in); Kunde *m*, Kundin *f*, Auftraggeber(in)
**cliff** Klippe *f*, Felsen *m*
**cli·mate** Klima *n*
**cli·max** Höhepunkt *m*; Orgasmus *m*
**climb** klettern; (er-, be)steigen; **~ (*up*) *a tree*** auf e-n Baum klettern
**climb·er** Kletterer *m*, Bergsteiger(in); BOT Kletterpflanze *f*
**clinch 1.** TECH sicher befestigen; (ver)nieten; *boxing*: umklammern (*v/i* clinchen); *fig* entscheiden; ***that ~ed it*** damit war die Sache entschieden; **2.** *boxing*: Clinch *m*
**cling (*to*)** festhalten (an *dat*), sich klammern (an *acc*); sich (an)schmiegen (an *acc*)
**cling·film**® *esp Br* Frischhaltefolie *f*
**clin·ic** Klinik *f*
**clin·i·cal** klinisch
**clink 1.** Klirren *n*, Klingen *n*; *sl* Knast *m*; **2.** klingen *or* klirren (lassen); klimpern mit
**clip**[1] **1.** ausschneiden; *Schafe etc* scheren; **2.** Schnitt *m*; Schur *f*; (*Film- etc* -) Ausschnitt *m*; (*Video*)Clip *m*
**clip**[2] **1.** (Heft-, Büro- *etc*)Klammer *f*; (*Ohr*)Klipp *m*; **2.** *a.* **~ on** anklammern
**clip·per: (*a pair of*) ~s** (e-e) (*Nagel- etc*)Schere *f*, Haarschneidemaschine *f*
**clip·pings** Abfälle *pl*, Schnitzel *pl*; (*Zeitungs- etc*)Ausschnitte *pl*
**clit·o·ris** ANAT Klitoris *f*
**cloak 1.** Umhang *m*; **2.** *fig* verhüllen
**cloak·room** *Br* Garderobe *f*; Toilette *f*
**clock 1.** (*Wand-*, *Stand-*, *Turm*)Uhr *f*; ***9 o'clock*** 9 Uhr; **2.** SPORT Zeit stoppen; **~ *in*, ~ *on*** einstempeln; **~ *out*, ~ *off*** ausstempeln; **~ ra·di·o** Radiowecker *m*
**clock·wise** im Uhrzeigersinn
**clock·work** Uhrwerk *n*; ***like ~*** wie am Schnürchen
**clod** (Erd)Klumpen *m*
**clog 1.** (Holz)Klotz *m*; Holzschuh *m*; **2.** *a.* **~ *up*** verstopfen
**clois·ter** ARCH Kreuzgang *m*; REL Kloster *n*
**close 1.** *adj* geschlossen; knapp (*result*

*etc*); genau, gründlich (*inspection etc*); eng (anliegend); stickig, schwül; eng (*friend*), nah (*relative*); ***keep a ~ watch on*** scharf im Auge behalten (*acc*); **2.** *adv* eng, nahe, dicht; ***~ by*** ganz in der Nähe, nahe *or* dicht bei; **3.** Ende *n*, (Ab)Schluss *m*; ***come*** *or* ***draw to a ~*** sich dem Ende nähern; Einfriedung *f*; **4.** *v/t* (ab-, ver-, zu)schließen, zumachen; ECON schließen; *Straße* (ab)sperren; *v/i* sich schließen; schließen, zumachen; enden, zu Ende gehen; ***~ down*** *Geschäft etc* schließen, *Betrieb* stilllegen; *radio*, TV das Programm beenden, Sendeschluss haben; ***~ in*** bedrohlich nahe kommen; hereinbrechen (*night*); ***~ up*** (ab-, ver-, zu)schließen; aufschließen, aufrücken

**closed** geschlossen, F *pred* zu

**clos·et** (Wand)Schrank *m*

**close-up** PHOT, *film*: Großaufnahme *f*

**clos·ing date** Einsendeschluss *m*

**clos·ing time** Laden-, Geschäftsschluss *m*; Polizeistunde *f* (*of a pub*)

**clot 1.** Klumpen *m*, Klümpchen *n*; ***~ of blood*** MED Blutgerinnsel *n*; **2.** gerinnen; Klumpen bilden

**cloth** Stoff *m*, Tuch *n*; Lappen *m*

**cloth·bound** in Leinen gebunden

**clothe** (an-, be)kleiden; einkleiden

**clothes** Kleider *pl*, Kleidung *f*; Wäsche *f*

**clothes bas·ket** Wäschekorb *m*

**clothes·horse** Wäscheständer *m*

**clothes·line** Wäscheleine *f*

**clothes peg** *Br*, **clothes·pin** Wäscheklammer *f*

**cloth·ing** (Be)Kleidung *f*

**cloud 1.** Wolke *f*; *fig* Schatten *m*; **2.** (sich) bewölken; (sich) trüben

**cloud·burst** Wolkenbruch *m*

**cloud·less** wolkenlos

**cloud·y** bewölkt; trüb; *fig* unklar

**clout** F Schlag *m*; POL Einfluss *m*

**clove**[1] GASTR (Gewürz)Nelke *f*; ***~ of garlic*** Knoblauchzehe *f*

**clo·ven hoof** ZO Huf *m* der Paarzeher

**clo·ver** BOT Klee *m*

**clown** Clown *m*, Hanswurst *m*

**club 1.** Keule *f*; Knüppel *m*; SPORT Schlagholz *n*; (*Golf*)Schläger *m*; Klub *m*; *pl card game*: Kreuz *n*; **2.** einknüppeln auf (*acc*), niederknüppeln

**club·foot** MED Klumpfuß *m*

**cluck** ZO **1.** gackern; glucken; **2.** Gackern *n*; Glucken *n*

**clue** Anhaltspunkt *m*, Fingerzeig *m*, Spur *f*

**clump 1.** Klumpen *m*; (*Baum- etc* -) Gruppe *f*; **2.** trampeln

**clum·sy** unbeholfen, ungeschickt, plump

**clus·ter 1.** BOT Traube *f*, Büschel *n*; Haufen *m*; **2.** sich drängen

**clutch 1.** Griff *m*; TECH Kupplung *f*; *fig* Klaue *f*; **2.** (er)greifen; umklammern

**clut·ter** *fig* überladen

**c/o** ABBR *of* ***care of*** c/o, (wohnhaft) bei

**Co** ABBR *of* ***company*** ECON Gesellschaft *f*

**coach 1.** Reisebus *m*; *Br* RAIL (Personen)Wagen *m*; Kutsche *f*; SPORT Trainer(in); PED Nachhilfelehrer(in); **2.** SPORT trainieren; PED *j-m* Nachhilfeunterricht geben

**coach·man** Kutscher *m*

**co·ag·u·late** gerinnen (lassen)

**coal** (Stein)Kohle *f*; ***carry ~s to Newcastle*** F *Br* Eulen nach Athen tragen

**co·a·li·tion** POL Koalition *f*; Bündnis *n*, Zusammenschluss *m*

**coal·mine, coal·pit** Kohlengrube *f*

**coarse** grob; rau; derb; ungeschliffen; gemein

**coast 1.** Küste *f*; **2.** MAR die Küste entlangfahren; im Leerlauf (*car*) *or* im Freilauf (*bicycle*) fahren; rodeln

**coast·er brake** Rücktritt(bremse *f*) *m*

**coast·guard** (Angehörige *m* der) Küstenwache *f*

**coast·line** Küstenlinie *f*, -strich *m*

**coat 1.** Mantel *m*; ZO Pelz *m*, Fell *n*; (*Farb- etc*)Überzug *m*, Anstrich *m*, Schicht *f*; **2.** (an)streichen, überziehen, beschichten

**coat hang·er** Kleiderbügel *m*

**coat·ing** (*Farb- etc*)Überzug *m*, Anstrich *m*; Schicht *f*; Mantelstoff *m*

**coat of arms** Wappen(schild *m*, *n*) *n*

**coax** überreden, beschwatzen

**cob** Maiskolben *m*

**cob·bled:** ***~ street*** Straße *f* mit Kopfsteinpflaster

**cob·bler** (Flick)Schuster *m*

**cob·web** Spinn(en)gewebe *n*

**co·caine** Kokain *n*

**cock 1.** ZO Hahn *m*; V Schwanz *m*; **2.** aufrichten; ***~ one's ears*** die Ohren spitzen

**cock·a·too** ZO Kakadu *m*
**cock·chaf·er** ZO Maikäfer *m*
**cock·eyed** F schielend; (krumm und) schief
**Cock·ney** Cockney *m*, waschechter Londoner
**cock·pit** AVIAT Cockpit *n*
**cock·roach** ZO Schabe *f*
**cock·sure** F übertrieben selbstsicher
**cock·tail** Cocktail *m*
**cock·y** großspurig, anmaßend
**co·co** BOT Kokospalme *f*
**co·coa** Kakao *m*
**co·co·nut** BOT Kokosnuss *f*
**co·coon** (*Seiden*)Kokon *m*
**cod** ZO Kabeljau *m*, Dorsch *m*
**COD** ABBR *of* ***collect*** (*Br* ***cash***) ***on delivery*** per Nachnahme
**cod·dle** verhätscheln, verzärteln
**code 1.** Kode *m*; **2.** verschlüsseln, chiffrieren; kodieren
**cod·fish** → ***cod***
**cod·ing** Kodierung *f*
**cod-liv·er oil** Lebertran *m*
**co·ed·u·ca·tion** PED Gemeinschaftserziehung *f*
**co·ex·ist** gleichzeitig *or* nebeneinander bestehen *or* leben
**co·ex·ist·ence** Koexistenz *f*
**cof·fee** Kaffee *m*; ***black*** (***white***) ~ Kaffee ohne (mit) Milch; ~ **bar** *Br* Café *n*; Imbissstube *f*; ~ **bean** Kaffeebohne *f*; ~ **grind·er** Kaffeemühle *f*; ~ **ma·chine** Kaffeeautomat *m*
**cof·fee·mak·er** Kaffeemaschine *f*
**cof·fee| pot** Kaffeekanne *f*; ~ **shop** Café *n*; Imbissstube *f*; ~ **ta·ble** Couchtisch *m*
**cof·fin** Sarg *m*
**cog** TECH (Rad)Zahn *m*; → **cog·wheel** TECH Zahnrad *n*
**co·her·ence, co·her·en·cy** Zusammenhang *m*
**co·her·ent** zusammenhängend
**co·he·sion** Zusammenhalt *m*
**co·he·sive** (fest) zusammenhaltend
**coif·fure** Frisur *f*
**coil 1.** *a.* ~ ***up*** aufrollen, (auf)wickeln; sich zusammenrollen; **2.** Spirale *f* (*a.* TECH, MED); Rolle *f*, Spule *f*
**coin 1.** Münze *f*; **2.** prägen
**co·in·cide** zusammentreffen; übereinstimmen; **co·in·ci·dence** (zufälliges) Zusammentreffen; Zufall *m*
**coin-op·e·rat·ed:** ~ (***gas***, *Br* ***petrol***) ***pump*** Münztank(automat) *m*
**coke** Koks *m* (*a.* F *cocaine*)
**Coke**® F Coke *n*, Cola *n*, *f*, Coca *n*, *f*
**cold 1.** kalt; **2.** Kälte *f*; MED Erkältung *f*; ***catch*** (***a***) ~ sich erkälten; ***have a*** ~ erkältet sein
**cold-blood·ed** kaltblütig
**cold cuts** GASTR Aufschnitt *m*
**cold-heart·ed** kaltherzig
**cold·ness** Kälte *f*
**cold sweat** Angstschweiß *m*; ***he broke out in a*** ~ ihm brach der Angstschweiß aus
**cold war** POL kalter Krieg
**cold wave** METEOR Kältewelle *f*
**cole·slaw** Krautsalat *m*
**col·ic** MED Kolik *f*
**col·lab·o·rate** zusammenarbeiten
**col·lab·o·ra·tion** Zusammenarbeit *f*; ***in*** ~ ***with*** gemeinsam mit
**col·lapse 1.** zusammenbrechen (*a. fig*), einstürzen; umfallen; *fig* scheitern; **2.** Einsturz *m*; *fig* Zusammenbruch *m*
**col·lap·si·ble** Klapp..., zusammenklappbar
**col·lar 1.** Kragen *m*; (*Hunde- etc*)Halsband *n*; **2.** beim Kragen packen; *j-n* festnehmen, F schnappen
**col·lar·bone** ANAT Schlüsselbein *n*
**col·league** Kollege *m*, Kollegin *f*, Mitarbeiter(in)
**col·lect** *v/t* (ein)sammeln; *Daten* erfassen; *Geld* kassieren; *j-n or et.* abholen; *Gedanken etc* sammeln; *v/i* sich (ver)sammeln; **col·lect·ed** *fig* gefasst
**col·lect·ing box** Sammelbüchse *f*
**col·lec·tion** Sammlung *f*; ECON Eintreibung *f*; REL Kollekte *f*; Abholung *f*
**col·lec·tive** gesammelt; Sammel...; ~ ***bargaining*** ECON Tarifverhandlungen
**col·lec·tive·ly** insgesamt; zusammen
**col·lec·tor** Sammler(in); Steuereinnehmer *m*; ELECTR Stromabnehmer *m*
**col·lege** College *n*; Hochschule *f*; höhere Lehranstalt
**col·lide** zusammenstoßen, kollidieren (*a. fig*)
**col·lie·ry** Kohlengrube *f*
**col·li·sion** Zusammenstoß *m*, Kollision *f* (*a. fig*)
**col·lo·qui·al** umgangssprachlich
**co·lon** LING Doppelpunkt *m*
**colo·nel** MIL Oberst *m*

**co·lo·ni·al·is·m** POL Kolonialismus *m*
**col·o·nize** kolonisieren, besiedeln
**col·o·ny** Kolonie *f*
**col·o(u)r 1.** Farbe *f*; *pl* MIL Fahne *f*; MAR Flagge *f*; ***what ~ is ...?*** welche Farbe hat ...?; **2.** *v/t* färben; anmalen, bemalen, anstreichen; *fig* beschönigen; *v/i* sich (ver)färben; erröten
**col·o(u)r bar** Rassenschranke *f*
**col·o(u)r-blind** farbenblind
**col·o(u)red** bunt; farbig
**col·o(u)r·fast** farbecht
**col·o(u)r film** PHOT Farbfilm *m*
**col·o(u)r·ful** farbenprächtig; *fig* farbig, bunt
**col·o(u)r·ing** Färbung *f*; Farbstoff *m*; Gesichtsfarbe *f*
**col·o(u)r·less** farblos
**col·o(u)r line** Rassenschranke *f*
**col·o(u)r| set** Farbfernseher *m*; **~ tel·e·vi·sion** Farbfernsehen *n*
**colt** ZO (Hengst)Fohlen *n*
**col·umn** Säule *f*; PRINT Spalte *f*; MIL Kolonne *f*
**col·umn·ist** Kolumnist(in)
**comb 1.** Kamm *m*; **2.** kämmen; striegeln
**com·bat 1.** Kampf *m*; ***single ~*** Zweikampf *m*; **2.** kämpfen gegen, bekämpfen; **com·ba·tant** MIL Kämpfer *m*
**com·bi·na·tion** Verbindung *f*, Kombination *f*; **com·bine 1.** (sich) verbinden; **2.** ECON Konzern *m*; AGR *a.* ***~ harvester*** Mähdrescher *m*
**com·bus·ti·ble 1.** brennbar; **2.** Brennstoff *m*, Brennmaterial *n*
**com·bus·tion** Verbrennung *f*
**come** kommen; ***to ~*** künftig, kommend; ***~ and go*** kommen und gehen; ***~ to see*** besuchen; ***~ about*** geschehen, passieren; ***~ across*** auf *j-n or et.* stoßen; ***~ along*** mitkommen, mitgehen; ***~ apart*** auseinander fallen; ***~ away*** sich lösen, ab-, losgehen (*button etc*); ***~ back*** zurückkommen; ***~ by s.th.*** zu et. kommen; ***~ down*** herunterkommen (*a. fig*); einstürzen; sinken (*prices*); überliefert werden; ***~ down with*** F erkranken an (*dat*); ***~ for*** abholen kommen, kommen wegen; ***~ forward*** sich melden; ***~ from*** kommen aus; kommen von; ***~ home*** nach Hause (*Austrian, Swiss a.* nachhause) kommen; ***~ in*** hereinkommen; eintreffen (*news*); einlaufen (*train*); ***~ in!*** herein!; ***~ loose*** sich ablösen, abgehen; ***~ off*** ab-, losgehen (*button etc*); ***~ on!*** los!, vorwärts!, komm!; ***~ out*** herauskommen; ***~ over*** vorbeikommen (*visitor*); ***~ round*** vorbeikommen (*visitor*); wieder zu sich kommen; ***~ through*** durchkommen; *Krankheit etc* überstehen, überleben; ***~ to*** sich belaufen auf (*acc*); wieder zu sich kommen; ***~ up to*** entsprechen (*dat*), heranreichen an (*acc*)
**come·back** Come-back *n*
**co·me·di·an** Komiker *m*
**com·e·dy** Komödie *f*, Lustspiel *n*
**come·ly** attraktiv, gut aussehend
**com·fort 1.** Komfort *m*, Bequemlichkeit *f*; Trost *m*; ***cold ~*** schwacher Trost; **2.** trösten
**com·for·ta·ble** komfortabel, behaglich, bequem; tröstlich
**com·fort·er** Tröster *m*; *esp Br* Schnuller *m*; Steppdecke *f*
**com·fort·less** unbequem; trostlos
**com·fort sta·tion** Bedürfnisanstalt *f*
**com·ic** komisch; Komödien..., Lustspiel...; **com·i·cal** komisch, spaßig
**com·ics** Comics *pl*, Comic-Hefte *pl*
**com·ma** LING Komma *n*
**com·mand 1.** Befehl *m*; Beherrschung *f*; MIL Kommando *n*; **2.** befehlen; MIL kommandieren; verfügen über (*acc*); beherrschen
**com·mand·er** MIL Kommandeur *m*, Befehlshaber *m*; **~ in chief** MIL Oberbefehlshaber *m*
**com·mand·ment** REL Gebot *n*
**com·mand mod·ule** Kommandokapsel *f*
**com·man·do** MIL Kommando *n*
**com·mem·o·rate** gedenken (*gen*)
**com·mem·o·ra·tion: *in ~ of*** zum Gedenken *or* Gedächtnis an (*acc*)
**com·mem·o·ra·tive** Gedenk..., Erinnerungs...
**com·ment 1.** (**on**) Kommentar *m* (zu); Bemerkung *f* (zu); Anmerkung *f* (zu); ***no ~!*** kein Kommentar!; **2.** *v/i* ***~ on*** e-n Kommentar abgeben zu, sich äußern über (*acc*); *v/t* bemerken (***that*** dass)
**com·men·ta·ry** Kommentar *m* (**on** zu)
**com·men·ta·tor** Kommentator *m*, *radio*, TV *a.* Reporter *m*
**com·merce** ECON Handel *m*
**com·mer·cial 1.** ECON Handels..., Ge-

schäfts...; kommerziell, finanziell; **2.** *radio*, TV Werbespot *m*, Werbesendung *f*; ~ **art** Gebrauchsgrafik *f*; ~ **art·ist** Gebrauchsgrafiker(in)

**com·mer·cial·ize** kommerzialisieren

**com·mer·cial tel·e·vi·sion** Werbefernsehen *n*; kommerzielles Fernsehen

**com·mis·e·rate:** ~ ***with*** Mitleid empfinden mit

**com·mis·e·ra·tion** Mitleid *n* (***for*** mit)

**com·mis·sion 1.** Auftrag *m*; Kommission *f*, Ausschuss *m*; ECON Kommission *f*, Provision *f*; Begehung *f* (*of a crime*); **2.** beauftragen; *et.* in Auftrag geben

**com·mis·sion·er** Beauftragte *m*, *f*; Kommissar(in)

**com·mit** anvertrauen, übergeben (***to*** *dat*); JUR *j-n* einweisen (***to*** in *acc*); *Verbrechen* begehen; *j-n* verpflichten (***to*** zu), *j-n* festlegen (***to*** auf *acc*)

**com·mit·ment** Verpflichtung *f*; Engagement *n*

**com·mit·tal** JUR Einweisung *f*

**com·mit·tee** Komitee *n*, Ausschuss *m*

**com·mod·i·ty** ECON Ware *f*, Artikel *m*

**com·mon 1.** gemeinsam, gemeinschaftlich; allgemein; alltäglich; gewöhnlich, einfach; **2.** Gemeindeland *n*; ***in*** ~ gemeinsam (***with*** mit)

**com·mon·er** Bürgerliche *m*, *f*

**com·mon law** (ungeschriebenes englisches) Gewohnheitsrecht

**Com·mon Mar·ket** ECON, POL HIST Gemeinsamer Markt

**com·mon·place 1.** Gemeinplatz *m*; **2.** alltäglich; abgedroschen

**Com·mons:** ***the*** ~, ***the House of*** ~ *Br* PARL das Unterhaus

**com·mon sense** gesunder Menschenverstand

**Com·mon·wealth:** ***the*** ~ (***of Nations***) das Commonwealth

**com·mo·tion** Aufregung *f*; Aufruhr *m*, Tumult *m*

**com·mu·nal** Gemeinde...; Gemeinschafts...; **com·mune** Kommune *f*

**com·mu·ni·cate** *v/t* mitteilen; *v/i* sich besprechen; sich in Verbindung setzen (***with s.o.*** mit j-m); (durch e-e Tür) verbunden sein

**com·mu·ni·ca·tion** Mitteilung *f*; Verständigung *f*, Kommunikation *f*; Verbindung *f*; *pl* Kommunikationsmittel *pl*; Verkehrswege *pl*

**com·mu·ni·ca·tions sat·el·lite** Nachrichtensatellit *m*

**com·mu·ni·ca·tive** mitteilsam, gesprächig

**Com·mu·nion** *a.* ***Holy*** ~ REL (heilige) Kommunion, Abendmahl *n*

**com·mu·nis·m** POL Kommunismus *m*

**com·mu·nist** POL **1.** Kommunist(in); **2.** kommunistisch

**com·mu·ni·ty** Gemeinschaft *f*; Gemeinde *f*

**com·mute** JUR Strafe *mildernd* umwandeln; RAIL *etc* pendeln

**com·mut·er** Pendler(in); ~ **train** Pendlerzug *m*, Nahverkehrszug *m*

**com·pact 1.** Puderdose *f*; MOT Kleinwagen *m*; **2.** *adj* kompakt; eng, klein; knapp (*style*); ~ **car** MOT Kleinwagen *m*; ~ **disk** (ABBR ***CD***) Compact Disc *f*, CD *f*; ~ **disk play·er** CD-Player *m*, CD-Spieler *m*

**com·pan·ion** Begleiter(in); Gefährte *m*, Gefährtin *f*; Gesellschafter(in); Handbuch *n*, Leitfaden *m*

**com·pan·ion·ship** Gesellschaft *f*

**com·pa·ny** Gesellschaft *f*, ECON *a.* Firma *f*; MIL Kompanie *f*; THEA Truppe *f*; ***keep s.o.*** ~ j-m Gesellschaft leisten

**com·pa·ra·ble** vergleichbar

**com·par·a·tive 1.** vergleichend; verhältnismäßig; **2.** *a.* ~ ***degree*** LING Komparativ *m*; **com·par·a·tive·ly** vergleichsweise; verhältnismäßig

**com·pare 1.** *v/t* vergleichen; ~***d with*** im Vergleich zu; *v/i* sich vergleichen lassen; **2.** ***beyond*** ~, ***without*** ~ unvergleichlich

**com·pa·ri·son** Vergleich *m*

**com·part·ment** Fach *n*; RAIL Abteil *n*

**com·pass** Kompass *m*; ***pair of*** ~***es*** Zirkel *m*

**com·pas·sion** Mitleid *n*

**com·pas·sion·ate** mitleidig

**com·pat·i·ble** vereinbar; ***be*** ~ (***with***) passen (zu), zusammenpassen; EDP *etc* kompatibel sein (mit)

**com·pat·ri·ot** Landsmann *m*, Landsmännin *f*

**com·pel** (er)zwingen

**com·pel·ling** bezwingend

**com·pen·sate** *j-n* entschädigen; *et.* ersetzen; ausgleichen

**com·pen·sa·tion** Ersatz *m*; Ausgleich

*m*; Schadenersatz *m*, Entschädigung *f*; Bezahlung *f*, Gehalt *n*
**com·pere** *Br* Conférencier *m*
**com·pete** sich (mit)bewerben (***for*** um); konkurrieren; SPORT (am Wettkampf) teilnehmen
**com·pe·tence** Können *n*, Fähigkeit *f*
**com·pe·tent** fähig, tüchtig; fachkundig, sachkundig
**com·pe·ti·tion** Wettbewerb *m*; Konkurrenz *f*
**com·pet·i·tive** konkurrierend
**com·pet·i·tor** Mitbewerber(in); Konkurrent(in); SPORT (Wettbewerbs)Teilnehmer(in)
**com·pile** kompilieren, zusammentragen, zusammenstellen
**com·pla·cence, com·pla·cen·cy** Selbstzufriedenheit *f*, Selbstgefälligkeit *f*; **com·pla·cent** selbstzufrieden, selbstgefällig
**com·plain** sich beklagen *or* beschweren (***about*** über *acc*; ***to*** bei); klagen (***of*** über *acc*)
**com·plaint** Klage *f*, Beschwerde *f*; MED Leiden *n*, *pl* MED *a.* Beschwerden *pl*
**com·ple·ment 1.** Ergänzung *f*; **2.** ergänzen
**com·ple·men·ta·ry** (sich) ergänzend
**com·plete 1.** vollständig; vollzählig; **2.** vervollständigen; beenden, abschließen
**com·ple·tion** Vervollständigung *f*; Abschluss *m*; **~ test** PSYCH Lückentext *m*
**com·plex 1.** zusammengesetzt; komplex, vielschichtig; **2.** Komplex *m* (*a.* PSYCH)
**com·plex·ion** Gesichtsfarbe *f*, Teint *m*
**com·plex·i·ty** Komplexität *f*, Vielschichtigkeit *f*
**com·pli·ance** Einwilligung *f*; Befolgung *f*; ***in ~ with*** gemäß (*dat*)
**com·pli·ant** willfährig
**com·pli·cate** komplizieren
**com·pli·cat·ed** kompliziert
**com·pli·ca·tion** Komplikation *f* (*a.* MED)
**com·plic·i·ty** JUR Mitschuld *f*, Mittäterschaft *f* (***in*** an *dat*)
**com·pli·ment 1.** Kompliment *n*; Empfehlung *f*; Gruß *m*; **2.** *v/t j-m* ein Kompliment *or* Komplimente machen (***on*** über *acc*)
**com·ply** (***with***) einwilligen (in *acc*); (*e-e Abmachung etc*) befolgen
**com·po·nent** Bestandteil *m*; TECH, ELECTR Bauelement *n*
**com·pose** zusammensetzen, -stellen; MUS komponieren; verfassen; ***be ~d of*** bestehen *or* sich zusammensetzen aus; ***~ o.s.*** sich beruhigen
**com·posed** ruhig, gelassen
**com·pos·er** MUS Komponist(in)
**com·po·si·tion** Zusammensetzung *f*; MUS Komposition *f*; PED Aufsatz *m*
**com·po·sure** Fassung *f*, (Gemüts)Ruhe *f*
**com·pound¹** Lager *n*; Gefängnishof *m*; (Tier)Gehege *n*
**com·pound² 1.** Zusammensetzung *f*; Verbindung *f*; LING zusammengesetztes Wort; **2.** zusammengesetzt; ***~ interest*** ECON Zinseszinsen *pl*; **3.** *v/t* zusammensetzen; steigern, *esp* verschlimmern
**com·pre·hend** begreifen, verstehen
**com·pre·hen·si·ble** verständlich
**com·pre·hen·sion** Verständnis *n*; Begriffsvermögen *n*, Verstand *m*; ***past ~*** unfassbar, unfasslich
**com·pre·hen·sive 1.** umfassend; **2.** *a.* ***~ school*** *Br* Gesamtschule *f*
**com·press** zusammendrücken, -pressen; ***~ed air*** Druckluft *f*
**com·pres·sion** PHYS Verdichtung *f*; TECH Druck *m*
**com·prise** einschließen, umfassen; bestehen aus
**com·pro·mise 1.** Kompromiss *m*; **2.** *v/t* bloßstellen, kompromittieren; *v/i* e-n Kompromiss schließen
**com·pro·mis·ing** kompromittierend; verfänglich
**com·pul·sion** Zwang *m*
**com·pul·sive** zwingend, Zwangs...; PSYCH zwanghaft
**com·pul·so·ry** obligatorisch; Pflicht..., Zwangs...
**com·punc·tion** Gewissensbisse *pl*; Reue *f*; Bedenken *pl*
**com·pute** berechnen; schätzen
**com·put·er** Computer *m*, Rechner *m*
**com·put·er|-aid·ed** computergestützt; **~-con·trolled** computergesteuert
**com·put·er| game** Computerspiel *n*; **~ graph·ics** Computergrafik *f*
**com·put·er·ize** (sich) auf Computer umstellen; computerisieren; mit Hilfe

C

e-s Computers errechnen *or* zusammenstellen
**com·put·er| pre·dic·tion** Hochrechnung *f*; ~ **sci·ence** Informatik *f*; ~ **sci·en·tist** Informatiker *m*; ~ **vi·rus** EDP Computervirus *m*
**com·rade** Kamerad *m*; (Partei)Genosse *m*
**con**[1] → ***contra***
**con**[2] F reinlegen, betrügen
**con·ceal** verbergen; verheimlichen
**con·cede** zugestehen, einräumen
**con·ceit** Einbildung *f*, Dünkel *m*
**con·ceit·ed** eingebildet (***of*** auf *acc*)
**con·cei·va·ble** denkbar, begreiflich
**con·ceive** *v/i* schwanger werden; *v/t Kind* empfangen; sich *et.* vorstellen *or* denken
**con·cen·trate** (sich) konzentrieren
**con·cept** Begriff *m*; Gedanke *m*
**con·cep·tion** Vorstellung *f*, Begriff *m*; BIOL Empfängnis *f*
**con·cern 1.** Angelegenheit *f*; Sorge *f*; ECON Geschäft *n*, Unternehmen *n*; **2.** betreffen, angehen; beunruhigen
**con·cerned** besorgt; beteiligt (***in*** an *dat*)
**con·cern·ing** *prp* betreffend, hinsichtlich (*gen*), was ... (*acc*) (an)betrifft
**con·cert** MUS Konzert *n*
**con·cert hall** Konzerthalle *f*, -saal *m*
**con·ces·sion** Zugeständnis *n*; Konzession *f*
**con·cil·i·a·to·ry** versöhnlich, vermittelnd
**con·cise** kurz, knapp
**con·cise·ness** Kürze *f*
**con·clude** schließen, beenden; *Vertrag etc* abschließen; *et.* folgern, schließen (***from*** aus); ***to be ~d*** Schluss folgt
**con·clu·sion** (Ab)Schluss *m*, Ende *n*; Abschluss *m* (*of a contract etc*); (Schluss)Folgerung *f*; → ***jump***
**con·clu·sive** schlüssig
**con·coct** (zusammen)brauen; *fig* aushecken, ausbrüten
**con·coc·tion** Gebräu *n*; *fig* Erfindung *f*
**con·crete**[1] konkret
**con·crete**[2] **1.** Beton *m*; **2.** Beton...; **3.** betonieren
**con·cur** übereinstimmen
**con·cur·rence** Zusammentreffen *n*; Übereinstimmung *f*
**con·cus·sion** MED Gehirnerschütterung *f*
**con·demn** verurteilen (*a.* JUR); verdammen; für unbrauchbar *or* unbewohnbar *etc* erklären; ~ ***to death*** JUR zum Tode verurteilen; **con·dem·na·tion** Verurteilung *f* (*a.* JUR); Verdammung *f*
**con·den·sa·tion** Kondensation *f*; Zusammenfassung *f*
**con·dense** kondensieren; zusammenfassen
**con·densed milk** Kondensmilch *f*
**con·dens·er** TECH Kondensator *m*
**con·de·scend** sich herablassen
**con·de·scend·ing** herablassend, gönnerhaft
**con·di·ment** Gewürz *n*, Würze *f*
**con·di·tion 1.** Zustand *m*; (*körperlicher or* Gesundheits)Zustand *m*; SPORT Kondition *f*, Form *f*; Bedingung *f*; *pl* Verhältnisse *pl*, Umstände *pl*; ***on ~ that*** unter der Bedingung, dass; ***out of ~*** in schlechter Verfassung, in schlechtem Zustand; **2.** bedingen; in Form bringen
**con·di·tion·al 1.** (***on***) bedingt (durch), abhängig (von); **2.** *a.* ~ ***clause*** LING Bedingungs-, Konditionalsatz *m*; *a.* ~ ***mood*** LING Konditional *m*
**con·do** → ***condominium***
**con·dole** kondolieren (***with*** *dat*)
**con·do·lence** Beileid *n*
**con·dom** Kondom *n*, *m*
**con·do·min·i·um** Eigentumswohnanlage *f*; Eigentumswohnung *f*
**con·done** verzeihen, vergeben
**con·du·cive** dienlich, förderlich (***to*** *dat*)
**con·duct 1.** Führung *f*; Verhalten *n*, Betragen *n*; **2.** führen; PHYS leiten; MUS dirigieren; ***~ed tour*** Führung *f* (***of*** durch); **con·duc·tor** Führer *m*, Leiter *m*; (*Bus-, Straßenbahn*)Schaffner *m*; RAIL Zugbegleiter *m*; MUS Dirigent *m*; PHYS Leiter *m*; ELECTR Blitzableiter *m*
**cone** Kegel *m*; GASTR Eistüte *f*; BOT Zapfen *m*
**con·fec·tion** Konfekt *n*
**con·fec·tion·er** Konditor *m*
**con·fec·tion·e·ry** Süßigkeiten *pl*, Süß-, Konditoreiwaren *pl*; Konfekt *n*; Konditorei *f*; Süßwarengeschäft *n*
**con·fed·e·ra·cy** (Staaten)Bund *m*; ***the Confederacy*** HIST die Konföderation
**con·fed·er·ate 1.** verbündet; **2.** Verbündete *m*, Bundesgenosse *m*; **3.** (sich) verbünden

**con·fed·er·a·tion** Bund *m*, Bündnis *n*; (Staaten)Bund *m*
**con·fer** *v/t Titel etc* verleihen (**on** *dat*); *v/i* sich beraten
**con·fe·rence** Konferenz *f*
**con·fess** gestehen; beichten
**con·fes·sion** Geständnis *n*; REL Beichte *f*
**con·fes·sion·al** REL Beichtstuhl *m*
**con·fes·sor** REL Beichtvater *m*
**con·fi·dant(e)** Vertraute *m (f)*
**con·fide:** ~ ***s.th. to s.o.*** j-m et. anvertrauen; ~ ***in s.o.*** sich j-m anvertrauen
**con·fi·dence** Vertrauen *n*; Selbstvertrauen *n*; ~ **man** → ***conman***; ~ **trickster** Trickbetrüger *m*
**con·fi·dent** überzeugt, zuversichtlich
**con·fi·den·tial** vertraulich
**con·fine** begrenzen, beschränken; einsperren; ***be ~d of*** entbunden werden von; **con·fine·ment** Haft *f*; Beschränkung *f*; MED Entbindung *f*
**con·firm** bestätigen; bekräftigen; REL konfirmieren, firmen
**con·fir·ma·tion** Bestätigung *f*; REL Konfirmation *f*, Firmung *f*
**con·fis·cate** beschlagnahmen
**con·fis·ca·tion** Beschlagnahme *f*
**con·flict 1.** Konflikt *m*, Zwiespalt *m*; **2.** im Widerspruch stehen (***with*** zu)
**con·flict·ing** widersprüchlich, zwiespältig
**con·form** (sich) anpassen (***to*** *dat*, an *acc*)
**con·found** verwirren, durcheinander bringen
**con·front** gegenübertreten, -stehen (*dat*); sich stellen (*dat*); konfrontieren
**con·fron·ta·tion** Konfrontation *f*
**con·fuse** verwechseln; verwirren; **con·fused** verwirrt; verlegen; verworren; **con·fu·sion** Verwirrung *f*; Verlegenheit *f*; Verwechslung *f*
**con·geal** erstarren (lassen); gerinnen (lassen)
**con·gest·ed** überfüllt; verstopft
**con·ges·tion** MED Blutandrang *m*; *a.* ***traffic*** ~ Verkehrsstockung *f*, Verkehrsstörung *f*, Verkehrsstau *m*
**con·grat·u·late** beglückwünschen, *j-m* gratulieren
**con·grat·u·la·tion** Glückwunsch *m*; ***~s!*** ich gratuliere!, herzlichen Glückwunsch!
**con·gre·gate** (sich) versammeln
**con·gre·ga·tion** REL Gemeinde *f*
**con·gress** Kongress *m*; ***Congress*** PARL der Kongress
**Con·gress·man** PARL Kongressabgeordnete *m*; **Con·gress·wom·an** PARL Kongressabgeordnete *f*
**con·ic, con·i·cal** *esp* TECH konisch, kegelförmig
**co·ni·fer** BOT Nadelbaum *m*
**con·jec·ture 1.** Vermutung *f*; **2.** vermuten
**con·ju·gal** ehelich
**con·ju·gate** LING konjugieren, beugen
**con·ju·ga·tion** LING Konjugation *f*, Beugung *f*
**con·junc·tion** Verbindung *f*; LING Konjunktion *f*, Bindewort *n*
**con·junc·ti·vi·tis** MED Bindehautentzündung *f*
**con·jure** zaubern; *Teufel etc* beschwören; ~ ***up*** heraufbeschwören (*a. fig*)
**con·jur·er** *esp Br* → ***conjuror***
**con·jur·ing trick** Zauberkunststück *n*
**con·jur·or** Zauberer *m*, Zauberin *f*, Zauberkünstler(in)
**con·man** Betrüger *m*; Hochstapler *m*
**con·nect** verbinden; ELECTR anschließen, zuschalten; RAIL, AVIAT *etc* Anschluss haben (***with*** an *acc*)
**con·nect·ed** verbunden; (logisch) zusammenhängend (*speech etc*); ***be well*** ~ gute Beziehungen haben
**con·nec·tion,** *Br* **con·nex·ion** Verbindung *f*, Anschluss *m* (*a.* ELECTR, RAIL, AVIAT, TEL); Zusammenhang *m*; *mst pl* Beziehungen *pl*, Verbindungen *pl*; Verwandte *pl*
**con·quer** erobern; (be)siegen
**con·quer·or** Eroberer *m*
**con·quest** Eroberung *f* (*a. fig*); erobertes Gebiet
**con·science** Gewissen *n*
**con·sci·en·tious** gewissenhaft; Gewissens...; **con·sci·en·tious·ness** Gewissenhaftigkeit *f*
**con·sci·en·tious ob·jec·tor** MIL Wehrdienstverweigerer *m*
**con·scious** MED bei Bewusstsein; bewusst; ***be ~ of*** sich bewusst sein (*gen*)
**con·scious·ness** Bewusstsein *n* (*a.* MED)
**con·script** MIL **1.** einberufen; **2.** Wehrpflichtige *m*; **con·scrip·tion** MIL Einberufung *f*; Wehrpflicht *f*

C

**con·se·crate** REL weihen; widmen
**con·se·cra·tion** REL Weihe *f*
**con·sec·u·tive** aufeinander folgend; fortlaufend
**con·sent 1.** Zustimmung *f*; **2.** einwilligen, zustimmen
**con·se·quence** Folge *f*, Konsequenz *f*; Bedeutung *f*
**con·se·quent·ly** folglich, daher
**con·ser·va·tion** Erhaltung *f*; Naturschutz *m*; Umweltschutz *m*; ~ ***area*** (Natur)Schutzgebiet *n*
**con·ser·va·tion·ist** Naturschützer(in); Umweltschützer(in)
**con·ser·va·tive 1.** erhaltend; konservativ; vorsichtig; **2.** ***Conservative*** POL Konservative *m, f*
**con·ser·va·to·ry** Treibhaus *n*, Gewächshaus *n*; Wintergarten *m*
**con·serve** erhalten
**con·sid·er** *v/t* nachdenken über (*acc*); betrachten als, halten für; sich überlegen, erwägen; in Betracht ziehen, berücksichtigen; *v/i* nachdenken, überlegen
**con·sid·e·ra·ble** ansehnlich, beträchtlich; **con·sid·e·ra·bly** bedeutend, ziemlich, (sehr) viel
**con·sid·er·ate** rücksichtsvoll
**con·sid·e·ra·tion** Erwägung *f*, Überlegung *f*; Berücksichtigung *f*; Rücksicht(nahme) *f*; ***take into*** ~ in Erwägung *or* in Betracht ziehen
**con·sid·er·ing** in Anbetracht (der Tatsache, dass)
**con·sign** ECON *Waren* zusenden
**con·sign·ment** ECON (Waren)Sendung *f*; Zusendung *f*
**con·sist:** ~ ***in*** bestehen in (*dat*); ~ ***of*** bestehen aus
**con·sis·tence, con·sis·ten·cy** Konsistenz *f*, Beschaffenheit *f*; Übereinstimmung *f*; Konsequenz *f*
**con·sis·tent** übereinstimmend, vereinbar (***with*** mit); konsequent; SPORT *etc*: beständig
**con·so·la·tion** Trost *m*
**con·sole** trösten
**con·sol·i·date** festigen; *fig* zusammenschließen, -legen
**con·so·nant** LING Konsonant *m*, Mitlaut *m*
**con·spic·u·ous** deutlich sichtbar; auffallend
**con·spi·ra·cy** Verschwörung *f*
**con·spi·ra·tor** Verschwörer *m*
**con·spire** sich verschwören
**con·sta·ble** *Br* Polizist *m*
**con·stant** konstant, gleich bleibend; (be)ständig, (an)dauernd
**con·stant-care pa·tient** MED Pflegefall *m*
**con·ster·na·tion** Bestürzung *f*
**con·sti·pat·ed** MED verstopft
**con·sti·pa·tion** MED Verstopfung *f*
**con·sti·tu·en·cy** POL *Br* Wählerschaft *f*; Wahlkreis *m*
**con·sti·tu·ent** (wesentlicher) Bestandteil; POL Wähler(in)
**con·sti·tute** ernennen, einsetzen; bilden, ausmachen
**con·sti·tu·tion** POL Verfassung *f*; Konstitution *f*, körperliche Verfassung
**con·sti·tu·tion·al** konstitutionell; POL verfassungsmäßig
**con·strained** gezwungen, unnatürlich
**con·strict** zusammenziehen
**con·stric·tion** Zusammenziehung *f*
**con·struct** bauen, errichten, konstruieren
**con·struc·tion** Konstruktion *f*; Bau *m*, Bauwerk *n*; ***under*** ~ im Bau (befindlich); ~ **site** Baustelle *f*
**con·struc·tive** konstruktiv
**con·struc·tor** Erbauer *m*, Konstrukteur *m*
**con·sul** Konsul *m*
**con·su·late** Konsulat *n*; ~ **gen·e·ral** Generalkonsulat *n*
**con·sul gen·e·ral** Generalkonsul *m*
**con·sult** *v/t* konsultieren, um Rat fragen; in *e-m Buch* nachschlagen; *v/i* (sich) beraten
**con·sul·tant** (fachmännischer) Berater; *Br* Facharzt *m*
**con·sul·ta·tion** Konsultation *f*, Beratung *f*, Rücksprache *f*
**con·sult·ing** beratend; ~ **hours** *Br* MED Sprechstunde *f*; ~ **room** *Br* MED Sprechzimmer *n*
**con·sume** *v/t Essen etc* zu sich nehmen, verzehren (*a. fig*); verbrauchen, konsumieren; zerstören, vernichten
**con·sum·er** ECON Verbraucher(in); ~ **so·ci·e·ty** Konsumgesellschaft *f*
**con·sum·mate 1.** vollendet; **2.** vollenden; *Ehe* vollziehen
**con·sump·tion** Verbrauch *m*

**cont** ABBR *of* ***continued*** Forts., Fortsetzung *f*; fortgesetzt
**con·tact 1.** Berührung *f*; Kontakt *m*; Ansprechpartner(in), Kontaktperson *f* (*a.* MED); ***make ~s*** Verbindungen anknüpfen *or* herstellen; **2.** sich in Verbindung setzen mit, Kontakt aufnehmen mit; **~ lens** Kontaktlinse *f*, -schale *f*, Haftschale *f*
**con·ta·gious** MED ansteckend (*a. fig*)
**con·tain** enthalten; *fig* zügeln, zurückhalten; **con·tain·er** Behälter *m*; ECON Container *m*; **con·tain·er·ize** ECON auf Containerbetrieb umstellen; in Containern transportieren
**con·tam·i·nate** verunreinigen; infizieren, vergiften; (*a.* radioaktiv) verseuchen; ***radioactively ~d*** verstrahlt; ***~d soil*** Altlasten *pl*; **con·tam·i·na·tion** Verunreinigung *f*; Vergiftung *f*; (*a.* radioaktive) Verseuchung
**contd** ABBR *of* ***continued*** (→ ***cont***)
**con·tem·plate** (nachdenklich) betrachten; nachdenken über (*acc*); erwägen, beabsichtigen
**con·tem·pla·tion** (nachdenkliche) Betrachtung; Nachdenken *n*
**con·tem·pla·tive** nachdenklich
**con·tem·po·ra·ry 1.** zeitgenössisch; **2.** Zeitgenosse *m*, Zeitgenossin *f*
**con·tempt** Verachtung *f*
**con·temp·ti·ble** verachtenswert
**con·temp·tu·ous** geringschätzig, verächtlich
**con·tend** kämpfen, ringen (***for*** um; ***with*** mit); **con·tend·er** *esp* SPORT Wettkämpfer(in)
**con·tent**[1] Gehalt *m*, Aussage *f*, *pl* Inhalt *m*; (***table of***) ***~s*** Inhaltsverzeichnis *n*
**con·tent**[2] **1.** zufrieden; **2.** befriedigen; ***~ o.s.*** sich begnügen
**con·tent·ed** zufrieden
**con·tent·ment** Zufriedenheit *f*
**con·test 1.** (Wett)Kampf *m*; Wettbewerb *m*; **2.** sich bewerben um; bestreiten, *a.* JUR anfechten
**con·tes·tant** Wettkämpfer(in), (Wettkampf)Teilnehmer(in)
**con·text** Zusammenhang *m*
**con·ti·nent** Kontinent *m*, Erdteil *m*; ***the Continent*** *Br* das (europäische) Festland; **con·ti·nen·tal** kontinental, Kontinental...
**con·tin·gen·cy** Möglichkeit *f*, Eventualität *f*; **~ *plan*** Notplan *m*
**con·tin·gent 1.** ***be ~ on*** abhängen von; **2.** Kontingent *n* (*a.* MIL)
**con·tin·u·al** fortwährend, unaufhörlich
**con·tin·u·a·tion** Fortsetzung *f*; Fortbestand *m*, Fortdauer *f*
**con·tin·ue** *v/t* fortsetzen, fortfahren mit; beibehalten; ***to be ~d*** Fortsetzung folgt; *v/i* fortdauern; andauern, anhalten; fortfahren, weitermachen
**con·ti·nu·i·ty** Kontinuität *f*
**con·tin·u·ous** ununterbrochen; **~ form** LING Verlaufsform *f*
**con·tort** verdrehen; verzerren
**con·tor·tion** Verdrehung *f*; Verzerrung *f*
**con·tour** Umriss *m*
**con·tra** wider, gegen
**con·tra·band** ECON Schmuggelware *f*
**con·tra·cep·tion** MED Empfängnisverhütung *f*
**con·tra·cep·tive** MED **1.** empfängnisverhütend; **2.** Verhütungsmittel *n*
**con·tract 1.** Vertrag *m*; **2.** (sich) zusammenziehen; sich *e-e Krankheit* zuziehen; e-n Vertrag abschließen; sich vertraglich verpflichten
**con·trac·tion** Zusammenziehung *f*
**con·trac·tor** *a.* ***building ~*** Bauunternehmer *m*
**con·tra·dict** widersprechen (*dat*)
**con·tra·dic·tion** Widerspruch *m*
**con·tra·dic·to·ry** (sich) widersprechend
**con·tra·ry 1.** entgegengesetzt (***to*** *dat*); gegensätzlich; ***~ to expectations*** wider Erwarten; **2.** Gegenteil *n*; ***on the ~*** im Gegenteil
**con·trast 1.** Gegensatz *m*; Kontrast *m*; **2.** *v/t* gegenüberstellen, vergleichen; *v/i* sich abheben (***with*** von, gegen); im Gegensatz stehen (***with*** zu)
**con·trib·ute** beitragen, beisteuern; spenden (***to*** für)
**con·tri·bu·tion** Beitrag *m*; Spende *f*
**con·trib·u·tor** Beitragende *m, f*; Mitarbeiter(in)
**con·trib·u·to·ry** beitragend
**con·trite** zerknirscht
**con·trive** zustande bringen; es fertig bringen
**con·trol 1.** Kontrolle *f*, Herrschaft *f*, Macht *f*, Gewalt *f*, Beherrschung *f*; Aufsicht *f*; TECH Steuerung *f*; *mst pl*

C

TECH Steuervorrichtung *f*; ***get*** (***have, keep***) ***under*** ~ unter Kontrolle bringen (haben, halten); ***get out of*** ~ außer Kontrolle geraten; ***lose*** ~ ***of*** die Herrschaft *or* Gewalt *or* Kontrolle verlieren über; **2.** beherrschen, die Kontrolle haben über (*acc*); *e-r Sache* Herr werden, (erfolgreich) bekämpfen; kontrollieren, überwachen; ECON (staatlich) lenken, *Preise* binden; ELECTR, TECH steuern, regeln, regulieren; ~ **desk** ELECTR Schalt-, Steuerpult *n*; ~ **pan·el** ELECTR Schalttafel *f*; ~ **tow·er** AVIAT Kontrollturm *m*, Tower *m*

**con·tro·ver·sial** umstritten

**con·tro·ver·sy** Kontroverse *f*, Streit *m*

**con·tuse** MED sich *et.* prellen *or* quetschen; **con·tu·sion** MED Prellung *f*, Quetschung *f*

**con·va·lesce** gesund werden, genesen

**con·va·les·cence** Rekonvaleszenz *f*, Genesung *f*

**con·va·les·cent 1.** genesend; **2.** Rekonvaleszent(in), Genesende *m, f*

**con·vene** (sich) versammeln; zusammenkommen; *Versammlung* einberufen

**con·ve·ni·ence** Annehmlichkeit *f*, Bequemlichkeit *f*; *Br* Toilette *f*; ***all*** (***modern***) ~***s*** aller Komfort; ***at your earliest*** ~ möglichst bald; **con·ve·ni·ent** bequem; günstig, passend

**con·vent** REL (Nonnen)Kloster *n*

**con·ven·tion** Zusammenkunft *f*, Tagung *f*, Versammlung *f*; Abkommen *n*; Konvention *f*, Sitte *f*; **con·ven·tion·al** herkömmlich, konventionell

**con·verge** konvergieren; zusammenlaufen, -strömen

**con·ver·sa·tion** Gespräch *n*, Unterhaltung *f*

**con·ver·sa·tion·al** Unterhaltungs...; ~ ***English*** Umgangsenglisch *n*

**con·verse** sich unterhalten

**con·ver·sion** Umwandlung *f*, Verwandlung *f*; Umbau *m*; Umstellung *f* (***to*** auf *acc*); REL Bekehrung *f*, Übertritt *m*; MATH Umrechnung *f*; ~ **ta·ble** Umrechnungstabelle *f*

**con·vert** (sich) umwandeln *or* verwandeln; umbauen (***into*** zu); umstellen (***to*** auf *acc*); REL *etc* (sich) bekehren; MATH umrechnen

**con·vert·er** ELECTR Umformer *m*

**con·ver·ti·ble 1.** umwandelbar, verwandelbar; ECON konvertierbar; **2.** MOT Kabrio(lett) *n*

**con·vey** befördern, transportieren, bringen; überbringen, übermitteln; *Ideen etc* mitteilen, vermitteln

**con·vey·ance** Beförderung *f*, Transport *m*; Übermittlung *f*; Verkehrsmittel *n*

**con·vey·or belt** TECH Förderband *n*

**con·vict 1.** Verurteilte *m, f*; Strafgefangene *m, f*; **2.** JUR (***of***) überführen (*gen*); verurteilen (wegen)

**con·vic·tion** Überzeugung *f*; JUR Verurteilung *f*

**con·vince** überzeugen

**con·voy 1.** MAR Geleitzug *m*, Konvoi *m*; MOT (Wagen)Kolonne *f*; (Geleit-) Schutz *m*; **2.** Geleitschutz geben (*dat*), eskortieren

**con·vul·sion** MED Zuckung *f*, Krampf *m*; **con·vul·sive** MED krampfhaft, krampfartig, konvulsiv

**coo** ZO gurren (*a. fig*)

**cook 1.** Koch *m*; Köchin *f*; **2.** kochen; F *Bericht etc* frisieren; ~ ***up*** F sich ausdenken, erfinden

**cook·book** Kochbuch *n*

**cook·er** *Br* Ofen *m*, Herd *m*

**cook·e·ry** Kochen *n*; Kochkunst *f*

**cook·e·ry book** *Br* Kochbuch *n*

**cook·ie** (süßer) Keks, Plätzchen *n*

**cook·ing** GASTR Küche *f*

**cook·y** → ***cookie***

**cool 1.** kühl; *fig* kalt(blütig), gelassen; abweisend; gleichgültig; F klasse, prima, cool; **2.** Kühle *f*; F (Selbst)Beherrschung *f*; **3.** (sich) abkühlen; ~ ***down***, ~ ***off*** sich beruhigen

**coon** F ZO Waschbär *m*

**coop 1.** Hühnerstall *m*; **2.** ~ ***up***, ~ ***in*** einsperren, einpferchen

**co-op** F Co-op *m*

**co·op·e·rate** zusammenarbeiten; mitwirken, helfen

**co·op·e·ra·tion** Zusammenarbeit *f*; Mitwirkung *f*, Hilfe *f*

**co·op·e·ra·tive 1.** zusammenarbeitend; kooperativ, hilfsbereit; ECON Gemeinschafts..., Genossenschafts...; **2.** *a.* ~ ***society*** Genossenschaft *f*; Co-op *m*, Konsumverein *m*; *a.* ~ ***store*** Co-op *m*, Konsumladen *m*

**co·or·di·nate 1.** koordinieren, aufeinander abstimmen; **2.** koordiniert, gleichgeordnet; **co·or·di·na·tion** Koordinierung *f*, Koordination *f*; harmonisches Zusammenspiel

**cop** F Bulle *m*

**cope:** *~ with* gewachsen sein (*dat*), fertig werden mit

**cop·i·er** Kopiergerät *n*, Kopierer *m*

**co·pi·ous** reich(lich); weitschweifig

**cop·per 1.** MIN Kupfer *n*; Kupfermünze *f*; **2.** kupfern, Kupfer...

**cop·pice, copse** Gehölz *n*

**cop·y 1.** Kopie *f*; Abschrift *f*; Nachbildung *f*; Durchschlag *m*; Exemplar *n*; (*Zeitungs*)Nummer *f*; PRINT Satzvorlage *f*; ***fair ~*** Reinschrift *f*; **2.** kopieren; abschreiben, e-e Kopie anfertigen von; EDP *Daten* übertragen; nachbilden; nachahmen

**cop·y·book** Schreibheft *n*

**cop·y·ing** Kopier...

**cop·y·right** Urheberrecht *n*, Copyright *n*

**cor·al** ZO Koralle *f*

**cord 1.** Schnur *f* (*a.* ELECTR), Strick *m*; Kordsamt *m*; **2.** ver-, zuschnüren

**cor·di·al**[1] Fruchtsaftkonzentrat *n*; MED Stärkungsmittel *n*

**cor·di·al**[2] herzlich

**cor·di·al·i·ty** Herzlichkeit *f*

**cord·less** schnurlos

**cord·less phone** schnurloses Telefon

**cor·don 1.** Kordon *m*, Postenkette *f*; **2.** *~* ***off*** abriegeln, absperren

**cor·du·roy** Kord *m*; (***a pair of***) *~**s*** (e-e) Kordhose

**core 1.** Kerngehäuse *n*; Kern *m*, *fig a. das* Innerste; **2.** entkernen

**core time** ECON Kernzeit *f*

**cork 1.** Kork(en) *m*; **2.** *a.* *~* ***up*** zu-, verkorken; **cork·screw** Korkenzieher *m*

**corn**[1] **1.** Korn *n*, Getreide *n*; *a.* ***Indian ~*** Mais *m*; **2.** pökeln

**corn**[2] MED Hühnerauge *n*

**cor·ner 1.** Ecke *f*; Winkel *m*; *esp* MOT Kurve *f*; *soccer*: Eckball *m*, Ecke *f*; *fig* schwierige Lage, Klemme *f*; **2.** Eck...; **3.** in die Ecke (*fig* Enge) treiben; **~ kick** *soccer*: Eckball *m*, Eckstoß *m*; **~ shop** *Br* Tante-Emma-Laden *m*

**cor·net** MUS Kornett *n*; *Br* GASTR Eistüte *f*

**corn·flakes** Cornflakes *pl*

**cor·nice** ARCH Gesims *n*, Sims *m*

**cor·o·na·ry 1.** ANAT Koronar...; **2.** F MED Herzinfarkt *m*

**cor·o·na·tion** Krönung *f*

**cor·o·net** Adelskrone *f*

**cor·po·ral** MIL Unteroffizier *m*

**cor·po·ral pun·ish·ment** körperliche Züchtigung

**cor·po·rate** gemeinsam; Firmen...

**cor·po·ra·tion** JUR Körperschaft *f*; Stadtverwaltung *f*; ECON (Aktien)Gesellschaft *f*

**corpse** Leichnam *m*, Leiche *f*

**cor·pu·lent** beleibt

**cor·ral 1.** Korral *m*, Hürde *f*, Pferch *m*; **2.** *Vieh* in e-n Pferch treiben

**cor·rect 1.** korrekt, richtig, *a.* genau (*time*); **2.** korrigieren, verbessern, berichtigen

**cor·rec·tion** Korrektur *f*, Verbess(e)rung *f*; Bestrafung *f*

**cor·rect·ness** Richtigkeit *f*

**cor·re·spond** (***with, to***) entsprechen (*dat*), übereinstimmen (mit); korrespondieren (***with*** mit)

**cor·re·spon·dence** Übereinstimmung *f*; Korrespondenz *f*, Briefwechsel *m*; **~ course** Fernkurs *m*

**cor·re·spon·dent 1.** entsprechend; **2.** Briefpartner(in); Korrespondent(in)

**cor·re·spon·ding** entsprechend

**cor·ri·dor** Korridor *m*, Gang *m*

**cor·rob·o·rate** bekräftigen, bestätigen

**cor·rode** zerfressen; CHEM korrodieren; rosten; **cor·ro·sion** CHEM Korrosion *f*; Rost *m*; **cor·ro·sive** CHEM ätzend; *fig* nagend, zersetzend

**cor·ru·gat·ed i·ron** Wellblech *n*

**cor·rupt 1.** korrupt, bestechlich, käuflich; *moralisch* verdorben; **2.** bestechen; *moralisch* verderben

**cor·rupt·i·ble** korrupt, bestechlich, käuflich

**cor·rup·tion** Verdorbenheit *f*; Unredlichkeit *f*; Korruption *f*; Bestechlichkeit *f*; Bestechung *f*

**cor·set** Korsett *n*

**cos·met·ic 1.** kosmetisch, Schönheits...; **2.** kosmetisches Mittel, Schönheitsmittel *n*

**cos·me·ti·cian** Kosmetiker(in)

**cos·mo·naut** Kosmonaut *m*, (Welt-)Raumfahrer *m*

**cos·mo·pol·i·tan 1.** kosmopolitisch; **2.** Weltbürger(in)

C

**cost** **1.** Preis *m*; Kosten *pl*; Schaden *m*; **2.** kosten
**cost·ly** kostspielig; teuer erkauft
**cost of liv·ing** Lebenshaltungskosten *pl*
**cos·tume** Kostüm *n*, Kleidung *f*, Tracht *f*; ~ **jew·el·(le)ry** Modeschmuck *m*
**co·sy** *Br* → ***cozy***
**cot** Feldbett *n*; *Br* Kinderbett *n*
**cot·tage** Cottage *n*, (kleines) Landhaus; Ferienhaus *n*, Ferienhäuschen *n*
**cot·ton** **1.** Baumwolle *f*; Baumwollstoff *m*; (Baumwoll)Garn *n*, (Baumwoll-) Zwirn *m*; (Verband)Watte *f*; **2.** baumwollen, Baumwoll...
**cot·ton·wood** BOT *e-e* amer. Pappel
**cot·ton wool** *Br* (Verband)Watte *f*
**couch** Couch *f*, Sofa *n*; Liege *f*
**cou·chette** RAIL Liegewagenplatz *m*; *a.* ~ ***coach*** Liegewagen *m*
**cou·gar** ZO Puma *m*
**cough** **1.** Husten *m*; **2.** husten
**coun·cil** Rat *m*, Ratsversammlung *f*; ~ **house** *Br* gemeindeeigenes Wohnhaus
**coun·cil·(l)or** Ratsmitglied *n*, Stadtrat *m*, Stadträtin *f*
**coun·sel** **1.** Beratung *f*; Rat(schlag) *m*; *Br* JUR (Rechts)Anwalt *m*; ~ ***for the defense*** (*Br* ***defence***) Verteidiger *m*; ~ ***for the prosecution*** Anklagevertreter *m*; **2.** *j-m* raten; zu *et*. raten; ~***ing center*** (*Br* ~***ing centre***) Beratungsstelle *f*
**coun·sel·(l)or** (*Berufs- etc*)Berater(in); JUR (Rechts)Anwalt *m*
**count**[1] Graf *m*
**count**[2] **1.** Zählung *f*; JUR Anklagepunkt *m*; **2.** *v/t* (ab-, auf-, aus-, nach-, zusammen)zählen; aus-, berechnen; *fig* halten für, betrachten als; *v/i* zählen; gelten; ~ ***ten*** bis zehn zählen; ~ ***down*** *Geld* hinzählen; den Count-down durchführen für, letzte (Start)Vorbereitungen treffen für; ~ ***on*** zählen auf (*acc*), sich verlassen auf (*acc*), sicher rechnen mit
**count·down** Count-down *m*, *n*, letzte (Start)Vorbereitungen *pl*
**coun·te·nance** Gesichtsausdruck *m*; Fassung *f*, Haltung *f*
**count·er**[1] TECH Zähler *m*; *Br* Spielmarke *f*
**coun·ter**[2] Ladentisch *m*; Theke *f*; (Bank-, Post)Schalter *m*
**coun·ter**[3] **1.** (ent)gegen, Gegen...; **2.** entgegentreten (*dat*), entgegnen (*dat*), bekämpfen; abwehren
**coun·ter·act** entgegenwirken (*dat*); neutralisieren
**coun·ter·bal·ance** **1.** Gegengewicht *n*; **2.** ein Gegengewicht bilden zu, ausgleichen
**coun·ter·clock·wise** entgegen dem Uhrzeigersinn
**coun·ter·es·pi·o·nage** Spionageabwehr *f*
**coun·ter·feit** **1.** falsch, gefälscht; **2.** Fälschung *f*; **3.** *Geld, Unterschrift etc* fälschen; ~ **mon·ey** Falschgeld *n*
**coun·ter·foil** Kontrollabschnitt *m*
**coun·ter·mand** *Befehl etc* widerrufen; *Ware* abbestellen
**coun·ter·pane** Tagesdecke *f*
**coun·ter·part** Gegenstück *n*; genaue Entsprechung
**coun·ter·sign** gegenzeichnen
**coun·tess** Gräfin *f*
**count·less** zahllos
**coun·try** **1.** Land *n*, Staat *m*; Gegend *f*, Landschaft *f*; ***in the*** ~ auf dem Lande; **2.** Land..., ländlich
**coun·try·man** Landbewohner *m*; Bauer *m*; *a.* ***fellow*** ~ Landsmann *m*
**coun·try road** Landstraße *f*
**coun·try·side** (ländliche) Gegend; Landschaft *f*
**coun·try·wom·an** Landbewohnerin *f*; Bäuerin *f*; *a.* ***fellow*** ~ Landsmännin *f*
**coun·ty** (Land)Kreis *m*; *Br* Grafschaft *f*; ~ **seat** Kreis(haupt)stadt *f*; ~ **town** *Br* Grafschaftshauptstadt *f*
**coup** Coup *m*; Putsch *m*
**cou·ple** **1.** Paar *n*; ***a*** ~ ***of*** F ein paar; **2.** (zusammen)koppeln; TECH kuppeln; ZO (sich) paaren
**cou·pon** Gutschein *m*; Kupon *m*, Bestellzettel *m*
**cour·age** Mut *m*
**cou·ra·geous** mutig, beherzt
**cou·ri·er** Kurier *m*, Eilbote *m*; Reiseleiter *m*
**course** AVIAT, MAR Kurs *m* (*a. fig*); SPORT (*Renn*)Bahn *f*, (*Renn*)Strecke *f*, (*Golf*)Platz *m*; Verlauf *m*; GASTR Gang *m*; Reihe *f*, Zyklus *m*; Kurs *m*, Lehrgang *m*; ***of*** ~ natürlich, selbstverständlich; ***the*** ~ ***of events*** der Gang der Ereignisse, der Lauf der Dinge
**court** **1.** Hof *m*; kleiner Platz; SPORT

Platz *m*, (Spiel)Feld *n*; JUR Gericht *n*, Gerichtshof *m*; ***go to ~*** JUR prozessieren; ***take s.o. to ~*** JUR gegen j-n prozessieren; j-m den Prozess machen; **2.** *j-m* den Hof machen; werben um

**cour·te·ous** höflich; **cour·te·sy** Höflichkeit *f*; ***by ~ of*** mit freundlicher Genehmigung von (*or gen*)

**court·house** Gerichtsgebäude *n*

**court·ier** Höfling *m*

**court·ly** höfisch; höflich

**court mar·tial** MIL Kriegsgericht *n*

**court-mar·tial** MIL vor ein Kriegsgericht stellen

**court·room** Gerichtssaal *m*

**court·ship** Werben *n*

**court·yard** Hof *m*

**cous·in** Cousin *m*, Vetter *m*; Cousine *f*, Kusine *f*

**cove** kleine Bucht

**cov·er 1.** Decke *f*; Deckel *m*; (Buch)Deckel *m*, Einband *m*; Umschlag *m*; Titelseite *f*; Hülle *f*; Überzug *m*, Bezug *m*; Schutzhaube *f*, Schutzplatte *f*; Abdeckhaube *f*; Briefumschlag *m*; GASTR Gedeck *n*; Deckung *f*; Schutz *m*; *fig* Tarnung *f*; ***take ~*** in Deckung gehen; ***under plain ~*** in neutralem Umschlag; ***under separate ~*** mit getrennter Post; **2.** (be-, zu)decken; einschlagen, einwickeln; verbergen; decken, schützen; ECON (ab)decken; versichern; *Thema* erschöpfend behandeln; *radio*, TV berichten über (*acc*); sich über *e-e Fläche etc* erstrecken; *Strecke* zurücklegen; SPORT *Gegenspieler* decken; *j-n* beschatten; ***~ up*** ab-, zudecken; *fig* verheimlichen, vertuschen; ***~ up for s.o.*** j-n decken

**cov·er·age** Berichterstattung *f* (***of*** über *acc*)

**cov·er girl** Covergirl *n*, Titelblattmädchen *n*

**cov·er·ing** Decke *f*; Überzug *m*; Hülle *f*; (*Fußboden*)Belag *m*

**cov·er sto·ry** Titelgeschichte *f*

**cow**[1] ZO Kuh *f*

**cow**[2] einschüchtern

**cow·ard 1.** feig(e); **2.** Feigling *m*

**cow·ard·ice** Feigheit *f*

**cow·ard·ly** feig(e)

**cow·boy** Cowboy *m*

**cow·er** kauern; sich ducken

**cow·herd** Kuhhirt *m*

**cow·hide** Rind(s)leder *n*

**cow·house** Kuhstall *m*

**cowl** Mönchskutte *f*; Kapuze *f*; TECH Schornsteinkappe *f*

**cow·shed** Kuhstall *m*

**cow·slip** BOT Schlüsselblume *f*; Sumpfdotterblume *f*

**cox, cox·swain** Bootsführer *m*; *rowing*: Steuermann *m*

**coy** schüchtern, scheu

**coy·ote** ZO Kojote *m*, Präriewolf *m*

**co·zy 1.** behaglich, gemütlich; **2.** → ***egg cosy, tea cosy***

**CPU** ABBR *of* ***central processing unit*** EDP Zentraleinheit *f*

**crab** ZO Krabbe *f*, Taschenkrebs *m*

**crack 1.** Knall *m*; Sprung *m*, Riss *m*; Spalt(e *f*) *m*, Ritze *f*; (heftiger) Schlag; **2.** erstklassig; **3.** *v/i* krachen, knallen, knacken; (zer)springen; überschnappen (*voice*); *a.* ***~ up*** zusammenbrechen; F ***~ up*** überschnappen; ***get ~ing*** F loslegen; *v/t* knallen mit (*Peitsche*), knacken mit (*Fingern*); zerbrechen; *Nuss*, F *Kode*, *Safe etc* knacken; ***~ a joke*** e-n Witz reißen; **crack·er** GASTR Cracker *m*, Kräcker *m*; Schwärmer *m*, Knallfrosch *m*, Knallbonbon *m*, *n*

**crack·le** knattern, knistern, prasseln

**cra·dle 1.** Wiege *f*; **2.** wiegen; betten

**craft**[1] Boot(e *pl*) *n*, Schiff(e *pl*) *n*; Flugzeug(e *pl*) *n*; (Welt)Raumfahrzeug(e *pl*) *n*

**craft**[2] Handwerk *n*, Gewerbe *n*; Schlauheit *f*, List *f*

**crafts·man** (Kunst)Handwerker *m*

**craft·y** gerissen, listig, schlau

**crag** Klippe *f*, Felsenspitze *f*

**cram** *v/t* (voll)stopfen; nudeln, mästen; mit *j-m* pauken; *v/i* pauken, büffeln (***for*** für)

**cramp 1.** MED Krampf *m*; TECH Klammer *f*; *fig* Fessel *f*; **2.** einengen, hemmen

**cran·ber·ry** BOT Preiselbeere *f*

**crane**[1] TECH Kran *m*

**crane**[2] **1.** ZO Kranich *m*; **2.** den Hals recken; ***~ one's neck*** sich den Hals verrenken (***for*** nach)

**crank 1.** TECH Kurbel *f*; TECH Schwengel *m*; F Spinner *m*, komischer Kauz; **2.** (an)kurbeln

**crank·shaft** TECH Kurbelwelle *f*

**crank·y** wack(e)lig; verschroben; schlecht gelaunt

C

**cran·ny** Riss *m*, Ritze *f*
**crape** Krepp *m*, Flor *m*
**crash 1.** Krach *m*, Krachen *n*; MOT Unfall *m*, Zusammenstoß *m*; AVIAT Absturz *m*; ECON Zusammenbruch *m*, (Börsen)Krach *m*; **2.** *v/t* zertrümmern; e-n Unfall haben mit; AVIAT abstürzen mit; *v/i* krachend einstürzen, zusammenkrachen; *esp* ECON zusammenbrechen; krachen (***against, into*** gegen); MOT zusammenstoßen, verunglücken; AVIAT abstürzen; **3.** Schnell..., Sofort...; **~ bar·ri·er** MOT Leitplanke *f*; **~ course** Schnell-, Intensivkurs *m*; **~ di·et** radikale Schlankheitskur; **~ hel·met** Sturzhelm *m*
**crash-land** AVIAT e-e Bruchlandung machen (mit); **crash land·ing** AVIAT Bruchlandung *f*
**crate** (Latten)Kiste *f*
**cra·ter** Krater *m*; Trichter *m*
**crave** sich sehnen (***for, after*** nach)
**crav·ing** heftiges Verlangen
**craw·fish** → ***crayfish***
**crawl 1.** Kriechen *n*; **2.** kriechen; krabbeln; kribbeln; wimmeln (***with*** von); *swimming*: kraulen; ***it makes my skin ~*** F mir läuft e-e Gänsehaut über den Rücken
**cray·fish** ZO Flusskrebs *m*
**cray·on** Zeichen-, Buntstift *m*
**craze** Verrücktheit *f*, F Fimmel *m*; ***be the ~*** Mode sein
**cra·zy** verrückt (***about*** nach)
**creak** knarren, quietschen
**cream 1.** GASTR Rahm *m*, Sahne *f*; Creme *f*; *fig* Auslese *f*, Elite *f*; **2.** creme(farben); **cream·y** sahnig; weich
**crease 1.** (Bügel)Falte *f*; **2.** (zer)knittern
**cre·ate** (er)schaffen; hervorrufen; verursachen
**cre·a·tion** Schöpfung *f*
**cre·a·tive** schöpferisch
**cre·a·tor** Schöpfer *m*
**crea·ture** Geschöpf *n*; Kreatur *f*
**crèche** (Kinder)Krippe *f*; (Weihnachts)Krippe *f*
**cre·den·tials** Beglaubigungsschreiben *n*; Referenzen *pl*; Zeugnis *n*; Ausweis *m*, Ausweispapiere *pl*
**cred·i·ble** glaubwürdig
**cred·it 1.** Glaube(n) *m*; Ruf *m*, Ansehen *n*; Verdienst *n*; ECON Kredit *m*; Guthaben *n*; **~ (*side*)** Kredit(seite *f*) *n*, Haben *n*; ***on ~*** auf Kredit; **2.** *j-m* glauben; *j-m* trauen; ECON gutschreiben; ***~ s.o. with s.th.*** j-m et. zutrauen; j-m et. zuschreiben
**cred·i·ta·ble** achtbar, ehrenvoll (***to*** für)
**cred·it card** ECON Kreditkarte *f*
**cred·i·tor** ECON Gläubiger *m*
**cred·its** *film*: Vorspann *m*, Nachspann *m*
**cred·it·wor·thy** ECON kreditwürdig
**cred·u·lous** leichtgläubig
**creed** REL Glaubensbekenntnis *n*
**creek** Bach *m*; *Br* kleine Bucht
**creep** kriechen; schleichen (*a. fig*); **~ *in*** (sich) hinein- *or* hereinschleichen; sich einschleichen (*mistake etc*); ***it makes my flesh ~*** mir läuft e-e Gänsehaut über den Rücken
**creep·er** BOT Kriech-, Kletterpflanze *f*
**creep·y** unheimlich
**cre·mate** verbrennen, einäschern
**cres·cent** Halbmond *m*
**cress** BOT Kresse *f*
**crest** ZO Haube *f*, Büschel *n*; (*Hahnen-*) Kamm *m*; Bergrücken *m*, Kamm *m*; (*Wellen*)Kamm *m*; Federbusch *m*; ***family ~*** Familienwappen *n*
**crest·fal·len** niedergeschlagen
**cre·vasse** GEOL (Gletscher)Spalte *f*
**crev·ice** GEOL Riss *m*, Spalte *f*
**crew** AVIAT, MAR Besatzung *f*, Crew *f*, MAR Mannschaft *f*
**crib 1.** (Futter)Krippe *f*; Kinderbettchen *n*; *esp Br* (Weihnachts)Krippe *f*; F PED Spickzettel *m*; **2.** F abschreiben, spicken
**crick: *a ~ in one's back*** (***neck***) ein steifer Rücken (Hals)
**crick·et**[1] ZO Grille *f*
**crick·et**[2] SPORT Kricket *n*
**crime** JUR Verbrechen *n*; *coll* Verbrechen *pl*; **~ nov·el** Kriminalroman *m*
**crim·i·nal 1.** kriminell; Kriminal..., Straf...; **2.** Verbrecher(in), Kriminelle *m, f*
**crimp** kräuseln
**crim·son** karmesinrot; puterrot
**cringe** sich ducken
**crin·kle 1.** Falte *f*, Fältchen *n*; **2.** (sich) kräuseln; knittern
**crip·ple 1.** Krüppel *m*; **2.** zum Krüppel machen; *fig* lähmen
**cri·sis** Krise *f*

**crisp** knusp(e)rig, mürbe; frisch, knackig (*vegetable*); scharf, frisch (*air*); kraus (*hair*)
**crisp·bread** Knäckebrot *n*
**crisps** *a.* ***potato*** ~ *Br* (Kartoffel)Chips *pl*
**criss-cross 1.** Netz *n* sich schneidender Linien; **2.** kreuz und quer ziehen durch; kreuz und quer (ver)laufen
**cri·te·ri·on** Kriterium *n*
**crit·ic** Kritiker(in)
**crit·i·cal** kritisch; bedenklich
**crit·i·cis·m** Kritik *f* (***of*** an *dat*)
**crit·i·cize** kritisieren; kritisch beurteilen; tadeln
**cri·tique** Kritik *f*, Besprechung *f*, Rezension *f*
**croak** ZO krächzen; quaken (*both a. fig*)
**cro·chet 1.** Häkelei *f*; Häkelarbeit *f*; **2.** häkeln
**crock·e·ry** Geschirr *n*
**croc·o·dile** ZO Krokodil *n*
**cro·ny** F alter Freund
**crook 1.** Krümmung *f*; Hirtenstab *m*; F Gauner *m*; **2.** (sich) krümmen *or* biegen; **crook·ed** gekrümmt, krumm; F unehrlich, betrügerisch
**croon** schmachtend singen; summen
**croon·er** Schnulzensänger(in)
**crop 1.** AGR (Feld)Frucht *f*; Ernte *f*; ZO Kropf *m*; kurzer Haarschnitt; kurz geschnittenes Haar; **2.** ZO abfressen, abweiden; *Haar* kurz schneiden; ~ ***up*** *fig* plötzlich auftauchen
**cross 1.** Kreuz *n* (*a. fig*); BIOL Kreuzung *f*; *soccer*: Flanke *f*; **2.** böse, ärgerlich; **3.** (sich) kreuzen; *Straße* überqueren; *Plan etc* durchkreuzen; BIOL kreuzen; ~ ***off***, ~ ***out*** ausstreichen, durchstreichen; ~ ***o.s.*** sich bekreuzigen; ~ ***one's arms*** die Arme verschränken; ~ ***one's legs*** die Beine übereinander schlagen; ***keep one's fingers*** ~***ed*** den Daumen drücken
**cross·bar** SPORT Tor-, Querlatte *f*
**cross·breed** Mischling *m*, Kreuzung *f*
**cross-coun·try** Querfeldein..., Gelände...; ~ ***skiing*** Skilanglauf *m*
**cross-ex·am·i·na·tion** JUR Kreuzverhör *n*; **cross-ex·am·ine** JUR ins Kreuzverhör nehmen
**cross-eyed:** ***be*** ~ schielen
**cross·ing** (*Straßen- etc*)Kreuzung *f*; Straßenübergang *m*; *Br* Fußgängerüberweg *m*; MAR Überfahrt *f*
**cross·road** Querstraße *f*
**cross·roads** (Straßen)Kreuzung *f*; *fig* Scheideweg *m*
**cross-sec·tion** Querschnitt *m*
**cross·walk** Fußgängerüberweg *m*
**cross·wise** kreuzweise
**cross·word (puz·zle)** Kreuzworträtsel *n*
**crotch** ANAT Schritt *m*
**crotch·et** MUS *Br* Viertelnote *f*
**crouch 1.** sich ducken; **2.** Hockstellung *f*
**crow 1.** ZO Krähe *f*; Krähen *n*; **2.** krähen
**crow·bar** TECH Brecheisen *n*
**crowd 1.** (Menschen)Menge *f*; Masse *f*; Haufen *m*; **2.** sich drängen; *Straßen etc* bevölkern; voll stopfen
**crowd·ed** überfüllt, voll
**crown 1.** Krone *f*; **2.** krönen; *Zahn* überkronen; ***to*** ~ ***it all*** zu allem Überfluss
**cru·cial** entscheidend, kritisch
**cru·ci·fix** REL Kruzifix *n*
**cru·ci·fix·ion** REL Kreuzigung *f*
**cru·ci·fy** REL kreuzigen
**crude** roh, unbearbeitet; *fig* roh, grob
**crude (oil)** Rohöl *n*
**cru·el** grausam; roh, gefühllos
**cru·el·ty** Grausamkeit *f*; ~ ***to animals*** Tierquälerei *f*; ***society for the prevention of*** ~ ***to animals*** Tierschutzverein *m*; ~ ***to children*** Kindesmisshandlung *f*
**cru·et** Essig-, Ölfläschchen *n*
**cruise 1.** Kreuzfahrt *f*, Seereise *f*; **2.** kreuzen, e-e Kreuzfahrt *or* Seereise machen; AVIAT, MOT mit Reisegeschwindigkeit fliegen *or* fahren; ~ **mis·sile** MIL Marschflugkörper *m*
**cruis·er** Kreuzfahrtschiff *n*; MIL MAR Kreuzer *m*; (Funk)Streifenwagen *m*
**crumb** Krume *f*, Krümel *m*
**crum·ble** zerkrümeln, zerbröckeln
**crum·ple** *v/t* zerknittern; *v/i* knittern; zusammengedrückt werden; ~ **zone** MOT Knautschzone *f*
**crunch** geräuschvoll (zer)kauen; knirschen
**cru·sade** HIST Kreuzzug *m* (*a. fig*)
**crush 1.** Gedränge *n*; ***have a*** ~ ***on s.o.*** für j-n schwärmen, F in j-n verknallt sein; **2.** *v/t* zerquetschen, zermalmen, zerdrücken; TECH zerkleinern, zermahlen; auspressen; *fig* nieder-, zerschmet-

tern, vernichten; *v/i* sich drängen; ~ **bar·ri·er** Barriere *f*, Absperrung *f*
**crust** (Brot)Kruste *f*, (Brot)Rinde *f*
**crus·ta·cean** ZO Krebs-, Krusten-, Schalentier *n*
**crust·y** krustig
**crutch** Krücke *f*
**cry 1.** Schrei *m*, Ruf *m*; Geschrei *n*; Weinen *n*; **2.** schreien, rufen (***for*** nach); weinen; heulen, jammern
**crypt** Gruft *f*, Krypta *f*
**crys·tal** Kristall *m*; Uhrglas *n*
**crys·tal·line** kristallen
**crys·tal·lize** kristallisieren
**cub** ZO Junge *n*
**cube** Würfel *m* (*a.* MATH); PHOT Blitzwürfel *m*; MATH Kubikzahl *f*
**cube root** MATH Kubikwurzel *f*
**cu·bic, cu·bi·cal** würfelförmig; kubisch; Kubik...
**cu·bi·cle** Kabine *f*
**cuck·oo** ZO Kuckuck *m*
**cu·cum·ber** BOT Gurke *f*; (***as***) ***cool as a*** ~ F eiskalt, kühl und gelassen
**cud** AGR wiedergekäutes Futter; ***chew the*** ~ wiederkäuen; *fig* überlegen
**cud·dle** *v/t* an sich drücken; schmusen mit; *v/i*: ~ ***up*** sich kuscheln *or* schmiegen (***to*** an *acc*)
**cud·gel 1.** Knüppel *m*; **2.** prügeln
**cue**[1] THEA *etc* Stichwort *n* (*a. fig*); *fig* Wink *m*
**cue**[2] *billiards*: Queue *n*
**cuff**[1] Manschette *f*; (Hosen-, *Br* Ärmel-) Aufschlag *m*
**cuff**[2] **1.** Klaps *m*; **2.** *j-m* e-n Klaps geben
**cuff link** Manschettenknopf *m*
**cui·sine** GASTR Küche *f*
**cul·mi·nate** gipfeln (***in*** in *dat*)
**cu·lottes** (***a pair of*** ein) Hosenrock
**cul·prit** Schuldige *m, f*, Täter(in)
**cul·ti·vate** AGR anbauen, bebauen; kultivieren; *Freundschaft etc* pflegen
**cul·ti·vat·ed** AGR bebaut; *fig* gebildet, kultiviert
**cul·ti·va·tion** AGR Kultivierung *f*, Anbau *m*; *fig* Pflege *f*
**cul·tu·ral** kulturell; Kultur...
**cul·ture** Kultur *f* (*a.* BIOL); ZO Zucht *f*
**cul·tured** kultiviert; gezüchtet, Zucht...
**cum·ber·some** lästig, hinderlich; klobig
**cu·mu·la·tive** sich (an)häufend, anwachsend; Zusatz...
**cun·ning 1.** schlau, listig; **2.** List *f*, Schlauheit *f*
**cup 1.** Tasse *f*; Becher *m*; Schale *f*; Kelch *m*; SPORT Cup *m*, Pokal *m*; **2.** *die Hand* hohl machen; ***she ~ped her chin in her hand*** sie stützte das Kinn in die Hand
**cup·board** (Geschirr-, Speise-, *Br a.* Wäsche-, Kleider)Schrank *m*
**cup·board bed** Schrankbett *n*
**cup fi·nal** SPORT Pokalendspiel *n*
**cu·po·la** ARCH Kuppel *f*
**cup tie** SPORT Pokalspiel *n*
**cup win·ner** SPORT Pokalsieger *m*
**cur** Köter *m*; Schurke *m*
**cu·ra·ble** MED heilbar
**cu·rate** REL Hilfsgeistliche *m*
**cu·ra·tive** heilkräftig; ~ ***power*** Heilkraft *f*
**curb 1.** Kandare *f* (*a. fig*); Bordstein *m*; **2.** an die Kandare legen (*a. fig*); *fig* zügeln
**curd** *a. pl* Dickmilch *f*, Quark *m*
**cur·dle** *v/t Milch* gerinnen lassen; *v/i* gerinnen, dick werden; ***the sight made my blood*** ~ bei dem Anblick erstarrte mir das Blut in den Adern
**cure 1.** MED Kur *f*; (Heil)Mittel *n*; Heilung *f*; **2.** MED heilen; GASTR pökeln; räuchern; trocknen
**cur·few** MIL Ausgangsverbot *n*, -sperre *f*
**cu·ri·o** Rarität *f*
**cu·ri·os·i·ty** Neugier *f*; Rarität *f*
**cu·ri·ous** neugierig; wissbegierig; seltsam, merkwürdig
**curl 1.** Locke *f*; **2.** (sich) kräuseln *or* locken; **curl·er** Lockenwickler *m*; **curl·y** gekräuselt; gelockt, lockig
**cur·rant** BOT Johannisbeere *f*; GASTR Korinthe *f*
**cur·ren·cy** ECON Währung *f*; ***foreign*** ~ Devisen *pl*
**cur·rent 1.** laufend; gegenwärtig, aktuell; üblich, gebräuchlich; ~ ***events*** Tagesereignisse *pl*; **2.** Strömung *f*, Strom *m* (*both a. fig*); ELECTR Strom *m*; ~ **ac·count** *Br* ECON Girokonto *n*
**cur·ric·u·lum** Lehr-, Stundenplan *m*; ~ **vi·tae** Lebenslauf *m*
**cur·ry**[1] GASTR Curry *m, n*
**cur·ry**[2] *Pferd* striegeln
**curse 1.** Fluch *m*, Verwünschung *f*; **2.** (ver)fluchen, verwünschen
**curs·ed** verflucht
**cur·sor** EDP Cursor *m*

**cur·so·ry** flüchtig, oberflächlich
**curt** knapp; barsch, schroff
**cur·tail** *Ausgaben etc* kürzen; *Rechte* beschneiden
**cur·tain 1.** Vorhang *m*, Gardine *f*; ***draw the ~s*** die Vorhänge auf- *or* zuziehen; **2.** ***~ off*** mit Vorhängen abteilen
**curt·s(e)y 1.** Knicks *m*; **2.** knicksen (***to*** vor *dat*)
**cur·va·ture** Krümmung *f*
**curve 1.** Kurve *f*; Krümmung *f*, Biegung *f*; **2.** (sich) krümmen *or* biegen
**cush·ion 1.** Kissen *n*, Polster *n*; **2.** polstern; *Stoß etc* dämpfen
**cuss 1.** Fluch *m*; **2.** (ver)fluchen
**cus·tard** Eiercreme *f*, Vanillesoße *f*
**cus·to·dy** JUR Haft *f*; Sorgerecht *n*
**cus·tom** Brauch *m*, Gewohnheit *f*; ECON Kundschaft *f*
**cus·tom·a·ry** üblich
**cus·tom-built** nach Kundenangaben gefertigt
**cus·tom·er** Kunde *m*, Kundin *f*, Auftraggeber(in)
**cus·tom house** Zollamt *n*
**cus·tom-made** maßgefertigt, Maß...
**cus·toms** Zoll *m*; **~ clear·ance** Zollabfertigung *f*; **~ of·fi·cer, ~ of·fi·cial** Zollbeamte *m*
**cut 1.** Schnitt *m*; MED Schnittwunde *f*; GASTR Schnitte *f*, Stück *n*; (Zu)Schnitt *m* (*clothes*); TECH Schnitt *m*, Schliff *m*; Haarschnitt *m*; *fig* Kürzung *f*, Senkung *f*; *cards*: Abheben *n*; **2.** schneiden; ab-, an-, auf-, aus-, be-, durch-, zer-, zuschneiden; *Edelstein etc* schleifen; *Gras* mähen, *Bäume* fällen, *Holz* hacken; MOT *Kurve* schneiden; *Löhne etc* kürzen; *Preise* herabsetzen, senken; *Karten* abheben; ***~ one's teeth*** Zähne bekommen, zahnen; ***~ s.o.*** (***dead***) *fig* F j-n schneiden; ***~ s.o.*** *or* ***s.th. short*** j-n *or* et. unterbrechen, j-m ins Wort fallen; ***~ across*** quer durch ... gehen; ***~ back*** *Pflanze* beschneiden, stutzen; einschränken; ***~ down*** *Bäume* fällen; verringern, einschränken, reduzieren; ***~ in*** F sich einmischen, unterbrechen; ***~ in on s.o.*** MOT j-n schneiden; ***~ off*** abschneiden; unterbrechen, trennen; *Strom etc* sperren; ***~ out*** (her)ausschneiden; *Kleid etc* zuschneiden; ***be ~ out for*** wie geschaffen sein für; ***~ up*** zerschneiden
**cut·back** Kürzung *f*
**cute** F schlau; niedlich, süß
**cu·ti·cle** Nagelhaut *f*
**cut·le·ry** (Ess)Besteck *n*
**cut·let** GASTR Kotelett *n*; (*Kalbs-, Schweine*)Schnitzel *n*; Hacksteak *n*
**cut·off date** Stichtag *m*
**cut-price, cut-rate** ECON herabgesetzt, ermäßigt; Billig...
**cut·ter** Zuschneider *m*; (*Glas-, Diamant*)Schleifer *m*; Schneidemaschine *f*, -werkzeug *n*; *film*: Cutter(in); MAR Kutter *m*
**cut·throat 1.** Mörder *m*; Killer *m*; **2.** mörderisch
**cut·ting 1.** schneidend; scharf; TECH Schneid(e)..., Fräs...; **2.** Schneiden *n*; BOT Steckling *m*; *esp Br* Ausschnitt *m*
**cut·tings** Schnipsel *pl*; Späne *pl*
**cut·ting torch** TECH Schneidbrenner *m*
**Cy·ber·space** → ***virtual reality***
**cy·cle**[1] Zyklus *m*; Kreis(lauf) *m*
**cy·cle**[2] **1.** Fahrrad *n*; **2.** Rad fahren
**cy·cle| path, ~ track** (Fahr)Radweg *m*
**cy·cling** Radfahren *n*
**cy·clist** Radfahrer(in); Motorradfahrer(in)
**cy·clone** Wirbelsturm *m*
**cyl·in·der** Zylinder *m*, TECH *a.* Walze *f*, Trommel *f*
**cyn·ic** Zyniker(in); **cyn·i·cal** zynisch; **cyn·i·cism** Zynismus *m*
**cy·press** BOT Zypresse *f*
**cyst** MED Zyste *f*
**czar** → ***tsar***
**Czech 1.** tschechisch; ***~ Republic*** Tschechien *n*, Tschechische Republik; **2.** Tscheche *m*, Tschechin *f*; LING Tschechisch *n*

# D



**D, d** D, d *n*
**d** ABBR *of* ***died*** gest., gestorben
**dab 1.** Klecks *m*, Spritzer *m*; **2.** betupfen, abtupfen
**dab·ble** bespritzen; ***~ at, ~ in*** sich oberflächlich *or contp* in dilettantischer Weise beschäftigen mit
**dachs·hund** ZO Dackel *m*
**dad** F, **dad·dy** F Papa *m*, Vati *m*
**dad·dy long·legs** ZO Schnake *f*; Weberknecht *m*
**daf·fo·dil** BOT gelbe Narzisse
**dag·ger** Dolch *m*; ***be at ~s drawn*** *fig* auf Kriegsfuß stehen (***with*** mit)
**dai·ly 1.** täglich; ***the ~ grind*** *or* ***rut*** das tägliche Einerlei; **2.** Tageszeitung *f*; Putzfrau *f*
**dain·ty 1.** zierlich, reizend; wählerisch; **2.** Leckerbissen *m*
**dair·y** Molkerei *f*; Milchwirtschaft *f*; Milchgeschäft *n*
**dai·sy** BOT Gänseblümchen *n*
**dal·ly:** ***~ about*** herumtrödeln
**dam 1.** (Stau)Damm *m*; **2.** *a.* ***~ up*** stauen, eindämmen
**dam·age 1.** Schaden *m*, (Be)Schädigung *f*; *pl* JUR Schadenersatz *m*; **2.** (be)schädigen
**dam·ask** Damast *m*
**damn 1.** verdammen; verurteilen; ***~ (it)!*** F verflucht!, verdammt!; **2.** *adj and adv* F → ***damned***; **3.** ***I don't care a ~*** F das ist mir völlig gleich(gültig) *or* egal
**dam·na·tion** Verdammung *f*; REL Verdammnis *f*
**damned** F verdammt
**damn·ing** vernichtend, belastend
**damp 1.** feucht, klamm; **2.** Feuchtigkeit *f*; **3.** *a.* **damp·en** an-, befeuchten; dämpfen; **damp·ness** Feuchtigkeit *f*
**dance 1.** Tanz *m*; Tanzveranstaltung *f*; **2.** tanzen
**danc·er** Tänzer(in)
**danc·ing 1.** Tanzen *n*; **2.** Tanz...
**dan·de·li·on** BOT Löwenzahn *m*
**dan·druff** (Kopf)Schuppen *pl*
**Dane** Däne *m*, Dänin *f*
**dan·ger** Gefahr *f*; ***be out of ~*** außer Lebensgefahr sein; ***~*** **ar·e·a** Gefahrenzone *f*, Gefahrenbereich *m*
**dan·ger·ous** gefährlich
**dan·ger zone** → ***danger area***
**dan·gle** baumeln (lassen)
**Da·nish 1.** dänisch; **2.** LING Dänisch *n*
**dank** feucht, nass(kalt)
**dare** *v/i* es wagen, sich (ge)trauen; ***I ~ say*** ich glaube wohl; allerdings; ***how ~ you!*** was fällt dir ein!; untersteh dich!; *v/t et.* wagen
**dare·dev·il** Draufgänger *m*
**dar·ing 1.** kühn, verwegen, waghalsig; **2.** Mut *m*, Kühnheit *f*, Verwegenheit *f*
**dark 1.** dunkel; finster; *fig* düster, trüb(e); geheim(nisvoll); **2.** Dunkel *n*, Dunkelheit *f*; ***before (at, after) ~*** vor (bei, nach) Einbruch der Dunkelheit; ***keep s.o. in the ~ about s.th.*** j-n über et. im Ungewissen lassen
**Dark Ag·es** *das* frühe Mittelalter
**dark·en** (sich) verdunkeln *or* verfinstern
**dark·ness** Dunkelheit *f*, Finsternis *f*
**dark·room** PHOT Dunkelkammer *f*
**dar·ling 1.** Liebling *m*; **2.** lieb; F goldig
**darn** stopfen, ausbessern
**dart 1.** Wurfpfeil *m*; Sprung *m*, Satz *m*; ***~s*** Darts *n*; **2.** *v/t* werfen, schleudern; *v/i* schießen, stürzen
**dart·board** Dartsscheibe *f*
**dash 1.** Schlag *m*; Klatschen *n*; GASTR Prise *f* (*of salt*), Schuss *m* (*of rum etc*), Spritzer *m* (*of lemon etc*); Gedankenstrich *m*; SPORT Sprint *m*; *fig* Anflug *m*; ***a ~ of blue*** ein Stich ins Blaue; ***make a ~ for*** losstürzen auf (*acc*); **2.** *v/t* schleudern, schmettern; *Hoffnung etc* zerstören, zunichte machen; *v/i* stürmen; ***~ off*** davonstürzen
**dash·board** MOT Armaturenbrett *n*
**dash·ing** schneidig, forsch
**da·ta** Daten *pl* (*a.* EDP), Angaben *pl*; ~ **bank, ~·base** EDP Datenbank *f*; ~ **cap·ture** Datenerfassung *f*; ~ **car·ri·er** Datenträger *m*; ~ **in·put** Dateneingabe *f*; ~ **me·di·um** Datenträger *m*; ~ **mem·o·ry** Datenspeicher *m*; ~ **out·put** Datenausgabe *f*; ~ **pro·cess·ing** Datenverarbeitung *f*; ~ **pro·tec·tion** JUR Datenschutz *m*; ~ **stor·age** Da-

tenspeicher *m*; ~ **trans·fer** Datenübertragung *f*
**date¹** BOT Dattel *f*
**date²** Datum *n*; Zeit *f*, Zeitpunkt *m*; Termin *m*; Verabredung *f*; F (Verabredungs)Partner(in); ***out of*** ~ veraltet, unmodern; ***up to*** ~ zeitgemäß, modern, auf dem Laufenden; **2.** datieren; F sich verabreden mit, (aus)gehen mit
**dat·ed** veraltet, überholt
**da·tive** *a.* ~ ***case*** LING Dativ *m*, dritter Fall
**daub** (be)schmieren
**daugh·ter** Tochter *f*
**daugh·ter-in-law** Schwiegertochter *f*
**daunt** entmutigen
**dav·en·port** Sofa *n*
**daw** zo Dohle *f*
**daw·dle** F (herum)trödeln
**dawn 1.** (Morgen)Dämmerung *f*; ***at*** ~ bei Tagesanbruch; **2.** dämmern; ~ ***on*** *fig j-m* dämmern
**day** Tag *m*; *often pl* (Lebens)Zeit *f*; ***any*** ~ jederzeit; ***these*** ~***s*** heutzutage; ***the other*** ~ neulich; ***the*** ~ ***after tomorrow*** übermorgen; ***the*** ~ ***before yesterday*** vorgestern; ***open all*** ~ durchgehend geöffnet; ***let's call it a*** ~***!*** machen wir Schluss für heute!, Feierabend!
**day·break** Tagesanbruch *m*
**day care cen·ter** (*Br* **cen·tre**) → ***day nursery***
**day·dream 1.** Tag-, Wachtraum *m*; **2.** (mit offenen Augen) träumen
**day·dream·er** Träumer(in)
**day·light** Tageslicht *n*; ***in broad*** ~ am helllichten Tag
**day nur·se·ry** (Kinder)Tagesstätte *f*
**day off** freier Tag
**day re·turn** *Br* Tagesrückfahrkarte *f*
**day·time:** ***in the*** ~ am Tag, bei Tage
**daze 1.** blenden; betäuben; **2.** ***in a*** ~ benommen, betäubt
**dead 1.** tot; unempfindlich (***to*** für); matt; blind (*window etc*); erloschen; ECON flau; tot (*capital etc*); völlig, total; ~ ***stop*** völliger Stillstand; ***drop*** ~ tot umfallen; **2.** *adv* völlig, total; plötzlich, abrupt; genau, direkt; ~ ***slow*** MOT Schritt fahren!; ~ ***tired*** todmüde; **3.** ***the*** ~ die Toten *pl*; ***in the*** ~ ***of winter*** im tiefsten Winter; ***in the*** ~ ***of night*** mitten in der Nacht
**dead·en** abstumpfen; (ab)schwächen; dämpfen
**dead end** Sackgasse *f* (*a. fig*)
**dead heat** SPORT totes Rennen
**dead·line** letzter (Ablieferungs)Termin; Stichtag *m*
**dead·lock** *fig* toter Punkt
**dead·locked** *fig* festgefahren
**dead loss** Totalverlust *m*; F ***he's a*** ~ er ist e-e Niete
**dead·ly** tödlich
**deaf 1.** taub; **2.** ***the*** ~ die Tauben *pl*
**deaf-and-dumb** taubstumm
**deaf·en** taub machen; betäuben
**deaf-mute** Taubstumme *m, f*
**deal 1.** F Geschäft *n*, Handel *m*; Menge *f*; ***it's a*** ~***!*** abgemacht!; ***a good*** ~ ziemlich viel; ***a great*** ~ sehr viel; **2.** *v/t* (aus-, ver-, zu)teilen; *j-m Karten* geben; *j-m e-n Schlag* versetzen; *v/i* handeln (***in*** mit *e-r Ware*); *sl* dealen; *cards*: geben; ~ ***with*** sich befassen mit, behandeln; ECON Handel treiben mit, Geschäfte machen mit; **deal·er** ECON Händler(in); *cards*: Geber(in); *sl* Dealer *m*;
**deal·ing** *mst pl* Umgang *m*, Beziehungen *pl*
**dean** REL, UNIV Dekan *m*
**dear 1.** teuer; lieb; ***Dear Sir*** Sehr geehrter Herr ...; **2.** Liebste *m, f*, Schatz *m*; ***my*** ~ m-e Liebe, mein Lieber; **3.** *int* (***oh***) ~***!***, ~ ~***!***, ~ ***me!*** F du liebe Zeit!, ach herrje!; **dear·est** sehnlichst; **dear·ly** innig, von ganzem Herzen; ECON teuer
**death** Tod *m*; Todesfall *m*
**death·bed** Sterbebett *n*
**death cer·tif·i·cate** Totenschein *m*
**death·ly** tödlich; ~ ***still*** totenstill
**death war·rant** JUR Hinrichtungsbefehl *m*; *fig* Todesurteil *n*
**de·bar:** ~ ***s.o. from*** j-n ausschließen aus
**de·base** erniedrigen; mindern
**de·ba·ta·ble** umstritten
**de·bate 1.** Debatte *f*, Diskussion *f*; **2.** debattieren, diskutieren
**deb·it** ECON **1.** Soll *n*; (Konto)Belastung *f*; ~ ***and credit*** Soll und Haben *n*; **2.** *j-n, ein Konto* belasten
**deb·ris** Trümmer *pl*, Schutt *m*
**debt** Schuld *f*; ***be in*** ~ Schulden haben, verschuldet sein; ***be out of*** ~ schuldenfrei sein; ***get into*** ~ sich verschulden, Schulden machen
**debt·or** Schuldner(in)
**de·bug** TECH, EDP Fehler beseitigen
**de·but** Debüt *n*

D

**Dec** ABBR *of* ***December*** Dez., Dezember *m*
**dec·ade** Jahrzehnt *n*
**dec·a·dent** dekadent
**de·caf·fein·at·ed** koffeinfrei
**de·camp** F verschwinden
**de·cant** abgießen; umfüllen
**de·cant·er** Karaffe *f*
**de·cath·lete** SPORT Zehnkämpfer *m*
**de·cath·lon** SPORT Zehnkampf *m*
**de·cay 1.** zerfallen; verfaulen; kariös *or* schlecht werden (*tooth*); **2.** Zerfall *m*; Verfaulen *n*
**de·cease** *esp* JUR Tod *m*, Ableben *n*
**de·ceased** *esp* JUR **1.** ***the*** ~ der *or* die Verstorbene; die Verstorbenen *pl*; **2.** verstorben
**de·ceit** Betrug *m*; Täuschung *f*
**de·ceit·ful** betrügerisch
**de·ceive** betrügen; täuschen
**de·ceiv·er** Betrüger(in)
**De·cem·ber** (ABBR ***Dec***) Dezember *m*
**de·cen·cy** Anstand *m*
**de·cent** anständig; F annehmbar, (ganz) anständig; F nett
**de·cep·tion** Täuschung *f*
**de·cep·tive** trügerisch; ***be*** ~ täuschen, trügen
**de·cide** (sich) entscheiden; bestimmen; beschließen, sich entschließen
**de·cid·ed** entschieden; bestimmt; entschlossen
**dec·i·mal** MATH **1.** *a.* ~ ***fraction*** Dezimalbruch *m*; **2.** Dezimal...
**de·ci·pher** entziffern
**de·ci·sion** Entscheidung *f*; Entschluss *m*; Entschlossenheit *f*; ***make a*** ~ e-e Entscheidung treffen; ***reach*** *or* ***come to a*** ~ zu e-m Entschluss kommen
**de·ci·sive** entscheidend; ausschlaggebend; entschieden
**deck 1.** MAR Deck *n*; Spiel *n*, Pack *m* (Spiel)Karten; **2.** ~ ***out*** schmücken
**deck·chair** Liegestuhl *m*
**dec·la·ra·tion** Erklärung *f*; Zollerklärung *f*; **de·clare** erklären; deklarieren, verzollen
**de·clen·sion** LING Deklination *f*
**de·cline 1.** abnehmen, zurückgehen; fallen; verfallen; (höflich) ablehnen; LING deklinieren; **2.** Abnahme *f*, Rückgang *m*, Verfall *m*
**de·cliv·i·ty** (Ab)Hang *m*
**de·clutch** MOT auskuppeln
**de·code** entschlüsseln
**de·com·pose** zerlegen; (sich) zersetzen; verwesen
**de·con·tam·i·nate** entgasen, entgiften, entseuchen, entstrahlen
**de·con·tam·i·na·tion** Entseuchung *f*
**dec·o·rate** verzieren, schmücken; tapezieren; (an)streichen; dekorieren
**dec·o·ra·tion** Verzierung *f*, Schmuck *m*, Dekoration *f*; Orden *m*
**dec·o·ra·tive** dekorativ; Zier...
**dec·o·ra·tor** Dekorateur *m*; Maler *m* und Tapezierer *m*
**dec·o·rous** anständig
**de·co·rum** Anstand *m*
**de·coy 1.** Lockvogel *m* (*a. fig*); Köder *m* (*a. fig*); **2.** ködern; locken (***into*** in *acc*); verleiten (***into*** zu)
**de·crease 1.** Abnahme *f*; **2.** abnehmen; (sich) vermindern
**de·cree 1.** Dekret *n*, Erlass *m*, Verfügung *f*; *esp* JUR Entscheid *m*, Urteil *n*; **2.** verfügen
**ded·i·cate** widmen
**ded·i·cat·ed** engagiert
**ded·i·ca·tion** Widmung *f*; Hingabe *f*
**de·duce** ableiten; folgern
**de·duct** *Betrag* abziehen (***from*** von); **de·duct·i·ble:** ***tax***-~ steuerlich absetzbar; **de·duc·tion** Abzug *m*; (Schluss)Folgerung *f*, Schluss *m*
**deed** Tat *f*; Heldentat *f*; JUR (Übertragungs)Urkunde *f*
**deep 1.** tief (*a. fig*); **2.** Tiefe *f*
**deep·en** (sich) vertiefen, *fig a.* (sich) verstärken
**deep freeze 1.** tiefkühlen, einfrieren; **2.** Tiefkühl-, Gefriertruhe *f*
**deep-fro·zen** tiefgefroren
**deep fry** frittieren
**deep·ness** Tiefe *f*
**deer** ZO Hirsch *m*; Reh *n*
**de·face** entstellen; unleserlich machen; ausstreichen
**def·a·ma·tion** Verleumdung *f*
**de·fault 1.** JUR Nichterscheinen *n* vor Gericht; SPORT Nichtantreten *n*; ECON Verzug *m*; **2.** s-n Verpflichtungen nicht nachkommen, ECON *a.* im Verzug sein; JUR nicht vor Gericht erscheinen; SPORT nicht antreten
**de·feat 1.** Niederlage *f*; **2.** besiegen, schlagen; vereiteln, zunichte machen
**de·fect** Defekt *m*, Fehler *m*; Mangel *m*

**de·fec·tive** mangelhaft; schadhaft, defekt
**de·fence** *Br* → ***defense***
**de·fence·less** *Br* → ***defenseless***
**de·fend** (***from, against***) verteidigen (gegen), schützen (vor *dat*, gegen)
**de·fen·dant** Angeklagte *m, f*; Beklagte *m, f*
**de·fend·er** Verteidiger(in); SPORT Abwehrspieler(in)
**de·fense** Verteidigung *f* (*a.* MIL, JUR, SPORT), Schutz *m*; SPORT Abwehr *f*; ***witness for the ~*** Entlastungszeuge *m*
**de·fense·less** schutzlos, wehrlos
**de·fen·sive 1.** Defensive *f*, Verteidigung *f*, Abwehr *f*; **2.** defensiv; Verteidigungs..., Abwehr...
**de·fer** aufschieben, verschieben
**de·fi·ance** Herausforderung *f*; Trotz *m*
**de·fi·ant** herausfordernd; trotzig
**de·fi·cien·cy** Unzulänglichkeit *f*; Mangel *m*
**de·fi·cient** mangelhaft, unzureichend
**def·i·cit** ECON Defizit *n*, Fehlbetrag *m*
**de·file** beschmutzen
**de·fine** definieren; erklären, bestimmen
**def·i·nite** bestimmt; endgültig, definitiv
**def·i·ni·tion** Definition *f*, Bestimmung *f*, Erklärung *f*
**de·fin·i·tive** endgültig, definitiv
**de·flect** *v/t* ablenken; *Ball* abfälschen; *v/i* abweichen
**de·form** entstellen, verunstalten
**de·formed** deformiert, verunstaltet; verwachsen
**de·for·mi·ty** Missbildung *f*
**de·fraud** betrügen (***of*** um)
**de·frost** *v/t Windschutzscheibe etc* entfrosten; *Kühlschrank etc* abtauen, *Tiefkühlkost etc* auftauen; *v/i* ab-, auftauen
**deft** geschickt, gewandt
**de·fy** herausfordern; trotzen (*dat*)
**de·gen·e·rate 1.** entarten; **2.** entartet
**deg·ra·da·tion** Erniedrigung *f*
**de·grade** erniedrigen, demütigen
**de·gree** Grad *m*; Stufe *f*; (akademischer) Grad; ***by ~s*** allmählich; ***take one's ~*** e-n akademischen Grad erwerben, promovieren
**de·hy·drate** austrocknen; TECH das Wasser entziehen (*dat*)
**de·i·fy** vergöttern; vergöttlichen
**deign** sich herablassen
**de·i·ty** Gottheit *f*
**de·jec·ted** niedergeschlagen, mutlos, deprimiert
**de·jec·tion** Niedergeschlagenheit *f*
**de·lay 1.** Aufschub *m*; Verzögerung *f*; RAIL *etc* Verspätung *f*; **2.** ver-, aufschieben; verzögern; aufhalten; ***be ~ed*** sich verzögern; RAIL *etc* Verspätung haben
**del·e·gate 1.** abordnen, delegieren; *Vollmachten etc* übertragen; **2.** Delegierte *m, f*, bevollmächtigter Vertreter
**del·e·ga·tion** Übertragung *f*; Abordnung *f*, Delegation *f*
**de·lete** (aus)streichen; EDP löschen
**de·lib·e·rate** absichtlich, vorsätzlich; bedächtig, besonnen
**de·lib·e·ra·tion** Überlegung *f*; Beratung *f*; Bedächtigkeit *f*
**del·i·ca·cy** Delikatesse *f*, Leckerbissen *m*; Zartheit *f*; Feingefühl *n*, Takt *m*
**del·i·cate** delikat (*a. fig*), schmackhaft; zart; fein; zierlich; zerbrechlich; heikel; empfindlich
**del·i·ca·tes·sen** Delikatessen *pl*, Feinkost *f*; Feinkostgeschäft *n*
**de·li·cious** köstlich
**de·light 1.** Vergnügen *n*, Entzücken *n*; **2.** entzücken, erfreuen; ***~ in*** (große) Freude haben an (*dat*)
**de·light·ful** entzückend
**de·lin·quen·cy** Kriminalität *f*
**de·lin·quent 1.** straffällig; **2.** Straffällige *m, f*; → ***juvenile*** 1
**de·lir·i·ous** MED im Delirium, fantasierend; **de·lir·i·um** MED Delirium *n*
**de·liv·er** ausliefern, (ab)liefern; *Briefe* zustellen; *Rede etc* halten; befreien, erlösen; ***be ~ed of*** MED entbunden werden von
**de·liv·er·ance** Befreiung *f*
**de·liv·er·er** Befreier(in)
**de·liv·er·y** (Ab-, Aus)Lieferung *f*; *post* Zustellung *f*; Halten *n* (*e-r Rede*); Vortrag(sweise *f*) *m*; MED Entbindung *f*
**de·liv·er·y van** *Br* MOT Lieferwagen *m*
**dell** kleines Tal
**de·lude** täuschen
**del·uge** Überschwemmung *f*; *fig* Flut *f*
**de·lu·sion** Täuschung *f*; Wahn(vorstellung *f*) *m*
**de·mand 1.** Forderung *f* (***for*** nach); Anforderung *f* (***on*** an *acc*); Nachfrage *f* (***for*** nach), Bedarf *m* (***for*** an *dat*); ***on ~*** auf Verlangen; **2.** verlangen, fordern; (*fordernd*) fragen nach; erfordern

**de·mand·ing** anspruchsvoll
**de·men·ted** wahnsinnig
**dem·i...** Halb..., halb...
**de·mil·i·ta·rize** entmilitarisieren
**dem·o** F Demo *f*
**de·mo·bi·lize** demobilisieren
**de·moc·ra·cy** Demokratie *f*
**dem·o·crat** Demokrat(in)
**dem·o·crat·ic** demokratisch
**de·mol·ish** demolieren; ab-, ein-, niederreißen; zerstören
**dem·o·li·tion** Demolierung *f*; Niederreißen *n*, Abbruch *m*
**de·mon** Dämon *m*; Teufel *m*
**dem·on·strate** demonstrieren; beweisen; zeigen; vorführen
**dem·on·stra·tion** Demonstration *f*, *a.* Kundgebung *f*, *a.* Vorführung *f*; **~ car** *Br* Vorführwagen *m*
**de·mon·stra·tive:** ***be* ~** s-e Gefühle (offen) zeigen
**dem·on·stra·tor** Demonstrant(in); Vorführer(in); MOT Vorführwagen *m*
**de·mor·al·ize** demoralisieren
**de·mote** degradieren
**de·mure** ernst, zurückhaltend
**den** zo Höhle *f* (*a. fig*); F Bude *f*
**de·ni·al** Ablehnung *f*; Leugnen *n*; Verweigerung *f*; ***official* ~** Dementi *n*
**den·ims** Jeans *pl*
**Den·mark** Dänemark *n*
**de·nom·i·na·tion** REL Konfession *f*; ECON Nennwert *m*
**de·note** bezeichnen; bedeuten
**de·nounce** (öffentlich) anprangern
**dense** dicht; *fig* beschränkt, begriffsstutzig; **den·si·ty** Dichte *f*
**dent 1.** Beule *f*, Delle *f*; **2.** ver-, einbeulen
**den·tal** Zahn...; **~ plaque** Zahnbelag *m*; **~ plate** (Zahn)Prothese *f*; **~ surgeon** Zahnarzt *m*, Zahnärztin *f*
**den·tist** Zahnarzt *m*, Zahnärztin *f*
**den·tures** (Zahn)Prothese *f*, (künstliches) Gebiss
**de·nun·ci·a·tion** Denunziation *f*
**de·nun·ci·a·tor** Denunziant(in)
**de·ny** abstreiten, bestreiten, dementieren, (ab)leugnen; *j-m et.* verweigern, abschlagen
**de·o·do·rant** De(s)odorant *n*, Deo *n*
**de·part** abreisen; abfahren, abfliegen; abweichen (***from*** von)
**de·part·ment** Abteilung *f*, UNIV *a.* Fachbereich *m*; POL Ministerium *n*
**De·part·ment| of De·fense** Verteidigungsministerium *n*; **~ of the En·vi·ron·ment** *Br* Umweltministerium *n*; **~ of the In·te·ri·or** Innenministerium *n*; **~ of State** *a.* ***State Department*** Außenministerium *n*
**de·part·ment store** Kaufhaus *n*, Warenhaus *n*
**de·par·ture** Abreise *f*; RAIL *etc* Abfahrt *f*; AVIAT Abflug *m*; *fig* Abweichung *f*; **~*s*** 'Abfahrt'; **~ gate** AVIAT Flugsteig *m*; **~ lounge** AVIAT Abflughalle *f*
**de·pend: ~ *on*** sich verlassen auf (*acc*); abhängen von; angewiesen sein auf (*acc*); ***that* ~*s*** das kommt darauf an
**de·pend·a·ble** zuverlässig
**de·pend·a·bil·i·ty** Zuverlässigkeit *f*
**de·pen·dant** Angehörige *m*, *f*
**de·pen·dence** Abhängigkeit *f*; Vertrauen *n*
**de·pen·dent 1.** (***on***) abhängig (von); angewiesen (auf *acc*); **2.** → ***dependant***
**de·plor·a·ble** bedauerlich, beklagenswert; **de·plore** beklagen, bedauern
**de·pop·u·late** entvölkern
**de·port** ausweisen, *Ausländer a.* abschieben; deportieren
**de·pose** *j-n* absetzen; JUR unter Eid erklären
**de·pos·it 1.** absetzen, abstellen; CHEM, GEOL (sich) ablagern *or* absetzen; deponieren, hinterlegen; ECON *Betrag* anzahlen; **2.** CHEM Ablagerung *f*, GEOL *a.* (*Erz- etc*)Lager *n*; Deponierung *f*, Hinterlegung *f*; ECON Anzahlung *f*; ***make a* ~** e-e Anzahlung leisten (***on*** für)
**dep·ot** Depot *n*; Bahnhof *m*
**de·prave** *moralisch* verderben
**de·pre·ci·ate** an Wert verlieren
**de·press** (nieder)drücken; deprimieren, bedrücken
**de·pressed** deprimiert, niedergeschlagen; ECON flau (*market*); Not leidend (*industry*); **~ ar·e·a** ECON Notstandsgebiet *n*
**de·press·ing** deprimierend, bedrückend
**de·pres·sion** Depression *f*, Niedergeschlagenheit *f*; ECON Depression *f*, Flaute *f*; Senke *f*, Vertiefung *f*; METEOR Tief(druckgebiet) *n*
**de·prive: ~ *s.o. of s.th.*** j-m et. entziehen *or* nehmen; **de·prived** benachteiligt

**dept, Dept** ABBR *of* ***department*** Abt., Abteilung *f*
**depth 1.** Tiefe *f*; **2.** Tiefen...
**dep·u·ta·tion** Abordnung *f*
**dep·u·tize:** *~ **for s.o.*** j-n vertreten
**dep·u·ty** (Stell)Vertreter(in); PARL Abgeordnete *m, f*; *a.* *~ **sheriff*** Hilfssheriff *m*
**de·rail:** ***be ~ed*** entgleisen
**de·ranged** geistesgestört
**der·by** F Melone *f*
**der·e·lict** heruntergekommen, baufällig
**de·ride** verhöhnen, verspotten
**de·ri·sion** Hohn *m*, Spott *m*
**de·ri·sive** höhnisch, spöttisch
**de·rive** herleiten (***from*** von); (sich) ableiten (***from*** von); abstammen (***from*** von); *~ **pleasure from*** Freude finden *or* haben an (*dat*)
**der·ma·tol·o·gist** Dermatologe *m*, Hautarzt *m*
**de·rog·a·to·ry** abfällig, geringschätzig
**der·rick** TECH Derrickkran *m*; MAR Ladebaum *m*; TECH Bohrturm *m*
**de·scend** herab-, hinabsteigen, herunter-, hinuntersteigen, -gehen, -kommen; AVIAT niedergehen; abstammen, herkommen (***from*** von); *~ **on*** herfallen über (*acc*); überfallen (*acc*) (*visitor etc*)
**de·scen·dant** Nachkomme *m*
**de·scent** Herab-, Hinuntersteigen *n*, -gehen *n*; AVIAT Niedergehen *n*; Gefälle *n*; Abstammung *f*, Herkunft *f*
**de·scribe** beschreiben
**de·scrip·tion** Beschreibung *f*, Schilderung *f*; Art *f*, Sorte *f*; **de·scrip·tive** beschreibend; anschaulich
**des·e·crate** entweihen
**de·seg·re·gate** die Rassentrennung aufheben in (*dat*); **de·seg·re·ga·tion** Aufhebung *f* der Rassentrennung
**des·ert**[1] **1.** Wüste *f*; **2.** Wüsten...
**de·sert**[2] *v/t* verlassen, im Stich lassen; *v/i* MIL desertieren
**de·sert·er** MIL Deserteur *m*
**de·ser·tion** (JUR *a.* böswilliges) Verlassen; MIL Fahnenflucht *f*
**de·serve** verdienen
**de·serv·ed·ly** verdientermaßen
**de·serv·ing** verdienstvoll
**de·sign 1.** Design *n*, Entwurf *m*, (TECH Konstruktions)Zeichnung *f*; Design *n*, Muster *n*; (*a.* böse)Absicht; **2.** entwerfen, TECH konstruieren; gestalten; ausdenken; bestimmen, vorsehen (***for*** für)
**des·ig·nate** *et. or j-n* bestimmen
**de·sign·er** Designer(in); TECH Konstrukteur *m*; (*Mode*)Schöpfer(in)
**de·sir·a·ble** erwünscht, wünschenswert; begehrenswert
**de·sire 1.** Wunsch *m*, Verlangen *n*, Begierde *f* (***for*** nach); **2.** wünschen; begehren
**de·sist** Abstand nehmen (***from*** von)
**desk** Schreibtisch *m*; Pult *n*; Empfang *m*, Rezeption *f*; Schalter *m*
**desk·top| com·put·er** Desktop-Computer *m*, Tischcomputer *m*, Tischrechner *m*; *~* **pub·lish·ing** (ABBR ***DTP***) EDP Desktop-Publishing *n*
**des·o·late** einsam, verlassen; trostlos
**de·spair 1.** Verzweiflung *f*; ***drive s.o. to ~*** j-n zur Verzweiflung bringen; **2.** verzweifeln (***of*** an *dat*)
**de·spair·ing** verzweifelt
**de·spatch** → ***dispatch***
**des·per·ate** verzweifelt; F hoffnungslos, schrecklich
**des·per·a·tion** Verzweiflung *f*
**des·pic·a·ble** verachtenswert, verabscheuungswürdig
**de·spise** verachten
**de·spite** trotz (*gen*)
**de·spon·dent** mutlos, verzagt
**des·pot** Despot *m*, Tyrann *m*
**des·sert** Nachtisch *m*, Dessert *n*
**des·ti·na·tion** Bestimmung *f*; Bestimmungsort *m*
**des·tined** bestimmt; MAR *etc* unterwegs (***for*** nach)
**des·ti·ny** Schicksal *n*
**des·ti·tute** mittellos
**de·stroy** zerstören, vernichten; *Tier* töten, einschläfern; **de·stroy·er** Zerstörer(in); MAR MIL Zerstörer *m*
**de·struc·tion** Zerstörung *f*, Vernichtung *f*; **de·struc·tive** zerstörend, vernichtend; zerstörerisch
**de·tach** (ab-, los)trennen, (los)lösen
**de·tached** einzeln, frei *or* allein stehend; unvoreingenommen; distanziert; *~ **house*** Einzelhaus *n*
**de·tach·ment** (Los)Lösung *f*, (Ab-) Trennung *f*; MIL (Sonder)Kommando *n*
**de·tail 1.** Detail *n*, Einzelheit *f*; MIL (Sonder)Kommando *n*; ***in ~*** ausführ-

lich; **2.** genau schildern; MIL abkommandieren
**de·tailed** detailliert, ausführlich
**de·tain** aufhalten; JUR in (Untersuchungs)Haft behalten

D

**de·tect** entdecken, (heraus)finden
**de·tec·tion** Entdeckung *f*
**de·tec·tive** Kriminalbeamte *m*, Detektiv *m*; ~ **nov·el,** ~ **sto·ry** Kriminalroman *m*
**de·ten·tion** JUR Haft *f*; PED Nachsitzen *n*
**de·ter** abschrecken (***from*** von)
**de·ter·gent** Reinigungs-, Wasch-, Geschirrspülmittel *n*
**de·te·ri·o·rate** (sich) verschlechtern, nachlassen; verderben
**de·ter·mi·na·tion** Entschlossenheit *f*, Bestimmtheit *f*; Entschluss *m*; Feststellung *f*, Ermittlung *f*; **de·ter·mine** *et.* beschließen, bestimmen; feststellen, ermitteln; (sich) entscheiden; sich entschließen; **de·ter·mined** entschlossen
**de·ter·rence** Abschreckung *f*
**de·ter·rent 1.** abschreckend; **2.** Abschreckungsmittel *n*
**de·test** verabscheuen
**de·throne** entthronen
**de·to·nate** *v/t* zünden; *v/i* detonieren, explodieren
**de·tour** Umweg *m*; Umleitung *f*
**de·tract:** ~ ***from*** ablenken von; schmälern (*acc*)
**de·tri·ment** Nachteil *m*, Schaden *m*
**deuce** *cards etc*: Zwei *f*; *tennis*: Einstand *m*
**de·val·u·a·tion** Abwertung *f*
**de·val·ue** abwerten
**dev·a·state** verwüsten
**dev·a·stat·ing** verheerend, vernichtend; F umwerfend, toll
**de·vel·op** (sich) entwickeln; *Naturschätze*, *Bauland* erschließen, *Altstadt etc* sanieren; **de·vel·op·er** PHOT Entwickler *m*; (Stadt)Planer *m*
**de·vel·op·ing** Entwicklungs...; ~ **coun·try,** ~ **na·tion** Entwicklungsland *n*
**de·vel·op·ment** Entwicklung *f*; Erschließung *f*, Sanierung *f*
**de·vi·ate** abweichen (***from*** von)
**de·vi·a·tion** Abweichung *f*
**de·vice** Vorrichtung *f*, Gerät *n*; Plan *m*, Trick *m*; ***leave s.o. to his own*** ~***s*** j-n sich selbst überlassen
**dev·il** Teufel *m* (*a. fig*)
**dev·il·ish** teuflisch
**de·vi·ous** abwegig; gewunden; unaufrichtig; ~ ***route*** Umweg *m*
**de·vise** (sich) ausdenken
**de·void:** ~ ***of*** ohne (*acc*)
**de·vote** widmen (***to*** *dat*); **de·vot·ed** ergeben; hingebungsvoll; eifrig, begeistert; **dev·o·tee** begeisterter Anhänger; **de·vo·tion** Ergebenheit *f*; Hingabe *f*; Frömmigkeit *f*, Andacht *f*
**de·vour** verschlingen
**de·vout** fromm; sehnlichst, innig
**dew** Tau *m*; **dew·y** taufeucht, taufrisch
**dex·ter·i·ty** Gewandtheit *f*
**dex·ter·ous, dex·trous** gewandt
**di·a·bol·i·cal** teuflisch
**di·ag·nose** diagnostizieren
**di·ag·no·sis** Diagnose *f*
**di·ag·o·nal 1.** diagonal; **2.** Diagonale *f*
**di·a·gram** Diagramm *n*, grafische Darstellung
**di·al 1.** Zifferblatt *n*; TEL Wählscheibe *f*; TECH Skala *f*; **2.** TEL wählen; ~ ***direct*** durchwählen (***to*** nach); ***direct*** ~***(l)ing*** Durchwahl *f*
**di·a·lect** Dialekt *m*, Mundart *f*
**di·al·ling code** *Br* TEL Vorwahl(nummer) *f*
**di·a·log,** *Br* **di·a·logue** Dialog *m*, (Zwie)Gespräch *n*
**di·am·e·ter** Durchmesser *m*; ***in*** ~ im Durchmesser
**di·a·mond** Diamant *m*; Raute *f*, Rhombus *m*; *cards*: Karo *n*
**di·a·per** Windel *f*
**di·a·phragm** ANAT Zwerchfell *n*; OPT Blende *f*; TEL Membran(e) *f*
**di·ar·rh(o)e·a** MED Durchfall *m*
**di·a·ry** Tagebuch *n*
**dice 1.** Würfel *m*; **2.** GASTR in Würfel schneiden; würfeln
**dic·tate** diktieren; *fig* vorschreiben
**dic·ta·tion** Diktat *n*
**dic·ta·tor** Diktator *m*
**dic·ta·tor·ship** Diktatur *f*
**dic·tion** Ausdrucksweise *f*, Stil *m*
**dic·tion·a·ry** Wörterbuch *n*
**die**[1] sterben; zo eingehen, verenden; ~ ***of hunger*** verhungern; ~ ***of thirst*** verdursten; ~ ***away*** sich legen (*wind*); verklingen (*sound*); ~ ***down*** nachlassen; herunterbrennen; schwächer werden; ~ ***out*** aussterben (*a. fig*)

**die²** Würfel *m*
**di·et 1.** Diät *f*; Nahrung *f*, Kost *f*; ***be on a ~*** Diät leben; ***put s.o. on a ~*** j-m e-e Diät verordnen; **2.** Diät leben
**di·e·ti·cian** Diätassistent(in)
**dif·fer** sich unterscheiden; anderer Meinung sein (***with, from*** als); abweichen
**dif·fe·rence** Unterschied *m*; Differenz *f*; Meinungsverschiedenheit *f*
**dif·fe·rent** verschieden; andere(r, -s); anders (***from*** als)
**dif·fe·ren·ti·ate** (sich) unterscheiden
**dif·fi·cult** schwierig
**dif·fi·cul·ty** Schwierigkeit *f*, *pl* Unannehmlichkeiten *pl*
**dif·fi·dence** Schüchternheit *f*
**dif·fi·dent** schüchtern
**dif·fuse 1.** *fig* verbreiten; **2.** diffus; *esp* PHYS zerstreut; weitschweifig
**dif·fu·sion** CHEM, PHYS (Zer)Streuung *f*
**dig 1.** graben; ~ (***up***) umgraben; ~ (***up or out***) ausgraben (*a. fig*); ***~ s.o. in the ribs*** j-m e-n Rippenstoß geben; **2.** F Puff *m*, Stoß *m*; Seitenhieb *m* (***at*** auf *acc*)
**di·gest 1.** verdauen; ***~ well*** leicht verdaulich sein; **2.** Abriss *m*; Auslese *f*, Auswahl *f*; **di·gest·i·ble** verdaulich; **di·ges·tion** Verdauung *f*; **di·ges·tive** verdauungsfördernd; Verdauungs...
**dig·ger** (*esp* Gold)Gräber *m*
**di·git** Ziffer *f*; ***three-~ number*** dreistellige Zahl
**di·gi·tal** digital, Digital...
**dig·i·tal| clock, ~ watch** Digitaluhr *f*
**dig·ni·fied** würdevoll, würdig
**dig·ni·ta·ry** Würdenträger(in)
**dig·ni·ty** Würde *f*
**di·gress** abschweifen
**dike¹ 1.** Deich *m*, Damm *m*; Graben *m*; **2.** eindeichen, eindämmen
**dike²** *sl* Lesbe *f*
**di·lap·i·dat·ed** verfallen, baufällig, klapp(e)rig
**di·late** (sich) ausdehnen *or* (aus)weiten; *Augen* weit öffnen
**dil·a·to·ry** verzögernd, hinhaltend; langsam
**dil·i·gence** Fleiß *m*
**dil·i·gent** fleißig, emsig
**di·lute 1.** verdünnen; *fig* verwässern; **2.** verdünnt; *fig* verwässert
**dim 1.** (halb)dunkel, düster; undeutlich, verschwommen; schwach, trüb(e) (*light*); **2.** (sich) verdunkeln *or* verdüstern; (sich) trüben; undeutlich werden; ***~ one's headlights*** MOT abblenden
**dime** Zehncentstück *n*
**di·men·sion** Dimension *f*, Maß *n*, Abmessung *f*; *pl a.* Ausmaß *n*
**di·min·ish** (sich) vermindern *or* verringern
**di·min·u·tive** klein, winzig
**dim·ple** Grübchen *n*
**din** Getöse *n*, Lärm *m*
**dine** essen, speisen; ***~ in*** zu Hause essen; ***~ out*** auswärts essen, essen gehen
**din·er** Speisende *m, f*; Gast *m*; Speiselokal *n*; RAIL Speisewagen *m*
**din·ghy** MAR Jolle *f*; Dingi *n*; Beiboot *n*; Schlauchboot *n*
**din·gy** schmutzig, schmudd(e)lig
**din·ing car** RAIL Speisewagen *m*
**din·ing room** Ess-, Speisezimmer *n*
**din·ner** (Mittag-, Abend)Essen *n*; Diner *n*, Festessen *n*; **~ jack·et** Smoking *m*; **~ par·ty** Dinnerparty *f*, Abendgesellschaft *f*; **~ ser·vice, ~ set** Speiseservice *n*, Tafelgeschirr *n*
**din·ner·time** Essens-, Tischzeit *f*
**di·no** F → ***dinosaur***
**di·no·saur** ZO Dinosaurier *m*
**dip 1.** *v/t* (ein)tauchen; senken; schöpfen; ***~ one's headlights*** *Br* MOT abblenden; *v/i* (unter)tauchen; sinken; sich neigen, sich senken; **2.** (Ein-, Unter)Tauchen *n*; F kurzes Bad; Senkung *f*, Neigung *f*, Gefälle *n*; GASTR Dip *m*
**diph·ther·i·a** MED Diphtherie *f*
**di·plo·ma** Diplom *n*
**di·plo·ma·cy** Diplomatie *f*
**dip·lo·mat** Diplomat *m*
**dip·lo·mat·ic** diplomatisch
**dip·per** Schöpfkelle *f*
**dire** schrecklich; höchste(r, -s), äußerste(r, -s)
**di·rect 1.** *adj* direkt; gerade; unmittelbar; offen, aufrichtig; **2.** *adv* direkt, unmittelbar; **3.** richten; lenken, steuern; leiten; anordnen; *j-n* anweisen; *j-m* den Weg zeigen; *Brief* adressieren; Regie führen bei; **~ cur·rent** ELECTR Gleichstrom *m*; **~ train** durchgehender Zug
**di·rec·tion** Richtung *f*; Leitung *f*, Führung *f*; *film etc*: Regie *f*; *mst pl* Anweisung *f*, Anleitung *f*; ***~s for use*** Gebrauchsanweisung *f*; ***sense of ~*** Ortssinn *m*; **~ in·di·ca·tor** MOT Fahrtrichtungsanzeiger *m*, Blinker *m*

D

**di·rec·tive** Anweisung *f*
**di·rect·ly 1.** *adv* sofort; **2.** *cj* F sobald, sowie
**di·rec·tor** Direktor *m*; *film etc*: Regisseur(in)
**di·rec·to·ry** Adressbuch *n*
**di·rect speech** LING wörtliche Rede
**dirt** Schmutz *m*; (lockere) Erde
**dirt cheap** F spottbillig
**dirt·y 1.** schmutzig (*a. fig*); **2.** *v/t* beschmutzen; *v/i* schmutzig werden, schmutzen
**dis·a·bil·i·ty** Unfähigkeit *f*
**dis·a·bled 1.** arbeitsunfähig, erwerbsunfähig, invalid(e); MIL kriegsversehrt; *körperlich or geistig* behindert; **2. the ~** die Behinderten *pl*
**dis·ad·van·tage** Nachteil *m*; Schaden *m*; **dis·ad·van·ta·geous** nachteilig, ungünstig
**dis·a·gree** nicht übereinstimmen; uneinig sein; nicht bekommen (***with s.o.*** j-m); **dis·a·gree·a·ble** unangenehm; **dis·a·gree·ment** Verschiedenheit *f*, Unstimmigkeit *f*, Uneinigkeit *f*; Meinungsverschiedenheit *f*
**dis·ap·pear** verschwinden
**dis·ap·pear·ance** Verschwinden *n*
**dis·ap·point** *j-n* enttäuschen; *Hoffnungen etc* zunichte machen
**dis·ap·point·ing** enttäuschend
**dis·ap·point·ment** Enttäuschung *f*
**dis·ap·prov·al** Missbilligung *f*
**dis·ap·prove** missbilligen; dagegen sein
**dis·arm** *v/t* entwaffnen (*a. fig*); *v/i* MIL, POL abrüsten; **dis·ar·ma·ment** Entwaffnung *f*; MIL, POL Abrüstung *f*
**dis·ar·range** in Unordnung bringen
**dis·ar·ray** Unordnung *f*
**di·sas·ter** Unglück *n*, Unglücksfall *m*, Katastrophe *f*; **~ ar·e·a** Katastrophen-, Notstandsgebiet *n*; **~ con·trol** Katastrophenschutz *m*
**di·sas·trous** katastrophal, verheerend
**dis·be·lief** Unglaube *m*; Zweifel *m* (***in*** an *dat*); **dis·be·lieve** *et.* bezweifeln, nicht glauben
**disc** *Br* → ***disk***
**dis·card** *Karten* ablegen, *Kleidung etc a.* ausrangieren; *Freund etc* fallen lassen
**di·scern** wahrnehmen, erkennen
**di·scern·ing** kritisch, scharfsichtig
**di·scern·ment** Scharfblick *m*
**dis·charge 1.** *v/t* entladen, ausladen; *j-n* befreien, entbinden; *j-n* entlassen; *Gewehr etc* abfeuern; von sich geben, ausströmen, -senden, -stoßen; MED absondern; *Pflicht etc* erfüllen; *Zorn etc* auslassen (***on*** an *dat*); *v/i* ELECTR sich entladen; sich ergießen, münden (*river*); MED eitern; **2.** MAR Entladung *f*; MIL Abfeuern *n*; Ausströmen *n*; MED Absonderung *f*, Ausfluss *m*; Ausstoßen *n*; ELECTR Entladung *f*; Entlassung *f*; Erfüllung *f* (*e-r Pflicht*)
**di·sci·ple** Schüler *m*; Jünger *m*
**dis·ci·pline 1.** Disziplin *f*; **2.** disziplinieren; ***well ~d*** diszipliniert; ***badly ~d*** disziplinlos, undiszipliniert
**dis·claim** abstreiten, bestreiten; *Verantwortung* ablehnen; JUR verzichten auf (*acc*)
**dis·close** bekannt geben *or* machen; enthüllen, aufdecken
**dis·clo·sure** Enthüllung *f*
**dis·co** Disko *f*
**dis·col·o(u)r** (sich) verfärben
**dis·com·fort 1.** Unbehagen *n*; Unannehmlichkeit *f*; **2.** *j-m* Unbehagen verursachen
**dis·con·cert** aus der Fassung bringen
**dis·con·nect** trennen (*a.* ELECTR); TECH auskuppeln; ELECTR *Gerät* abschalten; *Gas, Strom, Telefon* abstellen; TEL *Gespräch* unterbrechen
**dis·con·nect·ed** zusammenhang(s)los
**dis·con·so·late** untröstlich
**dis·con·tent** Unzufriedenheit *f*
**dis·con·tent·ed** unzufrieden
**dis·con·tin·ue** aufgeben, aufhören mit; unterbrechen
**dis·cord** Uneinigkeit *f*, Zwietracht *f*, Zwist *m*; MUS Missklang *m*
**dis·cord·ant** nicht übereinstimmend; MUS unharmonisch, misstönend
**dis·co·theque** Diskothek *f*
**dis·count** ECON Diskont *m*; Preisnachlass *m*, Rabatt *m*, Skonto *m, n*
**dis·cour·age** entmutigen; abschrecken, abhalten, *j-m* abraten (***from*** von)
**dis·cour·age·ment** Entmutigung *f*; Abschreckung *f*
**dis·course 1.** Unterhaltung *f*, Gespräch *n*; Vortrag *m*; **2.** e-n Vortrag halten (***on*** über *acc*)
**dis·cour·te·ous** unhöflich
**dis·cour·te·sy** Unhöflichkeit *f*

**dis·cov·er** entdecken; ausfindig machen, (heraus)finden
**dis·cov·e·ry** Entdeckung *f*
**dis·cred·it** 1. Zweifel *m*; Misskredit *m*, schlechter Ruf; ***bring ~ (up)on*** in Verruf bringen; 2. nicht glauben; in Misskredit bringen
**di·screet** besonnen, vorsichtig; diskret, verschwiegen
**di·screp·an·cy** Diskrepanz *f*, Widerspruch *m*
**di·scre·tion** Ermessen *n*, Gutdünken *n*; Diskretion *f*, Verschwiegenheit *f*
**di·scrim·i·nate** unterscheiden; ***~ against*** benachteiligen, diskriminieren; **di·scrim·i·nat·ing** kritisch, urteilsfähig; **di·scrim·i·na·tion** unterschiedliche (*esp* nachteilige) Behandlung; Diskriminierung *f*, Benachteiligung *f*; Urteilsfähigkeit *f*
**dis·cus** SPORT Diskus *m*
**di·scuss** diskutieren, erörtern, besprechen; **di·scus·sion** Diskussion *f*, Besprechung *f*
**dis·cus| throw** SPORT Diskuswerfen *n*; **~ throw·er** SPORT Diskuswerfer(in)
**dis·ease** Krankheit *f*
**dis·eased** krank
**dis·em·bark** von Bord gehen (lassen); MAR *Waren* ausladen
**dis·en·chant·ed:** ***be ~ with*** sich keine Illusionen mehr machen über (*acc*)
**dis·en·gage** (sich) freimachen; losmachen; TECH auskuppeln, loskuppeln
**dis·en·tan·gle** entwirren; (sich) befreien
**dis·fa·vo(u)r** Missfallen *n*; Ungnade *f*
**dis·fig·ure** entstellen
**dis·grace** 1. Schande *f*; Ungnade *f*; 2. Schande bringen über (*acc*), *j-m* Schande bereiten
**dis·grace·ful** schändlich; skandalös
**dis·guise** 1. verkleiden (**as** als); *Stimme etc* verstellen; *et.* verbergen, verschleiern; 2. Verkleidung *f*; Verstellung *f*; Verschleierung *f*; ***in ~*** maskiert, verkleidet; *fig* verkappt; ***in the ~ of*** verkleidet als
**dis·gust** 1. Ekel *m*, Abscheu *m*; 2. (an)ekeln; empören, entrüsten
**dis·gust·ing** ekelhaft
**dish** 1. flache Schüssel; (Servier)Platte *f*; GASTR Gericht *n*, Speise *f*; ***the ~es*** das Geschirr; ***wash*** *or* ***do the ~es*** abspülen, abwaschen; 2. ***~ out*** F austeilen; *often* ***~ up*** *Speisen* anrichten, auftragen; F *Geschichte etc* auftischen
**dish·cloth** Geschirrtuch *n*
**dis·heart·en** entmutigen
**di·shev·el(l)ed** zerzaust
**dis·hon·est** unehrlich, unredlich
**dis·hon·est·y** Unehrlichkeit *f*; Unredlichkeit *f*
**dis·hon·o(u)r** 1. Schande *f*; 2. Schande bringen über (*acc*); ECON *Wechsel* nicht honorieren *or* einlösen
**dis·hon·o(u)·ra·ble** schändlich, unehrenhaft
**dish·wash·er** Tellerwäscher *m*, Spüler(in); TECH Geschirrspülmaschine *f*, Geschirrspüler *m*
**dish·wa·ter** Spülwasser *n*
**dis·il·lu·sion** 1. Ernüchterung *f*, Desillusion *f*; 2. ernüchtern, desillusionieren; ***be ~ed with*** sich keine Illusionen mehr machen über (*acc*)
**dis·in·clined** abgeneigt
**dis·in·fect** MED desinfizieren
**dis·in·fec·tant** Desinfektionsmittel *n*
**dis·in·her·it** JUR enterben
**dis·in·te·grate** (sich) auflösen; verfallen, zerfallen
**dis·in·terest·ed** uneigennützig, selbstlos; objektiv, unvoreingenommen
**disk** Scheibe *f*; (Schall)Platte *f*; Parkscheibe *f*; EDP Diskette *f*; ANAT Bandscheibe *f*; ***slipped ~*** MED Bandscheibenvorfall *m*
**disk drive** EDP Diskettenlaufwerk *n*
**disk·ette** EDP Floppy *f*, Diskette *f*
**disk jock·ey** Diskjockey *m*
**disk park·ing** MOT Parken *n* mit Parkscheibe
**dis·like** 1. Abneigung *f*, Widerwille *m* (***of, for*** gegen); ***take a ~ to s.o.*** gegen j-n e-e Abneigung fassen; 2. nicht leiden können, nicht mögen
**dis·lo·cate** MED sich *den Arm etc* verrenken *or* ausrenken
**dis·loy·al** treulos, untreu
**dis·mal** trüb(e), trostlos, elend
**dis·man·tle** TECH demontieren
**dis·may** 1. Schreck(en) *m*, Bestürzung *f*; ***in ~, with ~*** bestürzt; ***to my ~*** zu m-r Bestürzung; 2. *v/t* erschrecken, bestürzen
**dis·miss** *v/t* entlassen; wegschicken; ablehnen; *Thema etc* fallen lassen; JUR

abweisen; **dis·miss·al** Entlassung *f*; Aufgabe *f*; JUR Abweisung *f*
**dis·mount** *v/i* absteigen, absitzen (***from*** von); *v/t* demontieren; TECH auseinander nehmen
**dis·o·be·di·ence** Ungehorsam *m*
**dis·o·be·di·ent** ungehorsam
**dis·o·bey** nicht gehorchen, ungehorsam sein (gegen)
**dis·or·der** Unordnung *f*; Aufruhr *m*; MED Störung *f*
**dis·or·der·ly** unordentlich; ordnungswidrig; unruhig; aufrührerisch
**dis·or·gan·ize** durcheinander bringen; desorganisieren
**dis·own** nicht anerkennen; *Kind* verstoßen; ablehnen
**di·spar·age** verächtlich machen, herabsetzen; gering schätzen
**di·spar·i·ty** Ungleichheit *f*; ~ ***of or in age*** Altersunterschied *m*
**dis·pas·sion·ate** leidenschaftslos; objektiv
**di·spatch 1.** schnelle Erledigung; (Ab)Sendung *f*; Abfertigung *f*; Eile *f*; (Eil)Botschaft *f*; Bericht *m*; **2.** schnell erledigen; absenden, abschicken, *Telegramm* aufgeben, abfertigen
**di·spel** *Menge etc* zerstreuen (*a. fig*), *Nebel* zerteilen
**di·spen·sa·ble** entbehrlich
**di·spen·sa·ry** Werks-, Krankenhaus-, Schul-, MIL Lazarettapotheke *f*
**dis·pen·sa·tion** Austeilung *f*; Befreiung *f*; Dispens *m*; *göttliche* Fügung
**di·spense** austeilen; *Recht* sprechen; *Arzneien* zubereiten und abgeben; ~ ***with*** auskommen ohne; überflüssig machen; **di·spens·er** Spender *m*, *a.* Abroller *m* (*for adhesive tape etc*), (*Briefmarken- etc*)Automat *m*
**di·sperse** verstreuen; (sich) zerstreuen
**di·spir·it·ed** entmutigt
**dis·place** verschieben; ablösen, entlassen; *j-n* verschleppen; ersetzen; verdrängen
**dis·play 1.** Entfaltung *f*; (Her)Zeigen *n*; (protzige) Zurschaustellung; EDP Display *n*, Bildschirm *m*, Datenanzeige *f*; ECON Display *n*, Auslage *f*; ***be on*** ~ ausgestellt sein; **2.** entfalten; zur Schau stellen; zeigen
**dis·please** *j-m* missfallen
**dis·pleased** ungehalten
**dis·plea·sure** Missfallen *n*
**dis·pos·a·ble** Einweg...; Wegwerf...
**dis·pos·al** Beseitigung *f*, Entsorgung *f*; Endlagerung *f*; Verfügung(srecht *n*) *f*; ***be*** (***put***) ***at s.o.'s*** ~ j-m zur Verfügung stehen (stellen)
**dis·pose** *v/t* (an)ordnen, einrichten; geneigt machen, bewegen; *v/i*: ~ ***of*** verfügen über (*acc*); erledigen; loswerden; wegschaffen, beseitigen; *Abfall, a. Atommüll etc* entsorgen
**dis·posed** geneigt; ...gesinnt
**dis·po·si·tion** Veranlagung *f*
**dis·pos·sess** enteignen, vertreiben; berauben (***of*** *gen*)
**dis·pro·por·tion·ate(·ly)** unverhältnismäßig
**dis·prove** widerlegen
**di·spute 1.** Disput *m*, Kontroverse *f*; Streit *m*; Auseinandersetzung *f*; **2.** streiten (über *acc*); bezweifeln
**dis·qual·i·fy** unfähig *or* untauglich machen; für untauglich erklären; SPORT disqualifizieren
**dis·re·gard 1.** Nichtbeachtung *f*; Missachtung *f*; **2.** nicht beachten
**dis·rep·u·ta·ble** übel; verrufen
**dis·re·pute** schlechter Ruf
**dis·re·spect** Respektlosigkeit *f*; Unhöflichkeit *f*
**dis·re·spect·ful** respektlos; unhöflich
**dis·rupt** unterbrechen
**dis·sat·is·fac·tion** Unzufriedenheit *f*
**dis·sat·is·fied** unzufrieden (***with*** mit)
**dis·sect** MED sezieren, zerlegen, zergliedern (*a. fig*)
**dis·sen·sion** Meinungsverschiedenheit(en *pl*) *f*, Differenz(en *pl*) *f*; Uneinigkeit *f*
**dis·sent 1.** abweichende Meinung; **2.** anderer Meinung sein (***from*** als)
**dis·sent·er** Andersdenkende *m*, *f*
**dis·si·dent** Andersdenkende *m*, *f*; POL Dissident(in), Regime-, Systemkritiker(in)
**dis·sim·i·lar** (***to***) unähnlich (*dat*); verschieden (von)
**dis·sim·u·la·tion** Verstellung *f*
**dis·si·pate** (sich) zerstreuen; verschwenden
**dis·si·pat·ed** ausschweifend, zügellos
**dis·so·ci·ate** trennen; ~ ***o.s.*** sich distanzieren (***from*** von)
**dis·so·lute** → ***dissipated***

**dis·so·lu·tion** Auflösung *f*
**dis·solve** (sich) auflösen
**dis·suade** *j-m* abraten (***from*** von)
**dis·tance 1.** Abstand *m*; Entfernung *f*; Ferne *f*; Strecke *f*; *fig* Distanz *f*, Zurückhaltung *f*; ***at a ~*** von weitem; in einiger Entfernung; ***keep s.o. at a ~*** j-m gegenüber reserviert sein; **2.** hinter sich lassen; **~ race** SPORT Langstreckenlauf *m*; **~ run·ner** SPORT Langstreckenläufer(in), Langstreckler(in)
**dis·tant** entfernt; fern, Fern...; distanziert
**dis·taste** Widerwille *m*, Abneigung *f*
**dis·taste·ful** Ekel erregend; unangenehm; ***be ~ to s.o.*** j-m zuwider sein
**dis·tem·per** VET Staupe *f*
**dis·tend** (sich) (aus)dehnen; (auf)blähen; sich weiten
**dis·til(l)** destillieren
**dis·tinct** verschieden; deutlich, klar
**dis·tinc·tion** Unterscheidung *f*; Unterschied *m*; Auszeichnung *f*; Rang *m*
**dis·tinc·tive** unterscheidend; kennzeichnend, bezeichnend
**dis·tin·guish** unterscheiden; auszeichnen; ***~ o.s.*** sich auszeichnen
**dis·tin·guished** berühmt; ausgezeichnet; vornehm
**dis·tort** verdrehen; verzerren
**dis·tract** ablenken; **dis·tract·ed** beunruhigt, besorgt; (***by, with*** vor *dat*) außer sich, wahnsinnig; **dis·trac·tion** Ablenkung *f*; Zerstreuung *f*; Wahnsinn *m*; ***drive s.o. to ~*** j-n wahnsinnig machen
**dis·traught** → ***distracted***
**dis·tress 1.** Leid *n*, Kummer *m*, Sorge *f*; Not(lage) *f*; **2.** beunruhigen, mit Sorge erfüllen
**dis·tressed** Not leidend; **~ ar·e·a** Notstandsgebiet *n*
**dis·tress·ing** Besorgnis erregend
**dis·trib·ute** ver-, aus-, zuteilen; ECON *Waren* vertreiben, absetzen; *Filme* verleihen; **dis·tri·bu·tion** Ver-, Aus-, Zuteilung *f*; ECON Vertrieb *m*, Absatz *m*; *film*: Verleih *m*
**dis·trict** Bezirk *m*; Gegend *f*
**dis·trust 1.** Misstrauen *n*; **2.** misstrauen (*dat*); **dis·trust·ful** misstrauisch
**dis·turb** stören; beunruhigen
**dis·turb·ance** Störung *f*; Unruhe *f*; ***~ of the peace*** JUR Störung *f* der öffentlichen Sicherheit und Ordnung; ***cause a ~*** für Unruhe sorgen; ruhestörenden Lärm machen
**dis·turbed** geistig gestört; verhaltensgestört
**dis·used** nicht mehr benutzt (*machinery etc*), stillgelegt (*colliery etc*)
**ditch** Graben *m*
**di·van** Diwan *m*; **~ bed** Bettcouch *f*
**dive 1.** (unter)tauchen; *vom Sprungbrett* springen; e-n Hecht- *or* Kopfsprung machen; hechten (***for*** nach); e-n Sturzflug machen; **2.** *swimming*: Springen *n*; Kopfsprung *m*, Hechtsprung *m*; *soccer*: Schwalbe *f*; AVIAT Sturzflug *m*; F Spelunke *f*; **div·er** Taucher(in); SPORT Wasserspringer(in)
**di·verge** auseinander laufen; abweichen; **di·ver·gence** Abweichung *f*; **di·ver·gent** abweichend
**di·verse** verschieden; mannigfaltig
**di·ver·si·fy** verschieden(artig) *or* abwechslungsreich gestalten
**di·ver·sion** Ablenkung *f*; Zeitvertreib *m*; *Br* MOT Umleitung *f*
**di·ver·si·ty** Verschiedenheit *f*; Mannigfaltigkeit *f*
**di·vert** ablenken; *j-n* zerstreuen, unterhalten; *Br Verkehr* umleiten
**di·vide 1.** *v/t* teilen; ver-, aus-, aufteilen; trennen; MATH dividieren, teilen (***by*** durch); *v/i* sich teilen; sich aufteilen; MATH sich dividieren *or* teilen lassen (***by*** durch); **2.** GEOGR Wasserscheide *f*
**di·vid·ed** geteilt; **~ *highway*** Schnellstraße *f*
**div·i·dend** ECON Dividende *f*
**di·vid·ers** (***a pair of ~*** ein) Stechzirkel *m*
**di·vine** göttlich
**di·vine ser·vice** REL Gottesdienst *m*
**div·ing 1.** Tauchen *n*; SPORT Wasserspringen *n*; **2.** Taucher...
**div·ing·board** Sprungbrett *n*
**div·ing·suit** Taucheranzug *m*
**di·vin·i·ty** Gottheit *f*; Göttlichkeit *f*; Theologie *f*
**di·vis·i·ble** teilbar
**di·vi·sion** Teilung *f*; Trennung *f*; Abteilung *f*; MIL, MATH Division *f*
**di·vorce 1.** (Ehe)Scheidung *f*; ***get a ~*** sich scheiden lassen (***from*** von); **2.** JUR *j-n*, *Ehe* scheiden; ***get ~d*** sich scheiden lassen; **di·vor·cee** Geschiedene *m, f*
**DIY** ABBR → ***do-it-yourself***

**DIY store** Baumarkt *m*
**diz·zy** schwind(e)lig
**do** *v/t* tun, machen; (zu)bereiten; *Zimmer* aufräumen; *Geschirr* abwaschen; *Wegstrecke* zurücklegen, schaffen; **~ *you know him? no, I don't*** kennst du ihn? nein; ***what can I ~ for you?*** was kann ich für Sie tun?, womit kann ich (Ihnen) dienen?; **~ *London*** F London besichtigen; ***have one's hair done*** sich die Haare machen *or* frisieren lassen; ***have done reading*** fertig sein mit Lesen; *v/i* tun, handeln; sich befinden; genügen; ***that will ~*** das genügt; ***how ~ you ~?*** guten Tag!; **~ *be quick*** beeil dich doch; **~ *you like New York? I ~*** gefällt Ihnen New York? ja; ***she works hard, doesn't she?*** sie arbeitet viel, nicht wahr?; **~ *well*** s-e Sache gut machen; gute Geschäfte machen; **~ *away with*** beseitigen, weg-, abschaffen; ***do s.o. in*** F j-n umlegen; ***I'm done in*** F ich bin geschafft; **~ *up*** *Kleid etc* zumachen; *Haus etc* instand setzen; *Päckchen* zurechtmachen; **~ *o.s. up*** sich zurechtmachen; ***I could ~ with ...*** ich könnte ... brauchen *or* vertragen; **~ *without*** auskommen *or* sich behelfen ohne
**doc** F → ***doctor***
**do·cile** gelehrig; fügsam
**dock**[1] stutzen, kupieren
**dock**[2] **1.** MAR Dock *n*; Kai *m*, Pier *m*; JUR Anklagebank *f*; **2.** *v/t* MAR (ein)docken; *Raumschiff* koppeln; *v/i* MAR anlegen; andocken, ankoppeln (*Raumschiff*)
**dock·er** Dock-, Hafenarbeiter *m*
**dock·ing** Docking *n*, Ankopp(e)lung *f*
**dock·yard** MAR Werft *f*
**doc·tor** Doktor *m* (*a.* UNIV), Arzt *m*, Ärztin *f*
**doc·tor·al:** **~ *thesis*** UNIV Doktorarbeit *f*
**doc·trine** Doktrin *f*, Lehre *f*
**doc·u·ment 1.** Urkunde *f*; **2.** (urkundlich) belegen; **doc·u·men·ta·ry 1.** urkundlich; *film etc*: Dokumentar...; **2.** Dokumentarfilm *m*
**dodge** (rasch) zur Seite springen, ausweichen; F sich drücken (vor *dat*)
**dodg·er** Drückeberger *m*
**doe** ZO (Reh)Geiß *f*, Ricke *f*
**dog 1.** ZO Hund *m*; **2.** *j-n* beharrlich verfolgen
**dog-eared** mit Eselsohren (*book*)
**dog·ged** verbissen, hartnäckig
**dog·ma** Dogma *n*; Glaubenssatz *m*
**dog·mat·ic** dogmatisch
**do-it-your·self 1.** Heimwerken *n*; **2.** Heimwerker...
**do-it-your·self·er** Heimwerker *m*
**dole 1.** milde Gabe; *Br* F Stempelgeld *n*; ***go or be on the ~*** *Br* F stempeln gehen; **2. ~ *out*** sparsam ver- *or* austeilen
**dole·ful** traurig, trübselig
**doll** Puppe *f*
**dol·lar** Dollar *m*
**dol·phin** ZO Delphin *m*
**dome** Kuppel *f*
**do·mes·tic 1.** häuslich; inländisch, einheimisch; zahm; **2.** Hausangestellte *m, f*; **~ an·i·mal** Haustier *n*
**do·mes·ti·cate** *Tier* zähmen
**do·mes·tic| flight** AVIAT Inlandsflug *m*; **~ mar·ket** ECON Binnenmarkt *m*; **~ trade** ECON Binnenhandel *m*; **~ vi·o·lence** häusliche Gewalt
**dom·i·cile** Wohnsitz *m*
**dom·i·nant** dominierend, (vor)herrschend
**dom·i·nate** beherrschen; dominieren
**dom·i·na·tion** (Vor)Herrschaft *f*
**dom·i·neer·ing** herrisch, tyrannisch
**do·nate** schenken; stiften; spenden (*a.* MED); **do·na·tion** Schenkung *f*
**done** getan; erledigt; fertig; GASTR gar
**don·key** ZO Esel *m*
**do·nor** Spender(in) (*a.* MED)
**do-noth·ing** F Nichtstuer *m*
**doom 1.** Schicksal *n*, Verhängnis *n*; **2.** verurteilen, verdammen
**Dooms·day** der Jüngste Tag
**door** Tür *f*; Tor *n*; ***next ~*** nebenan
**door·bell** Türklingel *f*
**door han·dle** Türklinke *f*
**door·keep·er** Pförtner *m*
**door·knob** Türknauf *m*
**door·mat** (Fuß)Abtreter *m*
**door·step** Türstufe *f*
**door·way** Türöffnung *f*
**dope 1.** F Stoff *m* (*Rauschgift*); Betäubungsmittel *n*; SPORT Dopingmittel *n*; *sl* Trottel *m*; **2.** F *j-m* Stoff geben; SPORT dopen; **~ test** SPORT Dopingkontrolle *f*
**dor·mant** schlafend, ruhend; untätig
**dor·mi·to·ry** Schlafsaal *m*; Studentenwohnheim *n*
**dor·mo·bile**® Campingbus *m*, Wohnmobil *n*

**dor·mouse** ZO Haselmaus *f*
**dose 1.** Dosis *f*; **2.** *j-m* e-e Medizin geben
**dot 1.** Punkt *m*; Fleck *m*; ***on the ~*** F auf die Sekunde pünktlich; **2.** punktieren; tüpfeln; *fig* sprenkeln; ***~ted line*** punktierte Linie
**dote:** ***~ on*** vernarrt sein in (*acc*)
**dot·ing** vernarrt
**doub·le 1.** doppelt; Doppel...; zweifach; **2.** Doppelte *n*; Doppelgänger(in); *film*, TV Double *n*; **3.** (sich) verdoppeln; *film*, TV *j-n* doubeln; *a.* ***~ up*** falten; *Decke* zusammenlegen; ***~ back*** kehrtmachen; ***~ up with*** sich krümmen vor (*dat*)
**dou·ble-breast·ed** zweireihig
**dou·ble-check** genau nachprüfen
**dou·ble chin** Doppelkinn *n*
**dou·ble-cross** ein doppeltes *or* falsches Spiel treiben mit
**dou·ble-deal·ing 1.** betrügerisch; **2.** Betrug *m*
**dou·ble-deck·er** Doppeldecker *m*
**dou·ble-edged** zweischneidig (*a. fig*); zweideutig
**dou·ble fea·ture** *film*: Doppelprogramm *n*
**dou·ble-park** MOT in zweiter Reihe parken
**dou·bles** *esp tennis*: Doppel *n*; ***men's ~*** Herrendoppel *n*; ***women's ~*** Damendoppel *n*
**dou·ble-sid·ed** EDP zweiseitig
**doubt 1.** *v/i* zweifeln; *v/t* bezweifeln; misstrauen (*dat*); **2.** Zweifel *m*; ***be in ~ about*** Zweifel haben an (*dat*); ***no ~*** ohne Zweifel
**doubt·ful** zweifelhaft
**doubt·less** ohne Zweifel
**douche 1.** Spülung *f* (*a.* MED); Spülapparat *m*; **2.** spülen (*a.* MED)
**dough** Teig *m*
**dough·nut** *appr* Krapfen *m*, Berliner Pfannkuchen, Schmalzkringel *m*
**dove** ZO Taube *f*
**dow·dy** unelegant; unmodern
**dow·el** TECH Dübel *m*
**down**[1] Daunen *pl*; Flaum *m*
**down**[2] **1.** *adv* nach unten, herunter, hinunter, herab, hinab, abwärts; unten; **2.** *prp* herab, hinab, herunter, hinunter; ***~ the river*** flussabwärts; **3.** *adj* nach unten gerichtet; deprimiert, niedergeschlagen; ***~ platform*** Abfahrtsbahnsteig *m* (*in London*); ***~ train*** Zug *m* (von London fort); **4.** *v/t* niederschlagen; *Flugzeug* abschießen; F *Getränk* runterkippen; ***~ tools*** die Arbeit niederlegen, in den Streik treten
**down·cast** niedergeschlagen
**down·fall** Platzregen *m*; *fig* Sturz *m*
**down·heart·ed** niedergeschlagen
**down·hill 1.** *adv* bergab; **2.** *adj* abschüssig; *skiing*: Abfahrts...; **3.** Abhang *m*; *skiing*: Abfahrt *f*
**down pay·ment** ECON Anzahlung *f*
**down·pour** Regenguss *m*, Platzregen *m*
**down·right 1.** *adv* völlig, ganz und gar, ausgesprochen; **2.** *adj* glatt (*lie etc*); ausgesprochen
**downs** Hügelland *n*
**down·stairs** die Treppe herunter *or* hinunter; (nach) unten
**down·stream** stromabwärts
**down-to-earth** realistisch
**down·town 1.** *adv* im *or* ins Geschäftsviertel; **2.** *adj* im Geschäftsviertel (gelegen *or* tätig); **3.** Geschäftsviertel *n*, Innenstadt *f*, City *f*
**down·ward(s)** abwärts, nach unten
**down·y** flaumig
**dow·ry** Mitgift *f*
**doze 1.** dösen, ein Nickerchen machen; **2.** Nickerchen *n*
**doz·en** Dutzend *n*
**drab** trist; düster; eintönig
**draft 1.** Entwurf *m*; (Luft)Zug *m*; Zugluft *f*; Zug *m*, Schluck *m*; MAR Tiefgang *m*; ECON Tratte *f*, Wechsel *m*; MIL Einberufung *f*; ***beer on ~, ~ beer*** Bier *n* vom Fass, Fassbier *n*; **2.** entwerfen; *Brief etc* aufsetzen; MIL einberufen
**draft·ee** MIL Wehr(dienst)pflichtige *m*
**drafts·man** TECH Zeichner *m*
**drafts·wom·an** TECH Zeichnerin *f*
**draft·y** zugig
**drag 1.** Schleppen *n*, Zerren *n*; *fig* Hemmschuh *m*; F *et.* Langweiliges; **2.** schleppen, zerren, ziehen, schleifen; *a.* ***~ behind*** zurückbleiben, nachhinken; ***~ on*** weiterschleppen; *fig* sich dahinschleppen; *fig* sich in die Länge ziehen
**drag lift** Schlepplift *m*
**drag·on** MYTH Drache *m*
**drag·on·fly** ZO Libelle *f*
**drain 1.** Abfluss(kanal) *m*, Abflussrohr *n*; Entwässerungsgraben *m*; **2.** *v/t* ab-

fließen lassen; entwässern; austrinken, leeren; *v/i*: **~ off, ~ away** abfließen, ablaufen; **drain·age** Abfließen *n*, Ablaufen *n*, Entwässerung *f*; Entwässerungsanlage *f*, -system *n*

D

**drain·pipe** Abflussrohr *n*

**drake** ZO Enterich *m*, Erpel *m*

**dram** Schluck *m*

**dra·ma** Drama *n*; **dra·mat·ic** dramatisch; **dram·a·tist** Dramatiker *m*; **dram·a·tize** dramatisieren

**drape 1.** drapieren; in Falten legen; **2.** *mst* **~s** Vorhänge *pl*

**drap·er·y** *Br* Textilien *pl*

**dras·tic** drastisch, durchgreifend

**draught** *Br* → **draft**

**draughts** *Br* Damespiel *n*

**draughts·man** *etc* → **draftsman** *etc*

**draugh·ty** *Br* → **drafty**

**draw 1.** *v/t* ziehen; *Vorhänge* auf-, zuziehen; *Atem* holen; *Tee* ziehen lassen; *fig Menge* anziehen; *Interesse* auf sich ziehen; zeichnen; *Geld* abheben; *Scheck* ausstellen; *v/i* ziehen; SPORT unentschieden spielen; **~ back** zurückweichen; **~ near** sich nähern; **~ out** *Geld* abheben; *fig* in die Länge ziehen; **~ up** *Schriftstück* aufsetzen; MOT (an)halten; vorfahren; **2.** Ziehen *n*; *lottery*: Ziehung *f*; SPORT Unentschieden *n*; Attraktion *f*, Zugnummer *f*

**draw·back** Nachteil *m*, Hindernis *n*

**draw·bridge** Zugbrücke *f*

**draw·er**[1] Schublade *f*, Schubfach *n*

**draw·er**[2] Zeichner(in); ECON Aussteller(in)

**draw·ing** Zeichnen *n*; Zeichnung *f*; **~ board** Reißbrett *n*; **~ pin** *Br* Reißzwecke *f*, Reißnagel *m*, Heftzwecke *f*; **~ room** → **living room**; Salon *m*

**drawl** gedehnt sprechen

**drawn** abgespannt; SPORT unentschieden

**dread 1.** (große) Angst, Furcht *f*; **2.** (sich) fürchten

**dread·ful** schrecklich, furchtbar

**dream 1.** Traum *m*; **2.** träumen

**dream·er** Träumer(in)

**dream·y** träumerisch, verträumt

**drear·y** trübselig; trüb(e); langweilig

**dredge 1.** (Schwimm)Bagger *m*; **2.** (aus)baggern

**dredg·er** (Schwimm)Bagger *m*

**dregs** Bodensatz *m*; *fig* Abschaum *m*

**drench** durchnässen

**dress 1.** Kleidung *f*; Kleid *n*; **2.** (sich) ankleiden *or* anziehen; schmücken, dekorieren; zurechtmachen; GASTR zubereiten, *Salat* anmachen; MED *Wunde* verbinden; *Haare* frisieren; **get ~ed** sich anziehen; **~ s.o. down** F j-m e-e Standpauke halten; **~ up** (sich) fein machen; sich kostümieren *or* verkleiden

**dress cir·cle** THEA erster Rang

**dress de·sign·er** Modezeichner(in)

**dress·er** Anrichte *f*; Toilettentisch *m*

**dress·ing** An-, Zurichten *n*; Ankleiden *n*; MED Verband *m*; GASTR Dressing *n*, Füllung *f*

**dressing-down** F Standpauke *f*

**dress·ing| gown** *esp Br* Morgenrock *m*, -mantel *m*; SPORT Bademantel *m*; **~ room** THEA *etc* (Künstler)Garderobe *f*; SPORT (Umkleide)Kabine *f*; **~ ta·ble** Toilettentisch *m*

**dress·mak·er** (Damen)Schneider(in)

**dress re·hears·al** THEA *etc* Generalprobe *f*

**drib·ble** tröpfeln (lassen); sabbern, geifern; *soccer*: dribbeln

**dried** getrocknet, Dörr...

**dri·er** → **dryer**

**drift 1.** (Dahin)Treiben *n*; (Schnee)Verwehung *f*; Schnee-, Sandwehe *f*; *fig* Tendenz *f*; **2.** (dahin)treiben; wehen; sich häufen

**drill 1.** TECH Bohrer *m*; MIL Drill *m* (*a. fig*), Exerzieren *n*; **2.** bohren; MIL drillen (*a. fig*); **drill·ing site** TECH Bohrgelände *n*, Bohrstelle *f*

**drink 1.** Getränk *n*; **2.** trinken; **~ to s.o.** j-m zuprosten *or* zutrinken

**drink-driv·ing** *Br* Trunkenheit *f* am Steuer

**drink·er** Trinker(in)

**drinks ma·chine** Getränkeautomat *m*

**drip 1.** Tröpfeln *n*; MED Tropf *m*; **2.** tropfen *or* tröpfeln (lassen); triefen

**drip-dry** bügelfrei

**drip·ping** Bratenfett *n*

**drive 1.** Fahrt *f*; Aus-, Spazierfahrt *f*; Zufahrt(sstraße) *f*; (private) Auffahrt; TECH Antrieb *m*; EDP Laufwerk *n*; MOT (*Links- etc*)Steuerung *f*; PSYCH Trieb *m*; *fig* Kampagne *f*; *fig* Schwung *m*, Elan *m*, Dynamik *f*; **2.** *v/t* treiben; *Auto etc* fahren, lenken, steuern; (im *Auto etc*) fahren; TECH (an)treiben; *a.* **~ off**

vertreiben; *v/i* treiben; (Auto) fahren; ~ ***off*** wegfahren; ***what are you driving at?*** F worauf wollen Sie hinaus?
**drive-in 1.** Auto...; ~ ***cinema*** *Br*, ~ ***motion-picture theater*** Autokino *n*; **2.** Autokino *n*; Drive-in-Restaurant *n*; Autoschalter *m*, Drive-in-Schalter *m*
**driv·el 1.** faseln; **2.** Geschwätz *n*, Gefasel *n*
**driv·er** MOT Fahrer(in); (*Lokomotiv-*) Führer *m*
**driv·er's li·cense** Führerschein *m*
**driv·ing** (an)treibend; TECH Antriebs..., Treib..., Trieb...; MOT Fahr...
**driv·ing force** *fig* Triebkraft *f*
**driv·ing li·cence** *Br* Führerschein *m*
**driv·ing test** Fahrprüfung *f*
**driz·zle 1.** Sprühregen *m*; **2.** sprühen, nieseln
**drone 1.** ZO Drohne *f* (*a. fig*); **2.** summen; dröhnen
**droop** (schlaff) herabhängen
**drop 1.** Tropfen *m*; Fallen *n*, Fall *m*; *fig* Fall *m*, Sturz *m*; Bonbon *m, n*; ***fruit ~s*** Drops *pl*; **2.** *v/t* tropfen (lassen); fallen lassen (*a. fig*); *Brief* einwerfen; *Fahrgast* absetzen; senken; ~ ***s.o. a few lines*** j-m ein paar Zeilen schreiben; *v/i* tropfen; herab-, herunterfallen; umsinken, fallen; ~ ***in*** (kurz) hereinschauen; ~ ***off*** abfallen; zurückgehen, nachlassen; F einnicken; ~ ***out*** herausfallen; aussteigen (***of*** aus); *a.* ~ ***out of school*** (***university***) die Schule (das Studium) abbrechen
**drop·out** Drop-out *m*, Aussteiger *m*; (Schul-, Studien)Abbrecher *m*
**drought** Trockenheit *f*, Dürre *f*
**drown** *v/t* ertränken; überschwemmen; *fig* übertönen; *v/i* ertrinken
**drow·sy** schläfrig; einschläfernd
**drudge** sich (ab)placken, schuften, sich schinden; **drudg·e·ry** (stumpfsinnige) Plackerei *or* Schinderei *or* Schufterei
**drug 1.** Arzneimittel *n*, Medikament *n*; Droge *f*, Rauschgift *n*; ***be on ~s*** drogenabhängig *or* drogensüchtig sein; ***be off ~s*** clean sein; **2.** *j-m* Medikamente geben; *j-n* unter Drogen setzen; ein Betäubungsmittel beimischen (*dat*); betäuben (*a. fig*); ~ **a·buse** Drogenmissbrauch *m*; Medikamentenmissbrauch *m*; ~ **ad·dict** Drogenabhängige *m, f*, Drogensüchtige *m, f*; ***be a*** ~ drogenabhängig *or* drogensüchtig sein
**drug·gist** Apotheker(in); Inhaber(in) e-s Drugstores
**drug·store** Apotheke *f*; Drugstore *m*
**drug vic·tim** Drogentote *m, f*
**drum 1.** MUS Trommel *f*; ANAT Trommelfell *n*; *pl* MUS Schlagzeug *n*; **2.** trommeln; **drum·mer** MUS Trommler *m*; Schlagzeuger *m*
**drunk 1.** *adj* betrunken; ***get*** ~ sich betrinken; **2.** Betrunkene *m, f*; → ***drunkard***
**drunk·ard** Trinker(in), Säufer(in)
**drunk driv·ing** Trunkenheit *f* am Steuer
**drunk·en** betrunken; ~ **driv·ing** *Br* Trunkenheit *f* am Steuer
**dry 1.** trocken, GASTR *a.* herb; F durstig; **2.** trocknen; dörren; ~ ***out*** trocknen; e-e Entziehungskur machen, F trocken werden; ~ ***up*** austrocknen; versiegen
**dry-clean** chemisch reinigen
**dry clean·er's** chemische Reinigung
**dry·er** TECH Trockner *m*
**dry goods** Textilien *pl*
**du·al** doppelt, Doppel...; ~ **car·riage·way** *Br* Schnellstraße *f*
**dub** *Film* synchronisieren
**du·bi·ous** zweifelhaft
**duch·ess** Herzogin *f*
**duck 1.** ZO Ente *f*; Ducken *n*; F Schatz *m*; **2.** (unter)tauchen; (sich) ducken
**duck·ling** ZO Entchen *n*
**due 1.** zustehend; gebührend; angemessen; ECON fällig; ~ ***to*** wegen (*gen*); ***be ~ to*** zurückzuführen sein auf (*acc*); **2.** *adv* direkt, genau (*nach Osten etc*)
**du·el** Duell *n*
**dues** Gebühren *pl*; Beitrag *m*
**du·et** MUS Duett *n*
**duke** Herzog *m*
**dull 1.** dumm; träge, schwerfällig; stumpf; matt (*eyes etc*); schwach (*hearing*); langweilig; abgestumpft, teilnahmslos; dumpf; trüb(e); ECON flau; **2.** stumpf machen *or* werden; (sich) trüben; mildern, dämpfen; *Schmerz* betäuben; *fig* abstumpfen
**du·ly** ordnungsgemäß; gebührend; rechtzeitig
**dumb** stumm; sprachlos; F doof, dumm, blöd
**dum(b)·found·ed** verblüfft, sprachlos
**dum·my** Attrappe *f*; Kleider-, Schau-

fensterpuppe *f*; MOT Dummy *m*, Puppe *f*; *Br* Schnuller *m*
**dump 1.** *v/t* (hin)plumpsen *or* (hin)fallen lassen; auskippen; *Schutt etc* abladen; *Schadstoffe in e-n Fluss etc* einleiten, *im Meer* verklappen (***into*** in); ECON *Waren* zu Dumpingpreisen verkaufen; **2.** Plumps *m*; Schuttabladeplatz *m*, Müllkippe *f*, Müllhalde *f*, (Müll)Deponie *f*; **dump·ing** ECON Dumping *n*, Ausfuhr *f* zu Schleuderpreisen
**dune** Düne *f*
**dung** AGR **1.** Dung *m*; **2.** düngen
**dun·geon** (Burg)Verlies *n*
**dupe** betrügen, täuschen
**du·plex 1.** doppelt, Doppel...; **2.** *a.* ~ ***apartment*** Maisonette *f*, Maisonettewohnung *f*; *a.* ~ ***house*** Doppel-, Zweifamilienhaus *n*
**du·pli·cate 1.** doppelt; ~ ***key*** Zweit-, Nachschlüssel *m*; **2.** Duplikat *n*; Zweit-, Nachschlüssel *m*; **3.** doppelt ausfertigen; kopieren, vervielfältigen
**du·plic·i·ty** Doppelzüngigkeit *f*
**dur·a·ble** haltbar; dauerhaft
**du·ra·tion** Dauer *f*
**du·ress** Zwang *m*
**dur·ing** während
**dusk** (Abend)Dämmerung *f*
**dusk·y** dämmerig, düster (*a. fig*); schwärzlich
**dust 1.** Staub *m*; **2.** *v/t* abstauben; (be)streuen; *v/i* Staub wischen, abstauben
**dust·bin** *Br* Abfall-, Mülleimer *m*; Abfall-, Mülltonne *f*; ~ **lin·er** *Br* Müllbeutel *m*
**dust·cart** *Br* Müllwagen *m*
**dust·er** Staubtuch *n*
**dust cov·er, dust jack·et** Schutzumschlag *m*
**dust·man** *Br* Müllmann *m*
**dust·pan** Kehrichtschaufel *f*
**dust·y** staubig
**Dutch 1.** *adj* holländisch, niederländisch; **2.** *adv*: ***go*** ~ getrennte Kasse machen; **3.** LING Holländisch *n*, Niederländisch *n*; ***the*** ~ die Holländer *pl*, die Niederländer *pl*
**Dutch·man** Holländer *m*, Niederländer *m*; **Dutch·wom·an** Holländerin *f*, Niederländerin *f*
**du·ti·a·ble** ECON zollpflichtig
**du·ty** Pflicht *f*; Ehrerbietung *f*; ECON Abgabe *f*; Zoll *m*; Dienst *m*; ***on*** ~ Dienst habend; ***be on*** ~ Dienst haben; ***be off*** ~ dienstfrei haben; **du·ty-free** zollfrei
**dwarf 1.** Zwerg(in); **2.** verkleinern, klein erscheinen lassen
**dwell** wohnen; *fig* verweilen (***on*** bei)
**dwell·ing** Wohnung *f*
**dwin·dle** (dahin)schwinden, abnehmen
**dye 1.** Farbe *f*; ***of the deepest*** ~ *fig* von der übelsten Sorte; **2.** färben
**dy·ing 1.** sterbend; Sterbe...; **2.** Sterben *n*; ~ ***of forests*** Waldsterben *n*
**dyke** → ***dike***[1,2]
**dy·nam·ic** dynamisch, kraftgeladen
**dy·nam·ics** Dynamik *f*
**dy·na·mite 1.** Dynamit *n*; **2.** (mit Dynamit) sprengen
**dys·en·te·ry** MED Ruhr *f*
**dys·pep·si·a** MED Verdauungsstörung *f*

# E

**E, e** E, e *n*
**each** jede(r, -s); ~ ***other*** einander, sich; je, pro Person, pro Stück
**ea·ger** begierig; eifrig
**ea·ger·ness** Begierde *f*; Eifer *m*
**ea·gle** ZO Adler *m*; HIST Zehndollarstück *n*; **ea·gle-eyed** scharfsichtig
**ear** BOT Ähre *f*; ANAT Ohr *n*; Öhr *n*; Henkel *m*; ***keep an*** ~ ***to the ground*** die Ohren offen halten
**ear·ache** Ohrenschmerzen *pl*
**ear·drum** ANAT Trommelfell *n*
**earl** *englischer* Graf
**ear·lobe** ANAT Ohrläppchen *n*
**ear·ly** früh; Früh...; Anfangs..., erste(r, -s); bald(ig); ***as*** ~ ***as May*** schon im

Mai; ***as ~ as possible*** so bald wie möglich; ~ ***on*** schon früh, frühzeitig
**ear·ly bird** Frühaufsteher(in)
**ear·ly warn·ing sys·tem** MIL Frühwarnsystem *n*
**ear·mark 1.** Kennzeichen *n*; Merkmal *n*; **2.** kennzeichnen; zurücklegen (***for*** für)
**earn** verdienen; einbringen
**ear·nest 1.** ernst, ernstlich, ernsthaft; ernst gemeint; **2.** Ernst *m*; ***in*** ~ im Ernst; ernsthaft
**earn·ings** Einkommen *n*
**ear·phones** Ohrhörer *pl*; Kopfhörer *pl*
**ear·piece** TEL Hörmuschel *f*
**ear·ring** Ohrring *m*
**ear·shot:** ***within*** (***out of***) ~ in (außer) Hörweite
**earth 1.** Erde *f*; Land *n*; **2.** *v/t* ELECTR erden
**earth·en** irden
**earth·en·ware** Steingut(geschirr) *n*
**earth·ly** irdisch, weltlich; F denkbar
**earth·quake** Erdbeben *n*
**earth·worm** ZO Regenwurm *m*
**ease 1.** Bequemlichkeit *f*; (Gemüts)Ruhe *f*; Sorglosigkeit *f*; Leichtigkeit *f*; ***at*** (***one's***) ~ ruhig, entspannt; unbefangen; ***be*** *or* ***feel ill at*** ~ sich (in s-r Haut) nicht wohl fühlen; **2.** *v/t* erleichtern; beruhigen; *Schmerzen* lindern; *v/i mst* ~ ***off***, ~ ***up*** nachlassen; sich entspannen (*situation etc*)
**ea·sel** Staffelei *f*
**east 1.** Ost, Osten *m*; **2.** *adj* östlich, Ost...; **3.** *adv* nach Osten, ostwärts
**Eas·ter** Ostern *n*; Oster...; ~ **bun·ny** Osterhase *m*; ~ **egg** Osterei *n*
**eas·ter·ly** östlich, Ost...
**east·ern** östlich, Ost...
**east·ward(s)** östlich, nach Osten
**eas·y** leicht; einfach; bequem; gemächlich, gemütlich; ungezwungen; ***go*** ~ ***on*** schonen, sparsam umgehen mit; ***go*** ~, ***take it*** ~ sich Zeit lassen; ***take it*** ~! immer mit der Ruhe!
**eas·y chair** Sessel *m*
**eas·y·go·ing** gelassen; ungezwungen
**eat** essen; (zer)fressen; ~ ***out*** essen gehen; ~ ***up*** aufessen
**eat·a·ble** essbar, genießbar
**eat·er** Esser(in)
**eaves** Dachrinne *f*, Traufe *f*
**eaves·drop** (heimlich) lauschen *or* horchen; ~ ***on*** belauschen
**ebb 1.** Ebbe *f*; **2.** zurückgehen; ~ ***away*** abnehmen; ~ **tide** Ebbe *f*
**eb·o·ny** Ebenholz *n*
**ec** ABBR *of* ***Eurocheque*** *Br* Eurocheque *m*
**ec·cen·tric 1.** exzentrisch; **2.** Exzentriker *m*, Sonderling *m*
**ec·cle·si·as·tic, ec·cle·si·as·ti·cal** geistlich, kirchlich
**ech·o 1.** Echo *n*; **2.** widerhallen; *fig* echoen, nachsprechen
**e·clipse** ASTR (*Sonnen-*, *Mond*)Finsternis *f*; *fig* Niedergang *m*
**e·co·cide** Umweltzerstörung *f*
**e·co·lo·gi·cal** ökologisch, Umwelt...
**e·col·o·gist** Ökologe *m*
**e·col·o·gy** Ökologie *f*
**ec·o·nom·ic** Wirtschafts..., wirtschaftlich; ~ ***growth*** Wirtschaftswachstum *n*
**e·co·nom·i·cal** wirtschaftlich, sparsam
**e·co·nom·ics** Volkswirtschaft(slehre) *f*
**e·con·o·mist** Volkswirt *m*
**e·con·o·mize** sparsam wirtschaften (mit)
**e·con·o·my 1.** Wirtschaft *f*; Wirtschaftlichkeit *f*, Sparsamkeit *f*; Einsparung *f*; **2.** Spar...
**e·co·sys·tem** Ökosystem *n*
**ec·sta·sy** Ekstase *f*, Verzückung *f*
**ec·stat·ic** verzückt
**ed·dy 1.** Wirbel *m*; **2.** wirbeln
**edge 1.** Schneide *f*; Rand *m*; Kante *f*; Schärfe *f*; ***be on*** ~ nervös *or* gereizt sein; **2.** schärfen; (um)säumen; (sich) drängen
**edge·ways, edge·wise** seitlich, von der Seite
**edg·ing** Einfassung *f*; Rand *m*
**edg·y** scharf(kantig); F nervös; F gereizt
**ed·i·ble** essbar, genießbar
**e·dict** Edikt *n*
**ed·i·fice** Gebäude *n*
**ed·it** *Text* herausgeben, redigieren; EDP editieren; *Zeitung* als Herausgeber leiten; **e·di·tion** (*Buch*)Ausgabe *f*; Auflage *f*; **ed·i·tor** Herausgeber(in); Redakteur(in); **ed·i·to·ri·al 1.** Leitartikel *m*; **2.** Redaktions...
**EDP** ABBR *of* ***electronic data processing*** EDV, elektronische Datenverarbeitung
**ed·u·cate** erziehen; unterrichten
**ed·u·cat·ed** gebildet
**ed·u·ca·tion** Erziehung *f*; (Aus)Bil-

E

dung *f*; Bildungs-, Schulwesen *n*; ***Ministry of Education*** *appr Unterrichtsministerium*
**ed·u·ca·tion·al** erzieherisch, pädagogisch, Erziehungs...; Bildungs...
**ed·u·ca·tion·(al·)ist** Pädagoge *m*
**eel** ZO Aal *m*
**ef·fect** (Aus)Wirkung *f*; Effekt *m*, Eindruck *m*; *pl* ECON Effekten *pl*; ***be in ~*** in Kraft sein; ***in ~*** in Wirklichkeit; ***take ~*** in Kraft treten; **ef·fec·tive** wirksam; eindrucksvoll; tatsächlich
**ef·fem·i·nate** verweichlicht; weibisch
**ef·fer·vesce** brausen, sprudeln
**ef·fer·ves·cent** sprudelnd, schäumend
**ef·fi·cien·cy** Leistung *f*; Leistungsfähigkeit *f*; ***~ measure*** ECON Rationalisierungsmaßnahme *f*; **ef·fi·cient** wirksam; leistungsfähig, tüchtig
**ef·flu·ent** Abwasser *n*, Abwässer *pl*
**ef·fort** Anstrengung *f*, Bemühung *f* (***at*** um); Mühe *f*; ***without ~*** → **ef·fort·less** mühelos, ohne Anstrengung
**ef·fron·te·ry** Frechheit *f*
**ef·fu·sive** überschwänglich
**egg**[1] Ei *n*; ***put all one's ~s in one basket*** alles auf eine Karte setzen
**egg**[2]**:** ***~ on*** anstacheln
**egg co·sy** *Br* Eierwärmer *m*
**egg·cup** Eierbecher *m*
**egg·head** F Eierkopf *m*
**egg·plant** BOT Aubergine *f*
**egg·shell** Eierschale *f*
**egg tim·er** Eieruhr *f*
**e·go·is·m** Egoismus *m*, Selbstsucht *f*
**e·go·ist** Egoist(in)
**E·gypt** Ägypten *n*; **E·gyp·tian 1.** ägyptisch; **2.** Ägypter(in)
**ei·der·down** Eiderdaunen *pl*; Daunendecke *f*
**eight 1.** acht; **2.** Acht *f*
**eigh·teen 1.** achtzehn; **2.** Achtzehn *f*
**eigh·teenth** achtzehnte(r, -s)
**eight·fold** achtfach
**eighth 1.** achte(r, -s); **2.** Achtel *n*
**eighth·ly** achtens
**eigh·ti·eth** achtzigste(r, -s)
**eigh·ty 1.** achtzig; ***the eighties*** die Achtzigerjahre; **2.** Achtzig *f*
**ei·ther** jede(r, -s) (*von zweien*); eine(r, -s) (*von zweien*); beides; ***~ ... or*** entweder ... oder; ***not ~*** auch nicht
**e·jac·u·late** *v/t Samen* ausstoßen; *v/i* ejakulieren, e-n Samenerguss haben
**e·jac·u·la·tion** Samenerguss *m*
**e·ject** *j-n* hinauswerfen; TECH ausstoßen, auswerfen
**eke:** ***~ out*** *Vorräte etc* strecken; *Einkommen* aufbessern; ***~ out a living*** sich (mühsam) durchschlagen
**e·lab·o·rate 1.** sorgfältig (aus)gearbeitet; kompliziert; **2.** sorgfältig ausarbeiten
**e·lapse** verfließen, verstreichen
**e·las·tic 1.** elastisch, dehnbar; ***~ band*** *Br* → **2.** Gummiring *m*, Gummiband *n*
**e·las·ti·ci·ty** Elastizität *f*
**e·lat·ed** begeistert (***at, by*** von)
**el·bow 1.** Ellbogen *m*; (scharfe) Biegung; TECH Knie *n*; ***at one's ~*** bei der Hand; **2.** mit dem Ellbogen (weg)stoßen; ***~ one's way through*** sich (mit den Ellbogen) e-n Weg bahnen durch
**el·der**[1] **1.** ältere(r, -s); **2.** der, die Ältere; (Kirchen)Älteste(r) *m*
**el·der**[2] BOT Holunder *m*
**el·der·ly** ältlich, ältere(r, -s)
**el·dest** älteste(r, -s)
**e·lect 1.** gewählt; **2.** (aus-, er)wählen
**e·lec·tion** Wahl *f*; **~ vic·to·ry** POL Wahlsieg *m*; **~ win·ner** POL Wahlsieger *m*
**e·lec·tor** Wähler(in); POL Wahlmann *m*; HIST Kurfürst *m*; **e·lec·to·ral** Wähler..., Wahl...; ***~ college*** POL Wahlmänner *pl*; ***~ district*** POL Wahlkreis *m*; **elec·to·rate** POL Wähler(schaft *f*) *pl*
**e·lec·tric** elektrisch, Elektro...
**e·lec·tri·cal** elektrisch; Elektro...; **~ en·gi·neer** Elektroingenieur *m*, Elektrotechniker *m*; **~ en·gi·neer·ing** Elektrotechnik *f*
**e·lec·tric chair** elektrischer Stuhl
**e·lec·tri·cian** Elektriker *m*
**e·lec·tri·ci·ty** Elektrizität *f*
**e·lec·tric ra·zor** Elektrorasierer *m*
**e·lec·tri·fy** elektrifizieren; elektrisieren (*a. fig*)
**e·lec·tro·cute** auf dem elektrischen Stuhl hinrichten; durch elektrischen Strom töten
**e·lec·tron** Elektron *n*
**e·lec·tron·ic** elektronisch, Elektronen...; **~ da·ta pro·cess·ing** elektronische Datenverarbeitung
**e·lec·tron·ics** Elektronik *f*
**el·e·gance** Eleganz *f*; **el·egant** elegant; geschmackvoll; erstklassig

**el·e·ment** CHEM Element *n*; Urstoff *m*; (Grund)Bestandteil *m*; *pl* Anfangsgründe *pl*, Grundlage(n *pl*) *f*; Elemente *pl*, Naturkräfte *pl*
**el·e·men·tal** elementar; wesentlich
**el·e·men·ta·ry** elementar; Anfangs...; **~ school** Grundschule *f*
**el·e·phant** ZO Elefant *m*
**el·e·vate** erhöhen; *fig* erheben
**el·evat·ed** erhöht; *fig* gehoben, erhaben
**el·e·va·tion** Erhebung *f*; Erhöhung *f*; Höhe *f*; Erhabenheit *f*
**el·e·va·tor** TECH Lift *m*, Fahrstuhl *m*, Aufzug *m*
**e·lev·en 1.** elf; **2.** Elf *f*
**e·leventh 1.** elfte(r, -s); **2.** Elftel *n*
**elf** Elf *m*, Elfe *f*; Kobold *m*
**e·li·cit** *et.* entlocken (***from*** *dat*); ans (Tages)Licht bringen
**el·i·gi·ble** infrage kommend, geeignet, annehmbar, akzeptabel
**e·lim·i·nate** entfernen, beseitigen; ausscheiden; **e·lim·i·na·tion** Entfernung *f*, Beseitigung *f*; Ausscheidung *f*
**é·lite** Elite *f*; Auslese *f*
**elk** ZO Elch *m*; Wapitihirsch *m*
**el·lipse** MATH Ellipse *f*
**elm** BOT Ulme *f*
**e·lon·gate** verlängern
**e·lope** (mit s-m *or* s-r Geliebten) ausreißen *or* durchbrennen
**el·o·quent** redegewandt, beredt
**else** sonst, weiter; andere(r, -s)
**else·where** anderswo(hin)
**e·lude** geschickt entgehen, ausweichen, sich entziehen (*all*: *dat*); *fig* nicht einfallen (*dat*)
**e·lu·sive** schwer fassbar
**e·ma·ci·ated** abgezehrt, ausgemergelt
**em·a·nate** ausströmen; ausgehen (***from*** von); **em·a·na·tion** Ausströmen *n*; *fig* Ausstrahlung *f*
**e·man·ci·pate** emanzipieren
**e·ma·ci·pa·tion** Emanzipation *f*
**em·balm** (ein)balsamieren
**em·bank·ment** (Bahn-, Straßen-) Damm *m*; (Erd)Damm *m*; Uferstraße *f*
**em·bar·go** ECON Embargo *n*, (Hafen-, Handels)Sperre *f*
**em·bark** AVIAT, MAR an Bord nehmen *or* gehen, MAR *a.* (sich) einschiffen; *Waren* verladen; **~ *on*** *et.* anfangen, *et.* beginnen
**em·bar·rass** in Verlegenheit bringen, verlegen machen, in e-e peinliche Lage bringen; **em·bar·rass·ing** unangenehm, peinlich; verfänglich
**em·bar·rass·ment** Verlegenheit *f*
**em·bas·sy** POL Botschaft *f*
**em·bed** (ein)betten, (ein)lagern
**em·bel·lish** verschönern; *fig* ausschmücken, beschönigen
**em·bers** Glut *f*
**em·bez·zle** unterschlagen
**em·bez·zle·ment** Unterschlagung *f*
**em·bit·ter** verbittern
**em·blem** Sinnbild *n*; Wahrzeichen *n*
**em·bod·y** verkörpern; enthalten
**em·bo·lis·m** MED Embolie *f*
**em·brace 1.** (sich) umarmen; einschließen; **2.** Umarmung *f*
**em·broi·der** (be)sticken; *fig* ausschmücken; **em·broi·der·y** Stickerei *f*; *fig* Ausschmückung *f*
**em·broil** verwickeln (***in*** in *acc*)
**e·mend** *Texte* verbessern, korrigieren
**em·e·rald 1.** Smaragd *m*; **2.** smaragdgrün
**e·merge** auftauchen; sich herausstellen *or* ergeben
**e·mer·gen·cy 1.** Not *f*, Notlage *f*, Notfall *m*, Notstand *m*; ***state of* ~** POL Ausnahmezustand *m*; **2.** Not...; **~ brake** Notbremse *f*; **~ call** Notruf *m*; **~ ex·it** Notausgang *m*; **~ land·ing** AVIAT Notlandung *f*; **~ num·ber** Notruf(nummer *f*) *m*; **~ room** MED Notaufnahme *f*
**em·i·grant** Auswanderer *m*, *esp* POL Emigrant(in)
**em·i·grate** auswandern, *esp* POL emigrieren
**em·i·gra·tion** Auswanderung *f*, *esp* POL Emigration *f*
**em·i·nence** Berühmtheit *f*, Bedeutung *f*; ***Eminence*** REL Eminenz *f*
**em·i·nent** hervorragend, berühmt; bedeutend; **~ly** ganz besonders, äußerst
**e·mis·sion** Ausstoß *m*, Ausstrahlung *f*, Ausströmen *n*; **~-free** abgasfrei
**e·mit** aussenden, ausstoßen, ausstrahlen, ausströmen; von sich geben
**e·mo·tion** (Gemüts)Bewegung *f*, Gefühl *n*, Gefühlsregung *f*; Rührung *f*
**e·mo·tion·al** emotional; gefühlsmäßig; gefühlsbetont
**e·mo·tion·al·ly** emotional, gefühlsmäßig; **~ *disturbed*** seelisch gestört

E

**e·mo·tion·less** gefühllos
**e·mo·tive word** PSYCH Reizwort *n*
**em·pe·ror** Kaiser *m*
**em·pha·sis** Gewicht *n*; Nachdruck *m*
**em·pha·size** nachdrücklich betonen
**em·phat·ic** nachdrücklich; deutlich; bestimmt
**em·pire** Reich *n*, Imperium *n*; Kaiserreich *n*
**em·pir·i·cal** erfahrungsgemäß
**em·ploy 1.** beschäftigen, anstellen; an-, verwenden, gebrauchen; **2.** Beschäftigung *f*; ***in the ~ of*** angestellt bei;
**em·ploy·ee** Angestellte *m, f*, Arbeitnehmer(in)
**em·ploy·er** Arbeitgeber(in)
**em·ploy·ment** Beschäftigung *f*, Arbeit *f*; **~ ad** Stellenanzeige *f*; **~ of·fice** Arbeitsamt *n*
**em·pow·er** ermächtigen; befähigen
**em·press** Kaiserin *f*
**emp·ti·ness** Leere *f* (*a. fig*)
**emp·ty 1.** leer (*a. fig*); **2.** leeren, ausleeren, entleeren; sich leeren
**em·u·late** wetteifern mit; nacheifern (*dat*); es gleichtun (*dat*)
**e·mul·sion** Emulsion *f*
**en·a·ble** befähigen, es *j-m* ermöglichen; ermächtigen
**en·act** *Gesetz* erlassen; verfügen
**e·nam·el 1.** Email *n*, Emaille *f*; ANAT (Zahn)Schmelz *m*; Glasur *f*, Lack *m*; Nagellack *m*; **2.** emaillieren; glasieren; lackieren
**en·am·o(u)red:** ***~ of*** verliebt in (*acc*)
**en·camp·ment** *esp* MIL (Feld)Lager *n*
**en·cased:** ***~ in*** gehüllt in (*acc*)
**en·chant** bezaubern; **en·chant·ing** bezaubernd; **en·chant·ment** Bezauberung *f*; Zauber *m*
**en·cir·cle** einkreisen, umzingeln; umfassen, umschlingen
**en·close** einschließen, umgeben; beilegen, beifügen
**en·clo·sure** Einzäunung *f*; Anlage *f*
**en·code** verschlüsseln, chiffrieren; kodieren
**en·com·pass** umgeben
**en·coun·ter 1.** Begegnung *f*; Gefecht *n*; **2.** begegnen (*dat*); auf *Schwierigkeiten etc* stoßen; mit *j-m feindlich* zusammenstoßen
**en·cour·age** ermutigen; fördern
**en·cour·age·ment** Ermutigung *f*; Anfeuerung *f*; Unterstützung *f*
**en·cour·ag·ing** ermutigend
**en·croach** (***on***) eingreifen (in *j-s Recht etc*), eindringen (in *acc*); über Gebühr in Anspruch nehmen (*acc*)
**en·croach·ment** Ein-, Übergriff *m*
**en·cum·ber** belasten; (be)hindern
**en·cum·brance** Belastung *f*
**en·cy·clo·p(a)e·di·a** Enzyklopädie *f*
**end 1.** Ende *n*; Ziel *n*, Zweck *m*; ***no ~ of*** unendlich viel(e), unzählige; ***at the ~ of May*** Ende Mai; ***in the ~*** am Ende, schließlich; ***on ~*** aufrecht; ***stand on ~*** zu Berge stehen (*hair*); ***to no ~*** vergebens; ***go off the deep ~*** F *fig* in die Luft gehen; ***make*** (***both***) ***~s meet*** durchkommen, finanziell über die Runden kommen; **2.** enden; beend(ig)en
**en·dan·ger** gefährden
**en·dear** beliebt machen (***to s.o.*** bei j-m); **en·dear·ing** gewinnend; liebenswert; **en·dear·ment:** ***words of ~, ~s*** zärtliche Worte *pl*
**en·deav·o(u)r 1.** Bestreben *n*, Bemühung *f*; **2.** sich bemühen
**end·ing** Ende *n*; Schluss *m*; LING Endung *f*
**en·dive** BOT Endivie *f*
**end·less** endlos, unendlich; TECH ohne Ende
**en·dorse** ECON *Scheck etc* indossieren; *et.* vermerken (***on*** auf der Rückseite); billigen; **en·dorse·ment** Vermerk *m*; ECON Indossament *n*, Giro *n*
**en·dow** *fig* ausstatten; ***~ s.o. with s.th.*** j-m et. stiften; **en·dow·ment** Stiftung *f*; *mst pl* Begabung *f*, Talent *n*
**en·dur·ance** Ausdauer *f*; ***beyond ~, past ~*** unerträglich; **en·dure** ertragen
**end us·er** Endverbraucher *m*
**en·e·my 1.** Feind *m*; **2.** feindlich
**en·er·get·ic** energisch; tatkräftig
**en·er·gy** Energie *f*
**en·er·gy cri·sis** Energiekrise *f*
**en·er·gy-sav·ing** energiesparend
**en·er·gy sup·ply** Energieversorgung *f*
**en·fold** einhüllen; umfassen
**en·force** (mit Nachdruck, *a.* gerichtlich) geltend machen; *Gesetz etc* durchführen; durchsetzen, erzwingen
**en·force·ment** ECON, JUR Geltendmachung *f*; Durchsetzung *f*, Erzwingung *f*
**en·fran·chise** *j-m* das Wahlrecht verleihen

**en·gage** *v/t j-s Aufmerksamkeit* auf sich ziehen; TECH einrasten lassen; MOT *e-n Gang* einlegen; *j-n* einstellen, anstellen, *Künstler* engagieren; *v/i* TECH einrasten, greifen; ~ ***in*** sich einlassen auf (*acc*) *or* in (*acc*); sich beschäftigen mit

**en·gaged** verlobt (***to*** mit); beschäftigt (***in, on*** mit); besetzt (*a. Br* TEL); ~ ***tone*** *or* ***signal*** *Br* TEL Besetztzeichen *n*

**en·gage·ment** Verlobung *f*; Verabredung *f*; MIL Gefecht *n*

**en·gag·ing** einnehmend; gewinnend

**en·gine** Maschine *f*; Motor *m*; RAIL Lokomotive *f*; ~ **driv·er** *Br* RAIL Lokomotivführer *m*

**en·gi·neer 1.** Ingenieur *m*, Techniker *m*, Mechaniker *m*; RAIL Lokomotivführer *m*; MIL Pionier *m*; **2.** bauen; *fig* (geschickt) in die Wege leiten

**en·gi·neer·ing** Technik *f*, Ingenieurwesen *n*, Maschinen- und Gerätebau *m*

**En·gland** England *n*

**En·glish 1.** englisch; **2.** LING Englisch *n*; ***the*** ~ die Engländer *pl*; ***in plain*** ~ *fig* unverblümt

**Eng·lish·man** Engländer *m*

**Eng·lish·wom·an** Engländerin *f*

**en·grave** (ein)gravieren, (ein)meißeln, (ein)schnitzen; *fig* einprägen

**en·grav·er** Graveur *m*

**en·grav·ing** (Kupfer-, Stahl)Stich *m*; Holzschnitt *m*

**en·grossed:** ~ ***in*** (voll) in Anspruch genommen von, vertieft *or* versunken in (*acc*)

**en·hance** erhöhen, verstärken, steigern

**e·nig·ma** Rätsel *n*

**en·ig·mat·ic** rätselhaft

**en·joy** sich erfreuen an (*dat*); genießen; ***did you*** ~ ***it?*** hat es Ihnen gefallen?; ~ ***o.s.*** sich amüsieren, sich gut unterhalten; ~ ***yourself!*** viel Spaß!; ***I*** ~ ***my dinner*** es schmeckt mir; **en·joy·a·ble** angenehm, erfreulich; **en·joy·ment** Vergnügen *n*, Freude *f*; Genuss *m*

**en·large** (sich) vergrößern *or* erweitern, ausdehnen; PHOT vergrößern; sich verbreiten *or* auslassen (***on*** über *acc*)

**en·large·ment** Erweiterung *f*; Vergrößerung *f* (*a.* PHOT)

**en·light·en** aufklären, belehren

**en·light·en·ment** Aufklärung *f*

**en·list** MIL *v/t* anwerben; *v/i* sich freiwillig melden; ~***ed men*** Unteroffiziere *pl* und Mannschaften *pl*

**en·liv·en** beleben

**en·mi·ty** Feindschaft *f*

**en·no·ble** adeln; veredeln

**e·nor·mi·ty** Ungeheuerlichkeit *f*

**e·nor·mous** ungeheuer

**e·nough** genug

**en·quire, en·qui·ry** → ***inquire, inquiry***

**en·rage** wütend machen

**en·raged** wütend (***at*** über *acc*)

**en·rap·ture** entzücken, hinreißen

**en·rap·tured** entzückt, hingerissen

**en·rich** bereichern; anreichern

**en·rol(l)** (sich) einschreiben *or* eintragen; UNIV (sich) immatrikulieren

**en·sign** MAR *esp* (National)Flagge *f*; MIL Leutnant *m* zur See

**en·sue** (darauf-, nach)folgen

**en·sure** sichern

**en·tail** mit sich bringen, zur Folge haben

**en·tan·gle** verwickeln

**en·ter** *v/t* hinein-, hereingehen, -kommen, -treten in (*acc*), eintreten, einsteigen in (*acc*), betreten; einreisen in (*acc*); MAR, RAIL einlaufen, einfahren in (*acc*); eindringen in (*acc*); *Namen etc* eintragen, einschreiben; SPORT melden, nennen (***for*** für); *fig* eintreten in (*acc*), beitreten (*dat*); EDP eingeben; *v/i* eintreten, herein-, hineinkommen, herein-, hineingehen; THEA auftreten; sich eintragen *or* einschreiben *or* anmelden (***for*** für); SPORT melden, nennen (***for*** für)

**en·ter key** EDP Eingabetaste *f*

**en·ter·prise** Unternehmen *n* (*a.* ECON); ECON Unternehmertum *n*; Unternehmungsgeist *m*; **en·ter·pris·ing** unternehmungslustig; wagemutig; kühn

**en·ter·tain** unterhalten; bewirten

**en·ter·tain·er** Entertainer(in), Unterhaltungskünstler(in)

**en·ter·tain·ment** Unterhaltung *f*; Entertainment *n*; Bewirtung *f*

**en·thral(l)** fesseln, bezaubern

**en·throne** inthronisieren

**en·thu·si·asm** Begeisterung *f*, Enthusiasmus *m*; **en·thu·si·ast** Enthusiast(in); **en·thu·si·as·tic** begeistert, enthusiastisch

**en·tice** (ver)locken

**en·tice·ment** Verlockung *f*, Reiz *m*

**en·tire** ganz, vollständig; ungeteilt
**en·tire·ly** völlig; ausschließlich
**en·ti·tle** betiteln; berechtigen (**to** zu)
**en·ti·ty** Einheit *f*
**en·trails** ANAT Eingeweide *pl*
**en·trance** Eintreten *n*, Eintritt *m*; Eingang *m*, Zugang *m*; Zufahrt *f*; Einlass *m*, Eintritt *m*, Zutritt *m*
**en·trance| ex·am(·i·na·tion)** Aufnahmeprüfung *f*; **~ fee** Eintritt *m*, Eintrittsgeld *n*; Aufnahmegebühr *f*
**en·treat** inständig bitten, anflehen
**en·trea·ty** dringende *or* inständige Bitte
**en·trench** MIL verschanzen (*a. fig*)
**en·tre·pre·neur** ECON Unternehmer(in); **en·tre·pre·neu·ri·al** ECON unternehmerisch
**en·trust** anvertrauen (***s.th. to s.o.*** j-m et.); *j-n* betrauen (***with*** mit)
**en·try** Eintreten *n*, Eintritt *m*; Einreise *f*; Beitritt *m* (***into*** zu); Einlass *m*, Zutritt *m*; Zugang *m*, Eingang *m*, Einfahrt *f*; Eintrag(ung *f*) *m*; Stichwort *n*; SPORT Nennung *f*, Meldung *f*; ***no ~!*** Zutritt verboten!, MOT keine Einfahrt!
**en·try per·mit** Einreiseerlaubnis *f*, -genehmigung *f*
**en·try·phone** Türsprechanlage *f*
**en·try vi·sa** Einreisevisum *n*
**en·twine** ineinander schlingen
**e·nu·me·rate** aufzählen
**en·vel·op** (ein)hüllen, einwickeln
**en·ve·lope** Briefumschlag *m*
**en·vi·a·ble** beneidenswert
**en·vi·ous** neidisch
**en·vi·ron·ment** Umgebung *f*, *a.* Milieu *n*; Umwelt *f*; **en·vi·ron·men·tal** Milieu...; Umwelt...; **en·vi·ron·men·tal·ist** Umweltschützer(in)
**en·vi·ron·men·tal| law** Umweltschutzgesetz *n*; **~ pol·lu·tion** Umweltverschmutzung *f*
**en·vi·ron·ment friend·ly** umweltfreundlich
**en·vi·rons** Umgebung *f*
**en·vis·age** sich *et.* vorstellen
**en·voy** Gesandte *m*, Gesandtin *f*
**en·vy 1.** Neid *m*; **2.** beneiden
**ep·ic 1.** episch; **2.** Epos *n*
**ep·i·dem·ic** MED **1.** seuchenartig; ***~ disease*** → **2.** Epidemie *f*, Seuche *f*
**ep·i·der·mis** ANAT Oberhaut *f*
**ep·i·lep·sy** MED Epilepsie *f*
**ep·i·log,** *Br* **ep·i·logue** Epilog *m*, Nachwort *n*
**e·pis·co·pal** REL bischöflich
**ep·i·sode** Episode *f*
**ep·i·taph** Grabinschrift *f*
**e·poch** Epoche *f*, Zeitalter *n*
**eq·ua·ble** ausgeglichen (*a.* METEOR)
**e·qual 1.** gleich; gleichmäßig; ***~ to fig*** gewachsen (*dat*); ***~ opportunities*** Chancengleichheit *f*; ***~ rights for women*** Gleichberechtigung *f* der Frau; **2.** Gleiche *m*, *f*; **3.** gleichen (*dat*)
**e·qual·i·ty** Gleichheit *f*
**e·qual·i·za·tion** Gleichstellung *f*; Ausgleich *m*; **e·qual·ize** gleichmachen, gleichstellen, angleichen; SPORT ausgleichen; **e·qual·iz·er** SPORT Ausgleich *m*, Ausgleichstor *n*, -treffer *m*
**eq·ua·nim·i·ty** Gleichmut *m*
**e·qua·tion** MATH Gleichung *f*
**e·qua·tor** Äquator *m*
**e·qui·lib·ri·um** Gleichgewicht *n*
**e·quip** ausrüsten
**e·quip·ment** Ausrüstung *f*, Ausstattung *f*; TECH Einrichtung *f*; *fig* Rüstzeug *n*
**e·quiv·a·lent 1.** gleichwertig, äquivalent; gleichbedeutend (**to** mit); **2.** Äquivalent *n*, Gegenwert *m*
**e·ra** Zeitrechnung *f*; Zeitalter *n*
**e·rad·i·cate** ausrotten
**e·rase** ausradieren, ausstreichen, löschen (*a.* EDP); *fig* auslöschen
**e·ras·er** Radiergummi *m*
**e·rect 1.** aufrecht; **2.** aufrichten; *Denkmal etc* errichten; aufstellen
**e·rec·tion** Errichtung *f*; MED Erektion *f*
**er·mine** zo Hermelin *n*
**e·rode** GEOL erodieren
**e·ro·sion** GEOL Erosion *f*
**e·rot·ic** erotisch
**err** (sich) irren
**er·rand** Botengang *m*, Besorgung *f*; ***go on an ~, run an ~*** e-e Besorgung machen; **~ boy** Laufbursche *m*
**er·rat·ic** sprunghaft, unstet, unberechenbar
**er·ro·ne·ous** irrig
**er·ror** Irrtum *m*, Fehler *m* (*a.* EDP); ***in ~*** irrtümlicherweise; ***~ of judg(e)ment*** Fehleinschätzung *f*; ***~s excepted*** ECON Irrtümer vorbehalten; **~ mes·sage** EDP Fehlermeldung *f*
**e·rupt** ausbrechen (*volcano etc*); durch-

brechen (*teeth*); **e·rup·tion** (*Vulkan-*) Ausbruch *m*; MED Ausschlag *m*
**ESA** ABBR *of* ***European Space Agency*** Europäische Weltraumbehörde
**es·ca·late** eskalieren; ECON steigen, in die Höhe gehen
**es·ca·la·tion** Eskalation *f*
**es·ca·la·tor** Rolltreppe *f*
**es·ca·lope** GASTR (*esp* Wiener) Schnitzel *n*
**es·cape 1.** entgehen (*dat*); entkommen, entrinnen (*both dat*); entweichen; *j-m* entfallen; **2.** Entrinnen *n*; Entweichen *n*, Flucht *f*; ***have a narrow*** ~ mit knapper Not davonkommen
**es·cape chute** AVIAT Notrutsche *f*
**es·cape key** EDP Escape-Taste *f*
**es·cort 1.** MIL Eskorte *f*; Geleit(schutz *m*) *n*; **2.** MIL eskortieren; AVIAT, MAR Geleit(schutz) geben; geleiten
**es·cutch·eon** Wappenschild *m*, *n*
**es·pe·cial** besondere(r, -s);
**es·pe·cial·ly** besonders
**es·pi·o·nage** Spionage *f*
**es·pla·nade** (*esp* Strand)Promenade *f*
**es·say** Aufsatz *m*, kurze Abhandlung, Essay *m*, *n*
**es·sence** Wesen *n*; Essenz *f*; Extrakt *m*
**es·sen·tial 1.** wesentlich; unentbehrlich; **2.** *mst pl das* Wesentliche
**es·sen·tial·ly** im Wesentlichen, in der Hauptsache
**es·tab·lish** einrichten, errichten; ~ ***o.s.*** sich etablieren *or* niederlassen; beweisen, nachweisen; **es·tab·lish·ment** Einrichtung *f*, Errichtung *f*; ECON Unternehmen *n*, Firma *f*; ***the Establishment*** das Establishment, die etablierte Macht, die herrschende Schicht
**es·tate** (großes) Grundstück, Landsitz *m*, Gut *n*; JUR Besitz *m*, (Erb)Masse *f*, Nachlass *m*; ***housing*** ~ (Wohn)Siedlung *f*; ***industrial*** ~ Industriegebiet *n*; ***real*** ~ Liegenschaften *pl*; ~ **a·gent** *Br* Grundstücks-, Immobilienmakler *m*; ~ **car** *Br* MOT Kombiwagen *m*
**es·teem 1.** Achtung *f*, Ansehen *n* (***with*** bei); **2.** achten, (hoch) schätzen
**es·thet·ic** ästhetisch
**es·thet·ics** Ästhetik *f*
**es·ti·mate 1.** (ab-, ein)schätzen; veranschlagen; **2.** Schätzung *f*; (Kosten)Voranschlag *m*; **es·ti·ma·tion** Meinung *f*; Achtung *f*, Wertschätzung *f*
**es·tranged** entfremdet
**es·trange·ment** Entfremdung *f*
**es·tu·a·ry** weite Flussmündung
**etch** ätzen; radieren
**etch·ing** Radierung *f*; Kupferstich *m*
**e·ter·nal** ewig
**e·ter·ni·ty** Ewigkeit *f*
**e·ther** Äther *m*
**e·the·re·al** ätherisch (*a. fig*)
**eth·i·cal** sittlich, ethisch
**eth·ics** Sittenlehre *f*, Ethik *f*
**eu·ro** Euro *m*
**Eu·ro·cheque** *Br* Eurocheque *m*
**Eu·rope** Europa *n*
**Eu·ro·pe·an 1.** europäisch; **2.** Europäer(in); ~ **Com·mu·ni·ty** (ABBR ***EC***) Europäische Gemeinschaft (ABBR EG)
**e·vac·u·ate** entleeren; evakuieren; *Haus etc* räumen
**e·vade** (geschickt) ausweichen (*dat*); umgehen
**e·val·u·ate** schätzen; abschätzen, bewerten, beurteilen
**e·vap·o·rate** verdunsten, verdampfen (lassen); ~***d milk*** Kondensmilch *f*
**e·vap·o·ra·tion** Verdunstung *f*, Verdampfung *f*
**e·va·sion** Umgehung *f*, Vermeidung *f*; (*Steuer*)Hinterziehung *f*; Ausflucht *f*
**e·va·sive** ausweichend; ***be*** ~ ausweichen
**eve** Vorabend *m*; Vortag *m*; ***on the*** ~ ***of*** unmittelbar vor (*dat*), am Vorabend (*gen*)
**e·ven 1.** *adj* eben, gleich; gleichmäßig; ausgeglichen; glatt; gerade (*Zahl*); ***get*** ~ ***with s.o.*** es j-m heimzahlen; **2.** *adv* selbst, sogar, auch; ***not*** ~ nicht einmal; ~ ***though***, ~ ***if*** wenn auch; **3.** ~ ***out*** sich einpendeln; sich ausgleichen
**eve·ning** Abend *m*; ***in the*** ~ am Abend, abends; ~ **class·es** Abendkurs *m*, Abendunterricht *m*; ~ **dress** Gesellschaftsanzug *m*; Frack *m*, Smoking *m*; Abendkleid *n*
**e·ven·song** REL Abendgottesdienst *m*
**e·vent** Ereignis *n*; Fall *m*; SPORT Disziplin *f*; SPORT Wettbewerb *m*; ***at all*** ~***s*** auf alle Fälle; ***in the*** ~ ***of*** im Falle (*gen*)
**e·vent·ful** ereignisreich
**e·ven·tu·al(·ly)** schließlich
**ev·er** immer (wieder); je(mals); ~ ***after***, ~ ***since*** seitdem; ~ ***so*** F sehr, noch so; ***for*** ~ für immer, auf ewig; ***Yours*** ~, ...,

***Ever yours, ...*** Viele Grüße, dein(e) *or* Ihr(e), ...; ***have you ~ been to Boston?*** bist du schon einmal in Boston gewesen?

**ev·er·green 1.** immergrün; unverwüstlich, *esp* immer wieder gern gehört; **2.** immergrüne Pflanze; MUS Evergreen *m, n*

E

**ev·er·last·ing** ewig

**ev·er·more:** (***for***) ~ für immer

**ev·ery** jede(r, -s); alle(r, -s); ***~ now and then*** von Zeit zu Zeit, dann und wann; ***~ one of them*** jeder von ihnen; ***~ other day*** jeden zweiten Tag, alle zwei Tage

**ev·ery·bod·y** jeder(mann)

**ev·ery·day** Alltags...

**ev·ery·one** jeder(mann)

**ev·ery·thing** alles

**ev·ery·where** überall(hin)

**e·vict** JUR zur Räumung zwingen; *j-n* gewaltsam vertreiben

**ev·i·dence** Beweis(material *n*) *m*, Beweise *pl*; (Zeugen)Aussage *f*; ***give ~*** (als Zeuge) aussagen; **ev·i·dent** augenscheinlich, offensichtlich

**e·vil 1.** übel, schlimm, böse; **2.** Übel *n*; *das* Böse; **e·vil-mind·ed** bösartig

**e·voke** (herauf)beschwören; *Erinnerungen* wachrufen

**ev·o·lu·tion** Entwicklung *f*; BIOL Evolution *f*

**e·volve** (sich) entwickeln

**ewe** ZO Mutterschaf *n*

**ex** *prp* ECON ab; ***~ works*** ab Werk

**ex...** Ex..., ehemalig

**ex·act 1.** exakt, genau; **2.** fordern, verlangen; **ex·act·ing** streng, genau; aufreibend, anstrengend; **ex·act·ly** exakt, genau; ***~!*** ganz recht!, genau!

**ex·act·ness** Genauigkeit *f*

**ex·ag·ge·rate** übertreiben

**ex·ag·ge·ra·tion** Übertreibung *f*

**ex·am** F Examen *n*

**ex·am·i·na·tion** Examen *n*, Prüfung *f*; Untersuchung *f*; JUR Vernehmung *f*, Verhör *n*; **ex·am·ine** untersuchen; JUR vernehmen, verhören; PED *etc* prüfen (***in*** in *dat*; ***on*** über *acc*)

**ex·am·ple** Beispiel *n*; Vorbild *n*, Muster *n*; ***for ~*** zum Beispiel

**ex·as·pe·rate** wütend machen

**ex·as·pe·rat·ing** ärgerlich

**ex·ca·vate** ausgraben, ausheben, ausschachten

**ex·ceed** überschreiten; übertreffen

**ex·ceed·ing** übermäßig

**ex·ceed·ing·ly** außerordentlich, überaus

**ex·cel** *v/t* übertreffen; *v/i* sich auszeichnen

**ex·cel·lence** ausgezeichnete Qualität

**Ex·cel·lency** Exzellenz *f*

**ex·cel·lent** ausgezeichnet, hervorragend

**ex·cept 1.** ausnehmen, ausschließen; **2.** *prp* ausgenommen, außer; ***~ for*** abgesehen von, bis auf (*acc*)

**ex·cept·ing** *prp* ausgenommen

**ex·cep·tion** Ausnahme *f*; Einwand *m* (***to*** gegen); ***make an ~*** e-e Ausnahme machen; ***take ~ to*** Anstoß nehmen an (*dat*); ***without ~*** ohne Ausnahme, ausnahmslos; **ex·cep·tion·al** außergewöhnlich; **ex·cep·tion·al·ly** ungewöhnlich, außergewöhnlich

**ex·cerpt** Auszug *m*

**ex·cess 1.** Übermaß *n*; Überschuss *m*; Ausschweifung *f*; **2.** Mehr...; **~ baggage** AVIAT Übergepäck *n*; **~ fare** (Fahrpreis)Zuschlag *m*

**ex·ces·sive** übermäßig, übertrieben

**ex·cess| lug·gage** → ***excess baggage***; **~ post·age** Nachgebühr *f*

**ex·change 1.** (aus-, ein-, um)tauschen (***for*** gegen); wechseln; **2.** (Aus-, Um-) Tausch *m*; (*esp* Geld)Wechsel *m*; ECON *a.* ***bill of ~*** Wechsel *m*; Börse *f*; Wechselstube *f*; TEL Fernsprechamt *n*; ECON ***foreign ~(s)*** Devisen *pl*; ***rate of ~*** → ***exchange rate***; **~ of·fice** Wechselstube *f*; **~ rate** Wechselkurs *m*; **~ student** Austauschschüler(in), Austauschstudent(in)

**Ex·cheq·uer:** ***Chancellor of the ~*** *Br* Finanzminister *m*

**ex·cise** Verbrauchssteuer *f*

**ex·ci·ta·ble** reizbar, (leicht) erregbar

**ex·cite** erregen, anregen; reizen

**ex·cit·ed** erregt, aufgeregt

**ex·cite·ment** Aufregung *f*, Erregung *f*

**ex·cit·ing** erregend, aufregend, spannend

**ex·claim** (aus)rufen

**ex·cla·ma·tion** Ausruf *m*, (Auf)Schrei *m*; **~ mark** *Br*, **~ point** Ausrufe-, Ausrufungszeichen *n*

**ex·clude** ausschließen

**ex·clu·sion** Ausschließung *f*, Ausschluss *m*; **ex·clu·sive** ausschließlich; exklusiv; Exklusiv...; ~ ***of*** abgesehen von, ohne

**ex·com·mu·ni·cate** REL exkommunizieren; **ex·com·mu·ni·ca·tion** REL Exkommunikation *f*

**ex·cre·ment** Kot *m*

**ex·crete** MED ausscheiden

**ex·cur·sion** Ausflug *m*

**ex·cu·sa·ble** entschuldbar

**ex·cuse 1.** entschuldigen; ~ ***me*** entschuldige(n Sie); **2.** Entschuldigung *f*

**ex-di·rec·to·ry num·ber** *Br* TEL Geheimnummer *f*

**ex·e·cute** ausführen; vollziehen; MUS vortragen; hinrichten; JUR *Testament* vollstrecken; **ex·e·cu·tion** Ausführung *f*; Vollziehung *f*; JUR (Zwangs-) Vollstreckung *f*; Hinrichtung *f*; MUS Vortrag *m*; ***put*** *or* ***carry a plan into*** ~ e-n Plan ausführen *or* verwirklichen

**ex·e·cu·tion·er** JUR Henker *m*, Scharfrichter *m*

**ex·ec·u·tive 1.** vollziehend, ausübend, POL Exekutiv...; ECON leitend; **2.** POL Exekutive *f*, vollziehende Gewalt; ECON *der*, *die* leitende Angestellte

**ex·em·pla·ry** vorbildlich

**ex·em·pli·fy** veranschaulichen

**ex·empt 1.** befreit, frei; **2.** ausnehmen, befreien

**ex·er·cise 1.** Übung *f*; Ausübung *f*; PED Übung(sarbeit) *f*, Schulaufgabe *f*; MIL Manöver *n*; (körperliche) Bewegung; ***do one's ~s*** Gymnastik machen; ***take*** ~ sich Bewegung machen; **2.** üben; ausüben; (sich) bewegen; sich Bewegung machen; MIL exerzieren

**ex·er·cise book** Schul-, Schreibheft *n*

**ex·ert** *Einfluss etc* ausüben; ~ ***o.s.*** sich anstrengen *or* bemühen; **ex·er·tion** Ausübung *f*; Anstrengung *f*, Strapaze *f*

**ex·hale** ausatmen; *Gas, Geruch etc* verströmen; *Rauch* ausstoßen

**ex·haust 1.** erschöpfen; *Vorräte* ver-, aufbrauchen; **2.** TECH Auspuff *m*; *a.* ~ ***fumes*** TECH Auspuff-, Abgase *pl*

**ex·haust·ed** erschöpft; aufgebraucht (*supplies*), vergriffen (*book*)

**ex·haus·tion** Erschöpfung *f*

**ex·haus·tive** erschöpfend

**ex·haust pipe** TECH Auspuffrohr *n*

**ex·hib·it 1.** ausstellen; vorzeigen; *fig* zeigen, zur Schau stellen; **2.** Ausstellungsstück *n*; JUR Beweisstück *n*

**ex·hi·bi·tion** Ausstellung *f*; Zurschaustellung *f*

**ex·hil·a·rat·ing** erregend, berauschend

**ex·hort** ermahnen

**ex·ile 1.** Exil *n*; im Exil Lebende *m, f*; **2.** ins Exil schicken

**ex·ist** existieren; vorhanden sein; leben; bestehen; **ex·ist·ence** Existenz *f*; Vorhandensein *n*, Vorkommen *n*; Leben *n*, Dasein *n*; **ex·ist·ent** vorhanden

**ex·it 1.** Abgang *m*; Ausgang *m*; (Autobahn)Ausfahrt *f*; Ausreise *f*; **2.** *v/i* verlassen; EDP (das Programm) beenden; ~ ***Macbeth*** THEA Macbeth (geht) ab

**ex·o·dus** Auszug *m*; Abwanderung *f*; ***general*** ~ allgemeiner Aufbruch

**ex·on·e·rate** entlasten, entbinden, befreien

**ex·or·bi·tant** übertrieben, maßlos; unverschämt (*price etc*)

**ex·or·cize** *böse Geister* beschwören, austreiben (***from*** aus); befreien (***of*** von)

**ex·ot·ic** exotisch; fremd(artig)

**ex·pand** ausbreiten; (sich) ausdehnen *or* erweitern; ECON *a.* expandieren

**ex·panse** weite Fläche, Weite *f*

**ex·pan·sion** Ausbreitung *f*; Ausdehnung *f*, Erweiterung *f*

**ex·pan·sive** mitteilsam

**ex·pat·ri·ate** *j-n* ausbürgern, *j-m* die Staatsangehörigkeit aberkennen

**ex·pect** erwarten; F annehmen; ***be ~ing*** in anderen Umständen sein

**ex·pec·tant** erwartungsvoll; ~ ***mother*** werdende Mutter

**ex·pec·ta·tion** Erwartung *f*; Hoffnung *f*, Aussicht *f*

**ex·pe·dient 1.** zweckdienlich, zweckmäßig; ratsam; **2.** (Hilfs)Mittel *n*, (Not)Behelf *m*

**ex·pe·di·tion** Expedition *f*, (Forschungs)Reise *f*

**ex·pe·di·tious** schnell

**ex·pel** (***from***) vertreiben (aus); ausweisen (aus); ausschließen (von, aus)

**ex·pen·di·ture** Ausgaben *pl*, (Kosten-) Aufwand *m*

**ex·pense** Ausgaben *pl*; *pl* ECON Unkosten *pl*, Spesen *pl*, Auslagen *pl*; ***at the*** ~ ***of*** auf Kosten (*gen*)

**ex·pen·sive** kostspielig, teuer

**ex·pe·ri·ence 1.** Erfahrung *f*; (Lebens)Praxis *f*; Erlebnis *n*; **2.** erfahren,

erleben; **ex·pe·rienced** erfahren
**ex·per·i·ment 1.** Versuch *m*; ~ ***with animals*** MED Tierversuch *m*; **2.** experimentieren; **ex·per·i·men·tal** Versuchs...
**ex·pert 1.** erfahren, geschickt; fachmännisch; **2.** Fachmann *m*; Sachverständige *m, f*

E

**ex·pi·ra·tion** Ablauf *m*, Ende *n*; Verfall *m*
**ex·pire** ablaufen, erlöschen; verfallen
**ex·plain** erklären
**ex·pla·na·tion** Erklärung *f*
**ex·pli·cit** ausdrücklich; ausführlich; offen, deutlich; (***sexually***) ~ freizügig (*film etc*)
**ex·plode** *v/t* zur Explosion bringen; *v/i* explodieren; *fig* ausbrechen (***with*** in *acc*), platzen (***with*** vor); *fig* sprunghaft ansteigen
**ex·ploit 1.** (Helden)Tat *f*; **2.** ausbeuten; *fig* ausnutzen
**ex·ploi·ta·tion** Ausbeutung *f*, Auswertung *f*, Verwertung *f*, Abbau *m*
**ex·plo·ra·tion** Erforschung *f*
**ex·plore** erforschen
**ex·plor·er** Forscher(in); Forschungsreisende *m, f*
**ex·plo·sion** Explosion *f*; *fig* Ausbruch *m*; *fig* sprunghafter Anstieg
**ex·plo·sive 1.** explosiv; *fig* aufbrausend; *fig* sprunghaft ansteigend; **2.** Sprengstoff *m*
**ex·po·nent** MATH Exponent *m*, Hochzahl *f*; Vertreter(in), Verfechter(in)
**ex·port** ECON **1.** exportieren, ausführen; **2.** Export *m*, Ausfuhr *f*; *mst pl* Export-, Ausfuhrartikel *m*
**ex·por·ta·tion** ECON Ausfuhr *f*
**ex·port·er** ECON Exporteur *m*
**ex·pose** aussetzen; PHOT belichten; *Waren* ausstellen; *j-n* entlarven, bloßstellen, *et.* aufdecken
**ex·po·si·tion** Ausstellung *f*
**ex·po·sure** Aussetzen *n*, Ausgesetztsein *n* (***to*** *dat*); *fig* Bloßstellung *f*, Aufdeckung *f*, Enthüllung *f*, Entlarvung *f*; PHOT Belichtung *f*; PHOT Aufnahme *f*; ***die of*** ~ an Unterkühlung sterben; ~ **me·ter** PHOT Belichtungsmesser *m*
**ex·press 1.** ausdrücklich, deutlich; Express..., Eil...; **2.** Eilbote *m*; Schnellzug *m*; ***by*** ~ → **3.** *adv* durch Eilboten; als Eilgut; **4.** äußern, ausdrücken
**ex·pres·sion** Ausdruck *m*
**ex·pres·sion·less** ausdruckslos
**ex·pres·sive** ausdrucksvoll; ***be*** ~ ***of*** *et.* ausdrücken
**ex·press let·ter** *Br* Eilbrief *m*
**ex·press·ly** ausdrücklich, eigens
**ex·press train** Schnellzug *m*
**ex·press·way** Schnellstraße *f*
**ex·pro·pri·ate** JUR enteignen
**ex·pul·sion** (***from***) Vertreibung *f* (aus); Ausweisung *f* (aus)
**ex·pur·gate** reinigen
**ex·qui·site** erlesen; fein
**ex·tant** noch vorhanden
**ex·tem·po·re** aus dem Stegreif
**ex·tem·po·rize** aus dem Stegreif sprechen *or* spielen
**ex·tend** (aus)dehnen, (aus)weiten; *Hand etc* ausstrecken; *Betrieb etc* vergrößern, ausbauen; *Frist*, *Pass etc* verlängern; sich ausdehnen *or* erstrecken
**ex·tend·ed fam·i·ly** Großfamilie *f*
**ex·ten·sion** Ausdehnung *f*; Vergrößerung *f*, Erweiterung *f*; (Frist)Verlängerung *f*; ARCH Erweiterung *f*, Anbau *m*; TEL Nebenanschluss *m*, (-)Apparat *m*; *a.* ~ ***cord*** (*Br* ***lead***) ELECTR Verlängerungskabel *n*, -schnur *f*
**ex·ten·sive** ausgedehnt, umfassend
**ex·tent** Ausdehnung *f*; Umfang *m*, (Aus)Maß *n*, Grad *m*; ***to some*** ~, ***to a certain*** ~ bis zu e-m gewissen Grade; ***to such an*** ~ ***that*** so sehr, dass
**ex·ten·u·ate** abschwächen, mildern; beschönigen; ***extenuating circumstances*** JUR mildernde Umstände *pl*
**ex·te·ri·or 1.** äußerlich, äußere(r, -s), Außen...; **2.** *das* Äußere; Außenseite *f*; äußere Erscheinung
**ex·ter·mi·nate** ausrotten (*a. fig*), vernichten, *Ungeziefer*, *Unkraut a.* vertilgen
**ex·ter·nal** äußere(r, -s), äußerlich, Außen...
**ex·tinct** erloschen; ausgestorben
**ex·tinc·tion** Erlöschen *n*; Aussterben *n*, Untergang *m*; Vernichtung *f*, Zerstörung *f*
**ex·tin·guish** (aus)löschen; vernichten
**ex·tin·guish·er** (*Feuer*)Löscher *m*
**ex·tort** erpressen (***from*** von)
**ex·tra 1.** *adj* zusätzlich, Extra..., Sonder...; ***be*** ~ gesondert berechnet werden; **2.** *adv* extra, besonders; ***charge*** ~

***for*** *et.* gesondert berechnen; **3.** Sonderleistung *f*; *esp* MOT Extra *n*; Zuschlag *m*; Extrablatt *n*; THEA, *film*: Statist(in)
**ex·tract 1.** Auszug *m*; **2.** (heraus)ziehen; herauslocken; ableiten, herleiten
**ex·trac·tion** (Heraus)Ziehen *n*; Herkunft *f*
**ex·tra·dite** ausliefern; *j-s* Auslieferung erwirken;
**ex·tra·di·tion** Auslieferung *f*
**extra·or·di·na·ry** außerordentlich; ungewöhnlich; Sonder...
**ex·tra pay** Zulage *f*
**ex·tra·ter·res·tri·al** außerirdisch
**ex·tra time** SPORT (Spiel)Verlängerung *f*
**ex·trav·a·gance** Übertriebenheit *f*; Verschwendung *f*; Extravaganz *f*
**ex·trav·a·gant** übertrieben, überspannt; verschwenderisch; extravagant
**ex·treme 1.** äußerste(r, -s), größte(r, -s), höchste(r, -s); außergewöhnlich; *~ right* POL rechtsextrem(istisch); *~ right wing* POL rechtsradikal; **2.** *das* Äußerste; Extrem *n*; höchster Grad
**ex·treme·ly** äußerst, höchst
**ex·trem·ism** POL Extremismus *m*
**ex·trem·ist** POL Extremist(in)
**ex·trem·i·ties** Gliedmaßen *pl*, Extremitäten *pl*
**ex·trem·i·ty** *das* Äußerste; höchste Not; äußerste Maßnahme
**ex·tri·cate** herauswinden, herausziehen, befreien
**ex·tro·vert** Extrovertierte *m, f*
**ex·u·be·rance** Fülle *f*; Überschwang *m*; **ex·u·be·rant** reichlich, üppig; überschwänglich; ausgelassen
**ex·ult** frohlocken, jubeln
**eye 1.** ANAT Auge *n*; Blick *m*; Öhr *n*; Öse *f*; ***see ~ to ~ with s.o.*** mit j-m völlig übereinstimmen; ***be up to the ~s in work*** bis über die Ohren in Arbeit stecken; ***with an ~ to s.th.*** im Hinblick auf et.; **2.** ansehen; mustern
**eye·ball** ANAT Augapfel *m*
**eye·brow** ANAT Augenbraue *f*
**eye-catch·ing** ins Auge fallend, auffallend
**eye doc·tor** F Augenarzt *m*, -ärztin *f*
**eye·glass·es** *a.* ***pair of ~*** Brille *f*
**eye·lash** ANAT Augenwimper *f*
**eye·lid** ANAT Augenlid *n*
**eye·lin·er** Eyeliner *m*
**eye-o·pen·er:** ***that was an ~ to me*** das hat mir die Augen geöffnet
**eye shad·ow** Lidschatten *m*
**eye·sight** Augen(licht *n*) *pl*, Sehkraft *f*
**eye·sore** F Schandfleck *m*
**eye spe·cial·ist** Augenarzt *m*, -ärztin *f*
**eye·strain** Ermüdung *f or* Überanstrengung *f* der Augen
**eye·wit·ness** Augenzeuge *m*, -zeugin *f*

# F

**F, f** F, f *n*
**fa·ble** Fabel *f*; Sage *f*
**fab·ric** Gewebe *n*, Stoff *m*; Struktur *f*
**fab·ri·cate** fabrizieren (*mst fig*)
**fab·u·lous** sagenhaft, der Sage angehörend; fabelhaft
**fa·cade, fa·çade** ARCH Fassade *f*
**face 1.** Gesicht *n*; Gesichtsausdruck *m*, Miene *f*; (Ober)Fläche *f*; Vorderseite *f*; Zifferblatt *n*; ***~ to ~ with*** Auge in Auge mit; ***save (lose) one's ~*** das Gesicht wahren (verlieren); ***on the ~ of it*** auf den ersten Blick; ***pull a long ~*** ein langes Gesicht machen; ***have the ~ to do s.th.*** die Stirn haben, et. zu tun; **2.** *v/t* ansehen; gegenüberstehen (*dat*); (hinaus)gehen auf (*acc*); die Stirn bieten (*dat*); einfassen; ARCH bekleiden; *v/i*: ***~ about*** sich umdrehen
**face·cloth,** *Br* **face flan·nel** Waschlappen *m*
**face·lift** Facelifting *n*, Gesichtsstraffung *f*; *fig* Renovierung *f*, Verschönerung *f*
**fa·ce·tious** witzig
**fa·cial 1.** Gesichts...; **2.** Gesichtsbehandlung *f*
**fa·cile** leicht; oberflächlich

**fa·cil·i·tate** erleichtern
**fa·cil·i·ty** Leichtigkeit *f*; Oberflächlichkeit *f*; *mst pl* Erleichterung(en *pl*) *f*; Einrichtung(en *pl*) *f*, Anlage(n *pl*) *f*
**fac·ing** TECH Verkleidung *f*; *pl* Besatz *m*
**fact** Tatsache *f*, Wirklichkeit *f*, Wahrheit *f*; Tat *f*; *pl* Daten; ***in ~*** in der Tat, tatsächlich
**fac·tion** *esp* POL Splittergruppe *f*; Zwietracht *f*
**fac·ti·tious** künstlich
**fac·tor** Faktor *m*
**fac·to·ry** Fabrik *f*
**fac·ul·ty** Fähigkeit *f*; Kraft *f*; *fig* Gabe *f*; UNIV Fakultät *f*; Lehrkörper *m*
**fad** Mode *f*, Modeerscheinung *f*, -torheit *f*; (vorübergehende) Laune
**fade** (ver)welken (lassen); verschießen, verblassen (*color*); schwinden; immer schwächer werden (*person*); *film, radio,* TV ***~ in*** auf- *or* eingeblendet werden; auf- *or* einblenden; ***~ out*** aus- *or* abgeblendet werden; aus- *or* abblenden; ***~d jeans*** ausgewaschene Jeans *pl*
**fail 1.** *v/i* versagen; misslingen, fehlschlagen; versiegen; nachlassen; durchfallen (*candidate*); *v/t* im Stich lassen; *j-n in e-r Prüfung* durchfallen lassen; **2. *without ~*** mit Sicherheit, ganz bestimmt; **fail·ure** Versagen *n*; Fehlschlag *m*, Misserfolg *m*; Versäumnis *n*; Versager *m*, F Niete *f*
**faint 1.** schwach, matt; **2.** ohnmächtig werden, in Ohnmacht fallen (***with*** vor); **3.** Ohnmacht *f*
**faint-heart·ed** verzagt
**fair**[1] gerecht, ehrlich, anständig, fair; recht gut, ansehnlich; schön (*weather*); klar (*sky*); blond (*hair*); hell (*skin*); ***play ~*** fair spielen; *fig* sich an die Spielregeln halten
**fair**[2] (Jahr)Markt *m*; Volksfest *n*; Ausstellung *f*, Messe *f*
**fair game** *fig* Freiwild *n*
**fair·ground** Rummelplatz *m*
**fair·ly** gerecht; ziemlich
**fair·ness** Gerechtigkeit *f*, Fairness *f*
**fair play** SPORT *and fig* Fair Play *n*, Fairness *f*
**fai·ry** Fee *f*; Zauberin *f*; Elf *m*, Elfe *f*
**fai·ry·land** Feen-, Märchenland *n*
**fai·ry| sto·ry, ~ tale** Märchen *n* (*a. fig*)
**faith** Glaube *m*; Vertrauen *n*; **faith·ful** treu (***to*** *dat*); ***Yours ~ly*** Hochachtungsvoll (*letter*); **faith·less** treulos
**fake 1.** Schwindel *m*; Fälschung *f*; Schwindler *m*; **2.** fälschen; imitieren, nachmachen; vortäuschen, simulieren; **3.** gefälscht; fingiert
**fal·con** ZO Falke *m*
**fall 1.** Fallen *n*, Fall *m*; Sturz *m*; Verfall *m*; Einsturz *m*; Herbst *m*; ECON Sinken *n* (*of prices etc*); Gefälle *n*; *mst pl* Wasserfall *m*; **2.** fallen, stürzen; ab-, einfallen; sinken; sich legen (*wind*); *in e-n Zustand* verfallen; ***~ ill, ~ sick*** krank werden; ***~ in love with*** sich verlieben in (*acc*); ***~ short of*** *den Erwartungen etc* nicht entsprechen; ***~ back*** zurückweichen; ***~ back on*** *fig* zurückgreifen auf (*acc*); ***~ for*** hereinfallen auf (*acc*); F sich in *j-n* verknallen; ***~ off*** zurückgehen (*business, demand etc*), nachlassen; ***~ on*** herfallen über (*acc*); ***~ out*** sich streiten (***with*** mit); ***~ through*** durchfallen (*a. fig*); ***~ to*** reinhauen, tüchtig zugreifen
**fal·la·cious** trügerisch
**fal·la·cy** Trugschluss *m*
**fall guy** F *der* Lackierte, *der* Dumme
**fal·li·ble** fehlbar
**fall·ing star** Sternschnuppe *f*
**fall·out** Fall-out *m*, radioaktiver Niederschlag
**fal·low** ZO falb; AGR brach(liegend)
**false** falsch
**false·hood, false·ness** Falschheit *f*; Unwahrheit *f*
**false start** Fehlstart *m*
**fal·si·fi·ca·tion** (Ver)Fälschung *f*
**fal·si·fy** (ver)fälschen
**fal·si·ty** Falschheit *f*, Unwahrheit *f*
**fal·ter** schwanken; stocken (*voice*); stammeln; *fig* zaudern
**fame** Ruf *m*, Ruhm *m*
**famed** berühmt (***for*** wegen)
**fa·mil·i·ar 1.** vertraut; gewohnt; familiär; **2.** Vertraute *m, f*
**fa·mil·i·ar·i·ty** Vertrautheit *f*; (plumpe) Vertraulichkeit
**fa·mil·i·ar·ize** vertraut machen
**fam·i·ly 1.** Familie *f*; **2.** Familien..., Haus...; ***be in the ~ way*** F in anderen Umständen sein; **~ al·low·ance** → ***child benefit***; **~ name** Familien-, Nachname *m*; **~ plan·ning** Familienplanung *f*; **~ tree** Stammbaum *m*
**fam·ine** Hungersnot *f*; Knappheit *f* (***of*** an *dat*)

**fam·ished** verhungert; ***be*** ~ F am Verhungern sein
**fa·mous** berühmt
**fan**[1] **1.** Fächer *m*; Ventilator *m*; **2.** (zu)fächeln; anfachen; *fig* entfachen
**fan**[2] (*Sport- etc*)Fan *m*
**fa·nat·ic** Fanatiker(in)
**fa·nat·i·cal** fanatisch
**fan belt** TECH Keilriemen *m*
**fan·ci·er** BOT, ZO Liebhaber(in), Züchter(in)
**fan·ci·ful** fantastisch
**fan club** Fanklub *m*
**fan·cy 1.** Fantasie *f*; Einbildung *f*; plötzlicher Einfall, Idee *f*; Laune *f*; Vorliebe *f*, Neigung *f*; **2.** ausgefallen; Fantasie...; **3.** sich vorstellen; sich einbilden; ***~ that!*** stell dir vor!, denk nur!; sieh mal einer an!
**fan·cy| ball** Kostümfest *n*, Maskenball *m*; **~ dress** (Masken)Kostüm *n*
**fan·cy-free** → ***footloose***
**fan·cy goods** Modeartikel *pl*, -waren *pl*
**fan·cy·work** Stickerei *f*
**fang** ZO Reiß-, Fangzahn *m*; Hauer *m*; Giftzahn *m*
**fan mail** Fanpost *f*, Verehrerpost *f*
**fan·tas·tic** fantastisch
**fan·ta·sy** Fantasie *f*
**far 1.** *adj* fern, entfernt, weit; **2.** *adv* fern; weit; (sehr) viel; ***as ~ as*** bis; ***in so ~ as*** insofern als
**far·a·way** weit entfernt
**fare 1.** Fahrgeld *n*; Fahrgast *m*; Verpflegung *f*, Kost *f*; **2.** *gut* leben; ***he ~d well*** es (er)ging ihm gut
**fare dodg·er** Schwarzfahrer(in)
**fare·well 1.** *int* lebe(n Sie) wohl!; **2.** Abschied *m*, Lebewohl *n*
**far·fetched** *fig* weit hergeholt, gesucht
**farm 1.** Bauernhof *m*, Gut *n*, Gehöft *n*, Farm *f*; **2.** *Land, Hof* bewirtschaften
**farm·er** Bauer *m*, Landwirt *m*, Farmer *m*
**farm·hand** Landarbeiter(in)
**farm·house** Bauernhaus *n*
**farm·ing 1.** Acker..., landwirtschaftlich; **2.** Landwirtschaft *f*
**farm·stead** Bauernhof *m*, Gehöft *n*
**farm·yard** Wirtschaftshof *m*
**far-off** entfernt, fern
**far right** POL rechtsgerichtet
**far·sight·ed** weitsichtig, *fig a.* weitblickend
**fas·ci·nate** faszinieren
**fas·ci·nat·ing** faszinierend
**fas·ci·na·tion** Zauber *m*, Reiz *m*, Faszination *f*
**fas·cism** POL Faschismus *m*
**fas·cist** POL **1.** Faschist *m*; **2.** faschistisch
**fash·ion** Mode *f*; Art *f* und Weise *f*; ***be in ~*** in Mode sein; ***out of ~*** unmodern; **2.** formen, gestalten; **fash·ion·a·ble** modisch, elegant; in Mode
**fash·ion| pa·rade, ~ show** Mode(n)schau *f*
**fast**[1] **1.** Fasten *n*; **2.** fasten
**fast**[2] schnell; fest; treu; echt, beständig (*color*); flott; ***be ~*** vorgehen (*watch*)
**fast·back** MOT (Wagen *m* mit) Fließheck *n*
**fast breed·er (re·ac·tor)** PHYS schneller Brüter
**fas·ten** befestigen, festmachen, anheften, anschnallen, anbinden, zuknöpfen, zu-, verschnüren; *Blick etc* richten (***on*** auf *acc*); sich festmachen *or* schließen lassen; **fas·ten·er** Verschluss *m*
**fast food** Schnellgericht(e *pl*) *n*
**fast-food res·tau·rant** Schnellimbiss *m*, Schnellgaststätte *f*
**fas·tid·i·ous** anspruchsvoll, heikel, wählerisch, verwöhnt
**fast lane** MOT Überholspur *f*
**fat 1.** fett; dick; fettig, fetthaltig; **2.** Fett *n*; ***be low in ~*** fettarm sein
**fa·tal** tödlich; verhängnisvoll, fatal (***to*** für); **fa·tal·i·ty** Verhängnis *n*; tödlicher Unfall; (Todes)Opfer *n*
**fate** Schicksal *n*; Verhängnis *n*
**fa·ther** Vater *m*
**Fa·ther Christ·mas** *esp Br* der Weihnachtsmann, der Nikolaus
**fa·ther·hood** Vaterschaft *f*
**fa·ther-in-law** Schwiegervater *m*
**fa·ther·less** vaterlos
**fa·ther·ly** väterlich
**fath·om 1.** MAR Faden *m*; **2.** MAR loten; *fig* ergründen
**fath·om·less** unergründlich
**fa·tigue 1.** Ermüdung *f*; Strapaze *f*; **2.** ermüden
**fat·ten** dick *or contp* fett machen *or* werden; mästen; **fat·ty** fett; fettig
**fau·cet** TECH (Wasser)Hahn *m*
**fault** Fehler *m*; Defekt *m*; Schuld *f*; ***find ~ with*** et. auszusetzen haben an (*dat*); ***be at ~*** Schuld haben

F

**fault·less** fehlerfrei, fehlerlos
**fault·y** fehlerhaft, TECH *a.* defekt
**fa·vo(u)r 1.** Gunst *f*; Gefallen *m*; Begünstigung *f*; ***in ~ of*** zu Gunsten von (*or gen*); ***do s.o. a ~*** j-m e-n Gefallen tun; **2.** begünstigen; bevorzugen, vorziehen; wohlwollend gegenüberstehen; SPORT favorisieren; **fa·vo(u)r·a·ble** günstig; **fa·vo(u)r·ite 1.** Liebling *m*; SPORT Favorit *m*; **2.** Lieblings...
**fawn 1.** ZO (Reh)Kitz *n*; Rehbraun *n*; **2.** rehbraun
**fax 1.** Fax *n*; **2.** faxen; ***~ s.th.*** (***through***) ***to s.o.*** j-m et. faxen
**fax (ma·chine)** Faxgerät *n*
**fear 1.** Furcht *f* (***of*** vor *dat*); Befürchtung *f*; Angst *f*; **2.** (be)fürchten; sich fürchten vor (*dat*)
**fear·ful** furchtsam; furchtbar
**fear·less** furchtlos
**fea·si·ble** durchführbar
**feast 1.** REL Fest *n*, Feiertag *m*; Festessen *n*; *fig* Fest *n*, (Hoch)Genuss *m*; **2.** *v/t* festlich bewirten; *v/i* sich gütlich tun (***on*** an *dat*), schlemmen
**feat** große Leistung; (Helden)Tat *f*
**fea·ther 1.** Feder *f*; *a. pl* Gefieder *n*; ***birds of a ~*** Leute vom gleichen Schlag; ***birds of a ~ flock together*** Gleich und Gleich gesellt sich gern; ***that is a ~ in his cap*** darauf kann er stolz sein; **2.** mit Federn polstern *or* schmücken; *Pfeil* fiedern
**feath·er·bed** verhätscheln
**feath·er·brained** F hohlköpfig
**feath·ered** ZO gefiedert
**feath·er·weight** SPORT Federgewicht *n*, Federgewichtler *m*; Leichtgewicht *n* (*person*)
**feath·er·y** gefiedert; federleicht
**fea·ture 1.** (Gesichts)Zug *m*; (charakteristisches) Merkmal; *radio*, TV *etc* Feature *n*; Haupt-, Spielfilm *m*; **2.** groß herausbringen; *film*: in der Hauptrolle zeigen; **~ film** Haupt-, Spielfilm *m*
**Feb** ABBR *of* ***February*** Febr., Februar *m*
**Feb·ru·a·ry** (ABBR ***Feb***) Februar *m*
**fed·e·ral** POL Bundes...
**Fed·e·ral Re·pub·lic of Ger·man·y** *die* Bundesrepublik Deutschland (ABBR ***BRD***)
**fed·e·ra·tion** POL Bundesstaat *m*; Föderation *f*, Staatenbund *m*; ECON, SPORT *etc* (Dach)Verband *m*
**fee** Gebühr *f*; Honorar *n*; (Mitglieds-) Beitrag *m*; Eintrittsgeld *n*
**fee·ble** schwach
**feed 1.** Futter *n*; Nahrung *f*; Fütterung *f*; TECH Zuführung *f*, Speisung *f*; **2.** *v/t* füttern; ernähren; TECH *Maschine* speisen; EDP eingeben; AGR weiden lassen; ***be fed up with s.o.*** (***s.th.***) j-n (et.) satt haben; ***well fed*** wohlgenährt; *v/i* (fr)essen; sich ernähren; weiden
**feed·back** ELECTR Feed-back *n*, Rückkoppelung *f*; *radio*, TV Reaktion *f*
**feed·er** Esser *m*
**feed·er road** Zubringer(straße *f*) *m*
**feed·ing bot·tle** (Saug)Flasche *f*
**feel 1.** (sich) fühlen; befühlen; empfinden; sich anfühlen; ***~ sorry for s.o.*** j-n bedauern *or* bemitleiden; **2.** Gefühl *n*; Empfindung *f*; **feel·er** ZO Fühler *m*;
**feel·ing** Gefühl *n*
**feign** *Interesse etc* vortäuschen, *Krankheit a.* simulieren
**feint** Finte *f*
**fell** niederschlagen; fällen
**fel·low 1.** Gefährte *m*, Gefährtin *f*, Kamerad(in); Gegenstück *n*; F Kerl *m*; ***old ~*** F alter Knabe; ***the ~ of a glove*** der andere Handschuh; **2.** Mit...; **~ be·ing** Mitmensch *m*; **~ cit·i·zen** Mitbürger *m*; **~ coun·try·man** Landsmann *m*
**fel·low·ship** Gemeinschaft *f*; Kameradschaft *f*
**fel·low trav·el·(l)er** Mitreisende *m, f*, Reisegefährte *m*, -gefährtin *f*; POL Mitläufer(in)
**fel·on** JUR Schwerverbrecher *m*
**fel·o·ny** JUR (schweres) Verbrechen, Kapitalverbrechen *n*
**felt** Filz *m*; **~ pen, ~ tip, ~-tip(ped) pen** Filzstift *m*, Filzschreiber *m*
**fe·male 1.** weiblich; **2.** *contp* Weib *n*, Weibsbild *n*; ZO Weibchen *n*
**fem·i·nine** weiblich, Frauen...; feminin
**fem·i·nism** Feminismus *m*
**fem·i·nist 1.** Feminist(in); **2.** feministisch
**fen** Fenn *n*, Sumpf-, Marschland *n*
**fence 1.** Zaun *m*; *sl* Hehler *m*; **2.** *v/t*: ***~ in*** einzäunen, umzäunen; einsperren; ***~ off*** abzäunen; *v/i* SPORT fechten; **fenc·er** SPORT Fechter *m*; **fenc·ing 1.** Einfriedung *f*; SPORT Fechten *n*; **2.** Fecht...
**fend**: ***~ off*** abwehren; ***~ for o.s.*** für sich selbst sorgen

**fend·er** Schutzvorrichtung *f*; Schutzblech *n*; MOT Kotflügel *m*; Kamingitter *n*, Kaminvorsetzer *m*
**fen·nel** BOT Fenchel *m*
**fer·ment 1.** Ferment *n*; Gärung *f*; **2.** gären (lassen)
**fer·men·ta·tion** Gärung *f*
**fern** BOT Farn(kraut *n*) *m*
**fe·ro·cious** wild; grausam
**fe·ro·ci·ty** Wildheit *f*
**fer·ret 1.** ZO Frettchen *n*; *fig* Spürhund *m*; **2.** herumstöbern; **~ *out*** aufspüren, aufstöbern
**fer·ry 1.** Fähre *f*; **2.** übersetzen
**fer·ry·boat** Fährboot *n*, Fähre *f*
**fer·ry·man** Fährmann *m*
**fer·tile** fruchtbar; reich (***of, in*** an *dat*)
**fer·til·i·ty** Fruchtbarkeit *f* (*a. fig*)
**fer·ti·lize** fruchtbar machen; befruchten; AGR düngen; **fer·ti·liz·er** AGR (*esp* Kunst)Dünger *m*, Düngemittel *n*
**fer·vent** glühend, leidenschaftlich
**fer·vo(u)r** Glut *f*; Inbrunst *f*
**fes·ter** MED eitern
**fes·ti·val** Fest *n*; Festival *n*, Festspiele *pl*
**fes·tive** festlich
**fes·tiv·i·ty** Festlichkeit *f*
**fes·toon** Girlande *f*
**fetch** holen; *Preis* erzielen; *Seufzer* ausstoßen; **fetch·ing** F reizend
**fete, fête 1.** Fest *n*; ***village* ~** Dorffest *n*; **2.** feiern
**fet·id** stinkend
**fet·ter 1.** Fessel *f*; **2.** fesseln
**feud** Fehde *f*
**feud·al** Feudal..., Lehns...
**feu·dal·ism** Feudalismus *m*, Feudal-, Lehnssystem *n*
**fe·ver** MED Fieber *n*; **fe·ver·ish** MED fieb(e)rig, fieberhaft (*a. fig*)
**few** wenige; ***a* ~** ein paar, einige; ***no fewer than*** nicht weniger als; ***quite a* ~, *a good* ~** e-e ganze Menge
**fi·an·cé** Verlobte *m*
**fi·an·cée** Verlobte *f*
**fi·as·co** Fiasko *n*
**fib** F **1.** Flunkerei *f*, Schwindelei *f*; **2.** schwindeln, flunkern
**fi·ber,** *Br* **fi·bre** Faser *f*
**fi·ber·glass** TECH Fiberglas *n*, Glasfaser *f*
**fi·brous** faserig
**fick·le** wankelmütig; unbeständig
**fic·tion** Erfindung *f*; Prosaliteratur *f*, Belletristik *f*; Romane *pl*
**fic·tion·al** erdichtet; Roman...
**fic·ti·tious** erfunden, fiktiv
**fid·dle 1.** Fiedel *f*, Geige *f*; ***play first (second)* ~** *esp fig* die erste (zweite) Geige spielen; **(*as*) *fit as a* ~** kerngesund; **2.** MUS fiedeln; *a.* **~ *about*** *or* ***around*** **(*with*)** herumfingern (an *dat*), spielen (mit)
**fid·dler** Geiger(in)
**fi·del·i·ty** Treue *f*; Genauigkeit *f*
**fid·get** F nervös machen; (herum)zappeln; **fid·get·y** zapp(e)lig, nervös
**field** Feld *n*; SPORT Spielfeld *n*; Arbeitsfeld *n*; Gebiet *n*; Bereich *m*; **~ *of vision*** OPT Gesichtsfeld *n*; **~ e·vents** SPORT Sprung- und Wurfdisziplinen *pl*; **~ glass·es** *a.* ***pair of* ~** Feldstecher *m*, Fernglas *n*; **~ mar·shal** MIL Feldmarschall *m*
**field·work** praktische (wissenschaftliche) Arbeit, *a.* Arbeit *f* im Gelände; ECON Feldarbeit *f*
**fiend** Satan *m*, Teufel *m*; F (*Frischluft- etc*)Fanatiker(in)
**fiend·ish** teuflisch, boshaft
**fierce** wild; scharf; heftig; **fierce·ness** Wildheit *f*, Schärfe *f*; Heftigkeit *f*
**fi·er·y** feurig; hitzig
**fif·teen 1.** fünfzehn; **2.** Fünfzehn *f*
**fif·teenth** fünfzehnte(r, -s)
**fifth 1.** fünfte(r, -s); **2.** Fünftel *n*
**fifth·ly** fünftens
**fif·ti·eth** fünfzigste(r, -s)
**fif·ty 1.** fünfzig; **2.** Fünfzig *f*
**fif·ty-fif·ty** F halbe-halbe
**fig** BOT Feige *f*
**fight 1.** Kampf *m*; MIL Gefecht *n*; Schlägerei *f*; *boxing*: Kampf *m*, Fight *m*; **2.** *v/t* bekämpfen; kämpfen gegen *or* mit, SPORT *a.* boxen gegen; *v/i* kämpfen, sich schlagen; SPORT boxen
**fight·er** Kämpfer *m*; SPORT Boxer *m*, Fighter *m*; *a.* **~ *plane*** MIL Jagdflugzeug *n*
**fight·ing** Kampf *m*
**fig·u·ra·tive** bildlich
**fig·ure 1.** Figur *f*; Gestalt *f*; Zahl *f*, Ziffer *f*; Preis *m*; ***be good at* ~*s*** ein guter Rechner sein; **2.** *v/t* abbilden, darstellen; F meinen, glauben; sich *et.* vorstellen; **~ *out*** *Problem* lösen, F rauskriegen; verstehen; **~ *up*** zusammenzählen; *v/i* erscheinen, vorkommen; **~**

*on* rechnen mit; ~ **skat·er** Eiskunstläufer(in); ~ **skat·ing** Eiskunstlauf *m*
**fil·a·ment** ELECTR Glühfaden *m*
**filch** F klauen, stibitzen
**file**[1] **1.** Ordner *m*; Karteikasten *m*; Akte *f*, Akten *pl*; Ablage *f*; EDP Datei *f*; Reihe *f*; MIL Rotte *f*; ***on*** ~ bei den Akten; **2.** *v/t Briefe etc* ablegen, zu den Akten nehmen, einordnen; *Antrag* einreichen, *Berufung* einlegen; *v/i* hintereinander marschieren
**file**[2] TECH **1.** Feile *f*; **2.** feilen
**file| man·age·ment** EDP Dateiverwaltung *f*; ~ **pro·tec·tion** EDP Schreibschutz *m*
**fil·et** GASTR Filet *n*
**fi·li·al** kindlich, Kindes...
**fil·ing** Ablegen *n*
**fil·ing cab·i·net** Aktenschrank *m*
**fill 1.** (sich) füllen; an-, aus-, erfüllen, voll füllen; *Pfeife* stopfen; *Zahn* füllen, plombieren; ~ ***in*** einsetzen; ~ ***out*** (*Br* ***in***) *Formular* ausfüllen; ~ ***up*** voll füllen; sich füllen; ~ ***her up!*** F MOT voll tanken, bitte!; **2.** Füllung *f*; ***eat one's*** ~ sich satt essen
**fil·let** → ***filet***
**fill·ing** Füllung *f*; MED (Zahn)Füllung *f*, Plombe *f*; ~ **sta·tion** Tankstelle *f*
**fil·ly** ZO Stutenfohlen *n*
**film 1.** Häutchen *n*; Membran(e) *f*; Film *m* (*a.* PHOT); ***take or shoot a*** ~ e-n Film drehen; **2.** (ver)filmen; sich verfilmen lassen; ~ **star** *esp Br* Filmstar *m*
**fil·ter 1.** Filter *m*; **2.** filtern
**fil·ter tip** Filter *m*; Filterzigarette *f*
**fil·ter-tipped:** ~ ***cigarette*** Filterzigarette *f*
**filth** Schmutz *m*
**filth·y** schmutzig; *fig* unflätig
**fin** ZO Flosse *f*; SPORT Schwimmflosse *f*
**fi·nal 1.** letzte(r, -s); End..., Schluss...; endgültig; **2.** SPORT Finale *n*; *mst pl* Schlussexamen *n*, -prüfung *f*
**fi·nal dis·pos·al** Endlagerung *f*
**fi·nal·ist** SPORT Finalist(in)
**fi·nal·ly** endlich, schließlich; endgültig
**fi·nal whis·tle** SPORT Schlusspfiff *m*, Abpfiff *m*
**fi·nance 1.** Finanzwesen *n*; *pl* Finanzen *pl*; **2.** finanzieren
**fi·nan·cial** finanziell
**fi·nan·cier** Finanzier *m*
**finch** ZO Fink *m*
**find 1.** finden; (an)treffen; herausfinden; JUR *j-n* für (*nicht*) *schuldig* erklären; beschaffen, besorgen; ~ ***out*** *v/t et.* herausfinden; *v/i* es herausfinden; **2.** Fund *m*, Entdeckung *f*; **find·ings** Befund *m*; JUR Feststellung *f*, Spruch *m*
**fine**[1] **1.** *adj* fein; schön; ausgezeichnet, großartig; ***I'm*** ~ mir geht es gut; **2.** *adv* F sehr gut, bestens
**fine**[2] **1.** Geldstrafe *f*, Bußgeld *n*; **2.** zu e-r Geldstrafe verurteilen
**fin·ger 1.** ANAT Finger *m*; → ***cross*** 3; **2.** betasten, (herum)fingern an (*dat*)
**fin·ger·nail** ANAT Fingernagel *m*
**fin·ger·print** Fingerabdruck *m*
**fin·ger·tip** Fingerspitze *f*
**fin·i·cky** pedantisch; wählerisch
**fin·ish 1.** (be)enden, aufhören (mit); *a.* ~ ***off*** vollenden, zu Ende führen, erledigen, *Buch etc* auslesen; *a.* ~ ***off***, ~ ***up*** aufessen, austrinken; **2.** Ende *n*, Schluss *m*; SPORT Endspurt *m*, Finish *n*; Ziel *n*; Vollendung *f*, letzter Schliff
**fin·ish·ing line** SPORT Ziellinie *f*
**Fin·land** Finnland *n*
**Finn** Finne *m*, Finnin *f*
**Finn·ish 1.** finnisch; **2.** LING Finnisch *n*
**fir** *a.* ~ ***tree*** BOT Tanne *f*
**fir cone** BOT Tannenzapfen *m*
**fire 1.** Feuer *n*; ***be on*** ~ in Flammen stehen, brennen; ***catch*** ~ Feuer fangen, in Brand geraten; ***set on*** ~, ***set*** ~ ***to*** anzünden; **2.** *v/t* anzünden, entzünden; *fig* anfeuern; abfeuern; *Ziegel etc* brennen; F *j-n* rausschmeißen; heizen; *v/i* Feuer fangen (*a. fig*); feuern
**fire a·larm** Feueralarm *m*; Feuermelder *m*
**fire·arms** Schusswaffen *pl*
**fire bri·gade** *Br* Feuerwehr *f*
**fire·bug** F Feuerteufel *m*
**fire·crack·er** Knallfrosch *m*; Knallbonbon *m, n*
**fire de·part·ment** Feuerwehr *f*
**fire en·gine** *Br* Löschfahrzeug *n*
**fire es·cape** Feuerleiter *f*, -treppe *f*
**fire ex·tin·guish·er** Feuerlöscher *m*
**fire fight·er** Feuerwehrmann *m*
**fire·guard** *Br* Kamingitter *n*
**fire hy·drant** *Br* Hydrant *m*
**fire·man** Feuerwehrmann *m*; Heizer *m*
**fire·place** (offener) Kamin
**fire·plug** Hydrant *m*
**fire·proof** feuerfest

**fire-rais·ing** *Br* Brandstiftung *f*
**fire·screen** Kamingitter *n*
**fire ser·vice** *Br* Feuerwehr *f*
**fire·side** (offener) Kamin
**fire sta·tion** Feuerwache *f*
**fire truck** Löschfahrzeug *n*
**fire·wood** Brennholz *n*
**fire·works** Feuerwerk *n*
**fir·ing squad** MIL Exekutionskommando *n*
**firm**[1] fest; hart; standhaft
**firm**[2] Firma *f*
**first 1.** *adj* erste(r, -s); beste(r, -s); **2.** *adv* erstens; zuerst; ~ ***of all*** an erster Stelle; zu allererst; **3.** Erste(r, -s); ***at*** ~ zuerst, anfangs; ***from the*** ~ von Anfang an
**first aid** MED erste Hilfe; ~ **box,** ~ **kit** Verband(s)kasten *m*
**first·born** erstgeborene(r, -s), älteste(r, -s)
**first class** RAIL *etc* 1. Klasse
**first-class** erstklassig
**first floor** Erdgeschoss *n*, *Br* erster Stock; → ***second floor***
**first·hand** aus erster Hand
**first leg** SPORT Hinspiel *n*
**first·ly** erstens
**first name** Vorname *m*
**first-rate** erstklassig
**firth** Förde *f*, Meeresarm *m*
**fish 1.** ZO Fisch *m*; **2.** fischen, angeln
**fish·bone** Gräte *f*
**fish·er·man** Fischer *m*
**fish·e·ry** Fischerei *f*
**fish fin·ger** *Br* GASTR Fischstäbchen *n*
**fish·hook** Angelhaken *m*
**fish·ing** Fischen *n*, Angeln *n*; ~ **line** Angelschnur *f*; ~ **rod** Angelrute *f*; ~ **tack·le** Angelgerät *n*
**fish·mon·ger** *esp Br* Fischhändler *m*
**fish stick** GASTR Fischstäbchen *n*
**fish·y** Fisch...; F verdächtig
**fis·sion** PHYS Spaltung *f*
**fis·sure** GEOL Spalt *m*, Riss *m*
**fist** Faust *f*
**fit**[1] **1.** geeignet, passend; tauglich; SPORT fit, (gut) in Form; ***keep*** ~ sich fit halten; **2.** *v/t* passend machen (***for*** für), anpassen; TECH einpassen, einbauen; anbringen; ~ ***in*** *j-m* e-n Termin geben, *j-n*, *et.* einschieben; *a.* ~ ***on*** anprobieren; *a.* ~ ***out*** ausrüsten, ausstatten, einrichten (***with*** mit); *a.* ~ ***up*** einrichten (***with*** mit); montieren, installieren; *v/i* passen, sitzen (*dress etc*); **3.** Sitz *m*
**fit**[2] MED Anfall *m*; ***give s.o. a*** ~ F j-n auf die Palme bringen; j-m e-n Schock versetzen
**fit·ful** unruhig (*sleep etc*)
**fit·ness** Tauglichkeit *f*; *esp* SPORT Fitness *f*, (gute) Form; ~ **cen·ter** (*Br* **cen·tre**) Fitnesscenter *n*
**fit·ted** zugeschnitten; ~ ***carpet*** Spannteppich *m*, Teppichboden *m*; ~ ***kitchen*** Einbauküche *f*
**fit·ter** Monteur *m*; Installateur *m*
**fit·ting 1.** passend; schicklich; **2.** Montage *f*, Installation *f*; *pl* Ausstattung *f*; Armaturen *pl*
**five 1.** fünf; **2.** Fünf *f*
**fix 1.** befestigen, anbringen (***to*** an *dat*); *Preis* festsetzen; fixieren; *Blick etc* richten (***on*** auf *acc*); *Aufmerksamkeit etc* fesseln; reparieren, in Ordnung bringen (*a. fig*); *Essen* zubereiten; **2.** F Klemme *f*; *sl* Fix *m*
**fixed** fest; starr
**fix·ings** GASTR Beilagen *pl*
**fix·ture** Inventarstück *n*; ***lighting*** ~ Beleuchtungskörper *m*
**fizz** zischen, sprudeln
**flab·ber·gast** F verblüffen; ***be*** ~***ed*** F platt sein
**flab·by** schlaff
**flac·cid** schlaff, schlapp
**flag**[1] **1.** Fahne *f*, Flagge *f*; **2.** beflaggen
**flag**[2] **1.** (Stein)Platte *f*, Fliese *f*; **2.** mit (Stein)Platten *or* Fliesen belegen, fliesen
**flag**[3] nachlassen, erlahmen
**flag·pole, flag·staff** Fahnenstange *f*
**flag·stone** (Stein)Platte *f*, Fliese *f*
**flake 1.** Flocke *f*; Schuppe *f*; **2.** *mst* ~ ***off*** abblättern; F ~ ***out*** schlappmachen
**flak·y** flockig; blätt(e)rig
**flak·y pas·try** GASTR Blätterteig *m*
**flame 1.** Flamme *f* (*a. fig*); ***be in*** ~***s*** in Flammen stehen; **2.** flammen, lodern
**flam·ma·ble** TECH brennbar, leicht entzündlich, feuergefährlich
**flan** GASTR Obst-, Käsekuchen *m*
**flank 1.** Flanke *f*; **2.** flankieren
**flan·nel** Flanell *m*; *Br* Waschlappen *m*; *pl Br* Flanellhose *f*
**flap 1.** Flattern *n*, (Flügel)Schlag *m*; Klappe *f*; **2.** mit *den Flügeln etc* schlagen; flattern
**flare 1.** flackern; sich weiten; ~ ***up*** auf-

F

flammen; *fig* aufbrausen; **2.** Lichtsignal *n*
**flash 1.** Aufblitzen *n*, Aufleuchten *n*, Blitz *m*; *radio etc*: Kurzmeldung *f*; PHOT F Blitz *m*; F Taschenlampe *f*; ***like a ~*** wie der Blitz; ***in a ~*** im Nu; ***a ~ of lightning*** ein Blitz; **2.** (auf)blitzen *or* aufleuchten (lassen); zucken; rasen, flitzen
**flash·back** *film*: Rückblende *f*
**flash freeze** GASTR schnell einfrieren
**flash·light** PHOT Blitzlicht *n*; Taschenlampe *f*
**flash·y** protzig; auffallend
**flask** Taschenflasche *f*
**flat¹ 1.** flach, eben, platt; schal; ECON flau; MOT platt (*tire*); **2.** *adv* ***fall ~*** danebengehen; ***sing ~*** zu tief singen; **3.** Fläche *f*, Ebene *f*; flache Seite; Flachland *n*, Niederung *f*; MOT Reifenpanne *f*
**flat²** *Br* Wohnung *f*
**flat-foot·ed** plattfüßig
**flat·mate** *Br* Mitbewohner(in)
**flat·ten** (ein)ebnen; abflachen; *a.* ***~ out*** flach(er) werden
**flat·ter** schmeicheln (*dat*)
**flat·ter·er** Schmeichler(in)
**flat·ter·y** Schmeichelei *f*
**fla·vo(u)r 1.** Geschmack *m*; Aroma *n*; Blume *f*; *fig* Beigeschmack *m*; Würze *f*; **2.** würzen
**fla·vo(u)r·ing** Würze *f*, Aroma *n*
**flaw** Fehler *m*, TECH *a.* Defekt *m*
**flaw·less** einwandfrei, tadellos
**flax** BOT Flachs *m*
**flea** ZO Floh *m*
**flea mar·ket** Flohmarkt *m*
**fleck** Fleck(en) *m*; Tupfen *m*
**fledged** ZO flügge
**fledg(e)·ling** ZO Jungvogel *m*; *fig* Grünschnabel *m*
**flee** fliehen; meiden
**fleece 1.** Vlies *n*, *esp* Schafsfell *n*; **2.** F *j-n* neppen
**fleet** MAR Flotte *f*
**flesh** Fleisch *n*; **flesh·y** fleischig; dick
**flex¹** *esp* ANAT biegen
**flex²** *esp Br* ELECTR (Anschluss-, Verlängerungs)Kabel *n*, (-)Schnur *f*
**flex·i·ble** flexibel, biegsam; *fig* anpassungsfähig; ***~ working hours*** Gleitzeit *f*
**flex·i·time** *Br*, **flex·time** Gleitzeit *f*
**flick** schnippen; schnellen
**flick·er 1.** flackern; TV flimmern; **2.** Flackern *n*; TV Flimmern *n*
**fli·er** AVIAT Flieger *m*; Reklamezettel *m*
**flight** Flucht *f*; Flug *m* (*a. fig*); ZO Schwarm *m*; *a.* ***~ of stairs*** Treppe *f*; ***put to ~*** in die Flucht schlagen; ***take*** (***to***) ***~*** die Flucht ergreifen; **~ at·tend·ant** AVIAT Flugbegleiter(in)
**flight·less** ZO flugunfähig
**flight re·cord·er** AVIAT Flugschreiber *m*
**flight·y** flatterhaft
**flim·sy** dünn; zart; *fig* fadenscheinig
**flinch** (zurück)zucken, zusammenfahren; zurückschrecken (***from*** vor *dat*)
**fling 1.** werfen, schleudern; ***~ o.s.*** sich stürzen; ***~ open*** (***to***) *Tür etc* aufreißen (zuschlagen); **2.** ***have a ~*** sich austoben; ***have a ~ at*** es versuchen *or* probieren mit
**flint** Feuerstein *m*
**flip** schnippen, schnipsen; *Münze* hochwerfen
**flip·pant** respektlos, F schnodd(e)rig
**flip·per** ZO Flosse *f*; Schwimmflosse *f*
**flirt 1.** flirten; **2.** ***be a ~*** gern flirten
**flir·ta·tion** Flirt *m*
**flit** flitzen, huschen
**float 1.** *v/i* (auf dem Wasser) schwimmen, (im Wasser) treiben; schweben; *a.* ECON in Umlauf sein; *v/t* schwimmen *or* treiben lassen; MAR flottmachen; ECON *Wertpapiere etc* in Umlauf bringen; *Währung* floaten, den Wechselkurs (*gen*) freigeben; **2.** Festwagen *m*
**float·ing 1.** schwimmend, treibend; ECON umlaufend; frei (*exchange rate*); frei konvertierbar (*currency*); **2.** ECON Floating *n*
**float·ing vot·er** POL Wechselwähler(in)
**flock 1.** ZO Herde *f* (*a.* REL); Menge *f*, Schar *f*; **2.** *fig* strömen
**floe** (treibende) Eisscholle
**flog** prügeln, schlagen
**flog·ging** Tracht *f* Prügel
**flood 1.** *a.* ***~ tide*** Flut *f*; Überschwemmung *f*; **2.** überfluten, überschwemmen
**flood·gate** Schleusentor *n*
**flood·lights** ELECTR Flutlicht *n*
**floor 1.** (Fuß)Boden *m*; Stock *m*, Stockwerk *n*, Etage *f*; Tanzfläche *f*; → ***first floor, second floor***; ***take the ~*** das Wort ergreifen; **2.** e-n (Fuß)Boden legen in; zu Boden schlagen; *fig* F *j-n* umhauen

**floor·board** (Fußboden)Diele *f*
**floor cloth** Putzlappen *m*
**floor·ing** (Fuß)Bodenbelag *m*
**floor lamp** Stehlampe *f*
**floor lead·er** PARL Fraktionsführer *m*
**floor-length** bodenlang
**floor show** Nachtklubvorstellung *f*
**floor·walk·er** Aufsicht *f*
**flop 1.** sich (hin)plumpsen lassen; F durchfallen, danebengehen, ein Reinfall sein; **2.** Plumps *m*; F Flop *m*, Reinfall *m*, Pleite *f*; Versager *m*
**flop·py (disk)** EDP Floppy Disk *f*, Diskette *f*
**flor·id** rot, gerötet
**flor·ist** Blumenhändler(in)
**floun·der**[1] ZO Flunder *f*
**floun·der**[2] zappeln; strampeln; *fig* sich verhaspeln
**flour** (feines) Mehl
**flour·ish 1.** Schnörkel *m*; MUS Tusch *m*; **2.** *v/i* blühen, gedeihen; *v/t* schwenken
**flow 1.** fließen, strömen; wallen; **2.** Fluß *m*, Strom *m* (*both a. fig*)
**flow·er 1.** Blume *f*; Blüte *f* (*a. fig*); **2.** blühen
**flow·er·bed** Blumenbeet *n*
**flow·er·pot** Blumentopf *m*
**fluc·tu·ate** schwanken
**fluc·tu·a·tion** Schwankung *f*
**flu** F MED Grippe *f*
**flue** Rauchfang *m*, Esse *f*
**flu·en·cy** Flüssigkeit *f*; (Rede)Gewandtheit *f*; **flu·ent** flüssig; gewandt; ***speak ~ French*** fließend Französisch sprechen
**fluff 1.** Flaum *m*; Staubflocke *f*; **2.** ZO aufplustern; **fluff·y** flaumig
**flu·id 1.** flüssig; **2.** Flüssigkeit *f*
**flunk** F durchfallen (lassen)
**flu·o·res·cent** fluoreszierend
**flu·o·ride** CHEM Fluor *n*
**flu·o·rine** CHEM Fluor *n*
**flur·ry** Windstoß *m*; (*Regen-*, *Schnee-*) Schauer *m*; *fig* Aufregung *f*, Unruhe *f*
**flush 1.** (Wasser)Spülung *f*; Erröten *n*; Röte *f*; **2.** *v/t a.* ***~ out*** (aus)spülen; ***~ down*** hinunterspülen; ***~ the toilet*** spülen; *v/i* erröten, rot werden; spülen; **3.** ***be ~*** F gut bei Kasse sein
**flus·ter 1.** nervös machen *or* werden; **2.** Nervosität *f*
**flute** MUS **1.** Flöte *f*; **2.** (auf der) Flöte spielen
**flut·ter 1.** flattern; **2.** Flattern *n*; *fig* Erregung *f*
**flux** *fig* Fluss *m*
**fly**[1] ZO Fliege *f*
**fly**[2] Hosenschlitz *m*; Zeltklappe *f*
**fly**[3] fliegen (lassen); stürmen, stürzen; flattern, wehen; (ver)fliegen (*time*); *Drachen* steigen lassen; ***~ at s.o.*** auf j-n losgehen; ***~ into a passion*** *or* ***rage*** in Wut geraten; **fly·er** → ***flier***
**fly·ing** fliegend; Flug...; **~ sau·cer** fliegende Untertasse; **~ squad** Überfallkommando *n*; **~ vis·it** F Stippvisite *f*
**fly·o·ver** *Br* (Straßen-, Eisenbahn-) Überführung *f*
**fly·screen** Fliegenfenster *n*
**fly·weight** *boxing*: Fliegengewicht *n*, Fliegengewichtler *m*
**fly·wheel** TECH Schwungrad *n*
**foal** ZO Fohlen *n*
**foam 1.** Schaum *m*; **2.** schäumen; **~ ex·tin·guish·er** Schaumlöscher *m*, -löschgerät *n*; **~ rub·ber** Schaumgummi *m*
**foam·y** schaumig
**fo·cus 1.** Brennpunkt *m*, *fig a.* Mittelpunkt *m*; OPT, PHOT Scharfeinstellung *f*; **2.** OPT, PHOT scharf einstellen; *fig* konzentrieren (***on*** auf *acc*)
**fod·der** AGR (Trocken)Futter *n*
**foe** POET Feind *m*, Gegner *m*
**fog** (dichter) Nebel
**fog·gy** neb(e)lig; *fig* nebelhaft
**foi·ble** (kleine) Schwäche
**foil**[1] Folie *f*; *fig* Hintergrund *m*
**foil**[2] vereiteln
**foil**[3] *fencing*: Florett *n*
**fold**[1] **1.** Falte *f*; Falz *m*; **2.** ...fach, ...fältig; **3.** (sich) falten; falzen; *Arme* verschränken; einwickeln; *often* ***~ up*** zusammenfalten, -legen, -klappen
**fold**[2] AGR Schafhürde *f*, Pferch *m*; REL Herde *f*
**fold·er** Aktendeckel *m*; Schnellhefter *m*; Faltprospekt *m*, -blatt *n*, Broschüre *f*
**fold·ing** zusammenlegbar; Klapp...; **~ bed** Klappbett *n*; **~ bi·cy·cle** Klapprad *n*; **~ boat** Faltboot *n*; **~ chair** Klappstuhl *m*; **~ door(s)** Falttür *f*
**fo·li·age** BOT Laub *n*, Laubwerk *n*
**folk 1.** Leute *pl*; *pl* F *m-e etc* Leute *pl*; **2.** Volks...
**folk·lore** Volkskunde *f*; Volkssagen *pl*; Folklore *f*

**folk mu·sic** Volksmusik *f*
**folk song** Volkslied *n*; Folksong *m*
**fol·low** folgen (*dat*); folgen auf (*acc*); befolgen; verfolgen; *s-m Beruf etc* nachgehen; ~ ***through*** *Plan etc* bis zum Ende durchführen; ~ ***up*** *e-r Sache* nachgehen; *e-e Sache* weiterverfolgen; ***as*** ~***s*** wie folgt; **fol·low·er** Nachfolger(in); Verfolger(in); Anhänger(in); **fol·low·ing 1.** Anhängerschaft *f*, Anhänger *pl*; Gefolge *n*; ***the*** ~ das Folgende; die Folgenden *pl*; **2.** folgende(r, -s); **3.** im Anschluss an (*acc*)
**fol·ly** Torheit *f*
**fond** zärtlich; vernarrt (***of*** in *acc*); ***be*** ~ ***of*** gern haben, lieben
**fon·dle** liebkosen; streicheln; (ver)hätscheln
**fond·ness** Zärtlichkeit *f*; Vorliebe *f*
**font** REL Taufstein *m*, Taufbecken *n*
**food** Nahrung *f*, Essen *n*; Nahrungs-, Lebensmittel *pl*; AGR Futter *n*
**fool 1.** Narr *m*, Närrin *f*, Dummkopf *m*; ***make a*** ~ ***of s.o.*** j-n zum Narren halten; ***make a*** ~ ***of o.s.*** sich lächerlich machen; **2.** zum Narren halten; betrügen (***out of*** um); ~ ***about,*** ~ ***around*** herumtrödeln; Unsinn machen, herumalbern
**fool·har·dy** tollkühn
**fool·ish** dumm, töricht; unklug
**fool·ish·ness** Dummheit *f*
**fool·proof** kinderleicht; todsicher
**foot 1.** ANAT Fuß *m* (*a. linear measure = 30,48 cm*); Fußende *n*; ***on*** ~ zu Fuß; **2.** F *Rechnung* bezahlen; ***have to*** ~ ***the bill*** die Zeche bezahlen müssen; ~ ***it*** zu Fuß gehen
**foot·ball** Football(spiel *n*) *m*; *Br* Fußball(spiel *n*) *m*; Football-Ball *m*; *Br* Fußball *m*
**foot·bal·ler** *Br* Fußballer *m*
**foot·ball| hoo·li·gan** *Br* Fußballrowdy *m*; ~ **play·er** *Br* Fußballspieler *m*
**foot·bridge** Fußgängerbrücke *f*
**foot·fall** Tritt *m*, Schritt *m*
**foot·hold** fester Stand, Halt *m*
**foot·ing** Halt *m*, Stand *m*; *fig* Grundlage *f*, Basis *f*; ***be on a friendly*** ~ ***with s.o.*** ein gutes Verhältnis zu j-m haben; ***lose one's*** ~ den Halt verlieren
**foot·lights** THEA Rampenlicht(er *pl*) *n*
**foot·loose** frei, unbeschwert; ~ ***and fancy-free*** frei und ungebunden
**foot·note** Fußnote *f*
**foot·path** (Fuß)Pfad *m*, (Fuß)Weg *m*
**foot·print** Fußabdruck *m*, *pl a.* Fußspur(en *pl*) *f*
**foot·sore:** ***be*** ~ wunde Füße haben
**foot·step** Tritt *m*, Schritt *m*; Fußstapfe *f*
**foot·wear** Schuhwerk *n*, Schuhe *pl*
**fop** Geck *m*, F Fatzke *m*
**for 1.** *prp mst* für; *purpose, direction*: zu; nach; *warten, hoffen etc* auf (*acc*); *sich sehnen etc* nach; *cause*: aus, vor (*dat*), wegen; *time*: ~ ***three days*** drei Tage (lang); seit drei Tagen; *distance*: ***I walked*** ~ ***a mile*** ich ging eine Meile (weit); *exchange*: (an)statt; als; ***I*** ~ ***one*** ich zum Beispiel; ~ ***sure*** sicher!, gewiss!; **2.** *cj* denn, weil
**for·age** *a.* ~ ***about*** (herum)stöbern, (-)wühlen (***in*** in *dat*; ***for*** nach)
**for·ay** MIL Einfall *m*, Überfall *m*; *fig* Ausflug *m* (***into*** *politics* in *die Politik*)
**for·bid** verbieten; hindern
**for·bid·ding** abstoßend
**force 1.** Stärke *f*, Kraft *f*, Gewalt *f*, Wucht *f*; ***the*** (***police***) ~ die Polizei; (***armed***) ~***s*** MIL Streitkräfte *pl*; ***by*** ~ mit Gewalt; ***come*** *or* ***put into*** ~ in Kraft treten *or* setzen; **2.** *j-n* zwingen; *et.* erzwingen; zwängen; drängen; *Tempo* beschleunigen; ~ ***s.th. on s.o.*** j-m et. aufzwingen *or* aufdrängen; ~ ***o.s. on s.o.*** sich j-m aufdrängen; ~ ***open*** aufbrechen
**forced** erzwungen; gezwungen, gequält; ~ **land·ing** AVIAT Notlandung *f*
**force·ful** energisch, kraftvoll; eindrucksvoll, überzeugend
**for·ceps** MED Zange *f*
**for·ci·ble** gewaltsam; eindringlich
**ford 1.** Furt *f*; **2.** durchwaten
**fore 1.** vorder, Vorder...; vorn; **2.** Vorderteil *m*, Vorderseite *f*, Front *f*
**fore·arm** ANAT Unterarm *m*
**fore·bear** *mst pl* Vorfahren *pl*, Ahnen *pl*
**fore·bod·ing** (böses) Vorzeichen; (*böse*) (Vor)Ahnung
**fore·cast 1.** voraussagen, vorhersehen; *Wetter* vorhersagen; **2.** Voraussage *f*; METEOR Vorhersage *f*
**fore·fa·ther** Vorfahr *m*
**fore·fin·ger** ANAT Zeigefinger *m*
**fore·foot** zo Vorderfuß *m*
**fore·gone con·clu·sion** ausgemachte Sache; ***be a*** ~ *a.* von vornherein feststehen

**fore·ground** Vordergrund *m*
**fore·hand** SPORT **1.** Vorhand *f*, Vorhandschlag *m*; **2.** Vorhand...
**fore·head** ANAT Stirn *f*
**for·eign** fremd, ausländisch, Außen..., Auslands...; **~ af·fairs** Außenpolitik *f*; **~ aid** Auslandshilfe *f*
**for·eign·er** Ausländer(in)
**for·eign| lan·guage** Fremdsprache *f*; **~ min·is·ter** POL Außenminister *m*
**For·eign Of·fice** *Br* POL Außenministerium *n*
**for·eign pol·i·cy** Außenpolitik *f*
**For·eign Sec·re·ta·ry** *Br* POL Außenminister *m*
**for·eign trade** ECON Außenhandel *m*
**for·eign work·er** Gastarbeiter(in)
**fore·knowl·edge** vorherige Kenntnis
**fore·leg** ZO Vorderbein *n*
**fore·man** TECH Vorarbeiter *m*, Polier *m*; Werkmeister *m*; JUR Sprecher *m*
**fore·most** vorderste(r, -s), erste(r, -s)
**fore·name** Vorname *m*
**fo·ren·sic** JUR Gerichts...; **~ me·di·cine** Gerichtsmedizin *f*
**fore·run·ner** Vorläufer(in)
**fore·see** vorhersehen, voraussehen
**fore·see·a·ble** vorhersehbar
**fore·shad·ow** ahnen lassen, andeuten
**fore·sight** Weitblick *m*; (weise) Voraussicht
**for·est** Wald *m* (*a. fig*); Forst *m*
**fore·stall** *et.* vereiteln; *j-m* zuvorkommen
**for·est·er** Förster *m*
**for·est·ry** Forstwirtschaft *f*
**fore·taste** Vorgeschmack *m*
**fore·tell** vorhersagen
**for·ev·er, for ev·er** für immer
**fore·wom·an** TECH Vorarbeiterin *f*
**fore·word** Vorwort *n*
**for·feit** verwirken; einbüßen
**forge 1.** Schmiede *f*; **2.** fälschen; schmieden
**forg·er** Fälscher *m*
**for·ge·ry** Fälschen *n*; Fälschung *f*
**for·ge·ry-proof** fälschungssicher
**for·get** vergessen
**for·get·ful** vergesslich
**for·get-me-not** BOT Vergissmeinnicht *n*
**for·give** vergeben, verzeihen
**for·give·ness** Verzeihung *f*; Vergebung *f*
**for·giv·ing** versöhnlich; nachsichtig
**fork 1.** Gabel *f*; **2.** (sich) gabeln
**fork·lift truck** MOT Gabelstapler *m*
**form 1.** Form *f*; Gestalt *f*; Formular *n*, Vordruck *m*; *Br* (Schul)Klasse *f*; Formalität *f*; Kondition *f*, Verfassung *f*; ***in great ~*** gut in Form; **2.** (sich) formen, (sich) bilden, gestalten
**for·mal** förmlich; formell
**for·mal dress** Gesellschaftskleidung *f*
**for·mal·i·ty** Förmlichkeit *f*; Formalität *f*
**for·mat 1.** Aufmachung *f*; Format *n*; **2.** EDP formatieren
**for·ma·tion** Bildung *f*
**form·a·tive** bildend; gestaltend; ***~ years*** Entwicklungsjahre *pl*
**for·mat·ting** EDP Formatierung *f*
**for·mer 1.** früher; ehemalig; **2. *the ~*** der *or* die *or* das Erstere
**for·mer·ly** früher
**for·mi·da·ble** Furcht erregend; gewaltig, riesig, gefährlich, schwierig
**form| mas·ter** *Br* Klassenlehrer *m*, -leiter *m*; **~ mis·tress** *Br* Klassenlehrerin *f*, -leiterin *f*; **~ teach·er** *Br* Klassenlehrer(in), Klassenleiter(in)
**for·mu·la** Formel *f*; Rezept *n*
**for·mu·late** formulieren
**for·sake** aufgeben; verlassen
**for·swear** abschwören, entsagen (*dat*)
**fort** MIL Fort *n*, Festung *f*
**forth** weiter, fort; (her)vor; ***and so ~*** und so weiter
**forth·com·ing** bevorstehend, kommend; in Kürze erscheinend (*book*) *or* anlaufend (*film*)
**for·ti·eth** vierzigste(r, -s)
**for·ti·fi·ca·tion** Befestigung *f*
**for·ti·fy** MIL befestigen; *fig* (ver)stärken
**for·ti·tude** (innere) Kraft *or* Stärke
**fort·night** *esp Br* vierzehn Tage
**for·tress** MIL Festung *f*
**for·tu·i·tous** zufällig
**for·tu·nate** glücklich; ***be ~*** Glück haben; **for·tu·nate·ly** glücklicherweise
**for·tune** Vermögen *n*; (glücklicher) Zufall, Glück *n*; Schicksal *n*
**for·tune-tell·er** Wahrsager(in)
**for·ty 1.** vierzig; ***have ~ winks*** F ein Nickerchen machen; **2.** Vierzig *f*
**for·ward 1.** *adv* nach vorn, vorwärts; **2.** *adj* Vorwärts...; fortschrittlich; vorlaut, dreist; **3.** *soccer*: Stürmer *m*; **4.** befördern, (ver)senden, schicken; *Brief etc* nachsenden

**for·ward·ing a·gent** Spediteur *m*
**fos·sil** GEOL Fossil *n* (*a.* F), Versteinerung *f*
**fos·ter-child** Pflegekind *n*
**fos·ter-par·ents** Pflegeeltern *pl*
**foul 1.** stinkend, widerlich; verpestet, schlecht (*air, water*); GASTR verdorben, faul; schmutzig, verschmutzt; METEOR stürmisch, schlecht; SPORT regelwidrig; *esp Br* F mies; **2.** SPORT Foul *n*, Regelverstoß *m*; ***vicious ~*** böses *or* übles Foul; **3.** beschmutzen, verschmutzen; SPORT foulen
**found**[1] gründen; stiften
**found**[2] TECH gießen
**foun·da·tion** ARCH Grundmauer *f*, Fundament *n*; *fig* Gründung *f*, Errichtung *f*; (gemeinnützige) Stiftung; *fig* Grundlage *f*, Basis *f*
**found·er**[1] Gründer(in); Stifter(in)
**foun·der**[2] MAR sinken; *fig* scheitern
**found·ling** JUR Findelkind *n*
**foun·dry** TECH Gießerei *f*
**foun·tain** Springbrunnen *m*; (*Wasser-*)Strahl *m*; **~ pen** Füllfederhalter *m*
**four 1.** vier; **2.** Vier *f*; *rowing*: Vierer *m*; ***on all ~s*** auf allen vieren
**four star** *Br* F Super *n*
**four-star pet·rol** *Br* Superbenzin *n*
**four-stroke en·gine** Viertaktmotor *m*
**four·teen 1.** vierzehn; **2.** Vierzehn *f*
**four·teenth** vierzehnte(r, -s)
**fourth 1.** vierte(r, -s); **2.** Viertel *n*
**fourth·ly** viertens
**four-wheel drive** MOT Vierradantrieb *m*
**fowl** ZO Geflügel *n*
**fox** ZO Fuchs *m*
**fox·glove** BOT Fingerhut *m*
**fox·y** schlau, gerissen
**frac·tion** Bruchteil *m*; MATH Bruch *m*
**frac·ture** MED **1.** (Knochen)Bruch *m*; **2.** brechen
**fra·gile** zerbrechlich
**frag·ment** Bruchstück *n*
**fra·grance** Wohlgeruch *m*, Duft *m*
**fra·grant** wohlriechend, duftend
**frail** gebrechlich; zerbrechlich; zart, schwach; **frail·ty** Zartheit *f*; Gebrechlichkeit *f*; Schwäche *f*
**frame 1.** Rahmen *m*; (*Brillen- etc*)Gestell *n*; Körper(bau) *m*; ***~ of mind*** (Gemüts)Verfassung *f*, (-)Zustand *m*; **2.** (ein)rahmen; bilden, formen, bauen; *a.* ***~ up*** F *j-m* et. anhängen
**frame-up** F abgekartetes Spiel; Intrige *f*
**frame·work** TECH Gerüst *n*; *fig* Struktur *f*, System *n*
**franc** Franc *m*; Franken *m*
**France** Frankreich *n*
**fran·chise** POL Wahlrecht *n*; ECON Konzession *f*
**frank 1.** frei(mütig), offen; ***~ly*** (***speaking***) offen gesagt; **2.** *Brief* freistempeln
**frank·fur·ter** GASTR Frankfurter (Würstchen *n*) *f*
**frank·ness** Offenheit *f*
**fran·tic** hektisch; ***be ~*** außer sich sein
**fra·ter·nal** brüderlich
**frat·er·nize** sich verbrüdern
**frat·er·ni·za·tion** Verbrüderung *f*
**fra·ter·ni·ty** Brüderlichkeit *f*; Vereinigung *f*, Zunft *f*; UNIV Verbindung *f*
**fraud** Betrug *m*; F Schwindel *m*
**fraud·u·lent** betrügerisch
**fray** ausfransen, (sich) durchscheuern
**freak 1.** Missgeburt *f*; Laune *f*; *in cpds* F ...freak *m*, ...fanatiker *m*; Freak *m*, irrer Typ; ***~ of nature*** Laune *f* der Natur; **2.** F *a.* ***~ out*** durchdrehen, die Nerven verlieren
**freck·le** Sommersprosse *f*
**freck·led** sommersprossig
**free 1.** frei; ungehindert; ungebunden; kostenlos, zum Nulltarif; freigebig; ***~ and easy*** zwanglos; sorglos; ***set ~*** freilassen; **2.** befreien; freilassen
**free·dom** Freiheit *f*
**free fares** Nulltarif *m*
**free·lance** frei, freiberuflich tätig, freischaffend
**Free·ma·son** Freimaurer *m*
**free skat·ing** Kür *f*
**free·style** SPORT Freistil *m*
**free time** Freizeit *f*
**free trade** ECON Freihandel *m*; **~ ar·e·a** ECON Freihandelszone *f*
**free·way** Schnellstraße *f*
**free·wheel** im Freilauf fahren
**freeze 1.** *v/i* (ge)frieren; erstarren; *v/t* gefrieren lassen; GASTR einfrieren (*a.* ECON), tiefkühlen; **2.** Frost *m*, Kälte *f*; ECON, POL Einfrieren *n*; ***wage ~, ~ on wages*** ECON Lohnstopp *m*
**freeze-dried** gefriergetrocknet
**freeze-dry** gefriertrocknen
**freez·er** Gefriertruhe *f*, Tiefkühl-, Gefriergerät *n*; Gefrierfach *n*
**freez·ing** eisig; Gefrier...; **~ com·part-**

**ment** Gefrierfach *n*; **~ point** Gefrierpunkt *m*
**freight 1.** Fracht *f*; Frachtgebühr *f*; **2.** Güter...; **3.** beladen; verfrachten
**freight car** RAIL Güterwagen *m*
**freight·er** MAR Frachter *m*, Frachtschiff *n*; AVIAT Transportflugzeug *n*
**freight train** Güterzug *m*
**French 1.** französisch; **2.** LING Französisch *n*; ***the*** **~** die Franzosen *pl*
**French doors** Terrassen-, Balkontür *f*
**French fries** GASTR Pommes frites *pl*
**French·man** Franzose *m*
**French win·dows** → ***French doors***
**French·wom·an** Französin *f*
**fren·zied** wahnsinnig, rasend (***with*** vor *dat*); hektisch; **fren·zy** Wahnsinn *m*; Ekstase *f*; Raserei *f*
**fre·quen·cy** Häufigkeit *f*; ELECTR Frequenz *f*
**fre·quent 1.** häufig; **2.** (oft) besuchen
**fresh** frisch; neu; unerfahren; frech; ***get*** **~** (***with s.o.***) (j-m gegenüber) zudringlich werden; **fresh·en** auffrischen (*wind*); **~** (***o.s.***) ***up*** sich frisch machen
**fresh·man** UNIV Student(in) im ersten Jahr
**fresh·ness** Frische *f*; Frechheit *f*
**fresh wa·ter** Süßwasser *n*
**fresh·wa·ter** Süßwasser...
**fret** sich Sorgen machen;
**fret·ful** verärgert, gereizt; quengelig
**FRG** ABBR *of* ***Federal Republic of Germany*** Bundesrepublik *f* Deutschland
**Fri** ABBR *of* ***Friday*** Fr., Freitag *m*
**fri·ar** REL Mönch *m*
**fric·tion** TECH *etc* Reibung *f* (*a. fig*)
**Fri·day** (ABBR ***Fri***) Freitag *m*; ***on*** **~** (am) Freitag; ***on ~s*** freitags
**fridge** F Kühlschrank *m*
**friend** Freund(in); Bekannte *m,f*; ***make ~s with*** sich anfreunden mit, Freundschaft schließen mit
**friend·ly 1.** freund(schaft)lich; **2.** *esp Br* SPORT Freundschaftsspiel *n*
**friend·ship** Freundschaft *f*
**fries** F GASTR Fritten *pl*
**frig·ate** MAR Fregatte *f*
**fright** Schreck(en) *m*; ***look a*** **~** F verboten aussehen; **fright·en** erschrecken; ***be ~ed*** erschrecken (***at, by, of*** vor *dat*); Angst haben (***of*** vor *dat*)
**fright·ful** schrecklich, fürchterlich
**fri·gid** PSYCH frigid(e); kalt, frostig
**frill** Krause *f*, Rüsche *f*
**fringe 1.** Franse *f*; Rand *m*; Pony *m*; **2.** mit Fransen besetzen; **~ ben·e·fits** ECON Gehalts-, Lohnnebenleistungen *pl*; **~ e·vent** Randveranstaltung *f*; **~ group** *soziale* Randgruppe *f*
**frisk** herumtollen; F *j-n* filzen, durchsuchen; **frisk·y** lebhaft, munter
**frit·ter:** **~ *away*** *Geld etc* vertun, *Zeit* vertrödeln, *Geld, Kräfte* vergeuden
**fri·vol·i·ty** Frivolität *f*, Leichtfertigkeit *f*; **friv·o·lous** frivol, leichtfertig
**friz·zle** F GASTR verbrutzeln
**frizz·y** gekräuselt, kraus
**fro:** ***to and*** **~** hin und her
**frock** REL Kutte *f*
**frog** ZO Frosch *m*
**frog·man** Froschmann *m*, MIL *a.* Kampfschwimmer *m*
**frol·ic** herumtoben, herumtollen
**from** von; aus; von ... aus *or* her; von ... (an), seit; aus, vor (*dat*); **~ *9 to 5*** (***o'clock***) von 9 bis 5 (Uhr)
**front 1.** Vorderseite *f*; Front *f* (*a.* MIL); ***at the ~, in ~*** vorn; ***in ~ of*** vor; ***be in ~*** in Führung sein; **2.** Vorder...; **3.** *a.* **~ *on,* ~ *to*(*wards*)** gegenüberstehen, gegenüberliegen
**front·age** ARCH (Vorder)Front *f*
**front cov·er** Titelseite *f*
**front door** Haustür *f*, Vordertür *f*
**front en·trance** Vordereingang *m*
**fron·tier 1.** (Landes)Grenze *f*; HIST Grenzland *n*, Grenze *f*; **2.** Grenz...
**front-page** F wichtig, aktuell
**front-wheel drive** MOT Vorderradantrieb *m*
**frost 1.** Frost *m*; *a.* ***hoar ~, white ~*** Reif *m*; **2.** mit Reif überziehen; *Glas* mattieren; GASTR glasieren, mit Zuckerguss überziehen; mit (Puder)Zucker bestreuen
**frost·bite** MED Erfrierung *f*
**frost·bit·ten** MED erfroren
**frost·ed glass** Matt-, Milchglas *n*
**frost·y** eisig, frostig (*a. fig*)
**froth 1.** Schaum *m*; **2.** schäumen; zu Schaum schlagen
**froth·y** schäumend; schaumig
**frown 1.** Stirnrunzeln *n*; ***with a ~*** stirnrunzelnd; **2.** *v/i* die Stirn runzeln
**fro·zen** *adj* (eis)kalt; (ein-, zu)gefroren; Gefrier...
**fro·zen foods** Tiefkühlkost *f*

F

**fru·gal** sparsam; bescheiden; einfach
**fruit** Frucht *f*; Früchte *pl*; Obst *n*
**fruit·er·er** Obsthändler *m*
**fruit·ful** fruchtbar
**fruit·less** unfruchtbar; erfolglos
**fruit juice** Fruchtsaft *m*
**fruit·y** fruchtartig; fruchtig (*wine*)
**frus·trate** vereiteln; frustrieren
**frus·tra·tion** Vereitelung *f*; Frustration *f*
**fry** braten; ***fried eggs*** Spiegeleier *pl*; ***fried potatoes*** Bratkartoffeln *pl*
**fry·ing pan** Bratpfanne *f*
**fuch·sia** BOT Fuchsie *f*
**fuck** V ficken, vögeln; *~ **off!*** verpiss dich!; ***get ~ed!*** der Teufel soll dich holen!; **fuck·ing** V Scheiß..., verflucht; *~ **hell!*** verdammte Scheiße!
**fudge** GASTR Fondant *m*
**fu·el 1.** Brennstoff *m*; MOT Treib-, Kraftstoff *m*; **2.** MOT, AVIAT (auf)tanken
**fu·el in·jec·tion en·gine** MOT Einspritzmotor *m*
**fu·gi·tive 1.** flüchtig (*a. fig*); **2.** Flüchtling *m*
**ful·fil** *Br*, **ful·fill** erfüllen; vollziehen; **ful·fil·(l)ing** befriedigend; **ful·fil(l)·ment** Erfüllung *f*, Ausführung *f*
**full 1.** voll; ganz; Voll...; *~ **of*** voll von, voller; *~ **(up)*** (voll) besetzt (*bus etc*); F voll, satt; ***house ~!*** THEA ausverkauft!; *~ **of o.s.*** (ganz) von sich eingenommen; **2.** *adv* völlig, ganz; **3.** ***in ~*** vollständig, ganz; ***write out in ~*** *Wort etc* ausschreiben
**full board** Vollpension *f*
**full dress** Gesellschaftskleidung *f*
**full-fledged** ZO flügge; *fig* richtig
**full-grown** ausgewachsen
**full-length** in voller Größe; bodenlang; abendfüllend (*film etc*)
**full moon** Vollmond *m*
**full stop** LING Punkt *m*
**full time** SPORT Spielende *n*
**full-time** ganztägig, Ganztags...; *~* **job** Ganztagsbeschäftigung *f*
**ful·ly** voll, völlig, ganz
**ful·ly-fledged** *Br* → ***full-fledged***
**ful·ly-'grown** *Br* → ***full-grown***
**fum·ble** tasten; fummeln
**fume** wütend sein
**fumes** Dämpfe *pl*, Rauch *m*; Abgase *pl*
**fum·ing** wutschnaubend
**fun** Scherz *m*, Spaß *m*; ***for ~*** aus *or* zum Spaß; ***make ~ of*** sich lustig machen über (*acc*), verspotten
**func·tion 1.** Funktion *f*; Aufgabe *f*; Veranstaltung *f*; **2.** funktionieren
**func·tion·a·ry** Funktionär *m*
**func·tion key** EDP Funktionstaste *f*
**fund** ECON Fonds *m*; Geld(mittel *pl*) *n*
**fun·da·men·tal 1.** Grund..., grundlegend; **2.** *~**s*** Grundlage *f*, Grundbegriffe *pl*
**fun·da·men·tal·ist** Fundamentalist *m*
**fu·ne·ral** Begräbnis *n*, Beerdigung *f*; *~* **march** MUS Trauermarsch *m*; *~* **o·ra·tion** Trauerrede *f*; *~* **pro·ces·sion** Trauerzug *m*; *~* **ser·vice** Trauerfeier *f*
**fun·fair** Rummelplatz *m*
**fun·gus** BOT Pilz *m*, Schwamm *m*
**fu·nic·u·lar** *a. ~ **railway*** (Draht)Seilbahn *f*
**funk·y** F irre, schräg, schrill
**fun·nel** Trichter *m*; MAR, RAIL Schornstein *m*
**fun·nies** F Comics *pl*
**fun·ny** komisch, lustig, spaßig; sonderbar
**fur** Pelz *m*, Fell *n*; MED Belag *m*; TECH Kesselstein *m*
**fu·ri·ous** wütend
**furl** *Fahne*, *Segel* aufrollen, einrollen; *Schirm* zusammenrollen
**fur·nace** TECH Schmelzofen *m*, Hochofen *m*; (Heiz)Kessel *m*
**fur·nish** einrichten, möblieren; liefern; versorgen, ausrüsten, ausstatten (***with*** mit)
**fur·ni·ture** Möbel *pl*; ***sectional ~*** Anbaumöbel *pl*
**furred** MED belegt, pelzig
**fur·ri·er** Kürschner *m*
**fur·row 1.** Furche *f*; **2.** furchen
**fur·ry** pelzig; flauschig
**fur·ther 1.** weiter; **2.** fördern, unterstützen; *~* **ed·u·ca·tion** *Br* Fortbildung *f*, Weiterbildung *f*
**fur·ther·more** *fig* weiter, überdies
**fur·ther·most** entfernteste(r, -s), äußerste(r, -s)
**fur·tive** heimlich, verstohlen
**fu·ry** Wut *f*, Zorn *m*
**fuse 1.** Zünder *m*; ELECTR Sicherung *f*; Zündschnur *f*; **2.** schmelzen; ELECTR durchbrennen
**fuse box** ELECTR Sicherungskasten *m*
**fu·se·lage** (Flugzeug)Rumpf *m*

**fu·sion** Verschmelzung *f*, Fusion *f*; PHYS ***nuclear*** ~ Kernfusion *f*
**fuss 1.** (unnötige) Aufregung; Wirbel *m*, F Theater *n*; **2.** sich (unnötig) aufregen; viel Aufhebens machen (***about*** um, von); **fuss·y** aufgeregt, hektisch; kleinlich, pedantisch; heikel, wählerisch
**fus·ty** muffig; *fig* verstaubt
**fu·tile** nutzlos, zwecklos
**fu·ture 1.** (zu)künftig; **2.** Zukunft *f*; LING Futur *n*, Zukunft *f*; ***in*** ~ in Zukunft, künftig
**fuzz** feiner Flaum
**fuzz·y** kraus, wuschelig; unscharf, verschwommen; flaumig, flauschig

# G

**G, g** G, g *n*
**gab** F Geschwätz *n*; ***have the gift of the*** ~ ein gutes Mundwerk haben
**gab·ar·dine** Gabardine *m*
**gab·ble 1.** Geschnatter *n*, Geschwätz *n*; **2.** schnattern, schwatzen
**ga·ble** ARCH Giebel *m*
**gad:** F ~ ***about*** (viel) unterwegs sein (in *dat*), sich herumtreiben
**gad·fly** ZO Bremse *f*
**gad·get** TECH Apparat *m*, Gerät *n*, Vorrichtung *f*; *often contp* technische Spielerei
**gag 1.** Knebel *m* (*a. fig*); F Gag *m*; **2.** knebeln; *fig* mundtot machen
**gage 1.** Eichmaß *n*; TECH Messgerät *n*, Lehre *f*; TECH Stärke *f*, Dicke *f*; RAIL Spur(weite) *f*; **2.** TECH eichen; (ab-, aus)messen
**gai·e·ty** Fröhlichkeit *f*
**gain 1.** gewinnen; erreichen, bekommen; zunehmen an (*dat*); vorgehen (um) (*watch*); ~ ***speed*** schneller werden; ~ ***5 pounds*** 5 Pfund zunehmen; ~ ***in*** zunehmen an (*dat*); **2.** Gewinn *m*; Zunahme *f*; ~ ***of time*** Zeitgewinn *m*
**gait** Gang *m*, Gangart *f*; Schritt *m*
**gai·ter** Gamasche *f*
**gal** F Mädchen *n*
**ga·la 1.** Festlichkeit *f*; Gala(veranstaltung) *f*; **2.** Gala...
**gal·ax·y** ASTR Milchstraße *f*, Galaxis *f*
**gale** Sturm *m*
**gall**[1] Frechheit *f*
**gall**[2] **1.** wund geriebene Stelle; **2.** wund reiben *or* scheuern; *fig* (ver)ärgern
**gal·lant** tapfer; galant, höflich
**gal·lan·try** Tapferkeit *f*; Galanterie *f*
**gall blad·der** ANAT Gallenblase *f*
**gal·le·ry** Galerie *f*; Empore *f*
**gal·ley** MAR Galeere *f*; Kombüse *f*; *a.* ~ ***proof*** PRINT Fahne *f*, Fahnenabzug *m*
**gal·lon** Gallone *f* (*3,79 l, Br 4,55 l*)
**gal·lop 1.** Galopp *m*; **2.** galoppieren (lassen)
**gal·lows** Galgen *m*
**gal·lows hu·mo(u)r** Galgenhumor *m*
**ga·lore** in rauen Mengen
**gam·ble 1.** (um Geld) spielen; **2.** Glücksspiel *n*
**gam·bler** (Glücks)Spieler(in)
**gam·bol 1.** Luftsprung *m*; **2.** (herum-) tanzen, (herum)hüpfen
**game** (Karten-, Ball- *etc*)Spiel *n*; (einzelnes) Spiel (*a. fig*); HUNT Wild *n*; Wildbret *n*; *pl* Spiele *pl*; PED Sport *m*
**game·keep·er** Wildhüter *m*
**game| park,** ~ **re·serve** Wildpark *m*; Wildreservat *n*
**gan·der** ZO Gänserich *m*
**gang 1.** (Arbeiter)Trupp *m*; Gang *f*, Bande *f*; Clique *f*; Horde *f*; **2.** ~ ***up*** sich zusammentun, *contp* sich zusammenrotten
**gan·gling** schlaksig
**gang·ster** Gangster *m*
**gang| war,** ~ **war·fare** Bandenkrieg *m*
**gang·way** Gang *m*; AVIAT, MAR Gangway *f*
**gaol, gaol·bird, gaol·er** *Br* → ***jail etc***
**gap** Lücke *f*; Kluft *f*; Spalte *f*
**gape** gähnen; klaffen; gaffen
**gar·age 1.** Garage *f*; (Reparatur)Werkstatt *f* (und Tankstelle *f*); **2.** *Auto* in e-r

Garage ab- *or* unterstellen; *Auto* in die Garage fahren
**gar·bage** Abfall *m*, Müll *m*; ~ **bag** Müllbeutel *m*; ~ **can** Abfalleimer *m*, Mülleimer *m*; Abfalltonne *f*, Mülltonne *f*; ~ **truck** Müllwagen *m*
**gar·den** Garten *m*
**gar·den·er** Gärtner(in)
**gar·den·ing** Gartenarbeit *f*
**gar·gle** gurgeln
**gar·ish** grell, auffallend
**gar·land** Girlande *f*
**gar·lic** BOT Knoblauch *m*
**gar·ment** Kleidungsstück *n*; Gewand *n*
**gar·nish** GASTR garnieren
**gar·ret** Dachkammer *f*
**gar·ri·son** MIL Garnison *f*
**gar·ter** Strumpfband *n*; Sockenhalter *m*; Strumpfhalter *m*, Straps *m*
**gas** Gas *n*; F Benzin *n*, Sprit *m*
**gas·e·ous** gasförmig
**gash** klaffende Wunde
**gas·ket** TECH Dichtung(sring *m*) *f*
**gas me·ter** Gasuhr *f*, Gaszähler *m*
**gas·o·lene, gas·o·line** Benzin *n*; ~ **pump** Zapfsäule *f*
**gasp 1.** keuchen, röcheln; ~ (***for breath***) nach Atem ringen, F nach Luft schnappen; **2.** Keuchen *n*, Röcheln *n*
**gas sta·tion** Tankstelle *f*
**gas stove** Gasofen *m*, Gasherd *m*
**gas·works** TECH Gaswerk *n*
**gate** Tor *n*; Pforte *f*; Schranke *f*, Sperre *f*; AVIAT Flugsteig *m*
**gate·crash** F uneingeladen kommen (zu); sich ohne zu bezahlen hineinschmuggeln (in *acc*)
**gate·post** Tor-, Türpfosten *m*
**gate·way** Tor(weg *m*) *n*, Einfahrt *f*
**gate·way drug** Einstiegsdroge *f*
**gath·er** *v/t* sammeln, *Informationen* einholen, einziehen; *Personen* versammeln; ernten, pflücken; zusammenziehen, kräuseln; *fig* folgern, schließen (***from*** aus); ~ ***speed*** schneller werden; *v/i* sich (ver)sammeln; sich (an)sammeln; **gath·er·ing** Versammlung *f*; Zusammenkunft *f*
**gau·dy** auffällig, bunt, grell; protzig
**gauge** *Br* → ***gage***
**gaunt** hager; ausgemergelt
**gaunt·let** Schutzhandschuh *m*
**gauze** Gaze *f*; MED Bandage *f*, Binde *f*
**gav·el** Hammer *m*
**gaw·ky** linkisch
**gay 1.** lustig, fröhlich; bunt, (farben-)prächtig; F schwul; **2.** F Schwule *m*
**gaze 1.** (starrer) Blick; **2.** starren; ~ ***at*** starren auf (*acc*), anstarren
**ga·zette** Amtsblatt *n*
**ga·zelle** ZO Gazelle *f*
**gear** TECH Getriebe *n*; MOT Gang *m*; *mst in cpds* Vorrichtung *f*, Gerät *n*; F Kleidung *f*, Aufzug *m*; ***shift*** (*esp Br* ***change***) ~(***s***) MOT schalten; ***shift*** (*esp Br* ***change***) ***into second*** ~ MOT in den zweiten Gang schalten
**gear·box** MOT Getriebe *n*
**gear le·ver** *Br*, **gear shift** , **gear stick** *Br* MOT Schalthebel *m*
**Gei·ger count·er** PHYS Geigerzähler *m*
**geld·ing** ZO Wallach *m*
**gem** Edelstein *m*
**Gem·i·ni** ASTR Zwillinge *pl*; ***he*** (***she***) ***is*** (***a***) ~ er (sie) ist (ein) Zwilling
**gen·der** LING Genus *n*, Geschlecht *n*
**gene** BIOL Gen *n*, Erbfaktor *m*
**gen·e·ral 1.** allgemein; Haupt..., General...; **2.** MIL General *m*; ***in*** ~ im Allgemeinen; ~ **de·liv·er·y:** (***in care of***) ~ postlagernd; ~ **e·lec·tion** *Br* POL Parlamentswahlen *pl*
**gen·e·ral·ize** verallgemeinern
**gen·er·al·ly** im Allgemeinen, allgemein
**gen·e·ral prac·ti·tion·er** (ABBR ***GP***) *appr* Arzt *m or* Ärztin *f* für Allgemeinmedizin
**gen·e·rate** erzeugen; **gen·e·ra·tion** Erzeugung *f*; Generation *f*
**gen·e·ra·tor** ELECTR Generator *m*; MOT Lichtmaschine *f*
**gen·e·ros·i·ty** Großzügigkeit *f*
**gen·e·rous** großzügig; reichlich
**ge·net·ic** genetisch; ~ **code** BIOL Erbanlage *f*; ~ **en·gin·eer·ing** Gentechnologie *f*; ~ **fin·ger·print** genetischer Fingerabdruck
**ge·net·ics** BIOL Genetik *f*, Vererbungslehre *f*
**ge·ni·al** freundlich
**gen·i·tive** *a.* ~ ***case*** LING Genitiv *m*, zweiter Fall
**ge·ni·us** Genie *n*
**gen·o·cide** Völkermord *m*
**gent** F *esp Br* Herr *m*; ***gents*** *Br* F Herrenklo *n*
**gen·tle** sanft, zart, sacht; mild
**gen·tle·man** Gentleman *m*; Herr *m*

**gen·tle·man·ly** gentlemanlike, vornehm
**gen·tle·ness** Sanftheit *f*, Zartheit *f*; Milde *f*
**gen·try** *Br* niederer Adel; Oberschicht *f*
**gen·u·ine** echt; aufrichtig
**ge·og·ra·phy** Geografie *f*
**ge·ol·o·gy** Geologie *f*
**ge·om·e·try** Geometrie *f*
**germ** BIOL, BOT Keim *m*; MED Bazillus *m*, Bakterie *f*, (Krankheits)Erreger *m*
**Ger·man 1.** deutsch; **2.** Deutsche *m, f*; LING Deutsch *n*; ~ **shep·herd** ZO Deutscher Schäferhund
**Ger·man·y** Deutschland *n*
**ger·mi·nate** BIOL, BOT keimen (lassen)
**ger·und** LING Gerundium *n*
**ges·tic·u·late** gestikulieren
**ges·ture** Geste *f*, Gebärde *f*
**get** *v/t* bekommen, erhalten; sich *et.* verschaffen *or* besorgen; erwerben, sich aneignen; holen; bringen; F erwischen; F kapieren, verstehen; *j-n* dazu bringen (***to do*** zu tun); *with pp*: lassen; ~ ***one's hair cut*** sich die Haare schneiden lassen; ~ ***going*** in Gang bringen; ~ ***s.th. by heart*** et. auswendig lernen; ~ ***s.th. ready*** et. fertig machen; ***have got*** haben; ***have got to*** müssen; *v/i* kommen, gelangen; *with pp or adj*: werden; ~ ***tired*** müde werden, ermüden; ~ ***going*** in Gang kommen; *fig* in Schwung kommen; ~ ***home*** nach Hause kommen; ~ ***ready*** sich fertig machen; ~ ***about*** herumkommen; sich herumsprechen *or* verbreiten (*rumor etc*); ~ ***ahead of*** übertreffen (*acc*); ~ ***along*** vorwärts-, vorankommen; auskommen (***with*** mit *j-m*); zurechtkommen (***with*** mit *et.*); ~ ***at*** herankommen an (*acc*); ***what is he getting at?*** worauf will er hinaus?; ~ ***away*** loskommen; entkommen; ~ ***away with*** davonkommen mit; ~ ***back*** zurückkommen; *et.* zurückbekommen; ~ ***in*** hinein-, hereinkommen; einsteigen (in *acc*); ~ ***off*** aussteigen (aus); davonkommen (***with*** mit); ~ ***on*** einsteigen (in *acc*); → ***get along***; ~ ***out*** herausgehen, hinausgehen; aussteigen (***of*** aus); *et.* herausbekommen; ~ ***over s.th.*** über et. hinwegkommen; ~ ***to*** kommen nach; ~ ***together*** zusammenkommen; ~ ***up*** aufstehen
**get·a·way** Flucht *f*; ~ ***car*** Fluchtauto *n*
**get·up** Aufmachung *f*
**gey·ser** GEOL Geysir *m*; *Br* TECH Durchlauferhitzer *m*
**ghast·ly** grässlich; schrecklich; (toten-) bleich
**gher·kin** Gewürzgurke *f*
**ghet·to** Getto *n*
**ghost** Geist *m*, Gespenst *n*; *fig* Spur *f*
**ghost·ly** geisterhaft
**gi·ant 1.** Riese *m*; **2.** riesig
**gibe** Stichelei *f*
**gib·ber·ish** Kauderwelsch *n*
**gib·bet** Galgen *m*
**gibe 1.** spotten (***at*** über *acc*); **2.** höhnische Bemerkung
**gib·lets** GASTR Hühner-, Gänseklein *n*
**gid·di·ness** MED Schwindel(gefühl *n*) *m*; **gid·dy** Schwindel erregend; ***I feel*** ~ mir ist schwind(e)lig
**gift** Geschenk *n*; Talent *n*
**gift·ed** begabt
**gig** F MUS Gig *m*, Auftritt *m*, Konzert *n*
**gi·gan·tic** gigantisch, riesenhaft, riesig, gewaltig
**gig·gle 1.** kichern; **2.** Gekicher *n*
**gild** vergolden
**gill** ZO Kieme *f*; BOT Lamelle *f*
**gim·mick** F Trick *m*; Spielerei *f*
**gin** Gin *m*
**gin·ger 1.** Ingwer *m*; **2.** rötlich *or* gelblich braun;
**gin·ger·bread** Lebkuchen *m*, Pfefferkuchen *m*
**gin·ger·ly** behutsam, vorsichtig
**gip·sy** *Br* → ***gypsy***
**gi·raffe** ZO Giraffe *f*
**gir·der** TECH Tragbalken *m*
**gir·dle** Hüfthalter *m*, Hüftgürtel *m*
**girl** Mädchen *n*
**girl·friend** Freundin *f*
**girl guide** *Br* Pfadfinderin *f*
**girl·hood** Mädchenjahre *pl*, Jugend *f*, Jugendzeit *f*
**girl·ish** mädchenhaft; Mädchen...
**girl scout** Pfadfinderin *f*
**gi·ro** *Br* Postgirodienst *m*
**gi·ro ac·count** *Br* Postgirokonto *n*
**gi·ro cheque** *Br* Postscheck *m*
**girth** (Sattel)Gurt *m*; (*a.* Körper)Umfang *m*
**gist** *das* Wesentliche, Kern *m*
**give** geben; schenken; spenden; *Leben* hingeben, opfern; *Befehl etc* geben, erteilen; *Hilfe* leisten; *Schutz* bieten;

*Grund etc* angeben; THEA *etc* geben, aufführen; *Vortrag* halten; *Schmerzen* bereiten, verursachen; *Grüße etc* übermitteln; **~ her my love** bestelle ihr herzliche Grüße von mir; **~ birth to** zur Welt bringen; **~ s.o. to understand that** j-m zu verstehen geben, dass; **~ way** nachgeben; *Br* MOT die Vorfahrt lassen (*dat*); **~ away** hergeben, weggeben, verschenken; *j-n, et.* verraten; **~ back** zurückgeben; **~ in** *Gesuch etc* einreichen; *Prüfungsarbeit etc* abgeben; nachgeben; aufgeben; **~ off** *Geruch* verbreiten; ausstoßen; ausströmen, verströmen; **~ on(to)** führen auf *or* nach, gehen nach; **~ out** aus-, verteilen; *esp Br* bekannt geben; zu Ende gehen (*supplies, strength etc*); F versagen (*engine etc*); **~ up** aufgeben; aufhören mit; *j-n* ausliefern; **~ o.s. up** sich (freiwillig) stellen (**to the police** der Polizei)

**give-and-take** beiderseitiges Entgegenkommen, Kompromiss(bereitschaft *f*) *m*

**giv·en: be ~ to** neigen zu (*dat*)

**giv·en name** Vorname *m*

**gla·cial** eisig; Eis...

**gla·ci·er** Gletscher *m*

**glad** froh, erfreut; **be ~ of** sich freuen über (*acc*); **glad·ly** gern(e)

**glam·o(u)r** Zauber *m*, Glanz *m*

**glam·o(u)r·ous** bezaubernd, reizvoll

**glance 1.** (schneller *or* flüchtiger) Blick (**at** auf *acc*); **at a ~** auf e-n Blick; **2.** (schnell *or* flüchtig) blicken (**at** auf *acc*)

**gland** ANAT Drüse *f*

**glare 1.** grell scheinen *or* leuchten; wütend starren; **~ at s.o.** j-n wütend anstarren; **2.** greller Schein, grelles Leuchten; wütender Blick

**glar·ing** *fig* schreiend

**glass 1.** Glas *n*; (Trink)Glas *n*; Glas(gefäß) *n*; (Fern-, Opern)Glas *n*; *Br* F Spiegel *m*; *Br* Barometer *n*; (**a pair of**) **~es** (e-e) Brille; **2.** gläsern; Glas...; **3. ~ in, ~ up** verglasen

**glass case** Vitrine *f*; Schaukasten *m*

**glass·ful** *ein* Glas (voll)

**glass·house** Gewächs-, Treibhaus *n*

**glass·ware** Glaswaren *pl*

**glass·y** gläsern; glasig

**glaze 1.** *v/t* verglasen; glasieren; *v/i: a.* **~ over** glasig werden (*eyes*); **2.** Glasur *f*

**gla·zi·er** Glaser *m*

**gleam 1.** schwacher Schein, Schimmer *m*; **2.** leuchten, schimmern

**glean** *v/t* sammeln; *v/i* Ähren lesen

**glee** Fröhlichkeit *f*

**glee club** Gesangverein *m*

**glee·ful** ausgelassen, fröhlich

**glen** enges Bergtal *n*

**glib** gewandt; schlagfertig

**glide 1.** gleiten; segeln; **2.** Gleiten *n*; AVIAT Gleitflug *m*; **glid·er** Segelflugzeug *n*; **glid·ing** Segelfliegen *n*

**glim·mer 1.** schimmern; **2.** Schimmer *m*

**glimpse 1.** (nur) flüchtig zu sehen bekommen; **2.** flüchtiger Blick

**glint 1.** glitzern, glänzen; **2.** Glitzern *n*, Glanz *m*

**glis·ten** glitzern, glänzen

**glit·ter 1.** glitzern, funkeln, glänzen; **2.** Glitzern *n*, Funkeln *n*, Glanz *m*

**gloat: ~ over** sich hämisch *or* diebisch freuen über (*acc*)

**gloat·ing** hämisch, schadenfroh

**glo·bal** Welt..., global, weltumspannend; umfassend; **~ warm·ing** Erwärmung *f* der Erdatmosphäre

**globe** (Erd)Kugel *f*; Globus *m*

**gloom** Düsterkeit *f*; Dunkelheit *f*; düstere *or* gedrückte Stimmung

**gloom·y** düster; hoffnungslos; niedergeschlagen; trübsinnig, trübselig

**glo·ri·fi·ca·tion** Verherrlichung *f*

**glo·ri·fy** verherrlichen

**glo·ri·ous** ruhmreich, glorreich; herrlich, prächtig

**glo·ry** Ruhm *m*; Herrlichkeit *f*, Pracht *f*

**gloss 1.** Glanz *m*; LING Glosse *f*; **2. ~ over** beschönigen, vertuschen

**glos·sa·ry** Glossar *n*

**gloss·y** glänzend

**glove** Handschuh *m*; **~ com·part·ment** MOT Handschuhfach *n*

**glow 1.** glühen; **2.** Glühen *n*; Glut *f*

**glow·er** finster blicken

**glow-worm** ZO Glühwürmchen *n*

**glu·cose** Traubenzucker *m*

**glue 1.** Leim *m*; **2.** kleben

**glum** bedrückt

**glut·ton** *fig* Vielfraß *m*

**glut·ton·ous** gefräßig, unersättlich

**gnarled** knorrig; knotig (*hands etc*)

**gnash** knirschen (mit)

**gnat** ZO (Stech)Mücke *f*

**gnaw** (zer)nagen; (zer)fressen

**gnome** Gnom *m*; Gartenzwerg *m*
**go 1.** gehen, fahren, reisen (***to*** nach); (fort)gehen; gehen, führen (***to*** nach) (*road etc*); sich erstrecken, gehen (***to*** bis zu); verkehren, fahren (*bus etc*); TECH gehen, laufen, funktionieren; vergehen (*time*); harmonieren (***with*** mit), passen (***with*** zu); ausgehen, ablaufen, ausfallen; werden (***~ mad; ~ blind***); ***be ~ing to*** *inf* im Begriff sein zu *inf*, *tun* wollen, *tun* werden; ***~ shares*** teilen; ***~ swimming*** schwimmen gehen; ***it is ~ing to rain*** es gibt Regen; ***I must be ~ing*** ich muss gehen; ***~ for a walk*** e-n Spaziergang machen, spazieren gehen; ***~ to bed*** ins Bett gehen; ***~ to school*** zur Schule gehen; ***~ to see*** besuchen; ***let ~*** loslassen; ***~ after*** nachlaufen (*dat*); sich bemühen um; ***~ ahead*** vorangehen; vorausgehen, vorausfahren; ***~ ahead with*** beginnen mit; fortfahren mit; ***~ at*** losgehen auf (*acc*); ***~ away*** weggehen; ***~ between*** vermitteln zwischen (*dat*); ***~ by*** vorbeigehen, vorbeifahren; vergehen (*time*); *fig* sich halten an (*acc*), sich richten nach; ***~ down*** untergehen (*sun*); ***~ for*** holen; ***~ in*** hineingehen; ***~ in for an examination*** e-e Prüfung machen; ***~ off*** fortgehen, weggehen; losgehen (*gun etc*); ***~ on*** weitergehen, weiterfahren; *fig* fortfahren (***doing*** zu tun); *fig* vor sich gehen, vorgehen; ***~ out*** hinausgehen; ausgehen (***with*** mit); ausgehen (*light etc*); ***~ through*** durchgehen, durchnehmen; durchmachen; ***~ up*** steigen; hinaufgehen, -steigen; ***~ without*** sich behelfen ohne, auskommen ohne; **2.** F Schwung *m*, Schmiss *m*; *esp Br* F Versuch *m*; ***it's my ~*** *esp Br* F ich bin dran *or* an der Reihe; ***it's a ~!*** F abgemacht!; ***have a ~ at s.th.*** *Br* F et. probieren; ***be all the ~*** *Br* F große Mode sein
**goad** *fig* anstacheln
**go-a·head[1]**: ***get the ~*** grünes Licht bekommen; ***give s.o. the ~*** j-m grünes Licht geben
**go-a·head[2]** *Br* zielstrebig; unternehmungslustig
**goal** Ziel *n* (*a. fig*); SPORT Tor *n*; ***keep ~*** im Tor stehen; ***score a ~*** ein Tor schießen *or* erzielen; ***consolation ~*** Ehrentreffer *m*; ***own ~*** Eigentor *n*, Eigentreffer *m*; ***shot at ~*** Torschuss *m*
**goal·ie** F, **goal·keep·er** SPORT Torwart *m*, Torhüter *m*
**goal kick** *soccer*: Abstoß *m*
**goal line** SPORT Torlinie *f*
**goal·mouth** SPORT Torraum *m*
**goal·post** SPORT Torpfosten *m*
**goat** ZO Ziege *f*, Geiß *f*
**gob·ble** schlingen; *mst* ***~ up*** verschlingen (*a. fig*)
**go-be·tween** Vermittler(in), Mittelsmann *m*
**gob·lin** Kobold *m*
**god** REL ***God*** Gott *m*; *fig* Abgott *m*
**god·child** Patenkind *n*
**god·dess** Göttin *f*
**god·fa·ther** Pate *m* (*a. fig*), Taufpate *m*
**god·for·sak·en** *contp* gottverlassen
**god·head** Gottheit *f*
**god·less** gottlos
**god·like** gottähnlich; göttlich
**god·moth·er** (Tauf)Patin *f*
**god·pa·rent** (Tauf)Pate, (Tauf)Patin *f*
**god·send** Geschenk *n* des Himmels
**gog·gle** glotzen
**gog·gle box** *Br* F TV Glotze *f*
**gog·gles** Schutzbrille *f*
**go·ings-on** F Treiben *n*, Vorgänge *pl*
**gold 1.** Gold *n*; **2.** golden
**gold·en** *mst fig* golden, goldgelb
**gold·finch** ZO Stieglitz *m*
**gold·fish** ZO Goldfisch *m*
**gold·smith** Goldschmied *m*
**golf 1.** Golf(spiel) *n*; **2.** Golf spielen
**golf club** Golfschläger *m*; Golfklub *m*
**golf course, golf links** Golfplatz *m*
**gon·do·la** Gondel *f*
**gone** *adj* fort; F futsch; vergangen; tot; F hoffnungslos
**good 1.** gut; artig; gütig; gründlich; ***~ at*** geschickt *or* gut in (*dat*); ***real ~*** F echt gut; **2.** Nutzen *m*, Wert *m*; *das* Gute; ***do (no) ~*** (nichts) nützen; ***for ~*** für immer; F ***what ~ is ...?*** was nützt ...?
**good·by(e) 1.** ***wish s.o. ~, say ~ to s.o.*** j-m Auf Wiedersehen sagen; **2.** *int* (auf) Wiedersehen!
**Good Fri·day** REL Karfreitag *m*
**good-hu·mo(u)red** gut gelaunt; gutmütig
**good·look·ing** gut aussehend
**good·na·tured** gutmütig
**good·ness** Güte *f*; ***thank ~!*** Gott sei Dank!; ***(my) ~!, ~ gracious!*** du meine Güte!, du lieber Himmel!; ***for ~' sake***

um Himmels willen!; ~ ***knows*** weiß der Himmel
**goods** ECON Waren *pl*, Güter *pl*
**good·will** gute Absicht, guter Wille; ECON Firmenwert *m*
**good·y** F Bonbon *m*, *n*
**goose** ZO Gans *f*
**goose·ber·ry** BOT Stachelbeere *f*
**goose·flesh, goose pim·ples** *fig* Gänsehaut *f*
**go·pher** ZO Taschenratte *f*; Ziesel *m*
**gore** durchbohren, aufspießen
**gorge 1.** ANAT Kehle *f*, Schlund *m*; GEOGR enge (Fels)Schlucht; **2.** verschlingen; schlingen, (sich) voll stopfen
**gor·geous** prächtig
**go·ril·la** ZO Gorilla *m*
**gor·y** F blutrünstig
**gosh** *int* F Mensch!, Mann!
**gos·ling** ZO junge Gans
**go-slow** *Br* ECON Bummelstreik *m*
**Gos·pel** REL Evangelium *n*
**gos·sa·mer** Altweibersommer *m*
**gos·sip 1.** Klatsch *m*, Tratsch *m*; Klatschbase *f*; **2.** klatschen, tratschen
**gos·sip·y** geschwätzig; voller Klatsch und Tratsch (*letter etc*)
**Goth·ic** ARCH **1.** gotisch; ~ ***novel*** Schauerroman *m*; **2.** Gotik *f*
**gourd** BOT Kürbis *m*
**gout** MED Gicht *f*
**gov·ern** *v/t* regieren; lenken, leiten; *v/i* herrschen
**gov·ern·ess** Erzieherin *f*
**gov·ern·ment** Regierung *f*; Staat *m*
**gov·er·nor** Gouverneur *m*; Direktor *m*, Leiter *m*; F Alte *m*
**gown** Kleid *n*; Robe *f*, Talar *m*
**grab 1.** packen, (hastig *or* gierig) ergreifen, fassen; **2.** (hastiger *or* gieriger) Griff; TECH Greifer *m*
**grace 1.** Anmut *f*, Grazie *f*; Anstand *m*; ECON Frist *f*, Aufschub *m*; Gnade *f*; REL Tischgebet *n*; **2.** zieren, schmücken
**grace·ful** anmutig
**grace·less** ungraziös
**gra·cious** gnädig
**gra·da·tion** Abstufung *f*
**grade 1.** Grad *m*, Rang *m*; Stufe *f*; ECON Qualität *f*; RAIL *etc* Steigung *f*, Gefälle *n*; PED Klasse *f*; Note *f*, Zensur *f*; **2.** sortieren, einteilen; abstufen
**grade cross·ing** RAIL schienengleicher Bahnübergang
**grade school** Grundschule *f*
**gra·di·ent** *Br* RAIL *etc* Steigung *f*, Gefälle *n*
**grad·u·al** stufenweise, allmählich
**grad·u·al·ly** nach und nach; allmählich
**grad·u·ate 1.** UNIV Hochschulabsolvent(in), Akademiker(in); Graduierte *m*, *f*; PED Schulabgänger(in); **2.** abstufen, staffeln; UNIV graduieren; PED die Abschlussprüfung bestehen
**grad·u·a·tion** Abstufung *f*, Staffelung *f*; UNIV Graduierung *f*; PED Absolvieren *n* (***from*** *gen*)
**graf·fi·ti** Graffiti *pl*, Wandschmierereien *pl*
**graft 1.** MED Transplantat *n*; AGR Pfropfreis *n*; **2.** MED *Gewebe* verpflanzen, transplantieren; AGR pfropfen
**grain** (Samen-, *esp* Getreide)Korn *n*; Getreide *n*; (*Sand- etc*)Körnchen *n*, (-)Korn *n*; Maserung *f*; ***go against the ~ for s.o.*** *fig* j-m gegen den Strich gehen
**gram** Gramm *n*
**gram·mar** Grammatik *f*
**gram·mar school** Grundschule *f*; *Br appr* (humanistisches) Gymnasium
**gram·mat·i·cal** grammatisch, Grammatik...
**gramme** → ***gram***
**gra·na·ry** Kornspeicher *m*
**grand 1.** *fig* großartig; erhaben; groß; Groß..., Haupt...; **2.** F Riese *m* (*1000 dollars or pounds*)
**grand·child** Enkel *m*, Enkelin *f*
**grand·daugh·ter** Enkelin *f*
**gran·deur** Größe *f*, Erhabenheit *f*; Großartigkeit *f*
**grand·fa·ther** Großvater *m*
**gran·di·ose** großartig
**grand·moth·er** Großmutter *f*
**grand·par·ents** Großeltern *pl*
**grand·son** Enkel *m*
**grand·stand** SPORT Haupttribüne *f*
**gran·ny** F Oma *f*
**grant 1.** bewilligen, gewähren; *Erlaubnis etc* geben; *Bitte etc* erfüllen; *et.* zugeben; ***take s.th. for ~ed*** et. als selbstverständlich betrachten *or* hinnehmen; **2.** Stipendium *n*; Bewilligung *f*, Unterstützung *f*
**gran·u·lat·ed** körnig, granuliert; ~ ***sugar*** Kristallzucker *m*
**gran·ule** Körnchen *n*
**grape** BOT Weinbeere *f*, Weintraube *f*

**grape·fruit** BOT Grapefruit *f*, Pampelmuse *f*
**grape·vine** BOT Weinstock *m*
**graph** grafische Darstellung
**graph·ic** grafisch; anschaulich; *~ **arts*** Grafik *f*; **graph·ics** EDP Grafik *f*
**grap·ple:** *~ **with*** kämpfen mit, *fig a.* sich herumschlagen mit
**grasp 1.** (er)greifen, packen; *fig* verstehen, begreifen; **2.** Griff *m*; Reichweite *f* (*a. fig*); *fig* Verständnis *n*
**grass** Gras *n*; Rasen *m*; Weide(land *n*) *f*; *sl.* Grass *n* (*marijuana*)
**grass·hop·per** ZO Heuschrecke *f*
**grass roots** POL Basis *f*
**grass wid·ow** Strohwitwe *f*
**grass wid·ow·er** Strohwitwer *m*
**gras·sy** grasbedeckt, Gras...
**grate 1.** (Kamin)Gitter *n*; (Feuer)Rost *m*; **2.** reiben, raspeln; knirschen (mit); *~ **on s.o.'s nerves*** an j-s Nerven zerren
**grate·ful** dankbar
**grat·er** Reibe *f*
**grat·i·fi·ca·tion** Befriedigung *f*; Freude *f*; **grat·i·fy** erfreuen; befriedigen
**grat·ing**[1] kratzend, knirschend, quietschend; schrill; unangenehm
**grat·ing**[2] Gitter(werk) *n*
**grat·i·tude** Dankbarkeit *f*
**gra·tu·i·tous** unentgeltlich; freiwillig
**gra·tu·i·ty** Abfindung *f*; Gratifikation *f*; Trinkgeld *n*
**grave**[1] ernst; (ge)wichtig; gemessen
**grave**[2] Grab *n*
**grave·dig·ger** Totengräber *m*
**grav·el 1.** Kies *m*; **2.** mit Kies bestreuen
**grave·stone** Grabstein *m*
**grave·yard** Friedhof *m*
**grav·i·ta·tion** PHYS Gravitation *f*, Schwerkraft *f*
**grav·i·ty** PHYS Schwerkraft *f*; Ernst *m*
**gra·vy** Bratensaft *m*; Bratensoße *f*
**gray 1.** grau; **2.** Grau *n*; **3.** grau machen *or* werden
**gray·hound** ZO Windhund *m*
**graze**[1] *Vieh* weiden (lassen); (ab)weiden; (ab)grasen
**graze**[2] **1.** streifen; schrammen; *Haut* (ab-, auf)schürfen, (auf)schrammen; **2.** Abschürfung *f*, Schramme *f*; Streifschuss *m*
**grease 1.** Fett *n*; TECH Schmierfett *n*, Schmiere *f*; **2.** (ein)fetten; TECH schmieren; **greas·y** fett(ig), ölig; speckig; schmierig
**great** groß; Ur(groß)...; F großartig, super
**Great Brit·ain** Großbritannien *n*
**great-grand·child** Urenkel(in)
**great-grand·par·ents** Urgroßeltern *pl*
**great·ly** sehr
**great·ness** Größe *f*
**Greece** Griechenland *n*
**greed** Gier *f*; **greed·y** gierig (***for*** auf *acc*, nach); habgierig; gefräßig
**Greek 1.** griechisch; **2.** Grieche *m*, Griechin *f*; LING Griechisch *n*
**green 1.** grün; *fig* grün, unerfahren; **2.** Grün *n*; Grünfläche *f*, Rasen *m*; *pl* grünes Gemüse, Blattgemüse *n*
**green·back** F Dollar *m*
**green belt** Grüngürtel *m*
**green card** Arbeitserlaubnis *f*
**green·gro·cer** *esp Br* Obst- und Gemüsehändler(in)
**green·horn** F Greenhorn *n*, Grünschnabel *m*
**green·house** Gewächs-, Treibhaus *n*; *~* **ef·fect** Treibhauseffekt *m*
**green·ish** grünlich
**greet** grüßen; **greet·ing** Begrüßung *f*, Gruß *m*; *pl* Grüße *pl*
**gre·nade** MIL Granate *f*
**grey** *Br* → ***gray***
**grid** Gitter *n*; ELECTR *etc* Versorgungsnetz *n*; Gitter(netz) *n* (*map etc*)
**grid·i·ron** Bratrost *m*
**grief** Kummer *m*
**griev·ance** (Grund *m* zur) Beschwerde *f*; Missstand *m*
**grieve** *v/t* betrüben, bekümmern; *v/i* bekümmert sein; *~ **for*** trauern um
**griev·ous** schwer, schlimm
**grill 1.** grillen; **2.** Grill *m*; Bratrost *m*; GASTR *das* Gegrillte *n*
**grim** grimmig; schrecklich; erbittert; F schlimm
**gri·mace 1.** Fratze *f*, Grimasse *f*; **2.** Grimassen schneiden
**grime** Schmutz *m*; Ruß *m*
**grim·y** schmutzig; rußig
**grin 1.** Grinsen *n*; **2.** grinsen
**grind 1.** *v/t* (zer)mahlen, zerreiben, zerkleinern; *Messer etc* schleifen; *Fleisch* durchdrehen; *~ **one's teeth*** mit den Zähnen knirschen; *v/i* F schuften; pau-

ken, büffeln; **2.** Schinderei *f*, F Schufterei *f*; ***the daily ~*** das tägliche Einerlei
**grind·er** (Messer- *etc*)Schleifer *m*; TECH Schleifmaschine *f*; TECH Mühle *f*
**grind·stone** Schleifstein *m*
**grip 1.** packen (*a. fig*); **2.** Griff *m*; *fig* Gewalt *f*, Herrschaft *f*; Reisetasche *f*
**grip·ping** spannend
**gris·ly** grässlich, schrecklich
**gris·tle** GASTR Knorpel *m*
**grit 1.** Kies *m*, (grober) Sand; *fig* Mut *m*; **2.** streuen; ***~ one's teeth*** die Zähne zusammenbeißen
**griz·zly (bear)** ZO Grislibär *m*, Graubär *m*
**groan 1.** stöhnen, ächzen; **2.** Stöhnen *n*, Ächzen *n*
**gro·cer** Lebensmittelhändler *m*
**gro·cer·ies** Lebensmittel *pl*
**gro·cer·y** Lebensmittelgeschäft *n*
**grog·gy** F groggy, schwach *or* wackelig (auf den Beinen)
**groin** ANAT Leiste *f*, Leistengegend *f*
**groom 1.** Pferdepfleger *m*, Stallbursche *m*; Bräutigam *m*; **2.** *Pferde* versorgen, striegeln; pflegen
**groove** Rinne *f*, Furche *f*; Rille *f*, Nut *f*
**grope** tasten; F *Mädchen* befummeln
**gross 1.** dick, feist; grob, derb; ECON Brutto...; **2.** Gros *n*
**gro·tesque** grotesk
**ground**[1] gemahlen (*coffee etc*); ***~ meat*** Hackfleisch *n*
**ground**[2] **1.** (Erd)Boden *m*, Erde *f*; Boden *m*, Gebiet *n*; SPORT (*Spiel*)Platz *m*; ELECTR Erdung *f*; (Boden)Satz *m*; *fig* Beweggrund *m*; *pl* Grundstück *n*, Park *m*, Gartenanlage *f*; ***on the ~(s) of*** aufgrund (*gen*); ***hold or stand one's ~*** sich behaupten; **2.** MAR auflaufen; ELECTR erden; *fig* gründen, stützen; **~ crew** AVIAT Bodenpersonal *n*; **~ floor** *esp Br* Erdgeschoss *n*; **~ forc·es** MIL Bodentruppen *pl*, Landstreitkräfte *pl*
**ground·hog** ZO Amer. Waldmurmeltier *n*
**ground·ing** ELECTR Erdung *f*; Grundlagen *pl*, Grundkenntnisse *pl*
**ground·keep·er** SPORT Platzwart *m*
**ground·less** grundlos
**ground·nut** *Br* BOT Erdnuss *f*
**grounds·man** *Br* SPORT Platzwart *m*
**ground| staff** *Br* AVIAT Bodenpersonal *n*; **~ sta·tion** Bodenstation *f*
**ground·work** *fig* Grundlage *f*, Fundament *n*
**group 1.** Gruppe *f*; **2.** (sich) gruppieren
**group·ie** F Groupie *n*
**group·ing** Gruppierung *f*
**grove** Wäldchen *n*, Gehölz *n*
**grov·el** (am Boden) kriechen
**grow** *v/i* wachsen; (allmählich) werden; ***~ up*** aufwachsen, heranwachsen; *v/t* BOT anpflanzen, anbauen, züchten; ***~ a beard*** sich e-n Bart wachsen lassen
**grow·er** Züchter *m*, Erzeuger *m*
**growl** knurren, brummen
**grown-up 1.** erwachsen; **2.** Erwachsene *m*, *f*
**growth** Wachsen *n*, Wachstum *n*; Wuchs *m*, Größe *f*; *fig* Zunahme *f*, Anwachsen *n*; MED Gewächs *n*, Wucherung *f*
**grub 1.** ZO Larve *f*, Made *f*; F Futter *n*; **2.** graben
**grub·by** schmudd(e)lig
**grudge 1.** missgönnen (***s.o. s.th.*** j-m et.); **2.** Groll *m*
**grudg·ing·ly** widerwillig
**gru·el** Haferschleim *m*
**gruff** grob, schroff, barsch, unwirsch
**grum·ble** murren, F meckern (***über*** *acc* about, at); ***~ at*** schimpfen über (*acc*)
**grump·y** F schlecht gelaunt, mürrisch, missmutig, verdrießlich, verdrossen
**grun·gy** F schmudd(e)lig-schlampig; MUS schlecht und laut
**grunt 1.** grunzen; brummen; stöhnen; **2.** Grunzen *n*; Stöhnen *n*
**guar·an·tee 1.** Garantie *f*; Kaution *f*, Sicherheit *f*; **2.** (sich ver)bürgen für; garantieren
**guar·an·tor** JUR Bürge *m*, Bürgin *f*
**guar·an·ty** JUR Garantie *f*; Sicherheit *f*
**guard 1.** Wache *f*, (Wacht)Posten *m*, Wächter *m*; Wärter *m*, Aufseher *m*; Wache *f*, Bewachung *f*; *Br* Zugbegleiter *m*; Schutz(vorrichtung *f*) *m*; Garde *f*; ***be on ~*** Wache stehen; ***be on (off) one's ~*** (nicht) auf der Hut sein; **2.** *v/t* bewachen, (be)schützen (***from*** vor *dat*); *v/i* sich hüten *or* in Acht nehmen *or* schützen (***against*** vor *dat*)
**guard·ed** vorsichtig, zurückhaltend
**guard·i·an 1.** JUR Vormund *m*; **2.** Schutz...
**guard·i·an·ship** JUR Vormundschaft *f*
**gue(r)·ril·la** MIL Guerilla *m*

**gue(r)·ril·la war·fare** Guerillakrieg *m*
**guess 1.** (er)raten; vermuten; schätzen; glauben, meinen; **2.** Vermutung *f*
**guess·work** (reine) Vermutung(en *pl*)
**guest** Gast *m*
**guest·house** (Hotel)Pension *f*, Fremdenheim *n*
**guest·room** Gäste-, Fremdenzimmer *n*
**guf·faw 1.** schallendes Gelächter; **2.** schallend lachen
**guid·ance** Führung *f*; (An)Leitung *f*
**guide 1.** (Reise-, Fremden)Führer(in); (Reise- *etc*)Führer *m* (*book*); Handbuch (***to*** *gen*); ***a ~ to London*** ein London-Führer; **2.** leiten; führen; lenken
**guide·book** (Reise- *etc*)Führer *m*
**guid·ed tour** Führung *f*
**guide·lines** Richtlinien *pl* (***on*** *gen*)
**guild** HIST Gilde *f*, Zunft *f*
**guile·less** arglos
**guilt** Schuld *f*
**guilt·less** schuldlos, unschuldig (***of*** an *dat*)
**guilt·y** schuldig (***of*** *gen*); schuldbewusst
**guin·ea pig** ZO Meerschweinchen *n*; *fig* Versuchsperson *f*, F Versuchskaninchen *n*
**guise** *fig* Gestalt *f*, Maske *f*
**gui·tar** MUS Gitarre *f*
**gulch** GEOGR tiefe Schlucht, Klamm *f*
**gulf** GEOGR Golf *m*; *fig* Kluft *f*
**gull** ZO Möwe *f*
**gul·let** ANAT Speiseröhre *f*; Gurgel *f*, Kehle *f*
**gulp 1.** (großer) Schluck; **2.** *often* ***~ down*** *Getränk* hinunterstürzen, *Speise* hinunterschlingen
**gum**[1] ANAT *mst pl* Zahnfleisch *n*
**gum**[2] **1.** Gummi *m*, *n*; Klebstoff *m*; Kaugummi *m*; (Frucht)Gummi *m*; **2.** kleben
**grump·tion** F Grips *m*; Schneid *m*
**gun 1.** Gewehr *n*; Pistole *f*, Revolver *m*; Geschütz *n*, Kanone *f*; **2.** ***~ down*** niederschießen
**gun·fight** Feuergefecht *n*, Schießerei *f*
**gun·fire** Schüsse *pl*; MIL Geschützfeuer *n*
**gun li·cence** *Br*, **gun li·cense** Waffenschein *m*
**gun·man** Bewaffnete *m*
**gun·point: *at ~*** mit vorgehaltener Waffe, mit Waffengewalt
**gun·pow·der** Schießpulver *n*
**gun·run·ner** Waffenschmuggler *m*
**gun·run·ning** Waffenschmuggel *m*
**gun·shot** Schuss *m*; ***within*** (***out of***) ~ in (außer) Schussweite
**gur·gle 1.** gurgeln, gluckern, glucksen; **2.** Gurgeln *n*, Gluckern *n*, Glucksen *n*
**gush 1.** strömen, schießen (***from*** aus); **2.** Schwall *m*, Strom *m* (*a. fig*)
**gust** Windstoß *m*, Bö *f*
**guts** F Eingeweide *pl*; Schneid *m*, Mumm *m*
**gut·ter** Gosse *f* (*a. fig*), Rinnstein *m*; Dachrinne *f*
**guy** F Kerl *m*, Typ *m*
**guz·zle** F saufen; fressen
**gym** F Fitnesscenter *n*; → ***gymnasium***; → ***gymnastics***
**gym·na·si·um** Turn-, Sporthalle *f*
**gym·nast** Turner(in)
**gym·nas·tics** Turnen *n*, Gymnastik *f*
**gym shirt** Turnhemd *n*
**gym shorts** Turnhose *f*
**gy·n(a)e·col·o·gist** Gynäkologe *m*, Gynäkologin *f*, Frauenarzt *m*, -ärztin *f*
**gy·n(a)e·col·o·gy** Gynäkologie *f*, Frauenheilkunde *f*
**gyp·sy** Zigeuner *m*, Zigeunerin *f*
**gy·rate** kreisen, sich (im Kreis) drehen, (herum)wirbeln

# H

**H, h** H, h *n*
**hab·it** (An)Gewohnheit *f*; *esp* (Ordens-)Tracht *f*; ***get into*** (***out of***) ***the ~ of smoking*** sich das Rauchen angewöhnen (abgewöhnen); **ha·bit·u·al** gewohnheitsmäßig, Gewohnheits...
**hack**[1] hacken
**hack**[2] *contp* Schreiberling *m*

**hack³** *contp* Klepper *m*
**hack·er** EDP Hacker *m*
**hack·neyed** abgedroschen
**had·dock** zo Schellfisch *m*
**h(a)e·mor·rhage** MED Blutung *f*
**hag** hässliches altes Weib, Hexe *f*
**hag·gard** abgespannt; verhärmt, abgehärmt; hager
**hag·gle** feilschen, handeln
**hail 1.** Hagel *m*; **2.** hageln
**hail·stone** Hagelkorn *n*
**hail·storm** Hagelschauer *m*
**hair** *einzelnes* Haar; *coll* Haar *n*, Haare *pl*; ***let one's ~ down*** F aus sich herausgehen; ***without turning a ~*** ohne mit der Wimper zu zucken
**hair·breadth** → ***hair's breadth***
**hair·brush** Haarbürste *f*
**hair·cut** Haarschnitt *m*
**hair·do** F Frisur *f*
**hair·dress·er** Friseur(in)
**hair·dri·er, hair·dry·er** Trockenhaube *f*; Haartrockner *m*, Föhn *m*
**hair·grip** *Br* Haarklammer *f*, Haarklemme *f*
**hair·less** ohne Haare, kahl
**hair·pin** Haarnadel *f*; **~ bend** MOT Haarnadelkurve *f*
**hair-rais·ing** haarsträubend
**hair's breadth:** ***by a ~*** um Haaresbreite
**hair slide** *Br* Haarspange *f*
**hair-split·ting** Haarspalterei *f*
**hair·spray** Haarspray *m, n*
**hair·style** Frisur *f*
**hair styl·ist** Hair-Stylist *m*, Damenfriseur *m*
**hair·y** behaart, haarig
**half 1.** Hälfte *f*; ***go halves*** halbe-halbe machen, teilen; **2.** halb; ***~ an hour*** e-e halbe Stunde; ***~ a pound*** ein halbes Pfund; ***~ past ten*** halb elf (Uhr); ***~ way up*** auf halber Höhe
**half-breed** Halbblut *n*
**half-broth·er** Halbbruder *m*
**half-caste** *esp contp* Mischling *m*
**half-heart·ed** halbherzig
**half time** SPORT Halbzeit *f*; **~ score** SPORT Halbzeitstand *m*
**half·way** halb; auf halbem Weg, in der Mitte; **~ line** *soccer*: Mittellinie *f*
**half-wit·ted** schwachsinnig
**hal·i·but** zo Heilbutt *m*
**hall** Halle *f*, Saal *m*; Flur *m*, Diele *f*; *esp Br* Herrenhaus *n*; *Br* UNIV Speisesaal *m*; *Br* ***~ of residence*** Studentenheim *n*
**hall·mark** *fig* Kennzeichen *n*
**Hal·low·e'en** Abend *m* vor Allerheiligen
**hal·lu·ci·na·tion** Halluzination *f*
**hall·way** Halle *f*, Diele *f*; Korridor *m*
**ha·lo** ASTR Hof *m*; Heiligenschein *m*
**halt 1.** Halt *m*; **2.** (an)halten
**hal·ter** Halfter *m, n*
**halt·ing** zögernd, stockend
**halve** halbieren
**ham** Schinken *m*; ***~ and eggs*** Schinken mit (Spiegel)Ei
**ham·burg·er** GASTR Hamburger *m*; Rinderhack *n*
**ham·let** Weiler *m*
**ham·mer 1.** Hammer *m*; **2.** hämmern
**ham·mock** Hängematte *f*
**ham·per¹** (Deckel)Korb *m*; Präsentkorb *m*; Wäschekorb *m*
**ham·per²** (be)hindern
**ham·ster** zo Hamster *m*
**hand 1.** Hand *f* (*a. fig*); Handschrift *f*; (Uhr)Zeiger *m*; *often in cpds* Arbeiter *m*; Fachmann *m*; *card game*: Blatt *n*, Karten *pl*; ***~ in glove*** ein Herz und eine Seele; ***change ~s*** den Besitzer wechseln; ***give*** *or* ***lend a ~*** mit zugreifen, *j-m* helfen (***with*** by); ***shake ~s with*** *j-m* die Hand schütteln *or* geben; ***at ~*** in Reichweite; nahe; bei der *or* zur Hand; ***at first ~*** aus erster Hand; ***by ~*** mit der Hand; ***on the one ~*** einerseits; ***on the other ~*** andererseits; ***on the right ~*** rechts; ***~s off!*** Hände weg!; ***~s up!*** Hände hoch!; **2.** aushändigen, (über)geben, (über)reichen; ***~ around*** herumreichen; ***~ down*** weitergeben, überliefern; ***~ in*** *Prüfungsarbeit etc* abgeben; *Bericht, Gesuch etc* einreichen; ***~ on*** weiterreichen, weitergeben; überliefern; ***~ out*** austeilen, verteilen; ***~ over*** übergeben, aushändigen (***to*** *dat*); ***~ up*** hinauf-, heraufreichen
**hand·bag** Handtasche *f*
**hand bag·gage** Handgepäck *n*
**hand·ball** SPORT Handball *m*; *soccer*: Handspiel *n*
**hand·book** Handbuch *n*
**hand·bill** Handzettel *m*, Flugblatt *n*
**hand·brake** TECH Handbremse *f*
**hand·cart** Handwagen *m*
**hand·cuffs** Handschellen *pl*

**hand·ful** Hand voll *f*; F Plage *f*
**hand gre·nade** MIL Handgranate *f*
**hand·i·cap 1.** Handikap *n*, MED *a.* Behinderung *f*, SPORT *a.* Vorgabe *f*; → ***mental handicap, physical handicap***; **2.** behindern, benachteiligen
**hand·i·capped 1.** gehandikapt, behindert, benachteiligt; → ***mental, physical***; **2. *the* ~** MED die Behinderten *pl*
**hand·ker·chief** Taschentuch *n*
**han·dle 1.** Griff *m*; Stiel *m*; Henkel *m*; Klinke *f*; ***fly off the* ~** F wütend werden; **2.** anfassen, berühren; hantieren *or* umgehen mit; behandeln
**han·dle·bar(s)** Lenkstange *f*
**hand lug·gage** Handgepäck *n*
**hand·made** handgearbeitet
**hand·out** Almosen *n*; Handzettel *m*; Hand-out *n*, Informationsmaterial *n*
**hand·rail** Geländer *n*
**hand·shake** Händedruck *m*
**hand·some** gut aussehend; *fig* ansehnlich, beträchtlich (*sum etc*)
**hands-on** praktisch
**hand·spring** Handstandüberschlag *m*
**hand·stand** Handstand *m*
**hand·writ·ing** Handschrift *f*
**hand·writ·ten** handgeschrieben
**hand·y** zur Hand; geschickt; handlich, praktisch; nützlich; ***come in* ~** sich als nützlich erweisen; (sehr) gelegen kommen; **hand·y·man** Handwerker *m*; ***be a* ~** *a.* handwerklich geschickt sein
**hang** (auf-, be-, ein)hängen; *Tapete* ankleben; *j-n* (auf)hängen; **~ *o.s.*** sich erhängen; **~ *about*, ~ *around*** herumlungern; **~ *on*** sich klammern (***to*** an *acc*) (*a. fig*), festhalten (***to*** *acc*); TEL am Apparat bleiben; **~ *up*** TEL einhängen, auflegen; ***she hung up on me*** sie legte einfach auf
**han·gar** Hangar *m*, Flugzeughalle *f*
**hang·er** Kleiderbügel *m*
**hang glid·er** SPORT (Flug)Drachen *m*; Drachenflieger(in)
**hang glid·ing** SPORT Drachenfliegen *n*
**hang·ing 1.** Hänge...; **2.** (Er)Hängen *n*
**hang·ings** Tapete *f*, Wandbehang *m*, Vorhang *m*
**hang·man** Henker *m*
**hang·nail** MED Niednagel *m*
**hang·o·ver** Katzenjammer *m*, Kater *m*
**han·ker** F sich sehnen (***after, for*** nach)
**han·kie, han·ky** F Taschentuch *n*
**hap·haz·ard** willkürlich, planlos, wahllos
**hap·pen** (zufällig) geschehen; sich ereignen, passieren, vorkommen
**hap·pen·ing** Ereignis *n*, Vorkommnis *n*; Happening *n*
**hap·pi·ly** glücklich(erweise)
**hap·pi·ness** Glück *n*
**hap·py** glücklich; erfreut
**hap·py-go-luck·y** unbekümmert, sorglos
**ha·rangue 1.** (Straf)Predigt *f*; **2.** *v/t j-m* e-e Strafpredigt halten
**har·ass** ständig belästigen; schikanieren; aufreiben, zermürben
**har·ass·ment** ständige Belästigung; Schikane(n *pl*) *f*; → ***sexual harassment***
**har·bo(u)r 1.** Hafen *m*; Zufluchtsort *m*; **2.** *j-m* Zuflucht *or* Unterschlupf gewähren; *Groll etc* hegen
**hard** hart (*a. fig*); fest; schwer, schwierig; heftig, stark; streng (*a. winter*); *fig* nüchtern (*facts etc*); ***give s.o. a* ~ *time*** j-m das Leben schwer machen; **~ *of hearing*** schwerhörig; ***be* ~ *on s.th.*** et. strapazieren; **~ *up*** F in (Geld)Schwierigkeiten, knapp bei Kasse; F ***the* ~ *stuff*** die harten Sachen (*alcohol, drugs*)
**hard·back** gebundene Ausgabe
**hard-boiled** GASTR hart (gekocht); F *fig* hart, unsentimental, nüchtern
**hard cash** Bargeld *n*; klingende Münze
**hard core** harter Kern; **hard-core** zum harten Kern gehörend; hart
**hard court** *tennis*: Hartplatz *m*
**hard·cov·er 1.** gebunden; **2.** Hard Cover *n*, gebundene Ausgabe
**hard cur·ren·cy** ECON harte Währung
**hard disk** EDP Festplatte *f*
**hard·en** härten; hart machen *or* werden; (sich) abhärten
**hard hat** Schutzhelm *m*
**hard-head·ed** nüchtern, praktisch; starrköpfig, dickköpfig
**hard-heart·ed** hartherzig
**hard la·bo(u)r** JUR Zwangsarbeit *f*
**hard line** *esp* POL harter Kurs
**hard-line** *esp* POL hart, kompromisslos
**hard·ly** kaum
**hard·ness** Härte *f*; Schwierigkeit *f*
**hard·ship** Not *f*; Härte *f*; Strapaze *f*
**hard shoul·der** *Br* MOT Standspur *f*
**hard·top** MOT Hardtop *n*, *m*

**hard·ware** Eisenwaren *pl*; Haushaltswaren *pl*; EDP Hardware *f*
**hard·wear·ing** strapazierfähig
**har·dy** zäh, robust, abgehärtet; BOT winterhart, winterfest
**hare** ZO Hase *m*
**hare·bell** BOT Glockenblume *f*
**hare·brained** verrückt
**hare·lip** MED Hasenscharte *f*
**harm 1.** Schaden *m*; **2.** verletzen; schaden (*dat*)
**harm·ful** schädlich
**harm·less** harmlos
**har·mo·ni·ous** harmonisch
**har·mo·nize** harmonieren; in Einklang sein *or* bringen
**har·mo·ny** Harmonie *f*
**har·ness 1.** (*Pferde- etc*)Geschirr *n*; ***die in ~*** *fig* in den Sielen sterben; **2.** anschirren; anspannen (***to*** an *acc*)
**harp 1.** MUS Harfe *f*; **2.** MUS Harfe spielen; F ***~ on*** (***about***) herumreiten auf (*dat*)
**har·poon 1.** Harpune *f*; **2.** harpunieren
**har·row** AGR **1.** Egge *f*; **2.** eggen
**har·row·ing** quälend, qualvoll, erschütternd
**harsh** rau; grell; streng; schroff, barsch
**hart** ZO Hirsch *m*
**har·vest 1.** Ernte(zeit) *f*; (Ernte)Ertrag *m*; **2.** ernten
**har·vest·er** MOT Mähdrescher *m*
**hash**[1] GASTR Haschee *n*; F ***make a ~ of s.th.*** et. verpfuschen
**hash**[2] F Hasch *n*
**hash browns** GASTR Brat-, Röstkartoffeln *pl*
**hash·ish** Haschisch *n*
**hasp** TECH Haspe *f*
**haste** Eile *f*, Hast *f*
**has·ten** *j-n* antreiben; (sich be)eilen; *et.* beschleunigen
**hast·y** eilig, hastig, überstürzt; voreilig
**hat** Hut *m*
**hatch**[1]**:** *a.* ***~ out*** ZO ausbrüten; ausschlüpfen
**hatch**[2] Durchreiche *f*; AVIAT, MAR Luke *f*
**hatch·back** MOT (Wagen *m* mit) Hecktür *f*
**hatch·et** Beil *n*; ***bury the ~*** das Kriegsbeil begraben
**hate 1.** Hass *m*; **2.** hassen
**hate·ful** verhasst; abscheulich
**ha·tred** Hass *m*
**haugh·ty** hochmütig, überheblich
**haul 1.** ziehen, zerren; schleppen; befördern, transportieren; **2.** Ziehen *n*; Fischzug *m*, *fig* F *a.* Fang *m*; Beförderung *f*, Transport *m*; Transportweg *m*
**haul·age** Beförderung *f*, Transport *m*
**haul·er,** *Br* **haul·i·er** Transportunternehmer *m*
**haunch** ANAT Hüfte *f*, Hüftpartie *f*, Hinterbacke *f*; GASTR Keule *f*
**haunt 1.** spuken in (*dat*); häufig besuchen; *fig* verfolgen, quälen; **2.** häufig besuchter Ort; Schlupfwinkel *m*
**haunt·ing** quälend; unvergesslich, eindringlich
**have** *v/t* haben; erhalten, bekommen; essen, trinken; ***~ breakfast*** frühstücken; ***~ a cup of tea*** e-n Tee trinken); *with inf*: müssen (***I ~ to go now*** ich muss jetzt gehen); *with object and pp*: lassen (***I had my hair cut*** ich ließ mir die Haare schneiden); ***~ back*** zurückbekommen; ***~ on*** *Kleidungsstück* anhaben, *Hut* aufhaben; *v/aux* haben; *v/i often* sein; ***I ~ come*** ich bin gekommen
**ha·ven** Hafen *m* (*mst fig*)
**hav·oc** Verwüstung *f*, Zerstörung *f*; ***play ~ with*** verwüsten, zerstören; *fig* verheerend wirken auf (*acc*)
**hawk**[1] ZO Habicht *m*, Falke *m*
**hawk**[2] hausieren mit; auf der Straße verkaufen; **hawk·er** Hausierer(in); Straßenhändler(in); Drücker(in)
**haw·thorn** BOT Weißdorn *m*
**hay** Heu *n*
**hay fe·ver** MED Heuschnupfen *m*
**hay·loft** Heuboden *m*
**hay·stack** Heuhaufen *m*
**haz·ard** Gefahr *f*, Risiko *n*
**haz·ard·ous** gewagt, gefährlich, riskant; **~ waste** Sonder-, Giftmüll *m*
**haze** Dunst(schleier) *m*
**ha·zel 1.** BOT Hasel(nuss)strauch *m*; **2.** (hasel)nussbraun
**ha·zel·nut** BOT Haselnuss *f*
**haz·y** dunstig, diesig; *fig* unklar, verschwommen
**H-bomb** H-Bombe *f*, Wasserstoffbombe *f*
**he 1.** er; **2.** Er *m*; ZO Männchen *n*; ***~-goat*** Ziegenbock *m*
**head 1.** Kopf *m*; (Ober)Haupt *n*; Chef *m*; (An)Führer(in), Leiter(in); Spitze *f*;

Kopf(ende *n*) *m*; Kopf *m* (*of a page, nail etc*); Vorderseite *f*; Überschrift *f*; ***20 dollars a ~ or per ~*** zwanzig Dollar pro Kopf *or* Person; ***40 ~ (of cattle)*** 40 Stück (Vieh); ***~s or tails?*** Kopf oder Zahl?; ***at the ~ of*** an der Spitze (*gen*); ***~ over heels*** kopfüber; bis über beide Ohren (*verliebt sein*); ***bury one's ~ in the sand*** den Kopf in den Sand stecken; ***get it into one's ~ that ...*** es sich in den Kopf setzen, dass; ***lose one's ~*** den Kopf *or* die Nerven verlieren; **2.** Ober..., Haupt..., Chef..., oberste(r, -s), erste(r, -s); **3.** *v/t* anführen, an der Spitze stehen von (*or gen*); voran-, vorausgehen (*dat*); (an)führen, leiten; *soccer*: köpfen; *v/i* (***for***) gehen, fahren (nach); lossteuern, losgehen (auf *acc*); MAR Kurs halten (auf *acc*)

**head·ache** Kopfweh *n*

**head·band** Stirnband *n*

**head·dress** Kopfschmuck *m*

**head·er** Kopfsprung *m*; *soccer*: Kopfball *m*

**head·first** kopfüber, mit dem Kopf voran; *fig* ungestüm, stürmisch

**head·gear** Kopfbedeckung *f*

**head·ing** Überschrift *f*, Titel(zeile *f*) *m*

**head·land** Landspitze *f*, Landzunge *f*

**head·light** MOT Scheinwerfer *m*

**head·line** Schlagzeile *f*; ***news ~s*** *radio*, TV *das* Wichtigste in Schlagzeilen

**head·long** kopfüber; *fig* ungestüm

**head·mas·ter** *Br* PED Direktor *m*, Rektor *m*

**head·mis·tress** *Br* PED Direktorin *f*, Rektorin *f*

**head-on** frontal, Frontal...; ***~ collision*** MOT Frontalzusammenstoß *m*

**head·phones** Kopfhörer *pl*

**head·quar·ters** (ABBR ***HQ***) MIL Hauptquartier *n*; Zentrale *f*

**head·rest** MOT Kopfstütze *f*

**head·set** Kopfhörer *pl*

**head start** SPORT Vorgabe *f*, Vorsprung *m* (*a. fig*)

**head·strong** halsstarrig

**head teach·er** → ***headmaster, headmistress, principal***

**head·wa·ters** GEOGR Quellgebiet *n*

**head·way** Fortschritt(e *pl*) *m*; ***make ~*** (gut) vorankommen

**head·word** Stichwort *n*

**head·y** zu Kopfe steigend, berauschend

**heal** heilen; ***~ over, ~ up*** (zu)heilen

**heal·ing** Heilung *f*; ***~ power*** Heilkraft *f*

**health** Gesundheit *f*; **~ cer·tif·i·cate** Gesundheitszeugnis *n*; **~ club** Fitnessklub *m*, Fitnesscenter *n*; **~ food** Reform-, Biokost *f*; **~ food shop** *Br*, **~ food store** Reformhaus *n*, Bioladen *m*

**health·ful** gesund; heilsam

**health| in·su·rance** Krankenversicherung *f*; **~ re·sort** Kurort *m*; **~ ser·vice** Gesundheitsdienst *m*

**health·y** gesund

**heap 1.** Haufe(n) *m*; **2.** *a.* ***~ up*** aufhäufen, *fig a.* anhäufen

**hear** hören; anhören, *j-m* zuhören; *Zeugen* vernehmen; *Lektion* abhören

**hear·er** (Zu)Hörer(in)

**hear·ing** Gehör *n*; Hören *n*; JUR Verhandlung *f*; JUR Vernehmung *f*; *esp* POL Hearing *n*, Anhörung *f*; ***within (out of) ~*** in (außer) Hörweite

**hear·ing aid** Hörgerät *n*

**hear·say** Gerede *n*; ***by ~*** vom Hörensagen *n*

**hearse** Leichenwagen *m*

**heart** ANAT Herz *n* (*a. fig*); Kern *m*; *card games*: Herz(karte *f*) *n*, *pl* Herz *n*; ***lose ~*** den Mut verlieren; ***take ~*** sich ein Herz fassen; ***take s.th. to ~*** sich et. zu Herzen nehmen; ***with a heavy ~*** schweren Herzens

**heart·ache** Kummer *m*

**heart at·tack** MED Herzanfall *m*; Herzinfarkt *m*

**heart·beat** Herzschlag *m*

**heart·break** Leid *n*, großer Kummer

**heart·break·ing** herzzerreißend

**heart·brok·en** gebrochen, verzweifelt

**heart·burn** MED Sodbrennen *n*

**heart·en** ermutigen

**heart fail·ure** MED Herzversagen *n*

**heart·felt** innig, tief empfunden

**hearth** Kamin *m*

**heart·less** herzlos

**heart·rend·ing** herzzerreißend

**heart trans·plant** MED Herzverpflanzung *f*, Herztransplantation *f*

**heart·y** herzlich; gesund; herzhaft

**heat 1.** Hitze *f*; PHYS Wärme *f*; Eifer *m*; ZO Läufigkeit *f*; SPORT (Einzel)Lauf *m*; ***preliminary ~*** Vorlauf *m*; **2.** *v/t* heizen; *a.* ***~ up*** erhitzen, aufwärmen; *v/i* sich erhitzen (*a. fig*); **heat·ed** geheizt; heizbar; erhitzt, *fig a.* erregt

H

**heat·er** Heizgerät *n*, Heizkörper *m*
**heath** Heide *f*, Heideland *n*
**hea·then** REL **1.** Heide *m*, Heidin *f*; **2.** heidnisch
**heath·er** BOT Heidekraut *n*; Erika *f*
**heat·ing 1.** Heizung *f*; **2.** Heiz...
**heat·proof** hitzebeständig
**heat shield** Hitzeschild *m*
**heat·stroke** MED Hitzschlag *m*
**heat wave** Hitzewelle *f*
**heave** *v/t* (hoch)stemmen, (hoch)hieven; *Anker* lichten; *Seufzer* ausstoßen; *v/i* sich heben und senken, wogen
**heav·en** Himmel *m*
**heav·en·ly** himmlisch
**heav·y** schwer; stark (*rain, smoker, drinker, traffic etc*); hoch (*fine, taxes etc*); schwer (verdaulich); drückend, lastend; Schwer...
**heav·y cur·rent** ELECTR Starkstrom *m*
**heav·y-du·ty** TECH Hochleistungs...; strapazierfähig
**heav·y-hand·ed** ungeschickt
**heav·y·weight** *boxing*: Schwergewicht *n*, Schwergewichtler *m*
**He·brew 1.** hebräisch; **2.** Hebräer(in); LING Hebräisch *n*
**heck·le** *Redner* durch Zwischenrufe *or* Zwischenfragen stören; **heck·ler** Zwischenrufer *m*; **heck·ling** Zwischenrufe
**hec·tic** hektisch
**hedge 1.** Hecke *f*; **2.** *v/t*: *a.* ~ ***in*** mit e-r Hecke einfassen; *v/i fig* ausweichen
**hedge·hog** ZO Stachelschwein *n*; *Br* Igel *m*
**hedge·row** Hecke *f*
**heed 1.** beachten, Beachtung schenken (*dat*); **2.** ***give*** *or* ***pay*** ~ ***to, take*** ~ ***of*** → 1
**heed·less:** ***be*** ~ ***of*** nicht beachten, *Warnung etc* in den Wind schlagen
**heel 1.** ANAT Ferse *f*; Absatz *m*; ***down at*** ~ *fig* abgerissen; heruntergekommen; **2.** Absätze machen auf (*acc*)
**hef·ty** kräftig, stämmig; mächtig (*blow etc*), gewaltig; F saftig (*prices, fine etc*)
**heif·er** ZO Färse *f*, junge Kuh
**height** Höhe *f*; (Körper)Größe *f*; Anhöhe *f*; *fig* Höhe(punkt *m*) *f*
**height·en** erhöhen; vergrößern
**heir** Erbe *m*; ~ ***to the throne*** Thronerbe *m*, Thronfolger *m*
**heir·ess** Erbin *f*
**heir·loom** Erbstück *n*
**hel·i·cop·ter** AVIAT Hubschrauber *m*, Helikopter *m*
**hel·i·port** AVIAT Hubschrauberlandeplatz *m*
**hell 1.** Hölle *f*; ***a*** ~ ***of a noise*** F ein Höllenlärm; ***what the*** ~ ***...?*** F was zum Teufel ...?; ***raise*** ~ F e-n Mordskrach schlagen; **2.** Höllen...; **3.** *int* F verdammt!, verflucht!; **hell·ish** F höllisch
**hel·lo** *int* hallo!
**helm** MAR Ruder *n*, Steuer *n*
**hel·met** Helm *m*
**helms·man** MAR Steuermann *m*
**help 1.** Hilfe *f*; Hausangestellte *f*; ***a call*** *or* ***cry for*** ~ ein Hilferuf, ein Hilfeschrei; **2.** helfen; ~ ***o.s.*** sich bedienen, zulangen; ***I cannot*** ~ ***it*** ich kann es nicht ändern; ***I could not*** ~ ***laughing*** ich musste einfach lachen
**help·er** Helfer(in)
**help·ful** hilfreich; nützlich
**help·ing** Portion *f*
**help·less** hilflos
**help·less·ness** Hilflosigkeit *f*
**help men·u** EDP Hilfemenü *n*
**hel·ter-skel·ter 1.** *adv* holterdiepolter, Hals über Kopf; **2.** *adj* überstürzt
**helve** Stiel *m*, Griff *m*
**Hel·ve·tian** Schweizer ...
**hem 1.** Saum *m*; **2.** säumen; ~ ***in*** einschließen
**hem·i·sphere** GEOGR Halbkugel *f*, Hemisphäre *f*
**hem·line** Saum *m*
**hem·lock** BOT Schierling *m*
**hemp** BOT Hanf *m*
**hem·stitch** Hohlsaum *m*
**hen** ZO Henne *f*, Huhn *n*; Weibchen *n*
**hence** daher; ***a week*** ~ in e-r Woche
**hence·forth** von nun an
**hen house** Hühnerstall *m*
**hen·pecked hus·band** Pantoffelheld *m*
**her** sie; ihr; ihr(e); sich
**her·ald 1.** HIST Herold *m*; **2.** ankündigen
**her·ald·ry** Wappenkunde *f*, Heraldik *f*
**herb** BOT Kraut *n*; Heilkraut *n*
**her·ba·ceous** BOT krautartig; ~ ***plant*** Staudengewächs *n*
**herb·al** BOT Kräuter..., Pflanzen...
**her·bi·vore** ZO Pflanzenfresser *m*
**herd 1.** Herde *f* (*a. fig*), Rudel *n*; **2.** *v/t*

H

*Vieh* hüten; *v/i*: *a.* ~ ***together*** in e-r Herde leben; sich zusammendrängen
**herds·man** Hirt *m*
**here** hier; hierher; ~ ***you are*** hier (bitte); ~***'s to you!*** auf dein Wohl!
**here·a·bout(s)** hier herum, in dieser Gegend
**here·af·ter 1.** künftig; **2.** *das* Jenseits
**here·by** hiermit
**he·red·i·ta·ry** BIOL erblich, Erb...
**he·red·i·ty** BIOL Erblichkeit *f*; ererbte Anlagen *pl*, Erbmasse *f*
**here·in** hierin
**here·of** hiervon
**her·e·sy** REL Ketzerei *f*
**her·e·tic** REL Ketzer(in)
**here·up·on** hierauf, darauf(hin)
**here·with** hiermit
**her·i·tage** Erbe *n*
**her·maph·ro·dite** BIOL Zwitter *m*
**her·met·ic** TECH hermetisch
**her·mit** Einsiedler *m*
**he·ro** Held *m*
**he·ro·ic** heroisch, heldenhaft, Helden...
**her·o·in** Heroin *n*
**her·o·ine** Heldin *f*
**her·o·is·m** Heldentum *n*
**her·on** ZO Reiher *m*
**her·ring** ZO Hering *m*
**hers** ihrs, ihre(r, -s)
**her·self** sie selbst, ihr selbst; sich (selbst); ***by*** ~ von selbst, allein, ohne Hilfe
**hes·i·tant** zögernd, zaudernd, unschlüssig; **hes·i·tate** zögern, zaudern, unschlüssig sein, Bedenken haben; **hes·i·ta·tion** Zögern *n*, Zaudern *n*, Unschlüssigkeit *f*; ***without*** ~ ohne zu zögern, bedenkenlos
**hew** hauen, hacken; ~ ***down*** fällen, umhauen
**hey** *int* F he!, heda!
**hey·day** Höhepunkt *m*, Gipfel *m*; Blüte(zeit) *f*
**hi** *int* F hallo!
**hi·ber·nate** ZO Winterschlaf halten
**hic·cough, hic·cup 1.** Schluckauf *m*; **2.** den Schluckauf haben
**hide**[1] (sich) verbergen, verstecken; verheimlichen
**hide**[2] Haut *f*, Fell *n*
**hide-and-seek** Versteckspiel *n*
**hide·a·way** F Versteck *n*
**hid·e·ous** abscheulich, scheußlich
**hide·out** Versteck *n*
**hid·ing**[1] F Tracht *f* Prügel
**hid·ing**[2]**:** ***be in*** ~ sich versteckt halten; ***go into*** ~ untertauchen
**hid·ing place** Versteck *n*
**hi-fi** Hi-Fi *n*, Hi-Fi-Gerät *n*, -Anlage *f*
**high 1.** hoch; groß (*hopes etc*); GASTR angegangen; F blau; F high; ***be in*** ~ ***spirits*** in Hochstimmung sein; ausgelassen *or* übermütig sein; **2.** METEOR Hoch *n*; Höchststand *m*; High School *f*
**high·brow** F **1.** Intellektuelle *m*, *f*; **2.** (betont) intellektuell
**high-cal·o·rie** kalorienreich
**high-class** erstklassig
**high·er ed·u·ca·tion** Hochschulausbildung *f*
**high fi·del·i·ty** High Fidelity *f*
**high·grade** hochwertig; erstklassig
**high-hand·ed** anmaßend, eigenmächtig
**high-heeled** hochhackig
**high jump** SPORT Hochsprung *m*
**high jump·er** SPORT Hochspringer(in)
**high·land** Hochland *n*
**high·light 1.** Höhe-, Glanzpunkt *m*; **2.** hervorheben
**high·ly** *fig* hoch; ***think*** ~ ***of*** viel halten von; **high·ly-strung** reizbar, nervös
**high·ness** *mst fig* Höhe *f*; ***Highness*** Hoheit *f* (*title*)
**high-pitched** schrill; steil (*roof*)
**high-pow·ered** TECH Hochleistungs...; *fig* dynamisch
**high-pres·sure** METEOR, TECH Hochdruck...
**high-rank·ing** hochrangig
**high rise** Hochhaus *n*
**high road** *esp Br* Hauptstraße *f*
**high school** High School *f*
**high sea·son** Hochsaison *f*
**high so·ci·e·ty** High Society *f*
**high-spir·it·ed** übermütig, ausgelassen
**high street** *Br* Hauptstraße *f*
**high tea** *Br* frühes Abendessen
**high tech·nol·o·gy** Hochtechnologie *f*
**high ten·sion** ELECTR Hochspannung *f*
**high tide** Flut *f*
**high time:** ***it is*** ~ es ist höchste Zeit
**high wa·ter** Hochwasser *n*
**high·way** Highway *m*, Haupt(verkehrs)straße *f*; **High·way Code** *Br* Straßenverkehrsordnung *f*
**hi·jack 1.** *Flugzeug* entführen; *j-n*, *Geld-*

*transport etc* überfallen; **2.** (Flugzeug-)Entführung *f*; Überfall *m*
**hi·jack·er** Räuber *m*; (Flugzeug)Entführer(in)
**hike 1.** wandern; **2.** Wanderung *f*
**hik·er** Wanderer *m*, Wanderin *f*
**hik·ing** Wandern *n*
**hi·lar·i·ous** ausgelassen
**hi·lar·i·ty** Ausgelassenheit *f*
**hill** Hügel *m*, Anhöhe *f*
**hill·bil·ly** *contp* Hinterwäldler *m*
**hill·ock** kleiner Hügel
**hill·side** (Ab)Hang *m*
**hill·top** Hügelspitze *f*
**hill·y** hügelig
**hilt** Heft *n*, Griff *m*
**him** ihn; ihm; F er; sich
**him·self** er *or* ihm *or* ihn selbst; sich; sich (selbst); ***by ~*** von selbst, allein, ohne Hilfe
**hind**[1] zo Hirschkuh *f*
**hind**[2] Hinter...
**hin·der** hindern (***from*** an *dat*); hemmen
**hind·most** hinterste(r, -s), letzte(r, -s)
**hin·drance** Hindernis *n*
**Hin·du** Hindu *m*
**Hin·du·ism** Hinduismus *m*
**hinge 1.** TECH (Tür)Angel *f*, Scharnier *n*; **2.** ***~ on*** *fig* abhängen von
**hint 1.** Wink *m*, Andeutung *f*; Tipp *m*; Anspielung *f*; ***take a ~*** e-n Wink verstehen; **2.** andeuten; anspielen (***at*** auf *acc*)
**hip**[1] ANAT Hüfte *f*
**hip**[2] BOT Hagebutte *f*
**hip·po** F → **hip·po·pot·a·mus** zo Flusspferd *n*, Nilpferd *n*
**hire 1.** *Br Auto etc* mieten, *Flugzeug etc* chartern; *j-n* anstellen; *j-n* engagieren, anheuern; ***~ out*** *Br* vermieten; **2.** Miete *f*; Lohn *m*; ***for ~*** zu vermieten; frei
**hire car** *Br* Leih-, Mietwagen *m*
**hire pur·chase: *on ~*** *Br* ECON auf Abzahlung, auf Raten
**his** sein(e); seins, seine(r, -s)
**hiss 1.** zischen; fauchen (*cat*); auszischen; **2.** Zischen *n*; Fauchen *n*
**his·to·ri·an** Historiker(in)
**his·tor·ic** historisch, geschichtlich (bedeutsam); **his·tor·i·cal** historisch, geschichtlich (belegt *or* überliefert); Geschichts...; ***~ novel*** historischer Roman
**his·to·ry** Geschichte *f*; ***~ of civilization*** Kulturgeschichte *f*; ***contemporary ~*** Zeitgeschichte *f*

**hit 1.** schlagen; treffen (*a. fig*); MOT *etc j-n*, *et.* anfahren, *et.* rammen; F ***~ it off*** (***with s.o.***) sich (mit j-m) gut vertragen; ***~ on*** (zufällig) auf *et.* stoßen, *et.* finden; **2.** Schlag *m*; *fig* (Seiten)Hieb *m*; (Glücks)Treffer *m*; Hit *m*
**hit-and-run: *~ driver*** (unfall)flüchtiger Fahrer; ***~ offense*** (*Br* ***offence***) Fahrerflucht *f*
**hitch 1.** befestigen, festmachen, festhaken, anbinden, ankoppeln (***to*** an *acc*); ***~ up*** hochziehen; ***~ a ride*** *or* ***lift*** im Auto mitgenommen werden; **2.** Ruck *m*, Zug *m*; Schwierigkeit *f*, Haken *m*; ***without a ~*** glatt, reibungslos;
**hitch·hike** per Anhalter fahren, trampen; **hitch·hik·er** Anhalter(in), Tramper(in)
**hi-tech** → ***high tech***
**HIV: *~ carrier*** HIV-Positive *m, f*; ***~ negative*** HIV-negativ; ***~ positive*** HIV-positiv
**hive** Bienenstock *m*; Bienenschwarm *m*
**hoard 1.** Vorrat *m*, Schatz *m*; **2.** *a.* ***~ up*** horten, hamstern; **hoard·ing** Bauzaun *m*; *Br* Reklametafel *f*
**hoar·frost** (Rau)Reif *m*
**hoarse** heiser, rau
**hoax 1.** Falschmeldung *f*; (übler) Scherz; **2.** *j-n* hereinlegen
**hob·ble** humpeln, hinken
**hob·by** Hobby *n*, Steckenpferd *n*
**hob·by·horse** Steckenpferd *n* (*a. fig*)
**hob·gob·lin** Kobold *m*
**ho·bo** F Landstreicher *m*
**hock**[1] weißer Rheinwein
**hock**[2] zo Sprunggelenk *n*
**hock·ey** SPORT Eishockey *n*; *esp Br* Hockey *n*
**hodge·podge** Mischmasch *m*
**hoe** AGR **1.** Hacke *f*; **2.** hacken
**hog** zo (Haus-, Schlacht)Schwein *n*
**hoist 1.** hochziehen; hissen; **2.** TECH Winde *f*, (Lasten)Aufzug *m*
**hold 1.** halten; festhalten; *Gewicht etc* tragen, aushalten; zurück-, abhalten (***from*** von); *Wahlen*, *Versammlung etc* abhalten; *Stellung* halten; SPORT *Meisterschaft etc* austragen; *Aktien*, *Rechte etc* besitzen; *Amt* bekleiden; *Platz* einnehmen; *Rekord* halten; fassen, enthalten; Platz bieten für; der Ansicht sein (***that*** dass); halten für; *fig* fesseln, in Spannung halten; (sich) festhalten; an-

halten, andauern (*a. fig*); ~ ***one's ground***, ~ ***one's own*** sich behaupten; ~ ***the line*** TEL am Apparat bleiben; ~ ***responsible*** verantwortlich machen; ~ ***still*** still halten; ~ ***s.th. against s.o.*** j-m et. vorhalten *or* vorwerfen; j-m et. übel nehmen *or* nachtragen; ~ ***back*** (sich) zurückhalten; *fig* zurückhalten mit; ~ ***on*** (sich) festhalten (***to*** an *dat*); aus-, durchhalten; andauern; TEL am Apparat bleiben; ~ ***out*** aus-, durchhalten; reichen (*supplies etc*); ~ ***up*** hochheben; hochhalten; hinstellen (**as** als); aufhalten, verzögern; *j-n, Bank etc* überfallen; **2.** Griff *m*, Halt *m*; Stütze *f*; Gewalt *f*, Macht *f*, Einfluss *m*; MAR Laderaum *m*, Frachtraum *m*; ***catch*** (***get, take***) ~ ***of s.th.*** et. ergreifen, et. zu fassen bekommen

**hold·er** TECH Halter *m*; *esp* ECON Inhaber(in)

**hold·ing** Besitz *m*; ~ **com·pa·ny** ECON Holding-, Dachgesellschaft *f*

**hold·up** (Verkehrs)Stockung *f*; (bewaffneter) (Raub)Überfall

**hole 1.** Loch *n*; Höhle *f*, Bau *m*; *fig* F Klemme *f*; **2.** durchlöchern

**hol·i·day** Feiertag *m*; freier Tag; *esp Br mst pl* Ferien *pl*, Urlaub *m*; ***be on*** ~ im Urlaub sein, Urlaub machen; ~ **home** Ferienhaus *n*, Ferienwohnung *f*

**hol·i·day·mak·er** Urlauber(in)

**hol·i·ness** Heiligkeit *f*; ***His Holiness*** Seine Heiligkeit

**hol·ler** F schreien

**hol·low 1.** hohl; **2.** Hohlraum *m*, (Aus)Höhlung *f*; Mulde *f*, Vertiefung *f*; **3.** ~ ***out*** aushöhlen

**hol·ly** BOT Stechpalme *f*

**hol·o·caust** Massenvernichtung *f*, Massensterben *n*, (*esp* Brand)Katastrophe *f*; ***the Holocaust*** HIST der Holocaust

**hol·ster** (Pistolen)Halfter *m*, *n*

**ho·ly** heilig

**ho·ly wa·ter** REL Weihwasser *n*

**Ho·ly Week** REL Karwoche *f*

**home 1.** Heim *n*; Haus *n*; Wohnung *f*; Zuhause *n*; Heimat *f*; ***at*** ~ zu Hause; ***make oneself at*** ~ es sich bequem machen; ***at*** ~ ***and abroad*** im In- und Ausland; **2.** *adj* häuslich, Heim... (*a.* SPORT); inländisch, Inlands...; Heimat...; **3.** *adv* heim, nach Hause; zu Hause; daheim; *fig* ins Ziel, ins Schwarze; ***return*** ~ heimkehren; ***strike*** ~ sitzen, treffen

**home ad·dress** Privatanschrift *f*

**home com·put·er** Heimcomputer *m*

**home·less** heimatlos; obdachlos; ~ ***person*** Obdachlose *m*, *f*; ***shelter for the*** ~ Obdachlosenasyl *n*

**home·ly** einfach; unscheinbar, reizlos

**home·made** selbst gemacht, Hausmacher...

**home mar·ket** ECON Binnenmarkt *m*

**Home| Of·fice** *Br* POL Innenministerium *n*; ~ **Sec·re·ta·ry** *Br* POL Innenminister *m*

**home·sick**: ***be*** ~ Heimweh haben

**home·sick·ness** Heimweh *n*

**home team** SPORT Gastgeber *pl*

**home·ward** *adj* Heim..., Rück...

**home·ward(s)** *adv* nach Hause

**home·work** Hausaufgabe(n *pl*) *f*; ***do one's*** ~ s-e Hausaufgaben machen (*a. fig*)

**hom·i·cide** JUR Mord *m*; Totschlag *m*; Mörder(in)

**hom·i·cide squad** Mordkommission *f*

**ho·mo·ge·ne·ous** homogen, gleichartig

**ho·mo·sex·u·al 1.** homosexuell; **2.** Homosexuelle *m*, *f*

**hone** TECH fein schleifen

**hon·est** ehrlich, rechtschaffen; aufrichtig; **hon·es·ty** Ehrlichkeit *f*, Rechtschaffenheit *f*; Aufrichtigkeit *f*

**hon·ey** Honig *m*; Liebling *m*, Schatz *m*

**hon·ey·comb** (Honig)Wabe *f*

**hon·eyed** *fig* honigsüß

**hon·ey·moon 1.** Flitterwochen *pl*, Hochzeitsreise *f*; **2.** ***be*** ~***ing*** auf Hochzeitsreise sein

**hon·ey·suck·le** BOT Geißblatt *n*

**honk** MOT hupen

**hon·or·ar·y** Ehren...; ehrenamtlich

**hon·o(u)r 1.** Ehre *f*; Ehrung *f*, Ehre(n *pl*) *f*; *pl* besondere Auszeichnung(en *pl*); ***Your Hono(u)r*** JUR Euer Ehren; **2.** ehren; auszeichnen; ECON *Scheck etc* honorieren, einlösen

**hon·o(u)r·a·ble** ehrenvoll, ehrenhaft; ehrenwert

**hood** Kapuze *f*; MOT Verdeck *n*; (Motor)Haube *f*; TECH (Schutz)Haube *f*

**hood·lum** F Rowdy *m*; Ganove *m*

**hood·wink** *j-n* hinters Licht führen

H

**hoof** ZO Huf *m*
**hook 1.** Haken *m*; Angelhaken *m*; ***by ~ or by crook*** F mit allen Mitteln; **2.** an-, ein-, fest-, zuhaken; angeln (*a. fig*)
**hooked** krumm, Haken...; F süchtig (***on*** nach) (*a. fig*); ***~ on heroin*** (***television***) heroinsüchtig (fernsehsüchtig)
**hook·er** F Nutte *f*
**hook·y: *play ~*** F (die Schule) schwänzen
**hoo·li·gan** Rowdy *m*
**hoo·li·gan·ism** Rowdytum *n*
**hoop** Reif(en) *m*
**hoot 1.** ZO Schrei *m* (*a. fig*); MOT Hupen *n*; **2.** *v/i* heulen; johlen; ZO schreien; MOT hupen; *v/t* auspfeifen, auszischen
**Hoo·ver®** *Br* **1.** Staubsauger *m*; **2.** *mst* ***hoover*** (staub)saugen
**hop¹ 1.** hüpfen, hopsen; hüpfen über (*acc*); ***be ~ping mad*** F e-e Stinkwut haben; **2.** Sprung *m*
**hop²** BOT Hopfen *m*
**hope 1.** Hoffnung *f* (***of*** auf *acc*); **2.** hoffen (***for*** auf *acc*); ***~ for the best*** das Beste hoffen; ***I ~ so, let's ~ so*** hoffentlich
**hope·ful: *be ~ that*** hoffen, dass
**hope·ful·ly** hoffnungsvoll; hoffentlich
**hope·less** hoffnungslos; verzweifelt
**horde** Horde *f* (*often contp*)
**ho·ri·zon** Horizont *m*
**hor·i·zon·tal** horizontal, waag(e)recht
**hor·mone** BIOL Hormon *n*
**horn** ZO Horn *n*, *pl* Geweih *n*; MOT Hupe *f*
**hor·net** ZO Hornisse *f*
**horn·y** schwielig; V geil
**hor·o·scope** Horoskop *n*
**hor·ri·ble** schrecklich, furchtbar, scheußlich
**hor·rid** *esp Br* grässlich, abscheulich; schrecklich
**hor·rif·ic** schrecklich, entsetzlich
**hor·ri·fy** entsetzen
**hor·ror** Entsetzen *n*; Abscheu *m*, Horror *m*; F Gräuel *m*
**horse** ZO Pferd *n*; Bock *m*, Gestell *n*; ***wild ~s couldn't drag me there*** keine zehn Pferde bringen mich dort hin
**horse·back: *on ~*** zu Pferde, beritten
**horse chest·nut** BOT Rosskastanie *f*
**horse·hair** Rosshaar *n*
**horse·man** (geübter) Reiter
**horse·pow·er** TECH Pferdestärke *f*
**horse race** Pferderennen *n*
**horse rac·ing** Pferderennen *n or pl*
**horse·rad·ish** BOT Meerrettich *m*
**horse·shoe** Hufeisen *n*
**horse·wom·an** (geübte) Reiterin
**hor·ti·cul·ture** Gartenbau *m*
**hose¹** Schlauch *m*
**hose²** Strümpfe *pl*, Strumpfwaren *pl*
**ho·sier·y** Strumpfwaren *pl*
**hos·pice** Sterbeklinik *f*
**hos·pi·ta·ble** gastfreundlich
**hos·pi·tal** Krankenhaus *n*, Klinik *f*; ***in the ~*** im Krankenhaus
**hos·pi·tal·i·ty** Gastfreundschaft *f*
**hos·pi·tal·ize** ins Krankenhaus einliefern *or* einweisen
**host¹ 1.** Gastgeber *m*; BIOL Wirt *m*; *radio*, TV Talkmaster *m*, Showmaster *m*, Moderator(in); ***your ~ was ...*** durch die Sendung führte Sie ...; **2.** *radio*, TV F *Sendung* moderieren
**host²** Menge *f*, Masse *f*
**host³** REL *often* ***Host*** Hostie *f*
**hos·tage** Geisel *m*, *f*; ***take s.o. ~*** j-n als Geisel nehmen
**hos·tel** *esp Br* UNIV (Wohn)Heim *n*; *mst* ***youth ~*** Jugendherberge *f*
**host·ess** Gastgeberin *f*; Hostess *f* (*a.* AVIAT); AVIAT Stewardess *f*
**hos·tile** feindlich; feindselig (***to*** gegen); ***~ to foreigners*** ausländerfeindlich
**hos·til·i·ty** Feindseligkeit *f* (***to*** gegen); ***~ to foreigners*** Ausländerfeindlichkeit *f*
**hot** heiß (*a. fig and sl*); GASTR scharf; warm (*meal*); *fig* hitzig, heftig; ganz neu *or* frisch (*news etc*); ***I am or feel ~*** mir ist heiß
**hot·bed** Mistbeet *n*; *fig* Brutstätte *f*
**hotch·potch** *Br* → ***hodgepodge***
**hot dog** GASTR Hot Dog *n*, *m*
**ho·tel** Hotel *n*
**hot·head** Hitzkopf *m*
**hot·house** Treib-, Gewächshaus *n*
**hot line** POL heißer Draht; TEL Hotline *f*
**hot·plate** Kochplatte *f*
**hot spot** *esp* POL Unruhe-, Krisenherd *m*
**hot spring** Thermalquelle *f*
**hot-tem·pered** jähzornig
**hot-wa·ter bot·tle** Wärmflasche *f*
**hound** ZO Jagdhund *m*
**hour** Stunde *f*; *pl* (*Arbeits*)Zeit *f*, (*Geschäfts*)Stunden *pl*; **hour·ly** stündlich
**house 1.** Haus *n*; **2.** unterbringen
**house·bound** ans Haus gefesselt

**house·break·ing** Einbruch *m*
**house·hold 1.** Haushalt *m*; **2.** Haushalts...
**house hus·band** Hausmann *m*
**house·keep·er** Haushälterin *f*
**house·keep·ing** Haushaltung *f*, Haushaltsführung *f*
**house·maid** Hausangestellte *f*, Hausmädchen *n*
**house·man** *Br* MED Assistenzarzt *m*, -ärztin *f*
**House of Lords** *Br* PARL Oberhaus *n*
**house plant** Zimmerpflanze *f*
**house-warm·ing** Hauseinweihung *f*, Einzugsparty *f*
**house·wife** Hausfrau *f*
**house·work** Hausarbeit *f*
**hous·ing** Wohnung *f*; **~ de·vel·op·ment,** *Br* **~ es·tate** Wohnsiedlung *f*
**hov·er** schweben; herumlungern; *fig* schwanken
**hov·er·craft** Hovercraft *n*, Luftkissenfahrzeug *n*
**how** wie; **~ *are you?*** wie geht es dir?; **~ *about ...?*** wie steht's mit ...?, wie wäre es mit ...?; **~ *do you do?*** guten Tag!; **~ *much?*** wie viel?; **~ *many*** wie viele?
**how·ev·er 1.** *adv* wie auch (immer); **2.** *cj* jedoch
**howl 1.** heulen; brüllen, schreien; **2.** Heulen *n*; **howl·er** F grober Schnitzer
**hub** TECH (Rad)Nabe *f*; *fig* Mittelpunkt *m*, Angelpunkt *m*
**hub·bub** Stimmengewirr *n*; Tumult *m*
**hub·by** F (Ehe)Mann *m*
**huck·le·ber·ry** BOT amerikanische Heidelbeere
**hud·dle: ~ *together*** (sich) zusammendrängen; **~*d up*** zusammengekauert
**hue¹** Farbe *f*; (Farb)Ton *m*
**hue²: ~ *and cry*** *fig* großes Geschrei, heftiger Protest
**huff: *in a* ~** verärgert, verstimmt
**hug 1.** (sich) umarmen; an sich drücken; **2.** Umarmung *f*
**huge** riesig, riesengroß
**hulk** F Koloss *m*; sperriges Ding; ***a* ~ *of a man*** ein ungeschlachter Kerl
**hull 1.** BOT Schale *f*, Hülse *f*; MAR Rumpf *m*; **2.** enthülsen, schälen
**hul·la·ba·loo** Lärm *m*, Getöse *n*
**hul·lo** *int* hallo!
**hum** summen; brummen
**hu·man 1.** menschlich, Menschen...; **2.** *a.* **~ *being*** Mensch *m*
**hu·mane** human, menschlich
**hu·man·i·tar·i·an** humanitär, menschenfreundlich
**hu·man·i·ty** die Menschheit, die Menschen *pl*; Humanität *f*, Menschlichkeit *f*; *pl* Geisteswissenschaften *pl*; Altphilologie *f*
**hu·man·ly: ~ *possible*** menschenmöglich
**hu·man rights** Menschenrechte *pl*
**hum·ble 1.** demütig; bescheiden; **2.** demütigen; **hum·ble·ness** Demut *f*
**hum·drum** eintönig, langweilig
**hu·mid** feucht, nass
**hu·mid·i·ty** Feuchtigkeit *f*
**hu·mil·i·ate** demütigen, erniedrigen
**hu·mil·i·a·tion** Demütigung *f*, Erniedrigung *f*
**hu·mil·i·ty** Demut *f*
**hum·ming·bird** ZO Kolibri *m*
**hu·mor·ous** humorvoll, komisch
**hu·mo(u)r 1.** Humor *m*; Komik *f*; **2.** *j-m* s-n Willen lassen; eingehen auf (*acc*)
**hump** ZO Höcker *m*; MED Buckel *m*
**hump·back(ed)** → ***hunchback(ed)***
**hunch 1.** → ***hump***; dickes Stück; (Vor)Ahnung *f*; **2.** *a.* **~ *up*** krümmen; **~ *one's shoulders*** die Schultern hochziehen
**hunch·back** Buckel *m*; Bucklige *m, f*
**hunch·backed** buck(e)lig
**hun·dred 1.** hundert; **2.** Hundert *f*
**hun·dredth 1.** hundertste(r, -s); **2.** Hundertstel *n*
**hun·dred·weight** *appr* Zentner *m* (= *50,8 kg*)
**Hun·ga·ri·an 1.** ungarisch; **2.** Ungar(in); LING Ungarisch *n*
**Hun·ga·ry** Ungarn *n*
**hun·ger 1.** Hunger *m* (*a. fig* ***for*** nach); **2.** *fig* hungern (***for, after*** nach)
**hun·ger strike** Hungerstreik *m*
**hun·gry** hungrig
**hunk** dickes *or* großes Stück
**hunt 1.** jagen; Jagd machen auf (*acc*); verfolgen; suchen (***for, after*** nach); **~ *down*** zur Strecke bringen; **~ *for*** Jagd machen auf (*acc*); **~ *out,* ~ *up*** aufspüren; **2.** Jagd *f* (*a. fig*), Jagen *n*; Verfolgung *f*; Suche *f* (***for, after*** nach)
**hunt·er** Jäger *m*; Jagdpferd *n*
**hunt·ing 1.** Jagen *n*; **2.** Jagd...

**hunt·ing ground** Jagdrevier *n*
**hur·dle** SPORT Hürde *f* (*a. fig*)
**hur·dler** SPORT Hürdenläufer(in)
**hur·dle race** SPORT Hürdenrennen *n*
**hurl** schleudern; ~ ***abuse at s.o.*** j-m Beleidigungen ins Gesicht schleudern
**hur·rah, hur·ray** *int* hurra!
**hur·ri·cane** Hurrikan *m*, Wirbelsturm *m*; Orkan *m*
**hur·ried** eilig, hastig, übereilt
**hur·ry 1.** *v/t* schnell *or* eilig befördern *or* bringen; *often* ~ ***up*** *j-n* antreiben, hetzen; *et.* beschleunigen; *v/i* eilen, hasten; ~ (***up***) sich beeilen; ~ ***up!*** (mach) schnell!; **2.** (große) Eile, Hast *f*; ***be in a*** ~ es eilig haben
**hurt** verletzen, verwunden (*a. fig*); schmerzen, wehtun; schaden (*dat*)
**hurt·ful** verletzend
**hus·band** (Ehe)Mann *m*
**hush 1.** *int* still!; **2.** Stille *f*; **3.** zum Schweigen bringen; ~ ***up*** vertuschen, totschweigen
**hush mon·ey** Schweigegeld *n*
**husk** BOT **1.** Hülse *f*, Schote *f*, Schale *f*; **2.** enthülsen, schälen
**hus·tle 1.** (*in aller Eile*) *wohin* bringen *or* schicken; hasten, hetzen; sich beeilen; **2.** ~ ***and bustle*** Gedränge *n*; Gehetze *n*; Betrieb *m*, Wirbel *m*
**hut** Hütte *f*
**hutch** Stall *m*
**hy·a·cinth** BOT Hyazinthe *f*
**hy·(a)e·na** ZO Hyäne *f*
**hy·brid** BIOL Mischling *m*, Kreuzung *f*
**hy·drant** Hydrant *m*
**hy·draul·ic** hydraulisch
**hy·draul·ics** Hydraulik *f*
**hy·dro...** Wasser...
**hy·dro·car·bon** CHEM Kohlenwasserstoff *m*
**hy·dro·chlor·ic ac·id** CHEM Salzsäure *f*
**hy·dro·foil** MAR Tragflächenboot *n*, Tragflügelboot *n*
**hy·dro·gen** CHEM Wasserstoff *m*; ~ **bomb** Wasserstoffbombe
**hy·dro·plane** AVIAT Wasserflugzeug *n*; MAR Gleitboot *n*
**hy·dro·plan·ing** MOT Aquaplaning *n*
**hy·e·na** ZO Hyäne *f*
**hy·giene** Hygiene *f*
**hy·gien·ic** hygienisch
**hymn** Kirchenlied *n*, Choral *m*
**hype** F **1.** *a.* ~ ***up*** (übersteigerte) Publicity machen für; **2.** (übersteigerte) Publicity; ***media*** ~ Medienrummel *m*
**hy·per...** hyper..., übermäßig
**hy·per·mar·ket** *Br* Groß-, Verbrauchermarkt *m*
**hy·per·sen·si·tive** überempfindlich (***to*** gegen)
**hy·phen** Bindestrich *m*
**hy·phen·ate** mit Bindestrich schreiben
**hyp·no·tize** hypnotisieren
**hy·po·chon·dri·ac** Hypochonder *m*
**hy·poc·ri·sy** Heuchelei *f*
**hyp·o·crite** Heuchler(in)
**hyp·o·crit·i·cal** heuchlerisch, scheinheilig
**hy·poth·e·sis** Hypothese *f*
**hys·te·ri·a** MED Hysterie *f*
**hys·ter·i·cal** hysterisch
**hys·ter·ics** hysterischer Anfall; ***go into*** ~ hysterisch werden

# I

**I, i** I, i *n*
**I** ich; ***it is*** ~ ich bin es
**ice 1.** Eis *n*; **2.** *Getränke etc* mit *or* in Eis kühlen; GASTR glasieren, mit Zuckerguss überziehen; ~***d over*** zugefroren (*lake etc*); ~***d up*** vereist (*road*)
**ice age** Eiszeit *f*
**ice·berg** Eisberg *m* (*a. fig*)
**ice·bound** eingefroren
**ice cream** (Speise)Eis *n*
**ice-cream par·lo(u)r** Eisdiele *f*
**ice cube** Eiswürfel *m*
**iced** eisgekühlt
**ice floe** Eisscholle *f*
**ice hock·ey** SPORT Eishockey *n*
**ice lol·ly** *Br* Eis *n* am Stiel

**ice rink** (Kunst)Eisbahn *f*
**ice skate** Schlittschuh *m*
**ice-skate** Schlittschuh laufen
**ice show** Eisrevue *f*
**i·ci·cle** Eiszapfen *m*
**ic·ing** GASTR Glasur *f*, Zuckerguss *m*; ***the ~ on the cake*** das Tüpfelchen auf dem i
**i·con** REL Ikone *f*; EDP Ikone *f*, (Bild)Symbol *n*
**i·cy** eisig; vereist
**ID** ABBR *of* ***identity*** Identität *f*; ***ID card*** (Personal)Ausweis *m*
**i·dea** Idee *f*, Vorstellung *f*, Begriff *m*; Gedanke *m*, Idee *f*; ***have no ~*** keine Ahnung haben
**i·deal 1.** ideal; **2.** Ideal *n*
**i·deal·ism** Idealismus *m*
**i·deal·ize** idealisieren
**i·den·ti·cal** identisch (***to, with*** mit); **~ twins** eineiige Zwillinge *pl*
**i·den·ti·fi·ca·tion** Identifizierung *f*; **~ (pa·pers)** Ausweis(papiere *pl*) *m*
**i·den·ti·fy** identifizieren; ***~ o.s.*** sich ausweisen
**i·den·ti·kit® pic·ture** *Br* JUR Phantombild *n*
**i·den·ti·ty** Identität *f*; **~ card** (Personal)Ausweis *m*
**i·de·o·log·i·cal** ideologisch
**i·de·ol·o·gy** Ideologie *f*
**id·i·om** Idiom *n*, idiomatischer Ausdruck, Redewendung *f*
**id·i·o·mat·ic** idiomatisch
**id·i·ot** MED Idiot(in), *contp a.* Trottel *m*
**id·i·ot·ic** MED idiotisch, F *a.* blödsinnig, schwachsinnig
**i·dle 1.** untätig; faul, träge; nutzlos; leer, hohl (*talk*); TECH stillstehend, außer Betrieb; MOT leer laufend, im Leerlauf; **2.** faulenzen; MOT leer laufen; *mst* ***~ away*** *Zeit* vertrödeln
**i·dol** Idol *n* (*a. fig*); Götzenbild *n*
**i·dol·ize** abgöttisch verehren, vergöttern
**i·dyl·lic** idyllisch
**if** wenn, falls; ob; ***~ I were you*** wenn ich du wäre
**ig·loo** Iglu *m*, *n*
**ig·nite** anzünden, (sich) entzünden; MOT zünden; **ig·ni·tion** MOT Zündung *f*
**ig·ni·tion key** MOT Zündschlüssel *m*
**ig·no·rance** Unkenntnis *f*, Unwissenheit *f*; **ig·no·rant:** ***be ~ of s.th.*** et. nicht wissen *or* kennen, nichts wissen von et.
**ig·nore** ignorieren, nicht beachten
**ill** krank; schlimm, schlecht; ***fall ~, be taken ~*** krank werden, erkranken
**ill-ad·vised** schlecht beraten; unklug
**ill-bred** schlecht erzogen; ungezogen
**il·le·gal** verboten; JUR illegal, ungesetzlich; ***~ parking*** Falschparken *n*
**il·le·gi·ble** unleserlich
**il·le·git·i·mate** unehelich; unrechtmäßig
**ill feel·ing** Verstimmung *f*; ***cause ~*** böses Blut machen
**ill-hu·mo(u)red** schlecht gelaunt
**il·li·cit** unerlaubt, verboten
**il·lit·e·rate** ungebildet
**ill-man·nered** ungehobelt, ungezogen
**ill-na·tured** boshaft, bösartig
**ill·ness** Krankheit *f*
**ill-tem·pered** schlecht gelaunt
**ill-timed** ungelegen, unpassend
**il·lu·mi·nate** beleuchten
**il·lu·mi·nat·ing** aufschlussreich
**il·lu·mi·na·tion** Beleuchtung *f*; *pl* Illumination *f*, Festbeleuchtung *f*
**il·lu·sion** Illusion *f*, Täuschung *f*
**il·lu·sive, il·lu·so·ry** illusorisch, trügerisch
**il·lus·trate** illustrieren; bebildern; erläutern, veranschaulichen
**il·lus·tra·tion** Erläuterung *f*; Illustration *f*; Bild *n*, Abbildung *f*
**il·lus·tra·tive** erläuternd
**il·lus·tri·ous** berühmt
**ill will** Feindschaft *f*
**im·age** Bild *n*; Ebenbild *n*; Image *n*; bildlicher Ausdruck, Metapher *f*
**im·age·ry** Bildersprache *f*, Metaphorik *f*
**i·ma·gi·na·ble** vorstellbar, denkbar
**i·ma·gi·na·ry** eingebildet, imaginär
**i·ma·gi·na·tion** Einbildung(skraft) *f*; Vorstellungskraft *f*, -vermögen *n*
**i·ma·gi·na·tive** ideenreich, einfallsreich; fantasievoll
**i·ma·gine** sich *j-n or et.* vorstellen; sich *et.* einbilden
**im·bal·ance** Unausgewogenheit *f*; POL *etc* Ungleichgewicht *n*
**im·be·cile** Idiot *m*, Trottel *m*
**im·i·tate** nachahmen, nachmachen, imitieren; **im·i·ta·tion 1.** Nachahmung *f*, Imitation *f*; **2.** nachgemacht, unecht, künstlich, Kunst...

I

**im·mac·u·late** unbefleckt, makellos; tadellos, fehlerlos
**im·ma·te·ri·al** unwesentlich, unerheblich (*to* für)
**im·ma·ture** unreif
**im·mea·su·ra·ble** unermesslich
**im·me·di·ate** unmittelbar; sofortig, umgehend; nächste(r, -s) (*family*)
**im·me·di·ate·ly** unmittelbar; sofort
**im·mense** riesig, *fig a.* enorm, immens
**im·merse** (ein)tauchen; **~ *o.s. in*** sich vertiefen in (*acc*)
**im·mer·sion** Eintauchen *n*
**im·mer·sion heat·er** Tauchsieder *m*
**im·mi·grant** Einwanderer *m*, Einwanderin *f*, Immigrant(in); **im·mi·grate** einwandern, immigrieren (***into*** in *dat*); **im·mi·gra·tion** Einwanderung *f*, Immigration *f*
**im·mi·nent** nahe bevorstehend; **~ *danger*** drohende Gefahr
**im·mo·bile** unbeweglich
**im·mod·e·rate** maßlos
**im·mod·est** unbescheiden; schamlos, unanständig
**im·mor·al** unmoralisch
**im·mor·tal 1.** unsterblich; **2.** Unsterbliche *m*, *f*
**im·mor·tal·i·ty** Unsterblichkeit *f*
**im·mo·va·ble** unbeweglich; *fig* unerschütterlich; hart, unnachgiebig
**im·mune** MED immun (***to*** gegen); geschützt (***from*** vor, gegen); **~ sys·tem** MED Immunsystem *n*
**im·mu·ni·ty** MED Immunität *f*
**im·mu·nize** MED immunisieren, immun machen (***against*** gegen)
**imp** Kobold *m*; F Racker *m*
**im·pact** Zusammenprall *m*, Anprall *m*; Aufprall *m*; Wucht *f*; *fig* (Ein)Wirkung *f*, (starker) Einfluss (***on*** auf *acc*)
**im·pair** beeinträchtigen
**im·part** (***to*** *dat*) mitteilen; vermitteln
**im·par·tial** unparteiisch, unvoreingenommen; **im·par·ti·al·i·ty** Unparteilichkeit *f*, Objektivität *f*
**im·pass·a·ble** unpassierbar
**im·passe** *fig* Sackgasse *f*; ***reach an ~*** in e-e Sackgasse geraten
**im·pas·sioned** leidenschaftlich
**im·pas·sive** teilnahmslos; ungerührt; gelassen
**im·pa·tience** Ungeduld *f*
**im·pa·tient** ungeduldig
**im·peach** JUR anklagen (***for, of, with*** *gen*); JUR anfechten; infrage stellen, in Zweifel ziehen
**im·pec·ca·ble** untadelig, einwandfrei
**im·pede** (be)hindern
**im·ped·i·ment** Hindernis *n* (***to*** für); Behinderung *f*
**im·pel** antreiben; zwingen
**im·pend·ing** nahe bevorstehend, drohend
**im·pen·e·tra·ble** undurchdringlich; *fig* unergründlich
**im·per·a·tive 1.** unumgänglich, unbedingt erforderlich; gebieterisch; LING Imperativ...; **2.** *a.* **~ *mood*** LING Imperativ *m*, Befehlsform *f*
**im·per·cep·ti·ble** nicht wahrnehmbar, unmerklich
**im·per·fect 1.** unvollkommen; mangelhaft; **2.** *a.* **~ *tense*** LING Imperfekt *n*, 1. Vergangenheit
**im·pe·ri·al·ism** POL Imperialismus
**im·pe·ri·al·ist** POL Imperialist *m*
**im·per·il** gefährden
**im·pe·ri·ous** herrisch, gebieterisch
**im·per·me·a·ble** undurchlässig
**im·per·son·al** unpersönlich
**im·per·so·nate** *j-n* imitieren, nachahmen; verkörpern, THEA *etc* darstellen
**im·per·ti·nence** Unverschämtheit *f*, Frechheit *f*
**im·per·ti·nent** unverschämt, frech
**im·per·tur·ba·ble** unerschütterlich, gelassen
**im·per·vi·ous** undurchlässig; *fig* unzugänglich (***to*** für)
**im·pe·tu·ous** ungestüm, heftig; impulsiv; vorschnell
**im·pe·tus** TECH Antrieb *m*, Impuls *m*
**im·pi·e·ty** Gottlosigkeit *f*; Pietätlosigkeit *f*, Respektlosigkeit *f* (***to*** gegenüber)
**im·pinge: ~ *on*** sich auswirken auf (*acc*), beeinflussen (*acc*)
**im·pi·ous** gottlos; pietätlos, respektlos (***to*** gegenüber)
**im·plac·a·ble** unversöhnlich
**im·plant** MED implantieren, einpflanzen; *fig* einprägen
**im·plau·si·ble** unglaubwürdig
**im·ple·ment 1.** Werkzeug *n*, Gerät *n*; **2.** ausführen
**im·pli·cate** *j-n* verwickeln, hineinziehen (***in*** in *acc*); **im·pli·ca·tion** Verwicklung *f*; Folge *f*; Andeutung *f*

**im·pli·cit** vorbehaltlos, bedingungslos; impliziert, (stillschweigend *or* mit) inbegriffen
**im·plore** *j-n* anflehen; *et.* erflehen
**im·ply** implizieren, einbeziehen, mit enthalten; andeuten; bedeuten
**im·po·lite** unhöflich
**im·pol·i·tic** unklug
**im·port** ECON **1.** importieren, einführen; **2.** Import *m*, Einfuhr *f*
**im·por·tance** Wichtigkeit *f*, Bedeutung *f*; **im·por·tant** wichtig, bedeutend
**im·por·ta·tion** → ***import*** 2
**im·port du·ty** ECON Einfuhrzoll *m*
**im·port·er** ECON Importeur *m*
**im·pose** auferlegen, aufbürden (**on** *dat*); *Strafe* verhängen (**on** gegen); *et.* aufdrängen, aufzwingen (**on** *dat*); **~ *o.s. on s.o.*** sich j-m aufdrängen
**im·pos·ing** imponierend, eindrucksvoll, imposant
**im·pos·si·bil·i·ty** Unmöglichkeit *f*
**im·pos·si·ble** unmöglich
**im·pos·ter,** *Br* **im·pos·tor** Betrüger(in), *esp* Hochstapler(in)
**im·po·tence** Unvermögen *n*, Unfähigkeit *f*; Hilflosigkeit *f*; MED Impotenz *f*
**im·po·tent** unfähig; hilflos; MED impotent
**im·pov·e·rish** arm machen; ***be ~ed*** verarmen; verarmt sein
**im·prac·ti·ca·ble** undurchführbar; unpassierbar
**im·prac·ti·cal** unpraktisch; undurchführbar
**im·preg·na·ble** uneinnehmbar
**im·preg·nate** imprägnieren, tränken; BIOL schwängern
**im·press** aufdrücken, einprägen (*a. fig*); *j-n* beeindrucken; ***be ~ed with*** beeindruckt sein von
**im·pres·sion** Eindruck *m*; Abdruck *m*; ***under the ~ that*** in der Annahme, dass
**im·pres·sive** eindrucksvoll
**im·print 1.** (auf)drücken (**on** auf *acc*); **~ *s.th. on s.o.'s memory*** j-m et. ins Gedächtnis einprägen; **2.** Abdruck *m*, Eindruck *m*; PRINT Impressum *n*
**im·pris·on** JUR inhaftieren
**im·pris·on·ment** Freiheitsstrafe *f*, Gefängnis(strafe *f*) *n*, Haft *f*
**im·prob·a·ble** unwahrscheinlich
**im·prop·er** ungeeignet, unpassend; unanständig, unschicklich; unrichtig
**im·pro·pri·e·ty** Unschicklichkeit *f*
**im·prove** *v/t* verbessern; *Wert etc* erhöhen, steigern; **~ *on*** übertreffen; *v/i* sich (ver)bessern, besser werden, sich erholen; **im·prove·ment** (Ver)Bess(e)rung *f*; Steigerung *f*; Fortschritt *m* (**on** gegenüber *dat*)
**im·pro·vise** improvisieren
**im·pru·dent** unklug
**im·pu·dence** Unverschämtheit *f*
**im·pu·dent** unverschämt
**im·pulse** Impuls *m* (*a. fig*); Anstoß *m*, Anreiz *m*; **im·pul·sive** impulsiv
**im·pu·ni·ty: *with ~*** straflos, ungestraft
**im·pure** unrein (*a.* REL), schmutzig; *fig* schlecht, unmoralisch
**im·pu·ri·ty** Unreinheit *f*
**im·pute: ~ *s.th. to s.o.*** j-n e-r Sache bezichtigen; j-m et. unterstellen
**in 1.** *prp place*: in (*dat or acc*), an (*dat*), auf (*dat*): **~ *New York*** in New York; **~ *the street*** auf der Straße; ***put it ~ your pocket*** steck es in deine Tasche; *time*: in (*dat*), an (*dat*): **~ *1999*** 1999; **~ *two hours*** in zwei Stunden; **~ *the morning*** am Morgen; *state, manner*: in (*dat*), auf (*acc*), mit; **~ *English*** auf Englisch; *activity*: in (*dat*), bei, auf (*dat*): **~ *crossing the road*** beim Überqueren der Straße; *author*: bei: **~ *Shakespeare*** bei Shakespeare; *direction*: in (*acc, dat*), auf (*acc*), zu: ***have confidence ~*** Vertrauen haben zu; *purpose*: in (*dat*), zu, als: **~ *defense of*** zur Verteidigung *or* zum Schutz von; *material*: in (*dat*), aus, mit: ***dressed ~ blue*** in Blau (gekleidet); *amount etc*: in, von, aus, zu: ***three ~ all*** insgesamt *or* im Ganzen drei; ***one ~ ten*** eine(r, -s) von zehn; nach, gemäß: **~ *my opinion*** m-r Meinung nach; **2.** *adv* innen, drinnen; hinein, herein; da, (an)gekommen; da, zu Hause; **3.** *adj* F in (Mode)
**in·a·bil·i·ty** Unfähigkeit *f*
**in·ac·ces·si·ble** unzugänglich, unerreichbar (**to** für *or dat*)
**in·ac·cu·rate** ungenau
**in·ac·tive** untätig
**in·ac·tiv·i·ty** Untätigkeit *f*
**in·ad·e·quate** unangemessen; unzulänglich, ungenügend
**in·ad·mis·si·ble** unzulässig, unstatthaft
**in·ad·ver·tent** unbeabsichtigt, versehentlich; **~ly** *a.* aus Versehen

**in·an·i·mate** leblos; langweilig
**in·ap·pro·pri·ate** unpassend, ungeeignet (***for, to*** für)
**in·apt** ungeeignet, unpassend
**in·ar·tic·u·late** unartikuliert, undeutlich (ausgesprochen), unverständlich; unfähig(, deutlich) zu sprechen
**in·at·ten·tive** unaufmerksam
**in·au·di·ble** unhörbar
**in·au·gu·ral** **1.** Eröffnungs..., Antritts...; ~ ***speech*** → **2.** Antrittsrede *f*
**in·au·gu·rate** *j-n* (feierlich) (in sein Amt) einführen; einweihen, eröffnen; einleiten; **in·au·gu·ra·tion** Amtseinführung *f*; Einweihung *f*, Eröffnung *f*; Beginn *m*; ***Inauguration Day*** Tag *m* der Amtseinführung des neu gewählten Präsidenten der USA
**in·born** angeboren
**in·cal·cu·la·ble** unberechenbar; unermesslich
**in·can·des·cent** (weiß) glühend
**in·ca·pa·ble** unfähig (***of*** zu *inf or gen*), nicht imstande (***of doing*** zu tun)
**in·ca·pa·ci·tate** unfähig *or* untauglich machen; **in·ca·pac·i·ty** Unfähigkeit *f*, Untauglichkeit *f*
**in·car·nate** leibhaftig; personifiziert
**in·cau·tious** unvorsichtig
**in·cen·di·a·ry** Brand...; *fig* aufwiegelnd, aufhetzend
**in·cense**[1] REL Weihrauch *m*
**in·cense**[2] in Wut bringen, erbosen
**in·cen·tive** Ansporn *m*, Anreiz *m*
**in·ces·sant** ständig, unaufhörlich
**in·cest** Inzest *m*, Blutschande *f*
**inch 1.** Inch *m* (*2,54 cm*), Zoll *m* (*a. fig*); ***by ~es, ~ by ~*** allmählich; ***every ~*** durch und durch; **2.** (sich) zentimeterweise *or* sehr langsam bewegen
**in·ci·dence** Vorkommen *n*
**in·ci·dent** Vorfall *m*, Ereignis *n*; POL Zwischenfall *m*
**in·ci·den·tal** nebensächlich, Neben...; beiläufig; **in·ci·den·tal·ly** nebenbei bemerkt, übrigens
**in·cin·e·rate** verbrennen
**in·cin·e·ra·tor** TECH Verbrennungsofen *m*; Verbrennungsanlage *f*
**in·cise** einschneiden; aufschneiden; einritzen, einschnitzen
**in·ci·sion** (Ein)Schnitt *m*
**in·ci·sive** schneidend, scharf; *fig* treffend
**in·ci·sor** ANAT Schneidezahn *m*
**in·cite** anstiften; aufwiegeln, aufhetzen
**in·cite·ment** Anstiftung *f*; Aufhetzung *f*, Aufwieg(e)lung *f*
**in·clem·ent** rau
**in·cli·na·tion** Neigung *f* (*a. fig*)
**in·cline 1.** *v/i* sich neigen (***to, towards*** nach); *fig* neigen (***to, towards*** zu); *v/t* neigen; *fig* veranlassen; **2.** Gefälle *n*; (Ab)Hang *m*
**in·close, in·clos·ure** → ***enclose, enclosure***
**in·clude** einschließen, enthalten; aufnehmen (***in*** in *e-e Liste etc*); ***the group ~d several ...*** zu der Gruppe gehörten einige ...; ***tax ~d*** inklusive Steuer
**in·clud·ing** einschließlich
**in·clu·sion** Einschluss *m*, Einbeziehung *f*; **in·clu·sive** einschließlich, inklusive (***of*** *gen*); ***be ~ of*** einschließen (*acc*)
**in·co·her·ent** unzusammenhängend, unklar, unverständlich
**in·come** ECON Einkommen *n*, Einkünfte *pl*; **~ tax** ECON Einkommensteuer *f*
**in·com·ing** hereinkommend; ankommend; nachfolgend, neu; ~ ***mail*** Posteingang *m*
**in·com·mu·ni·ca·tive** verschlossen
**in·com·pa·ra·ble** unvergleichlich; unvergleichbar
**in·com·pat·i·ble** unvereinbar; unverträglich; inkompatibel
**in·com·pe·tence** Unfähigkeit *f*; Inkompetenz *f*; **in·com·pe·tent** unfähig; nicht fachkundig *or* sachkundig; unzuständig, inkompetent
**in·com·plete** unvollständig; unvollendet
**in·com·pre·hen·si·ble** unbegreiflich, unfassbar
**in·com·pre·hen·sion** Unverständnis *n*
**in·con·cei·va·ble** unbegreiflich, unfassbar; undenkbar
**in·con·clu·sive** nicht überzeugend; ergebnislos, erfolglos
**in·con·gru·ous** nicht übereinstimmend; unvereinbar
**in·con·se·quen·tial** unbedeutend
**in·con·sid·e·ra·ble** unbedeutend
**in·con·sid·er·ate** unüberlegt; rücksichtslos
**in·con·sis·tent** unvereinbar; widersprüchlich; inkonsequent
**in·con·so·la·ble** untröstlich

**in·con·spic·u·ous** unauffällig
**in·con·stant** unbeständig, wankelmütig
**in·con·test·a·ble** unanfechtbar
**in·con·ti·nent** MED inkontinent
**in·con·ve·ni·ence 1.** Unbequemlichkeit *f*; Unannehmlichkeit *f*, Ungelegenheit *f*; **2.** *j-m* lästig sein; *j-m* Umstände machen; **in·con·ve·ni·ent** unbequem; ungelegen, lästig
**in·cor·po·rate** (sich) vereinigen *or* zusammenschließen; (mit) einbeziehen; enthalten; eingliedern; *Ort* eingemeinden; ECON, JUR als Aktiengesellschaft eintragen (lassen)
**in·cor·po·rat·ed com·pa·ny** ECON Aktiengesellschaft *f*
**in·cor·po·ra·tion** Vereinigung *f*, Zusammenschluss *m*; Eingliederung *f*; Eingemeindung *f*; ECON, JUR Eintragung *f* als Aktiengesellschaft
**in·cor·rect** unrichtig, falsch; inkorrekt
**in·cor·ri·gi·ble** unverbesserlich
**in·cor·rup·ti·ble** unbestechlich
**in·crease 1.** zunehmen, (an)wachsen; steigen; vergrößern, vermehren, erhöhen; **2.** Vergrößerung *f*, Erhöhung *f*, Zunahme *f*, Zuwachs *m*, (An)Wachsen *n*, Steigerung *f*; **in·creas·ing·ly** immer mehr; ~ ***difficult*** immer schwieriger
**in·cred·i·ble** unglaublich
**in·cre·du·li·ty** Ungläubigkeit *f*
**in·cred·u·lous** ungläubig, skeptisch
**in·crim·i·nate** *j-n* belasten
**in·cu·bate** ausbrüten; **in·cu·ba·tor** Brutapparat *m*; MED Brutkasten *m*
**in·cur** sich *et.* zuziehen, auf sich laden; *Schulden* machen; *Verluste* erleiden
**in·cu·ra·ble** unheilbar
**in·cu·ri·ous** nicht neugierig, gleichgültig, uninteressiert
**in·cur·sion** (feindlicher) Einfall; Eindringen *n*
**in·debt·ed** (zu Dank) verpflichtet; ECON verschuldet
**in·de·cent** unanständig, anstößig; JUR unsittlich, unzüchtig; ~ ***assault*** JUR Sittlichkeitsverbrechen *n*
**in·de·ci·sion** Unentschlossenheit *f*
**in·de·ci·sive** unentschlossen; unentschieden; unbestimmt, ungewiss
**in·deed 1.** *adv* in der Tat, tatsächlich, wirklich; allerdings; ***thank you very much*** ~**!** vielen herzlichen Dank!; **2.** *int* ach wirklich?
**in·de·fat·i·ga·ble** unermüdlich
**in·de·fen·si·ble** unhaltbar
**in·de·fi·na·ble** undefinierbar, unbestimmbar
**in·def·i·nite** unbestimmt; unbegrenzt
**in·def·i·nite·ly** auf unbestimmte Zeit
**in·del·i·ble** unauslöschlich (*a. fig*); ~ ***pencil*** Tintenstift *m*
**in·del·i·cate** taktlos; unfein, anstößig
**in·dem·ni·fy** *j-n* entschädigen, *j-m* Schadenersatz leisten (***for*** für)
**in·dem·ni·ty** Entschädigung *f*
**in·dent** (ein)kerben, auszacken; PRINT *Zeile* einrücken
**in·de·pen·dence** Unabhängigkeit *f*; Selbstständigkeit *f*; ***Independence Day*** Unabhängigkeitstag *m*
**in·de·pen·dent** unabhängig; selbstständig
**in·de·scri·ba·ble** unbeschreiblich
**in·de·struc·ti·ble** unzerstörbar; unverwüstlich
**in·de·ter·mi·nate** unbestimmt; unklar, vage
**in·dex** Index *m*, (Inhalts-, Namens-, Stichwort)Verzeichnis *n*, (Sach)Register *n*; (An)Zeichen *n*; ***cost of living*** ~ Lebenshaltungsindex *m*
**in·dex card** Karteikarte *f*
**in·dex fin·ger** ANAT Zeigefinger *m*
**In·di·a** Indien *n*
**In·di·an 1.** indisch; *neg!* indianisch, Indianer...; **2.** Inder(in); ***American*** ~ Indianer(in); ~ **corn** BOT Mais *m*; ~ **file:** ***in*** ~ im Gänsemarsch; ~ **sum·mer** Altweibersommer *m*, Nachsommer *m*
**in·di·a rub·ber** Gummi *n*, *m*; Radiergummi *m*
**in·di·cate** deuten *or* zeigen auf (*acc*); TECH anzeigen; MOT blinken; *fig* hinweisen *or* hindeuten auf (*acc*); andeuten; **in·di·ca·tion** (An)Zeichen *n*, Hinweis *m*, Andeutung *f*, Indiz *n*
**in·dic·a·tive** *a.* ~ ***mood*** LING Indikativ *m*
**in·di·ca·tor** TECH Anzeiger *m*; MOT Richtungsanzeiger *m*, Blinker *m*
**in·dict** JUR anklagen (***for*** wegen)
**in·dict·ment** JUR Anklage *f*
**in·dif·fer·ence** Gleichgültigkeit *f*
**in·dif·fer·ent** gleichgültig (***to*** gegen); mittelmäßig
**in·di·gent** arm
**in·di·ges·ti·ble** unverdaulich

**in·di·ges·tion** MED Verdauungsstörung *f*, Magenverstimmung *f*
**in·dig·nant** entrüstet, empört, ungehalten (***about, at, over*** über *acc*)
**in·dig·na·tion** Entrüstung *f*, Empörung *f* (***about, at, over*** über *acc*)
**in·dig·ni·ty** Demütigung *f*, unwürdige Behandlung
**in·di·rect** indirekt; ***by ~ means*** *fig* auf Umwegen
**in·dis·creet** unbesonnen, unbedacht; indiskret; **in·dis·cre·tion** Unbesonnenheit *f*; Indiskretion *f*
**in·dis·crim·i·nate** kritiklos; wahllos
**in·di·spen·sa·ble** unentbehrlich, unerlässlich
**in·dis·posed** indisponiert, unpässlich; abgeneigt; **in·dis·po·si·tion** Unpässlichkeit *f*; Abneigung *f* (***to do*** zu tun)
**in·dis·pu·ta·ble** unbestreitbar, unstreitig
**in·dis·tinct** undeutlich; unklar, verschwommen
**in·dis·tin·guish·a·ble** nicht zu unterscheiden(d) (***from*** von)
**in·di·vid·u·al** **1.** individuell, einzeln, Einzel...; persönlich; **2.** Individuum *n*, Einzelne *m, f*
**in·di·vid·u·al·ism** Individualismus *m*
**in·di·vid·u·al·ist** Individualist(in)
**in·di·vid·u·al·i·ty** Individualität *f*, (persönliche) Note
**in·di·vid·u·al·ly** einzeln, jede(r, -s) für sich; individuell
**in·di·vis·i·ble** unteilbar
**in·dom·i·ta·ble** unbezähmbar, nicht unterzukriegen(d)
**in·door** Haus..., Zimmer..., Innen..., SPORT Hallen...
**in·doors** im Haus, drinnen; ins Haus (hinein); SPORT in der Halle
**in·dorse** → ***endorse etc***
**in·duce** *j-n* veranlassen; verursachen, bewirken; **in·duce·ment** Anreiz *m*
**in·duct** einführen, -setzen; **in·duc·tion** Herbeiführung *f*; Einführung *f*, Einsetzung *f*; ELECTR Induktion *f*
**in·dulge** nachsichtig sein gegen; *e-r Neigung etc* nachgeben; ***~ in s.th.*** sich et. gönnen *or* leisten; **in·dul·gence** Nachsicht *f*; Luxus *m*; REL Ablass *m*
**in·dul·gent** nachsichtig, nachgiebig
**in·dus·tri·al** industriell, Industrie..., Gewerbe..., Betriebs...
**in·dus·tri·al ar·e·a** Industriegebiet *n*
**in·dus·tri·al·ist** Industrielle *m, f*
**in·dus·tri·al·ize** industrialisieren
**in·dus·tri·ous** fleißig
**in·dus·try** Industrie(zweig *m*) *f*; Gewerbe(zweig *m*) *n*; Fleiß *m*
**in·ed·i·ble** ungenießbar, nicht essbar
**in·ef·fec·tive, in·ef·fec·tu·al** unwirksam, wirkungslos; unfähig, untauglich
**in·ef·fi·cient** ineffizient; unfähig, untauglich; unrationell, unwirtschaftlich
**in·el·e·gant** unelegant
**in·el·i·gi·ble** nicht berechtigt
**in·ept** unpassend; ungeschickt; albern, töricht
**in·e·qual·i·ty** Ungleichheit *f*
**in·ert** PHYS träge (*a. fig*); inaktiv
**in·er·tia** PHYS Trägheit *f* (*a. fig*)
**in·es·cap·a·ble** unvermeidlich
**in·es·sen·tial** unwesentlich, unwichtig (***to*** für)
**in·es·ti·ma·ble** unschätzbar
**in·ev·i·ta·ble** unvermeidlich
**in·ev·i·ta·bly** zwangsläufig
**in·ex·act** ungenau
**in·ex·cu·sa·ble** unverzeihlich, unentschuldbar
**in·ex·haus·ti·ble** unerschöpflich; unermüdlich
**in·ex·o·ra·ble** unerbittlich
**in·ex·pe·di·ent** unzweckmäßig; nicht ratsam
**in·ex·pen·sive** billig, preiswert
**in·ex·pe·ri·ence** Unerfahrenheit *f*
**in·ex·pe·ri·enced** unerfahren
**in·ex·pert** unerfahren; ungeschickt
**in·ex·plic·a·ble** unerklärlich
**in·ex·pres·si·ble** unaussprechlich, unbeschreiblich
**in·ex·pres·sive** ausdruckslos
**in·ex·tri·ca·ble** unentwirrbar
**in·fal·li·ble** unfehlbar
**in·fa·mous** berüchtigt; schändlich, niederträchtig; **in·fa·my** Ehrlosigkeit *f*; Schande *f*; Niedertracht *f*
**in·fan·cy** frühe Kindheit; ***be in its ~*** *fig* in den Kinderschuhen stecken
**in·fant** Säugling *m*; kleines Kind, Kleinkind *n*; **in·fan·tile** kindlich; Kindes..., Kinder...; infantil, kindisch
**in·fan·try** MIL Infanterie *f*
**in·fat·u·at·ed** vernarrt (***with*** in *acc*)
**in·fect** MED *j-n, et.* infizieren, *j-n* anstecken (*a. fig*); verseuchen, verunreini-

gen; **in·fec·tion** MED Infektion *f*, Ansteckung *f* (*a. fig*); **in·fec·tious** MED infektiös, ansteckend (*a. fig*)

**in·fer** folgern, schließen (***from*** aus)

**in·fer·ence** (Schluss)Folgerung *f*, (Rück)Schluss *m*

**in·fe·ri·or 1.** untergeordnet (***to*** *dat*), niedriger (***to*** als); weniger wert (***to*** als); minderwertig; ***be ~ to s.o.*** j-m untergeordnet sein; j-m unterlegen sein; **2.** Untergebene *m, f*

**in·fe·ri·or·i·ty** Unterlegenheit *f*; Minderwertigkeit *f*; **~ com·plex** PSYCH Minderwertigkeitskomplex *m*

**in·fer·nal** höllisch, Höllen...

**in·fer·no** Inferno *n*, Hölle *f*

**in·fer·tile** unfruchtbar

**in·fest** verseuchen, befallen; *fig* überschwemmen (***with*** mit)

**in·fi·del·i·ty** (*esp* eheliche) Untreue

**in·fil·trate** einsickern in (*acc*); einschleusen (***into*** in *acc*); POL unterwandern

**in·fi·nite** unendlich

**in·fin·i·tive** *a.* ***~ mood*** LING Infinitiv *m*, Nennform *f*

**in·fin·i·ty** Unendlichkeit *f*

**in·firm** schwach, gebrechlich

**in·fir·ma·ry** Krankenhaus *n*; PED *etc* Krankenzimmer *n*

**in·fir·mi·ty** Schwäche *f*, Gebrechlichkeit *f*

**in·flame** entflammen (*mst fig*); erregen; ***become ~d*** MED sich entzünden

**in·flam·ma·ble** brennbar, leicht entzündlich; feuergefährlich

**in·flam·ma·tion** MED Entzündung *f*

**in·flam·ma·to·ry** MED entzündlich; *fig* aufrührerisch, Hetz...

**in·flate** aufpumpen, aufblasen, aufblähen (*a. fig*); ECON *Preise etc* in die Höhe treiben

**in·fla·tion** ECON Inflation *f*

**in·flect** LING flektieren, beugen

**in·flec·tion** LING Flexion *f*, Beugung *f*

**in·flex·i·ble** unbiegsam, starr (*a. fig*); *fig* inflexibel, unbeweglich, unbeugsam

**in·flex·ion** *Br* → ***inflection***

**in·flict** (**on**) *Leid, Schaden etc* zufügen (*dat*); *Wunde etc* beibringen (*dat*); *Strafe* auferlegen (*dat*), verhängen (über *acc*); aufbürden, aufdrängen (*dat*)

**in·flic·tion** Zufügung *f*; Verhängung *f*; Plage *f*

**in·flu·ence 1.** Einfluss *m*; **2.** beeinflussen; **in·flu·en·tial** einflussreich

**in·flux** Zustrom *m*, Zufluss *m*, (*Waren-*)Zufuhr *f*

**in·form** benachrichtigen, unterrichten (***of*** von), informieren (***of*** über *acc*); ***~ against*** *or* ***on s.o.*** j-n anzeigen; j-n denunzieren

**in·for·mal** formlos, zwanglos

**in·for·mal·i·ty** Formlosigkeit *f*; Ungezwungenheit *f*

**in·for·ma·tion** Auskunft *f*, Information *f*; Nachricht *f*; **~ (su·per·)high·way** EDP Datenautobahn *f*

**in·for·ma·tive** informativ; lehrreich; mitteilsam

**in·form·er** Denunziant(in); Spitzel *m*

**in·fra·struc·ture** Infrastruktur *f*

**in·fre·quent** selten

**in·fringe:** ***~ on*** *Rechte, Vertrag etc* verletzen, verstoßen gegen

**in·fu·ri·ate** wütend machen

**in·fuse** *Tee* aufgießen

**in·fu·sion** Aufguss *m*; MED Infusion *f*

**in·ge·ni·ous** genial; einfallsreich; raffiniert; **in·ge·nu·i·ty** Genialität *f*; Einfallsreichtum *m*

**in·gen·u·ous** offen, aufrichtig; naiv

**in·got** (*Gold- etc*)Barren *m*

**in·gra·ti·ate:** ***~ o.s. with s.o.*** sich bei j-m beliebt machen

**in·grat·i·tude** Undankbarkeit *f*

**in·gre·di·ent** Bestandteil *m*; GASTR Zutat *f*

**in·hab·it** bewohnen, leben in (*dat*)

**in·hab·it·a·ble** bewohnbar

**in·hab·i·tant** Bewohner(in); Einwohner(in)

**in·hale** einatmen, MED *a.* inhalieren

**in·her·ent** innewohnend, eigen (***in*** *dat*)

**in·her·it** erben; **in·her·i·tance** Erbe *n*

**in·hib·it** hemmen (*a.* PSYCH), (ver)hindern; **in·hib·it·ed** PSYCH gehemmt; **in·hi·bi·tion** PSYCH Hemmung *f*

**in·hos·pi·ta·ble** ungastlich; unwirtlich (*region etc*)

**in·hu·man** unmenschlich

**in·hu·mane** inhuman, menschenunwürdig

**in·im·i·cal** feindselig (***to*** gegen); nachteilig (***to*** für)

**in·im·i·ta·ble** unnachahmlich

**i·ni·tial 1.** anfänglich, Anfangs...; **2.** Initiale *f*, (großer) Anfangsbuchstabe

**i·ni·tial·ly** am *or* zu Anfang, anfänglich
**i·ni·ti·ate** in die Wege leiten, ins Leben rufen; einführen
**i·ni·ti·a·tion** Einführung *f*
**i·ni·tia·tive** Initiative *f*, erster Schritt; ***take the*** ~ die Initiative ergreifen; ***on one's own*** ~ aus eigenem Antrieb
**in·ject** MED injizieren, einspritzen
**in·jec·tion** MED Injektion *f*, Spritze *f*
**in·ju·di·cious** unklug, unüberlegt
**in·junc·tion** JUR gerichtliche Verfügung
**in·jure** verletzen, verwunden; schaden (*dat*); kränken; **in·jured 1.** verletzt; **2.** ***the*** ~ die Verletzten *pl*
**in·ju·ri·ous** schädlich; ***be*** ~ ***to*** schaden (*dat*); ~ ***to health*** gesundheitsschädlich
**in·ju·ry** MED Verletzung *f*; Kränkung *f*; ~ **time** *Br esp soccer*: Nachspielzeit *f*
**in·jus·tice** Ungerechtigkeit *f*; Unrecht *n*; ***do s.o. an*** ~ j-m unrecht tun
**ink** Tinte *f*
**ink·ling** Andeutung *f*; dunkle *or* leise Ahnung
**ink pad** Stempelkissen *n*
**ink·y** Tinten...; tinten-, pechschwarz
**in·laid** eingelegt, Einlege...; ~ ***work*** Einlegearbeit *f*
**in·land 1.** *adj* inländisch, einheimisch; ECON Binnen...; **2.** *adv* landeinwärts
**In·land Rev·e·nue** *Br* Finanzamt *n*
**in·lay** Einlegearbeit *f*; MED (Zahn)Füllung *f*, Plombe *f*
**in·let** GEOGR schmale Bucht; TECH Eingang *m*, Einlass *m*
**in-line skate** Inliner *m*, Inline Skate *m*
**in·mate** Insasse *m*, Insassin *f*; Mitbewohner(in)
**in·most** innerste(r, -s) (*a. fig*)
**inn** Gasthaus *n*, Wirtshaus *n*
**in·nate** angeboren
**in·ner** innere(r, -s); Innen...; verborgen
**in·ner·most** → ***inmost***
**in·nings** *cricket*, *baseball*: Spielzeit *f*
**inn·keep·er** Gastwirt(in)
**in·no·cence** Unschuld *f*; Harmlosigkeit *f*; Naivität *f*; **in·no·cent** unschuldig; harmlos; arglos, naiv
**in·noc·u·ous** harmlos
**in·no·va·tion** Neuerung *f*
**in·nu·en·do** (versteckte) Andeutung *f*
**in·nu·me·ra·ble** unzählig, zahllos
**i·noc·u·late** MED impfen
**i·noc·u·la·tion** MED Impfung *f*
**in·of·fen·sive** harmlos
**in·op·e·ra·ble** MED inoperabel, nicht operierbar; undurchführbar (*plan etc*)
**in·op·por·tune** inopportun, unangebracht, ungelegen
**in·or·di·nate** unmäßig
**in·pa·tient** MED stationärer Patient, stationäre Patientin
**in·put** Input *m, n*, EDP *a.* (Daten)Eingabe *f*, ELECTR *a.* Eingangsleistung *f*
**in·quest** JUR gerichtliche Untersuchung
**in·quire** fragen *or* sich erkundigen (nach); ~ ***into*** *et.* untersuchen, prüfen
**in·quir·ing** forschend; wissbegierig
**in·quir·y** Erkundigung *f*, Nachfrage *f*; Untersuchung *f*; Ermittlung *f*; ***make inquiries*** Erkundigungen einziehen
**in·qui·si·tion** (amtliche) Untersuchung; Verhör *n*; ***Inquisition*** REL HIST Inquisition *f*
**in·quis·i·tive** neugierig, wissbegierig
**in·roads** (***in***[***to***], ***on***) Eingriff *m* (in *acc*), Übergriff *m* (auf *acc*)
**in·sane** geisteskrank, wahnsinnig
**in·san·i·ta·ry** unhygienisch
**in·san·i·ty** Geisteskrankheit *f*, Wahnsinn *m*
**in·sa·tia·ble** unersättlich
**in·scrip·tion** Inschrift *f*, Aufschrift *f*; Widmung *f*
**in·scru·ta·ble** unerforschlich, unergründlich
**in·sect** ZO Insekt *n*; **in·sec·ti·cide** Insektenvertilgungsmittel *n*, Insektizid *n*
**in·se·cure** unsicher; nicht sicher *or* fest
**in·sen·si·ble** unempfindlich (***to*** gegen); bewusstlos; unempfänglich (***of, to*** für), gleichgültig (***of, to*** gegen); unmerklich
**in·sen·si·tive** unempfindlich (***to*** gegen); unempfänglich (***of, to*** für), gleichgültig (***of, to*** gegen)
**in·sep·a·ra·ble** untrennbar; unzertrennlich
**in·sert 1.** einfügen, einsetzen, einführen, (hinein)stecken, *Münze* einwerfen; inserieren; **2.** (Zeitungs)Beilage *f*, (Buch)Einlage *f*
**in·ser·tion** Einfügen *n*, Einsetzen *n*, Einführen *n*, Hineinstecken *n*; Einfügung *f*; Einwurf *m*; Anzeige *f*, Inserat *n*
**in·sert key** EDP Einfügetaste *f*
**in·shore** an *or* nahe der Küste; Küsten...
**in·side 1.** Innenseite *f*; *das* Innere; ***turn*** ~ ***out*** umkrempeln; auf den Kopf stel-

len; **2.** *adj* innere(r, -s), Innen...; Insider...; **3.** *adv* im Inner(e)n, innen, drinnen; ~ ***of*** F innerhalb (*gen*); **4.** *prp* innerhalb, im Inner(e)n
**in·sid·er** Insider(in), Eingeweihte *m, f*
**in·sid·i·ous** heimtückisch
**in·sight** Einsicht *f*, Einblick *m*; Verständnis *n*
**in·sig·ni·a** Insignien *pl*; Abzeichen *pl*
**in·sig·nif·i·cant** bedeutungslos; unbedeutend
**in·sin·cere** unaufrichtig
**in·sin·u·ate** andeuten, anspielen auf (*acc*); unterstellen; ~ ***that s.o. ...*** j-m unterstellen, dass er ...
**in·sin·u·a·tion** Anspielung *f*, Andeutung *f*, Unterstellung *f*
**in·sip·id** geschmacklos, fad
**in·sist** bestehen, beharren (***on*** auf *dat*)
**in·sis·tence** Bestehen *n*, Beharren *n*; Beharrlichkeit *f*
**in·sis·tent** beharrlich, hartnäckig
**in·sole** Einlegesohle *f*; Brandsohle *f*
**in·so·lent** unverschämt
**in·sol·u·ble** unlöslich (*substance etc*); unlösbar (*problem etc*)
**in·sol·vent** ECON zahlungsunfähig, insolvent
**in·som·ni·a** Schlaflosigkeit *f*
**in·spect** untersuchen, prüfen, nachsehen; besichtigen, inspizieren
**in·spec·tion** Prüfung *f*, Untersuchung *f*, Kontrolle *f*; Inspektion *f*
**in·spec·tor** Aufsichtsbeamte *m*, Inspektor *m*; (Polizei)Inspektor *m*, (Polizei)Kommissar *m*
**in·spi·ra·tion** Inspiration *f*, (plötzlicher) Einfall; **in·spire** inspirieren, anregen; *Gefühl etc* auslösen
**in·stall** TECH installieren, einrichten, aufstellen, einbauen, *Leitung* legen; *j-n in ein Amt etc* einsetzen
**in·stal·la·tion** TECH Installation *f*, Einrichtung *f*, Einbau *m*; TECH *fertige* Anlage *f*; *fig* Einsetzung *f*, Einführung *f*
**in·stall·ment, in·stal·ment** *Br* ECON Rate *f*; (Teil)Lieferung *f*; Fortsetzung *f*; *radio*, TV Folge *f*
**in·stall·ment plan:** ***buy on the*** ~ ECON auf Abzahlung *or* Raten kaufen
**in·stance** Beispiel *n*; (besonderer) Fall; JUR Instanz *f*; ***for*** ~ zum Beispiel
**in·stant 1.** Moment *m*, Augenblick *m*; **2.** sofortig, augenblicklich
**in·stan·ta·ne·ous** sofortig, augenblicklich; ***death was*** ~ der Tod trat sofort ein
**in·stant| cam·e·ra** PHOT Sofortbildkamera *f*; ~ **cof·fee** GASTR Pulver-, Instantkaffee *m*
**in·stant·ly** sofort, augenblicklich
**in·stead** stattdessen, dafür; ~ ***of*** anstelle von, (an)statt
**in·step** ANAT Spann *m*, Rist *m*
**in·sti·gate** anstiften; aufhetzen; veranlassen; **in·sti·ga·tor** Anstifter(in); (Auf)Hetzer(in)
**in·stil** *Br*, **in·still** beibringen, einflößen (***into*** *dat*)
**in·stinct** Instinkt *m*
**in·stinc·tive** instinktiv
**in·sti·tute** Institut *n*
**in·sti·tu·tion** Institution *f*, Einrichtung *f*; Institut *n*; Anstalt *f*
**in·struct** unterrichten, -weisen; ausbilden, schulen; informieren; anweisen
**in·struc·tion** Unterricht *m*; Ausbildung *f*, Schulung *f*, Unterweisung *f*; Anweisung *f*, Instruktion *f*; EDP Befehl *m*; ~***s for use*** Gebrauchsanweisung *f*; ***operating*** ~***s*** Bedienungsanleitung *f*
**in·struc·tive** instruktiv, lehrreich
**in·struc·tor** Lehrer *m*; Ausbilder *m*
**in·struc·tress** Lehrerin *f*; Ausbilderin *f*
**in·stru·ment** Instrument *n* (*a.* MUS); Werkzeug *n* (*a. fig*)
**in·stru·men·tal** MUS Instrumental...; behilflich; ***be*** ~ ***in*** beitragen zu
**in·sub·or·di·nate** aufsässig
**in·sub·or·di·na·tion** Auflehnung *f*, Aufsässigkeit *f*
**in·suf·fe·ra·ble** unerträglich, unausstehlich
**in·suf·fi·cient** unzulänglich, ungenügend
**in·su·lar** Insel...; *fig* engstirnig
**in·su·late** isolieren; **in·su·la·tion** Isolierung *f*; Isoliermaterial *n*
**in·sult 1.** Beleidigung *f*; **2.** beleidigen
**in·sur·ance** Versicherung *f*; Versicherungssumme *f*; Absicherung *f* (***against*** gegen); ~ **com·pa·ny** Versicherungsgesellschaft *f*; ~ **pol·i·cy** Versicherungspolice *f*
**in·sure** versichern (***against*** gegen)
**in·sured:** ***the*** ~ der *or* die Versicherte
**in·sur·gent 1.** aufständisch; **2.** Aufständische *m, f*

I

**in·sur·moun·ta·ble** *fig* unüberwindlich
**in·sur·rec·tion** Aufstand *m*
**in·tact** intakt, unversehrt, unbeschädigt, ganz
**in·take** (*Nahrungs- etc*)Aufnahme *f*; (Neu)Aufnahme(n *pl*) *f*, (Neu)Zugänge *pl*; TECH Einlass(öffnung *f*) *m*
**in·te·gral** ganz, vollständig; wesentlich
**in·te·grate** (sich) integrieren; zusammenschließen; eingliedern, einbeziehen; ***~d circuit*** ELECTR integrierter Schaltkreis
**in·te·gra·tion** Integration *f*
**in·teg·ri·ty** Integrität *f*; Vollständigkeit *f*; Einheit *f*
**in·tel·lect** Intellekt *m*, Verstand *m*
**in·tel·lec·tual 1.** intellektuell, Verstandes..., geistig; **2.** Intellektuelle *m*, *f*
**in·tel·li·gence** Intelligenz *f*; nachrichtendienstliche Informationen *pl*
**in·tel·li·gent** intelligent, klug
**in·tel·li·gi·ble** verständlich (***to*** für)
**in·tem·per·ate** unmäßig
**in·tend** beabsichtigen, vorhaben, planen; ***~ed for*** bestimmt für *or* zu
**in·tense** intensiv, stark, heftig
**in·ten·si·fy** intensivieren; (sich) verstärken
**in·ten·si·ty** Intensität *f*
**in·ten·sive** intensiv, gründlich; **~ care u·nit** MED Intensivstation *f*
**in·tent 1.** gespannt, aufmerksam; ***~ on*** fest entschlossen zu (*dat*); konzentriert auf (*acc*); **2.** Absicht *f*, Vorhaben *n*
**in·ten·tion** Absicht *f*; JUR Vorsatz *m*
**in·ten·tion·al** absichtlich, vorsätzlich
**in·ter** bestatten
**in·ter...** zwischen, Zwischen...; gegenseitig, einander
**in·ter·act** aufeinander (ein)wirken, sich gegenseitig beeinflussen
**in·ter·ac·tion** Wechselwirkung *f*
**in·ter·cede** vermitteln, sich einsetzen (***with*** bei; ***for*** für)
**in·ter·cept** abfangen
**in·ter·ces·sion** Fürsprache *f*
**in·ter·change 1.** austauschen; **2.** Austausch *m*; MOT Autobahnkreuz *n*
**in·ter·com** Sprechanlage *f*
**in·ter·course** Verkehr *m*; *a.* ***sexual ~*** (Geschlechts)Verkehr *m*
**in·terest 1.** Interesse *n* (***in*** an *dat*, für); Wichtigkeit *f*, Bedeutung *f*; Vorteil *m*, Nutzen *m*; ECON Anteil *m*, Beteiligung *f*; ECON Zins(en *pl*) *m*; ***take an ~ in*** sich interessieren für; **2.** interessieren (***in*** für *et*); **in·terest·ed** interessiert (***in*** an *dat*); ***be ~ in*** sich interessieren für
**in·terest·ing** interessant
**in·terest rate** ECON Zinssatz *m*
**in·ter·face** EDP Schnittstelle *f*
**in·ter·fere** sich einmischen (***with*** in *acc*); stören; **in·ter·fer·ence** Einmischung *f*; Störung *f*
**in·te·ri·or 1.** innere(r, -s), Innen...; Binnen...; Inlands...; **2.** *das* Innere; Interieur *n*; POL innere Angelegenheiten *pl*; → ***Department of the Interior***; **~ dec·o·ra·tor** Innenarchitekt(in)
**in·ter·ject** *Bemerkung* einwerfen
**in·ter·jec·tion** Einwurf *m*; Ausruf *m*; LING Interjektion *f*
**in·ter·lace** (sich) (ineinander) verflechten
**in·ter·lop·er** Eindringling *m*
**in·ter·lude** Zwischenspiel *n*; Pause *f*; ***~s of bright weather*** zeitweilig schön
**in·ter·me·di·a·ry** Vermittler(in), Mittelsmann *m*
**in·ter·me·di·ate** in der Mitte liegend, Mittel..., Zwischen...; PED für fortgeschrittene Anfänger
**in·ter·ment** Beerdigung *f*, Bestattung *f*
**in·ter·mi·na·ble** endlos
**in·ter·mis·sion** Unterbrechung *f*; THEA *etc* Pause *f*
**in·ter·mit·tent** mit Unterbrechungen, periodisch (auftretend); ***~ fever*** MED Wechselfieber *n*
**in·tern¹** internieren
**in·tern²** Assistenzarzt *m*, -ärztin *f*
**in·ter·nal** innere(r, -s); einheimisch, Inlands...
**in·ter·nal-com·bus·tion en·gine** Verbrennungsmotor *m*
**in·ter·na·tion·al 1.** international; Auslands...; **2.** SPORT Internationale *m*, *f*, Nationalspieler(in); internationaler Wettkampf; Länderspiel *n*; **~ call** TEL Auslandsgespräch *n*; **~ law** JUR Völkerrecht *n*
**in·tern·ist** MED Internist *m*
**in·ter·per·son·al** zwischenmenschlich
**in·ter·pret** interpretieren, auslegen, erklären; dolmetschen
**in·ter·pre·ta·tion** Interpretation *f*, Auslegung *f*

**in·ter·pret·er** Dolmetscher(in)
**in·ter·ro·gate** verhören, vernehmen; (be)fragen; **in·ter·ro·ga·tion** Verhör *n*, Vernehmung *f*; Frage *f*
**in·ter·rog·a·tive** LING Interrogativ..., Frage...
**in·ter·rupt** unterbrechen
**in·ter·rup·tion** Unterbrechung *f*
**in·ter·sect** (durch)schneiden; sich schneiden *or* kreuzen; **in·ter·sec·tion** Schnittpunkt *m*; (Straßen)Kreuzung *f*
**in·ter·sperse** einstreuen, hier und da einfügen
**in·ter·state 1.** zwischenstaatlich; **2.** *a.* **~ *highway*** Autobahn *f*
**in·ter·twine** (sich ineinander) verschlingen, sich verflechten
**in·ter·val** Intervall *n* (*a.* MUS), Abstand *m*; *Br* Pause *f* (*a.* THEA *etc*); ***at regular ~s*** in regelmäßigen Abständen
**in·ter·vene** eingreifen, einschreiten, intervenieren; dazwischenkommen
**in·ter·ven·tion** Eingreifen *n*, Einschreiten *n*, Intervention *f*
**in·ter·view 1.** Interview *n*; Einstellungsgespräch *n*; **2.** interviewen; ein Einstellungsgespräch führen mit
**in·ter·view·ee** Interviewte *m*, *f*
**in·ter·view·er** Interviewer(in)
**in·ter·weave** (miteinander) verweben *or* verflechten
**in·tes·tate: *die ~*** JUR ohne Hinterlassung e-s Testaments sterben
**in·tes·tine** ANAT Darm *m*; *pl* Eingeweide *pl*; ***large ~*** Dickdarm *m*; ***small ~*** Dünndarm *m*
**in·ti·ma·cy** Intimität *f*, Vertrautheit *f*; (*a. plumpe*) Vertraulichkeit; intime (*sexuelle*) Beziehungen *pl*
**in·ti·mate 1.** intim (*a. sexually*); vertraut, eng (*friends etc*); (*a.* plump)vertraulich; innerste(r, -s); gründlich, genau (*knowledge etc*); **2.** Vertraute *m*, *f*
**in·tim·i·date** einschüchtern
**in·tim·i·da·tion** Einschüchterung *f*
**in·to** in (*acc*), in (*acc*) ... hinein; gegen (*acc*); MATH in (*acc*); ***4 ~ 20 goes five times*** 4 geht fünfmal in 20
**in·tol·e·ra·ble** unerträglich
**in·tol·e·rance** Intoleranz *f*, Unduldsamkeit (***of*** gegen)
**in·tol·e·rant** intolerant, unduldsam (***of*** gegen)
**in·to·na·tion** MUS Intonation *f*, LING *a.* Tonfall *m*
**in·tox·i·cat·ed** berauscht, betrunken
**in·tox·i·ca·tion** Rausch *m* (*a. fig*)
**in·trac·ta·ble** eigensinnig; schwer zu handhaben(d)
**in·tran·si·tive** LING intransitiv
**in·tra·ve·nous** MED intravenös
**in tray: *in the ~*** im Posteingang *etc*
**in·trep·id** unerschrocken
**in·tri·cate** verwickelt, kompliziert
**in·trigue 1.** Intrige *f*; **2.** faszinieren, interessieren; intrigieren
**in·tro·duce** vorstellen (***to*** *dat*), *j-n* bekannt machen (***to*** mit); einführen
**in·tro·duc·tion** Vorstellung *f*; Einführung *f*; Einleitung *f*, Vorwort *n*; ***letter of ~*** Empfehlungsschreiben *n*
**in·tro·duc·to·ry** Einführungs...; einleitend, Einleitungs...
**in·tro·spec·tion** Selbstbeobachtung *f*
**in·tro·vert** PSYCH introvertierter Mensch; **in·tro·vert·ed** PSYCH introvertiert, in sich gekehrt
**in·trude** (sich) aufdrängen; stören; ***am I intruding?*** störe ich?; **in·trud·er** Eindringling *m*, Störenfried *m*
**in·tru·sion** Störung *f*
**in·tru·sive** aufdringlich
**in·tu·i·tion** Intuition *f*
**in·tu·i·tive** intuitiv
**In·u·it** *a.* ***Innuit*** Inuit *m*, Eskimo *m*
**in·un·date** überschwemmen, überfluten (*a. fig*)
**in·vade** eindringen in (*acc*), einfallen in (*acc*), MIL *a.* einmarschieren in (*acc*); *fig* überlaufen, überschwemmen
**in·vad·er** Eindringling *m*
**in·va·lid[1] 1.** krank; invalid(e); **2.** Kranke *m*; *f*; Invalide *m*, *f*
**in·val·id[2]** (rechts)ungültig
**in·val·i·date** JUR für ungültig erkären
**in·val·u·a·ble** *fig* unschätzbar, unbezahlbar
**in·var·i·a·ble** unveränderlich
**in·var·i·a·bly** ausnahmslos
**in·va·sion** Invasion *f* (*a.* MIL), Einfall *m*, MIL *a.* Einmarsch *m*; *fig* Eingriff *m*, Verletzung *f*
**in·vec·tive** Schmähung(en *pl*) *f*, Beschimpfung(en *pl*) *f*
**in·vent** erfinden
**in·ven·tion** Erfindung *f*
**in·ven·tive** erfinderisch; einfallsreich
**in·ven·tor** Erfinder(in)

I

**in·ven·to·ry** Inventar *n*, Bestand *m*; Bestandsliste *f*; Inventur *f*
**in·verse 1.** umgekehrt; **2.** Umkehrung *f*, Gegenteil *n*; **in·ver·sion** Umkehrung *f*; LING Inversion *f*; **in·vert** umkehren
**in·ver·te·brate** ZO **1.** wirbellos; **2.** wirbelloses Tier
**in·vert·ed com·mas** LING Anführungszeichen *pl*
**in·vest** ECON investieren, anlegen
**in·ves·ti·gate** untersuchen; überprüfen; Untersuchungen *or* Ermittlungen anstellen (***into*** über *acc*), nachforschen
**in·ves·ti·ga·tion** Untersuchung *f*; Ermittlung *f*, Nachforschung *f*
**in·ves·ti·ga·tor:** ***private ~*** Privatdetektiv *m*
**in·vest·ment** ECON Investition *f*, (Kapital)Anlage *f*
**in·ves·tor** ECON Anleger *m*
**in·vet·e·rate** unverbesserlich; hartnäckig
**in·vid·i·ous** gehässig, boshaft, gemein
**in·vig·o·rate** stärken, beleben
**in·vin·ci·ble** unbesiegbar; unüberwindlich
**in·vi·o·la·ble** unantastbar
**in·vis·i·ble** unsichtbar
**in·vi·ta·tion** Einladung *f*; Aufforderung *f*
**in·vite** einladen; auffordern; *Gefahr etc* herausfordern; ***~ s.o. in*** j-n hereinbitten; **in·vit·ing** einladend, verlockend
**in·voice** ECON **1.** (Waren)Rechnung *f*; **2.** in Rechnung stellen, berechnen
**in·voke** flehen um; *Gott etc* anrufen; beschwören
**in·vol·un·ta·ry** unfreiwillig; unabsichtlich; unwillkürlich
**in·volve** verwickeln, hineinziehen (***in*** in *acc*); *j-n, et.* angehen, betreffen; zur Folge haben, mit sich bringen
**in·volved** kompliziert, verworren
**in·volve·ment** Verwicklung *f*; Beteiligung *f*
**in·vul·ne·ra·ble** unverwundbar; *fig* unanfechtbar
**in·ward 1.** *adj* innere(r, -s), innerlich; **2.** *adv mst* ***~s*** einwärts, nach innen
**i·o·dine** CHEM Jod *n*
**i·on** PHYS Ion *n*
**IOU** (= ***I owe you***) Schuldschein *m*
**IQ** ABBR *of* ***intelligence quotient*** IQ, Intelligenzquotient *m*
**I·ran** Iran *m*; **I·ra·ni·an 1.** iranisch; **2.** Iraner(in); LING Iranisch *n*
**I·raq** Irak *m*; **I·ra·qi 1.** irakisch; **2.** Iraker(in); LING Irakisch *n*
**i·ras·ci·ble** jähzornig
**i·rate** zornig, wütend
**Ire·land** Irland *n*
**ir·i·des·cent** schillernd
**i·ris** ANAT Regenbogenhaut *f*, Iris *f*; BOT Schwertlilie *f*, Iris *f*
**I·rish 1.** irisch; **2.** LING Irisch *n*; ***the ~*** die Iren *pl*
**I·rish·man** Ire *m*
**I·rish·wom·an** Irin *f*
**i·ron 1.** Eisen *n*; Bügeleisen *n*; ***strike while the ~ is hot*** *fig* das Eisen schmieden, solange es heiß ist; **2.** eisern (*a. fig*), Eisen..., aus Eisen; **3.** bügeln; ***~ out*** ausbügeln
**I·ron Cur·tain** POL HIST Eiserner Vorhang
**i·ron·ic, i·ron·i·cal** ironisch, spöttisch
**i·ron·ing board** Bügelbrett *n*
**i·ron·mon·ger** *Br* Eisenwarenhändler *m*
**i·ron·works** TECH Eisenhütte *f*
**i·ron·y** Ironie *f*
**ir·ra·tion·al** irrational, unvernünftig
**ir·rec·on·ci·la·ble** unversöhnlich; unvereinbar
**ir·re·cov·e·ra·ble** unersetzlich; unwiederbringlich
**ir·re·fut·a·ble** unwiderlegbar
**ir·reg·u·lar** unregelmäßig; ungleichmäßig; regelwidrig, vorschriftswidrig
**ir·rel·e·vant** irrelevant, unerheblich, belanglos (***to*** für)
**ir·rep·a·ra·ble** irreparabel, nicht wieder gutzumachen(d)
**ir·re·place·a·ble** unersetzlich
**ir·re·pres·si·ble** nicht zu unterdrücken(d); unbezähmbar
**ir·re·proach·a·ble** einwandfrei, untadelig
**ir·re·sist·i·ble** unwiderstehlich
**ir·res·o·lute** unentschlossen
**ir·re·spec·tive:** ***~ of*** ohne Rücksicht auf (*acc*); unabhängig von
**ir·re·spon·si·ble** unverantwortlich; verantwortungslos
**ir·re·trie·va·ble** unwiederbringlich, unersetzlich
**ir·rev·e·rent** respektlos

**ir·rev·o·ca·ble** unwiderruflich, endgültig
**ir·ri·gate** bewässern
**ir·ri·ga·tion** Bewässerung *f*
**ir·ri·ta·ble** reizbar
**ir·ri·tant** Reizmittel *n*
**ir·ri·tate** reizen; (ver)ärgern
**ir·ri·tat·ing** ärgerlich
**ir·ri·ta·tion** Reizung *f*; Verärgerung *f*; Ärger *m* (**at** über *acc*)
**is** *er*, *sie*, *es* ist
**Is·lam** der Islam
**is·land** Insel *f*; *a.* ***traffic*** ~ Verkehrsinsel *f*; **is·land·er** Inselbewohner(in)
**isle** POET Insel *f*
**i·so·late** absondern; isolieren
**i·so·lat·ed** isoliert, abgeschieden; einzeln; ***become*** ~ vereinsamen
**i·so·la·tion** Isolierung *f*, Absonderung *f*; ~ **ward** MED Isolierstation *f*
**Is·rael** Israel *n*
**Is·rae·li** **1.** israelisch; **2.** Israeli *m*, *f*
**is·sue** **1.** Streitfrage *f*, Streitpunkt *m*; Ausgabe *f*; Erscheinen *n*; JUR Nachkommen(schaft *f*) *pl*; *fig* Ausgang *m*, Ergebnis *n*; ***be at*** ~ zur Debatte stehen; ***point at*** ~ strittiger Punkt; ***die without*** ~ kinderlos sterben; **2.** *v/t Zeitung etc* herausgeben; *Banknoten etc* ausgeben; *Dokument etc* ausstellen; *v/i* herauskommen, hervorkommen; herausfließen, herausströmen
**it** es; *s.th. previously mentioned*: es, er, ihn, sie
**I·tal·i·an** **1.** italienisch; **2.** Italiener(in); LING Italienisch *n*
**i·tal·ics** PRINT Kursivschrift *f*
**It·a·ly** Italien *n*
**itch** **1.** Jucken *n*, Juckreiz *m*; **2.** jucken, kratzen; ***I ~ all over*** es juckt mich überall; ***be ~ing for s.th.*** F et. unbedingt (haben) wollen; ***be ~ing to*** *inf* F darauf brennen zu *inf*
**itch·y** juckend; kratzend
**i·tem** Punkt *m* (*on the agenda etc*), Posten *m* (*on a list*); Artikel *m*, Gegenstand *m*; (*Presse-*, *Zeitungs*)Notiz *f*, (*a. radio*, TV) Nachricht *f*, Meldung *f*
**i·tem·ize** einzeln angeben *or* aufführen
**i·tin·e·ra·ry** Reiseweg *m*, Reiseroute *f*; Reiseplan *m*
**its** sein(e), ihr(e)
**it·self** sich; sich selbst; selbst; ***by*** ~ (für sich) allein; von selbst; ***in*** ~ an sich
**i·vo·ry** Elfenbein *n*
**i·vy** BOT Efeu *m*

# J

**J, j** J, j *n*
**jab** **1.** (hinein)stechen, (hinein)stoßen; **2.** Stich *m*, Stoß *m*
**jab·ber** F (daher)plappern
**jack** **1.** TECH Hebevorrichtung *f*; MOT Wagenheber *m*; *cards*: Bube *m*; **2.** ~ ***up*** *Auto* aufbocken
**jack·al** ZO Schakal *m*
**jack·ass** ZO Esel *m* (*a. fig*)
**jack·daw** ZO Dohle *f*
**jack·et** Jacke *f*, Jackett *n*; TECH Mantel *m*; (Schutz)Umschlag *m*; (*Platten*)Hülle *f*; ~ ***potatoes, potatoes*** (***boiled***) ***in their ~s*** Pellkartoffeln *pl*
**jack knife** **1.** Klappmesser *n*; **2.** zusammenklappen, -knicken
**jack-of-all-trades** Hansdampf *m* in allen Gassen
**jack·pot** Jackpot *m*, Haupttreffer *m*; ***hit the*** ~ F den Jackpot gewinnen; *fig* das große Los ziehen
**jade** MIN Jade *m*, *f*; Jadegrün *n*
**jag** Zacken *m*
**jag·ged** gezackt, zackig; schartig
**jag·u·ar** ZO Jaguar *m*
**jail** **1.** Gefängnis *n*; **2.** einsperren
**jail·bird** F Knastbruder *m*
**jail·er** Gefängnisaufseher *m*
**jail·house** Gefängnis *n*
**jam¹** Konfitüre *f*, Marmelade *f*
**jam²** **1.** *v/t* (hinein)pressen, (hinein-)quetschen, (hinein)zwängen, *Menschen a.* (hinein)pferchen; (ein)klemmen, (ein)quetschen; *a.* ~ ***up*** blockieren, ver-

stopfen; *Funkempfang* stören; ~ ***on the brakes*** MOT voll auf die Bremse treten; *v/i* sich (hinein)drängen *or* (hinein-) quetschen; TECH sich verklemmen, *brake*: blockieren; **2.** Gedränge *n*; TECH Blockierung *f*; Stauung *f*, Stockung *f*; ***traffic*** ~ Verkehrsstau *m*; ***be in a*** ~ F in der Klemme stecken

**jamb** (Tür-, Fenster)Pfosten *m*

**jam·bo·ree** Jamboree *n*, Pfadfindertreffen *n*; Fest *n*

**Jan** ABBR *of* ***January*** Jan., Januar *m*

**jan·gle** klimpern *or* klirren (mit)

**jan·i·tor** Hausmeister *m*

**Jan·u·a·ry** (ABBR *of* ***Jan***) Januar *m*

**Ja·pan** Japan *n*; **Jap·a·nese 1.** japanisch; **2.** Japaner(in); LING Japanisch *n*; ***the*** ~ die Japaner *pl*

**jar[1] 1.** Gefäß *n*, Krug *m*; (Marmelade- *etc*)Glas *n*

**jar[2]:** ~ ***on*** wehtun (*dat*)

**jar·gon** Jargon *m*, Fachsprache *f*

**jaun·dice** MED Gelbsucht *f*

**jaunt 1.** Ausflug *m*, MOT Spritztour *f*; **2.** e-n Ausflug *or* e-e Spritztour machen

**jaun·ty** unbeschwert, unbekümmert; flott

**jav·e·lin** SPORT Speer *m*; ~ (***throw***), ***throwing the*** ~ SPORT Speerwerfen *n*

**jav·e·lin throw·er** SPORT Speerwerfer(in)

**jaw** ANAT Kiefer *m*; *pl* ZO Rachen *m*, Maul *n*; TECH Backen *pl*; ***lower*** ~ ANAT Unterkiefer *m*; ***upper*** ~ ANAT Oberkiefer; **jaw·bone** ANAT Kieferknochen *m*

**jay** ZO Eichelhäher *m*

**jay·walk·er** unachtsamer Fußgänger

**jazz** MUS Jazz *m*

**jazz·y** F poppig

**jeal·ous** eifersüchtig (***of*** auf *acc*); neidisch; **jeal·ous·y** Eifersucht *f*; Neid *m*

**jeans** Jeans *pl*

**jeer 1.** (***at***) höhnische Bemerkung(en) machen (über *acc*); höhnisch lachen (über *acc*); ~ (***at***) verhöhnen; **2.** höhnische Bemerkung; Hohngelächter *n*

**jel·lied** GASTR in Aspik, in Sülze

**jel·ly** Gallert(e *f*) *n*; GASTR Gelee *n*; Aspik *m*, *n*, Sülze *f*; Götterspeise *f*; ~ **ba·by** *Br* Gummibärchen *n*; ~ **bean** Gummi-, Geleebonbon *m*, *n*

**jel·ly·fish** ZO Qualle *f*

**jeop·ar·dize** gefährden

**jerk 1.** ruckartig ziehen an (*dat*); (zusammen)zucken; sich ruckartig bewegen; **2.** (plötzlicher) Ruck; Sprung *m*, Satz *m*; MED Zuckung *f*

**jerk·y** ruckartig; holprig; rüttelnd

**jer·sey** Pullover *m*

**jest 1.** Scherz *m*, Spaß *m*; **2.** scherzen, spaßen; **jest·er** HIST (Hof)Narr *m*

**jet 1.** (Wasser-, Gas- *etc*)Strahl *m*; TECH Düse *f*; AVIAT Jet *m*; **2.** (heraus-, hervor)schießen (***from*** aus); AVIAT F jetten; ~ **en·gine** AVIAT Düsen-, Strahltriebwerk *n*; ~ **plane** AVIAT Düsenflugzeug *n*, Jet *m*

**jet-pro·pelled** AVIAT mit Düsenantrieb, Düsen...

**jet pro·pul·sion** AVIAT Düsen-, Strahlantrieb *m*

**jet·ty** MAR (Hafen)Mole *f*

**Jew** Jude *m*, Jüdin *f*

**jew·el** Juwel *n*, *m*, Edelstein *m*

**jew·el·er,** *Br* **jew·el·ler** Juwelier *m*

**jew·el·lery** *Br*, **jew·el·ry** Juwelen *pl*; Schmuck *m*

**Jew·ess** Jüdin *f*

**Jew·ish** jüdisch

**jif·fy:** F ***in a*** ~ im Nu, sofort

**jig·saw** Laubsäge *f*; → **jig·saw puz·zle** Puzzle(spiel) *n*

**jilt** *Mädchen* sitzen lassen; *e-m Liebhaber* den Laufpass geben

**jin·gle 1.** klimpern (mit), bimmeln (lassen); **2.** Klimpern *n*, Bimmeln *n*; Werbesong *m*, Werbespruch *m*

**jit·ters:** F ***the*** ~ Bammel *m*, e-e Heidenangst; **jit·ter·y** F nervös; ängstlich

**job 1.** (*einzelne*) Arbeit; Beruf *m*, Beschäftigung *f*, Stellung *f*, Stelle *f*, Arbeit *f*, Job *m* (*a.* EDP); Arbeitsplatz *m*; Aufgabe *f*, Sache *f*, Angelegenheit *f*; *a.* ~ ***work*** Akkordarbeit *f*; ***by the*** ~ im Akkord; ***out of a*** ~ arbeitslos; **2.** ~ ***around*** jobben; ~ **ad,** ~ **ad·ver·tise·ment** Stellenanzeige *f*

**job·ber** *Br* ECON Börsenspekulant *m*

**job cen·tre** *Br* Arbeitsamt *n*

**job hop·ping** häufiger Arbeitsplatzwechsel

**job·hunt·ing** Arbeitssuche *f*; ***be*** ~ auf Arbeitssuche sein

**job·less** arbeitslos

**jock·ey** Jockei *m*

**jog 1.** stoßen an (*acc*) *or* gegen, *j-n* anstoßen; *mst* ~ ***along,*** ~ ***on*** dahintrotten, dahinzuckeln; SPORT joggen; **2.** (leich-

ter) Stoß, Stups *m*; Trott *m*; SPORT Trimmtrab *m*
**jog·ger** SPORT Jogger(in)
**jog·ging** SPORT Joggen *n*, Jogging *n*
**join 1.** *v/t* verbinden, vereinigen, zusammenfügen; sich anschließen (*dat or* an *acc*), sich gesellen zu; eintreten in (*acc*), beitreten; teilnehmen *or* sich beteiligen an (*dat*), mitmachen bei; ~ ***in*** einstimmen in; *v/i* sich vereinigen *or* verbinden; ~ ***in*** teilnehmen *or* sich beteiligen (an *dat*), mitmachen (bei); **2.** Verbindungsstelle *f*, Naht *f*
**join·er** Tischler *m*, Schreiner *m*
**joint 1.** Verbindungs-, Nahtstelle *f*; ANAT, TECH Gelenk *n*; BOT Knoten *m*; *Br* GASTR Braten *m*; F Laden *m*, Bude *f*, Spelunke *f*; *sl* Joint *m*; ***out of*** ~ MED ausgerenkt; *fig* aus den Fugen; **2.** gemeinsam, gemeinschaftlich; Mit...
**joint·ed** gegliedert; Glieder...
**joint-stock com·pa·ny** *Br* ECON Kapital- *or* Aktiengesellschaft *f*
**joint ven·ture** ECON Gemeinschaftsunternehmen *n*
**joke 1.** Witz *m*; Scherz *m*, Spaß *m*; ***practical*** ~ Streich *m*; ***play a*** ~ ***on s.o.*** j-m e-n Streich spielen; **2.** scherzen, Witze machen; **jok·er** Spaßvogel *m*, Witzbold *m*; *cards*: Joker *m*
**jol·ly 1.** *adj* lustig, fröhlich, vergnügt; **2.** *adv Br* F ganz schön; ~ ***good*** prima
**jolt 1.** e-n Ruck *or* Stoß geben; durchrütteln, durchschütteln; rütteln, holpern (*vehicle*); *fig* aufrütteln; **2.** Ruck *m*, Stoß *m*; *fig* Schock *m*
**joss stick** Räucherstäbchen *n*
**jos·tle** (an)rempeln; dränge(l)n
**jot 1.** ***not a*** ~ keine Spur; **2.** ~ ***down*** sich schnell *et.* notieren
**joule** PHYS Joule *n*
**jour·nal** Journal *n*; (Fach)Zeitschrift *f*; Tagebuch *n*
**jour·nal·ism** Journalismus *m*
**jour·nal·ist** Journalist(in)
**jour·ney 1.** Reise *f*; **2.** reisen
**jour·ney·man** Geselle *m*
**joy** Freude *f*; ***for*** ~ vor Freude
**joy·ful** freudig; erfreut
**joy·less** freudlos, traurig
**joy·stick** AVIAT Steuerknüppel *m*; EDP Joystick *m*
**jub·i·lant** jubelnd, überglücklich
**ju·bi·lee** Jubiläum *n*
**judge 1.** JUR Richter(in); SPORT Kampf-, Schieds-, Preisrichter(in); *fig* Kenner(in); **2.** JUR *Fall* verhandeln; urteilen, ein Urteil fällen; beurteilen, einschätzen
**judg·ment** JUR Urteil *n*; Urteilsvermögen *n*; Meinung *f*, Ansicht *f*; göttliches (Straf)Gericht; ***the Last Judgment*** REL das Jüngste Gericht
**Judgment Day,** *a.* ***Day of Judgment*** REL Tag *m* des Jüngsten Gerichts, Jüngster Tag
**ju·di·cial** JUR gerichtlich, Justiz...; richterlich
**ju·di·cia·ry** JUR Richter *pl*
**ju·di·cious** klug, weise
**ju·do** SPORT Judo *n*
**jug** Krug *m*; Kanne *f*, Kännchen *n*
**jug·gle** jonglieren (mit); ECON *Bücher etc* frisieren; **jug·gler** Jongleur *m*
**juice** Saft *m*; MOT F Sprit *m*
**juic·y** saftig; F pikant (*story etc*); F gepfeffert (*price etc*)
**juke·box** Musikbox *f*, Musikautomat *m*
**Jul** ABBR *of* ***July*** Juli *m*
**Ju·ly** (ABBR ***Jul***) Juli *m*
**jum·ble 1.** *a.* ~ ***together,*** ~ ***up*** durcheinander bringen *or* werfen; **2.** Durcheinander *n*; ~ **sale** *Br* Wohltätigkeitsbasar *m*
**jum·bo 1.** riesig, Riesen...; **2.** AVIAT F Jumbo *m*; ~ **jet** AVIAT Jumbo-Jet *m*
**jum·bo-sized** riesig
**jump 1.** *v/i* springen; hüpfen; zusammenzucken, -fahren, hochfahren (***at*** bei); ~ ***at the chance*** mit beiden Händen zugreifen; ~ ***to conclusions*** voreilige Schlüsse ziehen; *v/t* (hinweg)springen über (*acc*); überspringen; ~ ***the queue*** *Br* sich vordränge(l)n; ~ ***the lights*** bei Rot über die Kreuzung fahren; **2.** Sprung *m*
**jump·er**[1] SPORT (*Hoch- etc*)Springer(in)
**jump·er**[2] Trägerrock *m*, Trägerkleid *n*; *Br* Pullover *m*
**jump·ing jack** Hampelmann *m*
**jump·y** nervös
**Jun** ABBR *of* ***June*** Juni *m*
**junc·tion** (Straßen)Kreuzung *f*; RAIL Knotenpunkt *m*
**junc·ture:** ***at this*** ~ zu diesem Zeitpunkt
**June** (ABBR ***Jun***) Juni *m*
**jun·gle** Dschungel *m*

J

**ju·ni·or 1.** junior; jüngere(r, -s); untergeordnet; SPORT Junioren..., Jugend...; **2.** Jüngere *m, f*; **~ school** *Br* Grundschule *f* (*for children aged 7 to 11*)
**junk**[1] MAR Dschunke *f*
**junk**[2] F Trödel *m*; Schrott *m*; Abfall *m*; *sl* Stoff *m*
**junk food** F Junk-Food *n*
**junk·ie, junk·y** *sl* Junkie *m*, Fixer(in)
**junk·yard** Schuttabladeplatz *m*; Schrottplatz *m*; ***auto*** **~** Autofriedhof *m*
**jur·is·dic·tion** JUR Gerichtsbarkeit *f*; Zuständigkeit(sbereich *m*) *f*
**ju·ris·pru·dence** Rechtswissenschaft *f*
**ju·ror** JUR Geschworene *m, f*
**ju·ry** JUR *die* Geschworenen *pl*; SPORT *etc* Jury *f*, Preisrichter *pl*
**ju·ry·man** JUR Geschworene *m*
**ju·ry·wom·an** JUR Geschworene *f*
**just 1.** *adj* gerecht; berechtigt; angemessen; **2.** *adv* gerade, (so)eben; genau, eben; gerade (noch), ganz knapp; nur, bloß; **~ *about*** ungefähr, etwa; **~ *like that*** einfach so; **~ *now*** gerade (jetzt), (so)eben
**jus·tice** Gerechtigkeit *f*; JUR Richter *m*; ***Justice of the Peace*** Friedensrichter *m*; ***court of*** **~** Gericht *n*, Gerichtshof *m*
**jus·ti·fi·ca·tion** Rechtfertigung *f*
**jus·ti·fy** rechtfertigen
**just·ly** mit *or* zu Recht
**jut:** **~ *out*** vorspringen, herausragen
**ju·ve·nile 1.** jugendlich; Jugend...; **2.** Jugendliche *m, f*; **~ court** JUR Jugendgericht *n*; **~ de·lin·quen·cy** JUR Jugendkriminalität *f*; **~ de·lin·quent** JUR straffälliger Jugendlicher, jugendlicher Straftäter

K

# K

**K, k** K, k *n*
**kan·ga·roo** ZO Känguru *n*
**ka·ra·te** SPORT Karate *n*
**keel** MAR **1.** Kiel *m*; **2.** **~ *over*** umschlagen, kentern
**keen** scharf (*a. fig*); schneidend (*cold*); heftig, stark; lebhaft (*interest*); groß (*appetite etc*); begeistert, leidenschaftlich; **~ *on*** versessen *or* scharf auf (*acc*)
**keep 1.** *v/t* (auf-, fest-, zurück)halten; (bei)behalten, bewahren; *Gesetze etc* einhalten, befolgen; *Ware* führen; *Geheimnis* für sich behalten; *Versprechen, Wort* halten; ECON *Buch* führen; aufheben, aufbewahren; abhalten, hindern (***from*** von); *Tiere* halten; *Bett* hüten; ernähren, erhalten, unterhalten; **~ *early hours*** früh zu Bett gehen; **~ *one's head*** die Ruhe bewahren; **~ *one's temper*** sich beherrschen; **~ *s.o. company*** j-m Gesellschaft leisten; **~ *s.th. from s.o.*** j-m et. vorenthalten *or* verschweigen *or* verheimlichen; **~ *time*** richtig gehen (*watch*); MUS Takt halten; *v/i* bleiben; sich halten; **~ *going*** weitergehen; **~ *smiling*** immer nur lächeln!; **~ (*on*) *talking*** weitersprechen; **~ (*on*) *trying*** es weiterversuchen, es immer wieder versuchen; **~ *s.o. waiting*** j-n warten lassen; **~ *away*** (sich) fern halten (***from*** von); **~ *back*** zurückhalten (*a. fig*); **~ *from doing s.th.*** et. nicht tun; **~ *in*** *Schüler(in)* nachsitzen lassen; **~ *off*** (sich) fern halten; **~ *off!*** Betreten verboten!; **~ *on*** *Kleidungsstück* anbehalten, anlassen, *Hut* aufbehalten; *Licht* brennen lassen; ***keep on doing*** fortfahren zu tun; **~ *out*** nicht hinein- *or* hereinlassen; **~ *out!*** Zutritt verboten!; **~ *to*** sich halten an (*acc*); **~ *up*** *fig* aufrechterhalten; *Mut* nicht sinken lassen; fortfahren mit, weitermachen; **~ *s.o. up*** j-n nicht schlafen lassen; **~ *it up*** so weitermachen; **~ *up with*** Schritt halten mit; **~ *up with the Joneses*** nicht hinter den Nachbarn zurückstehen (wollen); **2.** (Lebens)Unterhalt *m*; ***for*** **~*s*** F für immer
**keep·er** Wärter(in), Wächter(in), Aufseher(in); *mst in cpds*: Inhaber(in), Besitzer(in); **keep·ing** Verwahrung *f*; Obhut *f*; ***be in*** (***out of***) **~ *with ...*** (nicht) übereinstimmen mit ...

**keep·sake** Andenken *n*
**keg** Fässchen *n*, kleines Fass
**ken·nel** Hundehütte *f*; **~s** Hundezwinger *m*; Hundepension *f*
**kerb** *Br* → **curb**
**ker·chief** (Hals-, Kopf)Tuch *n*
**ker·nel** BOT Kern *m* (*a. fig*)
**ker·o·sene** Petroleum *n*
**ket·tle** Kessel *m*
**ket·tle·drum** MUS (Kessel)Pauke *f*
**key 1.** Schlüssel *m* (*a. fig*); (*Schreibmaschinen-*, *Klavier- etc*)Taste *f*; MUS Tonart *f*; **2.** Schlüssel...; **3.** anpassen (**to** an *acc*); **~ in** EDP *Daten* eingeben; **~ed up** nervös, aufgeregt, überdreht
**key·board** Tastatur *f*
**key·hole** Schlüsselloch *n*
**key·note** MUS Grundton *m*; *fig* Grundgedanke *m*, Tenor *m*
**key ring** Schlüsselring *m*
**key·stone** ARCH Schlussstein *m*; *fig* Grundpfeiler *m*
**key·word** Schlüssel-, Stichwort *n*
**kick 1.** (mit dem Fuß) stoßen, treten, e-n Tritt geben *or* versetzen (*dat*); *soccer*: schießen, treten, kicken; strampeln; ausschlagen (*horse*); **~ off** von sich schleudern; *soccer*: anstoßen; **~ out** F rausschmeißen; **~ up** hochschleudern; **~ up a fuss** *or* **row** F Krach schlagen; **2.** (Fuß)Tritt *m*; Stoß *m*; *soccer*: Schuss *m*; **free ~** Freistoß *m*; **for ~s** F zum Spaß; **they get a ~ out of it** es macht ihnen e-n Riesenspaß
**kick·off** *soccer*: Anstoß *m*
**kick·out** *soccer*: Abschlag *m*
**kid**[1] ZO Zicklein *n*, Kitz *n*; Ziegenleder *n*; F Kind *n*; **~ brother** F kleiner Bruder
**kid**[2] *v/t j-n* auf den Arm nehmen; **~ s.o.** j-m et. vormachen; *v/i* Spaß machen; **he is only ~ding** er macht ja nur Spaß; **no ~ding!** im Ernst!
**kid gloves** Glacéhandschuhe *pl* (*a. fig*)
**kid·nap** entführen, kidnappen
**kid·nap·(p)er** Entführer(in), Kidnapper(in)
**kid·nap·(p)ing** Entführung *f*, Kidnapping *n*
**kid·ney** ANAT Niere *f*; **~ bean** BOT Kidneybohne *f*, rote Bohne; **~ ma·chine** MED künstliche Niere
**kill** töten (*a. fig*), umbringen, ermorden; vernichten; ZO schlachten; HUNT erlegen, schießen; **be ~ed in an accident** tödlich verunglücken; **~ time** die Zeit totschlagen; **kill·er** Mörder(in), Killer(in); **kill·ing** mörderisch, tödlich
**kill·joy** Spielverderber *m*
**kiln** TECH Brennofen *m*
**ki·lo** F Kilo *n*
**kil·o·gram(me)** Kilogramm *n*
**kil·o·me·ter**, *Br* **kil·o·me·tre** Kilometer *m*
**kilt** Kilt *m*, Schottenrock *m*
**kin** Verwandtschaft *f*, Verwandte *pl*; **next of ~** *der*, *die* nächste Verwandte, *die* nächsten Angehörigen *pl*
**kind**[1] freundlich, liebenswürdig, nett; herzlich
**kind**[2] Art *f*, Sorte *f*; Wesen *n*; **all ~s of** alle möglichen, allerlei; **nothing of the ~** nichts dergleichen; **~ of** F ein bisschen
**kin·der·gar·ten** Kindergarten *m*
**kind-heart·ed** gütig
**kin·dle** anzünden, (sich) entzünden; *Interesse etc* wecken
**kind·ly 1.** *adj* freundlich, liebenswürdig, nett; **2.** *adv* → 1; freundlicherweise, liebenswürdigerweise, netterweise
**kind·ness** Freundlichkeit *f*, Liebenswürdigkeit *f*; Gefälligkeit *f*
**kin·dred** verwandt; **~ spirits** Gleichgesinnte *pl*
**king** König *m*
**king·dom** Königreich *n*; REL Reich *n* Gottes; *fig* Reich *n*; **animal ~** Tierreich *n*; **vegetable ~** Pflanzenreich *n*
**king·ly** königlich
**king-size(d)** Riesen...
**kink** Knick *m*; *fig* Tick *m*, Spleen *m*
**kink·y** spleenig; pervers
**ki·osk** Kiosk *m*; *Br* Telefonzelle *f*
**kip·per** GASTR Räucherhering *m*
**kiss 1.** Kuss *m*; **2.** (sich) küssen
**kit** Ausrüstung *f*; Arbeitsgerät *n*, Werkzeug(e *pl*) *n*; Werkzeugtasche *f*, -kasten *m*; Bastelsatz *m*; **kit bag** Seesack *m*
**kitch·en 1.** Küche *f*; **2.** Küchen...
**kitch·en·ette** Kleinküche *f*, Kochnische *f*
**kitch·en gar·den** Küchen-, Gemüsegarten *m*
**kite** Drachen *m*; ZO Milan *m*; **fly a ~** e-n Drachen steigen lassen
**kit·ten** ZO Kätzchen *n*
**knack** Kniff *m*, Trick *m*, F Dreh *m*; Geschick *n*, Talent *n*
**knave** *card games*: Bube *m*, Unter *m*

K

**knead** kneten; massieren
**knee** ANAT Knie *n*; TECH Knie(stück) *n*
**knee·cap** ANAT Kniescheibe *f*
**knee-deep** knietief, bis an die Knie (reichend)
**knee joint** ANAT Kniegelenk *n* (*a.* TECH)
**kneel** knien (**to** vor *dat*)
**knee-length** knielang
**knell** Totenglocke *f*
**knick·er·bock·ers** Knickerbocker *pl*, Kniehosen *pl*
**knick·ers** *Br* F (Damen)Schlüpfer *m*
**knick-knack** Nippsache *f*
**knife 1.** Messer *n*; **2.** mit e-m Messer stechen *or* verletzen; erstechen
**knight 1.** Ritter *m*; *chess*: Springer *m*; **2.** zum Ritter schlagen
**knight·hood** Ritterwürde *f*, -stand *m*
**knit** *v/t* stricken; *a.* **~ *together*** zusammenfügen, verbinden; **~ *one's brows*** die Stirn runzeln; *v/i* stricken; MED zusammenwachsen
**knit·ting 1.** Stricken *n*; Strickzeug *n*; **2.** Strick...; **~ nee·dle** Stricknadel *f*
**knit·wear** Strickwaren *pl*
**knob** Knopf *m*, Knauf *m*, *runder* Griff; GASTR Stück(chen) *n*
**knock 1.** schlagen, stoßen; pochen, klopfen; **~ *at the door*** an die Tür klopfen; **~ *about*, ~ *around*** herumstoßen; F sich herumtreiben; F herumliegen; **~ *down*** *Gebäude etc* abreißen; umstoßen, umwerfen; niederschlagen; anfahren, umfahren; überfahren; mit *dem Preis* heruntergehen; *auction*: *et.* zuschlagen (**to s.o.** j-m); ***be ~ed down*** überfahren werden; **~ *off*** herunter-, abschlagen; F *et.* hinhauen; F aufhören (mit); F Feierabend *or* Schluss machen; **~ *out*** herausschlagen, -klopfen, *Pfeife* ausklopfen; *j-n* bewusstlos schlagen; *boxing*: k.o. schlagen; *fig* betäuben (*drug etc*); *fig* F umhauen, schocken; **~ *over*** umwerfen, umstoßen; überfahren; ***be ~ed over*** überfahren werden; **2.** Schlag *m*, Stoß *m*; Klopfen *n*; ***there is a ~* (*on* [*Br at*] *the door*)** es klopft
**knock·er** Türklopfer *m*
**knock-kneed** x-beinig
**knock·out** *boxing*: K.o. *m*
**knoll** Hügel *m*
**knot 1.** Knoten *m*; BOT Astknoten *m*; MAR Knoten *m*, Seemeile *f*; **2.** (ver)knoten, (ver)knüpfen; **knot·ty** knotig; knorrig; *fig* verwickelt, kompliziert
**know** wissen; können; kennen; erfahren, erleben; (wieder) erkennen; verstehen; **~ *French*** Französisch können; **~ *one's way around*** sich auskennen in (*a place etc*); **~ *all about it*** genau Bescheid wissen; ***get to ~*** kennen lernen; **~ *one's business*, ~ *the ropes*, ~ *a thing or two*, ~ *what's what*** F sich auskennen, Erfahrung haben; ***you ~*** wissen Sie
**know-how** Know-how *n*, (Sach-, Spezial)Kenntnis(se *pl*) *f*
**know·ing** klug, gescheit; schlau; verständnisvoll; **know·ing·ly** wissend; wissentlich, absichtlich, bewusst
**knowl·edge** Kenntnis(se *pl*) *f*; Wissen *n*; ***to my ~*** meines Wissens; ***have a good ~ of*** viel verstehen von, sich gut auskennen in (*dat*)
**knowl·edge·a·ble: *be very ~ about*** viel verstehen von
**knuck·le 1.** ANAT (Finger)Knöchel *m*; **2. ~ *down to work*** sich an die Arbeit machen
**Krem·lin:** POL ***the ~*** der Kreml

# L

**L, l** L, l *n*
**L** ABBR *of* ***large* (*size*)** groß
**lab** F Labor *n*
**la·bel 1.** Etikett *n*, (Klebe- *etc*)Zettel *m*, (-)Schild(chen) *n*; (Schall)Plattenfirma *f*; **2.** etikettieren, beschriften; *fig* abstempeln als
**la·bor·a·to·ry** Labor(atorium) *n*; **~ as·sis·tant** Laborant(in)
**la·bo·ri·ous** mühsam; schwerfällig

**la·bor 1.** (schwere) Arbeit; Mühe *f*; Arbeiter *pl*, Arbeitskräfte *pl*; MED Wehen *pl*; **2.** (schwer) arbeiten; sich bemühen, sich abmühen, sich anstrengen
**la·bored** schwerfällig (*style etc*); mühsam (*breathing etc*)
**la·bor·er** (*esp* Hilfs)Arbeiter *m*
**la·bor u·ni·on** Gewerkschaft *f*
**la·bour** *Br* → ***labor***
**Labour** *Br* POL die Labour Party
**la·boured, la·bour·er** *Br* → ***labored, laborer***
**La·bour Par·ty** *Br* POL Labour Party *f*
**lace 1.** Spitze *f*; Borte *f*; Schnürsenkel *m*; **2.** ~ ***up*** (zu-, zusammen)schnüren; *Schuh* zubinden; ***~d with brandy*** mit e-m Schuss Weinbrand
**la·ce·rate** zerschneiden, zerkratzen, aufreißen; *j-s Gefühle* verletzen
**lack 1.** (***of***) Fehlen *n* (von), Mangel *m* (an *dat*); **2.** *v/t* nicht haben; ***he ~s money*** es fehlt ihm an Geld; *v/i* ***be ~ing*** fehlen; ***he is ~ing in courage*** ihm fehlt der Mut
**lack·lus·ter,** *Br* **lack·lus·tre** glanzlos, matt
**la·con·ic** lakonisch, wortkarg
**lac·quer 1.** Lack *m*; Haarspray *m, n*; **2.** lackieren
**lad** Bursche *m*, Junge *m*
**lad·der** Leiter *f*; *Br* Laufmasche *f*
**lad·der·proof** (lauf)maschenfest
**la·den** (schwer) beladen
**la·dle 1.** (Schöpf-, Suppen)Kelle *f*, Schöpflöffel *m*; **2.** ~ ***out*** *Suppe* austeilen
**la·dy** Dame *f*; ***Lady*** Lady *f*; ~ ***doctor*** Ärztin *f*; ***Ladies' room,*** *Br* ***Ladies***(') Damentoilette *f*
**la·dy·bird** ZO Marienkäfer *m*
**la·dy·like** damenhaft
**lag 1.** *mst* ~ ***behind*** zurückbleiben; **2.** → ***time lag***
**la·ger** Lagerbier *n*
**la·goon** Lagune *f*
**lair** ZO Lager *n*, Höhle *f*, Bau *m*
**la·i·ty** Laien *pl*
**lake** See *m*
**lamb** ZO **1.** Lamm *n*; **2.** lammen
**lame 1.** lahm (*a. fig*); **2.** lähmen
**la·ment 1.** jammern, (weh)klagen; trauern; **2.** Jammer *m*, (Weh)Klage *f*
**lam·en·ta·ble** beklagenswert; kläglich
**lam·en·ta·tion** (Weh)Klage *f*
**lam·i·nat·ed** laminiert, geschichtet, beschichtet; ~ ***glass*** Verbundglas *n*
**lamp** Lampe *f*; Laterne *f*
**lamp·post** Laternenpfahl *m*
**lamp·shade** Lampenschirm *m*
**lance** Lanze *f*
**land 1.** Land *n*, AGR *a.* Boden *m*, POL *a.* Staat *m*; ***by*** ~ auf dem Landweg; **2.** landen, MAR *a.* anlegen; *Güter* ausladen, MAR *a.* löschen
**land a·gent** AGR Gutsverwalter *m*
**land·ed** Land..., Grund...; ~ ***gentry*** Landadel *m*; ~ ***property*** Grundbesitz *m*
**land·ing** AVIAT Landung *f*, Landen *n*, MAR *a.* Anlegen *n*; Treppenabsatz *m*; ~ ***field*** AVIAT Landeplatz *m*; ~ ***gear*** AVIAT Fahrgestell *n*; ~ ***stage*** MAR Landungsbrücke *f*, -steg *m*; ~ ***strip*** AVIAT Landeplatz *m*
**land·la·dy** Vermieterin *f*; Wirtin *f*
**land·lord** Vermieter *m*; Wirt *m*; Grundbesitzer *m*
**land·lub·ber** MAR *contp* Landratte *f*
**land·mark** Wahrzeichen *n*; *fig* Meilenstein *m*
**land·own·er** Grundbesitzer(in)
**land·scape** Landschaft *f* (*a. paint*)
**land·slide** Erdrutsch *m* (*a.* POL); ***a*** ~ ***victory*** POL ein überwältigender Wahlsieg
**land·slip** (kleiner) Erdrutsch
**lane** (Feld)Weg *m*; Gasse *f*, Sträßchen *n*; MAR Fahrrinne *f*; AVIAT Flugschneise *f*; SPORT (*einzelne*) Bahn; MOT (Fahr-) Spur *f*; ***change ~s*** MOT die Spur wechseln; ***get in*** ~ MOT sich einordnen
**lan·guage** Sprache *f*; ~ **la·bor·a·to·ry** Sprachlabor *n*
**lan·guid** matt; träg(e)
**lank** glatt
**lank·y** schlaksig
**lan·tern** Laterne *f*
**lap**[1] Schoß *m*
**lap**[2] SPORT **1.** Runde *f*; ~ ***of hono(u)r*** Ehrenrunde *f*; **2.** *Gegner* überrunden; e-e Runde zurücklegen
**lap**[3] *v/t*: ~ ***up*** auflecken, aufschlecken; *v/i* plätschern
**la·pel** Revers *n, m*, Aufschlag *m*
**lapse 1.** Versehen *n*, (kleiner) Fehler *or* Irrtum; Vergehen *n*; Zeitspanne *f*; JUR Verfall *m*; ~ ***of memory, memory*** ~ Gedächtnislücke *f*; **2.** verfallen; JUR verfallen, erlöschen
**lar·ce·ny** JUR Diebstahl *m*

L

**larch** BOT Lärche *f*
**lard** **1.** Schweinefett *n*, Schweineschmalz *n*; **2.** *Fleisch* spicken
**lar·der** Speisekammer *f*, -schrank *m*
**large** groß; beträchtlich, reichlich; umfassend, weitgehend; ***at ~*** in Freiheit, auf freiem Fuß; *fig* (sehr) ausführlich; in der Gesamtheit
**large·ly** großenteils, größtenteils
**large-mind·ed** aufgeschlossen, tolerant
**large·ness** Größe *f*
**lar·i·at** Lasso *n*, *m*
**lark**[1] ZO Lerche *f*
**lark**[2] F Jux *m*, Spaß *m*
**lark·spur** BOT Rittersporn *m*
**lar·va** ZO Larve *f*
**lar·yn·gi·tis** MED Kehlkopfentzündung *f*; **lar·ynx** ANAT Kehlkopf *m*
**las·civ·i·ous** geil, lüstern
**la·ser** PHYS Laser *m*; **~ beam** PHYS Laserstrahl *m*; **~ print·er** EDP Laserdrucker *m*; **~ tech·nol·o·gy** Lasertechnik *f*
**lash** **1.** Peitschenschnur *f*; (Peitschen-) Hieb *m*; Wimper *f*; **2.** peitschen (mit); (fest)binden; schlagen; ***~ out*** (wild) um sich schlagen
**las·so** Lasso *n*, *m*
**last**[1] **1.** *adj* letzte(r, -s); vorige(r, -s); ***~ but one*** vorletzte(r, -s); ***~ night*** gestern Abend; letzte Nacht; **2.** *adv* zuletzt, an letzter Stelle; ***~ but not least*** nicht zuletzt, nicht zu vergessen; **3.** *der*, *die*, *das* Letzte; ***at ~*** endlich; ***to the ~*** bis zum Schluss
**last**[2] (an-, fort)dauern; (sich) halten; (aus)reichen
**last**[3] (Schuhmacher)Leisten *m*
**last·ing** dauerhaft; beständig
**last·ly** zuletzt, zum Schluss
**latch** **1.** Schnappriegel *m*; Schnappschloss *n*; **2.** einklinken, zuklinken
**latch·key** Haus-, Wohnungsschlüssel *m*
**late** spät; jüngste(r, -s), letzte(r, -s), frühere(r, -s), ehemalig; verstorben; ***be ~*** zu spät kommen, sich verspäten; RAIL *etc* Verspätung haben; ***as ~ as*** noch, erst; ***of ~*** kürzlich; ***later on*** später
**late·ly** kürzlich
**lath** Latte *f*, Leiste *f*
**lathe** TECH Drehbank *f*
**la·ther** **1.** (Seifen)Schaum *m*; **2.** *v/t* einseifen; *v/i* schäumen
**Lat·in** LING **1.** lateinisch; südländisch; **2.** Latein(isch) *n*; **~ A·mer·i·ca** Lateinamerika *n*; **~ A·mer·i·can** **1.** lateinamerikanisch; **2.** Lateinamerikaner(in)
**lat·i·tude** GEOGR Breite *f*
**lat·ter** Letztere(r, -s)
**lat·tice** Gitter(werk) *n*
**lau·da·ble** lobenswert
**laugh** **1.** lachen (***at*** über *acc*); ***~ at s.o.*** *a.* j-n auslachen; **2.** Lachen *n*, Gelächter *n*
**laugh·a·ble** lächerlich, lachhaft
**laugh·ter** Lachen *n*, Gelächter *n*
**launch**[1] **1.** MAR vom Stapel lassen; MIL abschießen, *Rakete a.* starten; *fig Projekt etc* in Gang setzen, starten; **2.** MAR Stapellauf *m*; MIL Abschuss *m*, Start *m*
**launch**[2] MAR Barkasse *f*
**launch pad** → ***launching pad***
**launch·ing** → ***launch***[1] 2; **~ pad** Abschussrampe *f*; **~ site** Abschussbasis *f*
**laun·der** *Wäsche* waschen (und bügeln); F *esp Geld* waschen
**laun·der·ette, laun·drette** *esp Br*, **laun·dro·mat**® Waschsalon *m*
**laun·dry** Wäscherei *f*; Wäsche *f*
**laur·el** BOT Lorbeer *m* (*a. fig*)
**la·va** GEOL Lava *f*
**lav·a·to·ry** Toilette *f*, Klosett *n*; ***public ~*** Bedürfnisanstalt *f*
**lav·en·der** BOT Lavendel *m*
**lav·ish** **1.** sehr freigebig, verschwenderisch; **2.** **~ *s.th. on s.o.*** j-n mit et. überhäufen *or* überschütten
**law** Gesetz(e *pl*) *n*; Recht *n*, Rechtssystem *n*; Rechtswissenschaft *f*, Jura; F Bullen *pl* (*police*); F Bulle *m* (*policeman*); Gesetz *n*, Vorschrift *f*; ***~ and order*** Recht *or* Ruhe und Ordnung
**law-a·bid·ing** gesetzestreu
**law·court** Gericht *n*, Gerichtshof *m*
**law·ful** gesetzlich; rechtmäßig, legitim; rechtsgültig
**law·less** gesetzlos; gesetzwidrig; zügellos
**lawn** Rasen *m*
**lawn·mow·er** Rasenmäher *m*
**law·suit** JUR Prozess *m*
**law·yer** JUR (Rechts)Anwalt *m*, (Rechts)Anwältin *f*
**lax** locker, schlaff; lax, lasch
**lax·a·tive** MED **1.** abführend; **2.** Abführmittel *n*
**lay**[1] REL weltlich; Laien...
**lay**[2] *v/t* legen; *Teppich* verlegen; belegen,

L

auslegen (***with*** mit); *Tisch* decken; ZO *Eier* legen; vorlegen (***before*** *dat*), bringen (***before*** vor *acc*); *Schuld etc* zuschreiben, zur Last legen (*dat*); *v/i* ZO (Eier) legen; ~ ***aside*** beiseite legen, zurücklegen; ~ ***off*** *Arbeiter* (*esp* vorübergehend) entlassen; *Arbeit* einstellen; ~ ***open*** darlegen; ~ ***out*** ausbreiten, auslegen; *Garten etc* anlegen; entwerfen, planen; PRINT das Layout (*gen*) machen; ~ ***up*** anhäufen, (an)sammeln; ***be laid up*** das Bett hüten müssen

**lay-by** *Br* MOT Parkbucht *f*, Parkstreifen *m*; Parkplatz *m*, Rastplatz *m*

**lay·er** Lage *f*, Schicht *f*; BOT Ableger *m*

**lay·man** Laie *m*

**lay-off** ECON (*esp* vorübergehende) Entlassung

**lay·out** Grundriss *m*, Lageplan *m*; PRINT Layout *n*, Gestaltung *f*

**la·zy** faul, träg(e)

**LCD** ABBR *of* ***liquid crystal display*** Flüssigkristallanzeige *f*

**lead**[1] **1.** *v/t* führen; (an)führen, leiten; dazu bringen, veranlassen (***to do*** zu tun); *v/i* führen; vorangehen; SPORT an der Spitze *or* in Führung liegen; ~ ***off*** anfangen, beginnen; ~ ***on*** *j-m* et. vormachen *or* weismachen; ~ ***to*** *fig* führen zu; ~ ***up to*** *fig* (allmählich) führen zu; **2.** Führung *f*; Leitung *f*; Spitzenposition *f*; Vorbild *n*, Beispiel *n*; THEA Hauptrolle *f*; Hauptdarsteller(in); (Hunde)Leine *f*; Hinweis *m*, Tipp *m*, Anhaltspunkt *m*; SPORT *and fig* Führung *f*, Vorsprung *m*; ***be in the*** ~ in Führung sein; ***take the*** ~ in Führung gehen, die Führung übernehmen

**lead**[2] CHEM Blei *n*; MAR Lot *n*

**lead·ed** verbleit, bleihaltig

**lead·en** bleiern (*a. fig*), Blei...

**lead·er** (An)Führer(in), Leiter(in); Erste *m, f*; *Br* Leitartikel *m*

**lead·er·ship** Führung *f*, Leitung *f*

**lead-free** bleifrei

**lead·ing** leitend; führend; Haupt...

**leaf 1.** BOT, PRINT Blatt *n*; (*Tür- etc*)Flügel *m*; (*Tisch*)Klappe *f*, Ausziehplatte *f*; **2.** ~ ***through*** durchblättern

**leaf·let** Hand-, Reklamezettel *m*; Prospekt *m*

**league** POL Bund *m*; SPORT Liga *f*

**leak 1.** lecken, leck sein; tropfen; ~ ***out*** auslaufen; *fig* durchsickern; **2.** Leck *n*, undichte Stelle (*a. fig*)

**leak·age** Auslaufen *n*

**leak·y** leck, undicht

**lean**[1] (sich) lehnen; (sich) neigen; ~ ***on*** sich verlassen auf (*acc*)

**lean**[2] **1.** mager (*a. fig*); **2.** GASTR das Magere; ~ **man·age·ment** ECON schlanke Unternehmensstruktur

**leap 1.** springen; ~ ***at*** *fig* sich stürzen auf (*acc*); **2.** Sprung *m*

**leap·frog** Bockspringen *n*

**leap year** Schaltjahr *n*

**learn** (er)lernen; erfahren, hören

**learn·ed** gelehrt

**learn·er** Anfänger(in); Lernende *m, f*; ~ ***driver*** *Br* MOT Fahrschüler(in)

**learn·ing** Gelehrsamkeit *f*

**lease 1.** Pacht *f*, Miete *f*; Pacht-, Mietvertrag *m*; **2.** pachten, mieten; leasen; ~ ***out*** verpachten, vermieten

**leash** (Hunde)Leine *f*

**least 1.** *adj* geringste(r, -s), mindeste(r, -s), wenigste(r, -s); **2.** *adv* am wenigsten; ~ ***of all*** am allerwenigsten; **3.** *das* Mindeste, *das* wenigste; ***at*** ~ wenigstens; ***to say the*** ~ gelinde gesagt

**leath·er 1.** Leder *n*; **2.** ledern; Leder...

**leave 1.** *v/t* (hinter-, über-, ver-, zurück)lassen, übrig lassen; liegen *or* stehen lassen, vergessen; vermachen, vererben; ***be left*** übrig bleiben, übrig sein; *v/i* (fort-, weg)gehen, abreisen, abfahren, abfliegen; ~ ***alone*** allein lassen; *j-n, et.* in Ruhe lassen; ~ ***behind*** zurücklassen; ~ ***on*** anlassen; ~ ***out*** draußen lassen; auslassen, weglassen; **2.** Erlaubnis *f*; Urlaub *m*; Abschied *m*; ***on*** ~ auf Urlaub

**leav·en** Sauerteig *m*

**leaves** BOT Laub *n*

**leav·ings** Überreste *pl*

**lech·er·ous** geil, lüstern

**lec·ture 1.** UNIV Vorlesung *f* (***über*** *acc* on); Vortrag *m*; Strafpredigt *f*; **2.** *v/i* UNIV e-e Vorlesung *or* Vorlesungen halten (***über*** *acc* on; ***vor*** *dat* to); e-n Vortrag *or* Vorträge halten; *v/t j-m* e-e Strafpredigt halten

**lec·tur·er** UNIV Dozent(in); Redner(in)

**ledge** Leiste *f*, Sims *m, n*

**leech** ZO Blutegel *m*

**leek** BOT Lauch *m*, Porree *m*

**leer 1.** anzüglicher *or* lüsterner Seiten-

L

blick; **2.** anzüglich *or* lüstern blicken *or* schielen (**at** nach)

**left 1.** *adj* linke(r, -s), Links...; **2.** *adv* links; ***turn*** ~ (sich) nach links wenden; MOT links abbiegen; **3.** *die* Linke (*a.* POL, *boxing*), linke Seite; ***on the*** ~ links, auf der linken Seite; ***to the*** ~ (nach) links; ***keep to the*** ~ sich links halten; links fahren

**left-hand** linke(r, -s)

**left-hand drive** MOT Linkssteuerung *f*

**left-hand·ed** linkshändig; für Linkshänder; ***be*** ~ Linkshänder(in) sein

**left lug·gage of·fice** *Br* RAIL Gepäckaufbewahrung *f*

**left·o·vers** (Speise)Reste *pl*

**left-wing** POL dem linken Flügel angehörend, links..., Links...

**leg** ANAT Bein *n*; GASTR Keule *f*; MATH Schenkel *m*; ***pull s.o.'s*** ~ F j-n auf den Arm nehmen; ***stretch one's*** **~s** sich die Beine vertreten

**leg·a·cy** *fig* Vermächtnis *n*, Erbe *n*

**le·gal** legal, gesetzmäßig; gesetzlich, rechtlich; juristisch, Rechts...

**le·gal·ize** legalisieren

**le·gal·i·za·tion** Legalisierung *f*

**le·gal pro·tec·tion** Rechtsschutz *m*

**le·ga·tion** POL Gesandtschaft *f*

**le·gend** Legende *f*, Sage *f*

**le·gen·da·ry** legendär

**le·gi·ble** leserlich

**le·gis·la·tion** Gesetzgebung *f*

**le·gis·la·tive** POL **1.** gesetzgebend, legislativ; **2.** Legislative *f*, gesetzgebende Gewalt

**le·gis·la·tor** POL Gesetzgeber *m*

**le·git·i·mate** legitim; gesetzmäßig, rechtmäßig; ehelich

**lei·sure** freie Zeit; Muße *f*; ***at*** ~ ohne Hast; ~ **cen·tre** *Br* Freizeitzentrum *n*

**lei·sure·ly** gemächlich

**lei·sure time** Freizeit *f*

**lei·sure-time ac·tiv·i·ties** Freizeitbeschäftigung *f*, -gestaltung *f*

**lei·sure·wear** Freizeitkleidung *f*

**lem·on** BOT **1.** Zitrone *f*; **2.** Zitronen...

**lem·on·ade** Zitronenlimonade *f*

**lend** *j-m et.* (ver-, aus)leihen

**length** Länge *f*; Strecke *f*; (Zeit)Dauer *f*; ***at*** ~ ausführlich

**length·en** verlängern, länger machen; länger werden

**length·ways, length·wise** der Länge nach

**length·y** sehr lang

**le·ni·ent** mild(e), nachsichtig

**lens** ANAT, PHOT, PHYS Linse *f*; PHOT Objektiv *n*

**Lent** REL Fastenzeit *f*

**len·til** BOT Linse *f*

**Le·o** ASTR Löwe *m*; ***he*** (***she***) ***is*** (***a***) ~ er (sie) ist (ein) Löwe

**leop·ard** ZO Leopard *m*

**le·o·tard** (Tänzer)Trikot *n*

**lep·ro·sy** MED Lepra *f*

**les·bi·an 1.** lesbisch; **2.** Lesbierin *f*, F Lesbe *f*

**less 1.** *adj and adv* kleiner, geringer, weniger; **2.** *prp* weniger, minus, abzüglich

**less·en** (sich) vermindern *or* verringern; abnehmen; herabsetzen

**less·er** kleiner, geringer

**les·son** Lektion *f*; (Unterrichts)Stunde *f*; *fig* Lehre *f*; *pl* Unterricht *m*

**let** lassen; *esp Br* vermieten, verpachten; ~ ***alone*** *j-n, et.* in Ruhe lassen; geschweige denn; ~ ***down*** hinunterlassen, herunterlassen; *Kleider* verlängern; *j-n* im Stich lassen, F *j-n* sitzen lassen; enttäuschen; ~ ***go*** loslassen; ~ ***o.s. go*** sich gehen lassen; **~'s go** gehen wir!; ~ ***in*** (her)einlassen; ~ ***o.s. in for s.th.*** sich et. einbrocken, sich auf et. einlassen

**le·thal** tödlich; Todes...

**leth·ar·gy** Lethargie *f*

**let·ter** Buchstabe *m*; PRINT Type *f*; Brief *m*

**let·ter·box** *esp Br* Briefkasten *m*

**let·ter car·ri·er** Briefträger *m*

**let·tuce** BOT (*esp* Kopf)Salat *m*

**leu·k(a)e·mia** MED Leukämie *f*

**lev·el 1.** *adj* eben; gleich (*a. fig*); ausgeglichen; ***be*** ~ ***with*** auf gleicher Höhe sein mit; ***my*** ~ ***best*** F mein Möglichstes; **2.** Ebene *f* (*a. fig*), ebene Fläche; Höhe *f* (*a.* GEOGR), (*Wasser- etc*)Spiegel *m*, (-)Stand *m*, (-)Pegel *m*; Wasserwaage *f*; *fig* Niveau *n*, Stufe *f*; ***sea*** ~ Meeresspiegel *m*; ***on the*** ~ F ehrlich, aufrichtig; **3.** (ein)ebnen, planieren; dem Erdboden gleichmachen; ~ ***at*** *Waffe* richten auf (*acc*); *Beschuldigungen* erheben gegen (*acc*); **4.** *adv*: ~ ***with*** in Höhe (*gen*)

**lev·el cross·ing** *Br* schienengleicher Bahnübergang

**lev·el-head·ed** vernünftig, nüchtern
**le·ver** Hebel *m*
**lev·y 1.** Steuer *f*, Abgabe *f*; **2.** *Steuern* erheben
**lewd** geil, lüstern; unanständig, obszön
**li·a·bil·i·ty** ECON, JUR Verpflichtung *f*, Verbindlichkeit *f*; ECON, JUR Haftung *f*, Haftpflicht *f*; Neigung *f* (***to*** zu), Anfälligkeit *f* (***to*** für); **li·a·ble** ECON, JUR haftbar, haftpflichtig; ***be ~ for*** haften für; ***be ~ to*** neigen zu, anfällig sein für
**li·ar** Lügner(in)
**li·bel** JUR **1.** (*schriftliche*) Verleumdung *or* Beleidigung; **2.** (*schriftlich*) verleumden *or* beleidigen
**lib·e·ral 1.** liberal (*a.* POL), aufgeschlossen; großzügig; reichlich; **2.** Liberale *m, f* (*a.* POL)
**lib·e·rate** befreien; **lib·e·ra·tion** Befreiung *f*; **lib·e·ra·tor** Befreier *m*
**lib·er·ty** Freiheit *f*; ***take liberties with*** sich Freiheiten gegen *j-n* herausnehmen; willkürlich mit *et.* umgehen; ***be at ~*** frei sein
**Li·bra** ASTR Waage *f*; ***he*** (***she***) ***is*** (***a***) *~* er (sie) ist (eine) Waage
**li·brar·i·an** Bibliothekar(in)
**li·bra·ry** Bibliothek *f*; Bücherei *f*
**li·cence 1.** *Br* → ***license*** 1; **2.** e-e Lizenz *or* Konzession erteilen (*dat*); *behördlich* genehmigen
**li·cense 1.** Lizenz *f*, Konzession *f*; (*Führer-, Jagd-, Waffen- etc*)Schein *m*; **2.** *Br* → ***licence*** 2
**li·cense plate** MOT Nummernschild *n*
**li·chen** BOT Flechte *f*
**lick 1.** Lecken *n*; Salzlecke *f*; **2.** *v/t* ab-, auflecken; F verdreschen, verprügeln; F schlagen, besiegen; *v/i* lecken; züngeln (*flames*)
**lic·o·rice** Lakritze *f*
**lid** Deckel *m*; ANAT (Augen)Lid *n*
**lie[1] 1.** lügen; ***~ to s.o.*** j-n belügen, j-n anlügen; **2.** Lüge *f*; ***tell ~s, tell a ~*** lügen; ***give the ~ to*** *j-n, et.* Lügen strafen
**lie[2] 1.** liegen; ***let sleeping dogs ~*** schlafende Hunde soll man nicht wecken; ***~ behind*** *fig* dahinter stecken; ***~ down*** sich hinlegen; **2.** Lage *f* (*a. fig*)
**lie-down** *Br* F Nickerchen *n*
**lie-in:** ***have a ~*** *esp Br* F sich gründlich ausschlafen
**lieu:** ***in ~ of*** anstelle von (*or gen*)
**lieu·ten·ant** MIL Leutnant *m*
**life** Leben *n*; JUR lebenslängliche Freiheitsstrafe; ***all her ~*** ihr ganzes Leben lang; ***for ~*** fürs (ganze) Leben; *esp* JUR lebenslänglich
**life as·sur·ance** *Br* → ***life insurance***
**life belt** Rettungsgürtel *m*
**life·boat** Rettungsboot *n*
**life·guard** Bademeister *m*; Rettungsschwimmer *m*
**life im·pris·on·ment** JUR lebenslängliche Freiheitsstrafe
**life in·sur·ance** Lebensversicherung *f*
**life jack·et** Schwimmweste *f*
**life·less** leblos; matt, schwung-, lustlos
**life·like** lebensecht
**life·long** lebenslang
**life pre·serv·er** Schwimmweste *f*; Rettungsgürtel *m*
**life sen·tence** JUR lebenslängliche Freiheitsstrafe
**life·time** Lebenszeit *f*
**lift 1.** *v/t* (hoch-, auf)heben; erheben; *Verbot etc* aufheben; *Gesicht etc* liften, straffen; F klauen; *v/i* sich heben, steigen (*a. fog*); ***~ off*** starten (*rocket*), AVIAT abheben; **2.** (Hoch-, Auf)Heben *n*; PHYS, AVIAT Auftrieb *m*; *Br* Lift *m*, Aufzug *m*, Fahrstuhl *m*; ***give s.o. a ~*** j-n (im Auto) mitnehmen; F j-n aufmuntern, j-m Auftrieb geben
**lift-off** Start *m*, Abheben *n*
**lig·a·ment** ANAT Band *n*
**light[1] 1.** Licht *n* (*a. fig*); Beleuchtung *f*; Schein *m*; Feuer *n*; *fig* Aspekt *m*; *Br mst pl* (Verkehrs)Ampel *f*; ***do you have*** (*Br* ***have you got***) ***a ~?*** haben Sie Feuer?; **2.** *v/t* beleuchten, erleuchten; *a.* ***~ up*** anzünden; *v/i* sich entzünden; ***~ up*** *fig* aufleuchten; **3.** hell, licht
**light[2]** leicht (*a. fig*); ***make ~ of s.th.*** et. leicht nehmen; et. bagatellisieren
**light·en[1]** *v/t* erhellen; aufhellen; *v/i* hell(er) werden, sich aufhellen
**light·en[2]** leichter machen *or* werden; erleichtern
**light·er** Anzünder *m*; Feuerzeug *n*
**light-head·ed** (leicht) benommen; leichtfertig, töricht
**light-heart·ed** fröhlich, unbeschwert
**light·house** Leuchtturm *m*
**light·ing** Beleuchtung *f*
**light·ness** Leichtheit *f*; Leichtigkeit *f*
**light·ning** Blitz *m*; ***like ~*** wie der Blitz; (***as***) ***quick as ~*** blitzschnell

**light·ning| con·duc·tor** *Br*, ~ **rod** ELECTR Blitzableiter *m*
**light·weight** SPORT Leichtgewicht *n*, Leichtgewichtler *m*
**like¹ 1.** *v/t* gern haben, mögen; ***I ~ it*** es gefällt mir; ***I ~ her*** ich kann sie gut leiden; ***how do you ~ it?*** wie gefällt es dir?, wie findest du es?; ***I ~ that!*** *iro* das hab ich gern!; ***I should*** *or* ***would ~ to know*** ich möchte gern wissen; *v/i* wollen; (***just***) ***as you ~*** (ganz) wie du willst; ***if you ~*** wenn du willst; **2.** ***~s and dislikes*** Neigungen und Abneigungen *pl*
**like² 1.** gleich; wie; ähnlich; ***~ that*** so; ***feel ~*** Lust haben auf (*acc*) *or* zu; ***what is he ~?*** wie ist er?; ***that is just ~ him!*** das sieht ihm ähnlich!; **2.** *der, die, das* Gleiche; ***his ~*** seinesgleichen; ***the ~*** dergleichen; ***the ~s of you*** Leute wie du
**like·li·hood** Wahrscheinlichkeit *f*
**like·ly 1.** *adj* wahrscheinlich; geeignet; **2.** *adv* wahrscheinlich; ***not ~!*** F bestimmt nicht!
**like·ness** Ähnlichkeit *f*; Abbild *n*
**like·wise** ebenso
**lik·ing** Vorliebe *f*
**li·lac 1.** lila; **2.** BOT Flieder *m*
**lil·y** BOT Lilie *f*
**lil·y of the val·ley** BOT Maiglöckchen *n*
**limb** ANAT (*Körper*)Glied *n*; BOT Ast *m*
**lime¹** Kalk *m*
**lime²** BOT Linde *f*; Limone *f*
**lime·light** *fig* Rampenlicht *n*
**lim·it 1.** Limit *n*, Grenze *f*; ***within ~s*** in Grenzen; ***off ~s*** Zutritt verboten (***to*** für); ***that is the ~!*** F das ist der Gipfel!, das ist (doch) die Höhe!; ***go to the ~*** bis zum Äußersten gehen; **2.** beschränken (***to*** auf *acc*)
**lim·i·ta·tion** Beschränkung *f*; *fig* Grenze *f*; JUR Verjährung *f*
**lim·it·ed** beschränkt, begrenzt; ~ (***liability***) ***company*** *Br* ECON Gesellschaft *f* mit beschränkter Haftung
**lim·it·less** grenzenlos
**limp¹ 1.** hinken, humpeln; **2.** Hinken *n*, Humpeln *n*
**limp²** schlaff, schlapp, F lappig
**line¹ 1.** Linie *f*, Strich *m*; Zeile *f*; Falte *f*, Runzel *f*; Reihe *f*; (Menschen-, *a.* Auto)Schlange *f*; (Abstammungs)Linie *f*; (*Verkehrs-*, *Eisenbahn- etc*)Linie *f*, Strecke *f*; (*Flug- etc*)Gesellschaft *f*; *esp* TEL Leitung *f*; MIL Linie *f*; Fach *n*, Gebiet *n*, Branche *f*; SPORT (*Ziel- etc*)Linie *f*; Leine *f*; Schnur *f*; Linie *f*, Richtung *f*; *fig* Grenze *f*; *pl* THEA Rolle *f*, Text *m*; ***the ~*** der Äquator; ***draw the ~*** Halt machen, die Grenze ziehen (***at*** bei); ***the ~ is busy*** *or* ***engaged*** TEL die Leitung ist besetzt; ***hold the ~*** TEL bleiben Sie am Apparat; ***stand in ~*** anstehen, Schlange stehen (***for*** um, nach); **2.** lin(i)ieren; *Gesicht* zeichnen, (zer)furchen; *Straße etc* säumen; ***~ up*** (sich) in e-r Reihe *or* Linie aufstellen, SPORT sich aufstellen; sich anstellen (***for*** um, nach)
**line²** *Kleid etc* füttern; TECH auskleiden, ausschlagen; MOT *Bremsen etc* belegen
**lin·e·ar** linear; Längen...
**lin·en 1.** Leinen *n*; (*Bett-*, *Tisch- etc* -) Wäsche *f*; **2.** leinen, Leinen...
**lin·en| clos·et**, *Br* ~ **cup·board** Wäscheschrank *m*
**lin·er** MAR Linienschiff *n*; AVIAT Verkehrsflugzeug *n*
**lines·man** SPORT Linienrichter *m*
**lines·wom·an** SPORT Linienrichterin *f*
**line-up** SPORT Aufstellung *f*; Gegenüberstellung *f* (zur Identifizierung)
**lin·ger** verweilen, sich aufhalten; *a.* ***~ on*** dahinsiechen; ***~ on*** noch dableiben; *fig* fortleben
**lin·ge·rie** Damenunterwäsche *f*
**lin·ing** Futter(stoff *m*) *n*; TECH Auskleidung *f*; MOT (*Brems- etc*)Belag *m*
**link 1.** (Ketten)Glied *n*; Manschettenknopf *m*; *fig* (Binde)Glied *n*, Verbindung *f*; **2.** *a.* ***~ up*** (sich) verbinden
**links** → ***golf links***
**link·up** Verbindung *f*
**lin·seed** BOT Leinsamen *m*
**lin·seed oil** Leinöl *n*
**li·on** ZO Löwe *m*
**li·on·ess** ZO Löwin *f*
**lip** ANAT Lippe *f*; (*Tassen- etc*)Rand *m*; F Unverschämtheit *f*
**lip·stick** Lippenstift *m*
**liq·ue·fy** (sich) verflüssigen
**liq·uid 1.** Flüssigkeit *f*; **2.** flüssig
**liq·ui·date** liquidieren (*a.* ECON); *Schulden* tilgen
**liq·uid·ize** zerkleinern, pürieren
**liq·uid·iz·er** Mixgerät *n*, Mixer *m*
**liq·uor** *Br* alkoholische Getränke *pl*, Alkohol *m*; Schnaps *m*, Spirituosen *pl*
**liq·uo·rice** *Br* → ***licorice***
**lisp 1.** lispeln; **2.** Lispeln *n*

**list 1.** Liste *f*, Verzeichnis *n*; MAR Schlagseite *f*; **2.** (in e-e Liste) eintragen, erfassen; MAR ***be ~ing*** Schlagseite haben
**lis·ten** hören; ***~ in*** Radio hören; ***~ in to*** *et.* im Radio (an)hören; ***~ in on*** *Telefongespräch etc* abhören *or* mithören; ***~ to*** anhören (*acc*), zuhören (*dat*); hören auf (*acc*)
**lis·ten·er** Zuhörer(in); (Rundfunk)Hörer(in)
**list·less** teilnahmslos, lustlos
**li·ter** Liter *m*, *n*
**lit·e·ral** (wort)wörtlich; genau; prosaisch
**lit·e·ra·ry** literarisch, Literatur...
**lit·e·ra·ture** Literatur *f*
**lithe** geschmeidig, gelenkig
**li·tre** *Br* → ***liter***
**lit·ter 1.** (*esp Papier*)Abfall *m*; AGR Streu *f*; ZO Wurf *m*; Trage *f*; Sänfte *f*; **2.** *et.* herumliegen lassen in (*dat*) *or* auf (*dat*); ***be ~ed with*** übersät sein mit
**lit·ter| bas·ket, ~ bin** Abfallkorb *m*
**lit·tle 1.** *adj* klein; wenig; ***the ~ ones*** die Kleinen *pl*; **2.** *adv* wenig, kaum; **3.** Kleinigkeit *f*; ***a ~*** ein wenig, ein bisschen; ***~ by ~*** (ganz) allmählich, nach und nach; ***not a ~*** nicht wenig
**live[1]** leben; wohnen (***with*** bei); ***~ to see*** erleben; ***~ on*** leben von; weiterleben; ***~ up to*** *s-n Grundsätzen etc* gemäß leben; *Erwartungen etc* entsprechen; ***~ with*** mit *j-m* zusammenleben; mit *et.* leben
**live[2] 1.** *adj* lebend, lebendig; richtig, echt; ELECTR Strom führend; *radio*, TV Direkt..., Live-...; **2.** *adv* direkt, original, live
**live·li·hood** (Lebens)Unterhalt *m*
**live·li·ness** Lebhaftigkeit *f*
**live·ly** lebhaft, lebendig; aufregend
**liv·er** ANAT Leber *f* (*a.* GASTR)
**liv·e·ry** Livree *f*
**live·stock** Vieh *n*, Viehbestand *m*
**liv·id** bläulich; F fuchsteufelswild
**liv·ing 1.** lebend; ***the ~ image of*** das genaue Ebenbild (*gen*); **2.** Leben *n*, Lebensweise *f*; Lebensunterhalt *m*; ***the ~*** die Lebenden *pl*; ***standard of ~*** Lebensstandard *m*; ***earn or make a ~*** (sich) s-n Lebensunterhalt verdienen
**liv·ing room** Wohnzimmer *n*
**liz·ard** ZO Eidechse *f*
**load 1.** Last *f* (*a. fig*); Ladung *f*; Belastung *f*; **2.** *j-n* überhäufen (***with*** mit); *Schusswaffe* laden; ***~ a camera*** e-n Film einlegen; *a.* ***~ up*** (auf-, be-, ein)laden
**loaf[1]** Laib *m* (Brot); Brot *n*
**loaf[2]** *a.* ***~ about, ~ around*** F herumlungern
**loaf·er** Müßiggänger(in)
**loam** Lehm *m*; **loam·y** lehmig
**loan 1.** (Ver)Leihen *n*; ECON Kredit *m*, Darlehen *n*; Leihgabe *f*; ***on ~*** leihweise; **2.** ***~ s.o. s.th., ~ s.th. to s.o.*** j-m et. (aus)leihen; et. an j-n verleihen
**loan shark** ECON Kredithai *m*
**loath: *be ~ to do s.th.*** et. nur (sehr) ungern tun
**loathe** verabscheuen, hassen
**loath·ing** Abscheu *m*
**lob** *esp tennis*: Lob *m*
**lob·by 1.** Vorhalle *f*; THEA, *film*: Foyer *n*; Wandelhalle *f*; POL Lobby *f*, Interessengruppe *f*; **2.** POL *Abgeordnete etc* beeinflussen
**lobe** ANAT, BOT Lappen *m*
**lob·ster** ZO Hummer *m*
**lo·cal 1.** örtlich, Orts..., lokal, Lokal...; **2.** Ortsansässige *m*, *f*, Einheimische *m*, *f*; *Br* F Stammkneipe *f*; **~ call** TEL Ortsgespräch *n*; **~ e·lec·tions** POL Kommunalwahlen *pl*; **~ gov·ern·ment** Gemeindeverwaltung *f*; **~ time** Ortszeit *f*; **~ traf·fic** Orts-, Nahverkehr *m*
**lo·cate** ausfindig machen; orten; ***be ~d*** gelegen sein, liegen, sich befinden
**lo·ca·tion** Lage *f*; Standort *m*; Platz *m* (***for*** für); *film*, TV Gelände *n* für Außenaufnahmen; ***on ~*** auf Außenaufnahme
**lock[1] 1.** (*Tür-*, *Gewehr- etc*)Schloss *n*; Schleuse(nkammer) *f*; Verschluss *m*; Sperrvorrichtung *f*; **2.** *v/t* zu-, verschließen, zu-, versperren (*a.* ***~ up***); umschlingen, umfassen; TECH sperren; *v/i* schließen; abschließbar *or* verschließbar sein; MOT *etc* blockieren; ***~ away*** wegschließen; ***~ in*** einschließen, einsperren; ***~ out*** aussperren; ***~ up*** abschließen; wegschließen; einsperren
**lock[2]** (Haar)Locke *f*
**lock·er** Spind *m*, Schrank *m*; Schließfach *n*; **~ room** *esp* SPORT Umkleidekabine *f*, Umkleideraum *m*
**lock·et** Medaillon *n*
**lock·out** ECON Aussperrung *f*
**lock·smith** Schlosser *m*
**lock·up** Arrestzelle *f*

**lo·cust** zo Heuschrecke *f*
**lodge 1.** Portier-, Pförtnerloge *f*; (*Jagd-, Ski- etc*)Hütte *f*; Sommer-, Gartenhaus *n*; (*Freimaurer*)Loge *f*; **2.** *v/i* logieren, (*esp* vorübergehend *or* in Untermiete) wohnen; stecken (bleiben) (*bullet etc*); *v/t* aufnehmen, beherbergen, (für die Nacht) unterbringen; *Beschwerde etc* einreichen; *Berufung, Protest* einlegen
**lodg·er** Untermieter(in); **lodg·ing** Unterkunft *f*; *pl esp* möbliertes Zimmer
**loft** (Dach)Boden *m*; Heuboden *m*; Empore *f*; (***converted***) ~ Loft *m*, Fabriketage *f*
**loft·y** hoch; erhaben; stolz, hochmütig
**log** (Holz)Klotz *m*; (*gefällter*) Baumstamm; (Holz)Scheit *n*; → **log·book** MAR Logbuch *n*; AVIAT Bordbuch *n*; MOT Fahrtenbuch *n*
**log cab·in** Blockhaus *n*, Blockhütte *f*
**log·ger·heads: *be at*** ~ sich streiten, sich in den Haaren liegen (***with*** mit)
**lo·gic** Logik *f*; **lo·gic·al** logisch
**loin** GASTR Lende(nstück *n*) *f*; *pl* ANAT Lende *f*
**loi·ter** trödeln; herumlungern
**loll** hängen (*head*), heraushängen (*tongue*); ~ ***around*** *or* ***about*** F sich rekeln *or* lümmeln
**lol·li·pop** GASTR Lutscher *m*; *esp Br* Eis *n* am Stiel; ~ ***man*** *Br* Schülerlotse *m*; ~ ***woman,*** ~ ***lady*** *Br* Schülerlotsin *f*
**lol·ly** GASTR F Lutscher *m*; ***ice*** ~ Eis *n* am Stiel
**lone·li·ness** Einsamkeit *f*
**lone·ly** einsam; ***become*** ~ vereinsamen
**lone·some** einsam
**long**[1] **1.** *adj* lang; weit; langfristig; **2.** *adv* lang(e); ***as*** *or* ***so*** ~ ***as*** solange wie; vorausgesetzt, dass; ~ ***ago*** vor langer Zeit; ***so*** ~*!* F bis dann!, tschüs(s)!; **3.** (e-e) lange Zeit; ***for*** ~ lange; ***take*** ~ lange brauchen *or* dauern
**long**[2] sich sehnen (***for*** nach)
**long-dis·tance** Fern..., Langstrecken...; ~ **call** TEL Ferngespräch *n*; ~ **run·ner** SPORT Langstreckenläufer(in)
**long·hand** Schreibschrift *f*
**long·ing 1.** sehnsüchtig; **2.** Sehnsucht *f*, Verlangen *n*
**lon·gi·tude** GEOGR Länge *f*
**long johns** lange Unterhose
**long jump** SPORT Weitsprung *m*
**long-life milk** *esp Br* H-Milch *f*
**long-play·er, long-play·ing rec·ord** Langspielplatte *f*
**long-range** MIL, AVIAT Fern..., Langstrecken...; langfristig
**long·shore·man** Dock-, Hafenarbeiter *m*
**long·sight·ed** *esp Br* weitsichtig, *fig a.* weitblickend
**long-stand·ing** seit langer Zeit bestehend; alt
**long-term** langfristig, auf lange Sicht
**long wave** ELECTR Langwelle *f*
**long·wear·ing** strapazierfähig
**long·wind·ed** langatmig
**look 1.** sehen, blicken, schauen (***at, on*** auf *acc*, nach); nachschauen, nachsehen; *krank etc* aussehen; nach *e-r Richtung* liegen, gehen (*window etc*); ~ ***here!*** schau mal (her); hör mal (zu)!; ~ ***like*** aussehen wie; ***it*** ~***s as if*** es sieht (so) aus, als ob; ~ ***after*** aufpassen auf (*acc*); sich kümmern um, sorgen für, *den Haushalt etc* versehen; ~ ***ahead*** nach vorne sehen; *fig* vorausschauen; ~ ***around*** sich umsehen; ~ ***at*** ansehen; ~ ***back*** sich umsehen; *fig* zurückblicken; ~ ***down*** herab-, heruntersehen (*a. fig* ***on s.o.*** auf j-n); ~ ***for*** suchen; ~ ***forward to*** sich freuen auf (*acc*); ~ ***in*** F hereinschauen (***on*** bei); ~ ***into*** untersuchen, prüfen; ~ ***on*** zusehen, zuschauen (*dat*); betrachten, ansehen (***as*** als); ~ ***onto*** liegen zu, (hinaus)gehen auf (*acc*) (*window etc*); ~ ***out*** hinaus-, heraussehen; aufpassen, sich vorsehen; ausschauen *or* Ausschau halten (***for*** nach); ~ ***over*** *et.* durchsehen; *j-n* mustern; ~ ***round*** sich umsehen; ~ ***through*** *et.* durchsehen; ~ ***up*** aufblicken, aufsehen; *et.* nachschlagen; *j-n* aufsuchen; **2.** Blick *m*; Miene *f*, (Gesichts)Ausdruck *m*; (***good***) ~***s*** gutes Aussehen; ***have a*** ~ ***at s.th.*** sich et. ansehen; ***I don't like the*** ~ ***of it*** es gefällt mir nicht
**look·ing glass** Spiegel *m*
**look·out** Ausguck *m*; Ausschau *f*; *fig* F Aussicht(en *pl*) *f*; ***be on the*** ~ ***for*** Ausschau halten nach; ***that's his own*** ~ F das ist allein seine Sache
**loom**[1] Webstuhl *m*
**loom**[2] *a.* ~ ***up*** undeutlich sichtbar werden *or* auftauchen
**loop 1.** Schlinge *f*, Schleife *f*; Schlaufe *f*;

Öse *f*; AVIAT Looping *m, n*; EDP Schleife *f*; **2.** (sich) schlingen
**loop·hole** MIL Schießscharte *f*; *fig* Hintertürchen *n*; ***a ~ in the law*** e-e Gesetzeslücke
**loose 1.** los(e); locker; weit; frei; ***let ~*** loslassen; freilassen; **2.** ***be on the ~*** frei herumlaufen
**loos·en** (sich) lösen *or* lockern; ***~ up*** SPORT Lockerungsübungen machen
**loot 1.** Beute *f*; **2.** plündern
**lop** *Baum* beschneiden, stutzen; ***~ off*** abhauen, abhacken
**lop·sid·ed** schief; *fig* einseitig
**lord** Herr *m*, Gebieter *m*; *Br* Lord *m*; ***the Lord*** REL Gott *m* (der Herr); ***the Lord's Prayer*** REL das Vaterunser; ***the Lord's Supper*** REL das (heilige) Abendmahl; ***House of Lords*** *Br* POL Oberhaus *n*
**Lord Mayor** *Br* Oberbürgermeister *m*
**lor·ry** *Br* MOT Last(kraft)wagen *m*, Lastauto *n*, Laster *m*
**lose** verlieren; verpassen, versäumen; nachgehen (*watch*); ***~ o.s.*** sich verirren; sich verlieren; **los·er** Verlierer(in); **loss** Verlust *m*; Schaden *m*; ***at a ~*** ECON mit Verlust; ***be at a ~*** in Verlegenheit sein (***for*** um); **lost** verloren; ***be ~*** sich verirrt haben, sich nicht mehr zurechtfinden (*a. fig*); ***be ~ in thought*** in Gedanken versunken sein; ***get ~*** sich verirren; ***get ~!*** *sl* hau ab!
**lost-and-found (of·fice),** *Br* **lost prop·er·ty of·fice** Fundbüro *n*
**lot** Los *n*; Parzelle *f*; Grundstück *n*; ECON Partie *f*, Posten *m*; Gruppe *f*, Gesellschaft *f*; Menge *f*, Haufen *m*; Los *n*, Schicksal *n*; ***the ~*** alles, das Ganze; ***a ~ of*** F, ***~s of*** F viel, e-e Menge; ***a bad ~*** F ein übler Kerl; ***cast or draw ~s*** losen
**loth** → ***loath***
**lo·tion** Lotion *f*
**lot·te·ry** Lotterie *f*
**loud** laut; *fig* schreiend, grell
**loud·mouth** *contp* Schwätzer *m*
**loud·speak·er** Lautsprecher *m*
**lounge 1.** Wohnzimmer *n*; Aufenthaltsraum *m*, Lounge *f* (*a.* AVIAT); Wartehalle *f*; **2.** F *contp* sich flegeln; ***~ about, ~ around*** herumlungern
**louse** ZO Laus *f*
**lou·sy** verlaust; F miserabel, saumäßig
**lout** Flegel *m*, Lümmel *m*, Rüpel *m*
**lov·a·ble** liebenswert; reizend
**love 1.** Liebe *f* (***of, for, to, towards*** zu); Liebling *m*, Schatz *m*; *tennis*: null; ***be in ~ with s.o.*** in j-n verliebt sein; ***fall in ~ with s.o.*** sich in j-n verlieben; ***make ~*** sich lieben, miteinander schlafen; ***give my ~ to her*** grüße sie herzlich von mir; ***send one's ~ to*** *j-n* grüßen lassen; ***~ from ...*** herzliche Grüße von ...; **2.** lieben; gern mögen
**love af·fair** Liebesaffäre *f*
**love·ly** (wunder)schön; nett, reizend; F prima
**lov·er** Liebhaber *m*, Geliebte *m, f*; (*Musik- etc*)Liebhaber(in), (-)Freund(in); *pl* Liebende *pl*, Liebespaar *n*
**lov·ing** liebevoll, liebend
**low 1.** *adj* niedrig (*a. fig*); tief (*a. fig*); knapp (*supplies etc*); gedämpft, schwach (*light*); tief (*sound*); leise (*sound, voice*); *fig* gering(schätzig); ordinär; niedergeschlagen, deprimiert; **2.** *adv* niedrig; tief (*a. fig*); leise; **3.** METEOR Tief(druckgebiet) *n*; *fig* Tief(punkt *m*) *n*
**low·brow** F **1.** geistig Anspruchslose *m, f*, Unbedarfte *m, f*; **2.** geistig anspruchslos, unbedarft
**low-cal·o·rie** kalorienarm, -reduziert
**low-e·mis·sion** schadstoffarm
**low·er 1.** niedriger; tiefer; untere(r, -s), Unter...; **2.** niedriger machen; herab-, herunterlassen; *Augen, Stimme, Preis etc* senken; *Standard* herabsetzen; *fig* erniedrigen
**low-fat** fettarm
**low-fly·ing plane** AVIAT Tiefflieger *m*
**low·land** Tief-, Flachland *n*
**low·ly** niedrig
**low-necked** (tief) ausgeschnitten
**low-pitched** MUS tief
**low-pres·sure** METEOR Tiefdruck...; TECH Niederdruck...
**low-rise** ARCH niedrig (gebaut)
**low-spir·it·ed** niedergeschlagen
**low tide** Ebbe *f*
**low wa·ter** Niedrigwasser *n*
**loy·al** loyal, treu
**loy·al·ty** Loyalität *f*, Treue *f*
**loz·enge** MATH Raute *f*, Rhombus *m*; GASTR Pastille *f*
**lu·bri·cant** TECH Schmiermittel *n*
**lu·bri·cate** TECH schmieren, ölen
**lu·bri·ca·tion** TECH Schmieren *n*, Ölen *n*
**lu·cid** klar

**luck** Schicksal *n*; Glück *n*; ***bad ~, hard ~, ill ~*** Unglück *n*, Pech *n*; ***good ~*** Glück *n*; ***good ~!*** viel Glück!; ***be in*** (***out of***) ***~*** (kein) Glück haben

**luck·i·ly** glücklicherweise, zum Glück

**luck·y** glücklich, Glücks...; ***be ~*** Glück haben; ***~ day*** Glückstag *m*; ***~ fellow*** Glückspilz *m*

**lu·cra·tive** einträglich, lukrativ

**lu·di·crous** lächerlich

**lug** zerren, schleppen

**luge** SPORT Rennrodeln *n*; Rennrodel *m*, Rennschlitten *m*

**lug·gage** *esp Br* (Reise)Gepäck *n*; **~ rack** *esp Br* RAIL *etc* Gepäcknetz *n*, Gepäckablage *f*; **~ van** *Br* RAIL Gepäckwagen *m*

**luke·warm** lau(warm); *fig* lau, mäßig, halbherzig

**lull 1.** beruhigen; sich legen (*storm*); *mst* ***~ to sleep*** einlullen; **2.** Pause *f*; MAR Flaute *f* (*a. fig*)

**lul·la·by** Wiegenlied *n*

**lum·ba·go** MED Hexenschuss *m*

**lum·ber**[1] schwerfällig gehen; (dahin-) rumpeln (*vehicle*)

**lum·ber**[2] **1.** Bau-, Nutzholz *n*; *esp Br* Gerümpel *n*; **2.** *v/t* ***~ s.o. with s.th.*** *Br* F j-m et. aufhalsen

**lum·ber·jack** Holzfäller *m*, -arbeiter *m*

**lum·ber mill** Sägewerk *n*

**lum·ber room** *esp Br* Rumpelkammer *f*

**lum·ber·yard** Holzplatz *m*, Holzlager *n*

**lu·mi·na·ry** *fig* Leuchte *f*, Koryphäe *f*

**lu·mi·nous** leuchtend, Leucht...

**lu·mi·nous di·splay** Leuchtanzeige *f*

**lu·mi·nous paint** Leuchtfarbe *f*

**lump 1.** Klumpen *m*; Schwellung *f*, Beule *f*; MED Geschwulst *f*, Knoten *m*; GASTR Stück *n*; ***in the ~*** in Bausch und Bogen, pauschal; **2.** *v/t*: ***~ together*** *fig* zusammenwerfen; in e-n Topf werfen; *v/i* Klumpen bilden, klumpen

**lump sug·ar** Würfelzucker *m*

**lump sum** Pauschalsumme *f*

**lump·y** klumpig

**lu·na·cy** Wahnsinn *m*

**lu·nar** ASTR Mond...

**lu·nar mod·ule** Mond(lande)fähre *f*

**lu·na·tic** *fig* **1.** wahnsinnig, verrückt; **2.** Wahnsinnige *m, f*, Verrückte *m, f*

**lunch,** *formal* **lun·cheon 1.** Lunch *m*, Mittagessen *n*; **2.** zu Mittag essen

**lunch hour, lunch time** Mittagszeit *f*, Mittagspause *f*

**lung** ANAT Lungenflügel *m*; *pl* die Lunge

**lunge** sich stürzen (***at*** auf *acc*)

**lurch 1.** taumeln, torkeln; **2.** ***leave s.o. in the ~*** j-n im Stich lassen, F j-n sitzen lassen

**lure 1.** Köder *m*; *fig* Lockung *f*; **2.** ködern, (an)locken

**lu·rid** grell; grässlich, schauerlich

**lurk** lauern; ***~ about, ~ around*** herumschleichen

**lus·cious** köstlich, lecker; üppig; F knackig

**lush** saftig, üppig

**lust 1.** sinnliche Begierde, Lust *f*; Gier *f*; **2.** ***~ after, ~ for*** begehren; gierig sein nach

**lus·ter,** *Br* **lus·tre** Glanz *m*, Schimmer *m*; **lus·trous** glänzend, schimmernd

**lust·y** kräftig, robust, vital

**lute** MUS Laute *f*

**Lu·ther·an** REL lutherisch

**lux·u·ri·ant** üppig

**lux·u·ri·ate** schwelgen (***in*** in *dat*)

**lux·u·ri·ous** luxuriös, Luxus...

**lux·u·ry 1.** Luxus *m*; Komfort *m*; Luxusartikel *m*; **2.** Luxus...

**lye** Lauge *f*

**ly·ing** lügnerisch, verlogen

**lymph** MED Lymphe *f*

**lynch** lynchen; **~ law** Lynchjustiz *f*

**lynx** ZO Luchs *m*

**lyr·ic 1.** lyrisch; **2.** lyrisches Gedicht; *pl* Lyrik *f*; (Lied)Text *m*

**lyr·i·cal** lyrisch, gefühlvoll; schwärmerisch

# M

**M, m** M, m *n*
**M** ABBR *of* ***medium*** (***size***) mittelgroß
**ma** F Mama *f*, Mutti *f*
**ma'am** → ***madam***
**ma·cad·am** Asphalt *m*
**mac·a·ro·ni** Makkaroni *pl*
**ma·chine 1.** Maschine *f*; **2.** maschinell herstellen
**ma·chine·gun** Maschinengewehr *n*
**ma·chine-read·a·ble** EDP maschinenlesbar
**ma·chin·e·ry** Maschinen *pl*; Maschinerie *f*
**ma·chin·ist** TECH Maschinist *m*
**mach·o** *contp* Macho *m*
**mack·e·rel** ZO Makrele *f*
**mac·ro...** Makro..., (sehr) groß
**mad** wahnsinnig, verrückt; VET tollwütig; F wütend; *fig* ***be ~ about*** wild *or* versessen sein auf (*acc*), verrückt sein nach; ***drive s.o. ~*** j-n verrückt machen; ***go ~*** verrückt werden; ***like ~*** wie verrückt
**mad·am** gnädige Frau
**mad·cap** verrückt
**mad cow dis·ease** VET Rinderwahn(sinn) *m*
**mad·den** verrückt *or* rasend machen
**mad·den·ing** unerträglich; verrückt *or* rasend machend
**made:** ***~ of gold*** aus Gold
**made-to-meas·ure** maßgeschneidert
**made-up** geschminkt; erfunden
**mad·house** *fig* F Irrenhaus *n*
**mad·ly** wie verrückt; F wahnsinnig, schrecklich
**mad·man** Verrückte *m*
**mad·ness** Wahnsinn
**mad·wom·an** Verrückte *f*
**mag·a·zine** Magazin *n* (*a.* PHOT, MIL), Zeitschrift *f*; Lagerhaus *n*
**mag·got** ZO Made *f*
**Ma·gi:** ***the*** (***three***) ~ die (drei) Weisen aus dem Morgenland, die Heiligen Drei Könige
**ma·gic 1.** Magie *f*, Zauberei *f*; Zauber *m*; *fig* Wunder *n*; **2.** *a.* ***magical*** magisch, Zauber...
**ma·gi·cian** Magier *m*, Zauberer *m*; Zauberkünstler *m*
**ma·gis·trate** (Friedens)Richter(in)
**mag·na·nim·i·ty** Großmut *f*
**mag·nan·i·mous** großmütig
**mag·net** Magnet *m*
**mag·net·ic** magnetisch, Magnet...
**mag·nif·i·cent** großartig, prächtig
**mag·ni·fy** vergrößern
**mag·ni·fy·ing glass** Vergrößerungsglas *n*, Lupe *f*
**mag·ni·tude** Größe *f*; Wichtigkeit *f*
**mag·pie** ZO Elster *f*
**ma·hog·a·ny** Mahagoni(holz) *n*
**maid** (Dienst)Mädchen *n*, Hausangestellte *f*; ***~ of all work*** *esp fig* Mädchen *n* für alles; ***~ of hono(u)r*** Hofdame *f*; (erste) Brautjungfer
**maid·en** Jungfern..., Erstlings...
**maid·en name** Mädchenname *m*
**mail 1.** Post(sendung) *f*; ***by ~*** mit der Post; **2.** mit der Post (zu)schicken, aufgeben, *Brief* einwerfen
**mail·bag** Postsack *m*; Posttasche *f*
**mail·box** Briefkasten *m*
**mail car·ri·er, mail·man** Briefträger *m*, Postbote *m*
**mail or·der** Bestellung *f* bei e-m Versandhaus
**mail-or·der| firm, ~ house** Versandhaus *n*
**maim** verstümmeln
**main 1.** Haupt..., wichtigste(r, -s); hauptsächlich; ***by ~ force*** mit äußerster Kraft; **2.** *mst pl* Hauptleitung *f*, Hauptgas-, Hauptwasser-, Hauptstromleitung *f*; (Strom)Netz *n*; ***in the ~*** in der Hauptsache, im Wesentlichen
**main·frame** EDP Großrechner *m*
**main·land** Festland *n*
**main·ly** hauptsächlich
**main mem·o·ry** EDP Hauptspeicher *m*; Arbeitsspeicher *m*
**main men·u** EDP Hauptmenü *n*
**main road** Haupt(verkehrs)straße *f*
**main·spring** TECH Hauptfeder *f*; *fig* (Haupt)Triebfeder *f*
**main·stay** *fig* Hauptstütze *f*
**main street** Hauptstraße *f*
**main·tain** (aufrecht)erhalten, beibehalten; instand halten, pflegen, TECH *a.* warten; *Familie etc* unterhalten, versorgen; *et.* behaupten

**main·te·nance** (Aufrecht)Erhaltung *f*; Instandhaltung *f*, Pflege *f*, TECH *a.* Wartung *f*; Unterhalt *m*

**maize** *esp Br* BOT Mais *m*

**ma·jes·tic** majestätisch

**ma·jes·ty** Majestät *f*; ***His*** (***Her, Your***) ***Majesty*** Seine (Ihre, Eure) Majestät

**ma·jor 1.** größere(r, -s), *fig a.* bedeutend, wichtig; JUR volljährig; ***C ~*** MUS C-Dur *n*; **2.** MIL Major *m*; JUR Volljährige *m,f*; UNIV Hauptfach *n*; MUS Dur *n*; **~ gen·e·ral** MIL Generalmajor *m*

**ma·jor·i·ty** Mehrheit *f*, Mehrzahl *f*; JUR Volljährigkeit *f*

**ma·jor league** *baseball*: oberste Spielklasse

**ma·jor road** Haupt(verkehrs)straße *f*

**make 1.** machen; anfertigen, herstellen, erzeugen; (zu)bereiten; (er)schaffen; ergeben, bilden; machen zu; ernennen zu; *Geld* verdienen; sich erweisen als, abgeben (*person*); schätzen auf (*acc*); *Geschwindigkeit* erreichen; *Fehler* machen; *Frieden etc* schließen; *e-e Rede* halten; F *Strecke* zurücklegen; *with inf*: *j-n* lassen, veranlassen zu, bringen zu, zwingen zu; ***~ it*** es schaffen; ***~ do with s.th.*** mit et. auskommen, sich mit et. behelfen; ***do you ~ one of us?*** machen Sie mit?; ***what do you ~ of it?*** was halten Sie davon?; ***~ believe*** vorgeben; ***~ friends with*** sich anfreunden mit; ***~ good*** wieder gutmachen; *Versprechen etc* halten; ***~ haste*** sich beeilen; ***~ way*** Platz machen; ***~ for*** zugehen auf (*acc*); sich aufmachen nach; ***~ into*** verarbeiten zu; ***~ off*** sich davonmachen, sich aus dem Staub machen; ***~ out*** *Rechnung, Scheck etc* ausstellen; ausmachen, erkennen; aus *j-m, e-r Sache* klug werden; ***~ over*** *Eigentum* übertragen; ***~ up*** *et.* zusammenstellen; sich *et.* ausdenken, *et.* erfinden; (sich) zurechtmachen *or* schminken; ***~ it up*** sich versöhnen *or* wieder vertragen (***with*** mit); ***~ up one's mind*** sich entschließen; ***be made up of*** bestehen aus, sich zusammensetzen aus; ***~ up for*** nachholen, aufholen; für *et.* entschädigen; **2.** Machart *f*, Bauart *f*; Fabrikat *n*, Marke *f*

**make-be·lieve** Schein *m*, Fantasie *f*

**mak·er** Hersteller *m*; ***Maker*** REL Schöpfer *m*

**make·shift 1.** Notbehelf *m*; **2.** behelfsmäßig, Behelfs...

**make-up** Make-up *n*, Schminke *f*; Aufmachung *f*; Zusammensetzung *f*

**mak·ing** Erzeugung *f*, Herstellung *f*, Fabrikation *f*; ***be in the ~*** noch in Arbeit sein; ***have the ~s of*** das Zeug haben zu

**mal·ad·just·ed** nicht angepasst, verhaltensgestört, milieugestört

**mal·ad·min·i·stra·tion** schlechte Verwaltung; POL Misswirtschaft *f*

**mal·con·tent 1.** unzufrieden; **2.** Unzufriedene *m,f*

**male 1.** männlich; **2.** Mann *m*; ZO Männchen *n*

**male nurse** (Kranken)Pfleger *m*

**mal·for·ma·tion** Missbildung *f*

**mal·ice** Bosheit *f*; Groll *m*; JUR böse Absicht, Vorsatz *m*

**ma·li·cious** boshaft; böswillig

**ma·lign** verleumden

**ma·lig·nant** bösartig (*a.* MED); boshaft

**mall** Einkaufszentrum *n*

**mal·le·a·ble** TECH verformbar; *fig* formbar

**mal·let** Holzhammer *m*; (Krocket-, Polo)Schläger *m*

**mal·nu·tri·tion** Unterernährung *f*; Fehlernährung *f*

**mal·o·dor·ous** übel riechend

**mal·prac·tice** Vernachlässigung *f* der beruflichen Sorgfalt; MED falsche Behandlung, (ärztlicher) Kunstfehler

**malt** Malz *n*

**mal·treat** schlecht behandeln; misshandeln

**mam·mal** ZO Säugetier *n*

**mam·moth 1.** ZO Mammut *n*; **2.** Mammut..., Riesen..., riesig

**mam·my** F Mami *f*

**man 1.** Mann *m*; Mensch(en *pl*) *m*; Menschheit *f*; F (Ehe)Mann *m*; F Geliebte *m*; (*Schach*)Figur *f*; (*Dame*)Stein *m*; ***the ~ on*** (*Br* ***in***) ***the street*** der Mann auf der Straße; **2.** (*Raum*)*Schiff etc* bemannen; *Büro etc* besetzen

**man·age** *v/t Betrieb etc* leiten, führen; *Künstler, Sportler etc* managen; *et.* zustande bringen; es fertig bringen (***to do*** zu tun); umgehen (können) mit; mit *j-m, et.* fertig werden; F *Arbeit, Essen etc* bewältigen, schaffen; *v/i* auskommen (***with*** mit; ***without*** ohne); F es

M

schaffen, zurechtkommen; F es einrichten, es ermöglichen
**man·age·a·ble** handlich; lenksam
**man·age·ment** Verwaltung *f*; ECON Management *n*, Unternehmensführung *f*; Geschäftsleitung *f*, Direktion *f*
**man·ag·er** Verwalter *m*; ECON Manager *m* (*a.* THEA *etc*); Geschäftsführer *m*, Leiter *m*, Direktor *m*; SPORT (Chef-) Trainer *m*; ***be a good ~*** gut *or* sparsam wirtschaften können
**man·a·ge·ri·al** ECON geschäftsführend, leitend; ***~ position*** leitende Stellung; ***~ staff*** leitende Angestellte *pl*
**man·ag·ing** ECON geschäftsführend, leitend; **~ di·rec·tor** Generaldirektor *m*, leitender Direktor
**man·date** Mandat *n*; Auftrag *m*; Vollmacht *f*
**man·da·to·ry** obligatorisch, zwingend
**mane** ZO Mähne *f* (*a.* F)
**ma·neu·ver** *a. fig* **1.** Manöver *n*; **2.** manövrieren
**mange** VET Räude *f*
**man·ger** AGR Krippe *f*
**man·gle 1.** (Wäsche)Mangel *f*; **2.** mangeln; *j-n* übel zurichten, zerfleischen; *fig Text* verstümmeln
**mang·y** VET räudig; *fig* schäbig
**man·hood** Mannesalter *n*; Männlichkeit *f*
**ma·ni·a** Wahnsinn *m*; *fig* (***for***) Sucht *f* (nach), Leidenschaft *f* (für), Manie *f*, Fimmel *m*; **ma·ni·ac** F Wahnsinnige *m, f*, Verrückte *m, f*; *fig* Fanatiker(in)
**man·i·cure** Maniküre *f*, Handpflege *f*
**man·i·fest 1.** offenkundig; **2.** *v/t* offenbaren, manifestieren
**man·i·fold** mannigfaltig, vielfältig
**ma·nip·u·late** manipulieren; (geschickt) handhaben
**ma·nip·u·la·tion** Manipulation *f*
**man·kind** die Menschheit, die Menschen *pl*
**man·ly** männlich
**man-made** vom Menschen geschaffen, künstlich; ***~ fiber*** Kunstfaser *f*
**man·ner** Art *f* (und Weise *f*); Betragen *n*, Auftreten *n*; *pl* Benehmen *n*, Umgangsformen *pl*, Manieren *pl*; Sitten *pl*
**ma·noeu·vre** *Br* → ***maneuver***
**man·or** *Br* (Land)Gut *n*; → **man·or house** Herrenhaus *n*
**man·pow·er** menschliche Arbeitskraft; Arbeitskräfte *pl*
**man·sion** (herrschaftliches) Wohnhaus
**man·slaugh·ter** JUR Totschlag *m*, fahrlässige Tötung
**man·tel·piece, man·tel·shelf** Kaminsims *m*
**man·u·al 1.** Hand...; mit der Hand (gemacht); **2.** Handbuch *n*
**man·u·fac·ture 1.** erzeugen, herstellen; **2.** Herstellung *f*, Fertigung *f*; Erzeugnis *n*, Fabrikat *n*
**man·u·fac·tur·er** Hersteller *m*, Erzeuger *m*
**man·u·fac·tur·ing** Herstellungs...
**ma·nure** AGR **1.** Dünger *m*, Mist *m*, Dung *m*; **2.** düngen
**man·u·script** Manuskript *n*
**man·y 1.** viel(e); ***~ a*** manche(r, -s), manch eine(r, -s); ***~ times*** oft; ***as ~*** ebenso viel(e); **2.** viele; ***a good ~*** ziemlich viel(e); ***a great ~*** sehr viele
**map 1.** (Land- *etc*)Karte *f*; (Stadt-*etc*)Plan *m*; **2.** e-e Karte machen von; auf e-r Karte eintragen; ***~ out*** *fig* (bis in die Einzelheiten) (voraus)planen
**ma·ple** BOT Ahorn *m*
**mar** beeinträchtigen; verderben
**Mar** ABBR *of* ***March*** März *m*
**mar·a·thon** SPORT **1.** *a.* ***~ race*** Marathonlauf *m*; **2.** Marathon... (*a. fig*)
**ma·raud** plündern
**mar·ble 1.** Marmor *m*; Murmel *f*; **2.** marmorn
**march 1.** marschieren; *fig* fortschreiten; **2.** Marsch *m*; *fig* (Fort)Gang *m*; ***the ~ of events*** der Lauf der Dinge
**March** (ABBR ***Mar***) März *m*
**mare** ZO Stute *f*
**mar·ga·rine,** *Br* F **marge** Margarine *f*
**mar·gin** Rand *m* (*a. fig*); Grenze *f* (*a. fig*); *fig* Spielraum *m*; (*Gewinn-, Verdienst*)Spanne *f*; ***by a wide ~*** mit großem Vorsprung; **mar·gin·al** Rand...; ***~ note*** Randbemerkung *f*
**mar·i·hua·na, mar·i·jua·na** Marihuana *n*
**ma·ri·na** Boots-, Jachthafen *m*
**ma·rine** Marine *f*; MIL Marineinfanterist *m*
**mar·i·ner** Seemann *m*
**mar·i·tal** ehelich, Ehe...
**mar·i·tal sta·tus** Familienstand *m*
**mar·i·time** See...; Küsten...; Schifffahrts...

**mark**[1] (Deutsche) Mark
**mark**[2] **1.** Marke *f*, Markierung *f*; (Kenn)Zeichen *n*, Merkmal *n*; (Körper)Mal *n*; Ziel *n* (*a. fig*); Spur *f* (*a. fig*); Fleck *m*; (*Fabrik-*, *Waren*)Zeichen *n*, (*Schutz-*, *Handels*)Marke *f*; ECON Preisangabe *f*; PED Note *f*, Zensur *f*, Punkt *m*; SPORT Startlinie *f*; *fig* Zeichen *n*; *fig* Norm *f*; ***be up to the ~*** den Anforderungen gewachsen sein (*person*) *or* genügen (*performance etc*); *gesundheitlich* auf der Höhe sein; ***be wide of the ~*** weit danebenschießen; *fig* sich gewaltig irren; weit danebenliegen (*estimate etc*); ***hit the ~*** (das Ziel) treffen; *fig* ins Schwarze treffen; ***miss the ~*** danebenschießen, das Ziel verfehlen (*a. fig*); **2.** markieren, anzeichnen; anzeigen; kennzeichnen; *Waren* auszeichnen; *Preis* festsetzen; Spuren hinterlassen auf (*dat*); Flecken machen auf (*dat*); PED benoten, zensieren; SPORT *Gegenspieler* decken, markieren; ***~ my words*** denk an m-e Worte; ***to ~ the occasion*** zur Feier des Tages; ***~ time*** auf der Stelle treten (*a. fig*); ***~ down*** notieren, vermerken; *im Preis* herabsetzen; ***~ off*** abgrenzen; *auf e-r Liste* abhaken; ***~ out*** *durch Striche etc* markieren; bestimmen (***for*** für); ***~ up*** *im Preis* heraufsetzen
**marked** deutlich, ausgeprägt
**mark·er** Markierstift *m*; Lesezeichen *n*; SPORT Bewacher(in)
**mar·ket 1.** Markt *m*; Marktplatz *m*; (Lebensmittel)Geschäft *n*, Laden *m*; ECON Absatz *m*; (***for***) Nachfrage *f* (nach), Bedarf *m* (an *dat*); ***on the ~*** auf dem Markt *or* im Handel; ***put on the ~*** auf den Markt *or* in den Handel bringen; (zum Verkauf) anbieten; **2.** *v/t* auf den Markt *or* in den Handel bringen; verkaufen, vertreiben
**mar·ket·a·ble** ECON marktgängig
**mar·ket gar·den** *Br* Gemüse- und Obstgärtnerei *f*
**mar·ket·ing** ECON Marketing *n*
**mark·ing** Markierung *f*; zo Zeichnung *f*; SPORT Deckung *f*; ***man-to-man ~*** Manndeckung *f*
**marks·man** guter Schütze
**mar·ma·lade** *esp* Orangenmarmelade *f*
**mar·mot** zo Murmeltier *n*
**ma·roon 1.** kastanienbraun; **2.** *auf e-r einsamen Insel* aussetzen; **3.** Leuchtrakete *f*
**mar·quee** Festzelt *n*
**mar·quis** Marquis *m*
**mar·riage** Heirat *f*, Hochzeit *f* (***to*** mit); Ehe *f*; ***civil ~*** standesamtliche Trauung
**mar·ria·ge·a·ble** heiratsfähig
**mar·riage cer·tif·i·cate** Trauschein *m*, Heiratsurkunde *f*
**mar·ried** verheiratet; ehelich, Ehe...; ***~ couple*** Ehepaar *n*; ***~ life*** Ehe(leben *n*) *f*
**mar·row** ANAT (Knochen)Mark *n*; *fig* Kern *m*, *das* Wesentliche
**mar·ry** *v/t* heiraten; *Paar* trauen; ***be married*** verheiratet sein (***to*** mit); ***get married*** heiraten; sich verheiraten (***to*** mit); *v/i* heiraten
**marsh** Sumpf(land *n*) *m*, Marsch *f*
**mar·shal 1.** MIL Marschall *m*; Bezirkspolizeichef *m*; **2.** ordnen; führen
**marsh·y** sumpfig
**mar·ten** zo Marder *m*
**mar·tial** kriegerisch; Kriegs..., Militär...; **~ arts** asiatische Kampfsportarten *pl*; **~ law** Kriegsrecht *n*
**mar·tyr** REL Märtyrer(in) (*a. fig*)
**mar·vel 1.** Wunder *n*; **2.** sich wundern, staunen; **mar·vel·(l)ous** wunderbar; fabelhaft, fantastisch
**mar·zi·pan** Marzipan *n*, *m*
**mas·ca·ra** Wimperntusche *f*
**mas·cot** Maskottchen *n*
**mas·cu·line** männlich; Männer...; maskulin (*a.* LING)
**mash** zerdrücken, zerquetschen
**mashed po·ta·toes** Kartoffelbrei *m*
**mask 1.** Maske *f* (*a.* EDP); **2.** maskieren; *fig* verbergen, verschleiern
**masked** maskiert; ***~ ball*** Maskenball *m*
**ma·son** Steinmetz *m*; *mst* ***Mason*** Freimaurer *m*; **ma·son·ry** Mauerwerk *n*
**masque** THEA HIST Maskenspiel *n*
**mas·que·rade 1.** Maskerade *f* (*a. fig*); Verkleidung *f*; **2.** sich ausgeben (**as** als, für)
**mass 1.** Masse *f*; Menge *f*; Mehrzahl *f*; ***the ~es*** die (breite) Masse; **2.** (sich) (an)sammeln *or* (an)häufen; **3.** Massen...
**Mass** REL Messe *f*
**mas·sa·cre 1.** Massaker *n*; **2.** niedermetzeln
**mas·sage 1.** Massage *f*; **2.** massieren
**mas·seur** Masseur *m*

**mas·seuse** Masseurin *f*, Masseuse *f*
**mas·sif** (Gebirgs)Massiv *n*
**mas·sive** massiv; groß, gewaltig
**mass me·di·a** Massenmedien *pl*
**mass-pro·duce** serienmäßig herstellen
**mass pro·duc·tion** Massen-, Serienproduktion *f*
**mast** MAR Mast *m*; *Br* ELECTR Sendemast *m*
**mas·ter 1.** Meister *m* (*a.* PAINT); Herr *m*; *esp Br* Lehrer *m*; Original(kopie *f*) *n*; UNIV Magister *m*; ***Master of Arts*** (ABBR ***MA***) Magister *m* Artium; ~ ***of ceremonies*** Conférencier *m*; **2.** Meister...; Haupt...; ~ ***copy*** Originalkopie *f*; ~ ***tape*** TECH Mastertape *n*, Originaltonband *n*; **3.** Herr sein über (*acc*); *Sprache etc* beherrschen; *Aufgabe etc* meistern
**mas·ter key** Hauptschlüssel *m*
**mas·ter·ly** meisterhaft, virtuos
**mas·ter·piece** Meisterstück *n*, -werk *n*
**mas·ter·y** Herrschaft *f*; Oberhand *f*; Beherrschung *f*
**mas·tur·bate** masturbieren, onanieren
**mat[1] 1.** Matte *f*; Untersetzer *m*; **2.** sich verfilzen
**mat[2]** mattiert, matt
**match[1]** Streichholz *n*, Zündholz *n*
**match[2] 1.** *der, die, das* Gleiche; (dazu) passende Sache *or* Person, Gegenstück *n*; (*Fußball- etc*)Spiel *n*, (*Box- etc* -)Kampf *m*, (*Tennis- etc*)Match *n*, *m*; Heirat *f*; *gute etc* Partie (*person*); ***be a*** (***no***) ~ ***for s.o.*** j-m (nicht) gewachsen sein; ***find*** *or* ***meet one's*** ~ s-n Meister finden; **2.** *v/t j-m, e-r Sache* ebenbürtig *or* gewachsen sein, gleichkommen; *j-m, e-r Sache* entsprechen, passen zu; *v/i* zusammenpassen, übereinstimmen, entsprechen; ***gloves to*** ~ dazu passende Handschuhe
**match·box** Streichholz-, Zündholzschachtel *f*
**match·less** unvergleichlich, einzigartig
**match·mak·er** Ehestifter(in)
**match point** *tennis etc*: Matchball *m*
**mate[1]** → ***checkmate***
**mate[2] 1.** (Arbeits)Kamerad *m*, (-)Kollege *m*; ZO Männchen *n*, Weibchen *n*; MAR Maat *m*; **2.** ZO (sich) paaren
**ma·te·ri·al 1.** Material *n*, Stoff *m*; ***writing*** ~***s*** Schreibmaterial(ien *pl*) *n*; **2.** materiell; leiblich; wesentlich
**ma·ter·nal** mütterlich, Mutter...; mütterlicherseits
**ma·ter·ni·ty 1.** Mutterschaft *f*; **2.** Schwangerschafts..., Umstands...
**ma·ter·ni·ty| leave** Mutterschaftsurlaub *m*; ~ **ward** Entbindungsstation *f*
**math** F Mathe *f*
**math·e·ma·ti·cian** Mathematiker *m*
**math·e·mat·ics** Mathematik *f*
**maths** *Br* F Mathe *f*
**mat·i·née** THEA *etc* Nachmittagsvorstellung *f*
**ma·tric·u·late** (sich) immatrikulieren
**mat·ri·mo·ni·al** ehelich, Ehe...
**mat·ri·mo·ny** Ehe *f*, Ehestand *m*
**ma·trix** TECH Matrize *f*
**ma·tron** *Br* MED Oberschwester *f*; Hausmutter *f*; Matrone *f*
**mat·ter 1.** Materie *f*, Material *n*, Substanz *f*, Stoff *m*; MED Eiter *m*; Sache *f*, Angelegenheit *f*; ***printed*** ~ Drucksache *f*; ***what's the*** ~ (***with you***)***?*** was ist los (mit dir)?; ***no*** ~ ***who*** gleichgültig, wer; ***for that*** ~ was das betrifft; ***a*** ~ ***of course*** e-e Selbstverständlichkeit; ***a*** ~ ***of fact*** e-e Tatsache; ***as a*** ~ ***of fact*** tatsächlich, eigentlich; ***a*** ~ ***of form*** e-e Formsache; ***a*** ~ ***of time*** e-e Frage der Zeit; **2.** von Bedeutung sein (***to*** für); ***it doesn't*** ~ es macht nichts
**mat·ter-of-fact** sachlich, nüchtern
**mat·tress** Matratze *f*
**ma·ture 1.** reif (*a. fig*); **2.** (heran)reifen, reif werden
**ma·tu·ri·ty** Reife *f* (*a. fig*)
**maud·lin** rührselig
**maul** übel zurichten; *fig* verreißen
**Maun·dy Thurs·day** Gründonnerstag *m*
**mauve** malvenfarbig, mauve
**mawk·ish** rührselig
**max·i...** Maxi..., riesig, Riesen...
**max·im** Grundsatz *m*
**max·i·mum 1.** Maximum *n*; **2.** maximal, Maximal..., Höchst...
**May** Mai *m*
**may** *v/aux ich* kann/mag/darf *etc*, *du* kannst/magst/darfst *etc*
**may·be** vielleicht
**may·bug** ZO Maikäfer *m*
**May Day** der 1. Mai
**may·on·naise** Mayonnaise *f*
**mayor** Bürgermeister *m*
**may·pole** Maibaum *m*
**maze** Irrgarten *m*, Labyrinth *n* (*a. fig*)

**me** mich; mir; F ich
**mead·ow** Wiese *f*, Weide *f*
**mea·ger,** *Br* **mea·gre** mager (*a. fig*), dürr; dürftig
**meal**[1] Mahl(zeit *f*) *n*; Essen *n*
**meal**[2] Schrotmehl *n*
**mean**[1] gemein, niederträchtig; geizig, knauserig; schäbig
**mean**[2] meinen; sagen wollen; bedeuten; beabsichtigen, vorhaben; ***be meant for*** bestimmt sein für; ~ ***well*** (***ill***) es gut (schlecht) meinen
**mean**[3] **1.** Mitte *f*, Mittel *n*, Durchschnitt *m*; **2.** mittlere(r, -s), Mittel..., durchschnittlich, Durchschnitts...
**mean·ing 1.** Sinn *m*, Bedeutung *f*; **2.** bedeutungsvoll, bedeutsam
**mean·ing·ful** bedeutungsvoll; sinnvoll
**mean·ing·less** sinnlos
**means** Mittel *n or pl*, Weg *m*; ECON Mittel *pl*, Vermögen *n*; ***by all*** ~***s*** auf alle Fälle, unbedingt; ***by no*** ~***s*** keineswegs, auf keinen Fall; ***by*** ~***s of*** durch, mit
**mean·time 1.** inzwischen; **2.** ***in the*** ~ inzwischen
**mean·while** inzwischen
**mea·sles** MED Masern *pl*
**mea·sur·a·ble** messbar
**mea·sure 1.** Maß *n* (*a. fig*); TECH Messgerät *n*; MUS Takt *m*; *fig* Maßnahme *f*; ***beyond*** ~ über alle Maßen; ***in a great*** ~ großenteils; ***take*** ~***s*** Maßnahmen treffen *or* ergreifen; **2.** (ab-, aus-, ver)messen; *j-m* Maß nehmen; ~ ***up to*** den Ansprüchen (*gen*) genügen; **mea·sured** gemessen; wohl überlegt; maßvoll
**mea·sure·ment** (Ver)Messung *f*; Maß *n*; ~ **of ca·pac·i·ty** Hohlmaß *n*
**mea·sur·ing tape** → ***tape measure***
**meat** GASTR Fleisch *n*; ***cold*** ~ kalter Braten
**meat·ball** GASTR Fleischklößchen *n*
**me·chan·ic** Mechaniker *m*
**me·chan·i·cal** mechanisch; Maschinen...
**me·chan·ics** PHYS Mechanik *f*
**mech·a·nism** Mechanismus *m*
**mech·a·nize** mechanisieren
**med·al** Medaille *f*; Orden *m*
**med·al·(l)ist** SPORT Medaillengewinner(in)
**med·dle** sich einmischen (***with, in*** in *acc*); **med·dle·some** aufdringlich
**me·di·a** Medien *pl*
**med·i·ae·val** → ***medieval***
**me·di·an** *a.* ~ ***strip*** MOT Mittelstreifen *m*
**me·di·ate** vermitteln
**me·di·a·tion** Vermittlung *f*
**me·di·a·tor** Vermittler *m*
**med·ic** MIL Sanitäter *m*
**med·i·cal 1.** medizinisch, ärztlich; **2.** ärztliche Untersuchung
**med·i·cal cer·tif·i·cate** ärztliches Attest
**med·i·cated** medizinisch
**me·di·ci·nal** medizinisch, heilkräftig, Heil...
**medi·cine** Medizin *f*, *a.* Arznei *f*, *a.* Heilkunde *f*
**med·i·e·val** mittelalterlich
**me·di·o·cre** mittelmäßig
**med·i·tate** *v/i* (***on***) nachdenken (über *acc*); meditieren (über *acc*); *v/t* erwägen
**med·i·ta·tion** Nachdenken *n*; Meditation *f*
**med·i·ta·tive** nachdenklich
**Med·i·ter·ra·ne·an** Mittelmeer...
**me·di·um 1.** Mitte *f*; Mittel *n*; Medium *n*; **2.** mittlere(r, -s), Mittel..., *a.* mittelmäßig; GASTR medium, halb gar
**med·ley** Gemisch *n*; MUS Medley *n*, Potpourri *n*
**meek** sanft(mütig), bescheiden
**meet** *v/t* treffen, sich treffen mit; begegnen (*dat*); *j-n* kennen lernen; *j-n* abholen; zusammentreffen mit, stoßen *or* treffen auf (*acc*); *Wünschen* entgegenkommen, entsprechen; *e-r Forderung, Verpflichtung* nachkommen; *v/i* zusammenkommen, -treten; sich begegnen, sich treffen; (*feindlich*) zusammenstoßen; SPORT aufeinander treffen; sich kennen lernen; ~ ***with*** zusammentreffen mit; sich treffen mit; stoßen auf (*Schwierigkeiten etc*); erleben, erleiden
**meet·ing** Begegnung *f*, (Zusammen-) Treffen *n*; Versammlung *f*, Konferenz *f*, Tagung *f*; ~ **place** Tagungs-, Versammlungsort *m*; Treffpunkt *m*
**mel·an·chol·y 1.** Melancholie *f*, Schwermut *f*, Trübsinn *m*; **2.** melancholisch, traurig, trübsinnig, wehmütig
**mel·low 1.** reif, weich; sanft, mild (*light*), zart (*colors*); *fig* gereift (*person*); **2.** reifen (lassen) (*a. fig*); weich *or* sanft werden
**me·lo·di·ous** melodisch

**mel·o·dra·mat·ic** melodramatisch
**mel·o·dy** MUS Melodie *f*
**mel·on** BOT Melone *f*
**melt** (zer)schmelzen; *~ **down*** einschmelzen
**mem·ber** Mitglied *n*, Angehörige *m, f*; ANAT Glied *n*, Gliedmaße *f*; (männliches) Glied; ***Member of Parliament*** *Br* Mitglied *n* des Unterhauses, Unterhausabgeordnete *m, f*; **mem·ber·ship** Mitgliedschaft *f*; Mitgliederzahl *f*
**mem·brane** Membran(e) *f*
**mem·o** Memo *n*
**mem·oirs** Memoiren *pl*
**mem·o·ra·ble** denkwürdig
**me·mo·ri·al** Denkmal *n*, Ehrenmal *n*, Gedenkstätte *f* (***to*** für); Gedenkfeier *f* (***to*** für)
**mem·o·rize** auswendig lernen, sich *et.* einprägen
**mem·o·ry** Gedächtnis *n*; Erinnerung *f*; Andenken *n*; EDP Speicher *m*; ***in ~ of*** zum Andenken an (*acc*); *~* **ca·pac·i·ty** EDP Speicherkapazität *f*
**men·ace 1.** (be)drohen; **2.** (Be)Drohung *f*
**mend 1.** *v/t* (ver)bessern; ausbessern, reparieren, flicken; *~ **one's ways*** sich bessern; *v/i* sich bessern; **2.** ausgebesserte Stelle; ***on the*** *~* auf dem Wege der Bess(e)rung
**men·di·cant** REL Bettelmönch *m*
**me·ni·al** niedrig, untergeordnet
**men·in·gi·tis** MED Meningitis *f*, Hirnhautentzündung *f*
**men·o·pause** MED Wechseljahre *pl*
**men·stru·ate** menstruieren
**men·stru·a·tion** Menstruation *f*
**men·tal** geistig, Geistes...; seelisch, psychisch; *~* **a·rith·me·tic** Kopfrechnen *n*; *~* **hand·i·cap** geistige Behinderung; *~* **hos·pi·tal** psychiatrische Klinik
**men·tal·i·ty** Mentalität *f*
**men·tal·ly:** *~ **handicapped*** geistig behindert; *~ **ill*** geisteskrank
**men·tion 1.** erwähnen; ***don't ~ it!*** keine Ursache!; **2.** Erwähnung *f*
**men·u** Speise(n)karte *f*; EDP Menü *n*
**me·ow** ZO miauen
**mer·can·tile** Handels...
**mer·ce·na·ry 1.** geldgierig; **2.** MIL Söldner *m*
**mer·chan·dise 1.** Ware(n *pl*) *f*; **2.** vermarkten
**mer·chan·dis·ing** Vermarktung *f*
**mer·chant 1.** (Groß)Händler *m*, (Groß-) Kaufmann *m*; **2.** Handels...
**mer·ci·ful** barmherzig, gnädig
**mer·ci·less** unbarmherzig, erbarmungslos
**mer·cu·ry** CHEM Quecksilber *n*
**mer·cy** Barmherzigkeit *f*, Erbarmen *n*, Gnade *f*
**mere, mere·ly** bloß, nur
**merge** verschmelzen (***into, with*** mit); ECON fusionieren
**merg·er** ECON Fusion *f*
**me·rid·i·an** GEOGR Meridian *m*; *fig* Gipfel *m*, Höhepunkt *m*
**mer·it 1.** Verdienst *n*; Wert *m*; Vorzug *m*; **2.** verdienen
**mer·maid** Meerjungfrau *f*, Nixe *f*
**mer·ri·ment** Fröhlichkeit *f*; Gelächter *n*, Heiterkeit *f*
**mer·ry** lustig, fröhlich, ausgelassen; ***Merry Christmas!*** fröhliche *or* frohe Weihnachten
**mer·ry-go-round** Karussell *n*
**mesh 1.** Masche *f*; *fig often pl* Netz *n*, Schlingen *pl*; ***be in ~*** TECH (ineinander) greifen; **2.** TECH (ineinander) greifen; *fig* passen (***with*** zu), zusammenpassen
**mess 1.** Unordnung *f*, Durcheinander *n*; Schmutz *m*, F Schweinerei *f*; F Patsche *f*, Klemme *f*; MIL Messe *f*, Kasino *n*; ***make a ~ of*** F *fig* verpfuschen, ruinieren, *Pläne etc* über den Haufen werfen; **2.** *~ **about**, ~ **around*** F herumspielen, herumbasteln (***with*** an *dat*); herumgammeln; *~ **up*** in Unordnung bringen, durcheinander bringen; *fig* F verpfuschen, ruinieren, *Pläne etc* über den Haufen werfen
**mes·sage** Mitteilung *f*, Nachricht *f*; Anliegen *n*, Aussage *f*; ***can I take a ~?*** kann ich etwas ausrichten?; ***get the ~*** F kapieren; **mes·sen·ger** Bote *m*
**mess·y** unordentlich; unsauber, schmutzig
**me·tab·o·lis·m** MED Stoffwechsel *m*
**met·al** Metall *n*
**me·tal·lic** metallisch; Metall...
**met·a·mor·pho·sis** Metamorphose *f*, Verwandlung *f*
**met·a·phor** Metapher *f*
**me·tas·ta·sis** MED Metastase *f*
**me·te·or** Meteor *m*
**me·te·or·o·log·i·cal** meteorologisch,

M

Wetter..., Witterungs...; ~ **of·fice** Wetteramt *n*
**me·te·o·rol·o·gy** Meteorologie *f*, Wetterkunde *f*
**me·ter**[1] TECH Messgerät *n*, Zähler *m*
**me·ter**[2] Meter *m, n*; Versmaß *n*
**meth·od** Methode *f*, Verfahren *n*; System *n*; **me·thod·i·cal** methodisch, systematisch, planmäßig
**me·tic·u·lous** peinlich genau, übergenau
**me·tre** *Br* → ***meter***[2]
**met·ric** metrisch; ~ **sys·tem** metrisches (Maß- und Gewichts)System
**met·ro·pol·i·tan** ... der Hauptstadt
**me·trop·o·lis** Weltstadt *f*
**met·tle** Eifer *m*, Mut *m*, Feuer *n*
**mew** ZO miauen
**Mex·i·can 1.** mexikanisch; **2.** Mexikaner(in)
**Mex·i·co** Mexiko *n*
**mi·aow** ZO miauen
**mi·cro...** Mikro..., (sehr) klein
**mi·cro·chip** Mikrochip *m*
**mi·cro·e·lec·tron·ics** Mikroelektronik *f*
**mi·cro·film** Mikrofilm *m*
**mi·cro·or·gan·ism** BIOL Mikroorganismus *m*
**mi·cro·phone** Mikrofon *n*
**mi·cro·pro·ces·sor** Mikroprozessor *m*
**mi·cro·scope** Mikroskop *n*
**mi·cro·scop·ic** mikroskopisch
**mi·cro·wave** Mikrowelle *f*; ~ **ov·en** Mikrowellenherd *m*
**mid** mittlere(r, -s), Mitt(el)...
**mid·air:** ***in*** ~ in der Luft
**mid·day 1.** Mittag *m*; **2.** mittägig, Mittag(s)...
**mid·dle 1.** mittlere(r, -s), Mittel...; **2.** Mitte *f*
**mid·dle-aged** mittleren Alters
**Mid·dle Ag·es** HIST Mittelalter *n*
**mid·dle class(·es)** Mittelstand *m*
**mid·dle·man** ECON Zwischenhändler *m*; Mittelsmann *m*
**mid·dle name** zweiter Vorname *m*
**mid·dle-sized** mittelgroß
**mid·dle·weight** *boxing*: Mittelgewicht *n*, Mittelgewichtler *m*
**mid·dling** F mittelmäßig, Mittel...; leidlich
**mid·field** *esp soccer*: Mittelfeld *n*
**mid·field·er, mid·field play·er** *esp soccer*: Mittelfeldspieler *m*
**midge** ZO Mücke *f*
**midg·et** Zwerg *m*, Knirps *m*
**mid·night** Mitternacht *f*; ***at*** ~ um Mitternacht
**midst:** ***in the*** ~ ***of*** mitten in (*dat*)
**mid·sum·mer** Hochsommer *m*; ASTR Sommersonnenwende *f*
**mid·way** auf halbem Wege
**mid·wife** Hebamme *f*
**mid·win·ter** Mitte *f* des Winters; ASTR Wintersonnenwende *f*; ***in*** ~ mitten im Winter
**might** Macht *f*, Gewalt *f*; Kraft *f*
**might·y** mächtig, gewaltig
**mi·grate** (aus)wandern, (fort)ziehen (*a.* ZO)
**mi·gra·tion** Wanderung *f* (*a.* ZO)
**mi·gra·to·ry** Wander...; ZO Zug...
**mike** F Mikrofon *n*
**mild** mild, sanft, leicht
**mil·dew** BOT Mehltau *m*
**mild·ness** Milde *f*
**mile** Meile *f* (*1,6 km*)
**mile·age** zurückgelegte Meilenzahl *or* Fahrtstrecke; Meilenstand *m*; *a.* ~ ***allowance*** Meilengeld *n*, *appr* Kilometergeld *n*
**mile·stone** Meilenstein *m* (*a. fig*)
**mil·i·tant** militant; streitbar, kriegerisch
**mil·i·ta·ry 1.** militärisch, Militär...; **2.** ***the*** ~ das Militär; ~ **gov·ern·ment** Militärregierung *f*; ~ **po·lice** (ABBR ***MP***) Militärpolizei *f*
**mi·li·tia** Miliz *f*, Bürgerwehr *f*
**milk 1.** Milch *f*; ***it's no use crying over spilt*** ~ geschehen ist geschehen; **2.** *v/t* melken; *v/i* Milch geben; ~ **choc·o·late** Vollmilchschokolade *f*
**milk·man** Milchmann *m*
**milk pow·der** Milchpulver *n*, Trockenmilch *f*
**milk shake** Milchmixgetränk *n*
**milk tooth** ANAT Milchzahn *m*
**milk·y** milchig; Milch...
**Milky Way** ASTR Milchstraße *f*
**mill 1.** Mühle *f*; Fabrik *f*; **2.** *Korn etc* mahlen; *Metall* verarbeiten; *Münze* rändeln
**mil·le·pede** → ***millipede***
**mill·er** Müller *m*
**mil·let** BOT Hirse *f*

**mil·li·ner** Hutmacherin *f*, Putzmacherin *f*, Modistin *f*

**mil·lion** Million *f*

**mil·lion·aire** Millionär(in)

**mil·lionth 1.** millionste(r, -s); **2.** Millionstel *n*

**mil·li·pede** ZO Tausendfüß(l)er *m*

**mill·stone** Mühlstein *m*; ***be a ~ round s.o.'s neck*** *fig* j-m ein Klotz am Bein sein

**milt** ZO Milch *f*

**mime 1.** Pantomime *f*; Pantomime *m*; **2.** (panto)mimisch darstellen; **mim·ic 1.** mimisch; Schein...; **2.** Imitator *m*; **3.** nachahmen; nachäffen; **mim·ic·ry** Nachahmung *f*; ZO Mimikry *f*

**mince 1.** *v/t* zerhacken, (zer)schneiden; ***he does not ~ matters*** *or* ***his words*** er nimmt kein Blatt vor den Mund; *v/i* tänzeln, trippeln; **2.** *a.* ***~d meat*** Hackfleisch *n*; **minc·er** Fleischwolf *m*

**mind 1.** Sinn *m*, Gemüt *n*, Herz *n*; Verstand *m*, Geist *m*; Ansicht *f*, Meinung *f*; Absicht *f*, Neigung *f*, Lust *f*; Erinnerung *f*, Gedächtnis *n*; ***be out of one's ~*** nicht (recht) bei Sinnen sein; ***bear*** *or* ***keep in ~*** (immer) denken an (*acc*), *et.* nicht vergessen; ***change one's ~*** es sich anders überlegen, s-e Meinung ändern; ***enter s.o.'s ~*** j-m in den Sinn kommen; ***give s.o. a piece of one's ~*** j-m gründlich die Meinung sagen; ***have*** (***half***) ***a ~ to*** *inf* (nicht übel) Lust haben zu *inf*; ***lose one's ~*** den Verstand verlieren; ***make up one's ~*** sich entschließen, e-n Entschluss fassen; ***to my ~*** meiner Ansicht nach; **2.** *v/t* Acht geben auf (*acc*); sehen nach, aufpassen auf (*acc*); et. haben gegen; ***~ the step!*** Vorsicht, Stufe!; ***~ your own business!*** kümmere dich um deine eigenen Angelegenheiten!; ***do you ~ if I smoke?, do you ~ my smoking?*** haben Sie et. dagegen *or* stört es Sie, wenn ich rauche?; ***would you ~ opening the window?*** würden Sie bitte das Fenster öffnen?; ***would you ~ coming*** würden Sie bitte kommen?; *v/i* aufpassen; et. dagegen haben; ***~*** (***you***) wohlgemerkt, allerdings; ***never ~!*** macht nichts!, ist schon gut!; ***I don't ~*** meinetwegen, von mir aus

**mind·less** gedankenlos, blind; unbekümmert (***of*** um), ohne Rücksicht (***of*** auf *acc*)

**mine[1]** meins; ***that's ~*** das gehört mir

**mine[2] 1.** Bergwerk *n*, Mine *f*, Zeche *f*, Grube *f*; MIL Mine *f*; *fig* Fundgrube *f*; **2.** *v/i* schürfen, graben (***for*** nach); *v/t* *Erz*, *Kohle* abbauen; MIL verminen

**min·er** Bergmann *m*, Kumpel *m*

**min·e·ral 1.** Mineral *n*; *pl Br* Mineralwasser *n*; **2.** Mineral...; **~ oil** Mineralöl *n*; **~ wa·ter** Mineralwasser *n*

**min·gle** *v/t* (ver)mischen; *v/i* sich mischen *or* mengen (***with*** unter)

**min·i...** Mini..., Klein(st)...; → ***miniskirt***

**min·i·a·ture 1.** Miniatur(gemälde *n*) *f*; **2.** Miniatur...; Klein...; **~ cam·e·ra** Kleinbildkamera *f*

**min·i·mize** auf ein Mindestmaß herabsetzen; herunterspielen, bagatellisieren

**min·i·mum 1.** Minimum *n*, Mindestmaß *n*; **2.** minimal, Mindest...

**min·ing 1.** Bergbau *m*; **2.** Berg(bau)..., Bergwerks...; Gruben...

**min·i·skirt** Minirock *m*

**min·is·ter** POL Minister(in); Gesandte *m*; REL Geistliche *m*; **min·is·try** POL Ministerium *n*; REL geistliches Amt

**mink** ZO Nerz *m*

**mi·nor 1.** kleinere(r, -s), *fig a.* unbedeutend, geringfügig; JUR minderjährig; ***A ~*** MUS a-Moll *n*; ***~ key*** MUS Moll(tonart *f*) *n*; **2.** JUR Minderjährige *m, f*; UNIV Nebenfach *n*; MUS Moll *n*; **mi·nor·i·ty** Minderheit *f*; JUR Minderjährigkeit *f*

**min·ster** *Br* Münster *n*

**mint[1] 1.** Münze *f*, Münzanstalt *f*; **2.** prägen

**mint[2]** BOT Minze *f*

**min·u·et** MUS Menuett *n*

**mi·nus 1.** *prp* minus, weniger; F ohne; **2.** *adj* Minus...; **3.** Minus *n*, *fig a.* Nachteil *m*

**min·ute[1]** Minute *f*; Augenblick *m*; ***in a ~*** sofort; ***just a ~!*** Moment mal!

**mi·nute[2]** winzig; sehr genau

**min·utes** Protokoll *n*; ***take*** (*or* ***keep***) ***the ~*** (das) Protokoll führen

**mir·a·cle** Wunder *n*

**mi·rac·u·lous** wunderbar

**mi·rac·u·lous·ly** wie durch ein Wunder

**mi·rage** Luftspiegelung *f*, Fata Morgana *f*

**mire** Schlamm *m*; ***drag through the ~*** *fig* in den Schmutz ziehen

**mir·ror 1.** Spiegel *m*; **2.** (wider)spiegeln (*a. fig*)

**mis...** miss..., falsch, schlecht
**mis·ad·ven·ture** Missgeschick *n*; Unglück *n*, Unglücksfall *m*
**mis·an·thrope, mis·an·thro·pist** Menschenfeind(in)
**mis·ap·ply** falsch an- *or* verwenden
**mis·ap·pre·hend** missverstehen
**mis·ap·pro·pri·ate** unterschlagen, veruntreuen
**mis·be·have** sich schlecht benehmen
**mis·cal·cu·late** falsch berechnen; sich verrechnen (in *dat*)
**miscar·riage** MED Fehlgeburt *f*; Misslingen *n*, Fehlschlag(en *n*) *m*; **~ of justice** JUR Fehlurteil *n*
**mis·car·ry** MED e-e Fehlgeburt haben; misslingen, scheitern
**mis·cel·la·ne·ous** gemischt, vermischt; verschiedenartig
**mis·cel·la·ny** Gemisch *n*; Sammelband *m*
**mis·chief** Schaden *m*; Unfug *m*; Übermut *m*; **~-mak·er** Unruhestifter(in)
**mis·chie·vous** boshaft, mutwillig; schelmisch
**mis·con·ceive** falsch auffassen, missverstehen
**mis·con·duct** schlechtes Benehmen; schlechte Führung; Verfehlung *f*
**mis·con·strue** falsch auslegen, missdeuten
**mis·de·mea·no(u)r** JUR Vergehen *n*
**mis·di·rect** fehlleiten, irreleiten; *Brief etc* falsch adressieren
**mise-en-scène** THEA Inszenierung *f*
**mi·ser** Geizhals *m*
**mis·e·ra·ble** erbärmlich, kläglich, elend; unglücklich
**mi·ser·ly** geizig, F knick(e)rig
**mis·e·ry** Elend *n*, Not *f*
**mis·fire** versagen (*gun*); MOT fehlzünden, aussetzen; *fig* danebengehen
**mis·fit** Außenseiter(in)
**mis·for·tune** Unglück *n*, Unglücksfall *m*; Missgeschick *n*
**mis·giv·ing** Befürchtung *f*, Zweifel *m*
**mis·guid·ed** irregeleitet, irrig, unangebracht
**mis·hap** Unglück *n*; Missgeschick *n*; **without ~** ohne Zwischenfälle
**mis·in·form** falsch unterrichten
**mis·in·ter·pret** missdeuten, falsch auffassen *or* auslegen
**mis·lay** *et.* verlegen
**mis·lead** irreführen, täuschen; verleiten
**mis·man·age** schlecht verwalten *or* führen *or* handhaben
**mis·place** *et.* an e-e falsche Stelle legen *or* setzen; *et.* verlegen; **~d** *fig* unangebracht, deplatziert
**mis·print 1.** verdrucken; **2.** Druckfehler *m*
**mis·read** falsch lesen; falsch deuten, missdeuten
**mis·rep·re·sent** falsch darstellen; entstellen, verdrehen
**miss 1.** *v/t* verpassen, versäumen, verfehlen; übersehen, nicht bemerken; überhören; nicht verstehen *or* begreifen; vermissen; *a.* **~ out** auslassen, übergehen, überspringen; *v/i* nicht treffen; missglücken; **~ out on** *et.* verpassen; **2.** Fehlschuss *m*, Fehlstoß *m*, Fehlwurf *m etc*; Verpassen *n*, Verfehlen *n*
**Miss** Fräulein *n*
**mis·shap·en** missgebildet
**mis·sile 1.** Geschoss *n*; Rakete *f*; **2.** Raketen...
**miss·ing** fehlend; **be ~** fehlen, verschwunden *or* weg sein; (MIL *a.* **~ in action**) vermisst; **be ~** MIL vermisst sein *or* werden
**mis·sion** (*Militär- etc*)Mission *f*; *esp* POL Auftrag *m*, Mission *f* (*a.* REL); MIL, AVIAT Einsatz *m*
**mis·sion·a·ry** REL Missionar *m*
**mis·spell** falsch buchstabieren *or* schreiben
**mis·spend** falsch verwenden; vergeuden
**mist 1.** (feiner *or* leichter) Nebel; **2. ~ over** sich trüben; **~ up** (sich) beschlagen
**mis·take 1.** verwechseln (**for** mit); verkennen, sich irren in (*dat*); falsch verstehen, missverstehen; **2.** Irrtum *m*, Versehen *n*, Fehler *m*; **by ~** aus Versehen, irrtümlich; **mis·tak·en** irrig, falsch (verstanden); **be ~** sich irren
**mis·tle·toe** BOT Mistel *f*
**mis·tress** Herrin *f*; *esp Br* Lehrerin *f*; Geliebte *f*
**mis·trust 1.** misstrauen (*dat*); **2.** Misstrauen *n* (**of** gegen)
**mis·trust·ful** misstrauisch
**mist·y** (leicht) neb(e)lig; *fig* unklar, verschwommen

M

**mis·un·der·stand** missverstehen; *j-n* nicht verstehen; **mis·un·der·stand·ing** Missverständnis *n*
**mis·use 1.** missbrauchen; falsch gebrauchen; **2.** Missbrauch *m*
**mite** ZO Milbe *f*; kleines Ding, Würmchen *n*; ***a*** ~ F ein bisschen
**mi·ter,** *Br* **mi·tre** REL Mitra *f*, Bischofsmütze *f*
**mitt** *baseball*: Fanghandschuh *m*; → **mit·ten** Fausthandschuh *m*
**mix 1.** (ver)mischen, vermengen; *Getränke* mixen; sich (ver)mischen; sich mischen lassen; verkehren (***with*** mit); ~ ***well*** kontaktfreudig sein; ~ ***up*** zusammenmischen, durcheinander mischen; (völlig) durcheinander bringen; verwechseln (***with*** mit); ***be*** ~***ed up*** verwickelt sein *or* werden (***in*** in *acc*); (*geistig*) ganz durcheinander sein; **2.** Mischung *f*
**mixed** gemischt (*a. fig*); vermischt, Misch...
**mix·er** Mixer *m*; TECH Mischmaschine *f*; *radio*, TV *etc*: Mischpult *n*
**mix·ture** Mischung *f*; Gemisch *n*
**mix-up** F Verwechs(e)lung *f*
**moan 1.** Stöhnen *n*; **2.** stöhnen
**moat** (Burg-, Stadt)Graben *m*
**mob 1.** Mob *m*, Pöbel *m*; **2.** herfallen über (*acc*); *j-n* bedrängen, belagern
**mo·bile 1.** beweglich; MIL mobil, motorisiert; *fig* lebhaft; **2.** → ***mobile phone*** *or* ***telephone***; ~ **home** Wohnwagen *m*; ~ **phone,** ~ **tel·e·phone** Mobiltelefon *n*, Handy *n*
**mo·bil·ize** mobilisieren, MIL *a.* mobil machen
**moc·ca·sin** Mokassin *m*
**mock 1.** *v/t* verspotten; nachäffen; *v/i* sich lustig machen, spotten (***at*** über *acc*); **2.** nachgemacht, Schein...
**mock·e·ry** Spott *m*, Hohn *m*; Gespött *n*
**mock·ing·bird** ZO Spottdrossel *f*
**mode** (Art *f* und) Weise *f*; EDP Modus *m*, Betriebsart *f*
**mod·el 1.** Modell *n*; Muster *n*; Vorbild *n*; Mannequin *n*; Model *n*, (Foto)Modell *n*; TECH Modell *n*, Typ *m*; ***male*** ~ Dressman *m*; **2.** Modell..., Muster...; **3.** *v/t* modellieren, *a. fig* formen; *Kleider etc* vorführen; *v/i* Modell stehen *or* sitzen; als Mannequin *or* (Foto)Modell *or* Dressman arbeiten
**mo·dem** EDP Modem *m*, *n*
**mod·e·rate 1.** (mittel)mäßig; gemäßigt; vernünftig, angemessen; **2.** (sich) mäßigen
**mod·e·ra·tion** Mäßigung *f*
**mod·ern** modern, neu
**mod·ern·ize** modernisieren
**mod·est** bescheiden
**mod·es·ty** Bescheidenheit *f*
**mod·i·fi·ca·tion** (Ab-, Ver)Änderung *f*
**mod·i·fy** (ab-, ver)ändern
**mod·u·late** modulieren
**mod·ule** TECH Modul *n*, ELECTR *a.* Baustein *m*; (*Kommando- etc*)Kapsel *f*
**moist** feucht
**moist·en** *v/t* anfeuchten, befeuchten; *v/i* feucht werden
**mois·ture** Feuchtigkeit *f*
**mo·lar** ANAT Backenzahn *m*
**mo·las·ses** Sirup *m*
**mold**[1] Schimmel *m*; Moder *m*; Humus(boden) *m*
**mold**[2] TECH **1.** (Gieß-, Guss-, Press-) Form *f*; **2.** gießen; formen
**mol·der** *a.* ~ ***away*** vermodern; zerfallen
**mold·y** verschimmelt, schimm(e)lig; mod(e)rig
**mole**[1] ZO Maulwurf *m*
**mole**[2] Muttermal *n*, Leberfleck *m*
**mole**[3] Mole *f*, Hafendamm *m*
**mol·e·cule** Molekül *n*
**mole·hill** Maulwurfshügel *m*; ***make a mountain out of a*** ~ aus e-r Mücke e-n Elefanten machen
**mo·lest** belästigen
**mol·li·fy** besänftigen, beschwichtigen
**mol·lusc** *Br*, **mol·lusk** ZO Weichtier *n*
**mol·ly·cod·dle** F verhätscheln, verzärteln
**molt** (sich) mausern; *Haare* verlieren
**mol·ten** geschmolzen
**mom** F Mami *f*, Mutti *f*
**mom-and-pop store** Tante-Emma-Laden *m*
**mo·ment** Moment *m*, Augenblick *m*; Bedeutung *f*; PHYS Moment *n*
**mo·men·ta·ry** momentan, augenblicklich
**mo·men·tous** bedeutsam, folgenschwer
**mo·men·tum** PHYS Moment *n*; Schwung *m*
**Mon** ABBR *of* ***Monday*** Mo., Montag *m*
**mon·arch** Monarch(in), Herrscher(in)

**mon·ar·chy** Monarchie *f*
**mon·as·tery** REL (Mönchs)Kloster *n*
**Mon·day** (ABBR ***Mon***) Montag *m*; ***on ~*** (am) Montag; ***on ~s*** montags
**mon·e·ta·ry** ECON Währungs...; Geld...
**mon·ey** Geld *n*
**mon·ey·box** *Br* Sparbüchse *f*
**mon·ey·chang·er** (Geld)Wechsler *m*; TECH Wechselautomat *m*
**mon·ey or·der** Post- *or* Zahlungsanweisung *f*
**mon·grel** ZO Bastard *m*, *esp* Promenadenmischung *f*
**mon·i·tor 1.** Monitor *m*; Kontrollgerät *n*, -schirm *m*; **2.** abhören; überwachen
**monk** REL Mönch *m*
**mon·key 1.** ZO Affe *m*; F (kleiner) Schlingel; ***make a ~ (out) of s.o.*** F j-n zum Deppen machen; **2.** ***~ about, ~ around*** F (herum)albern; ***~ about*** *or* ***around with*** F herumspielen mit *or* an (*dat*), herummurksen an (*dat*); ***~ wrench*** TECH Engländer *m*, Franzose *m*; ***throw a ~ into s.th.*** F et. behindern
**mon·o 1.** Mono *n*; F Monogerät *n*; F Monoschallplatte *f*; **2.** Mono...
**mon·o...** ein..., mono...
**mon·o·log,** *esp Br* **mon·o·logue** Monolog *m*
**mo·nop·o·lize** monopolisieren; *fig* an sich reißen
**mo·nop·o·ly** Monopol *n* (***of*** auf *acc*)
**mo·not·o·nous** monoton, eintönig
**mo·not·o·ny** Monotonie *f*
**mon·soon** Monsun *m*
**mon·ster 1.** Monster *n*, Ungeheuer *n* (*a. fig*); Monstrum *n*; **2.** Riesen...
**mon·stros·i·ty** Ungeheuerlichkeit *f*; Monstrum *n*; **mon·strous** ungeheuer; *mst contp* ungeheuerlich; scheußlich
**month** Monat *m*; **month·ly 1.** monatlich; Monats...; **2.** Monatsschrift *f*
**mon·u·ment** Monument *n*, Denkmal *n*
**mon·u·ment·al** monumental; F kolossal, Riesen...; Gedenk...
**moo** ZO muhen
**mooch** F schnorren
**mood** Stimmung *f*, Laune *f*; ***be in a good (bad) ~*** gute (schlechte) Laune haben, gut (schlecht) aufgelegt sein
**mood·y** launisch; schlecht gelaunt
**moon 1.** ASTR Mond *m*; **2.** ***~ about, ~ around*** F herumtrödeln; F ziellos herumstreichen
**moon·light** Mondlicht *n*, -schein *m*
**moon·lit** mondhell
**moor**[1] (Hoch)Moor *n*
**moor**[2] MAR vertäuen, festmachen
**moor·ings** MAR Vertäuung *f*; Liegeplatz *m*
**moose** ZO *nordamerikanischer* Elch
**mop 1.** Mopp *m*; F (Haar)Wust *m*; **2.** wischen; ***~ up*** aufwischen
**mope** Trübsal blasen
**mo·ped** *Br* MOT Moped *n*
**mor·al 1.** moralisch; Moral..., Sitten...; **2.** Moral *f*, Lehre *f*; *pl* Moral *f*, Sitten *pl*
**mo·rale** Moral *f*, Stimmung *f*
**mor·al·ize** moralisieren (***about, on*** über *acc*)
**mor·bid** morbid, krankhaft
**more 1.** *adj* mehr; noch (mehr); ***some ~ tea*** noch etwas Tee; **2.** *adv* mehr; noch; ***~ and ~*** immer mehr; ***~ or less*** mehr oder weniger; ***once ~*** noch einmal; ***the ~ so because*** umso mehr, da; ***~ important*** wichtiger; ***~ often*** öfter; **3.** Mehr *n* (***of*** an *dat*); ***a little ~*** etwas mehr
**mo·rel** BOT Morchel *f*
**more·o·ver** außerdem, weiter, ferner
**morgue** Leichenschauhaus *n*; F (Zeitungs)Archiv *n*
**morn·ing** Morgen *m*; Vormittag *m*; ***good ~!*** guten Morgen!; ***in the ~*** morgens, am Morgen; vormittags, am Vormittag; ***tomorrow ~*** morgen früh *or* Vormittag
**mo·rose** mürrisch, verdrießlich
**mor·phi·a, mor·phine** PHARM Morphium *n*
**mor·sel** Bissen *m*, Happen *m*; ***a ~ of*** ein bisschen
**mor·tal 1.** sterblich; tödlich; Tod(es)...; **2.** Sterbliche *m, f*
**mor·tal·i·ty** Sterblichkeit *f*
**mor·tar**[1] Mörtel *m*
**mor·tar**[2] Mörser *m*
**mort·gage 1.** Hypothek *f*; **2.** mit e-r Hypothek belasten, e-e Hypothek aufnehmen auf (*acc*)
**mor·ti·cian** Leichenbestatter *m*
**mor·ti·fi·ca·tion** Kränkung *f*; Ärger *m*, Verdruss *m*
**mor·ti·fy** kränken; ärgern, verdrießen
**mor·tu·a·ry** Leichenhalle *f*
**mo·sa·ic** Mosaik *n*
**Mos·lem** → ***Muslim***
**mosque** Moschee *f*

M

**mos·qui·to** zo Moskito *m*; Stechmücke *f*
**moss** BOT Moos *n*
**moss·y** BOT moosig, bemoost
**most 1.** *adj* meiste(r, -s), größte(r, -s); die meisten; ~ ***people*** die meisten Leute; **2.** *adv* am meisten; ~ ***of all*** am allermeisten; *before adj*: höchst, äußerst; ***the*** ~ ***important point*** der wichtigste Punkt; **3.** *das* meiste, *das* Höchste; das meiste, der größte Teil; die meisten *pl*; ***at*** (***the***) ~ höchstens; ***make the*** ~ ***of*** *et.* nach Kräften ausnutzen, das Beste herausholen aus
**most·ly** hauptsächlich, meist(ens)
**mo·tel** Motel *n*
**moth** zo Motte *f*
**moth-eat·en** mottenzerfressen
**moth·er 1.** Mutter *f*; **2.** bemuttern
**moth·er coun·try** Vaterland *n*, Heimatland *n*; Mutterland *n*
**moth·er·hood** Mutterschaft *f*
**moth·er-in-law** Schwiegermutter *f*
**moth·er·ly** mütterlich
**moth·er-of-pearl** Perlmutter *f*, *n*, Perlmutt *n*
**moth·er tongue** Muttersprache *f*
**mo·tif** Motiv *n*
**mo·tion 1.** Bewegung *f*; PARL Antrag *m*; ***in quick*** ~ *film*: im Zeitraffer; ***in slow*** ~ *film*: in Zeitlupe; ***put*** *or* ***set in*** ~ in Gang bringen (*a. fig*), in Bewegung setzen; **2.** *v/t j-n* durch e-n Wink auffordern, *j-m* ein Zeichen geben; *v/i* winken
**mo·tion·less** bewegungslos, unbeweglich
**mo·tion pic·ture** Film *m*
**mo·ti·vate** motivieren, anspornen
**mo·ti·va·tion** Motivation *f*, Ansporn *m*
**mo·tive 1.** Motiv *n*, Beweggrund *m*; **2.** treibend (*a. fig*)
**mot·ley** bunt
**mo·to·cross** SPORT Motocross *n*
**mo·tor 1.** Motor *m*, *fig a.* treibende Kraft; **2.** Motor...
**mo·tor·bike** Moped *n*; *Br* F Motorrad *n*
**mo·tor·boat** Motorboot *n*
**mo·tor·cade** Auto-, Wagenkolonne *f*
**mo·tor·car** *Br* Kraftfahrzeug *n*
**mo·tor car·a·van** *Br* Wohnmobil *n*
**mo·tor·cy·cle** Motorrad *n*
**mo·tor·cy·clist** Motorradfahrer(in)
**mo·tor home** Wohnmobil *n*
**mo·tor·ing** Autofahren *n*; ***school of*** ~ Fahrschule *f*
**mo·tor·ist** Autofahrer(in)
**mo·tor·ize** motorisieren
**mo·tor launch** Motorbarkasse *f*
**mo·tor·way** *Br* Autobahn *f*
**mot·tled** gefleckt, gesprenkelt
**mould**[1] *Br* → ***mold***[1]
**mould**[2] *Br* → ***mold***[2]
**moul·der** *Br* → ***molder***
**mould·y** *Br* → ***moldy***
**moult** *Br* → ***molt***
**mound** Erdhügel *m*, Erdwall *m*
**mount 1.** *v/t Pferd etc* besteigen, steigen auf (*acc*); montieren; anbringen, befestigen; *Bild etc* aufziehen, aufkleben; *Edelstein* fassen; ~***ed police*** berittene Polizei; *v/i* aufsitzen (*rider*); steigen, *fig a.* (an)wachsen; ~ ***up to*** sich belaufen auf (*acc*); **2.** Gestell *n*; Fassung *f*; Reittier *n*, Reitpferd *n*
**moun·tain 1.** Berg *m*, *pl a.* Gebirge *n*; **2.** Berg..., Gebirgs...
**moun·tain bike** Mountainbike *n*
**moun·tain·eer** Bergsteiger(in)
**moun·tain·eer·ing** Bergsteigen *n*
**moun·tain·ous** bergig, gebirgig
**mourn** *v/i* trauern (***for, over*** um); *v/t* betrauern, trauern um
**mourn·er** Trauernde *m*, *f*
**mourn·ful** traurig
**mourn·ing** Trauer *f*; Trauerkleidung *f*
**mouse** zo Maus *f* (*a.* EDP)
**mous·tache** → ***mustache***
**mouth** Mund *m*; zo Maul *n*, Schnauze *f*; GEOGR Mündung *f*; Öffnung *f*
**mouth·ful** *ein* Mund voll ; Bissen *m*
**mouth or·gan** F Mundharmonika *f*
**mouth·piece** Mundstück *n*; *fig* Sprachrohr *n*
**mouth·wash** Mundwasser *n*
**mo·va·ble** beweglich
**move 1.** *v/t* (weg)rücken; transportieren; bewegen, rühren (*both a. fig*); *chess etc*: e-n Zug machen mit; PARL beantragen; ~ ***house*** umziehen; ~ ***heaven and earth*** Himmel und Hölle in Bewegung setzen; *v/i* sich (fort)bewegen; sich rühren; umziehen (***to*** nach); *chess etc*: e-n Zug machen; ~ ***away*** weg-, fortziehen; ~ ***in*** einziehen; ~ ***off*** sich in Bewegung setzen; ~ ***on*** weitergehen; ~ ***out*** ausziehen; **2.** Bewegung *f*; Umzug *m*; *chess etc*: Zug *m*; *fig* Schritt *m*; ***on the*** ~ in Bewegung; auf den Beinen; ***get a*** ~ ***on!*** F Tempo!, mach(t) schon!, los!

M

**move·a·ble** → ***movable***
**move·ment** Bewegung *f* (*a. fig*); MUS Satz *m*; TECH Werk *n*
**mov·ie 1.** Film *m*; Kino *n*; **2.** Film..., Kino...; ~ **cam·e·ra** Filmkamera *f*; ~ **star** Filmstar *m*; ~ **thea·ter** Kino *n*
**mov·ing** sich bewegend, beweglich; *fig* rührend; ~ **stair·case** Rolltreppe *f*; ~ **van** Möbelwagen *m*
**mow** mähen
**mow·er** Mähmaschine *f*, *esp* Rasenmäher *m*
**Mr.** ABBR *of* ***Mister*** Herr *m*
**Mrs.** Frau *f*
**Ms.** Frau *f*
**much 1.** *adj* viel; **2.** *adv* sehr; viel; ~ ***better*** viel besser; ***very*** ~ sehr; ***I thought as*** ~ das habe ich mir gedacht; **3.** große Sache; ***nothing*** ~ nichts Besonderes; ***make*** ~ ***of*** viel Wesens machen von; ***think*** ~ ***of*** viel halten von; ***I am not*** ~ ***of a dancer*** F ich bin kein großer Tänzer
**muck** F *Br* AGR Mist *m*, Dung *m*; *fig* Dreck *m*, Schmutz *m*; F *contp* Fraß *m*
**mu·cus** (Nasen)Schleim *m*
**mud** Schlamm *m*, Matsch *m*; Schmutz *m* (*a. fig*)
**mud·dle 1.** Durcheinander *n*; ***be in a*** ~ durcheinander sein; **2.** *a.* ~ ***up*** durcheinander bringen; ~ ***through*** F sich durchwursteln
**mud·dy** schlammig, trüb; schmutzig; *fig* wirr
**mud·guard** Kotflügel *m*; Schutzblech *n*
**mues·li** Müsli *n*
**muff** Muff *m*
**muf·fle** *Ton etc* dämpfen; *often* ~ ***up*** einhüllen, einwickeln
**muf·fler** (dicker) Schal; MOT Auspufftopf *m*
**mug**[1] Krug *m*; Becher *m*; große Tasse; F Visage *f*; V Fresse *f*
**mug**[2] F überfallen und ausrauben
**mug·ger** F (Straßen)Räuber *m*
**mug·ging** F Raubüberfall *m*, *esp* Straßenraub *m*
**mug·gy** schwül
**mul·ber·ry** BOT Maulbeerbaum *m*; Maulbeere *f*
**mule** zo Maultier *n*; Maulesel *m*
**mulled:** ~ ***wine*** Glühwein *m*
**mul·li·on** ARCH Mittelpfosten *m*
**mul·ti...** viel..., mehr..., Mehrfach..., Multi...
**mul·ti·cul·tur·al** multikulturell
**mul·ti·far·i·ous** mannigfaltig, vielfältig
**mul·ti·lat·e·ral** vielseitig; POL multilateral, mehrseitig
**mul·ti·me·di·a** multimedial
**mul·ti·na·tion·al** ECON multinationaler Konzern, F Multi *m*
**mul·ti·ple 1.** vielfach, mehrfach; **2.** MATH Vielfache *n*
**mul·ti·pli·ca·tion** Vermehrung *f*; MATH Multiplikation *f*; ~ **table** Einmaleins *n*
**mul·ti·pli·ci·ty** Vielfalt *f*; Vielzahl *f*
**mul·ti·ply** (sich) vermehren, (sich) vervielfachen; MATH multiplizieren, malnehmen (***by*** mit)
**mul·ti·pur·pose** Mehrzweck...
**mul·ti·sto·rey** *Br* mehrstöckig; ~ **car park** *Br* Park(hoch)haus *n*
**mul·ti·tude** Vielzahl *f*
**mul·ti·tu·di·nous** zahlreich
**mum**[1] *Br* F Mami *f*, Mutti *f*
**mum**[2] **1.** *int*: ~***'s the word*** Mund halten!, kein Wort darüber!; **2.** *adj*: ***keep*** ~ nichts verraten, den Mund halten
**mum·ble** murmeln, F nuscheln; mümmeln
**mum·mi·fy** mumifizieren
**mum·my**[1] Mumie *f*
**mum·my**[2] *Br* F Mami *f*, Mutti *f*
**mumps** MED Ziegenpeter *m*, Mumps *m*
**munch** mampfen
**mun·dane** alltäglich; weltlich
**mu·ni·ci·pal** städtisch, Stadt..., kommunal, Gemeinde...; ~ ***council*** Stadt-, Gemeinderat *m*
**mu·ni·ci·pal·i·ty** Kommunalbehörde *f*; Stadtverwaltung *f*
**mu·ral** Wandgemälde *n*
**mur·der 1.** Mord *m*, Ermordung *f*; **2.** Mord...; **3.** ermorden; F verschandeln
**mur·der·er** Mörder *m*
**mur·der·ess** Mörderin *f*
**mur·der·ous** mörderisch
**murk·y** dunkel, finster
**mur·mur 1.** Murmeln *n*; Gemurmel *n*; Murren *n*; **2.** murmeln; murren
**mus·cle** Muskel *m*
**mus·cu·lar** Muskel...; muskulös
**muse**[1] (nach)sinnen, (nach)grübeln (***on, over*** über *acc*)
**muse**[2] *a.* ***Muse*** Muse *f*
**mu·se·um** Museum *n*
**mush** Brei *m*, Mus *n*; Maisbrei *m*
**mush·room 1.** BOT Pilz *m*, *esp* Cham-

pignon *m*; **2.** rasch wachsen; ~ ***up*** *fig* (wie Pilze) aus dem Boden schießen
**mu·sic** Musik *f*; Noten *pl*; ***put*** *or* ***set to*** ~ vertonen
**mu·sic·al 1.** musikalisch; Musik...; **2.** Musical *n*; ~ **box** *esp Br* Spieldose *f*; ~ **in·stru·ment** Musikinstrument *n*
**mu·sic| box** Spieldose *f*; ~ **cen·ter** (*Br* **cen·tre**) Kompaktanlage *f*; ~ **hall** *Br* Varietee(theater) *n*
**mu·si·cian** Musiker(in)
**mu·sic stand** Notenständer *m*
**musk** Moschus *m*
**musk·rat** ZO Bisamratte *f*; Bisampelz *m*
**Mus·lim 1.** Muslim *m*, Moslem *m*; **2.** muslimisch, moslemisch
**mus·sel** ZO (Mies)Muschel *f*
**must**[1] **1.** *v/aux ich* muss, *du* musst *etc*; ***you*** ~ ***not*** (F ***mustn't***) du darfst nicht; **2.** Muss *n*
**must**[2] Most *m*
**mus·tache** Schnurrbart *m*
**mus·tard** Senf *m*
**mus·ter 1.** ~ ***up*** *s-e Kraft etc* aufbieten; *s-n Mut* zusammennehmen; **2.** ***pass*** ~ *fig* Zustimmung finden (***with*** bei); den Anforderungen genügen
**must·y** mod(e)rig, muffig
**mu·ta·tion** Veränderung *f*; BIOL Mutation *f*
**mute 1.** stumm; **2.** Stumme *m*, *f*; MUS Dämpfer *m*
**mu·ti·late** verstümmeln
**mu·ti·la·tion** Verstümmelung *f*
**mu·ti·neer** Meuterer *m*
**mu·ti·nous** meuternd; rebellisch
**mu·ti·ny 1.** Meuterei *f*; **2.** meutern
**mut·ter 1.** murmeln; murren; **2.** Murmeln *n*; Murren *n*
**mut·ton** GASTR Hammel-, Schaffleisch *n*; ***leg of*** ~ Hammelkeule *f*
**mut·ton chop** GASTR Hammelkotelett *n*
**mu·tu·al** gegenseitig; gemeinsam
**muz·zle 1.** ZO Maul *n*, Schnauze *f*; Mündung *f* (*of a gun*); Maulkorb *m*; **2.** e-n Maulkorb anlegen (*dat*), *fig a. j-n* mundtot machen
**my** mein(e)
**myrrh** BOT Myrrhe *f*
**myr·tle** BOT Myrte *f*
**my·self** ich, mich *or* mir selbst; mich; mich (selbst); ***by*** ~ allein
**mys·te·ri·ous** rätselhaft, unerklärlich; geheimnisvoll, mysteriös
**mys·te·ry** Geheimnis *n*, Rätsel *n*; REL Mysterium *n*; ~ ***tour*** Fahrt *f* ins Blaue
**mys·tic 1.** Mystiker(in); **2.** → **mys·tic·al** mystisch
**mys·ti·fy** verwirren, vor ein Rätsel stellen; ***be mystified*** vor e-m Rätsel stehen
**myth** Mythos *m*, Sage *f*
**my·thol·o·gy** Mythologie *f*

N

# N

**N, n** N, n *n*
**nab** F schnappen, erwischen
**na·dir** ASTR Nadir *m*; *fig* Tiefpunkt *m*
**nag**[1] **1.** nörgeln; ~ (***at***) herumnörgeln an (*dat*); **2.** Nörgler(in)
**nag**[2] F Gaul *m*, Klepper *m*
**nail 1.** ANAT, TECH Nagel *m*; **2.** (an)nageln (***to*** an *acc*); ~ **pol·ish** Nagellack *m*; ~ **scis·sors** Nagelschere *f*; ~ **var·nish** *Br* Nagellack *m*
**na·ive, na·ïve** naiv (*a. art*)
**na·ked** nackt, bloß; kahl; *fig* ungeschminkt; **nak·ed·ness** Nacktheit *f*
**name 1.** Name *m*; Ruf *m*; ***by*** ~ mit Namen, namentlich; ***by the*** ~ ***of ...*** namens ...; ***what's your*** ~***?*** wie heißen Sie?; ***call s.o.*** ~***s*** j-n beschimpfen; **2.** (be)nennen; erwähnen; ernennen zu
**name·less** namenlos; unbekannt
**name·ly** nämlich
**name·plate** Namens-, Tür-, Firmenschild *n*
**name·sake** Namensvetter *m*, Namensschwester *f*
**name tag** Namensschild *n*
**nan·ny** Kindermädchen *n*
**nan·ny goat** ZO Geiß *f*, Ziege *f*

**nap 1.** Schläfchen *n*; ***have** or **take a ~*** → **2.** ein Nickerchen machen
**nape** *mst* ***~ of the neck*** ANAT Genick *n*, Nacken *m*
**nap·kin** Serviette *f*
**nap·py** *Br* Windel *f*
**nar·co·sis** MED Narkose *f*
**nar·cot·ic 1.** narkotisch, betäubend, einschläfernd; Rauschgift...; ***~ addiction*** Rauschgiftsucht *f*; **2.** Narkotikum *n*, Betäubungsmittel *n*; *often pl* Rauschgift *n*; ***~s squad*** Rauschgiftdezernat *n*
**nar·rate** erzählen; berichten, schildern
**nar·ra·tion** Erzählung *f*
**nar·ra·tive 1.** Erzählung *f*; Bericht *m*, Schilderung *f*; **2.** erzählend
**nar·ra·tor** Erzähler(in)
**nar·row 1.** eng, schmal; beschränkt; knapp; **2.** enger *or* schmäler werden *or* machen, (sich) verengen; beschränken, einschränken; **nar·row·ly** mit knapper Not; **nar·row-mind·ed** engstirnig, beschränkt; **nar·row·ness** Enge *f*; Beschränktheit *f*
**na·sal** nasal; Nasen...
**nas·ty** ekelhaft, eklig, widerlich (*smell, sight etc*); abscheulich (*weather etc*); böse, schlimm (*accident etc*); hässlich (*character, behavior etc*); gemein, fies; schmutzig, zotig (*language*)
**na·tal** Geburts...
**na·tion** Nation *f*, Volk *n*
**na·tion·al 1.** national, National..., Landes..., Volks...; **2.** Staatsangehörige *m*, *f*; **~ an·them** Nationalhymne *f*
**na·tion·al·i·ty** Nationalität *f*, Staatsangehörigkeit *f*
**na·tion·al·ize** ECON verstaatlichen
**na·tion·al| park** Nationalpark *m*; **~ so·cial·ism** HIST POL Nationalsozialismus *m*; **~ so·cial·ist** HIST POL Nationalsozialist *m*; **~ team** SPORT Nationalmannschaft *f*
**na·tion-wide** landesweit
**na·tive 1.** einheimisch, Landes...; heimatlich, Heimat...; eingeboren, Eingeborenen...; angeboren; **2.** Eingeborene *m, f*; Einheimische *m, f*; **~ lan·guage** Muttersprache *f*; **~ speak·er** Muttersprachler(in)
**Na·tiv·i·ty** REL *die* Geburt Christi
**nat·ty** F schick, *Austrian* fesch
**nat·u·ral** natürlich; angeboren; Natur...; **~ gas** Erdgas *n*
**nat·u·ral·ize** naturalisieren, einbürgern
**nat·u·ral·ly** natürlich; von Natur (aus)
**nat·u·ral| re·sourc·es** Boden- u. Naturschätze *pl*; **~ sci·ence** Naturwissenschaft *f*
**na·ture** Natur *f*; **~ con·ser·va·tion** Naturschutz *m*; **~ re·serve** Naturschutzgebiet *n*; **~ trail** Naturlehrpfad *m*
**naugh·ty** unartig; unanständig
**nau·se·a** Übelkeit *f*, Brechreiz *m*
**nau·se·ate: *~ s.o.*** j-m Übelkeit verursachen; *fig* j-n anwidern
**nau·se·at·ing** Ekel erregend, widerlich
**nau·ti·cal** nautisch, See...
**na·val** MIL Flotten..., Marine...; See...; **~ base** MIL Flottenstützpunkt *m*; **~ of·fi·cer** MIL Marineoffizier *m*; **~ pow·er** MIL Seemacht *f*
**nave** ARCH Mittel-, Hauptschiff *n*
**na·vel** ANAT Nabel *m* (*a. fig*)
**nav·i·ga·ble** schiffbar
**nav·i·gate** MAR befahren; AVIAT, MAR steuern, lenken
**nav·i·ga·tion** Schifffahrt *f*; AVIAT, MAR Navigation *f*
**nav·i·ga·tor** AVIAT, MAR Navigator *m*
**na·vy** (Kriegs)Marine *f*; Kriegsflotte *f*
**na·vy blue** Marineblau *n*
**nay** PARL Gegen-, Neinstimme *f*
**Na·zi** HIST POL *contp* Nazi *m*
**Na·zism** HIST POL *contp* Nazismus *m*
**near 1.** *adj* nahe; kurz; nahe (verwandt); ***in the ~ future*** in naher Zukunft; ***be a ~ miss*** knapp scheitern; **2.** *adv* nahe, in der Nähe (*a.* ***~ at hand***); nahe (bevorstehend) (*a.* ***~ at hand***); beinahe, fast; ***~ the station*** *etc* in der Nähe des Bahnhofs *etc*; ***~ you*** in deiner Nähe; **3.** *prp* nahe (*dat*), in der Nähe von (*or gen*); **4.** sich nähern, näher kommen (*dat*)
**near·by 1.** *adj* nahe (gelegen); **2.** *adv* in der Nähe
**near·ly** beinahe, fast; annähernd
**near·sight·ed** kurzsichtig
**neat** ordentlich; sauber; gepflegt; pur (*whisky etc*)
**neb·u·lous** verschwommen
**ne·ces·sar·i·ly** notwendigerweise; ***not ~*** nicht unbedingt
**ne·ces·sa·ry** notwendig, nötig; unvermeidlich

N

**ne·ces·si·tate** *et.* erfordern, verlangen
**ne·ces·si·ty** Notwendigkeit *f*; (dringendes) Bedürfnis; Not *f*
**neck 1.** ANAT Hals *m* (*a. of bottle etc*); Genick *n*, Nacken *m*; ***be ~ and ~*** F Kopf an Kopf liegen (*a. fig*); ***be up to one's ~ in debt*** F bis zum Hals in Schulden stecken; **2.** F knutschen, schmusen
**neck·er·chief** Halstuch *n*
**neck·lace** Halskette *f*
**neck·let** Halskettchen *n*
**neck·line** Ausschnitt *m*
**neck·tie** Krawatte *f*, Schlips *m*
**née:** ***~ Smith*** geborene Smith
**need 1.** (***of, for***) (dringendes) Bedürfnis (nach), Bedarf *m* (an *dat*); Notwendigkeit *f*; Mangel *m* (***of, for*** an *dat*); Not *f*; ***be in ~ of s.th.*** et. dringend brauchen; ***in ~*** in Not; ***in ~ of help*** hilfs-, hilfebedürftig; **2.** *v/t* benötigen, brauchen; *v/aux* brauchen, müssen
**nee·dle 1.** Nadel *f* (*a.* BOT, MED); Zeiger *m*; **2.** F *j-n* aufziehen, hänseln
**need·less** unnötig, überflüssig
**nee·dle·wom·an** Näherin *f*
**nee·dle·work** Handarbeit *f*
**need·y** bedürftig, arm
**ne·ga·tion** Verneinung *f*
**neg·a·tive 1.** negativ; verneinend; **2.** Verneinung *f*; PHOT Negativ *n*; ***answer in the ~*** verneinen
**ne·glect 1.** vernachlässigen; es versäumen (***doing, to do*** zu tun); **2.** Vernachlässigung *f*; Nachlässigkeit *f*
**neg·li·gence** Nachlässigkeit *f*, Unachtsamkeit *f*; **neg·li·gent** nachlässig, unachtsam; lässig, salopp
**neg·li·gi·ble** unbedeutend
**ne·go·ti·ate** verhandeln (über *acc*)
**ne·go·ti·a·tion** Verhandlung *f*
**ne·go·ti·a·tor** Unterhändler(in)
**neigh** zo **1.** wiehern; **2.** Wiehern *n*
**neigh·bo(u)r** Nachbar(in)
**neigh·bo(u)r·hood** Nachbarschaft *f*, Umgebung *f*
**neigh·bo(u)r·ing** benachbart, Nachbar..., angrenzend
**neigh·bo(u)r·ly** (gut)nachbarlich
**nei·ther 1.** *adj and pron* keine(r, -s) (von beiden); **2.** *cj* ***~ ... nor*** weder ... noch
**ne·on** CHEM Neon *n*; **~ lamp** Neonlampe *f*; **~ sign** Neon-, Leuchtreklame *f*
**neph·ew** Neffe *m*
**nep·o·tism** *contp* Vetternwirtschaft *f*
**nerd** F Trottel *m*; Computerfreak *m*
**nerve** Nerv *m*; Mut *m*, Stärke *f*, Selbstbeherrschung *f*; F Frechheit *f*; ***get on s.o.'s ~s*** j-m auf die Nerven gehen *or* fallen; ***lose one's ~*** den Mut *or* die Nerven verlieren; ***you've got a ~!*** F Sie haben Nerven!; **nerve·less** kraftlos; mutlos; ohne Nerven, kaltblütig
**ner·vous** nervös; Nerven...
**ner·vous·ness** Nervosität *f*
**nest 1.** Nest *n*; **2.** nisten
**nes·tle** (sich) schmiegen *or* kuscheln (***against, on*** an *acc*); *a.* ***~ down*** sich behaglich niederlassen, es sich bequem machen (***in*** in *dat*)
**net[1] 1.** Netz *n*; ***~ curtain*** Store *m*; **2.** mit e-m Netz fangen *or* abdecken
**net[2] 1.** netto, Netto..., Rein...; **2.** netto einbringen
**Neth·er·lands** *die* Niederlande *pl*
**net·tle 1.** BOT Nessel *f*; **2.** F *j-n* ärgern
**net·work** Netz *n* (*a.* EDP), Netzwerk *n*; (*Straßen- etc*)Netz *n*; *radio*, TV Sendernetz *n*; ***be in the ~*** EDP am Netz sein
**neu·ro·sis** MED Neurose *f*; **neu·rot·ic** MED **1.** neurotisch; **2.** Neurotiker(in)
**neu·ter 1.** LING sächlich; geschlechtslos; **2.** LING Neutrum *n*
**neu·tral 1.** neutral; **2.** Neutrale *m, f*; *a.* ***~ gear*** MOT Leerlauf(stellung *f*) *m*
**neu·tral·i·ty** Neutralität *f*
**neu·tral·ize** neutralisieren
**neu·tron** PHYS Neutron *n*
**nev·er** nie, niemals; **nev·er-end·ing** endlos, nicht enden wollend, unendlich
**nev·er·the·less** nichtsdestoweniger, dennoch, trotzdem
**new** neu; frisch; unerfahren; ***nothing ~*** nichts Neues
**new·born** neugeboren
**new·com·er** Neuankömmling *m*; Neuling *m*
**new·ly** kürzlich; neu
**news** Neuigkeit(en *pl*) *f*, Nachricht(en *pl*) *f*
**news·a·gent** Zeitungshändler(in)
**news·boy** Zeitungsjunge *m*, Zeitungsausträger *m*
**news bul·le·tin** Kurznachricht(en *pl*) *f*
**news·cast** *radio*, TV Nachrichtensendung *f*; **news·cast·er** *radio*, TV Nachrichtensprecher(in)
**news deal·er** Zeitungshändler(in)
**news·flash** *radio*, TV Kurzmeldung *f*

N

**news·let·ter** Rundschreiben *n*
**news·pa·per** Zeitung *f*
**news·print** Zeitungspapier *n*
**news·read·er** *esp Br* → ***newscaster***
**news·reel** *film*: Wochenschau *f*
**news·room** Nachrichtenredaktion *f*
**news·stand** Zeitungskiosk *m*, -stand *m*
**news·ven·dor** *esp Br* Zeitungsverkäufer(in)
**new year** Neujahr *n*, *das* neue Jahr; ***New Year's Day*** Neujahrstag *m*; ***New Year's Eve*** Silvester(abend *m*) *m*, *n*
**next 1.** *adj* nächste(r, -s); **(*the*) *~ day*** am nächsten Tag; ***~ door*** nebenan; ***~ but one*** übernächste(r, -s); ***~ to*** gleich neben *or* nach; beinahe, fast *unmöglich etc*; **2.** *adv* als Nächste(r, -s); demnächst, das nächste Mal; **3.** *der*, *die*, *das* Nächste; → ***kin***
**next-door** (von) nebenan
**nib·ble** *v/i* knabbern (***at*** an *dat*); *v/t* *Loch etc* nagen, knabbern (***in*** in *acc*)
**nice** nett, freundlich; hübsch, schön; *fig* fein (*detail etc*)
**nice·ly** gut, fein; genau, sorgfältig
**ni·ce·ty** Feinheit *f*; Genauigkeit *f*
**niche** Nische *f*
**nick 1.** Kerbe *f*; ***in the ~ of time*** gerade noch rechtzeitig, im letzten Moment; **2.** (ein)kerben; *j-n* streifen (*bullet*); *Br* F *et.* klauen; *Br* F *j-n* schnappen
**nick·el 1.** MIN Nickel *n*; Fünfcentstück *n*; **2.** TECH vernickeln
**nick·el-plate** TECH vernickeln
**nick-nack** → ***knick-knack***
**nick·name 1.** Spitzname *m*; **2.** *j-m* den Spitznamen ... geben
**niece** Nichte *f*
**nig·gard** Geizhals *m*
**nig·gard·ly** geizig, knaus(e)rig; schäbig, kümmerlich
**night** Nacht *f*; Abend *m*; ***at ~, by ~, in the ~*** in der Nacht, nachts
**night·cap** Schlummertrunk *m*
**night·club** Nachtklub *m*, Nachtlokal *n*
**night·dress** (Damen-, Kinder)Nachthemd *n*
**night·fall:** ***at ~*** bei Einbruch der Dunkelheit
**night·gown** → ***nightdress***
**night·ie** F → ***nightdress***
**nigh·tin·gale** ZO Nachtigall *f*
**night·ly** (all)nächtlich; (all)abendlich; jede Nacht; jeden Abend
**night·mare** Albtraum *m* (*a. fig*)
**night school** Abendschule *f*
**night shift** Nachtschicht *f*
**night·shirt** (Herren)Nachthemd *n*
**night·time:** ***in the ~, at ~*** nachts
**night watch·man** Nachtwächter *m*
**night·y** F → ***nightdress***
**nil** Nichts *n*, Null *f*; ***our team won two to ~ or by two goals to ~*** **(*2-0*)** unsere Mannschaft gewann zwei zu null (2:0)
**nim·ble** flink, gewandt; geistig beweglich
**nine 1.** neun; ***~ to five*** normale Dienststunden (von 9-5); ***a ~-to-five job*** e-e (An)Stellung mit geregelter Arbeitszeit; **2.** Neun *f*
**nine·pins** Kegeln *n*
**nine·teen 1.** neunzehn; **2.** Neunzehn *f*
**nine·teenth** neunzehnte(r, -s)
**nine·ti·eth** neunzigste(r, -s)
**nine·ty 1.** neunzig; **2.** Neunzig *f*
**ninth 1.** neunte(r, -s); **2.** Neuntel *n*
**ninth·ly** neuntens
**nip[1] 1.** kneifen, zwicken; F flitzen, sausen; ***~ off*** F abknipsen; ***~ in the bud*** *fig* im Keim ersticken; **2.** Kneifen *n*, Zwicken *n*; ***it was ~ and tuck*** F es war ganz knapp; ***there's a ~ in the air today*** heute ist es ganz schön kalt
**nip[2]** Schlückchen *n* (*of brandy etc*)
**nip·per:** **(*a pair of*) *~s*** (e-e) (Kneif)Zange *f*
**nip·ple** ANAT Brustwarze *f*; (Gummi-)Sauger *m*; TECH Nippel *m*
**ni·ter,** *Br* **ni·tre** CHEM Salpeter *m*
**ni·tro·gen** CHEM Stickstoff *m*
**no 1.** *adv* nein; nicht; **2.** *adj* kein(e); ***~ one*** keiner, niemand; ***in ~ time*** im Nu, im Handumdrehen; **3.** Nein *n*
**no·bil·i·ty** (Hoch)Adel *m*; *fig* Adel *m*
**no·ble** adlig; edel, nobel; prächtig
**no·ble·man** Adlige *m*
**no·ble·wom·an** Adlige *f*
**no·bod·y 1.** niemand, keiner; **2.** *fig* Niemand *m*, Null *f*
**no-cal·o·rie di·et** Nulldiät *f*
**noc·tur·nal** nächtlich, Nacht...
**nod 1.** nicken (mit); ***~ off*** einnicken; ***have a ~ding acquaintance with s.o.*** j-n flüchtig kennen; **2.** Nicken *n*
**node** BOT, MED Knoten *m*
**noise 1.** Krach *m*, Lärm *m*; Geräusch *n*; **2.** ***~ about*** **(*abroad, around*)** *Gerücht etc* verbreiten; **noise·less** geräuschlos; **nois·y** laut, geräuschvoll

**no·mad** Nomade *m*, Nomadin *f*
**nom·i·nal** nominell; ~ ***value*** ECON Nennwert *m*
**nom·i·nate** ernennen; nominieren, (zur Wahl) vorschlagen; **nom·i·na·tion** Ernennung *f*; Nominierung *f*
**nom·i·na·tive** *a.* ~ ***case*** LING Nominativ *m*, erster Fall
**nom·i·nee** Kandidat(in)
**non...** nicht..., Nicht..., un...
**non·al·co·hol·ic** alkoholfrei
**non·a·ligned** POL blockfrei
**non·com·mis·sioned of·fi·cer** MIL Unteroffizier *m*
**non·com·mit·tal** unverbindlich
**non·con·duc·tor** ELECTR Nichtleiter *m*
**non·de·script** nichts sagend; unauffällig
**none 1.** *pron* keine(r, -s), niemand; **2.** *adv* in keiner Weise, keineswegs
**non·en·ti·ty** *fig* Null *f*
**none·the·less** nichtsdestoweniger, dennoch, trotzdem
**non·ex·ist·ence** Nichtvorhandensein *n*, Fehlen *n*
**non·ex·ist·ent** nicht existierend
**non·fic·tion** Sachbücher *pl*
**non·flam·ma·ble, non·in·flam·ma·ble** nicht brennbar
**non·in·ter·fer·ence, non·in·ter·ven·tion** POL Nichteinmischung *f*
**non-i·ron** bügelfrei
**no-non·sense** nüchtern, sachlich
**non·par·ti·san** POL überparteilich; unparteiisch
**non·pay·ment** ECON Nicht(be)zahlung *f*
**non·plus** verblüffen
**non·pol·lut·ing** umweltfreundlich
**non·prof·it,** *Br* **non-prof·it·mak·ing** gemeinnützig
**non·res·i·dent 1.** nicht (orts)ansässig; nicht im Hause wohnend; **2.** Nichtansässige *m,f*; nicht im Hause Wohnende *m, f*
**non·re·turn·a·ble** Einweg...; ~ **bot·tle** Einwegflasche *f*
**non·sense** Unsinn *m*, dummes Zeug
**non-skid** rutschfest, rutschsicher
**non·smok·er** Nichtraucher(in)
**non·smok·ing** Nichtraucher...
**non·stick** mit Antihaftbeschichtung
**non·stop** nonstop, ohne Unterbrechung; RAIL durchgehend; AVIAT ohne Zwischenlandung; ~ ***flight*** *a.* Non--Stop-Flug *m*
**non·u·nion** nicht (gewerkschaftlich) organisiert
**non·vi·o·lence** (Politik *f* der) Gewaltlosigkeit *f*
**non·vi·o·lent** gewaltlos
**noo·dle** Nudel *f*
**nook** Ecke *f*, Winkel *m*
**noon** Mittag(szeit *f*) *m*; **at** ~ um 12 Uhr (mittags)
**noose** Schlinge *f*
**nope** F ne(e), nein
**nor** → ***neither*** 2; auch nicht
**norm** Norm *f*
**nor·mal** normal
**nor·mal·ize** (sich) normalisieren
**north 1.** Nord, Norden *m*; **2.** *adj* nördlich, Nord...; **3.** *adv* nach Norden, nordwärts
**north·east 1.** Nordost, Nordosten *m*; **2.** *a.* ***northeastern*** nordöstlich
**nor·ther·ly, nor·thern** Nord..., nördlich
**North Pole** Nordpol *m*
**north·ward(s)** *adv* nördlich, nach Norden
**north·west 1.** Nordwest, Nordwesten *m*; **2.** *a.* ***northwestern*** nordwestlich
**Nor·way** Norwegen *n*
**Nor·we·gian 1.** norwegisch; **2.** Norweger(in); LING Norwegisch *n*
**nose 1.** Nase *f*; ZO Schnauze *f*; *fig* Gespür *n*; **2.** *Auto etc* vorsichtig fahren; *a.* ~ ***about,*** ~ ***around*** *fig* F herumschnüffeln (in *dat*) (***for*** nach)
**nose·bleed** Nasenbluten *n*; ***have a*** ~ Nasenbluten haben
**nose·dive** AVIAT Sturzflug *m*
**nos·ey** → ***nosy***
**nos·tal·gia** Nostalgie *f*
**nos·tril** ANAT Nasenloch *n*, *esp* ZO Nüster *f*
**nos·y** F neugierig
**not** nicht; ~ ***a*** kein(e)
**no·ta·ble** bemerkenswert; beachtlich
**no·ta·ry** *mst* ~ ***public*** Notar *m*
**notch 1.** Kerbe *f*; GEOL Engpass *m*; **2.** (ein)kerben
**note** (*mst pl*) Notiz *f*, Aufzeichnung *f*; Anmerkung *f*; Vermerk *m*; Briefchen *n*, Zettel *m*; (diplomatische) Note; Banknote *f*, Geldschein *m*; MUS Note *f*; *fig* Ton *m*; ***take*** ~***s*** (***of***) sich Notizen ma-

N

chen (über *acc*); **note·book** Notizbuch *n*; EDP Notebook *n*
**not·ed** bekannt, berühmt (***for*** wegen)
**note·pa·per** Briefpapier *n*
**note·wor·thy** bemerkenswert
**noth·ing** nichts; ~ ***but*** nichts als, nur; ~ ***much*** F nicht viel; ***for*** ~ umsonst; ***to say*** ~ ***of*** ganz zu schweigen von; ***there is*** ~ ***like*** es geht nichts über (*acc*)
**no·tice 1.** Ankündigung *f*, Bekanntgabe *f*, Mitteilung *f*, Anzeige *f*; Kündigung(sfrist) *f*; Beachtung *f*; ***give*** *or* ***hand in one's*** ~ kündigen (***to*** bei); ***give s.o.*** ~ j-m kündigen; ***give s.o.*** ~ ***to quit*** j-m kündigen; ***at six months'*** ~ mit halbjährlicher Kündigungsfrist; ***take*** (***no***) ~ ***of*** (keine) Notiz nehmen von, (nicht) beachten; ***at short*** ~ kurzfristig; ***until further*** ~ bis auf weiteres; ***without*** ~ fristlos; **2.** (es) bemerken; (besonders) beachten *or* achten auf (*acc*)
**no·tice·a·ble** erkennbar, wahrnehmbar; bemerkenswert
**no·tice·board** *Br* schwarzes Brett
**no·ti·fy** *et.* anzeigen, melden, mitteilen; *j-n* benachrichtigen
**no·tion** Begriff *m*, Vorstellung *f*; Idee *f*
**no·tions** Kurzwaren *pl*
**no·to·ri·ous** berüchtigt (***for*** für)
**not·with·stand·ing** trotz (*gen*)
**nought** *Br*: ***0.4*** (~ ***point four***) 0,4
**noun** LING Substantiv *n*, Hauptwort *n*
**nour·ish** (er)nähren; *fig* hegen
**nour·ish·ing** nahrhaft
**nour·ish·ment** Ernährung *f*; Nahrung *f*
**Nov** ABBR *of* ***November*** Nov., November *m*
**nov·el 1.** Roman *m*; **2.** (ganz) neu(artig)
**nov·el·ist** Romanschriftsteller(in)
**no·vel·la** Novelle *f*
**nov·el·ty** Neuheit *f*
**No·vem·ber** (ABBR ***Nov***) November *m*
**nov·ice** Anfänger(in), Neuling *m*; REL Novize *m*, Novizin *f*
**now 1.** *adv* nun, jetzt; ~ ***and again***, (***every***) ~ ***and then*** von Zeit zu Zeit, dann und wann; ***by*** ~ inzwischen; ***from*** ~ (***on***) von jetzt an; ***just*** ~ gerade eben; **2.** *cj a.* ~ ***that*** nun da; **now·a·days** heutzutage
**no·where** nirgends
**nox·ious** schädlich
**noz·zle** TECH Schnauze *f*; Stutzen *m*; Düse *f*; Zapfpistole *f*

**nu·ance** Nuance *f*
**nub** springender Punkt
**nu·cle·ar** Kern..., Atom..., atomar, nuklear, Nuklear...; ~ **en·er·gy** PHYS Atomenergie *f*, Kernenergie *f*; ~ **fam·i·ly** Kern-, Kleinfamilie *f*; ~ **fis·sion** PHYS Kernspaltung *f*
**nu·cle·ar-free** atomwaffenfrei
**nu·cle·ar| fu·sion** PHYS Kernfusion *f*; ~ **phys·ics** Kernphysik *f*; ~ **pow·er** PHYS Atomkraft *f*, Kernkraft *f*
**nu·cle·ar-pow·ered** atomgetrieben
**nu·cle·ar| pow·er plant** ELECTR Atomkraftwerk *n*, Kernkraftwerk *n*; ~ **re·ac·tor** PHYS Atomreaktor *m*, Kernreaktor *m*; ~ **war** Atomkrieg *m*; ~ **war·head** MIL Atomsprengkopf *m*; ~ **waste** Atommüll *m*; ~ **weap·ons** MIL Atomwaffen *pl*, Kernwaffen *pl*
**nu·cle·us** BIOL, PHYS Kern *m* (*a. fig*)
**nude 1.** nackt; **2.** *art*: Akt *m*
**nudge 1.** *j-n* anstoßen, (an)stupsen; **2.** Stups(er) *m*
**nug·get** (*esp* Gold)Klumpen *m*
**nui·sance** Plage *f*, Ärgernis *n*; Nervensäge *f*, Quälgeist *m*; ***what a*** ~***!*** wie ärgerlich!; ***be a*** ~ ***to s.o.*** j-m lästig fallen, F j-n nerven; ***make a*** ~ ***of o.s.*** den Leuten auf die Nerven gehen *or* fallen
**nukes** F Atom-, Kernwaffen *pl*
**null:** ~ ***and void*** *esp* JUR null und nichtig
**numb 1.** starr (***with*** vor), taub; *fig* wie betäubt (***with*** vor); **2.** starr *or* taub machen
**num·ber 1.** Zahl *f*, Ziffer *f*; Nummer *f*; (An)Zahl *f*; Ausgabe *f*; (*Bus- etc*)Linie *f*; ***sorry, wrong*** ~ TEL falsch verbunden!; **2.** nummerieren; zählen; sich belaufen auf (*acc*)
**num·ber·less** zahllos
**num·ber·plate** *esp Br* MOT Nummernschild *n*
**nu·me·ral** Ziffer *f*; LING Zahlwort *n*
**nu·me·ra·tor** MATH Zähler *m*
**nu·me·rous** zahlreich
**nun** REL Nonne *f*
**nun·ne·ry** REL Nonnenkloster *n*
**nurse 1.** (Kranken-, Säuglings)Schwester *f*, Kindermädchen *n*; (Kranken-)Pflegerin *f*; → ***male nurse***; *a.* ***wet*** ~ Amme *f*; **2.** stillen; pflegen; hegen; als Krankenschwester *or* -pfleger arbeiten; ~ ***s.o. back to health*** j-n gesund pflegen
**nur·se·ry** Tagesheim *n*, Tagesstätte *f*;

Baum-, Pflanzschule *f*; ~ **rhyme** Kinderlied *n*, Kinderreim *m*; ~ **school** *Br* Vorschule *f*; ~ **slope** *skiing*: F Idiotenhügel *m*

**nurs·ing** Stillen *n*; (Kranken)Pflege *f*; ~ **bot·tle** (Saug)Flasche *f*; ~ **home** Pflegeheim *n*

**nut** BOT Nuss *f*; TECH (Schrauben)Mutter *f*; F verrückter Kerl; F Birne *f* (*head*); ***be off one's*** ~ F spinnen

**nut·crack·er(s)** Nussknacker *m*

**nut·meg** BOT Muskatnuss *f*

**nu·tri·ent 1.** Nährstoff *m*; **2.** nahrhaft

**nu·tri·tion** Ernährung *f*

**nu·tri·tious, nu·tri·tive** nahrhaft

**nut·shell** Nussschale *f*; (***to put it***) ***in a*** ~ F kurz gesagt, mit e-m Wort

**nut·ty** voller Nüsse; Nuss...; F verrückt

**ny·lon** Nylon *n*; ~ **stock·ings** Nylonstrümpfe *pl*

**nymph** Nymphe *f*

# O

**O, o** O, o *n*

**o** Null *f*

**oaf** Lümmel *m*, Flegel *m*

**oak** BOT Eiche *f*

**oar** Ruder *n*

**oars·man** SPORT Ruderer *m*

**oars·wom·an** SPORT Ruderin *f*

**o·a·sis** Oase *f* (*a. fig*)

**oath** Eid *m*, Schwur *m*; Fluch *m*; ***take an*** ~ e-n Eid leisten *or* schwören; ***be on*** *or* ***under*** ~ JUR unter Eid stehen; ***take the*** ~ JUR schwören

**oat·meal** Hafermehl *n*, Hafergrütze *f*

**oats** BOT Hafer *m*; ***sow one's wild*** ~ sich die Hörner abstoßen

**o·be·di·ence** Gehorsam *m*

**o·be·di·ent** gehorsam

**o·bese** fett, fettleibig

**o·bes·i·ty** Fettleibigkeit *f*

**o·bey** gehorchen (*dat*), folgen (*dat*); *Befehl etc* befolgen

**o·bit·u·a·ry** Nachruf *m*; *a.* ~ ***notice*** Todesanzeige *f*

**ob·ject 1.** Objekt *n* (*a.* LING); Gegenstand *m*; Ziel *n*, Zweck *m*, Absicht *f*; **2.** einwenden; et. dagegen haben

**ob·jec·tion** Einwand *m*, Einspruch *m* (*a.* JUR); **ob·jec·tion·a·ble** nicht einwandfrei; unangenehm; anstößig

**ob·jec·tive 1.** objektiv, sachlich; **2.** Ziel *n*; **ob·jec·tive·ness** Objektivität *f*

**ob·li·ga·tion** Verpflichtung *f*; ***be under an*** ~ ***to s.o.*** j-m (zu Dank) verpflichtet sein; ***be under an*** ~ ***to do*** verpflichtet sein, *et.* zu tun; **ob·lig·a·to·ry** verpflichtend, verbindlich

**o·blige** nötigen, zwingen; (zu Dank) verpflichten; ~ ***s.o.*** j-m e-n Gefallen tun; ***much*** **~*d*** besten Dank

**o·blig·ing** entgegenkommend, gefällig

**o·blique** schief, schräg; *fig* indirekt

**o·blit·er·ate** auslöschen; vernichten, völlig zerstören; verdecken

**o·bliv·i·on** Vergessen(heit *f*) *n*; ***fall into*** ~ in Vergessenheit geraten

**o·bliv·i·ous:** ***be*** ~ ***of*** *or* ***to s.th.*** sich e-r Sache nicht bewusst sein; et. nicht bemerken *or* wahrnehmen

**ob·long** rechteckig; länglich

**ob·nox·ious** widerlich

**ob·scene** obszön, unanständig

**ob·scure 1.** dunkel, *fig a.* unklar; unbekannt; **2.** verdunkeln, verdecken

**ob·scu·ri·ty** Unbekanntheit *f*; Unklarheit *f*

**ob·se·quies** Trauerfeier(lichkeiten *pl*) *f*

**ob·ser·va·ble** wahrnehmbar, merklich; **ob·ser·vance** Beachtung *f*, Befolgung *f*; **ob·ser·vant** aufmerksam; **ob·ser·va·tion** Beobachtung *f*, Überwachung *f*; Bemerkung *f* (***on*** über *acc*); **ob·ser·va·to·ry** Observatorium *n*, Sternwarte *f*; **ob·serve** beobachten; überwachen; *Vorschrift etc* beachten, befolgen, einhalten; bemerken, äußern; **ob·serv·er** Beobachter(in)

**ob·sess:** ***be*** **~*ed by*** *or* ***with*** besessen sein von; **ob·ses·sion** PSYCH Beses-

senheit *f*, fixe Idee, Zwangsvorstellung *f*; **ob·ses·sive** PSYCH zwanghaft
**ob·so·lete** veraltet
**ob·sta·cle** Hindernis *n*
**ob·sti·na·cy** Starrsinn *m*
**ob·sti·nate** hartnäckig; halsstarrig, eigensinnig, starrköpfig
**ob·struct** verstopfen, versperren; blockieren; behindern
**ob·struc·tion** Verstopfung *f*; Blockierung *f*; Behinderung *f*
**ob·struc·tive** blockierend; hinderlich
**ob·tain** erhalten, bekommen, sich *et.* beschaffen; **ob·tain·a·ble** erhältlich
**ob·tru·sive** aufdringlich
**ob·tuse** MATH stumpf; *fig* begriffsstutzig; ***be ~*** sich dumm stellen
**ob·vi·ous** offensichtlich, klar, einleuchtend
**oc·ca·sion** Gelegenheit *f*; Anlass *m*; Veranlassung *f*; (festliches) Ereignis; ***on the ~ of*** anlässlich (*gen*)
**oc·ca·sion·al** gelegentlich; vereinzelt
**oc·ca·sion·al·ly** gelegentlich, manchmal
**Oc·ci·dent** *der* Westen, *der* Okzident, *das* Abendland
**oc·ci·den·tal** abendländisch, westlich
**oc·cu·pant** Bewohner(in); Insasse *m*, Insassin *f*
**oc·cu·pa·tion** Beruf *m*; Beschäftigung *f*; MIL, POL Besetzung *f*, Besatzung *f*, Okkupation *f*
**oc·cu·py** in Besitz nehmen, MIL, POL besetzen; *Raum* einnehmen; in Anspruch nehmen; beschäftigen; ***be occupied*** bewohnt sein; besetzt sein (*seat*)
**oc·cur** sich ereignen; vorkommen; ***it ~red to me that*** es fiel mir ein *or* mir kam der Gedanke, dass
**oc·cur·rence** Vorkommen *n*; Ereignis *n*; Vorfall *m*
**o·cean** Ozean *m*, (Welt)Meer *n*
**o'clock:** (***at***) ***five ~*** (um) fünf Uhr
**Oct** ABBR *of* ***October*** Okt., Oktober *m*
**Oc·to·ber** (ABBR ***Oct***) Oktober *m*
**oc·u·lar** Augen...
**oc·u·list** Augenarzt *m*, Augenärztin *f*
**OD** F *v/i*: ***~ on heroin*** an e-r Überdosis Heroin sterben
**odd** sonderbar, seltsam, merkwürdig; einzeln, Einzel...; ungerade (*number*); gelegentlich, Gelegenheits...; ***~ jobs*** Gelegenheitsarbeiten *pl*; F ***30 ~*** (et.) über 30, einige 30
**odds** (Gewinn)Chancen *pl*; ***the ~ are 10 to 1*** die Chancen stehen 10 zu 1; ***the ~ are that*** es ist sehr wahrscheinlich, dass; ***against all ~*** wider Erwarten, entgegen allen Erwartungen; ***be at ~*** uneins sein (***with*** mit); ***~ and ends*** Krimskrams *m*; **odds-on** hoch, klar (*favorite*), aussichtsreichst (*candidate etc*); F ***it's ~ that*** es sieht ganz so aus, als ob ...
**ode** Ode *f*
**o·do(u)r** Geruch *m*
**o·do(u)r·less** geruchlos
**of** *prp* von; *origin*: von, aus; *material*: aus; um (***cheat s.o. ~ s.th.*** j-n um et. betrügen); *cause*: an (*dat*) (***die ~*** sterben an); aus (***~ charity*** aus Nächstenliebe); vor (*dat*) (***be afraid ~*** Angst haben vor); auf (*acc*) (***be proud ~*** stolz sein auf); über (*acc*) (***be glad ~*** sich freuen über); nach (***smell ~*** riechen nach); von, über (*acc*) (***speak ~ s.th.*** von *or* über et. sprechen); an (*acc*) (***think ~ s.th.*** an et. denken); ***the city ~ London*** die Stadt London; ***the works ~ Dickens*** Dickens' Werke; ***your letter ~ ...*** Ihr Schreiben vom ...; ***five minutes ~ twelve*** fünf Minuten vor zwölf
**off 1.** *adv* fort(...), weg(...); ab(...), ab, abgegangen (*button etc*); weg, entfernt (***3 miles ~***); ELECTR *etc* aus(...), aus-, abgeschaltet; TECH zu; aus(gegangen), alle; aus, vorbei; verdorben (*food*); frei; ***I must be ~*** ich muss gehen *or* weg; ***~ with you!*** fort mit dir!; ***be ~*** ausfallen, nicht stattfinden; ***10% ~*** ECON 10% Nachlass; ***~ and on*** ab und zu, hin und wieder; ***take a day ~*** sich e-n Tag freinehmen; ***be well*** (***badly***) ***~*** gut (schlecht) d(a)ran *or* gestellt *or* situiert sein; **2.** *prp* fort von, weg von, von (... ab, weg, herunter); abseits von (*or gen*), von ... weg; MAR vor *der Küste etc*; ***be ~ duty*** nicht im Dienst sein, dienstfrei haben; ***be ~ smoking*** nicht mehr rauchen; **3.** *adj* frei, arbeits-, dienstfrei; *fig* ***have an ~ day*** e-n schlechten Tag haben
**of·fal** GASTR Innereien *pl*
**off-col·o(u)r** schlüpfrig, zweideutig
**of·fence** *Br* → ***offense***
**of·fend** beleidigen, kränken; verstoßen (***against*** gegen); **of·fend·er** (Übel-,

Misse)Täter(in); ***first ~*** JUR nicht Vorbestrafte *m*, *f*, Ersttäter(in)
**of·fense** Vergehen *n*, Verstoß *m*; JUR Straftat *f*; Beleidigung *f*, Kränkung *f*; ***take ~*** Anstoß nehmen (***at*** an *dat*)
**of·fen·sive 1.** beleidigend, anstößig; widerlich (*smell etc*); MIL Offensiv..., Angriffs...; **2.** MIL Offensive *f* (*a. fig*)
**of·fer 1.** *v/t* anbieten (*a.* ECON); *Preis, Möglichkeit etc* bieten; *Preis, Belohnung* aussetzen; sich bereit erklären (***to do*** zu tun); *Widerstand* leisten; *v/i* es *or* sich anbieten; **2.** Angebot *n*
**off·hand 1.** *adj* lässig; Stegreif...; ***be ~ with s.o.*** F mit j-m kurz angebunden sein; **2.** *adv* auf Anhieb, so ohne weiteres
**of·fice** Büro *n*, Geschäftsstelle *f*, (*Anwalts*)Kanzlei *f*; (*esp* öffentliches) Amt, Posten *m*; *mst* ***Office*** *esp Br* Ministerium *n*; **~ block** *Br*, **~ build·ing** Bürohaus *n*; **~ hours** Dienstzeit *f*; Geschäfts-, Öffnungszeiten *pl*
**of·fi·cer** MIL Offizier *m*; (*Polizei- etc*)Beamte *m*, (-)Beamtin *f*
**of·fi·cial 1.** Beamte *m*, Beamtin *f*; **2.** offiziell, amtlich, dienstlich
**of·fi·ci·ate** amtieren
**of·fi·cious** übereifrig
**off-licence** *Br* Wein- und Spirituosenhandlung *f*
**off·line** EDP offline, Offline..., rechnerunabhängig
**off-peak:** ***~ electricity*** Nachtstrom *m*; ***~ hours*** verkehrsschwache Stunden *pl*
**off sea·son** Nebensaison *f*
**off·set** ECON ausgleichen; verrechnen (***against*** mit)
**off·shoot** BOT Ableger *m*, Spross *m*
**off·shore** vor der Küste
**off·side** SPORT abseits; ***~ position*** Abseitsposition *f*, Abseitsstellung *f*; ***~ trap*** Abseitsfalle *f*
**off·spring** Nachkomme *m*, Nachkommenschaft *f*
**off-the-peg** *Br*, **off-the-rack** Konfektions..., ... von der Stange
**off-the-rec·ord** inoffiziell
**of·ten** oft(mals), häufig
**oh** *int* oh!
**oil 1.** Öl *n*; Erdöl *n*; **2.** (ein)ölen, schmieren (*a. fig*)
**oil change** MOT Ölwechsel *m*
**oil·cloth** Wachstuch *n*
**oil·field** Ölfeld *n*
**oil paint·ing** Ölmalerei *f*; Ölgemälde *n*
**oil pan** MOT Ölwanne *f*
**oil plat·form** → ***oilrig***
**oil pol·lu·tion** Ölpest *f*
**oil pro·duc·tion** Ölförderung *f*
**oil-pro·duc·ing coun·try** Ölförderland *n*
**oil re·fin·e·ry** Erdölraffinerie *f*
**oil·rig** (Öl)Bohrinsel *f*
**oil·skins** Ölzeug *n*
**oil slick** Ölteppich *m*
**oil well** Ölquelle *f*
**oil·y** ölig; *fig* schmierig, schleimig
**oint·ment** Salbe *f*
**OK, o·kay** F **1.** *adj and int* okay(!), o.k.(!), in Ordnung(!); **2.** genehmigen, *e-r Sache* zustimmen; **3.** Okay *n*, O.K. *n*, Genehmigung *f*, Zustimmung *f*
**old 1.** alt; **2.** ***the ~*** die Alten *pl*
**old age** (hohes) Alter; **~ pen·sion** Rente *f*, Pension *f*; **~ pen·sion·er** Rentner(in), Pensionär(in)
**old-fash·ioned** altmodisch
**old·ish** ältlich
**old peo·ple's home** Altersheim *n*, Altenheim *n*
**ol·ive** BOT Olive *f*; Olivgrün *n*
**O·lym·pic Games** SPORT Olympische Spiele *pl*
**om·i·nous** unheilvoll
**o·mis·sion** Auslassung *f*; Unterlassung *f*; Versäumnis *n*
**o·mit** auslassen, weglassen; unterlassen
**om·nip·o·tent** allmächtig
**om·nis·ci·ent** allwissend
**on 1.** *prp* auf (*acc or dat*) (***~ the table*** auf dem *or* den Tisch); an (*dat*) (***~ the wall*** an der Wand); in (***~ TV*** im Fernsehen); *direction, target*: auf (*acc*) ... (hin), an (*acc*), nach (*dat*) ... (hin) (***march ~ London*** nach London marschieren); *fig* auf (*acc*) ... (hin) (***~ demand*** auf Anfrage); *time*: an (*dat*) (***~ Sunday*** am Sonntag; ***~ the 1st of April*** am 1. April); (gleich) nach, bei (***~ his arrival***); *gehörig* zu, *beschäftigt* bei (***be ~ a committee*** e-m Ausschuss angehören; ***be ~ the "Daily Mail"*** bei der "Daily Mail" beschäftigt sein); *state*: in (*dat*), auf (*dat*) (***~ duty*** im Dienst; ***be ~ fire*** in Flammen stehen); *subject*: über (*acc*) (***talk ~ a subject*** über ein Thema sprechen); nach (*dat*) (***~ this model*** nach diesem Modell);

O

von (*dat*) (***live ~ s.th.*** von et. leben); ***~ the street*** auf der Straße; ***~ a train*** in e-m Zug; ***~ hearing it*** als ich *etc* es hörte; ***have you any money ~ you?*** hast du Geld bei dir?; **2.** *adj and adv* an(geschaltet) (*light etc*), eingeschaltet (*radio etc*), auf (*faucet etc*); (dar)auf(*legen, -schrauben etc*); an(*haben, -ziehen*) (***have a coat ~*** e-n Mantel anhaben); auf(*behalten*) (***keep one's hat ~*** den Hut aufbehalten); weiter(*gehen, -sprechen etc*); ***and so ~*** und so weiter; ***~ and ~*** immer weiter; ***from this day ~*** von dem Tage an; ***be ~*** THEA gegeben werden; *film*: laufen; *radio*, TV gesendet werden; ***what's ~?*** was ist los?

**once 1.** einmal; einst; ***~ again, ~ more*** noch einmal; ***~ in a while*** ab und zu, hin und wieder; ***~ and for all*** ein für alle Mal; ***not ~*** kein einziges Mal, keinmal; ***at ~*** sofort; auf einmal, gleichzeitig; ***all at ~*** plötzlich; ***for ~*** diesmal, ausnahmsweise; ***this ~*** dieses eine Mal; ***~ upon a time there was ...*** es war einmal ...; **2.** sobald

**one** ein(e); einzig; man; Eins *f*, eins; ***~'s*** sein(e); ***~ day*** eines Tages; ***~ Smith*** ein gewisser Smith; ***~ another*** sich (gegenseitig), einander; ***~ by ~, ~ after another, ~ after the other*** e-r nach dem andern; ***I for ~*** ich zum Beispiel; ***the little ~s*** die Kleinen *pl*

**one-horse town** F *contp* Nest *n*

O

**one·self** sich (selbst); sich selbst; (***all***) ***by ~*** ganz allein; ***to ~*** ganz für sich (allein)

**one-sid·ed** einseitig

**one·time** ehemalig, früher

**one-track mind:** ***have a ~*** immer nur dasselbe im Kopf haben

**one-two** *soccer*: Doppelpass *m*

**one-way** Einbahn...; **~ street** Einbahnstraße *f*; **~ tick·et** RAIL *etc* einfache Fahrkarte, AVIAT einfaches Ticket; **~ traf·fic** MOT Einbahnverkehr *m*

**on·ion** BOT Zwiebel *f*

**on·line** EDP online, Online..., rechnerabhängig

**on·look·er** Zuschauer(in)

**on·ly 1.** *adj* einzige(r, -s); **2.** *adv* nur, bloß; erst; ***~ yesterday*** erst gestern; **3.** *cj* F nur, bloß

**on·rush** Ansturm *m*

**on·set** Beginn *m*; MED Ausbruch *m*

**on·slaught** (heftiger) Angriff (*a. fig*)

**on·to** auf (*acc*)

**on·ward(s)** *adv* vorwärts, weiter; ***from now ~*** von nun an

**ooze** *v/i* sickern; ***~ away*** *fig* schwinden; *v/t* absondern; *fig* ausstrahlen, verströmen

**o·paque** undurchsichtig; *fig* unverständlich

**o·pen 1.** offen, *a.* geöffnet, *a.* frei (*country etc*); öffentlich; *fig* offen, *a.* unentschieden, *a.* freimütig; *fig* zugänglich, aufgeschlossen (**to** für *or dat*); ***~ all day*** durchgehend geöffnet; ***in the ~ air*** im Freien; **2.** *golf, tennis*: offenes Turnier; ***in the ~*** im Freien; ***come out into the ~*** *fig* an die Öffentlichkeit treten; **3.** *v/t* öffnen, aufmachen, *Buch etc a.* aufschlagen; eröffnen; *v/i* sich öffnen, aufgehen; öffnen, aufmachen (*store*); anfangen, beginnen; ***~ into*** führen nach *or* in (*acc*); ***~ onto*** hinausgehen auf (*acc*)

**o·pen-air** im Freien

**o·pen-end·ed** zeitlich unbegrenzt

**o·pen·er** (*Dosen- etc*)Öffner *m*

**o·pen-eyed** mit großen Augen, staunend

**o·pen-hand·ed** freigebig, großzügig

**o·pen-heart·ed** offenherzig

**o·pen·ing 1.** Öffnung *f*; ECON freie Stelle; Eröffnung *f*, Erschließung *f*, Einstieg *m*; **2.** Eröffnungs...; Öffnungs...

**o·pen-mind·ed** aufgeschlossen

**o·pen·ness** Offenheit *f*

**op·e·ra** Oper *f*; **~ glass·es** Opernglas *n*; **~ house** Opernhaus *n*, Oper *f*

**op·e·rate** *v/i* wirksam sein *or* werden; TECH arbeiten, in Betrieb sein, laufen (*machine etc*); MED operieren (***on s.o.*** j-n); *v/t Maschine* bedienen, *Schalter etc* betätigen; *Unternehmen, Geschäft* betreiben, führen

**op·e·rat·ing| room** MED Operationssaal *m*; **~ sys·tem** EDP Betriebssystem *n*; **~ thea·tre** *Br* MED Operationssaal *m*

**op·e·ra·tion** TECH Betrieb *m*, Lauf *m*; Bedienung *f*; ECON Tätigkeit *f*, Unternehmen *n*; MED, MIL Operation *f*; ***in ~*** TECH in Betrieb; ***have an ~*** MED operiert werden

**op·e·ra·tive** wirksam; MED operativ

**op·e·ra·tor** TECH Bedienungsperson *f*; EDP Operator *m*; TEL Vermittlung *f*

**o·pin·ion** Meinung *f*, Ansicht *f*; Gut-

achten *n* (***on*** über *acc*); ***in my ~*** meines Erachtens
**op·po·nent** Gegner(in)
**op·por·tune** günstig, passend; rechtzeitig
**op·por·tu·ni·ty** (günstige) Gelegenheit
**op·pose** sich widersetzen (*dat*)
**op·posed** entgegengesetzt; ***be ~ to*** gegen ... sein
**op·po·site 1.** Gegenteil *n*, Gegensatz *m*; **2.** *adj* gegenüberliegend; entgegengesetzt; **3.** *adv* gegenüber (***to*** *dat*); **4.** *prp* gegenüber (*dat*)
**op·po·si·tion** Widerstand *m*, Opposition *f* (*a.* PARL); Gegensatz *m*
**op·press** unterdrücken
**op·pres·sion** Unterdrückung *f*
**op·pres·sive** (be)drückend; hart, grausam; schwül (*weather*)
**op·tic** Augen..., Seh...; → **op·ti·cal** optisch; **op·ti·cian** Optiker(in)
**op·ti·mism** Optimismus *m*
**op·ti·mist** Optimist(in)
**op·ti·mis·tic** optimistisch
**op·tion** Wahl *f*; ECON Option *f*, Vorkaufsrecht *n*; MOT Extra *n*
**op·tion·al** freiwillig; Wahl...; ***be an ~ extra*** MOT gegen Aufpreis erhältlich sein; **~ sub·ject** PED *etc* Wahlfach *n*
**or** oder; ***~ else*** sonst
**o·ral** mündlich; Mund...
**or·ange 1.** BOT Orange *f*, Apfelsine *f*; **2.** orange(farben)
**or·ange·ade** Orangenlimonade *f*
**o·ra·tion** Rede *f*, Ansprache *f*
**or·a·tor** Redner(in)
**or·bit 1.** Kreisbahn *f*, Umlaufbahn *f*; ***get*** *or* ***put into ~*** in e-e Umlaufbahn gelangen *or* bringen; **2.** *v/t die Erde etc* umkreisen; *v/i* die Erde *etc* umkreisen, sich auf e-r Umlaufbahn bewegen
**or·chard** Obstgarten *m*
**or·ches·tra** MUS Orchester *n*; THEA Parkett *n*
**or·chid** BOT Orchidee *f*
**or·dain: *~ s.o.* (*priest*)** j-n zum Priester weihen
**or·deal** Qual *f*, Tortur *f*
**or·der 1.** Ordnung *f*; Reihenfolge *f*; Befehl *m*, Anordnung *f*; ECON Bestellung *f*, Auftrag *m*; PARL *etc* (Geschäfts)Ordnung *f*; REL *etc* Orden *m*; ***~ to pay*** ECON Zahlungsanweisung *f*; ***in ~ to*** *inf* um zu *inf*; ***out of ~*** TECH nicht in Ordnung, defekt; außer Betrieb; ***make to ~*** auf Bestellung *or* nach Maß anfertigen; **2.** *v/t j-m* befehlen (***to do*** zu tun), *et.* befehlen, anordnen; *j-n* schicken, beordern; MED *j-m et.* verordnen; ECON bestellen; *fig* ordnen, in Ordnung bringen; *v/i* bestellen (*in restaurant*)
**or·der·ly 1.** ordentlich; *fig* gesittet, friedlich; **2.** MED Hilfspfleger *m*
**or·di·nal** *a.* ***~ number*** MATH Ordnungszahl *f*
**or·di·nary** üblich, gewöhnlich, normal
**ore** MIN Erz *n*
**or·gan** ANAT Organ *n* (*a. fig*); MUS Orgel *f*; **~ do·nor** MED Organspender *m*; **~ grind·er** Leierkastenmann *m*; **~ re·cip·i·ent** MED Organempfänger *m*
**or·gan·ic** organisch
**or·gan·ism** Organismus *m*
**or·gan·i·za·tion** Organisation *f*
**or·gan·ize** organisieren; sich (gewerkschaftlich) organisieren
**or·gan·iz·er** Organisator(in)
**or·gasm** Orgasmus *m*
**o·ri·ent 1.** ***Orient*** *der* Osten, *der* Orient, *das* Morgenland; **2.** orientieren
**o·ri·en·tal 1.** orientalisch, östlich; **2.** ***Oriental*** Orientale *m*, Orientalin *f*
**o·ri·en·tate** orientieren
**or·i·gin** Ursprung *m*, Abstammung *f*, Herkunft *f*
**o·rig·i·nal 1.** ursprünglich; Original...; originell; **2.** Original *n*
**o·rig·i·nal·i·ty** Originalität *f*
**o·rig·i·nal·ly** ursprünglich; originell
**o·rig·i·nate** *v/t* schaffen, ins Leben rufen; *v/i* zurückgehen (***from*** auf *acc*), (her)stammen (***from*** von, aus)
**or·na·ment 1.** Ornament(e *pl*) *n*, Verzierung(en *pl*) *f*, Schmuck *m*; *fig* Zier(de) *f* (***to*** für *or gen*); **2.** verzieren, schmücken (***with*** mit)
**or·na·men·tal** dekorativ, schmückend, Zier...
**or·nate** *fig* überladen
**or·phan 1.** Waise *f*, Waisenkind *n*; **2. *be ~ed*** Waise werden
**or·phan·age** Waisenhaus *n*
**or·tho·dox** orthodox
**os·cil·late** PHYS schwingen; *fig* schwanken (***between*** zwischen *dat*)
**os·prey** ZO Fischadler *m*
**os·ten·si·ble** angeblich, vorgeblich
**os·ten·ta·tion** (protzige) Zurschaustellung; Protzerei *f*, Prahlerei *f*

**os·ten·ta·tious** protzend, prahlerisch
**os·tra·cize** ächten
**os·trich** zo Strauß *m*
**oth·er** andere(r, -s); ***the ~ day*** neulich; ***the ~ morning*** neulich morgens; ***every ~ day*** jeden zweiten Tag, alle zwei Tage
**oth·er·wise** anders; sonst
**ot·ter** zo Otter *m*
**ought** *v/aux ich* sollte, *du* solltest *etc*; ***you ~ to have done it*** Sie hätten es tun sollen
**ounce** Unze *f* (*28,35 g*)
**our** unser
**ours** unsere(r, -s)
**our·selves** wir *or* uns selbst; uns (selbst)
**oust** verdrängen, hinauswerfen (***from*** aus); *j-n s-s Amtes* entheben
**out 1.** *adv*, *adj* aus; hinaus(*gehen*, *-werfen etc*); heraus(*kommen etc*); aus(*brechen etc*); draußen, im Freien; nicht zu Hause; SPORT aus, draußen; aus, vorbei; aus, erloschen; ausverkauft; F out, aus der Mode; ***~ of*** aus (... heraus); zu ... hinaus; außerhalb von (*or gen*); außer *Reichweite etc*; außer *Atem*, *Übung etc*; (hergestellt) aus; aus *Furcht etc*; ***be ~ of bread*** kein Brot mehr haben; ***in nine ~ of ten cases*** in neun von zehn Fällen; **2.** *prp* F aus (... heraus); zu ... hinaus; **3.** outen
**out·bal·ance** überwiegen
**out·bid** überbieten
**out·board mo·tor** Außenbordmotor *m*
**out·break** MED, MIL Ausbruch *m*
**out·build·ing** Nebengebäude *n*
**out·burst** *fig* Ausbruch *m*
**out·cast 1.** ausgestoßen; **2.** Ausgestoßene *m, f*, Verstoßene *m, f*
**out·come** Ergebnis *n*
**out·cry** Aufschrei *m*, Schrei *m* der Entrüstung
**out·dat·ed** überholt, veraltet
**out·dis·tance** hinter sich lassen
**out·do** übertreffen
**out·door** *adj* im Freien, draußen
**out·doors** *adv* draußen, im Freien
**out·er** äußere(r, -s)
**out·er·most** äußerste(r,-s)
**out·er space** Weltraum *m*
**out·fit** Ausrüstung *f*, Ausstattung *f*; Kleidung *f*; F (Arbeits)Gruppe *f*
**out·fit·ter** Ausstatter *m*; ***men's ~*** Herrenausstatter *m*
**out·go·ing** (aus dem Amt) scheidend
**out·grow** herauswachsen aus (*dat*); *Angewohnheit etc* ablegen; größer werden als
**out·house** Nebengebäude *n*
**out·ing** Ausflug *m*; Outing *n*
**out·land·ish** befremdlich, sonderbar
**out·last** überdauern, überleben
**out·law** HIST Geächtete *m, f*
**out·lay** (Geld)Auslagen *pl*, Ausgaben *pl*
**out·let** Abfluss *m*, Abzug *m*; *fig* Ventil *n*
**out·line 1.** Umriss *m*; Überblick *m*; **2.** umreißen, skizzieren
**out·live** überleben
**out·look** (Aus)Blick *m*, (Aus)Sicht *f*; Einstellung *f*, Auffassung *f*
**out·ly·ing** abgelegen, entlegen
**out·num·ber** in der Überzahl sein; ***be ~ed by s.o.*** j-m zahlenmäßig unterlegen sein
**out-of-date** veraltet, überholt
**out-of-the-way** abgelegen, entlegen; *fig* ungewöhnlich
**out·pa·tient** MED ambulanter Patient, ambulante Patientin
**out·post** Vorposten *m*
**out·pour·ing** (Gefühls)Erguss *m*
**out·put** ECON Output *m*, Produktion *f*, Ausstoß *m*, Ertrag *m*; EDP (Daten)Ausgabe *f*
**out·rage 1.** Gewalttat *f*, Verbrechen *n*; Empörung *f*; **2.** grob verletzen; *j-n* empören; **out·ra·geous** abscheulich; empörend, unerhört
**out·right 1.** *adj* völlig, gänzlich, glatt (*lie etc*); **2.** *adv* auf der Stelle, sofort; ohne Umschweife
**out·run** schneller laufen als; *fig* übersteigen, übertreffen
**out·set** Anfang *m*, Beginn *m*
**out·shine** überstrahlen, *fig a.* in den Schatten stellen
**out·side 1.** Außenseite *f*; SPORT Außenstürmer(in); ***at the*** (***very***) ***~*** (aller-) höchstens; ***~ left*** (***right***) SPORT Linksaußen (Rechtsaußen) *m*; **2.** *adj* äußere(r, -s), Außen...; **3.** *adv* draußen; heraus, hinaus; **4.** *prp* außerhalb
**out·sid·er** Außenseiter(in)
**out·size 1.** Übergröße *f*; **2.** übergroß
**out·skirts** Stadtrand *m*, Außenbezirke *pl*
**out·spo·ken** offen, freimütig
**out·spread** ausgestreckt, ausgebreitet

O

**out·stand·ing** hervorragend; ECON ausstehend; ungeklärt (*problem*); unerledigt (*work*)
**out·stay** länger bleiben als; → ***welcome*** 4
**out·stretched** ausgestreckt
**out·strip** überholen; *fig* übertreffen
**out tray:** ***in the ~*** im Postausgang *etc*
**out·vote** überstimmen
**out·ward 1.** äußere(r, -s); äußerlich; **2.** *adv mst* ***outwards*** auswärts, nach außen; **out·ward·ly** äußerlich
**out·weigh** *fig* überwiegen
**out·wit** überlisten, F reinlegen
**out·worn** veraltet, überholt
**o·val 1.** oval; **2.** Oval *n*
**o·va·tion** Ovation *f*; ***give s.o. a standing ~*** j-m stehende Ovationen bereiten, j-m stehend Beifall klatschen
**ov·en** Backofen *m*, Bratofen *m*
**ov·en-read·y** bratfertig
**o·ver 1.** *prp* über; über (*acc*), über (*acc*) ... (hin)weg; über (*dat*), auf der anderen Seite von (*or gen*); über (*acc*), mehr als; **2.** *adv* hinüber, herüber (**to** zu); drüben; darüber, mehr; zu Ende, vorüber, vorbei; über..., um...: *et.* über(*geben etc*); über(*kochen etc*); um(*fallen, -werfen etc*); herum(*drehen etc*); von Anfang bis Ende, durch(*lesen etc*); (gründlich) über(*legen etc*); (***all***) ***~ again*** noch einmal; ***all ~*** ganz vorbei; ***~ and ~*** (***again***) immer wieder; ***~ and above*** obendrein, überdies
**o·ver·age** zu alt
**o·ver·all 1.** gesamt, Gesamt...; allgemein; insgesamt; **2.** *Br* Arbeitsmantel *m*, Kittel *m*; (*Br* ***~s***) Overall *m*, Arbeitsanzug *m*; Arbeitshose *f*
**o·ver·awe** einschüchtern
**o·ver·bal·ance** umstoßen, umkippen; das Gleichgewicht verlieren
**o·ver·bear·ing** anmaßend
**o·ver·board** MAR über Bord
**o·ver·bur·den** *fig* überlasten
**o·ver·cast** bewölkt, bedeckt
**o·ver·charge** überlasten, ELECTR *a.* überladen; ECON *j-m* zu viel berechnen; *Betrag* zu viel verlangen
**o·ver·coat** Mantel *m*
**o·ver·come** überwinden, überwältigen; ***be ~ with emotion*** von s-n Gefühlen übermannt werden
**o·ver·crowd·ed** überfüllt; überlaufen
**o·ver·do** übertreiben; GASTR zu lange kochen *or* braten; ***overdone*** *a.* übergar
**o·ver·dose** Überdosis *f*
**o·ver·draft** ECON (Konto)Überziehung *f*; *a.* ***~ facility*** Überziehungskredit *m*
**o·ver·draw** ECON *Konto* überziehen (***by*** um)
**o·ver·dress** (sich) zu fein anziehen; ***~ed*** overdressed, zu fein angezogen
**o·ver·drive** MOT Overdrive *m*, Schongang *m*
**o·ver·due** überfällig
**o·ver·eat** zu viel essen
**o·ver·es·ti·mate** zu hoch schätzen *or* veranschlagen; *fig* überschätzen
**o·ver·ex·pose** PHOT überbelichten
**o·ver·feed** überfüttern
**o·ver·flow 1.** *v/t* überfluten, überschwemmen; *v/i* überlaufen, überfließen; überquellen (***with*** von); **2.** TECH Überlauf *m*; Überlaufen *n*, -fließen *n*
**o·ver·grown** BOT überwachsen, überwuchert
**o·ver·hang** *v/t* über (*dat*) hängen; *v/i* überhängen
**o·ver·haul** *Maschine* überholen
**o·ver·head 1.** *adv* oben, droben; **2.** *adj* Hoch..., Ober...; ECON ***~ expenses*** *or* ***costs*** Gemeinkosten *pl*; SPORT Überkopf...; ***~ kick*** *soccer*: Fallrückzieher *m*; **3.** ECON *esp Br a. pl* Gemeinkosten *pl*
**o·ver·hear** (zufällig) hören
**o·ver·heat·ed** überhitzt, überheizt; TECH heißgelaufen
**o·ver·joyed** überglücklich
**o·ver·lap** (sich) überlappen; sich überschneiden
**o·ver·leaf** umseitig, umstehend
**o·ver·load** überlasten (*a.* ELECTR), überladen
**o·ver·look** übersehen; ***~ing the sea*** mit Blick aufs Meer
**o·ver·night 1.** über Nacht; ***stay ~*** über Nacht bleiben, übernachten; **2.** Nacht..., Übernachtungs...; ***~ bag*** Reisetasche *f*
**o·ver·pass** (Straßen-, Eisenbahn-) Überführung *f*
**o·ver·pay** zu viel (be)zahlen
**o·ver·pop·u·lat·ed** übervölkert
**o·ver·pow·er** überwältigen; ***~ing*** *fig* überwältigend
**o·ver·rate** überbewerten, überschätzen
**o·ver·reach:** ***~ o.s.*** sich übernehmen

**o·ver·re·act** überreagieren, überzogen reagieren (***to*** auf *acc*)
**o·ver·re·ac·tion** Überreaktion *f*, überzogene Reaktion
**o·ver·ride** sich hinwegsetzen über (*acc*)
**o·ver·rule** *Entscheidung etc* aufheben, *Einspruch etc* abweisen
**o·ver·run** länger dauern als vorgesehen; *Signal* überfahren; ***be ~ with*** wimmeln von
**o·ver·seas** 1. *adj* überseeisch, Übersee...; **2.** *adv* in *or* nach Übersee
**o·ver·see** beaufsichtigen, überwachen
**o·ver·shad·ow** *fig* überschatten, in den Schatten stellen
**o·ver·sight** Versehen *n*
**o·ver·size(d)** übergroß, überdimensional, in Übergröße(n)
**o·ver·sleep** verschlafen
**o·ver·staffed** (personell) überbesetzt
**o·ver·state** übertreiben
**o·ver·state·ment** Übertreibung *f*
**o·ver·stay** länger bleiben als; → ***welcome*** 4
**o·ver·step** *fig* überschreiten
**o·ver·take** überholen; *j-n* überraschen
**o·ver·tax** zu hoch besteuern; *fig* überbeanspruchen, überfordern
**o·ver·throw 1.** *Regierung etc* stürzen; **2.** (Um)Sturz *m*
**o·ver·time** ECON Überstunden *pl*; SPORT (Spiel)Verlängerung *f*; ***be on ~, do ~, work ~*** Überstunden machen
**o·ver·tired** übermüdet
**o·ver·ture** MUS Ouvertüre *f*; Vorspiel *n*
**o·ver·turn** *v/t* umwerfen, umstoßen; *Regierung etc* stürzen; *v/i* umkippen, MAR kentern
**o·ver·view** *fig* Überblick *m* (***of*** über *acc*)
**o·ver·weight 1.** Übergewicht *n*; **2.** übergewichtig (*person*), zu schwer (***by*** um); ***be five pounds ~*** fünf Pfund Übergewicht haben
**o·ver·whelm** überwältigen (*a. fig*)
**o·ver·whelm·ing** überwältigend
**o·ver·work** sich überarbeiten; überanstrengen
**o·ver·wrought** überreizt
**o·ver·zeal·ous** übereifrig
**owe** *j-m et.* schulden, schuldig sein; *et.* verdanken
**ow·ing:** ***~ to*** infolge, wegen
**owl** ZO Eule *f*
**own 1.** eigen; ***my ~*** mein Eigentum; (***all***) ***on one's ~*** allein; **2.** besitzen; zugeben, (ein)gestehen
**own·er** Eigentümer(in), Besitzer(in)
**own·er-oc·cu·pied** *esp Br* eigengenutzt; ***~ flat*** Eigentumswohnung *f*
**own·er·ship** Besitz *m*; Eigentum *n*; Eigentumsrecht *n*
**ox** ZO Ochse *m*
**ox·ide** CHEM Oxid *n*, Oxyd *n*
**ox·i·dize** CHEM oxidieren
**ox·y·gen** CHEM Sauerstoff *m*; **~ ap·pa·ra·tus** MED Sauerstoffgerät *n*; **~ tent** MED Sauerstoffzelt *n*
**oy·ster** ZO Auster *f*
**o·zone** CHEM Ozon *n*
**o·zone-friend·ly** FCKW-frei, ohne Treibgas
**o·zone| hole** Ozonloch *n*; **~ lay·er** Ozonschicht *f*; **~ lev·els** Ozonwerte *pl*; **~ shield** Ozonschild *m*

P

# P

**P, p** P, p *n*
**pace 1.** Tempo *n*, Geschwindigkeit *f*; Schritt *m*; Gangart *f* (*of a horse*); **2.** *v/t* *Zimmer etc* durchschreiten; *a.* ***~ out*** abschreiten; *v/i* (einher)schreiten; ***~ up and down*** auf und ab gehen
**pace·mak·er** SPORT Schrittmacher(in); MED Herzschrittmacher *m*
**pace·set·ter** SPORT Schrittmacher(in)
**Pa·cif·ic** *a.* ***~ Ocean*** *der* Pazifik, *der* Pazifische *or* Stille Ozean
**pac·i·fi·er** Schnuller *m*
**pac·i·fist** Pazifist(in)
**pac·i·fy** beruhigen, besänftigen
**pack 1.** Pack(en) *m*, Paket *n*, Bündel *n*; Packung *f*, Schachtel *f*; ZO Meute *f*;

Rudel *n*; *contp* Pack *n*, Bande *f*; MED *etc* Packung *f*; (Karten)Spiel *n*; ***a ~ of lies*** ein Haufen Lügen; **2.** *v/t* ein-, zusammenpacken, abpacken, verpacken (*a.* ***~ up***); zusammenpferchen; voll stopfen; *Koffer etc* packen; ***~ off*** F fort-, wegschicken; *v/i* packen; (sich) drängen (***into*** in *acc*); ***~ up*** zusammenpacken; ***send s.o. ~ing*** j-n fort- *or* wegjagen

**pack·age** Paket *n*; Packung *f*; ***software ~*** EDP Software-, Programmpaket *n*

**pack·age| deal** F Pauschalangebot *n*, -arrangement *n*; **~ hol·i·day** Pauschalurlaub *m*; **~ tour** Pauschalreise *f*

**pack·et** Päckchen *n*; Packung *f*, Schachtel *f*

**pack·ing** Packen *n*; Verpackung *f*

**pact** Pakt *m*, POL *a.* Vertrag *m*

**pad 1.** Polster *n*; SPORT (*Knie- etc*)Schützer *m*; (*Schreib- etc*)Block *m*; (*Stempel*)Kissen *n*; ZO Ballen *m*; (*Abschuss-*) Rampe *f*; **2.** (aus)polstern, wattieren

**pad·ding** Polsterung *f*, Wattierung *f*

**pad·dle 1.** Paddel *n*; MAR (Rad)Schaufel *f*; **2.** paddeln; plan(t)schen

**pad·dock** (Pferde)Koppel *f*

**pad·lock** Vorhängeschloss *n*

**pa·gan 1.** Heide *m*, Heidin *f*; **2.** heidnisch

**page[1] 1.** Seite *f*; **2.** paginieren

**page[2] 1.** (Hotel)Page *m*; **2.** *j-n* ausrufen (lassen)

**pag·eant** (*a.* historischer) Festzug

**pa·gin·ate** paginieren

**pail** Eimer *m*, Kübel *m*

**pain 1.** Schmerz(en *pl*) *m*; Kummer *m*; *pl* Mühe *f*, Bemühungen *pl*; ***be in (great) ~*** (große) Schmerzen haben; ***be a ~ (in the neck)*** F e-m auf den Wecker gehen; ***take ~s*** sich Mühe geben; **2.** *esp fig* schmerzen; **pain·ful** schmerzhaft, schmerzend; *fig* schmerzlich; peinlich

**pain·kill·er** Schmerzmittel *n*

**pain·less** schmerzlos

**pains·tak·ing** sorgfältig, gewissenhaft

**paint 1.** Farbe *f*; Anstrich *m*; **2.** *v/t* anmalen, bemalen; (an)streichen; *Auto etc* lackieren; *v/i* malen

**paint·box** Malkasten *m*

**paint·brush** (Maler)Pinsel *m*

**paint·er** (*a.* Kunst)Maler(in), Anstreicher(in)

**paint·ing** Malerei *f*; Gemälde *n*, Bild *n*

**pair 1.** Paar *n*; ***a ~ of ...*** ein Paar ..., ein(e) ...; ***a ~ of scissors*** e-e Schere; **2.** *v/i* zo sich paaren; *a.* ***~ off, ~ up*** Paare bilden; *v/t a.* ***~ off, ~ up*** paarweise anordnen; ***~ off*** *zwei Leute* zusammenbringen, verkuppeln

**pa·ja·ma(s)** (***a pair of***) ~ (ein) Schlafanzug *m*, (ein) Pyjama *m*

**pal** Kamerad *m*, F Kumpel *m*, Spezi *m*

**pal·ace** Palast *m*, Schloss *n*

**pal·a·ta·ble** schmackhaft (*a. fig*)

**pal·ate** ANAT Gaumen *m*; *fig* Geschmack *m*

**pale[1] 1.** blass, *a.* bleich, *a.* hell (*color*); **2.** blass *or* bleich werden

**pale[2]** Pfahl *m*; *fig* Grenzen *pl*

**pale·ness** Blässe *f*

**Pal·es·tin·i·an 1.** palästinensisch; **2.** Palästinenser(in)

**pal·ings** Lattenzaun *m*

**pal·i·sade** Palisade *f*; *pl* Steilufer *n*

**pal·let** TECH Palette *f*

**pal·lid** blass; **pal·lor** Blässe *f*

**palm[1]** *a.* ***~ tree*** BOT Palme *f*

**palm[2] 1.** ANAT Handfläche *f*; **2.** *et.* in der Hand verschwinden lassen; ***~ s.th. off on s.o.*** F j-m et. andrehen

**pal·pa·ble** fühlbar, greifbar

**pal·pi·tate** MED klopfen, pochen

**pal·pi·ta·tions** MED Herzklopfen *n*

**pal·sy** MED Lähmung *f*

**pal·try** armselig

**pam·per** verwöhnen

**pam·phlet** Broschüre *f*

**pan** Pfanne *f*; Topf *m*

**pan·a·ce·a** Allheilmittel *n*

**pan·cake** Pfannkuchen *m*

**pan·da** ZO Panda *m*

**pan·da car** *Br* (Funk)Streifenwagen *m*

**pan·de·mo·ni·um** Hölle *f*, Höllenlärm *m*, Tumult *m*, Chaos *n*

**pan·der** Vorschub leisten (***to*** *dat*)

**pane** (*Fenster*)Scheibe *f*

**pan·el 1.** (*Tür*)Füllung *f*, (*Wand*)Täfelung *f*; ELECTR, TECH Instrumentenbrett *n*, (*Schalt-, Kontroll- etc*)Tafel *f*; JUR Liste *f* der Geschworenen; Diskussionsteilnehmer *pl*, Diskussionsrunde *f*; Rateteam *n*; **2.** täfeln

**pang** stechender Schmerz; ***~s of hunger*** nagender Hunger; ***~s of conscience*** Gewissensbisse *pl*

**pan·han·dle 1.** Pfannenstiel *m*; GEOGR schmaler Fortsatz; **2.** F betteln

**pan·ic 1.** panisch; **2.** Panik *f*; **3.** in Panik versetzen *or* geraten
**pan·ick·y:** F ***be** ~* in Panik sein
**pan·ic-strick·en** von Panik erfasst *or* erfüllt
**pan·o·ra·ma** Panorama *n*, Ausblick *m*
**pan·sy** BOT Stiefmütterchen *n*
**pant** keuchen, schnaufen, nach Luft schnappen
**pan·ther** ZO Panther *m*; Puma *m*; Jaguar *m*
**pan·ties** (Damen)Schlüpfer *m*, Slip *m*; Höschen *n*
**pan·to·mime** THEA Pantomime *f*; *Br* F Weihnachtsspiel *n*
**pan·try** Speisekammer *f*
**pants** Hose *f*; *Br* Unterhose *f*; *Br* Schlüpfer *m*
**pant·suit** Hosenanzug *m*
**pan·ty·hose** Strumpfhose *f*
**pan·ty·lin·er** Slipeinlage *f*
**pap** Brei *m*
**pa·pal** päpstlich
**pa·per 1.** Papier *n*; Zeitung *f*; (Prüfungs)Arbeit *f*; UNIV Klausur(arbeit) *f*; Aufsatz *m*; Referat *n*; Tapete *f*; *pl* (Ausweis)Papiere *pl*; **2.** tapezieren
**pa·per·back** Taschenbuch *n*, Paperback *n*
**pa·per bag** (Papier)Tüte *f*
**pa·per·boy** Zeitungsjunge *m*
**pa·per clip** Büro-, Heftklammer *f*
**pa·per cup** Pappbecher *m*
**pa·per·hang·er** Tapezierer *m*
**pa·per knife** *Br* Brieföffner *m*
**pa·per mon·ey** Papiergeld *n*
**pa·per·weight** Briefbeschwerer *m*
**par:** ***at** ~* zum Nennwert; ***be on a ~ with*** gleich *or* ebenbürtig sein (*dat*)
**par·a·ble** Parabel *f*, Gleichnis *n*
**par·a·chute** Fallschirm *m*
**par·a·chut·ist** Fallschirmspringer(in)
**pa·rade 1.** Umzug *m*, *esp* MIL Parade *f*; *fig* Zurschaustellung *f*; ***make a ~ of*** *fig* zur Schau stellen; **2.** ziehen (***through*** durch); MIL antreten (lassen), vorbeimarschieren (lassen); zur Schau stellen; *~ (**through**)* stolzieren durch
**par·a·dise** Paradies *n*
**par·af·fin** *Br* Petroleum *n*
**par·a·glid·er** SPORT Gleitschirm *m*; Gleitschirmflieger(in); **par·a·glid·ing** SPORT Gleitschirmfliegen *n*
**par·a·gon** Muster *n* (***of*** an *dat*)
**par·a·graph** Absatz *m*, Abschnitt *m*; (Zeitungs)Notiz *f*
**par·al·lel 1.** parallel (***to, with*** zu); **2.** MATH Parallele *f* (*a. fig*); ***without** ~* ohne Parallele, ohnegleichen; **3.** entsprechen (*dat*), gleichkommen (*dat*)
**par·a·lyse** *Br*, **par·a·lyze** MED lähmen, *fig a.* lahm legen, zum Erliegen bringen; ***~d with*** *fig* starr *or* wie gelähmt vor (*dat*)
**pa·ral·y·sis** MED Lähmung *f*, *fig a.* Lahmlegung *f*
**par·a·med·ic** MED Sanitäter *m*
**par·a·mount** größte(r, -s), übergeordnet; ***of ~ importance*** von (aller)größter Bedeutung *or* Wichtigkeit
**par·a·pet** Brüstung *f*
**par·a·pher·na·li·a** (persönliche) Sachen *pl*; Ausrüstung *f*; *esp Br* F Scherereien *pl*
**par·a·phrase 1.** umschreiben; **2.** Umschreibung *f*
**par·a·site** Parasit *m*, Schmarotzer *m*
**par·a·troop·er** MIL Fallschirmjäger *m*; *pl* Fallschirmjägertruppe *f*
**par·boil** halb gar kochen, ankochen
**par·cel 1.** Paket *n*; Parzelle *f*; **2.** *~ **out*** aufteilen; *~ **up*** (als Paket) verpacken
**parch** ausdörren, austrocknen; vertrocknen
**parch·ment** Pergament *n*
**par·don 1.** JUR Begnadigung *f*; ***I beg your** ~* Entschuldigung!, Verzeihung!; erlauben Sie mal!, ich muss doch sehr bitten!; *a. ~?* F (wie) bitte?; **2.** verzeihen; vergeben; JUR begnadigen; *~ **me*** → ***I beg your pardon***; F (wie) bitte?
**par·don·a·ble** verzeihlich
**pare** sich *die Nägel* schneiden; *Apfel etc* schälen
**par·ent** Elternteil *m*, Vater *m*, Mutter *f*; *pl* Eltern *pl*; **par·ent·age** Abstammung *f*, Herkunft *f*; **pa·ren·tal** elterlich
**pa·ren·the·ses** (runde) Klammer
**par·ents-in-law** Schwiegereltern *pl*
**par·ent-teach·er meet·ing** PED Elternabend *m*
**par·ings** Schalen *pl*
**par·ish** REL Gemeinde *f*
**par·ish church** REL Pfarrkirche *f*
**pa·rish·ion·er** REL Gemeindemitglied *n*
**park 1.** Park *m*, (Grün)Anlage(n *pl*) *f*; **2.** MOT parken; ***look for somewhere to ~ the car*** e-n Parkplatz suchen

**par·ka** Parka *m, f*
**park·ing** MOT Parken *n*; ***no ~*** Parkverbot, Parken verboten; **~ disk** Parkscheibe *f*; **~ fee** Parkgebühr *f*; **~ garage** Park(hoch)haus *n*; **~ lot** Parkplatz *m*; **~ lot at·tend·ant** Parkwächter *m*; **~ me·ter** Parkuhr *f*; **~ of·fend·er** Parksünder(in); **~ space** Parkplatz *m*, Parklücke *f*; **~ tick·et** Strafzettel *m*
**par·ley** *esp* MIL Verhandlung *f*
**par·lia·ment** Parlament *n*
**par·lia·men·tar·i·an** Parlamentarier(in)
**par·lia·men·ta·ry** parlamentarisch, Parlaments...
**par·lo(u)r** *mst in cpds* Salon *m*
**pa·ro·chi·al** REL Pfarr..., Gemeinde...; *fig* engstirnig, beschränkt
**par·o·dy 1.** Parodie *f*; **2.** parodieren
**pa·role** JUR **1.** Hafturlaub *m*; bedingte Haftentlassung; ***he is out on ~*** er hat Hafturlaub; er wurde bedingt entlassen; **2. *~ s.o.*** j-m Hafturlaub gewähren; j-n bedingt entlassen
**par·quet** Parkett *n* (*a.* THEA)
**par·quet floor** Parkett(fuß)boden *m*
**par·rot 1.** ZO Papagei *m* (*a. fig*); **2.** *et.* (wie ein Papagei) nachplappern
**par·ry** abwehren, parieren
**par·si·mo·ni·ous** geizig
**pars·ley** BOT Petersilie *f*
**par·son** REL Pfarrer *m*
**par·son·age** REL Pfarrhaus *n*
**part 1.** Teil *m*; TECH Teil *n*, Bau-, Ersatzteil *n*; Anteil *m*; Seite *f*, Partei *f*; THEA, *fig* Rolle *f*; MUS Stimme *f*, Partie *f*; GEOGR Gegend *f*, Teil *m*; (Haar)Scheitel *m*; ***for my ~*** was mich betrifft; ***for the most ~*** größtenteils; meistens; ***in ~*** teilweise, zum Teil; ***on the ~ of*** vonseiten, seitens (*gen*); ***on my ~*** von m-r Seite; ***take ~ in s.th.*** an e-r Sache teilnehmen; ***take s.th. in good ~*** et. nicht übel nehmen; **2.** *v/t* trennen; (ab-, zer)teilen; einteilen; *Haar* scheiteln; ***~ company*** sich trennen (***with*** von); *v/i* sich trennen (***with*** von); **3.** *adj* Teil...; **4.** *adv*: ***~ ..., ~*** teils ..., teils
**par·tial** Teil..., teilweise; parteiisch, voreingenommen (***to*** für)
**par·ti·al·i·ty** Parteilichkeit *f*, Voreingenommenheit *f*; Schwäche *f*, besondere Vorliebe (***for*** für)
**par·tial·ly** teilweise, zum Teil
**par·tic·i·pant** Teilnehmer(in)
**par·tic·i·pate** teilnehmen, sich beteiligen (*both*: ***in*** an *dat*)
**par·tic·i·pa·tion** Teilnahme *f*, Beteiligung *f*
**par·ti·ci·ple** LING Partizip *n*, Mittelwort *n*
**par·ti·cle** Teilchen *n*
**par·tic·u·lar 1.** besondere(r, -s), speziell; genau, eigen, wählerisch; **2.** Einzelheit *f*; *pl* nähere Umstände *pl or* Angaben *pl*; Personalien *pl*; ***in ~*** insbesondere; **par·tic·u·lar·ly** besonders
**part·ing 1.** Trennung *f*, Abschied *m*; *esp Br* (Haar)Scheitel *m*; **2.** Abschieds...
**par·ti·san 1.** Parteigänger(in); MIL Partisan(in); **2.** parteiisch
**par·ti·tion 1.** Teilung *f*; Trennwand *f*; **2.** ***~ off*** abteilen, abtrennen
**part·ly** teilweise, zum Teil
**part·ner** Partner(in), ECON *a.* Teilhaber(in); **part·ner·ship** Partnerschaft *f*, ECON *a.* Teilhaberschaft *f*
**part-own·er** Miteigentümer(in)
**par·tridge** ZO Rebhuhn *n*
**part-time 1.** *adj* Teilzeit..., Halbtags...; ***~ worker → part-timer***; **2.** *adv* halbtags
**part-tim·er** F Teilzeitbeschäftigte *m, f*, Halbtagskraft *f*
**par·ty** Partei *f* (*a.* POL); (*Arbeits-, Reise-*) Gruppe *f*; (*Rettungs- etc*)Mannschaft *f*; MIL Kommando *n*, Trupp *m*; Party *f*, Gesellschaft *f*; Teilnehmer(in), Beteiligte *m, f*; **~ line** POL Parteilinie *f*; **~ pol·i·tics** Parteipolitik *f*
**pass 1.** *v/i* vorbeigehen, -fahren, -kommen, -ziehen *etc* (***by*** an *dat*); übergehen (***to*** auf *acc*), fallen (***to*** an *acc*); vergehen (*pain etc, time*); durchkommen, (die Prüfung) bestehen; gelten (***as, for*** als), gehalten werden (***as, for*** für); PARL Rechtskraft erlangen; unbeanstandet bleiben; SPORT (den Ball) abspielen *or* passen (***to*** zu); *card game*: passen (*a. fig*); ***let s.o. ~*** j-n vorbeilassen; ***let s.th. ~*** et. durchgehen lassen; *v/t* vorbeigehen, -fahren, -fließen, -kommen, -ziehen *etc* an (*dat*); überholen; *Prüfung* bestehen; *Prüfling* durchkommen lassen; (*mit der Hand*) streichen (***over*** über *acc*); *j-m et.* reichen, geben, *et.* weitergeben; SPORT *Ball* abspielen, passen (***to*** zu); *Zeit* verbringen; PARL *Gesetz* verabschieden; *Urteil* abgeben, fäl-

P

len, JUR *a.* sprechen (**on** über *acc*); *fig* hinausgehen über (*acc*), übersteigen, übertreffen; **~ away** sterben; **~ off** *j-n, et.* ausgeben (**as** als); *gut etc* verlaufen; **~ out** ohnmächtig werden; **2.** Passierschein *m*; Bestehen *n* (*examination*); SPORT Pass *m*, Zuspiel *n*; (*Gebirgs*)Pass *m*; **free ~** Frei(fahr)karte *f*; **things have come to such a ~ that** F die Dinge haben sich derart zugespitzt, dass; **make a ~ at** F Annäherungsversuche machen bei

**pass·a·ble** passierbar, befahrbar; passabel, leidlich

**pas·sage** Passage *f*, Korridor *m*, Gang *m*; Durchgang *m*; (See-, Flug)Reise *f*; Durchfahrt *f*, Durchreise *f*; Passage *f* (*a.* MUS), Stelle *f*; **bird of ~** Zugvogel *m*

**pass·book** ECON Sparbuch *n*

**pas·sen·ger** Passagier *m*, Fahrgast *m*, Fluggast *m*, Reisende *m, f*, MOT Insasse *m*, Insassin *f*

**pass·er·by** Passant(in)

**pas·sion** Leidenschaft *f*; Wut *f*, Zorn *m*; **Passion** REL Passion *f*; **~s ran high** die Erregung schlug hohe Wellen

**pas·sion·ate** leidenschaftlich

**pas·sive** passiv; LING passivisch

**Pass·o·ver** REL Passah(fest) *n*

**pass·port** (Reise)Pass *m*

**pass·word** Kennwort *n* (*a.* EDP), MIL *a.* Parole *f*, Losung *f*

**past 1.** *adj* vergangen; frühere(r, -s); **be ~** *a.* vorüber sein; **for some time ~** seit einiger Zeit; **~ tense** LING Vergangenheit *f*, Präteritum *n*; **2.** *adv* vorüber, vorbei; **go ~** vorbeigehen; **3.** *prp time*: nach, über (*acc*); über ... (*acc*) hinaus; an ... (*dat*) vorbei; **half ~ two** halb drei; **~ hope** hoffnungslos; **4.** Vergangenheit *f* (*a.* LING)

**pas·ta** Teigwaren *pl*

**paste 1.** Paste *f*; Kleister *m*; Teig *m*; **2.** kleben (**to, on** an *acc*); **~ up** ankleben

**paste·board** Karton *m*, Pappe *f*

**pas·tel** Pastell(zeichnung *f*) *n*

**pas·teur·ize** pasteurisieren

**pas·time** Zeitvertreib *m*, Freizeitbeschäftigung *f*

**pas·tor** REL Pastor *m*, Pfarrer *m*, Seelsorger *m*; **pas·tor·al** REL seelsorgerisch, pastoral; **~ care** Seelsorge *f*

**pas·try** GASTR (*Blätter-, Mürbe*)Teig *m*; Feingebäck *n*; **~ cook** Konditor *m*

**pas·ture 1.** Weide(land *n*) *f*; **2.** *v/t* weiden (lassen); *v/i* grasen, weiden

**pas·ty**[1] *esp Br* GASTR (Fleisch)Pastete *f*

**past·y**[2] blass, F käsig

**pat 1.** Klaps *m*; GASTR Portion *f*; **2.** tätscheln; klopfen

**patch 1.** Fleck *m*; Flicken *m*; kleines Stück Land; **in ~es** stellenweise; **2.** flicken

**pa·tent 1.** offenkundig; patentiert; Patent...; **2.** Patent *n*; **take out a ~ for s.th.** (sich) et. patentieren lassen; **3.** *et.* patentieren lassen

**pa·tent·ee** Patentinhaber(in)

**pa·tent leath·er** Lackleder *n*

**pa·ter·nal** väterlich; väterlicherseits

**pa·ter·ni·ty** JUR Vaterschaft *f*

**path** Pfad *m*; Weg *m*

**pa·thet·ic** Mitleid erregend; kläglich, miserabel

**pa·tience** Geduld *f*; *esp Br* Patience *f*

**pa·tient**[1] geduldig

**pa·tient**[2] MED Patient(in)

**pat·i·o** Terrasse *f*; Innenhof *m*, Patio *m*

**pat·ri·ot** Patriot(in)

**pat·ri·ot·ic** patriotisch

**pa·trol 1.** Patrouille *f* (*a.* MIL), Streife *f*, Runde *f*; **on ~** auf Patrouille, auf Streife; **2.** abpatrouillieren, auf Streife sein in (*dat*), s-e Runde machen in (*dat*)

**pa·trol car** (Funk)Streifenwagen *m*

**pa·trol·man** Streifenpolizist *m*; *Br* motorisierter Pannenhelfer

**pa·tron** Schirmherr *m*; Gönner *m*, Förderer *m*; (Stamm)Kunde *m*; Stammgast *m*; **pat·ron·age** Schirmherrschaft *f*; Förderung *f*; **pat·ron·ess** Schirmherrin *f*; Gönnerin *f*, Förderin *f*; **pat·ron·ize** fördern; (Stamm)Kunde *or* Stammgast sein bei *or* in (*dat*); gönnerhaft *or* herablassend behandeln

**pa·tron saint** REL Schutzheilige *m, f*

**pat·ter** prasseln (*rain*); trappeln (*feet*)

**pat·tern 1.** Muster *n* (*a. fig*); Schema *n*; **2.** bilden, formen (**after, on** nach)

**paunch** (dicker) Bauch

**pau·per** Arme *m, f*

**pause 1.** Pause *f*; **2.** innehalten, e-e Pause machen

**pave** pflastern; **~ the way for** *fig* den Weg ebnen für

**pave·ment** Fahrbahn *f*; Belag *m*, Pflaster *n*; *Br* Bürgersteig *m*, Gehsteig *m*

**pave·ment ca·fé** *Br* Straßencafé *n*

**paw 1.** ZO Pfote *f*, Tatze *f*; **2.** *v/t Boden* scharren; scharren an (*dat*); F betatschen; *v/i* scharren (**at** an *dat*)
**pawn**[1] *chess*: Bauer *m*; *fig* Schachfigur *f*
**pawn**[2] **1.** verpfänden, versetzen; **2.** ***be in ~*** verpfändet *or* versetzt sein
**pawn·bro·ker** Pfandleiher *m*
**pawn·shop** Leihhaus *n*, Pfandhaus *n*
**pay 1.** *v/t et.* (be)zahlen; *j-n* bezahlen; *Aufmerksamkeit* schenken; *Besuch* abstatten; *Kompliment* machen; ***~ attention*** Acht geben auf (*acc*); PED aufpassen; ***~ cash*** bar bezahlen; *v/i* zahlen; *fig* sich lohnen; ***~ for*** (*fig* für) *et.* bezahlen; *fig* büßen; ***~ in*** einzahlen; ***~ into*** einzahlen auf (*acc*); ***~ off*** *et.* ab(be)zahlen; *j-n* auszahlen; **2.** Bezahlung *f*, Gehalt *n*, Lohn *m*
**pay·a·ble** zahlbar, fällig
**pay·day** Zahltag *m*
**pay·ee** Zahlungsempfänger(in)
**pay en·ve·lope** Lohntüte *f*
**pay·ing** lohnend
**pay·mas·ter** MIL Zahlmeister *m*
**pay·ment** (Be)Zahlung *f*
**pay pack·et** *Br* Lohntüte *f*
**pay phone** *Br* Münzfernsprecher *m*
**pay·roll** Lohnliste *f*
**pay·slip** Lohn-, Gehaltsstreifen *m*
**PC** ABBR *of* ***personal computer*** PC *m*, Personalcomputer *m*; ***PC user*** PC-Benutzer *m*
**pea** BOT Erbse *f*
**peace** Friede(n) *m*; Ruhe *f*; JUR öffentliche Ruhe und Ordnung; ***at ~*** in Frieden
**peace·a·ble** friedlich, friedfertig
**peace·ful** friedlich
**peace·lov·ing** friedliebend
**peace move·ment** Friedensbewegung *f*
**peace·time** Friedenszeiten *pl*
**peach** BOT Pfirsich(baum) *m*
**pea·cock** ZO Pfau *m*, Pfauhahn *m*
**pea·hen** ZO Pfauhenne *f*
**peak** Spitze *f*, Gipfel *m*; Schirm *m*; *fig* Höhepunkt *m*, Höchststand *m*
**peaked cap** Schirmmütze *f*
**peak hours** Hauptverkehrszeit *f*, Stoßzeit *f*; ELECTR Hauptbelastungszeit *f*
**peak| time, ~ viewing hours** *Br* TV Haupteinschaltzeit *f*, Hauptsendezeit *f*, beste Sendezeit
**peal 1.** (*Glocken*)Läuten *n*; (*Donner-*)Schlag *m*; ***~s of laughter*** schallendes Gelächter; **2.** *a.* ***~ out*** läuten; krachen
**pea·nut** BOT Erdnuss *f*; *pl* F lächerliche Summe
**pear** BOT Birne *f*; Birnbaum *m*
**pearl 1.** Perle *f*; Perlmutter *f*, Perlmutt *n*; **2.** Perlen...
**pearl·y** perlenartig, Perlen...
**peas·ant** Kleinbauer *m*
**peat** Torf *m*
**peb·ble** Kiesel(stein) *m*
**peck** picken, hacken; ***~ at one's food*** im Essen herumstochern
**pe·cu·li·ar** eigen, eigentümlich, typisch; eigenartig, seltsam
**pe·cu·li·ar·i·ty** Eigenheit *f*; Eigentümlichkeit *f*
**ped·a·go·gic** pädagogisch
**ped·al 1.** Pedal *n*; **2.** das Pedal treten; (mit dem Rad) fahren, strampeln
**pe·dan·tic** pedantisch
**ped·dle** hausieren (gehen) mit; ***~ drugs*** mit Drogen handeln
**ped·dler** Hausierer(in)
**ped·es·tal** Sockel *m*
**pe·des·tri·an 1.** Fußgänger(in); **2.** Fußgänger...; **~ cross·ing** Fußgängerübergang *m*; **~ mall,** *esp Br* **~ pre·cinct** Fußgängerzone *f*
**ped·i·cure** Pediküre *f*
**ped·i·gree** Stammbaum *m* (*a.* ZO)
**ped·lar** *Br* → ***peddler***
**pee** F **1.** pinkeln; **2.** ***have*** (*or* ***go for***) ***a ~*** pinkeln (gehen)
**peek 1.** kurz *or* verstohlen gucken (**at** auf *acc*); **2.** ***have*** *or* ***take a ~ at*** e-n kurzen *or* verstohlenen Blick werfen auf (*acc*)
**peel 1.** *v/t* schälen; *a.* ***~ off*** abschälen, *Folie*, *Tapete etc* abziehen, ablösen; *Kleid* abstreifen; *v/i a.* ***~ off*** sich lösen (*wallpaper etc*), abblättern (*paint etc*), sich schälen (*skin*); **2.** BOT Schale *f*
**peep**[1] **1.** kurz *or* verstohlen gucken (**at** auf *acc*); *mst* ***~ out*** (her)vorschauen; **2.** ***take a ~ at*** e-n kurzen *or* verstohlenen Blick werfen auf (*acc*)
**peep**[2] **1.** Piep(s)en *n*; F Piepser *m*; **2.** piep(s)en
**peep·hole** Guckloch *n*; (Tür)Spion *m*
**peer** angestrengt schauen, spähen; ***~ at s.o.*** j-n anstarren
**peer·less** unvergleichlich, einzigartig
**peev·ish** verdrießlich, gereizt

**peg 1.** (Holz)Stift *m*, Zapfen *m*, Pflock *m*; (Kleider)Haken *m*; *Br* (*Wäsche-*) Klammer *f*; (*Zelt*)Hering *m*; ***take s.o. down a ~*** (***or two***) F j-m e-n Dämpfer aufsetzen; **2.** anpflocken; *Wäsche* anklammern, festklammern
**pel·i·can** zo Pelikan *m*; **~ cross·ing** *Br* Ampelübergang *m*
**pel·let** Kügelchen *n*; Schrotkorn *n*
**pelt**[1] *v/t* bewerfen; *v/i*: ***it's ~ing*** (***down***), *esp Br* ***it's ~ing with rain*** es gießt in Strömen
**pelt**[2] zo Fell *n*, Pelz *m*
**pel·vis** ANAT Becken *n*
**pen**[1] (*Schreib*)Feder *f*; Füller *m*; Kugelschreiber *m*
**pen**[2] **1.** Pferch *m*, (*Schaf*)Hürde *f*; **2.** ***~ in, ~ up*** *Tiere* einpferchen, *Personen* zusammenpferchen
**pe·nal** JUR Straf...; strafbar
**pe·nal code** JUR Strafgesetzbuch *n*
**pe·nal·ize** bestrafen
**pen·al·ty** Strafe *f*, SPORT *a.* Strafpunkt *m*; *soccer*: Elfmeter *m*; **~ ar·e·a, ~ box** F *soccer*: Strafraum *m*; **~ goal** *soccer*: Elfmetertor *n*; **~ kick** *soccer*: Elfmeter *m*, Strafstoß *m*; **~ shoot-out** *soccer*: Elfmeterschießen *n*; **~ spot** *soccer*: Elfmeterpunkt *m*
**pen·ance** REL Buße *f*
**pen·cil 1.** Bleistift *m*; **2.** (mit Bleistift) markieren *or* schreiben *or* zeichnen; *Augenbrauen* nachziehen
**pen·cil case** Federmäppchen *n*
**pen·cil sharp·en·er** Bleistiftspitzer *m*
**pen·dant, pen·dent** (Schmuck)Anhänger *m*
**pend·ing 1.** *prp* bis zu; **2.** *adj esp* JUR schwebend
**pen·du·lum** Pendel *n*
**pen·e·trate** *v/t* eindringen in (*acc*); dringen durch, durchdringen; *v/i* eindringen (***into*** in *acc*); **pen·e·trat·ing** durchdringend; *fig* scharf; scharfsinnig; **pen·e·tra·tion** Durchdringen *n*, Eindringen *n*; *fig* Scharfsinn *m*
**pen friend** *Br* Brieffreund(in)
**pen·guin** zo Pinguin *m*
**pe·nin·su·la** Halbinsel *f*
**pe·nis** ANAT Penis *m*
**pen·i·tence** Buße *f*, Reue *f*
**pen·i·tent 1.** reuig, bußfertig; **2.** REL Büßer(in)
**pen·i·ten·tia·ry** (Staats)Gefängnis *n*, Strafanstalt *f*
**pen·knife** Taschenmesser *n*
**pen name** Schriftstellername *m*, Pseudonym *n*
**pen·nant** Wimpel *m*
**pen·ni·less** (völlig) mittellos
**pen·ny** *a.* ***new ~*** *Br* Penny *m*
**pen pal** Brieffreund(in)
**pen·sion 1.** Rente *f*, Pension *f*; **2.** ***~ off*** pensionieren, in den Ruhestand versetzen
**pen·sion·er** Rentner(in), Pensionär(in)
**pen·sive** nachdenklich
**pen·tath·lete** SPORT Fünfkämpfer(in)
**pen·tath·lon** SPORT Fünfkampf *m*
**Pen·te·cost** REL Pfingsten *n*
**pent·house** Penthouse *n*, Penthaus *n*
**pent-up** auf-, angestaut (*emotions*)
**pe·o·ny** BOT Pfingstrose *f*
**peo·ple 1.** Volk *n*, Nation *f*; die Menschen *pl*, die Leute *pl*; Leute *pl*, Personen *pl*; man; ***the ~*** das (*gemeine*) Volk; **2.** besiedeln, bevölkern (***with*** mit)
**peo·ple's re·pub·lic** Volksrepublik *f*
**pep** F **1.** Pep *m*, Schwung *m*; **2.** *mst* ***~ up*** *j-n or et.* in Schwung bringen, aufmöbeln
**pep·per 1.** Pfeffer *m*; BOT Paprikaschote *f*; **2.** pfeffern
**pep·per cast·er** Pfefferstreuer *m*
**pep·per·mint** BOT Pfefferminze *f*; Pfefferminz *n*
**pep·per·y** pfeff(e)rig; *fig* hitzig
**pep pill** F Aufputschpille *f*
**per** per, durch; pro, für, je
**per·ceive** (be)merken, wahrnehmen; erkennen
**per cent, per·cent** Prozent *n*
**per·cen·tage** Prozentsatz *m*; F Prozente *pl*, (An)Teil *m*
**per·cep·ti·ble** wahrnehmbar, merklich; **per·cep·tion** Wahrnehmung *f*; Auffassung *f*, Auffassungsgabe *f*
**perch**[1] **1.** (Sitz)Stange *f*; **2.** (***on***) sich setzen (auf *acc*), sich niederlassen (auf *acc, dat*); F hocken (***on*** auf *dat*); ***~ o.s.*** F sich hocken (***on*** auf *acc*)
**perch**[2] zo Barsch *m*
**per·co·la·tor** Kaffeemaschine *f*
**per·cus·sion** Schlag *m*; Erschütterung *f*; MUS Schlagzeug *n*; **~ drill** TECH Schlagbohrer *m*; **~ in·stru·ment** MUS Schlaginstrument *n*

**pe·remp·to·ry** herrisch
**pe·ren·ni·al** ewig, immer während; BOT mehrjährig
**per·fect 1.** perfekt, vollkommen, vollendet; gänzlich, völlig; **2.** vervollkommnen; **3.** *a.* ~ ***tense*** LING Perfekt *n*
**per·fec·tion** Vollendung *f*; Vollkommenheit *f*, Perfektion *f*
**per·fo·rate** durchbohren, -löchern
**per·form** *v/t* verrichten, durchführen, tun; *Pflicht etc* erfüllen; THEA, MUS aufführen, spielen, vortragen; *v/i* THEA *etc* e-e Vorstellung geben, auftreten, spielen; **per·form·ance** Verrichtung *f*, Durchführung *f*; Leistung *f*; THEA, MUS Aufführung *f*, Vorstellung *f*, Vortrag *m*; **per·form·er** THEA, MUS Darsteller(in), Künstler(in)
**per·fume 1.** Duft *m*; Parfüm *n*; **2.** parfümieren; **per·fum·er·y** Parfümerie *f*
**per·haps** vielleicht
**per·il** Gefahr *f*; **per·il·ous** gefährlich
**pe·ri·od** Periode *f*, Zeit *f*, Zeitdauer *f*, Zeitraum *m*, Zeitspanne *f*; (Unterrichts)Stunde *f*; MED Periode *f*; LING Punkt *m*; ~ **fur·ni·ture** Stilmöbel *pl*
**pe·ri·od·ic** periodisch
**pe·ri·od·i·cal 1.** periodisch; **2.** Zeitschrift *f*
**pe·riph·e·ral** EDP Peripheriegerät *n*; ~ **e·quip·ment** EDP Peripheriegeräte *pl*
**pe·riph·e·ry** Peripherie *f*, Rand *m*
**per·ish** umkommen; GASTR schlecht werden, verderben; TECH verschleißen
**per·ish·a·ble** leicht verderblich
**per·ish·a·bles** leicht verderbliche Lebensmittel
**per·jure:** ~ ***o.s.*** JUR e-n Meineid leisten
**per·ju·ry** JUR Meineid *m*; ***commit*** ~ e-n Meineid leisten
**perk:** ~ ***up*** *v/i* aufleben, munter werden; *v/t j-n* munter machen, F aufmöbeln
**perk·y** F munter, lebhaft; keck, selbstbewusst
**perm 1.** Dauerwelle *f*; ***get a*** ~ → **2.** ***get one's hair*** ~***ed*** sich e-e Dauerwelle machen lassen
**per·ma·nent 1.** (be)ständig, dauerhaft, Dauer...; **2.** *a.* ~ ***wave*** Dauerwelle *f*
**per·me·a·ble** durchlässig (***to*** für)
**per·me·ate** durchdringen; dringen (***into*** in *acc*; ***through*** durch)
**per·mis·si·ble** zulässig, erlaubt
**per·mis·sion** Erlaubnis *f*
**per·mis·sive** liberal; (sexuell) freizügig; ~ **so·ci·e·ty** tabufreie Gesellschaft
**per·mit 1.** erlauben, gestatten; **2.** Genehmigung *f*
**per·pen·dic·u·lar** senkrecht; rechtwink(e)lig (***to*** zu)
**per·pet·u·al** fortwährend, ständig, ewig
**per·plex** verwirren
**per·plex·i·ty** Verwirrung *f*
**per·se·cute** verfolgen
**per·se·cu·tion** Verfolgung *f*
**per·se·cu·tor** Verfolger(in)
**per·se·ver·ance** Ausdauer *f*, Beharrlichkeit *f*
**per·se·vere** beharrlich weitermachen
**per·sist** beharren (***in*** auf *dat*); anhalten
**per·sis·tence** Beharrlichkeit *f*
**per·sis·tent** beharrlich; anhaltend
**per·son** Person *f* (*a.* LING)
**per·son·al** persönlich (*a.* LING); Personal...; Privat...; ~ **com·pu·ter** (ABBR ***PC***) Personalcomputer *m*; ~ **da·ta** Personalien *pl*
**per·son·al·i·ty** Persönlichkeit *f*; *pl* anzügliche *or* persönliche Bemerkungen *pl*
**per·son·al| or·ga·ni·zer** Notizbuch *n*, Adressbuch *n* und Taschenkalender *m etc* (*in einem*); ~ **pro·noun** LING Personalpronomen *n*; ~ **ster·e·o** Walkman® *m*
**per·son·i·fy** personifizieren, verkörpern
**per·son·nel** Personal *n*, Belegschaft *f*; die Personalabteilung; ~ **de·part·ment** Personalabteilung *f*; ~ **man·ag·er** Personalchef *m*
**per·spec·tive** Perspektive *f*; Fernsicht *f*
**per·spi·ra·tion** Transpirieren *n*, Schwitzen *n*; Schweiß *m*
**per·spire** transpirieren, schwitzen
**per·suade** überreden; überzeugen
**per·sua·sion** Überredung(skunst) *f*; Überzeugung *f*
**per·sua·sive** überzeugend
**pert** keck, kess; schnippisch
**per·tain:** ~ ***to s.th.*** et. betreffen
**per·ti·nent** sachdienlich, relevant, zur Sache gehörig
**per·turb** beunruhigen
**per·vade** durchdringen, erfüllen
**per·verse** pervers; eigensinnig

**per·ver·sion** Verdrehung *f*; Perversion *f*
**per·ver·si·ty** Perversität *f*; Eigensinn *m*
**per·vert 1.** pervertieren; verdrehen; **2.** perverser Mensch
**pes·sa·ry** MED Pessar *n*
**pes·si·mism** Pessimismus *m*
**pes·si·mist** Pessimist(in)
**pes·si·mis·tic** pessimistisch
**pest** ZO Schädling *m*; F Nervensäge *f*; F Plage *f*; **~ con·trol** Schädlingsbekämpfung *f*
**pes·ter** F *j-n* belästigen, *j-m* keine Ruhe lassen
**pes·ti·cide** Pestizid *n*, Schädlingsbekämpfungsmittel *n*
**pet 1.** (zahmes) (Haus)Tier; *often contp* Liebling *m*; **2.** Lieblings...; Tier...; **3.** streicheln; F Petting machen
**pet·al** BOT Blütenblatt *n*
**pet food** Tiernahrung *f*
**pe·ti·tion 1.** Eingabe *f*, Gesuch *n*, (schriftlicher) Antrag; **2.** ersuchen; ein Gesuch einreichen (***for*** um), e-n Antrag stellen (***for*** auf *acc*)
**pet name** Kosename *m*
**pet·ri·fy** versteinern
**pet·rol** *Br* Benzin *n*
**pe·tro·le·um** Erdöl *n*, Mineralöl *n*
**pet·rol| pump** *Br* Zapfsäule *f*; **~ sta·tion** *Br* Tankstelle *f*
**pet shop** Tierhandlung *f*, Zoogeschäft *n*
**pet·ti·coat** Unterrock *m*
**pet·ting** F Petting *n*
**pet·tish** launisch, gereizt
**pet·ty** belanglos, unbedeutend, JUR *a.* geringfügig; engstirnig; **~ cash** Portokasse *f*; **~ lar·ce·ny** JUR einfacher Diebstahl
**pet·u·lant** launisch, gereizt
**pew** (Kirchen)Bank *f*
**pew·ter** Zinn *n*; *a.* ***~ ware*** Zinn(geschirr) *n*
**phan·tom** Phantom *n*; Geist *m*
**phar·ma·cist** Apotheker(in)
**phar·ma·cy** Apotheke *f*
**phase** Phase *f*
**pheas·ant** ZO Fasan *m*
**phe·nom·e·non** Phänomen *n*, Erscheinung *f*
**phi·lan·thro·pist** Philanthrop(in), Menschenfreund(in)
**phil·is·tine** F *contp* **1.** Spießer *m*; **2.** spießig
**phi·lol·o·gist** Philologe *m*, Philologin *f*
**phi·lol·o·gy** Philologie *f*
**phi·los·o·pher** Philosoph(in)
**phi·los·o·phy** Philosophie *f*
**phlegm** MED Schleim *m*
**phone 1.** Telefon *n*; ***answer the ~*** ans Telefon gehen; ***by ~*** telefonisch; ***on the ~*** am Telefon; ***be on the ~*** Telefon haben; am Telefon sein; **2.** telefonieren, anrufen; **~ book** Telefonbuch *n*; **~ booth,** *Br* **~ box** Telefonzelle *f*; **~ call** Anruf *m*, Gespräch *n*
**phone·card** Telefonkarte *f*
**phone-in** *radio*, TV Sendung *f* mit telefonischer Zuhörer- *or* Zuschauerbeteiligung
**phone num·ber** Telefonnummer *f*
**pho·net·ics** Phonetik *f*
**pho·n(e)y** F **1.** Fälschung *f*; Schwindler(in); **2.** falsch, gefälscht, unecht; Schein...
**phos·pho·rus** CHEM Phosphor *m*
**pho·to** F Foto *n*, Bild *n*; ***in the ~*** auf dem Foto; ***take a ~*** ein Foto machen (***of*** von)
**pho·to·cop·i·er** Fotokopiergerät *n*
**pho·to·cop·y 1.** Fotokopie *f*; **2.** fotokopieren
**pho·to·graph 1.** Fotografie *f*; **2.** fotografieren
**pho·tog·ra·pher** Fotograf(in)
**pho·tog·ra·phy** Fotografie *f*
**phras·al verb** LING Verb *n* mit Adverb (und Präposition)
**phrase 1.** (Rede)Wendung *f*, Redensart *f*, idiomatischer Ausdruck; **2.** ausdrücken; **phrase·book** Sprachführer *m*
**phys·i·cal 1.** physisch, körperlich; physikalisch; ***~ly handicapped*** körperbehindert; **2.** ärztliche Untersuchung; **~ ed·u·ca·tion** Leibeserziehung *f*, Sport *m*; **~ ex·am·i·na·tion** ärztliche Untersuchung; **~ hand·i·cap** Körperbehinderung *f*; **~ train·ing** Leibeserziehung *f*, Sport *m*
**phy·si·cian** Arzt *m*, Ärztin *f*
**phys·i·cist** Physiker(in)
**phys·ics** Physik *f*
**phy·sique** Körper(bau) *m*, Statur *f*
**pi·a·nist** MUS Pianist(in)
**pi·an·o** MUS Klavier *n*
**pick 1.** (auf)hacken; (auf)picken; auflesen, aufnehmen; pflücken; *Knochen* abnagen; bohren *or* stochern in (*dat*); F

P

*Schloss* knacken; aussuchen, auswählen; ~ ***one's nose*** in der Nase bohren; ~ ***one's teeth*** in den Zähnen (herum)stochern; ~ ***s.o.'s pocket*** j-n bestehlen; ***have a bone to ~ with s.o.*** mit j-m ein Hühnchen zu rupfen haben; ~ ***out*** (sich) *et.* auswählen; ausmachen, erkennen; ~ ***up*** aufheben, auflesen, aufnehmen; aufpicken; *Spur* aufnehmen; *j-n* abholen; *Anhalter* mitnehmen; F *Mädchen* aufreißen; *Kenntnisse, Informationen etc* aufschnappen; sich *e-e Krankheit etc* holen; *a.* ~ ***up speed*** MOT schneller werden; **2.** (Spitz)Hacke *f*, Pickel *m*; (Aus)Wahl *f*; ***take your ~*** suchen Sie sich etwas aus

**pick-a-back** huckepack

**pick·ax,** *Br* **pick·axe** (Spitz)Hacke *f*, Pickel *m*

**pick·et 1.** Pfahl *m*; Streikposten *m*; **2.** Streikposten aufstellen vor (*dat*), mit Streikposten besetzen; Streikposten stehen; ~ **fence** Lattenzaun *m*; ~ **line** Streikpostenkette *f*

**pick·le** GASTR **1.** Salzlake *f*; Essigsoße *f*; Essig-, Gewürzgurke *f*; *mst pl esp Br* Pickles *pl*; ***be in a*** (***pretty***) ~ F (ganz schön) in der Patsche sitzen *or* sein *or* stecken; **2.** einlegen

**pick·lock** Einbrecher *m*; TECH Dietrich *m*

**pick·pock·et** Taschendieb(in)

**pick-up** Tonabnehmer *m*; Kleintransporter *m*; F (Zufalls)Bekanntschaft *f*

**pick·y** F wählerisch (*in dat* about)

**pic·nic 1.** Picknick *n*; **2.** ein Picknick machen, picknicken

**pic·ture 1.** Bild *n*; Gemälde *n*; PHOT Aufnahme *f*; Film *m*; *pl esp Br* Kino *n*; **2.** darstellen, malen; *fig* sich *j-n, et.* vorstellen; ~ **book** Bilderbuch *n*; ~ **post·card** Ansichtskarte *f*

**pic·tur·esque** malerisch

**pie** (*Fleisch- etc*)Pastete *f*; (*mst* gedeckter) (*Apfel- etc*)Kuchen

**piece 1.** Stück *n*; Teil *n* (*of a machine etc*); Teil *m* (*of a set etc*); *chess*: Figur *f*; *board game*: Stein *m*; (Zeitungs)Artikel *m*, (-)Notiz *f*; ***by the ~*** stückweise; ***a ~ of advice*** ein Rat; ***a ~ of news*** e-e Neuigkeit; ***give s.o. a ~ of one's mind*** j-m gründlich die Meinung sagen; ***go to ~s*** F zusammenbrechen; ***take to ~s*** auseinander nehmen; **2.** ~ ***together*** zusammensetzen, -stückeln; *fig* zusammenfügen

**piece·meal** schrittweise

**piece·work** Akkordarbeit *f*; ***do ~*** im Akkord arbeiten

**pier** MAR Pier *m*, Landungsbrücke *f*; TECH Pfeiler *m*

**pierce** durchbohren, durchstechen, durchstoßen; durchdringen

**pierc·ing** durchdringend, (*Kälte etc a.*) schneidend, (*Schrei a.*) gellend, (*Blick, Schmerz etc a.*) stechend

**pi·e·ty** Frömmigkeit *f*

**pig** ZO Schwein *n* (*a.* F); F Ferkel *n*; *sl contp* Bulle *m*

**pi·geon** ZO Taube *f*

**pi·geon·hole 1.** Fach *n*; **2.** ablegen

**pig·gy** F Schweinchen *n*

**pig·gy·back** huckepack

**pig·gy bank** Sparschwein(chen) *n*

**pig·head·ed** dickköpfig, stur

**pig·let** ZO Ferkel *n*

**pig·sty** Schweinestall *m*, F *contp* Saustall *m*

**pig·tail** Zopf *m*

**pike**[1] ZO Hecht *m*

**pike**[2] → ***turnpike***

**pile**[1] **1.** Stapel *m*, Stoß *m*; F Haufen *m*, Menge *f*; (**atomic**) ~ Atommeiler *m*; **2.** ~ ***up*** (an-, auf)häufen, (auf)stapeln, aufschichten; sich anhäufen; MOT F aufeinander auffahren

**pile**[2] Flor *m*

**pile**[3] Pfahl *m*

**piles** *Br* F MED Hämorrhoiden *pl*

**pile-up** MOT Massenkarambolage *f*

**pil·fer** stehlen, klauen

**pil·grim** Pilger(in)

**pil·grim·age** Pilgerfahrt *f*, Wallfahrt *f*

**pill** PHARM Pille *f*; ***the ~*** F die (*Antibaby*)Pille; ***be on the ~*** die Pille nehmen

**pil·lar** Pfeiler *m*; Säule *f*

**pil·li·on** MOT Soziussitz *m*

**pil·lo·ry 1.** HIST Pranger *m*; **2.** *fig* anprangern

**pil·low** (Kopf)Kissen *n*

**pil·low·case, pil·low slip** (Kopf)Kissenbezug *m*

**pi·lot 1.** AVIAT Pilot *m*; MAR Lotse *m*; **2.** Versuchs..., Pilot...; **3.** lotsen; steuern; ~ **film** TV Pilotfilm *m*; ~ **scheme** Versuchs-, Pilotprojekt *n*

**pimp** Zuhälter *m*

**pim·ple** MED Pickel *m*, Pustel *f*

P

**pin 1.** (Steck)Nadel *f*; (*Haar-, Krawatten- etc*)Nadel *f*; Brosche *f*; TECH Bolzen *m*, Stift *m*; *bowling*: Kegel *m*; Pin *m*; (*Wäsche*)Klammer *f*; *Br* (*Reiß*)Nagel *m*, (-)Zwecke *f*; **2.** (an)heften, anstecken (***to*** an *acc*), befestigen (***to*** an *dat*); pressen, drücken (***against, to*** gegen, an *acc*)
**PIN** *a.* ~ ***number*** ABBR *of* ***personal identification number*** PIN, persönliche Geheimzahl
**pin·a·fore** Schürze *f*
**pin·ball** Flippern *n*; ***play*** ~ flippern
**pin·ball ma·chine** Flipper(automat) *m*
**pin·cers:** (***a pair of*** ~ e-e) (Kneif)Zange
**pinch 1.** *v/t* kneifen, zwicken; F klauen; *v/i* drücken; **2.** Kneifen *n*, Zwicken *n*; Prise *f*; *fig* Not(lage) *f*
**pin·cush·ion** Nadelkissen *n*
**pine¹** BOT Kiefer *f*, Föhre *f*
**pine²** sich sehnen (***for*** nach)
**pine·ap·ple** BOT Ananas *f*
**pine cone** BOT Kiefernzapfen *m*
**pine·tree** BOT Kiefer *f*, Föhre *f*
**pin·ion** ZO Schwungfeder *f*
**pink 1.** rosa(farben); **2.** Rosa *n*; BOT Nelke *f*
**pint** Pint *n* (*0,47 l*, *Br 0,57 l*); *Br* F Halbe *f*
**pi·o·neer 1.** Pionier *m*; **2.** den Weg bahnen (für)
**pi·ous** fromm, religiös
**pip¹** *Br* (*Apfel-, Orangen- etc*)Kern *m*
**pip²** (Piep)Ton *m*
**pip³** *on cards etc*: Auge *n*, Punkt *m*
**pipe 1.** TECH Rohr *n*, Röhre *f*; (*Tabaks*)Pfeife *f*; MUS (*Orgel*)Pfeife *f*; *pl Br* F Dudelsack *m*; **2.** (durch Rohre) leiten
**pipe·line** Rohrleitung *f*; Pipeline *f*
**pip·er** MUS Dudelsackpfeifer *m*
**pip·ing 1.** Rohrleitung *f*, Rohrnetz *n*; **2.** ~ ***hot*** kochend heiß, siedend heiß
**pi·quant** pikant (*a. fig*)
**pique 1.** ***in a fit of*** ~ gekränkt, verletzt, pikiert; **2.** kränken, verletzen; ***be*** ~***d*** *a.* pikiert sein
**pi·rate 1.** Pirat *m*, Seeräuber *m*; **2.** unerlaubt kopieren *or* nachdrucken *or* nachpressen
**pi·rate ra·di·o** Piratensender *m or pl*
**Pis·ces** ASTR Fische *pl*; ***he*** (***she***) ***is*** (***a***) ~ er (sie) ist (ein) Fisch
**piss** V **1.** Pisse *f*; ***take the*** ~ ***out of s.o.*** j-n verarschen; **2.** pissen; ~ ***off!*** verpiss dich!
**pis·tol** Pistole *f*
**pis·ton** TECH Kolben *m*
**pit¹ 1.** Grube *f* (*a.* ANAT), MIN *a.* Zeche *f*; *esp Br* THEA Parkett *n*; *a.* ***orchestra*** ~ THEA Orchestergraben *m*; MED (*esp* Pocken)Narbe *f*; *car racing*: Box *f*; ~ ***stop*** Boxenstopp *m*; **2.** mit Narben bedecken
**pit² 1.** BOT Kern *m*, Stein *m*; **2.** entkernen, entsteinen
**pitch¹ 1.** *v/t Zelt*, *Lager* aufschlagen; werfen, schleudern; MUS (an)stimmen; *v/i* stürzen, fallen; MAR stampfen; sich neigen (*roof etc*); ~ ***in*** F sich ins Zeug legen; kräftig zulangen; **2.** *esp Br* SPORT (Spiel)Feld *n*; MUS Tonhöhe *f*; *fig* Grad *m*, Stufe *f*; *esp Br* Stand(platz) *m*; MAR Stampfen *n*; Neigung *f* (*of a roof etc*)
**pitch²** Pech *n*
**pitch-black, pitch-dark** pechschwarz; stockdunkel
**pitch·er¹** Krug *m*
**pitch·er²** *baseball*: Werfer *m*
**pitch·fork** Heugabel *f*, Mistgabel *f*
**pit·e·ous** kläglich
**pit·fall** Fallgrube *f*; *fig* Falle *f*
**pith** BOT Mark *n*; weiße innere Haut; *fig* Kern *m*; **pith·y** markig, prägnant
**pit·i·a·ble** → ***pitiful***
**pit·i·ful** Mitleid erregend, bemitleidenswert; erbärmlich, jämmerlich
**pit·i·less** unbarmherzig, erbarmungslos
**pit·ta bread** Fladenbrot *n*
**pit·y 1.** Mitleid *n* (***on*** mit); ***it is a*** (***great***) ~ es ist (sehr) schade; ***what a*** ~***!*** wie schade!; **2.** bemitleiden, bedauern
**piv·ot 1.** TECH Drehzapfen *m*; *fig* Dreh- und Angelpunkt *m*; **2.** sich drehen; ~ ***on*** *fig* abhängen von
**pix·el** EDP Pixel *m*
**piz·za** Pizza *f*
**plac·ard 1.** Plakat *n*; Transparent *n*; **2.** mit Plakaten bekleben
**place 1.** Platz *m*, Ort *m*, Stelle *f*; Stätte *f*; Haus *n*, Wohnung *f*; Wohnort *m*; (*Arbeits-, Lehr*)Stelle *f*; ***in the first*** ~ erstens; ***in third*** ~ SPORT *etc* auf dem dritten Platz; ***in*** ~ ***of*** anstelle von (*or gen*); ***out of*** ~ fehl am Platz; ***take*** ~ stattfinden; ***take s.o.'s*** ~ j-s Stelle einnehmen; **2.** stellen, legen, setzen; *Auftrag* erteilen (***with*** *dat*), *Bestellung* aufgeben (***with*** bei); ***be*** ~***d*** SPORT sich platzieren (***second*** an zweiter Stelle)

**place mat** Platzdeckchen *n*, Set *n*, *m*
**place·ment test** Einstufungsprüfung *f*
**place name** Ortsname *m*
**plac·id** ruhig; gelassen
**pla·gia·rize** plagiieren
**plague 1.** Seuche *f*; Pest *f*; Plage *f*; **2.** plagen
**plaice** ZO Scholle *f*
**plaid** Plaid *n or m*
**plain 1.** *adj* einfach, schlicht; klar (und deutlich); offen (und ehrlich); unscheinbar, wenig anziehend; rein, völlig (*nonsense etc*); **2.** *adv* F (ganz) einfach; **3.** Ebene *f*, Flachland *n*
**plain choc·olate** *Br* (zart)bittere Schokolade
**plain-clothes** ... in Zivil
**plain·tiff** JUR Kläger(in)
**plain·tive** traurig, klagend
**plait** *esp Br* **1.** Zopf *m*; **2.** flechten
**plan 1.** Plan *m*; **2.** planen; beabsichtigen
**plane**[1] Flugzeug *n*; ***by ~*** mit dem Flugzeug; ***go by ~*** fliegen
**plane**[2] **1.** flach, eben; **2.** MATH Ebene *f*; *fig* Stufe *f*, Niveau *n*
**plane**[3] **1.** Hobel *m*; **2.** hobeln; ***~ down*** abhobeln
**plan·et** ASTR Planet *m*
**plank** Planke *f*, Bohle *f*; **~bed** Pritsche *f*
**plank·ing** Planken *pl*
**plant 1.** BOT Pflanze *f*; ECON Werk *n*, Betrieb *m*, Fabrik *f*; **2.** (an-, ein)pflanzen; bepflanzen; *Garten etc* anlegen; aufstellen, postieren; ***~ s.th. on s.o.*** F j-m et. (*Belastendes*) unterschieben
**plan·ta·tion** Plantage *f*, Pflanzung *f*; Schonung *f*
**plant·er** Plantagenbesitzer(in), Pflanzer(in); Pflanzmaschine *f*; Übertopf *m*
**plaque** Gedenktafel *f*; MED Zahnbelag *m*
**plas·ter 1.** MED Pflaster *n*; (Ver)Putz *m*; *a.* ***~ of Paris*** Gips *m*; ***have one's leg in ~*** MED das Bein in Gips haben; **2.** verputzen; bekleben; **~ cast** Gipsabguss *m*, Gipsmodell *n*; MED Gipsverband *m*
**plas·tic 1.** plastisch; Plastik...; **2.** Plastik *n*, Kunststoff *m*; → **~ mon·ey** F Plastikgeld *n*, Kreditkarten *pl*; **~ wrap** Frischhaltefolie *f*
**plate 1.** Teller *m*; Platte *f*; (*Namens-, Nummern- etc*)Schild *n*; (Bild)Tafel *f*; (Druck)Platte *f*; Gegenstände *pl* aus Edelmetall; Doublé *n*, Dublee *n*; **2.** ***~d with gold, gold-plated*** vergoldet
**plat·form** Plattform *f*; RAIL Bahnsteig *m*; (Redner)Tribüne *f*, Podium *n*; POL Plattform *f*; MOT Pritsche *f*; ***party ~*** POL Parteiprogramm *n*; ***election ~*** POL Wahlprogramm *n*
**plat·i·num** CHEM Platin *n*
**pla·toon** MIL Zug *m*
**plat·ter** (Servier)Platte *f*
**plau·si·ble** plausibel, glaubhaft
**play 1.** Spiel *n*; Schauspiel *n*, (Theater)Stück *n*; TECH Spiel *n*; *fig* Spielraum *m*; ***at ~*** beim Spiel(en); ***in ~*** im Spiel (*ball*); ***out of ~*** im Aus (*ball*); **2.** *v/i* spielen (*a.* SPORT, THEA *etc*); *v/t Karten, Rolle, Stück etc* spielen, SPORT *Spiel* austragen; **~ s.o.** SPORT gegen j-n spielen; ***~ the guitar*** Gitarre spielen; ***~ a trick on s.o.*** j-m e-n Streich spielen; ***~ back*** *Ball* zurückspielen (**to** zu); *Tonband* abspielen; *~ s.th.* ***down*** verharmlosen, herunterspielen; ***~ off*** *fig* ausspielen (***against*** gegen); ***~ on*** *fig j-s Schwächen* ausnutzen
**play·back** Play-back *n*, Wiedergabe *f*, Abspielen *n*
**play·boy** Playboy *m*
**play·er** MUS, SPORT Spieler(in); TECH Plattenspieler *m*
**play·fel·low** *Br* → ***playmate***
**play·ful** verspielt; scherzhaft
**play·go·er** Theaterbesucher(in)
**play·ground** Spielplatz *m* (*a. fig*); Schulhof *m*
**play·group** *Br* Spielgruppe *f*
**play·house** THEA Schauspielhaus *n*; Spielhaus *n* (*for children*)
**play·ing card** Spielkarte *f*
**play·ing field** Sportplatz *m*, Spielfeld *n*
**play·mate** Spielkamerad(in)
**play·pen** Laufgitter *n*, Laufstall *m*
**play·thing** Spielzeug *n*
**play·wright** Dramatiker(in)
**plc, PLC** *Br* ECON ABBR *of* ***public limited company*** AG, Aktiengesellschaft *f*
**plea:** ***enter a ~ of*** (***not***) ***guilty*** JUR sich schuldig bekennen (s-e Unschuld erklären)
**plead** *v/i* (dringend) bitten (***for*** um); ***~*** (***not***) ***guilty*** JUR sich schuldig bekennen (s-e Unschuld erklären); *v/t a.* JUR zu s-r Verteidigung *or* Entschuldigung anführen, geltend machen; ***~ s.o.'s case*** sich für j-n einsetzen; JUR j-n vertreten

P

**pleas·ant** angenehm, erfreulich; freundlich; sympathisch
**please 1.** *j-m* gefallen; *j-m* zusagen, *j-n* erfreuen; zufrieden stellen; ***only to ~ you*** nur dir zuliebe; **~ *o.s.*** tun, was man will; **~ *yourself!*** mach, was du willst!; **2.** *int* bitte; (***yes,***) **~** (ja,) bitte; (oh ja,) gerne; **~ *come in!*** bitte, treten Sie ein!
**pleased** erfreut, zufrieden; ***be ~ about*** sich freuen über (*acc*); ***be ~ with*** zufrieden sein mit; ***I am ~ with it*** es gefällt mir; ***be ~ to do s.th.*** et. gern tun; **~ *to meet you!*** angenehm!
**pleas·ing** angenehm
**plea·sure** Vergnügen *n*; ***at*** (***one's***) **~** nach Belieben
**pleat** (Plissee)Falte *f*
**pleat·ed skirt** Faltenrock *m*
**pledge 1.** Pfand *n*; *fig* Unterpfand *n*; Versprechen *n*; **2.** versprechen, zusichern
**plen·ti·ful** reichlich
**plen·ty 1.** Überfluss *m*; ***in ~*** im Überfluss, in Hülle und Fülle; **~ *of*** e-e Menge, viel(e), reichlich; **2.** F reichlich
**pleu·ri·sy** MED Brustfell-, Rippenfellentzündung *f*
**pli·a·ble, pli·ant** biegsam; *fig* flexibel; *fig* leicht beeinflussbar
**pli·ers** (***a pair of ~*** e-e) Beißzange *f*
**plight** Not *f*, Notlage *f*
**plim·soll** *Br* Turnschuh *m*
**plod** *a.* **~ *along*** sich dahinschleppen; **~ *away*** sich abplagen (***at*** mit), schuften
**plop** F **1.** Plumps *m*, Platsch *m*; **2.** plumpsen, (*ins Wasser*) platschen
**plot 1.** Stück *n* Land, Parzelle *f*, Grundstück *n*; THEA, *film etc*: Handlung *f*; Komplott *n*, Verschwörung *f*; EDP grafische Darstellung; **2.** *v/i* sich verschwören (***against*** gegen); *v/t* planen; einzeichnen
**plot·ter** EDP Plotter *m*
**plough** *Br*, **plow** AGR **1.** Pflug *m*; **2.** (um)pflügen; **plough·share** *Br*, **plow·share** AGR Pflugschar *f*
**pluck 1.** *v/t Geflügel* rupfen; *mst* **~ *out*** ausreißen, ausrupfen, auszupfen; MUS *Saiten* zupfen; **~ *up*** (***one's***) ***courage*** Mut *or* sich ein Herz fassen; *v/i* zupfen (***at*** an *dat*); **2.** F Mut *m*, Schneid *m*
**pluck·y** F mutig
**plug 1.** Stöpsel *m*; ELECTR Stecker *m*, F Steckdose *f*; F MOT (*Zünd*)Kerze *f*; **2.** *v/t* F für *et.* Schleichwerbung machen; *a.* **~ *up*** zustöpseln; zustopfen, verstopfen; **~ *in*** ELECTR anschließen, einstecken
**plug·ging** F Schleichwerbung *f*
**plum** BOT Pflaume *f*; Zwetsch(g)e *f*
**plum·age** Gefieder *n*
**plumb 1.** (Blei)Lot *n*; **2.** ausloten, *fig a.* ergründen; **~ *in*** *esp Br Waschmaschine etc* anschließen; **3.** *adj* lotrecht, senkrecht; **4.** *adv* F (haar)genau
**plumb·er** Klempner *m*, Installateur *m*
**plumb·ing** Klempner-, Installateurarbeit *f*; Rohre *pl*, Rohrleitungen *pl*
**plume** (Schmuck)Feder *f*; Federbusch *m*; (*Rauch*)Fahne *f*
**plump 1.** *adj* drall, mollig, rund(lich), F pumm(e)lig; **2.** **~ *down*** fallen *or* plumpsen (lassen)
**plum pud·ding** *Br* Plumpudding *m*
**plun·der 1.** plündern; **2.** Plünderung *f*; Beute *f*
**plunge 1.** (ein-, unter)tauchen; (sich) stürzen (***into*** in *acc*); MAR stampfen; **2.** (Kopf)Sprung *m*; ***take the ~*** *fig* den entscheidenden Schritt wagen
**plu·per·fect** *a.* **~ *tense*** LING Plusquamperfekt *n*, Vorvergangenheit *f*
**plu·ral** LING Plural *m*, Mehrzahl *f*
**plus 1.** *prp* plus, und, *esp* ECON zuzüglich; **2.** *adj* Plus...; **~ *sign*** MATH Plus *n*, Pluszeichen *n*; **3.** MATH Plus *n* (*a.* F), Pluszeichen *n*; F Vorteil *m*
**plush** Plüsch *m*
**ply**[1] *regelmäßig* verkehren, fahren (***between*** zwischen *dat*)
**ply**[2] *mst in cpds* TECH Lage *f*, Schicht *f*; ***three-~*** dreifach (*thread etc*); dreifach gewebt (*carpet*)
**ply·wood** Sperrholz *n*
**pm, PM** ABBR *of* ***after noon*** (*Latin* ***post meridiem***) nachm., nachmittags, abends
**pneu·mat·ic** Luft..., pneumatisch; TECH Druck..., Pressluft...
**pneu·mat·ic drill** Pressluftbohrer *m*
**pneu·mo·ni·a** MED Lungenentzündung *f*
**poach**[1] GASTR pochieren; **~*ed eggs*** verlorene Eier *pl*
**poach**[2] wildern
**poach·er** Wilddieb *m*, Wilderer *m*
**PO Box** Postfach *n*; ***write to ~ 225*** schreiben Sie an Postfach 225

**pock** MED Pocke *f*, Blatter *f*
**pock·et 1.** (Hosen- *etc*)Tasche *f*; **2.** *adj* Taschen...; **3.** einstecken, in die Tasche stecken; *fig* in die eigene Tasche stecken; **pock·et·book** Notizbuch *n*; Brieftasche *f*
**pock·et| cal·cu·la·tor** Taschenrechner *m*; **~ knife** Taschenmesser *n*; **~ mon·ey** Taschengeld *n*
**pod** BOT Hülse *f*, Schote *f*
**po·di·a·trist** Fußpfleger(in)
**po·em** Gedicht *n*
**po·et** Dichter(in)
**po·et·ic** dichterisch
**po·et·i·cal** dichterisch
**po·et·ic jus·tice** *fig* ausgleichende Gerechtigkeit
**po·et·ry** Gedichte *pl*; Poesie *f* (*a. fig*), Dichtkunst *f*, Dichtung *f*
**poi·gnant** schmerzlich; ergreifend
**point 1.** Spitze *f*; GEOGR Landspitze *f*; LING, MATH, PHYS, SPORT *etc* Punkt *m*; MATH (Dezimal)Punkt *m*; Grad *m*; MAR (*Kompass*)Strich *m*; *fig* Punkt *m*, Stelle *f*, Ort *m*; Zweck *m*; Ziel *n*, Absicht *f*; springender Punkt; Pointe *f*; ***two ~ five*** (**2.5**) 2,5; ***~ of view*** Stand-, Gesichtspunkt *m*; ***be on the ~ of doing s.th.*** im Begriff sein, et. zu tun; ***to the ~*** zur Sache gehörig; ***off*** *or* ***beside the ~*** nicht zur Sache gehörig; ***come to the ~*** zur Sache kommen; ***that's not the ~*** darum geht es nicht; ***what's the ~?*** wozu?; ***win on ~s*** SPORT nach Punkten gewinnen; ***winner on ~s*** SPORT Punktsieger *m*; **2.** *v/t* (zu)spitzen; *Waffe etc* richten (***at*** auf *acc*); ***~ one's finger at s.o.*** (mit dem Finger) auf j-n zeigen; ***~ out*** zeigen; *fig* hinweisen *or* aufmerksam machen auf (*acc*); *v/i* (mit dem Finger) zeigen (***at, to*** auf *acc*); ***~ to*** nach *e-r Richtung* weisen *or* liegen; *fig* hinweisen auf (*acc*)
**point·ed** spitz; Spitz...; *fig* scharf (*remark etc*); ostentativ
**point·er** Zeiger *m*; Zeigestock *m*; ZO Pointer *m*, Vorstehhund *m*
**point·less** sinnlos, zwecklos
**points** *Br* RAIL Weiche *f*
**poise 1.** (Körper)Haltung *f*; *fig* Gelassenheit *f*; **2.** balancieren; ***be ~d*** schweben
**poi·son 1.** Gift *n*; **2.** vergiften
**poi·son·ous** giftig (*a. fig*)
**poke 1.** *v/t* stoßen; *Feuer* schüren; stecken; *v/i* ***~ about, ~ around*** F (herum-) stöbern, (-)wühlen (***in*** in *dat*); **2.** Stoß *m*
**pok·er** Schürhaken *m*
**pok·y** F eng; schäbig
**Po·land** Polen *n*
**po·lar** polar; **~ bear** ZO Eisbär *m*
**pole**[1] GEOGR Pol *m*
**pole**[2] Stange *f*; Mast *m*; Deichsel *f*; SPORT (Sprung)Stab *m*
**Pole** Pole *m*, Polin *f*
**pole·cat** ZO Iltis *m*; F Skunk *m*, Stinktier *n*
**po·lem·ic, po·lem·i·cal** polemisch
**pole star** ASTR Polarstern *m*
**pole vault** SPORT Stabhochsprung *m*, Stabhochspringen *n*
**pole-vault** SPORT stabhochspringen
**pole vault·er** SPORT Stabhochspringer(in)
**po·lice 1.** Polizei *f*; **2.** überwachen
**po·lice car** Polizeiauto *n*
**po·lice·man** Polizist *m*
**po·lice| of·fi·cer** Polizeibeamte *m*, -beamtin *f*, Polizist(in); **~ sta·tion** Polizeiwache *f*, Polizeirevier *n*
**po·lice·wom·an** Polizistin *f*
**pol·i·cy** Politik *f*; Taktik *f*; Klugheit *f*; (Versicherungs)Police *f*
**po·li·o** MED Polio *f*, Kinderlähmung *f*
**pol·ish 1.** polieren; *Schuhe* putzen; ***~ up*** aufpolieren (*a. fig*); **2.** Politur *f*; (*Schuh*)Creme *f*; *fig* Schliff *m*
**Pol·ish 1.** polnisch; **2.** LING Polnisch *n*
**po·lite** höflich
**po·lite·ness** Höflichkeit *f*
**po·lit·i·cal** politisch
**pol·i·ti·cian** Politiker(in)
**pol·i·tics** Politik *f*
**pol·ka** MUS Polka *f*
**pol·ka-dot** gepunktet, getupft
**poll 1.** (*Meinungs*)Umfrage *f*; Wahlbeteiligung *f*; *a. pl* Stimmabgabe *f*, Wahl *f*; **2.** befragen; *Stimmen* erhalten
**pol·len** BOT Pollen *m*, Blütenstaub *m*
**poll·ing** Stimmabgabe *f*; Wahlbeteiligung *f*; **~ booth** *esp Br* Wahlkabine *f*; **~ day** Wahltag *m*; **~ place,** *esp Br* **~ sta·tion** Wahllokal *n*
**polls** Wahl *f*; Wahllokal *n*
**poll·ster** Demoskop(in), Meinungsforscher(in)
**pol·lut·ant** Schadstoff *m*; **pol·lute** beschmutzen, verschmutzen; verunreinigen; **pol·lut·er** *a.* ***environmental ~***

P

Umweltsünder(in); **pol·lu·tion** (*Luft-*, *Wasser- etc*)Verschmutzung *f*; Verunreinigung *f*
**po·lo** SPORT Polo *n*
**po·lo neck** *a.* ~ ***sweater*** *esp Br* Rollkragenpullover *m*
**pol·yp** ZO, MED Polyp *m*
**pol·y·sty·rene** Styropor® *n*
**pom·mel** (Sattel- *etc*)Knopf *m*
**pomp** Pomp *m*, Prunk *m*
**pom·pous** aufgeblasen, wichtigtuerisch; schwülstig (*speech*)
**pond** Teich *m*, Weiher *m*
**pon·der** *v/i* nachdenken (***on, over*** über *acc*); *v/t* überlegen
**pon·der·ous** schwerfällig; schwer
**pon·toon** Ponton *m*
**pon·toon bridge** Pontonbrücke *f*
**po·ny** ZO Pony *n*
**po·ny·tail** Pferdeschwanz *m*
**poo·dle** ZO Pudel *m*
**pool**[1] Teich *m*, Tümpel *m*; Pfütze *f*, (*Blut- etc*)Lache *f*; (*Schwimm*)Becken *n*, (*Swimming*)Pool *m*
**pool**[2] **1.** (*Arbeits-*, *Fahr*)Gemeinschaft *f*; (*Mitarbeiter- etc*)Stab *m*; (*Fuhr*)Park *m*; (*Schreib*)Pool *m*; ECON Pool *m*, Kartell *n*; *card games*: Gesamteinsatz *m*; Poolbillard *n*; **2.** *Geld, Unternehmen etc* zusammenlegen; *Kräfte etc* vereinen
**pool hall, pool·room** Billardspielhalle *f*
**pools** *a.* ***football*** ~ *Br* (Fußball)Toto *n*, *m*
**poor 1.** arm; dürftig, mangelhaft, schwach; **2.** ***the*** ~ die Armen *pl*
**poor·ly 1.** *adj esp Br* F kränklich, unpässlich; **2.** *adv* ärmlich, dürftig, schlecht, schwach
**pop**[1] **1.** *v/t* zerknallen; F schnell *wohin* tun *or* stecken; *v/i* knallen; (zer)platzen; ~ ***in*** F auf e-n Sprung vorbeikommen; ~ ***off*** F (plötzlich) den Löffel weglegen; ~ ***up*** (plötzlich) auftauchen; **2.** Knall *m*; F Limo *f*
**pop**[2] MUS **1.** Pop *m*; **2.** Schlager...; Pop...
**pop**[3] F Paps *m*, Papa *m*
**pop**[4] ABBR *of* ***population*** Einw., Einwohner(zahl *f*) *pl*
**pop con·cert** MUS Popkonzert *n*
**pop·corn** Popcorn *n*, Puffmais *m*
**Pope** REL Papst *m*
**pop-eyed** F glotzäugig
**pop group** MUS Popgruppe *f*
**pop·lar** BOT Pappel *f*
**pop mu·sic** Popmusik *f*
**pop·py** BOT Mohn *m*
**pop·u·lar** populär, beliebt; volkstümlich; allgemein
**pop·u·lar·i·ty** Popularität *f*, Beliebtheit *f*; Volkstümlichkeit *f*
**pop·u·late** bevölkern, besiedeln; bewohnen
**pop·u·la·tion** Bevölkerung *f*
**pop·u·lous** dicht besiedelt, dicht bevölkert
**porce·lain** Porzellan *n*
**porch** überdachter Vorbau; Portal *n*; Veranda *f*
**por·cu·pine** ZO Stachelschwein *n*
**pore**[1] Pore *f*
**pore**[2]**:** ~ ***over*** vertieft sein in (*acc*), *et.* eifrig studieren
**pork** GASTR Schweinefleisch *n*
**porn** F → ***porno***
**por·no** F **1.** Porno *m*; **2.** Porno...
**por·nog·ra·phy** Pornografie *f*
**po·rous** porös
**por·poise** ZO Tümmler *m*
**por·ridge** Porridge *m*, *n*, Haferbrei *m*
**port**[1] Hafen *m*; Hafenstadt *f*
**port**[2] AVIAT, MAR Backbord *n*
**port**[3] EDP Port *m*, Anschluss *m*
**port**[4] Portwein *m*
**por·ta·ble** tragbar
**por·ter** (Gepäck)Träger *m*; *esp Br* Pförtner *m*, Portier *m*; RAIL Schlafwagenschaffner *m*
**port·hole** MAR Bullauge *n*
**por·tion 1.** (An)Teil *m*; GASTR Portion *f*; **2.** ~ ***out*** aufteilen, verteilen (***among, between*** unter *acc*)
**port·ly** korpulent
**por·trait** Porträt *n*, Bild *n*, Bildnis *n*
**por·tray** porträtieren; darstellen; schildern; **por·tray·al** THEA Verkörperung *f*, Darstellung *f*; Schilderung *f*
**Por·tu·gal** Portugal *n*
**Por·tu·guese 1.** portugiesisch; **2.** Portugiese *m*, Portugiesin *f*; LING Portugiesisch *n*; ***the*** ~ die Portugiesen *pl*
**pose 1.** *v/t* aufstellen; *Problem, Frage* aufwerfen, *Bedrohung, Gefahr etc* darstellen; *v/i* Modell sitzen *or* stehen; ~ ***as*** sich ausgeben als *or* für; **2.** Pose *f*
**posh** *esp Br* F schick, piekfein
**po·si·tion 1.** Position *f*, Lage *f*, Stellung *f* (*a. fig*); Stand *m*; *fig* Standpunkt *m*; **2.** (auf)stellen

P

**pos·i·tive 1.** positiv; bestimmt, sicher, eindeutig; greifbar, konkret; konstruktiv; **2.** PHOT Positiv *n*
**pos·sess** besitzen; *fig* beherrschen
**pos·sessed** *fig* besessen
**pos·ses·sion** Besitz *m*; *fig* Besessenheit *f*
**pos·ses·sive** besitzergreifend; LING possessiv, besitzanzeigend
**pos·si·bil·i·ty** Möglichkeit *f*
**pos·si·ble** möglich
**pos·si·bly** möglicherweise, vielleicht; ***if I ~ can*** wenn ich irgend kann; ***I can't ~ do this*** ich kann das unmöglich tun
**post¹** (*Tür-*, *Tor-*, *Ziel- etc*)Pfosten *m*; Pfahl *m*; **2.** *a.* ***~ up*** *Plakat etc* anschlagen, ankleben; ***be ~ed missing*** AVIAT, MAR als vermisst gemeldet werden
**post²** *esp Br* **1.** Post *f*; Postsendung *f*; ***by ~*** mit der Post; **2.** mit der Post (zu-)schicken, aufgeben, *Brief* einwerfen
**post³ 1.** Stelle *f*, Job *m*; Posten *m*; **2.** aufstellen, postieren; *esp Br* versetzen, MIL abkommandieren (***to*** nach)
**post...** nach..., Nach...
**post·age** Porto *n*; **~ stamp** Postwertzeichen *n*, Briefmarke *f*
**post·al** postalisch, Post...; **~ or·der** *Br* ECON Postanweisung *f*; **~ vote** POL Briefwahl *f*
**post·bag** *esp Br* Postsack *m*
**post·box** *esp Br* Briefkasten *m*
**post·card** Postkarte *f*; *a.* ***picture ~*** Ansichtskarte *f*
**post·code** *Br* Postleitzahl *f*
**post·er** Plakat *n*; Poster *n*, *m*
**poste res·tante** *Br* **1.** Abteilung *f* für postlagernde Sendungen; **2.** postlagernd
**pos·te·ri·or** HUMOR Hinterteil *n*
**pos·ter·i·ty** die Nachwelt
**post-free** *esp Br* portofrei
**post·hu·mous** post(h)um
**post·man** *esp Br* Briefträger *m*, Postbote *m*
**post·mark 1.** Poststempel *m*; **2.** (ab)stempeln
**post·mas·ter** Postamtsvorsteher *m*
**post of·fice** Post *f*; Postamt *n*, -filiale *f*
**post of·fice box** → ***PO Box***
**post-paid** portofrei
**post·pone** verschieben, aufschieben
**post·pone·ment** Verschiebung *f*, Aufschub *m*
**post·script** Postskript(um) *n*, Nachschrift *f*
**pos·ture 1.** (Körper)Haltung *f*; Stellung *f*; **2.** *fig* sich aufspielen
**post·war** Nachkriegs...
**post·wom·an** *esp Br* Briefträgerin *f*, Postbotin *f*
**po·sy** Sträußchen *n*
**pot 1.** Topf *m*; Kanne *f*; Kännchen *n* (*Tee etc*); SPORT F Pokal *m*; **2.** *Pflanze* eintopfen
**po·tas·si·um cy·a·nide** CHEM Zyankali *n*
**po·ta·to** Kartoffel *f*; → ***chips, crisps***
**pot·bel·ly** Schmerbauch *m*
**po·ten·cy** Stärke *f*; Wirksamkeit *f*, Wirkung *f*; MED Potenz *f*
**po·tent** PHARM stark; MED potent
**po·ten·tial 1.** potenziell, möglich; **2.** Potenzial *n*, Leistungsfähigkeit *f*
**pot·hole** MOT Schlagloch *n*
**po·tion** Trank *m*
**pot·ter¹** *Br*: ***~ about*** herumwerkeln
**pot·ter²** Töpfer(in)
**pot·ter·y** Töpferei *f*; Töpferware(n *pl*) *f*
**pouch** Beutel *m* (*a.* ZO); ZO (*Backen*)Tasche *f*
**poul·tice** MED (warmer) Umschlag *m*
**poul·try** Geflügel *n*
**pounce 1.** sich stürzen (***on*** auf *acc*); **2.** Satz *m*, Sprung *m*
**pound¹** Pfund *n* (*453,59 g*); ***~ (sterling)*** (ABBR **£**) Pfund *n*
**pound²** Tierheim *n*; Abstellplatz *m* für (polizeilich) abgeschleppte Fahrzeuge
**pound³** *v/t* zerstoßen, zerstampfen; trommeln *or* hämmern auf (*acc*) *or* an (*acc*) *or* gegen; *v/i* hämmern (***with*** vor *dat*)
**pour** *v/t* gießen, schütten; ***~ out*** ausgießen, ausschütten; *Getränk* eingießen; *v/i* strömen (*a. fig*)
**pout** *v/t* *Lippen* schürzen; *v/i* e-n Schmollmund machen; schmollen
**pov·er·ty** Armut *f*
**pow·der 1.** Pulver *n*; Puder *m*; **2.** pulverisieren; (sich) pudern; **~ puff** Puderquaste *f*; **~ room** (Damen)Toilette *f*
**pow·er 1.** Kraft *f*; Macht *f*; Fähigkeit *f*, Vermögen *n*; Gewalt *f*; JUR Befugnis *f*, Vollmacht *f*; MATH Potenz *f*; ELECTR Strom *m*; ***in ~*** POL an der Macht; **2.** TECH antreiben; **~ cut** ELECTR Stromsperre *f*; **~ fail·ure** ELECTR Stromausfall *m*, Netzausfall *m*

**pow·er·ful** stark, kräftig; mächtig
**pow·er·less** kraftlos; machtlos
**pow·er| plant** Elektrizitäts-, Kraftwerk *n*; **~ pol·i·tics** Machtpolitik *f*; **~ sta·tion** *Br* Elektrizitäts-, Kraftwerk *n*
**prac·ti·ca·ble** durchführbar
**prac·ti·cal** praktisch; **~ joke** Streich *m*
**prac·ti·cal·ly** so gut wie
**prac·tice 1.** Praxis *f*; Übung *f*; Gewohnheit *f*, Brauch *m*; ***it is common ~*** es ist allgemein üblich; ***put into ~*** in die Praxis umsetzen; **2.** *v/t* (ein)üben; *als Beruf* ausüben; **~ *law*** (***medicine***) als Anwalt (Arzt) praktizieren; *v/i* praktizieren; üben
**prac·ticed** geübt (***in*** in *dat*)
**prac·tise** *Br* → ***practice*** 2
**prac·tised** → ***practiced***
**prac·ti·tion·er:** ***general ~*** praktischer Arzt
**prai·rie** Prärie *f*
**prai·rie schoo·ner** HIST Planwagen *m*
**praise 1.** loben, preisen; **2.** Lob *n*
**praise·wor·thy** lobenswert
**pram** *Br* Kinderwagen *m*
**prance** sich aufbäumen, steigen (*horse*); tänzeln (*horse*); stolzieren
**prank** Streich *m*
**prat·tle:** **~ *on*** plappern (***about*** von)
**prawn** ZO Garnele *f*
**pray** beten (***to*** zu; ***for*** für, um)
**prayer** REL Gebet *n*; *often pl* Andacht *f*; ***the Lord's Prayer*** das Vaterunser
**prayer book** REL Gebetbuch *n*
**preach** predigen (***to*** zu, vor *dat*)
**preach·er** Prediger(in)
**pre·am·ble** Einleitung *f*
**pre·ar·range** vorher vereinbaren
**pre·car·i·ous** prekär, unsicher; gefährlich
**pre·cau·tion** Vorsichtsmaßnahme *f*; ***as a ~*** vorsorglich; ***take ~s*** Vorsichtsmaßnahmen treffen; **pre·cau·tion·a·ry** vorbeugend; vorsorglich
**pre·cede** voraus-, vorangehen (*dat*)
**pre·ce·dence** Vorrang *m*
**pre·ce·dent** Präzedenzfall *m*
**pre·cept** Regel *f*, Richtlinie *f*
**pre·cinct** (*Wahl*)Bezirk *m*; (*Polizei*)Revier *n*; *pl* Gelände *n*; *esp Br* (*Einkaufs*)Viertel *n*; (*Fußgänger*)Zone *f*
**pre·cious 1.** *adj* kostbar, wertvoll; Edel... (*stone etc*); **2.** *adv*: **~ *little*** F herzlich wenig
**pre·ci·pice** Abgrund *m*
**pre·cip·i·tate 1.** *v/t* (hinunter-, herunter)schleudern; CHEM ausfällen; beschleunigen; stürzen (***into*** in *acc*); *v/i* CHEM ausfallen; **2.** *adj* überstürzt; **3.** CHEM Niederschlag *m*
**pre·cip·i·ta·tion** CHEM Ausfällung *f*; METEOR Niederschlag *m*; Überstürzung *f*, Hast *f*
**pre·cip·i·tous** steil (abfallend); überstürzt
**pré·cis** Zusammenfassung *f*
**pre·cise** genau, präzis
**pre·ci·sion** Genauigkeit *f*; Präzision *f*
**pre·clude** ausschließen
**pre·co·cious** frühreif; altklug
**pre·con·ceived** vorgefasst
**pre·con·cep·tion** vorgefasste Meinung
**pre·cur·sor** Vorläufer(in)
**pred·a·to·ry** ZO Raub...
**pre·de·ces·sor** Vorgänger(in)
**pre·des·ti·na·tion** Vorherbestimmung *f*; **pre·des·tined** prädestiniert, vorherbestimmt (***to*** für, zu)
**pre·de·ter·mine** vorherbestimmen; vorher vereinbaren
**pre·dic·a·ment** missliche Lage, Zwangslage *f*
**pred·i·cate** LING Prädikat *n*, Satzaussage *f*; **pre·dic·a·tive** LING prädikativ
**pre·dict** vorhersagen, voraussagen
**pre·dic·tion** Vorhersage *f*, Voraussage *f*; ***computer ~*** Hochrechnung *f*
**pre·dis·pose** geneigt machen, einnehmen (***in favor of*** für); *esp* MED anfällig machen (***to*** für)
**pre·dis·po·si·tion:** **~ *to*** Neigung *f* zu, *esp* MED *a.* Anfälligkeit *f* für
**pre·dom·i·nant** (vor)herrschend, überwiegend
**pre·dom·i·nate** vorherrschen, überwiegen; die Oberhand haben
**pre·em·i·nent** hervorragend, überragend
**pre·emp·tive** ECON Vorkaufs...; MIL Präventiv...
**preen** ZO *sich or das Gefieder* putzen
**pre·fab** F Fertighaus *n*
**pre·fab·ri·cate** vorfabrizieren, vorfertigen; ***~d house*** Fertighaus *n*
**pref·ace 1.** Vorwort *n* (***to*** zu); **2.** *Buch, Rede etc* einleiten (***with*** mit)
**pre·fect** *Br* PED Aufsichts-, Vertrauensschüler(in)

**pre·fer** vorziehen (***to*** *dat*), lieber mögen (***to*** als), bevorzugen
**pref·e·ra·ble:** ***be ~*** (***to***) vorzuziehen sein (*dat*), besser sein (als)
**pref·e·ra·bly** vorzugsweise, lieber, am liebsten
**pref·e·rence** Vorliebe *f* (***for*** für); Vorzug *m*
**pre·fix** LING Präfix *n*, Vorsilbe *f*
**preg·nan·cy** MED Schwangerschaft *f*; ZO Trächtigkeit *f*
**preg·nant** MED schwanger; ZO trächtig
**pre·heat** *Backofen etc* vorheizen
**pre·judge** *j-n* vorverurteilen; vorschnell beurteilen
**prej·u·dice 1.** Vorurteil *n*, Voreingenommenheit *f*, Befangenheit *f*; ***to the ~ of*** zum Nachteil *or* Schaden (*gen*); **2.** einnehmen (***in favo***[***u***]***r of*** für; ***against*** gegen); schaden (*dat*), beeinträchtigen
**prej·u·diced** (vor)eingenommen, befangen
**pre·lim·i·na·ry 1.** vorläufig, einleitend, Vor...; **2.** *pl* Vorbereitungen *pl*
**prel·ude** Vorspiel *n* (*a.* MUS)
**pre·mar·i·tal** vorehelich
**pre·ma·ture** vorzeitig, verfrüht; *fig* voreilig
**pre·med·i·tat·ed** JUR vorsätzlich
**pre·med·i·ta·tion:** ***with ~*** JUR vorsätzlich
**prem·i·er** POL Premier(minister) *m*
**prem·i·ere, prem·i·ère** THEA *etc* Premiere *f*, Ur-, Erstaufführung *f*
**prem·is·es** Gelände *n*, Grundstück *n*, (*Geschäfts*)Räume *pl*; ***on the ~*** an Ort und Stelle, im Haus, im Lokal
**pre·mi·um** Prämie *f*, Bonus *m*
**pre·mi·um (gas·o·line)** MOT Super *n*, Superbenzin *n*
**pre·mo·ni·tion** (böse) Vorahnung
**pre·oc·cu·pa·tion** Beschäftigung *f* (***with*** mit)
**pre·oc·cu·pied** gedankenverloren, geistesabwesend
**pre·oc·cu·py** (stark) beschäftigen
**prep** *Br* F PED Hausaufgabe(n *pl*) *f*
**pre·packed, pre·pack·aged** abgepackt
**pre·paid** *post* frankiert, freigemacht; ***~ envelope*** Freiumschlag *m*
**prep·a·ra·tion** Vorbereitung *f* (***for*** auf *acc*, für); Zubereitung *f*; CHEM, MED Präparat *n*
**pre·par·a·to·ry** vorbereitend
**pre·pare** *v/t* vorbereiten; GASTR zubereiten; *v/i*: ***~ for*** sich vorbereiten auf (*acc*); Vorbereitungen treffen für; sich gefasst machen auf (*acc*)
**pre·pared** vorbereitet; bereit
**prep·o·si·tion** LING Präposition *f*, Verhältniswort *n*
**pre·pos·sess·ing** einnehmend, anziehend
**pre·pos·ter·ous** absurd; lächerlich, grotesk
**pre·pro·gram(me)** vorprogrammieren
**pre·req·ui·site** Vorbedingung *f*, Voraussetzung *f*
**pre·rog·a·tive** Vorrecht *n*
**pre·school** Vorschule *f*
**pre·scribe** *et.* vorschreiben; MED *j-m et.* verschreiben; **pre·scrip·tion** Verordnung *f*, Vorschrift *f*; MED Rezept *n*
**pres·ence** Gegenwart *f*, Anwesenheit *f*; ***~ of mind*** Geistesgegenwart *f*
**pres·ent**[1] Geschenk *n*
**pre·sent**[2] präsentieren; (über)reichen, (über)bringen, (über)geben; schenken; vorbringen, vorlegen; zeigen, vorführen, THEA *etc* aufführen; schildern, darstellen; *j-n*, *Produkt etc* vorstellen; *Programm etc* moderieren
**pres·ent**[3] **1.** anwesend; vorhanden; gegenwärtig, jetzig; laufend; vorliegend (*case etc*); ***~ tense*** LING Präsens *n*, Gegenwart *f*; **2.** Gegenwart *f*, LING *a.* Präsens *n*; ***at ~*** gegenwärtig, zurzeit; ***for the ~*** vorerst, vorläufig
**pre·sen·ta·tion** Präsentation *f*; Überreichung *f*; Vorlage *f*; Vorführung *f*, THEA *etc* Aufführung *f*; Schilderung *f*, Darstellung *f*; Vorstellung *f*; *radio*, TV Moderation *f*
**pres·ent-day** heutig, gegenwärtig, modern
**pre·sent·er** *esp Br radio*, TV Moderator(in)
**pre·sen·ti·ment** (böse) Vorahnung
**pres·ent·ly** zurzeit, jetzt; *Br* bald
**pres·er·va·tion** Bewahrung *f*; Erhaltung *f*; GASTR Konservierung *f*
**pre·ser·va·tive** GASTR Konservierungsmittel *n*
**pre·serve 1.** bewahren, (be)schützen; erhalten; GASTR konservieren, *Obst etc* einmachen, einkochen; **2.** (*Jagd*)Revier

P

*n*; *fig* Ressort *n*, Reich *n*; *mst pl* GASTR *das* Eingemachte
**pre·side** den Vorsitz haben (***at, over*** bei); **pres·i·den·cy** POL Präsidentschaft *f*; Amtszeit *f*; **pres·i·dent** Präsident *m*; ECON Generaldirektor *m*
**press 1.** *v/t* drücken, pressen; *Frucht* (aus)pressen; drücken auf (*acc*); bügeln; drängen; *j-n* (be)drängen; bestehen auf (*dat*); *v/i* drücken; drängen (*time etc*); (sich) drängen; **~ *for*** dringen *or* drängen auf (*acc*); **~ *on*** (zügig) weitermachen; **2.** Druck *m* (*a. fig*); (Wein-*etc*)Presse *f*; Bügeln *n*; *die* Presse; *a.* ***printing*** **~** Druckerpresse *f*
**press a·gen·cy** Presseagentur *f*
**press box** Pressetribüne *f*
**press con·fe·rence** Pressekonferenz *f*
**press of·fice** Pressebüro *n*, Pressestelle *f*; **press of·fi·cer** Pressereferent(in)
**press·ing** dringend
**press re·lease** Pressemitteilung *f*
**press stud** *Br* Druckknopf *m*
**press-up** *esp Br* SPORT Liegestütz *m*
**pres·sure** PHYS, TECH *etc* Druck *m* (*a. fig*); **~ cook·er** Dampfkochtopf *m*, Schnellkochtopf *m*
**pres·tige** Prestige *n*, Ansehen *n*
**pre·su·ma·bly** vermutlich
**pre·sume** *v/t* annehmen, vermuten; sich erdreisten *or* anmaßen (***to do*** zu tun); *v/i* annehmen, vermuten; anmaßend sein; **~ *on*** *et.* ausnützen, *et.* missbrauchen
**pre·sump·tion** Annahme *f*, Vermutung *f*; Anmaßung *f*
**pre·sump·tu·ous** anmaßend, vermessen
**pre·sup·pose** voraussetzen
**pre·sup·po·si·tion** Voraussetzung *f*
**pre·tence** *Br* → ***pretense***; **pre·tend** vortäuschen, vorgeben; sich verstellen; Anspruch erheben (***to*** auf *acc*); ***she is only ~ing*** sie tut nur so; **pre·tend·ed** vorgetäuscht, gespielt; **pre·tense** Verstellung *f*, Vortäuschung *f*; Anspruch *m* (***to*** auf *acc*); **pre·ten·sion** Anspruch *m* (***to*** auf *acc*); Anmaßung *f*
**pre·ter·it(e)** LING Präteritum *n*
**pre·text** Vorwand *m*
**pret·ty 1.** *adj* hübsch; **2.** *adv* ziemlich, ganz schön
**pret·zel** Brezel *f*
**pre·vail** vorherrschen, weit verbreitet sein; siegen (***over, against*** über *acc*)
**pre·vail·ing** (vor)herrschend
**pre·vent** verhindern, verhüten, *e-r Sache* vorbeugen; *j-n* hindern (***from*** an *dat*)
**pre·ven·tion** Verhinderung *f*, Verhütung *f*, Vorbeugung *f*
**pre·ven·tive** vorbeugend
**pre·view** *film*, TV Voraufführung *f*; Vorbesichtigung *f*; *film*, TV *etc*: Vorschau *f* (***of*** auf *acc*)
**pre·vi·ous** vorhergehend, vorausgehend, vorherig, vorig; **~ *to*** bevor, vor (*dat*); **~ *knowledge*** Vorkenntnisse *pl*
**pre·vi·ous·ly** vorher, früher
**pre-war** Vorkriegs...
**prey 1.** ZO Beute *f*, Opfer *n* (*a. fig*); ***be easy ~ for*** *or* ***to*** *fig* e-e leichte Beute sein für; **2. ~ *on*** ZO Jagd machen auf (*acc*); *fig* nagen an (*dat*); **~ *on s.o.'s mind*** j-m keine Ruhe lassen
**price 1.** Preis *m*; **2.** den Preis festsetzen für; auszeichnen (***at*** mit)
**price·less** unbezahlbar
**price tag** Preisschild *n*
**prick 1.** Stich *m*; V Schwanz *m*; ***~s of conscience*** Gewissensbisse *pl*; **2.** *v/t* (auf-, durch)stechen, stechen in (*acc*); ***her conscience ~ed her*** sie hatte Gewissensbisse; **~ *up one's ears*** die Ohren spitzen; *v/i* stechen
**prick·le** BOT, ZO Stachel *m*, Dorn *m*
**prick·ly** stach(e)lig; prickelnd, kribbelnd
**pride 1.** Stolz *m*; Hochmut *m*; ***take*** (***a***) **~ *in*** stolz sein auf (*acc*); **2. ~ *o.s. on*** stolz sein auf (*acc*)
**priest** REL Priester *m*
**prig** Tugendbold *m*
**prig·gish** tugendhaft
**prim** steif; prüde
**pri·mae·val** *esp Br* → ***primeval***
**pri·ma·ri·ly** in erster Linie, vor allem
**pri·ma·ry 1.** wichtigste(r, -s), Haupt...; grundlegend, elementar, Grund...; Anfangs..., Ur...; **2.** POL Vorwahl *f*
**pri·ma·ry school** *Br* Grundschule *f*
**prime 1.** MATH Primzahl *f*; *fig* Blüte(zeit) *f*; ***in the ~ of life*** in der Blüte s-r Jahre; ***be past one's ~*** s-e besten Jahre hinter sich haben; **2.** *adj* erste(r, -s), wichtigste(r, -s), Haupt...; erstklassig; **3.** *v/t* TECH grundieren; *j-n* instruieren, vorbereiten; **~ min·is·ter** (ABBR POL F

***PM***) Premierminister(in), Ministerpräsident(in); ~ **num·ber** MATH Primzahl *f*
**prim·er** Fibel *f*, Elementarbuch *n*
**prime time** TV Haupteinschaltzeit *f*, Hauptsendezeit *f*, beste Sendezeit
**pri·me·val** urzeitlich, Ur...
**prim·i·tive** erste(r, -s), ursprünglich, Ur...; primitiv
**prim·rose** BOT Primel *f*, *esp* Schlüsselblume *f*
**prince** Fürst *m*; Prinz *m*
**prin·cess** Fürstin *f*; Prinzessin *f*
**prin·ci·pal 1.** wichtigste(r, -s), hauptsächlich, Haupt...; **2.** PED Direktor(in), Rektor(in); THEA Hauptdarsteller(in); MUS Solist(in)
**prin·ci·pal·i·ty** Fürstentum *n*
**prin·ci·ple** Prinzip *n*, Grundsatz *m*; ***on*** ~ grundsätzlich, aus Prinzip
**print 1.** PRINT Druck *m* (*a. art*); Gedruckte *n*; (*Finger- etc*)Abdruck *m*; PHOT Abzug *m*; bedruckter Stoff; ***in*** ~ gedruckt; ***out of*** ~ vergriffen; **2.** *v/i* drucken; *v/t* (ab-, auf-, be)drucken; in Druckbuchstaben schreiben; *fig* einprägen (***on*** *dat*); *a.* ~ ***off*** PHOT abziehen; ~ ***out*** EDP ausdrucken
**print·ed mat·ter** *post* Drucksache *f*
**print·er** Drucker *m* (*a.* TECH); ***~'s error*** Druckfehler *m*; ***~'s ink*** Druckerschwärze *f*; **print·ers** Druckerei *f*
**print·ing** Drucken *n*; Auflage *f*; ~ **ink** Druckerschwärze *f*; ~ **press** Druckerpresse *f*
**print·out** EDP Ausdruck *m*
**pri·or** frühere(r, -s); vorrangig
**pri·or·i·ty** Priorität *f*, Vorrang *m*; MOT Vorfahrt *f*; ***give s.th.*** ~ et. vordringlich behandeln
**prise** *esp Br* → ***prize²***
**prism** Prisma *n*
**pris·on** Gefängnis *n*, Strafanstalt *f*
**pris·on·er** Gefangene *m,f*, Häftling *m*; ***hold*** ~, ***keep*** ~ gefangen halten; ***take*** ~ gefangen nehmen
**pri·va·cy** Intim-, Privatsphäre *f*; Geheimhaltung *f*
**pri·vate 1.** privat, Privat...; vertraulich; geheim; ~ ***parts*** Geschlechtsteile *pl*; **2.** MIL gemeiner Soldat; ***in*** ~ privat; unter vier Augen
**pri·va·tion** Entbehrung *f*
**priv·i·lege** Privileg *n*; Vorrecht *n*
**priv·i·leged** privilegiert
**priv·y:** ***be*** ~ ***to*** eingeweiht sein in (*acc*)
**prize¹ 1.** (Sieger-, Sieges)Preis *m*, Prämie *f*, Auszeichnung *f*; (*Lotterie*)Gewinn *m*; **2.** preisgekrönt; Preis...; **3.** (hoch) schätzen
**prize²:** ~ ***open*** aufbrechen, aufstemmen
**prize·win·ner** Preisträger(in)
**pro¹** F Profi *m*
**pro²:** ***the ~s and cons*** das Pro und Kontra, das Für und Wider
**prob·a·bil·i·ty** Wahrscheinlichkeit *f*; ***in all*** ~ höchstwahrscheinlich
**prob·a·ble** *adj* wahrscheinlich
**prob·a·bly** *adv* wahrscheinlich
**pro·ba·tion** Probe *f*, Probezeit *f*; JUR Bewährung *f*, Bewährungsfrist *f*
**pro·ba·tion of·fi·cer** JUR Bewährungshelfer(in)
**probe 1.** MED, TECH Sonde *f*; *fig* Untersuchung *f* (***into*** *gen*); **2.** sondieren; (gründlich) untersuchen
**prob·lem** Problem *n*; MATH *etc* Aufgabe *f*; **prob·lem·at·ic, prob·lem·at·i·cal** problematisch
**pro·ce·dure** Verfahren *n*, Verfahrensweise *f*, Vorgehen *n*
**pro·ceed** (weiter)gehen, (weiter)fahren; sich begeben (***to*** nach, zu); *fig* weitergehen; *fig* fortfahren; *fig* vorgehen; ~ ***from*** kommen *or* herrühren von; ~ ***to do s.th.*** sich anschicken *or* daranmachen, et. zu tun
**pro·ceed·ing** Verfahren *n*, Vorgehen *n*
**pro·ceed·ings** Vorgänge *pl*, Geschehnisse *pl*; ***start*** *or* ***take*** (***legal***) ~ ***against*** JUR (gerichtlich) vorgehen gegen
**pro·ceeds** ECON Erlös *m*, Ertrag *m*, Einnahmen *pl*
**pro·cess 1.** Prozess *m*, Verfahren *n*, Vorgang *m*; ***in the*** ~ dabei; ***be in*** ~ im Gange sein; ***in*** ~ ***of construction*** im Bau (befindlich); **2.** TECH *etc* bearbeiten, behandeln; EDP *Daten* verarbeiten; PHOT *Film* entwickeln
**pro·ces·sion** Prozession *f*
**pro·ces·sor** EDP Prozessor *m*; (*Wort-, Text*)Verarbeitungsgerät *n*
**pro·claim** proklamieren, ausrufen
**proc·la·ma·tion** Proklamation *f*, Bekanntmachung *f*
**pro·cure** (sich) *et.* beschaffen *or* besorgen; verkuppeln
**prod 1.** stoßen; *fig* anstacheln, anspornen (***into*** zu); **2.** Stoß *m*

**prod·i·gal** 1. verschwenderisch; 2. F Verschwender(in)
**pro·di·gious** erstaunlich, großartig
**prod·i·gy** Wunder *n*; ***child*** ~ Wunderkind *n*
**pro·duce**[1] ECON produzieren (*a. film*, TV), herstellen, erzeugen (*a. fig*); hervorholen (***from*** aus); *Ausweis etc* (vor)zeigen; *Beweise etc* vorlegen; *Zeugen etc* beibringen; *Gewinn etc* (er)bringen, abwerfen; THEA inszenieren; *fig* hervorrufen, *Wirkung* erzielen
**prod·uce**[2] *esp* (*Agrar*)Produkt(e *pl*) *n*, (*Agrar*)Erzeugnis(se *pl*) *n*
**pro·duc·er** Produzent(in) (*a. film*, TV), Hersteller(in); THEA Regisseur(in)
**prod·uct** Produkt *n*, Erzeugnis *n*
**pro·duc·tion** ECON Produktion *f* (*a. film*, TV), Erzeugung *f*, Herstellung *f*; Produkt *n*, Erzeugnis *n*; Hervorholen *n*; Vorzeigen *n*, Vorlegen *n*, Beibringung *f*; THEA Inszenierung *f*
**pro·duc·tive** produktiv (*a. fig*), ergiebig, rentabel; *fig* schöpferisch
**pro·duc·tiv·i·ty** Produktivität *f*
**prof** F Prof *m*
**pro·fa·na·tion** Entweihung *f*
**pro·fane** 1. (gottes)lästerlich; profan, weltlich; 2. entweihen
**pro·fan·i·ty**: ***profanities*** Flüche *pl*, Lästerungen *pl*
**pro·fess** vorgeben, vortäuschen; behaupten (***to be*** zu sein); erklären
**pro·fessed** erklärt (*enemy etc*); angeblich
**pro·fes·sion** (*esp akademischer*) Beruf; Berufsstand *m*
**pro·fes·sion·al** 1. Berufs..., beruflich; Fach..., fachlich; fachmännisch; professionell; 2. Fachmann *m*, Profi *m*; Berufsspieler(in), -sportler(in), Profi *m*
**pro·fes·sor** Professor(in); Dozent(in)
**pro·fi·cien·cy** Können *n*, Tüchtigkeit *f*
**pro·fi·cient** tüchtig (***at, in*** in *dat*)
**pro·file** Profil *n*; ***keep a low*** ~ Zurückhaltung üben
**prof·it** 1. Gewinn *m*, Profit *m*; Vorteil *m*, Nutzen *m*; 2. ~ ***by***, ~ ***from*** Nutzen ziehen aus, profitieren von
**prof·it·a·ble** Gewinn bringend, einträglich; nützlich, vorteilhaft
**prof·it·eer** *contp* Profitmacher *m*, Schieber *m*
**prof·it shar·ing** ECON Gewinnbeteiligung *f*
**prof·li·gate** verschwenderisch
**pro·found** *fig* tief; tiefgründig; profund (*knowledge etc*)
**pro·fuse** (über)reich; verschwenderisch; **pro·fu·sion** Überfülle *f*; ***in*** ~ in Hülle und Fülle
**prog·e·ny** Nachkommen(schaft *f*) *pl*
**prog·no·sis** MED Prognose *f*
**pro·gram** 1. Programm *n* (*a.* EDP); *radio*, TV *a.* Sendung *f*; 2. (vor)programmieren; planen; EDP programmieren
**pro·gram·er** EDP Programmierer(in)
**pro·gramme** *Br* → ***program***
**ˈpro·gram·mer** *Br* → ***programer***
**pro·gress** 1. Fortschritt(e *pl*) *m*; ***make slow*** ~ (nur) langsam vorankommen; ***be in*** ~ im Gange sein; 2. fortschreiten; Fortschritte machen
**pro·gres·sive** progressiv, fortschreitend; fortschrittlich
**pro·hib·it** verbieten; verhindern
**pro·hi·bi·tion** Verbot *n*
**pro·hib·i·tive** Schutz... (*Zoll etc*); unerschwinglich
**proj·ect**[1] Projekt *n*, Vorhaben *n*
**pro·ject**[2] *v/i* vorspringen, vorragen, vorstehen; *v/t* werfen, schleudern; planen; projizieren
**pro·jec·tile** Projektil *n*, Geschoss *n*
**pro·jec·tion** Vorsprung *m*, vorspringender Teil; Werfen *n*, Schleudern *n*; Planung *f*; *film*: Projektion *f*
**pro·jec·tion·ist** Filmvorführer *m*
**pro·jec·tor** *film*: Projektor *m*
**pro·le·tar·i·an** 1. proletarisch; 2. Proletarier(in)
**pro·lif·ic** fruchtbar
**pro·log**, *esp Br* **pro·logue** Prolog *m*
**pro·long** verlängern
**prom·e·nade** 1. (Strand)Promenade *f*; 2. promenieren
**prom·i·nent** vorspringend, vorstehend; *fig* prominent
**pro·mis·cu·ous** sexuell freizügig
**prom·ise** 1. Versprechen *n*; *fig* Aussicht *f*; 2. versprechen
**prom·is·ing** viel versprechend
**prom·on·to·ry** GEOGR Vorgebirge *n*
**pro·mote** *j-n* befördern; *Schüler* versetzen; ECON werben für; *Boxkampf*, *Konzert etc* veranstalten; *et.* fördern; ***be*** ~***d*** SPORT *esp Br* aufsteigen (***to*** in *acc*)

**pro·mot·er** Promoter(in), Veranstalter(in); ECON Verkaufsförderer *m*
**pro·mo·tion** Beförderung *f*; PED Versetzung *f*; SPORT Aufstieg *m*; ECON Verkaufsförderung *f*, Werbung *f*
**pro·mo·tion(·al) film** Werbefilm *m*
**prompt 1.** *j-n* veranlassen (***to do*** zu tun); führen zu, *Gefühle etc* wecken; *j-m* vorsagen; THEA *j-m* soufflieren; **2.** prompt, umgehend, unverzüglich; pünktlich
**prompt·er** THEA Souffleur *m*, Souffleuse *f*
**prone** auf dem Bauch *or* mit dem Gesicht nach unten liegend; ***be ~ to*** *a.* MED neigen zu, anfällig sein für
**prong** Zinke *f*; (*Geweih*)Sprosse *f*
**pro·noun** LING Pronomen *n*, Fürwort *n*
**pro·nounce** aussprechen; erklären für; JUR *Urteil* verkünden
**pro·nun·ci·a·tion** Aussprache *f*
**proof 1.** Beweis(e *pl*) *m*, Nachweis *m*; Probe *f*; PRINT Korrekturfahne *f*, *a.* PHOT Probeabzug *m*; **2.** *adj in cpds* ...fest, ...beständig, ...dicht, ...sicher; → ***heatproof, soundproof, waterproof***; ***be ~ against*** geschützt sein vor (*dat*); **3.** imprägnieren
**proof·read** PRINT Korrektur lesen
**proof·read·er** PRINT Korrektor(in)
**prop 1.** Stütze *f* (*a. fig*); **2.** *a.* ***~ up*** stützen; *sich or et.* lehnen (***against*** gegen)
**prop·a·gate** BIOL sich fortpflanzen *or* vermehren; verbreiten
**prop·a·ga·tion** Fortpflanzung *f*, Vermehrung *f*; Verbreitung *f*
**pro·pel** (an)treiben; **pro·pel·lant, pro·pel·lent** Treibstoff *m*; Treibgas *n*
**pro·pel·ler** AVIAT Propeller *m*, MAR *a.* Schraube *f*
**pro·pel·ling pen·cil** Drehbleistift *m*
**pro·pen·si·ty** *fig* Neigung *f*
**prop·er** richtig, passend, geeignet; anständig, schicklich; echt, wirklich, richtig; eigentlich; eigen(tümlich); *esp Br* F ordentlich, tüchtig, gehörig
**prop·er| name, ~ noun** Eigenname *m*
**prop·er·ty** Eigentum *n*, Besitz *m*; Landbesitz *m*, Grundbesitz *m*; Grundstück *n*; *fig* Eigenschaft *f*
**proph·e·cy** Prophezeiung *f*
**proph·e·sy** prophezeien
**proph·et** Prophet *m*
**pro·por·tion 1.** Verhältnis *n*; (An)Teil *m*; *pl* Größenverhältnisse *pl*, Proportionen *pl*; ***in ~ to*** im Verhältnis zu; **2.** (***to***) in das richtige Verhältnis bringen (mit, zu); anpassen (*dat*)
**pro·por·tion·al** proportional; → ***proportionate***
**pro·por·tion·ate** (***to***) im richtigen Verhältnis (zu), entsprechend (*dat*)
**pro·pos·al** Vorschlag *m*; (Heirats)Antrag *m*; **pro·pose** *v/t* vorschlagen; beabsichtigen, vorhaben; *Toast* ausbringen (***to*** auf *acc*); ***~ s.o.'s health*** auf j-s Gesundheit trinken; *v/i*: ***~ to*** *j-m* e-n (Heirats)Antrag machen
**prop·o·si·tion** Behauptung *f*; Vorschlag *m*, ECON *a.* Angebot *n*
**pro·pri·e·ta·ry** ECON gesetzlich *or* patentrechtlich geschützt; *fig* besitzergreifend
**pro·pri·e·tor** Eigentümer *m*, Besitzer *m*, Geschäftsinhaber *m*
**pro·pri·e·tress** Eigentümerin *f*, Besitzerin *f*, Geschäftsinhaberin *f*
**pro·pri·e·ty** Anstand *m*; Richtigkeit *f*
**pro·pul·sion** TECH Antrieb *m*
**pro·sa·ic** prosaisch, nüchtern, sachlich
**prose** Prosa *f*
**pros·e·cute** JUR strafrechtlich verfolgen, (gerichtlich) belangen (***for*** wegen)
**pros·e·cu·tion** JUR strafrechtliche Verfolgung, Strafverfolgung *f*; ***the ~*** die Staatsanwaltschaft, die Anklage(behörde)
**pros·e·cu·tor** *a.* ***public ~*** JUR Staatsanwalt *m*, Staatsanwältin *f*
**pros·pect 1.** Aussicht *f* (*a. fig*); Interessent *m*, ECON möglicher Kunde, potenzieller Käufer; **2.** ***~ for*** *mining*: schürfen nach; bohren nach
**pro·spec·tive** voraussichtlich
**pro·spec·tus** (Werbe)Prospekt *m*
**pros·per** gedeihen; ECON blühen, florieren; **pros·per·i·ty** Wohlstand *m*; **pros·per·ous** ECON erfolgreich, blühend, florierend; wohlhabend
**pros·ti·tute** Prostituierte *f*, Dirne *f*; ***male ~*** Strichjunge *m*
**pros·trate 1.** hingestreckt; *fig* am Boden liegend; erschöpft; ***~ with grief*** gramgebeugt; **2.** niederwerfen; *fig* erschöpfen; *fig* niederschmettern
**pros·y** langweilig; weitschweifig
**pro·tag·o·nist** Vorkämpfer(in); THEA Hauptfigur *f*, Held(in)

**pro·tect** (be)schützen (***from*** vor *dat*; ***against*** gegen)
**pro·tec·tion** Schutz *m*; F Schutzgeld *n*; ~ ***of animals*** Tierschutz; ~ ***of endangered species*** Artenschutz *m*; ~ **money** F Schutzgeld *n*; ~ **rack·et** F Schutzgelderpressung *f*
**pro·tec·tive** (be)schützend; Schutz...; ~ **cloth·ing** Schutzkleidung *f*; ~ **cus·to·dy** JUR Schutzhaft *f*; ~ **du·ty,** ~ **tar·iff** ECON Schutzzoll *m*
**pro·tec·tor** Beschützer *m*; (*Brust- etc -*) Schutz *m*
**pro·tec·to·rate** POL Protektorat *n*
**pro·test 1.** Protest *m*; Einspruch *m*; **2.** *v/i* protestieren (***against*** gegen); *v/t* protestieren gegen; beteuern
**Prot·es·tant** REL **1.** protestantisch; **2.** Protestant(in)
**prot·es·ta·tion** Beteuerung *f*; Protest *m* (***against*** gegen)
**pro·to·col** Protokoll *n*
**pro·to·type** Prototyp *m*
**pro·tract** in die Länge ziehen, hinziehen
**pro·trude** herausragen, vorstehen (***from*** aus); **pro·trud·ing** vorstehend (*a. teeth*), vorspringend (*chin*)
**proud** stolz (***of*** auf *acc*)
**prove** *v/t* be-, er-, nachweisen; *v/i*: ~ (***to be***) sich herausstellen *or* erweisen als
**prov·en** bewährt
**prov·erb** Sprichwort *n*
**pro·vide** *v/t* versehen, versorgen, beliefern; zur Verfügung stellen, bereitstellen; JUR vorsehen, vorschreiben (***that*** dass); *v/i*: ~ ***against*** Vorsorge treffen gegen; JUR verbieten; ~ ***for*** sorgen für; vorsorgen für; JUR *et.* vorsehen
**pro·vid·ed:** ~ (***that***) vorausgesetzt(, dass)
**pro·vid·er** Ernährer(in)
**prov·ince** Provinz *f*; (Aufgaben-, Wissens)Gebiet *n*; **pro·vin·cial 1.** Provinz..., provinziell, *contp* provinzlerisch; **2.** *contp* Provinzler(in)
**pro·vi·sion** Bereitstellung *f*, Beschaffung *f*; Vorkehrung *f*, Vorsorge *f*; Bestimmung *f*, Vorschrift *f*; *pl* Proviant *m*, Verpflegung *f*; ***with the*** ~ ***that*** unter der Bedingung, dass
**pro·vi·sion·al** provisorisch, vorläufig
**pro·vi·so** Bedingung *f*, Vorbehalt *m*; ***with the*** ~ ***that*** unter der Bedingung, dass
**prov·o·ca·tion** Provokation *f*
**pro·voc·a·tive** provozierend, (*a. sexually*) aufreizend
**pro·voke** provozieren, reizen
**prowl 1.** *v/i a.* ~ ***about,*** ~ ***around*** herumschleichen, herumstreifen; *v/t* durchstreifen; **2.** Herumstreifen *n*
**prowl car** (Funk)Streifenwagen *m*
**prox·im·i·ty** Nähe *f*
**prox·y** (Handlungs)Vollmacht *f*; (Stell)Vertreter(in), Bevollmächtigte *m, f*; ***by*** ~ durch e-n Bevollmächtigten
**prude:** ***be a*** ~ prüde sein
**pru·dence** Klugheit *f*, Vernunft *f*; Besonnenheit *f*
**pru·dent** klug, vernünftig; besonnen
**prud·ish** prüde
**prune**[1] BOT (be)schneiden
**prune**[2] Backpflaume *f*
**prus·sic ac·id** CHEM Blausäure *f*
**pry**[1] neugierig sein; ~ ***about*** herumschnüffeln; ~ ***into*** s-e Nase stecken in (*acc*)
**pry**[2] → ***prize***[2]
**psalm** REL Psalm *m*
**pseu·do·nym** Pseudonym *n*, Deckname *m*
**psy·chi·a·trist** Psychiater(in)
**psy·chi·a·try** Psychiatrie *f*
**psy·cho·a·nal·y·sis** Psychoanalyse *f*
**psy·cho·log·i·cal** psychologisch
**psy·chol·o·gist** Psychologe *m*, Psychologin *f*
**psy·chol·o·gy** Psychologie *f*
**psy·cho·so·mat·ic** psychosomatisch
**pub** *Br* Pub *n, m*, Kneipe *f*
**pu·ber·ty** Pubertät *f*
**pu·bic hair** Schamhaare *pl*
**pub·lic 1.** öffentlich; allgemein bekannt; ***make*** ~ bekannt machen, an die Öffentlichkeit bringen; **2.** *die* Öffentlichkeit, *das* Publikum; ***in*** ~ öffentlich, in aller Öffentlichkeit
**pub·li·ca·tion** Bekanntgabe *f*, Bekanntmachung *f*; Publikation *f*, Veröffentlichung *f*
**pub·lic| con·ve·ni·ence** *Br* öffentliche Bedürfnisanstalt; ~ **en·e·my** Staatsfeind *m*; ~ **health** öffentliches Gesundheitswesen; ~ **hol·i·day** gesetzlicher Feiertag
**pub·lic·i·ty** Publicity *f*, *a.* Bekanntheit *f*, ECON *a.* Reklame *f*, Werbung *f*; ~ **de·part·ment** Werbeabteilung *f*

**pub·lic| li·bra·ry** Leihbücherei *f*; **~ re·la·tions** (ABBR ***PR***) Public Relations *pl*, Öffentlichkeitsarbeit *f*; **~ school** staatliche Schule; *Br* Public School *f*; **~ trans·port** *esp Br*, **~ trans·por·ta·tion** öffentliche Verkehrsmittel *pl*
**pub·lish** bekannt geben *or* machen; publizieren, veröffentlichen; *Buch etc* verlegen, herausgeben
**pub·lish·er** Verleger(in), Herausgeber(in); Verlag *m*, Verlagshaus *n*
**pub·lish·er's, pub·lish·ers, pub·lish·ing house** Verlag *m*, Verlagshaus *n*
**puck·er** *a.* **~ *up*** (sich) verziehen, (sich) runzeln
**pud·ding** *Br* GASTR Nachspeise *f*, Nachtisch *m*; (*Reis- etc*)Auflauf *m*; (*Art*) Fleischpastete *f*; Pudding *m*
**pud·dle** Pfütze *f*
**pu·er·ile** infantil, kindisch
**puff 1.** *v/i* schnaufen, keuchen; *a.* **~ *away*** paffen (***at*** an *dat*); **~ *up*** (an)schwellen; *v/t Rauch* blasen; **~ *out*** *Kerze etc* ausblasen; *Rauch etc* ausstoßen; *Brust* herausdrücken; **2.** Zug *m*; (*Wind-*) Hauch *m*, (*Wind*)Stoß *m*; (*Puder*)Quaste *f*; F Puste *f*
**puffed sleeve** Puffärmel *m*
**puff pas·try** GASTR Blätterteig *m*
**puff·y** (an)geschwollen; aufgedunsen
**pug** ZO Mops *m*
**puke** F (aus)kotzen
**pull 1.** Ziehen *n*; Zug *m*, Ruck *m*; Anstieg *m*, Steigung *f*; Zuggriff *m*, Zugleine *f*; F Beziehungen *pl*; **2.** ziehen; ziehen an (*dat*); zerren; reißen; *Pflanze* ausreißen; *esp Br Bier* zapfen; *fig* anziehen; **~ *ahead of*** vorbeiziehen an (*dat*), MOT überholen (*acc*); **~ *away*** anfahren (*bus etc*); **~ *down*** *Gebäude* abreißen; **~ *in*** einfahren (*train*); anhalten; **~ *off*** F *et.* zustande bringen, schaffen; **~ *out*** herausziehen (***of*** aus); *Tisch* ausziehen; RAIL abfahren; MOT ausscheren; *fig* sich zurückziehen, aussteigen (***of*** aus); **~ *over*** (s-n Wagen) an die *or* zur Seite fahren; **~ *round*** MED durchbringen; durchkommen; **~ *through*** *j-n* durchbringen; **~ *o.s. together*** sich zusammennehmen, F sich zusammenreißen; **~ *up*** MOT anhalten; (an)halten; **~ *up to***, **~ *up with*** SPORT *j-n* einholen
**pull date** Mindesthaltbarkeitsdatum *n*
**pul·ley** TECH Flaschenzug *m*
**pull-in** *Br* F Raststätte *f*, Rasthaus *n*
**pull·o·ver** Pullover *m*
**pull-up** SPORT Klimmzug *m*; ***do a*** **~** e-n Klimmzug machen
**pulp 1.** Fruchtfleisch *n*; Brei *m*; **2.** Schund...; **~ *novel*** Schundroman *m*
**pul·pit** Kanzel *f*
**pulp·y** breiig
**pul·sate** pulsieren, vibrieren
**pulse** Puls *m*; Pulsschlag *m*
**pul·ver·ize** pulverisieren
**pu·ma** ZO Puma *m*
**pum·mel** mit den Fäusten bearbeiten
**pump 1.** Pumpe *f*; (*Zapf*)Säule *f*; **2.** pumpen; F *j-n* aushorchen; **~ *up*** aufpumpen; **~ at·tend·ant** Tankwart *m*
**pump·kin** BOT Kürbis *m*
**pun 1.** Wortspiel *n*; **2.** Wortspiele *or* ein Wortspiel machen
**punch**[1] **1.** boxen, (mit der Faust) schlagen; **2.** (Faust)Schlag *m*
**punch**[2] **1.** lochen; *Loch* stanzen (***in*** in *acc*); **~ *in*** einstempeln; **~ *out*** ausstempeln; **2.** Locher *m*; Lochzange *f*; Locheisen *n*
**punch**[3] Punsch *m*
**Punch** *appr* Kasper *m*, Kasperle *n*, *m*; ***be as pleased or proud as*** **~** sich freuen wie ein Schneekönig; **~ and Ju·dy show** Kasperletheater *n*
**punc·tu·al** pünktlich
**punc·tu·al·i·ty** Pünktlichkeit *f*
**punc·tu·ate** interpunktieren
**punc·tu·a·tion** LING Interpunktion *f*; **~ mark** LING Satzzeichen *n*
**punc·ture 1.** (Ein)Stich *m*, Loch *n*; MOT Reifenpanne *f*; **2.** durchstechen, durchbohren; ein Loch bekommen, platzen; MOT e-n Platten haben
**pun·gent** scharf, stechend, beißend (*smell, taste*); scharf, bissig (*remark etc*)
**pun·ish** *j-n* (be)strafen
**pun·ish·a·ble** strafbar
**pun·ish·ment** Strafe *f*; Bestrafung *f*
**punk** Punk *m* (*a.* MUS); Punk(er) *m*
**pu·ny** schwächlich
**pup** ZO Welpe *m*, junger Hund
**pu·pa** ZO Puppe *f*
**pu·pil**[1] Schüler(in)
**pu·pil**[2] ANAT Pupille *f*
**pup·pet** Handpuppe *f*; Marionette *f* (*a. fig*); **~ show** Marionettentheater *n*, Puppenspiel *n*

**pup·pe·teer** Puppenspieler(in)
**pup·py** zo Welpe *m*, junger Hund
**pur·chase 1.** kaufen; *fig* erkaufen; **2.** Kauf *m*; ***make ~s*** Einkäufe machen
**pur·chas·er** Käufer(in)
**pure** rein; pur
**pure·bred** zo reinrassig
**pur·ga·tive** MED **1.** abführend; **2.** Abführmittel *n*
**pur·ga·to·ry** REL Fegefeuer *n*
**purge 1.** *Partei etc* säubern (**of** von); **2.** Säuberung *f*, Säuberungsaktion *f*
**pu·ri·fy** reinigen
**pu·ri·tan** (HIST ***Puritan***) **1.** Puritaner(in); **2.** puritanisch
**pu·ri·ty** Reinheit *f*
**purl 1.** linke Masche; **2.** links stricken
**pur·ple** purpurn, purpurrot
**pur·pose 1.** Absicht *f*, Vorsatz *m*; Zweck *m*, Ziel *n*; Entschlossenheit *f*; ***on ~*** absichtlich; ***to no ~*** vergeblich; **2.** beabsichtigen, vorhaben
**pur·pose·ful** entschlossen, zielstrebig
**pur·pose·less** zwecklos; ziellos
**pur·pose·ly** absichtlich
**purr** zo schnurren; MOT summen, surren
**purse**[1] Geldbeutel *m*, Geldbörse *f*, Portemonnaie *n*; Handtasche *f*; SPORT Siegprämie *f*; *boxing*: Börse *f*
**purse**[2]**:** *~* (***up***) ***one's lips*** die Lippen schürzen
**purs·er** MAR Zahlmeister *m*
**pur·su·ance:** ***in*** (***the***) ***~ of his duty*** in Ausübung s-r Pflicht
**pur·sue** verfolgen; *s-m Studium etc* nachgehen; *Absicht*, *Politik etc* verfolgen; *Angelegenheit etc* weiterführen
**pur·su·er** Verfolger(in)
**pur·suit** Verfolgung *f*; Weiterführung *f*
**pur·vey** *Lebensmittel etc* liefern
**pur·vey·or** Lieferant *m*
**pus** MED Eiter *m*
**push 1.** stoßen, F schubsen; schieben; *Taste etc* drücken; drängen; (an)treiben; F *Rauschgift* pushen; *fig j-n* drängen (***to do*** zu tun); *fig* Reklame machen für; ***~ one's way*** sich drängen (***through*** durch); ***~ ahead with*** *Plan etc* vorantreiben; ***~ along*** F sich auf die Socken machen; ***~ around*** F herumschubsen; ***~ for*** drängen auf (*acc*); ***~ forward with*** → ***push ahead with***; ***~ o.s. forward*** *fig* sich in den Vordergrund drängen *or* schieben; ***~ in*** F sich vordrängeln; ***~ off!*** F hau ab!; ***~ on with*** → ***push ahead with***; ***~ out*** *fig j-n* hinausdrängen; ***~ through*** *et.* durchsetzen; ***~ up*** *Preise etc* hochtreiben; **2.** Stoß *m*, F Schubs *m*; (*Werbe*)Kampagne *f*; F Durchsetzungsvermögen *n*, Energie *f*, Tatkraft *f*
**push but·ton** TECH Druckknopf *m*, Drucktaste *f*; **push-but·ton** TECH (Druck)Knopf..., (Druck)Tasten...; ***~*** (***tele***)***phone*** Tastentelefon *n*
**push·chair** *Br* Sportwagen *m*
**push·er** F *contp* Rauschgifthändler *m*
**push·o·ver** F Kinderspiel *n*
**push-up** SPORT Liegestütz *m*
**puss** F zo Mieze *f*
**pus·sy** *a.* ***~ cat*** F Miezekatze *f*
**pus·sy·foot:** F ***~ about, ~ around*** leisetreten, sich nicht festlegen wollen
**put** legen, setzen, stecken, stellen, tun; *j-n in e-e Lage etc, et. auf den Markt, in Ordnung etc* bringen; *et. in Kraft, in Umlauf etc* setzen; SPORT *Kugel* stoßen; unterwerfen, unterziehen (**to** *dat*); *et.* ausdrücken, *in Worte* fassen; übersetzen (***into German*** ins Deutsche); *Schuld* geben (**on** *dat*); ***~ right*** in Ordnung bringen; ***~ s.th. before s.o.*** *fig* j-m et. vorlegen; ***~ to bed*** ins Bett bringen; ***~ to school*** zur Schule schicken; ***~ about*** *Gerüchte* verbreiten, in Umlauf setzen; ***~ across*** *et.* verständlich machen; ***~ ahead*** SPORT in Führung bringen; ***~ aside*** beiseite legen; *Ware* zurücklegen; *fig* beiseite schieben; ***~ away*** weglegen, wegtun; auf-, wegräumen; ***~ back*** zurücklegen, -stellen, -tun; *Uhr* zurückstellen (**by** um); ***~ by*** *Geld* zurücklegen; ***~ down*** *v/t* hinlegen, niederlegen, hinsetzen, hinstellen; *j-n* absetzen, aussteigen lassen; (auf-, nieder-) schreiben, eintragen; zuschreiben (**to** *dat*); *Aufstand* niederschlagen; (*a. v/i*) AVIAT landen; ***~ forward*** *Plan etc* vorlegen; *Uhr* vorstellen (**by** um); *fig* vorverlegen (***two days*** um zwei Tage; ***to*** auf *acc*); ***~ in*** *v/t* hineinlegen, -stecken, -stellen, *Kassette etc* einlegen; installieren; *Gesuch etc* einreichen, *Forderung etc a.* geltend machen; *Antrag* stellen; *Arbeit*, *Zeit* verbringen (**on** mit); *Bemerkung* einwerfen; *v/i* MAR einlaufen (**at** in *acc*); ***~ off*** *et.* verschieben (***until*** auf *acc*); *j-m* absagen; *j-n* hinhalten (**with** mit), *j-n* vertrösten; *j-n* aus dem

Konzept bringen; ~ ***on*** *Kleider etc* anziehen, *Hut, Brille* aufsetzen; *Licht, Radio etc* anmachen, einschalten; *Sonderzug* einsetzen; THEA *Stück etc* herausbringen; *et.* vortäuschen; F *j-n* auf den Arm nehmen; ~ ***on airs*** sich aufspielen; ~ ***on weight*** zunehmen; ~ ***out*** *v/t* hinauslegen, -setzen, -stellen; *Hand etc* ausstrecken; *Feuer* löschen; *Licht, Radio etc* ausmachen (*a. cigarette*), ab-, ausschalten; veröffentlichen, herausgeben; *radio*, TV bringen, senden; *j-n* aus der Fassung bringen; *j-n* verärgern; *j-m* Ungelegenheiten bereiten; *j-m* Umstände machen; sich *den Arm etc* verrenken *or* ausrenken; *v/i* MAR auslaufen; ~ ***over*** → ***put across;*** ~ ***through*** TEL *j-n* verbinden (***to*** mit); durch-, ausführen; ~ ***together*** zusammenbauen, -setzen, -stellen; ~ ***up*** *v/t* hinauflegen, -stellen; *Hand* (hoch)heben; *Zelt etc* aufstellen; *Gebäude* errichten; *Bild etc* aufhängen; *Plakat, Bekanntmachung etc* anschlagen; *Schirm* aufspannen; *zum Verkauf* anbieten; *Preis* erhöhen; *Widerstand* leisten; *Kampf* liefern; *j-n* unterbringen, (bei sich) aufnehmen; *v/i* ~ ***up at*** absteigen in (*dat*); ~ ***up with*** sich gefallen lassen; sich abfinden mit

**pu·tre·fy** (ver)faulen, verwesen

**pu·trid** faul, verfault, verwest; F scheußlich, saumäßig

**put·ty 1.** Kitt *m*; **2.** kitten

**put-up job** F abgekartetes Spiel

**puz·zle 1.** Rätsel *n*; Geduld(s)spiel *n*; **2.** *v/t j-n* vor ein Rätsel stellen; verwirren; ***be*** ~***d*** vor e-m Rätsel stehen; ~ ***out*** herausfinden, herausbringen, F austüfteln; *v/i* sich den Kopf zerbrechen (***about, over*** über *dat or acc*)

**pyg·my 1.** Pygmäe *m*, Pygmäin *f*; Zwerg(in); **2.** *esp* ZO Zwerg...

**py·ja·mas** *Br* → ***pajamas***

**py·lon** TECH Hochspannungsmast *m*

**pyr·a·mid** Pyramide *f*

**pyre** Scheiterhaufen *m*

**py·thon** ZO Python(schlange) *f*

**pyx** REL Hostienbehälter *m*

# Q

**Q, q** Q, q *n*

**quack**[1] ZO **1.** quaken; **2.** Quaken *n*

**quack**[2] *a.* ~ ***doctor*** Quacksalber *m*, Kurpfuscher *m*; **quack·er·y** Quacksalberei *f*, Kurpfuscherei *f*

**quad·ran·gle** Viereck *n*

**quad·ran·gu·lar** viereckig

**quad·ra·phon·ic** quadrophon(isch)

**quad·rat·ic** MATH quadratisch

**quad·ri·lat·er·al** MATH **1.** vierseitig; **2.** Viereck *n*

**quad·ro·phon·ic** → ***quadraphonic***

**quad·ru·ped** ZO Vierfüß(l)er *m*; Vierbeiner *m*

**quad·ru·ple 1.** vierfach; **2.** (sich) vervierfachen

**quad·ru·plets** Vierlinge *pl*

**quads** Vierlinge *pl*

**quag·mire** Morast *m*, Sumpf *m*

**quail** ZO Wachtel *f*

**quaint** idyllisch, malerisch

**quake 1.** zittern, beben (***with, for*** vor *dat*; ***at*** bei); **2.** F Erdbeben *n*

**Quak·er** REL Quäker(in)

**qual·i·fi·ca·tion** Qualifikation *f*, Befähigung *f*, Eignung *f* (***for*** für, zu); Voraussetzung *f*; Einschränkung *f*

**qual·i·fied** qualifiziert, geeignet, befähigt (***for*** für); berechtigt; bedingt, eingeschränkt; **qual·i·fy** *v/t* qualifizieren, befähigen (***for*** für, zu); berechtigen (***to do*** zu tun); einschränken, abschwächen, mildern; *v/i* sich qualifizieren *or* eignen (***for*** für; ***as*** als); SPORT sich qualifizieren (***for*** für)

**qual·i·ty** Qualität *f*; Eigenschaft *f*

**qualms** Bedenken *pl*, Skrupel *pl*

**quan·da·ry: *be in a*** ~ ***about what to do*** nicht wissen, was man tun soll

**quan·ti·ty** Quantität *f*, Menge *f*

**quan·tum** PHYS **1.** Quant *n*; **2.** Quanten...

**quar·an·tine 1.** Quarantäne *f*; **2.** unter Quarantäne stellen
**quar·rel 1.** Streit *m*, Auseinandersetzung *f*; **2.** (sich) streiten
**quar·rel·some** streitsüchtig, zänkisch
**quar·ry**[1] Steinbruch *m*
**quar·ry**[2] HUNT Beute *f*, *a. fig* Opfer *n*
**quart** Quart *n* (ABBR **qt**) (*0,95 l, Br 1,14 l*)
**quar·ter 1.** Viertel *n*, vierter Teil; Quartal *n*, Vierteljahr *n*; Viertelpfund *n*; Vierteldollar *m*; SPORT (Spiel)Viertel *n*; (Himmels)Richtung *f*; Gegend *f*, Teil *m*; (Stadt)Viertel *n*; GASTR (*esp* Hinter)Viertel *n*; Gnade *f*, Pardon *m*; *pl* Quartier *n*, Unterkunft *f* (*a.* MIL); ***a ~ of an hour*** e-e Viertelstunde; ***a ~ of*** (*Br* ***to***) ***five*** (ein) Viertel vor fünf (*4.45*); ***a ~ after*** (*Br* ***past***) ***five*** (ein) Viertel nach fünf (*5.15*); ***at close ~s*** in *or* aus nächster Nähe; ***from official ~s*** von amtlicher Seite; **2.** vierteln; *esp* MIL einquartieren (**on** bei)
**quar·ter·deck** MAR Achterdeck *n*
**quar·ter·fi·nals** SPORT Viertelfinale *n*
**quar·ter·ly 1.** vierteljährlich; **2.** Vierteljahresschrift *f*
**quar·tet(te)** MUS Quartett *n*
**quartz** MIN Quarz *m*; **~ clock** Quarzuhr *f*; **~ watch** Quarz(armband)uhr *f*
**qua·ver 1.** *v/i* zittern; *v/t et.* mit zitternder Stimme sagen; **2.** Zittern *n*
**quay** MAR Kai *m*
**quea·sy: *I feel ~*** mir ist übel *or* F mulmig
**queen** Königin *f*; *card game, chess*: Dame *f*; F Schwule *m*, Homo *m*
**queen bee** ZO Bienenkönigin *f*
**queen·ly** wie e-e Königin, königlich
**queer** komisch, seltsam; F wunderlich; F schwul
**quench** *Durst* löschen, stillen
**quer·u·lous** nörglerisch
**que·ry 1.** Frage *f*; Zweifel *m*; **2.** infrage stellen, in Zweifel ziehen
**quest 1.** Suche *f* (***for*** nach); ***in ~ of*** auf der Suche nach; **2.** suchen (***after, for*** nach)
**ques·tion 1.** Frage *f*, *a.* Problem *n*, *a.* Sache *f*, *a.* Zweifel *m*; ***only a ~ of time*** nur e-e Frage der Zeit; ***this is not the point in ~*** darum geht es nicht; ***there is no ~ that, it is beyond ~ that*** es steht außer Frage, dass; ***there is no ~ about this*** daran besteht kein Zweifel; ***be out of the ~*** nicht infrage kommen; **2.** befragen (***about*** über *acc*); JUR vernehmen, verhören (***about*** zu); bezweifeln, in Zweifel ziehen, infrage stellen
**ques·tion·a·ble** fraglich, zweifelhaft; fragwürdig
**ques·tion·er** Fragesteller(in)
**ques·tion| mark** Fragezeichen *n*; **~ mas·ter** *esp Br* Quizmaster *m*
**ques·tion·naire** Fragebogen *m*
**queue** *esp Br* **1.** Schlange *f*; → ***jump***; **2.** *mst* ***~ up*** Schlange stehen, anstehen, sich anstellen
**quib·ble** sich herumstreiten (***with*** mit; ***about, over*** wegen)
**quick 1.** *adj* schnell, rasch; aufbrausend, hitzig (*temper*); ***be ~!*** mach schnell!, beeil dich!; **2.** *adv* schnell, rasch; **3. *cut s.o. to the ~*** *fig* j-n tief verletzen
**quick·en** (sich) beschleunigen
**quick·sand** Treibsand *m*
**quick-tem·pered** aufbrausend, hitzig
**quick-wit·ted** schlagfertig; geistesgegenwärtig
**qui·et 1.** ruhig, still; ***~, please*** Ruhe, bitte; ***be ~!*** sei still!; **2.** Ruhe *f*, Stille *f*; ***on the ~*** F heimlich; **3.** *v/t a.* ***~ down*** *j-n* beruhigen; *v/i a.* ***~ down*** sich beruhigen
**qui·et·en** *Br* → ***quiet*** 3
**qui·et·ness** Ruhe *f*, Stille *f*
**quill** ZO (Schwung-, Schwanz)Feder *f*; Stachel *m*
**quilt** Steppdecke *f*; **quilt·ed** Stepp...
**quince** BOT Quitte *f*
**quin·ine** PHARM Chinin *n*
**quint** F Fünfling *m*
**quin·tes·sence** Quintessenz *f*; Inbegriff *m*
**quin·tet(te)** MUS Quintett *n*
**quin·tu·ple 1.** fünffach; **2.** (sich) verfünffachen
**quin·tu·plets** Fünflinge *pl*
**quip 1.** geistreiche *or* witzige Bemerkung; **2.** witzeln, spötteln
**quirk** Eigenart *f*, Schrulle *f*; ***by some ~ of fate*** durch e-e Laune des Schicksals, durch e-n verrückten Zufall
**quit** F *v/t* aufhören mit; ***~ one's job*** kündigen; *v/i* aufhören; kündigen
**quite** ganz, völlig; ziemlich; ***~ a few*** ziemlich viele; ***~ nice*** ganz nett, recht nett; **~ (*so*)!** *esp Br* genau, ganz recht; ***be ~ right*** völlig Recht haben; ***she's ~ a***

***beauty*** sie ist e-e wirkliche Schönheit
**quits** F quitt (***with*** mit); ***call it ~*** es gut sein lassen
**quit·ter:** F ***be a ~*** schnell aufgeben
**quiv·er¹** zittern (***with*** vor *dat*; ***at*** bei)
**quiv·er²** Köcher *m*
**quiz 1.** Quiz *n*; Prüfung *f*, Test *m*; **2.** ausfragen (***about*** über *acc*)
**quiz·mas·ter** Quizmaster *m*
**quiz·zi·cal** spöttisch-fragend
**quo·ta** Quote *f*, Kontingent *n*
**quo·ta·tion** Zitat *n*; ECON Notierung *f*; Kostenvoranschlag *m*; **~ marks** LING Anführungszeichen *pl*
**quote** zitieren; *Beispiel etc* anführen; *Preis* nennen; ***be ~d at*** ECON notieren mit
**quo·tient** MATH Quotient *m*

# R

**R, r** R, r *n*
**rab·bi** REL Rabbiner *m*
**rab·bit** ZO Kaninchen *n*
**rab·ble** Pöbel *m*, Mob *m*
**rab·ble-rous·ing** Hetz..., aufwieglerisch
**rab·id** VET tollwütig; *fig* fanatisch
**ra·bies** VET Tollwut *f*
**rac·coon** ZO Waschbär *m*
**race¹** Rasse *f*, Rassenzugehörigkeit *f*; (*Menschen*)Geschlecht *n*
**race² 1.** (Wett)Rennen *n*, (Wett)Lauf *m*; **2.** *v/i* an (e-m) Rennen teilnehmen; um die Wette laufen *or* fahren *etc*; rasen, rennen; MOT durchdrehen; *v/t* um die Wette laufen *or* fahren *etc* mit; rasen mit
**race car** MOT Rennwagen *m*
**race·course** Rennbahn *f*
**race·horse** Rennpferd *n*
**rac·er** Rennpferd *n*; Rennrad *n*, Rennwagen *m*
**race ri·ots** Rassenunruhen *pl*
**race·track** Rennbahn *f*
**ra·cial** rassisch, Rassen...
**rac·ing 1.** Rennsport *m*; **2.** Renn...
**rac·ing car** *Br* MOT Rennwagen *m*
**ra·cism** Rassismus *m*
**ra·cist 1.** Rassist(in); **2.** rassistisch
**rack 1.** Gestell *n*, (*Geschirr-, Zeitungs- etc*)Ständer *m*, RAIL (*Gepäck*)Netz *n*, MOT (*Dach*)Gepäckständer *m*; HIST Folter(bank) *f*; **2.** ***be ~ed by or with*** geplagt *or* gequält werden von; ***~ one's brains*** sich das Hirn zermartern, sich den Kopf zerbrechen
**rack·et¹** *tennis etc*: Schläger *m*
**rack·et²** F Krach *m*, Lärm *m*; Schwindel *m*, Gaunerei *f*; (*Drogen- etc*)Geschäft *n*; organisierte Erpressung
**rack·et·eer** Gauner *m*; Erpresser *m*
**ra·coon** → ***raccoon***
**rac·y** spritzig, lebendig; gewagt (*joke*)
**ra·dar** TECH Radar *m, n*; **~ screen** Radarschirm *m*; **~ speed check** MOT Radarkontrolle *f*; **~ sta·tion** Radarstation *f*; **~ trap** MOT Radarkontrolle *f*
**ra·di·al 1.** radial, Radial..., strahlenförmig; **2.** MOT Gürtelreifen *m*
**ra·di·al| tire,** *Br* **~ tyre** → ***radial*** 2
**ra·di·ant** strahlend, leuchtend (*a. fig* ***with*** vor *dat*)
**ra·di·ate** ausstrahlen; strahlenförmig ausgehen (***from*** von)
**ra·di·a·tion** Ausstrahlung *f*
**ra·di·a·tor** Heizkörper *m*; MOT Kühler *m*
**rad·i·cal 1.** radikal (*a.* POL); MATH Wurzel...; **2.** POL Radikale *m, f*
**ra·di·o 1.** Radio(apparat *m*) *n*; Funk *m*; Funkgerät *n*; ***by ~*** über Funk; ***on the ~*** im Radio; **2.** funken
**ra·di·o·ac·tive** radioaktiv; **~ waste** Atommüll *m*, radioaktiver Abfall
**ra·di·o·ac·tiv·i·ty** Radioaktivität *f*
**ra·di·o| ham** Funkamateur *m*; **~ play** Hörspiel *n*; **~ set** Radioapparat *m*; **~ sta·tion** Funkstation *f*; Rundfunksender *m*, -station *f*; **~ ther·a·py** MED Strahlentherapie *f*, Röntgentherapie *f*; **~ tow·er** Funkturm *m*
**rad·ish** BOT Rettich *m*; Radieschen *n*

R

**ra·di·us** MATH Radius *m*
**raf·fle 1.** Tombola *f*; **2.** *a.* **~ off** verlosen
**raft** Floß *n*
**raf·ter** (Dach)Sparren *m*
**rag** Lumpen *m*, Fetzen *m*; Lappen *m*; **in ~s** zerlumpt
**rage 1.** Wut *f*, Zorn *m*; **fly into a ~** wütend werden; **the latest ~** F der letzte Schrei; **be all the ~** F große Mode sein; **2.** wettern (**against, at** gegen); wüten, toben
**rag·ged** zerlumpt; struppig; *fig* stümperhaft
**raid 1.** (**on**) Überfall *m* (auf *acc*), MIL *a.* Angriff *m* (gegen); Razzia *f* (in *dat*); **2.** überfallen, MIL *a.* angreifen; e-e Razzia machen in (*dat*)
**rail 1.** Geländer *n*; Stange *f*; (*Handtuch*)Halter *m*; (Eisen)Bahn *f*; RAIL Schiene *f*, *pl a.* Gleis *n*; **by ~** mit der Bahn; **2. ~ in** einzäunen; **~ off** abzäunen
**rail·ing** *often pl* (Gitter)Zaun *m*
**rail·road** Eisenbahn *f*; **~ line** Bahnlinie *f*; **~·man** Eisenbahner *m*; **~ sta·tion** Bahnhof *m*
**rail·way** *Br* → **railroad**
**rain 1.** Regen *m*, *pl* Regenfälle *pl*; **the ~s** die Regenzeit; (**come**) **~ or shine** *fig* was immer auch geschieht; **2.** regnen; **it is ~ing cats and dogs** F es gießt in Strömen; **it never ~s but it pours** es kommt immer gleich knüppeldick, ein Unglück kommt selten allein
**rain·bow** Regenbogen *m*
**rain·coat** Regenmantel *m*
**rain·fall** Niederschlag(smenge *f*) *m*
**rain for·est** GEOGR Regenwald *m*
**rain·proof** regendicht, wasserdicht
**rain·y** regnerisch, verregnet, Regen...; **save s.th. for a ~ day** et. für schlechte Zeiten zurücklegen
**raise 1.** heben; hochziehen; erheben; *Denkmal etc* errichten; *Staub etc* aufwirbeln; *Gehalt, Miete etc* erhöhen; *Geld* zusammenbringen, beschaffen; *Kinder* aufziehen, großziehen; *Tiere* züchten; *Getreide etc* anbauen; *Frage* aufwerfen, *et.* zur Sprache bringen; *Blockade etc, a. Verbot* aufheben; **2.** Lohn- *or* Gehaltserhöhung *f*
**rai·sin** Rosine *f*
**rake 1.** Rechen *m*, Harke *f*; **2.** *v/t*: **~** (**up**) (zusammen)rechen, (zusammen)harken; F **~ in** scheffeln; *v/i*: **~ about, ~ around** herumstöbern
**rak·ish** flott, keck, verwegen
**ral·ly 1.** (sich) (wieder) sammeln; sich erholen (**from** von) (*a.* ECON); **~ round** sich scharen um; **2.** Kundgebung *f*, (Massen)Versammlung *f*; MOT Rallye *f*; *tennis etc*: Ballwechsel *m*
**ram 1.** ZO Widder *m*, Schafbock *m*; TECH Ramme *f*; **2.** rammen
**ram·ble 1.** wandern, umherstreifen; abschweifen; **2.** Wanderung *f*; **ram·bler** Wanderer *m*; BOT Kletterrose *f*
**ram·bling** weitschweifig; weitläufig; **~ rose** BOT Kletterrose *f*
**ramp** Rampe *f*; MOT (Autobahn)Auffahrt *f*; (Autobahn)Ausfahrt *f*
**ram·page 1. ~ through** (wild *or* aufgeregt) trampeln durch (*elephant etc*); → **2. go on the ~ through** randalierend ziehen durch
**ram·pant: be ~** wuchern (*plant*); grassieren (**in** in *dat*)
**ram·shack·le** baufällig (*building*); klapp(e)rig (*vehicle*)
**ranch** Ranch *f*; (*Geflügel- etc*)Farm *f*
**ranch·er** Rancher *m*; (*Geflügel- etc*) Züchter *m*
**ran·cid** ranzig
**ran·co(u)r** Groll *m*, Erbitterung *f*
**ran·dom 1.** *adj* ziellos, wahllos; zufällig, Zufalls...; **~ sample** Stichprobe *f*; **2. at ~** aufs Geratewohl
**range 1.** Reich-, Schuss-, Tragweite *f*; Entfernung *f*; *fig* Bereich *m*, *a.* Spielraum *m*, *a.* Gebiet *n*; (*Schieß*)Stand *m*, (-)Platz *m*; (*Berg*)Kette *f*; offenes Weidegebiet; ECON Kollektion *f*, Sortiment *n*; Küchenherd *m*; **at close ~** aus nächster Nähe; **within ~ of vision** in Sichtweite; **a wide ~ of ...** eine große Auswahl an ... (*dat*); **2.** *v/i*: **~ from ... to ..., ~ between ... and ...** sich zwischen ... und ... bewegen (*prices etc*); *v/t* aufstellen, anordnen
**range find·er** PHOT Entfernungsmesser *m*
**rang·er** Förster *m*; Ranger *m*
**rank**[1] **1.** Rang *m* (*a.* MIL), (soziale) Stellung; Reihe *f*; (*Taxi*)Stand *m*; **of the first ~** *fig* erstklassig; **the ~ and file** *fig* die Basis; **the ~s** *fig* das Heer, die Masse; **2.** *v/t* rechnen, zählen (**among** zu); stellen (**above** über *acc*); *v/i* zählen, gehören (**among** zu); gelten (**as** als)

**rank²** BOT (üppig) wuchernd; übel riechend, übel schmeckend; *fig* krass (*outsider*), blutig (*beginner*)
**ran·kle** *fig* nagen, wehtun, F wurmen
**ran·sack** durchwühlen, durchsuchen; plündern
**ran·som 1.** Lösegeld *n*; **2.** freikaufen, auslösen
**rant:** ~ (**on**) ***about,*** ~ ***and rave about*** eifern gegen
**rap 1.** Klopfen *n*; Klaps *m*; **2.** klopfen (an *acc*, auf *acc*)
**ra·pa·cious** habgierig
**rape¹ 1.** vergewaltigen; **2.** Vergewaltigung *f*
**rape²** BOT Raps *m*
**rap·id** schnell, rasch
**ra·pid·i·ty** Schnelligkeit *f*
**rap·ids** GEOGR Stromschnellen *pl*
**rapt:** ***with*** ~ ***attention*** mit gespannter Aufmerksamkeit
**rap·ture** Entzücken *n*, Verzückung *f*; ***go into*** ~***s*** in Verzückung geraten
**rare¹** selten, rar; dünn (*air*); F Mords...
**rare²** GASTR blutig (*steak*)
**rar·e·fied** dünn (*air*)
**rar·i·ty** Seltenheit *f*; Rarität *f*
**ras·cal** Schlingel *m*
**rash¹** voreilig, vorschnell, unbesonnen
**rash²** MED (Haut)Ausschlag *m*
**rash·er** dünne Speckscheibe
**rasp 1.** raspeln; kratzen; **2.** Raspel *f*; Kratzen *n*
**rasp·ber·ry** BOT Himbeere *f*
**rat** ZO Ratte *f* (*a. contp*); F ***smell a*** ~ Lunte *or* den Braten riechen
**rate 1.** Quote *f*, Rate *f*, (*Geburten-, Sterbe*)Ziffer *f*; (*Steuer-, Zins- etc*)Satz *m*; (*Wechsel*)Kurs *m*; Geschwindigkeit *f*, Tempo *n*; ***at any*** ~ auf jeden Fall; **2.** einschätzen, halten (**as** für); *Lob etc* verdienen; ***be*** ~***d as*** gelten als
**rate of ex·change** ECON (Umrechnungs-, Wechsel)Kurs *m*
**rate of in·terest** ECON Zinssatz *m*
**ra·ther** ziemlich; eher, vielmehr, besser gesagt; ~***!*** *esp Br* F und ob!; ***I would*** *or* ***had*** ~ ***go*** ich möchte lieber gehen
**rat·i·fy** POL ratifizieren
**rat·ing** Einschätzung *f*; *radio*, TV Einschaltquote *f*
**ra·ti·o** MATH Verhältnis *n*
**ra·tion 1.** Ration *f*; **2.** *et.* rationieren; ~ ***out*** zuteilen (**to** *dat*)
**ra·tion·al** rational; vernunftbegabt; vernünftig; verstandesmäßig
**ra·tion·al·i·ty** Vernunft *f*
**ra·tion·al·ize** rational erklären; ECON rationalisieren
**rat race** F endloser Konkurrenzkampf
**rat·tle 1.** klappern; rasseln *or* klimpern (mit); prasseln (**on** auf *acc*) (*rain etc*); rattern, knattern (*vehicle*); rütteln an (*dat*); F *j-n* verunsichern; ~ ***at*** rütteln an (*dat*); ~ ***off*** F *Gedicht etc* herunterrasseln; F ~ ***on*** quasseln (***about*** über *acc*); F ~ ***through*** *Rede etc* herunterrasseln; **2.** Klappern *n* (*etc* → 1); Rassel *f*, Klapper *f*
**rat·tle·snake** ZO Klapperschlange *f*
**rau·cous** heiser, rau
**rav·age** verwüsten
**rav·ag·es** Verwüstungen *pl*, *a. fig* verheerende Auswirkungen *pl*
**rave** fantasieren, irrereden; toben; wettern (***against, at*** gegen); schwärmen (***about*** von)
**rav·el** (sich) verwickeln *or* verwirren
**ra·ven** ZO Rabe *m*
**rav·e·nous** ausgehungert, heißhungrig
**ra·vine** Schlucht *f*, Klamm *f*
**rav·ing mad** tobsüchtig
**rav·ings** irres Gerede, Delirien *pl*
**rav·ish·ing** *fig* hinreißend
**raw** GASTR roh, ECON, TECH *a.* Roh...; MED wund; METEOR nasskalt; *fig* unerfahren; ~ ***vegetables and fruit*** Rohkost *f*
**raw-boned** knochig, hager
**raw·hide** Rohleder *n*
**raw ma·te·ri·al** Rohstoff *m*
**ray** Strahl *m*; *fig* Schimmer *m*
**ray·on** Kunstseide *f*
**ra·zor** Rasiermesser *n*; Rasierapparat *m*; ***electric*** ~ Elektrorasierer *m*
**ra·zor blade** Rasierklinge *f*
**ra·zor('s) edge** *fig* kritische Lage; ***be on a*** ~ auf des Messers Schneide stehen
**re...** wieder, noch einmal, neu
**reach 1.** *v/t* erreichen; reichen *or* gehen bis an (*acc*) *or* zu; ~ ***down*** herunter-, hinunterreichen (***from*** von); ~ ***out*** *Arm etc* ausstrecken; *v/i* reichen, gehen, sich erstrecken; *a.* ~ ***out*** greifen, langen (***for*** nach); ~ ***out*** die Hand ausstrecken; **2.** Reichweite *f*; ***within*** (***out of***) ~ in (außer) Reichweite; ***within easy*** ~ leicht erreichbar

**re·act** reagieren (***to*** auf *acc*; CHEM ***with*** mit); **re·ac·tion** Reaktion *f* (*a.* CHEM)
**re·ac·tor** PHYS Reaktor *m*
**read** lesen; TECH (an)zeigen; *Zähler etc* ablesen; UNIV studieren; deuten, verstehen (***as*** als); sich *gut etc* lesen (lassen); lauten; ~ (***s.th.***) ***to s.o.*** j-m (et.) vorlesen; ~ ***medicine*** Medizin studieren
**read·a·ble** lesbar; leserlich; lesenswert
**read·er** Leser(in); Lektor(in); Lesebuch *n*
**read·i·ly** bereitwillig, gern; leicht, ohne weiteres
**read·i·ness** Bereitschaft *f*
**read·ing 1.** Lesen *n*; Lesung *f* (*a.* PARL); TECH Anzeige *f*, (*Thermometer- etc* -) Stand *m*; Auslegung *f*; **2.** Lese...; ~ ***matter*** Lesestoff *m*
**re·ad·just** TECH nachstellen, korrigieren; ~ (***o.s.***) ***to*** sich wieder anpassen (*dat*) *or* an (*acc*), sich wieder einstellen auf (*acc*)
**read·y** bereit, fertig; bereitwillig; im Begriff (***to do*** zu tun); schnell, schlagfertig; ~ ***for use*** gebrauchsfertig; ***get*** ~ (sich) fertig machen
**read·y cash** → ***ready money***
**read·y-made** Konfektions...
**read·y meal** Fertiggericht *n*
**read·y mon·ey** Bargeld *n*
**real** echt; wirklich, tatsächlich, real; F ***for*** ~ echt, im Ernst
**real es·tate** Grundbesitz *m*, Immobilien *pl*; ~ **a·gent** Grundstücks-, Immobilienmakler *m*
**re·a·lism** Realismus *m*
**re·al·ist** Realist(in)
**re·al·is·tic** realistisch
R
**re·al·i·ty** Realität *f*, Wirklichkeit *f*
**re·a·li·za·tion** Erkenntnis *f*; Realisierung *f* (*a.* ECON), Verwirklichung *f*
**re·al·ize** sich klarmachen, erkennen, begreifen, einsehen; realisieren (*a.* ECON), verwirklichen
**real·ly** wirklich, tatsächlich; ***well,*** ~***!*** ich muss schon sagen!; ~***?*** im Ernst?
**realm** Königreich *n*; *fig* Reich *n*
**real·tor** Grundstücks-, Immobilienmakler *m*
**reap** *Getreide etc* schneiden; *Feld* abernten; *fig* ernten
**re·ap·pear** wieder erscheinen
**rear 1.** *v/t Kind, Tier* aufziehen, großziehen; *Kopf* heben; *v/i* sich aufbäumen (*horse*); **2.** Rückseite *f*, Hinterseite *f*, MOT Heck *n*; ***in*** (*Br* ***at***) ***the*** ~ ***of*** hinter (*dat*); ***bring up the*** ~ die Nachhut bilden; **3.** hinter, Hinter..., Rück..., MOT *a.* Heck...
**rear-end col·li·sion** MOT Auffahrunfall *m*
**rear·guard** MIL Nachhut *f*
**rear light** MOT Rücklicht *n*
**re·arm** MIL (wieder) aufrüsten
**re·ar·ma·ment** MIL (Wieder)Aufrüstung *f*
**rear·most** hinterste(r, -s)
**rear·view mir·ror** MOT Rückspiegel *m*
**rear·ward 1.** *adj* hintere(r, -s), rückwärtig; **2.** *adv a.* ***rearwards*** rückwärts
**rear-wheel drive** MOT Hinterradantrieb *m*
**rear win·dow** MOT Heckscheibe *f*
**rea·son 1.** Grund *m*; Verstand *m*; Vernunft *f*; ***by*** ~ ***of*** wegen; ***for this*** ~ aus diesem Grund; ***listen to*** ~ Vernunft annehmen; ***it stands to*** ~ ***that*** es leuchtet ein, dass; **2.** *v/i* vernünftig *or* logisch denken; vernünftig reden (***with*** mit); *v/t* folgern, schließen (***that*** dass); ~ ***s.o. into*** (***out of***) ***s.th.*** j-m et. einreden (ausreden); **rea·son·a·ble** vernünftig; günstig (*price*); ganz gut, nicht schlecht
**re·as·sure** beruhigen
**re·bate** ECON Rabatt *m*, (Preis)Nachlass *m*; Rückzahlung *f*
**reb·el**[1] **1.** Rebell(in); Aufständische *m*, *f*; **2.** aufständisch
**re·bel**[2] rebellieren, sich auflehnen (***against*** gegen)
**re·bel·lion** Rebellion *f*, Aufstand *m*
**re·bel·lious** rebellisch, aufständisch
**re·birth** Wiedergeburt *f*
**re·bound 1.** abprallen, zurückprallen (***from*** von); *fig* zurückfallen (***on*** auf *acc.*); **2.** SPORT Abpraller *m*
**re·buff 1.** schroffe Abweisung, Abfuhr *f*; **2.** schroff abweisen
**re·build** wieder aufbauen (*a. fig*)
**re·buke 1.** rügen, tadeln; **2.** Rüge *f*, Tadel *m*
**re·call 1.** zurückrufen, abberufen; MOT (in die Werkstatt) zurückrufen; sich erinnern an (*acc*); erinnern an (*acc*); **2.** Zurückrufung *f*, Abberufung *f*; Rückrufaktion *f*; ***have total*** ~ das absolute Gedächtnis haben; ***beyond*** ~, ***past*** ~

unwiederbringlich *or* unwiderruflich vorbei
**re·ca·pit·u·late** rekapitulieren, (kurz) zusammenfassen
**re·cap·ture** wieder einfangen (*a. fig*); *Häftling* wieder fassen; MIL zurückerobern
**re·cast** TECH umgießen; umformen, neu gestalten; THEA *etc* umbesetzen, neu besetzen
**re·cede** schwinden; ***receding chin*** fliehendes Kinn
**re·ceipt** *esp* ECON Empfang *m*, Eingang *m*; Quittung *f*; *pl* Einnahmen *pl*
**re·ceive** bekommen, erhalten; empfangen; *j-n* aufnehmen (***into*** in *acc*); *radio*, TV empfangen; **re·ceiv·er** Empfänger(in); TEL Hörer *m*; JUR Hehler(in); *a.* ***official*** ~ *Br* JUR Konkursverwalter *m*
**re·cent** neuere(r, -s); jüngste(r, -s)
**re·cent·ly** kürzlich, vor kurzem
**re·cep·tion** Empfang *m*; Aufnahme *f* (***into*** in *acc*); *radio*, TV Empfang *m*; *a.* ~ ***desk*** *hotel*: Rezeption *f*, Empfang *m*
**re·cep·tion·ist** Empfangsdame *f*, -chef *m*; MED Sprechstundenhilfe *f*
**re·cep·tive** aufnahmefähig; empfänglich (***to*** für)
**re·cess** Unterbrechung *f*, (Schul)Pause *f*; PARL, JUR Ferien *pl*; Nische *f*
**re·ces·sion** ECON Rezession *f*
**re·ci·pe** (Koch)Rezept *n*
**re·cip·i·ent** Empfänger(in)
**re·cip·ro·cal** wechselseitig, gegenseitig
**re·cip·ro·cate** *v/i* TECH sich hin- und herbewegen; sich revanchieren; *v/t Einladung etc* erwidern
**re·cit·al** Vortrag *m*, (*Klavier- etc*)Konzert *n*, (*Lieder*)Abend *m*; Schilderung *f*; **re·ci·ta·tion** Aufsagen *n*, Hersagen *n*; Vortrag *m*; **re·cite** aufsagen, hersagen; vortragen; aufzählen
**reck·less** rücksichtslos
**reck·on** *v/t* (aus-, be)rechnen; glauben, schätzen; ~ ***up*** zusammenrechnen; *v/i*: ~ ***on*** rechnen mit; ~ ***with*** rechnen mit; ~ ***without*** nicht rechnen mit
**reck·on·ing** (Be)Rechnung *f*; ***be out in one's*** ~ sich verrechnet haben
**re·claim** zurückfordern; *Gepäck etc* abholen; *dem Meer etc Land* abgewinnen; TECH wiedergewinnen
**re·cline** sich zurücklehnen
**re·cluse** Einsiedler(in)
**rec·og·ni·tion** (Wieder)Erkennen *n*; Anerkennung *f*
**rec·og·nize** (wieder) erkennen; anerkennen; zugeben, eingestehen
**re·coil 1.** zurückschrecken (***from*** vor *dat*); **2.** Rückstoß *m*
**rec·ol·lect** sich erinnern an (*acc*)
**rec·ol·lec·tion** Erinnerung *f* (***of*** an *acc*)
**rec·om·mend** empfehlen (***as*** als; ***for*** für)
**rec·om·men·da·tion** Empfehlung *f*
**rec·om·pense 1.** entschädigen (***for*** für); **2.** Entschädigung *f*
**rec·on·cile** versöhnen, aussöhnen; in Einklang bringen (***with*** mit)
**rec·on·cil·i·a·tion** Versöhnung *f*, Aussöhnung *f* (***between*** zwischen *dat*; ***with*** mit)
**re·con·di·tion** TECH (general)überholen
**re·con·nais·sance** MIL Aufklärung *f*, Erkundung *f*
**re·con·noi·ter**, *Br* **re·con·noi·tre** MIL erkunden, auskundschaften
**re·con·sid·er** noch einmal überdenken
**re·con·struct** wieder aufbauen (*a. fig*); *Verbrechen etc* rekonstruieren
**re·con·struc·tion** Wiederaufbau *m*; Rekonstruktion *f*
**rec·ord¹** Aufzeichnung *f*; JUR Protokoll *n*; Akte *f*; (Schall)Platte *f*; SPORT Rekord *m*; ***off the*** ~ inoffiziell; ***have a criminal*** ~ vorbestraft sein
**re·cord²** aufzeichnen, aufschreiben, schriftlich niederlegen; JUR protokollieren, zu Protokoll nehmen; *auf Schallplatte, Tonband etc* aufnehmen, *Sendung a.* aufzeichnen, mitschneiden
**re·cord·er** (*Kassetten*)Rekorder *m*; (*Tonband*)Gerät *n*; MUS Blockflöte *f*
**re·cord·ing** Aufnahme *f*, Aufzeichnung *f*, Mitschnitt *m*
**rec·ord play·er** Plattenspieler *m*
**re·count** erzählen
**re·cov·er** *v/t* wiedererlangen, wiederbekommen, wieder finden; *Kosten etc* wiedereinbringen; *Fahrzeug, Verunglückten etc* bergen; ~ ***consciousness*** MED wieder zu sich kommen, das Bewusstsein wiedererlangen; *v/i* sich erholen (***from*** von); **re·cov·er·y** Wiedererlangen *n*; Wiederfinden *n*; Bergung *f*; Genesung *f*; Erholung *f*
**rec·re·a·tion** Entspannung *f*; Unter-

haltung *f*, Freizeitbeschäftigung *f*
**re·cruit 1.** MIL Rekrut *m*; Neue *m, f*, neues Mitglied; **2.** MIL rekrutieren; *Personal* einstellen; *Mitglieder* werben
**rec·tan·gle** MATH Rechteck *n*
**rec·tan·gu·lar** rechteckig
**rec·ti·fy** ELECTR gleichrichten
**rec·tor** REL Pfarrer *m*
**rec·to·ry** REL Pfarrhaus *n*
**re·cu·pe·rate** sich erholen (***from*** von) (*a. fig*)
**re·cur** wiederkehren, wieder auftreten
**re·cur·rence** Wiederkehr *f*
**re·cur·rent** wiederkehrend
**re·cy·cla·ble** TECH recycelbar, wieder verwertbar; **re·cy·cle** TECH *Abfälle* recyceln, wieder verwerten; ***~d paper*** Recyclingpapier *n*, Umwelt(schutz)papier *n*; **re·cy·cling** TECH Recycling *n*, Wiederverwertung *f*
**red 1.** rot; **2.** Rot *n*; ***be in the ~*** ECON in den roten Zahlen sein
**red·breast** → ***robin***
**Red Cres·cent** Roter Halbmond
**Red Cross** Rotes Kreuz
**red·cur·rant** BOT Rote Johannisbeere
**red·den** röten, rot färben; rot werden
**red·dish** rötlich
**re·dec·o·rate** *Zimmer etc* neu streichen *or* tapezieren
**re·deem** *Pfand, Versprechen etc* einlösen; REL erlösen
**Re·deem·er** REL Erlöser *m*, Heiland *m*
**re·demp·tion** Einlösung *f*; REL Erlösung *f*
**re·de·vel·op** *Gebäude, Stadtteil* sanieren
**red-faced** verlegen, mit rotem Kopf
**red-hand·ed: *catch s.o. ~*** j-n auf frischer Tat ertappen
**red·head** F Rotschopf *m*, Rothaarige *f*
**red-head·ed** rothaarig
**red her·ring** *fig* falsche Fährte *or* Spur
**red-hot** rot glühend; *fig* glühend; F brandaktuell (*news etc*)
**Red In·di·an** *contp* Indianer(in)
**red-let·ter day** Freuden-, Glückstag *m*
**red·ness** Röte *f*
**re·dou·ble** verdoppeln
**red tape** Bürokratismus *m*, F Amtsschimmel *m*
**re·duce** verkleinern; *Geschwindigkeit, Risiko etc* verringern, *Steuern etc* senken, *Preis, Waren etc* herabsetzen, reduzieren (***from ... to*** von ... auf *acc*), *Gehalt etc* kürzen; verwandeln (***to*** in *acc*), machen (***to*** zu); reduzieren, zurückführen (***to*** auf *acc*); **re·duc·tion** Verkleinerung *f*, Verringerung *f*, Senkung *f*, Herabsetzung *f*, Reduzierung *f*, Kürzung *f*
**re·dun·dant** überflüssig
**reed** BOT Schilf(rohr) *n*
**re·ed·u·cate** umerziehen
**re·ed·u·ca·tion** Umerziehung *f*
**reef** (Felsen)Riff *n*
**reek 1.** Gestank *m*; **2.** stinken (***of*** nach)
**reel**[1] 1. Rolle *f*, Spule *f*; **2. *~ off*** abrollen, abspulen; *fig* herunterrasseln
**reel**[2] sich drehen; (sch)wanken, taumeln, torkeln; ***my head ~ed*** mir drehte sich alles
**re-e·lect** wieder wählen
**re-en·ter** wieder eintreten in (*acc*), wieder betreten; **re-en·try** Wiedereintreten *n*, Wiedereintritt *m*
**ref** F SPORT Schiri *m*
**re·fer: *~ to*** verweisen *or* hinweisen auf (*acc*); *j-n* verweisen an (*acc*); sich beziehen auf (*acc*); anspielen auf (*acc*); erwähnen (*acc*); nachschlagen in (*dat*)
**ref·er·ee** SPORT Schiedsrichter *m*, Unparteiische *m*; *boxing*: Ringrichter *m*
**ref·er·ence** Verweis *m*, Hinweis *m* (***to*** auf *acc*); Verweisstelle *f*; Referenz *f*, Empfehlung *f*, Zeugnis *n*; Bezugnahme *f* (***to*** auf *acc*); Anspielung *f* (***to*** auf *acc*); Erwähnung *f* (***to*** *gen*); Nachschlagen *n* (***to*** in *dat*); ***list of ~s*** Quellenangabe *f*; **~ book** Nachschlagewerk *n*; **~ li·bra·ry** Handbibliothek *f*; **~ num·ber** Aktenzeichen *n*
**ref·e·ren·dum** POL Referendum *n*, Volksentscheid *m*
**re·fill 1.** wieder füllen, nachfüllen, auffüllen; **2.** (*Ersatz*)Mine *f*; (*Ersatz*)Patrone *f*
**re·fine** TECH raffinieren; *fig* verfeinern, kultivieren; ***~ on*** verbessern, verfeinern
**re·fined** TECH raffiniert; *fig* kultiviert, vornehm
**re·fine·ment** TECH Raffinierung *f*; *fig* Verbess(e)rung *f*, Verfeinerung *f*; Kultiviertheit *f*, Vornehmheit *f*
**re·fin·e·ry** TECH Raffinerie *f*
**re·flect** *v/t* reflektieren, zurückwerfen, -strahlen, (wider)spiegeln; ***be ~ed in*** sich (wider)spiegeln in (*dat*) (*a. fig*); *v/i*

R

nachdenken (***on*** über *acc*); ~ (***badly***) ***on*** sich nachteilig auswirken auf (*acc*); ein schlechtes Licht werfen auf (*acc*)
**re·flec·tion** Reflexion *f*, Zurückwerfung *f*, -strahlung *f*, (Wider)Spiegelung *f* (*a. fig*); Spiegelbild *n*; Überlegung *f*; Betrachtung *f*; ***on*** ~ nach einigem Nachdenken
**re·flec·tive** reflektierend; nachdenklich
**re·flex** Reflex *m*; ~ **ac·tion** Reflexhandlung *f*; ~ **cam·e·ra** PHOT Spiegelreflexkamera *f*
**re·flex·ive** LING reflexiv, rückbezüglich
**re·form 1.** reformieren, verbessern; sich bessern; **2.** Reform *f* (*a.* POL), Besserung *f*; **ref·or·ma·tion** Reformierung *f*; Besserung *f*; ***the Reformation*** REL die Reformation; **re·form·er** *esp* POL Reformer *m*; REL Reformator *m*
**re·fract** *Strahlen etc* brechen
**re·frac·tion** (*Strahlen- etc*)Brechung *f*
**re·frain[1]:** ~ ***from*** sich enthalten (*gen*), unterlassen (*acc*)
**re·frain[2]** Kehrreim *m*, Refrain *m*
**re·fresh** (**o.s.** sich) erfrischen, stärken; *Gedächtnis* auffrischen
**re·fresh·ing** erfrischend (*a. fig*)
**re·fresh·ment** Erfrischung *f*
**re·fri·ge·rate** TECH kühlen
**re·fri·ge·ra·tor** Kühlschrank *m*
**re·fu·el** auftanken
**ref·uge** Zuflucht *f*, Zufluchtsstätte *f*; *Br* Verkehrsinsel *f*
**ref·u·gee** Flüchtling *m*
**ref·u·gee camp** Flüchtlingslager *n*
**re·fund 1.** Rückzahlung *f*, Rückerstattung *f*; **2.** *Geld* zurückzahlen, zurückerstatten; *Auslagen* ersetzen
**re·fur·bish** aufpolieren (*a. fig*); renovieren
**re·fus·al** Ablehnung *f*; Weigerung *f*; Verweigerung *f*
**re·fuse[1]** *v/t* ablehnen; verweigern; sich weigern, es ablehnen (***to do*** zu tun); *v/i* ablehnen; sich weigern
**ref·use[2]** Abfall *m*, Abfälle *pl*, Müll *m*
**ref·use dump** Müllabladeplatz *m*
**re·fute** widerlegen
**re·gain** wieder-, zurückgewinnen
**re·gale:** ~ ***s.o. with s.th.*** j-n mit et. erfreuen *or* ergötzen
**re·gard 1.** Achtung *f*; Rücksicht *f*; *pl* Grüße *pl*; ***in this*** ~ in dieser Hinsicht; ***with*** ~ ***to*** im Hinblick auf (*acc*); hinsichtlich (*gen*); ***with kind*** ~***s*** mit freundlichen Grüßen; **2.** betrachten (*a. fig*), ansehen; ~ ***as*** betrachten als, halten für; ***as*** ~***s ...*** was ... betrifft
**re·gard·ing** bezüglich, hinsichtlich (*gen*)
**re·gard·less:** ~ ***of*** ohne Rücksicht auf (*acc*), ungeachtet (*gen*)
**regd** ABBR *of* ***registered*** ECON eingetragen; *post* eingeschrieben
**re·gen·e·rate** (sich) erneuern *or* regenerieren
**re·gent** Regent(in)
**re·gi·ment 1.** MIL Regiment *n*, *fig a.* Schar *f*; **2.** reglementieren, bevormunden
**re·gion** Gegend *f*, Gebiet *n*, Region *f*
**re·gion·al** regional, örtlich, Orts...
**re·gis·ter 1.** Register *n*, Verzeichnis *n*, (*Wähler- etc*)Liste *f*; **2.** *v/t* registrieren, eintragen (lassen); *Messwerte* anzeigen; *Brief etc* einschreiben lassen; *v/i* sich eintragen (lassen)
**re·gis·tered let·ter** Einschreib(e)brief *m*, Einschreiben *n*
**re·gis·tra·tion** Registrierung *f*, Eintragung *f*; MOT Zulassung *f*; ~ **fee** Anmeldegebühr *f*; ~ **num·ber** MOT (polizeiliches) Kennzeichen
**re·gis·try** Registratur *f*
**re·gis·try of·fice** *esp Br* Standesamt *n*
**re·gret 1.** bedauern; bereuen; **2.** Bedauern *n*; Reue *f*; **re·gret·ful** bedauernd; **re·gret·ta·ble** bedauerlich
**reg·u·lar 1.** regelmäßig; geregelt, geordnet; richtig; normal; MIL Berufs...; ~ ***gas*** (*Br* ***petrol***) MOT Normalbenzin *n*; **2.** F Stammkunde *m*, Stammkundin *f*; Stammgast *m*; SPORT Stammspieler(in); MIL Berufssoldat *m*; MOT Normal(benzin) *n*
**reg·u·lar·i·ty** Regelmäßigkeit *f*
**reg·u·late** regeln, regulieren; TECH einstellen, regulieren
**reg·u·la·tion** Reg(e)lung *f*, Regulierung *f*; TECH Einstellung *f*; Vorschrift *f*
**reg·u·la·tor** TECH Regler *m*
**re·hears·al** MUS, THEA Probe *f*
**re·hearse** MUS, THEA proben
**reign 1.** Regierung *f*, *a. fig* Herrschaft *f*; **2.** herrschen, regieren
**re·im·burse** *Auslagen* erstatten, vergüten
**rein 1.** Zügel *m*; **2.** ~ ***in*** *Pferd etc* zügeln; *fig* bremsen

**rein·deer** ZO Ren *n*, Rentier *n*
**re·in·force** verstärken
**re·in·force·ment** Verstärkung *f*
**re·in·state** *j-n* wieder einstellen (***as*** als; ***in*** in *dat*)
**re·in·sure** rückversichern
**re·it·e·rate** (ständig) wiederholen
**re·ject** *j-n, et.* ablehnen, *Bitte* abschlagen, *Plan etc* verwerfen; *j-n* ab-, zurückweisen; MED *Organ etc* abstoßen
**re·jec·tion** Ablehnung *f*; Verwerfung *f*; Zurückweisung *f*; MED Abstoßung *f*
**re·joice** sich freuen, jubeln (***at, over*** über *acc*); **re·joic·ing(s)** Jubel *m*
**re·join**[1] wieder zusammenfügen; wieder zurückkehren zu
**re·join**[2] erwidern
**re·ju·ve·nate** verjüngen
**re·kin·dle** *Feuer* wieder anzünden; *fig* wieder entfachen
**re·lapse 1.** zurückfallen, wieder verfallen (***into*** in *acc*); rückfällig werden; MED e-n Rückfall bekommen; **2.** Rückfall *m*
**re·late** *v/t* erzählen, berichten; in Verbindung *or* Zusammenhang bringen (***to*** mit); *v/i* sich beziehen (***to*** auf *acc*); zusammenhängen (***to*** mit)
**re·lat·ed** verwandt (***to*** mit)
**re·la·tion** Verwandte *m, f*; Beziehung *f* (***between*** zwischen *dat*; ***to*** zu); *pl diplomatische, geschäftliche* Beziehungen *pl*; ***in*** *or* ***with ~ to*** in Bezug auf (*acc*)
**re·la·tion·ship** Verwandtschaft *f*; Beziehung *f*, Verhältnis *n*
**rel·a·tive**[1] Verwandte *m, f*
**rel·a·tive**[2] relativ, verhältnismäßig; bezüglich (***to*** *gen*); LING Relativ..., bezüglich
**rel·a·tive pro·noun** LING Relativpronomen *n*, bezügliches Fürwort
**re·lax** *v/t Muskeln etc* entspannen; *Griff etc* lockern; *fig* nachlassen in (*dat*); *v/i* sich entspannen, *fig a.* ausspannen; sich lockern
**re·lax·a·tion** Entspannung *f*; Erholung *f*; Lockerung *f*
**re·laxed** entspannt, zwanglos
**re·lay**[1] **1.** Ablösung *f*; SPORT Staffel *f*; *radio*, TV Übertragung *f*; ELECTR Relais *n*; **2.** *radio*, TV übertragen
**re·lay**[2] *Kabel, Teppich* neu verlegen
**re·lay race** SPORT Staffel *f*
**re·lease 1.** entlassen, freilassen; loslassen; freigeben, herausbringen, veröffentlichen; MOT *Handbremse* lösen; *fig* befreien, erlösen; **2.** Entlassung *f*, Freilassung *f*; Befreiung *f*; Freigabe *f*; Veröffentlichung *f*; TECH, PHOT Auslöser *m*; *film*: *often* ***first ~*** Uraufführung *f*
**rel·e·gate** verbannen; ***be ~d*** SPORT absteigen (***to*** in *acc*)
**re·lent** nachgeben; nachlassen
**re·lent·less** unbarmherzig; anhaltend
**rel·e·vant** relevant, erheblich, wichtig; sachdienlich, zutreffend
**re·li·a·bil·i·ty** Zuverlässigkeit *f*
**re·li·a·ble** zuverlässig
**re·li·ance** Vertrauen *n*; Abhängigkeit *f* (***on*** von)
**rel·ic** Relikt *n*, Überrest *m*; REL Reliquie *f*
**re·lief** Erleichterung *f*; Unterstützung *f*, Hilfe *f*; Sozialhilfe *f*; Ablösung *f*; Relief *n*; **~ map** GEOGR Reliefkarte *f*
**re·lieve** *Schmerz, Not* lindern, *j-n, Gewissen* erleichtern; *j-n* ablösen
**re·li·gion** Religion *f*
**re·li·gious** Religions...; religiös; gewissenhaft
**rel·ish 1.** *fig* Gefallen *m*, Geschmack *m* (***for*** an *dat*); GASTR Würze *f*; Soße *f*; ***with ~*** mit Genuss; **2.** genießen, sich *et.* schmecken lassen; Geschmack *or* Gefallen finden an (*dat*)
**re·luc·tance** Widerstreben *n*; ***with ~*** widerwillig, ungern
**re·luc·tant** widerstrebend, widerwillig
**re·ly:** ***~ on*** sich verlassen auf (*acc*)
**re·main 1.** (ver)bleiben; übrig bleiben; **2.** *pl* (Über)Reste *pl*
**re·main·der** Rest *m*; Restbetrag *m*
**re·make 1.** wieder *or* neu machen; **2.** Remake *n*, Neuverfilmung *f*
**re·mand** JUR **1.** ***be ~ed in custody*** in Untersuchungshaft bleiben; **2.** ***be on ~*** in Untersuchungshaft sein; ***prisoner on ~*** Untersuchungsgefangene *m, f*
**re·mark 1.** *v/t* bemerken, äußern; *v/i* sich äußern (***on*** über *acc*, zu); **2.** Bemerkung *f*
**re·mark·a·ble** bemerkenswert; außergewöhnlich
**rem·e·dy 1.** (Heil-, Hilfs-, Gegen)Mittel *n*; (Ab)Hilfe *f*; **2.** *Schaden etc* beheben; *Missstand* abstellen; *Situation* bereinigen
**re·mem·ber** sich erinnern an (*acc*); denken an (*acc*); ***please ~ me to her*** grüße sie bitte von mir

R

**re·mem·brance** Erinnerung *f*; ***in ~ of*** zur Erinnerung an (*acc*)
**re·mind** erinnern (***of*** an *acc*)
**re·mind·er** Mahnung *f*
**rem·i·nis·cences** Erinnerungen *pl* (***of*** an *acc*); **rem·i·nis·cent:** ***be ~ of*** erinnern an (*acc*)
**re·mit** *Schulden, Strafe* erlassen; *Sünden* vergeben; *Geld* überweisen (***to*** *dat or* an *acc*); **re·mit·tance** ECON Überweisung *f* (***to*** an *acc*)
**rem·nant** (Über)Rest *m*
**re·mod·el** umformen, umgestalten
**re·morse** Gewissensbisse *pl*, Reue *f* (***über*** *acc* for)
**re·morse·ful** zerknirscht, reumütig
**re·morse·less** unbarmherzig
**re·mote** fern, entfernt; abgelegen, entlegen; **~ con·trol** TECH Fernlenkung *f*, Fernsteuerung *f*; Fernbedienung *f*
**re·mov·al** Entfernung *f*; Umzug *m*
**re·mov·al van** Möbelwagen *m*
**re·move** *v/t* entfernen (***from*** von); *Hut, Deckel etc* abnehmen; *Kleidung* ablegen; beseitigen, aus dem Weg räumen; *v/i* (um)ziehen (***from*** von; ***to*** nach)
**re·mov·er** (*Flecken- etc*)Entferner *m*
**Re·nais·sance** *die* Renaissance
**ren·der** *berühmt, schwierig, möglich etc* machen; *Dienst* erweisen; *Gedicht, Musikstück* vortragen; übersetzen, übertragen (***into*** in *acc*); *mst* ***~ down*** *Fett* auslassen
**ren·der·ing** *esp Br* → ***rendition***
**ren·di·tion** MUS *etc* Vortrag *m*; Übersetzung *f*, Übertragung *f*
**re·new** erneuern; *Gespräch etc* wieder aufnehmen; *Kraft etc* wiedererlangen; *Vertrag, Pass* verlängern (lassen)
**re·new·al** Erneuerung *f*; Verlängerung *f*
**re·nounce** verzichten auf (*acc*); *s-m Glauben etc* abschwören
**ren·o·vate** renovieren
**re·nown** Ruhm *m*; **re·nowned** berühmt (***as*** als; ***for*** wegen, für)
**rent¹** **1.** Miete *f*; Pacht *f*; Leihgebühr *f*; ***for ~*** zu vermieten, zu verleihen; **2.** mieten, pachten (***from*** von); *a.* ***~ out*** vermieten, verpachten (***to*** an *acc*); ***~ed car*** Miet-, Leihwagen *m*
**rent²** Riss *m*
**rent·al** Miete *f*; Pacht *f*; Leihgebühr *f*; ***~ car*** Miet-, Leihwagen *m*
**re·nun·ci·a·tion** Verzicht *m* (***of*** auf *acc*); Abschwören *n*
**re·pair** **1.** reparieren, ausbessern; *fig* wieder gutmachen; **2.** Reparatur *f*; Ausbesserung *f*; *pl* Instandsetzungsarbeiten *pl*; ***beyond ~*** nicht mehr zu reparieren; ***in good*** (***bad***) ***~*** in gutem (schlechtem) Zustand; ***be under ~*** in Reparatur sein; ***the road is under ~*** an der Straße wird gerade gearbeitet
**rep·a·ra·tion** Wiedergutmachung *f*; Entschädigung *f*; *pl* POL Reparationen *pl*
**rep·ar·tee** Schlagfertigkeit *f*; schlagfertige Antwort(en *pl*) *f*
**re·pay** *et.* zurückzahlen; *Besuch* erwidern; *et.* vergelten; *j-n* entschädigen
**re·pay·ment** Rückzahlung *f*
**re·peal** *Gesetz etc* aufheben
**re·peat** **1.** *v/t* wiederholen; nachsprechen; ***~ o.s.*** sich wiederholen; *v/i* F aufstoßen (***on s.o.*** j-m) (*food*); **2.** *radio*, TV Wiederholung *f*; **re·peat·ed** wiederholt; **re·peat·ed·ly** verschiedentlich
**re·pel** *Angriff, Feind* zurückschlagen; *Wasser etc, fig j-n* abstoßen
**re·pel·lent** abstoßend
**re·pent** bereuen
**re·pent·ance** Reue *f* (***for*** über *acc*)
**re·pen·tant** reuig, reumütig
**re·per·cus·sion** *mst pl* Auswirkungen *pl* (***on*** auf *acc*)
**rep·er·toire** THEA *etc* Repertoire *n*
**rep·er·to·ry the·a·ter** (*Br* **the·a·tre**) Repertoiretheater *n*
**rep·e·ti·tion** Wiederholung *f*
**re·place** an *j-s* Stelle treten, *j-n*, *et.* ersetzen; TECH austauschen, ersetzen
**re·place·ment** TECH Austausch *m*; Ersatz *m*
**re·plant** umpflanzen
**re·play** **1.** SPORT *Spiel* wiederholen; *Tonband-, Videoaufname etc* abspielen; **2.** SPORT Wiederholung *f*
**re·plen·ish** (wieder) auffüllen
**re·plete** satt; angefüllt, ausgestattet (***with*** mit)
**rep·li·ca** *art*: Originalkopie *f*; Kopie *f*, Nachbildung *f*
**re·ply** **1.** antworten, erwidern (***to*** auf *acc*); **2.** Antwort *f*, Erwiderung *f* (***to*** auf *acc*); ***in ~ to*** (als Antwort) auf (*acc*)
**re·ply cou·pon** Rückantwortschein *m*
**re·ply-paid en·ve·lope** Freiumschlag *m*

**re·port 1.** Bericht *m*; Meldung *f*, Nachricht *f*; Gerücht *n*; Knall *m*; ***~card*** PED Zeugnis *n*; **2.** berichten (über *acc*); (sich) melden; anzeigen; ***it is ~ed that*** es heißt, dass; ***~ed speech*** LING indirekte Rede; **re·port·er** Reporter(in), Berichterstatter(in)

**re·pose** Ruhe *f*; Gelassenheit *f*

**re·pos·i·to·ry** (Waren)Lager *n*; *fig* Fundgrube *f*, Quelle *f*

**rep·re·sent** *j-n*, *Wahlbezirk* vertreten; darstellen; hinstellen (***as, to be*** als)

**rep·re·sen·ta·tion** Vertretung *f*; Darstellung *f*

**rep·re·sen·ta·tive 1.** repräsentativ (*a.* POL), typisch (***of*** für); **2.** (Stell)Vertreter(in); ECON (Handels)Vertreter(in); PARL Abgeordnete *m, f*; ***House of Representatives*** Repräsentantenhaus *n*

**re·press** unterdrücken; PSYCH verdrängen; **re·pres·sion** Unterdrückung *f*; PSYCH Verdrängung *f*

**re·prieve** JUR **1.** ***he was ~d*** er wurde begnadigt; s-e Urteilsvollstreckung wurde ausgesetzt; **2.** Begnadigung *f*; Vollstreckungsaufschub *m*

**rep·ri·mand 1.** rügen, tadeln (***for*** wegen); **2.** Rüge *f*, Tadel *m*, Verweis *m*

**re·print 1.** neu auflegen *or* drucken, nachdrucken; **2.** Neuauflage *f*, Nachdruck *m*

**re·pri·sal** Repressalie *f*, Vergeltungsmaßnahme *f*

**re·proach 1.** Vorwurf *m*; **2.** vorwerfen (***s.o. with s.th.*** j-m et.); Vorwürfe machen; **re·proach·ful** vorwurfsvoll

**rep·ro·bate** verkommenes Subjekt

**re·pro·cess** NUCL wieder aufbereiten

**re·pro·cess·ing** TECH Wiederaufbereitung *f*; **~ plant** TECH Wiederaufbereitungsanlage *f*

**re·pro·duce** *v/t Ton etc* wiedergeben; *Bild etc* reproduzieren; ***~o.s.*** → *v/i* BIOL sich fortpflanzen, sich vermehren

**re·pro·duc·tion** BIOL Fortpflanzung *f*; Reproduktion *f*; Wiedergabe *f*; PED Nacherzählung *f*

**re·pro·duc·tive** BIOL Fortpflanzungs...

**re·proof** Rüge *f*, Tadel *m*

**re·prove** rügen, tadeln (***for*** wegen)

**rep·tile** ZO Reptil *n*

**re·pub·lic** Republik *f*

**re·pub·li·can 1.** republikanisch; **2.** Republikaner(in)

**re·pug·nant** widerlich, abstoßend

**re·pulse 1.** *j-n*, *Angebot etc* zurückweisen; MIL *Angriff* zurückschlagen; **2.** MIL Zurückschlagen *n*; Zurückweisung *f*

**re·pul·sion** Abscheu *m*, Widerwille *m*; PHYS Abstoßung *f*

**re·pul·sive** abstoßend, widerlich, widerwärtig; PHYS abstoßend

**rep·u·ta·ble** angesehen

**rep·u·ta·tion** (guter) Ruf, Ansehen *n*

**re·pute** (guter) Ruf

**re·put·ed** angeblich

**re·quest 1.** (***for***) Bitte *f* (um), Wunsch *m* (nach); ***at the ~ of s.o., at s.o.'s ~*** auf j-s Bitte hin; ***on ~*** auf Wunsch; **2.** um *et.* bitten *or* ersuchen; *j-n* bitten, ersuchen (***to do*** zu tun)

**re·quest stop** *Br* Bedarfshaltestelle *f*

**re·quire** erfordern; benötigen, brauchen; verlangen; ***if ~d*** wenn nötig

**re·quire·ment** Erfordernis *n*, Bedürfnis *n*; Anforderung *f*

**req·ui·site 1.** erforderlich; **2.** *mst pl* Artikel *pl*; ***toilet ~s*** Toilettenartikel *pl*

**req·ui·si·tion 1.** Anforderung *f*; MIL Requisition *f*, Beschlagnahme *f*; ***make a ~ for*** *et.* anfordern; **2.** anfordern; MIL requirieren, beschlagnahmen

**re·sale** Wieder-, Weiterverkauf *m*

**re·scind** JUR *Gesetz*, *Urteil etc* aufheben

**res·cue 1.** retten (***from*** aus, vor *dat*); **2.** Rettung *f*; Hilfe *f*; **3.** Rettungs...

**re·search 1.** Forschung *f*; **2.** forschen; *et.* erforschen

**re·search·er** Forscher(in)

**re·sem·blance** Ähnlichkeit *f* (***to*** mit; ***between*** zwischen *dat*)

**re·sem·ble** ähnlich sein, ähneln (*both*: *dat*)

**re·sent** übel nehmen, sich ärgern über (*acc*); **re·sent·ful** ärgerlich (***of, at*** über *acc*); **re·sent·ment** Ärger *m* (***against, at*** über *acc*)

**res·er·va·tion** Reservierung *f*, Vorbestellung *f*; Vorbehalt *m*; (*Indianer*)Reservat(ion *f*) *n*; (*Wild*)Reservat *n*

**re·serve 1.** (sich) *et.* aufsparen (***for*** für); sich vorbehalten; reservieren (lassen), vorbestellen; **2.** Reserve *f* (*a.* MIL); Vorrat *m*; (*Naturschutz-*, *Wild*)Reservat *n*; SPORT Reservespieler(in); Reserviertheit *f*, Zurückhaltung *f*

**re·served** zurückhaltend, reserviert

**res·er·voir** Reservoir *n* (*a. fig* ***of*** an *dat*)
**re·set** *Uhr* umstellen; *Zeiger etc* zurückstellen (***to*** auf *acc*)
**re·set·tle** umsiedeln
**re·side** wohnen, ansässig sein, s-n Wohnsitz haben
**res·i·dence** Wohnsitz *m*, Wohnort *m*; Aufenthalt *m*; Residenz *f*; ***official ~*** Amtssitz *m*; **~ per·mit** Aufenthaltsgenehmigung *f*, -erlaubnis *f*
**res·i·dent 1.** wohnhaft, ansässig; **2.** Bewohner(in), *in a town etc a.* Einwohner(in); (Hotel)Gast *m*; MOT Anlieger(in)
**res·i·den·tial** Wohn...; **~ ar·e·a** Wohngebiet *n*, Wohngegend *f*
**re·sid·u·al** übrig (geblieben), restlich, Rest...; **~ pol·lu·tion** Altlasten *pl*
**res·i·due** Rest *m*, CHEM A. Rückstand *m*
**re·sign** *v/i* zurücktreten (***from*** von); *v/t Amt etc* niederlegen; aufgeben; verzichten auf (*acc*); ***~ o.s. to*** sich fügen in (*acc*), sich abfinden mit
**res·ig·na·tion** Rücktritt *m*; Resignation *f*
**re·signed** ergeben, resigniert
**re·sil·i·ence** Elastizität *f*; *fig* Zähigkeit *f*; **re·sil·i·ent** elastisch; *fig* zäh
**res·in** Harz *n*
**re·sist** widerstehen (*dat*); Widerstand leisten, sich widersetzen (*both*: *dat*)
**re·sist·ance** Widerstand *m* (*a.* ELECTR); MED Widerstandskraft *f*; (*Hitze- etc* -)Beständigkeit *f*, (*Stoß- etc*)Festigkeit *f*; ***line of least ~*** Weg *m* des geringsten Widerstands
**re·sist·ant** widerstandsfähig; (*hitze- etc*)beständig, (*stoß- etc*)fest
**res·o·lute** resolut, entschlossen
**res·o·lu·tion** Beschluss *m*, PARL *etc a.* Resolution *f*; Vorsatz *m*; Entschlossenheit *f*; Lösung *f*
**re·solve 1.** beschließen; *Problem etc* lösen; (sich) auflösen; ***~ on*** sich entschließen zu; **2.** Vorsatz *m*; Entschlossenheit *f*
**res·o·nance** Resonanz *f*; voller Klang
**res·o·nant** voll(tönend); widerhallend
**re·sort 1.** Erholungsort *m*, Urlaubsort *m*; ***have ~ to*** → **2. *~ to*** Zuflucht nehmen zu
**re·sound** widerhallen (***with*** von)
**re·source** Mittel *n*, Zuflucht *f*; Ausweg *m*; Einfallsreichtum *m*; *pl* Mittel *pl*; (*natürliche*) Reichtümer *pl*, (*Boden-, Natur*)Schätze *pl*
**re·source·ful** einfallsreich, findig
**re·spect 1.** Achtung *f*, Respekt *m* (*both*: ***for*** vor *dat*); Rücksicht *f* (***for*** auf *acc*); Beziehung *f*, Hinsicht *f*; ***with ~ to ...*** was ... anbelangt *or* betrifft; ***in this ~*** in dieser Hinsicht; ***give my ~s to ...*** e-e Empfehlung an ... (*acc*); **2.** *v/t* respektieren, *a.* achten, *a.* berücksichtigen, beachten
**re·spect·a·ble** ehrbar, anständig, geachtet; F ansehnlich, beachtlich
**re·spect·ful** respektvoll, ehrerbietig
**re·spec·tive** jeweilig; ***we went to our ~ places*** jeder ging zu seinem Platz
**re·spec·tive·ly** beziehungsweise
**res·pi·ra·tion** Atmung *f*
**res·pi·ra·tor** Atemschutzgerät *n*
**re·spite** Pause *f*; Aufschub *m*, Frist *f*; ***without ~*** ohne Unterbrechung
**re·splen·dent** glänzend, strahlend
**re·spond** antworten, erwidern (***to*** auf *acc*; ***that*** dass); reagieren, MED *a.* ansprechen (***to*** auf *acc*)
**re·sponse** Antwort *f*, Erwiderung *f* (***to*** auf *acc*); *fig* Reaktion *f* (***to*** auf *acc*)
**re·spon·si·bil·i·ty** Verantwortung *f*; ***on one's own ~*** auf eigene Verantwortung; ***sense of ~*** Verantwortungsgefühl *n*; ***take*** (***full***) ***~ for*** die (volle) Verantwortung übernehmen für
**re·spon·si·ble** verantwortlich; verantwortungsbewusst; verantwortungsvoll
**rest**[1] **1.** Ruhe(pause) *f*; Erholung *f*; TECH Stütze *f*; (*Telefon*)Gabel *f*; ***have or take a ~*** sich ausruhen; ***set s.o.'s mind at ~*** j-n beruhigen; **2.** *v/i* ruhen; sich ausruhen; lehnen (***against, on*** an *dat*); ***let s.th. ~*** et. auf sich beruhen lassen; ***~ on*** ruhen auf (*dat*) (*a. fig*); *fig* beruhen auf (*dat*); *v/t* (aus)ruhen (lassen); lehnen (***against*** gegen; ***on*** an *acc*)
**rest**[2] Rest *m*; ***all the ~ of them*** alle Übrigen; ***for the ~*** im Übrigen
**rest ar·e·a** MOT Rastplatz *m*
**res·tau·rant** Restaurant *n*, Gaststätte *f*
**rest·ful** ruhig, erholsam
**rest home** Altenpflegeheim *n*; Erholungsheim *n*
**res·ti·tu·tion** ECON Rückgabe *f*, Rückerstattung *f*
**res·tive** unruhig, nervös
**rest·less** ruhelos, rastlos; unruhig

**res·to·ra·tion** Wiederherstellung *f*; Restaurierung *f*; Rückgabe *f*, Rückerstattung *f*; **re·store** wiederherstellen; restaurieren; zurückgeben, -erstatten; ***be ~d*** (***to health***) wieder gesund sein
**re·strain** (***from***) zurückhalten (von), hindern an (*dat*); ***I had to ~ myself*** ich musste mich beherrschen (***from doing s.th.*** um nicht et. zu tun)
**re·strained** beherrscht; dezent (*color*)
**re·straint** Beherrschung *f*, Zurückhaltung *f*; ECON Be-, Einschränkung *f*
**re·strict** ECON beschränken (***to*** auf *acc*), einschränken
**re·stric·tion** ECON Be-, Einschränkung *f*; ***without ~s*** uneingeschränkt
**rest room** Toilette *f*
**re·struc·ture** umstrukturieren
**re·sult 1.** Ergebnis *n*, Resultat *n*; Folge *f*; ***as a ~ of*** als Folge von (*or gen*); ***without ~*** ergebnislos; **2.** folgen, sich ergeben (***from*** aus); ***~ in*** zur Folge haben (*acc*), führen zu
**re·sume** wieder aufnehmen; fortsetzen; *Platz* wieder einnehmen
**re·sump·tion** Wiederaufnahme *f*; Fortsetzung *f*
**Res·ur·rec·tion** REL Auferstehung *f*
**re·sus·ci·tate** MED wieder beleben
**re·sus·ci·ta·tion** MED Wiederbelebung *f*
**re·tail** ECON **1.** Einzelhandel *m*; ***by ~*** im Einzelhandel; **2.** Einzelhandels...; **3.** *adv* im Einzelhandel; **4.** *v/t* im Einzelhandel verkaufen (***at, for*** für); *v/i* im Einzelhandel verkauft werden (***at, for*** für); **re·tail·er** ECON Einzelhändler(in)
**re·tain** (be)halten, bewahren; *Wasser, Wärme* speichern
**re·tal·i·ate** Vergeltung üben, sich revanchieren; **re·tal·i·a·tion** Vergeltung *f*, Vergeltungsmaßnahmen *pl*
**re·tard** verzögern, aufhalten, hemmen; (***mentally***) ***~ed*** (geistig) zurückgeblieben
**retch** würgen
**re·tell** nacherzählen
**re·think** *et.* noch einmal überdenken
**re·ti·cent** schweigsam, zurückhaltend
**ret·i·nue** Gefolge *n*
**re·tire** *v/i* in Rente *or* Pension gehen, sich pensionieren lassen; sich zurückziehen; ***~ from business*** sich zur Ruhe setzen; *v/t* in den Ruhestand versetzen, pensionieren; **re·tired** pensioniert, im Ruhestand (lebend); ***be ~ a.*** in Rente *or* Pension sein; **re·tire·ment** Pensionierung *f*, Ruhestand *m*
**re·tir·ing** zurückhaltend
**re·tort 1.** (scharf) entgegnen *or* erwidern; **2.** (scharfe) Entgegnung *or* Erwiderung
**re·touch** PHOT retuschieren
**re·trace** *Tathergang etc* rekonstruieren; ***~ one's steps*** denselben Weg zurückgehen
**re·tract** *v/t Angebot* zurückziehen; *Behauptung* zurücknehmen; *Geständnis* widerrufen; TECH, ZO einziehen; *v/i* TECH, ZO eingezogen werden
**re·train** umschulen
**re·tread** MOT **1.** *Reifen* runderneuern; **2.** runderneuerter Reifen
**re·treat 1.** MIL Rückzug *m*; Zufluchtsort *m*; ***beat a*** (***hasty***) ***~*** das Feld räumen, F abhauen; **2.** sich zurückziehen; zurückweichen (***from*** vor *dat*)
**ret·ri·bu·tion** Vergeltung *f*
**re·trieve** zurückholen, wiederbekommen; *Fehler, Verlust etc* wieder gutmachen; HUNT apportieren
**ret·ro·ac·tive** JUR rückwirkend
**ret·ro·grade** rückschrittlich
**ret·ro·spect:** ***in ~*** im Rückblick
**ret·ro·spec·tive** rückblickend; JUR rückwirkend
**re·try** JUR *Fall* erneut verhandeln; neu verhandeln gegen *j-n*
**re·turn 1.** *v/i* zurückkehren, zurückkommen; zurückgehen; ***~ to*** auf *ein Thema etc* zurückkommen; in *e-e Gewohnheit etc* zurückfallen; in *e-n Zustand etc* zurückkehren; *v/t* zurückgeben (***to*** *dat*); zurückbringen (***to*** *dat*); zurückschicken, -senden (***to*** *dat or* an *acc*); zurücklegen, -stellen; erwidern; *Gewinn etc* abwerfen; → ***verdict*; 2.** Rückkehr *f*; *fig* Wiederauftreten *n*; Rückgabe *f*; Zurückbringen *n*; Zurückschicken *n*, -senden *n*; Zurücklegen *n*, -stellen *n*; Erwiderung *f*; (*Steuer*)Erklärung *f*; *tennis etc*: Return *m*, Rückschlag *m*; ECON *a. pl* Gewinn *m*; *Br* → ***return ticket***; *Br* ***many happy ~s*** (***of the day***) herzlichen Glückwunsch zum Geburtstag; ***by ~*** (***of post***) umgehend, postwendend; ***in ~ for*** (als Gegenleistung) für; **3.** *adj* Rück...

**re·turn·a·ble** *in cpds* Mehrweg...; **~ bottle** Pfandflasche *f*
**re·turn| key** EDP Eingabetaste *f*; **~ game, ~ match** SPORT Rückspiel *n*; **~ tick·et** *Br* RAIL Rückfahrkarte *f*; AVIAT Rückflugticket *n*
**re·u·ni·fi·ca·tion** POL Wiedervereinigung *f*
**re·u·nion** Treffen *n*, Wiedersehensfeier *f*; Wiedervereinigung *f*
**re·us·a·ble** wieder verwendbar
**rev** F MOT **1.** Umdrehung *f*; **~ counter** Drehzahlmesser *m*; **2.** *a.* **~ up** aufheulen (lassen)
**re·val·ue** ECON *Währung* aufwerten
**re·veal** den Blick freigeben auf (*acc*), zeigen; *Geheimnis etc* enthüllen, aufdecken; **re·veal·ing** aufschlussreich (*remark etc*); offenherzig (*dress etc*)
**rev·el:** **~ in** schwelgen in (*dat*); sich weiden an (*dat*)
**rev·e·la·tion** Enthüllung *f*; REL Offenbarung *f*
**re·venge 1.** Rache *f*; *esp* SPORT Revanche *f*; **in ~ for** aus Rache für; **take ~ on s.o. for s.th.** sich an j-m für et. rächen; **2.** rächen; **re·venge·ful** rachsüchtig
**rev·e·nue** Staatseinkünfte *pl*, Staatseinnahmen *pl*
**re·ver·be·rate** nach-, widerhallen
**re·vere** (ver)ehren; **rev·e·rence** Verehrung *f*; Ehrfurcht *f* (**for** vor *dat*)
**Rev·e·rend** REL Hochwürden *m*
**rev·e·rent** ehrfürchtig, ehrfurchtsvoll
**rev·er·ie** (Tag)Träumerei *f*
**re·vers·al** Umkehrung *f*; Rückschlag *m*
**re·verse 1.** *adj* umgekehrt; **in ~ order** in umgekehrter Reihenfolge; **2.** *Wagen* im Rückwärtsgang *or* rückwärts fahren; *Reihenfolge etc* umkehren; *Urteil etc* aufheben; *Entscheidung etc* umstoßen; **3.** Gegenteil *n*; MOT Rückwärtsgang *m*; Rückseite *f*, Kehrseite *f* (*of a coin*); Rückschlag *m*; **~ gear** MOT Rückwärtsgang *m*; **~ side** linke (*Stoff*)Seite
**re·vers·i·ble** doppelseitig (tragbar)
**re·vert:** **~ to** in *e-n Zustand* zurückkehren; in *e-e Gewohnheit etc* zurückfallen; auf *ein Thema* zurückkommen
**re·view 1.** Überprüfung *f*; Besprechung *f*, Kritik *f*, Rezension *f*; MIL Parade *f*; PED (Stoff)Wiederholung *f* (**for** für *e-e Prüfung*); **2.** überprüfen; besprechen, rezensieren; MIL besichtigen, inspizieren; PED *Stoff* wiederholen (**for** für *e-e Prüfung*)
**re·view·er** Kritiker(in), Rezensent(in)
**re·vise** revidieren, *Ansicht* ändern, *Buch etc* überarbeiten; *Br* PED *Stoff* wiederholen (**for** für *e-e Prüfung*)
**re·vi·sion** Revision *f*, Überarbeitung *f*; überarbeitete Ausgabe; *Br* PED (Stoff-)Wiederholung *f* (**for** für *e-e Prüfung*)
**re·viv·al** Wiederbelebung *f*; Wiederaufleben *n*
**re·vive** wieder beleben; wieder aufleben (lassen); *Erinnerungen* wachrufen; MED wieder zu sich kommen; sich erholen
**re·voke** widerrufen, zurücknehmen, rückgängig machen
**re·volt 1.** *v/i* sich auflehnen, revoltieren (**against** gegen); Abscheu empfinden, empört sein (**against, at, from** über *acc*); *v/t* mit Abscheu erfüllen, abstoßen; **2.** Revolte *f*, Aufstand *m*
**re·volt·ing** abscheulich, abstoßend
**rev·o·lu·tion** Revolution *f*, Umwälzung *f*; ASTR Umlauf *m* (**round** um); TECH Umdrehung *f*; **number of ~s** Drehzahl *f*; **~ counter** Drehzahlmesser *m*; **rev·o·lu·tion·a·ry 1.** revolutionär; Revolutions...; **2.** POL Revolutionär(in)
**rev·o·lu·tion·ize** revolutionieren
**re·volve** sich drehen (**on, round** um); **~ around** *fig* sich drehen um
**re·volv·er** Revolver *m*
**re·volv·ing** Dreh...; **~ door(s)** Drehtür *f*
**re·vue** THEA Revue *f*; Kabarett *n*
**re·vul·sion** Abscheu *m*
**re·ward 1.** Belohnung *f*; **2.** belohnen
**re·ward·ing** lohnend
**re·write** neu schreiben, umschreiben
**rhap·so·dy** MUS Rhapsodie *f*
**rhe·to·ric** Rhetorik *f*
**rheu·ma·tism** MED Rheumatismus *m*, F Rheuma *n*
**rhi·no** F, **rhi·no·ce·ros** ZO Rhinozeros *n*, Nashorn *n*
**rhu·barb** BOT Rhabarber *m*
**rhyme 1.** Reim *m*; Vers *m*; **without ~ or reason** ohne Sinn und Verstand; **2.** (sich) reimen
**rhyth·m** Rhythmus *m*
**rhyth·mic, rhyth·mi·cal** rhythmisch
**rib** ANAT Rippe *f*

**rib·bon** (*a.* Farb-, Ordens)Band *n*; Streifen *m*; Fetzen *m*
**rib cage** ANAT Brustkorb *m*
**rice** BOT Reis *m*
**rice pud·ding** GASTR Milchreis *m*
**rich 1.** reich (*in* an *dat*); prächtig, kostbar; GASTR schwer; AGR fruchtbar, fett (*soil*); voll (*sound*); satt (*color*); ~ (*in calories*) kalorienreich; **2.** *the* ~ die Reichen *pl*
**rick** (Stroh-, Heu)Schober *m*
**rick·ets** MED Rachitis *f*
**rick·et·y** F *fig* gebrechlich; wack(e)lig
**rid** befreien (*of* von); *get* ~ *of* loswerden
**rid·dance:** F *good* ~! den (die, das) sind wir Gott sei Dank los!
**rid·den** *in cpds* geplagt von
**rid·dle**[1] Rätsel *n*
**rid·dle**[2] **1.** grobes Sieb, Schüttelsieb *n*; **2.** sieben; durchlöchern, durchsieben
**ride 1.** *v/i* reiten; fahren (*on* auf *e-m Fahrrad etc*; *on or Br in* in *e-m Bus etc*); *v/t* reiten (auf *dat*); *Fahrrad, Motorrad* fahren, fahren auf (*dat*); **2.** Ritt *m*; Fahrt *f*; **rid·er** Reiter(in); (*Motorrad-, Rad*)Fahrer(in)
**ridge** GEOGR (*Gebirgs*)Kamm *m*, Grat *m*; ARCH (*Dach*)First *m*
**rid·i·cule 1.** Spott *m*; **2.** lächerlich machen, spotten über (*acc*), verspotten
**ri·dic·u·lous** lächerlich
**rid·ing** Reit...
**riff-raff** *contp* Gesindel *n*
**ri·fle**[1] Gewehr *n*
**ri·fle**[2] durchwühlen
**rift** Spalt *m*, Spalte *f*; *fig* Riss *m*
**rig 1.** *Schiff* auftakeln; ~ *out j-n* ausstaffieren; ~ *up* F (behelfsmäßig) zusammenbauen (*from* aus); **2.** MAR Takelage *f*; TECH Bohrinsel *f*; F Aufmachung *f*
**rig·ging** MAR Takelage *f*
**right 1.** *adj* recht; richtig; rechte(r, -s), Rechts...; *all* ~! in Ordnung!, gut!; *that's all* ~! das macht nichts!, schon gut!, bitte!; *that's* ~! richtig!, ganz recht!, stimmt!; *be* ~ Recht haben; *put* ~, *set* ~ in Ordnung bringen; berichtigen, korrigieren; **2.** *adv* (nach) rechts; richtig, recht; genau; gerade(wegs), direkt; ganz, völlig; ~ *away* sofort; ~ *now* im Moment; sofort; ~ *on* geradeaus; *turn* ~ (sich) nach rechts wenden; MOT rechts abbiegen; **3.** Recht *n*; *die* Rechte (*a.* POL, *boxing*), rechte Seite; *on the* ~ rechts, auf der rechten Seite; *to the* ~ (nach) rechts; *keep to the* ~ sich rechts halten; MOT rechts fahren; **4.** aufrichten; *et.* wieder gutmachen; in Ordnung bringen
**right an·gle** MATH rechter Winkel
**right-an·gled** MATH rechtwink(e)lig
**right·eous** gerecht (*anger etc*)
**right·ful** rechtmäßig
**right-hand** rechte(r, -s); ~ **drive** MOT Rechtssteuerung *f*
**right-hand·ed** rechtshändig; für Rechtshänder; *be* ~ Rechtshänder(in) sein
**right·ly** richtig; mit Recht
**right of way** MOT Vorfahrt *f*, Vorfahrtsrecht *n*; Durchgangsrecht *n*
**right-wing** POL dem rechten Flügel angehörend, Rechts...
**rig·id** starr, steif; *fig* streng, strikt
**rig·a·ma·role** Geschwätz *n*; *fig* Theater *n*, Zirkus *m*
**rig·or·ous** streng; genau
**rig·o(u)r** Strenge *f*, Härte *f*
**rile** F ärgern, reizen
**rim** Rand *m*; TECH Felge *f*
**rim·less** randlos
**rind** (*Zitronen- etc*)Schale *f*; (*Käse*)Rinde *f*; (*Speck*)Schwarte *f*
**ring**[1] **1.** Ring *m*; Kreis *m*; Manege *f*; (Box)Ring *m*; (Spionage- *etc*)Ring *m*; **2.** umringen, umstellen; *Vogel* beringen
**ring**[2] **1.** läuten; klingeln; klingen (*a. fig*); *Br* TEL anrufen; *the bell is* ~*ing* es läutet *or* klingelt; ~ *the bell* läuten, klingeln; ~ *back Br* TEL zurückrufen; ~ *for* nach *j-m, et.* läuten; *Arzt etc* rufen; ~ *off Br* TEL (den Hörer) auflegen, Schluss machen; ~ *s.o.* (*up*) j-n *or* bei j-m anrufen; **2.** Läuten *n*, Klingeln *n*; *fig* Klang *m*; *Br* TEL Anruf *m*; F *give s.o. a* ~ j-n anrufen
**ring bind·er** Ringbuch *n*
**ring fin·ger** Ringfinger *m*
**ring·lead·er** Rädelsführer(in)
**ring·let** (Ringel)Löckchen *n*
**ring road** *Br* Umgehungsstraße *f*; Ringstraße *f*
**ring·side:** *at the* ~ *boxing*: am Ring
**rink** (Kunst)Eisbahn *f*; Rollschuhbahn *f*
**rinse** *a.* ~ *out* (aus)spülen
**ri·ot 1.** Aufruhr *m*; Krawall *m*; *run* ~ randalieren; *run* ~ *through* randalie-

R

rend ziehen durch; **2.** Krawall machen, randalieren; **ri·ot·er** Aufrührer(in); Randalierer(in); **ri·ot·ous** aufrührerisch; randalierend; ausgelassen, wild
**rip 1.** *a.* ~ ***up*** zerreißen; ~ ***open*** aufreißen; F ~ ***s.o. off*** j-n neppen; **2.** Riss *m*
**ripe** reif; **rip·en** reifen (lassen)
**rip-off** F Nepp *m*
**rip·ple 1.** (sich) kräuseln; plätschern, rieseln; **2.** kleine Welle; Kräuselung *f*; Plätschern *n*, Rieseln *n*
**rise 1.** aufstehen, sich erheben; REL auferstehen; aufsteigen (*smoke etc*); sich heben (*curtain, spirits*); ansteigen (*road, river etc*), anschwellen (*river etc*); (an)steigen (*temperature etc*), *prices etc*: *a.* anziehen; stärker werden (*wind etc*); aufgehen (*sun etc, bread etc*); entspringen (*river etc*); *fig* aufsteigen; *fig* entstehen (***from, out of*** aus); *a.* ~ ***up*** sich erheben (***against*** gegen); ~ ***to the occasion*** sich der Lage gewachsen zeigen; **2.** (An)Steigen *n*; Steigung *f*; Anhöhe *f*; ASTR Aufgang *m*; *Br* Lohn- *or* Gehaltserhöhung *f*; *fig* Anstieg *m*; Aufstieg *m*; ***give*** ~ ***to*** verursachen, führen zu
**ris·er: *early*** ~ Frühaufsteher(in)
**ris·ing 1.** Aufstand *m*; **2.** aufstrebend
**risk 1.** Gefahr *f*, Risiko *n*; ***at one's own*** ~ auf eigene Gefahr; ***at the*** ~ ***of doing s.th.*** auf die Gefahr hin, et. zu tun; ***be at*** ~ gefährdet sein; ***run the*** ~ ***of doing s.th.*** Gefahr laufen, et. zu tun; ***run a*** ~, ***take a*** ~ ein Risiko eingehen; **2.** wagen, riskieren; **risk·y** riskant
**rite** Ritus *m*; Zeremonie *f*
**rit·u·al 1.** rituell; Ritual...; **2.** Ritual *n*
**ri·val 1.** Rivale *m*, Rivalin *f*, Konkurrent(in); **2.** Konkurrenz..., rivalisierend; **3.** rivalisieren *or* konkurrieren mit; **ri·val·ry** Rivalität *f*; Konkurrenz *f*; Konkurrenzkampf *m*
**riv·er** Fluss *m*; Strom *m*; **riv·er·side** Flussufer *n*; ***by the*** ~ am Fluss
**riv·et 1.** TECH Niet *m*, *n*, Niete *f*; **2.** TECH (ver)nieten; *fig Aufmerksamkeit, Blick* richten (***on*** auf *acc*)
**road** (Auto-, Land)Straße *f*; *fig* Weg *m*; ***on the*** ~ auf der Straße; unterwegs; THEA auf Tournee
**road ac·ci·dent** Verkehrsunfall *m*
**road·block** Straßensperre *f*
**road hog** F Verkehrsrowdy *m*
**road map** Straßenkarte *f*
**road safe·ty** Verkehrssicherheit *f*
**road·side** Straßenrand *m*; ***at the*** ~, ***by the*** ~ am Straßenrand
**road toll** Straßenbenutzungsgebühr *f*
**road·way** Fahrbahn *f*
**road works** Straßenarbeiten *pl*
**road·wor·thi·ness** Verkehrssicherheit *f*; **road·wor·thy** verkehrssicher
**roam** *v/i* (umher)streifen, (-)wandern; *v/t* streifen *or* wandern durch
**roar 1.** Brüllen *n*, Gebrüll *n*; Brausen *n*, Krachen *n*, Donnern *n*; ~***s of laughter*** brüllendes Gelächter; **2.** brüllen; brausen; donnern (*truck, gun etc*)
**roast** GASTR **1.** *v/t* braten (*a. v/i*); *Kaffee etc* rösten; **2.** Braten *m*; **3.** *adj* gebraten
**roast beef** GASTR Rinderbraten *m*
**rob** *Bank etc* überfallen; *j-n* berauben
**rob·ber** Räuber *m*
**rob·ber·y** Raubüberfall *m*, (*Bank-*)Raub *m*, (*Bank*)Überfall *m*
**robe** *a. pl* Robe *f*, Talar *m*
**rob·in** ZO Rotkehlchen *n*
**ro·bot** Roboter *m*
**ro·bust** robust, kräftig
**rock**[1] schaukeln, wiegen; erschüttern (*a. fig*)
**rock**[2] Fels(en) *m*; Felsen *pl*; GEOL Gestein *n*; Felsbrocken *m*; Stein *m*; *Br* Zuckerstange *f*; *pl* Klippen *pl*; F ***on the*** ~***s*** in ernsten Schwierigkeiten (*business etc*); kaputt (*marriage etc*); GASTR mit Eis
**rock**[3] *a.* ~ ***music*** Rock(musik *f*) *m*; → ***rock 'n' roll***
**rock·er** Kufe *f*; Schaukelstuhl *m*; *Br* Rocker *m*; ***off one's*** ~ F übergeschnappt
**rock·et 1.** Rakete *f*; **2.** rasen, schießen; *a.* ~ ***up*** hochschnellen, in die Höhe schießen (*prices*)
**rock·ing chair** Schaukelstuhl *m*
**rock·ing horse** Schaukelpferd *n*
**rock 'n' roll** MUS Rock 'n' Roll *m*
**rock·y** felsig; steinhart
**rod** Rute *f*; TECH Stab *m*, Stange *f*
**ro·dent** ZO Nagetier *n*
**ro·de·o** Rodeo *m*, *n*
**roe** ZO *a.* ***hard*** ~ Rogen *m*; *a.* ***soft*** ~ Milch *f*
**roe·buck** ZO Rehbock *m*
**roe deer** ZO Reh *n*
**rogue** Schurke *m*, Gauner *m*; Schlingel *m*, Spitzbube *m*

**ro·guish** schelmisch, spitzbübisch
**role** THEA *etc* Rolle *f* (*a. fig*)
**roll 1.** *v/i* rollen; sich wälzen; fahren; MAR schlingern; (g)rollen (*thunder*); *v/t et.* rollen; auf-, zusammenrollen; *Zigarette* drehen; ~ ***down*** *Ärmel* herunterkrempeln; MOT *Fenster* herunterkurbeln; ~ ***out*** ausrollen; ~ ***up*** aufrollen; (sich) zusammenrollen; *Ärmel* hochkrempeln; MOT *Fenster* hochkurbeln; **2.** Rolle *f*; GASTR Brötchen *n*, Semmel *f*; Namens-, Anwesenheitsliste *f*; (G)Rollen *n* (*of thunder*); (*Trommel*)Wirbel *m*; MAR Schlingern *n*
**roll call** Namensaufruf *m*
**roll·er** (Locken)Wickler *m*; TECH Rolle *f*, Walze *f*
**roll·er coast·er** Achterbahn *f*
**roll·er skate** Rollschuh *m*
**roll·er-skate** Rollschuh laufen
**roll·er-skat·ing** Rollschuhlaufen *n*
**roll·er tow·el** Rollhandtuch *n*
**roll·ing pin** Nudelholz *n*
**roll-on** Deoroller *m*
**Ro·man 1.** römisch; **2.** Römer(in)
**ro·mance** Abenteuer-, Liebesroman *m*; Romanze *f*; Romantik *f*
**Ro·mance** LING romanisch
**Ro·ma·ni·a** Rumänien *n*
**Ro·ma·ni·an 1.** rumänisch; **2.** Rumäne *m*, Rumänin *f*; LING Rumänisch *n*
**ro·man·tic 1.** romantisch; **2.** Romantiker(in)
**ro·man·ti·cism** Romantik *f*
**romp** *a.* ~ ***about,*** ~ ***around*** herumtollen, herumtoben
**romp·ers** Spielanzug *m*
**roof 1.** Dach *n*; MOT Verdeck *n*; **2.** mit e-m Dach versehen; ~ ***in,*** ~ ***over*** überdachen
**roof·ing felt** Dachpappe *f*
**roof-rack** MOT Dachgepäckträger *m*
**rook[1]** ZO Saatkrähe *f*
**rook[2]** *chess*: Turm *m*
**rook[3]** F *j-n* betrügen (***of*** um)
**room 1.** Raum *m*, *a.* Zimmer *n*, *a.* Platz *m*; *fig* Spielraum *m*; **2.** wohnen
**room·er** Untermieter(in)
**room·ing-house** Fremdenheim *n*, Pension *f*
**room·mate** Zimmergenosse *m*, -genossin *f*
**room ser·vice** Zimmerservice *m*
**room·y** geräumig
**roost 1.** (Hühner)Stange *f*; ZO Schlafplatz *m*; **2.** auf der Stange *etc* sitzen *or* schlafen
**roost·er** ZO (Haus)Hahn *m*
**root 1.** Wurzel *f*; ***take*** ~ Wurzeln schlagen (*a. fig*); **2.** *v/i* Wurzeln schlagen; wühlen (***for*** nach); ~ ***about*** herumwühlen (***among*** in *dat*); *v/t* ~ ***out*** *fig* ausrotten; ~ ***up*** mit der Wurzel ausreißen
**root·ed:** ***deeply*** ~ *fig* tief verwurzelt; ***stand*** ~ ***to the spot*** wie angewurzelt dastehen
**rope 1.** Seil *n*; MAR Tau *n*; Strick *m*; (*Perlen- etc*)Schnur *f*; ***give s.o. plenty of*** ~ j-m viel Freiheit *or* Spielraum lassen; ***know the*** ~***s*** F sich auskennen; ***show s.o. the*** ~***s*** F j-n einarbeiten; **2.** festbinden (***to*** an *dat or acc*); ~ ***off*** (durch ein Seil) absperren *or* abgrenzen; ~ **lad·der** Strickleiter *f*
**ro·sa·ry** REL Rosenkranz *m*
**rose 1.** BOT Rose *f*; Brause *f*; **2.** rosarot, rosenrot
**ros·trum** Redner-, Dirigentenpult *n*
**ros·y** rosig (*a. fig*)
**rot 1.** *v/t* (ver)faulen *or* verrotten lassen; *v/i a.* ~ ***away*** (ver)faulen, verrotten, morsch werden; **2.** Fäulnis *f*
**ro·ta·ry** rotierend, sich drehend; Rotations..., Dreh...; **ro·tate** rotieren (lassen), (sich) drehen; turnusmäßig (aus-) wechseln; **ro·ta·tion** Rotation *f*, Drehung *f*; Wechsel *m*
**ro·tor** TECH Rotor *m*
**rot·ten** verfault, faul; verrottet, morsch; *fig* miserabel; gemein; ***feel*** ~ F sich mies fühlen
**ro·tund** rund und dick
**rough 1.** *adj* rau; uneben (*road etc*); stürmisch (*sea, crossing, weather*); grob; barsch; hart; grob, ungefähr (*estimate etc*); roh, Roh...; **2.** *adv* ***sleep*** ~ im Freien übernachten; ***play*** ~ SPORT hart spielen; **3.** *golf*: Rough *n*; ***write it out in*** ~ ***first*** zuerst ins Unreine schreiben; **4.** ~ ***it*** F primitiv *or* anspruchslos leben; ~ ***out*** entwerfen, skizzieren; ~ ***up*** F *j-n* zusammenschlagen
**rough·age** MED Ballaststoffe *pl*
**rough·cast** ARCH Rauputz *m*
**rough| cop·y** Rohentwurf *m*, Konzept *n*; ~ **draft** Rohfassung *f*
**rough·en** rau werden; rau machen, anrauen, aufrauen

**rough·ly** grob, *fig a.* ungefähr
**rough·neck** F Schläger *m*
**rough·shod:** ***ride ~ over** j-n* rücksichtslos behandeln; sich rücksichtslos über *et.* hinwegsetzen
**round 1.** *adj* rund; ***a ~ dozen*** ein rundes Dutzend; ***in ~ figures*** aufgerundet, abgerundet, rund(e) ...; **2.** *adv* rund(her)um, rings(her)um; überall, auf *or* von *or* nach allen Seiten; ***turn ~*** sich umdrehen; ***invite s.o. ~*** j-n zu sich einladen; ***~ about*** F ungefähr; ***all (the) year ~*** das ganze Jahr hindurch *or* über; ***the other way ~*** umgekehrt; **3.** *prp* (rund) um, um (*acc* ... herum); in *or* auf (*dat*) ... herum; ***trip ~ the world*** Weltreise *f*; **4.** Runde *f*, *a.* Rundgang *m*, MED Visite *f*, *a.* Lage *f* (*beer etc*); Schuss *m*; *esp Br* Scheibe *f* (*bread etc*); MUS Kanon *m*; **5.** rund machen, (ab)runden, *Lippen* spitzen; umfahren, fahren um, *Kurve* nehmen; ***~ down*** *Zahl etc* abrunden (***to*** auf *acc*); ***~ off*** *Essen etc* abrunden, beschließen (***with*** mit); *Zahl etc* auf- *or* abrunden (***to*** auf *acc*); ***~ up*** *Vieh* zusammentreiben; *Leute etc* zusammentrommeln; *Zahl etc* aufrunden (***to*** auf *acc*)
**round·a·bout 1.** *Br* MOT Kreisverkehr *m*; *Br* Karussell *n*; **2.** ***take a ~ route*** e-n Umweg machen; ***in a ~ way*** *fig* auf Umwegen
**round trip** Hin- und Rückfahrt *f*; Hin- und Rückflug *m*
**round-trip tick·et** Rückfahrkarte *f*; Rückflugticket *n*
**round·up** Razzia *f*
**rouse** *j-n* wecken; *fig j-n* aufrütteln, wachrütteln; *j-n* erzürnen, reizen
**route** Route *f*, Strecke *f*, Weg *m*, (*Bus-etc*)Linie *f*
**rou·tine 1.** Routine *f*; ***the same old (daily) ~*** das (tägliche) ewige Einerlei; **2.** üblich, routinemäßig, Routine...
**rove** (umher)streifen, (umher)wandern
**row¹** Reihe *f*
**row² 1.** rudern; **2.** Kahnfahrt *f*
**row³** *Br* F **1.** Krach *m*; (lauter) Streit; **2.** (sich) streiten
**row·boat** Ruderboot *n*
**row·er** Ruderer *m*, Ruderin *f*
**row house** Reihenhaus *n*
**row·ing boat** *Br* Ruderboot *n*
**roy·al** königlich, Königs...
**roy·al·ty** die königliche Familie; Tantieme *f* (***on*** auf *acc*)
**rub 1.** *v/t* reiben; abreiben; polieren; ***~ dry*** trocken reiben; ***~ it in*** *fig* F darauf herumreiten; ***~ shoulders with*** F verkehren mit; *v/i* reiben, scheuern (***against, on*** an *dat*); ***~ down*** abreiben, trocken reiben; abschmirgeln, abschleifen; ***~ off*** abreiben; abgehen (*paint etc*); ***~ off on(to)*** *fig* abfärben auf (*acc*); ***~ out*** *Br* ausradieren; **2.** ***give s.th. a ~*** et. abreiben *or* polieren
**rub·ber** Gummi *n*, *m*; *esp Br* Radiergummi *m*; Wischtuch *n*; F Gummi *m*
**rub·ber band** Gummiband *n*
**rub·ber din·ghy** Schlauchboot *n*
**rub·ber·neck** F **1.** neugierig gaffen; **2.** *a.* ***rubbernecker*** Gaffer(in), Schaulustige *m*, *f*
**rub·ber·y** gummiartig; zäh
**rub·bish** *Br* Abfall *m*, Abfälle *pl*, Müll *m*; F Schund *m*; Quatsch *m*, Blödsinn *m*; **~ bin** *Br* Mülleimer *m*; **~ chute** *Br* Müllschlucker *m*
**rub·ble** Schutt *m*; Trümmer *pl*
**ru·by** Rubin *m*; Rubinrot *n*
**ruck·sack** *esp Br* Rucksack *m*
**rud·der** AVIAT, MAR Ruder *n*
**rud·dy** frisch, gesund
**rude** unhöflich, grob; unanständig (*joke etc*); bös (*shock etc*)
**ru·di·men·ta·ry** elementar, Anfangs...; primitiv
**ru·di·ments** Anfangsgründe *pl*
**rue·ful** reuevoll, reumütig
**ruff** Halskrause *f* (*a.* ZO)
**ruf·fle 1.** kräuseln; *Haar* zerzausen; *Federn* sträuben; ***~ s.o.'s composure*** j-n aus der Fassung bringen; **2.** Rüsche *f*
**rug** Vorleger *m*, Brücke *f*; *esp Br* dicke Wolldecke
**rug·by** *a.* ***~ football*** SPORT Rugby *n*
**rug·ged** GEOGR zerklüftet, schroff; TECH robust, stabil; zerfurcht (*face*)
**ru·in 1.** Ruin *m*; *mst pl* Ruine(n *pl*) *f*, Trümmer *pl*; **2.** ruinieren, zerstören
**ru·in·ous** ruinös
**rule 1.** Regel *f*; Spielregel *f*; Vorschrift *f*; Herrschaft *f*; Lineal *n*; ***against the ~s*** regelwidrig; verboten; ***as a ~*** in der Regel; ***as a ~ of thumb*** als Faustregel; ***work to ~*** Dienst nach Vorschrift tun; **2.** *v/t* herrschen über (*acc*); *esp* JUR entscheiden; *Papier* lin(i)ieren; *Linie* zie-

hen; ***be ~d by*** *fig* sich leiten lassen von; beherrscht werden von; ***~ out*** *et.* ausschließen; *v/i* herrschen (***over*** über *acc*); *esp* JUR entscheiden

**rul·er** Herrscher(in); Lineal *n*

**rum** Rum *m*

**rum·ble** rumpeln (*vehicle*); (g)rollen (*thunder*); knurren (*stomach*)

**ru·mi·nant** zo Wiederkäuer *m*

**ru·mi·nate** zo wiederkäuen

**rum·mage** F **1.** *a.* ***~ about*** herumstöbern, herumwühlen (***among, in, through*** in *dat*); **2.** Ramsch *m*; **~ sale** Wohltätigkeitsbasar *m*

**ru·mo(u)r 1.** Gerücht *n*; ***~ has it that*** es geht das Gerücht, dass; **2.** ***it is ~ed that*** es geht das Gerücht, dass; ***he is ~ed to be ...*** man munkelt, er sei ...

**rump** F Hinterteil *n*

**rum·ple** zerknittern, zerknüllen, zerwühlen; *Haar* zerzausen

**run 1.** *v/i* laufen (*a.* SPORT), rennen; fahren, verkehren, gehen (*train, bus etc*); laufen, fließen; zerfließen, zerlaufen (*butter, paint etc*); TECH laufen (*engine*), in Betrieb *or* Gang sein; verlaufen (*road etc*); *esp* JUR gelten, laufen (***for one year*** ein Jahr); THEA *etc* laufen (***for three months*** drei Monate lang); lauten (*text*); gehen (*melody*); POL kandidieren (***for*** für); ***~ dry*** austrocknen; ***~ low*** knapp werden; ***~ short*** knapp werden; ***~ short of gas*** (*Br* ***petrol***) kein Benzin mehr haben; *v/t Strecke*, *Rennen* laufen; *Zug*, *Bus* fahren *or* verkehren lassen; *Wasser*, *Maschine etc* laufen lassen; *Geschäft*, *Hotel etc* führen, leiten; *Zeitungsartikel etc* abdrucken, bringen; ***~ s.o. home*** F j-n nach Hause bringen *or* fahren; ***be ~ning a temperature*** erhöhte Temperatur *or* Fieber haben; → ***errand***; ***~ across*** *j-n* zufällig treffen; stoßen auf (*acc*); ***~ after*** hinterherlaufen, nachlaufen (*dat*); ***~ along!*** F ab mit dir!; ***~ away*** davonlaufen (***from*** vor *dat*); ***~ away with*** durchbrennen mit; durchgehen mit (*feelings etc*); ***~ down*** MOT anfahren, umfahren; F schlecht machen; ausfindig machen; ablaufen (*watch*); leer werden (*battery*); ***~ in*** *Wagen etc* einfahren; F *Verbrecher* schnappen; ***~ into*** laufen *or* fahren gegen; *j-n* zufällig treffen; *fig* geraten in (*acc*); *fig* sich belaufen auf (*acc*); ***~ off with*** → ***run away with***; ***~ on*** weitergehen, sich hinziehen (***until*** bis); F unaufhörlich reden (***about*** über *acc*, von); ***~ out*** ablaufen (*time etc*); ausgehen, zu Ende gehen (*supplies etc*); ***~ out of gas*** (*Br* ***petrol***) kein Benzin mehr haben; ***~ over*** MOT überfahren; überlaufen, überfließen; ***~ through*** überfliegen, durchgehen, durchlesen; ***~ up*** *Flagge* hissen; *hohe Rechnung*, *Schulden* machen; ***~ up against*** stoßen auf (*acc*); **2.** Lauf *m* (*a.* SPORT); Fahrt *f*; Spazierfahrt *f*; Ansturm *m*, ECON *a.* Run *m* (***on*** auf *acc*); THEA *etc* Laufzeit *f*; Laufmasche *f*; Gehege *n*; Auslauf *m*, (*Hühner*)Hof *m*; SPORT (*Bob-*, *Rodel-*) Bahn *f*; (*Ski*)Hang *m*; ***~ of good*** (***bad***) ***luck*** Glückssträhne *f* (Pechsträhne *f*); ***in the long ~*** auf die Dauer; ***in the short ~*** zunächst; ***on the ~*** auf der Flucht

**run·a·bout** F MOT Stadt-, Kleinwagen *m*

**run·a·way** Ausreißer(in)

**rung** Sprosse *f*

**run·ner** SPORT Läufer(in); Rennpferd *n*; *mst in cpds* Schmuggler(in); (*Schlitten-*, *Schlittschuh*)Kufe *f*; Tischläufer *m*; TECH (Gleit)Schiene *f*; BOT Ausläufer *m*; **~ bean** *Br* BOT grüne Bohne

**run-up** SPORT Zweite *m*, *f*, Vizemeister(in)

**run·ning 1.** Laufen *n*, Rennen *n*; Führung *f*, Leitung *f*; **2.** fließend; SPORT Lauf...; ***two days ~*** zwei Tage hintereinander; **~ costs** ECON Betriebskosten *pl*, laufende Kosten *pl*

**run·ny** F flüssig; laufend (*nose*), tränend (*eyes*)

**run-off** POL Stichwahl *f*

**run·way** AVIAT Start- und Landebahn *f*, Rollbahn *f*, Piste *f*

**rup·ture 1.** Bruch *m* (*a.* MED *and fig*), Riss *m*; **2.** bersten, platzen; (zer)reißen; ***~ o.s.*** MED sich e-n Bruch heben *or* zuziehen

**ru·ral** ländlich

**ruse** List *f*, Trick *m*

**rush[1] 1.** *v/i* hasten, hetzen, stürmen, rasen; ***~ at*** losstürzen *or* sich stürzen auf (*acc*); ***~ in*** hineinstürzen, hineinstürmen, hereinstürzen, hereinstürmen; ***~ into*** *fig* sich stürzen in (*acc*); *et.* überstürzen; *v/t* antreiben, drängen, hetzen; schnell bringen; *Essen* hinunterschlingen; losstürmen auf (*acc*); ***don't ~ it*** lass

R

dir Zeit dabei; **2.** Ansturm *m*; Hast *f*, Hetze *f*; Hochbetrieb *m*; ECON stürmische Nachfrage; ***what's all the ~?*** wozu diese Eile *or* Hetze?
**rush**[2] BOT Binse *f*
**rush hour** Rushhour *f*, Hauptverkehrszeit *f*, Stoßzeit *f*
**rush-hour traf·fic** Stoßverkehr *m*
**rusk** *esp Br* Zwieback *m*
**Rus·sia** Russland *n*
**Rus·sian 1.** russisch; **2.** Russe *m*, Russin *f*; LING Russisch *n*
**rust 1.** Rost *m*; **2.** *v/t* (ein-, ver)rosten lassen; *v/i* (ein-, ver)rosten
**rus·tic** ländlich, bäuerlich; rustikal
**rus·tle 1.** rascheln (mit), knistern; *Vieh* stehlen; **2.** Rascheln *n*
**rust·proof** rostfrei, nicht rostend
**rust·y** rostig; *fig* eingerostet
**rut**[1] **1.** (Rad)Spur *f*, Furche *f*; *fig* (alter) Trott; ***the daily ~*** das tägliche Einerlei; **2.** furchen; ***rutted*** ausgefahren
**rut**[2] ZO Brunft *f*, Brunst *f*
**ruth·less** unbarmherzig; rücksichtslos, skrupellos
**rye** BOT Roggen *m*

# S

**S, s** S, s *n*
**S** ABBR *of* ***small*** (***size***) klein
**sa·ber,** *Br* **sa·bre** Säbel *m*
**sa·ble** ZO Zobel *m*; Zobelpelz *m*
**sab·o·tage 1.** Sabotage *f*; **2.** sabotieren
**sack 1.** Sack *m*; ***get the ~*** *Br* F rausgeschmissen werden; ***give s.o. the ~*** *Br* F j-n rausschmeißen; ***hit the ~*** F sich in die Falle *or* Klappe hauen; **2.** in Säcke füllen, einsacken; *Br* F *j-n* rausschmeißen
**sack·cloth, sack·ing** Sackleinen *n*
**sac·ra·ment** REL Sakrament *n*
**sa·cred** geistlich (*music etc*); heilig
**sac·ri·fice 1.** Opfer *n*; **2.** opfern
**sac·ri·lege** REL Sakrileg *n*; Frevel *m*
**sac·ris·ty** REL Sakristei *f*
**sad** traurig; schmerzlich; schlimm
**sad·dle 1.** Sattel *m*; **2.** satteln
**sa·dism** Sadismus *m*
**sa·dist** Sadist(in)
**sa·dis·tic** sadistisch
**sad·ness** Traurigkeit *f*
**sa·fa·ri** Safari *f*; **~ park** Safaripark *m*
**safe 1.** sicher; **2.** Safe *m*, *n*, Tresor *m*, Geldschrank *m*
**safe con·duct** freies Geleit
**safe de·pos·it** Tresor *m*
**safe-de·pos·it box** Schließfach *n*
**safe·guard 1.** Schutz *m* (***against*** gegen, vor *dat*); **2.** schützen (***against, from*** gegen, vor *dat*)
**safe·keep·ing** sichere Verwahrung
**safe·ty 1.** Sicherheit *f*; **2.** Sicherheits...; **~ belt** → ***seat belt***; **~ is·land** Verkehrsinsel *f*; **~ lock** Sicherheitsschloss *n*; **~ mea·sure** Sicherheitsmaßnahme *f*; **~ pin** Sicherheitsnadel *f*; **~ ra·zor** Rasierapparat *m*
**sag** sich senken, absacken; durchhängen; (herab)hängen (*shoulders*); *fig* sinken (*morale*); nachlassen (*interest etc*)
**sa·ga·cious** scharfsinnig
**sa·ga·ci·ty** Scharfsinn *m*
**sage** BOT Salbei *m*, *f*
**Sa·git·tar·i·us** ASTR Schütze *m*; ***he*** (***she***) ***is*** (***a***) **~** er (sie) ist (ein) Schütze
**sail 1.** Segel *n*; Segelfahrt *f*; (*Windmühlen*)Flügel *m*; ***set ~*** auslaufen (***for*** nach); ***go for a ~*** segeln gehen; **2.** *v/i* MAR segeln, fahren; auslaufen (***for*** nach); gleiten, schweben; ***go ~ing*** segeln gehen; *v/t* MAR befahren; *Schiff* steuern, *Boot* segeln
**sail·board** Surfbrett *n*
**sail·boat** Segelboot *n*
**sail·ing** Segeln *n*; Segelsport *m*; ***when is the next ~ to ...?*** wann fährt das nächste Schiff nach ...?; **~ boat** *Br* Segelboot *n*; **~ ship** Segelschiff *n*
**sail·or** Seemann *m*, Matrose *m*; ***be a good*** (***bad***) **~** (nicht) seefest sein
**sail·plane** Segelflugzeug *n*
**saint** Heilige *m*, *f*

**saint·ly** heilig, fromm
**sake:** ***for the ~ of ...*** um ... (*gen*) willen; ***for my ~*** meinetwegen; ***for God's ~*** F um Gottes willen
**sal·a·ble** verkäuflich
**sal·ad** Salat *m*; **~ dress·ing** Dressing *n*, Salatsoße *f*
**sal·a·ried:** ***~ employee*** Angestellte *m*, *f*, Gehaltsempfänger(in)
**sal·a·ry** Gehalt *n*
**sale** Verkauf *m*; Absatz *m*, Umsatz *m*; (Saison)Schlussverkauf *m*; Auktion *f*, Versteigerung *f*; ***for ~*** zu verkaufen; ***not for ~*** unverkäuflich; ***be on ~*** verkauft werden, erhältlich sein
**sale·a·ble** → ***salable***
**sales·clerk** (Laden)Verkäufer(in)
**sales·girl** (Laden)Verkäuferin *f*
**sales·man** Verkäufer *m*; (Handels-) Vertreter *m*
**sales rep·re·sen·ta·tive** Handlungsreisende *m*, *f*; (Handels)Vertreter(in)
**sales slip** ECON Quittung *f*
**sales tax** ECON Umsatzsteuer *f*
**sales·wom·an** Verkäuferin *f*; (Handels)Vertreterin *f*
**sa·line** salzig, Salz...
**sa·li·va** Speichel *m*
**sal·low** gelblich
**salm·on** ZO Lachs *m*
**sal·on** (*Schönheits- etc*)Salon *m*
**sa·loon** *Br* MOT Limousine *f*; HIST Saloon *m*; MAR Salon *m*
**sa·loon car** *Br* MOT Limousine *f*
**salt 1.** Salz *n*; **2.** salzen; (ein)pökeln, einsalzen (*a.* ***~ down***); *Straße etc* (mit Salz) streuen; **3.** Salz...; gepökelt; salzig, gesalzen
**salt·cel·lar** *Br* Salzstreuer *m*
**salt·pe·ter,** *esp Br* **salt·pe·tre** CHEM Salpeter *m*
**salt shak·er** Salzstreuer *m*
**salt wa·ter** Salzwasser *n*
**salt·y** salzig
**sal·u·ta·tion** Gruß *m*, Begrüßung *f*; Anrede *f*; **sa·lute 1.** MIL salutieren; (be)grüßen; **2.** Gruß *m*; MIL Ehrenbezeugung *f*; Salut *m*
**sal·vage 1.** Bergung *f*; Bergungsgut *n*; **2.** bergen (***from*** aus); retten (*a. fig*)
**sal·va·tion** Rettung *f*; REL Erlösung *f*; (Seelen)Heil *n*
**Sal·va·tion Ar·my** Heilsarmee *f*
**salve** (Heil)Salbe *f*
**same:** ***the ~*** derselbe, dieselbe, dasselbe; ***all the ~*** trotzdem; ***it is all the ~ to me*** es ist mir ganz egal
**sam·ple 1.** Muster *n*, Probe *f*; **2.** kosten, probieren
**san·a·to·ri·um** Sanatorium *n*
**sanc·ti·fy** heiligen
**sanc·tion 1.** Billigung *f*, Zustimmung *f*; *mst pl* Sanktionen *pl*; **2.** billigen, sanktionieren
**sanc·ti·ty** Heiligkeit *f*
**sanc·tu·a·ry** Zuflucht *f*, Asyl *n*; ZO Schutzgebiet *n*
**sand 1.** Sand *m*; *pl* Sandfläche *f*; **2.** *Straße etc* mit Sand (be)streuen; TECH schmirgeln
**san·dal** Sandale *f*
**sand·bag** Sandsack *m*
**sand·bank** GEOGR Sandbank *f*
**sand·box** Sandkasten *m*
**sand·cas·tle** Sandburg *f*
**sand·man** Sandmännchen *n*
**sand·pa·per** Sand-, Schmirgelpapier *n*
**sand·pip·er** ZO Strandläufer *m*
**sand·pit** *Br* Sandkasten *m*; Sandgrube *f*
**sand·stone** GEOL Sandstein *m*
**sand·storm** Sandsturm *m*
**sand·wich 1.** Sandwich *n*; **2.** ***be ~ed between*** eingekeilt sein zwischen (*dat*); ***~ s.th. in between*** *fig* et. einschieben zwischen (*acc or dat*)
**sand·y** sandig; rotblond
**sane** geistig gesund; JUR zurechnungsfähig; vernünftig
**san·i·tar·i·um** → ***sanatorium***
**san·i·ta·ry** hygienisch; Gesundheits...; **~ nap·kin,** *Br* **~ tow·el** (Damen)Binde *f*
**san·i·ta·tion** sanitäre Einrichtungen *pl*; Kanalisation *f*
**san·i·ty** geistige Gesundheit; JUR Zurechnungsfähigkeit *f*
**San·ta Claus** der Weihnachtsmann, der Nikolaus
**sap**[1] BOT Saft *m*
**sap**[2] schwächen
**sap·phire** Saphir *m*
**sar·casm** Sarkasmus *m*
**sar·cas·tic** sarkastisch
**sar·dine** ZO Sardine *f*
**sash**[1] Schärpe *f*
**sash**[2] Fensterrahmen *m*
**sash win·dow** Schiebefenster *n*
**sas·sy** frech

**Sat** ABBR *of* ***Saturday*** Sa., Samstag *m*, Sonnabend *m*
**Sa·tan** der Satan
**satch·el** (Schul)Ranzen *m*; Schultasche *f*
**sat·ed** *fig* übersättigt
**sat·el·lite 1.** Satellit *m*; ***by*** *or* ***via*** ~ über Satellit; **2.** Satelliten...; ~ ***dish*** F Satellitenschüssel *f*
**sat·in** Satin *m*
**sat·ire** Satire *f*
**sat·ir·ic, sat·ir·i·cal** satirisch
**sat·i·rist** Satiriker(in)
**sat·ir·ize** verspotten
**sat·is·fac·tion** Befriedigung *f*; Genugtuung *f*, Zufriedenheit *f*
**sat·is·fac·to·ry** befriedigend, zufrieden stellend
**sat·is·fy** befriedigen, zufrieden stellen; überzeugen; ***be satisfied that*** davon überzeugt sein, dass
**sat·u·rate** (durch)tränken (***with*** mit); CHEM sättigen (*a. fig*)
**Sat·ur·day** Sonnabend *m*, Samstag *m*; ***on*** ~ (am) Sonnabend *or* Samstag; ***on*** ~***s*** sonnabends, samstags
**sauce** Soße *f*
**sauce·pan** Kochtopf *m*
**sau·cer** Untertasse *f*
**sauc·y** *Br* frech
**saun·ter** bummeln, schlendern
**saus·age** Wurst *f*; *a.* ***small*** ~ Würstchen *n*
**sav·age 1.** wild; unzivilisiert; **2.** Wilde *m, f*; **sav·ag·e·ry** Wildheit *f*; Rohheit *f*, Grausamkeit *f*
**save 1.** retten (***from*** vor *dat*); *Geld, Zeit etc* (ein)sparen; *et.* aufheben, aufsparen (***for*** für); *j-m et.* ersparen; EDP (ab)speichern, sichern; SPORT *Schuss* halten, parieren, *Tor* verhindern; **2.** SPORT Parade *f*
**sav·er** Retter(in); ECON Sparer(in)
**sav·ings** ECON Ersparnisse *pl*; ~ **ac·count** Sparkonto *n*; ~ **bank** Sparkasse *f*; ~ **de·pos·it** Spareinlage *f*
**sa·vio(u)r** Retter(in); ***the Savio(u)r*** REL der Erlöser, der Heiland
**sa·vo(u)r** mit Genuss essen *or* trinken; ~ ***of*** *fig* e-n Beigeschmack haben von
**sa·vo(u)r·y** schmackhaft
**saw 1.** Säge *f*; **2.** sägen
**saw·dust** Sägemehl *n*, Sägespäne *pl*
**saw·mill** Sägewerk *n*
**Sax·on 1.** (Angel)Sachse *m*, (Angel-) Sächsin *f*; **2.** (angel)sächsisch
**say 1.** sagen; aufsagen; *Gebet* sprechen, *Vaterunser* beten; ~ ***grace*** das Tischgebet sprechen; ***what does your watch*** ~***?*** wie spät ist es auf deiner Uhr?; ***he is said to be ...*** er soll ... sein; ***it*** ~***s*** es lautet (*letter etc*); ***it*** ~***s here*** hier heißt es; ***it goes without*** ~***ing*** es versteht sich von selbst; ***no sooner said than done*** gesagt, getan; ***that is to*** ~ das heißt; (***and***) ***that's*** ~***ing s.th.*** (und) das will was heißen; ***you said it*** du sagst es; ***you can*** ~ ***that again!*** das kannst du laut sagen!; ***you don't*** ~ (***so***)***!*** was du nicht sagst!; ***I*** ~ sag(en Sie) mal!; ich muss schon sagen!; ***I can't*** ~ das kann ich nicht sagen; **2.** Mitspracherecht *n* (***in*** bei); ***have one's*** ~ s-e Meinung äußern, zu Wort kommen; ***he always has to have his*** ~ er muss immer mitreden
**say·ing** Sprichwort *n*, Redensart *f*; ***as the*** ~ ***goes*** wie man so (schön) sagt
**scab** MED, BOT Schorf *m*; *contp* Streikbrecher(in)
**scaf·fold** (Bau)Gerüst *n*; Schafott *n*
**scaf·fold·ing** (Bau)Gerüst *n*
**scald 1.** sich *die Zunge etc* verbrühen; *Milch* abkochen; ~***ing hot*** kochend heiß; **2.** MED Verbrühung *f*
**scale[1] 1.** Skala *f* (*a. fig*), Grad- *or* Maßeinteilung *f*; MATH, TECH Maßstab *m* (*a. fig*); Waage *f*; MUS Skala *f*, Tonleiter *f*; *fig* Ausmaß *n*, Umfang *m*; **2.** erklettern; ~ ***down*** *fig* verringern; ~ ***up*** *fig* erhöhen
**scale[2]** Waagschale *f*; (***a pair of***) ~***s*** (e-e) Waage
**scale[3] 1.** ZO Schuppe *f*; TECH Kesselstein *m*; ***the*** ~***s fell from my eyes*** es fiel mir wie Schuppen von den Augen; **2.** *Fisch* (ab)schuppen
**scal·lop** ZO Kammmuschel *f*
**scalp 1.** Kopfhaut *f*; Skalp *m*; **2.** skalpieren
**scal·y** ZO schuppig (*a. fig*)
**scamp** F Schlingel *m*, (kleiner) Strolch
**scam·per** trippeln; huschen
**scan 1.** *et.* absuchen (***for*** nach); *Zeitung etc* überfliegen; EDP, *radar*, TV abtasten, scannen; **2.** MED *etc* Scanning *n*
**scan·dal** Skandal *m*; Klatsch *m*
**scan·dal·ize:** ***be*** ~***d at s.th.*** über et. empört *or* entrüstet sein

**scan·dal·ous** skandalös; ***be ~*** *a.* ein Skandal sein (***that*** dass)
**Scan·di·na·vi·a** Skandinavien *n*
**Scan·di·na·vi·an** **1.** skandinavisch; **2.** Skandinavier(in)
**scan·ner** TECH Scanner *m*
**scant** dürftig, gering
**scant·y** dürftig, kärglich, knapp
**scape·goat** Sündenbock *m*
**scar** MED **1.** Narbe *f* (*a. fig*); **2.** e-e Narbe *or* Narben hinterlassen auf (*dat*) *or fig* bei *j-m*; ***~ over*** vernarben
**scarce** knapp (*food etc*); selten; ***be ~*** Mangelware sein (*a. fig*); **scarce·ly** kaum; **scar·ci·ty** Mangel *m*, Knappheit *f* (***of*** an *dat*)
**scare** **1.** erschrecken; ***be ~d*** Angst haben (***of*** vor *dat*); ***~ away, ~ off*** verjagen, -scheuchen; **2.** Schreck(en) *m*; Panik *f*
**scare·crow** Vogelscheuche *f* (*a. fig*)
**scarf** Schal *m*; Hals-, Kopf-, Schultertuch *n*
**scar·let** scharlachrot; **~ fe·ver** MED Scharlach *m*
**scarred** narbig
**scath·ing** bissig (*remark etc*); vernichtend (*criticism etc*)
**scat·ter** (sich) zerstreuen (*crowd*); ausstreuen, verstreuen; auseinander stieben (*birds etc*)
**scat·ter·brained** F schusselig, schusslig
**scat·tered** verstreut; vereinzelt
**scav·enge:** ***~ on*** zo leben von; ***~ for*** suchen (nach)
**scene** Szene *f*; Schauplatz *m*; *pl* THEA Kulissen *pl*
**sce·ne·ry** Landschaft *f*, Gegend *f*; THEA Bühnenbild *n*, Kulissen *pl*
**scent** **1.** Duft *m*, Geruch *m*; *esp Br* Parfüm *n*; HUNT Witterung *f*; Fährte *f*, Spur *f* (*a. fig*); **2.** wittern; *esp Br* parfümieren; **scent·less** geruchlos
**scep·ter,** *Br* **scep·tre** Zepter *n*
**scep·tic, scep·ti·cal** *Br* → ***skeptic*** *etc*
**sched·ule** **1.** Aufstellung *f*, Verzeichnis *n*; (*Arbeits-, Stunden-, Zeit- etc*)Plan *m*; Fahr-, Flugplan *m*; ***ahead of ~*** dem Zeitplan voraus, früher als vorgesehen; ***be behind ~*** Verspätung haben; im Verzug *or* Rückstand sein; ***on ~*** (fahr-)planmäßig, pünktlich; **2.** ***the meeting is ~d for Monday*** die Sitzung ist für Montag angesetzt; ***it is ~d to take place tomorrow*** es soll morgen stattfinden
**sched·uled| de·par·ture** (fahr)planmäßige Abfahrt; **~ flight** Linienflug *m*
**scheme** **1.** *esp Br* Programm *n*, Projekt *n*; Schema *n*, System *n*; Intrige *f*, Machenschaft *f*; **2.** intrigieren
**schmaltz·y** F schnulzig
**schnit·zel** GASTR Wiener Schnitzel *n*
**schol·ar** Gelehrte *m*, *f*; UNIV Stipendiat(in); **schol·ar·ly** gelehrt
**schol·ar·ship** Gelehrsamkeit *f*; UNIV Stipendium *n*
**school**[1] **1.** Schule *f* (*a. fig*); UNIV Fakultät *f*; Hochschule *f*; ***at ~*** auf *or* in der Schule; ***go to ~*** in die *or* zur Schule gehen; **2.** *j-n* schulen, unterrichten; *Tier* dressieren
**school**[2] zo Schule *f*, Schwarm *m*
**school·bag** Schultasche *f*
**school·boy** Schüler *m*
**school·child** Schulkind *n*
**school·fel·low** → ***schoolmate***
**school·girl** Schülerin *f*
**school·ing** (Schul)Ausbildung *f*
**school·mate** Mitschüler(in), Schulkamerad(in)
**school·teach·er** (Schul)Lehrer(in)
**school·yard** Schulhof *m*
**schoo·ner** MAR Schoner *m*
**sci·ence** Wissenschaft *f*; *a.* ***natural ~*** Naturwissenschaft(en *pl*) *f*; **~ fic·tion** (ABBR ***SF***) Sciencefiction *f*
**sci·en·tif·ic** (natur)wissenschaftlich; exakt, systematisch
**sci·en·tist** (Natur)Wissenschaftler(in)
**sci-fi** F Sciencefiction *f*
**scis·sors:** (***a pair of ~*** e-e) Schere
**scoff** **1.** spotten (***at*** über *acc*); **2.** spöttische Bemerkung
**scold** schimpfen (mit)
**scoop** **1.** Schöpfkelle *f*; (*Mehl- etc* -)Schaufel *f*; (*Eis- etc*)Portionierer *m*; Kugel *f* (*icecream*); *newspaper, radio,* TV Exklusivmeldung *f*, F Knüller *m*; **2.** schöpfen, schaufeln; ***~ up*** aufheben, hochheben
**scoot·er** (Kinder)Roller *m*; (*Motor-*)Roller *m*
**scope** Bereich *m*; Spielraum *m*
**scorch** *v/t* ansengen, versengen, verbrennen; ausdörren; *v/i Br* MOT F rasen
**score** **1.** SPORT (Spiel)Stand *m*, (-)Ergebnis *n*; MUS Partitur *f*; Musik *f*; 20

(Stück); *a.* ~ **mark** Kerbe *f*, Rille *f*; **what is the ~?** wie steht es *or* das Spiel?; **the ~ stood at** *or* **was 3-2** das Spiel stand 3:2; **keep (the) ~** anschreiben; **~s of** e-e Menge; **four ~ and ten** neunzig; **on that ~** deshalb, in dieser Hinsicht; **have a ~ to settle with s.o.** e-e alte Rechnung mit j-m zu begleichen haben; **2.** *v/t* SPORT *Punkte, Treffer* erzielen, *Tor a.* schießen; *Erfolg, Sieg* erringen; MUS instrumentieren; die Musik schreiben zu *or* für; einkerben; *v/i* SPORT e-n Treffer *etc* erzielen, ein Tor schießen; erfolgreich sein

**score·board** SPORT Anzeigetafel *f*

**scor·er** SPORT Torschütze *m*, Torschützin *f*; Anschreiber(in)

**scorn** Verachtung *f*

**scorn·ful** verächtlich

**Scor·pi·o** ASTR Skorpion *m*; **he (she) is (a) ~** er (sie) ist (ein) Skorpion

**Scot** Schotte *m*, Schottin *f*

**Scotch 1.** schottisch; **2.** Scotch *m*

**scot-free:** F **get off ~** ungeschoren davonkommen

**Scot·land** Schottland *n*

**Scots** schottisch; **Scotsman** Schotte *m*; **Scots·wom·an** Schottin *f*

**Scot·tish** schottisch

**scoun·drel** Schurke *m*

**scour**[1] scheuern, schrubben

**scour**[2] *Gegend* absuchen, durchkämmen (**for** nach)

**scourge 1.** Geißel *f* (*a. fig*); **2.** geißeln, *fig a.* heimsuchen

**scout 1.** *esp* MIL Kundschafter *m*; *Br* motorisierter Pannenhelfer; *a.* **boy ~** Pfadfinder *m*; *a.* **girl ~** Pfadfinderin *f*; *a.* **talent ~** Talentsucher(in); **2. ~ about, ~ around** sich umsehen (**for** nach); *a.* **~ out** MIL auskundschaften

**scowl 1.** finsteres Gesicht; **2.** finster blicken; **~ at s.o.** j-n böse *or* finster anschauen

**scram·ble 1.** klettern; sich drängeln (**for** zu); **2.** Kletterei *f*; Drängelei *f*

**scram·bled eggs** Rührei(er *pl*) *n*

**scrap**[1] **1.** Stückchen *n*, Fetzen *m*; Altmaterial *n*; Schrott *m*; *pl* Abfall *m*, Speisereste *pl*; **2.** verschrotten; ausrangieren; *Plan etc* aufgeben, fallen lassen

**scrap**[2] F **1.** Streiterei *f*; Balgerei *f*; **2.** sich streiten; sich balgen

**scrap·book** Sammelalbum *n*

**scrape 1.** (ab)kratzen, (ab)schaben; sich *die Knie etc* aufschürfen; *Wagen etc* ankratzen; scheuern (**against** an *dat*); (entlang)streifen; scharren; **2.** Kratzen *n*; Kratzer *m*, Schramme *f*; *fig* Klemme *f*

**scrap heap** Schrotthaufen *m*

**scrap met·al** Altmetall *n*, Schrott *m*

**scrap pa·per** *esp Br* Schmierpapier *n*

**scrap val·ue** Schrottwert *m*

**scrap·yard** Schrottplatz *m*

**scratch 1.** (zer)kratzen; abkratzen; *s-n Namen etc* einkratzen; (sich) kratzen; scharren; **2.** Kratzer *m*, Schramme *f*; Gekratze *n*; Kratzen *n*; **from ~** F ganz von vorn; **3.** (bunt) zusammengewürfelt

**scratch·pad** Notiz-, Schmierblock *m*

**scratch pa·per** Schmierpapier *n*

**scrawl 1.** kritzeln; **2.** Gekritzel *n*

**scraw·ny** dürr

**scream 1.** schreien (**with** vor *dat*); *a.* **~ out** schreien; **~ with laughter** vor Lachen brüllen; **2.** Schrei *m*; **~s of laughter** brüllendes Gelächter; **be a ~** F zum Schreien (komisch) sein

**screech 1.** kreischen (*a. fig*), (gellend) schreien; **2.** Kreischen *n*; (gellender) Schrei

**screen 1.** Wand-, Ofen-, Schutzschirm *m*; *film*: Leinwand *f*; *radar*, TV, EDP Bildschirm *m*; Fliegenfenster *n*, -gitter *n*; *fig* Tarnung *f*; **2.** abschirmen; *film* zeigen, *Fernsehprogramm a.* senden; *fig j-n* decken; *fig j-n* überprüfen; **~ off** abtrennen

**screen·play** Drehbuch *n*

**screen sav·er** EDP Bildschirmschoner *m*

**screw 1.** TECH Schraube *f*; **he has a ~ loose** F bei ihm ist e-e Schraube locker; **2.** (an)schrauben (**to** an *acc*); V bumsen, vögeln; **~ up** *Gesicht* verziehen; *Augen* zusammenkneifen; **~ up one's courage** sich ein Herz fassen

**screw·ball** F Spinner(in)

**screw·driv·er** Schraubenzieher *m*

**screw top** Schraubverschluss *m*

**scrib·ble 1.** (hin)kritzeln; **2.** Gekritzel *n*

**scrimp: ~ and save** jeden Pfennig zweimal umdrehen

**script** Manuskript *n*; *film*, TV Drehbuch *n*, Skript *n*; THEA Text *m*, Textbuch *n*; Schrift(zeichen *pl*) *f*; *Br* UNIV (schriftliche) Prüfungsarbeit

**Scrip·ture** *a.* **the ~s** REL die Heilige Schrift
**scroll 1.** Schriftrolle *f*; **2. ~ down (up)** EDP zurückrollen (vorrollen)
**scro·tum** ANAT Hodensack *m*
**scrub[1] 1.** schrubben, scheuern; **2.** Schrubben *n*, Scheuern *n*
**scrub[2]** Gebüsch *n*, Gestrüpp *n*
**scru·ple 1.** Skrupel *m*, Zweifel *m*, Bedenken *pl*; **2.** Bedenken haben
**scru·pu·lous** gewissenhaft
**scru·ti·nize** genau prüfen; mustern
**scru·ti·ny** genaue Prüfung; prüfender Blick
**scu·ba div·ing** (Sport)Tauchen *n*
**scuf·fle 1.** Handgemenge *n*, Rauferei *f*; **2.** sich raufen
**scull 1.** Skull *n*; Skullboot *n*; **2.** rudern, skullen
**sculp·tor** Bildhauer *m*
**sculp·ture 1.** Bildhauerei *f*; Skulptur *f*, Plastik *f*; **2.** hauen, meißeln, formen
**scum** Schaum *m*; *fig* Abschaum *m*; **the ~ of the earth** *fig* der Abschaum der Menschheit
**scurf** (Kopf)Schuppen *pl*
**scur·ri·lous** beleidigend; verleumderisch
**scur·ry** huschen; trippeln
**scur·vy** MED Skorbut *m*
**scut·tle: ~ away, ~ off** davonhuschen
**scythe** Sense *f*
**sea** Meer *n* (*a. fig*), See *f*; **at ~** auf See; **be all** *or* **completely at ~** *fig* F völlig ratlos sein; **by ~** auf dem Seeweg; **by the ~** am Meer
**sea·food** GASTR Meeresfrüchte *pl*
**sea·gull** ZO Seemöwe *f*
**seal[1]** ZO Robbe *f*, Seehund *m*
**seal[2] 1.** Siegel *n*; TECH Plombe *f*; TECH Dichtung *f*; **2.** (ver)siegeln; TECH plombieren; abdichten; *fig* besiegeln; **~ed envelope** verschlossener Briefumschlag; **~ off** *Gegend etc* abriegeln
**sea lev·el: above (below) ~** über (unter) dem Meeresspiegel
**seal·ing wax** Siegellack *m*
**seam** Naht *f*; Fuge *f*; GEOL Flöz *n*
**sea·man** Seemann *m*
**seam·stress** Näherin *f*
**sea·plane** Wasserflugzeug *n*
**sea·port** Seehafen *m*; Hafenstadt *f*
**sea pow·er** Seemacht *f*
**search 1.** *v/i* suchen (**for** nach); **~ through** durchsuchen; *v/t j-n, et.* durchsuchen (**for** nach); **~ me!** F keine Ahnung!; **2.** Suche *f* (**for** nach); Fahndung *f* (**for** nach); Durchsuchung *f*; **in ~ of** auf der Suche nach; **search·ing** prüfend (*look*); eingehend (*examination*)
**search·light** (Such)Scheinwerfer *m*
**search par·ty** Suchmannschaft *f*
**search war·rant** JUR Haussuchungs-, Durchsuchungsbefehl *m*
**sea·shore** Meeresküste *f*
**sea·sick** seekrank
**sea·side: at** *or* **by the ~** am Meer; **go to the ~** ans Meer fahren
**sea·side re·sort** Seebad *n*
**sea·son[1]** Jahreszeit *f*; Saison *f*, THEA *etc a.* Spielzeit *f*, (*Jagd-, Urlaubs- etc*)Zeit *f*; **in (out of) ~** in (außerhalb) der (Hoch)Saison; **cherries are now in ~** jetzt ist Kirschenzeit; **Season's Greetings!** Frohe Weihnachten!; **with the compliments of the ~** mit den besten Wünschen zum Fest
**sea·son[2]** *Speise* würzen (**with** mit); *Holz* ablagern
**sea·son·al** saisonbedingt, Saison...
**sea·son·ing** GASTR Gewürz *n*
**sea·son tick·et** RAIL *etc* Dauer-, Zeitkarte *f*; THEA Abonnement *n*
**seat 1.** Sitz(gelegenheit *f*) *m*; (Sitz)Platz *m*; Sitz(fläche *f*) *m*; Hosenboden *m*; Hinterteil *n*; (*Geschäfts-, Regierungs- etc*)Sitz *m*; PARL Sitz *m*; **take a ~** Platz nehmen; **take one's ~** s-n Platz einnehmen; **2.** *j-n* setzen; Sitzplätze bieten für; **be ~ed** sitzen; **please be ~ed** bitte nehmen Sie Platz; **remain ~ed** sitzen bleiben
**seat belt** AVIAT, MOT Sicherheitsgurt *m*; **fasten one's ~** sich anschnallen
**sea ur·chin** ZO Seeigel *m*
**sea·ward(s)** seewärts
**sea·weed** BOT (See)Tang *m*
**sea·wor·thy** seetüchtig
**sec** F Augenblick *m*, Sekunde *f*; **just a ~** Augenblick(, bitte)!
**se·cede** sich abspalten (**from** von)
**se·ces·sion** Abspaltung *f*, Sezession *f* (**from** von)
**se·clud·ed** abgelegen, abgeschieden (*place*); zurückgezogen (*life*)
**se·clu·sion** Abgeschiedenheit *f*; Zurückgezogenheit *f*

**sec·ond**[1] **1.** *adj* zweite(r, -s); ***every ~ day*** jeden zweiten Tag, alle zwei Tage; ***~ to none*** unerreicht, unübertroffen; ***but on ~ thought*** (*Br* ***thoughts***) aber wenn ich es mir so überlege; **2.** *adv* als Zweite(r, -s); **3.** *der, die, das* Zweite; MOT zweiter Gang; Sekundant *m*; *pl* F ECON Waren *pl* zweiter Wahl; **4.** *Antrag etc* unterstützen

**sec·ond**[2] Sekunde *f*; *fig* Augenblick *m*, Sekunde *f*; ***just a ~*** Augenblick(, bitte)!

**sec·ond·a·ry** sekundär, zweitrangig; PED höher

**sec·ond-best** zweitbeste(r, -s)

**sec·ond class** RAIL *etc* zweiter Klasse

**sec·ond-class** zweitklassig

**sec·ond floor** erster (*Br* zweiter) Stock

**sec·ond hand** Sekundenzeiger *m*

**sec·ond-hand** aus zweiter Hand; gebraucht; antiquarisch

**sec·ond·ly** zweitens

**sec·ond-rate** zweitklassig

**se·cre·cy** Verschwiegenheit *f*; Geheimhaltung *f*

**se·cret 1.** geheim, Geheim...; heimlich; verschwiegen; **2.** Geheimnis *n*; ***in ~*** heimlich, im Geheimen; ***keep s.th. a ~*** et. geheim halten (***from*** vor *dat*); ***can you keep a ~?*** kannst du schweigen?

**se·cret a·gent** Geheimagent(in)

**sec·re·ta·ry** Sekretär(in); POL Minister(in)

**Sec·re·ta·ry of State** POL Außenminister(in); *Br* Minister(in)

**se·crete** MED absondern; **se·cre·tion** MED Sekret *n*; Absonderung *f*

**se·cre·tive** verschlossen

**se·cret·ly** heimlich

**se·cret ser·vice** Geheimdienst *m*

**sec·tion** Teil *m*; Abschnitt *m*; JUR Paragraf *m*; Abteilung *f*; MATH, TECH Schnitt *m*

**sec·tor** Sektor *m*, Bereich *m*

**sec·u·lar** weltlich

**se·cure 1.** sicher (***against, from*** vor *dat*); **2.** *Tür etc* fest verschließen; *et.* sichern (***against, from*** vor *dat*)

**se·cu·ri·ty** Sicherheit *f*; *pl* ECON Wertpapiere *pl*; **~ check** Sicherheitskontrolle *f*; **~ mea·sure** Sicherheitsmaßnahme *f*; **~ risk** Sicherheitsrisiko *n*

**se·dan** MOT Limousine *f*

**se·date** ruhig, gelassen

**sed·a·tive** *mst* MED **1.** beruhigend; **2.** Beruhigungsmittel *n*

**sed·i·ment** (Boden)Satz *m*

**se·duce** verführen

**se·duc·er** Verführer(in)

**se·duc·tion** Verführung *f*

**se·duc·tive** verführerisch

**see**[1] *v/i* sehen; nachsehen; ***I ~!*** (ich) verstehe!, ach so!; ***you ~*** weißt du; ***let me ~*** warte mal, lass mich überlegen; ***we'll ~*** mal sehen; *v/t* sehen; besuchen; *j-n* aufsuchen, *j-n* konsultieren; ***~ s.o. home*** j-n nach Hause bringen *or* begleiten; ***~ you!*** bis dann!, auf bald!; ***~ about*** sehen nach, sich kümmern um; ***~ off*** *j-n* verabschieden (***at*** am *Bahnhof etc*); ***~ out*** *j-n* hinausbringen, hinausbegleiten; ***~ through*** *j-n, et.* durchschauen; *j-m* hinweghelfen über (*acc*); ***~ to it that*** dafür sorgen, dass

**see**[2] REL Bistum *n*, Diözese *f*; ***Holy See*** *der* Heilige Stuhl

**seed 1.** BOT Same(n) *m*; AGR Saat *f*, Saatgut *n*; (*Apfel- etc*)Kern *m*; SPORT gesetzter Spieler, gesetzte Spielerin; ***go*** *or* ***run to ~*** BOT schießen; ***go to ~*** F herunterkommen, verkommen; **2.** *v/t* besäen; entkernen; SPORT *Spieler* setzen; *v/i* BOT in Samen schießen

**seedless** BOT kernlos

**seed·y** F heruntergekommen

**seek** *Schutz, Wahrheit etc* suchen

**seem** scheinen; **seem·ing** scheinbar

**seep** sickern

**see·saw** Wippe *f*, Wippschaukel *f*

**seethe** schäumen (*a. fig*); *fig* kochen

**see-through** durchsichtig

**seg·ment** Teil *m, n*; Stück *n*; Abschnitt *m*; Segment *n*

**seg·re·gate** trennen

**seg·re·ga·tion** Rassentrennung *f*

**seize** *j-n, et.* packen, ergreifen; *Macht etc* an sich reißen; *et.* beschlagnahmen; *et.* pfänden; **sei·zure** Beschlagnahme *f*; Pfändung *f*; MED Anfall *m*

**sel·dom** *adv* selten

**se·lect 1.** (aus)wählen; **2.** ausgewählt; exklusiv; **se·lec·tion** (Aus)Wahl *f*; ECON Auswahl *f* (***of*** an *dat*)

**self** Ich *n*, Selbst *n*

**self-as·sured** selbstbewusst, -sicher

**self-cen·tered,** *Br* **self-cen·tred** egozentrisch

**self-col·o(u)red** einfarbig

**self-con·fi·dence** Selbstbewusstsein *n*, Selbstvertrauen *n*
**self-con·fi·dent** selbstbewusst
**self-con·scious** befangen, gehemmt, unsicher
**self-con·tained** (in sich) abgeschlossen; *fig* verschlossen; **~ flat** *Br* abgeschlossene Wohnung
**self-con·trol** Selbstbeherrschung *f*
**self-crit·i·cal** selbstkritisch
**self-de·fence** *Br*, **self-de·fense** Selbstverteidigung *f*; **in ~** in *or* aus Notwehr
**self-de·ter·mi·na·tion** POL Selbstbestimmung *f*
**self-em·ployed** selbstständig
**self-es·teem** Selbstachtung *f*
**self-ev·i·dent** selbstverständlich; offensichtlich
**self-gov·ern·ment** POL Selbstverwaltung *f*
**self-help** Selbsthilfe *f*; **~ group** Selbsthilfegruppe *f*
**self-im·por·tant** überheblich
**self-in·dul·gent** nachgiebig gegen sich selbst; zügellos
**self-in·terest** Eigennutz *m*
**self·ish** selbstsüchtig, egoistisch
**self-knowl·edge** Selbsterkenntnis *f*
**self-pit·y** Selbstmitleid *n*
**self-por·trait** Selbstportät *n*
**self-pos·sessed** selbstbeherrscht
**self-re·li·ant** selbstständig
**self-re·spect** Selbstachtung *f*
**self-right·eous** selbstgerecht
**self-sat·is·fied** selbstzufrieden
**self-serv·ice 1.** mit Selbstbedienung, Selbstbedienungs...; **2.** Selbstbedienung *f*
**self-stud·y** Selbststudium *n*
**self-suf·fi·cient** ECON autark
**self-sup·port·ing** finanziell unabhängig
**self-willed** eigensinnig, eigenwillig
**sell** *v/t* verkaufen; *v/i* verkauft werden (**at, for** für); sich *gut etc* verkaufen (lassen), gehen; **~ by ...** mindestens haltbar bis ...; **~ off** (*esp* billig) abstoßen; **~ out** ausverkaufen; **be sold out** ausverkauft sein; **~ up** *esp Br sein Geschäft etc* verkaufen; **sell-by date** Mindesthaltbarkeitsdatum *n*; **sell·er** Verkäufer(in); **good ~** ECON gut gehender Artikel
**sem·blance** Anschein *m* (**of** von)
**se·men** MED Samen(flüssigkeit *f*) *m*, Sperma *n*
**se·mes·ter** UNIV Semester *n*
**sem·i...** halb..., Halb...
**sem·i·cir·cle** Halbkreis *m*
**sem·i·co·lon** LING Semikolon *n*, Strichpunkt *m*
**sem·i·con·duc·tor** ELECTR Halbleiter *m*
**sem·i·de·tached (house)** *Br* Doppelhaushälfte *f*
**sem·i·fi·nals** SPORT Semi-, Halbfinale *n*
**sem·i·nar·y** Priesterseminar *n*
**sem·i-pre·cious: ~ stone** Halbedelstein *m*
**sem·i-skilled** angelernt
**sem·o·li·na** Grieß *m*
**sen·ate** POL Senat *m*
**sen·a·tor** POL Senator *m*
**send** *et., a. Grüße, Hilfe etc* senden, schicken (**to** *dat or* an *acc*); *Ware etc* versenden, verschicken (**to** an *acc*); *j-n* schicken (**to** ins *Bett etc*); *with adj or pp*: machen: **~ s.o. mad** j-n wahnsinnig machen; **~ word to s.o.** j-m Nachricht geben; **~ away** fort-, wegschicken; *Brief etc* absenden, abschicken; **~ down** *Preise etc* fallen lassen; **~ for** nach *j-m* schicken, *j-n* kommen lassen; sich *et.* kommen lassen, *et.* anfordern; **~ in** einsenden, einschicken, einreichen; **~ off** fort-, wegschicken; *Brief etc* absenden, abschicken; SPORT *j-n* vom Platz stellen; **~ on** *Brief etc* nachsenden, nachschicken (**to** an *acc*); *Gepäck etc* vorausschicken; **~ out** hinausschicken; *Einladungen etc* verschicken; **~ up** *Preise etc* steigen lassen
**send·er** Absender(in)
**se·nile** senil; **se·nil·i·ty** Senilität *f*
**se·ni·or 1.** senior; älter (**to** als); dienstälter; rangälter; Ober...; **2.** Ältere *m, f*; UNIV Student(in) im letzten Jahr; **he is my ~ by a year** er ist ein Jahr älter als ich; **~ cit·i·zens** ältere Mitbürger *pl*, Senioren *pl*
**se·ni·or·i·ty** (höheres) Alter; (höheres) Dienstalter; (höherer) Rang
**se·ni·or part·ner** ECON Seniorpartner *m*
**sen·sa·tion** Empfindung *f*; Gefühl *n*; Sensation *f*
**sen·sa·tion·al** F großartig, fantastisch; sensationell, Sensations...

S

**sense 1.** Sinn *m*; Verstand *m*; Vernunft *f*; Gefühl *n*; Bedeutung *f*; ***bring s.o. to his ~s*** j-n zur Besinnung *or* Vernunft bringen; ***come to one's ~s*** zur Besinnung *or* Vernunft kommen; ***in a ~*** in gewisser Hinsicht; ***make ~*** e-n Sinn ergeben; vernünftig sein; ***~ of duty*** Pflichtgefühl *n*; ***~ of security*** Gefühl *n* der Sicherheit; **2.** fühlen, spüren

**sense·less** bewusstlos; sinnlos

**sen·si·bil·i·ty** Empfindlichkeit *f*; *a. pl* Empfindsamkeit *f*, Zartgefühl *n*

**sen·si·ble** vernünftig; spürbar, merklich; *esp Br* praktisch (*clothes etc*)

**sen·si·tive** empfindlich; sensibel, empfindsam, feinfühlig

**sen·sor** TECH Sensor *m*

**sen·su·al** sinnlich

**sen·su·ous** sinnlich

**sen·tence 1.** LING Satz *m*; JUR Strafe *f*, Urteil *n*; ***pass*** *or* ***pronounce ~*** das Urteil fällen (***on*** über *acc*); **2.** JUR verurteilen (***to*** zu)

**sen·ti·ment** Gefühle *pl*; Sentimentalität *f*; *a. pl* Ansicht *f*, Meinung *f*

**sen·ti·ment·al** sentimental; gefühlvoll

**sen·ti·men·tal·i·ty** Sentimentalität *f*

**sen·try** MIL Wache *f*, (Wach[t])Posten *m*

**sep·a·ra·ble** trennbar; **sep·a·rate 1.** (sich) trennen; (auf-, ein-, zer)teilen (***into*** in *acc*); **2.** getrennt, separat; einzeln; **sep·a·ra·tion** Trennung *f*; (Auf-, Ein-, Zer)Teilung *f*

**Sept** ABBR *of* ***September*** Sept., September *m*

**Sep·tem·ber** September *m*

**sep·tic** MED vereitert, septisch

**se·quel** Nachfolgeroman *m*, -film *m*, Fortsetzung *f*; *fig* Folge *f*; Nachspiel *n*

**se·quence** (Aufeinander-, Reihen)Folge *f*; *film*, TV Sequenz *f*, Szene *f*; ***~ of tenses*** LING Zeitenfolge *f*

**ser·e·nade** MUS **1.** Serenade *f*, Ständchen *n*; **2.** *j-m* ein Ständchen bringen

**se·rene** klar; heiter; gelassen

**ser·geant** MIL Feldwebel *m*; (Polizei-) Wachtmeister *m*

**se·ri·al 1.** Fortsetzungsroman *m*; (*Rundfunk-*, *Fernseh*)Serie *f*; **2.** serienmäßig, Serien..., Fortsetzungs...

**se·ries** Serie *f*, Reihe *f*, Folge *f*; (*Buch*)Reihe *f*; (*Rundfunk-*, *Fernseh*)Serie *f*, Sendereihe *f*

**se·ri·ous** ernst, ernsthaft; ernstlich; schwer (*illness*, *damage*, *crime etc*); ***be ~*** es ernst meinen (***about*** mit)

**se·ri·ous·ness** Ernst *m*, Ernsthaftigkeit *f*; Schwere *f*

**ser·mon** REL Predigt *f*; F Moral-, Strafpredigt *f*

**ser·pen·tine** gewunden, kurvenreich

**ser·rat·ed** zackig, gezackt

**se·rum** MED Serum *n*

**ser·vant** Diener(in) (*a. fig*); Dienstmädchen *n*; → ***civil servant***

**serve 1.** *v/t j-m*, *s-m Land etc* dienen; *Dienstzeit* (*a.* MIL) ableisten, *Amtszeit etc* durchlaufen; *j-n*, *et.* versorgen (***with*** mit); *Essen* servieren; *Alkohol* ausschenken; *j-n* (*im Laden*) bedienen; JUR *Strafe* verbüßen; *e-m Zweck* dienen; *e-n Zweck* erfüllen; JUR *Vorladung etc* zustellen (***on s.o.*** j-m); *tennis etc*: aufschlagen; ***are you being ~d?*** werden Sie schon bedient?; (***it***) ***~s him right*** F (das) geschieht ihm ganz recht; *v/i esp* MIL dienen; servieren; dienen (***as, for*** als); *tennis etc*: aufschlagen; ***XY to ~*** *tennis etc*: Aufschlag XY; ***~ on a committee*** e-m Ausschuss angehören; **2.** *tennis etc*: Aufschlag *m*

**serv·er** *tennis etc*: Aufschläger(in); GASTR Servierlöffel *m*

**ser·vice 1.** Dienst *m* (***to*** an *dat*); Dienstleistung *f*; (*Post-*, *Staats-*, *Telefon- etc* -) Dienst *m*; (*Zug- etc*)Verkehr *m*; ECON Service *m*, Kundendienst *m*; Bedienung *f*; Betrieb *m*; REL Gottesdienst *m*; TECH Wartung *f*, MOT *a.* Inspektion *f*; (*Tee- etc*)Service *n*; JUR Zustellung *f* (*e-r Vorladung*); *tennis etc*: Aufschlag *m*; *pl* MIL Streitkräfte *pl*; **2.** TECH warten

**ser·vice·a·ble** brauchbar; strapazierfähig

**ser·vice| ar·e·a** MOT (Autobahn)Raststätte *f*; **~ charge** Bedienung *f*, Bedienungszuschlag *m*; **~ sta·tion** Tankstelle *f*; (Reparatur)Werkstatt *f*

S

**ser·vi·ette** *esp Br* Serviette *f*

**ser·vile** sklavisch (*a. fig*); servil, unterwürfig

**serv·ing** Portion *f*

**ser·vi·tude** Knechtschaft *f*; Sklaverei *f*

**ses·sion** Sitzung *f*; Sitzungsperiode *f*; ***be in ~*** JUR, PARL tagen

**set 1.** *v/t* setzen, stellen, legen; *in e-n Zustand* versetzen; veranlassen (***doing*** zu tun); TECH einstellen, *Uhr* stellen (***by***

nach), *Wecker* stellen (***for*** auf *acc*); *Tisch* decken; *Preis, Termin etc* festsetzen, festlegen; *Rekord* aufstellen; *Edelstein* fassen (***in*** in *dat*); *Ring etc* besetzen (***with*** mit); *Flüssigkeit* erstarren lassen; *Haar* legen; *Knochen* einrenken, einrichten; MUS vertonen; PRINT absetzen; *Aufgabe, Frage* stellen; ~ ***at ease*** beruhigen; ~ ***an example*** ein Beispiel geben; ~ ***s.o. free*** j-n freilassen; ~ ***going*** in Gang setzen; ~ ***s.o. thinking*** j-m zu denken geben; ~ ***one's hopes on*** s-e Hoffnung setzen auf (*acc*); ~ ***s.o.'s mind at rest*** j-n beruhigen; ~ ***great*** (***little***) ***store by*** großen (geringen) Wert legen auf (*acc*); ***the novel is*** ~ ***in*** der Roman spielt in (*dat*); *v/i* ASTR untergehen; fest werden, erstarren; HUNT vorstehen; ~ ***about doing s.th.*** sich daranmachen, et. zu tun; ~ ***about s.o.*** F über j-n herfallen; ~ ***aside*** beiseite legen; JUR *Urteil etc* aufheben; ~ ***back*** verzögern; *j-n, et.* zurückwerfen (***by two months*** um zwei Monate); ~ ***in*** einsetzen; ~ ***off*** aufbrechen, sich aufmachen; hervorheben, betonen; *et.* auslösen; ~ ***out*** arrangieren, herrichten; aufbrechen, sich aufmachen; ~ ***out to do s.th.*** sich daranmachen, et. zu tun; ~ ***up*** errichten; *Gerät etc* aufbauen; *Firma etc* gründen; *et.* auslösen, verursachen; *j-n* versorgen (***with*** mit); sich niederlassen; ~ ***o.s. up as*** sich ausgeben für; **2.** *adj* festgesetzt, festgelegt; F bereit, fertig; starr (*smile etc*); ~ ***lunch*** *or* ***meal*** *Br* Menü *n*; ~ ***phrase*** feststehender Ausdruck; ***be*** ~ ***on doing s.th.*** (fest) entschlossen sein, et. zu tun; ***be all*** ~ F startklar sein; **3.** Satz *m*; (*Möbel- etc*)Garnitur *f*, (*Tee- etc*)Service *n*; (*Fernseh-, Rundfunk*)Apparat *m*, (-)Gerät *n*; THEA Bühnenbild *n*; *film*, TV Set *n, m*; *tennis etc*: Satz *m*; (Personen)Kreis *m*, Clique *f*; (*Kopf- etc*)Haltung *f*; ***have a shampoo and*** ~ sich die Haare waschen und legen lassen

**set·back** Rückschlag *m* (***to*** für)

**set·square** *Br* Winkel *m*, Zeichendreieck *n*

**set·tee** Sofa *n*

**set the·o·ry** MATH Mengenlehre *f*

**set·ting** ASTR Untergang *m*; TECH Einstellung *f*; Umgebung *f*; *film etc*: Schauplatz *m*; (*Gold- etc*)Fassung *f*

**set·ting lo·tion** Haarfestiger *m*

**set·tle** *v/i* sich niederlassen (***on*** auf *acc or dat*), sich setzen (***on*** auf *acc*) (*a.* ~ ***down***); sich niederlassen (***in*** in *dat*); sich legen (*dust*); sich setzen (*coffee etc*); sich senken (*building etc*); sich beruhigen (*person, stomach etc*), sich legen (*a.* ~ ***down***); sich einigen; *v/t j-n, Nerven etc* beruhigen; vereinbaren; *Frage etc* klären, entscheiden; *Streit etc* beilegen; *Land* besiedeln; *Leute* ansiedeln; *Rechnung* begleichen, bezahlen; *Konto* ausgleichen; *Schaden* regulieren; *s-e Angelegenheiten* in Ordnung bringen; ~ ***o.s.*** sich niederlassen (***on*** auf *acc or dat*), sich setzen (***on*** auf *acc*); ***that*** ~***s it*** damit ist der Fall erledigt; ***that's*** ~***d then*** das ist also klar; ~ ***back*** sich (gemütlich) zurücklehnen; ~ ***down*** → *v/i*; sesshaft werden; ~ ***down to*** sich widmen (*dat*); ~ ***for*** sich zufrieden geben *or* begnügen mit; ~ ***in*** sich einleben *or* eingewöhnen; ~ ***on*** sich einigen auf (*acc*); ~ ***up*** (be)zahlen; abrechnen (***with*** mit)

**set·tled** fest (*ideas etc*); geregelt (*life*); beständig (*weather*)

**set·tle·ment** Vereinbarung *f*; Klärung *f*; Beilegung *f*; Einigung *f*; Siedlung *f*; Besiedlung *f*; Begleichung *f*, Bezahlung *f*; ***reach a*** ~ sich einigen

**set·tler** Siedler(in)

**sev·en 1.** sieben; **2.** Sieben *f*

**sev·en·teen 1.** siebzehn; **2.** Siebzehn *f*

**sev·en·teenth** siebzehnte(r, -s)

**sev·enth 1.** siebente(r, -s), siebte(r, -s); **2.** Siebentel *n*, Siebtel *n*

**sev·enth·ly** siebentens, siebtens

**sev·en·ti·eth** siebzigste(r, -s)

**sev·en·ty 1.** siebzig; **2.** Siebzig *f*

**sev·er** durchtrennen; abtrennen; *Beziehungen* abbrechen; (zer)reißen

**sev·er·al** mehrere

**sev·er·al·ly** einzeln, getrennt

**se·vere** schwer (*injuries, setback etc*); stark (*pain*); hart, streng (*winter*); streng (*person, discipline etc*); scharf (*criticism etc*); **se·ver·i·ty** Schwere *f*; Stärke *f*; Härte *f*; Strenge *f*; Schärfe *f*

**sew** nähen

**sew·age** Abwasser *n*

**sew·age works** Kläranlage *f*

**sew·er** Abwasserkanal *m*

**sew·er·age** Kanalisation *f*

**sew·ing 1.** Nähen *n*; Näharbeit *f*; **2.** Näh...; ~ **ma·chine** Nähmaschine *f*

S

**sex** Geschlecht *n*; Sexualität *f*; Sex *m*; Geschlechtsverkehr *m*
**sex·ism** Sexismus *m*
**sex·ist 1.** sexistisch; **2.** Sexist(in)
**sex·ton** Küster *m* (und Totengräber *m*)
**sex·u·al** sexuell, Sexual..., geschlechtlich, Geschlechts...; **~ har·ass·ment** sexuelle Belästigung; **~ in·ter·course** Geschlechtsverkehr *m*
**sex·u·al·i·ty** Sexualität *f*
**sex·y** F sexy, aufreizend
**shab·by** schäbig
**shack** Hütte *f*, Bude *f*; F *contp* Schuppen *m*
**shack·les** Fesseln *pl*, Ketten *pl* (*both a. fig*)
**shade 1.** Schatten *m* (*a. fig*); (*Lampen-*)Schirm *m*; Schattierung *f*; Rouleau *n*; *fig* Nuance *f*; ***a ~ fig*** ein kleines bisschen, e-e Spur; **2.** abschirmen (***from*** gegen); schattieren; ***~ off*** allmählich übergehen (***into*** in *acc*)
**shad·ow 1.** Schatten *m* (*a. fig*); ***there's not a*** *or* ***the ~ of a doubt about it*** daran besteht nicht der geringste Zweifel; **2.** *j-n* beschatten
**shad·ow·y** schattig, dunkel; verschwommen, vage, schemenhaft
**shad·y** schattig; Schatten spendend; F zwielichtig, fragwürdig
**shaft** (*Pfeil- etc*)Schaft *m*; (*Hammer- etc*)Stiel *m*; TECH Welle *f*; (*Aufzugs-, Bergwerks- etc*)Schacht *m*; (*Sonnen- etc*)Strahl *m*
**shag·gy** zottig, struppig
**shake 1.** *v/t* schütteln; rütteln an (*dat*); erschüttern; ***~ hands*** sich die Hand geben *or* schütteln; *v/i* zittern, beben, wackeln (***with*** vor *dat*); ***~ down*** herunterschütteln; durchsuchen, F filzen; *Br* F kampieren; ***~ off*** abschütteln; *Erkältung etc* loswerden; ***~ up*** *Kissen etc* aufschütteln; *Flasche, Flüssigkeit* (durch-)schütteln; *fig* erschüttern; **2.** Schütteln *n*; F Milchshake *m*; ***~ of the head*** Kopfschütteln *n*
**shake·down** F Erpressung *f*; Durchsuchung *f*, Filzung *f*; *Br* (Not)Lager *n*
**shak·en** *a.* ***~ up*** erschüttert
**shak·y** wack(e)lig; zitt(e)rig
**shall** *v/aux future*: *ich* werde, *wir* werden; *in questions*: soll *ich* ...?, sollen *wir* ...?; ***~ we go?*** gehen wir?
**shal·low** seicht, flach, *fig a.* oberflächlich; **shal·lows** seichte *or* flache Stelle, Untiefe *f*
**sham 1.** Farce *f*; Heuchelei *f*; **2.** unecht, falsch; vorgetäuscht, geheuchelt; **3.** *v/t Mitgefühl etc* vortäuschen, heucheln; *Krankheit etc* simulieren; *v/i* sich verstellen, heucheln; ***he's only ~ming*** er tut nur so
**sham·bles** F Schlachtfeld *n*, wüstes Durcheinander, Chaos *n*
**shame 1.** Scham *f*, Schamgefühl *n*; Schande *f*; ***~!*** pfui!; ***~ on you!*** pfui!; schäm dich!; ***put to ~*** → **2.** beschämen; Schande machen (*dat*)
**shame·faced** betreten, verlegen
**shame·ful** beschämend; schändlich
**shame·less** schamlos
**sham·poo 1.** Shampoo *n*, Schampon *n*, Schampun *n*; Haarwäsche *f*; → ***set*** 3; **2.** *Haare* waschen; *j-m* die Haare waschen; *Teppich etc* schamponieren
**shank** TECH Schaft *m*; GASTR Hachse *f*
**shan·ty**[1] Hütte *f*, Bude *f*
**shan·ty**[2] Shanty *n*, Seemannslied *n*
**shan·ty·town** Elendsviertel *n*
**shape 1.** Form *f*; Gestalt *f*; Verfassung *f*, Zustand *m*; ***in good*** (***bad***) ***~*** in gutem (schlechtem) Zustand; ***in*** (***out of***) ***~*** SPORT (nicht) gut in Form; ***take ~*** *fig* Gestalt annehmen; **2.** *v/t* formen; gestalten; *v/i a.* ***~ up*** sich *gut etc* machen
**shape·less** formlos; ausgebeult
**shape·ly** wohlgeformt
**share 1.** Anteil *m* (***in, of*** an *dat*); *esp Br* ECON Aktie *f*; ***go ~s*** teilen; ***have a*** (***no***) ***~ in*** (nicht) beteiligt sein an (*dat*); **2.** *v/t* (sich) *et.* teilen (***with*** mit); *a.* ***~ out*** verteilen (***among, between*** an *acc*, unter *acc*); *v/i* teilen; ***~ in*** sich teilen in (*acc*)
**share·hold·er** *esp Br* ECON Aktionär(in)
**shark** ZO Hai(fisch) *m*; → ***loan shark***
**sharp 1.** *adj* scharf (*a. fig*); spitz; abrupt; schneidend (*wind, frost, command, voice, etc*); beißend (*cold, smell etc*); stechend, heftig (*pain*); gescheit; MUS (*um e-n Halbton*) erhöht; ***C ~*** MUS Cis *n*; **2.** *adv* scharf, abrupt; MUS zu hoch; pünktlich, genau; ***at eight o'clock ~*** Punkt 8 (Uhr); ***look ~*** F sich beeilen; ***look ~!*** F mach schnell!, Tempo!; F pass auf!, gib Acht!
**sharp·en** *Messer etc* schärfen, schleifen; *Bleistift etc* spitzen

S

**sharp·en·er** (*Messer- etc*)Schärfer *m*; (*Bleistift*)Spitzer *m*
**sharp·ness** Schärfe *f* (*a. fig*)
**sharp·shoot·er** Scharfschütze *m*
**sharp-sight·ed** scharfsichtig
**sharp-wit·ted** scharfsinnig
**shat·ter** *v/t* zerschmettern, zerschlagen; *Hoffnungen etc* zerstören; *v/i* zerspringen, zersplittern
**shat·ter·ing** vernichtend; erschütternd
**shat·ter·proof** splitterfrei
**shave 1.** (sich) rasieren; (glatt) hobeln; *j-n, et.* streifen; **2.** Rasur *f*; ***have a* ~** sich rasieren; ***that was a close* ~** das war knapp, das ist gerade noch einmal gut gegangen!; **shav·en** kahl geschoren
**shav·er** (*esp* elektrischer) Rasierapparat *m*
**shav·ing 1.** Rasieren *n*; **2.** Rasier...; **~ bag** Kulturbeutel *m*; **~ brush** Rasierpinsel *m*; **~ cream** Rasiercreme *f*
**shav·ings** Späne *pl*
**shawl** Umhängetuch *n*; Kopftuch *n*
**she 1.** *pron* sie; **2.** Sie *f*; ZO Weibchen *n*; **3.** *adj in cpds* ZO ...weibchen *n*; ***~-bear*** Bärin *f*
**sheaf** Bündel *n*; AGR Garbe *f*
**shear 1.** scheren; **2.** (***a pair of***) ***~s*** (e-e) große Schere
**sheath** (*Schwert- etc*)Scheide *f*; Hülle *f*; *Br* Kondom *n, m*; **sheathe** *Schwert etc* in die Scheide stecken; TECH umhüllen, verkleiden, ummanteln
**shed**[1] Schuppen *m*; Stall *m*
**shed**[2] *Tränen etc* vergießen; *Blätter etc* verlieren; *fig Hemmungen etc* ablegen; ***~ its skin*** sich häuten; ***~ a few pounds*** ein paar Pfund abnehmen
**sheen** Glanz *m*
**sheep** ZO Schaf *n*
**sheep·dog** ZO Schäferhund *m*
**sheep·ish** verlegen
**sheep·skin** Schaffell *n*
**sheer** rein, bloß; steil, (fast) senkrecht; hauchdünn
**sheet** Betttuch *n*, (Bett)Laken *n*, Leintuch *n*; (*Glas-, Metall- etc*)Platte *f*; Blatt *n*, Bogen *m*; weite (*Eis- etc*)Fläche; ***the rain was coming down in ~s*** es regnete in Strömen
**sheet light·ning** Wetterleuchten *n*
**shelf** (Bücher-, Wand- *etc*)Brett *n*, (-)Bord *n*; GEOGR Riff *n*; *pl* Regal *n*; ***off the ~*** gleich zum Mitnehmen
**shell 1.** (*Austern-, Eier-, Nuss- etc*)Schale *f*; BOT (*Erbsen- etc*)Hülse *f*; ZO Muschel *f*; (*Schnecken*)Haus *n*; ZO Panzer *m*; MIL Granate *f*; (Geschoss-, Patronen)Hülse *f*; Patrone *f*; TECH Rumpf *m*, Gerippe *n*, ARCH *a.* Rohbau *m*; **2.** schälen, enthülsen; mit Granaten beschießen
**shell·fish** ZO Schal(en)tier *n*
**shel·ter 1.** Zuflucht *f*, Schutz *m*; Unterkunft *f*, Obdach *n*; MIL Unterstand *m*; ***run for ~*** Schutz suchen; ***take ~*** sich unterstellen (***under*** unter *dat*); ***bus ~*** Wartehäuschen *n*; **2.** *v/t* schützen (***from*** vor *dat*); *v/i* sich unterstellen
**shelve** *v/t Bücher* in ein Regal stellen; *Plan etc* aufschieben, zurückstellen; *v/i* sanft abfallen (*garden etc*)
**shep·herd 1.** Schäfer *m*, Hirt *m*; **2.** *j-n* führen
**sher·iff** Sheriff *m*
**shield 1.** Schild *m*; **2.** *j-n* (be)schützen (***from*** vor *dat*); *j-n* decken
**shift 1.** *v/t et.* bewegen, schieben, *Möbelstück a.* (ver)rücken; *Schuld etc* (ab-) schieben (***onto*** auf *acc*); ***~ gear(s)*** MOT schalten; *v/i* sich bewegen; umspringen (*wind*); *fig* sich verlagern *or* verschieben *or* wandeln; MOT schalten (***into, to*** in *acc*); ***~ from one foot to the other*** von e-m Fuß auf den anderen treten; ***~ on one's chair*** auf s-m Stuhl *ungeduldig etc* hin und her rutschen; **2.** *fig* Verlagerung *f*, Verschiebung *f*, Wandel *m*; ECON Schicht *f*; **~ key** TECH Umschalttaste *f*; **~ work·er** Schichtarbeiter(in)
**shift·y** F verschlagen
**shim·mer** schimmern; flimmern
**shin 1.** *a.* ***~bone*** ANAT Schienbein *n*; **2.** ***~ up*** hinaufklettern; ***~ down*** herunterklettern
**shine 1.** *v/i* scheinen; leuchten; glänzen (*a. fig*); *v/t Schuhe etc* polieren; **2.** Glanz *m*
**shin·gle**[1] grober Strandkies
**shin·gle**[2] (Dach)Schindel *f*
**shin·gles** MED Gürtelrose *f*
**shin·y** blank, glänzend
**ship 1.** Schiff *n*; **2.** verschiffen; ECON verfrachten, versenden
**ship·ment** ECON Ladung *f*; Verschiffung *f*, Verfrachtung *f*, Versand *m*
**ship·own·er** Reeder *m*; Schiffseigner *m*

**ship·ping** Schifffahrt *f*; Schiffsbestand *m*; ECON Verschiffung *f*, Verfrachtung *f*, Versand *m*
**ship·wreck** Schiffbruch *m*
**ship·wrecked 1.** ***be ~*** Schiffbruch erleiden; **2.** schiffbrüchig
**ship·yard** (Schiffs)Werft *f*
**shirk** sich drücken (vor *dat*)
**shirk·er** Drückeberger(in)
**shirt** Hemd *n*
**shirt·sleeve 1.** Hemdsärmel *m*; ***in (one's) ~s*** in Hemdsärmeln, hemdsärmelig; **2.** hemdsärmelig
**shish ke·bab** GASTR Schaschlik *m*, *n*
**shit** V **1.** Scheiße *f* (*a. fig*); *fig* Scheiß *m*; **2.** (voll)scheißen
**shiv·er 1.** zittern (***with*** vor *dat*); **2.** Schauer *m*; *pl* MED F Schüttelfrost *m*; ***the sight send ~s (up and) down my spine*** bei dem Anblick überlief es mich eiskalt
**shoal**[1] Untiefe *f*; Sandbank *f*
**shoal**[2] ZO Schwarm *m*
**shock**[1] **1.** Schock *m* (*a.* MED); Wucht *f*; ELECTR Schlag *m*, (*a.* MED Elektro-) Schock *m*; ***be in (a state of) ~*** unter Schock stehen; **2.** schockieren, empören; *j-m* e-n Schock versetzen
**shock**[2] (***~ of hair*** Haar)Schopf *m*
**shock ab·sorb·er** TECH Stoßdämpfer *m*
**shock·ing** schockierend, empörend, anstößig; F scheußlich
**shod·dy** minderwertig (*goods*); gemein, schäbig (*trick etc*)
**shoe 1.** Schuh *m*; Hufeisen *n*; **2.** *Pferd* beschlagen
**shoe·horn** Schuhanzieher *m*, -löffel *m*
**shoe·lace** Schnürsenkel *m*
**shoe·mak·er** Schuhmacher *m*, Schuster *m*
**shoe·shine boy** Schuhputzer *m*
**shoe store** (*Br* **shop**) Schuhgeschäft *n*
**shoe·string** Schnürsenkel *m*
**shoot 1.** *v/t* schießen, HUNT *a.* erlegen; abfeuern, abschießen; erschießen; *Riegel* vorschieben; *j-n* fotografieren, aufnehmen, *Film* drehen; *Heroin etc* spritzen; ***~ the lights*** MOT bei Rot fahren; *v/i* schießen (***at*** auf *acc*); jagen; *fig* schießen, rasen; *film*, TV drehen, filmen; BOT sprießen, treiben; **2.** BOT Trieb *m*; Jagd *f*; Jagdrevier *n*
**shoot·er** F Schießeisen *n*
**shoot·ing 1.** Schießen *n*; Schießerei *f*; Erschießung *f*; Anschlag *m*; Jagd *f*; *film*, TV Dreharbeiten *pl*, Aufnahmen *pl*; **2.** stechend (*pain*); **~ gal·le·ry** Schießbude *f*; **~ range** Schießstand *m*; **~ star** ASTR Sternschnuppe *f*
**shop 1.** *Br* Laden *m*, Geschäft *n*; Werkstatt *f*; Betrieb *m*; ***talk ~*** fachsimpeln; **2.** *mst* ***go shopping*** einkaufen gehen
**shop as·sis·tant** *Br* Verkäufer(in)
**shop·keep·er** *Br* Ladenbesitzer(in), Ladeninhaber(in)
**shop·lift·er** Ladendieb(in)
**shop·lift·ing** Ladendiebstahl *m*
**shop·per** Käufer(in)
**shop·ping 1.** Einkauf *m*, Einkaufen *n*; Einkäufe *pl* (*items bought*); ***do one's ~*** *Br* einkaufen, (s-e) Einkäufe machen; **2.** Einkaufs...; **~ bag** Einkaufsbeutel *m*, -tasche *f*; **~ cart** Einkaufswagen *m*; **~ cen·ter** (*Br* **cen·tre**) Einkaufszentrum *n*; **~ list** Einkaufsliste *f*, -zettel *m*; **~ mall** Einkaufszentrum *n*; **~ pre·cinct** *Br* Fußgängerzone *f*; **~ street** Geschäfts-, Ladenstraße *f*
**shop stew·ard** ECON gewerkschaftlicher Vertrauensmann
**shop·walk·er** *Br* Aufsicht(sperson) *f*
**shop win·dow** Schaufenster *n*
**shore**[1] Küste *f*; (*See*)Ufer *n*; ***on ~*** an Land
**shore**[2]**:** ***~ up*** (ab)stützen
**short 1.** *adj* kurz; klein (*person*); kurz angebunden, barsch, schroff (***with*** zu); GASTR mürbe; ***be ~ for*** die Kurzform sein von; ***be ~ of ...*** nicht genügend ... haben; **2.** *adv* plötzlich, abrupt; ***~ of*** außer; ***cut ~*** plötzlich unterbrechen; ***fall ~ of*** *et.* nicht erreichen; ***stop ~*** plötzlich innehalten, stutzen; ***stop ~ of or at*** zurückschrecken vor (*dat*); → ***run*** 1; **3.** F Kurzfilm *m*; ELECTR Kurze *m*; ***called ... for ~*** kurz ... genannt; ***in ~*** kurz(um)
**short·age** Knappheit *f*, Mangel *m* (***of*** an *dat*)
**short·com·ings** Unzulänglichkeiten *pl*, Mängel *pl*, Fehler *pl*
**short cut** Abkürzung *f*; ***take a ~*** (den Weg) abkürzen
**short·en** *v/t* (ab-, ver)kürzen; *v/i* kürzer werden
**short·hand** Kurzschrift *f*, Stenografie *f*; **~ typ·ist** Stenotypistin *f*
**short·ly** bald; barsch, schroff; mit wenigen Worten

**short·ness** Kürze *f*; Schroffheit *f*
**shorts** *a. **pair of** ~* Shorts *pl*; (Herren)Unterhose *f*
**short·sight·ed** *esp Br* kurzsichtig (*a. fig*)
**short sto·ry** Kurzgeschichte *f*
**short-tem·pered** aufbrausend, hitzig
**short-term** ECON kurzfristig
**short time** ECON Kurzarbeit *f*
**short wave** ELECTR Kurzwelle *f*
**short-wind·ed** kurzatmig
**shot** Schuss *m*; Schrot(kugeln *pl*) *m, n*; SPORT Kugel *f*; *guter etc* Schütze *m*; *soccer etc*: Schuss *m*; *basketball etc*: Wurf *m*; *tennis, golf*: Schlag *m*; PHOT Schnappschuss *m*, Aufnahme *f*; *film*, TV Aufnahme *f*, Einstellung *f*; MED F Spritze *f*; F Schuss *m* (*of drugs*); *fig* F Versuch *m*; ***a ~ of rum*** ein Schluck Rum; ***I'll have a ~ at it*** ich probier's mal; ***not by a long ~*** F noch lange nicht; → ***big shot***
**shot·gun** Schrotflinte *f*
**shot·gun wed·ding** F Mussheirat *f*
**shot put** SPORT Kugelstoßen *n*
**shot put·ter** SPORT Kugelstoßer(in)
**shoul·der 1.** ANAT Schulter *f*; MOT Standspur *f*; **2.** schultern; *Kosten, Verantwortung etc* übernehmen; (mit der Schulter) stoßen; **~ bag** Schulter-, Umhängetasche *f*; **~ blade** ANAT Schulterblatt *n*; **~ strap** Träger *m*; Tragriemen *m*
**shout 1.** *v/i* rufen, schreien (***for*** nach; ***for help*** um Hilfe); ***~ at s.o.*** j-n anschreien; *v/t* rufen, schreien; **2.** Ruf *m*, Schrei *m*
**shove 1.** stoßen, F schubsen; *et.* schieben, stopfen; **2.** Stoß *m*, F Schubs *m*
**shov·el 1.** Schaufel *f*; **2.** schaufeln
**show 1.** *v/t* zeigen, vorzeigen, anzeigen; *j-n* bringen, führen (***to*** zu); ausstellen; zeigen, *film etc a.* vorführen, TV *a.* bringen; *v/i* zu sehen sein; ***be ~ing*** gezeigt werden, laufen; ***~ around*** herumführen; ***~ in*** herein-, hineinführen, herein-, hineinbringen; ***~ off*** angeben *or* protzen (mit); vorteilhaft zur Geltung bringen; ***~ out*** heraus-, hinausführen, heraus-, hinausbringen; ***~ round*** herumführen; ***~ up*** *v/t* herauf-, hinaufführen, herauf-, hinaufbringen; sichtbar machen; *j-n* entlarven, bloßstellen; *et.* aufdecken; *j-n* in Verlegenheit bringen; *v/i* zu sehen sein; F aufkreuzen, auftauchen; **2.** THEA *etc* Vorstellung *f*; Show *f*; *radio*, TV Sendung *f*; Ausstellung *f*; Zurschaustellung *f*, Demonstration *f*; *fig leerer* Schein; ***be on ~*** ausgestellt *or* zu besichtigen sein; ***steal the ~ from s.o.*** *fig* j-m die Schau stehlen; ***make a ~ of*** *Anteilnahme, Interesse etc* heucheln; ***put up a poor ~*** F e-e schwache Leistung zeigen; ***be in charge of the whole ~*** F den ganzen Laden schmeißen; **3.** Muster...
**show·biz** F, **show busi·ness** Showbusiness *n*, Showgeschäft *n*, Unterhaltungsindustrie *f*
**show·case** Schaukasten *m*, Vitrine *f*
**show·down** Kraft-, Machtprobe *f*
**show·er 1.** (Regen- *etc*)Schauer *m*; (*Funken*)Regen *m*; (*Wasser-, Wort-etc*)Schwall *m*; Dusche *f*; (Geschenk-) Party *f*; ***have** or **take a ~*** duschen; **2.** *v/t j-n mit et.* überschütten *or* überhäufen; *v/i* duschen; ***~ down*** niederprasseln
**show jump·er** SPORT Springreiter(in)
**show jump·ing** SPORT Springreiten *n*
**show-off** F Angeber(in)
**show·room** Ausstellungsraum *m*
**show tri·al** JUR Schauprozess *m*
**show·y** auffallend
**shred 1.** Fetzen *m*; **2.** zerfetzen; in (schmale) Streifen schneiden, schnitzeln, schnetzeln; in den Papier- *or* Reißwolf geben; **shred·der** Schnitzelmaschine *f*; Papier-, Reißwolf *m*
**shrewd** scharfsinnig; schlau
**shriek 1.** (gellend) aufschreien; ***~ with laughter*** vor Lachen kreischen; **2.** (schriller) Schrei
**shrill** schrill; *fig* heftig, scharf, lautstark
**shrimp** ZO Garnele *f*; *fig contp* Knirps *m*
**shrine** Schrein *m*
**shrink 1.** (ein-, zusammen)schrumpfen (lassen); einlaufen; *fig* abnehmen; **2.** F Klapsdoktor *m*
**shrink·age** Schrumpfung *f*; Einlaufen *n*; *fig* Abnahme *f*
**shrink-wrap** einschweißen
**shriv·el** schrumpfen (lassen); runz(e)lig werden (lassen)
**shroud 1.** Leichentuch *n*; **2.** *fig* hüllen
**Shrove Tues·day** Fastnachts-, Faschingsdienstag *m*
**shrub** Strauch *m*, Busch *m*
**shrub·be·ry** BOT Strauch-, Buschwerk *n*, Gebüsch *n*
**shrug 1.** *a. **~ one's shoulders*** mit den

Achseln *or* Schultern zucken; **2.** Achselzucken *n*, Schulterzucken *n*
**shuck** BOT **1.** Hülse *f*, Schote *f*; Schale *f*; **2.** enthülsen; schälen
**shud·der 1.** schaudern; **2.** Schauder *m*
**shuf·fle 1.** *v/t Karten* mischen; *Papiere etc* umordnen, hierhin oder dorthin legen; **~ *one's feet*** schlurfen; *v/i* schlurfen; *Karten* mischen; **2.** Schlurfen *n*, schlurfender Gang; Mischen *n*
**shun** *j-n*, *et.* meiden
**shunt** *Zug etc* rangieren, verschieben; *a.* **~ *off*** F *j-n* abschieben (***to*** in *acc*, nach)
**shut** (sich) schließen; zumachen; **~ *down*** *Fabrik etc* schließen; **~ *off*** *Wasser*, *Gas*, *Maschine etc* abstellen; **~ *up*** einschließen; einsperren; *Geschäft* schließen; **~ *up!*** F halt die Klappe!
**shut·ter** Fensterladen *m*; PHOT Verschluss *m*
**shut·tle 1.** Pendelverkehr *m*; (*Raum-*) Fähre *f*, (-)Transporter *m*; TECH Schiffchen *n*; **2.** hin- und herbefördern
**shut·tle·cock** SPORT Federball *m*
**shut·tle ser·vice** Pendelverkehr *m*
**shy 1.** scheu; schüchtern; **2.** scheuen (***at*** vor *dat*); **~ *away from*** *fig* zurückschrecken vor (*dat*)
**shy·ness** Scheu *f*; Schüchternheit *f*
**sick 1.** krank; ***be* ~** *esp Br* sich übergeben; ***she was*** *or* ***felt* ~** ihr war schlecht; ***get* ~** krank werden; ***be off* ~** krank (geschrieben) sein; ***report* ~** sich krank melden; ***be* ~ *of s.th.*** F et. satt haben; ***it makes me* ~** F mir wird schlecht davon, *a. fig* es ekelt *or* widert mich an; **2. *the* ~** die Kranken *pl*
**sick·bed** Krankenbett *n*
**sick·en** *v/t j-n* anekeln, anwidern; *v/i esp Br* krank werden
**sick·le** ['sɪkl] Sichel *f*
**sick leave: *be on* ~** krank (geschrieben) sein, wegen Krankheit fehlen
**sick·ly** kränklich; ungesund; matt; widerlich (*smell etc*)
**sick·ness** Krankheit *f*; Übelkeit *f*; **~ ben·e·fit** *Br* Krankengeld *n*
**side 1.** Seite *f*; *esp Br* SPORT Mannschaft *f*; **~ *by* ~** nebeneinander; ***take* ~*s*** Partei ergreifen (***with*** für; ***against*** gegen); **2.** Seiten...; Neben...; **3.** Partei ergreifen (***with*** für; ***against*** gegen)
**side·board** Anrichte *f*, Sideboard *n*
**side·car** MOT Bei-, Seitenwagen *m*
**side dish** GASTR Beilage *f*
**side·long** seitlich; Seiten...; **~ glance** Seitenblick *m*
**side street** Nebenstraße *f*
**side·swipe** Seitenhieb *m*
**side·track** *j-n* ablenken; F *et.* abbiegen; RAIL *etc* rangieren, verschieben
**side·walk** Bürgersteig *m*, Gehsteig *m*
**side·walk ca·fé** Straßencafé *n*
**side·ways** seitlich; seitwärts, nach der *or* zur Seite
**sid·ing** RAIL Nebengleis *n*
**si·dle: ~ *up to s.o.*** sich an j-n heranschleichen
**siege** MIL Belagerung *f*; ***lay* ~ *to*** belagern (*a. fig*)
**sieve 1.** Sieb *n*; **2.** (durch)sieben
**sift** (durch)sieben; *a.* **~ *through*** *fig* sichten, durchsehen, prüfen
**sigh 1.** seufzen; **2.** Seufzer *m*
**sight 1.** Sehvermögen *n*, Sehkraft *f*, Augenlicht *n*; Anblick *m*; Sicht(weite) *f*; *pl* Visier *n*; Sehenswürdigkeiten *pl*; ***at* ~, *on* ~** sofort; ***at the* ~ *of*** beim Anblick von (*or gen*); ***at first* ~** auf den ersten Blick; ***catch* ~ *of*** erblicken; ***know by* ~** vom Sehen kennen; ***lose* ~ *of*** aus den Augen verlieren; ***be*** (***with***)***in* ~** in Sicht sein (*a. fig*); **2.** sichten
**sight-read** MUS vom Blatt singen *or* spielen
**sight·see·ing** Sightseeing *n*, Besichtigung *f* von Sehenswürdigkeiten; ***go* ~** sich die Sehenswürdigkeiten anschauen; **~ tour** Sightseeingtour *f*, Besichtigungstour *f*, (Stadt)Rundfahrt *f*
**sight·se·er** Tourist(in)
**sight test** Sehtest *m*
**sign 1.** Zeichen *n*; (*Hinweis-*, *Warn-etc*)Schild *n*; *fig* (An)Zeichen *n*; **2.** unterschreiben, unterzeichnen; *Scheck* ausstellen; **~ *in*** sich eintragen; **~ *out*** sich austragen
**sig·nal 1.** Signal *n* (*a. fig*); Zeichen *n* (*a. fig*); **2.** (ein) Zeichen geben; signalisieren
**sig·na·to·ry** Unterzeichner(in)
**sig·na·ture** Unterschrift *f*; Signatur *f*; **~ tune** *radio*, TV Kennmelodie *f*
**sign·board** (Aushänge)Schild *n*
**sign·er** Unterzeichnete *m*, *f*
**sig·net** Siegel *n*
**sig·nif·i·cance** Bedeutung *f*, Wichtigkeit *f*; **sig·nif·i·cant** bedeutend, bedeutsam, wichtig; bezeichnend

S

**sig·ni·fy** bedeuten; andeuten
**sign·post** Wegweiser *m*
**si·lence 1.** Stille *f*; Schweigen *n*; **~!** Ruhe!; ***in ~*** schweigend; ***reduce to ~*** → **2.** zum Schweigen bringen
**si·lenc·er** TECH Schalldämpfer *m*; *Br* MOT Auspufftopf *m*
**si·lent** still; schweigend; schweigsam; stumm; **~ part·ner** ECON stiller Teilhaber
**sil·i·con** CHEM Silizium *n*
**sil·i·cone** CHEM Silikon *n*
**silk 1.** Seide *f*; **2.** Seiden...
**silk·worm** ZO Seidenraupe *f*
**silk·y** seidig; samtig (*voice*)
**sill** (*Fenster*)Brett *n*
**sil·ly 1.** albern, töricht, dumm; **2.** F Dummerchen *n*
**sil·ver 1.** Silber *n*; **2.** silbern, Silber...; **3.** versilbern
**sil·ver-plat·ed** versilbert
**sil·ver·ware** Tafelsilber *n*
**sil·ver·y** silberglänzend; *fig* silberhell
**sim·i·lar** ähnlich (**to** *dat*)
**sim·i·lar·i·ty** Ähnlichkeit *f*
**sim·i·le** Gleichnis *n*, Vergleich *m*
**sim·mer** leicht kochen, köcheln; ***~ with*** *fig* kochen vor (*rage etc*), fiebern vor (*excitement etc*); ***~ down*** F sich beruhigen, F sich abregen
**sim·per** albern *or* affektiert lächeln
**sim·ple** einfach, schlicht; leicht; dumm, einfältig; naiv; ***the ~ fact is that ...*** es ist einfach e-e Tatsache, dass ...
**sim·ple-mind·ed** dumm; naiv
**sim·pli·ci·ty** Einfachheit *f*, Schlichtheit *f*; Dummheit *f*; Naivität *f*
**sim·pli·fi·ca·tion** Vereinfachung *f*
**sim·pli·fy** vereinfachen
**sim·ply** einfach; bloß, nur
**sim·u·late** vortäuschen; MIL, TECH simulieren
**sim·ul·ta·ne·ous** simultan, gleichzeitig
**sin 1.** Sünde *f*; **2.** sündigen
**since 1.** *adv a.* ***ever ~*** seitdem, seither; **2.** *prp* seit (*dat*); **3.** *cj* seit(dem); da
**sin·cere** aufrichtig, ehrlich, offen
**sin·cer·i·ty** Aufrichtigkeit *f*; Offenheit *f*
**sin·ew** ANAT Sehne *f*
**sin·ew·y** sehnig; *fig* kraftvoll
**sin·ful** sündig, sündhaft
**sing** singen; ***~ s.th. to s.o.*** j-m et. vorsingen
**singe** (sich *et.*) ansengen *or* versengen
**sing·er** Sänger(in)
**sing·ing** Singen *n*, Gesang *m*
**sin·gle 1.** einzig; einzeln, Einzel...; einfach; ledig, unverheiratet; ***in ~ file*** im Gänsemarsch; **2.** *Br* RAIL *etc* einfache Fahrkarte, AVIAT einfaches Ticket (*both a.* ***~ ticket***); Single *f*; Single *m*, Unverheiratete *m*, *f*; **3. *~ out*** sich herausgreifen
**sin·gle-breast·ed** einreihig
**sin·gle-en·gined** AVIAT einmotorig
**sin·gle fam·i·ly home** Einfamilienhaus *n*
**sin·gle fa·ther** allein erziehender Vater
**sin·gle-hand·ed** eigenhändig, allein
**sin·gle-lane** MOT einspurig
**sin·gle-mind·ed** zielstrebig, -bewusst
**sin·gle moth·er** allein erziehende Mutter
**sin·gle pa·rent** Alleinerziehende *m*, *f*
**sin·gle room** Einzelzimmer *n*
**sin·gles** *esp tennis*: Einzel *n*; ***a ~ match*** ein Einzel; ***men's ~*** Herreneinzel *n*; ***women's ~*** Dameneinzel *n*
**sin·glet** *Br* ärmelloses Unterhemd *or* Trikot
**sin·gle-track** eingleisig, einspurig
**sin·gu·lar 1.** einzigartig, einmalig; **2.** LING Singular *m*, Einzahl *f*
**sin·is·ter** finster, unheimlich
**sink 1.** *v/i* sinken, untergehen; sich senken; ***~ in*** eindringen (*a. fig*); *v/t* versenken; *Brunnen etc* bohren; *Zähne etc* vergraben (***into*** in *acc*); **2.** Spülbecken *n*, Spüle *f*; Waschbecken *n*
**sin·ner** Sünder(in)
**sip 1.** Schlückchen *n*; **2.** *v/t* nippen an (*dat*) *or* von; schlückchenweise trinken; *v/i* nippen (***at*** an *dat or* von)
**sir** mein Herr; ***Dear Sir or Madam*** Sehr geehrte Damen und Herren (*address in letters*)
**sire** ZO Vater *m*, Vatertier *n*
**si·ren** Sirene *f*
**sis·sy** F Weichling *m*
**sis·ter** Schwester *f*; *Br* MED Oberschwester *f*; REL (Ordens)Schwester *f*
**sis·ter·hood** Schwesternschaft *f*
**sis·ter-in-law** Schwägerin *f*
**sis·ter·ly** schwesterlich
**sit** *v/i* sitzen; sich setzen; tagen; *v/t j-n* setzen; *esp Br Prüfung* ablegen, machen; ***~ down*** sich setzen; ***~ for*** *Br Prüfung* ablegen, machen; ***~ in*** ein Sit-in

veranstalten; an e-m Sit-in teilnehmen; ~ ***in for*** *j-n* vertreten; ~ ***in on*** als Zuhörer teilnehmen an (*dat*); ~ ***on*** sitzen auf (*dat*) (*a. fig*); ~ ***on a committee*** e-m Ausschuss angehören; ~ ***out*** *Tanz* auslassen; das Ende (*gen*) abwarten; *Krise etc* aussitzen; ~ ***up*** sich *or j-n* aufrichten *or* aufsetzen; aufrecht sitzen; aufbleiben

**sit·com** → ***situation comedy***

**sit-down** *a.* ~ ***strike*** Sitzstreik *m*; *a.* ~ ***demonstration*** *or* F ***demo*** Sitzblockade *f*

**site** Platz *m*, Ort *m*, Stelle *f*; (*Ausgrabungs*)Stätte *f*; Baustelle *f*

**sit-in** Sit-in *n*, Sitzstreik *m*

**sit·ting** Sitzung *f*

**sit·ting room** *esp Br* Wohnzimmer *n*

**sit·u·at·ed:** ***be*** ~ liegen, gelegen sein

**sit·u·a·tion** Lage *f*, Situation *f*; ~ **com·e·dy** TV *etc* Situationskomödie *f*

**six 1.** sechs; **2.** Sechs *f*

**six·teen 1.** sechzehn; **2.** Sechzehn *f*

**six·teenth** sechzehnte(r, -s)

**sixth 1.** sechste(r, -s); **2.** Sechstel *n*

**sixth·ly** sechstens

**six·ti·eth** sechzigste(r, -s)

**six·ty 1.** sechzig; **2.** Sechzig *f*

**size 1.** Größe *f*, *fig a.* Ausmaß *n*, Umfang *m*; **2.** ~ ***up*** F abschätzen

**siz(e)·a·ble** beträchtlich

**siz·zle** brutzeln

**skate 1.** Schlittschuh *m*; Rollschuh *m*; **2.** Schlittschuh laufen, Eis laufen; Rollschuh laufen

**skate·board** Skateboard *n*

**skat·er** Eisläufer(in), Schlittschuhläufer(in); Rollschuhläufer(in)

**skat·ing** Eislaufen *n*, Schlittschuhlaufen *n*; Rollschuhlaufen *n*; ***free*** ~ Kür *f*, Kürlauf *m*; ~ **rink** (Kunst)Eisbahn *f*; Rollschuhbahn *f*

**skel·e·ton** Skelett *n*, Gerippe *n*

**skep·tic** Skeptiker(in)

**skep·ti·cal** skeptisch

**sketch 1.** Skizze *f*; THEA *etc* Sketch *m*; **2.** skizzieren

**skew·er 1.** (Brat)Spieß *m*; **2.** (auf)spießen

**ski 1.** Ski *m*; **2.** Ski...; **3.** Ski fahren *or* laufen

**skid 1.** MOT rutschen, schleudern; **2.** MOT Rutschen *n*, Schleudern *n*; TECH Kufe *f*

**skid mark(s)** MOT Bremsspur *f*

**ski·er** Skifahrer(in), Skiläufer(in)

**ski·ing** Skifahren *n*, Skilaufen *n*, Skisport *m*

**ski jump** (Sprung)Schanze *f*

**ski jump·er** Skispringer *m*

**ski jump·ing** Skispringen *n*

**skil·ful** *Br* → ***skillful***

**ski lift** Skilift *m*

**skill** Geschicklichkeit *f*, Fertigkeit *f*

**skilled** geschickt (***at, in*** in *dat*)

**skilled work·er** Facharbeiter(in)

**skill·ful** geschickt

**skim** *Fett etc* abschöpfen (*a.* ~ ***off***); *Milch* entrahmen; (hin)gleiten über (*acc*); *a.* ~ ***over,*** ~ ***through*** *Bericht etc* überfliegen

**skim(med) milk** Magermilch *f*

**skimp** *a.* ~ ***on*** sparen an (*dat*)

**skimp·y** dürftig; knapp

**skin 1.** ANAT Haut *f*; ZO Fell *n*; BOT Schale *f*; **2.** *Tier* abhäuten; *Zwiebel etc* schälen; sich *das Knie etc* aufschürfen

**skin-deep** (nur) oberflächlich

**skin div·ing** Sporttauchen *n*

**skin·flint** Geizhals *m*

**skin·ny** F dürr, mager

**skin·ny-dip** F nackt baden

**skip 1.** *v/i* hüpfen, springen; seilhüpfen, seilspringen; *v/t et.* überspringen, auslassen; **2.** Hüpfer *m*

**skip·per** MAR, SPORT Kapitän *m*

**skir·mish** Geplänkel *n*

**skirt 1.** Rock *m*; **2.** *a.* ~ ***(a)round*** umgeben; *Problem etc* umgehen

**skirt·ing board** *Br* Scheuerleiste *f*

**ski| run** Skipiste *f*; ~ **tow** Schlepplift *m*

**skit·tle** Kegel *m*

**skulk** sich herumdrücken, herumschleichen

**skull** ANAT Schädel *m*

**skul(l)·dug·ge·ry** F fauler Zauber

**skunk** ZO Skunk *m*, Stinktier *n*

**sky** *a.* ***skies*** Himmel *m*

**sky·jack** *Flugzeug* entführen

**sky·jack·er** Flugzeugentführer(in)

**sky·lark** ZO Feldlerche *f*

**sky·light** Dachfenster *n*

**sky·line** Skyline *f*, Silhouette *f*

**sky·rock·et** F hochschnellen, in die Höhe schießen

**sky·scrap·er** Wolkenkratzer *m*

**slab** (*Stein- etc*)Platte *f*; dickes Stück

**slack 1.** locker; ECON flau; *fig* lax, lasch, nachlässig; **2.** bummeln; ~ ***off,*** ~ ***up*** *fig* nachlassen, (*person a.*) abbauen

**slack·en** *v/t* lockern; verringern; ~ ***speed*** langsamer werden; *v/i* locker werden; *a.* ~ ***off*** nachlassen
**slacks** F Hose *f*
**slag** TECH Schlacke *f*
**sla·lom** SPORT Slalom *m*
**slam 1.** *a.* ~ ***shut*** zuschlagen, F zuknallen; *a.* ~ ***down*** F *et.* knallen (***on*** auf *acc*); ~ ***on the brakes*** F MOT auf die Bremse steigen; **2.** Zuschlagen *n*; Knall *m*
**slan·der 1.** Verleumdung *f*; **2.** verleumden; **slan·der·ous** verleumderisch
**slang 1.** Slang *m*; Jargon *m*; **2.** *esp Br* F *j-n* wüst beschimpfen
**slant 1.** schräg legen *or* liegen; sich neigen; **2.** schräge Fläche; Abhang *m*; *fig* Einstellung *f*; ***at*** *or* ***on a*** ~ schräg
**slant·ing** schräg
**slap 1.** Klaps *m*, Schlag *m*; **2.** e-n Klaps geben (*dat*); schlagen; klatschen (***down on*** auf *acc*; ***against*** gegen)
**slap·stick** THEA Slapstick *m*, Klamauk *m*; ~ **com·e·dy** Slapstickkomödie *f*
**slash 1.** auf-, zerschlitzen; *Preise* drastisch herabsetzen; *Ausgaben etc* drastisch kürzen; ~ ***at*** schlagen nach; **2.** Hieb *m*; Schlitz *m*
**slate 1.** Schiefer *m*; Schiefertafel *f*; POL Kandidatenliste *f*; **2.** mit Schiefer decken; *j-n* vorschlagen (***for, to be*** als); *et.* planen (***for*** für)
**slaugh·ter 1.** Schlachten *n*; *fig* Blutbad *n*, Gemetzel *n*; **2.** schlachten; *fig* niedermetzeln; **slaugh·ter·house** Schlachthaus *n*, Schlachthof *m*
**Slav 1.** Slawe *m*, Slawin *f*; **2.** slawisch
**slave 1.** Sklave *m*, Sklavin *f* (*a. fig*); **2.** *a.* ~ ***away*** sich abplagen, F schuften
**slav·er** geifern, sabbern
**sla·ve·ry** Sklaverei *f*
**slav·ish** sklavisch
**sleaze** unsaubere Machenschaften; Kumpanei *f*; F POL Filz *m*
**slea·zy** schäbig, heruntergekommen; anrüchig
**sled 1.** (*a.* Rodel)Schlitten *m*; **2.** Schlitten fahren, rodeln
**sledge** *Br* → ***sled***
**sledge·ham·mer** TECH Vorschlaghammer *m*
**sleek 1.** glatt, glänzend; geschmeidig; MOT schnittig; **2.** glätten
**sleep 1.** Schlaf *m*; ***I couldn't get to*** ~ ich konnte nicht einschlafen; ***go to*** ~ einschlafen (F *a. leg etc*); ***put to*** ~ *Tier* einschläfern; **2.** *v/i* schlafen; ~ ***late*** lang *or* länger schlafen; ~ ***on*** *Problem etc* überschlafen; ~ ***with s.o.*** mit j-m schlafen; *v/t* Schlafgelegenheit bieten für
**sleep·er** Schlafende *m, f*, Schläfer(in); *Br* RAIL Schwelle *f*; RAIL Schlafwagen *m*
**sleep·ing bag** Schlafsack *m*
**Sleep·ing Beau·ty** Dornröschen *n*
**sleep·ing| car** RAIL Schlafwagen *m*; ~ **part·ner** *Br* ECON stiller Teilhaber; ~ **pill** PHARM Schlaftablette *f*, -mittel *n*; ~ **sick·ness** MED Schlafkrankheit *f*
**sleep·less** schlaflos
**sleep·walk·er** Schlafwandler(in)
**sleep·y** schläfrig, müde; verschlafen
**sleep·y·head** F Schlafmütze *f*
**sleet 1.** Schneeregen *m*; Graupelschauer *m*; **2.** ***it's ~ing*** es gibt Schneeregen; es graupelt
**sleeve** Ärmel *m*; TECH Manschette *f*, Muffe *f*; *esp Br* (*Platten*)Hülle *f*
**sleeve·less** ärmellos
**sleigh** (*esp* Pferde)Schlitten *m*
**sleight of hand** Fingerfertigkeit *f*; *fig* (Taschenspieler)Trick *m*
**slen·der** schlank; *fig* mager, dürftig; schwach (*hope etc*)
**slice 1.** Scheibe *f*, Stück *n*; *fig* Anteil *m* (***of*** an *dat*); **2.** *a.* ~ ***up*** in Scheiben *or* Stücke schneiden; ~ ***off*** *Stück* abschneiden (***from*** von)
**slick 1.** gekonnt; geschickt, raffiniert; glatt (*road etc*); **2.** F (*Öl*)Teppich *m*; **3.** ~ ***down*** *Haar* glätten, F anklatschen
**slick·er** Regenmantel *m*
**slide 1.** gleiten (lassen); rutschen; schlüpfen; schieben; ***let things*** ~ *fig* die Dinge schleifen lassen; **2.** Gleiten *n*, Rutschen *n*; Rutsche *f*, Rutschbahn *f*; TECH Schieber *m*; PHOT Dia *n*; Objektträger *m*; (*Erd- etc*)Rutsch *m*; *Br* (*Haar*)Spange *f*; ~ **rule** Rechenschieber *m*; ~ **tack·le** *soccer*: Grätsche *f*
**slid·ing door** Schiebetür *f*
**slight 1.** leicht, gering(fügig), unbedeutend; **2.** beleidigen, kränken; **3.** Beleidigung *f*, Kränkung *f*
**slim 1.** schlank; *fig* gering; **2.** *a.* ***be slimming, be on a slimming diet*** e-e Schlankheitskur machen, abnehmen
**slime** Schleim *m*
**slim·y** schleimig (*a. fig*)

**sling 1.** aufhängen; F schleudern; **2.** Schlinge *f*; Tragriemen *m*; Tragetuch *n*; Schleuder *f*
**slip**[1] **1.** *v/i* rutschen, schlittern; ausgleiten, ausrutschen; schlüpfen; *v/t* sich losreißen von; **~ s.th. into s.o.'s hand** j-m et. in die Hand schieben; **~ s.o. s.th.** j-m et. zuschieben; **~ s.o.'s attention** j-m *or* j-s Aufmerksamkeit entgehen; **~ s.o.'s mind** j-m entfallen; **she has ~ped a disk** MED sie hat e-n Bandscheibenvorfall; **~ by, ~ past** verstreichen (*time*); **~ off, ~ out of** schlüpfen aus; **~ on** überstreifen, schlüpfen in (*acc*); **2.** Ausgleiten *n*, (Aus)Rutschen *n*; Versehen *n*; Unterrock *m*; (*Kissen*)Bezug *m*; **~ of the tongue** Versprecher *m*; **give s.o. the ~** F j-m entwischen
**slip**[2] *a.* **~ of paper** Zettel *m*
**slip·case** Schuber *m*
**slip-on 1.** *adj* **~ shoe** → **2.** Slipper *m*
**slipped disk** MED Bandscheibenvorfall *m*
**slip·per** Hausschuh *m*, Pantoffel *m*
**slip·per·y** glatt, rutschig, glitschig
**slip road** *Br* MOT → **ramp**
**slip·shod** schlampig
**slit 1.** Schlitz *m*; **2.** schlitzen; **~ open** aufschlitzen
**slith·er** gleiten, rutschen
**sliv·er** (*Glas- etc*)Splitter *m*
**slob·ber** sabbern
**slo·gan** Slogan *m*
**sloop** MAR Schaluppe *f*
**slop 1.** *v/t* verschütten; *v/i* überschwappen; schwappen (**over** über *acc*); **2.** *a. pl* schlabb(e)riges Zeug; (*Tee-*, *Kaffee-*) Rest(e *pl*) *m*; *esp Br* Schmutzwasser *n*
**slope 1.** (Ab)Hang *m*; Neigung *f*, Gefälle *n*; **2.** sich neigen, abfallen
**slop·py** schlampig; F gammelig; F rührselig
**slot** Schlitz *m*, (Münz)Einwurf *m*; EDP Steckplatz *m*
**sloth** ZO Faultier *n*
**slot ma·chine** (Waren-, Spiel)Automat *m*
**slouch 1.** krumme Haltung; F latschiger Gang; **2.** krumm dasitzen *or* dastehen; F latschen
**slough**[1]**: ~ off** *Haut* abstreifen, ZO sich häuten
**slough**[2] Sumpf *m*, Sumpfloch *n*
**Slo·vak 1.** slowakisch; **2.** Slowake *m*, Slowakin *f*; LING Slowakisch *n*
**Slo·va·ki·a** Slowakei *f*
**slov·en·ly** schlampig
**slow 1.** *adj* langsam; begriffsstutzig; ECON schleppend; **be (ten minutes) ~** (zehn Minuten) nachgehen; **2.** *adv* langsam; **3.** *v/t often* **~ down, ~ up** *Geschwindigkeit* verringern; *v/i often* **~ down, ~ up** langsamer fahren *or* gehen *or* werden
**slow·coach** *Br* → **slowpoke**
**slow·down** ECON Bummelstreik *m*
**slow lane** MOT Kriechspur *f*
**low mo·tion** PHOT Zeitlupe *f*
**slow-mov·ing** kriechend (*traffic*)
**slow·poke** Langweiler(in)
**slow·worm** ZO Blindschleiche *f*
**sludge** Schlamm *m*
**slug**[1] ZO Nacktschnecke *f*
**slug**[2] F (*Gewehr- etc*)Kugel *f*; Schluck *m* (*whisky etc*)
**slug**[3] F *j-m* e-n Faustschlag versetzen
**slug·gish** träge; ECON schleppend
**sluice** TECH Schleuse *f*
**slum** *a. pl* Slums *pl*, Elendsviertel *n or pl*
**slum·ber** POET **1.** schlummern; **2.** *a. pl* Schlummer *m*
**slump 1.** ECON stürzen (*prices*), stark zurückgehen (*sales etc*); **sit ~ed over** zusammengesunken sitzen über (*dat*); **~ into a chair** sich in e-n Sessel fallen lassen; **2.** ECON starker Konjunkturrückgang; **~ in prices** Preissturz *m*
**slur**[1] **1.** MUS *Töne* binden; **~ one's speech** undeutlich sprechen; lallen; **2.** undeutliche Aussprache
**slur**[2] **1.** verleumden; **2. ~ on s.o.'s reputation** Rufschädigung *f*
**slurp** F schlürfen
**slush** Schneematsch *m*; F Kitsch *m*
**slush·y** F kitschig
**slut** Schlampe *f*; Nutte *f*
**sly** gerissen, schlau, listig; **on the ~** heimlich
**smack**[1] **1.** *j-m* e-n Klaps geben; **~ one's lips** sich (geräuschvoll) die Lippen lecken; **~ down** F *et.* hinklatschen; **2.** klatschendes Geräusch, Knall *m*; F Schmatz *m* (*kiss*); F Klaps *m*
**smack**[2]**: ~ of** *fig* schmecken *or* riechen nach
**small 1.** *adj and adv* klein; **~ wonder (that)** kein Wunder, dass; **feel ~** *fig* sich klein (und hässlich) vorkommen; **2. ~**

***of the back*** ANAT Kreuz *n*; **~ ad** Kleinanzeige *f*; **~ arms** Handfeuerwaffen *pl*; **~ change** Kleingeld *n*; **~ hours:** ***in the ~*** in den frühen Morgenstunden
**small-mind·ed** engstirnig; kleinlich
**small·pox** MED Pocken *pl*
**small print** *das* Kleingedruckte
**small talk** Small Talk *m, n,* oberflächliche Konversation; ***make ~*** plaudern
**small-time** F klein, unbedeutend; *in cpds* Schmalspur...
**small town** Kleinstadt *f*
**smart 1.** schick, fesch; smart, schlau, clever; **2.** wehtun; brennen; **3.** (brennender) Schmerz; **~ al·eck** F Besserwisser(in), Klugscheißer(in)
**smart·ness** Schick *m*; Schlauheit *f*, Cleverness *f*
**smash 1.** *v/t* zerschlagen (*a.* ***~ up***); schmettern (*a. tennis etc*); *Aufstand etc* niederschlagen, *Drogenring etc* zerschlagen; ***~ up one's car*** s-n Wagen zu Schrott fahren; *v/i* zerspringen; ***~ into*** prallen an (*acc*) *or* gegen, krachen gegen; **2.** Schlag *m*; *tennis etc*: Schmetterball *m*; → ***smash hit, smash-up***
**smash hit** Hit *m*
**smash-up** MOT, RAIL schwerer Unfall
**smat·ter·ing:** ***have a ~ of English*** ein paar Brocken Englisch können
**smear 1.** Fleck *m*; MED Abstrich *m*; Verleumdung *f*; **2.** (ein-, ver)schmieren; (sich) verwischen; verleumden
**smell 1.** *v/i* riechen (***at*** an *dat*); duften; stinken; *v/t* riechen (an *dat*); **2.** Geruch *m*; Gestank *m*; Duft *m*
**smell·y** übel riechend, stinkend
**smelt** *Erz* schmelzen
**smile 1.** Lächeln *n*; **2.** lächeln; ***~ at*** *j-n* anlächeln, *j-m* zulächeln; *j-n, et.* belächeln, lächeln über (*acc*); ***~ to o.s.*** schmunzeln
**smirk** (selbstgefällig *or* schadenfroh) grinsen
**smith** Schmied *m*
**smith·e·reens:** ***smash (in)to ~*** F in tausend Stücke schlagen *or* zerspringen
**smith·y** Schmiede *f*
**smit·ten** verliebt, F verknallt (***with*** in *acc*); ***be ~ by*** *or* ***with*** *fig* gepackt werden von
**smock** Kittel *m*
**smog** Smog *m*
**smoke 1.** Rauch *m*; ***have a ~*** eine rauchen; **2.** rauchen; räuchern
**smok·er** Raucher(in); RAIL Raucher *m*, Raucherabteil *n*
**smoke·stack** Schornstein *m*
**smok·ing** Rauchen *n*; ***no ~*** Rauchen verboten; **~ com·part·ment** RAIL Raucher *m*, Raucherabteil *n*
**smok·y** rauchig; verräuchert
**smooch** F schmusen
**smooth 1.** glatt (*a. fig*); ruhig (*a. journey etc*); mild (*wine*); *fig* (aal)glatt; **2.** *a.* ***~ out*** glätten, glatt streichen; ***~ away*** *Falten etc* glätten; *Schwierigkeiten etc* aus dem Weg räumen; ***~ down*** glatt streichen
**smoth·er** ersticken
**smo(u)l·der** glimmen, schwelen
**smudge 1.** Schmutzfleck *m*; **2.** (be-, ver)schmieren; (sich) verwischen
**smug** selbstgefällig
**smug·gle** schmuggeln (***into*** nach; in *acc*); **smug·gler** Schmuggler(in)
**smut** Rußflocke *f*; Schmutz *m* (*a. fig*)
**smut·ty** *fig* schmutzig
**snack** Snack *m*, Imbiss *m*; ***have a ~*** e-e Kleinigkeit essen
**snack bar** Snackbar *f*, Imbissstube *f*
**snag 1.** *fig* Haken *m*; **2.** mit *et.* hängen bleiben (***on*** an *dat*)
**snail** ZO Schnecke *f*
**snake** ZO Schlange *f*
**snap 1.** *v/i* (zer)brechen, (zer)reißen; *a.* ***~ shut*** zuschnappen; ***~ at*** schnappen nach; *j-n* anschnauzen; ***~ out of it!*** F Kopf hoch!, komm, komm!; ***~ to it!*** mach fix!; *v/t* zerbrechen; PHOT F knipsen; ***~ one's fingers*** mit den Fingern schnalzen; ***~ one's fingers at*** *fig* keinen Respekt haben vor (*dat*), sich hinwegsetzen über (*acc*); ***~ off*** abbrechen; ***~ up*** *et.* schnell entschlossen kaufen; ***~ it up!*** mach fix!; **2.** Krachen *n*, Knacken *n*, Knall *m*; PHOT F Schnappschuss *m*; Druckknopf *m*; F Schwung *m*; ***cold ~*** Kälteeinbruch *m*
**snap fas·ten·er** Druckknopf *m*
**snap·pish** *fig* bissig
**snap·py** modisch, schick; ***make it ~!*** F mach fix!
**snap·shot** PHOT Schnappschuss *m*
**snare 1.** Schlinge *f*, Falle *f* (*a. fig*); **2.** in der Schlinge fangen; F *et.* ergattern
**snarl 1.** knurren; ***~ at s.o.*** j-n anknurren; **2.** Knurren *n*

S

**snatch 1.** *v/t et.* packen; *Gelegenheit* ergreifen; *ein paar Stunden Schlaf etc* ergattern; ~ ***s.o.'s handbag*** j-m die Handtasche entreißen; *v/i* ~ ***at*** (schnell) greifen nach; *Gelegenheit* ergreifen; **2.** ***make a*** ~ ***at*** (schnell) greifen nach; ~ ***of conversation*** Gesprächsfetzen *m*

**sneak 1.** *v/i* (sich) schleichen; *Br* F petzen; *v/t* F stibitzen; **2.** *Br* F Petze *f*

**sneak·er** Turnschuh *m*

**sneer 1.** höhnisch *or* spöttisch grinsen (***at*** über *acc*); spotten (***at*** über *acc*); **2.** höhnisches *or* spöttisches Grinsen; höhnische *or* spöttische Bemerkung

**sneeze 1.** niesen; **2.** Niesen *n*

**snick·er** kichern (***at*** über *acc*)

**sniff 1.** *v/i* schniefen; schnüffeln (***at*** an *dat*); ~ ***at*** *fig* die Nase rümpfen über (*acc*); *v/t Klebstoff etc* schnüffeln, *Kokain etc* schnupfen; **2.** Schniefen *n*

**snif·fle 1.** schniefen; **2.** Schniefen *n*; ***she's got the*** ~***s*** F ihr läuft dauernd die Nase

**snig·ger** *esp Br* → ***snicker***

**snip 1.** Schnitt *m*; **2.** durchschnippeln; ~ ***off*** abschnippeln

**snipe**[1] zo Schnepfe *f*

**snipe**[2] aus dem Hinterhalt schießen (***at*** auf *acc*)

**snip·er** Heckenschütze *m*

**sniv·el** greinen, jammern

**snob** Snob *m*; **snob·bish** versnobt

**snoop:** ~ ***about***, ~ ***around*** F herumschnüffeln

**snoop·er** F Schnüffler(in)

**snooze** F **1.** ein Nickerchen machen; **2.** Nickerchen *n*

**snore 1.** schnarchen; **2.** Schnarchen *n*

**snor·kel 1.** Schnorchel *m*; **2.** schnorcheln

**snort 1.** schnauben; **2.** Schnauben *n*

**snot·ty nose** F Rotznase *f*

**snout** zo Schnauze *f*, Rüssel *m*

**snow 1.** Schnee *m* (*a. sl cocaine*); **2.** schneien; ***be*** ~***ed in*** *or* ***up*** eingeschneit sein

**snow·ball** Schneeball *m*; ~ **fight** Schneeballschlacht *f*

**snow·bound** eingeschneit

**snow-capped** schneebedeckt

**snow·drift** Schneewehe *f*

**snow·drop** BOT Schneeglöckchen *n*

**snow·fall** Schneefall *m*

**snow·flake** Schneeflocke *f*

**snow line** Schneegrenze *f*

**snow·man** Schneemann *m*

**snow·mo·bile** Schneemobil *n*

**snow·plough** *Br*, **snow·plow** Schneepflug *m*

**snow·storm** Schneesturm *m*

**snow-white** schneeweiß

**Snow White** Schneewittchen *n*

**snow·y** schneereich; verschneit

**snub** *j-n* brüskieren, *j-n* vor den Kopf stoßen

**snub nose** Stupsnase *f*

**snuff**[1] Schnupftabak *m*

**snuff**[2] *Kerze* ausdrücken, löschen; ~ ***out*** *Leben* auslöschen

**snuf·fle** schnüffeln, schniefen

**snug** gemütlich, behaglich; *clothing*: gut sitzend; eng (anliegend)

**snug·gle:** ~ ***up to s.o.*** sich an j-n kuscheln; ~ ***down in bed*** sich ins Bett kuscheln

**so** so; deshalb; → ***hope*** 2, ***think; is that*** ~***?*** wirklich?; ***an hour or*** ~ etwa e-e Stunde; ***she is tired -*** ~ ***am I*** sie ist müde - ich auch; ~ ***far*** bisher

**soak** *v/t* einweichen (***in*** in *dat*); durchnässen; ~ ***up*** aufsaugen; *v/i* sickern

**soak·ing** *a.* ~ ***wet*** völlig durchnässt, F klatschnass

**soap 1.** Seife *f*; F → ***soap opera***; **2.** (sich) einseifen

**soap op·e·ra** *radio*, TV Seifenoper *f*

**soap·y** Seifen...; seifig; *fig* F schmeichlerisch

**soar** (hoch) aufsteigen; hochragen; zo, AVIAT segeln, gleiten; *fig* in die Höhe schnellen (*prices etc*)

**sob 1.** schluchzen; **2.** Schluchzen *n*

**so·ber 1.** nüchtern (*a. fig*); **2.** ernüchtern; ~ ***up*** nüchtern machen *or* werden

**so-called** so genannt

**soc·cer** Fußball *m*

**soc·cer hoo·li·gan** Fußballrowdy *m*

**so·cia·ble** gesellig

**so·cial** sozial, Sozial...; gesellschaftlich, Gesellschafts...; zo gesellig; ~ **dem·o·crat** POL Sozialdemokrat(in); ~ **in·sur·ance** Sozialversicherung *f*

**so·cial·ism** Sozialismus *m*

**so·cial·ist 1.** Sozialist(in); **2.** sozialistisch

**so·cial·ize** *v/i* gesellschaftlich verkehren (***with*** mit); *v/t* sozialisieren

**so·cial| sci·ence** Sozialwissenschaft *f*;

S

~ **se·cu·ri·ty** *Br* Sozialhilfe *f*; **be on ~** Sozialhilfe beziehen; **~ ser·vic·es** *esp Br* Sozialeinrichtungen; **~ work** Sozialarbeit *f*; **~ work·er** Sozialarbeiter(in)
**so·ci·e·ty** Gesellschaft *f*; Verein *m*
**so·ci·ol·o·gy** Soziologie *f*
**sock** Socke *f*
**sock·et** ELECTR Steckdose *f*; Fassung *f*; (Anschluss)Buchse *f*; ANAT (*Augen-*)Höhle *f*
**so·da** Soda(wasser) *n*; (*Orangen- etc*)Limonade *f*
**sod·den** aufgeweicht (*ground*); durchweicht (*clothes*)
**so·fa** Sofa *n*
**soft** weich ; sanft; leise; gedämpft (*light etc*); F leicht, angenehm, ruhig (*job etc*); alkoholfrei (*drink*); F verweichlicht
**soft drink** Soft Drink *m*, alkoholfreies Getränk
**soft·en** *v/t* weich machen; *Wasser* enthärten; *Ton, Licht, Stimme etc* dämpfen; **~ up** F *j-n* weich machen; *v/i* weich(er) *or* sanft(er) *or* mild(er) werden
**soft·heart·ed** weichherzig
**soft land·ing** weiche Landung
**soft·ware** EDP Software *f*; **~ pack·age** EDP Softwarepaket *n*
**soft·y** F Softie *m*, Weichling *m*
**sog·gy** aufgeweicht, matschig
**soil**[1] Boden *m*, Erde *f*
**soil**[2] beschmutzen, schmutzig machen
**so·lar** Sonnen...; **~ en·er·gy** Solar-, Sonnenenergie *f*; **~ pan·el** Sonnenkollektor *m*; **~ sys·tem** Sonnensystem *n*
**sol·der** TECH (ver)löten
**sol·dier** Soldat *m*
**sole**[1] **1.** (Fuß-, Schuh)Sohle *f*; **2.** besohlen
**sole**[2] ZO Seezunge *f*
**sole**[3] einzig; alleinig, Allein...
**sole·ly** (einzig und) allein, ausschließlich
**sol·emn** feierlich; ernst
**so·lic·it** bitten um
**so·lic·i·tous** besorgt (**about, for** um)
**sol·id 1.** fest; stabil; massiv; MATH körperlich; gewichtig, triftig (*reason etc*), stichhaltig (*argument etc*); solid(e), gründlich (*work etc*); einmütig, geschlossen; **a ~ hour** F e-e geschlagene Stunde; **2.** MATH Körper *m*; *pl* feste Nahrung
**sol·i·dar·i·ty** Solidarität *f*
**so·lid·i·fy** fest werden (lassen); *fig* (sich) festigen
**so·lil·o·quy** Selbstgespräch *n*, *esp* THEA Monolog *m*
**sol·i·taire** Solitär *m*; Patience *f*
**sol·i·ta·ry** einsam, (*Leben a.*) zurückgezogen, (*Ort etc a.*) abgelegen; einzig; **~ con·fine·ment** JUR Einzelhaft *f*
**so·lo** MUS Solo *n*; AVIAT Alleinflug *m*
**so·lo·ist** MUS Solist(in)
**sol·u·ble** CHEM löslich; *fig* lösbar
**so·lu·tion** CHEM Lösung *f*; *fig* (Auf)Lösung *f*
**solve** *Fall etc* lösen
**sol·vent 1.** ECON zahlungsfähig; **2.** CHEM Lösungsmittel *n*
**som·ber,** *Br* **som·bre** düster, trüb(e); *fig* trübsinnig
**some** (irgend)ein; *pl* einige, ein paar; manche; etwas, ein wenig, ein bisschen; ungefähr; **~ 20 miles** etwa 20 Meilen; **~ more cake** noch ein Stück Kuchen; **to ~ extent** bis zu e-m gewissen Grade
**some·bod·y** jemand
**some·day** eines Tages
**some·how** irgendwie
**some·one** jemand
**some·place** irgendwo, irgendwohin
**som·er·sault 1.** Salto *m*; Purzelbaum *m*; **turn a ~** → **2.** e-n Salto machen; e-n Purzelbaum schlagen
**some·thing** etwas; **~ like** ungefähr
**some·time** irgendwann
**some·times** manchmal
**some·what** ein bisschen, ein wenig
**some·where** irgendwo(hin)
**son** Sohn *m*; **~ of a bitch** V Scheißkerl *m*
**so·na·ta** MUS Sonate *f*
**song** MUS Lied *n*; Gesang *m*; **for a ~** F für ein Butterbrot
**song·bird** ZO Singvogel *m*
**son·ic** Schall...; **~ bang** *Br*, **~ boom** Überschallknall *m*
**son-in-law** Schwiegersohn *m*
**son·net** Sonett *n*
**so·nor·ous** sonor, volltönend
**soon** bald; **as ~ as** sobald; **as ~ as possible** so bald wie möglich
**soon·er** eher, früher; **~ or later** früher oder später; **the ~ the better** je eher, desto besser; **no ~ ... than** kaum ... als;

***no ~ said than done*** gesagt, getan
**soot** Ruß *m*
**soothe** beruhigen, beschwichtigen (*a.* **~ *down***); *Schmerzen* lindern, mildern
**sooth·ing** beruhigend; lindernd
**soot·y** rußig
**sop**[1] Beschwichtigungsmittel *n* (***to*** für)
**sop**[2]**: ~ *up*** aufsaugen
**so·phis·ti·cat·ed** anspruchsvoll, kultiviert; intellektuell; TECH raffiniert, hoch entwickelt
**soph·o·more** Student(in) im zweiten Jahr
**sop·o·rif·ic** einschläfernd
**sop·ping** *a.* ***~ wet*** F klatschnass
**sor·cer·er** Zauberer *m*, Hexenmeister *m*, Hexer *m*
**sor·cer·ess** Zauberin *f*, Hexe *f*
**sor·cer·y** Zauberei *f*, Hexerei *f*
**sor·did** schmutzig; schäbig
**sore 1.** weh, wund (*a. fig*); entzündet; F *fig* sauer; ***I'm ~ all over*** mir tut alles weh; ***~ throat*** Halsentzündung *f*; ***have a ~ throat*** *a.* Halsschmerzen haben; **2.** wunde Stelle, Wunde *f*
**sor·rel**[1] BOT Sauerampfer *m*
**sor·rel**[2] **1.** ZO Fuchs *m* (*horse*); **2.** rotbraun
**sor·row** Kummer *m*, Leid *n*, Schmerz *m*, Trauer *f*
**sor·row·ful** traurig, betrübt
**sor·ry 1.** *adj* traurig, jämmerlich; ***be** or **feel ~ for s.o.*** j-n bedauern *or* bemitleiden; ***I'm ~ for her*** sie tut mir leid; ***I am ~ to say*** ich muss leider sagen; ***I'm ~*** → **2.** *int* (es) tut mir leid!; Entschuldigung!, Verzeihung!; ***~?*** *esp Br* wie bitte?
**sort 1.** Sorte *f*, Art *f*; ***~ of*** F irgendwie; ***of a ~, of ~s*** F so etwas Ähnliches wie; ***all ~s of things*** alles Mögliche; ***nothing of the ~*** nichts dergleichen; ***what ~ of (a) man is he?*** wie ist er?; ***be out of ~s*** F nicht auf der Höhe *or* auf dem Damm sein; ***be completely out of ~s*** SPORT F völlig außer Form sein; **2.** sortieren; ***~ out*** aussortieren; *Problem etc* lösen, *Frage etc* klären
**SOS** SOS *n*; ***send an ~*** ein SOS funken; ***~ call** or **message*** SOS-Ruf *m*
**soul** Seele *f* (*a. fig*); MUS Soul *m*
**sound**[1] **1.** Geräusch *n*; Laut *m*; PHYS Schall *m*; *radio*, TV Ton *m*; MUS Klang *m*, Sound *m*; **2.** *v/i* (er)klingen, (er)tönen; sich *gut etc* anhören; *v/t* LING (aus)sprechen; MAR (aus)loten; MED abhorchen; ***~ one's horn*** MOT hupen
**sound**[2] gesund; intakt, in Ordnung; solid(e), stabil, sicher; klug, vernünftig (*person, advice etc*); gründlich (*training etc*); gehörig (*beating*); vernichtend (*defeat*); fest, tief (*sleep*)
**sound| bar·ri·er** Schallgrenze *f*, Schallmauer *f*; **~ film** Tonfilm *m*
**sound·less** lautlos
**sound·proof** schalldicht
**sound·track** Filmmusik *f*; Tonspur *f*
**sound wave** Schallwelle *f*
**soup 1.** Suppe *f*; **2.** ***~ up*** F *Motor* frisieren
**sour 1.** sauer; *fig* mürrisch; **2.** sauer werden (lassen); *fig* trüben, verbittern
**source** Quelle *f*, *fig a.* Ursache *f*, Ursprung *m*
**south 1.** Süd, Süden *m*; **2.** *adj* südlich, Süd...; **3.** *adv* nach Süden, südwärts
**south·east 1.** Südost, Südosten *m*; **2.** *a.* **south·east·ern** südöstlich
**south·er·ly, south·ern** südlich, Süd...
**south·ern·most** südlichste(r, -s)
**South Pole** Südpol *m*
**south·ward(s)** südlich, nach Süden
**south·west 1.** Südwest, Südwesten *m*; **2.** *a.* **south·west·ern** südwestlich
**sou·ve·nir** Souvenir *n*, Andenken *n* (***of*** an *acc*)
**sove·reign 1.** Monarch(in), Landesherr(in); **2.** POL souverän
**sove·reign·ty** Souveränität *f*
**So·vi·et** HIST POL sowjetisch, Sowjet...
**sow**[1] (aus)säen
**sow**[2] ZO Sau *f*
**soy bean** BOT Sojabohne *f*
**spa** (Heil)Bad *n*
**space 1.** Raum *m*, Platz *m*; (Welt-) Raum *m*; Zwischenraum *m*; Zeitraum *m*; **2.** *a.* ***~ out*** in Abständen anordnen; PRINT sperren
**space age** Weltraumzeitalter *n*
**space bar** TECH Leertaste *f*
**space cap·sule** Raumkapsel *f*
**space cen·ter** (*Br* **cen·tre**) Raumfahrtzentrum *n*
**space·craft** (Welt)Raumfahrzeug *n*
**space flight** (Welt)Raumflug *m*
**space·lab** Raumlabor *n*
**space·man** F Raumfahrer *m*; Außerirdische *m*
**space probe** (Welt)Raumsonde *f*

**space re·search** (Welt)Raumforschung *f*
**space·ship** Raumschiff *n*
**space shut·tle** Raumfähre *f*, Raumtransporter *m*
**space sta·tion** (Welt)Raumstation *f*
**space·suit** Raumanzug *m*
**space walk** Weltraumspaziergang *m*
**space·wom·an** F (Welt)Raumfahrerin *f*; Außerirdische *f*
**spa·cious** geräumig
**spade** Spaten *m*; *card game*: Pik *n*, Grün *n*; ***king of ~s*** Pikkönig *m*; ***call a ~ a ~*** das Kind beim (rechten) Namen nennen
**Spain** Spanien *n*
**span 1.** Spanne *f*; Spannweite *f*; **2.** *Fluss etc* überspannen; *fig* sich erstrecken über (*acc*)
**span·gle 1.** Flitter *m*, Paillette *f*; **2.** mit Flitter *or* Pailletten besetzen; *fig* übersäen (***with*** mit)
**Span·iard** Spanier(in)
**span·iel** ZO Spaniel *m*
**Span·ish 1.** spanisch; **2.** LING Spanisch *n*; ***the ~*** die Spanier *pl*
**spank** *j-m* den Hintern versohlen
**spank·ing** Tracht *f* Prügel
**span·ner** *esp Br* Schraubenschlüssel *m*; ***put*** *or* ***throw a ~ in the works*** F j-m in die Quere kommen
**spar** *boxing*: sparren (***with*** mit); *fig* sich ein Wortgefecht liefern (***with*** mit)
**spare 1.** *j-n*, *et*. entbehren; *Geld*, *Zeit etc* übrig haben; *keine Kosten*, *Mühen etc* scheuen; **~ *s.o. s.th.*** j-m et. ersparen; **2.** Ersatz..., Reserve...; überschüssig; **3.** MOT Ersatz-, Reservereifen *m*; *esp Br* → **~ part** TECH Ersatzteil *n*, *m*
**spare room** Gästezimmer *n*
**spare time** Freizeit *f*
**spar·ing** sparsam; ***use ~ly*** sparsam umgehen mit
**spark 1.** Funke(n) *m* (*a. fig*); **2.** Funken sprühen
**spark·ing plug** *Br* → ***spark plug***
**spar·kle 1.** funkeln, blitzen (***with*** vor *dat*); perlen (*drink*); **2.** Funkeln *n*, Blitzen *n*; **spar·kling** funkelnd, blitzend; (geist)sprühend, spritzig; **~ *wine*** Sekt *m*, Schaumwein *m*
**spark plug** MOT Zündkerze *f*
**spar·row** ZO Spatz *m*, Sperling *m*
**spar·row·hawk** ZO Sperber *m*
**sparse** spärlich, dünn
**spasm** MED Krampf *m*; Anfall *m*
**spas·mod·ic** MED krampfartig; *fig* sporadisch, unregelmäßig
**spas·tic** MED **1.** spastisch; **2.** Spastiker(in)
**spa·tial** räumlich
**spat·ter** (be)spritzen
**spawn 1.** ZO laichen; *fig* hervorbringen; **2.** ZO Laich *m*
**speak** *v/i* sprechen, reden (***to, with*** mit; ***about*** über *acc*); sprechen (***to*** vor *dat*; ***about, on*** über *acc*); ***so to ~*** sozusagen; ***speaking!*** TEL am Apparat!; **~ *up*** lauter sprechen; *v/t* sprechen, sagen; *Sprache* sprechen
**speak·er** Sprecher(in), Redner(in)
**spear 1.** Speer *m*; **2.** aufspießen; durchbohren
**spear·head** Speerspitze *f*; MIL Angriffsspitze *f*; SPORT (Sturm-, Angriffs)Spitze *f*
**spear·mint** BOT Grüne Minze
**spe·cial 1.** besondere(r, -s); speziell; Sonder...; Spezial...; **2.** Sonderbus *m*, Sonderzug *m*; *radio*, TV Sondersendung *f*; ECON F Sonderangebot *n*; ***be on ~*** ECON im Angebot sein
**spe·cial·ist** Spezialist(in), MED *a.* Facharzt *m*, Fachärztin *f* (***in*** für)
**spe·ci·al·i·ty** *Br* → ***specialty***
**spe·cial·ize** sich spezialisieren (***in*** auf *acc*)
**spe·cial·ty** Spezialgebiet *n*; GASTR Spezialität *f*
**spe·cies** Art *f*, Spezies *f*
**spe·cif·ic** konkret, präzis; spezifisch, speziell, besondere(r, -s); eigen (***to*** *dat*)
**spe·ci·fy** genau beschreiben *or* angeben *or* festlegen
**spe·ci·men** Exemplar *n*; Probe *f*, Muster *n*
**speck** kleiner Fleck, (*Staub*)Korn *n*; Punkt *m* (***on the horizon*** am Horizont)
**speck·led** gefleckt, gesprenkelt
**spec·ta·cle** Schauspiel *n*; Anblick *m*; (***a pair of***) **~s** (e-e) Brille
**spec·tac·u·lar 1.** spektakulär; **2.** große (*Fernseh- etc*)Show
**spec·ta·tor** Zuschauer(in)
**spec·ter** (*fig a. Schreck*)Gespenst *n*
**spec·tral** geisterhaft, gespenstisch
**spec·tre** *Br* → ***specter***
**spec·u·late** spekulieren, Vermutungen

anstellen (***about, on*** über *acc*); ECON spekulieren (***in*** mit); **spec·u·la·tion** Spekulation *f* (*a.* ECON), Vermutung *f*; **spec·u·la·tive** spekulativ, ECON *a.* Spekulations...; **spec·u·la·tor** ECON Spekulant(in)

**speech** Sprache *f*; Rede *f*, Ansprache *f*; ***make a ~*** e-e Rede halten

**speech day** *Br* PED (Jahres)Schlussfeier *f*

**speech·less** sprachlos (***with*** vor *dat*)

**speed 1.** Geschwindigkeit *f*, Tempo *n*, Schnelligkeit *f*; TECH Drehzahl *f*; PHOT Lichtempfindlichkeit *f*; *sl* Speed *n*; MOT *etc* Gang *m*; ***five-speed gearbox*** Fünfganggetriebe *n*; ***at a ~ of*** mit e-r Geschwindigkeit von; ***at full*** *or* ***top ~*** mit Höchstgeschwindigkeit; **2.** *v/i* rasen; ***be ~ing*** MOT zu schnell fahren; ***~ up*** beschleunigen, schneller werden; *v/t* rasch bringen *or* befördern; ***~ up*** *et.* beschleunigen

**speed·boat** Rennboot *n*

**speed·ing** MOT zu schnelles Fahren, Geschwindigkeitsüberschreitung *f*

**speed lim·it** MOT Geschwindigkeitsbegrenzung *f*, Tempolimit *n*

**speed·om·e·ter** MOT Tachometer *m*, *n*

**speed trap** MOT Radarfalle *f*

**speed·y** schnell, (*reply etc a.*) prompt

**spell**[1] *a.* ***~ out*** buchstabieren; (*orthographisch* richtig) schreiben

**spell**[2] Weile *f*; (*Husten- etc*)Anfall *m*; ***for a ~*** e-e Zeit lang; ***a ~ of fine weather*** e-e Schönwetterperiode; ***hot ~*** Hitzewelle *f*

**spell**[3] Zauber *m* (*a. fig*)

**spell·bound** wie gebannt

**spell·er** EDP Speller *m*, Rechtschreibsystem *n*; ***be a good*** (***bad***) ***~*** in Rechtschreibung gut (schlecht) sein

**spell·ing** Buchstabieren *n*; Rechtschreibung *f*; Schreibung *f*, Schreibweise *f*; **~ mis·take** (Recht)Schreibfehler *m*

**spend** *Geld* ausgeben (***on*** für); *Urlaub, Zeit* verbringen

**spend·ing** Ausgaben *pl*

**spend·thrift** Verschwender(in)

**spent** verbraucht

**sperm** BIOL Sperma *n*, Samen *m*

**sphere** Kugel *f*; *fig* (*Einfluss- etc*)Sphäre *f*, (*Einfluss- etc*)Bereich *m*, Gebiet *n*

**spher·i·cal** kugelförmig

**spice 1.** Gewürz *n*; *fig* Würze *f*; **2.** würzen

**spick-and-span** blitzsauber

**spic·y** gut gewürzt, würzig; *fig* pikant

**spi·der** ZO Spinne *f*

**spike 1.** Spitze *f*; Dorn *m*; Stachel *m*; SPORT Spike *m*, Dorn *m*; *pl* Spikes *pl*, Rennschuhe *pl*; **2.** aufspießen

**spill 1.** *v/t* ausschütten, verschütten; ***~ the beans*** F alles ausplaudern, singen; → ***milk*** 1; *v/i fig* strömen (***out of*** aus); ***~ over*** überlaufen; *fig* übergreifen (***into*** auf *acc*); **2.** F Sturz *m*

**spin 1.** *v/t* drehen; *Wäsche* schleudern; *Münze* hochwerfen; *Fäden, Wolle etc* spinnen; ***~ out*** *Arbeit etc* in die Länge ziehen; *Geld etc* strecken; *v/i* sich drehen; spinnen; ***my head was ~ning*** mir drehte sich alles; ***~ along*** MOT dahinrasen; ***~ round*** herumwirbeln; **2.** (schnelle) Drehung; SPORT Effet *m*; TECH Schleudern *n*; AVIAT Trudeln *n*; ***be in a*** (***flat***) ***~*** *esp Br* F am Rotieren sein; ***go for a ~*** MOT F e-e Spritztour machen

**spin·ach** BOT Spinat *m*

**spin·al** ANAT Rückgrat...; **~ col·umn** ANAT Wirbelsäule *f*, Rückgrat *n*; **~ cord, ~ mar·row** ANAT Rückenmark *n*

**spin·dle** Spindel *f*

**spin-dri·er** (Wäsche)Schleuder *f*

**spin-dry** *Wäsche* schleudern

**spin-dry·er** → ***spin-drier***

**spine** ANAT Wirbelsäule *f*, Rückgrat *n*; ZO Stachel *m*, BOT *a.* Dorn *m*; (*Buch-*) Rücken *m*

**spin·ning| mill** TECH Spinnerei *f*; **~ top** Kreisel *m*; **~ wheel** Spinnrad *n*

**spin·ster** ältere unverheiratete Frau, *contp* alte Jungfer, spätes Mädchen

**spin·y** ZO stach(e)lig, BOT *a.* dornig

**spi·ral 1.** spiralförmig, Spiral...; **2.** (*a.* ECON *Preis- etc*)Spirale *f*

**spi·ral stair·case** Wendeltreppe *f*

**spire** (*Kirch*)Turmspitze *f*

**spir·it** Geist *m*; Stimmung *f*, Einstellung *f*; Schwung *m*, Elan *m*; CHEM Spiritus *m*; *mst pl* Spirituosen *pl*

**spir·it·ed** energisch; erregt (*debate etc*)

**spir·it·less** temperamentlos; mutlos

**spir·its** Laune *f*, Stimmung *f*; ***be in high ~*** in Hochstimmung sein; ausgelassen *or* übermütig sein; ***be in low ~*** niedergeschlagen sein

**spir·i·tu·al 1.** geistig; geistlich; **2.** MUS Spiritual *n*
**spit¹ 1.** spucken; knistern (*fire*), brutzeln (*meat etc*); *a.* **~ out** ausspucken; **~ at s.o.** j-n anspucken; ***it is ~ting*** (***with rain***) es tröpfelt; **2.** Spucke *f*
**spit²** (Brat)Spieß *m*; GEOGR Landzunge *f*
**spite 1.** Bosheit *f*, Gehässigkeit *f*; ***out of*** *or* ***from pure ~*** aus reiner Bosheit; ***in ~ of*** trotz (*gen*); **2.** *j-n* ärgern
**spite·ful** boshaft, gehässig
**spit·ting im·age** Ebenbild *n*; ***she is the ~ of her mother*** sie ist ihrer Mutter wie aus dem Gesicht geschnitten
**spit·tle** Speichel *m*, Spucke *f*
**splash 1.** (be)spritzen; klatschen; plan(t)schen; platschen; **~ down** wassern; **2.** Klatschen *n*, Platschen *n*; Spritzer *m*, Spritzfleck *m*; *esp Br* GASTR Spritzer *m*, Schuss *m*
**splash·down** Wasserung *f*
**splay** *a.* **~ out** *Finger*, *Zehen* spreizen
**spleen** ANAT Milz *f*
**splen·did** großartig, herrlich, prächtig
**splen·do(u)r** Pracht *f*
**splice** miteinander verbinden, *Film etc* (zusammen)kleben
**splint** MED Schiene *f*; ***put in a ~, put in ~s*** schienen
**splin·ter 1.** Splitter *m*; **2.** (zer)splittern; **~ off** absplittern; *fig* sich abspalten (***from*** von)
**split 1.** *v/t* (zer)spalten; zerreißen; *a.* **~ up** aufteilen (***between*** unter *acc*; ***into*** in *acc*); sich *et.* teilen; **~ *hairs*** Haarspalterei treiben; **~ *one's sides*** F sich vor Lachen biegen; *v/i* sich spalten; zerreißen; sich teilen (***into*** in *acc*); *a.* **~ up** (***with***) Schluss machen (mit), sich trennen (von); **2.** Riss *m*; Spalt *m*; Aufteilung *f*; *fig* Bruch *m*; *fig* Spaltung *f*
**split·ting** heftig, rasend (*headache etc*)
**splut·ter** stottern (*a.* MOT); zischen
**spoil 1.** *v/t* verderben; ruinieren; *j-n* verwöhnen, *Kind a.* verziehen; *v/i* verderben, schlecht werden; **2.** *mst pl* Beute *f*
**spoil·er** MOT Spoiler *m*
**spoil·sport** F Spielverderber(in)
**spoke** TECH Speiche *f*
**spokes·man** Sprecher *m*
**spokes·wom·an** Sprecherin *f*
**sponge 1.** Schwamm *m*; Schnorrer(in); *Br* → **sponge cake; 2.** *v/t a.* **~ down** (mit e-m Schwamm) abwaschen; **~ *off*** weg-, abwischen; **~ (*up*)** aufsaugen, aufwischen (***from*** von); *et.* schnorren (***from, off, on*** von, bei); *v/i* schnorren (***from, off, on*** bei)
**sponge cake** Biskuitkuchen *m*
**spong·er** Schnorrer(in)
**spong·y** schwammig; weich
**spon·sor 1.** Bürge *m*, Bürgin *f*; Sponsor(in), Geldgeber(in); Spender(in); **2.** bürgen für; sponsern
**spon·ta·ne·ous** spontan
**spook** F Geist *m*
**spook·y** F gespenstisch, unheimlich
**spool** Spule *f*; ***~ of thread*** Garnrolle *f*
**spoon 1.** Löffel *m*; **2.** löffeln
**spoon-feed** *Kind etc* füttern
**spoon·ful** (*ein*) Löffel (voll)
**spo·rad·ic** sporadisch, gelegentlich
**spore** BOT Spore *f*
**sport 1.** Sport *m*; Sportart *f*; F feiner Kerl; *pl* Sport *m*; **2.** herumlaufen mit; protzen mit
**sports** Sport...; **~ car** MOT Sportwagen *m*; **~ cen·ter** (*Br* **cen·tre**) Sportzentrum *n*
**sports·man** Sportler *m*
**sports·wear** Sportkleidung *f*
**sports·wom·an** Sportlerin *f*
**spot 1.** Punkt *m*, Tupfen *m*; Fleck *m*; MED Pickel *m*; Ort *m*, Platz *m*, Stelle *f*; *radio*, TV (Werbe)Spot *m*; F Spot *m*; ***a ~ of*** *Br* F ein bisschen; ***on the ~*** auf der Stelle, sofort; zur Stelle; an Ort und Stelle, vor Ort; auf der Stelle; ***be in a ~*** F in Schwulitäten sein; ***soft ~*** *fig* Schwäche *f* (***for*** für); ***tender ~*** empfindliche Stelle; ***weak ~*** schwacher Punkt; Schwäche *f*; **2.** entdecken, sehen
**spot check** Stichprobe *f*
**spot·less** tadellos sauber; *fig* untad(e)lig
**spot·light** Spotlight *n*, Scheinwerfer *m*; Scheinwerferlicht *n*
**spot·ted** getüpfelt; fleckig
**spot·ter** Beobachter *m*
**spot·ty** pick(e)lig
**spouse** Gatte *m*, Gattin *f*, Gemahl(in)
**spout 1.** *v/t Wasser etc* (heraus)spritzen; *v/i* spritzen (***from*** aus); **2.** Schnauze *f*, Tülle *f*; (*Wasser- etc*)Strahl *m*
**sprain** MED **1.** sich *et.* verstauchen; **2.** Verstauchung *f*
**sprat** ZO Sprotte *f*

**sprawl** ausgestreckt liegen *or* sitzen (*a.* ~ ***out***); sich ausbreiten

**spray 1.** (be)sprühen; spritzen; sich *die Haare* sprayen; *Parfüm etc* versprühen, zerstäuben; **2.** Sprühnebel *m*; Gischt *m, f*; Spray *m, n*; → ***sprayer***

**spray can** → **spray·er** Sprüh-, Spraydose *f*, Zerstäuber *m*

**spread 1.** *v/t* ausbreiten, *Arme a.* ausstrecken, *Finger etc* spreizen (*all a.* ~ ***out***); *Furcht, Krankheit, Nachricht etc* verbreiten, *Gerücht a.* ausstreuen; *Butter etc* streichen (***on*** auf *acc*); *Brot etc* (be)streichen (***with*** mit); *v/i* sich ausbreiten (*a.* ~ ***out***); sich erstrecken (***over*** über *acc*); sich verbreiten, übergreifen (***to*** auf *acc*); sich streichen lassen (*butter etc*); **2.** Ausbreitung *f*, Verbreitung *f*; Ausdehnung *f*; Spannweite *f*; GASTR Aufstrich *m*

**spread·sheet** EDP Tabellenkalkulation *f*, Tabellenkalkulationsprogramm *n*

**spree: *go* (*out*) *on a*** ~ F e-e Sauftour machen; ***go on a buying*** (*or* ***shopping, spending***) ~ wie verrückt einkaufen

**sprig** BOT kleiner Zweig

**spright·ly** lebhaft; rüstig

**spring 1.** *v/i* springen; ~ ***from*** herrühren von; ~ ***up*** aufkommen (*wind*); aus dem Boden schießen (*building etc*); *v/t*: ~ ***a leak*** ein Leck bekommen; ~ ***a surprise on s.o.*** j-n überraschen; **2.** Frühling *m*, Frühjahr *n*; Quelle *f*; TECH Feder *f*; Elastizität *f*; Federung *f*; Sprung *m*, Satz *m*; ***in*** (***the***) ~ im Frühling

**spring·board** Sprungbrett *n*

**spring-clean** gründlich putzen, Frühjahrsputz machen (in *dat*)

**spring tide** Springflut *f*

**spring·time** Frühling *m*, Frühlingszeit *f*, Frühjahr *n*

**spring·y** elastisch, federnd

**sprin·kle 1.** *Wasser etc* sprengen (***on*** auf *acc*); *Salz etc* streuen (***on*** auf *acc*); *et.* (be)sprengen *or* bestreuen (***with*** mit); ***it is sprinkling*** es tröpfelt; **2.** Sprühregen *m*

**sprin·kler** (*Rasen*)Sprenger *m*; Sprinkler *m*, Berieselungsanlage *f*

**sprin·kling: *a*** ~ ***of*** ein bisschen, ein paar

**sprint** SPORT **1.** sprinten; spurten; **2.** Sprint *m*; Spurt *m*

**sprint·er** SPORT Sprinter(in)

**sprite** Kobold *m*

**sprout** BOT **1.** sprießen (*a. fig*), keimen; wachsen lassen; **2.** Spross *m*; (***Brussels***) ~***s*** Rosenkohl *m*

**spruce**[1] BOT Fichte *f*; Rottanne *f*

**spruce**[2] adrett

**spry** rüstig, lebhaft

**spur 1.** Sporn *m* (*a.* ZO); *fig* Ansporn *m* (***to*** zu); ***on the*** ~ ***of the moment*** spontan; **2.** *e-m Pferd* die Sporen geben; *often* ~ ***on*** *fig* anspornen (***to*** zu)

**spurt**[1] **1.** spurten, sprinten; **2.** plötzliche Aktivität, (*Arbeits*)Anfall *m*; Spurt *m*, Sprint *m*

**spurt**[2] **1.** spritzen (***from*** aus); **2.** (*Wasser- etc*)Strahl *m*

**sput·ter** stottern (*a.* MOT); zischen

**spy 1.** Spion(in); **2.** spionieren, Spionage treiben (***for*** für); ~ ***into*** *fig* herumspionieren in (*dat*); ~ ***on*** *j-m* nachspionieren

**spy·hole** (Tür)Spion *m*

**squab·ble** (sich) streiten (***about, over*** um, wegen)

**squad** Mannschaft *f*, Trupp *m*; (*Überfall- etc*)Kommando *n*; Dezernat *n*

**squad car** (Funk)Streifenwagen *m*

**squad·ron** MIL, AVIAT Staffel *f*; MAR Geschwader *n*

**squal·id** schmutzig, verwahrlost, verkommen, armselig

**squall** Bö *f*

**squan·der** *Geld, Zeit etc* verschwenden, *Chance* vertun

**square 1.** Quadrat *n*; Viereck *n*; *öffentlicher* Platz; MATH Quadrat(zahl *f*) *n*; *board game*: Feld *n*; TECH Winkel(maß *n*) *m*; **2.** quadratisch, Quadrat...; viereckig; rechtwink(e)lig; eckig (*shoulders etc*); *fig* fair, gerecht; ***be*** (***all***) ~ quitt sein; **3.** quadratisch *or* rechtwink(e)lig machen (*a.* ~ ***off*** *or* ***up***); in Quadrate einteilen (*a.* ~ ***off***); MATH *Zahl* ins Quadrat erheben; *Schultern* straffen; *Konto* ausgleichen; *Schulden* begleichen; *fig* in Einklang bringen *or* stehen (***with*** mit); ~ ***up*** F abrechnen; ~ ***up to*** sich *j-m, e-m Problem etc* stellen

**square root** MATH Quadratwurzel *f*

**squash**[1] **1.** zerdrücken, zerquetschen; quetschen, zwängen (***into*** in *acc*); ~ ***flat*** flach drücken, F platt walzen; **2.** Gedränge *n*; SPORT Squash *n*

**squash**[2] BOT Kürbis *m*

S

**squat 1.** hocken, kauern; *leer stehendes Haus* besetzen; ~ ***down*** sich (hin)kauern *or* (hin)hocken; **2.** gedrungen, untersetzt; **squat·ter** Hausbesetzer(in)
**squaw** Squaw *f*
**squawk** kreischen, schreien; F lautstark protestieren (***about*** gegen)
**squeak 1.** piep(s)en (*mouse etc*); quietschen (*door etc*); **2.** Piep(s)en *n*; Piep(s) *m*; Quietschen *n*; **squeak·y** piepsig (*voice*); quietschend (*door etc*)
**squeal 1.** kreischen (***with*** vor *dat*); ~ ***on s.o.*** *fig* F j-n verpfeifen; **2.** Kreischen *n*; Schrei *m*
**squeam·ish** empfindlich, zart besaitet
**squeeze 1.** drücken; auspressen, ausquetschen; (sich) quetschen *or* zwängen (***into*** in *acc*); **2.** Druck *m*; GASTR Spritzer *m*; Gedränge *n*
**squeez·er** (Frucht)Presse *f*
**squid** ZO Tintenfisch *m*
**squint** schielen; blinzeln
**squirm** sich winden
**squir·rel** ZO Eichhörnchen *n*
**squirt 1.** (be)spritzen; **2.** Strahl *m*
**stab 1.** *v/t* niederstechen; ***be ~bed in the arm*** e-n Stich in den Arm bekommen; *v/i* stechen (***at*** nach); **2.** Stich *m*
**sta·bil·i·ty** Stabilität *f*; *fig* Dauerhaftigkeit *f*; Ausgeglichenheit *f*
**sta·bil·ize** (sich) stabilisieren
**sta·ble¹** stabil; *fig* dauerhaft; ausgeglichen
**sta·ble²** Stall *m*
**stack 1.** Stapel *m*, Stoß *m*; ***~s of, a ~ of*** F jede Menge *Arbeit etc*; **2.** stapeln; voll stapeln (***with*** mit); ~ ***up*** aufstapeln
**sta·di·um** SPORT Stadion *n*
**staff 1.** Stab *m*; Mitarbeiter(stab *m*) *pl*; Personal *n*, Belegschaft *f*; Lehrkörper *m*; MIL Stab *m*; **2.** besetzen (***with*** mit)
**staff room** Lehrerzimmer *n*
**stag** ZO Hirsch *m*
**stage 1.** THEA Bühne *f* (*a. fig*); Etappe *f* (*a. fig*), (Reise)Abschnitt *m*; Teilstrecke *f*, Fahrzone *f* (*bus etc*); *fig* Stufe *f*, Stadium *n*, Phase *f*; **2.** THEA inszenieren; veranstalten
**stage·coach** Postkutsche *f*
**stage| di·rec·tion** THEA Regieanweisung *f*; ~ **fright** Lampenfieber *n*; ~ **man·ag·er** THEA Inspizient *m*
**stag·ger 1.** *v/i* (sch)wanken, taumeln, torkeln; *v/t* *j-n* sprachlos machen, F umhauen; *Arbeitszeit etc* staffeln; **2.** Wanken *n*, Schwanken *n*, Taumeln *n*
**stag·nant** stehend (*water*); *esp* ECON stagnierend
**stag·nate** *esp* ECON stagnieren
**stain 1.** *v/t* beflecken; (ein)färben; *Holz* beizen; *Glas* bemalen; *v/i* Flecken bekommen, schmutzen; **2.** Fleck *m*; TECH Färbemittel *n*; (*Holz*)Beize *f*; Makel *m*
**stained glass** Bunt-, Farbglas *n*
**stain·less** nicht rostend, rostfrei
**stair** (Treppen)Stufe *f*; *pl* Treppe *f*
**stair·case, stair·way** Treppe *f*; Treppenhaus *n*
**stake¹ 1.** Pfahl *m*, Pfosten *m*; HIST Marterpfahl *m*; **2.** ~ ***off***, ~ ***out*** abstecken
**stake² 1.** Anteil *m*, Beteiligung *f* (***in*** an *dat*) (*a.* ECON); (Wett- *etc*)Einsatz *m*; ***be at ~*** *fig* auf dem Spiel stehen; **2.** *Geld etc* setzen (***on*** auf *acc*); *Ruf etc* riskieren, aufs Spiel setzen
**stale** alt(backen); abgestanden, *beer etc*: *a.* schal, *air etc*: *a.* verbraucht
**stalk¹** BOT Stängel *m*, Stiel *m*, Halm *m*
**stalk²** *v/t* sich heranpirschen an (*acc*); verfolgen, hinter *j-m*, *et.* herschleichen; *v/i* stolzieren
**stall¹ 1.** (*Obst- etc*)Stand *m*, (*Markt*)Bude *f*; AGR Box *f*; *pl* REL Chorgestühl *n*; *Br* THEA Parkett *n*; **2.** *v/t Motor* abwürgen; *v/i* MOT absterben
**stall²** *v/i* Ausflüchte machen; Zeit schinden; *v/t j-n* hinhalten; *et.* hinauszögern
**stal·li·on** ZO (Zucht)Hengst *m*
**stal·wart** kräftig, robust; *esp* POL treu
**stam·i·na** Ausdauer *f*; Durchhaltevermögen *n*, Kondition *f*
**stam·mer 1.** stottern, stammeln; **2.** Stottern *n*, Stammeln *n*
**stamp 1.** *v/i* sta(m)pfen, trampeln; *v/t Pass etc* (ab)stempeln; *Datum etc* aufstempeln (***on*** auf *acc*); *Brief etc* frankieren; *fig j-n* abstempeln (***as*** als, zu); ~ ***one's foot*** aufstampfen; ~ ***out*** *Feuer* austreten; TECH ausstanzen; **2.** (Brief-) Marke *f*; (*Steuer- etc*)Marke *f*; Stempel *m*; ***~ed addressed envelope*** Freiumschlag *m*
**stam·pede 1.** ZO wilde Flucht; wilder Ansturm, Massenansturm *m* (***for*** auf *acc*); **2.** *v/i* ZO durchgehen; *v/t* in Panik versetzen
**stanch** treu, zuverlässig
**stand 1.** *v/i* stehen; aufstehen; *fig fest-*

S

*etc* bleiben; ~ ***still*** still stehen; *v/t* stellen (***on*** auf *acc*); aushalten, ertragen; *e-r Prüfung etc* standhalten; *Probe* bestehen; *Chance* haben; *Drink etc* spendieren; ***I can't ~ him*** (*or* ***it***) ich kann ihn (*or* das) nicht ausstehen *or* leiden; ~ ***around*** herumstehen; ~ ***back*** zurücktreten; ~ ***by*** danebenstehen; *fig* zu *j-m* halten; zu *et.* stehen; ~ ***idly by*** tatenlos zusehen; ~ ***down*** verzichten; zurücktreten; JUR den Zeugenstand verlassen; ~ ***for*** stehen für, bedeuten; sich *et.* gefallen lassen, *et.* dulden; *esp Br* kandidieren für; ~ ***in*** einspringen (***for*** für); ~ ***in for s.o.*** *a.* j-n vertreten; ~ ***on*** (*fig* be)stehen auf (*dat*); ~ ***out*** hervorstechen; sich abheben (***against*** gegen, von); ~ ***over*** überwachen, aufpassen auf (*acc*); ~ ***together*** zusammenhalten, -stehen; ~ ***up*** aufstehen, sich erheben; ~ ***up for*** eintreten *or* sich einsetzen für; ~ ***up to*** *j-m* mutig gegenübertreten, *j-m* die Stirn bieten; **2.** (*Obst-, Messe- etc*)Stand *m*; (*Schirm-, Noten- etc*)Ständer *m*; SPORT *etc* Tribüne *f*; (*Taxi*)Stand(platz) *m*; JUR Zeugenstand *m*; ***take a ~*** *fig* Position beziehen (***on*** zu)

**stan·dard¹ 1.** Norm *f*, Maßstab *m*; Standard *m*, Niveau *n*; ~ ***of living, living ~*** Lebensstandard *m*; **2.** normal, Normal...; durchschnittlich, Durchschnitts...; Standard...

**stan·dard²** Standarte *f*, MOT Stander *m*; HIST Banner *n*

**stan·dard·ize** vereinheitlichen, *esp* TECH standardisieren, normen

**stan·dard lamp** *Br* Stehlampe *f*

**stand·by 1.** Reserve *f*; AVIAT Stand-by *n*; ***be on ~*** in Bereitschaft stehen; **2.** Reserve..., Not...; AVIAT Stand-by...

**stand-in** *film*, TV Double *n*; Ersatzmann *m*; Vertreter(in)

**stand·ing 1.** stehend; *fig* ständig; → ***ovation***; **2.** Rang *m*, Stellung *f*; Ansehen *n*, Ruf *m*; Dauer *f*; ***of long ~*** alt, seit langem bestehend; ~ **or·der** ECON Dauerauftrag *m*; ~ **room:** ~ ***only*** nur noch Stehplätze

**stand·off·ish** F (sehr) ablehnend, hochnäsig

**stand·point** *fig* Standpunkt *m*

**stand·still** Stillstand *m*; ***be at a ~*** stehen (*car etc*); ruhen (*production etc*); ***bring to a ~*** *Auto etc* zum Stehen bringen; *Produktion etc* zum Erliegen bringen

**stand-up** Steh...; ~ ***fight*** Schlägerei *f*

**stan·za** Strophe *f*

**sta·ple¹ 1.** Hauptnahrungsmittel *n*; ECON Haupterzeugnis *n*; **2.** Haupt...; üblich

**sta·ple² 1.** Heftklammer *f*; Krampe *f*; **2.** heften

**sta·pler** TECH (Draht)Hefter *m*

**star 1.** ASTR Stern *m*; PRINT Sternchen *n*; THEA, SPORT *etc* Star *m*; **2.** *v/t* PRINT mit e-m Sternchen kennzeichnen; ***~ring ...*** in der Hauptrolle *or* in den Hauptrollen ...; ***a film ~ring ...*** ein Film mit ... in der Hauptrolle *or* den Hauptrollen; *v/i* die *or* e-e Hauptrolle spielen (***in*** in *dat*)

**star·board** AVIAT, MAR Steuerbord *n*

**starch 1.** (*Kartoffel- etc*)Stärke *f*; stärkereiches Nahrungsmittel; (*Wäsche-*) Stärke *f*; **2.** *Wäsche* stärken

**stare 1.** starren; ~ ***at*** *j-n* anstarren; **2.** (starrer) Blick, Starren *n*

**stark 1.** *adj fig* nackt; ***be in ~ contrast to*** in krassem Gegensatz stehen zu; **2.** *adv*: F ~ ***naked*** splitternackt; ~ ***raving mad***, ~ ***staring mad*** total verrückt

**star·light** ASTR Sternenlicht *n*

**star·ling** ZO Star *m*

**star·lit** stern(en)klar

**star·ry** Stern..., Sternen...

**star·ry-eyed** F blauäugig, naiv

**start 1.** *v/i* anfangen, beginnen (*a.* ~ ***off***); aufbrechen (***for*** nach) (*a.* ~ ***off***, ~ ***out***); RAIL *etc* abfahren, MAR ablegen, AVIAT abfliegen, starten; MOT anspringen; TECH anlaufen; SPORT starten; zusammenfahren, -zucken (***at*** bei); ***to ~ with*** anfangs, zunächst; erstens; ~ ***from scratch*** ganz von vorn anfangen; *v/t* anfangen, beginnen (*a.* ~ ***off***); in Gang setzen *or* bringen, *Motor etc a.* anlassen, starten; **2.** Anfang *m*, Beginn *m*, (*esp* SPORT) Start *m*; Aufbruch *m*; Auffahren *n*, Aufschrecken *n*; ***at the ~*** am Anfang; SPORT am Start; ***for a ~*** erstens; ***from ~ to finish*** von Anfang bis Ende

**start·er** SPORT Starter(in); MOT Anlasser *m*, Starter *m*; *esp Br* GASTR F Vorspeise *f*; ***for ~s*** zunächst einmal

**start·le** erschrecken; überraschen, bestürzen

**starv·a·tion** Hungern *n*; ***die of ~*** verhungern; ~ ***diet*** F Fasten-, Hungerkur *f*, Nulldiät *f*

S

**starve** hungern (lassen); ~ (**to death**) verhungern (lassen); ***I'm starving!*** *Br* F, ***I'm ~d!*** F ich komme um vor Hunger!

**state 1.** Zustand *m*; Stand *m*, Lage *f*; POL (Bundes-, Einzel)Staat *m*; *often* ***State*** POL Staat *m*; **2.** Staats..., staatlich; **3.** angeben, nennen; erklären, JUR aussagen (***that*** dass); festlegen, festsetzen

**State De·part·ment** POL Außenministerium *n*

**state·ly** gemessen, würdevoll; prächtig

**state·ment** Statement *n*, Erklärung *f*; Angabe *f*; JUR Aussage *f*; ECON (*Bank-*, *Konto*)Auszug *m*; ***make a ~*** e-e Erklärung abgeben

**state-of-the-art** TECH neuest, modernst

**states·man** POL Staatsmann *m*

**stat·ic** statisch

**sta·tion 1.** (*a. Bus-*, *U-*)Bahnhof *m*, Station *f*; (*Forschungs-*, *Rettungs- etc*)Station *f*; Tankstelle *f*; (*Feuer*)Wache *f*; (*Polizei*)Revier *n*; (*Wahl*)Lokal *n*; *radio*, TV Sender *m*, Station *f*; **2.** aufstellen, postieren; MIL stationieren

**sta·tion·ar·y** stehend

**sta·tion·er** Schreibwarenhändler(in); **sta·tion·er's (shop)** Schreibwarenhandlung *f*; **sta·tion·er·y** Schreibwaren *pl*; Briefpapier *n*

**sta·tion·mas·ter** RAIL Stations-, Bahnhofsvorsteher *m*

**sta·tion wag·on** MOT Kombiwagen *m*

**sta·tis·ti·cal** statistisch

**stat·is·ti·cian** Statistiker *m*

**sta·tis·tics** Statistik(en *pl*) *f*

**stat·ue** Statue *f*, Standbild *n*

**sta·tus** Status *m*, Rechtsstellung *f*; (*Familien*)Stand *m*; Stellung *f*, Rang *m*, Status *m*; **~ line** EDP Statuszeile *f*

**stat·ute** Gesetz *n*; Statut *n*, Satzung *f*

**stat·ute of lim·i·ta·tions** JUR Verjährungsfrist *f*; ***come under the ~*** verjähren

**staunch**[1] *Br* → ***stanch***

**staunch**[2] *Blutung* stillen

**stay 1.** bleiben (***with s.o.*** bei j-m); wohnen (***at*** in *dat*; ***with s.o.*** bei j-m); ***~ put*** F sich nicht (vom Fleck) rühren; ***~ away*** wegbleiben, sich fern halten (***from*** von); ***~ up*** aufbleiben; **2.** Aufenthalt *m*; JUR Aussetzung *f*, Aufschub *m*

**stead·fast** treu, zuverlässig; fest

**stead·y 1.** *adj* fest; stabil; ruhig (*hand*), gut (*nerves*); gleichmäßig; **2.** (sich) beruhigen; **3.** *int a.* ***~ on!*** *Br* F Vorsicht!; **4.** *adv*: ***go ~ with s.o.*** (fest) mit j-m gehen; **5.** feste Freundin, fester Freund

**steak** GASTR Steak *n*; (*Fisch*)Filet *n*

**steal** stehlen (*a. fig*); sich stehlen, (sich) schleichen (***out of*** aus)

**stealth:** ***by ~*** heimlich, verstohlen

**stealth·y** heimlich, verstohlen

**steam 1.** Dampf *m*; Dunst *m*; ***let off ~*** Dampf ablassen, *fig a.* sich Luft machen; **2.** Dampf...; **3.** *v/i* dampfen; ***~ up*** beschlagen (*mirror etc*); *v/t* GASTR dünsten, dämpfen

**steam·boat** Dampfboot *n*, Dampfer *m*

**steam·er** Dampfer *m*, Dampfschiff *n*; Dampf-, Schnellkochtopf *m*

**steam·ship** Dampfer *m*, Dampfschiff *n*

**steel 1.** Stahl *m*; **2.** ***~ o.s. for*** sich wappnen gegen

**steel·work·er** Stahlarbeiter *m*

**steel·works** Stahlwerk *n*

**steep**[1] steil; *fig* stark (*rise etc*); F happig

**steep**[2] eintauchen (***in*** in *acc*); *Wäsche* (ein)weichen

**stee·ple** Kirchturm *m*

**stee·ple·chase** *horse racing*: Hindernisrennen *n*; SPORT Hindernislauf *m*

**steer**[1] ZO (junger) Ochse

**steer**[2] steuern, lenken

**steer·ing col·umn** MOT Lenksäule *f*

**steer·ing wheel** MOT Lenkrad *n*, *a.* MAR Steuerrad *n*

**stein** Maßkrug *m*

**stem 1.** BOT Stiel *m* (*a. of a wine glass etc*), Stängel *m*; LING Stamm *m*; **2.** ***~ from*** stammen *or* herrühren von

**stench** Gestank *m*

**sten·cil** Schablone *f*; PRINT Matrize *f*

**ste·nog·ra·pher** Stenotypistin *f*

**step 1.** Schritt *m* (*a. fig*); Stufe *f*; Sprosse *f*; (***a pair of***) ***~s*** (e-e) Tritt- *or* Stufenleiter; ***mind the ~!*** Vorsicht, Stufe!; ***~ by ~*** Schritt für Schritt; ***take ~s*** Schritte *or* et. unternehmen; **2.** gehen; treten (***in*** in *acc*; ***on*** auf *acc*); ***~ on it, ~ on the gas*** MOT F Gas geben, auf die Tube drücken; ***~ aside*** zur Seite treten; *fig* Platz machen; ***~ down*** *fig* Platz machen; ***~ up*** *Produktion etc* steigern

**step-by-step** *fig* schrittweise

**step·fa·ther** Stiefvater *m*

**step·lad·der** Tritt-, Stufenleiter *f*

S

**step·moth·er** Stiefmutter *f*
**steppes** GEOGR Steppe *f*
**step·ping-stone** *fig* Sprungbrett *n* (**to** für)
**ster·e·o 1.** Stereo *n*; Stereogerät *n*, Stereoanlage *f*; **2.** Stereo...; ~ **sys·tem** MUS Kompaktanlage *f*
**ster·ile** steril (*a. fig*), *a.* unfruchtbar, MED *a.* keimfrei
**ste·ril·i·ty** Sterilität *f* (*a. fig*), Unfruchtbarkeit *f*
**ster·il·ize** MED sterilisieren
**ster·ling** das Pfund Sterling
**stern**[1] streng
**stern**[2] MAR Heck *n*
**stew 1.** *Fleisch, Gemüse* schmoren, *Obst* dünsten; ~***ed apples*** Apfelkompott *n*; **2.** Eintopf *m*; ***be in a*** ~ in heller Aufregung sein
**stew·ard** Ordner *m*; AVIAT, MAR Steward *m*
**stew·ard·ess** AVIAT, MAR Stewardess *f*
**stick**[1] trockener Zweig; Stock *m*; ([*Eis*]*Hockey*)Schläger *m*; (*Besen- etc* -)Stiel *m*; AVIAT (*Steuer*)Knüppel *m*; Stück *n*, Stange *f*, (*Lippen- etc*)Stift *m*, Stäbchen *n*
**stick**[2] *v/t* mit *e-r Nadel etc* stechen (**into** in *acc*); *et.* kleben (**on** auf, an *acc*); an-, festkleben (***with*** mit); stecken; F tun, stellen, setzen, legen; ***I can't*** ~ ***him*** (*or* ***it***) *esp Br* F ich kann ihn (*or* das) nicht ausstehen *or* leiden; *v/i* kleben; kleben bleiben (**to** an *dat*); stecken bleiben; ~ ***at nothing*** vor nichts zurückschrecken; ~ ***by*** F bleiben bei; F zu *j-m* halten; ~ ***out*** vorstehen; abstehen; *et.* ausstrecken *or* vorstrecken; ~ ***to*** bleiben bei
**stick·er** Aufkleber *m*
**stick·ing plas·ter** *Br* Heftpflaster *n*
**stick·y** klebrig (***with*** von); F heikel, unangenehm
**stiff 1.** *adj* steif; F stark (*drink etc*); schwer, hart (*task, penalty etc*); hartnäckig (*resistance*); F happig, gepfeffert, gesalzen (*price*); ***keep a*** ~ ***upper lip*** *fig* Haltung bewahren; **2.** *adv* äußerst; höchst; ***be bored*** ~ F sich zu Tode langweilen; ***be scared*** ~ e-e wahnsinnige Angst haben; ***be worried*** ~ sich furchtbare Sorgen machen
**stiff·en** *v/t* *Wäsche* stärken; versteifen; verstärken; *v/i* steif werden; sich verhärten *or* versteifen

**sti·fle** ersticken; *fig* unterdrücken
**stile** Zauntritt *m*
**sti·let·to** Stilett *n*; ~ **heel** Bleistift-, Pfennigabsatz *m*
**still**[1] **1.** *adv* (immer) noch, noch immer; *with comparative*: noch; **2.** *cj* dennoch, trotzdem
**still**[2] **1.** *adj* still; ruhig; GASTR ohne Kohlensäure; **2.** *film*, TV Standfoto *n*
**still·born** MED tot geboren
**still life** PAINT Stillleben *n*
**stilt** Stelze *f*; **stilt·ed** *fig* gestelzt
**stim·u·lant** MED Stimulans *n*, Anregungs-, Aufputschmittel *n*; *fig* Anreiz *m*, Ansporn *m* (**to** für)
**stim·u·late** MED stimulieren (*a. fig*), anregen, *fig a.* anspornen
**stim·u·lus** Reiz *m*; *fig* Anreiz *m*, Ansporn *m* (**to** für)
**sting 1.** stechen (*insect*); brennen (auf *or* in *dat*); **2.** Stachel *m*; Stich *m*; Brennen *n*, brennender Schmerz
**stin·gy** F knaus(e)rig, knick(e)rig (*person*); mick(e)rig (*meal etc*)
**stink 1.** stinken (**of** nach); ~ ***up*** (*Br* ***out***) verpesten; **2.** Gestank *m*
**stint:** ~ ***o.s.*** (***of s.th.***) sich einschränken (mit et.); ~ (***on***) ***s.th.*** sparen mit et.
**stip·u·late** zur Bedingung machen; festsetzen, vereinbaren; **stip·u·la·tion** Bedingung *f*; Vereinbarung *f*
**stir 1.** (um)rühren; (sich) rühren *or* bewegen; *j-n* aufwühlen; ~ ***up*** *Unruhe* stiften; *Streit* entfachen; *Erinnerungen* wachrufen; **2.** ***give s.th. a*** ~ et. umrühren; ***cause*** (*or* ***create***) ***a*** ~ für Aufsehen sorgen
**stir·rup** Steigbügel *m*
**stitch 1.** Stich *m*; Masche *f*; MED Seitenstechen *n*; **2.** zunähen, *Wunde* nähen (*a.* ~ ***up***); heften
**stock 1.** Vorrat *m* (**of** an *dat*); GASTR Brühe *f*; *a.* ***live***~ Viehbestand *m*; (*Gewehr*)Schaft *m*; *fig* Abstammung *f*, Herkunft *f*; ECON Aktie(n *pl*) *f*; *pl* Aktien *pl*, Wertpapiere *pl*; ***have s.th. in*** ~ ECON et. vorrätig *or* auf Lager haben; ***take*** ~ ECON Inventur machen; ***take*** ~ ***of*** *fig* sich klar werden über (*acc*); **2.** ECON *Ware* vorrätig haben, führen; ~ ***up*** sich eindecken *or* versorgen (***on, with*** mit); **3.** Serien...; Standard...; stereotyp
**stock·breed·er** AGR Viehzüchter *m*
**stock·breed·ing** AGR Viehzucht *f*

S

**stock·brok·er** ECON Börsenmakler *m*
**stock ex·change** ECON Börse *f*
**stock·hold·er** ECON Aktionär(in)
**stock·ing** Strumpf *m*
**stock mar·ket** ECON Börse *f*
**stock·pile 1.** Vorrat *m* (**of** an *dat*); **2.** e-n Vorrat anlegen an (*dat*)
**stock·still** regungslos
**stock·tak·ing** ECON Inventur *f*; *fig* Bestandsaufnahme *f*
**stock·y** stämmig, untersetzt
**stol·id** gleichmütig
**stom·ach 1.** ANAT Magen *m*; Bauch *m*; *fig* Appetit *m* (**for** auf *acc*); **2.** vertragen (*a. fig*)
**stom·ach·ache** MED Magenschmerzen *pl*, Bauchschmerzen *pl*, Bauchweh *n*
**stom·ach up·set** MED Magenverstimmung *f*
**stone 1.** Stein *m*, BOT *a.* Kern *m*; (*Hagel*)Korn *n*; **2.** mit Steinen bewerfen; steinigen; entkernen, entsteinen
**stone·ma·son** Steinmetz *m*
**stone·ware** Steingut *n*
**ston·y** steinig; steinern (*face etc*), eisig (*silence*)
**stool** Hocker *m*, Schemel *m*; MED Stuhl *m*, Stuhlgang *m*
**stool·pi·geon** F (Polizei)Spitzel *m*
**stoop 1.** *v/i* sich bücken (*a.* ~ **down**); gebeugt gehen; ~ **to** *fig* sich herablassen *or* hergeben zu; **2.** gebeugte Haltung
**stop 1.** *v/i* (an)halten, stehen bleiben (*a. watch etc*), stoppen; aufhören; *esp Br* bleiben; ~ **dead** plötzlich *or* abrupt stehen bleiben; ~ **at nothing** vor nichts zurückschrecken; ~ **short of** *doing*, ~ **short at** *s.th.* zurückschrecken vor (*dat*); *v/t* anhalten, stoppen; aufhören mit; ein Ende machen *or* setzen (*dat*); *Blutung* stillen; *Arbeiten*, *Verkehr etc* zum Erliegen bringen; *et.* verhindern; *j-n* abhalten (**from** von), hindern (**from** an *dat*); *Rohr etc* verstopfen (*a.* ~ **up**); *Zahn* füllen, plombieren; *Scheck* sperren (lassen); ~ **by** vorbeischauen; ~ **in** vorbeischauen (**at** bei); ~ **off** F kurz Halt machen; ~ **over** kurz Halt machen; Zwischenstation machen; **2.** Halt *m*; (*Bus*)Haltestelle *f*; PHOT Blende *f*; *mst* **full** ~ LING Punkt *m*
**stop·gap** Notbehelf *m*
**stop·light** MOT Bremslicht *n*; rotes Licht
**stop·o·ver** Zwischenstation *f*; AVIAT Zwischenlandung *f*
**stop·page** Unterbrechung *f*, Stopp *m*; Verstopfung *f*; Streik *m*; *Br* (Gehalts-, Lohn)Abzug *m*
**stop·per** Stöpsel *m*
**stop sign** MOT Stoppschild *n*
**stop·watch** Stoppuhr *f*
**stor·age** ECON Lagerung *f*; Lagergeld *n*; EDP Speicher *m*
**store 1.** (ein)lagern; *Energie* speichern; EDP (ab)speichern, sichern; *a.* ~ **up** sich e-n Vorrat anlegen an (*dat*); **2.** Vorrat *m*; Lager *n*, Lagerhalle *f*, Lagerhaus *n*; Laden *m*, Geschäft *n*, *esp Br* Kaufhaus *n*, Warenhaus *n*; **set great** ~ **by** großen Wert legen auf (*acc*)
**store·house** Lagerhaus *n*; *fig* Fundgrube *f*
**store·keep·er** Ladenbesitzer(in)
**store·room** Lagerraum *m*
**sto·rey** *Br* → **story²**
**...sto·reyed** *Br*, **...sto·ried** mit ... Stockwerken, ...stöckig
**stork** ZO Storch *m*
**storm 1.** Unwetter *n*; Gewitter *n*; Sturm *m*; **2.** *v/t* MIL *etc* stürmen; *v/i* stürmen, stürzen; **storm·y** stürmisch
**sto·ry¹** Geschichte *f*; Märchen *n* (*a. fig*); Story *f*, *a.* Handlung *f*, *a.* Bericht *m* (**on** über *acc*)
**sto·ry²** Stock *m*, Stockwerk *n*, Etage *f*
**stout** korpulent, vollschlank; *fig* unerschrocken; entschieden
**stove** Ofen *m*, Herd *m*
**stow** *a.* ~ **away** verstauen
**stow·a·way** AVIAT, MAR blinder Passagier
**strad·dle** rittlings sitzen auf (*dat*)
**strag·gle** verstreut liegen *or* stehen; BOT *etc* wuchern; ~ **in** F einzeln eintrudeln
**strag·gler** Nachzügler(in)
**strag·gly** verstreut (liegend); BOT *etc* wuchernd; struppig (*mustache etc*)
**straight 1.** *adj* gerade; glatt (*hair*); pur (*whisky etc*); aufrichtig, offen, ehrlich; *sl* hetero(*sexuell*); *sl* clean, sauber; **put** ~ in Ordnung bringen; **2.** *adv* gerade; genau, direkt; klar; ehrlich, anständig; ~ **ahead** geradeaus; ~ **off** F sofort; ~ **on** geradeaus; ~ **out** F offen, rundheraus; **3.** SPORT (*Gegen-*, *Ziel*)Gerade *f*
**straight·en** *v/t* gerade machen, (gerade) richten; ~ **out** in Ordnung bringen;

S

*v/i a.* ~ ***out*** gerade werden; ~ ***up*** sich aufrichten

**straight·for·ward** aufrichtig; einfach

**strain 1.** *v/t Seil etc* (an)spannen; *sich, Augen etc* überanstrengen; sich *e-n Muskel etc* zerren; *Gemüse, Tee etc* abgießen; *v/i* sich anstrengen; ~ ***at*** zerren *or* ziehen an (*dat*); **2.** Spannung *f*; Anspannung *f*; Strapaze *f*; *fig* Belastung *f*; MED Zerrung *f*; **strained** MED gezerrt; gezwungen (*smile etc*); gespannt (*relations*); ***look*** ~ abgespannt aussehen

**strain·er** Sieb *n*

**strait** GEOGR Meerenge *f*, Straße *f*; *pl fig* Notlage *f*

**strait·ened:** ***live in*** ~ ***circumstances*** in beschränkten Verhältnissen leben

**strand** Strang *m*; Faden *m*; (*Kabel-*) Draht *m*; (*Haar*)Strähne *f*

**strand·ed:** ***be*** ~ MAR gestrandet sein; ***be*** (***left***) ~ *fig* festsitzen (***in*** in *dat*)

**strange** merkwürdig, seltsam, sonderbar; fremd; **strang·er** Fremde *m, f*

**stran·gle** erwürgen

**strap 1.** Riemen *m*, Gurt *m*; (*Uhr*)Armband *n*; Träger *m*; **2.** festschnallen; anschnallen

**stra·te·gic** strategisch

**strat·e·gy** Strategie *f*

**stra·tum** GEOL Schicht *f* (*a. fig*)

**straw** Stroh *n*; Strohhalm *m*

**straw·ber·ry** BOT Erdbeere *f*

**stray 1.** (herum)streunen; sich verirren; *fig* abschweifen (***from*** von); **2.** verirrtes *or* streunendes Tier; **3.** verirrt (*bullet, dog etc*); streunend (*dog etc*); vereinzelt

**streak 1.** Streifen *m*; Strähne *f*; (Charakter)Zug *m*; ***a*** ~ ***of lightning*** ein Blitz; ***lucky*** ~ Glückssträhne *f*; **2.** flitzen; streifen

**streak·y** streifig; GASTR durchwachsen

**stream 1.** Bach *m*; Strömung *f*; *fig* Strom *m*; **2.** strömen; flattern, wehen

**stream·er** Luft-, Papierschlange *f*; Wimpel *m*; EDP Streamer *m*

**street 1.** Straße *f*; ***on*** (*esp Br* ***in***) ***the*** ~ auf der Straße; **2.** Straßen...

**street·car** Straßenbahn(wagen *m*) *f*

**street sweep·er** Straßenkehrer *m*

**strength** Stärke *f*, Kraft *f*, Kräfte *pl*

**strength·en** *v/t* (ver)stärken; *v/i* stärker werden

**stren·u·ous** anstrengend, strapaziös; unermüdlich

**stress 1.** *fig* Stress *m*; PHYS, TECH Beanspruchung *f*, Belastung *f*, Druck *m*; LING Betonung *f*; *fig* Nachdruck *m*; **2.** betonen

**stress·ful** stressig, aufreibend

**stretch 1.** *v/t* strecken; (aus)weiten, dehnen; spannen; *fig* es nicht allzu genau nehmen mit; ~ ***out*** ausstrecken; ***be fully*** ~***ed*** *fig* richtig gefordert werden; voll ausgelastet sein; *v/i* sich dehnen, *a.* länger *or* weiter werden; sich dehnen *or* recken *or* strecken; sich erstrecken; ~ ***out*** sich ausstrecken; **2.** Dehnbarkeit *f*, Elastizität *f*; Strecke *f*; SPORT (*Gegen-, Ziel*)Gerade *f*; Zeit *f*, Zeitraum *m*, Zeitspanne *f*; ***have a*** ~ sich dehnen *or* recken *or* strecken

**stretch·er** Trage *f*

**strick·en** schwer betroffen; ~ ***with*** befallen *or* ergriffen von

**strict** streng, strikt; genau; ~***ly*** (***speaking***) genau genommen

**strict·ness** Strenge *f*

**stride 1.** schreiten, mit großen Schritten gehen; **2.** großer Schritt

**strife** Streit *m*

**strike 1.** *v/t* schlagen; treffen; einschlagen in (*acc*) (*lightning*); *Streichholz* anzünden; MAR auflaufen auf (*acc*); streichen (***from, off*** aus *dat*, von); stoßen auf (*acc*); *j-n* beeindrucken; *j-m* einfallen, in den Sinn kommen; *Münze* prägen; *Saite etc* anschlagen; *Lager, Zelt* abbrechen; *Flagge, Segel* streichen; ~ ***out*** (aus)streichen; ~ ***up*** *Lied etc* anstimmen; *Freundschaft etc* schließen; *v/i* schlagen; einschlagen; ECON streiken; ~ (***out***) ***at s.o.*** auf j-n einschlagen; **2.** ECON Streik *m*; (*Öl- etc*)Fund *m*; MIL Angriff *m*; *soccer*: Schuss *m*; ***be on*** ~ streiken; ***go on*** ~ streiken, in den Streik treten; ***a lucky*** ~ ein Glückstreffer

**strik·er** ECON Streikende *m, f*; *soccer*: Stürmer(in)

**strik·ing** apart; auffallend

**string 1.** Schnur *f*, Bindfaden *m*; (*Schürzen-, Schuh- etc*)Band *n*; (*Puppenspiel-*) Faden *m*, Draht *m*; (*Perlen- etc*)Schnur *f*; MUS, SPORT Saite *f*; (*Bogen*)Sehne *f*; BOT Faser *f*; EDP Zeichenfolge *f*; *fig* Reihe *f*, Serie *f*; ***the*** ~***s*** MUS die Streichinstrumente *pl*, die Streicher *pl*; ***pull a few*** ~***s*** *fig* ein paar Beziehungen spielen lassen; ***with no*** ~***s attached*** *fig* ohne

Bedingungen; **2.** *Perlen etc* aufreihen; *Gitarre etc* besaiten, *Tennisschläger etc* bespannen; *Bohnen* abziehen; **3.** MUS Streich...; **~ bean** BOT grüne Bohne
**strin·gent** streng
**string·y** fas(e)rig
**strip 1.** *v/i*: *a.* **~ *off*** sich ausziehen (***to*** bis auf *acc*); *v/t* ausziehen; *Farbe etc* abkratzen, *Tapete etc* abreißen (***from, off*** von); *a.* **~ *down*** TECH zerlegen, auseinander nehmen; **~ *s.o. of s.th.*** j-m et. rauben *or* wegnehmen; **2.** (*Land-, Papier- etc*)Streifen *m*; Strip *m*
**stripe** Streifen *m*; **striped** gestreift
**strive:** **~ *for*** *or* ***after*** streben nach
**stroke 1.** streicheln; streichen über (*acc*); **2.** Schlag *m* (*a.* SPORT); MED Schlag(anfall) *m*; (*Pinsel*)Strich *m*; *swimming*: Zug *m*; TECH Hub *m*; → ***four-stroke engine***; **~ *of lightning*** Blitzschlag *m*; ***a ~ of luck*** *fig* ein glücklicher Zufall, ein Glücksfall
**stroll 1.** bummeln, spazieren; **2.** Bummel *m*, Spaziergang *m*
**stroll·er** Bummler(in), Spaziergänger(in); Sportwagen *m*
**strong** stark (*a.* GASTR, PHARM); kräftig; mächtig; stabil; fest; robust
**strong·box** (Geld-, Stahl)Kassette *f*
**strong·hold** Festung *f*; Stützpunkt *m*; *fig* Hochburg *f*
**strong-mind·ed** willensstark
**strong room** Tresor(raum) *m*
**struc·ture** Struktur *f*; (Auf)Bau *m*, Gliederung *f*; Bau *m*, Konstruktion *f*
**strug·gle 1.** kämpfen, ringen (***with*** mit; ***for*** um); sich abmühen; sich winden, zappeln; **~ *against*** sich sträuben gegen; **2.** Kampf *m*
**strum** klimpern auf (*dat*) (*or* ***on*** auf *dat*)
**strut**[1] stolzieren
**strut**[2] TECH Strebe *f*; Stütze *f*
**stub 1.** (*Bleistift-, Zigaretten- etc*) Stummel *m*; Kontrollabschnitt *m*; **2.** sich *die Zehe* anstoßen; **~ *out*** *Zigarette* ausdrücken
**stub·ble** Stoppeln *pl*
**stub·bly** stoppelig
**stub·born** eigensinnig, stur; hartnäckig
**stub·born·ness** Starrsinn *m*
**stuck-up** F hochnäsig
**stud**[1] **1.** (*Kragen-, Manschetten*)Knopf *m*; *soccer*: Stollen *m*; Beschlagnagel *m*; Ziernagel *m*; *pl* MOT Spikes *pl*; **2.** ***be ~ded with*** besetzt sein mit; übersät sein mit; ***~ded tires*** Spikesreifen *pl*
**stud**[2] Gestüt *n*
**stu·dent** Student(in); Schüler(in)
**stud farm** Gestüt *n*
**stud horse** ZO Zuchthengst *m*
**stud·ied** wohl überlegt; gesucht
**stu·di·o** Studio *n*; Atelier *n*; *a.* **~ *apartment***, *Br* **~ *flat*** Studio *n*, Einzimmerappartement *n*; **~ couch** Schlafcouch *f*
**stu·di·ous** fleißig
**stud·y 1.** Studium *n*; Studie *f*, Untersuchung *f*; Arbeitszimmer *n*; *pl* Studium *n*; ***be in a brown ~*** in Gedanken versunken *or* geistesabwesend sein; **2.** studieren; lernen (***for*** für)
**stuff 1.** Zeug *n*; **2.** (aus)stopfen, (voll) stopfen; füllen (*a.* GASTR); **~ *o.s.*** F sich voll stopfen; **stuff·ing** Füllung *f* (*a.* GASTR)
**stuff·y** stickig; spießig; prüde
**stum·ble 1.** stolpern (***on, over***, *fig* ***at, over*** über *acc*); **~ *across***, **~ *on*** stoßen auf (*acc*); **2.** Stolpern *n*
**stump 1.** Stumpf *m*; Stummel *m*; **2.** stampfen, stapfen
**stump·y** F kurz und dick
**stun** betäuben; *fig* sprachlos machen
**stun·ning** fantastisch; unglaublich
**stunt**[1] (das Wachstum *gen*) hemmen; ***~ed*** BIOL verkümmert; ***become ~ed*** BIOL verkümmern
**stunt**[2] (*Film*)Stunt *m*; (*gefährliches*) Kunststück; (*Reklame*)Gag *m*
**stunt| man** *film*, TV Stuntman *m*, Double *n*; **~ wom·an** *film*, TV Stuntwoman *f*, Double *n*
**stu·pid** dumm; F blöd
**stu·pid·i·ty** Dummheit *f*
**stu·por** Betäubung *f*; ***in a drunken ~*** im Vollrausch
**stur·dy** kräftig, stämmig; *fig* entschlossen, hartnäckig
**stut·ter 1.** stottern (*a.* MOT); stammeln; **2.** Stottern *n*, Stammeln *n*
**sty**[1] → ***pigsty***
**sty**[2], **stye** MED Gerstenkorn *n*
**style 1.** Stil *m*; Ausführung *f*; Mode *f*; **2.** entwerfen; gestalten
**styl·ish** stilvoll; modisch, elegant
**styl·ist** Stilist(in)
**Sty·ro·foam**® Styropor® *n*
**suave** verbindlich
**sub·con·scious** Unterbewusstsein *n*;

~**ly** im Unterbewusstsein
**sub·di·vi·sion** Unterteilung *f*; Unterabteilung *f*
**sub·due** unterwerfen; *Ärger etc* unterdrücken; **sub·dued** gedämpft (*light, voice etc*); ruhig, still (*person*)
**sub·ject 1.** Thema *n*; PED, UNIV Fach *n*; LING Subjekt *n*, Satzgegenstand *m*; Untertan(in); Staatsangehörige *m,f*, -bürger(in); **2.** *adj*: ~ **to** anfällig für; **be ~ to** *a.* neigen zu; **be ~ to** unterliegen (*dat*); abhängen von; **prices ~ to change** Preisänderungen vorbehalten; **3.** unterwerfen; ~ **to** *e-m Test etc* unterziehen; *der Kritik etc* aussetzen
**sub·jec·tion** Unterwerfung *f*; Abhängigkeit *f* (**to** von)
**sub·ju·gate** unterjochen, unterwerfen
**sub·junc·tive** LING *a.* ~ **mood** Konjunktiv *m*
**sub·lease, sub·let** untervermieten, weitervermieten
**sub·lime** großartig; *fig* total
**sub·ma·chine gun** Maschinenpistole *f*
**sub·ma·rine 1.** unterseeisch; **2.** Unterseeboot *n*, U-Boot *n*
**sub·merge** tauchen; (ein)tauchen (**in** in *acc*)
**sub·mis·sion** Einreichung *f*; *boxing etc*: Aufgabe *f*; Unterwerfung *f* (**to** unter); **sub·mis·sive** unterwürfig
**sub·mit** *Gesuch etc* einreichen (**to** *dat or* bei); sich fügen (**to** *dat or* in *acc*); *boxing etc*: aufgeben
**sub·or·di·nate 1.** untergeordnet (**to** *dat*); **2.** Untergebene *m,f*; **3.** ~ **to** unterordnen (*dat*), zurückstellen (hinter *acc*); ~ **clause** LING Nebensatz *m*
**sub·scribe** *v/t Geld* geben, spenden (**to** für); *v/i*: ~ **to** *Zeitung etc* abonnieren; **sub·scrib·er** Abonnent(in); TEL Teilnehmer(in); **sub·scrip·tion** Abonnement *n*; (Mitglieds)Beitrag *m*
**sub·se·quent** später
**sub·side** sich senken (*building, road etc*); zurückgehen (*flood, demand etc*), sich legen (*storm, anger etc*)
**sub·sid·i·a·ry 1.** Neben...; ~ **question** Zusatzfrage *f*; **2.** ECON Tochtergesellschaft *f*
**sub·si·dize** subventionieren
**sub·si·dy** Subvention *f*
**sub·sist** leben, existieren (**on** von)
**sub·sis·tence** Existenz *f*
**sub·stance** Substanz *f* (*a. fig*), Stoff *m*; *das* Wesentliche, Kern *m*
**sub·stan·dard** minderwertig
**sub·stan·tial** solid (*furniture etc*); beträchtlich (*salary etc*), (*changes etc a.*) wesentlich; reichlich, kräftig (*meal*)
**sub·stan·ti·ate** beweisen
**sub·stan·tive** LING Substantiv *n*, Hauptwort *n*
**sub·sti·tute 1.** Ersatz *m*; Stellvertreter(in), Vertretung *f*; SPORT Auswechselspieler(in), Ersatzspieler(in); **2.** ~ **s.th. for s.th.** et. durch et. ersetzen, et. gegen et. austauschen *or* auswechseln; ~ **for** einspringen für, *j-n* vertreten
**sub·sti·tu·tion** Ersatz *m*; SPORT Austausch *m*, Auswechslung *f*
**sub·ter·fuge** List *f*
**sub·ter·ra·ne·an** unterirdisch
**sub·ti·tle** Untertitel *m*
**sub·tle** fein (*differences etc*); raffiniert (*plan etc*); scharf (*mind*); scharfsinnig
**sub·tract** MATH abziehen, subtrahieren (**from** von); **sub·trac·tion** MATH Abziehen *n*, Subtraktion *f*
**sub·trop·i·cal** subtropisch
**sub·urb** Vorort *m*, Vorstadt *f*
**sub·ur·ban** Vorort..., vorstädtisch, Vorstadt...
**sub·ver·sive** umstürzlerisch, subversiv
**sub·way** Unterführung *f*; U-Bahn *f*
**suc·ceed** *v/i* Erfolg haben, erfolgreich sein, (*plan etc a.*) gelingen; ~ **to** in *e-m Amt* nachfolgen; ~ **to the throne** auf dem Thron folgen; *v/t*: ~ **s.o. as** j-s Nachfolger werden als
**suc·cess** Erfolg *m*
**suc·cess·ful** erfolgreich
**suc·ces·sion** Folge *f*; Erb-, Nach-, Thronfolge *f*; **five times in ~** fünfmal hintereinander; **in quick ~** in rascher Folge; **suc·ces·sive** aufeinander folgend; **suc·ces·sor** Nachfolger(in); Thronfolger(in)
**suc·cu·lent** GASTR saftig
**such** solche(r, -s); derartige(r, -s); so; derart; ~ **a** so ein(e)
**suck 1.** *v/t* saugen; lutschen (an *dat*); *v/i* saugen (**at** an *dat*); **2. have** *or* **take a ~ at** saugen *or* lutschen an (*dat*)
**suck·er** ZO Saugnapf *m*, Saugorgan *n*; TECH Saugfuß *m*; BOT Wurzelschössling *m*, Wurzelspross *m*; F Trottel *m*, Simpel *m*; Lutscher *m*

S

**suck·le** säugen, stillen
**suc·tion** (An)Saugen *n*; Saugwirkung *f*; **~ pump** TECH Saugpumpe *f*
**sud·den** plötzlich, unvermittelt; ***all of a ~*** F ganz plötzlich
**sud·den·ly** plötzlich
**suds** Seifenschaum *m*
**sue** JUR *j-n* verklagen (***for*** auf *acc*, wegen); klagen (***for*** auf *acc*)
**suede, suède** Wildleder *n*, Velours(leder) *n*
**su·et** GASTR Nierenfett *n*, Talg *m*
**suf·fer** *v/i* leiden (***from*** an *dat*, unter *dat*); darunter leiden; *v/t* erleiden; *Folgen* tragen; **suf·fer·er** Leidende *m, f*; **suf·fer·ing** Leiden *n*; Leid *n*
**suf·fi·cient** genügend, genug, ausreichend; ***be ~*** genügen, (aus)reichen
**suf·fix** LING Suffix *n*, Nachsilbe *f*
**suf·fo·cate** ersticken
**suf·frage** POL Wahl-, Stimmrecht *n*
**suf·fuse** durchfluten (*light etc*); überziehen (*color etc*)
**sug·ar 1.** Zucker *m*; **2.** zuckern
**sug·ar beet** BOT Zuckerrübe *f*
**sug·ar bowl** Zuckerdose *f*
**sug·ar·cane** BOT Zuckerrohr *n*
**sug·ar tongs** Zuckerzange *f*
**sug·ar·y** süß; *fig* süßlich
**sug·gest** vorschlagen, anregen; hindeuten *or* hinweisen auf (*acc*), schließen lassen auf (*acc*); andeuten
**sug·ges·tion** Vorschlag *m*, Anregung *f*; Anflug *m*, Spur *f*; Andeutung *f*; PSYCH Suggestion *f*
**sug·ges·tive** zweideutig (*remark etc*), viel sagend (*look etc*)
**su·i·cide** Selbstmord *m*; Selbstmörder(in); ***commit ~*** Selbstmord begehen
**suit 1.** Anzug *m*; Kostüm *n*; *card game*: Farbe *f*; JUR Prozess *m*; ***follow ~*** *fig* dem Beispiel folgen, dasselbe tun; **2.** *v/t j-m* passen (*date etc*); *j-n* kleiden, *j-m* stehen; *et.* anpassen (***to*** *dat*); ***~ s.th., be ~ed to s.th.*** geeignet sein *or* sich eignen für; ***~ yourself!*** mach, was du willst!
**sui·ta·ble** passend, geeignet (***for, to*** für)
**suit·case** Koffer *m*
**suite** (*Möbel-, Sitz*)Garnitur *f*; Suite *f*, Zimmerflucht *f*; MUS Suite *f*; Gefolge *n*
**sul·fur** CHEM Schwefel *m*
**sul·fu·ric ac·id** CHEM Schwefelsäure *f*
**sulk** schmollen, F eingeschnappt sein
**sulk·y** schmollend, F eingeschnappt
**sul·len** mürrisch, verdrossen
**sul·phur** *Br* → ***sulfur***
**sul·phu·ric ac·id** *Br* → ***sulfuric acid***
**sul·try** schwül; aufreizend (*look etc*)
**sum 1.** Summe *f*; Betrag *m*; (einfache) Rechenaufgabe; ***do ~s*** rechnen; **2.** ***~ up*** zusammenfassen; *j-n, et.* abschätzen
**sum·mar·ize** zusammenfassen
**sum·ma·ry** Zusammenfassung *f*, (kurze) Inhaltsangabe
**sum·mer** Sommer *m*; ***in*** (***the***) ~ im Sommer; **~ camp** Ferienlager *n*; **~ hol·i·days** *Br* Sommerferien *pl*; **~ re·sort** Sommerfrische *f*; **~ school** Ferienkurs *m*
**sum·mer·time** Sommer *m*, Sommerszeit *f*; ***in*** (***the***) ~ im Sommer
**sum·mer| time** *esp Br* Sommerzeit *f*; **~ va·ca·tion** Sommerferien *pl*
**sum·mer·y** sommerlich, Sommer...
**sum·mit** Gipfel *m* (*a.* ECON, POL, *fig*); **~ con·fe·rence** POL Gipfelkonferenz *f*; **~ meet·ing** POL Gipfeltreffen *n*
**sum·mon** auffordern; *Versammlung etc* einberufen; JUR vorladen; ***~ up*** *Kraft, Mut etc* zusammennehmen
**sum·mons** JUR Vorladung *f*
**sump** *Br* MOT Ölwanne *f*
**sump·tu·ous** luxuriös, aufwändig
**sun 1.** Sonne *f*; **2.** Sonnen...; **3.** ***~ o.s.*** sich sonnen
**Sun** ABBR *of* ***Sunday*** So., Sonntag *m*
**sun·bathe** sich sonnen, ein Sonnenbad nehmen
**sun·beam** Sonnenstrahl *m*
**sun·bed** Sonnenbank *f*
**sun·burn** Sonnenbrand *m*
**sun cream** Sonnencreme *f*
**sun·dae** GASTR Eisbecher *m*
**Sun·day** (ABBR ***Sun***) Sonntag *m*; ***on ~*** (am) Sonntag; ***on ~s*** sonntags
**sun·dial** Sonnenuhr *f*
**sun·dries** Diverses, Verschiedenes
**sun·dry** diverse, verschiedene
**sun·glass·es** (***a pair of ~*** e-e) Sonnenbrille *f*
**sunk·en** MAR gesunken, versunken; versenkt; tief liegend; eingefallen (*cheeks*), (*a. eyes*) eingesunken
**sun·light** Sonnenlicht *n*
**sun·lit** sonnenbeschienen
**sun·ny** sonnig
**sun·rise** Sonnenaufgang *m*; ***at ~*** bei Sonnenaufgang

**sun·roof** Dachterrasse *f*; MOT Schiebedach *n*
**sun·set** Sonnenuntergang *m*; ***at ~*** bei Sonnenuntergang
**sun·shade** Sonnenschirm *m*
**sun·shine** Sonnenschein *m*
**sun·stroke** MED Sonnenstich *m*
**sun·tan** (Sonnen)Bräune *f*; **~ lo·tion** Sonnenschutz *m*, Sonnencreme *f*; **~ oil** Sonnenöl *n*
**su·per** F super, spitze, klasse
**su·per...** Über..., über...
**su·per·a·bun·dant** überreichlich
**su·per·an·nu·at·ed** pensioniert, im Ruhestand
**su·perb** ausgezeichnet
**su·per·charg·er** MOT Kompressor *m*
**su·per·cil·i·ous** hochmütig, F hochnäsig
**su·per·fi·cial** oberflächlich
**su·per·flu·ous** überflüssig
**su·per·hu·man** übermenschlich
**su·per·im·pose** überlagern; *Bild etc* einblenden (***on*** in *acc*)
**su·per·in·tend** die (Ober)Aufsicht haben über (*acc*), überwachen; leiten
**su·per·in·tend·ent** Aufsicht *f*, Aufsichtsbeamter *m*, -beamtin *f*; *Br* Kriminalrat *m*
**su·pe·ri·or 1.** ranghöher (***to*** als); überlegen (***to*** *dat*), besser (***to*** als); ausgezeichnet, hervorragend; überheblich, überlegen; ***Father Superior*** REL Superior *m*; ***Mother Superior*** REL Oberin *f*; **2.** Vorgesetzte *m, f*; **su·pe·ri·or·i·ty** Überlegenheit *f* (***over*** gegenüber)
**su·per·la·tive 1.** höchste(r, -s), überragend; **2.** *a.* ***~ degree*** LING Superlativ *m*
**su·per·mar·ket** Supermarkt *m*
**su·per·nat·u·ral** übernatürlich
**su·per·nu·me·ra·ry** zusätzlich
**su·per·sede** ablösen, ersetzen, verdrängen
**su·per·son·ic** AVIAT, PHYS Überschall...
**su·per·sti·tion** Aberglaube *m*
**su·per·sti·tious** abergläubisch
**su·per·store** Großmarkt *m*
**su·per·vene** dazwischenkommen
**su·per·vise** beaufsichtigen, überwachen; **su·per·vi·sion** Beaufsichtigung *f*, Überwachung *f*; ***under s.o.'s ~*** unter j-s Aufsicht; **su·per·vi·sor** Aufseher(in), Aufsicht *f*
**sup·per** Abendessen *n*; ***have ~*** zu Abend essen; → ***lord***
**sup·plant** verdrängen
**sup·ple** gelenkig, geschmeidig, biegsam
**sup·ple·ment 1.** Ergänzung *f*; Nachtrag *m*, Anhang *m*; Ergänzungsband *m*; (*Zeitungs- etc*)Beilage *f*; **2.** ergänzen; **sup·ple·men·ta·ry** ergänzend, zusätzlich
**sup·pli·er** ECON Lieferant(in), *a. pl* Lieferfirma *f*
**sup·ply 1.** liefern; stellen, sorgen für; *j-n, et.* versorgen, ECON beliefern (***with*** mit); **2.** Lieferung *f* (***to*** an *acc*); Versorgung *f*; ECON Angebot *n*; *mst pl* Vorrat *m* (***of*** an *dat*), *a.* Proviant *m*, MIL Nachschub *m*; ***~ and demand*** ECON Angebot und Nachfrage
**sup·port 1.** (ab)stützen, *Gewicht etc* tragen; *Währung* stützen; unterstützen; unterhalten, sorgen für; **2.** Stütze *f*; TECH Träger *m*; *fig* Unterstützung *f*
**sup·port·er** Anhänger(in) (*a.* SPORT), Befürworter(in)
**sup·pose 1.** annehmen, vermuten; ***be ~d to ...*** sollen; ***what is that ~d to mean?*** was soll denn das?; ***I ~ so*** ich nehme es an, vermutlich; **2.** *cj* angenommen; wie wäre es, wenn
**sup·posed** angeblich, vermeintlich
**sup·pos·ing** → ***suppose*** 2
**sup·po·si·tion** Annahme *f*, Vermutung *f*
**sup·pos·i·to·ry** PHARM Zäpfchen *n*
**sup·press** unterdrücken
**sup·pres·sion** Unterdrückung *f*
**sup·pu·rate** MED eitern
**su·prem·a·cy** Vormachtstellung *f*
**su·preme** höchste(r, -s), oberste(r, -s), Ober...; größte(r, -s)
**sur·charge 1.** Nachporto *or* e-n Zuschlag erheben (***on*** auf *acc*); **2.** Aufschlag *m*, Zuschlag *m* (***on*** auf *acc*); Nach-, Strafporto *n* (***on*** auf *acc*)
**sure 1.** *adj* sicher; ***~ of o.s.*** selbstsicher; ***~ of winning*** siegessicher; ***~ thing!*** F (aber) klar!; ***be or feel ~*** sicher sein; ***be ~ to ...*** vergiss nicht zu ...; ***for ~*** ganz sicher *or* bestimmt; ***make ~ that*** sich (davon) überzeugen, dass; ***to be ~*** sicher(lich); **2.** *adv* F sicher, klar; ***~ enough*** tatsächlich
**sure·ly** sicher(lich)
**sur·e·ty** JUR Bürge *m*, Bürgin *f*; Bürg-

S

schaft *f*, Sicherheit *f*; ***stand ~ for s.o.*** für j-n bürgen
**surf 1.** Brandung *f*; **2.** SPORT surfen
**sur·face 1.** Oberfläche *f*; (*Straßen*)Belag *m*; **2.** auftauchen; *Straße* mit e-m Belag versehen; **3.** Oberflächen...; *fig* oberflächlich; ***~ mail*** gewöhnliche Post
**surf·board** Surfboard *n*, Surfbrett *n*
**surf·er** Surfer(in), Wellenreiter(in)
**surf·ing** Surfen *n*, Wellenreiten *n*
**surge 1.** *fig* Welle *f*, Woge *f*, (*Gefühls*)Aufwallung *f*; **2.** (vorwärts) drängen; ***~ (up)*** aufwallen
**sur·geon** MED Chirurg(in)
**sur·ge·ry** MED Chirurgie *f*; operativer Eingriff, Operation *f*; *Br* Sprechzimmer *n*; *Br* Sprechstunde *f*; *a.* ***doctor's ~*** Arztpraxis *f*; **~ hours** MED *Br* Sprechstunde(n *pl*) *f*
**sur·gi·cal** MED chirurgisch
**sur·ly** mürrisch, unwirsch
**sur·name** Familienname *m*, Nachname *m*, Zuname *m*
**sur·pass** *Erwartungen etc* übertreffen
**sur·plus 1.** Überschuss *m* (***of*** an *dat*); **2.** überschüssig
**sur·prise 1.** Überraschung *f*, Verwunderung *f*; ***take s.o. by ~*** j-n überraschen; **2.** überraschen; ***be ~d at*** *or* ***by*** überrascht sein über (*acc*)
**sur·ren·der 1.** *v/i* ***~ to*** MIL, *a. fig* sich ergeben (*dat*), kapitulieren vor (*dat*); ***~ to the police*** sich der Polizei stellen; *v/t et.* übergeben, ausliefern (***to*** *dat*); aufgeben, verzichten auf (*acc*); ***~ o.s. to the police*** sich der Polizei stellen; **2.** MIL Kapitulation *f* (*a. fig*); Aufgabe *f*, Verzicht *m*
**sur·ro·gate** Ersatz *m*
**sur·ro·gate moth·er** Leihmutter *f*
**sur·round** umgeben; umstellen
**sur·round·ing** umliegend
**sur·round·ings** Umgebung *f*
**sur·vey 1.** (sich) *et.* betrachten (*a. fig*); *Haus etc* begutachten; *Land* vermessen; **2.** Umfrage *f*; Überblick *m* (***of*** über *acc*); Begutachtung *f*; Vermessung *f*
**sur·vey·or** Gutachter *m*; Land(ver)messer *m*
**sur·viv·al** Überleben *n* (*a. fig*); Überbleibsel *n*; **~ in·stinct** Selbsterhaltungstrieb *m*; **~ kit** Überlebensausrüstung *f*; **~ train·ing** Überlebenstraining *n*
**sur·vive** überleben; *Feuer etc* überstehen; erhalten bleiben *or* sein
**sur·vi·vor** Überlebende *m, f* (***from, of*** *gen*)
**sus·cep·ti·ble** empfänglich, anfällig (*both*: ***to*** für)
**sus·pect 1.** *j-n* verdächtigen (***of*** *gen*); *et.* vermuten; *et.* anzweifeln, *et.* bezweifeln; **2.** Verdächtige *m, f*; **3.** verdächtig, suspekt
**sus·pend** *Verkauf*, *Zahlungen etc* (vorübergehend) einstellen; JUR *Verfahren*, *Urteil* aussetzen, *Strafe* zur Bewährung aussetzen; *j-n* suspendieren; vorübergehend ausschließen (***from*** aus); SPORT *j-n* sperren; (auf)hängen; ***be ~ed*** schweben; **sus·pend·er** *Br* Strumpfhalter *m*, Straps *m*; Sockenhalter *m*; (*a.* ***a pair of***) ***~s*** Hosenträger *pl*
**sus·pense** Spannung *f*; ***in ~*** gespannt, voller Spannung
**sus·pen·sion** (vorübergehende) Einstellung; Suspendierung *f*; vorübergehender Ausschluss; SPORT Sperre *f*; MOT *etc* Aufhängung *f*; **~ bridge** Hängebrücke *f*; **~ rail·way** *esp Br* Schwebebahn *f*
**sus·pi·cion** Verdacht *m*; Verdächtigung *f*; Argwohn *m*, Misstrauen *n*; *fig* Hauch *m*, Spur *f*; **sus·pi·cious** verdächtig; argwöhnisch, misstrauisch; ***become ~*** Verdacht schöpfen
**sus·tain** *j-n* stärken; *Interesse etc* aufrechterhalten; *Schaden*, *Verlust* erleiden; JUR *e-m Einspruch etc* stattgeben
**swab** MED **1.** Tupfer *m*; Abstrich *m*; **2.** *Wunde* abtupfen
**swad·dle** *Baby* wickeln
**swag·ger** stolzieren
**swal·low**[1] **1.** schlucken (*a.* F); hinunterschlucken; ***~ up*** *fig* schlucken, verschlingen; **2.** Schluck *m*
**swal·low**[2] ZO Schwalbe *f*
**swamp 1.** Sumpf *m*; **2.** überschwemmen; ***be ~ed with*** *fig* überschwemmt werden mit; **swamp·y** sumpfig
**swan** ZO Schwan *m*
**swank 1.** F *esp Br* angeben; **2.** F *esp Br* Angeber(in); Angabe *f*; **3.** F piekfein
**swank·y** F piekfein; *esp Br* angeberisch
**swap** F **1.** (ein)tauschen; **2.** Tausch *m*
**swarm 1.** ZO Schwarm *m* (*a. fig*); **2.** ZO schwärmen, *fig a.* strömen; *a. fig* wimmeln (***with*** von)

**swar·thy** dunkel (*skin*), dunkelhäutig (*person*)
**swas·ti·ka** Hakenkreuz *n*
**swat** *Fliege etc* totschlagen
**sway 1.** *v/i* sich wiegen, schaukeln; **~ *between*** *fig* schwanken zwischen (*dat*); *v/t* hin- und herbewegen, schwenken, *s-n Körper* wiegen; beeinflussen; **2.** Schwanken *n*, Schaukeln *n*
**swear** fluchen; schwören; **~ *at s.o.*** j-n wüst beschimpfen; **~ *by*** *fig* F schwören auf (*acc*); **~ *s.o. in*** JUR j-n vereidigen
**sweat 1.** *v/i* schwitzen (***with*** vor *dat*); *v/t*: **~ *out*** *Krankheit* ausschwitzen; **~ *blood*** F sich abrackern (***over*** mit); **2.** Schweiß *m*; F Schufterei *f*; ***get in(to) a ~*** *fig* F ins Schwitzen geraten *or* kommen
**sweat·er** Pullover *m*
**sweat·shirt** Sweatshirt *n*
**sweat·y** schweißig, verschwitzt; nach Schweiß riechend, Schweiß...; schweißtreibend
**Swede** Schwede *m*, Schwedin *f*
**Swe·den** Schweden *n*
**Swe·dish 1.** schwedisch; **2.** LING Schwedisch *n*
**sweep 1.** *v/t* kehren, fegen; *fig* fegen über (*acc*) (*storm etc*); *Horizont etc* absuchen (***for*** nach); *fig Land etc* überschwemmen; **~ *along*** mitreißen; *v/i* kehren, fegen; rauschen (*person*); **2.** Kehren *n*, Fegen *n*; Hieb *m*, Schlag *m*; F Schornsteinfeger *m*, Kaminkehrer *m*; ***give the floor a good ~*** den Boden gründlich kehren *or* fegen; ***make a clean ~*** gründlich aufräumen; SPORT gründlich abräumen
**sweep·er** (*Straßen*)Kehrer *m*; Kehrmaschine *f*; *soccer*: Libero *m*
**sweep·ing** durchgreifend (*changes etc*); pauschal, zu allgemein
**sweep·ings** Kehricht *m*
**sweet 1.** süß (*a. fig*); lieblich; lieb; **~ *nothings*** Zärtlichkeiten *pl*; ***have a ~ tooth*** gern naschen; **2.** *Br* Süßigkeit *f*, Bonbon *m, n*; *Br* Nachtisch *m*; **~ corn** *esp Br* BOT Zuckermais *m*
**sweet·en** süßen
**sweet·heart** Schatz *m*, Liebste *m, f*
**sweet pea** BOT Gartenwicke *f*
**sweet shop** *esp Br* Süßwarengeschäft *n*
**swell 1.** *v/i a.* **~ *up*** MED (an)schwellen; *a.* **~ *out*** sich blähen; *v/t fig Zahl etc* anwachsen lassen; *a.* **~ *out*** *Segel* blähen; **2.** MAR Dünung *f*; **3.** F klasse
**swell·ing** MED Schwellung *f*
**swel·ter** vor Hitze fast umkommen
**swerve 1.** schwenken (***to the left*** nach links), e-n Schwenk machen; *fig* abweichen (***from*** von); **2.** Schwenk *m*, Schwenkung *f*, MOT *etc a.* Schlenker *m*
**swift** schnell
**swim 1.** *v/i* schwimmen; *fig* verschwimmen; ***my head was ~ming*** mir drehte sich alles; *v/t* *Strecke* schwimmen; *Fluss etc* durchschwimmen; **2.** Schwimmen *n*; ***go for a ~*** schwimmen gehen
**swim·mer** Schwimmer(in)
**swim·ming** Schwimmen *n*; **~ bath(s)** *Br* Schwimmbad *n*, *esp* Hallenbad *n*; **~ cap** Badekappe *f*, Bademütze *f*; **~ costume** Badeanzug *m*; **~ pool** Swimmingpool *m*, Schwimmbecken *n*; **~ trunks** Badehose *f*
**swim·suit** Badeanzug *m*
**swin·dle 1.** *j-n* beschwindeln (***out of*** um); **2.** Schwindel *m*
**swine** ZO Schwein *n* (*a.* F *fig*)
**swing 1.** *v/i* (hin- und her)schwingen; sich schwingen; einbiegen, -schwenken (***into*** in *acc*); MUS schwungvoll spielen (*band etc*); Schwung haben (*music*); **~ *round*** sich ruckartig umdrehen; **~ *shut*** zuschlagen (*door etc*); *v/t et., die Arme etc* schwingen; **2.** Schwingen *n*; Schaukel *f*; *fig* Schwung *m*; *fig* Umschwung *m*; ***in full ~*** in vollem Gang
**swing door** Pendeltür *f*
**swin·ish** ekelhaft
**swipe 1.** Schlag *m*; **2.** schlagen (***at*** nach)
**swirl 1.** wirbeln; **2.** Wirbel *m*
**swish[1] 1.** *v/i* sausen, zischen; rascheln (*silk etc*); *v/t* mit *dem Schwanz* schlagen; **2.** Sausen *n*, Zischen *n*; Rascheln *n*; Schlagen *n*
**swish[2]** *Br* feudal, schick
**Swiss 1.** schweizerisch, eidgenössisch, Schweizer...; **2.** Schweizer(in); ***the ~*** die Schweizer *pl*
**switch 1.** ELECTR, TECH Schalter *m*; RAIL Weiche *f*; Gerte *f*, Rute *f*; *fig* Umstellung *f*; **2.** ELECTR, TECH (um)schalten (*a.* **~ *over***) (***to*** auf *acc*); RAIL rangieren; wechseln (***to*** zu); **~ *off*** abschalten, ausschalten; **~ *on*** anschalten, einschalten
**switch·board** ELECTR Schalttafel *f*; (Telefon)Zentrale *f*

**Swit·zer·land** die Schweiz
**swiv·el** (sich) drehen
**swiv·el chair** Drehstuhl *m*
**swoon** in Ohnmacht fallen
**swoop 1.** *fig* F zuschlagen (*police etc*); *a.* ~ ***down*** ZO herabstoßen (**on** auf *acc*); ~ ***on*** F herfallen über (*acc*); **2.** Razzia *f*
**swop** F → ***swap***
**sword** Schwert *n*
**syc·a·more** BOT Bergahorn *m*; Platane *f*
**syl·la·ble** Silbe *f*
**syl·la·bus** PED, UNIV Lehrplan *m*
**sym·bol** Symbol *n*
**sym·bol·ic** symbolisch
**sym·bol·is·m** Symbolik *f*
**sym·bol·ize** symbolisieren
**sym·met·ri·cal** symmetrisch
**sym·me·try** Symmetrie *f*
**sym·pa·thet·ic** mitfühlend; verständnisvoll; wohlwollend
**sym·pa·thize** mitfühlen; sympathisieren
**sym·pa·thiz·er** Sympathisant(in)
**sym·pa·thy** Mitgefühl *n*; Verständnis *n*
**sym·pho·ny** MUS Sinfonie *f*; ~ **or·ches·tra** MUS Sinfonieorchester *n*
**symp·tom** Symptom *n*
**syn·chro·nize** *v/t* aufeinander abstimmen; *Uhren*, *Film* synchronisieren; *v/i* synchron gehen *or* sein
**syn·o·nym** Synonym *n*
**sy·non·y·mous** synonym; gleichbedeutend
**syn·tax** LING Syntax *f*, Satzlehre *f*
**syn·the·sis** Synthese *f*
**syn·thet·ic** CHEM synthetisch; ~ **fi·ber** (*Br* **fi·bre**) Kunstfaser *f*
**Syr·i·a** Syrien *n*
**sy·ringe** MED Spritze *f*
**syr·up** Sirup *m*
**sys·tem** System *n*; (*Straßen- etc*)Netz *n*; Organismus *m*
**sys·te·mat·ic** systematisch
**sys·tem er·ror** EDP Systemfehler *m*

# T

**T, t** T, t *n*
**tab** Aufhänger *m*, Schlaufe *f*; Lasche *f*; Etikett *n*, Schildchen *n*; Reiter *m*; F Rechnung *f*
**ta·ble 1.** Tisch *m*; (Tisch)Runde *f*; Tabelle *f*, Verzeichnis *n*; MATH Einmaleins *n*; ***at*** ~ bei Tisch; ***at the*** ~ am Tisch; ***turn the*** ~***s*** (**on s.o.**) *fig* den Spieß umdrehen; **2.** *fig* auf den Tisch legen; *esp fig* zurückstellen
**ta·ble·cloth** Tischdecke *f*, Tischtuch *n*
**ta·ble·land** GEOGR Tafelland *n*, Plateau *n*, Hochebene *f*
**ta·ble lin·en** Tischwäsche *f*
**ta·ble·mat** Untersetzer *m*
**ta·ble·spoon** Esslöffel *m*
**tab·let** PHARM Tablette *f*; Stück *n*; (*Stein- etc*)Tafel *f*
**ta·ble ten·nis** SPORT Tischtennis *n*
**ta·ble·top** Tischplatte *f*
**ta·ble·ware** Geschirr *n* und Besteck *n*
**tab·loid** Boulevardblatt *n*, -zeitung *f*
**tab·loid press** Boulevardpresse *f*
**ta·boo 1.** tabu; **2.** Tabu *n*
**tab·u·lar** tabellarisch
**tab·u·late** tabellarisch (an)ordnen
**tab·u·la·tor** Tabulator *m*
**tach·o·graph** MOT Fahrtenschreiber *m*
**ta·chom·e·ter** MOT Drehzahlmesser *m*
**ta·cit** stillschweigend
**ta·ci·turn** schweigsam, wortkarg
**tack 1.** Stift *m*, (Reiß)Zwecke *f*; Heftstich *m*; **2.** heften (**to** an *acc*); ~ ***on*** anfügen (***to*** *dat*)
**tack·le 1.** *Problem etc* angehen; *soccer etc*: *ballführenden Gegner* angreifen; *j-n* zur Rede stellen (***about*** wegen); **2.** TECH Flaschenzug *m*; (*Angel*)Gerät(e *pl*) *n*; *soccer etc*: Angriff *m*
**tack·y** klebrig; F schäbig
**tact** Takt *m*, Feingefühl *n*
**tact·ful** taktvoll
**tac·tics** Taktik *f*
**tact·less** taktlos
**tad·pole** ZO Kaulquappe *f*
**taf·fe·ta** Taft *m*

**taf·fy** Sahnebonbon *m*, *n*, Toffee *n*

**tag 1.** Etikett *n*; (*Namens-*, *Preis*)Schild *n*; (Schnürsenkel)Stift *m*; stehende Redensart *f*; *a.* ***question ~*** LING Frageanhängsel *n*; **2.** etikettieren; *Waren* auszeichnen; anhängen; ***~ along*** F mitgehen, mitkommen; ***~ along behind s.o.*** F hinter j-m hertrotten

**tail 1.** Schwanz *m*; Schweif *m*; hinterer Teil; F Schatten *m*, Beschatter(in); *pl* Rück-, Kehrseite *f*; Frack *m*; ***put a ~ on*** *j-n* beschatten lassen; ***turn ~*** *fig* sich auf dem Absatz umdrehen; ***with one's ~ between one's legs*** *fig* mit eingezogenem Schwanz; **2.** F *j-n* beschatten; ***~ back*** *esp Br* MOT sich stauen (***to*** bis zu); ***~ off*** schwächer werden, abnehmen, nachlassen

**tail·back** *esp Br* MOT Rückstau *m*

**tail·coat** Frack *m*

**tail end** Ende *n*, Schluss *m*

**tail·light** MOT Rücklicht *n*

**tai·lor 1.** Schneider *m*; **2.** schneidern

**tai·lor-made** Maß...; maßgeschneidert (*a. fig*)

**tail pipe** TECH Auspuffrohr *n*

**tail·wind** Rückenwind *m*

**taint·ed** GASTR verdorben

**take 1.** *v/t* nehmen; (weg)nehmen; mitnehmen; bringen; MIL, MED einnehmen; *chess etc*: *Figur*, *Stein* schlagen; *Gefangene*, *Prüfung etc* machen; UNIV studieren; *Preis etc* erringen; *Scheck etc* (an)nehmen; *Rat* annehmen; *et.* hinnehmen; fassen, Platz bieten für; *et.* aushalten, ertragen; PHOT *et.* aufnehmen, *Aufnahme* machen; *Temperatur* messen; *Notiz* machen, niederschreiben; *ein Bad*, *Zug*, *Bus*, *Weg etc* nehmen; *Gelegenheit*, *Maßnahmen* ergreifen; *Mut* fassen; *Zeit*, *Geduld etc* erfordern, brauchen; *Zeit* dauern; ***it took her four hours*** sie brauchte vier Stunden; ***I ~ it that*** ich nehme an, dass; ***~ it or leave it*** F mach, was du willst; ***~n all in all*** im Großen (und) Ganzen; ***this seat is ~n*** dieser Platz ist besetzt; ***be ~n by*** *or* ***with*** angetan sein von; ***be ~n ill*** *or* ***sick*** erkranken, krank werden; ***~ to bits*** *or* ***pieces*** *et.* auseinander nehmen, zerlegen; ***~ the blame*** die Schuld auf sich nehmen; ***~ care*** vorsichtig sein, aufpassen; ***~ care!*** F mach's gut!; → ***care*** 1; ***~ hold of*** ergreifen; ***~ part*** teilnehmen (***in*** an *dat*); → ***part*** 1; ***~ pity on*** Mitleid haben mit; ***~ a walk*** e-n Spaziergang machen; ***~ my word for it*** verlass dich drauf; → ***advice, bath*** 1, ***break*** 1, ***lead***[1] 2, ***message, oath, offense, place*** 1, ***prisoner, risk*** 1, ***seat*** 1, ***step*** 1, ***trouble*** 1, ***turn*** 2, *etc*; *v/i* MED wirken, anschlagen; ***~ after*** *j-m* nachschlagen, ähneln; ***~ along*** mitnehmen; ***~ apart*** auseinander nehmen (*a. fig* F), zerlegen; ***~ away*** wegnehmen (***from s.o.*** j-m); ***... to ~ away*** *Br* ... zum Mitnehmen; ***~ back*** zurückbringen; zurücknehmen; bei *j-m* Erinnerungen wachrufen; *j-n* zurückversetzen (***to*** in *acc*); ***~ down*** herunternehmen, abnehmen; *Hose* herunterlassen; auseinander nehmen, zerlegen; (sich) *et.* aufschreiben *or* notieren; sich *Notizen* machen; ***what do you ~ me for?*** wofür hältst du mich eigentlich?; ***~ from*** *j-m et.* wegnehmen; MATH abziehen von; ***~ in*** *j-n* (bei sich) aufnehmen; *fig et.* einschließen; *Kleidungsstück* enger machen; *et.* begreifen; *j-n* hereinlegen, F *j-n* aufs Kreuz legen; ***be ~n in by*** hereinfallen auf (*acc*); ***~ off*** *Kleidungsstück* ablegen, ausziehen, *Hut etc* abnehmen; *et.* ab-, wegnehmen; abziehen; AVIAT abheben; SPORT abspringen; F sich davonmachen; ***~ a day off*** sich e-n Tag freinehmen; ***~ on*** *j-n* einstellen; *Arbeit etc* annehmen, übernehmen; *Farbe*, *Ausdruck etc* annehmen; sich anlegen mit; ***~ out*** herausnehmen, *Zahn* ziehen; *j-n* ausführen, ausgehen mit *j-m*; *Versicherung* abschließen; *s-n Frust etc* auslassen (***on*** an *dat*); ***~ over*** *Amt*, *Macht*, *Verantwortung etc* übernehmen; die Macht übernehmen; ***~ to*** Gefallen finden an (*dat*); ***~ to doing s.th.*** anfangen, et. zu tun; ***~ up*** *Vorschlag etc* aufgreifen; *Zeit etc* in Anspruch nehmen, *Platz* einnehmen; *Erzählung etc* aufnehmen; ***~ up doing s.th.*** anfangen, sich mit et. zu beschäftigen; ***~ up with*** sich einlassen mit; **2.** *film*, TV Einstellung *f*; F Einnahmen *pl*

**take·a·way** *Br* **1.** Essen *n* zum Mitnehmen; **2.** Restaurant *n* mit Straßenverkauf

**take·off** AVIAT Abheben *n*, Start *m*; SPORT Absprung *m*

**tak·ings** Einnahmen *pl*

**tale** Erzählung *f*; Geschichte *f*; Lüge *f*, Lügengeschichte *f*, Märchen *n*; ***tell ~s*** petzen
**tal·ent** Talent *n*, Begabung *f*
**tal·ent·ed** talentiert, begabt
**tal·is·man** Talisman *m*
**talk 1.** *v/i* reden, sprechen, sich unterhalten (***to, with*** mit; ***about*** über *acc*; ***of*** von); ***~ about s.th.*** *a.* et. besprechen; ***s.o. to ~ to*** Ansprechpartner(in); *v/t Unsinn etc* reden; reden *or* sprechen *or* sich unterhalten über (*acc*); ***~ s.o. into s.th.*** j-n zu et. überreden; ***~ s.o. out of s.th.*** j-m et. ausreden; ***~ s.th. over*** *Problem etc* besprechen (***with*** mit); ***~ round*** *j-n* bekehren (***to*** zu), umstimmen; **2.** Gespräch *n*, Unterhaltung *f* (***with*** mit; ***about*** über *acc*); Vortrag *m*; Sprache *f*, Sprechweise *f*; Gerede *n*, Geschwätz *n*; ***give a ~*** e-n Vortrag halten (***to*** vor *dat*; ***about, on*** über *acc*); ***be the ~ of the town*** Stadtgespräch sein; ***baby ~*** Babysprache *f*, kindliches Gebabbel; → ***small talk***
**talk·a·tive** gesprächig, redselig
**talk·er:** ***be a good ~*** gut reden können
**talk·ing-to** F Standpauke *f*; ***give s.o. a ~*** j-m e-e Standpauke halten
**talk show** TV Talkshow *f*
**talk-show host** TV Talkmaster *m*
**tall** groß (*person*), hoch (*building etc*)
**tal·low** Talg *m*
**tal·ly**[1] SPORT *etc* Stand *m*; ***keep a ~ of*** Buch führen über (*acc*)
**tal·ly**[2] übereinstimmen (***with*** mit); *a.* ***~ up*** zusammenrechnen, -zählen
**tal·on** ZO Kralle *f*, Klaue *f*
**tame 1.** ZO zahm; *fig* fad(e), lahm; **2.** ZO zähmen (*a. fig*)
**tam·per:** ***~ with*** sich zu schaffen machen an (*dat*)
**tam·pon** MED Tampon *m*
**tan 1.** *Fell* gerben; bräunen; braun werden; **2.** Gelbbraun *n*; (Sonnen)Bräune *f*; **3.** gelbbraun
**tang** (scharfer) Geruch *or* Geschmack
**tan·gent** MATH Tangente *f*; ***fly or go off at a ~*** plötzlich (vom Thema) abschweifen
**tan·ge·rine** BOT Mandarine *f*
**tan·gi·ble** greifbar, *fig a.* handfest, klar
**tan·gle 1.** (sich) verwirren *or* verheddern, durcheinander bringen; durcheinander kommen; **2.** Gewirr *n*, *fig a.* Wirrwarr *m*, Durcheinander *n*
**tank** MOT *etc* Tank *m*; MIL Panzer *m*
**tank·ard** (Bier)Humpen *m*
**tank·er** MAR Tanker *m*, Tankschiff *n*; AVIAT Tankflugzeug *n*; MOT Tankwagen *m*
**tan·ner** Gerber *m*
**tan·ne·ry** Gerberei *f*
**tan·ta·lize** *j-n* aufreizen
**tan·ta·liz·ing** verlockend
**tan·ta·mount:** ***be ~ to*** gleichbedeutend sein mit, hinauslaufen auf (*acc*)
**tan·trum** Wut-, Tobsuchtsanfall *m*
**tap**[1] **1.** TECH Hahn *m*; ***beer on ~*** Bier *n* vom Fass; **2.** *Naturschätze etc* erschließen; *Vorräte etc* angreifen; *Telefon*(*leitung*) abhören, F anzapfen; *Fass* anzapfen, anstechen
**tap**[2] **1.** mit *den Fingern*, *Füßen* klopfen, mit *den Fingern* trommeln (***on*** auf *acc*); antippen; ***~ s.o. on the shoulder*** j-m auf die Schulter klopfen; ***~ on*** (leicht) klopfen an (*acc*) *or* auf (*acc*) *or* gegen; **2.** (leichtes) Klopfen; Klaps *m*
**tap dance** Stepptanz *m*
**tape 1.** (schmales) Band; Kleb(e)streifen *m*; (Magnet-, Video-, Ton)Band *n*; (*Video- etc*)Kassette *f*; (Band)Aufnahme *f*; TV Aufzeichnung *f*; SPORT Zielband *n*; → ***red tape*; 2.** (auf Band) aufnehmen; TV aufzeichnen; *a.* ***~ up*** (mit Klebeband) zukleben
**tape deck** Tapedeck *n*
**tape meas·ure** Bandmaß *n*, Maßband *n*, Messband *n*
**ta·per** *a.* ***~ off*** spitz zulaufen, sich verjüngen; *fig* langsam nachlassen
**tape re·cord·er** Tonbandgerät *n*
**tape re·cord·ing** Tonbandaufnahme *f*
**ta·pes·try** Gobelin *m*, Wandteppich *m*
**tape·worm** ZO Bandwurm *m*
**taps** MIL Zapfenstreich *m*
**tap wa·ter** Leitungswasser *n*
**tar 1.** Teer *m*; **2.** teeren
**tare** ECON Tara *f*
**tar·get** (Schieß-, Ziel)Scheibe *f*; MIL Ziel *n* (*a. fig*), ECON *a.* Soll *n*; *fig* Zielscheibe *f*; ***~ ar·e·a*** MIL Zielbereich *m*; ***~ group*** Zielgruppe *f*
**tar·iff** ECON Zoll(tarif) *m*; *esp Br* Preisverzeichnis *n*
**tar·mac** Asphalt *m*; AVIAT Rollfeld *n*, Rollbahn *f*

**tar·nish** *v/i* anlaufen; *v/t Ansehen etc* beflecken
**tart**[1] *esp Br* Obstkuchen *m*; Obsttörtchen *n*; F Flittchen *n*, *sl* Nutte *f*
**tart**[2] herb, sauer; scharf (*a. fig*)
**tar·tan** Tartan *m*; Schottenstoff *m*; Schottenmuster *n*
**tar·tar** MED Zahnstein *m*; CHEM Weinstein *m*
**task** Aufgabe *f*; ***take s.o. to ~ fig*** j-n zurechtweisen (***for*** wegen); **~ force** MIL *etc* Sonder-, Spezialeinheit *f*
**tas·sel** Troddel *f*, Quaste *f*
**taste 1.** Geschmack *m* (*a. fig*), Geschmackssinn *m*; Kostprobe *f*; Vorliebe *f* (***for*** für); **2.** *v/t* kosten, probieren; schmecken; *v/i* schmecken (***of*** nach)
**taste·ful** *fig* geschmackvoll
**taste·less** geschmacklos (*a. fig*)
**tast·y** schmackhaft
**tat·tered** zerlumpt
**tat·ters** Fetzen *pl*; ***in ~*** zerfetzt, in Fetzen; *fig* ruiniert
**tat·too**[1] **1.** Tätowierung *f*; **2.** (ein)tätowieren
**tat·too**[2] MIL Zapfenstreich *m*
**taunt 1.** verhöhnen, verspotten; **2.** höhnische *or* spöttische Bemerkung
**Tau·rus** ASTR Stier *m*; ***he*** (***she***) ***is*** (***a***) **~** er (sie) ist (ein) Stier
**taut** straff; *fig* angespannt
**taw·dry** (billig und) geschmacklos
**taw·ny** gelbbraun
**tax 1.** Steuer *f* (***on*** auf *acc*); **2.** besteuern; *j-s Geduld etc* strapazieren
**tax·a·ble** steuerpflichtig
**tax·a·tion** Besteuerung *f*
**tax e·va·sion** Steuerhinterziehung *f*
**tax·i 1.** Taxi *n*, Taxe *f*; **2.** AVIAT rollen
**tax·i driv·er** Taxifahrer(in)
**tax·i rank, tax·i stand** Taxistand *m*
**tax of·fi·cer** Finanzbeamte *m*
**tax·pay·er** Steuerzahler(in)
**tax re·duc·tion** Steuersenkung *f*
**tax re·turn** Steuererklärung *f*
**T-bar** Bügel *m*; *a.* ***~ lift*** Schlepplift *m*
**tea** Tee *m*; ***have a cup of ~*** e-n Tee trinken; ***make some ~*** e-n Tee machen *or* kochen
**tea·bag** Teebeutel *m*, Aufgussbeutel *m*
**teach** lehren, unterrichten (in *dat*); *j-m et.* beibringen; unterrichten (***at*** an *dat*)
**teach·er** Lehrer(in)
**tea co·sy** Teewärmer *m*
**tea·cup** Teetasse *f*; ***a storm in a ~ fig*** ein Sturm im Wasserglas
**team** Team *n*, *a.* Arbeitsgruppe *f*, SPORT *a.* Mannschaft *f*, *soccer*: *a.* Elf *f*
**team·ster** MOT LKW-Fahrer *m*
**team·work** Zusammenarbeit *f*, Teamwork *n*; Zusammenspiel *n*
**tea·pot** Teekanne *f*
**tear**[1] Träne *f*; ***in ~s*** weinend, in Tränen (aufgelöst)
**tear**[2] **1.** *v/t* zerreißen; sich *et.* zerreißen (***on*** an *dat*); weg-, losreißen (***from*** von); *v/i* (zer)reißen; F rasen, sausen; ***~ down*** *Plakat etc* herunterreißen; *Haus etc* abreißen; ***~ off*** abreißen; sich *Kleidung* vom Leib reißen; ***~ out*** (her)ausreißen; ***~ up*** aufreißen; zerreißen; **2.** Riss *m*
**tear·drop** Träne *f*
**tear·ful** weinend; tränenreich
**tear·jerk·er** F Schnulze *f*
**tea·room** Teestube *f*
**tease** necken, hänseln; ärgern
**tea·spoon** Teelöffel *m*
**teat** zo Zitze *f*; *Br* (Gummi)Sauger *m*
**tech·ni·cal** technisch; fachlich, Fach...
**tech·ni·cal·i·ty** technische Einzelheit; reine Formsache
**tech·ni·cian** Techniker(in)
**tech·nique** Technik *f*, Verfahren *n*
**tech·nol·o·gy** Technologie *f*; Technik *f*
**ted·dy bear** Teddybär *m*
**te·di·ous** langweilig, ermüdend
**teem: *~ with*** wimmeln von, strotzen von *or* vor (*dat*)
**teen·age(d)** im Teenageralter; für Teenager; **teen·ag·er** Teenager *m*
**teens: *be in one's ~*** im Teenageralter sein
**tee·ny(-wee·ny)** F klitzeklein, winzig
**tee shirt** → ***T-shirt***
**teethe** zahnen
**tee·to·tal·(l)er** Abstinenzler(in)
**tel·e·cast** Fernsehsendung *f*
**tel·e·com·mu·ni·ca·tions** Telekommunikation *f*, Fernmeldewesen *n*
**tel·e·gram** Telegramm *n*
**tel·e·graph 1.** ***by ~*** telegrafisch; **2.** telegrafieren
**tel·e·graph·ic** telegrafisch
**te·leg·ra·phy** Telegrafie *f*
**tel·e·phone 1.** Telefon *n*; **2.** telefonieren; anrufen; **~ booth, ~ box** *Br* Telefonzelle *f*, Fernsprechzelle *f*; **~ call** Telefonanruf *n*, Telefongespräch *n*; **~**

**di·rec·to·ry** → ***phone book***; ~ **ex·change** Fernsprechamt *n*; ~ **num·ber** Telefonnummer *f*
**te·leph·o·nist** *esp Br* Telefonist(in)
**tel·e·pho·to lens** PHOT Teleobjektiv *n*
**tel·e·print·er** Fernschreiber *m*
**tel·e·scope** Teleskop *n*, Fernrohr *n*
**tel·e·text** Teletext *m*, Videotext *m*
**tel·e·type·writ·er** Fernschreiber *m*
**tel·e·vise** im Fernsehen übertragen *or* bringen; **tel·e·vi·sion 1.** Fernsehen *n*; *a.* ~ ***set*** Fernsehapparat *m*, -gerät *n*, F Fernseher *m*; ***on*** ~ im Fernsehen; ***watch*** ~ fernsehen; **2.** Fernseh...
**tel·ex 1.** Telex *n*, Fernschreiben *n*; **2.** telexen (***to*** an *acc*), ein Telex schicken (*dat*)
**tell** *v/t* sagen; erzählen; erkennen (***by*** an *dat*); *Namen etc* nennen; *et.* anzeigen; *j-m* sagen, befehlen (***to do*** zu tun); ***I can't*** ~ ***one from the other, I can't*** ~ ***them apart*** ich kann sie nicht auseinander halten; *v/i* sich auswirken (***on*** bei, auf *acc*), sich bemerkbar machen; ***who can*** ~***?*** wer weiß?; ***you can never*** ~, ***you never can*** ~ man kann nie wissen; ~ ***against*** sprechen gegen; von Nachteil sein für; ~ ***s.o. off*** F mit j-m schimpfen (***for*** wegen); ~ ***on s.o.*** j-n verpetzen *or* verraten
**tell·er** Kassierer(in)
**tell·ing** aufschlussreich
**tell·tale 1.** verräterisch; **2.** F Petze *f*
**tel·ly** *Br* F Fernseher *m*
**te·mer·i·ty** Frechheit *f*, Kühnheit *f*
**tem·per 1.** Temperament *n*, Wesen *n*, Wesensart *f*; Laune *f*, Stimmung *f*; TECH Härte(grad *m*) *f*; ***keep one's*** ~ sich beherrschen, ruhig bleiben; ***lose one's*** ~ die Beherrschung verlieren; **2.** TECH *Stahl* härten
**tem·pe·ra·ment** Temperament *n*, Naturell *n*, Wesen *n*, Wesensart *f*
**tem·pe·ra·men·tal** launisch; von Natur aus
**tem·pe·rate** gemäßigt (*climate, region*)
**tem·pe·ra·ture** Temperatur *f*; ***have*** *or* ***be running a*** ~ MED erhöhte Temperatur *or* Fieber haben
**tem·pest** POET (heftiger) Sturm
**tem·ple**[1] Tempel *m*
**tem·ple**[2] ANAT Schläfe *f*
**tem·po·ral** weltlich; LING temporal, der Zeit
**tem·po·ra·ry** vorübergehend, zeitweilig
**tempt** *j-n* in Versuchung führen; *j-n* verführen (***to*** zu); **temp·ta·tion** Versuchung *f*, Verführung *f*; **tempt·ing** verführerisch
**ten 1.** zehn; **2.** Zehn *f*
**ten·a·ble** *fig* haltbar
**te·na·cious** hartnäckig, zäh
**ten·ant** Pächter(in), Mieter(in)
**tend** neigen, tendieren (***to*** zu); ~ ***upwards*** e-e steigende Tendenz haben
**ten·den·cy** Tendenz *f*; Neigung *f*
**ten·der**[1] empfindlich, *fig a.* heikel; GASTR zart, weich; sanft, zart, zärtlich
**ten·der**[2] RAIL, MAR Tender *m*
**ten·der**[3] ECON **1.** Angebot *n*; ***legal*** ~ gesetzliches Zahlungsmittel; **2.** ein Angebot machen (***for*** für)
**ten·der·foot** F Neuling *m*, Anfänger *m*
**ten·der·loin** GASTR zartes Lendenstück
**ten·der·ness** Zartheit *f*; Zärtlichkeit *f*
**ten·don** ANAT Sehne *f*
**ten·dril** BOT Ranke *f*
**ten·e·ment** Mietshaus *n*, *contp* Mietskaserne *f*
**ten·nis** Tennis *n*; ~ **court** Tennisplatz *m*; ~ **play·er** Tennisspieler(in)
**ten·or** MUS, JUR Tenor *m*, JUR *a.* Wortlaut *m*, Sinn *m*; Verlauf *m*
**tense**[1] LING Zeit(form) *f*, Tempus *n*
**tense**[2] gespannt, straff (*rope etc*), (an)gespannt (*a. fig*); (über)nervös, verkrampft (*person*)
**ten·sion** Spannung *f* (*a.* ELECTR)
**tent** Zelt *n*
**ten·ta·cle** ZO Tentakel *m*, *n*, Fangarm *m*
**ten·ta·tive** vorläufig; vorsichtig, zaghaft
**ten·ter·hooks:** ***be on*** ~ wie auf (glühenden) Kohlen sitzen
**tenth 1.** zehnte(r, -s); **2.** Zehntel *n*
**tenth·ly** zehntens
**ten·u·ous** *fig* lose (*link, relationship etc*)
**ten·ure** Besitz *m*, Besitzdauer *f*; ~ ***of office*** Amtsdauer *f*, Dienstzeit *f*
**tep·id** lau(warm)
**term 1.** Zeit *f*, Zeitraum *m*, Dauer *f*; JUR Laufzeit *f*; PED, UNIV Semester *n*, *esp Br* Trimester *n*; Ausdruck *m*, Bezeichnung *f*; ~ ***of office*** Amtsdauer *f*, Amtsperiode *f*, Amtszeit *f*; *pl* Bedingungen *pl*; ***be on good*** (***bad***) ~***s with*** gut (schlecht) aus-

kommen mit; ***they are not on speaking ~s*** sie sprechen nicht (mehr) miteinander; ***come to ~s*** sich einigen (***with*** mit); **2.** nennen, bezeichnen als

**ter·mi·nal 1.** End...; letzte(r, -s); MED unheilbar; im Endstadium; ***~ly ill*** unheilbar krank; **2.** RAIL *etc* Endstation *f*; Terminal *m, n*; ELECTR Pol *m*; EDP Terminal *n*, Datenendstation *f*

**ter·mi·nate** *v/t* beenden; *Vertrag* kündigen, lösen; MED *Schwangerschaft* unterbrechen; *v/i* enden; ablaufen (*contract*)

**ter·mi·na·tion** Beendigung *f*; Kündigung *f*, Lösung *f*; Ende *n*; Ablauf *m*

**ter·mi·nus** RAIL *etc* Endstation *f*

**ter·race** Terrasse *f*; Häuserreihe *f*; *mst pl esp Br* SPORT Ränge *pl*

**ter·raced house** *Br* Reihenhaus *n*

**ter·res·tri·al** irdisch; Erd...; *esp* BOT, ZO Land...

**ter·ri·ble** schrecklich

**ter·rif·ic** F toll, fantastisch; irre (*speed, heat etc*)

**ter·ri·fy** *j-m* schreckliche Angst einjagen

**ter·ri·to·ri·al** territorial, Gebiets...

**ter·ri·to·ry** Territorium *n*, (*a.* Hoheits-, Staats)Gebiet *n*

**ter·ror** Entsetzen *n*; Schrecken *m*; POL Terror *m*; F Landplage *f*; ***in ~*** in panischer Angst

**ter·ror·is·m** Terrorismus *m*

**ter·ror·ist** Terrorist(in)

**ter·ror·ize** terrorisieren

**terse** *fig* knapp, kurz (und bündig)

**test 1.** Test *m*, Prüfung *f*; Probe *f*; **2.** testen, prüfen; probieren; *j-s Geduld etc* auf e-e harte Probe stellen

**tes·ta·ment: *last will and ~*** JUR letzter Wille, Testament *n*

**test an·i·mal** Versuchstier *n*

**test card** TV Testbild *n*

**test drive** MOT Probefahrt *f*

**tes·ti·cle** ANAT Hoden *m*

**tes·ti·fy** JUR aussagen

**tes·ti·mo·ni·al** Referenz *f*

**tes·ti·mo·ny** JUR Aussage *f*; Beweis *m*

**test pi·lot** AVIAT Testpilot *m*

**test tube** CHEM Reagenzglas *n*

**tes·ty** gereizt

**tet·a·nus** MED Tetanus *m*, Wundstarrkrampf *m*

**teth·er 1.** Strick *m*; Kette *f*; ***at the end of one's ~*** *fig* mit s-n Kräften *or* Nerven am Ende sein; **2.** *Tier* anbinden; anketten

**text** Text *m*

**text·book** Lehrbuch *n*

**tex·tile 1.** Stoff *m*, *pl* Textilien *pl*; **2.** Textil...

**tex·ture** Textur *f*, Gewebe *n*; Beschaffenheit *f*; Struktur *f*

**than** als

**thank 1.** *j-m* danken, sich bei *j-m* bedanken (***for*** für); ***~ you*** danke; ***~ you very much*** vielen Dank; ***no, ~ you*** nein, danke; (***yes,***) ***~ you*** ja, bitte; **2.** ***~s*** Dank *m*; ***~s*** danke (schön); ***no, ~s*** nein, danke; ***~s to*** dank (*gen*), wegen (*gen*)

**thank·ful** dankbar

**thank·less** undankbar

**that 1.** *pron and adj* das; jene(r, -s), der, die, das, derjenige, diejenige, dasjenige; **2.** *relative pron* der, die, das, welche(r, -s); **3.** *cj* dass; **4.** *adv* F so, dermaßen; ***it's ~ simple*** so einfach ist das

**thatch 1.** mit Stroh *or* Reet decken; **2.** (Dach)Stroh *n*, Reet *n*; Strohdach *n*, Reetdach *n*

**thaw 1.** (auf)tauen; **2.** Tauwetter *n*; (Auf)Tauen *n*

**the 1.** der, die, das, *pl* die; **2.** *adv*: ***~ ... ~ ...*** je ... desto ...; ***~ sooner ~ better*** je eher, desto besser

**the·a·ter** Theater *n*; UNIV (*Hör*)Saal *m*; MIL (Kriegs)Schauplatz *m*

**the·a·ter·go·er** Theaterbesucher(in)

**the·a·tre** *Br* → ***theater***; MED Operationssaal *m*

**the·at·ri·cal** Theater...; *fig* theatralisch

**theft** Diebstahl *m*

**their** ihr(e)

**theirs** der (die, das) ihrige *or* ihre

**them** sie (*acc pl*); ihnen (*dat*)

**theme** Thema *n*

**them·selves** sie (*acc pl*) selbst; sich (selbst)

**then 1.** *adv* dann; da; damals; ***by ~*** bis dahin; ***from ~ on*** von da an; → ***every, now*** 1, ***there***; **2.** *adj* damalig

**the·o·lo·gian** Theologe *m*, Theologin *f*

**the·ol·o·gy** Theologie *f*

**the·o·ret·i·cal** theoretisch

**the·o·rist** Theoretiker *m*

**the·o·ry** Theorie *f*

**ther·a·peu·tic** therapeutisch; F wohltuend; gesund

**ther·a·pist** Therapeut(in)

T

**ther·a·py** Therapie *f*
**there 1.** da, dort; (da-, dort)hin; ~ ***is***, ~ ***are*** es gibt, es ist, *pl* es sind; ~ ***and then*** auf der Stelle; ~ ***you are*** hier bitte; siehst du!, na also!; **2.** *int* so; siehst du!, na also!; ~, ~ ist ja gut!
**there·a·bout(s)** so ungefähr
**there·af·ter** danach
**there·by** dadurch
**there·fore** deshalb, daher; folglich
**there·up·on** darauf(hin)
**ther·mal 1.** thermisch, Thermo..., Wärme...; **2.** Thermik *f*
**ther·mom·e·ter** Thermometer *n*
**ther·mos®** Thermosflasche® *f*
**the·sis** These *f*; UNIV Dissertation *f*, Doktorarbeit *f*
**they** sie *pl*; man
**thick 1.** *adj* dick, (*fog etc a.*) dicht; F dumm; F dick befreundet; ***be ~ with*** wimmeln von; ~ ***with smoke*** verräuchert; ***that's a bit ~!*** *esp Br* F das ist ein starkes Stück!; **2.** *adv* dick, dicht; ***lay it on ~*** F dick auftragen; **3.** ***in the ~ of*** mitten in (*dat*); ***through ~ and thin*** durch dick und dünn; **thick·en** dicker werden, (*fog etc a.*) dichter werden; GASTR eindicken, binden
**thick·et** Dickicht *n*
**thick·head·ed** F strohdumm
**thick·ness** Dicke *f*; Lage *f*, Schicht *f*
**thick·set** gedrungen, untersetzt
**thick-skinned** *fig* dickfellig
**thief** Dieb(in)
**thigh** ANAT (Ober)Schenkel *m*
**thim·ble** Fingerhut *m*
**thin 1.** *adj* dünn; dürr; spärlich, dürftig; schütter (*hair*); schwach, (*excuse etc a.*) fadenscheinig; **2.** *adv* dünn; **3.** verdünnen; dünner werden, (*fog*, *hair a.*) sich lichten
**thing** Ding *n*; Sache *f*; *pl* Sachen *pl*, Zeug *n*; *fig* Dinge *pl*, Lage *f*, Umstände *pl*; ***I couldn't see a ~*** ich konnte überhaupt nichts sehen; ***another ~*** et. anderes; ***the right ~*** das Richtige
**thing·a·ma·jig** F Dings(bums) *m*, *f*, *n*
**think** *v/i* denken (***of*** an *acc*); nachdenken (***about*** über *acc*); ***I ~ so*** ich glaube *or* denke schon; ***I'll ~ about it*** ich überlege es mir; ~ ***of*** sich erinnern an (*acc*); ~ ***of doing s.th.*** beabsichtigen *or* daran denken, et. zu tun; ***what do you ~ of*** *or* ***about ...?*** was halten Sie von ...?; *v/t* denken, glauben, meinen; *j-n*, *et.* halten für; ~ ***over*** nachdenken über (*acc*), sich *et.* überlegen; ~ ***up*** sich *et.* ausdenken
**think tank** Beraterstab *m*, Sachverständigenstab *m*, Denkfabrik *f*
**third 1.** dritte(r, -s); **2.** Drittel *n*
**third·ly** drittens
**third-rate** drittklassig
**Third World** Dritte Welt
**thirst** Durst *m*
**thirst·y** durstig; ***be ~*** Durst haben, durstig sein
**thir·teen 1.** dreizehn; **2.** Dreizehn *f*
**thir·teenth** dreizehnte(r, -s)
**thir·ti·eth** dreißigste(r, -s)
**thir·ty 1.** dreißig; **2.** Dreißig *f*
**this** diese(r, -s); ~ ***morning*** heute Morgen; ~ ***is John speaking*** TEL hier (spricht) John
**this·tle** BOT Distel *f*
**thong** (Leder)Riemen *m*
**thorn** Dorn *m*
**thorn·y** dornig; *fig* schwierig, heikel
**thor·ough** gründlich, genau; fürchterlich (*mess etc*)
**thor·ough·bred** zo Vollblüter *m*
**thor·ough·fare** Hauptverkehrsstraße *f*; ***no ~!*** Durchfahrt verboten!
**though 1.** *cj* obwohl; (je)doch; ***as ~*** als ob; **2.** *adv* dennoch, trotzdem
**thought** Denken *n*; Gedanke *m* (***of*** an *acc*); ***on second ~*** wenn ich es mir (recht) überlege
**thought·ful** nachdenklich; rücksichtsvoll, aufmerksam
**thought·less** gedankenlos; rücksichtslos
**thou·sand 1.** tausend; **2.** Tausend *n*
**thou·sandth 1.** tausendste(r, -s); **2.** Tausendstel *n*
**thrash** verdreschen, verprügeln; SPORT F *j-m* e-e Abfuhr erteilen; ~ ***about***, ~ ***around*** sich *im Bett etc* hin und her werfen; um sich schlagen; zappeln (*fish*); ~ ***out*** *Problem etc* ausdiskutieren
**thrash·ing** Dresche *f*, Tracht *f* Prügel
**thread 1.** Faden *m* (*a. fig*); Garn *n*; TECH Gewinde *n*; **2.** *Nadel* einfädeln; *Perlen etc* auffädeln, aufreihen
**thread·bare** abgewetzt, abgetragen; *fig* abgedroschen
**threat** Drohung *f*; Bedrohung *f*, Gefahr *f* (***to*** *gen or* für)
**threat·en** (be)drohen

**threat·en·ing** drohend
**three** 1. drei; 2. Drei *f*
**three·fold** dreifach
**three-ply** → ***ply***[2]
**three·score** sechzig
**three-stage** dreistufig
**thresh** AGR dreschen
**thresh·ing ma·chine** AGR Dreschmaschine *f*
**thresh·old** Schwelle *f*
**thrift** Sparsamkeit *f*
**thrift·y** sparsam
**thrill** 1. prickelndes Gefühl; Nervenkitzel *m*; aufregendes Erlebnis; 2. *v/t* ***be ~ed*** (ganz) hingerissen sein (***at, about*** von)
**thrill·er** Thriller *m*, F Reißer *m*
**thrill·ing** spannend, fesselnd, packend
**thrive** gedeihen; *fig* blühen, florieren
**throat** ANAT Kehle *f*, Gurgel *f*; Rachen *m*; Hals *m*; ***clear one's ~*** sich räuspern; → ***sore*** 1
**throb** 1. hämmern (*machine*), (*heart etc a.*) pochen, schlagen; pulsieren (*pain*); 2. Hämmern *n*, Pochen *n*, Schlagen *n*
**throm·bo·sis** MED Thrombose *f*
**throne** Thron *m*
**throng** 1. Schar *f*, Menschenmenge *f*; 2. sich drängen (in *dat*)
**throt·tle** 1. erdrosseln; ***~ down*** MOT, TECH drosseln, Gas wegnehmen; 2. TECH Drosselklappe *f*
**through** 1. *prp* durch (*acc*); bis (einschließlich); ***Monday ~ Friday*** von Montag bis Freitag; 2. *adv* durch; ***~ and ~*** durch und durch; ***put s.o. ~ to*** TEL j-n verbinden mit; ***wet ~*** völlig durchnässt; 3. *adj* durchgehend (*train etc*); Durchgangs...
**through·out** 1. *prp*: ***~ the night*** die ganze Nacht hindurch; ***~ the country*** im ganzen Land, überall im Land; 2. *adv* ganz, überall; die ganze Zeit (hindurch)
**through traf·fic** Durchgangsverkehr *m*
**through·way** *Br* → ***thruway***
**throw** 1. werfen; *Hebel etc* betätigen; *Reiter* abwerfen; *Party* geben, F schmeißen; ***~ a four*** e-e Vier würfeln; ***~ off*** *Jacke etc* abwerfen; *Verfolger* abschütteln; *Krankheit* loswerden; ***~ on*** sich *e-e Jacke etc* (hastig) überwerfen; ***~ out*** hinauswerfen; wegwerfen; ***~ up*** *v/t* hochwerfen; F *Job etc* hinschmeißen; F (er)brechen; *v/i* F (sich er)brechen; 2. Wurf *m*
**throw·a·way** Wegwerf..., Einweg...; ***~ pack*** Einwegpackung *f*
**throw-in** *soccer*: Einwurf *m*
**thru** F → ***through***
**thrum** → ***strum***
**thrush** ZO Drossel *f*
**thrust** 1. *j-n*, *et.* stoßen (***into*** in *acc*); *et.* stecken, schieben (***into*** in *acc*); ***~ at*** stoßen nach; ***~ s.th. upon s.o.*** j-m et. aufdrängen; 2. Stoß *m*; MIL Vorstoß *m*; PHYS Schub *m*, Schubkraft *f*
**thru·way** Schnellstraße *f*
**thud** 1. dumpfes Geräusch, Plumps *m*; 2. plumpsen
**thug** Verbrecher *m*, Schläger *m*
**thumb** 1. ANAT Daumen *m*; 2. ***~ a lift*** *or* ***ride*** per Anhalter fahren, trampen (***to*** nach); ***~ through a book*** ein Buch durchblättern; ***well-thumbed*** abgegriffen
**thumb·tack** Reißzwecke *f*, Reißnagel *m*, Heftzwecke *f*
**thump** 1. *v/t j-m* e-n Schlag versetzen; ***~ out*** *Melodie* herunterhämmern (***on the piano*** auf dem Klavier); *v/i* (heftig) schlagen *or* hämmern *or* pochen (*a. heart*); plumpsen; trampeln; 2. dumpfes Geräusch, Plumps *m*; Schlag *m*
**thun·der** 1. Donner *m*, Donnern *n*; 2. donnern
**thun·der·bolt** Blitz *m* und Donner *m*
**thun·der·clap** Donnerschlag *m*
**thun·der·cloud** Gewitterwolke *f*
**thun·der·ous** donnernd (*applause*)
**thun·der·storm** Gewitter *n*, Unwetter *n*
**thun·der·struck** wie vom Donner gerührt
**Thur(s)** ABBR *of* ***Thursday*** Do., Donnerstag *m*
**Thurs·day** (ABBR ***Thur, Thurs***) Donnerstag *m*; ***on ~*** (am) Donnerstag; ***on ~s*** donnerstags
**thus** so, auf diese Weise; folglich, somit; ***~ far*** bisher
**thwart** durchkreuzen, vereiteln
**thyme** BOT Thymian *m*
**thy·roid (gland)** ANAT Schilddrüse *f*
**tick**[1] 1. Ticken *n*; Haken *m*, Häkchen *n*; 2. *v/i* ticken; *v/t mst* ***~ off*** ab-, anhaken
**tick**[2] zo Zecke *f*
**tick**[3]: ***on ~*** *Br* F auf Pump

**tick·er·tape pa·rade** Konfettiparade *f*
**tick·et 1.** Fahrkarte *f*, Fahrschein *m*; Flugkarte *f*, Flugschein *m*, Ticket *n*; (*Eintritts-, Theater- etc*)Karte *f*; (*Gepäck*)Schein *m*; Etikett *n*, (*Preis- etc -*) Schild *n*; POL Wahl-, Kandidatenliste *f*; (*a.* ***parking*** ~) MOT Strafzettel *m*; **2.** etikettieren; bestimmen, vorsehen (***for*** für)
**tick·et-can·cel·(l)ing ma·chine** (Fahrschein)Entwerter *m*
**tick·et| col·lec·tor** (Bahnsteig)Schaffner(in); ~ **machine** Fahrkartenautomat *m*; ~ **of·fice** RAIL Fahrkartenschalter *m*
**tick·ing** Inlett *n*; Matratzenbezug *m*
**tick·le** kitzeln
**tick·lish** kitz(e)lig, *fig a.* heikel
**tid·al wave** Flutwelle *f*
**tid·bit** Leckerbissen *m*
**tide 1.** Gezeiten *pl*; Flut *f*; *fig* Strömung *f*, Trend *m*; ***high*** ~ Flut *f*; ***low*** ~ Ebbe *f*; **2.** ~ ***over*** *fig j-m* hinweghelfen über (*acc*); *j-n* über Wasser halten
**ti·dy 1.** sauber, ordentlich, aufgeräumt; F hübsch, beträchtlich (*sum etc*); **2.** *a.* ~ ***up*** in Ordnung bringen, (*Zimmer a.*) aufräumen; ~ ***away*** wegräumen, aufräumen
**tie 1.** Krawatte *f*, Schlips *m*; Band *n*; Schnur *f*; Stimmengleichheit *f*; SPORT Unentschieden *n*; (*Pokal*)Spiel *n*; RAIL Schwelle *f*; *mst pl fig* Bande *pl*; **2.** *v/t* an-, festbinden; (sich) *Krawatte etc* binden; *fig* verbinden; ***the game was*** ~***d*** SPORT das Spiel ging unentschieden aus; *v/i*: ***they*** ~***d for second place*** SPORT *etc* sie belegten gemeinsam den zweiten Platz; ~ ***down*** *fig* (an)binden; *j-n* festlegen (***to*** auf *acc*); ~ ***in with*** übereinstimmen mit, passen zu; verbinden *or* koppeln mit; ~ ***up*** *Paket etc* verschnüren; *et.* in Verbindung bringen (***with*** mit); *Verkehr etc* lahm legen; ***be*** ~***d up*** ECON fest angelegt sein (***in*** in *dat*)
**tie·break(·er)** *tennis*: Tie-Break *m, n*
**tie-in** (enge) Verbindung, (enger) Zusammenhang; ECON Kopplungsgeschäft *n*; ***a book movie*** ~ *appr* das Buch zum Film
**tie-on** Anhänge...
**tie·pin** Krawattennadel *f*
**tier** (Sitz)Reihe *f*; Lage *f*, Schicht *f*; *fig* Stufe *f*
**tie-up** (enge) Verbindung, (enger) Zusammenhang; ECON Fusion *f*
**ti·ger** ZO Tiger *m*
**tight 1.** *adj* fest (sitzend), fest angezogen; straff (*rope etc*); eng (*a. dress etc*); knapp (*a. fig*); F knick(e)rig; F blau; ***be in a*** ~ ***corner*** in der Klemme sein *or* sitzen *or* stecken; **2.** *adv* fest; F gut; ***hold*** ~ festhalten; ***sleep*** ~***!*** F schlaf gut!
**tight·en** festziehen, anziehen; *Seil etc* straffen; ~ ***one's belt*** *fig* den Gürtel enger schnallen; ~ ***up*** (***on***) *Gesetz etc* verschärfen
**tight·fist·ed** F knick(e)rig
**tights** (*Tänzer-, Artisten*)Trikot *n*; *esp Br* Strumpfhose *f*
**ti·gress** ZO Tigerin *f*
**tile 1.** (Dach)Ziegel *m*; Fliese *f*, Kachel *f*; **2.** (mit Ziegeln) decken; fliesen, kacheln
**til·er** Dachdecker *m*; Fliesenleger *m*
**till**[1] → ***until***
**till**[2] (Laden)Kasse *f*
**tilt 1.** kippen; sich neigen; **2.** Kippen *n*; ***at a*** ~ schief, schräg; (***at***) ***full*** ~ F mit Volldampf
**tim·ber** *Br* Bau-, Nutzholz *n*; Baumbestand *m*, Bäume *pl*; Balken *m*
**time 1.** Zeit *f*; Uhrzeit *f*; MUS Takt *m*; Mal *n*; ~ ***after*** ~, ~ ***and again*** immer wieder; ***every*** ~ ***I ...*** jedes Mal, wenn ich ...; ***how many*** ~***s?*** wie oft?; ***next*** ~ nächstes Mal; ***this*** ~ diesmal; ***three*** ~***s*** dreimal; ***three*** ~***s four equals*** *or* ***is twelve*** drei mal vier ist zwölf; ***what's the*** ~***?*** wie spät ist es?; ***what*** ~***?*** um wie viel Uhr?; ***all the*** ~ die ganze Zeit; ***at all*** ~***s, at any*** ~ jederzeit; ***at the*** ~ damals; ***at the same*** ~ gleichzeitig; ***at*** ~***s*** manchmal; ***by the*** ~ wenn; als; ***for a*** ~ e-e Zeit lang; ***for the*** ~ ***being*** vorläufig, fürs Erste; ***from*** ~ ***to*** ~ von Zeit zu Zeit; ***have a good*** ~ sich gut unterhalten *or* amüsieren; ***in*** ~ rechtzeitig; ***in no*** ~ (***at all***) im Nu; ***on*** ~ pünktlich; ***some*** ~ ***ago*** vor einiger Zeit; ***to pass the*** ~ zum Zeitvertreib; ***take one's*** ~ sich Zeit lassen; **2.** *et.* timen (*a.* SPORT); (ab)stoppen; zeitlich abstimmen, den richtigen Zeitpunkt wählen *or* bestimmen für
**time| card** Stechkarte *f*; ~ **clock** Stechuhr *f*; ~ **lag** Zeitdifferenz *f*
**time-lapse** *film*: Zeitraffer...
**time·less** immer während, ewig; zeitlos

T

**time lim·it** Frist *f*
**time·ly** (recht)zeitig
**time sheet** Stechkarte *f*
**time sig·nal** *radio*: Zeitzeichen *n*
**time·ta·ble** *Br* Fahrplan *m*, Flugplan *m*; Stundenplan *m*; Zeitplan *m*
**tim·id** ängstlich, furchtsam, zaghaft
**tim·ing** Timing *n*
**tin 1.** Zinn *n*; *Br* (Blech-, Konserven)Dose *f*, (-)Büchse *f*; **2.** verzinnen; *Br* einmachen, eindosen
**tinc·ture** Tinktur *f*
**tin·foil** Stanniol(papier) *n*; Alufolie *f*
**tinge 1.** tönen; ***be ~d with*** *fig* e-n Anflug haben von; **2.** Tönung *f*; *fig* Anflug *m*, Spur *f* (***of*** von)
**tin·gle** prickeln, kribbeln
**tink·er** herumpfuschen, herumbasteln (***at*** an *dat*)
**tin·kle** bimmeln; klirren
**tinned** *Br* Dosen..., Büchsen...
**tinned fruit** *Br* Obstkonserven *pl*
**tin o·pen·er** *Br* Dosenöffner *m*, Büchsenöffner *m*
**tin·sel** Lametta *n*; Flitter *m*
**tint 1.** (Farb)Ton *m*, Tönung *f*; **2.** tönen
**ti·ny** winzig
**tip[1] 1.** Spitze *f*; Filter *m*; ***it's on the ~ of my tongue*** *fig* es liegt mir auf der Zunge; **2.** mit e-r Spitze versehen
**tip[2] 1.** *esp Br* (aus)kippen, schütten; kippen; ***~ over*** umkippen; **2.** *esp Br* (*Schutt- etc*)Abladeplatz *m*, (-)Halde *f*; *Br fig* F Saustall *m*
**tip[3] 1.** Trinkgeld *n*; **2.** *j-m* ein Trinkgeld geben
**tip[4] 1.** Tipp *m*, Rat(schlag) *m*; **2.** tippen auf (*acc*) (***as*** als); ***~ s.o. off*** j-m e-n Tipp *or* Wink geben
**tip·sy** angeheitert
**tip·toe 1.** ***on ~*** auf Zehenspitzen; **2.** auf Zehenspitzen gehen
**tire[1]** MOT Reifen *m*
**tire[2]** ermüden, müde machen *or* werden
**tired** müde; ***be ~ of*** *j-n, et.* satt haben
**tire·less** unermüdlich
**tire·some** ermüdend; lästig
**tis·sue** BIOL Gewebe *n*; Papier(taschen)tuch *n*; → ***~*** **pa·per** Seidenpapier *n*
**tit[1]** F *contp* Titte *f*
**tit[2]** ZO Meise *f*
**tit·bit** *esp Br* → ***tidbit***
**tit·il·late** *j-n* (*sexuell*) anregen
**ti·tle** Titel *m*; JUR (Rechts)Anspruch *m* (***to*** auf *acc*)
**ti·tle·hold·er** SPORT Titelhalter(in)
**ti·tle page** Titelseite *f*
**ti·tle role** THEA *etc* Titelrolle *f*
**tit·mouse** ZO Meise *f*
**tit·ter 1.** kichern; **2.** Kichern *n*
**to 1.** *prp* zu; an (*acc*), auf (*acc*), für, in (*acc*), in (*dat*), nach; (im Verhältnis *or* im Vergleich) zu, gegen(über); *extent, limit, degree*: bis, (bis) zu, (bis) an (*acc*); *time*: bis, bis zu, bis gegen, vor (*dat*); ***from Monday ~ Friday*** von Montag bis Freitag; ***a quarter ~ one*** (ein) Viertel vor eins, drei viertel eins; ***go ~ Italy*** nach Italien fahren; ***go ~ school*** in die *or* zur Schule gehen; ***have you ever been ~ Rome?*** bist du schon einmal in Rom gewesen?; ***~ me*** *etc* mir *etc*; ***here's ~ you!*** auf Ihr Wohl!, prosit!; **2.** *adv* zu; ***pull ~*** *Tür etc* zuziehen; ***come ~*** (wieder) zu sich kommen; ***~ and fro*** hin und her, auf und ab; **3.** *with infinitive*: zu; *intention, aim*: um zu; ***~ go*** gehen; ***easy ~ learn*** leicht zu lernen; ***... ~ earn money*** ... um Geld zu verdienen
**toad** ZO Kröte *f*, Unke *f*
**toad·stool** BOT ungenießbarer Pilz; Giftpilz *m*
**toad·y 1.** Kriecher(in); **2.** ***~ to s.o.*** *fig* vor j-m kriechen
**toast[1] 1.** Toast *m*; **2.** toasten; rösten
**toast[2] 1.** Toast *m*, Trinkspruch *m*; **2.** auf *j-n or j-s* Wohl trinken
**toast·er** TECH Toaster *m*
**to·bac·co** Tabak *m*; **to·bac·co·nist** Tabak(waren)händler(in)
**to·bog·gan 1.** (Rodel)Schlitten *m*; **2.** Schlitten fahren, rodeln
**to·day 1.** *adv* heute; heutzutage; ***a week ~, ~ week*** heute in e-r Woche, heute in acht Tagen; **2.** ***~'s paper*** die heutige Zeitung, die Zeitung von heute; ***of ~, ~'s*** von heute, heutig
**tod·dle** auf wack(e)ligen *or* unsicheren Beinen gehen
**to-do** F *fig* Theater *n*
**toe** ANAT Zehe *f*; Spitze *f*
**toe·nail** ANAT Zehennagel *m*
**tof·fee, tof·fy** Sahnebonbon *m*, *n*, Toffee *n*
**to·geth·er** zusammen; gleichzeitig
**toi·let** Toilette *f*; ***~*** **pa·per** Toilettenpapier *n*; ***~*** **roll** *esp Br* Rolle *f* Toilettenpapier

**to·ken** Zeichen *n*; ***as a ~, in ~ of*** als *or* zum Zeichen (*gen*); zum Andenken an (*acc*); **~ strike** Warnstreik *m*
**tol·e·ra·ble** erträglich
**tol·e·rance** Toleranz *f*; Nachsicht *f*
**tol·e·rant** tolerant (***of, towards*** gegenüber)
**tol·e·rate** tolerieren, dulden; ertragen
**toll**[1] Benutzungsgebühr *f*, Maut *f*; ***heavy death ~*** große Zahl an Todesopfern; ***take its ~ (on)*** *fig* s-n Tribut fordern (von); s-e Spuren hinterlassen (bei)
**toll**[2] läuten
**toll-free** TEL gebührenfrei
**toll road** gebührenpflichtige Straße, Mautstraße *f*
**tom** F → ***tomcat***
**to·ma·to** BOT Tomate *f*
**tomb** Grab *n*; Grabmal *n*; Gruft *f*
**tom·boy** Wildfang *m*
**tomb·stone** Grabstein *m*
**tom·cat** ZO Kater *m*
**tom·fool·e·ry** Unsinn *m*
**to·mor·row** **1.** *adv* morgen; ***a week ~, ~ week*** morgen in e-r Woche, morgen in acht Tagen; ***~ morning*** morgen früh; ***~ night*** morgen Abend; **2.** ***the day after ~*** übermorgen; ***of ~, ~'s*** von morgen
**ton** (ABBR ***t, tn***) Tonne *f*
**tone** **1.** Ton *m*; Klang *m*; (Farb)Ton *m*; MUS Note *f*; MED Tonus *m*; *fig* Niveau *n*; **2.** ***~ down*** abschwächen; ***~ up*** *Muskeln etc* kräftigen
**tongs** (***a pair of ~*** e-e) Zange *f*
**tongue** ANAT, TECH Zunge *f*; (*Mutter*)Sprache *f*; Klöppel *m* (*e-r Glocke*); ***hold one's ~*** den Mund halten
**ton·ic** Tonikum *n*, Stärkungsmittel *n*; Tonic *n*; MUS Grundton *m*
**to·night** heute Abend *or* Nacht
**ton·sil** ANAT Mandel *f*
**ton·sil·li·tis** MED Mandelentzündung *f*; Angina *f*
**too** zu; zu, sehr; auch (noch)
**tool** Werkzeug *n*, Gerät *n*; **~ bag** Werkzeugtasche *f*; **~ box** Werkzeugkasten *m*; **~ kit** Werkzeug *n*
**tool·mak·er** Werkzeugmacher *m*
**tool·shed** Geräteschuppen *m*
**toot** *esp* MOT hupen
**tooth** Zahn *m*
**tooth·ache** Zahnschmerzen *pl*, Zahnweh *n*
**tooth·brush** Zahnbürste *f*
**tooth·less** zahnlos
**tooth·paste** Zahncreme *f*, Zahnpasta *f*
**tooth·pick** Zahnstocher *m*
**top**[1] **1.** oberer Teil; GEOGR Gipfel *m*, Spitze *f*; BOT Krone *f*, Wipfel *m*; Kopfende *n*, oberes Ende; Oberteil *n*; Oberfläche *f*; Deckel *m*; Verschluss *m*; MOT Verdeck *n*; MOT höchster Gang; ***at the ~ of the page*** oben auf der Seite; ***at the ~ of one's voice*** aus vollem Hals; ***on ~*** oben(auf); darauf, F drauf; ***on ~ of*** (oben) auf (*dat or acc*), über (*dat or acc*); **2.** oberste(r, -s); Höchst..., Spitzen..., Top...; **3.** bedecken (***with*** mit); *fig* übersteigen, übertreffen; ***~ up*** *Tank etc* auffüllen; F *j-m* nachschenken
**top**[2] Kreisel *m* (*toy*)
**top hat** Zylinder *m*
**top-heav·y** kopflastig (*a. fig*)
**top·ic** Thema *n*; **top·ic·al** aktuell
**top·ple:** *mst* ***~ over*** umkippen; ***~ the government*** die Regierung stürzen
**top·sy-tur·vy** in e-r heillosen Unordnung
**torch** *Br* Taschenlampe *f*; Fackel *f*
**torch·light** Fackelschein *m*; ***~ procession*** Fackelzug *m*
**tor·ment** **1.** Qual *f*; **2.** quälen, peinigen, plagen
**tor·na·do** Tornado *m*, Wirbelsturm *m*
**tor·pe·do** MIL **1.** Torpedo *m*; **2.** torpedieren (*a. fig*)
**tor·rent** reißender Strom; *fig* Schwall *m*
**tor·ren·tial:** ***~ rain*** sintflutartige Regenfälle *pl*
**tor·toise** ZO Schildkröte *f*
**tor·tu·ous** gewunden
**tor·ture** **1.** Folter *f*, Folterung *f*; *fig* Qual *f*, Tortur *f*; **2.** foltern; *fig* quälen
**toss** **1.** *v/t* werfen; *Münze* hochwerfen; GASTR schwenken; ***~ off*** F *Bild etc* hinhauen; *v/i a.* ***~ about, ~ and turn*** sich *im Schlaf* hin und her werfen; *a.* ***~ up*** e-e Münze hochwerfen; ***~ for s.th.*** um et. losen; ***~ one's head*** den Kopf zurückwerfen; **2.** Wurf *m*; Zurückwerfen *n*; Hochwerfen *n*
**tot** F Knirps *m*
**to·tal** **1.** völlig, total; ganz, gesamt, Gesamt...; **2.** Gesamtbetrag *m*, -menge *f*; **3.** sich belaufen auf (*acc*); ***~ up*** zusammenrechnen, -zählen
**tot·ter** schwanken, wanken

**touch 1.** (sich) berühren; anfassen; *Essen etc* anrühren; *fig* herankommen an (*acc*); *fig* rühren; **~ wood!** toi, toi, toi!; **~ down** AVIAT aufsetzen; **~ up** ausbessern; PHOT retuschieren; **2.** Tastempfindung *f*; Berührung *f*, MUS *etc* Anschlag *m*; (*Pinsel- etc*)Strich *m*; GASTR Spur *f*; Verbindung *f*, Kontakt *m*; *fig* Note *f*; *fig* Anflug *m*; **a ~ of flu** e-e leichte Grippe; **get in ~ with s.o.** sich mit j-m in Verbindung setzen
**touch-and-go** F kritisch, riskant, prekär; **it was ~ whether** es stand auf des Messers Schneide, ob
**touch·down** AVIAT Aufsetzen *n*, Landung *f*
**touched** gerührt; F leicht verrückt
**touch·ing** rührend
**touch·line** *soccer*: Seitenlinie *f*
**touch·stone** Prüfstein *m* (**of** für)
**touch·y** empfindlich; heikel (*subject etc*)
**tough** zäh; widerstandsfähig; *fig* hart; schwierig (*problem, negotiations etc*)
**tough·en** *a.* **~ up** hart *or* zäh machen *or* werden
**tour 1.** Tour *f* (**of** durch), (Rund)Reise *f*, (Rund)Fahrt *f*; Ausflug *m*; Rundgang *m* (**of** durch); THEA Tournee *f* (*a.* SPORT); **go on ~** auf Tournee gehen; → **conduct** 2; **2.** bereisen, reisen durch
**tour·is·m** Tourismus *m*, Fremdenverkehr *m*
**tour·ist 1.** Tourist(in); **2.** Touristen...; **~ class** AVIAT, MAR Touristenklasse *f*; **~ in·dus·try** Tourismusgeschäft *n*; **~ in·for·ma·tion of·fice, ~ of·fice** Verkehrsverein *m*; **~ sea·son** Reisesaison *f*, Reisezeit *f*
**tour·na·ment** Turnier *n*
**tou·sled** zerzaust
**tow 1.** *Boot etc* schleppen, *Auto etc a.* abschleppen; **2. give s.o. a ~** j-n abschleppen; **take in ~** *Auto etc* abschleppen
**to·ward,** *esp Br* **to·wards** auf (*acc*) ... zu, (in) Richtung, zu; *time*: gegen; *fig* gegenüber
**tow·el 1.** Handtuch *n*, (*Bade- etc*)Tuch *n*; **2.** (mit e-m Handtuch) abtrocknen *or* abreiben
**tow·er 1.** Turm *m*; **2. ~ above, ~ over** überragen; **~ block** *Br* Hochhaus *n*
**tow·er·ing** turmhoch; *fig* überragend; **in a ~ rage** rasend vor Zorn
**town** Stadt *f*; Kleinstadt *f*; **go into ~** in die Stadt gehen; **~ cen·tre** *Br* Innenstadt *f*, City *f*; **~ coun·cil** *Br* Stadtrat *m*; **~ coun·ci(l)·lor** *Br* Stadtrat *m*, Stadträtin *f*; **~ hall** Rathaus *n*
**town·ie** F Städter(in), Stadtmensch *m*
**town| plan·ner** Stadtplaner(in); **~ plan·ning** Stadtplanung *f*
**towns·peo·ple** Städter *pl*, Stadtbevölkerung *f*
**tow·rope** MOT Abschleppseil *n*
**tox·ic** toxisch, giftig; Gift...
**tox·ic waste** Giftmüll *m*
**tox·ic waste dump** Giftmülldeponie *f*
**toy 1.** Spielzeug *n*, *pl a.* Spielsachen *pl*, ECON Spielwaren *pl*; **2.** Spielzeug...; Miniatur...; Zwerg...; **3. ~ with** spielen mit (*a. fig*)
**trace 1.** (durch)pausen; *j-n*, *et.* ausfindig machen, aufspüren, *et.* finden; *a.* **~ back** *et.* zurückverfolgen (**to** bis zu); **~ s.th. to** et. zurückführen auf (*acc*); **2.** Spur *f* (*a. fig*)
**track 1.** Spur *f* (*a. fig*), Fährte *f*; Pfad *m*, Weg *m*; RAIL Gleis *n*, Geleise *n*; TECH Raupe *f*, Raupenkette *f*; SPORT (Renn-, Aschen)Bahn *f*, (*Renn*)Strecke *f*; *tape etc*: Spur *f*; Nummer *f* (*on an LP etc*); **2.** verfolgen; **~ down** aufspüren; auftreiben
**track and field** SPORT Leichtathletik *f*
**track e·vent** SPORT Laufdisziplin *f*
**track·ing sta·tion** Bodenstation *f*
**track·suit** Trainingsanzug *m*
**tract** Fläche *f*, Gebiet *n*; ANAT (*Verdauungs*)Trakt *m*, (*Atem*)Wege *pl*
**trac·tion** Ziehen *n*, Zug *m*
**trac·tion en·gine** Zugmaschine *f*
**trac·tor** Traktor *m*, Trecker *m*
**trade 1.** Handel *m*; Branche *f*, Gewerbe *n*; (*esp* Handwerks)Beruf *m*; **2.** Handel treiben, handeln; **~ on** ausnutzen; **~ a·gree·ment** Handelsabkommen *n*
**trade·mark** Warenzeichen *n*
**trade name** Markenname *m*, Handelsbezeichnung *f*
**trade price** Großhandelspreis *m*
**trad·er** Händler(in)
**trades·man** (Einzel)Händler *m*; Ladeninhaber *m*; Lieferant *m*
**trade(s** *Br*)**| u·nion** Gewerkschaft *f*; **~ u·nion·ist** Gewerkschaftler(in)
**tra·di·tion** Tradition *f*; Überlieferung *f*
**tra·di·tion·al** traditionell

**traf·fic 1.** Verkehr *m*; (*esp* illegaler) Handel (***in*** mit); **2.** (*esp* illegal) handeln (***in*** mit); **~ cir·cle** MOT Kreisverkehr *m*; **~ in·struc·tion** Verkehrsunterricht *m*; **~ is·land** Verkehrsinsel *f*; **~ jam** (Verkehrs)Stau *m*, Verkehrsstockung *f*; **~ light(s)** Verkehrsampel *f*; **~ of·fense** (*Br* **of·fence**) Verkehrsdelikt *n*; **~ of·fend·er** Verkehrssünder(in); **~ reg·u·la·tions** Straßenverkehrsordnung *f*; **~ sign** Verkehrszeichen *n*, -schild *n*; **~ sig·nal** → ***traffic light(s)***; **~ war·den** *Br* Parküberwacher *m*, Politesse *f*
**tra·ge·dy** Tragödie *f*
**tra·gic** tragisch
**trail 1.** *v/t et.* nachschleifen lassen; verfolgen; SPORT zurückliegen hinter (*dat*) (***by*** um); *v/i* sich schleppen; BOT kriechen; SPORT zurückliegen (***by 3-0*** 0:3); **~** (***along***) ***behind s.o.*** hinter j-m herschleifen; **2.** Spur *f* (*a. fig*), Fährte *f*; Pfad *m*, Weg *m*; **~ *of blood*** Blutspur *f*; **~ *of dust*** Staubwolke *f*
**trail·er** MOT Anhänger *m*; Wohnwagen *m*, Caravan *m*; *film*, TV Trailer *m*, Vorschau *f*; **~ park** Standplatz *m* für Wohnwagen
**train 1.** RAIL Zug *m*; Kolonne *f*, Schlange *f*; Schleppe *f*; *fig* Folge *f*, Kette *f*; ***by ~*** mit der Bahn, mit dem Zug; **~ *of thought*** Gedankengang *m*; **2.** *v/t j-n* ausbilden (***as*** als, zum), schulen; SPORT trainieren; *Tier* abrichten, dressieren; *Kamera etc* richten (***on*** auf *acc*); *v/i* ausgebildet werden (***as*** als, zum); SPORT trainieren (***for*** für)
**train·ee** Auszubildende *m, f*
**train·er** Ausbilder(in); ZO Abrichter(in), Dompteur *m*, Dompteuse *f*; SPORT Trainer(in); *Br* Turnschuh *m*
**train·ing** Ausbildung *f*, Schulung *f*; Abrichten *n*, Dressur *f*; SPORT Training *n*
**trait** (Charakter)Zug *m*
**trai·tor** Verräter *m*
**tram** *Br* Straßenbahn(wagen *m*) *f*
**tram·car** *Br* Straßenbahnwagen *m*
**tramp 1.** sta(m)pfen *or* trampeln (durch); **2.** Tramp *m*, Landstreicher *m*, Vagabund *m*; Wanderung *f*; Flittchen *n*; **tram·ple** (zer)trampeln
**trance** Trance *f*
**tran·quil** ruhig, friedlich
**tran·quil·(l)i·ty** Ruhe *f*, Frieden *m*
**tran·quil·(l)ize** beruhigen
**tran·quil·(l)iz·er** PHARM Beruhigungsmittel *n*
**trans·act** *Geschäft* abwickeln, *Handel* abschließen
**trans·ac·tion** Abwicklung *f*, Abschluss *m*; Geschäft *n*, Transaktion *f*
**trans·at·lan·tic** transatlantisch, Transatlantik..., Übersee...
**tran·scribe** abschreiben, kopieren; *Stenogramm etc* übertragen
**tran·script** Abschrift *f*, Kopie *f*
**tran·scrip·tion** Umschreibung *f*, Umschrift *f*; Abschrift *f*, Kopie *f*
**trans·fer 1.** *v/t* (***to***) *Betrieb etc* verlegen (nach); *j-n* versetzen (nach); SPORT *Spieler* transferieren (zu), abgeben (an *acc*); *Geld* überweisen (an *acc*, auf *acc*); JUR *Eigentum*, *Recht* übertragen (auf *acc*); *v/i* SPORT wechseln (***to*** zu); umsteigen (***from ... to ...*** von ... auf ... *acc*); **2.** Verlegung *f*; Versetzung *f*; SPORT Transfer *m*, Wechsel *m*; ECON Überweisung *f*; JUR Übertragung *f*; Umsteige(fahr)karte *f*
**trans·fer·a·ble** übertragbar
**trans·fixed** *fig* versteinert, starr
**trans·form** umwandeln, verwandeln
**trans·for·ma·tion** Umwandlung *f*, Verwandlung *f*
**trans·form·er** ELECTR Transformator *m*
**trans·fu·sion** MED Bluttransfusion *f*, Blutübertragung *f*
**trans·gress** verletzen, verstoßen gegen
**tran·sient** flüchtig, vergänglich
**tran·sis·tor** Transistor *m*
**tran·sit** Transit-, Durchgangsverkehr *m*; ECON Transport *m*; ***in ~*** unterwegs, auf dem Transport
**tran·si·tion** Übergang *m*
**tran·si·tive** LING transitiv
**tran·si·to·ry** → ***transient***
**trans·late** übersetzen (***from English into German*** aus dem Englischen ins Deutsche)
**trans·la·tion** Übersetzung *f*
**trans·la·tor** Übersetzer(in)
**trans·lu·cent** lichtdurchlässig
**trans·mis·sion** MED Übertragung *f*; *radio*, TV Sendung *f*; MOT Getriebe *n*
**trans·mit** *Signale* (aus)senden; *radio*, TV senden; PHYS *Wärme etc* leiten, *Licht etc* durchlassen; MED *Krankheit* übertragen

**trans·mit·ter** Sender *m*
**trans·par·en·cy** Durchsichtigkeit *f* (*a. fig*); *fig* Durchschaubarkeit *f*; Dia(positiv) *n*; Folie *f*; **trans·par·ent** durchsichtig (*a. fig*); *fig* durchschaubar
**tran·spire** transpirieren, schwitzen; *fig* durchsickern; F passieren
**trans·plant 1.** umpflanzen, verpflanzen (*a.* MED); MED transplantieren; **2.** MED Transplantation *f*, Verpflanzung *f*; Transplantat *n*
**trans·port 1.** Transport *m*, Beförderung *f*; Beförderungs-, Verkehrsmittel *n or pl*; MIL Transportschiff *n*, -flugzeug *n*, (*Truppen*)Transporter *m*; **2.** transportieren, befördern
**trans·port·a·ble** transportabel, transportfähig
**trans·por·ta·tion** Transport *m*, Beförderung *f*
**trap 1.** Falle *f* (*a. fig*); ***set a ~ for s.o.*** j-m e-e Falle stellen; ***shut one's ~, keep one's ~ shut*** F die Schnauze halten; **2.** (in *or* mit e-r Falle) fangen; *fig* in e-e Falle locken; ***be ~ped*** eingeschlossen sein
**trap·door** Falltür *f*; THEA Versenkung *f*
**tra·peze** Trapez *n*
**trap·per** Trapper *m*, Fallensteller *m*, Pelztierjäger *m*
**trap·pings** Rangabzeichen *pl*; *fig* Drum und Dran *n*
**trash** F Schund *m*; Quatsch *m*, Unsinn *m*; Abfall *m*, Abfälle *pl*, Müll *m*; Gesindel *n*
**trash·can** Abfall-, Mülleimer *m*; Abfall-, Mülltonne *f*
**trash·y** Schund...
**trav·el 1.** *v/i* reisen; fahren; TECH *etc* sich bewegen; *fig* sich verbreiten; *fig* schweifen, wandern; *v/t* bereisen; *Strecke* zurücklegen, fahren; **2.** Reisen *n*; *pl* (*esp* Auslands)Reisen *pl*; **~ a·gen·cy** Reisebüro *n*; **~ a·gent** Reisebüroinhaber(in); Angestellte *m, f* in e-m Reisebüro; **~ a·gent's, ~ bu·reau** Reisebüro *n*
**trav·el·(l)er** Reisende *m, f*
**trav·el·(l)er's check** (*Br* **cheque**) Reise-, Travellerscheck *m*
**trav·el·(l)ing| bag** Reisetasche *f*; **~ ex·pens·es** Reisekosten *pl*
**trav·el sick·ness** Reisekrankheit *f*
**trav·es·ty** Zerrbild *n*
**trawl 1.** Schleppnetz *n*; **2.** mit dem Schleppnetz fischen
**trawl·er** MAR Trawler *m*
**tray** Tablett *n*; Ablagekorb *m*
**treach·er·ous** verräterisch; tückisch
**treach·er·y** Verrat *m*
**trea·cle** *esp Br* Sirup *m*
**tread 1.** treten (***on*** auf *acc*; in *acc*); *Pfad etc* treten; **2.** Gang *m*; Schritt(e *pl*) *m*; (Reifen)Profil *n*
**tread·mill** Tretmühle *f* (*a. fig*)
**trea·son** Landesverrat *m*
**trea·sure 1.** Schatz *m*; **2.** sehr schätzen; in Ehren halten
**trea·sur·er** Schatzmeister(in)
**trea·sure trove** Schatzfund *m*
**Trea·su·ry** *Br*, **~ De·part·ment** Finanzministerium *n*
**treat 1.** *j-n*, *et.* behandeln; umgehen mit; *et.* ansehen, betrachten (***as*** als); MED *j-n* behandeln (***for*** gegen); *j-n* einladen (***to*** zu); ***~ s.o. to s.th.*** *a.* j-m et. spendieren; ***~ o.s. to s.th.*** sich et. leisten *or* gönnen; ***be ~ed for*** MED in ärztlicher Behandlung sein wegen; **2.** (besondere) Freude *or* Überraschung; ***this is my ~*** das geht auf meine Rechnung, ich lade dich *etc* ein
**trea·tise** Abhandlung *f*
**treat·ment** Behandlung *f*
**treat·y** Vertrag *m*
**tre·ble[1] 1.** dreifach; **2.** (sich) verdreifachen
**tre·ble[2]** MUS Knabensopran *m*; *radio*: (Ton)Höhe *f*
**tree** BOT Baum *m*
**tre·foil** BOT Klee *m*
**trel·lis** BOT Spalier *n*
**trem·ble** zittern (***with*** vor *dat*)
**tre·men·dous** gewaltig, enorm; F klasse, toll
**trem·or** Zittern *n*; Beben *n*
**trench** Graben *m*; MIL Schützengraben *m*
**trend** Trend *m*, Entwicklung *f*, Tendenz *f*; Mode *f*
**trend·y** F **1.** modern, modisch; ***be ~*** als schick gelten, in sein; **2.** *esp Br contp* Schickimicki *m*
**tres·pass 1. *~ on*** *Grundstück etc* unbefugt betreten; *j-s Zeit etc* über Gebühr in Anspruch nehmen; ***no ~ing*** Betreten verboten!; **2.** unbefugtes Betreten
**tres·pass·er: *~s will be prosecuted*** Betreten bei Strafe verboten!

T

**tres·tle** Bock *m*, Gestell *n*
**tri·al 1.** JUR Prozess *m*, (Gerichts)Verhandlung *f*, (-)Verfahren *n*; Erprobung *f*, Probe *f*, Prüfung *f*, Test *m*; Plage *f*; ***on ~*** auf *or* zur Probe; ***be on ~*** erprobt *or* getestet werden; ***be on ~, stand ~*** vor Gericht stehen (***for*** wegen); ***by way of ~*** versuchsweise; **2.** Versuchs..., Probe...
**tri·an·gle** Dreieck *n*; Winkel *m*, Zeichendreieck *n*
**tri·an·gu·lar** dreieckig
**tri·ath·lon** SPORT Triathlon *n*, *m*, Dreikampf *m*
**trib·al** Stammes...
**tribe** (Volks)Stamm *m*
**tri·bu·nal** JUR Gericht(shof *m*) *n*
**trib·u·ta·ry** GEOGR Nebenfluss *m*
**trib·ute:** ***be a ~ to*** *j-m* Ehre machen; ***pay ~ to*** *j-m* Anerkennung zollen
**trick 1.** Trick *m*; (*Karten- etc*)Kunststück *n*; Streich *m*; *card game*: Stich *m*; (merkwürdige) Angewohnheit, Eigenart *f*; ***play a ~ on s.o.*** j-m e-n Streich spielen; **2.** Trick...; ***~ question*** Fangfrage *f*; **3.** überlisten, F reinlegen
**trick·e·ry** Tricks *pl*
**trick·le 1.** tröpfeln; rieseln; **2.** Tröpfeln *n*; Rinnsal *n*
**trick·ster** Betrüger(in), Schwindler(in)
**trick·y** heikel, schwierig; durchtrieben, raffiniert
**tri·cy·cle** Dreirad *n*
**tri·dent** Dreizack *m*
**tri·fle 1.** Kleinigkeit *f*; Lappalie *f*; ***a ~*** ein bisschen, etwas; **2.** ***~ with*** *fig* spielen mit; ***he is not to be ~d with*** er lässt nicht mit sich spaßen
**tri·fling** geringfügig, unbedeutend
**trig·ger** Abzug *m*; ***pull the ~*** abdrücken
**trig·ger-hap·py** F schießwütig
**trill 1.** Triller *m*; **2.** trillern
**trim 1.** *Hecke etc* stutzen, beschneiden, sich *den Bart etc* stutzen; *Kleidungsstück* besetzen (***with*** mit); ***~med with fur*** pelzbesetzt, mit Pelzbesatz; ***~ off*** abschneiden; **2.** ***give s.th. a ~*** et. stutzen, et. (be)schneiden; ***be in good ~*** F gut in Form sein; **3.** gepflegt
**trim·mings** Besatz *m*; GASTR Beilagen *pl*
**Trin·i·ty** REL Dreieinigkeit *f*
**trin·ket** (*esp* billiges) Schmuckstück
**trip 1.** *v/i* stolpern (***over*** über *acc*); (e-n) Fehler machen; *v/t a.* ***~ up*** *j-m* ein Bein stellen (*a. fig*); **2.** (kurze) Reise; Ausflug *m*, Trip *m* (*a. sl*); Stolpern *n*, Fallen *n*
**tripe** GASTR Kaldaunen *pl*, Kutteln *pl*
**trip·le 1.** dreifach; **2.** verdreifachen
**trip·le jump** SPORT Dreisprung *m*
**trip·lets** Drillinge *pl*
**trip·li·cate 1.** dreifach; **2.** ***in ~*** in dreifacher Ausfertigung
**tri·pod** PHOT Stativ *n*
**trip·per** *esp Br* (*esp Tages*)Ausflügler(in)
**trite** abgedroschen, banal
**tri·umph 1.** Triumph *m*, *fig* Sieg *m* (***over*** über *acc*); **2.** triumphieren (***over*** über *acc*)
**tri·um·phal** Triumph...
**tri·um·phant** triumphierend
**triv·i·al** unbedeutend, bedeutungslos; trivial, alltäglich
**trol·ley** *esp Br* Einkaufswagen *m*; Gepäckwagen *m*, Kofferkuli *m*; (*Tee- etc*)Wagen *m*; (***supermarket***) ***~*** Einkaufswagen *m*; ***shopping ~*** Einkaufsroller *m*
**trol·ley·bus** Oberleitungsbus *m*, Obus *m*
**trom·bone** MUS Posaune *f*
**troop 1.** Schar *f*; *pl* MIL Truppen *pl*; **2.** (*herein- etc*)strömen; ***~ the colour*** *Br* MIL e-e Fahnenparade abhalten
**troop·er** MIL Kavallerist *m*; Panzerjäger *m*; Polizist *m*
**tro·phy** Trophäe *f*
**trop·ic** ASTR, GEOGR Wendekreis *m*; ***the ~ of Cancer*** der Wendekreis des Krebses; ***the ~ of Capricorn*** der Wendekreis des Steinbocks
**trop·i·cal** tropisch, Tropen...
**trop·ics** Tropen *pl*
**trot 1.** Trab *m*; Trott *m*; **2.** traben (lassen); ***~ along*** F losziehen
**trou·ble 1.** Schwierigkeit *f*, Problem *n*, Ärger *m*; Mühe *f*; MED Beschwerden *pl*; *a. pl* POL Unruhen *pl*; *pl* Unannehmlichkeiten *pl*; ***be in ~*** in Schwierigkeiten sein; ***get into ~*** Schwierigkeiten *or* Ärger bekommen; *j-n* in Schwierigkeiten bringen; ***get*** *or* ***run into ~*** in Schwierigkeiten geraten; ***have ~ with*** Schwierigkeiten *or* Ärger haben mit; ***put s.o. to ~*** j-m Mühe *or* Umstände machen; ***take the ~ to do s.th.*** sich die Mühe machen, et. zu tun; **2.** *v/t j-n* beunruhigen; *j-m*

Mühe *or* Umstände machen; *j-n* bemühen (**for** um), bitten (**for** um; ***to do*** zu tun); ***be ~d by*** geplagt werden von, leiden an (*dat*); *v/i* sich bemühen (***to do*** zu tun), sich Umstände machen (***about*** wegen)

**trou·ble·mak·er** Störenfried *m*, Unruhestifter(in)

**trou·ble·some** lästig

**trou·ble spot** *esp* POL Krisenherd *m*

**trough** Trog *m*; Wellental *n*

**trounce** SPORT haushoch besiegen

**troupe** THEA Truppe *f*

**trou·ser:** (***a pair of***) ***~s*** (e-e) Hose *f*

**trou·ser suit** *Br* Hosenanzug *m*

**trous·seau** Aussteuer *f*

**trout** ZO Forelle *f*

**trow·el** (Maurer)Kelle *f*

**tru·ant** Schulschwänzer(in); ***play ~*** *Br* (die Schule) schwänzen

**truce** MIL Waffenstillstand *m* (*a. fig*)

**truck 1.** MOT Lastwagen *m*; Fernlaster *m*; *Br* RAIL (offener) Güterwagen; Transportkarren *m*; **2.** auf *or* mit Lastwagen transportieren

**truck driv·er, truck·er** MOT Lastwagenfahrer *m*; Fernfahrer *m*

**truck farm** ECON Gemüse- und Obstgärtnerei *f*

**trudge** (mühsam) stapfen

**true** wahr; echt, wirklich; treu (**to** *dat*); ***be ~*** wahr sein, stimmen; ***come ~*** in Erfüllung gehen; wahr werden; ***~ to life*** lebensecht

**tru·ly** wahrheitsgemäß; wirklich, wahrhaft; aufrichtig

**trump 1.** Trumpf(karte *f*) *m*; *pl* Trumpf *m*; **2.** mit e-m Trumpf stechen; ***~ up*** erfinden

**trum·pet 1.** MUS Trompete *f*; **2.** trompeten; *fig* ausposaunen

**trun·cheon** (Gummi)Knüppel *m*, Schlagstock *m*

**trun·dle** *Karren etc* ziehen

**trunk** (Baum)Stamm *m*; Schrankkoffer *m*; ZO Rüssel *m*; ANAT Rumpf *m*; MOT Kofferraum *m*; **~ road** *Br* Fernstraße *f*

**trunks** (*a.* ***a pair of ~*** e-e) (*Bade*)Hose *f*; SPORT Shorts *pl*

**truss 1.** *a.* ***~ up*** *j-n* fesseln; GASTR *Geflügel etc* dressieren; **2.** MED Bruchband *n*

**trust 1.** Vertrauen *n* (***in*** zu); JUR Treuhand *f*; ECON Trust *m*; Großkonzern *m*; ***hold s.th. in ~*** et. treuhänderisch verwalten (**for** für); ***place s.th. in s.o.'s ~*** j-m et. anvertrauen; **2.** *v/t* (ver)trauen (*dat*); sich verlassen auf (*acc*); (zuversichtlich) hoffen; ***~ him!*** das sieht ihm ähnlich!; *v/i*: ***~ in*** vertrauen auf (*acc*); ***~ to*** sich verlassen auf (*acc*)

**trust·ee** JUR Treuhänder(in); Sachverwalter(in)

**trust·ful, trust·ing** vertrauensvoll

**trust·wor·thy** vertrauenswürdig, zuverlässig

**truth** Wahrheit *f*

**truth·ful** wahr; wahrheitsliebend

**try 1.** *v/t* versuchen; *et.* (aus)probieren; JUR (über) *e-e Sache* verhandeln; *j-m* den Prozess machen (***for*** wegen); *j-n, j-s Geduld, Nerven etc* auf e-e harte Probe stellen; ***~*** *s.th.* ***on*** *Kleid etc* anprobieren; ***~*** *s.th.* ***out*** *et.* ausprobieren; *v/i* es versuchen; ***~ for*** *Br*, ***~ out for*** sich bemühen um; **2.** Versuch *m*; ***give*** *s.o., s.th.* ***a ~*** es mit *j-m, et.* versuchen; ***have a ~*** es versuchen; **try·ing** anstrengend

**tsar** HIST Zar *m*

**T-shirt** T-Shirt *n*

**tub** Bottich *m*, Zuber *m*, Tonne *f*; Becher *m*; F (Bade)Wanne *f*

**tub·by** F pumm(e)lig

**tube** Röhre *f* (*a.* ANAT), Rohr *n*; Schlauch *m*; Tube *f*; *Br* F U-Bahn *f* (*in London*); F Röhre *f*, Glotze *f*

**tube·less** schlauchlos

**tu·ber** BOT Knolle *f*

**tu·ber·cu·lo·sis** MED Tuberkulose *f*

**tu·bu·lar** röhrenförmig

**tuck 1.** stecken; ***~ away*** F wegstecken; ***~ in*** *esp Br* F reinhauen, zulangen; ***~ up*** (***in bed***) *Kind* ins Bett packen; **2.** Biese *f*; Saum *m*; Abnäher *m*

**Tue(s)** ABBR *of* ***Tuesday*** Di., Dienstag *m*

**Tues·day** (ABBR ***Tue, Tues***) Dienstag *m*; ***on ~*** (am) Dienstag; ***on ~s*** dienstags

**tuft** (*Gras-, Haar- etc*)Büschel *n*

**tug 1.** zerren *or* ziehen (an *dat or* **at** an *dat*); **2.** ***give*** *s.th.* ***a ~*** zerren *or* ziehen an (*dat*)

**tug-of-war** SPORT Tauziehen *n* (*a. fig*)

**tu·i·tion** Unterricht *m*; Unterrichtsgebühr(en *pl*) *f*

**tu·lip** BOT Tulpe *f*

**tum·ble 1.** fallen, stürzen; purzeln (*a. fig*); **2.** Fall *m*, Sturz *m*

**tum·ble·down** baufällig

**tum·bler** (Trink)Glas *n*

**tu·mid** MED geschwollen

**tum·my** F Bauch *m*, Bäuchlein *n*

**tu·mo(u)r** MED Tumor *m*

**tu·mult** Tumult *m*

**tu·mul·tu·ous** tumultartig, (*applause etc*) stürmisch

**tu·na** ZO Thunfisch *m*

**tune 1.** MUS Melodie *f*; ***be out of ~*** verstimmt sein; **2.** *v/t mst* ***~ in*** *Radio etc* einstellen (***to*** auf *acc*); *a.* ***~ up*** MUS stimmen; *a.* ***~ up*** *Motor* tunen; *v/i*: ***~ in*** (das Radio *etc*) einschalten; ***~ up*** MUS (die Instrumente) stimmen

**tune·ful** melodisch

**tune·less** unmelodisch

**tun·er** *radio*, TV Tuner *m*

**tun·nel 1.** Tunnel *m*; **2.** *Berg* durchtunneln; *Fluss etc* untertunneln

**tun·ny** ZO Thunfisch *m*

**tur·ban** Turban *m*

**tur·bid** trüb (*water*); dick, dicht (*smoke etc*); *fig* verworren, wirr

**tur·bine** TECH Turbine *f*

**tur·bo** F, **tur·bo·charg·er** MOT Turbolader *m*

**tur·bot** ZO Steinbutt *m*

**tur·bu·lent** turbulent

**tu·reen** (Suppen)Terrine *f*

**turf 1.** Rasen *m*; Sode *f*, Rasenstück *n*; ***the ~*** die (Pferde)Rennbahn; der Pferderennsport; **2.** mit Rasen bedecken

**tur·gid** MED geschwollen

**Turk** Türke *m*, Türkin *f*

**Tur·key** die Türkei

**tur·key** ZO Truthahn *m*, Truthenne *f*, Pute *f*, Puter *m*; ***talk ~*** F offen *or* sachlich reden

**Turk·ish 1.** türkisch; **2.** LING Türkisch *n*

**tur·moil** Aufruhr *m*

**turn 1.** *v/t* drehen, herum-, umdrehen; (um)wenden; *Seite* umblättern; *Schlauch etc* richten (***on*** auf *acc*); *Antenne* ausrichten (***toward*[*s*]** auf *acc*); *Aufmerksamkeit* zuwenden (***to*** *dat*); verwandeln (***into*** in *acc*); *Laub etc* färben; *Milch* sauer werden lassen; TECH formen, drechseln; ***~ the corner*** um die Ecke biegen; ***~ loose*** los-, freilassen; ***~ s.o.'s stomach*** j-m den Magen umdrehen; → ***inside*** 1, ***upside down, somersault*** 1; *v/i* sich (um)drehen; abbiegen; einbiegen (***onto*** auf *acc*; ***into*** in *acc*); MOT wenden; *blass, sauer etc* werden; sich verwandeln, *fig a.* umschlagen (***into, to*** in *acc*); → ***left*** 2, ***right*** 2; ***~ against*** *j-n* aufbringen *or* aufhetzen gegen; *fig* sich wenden gegen; ***~ away*** (sich) abwenden (***from*** von); *j-n* abweisen, wegschicken; ***~ back*** umkehren; *j-n* zurückschicken; *Uhr* zurückstellen; ***~ down*** *Radio etc* leiser stellen; *Gas etc* klein(er) stellen; *Heizung etc* runterschalten; *j-n*, *Angebot etc* ablehnen; *Kragen* umschlagen; *Bettdecke* zurückschlagen; ***~ in*** *v/t* zurückgeben; *Gewinn etc* erzielen, machen; *Arbeit* einreichen, abgeben; ***~ o.s. in*** sich stellen; *v/i* F sich aufs Ohr legen; ***~ off*** *v/t Gas, Wasser etc* abdrehen; *Licht*, *Radio etc* ausmachen, ausschalten; *Motor* abstellen; F *j-n* anwidern; F *j-m* die Lust nehmen; *v/i* abbiegen; ***~ on*** *Gas*, *Wasser etc* aufdrehen; *Gerät* anstellen; *Licht*, *Radio etc* anmachen, an-, einschalten; F *j-n* antörnen, anmachen; ***~ out*** *v/t Licht* ausmachen, ausschalten; *j-n* hinauswerfen; F *Waren* ausstoßen; *Tasche etc* (aus)leeren; *v/i* kommen (***for*** zu); sich erweisen *or* herausstellen als; ***~ over*** (sich) umdrehen; *Seite* umblättern; wenden; *et.* umkippen; sich *et.* überlegen; *j-n*, *et.* übergeben (***to*** *dat*); *Waren* umsetzen; ***~ round*** sich umdrehen; ***~ one's car round*** wenden; ***~ to*** sich an *j-n* wenden; sich zuwenden (*dat*); ***~ up*** *Kragen* hochschlagen; *Ärmel*, *Saum etc* umschlagen; *Radio etc* lauter stellen; *Gas etc* aufdrehen; *fig* auftauchen; **2.** (Um)Drehung *f*; Biegung *f*, Kurve *f*, Kehre *f*; Abzweigung *f*; *fig* Wende *f*, Wendung *f*; ***at every ~*** auf Schritt und Tritt; ***by ~s*** abwechselnd; ***in ~*** der Reihe nach; abwechselnd; ***it is my ~*** ich bin an der Reihe *or* F dran; ***make a left ~*** (nach) links abbiegen; ***take ~s*** sich abwechseln (***at*** bei); ***take a ~ for the better*** (***worse***) sich bessern (sich verschlimmern); ***do s.o. a good*** (***bad***) ***~*** j-m e-n guten (schlechten) Dienst erweisen

**turn·coat** Abtrünnige *m*, *f*, Überläufer(in); (***political***) ***~*** F Wendehals *m*

**turn·er** Drechsler *m*; Dreher *m*

**turn·ing** *esp Br* Abzweigung *f*

**turn·ing cir·cle** MOT Wendekreis *m*

**turn·ing point** *fig* Wendepunkt *m*

**tur·nip** BOT Rübe *f*

**turn-off** Abzweigung *f*
**turn·out** Besucher(zahl *f*) *pl*, Beteiligung *f*; Wahlbeteiligung *f*; F Aufmachung *f*
**turn·o·ver** ECON Umsatz *m*; Personalwechsel *m*, Fluktuation *f*
**turn·pike (road)** gebührenpflichtige Schnellstraße
**turn·stile** Drehkreuz *n*
**turn·ta·ble** Plattenteller *m*
**turn-up** *Br* (Hosen)Aufschlag *m*
**tur·pen·tine** CHEM Terpentin *n*
**tur·quoise** MIN Türkis *m*
**tur·ret** ARCH Ecktürmchen *n*; MIL (Panzer)Turm *m*; MAR Gefechtsturm *m*, Geschützturm *m*
**tur·tle** ZO (See)Schildkröte *f*
**tur·tle·dove** ZO Turteltaube *f*
**tur·tle·neck** Rollkragen(pullover) *m*
**tusk** ZO Stoßzahn *m*; Hauer *m*
**tus·sle** F Gerangel *n*
**tus·sock** Grasbüschel *n*
**tu·te·lage** (An)Leitung *f*; JUR Vormundschaft *f*
**tu·tor** Privat-, Hauslehrer(in); *Br* UNIV Tutor(in), Studienleiter(in)
**tu·to·ri·al** *Br* UNIV Tutorenkurs *m*
**tux·e·do** Smoking *m*
**TV 1.** TV *n*, Fernsehen *n*; Fernsehgerät *n*, F Fernseher *m*; ***on ~*** im Fernsehen; ***watch ~*** fernsehen; **2.** Fernseh...
**twang 1.** Schwirren *n*; *mst* ***nasal ~*** näselnde Aussprache; **2.** schwirren (lassen)
**tweak** F zwicken, kneifen
**tweet** ZO piep(s)en
**tweez·ers** (***a pair of ~*** e-e) Pinzette *f*
**twelfth 1.** zwölfte(r, -s); **2.** Zwölftel *n*
**twelve 1.** zwölf; **2.** Zwölf *f*
**twen·ti·eth** zwanzigste(r, -s)
**twen·ty 1.** zwanzig; **2.** Zwanzig *f*
**twice** zweimal
**twid·dle** (herum)spielen mit (*or* ***with*** mit); ***~ one's thumbs*** Däumchen drehen
**twig** BOT dünner Zweig, Ästchen *n*
**twi·light** (*esp* Abend)Dämmerung *f*; Zwielicht *n*, Dämmerlicht *n*
**twin 1.** Zwilling *m*; *pl* Zwillinge *pl*; **2.** Zwillings...; doppelt; **3.** ***be ~ned with*** die Partnerstadt sein von
**twin-bed·ded room** Zweibettzimmer *n*
**twin beds** zwei Einzelbetten
**twin broth·er** Zwillingsbruder *m*
**twine 1.** Bindfaden *m*, Schnur *f*; **2.** (sich) schlingen *or* winden (***round*** um); *a.* ***~ together*** zusammendrehen
**twin-en·gined** AVIAT zweimotorig
**twinge** stechender Schmerz, Stechen *n*; ***a ~ of conscience*** Gewissensbisse *pl*
**twin·kle 1.** glitzern (*stars*), (*a. eyes*) funkeln (***with*** vor *dat*); **2.** Glitzern *n*, Funkeln *n*; ***with a ~ in one's eye*** augenzwinkernd
**twin sis·ter** Zwillingsschwester *f*
**twin town** Partnerstadt *f*
**twirl 1.** (herum)wirbeln; wirbeln (***round*** über *acc*); **2.** Wirbel *m*
**twist 1.** *v/t* drehen; wickeln (***round*** um); *fig* verdrehen; ***~ off*** abdrehen, *Deckel* abschrauben; ***~ one's ankle*** (mit dem Fuß) umknicken, sich den Fuß vertreten; ***her face was ~ed with pain*** ihr Gesicht war schmerzverzerrt; *v/i* sich winden, (*river etc a.*) sich schlängeln; **2.** Drehung *f*; Biegung *f*; (*überraschende*) Wendung; MUS Twist *m*
**twitch 1.** *v/t* zucken (mit); *v/i* zucken (***with*** vor); zupfen (***at*** an *dat*); **2.** Zucken *n*; Zuckung *f*
**twit·ter 1.** zwitschern; **2.** Zwitschern *n*, Gezwitscher *n*; ***be all of a ~*** F ganz aufgeregt sein
**two 1.** zwei; ***the ~ cars*** die beiden Autos; ***the ~ of us*** wir beide; ***in ~s*** zu zweit, paarweise; ***cut in ~*** in zwei Teile schneiden; ***put ~ and ~ together*** zwei und zwei zusammenzählen; **2.** Zwei *f*
**two-edged** zweischneidig
**two-faced** falsch, heuchlerisch
**two·fold** zweifach
**two·pence** *Br* zwei Pence *pl*
**two·pen·ny** *Br* F für zwei Pence
**two-piece** zweiteilig; ***~ dress*** Jackenkleid *n*
**two-seat·er** AVIAT, MOT Zweisitzer *m*
**two-sid·ed** zweiseitig
**two-sto·ried,** *Br* **two-sto·rey** zweistöckig
**two-way traf·fic** MOT Gegenverkehr *m*
**ty·coon** (*Industrie- etc*)Magnat *m*
**type 1.** Art *f*, Sorte *f*; Typ *m*; PRINT Type *f*, Buchstabe *m*; **2.** *v/t et.* mit der Maschine schreiben, tippen; *v/i* Maschine schreiben, tippen
**type·writ·er** Schreibmaschine *f*
**type·writ·ten** maschine(n)geschrieben

**ty·phoid (fe·ver)** MED Typhus *m*
**ty·phoon** Taifun *m*
**ty·phus** MED Flecktyphus *m*, -fieber *n*
**typ·i·cal** typisch, bezeichnend (**of** für)
**typ·i·fy** typisch sein für, kennzeichnen; verkörpern
**typ·ing er·ror** Tippfehler *m*
**typ·ing pool** ECON Schreibzentrale *f*
**typ·ist** Schreibkraft *f*; Maschinenschreiber(in)
**ty·ran·ni·cal** tyrannisch
**tyr·an·nize** tyrannisieren
**tyr·an·ny** Tyrannei *f*
**ty·rant** Tyrann(in)
**tyre** *Br* → ***tire***[1]
**tzar** → ***tsar***

# U

**U, u** U, u *n*
**ud·der** ZO Euter *n*
**ug·ly** hässlich (*a. fig*); bös(e), schlimm (*wound etc*)
**ul·cer** MED Geschwür *n*
**ul·te·ri·or:** ~ ***motive*** Hintergedanke *m*
**ul·ti·mate** letzte(r, -s), End...; höchste(r, -s)
**ul·ti·mate·ly** letztlich; schließlich
**ul·ti·ma·tum** Ultimatum *n*; ***deliver an ~ to s.o.*** j-m ein Ultimatum stellen
**ul·tra·high fre·quen·cy** ELECTR Ultrakurzwelle *f*
**ul·tra·ma·rine** ultramarin
**ul·tra·son·ic** Ultraschall...
**ul·tra·sound** PHYS Ultraschall *m*
**ul·tra·vi·o·let** ultraviolett
**um·bil·i·cal cord** ANAT Nabelschnur *f*
**um·brel·la** (Regen)Schirm *m*; *fig* Schutz *m*
**um·pire** SPORT **1.** Schiedsrichter(in); **2.** als Schiedsrichter(in) fungieren (bei)
**un·a·bashed** unverfroren
**un·a·bat·ed** unvermindert
**un·a·ble** unfähig, außerstande, nicht in der Lage
**un·ac·cept·a·ble** unzumutbar
**un·ac·count·a·ble** unerklärlich
**un·ac·cus·tomed** ungewohnt
**un·ac·quaint·ed:** ***be ~ with s.th.*** et. nicht kennen, mit e-r Sache nicht vertraut sein
**un·ad·vised** unbesonnen, unüberlegt
**un·af·fect·ed** natürlich, ungekünstelt; ***be ~ by*** nicht betroffen sein von
**un·aid·ed** ohne Unterstützung, (ganz) allein
**un·al·ter·a·ble** unabänderlich
**u·nan·i·mous** einmütig; einstimmig
**un·an·nounced** unangemeldet
**un·an·swer·a·ble** unwiderlegbar; nicht zu beantworten(d)
**un·ap·pe·tiz·ing** unappetitlich
**un·ap·proach·a·ble** unnahbar
**un·armed** unbewaffnet
**un·asked** ungestellt (*question*); unaufgefordert, ungebeten (*guest etc*)
**un·as·sist·ed** ohne (fremde) Hilfe, (ganz) allein
**un·as·sum·ing** bescheiden
**un·at·tached** ungebunden, frei
**un·at·tend·ed** unbeaufsichtigt
**un·at·trac·tive** unattraktiv, wenig anziehend, reizlos
**un·au·thor·ized** unberechtigt, unbefugt
**un·a·void·a·ble** unvermeidlich
**un·a·ware:** ***be ~ of s.th.*** sich e-r Sache nicht bewusst sein, et. nicht bemerken
**un·a·wares:** ***catch*** *or* ***take s.o. ~*** j-n überraschen
**un·bal·ance** *j-n* aus dem (seelischen) Gleichgewicht bringen
**un·bal·anced** unausgeglichen, labil
**un·bar** aufriegeln, entriegeln
**un·bear·a·ble** unerträglich; *person*: unausstehlich
**un·beat·a·ble** unschlagbar
**un·beat·en** ungeschlagen, unbesiegt
**un·be·com·ing** unvorteilhaft
**un·be·known(st):** ~ ***to s.o.*** ohne j-s Wissen
**un·be·liev·a·ble** unglaublich
**un·bend** gerade biegen; sich aufrichten;

*fig* aus sich herausgehen, auftauen
**un·bend·ing** unbeugsam
**un·bi·as(s)ed** unvoreingenommen; JUR unbefangen
**un·bind** losbinden
**un·blem·ished** makellos
**un·born** ungeboren
**un·break·a·ble** unzerbrechlich
**un·bri·dled** *fig* ungezügelt, zügellos; ~ ***tongue*** lose Zunge
**un·bro·ken** ununterbrochen; heil, unversehrt; nicht zugeritten (*horse*)
**un·buck·le** aufschnallen, losschnallen
**un·bur·den:** ~ ***o.s. to s.o.*** j-m sein Herz ausschütten
**un·but·ton** aufknöpfen
**un·called-for** ungerechtfertigt; unnötig; unpassend
**un·can·ny** unheimlich
**un·cared-for** vernachlässigt
**un·ceas·ing** unaufhörlich
**un·ce·re·mo·ni·ous** brüsk, unhöflich; überstürzt
**un·cer·tain** unsicher, ungewiss, unbestimmt; vage; METEOR unbeständig
**un·cer·tain·ty** Unsicherheit *f*, Ungewissheit *f*
**un·chain** losketten
**un·changed** unverändert
**un·chang·ing** unveränderlich
**un·char·i·ta·ble** unfair
**un·checked** ungehindert; ungeprüft
**un·chris·tian** unchristlich
**un·civ·il** unhöflich
**un·civ·i·lized** unzivilisiert
**un·cle** Onkel *m*
**un·com·fort·a·ble** unbequem; ***feel*** ~ sich unbehaglich fühlen
**un·com·mon** ungewöhnlich
**un·com·mu·ni·ca·tive** wortkarg, verschlossen
**un·com·pre·hend·ing** verständnislos
**un·com·pro·mis·ing** kompromisslos
**un·con·cerned:** ***be*** ~ ***about*** sich keine Gedanken *or* Sorgen machen über (*acc*); ***be*** ~ ***with*** uninteressiert sein an (*dat*)
**un·con·di·tion·al** bedingungslos
**un·con·firmed** unbestätigt
**un·con·scious** unbewusst; unbeabsichtigt; MED bewusstlos; ***be*** ~ ***of*** sich *e-r Sache* nicht bewusst sein, nicht bemerken; **un·con·scious·ness** MED Bewusstlosigkeit *f*
**un·con·sti·tu·tion·al** verfassungswidrig
**un·con·trol·la·ble** unkontrollierbar; nicht zu bändigen(d); unbändig (*rage etc*); **un·con·trolled** unkontrolliert
**un·con·ven·tion·al** unkonventionell
**un·con·vinced:** ***be*** ~ nicht überzeugt sein (***about*** von)
**un·con·vinc·ing** nicht überzeugend
**un·cooked** ungekocht, roh
**un·cork** entkorken
**un·count·a·ble** unzählbar
**un·coup·le** abkoppeln
**un·couth** *fig* ungehobelt
**un·cov·er** aufdecken, *fig a.* enthüllen
**un·crit·i·cal** unkritisch; ***be*** ~ ***of s.th.*** e-r Sache unkritisch gegenüberstehen
**unc·tion** REL Salbung *f*
**unc·tu·ous** salbungsvoll
**un·cut** ungekürzt (*film, novel etc*); ungeschliffen (*diamond etc*)
**un·dam·aged** unbeschädigt, unversehrt, heil
**un·dat·ed** undatiert, ohne Datum
**un·daunt·ed** unerschrocken, furchtlos
**un·de·cid·ed** unentschieden, offen; unentschlossen
**un·de·mon·stra·tive** zurückhaltend, reserviert
**un·de·ni·a·ble** unbestreitbar
**un·der 1.** *prp* unter (*dat or acc*); **2.** *adv* unten; darunter
**un·der·age** minderjährig
**un·der·bid** unterbieten
**un·der·brush** → ***undergrowth***
**un·der·car·riage** AVIAT Fahrwerk *n*, Fahrgestell *n*
**un·der·charge** zu wenig berechnen; zu wenig verlangen
**un·der·clothes, un·der·cloth·ing** → ***underwear***
**un·der·coat** Grundierung *f*
**un·der·cov·er:** ~ ***agent*** verdeckter Ermittler
**un·der·cut** *j-n* (im Preis) unterbieten
**un·der·de·vel·oped** unterentwickelt; ~ ***country*** Entwicklungsland *n*
**un·der·dog** Benachteiligte *m, f*
**un·der·done** nicht durchgebraten
**un·der·es·ti·mate** zu niedrig schätzen *or* veranschlagen; *fig* unterschätzen
**un·der·ex·pose** PHOT unterbelichten
**un·der·fed** unterernährt
**un·der·go** erleben, durchmachen; MED sich *e-r Operation etc* unterziehen

**un·der·grad** F, **un·der·grad·u·ate** Student(in)
**un·der·ground 1.** *adv* unterirdisch, unter der Erde; **2.** *adj* unterirdisch; *fig* Untergrund...; **3.** *esp Br* Untergrundbahn *f*, U-Bahn *f*; ***by ~*** mit der U-Bahn
**un·der·growth** Unterholz *n*
**un·der·hand, un·der·hand·ed** heimlich; hinterhältig
**un·der·line** unterstreichen (*a. fig*)
**un·der·ling** *contp* Untergebene *m, f*
**un·der·ly·ing** zugrunde liegend
**un·der·mine** unterspülen; *fig* untergraben, unterminieren
**un·der·neath 1.** *prp* unter (*dat or acc*); **2.** *adv* darunter
**un·der·nour·ished** unterernährt
**un·der·pants** Unterhose *f*
**un·der·pass** Unterführung *f*
**un·der·pay** *j-m* zu wenig bezahlen, *j-n* unterbezahlen
**un·der·priv·i·leged** unterprivilegiert, benachteiligt
**un·der·rate** unterbewerten, -schätzen
**un·der·sec·re·ta·ry** POL Staatssekretär *m*
**un·der·sell** ECON *Ware* verschleudern, unter Wert verkaufen; ***~ o.s.*** *fig* sich schlecht verkaufen
**un·der·shirt** Unterhemd *n*
**un·der·side** Unterseite *f*
**un·der·signed: *the ~*** der *or* die Unterzeichnete, die Unterzeichneten *pl*
**un·der·size(d)** zu klein
**un·der·staffed** (personell) unterbesetzt
**un·der·stand** verstehen; erfahren *or* gehört haben (***that*** dass); ***make o.s. understood*** sich verständlich machen; ***am I to ~ that*** soll das heißen, dass; ***give s.o. to ~ that*** j-m zu verstehen geben, dass
**un·der·stand·a·ble** verständlich
**un·der·stand·ing 1.** Verstand *m*; Verständnis *n*; Abmachung *f*; Verständigung *f*; ***come to an ~*** e-e Abmachung treffen (***with*** mit); ***on the ~ that*** unter der Voraussetzung, dass; **2.** verständnisvoll
**un·der·state** untertreiben, untertrieben darstellen; **un·der·state·ment** Understatement *n*, Untertreibung *f*
**un·der·take** *et.* übernehmen; sich verpflichten (***to do*** zu tun)
**un·der·tak·er** Leichenbestatter *m*; Beerdigungs-, Bestattungsinstitut *n*
**un·der·tak·ing** Unternehmen *n*; Zusicherung *f*
**un·der·tone** *fig* Unterton *m*; ***in an ~*** mit gedämpfter Stimme
**un·der·val·ue** unterbewerten
**un·der·wa·ter 1.** *adj* Unterwasser...; **2.** *adv* unter Wasser
**un·der·wear** Unterwäsche *f*
**un·der·weight 1.** Untergewicht *n*; **2.** untergewichtig, zu leicht (***by*** um); ***she is five pounds ~*** sie hat fünf Pfund Untergewicht
**un·der·world** Unterwelt *f*
**un·de·served** unverdient
**un·de·sir·a·ble** unerwünscht
**un·de·vel·oped** unerschlossen (*area*); unentwickelt
**un·dies** F (Damen)Unterwäsche *f*
**un·dig·ni·fied** würdelos
**un·di·min·ished** unvermindert
**un·dis·ci·plined** undiszipliniert
**un·dis·cov·ered** unentdeckt
**un·dis·guised** unverhohlen
**un·dis·put·ed** unbestritten
**un·dis·turbed** ungestört
**un·di·vid·ed** ungeteilt
**un·do** aufmachen, öffnen; *fig* zunichte machen; **un·do·ing: *be s.o.'s ~*** j-s Ruin *or* Verderben sein; **un·done** unerledigt; offen; ***come ~*** aufgehen
**un·doubt·ed** unbestritten
**un·doubt·ed·ly** zweifellos, ohne (jeden) Zweifel
**un·dreamed-of, un·dreamt-of** ungeahnt
**un·dress** sich ausziehen; *j-n* ausziehen
**un·due** übermäßig
**un·du·lat·ing** sanft (*hills*)
**un·dy·ing** ewig
**un·earned** *fig* unverdient
**un·earth** ausgraben, *fig a.* ausfindig machen, aufstöbern
**un·earth·ly** überirdisch; unheimlich; ***at an ~ hour*** F zu e-r unchristlichen Zeit
**un·eas·i·ness** Unbehagen *n*
**un·eas·y** unruhig (*sleep*); unsicher (*peace*); ***feel ~*** sich unbehaglich fühlen; ***I'm ~ about*** mir ist nicht wohl bei
**un·e·co·nom·ic** unwirtschaftlich
**un·ed·u·cat·ed** ungebildet
**un·e·mo·tion·al** leidenschaftslos, kühl, beherrscht
**un·em·ployed 1.** arbeitslos; **2. *the ~*** die Arbeitslosen *pl*

**un·em·ploy·ment** Arbeitslosigkeit *f*; ~ **ben·e·fit** *Br*, ~ **com·pen·sa·tion** Arbeitslosengeld *n*
**un·end·ing** endlos
**un·en·dur·a·ble** unerträglich
**un·en·vi·a·ble** wenig beneidenswert
**un·e·qual** ungleich (*a. fig*), unterschiedlich; *fig* einseitig; **be** ~ **to** *e-r Aufgabe etc* nicht gewachsen sein
**un·e·qual(l)ed** unerreicht, unübertroffen
**un·er·ring** unfehlbar
**un·e·ven** uneben; ungleich(mäßig); ungerade (*number*)
**un·e·vent·ful** ereignislos
**un·ex·am·pled** beispiellos
**un·ex·pec·ted** unerwartet
**un·ex·posed** PHOT unbelichtet
**un·fail·ing** unerschöpflich; nie versagend
**un·fair** unfair, ungerecht
**un·faith·ful** untreu (***to*** *dat*)
**un·fa·mil·i·ar** ungewohnt; unbekannt; nicht vertraut (***with*** mit)
**un·fas·ten** aufmachen, öffnen; losbinden
**un·fa·vo(u)r·a·ble** ungünstig; unvorteilhaft (***for, to*** für); negativ, ablehnend
**un·feel·ing** gefühllos, herzlos
**un·fin·ished** unvollendet; unfertig; unerledigt
**un·fit** nicht fit, nicht in Form; ungeeignet, untauglich; unfähig
**un·flag·ging** unermüdlich, unentwegt
**un·flap·pa·ble** F nicht aus der Ruhe zu bringen(d)
**un·fold** auffalten, auseinander falten; darlegen, enthüllen; sich entfalten
**un·fore·seen** unvorhergesehen, unerwartet
**un·for·get·ta·ble** unvergesslich
**un·for·got·ten** unvergessen
**un·for·tu·nate** unglücklich; unglückselig; bedauerlich
**un·for·tu·nate·ly** leider
**un·found·ed** unbegründet
**un·friend·ly** unfreundlich (***to, towards*** zu)
**un·furl** *Fahne* aufrollen, entrollen, *Segel* losmachen
**un·fur·nished** unmöbliert
**un·gain·ly** linkisch, unbeholfen
**un·god·ly** gottlos; ***at an*** ~ ***hour*** F zu e-r unchristlichen Zeit
**un·gra·cious** ungnädig; unfreundlich
**un·grate·ful** undankbar
**un·guard·ed** unbewacht; unbedacht, unüberlegt
**un·hap·pi·ly** unglücklicherweise, leider; **un·hap·py** unglücklich
**un·harmed** unversehrt
**un·health·y** kränklich, nicht gesund; ungesund; *contp* krankhaft, unnatürlich
**un·heard:** ***go*** ~ keine Beachtung finden, unbeachtet bleiben; **un·heard-of** noch nie da gewesen, beispiellos
**un·hinge:** ~ ***s.o.('s mind)*** *fig* j-n völlig aus dem Gleichgewicht bringen
**un·ho·ly** F furchtbar, schrecklich
**un·hoped-for** unverhofft, unerwartet
**un·hurt** unverletzt
**u·ni·corn** Einhorn *n*
**un·i·den·ti·fied** unbekannt, nicht identifiziert
**u·ni·fi·ca·tion** Vereinigung *f*
**u·ni·form 1.** Uniform *f*; **2.** gleichmäßig; einheitlich
**u·ni·form·i·ty** Einheitlichkeit *f*
**u·ni·fy** verein(ig)en; vereinheitlichen
**u·ni·lat·e·ral** *fig* einseitig
**un·i·ma·gin·a·ble** unvorstellbar
**un·i·ma·gin·a·tive** fantasielos, einfallslos
**un·im·por·tant** unwichtig
**un·im·pressed:** ***remain*** ~ unbeeindruckt bleiben (***by*** von)
**un·in·formed** nicht unterrichtet *or* eingeweiht
**un·in·hab·it·a·ble** unbewohnbar
**un·in·hab·it·ed** unbewohnt
**un·in·jured** unverletzt
**un·in·tel·li·gi·ble** unverständlich
**un·in·ten·tion·al** unabsichtlich, unbeabsichtigt
**un·in·terest·ed** uninteressiert (***in*** an *dat*); **be** ~ ***in a.*** sich nicht interessieren für; **un·in·terest·ing** uninteressant
**un·in·ter·rupt·ed** ununterbrochen
**u·nion** Vereinigung *f*; Union *f*; Gewerkschaft *f*; **u·nion·ist** Gewerkschaftler(in); **u·nion·ize** (sich) gewerkschaftlich organisieren
**u·nique** einzigartig; einmalig
**u·ni·son:** ***in*** ~ gemeinsam
**u·nit** Einheit *f*; PED Unit *f*, Lehreinheit *f*; MATH Einer *m*; TECH (Anbau)Element *n*, Teil *n*; ~ ***furniture*** Anbaumöbel *pl*

**u·nite** verbinden, vereinigen; sich vereinigen *or* zusammentun
**u·nit·ed** vereinigt, vereint
**U·nit·ed King·dom** *das* Vereinigte Königreich (*England, Scotland, Wales and Northern Ireland*)
**U·nit·ed States of A·mer·i·ca** *die* Vereinigten Staaten von Amerika
**u·ni·ty** Einheit *f*; MATH Eins *f*
**u·ni·ver·sal** allgemein; universal, universell; Welt...
**u·ni·verse** Universum *n*, Weltall *n*
**u·ni·ver·si·ty** Universität *f*, Hochschule *f*; **~ grad·u·ate** Akademiker(in)
**un·just** ungerecht
**un·kempt** ungekämmt (*hair*); ungepflegt (*clothes etc*)
**un·kind** unfreundlich
**un·known 1.** unbekannt (**to** *dat*); **2.** *der, die, das* Unbekannte; **~ quan·ti·ty** MATH unbekannte Größe (*a. fig*), Unbekannte *f*
**un·law·ful** ungesetzlich, gesetzwidrig
**un·lead·ed** bleifrei
**un·learn** *Ansichten etc* ablegen, aufgeben
**un·less** wenn ... nicht, außer wenn ..., es sei denn ...
**un·like** *prp* im Gegensatz zu; ***he is very ~ his father*** er ist ganz anders als sein Vater; ***that is very ~ him*** das sieht ihm gar nicht ähnlich
**un·like·ly** unwahrscheinlich
**un·lim·it·ed** unbegrenzt
**un·list·ed: *be ~*** nicht im Telefonbuch stehen; **~ num·ber** TEL Geheimnummer *f*
**un·load** entladen, abladen, ausladen; MAR *Ladung* löschen
**un·lock** aufschließen
**un·loos·en** losmachen; lockern; lösen
**un·loved** ungeliebt
**un·luck·y** unglücklich; ***be ~*** Pech haben
**un·made** ungemacht
**un·manned** unbemannt
**un·marked** nicht gekennzeichnet; SPORT ungedeckt, frei
**un·mar·ried** unverheiratet, ledig
**un·mask** *fig* entlarven
**un·matched** unübertroffen, unvergleichlich
**un·men·tio·na·ble** Tabu...; ***be ~*** tabu sein
**un·mis·tak·a·ble** unverkennbar, unverwechselbar, untrüglich
**un·mo·lest·ed** unbehelligt
**un·moved** ungerührt; ***she remained ~ by it*** es ließ sie kalt
**un·mu·si·cal** unmusikalisch
**un·named** ungenannt
**un·nat·u·ral** unnatürlich; widernatürlich
**un·ne·ces·sa·ry** unnötig
**un·nerve** entnerven
**un·no·ticed** unbemerkt
**un·num·bered** unnummeriert
**un·ob·tru·sive** unauffällig, unaufdringlich
**un·oc·cu·pied** leer (stehend), unbewohnt; unbeschäftigt
**un·of·fi·cial** inoffiziell
**un·pack** auspacken
**un·paid** unbezahlt; *post* unfrei
**un·par·al·leled** einmalig, beispiellos
**un·par·don·a·ble** unverzeihlich
**un·per·turbed** gelassen, ruhig
**un·pick** *Naht etc* auftrennen
**un·placed: *be ~*** SPORT sich nicht platzieren können
**un·play·a·ble** SPORT unbespielbar
**un·pleas·ant** unangenehm, unerfreulich; unfreundlich
**un·plug** den Stecker (*gen*) herausziehen
**un·pol·ished** unpoliert; *fig* ungehobelt
**un·pol·lut·ed** sauber, unverschmutzt
**un·pop·u·lar** unpopulär, unbeliebt
**un·pop·u·lar·i·ty** Unbeliebtheit *f*
**un·prac·ti·cal** unpraktisch
**un·prac·ticed,** *Br* **un·prac·tised** ungeübt
**un·pre·ce·dent·ed** beispiellos, noch nie da gewesen
**un·pre·dict·a·ble** unvorhersehbar; unberechenbar (*person*)
**un·prej·u·diced** unvoreingenommen; JUR unbefangen
**un·pre·med·i·tat·ed** nicht vorsätzlich; unüberlegt
**un·pre·pared** unvorbereitet
**un·pre·ten·tious** bescheiden, einfach, schlicht
**un·prin·ci·pled** skrupellos, gewissenlos
**un·prin·ta·ble** nicht druckfähig *or* druckreif
**un·pro·duc·tive** unproduktiv, unergiebig
**un·pro·fes·sion·al** unprofessionell; unfachmännisch

**un·prof·it·a·ble** unrentabel
**un·pro·nounce·a·ble** unaussprechbar
**un·pro·tect·ed** ungeschützt
**un·proved, un·prov·en** unbewiesen
**un·pro·voked** grundlos
**un·pun·ished** unbestraft, ungestraft; ***go ~*** straflos bleiben
**un·qual·i·fied** unqualifiziert, ungeeignet (***for*** für); uneingeschränkt
**un·ques·tion·a·ble** unbestritten
**un·ques·tion·ing** bedingungslos
**un·quote:** ***quote ... ~*** Zitat ... Zitat Ende
**un·rav·el** (sich) auftrennen (*pullover etc*); entwirren
**un·read·a·ble** nicht lesenswert, unlesbar, *a.* unleserlich
**un·re·al** unwirklich
**un·rea·lis·tic** unrealistisch
**un·rea·son·a·ble** unvernünftig; übertrieben, unzumutbar
**un·rec·og·niz·a·ble** nicht wieder zu erkennen(d)
**un·re·lat·ed:** ***be ~*** in keinem Zusammenhang stehen (***to*** mit)
**un·re·lent·ing** unvermindert
**un·re·li·a·ble** unzuverlässig
**un·re·lieved** ununterbrochen, ständig
**un·re·mit·ting** unablässig, unaufhörlich
**un·re·quit·ed:** ***~ love*** unerwiderte Liebe
**un·re·served** uneingeschränkt; nicht reserviert
**un·rest** POL *etc* Unruhen *pl*
**un·re·strained** hemmungslos, ungezügelt
**un·re·strict·ed** uneingeschränkt
**un·ripe** unreif
**un·ri·val(l)ed** unerreicht, unübertroffen, einzigartig
**un·roll** (sich) aufrollen *or* entrollen; sich entfalten
**un·ruf·fled** gelassen, ruhig
**un·ru·ly** ungebärdig, wild; widerspenstig (*hair*)
**un·sad·dle** *Pferd* absatteln; *Reiter* abwerfen
**un·safe** unsicher, nicht sicher
**un·said** unausgesprochen
**un·sal(e)·a·ble** unverkäuflich
**un·salt·ed** ungesalzen
**un·san·i·tar·y** unhygienisch
**un·sat·is·fac·to·ry** unbefriedigend
**un·sat·u·rat·ed** CHEM ungesättigt
**un·sa·vo(u)r·y** anrüchig, unerfreulich
**un·scathed** unversehrt, unverletzt
**un·screw** abschrauben, losschrauben
**un·scru·pu·lous** skrupellos, gewissenlos
**un·seat** *Reiter* abwerfen; *j-n* s-s Amtes entheben
**un·seem·ly** ungebührlich
**un·self·ish** selbstlos, uneigennützig
**un·set·tle** durcheinander bringen; beunruhigen; aufregen
**un·set·tled** ungeklärt, offen (*question etc*); unsicher (*situation etc*); METEOR unbeständig
**un·shak(e)·a·ble** unerschütterlich
**un·shav·en** unrasiert
**un·shrink·a·ble** nicht eingehend *or* einlaufend
**un·sight·ly** unansehnlich; hässlich
**un·skilled:** ***~ worker*** ungelernter Arbeiter
**un·so·cia·ble** ungesellig
**un·so·cial:** ***work ~ hours*** außerhalb der normalen Arbeitszeit arbeiten
**un·so·lic·it·ed** unaufgefordert ein- *or* zugesandt, ECON *a.* unbestellt
**un·solved** ungelöst (*problem etc*)
**un·so·phis·ti·cat·ed** einfach, schlicht; TECH unkompliziert
**un·sound** nicht gesund; nicht in Ordnung; morsch; unsicher, schwach; nicht stichhaltig (*argument etc*); ***of ~ mind*** JUR unzurechnungsfähig
**un·spar·ing** großzügig, freigebig, verschwenderisch; schonungslos, unbarmherzig
**un·speak·a·ble** unbeschreiblich, entsetzlich
**un·spoiled, un·spoilt** unverdorben; nicht verwöhnt *or* verzogen
**un·sta·ble** instabil; unsicher, schwankend; labil (*person*)
**un·stead·y** wack(e)lig, schwankend, unsicher; unbeständig; ungleichmäßig, unregelmäßig
**un·stop** *Abfluss etc* freimachen; *Flasche* entstöpseln
**un·stressed** LING unbetont
**un·stuck:** ***come ~*** abgehen, sich lösen; *fig* scheitern
**un·stud·ied** ungekünstelt, natürlich
**un·suc·cess·ful** erfolglos, ohne Erfolg; vergeblich
**un·suit·a·ble** unpassend, ungeeignet; unangemessen

U

**un·sure** unsicher; ~ ***of o.s.*** unsicher
**un·sur·passed** unübertroffen
**un·sus·pect·ed** unverdächtig; unvermutet; **un·sus·pect·ing** nichts ahnend, ahnungslos
**un·sus·pi·cious** arglos; unverdächtig, harmlos
**un·sweet·ened** ungesüßt
**un·swerv·ing** unbeirrbar, unerschütterlich
**un·tan·gle** entwirren (*a. fig*)
**un·tapped** unerschlossen (*resource etc*)
**un·teach·a·ble** unbelehrbar (*person*); nicht lehrbar
**un·ten·a·ble** unhaltbar (*theory etc*)
**un·think·a·ble** undenkbar, unvorstellbar; **un·think·ing** gedankenlos
**un·ti·dy** unordentlich
**un·tie** aufknoten, *Knoten etc* lösen; losbinden
**un·til** *prp*, *cj* bis; ***not*** ~ erst; erst wenn, nicht bevor
**un·time·ly** vorzeitig, verfrüht; unpassend, ungelegen
**un·tir·ing** unermüdlich
**un·told** *fig* unermesslich
**un·touched** unberührt, unangetastet
**un·true** unwahr, falsch
**un·trust·wor·thy** unzuverlässig, nicht vertrauenswürdig
**un·used**[1] unbenutzt, ungebraucht
**un·used**[2]: ***be ~ to s.th.*** an et. nicht gewöhnt sein, et. nicht gewohnt sein; ***be ~ to doing s.th.*** es nicht gewohnt sein, et. zu tun
**un·u·su·al** ungewöhnlich
**un·var·nished** *fig* ungeschminkt
**un·var·y·ing** unveränderlich, gleich bleibend
**un·veil** *Denkmal etc* enthüllen
**un·versed** unbewandert, unerfahren (***in*** in *dat*)
**un·voiced** unausgesprochen
**un·want·ed** unerwünscht, ungewollt
**un·war·rant·ed** ungerechtfertigt
**un·washed** ungewaschen
**un·wel·come** unwillkommen
**un·well:** ***be*** *or* ***feel*** ~ sich unwohl *or* nicht wohl fühlen
**un·whole·some** ungesund (*a. fig*)
**un·wield·y** unhandlich, sperrig
**un·will·ing** widerwillig; ungern; ***be ~ to do s.th.*** et. nicht tun wollen
**un·wind** (sich) abwickeln; F abschalten, sich entspannen
**un·wise** unklug
**un·wit·ting** unwissentlich; unbeabsichtigt
**un·wor·thy** unwürdig; ***he*** (***she***) ***is ~ of it*** er (sie) verdient es nicht, er (sie) ist es nicht wert
**un·wrap** auswickeln, auspacken
**un·writ·ten** ungeschrieben
**un·yield·ing** unnachgiebig
**un·zip** den Reißverschluss (*gen*) aufmachen
**up 1.** *adv* herauf, hinauf, aufwärts, nach oben, hoch, in die Höhe; oben; ***~ there*** dort oben; ***jump ~ and down*** hüpfen; ***walk ~ and down*** auf und ab gehen, hin und her gehen; ***~ to*** bis zu; ***be ~ to s.th.*** F et. vorhaben, et. im Schilde führen; ***not to be ~ to s.th.*** e-r Sache nicht gewachsen sein; ***it's ~ to you*** das liegt bei dir; **2.** *prp* herauf, hinauf; oben auf (*dat*); ***~ the river*** flussaufwärts; **3.** *adj* nach oben (gerichtet), Aufwärts...; ASTR aufgegangen; ECON gestiegen; *time*: abgelaufen, um; aufgestanden, F auf; ***the ~ train*** der Zug nach London; ***be ~ and about*** F wieder auf den Beinen sein; ***what's ~?*** F was ist los?; **4.** F *v/t Angebot*, *Preis etc* erhöhen; **5.** ***the ~s and downs*** F die Höhen und Tiefen *pl* (***of life*** des Lebens)
**up-and-com·ing** aufstrebend, viel versprechend
**up·bring·ing** Erziehung *f*
**up·com·ing** bevorstehend
**up·coun·try** landeinwärts; im Landesinneren
**up·date 1.** auf den neuesten Stand bringen; aktualisieren; **2.** Lagebericht *m*
**up·end** hochkant stellen
**up·grade** *j-n* befördern
**up·heav·al** *fig* Umwälzung *f*
**up·hill** aufwärts, bergan; bergauf führend; *fig* mühsam
**up·hold** *Rechte etc* schützen, wahren; JUR *Urteil* bestätigen
**up·hol·ster** *Möbel* polstern
**up·hol·ster·er** Polsterer *m*
**up·hol·ster·y** Polsterung *f*; Bezug *m*; Polsterei *f*
**up·keep** Instandhaltung(skosten *pl*) *f*; Unterhalt(ungskosten *pl*) *m*
**up·land** *mst pl* Hochland *n*

**up·lift 1.** *j-n* aufrichten, *j-m* Auftrieb geben; **2.** Auftrieb *m*
**up·on** → ***on, once*** 1
**up·per** obere(r, -s), Ober...;
**up·per·most 1.** *adj* oberste(r, -s), größte(r, -s), höchste(r, -s); ***be ~*** oben sein; *fig* an erster Stelle stehen; **2.** *adv* nach oben
**up·right** aufrecht, *a.* gerade, *fig a.* rechtschaffen
**up·ris·ing** Aufstand *m*
**up·roar** Aufruhr *m*; **up·roar·i·ous** lärmend, laut; schallend (*laughter*)
**up·root** ausreißen, entwurzeln; *fig j-n* herausreißen (***from*** aus)
**up·set** umkippen, umstoßen, umwerfen; *Pläne etc* durcheinander bringen, stören; *j-n* aus der Fassung bringen; ***the fish has ~ me*** *or* ***my stomach*** ich habe mir durch den Fisch den Magen verdorben; ***be ~*** aufgeregt sein; aus der Fassung *or* durcheinander sein; gekränkt *or* verletzt sein
**up·shot** Ergebnis *n*
**up·side down** verkehrt herum; *fig* drunter und drüber; ***turn ~*** umdrehen, *a. fig* auf den Kopf stellen
**up·stairs 1.** die Treppe herauf *or* hinauf, nach oben; oben; **2.** im oberen Stockwerk (gelegen), obere(r, -s)
**up·start** Emporkömmling *m*
**up·state** im Norden (e-s Bundesstaats)
**up·stream** fluss-, stromaufwärts
**up·take:** F ***be quick*** (***slow***) ***on the ~*** schnell begreifen (schwer von Begriff sein)
**up-to-date** modern; aktuell, auf dem neuesten Stand
**up·town** in den Wohnvierteln; in die Wohnviertel
**up·turn** Aufschwung *m*
**up·ward(s)** aufwärts, nach oben
**u·ra·ni·um** CHEM Uran *n*
**ur·ban** städtisch, Stadt...
**ur·ban·i·za·tion** Verstädterung *f*
**ur·chin** Bengel *m*
**urge 1.** *j-n* drängen (***to do*** zu tun); drängen auf (*acc*); *a.* ***~ on*** *j-n* drängen, antreiben; **2.** Drang *m*, Verlangen *n*
**ur·gen·cy** Dringlichkeit *f*
**ur·gent** dringend; ***be ~*** *a.* eilen
**u·ri·nate** urinieren; **u·rine** Urin *m*
**urn** Urne *f*; Großteemaschine *f*, Großkaffeemaschine *f*
**us** uns; ***all of ~*** wir alle; ***both of ~*** wir beide
**us·age** Sprachgebrauch *m*; Behandlung *f*; Verwendung *f*, Gebrauch *m*
**use 1.** *v/t* benutzen, gebrauchen, anwenden, verwenden; (ver)brauchen; ***~ up*** auf-, verbrauchen; *v/i*: ***I ~d to live here*** ich habe früher hier gewohnt; **2.** Benutzung *f*, Gebrauch *m*, Verwendung *f*; Nutzen *m*; ***be of ~*** nützlich *or* von Nutzen sein (***to*** für); ***it's no ~*** *doing* es ist nutzlos *or* zwecklos *zu inf*; → ***milk*** 1
**used[1]:** ***be ~ to s.th.*** an et. gewöhnt sein, et. gewohnt sein; ***be ~ to doing s.th.*** es gewohnt sein, et. zu tun
**used[2]** gebraucht; **~ car** Gebrauchtwagen *m*; **~ car deal·er** Gebrauchtwagenhändler(in)
**use·ful** nützlich
**use·less** nutzlos, zwecklos
**us·er** Benutzer(in); Verbraucher(in)
**us·er-friend·ly** benutzer- *or* verbraucherfreundlich
**us·er in·ter·face** EDP Benutzeroberfläche *f*
**ush·er 1.** Platzanweiser *m*; Gerichtsdiener *m*; **2.** *j-n* führen, geleiten (***into*** in *acc*; ***to*** zu)
**ush·er·ette** Platzanweiserin *f*
**u·su·al** gewöhnlich, üblich
**u·su·al·ly** (für) gewöhnlich, normalerweise
**u·sur·er** Wucherer *m*
**u·su·ry** Wucher *m*
**u·ten·sil** Gerät *n*
**u·te·rus** ANAT Gebärmutter *f*
**u·til·i·ty** Nutzen *m*; *pl* Leistungen *pl* der öffentlichen Versorgungsbetriebe
**u·til·ize** nutzen
**ut·most** äußerste(r, -s), größte(r, -s), höchste(r,- s)
**u·to·pi·an** utopisch
**ut·ter[1]** total, völlig
**ut·ter[2]** äußern, *Seufzer etc* ausstoßen, *Wort* sagen
**U-turn** MOT Wende *f*; *fig* Kehrtwendung *f*
**u·vu·la** ANAT (Gaumen)Zäpfchen *n*

# V

**V, v** V, v *n*
**va·can·cy** freie *or* offene Stelle; ***vacancies*** Zimmer frei; ***no vacancies*** belegt
**va·cant** leer stehend, unbewohnt; frei (*seat etc*); frei, offen (*job*); *fig* leer (*expression, stare etc*)
**va·cate** *Hotelzimmer* räumen; *Stelle etc* aufgeben
**va·ca·tion 1.** Ferien *pl*, Urlaub *m*; *esp Br* UNIV Semesterferien *pl*; JUR Gerichtsferien *pl*; ***be on ~*** im Urlaub sein, Urlaub machen; **2.** Urlaub machen, die Ferien verbringen
**va·ca·tion·er, va·ca·tion·ist** Urlauber(in)
**vac·cin·ate** MED impfen
**vac·cin·a·tion** MED (Schutz)Impfung *f*
**vac·cine** MED Impfstoff *m*
**vac·il·late** *fig* schwanken
**vac·u·um 1.** PHYS Vakuum *n*; **2.** F *Teppich, Zimmer etc* saugen; **~ bot·tle** Thermosflasche® *f*; **~ clean·er** Staubsauger *m*; **~ flask** *Br* Thermosflasche® *f*; **~-packed** vakuumverpackt
**vag·a·bond** Vagabund *m*, Landstreicher(in)
**va·ga·ry** *mst pl* Laune *f*; wunderlicher Einfall
**va·gi·na** ANAT Vagina *f*, Scheide *f*
**va·gi·nal** ANAT vaginal, Scheiden...
**va·grant** Nichtsesshafte *m, f*, Landstreicher(in)
**vague** verschwommen; vage; unklar
**vain** eingebildet, eitel; vergeblich; ***in ~*** vergebens, vergeblich
**val·en·tine** Valentinskarte *f*
**va·le·ri·an** BOT, PHARM Baldrian *m*
**val·et** (Kammer)Diener *m*
**val·id** stichhaltig, triftig; gültig (***for two weeks*** zwei Wochen); JUR rechtsgültig, rechtskräftig; ***be ~ a.*** gelten
**va·lid·i·ty** (JUR Rechts)Gültigkeit *f*; Stichhaltigkeit *f*, Triftigkeit *f*
**val·ley** Tal *n*
**val·u·a·ble 1.** wertvoll; **2.** *pl* Wertgegenstände *pl*, Wertsachen *pl*
**val·u·a·tion** Schätzung *f*; Schätzwert *m* (***on*** *gen*)
**val·ue 1.** Wert *m*; ***be of ~*** wertvoll sein (***to*** für); ***get ~ for money*** reell bedient werden; **2.** *Haus etc* schätzen (***at*** auf *acc*); *j-n, j-s Rat etc* schätzen
**val·ue-ad·ded tax** *Br* ECON (ABBR ***VAT***) Mehrwertsteuer *f*
**val·ue·less** wertlos
**valve** TECH, MUS Ventil *n*; ANAT (*Herz-etc*)Klappe *f*
**vam·pire** Vampir *m*
**van** MOT Lieferwagen *m*, Transporter *m*; *Br* RAIL (geschlossener) Güterwagen
**van·dal** Wandale *m*, Vandale *m*
**van·dal·ism** Wandalismus *m*, Vandalismus *m*
**van·dal·ize** mutwillig beschädigen *or* zerstören
**vane** TECH (*Propeller- etc*)Flügel *m*; (*Wetter*)Fahne *f*
**van·guard** MIL Vorhut *f*
**va·nil·la** Vanille *f*
**van·ish** verschwinden
**van·i·ty** Eitelkeit *f*; **~ bag** Kosmetiktäschchen *n*; **~ case** Kosmetikkoffer *m*
**van·tage·point** Aussichtspunkt *m*; ***from my ~*** *fig* aus m-r Sicht
**va·por·ize** verdampfen; verdunsten (lassen)
**va·po(u)r** Dampf *m*, Dunst *m*; **~ trail** AVIAT Kondensstreifen *m*
**var·i·a·ble 1.** variabel, veränderlich; unbeständig, wechselhaft; TECH einstellbar, regulierbar; **2.** MATH, PHYS Variable *f*, veränderliche Größe (*both a. fig*)
**var·i·ance: *be at ~ with*** im Gegensatz *or* Widerspruch stehen zu
**var·i·ant 1.** abweichend, verschieden; **2.** Variante *f*; **var·i·a·tion** Abweichung *f*; Schwankung *f*; MUS Variation *f*
**var·i·cose veins** MED Krampfadern *pl*
**var·ied** unterschiedlich; abwechslungsreich
**va·ri·e·ty** Abwechslung *f*; Vielfalt *f*; ECON Auswahl *f*, Sortiment *n* (***of*** an *dat*); BOT, ZO Art *f*; Varietee *n*; ***for a ~ of reasons*** aus den verschiedensten Gründen; **~ show** Varieteevorstellung *f*; **~ thea·ter** (*Br* **thea·tre**) Varietee(theater) *n*
**var·i·ous** verschieden; mehrere, verschiedene

**var·nish 1.** Lack *m*; **2.** lackieren
**var·si·ty team** SPORT Universitäts-, College-, Schulmannschaft *f*
**var·y** *v/i* sich (ver)ändern; variieren, auseinander gehen (*opinions etc*) (**on** über *acc*); **~ in size** verschieden groß sein; *v/t* (ver)ändern; variieren
**vase** Vase *f*
**vast** gewaltig, riesig, (*area a.*) ausgedehnt, weit; **vast·ly** gewaltig, weitaus
**vat** (großes) Fass, Bottich *m*
**VAT** ABBR *of* **value-added tax** ECON Mehrwertsteuer *f*
**vau·de·ville** Varietee(theater) *n*
**vault**[1] ARCH Gewölbe *n*; *a. pl* Stahlkammer *f*, Tresorraum *m*; (Keller)Gewölbe *n*; Gruft *f*
**vault**[2] **1. ~** (**over**) springen über (*acc*); **2.** *esp* SPORT Sprung *m*
**vault·ing| horse** *gymnastics*: Pferd *n*; **~ pole** SPORT Sprungstab *m*
**VCR** ABBR *of* **video cassette recorder** Videorekorder *m*, Videogerät *n*
**veal** GASTR Kalbfleisch *n*; **~ chop** Kalbskotelett *n*; **~ cutlet** Kalbsschnitzel *n*; **roast ~** Kalbsbraten *m*
**veer** (sich) drehen; MOT ausscheren; **~ to the right** das Steuer nach rechts reißen
**veg·e·ta·ble 1.** *mst pl* Gemüse *n*; **2.** Gemüse...; Pflanzen...
**veg·e·tar·i·an 1.** Vegetarier(in); **2.** vegetarisch
**veg·e·tate** (dahin)vegetieren
**veg·e·ta·tion** Vegetation *f*
**ve·he·mence** Vehemenz *f*, Heftigkeit *f*; **ve·he·ment** vehement, heftig
**ve·hi·cle** Fahrzeug *n*; *fig* Medium *n*
**veil 1.** Schleier *m*; **2.** verschleiern (*a. fig*)
**vein** ANAT Vene *f*, Ader *f* (*a.* BOT, GEOL, *fig*); *fig* (*Charakter*)Zug *m*; Stimmung *f*
**ve·loc·i·ty** TECH Geschwindigkeit *f*
**ve·lour(s)** Velours *m*
**vel·vet** Samt *m*; **vel·vet·y** samtig
**vend·er** → **vendor**
**vend·ing ma·chine** (Verkaufs-, Waren)Automat *m*
**vend·or** (*Straßen*)Händler(in), (*Zeitungs- etc*)Verkäufer(in)
**ve·neer 1.** Furnier *n*; *fig* Fassade *f*; **2.** furnieren
**ven·e·ra·ble** ehrwürdig
**ven·e·rate** verehren
**ven·e·ra·tion** Verehrung *f*
**ve·ne·re·al dis·ease** MED Geschlechtskrankheit *f*
**Ve·ne·tian 1.** Venezianer(in); **2.** venezianisch; **~ blind** (Stab)Jalousie *f*
**ven·geance** Rache *f*; **take ~ on** sich rächen an (*dat*); **with a ~** mächtig, F wie verrückt
**ve·ni·al** entschuldbar, verzeihlich; REL lässlich
**ven·i·son** GASTR Wildbret *n*
**ven·om** ZO Gift *n*, *fig a.* Gehässigkeit *f*
**ven·om·ous** giftig, *fig a.* gehässig
**ve·nous** MED venös
**vent 1.** *v/t s-m Zorn etc* Luft machen, *s-e Wut etc* auslassen, abreagieren (**on** an *dat*); **2.** Schlitz *m* (*in a coat etc*); TECH (Abzugs)Öffnung *f*; **give ~ to** *s-m Ärger etc* Luft machen
**ven·ti·late** (be)lüften; *fig* äußern
**ven·ti·la·tion** (Be)Lüftung *f*, Ventilation *f*
**ven·ti·la·tor** Ventilator *m*
**ven·tri·cle** ANAT Herzkammer *f*
**ven·tril·o·quist** Bauchredner(in)
**ven·ture 1.** *esp* ECON Wagnis *n*, Risiko *n*; ECON Unternehmen *n*; → **joint venture**; **2.** sich wagen; riskieren
**ven·ue** SPORT Austragungsort *m*
**verb** LING Verb *n*, Zeitwort *n*
**verb·al** mündlich; wörtlich, Wort...
**ver·dict** JUR (Urteils)Spruch *m*; *fig* Urteil *n*; **bring in** *or* **return a ~ of** (**not**) **guilty** JUR auf (nicht) schuldig erkennen
**ver·di·gris** Grünspan *m*
**verge 1.** Rand *m* (*a. fig*); **be on the ~ of** kurz vor (*dat*) stehen; **be on the ~ of despair** (**tears**) der Verzweiflung (den Tränen) nahe sein; **2. ~ on** *fig* grenzen an (*acc*)
**ver·i·fy** bestätigen; nachweisen; (über-) prüfen
**ver·i·ta·ble** wahr
**ver·mi·cel·li** Fadennudeln *pl*
**ver·mi·form ap·pen·dix** ANAT Wurmfortsatz *m*, Blinddarm *m*
**ver·mil·i·on 1.** zinnoberrot; **2.** Zinnoberrot *n*
**ver·min** Ungeziefer *n*; Schädlinge *pl*; *fig* Gesindel *n*, Pack *n*
**ver·min·ous** voller Ungeziefer
**ver·nac·u·lar** Dialekt *m*, Mundart *f*; **in the ~** im Volksmund
**ver·sa·tile** vielseitig; vielseitig verwendbar

**verse** Versdichtung *f*; Vers *m*; Strophe *f*
**versed:** ***be*** (***well***) ***~ in*** beschlagen *or* bewandert sein in (*dat*)
**ver·sion** Version *f*; TECH Ausführung *f*; Darstellung *f* (*of an event*); Fassung *f* (*of a film etc*); Übersetzung *f*
**ver·sus** (ABBR ***v., vs.***) SPORT, JUR gegen
**ver·te·bra** ANAT Wirbel *m*
**ver·te·brate** ZO Wirbeltier *n*
**ver·ti·cal** vertikal, senkrecht
**ver·ti·go** MED Schwindel *m*; ***suffer from ~*** an *or* unter Schwindel leiden
**verve** Elan *m*, Schwung *m*
**ver·y 1.** *adv* sehr; aller...; ***I ~ much hope that*** ich hoffe sehr, dass; ***the ~ best*** das Allerbeste; ***for the ~ last time*** zum allerletzten Mal; **2.** *adj* ***the ~*** genau der *or* die *or* das; ***the ~ opposite*** genau das Gegenteil; ***the ~ thing*** genau das Richtige; ***the ~ thought of*** schon der *or* der bloße Gedanke an (*acc*)
**ves·i·cle** MED Bläschen *n*
**ves·sel** ANAT, BOT Gefäß *n*; Schiff *n*
**vest** Weste *f*; *Br* Unterhemd *n*; *kugelsichere* Weste
**ves·ti·bule** (Vor)Halle *f*
**ves·tige** *fig* Spur *f*
**vest·ment** Ornat *n*, Gewand *n*, Robe *f*
**ves·try** REL Sakristei *f*
**vet**[1] F Tierarzt *m*, Tierärztin *f*
**vet**[2] *esp Br* F überprüfen
**vet**[3] MIL F Veteran *m*
**vet·e·ran 1.** MIL Veteran *m* (*a. fig*); **2.** altgedient; erfahren; **~ car** *Br* Oldtimer *m* (*built before 1905*)
**vet·e·ri·nar·i·an** Tierarzt *m*, -ärztin *f*
**vet·e·ri·na·ry** tierärztlich; **~ sur·geon** *Br* Tierarzt *m*, Tierärztin *f*
**ve·to 1.** Veto *n*; **2.** sein Veto einlegen gegen
**vexed ques·tion** leidige Frage
**vi·a** über (*acc*), via
**vi·a·duct** Viadukt *m*, *n*
**vi·al** (*esp* Arznei)Fläschchen *n*
**vibes** F Atmosphäre *f*
**vi·brant** kräftig (*color etc*); pulsierend (*city etc*)
**vi·brate** *v/i* vibrieren, zittern; flimmern; *fig* pulsieren; *v/t* in Schwingungen versetzen; **vi·bra·tion** Vibrieren *n*, Zittern *n*; *pl* F Atmosphäre *f*
**vic·ar** REL Pfarrer *m*
**vic·ar·age** Pfarrhaus *n*
**vice**[1] Laster *n*
**vice**[2] *esp Br* Schraubstock *m*
**vice...** Vize..., stellvertretend
**vice squad** Sittendezernat *n*, Sittenpolizei *f*; Rauschgiftdezernat *n*
**vi·ce ver·sa:** ***and ~*** und umgekehrt
**vi·cin·i·ty** Nähe *f*; Nachbarschaft *f*
**vi·cious** brutal; bösartig
**vi·cis·si·tudes** *das* Auf und Ab, *die* Wechselfälle *pl*
**vic·tim** Opfer *n*
**vic·tim·ize** (ungerechterweise) bestrafen, ungerecht behandeln; schikanieren
**vic·to·ri·ous** siegreich
**vic·to·ry** Sieg *m*
**vid·e·o 1.** Video *n*; Videokassette *f*; F Videoband *n*; *esp Br* Videorekorder *m*, Videogerät *n*; ***on ~*** auf Video; **2.** Video...; **3.** *esp Br* auf Video aufnehmen, aufzeichnen; **~ cam·e·ra** Videokamera *f*; **~ cas·sette** Videokassette *f*; **~ cas·sette re·cord·er** → ***video recorder***; **~ clip** Videoclip *m*
**vid·eo·disk** Bildplatte *f*
**vid·e·o| game** Videospiel *n*; **~ li·bra·ry** Videothek *f*; **~ re·cord·er** Videorekorder *m*, Videogerät *n*; **~ re·cord·ing** Videoaufnahme *f*, Videoaufzeichnung *f*; **~ shop** *Br*, **~ store** Videothek *f*
**vid·e·o·tape 1.** Videokassette *f*; Videoband *n*; **2.** auf Video aufnehmen, aufzeichnen
**vid·e·o·text** Bildschirmtext *m*
**vie** wetteifern (***with*** mit; ***for*** um)
**Vi·en·nese 1.** Wiener(in); **2.** wienerisch, Wiener...
**view1.** Sicht *f* (***of*** auf *acc*); Aussicht *f*, (Aus)Blick *m* (***of*** auf *acc*); Ansicht *f* (*a.* PHOT), Meinung *f* (***about, on*** über *acc*); *fig* Überblick *m* (***of*** über *acc*); ***a room with a ~*** ein Zimmer mit schöner Aussicht; ***be on ~*** ausgestellt *or* zu besichtigen sein; ***be hidden from ~*** nicht zu sehen sein; ***come into ~*** in Sicht kommen; ***in full ~ of*** direkt vor *j-s* Augen; ***in ~ of*** *fig* angesichts (*gen*); ***in my ~*** m-r Ansicht nach; ***keep in ~*** *et.* im Auge behalten; ***with a ~ to*** *fig* mit Blick auf (*acc*); **2.** *v/t Haus etc* besichtigen; *fig* betrachten (***as*** als); *v/i* fernsehen
**view·da·ta** Bildschirmtext *m*
**view·er** Fernsehzuschauer(in), F Fernseher(in); TECH (*Dia*)Betrachter *m*
**view·find·er** PHOT Sucher *m*

**view·point** Gesichts-, Standpunkt *m*
**vig·il** (Nacht)Wache *f*
**vig·i·lance** Wachsamkeit *f*
**vig·i·lant** wachsam
**vig·or·ous** energisch; kräftig
**vig·o(u)r** Energie *f*
**Vi·king 1.** Wikinger *m*; **2.** Wikinger...
**vile** gemein, niederträchtig; F scheußlich
**vil·lage** Dorf *n*; **~ green** Dorfanger *m*
**vil·lag·er** Dorfbewohner(in)
**vil·lain** Bösewicht *m*, Schurke *m*; *Br* F Ganove *m*
**vin·di·cate** *j-n* rehabilitieren; *et.* rechtfertigen; *et.* bestätigen
**vin·dic·tive** rachsüchtig, nachtragend
**vine** BOT (Wein)Rebe *f*; Kletterpflanze *f*
**vin·e·gar** Essig *m*
**vine·grow·er** Winzer *m*
**vine·yard** Weinberg *m*
**vin·tage 1.** Weinernte *f*, Weinlese *f*; GASTR Jahrgang *m*; **2.** GASTR Jahrgangs...; *fig* hervorragend, glänzend; ***a 1994 ~*** ein 1994er Jahrgang *or* Wein
**vin·tage car** *esp Br* Oldtimer *m* (*built between 1919 and 1930*)
**vi·o·la** MUS Bratsche *f*
**vi·o·late** *Vertrag etc* verletzen, *a. Versprechen* brechen, *Gesetz etc* übertreten; *Ruhe etc* stören; *Grab etc* schänden; **vi·o·la·tion** Verletzung *f*, Bruch *m*, Übertretung *f*
**vi·o·lence** Gewalt *f*; Gewalttätigkeit *f*; Ausschreitungen *pl*; Heftigkeit *f*
**vi·o·lent** gewalttätig; gewaltsam; heftig
**vi·o·let 1.** BOT Veilchen *n*; **2.** violett
**vi·o·lin** MUS Geige *f*, Violine *f*
**vi·o·lin·ist** Geiger(in), Violinist(in)
**VIP** ABBR *of* ***very important person*** VIP *f*; **~ lounge** AVIAT *etc* VIP-Lounge *f*; SPORT Ehrentribüne *f*
**vi·per** ZO Viper *f*, Natter *f*
**vir·gin 1.** Jungfrau *f*; **2.** jungfräulich, unberührt (*both a. fig*)
**Vir·go** ASTR Jungfrau *f*; ***he*** (***she***) ***is*** (***a***) **~** er (sie) ist Jungfrau
**vir·ile** männlich; potent
**vi·ril·i·ty** Männlichkeit *f*; Potenz *f*
**vir·tu·al** eigentlich, praktisch
**vir·tu·al·ly** praktisch, so gut wie
**vir·tu·al re·al·i·ty** EDP virtuelle Realität
**vir·tue** Tugend *f*; Vorzug *m*, Vorteil *m*; ***by*** *or* ***in ~ of*** aufgrund (*gen*), kraft (*gen*); ***make a ~ of necessity*** aus der Not e-e Tugend machen
**vir·tu·ous** tugendhaft
**vir·u·lent** MED (akut und) bösartig; schnell wirkend (*poison*); *fig* bösartig, gehässig
**vi·rus** MED Virus *n*, *m*
**vi·sa** Visum *n*, Sichtvermerk *m*
**vis·cose** Viskose *f*
**vis·cous** dickflüssig, zähflüssig
**vise** TECH Schraubstock *m*
**vis·i·bil·i·ty** Sicht *f*, Sichtverhältnisse *pl*, Sichtweite *f*
**vis·i·ble** sichtbar; (er)sichtlich
**vi·sion** Sehkraft *f*; Weitblick *m*; Vision *f*
**vi·sion·a·ry 1.** weitblickend; eingebildet, unwirklich; **2.** Fantast(in), Träumer(in); Seher(in)
**vis·it 1.** *v/t j-n* besuchen, *Schloss etc a.* besichtigen; *et.* inspizieren; *v/i*: ***be ~ing*** auf Besuch sein (***with*** bei); **~ *with*** plaudern mit; **2.** Besuch *m*, Besichtigung *f* (***to*** *gen*); Plauderei *f*; ***for*** *or* ***on a ~*** auf Besuch; ***have a ~ from*** Besuch haben von; ***pay a ~ to*** *j-n* besuchen, *j-m* e-n Besuch abstatten; *Arzt* aufsuchen
**vis·it·ing hours** MED Besuchszeit *f*
**vis·it·or** Besucher(in), Gast *m*
**vi·sor** Visier *n*; Schirm *m*; MOT (*Sonnen-*) Blende *f*
**vis·u·al** Seh...; visuell; **~ aids** PED Anschauungsmaterial *n*, Lehrmittel *pl*; **~ dis·play u·nit** EDP Bildschirmgerät *n*, Datensichtgerät *n*; **~ in·struc·tion** PED Anschauungsunterricht *m*
**vis·u·al·ize** sich *et.* vorstellen
**vi·tal** vital, Lebens...; lebenswichtig; unbedingt notwendig; ***of ~ importance*** von größter Wichtigkeit
**vi·tal·i·ty** Vitalität *f*
**vit·a·min** Vitamin *n*; **~ de·fi·cien·cy** Vitaminmangel *m*
**vit·re·ous** Glas...
**vi·va·cious** lebhaft, temperamentvoll
**viv·id** hell (*light*); kräftig, leuchtend (*color*); anschaulich (*description*); lebhaft (*imagination*)
**vix·en** ZO Füchsin *f*
**V-neck** V-Ausschnitt *m*
**V-necked** mit V-Ausschnitt
**vo·cab·u·la·ry** Vokabular *n*, Wortschatz *m*; Wörterverzeichnis *n*
**vo·cal** Stimm...; F lautstark; MUS Vokal..., Gesang...; **~ cords** ANAT Stimmbänder *pl*

**vo·cal·ist** Sänger(in)
**vo·ca·tion** Begabung *f* (**for** für); Berufung *f*
**vo·ca·tion·al** Berufs...; **~ ed·u·ca·tion** Berufsausbildung *f*; **~ guid·ance** Berufsberatung *f*; **~ train·ing** Berufsausbildung *f*
**vogue** Mode *f*; ***be in ~*** Mode sein
**voice 1.** Stimme *f*; ***active ~*** LING Aktiv *n*; ***passive ~*** LING Passiv *n*; **2.** zum Ausdruck bringen; LING (stimmhaft) aussprechen; **voiced** LING stimmhaft; **voice·less** LING stimmlos
**void 1.** leer; JUR ungültig; **~ *of*** ohne; **2.** (Gefühl *n* der) Leere *f*
**vol** ABBR *of* ***volume*** Bd., Band *m*
**vol·a·tile** cholerisch (*person*); explosiv (*situation etc*); CHEM flüchtig
**vol·ca·no** Vulkan *m*
**vol·ley 1.** Salve *f*; (*Geschoss- etc*)Hagel *m* (*a. fig*); *tennis*: Volley *m*, Flugball *m*; *soccer*: Volleyschuss *m*; **2.** *Ball* volley schießen
**vol·ley·ball** SPORT Volleyball *m*
**volt** ELECTR Volt *n*
**volt·age** ELECTR Spannung *f*
**vol·u·ble** redselig; wortreich
**vol·ume** Band *m*; Volumen *n*, Rauminhalt *m*; Umfang *m*, große Menge; Lautstärke *f*
**vo·lu·mi·nous** bauschig (*dress etc*); geräumig; umfangreich (*notes etc*)
**vol·un·ta·ry** freiwillig; unbezahlt
**vol·un·teer 1.** *v/i* sich freiwillig melden (**for** zu) (*a.* MIL); *v/t Hilfe etc* anbieten; *et.* von sich aus sagen, F herausrücken mit; **2.** Freiwillige *m,f*; freiwilliger Helfer
**vo·lup·tu·ous** sinnlich (*lips etc*); aufreizend (*gesture etc*); üppig (*body etc*); kurvenreich (*woman*)
**vom·it 1.** *v/t* erbrechen; *v/i* (sich er)brechen, sich übergeben; **2.** Erbrochene *n*
**vo·ra·cious** unersättlich (*appetite etc*)
**vote 1.** Abstimmung *f* (***about, on*** über *acc*); (Wahl)Stimme *f*; Stimmzettel *m*; *a. pl* Wahlrecht *n*; ***~ of no confidence*** Misstrauensvotum *n*; ***take a ~ on s.th.*** über et. abstimmen; **2.** *v/i* wählen; ***~ for (against)*** stimmen für (gegen); ***~ on*** abstimmen über (*acc*); *v/t* wählen; *et.* bewilligen; ***~ out of office*** abwählen
**vot·er** Wähler(in)
**vot·ing booth** Wahlkabine *f*
**vouch:** ***~ for*** (sich ver)bürgen für
**vouch·er** Gutschein *m*, Kupon *m*
**vow 1.** Gelöbnis *n*; Gelübde *n*; ***take a ~, make a ~*** ein Gelöbnis *or* Gelübde ablegen; **2.** geloben, schwören (***to do*** zu tun)
**vow·el** LING Vokal *m*, Selbstlaut *m*
**voy·age** (See)Reise *f*
**vul·gar** vulgär, ordinär; geschmacklos
**vul·ne·ra·ble** *fig* verletzbar, verwundbar; verletzlich; anfällig (**to** für)
**vul·ture** ZO Geier *m*

# W

**W, w** W, w *n*
**wad** (*Watte- etc*)Bausch *m*; Bündel *n*; (*Papier- etc*)Knäuel *m, n*
**wad·ding** Einlage *f*, Füllmaterial *n*
**wad·dle** watscheln
**wade** *v/i* waten; ***~ through*** waten durch; F sich durchkämpfen durch, *et.* durchackern; *v/t* durchwaten
**wa·fer** (*esp* Eis)Waffel *f*; Oblate *f*; REL Hostie *f*
**waf·fle**[1] Waffel *f*
**waf·fle**[2] *Br* F schwafeln
**waft** *v/i* ziehen (*smell etc*); *v/t* wehen
**wag 1.** wedeln (mit); **2.** ***with a ~ of its tail*** schwanzwedelnd
**wage**[1] *mst pl* (Arbeits)Lohn *m*
**wage**[2]**:** **~ (*a*) *war against*** *or* ***on*** MIL Krieg führen gegen; *fig* e-n Feldzug führen gegen
**wage| earn·er** Lohnempfänger(in); Verdiener(in); **~ freeze** Lohnstopp *m*; **~ ne·go·ti·a·tions** Tarifverhandlungen *pl*; **~ pack·et** Lohntüte *f*; **~ rise** Lohnerhöhung *f*

**wa·ger** Wette *f*
**wag·gle** F wackeln (mit)
**wag·gon** *Br* → **wag·on** Fuhrwerk *n*, Wagen *m*; *Br* RAIL (offener) Güterwagen; (*Tee- etc*)Wagen *m*
**wag·tail** zo Bachstelze *f*
**wail 1.** jammern; heulen (*siren, wind*); **2.** Jammern *n*; Heulen *n*
**wain·scot** (Wand)Täfelung *f*
**waist** Taille *f*
**waist·coat** *esp Br* Weste *f*
**waist·line** Taille *f*
**wait 1.** *v/i* warten (***for, on*** auf *acc*); ~ ***for s.o.*** *a.* j-n erwarten; ***keep s.o. ~ing*** j-n warten lassen; ~ ***and see!*** warte es ab!; ~ ***on*** (*Br* ***at***) ***table*** bedienen, servieren; ~ ***on s.o.*** j-n bedienen; ~ ***up*** F aufbleiben (***for*** wegen); *v/t:* ~ ***one's chance*** auf e-e günstige Gelegenheit warten (***to do*** zu tun); ~ ***one's turn*** warten, bis man an der Reihe ist; **2.** Wartezeit *f*; ***have a long*** ~ lange warten müssen; ***lie in ~ for s.o.*** j-m auflauern
**wait·er** Kellner *m*, Ober *m*; ~, ***the check*** (*Br* ***bill***), ***please!*** (Herr) Ober, bitte zahlen!
**wait·ing** Warten *n*; ***no*** ~ MOT Halt(e)verbot *n*; ~ **list** Warteliste *f*; ~ **room** MED *etc* Wartezimmer *n*; RAIL Wartesaal *m*
**wait·ress** Kellnerin *f*, Bedienung *f*; ~, ***the check*** (*Br* ***bill***), ***please!*** Fräulein, bitte zahlen!
**wake**[1] *v/i a.* ~ ***up*** aufwachen, wach werden; *v/t a.* ~ ***up*** (auf)wecken; *fig* wachrufen, wecken
**wake**[2] MAR Kielwasser *n*; ***follow in the ~ of*** *fig* folgen auf (*acc*)
**wake·ful** schlaflos
**wak·en** *v/i a.* ~ ***up*** aufwachen, wach werden; *v/t a.* ~ ***up*** (auf)wecken
**walk 1.** *v/i* (zu Fuß) gehen, laufen; spazieren gehen; wandern; *v/t Strecke* gehen, laufen; *j-n* bringen (***to*** zu; ***home*** nach Hause); *Hund* ausführen; *Pferd* im Schritt gehen lassen; ~ ***away*** → ***walk off***; ~ ***in*** hineingehen, hereinkommen; ~ ***off*** fort-, weggehen; ~ ***off with*** F abhauen mit; F *Preis etc* locker gewinnen; ~ ***out*** hinausgehen; (unter Protest) den Saal *etc* verlassen; ECON streiken, in (den) Streik treten; ~ ***out on s.o.*** F j-n verlassen, j-n im Stich lassen; ~ ***up*** hinaufgehen, heraufkommen; ~ ***up to s.o.*** auf j-n zugehen; ~ ***up!*** treten Sie näher!; **2.** Spaziergang *m*; Wanderung *f*; Spazier-, Wanderweg *m*; ***go for a*** ~, ***take a*** ~ e-n Spaziergang machen, spazieren gehen; ***an hour's*** ~ e-e Stunde Fußweg *or* zu Fuß; ***from all ~s of life*** *Leute* aus allen Berufen *or* Schichten
**walk·a·way** F Spaziergang *m*, leichter Sieg
**walk·er** Spaziergänger(in); Wanderer *m*, Wand(r)erin *f*; SPORT Geher(in); ***be a good*** ~ gut zu Fuß sein
**walk·ie-talk·ie** Walkie-Talkie *n*, tragbares Funksprechgerät
**walk·ing** Gehen *n*, Laufen *n*; Spazierengehen *n*; Wandern *n*; ~ **pa·pers: *get one's*** ~ F den Laufpass bekommen; ~ **shoes** Wanderschuhe *pl*; ~ **stick** Spazierstock *m*; ~ **tour** Wanderung *f*
**Walk·man**® Walkman® *m*
**walk·out** Auszug *m* (***by, of*** *e-r Delegation etc*); ECON Ausstand *m*, Streik *m*
**walk·over** → ***walkaway***
**walk-up** F (Miets)Haus *n* ohne Fahrstuhl; Wohnung *f or* Büro *n etc* in e-m Haus ohne Fahrstuhl
**wall 1.** Wand *f*; Mauer *f*; **2.** *a.* ~ ***in*** mit e-r Mauer umgeben; ~ ***up*** zumauern
**wall cal·en·dar** Wandkalender *m*
**wall·chart** Wandkarte *f*
**wal·let** Brieftasche *f*
**wall·flow·er** F Mauerblümchen *n*
**wal·lop** F *j-m* ein Ding verpassen; SPORT *j-n* erledigen, vernichten (***at*** in *dat*)
**wal·low** sich wälzen; *fig* schwelgen, sich baden (***in*** in *dat*)
**wall·pa·per 1.** Tapete *f*; **2.** tapezieren
**wall-to-wall:** ~ ***carpet***(***ing***) Spannteppich *m*, Teppichboden *m*
**wal·nut** BOT Walnuss(baum *m*) *f*
**wal·rus** zo Walross *n*
**waltz 1.** Walzer *m*; **2.** Walzer tanzen
**wand** (*Zauber*)Stab *m*
**wan·der** (herum)wandern, herumlaufen, umherstreifen; *fig* abschweifen; fantasieren
**wane 1.** ASTR abnehmen; *fig* schwinden; **2.** ***be on the*** ~ *fig* im Schwinden begriffen sein
**wan·gle** F deichseln, hinkriegen; ~ ***s.th. out of s.o.*** j-m et. abluchsen; ~ ***one's way out of*** sich herauswinden aus
**want 1.** *v/t et.* wollen; *j-n* brauchen; *j-n* sprechen wollen; F *et.* brauchen, nötig

haben; ***be ~ed*** (*polizeilich*) gesucht werden (***for*** wegen); *v/i* wollen; ***I don't ~ to*** ich will nicht; ***he does not ~ for anything*** es fehlt ihm an nichts; **2.** Mangel *m* (***of*** an *dat*); Bedürfnis *n*, Wunsch *m*; Not *f*; **~ ad** Kleinanzeige *f*
**want·ed** (*polizeilich*) gesucht
**wan·ton** mutwillig
**war** Krieg *m* (*a. fig*); *fig* Kampf *m* (***against*** gegen)
**war·ble** ZO trillern
**ward 1.** MED Station *f*; *Br* POL Stadtbezirk *m*; JUR Mündel *n*; **2. *~ off*** *Schlag etc* abwehren, *Gefahr etc* abwenden
**war·den** Aufseher(in); Heimleiter(in); (Gefängnis)Direktor(in)
**ward·er** *Br* Aufsichtsbeamte *m*, -beamtin *f*
**war·drobe** Kleiderschrank *m*; Garderobe *f*
**ware·house** Lager(haus) *n*
**war·fare** Krieg *m*; Kriegführung *f*
**war·head** MIL Spreng-, Gefechtskopf *m*
**war·like** kriegerisch; Kriegs...
**warm 1.** *adj* warm, *fig a.* herzlich; ***I am ~, I feel ~*** mir ist warm; **2.** *v/t a.* ***~ up*** wärmen, sich *die Hände etc* wärmen; *Motor* warm laufen lassen; *v/i a.* ***~ up*** warm *or* wärmer werden, sich erwärmen; **warmth** Wärme *f*
**warm-up** SPORT Aufwärmen *n*
**warn** warnen (***against, of*** vor *dat*); *j-n* verständigen
**warn·ing** Warnung *f* (***of*** vor *dat*); Verwarnung *f*; ***without ~*** ohne Vorwarnung; **~ sig·nal** Warnsignal *n*
**warp** sich verziehen *or* werfen
**war·rant 1.** JUR (Durchsuchungs-, Haft- *etc*)Befehl *m*; **2.** *et.* rechtfertigen; **~ of ar·rest** JUR Haftbefehl *m*
**war·ran·ty** ECON Garantie(erklärung) *f*; ***it's still under ~*** darauf ist noch Garantie
**war·ri·or** Krieger *m*
**war·ship** Kriegsschiff *n*
**wart** MED Warze *f*
**war·y** vorsichtig
**was** *ich, er, sie, es* war; *passive*: *ich, er, sie, es* wurde
**wash 1.** *v/t* waschen, sich *die Hände etc* waschen; *v/i* sich waschen; sich *gut etc* waschen (lassen); ***~ up*** *v/i Br* abwaschen, (das) Geschirr spülen; *v/t* anschwemmen, anspülen; ***~ one's dirty linen*** schmutzige Wäsche waschen; **2.** Wäsche *f*; MOT Waschanlage *f*, Waschstraße *f*; ***be in the ~*** in der Wäsche sein; ***give s.th. a ~*** et. waschen; ***have a ~*** sich waschen
**wash·a·ble** (ab)waschbar
**wash-and-wear** bügelfrei; pflegeleicht
**wash·ba·sin** *Br*, **wash·bowl** Waschbecken *n*
**wash·cloth** Waschlappen *m*
**wash·er** Waschmaschine *f*; TECH Unterlegscheibe *f*
**wash·ing 1.** Wäsche *f*; **2.** Wasch...
**wash·ing| ma·chine** Waschmaschine *f*; **~ pow·der** Waschpulver *n*, -mittel *n*
**washing-up** *Br* Abwasch *m*; ***do the ~*** den Abwasch machen
**wash·room** Toilette *f*
**wasp** ZO Wespe *f*
**waste 1.** Verschwendung *f*; Abfall *m*; Müll *m*; ***~ of time*** Zeitverschwendung *f*; ***hazardous ~, special toxic ~*** Sondermüll *m*; ***special ~ dump*** Sondermülldeponie *f*; **2.** *v/t* verschwenden, vergeuden; *j-n* auszehren; *v/i* ***~ away*** immer schwächer werden (*person*); **3.** überschüssig; Abfall...; brachliegend, öde; ***lay ~*** verwüsten
**waste dis·pos·al** Abfall-, Müllbeseitigung *f*; Entsorgung *f*; **~ site** Deponie *f*
**waste·ful** verschwenderisch
**waste| gas** Abgas *n*; **~ pa·per** Abfallpapier *n*; Altpapier *n*
**waste·pa·per bas·ket** Papierkorb *m*
**waste pipe** Abflussrohr *n*
**watch 1.** *v/i* zuschauen; ***~ for*** warten auf (*acc*); ***~ out!*** pass auf!, Vorsicht!; ***~ out for*** Ausschau halten nach; sich in Acht nehmen vor (*dat*); *v/t* beobachten; zuschauen bei, sich *et.* ansehen; → ***television***; **2.** (*Armband-, Taschen*)Uhr *f*; Wache *f*; ***keep ~*** Wache halten, wachen (***over*** über *acc*); ***be on the ~ for*** Ausschau halten nach; auf der Hut sein vor (*dat*); ***keep (a) careful*** *or* ***close ~ on*** genau beobachten, scharf im Auge behalten
**watch·dog** Wachhund *m*
**watch·ful** wachsam
**watch·mak·er** Uhrmacher(in)
**watch·man** Wachmann *m*, Wächter *m*
**watch·tow·er** Wach(t)turm *m*
**wa·ter 1.** Wasser *n*; **2.** *v/t Blumen* gießen, *Rasen etc* sprengen; *Vieh* tränken;

~ ***down*** verdünnen, verwässern; *fig* abschwächen; *v/i* tränen (*eyes*); ***make s.o.'s mouth*** ~ j-m den Mund wässerig machen
**wa·ter bird** ZO Wasservogel *m*
**wa·ter·col·o(u)r** Wasser-, Aquarellfarbe *f*; Aquarellmalerei *f*; Aquarell *n*
**wa·ter·course** Wasserlauf *m*
**wa·ter·cress** BOT Brunnenkresse *f*
**wa·ter·fall** Wasserfall *m*
**wa·ter·front** Hafenviertel *n*; ***along the*** ~ am Wasser entlang
**wa·ter·hole** Wasserloch *n*
**wa·ter·ing can** Gießkanne *f*
**wa·ter jump** SPORT Wassergraben *m*
**wa·ter lev·el** Wasserstand *m*
**wa·ter lil·y** BOT Seerose *f*
**wa·ter·mark** Wasserzeichen *n*
**wa·ter·mel·on** BOT Wassermelone *f*
**wa·ter| pol·lu·tion** Wasserverschmutzung *f*; ~ **po·lo** SPORT Wasserball(spiel *n*) *m*
**wa·ter·proof 1.** wasserdicht; **2.** *Br* Regenmantel *m*; **3.** imprägnieren
**wa·ters** Gewässer *pl*; Wasser *pl*
**wa·ter·shed** GEOGR Wasserscheide *f*; *fig* Wendepunkt *m*
**wa·ter·side** Ufer *n*
**wa·ter ski·ing** SPORT Wasserskilaufen *n*
**wa·ter·tight** wasserdicht, *fig a.* hieb- und stichfest
**wa·ter·way** Wasserstraße *f*
**wa·ter·works** Wasserwerk *n*; ***turn on the*** ~ F zu heulen anfangen
**wa·ter·y** wäss(e)rig
**watt** ELECTR Watt *n*
**wave 1.** *v/t* schwenken; winken mit; *Haar* wellen, in Wellen legen; ~ ***one's hand*** winken; ~ ***s.o. aside*** j-n beiseite winken; *v/i* winken; wehen (*flag etc*); sich wellen (*hair*); ~ ***at s.o.***, ~ ***to s.o.*** j-m zuwinken; **2.** Welle *f* (*a. fig*); Winken *n*
**wave·length** PHYS Wellenlänge *f* (*a. fig*)
**wa·ver** flackern; schwanken
**wav·y** wellig, gewellt
**wax[1] 1.** Wachs *n*; (*Ohren*)Schmalz *n*; **2.** wachsen; bohnern
**wax[2]** ASTR zunehmen
**wax·en** wächsern
**wax·works** Wachsfigurenkabinett *n*
**wax·y** wächsern
**way 1.** Weg *m*; Richtung *f*, Seite *f*; Entfernung *f*, Strecke *f*; Art *f*, Weise *f*; ~***s and means*** Mittel und Wege *pl*; ~ ***back*** Rückweg *m*, Rückfahrt *f*; ~ ***home*** Heimweg *m*; ~ ***in*** Eingang *m*; ~ ***out*** Ausgang *m*; ***be on the*** ~ ***to***, ***be on one's*** ~ ***to*** unterwegs sein nach; ***by*** ~ ***of*** über (*acc*), via; *esp Br* statt; ***by the*** ~ übrigens; ***give*** ~ nachgeben; *Br* MOT die Vorfahrt lassen; ***in a*** ~ in gewisser Hinsicht; ***in no*** ~ in keiner Weise; ***lead the*** ~ vorangehen; ***let s.o. have his*** (***own***) ~ j-m s-n Willen lassen; ***lose one's*** ~ sich verlaufen *or* verirren; ***make*** ~ Platz machen (***for*** für); ***no*** ~! F kommt überhaupt nicht in Frage!; ***out of the*** ~ ungewöhnlich; ***this*** ~ hierher; hier entlang; **2.** *adv* weit
**way·bill** ECON Frachtbrief *m*
**way·lay** *j-m* auflauern; *j-n* abfangen, abpassen
**way·ward** eigensinnig, launisch
**we** wir *pl*
**weak** schwach (***at***, ***in*** in *dat*), GASTR *a.* dünn; **weak·en** *v/t* schwächen (*a. fig*); *v/i* schwächer werden; *fig* nachgeben; **weak·ling** Schwächling *m*, F Schlappschwanz *n*; **weak·ness** Schwäche *f*
**weal** Striemen *m*
**wealth** Reichtum *m*; *fig* Fülle *f* (***of*** von)
**wealth·y** reich
**wean** entwöhnen; ~ ***s.o. from*** *or* ***off s.th.*** j-m et. abgewöhnen
**weap·on** Waffe *f* (*a. fig*)
**wear 1.** *v/t Bart*, *Brille*, *Schmuck etc* tragen, *Mantel etc a.* anhaben, *Hut etc a.* aufhaben; abnutzen, abtragen; ~ ***the pants*** (*Br* ***trousers***) F die Hosen anhaben; ~ ***an angry expression*** verärgert dreinschauen; *v/i* sich abnutzen, verschleißen; sich *gut etc* halten; ***s.th. to*** ~ et. zum Anziehen; ~ ***away*** (sich) abtragen *or* abschleifen; ~ ***down*** (sich) abtreten (*stairs*), (sich) ablaufen (*heels*), (sich) abfahren (*tires*); abschleifen; *j-n* zermürben; ~ ***off*** nachlassen (*pain etc*); ~ ***on*** sich hinziehen (***all day*** über den ganzen Tag); ~ ***out*** (sich) abnutzen *or* abtragen; *fig j-n* erschöpfen; **2.** *often in cpds* Kleidung *f*; *a.* ~ ***and tear*** Abnutzung *f*, Verschleiß *m*; ***the worse for*** ~ abgenutzt, verschlissen; F lädiert
**wear·i·some** ermüdend; langweilig; lästig
**wear·y** erschöpft, müde; ermüdend, an-

strengend; ***be ~ of s.th.*** F et. satt haben
**wea·sel** zo Wiesel *n*
**weath·er 1.** Wetter *n*; Witterung *f*; **2.** *v/t* dem Wetter aussetzen; *fig Krise etc* überstehen; *v/i* verwittern
**weath·er-beat·en** verwittert
**weath·er| chart** METEOR Wetterkarte *f*; **~ fore·cast** METEOR Wettervorhersage *f*; Wetterbericht *m*
**weath·er·man** *radio*, TV Wetteransager *m*
**weath·er·proof 1.** wetterfest; **2.** wetterfest machen
**weath·er| re·port** METEOR Wetterbericht *m*; **~ sta·tion** METEOR Wetterwarte *f*; **~ vane** Wetterfahne *f*
**weave** weben; *Netz* spinnen; *Korb* flechten; ***~ one's way through*** sich schlängeln durch; **weav·er** Weber(in)
**web** Netz *n* (*a. fig*), Gewebe *n*; zo Schwimmhaut *f*
**wed** heiraten
**Wed(s)** ABBR *of* ***Wednesday*** Mi., Mittwoch *m*
**wed·ding 1.** Hochzeit *f*; **2.** Hochzeits..., Braut..., Ehe..., Trau...
**wed·ding ring** Ehering *m*, Trauring *m*
**wedge 1.** Keil *m*; **2.** verkeilen, mit e-m Keil festklemmen; ***~ in*** einkeilen, einzwängen
**wed·lock:** ***born in*** (***out of***) ~ ehelich (unehelich) geboren
**Wednes·day** (ABBR ***Wed, Weds***) Mittwoch *m*; ***on ~*** (am) Mittwoch; ***on ~s*** mittwochs
**wee**[1] F klein, winzig; ***a ~ bit*** ein (kleines) bisschen
**wee**[2] F **1.** Pipi machen; **2.** ***do*** *or* ***have a ~*** Pipi machen
**weed 1.** Unkraut *n*; **2.** jäten
**weed·kill·er** Unkrautvertilgungsmittel *n*
**weed·y** voll Unkraut; F schmächtig; F rückgratlos
**week** Woche *f*; ***~ after ~*** Woche um Woche; ***a ~ today, today ~*** heute in e-r Woche *or* in acht Tagen; ***every other ~*** jede zweite Woche; ***for ~s*** wochenlang; ***four times a ~*** viermal die Woche; ***in a ~('s time)*** in e-r Woche
**week·day** Wochentag *m*
**week·end** Wochenende *n*; ***on*** (*Br* ***at***) ***the ~*** am Wochenende; **week·end·er** Wochenendausflügler(in)
**week·ly 1.** Wochen...; wöchentlich; **2.** Wochenblatt *n*, Wochen(zeit)schrift *f*, Wochenzeitung *f*
**weep** weinen (***for*** um *j-n*; ***over*** über *acc*); MED nässen
**weep·ing wil·low** BOT Trauerweide *f*
**weep·y** F weinerlich; rührselig
**wee-wee** F → ***wee***[2]
**weigh** *v/t* (ab)wiegen; *fig* abwägen (***against*** gegen); ***~ anchor*** MAR den Anker lichten; ***be ~ed down with*** *fig* niedergedrückt werden von; *v/i ... Kilo etc* wiegen; ***~ on*** *fig* lasten auf (*dat*)
**weight 1.** Gewicht *n*; Last *f* (*a. fig*); *fig* Bedeutung *f*; ***gain ~, put on ~*** zunehmen; ***lose ~*** abnehmen; **2.** beschweren
**weight·less** schwerelos
**weight·less·ness** Schwerelosigkeit *f*
**weight lift·er** SPORT Gewichtheber *m*
**weight lift·ing** SPORT Gewichtheben *n*
**weight·y** schwer; *fig* schwerwiegend
**weir** Wehr *n*
**weird** unheimlich; F sonderbar, verrückt
**wel·come 1.** *int* ***~ back!, ~ home!*** willkommen zu Hause!; ***~ to England!*** willkommen in England!; **2.** *v/t* begrüßen (*a. fig*), willkommen heißen; **3.** *adj* willkommen; ***you are ~ to do it*** Sie können es gerne tun; ***you're ~!*** nichts zu danken!, keine Ursache!, bitte sehr!; **4.** Empfang *m*, Willkommen *n*; ***outstay*** *or* ***overstay one's ~*** j-s Gastfreundschaft überstrapazieren *or* zu lange in Anspruch nehmen
**weld** TECH schweißen
**wel·fare** Wohl(ergehen) *n*; Sozialhilfe *f*; ***be on ~*** Sozialhilfe beziehen; **~ state** Wohlfahrtsstaat *m*; **~ work** Sozialarbeit *f*; **~ work·er** Sozialarbeiter(in)
**well**[1] **1.** *adv* gut; gründlich; ***as ~*** ebenso, auch; ***as ~ as ...*** sowohl ... als auch ...; nicht nur ..., sondern auch ...; ***very ~*** also gut, na gut; ***~ done!*** bravo!; → ***off*** 1; **2.** *int* nun, also; ***~, ~!*** na so was!; **3.** *adj* gesund; ***feel ~*** sich wohl fühlen
**well**[2] **1.** Brunnen *m*; (*Öl*)Quelle *f*; (*Aufzugs- etc*)Schacht *m*; **2.** *a.* ***~ out*** quellen (***from*** aus); ***tears ~ed*** (***up***) ***in their eyes*** die Tränen stiegen ihnen in die Augen
**well-bal·anced** ausgeglichen (*person*); ausgewogen (*diet*)
**well-be·haved** artig, gut erzogen
**well-be·ing** Wohl(befinden) *n*

**well-dis·posed:** ***be ~ towards s.o.*** j-m wohlgesinnt sein
**well-done** GASTR durchgebraten
**well-earned** wohlverdient
**well-fed** gut genährt
**well-found·ed** (wohl) begründet
**well-in·formed** gut unterrichtet; gebildet
**well-known** (wohl) bekannt
**well-mean·ing** wohlmeinend, gut gemeint; **well-meant** gut gemeint
**well-off** **1.** wohlhabend, vermögend, besser gestellt; ***be ~ for*** gut versorgt sein mit; **2.** ***the ~*** die Wohlhabenden *pl*
**well-read** belesen
**well-timed** (zeitlich) günstig, im richtigen Augenblick
**well-to-do** wohlhabend, reich
**well-worn** abgetragen; *fig* abgedroschen
**Welsh** **1.** walisisch; **2.** LING Walisisch *n*; ***the ~*** die Waliser *pl*
**welt** Striemen *m*
**wel·ter** Wirrwarr *m*, Durcheinander *n*
**wel·ter·weight** SPORT Weltergewicht *n*; Weltergewichtler *m*
**were** *du* warst, *Sie* waren, *wir*, *sie* waren, *ihr* wart
**west** **1.** West, Westen *m*; ***the West*** POL der Westen; die Weststaaten *pl*; **2.** *adj* westlich, West...; **3.** *adv* nach Westen, westwärts; **west·er·ly** West..., westlich; **west·ern** **1.** westlich, West...; **2.** Western *m*; **west·ward(s)** westlich, nach Westen
**wet** **1.** nass, feucht; **2.** Nässe *f*; **3.** nass machen, anfeuchten
**weth·er** ZO Hammel *m*
**wet nurse** Amme *f*
**whack** (knallender) Schlag; F Anteil *m*
**whacked** F fertig, erledigt
**whack·ing** **1.** *Br* F Mords...; **2.** (Tracht *f*) Prügel *pl*
**whale** ZO Wal *m*
**wharf** Kai *m*
**what** **1.** *pron* was; ***~ about ...?*** wie wärs mit ...?; ***~ for?*** wozu?; ***so ~?*** na und?; ***know ~'s ~*** F wissen, was Sache ist; **2.** *adj* was für ein(e), welche(r, -s); alle, die; alles, was
**what·cha·ma·call·it** F → ***whatsit***
**what·ev·er** **1.** *pron* was (auch immer); alles, was; egal, was; **2.** *adj* welche(r, -s) ... auch (immer); ***no ... ~*** überhaupt kein(e) ...
**whats·it** F Dings(bums, -da) *m*, *f*, *n*
**what·so·ev·er** → ***whatever***
**wheat** BOT Weizen *m*
**whee·dle** beschwatzen; ***~ s.th. out of s.o.*** j-m et. abschwatzen
**wheel** **1.** Rad *n*; MOT, MAR Steuer *n*; **2.** schieben, rollen; kreisen; ***~ about, ~ (a)round*** herumfahren, herumwirbeln
**wheel·bar·row** Schubkarre(n *m*) *f*
**wheel·chair** Rollstuhl *m*
**wheel clamp** MOT Parkkralle *f*
**wheeled** mit Rädern; fahrbar; *in cpds* ...räd(e)rig
**wheeze** keuchen, pfeifend atmen
**whelp** ZO Welpe *m*, Junge *n*
**when** wann; als; wenn; obwohl; ***since ~?*** seit wann?
**when·ev·er** wann auch (immer); jedes Mal, wenn
**where** wo; wohin; ***~ ... (from)?*** woher?; ***~ ... (to)?*** wohin?; **where·a·bouts** **1.** *adv* wo etwa; **2.** Verbleib *m*; Aufenthalt *m*, Aufenthaltsort *m*
**where·as** während, wohingegen
**where·by** wodurch, womit; wonach
**where·u·pon** worauf, woraufhin
**wher·ev·er** wo *or* wohin auch (immer); ganz gleich wo *or* wohin
**whet** *Messer etc* schärfen; *fig Appetit* anregen
**wheth·er** ob
**whey** Molke *f*
**which** welche(r, -s); der, die, das; was; ***~ of you?*** wer von euch?
**which·ev·er** welche(r, -s) auch (immer); ganz gleich, welche(r, -s)
**whiff** Luftzug *m*; Hauch *m* (*a. fig* ***of*** von); Duft *m*, Duftwolke *f*
**while** **1.** Weile *f*; ***for a ~*** e-e Zeit lang; **2.** *cj* während; obwohl; **3.** *mst* ***~ away*** sich *die Zeit* vertreiben (***by doing s.th.*** mit et.)
**whim** Laune *f*
**whim·per** **1.** wimmern; ZO winseln; **2.** Wimmern *n*; ZO Winseln *n*
**whim·si·cal** wunderlich; launisch
**whine** **1.** ZO jaulen; jammern (***about*** über *acc*); **2.** ZO Jaulen *n*; Gejammer *n*
**whin·ny** ZO **1.** wiehern; **2.** Wiehern *n*
**whip** **1.** Peitsche *f*; GASTR Creme *f*; **2.** *v/t* (aus)peitschen; GASTR schlagen; *v/i* sausen, flitzen, (*wind*) fegen
**whipped| cream** Schlagsahne *f*, Schlagrahm *m*; **~ eggs** Eischnee *m*

**whip·ping** (Tracht *f*) Prügel *pl*
**whip·ping boy** Prügelknabe *m*
**whip·ping cream** Schlagsahne *f*, Schlagrahm *m*
**whir** → ***whirr***
**whirl 1.** wirbeln; ***my head is ~ing*** mir schwirrt der Kopf; **2.** Wirbeln *n*; Wirbel *m* (*a. fig*); ***my head's in a ~*** mir schwirrt der Kopf
**whirl·pool** Strudel *m*; Whirlpool *m*
**whirl·wind** Wirbelsturm *m*
**whirr** schwirren
**whisk 1.** schnelle Bewegung; Wedel *m*; GASTR Schneebesen *m*; **2.** GASTR schlagen; ***~ its tail*** ZO mit dem Schwanz schlagen; ***~ away*** *Fliegen etc* verscheuchen *or* wegscheuchen; *et.* schnell verschwinden lassen *or* wegnehmen
**whis·ker** ZO Schnurr- *or* Barthaar *n*; *pl* Backenbart *m*
**whis·k(e)y** Whisky *m*
**whis·per 1.** flüstern; **2.** Flüstern *n*; ***say s.th. in a ~*** et. im Flüsterton sagen
**whis·tle 1.** Pfeife *f*; Pfiff *m*; **2.** pfeifen
**white 1.** weiß; **2.** Weiß(e) *n*; Weiße *m, f*; Eiweiß *n*; **~ bread** Weißbrot *n*; **~ coffee** *Br* Milchkaffee *m*, Kaffee *m* mit Milch
**white-col·lar work·er** (Büro)Angestellte *m, f*
**white lie** Notlüge *f*
**whit·en** weiß machen *or* werden
**white·wash 1.** Tünche *f*; **2.** tünchen, anstreichen; weißen; *fig* beschönigen
**whit·ish** weißlich
**Whit·sun** Pfingstsonntag *m*; Pfingsten *n or pl*
**Whit Sunday** Pfingstsonntag *m*
**Whit·sun·tide** Pfingsten *n or pl*
**whit·tle** (zurecht)schnitzen; ***~ away*** *Gewinn etc* allmählich aufzehren; ***~ down*** *et.* reduzieren (***to*** auf *acc*)
**whiz(z)** F **1.** ***~ by, ~ past*** vorbeizischen, vorbeidüsen; **2.** Ass *n*, Kanone *f* (***at*** in *dat*); **~ kid** F Senkrechtstarter(in)
**who** wer; wen; wem; welche(r, -s); der, die, das
**who·dun·(n)it** F Krimi *m*
**who·ev·er** wer *or* wen *or* wem auch (immer); egal, wer *or* wen *or* wem
**whole 1.** *adj* ganz; **2.** *das* Ganze; ***the ~ of London*** ganz London; ***on the ~*** im Großen (und) Ganzen
**whole-heart·ed** ungeteilt (*attention*), voll (*support*), ernsthaft (*effort etc*)
**whole-heart·ed·ly** uneingeschränkt, voll und ganz
**whole·meal** Vollkorn...; ***~ bread*** Vollkornbrot *n*
**whole·sale** ECON **1.** Großhandel *m*; **2.** Großhandels...; **~ mar·ket** ECON Großmarkt *m*
**whole·sal·er** ECON Großhändler *m*
**whole·some** gesund
**whole wheat** → ***wholemeal***
**whol·ly** gänzlich, völlig
**whoop 1.** schreien, *esp* jauchzen; ***~ it up*** F auf den Putz hauen; **2.** (*esp* Freuden)Schrei *m*
**whoop·ee:** F ***make ~*** auf den Putz hauen
**whoop·ing cough** MED Keuchhusten *m*
**whore** Hure *f*
**why** warum, weshalb; ***that's ~*** deshalb
**wick** Docht *m*
**wick·ed** gemein, niederträchtig
**wick·er·work** Korbwaren *pl*
**wick·et** *cricket*: Tor *n*
**wide 1.** *adj* breit; weit offen, aufgerissen (*eyes*); *fig* umfangreich (*knowledge etc*), vielfältig (*interests etc*); **2.** *adv* weit; ***go ~*** danebengehen; ***go ~ of the goal*** SPORT am Tor vorbeigehen
**wide-an·gle lens** PHOT Weitwinkelobjektiv *n*
**wide-a·wake** hellwach; *fig* aufgeweckt, wach
**wide-eyed** mit großen *or* aufgerissenen Augen; naiv
**wid·en** verbreitern; breiter werden
**wide-o·pen** weit offen, aufgerissen (*eyes*)
**wide·spread** weit verbreitet
**wid·ow** Witwe *f*
**wid·owed** verwitwet; ***be ~*** verwitwet sein; Witwe(r) werden
**wid·ow·er** Witwer *m*
**width** Breite *f*; Bahn *f*
**wield** *Einfluss etc* ausüben
**wife** (Ehe)Frau *f*, Gattin *f*
**wig** Perücke *f*
**wild 1.** *adj* wild; stürmisch (*wind, applause etc*); außer sich (***with*** vor *dat*); verrückt (*idea etc*); ***make a ~ guess*** einfach drauflosraten; ***be ~ about*** (ganz) verrückt sein nach; **2.** *adv*: ***go ~*** ausflippen; ***let one's children run ~*** s-e

Kinder machen lassen, was sie wollen; **3.** ***in the*** ~ in freier Wildbahn; ***the ~s*** die Wildnis
**wild·cat** ZO Wildkatze *f*
**wild·cat strike** ECON wilder Streik
**wil·der·ness** Wildnis *f*
**wild·fire:** ***spread like*** ~ sich wie ein Lauffeuer verbreiten
**wild·life** Tier- und Pflanzenwelt *f*
**wil·ful** *Br* → ***willful***
**will**[1] *v/aux ich, du* will(st) *etc*; *ich* werde ... *etc*
**will**[2] Wille *m*; Testament *n*; ***of one's own free*** ~ aus freien Stücken
**will**[3] durch Willenskraft erzwingen; JUR vermachen
**will·ful** eigensinnig; absichtlich, *esp* JUR vorsätzlich
**will·ing** bereit (***to do*** zu tun); (bereit)willig
**will-o'-the-wisp** Irrlicht *n*
**wil·low** BOT Weide *f*
**wil·low·y** *fig* gertenschlank
**will·pow·er** Willenskraft *f*
**wil·ly-nil·ly** wohl oder übel
**wilt** verwelken, welk werden
**wi·ly** gerissen, raffiniert
**wimp** F Schlappschwanz *m*
**win 1.** *v/t* gewinnen; ~ ***s.o. over*** *or* ***round to*** j-n gewinnen für; *v/i* gewinnen, siegen; ***OK, you*** ~ okay, du hast gewonnen; **2.** *esp* SPORT Sieg *m*
**wince** zusammenzucken (***at*** bei)
**winch** TECH Winde *f*
**wind**[1] **1.** Wind *m*; Atem *m*, Luft *f*; MED Blähungen *pl*; ***the*** ~ MUS die Bläser *pl*; **2.** *j-m* den Atem nehmen *or* verschlagen; HUNT wittern
**wind**[2] **1.** *v/t* drehen (an *dat*); *Uhr etc* aufziehen; wickeln (***round*** um); *v/i* sich winden *or* schlängeln; ~ ***back*** *Film etc* zurückspulen; ~ ***down*** *Autofenster etc* herunterdrehen, -kurbeln; *Produktion etc* reduzieren; sich entspannen; ~ ***forward*** *Film etc* weiterspulen; ~ ***up*** *v/t Autofenster etc* hochdrehen, -kurbeln; *Uhr etc* aufziehen; *Versammlung etc* schließen (***with*** mit); *Unternehmen* liquidieren, auflösen; *v/i* F enden, landen; (*esp* s-e Rede) schließen (***by saying*** mit den Worten); **2.** Umdrehung *f*
**wind·bag** F Schwätzer(in)
**wind·fall** BOT Fallobst *n*; unverhofftes Geschenk; unverhoffter Gewinn
**wind·ing** gewunden
**wind·ing stairs** Wendeltreppe *f*
**wind in·stru·ment** MUS Blasinstrument *n*
**wind·lass** TECH Winde *f*
**wind·mill** Windmühle *f*
**win·dow** Fenster *n*; Schaufenster *n*; Schalter *m*; ~ **clean·er** Fensterputzer *m*; ~ **dress·er** Schaufensterdekorateur(in); ~ **dress·ing** Schaufensterdekoration *f*; *fig* F Mache *f*
**win·dow·pane** Fensterscheibe *f*
**win·dow seat** Fensterplatz *m*
**win·dow shade** Rouleau *n*
**win·dow-shop:** ***go window-shopping*** e-n Schaufensterbummel machen
**win·dow·sill** Fensterbank *f*, -brett *n*
**wind·pipe** ANAT Luftröhre *f*
**wind·screen** *Br* MOT Windschutzscheibe *f*; ~ **wip·er** *Br* MOT Scheibenwischer *m*
**wind·shield** MOT Windschutzscheibe *f*; ~ **wip·er** MOT Scheibenwischer *m*
**wind·surf·ing** SPORT Windsurfing *n*, Windsurfen *n*
**wind·y** windig; MED blähend
**wine** Wein *m*; ~ **cel·lar** Weinkeller *m*; ~ **list** Weinkarte *f*; ~ **mer·chant** Weinhändler *m*
**win·er·y** Weinkellerei *f*
**wine tast·ing** Weinprobe *f*
**wing** ZO Flügel *m*, Schwinge *f*; *Br* MOT Kotflügel *m*; AVIAT Tragfläche *f*; AVIAT MIL Geschwader *n*; *pl* THEA Seitenkulisse *f*
**wing·er** SPORT Außenstürmer(in), Flügelstürmer(in)
**wink 1.** zwinkern; ~ ***at*** *j-m* zuzwinkern; *et.* geflissentlich übersehen; ~ ***one's lights*** *Br* MOT blinken; **2.** Zwinkern *n*; ***I didn't get a*** ~ ***of sleep last night, I didn't sleep a*** ~ ***last night*** ich habe letzte Nacht kein Auge zugetan; → ***forty*** 1
**win·ner** Gewinner(in), *esp* SPORT Sieger(in)
**win·ning 1.** einnehmend, gewinnend; **2.** *pl* Gewinn *m*
**win·ter 1.** Winter *m*; ***in*** (***the***) ~ im Winter; **2.** überwintern; den Winter verbringen; ~ **sports** Wintersport *m*
**win·ter·time** Winter *m*; Winterzeit *f*; ***in*** (***the***) ~ im Winter

**win·try** winterlich; *fig* frostig
**wipe** (ab-, auf)wischen; ~ ***off*** ab-, wegwischen; ~ ***out*** auswischen; auslöschen, ausrotten; ~ ***up*** aufwischen
**wip·er** MOT (*Scheiben*)Wischer *m*
**wire 1.** Draht *m*; ELECTR Leitung *f*; Telegramm *n*; **2.** Leitungen verlegen in (*dat*) (*a.* ~ ***up***); *j-m* ein Telegramm schicken; *j-m et.* telegrafieren
**wire·less** drahtlos, Funk...
**wire net·ting** Maschendraht *m*
**wire-tap** *j-n*, *j-s Telefon* abhören
**wir·y** *fig* drahtig
**wis·dom** Weisheit *f*, Klugheit *f*
**wis·dom tooth** Weisheitszahn *m*
**wise** weise, klug
**wise·crack** F **1.** Witzelei *f*; **2.** witzeln
**wise guy** F Klugscheißer *m*
**wish 1.** wünschen; wollen; ~ ***s.o. well*** j-m alles Gute wünschen; ***if you*** ~ (***to***) wenn du willst; ~ ***for s.th.*** sich et. wünschen; **2.** Wunsch *m* (***for*** nach)
**wish·ful think·ing** Wunschdenken *n*
**wish·y-wash·y** F labb(e)rig, wäss(e)rig; *fig* lasch (*person*); verschwommen
**wisp** (*Gras-*, *Haar*)Büschel *n*
**wist·ful** wehmütig
**wit** Geist *m*, Witz *m*; geistreicher Mensch; *a. pl* Verstand *m*; ***be at one's*** ~***s' end*** mit s-r Weisheit am Ende sein; ***keep one's*** ~***s about one*** e-n klaren Kopf behalten
**witch** Hexe *f*
**witch·craft** Hexerei *f*
**with** mit; bei; vor (*dat*)
**with·draw** *v/t Geld* abheben (***from*** von); *Angebot etc* zurückziehen, *Anschuldigung etc* zurücknehmen; MIL *Truppen* zurückziehen, abziehen; *v/i* sich zurückziehen; zurücktreten (***from*** von)
**with·draw·al** Rücknahme *f*; *esp* MIL Abzug *m*, Rückzug *m*; Rücktritt *m* (***from*** von), Ausstieg *m* (***from*** aus); MED Entziehung *f*, Entzug *m*; ***make a*** ~ Geld abheben (***from*** von); ~ **cure** MED Entziehungskur *f*; ~ **symp·toms** MED Entzugserscheinungen *pl*
**with·er** eingehen *or* verdorren *or* (ver)welken (lassen)
**with·hold** zurückhalten; ~ ***s.th. from s.o.*** j-m et. vorenthalten
**with·in** innerhalb (*gen*)
**with·out** ohne (*acc*)
**with·stand** *e-m Angriff etc* standhalten; *Beanspruchung etc* aushalten
**wit·ness 1.** Zeuge *m*, Zeugin *f*; ~ ***for the defense*** (*Br* ***defence***) JUR Entlastungszeuge *m*, -zeugin *f*; ~ ***for the prosecution*** JUR Belastungszeuge *m*, -zeugin *f*; **2.** Zeuge sein von *et.*; *et.* bezeugen, *Unterschrift* beglaubigen; ~ **box** *Br*, ~ **stand** JUR Zeugenstand *m*
**wit·ti·cis·m** geistreiche *or* witzige Bemerkung; **wit·ty** geistreich, witzig
**wiz·ard** Zauberer *m*; *fig* Genie *n* (**at** in *dat*)
**wiz·ened** verhutzelt
**wob·ble** *v/i* wackeln, zittern (*a. voice*), schwabbeln; MOT flattern; *fig* schwanken; *v/t* wackeln an (*dat*)
**woe·ful** traurig; bedauerlich
**wolf 1.** ZO Wolf *m*; ***lone*** ~ *fig* Einzelgänger(in); **2.** *a.* ~ ***down*** F *Essen* hinunterschlingen
**wom·an** Frau *f*; ~ **doc·tor** Ärztin *f*; ~ **driv·er** Frau *f* am Steuer
**wom·an·ish** weibisch
**wom·an·ly** fraulich; weiblich
**womb** ANAT Gebärmutter *f*
**women's| lib·ber** F Emanze *f*; ~ **move·ment** Frauenbewegung *f*; ~ **ref·uge** *Br*, ~ **shel·ter** Frauenhaus *n*
**won·der 1.** neugierig *or* gespannt sein, gern wissen mögen; sich fragen, überlegen; sich wundern, erstaunt sein (***about*** über *acc*); ***I*** ~ ***if you could help me*** vielleicht können Sie mir helfen; **2.** Staunen *n*, Verwunderung *f*; Wunder *n*; ***do*** *or* ***work*** ~***s*** wahre Wunder vollbringen, Wunder wirken (***for*** bei)
**won·der·ful** wunderbar, wundervoll
**wont 1.** ***be*** ~ ***to do s.th.*** et. zu tun pflegen; **2.** ***as was his*** ~ wie es s-e Gewohnheit war
**woo** umwerben, werben um
**wood** Holz *n*; Holzfass *n*; *a. pl* Wald *m*, Gehölz *n*; ***touch*** ~***!*** unberufen!, toi, toi, toi!; ***he can't see the*** ~ ***for the trees*** er sieht den Wald vor lauter Bäumen nicht
**wood·cut** Holzschnitt *m*
**wood·cut·ter** Holzfäller *m*
**wood·ed** bewaldet
**wood·en** hölzern (*a. fig*), aus Holz, Holz...
**wood·peck·er** ZO Specht *m*
**wood·wind: *the*** ~ MUS die Holzblasinstrumente *pl*, die Holzbläser *pl*; ~ ***instrument*** Holzblasinstrument *n*

**wood·work** Holzarbeit *f*
**wood·y** waldig; BOT holzig
**wool** Wolle *f*
**wool·(l)en 1.** wollen, Woll...; **2.** *pl* Wollsachen *pl*, Wollkleidung *f*
**wool·(l)y 1.** wollig; *fig* schwammig; **2.** *pl* F Wollsachen *pl*
**word 1.** Wort *n*; Nachricht *f*; Losung *f*, Losungswort *n*; Versprechen *n*; Befehl *m*; *pl* MUS *etc* Text *m*; ***have a ~ or a few ~s with s.o.*** mit j-m sprechen; **2.** *et.* ausdrücken, *Text* abfassen, formulieren; **word·ing** Wortlaut *m*
**word| or·der** LING Wortstellung *f*; **~ pro·cess·ing** EDP Textverarbeitung *f*; **~ pro·ces·sor** EDP Textverarbeitungsgerät *n*
**word·y** wortreich, langatmig
**work 1.** Arbeit *f*; Werk *n*; *pl* TECH Werk *n*, Getriebe *n*; ECON Werk *n*, Fabrik *f*; ***at ~*** bei der Arbeit; ***be in ~*** Arbeit haben; ***be out of ~*** arbeitslos sein; ***go or set to ~*** an die Arbeit gehen; **2.** *v/i* arbeiten (***at, on*** an *dat*); TECH funktionieren (*a. fig*); wirken; ***~ to rule*** Dienst nach Vorschrift tun; *v/t j-n* arbeiten lassen; *Maschine etc* bedienen, *et.* betätigen; *et.* bearbeiten; bewirken, herbeiführen; ***~ one's way*** sich durcharbeiten *or* durchkämpfen; ***~ off*** *Schulden* abarbeiten; *Wut etc* abreagieren; ***~ out*** *v/t* ausrechnen; *Aufgabe* lösen; *Plan etc* ausarbeiten; *fig* sich *et.* zusammenreimen; *v/i* gut gehen, F klappen; aufgehen; F SPORT trainieren; ***~ up*** *Zuhörer etc* aufpeitschen, aufwühlen; *et.* ausarbeiten (***into*** zu); ***be ~ed up*** aufgeregt *or* nervös sein (***about*** wegen)
**work·a·ble** formbar; *fig* durchführbar
**work·a·day** Alltags...
**work·a·hol·ic** F Arbeitssüchtige *m, f*
**work·bench** TECH Werkbank *f*
**work·book** PED Arbeitsheft *n*
**work·day** Arbeitstag *m*; Werktag *m*; ***on ~s*** werktags
**work·er** Arbeiter(in); Angestellte *m, f*
**work ex·pe·ri·ence** Erfahrung *f*
**work·ing** werktätig; Arbeits...; ***~ knowledge*** Grundkenntnisse *pl*; ***in ~ order*** in betriebsfähigem Zustand; **~ class** Arbeiterklasse *f*; **~ day** → ***workday***; **~ hours** Arbeitszeit *f*; ***fewer ~*** Arbeitszeitverkürzung *f*; ***reduced ~*** Kurzarbeit *f*
**work·ings** Arbeits-, Funktionsweise *f*
**work·man** Handwerker *m*
**work·man·like** fachmännisch
**work·man·ship** fachmännische Arbeit
**work of art** Kunstwerk *n*
**work·out** F SPORT Training *n*
**work·place** Arbeitsplatz *m*; ***at the ~*** am Arbeitsplatz
**works coun·cil** Betriebsrat *m*
**work·sheet** PED *etc* Arbeitsblatt *n*
**work·shop** Werkstatt *f*; Workshop *m*
**work·shy** arbeitsscheu
**work·sta·tion** EDP Bildschirmarbeitsplatz *m*
**work-to-rule** *Br* Dienst *m* nach Vorschrift
**world 1.** Welt *f*; ***all over the ~*** in der ganzen Welt; ***bring into the ~*** auf die Welt bringen; ***do s.o. a or the ~ of good*** j-m unwahrscheinlich gut tun; ***mean all the ~ to s.o.*** j-m alles bedeuten; ***they are ~s apart*** zwischen ihnen liegen Welten; ***think the ~ of*** große Stücke halten von; ***what in the ~ ...?*** was um alles in der Welt ...?; **2.** Welt...; **~ cham·pi·on** SPORT Weltmeister *m*; **~ cham·pi·on·ship** SPORT Weltmeisterschaft *f*
**World Cup** Fußballweltmeisterschaft *f*; *skiing*: Weltcup *m*
**world-fa·mous** weltberühmt
**world lit·er·a·ture** Weltliteratur *f*
**world·ly** weltlich; irdisch
**world·ly-wise** weltklug
**world| mar·ket** ECON Weltmarkt *m*; **~ pow·er** POL Weltmacht *f*; **~ rec·ord** SPORT Weltrekord *m*; **~ trip** Weltreise *f*; **~ war** Weltkrieg *m*
**world·wide** weltweit; auf der ganzen Welt
**worm 1.** ZO Wurm *m*; **2.** *Hund etc* entwurmen; ***~ one's way through*** sich schlängeln *or* zwängen durch; ***~ o.s. into s.o.'s confidence*** sich in j-s Vertrauen einschleichen; ***~ s.th. out of s.o.*** j-m et. entlocken
**worm-eat·en** wurmstichig
**worm's-eye view** Froschperspektive *f*
**worn-out** abgenutzt, abgetragen; *fig* erschöpft
**wor·ried** besorgt, beunruhigt
**wor·ry 1.** beunruhigen; (sich) Sorgen machen; ***don't ~!*** keine Angst!, keine Sorge!; **2.** Sorge *f*
**worse** schlechter, schlimmer; ***~ still*** was

noch schlimmer ist; ***to make matters ~*** zu allem Übel
**wors·en** schlechter machen *or* werden, (sich) verschlechtern
**wor·ship 1.** Verehrung *f*; Gottesdienst *m*; **2.** *v/t* anbeten, verehren; *v/i* den Gottesdienst besuchen
**wor·ship·(p)er** Anbeter(in), Verehrer(in); Kirchgänger(in)
**worst 1.** *adj* schlechteste(r, -s), schlimmste(r, -s); **2.** *adv* am schlechtesten, am schlimmsten; **3.** *der, die, das* Schlechteste *or* Schlimmste; ***at (the) ~*** schlimmstenfalls
**wor·sted** Kammgarn *n*
**worth 1.** wert; ***~ reading*** lesenswert; **2.** Wert *m*; **worth·less** wertlos
**worth·while** lohnend; ***be ~*** sich lohnen
**worth·y** würdig
**would-be** Möchtegern...
**wound 1.** Wunde *f*, Verletzung *f*; **2.** verwunden, verletzen
**wow** *int* F wow!, Mensch!, toll!
**wran·gle 1.** (sich) streiten; **2.** Streit *m*
**wrap 1.** *v/t a.* ***~ up*** (ein)packen, (ein)wickeln (***in*** in *dat*); *et.* wickeln (***[a]round*** um); *v/i*: ***~ up*** sich warm anziehen; **2.** Umhang *m*
**wrap·per** (Schutz)Umschlag *m*
**wrap·ping** Verpackung *f*; **~ pa·per** Einwickel-, Pack-, Geschenkpapier *n*
**wrath** Zorn *m*
**wreath** Kranz *m*
**wreck 1.** MAR Wrack *n* (*a. fig*); **2.** *Pläne etc* zunichte machen; ***be ~ed*** MAR zerschellen; Schiffbruch erleiden
**wreck·age** Trümmer *pl* (*a. fig*), Wrackteile *pl*
**wreck·er** MOT Abschleppwagen *m*
**wreck·ing| com·pa·ny** Abbruchfirma *f*; **~ ser·vice** MOT Abschleppdienst *m*
**wren** ZO Zaunkönig *m*
**wrench 1.** MED sich *das Knie etc* verrenken; ***~ s.th. from*** *or* ***out of s.o.'s hands*** j-m et. aus den Händen winden, j-m et. entwinden; ***~ off*** *et.* mit e-m Ruck abreißen *or* wegreißen; ***~ open*** aufreißen; **2.** Ruck *m*; MED Verrenkung *f*; *Br* TECH Schraubenschlüssel *m*
**wrest**: ***~ s.th. from*** *or* ***out of s.o.'s hands*** j-m et. aus den Händen reißen, j-m et. entreißen *or* entwinden
**wres·tle** *v/i* SPORT ringen (***with*** mit), *fig a.* kämpfen (***with*** mit); *v/t* SPORT ringen gegen; **wres·tler** SPORT Ringer *m*; **wres·tling** SPORT Ringen *n*
**wretch** *often* HUMOR Schuft *m*, Wicht *m*; *a.* ***poor ~*** armer Teufel
**wretch·ed** elend; (tod)unglücklich; scheußlich; verdammt, verflixt
**wrig·gle** *v/i* sich winden; zappeln; ***~ out of*** *fig* F sich herauswinden aus; F sich drücken vor (*dat*); *v/t* mit *den Zehen* wackeln
**wring** *j-m die Hand* drücken; *die Hände* ringen; *den Hals* umdrehen; ***~ out*** *Wäsche etc* auswringen; ***~ s.o.'s heart*** j-m zu Herzen gehen
**wrin·kle 1.** Falte *f*, Runzel *f*; **2.** runzeln; *Nase* kraus ziehen, rümpfen; faltig *or* runz(e)lig werden
**wrist** ANAT Handgelenk *n*
**wrist·band** Bündchen *n*, (Hemd)Manschette *f*; Armband *n*
**wrist·watch** Armbanduhr *f*
**writ** JUR Befehl *m*, Verfügung *f*
**write** schreiben; ***~ down*** auf-, niederschreiben; ***~ off*** *j-n*, ECON *et.* abschreiben; ***~ out*** *Namen etc* ausschreiben; *Bericht etc* ausarbeiten; *j-m e-e Quittung etc* ausstellen; **~ pro·tec·tion** EDP Schreibschutz *m*
**writ·er** Schreiber(in), Verfasser(in), Autor(in); Schriftsteller(in)
**writhe** sich krümmen *or* winden (***in, with*** vor *dat*)
**writ·ing 1.** Schreiben *n*; (Hand)Schrift *f*; Schriftstück *n*; *pl* Werke *pl*; ***in ~*** schriftlich; **2.** Schreib...; **~ case** Schreibmappe *f*; **~ desk** Schreibtisch *m*; **~ pad** Schreibblock *m*; **~ pa·per** Briefpapier *n*, Schreibpapier *n*
**writ·ten** schriftlich
**wrong 1.** *adj* falsch; unrecht; ***be ~*** falsch sein, nicht stimmen; Unrecht haben; falsch gehen (*watch*); ***be on the ~ side of forty*** über 40 (Jahre alt) sein; ***is anything ~?*** ist et. nicht in Ordnung?; ***what's ~ with her?*** was ist los mit ihr?, was hat sie?; **2.** *adv* falsch; ***get ~*** *j-n, et.* falsch verstehen; ***go ~*** e-n Fehler machen; kaputtgehen; *fig* F schief gehen; **3.** Unrecht *n*; ***be in the ~*** im Unrecht sein; **4.** *j-m* unrecht tun
**wrong·ful** ungerechtfertigt; gesetzwidrig
**wrong-way driv·er** MOT F Geisterfahrer(in)

**wrought i·ron** Schmiedeeisen *n*
**wrought-i·ron** schmiedeeisern
**wry** süßsauer (*smile*); ironisch, sarkastisch (*humor etc*)
**wt** ABBR *of* ***weight*** Gew., Gewicht *n*
**WWF** ABBR *of* ***World Wide Fund for Nature*** WWF *m*
**WYSIWYG** ABBR *of* ***what you see is what you get*** EDP was du (*auf dem Bildschirm*) siehst, bekommst du (*auch ausgedruckt*)

# X

**X, x** X, x *n*
**xen·o·pho·bi·a** Fremdenhass *m*; Ausländerfeindlichkeit *f*
**XL** ABBR *of* ***extra large*** (***size***) extragroß
**X·mas** F → ***Christmas***
**X-ray** MED **1.** röntgen; **2.** Röntgenstrahl *m*; Röntgenaufnahme *f*, -bild *n*; Röntgenuntersuchung *f*
**xy·lo·phone** MUS Xylophon *n*

# Y

**Y, y** Y, y *n*
**yacht** MAR **1.** (Segel)Boot *n*; Jacht *f*; **2.** segeln; ***go ~ing*** segeln gehen
**yacht club** Segelklub *m*, Jachtklub *m*
**yacht·ing** Segeln *n*, Segelsport *m*
**Yan·kee** F Yankee *m*, Ami *m*
**yap** kläffen; F quasseln
**yard**[1] (ABBR ***yd***) Yard *n* (*91,44 cm*)
**yard**[2] Hof *m*; (*Bau-, Stapel- etc*)Platz *m*; Garten *m*
**yard·stick** *fig* Maßstab *m*
**yarn** Garn *n*; ***spin s.o. a ~ about*** j-m e-e abenteuerliche Geschichte *or* e-e Lügengeschichte erzählen von
**yawn 1.** gähnen; **2.** Gähnen *n*
**yeah** F ja
**year** Jahr *n*; ***all the ~ round*** das ganze Jahr hindurch; ***~ after ~*** Jahr für Jahr; ***~ in ~ out*** jahraus, jahrein; ***this ~*** dieses Jahr; ***this ~'s*** diesjährige(r, -s)
**year·ly** jährlich
**yearn** sich sehnen (***for*** nach; ***to do*** danach, zu tun); **yearn·ing 1.** Sehnsucht *f*; **2.** sehnsüchtig
**yeast** Hefe *f*
**yell 1.** schreien, brüllen (***with*** vor *dat*); ***~ at s.o.*** j-n anschreien *or* anbrüllen; ***~*** (***out***) *et.* schreien, brüllen; **2.** Schrei *m*
**yel·low 1.** gelb; F feig(e); **2.** Gelb *n*; ***at ~*** MOT bei Gelb; **3.** (sich) gelb färben; gelb werden; vergilben
**yel·low fe·ver** MED Gelbfieber *n*
**yel·low·ish** gelblich
**Yel·low Pag·es**® TEL *die* Gelben Seiten *pl*, Branchenverzeichnis *n*
**yel·low press** Sensationspresse *f*
**yelp 1.** (auf)jaulen; aufschreien; **2.** (Auf)Jaulen *n*; Aufschrei *m*
**yes 1.** ja; doch; **2.** Ja *n*
**yes·ter·day** gestern; ***~ morning*** (***afternoon***) gestern Morgen (Nachmittag); ***the day before ~*** vorgestern
**yet 1.** *adv in questions*: schon; noch; (doch) noch; doch, aber; ***as ~*** bis jetzt, bisher; ***not ~*** noch nicht; **2.** *cj* aber, doch
**yew** BOT Eibe *f*
**yield 1.** *v/t Früchte* tragen; *Gewinn* abwerfen; *Resultat etc* ergeben, liefern; *v/i* nachgeben; ***~ to*** MOT *j-m* die Vorfahrt lassen; **2.** Ertrag *m*
**yip·pee** *int* F hurra!

**yo·del 1.** jodeln; **2.** Jodler *m*
**yo·ga** Joga *m, n,* Yoga *m, n*
**yog·h(o)urt, yog·urt** Jog(h)urt *m, n*
**yoke** Joch *n (a. fig)*
**yolk** (Ei)Dotter *m, n,* Eigelb *n*
**you** du, ihr, Sie; (*dat*) dir, euch, Ihnen; (*acc*) dich, euch, Sie; man
**young 1.** jung; **2.** ZO Junge *pl*; ***with*** ~ ZO trächtig; ***the*** ~ die jungen Leute *pl*, die Jugend
**young·ster** Junge *m*
**your** dein(e); *pl* euer, eure; Ihr(e) (*a. pl*)
**yours** deine(r, -s); *pl* euer, eure(s); Ihre(r, -s) (*a. pl*); ***a friend of*** ~ ein Freund von dir; ***Yours, Bill*** Dein Bill
**your·self** selbst; dir, dich, sich; ***by*** ~ allein
**youth** Jugend *f*; Jugendliche *m*
**youth club** Jugendklub *m*
**youth·ful** jugendlich
**youth hos·tel** Jugendherberge *f*
**yuck·y** F *contp* scheußlich
**Yu·go·slav 1.** jugoslawisch; **2.** Jugoslawe *m*, Jugoslawin *f*; **Yu·go·sla·vi·a** Jugoslawien *n*
**yup·pie, yup·py** ABBR *of* ***young upwardly-mobile*** *or* ***urban professional*** junger, aufstrebender *or* städtischer Karrieremensch, Yuppie *m*

# Z

**Z, z** Z, z *n*
**zap** F *esp computer game etc*: abknallen, fertig machen; MOT beschleunigen (***from ... to ...*** von ... auf *acc* ...); jagen, hetzen; TV *Fernbedienung* bedienen; TV zappen, umschalten; ~ ***off*** abzischen; ~ ***to*** düsen *or* jagen *or* hetzen nach
**zap·per** TV F Fernbedienung *f*
**zap·py** *Br* F voller Pep, schmissig, fetzig
**zeal** Eifer *m*
**zeal·ot** Fanatiker(in), Eiferer *m*, Eiferin *f*; **zeal·ous** eifrig; ***be*** ~ ***to do s.th.*** eifrig darum bemüht sein, et. zu tun
**ze·bra** ZO Zebra *n*
**ze·bra cross·ing** *Br* Zebrastreifen *m*
**zen·ith** Zenit *m (a. fig)*
**ze·ro 1.** Null *f*; Nullpunkt *m*; ***20 degrees below*** ~ 20 Grad unter Null; **2.** Null...; ~ **growth** Nullwachstum *n*; ~ **in·terest: *have*** ~ ***in s.th.*** F null Bock auf et. haben; ~ **op·tion** POL Nulllösung *f*
**zest** *fig* Würze *f*; Begeisterung *f*; ~ ***for life*** Lebensfreude *f*
**zig·zag 1.** Zickzack *m*; **2.** Zickzack...; **3.** im Zickzack fahren, laufen *etc*, zickzackförmig verlaufen
**zinc** CHEM Zink *n*
**zip[1] 1.** Reißverschluss *m*; **2.** ~ ***the bag open*** (***shut***) den Reißverschluss der Tasche aufmachen (zumachen); ~ ***s.o. up*** j-m den Reißverschluss zumachen
**zip[2] 1.** Zischen *n*, Schwirren *n*; F Schwung *m*; **2.** zischen, schwirren; ~ ***by,*** ~ ***past*** vorbeiflitzen
**zip code** Postleitzahl *f*
**zip fas·ten·er** *esp Br* → ***zipper***
**zip·per** Reißverschluss *m*
**zo·di·ac** ASTR Tierkreis *m*; ***signs of the*** ~ Tierkreiszeichen *pl*
**zone** Zone *f*
**zoo** Zoo *m*, Tierpark *m*
**zo·o·log·i·cal** zoologisch; ~ **gar·dens** Tierpark *m*, zoologischer Garten
**zo·ol·o·gist** Zoologe *m*, Zoologin *f*
**zo·ol·o·gy** Zoologie *f*
**zoom 1.** surren; F sausen; F *fig* in die Höhe schnellen; PHOT zoomen; ~ ***by,*** ~ ***past*** F vorbeisausen; ~ ***in on*** PHOT *et.* heranholen; **2.** Surren *n*; *a.* ~ ***lens*** PHOT Zoom *n*, Zoomobjektiv *n*

# APPENDIX

# States of the Federal Republic of Germany

**Baden-Württemberg** ['ba:dən'vʏrtəmbɛrk] Baden-Württemberg
**Bayern** ['baɪɐn] Bavaria
**Berlin** [bɛr'li:n] Berlin
**Brandenburg** ['brandənbʊrk] Brandenburg
**Bremen** ['bre:mən] Bremen
**Hamburg** ['hambʊrk] Hamburg
**Hessen** ['hɛsən] Hesse
**Mecklenburg-Vorpommern** ['me:klənbʊrk'fo:ɐpɔmɐn] Mecklenburg-Western Pomerania
**Niedersachsen** ['ni:dɐzaksən] Lower Saxony
**Nordrhein-Westfalen** ['nɔrtraɪnvɛst'fa:lən] North Rhine-Westphalia
**Rheinland-Pfalz** ['raɪnlant'pfalts] Rhineland-Palatinate
**Saarland** ['za:ɐlant]: ***das*** ~ the Saarland
**Sachsen** ['zaksən] Saxony
**Sachsen-Anhalt** ['zaksən'anhalt] Saxony-Anhalt
**Schleswig-Holstein** ['ʃle:svɪç'hɔlʃtaɪn] Schleswig-Holstein
**Thüringen** ['ty:rɪŋən] Thuringia

# States of the Republic of Austria

**Burgenland** ['bʊrgənlant]: ***das*** ~ the Burgenland
**Kärnten** ['kɛrntən] Carinthia
**Niederösterreich** ['ni:dɐˀø:stəraɪç] Lower Austria
**Oberösterreich** ['o:bɐˀø:stəraɪç] Upper Austria
**Salzburg** ['zaltsbʊrk] Salzburg
**Steiermark** ['ʃtaɪɐmark]: ***die*** ~ Styria
**Tirol** [ti'ro:l] Tyrol
**Vorarlberg** ['fo:ɐˀarlbɛrk] Vorarlberg
**Wien** [vi:n] Vienna

# Cantons of the Swiss Confederation

**Aargau** ['a:ɐgaʊ]: ***der*** ~ the Aargau
**Appenzell** [apən'tsɛl] Appenzell
**Basel** ['ba:zəl] Basel, Basle
**Bern** [bɛrn] Bern(e)
**Freiburg** ['fraɪbʊrk], *French* **Fribourg** [fri'bu:r] Fribourg
**Genf** [gɛnf], *French* **Genève** [ʒə'nɛ:v] Geneva
**Glarus** ['gla:rʊs] Glarus
**Graubünden** [graʊ'bʏndən] Graubünden, Grisons
**Jura** ['ju:ra]: ***der*** ~ the Jura
**Luzern** [lu'tsɛrn] Lucerne
**Neuenburg** ['nɔʏənbʊrk], *French* **Neuchâtel** [nøʃa'tɛl] Neuchâtel
**St. Gallen** [zaŋkt 'galən] St Gallen, St Gall
**Schaffhausen** [ʃaf'haʊzən] Schaffhausen
**Schwyz** [ʃvi:ts] Schwyz
**Solothurn** ['zo:lotʊrn] Solothurn
**Tessin** [tɛ'si:n]: ***der*** ~ the Ticino, *Italian* **Ticino** [ti'tʃi:no]: ***das*** ~ the Ticino
**Thurgau** ['tu:ɐgaʊ]: ***der*** ~ the Thurgau
**Unterwalden** ['ʊntɐvaldən] Unterwalden
**Uri** ['u:ri] Uri
**Waadt** [va(:)t], *French* **Vaud** [vo] Vaud
**Wallis** ['valɪs], *French* **Valais** [va'lɛ]: ***das*** ~ the Valais, Wallis
**Zug** [tsu:k] Zug
**Zürich** ['tsy:rɪç] Zurich

## States of the Federal Republic of Germany

[illegible]

## [illegible]

[illegible]

## Cantons of the Swiss Confederation

[illegible]

# German and European Currency

## German Money

(*valid till December 31, 2001*)

1 DM = 100 Pfennig

### coins

1 Pf (=Pfennig)
5 Pf
10 Pf
50 Pf
1 DM (=Deutsche Mark)
2 DM
5 DM

### bills (*Br* bank notes)

5 DM (=Deutsche Mark)
10 DM
20 DM
50 DM
100 DM
1000 DM

## Euro

(*official European currency from January 1, 2002*)

### coins

1 Cent
2 Cent
5 Cent
10 Cent
20 Cent
50 Cent
1 Euro
2 Euro

### bills (*Br* bank notes)

5 Euro
10 Euro
20 Euro
50 Euro
100 Euro
200 Euro
500 Euro

# Numerals

## Cardinal Numbers

**0** null *nought, zero*
**1** eins *one*
**2** zwei *two*
**3** drei *three*
**4** vier *four*
**5** fünf *five*
**6** sechs *six*
**7** sieben *seven*
**8** acht *eight*
**9** neun *nine*
**10** zehn *ten*
**11** elf *eleven*
**12** zwölf *twelve*
**13** dreizehn *thirteen*
**14** vierzehn *fourteen*
**15** fünfzehn *fifteen*
**16** sechzehn *sixteen*
**17** siebzehn *seventeen*
**18** achtzehn *eighteen*
**19** neunzehn *nineteen*
**20** zwanzig *twenty*
**21** einundzwanzig *twenty-one*
**22** zweiundzwanzig *twenty-two*
**30** dreißig *thirty*
**31** einunddreißig *thirty-one*
**40** vierzig *forty*
**41** einundvierzig *forty-one*
**50** fünfzig *fifty*
**51** einundfünfzig *fifty-one*
**60** sechzig *sixty*
**61** einundsechzig *sixty-one*
**70** siebzig *seventy*
**71** einundsiebzig *seventy-one*
**80** achtzig *eighty*
**81** einundachtzig *eighty-one*
**90** neunzig *ninety*
**91** einundneunzig *ninety-one*
**100** hundert *a* or *one hundred*
**101** hunderteins *a hundred and one*
**200** zweihundert *two hundred*
**300** dreihundert *three hundred*
**572** fünfhundertzweiundsiebzig *five hundred and seventy-two*
**1000** tausend *a* or *one thousand*
**1999** neunzehnhundertneunundneunzig *nineteen hundred and ninety-nine*
**2000** zweitausend *two thousand*
**5044** TEL fünfzig vierundvierzig *five O* (or *zero*) *double four*
**1 000 000** eine Million *one million*
**2 000 000** zwei Millionen *two million*

## Ordinal Numbers

**1.** erste *first* (*1st*)
**2.** zweite *second* (*2nd*)
**3.** dritte *third* (*3rd*)
**4.** vierte *fourth* (*4th*)
**5.** fünfte *fifth* (*5th*) *etc.*
**6.** sechste *sixth*
**7.** siebente *seventh*
**8.** achte *eighth*
**9.** neunte *ninth*
**10.** zehnte *tenth*
**11.** elfte *eleventh*
**12.** zwölfte *twelfth*
**13.** dreizehnte *thirteenth*
**14.** vierzehnte *fourteenth*
**15.** fünfzehnte *fifteenth*
**16.** sechzehnte *sixteenth*
**17.** siebzehnte *seventeenth*
**18.** achtzehnte *eighteenth*
**19.** neunzehnte *nineteenth*
**20.** zwanzigste *twentieth*
**21.** einundzwanzigste *twenty-first*
**22.** zweiundzwanzigste *twenty-second*
**23.** dreiundzwanzigste *twenty-third*
**30.** dreißigste *thirtieth*
**31.** einunddreißigste *thirty-first*
**40.** vierzigste *fortieth*
**41.** einundvierzigste *forty-first*
**50.** fünfzigste *fiftieth*
**51.** einundfünfzigste *fifty-first*
**60.** sechzigste *sixtieth*
**61.** einundsechzigste *sixty-first*
**70.** siebzigste *seventieth*

**71.** einundsiebzigste *seventy-first*
**80.** achtzigste *eightieth*
**81.** einundachtzigste *eighty-first*
**90.** neunzigste *ninetieth*
**100.** hundertste (*one*) *hundredth*
**101.** hundert(und)erste (*one*) *hundred and first*
**200.** zweihundertste *two hundredth*
**300.** dreihundertste *three hundredth*
**572.** fünfhundert(und)zweiundsiebzigste *five hundred and seventy-second*
**1000.** tausendste (*one*) *thousandth*
**1970.** neunzehnhundert(und)siebzigste *nineteen hundred and seventieth*
**500 000.** fünfhunderttausendste *five hundred thousandth*
**1 000 000.** millionste (*one*) *millionth*

## Fractional Numbers and other Numerical Values

$\frac{1}{2}$ halb *one* or *a half*
$\frac{1}{2}$ eine halbe Meile *half a mile*
$1\frac{1}{2}$ anderthalb *or* eineinhalb *one and a half*
$2\frac{1}{2}$ zweieinhalb *two and a half*
$\frac{1}{3}$ ein Drittel *one* or *a third*
$\frac{2}{3}$ zwei Drittel *two thirds*
$\frac{1}{4}$ ein Viertel *one* or *a fourth*, *one* or *a quarter*
$\frac{3}{4}$ drei Viertel *three fourths*, *three quarters*
$1\frac{1}{4}$ ein und eine viertel Stunde *one hour and a quarter*
$\frac{1}{5}$ ein Fünftel *one* or *a fifth*
$3\frac{4}{5}$ drei vier Fünftel *three and four fifths*
0,4 null Komma vier *point four* (*.4*)
2,5 zwei Komma fünf *two point five* (*2.5*)

einfach *single*
zweifach *double*, *twofold*
dreifach *threefold*, *treble*, *triple*
vierfach *fourfold*, *quadruple*
fünffach *fivefold*, *quintuple*

einmal *once*
zweimal *twice*
drei-, vier-, fünfmal *three* or *four* or *five times*
zweimal so viel (so viele) *twice as much* (*many*)

erstens, zweitens, drittens *first*(*ly*), *secondly*, *thirdly*; *in the first* or *second* or *third place*

$2 \times 3 = 6$ zwei mal drei ist sechs, zwei multipliziert mit drei ist sechs *two threes are six*, *two multiplied by three is six*

$7 + 8 = 15$ sieben plus acht ist fünfzehn *seven plus eight is fifteen*

$10 - 3 = 7$ zehn minus drei ist sieben *ten minus three is seven*

$20 : 5 = 4$ zwanzig (dividiert) durch fünf ist vier *twenty divided by five is four*

# German Weights and Measures

## I Linear Measure

**1 mm** ***Millimeter*** millimeter, *Br* millimetre
= $\frac{1}{1000}$ meter (*Br* metre)
= 0.003 feet
= 0.039 inches

**1 cm** ***Zentimeter*** centimeter, *Br* centimetre
= $\frac{1}{100}$ meter (*Br* metre)
= 0.39 inches

**1 dm** ***Dezimeter*** decimeter, *Br* decimetre
= $\frac{1}{10}$ meter (*Br* metre)
= 3.94 inches

**1 m** ***Meter*** meter, *Br* metre
= 1.094 yards
= 3.28 feet
= 39.37 inches

**1 km** ***Kilometer*** kilometer, *Br* kilometre
= 1,000 meters (*Br* metres)
= 1,093.637 yards
= 0.621 (statute) miles

**1 sm** ***Seemeile*** nautical mile
= 1,852 meters (*Br* metres)

## II Square Measure

**1 mm²** ***Quadratmillimeter*** square millimeter (*Br* millimetre)
= 0.0015 square inches

**1 cm²** ***Quadratzentimeter*** square centimeter (*Br* centimetre)
= 0.155 square inches

**1 m²** ***Quadratmeter*** square meter (*Br* metre)
= 1.195 square yards
= 10.76 square feet

**1 a** ***Ar*** are
= 100 square meters (*Br* metres)
= 119.59 square yards
= 1,076.41 square feet

**1 ha** ***Hektar*** hectare
= 100 ares
= 10,000 square meters (*Br* metres)
= 11,959.90 square yards
= 2.47 acres

**1 km²** ***Quadratkilometer*** square kilometer (*Br* kilometre)
= 100 hectares
= 1,000,000 square meters (*Br* metres)
= 247.11 acres
= 0.386 square miles

## III Cubic Measure

**1 cm³** ***Kubikzentimeter*** cubic centimeter (*Br* centimetre)
= 1,000 cubic millimeters (*Br* millimetres)
= 0.061 cubic inches

**1 dm³** ***Kubikdezimeter*** cubic decimeter (*Br* decimetre)
= 1,000 cubic centimeters (*Br* centimetres)
= 61.025 cubic inches

**1 m³** ***Kubikmeter***
**1 rm** ***Raummeter***
**1 fm** ***Festmeter***
} cubic meter (*Br* metre)
= 1,000 cubic decimeters (*Br* decimetres)
= 1.307 cubic yards
= 35.31 cubic feet

**1 RT** ***Registertonne*** register ton
= 2.832 m³
= 100 cubic feet

## IV Measure of Capacity

**1 l** ***Liter*** liter, *Br* litre
= 10 deciliters (*Br* decilitres)
= 2.11 pints (*Am*)
= 8.45 gills (*Am*)
= 1.06 quarts (*Am*)
= 0.26 gallons (*Am*)
= 1.76 pints (*Br*)
= 7.04 gills (*Br*)
= 0.88 quarts (*Br*)
= 0.22 gallons (*Br*)

**1 hl** ***Hektoliter*** hectoliter, *Br* hectolitre
= 100 liters (*Br* litres)
= 26.42 gallons (*Am*)
= 2.84 bushels (*Am*)
= 22.009 gallons (*Br*)
= 2.75 bushels (*Br*)

## V Weight

**1 mg** ***Milligramm*** milligram(me)
= 1/1000 gram(me)
= 0.015 grains

**1 g** ***Gramm*** gram(me)
= 1/1000 kilogram(me)
= 15.43 grains

**1 Pfd** ***Pfund*** pound (German)
= ½ kilogram(me)
= 500 gram(me)s
= 1.102 pounds (lb)

**1 kg** ***Kilogramm, Kilo*** kilogram(me)
= 1,000 gram(me)s
= 2.204 pounds (lb)

**1 Ztr.** ***Zentner*** centner
= 100 pounds (German)
= 50 kilogram(me)s
= 110.23 pounds (lb)
= 1.102 US hundredweights
= 0.98 British hundredweights

**1 t** ***Tonne*** ton
= 1,000 kilogram(me)s
= 1.102 US tons
= 0.984 British tons

# Conversion Tables for Temperatures

| °C (Celsius) | °F (Fahrenheit) |
|---|---|
| 100 | 212 |
| 95 | 203 |
| 90 | 194 |
| 85 | 185 |
| 80 | 176 |
| 75 | 167 |
| 70 | 158 |
| 65 | 149 |
| 60 | 140 |
| 55 | 131 |
| 50 | 122 |
| 45 | 113 |
| 40 | 104 |
| 35 | 95 |
| 30 | 86 |
| 25 | 77 |
| 20 | 68 |
| 15 | 59 |
| 10 | 50 |
| 5 | 41 |
| 0 | 32 |
| −5 | 23 |
| −10 | 14 |
| −15 | 5 |
| −17.8 | 0 |
| −20 | −4 |
| −25 | −13 |
| −30 | −22 |
| −35 | −31 |
| −40 | −40 |
| −45 | −49 |
| −50 | −58 |

# Clinical Thermometer

| °C (Celsius) | °F (Fahrenheit) |
|---|---|
| 42.0 | 107.6 |
| 41.8 | 107.2 |
| 41.6 | 106.9 |
| 41.4 | 106.5 |
| 41.2 | 106.2 |
| 41.0 | 105.8 |
| 40.8 | 105.4 |
| 40.6 | 105.1 |
| 40.4 | 104.7 |
| 40.2 | 104.4 |
| 40.0 | 104.0 |
| 39.8 | 103.6 |
| 39.6 | 103.3 |
| 39.4 | 102.9 |
| 39.2 | 102.6 |
| 39.0 | 102.2 |
| 38.8 | 101.8 |
| 38.6 | 101.5 |
| 38.4 | 101.1 |
| 38.2 | 100.8 |
| 38.0 | 100.4 |
| 37.8 | 100.0 |
| 37.6 | 99.7 |
| 37.4 | 99.3 |
| 37.2 | 99.0 |
| 37.0 | 98.6 |
| 36.8 | 98.2 |
| 36.6 | 97.9 |

**Rules for Conversion**

$$°F = \frac{9}{5}\,°C + 32$$

$$°C = (°F - 32)\frac{5}{9}$$

# Alphabetical List of the German Irregular Verbs

### Infinitive – Past Tense – Past Participle

**backen** – backte – gebacken
**bedingen** – bedang (bedingte) – bedungen (*conditional*: bedingt)
**befehlen** – befahl – befohlen
**beginnen** – begann – begonnen
**beißen** – biss – gebissen
**bergen** – barg – geborgen
**bersten** – barst – geborsten
**bewegen** – bewog – bewogen
**biegen** – bog – gebogen
**bieten** – bot – geboten
**binden** – band – gebunden
**bitten** – bat – gebeten
**blasen** – blies – geblasen
**bleiben** – blieb – geblieben
**bleichen** – blich – geblichen
**braten** – briet – gebraten
**brauchen** – brauchte – gebraucht (*v*/*aux* brauchen)
**brechen** – brach – gebrochen
**brennen** – brannte – gebrannt
**bringen** – brachte – gebracht
**denken** – dachte – gedacht
**dreschen** – drosch – gedroschen
**dringen** – drang – gedrungen
**dürfen** – durfte – gedurft (*v*/*aux* dürfen)
**empfehlen** – empfahl – empfohlen
**erlöschen** – erlosch – erloschen
**erschrecken** – erschrak – erschrocken
**essen** – aß – gegessen
**fahren** – fuhr – gefahren
**fallen** – fiel – gefallen
**fangen** – fing – gefangen
**fechten** – focht – gefochten
**finden** – fand – gefunden
**flechten** – flocht – geflochten
**fliegen** – flog – geflogen
**fliehen** – floh – geflohen
**fließen** – floss – geflossen
**fressen** – fraß – gefressen
**frieren** – fror – gefroren
**gären** – gor (*esp fig* gärte) – gegoren (*esp fig* gegärt)
**gebären** – gebar – geboren
**geben** – gab – gegeben
**gedeihen** – gedieh – gediehen
**gehen** – ging – gegangen
**gelingen** – gelang – gelungen
**gelten** – galt – gegolten
**genesen** – genas – genesen
**genießen** – genoss – genossen
**geschehen** – geschah – geschehen
**gewinnen** – gewann – gewonnen
**gießen** – goss – gegossen
**gleichen** – glich – geglichen
**gleiten** – glitt – geglitten
**glimmen** – glomm – geglommen
**graben** – grub – gegraben
**greifen** – griff – gegriffen
**haben** – hatte – gehabt
**halten** – hielt – gehalten
**hängen** – hing – gehangen
**hauen** – haute (hieb) – gehauen
**heben** – hob – gehoben
**heißen** – hieß – geheißen
**helfen** – half – geholfen
**kennen** – kannte – gekannt
**klingen** – klang – geklungen
**kneifen** – kniff – gekniffen
**kommen** – kam – gekommen
**können** – konnte – gekonnt (*v*/*aux* können)
**kriechen** – kroch – gekrochen
**laden** – lud – geladen
**lassen** – ließ – gelassen (*v*/*aux* lassen)
**laufen** – lief – gelaufen
**leiden** – litt – gelitten
**leihen** – lieh – geliehen
**lesen** – las – gelesen
**liegen** – lag – gelegen
**lügen** – log – gelogen
**mahlen** – mahlte – gemahlen
**meiden** – mied – gemieden
**melken** – melkte (molk) – gemolken (gemelkt)
**messen** – maß – gemessen
**misslingen** – misslang – misslungen
**mögen** – mochte – gemocht (*v*/*aux* mögen)
**müssen** – musste – gemusst (*v*/*aux* müssen)
**nehmen** – nahm – genommen
**nennen** – nannte – genannt

**pfeifen** – pfiff – gepfiffen
**preisen** – pries – gepriesen
**quellen** – quoll – gequollen
**raten** – riet – geraten
**reiben** – rieb – gerieben
**reißen** – riss – gerissen
**reiten** – ritt – geritten
**rennen** – rannte – gerannt
**riechen** – roch – gerochen
**ringen** – rang – gerungen
**rinnen** – rann – geronnen
**rufen** – rief – gerufen
**salzen** – salzte – gesalzen (gesalzt)
**saufen** – soff – gesoffen
**saugen** – sog – gesogen
**schaffen** – schuf – geschaffen
**schallen** – schallte (scholl) – geschallt (*for* **erschallen** *a.* erschollen)
**scheiden** – schied – geschieden
**scheinen** – schien – geschienen
**scheißen** – schiss – geschissen
**scheren** – schor – geschoren
**schieben** – schob – geschoben
**schießen** – schoss – geschossen
**schinden** – schund – geschunden
**schlafen** – schlief – geschlafen
**schlagen** – schlug – geschlagen
**schleichen** – schlich – geschlichen
**schleifen** – schliff – geschliffen
**schließen** – schloss – geschlossen
**schlingen** – schlang – geschlungen
**schmeißen** – schmiss – geschmissen
**schmelzen** – schmolz – geschmolzen
**schneiden** – schnitt – geschnitten
**schrecken** – schrak – *rare* geschrocken
**schreiben** – schrieb – geschrieben
**schreien** – schrie – geschrie(e)n
**schreiten** – schritt – geschritten
**schweigen** – schwieg – geschwiegen
**schwellen** – schwoll – geschwollen
**schwimmen** – schwamm – geschwommen
**schwinden** – schwand – geschwunden
**schwingen** – schwang – geschwungen
**schwören** – schwor – geschworen
**sehen** – sah – gesehen
**sein** – war – gewesen
**senden** – sandte – gesandt
**sieden** – sott – gesotten
**singen** – sang – gesungen
**sinken** – sank – gesunken
**sinnen** – sann – gesonnen
**sitzen** – saß – gesessen
**sollen** – sollte – gesollt (*v/aux* sollen)
**spalten** – spaltete – gespalten (gespaltet)
**speien** – spie – gespie(e)n
**spinnen** – spann – gesponnen
**sprechen** – sprach – gesprochen
**sprießen** – spross – gesprossen
**springen** – sprang – gesprungen
**stechen** – stach – gestochen
**stecken** – steckte (stak) – gesteckt
**stehen** – stand – gestanden
**stehlen** – stahl – gestohlen
**steigen** – stieg – gestiegen
**sterben** – starb – gestorben
**stinken** – stank – gestunken
**stoßen** – stieß – gestoßen
**streichen** – strich – gestrichen
**streiten** – stritt – gestritten
**tragen** – trug – getragen
**treffen** – traf – getroffen
**treiben** – trieb – getrieben
**treten** – trat – getreten
**trinken** – trank – getrunken
**trügen** – trog – getrogen
**tun** – tat – getan
**verderben** – verdarb – verdorben
**verdrießen** – verdross – verdrossen
**vergessen** – vergaß – vergessen
**verlieren** – verlor – verloren
**verschleißen** – verschliss – verschlissen
**verzeihen** – verzieh – verziehen
**wachsen** – wuchs – gewachsen
**wägen** – wog (*rare* wägte) – gewogen (*rare* gewägt)
**waschen** – wusch – gewaschen
**weben** – wob – gewoben
**weichen** – wich – gewichen
**weisen** – wies – gewiesen
**wenden** – wandte – gewandt
**werben** – warb – geworben
**werden** – wurde – geworden (worden*)
**werfen** – warf – geworfen
**wiegen** – wog – gewogen
**winden** – wand – gewunden
**wissen** – wusste – gewusst
**wollen** – wollte – gewollt (*v/aux* wollen)
**wringen** – wrang – gewrungen
**ziehen** – zog – gezogen
**zwingen** – zwang – gezwungen

* only in connection with the past participles of other verbs, *e.g.* ***er ist gesehen worden*** he has been seen.

# Alphabetical List of the English Irregular Verbs

### Infinitive – Past Tense – Past Participle

**arise** – arose – arisen
**awake** – awoke – awoke*
**be** – was – been
**bear** – bore – *getragen*: borne – *geboren*: born
**beat** – beat – beaten, beat
**become** – became – become
**beget** – begot – begotten
**begin** – began – begun
**bend** – bent – bent
**bereave** – bereft* – bereft*
**beseech** – besought – besought
**bet** – bet* – bet*
**bid** – bade, bid – bidden, bid
**bide** – bode* – bided
**bind** – bound – bound
**bite** – bit – bitten
**bleed** – bled – bled
**bless** – blest* – blest*
**blow** – blew – blown
**break** – broke – broken
**breed** – bred – bred
**bring** – brought – brought
**build** – built – built
**burn** – burnt* – burnt*
**burst** – burst – burst
**buy** – bought – bought
**cast** – cast – cast
**catch** – caught – caught
**choose** – chose – chosen
**cleave** – cleft, clove* – cleft, cloven*
**cling** – clung – clung
**clothe** – clad* – clad*
**come** – came – come
**cost** – cost – cost
**creep** – crept – crept
**crow** – crew* – crowed
**cut** – cut – cut
**deal** – dealt – dealt
**dig** – dug – dug
**dive** – dived, *a.* dove – dived
**do** – did – done
**draw** – drew – drawn
**dream** – dreamt* – dreamt*
**drink** – drank – drunk
**drive** – drove – driven
**dwell** – dwelt* – dwelt*
**eat** – ate – eaten
**fall** – fell – fallen
**feed** – fed – fed
**feel** – felt – felt
**fight** – fought – fought
**find** – found – found
**fit** – fitted, *a.* fit – fitted, *a.* fit
**flee** – fled – fled
**fling** – flung – flung
**fly** – flew – flown
**forbid** – forbade – forbidden
**forget** – forgot – forgotten
**forsake** – forsook – forsaken
**freeze** – froze – frozen
**get** – got – got, *a.* gotten
**give** – gave – given
**go** – went – gone
**grind** – ground – ground
**grow** – grew – grown
**hang** – hung – hung
**have** – had – had
**hear** – heard – heard
**heave** – hove* – hove*
**hew** – hewed – hewn*
**hide** – hid – hidden
**hit** – hit – hit
**hold** – held – held
**hurt** – hurt – hurt
**keep** – kept – kept
**kneel** – knelt* – knelt*
**knit** – knit* – knit*
**know** – knew – known
**lay** – laid – laid
**lead** – led – led
**lean** – leant* – leant*
**leap** – leapt* – leapt*
**learn** – learnt* – learnt*
**leave** – left – left
**lend** – lent – lent
**let** – let – let
**lie** – lay – lain
**light** – lit* – lit*
**lose** – lost – lost
**make** – made – made
**mean** – meant – meant
**meet** – met – met
**mow** – mowed – mown*

**pay** – paid – paid
**plead** – pleaded, *a.* pled – pleaded, *a.* pled
**put** – put – put
**read** – read – read
**rid** – rid – rid
**ride** – rode – ridden
**ring** – rang – rung
**rise** – rose – risen
**run** – ran – run
**saw** – sawed – sawn*
**say** – said – said
**see** – saw – seen
**seek** – sought – sought
**sell** – sold – sold
**send** – sent – sent
**set** – set – set
**sew** – sewed – sewn*
**shake** – shook – shaken
**shave** – shaved – shaven*
**shear** – sheared – shorn
**shed** – shed – shed
**shine** – shone – shone
**shit** – shit – shit
**shoe** – shod – shod
**shoot** – shot – shot
**show** – showed – shown*
**shrink** – shrank – shrunk
**shut** – shut – shut
**sing** – sang – sung
**sink** – sank – sunk
**sit** – sat – sat
**slay** – slew – slain
**sleep** – slept – slept
**slide** – slid – slid
**sling** – slung – slung
**slink** – slunk – slunk
**slit** – slit – slit
**smell** – smelt* – smelt*
**sow** – sowed – sown*
**speak** – spoke – spoken
**speed** – sped* – sped*
**spell** – spelt* – spelt*
**spend** – spent – spent
**spill** – spilt* – spilt*
**spin** – spun – spun
**spit** – spat – spat
**split** – split – split
**spoil** – spoilt* – spoilt*
**spread** – spread – spread
**spring** – sprang, *a.* sprung – sprung
**stand** – stood – stood
**stave** – stove* – stove*
**steal** – stole – stolen
**stick** – stuck – stuck
**sting** – stung – stung
**stink** – stank, stunk – stunk
**strew** – strewed – strewn*
**stride** – strode – stridden
**strike** – struck – struck
**string** – strung – strung
**strive** – strove – striven
**swear** – swore – sworn
**sweat** – sweat* – sweat*
**sweep** – swept – swept
**swell** – swelled – swollen
**swim** – swam – swum
**swing** – swung – swung
**take** – took – taken
**teach** – taught – taught
**tear** – tore – torn
**tell** – told – told
**think** – thought – thought
**thrive** – throve* – thriven*
**throw** – threw – thrown
**thrust** – thrust – thrust
**tread** – trod – trodden, trod
**wake** – woke* – woke(n)*
**wear** – wore – worn
**weave** – wove – woven
**wed** – wedded, wed – wedded, wed
**weep** – wept – wept
**wet** – wet* – wet*
**win** – won – won
**wind** – wound – wound
**wring** – wrung – wrung
**write** – wrote – written

Irregular forms marked with asterisks (*) can be exchanged for the regular forms.

# Examples of German Declension and Conjugation

## A. Declension

Order of cases: *nom*, *gen*, *dat*, *acc*, *sg* and *pl*. – Compound nouns and adjectives (e.g. *Eisbär*, *Ausgang*, *abfällig* etc.) inflect like their last elements (*Bär*, *Gang*, *fällig*). *dem* = demonstrative, *imp* = imperative, *ind* = indicative, *perf* = perfect, *pres* = present, *pres p* = present participle, *rel* = relative, *su* = substantive.

### I. Nouns

**1** Bild ~(e)s[1] ~(e) ~
Bilder[2] ~ ~n ~

[1] **es *only*:** Geist, Geistes.
[2] **a, o, u > ä, ö, ü:** Rand, Ränder; Haupt, Häupter; Dorf; Dörfer; Wurm, Würmer.

---

**2** Reis* ~es ['-zəs] ~(e) ~
Reiser[1] ['-zɐ] ~ ~n ~

[1] **a, o > ä, ö:** Glas, Gläser ['glɛːzɐ]; Haus, Häuser ['hɔʏzɐ]; Fass, Fässer; Schloss, Schlösser.
* Fass, Fasse(s).

---

**3** Arm ~(e)s[1,2] ~(e)[1] ~
Arme[3] ~ ~n ~

[1] ***without* e:** Billard, Billard(s).
[2] **es *only*:** Maß, Maßes.
[3] **a, o, u > ä, ö, ü:** Gang, Gänge; Saal, Säle; Gebrauch, Gebräuche [gə'brɔʏçə]; Sohn, Söhne; Hut, Hüte.

---

**4** Greis[1]* ~es ['-zəs] ~(e) ~
Greise[2] ['-zə] ~ ~n ~

[1] **s > ss:** Kürbis, Kürbisse(s).
[2] **a, o, u > ä, ö, ü:** Hals, Hälse; Bass, Bässe; Schoß, Schöße; Fuchs, Füchse; Schuss, Schüsse.
* Ross, Rosse(s).

---

**5** Strahl ~(e)s[1,2] ~(e)[2] ~
Strahlen[3] ~ ~ ~

[1] **es *only*:** Schmerz, Schmerzes.
[2] ***without* e:** Juwel, Juwel(s).
[3] Sporn, Sporen.

---

**6** Lappen ~s ~ ~*
Lappen[1] ~ ~ ~

[1] **a, o > ä, ö:** Graben, Gräben; Boden, Böden.
* ***Infinitives used as nouns have no** pl*: Geschehen, Befinden etc.

---

**7** Maler ~s ~ ~
Maler[1] ~ ~n ~

[1] **a, o, u > ä, ö, ü:** Vater, Väter; Kloster, Klöster; Bruder, Brüder.

---

**8** Untertan ~s ~ ~
Untertanen[1,2] ~ ~ ~

[1] ***with change of accent*:** Pro'fessor, Profes'soren [-'soːrən]; 'Dämon ['dɛːmɔn], Dä'monen [dɛ'moːnən].
[2] *pl* **ien** [-jən]: Kolleg, Kollegien [-'leːgjən]; Mineral, Mineralien.

---

**9** Studium ~s ~ ~
Studien[1,2] ['-djən] ~ ~ ~

[1] **a *and* o(n) > en:** Drama, Dramen; Stadion, Stadien.
[2] **on *and* um > a:** Lexikon, Lexika; Neutrum, Neutra.

**10** Auge ~s ~ ~
Augen ~ ~ ~

**11** Genie ~s[1*] ~ ~
Genies[2*] ~ ~ ~

[1] ***without inflection*:** Bouillon etc.

[2] *pl* **s *or* ta:** Komma, Kommas ***or*** Kommata; ***but*:** 'Klima, Klimate [kli'ma:tə] (3).

* **s *is pronounced*:** [ʒe'ni:s].

**12** Bär* ~en[1] ~en[1] ~en[1]
Bären ~ ~ ~

[1] Herr, *sg mst* Herrn; Herz, *gen* Herzens, *acc* Herz.

* **...'log *as well as* ...'loge** (13), e.g. Biolog(e).

**13** Knabe ~n[1] ~n ~n
Knaben ~ ~ ~

[1] **ns:** Name, Namens.

**14** Trübsal ~ ~ ~
Trübsale[1,2,3] ~ ~n ~

[1] **a, o, u > ä, ö, ü:** Hand, Hände; Braut, Bräute; Not, Nöte; Luft, Lüfte; Nuss, Nüsse; ***without* e:** Tochter, Töchter; Mutter, Mütter.

[2] **s > ss:** Kenntnis, Kenntnisse; Nimbus, Nimbusse.

[3] **is *or* us > e:** Kultus, Kulte; ***with change of accent*:** Di'akonus, Dia'kone [-'ko:nə].

**15** Blume ~ ~ ~
Blumen ~ ~ ~

**...ee:** e:, *pl* e:ən, *e.g.* I'dee, I'deen.

**...ie** { ***stressed syllable*:** i:, *pl* i:ən, *e.g.* Batte'rie(n).
***unstressed syllable*:** jə, *pl* jən, *e.g.* Ar'terie(n).

**16** Frau ~ ~ ~
Frauen[1,2,3] ~ ~ ~

[1] **in > innen:** Freundin, Freundinnen.

[2] **a, is, os *and* us > en:** Firma, Firmen; Krisis, Krisen; Epos, Epen; Genius, Genien; ***with change of accent*:** 'Heros, He'roen [he'ro:ən]; Di'akonus, Dia'konen [-'ko:nən].

[3] **s > ss:** Kirmes, Kirmessen.

## II. Proper nouns

**17** ***In general proper nouns have no*** *pl*.

***The following form the*** *gen sg* ***with*** **s:**

1. ***Proper nouns without a definite article*:** Friedrichs, Paulas, (Friedrich von) Schillers, Deutschlands, Berlins;
2. ***Proper nouns, masculine and neuter*** **(*except the names of countries*)** ***with a definite article and an adjective*:** des braven Friedrichs Bruder, des jungen Deutschlands (Söhne).

***After* s, sch, ß, tz, x, *and* z *the*** *gen sg* ***ends in* -ens** *or* **' (*instead of* ' *it is more advisable to use the definite article or* von)**, e.g. die Werke des [*or* von] Sokrates, Voß *or* Sokrates', Voß' [***not*** Sokratessens, ***seldom*** Vossens] Werke; ***but*:** die Umgebung von Mainz.

***Feminine names ending in a consonant or the vowel* e *form the*** *gen sg* ***with*** **(en)s *or* (n)s; *in the*** *dat* ***and*** *acc sg* ***such names may end in*** **(e)n** (*pl* = **a**).

***If a proper noun is followed by a title, only the following forms are inflected*:**

1. ***the title when used*** with ***a definite article*:**

der Kaiser Karl (der Große)
des ~s ~ (des ~n)
etc.

| | |
|---|---|
| 2. ***the*** (***last***) ***name when used*** without ***an article***: | Kaiser Karl (der Große)<br>~ **~s** (des **~n**) etc.<br>(***but***: Herrn Lehmanns Brief). |

## III. Adjectives and participles (also used as nouns*), pronouns, etc.

**18**

| | *m* | *f* | *n* | *pl* | |
|---|---|---|---|---|---|
| **a**) gut | er[1,2] | ~e | ~es | ~e° | ***without article, after prepositions, personal pronouns, and invariables*** |
| | en** | ~er | ~en** | ~er | |
| | em | ~er | ~em | ~en | |
| | en | ~e | ~es | ~e | |
| **b**) gut | e[1,2] | ~e | ~e | ~en | ***with definite article*** (22) ***or with pronoun*** (21) |
| | en | ~en | ~en | ~en | |
| | en | ~en | ~en | ~en | |
| | en | ~e | ~e | ~en | |
| **c**) gut | er[1,2] | ~e | ~es | ~en | ***with indefinite article or with pronoun*** (20) |
| | en | ~en | ~en | ~en | |
| | en | ~en | ~en | ~en | |
| | en | ~e | ~es | ~en | |

[1] krass, krasse(r, ~s, ~st etc.).

[2] **a, o, u > ä, ö, ü *when forming the*** *comp* ***and*** *sup*: alt, älter(e, ~es etc.), ältest (der ~e, am ~en); grob, gröber(e, ~es etc.), gröbst (der ~e, am ~en); kurz, kürzer(e, ~es etc.), kürzest (der ~e, am ~en).

* e.g. Böse(r) *su*: der (die, eine) Böse, ein Böser; Böse(s) *n*: das Böse, ***without article*** Böses; ***in the same way*** Abgesandte(r) *su*, Angestellte(r) *su* etc.; ***in some cases the use varies.***

** ***Sometimes the*** *gen sg* ***ends in ~es instead of ~en:*** gutes (***or*** gut**en**) Mutes sein.

° ***In*** böse, böse(r, ~s, ~st etc.) ***one e is dropped.***

## The Grades of Comparison

***The endings of the*** *comparative* ***and*** *superlative* ***are:***

| | | | |
|---|---|---|---|
| | reich | schön | ***inflected according to*** (18²). |
| *comp* | reicher | schöner | |
| *sup* | reichst | schönst | |

***After vowels*** (***except* e** [18°]) ***and after*** d, s, sch, ß, st, t, tz, x, y, z ***the*** *sup* ***ends in ~est, but in unstressed syllables after* d, sch *and* t *generally in* ~st:** blau, 'blau**est**; rund, 'rund**est**; rasch, 'rasch**est** etc.; ***but***: 'dringend, 'dringend**st**; 'närrisch, 'närrisch**st**; ge'eignet, ge'eignet**st**.

*Note.* — ***The adjectives ending in ~el, ~en (except ~nen) and ~er*** (e.g. dunk**el**, eb**en**, heit**er**), ***and also the possessive adjectives*** uns**er** ***and*** eu**er** ***generally drop* e.**

| ***Inflection:*** | **~e** | **~em** | **~en** | **~er** | **~es,** ***and*** |
|---|---|---|---|---|---|
| **~el** > | ~le | ~lem* | ~len* | ~ler | ~les |
| **~en** > | ~(e)ne | ~(e)nem | ~(e)nen | ~(e)ner° | ~(e)nes |
| **~er** > | ~(e)re | ~rem* | ~ren* | ~(e)rer° | ~(e)res |

* ***or*** ~elm, ~eln, ~erm, ~ern; e.g. **dunk|el:** ~le, ~lem (***or*** ~elm), ~len (***or*** ~eln), ~ler, ~les; **eb|en:** ~(e)ne, ~(e)nem etc.; **heit|er:** ~(e)re, ~rem (***or*** ~erm) etc.

° ***The inflected*** *comp* ***ends in*** ~ner ***and*** ~rer ***only:*** eben, ebnere(r, ~s etc.); heiter, heitrere(r, ~s etc.); ***but*** *sup* ebenst, heiterst.

## 19

| | ***1st pers.*** *m, f, n* | ***2nd pers.*** *m, f, n* | ***3rd pers.*** *m* | *f* | *n* |
|---|---|---|---|---|---|
| *sg* | ich | du | er | sie | es |
| | meiner* | deiner* | seiner* | ihrer | seiner* |
| | mir | dir | ihm | ihr | ihm° |
| | mich | dich | ihn | sie | es° |
| *pl* | wir | ihr | sie | | (Sie) |
| | unser | euer | ihrer | | (Ihrer) |
| | uns | euch | ihnen | | (Ihnen)° |
| | uns | euch | sie | | (Sie)° |

* ***In poetry sometimes without inflection:*** gedenke mein!; ***also*** **es** ***instead of*** seiner *n* (= *e-r Sache*): ich bin es überdrüssig.

° ***Reflexive form:*** sich.

## 20

| *m* | | *f* | *n* | *pl* |
|---|---|---|---|---|
| mein | | ~e | ~ | ~e* |
| dein | es | ~er | ~es | ~er |
| sein | em | ~er | ~em | ~en |
| (k)ein | en | ~e | ~ | ~e |

* ***The indefinite article*** ein ***has no*** *pl.* — ***In poetry*** mein, dein ***and*** sein ***may stand behind the*** *su* ***without inflection:*** die Mutter (Kinder) mein, ***or as predicate:*** *der Hut* [*die Tasche, das Buch*] *ist* mein; ***without*** *su*: meiner *m*, meine *f*, mein(e)s *n*, meine *pl* etc.: *wem gehört der Hut* [*die Tasche, das Buch*]? *es ist* meiner (meine, mein[e]s); ***or with definite article:*** der (die, das) meine, *pl* die meinen (18b). ***Regarding*** unser ***and*** euer ***see note*** (18).

[1] **welche(r, s)** ***as*** *rel pron*: *gen sg* dessen, deren, *gen pl* deren, *dat pl* denen (23).

* ***Used as*** *su*, dies ***is preferable to*** dieses.

** manch, solch, welch ***frequently are uninflected:***

| | | | |
|---|---|---|---|
| manch | gut**er** | (ein gut**er**) | Mann |
| solch | **~en** | ( **~es** **~en**) | **~es** |
| welch | **~em** | ( **~em** **~en**) | **~e** |

etc. (18)

***Similarly*** all:

| | | |
|---|---|---|
| all der | (dies**er**, mein ) | Schmerz |
| ~ des | ( **~es**, **~es**) | **~es** |

## 21

| *m* | | *f* | *n* | *pl* |
|---|---|---|---|---|
| dies | er | ~e | ~es* | ~e** |
| jen | es | ~er | ~es | ~er[1] |
| manch | em | ~er | ~em | ~en[1] |
| welch | en | ~e | ~es* | ~e |

## 22

| *m* | *f* | *n* | *pl* | |
|---|---|---|---|---|
| der | die | das | die[1] | ***definite article*** |
| des | der | des | der | |
| dem | der | dem | den | |
| den | die | das | die | |

[1] derjenige, derselbe — desjenigen, demjenigen, desselben, demselben etc. (18b).

## 23 *Relative pronoun*

| *m* | *f* | *n* | *pl* |
|---|---|---|---|
| der | die | das | die |
| dessen* | deren | dessen* | deren[1] |
| dem | der | dem | denen |
| den | die | das | die |

[1] ***also*** derer, ***when used as*** *dem pron*
* ***also*** des.

## 24

| wer | was | jemand, niemand |
|---|---|---|
| wessen* | wessen | ~(e)s |
| wem | — | ~(em°) |
| wen | was | ~(en°) |

* ***also*** wes.
° ***preferably without inflection.***

# B. Conjugation

In the conjugation tables (25–30) only the simple verbs may be found; in the alphabetical list of the German irregular verbs compound verbs are only included when no simple verb exists (e.g. **beginnen;** *ginnen* does not exist). In order to find the conjugation of any compound verb (with separable or inseparable prefix, regular or irregular) look up the respective simple verb.

Verbs with separable and stressed prefixes such as **'ab-, 'an-, 'auf-, 'aus-, 'bei-, be'vor-, 'dar-, 'ein-, em'por-, ent'gegen-, 'fort-, 'her-, he'rab-** etc. and also *'klar-[legen], 'los-[schießen], 'sitzen [bleiben], über'hand [nehmen]* etc. (but not the verbs derived from compound nouns as *be'antragen* or *be'ratschlagen* from *Antrag* and *Ratschlag* etc.) take the preposition **zu** (in the *inf* and the *pres p*) and the syllable **ge** (in the *pp* and in the passive voice) between the stressed prefix and their root.

Verbs with inseparable and unstressed prefixes such as **be-, emp-, ent-, er-, ge-, ver-, zer-** and generally **miss-** (in spite of its being stressed) take the preposition **zu** before the prefix and drop the syllable **ge** in the *pp* and in the passive voice. The prefixes **durch-, hinter-, über-, um-, unter-, voll-, wi(e)der-** are separable when stressed and inseparable when unstressed, e.g.

**geben:** *zu geben, zu gebend; gegeben; ich gebe, du gibst* etc.;

**'abgeben:** *'abzugeben, 'abzugebend; 'abgegeben; ich gebe* (*du gibst* etc.) *ab*;

**ver'geben:** *zu ver'geben, zu ver'gebend; ver'geben; ich ver'gebe, du ver'gibst* etc.;

**'umgehen:** *'umzugehen, 'umzugehend; 'umgegangen; ich gehe* (*du gehst* etc.) *um*;

**um'gehen:** *zu um'gehen, zu um'gehend; um'gangen; ich um'gehe, du um'gehst* etc.

The same rules apply to verbs with two prefixes, e.g.

**zu'rückbehalten** [see *halten*]: *zu'rückzubehalten, zu'rückzubehaltend; zu'rückbehalten; ich behalte* (*du behältst* etc.) *zurück*;

**wieder 'aufheben** [see *heben*]: *wieder 'aufzuheben, wieder 'aufzuhebend; wieder 'aufgehoben; ich hebe* (*du hebst* etc.) *wieder auf.*

The forms in parentheses ( ) follow the same rules.

## a) 'Weak' Conjugation

### 25 loben

| | | | |
|---|---|---|---|
| *pres ind* | lobe | lobst | lobt |
| | loben | lobt | loben |
| *pres subj* | lobe | lobest | lobe |
| | loben | lobet | loben |
| *pret ind* and *subj* | lobte | lobtest | lobte |
| | lobten | lobtet | lobten |

*imp sg* lob(e), *pl* lob(e)t, loben Sie; *inf pres* loben; *inf perf* gelobt haben; *pres p* lobend; *pp* gelobt (18; 29**).

### 26 reden

| | | | |
|---|---|---|---|
| *pres ind* | rede | redest | redet |
| | reden | redet | reden |
| *pres subj* | rede | redest | rede |
| | reden | redet | reden |
| *pret ind* and *subj* | redete | redetest | redete |
| | redeten | redetet | redeten |

*imp sg* rede, *pl* redet, reden Sie; *inf pres* reden; *inf perf* geredet haben; *pres p* redend; *pp* geredet (18; 29**).

### 27 reisen

| | | | |
|---|---|---|---|
| *pres ind* | reise | rei(se)st* | reist |
| | reisen | reist | reisen |
| *pres subj* | reise | reisest | reise |
| | reisen | reiset | reisen |
| *pret ind* and *subj* | reiste | reistest | reisten |
| | reisten | reistet | reisten |

*imp sg* reise, *pl* reist, reisen Sie; *inf pres* reisen; *inf perf* gereist sein *or now rare* haben; *pres p* reisend; *pp* gereist (18; 29**).

* **sch:** naschen, nasch(e)st; **ß:** spaßen, spaßt (spaßest); **tz:** ritzen, ritzt (ritzest); **x:** hexen, hext (hexest); **z:** reizen, reizt (reizest); faulenzen, faulenzt (faulenzest).

### 28 fassen

| | | | |
|---|---|---|---|
| *pres ind* | fasse | fasst (fassest) | fasst |
| | fassen | fasst | fassen |
| *pres subj* | fasse | fassest | fasse |
| | fassen | fasset | fassen |
| *pret ind* and *subj* | fasste | fasstest | fasste |
| | fassten | fasstet | fassten |

*imp sg* fasse (fass), *pl* fasst, fassen Sie; *inf pres* fassen; *inf perf* gefasst haben; *pres p* fassend; *pp* gefasst (18; 29**).

### 29 handeln

| | | |
|---|---|---|
| | *pres ind* | |
| handle* | handelst | handelt |
| handeln | handelt | handeln |
| | *pres subj* | |
| handle* | handelst | handle* |
| handeln | handelt | handeln |
| | *pret ind* and *subj* | |
| handelte | handeltest | handelte |
| handelten | handeltet | handelten |

*imp sg* handle, *pl* handelt, handeln Sie; *inf pres* handeln; *inf perf* gehandelt haben; *pres p* handelnd; *pp* gehandelt (18).

* ***Also*** handele; wandern, wand(e)re; bessern, bessere (bessre); donnern, donnere.

** ***Without* ge*, when the first syllable is unstressed,*** e.g. be'grüßen, be'grüßt; ent'stehen, ent'standen; stu'dieren, stu'diert (***not*** gestudiert); trom'peten, trom'petet (***also when preceded by a stressed prefix:*** 'austrompeten, 'austrompetet, ***not*** 'ausgetrompetet). ***In some weak verbs the** pp **ends in* en *instead of* t,** e.g. mahlen, gemahlen. ***With the verbs*** brauchen, dürfen, heißen, helfen, hören, können, lassen, lehren, lernen, machen, mögen, müssen, sehen, sollen, wollen ***the** pp **is replaced by** inf **(without*** ge***), when used in connection with another** inf*, e.g. ich habe ihn singen hören, du hättest es tun können, er hat gehen müssen, ich hätte ihn laufen lassen sollen.

## b) 'Strong' Conjugation

### 30 fahren

| | | | |
|---|---|---|---|
| *pres ind* | fahre | fährst | fährt |
| | fahren | fahrt | fahren |
| *pres subj* | fahre | fahrest | fahre |
| | fahren | fahret | fahren |
| *pret ind* | fuhr | fuhr(e)st | fuhr |
| | fuhren | fuhrt | fuhren |
| *pret subj* | führe | führest | führe |
| | führen | führet | führen |

*imp sg* fahr(e), *pl* fahr(e)t, fahren Sie; *inf pres* fahren; *inf perf* gefahren haben **or** sein; *pres p* fahrend; *pp* gefahren (18; 29**).

# Proper Names

**Aachen** ['a:xən] Aachen, Aix-la-Chapelle
**Adler** ['a:dlɐ] *Austrian psychologist*
**Adria** ['a:dria]: ***die*** ~ the Adriatic (Sea)
**Afrika** ['a:frika] Africa
**Ägäis** [ɛ'gɛ:ɪs]: ***die*** ~ the Aegean (Sea)
**Ägypten** [ɛ'gʏptən] Egypt
**Albanien** [al'ba:njən] Albania
**Algerien** [al'ge:rjən] Algeria
**Algier** ['alʒi:ɐ] Algiers
**Allgäu** ['algɔʏ]: ***das*** ~ the Al(l)gäu (*region of Bavaria, Germany*)
**Alpen** ['alpən]: ***die*** ~ *pl* the Alps
**Amerika** [a'me:rika] America
**Anden** ['andən]: ***die*** ~ *pl* the Andes
**Antillen** [an'tɪlən]: ***die*** ~ *pl* the Antilles
**Antwerpen** [ant'vɛrpən] Antwerp
**Apenninen** [ape'ni:nən]: ***die*** ~ *pl* the Apennines
**Argentinien** [argɛn'ti:njən] Argentina, the Argentine
**Ärmelkanal** ['ɛrməlkana:l]: ***der*** ~ the English Channel, the Channel
**Asien** ['a:zjən] Asia
**Athen** [a'te:n] Athens
**Äthiopien** [ɛ'tjo:pjən] Ethiopia
**Atlantik** [at'lantɪk]: ***der*** ~ the Atlantic (Ocean)
**Australien** [aʊs'tra:ljən] Australia

**Bach** [bax] *German composer*
**Barlach** ['barlax] *German sculptor*
**Basel** ['ba:zəl] Basel, Basle
**Bayern** ['baɪɐn] Bavaria
**Beethoven** ['be:tho:fən] *German composer*
**Belgien** ['bɛlgjən] Belgium
**Belgrad** ['bɛlgra:t] Belgrade
**Berlin** [bɛr'li:n] *German city*
**Bern** [bɛrn] Bern(e)
**Bloch** [blɔx] *German philosopher*
**Böcklin** ['bœkli:n] *German painter*
**Bodensee** ['bo:dənze:]: ***der*** ~ Lake Constance
**Böhm** [bø:m] *Austrian conductor*
**Böhmen** ['bø:mən] HIST Bohemia
**Böll** [bœl] *German author*
**Bonn** [bɔn] *German city*
**Brahms** [bra:ms] *German composer*
**Brasilien** [bra'zi:ljən] Brazil
**Braunschweig** ['braʊnʃvaɪk] Braunschweig, Brunswick
**Brecht** [brɛçt] *German dramatist*
**Bremen** ['bre:mən] *German city*
**Bruckner** ['brʊknɐ] *Austrian composer*
**Brüssel** ['brʏsəl] Brussels
**Budapest** ['bu:dapɛst] *Hungarian city*
**Bukarest** ['bu:karɛst] Bucharest
**Bulgarien** [bʊl'ga:rjən] Bulgaria

**Calais** [ka'lɛ:]: ***die Straße von*** ~ the Straits of Dover
**Calvin** [kal'vi:n] *Swiss religious reformer*
**Chile** ['tʃi:le] Chile
**China** ['çi:na] China

**Daimler** ['daɪmlɐ] *German inventor*
**Dänemark** ['dɛ:nəmark] Denmark
**Deutschland** ['dɔʏtʃlant] Germany
**Diesel** ['di:zəl] *German inventor*
**Döblin** ['dø:bli:n] *German author*
**Dolomiten** [dolo'mi:tən]: ***die*** ~ *pl* the Dolomites
**Donau** ['do:naʊ]: ***die*** ~ the Danube
**Dortmund** ['dɔrtmʊnt] *German city*
**Dresden** ['dre:sdən] *German city*
**Dünkirchen** ['dy:nkɪrçən] Dunkirk
**Dürer** ['dy:rɐ] *German painter*
**Dürrenmatt** ['dʏrənmat] *Swiss dramatist*
**Düsseldorf** ['dʏsəldɔrf] *German city*

**Egk** [ɛk] *German composer*
**Eichendorff** ['aɪçəndɔrf] *German poet*
**Eiger** ['aɪgɐ] *Swiss mountain*
**Einstein** ['aɪnʃtaɪn] *German physicist*
**Elbe** ['ɛlbə]: ***die*** ~ (*German river*)
**Elsass** ['ɛlzas]: ***das*** ~ Alsace
**England** ['ɛŋlant] England
**Essen** ['ɛsən] *German city*
**Europa** [ɔʏ'ro:pa] Europe

**Finnland** ['fɪnlant] Finland

**Florenz** [flo'rɛnts] Florence
**Fontane** [fɔn'taːnə] *German author*
**Franken** ['fraŋkən] Franconia
**Frankfurt am Main** ['fraŋkfʊrt am 'maɪn] Frankfurt on the Main
**Frankfurt an der Oder** ['fraŋkfʊrt an deːɐ 'oːdɐ] Frankfurt on the Oder
**Frankreich** ['fraŋkraɪç] France
**Freud** [frɔʏt] *Austrian psychologist*
**Frisch** [frɪʃ] *Swiss author*

**Garmisch** ['garmɪʃ] *health resort in Bavaria, Germany*
**Genf** [gɛnf] Geneva; **~er See** Lake Geneva
**Genua** ['geːnua] Genoa
**Goethe** ['gøːtə] *German poet*
**Grass** [gras] *German author*
**Griechenland** ['griːçənlant] Greece
**Grillparzer** ['grɪlpartsɐ] *Austrian dramatist*
**Grönland** ['grøːnlant] Greenland
**Gropius** ['groːpjʊs] *German architect*
**Großbritannien** [groːsbri'tanjən] (Great) Britain
**Großglockner** ['groːsglɔknɐ]: ***der*** **~** (*Austrian mountain*)
**Grünewald** ['gryːnəvalt] *German painter*

**Haag** [haːk]: ***Den*** **~** The Hague
**Hahn** [haːn] *German chemist*
**Hamburg** ['hambʊrk] *German city*
**Händel** ['hɛndəl] Handel (*German composer*)
**Hannover** [ha'noːfɐ] Hanover
**Harz** [haːɐts]: ***der*** **~** the Harz (Mountains)
**Hauptmann** ['haʊptman] *German dramatist*
**Haydn** ['haɪdən] *Austrian composer*
**Hegel** ['heːgəl] *German philosopher*
**Heidegger** ['haɪdɛgɐ] *German philosopher*
**Heidelberg** ['haɪdəlbɛrk] *German city*
**Heine** ['haɪnə] *German poet*
**Heisenberg** ['haɪzənbɛrk] *German physicist*
**Heißenbüttel** ['haɪsənbʏtəl] *German poet*
**Helgoland** ['hɛlgolant] Hel(i)goland
**Helsinki** ['hɛlzɪŋkɪ] *Finnish city*
**Hesse** ['hɛsə] *German poet*
**Hindemith** ['hɪndəmɪt] *German composer*
**Hölderlin** ['hœldəliːn] *German poet*
**Holland** ['hɔlant] Holland

**Indien** ['ɪndjən] India
**Inn** [ɪn]: ***der*** **~** (*affluent of the Danube*)
**Innsbruck** ['ɪnsbrʊk] *Austrian city*
**Irak** [i'raːk]: ***der*** **~** Iraq
**Iran** [i'raːn]: ***der*** **~** Iran
**Irland** ['ɪrlant] Ireland
**Island** ['iːslant] Iceland
**Israel** ['ɪsraɛl] Israel
**Italien** [i'taːljən] Italy

**Japan** ['jaːpan] Japan
**Jaspers** ['jaspɐs] *German philosopher*
**Jordanien** [jɔr'daːnjən] Jordan
**Jugoslawien** [jugo'slaːvjən] Yugoslavia
**Jung** [jʊŋ] *Swiss psychologist*
**Jungfrau** ['jʊŋfraʊ]: ***die*** **~** (*Swiss mountain*)

**Kafka** ['kafka] *Czech author*
**Kanada** ['kanada] Canada
**Kant** [kant] *German philosopher*
**Karlsruhe** ['karlsruːə] *German city*
**Kärnten** ['kɛrntən] Carinthia
**Kästner** ['kɛstnɐ] *German author*
**Kiel** [kiːl] *German city*
**Klee** [kleː] *Swiss-born painter*
**Kleist** [klaɪst] *German poet*
**Koblenz** ['koːblɛnts] Koblenz, Coblenz
**Kokoschka** [ko'kɔʃka] *Austrian painter*
**Köln** [kœln] Cologne
**Kolumbien** [ko'lʊmbjən] Colombia
**Kolumbus** [ko'lʊmbʊs] Columbus
**Konstanz** ['kɔnstants] Constance
**Kopenhagen** [koːpən'haːgən] Copenhagen
**Kordilleren** [kɔrdɪl'jeːrən]: ***die*** **~** *pl* the Cordilleras
**Kreml** ['kreːməl]: ***der*** **~** the Kremlin

**Leibniz** ['laɪbnɪts] *German philosopher*
**Leipzig** ['laɪptsɪç] Leipzig, Leipsic
**Lessing** ['lɛsɪŋ] *German poet*
**Libanon** ['liːbanɔn]: ***der*** **~** (the) Lebanon
**Liebig** ['liːbɪç] *German chemist*
**Lissabon** ['lɪsabɔn] Lisbon
**London** ['lɔndɔn] London
**Lothringen** ['loːtrɪŋən] Lorraine
**Lübeck** ['lyːbɛk] *German city*
**Luther** ['lʊtɐ] *German religious reformer*

**Luxemburg** ['lʊksəmbʊrk] Luxemb(o)urg
**Luzern** [lu'tsɛrn] Lucerne

**Maas** [maːs]: ***die*** ~ the Meuse, the Maas
**Madrid** [ma'drɪt] Madrid
**Mahler** ['maːlɐ] *Austrian composer*
**Mailand** ['maɪlant] Milan
**Main** [maɪn]: ***der*** ~ (*German river*)
**Mainz** [maɪnts] *German city*
**Mann** [man] *name of three German authors*
**Marokko** [ma'rɔko] Morocco
**Matterhorn** ['matɐhɔrn]: ***das*** ~ (*Swiss mountain*)
**Meißen** ['maɪsən] Meissen
**Memel** ['meːməl]: ***die*** ~ (*frontier river in East Prussia*)
**Menzel** ['mɛntsəl] *German painter*
**Mexiko** ['mɛksiko] Mexico
**Mies van der Rohe** ['miːs fan deːɐ 'roːə] *German architect*
**Mittelmeer** ['mɪtəlmeːɐ]: ***das*** ~ the Mediterranean (Sea)
**Moldau** ['mɔldaʊ]: ***die*** ~ the Vltava; HIST the Moldau (*Bohemian river*)
**Mörike** ['mørɪkə] *German poet*
**Mosel** ['moːzəl]: ***die*** ~ the Moselle
**Mössbauer** ['mœsbaʊɐ] *German physicist*
**Moskau** ['mɔskaʊ] Moscow
**Mozart** ['moːtsart] *Austrian composer*
**München** ['mʏnçən] Munich

**Neapel** [ne'aːpəl] Naples
**Neiße** ['naɪsə]: ***die*** ~ (*German river*)
**Neufundland** [nɔʏ'fʊntlant] Newfoundland
**Neuseeland** [nɔʏ'zeːlant] New Zealand
**Niederlande** ['niːdɐlandə]: ***die*** ~ *pl* the Netherlands
**Nietzsche** ['niːtʃə] *German philosopher*
**Nil** [niːl]: ***der*** ~ the Nile
**Nordamerika** ['nɔrtʔa'meːrika] North America
**Nordsee** ['nɔrtzeː]: ***die*** ~ the North Sea
**Normandie** [nɔrman'diː]: ***die*** ~ Normandy
**Norwegen** ['nɔrveːgən] Norway
**Nürnberg** ['nʏrnbɛrk] Nuremberg

**Oder** ['oːdɐ]: ***die*** ~ (*German river*)
**Orff** [ɔrf] *German composer*
**Oslo** ['ɔslo] Oslo
**Ostende** [ɔst'ʔɛndə] Ostend
**Österreich** ['øːstəraɪç] Austria
**Ostsee** ['ɔstzeː]: ***die*** ~ the Baltic (Sea)

**Palästina** [palɛs'tiːna] Palestine
**Paris** [pa'riːs] Paris
**Pfalz** [pfalts]: ***die*** ~ the Palatinate
**Philippinen** [fɪlɪ'piːnən]: ***die*** ~ *pl* the Philippines
**Planck** [plaŋk] *German physicist*
**Polen** ['poːlən] Poland
**Porsche** ['pɔrʃə] *German inventor*
**Portugal** ['pɔrtugal] Portugal
**Prag** [praːk] Prague
**Preußen** ['prɔʏsən] HIST Prussia
**Pyrenäen** [pyre'nɛːən]: ***die*** ~ *pl* the Pyrenees

**Rhein** [raɪn]: ***der*** ~ the Rhine
**Rilke** ['rɪlkə] *Austrian poet*
**Rom** [roːm] Rome
**Röntgen** ['rœntgən] *German physicist*
**Ruhr** [ruːɐ]: ***die*** ~ (*German river*); **Ruhrgebiet** ['ruːɐgəbiːt]: ***das*** ~ (*industrial center of Germany*)
**Rumänien** [ru'mɛːnjən] Rumania, Ro(u)mania
**Russland** ['rʊslant] Russia

**Saale** ['zaːlə]: ***die*** ~ (*German river*)
**Saar** [zaːɐ]: ***die*** ~ (*affluent of the Moselle*)
**Salzburg** ['zaltsbʊrk] *Austrian city*
**Schiller** ['ʃɪlɐ] *German poet*
**Schönberg** ['ʃøːnbɛrk] *Austrian composer*
**Schottland** ['ʃɔtlant] Scotland
**Schubert** ['ʃuːbɐt] *Austrian composer*
**Schumann** ['ʃuːman] *German composer*
**Schwaben** ['ʃvaːbən] Swabia
**Schwarzwald** ['ʃvartsvalt]: ***der*** ~ the Black Forest
**Schweden** ['ʃveːdən] Sweden
**Schweiz** [ʃvaɪts]: ***die*** ~ Switzerland
**Sibirien** [zi'biːrjən] Siberia
**Siemens** ['ziːməns] *German inventor*
**Sizilien** [zi'tsiːljən] Sicily
**Skandinavien** [skandi'naːvjən] Scandinavia
**Slowakei** [slova'kai]: ***die*** ~ Slovakia
**Sofia** ['zɔfja] Sofia
**Spanien** ['ʃpaːnjən] Spain
**Spitzweg** ['ʃpɪtsveːk] *German painter*

**Spranger** ['ʃpraŋɐ] *German philosopher*
**Stifter** ['ʃtɪftɐ] *Austrian author*
**Stockholm** ['ʃtɔkhɔlm] Stockholm
**Storm** [ʃtɔrm] *German poet*
**Straßburg** ['ʃtra:sbʊrk] Strasbourg
**Strauß** [ʃtraʊs] *Austrian composer*
**Strauss** [ʃtraʊs] *German composer*
**Südamerika** ['zy:tʔa'me:rika] South America
**Syrien** ['zy:rjən] Syria

**Themse** ['tɛmzə]: ***die*** ~ the Thames
**Tirol** [ti'ro:l] (the) Tyrol
**Tschechien** ['tʃɛçjən] Czech Republic
**Türkei** [tʏr'kaɪ]: ***die*** ~ Turkey

**Ungarn** ['ʊŋgarn] Hungary
**Ural** [u'ra:l]: ***der*** ~ the Urals

**Venedig** [ve'ne:dɪç] Venice
**Vereinigte Staaten (von Amerika)** [fɛr'ʔaɪnɪçtə 'ʃta:tən (fɔn a'me:rika)]: ***die Vereinigten Staaten*** (***von Amerika***) the United States (of America)
**Vierwaldstätter See** [fi:ɐ'valtʃtɛtɐ 'ze:]: ***der*** ~ Lake Lucerne

**Wagner** ['va:gnɐ] *German composer*
**Wankel** ['vaŋkəl] *German inventor*
**Warschau** ['varʃaʊ] Warsaw
**Weichsel** ['vaɪksəl]: ***die*** ~ the Vistula
**Weiß** [vaɪs] *German dramatist*
**Werfel** ['vɛrfəl] *Austrian author*
**Weser** ['ve:zɐ]: ***die*** ~ (*German river*)
**Wien** [vi:n] Vienna
**Wiesbaden** ['vi:sba:dən] German city

**Zuckmayer** ['tsʊkmaɪɐ] *German dramatist*
**Zweig** [tsvaɪk] *Austrian author*
**Zürich** ['tsy:rɪç] Zurich
**Zypern** ['tsy:pɐn] Cyprus

# German Abbreviations

**Abb.** ***Abbildung*** illustration
**Abf.** ***Abfahrt*** departure, ABBR dep.
**Abt.** ***Abteilung*** department, ABBR dept.
**a. D.** ***außer Dienst*** retired
**ADAC** ***Allgemeiner Deutscher Automobil-Club*** General German Automobile Association
**AG** ***Aktiengesellschaft*** (stock) corporation, joint-stock company
**allg.** ***allgemein*** general
**Ank.** ***Ankunft*** arrival
**atü** ***Atmosphärenüberdruck*** atmospheric excess pressure

**Bd.** ***Band*** volume, ABBR vol.; **Bde.** ***Bände*** volumes, ABBR vols.
**Betr.** ***Betreff, betrifft*** *letter*: subject, re
**BRD** ***Bundesrepublik Deutschland*** Federal Republic of Germany

**CDU** ***Christlich-Demokratische Union*** Christian Democratic Union
**CSU** ***Christlich-Soziale Union*** Christian Social Union

**DB** ***Deutsche Bundesbahn*** German Federal Railway
**DDR** HIST ***Deutsche Demokratische Republik*** German Democratic Republic
**DGB** ***Deutscher Gewerkschaftsbund*** Federation of German Trade Unions
**d. h.** ***das heißt*** that is, ABBR i. e.
**DIN** ***Deutsche Industrie-Norm(en)*** German Industrial Standards
**DM** ***Deutsche Mark*** German Mark(s)
**dpa** ***Deutsche Presse-Agentur*** German Press Agency
**Dr.** ***Doktor*** Doctor, ABBR Dr.
**DRK** ***Deutsches Rotes Kreuz*** German Red Cross

**EDV** ***Elektronische Datenverarbeitung*** electronic data processing, ABBR EDP
**EG** ***Europäische Gemeinschaft*** European Community, ABBR EC
**EM** ***Europameisterschaft*** European championship(s)
**e. V.** ***eingetragener Verein*** registered association, incorporated, ABBR inc.

**FDP** ***Freie Demokratische Partei*** Liberal Democratic Party
**Forts.** ***Fortsetzung*** continuation

**geb.** ***geboren*** born; ***geborene ...*** née; ***gebunden*** bound
**Ges.** ***Gesellschaft*** association, company; society
**gez.** ***gezeichnet*** signed, ABBR sgd
**GmbH** ***Gesellschaft mit beschränkter Haftung*** private limited liability company

**h. c.** ***honoris causa*** = ehrenhalber; *academic title*: honorary
**Hrsg.** ***Herausgeber*** editor, ABBR ed.

**i. A.** ***im Auftrage*** for, by order, under instruction
**Ing.** ***Ingenieur*** engineer
**Inh.** ***Inhaber*** proprietor
**inkl.** ***inklusive, einschließlich*** inclusive
**'Interpol** ***Internationale Kriminalpolizeiliche Organisation*** International Criminal Police Commission
**IOK** ***Internationales Olympisches Komitee*** International Olympic Committee, ABBR IOC
**ISBN** ***Internationale Standardbuchnummer*** international standard book number, ABBR ISBN
**i. V.** ***in Vertretung*** by proxy, as a substitute

**jr., jun.** ***junior, der Jüngere*** junior ABBR jr, jun.

**Kat** ***Katalysator*** catalytic converter, catalyst, ABBR cat.
**Kfm.** ***Kaufmann*** merchant

**Kfz.** ***Kraftfahrzeug*** motor vehicle
**KG** ***Kommanditgesellschaft*** limited partnership
**Kl.** ***Klasse*** class; *school*: form
**'Kripo** ***Kriminalpolizei*** Criminal Investigation Department, ABBR CID
**Kto.** ***Konto*** account, ABBR a/c

**lfd.** ***laufend*** current, running
**Lfg., Lfrg.** ***Lieferung*** delivery; instal(l)ment, part
**Lit.** ***Literatur*** literature
**Lkw, LKW** ***Lastkraftwagen*** truck, lorry
**lt.** ***laut*** according to

**MdB** ***Mitglied des Bundestages*** Member of the Bundestag
**MEZ** ***mitteleuropäische Zeit*** Central European Time
**MS, Ms.** ***Manuskript*** manuscript, ABBR MS, ms.
**mtl.** ***monatlich*** monthly

**n. Chr.** ***nach Christus*** after Christ, ABBR AD
**No., Nr.** ***Numero, Nummer*** number, ABBR No., no
**NS** ***Nachschrift*** postscript, ABBR PS

**o. B.** ***ohne Befund*** MED without findings
**OEZ** ***osteuropäische Zeit*** Eastern European Time, ABBR EET

**PDS** ***Partei des Demokratischen Sozialismus*** Party of Democratic Socialism
**Pf** ***Pfennig*** *German coin*: pfennig
**Pfd.** ***Pfund*** *German weight*: pound
**PKW, Pkw** ***Personenkraftwagen*** car
**PLZ** ***Postleitzahl*** zip code, *Br* postcode
**Prof.** ***Professor*** professor
**PS** ***Pferdestärke(n)*** horse-power, ABBR HP, h.p.; ***postscriptum, Nachschrift*** postscript, ABBR PS

**Rel.** ***Religion*** religion

**S.** ***Seite*** page
**s.** ***siehe*** see, ABBR v., vid. (= vide)
**Sa.** ***Summa, Summe*** sum, total
**sen.** ***senior, der Ältere*** senior
**s. o.** ***siehe oben*** see above
**sog.** ***so genannt*** so-called
**SPD** ***Sozialdemokratische Partei Deutschlands*** Social Democratic Party of Germany
**St.** ***Stück*** piece; ***Sankt*** Saint
**Std.** ***Stunde*** hour, ABBR h
**Str.** ***Straße*** street, ABBR St.
**StVO** ***Straßenverkehrsordnung*** (road) traffic regulations, *in GB*: Highway Code
**s. u.** ***siehe unten*** see below

**tägl.** ***täglich*** daily, per day
**Tel.** ***Telefon*** telephone; ***Telegramm*** wire, cable
**TH** ***Technische Hochschule*** college *or* institute of technology
**TU** ***Technische Universität*** technical university; college *or* institute of technology
**TÜV** ***Technischer Überwachungs-Verein*** safety standards authority

**u. a.** ***und andere(s)*** and others; ***unter anderem*** *or* ***anderen*** among other things, inter alia
**UKW** ***Ultrakurzwelle*** ultra-short wave, very high frequency, ABBR VHF

**V** ***Volt*** volt; ***Volumen*** volume
**v. Chr.** ***vor Christus*** before Christ, ABBR BC
**vgl.** ***vergleiche*** confer, ABBR cf.
**v. H.** ***vom Hundert*** per cent
**v. T.** ***vom Tausend*** per thousand
**VW** ***Volkswagen*** Volkswagen, People's Car

**WAA** ***Wiederaufbereitungsanlage*** reprocessing plant
**WEZ** ***westeuropäische Zeit*** Greenwich Mean Time, ABBR GMT
**WG** ***Wohngemeinschaft*** flat share, flat sharing (community)
**WM** ***Weltmeisterschaft*** world championship(s); *soccer*: World Cup

**z. B.** ***zum Beispiel*** for instance, ABBR e.g.
**z. H(d).** ***zu Händen*** attention of, to be delivered to, care of, ABBR c/o
**z. T.** ***zum Teil*** partly
**zus.** ***zusammen*** together
**z. Z(t).** ***zur Zeit*** at the time, at present, for the time being